D1385093

The CHELSEA HOUSE LIBRARY of LITERARY CRITICISM

The

CHELSEA HOUSE LIBRARY
_of_ LITERARY CRITICISM

The

NEW MOULTON'S
LIBRARY _of_ LITERARY CRITICISM

Volume 3

Elizabethan—Caroline

General Editor

HAROLD BLOOM

1986
CHELSEA HOUSE PUBLISHERS
New York
New Haven   Philadelphia

MANAGING EDITOR
S. T. Joshi

ASSOCIATE EDITORS
Patrick Nielsen Hayden
Teresa Nielsen Hayden
Larson Powell
Daniel Carmi Sherer
Anna Williams

EDITORIAL COORDINATOR
Karyn Gullen Browne

EDITORIAL STAFF
Richard Fumosa
Perry King

RESEARCH
Anthony C. Coulter
Susan B. Hamburger

BIOGRAPHER
Jack Bishop

PICTURE RESEARCH
Catherine Ruello

DESIGN
Susan Lusk

Printed and bound in the United States of
America.

10 9 8 7 6 5 4 3 2

Library of Congress Cataloging in Publication
Data

The New Moulton's library of literary criticism.
    (The Chelsea House library of literary criti-
    cism)
    Cover title: The New Moulton's.
    Rev. ed. of: Moulton's library of literary
    criticism.
    Contents: v. 1. Medieval—early Renais-
sance—v. 3. Elizabethan—Caroline.
    1. English literature—History and criti-
cism—Collected   works.   2.   American
literature—History and criticism—Collected
works. I. Bloom, Harold. II. Title: Moulton's
library of literary criticism. III. Series.
PR85.N39   1985   820'.9   87-27429
ISBN 0-87754-779-3 (v. 1)
ISBN 0-87754-781-5 (v. 3)

CONTENTS

The Index to this series, *The New Moulton's Library of Literary Criticism*, appears in Volume 10.

ILLUSTRATIONS

FRANCIS BEAUMONT AND JOHN FLETCHER

1584–1616   1579–1625

Francis Beaumont was born in 1584 at Grace-Dieu, Leicestershire. The son of a judge and brother of the poet Sir John, Beaumont entered Broadgates Hall (later Pembroke College), Oxford, in 1597. He left Oxford in 1599 without taking a degree and briefly read law at the Inner Temple, London. Settling in London, Beaumont quickly began associating with other young playwrights in the so-called "Tribe of Ben." Both Beaumont and Fletcher wrote dedicatory verses to Jonson's *Volpone*. Their collaborative effort began in 1606 and lasted until Beaumont's marriage to Ursula Isley, a wealthy heiress, in 1613. Beaumont is thought to have written *Salmacis and Hermaphroditus*, a 1602 verse narrative. He is considered solely responsible for *The Woman Hater* (1605) and possibly also *The Knight of the Burning Pestle* (1607). He died on March 6, 1616, and was buried in Westminster Abbey near Chaucer and Spenser.

John Fletcher was born in December 1579 in Rye, Sussex. The son of a clergyman, who later served as the bishop of Bristol and London, Fletcher probably was educated at Benet (later Corpus Christi) College, Cambridge. Fletcher came from a literary family which included an uncle and two cousins who were contemporary poets. Fletcher's solo effort, *The Faithfull Shepheardesse* (1608), was later imitated by Milton in *Comus*. After Beaumont's retirement, Fletcher worked alternately with Massinger, Rowley, and Shakespeare, as well as by himself. Fletcher's noted collaborative efforts include *The Beggars' Bush* (1622), written with Massinger, and *Henry VIII* (1613) and *The Two Noble Kinsmen* (1613), written with Shakespeare. Fletcher died of the plague in 1625 and was buried on August 29 at St. Saviour's, Southwark.

The dramatic team of Beaumont and Fletcher is credited with having written some fifty-two plays. Their best-known collaborations include the tragicomedy *Philaster; Or, Love Lies A-Bleeding* (1610), *The Maides Tragedy* and *A King and No King*, both produced in 1611, and *Cupid's Revenge* (c. 1612). Beaumont and Fletcher's works were collected in folio editions published in 1647 and 1679, thus ranking them along with the most distinguished dramatists of the period, Shakespeare and Jonson.

Francis Beaumont

Personal

Thou should'st have followed me, but Death, to blame,
Miscounted years, and measured age by fame;
So dearly hast thou bought thy precious lines—
Their praise grew swiftly, so thy life declines:
Thy Muse, the hearer's queen, the reader's love,
All ears, all hearts—but Death's—could please and move.
　　　　—SIR JOHN BEAUMONT, "An Epitaph on My
　　　　　　Deare Brother, Francis Beaumont," c. 1616

Francis Beaumont loved too much himself & his own Verses.—BEN JONSON, *Conversations with William Drummond*, 1619

　　Excellent Beaumont, in the foremost rank
　　Of the rarest wits, was never more than *Frank*.
　　　　—THOMAS HEYWOOD, *The Hierarchy of the
　　　　　　Blessed Angels*, 1635

Beneath yon eastern ridge, the craggy bound,
Rugged and high, of Charnwood's forest ground,
Stand yet, but, Stranger! hidden from thy view,
The ivied Ruins of forlorn GRACE DIEU;
Erst a religious House, which day and night
With hymns resounded, and the chanted rite:
And when those rites had ceased, the Spot gave birth
To honourable Men of various worth:
There, on the margin of a streamlet wild,
Did Francis Beaumont sport, an eager child;
There, under shadow of the neighbouring rocks,
Sang youthful tales of shepherds and their flocks;

Unconscious prelude to heroic themes,
Heart-breaking tears, and melancholy dreams
Of slighted love, and scorn, and jealous rage,
With which his genius shook the buskined stage.
Communities are lost, and Empires die,
And things of holy use unhallowed lie;
They perish;—but the Intellect can raise,
From airy words alone, a Pile that ne'er decays.
　　　　—WILLIAM WORDSWORTH, "For a Seat in the
　　　　　　Groves of Coleorton," 1811

General

　　The strongest marble fears the smallest rain,
　　The rusting canker eats the purest gold.
　　Honour's best dye dreads envy's blackest stain;
　　The crimson badge of beauty must wax old:
　　But this fair issue of thy fruitful brain,
　　Nor dreads age, envy, cankering rust, or rain.
　　　　—JOHN FLETCHER, "To Beaumont on his
　　　　　　Poems," 1610

How I doe love thee BEAUMONT, and thy *Muse*,
That unto me do'st such religion use!
How I doe feare my selfe, that am not worth
The least indulgent thought thy pen drops forth!
At once thou mak'st me happie, and unmak'st;
And giving largely to me, more thou tak'st.
What fate is mine, that so it selfe bereaves?
What art is thine, that so thy friend deceives?

When even there where most thou praisest me,
For writing better, I must envy thee.
      —BEN JONSON, "To Mr Francis Beaumont,"
      c. 1616

Beaumont lyes here; and where now shall we have
A Muse like his to sigh upon his grave?
Ah! none to weepe this with a worthy teare,
But he that cannot, *Beaumont*, that lies here.
Who now shall pay thy Tombe with such a Verse
As thou that Ladies didst, faire *Rutlands* Herse?
A Monument that will then lasting be,
When all her Marble is more dust than she.
In thee all's lost: a sudden dearth and want
Hath seiz'd on Wit, good Epitaphs are scant;
We dare not write thy Elegie, whilst each feares
He nere shall match that coppy of thy teares.
Scarce in an Age a Poet, and yet he
Scarce lives the third part of his age to see,
But quickly taken off and only known,
Is in a minute shut as soone as showne.
Why should weake Nature tire her selfe in vaine
In such a peice, to dash it straight againe?
Why should she take such worke beyond her skill,
Which when she cannot perfect, she must kill?
Alas, what is't to temper slime or mire?
But Nature's puzled when she workes in fire:
Great Braines (like brightest glasse) crack straight, while those
Of Stone or Wood hold out, and feare not blowes.
And wee their Ancient hoary heads can see
Whose Wit was never their mortality:
Beaumont dies young, so *Sidney* did before,
There was not Poetry be could live to more,
He could not grow up higher, I scarce know
If th' art it selfe unto that pitch could grow,
Were't not in thee that hadst arriv'd the hight
Of all that wit could reach, or Nature might.
O when I read those excellent things of thine,
Such Strength, such sweetnesse coucht in every line,
Such life of Fancy, such high choise of braine,
Nought of the Vulgar wit or borrowed straine,
Such Passion, such expressions meet my eye,
Such Wit untainted with obscenity,
And these so unaffectedly exprest,
All in a language purely flowing drest,
And all so borne within thy selfe, thine owne,
So new, so fresh, so nothing trod upon.
I grieve not now that old *Menanders* veine
Is ruin'd to survive in thee againe;
Such in his time was he of the same peece,
The smooth, even naturall Wit, and Love of Greece. •
Those few sententious fragments shew more worth,
Then all the Poets *Athens* ere brought forth;
And I am sorry we have lost those houres
On them, whose quicknesse comes far short of ours,
And dwell not more on thee, whose every Page
May be a patterne for their Scene and Stage.
I will not yeeld thy Workes so meane a Prayse;
More pure, more chaste, more sainted then are Playes,
Nor with that dull supinenesse to be read,
To passe a fire, or laugh an houre in bed.
How doe the Muses suffer every where,
Taken in such mouthes censure, in such eares,
That twixt a whiffe, a Line or two rehearse,
And with their Rheume together spaule a Verse?
This all a Poems leisure after Play,

Drinke or Tabacco, it may keep the Day.
Whilst even their very idlenesse they thinke
Is lost in these, that lose their time in drinke.
Pity then dull we, we that better know,
Will a more serious houre on thee bestow,
Why should not *Beaumont* in the Morning please,
As well as *Plautus, Aristophanes?*
Who if my Pen may as my thoughts be free,
Were scurrill Wits and Buffons both to Thee;
Yet these our Learned of severest brow
Will deigne to looke on, and to note them too,
That will defie our owne, tis English stuffe,
And th' Author is not rotten long enough.
Alas what flegme are they, compared to thee,
In thy *Philaster*, and *Maids-Tragedy?*
Where's such an humour as thy *Bessus?* pray
Let them put all their *Thrasoes* in one Play,
He shall out-bid them; their conceit was poore,
All in a Circle of a Bawd or Whore;
A cozning dance, take the foole away,
And not a good jest extant in a Play.
Yet these are Wits, because they'r old, and now
Being Greeke and Latine, they are Learning too:
But those their owne Times were content t' allow
A thirsty fame, and thine is lowest now.
But thou shalt live, and when thy Name is growne
Six Ages older, shall be better knowne,
When th' art of *Chaucers* standing in the Tombe,
Thou shalt not share, but take up all his roome.
      —JOHN EARLE, "On Mr Beaumont," c. 1616

He that hath such acutenesse, and such witt,
As would aske ten good heads to husband it;
He that can write so well that no man dare
Refuse it for the best, let him beware:
    BEAUMONT is dead, by whose sole death appeares,
    Witt's a Disease consumes men in few yeares.
      —RICHARD CORBETT, "On Mr Francis Beau-
      mont," c. 1616

Francis Beaumont, an inseparable companion and coadjutor to *Fletcher* in the making of many of his Plays; besides what he made solely himself. There is also extant a poem of his, entitled, *Salmacis* and *Hermaphroditus*, a Fable taken out of *Ovid's Metamorphosis*.—EDWARD PHILLIPS, *Theatrum Poetarum Anglicanorum*, 1675

Compare with Beaumont's admirable farce of Bessus the wretched imitation of it attempted after his death in the *Nice Valour* of Fletcher; whose proper genius was neither for pure tragedy nor broad farce, but for high comedy and heroic romance—a field of his own invention; witness *Monsieur Thomas* and *The Knight of Malta*: while Beaumont has approved himself in tragedy all but the worthiest disciple of Shakespeare, in farce beyond all comparison the aptest pupil of Jonson. He could give us no *Fox* or *Alchemist*; but the inventor of Bessus and Calianax was worthy of the esteem and affection returned to him by the creator of Morise and Rabbi Busy.
—ALGERNON CHARLES SWINBURNE, *A Study of Shakespeare*, 1880, p. 89, Note

The history of the English drama from 1611 to 1642 may serve, when it is written, to illustrate the statement that, so far as this great national product had any single source, it sprang originally from the spirit of united patriotism; and the claim of Francis Beaumont to consideration in such a history would be partly at least the fact that he was more than any other man the link between the earlier and the later generation.—G. C.   MACAULAY, *Francis Beaumont: A Critical Study*, 1883, p. 194

John Fletcher

Personal

John Fletcher, son of Richard Fletcher, D. D. was (as by proportion of time is collectible) born in this county, before his
father was bishop of Bristol or London, and whilst as yet he was
dean of Peterborough. He had an excellent wit, which, the
back friends to stage-plays will say, was neither idle nor well
employed; for he and Francis Beaumont, esquire, like Castor
and Pollux (most happy when in conjunction) raised the English to equal the Athenian and Roman theatre; Beaumont
bringing the ballast of judgment, Fletcher the sail of phantasy;
both compounding a poet to admiration.

Meeting once in a tarvern, to contrive the rude draught of
a tragedy, Fletcher undertook to kill the king therein; whose
words being overheard by a listener (though his loyalty not to
be blamed herein), he was accused of high treason; till, the
mistake soon appearing, that the plot was only against a dramatic and scenical king, all wound off in merriment.

Nor could it be laid to Fletcher's charge, what Ajax doth
to Ulysses:

> *Nihil hic Diomede remoto.*
> When Diomede was gone,
> He could do nought alone.

For, surviving his partner, he wrote good comedies himself,
though inferior to the former; and no wonder, if a single thread
was not so strong as a twisted one. He died (as I am informed)
in London, of the plague, in the first of king Charles, 1625.
—THOMAS FULLER, *The History of the Worthies of England*,
1662

Oldwit: I knew *Fletcher*, my Friend *Fletcher*, and his Maid
Joan: Well, I shall never forget him, I have Supp'd with him, at
his House, on the *Bankside:* He lov'd a fat Loyn of Pork of all
things in the World: and *Joan*, his Maid, had her Beerglass of
Sack; and we all kiss'd her, i'faith, and were as merry as
pass'd.—THOMAS SHADWELL, *Bury-Fair*, 1689, Act I, Sc. 1

General

> Fletcher the Muses' darling, and choice love
> Of Phoebus, the delight of every Grove;
> Upon whose head the Laurel grew, whose wit
> Was the Times wonder, and example yet.
> —JAMES SHIRLEY, "Prologue" to *The Sisters*,
>   1640

> So shall we joy, when all whom Beasts and Wormes
> Had turn'd to their owne substances and formes,
> Whom Earth to Earth, or fire hath chang'd to fire,
> Wee shall behold more then at first intire
> As now we doe, to see all thine, thine owne
> In this thy Muses Resurrection,
> Whose scatter'd parts, from thy owne Race, more wounds
> Hath suffer'd, then *Acteon* from his hounds;
> Which first their Braines, and then their Bellies fed,
> And from their excrements new Poets bred.
> But now thy Muse inraged from her urne
> Like Ghosts of Murdred bodyes doth returne
> To accuse the Murderers, to right the Stage,
> And undeceive the long abused Age,
> Which casts thy praise on them, to whom thy Wit
> Gives not more Gold then they give drosse to it:

> Who not content like fellons to purloyne,
> Adde Treason to it, and debase thy Coyne.
>   But whither am I strayd? I need not raise
> Trophies to thee from other Mens dispraise;
> Nor is thy fame on lesser Ruines built,
> Nor needs thy juster title the foule guilt
> Of Easterne Kings, who to secure their Raigne,
> Must have their Brothers, Sonnes, and Kindred slaine.
> Then was wits Empire at the fatall height,
> When labouring and sinking with its weight,
> From thence a thousand lesser Poets sprong
> Like petty Princes from the fall of *Rome*.
> When JOHNSON, SHAKESPEARE, and thy selfe did sit,
> And sway'd in the Triumvirate of wit—
> Yet what from JOHNSONS oyle and sweat did flow,
> Or what more easie nature did bestow
> On SHAKESPEARES gentler Muse, in thee full growne
> Their Graces both appeare, yet so, that none
> Can say here Nature ends, and Art begins
> But mixt like th'Elements, and borne like twins,
> So interweav'd, so like, so much the same,
> None this meere Nature, that meere Art can name:
> 'Twas this the Ancients meant, Nature and Skill
> Are the two topps of their *Pernassus* Hill.
> —JOHN DENHAM, "On Mr. *John Fletcher's*
>   Workes," 1647

> Apollo sings, his harpe resounds; give roome,
> For now behold the golden Pompe is come,
> Thy Pompe of Playes which thousands come to see,
> With admiration both of them and thee,
> O Volume worthy leafe, by leafe and cover
> To be with juice of Cedar washt all over;
> Here's words with lines, and lines with Scenes consent,
> To raise an Act to full astonishment;
> Here melting numbers, words of power to move
> Young men to swoone, and Maides to dye for love.
> Love lyes a bleeding here, *Evadne* there
> Swells with brave rage, yet comely every where,
> Here's a *mad lover*, there that high designe
> Of *King and no King* (and the rare Plot thine)
> So that when 'ere wee circumvolve our Eyes,
> Such rich, such fresh, such sweet varietyes,
> Ravish our spirits, that entranc't we see
> None writes lov's passion in the world, like Thee.
> —ROBERT HERRICK, "Upon Master Fletchers
>   Incomparable Plays," 1647

> How have I been Religious? what strange Good
> Ha's scap't me that I never understood?
> Have I Hell guarded *Hæresie* o'rethrowne?
> Heald wounded States? made Kings and Kingdomes one?
> That *Fate* should be so mercifull to me,
> To let me live t'have said I have read thee.
>   Faire Star ascend! the Joy! the Life! the Light
> Of this tempestuous Age, this darke worlds sight!
> Oh from thy Crowne of Glory dart one flame
> May strike a sacred Reverence, whilest thy Name
> (Like holy *Flamens* to their God of Day)
> We bowing, sing; and whilst we praise, we pray.
>   Bright Spirit! whose Æternall motion

Of Wit, like *Time*, still in it selfe did runne;
Binding all others in it and did give
Commission, how far this, or that shall live:
Like *Destinie* of Poems, who, as she
Signes death to all, her selfe can never dye.

　　And now thy purple-robed *Tragoedie*,
In her imbroider'd Buskins, calls mine eye,
Where brave *Aëtius* we see betray'd,
T'obey his Death, whom thousand lives obey'd;
Whilst that the *Mighty Foole* his Scepter breakes,
And through his *Gen'rals* wounds his owne doome speaks,
Weaving thus richly *Valentinian*
The costliest Monarch with the cheapest man.

　　Souldiers may here to their old glories adde,
The Lover love, and be with reason *mad*:
Not as of old, *Alcides* furious,
Who wilder then his Bull did teare the house,
(Hurling his Language with the Canvas stone)
'Twas thought the Monster roar'd the sob'rer Tone.

　　But ah, when thou thy sorrow didst inspire
With Passions, blacke as is her darke attire,
Virgins as *Sufferers* have wept to see
So white a Soule, so red a Crueltie;
That thou hast griev'd, and with unthought redresse,
Dri'd their wet eyes who now thy mercy blesse;
Yet loth to lose thy watry jewell, when
Joy wip't it off, Laughter straight sprung't agen.

　　Now ruddy-cheeked *Mirth* with Rosie wings,
Fanns ev'ry brow with gladnesse, whilest she sings
Delight to all, and the whole Theatre
A Festivall in Heaven doth appeare:
Nothing but Pleasure, Love, and (like the Morne)
Each face a generall smiling doth adorne.

　　Heare ye foule Speakers, that pronounce the Aire
Of Stewes and Shores, I will informe you where
And how to cloathe aright your wanton wit,
Without her nasty Bawd attending it.
View here a loose thought said with such a grace,
Minerva might have spoke in *Venus* face;
So well disguis'd, that t'was conceiv'd by none
But *Cupid* had *Diana's* linnen on;
And all his naked parts so vail'd, th' expresse
The Shape with clowding the uncomlinesse;
That if this Reformation which we
Receiv'd, had not been buried with thee,
The Stage (as this work) might have liv'd and lov'd;
Her Lines; the austere Skarlet had approv'd,
And th' *Actors* wisely been from that offence
As cleare, as they are now from *Audience*.

　　Thus with thy *Genius* did the *Scœne* expire,
Wanting thy Active and inliv'ning fire,
That now (to spread a darknesse over all,)
Nothing remaines but *Poesie* to fall.
And though from these thy *Embers* we receive
Some warmth, so much as may be said, we live,
That we dare praise thee, blushlesse, in the head
Of the best piece *Hermes* to *Love* e're read,
That We rejoyce and glory in thy Wit,
And feast each other with remembring it,
That we dare speak thy thought, thy Acts recite:
Yet all men henceforth be afraid to write.
　　　　—RICHARD LOVELACE, "To *Fletcher* Reviv'd,"
　　　　　1647

Fletcher, to thee, wee doe not only owe
All these good Playes, but those of others too:

Thy wit repeated, does support the Stage,
Credits the last and entertaines this age.
No Worthies form'd by any Muse but thine
Could purchase Robes to make themselves so fine:
What brave Commander is not proud to see
Thy brave *Melantius* in his Gallantry,
Our greatest Ladyes love to see their scorne
Out done by Thine, in what themselves have worne:
Th'impatient Widow ere the yeare be done
Sees thy *Aspasia* weeping in her Gowne:
I never yet the Tragick straine assay'd
Deterr'd by that inimitable *Maid*:
And when I venture at the Comick stile
Thy *Scornfull Lady* seems to mock my toile:
Thus has thy Muse, at once, improv'd and marr'd
Our Sport in Playes, by rendring it too hard.
So when a sort of lusty Shepheards throw
The barre by turns, and none the rest outgoe
So farre, but that the best are measuring casts,
Their emulation and their pastime lasts;
But if some Brawny yeoman, of the guard
Step in and tosse the Axeltree a yard
Or more beyond the farthest Marke, the rest
Despairing stand, their sport is at the best.
　　　—EDMUND WALLER, "Upon Mr. *John Fletcher's*
　　　　　Playes," 1647

John Fletcher, one of the happy Triumvirate, (the other two being Jonson and Shakespeare,) of the chief dramatic poets of our nation, in the last foregoing age; among whom there might be said to be a symmetry of perfection, while each excelled in his own peculiar way: *Ben Jonson*, in his elaborate pains and knowlege of authors; *Shakespeare*, in his pure vein of wit, and natural poetic height; *Fletcher*, in a courtly elegance, and gentle familiarity of style; and withal a wit and invention so overflowing, that the luxuriant branches thereof were frequently thought convenient to be lopped off by his almost inseparable companion, *Francis Beaumont*.—EDWARD PHILLIPS, *Theatrum Poetarum Anglicanorum*, 1675

In easie Dialogue is *Fletcher's* Praise:
He mov'd the mind, but had not power to raise.
　　　—JOHN DRYDEN, "To my Dear Friend Mr. Congreve, on His Comedy, call'd, *The Double-Dealer*," 1693

The sentiments and style of Fletcher, where not concealed by obscurity, or corruption of the text, are very dramatic. We cannot deny that the depths of Shakspeare's mind were often unfathomable by an audience: the bow was drawn by a matchless hand; but the shaft went out of sight. All might listen to Fletcher's pleasing, though not profound or vigorous, language; his thoughts are noble, and tinged with the ideality of romance, his metaphors vivid, though sometimes too forced; he possesses the idiom of English without much pedantry, though in many passages he strains it beyond common use; his versification, though studiously irregular, is often rhythmical and sweet. Yet we are seldom arrested by striking beauties; good lines occur in every page, fine ones but rarely: we lay down the volume with a sense of admiration of what we have read, but little of it remains distinctly in the memory. Fletcher is not much quoted, and has not even afforded copious materials to those who cull the beauties of ancient lore.—HENRY HALLAM, *Introduction to the Literature of Europe*, 1837–39, Pt. 3, Ch. 6, Par. 83

No art in the poet, nor accomplishment in the performers, will again restore A *King and No King*, *Philaster* or *The Faithful*

Shepherdess to the repertoire of acting plays. But in proportion as Fletcher departed from the schools of Shakespeare and Jonson, he acquired a lower but more natural tone, and, with less ambition, was really more successful. He was an artist of the second order, constrained to unnatural and spasmodical movements while he remained in the higher regions of art, but moving gracefully and spontaneously when he descended to the lower.—WILLIAM BODHAM DONNE, "Beaumont and Fletcher" (1850), *Essays on the Drama*, 1858, p. 66

It might be supposed that the extreme susceptibility of Fletcher—the openness of his nature to all impressions, ludicrous, romantic, heroic, or indecent—would have made him a great delineator of the varieties of life and character. But the truth is, it made him versatile without making him universal. He wrote a greater number of plays than Shakespeare, and he has between five and six hundred names of characters; but two or three plays of Shakespeare cover a wider extent of human life than all of Fletcher's. To compare them is like comparing a planet with a comet,—a comet whose nucleus is only a few hundred miles in diameter, though its nebulous appendage flames millions of leagues behind. Fletcher's susceptibility to the surfaces of things was almost unlimited; his vital sympathy and inward vision were confined to a few kinds of character and a few aspects of life. His variety is not variety of character, but variety of incident and circumstance. He contrives rather than creates; and his contrivances, ingenious and exhilarating as they are, cannot hide his constant repetition of a few types of human nature. These types he conceived by a process essentially different from Shakespeare's. Shakespeare individualized classes; Fletcher generalized individuals. One of Shakespeare's characters includes a whole body of persons; one of Fletcher's is simply an idealized individual, and that often an exceptional individual. This individual, repeated in play after play, never covers so large a portion of humanity as Shakespeare's individualized class, which he disdains to repeat. But, more than this, the very faculties of Fletcher,—his wit, humor, understanding, fancy, imagination,—though we call them by the same words we use in naming Shakespeare's, differ from Shakespeare's both in kind and degree. Shakespeare was a great and comprehensive man, whose faculties all partook of his general greatness. The man Fletcher was so much smaller and narrower, and the materials on which his faculties worked so much more limited, that we are fooled by words if, following the example of his contemporaries, we place any one of his qualities or faculties above or on a level with Shakespeare's. —EDWIN P. WHIPPLE, *The Literature of the Age of Elizabeth*, 1869, pp. 173–75

Works

THE FAITHFUL SHEPHERDESS

The wise, and many-headed bench, that sits
Upon the life and death of plays and wits,
(Compos'd of gamester, captain, knight, knight's man,
Lady or pucelle, that wears mask or fan,
Velvet, or taffata cap, rank'd in the dark
With the shop's foreman, or some such brave spark
That may judge for his sixpence) had, before
They saw it half, damn'd thy whole play, and more:
Their motives were, since it had not to do
With vices, which they look'd for, and came to.
I, that am glad thy innocence was thy guilt,
And wish that all the Muses' blood were spilt
In such a martyrdom, to vex their eyes,
Do crown thy murder'd poem: which shall rise

A glorified work to time, when fire,
Or moths shall eat what all these fools admire.
—BEN JONSON,, "To Mr. John Fletcher, upon his *Faithful Shepherdess*" (c. 1610), *The Under-Woods*, 1640

If all the parts of this Play had been in unison with these innocent scenes, and sweet lyric intermixtures, it had been a Poem fit to vie with *Comus* or the *Arcadia*, to have been put into the hands of boys and virgins, to have made matter for young dreams, like the loves of Hermia and Lysander. But a spot is on the face of this moon.—Nothing short of infatuation could have driven Fletcher upon mixing up with this blessedness such an ugly deformity as Cloe: the wanton shepherdess! Coarse words do but wound the ears; but a character of lewdness affronts the mind. Female lewdness at once shocks nature and morality. If Cloe was meant to set off Clorin by contrast, Fletcher should have known that such weeds by juxtaposition do not set off, but kill sweet flowers.—CHARLES LAMB, *Specimens of English Dramatic Poets*, 1808

The *Faithful Shepherdess* . . . is 'a perpetual feast of nectar'd sweets, where no crude surfeit reigns.' The author has in it given a loose to his fancy, and his fancy was his most delightful and genial quality, where, to use his own words,

He takes most ease, and grows ambitious
Thro' his own wanton fire and pride delicious.

The songs and lyrical descriptions throughout are luxuriant and delicate in a high degree. He came near to Spenser in a certain tender and voluptuous sense of natural beauty; he came near to Shakespear in the playful and fantastic expression of it. The whole composition is an exquisite union of dramatic and pastoral poetry; where the local descriptions receive a tincture from the sentiments and purposes of the speaker, and each character, cradled in the lap of nature, paints 'her virgin fancies wild' with romantic grace and classic elegance. . . .

There are few things that can surpass in truth and beauty of allegorical description, the invocation of Amaryllis to the God of Shepherds, Pan, to save her from the violence of the Sullen Shepherd, for Syrinx' sake:

For her dear sake,
That loves the rivers' brinks, and still doth shake
In cold remembrance of thy quick pursuit!

Or again, the friendly Satyr promises Clorin—

Brightest, if there be remaining
Any service, without feigning
I will do it; were I set
To catch the nimble wind, or get
Shadows gliding on the green.

It would be a task no less difficult than this, to follow the flight of the poet's Muse, or catch her fleeting graces, fluttering her golden wings, and singing in notes angelical of youth, of love, and joy!

There is only one affected and ridiculous character in this drama, that of Thenot in love with Clorin. He is attached to her for her inviolable fidelity to her buried husband, and wishes her not to grant his suit, lest it should put an end to his passion. Thus he pleads to her against himself:

If you yield, I die
To all affection; 'tis that loyalty
You tie unto this grave I so admire;
And yet there's something else I would desire,
If you would hear me, but withal deny.
Oh Pan, what an uncertain destiny
Hangs over all my hopes! I will retire;

> For if I longer stay, this double fire
> Will lick my life up.

This is paltry quibbling. It is spurious logic, not genuine feeling. A pedant may hang his affections on the point of a dilemma in this manner; but nature does not sophisticate; or when she does, it is to gain her ends, not to defeat them.

The Sullen Shepherd turns out too dark a character in the end, and gives a shock to the gentle and pleasing sentiments inspired throughout.

The resemblance of *Comus* to this poem is not so great as has been sometimes contended, nor are the particular allusions important or frequent. Whatever Milton copied, he made his own. In reading the *Faithful Shepherdess*, we find ourselves breathing the moonlight air under the cope of heaven, and wander by forest side or fountain, among fresh dews and flowers, following our vagrant fancies, or smit with the love of nature's works. In reading Milton's *Comus*, and most of his other works, we seem to be entering a lofty dome raised over our heads and ascending to the skies, and as if nature and every thing in it were but a temple and an image consecrated by the poet's art to the worship of virtue and pure religion.—WILLIAM HAZLITT, *Lecture on the Dramatic Literature of the Age of Elizabeth*, 1820

The Faithful Shepherdess, deservedly among the most celebrated productions of Fletcher, stands alone in its class, and admits of no comparison with any other play. . . .

It is impossible to withhold our praise from the poetical beauties of this pastoral drama. Every one knows that it contains the germ of *Comus*: the benevolent Satyr, whose last proposition to "stray in the middle air, and stay the sailing rack, or nimbly take hold of the moon," is not much in the character of those sylvans, has been judiciously metamorphosed by Milton to an attendant spirit; and a more austere as well as more uniform language has been given to the speakers. But Milton has borrowed largely from the imagination of his predecessor; and, by quoting the lyric parts of the *Faithful Shepherdess*, it would be easy to deceive any one not accurately familiar with the songs of *Comus*. They abound with that rapid succession of ideal scenery, that darting of the poet's fancy from earth to heaven, those picturesque and novel metaphors, which distinguish much of the poetry of this age, and which are ulti-

mately, perhaps, in great measure referable to Shakspeare.—HENRY HALLAM, *Introduction to the Literature of Europe*, 1837–39, Pt. 3, Ch. 6, Pars. 76–77

As a poet he is best judged, perhaps, by his pastoral tragicomedy of *The Faithful Shepherdess*, the most elaborate and one of the earliest of his works. It failed on the stage, being, in his own phrase, "hissed to ashes"; but the merits which the many-headed monster of the pit could not discern so enchanted Milton that they were vividly in his memory when he wrote *Comus*. The melody, the romantic sweetness of fancy, the luxuriant and luxurious descriptions of nature, and the true lyric inspiration, of large portions of this drama, are not more striking than the deliberate desecration of its beauty by the introduction of impure sentiments and images. The hoofprints of unclean beasts are visible all over Fletcher's pastoral paradise; and they are there by design. Why they are there is a question which can be answered only by pointing out the primal defect of Fletcher's mind, which was an incapacity to conceive or represent goodness and innocence except as the ideal opposites of evil and depravity. He took depravity as the positive fact of life, and then framed from fancy a kind of goodness out of its negation. The result is, that, in the case of *The Faithful Shepherdess*, Chloe and the Sullen Shepherd, the depraved characters of the play, are the most natural and lifelike, while there is a sickliness and unreality in the very virtue of Amoret. It is not, therefore, as some critics suppose, the mere admission of vicious characters into the play that gives it its taint. Milton, whose conceptions both of good and evil were positive, and who represented them in their right spiritual relations, entirely avoided this error in *Comus*, while he availed himself of much in *The Faithful Shepherdess* that is excellent. In *Comus* it is virtue which seems most real and permanent, and the vice and wickedness represented in it do not mar the general impression of moral beauty left by the whole poem. But Fletcher, having no positive imaginative conception of the good, and feeling for depravity neither mental nor moral disgust, reverses this order. His vice is robust and prominent; his virtue is vague, characterless, and fantastic; and though his play has a formal moral, it has an essential impurity.—EDWIN P. WHIPPLE, *The Literature of the Age of Elizabeth*, 1869, pp. 175–77

Beaumont and Fletcher

Personal

Mr. Francis Beaumont was the son of Judge Beaumont. There was a wonderfull consimility of phansey between him and Mr. John Fletcher, which caused that dearnesse of frendship between them.

I thinke they were both of Queen's College in Cambridge.

I have heard Dr. John Earles, since Bishop of Sarum, who knew them, say, that Mr. Beaumont's maine Businesse was to lop the overflowings of Mr. Fletcher's luxuriant Fancy and flowing Witt.

They lived together on the Banke side, not far from the Play-house, both batchelors; lay together; had one Wench in the house between them, which they did so admire; the same cloathes and cloake, &c.; betweene them.

He writt (amongst many other) an admirable Elegie on the Countesse of Rutland. John Earles in his Verses on him, speaking of them,

> A monument that will then lasting bee,
> When all her Marble is more dust than shee.

Mr. Edm. Waller on him:

> I never yet the Tragick Scene assaid

> Deterr'd by thy inimitable *Mayd*:
> And when I striv'd to reach the Comick Stile
> Thy *Scornfull Lady* seem'd to mock my toile.

John Fletcher, invited to goe with a Knight into Norfolke or Suffolke in the Plague-time 1625, stayd but to make himselfe a suite of Cloathes, and while it was makeing, fell sick of the Plague and dyed. This I had (1668) from his Tayler, who is now a very old man, and Clarke of St. Mary Overy's in Southwark. Mr. Fletcher had an Issue in his arm (I thought it had not used so long ago). The Clarke (who was wont to bring him Ivyleaves to dresse it) when he came, found the Spotts upon him. Death stopped his Journey and laid him low here.—JOHN AUBREY, "Francis Beaumont and John Fletcher," *Brief Lives*, 1669–96

I am now arriv'd at a brace of Authors, who like the *Dioscuri*, *Castor* and *Pollux*, succeeded in Conjunction more happily than any Poets of their own, or this Age, to the reserve of the Venerable *Shakespear*, and the Learned and Judicious *Johnson*. 'Tis impossible for me to reach their Characters; and therefore, as the Witty Dr. *Fuller* cites *Bale*'s saying of *Randal Higden*, That 'tis no shame to crave aid in a Work too weighty for any ones back to bear;

I must have recourse to others. Assistance, for the Characters of this worthy pair of Authors. To speak first of Mr. *Beaumont*, he was Master of a good Wit, and a better Judgment; he so admirably well understood the Art of the Stage, that even *Johnson* himself thought it no disparagement to submit his Writings to his Correction. What a great Veneration *Ben.* had for him, is evident by those Verses he writ to him when living. Mr. *Fletcher*'s Wit was equal to Mr. *Beaumont*'s Judgment, and was so luxuriant, that like superfluous Branches, it was frequently prun'd by his Judicious Partner. These Poets perfectly understood Breeding, and therefore successfully copy'd the Conversation of Gentlemen. They knew how to describe the Manners of the Age; and *Fletcher* had a peculiar tallent in expressing all his thoughts, with Life and Briskness. No Man ever understood, or drew the Passions more lively than he; and his witty Raillery was so drest, that it rather pleas'd than disgusted the modest part of his Audience. In a word, *Fletcher*'s Fancy, and *Beaumont*'s Judgment combin'd, produc'd such Plays, as will remain Monuments of their Wit to all Posterity: Nay, Mr. *Fletcher* himself after Mr. *Beaumont*'s Decease, compos'd several Dramatick Pieces, which were well worthy the Pen of so great a Master.

. . . I am extreamly sorry, that I am not able to give any Account of the Affairs of these Great Men; Mr. *Beaumont*'s Parentage, Birth, County, Education, and Death, being wholly unknown to me: And as to Mr. *Fletcher*, all I know of him is, That he was Son to the Eminent *Richard Fletcher*, created Bishop of *Bristol*, by Queen *Elizabeth An.* 1559. and by her preferr'd to *London*, 1593. He died in *London* of the Plague in the First Year of King *Charles* the Martyr, 1625 being Nine and fourty Years of Age, and was bury'd in St. *Mary Overies* Church in *Southwarke*. —GERARD LANGBAINE, *An Account of the English Dramatick Poets*, 1691

General

Poetry is the Child of *Nature*, which regulated and made beautifull by *Art*, presenteth the most Harmonious of all other compositions; among which (if we rightly consider) the *Dramaticall* is the most absolute, in regard of those transcendent *Abilities*, which should waite upon the *Composer*; who must have more then the instruction of Libraries (which of it selfe is but a cold contemplative knowledge) there being required in him a *Soule miraculously* knowing, and conversing with all mankind, inabling him to expresse not onely the Phlegme and folly *of thick-skin'd men*, but the strength and maturity *of the wise*, the Aire and insinuations of the *Court*, the discipline and Resolution of the Soldier, the Vertues and passions of every noble condition, nay the councells and characters of the greatest Princes.

This you will say is a vast comprehension, and hath not hapned in many Ages. Be it then remembred to the Glory of our *owne*, that all these are Demonstrative and met in BEAUMONT & FLETCHER, whom but to mention is to throw a cloude upon all former names and benight Posterity; This Book being, without flattery, the greatest *Monument* of the *Scene* that Time and Humanity have produced, and must Live, not only the *Crowne* and sole *Reputation* of our owne, but the stayne of all other *Nations* and *Languages*, for it may be boldly averred, not one indiscretion hath branded this Paper in all the Lines, this being the Authentick witt that made Blackfriers an Academy, where the three howers spectacle while *Beaumont* and *Fletcher* were presented, were usually of more advantage to the hopefull young Heire, then a costly, dangerous, forraigne Travell, with the assistance of a governing Mounsieur, or Signior to boot; And it cannot be denied but that the young spirits of the Time, whose Birth & Quality made them impatient of the sowrer wayes of education, have from the attentive hearing these pieces, got ground in point of wit and carriage of the most severely employed Students, while these Recreations were digested into Rules, and the very Pleasure did edifie. How many passable discoursing dining witts stand yet in good credit upon the bare stock of two or three of these single Scenes.

And now Reader in this *Tragicall Age* where the *Theater* hath been so much out-acted, congratulate thy owne happinesse, that in this silence of the Stage, thou hast a liberty to reade these inimitable Playes, to dwell and converse in these immortall Groves, which were only shewd our Fathers in a conjuring glasse, as suddenly removed as represented, the Landscrap is now brought home by this optick, and the Presse thought too pregnant before, shall be now look'd upon as greatest Benefactor to Englishmen, that must *acknowledge* all the felicity of *witt* and *words* to this Derivation.

You may here find passions raised to that excellent pitch and by such insinuating degrees that you shall not chuse but consent, & go along with them, finding your self at last grown insensibly the very same person you read, and then stand admiring the subtile Trackes of your engagement. Fall on a Scene of love and you will never believe the writers could have the least roome left in their soules for another passion, peruse a Scene of manly Rage, and you would sweare they cannot be exprest by the same hands, but both are so excellently wrought, you must confesse none, but the same hands, could worke them.

Would thy Melancholy have a cure? thou shalt laugh at *Democritus* himselfe, and but reading one piece of this *Comick* variety, find thy exalted fancie in *Elizium*; And when thou art sick of this cure, (for the excesse of delight may too much dilate thy *soule*) thou shalt meete almost in every leafe a soft purling passion or *spring* of sorrow so powerfully wrought high by the teares of innocence, and *wronged Lovers*, it shall perswade thy eyes to weepe into the streame, and yet smile when they contribute to their owne ruines.

Infinitely more might be said of these rare Copies, but let the ingenuous Reader peruse them & he will finde them so able to speake their own worth, that they need not come into the world with a trumpet, since any one of these incomparable pieces well understood will prove a *Preface* to the rest, and if the Reader can tast the best wit ever trod our English Stage, he will be forced himselfe to become *a breathing Panegerick* to them all.

Not to detaine or prepare thee longer, be as capritious and sick-brain'd, as ignorance & malice can make thee, here thou art rectified, or be as healthfull as the inward calme of an honest *Heart*, *Learning*, and *Temper* can state thy disposition, yet this booke may be thy fortunate *concernement* and Companion.

It is not so remote in Time, but very many Gentlemen may remember these Authors & some familiar in their conversation deliver them upon every pleasant occasion so fluent, to talke a Comedy. He must be a bold man that dares undertake to write their Lives. What I have to say is, we have the precious *Remaines*, and as the wisest contemporaries acknowledge they Lived a *Miracle*, I am very confident this volume cannot die without one.

What more specially concerne these Authors and their workes is told thee by another hand in the following Epistle of the *Stationer to the Readers.*

Farwell, Reade, and feare not thine owne understanding, this Booke will create a cleare one in thee, and when thou hast considered thy purchase, thou wilt call the price of it a Charity to thy selfe, and at the same time forgive thy friend, and these Authors humble admirer.—JAMES SHIRLEY, "To the Reader,"

Comedies and Tragedies Written by Francis Beaumont and John Fletcher, Gentlemen, 1647

Gentlemen, before you engage farther, be pleased to take notice of these Particulars. You have here a *New Booke*; I can speake it clearly; for of all this large Volume of *Comedies* and *Tragedies*, not one, till now, was every printed before. A *Collection of Playes* is commonly but a *new Impression*, the scattered pieces which were printed single, being then onely Republished together: 'Tis otherwise here.

Next, as it is all New, so here is not any thing *Spurious* or *impos'd*; I had the Originalls from such as received them from the *Authours* themselves; by Those, and none other, I publish this Edition.

And as here's nothing but what is genuine and Theirs, so you will finde here are no *Omissions*; you have not onely All I could get, but All that you must ever expect. For (besides those which were formerly printed) there is not any Piece written by these *Authours*, either Joyntly or Severally, but what are now publish'd to the World in this *Volume*. One only Play I must except (for I meane to deale openly) 'tis a *COMEDY* called the *Wilde-goose Chase*, which hath beene long lost, and I feare irrecoverable; for a *Person of Quality* borrowed it from the *Actours* many yeares since, and (by the negligence of a Servant) it was never return'd; therefore now I put up this *Si quis*, that whosoever hereafter happily meetes with it, shall be thankfully satisfied if he please to send it home.

Some *Playes* (you know) written by these *Authors* were heretofore Printed: I thought not convenient to mix them with this *Volume*, which of it selfe is entirely New. And indeed it would have rendred the Booke so Voluminous, that *Ladies* and *Gentlewomen* would have found it scarce manageable, who in Workes of this nature must first be remembred. Besides, I considered those former Pieces had been so long printed and re-printed, that many Gentlemen were already furnished; and I would have none say, they pay twice for the same Booke.

One thing I must answer before it bee objected; 'tis this: When these *Comedies* and *Tragedies* were presented on the Stage, the *Actours* omitted some *Scenes* and Passages (with the *Authour's* consent) as occasion led them; and when private friends desir'd a Copy, they then (and justly too) transcribed what they *Acted*. But now you have both All that was *Acted*, and all that was not; even the perfect full Originalls without the least mutilation; So that were the *Authours* living, (and sure they can never dye) they themselves would challenge neither more nor lesse then what is here published; this Volume being now so complete and finish'd, that the Reader must expect no future Alterations.

For *literall Errours* committed by the Printer, 'tis the fashion to aske pardon, and as much in fashion to take no notice of him that asks it; but in this also I have done my endeavour. 'Twere vaine to mention the *Chargeablenesse* of this Work; for those who own'd the *Manuscripts*, too well knew their value to make a cheap estimate of any of these Pieces, and though another joyn'd with me in the *Purchase* and Printing, yet the *Care & Pains* was wholly mine, which I found to be more then you'l easily imagine, unlesse you knew into how many hands the Originalls were dispersed. They are all now happily met in this Book, having escaped these *Publike Troubles*, free and unmangled. Heretofore when Gentlemen desired but a Copy of any of these *Playes*, the meanest piece here (if any may be called Meane where every one is Best) cost them more then foure times the price you pay for the whole *Volume*.

I should scarce have adventured in these slippery times on such a work as this, if knowing persons had not generally assured mee that these *Authors* were the most unquestionable *Wits* this

Kingdome hath afforded. Mr. *Beaumont* was ever acknowledged a man of a most strong and searching braine; and (his yeares considered) the most *Judicious Wit* these later Ages have produced; he dyed young, for (which was an invaluable losse to this Nation) he left the world when hee was not full thirty yeares old. Mr. *Fletcher* survived, and lived till almost fifty; whereof the World now enjoyes the benefit. It was once in my thoughts to have Printed Mr. *Fletcher's* workes by themselves, because single & alone he would make a *Just Volume*: But since never parted while they lived, I conceived it not equitable to seperate their ashes.

It becomes not me to say (though it be a knowne Truth) that these *Authors* had not only High unexpressible gifts of *Nature*, but also excellent *acquired Parts*, being furnished with Arts and Sciences by that liberall education they had at the *University*, which sure is the best place to make a great Wit understand it selfe; this their workes will soone make evident. I was very ambitious to have got Mr. *Beaumonts* picture; but could not possibly, though I spared no enquirie in those *Noble Families* whence he was descended, as also among those Gentlemen that were his acquaintance when he was of the *Inner Temple*: the best pictures and those most like him you'l finde in this *Volume*. This figure of Mr. *Fletcher* was cut by severall *Originall Pieces*, which his friends lent me, but withall they tell me, that his unimitable Soule did shine through his countenance in such *Ayre* and *Spirit*, that the Painters confessed, it was not easie to expresse him: As much as could be, you have here, and the *Graver* hath done his part. What ever I have seene of Mr. *Fletchers* owne hand, is free from interlining; and his friends affirme he never writ any one thing twice: it seemes he had that rare felicity to prepare and perfect all first in his owne braine; to shape and attire his *Notions*, to adde or loppe off, before he committed one word to writing, and never touched pen till all was to stand as firme and immutable as if ingraven in Brasse or Marble.—HUMPHREY MOSELEY, "The Stationer to the Readers," *Comedies and Tragedies Written by Francis Beaumont and John Fletcher, Gentlemen, 1647*

What's here? another Library of prayse.
Met in a Troupe t'advance contemned Playes.
And bring exploded *Witt* againe in fashion?
I can't but wonder at this *Reformation*.
My skipping soule surfets with so much good,
To see my hopes into *fruition* budd.
A happy *Chimistry*! blest viper, *joy*!
That through thy mothers bowels gnawst thy way!
   Witts flock in sholes, and clubb to re-erect
In spight of *Ignorance* the Architect
Of Occidentall *Poesye*; and turne
Godds, to recall *witts* ashes from their urne.
Like huge *Collosses* they've together mett
Their shoulders, to support a world of Witt.
   The tale of *Atlas* (though of truth it misse)
We plainely read *Mythologiz'd* in this;
Orpheus and *Amphion* whose undying stories
Made *Athens* famous, are but *Allegories*.
'Tis Poetry has pow'r to civilize
Men, worse then stones, more blockish then the Trees.
I cannot chuse but thinke (now things so fall)
That witt is past its *Climactericall*;
And though the *Muses* have beene dead and gone
I know they'll finde a *Resurrection*.
   Tis vaine to prayse; they're to themselves a glory,
And silence is our sweetest *Oratory*.
For he that names but *FLETCHER* must needs be
Found guilty of a loud *hyperbole*.

His fancy so transcendently aspires,
He showes himselfe a witt, who but admires.
    Here are no volumes stuft with cheverle sence,
The very *Anagrams* of Eloquence,
Nor long-long-winded sentences that be,
Being rightly spelld, but Witts *Stenographie*.
Nor words, as voyd of Reason, as of Rithme,
Only cæsura'd to spin out the time.
But heer's a *Magazine* of purest sence
Cloath'd in the newest Garbe of Eloquence.
Scænes that are quick and sprightly, in whose veines
Bubbles the quintessence of sweet-high straines.
Lines like their *Authours*, and each word of it
Does say twas writ b' a *Gemini* of Witt.
    How happie is our age! how blest our men!
When such rare soules live themselves o're agen.
We erre, that thinke a Poet dyes; for this,
Shewes that tis but a *Metempsychosis*.
BEAUMONT and FLETCHER here at last we see
Above the reach of dull mortalitie,
    Or pow'r of fate: & thus the proverbe hitts
(That's so much crost) These men live by their witts.
        —ALEXANDER BROME, "Upon the unparalelld
            Playes written by those Renowned Twinnes of
            Poetry Beaumont and Fletcher," 1647

Beaumont and *Fletcher* of whom I am next to speak, had with the advantage of *Shakespeare's* wit, which was their precedent, great natural gifts, improv'd by study, *Beaumont* especially being so accurate a judge of Playes, that Ben. *Johnson* while he liv'd, submitted all his Writings to his Censure, and 'tis thought, us'd his judgement in correcting, if not contriving all his Plots. What value he had for him, appears by the Verses he writ to him; and therefore I need speak no farther of it. The first Play that brought *Fletcher* and him in esteem was their *Philaster*: for before that, they had written two or three very unsuccessfully: as the like is reported of *Ben. Johnson*, before he writ *Every Man in his Humour*. Their Plots were generally more regular then *Shakespeare's*, especially those which were made before *Beaumont's* death; and they understood and imitated the conversation of Gentlemen much better; whose wilde debaucheries, and quickness of wit in reparties, no Poet before them could paint as they have done. Humour, which *Ben. Johnson* deriv'd from particular persons, they made it not their business to describe: they represented all the passions very lively, but above all, Love. I am apt to believe the *English* Language in them arriv'd to its highest perfection; what words have since been taken in, are rather superfluous then ornamental. Their Playes are now the most pleasant and frequent entertainments of the Stage; two of theirs being acted through the year for one of *Shakespeare's* or *Johnsons*: the reason is, because there is a certain gayety in their Comedies, and Pathos in their more serious Playes, which suits generally with all mens humours. *Shakespeares* language is likewise a little obsolete, and *Ben. Johnson's* wit comes short of theirs.—JOHN DRYDEN, *An Essay of Dramatick Poesie*, 1668

    Enough to furnish al the Lewd Impeachers
    Of witty Beumonts Poetry, and Fletchers,
    Who, for a few Misprisions of wit,
    Are chargd by those, who ten times worse commit.
        —SAMUEL BUTLER, "Upon Critics Who judge of
            Modern Plays Precisely by the Rules of the
            Antients," c. 1680

Beaumont and Fletcher, men of remarkable talent, seemed to have followed Shakspeare's mode of composition, rather than

Jonson's, and thus to have altogether neglected that art which Jonson taught, and which Massinger in some sort practised. They may, indeed, be rather said to have taken for their model the boundless license of the Spanish stage, from which many of their pieces are expressly and avowedly derived. The acts of their plays are so detached from each other, in substance and consistency, that the plot scarce can be said to hang together at all, or to have, in any sense of the word, a beginning, progress, and conclusion. It seems as if the play began, because the curtain rose, and ended because it fell; the author, in the meantime, exerting his genius for the amusement of the spectators, pretty much in the same manner as in the *Scenario* of the Italians, by the actors filling up, with their extempore wit, the scenes chalked out for them. To compensate for this excess of irregularity, the plays of Beaumont and Fletcher have still a high poetical value. If character be sometimes violated, probability discarded, and the interest of the plot neglected, the reader is, on the other hand, often gratified by the most beautiful description, the most tender and passionate dialogue; a display of brilliant wit and gaiety, or a feast of comic humour. These attributes had so much effect on the public, that, during the end of the seventeenth and beginning of the eighteenth centuries, many of Beaumont and Fletcher's plays had possession of the stage, while those of Shakspeare were laid upon the shelf.—SIR WALTER SCOTT, "Essay on the Drama," 1814

In metre, B. and F. are inferior to Shakspeare, on the one hand, as expressing the poetic part of the drama, and to Massinger, on the other, in the art of reconciling metre with the natural rhythm of conversation,—in which, indeed, Massinger is unrivalled. Read him aright, and measure by time, not syllables, and no lines can be more legitimate,—none in which the substitution of equipollent feet, and the modifications by emphasis, are managed with such exquisite judgment. B. and F. are fond of the twelve syllable (not Alexandrine) line, as—

    Too many fears 'tis thought too: and to nourish
        those—

This has, often, a good effect, and is one of the varieties most common in Shakspeare. . . .
    B. and F. always write as if virtue or goodness were a sort of talisman, or strange something, that might be lost without the least fault on the part of the owner. In short, their chaste ladies value their chastity as a material thing,—not as an act or state of being; and this mere thing being imaginary, no wonder that all their women are represented with the minds of strumpets, except a few irrational humorists, far less capable of exciting our sympathy than a Hindoo, who has had a bason of cow-broth thrown over him;—for this, though a debasing superstition, is still real, and we might pity the poor wretch, though we cannot help despising him. But B. and F.'s Lucinas are clumsy fictions. It is too plain that the authors had no one idea of chastity as a virtue, but only such a conception as a blind man might have of the power of seeing, by handling an ox's eye. In *The Queen of Corinth*, indeed, they talk differently; but it is all talk, and nothing is real in it but the dread of losing a reputation. Hence the frightful contrast between their women (even those who are meant for virtuous) and Shakspeare's. So, for instance, *The Maid in the Mill*:—a woman must not merely have grown old in brothels, but have chuckled over every abomination committed in them with a rampant sympathy of imagination, to have had her fancy so drunk with the *minutiæ* of lechery as this icy chaste virgin evinces hers to have been.
    It would be worth while to note how many of these plays are founded on rapes,—how many on incestuous passions, and how many on mere lunacies. Then their virtuous women are

either crazy superstitions of a merely bodily negation of having been acted on, or strumpets in their imaginations and wishes, or, as in this *Maid in the Mill*, both at the same time. In the men, the love is merely lust in one direction,—exclusive preference of one object. The tyrant's speeches are mostly taken from the mouths of indignant denouncers of the tyrant's character, with the substitution of 'I' for 'he,' and the omission of the prefatory 'he acts as if he thought' so and so. The only feelings they can possibly excite are disgust at the Aeciuses, if regarded as sane loyalists, or compassion, if considered as Bedlamites. So much for their tragedies. But even their comedies are, most of them, disturbed by the fantasticalness, or gross caricature, of the persons or incidents. There are few characters that you can really like,—(even though you should have had erased from your mind all the filth, which bespatters the most likeable of them, as Piniero in *The Island Princess* for instance,)—scarcely one whom you can love. How different this from Shakspeare, who makes one have a sort of sneaking affection even for his Barnardines;—whose very Iagos and Richards are awful, and, by the counteracting power of profound intellects, rendered fearful rather than hateful;—and even the exceptions, as Goneril and Regan, are proofs of superlative judgment and the finest moral tact, in being left utter monsters, *nulla virtute redemptæ*, and in being kept out of sight as much as possible,—they being, indeed, only means for the excitement and deepening of noblest emotions towards the Lear, Cordelia, &c. and employed with the severest economy! But even Shakspeare's grossness—that which is really so, independently of the increase in modern times of vicious associations with things indifferent,—(for there is a state of manners conceivable so pure, that the language of Hamlet at Ophelia's feet might be a harmless rallying, or playful teazing, of a shame that would exist in Paradise)—at the worst, how diverse in kind is it from Beaumont and Fletcher's! In Shakspeare it is the mere generalities of sex, mere words for the most part, seldom or never distinct images, all head-work, and fancy-drolleries; there is no sensation supposed in the speaker. I need not proceed to contrast this with B. and F.

In respect of style and versification, ⟨*The Queen of Corinth*⟩ and . . . *Bonduca* may be taken as the best, and yet as characteristic, specimens of Beaumont and Fletcher's dramas. I particularly instance the first scene of the *Bonduca*. Take Shakspeare's *Richard II.*, and having selected some one scene of about the same number of lines, and consisting mostly of long speeches, compare it with the first scene in Bonduca,—not for the idle purpose of finding out which is the better, but in order to see and understand the difference. The latter, that of B. and F., you will find a well arranged bed of flowers, each having its separate root, and its position determined aforehand by the will of the gardener,—each fresh plant a fresh volition. In the former you see an Indian fig-tree, as described by Milton;—all is growth, evolution, γένεσις;—each line, each word almost, begets the following, and the will of the writer is an interfusion, a continuous agency, and not a series of separate acts. Shakspeare is the height, breadth, and depth of genius: Beaumont and Fletcher the excellent mechanism, in juxta-position and succession, of talent.—SAMUEL TAYLOR COLERIDGE, "Notes on Beaumont and Fletcher" (1818), *Literary Remains*, ed. Henry Nelson Coleridge, 1836, Vol. 2, pp. 306–16

There are such extremes of grossness and magnificence in their drama, so much sweetness and beauty interspersed with views of nature either falsely romantic, or vulgar beyond reality; there is so much to animate and amuse us, and yet so much that we would willingly overlook, that I cannot help comparing the contrasted impressions which they make, to those which we receive from visiting some great and ancient city, picturesquely but irregularly built, glittering with spires and surrounded with gardens, but exhibiting in many quarters the lanes and hovels of wretchedness. They have scenes of wealthy and high life which remind us of courts and palaces frequented by elegant females and high-spirited gallants, whilst their noble old martial characters, with Caractacus in the midst of them, may inspire us with the same sort of regard which we pay to the rough-hewn magnificence of an ancient fortress. Unhappily, the same simile, without being hunted down, will apply but too faithfully to the *nuisances* of their drama. Their language is often basely profligate. Shakspeare's and Jonson's indelicacies are but casual blots; whilst theirs are sometimes essential colours of their painting, and extend, in one or two instances, to entire and offensive scenes. This fault has deservedly injured their reputation; and, saving a very slight allowance for the fashion and taste of their age, admits of no sort of apology. —THOMAS CAMPBELL, *An Essay on English Poetry*, 1819

Beaumont and Fletcher, with all their prodigious merits, appear to me the first writers who in some measure departed from the genuine tragic style of the age of Shakespear. They thought less of their subject, and more of themselves, than some others. They had a great and unquestioned command over the stores both of fancy and passion; but they availed themselves too often of common-place extravagances and theatrical trick. Men at first produce effect by studying nature, and afterwards they look at nature only to produce effect. It is the same in the history of other arts, and of other periods of literature. With respect to most of the writers of this age, their subject was their master. Shakespear was alone, as I have said before, master of his subject; but Beaumont and Fletcher were the first who made a play-thing of it, or a convenient vehicle for the display of their own powers. The example of preceding or contemporary writers had given them facility; the frequency of dramatic exhibition had advanced the popular taste; and this facility of production, and the necessity for appealing to popular applause, tended to vitiate their own taste, and to make them willing to pamper that of the public for novelty and extraordinary effect. There wants something of the sincerity and modesty of the older writers. They do not wait nature's time, or work out her materials patiently and faithfully, but try to anticipate her, and so far defeat themselves. They would have a catastrophe in every scene; so that you have none at last: they would raise admiration to its height in every line; so that the impression of the whole is comparatively loose and desultory. They pitch the characters at first in too high a key, and exhaust themselves by the eagerness and impatience of their efforts. We find all the prodigality of youth, the confidence inspired by success, an enthusiasm bordering on extravagance, richness running riot, beauty dissolving in its own sweetness. They are like heirs just come to their estates, like lovers in the honey-moon. In the economy of nature's gifts, they 'misuse the bounteous Pan, and thank the Gods amiss.' Their productions shoot up in haste, but bear the marks of precocity and premature decay. Or they are two goodly trees, the stateliest of the forest, crowned with blossoms, and with the verdure springing at their feet; but they do not strike their roots far enough into the ground, and the fruit can hardly ripen for the flowers!

It cannot be denied that they are lyrical and descriptive poets of the first order; every page of their writings is a *florilegium*: they are dramatic poets of the second class, in point of knowledge, variety, vivacity, and effect; there is hardly a passion, character, or situation, which they have not touched in their devious range, and whatever they touched, they adorned with some new grace or striking feature; they are masters of style and versification in almost every variety of melting modulation or sounding pomp, of which they are capable: in comic wit and spirit, they are scarcely surpassed by any writers of any age. There they are in their element, 'like eagles newly baited'; but I speak rather of their serious poetry;—and this, I apprehend, with all its richness, sweetness, loftiness, and grace, wants something—stimulates more than its gratifies, and leaves the mind in a certain sense exhausted and unsatisfied. Their fault is a too ostentatious and indiscriminate display of power. Every thing seems in a state of fermentation and effervescence, and not to have settled and found its centre in their minds. The ornaments, through neglect or abundance, do not always appear sufficiently appropriate: there is evidently a rich wardrobe of words and images, to set off any sentiments that occur, but not equal felicity in the choice of the sentiments to be expressed; the characters in general do not take a substantial form, or excite a growing interest, or leave a permanent impression; the passion does not accumulate by the force of time, of circumstances, and habit, but wastes itself in the first ebullitions of surprise and novelty.

Besides these more critical objections, there is a too frequent mixture of voluptuous softness or effeminacy of character with horror in the subjects, a conscious weakness (I can hardly think it wantonness) of moral constitution struggling with wilful and violent situations, like the tender wings of the moth, attracted to the flame that dazzles and consumes it. In the hey-day of their youthful ardour, and the intoxication of their animal spirits, they take a perverse delight in tearing up some rooted sentiment, to make a mawkish lamentation over it; and fondly and gratuitously cast the seeds of crimes into forbidden grounds, to see how they will shoot up and vegetate into luxuriance, to catch the eye of fancy. They are not safe teachers of morality: they tamper with it, like an experiment tried *in corpore vili*; and seem to regard the decomposition of the common affections, and the dissolution of the strict bonds of society, as an agreeable study and a careless pastime. The tone of Shakespear's writings is manly and bracing; theirs is at once insipid and meretricious, in the comparison. Shakespear never disturbs the grounds of moral principle; but leaves his characters (after doing them heaped justice on all sides) to be judged of by our common sense and natural feeling. Beaumont and Fletcher constantly bring in equivocal sentiments and characters, as if to set them up to be debated by sophistical casuistry, or varnished over with the colours of poetical ingenuity. Or Shakespear may be said to 'cast the diseases of the mind, only to restore it to a sound and pristine health': the dramatic paradoxes of Beaumont and Fletcher are, to all appearance, tinctured with an infusion of personal vanity and laxity of principle. I do not say that this was the character of the men; but it strikes me as the character of their minds. The two things are very distinct. The greatest purists (hypocrisy apart) are often free-livers; and some of the most unguarded professors of a general license of behaviour, have been the last persons to take the benefit of their own doctrine, from which they reap nothing, but the obloquy and the pleasure of startling their 'wonder-wounded' hearers. There is a division of labour, even in vice. Some persons addict themselves to the speculation only, others to the practice. The peccant humours of the body or the mind break out in different ways. One man *sows his wild oats* in his neighbour's field: another on Mount Parnassus; from whence, borne on the breath of fame, they may hope to spread and fructify to distant times and regions. Of the latter class were our poets, who, I believe, led unexceptionable lives, and only indulged their imaginations in occasional unwarrantable liberties with the Muses. What makes them more inexcusable, and

confirms this charge against them, is, that they are always abusing 'wanton poets,' as if willing to shift suspicion from themselves.

Beaumont and Fletcher were the first also who laid the foundation of the artificial diction and tinselled pomp of the next generation of poets, by aiming at a profusion of ambitious ornaments, and by translating the commonest circumstances into the language of metaphor and passion. It is this misplaced and inordinate craving after striking effect and continual excitement that had at one time rendered our poetry the most vapid of all things, by not leaving the moulds of poetic diction to be filled up by the overflowings of nature and passion, but by swelling out ordinary and unmeaning topics to certain preconceived and indispensable standards of poetical elevation and grandeur.—WILLIAM HAZLITT, *Lectures on the Dramatic Literature of the Age of Elizabeth*, 1820

It is a pity that Beaumont and Fletcher had not been born earlier, and in the neighbourhood of Shakspeare, and become his playmates. The wholesome company of the juvenile yeoman (like a greater Sandford) might have rectified the refined spirits of the young gentlemen, and saved their Hippocrene from becoming ditch-water. Even as it is, they seem different men when writing in their own persons, and following the taste of the town. Compare, for example, Beaumont's exquisite verses on *Melancholy* with any one of their plays; or Fletcher's lines entitled *An Honest Man's Fortune* with the play of the same name, to which it is appended. The difference is so great, and indeed is discernible to such an equal degree in the poetry which startles you in the plays themselves (as if two different souls were writing one passage), that it appears unaccountable, except on some principle anterior to their town life, and to education itself. Little is known of either of their families, except that there were numerous poets in both; but Fletcher's father was that Dean of Peterborough (afterwards Bishop of London) who behaved with such unfeeling impertinence to the Queen of Scots in her last moments, and who is said (as became such a man) to have died of chagrin because Elizabeth was angry at his marrying a second time. Was poetry such a "drug" with "both their houses" that the friends lost their respect for it? or was Fletcher's mother some angel of a woman—some sequestered Miranda of the day—with whose spirit the "earth" of the Dean her husband but ill accorded?

Every devout lover of poetry must have experienced the wish of Coleridge, that Beaumont and Fletcher had written "poems instead of tragedies." Imagine as voluminous a set of the one as they have given us of the other! It would have been to sequestered real life what Spenser was to the land of Faery,—a retreat beyond all groves and gardens, a region of medicinal sweets of thought and feeling. Nor would plenty of fable have been wanting. What a loss! And this,—their birthright with posterity—these extraordinary men sold for the mess of the loathsome pottage of the praise and profligacy of the court of James I.

But let us blush to find fault with them, even for such a descent from their height, while listening to their diviner moods.—LEIGH HUNT, *Imagination and Fancy*, 1844

It is generally conceded that Beaumont and Fletcher are more effeminate and dissolute than the band of dramatic authors to which they must be still considered to belong. Their minds had not the grasp, tension, insight, and collected energy, which characterized others who possessed less fertility. Their tragic Muse carouses in crime, and reels out upon us with bloodshot eyes and dishevelled tresses. From this relaxation of intellect and looseness of principle comes, in a great degree, their habit of disturbing the natural relations of things in their representations of the sterner passions. The atmosphere of their tragedy is too often hot, thick, and filled with pestilential vapors. They pushed every thing to excess. Their weakness is most evident, when they strain the fiercest after power. Their strength is flushed, bloated, spasmodic, and furious. They pitch every thing in a high key, approaching to a scream. In what has been considered the most imaginative passage in their whole works,—the speech of Suetonius to his soldiers before battle, in *Bonduca,*—the lines seem torn from the throat of the speaker:—

> The gods of Rome fight for ye; loud Fame calls ye,
> Pitch'd on the topless Apennine, and blows
> To all the under world, all nations,
> The seas, and unfrequented deserts, where the snow
> 　　dwells;
> Wakens the ruined monuments, and there,
> Where nothing but eternal death and sleep is,
> Informs again the dead bones with your virtues.

Even their heroism has, generally, the lightness of romance; something framed from fancy, not from nature. Their heads grow giddy among the true horrors of tragedy, and their action becomes hurry and bustle instead of progress. The style of their dramas, where the text is not butchered by misprinting, is sweet, colloquial, voluble, and voluptuous, but rarely condensed and powerful. It has been finely said, in respect to their agency in weakening the diction of the drama, that "Shakspeare had bred up the English courser of the air to the highest wild condition, till his blood became fire, and his sinews Nemean; Ben Jonson put a curb into his mouth, subjected him to strict *manége,* and fed him on astringent food, that hardened his nerves to rigidity; but our two authors took the reins off, and let him run loose over a rank soil, relaxing all his fibres again." The flush and hectic heat of this unbitted racing is ever observable; but the bright hoofs of the courser strike off few lightning sparks, and he is a long time arriving at his goal.

The Maid's Tragedy, which Hallam gravely says is no tragedy for maids, and one which, with all its beauties, no respectable woman can read, contains much exquisite poetry among its portentous obscenities. The character of Aspatia is the model of a love-lorn, patient maiden,

> Whose weak brain is overladen
> With the sorrow of her love;

such as we meet, in a degraded state, among the Arabella Dieaways of old novels. Shirley probably refers to the vein of sentiment touched in this drama, when he says, "Thou shalt meet, almost in every leaf, a soft, purling passion, or spring of sorrow, so powerfully wrought high by the tears of innocence and wronged lovers, it shall persuade thy eyes to weep into the stream, and yet smile when they contribute to their own ruins." Lysippus thus describes Aspatia:

> 　　　　　This lady
> Walks discontented, with her watery eyes
> Bent on the earth: the unfrequented woods
> Are her delight; and when she sees a bank
> Stuck full of flowers, she with a sigh will tell
> Her servants what a pretty place it were
> To bury lovers in; and make her maids
> Pluck 'em, and strew her over like a corse.
> She carries with her an infectious grief
> That strikes all her beholders: *she will sing*
> *The mournfull'st things that ever ear have heard,*
> And sigh, and sing again; and when the rest
> Of our young ladies, in their wanton blood,
> Tell mirthful tales in course that fill the room

> With laughter, she will with so sad a look
> Bring forth a story of the silent death
> Of some forsaken virgin, which her grief
> Will put in such a phrase, that, ere she end,
> She'll send them weeping one by one away.

Amintor, in this play, forsakes Aspatia, and marries Evadne, at the command of the king. The scene in which his wife avows herself the mistress of the monarch, and tells Amintor that her marriage with him is merely one of convenience, is wrought out in Fletcher's most characteristic manner. That, also, in which the brother of Evadne compels her to promise to murder the king, is spirited and powerful. . . .

A *King and No King* is another play in which Beaumont and Fletcher's characteristic faults and beauties are displayed. Arbaces is well delineated, and so is Bessus,—both braggarts in different stations. Hallam and Hazlitt concur in admiring this drama. *Thierry and Theodoret* contains two female characters, Brunhalt and Ordella, representing the two phases under which Fletcher commonly delineated women. The latter Lamb pronounces, we think incorrectly, to be "the most perfect idea of the female heroic character, next to Calantha, in the *Broken Heart* of Ford, that has been embodied in fiction." The former is a monstrosity, compounded of fiend and beast. *Valentinian* is one of the best tragedies in the collection, though the plot is absurdly managed. There are three songs in it of peculiar merit, one relating to love, another to wine, and a third, full of solemn beauty, addressed to sleep, which we extract. Valentinian is brought in sick, in a chair, and the song is introduced as an expression of the deep and silent love of Eudoxia, the empress, who leans over him.

> Care-charming Sleep, thou easer of all woes,—
> Brother to Death, sweetly thyself dispose
> On this afflicted prince: fall like a cloud
> In gentle showers; give nothing that is loud
> Or painful to his slumbers;—easy, sweet,
> And as a purling stream, thou son of night,
> Pass by his troubled sense:—sing his pain,
> Like hollow murmuring wind, or silver rain:
> Into this prince gently, oh, gently slide,
> And kiss him into slumbers like a bride!

The scene which succeeds this reminds us of the last in *King John.* The ravings of the poisoned emperor, however, though clothed in a drapery of similar imagery, have not the intense grandeur of the death-scene of Shakspeare's monarch.

Fletcher's comedies are light, airy, fluttering, vivacious, full of diverting situations, and often sparkling with fancy and wit; but still superficial and farcical, compared with Shakspeare's and Jonson's. They have none of that intensity of humor, little of that substantial life, which we demand in English comedy. The gentleman, as understood by Fletcher, is of a different type from that indicated by old Decker. Beaumont and Fletcher, according to Dryden, understood and imitated much better than Shakspeare "the conversation of *gentlemen,* whose wild debaucheries, and quickness of wit in repartees, no poet can ever paint as they have done." We trust that they never will be equalled in this department of character. Their "studiously protracted" indecency, and their command of all the gibberish and slang of lust and vulgarity, make their comedies curious libels on the taste and morals of their audiences. Fletcher could not escape from the foul imp that had taken possession of his imagination, even in *The Faithful Shepherdess,* which, with all its poetic beauty and pastoral sweetness, is still so defiled in parts as to merit Schlegel's ironical comment, of its being an immodest defence of modesty. The tone and pitch of Fletcher's mind, as compared with Milton's, may be seen in the contrast between *The Faithful Shepherdess* and *Comus*. Milton is indebted to Fletcher for the suggestion of his subject, but this debt is paid a thousand fold in the treatment of it.—EDWIN P. WHIPPLE, "The Old English Dramatists," *North American Review*, July 1846, pp. 77–83

True greatness, whether in a poet, in a statesman, or in a man of science, consists in being above or before the age, and thus taking rank among its teachers. No greatness of this kind is recognisable in the monuments which remain to us of the dramatic genius of Beaumont and Fletcher. The littleness of their age, not its better aspirations, reflects itself in their plays. It was an age of tyrants and their favourites; of evil counsellors and evil counsels; of pandars and minions; of cloaked vices and bedizened grossness; of blatant theories and systems; of the decay of principles and beliefs. Its portraiture of course needs the addition of many other features besides these; but it cannot be denied that they are prominent among the signs of the times in and for which Beaumont and Fletcher wrote. The best safeguard of a national life, domestic virtue, and the most invigorating element in national feeling, a healthy national self-confidence, were endangered in many spheres of English society by the degeneracy and degradation to be found at its centre, to which public attention most eagerly directed itself. The rule of statesmen was succeeded by the sway of adventurers; and Court intrigues too often usurped the place of national endeavour. Beaumont and Fletcher breathed a corrupt atmosphere, without, so far as we can see, aspiring after rarer and purer air. The national history was to them a source neither of indignant contrast nor of cheering consolation; and of the book of nature they were contented to turn but a few leaves. They were moved by no supreme force of genius or of character to go deeper or soar higher than the age demanded; they neither inherited the divining-rod of Shakspere nor laboured with infinite diligence like Ben Jonson; their pathos is incidental rather than essential to their work, though they could move its spring at their wish, and their humour fails to penetrate very far beneath the surface. Their plays will never cease to dazzle and to delight, even though denied that representation on the stage which in many instances could not fail to attest their almost unparalleled theatrical effectiveness; but it may be questioned whether any one drama of theirs is capable of fully satisfying the mind which it stimulates into attention, or of thoroughly harmonising the feelings which it stirs into tumult. Nearly always brilliant, at times irresistibly attractive, the plays of Fletcher and his associate will never cease to be admired where they are read; but they are unlikely at any time to achieve the one kind of success to which they never seem to have attained, and to take deep root in the national heart.—ADOLPHUS WILLIAM WARD, *A History of English Dramatic Literature* (1875), 1899, Vol. 2, pp. 762–64

Coleridge wished that Beaumont and Fletcher had written poems instead of tragedies. It was a bold wish, though not an unfriendly one; but perhaps we should be readier to echo it if Coleridge had spoken of lyrics rather than of poems generally. The longer poems of Beaumont which remain to us are, on the whole, not remarkable. He composed a free paraphrase of Ovid's *Remedia Amoris*. *Salmacis and Hermaphroditus*, printed as early as 1602, when he was probably seventeen years old, is noteworthy chiefly on that account. In this poem, written in the same metre as Marlowe's *Hero and Leander*, and founded on a passage in Ovid's *Metamorphoses*, there is plenty of luxuriance and facility, but also a superabundance of mere voluptuous description and of frigid conceits. Some of Beaumont's memorial poems are marked by an almost incredible

want of taste. But the case is very different with the letter to Ben Jonson, in which 'their merry meetings at the Mermaid' are described with great animation and doubtless with truth. By Fletcher there are but three poems extant; but each has an interest of its own. Two of them are addressed to 'the true master in his art' and 'his worthy friend,' Ben Jonson; and the other, 'Upon an Honest Man's Fortune,' is more than worthy of its place at the end of the comedy which bears that name. In it we seem to come nearer than usual to the poet himself, who probably knew too much of 'want, the curse of man,' but never lost heart or belief in himself, and who has here described with admirable strength, what Goethe afterwards felt so keenly, the self-sufficience of the mind and its superiority to fortune.

> Man is his own star, and the soul that can
> Render an honest and a perfect man,
> Commands all light, all influence, all fate;
> Nothing to him falls early or too late;
> Our acts our angels are, or good or ill,
> Our fatal shadows that walk by us still.

These are fine lines, and there are others in the poem as good; yet we should hardly be willing to exchange one of the best of the plays for them. But when we come to the purely lyrical poems, the songs from the dramas and the speeches from *The Faithful Shepherdess*, we feel that we are standing on different ground. Of the passages here selected some belong indubitably to Fletcher alone, and one, certainly the grandest, to Beaumont alone. The great lines 'On the Tombs in Westminster' are written in the common rhyming couplets of four accents which have been so plentifully and so variously used in English poetry. It was a favourite metre of Fletcher's too, and it is interesting to compare the difference of its effect in the hands of the two poets. There is a grave strength in Beaumont's verse, and a concentrated vigour of imagination in such lines as

> Here are sands, ignoble things,
> Dropt from the ruin'd sides of kings,

which hardly belongs to Fletcher's lighter nature. On the other hand, all the qualities of his dramatic verse, its delightful ease and grace, and its overflowing fancifulness, come out in the lyrical speeches of the *Faithful Shepherdess*. Milton himself, though he put a greater volume of imagination and sound into the measure, never gave it such an airy lightness; and we must look onwards to Shelley's 'Ariel to Miranda' for an echo to these lyrics, still sweeter than their melody, and to his 'Music, when soft voices die' for a fellow to 'Weep no more.'

There is the same buoyant grace in Fletcher's songs, and something more. In that age of songs, many a playwright could produce a lyric or two of the stamp which seems to have been wellnigh lost since; but songs seem to flow by nature from Fletcher's pen in every style and on every occasion, and to be always right and beautiful. If he wants a drinking-song, he can rise to 'God Lyæus, ever young,' or can produce, what on a much lower level is hardly less perfect, the 'Drink to-day and drown all sorrow' of the *Bloody Brother*. The wonderful verses on Melancholy, which suggested 'Il Penseroso' and are hardly surpassed by it, come as easily to his call as the mad laughing-song of the same play. 'Sad songs,' like that quoted from *The Queen of Corinth*; dirges, like the 'Come you, whose loves are dead' of *The Knight of the Burning Pestle*, or the 'Lay a garland on my hearse'; invocations, prayers to Cupid, hymns to Pan,— each has its own charm, and Fletcher is as ready with his Beggars' or Broom-man's songs, or even with a dramatic battle-lyric like the tumultuous 'Arm, arm, arm, arm!' of *The Mad Lover*. Some of the best of these occur, indeed, in plays of which Beaumont was the joint author; but a comparison of those lyrics which undeniably belong to each poet alone is perhaps enough to convince us that Fletcher was the author of 'Lay a garland on my hearse,' if not also of 'Come you, whose loves are dead.' Probably however he has touched his highest point in the song from *Valentinian*, 'Hear, ye ladies that despise.' Here the reader will observe (what applies also to another fine song from the same play, 'Now the lusty spring is seen') that the rhythm exactly corresponds in the two stanzas without at all interfering with the spontaneous effect of the whole.

Fletcher was the sole author of *The Faithful Shepherdess*, the forerunner of Milton's *Comus*; and we may safely assume that no one of the extracts which follow is a joint production of the two poets. But this is not the case with their dramatic works. So complete was their poetical union that it is impossible, in the absence of external evidence, to say with any certainty what part of those plays which belong to both is due to each, or even to describe their separate characteristics. An old tradition contrasted the 'judgment' of the younger poet, who was Jonson's intimate friend, with the fancy and facility of the elder. That Fletcher possessed the latter qualities is certain; but we have no reason to attribute to Beaumont any of the deficiencies which the 'faint praise' of 'judgment' might seem to imply.—A. C. Bradley, "Beaumont and Fletcher," *The English Poets*, ed. Thomas Humphry Ward, 1880, Vol. 2, pp. 43–46

An hour ere sudden sunset fired the west,
   Arose two stars upon the pale deep east.
   The hall of heaven was clear for night's high feast,
Yet was not yet day's fiery heart at rest.
Love leapt up from his mother's burning breast
   To see those warm twin lights, as day decreased,
   Wax wider, till when all the sun had ceased
As suns they shone from evening's kindled crest.
Across them and between, a quickening fire,
Flamed Venus, laughing with appeased desire.
   Their dawn, scarce lovelier for the gleam of tears,
Filled half the hollow shell 'twixt heaven and earth
With sound like moonlight, mingling moan and mirth,
   Which rings and glitters down the darkling years.

     —Algernon Charles Swinburne, "Beaumont and Fletcher," *Sonnets on English Dramatic Poets*, 1882

The comparative depreciation which has come upon Beaumont and Fletcher naturally fixes on the defects. There is in the work of the pair, and especially in Fletcher's work when he wrought alone, a certain loose fluency, an ungirt and relaxed air, which contrasts very strongly with the strenuous ways of the elder playwrights. This exhibits itself not in plotting or playwork proper, but in style and in versification (the redundant syllable predominating, and every now and then the verse slipping away altogether into the strange medley between verse and prose, which we shall find so frequent in the next and last period), and also in the characters. We quit indeed the monstrous types of cruelty, of lust, of revenge, in which many of the Elizabethans proper and of Fletcher's own contemporaries delighted. But at the same time we find a decidedly lowered standard of general morality—a distinct approach towards the *fay ce que voudras* of the Restoration. We are also nearer to the region of the commonplace. Nowhere appears that attempt to grapple with the impossible, that wrestle with the hardest problems, which Marlowe began, and which he taught to some at least of his followers. And lastly—despite innumerable touches of tender and not a few of heroic poetry—the actual poetical value of the dramas at their best is below that of the best work of

the preceding time, and of such contemporaries as Webster and Dekker. Beaumont and Fletcher constantly delight, but they do not very often transport, and even when they do, it is with a less strange rapture than that which communicates itself to the reader of Shakespere *passim*, and to the readers of many of Shakespere's fellows here and there.

This, I think, is a fair allowance. But, when it is made, a goodly capital whereon to draw still remains to our poets. In the first place, no sound criticism can possibly overlook the astonishing volume and variety of their work. No doubt they did not often (if they ever did) invent their fables. But they have never failed to treat them in such a way as to make them original, and this of itself shows a wonderful faculty of invention and constitutes an inexhaustible source of pleasure. This pleasure is all the more pleasurable because the matter is always presented in a thoroughly workmanlike form. The shapelessness, the incoherence, the necessity for endless annotation and patching together, which mar so many even of the finest Elizabethan plays, have no place in Beaumont and Fletcher. Their dramatic construction is almost narrative in its clear and easy flow, in its absence of puzzles and piecings. Again, their stories are always interesting, and their characters (especially the lighter ones) always more or less attractive. It used to be fashionable to praise their "young men," probably because of the agreeable contrast which they present with the brutality of the Restoration hero; but their girls are more to my fancy. They were not straightlaced, and have left some sufficiently ugly and (let it be added) not too natural types of sheer impudence, such as the Megra of *Philaster*. Nor could they ever attain to the romantic perfection of Imogen in one kind, of Rosalind in another, of Juliet in a third. But for portraits of pleasant English girls not too squeamish, not at all afraid of love-making, quite convinced of the hackneyed assertion of the mythologists that jests and jokes go in the train of Venus, but true-hearted, affectionate, and of a sound, if not a very nice morality, commend me to Fletcher's Dorotheas, and Marys, and Celias. Add to this the excellence of their comedy (there is little better comedy of its kind anywhere than that of *A King and No King*, of the *Humorous Lieutenant*, of *Rule a Wife and Have a Wife*), their generally high standard of dialogue verse, their charming songs, and it will be seen that if they have not the daemonic virtue of a few great dramatic poets, they have at any rate very good, solid, pleasant, and plentiful substitutes for it.—George Saintsbury, *A History of Elizabethan Literature*, 1887, pp. 256–58

AUGUST WILHELM SCHLEGEL
From *Lectures on Dramatic Art and Literature*
tr. John Black
1809

Beaumont and Fletcher are always named together, as if they had been two inseparable poets, whose works were all planned and executed in common. This idea, however, is not altogether correct. We know, indeed, but little of the circumstances of their lives: this much however is known, that Beaumont died very young; and that Fletcher survived his younger friend ten years, and was so unremittingly active in his career as a dramatic poet, that several of his plays were first brought on the stage after his death, and some which he left unfinished were completed by another hand. The pieces collected under both names amount to upwards of fifty; and of this number it is probable that the half must be considered as the work of Fletcher alone. Beaumont and Fletcher's works did not make their appearance until a short time after the death of the latter; the publishers have not given themselves the trouble to distinguish critically the share which belonged to each, and still less to afford us any information respecting the diversity of their talents. Some of their contemporaries have attributed boldness of imagination to Fletcher, and a mature judgment to his friend: the former, according to their opinion, was the inventive genius; the latter, the directing and moderating critic. But this account rests on no foundation. It is now impossible to distinguish with certainty the hand of each; nor would the knowledge repay the labour. All the pieces ascribed to them, whether they proceed from one alone or from both, are composed in the same spirit and in the same manner. Hence it is probable that it was not so much the need of supplying the deficiencies of each other, as the great resemblance of their way of thinking, which induced them to continue so long and so inseparably united.

Beaumont and Fletcher began their career in the lifetime of Shakspeare: Beaumont even died before him, and Fletcher only survived him nine years. From some allusions in the way of parody, we may conclude that they entertained no very extravagant admiration of their great predecessor; from whom, nevertheless, they both learned much, and unquestionably borrowed many of their thoughts. In the whole form of their plays they followed his example, regardless of the different principles of Ben Jonson and of the imitation of the ancients. Like him they drew from novels and romances; they combined pathetic and burlesque scenes in the same play, and, by the concatenation of the incidents, endeavoured to excite the impression of the extraordinary and the wonderful. A wish to surpass Shakspeare in this species is often evident enough; contemporary eulogists, indeed, have no hesitation in ranking Shakspeare far below them, and assert that the English stage was first brought to perfection by Beaumont and Fletcher. And, in reality, Shakspeare's fame was in some degree eclipsed by them in the generation which immediately succeeded, and in the time of Charles II. they still enjoyed greater popularity: the progress of time, however, has restored all three to their due places. As on the stage the highest excellence will wear out by frequent repetition, and novelty always possesses a great charm, the dramatic art is, consequently, much influenced by fashion; it is more than other branches of literature and the fine arts exposed to the danger of passing rapidly from a grand and simple style to dazzling and superficial mannerism.

Beaumont and Fletcher were in fact men of the most distinguished talents; they scarcely wanted anything more than a profounder seriousness of mind, and that artistic sagacity which everywhere observes a due measure, to rank beside the greatest dramatic poets of all nations. They possessed extraordinary fecundity and flexibility of mind, and a facility which however too often degenerated into carelessness. The highest perfection they have hardly ever attained; and I should have little hesitation in affirming that they had not even an idea of it: however, on several occasions they have approached quite close to it. And why was it denied them to take this last step? Because with them poetry was not an inward devotion of the feeling and imagination, but a means to obtain brilliant results. Their first object was effect, which the great artist can hardly fail of attaining if he is determined above all things to satisfy himself. They were not like the most of their predecessors, players,[1] but they lived in the neighbourhood of the theatre, were in constant intercourse with it, and possessed a perfect understanding of theatrical matters. They were also thoroughly acquainted with their contemporaries; but they found it more convenient to lower themselves to the taste of the public than

to follow the example of Shakspeare, who elevated the public to himself. They lived in a vigorous age, which more willingly pardoned extravagancies of every description than feebleness and frigidity. They therefore never allowed themselves to be restrained by poetical or moral considerations; and in this confidence they found their account: they resemble in some measure somnambulists, who with closed eyes pass safely through the greatest dangers. Even when they undertake what is most depraved they handle it with a certain felicity. In the commencement of a degeneracy in the dramatic art, the spectators first lose the capability of judging of a play as a whole; hence Beaumont and Fletcher bestow very little attention on harmony of composition and the observance of due proportion between all the different parts. They not unfrequently lose sight of a happily framed plot, and appear almost to forget it; they bring something else forward equally capable of affording pleasure and entertainment, but without preparation, and in the particular place where it occurs without propriety. They always excite curiosity, frequently compassion—they hurry us along with them; they succeed better, however, in exciting than in gratifying our expectation. So long as we are reading them we feel ourselves keenly interested; but they leave very few imperishable impressions behind. They are least successful in their tragic attempts, because their feeling is not sufficiently drawn from the depths of human nature, and because they bestowed too little attention on the general consideration of human destinies: they succeed much better in Comedy, and in those serious and pathetic pictures which occupy a middle place betwixt Comedy and Tragedy. Their characters are often arbitrarily drawn, and, when it suits the momentary wants of the poet, become even untrue to themselves; in external matters they are tolerably in keeping. Beaumont and Fletcher employ the whole strength of their talents in pictures of passion; but they enter little into the secret history of the heart; they pass over the first emotions and the gradual heightening of a feeling; they seize it, as it were, in its highest maturity, and then develope its symptoms with the most overpowering illusion, though with an exaggerated strength and fulness. But though its expression does not always possess the strictest truth, nevertheless it still appears natural, every thing has free motion; nothing is labouriously constrained or far-fetched, however striking it may sometimes appear. In their dialogue they have completely succeeded in uniting the familiar tone of real conversation and the appearance of momentary suggestion with poetical elevation. They even run into that popular affectation of the natural which has ensured such great success to some dramatic poets of our own time; but as the latter sought it in the absence of all elevation of fancy, they could not help falling into insipidity. Beaumont and Fletcher generally couple nature with fancy; they succeed in giving an extraordinary appearance to what is common, and thus preserve a certain fallacious image of the ideal. The morality of these writers is ambiguous. Not that they failed in strong colours to contrast greatness of soul and goodness with baseness and wickedness, or did not usually conclude with the disgrace and punishment of the latter, but an ostentatious generosity is often favourably exhibited in lieu of duty and justice. Every thing good and excellent in their pictures arises more from transient ebullition than fixed principle; they seem to place the virtues in the blood; and close beside them impulses of merely a selfish and instinctive nature hold up their heads, as if they were of nobler origin. There is an incurable vulgar side of human nature which, when he cannot help but show it, the poet should never handle without a certain bashfulness; but instead of this Beaumont and Fletcher throw no veil whatever over nature. They express every thing bluntly in words; they make the spectator the unwilling confidant of all that more noble minds endeavour even to hide from themselves. The indecencies in which these poets indulged themselves go beyond conception. Licentiousness of language is the least evil; many scenes, nay, even whole plots, are so contrived that the very idea, not to mention the beholding of them, is a gross insult to modesty. Aristophanes is a bold mouth-piece of sensuality; but like the Grecian statuaries in the figures of satyrs, &c., he banishes them into the animal kingdom to which they wholly belong; and judging him by the morality of his times, he is much less offensive. But Beaumont and Fletcher hold up to view the impure and nauseous colours of vice in quite a different sphere; their compositions resemble the sheet, in the vision of the Apostle, full of pure and impure animals. This was the universal tendency of the dramatic poets under James and Charles I. They seem as if they purposely wished to justify the assertion of the Puritans, that theatres were so many schools of seduction and chapels of the Devil.

To those who merely read for amusement and general cultivation, we can only recommend the works of Beaumont and Fletcher with some limitation.[2] For the practical artist, however, and the critical judge of dramatic poetry, an infinite deal may be learned from them; as well from their merits as their extravagances. A minute dissection of one of their works, for which we have not here the necessary space, would serve to place this in the clearest light. With regard to representation, these pieces had, in their day, this advantage, that they did not require such great actors to fill the principal characters as Shakspeare's plays did. In order to bring them on the stage in our days, it would be necessary to re-cast most of them; which might be done with some of them by omitting, moderating, and purging various passages.[3]

The Two Noble Kinsmen is deserving of more particular mention, as it is the joint production of Shakspeare and Fletcher. I see no ground for calling this in question; the piece, it is true, did not make its appearance till after the death of both; but what could be the motive with the editor or printer for any deception, as Fletcher's name was at that time in as great, at least, if not greater celebrity than Shakspeare's? Were it the sole production of Fletcher, it would, undoubtedly, have to be ranked as the best of his serious and heroic pieces. However, it would be unfair to a writer of talent to take from him a work simply because it seems too good for him. Might not Fletcher, who in his thoughts and images not unfrequently shows an affinity to Shakspeare, have for once had the good fortune to approach closer to him than usual? It would still be more dangerous to rest on the similarity of separate passages to others in Shakspeare. This might rather arise from imitation. I rely therefore entirely on the historical statement, which, probably, originated in a tradition of the players. There are connoisseurs, who, in the pictures of Raphael, (which, as is well known, were not always wholly executed by himself,) take upon them to determine what parts were painted by Francesco Penni, or Giulio Romano, or some other scholar. I wish them success with the nicety of their discrimination; they are at least secure from contradiction, as we have no certain information on the subject. I would only remind these connoisseurs, that Giulio Romano was himself deceived by a copy from Raphael of Andrea del Sarto's, and that, too, with regard to a figure which he had himself assisted in painting. The case in point is, however, a much more complicated problem in criticism. The design of Raphael's figures was at least his own, and the execution only was distributed in part among his scholars. But to find out how much of *The Two Noble Kinsmen* may belong to Shakspeare, we must not only be able to tell the difference of hands in the

execution, but also to determine the influence of Shakspeare on the plan of the whole. When, however, he once joined another poet in the production of a work, he must also have accommodated himself, in a certain degree, to his views, and renounced the prerogative of unfolding his inmost peculiarity. Amidst so many grounds for doubting, if I might be allowed to hazard an opinion, I should say, that I think I can perceive the mind of Shakspeare in a certain ideal purity, which distinguishes this piece from all others of Fletcher's, and in the conscientious fidelity with which the story adheres to that of Chaucer's *Palamon and Arcite*. In the style Shakspeare's hand is at first discoverable in a brevity and fulness of thought bordering on obscurity; in the colour of the expression, almost all the poets of that time bear a strong resemblance to each other. The first acts are most carefully laboured; afterwards the piece is drawn out to too great a length and in an epic manner; the dramatic law of quickening the action towards the conclusion, is not sufficiently observed. The part of the jailor's daughter, whose insanity is artlessly conducted in pure monologues, is certainly not Shakspeare's; for, in that case, we must suppose him to have had an intention of arrogantly imitating his own Ophelia.

Moreover, it was then a very general custom for two or even three poets to join together in the production of one play. Besides the constant example of Beaumont and Fletcher, we have many others. The consultations, respecting the plan, were generally held at merry meetings in taverns. Upon one of these occasions it happened that one in a poetical intoxication calling out, "I will undertake to kill the king!" was immediately taken into custody as a traitor, till the misunderstanding was cleared up. This mode of composing may answer very well in the lighter species of the drama, which require to be animated by social wit. With regard to theatrical effect, four eyes may, in general, see better than two, and mutual objections may be of use in finding out the most suitable means. But the highest poetical inspiration is much more eremitical than communicative; for it always seeks to express something which sets language at defiance, which, therefore, can only be weakened and dissipated by detached words, and can only be attained by the common impression of the complete work, whose idea is hovering before it.

The Knight of the Burning Pestle, of Beaumont and Fletcher, is an incomparable work and singular in its kind. It is a parody of the chivalry romances; the thought is borrowed from *Don Quixote*, but the imitation is handled with freedom, and so particularly applied to Spenser's *Fairy Queen*, that it may pass for a second invention. But the peculiarly ingenious novelty of the piece consists in the combination of the irony of a chimerical abuse of poetry with another irony exactly the contrary, of the incapacity to comprehend any fable, and the dramatic form more particularly. A grocer and his wife come as spectators to the theatre: they are discontented with the piece which has just been announced; they demand a play in honour of the corporation, and Ralph, their apprentice, is to act a principal part in it. Their humour is complied with; but still they are not satisfied, make their remarks on every thing, and incessantly address themselves to the players. Ben Jonson had already exhibited imaginary spectators, but they were either benevolent expounders or awkward censures of the poet's views: consequently, they always conducted his, the poet's, own cause. But the grocer and his wife represent a whole genus, namely, those unpoetical spectators, who are destitute of a feeling for art. The illusion with them becomes a passive error; the subject represented has on them all the effect of reality, they accordingly resign themselves to the impression of each moment, and take part for or against the persons of the drama. On the other hand, they show themselves insensible to all genuine illusion, that is, of entering vividly into the spirit of the fable: for them Ralph, however, heroically and chivalrously he may conduct himself, is always Ralph their apprentice; and in the whim of the moment they take upon them to demand scenes which are quite inconsistent with the plan of the piece that has been commenced. In short, the views and demands with which poets are often oppressed by a prosaical public are very cleverly and amusingly personified in these caricatures of spectators.

The Faithful Shepherdess, a pastoral, is highly extolled by some English critics, as it is without doubt finished with great care, in rhymed, and partly, in lyrical verses. Fletcher wished also to be classical for once, and did violence to his natural talent. Perhaps he had the intention of surpassing Shakspeare's *Midsummer Night's Dream*; but the composition which he has ushered into the world is as heavy as that of the other was easy and aërial. The piece is overcharged with mythology and rural painting, is untheatrical, and so far from pourtraying the genuine ideality of a pastoral world, it even contains the greatest vulgarities. We might rather call it an immodest eulogy of chastity. I am willing to hope that Fletcher was unacquainted with the *Pastor Fido* of Guarini, for otherwise his failure would admit of less justification.

We are in want of space to speak in detail of the remaining works of Beaumont and Fletcher, although they might be made the subject of many instructive observations. On the whole, we may say of these writers that they have built a splendid palace, but merely in the suburbs of poetry, while Shakspeare has his royal residence in the very centre point of the capital.

The fame of Massinger has been lately revived by an edition of his works. Some literary men wish to rank him above Beaumont and Fletcher, as if he had approached more closely to the excellence of Shakspeare. I cannot see it. He appears to me to bear the greatest resemblance to Beaumont and Fletcher in the plan of the pieces, in the tone of manners, and even in the language and negligences of versification. I would not undertake to decide, from internal symptoms, whether a play belonged to Massinger, or Beaumont and Fletcher. This applies also to the other contemporaries; for instance, to Shirley, of whose pieces two are stated to have crept into the works ascribed to the two last-named poets. There was (as already said) at this time in England a school of dramatic art, a school of which Shakspeare was the invisible and too often unacknowledged head; for Ben Jonson remained almost without successors. It is a characteristic of what is called manner in art to efface the features of personal originality, and to make the productions of various artists bear a resemblance to each other; and from manner no dramatic poet of this age, who succeeded Shakspeare, can be pronounced altogether free. When, however, we compare their works with those of the succeeding age, we perceive between them something about the same relation as between the paintings of the school of Michel Angelo and those of the last half of the seventeenth and the first half of the eighteenth century. Both are tainted with manner; but the manner of the former bears the trace of a sublime origin in the first ages; in the latter, all is little, affected, empty, and superficial. I repeat it: in a general history of the dramatic art, the first period of the English theatre is the only one of importance. The plays of the least known writers of that time, (I venture to affirm this, though I am far from being acquainted with all of them) are more instructive for theory, and more remarkable, than the most celebrated of all the succeeding times.

Notes

1. In the privilege granted by James I. to the royal players, a *Laurence Fletcher* is named along with Shakspeare as manager of the company. The poet's name was John Fletcher. Perhaps the former might be his brother or near relation.
2. Hence I cannot approve of the undertaking, which has been recently commenced, of translating them into German. They are not at all adapted for our great public, and whoever makes a particular study of dramatic poetry will have little difficulty in finding his way to the originals.
3. So far as I know only one play has yet been brought on the German theatre, namely, *Rule a Wife and have a Wife*, re-written by Schröder under the title of *Stille Wasser sind tief* (Still Waters run deep) which, when well acted, has always been uncommonly well received.

EDMUND GOSSE
From *The Jacobean Poets*
1894, pp. 68–86

There is no body of poetical work which displays so characteristically—we may not add, perhaps, so favourably—the qualities of the Jacobean age as the mass of plays united under the names of Beaumont and Fletcher. These celebrated friends, who supply the most illustrious examples of the art of literary partnership now extant, would probably be as little known to us as several of their scarcely less-gifted contemporaries, if they had not so exactly gratified the taste of their time, and of the generation which succeeded theirs, as to induce the players to preserve and revise their writings. Only ten of their plays were printed during their lives, but the folio of 1647 saved forty-two others from a destruction which may have been imminent.

As the century proceeded, the writings of these friends advanced in popularity far beyond that of Shakespeare's or even of Ben Jonson's, and when the Restoration thought of the classic English drama, it thought principally of Beaumont and Fletcher. Dryden expressed the common opinion when he said that they reproduced the easy conversation of gentlefolks more ably than Shakespeare, and acquiesced in the common taste when he recorded that in his day "two of theirs were acted through the year, for one of Shakespeare's or Jonson's." Beaumont and Fletcher preserved their vogue until the classic reaction was completed, and then their romantic plots and easy verse went suddenly out of fashion. Towards the end of the eighteenth century their fame revived, but it has never again risen to its first commanding height. Yet the richness and abundance of these dramatists, their very high level of merit, and their perfect sympathy with the age in which they flourished, will always save them from critical neglect. To praise them unreservedly is no longer possible; but no one who loves poetry can fail to read them with delight.

Of the famous Heavenly Twins of Parnassus, John Fletcher was the elder. He was born in December, 1579, at Rye, of which parish his father, Richard Fletcher, was then incumbent. Dr. Fletcher became successively Bishop of Bristol, of Worcester, and of London, dying when his son was seventeen, and an inmate of Bene't College, Cambridge. Fletcher's career is entirely obscure to us, until he began to be a dramatist, in his thirtieth year; but it is probable that, though not rich, he never found himself so pinched by poverty as the majority of his dramatic colleagues were. Francis Beaumont was even more certainly in easy circumstances. He was born, the third son of the squire of Grace-Dieu in Leicestershire, towards the close of 1584. He was admitted to Broadgates Hall, Oxford, in 1597, and proceeded to the Inner Temple three years later. He was probably the author of *Salmacis and Hermaphrodite*, 1602, a luscious paraphrase of a story of Ovid told in heroic verse, a juvenile performance, but one of high poetic promise. Early in the century Beaumont became a prominent figure among the wits, and was little more than of age when Ben Jonson addressed him—

How do I love thee, Beaumont, and thy Muse,

in answer to the complimentary "religion" of a neatly turned copy of verses on *Volpone*. Fletcher wrote on the same occasion, and their names are thus for the first time connected. The famous meetings at the Mermaid may have begun soon after 1606, when Beaumont composed his "Letter to Ben Jonson," "written before he and Master Fletcher came to London." He says in the course of this admirable epistle:—

What things have we seen
Done at the Mermaid; heard words that have been
So nimble and so full of subtle flame,
As if that every one from whence they came,
Had meant to put his whole wit in a jest,
And had resolved to live a fool the rest
Of his dull life.

From this same poem, in which he speaks of "scenes" which are not yet perfect, we see that he was already a dramatist. The first appearance he is known to have made was in the comedy of *The Woman-Hater*, witten and anonymously printed in 1607. There is little doubt that this was the unaided work of Beaumont. It bears manifest signs of a young hand, and is a crude miscellany of prose patched with soft passages of romantic blank verse. *The Woman-Hater* is interesting as manifestly composed under the influence of Shakespeare. The central figure is a hungry courtier, Lazarillo, who studies greediness as a fine art, and indulges in exquisite rhapsodies of longing for the head of an "umbrano," which fishy delicacy evades him to the last. The fair adventuress Oriana is a species of Beatrice, and Gondarino an unseemly and extravagant Benedick. The scene is laid at Milan; the verse is primitive, and the knowledge of stage-craft as yet rudimentary. None the less, the germ of the whole Beaumont-and-Fletcher drama is to be traced in this lax and luxurious mixture of poetry and farce.

In 1608 Fletcher is believed to have made his first essay in authorship with the pastoral tragi-comedy of *The Faithful Shepherdess*, which is admitted to be, from the purely poetical point of view, one of the best, if not the very best thing of its kind in English. There is no reason to suppose that at this point he had begun to combine with Beaumont, and this poem has all the air of being Fletcher's unaided composition, in spite of a phrase of Jonson's to Drummond. *The Faithful Shepherdess* was an attempt to introduce into English literature the art of Tasso and Guarini. It is an artificial and exotic piece, of little dramatic propriety, and even when it was originally produced, it made the audience angry by its substitution of *renaissance* fancies for "Whitsun-ales, cream, wassail and morris-dances." It is an excursion into the very fairyland of imagination; but, unfortunately, Fletcher carries with him the grossness and the moral perversity which were his most unfortunate characteristics, and his wanton shepherdesses are scandalously indifferent to decorum. On the other hand, no work of the period abounds with finer lyrical beauties, truer touches of sympathy with nature, or more artfully artless turns of exquisite language. . . .

The famous partnership of Beaumont and Fletcher began about 1608, and lasted until 1611. During this brief period they wrote ten or eleven of the plays which still exist, and without doubt not a few of their productions are lost. In 1608[1]

they brought out on the stage *Four Plays in One, Love's Cure*, and probably *A King and No King*. In 1609 *The Scornful Lady*; in 1610 *The Knight of the Burning Pestle, The Coxcomb, Cupid's Revenge* and *Philaster*; in 1611 *The Two Noble Kinsmen*, in which Shakespeare may have collaborated, *The Maid's Tragedy*, and perhaps *Love's Pilgrimage*. In 1611 Beaumont, who seems to have always shrunk from the rough publicity of the stage, made up his mind to retire from play-writing; he had never allowed his name to appear on a title-page. He probably married Ursula Isley at this time, and withdrew to the country. Perhaps his health began to fail; at all events, on the 6th of March, 1616, at the early age of thirty-one, he died, and was buried, three days later, in Westminster Abbey.

It is in the plays which have just been mentioned that the peculiar qualities of the two playwrights are seen to the best advantage. In later years, whether alone, or in collaboration with others, Fletcher produced many very fine works, but they scarcely have the charm of those which he wrote with Beaumont. When the posthumous editor of 1647 came to arrange the dramas, he placed *The Maid's Tragedy* at the head, *Philaster* next to it, and *A King or No King* third. In these three plays, and in *The Knight of the Burning Pestle*, too, the hand of Beaumont appears to be paramount. There is, at least, very marked, a certain element which does not reappear after the retirement of Beaumont, and which may safely be attributed to that writer.

The seventeenth century admired *The Maid's Tragedy* to excess, and it is true that it is full of poetry which it would be hardly possible to overpraise, a poetry which is more delicate, more spontaneous than the declamatory genius of Fletcher could produce unaided. . . .

The plot of *The Maid's Tragedy*, the only play of Beaumont and Fletcher's which has been revived on the modern stage, is gross, painful, and improbable. Yet there is tragic interest in the distressing relation of Evadne and Amintor; while in the fifth act, where Evadne kills the king, a certain moral altitude of horror, unusual with these poets is distinctly reached. In almost every way, for good and ill, *The Maid's Tragedy* is a characteristic specimen of their theatre.

Modern taste prefers *Philaster*, in many ways an enchanting performance. The beauty of the imagery and the melody of the language here become something veritably astonishing. Nothing in Jacobean poetry outside Shakespeare is more charming than the sweet companionship, in the second act, of Philaster and the boy-maiden, Bellario-Eufrasia. . . .

Bellario's final speech to the king sums up the essence of the play, and explains the prettiest of those rather awkward disguises of boys as girls and girls as boys, in which Sidney and Shakespeare had indulged, but which Beaumont and Fletcher observed in a positive extravagance. Stronger than either of these graceful romances, is the tragi-comedy of *A King and No King*, which sacrifices force less to sweetness than is usual with its authors, and proceeds with great spirit. Arbaces, a finely designed character, moves the accomplished type of a vaunting egotist, the man who is unshaken in the belief in himself. Magnanimous as well as braggart, there is a life-like variety in Arbaces more attractive than the too-Jonsonian figure of Bessus, whose almost professional cowardice is so incessant as to grow tiresome.

Other plays of this first and greatest period which demand a special word are *The Knight of the Burning Pestle*, with its extremely early proof of the popularity of Cervantes; *Four Plays in One*, two by Beaumont and two by Fletcher, which seems to represent their first efforts at combined authorship; *Love's Cure*, a rattling, vigorous comedy of Seville manners, in which Lucio, a lad brought up as a girl, is contrasted with Clara, the martial maid, who dreams herself a man—Love curing them both, and bringing both back to nature; the sparkling English comedy of *The Scornful Lady*, with its domestic scenes; and *The Two Noble Kinsmen*, a stirring but ill-constructed dramatization of Chaucer, to which the shadow of the name of Shakespeare, and a certain indisputable strength in the first act, have directed a somewhat exaggerated amount of attention. . . .

Whether Beaumont withdrew entirely in 1611, or lingered on until 1613, his influence seems to be very slight in the second period of the collaborated plays. Fletcher may have used hints supplied by his friend, but in the main the plays of the last years of Beaumont's life seem to be exclusively Fletcher's. In 1612 he probably brought out *The Captain*. In 1613 *The Honest Man's Fortune* and *The Nice Valour*. In 1614 *The Night-Walker*, *Wit without Money*, *The Woman's Prize*, and *The Faithful Friend*. In 1615 *The Chances*. In 1616 *Bonduca*, *Valentinian*, and *The Bloody Brother*. In 1617 *The Knight of Malta* and *The Queen of Corinth*. In 1618 *The Mad Lover*, *The Loyal Subject*, and *The Humourous Lieutenant*. Of these sixteen plays there is not one which can be said to be so important, either poetically or dramatically, as several of the preceding series, nor did Fletcher fail, at a subsequent time, to rise to greater heights. The decline is so abrupt at first as to mark almost beyond question the sudden weakness produced by the withdrawal of Beaumont; Fletcher learned gradually, but not without difficulty, to stand alone. Here are one or two good tragedies—*Bonduca*, *The Bloody Brother*—but not a single comedy, unless it be *The Chances*, which can be ranked among the best of Fletcher's. Aubrey's phrase, repeated from Earle, that Beaumont's "main business was to correct the overflowings of Mr. Fletcher's wit," has often been quoted; but, in the presence of the phenomenon before us, it cannot be credited. Something very much more positive than a mere critical exercise of judgment was removed when Beaumont ceased to write, and the versification alone is enough to assure us of the abundance of his actual contributions. The prose-scenes in the plays of the earliest period were undoubtedly Beaumont's, and they testify to a vein of fancy very different from Fletcher's. It is noticeable, however, that this group of imperfect plays contains almost all Fletcher's most exquisite and imperishable songs.

In *Bonduca*, a romance of Roman Britain, Fletcher composed a tragedy which only just missed greatness, in the manner of Shakespeare. The patriot queen is well contrasted with the soldierly graces of Caratach. *The Bloody Brother* was greatly admired throughout the seventeenth century; Dryden described it as the only English tragedy "whose plot has that uniformity and unity of design in it which I have commended in the French," but to a modern taste it seems crude and harsh. *Valentinian*, another early favourite, told the story of Nero under the guise of new names and intrigues. This class of tragedies revealed the existence of masculine qualities of writing in Fletcher, and were composed with spirit and fervour. He was, however, to attain greater sureness of execution, and the plots of these melodramas display the results of haste and want of judgment. The individual speeches, and some scenes, possess great beauty; the general texture is improbable and disagreeable. The comedies of this group are marked by a sort of frenzied gaiety which is almost delirious, and which too frequently degenerates into horseplay. They seem all farce and whimsies, decked out, to be sure, in laces and ribands of very pretty poetry, but essentially volatile.

At the very moment when we become certain that the judgment of Beaumont was completely withdrawn from cen-

suring the productions of his friend, we are aware that another talent is summoned to Fletcher's assistance. About 1619 Philip Massinger, an Oxford man of mature years, adopted the profession of dramatist, and began to work in conjunction with Fletcher. The circumstances of his life will be dealt with in a later chapter, when we come to treat his independent work. It is certain that at first he aimed at nothing more ambitious than the alteration and the completion of the plays of others. His collaboration seems not merely to have been welcome to Fletcher, but extremely stimulating, and for two years he and Massinger wrote with great assiduity a group of plays which appear in the so-called Beaumont-and-Fletcher collection. The main plays of this conjectural third group (1619–20) are *Sir John van Olden Barnaveldt*, *The Laws of Candy*, *The Custom of the Country*, *The Double Marriage*, *The Little French Lawyer*, *The False One*, *Women Pleased*, and *A Very Woman*. Of these there is little to be said for the five first, in which Fletcher strikes us as careless and Massinger still timid. The three last deserve separate attention.

In *The False One*, which deals with the familiar story of Antony and Cleopatra, the oratorical poetry of Fletcher rises to its sublimest altitude. The action of the piece is slow, and we are constantly tempted to regret Shakespeare's magnificent evolution. But of the grasp of character, the elevated conception of the principal figures, and the charm of broad and melodious poetry thrown like antique raiment about them, there can be no two opinions. *Women Pleased*, though the scene is laid in Florence, is a comedy of contemporary English life, full of agreeable humours. Bomby, the Puritan, who dances to "the pipe of persecution," and tries to stop the morris-dances, is a delightful creation, and is not too mechanically insisted on. The whole of the fourth act is very poetically conceived. *A Very Woman* is now more commonly treated as mainly the work of Massinger.

According to Mr. Fleay's computation, the arrangement between Fletcher and Massinger was abruptly suspended from September, 1620, till March, 1622. If this be so, we may with a certain plausibility name a series of plays as having been written in those months by Fletcher unaided. These are *Monsieur Thomas*, *Thierry and Theodoret*, *The Island Princess*, *The Pilgrim*, and *The Wild Goose Chase*. It appears, at all events, that no hand but Fletcher's was at work on these five plays, and they are of so high an excellence as to make us regret that his haste or his idleness led him so often to lean upon others, instead of trusting to his own admirable resources. *Thierry and Theodoret* is commonly admitted to be the best of Fletcher's tragedies. The childless King of France, who is warned to slay the first woman whom he meets proceeding at sunrise from the temple of Diana, is confronted with the veiled figure of his own beloved wife, Ordella. This Lamb considered to be the finest scene in Fletcher, and Ordella his "most perfect idea of the female heroic character." *The Wild Goose Chase*, in like manner, is one of the brightest and most coherent of Fletcher's comedies, a play which it is impossible to read and not be in a good humour. The central incident of *Monsieur Thomas*, a middle-class Don Juan brought to summary justice, is too gross for modern readers; but the play is admirably worked out as a comical conception, and adorned with a bevy of pleasing and indignant girls.

The final group of the plays which are commonly bound up together as the works of Beaumont and Fletcher is the most difficult to arrange and appreciate. Massinger may have returned to Fletcher in 1622, and may have been concerned that year in *The Prophetess*, *The Sea Voyage*, *The Spanish Curate*, and *The Beggar's Bush*. Of these the last alone is important; it is a very odd play, full of curious and fantastic stuff, and has had warm admirers. Coleridge said of *The Beggar's Bush*, "I could read it from morning to night; how sylvan and sunshiny it is!" It is a Flemish comedy, in which the ragged regiment are introduced using their cant phrases and discovering their cozening tricks. In 1623 Fletcher seems to have joined with some one who was not Massinger, but whom it would be hazardous to name with certainty, in writing *Wit at Several Weapons* and *The Maid of the Mill*, the first an English, and the second a Spanish comedy, trembling on the borderland of farce.

At this point the career of Fletcher becomes indistinct to us, but it is very interesting to observe that his genius seems to have deepened and brightened to the last, for his very latest plays, probably produced in 1624, are second to nothing of the same kind written through the long course of his career. These are the comedies of *A Wife for a Month*, and *Rule a Wife and Have a Wife*. These are much less farcical than the comic pieces which had preceded them, and rest on a solid basis of invention. When the poet composed *Rule a Wife and Have a Wife*, he must have been worn with a career of persistent and laborious invention, yet nowhere in the mass of his voluminous writings is the wit more fresh, the language more exquisite, elastic, and unexpected, or the evolution of character more delicate.

We may be permitted to hope that his anxieties were relaxed for some months before his death. But all we know is what Aubrey has retailed, that Fletcher died of the plague on the 19th of August, 1625, and that, "staying for a suit of clothes before he retired into the country, Death stopped his journey and laid him low." He was buried in the Church of St. Saviour's, Southwark, in a grave which was opened fourteen years later to receive Philip Massinger. The epitaph of Sir Aston Cockayne relates that—

Plays they did write together, were great friends,
And now one grave includes them in their ends;
Two whom on earth nothing could part, beneath
Here in their fame they live, in spite of death.

Aubrey relates of Beaumont and Fletcher that "they lived together on the Bankside, not far from the playhouse, both bachelors, had the same clothes, cloak, etc. between them." Fuller tells a story of their joint composition, probably in some tavern, and the ejaculation, "I'll kill the king," being overheard and mistaken for high treason against James I.

The aims which actuated Beaumont and Fletcher were so lofty, and their actual performance so huge in extent, and uniformly ambitious in effort, that we are bound to judge them by no standard less exacting than the highest. Their resolute intention was to conquer a place in the very forefront of English literature, and for a time they seemed unquestionably to have succeeded in so doing. For a generation after the death of Fletcher, it might reasonably be mooted whether any British writer of poetry had excelled them. After the Restoration, although their popularity continued, their reputation with the critics began to decline, and no one will again name them with poets of the first class. They take, and will retain, an honourable position in the second rank, but in the first they can never again be placed. The conditions of their time seriously affected them. The highest point of poetic elevation had been reached, and the age, brilliant as it was, was one of decadence. It would have been possible to Beaumont and Fletcher—as still later on, when the incline was still more rapid, it yet was to Milton—to resist the elements of decay, to be pertinaciously distinguished, austere, and noble. But they had not enough strength of purpose for this; they gave way to the stream, and

were carried down it, contenting themselves with flinging on it, from full hands, profuse showers of lyrical blossoms. They had to deal with a public which had cultivated a taste for the drama, and liked it coarse, bustling, and crude. They made it their business to please this public, not to teach or lead it, and the consequence was that they sacrificed to the whimsies of the pit all the proprieties, intellectual, moral, and theatrical.

It is a testimony to the talents of Beaumont and Fletcher that we do not compare them with any one but Shakespeare. Yet this is a test which they endure with difficulty. There are many scenes in which the superficial resemblance is so striking that we cannot hesitate to suppose that they were writing in conscious rivalry with their greatest contemporary. But it would be hard to point to a single instance in which he had not a complete advantage over them. They move too suddenly or too slowly, they are too fantastic for nature, or too flat for art, they are "making up," while he seems simply painting straight from the heart. It may perhaps be said, without injustice to Beaumont and Fletcher, that they differ from Shakespeare in this, that he is true throughout, and in relation to all the parts of the piece, while they are satisfied if they are true in isolated instances. Their single studies of a passion are often just and valuable in themselves, but they are almost always false to the combination in which the poets place them. What could be fairer or more genuine than the virtuous enthusiasm of Leucippus, what more unnatural and ridiculous in relation to the other personages which animate the tragedy of *Cupid's Revenge?*

The great twin-brethren of Jacobean poetry have many tricks which sink into conventions, and soon cease to please us. The incessant masquerade of girls as men, and boys as maidens, is one of them; we are fortunate when the girl disguised as a man (and, of course, acted, in those days, by a boy), does not assume a still further disguise as a woman. Beaumont and Fletcher's violent statement of moral problems which they have not the imagination nor the knowledge of the heart needful to unravel is a constant source of weakness; the looseness of their desultory plots, their hasty scheme in which, as Hazlitt has said, "everything seems in a state of fermentation and effervescence," their brazen recommendation of purely sensuous forces, their terrible facility and carelessness—all these are qualities which hold them back when they attempt the highest things, and it is sadly true that these eminent poets and all-accomplished playwrights have not left a single play which can be called first-rate.

If, however, Beaumont and Fletcher are severely judged at the strictest literary tribunal, they are none the less poets of an admirable excellence. Coleridge wished that they had written none but non-dramatic poetry, an expression, no doubt, of his sense of the beauty and propriety of their serious verse as compared with the meretricious rattle of what they designed to tickle the groundlings. It is not merely that their lyrics—their songs and masques and dirges—are so peculiarly exquisite, but that their soliloquies, for pure poetry, are unsurpassed in English dramatic literature. The poetry does not always seem in place, nor does it aid the evolution of the scenes, but in itself, in its relaxed and palpitating beauty, its sweetness of the hothouse, it is a delicious thing. The germs of the ruin of English prosody, of the degeneracy of English fancy, are in it, and they soon begin to fructify, but in the meantime the perfumed exotic is charming. Few dramatists can be quoted from with so much effect as Beaumont and Fletcher, or in that form are more enticing, or excite curiosity more acutely. The air they breathe is warm and musky, their star is "Venus, laughing with appeased desire," to young readers they appear divinely satisfying and romantically perfect. But deeper study does not further endear them, and the adult reader turns from them, with regret, to cultivate sterner and purer students of the heart. They are not quiet enough; we weary of their incessant "tibia orichalco vincta," and turn to simpler and serener masters. Yet even in their noisiness and their turbidity they were children of their age, and, when all is said, they were of the brood of the giants.

Notes

1. The conjectural arrangement so ingeniously worked out by Mr. Fleay is here in the main adopted.

ALGERNON CHARLES SWINBURNE
"The Earlier Plays of Beaumont and Fletcher" (1910)
Contemporaries of Shakespeare
eds. Edmund Gosse and Thomas James Wise
1919, pp. 145–65

For any man born only a little lesser than the greatest, a little lower than the angels or the gods of song, it is the heaviest and most enduring of all conceivable misfortunes to have been rated for a time among them if not above them. That a Jephson or a Tate, a Cibber or an Ibsen, should for a moment be compared or preferred to Shakespeare by any howling dervish or laughing jackass of letters is a matter of no moment: that men of genius should ever have been thrust forward as claimants for so ridiculous a promotion is only too certain to impair or to imperil, it may be for only too many generations, the recognition of their genuine claims to honour. That typical Oxonicule, the Rev. William Cartwright, "the most florid and seraphical preacher in the university," not only damned himself to everlasting fame, but did what in him lay to damn the reputation of Fletcher by assuring his departed spirit that "Shakespeare to thee was dull," obscene, inartistic, and scurrilous: dull as compared to the author of *The Nice Valour*, obscene as compared to the author of *The Custom of the Country*, inartistic as compared to the author of *The Sea Voyage*, and scurrilous as compared to the author of *The Scornful Lady*. The criticism is worthy of Matthew Arnold: and even he could not have surpassed it in perversity of cultivated impertinence and audacity of self-erratic conceit. But time has always done justice, when time was needed to do justice, on the academic aberrations of complacent incompetence and overweening culture. It is of far more importance that justice should be done to the victims of their admiration. To be dispraised is nothing: to be mispraised may be dangerous. Justice has never been done to Beaumont and Fletcher since the days in which their work was set up against Shakespeare's. It is time to consider so rich and various a treasure as they have bequeathed us without consideration or recollection of the fact that their garnets were once preferred to Shakespeare's rubies, their pearls to his diamonds. No other dramatic treasury can boast of so magnificent a display in quantity, in quality, and in variety of jewels.

It must be allowed that no expert in gems would have given much for the first sample of their workshop. The generous and cordial friendship of Ben Jonson could hardly have applauded so crude and juvenile a study in his school of comedy as *The Woman-Hater*. It is readable, absurd, and amusing: I cannot think that much more can be said for it. The rather dreary and mouldy Spanish tradition of jocularity on the subject of hunger and gluttony revives here in a final renaissance of farcical effect which may charitably be found not altogether unworthy of a tolerant rather than of a sympathetic smile: but the protagonist is a mere monomaniac, and the heroine is too eccentric to pass muster except as a type of the very newest and oldest of new women whom we may meet in the pages of Aristophanes or the columns of the *Times*.

In the tragedy of *Theirry and Theodoret* a new touch is felt—a new voice is audible. There is here no trace of Jonson's influence; nor is there any sign of Shakespeare's except in so far as we may say that all subsequent good work in tragedy must inevitably bear witness to the effect of Marlowe's example and of his. For this is good work, as well as new: the impetuous and continuous rush of the fluent and fervent verse is only the outward and visible sign of the inward and spiritual ardour, headlong and heedless of reflection or restraint, which impels the writer's genius along its passionate and breathless course. Even if, as has been plausibly suggested, the staider and less vehement hand of Massinger may here and there be traced, this play is on the whole about the finest and the fullest evidence left us of Fletcher's magnificent but far from supreme power as a tragic poet. The men are nothing: at least they are but rough and rudely coloured sketches. The abnormal wickedness of Brunhalt, the abnormal goodness of Ordella, give all the life and interest to the tragic action that readers can ever find in it or that spectators ever can have found. It is not quite human life: for the interest excited is hardly in human nature. But, such as it is, the interest is unflaggingly sustained, and the style is as admirable in its impulsive fashion as is the style of Marlowe and Shakespeare and Webster in the nobler and more serious manner appropriate to higher and sincerer inspiration.

Something more of such inspiration is perceptible in Philaster: and yet, leaving Shakespeare out of the question, we find here no figures comparable for creative power and living truth to Faustus and Edward, to Vittoria and Bracciano, the Duchess and her brothers. The boyish or feminine incapacity to draw even in outline, to paint even in monochrome, the likeness of a man, which is here so unmistakably displayed, was evidently no evidence of inferior power, no reason for inferior regard, in the estimate of contemporary admiration. Among all their tragic or serious heroes we may look in vain for the lifelike figure of a conceivable and acceptable man. A gallant and roistering humorist they could paint better and more delightfully, with more contagious sympathy and more audacious truth, than even the great Dumas himself; but the finest type of heroic manhood imaginable by either is a knight of Malta; an Origen in armour; a hero who renounces manhood. Philaster is something worse: he is hardly the shadow, the phantom, the wraith of a living man. The she-page Bellario is simply the loveliest and most interesting of all dramatic hermaphrodites from Shakespeare's Viola down to Wycherley's Fidelia: it is curious and significant that Beaumont and Fletcher could never create a man or a woman so attractive as this fantastic and pathetic figure, whose unquestionable and inimitable charm of perfect purity and more than manly womanhood threw so strange a fascination over the stage that it was a less outrageously than pardonably extravagant exaggeration of the truth which Lamb allowed himself in the assertion that "for many years after the date of Philaster's first exhibition on the stage scarce a play can be found without one of these women pages in it." Certainly, as he adds, "our ancestors seem to have been wonderfully delighted with these transformations of sex." But after all it must be admitted that the vital and enduring fascination of this beautiful and famous play depends less on character or on incident than on the exquisite and living loveliness of the style—most attractive when least realistic, most memorable when least dramatic.

The authors of *The Maid's Tragedy* succeeded in showing themselves at all points superior to the authors of *Philaster*. Their poetic power is equal in charm and more perfectly adapted or subordinated to the demands of dramatic art, the laws of theatrical evolution or construction. That they could not draw even in outline the figure of a man—that a protagonist of heroic mould, such as Marlowe's Faustus or Webster's Virginius, was not only unpresentable, but inconceivable by the purely passionate and impulsive nature of their tragic genius—this masterpiece would suffice to prove, even without the evidence of their later tragedies. The heroes, or rather the passive and the braggart figures of manhood proposed for our acceptance as the heroes of the play, are not above the rather lamentable level of Philaster. But the sinners are better than their elders; Pharamond and his Megra are little more than the sketches of a hot-blooded and headlong boy if set against the vivid, vigorous outlines of Evadne and her king. Yet, exquisite though it is as a poem, this famous tragedy is the first example of an English play in which all other considerations are subordinate to the imperious demands, the dominant exactions, of stage effect. Evadne is the one thoroughly credible and thoroughly realized figure in the play: a bad woman who might not have made so bad a man. Of the two heroes it can only be further said that Amintor is abject and Melantius absurd: the king is now and then as theatrical in villainy as they are in virtue, and Aspatia is not so much a woman as a mouthpiece and a subject for poetry incomparable in its kind. Shakespeare and Webster did not find it necessary and did not feel impelled to make their heroines talk so lyrically and evoke from other and minor figures such effusion of elegiac eloquence. In the earlier scenes she says now and then something that could not have been bettered by Webster or even by Shakespeare: but she never has enough of life and truth in her to stand beside "one of Shakespeare's women"—or of Webster's.

That Fletcher or any of his friends should have thought it probable or possible for *The Faithful Shepherdess* to find favour on the stage is the most wonderful and unimaginable witness we could have to the delight of an English audience in pure and absolute poetry throughout the age of Shakespeare—during the generation that reaches from the sunrise of Marlowe to the sunset of Shirley. That the loveliest of all pastoral plays ever set by fancy in the frame of a fantastic Arcadia should have evoked by its failure such noble tributes of indignant admiration from contemporary poets is an accident which may well be held worthy of rejoicing and thanksgiving by all who believe that sympathy and gratitude rather than defamation and envy are natural to all men not utterly ignoble and all competitors not utterly incompetent. The difference between this poem and Milton's exquisitely imitative *Comus* is the difference between a rose with a leaf or two faded or falling, but still fragrant and radiant, and the faultless but scentless reproduction of a rose in academic wax for the admiration and imitation of such craftsmen as must confine their ambition to the laurels of a college or the plaudits of a school. The figures who play their parts on the woodland stage of this fairyland theatre are hardly amenable to criticism as actual or possible men and women. The lover whose love is curable by compliance and destructible by the destruction of his idol's ideal inaccessibility would be absurdly misplaced in the world of comedy or tragedy: in the world of fancy, a world made up of poetic artifice and tradition, he is a perfectly appropriate and coherent figure, native to his fantastic element. To the same world the constant Clorin and the wanton Cloe so unmistakably belong that the serious application of an ethical standard to their conduct or their characters is as inept as a poet's objection to the unimaginative

realism of mathematics or a mathematician's to the sterile impotence of poetry if applied to the proof of a theorem or the solution of a problem. The most exquisitely appreciative and the most nearly infallible of critics fell surely for once into inconsistent partiality and untenable paradox when he objected to the contrast of the lascivious with the virginal shepherdess on the score that "such weeds by juxtaposition do not set off but kill sweet flowers," and defended the outrageous obscenities of *The Virgin Martyr* on the plea that they "have a strength of contrast, a raciness and a glow in them which set off the religion of the rest, somehow as Caliban serves to show Miranda." Such dunghill weeds as those were never planted or watered by Fletcher.

It is curious from the historic or literary point of view that the first burlesque ever presented on our stage should still be so very much the best. *The Knight of the Burning Pestle* is at least as superior to *The Rehearsal* at all points as the fifth act of *The Chances* substituted by the author of *The Rehearsal* for Fletcher's original fifth act is superior in dramatic force, character, and humour to that hasty and headlong scrawl of a sketch. The seemingly incongruous interfusion of serious and sometimes noble poetry might have been expected to destroy the broad comic effect of parody and raillery which it actually heightens. The good old city poet whose Cockney heroics it made no unkindly fun of, and whose homely power of pathetic realism was a quality altogether beyond the reach of Beaumont or of Fletcher, might have smiled without wincing at so good-humoured and hurtless a caricature of his counter-jumping paladins.

In theatrical magnificence of incident and effect *A King and No King* is as supreme a triumph as is *Othello* or *King Lear* in poetic sublimity and spiritual intensity of truth made manifest and awful in beauty as in terror to all ages of mankind. To say that there is nothing more in it would be shamefully and stupidly false: there is much beautiful writing and much brilliant vivacity of charm. But all serious study of character, all rational or moral evolution of conduct, is wantonly if not shamelessly sacrificed to the immediate effect of vehement if not sometimes galvanic sensation or surprise. The outrages on human possibility in the parts of Gobrias and Arane, the magnanimous murderess in design and the virtuous promoter of a supposedly incestuous passion, would have been impossible to any other poet and even to any other playwright of genius in any way comparable either with Beaumont or with Fletcher. That any soldier king was ever such a blatant braggart and swaggering swashbuckler as Arbaces might surely have been questioned, as now perhaps it may not be, in the days of the poets who decked out his crazy and feather-headed vanity with the splendid plumage of rhetorical rhapsody which, as Macaulay long since observed, so singularly anticipates the discoveries of modern mechanism.

The peculiar boyishness which distinguishes alike the tragic and the comic genius of Beaumont and Fletcher, but more especially the tragic work of Fletcher and the comic work of Beaumont, displays itself most amusingly in the once-famous parts of the three beaten braggarts which in their day were classed with the incomparable figure of Bobadil. The far from subtle or exquisite humour of kicking and cudgelling may have been caught from the example of their illustrious friend and occasional model, Ben Jonson: but the lightness of touch, the buoyancy of burlesque, must be allowed to give it a tone of contagious pleasantry which the heavier hand of the more serious artist has not given and perhaps did not care to give. The veriest horse-play of farce in the broadest scenes of Beaumont and Fletcher has more of good-humour and harmless or, anyhow, spiteless merriment than is to be looked for in the elaborate and deliberate brutality of such an unsavoury masterpiece as *The Silent Woman*.

The eccentric tragedy of *Cupid's Revenge* has always been a butt for the shafts of sarcasm rather than criticism. It is certainly somewhat grotesque and amorphous if not abnormal; we cannot be surprised that both Campbell and Dyce should have dismissed it with a bitter word of scorn. But a far greater than they or than any other critic of our great dramatic poets has not only embalmed its noblest passages in the deathless amber of a priceless volume, but has selected it for the supreme honour of a condensed rendering into narrative prose after the fashion of his incomparable *Tales from Shakespeare*. The rough and ready improvisation which reduces to a far lower level all the huddled and headlong later part of the play is as evidently due to enforced haste or natural weariness of the work in hand as is the inferiority of the latter part of Marlowe's *Jew of Malta* to the magnificent beauty and power of its opening scenes. To imagine in either or in any such case the necessary or the probable intervention or intrusion of a foreign hand and a feebler touch is a facile and uncritical evasion rather than explanation of a problem suggested by the naturally inevitable inequality of the finished parts with the hurried parts of even a great writer's work, when casually compelled to write against time for the stage or for any other pulpit or tribune required for the utterance of whatever he has to say. But no pantomimic absurdity in the opening and no convulsive debility in the closing scenes of the play can efface or should be allowed to affect the impression of the two scenes between Leucippus and his mistress before and after his chivalrous and mendacious affirmation of her virtue has resulted, during his absence at the seat of war, in her marriage with his father: a situation treated with characteristic frankness, but handled with exceptional delicacy. It may be remembered that Mr. Samuel Pepys, on August 17, 1668, "saw *Cupid's Revenge*, under the new name of *Love Despised*, that hath something very good in it, though I like not the whole body of it." The somewhat eccentric judge who preferred Tuke as a dramatic poet to Shakespeare at his very highest was on this occasion exactly and excellently right. He and Lamb ("Powers eternal! such names mingled!") have alone been just in their expressed or implied judgment of this otherwise unlucky play.

There are some pretty lines thrown away here and there on the not very brilliant masque in celebration of the ill-omened nuptials of Prince Rupert's illstarred mother; but Beaumont would perhaps have done as well to leave such work to the stronger and more inventive hand of his friend Ben Jonson, whose influence for good and evil, or at least for better and for worse, is evident in Beaumont's part of the *Four Plays in One*, which we must regret to remember as the only surviving example of a form of dramatic entertainment to which a horrible as well as terrible little work of relentless and realistic genius never to be unquestioningly rejected from the Shakespearean Apocrypha must pretty certainly be admitted to belong. From what context of companion plays or playlets such an inhuman or at least such a merciless masterpiece of condensed and concentrated horror as *A Yorkshire Tragedy* can have been detached by its publisher or its author, no imaginable student above the lowest level of brainless and frontless duncery will care or will presume to conjecture. In the present unique instance it would not be difficult for the youngest possible reader of average intelligence to distinguish and to determine the parts assignable to Beaumont from the parts assignable to Fletcher. The Jonsonian induction is Beaumont's: he was never worse employed than in imitation of his great friend Ben: *exemplar vitiis imitabile* if ever there was one. No one but a poet born could have written *The Triumph of Honour*, though he could only have written it during a transitory eclipse or collapse of his better powers; no one but an imitator of Ben Jonson when least happily inspired could have scribbled the farcical part of it. *The Triumph of Love* should have been a beautiful and pathetic play instead of a beautiful and pathetic sketch: but as it is we must gladly acknowledge that one lovely scene in it has been overpraised neither by Charles Lamb nor by Leigh Hunt. *The Triumph of Death*, in which there certainly is no suggestion of loveliness or pathos, is a superb example of Fletcher's vehement and fervent, though neither gentle nor sublime, genius for passionate and headlong tragedy. *The Triumph of Time* is a survival of the unfittest—a revival of the obsolete morality play, not improved by a dash of the contemporary masque. It is by no means worthless: but its author would probably have been the first to admit that it was not worth very much.

The noble and cordial verses in which Ben Jonson expressed the fervour of his love for a younger friend who had shown such religious devotion towards him should be borne in mind by the reader who cannot but think that the "religion" so affectionately acknowledged and so generously requited did not bring forth any very sweet or savory fruit in the rather too Jonsonian comedy of *The Scornful Lady*. In all the curious and interesting history of opinion—or moral and intellectual change and progress and reaction—there is nothing more singular than the variations of view among intelligent and honourable men as to decency and indecency, morality and immorality. It must surely be now incomprehensible to any student of letters or of ethics that so unquestionably good and true a man as Dr. Johnson should have denounced the noble and natural story of *Tom Jones* as a "corrupt" book, and agreed with the clergy of his day in commending to decent readers the infamous and abominable story of *Pamela*. If the one is sometimes blunt, the other is always vile. *The Scornful Lady* is, of course, not so ignoble and impure an abortion of immorality as Richardson's shamelessly shameful book; and in a rough way it is a vigorous and memorable example of the very broadest comedy: but alike in matter and in manner, in language and in character, it is undeniably the coarsest work of its authors. And yet it was so long held comparatively blameless that this particular discredit has generally been transferred to a far less offensive work of more graceful if still somewhat graceless audacity in treatment and in humour. Even Wycherley, if at his worst more basely and brutally immoral, was hardly more impudent in theatrical invention or device of daringly and undeniably comic effect.

The strange and straggling tragicomedy of *The Coxcomb* is as unadvisedly and as singularly misnamed from the idiotic protagonist of the uninterestingly extravagant underplot as is a far more memorable example of dramatic poetry, the masterpiece at once of Middleton and of Rowley which was somehow most absurdly misbaptized as *The Changeling*. In the gentle and devoted heroine of the more serious part there is a touch of simplicity and sweetness, in devotion and submission, of daring and of patience, which distinguishes her as a daughter of Beaumont's genius from the more vehement and voluble children of Fletcher's. Another play which is no less obviously a compound work, not less interesting and not less insufficient to satisfy a serious and grateful admirer of their sometimes rather idle and irregular genius, is *The Honest Man's Fortune*. The hero is a nobler and manlier type of manhood than any of Fletcher's when left to work by himself; but the movement and ease and spontaneity of the action in all but his very worst and hastiest and most puerile plays, if not even in those rather pitiful puerilities of invention and execution, will hardly be found in this more serious and ambitious poem. The two heroines are admirably sketched rather than admirably painted: but the simplicity and nobility of nature apparent and consistent in them both would be not less hard to find in the more theatrical and conventional heroines of Fletcher's later plays. There are noble passages and magnificent couplets in the little poem appended to this play: it would be difficult if not impossible to match them for moral dignity and for majesty of expression in any other work of Fletcher's: but few readers will probably agree with Leigh Hunt that they suffice to corroborate or to justify the expressed regret of Coleridge that Beaumont and Fletcher had not devoted their genius and their time to writing poems rather than to writing plays.

The ingrained and ineradicable juvenility of mind which distinguishes them from all other men of true and splendid genius is or should be at once apologetically and amusingly patent if not obvious to the readers of that admirably written comedy so childishly misnamed *The Captain*: misnamed from a Jonsonian figure of farce who is once happily humanized by generous sympathy and pity for the supposed sufferings of an elder soldier. The monstrous and abnormal criminality of the almost incredible heroine is more like the impudent fancy of a naughty boy than the corrupt imagination of a depraved man. But so bright and lively a piece of work would in common scholastic justice be set down so decidedly to the youngster's credit as to be deservedly set against the discredit if not the disgrace due to the juvenile audacity of his immature imagination. And the first scene of cajolery in which the woman's magnificent art of passionate hypocrisy is brought to bear upon a half-conscious and half-reluctant victim, a would-be dupe who cannot dupe himself, is finer than anything I know of the kind in prose or poetry before the advent of Balzac's almighty and ever-living Valérie. Madame Marneffe is as matchless as Madame de Merteuil: but the patrician or the plebian she-devil of immortal fiction might have given a smile of sympathy if not a hand of sisterhood to the hardly less terrible harlot of an English poet's invention.

In the magnificent melodrama or tragicomedy of *The Little French Lawyer*, it would be impossible to overpraise the brilliance of invention, the deftness of composition, or the splendour of execution: but the brutality of boyhood is as evident as its joyfulness. From any other hand the ruffianly insolence which derides the infirmity of a veteran hero in the public street would be unendurable and unpardonable; but here the merciless infidelity of the bride who has played false to her earlier and younger lover makes it intelligible if inexcusable. And here the incomparable and inimitable lightness of touch which impairs the tragic work and glorifies the comic work of Fletcher must be allowed by all intelligent or æsthetic judges to redeem the offence which would else be given to the moral or ethical critic of the superb result or outcome of his weakness and his strength—his inevitable limitations and his magnificent capacities. The juvenile horse-play of practical jokes which animates at once the serious comedy and the rampant farce of this dazzling and delightful poem, a poem in which no alloy of grave or of humorous prose can anywhere be found latent or apparent, contrives in some inexplicable if not inexcusable but bewitching if not irresistible fashion to succeed somehow in fusing them together with such instinctive alchemy of inspiration as to yield by way of product or result a deathless if not blameless masterpiece of comic poetry.

It is impossible to imagine that the author of this most brilliant and buoyant and high-spirited piece of work can have had anything to do, or that his even more glorious friend and compeer can have had anything to do, with one of the dullest and feeblest plays surviving—another survival of the unfittest—from the marvellous and matchless harvest of their time. The Apocrypha of the Scripture bequeathed to us by Beaumont and Fletcher may be more easily and more decisively tested and gauged and disposed of than the Apocrypha of Shakespeare's. That the bright and pleasant comedy of *The Widow* is Middleton's work alone will hardly be questioned by any reader whose time would not be better spent on even the most futile of employments or diversions than in the study of poetic or comic drama: and the most conscientious examination will only find in *The Faithful Friends* a passage or a verse here and there which may charitably be thought not quite bad enough for an old Sharpham or a new Shakespeare. It is perhaps not so utterly worthless and hopeless a failure as *Cupid's Whirligig* or *Thomas Lord Cromwell*. But it is sad stuff.

The riotous and outrageous farce of *Wit at Several Weapons* is such a play as might conceivably have been written in his nonage by a bastard son of Ben Jonson who had inherited more of the worse than of the better qualities, intellectual and moral, of his illustrious father. Even Ben, whose indignant humour so often concerned itself with crime, would hardly have introduced at the very opening of the action as a figure of pure comedy a veteran in villainy who boasts to his own son of his early successes as a professional pimp, and his later gains by the robbery and ruin of little children confided to his guardianship. This is the most seriously and odiously revolting passage in all the various and voluminous work of these great dramatic poets—or of any that I can remember among their fellows. And this comes of taking life and character too lightly and too stagily. The play is throughout a very slight and rather childish piece of work, with some touches in it of fun rather than of humour—unless there be humour in a schoolboy's pillow-fight. But the intended fun of the opening could only seem funny to an exceptionally ill-conditioned schoolboy. It is only fair to add that some of the heroine's tricks and shifts to rid herself of an idiot suitor and attract a hesitating lover are really not unworthy to remind the reader of Molière in his broader and rougher mood of practical pleasantry.

The genius of Beaumont and Fletcher for pure comedy was at its nadir in *Wit at Several Weapons*: in *Wit without Money* it rises easily and visibly to its radiant zenith. The matchless instinct of expression, the incomparable lightness of touch, which distinguishes its best work from all other triumphs of poetic comedy in the language, carries off and sweeps away all too curious or serious consideration of character or conduct. But, indeed, if the protagonist is a somewhat too extravagant figure of humorous extravagance when he joyously makes away with his brother's fortune as well as his own, the younger brother is so noble a fellow when he refuses to resent his ruin, or to forget the finer qualities of his reckless and rapacious elder, that this single figure should suffice to confute all charges ever brought against his creator or his twin creators on the score of immoral incompetence to conceive or to present a morally attractive and admirable young English hero. Even Shakespeare—to say nothing of Jonson, who in this race is quite out of the running—can show no other to be set beside him.[1]

The curious laxity with which educated and able men will fling about epithets when engaged in critical comment is rather singularly exemplified in the terms applied by Dyce as well as by Hallam to so magnificent a work of comic and tragic genius as *The Custom of the Country*. Dryden's previous attack on it as compared with his own dirty and greasy comedies and those of his brighter but not less unsavoury rivals may be dismissed with a brief expression of regret that so great a writer should have shown himself so small a critic—so stupidly shameless in misjudgment alike from the moral or ethical and from the intelligent or æsthetic point of view. "The very grossest" (as Mr. Dyce unhappily miscalls it) of all these plays is beyond all question *The Scornful Lady*. *The Custom of the Country* is certainly almost as audacious a comic poem as is even the alarmingly fearless and morally rather than immorally impudent *Lysistrata*: but coarse or obscene it is not. There is not a dirty word in it: not a touch, not a whiff, of Swiftian or Carlylesque impurity.

When some forgotten fool observed to Byron that Italian was an easy language, the supreme and final and unapproachable master of serio-comic poetry replied with unusual good sense and accuracy: "A very easy language to know badly; a very difficult language to know well." It would be no less easy to pass judgment on Fletcher as a tragic poet in a sweeping and summary fashion: it is certainly no less difficult to adjust the due balance of praise and blame, whether positive or comparative, which must determine the verdict to be passed on the admirable, though anything but impeccable, author of such tragedies as *Bonduca*, *Valentinian*, and *The Double Marriage*. Brilliant even to splendid, ardent even to satiety, they most indisputably are. That their somewhat hectic and feverish glory cannot endure a moment's comparison with the sunlight or the starlight of Shakespeare's, of Marlowe's, and of Webster's is anything but a reproach to a poet whose fame, if eclipsed, is not and can never be effaced by theirs.

The dazzling tragedy of *Bonduca* is half lit up by the flame of the footlights and half by the radiance of a magnificent if uncertain day. That it wanes and withers into the dusk of an autumnal sunset before the deathless dawn of Tennyson's almost Æschylean *Boadicea* can only be acknowledged as inevitable. That more than one or two of his contemporaries might have made out of the subject a far more perfect and a far sublimer poem is as certain as that none of them could have turned it to such triumphant account from the not ignobly theatrical point of view. But the reader of Fletcher's tragedies can never quite get away from the besetting sense of the theatre. In this instance the incongruous and excessive admixture or immixture of broad and not always brilliant comedy deforms and degrades the tragic beauty of the nobler scenes. The death scene is splendid and memorable: but while reading it we must not remember such another and more magnificent example of poetic tribute to the sacred and heroic virtue of suicide in face of shame as Marston had set in the immolation of his Sophonisba. The best by far of Fletcher's martial heroes is Caratach: and his nephew is a much finer and more natural youngster than Shakespeare's far less lifelike and lovable Arthur in *King John*: who would have made us reasonably doubt whether the omnipotent hand of his creator could have created a living little boy if it had not left us at a later date the incomparable and unapproachable and adorable figure of Mamillius.

Notes

1. Why Frank should be sometimes called Francisco is as insoluble a mystery as why the word "else," a word as necessary to the sense as to the metre, should have been persistently omitted by all editors in the penultimate scene of this comedy. "Do not allure me," says Valentine when secure of his bride. "Thou art no widow of this world (else)!" Without this obvious little word the line is immetrical nonsense.

SIR WALTER RALEGH

c. 1552–1618

Sir Walter Ralegh was born around 1552 at Hayes Barton in Devonshire. In 1569 he served in the Huguenot army in France. Surviving records list him among the students at Oriel College, Oxford, in 1572, and at Middle Temple in 1575; in 1577 he described himself as "at court." Ralegh later undertook several expeditions to America. A court favorite for many years, he was knighted by Elizabeth I in 1585.

Eventually, however, Ralegh's court position became jeopardized by his relationship with Elizabeth Throckmorton, whom he later married. He therefore left England to reside in Ireland, where he became friendly with Spenser. There he wrote the long elegy *Cynthia, the Lady of the Sea* in an attempt to regain Elizabeth's favor. Although he eventually returned to court, this poem remained unpublished and was presumed lost until the discovery of a fragment among the Hatfield MSS. in 1870. Ralegh's other literary endeavors include an introductory sonnet to the *Faerie Queene* and several prose works based on his travels such as the *Report of the Truth of the Fight about the Iles of the Açores this last sommer* (1591) and *Discovery of the large, rich and beautiful Empire of Guiana, with a relation of the great and golden city of Manoa* (1596).

Accused of conspiring against James I, Ralegh narrowly avoided a death sentence and was imprisoned in the Tower with his wife and son in 1603. During his imprisonment he is thought to have written the poems "The Lie" and "The Pilgrimage." *The History of the World*, planned as the first part of a longer work, was Ralegh's greatest literary undertaking, and was published in 1614. The first and ultimately only volume chronicles the ancient Jews and Egyptians as well as the history of Greek and Roman civilization before 130 B.C. A popular success, this book was printed in ten successive folio editions between 1614 and 1678.

After a failed expedition to South America in search of gold, Ralegh was arrested in connection with the destruction of a Spanish settlement, San Tomás. He was executed on October 29, 1618, and his remains were buried at St. Margaret's, Westminster.

Personal

Good Mr. Vice Chamberlaine;—As soon as I came on boarde the Carick on Wednesday at one of clock, with the rest of Her Majesty's commissioners, within one halfe houre Sir Walter Ralegh arrived with hys keper Mr. Blunt; I assure you, Sir, hys poore servants, to the number of 140 goodly men, and all the mariners, came to him with such shouts and joy as I never saw a man more troubled to quiet them in my life. But his hart is broken, for he is very extreamly pensive longer than he is busied, in w^h he can toil terribly. But if you dyd heare him rage at the spoiles, finding all the short wares utterly devoured, you would laugh, as I do w^h I can not choose. The meeting betweene him and Sir John Gilbert, was with teares on Sr John's part; and he, belike finding it is knowen he hath a keper, whensoever he is saluted with congratulations for liberty, he doth answer no, I am stylle ye Queen of England's poore captive. I wished him to conceale it, because here it diminisheth his credite, w^h I do vowe to you before God is greater amongst the mariners than I thoght for: I do grace him as much as I may, for I find him marveilously greedy to do any thing to recover ye conceit of his brutish offence.—ROBERT CECIL, Letter (Sept. 21, 1592)

I will prove you the notoriest Traitor that ever came to the bar. . . . Thou art a monster; thou hast an English face, but a Spanish heart. . . . We have to deal to-day with a man of wit. . . . Thou hast a Spanish heart, and thyself art a Spider of Hell.—SIR EDWARD COKE, Trial of Sir Walter Ralegh (1603), *Cobbee's Collection of State Trials*, Vol. 2, No. 74

For myself, I am left of all men that have done good to many. All my good turns forgotten; all my errors revived and expounded to all extremity of ill. All my services, hazards, and expenses for my country—plantings, discoveries, fights, councils, and whatsoever else—malice hath now covered over. I am now made an enemy and traitor by the word of an unworthy man. He hath proclaimed me to be a partaker of his vain imaginations, notwithstanding the whole course of my life hath approved the contrary, as my death shall approve it. Woe, woe, woe be unto him by whose falsehood we are lost. He hath separated us asunder. He hath slain my honor; my fortune. He hath robbed thee of thy husband, thy child of his father, and me of you both. O God! thou dost know my wrongs. Know, then, thou my wife, and child;—know, then, thou my Lord and King, that I ever thought them too honest to betray, and too good to conspire against.—SIR WALTER RALEGH, Letter to Lady Ralegh (1603)

I was commanded by the Lords of the Counsayle to be with him, both in prison and att his death, and so sett downe the manner of his death as nere as I could. . . . He was the most fearlesse of death that ever was knowen; and the most resolute and confident, yet with reverence and conscience. When I begann to incourage him against the feare of death, he seemed to make so light of itt, that I wondered att him, and when I told him, that the deare servants of God, in better causes than his, had shrunke backe and trembled a little, he denyed not, but yet gave God thankes, he never feared death, and much lesse then, for it was but an opinion and imagination; and the manner of death though to others might seem greevous, yet he had rather dye so then of a burning fever. . . . He was very cheerefull that morning he dyed, eate his breakfast hertily, and tooke tobacco, and made no more of his death, then if he had bene to take a journey, and left a great impression in the minds of those that beheld him, inasmuch that Sir Lewis Stukely and the French man grow very odious. This was the newes a weeke

since: but now it is blowen over, and he allmost forgotten—ROBERT TOUNSON, Letter to Sir John Isham (Nov. 9, 1618).

Sir Walter Ralegh had the favour to be beheaded at Westminster, where he died with great applause of the beholders, most constantly, most Christianly, most religiously.—JOHN PYM, *Memorable Accidents*, 1618

Sir Walter Raleigh ⟨was⟩ a man known and well deserving to be known; a man endued not with common endowments, being stored with the best of nature's furniture; taught much by much experience, experienced in both fortunes so feelingly and apparently, that it may truly be controverted whether he were more happy or miserable; yet behold in him the strange character of a mere man, a man subject to as many changes of resolution as resolute to be the instrument of change; politic, and yet in policy so unsteady, that his too much apprehension was the foil of his judgment.—JOHN FORD, A *Line of Life*, 1620

Sir Walter Rawleigh was one, that (it seems) Fortune had pickt out of purpose, of whom to make an example, or to use as her Tennis-Ball, thereby to shew what she could doe; for she tost him up of nothing, and too and fro to greatnesse, and from thence down to little more than to that wherein she found him, (a bare Gentleman). Not that he was lesse, for he was well descended, and of good alliance, but poor in his beginnings. . . .

He had in the outward man, a good presence, in a handsome and well compacted person, a strong naturall wit, and a better judgment, with a bold and plausible tongue, whereby he could set out his parts to the best advantage; and to these he had the adjuncts of some generall Learning, which by diligence he enforced to a great augmentation, and perfection; for he was an indefatigable Reader, whether by Sea or Land, and none of the least observers both of men and the times.—SIR ROBERT NAUNTON, *Fragmenta Regalia*, c. 1630

. . . ⟨C⟩oming to the Court, ⟨Ralegh⟩ found some hopes of the Queen's favours reflecting upon him. This made him write in a glasse window, obvious to the Queen's eye,—"Fain would I climb, yet fear I to fall." Her Majesty, either espying or being shown it, did under-write—"If thy heart fails thee, climb not at all." . . .

Captain Raleigh, coming out of Ireland to the English court in good habit (his cloaths being then a considerable part of his estate), found the Queen walking till meeting with a *plashy place*, she seemed to scruple going thereon. Presently Raleigh cast and spread his new plush cloak on the ground; whereon the Queen trod gently, rewarding him afterwards with many *suits*, for his so free and seasonable tender of so fair a *foot-cloath*. Thus an advantageous admission into the first notice of a Prince is more than half a degree to preferment.—THOMAS FULLER, *The History of the Worthies of England*, 1662

He was a tall, handsome and bold man; but his *naeve* was that he was damnable proud. Old Sir Robert Harley, of Brampton Brian Castle, who knew him, would say it was a great question who was the proudest, Sir Walter or Sir Thomas Overbury, but the difference that was, was judged on Sir Thomas's side. . . .

He had a most remarkeable aspect, an exceeding high forehead, long-faced and sour eie-lidded, a king of pigge-eie. His Beard turnd up naturally.

Old Sir Thomas Malett, one of the Justices of the King's bench *tempore Caroli I et II*, knew Sir Walter, and I have heard him say, that notwithstanding his so great Mastership in Style and his conversation with the learnedest and politest persons, yet he spake broad Devonshire to his dying day. His voice was small, as likewise were my schoolfellowes his grand-nephewes. . . .

In his youthful time was one Charles Chester, that often kept company with his acquaintance: he was a bold, impertenent fellowe, and they could never be at quiet for him; a perpetuall talker, and made a noyse like a drumme in a roome. So one time at a taverne, Sir W. R. beates him and seales up his mouth, i.e. his upper and neather beard, with hard wax. From him Ben Jonson takes his Carlo Buffono (i.e. Jester) in *Every Man out of his Humour*.

He loved a wench well; and one time getting up one of the Mayds of Honour up against a tree in a Wood ('twas his first Lady) who seemed at first boarding to be something fearfull of her Honour, and modest, she cryed, sweet Sir Walter, what doe you me ask? Will you undoe me? Nay, sweet Sir Walter! Sweet Sir Walter! Sir Walter! At last, as the danger and the pleasure at the same time grew higher, she cryed in the extasey, Swisser Swatter Swisser Swatter. She proved with child, and I doubt not but this Hero tooke care of them both, as also that the Product was more than an ordinary mortal.

My old friend James Harrington, Esq., was well acquainted with Sir Benjamin Ruddyer, who was an acquaintance of Sir Walter Raleigh's. He told Mr. J. H. that Sir Walter Raleigh, being invited to dinner with some great person, where his son was to goe with him; He sayd to his Son, Thou art such a quarrelsome, affronting creature that I am ashamed to have such a Beare in my Company. Mr. Walt humbled himselfe to his Father, and promised he would behave himselfe mightily mannerly. So away they went, and Sir Benjamin, I thinke, with them. He sate next to his Father and was very demure at leaste halfe dinner time. Then sayd he, I this morning, not having the feare of God before my eies, but by the instigation of the devill, went to a Whore. I was very eager of her, kissed and embraced her, and went to enjoy her, but she thrust me from her, and vowed I should not, *For your father lay with me but an hower ago*. Sir Walt, being so strangely supprized and putt out of his countenance at so great a Table, gives his son a damned blow over the face; his son, as rude as he was, would not strike his father, but strikes over the face of the Gentleman that sate next to him, and sayed, *Box about, 'twill come to my Father anon.. 'Tis now a common used Proverb. . . .*

He was such a person (every way) that (as King Charles I sayes of Lord Strafford) a prince would rather be afrayd of then ashamed of. He had that awfulness and ascendency in his Aspect over other mortalls. . . .

He was scandalised with Atheisme; but he was a bold man, and would venture at discourse which was unpleasant to the Church-men. I remember my Lord Scudamour sayd, 'twas basely sayd of Sir W. R. to talke of the Anagramme of Dog. In his speech on the Scaffold, I have heard my cosen Whitney say (and I thinke 'tis printed) that he spake not one word of Christ, but of the great and incomprehensible God, with much zeale and adoration, so that he concluded that he was an a-christ, not an atheist. . . .

A Scaffold was erected in the old Palace yard, upon which after 14 yeares reprivement, his head was cutt off: at which time, such abundance of bloud issued from his veines, that shewed he had stock of nature enough left to have continued him many yeares in life, though now above three score yeares old, if it had not been taken away by the hand of Violence. And this was the end of the great Sir Walter Raleigh: great sometimes in the favour of Queen Elizabeth, and next to Sir Francis Drake, the great Scourge and hate of the Spaniard, who had many things to be commended in his life, but none more than

his constancy at his death, which he tooke with so undaunted a resolution that one might perceive that he had a certain expectation of a better life after it, so far he was from holding those Atheisticall opinions, an Aspersion whereof some had cast upon him.

On the famous Sir Walter Rawleigh, who fell a Sacrifice to Spanish Politicks:

> Here lieth, hidden in this Pitt,
> The Wonder of the World for Witt.
> It to small purpose did him serve;
> His Witt could not his Life preserve.
> Hee living, was belov'd of none,
> Yet in his death all did him moane.
> Heaven hath his Soule, the world his Fame,
> The grave his Corps; Stukley his shame.

—JOHN AUBREY, "Sir Walter Raleigh," *Brief Lives*, 1669–96

He shone in the senate as a patriot, and the remains we have of his speeches, leave us in doubt which we ought most to admire, the beauty of his eloquence, or the strength of his understanding. . . .

In regard to his private life, a beneficent master, a kind husband, an affectionate father; and, in respect to the world, a warm friend, a pleasant companion, and a fine gentleman. In a word, he may be truly styled the English Xenophon; for no man of his age did things more worthy of being recorded, and no man was more able to record them than himself; insomuch, that we may say of him, as Scaliger did of Cæsar, "that he fought, and wrote, with the same inimitable spirit." And thus I take my leave of one, whom it is impossible to praise enough.—JOHN CAMPBELL, *History and Lives of the British Admirals*, 1742

He was accused by Cobham alone, in a sudden fit of passion, upon hearing that Raleigh, when examined, had pointed out some circumstances, by which Cobham's guilt might be known and ascertained. This accusation Cobham afterwards retracted; and soon after he retracted his retraction. Yet upon the written evidence of this single witness, a man of no honour or understanding, and so contradictory in his testimony, not confronted with Raleigh, not supported by any concurring circumstance, was that great man, contrary to all law and equity, found guilty by the jury. His name was at that time extremely odious in England; and every man was pleased to give sentence against the capital enemy of Essex, the favourite of the people.—DAVID HUME, *History of England*, 1754–62

Rawleigh exercised in perfection incompatible talents, and his character connects the opposite extremes of our nature! His "Book of Life," with its incidents of prosperity and adversity, of glory and humiliation, was as chequered as the novelist would desire for a tale of fiction. Yet in this mighty genius there lies an unsuspected disposition, which requires to be demonstrated, before it is possible to conceive its reality. From his earliest days, probably by his early reading of the romantic incidents of the first Spanish adventures in the New World, he himself betrayed the genius of an *adventurer*, which prevailed in his character to the latest; and it often involved him in the practice of mean artifices and petty deceptions; which appear like folly in the wisdom of a sage; like ineptitude in the profound views of a politican; like cowardice in the magnanimity of a hero; and degrade by their littleness the grandeur of a character which was closed by a splendid death, worthy the life of the wisest and the greatest of mankind!—ISAAC DISRAELI, "Secret History of Sir Walter Rawleigh," *Curiosities of Literature*, 1791–1824

The versatility of Raleigh's genius and pursuits were strikingly exemplified in his acquaintance with the mechanical arts, and his addiction to experimental inquiries. His discourses on ship-building, the navy, and naval tactics, are, we believe, the earliest productions of the kind in the English language. We never have been able to account for his great knowledge of seamanship, in which he had but little practical training, nor had he made many considerable voyages. His favour at court, his captures at sea, and his brilliant courage, procured him the rank of admiral, and employment as such on several important occasions; for naval rank was not yet regulated by any fixed rules of promotion; but, in point of fact, he rose to a reputation as a seaman not surpassed by any man of his day. After Drake and Hawkins disappeared from the scene, he seems, indeed, to have enjoyed a preeminence over all his contemporaries. Strong native predilections, and a wonderfully versatile mind, can alone explain his extraordinary proficiency in maritime affairs.—MACVEY NAPIER, "Sir Walter Raleigh" (1840), *Lord Bacon and Sir Walter Raleigh*, 1853, p. 223

He went to his trial a man so unpopular that he was hooted and pelted on the road; he came out an object of general pity and admiration, and has held his place ever since as one of England's favorite and representative heroes; and yet, if we except his gallant bearing and splendid abilities (which were no new revelations), there was nothing in his case which could have tended either to excite popular sympathy or to command popular respect; nor has anything been discovered since that enables us to explain his connection with the plot in a way at all favorable to his character. By his own showing he had been in intimate and confidential relation with a man whom nobody liked or respected, and who was secretly seeking help from the hated Spaniard in a plot to dispossess James in favor of the Lady Arabella. By his own admission he had at least listened to an offer of a large sum of money,—certainly Spanish, and therefore presumably in consideration of some service to be rendered to Spain. And though it is true that we do not know with what purposes he listened, how much he knew, how far he acquiesced, or what he intended to do, it is impossible to believe that his intentions (whether treasonable or not) were, or were then supposed to be, either popular or patriotic. He did not himself attempt to put any such color upon his proceedings; declaring only that he did not know of the plot in which his confidential friends were engaged. His blindest advocates have not succeeded in doing it for him. And those who, though partial, have taken pains to examine and felt bound to respect the evidence, have scarcely succeeded even in believing him innocent.—JAMES SPEDDING, *An Account of the Life and Times of Francis Bacon*, 1878, Vol. 1, p. 436

> The New World's sons, from England's breasts we
>   drew
>   Such milk as bids remember whence we came;
> Proud of her Past, wherefrom our Present grew,
>   This window we inscribe with Raleigh's name.
>
>   —JAMES RUSSELL LOWELL, Inscription, Sir Walter Raleigh Memorial Window, Westminster Cathedral, 1882

Sir Walter Raleigh, in whose honour this window is given, was not one of the world's simple, blameless characters, like William Caxton of whom we spoke so recently. Men of splendid physique and genius, children of a splendid and passionate age, have temptations more intense and terrible than we who live our small humdrum lives in the petty routine of commonplace. Our faults may be as bad as theirs, though they are meaner and smaller faults. Their sins show large in the largeness of their lives, and in the fierce light which beats upon them. . . . If Walter Raleigh, in some things, sinned greatly, God loved him so well that he also suffered greatly and out of much tribulation washed his robes white in the blood of the Lamb. . . . Remember also that he must be ranked forever among the benefactors of his race, and that there are very few of us who have not done worse deeds than he, and have never done as good ones. It is strange to me that one paltry tablet should hitherto have been almost the only memorial of such a man. Great nations should have more pride in their few great sons. I think that Americans will rejoice with us that, after more than 280 years, he should have a worthier memorial of his immortal deeds in the Church under whose altar lies his headless corpse.—FREDERICK W. FARRAR, Sermon preached at the unveiling of the Raleigh Window, Westminster Cathedral, 1882

It is difficult for us at this distance of time to realise the feelings with which Raleigh was regarded by the great mass of his contemporaries. To us he is the man who had more genius than all the Privy Council put together. At the first mention of his name, there rises up before us the remembrance of the active mind, the meditative head, and the bold heart, which have stamped themselves indelibly upon the pages of history of two continents. Above all, we think of him as the victim of oppression, sobered down by the patient endurance of an undeserved imprisonment, and as finally passing into his bloody grave, struck down by an unjust sentence. To the greater number of the men amongst whom he moved, he was simply the most unpopular man in England. Here and there were to be found a few who knew his worth. Those who had served under him, like his faithful Captain Keymis, and those who, like Sir John Harington, merely met him occasionally in social intercourse, knew well what the loyal heart of the man really was. But by the multitude, whom he despised, and by the grave statesmen and showy courtiers with whom he jostled for Elizabeth's favour, he was regarded as an insolent and unprincipled wretch, who feared neither God nor man, and who would shrink from no crime if he could thereby satisfy his ambitious desires. There can be no doubt that these charges, frivolous as they must seem to those who know what Raleigh's true nature was, had some basis in his character. Looking down as he did from the eminence of genius upon the actions of lesser men, he was too apt to treat them with the arrogance and scorn which they seldom deserved, and which it was certain that they would resent.—SAMUEL R. GARDINER, *History of England*, 1883, Vol. 1, p. 88

There is a proposal now in the United States to erect a monument to Sir Walter Raleigh. . . . Such a man, such principles, such a career, ought not to be given to the youth of the American republic as ideally correct and æsthetically beautiful. Raleigh was a man of versatile talents, possessing in a high degree the gifts of courtiership; fond of power, of land, of money, of luxury, of adventure; unscrupulous, of low standard of morality, and in many respects more like our Aaron Burr than like the Bayard of France, without fear and without reproach. That the great empire of America is under the least obligation to him is not susceptible of proof. His motive in sending an expedition out here was purely commercial and selfish, so far as the proofs go. He was actuated by the same motives in going to Ireland. He was no worse a man than his time and the standards of the age in which he lived made it inevitable that he should be.—MARGARET F. SULLIVAN, "Concerning Sir Walter Raleigh," *Catholic World*, Aug. 1884, p. 636

He was essentially an acrid and despotic nature. Among the eminent men of his day he scarcely had a true friend, and it is painful to read in the letters of his contemporaries how frequent were the disparaging remarks his petulent and grasping disposition called forth. Yet, in spite of the faults and vices of his character, the name of Raleigh is one which the history of this island will never attempt to erase from its list of celebrities. The man was, in every sense of the word, a true patriot, confident in the prowess of his country, and keenly sensitive as to her honour. It was the staunchness of his English instincts that made him wax so wroth when he saw a miserable creature, like our first James truckle to foreign Powers and drag the flag of England through the mire of a base servility.—ALEXANDER CHARLES EWALD, *Studies Re-Studied*, 1885, p. 204

When I consider his busy and brilliant and perturbed life, with its wonderful adventures, its strange friendships, its toils, its quiet hours with Spenser upon the Mulla shore, its other hours amidst the jungles of the Orinoco, its lawless gallantries in the court of Elizabeth, its booty snatched from Spanish galleons he has set ablaze, its perils, its long captivities—it is the life itself that seems to me a great Elizabethan epic, with all its fires, its mated couples of rhythmic sentiment, its poetic splendors, its shortened beat and broken pauses and blind turns, and its noble climacteric in a bloody death that is without shame and full of the largest pathos.—DONALD G. MITCHELL, *English Lands, Letters, and Kings (From Elizabeth to Anne)*, 1890, p. 18

General

To the right noble and valorous knight,
  Sir Walter Raleigh, Lord Wardein of the
  Stanneryes, and lieftenaunt of Cornewaile.

To thee, that art the sommers Nightingale,
  Thy soveraine Goddesses most deare delight,
  Why doe I send this rusticke Madrigale,
  That may thy tunefull eare unseason quite?
Thou onely fit this Argument to write,
  In whose high thoughts Pleasure hath built her bowre,
  And dainty love learnd sweetly to endite.
My rimes I know unsavory and sowre,
To tast the streames that, like a golden showre,
  Flow from thy fruitfull head, of thy love's praise;
  Fitter, perhaps, to thonder Martiall stowre,
When so thee list thy lofty Muse to raise:
Yet, till that thou thy Poeme wilt make knowne,
Let thy faire Cinthias praises be thus rudely showne.

> —EDMUND SPENSER, "Verses Addressed by the Author to Various Noblemen, Etc.," *The Faerie Queene*, 1589, Bk. 1

Upon maritimal concerns he published no fewer than eight treatises, being, as he proudly announced, the first writer either ancient or modern that had treated on this subject. These works are written with great perspicuity, and, although the practices recommended in them be now obsolete, and the improvements and plans suggested, superseded by the rapid strides of modern science, they are interesting, as all compositions dictated by good sense and experience must ever be; and curious, as illustrating the comparative progress of navigation, and of the arts connected with it.—KATHERINE THOMSON, *Memoirs of the Life of Sir Walter Raleigh*, 1830, p. 259

When the vigour of debate passed from Parliament to the Press, no deceased writer rendered truer service to Britain than did Ralegh in supporting and lighting up the policy which is truly liberal, just because it builds upon old foundations, appeals to old instincts, and brings out what is true and vital in the national traditions. A passionate and untiring energy is not more characteristic of Ralegh the man, than a clinging to political development, rather than political construction, is the distinctive mark of Ralegh the publicist. Hence it is, as I believe, that his name figures so saliently and so continually in the political literature of the eighteenth century. In the seventeenth, his deeds and his endeavours were continually rising before the minds of men who were still fighting under the same banner and against the same enemies. Not a few of them had been the contemporaries of his closing years. In the eighteenth, all the outward circumstances of the political conflict had changed. New men are seen in the arena. The party combinations are new. The impulses and the aims of the strife are new. Yet Ralegh's writings are even more frequently appealed to. A large volume might be made of the quotations which were pressed into service during the bitter contests of the Georgian reigns, and of the commentaries which grew out of the quotations.—EDWARD EDWARDS, *The Life of Sir Walter Ralegh*, 1868, Vol. 1, p. 718

A writer of magnificent prose, itself full of religion and poetry both in thought and expressions. . . .

It would be very unfair to judge Sir Walter by his verse. His prose is infinitely better, and equally displays the devout tendency of his mind—a tendency common to all the great men of that age. The worst I know of him is the selfishly prudent advice he left behind for his son. No doubt he had his faults, we must not judge a man even by what he says in an over-anxiety for the prosperity of his child.—GEORGE MAC-DONALD, "Sir Walter Raleigh's Pilgrimage," *England's Antiphon*, 1868, pp. 71–76

It was not remarkable that while gazing upon the house where Sir Walter Raleigh smoked tobacco—until then unknown in Ireland—and on the garden in which he first planted the potato, the thoughts of the traveller should run away from potatoes to poetry. In yonder manor he tuned his lyre; over those hills he rode to visit Spenser when that carpet-bagger was also enjoying a confiscated Irish estate and writing the *Faerie Queene*, of which George Eliot has said, when speaking of German comedy, what we all have thought, but ne'er so well expressed: "You see no reason in its structure why it should even come to an end, and you accept the conclusion as an arrangement of Providence rather than of the author." As a matter of fact, it was not an arrangement of Providence but the Irish rebels that did bring it to a close and interrupted the poet before he approached the end he had set for himself. As a poet Raleigh belongs to the class about whom an artificial fame is maintained. Spenser, in a fulsome fit of admiration, doubtless mutual, described him as the "summer's nightingale."

> He pip'd, I sang; and when he sang, I pip'd;
>   By change of turns, each making other merry;
>   Neither envying other, nor envied;
>   So pip'd we until we both were weary.

Weary indeed will he be who reads much of Sir Walter; and he must be of demure imagination and sombre fancy who can read even his best without laughter. But makers of manuals on English literature continue—the fashion having been firmly set among those traditional styles in taste which do not change with seasons—to include him with Chaucer and Gower, Spenser and Sidney, Lyly and Greene, Marlowe and Donne; yet one may read his every authenticated line without finding in it a true melody, a spontaneous flower, an original metaphor, or what George Eliot calls Heine, "a real voice, not an echo." Raleigh wrote poetry because it was the genteel extravagance of the court, and raised him, like the story of spreading his cloak for the queen to tread upon, above the horde of hungry adventurers who sought, with coarse greed and unconcealed knavery, the rewards of a reign rich in confiscations, prodigal in giving away the riches of abbey and sept, of chief and churchman. His coquetry with the queen was witty, astute, and brilliant; and out of the spirit of airy hypocrisy thus bred he wrote most of his verse. Some, penned, it is believed, in the Tower, might be held tolerable as the stiff song of a caged bird, but it is only middling poetry at best. Here is ample evidence from "His Pilgrimage":

> Give me my scallop-shell of quiet,
>   My staff of faith to walk upon,
> My scrip of joy, immortal diet,
>   My bottle of salvation,
> My gown of glory, hope's true gage,
> And thus I'll take my pilgrimage.
>
> Blood must be my body's balmer;
>   No other balm will there be given;
> Whilst my soul, like quiet palmer,
>   Travelleth toward the land of heaven;
>   Over the silver mountains,
>   Where spring the nectar fountains,
>   There will I kiss
>   The bowl of bliss,
> And drink mine everlasting fill
> Upon every milken hill.
> My soul will be a-dry before;
> But after it will thirst no more.
>
> And when our bottles and all we
> Are filled with immortality (etc.)

The world is still afflicted with an abundance of bad poetry; but that style of it has gone for ever, like Sir Walter's starched ruff, plumed hat, and slashed doublet. As a poet he need trouble critics not at all.

Even his claim to have introduced the potato into Ireland is open to dispute. That momentous credit is assigned to Sir John Hawkins, the slaver who, when Christianity had all but abolished the traffic in human beings, secured Queen Elizabeth as a partner and added the commodity Man to British commerce.—S. MARGARET FULLER, "Concerning Sir Walter Raleigh," *Catholic World*, Aug. 1884, p. 628–30

Undoubtedly Bacon (Shakespeare in his person as he lived being in the main *nominis umbra*) is the grandest figure of the age; but Raleigh is the most fascinating. Of the versatility and daring of the Elizabethans he remains the chief representative. In a larger sense than that in which the words were afterwards applied, he was "not one but all mankind's epitome." Soldier, courtier, philosopher, and poet, he had carried the spirit of Sidney into the field, and discussed metres and myths with Spenser when it was won. Drake was his only master among the kings of the sea; Bacon himself his only superior in the work of the "Instauratio Magna." Known abroad as the champion of the Indians, as the great intercessor for civil and religious liberty at home, he could turn from writing verses, only surpassed in grace by the lyrics of the later Cavaliers, to study "the learning of the Egyptians," or what passed for such before the reign of criticism, and record with an equal credulity and eloquence the annals of antiquity as then accepted. Early among the pioneers of European civilisation in the New World, he was the first modern historian of the Old.—JOHN NICOL, *Francis Bacon: His Life and Philosophy*, 1888, Pt. 1, p. 170

Ralegh makes amazing show of systematic arrangement; but the analysis is often arbitrary and inexact. On the one hand this poor analysis, on the other his utterly unwieldy and elephantine periods, make him an exceedingly bad paragraphist. —EDWIN HERBERT LEWIS, *The History of the English Paragraph*, 1894, p. 89

Works

POETRY

And there that shepheard of the Ocean is,
That spends his wit in loves consuming smart:
Full sweetly tempered is that Muse of his,
That can empierce of Princes mightie hart.

—EDMUND SPENSER, *Colin Clouts Come Home Againe*, 1595

The English poems of Sr *Walter Raleigh* . . . are not easily to be mended.—EDMUND BOLTON, *Hypercritica*, 1624

Do I pronounce Raleigh a poet? Not, perhaps, in the judgment of a severe criticism. Raleigh, in his better days, was too much occupied in action to have cultivated all the powers of a poet, which require solitude and perpetual meditation, and a refinement of sensibility, such as intercourse with business and the world deadens! . . .

The production of an *Heroic Poem* would have nobly employed this illustrious Hero's mighty faculties, during the lamentable years of his unjust incarceration. But how could He delight to dwell on the tale of Heroes, to whom the result of Heroism had been oppression, imprisonment, ruin, and condemnation to death? We have no proof that Raleigh possessed the copious, vivid, and creative powers of Spenser; nor is it probable that any cultivation would have brought forth from him fruit equally rich. But even in the careless fragments now presented to the reader, I think we can perceive some traits of attraction and excellence which, perhaps, even Spenser wanted. If less diversified than that gifted bard, he would, I think, have sometimes been more forcible and sublime; his images would have been more gigantic, and his reflections more daring. With all his mental attention keenly bent on the best state of existing things in political society, the range of his thoughts had been lowered down to practical wisdom; but other habits of intellectual exercise, excursions into the ethereal fields of fiction, and converse with the spirits which inhabit those upper regions, would have given a grasp and a colour to his conceptions as magnificent as the fortitude of his soul. —SAMUEL EGERTON BRYDGES, "Preface" to *The Poems of Sir Walter Raleigh*, 1813, pp. 43–46

A higher strain of compliment cannot well be conceived than this ⟨sonnet⟩ which raises your idea even of that which it disparages in the comparison, and makes you feel that nothing could have torn the writer from his idolatrous enthusiasm for Petrarch and his Laura's tomb, but Spenser's magic verses and diviner *Faëry Queen*—the one lifted above mortality, the other brought from the skies!—WILLIAM HAZLITT, *Lectures on the Dramatic Literature of the Age of Elizabeth*, 1820

His poetry, which is not so commonly read as it deserves to be, is a striking testimony both of the social habits of the time, and of the character of the man himself. It is conspicuous for amatory sweetness coupled with pastoral simplicity. Raleigh was the most polished courtier who ever adorned the precincts of English royalty; fond perhaps, as Macaulay says, of whispering his love sonnets too near to the willing ears of Elizabeth's maids of honour, but too innately refined to relapse into vulgar debauchery. In fact, the Court of the maiden Queen was one of the least dissolute of any monarch in the history of England. Raleigh's sonnets are an admirable reflection of the manners of the society in which he lived.—GEORGE F. UNDERHILL, *Literary Epochs*, 1887, p. 94

His fancy could inspire in his "Pilgrimage" one of the loftiest appeals in all literature to Heaven from the pedantry of human justice or injustice.

    . . . The Court spoilt him for a national poet, as it spoilt Cowley; as it might, if it had been more generous, have spoilt Dryden. He desired to be read between the lines by a class which loved to think its own separate thoughts, and express its own separate feelings in its own diction, sometimes in its own jargon. He hunted for epigrams, and too often sparkled rather than burned. He was afraid not to be witty, to wrangle, as he himself has said,

           In tickle points of niceness.

Often he refined instead of soaring. In place of sympathising he was ever striving to concentrate men's regards on himself. —WILLIAM STEBBING, *Sir Walter Raleigh*, 1891, p. 78

Though his imagery is vivid and metaphorical, it is often homely; his thought is very plain and direct, and his poetry breathes a spirit of high disdain and fierce indignation, mixed with a strong feeling of religion, evidently the result of personal experience.

    . . . Though the authorship ⟨*The Lie*⟩ has been questioned, is certainly Raleigh's.—W. J. COURTHOPE, *A History of English Poetry*, 1897, Vol. 2, pp. 310–11

THE HISTORY OF THE WORLD

Sʳ W. Raughlye esteemed more of fame than conscience, The best wits of England were Employed for making of his historie. Ben himself had written to piece to him of ye punick warre which he altered and set into his booke.—BEN JONSON, *Conversations with William Drummond*, 1619

Recreate yourself with Sir Walter Raleigh's *History*, it is a body of history, and will add much more to your understanding than fragments of stones.—OLIVER CROMWELL, Letter to Richard Cromwell (1650)

His Booke sold very slowly at first, and the Booke-seller complayned of it, and told him that he should be a looser by it, which put Sir W. into a passion, and sayd that since the world did not understand it, they should not have the second part, which he tooke and threw into the fire, and burnt before his face.—JOHN AUBREY, "Sir Walter Raleigh," *Brief Lives*, 1696

Sir Walter Raleigh's *History of the World* is a work of so vast a compass, such endless variety, that no genius, but one adventurous as his own, durst have undertaken that great design. I do not apprehend any great difficulty in collecting and commonplacing an universal history from the whole body of historians; that is nothing but mechanic labour. But to digest the several authors in his mind; to take in all their majesty, strength, and beauty; to raise the spirit of meaner historians, and to equal all the excellencies of the best; this is sir Walter's peculiar praise. His style is the most perfect, the happiest, the most beautiful of the age he wrote in; majestic, clear, and manly; and he appears every where so superior rather than unequal to his subject, that the spirit of Rome and Athens seems to be breathed into his work.—HENRY FELTON, *Dissertation on Reading the Classics*, 1711

The attempt of *Raleigh* is deservedly celebrated for the labour of his researches, and the elegance of his style; but he has endeavoured to exert his judgment more than his genius, to select facts, rather than adorn them; and has produced an historical dissertation, but seldom risen to the majesty of history.—SAMUEL JOHNSON, *The Rambler*, No. 122 (May 18, 1751)

If the reader of Raleigh's *History* can have the patience to wade through the Jewish and Rabbinical learning which compose the half of the volume, he will find, when he comes to the Greek and Roman story, that his pains are not unrewarded. Raleigh is the best model of that ancient style which some writers would affect to revive at present.—DAVID HUME, "Appendix" to *History of England*, 1754–62

Raleigh's *History of the World* is a proof of the respect for laborious learning that had long distinguished Europe. We should expect from the prison-hours of a soldier, a courtier, a busy intriguer in state affairs, a poet and man of genius, something well worth our notice; but hardly a prolix history of the ancient world, hardly disquisitions on the site of Paradise and the travels of Cain. These are probably translated with little alteration from some of the learned writings of the Continent; they are by much the least valuable portion of Raleigh's work. The Greek and Roman story is told more fully and exactly than by any earlier English author, and with a plain eloquence, which has given this book a classical reputation in our language, though from its length, and the want of that critical sifting of facts which we now justly demand, it is not greatly read. Raleigh has intermingled political reflections, and illustrated his history by episodes from modern times, which perhaps are now the most interesting passages. It descends only to the second Macedonian war; the continuation might have been more generally valuable; but either the death of Prince Henry, as Raleigh himself tells us, or the new schemes of ambition which unfortunately opened upon his eyes, prevented the execution of the large plan he had formed. There is little now obsolete in the words of Raleigh, nor, to any great degree, in his turn of phrase; the periods, when pains have been taken with them, show that artificial structure which we find in Sydney and Hooker, he is less pedantic than most of his contemporaries, seldom low, never affected.—HENRY HALLAM, *Introduction to the Literature of Europe*, 1837–39, Pt. 3, Ch. 7, Par. 32

It is to the Greek and Roman story that we would direct the attention of any one wishing to acquaint himself with Raleigh's peculiar merits. The narrative is clear, spirited, and unembarrassed; replete with remarks disclosing the mind of the soldier and the statesman; and largely sprinkled and adorned with original, forcible, and graphic expressions. But this portion of the work has a still more remarkable distinction, when considered as the production of an age not yet formed to any high notions of international morality, from its invariable reprehension of wars of ambition, and its entire freedom from those illusions which have biassed both historians and their readers in regard to the perfidies and cruelties exhibited in ancient, particularly Roman history. In this respect, he appears to us to stand honourably distinguished from all preceding authors; but while he thus endeavours to moderate our admiration of the Romans by awakening us to a strong perception of their national crimes, he never fails to do justice to their manly virtues, their energy of character, and their public affections.—MACVEY NAPIER, "Sir Walter Raleigh" (1840), *Lord Bacon and Sir Walter Raleigh*, 1853, p. 213

A fine antique eloquence flows from his pen, enriched with a deep learning, which excites wonder when displayed by

Raleigh. The soldier, the sailor, or the courtier is hardly the man from whom we expect profound philosophy or deep research; yet Raleigh showed by this achievement a power of wielding the pen, at least not inferior to his skill with sword or compass. That part of the History which he was able to complete, opening with the Creation, closes with the second Macedonian war, about one hundred and sixty-eight years before Christ. A deep tinge of melancholy, caught from the sombre walls that were ever frowning on his task, pervades the pages of the great book.—WILLIAM FRANCIS COLLIER, A *History of English Literature*, 1861, p. 152

The style of the history is excellent,—clear, sweet, flexible, straightforward and business-like, discussing the question of the locality of Paradise as Raleigh would have discussed the question of an expedition against Spain at the council-table of Elizabeth.—EDWIN P. WHIPPLE, *The Literature of the Age of Elizabeth*, 1869, p. 276

. . . ⟨H⟩is masterpiece, the famous *History of the World*, is made up of short passages of the most extraordinary beauty, and long stretches of monotonous narration and digression, showing not much grace of style, and absolutely no sense of proportion or skill in arrangement. The contrast is so strange that some have sought to see in the undoubted facts that Raleigh, in his tedious prison labours, had assistants and helpers (Ben Jonson among others), a reason for the superior excellence of such set pieces as the Preface, the Epilogue, and others, which are scattered about the course of the work. But independently of the other fact that excellence of the most varied kind meets us at every turn, though it also deserts us at every turn, in Raleigh's varied literary work, and that it would be absurd to attribute all these passages to some "affable familiar ghost," there is the additional difficulty that in none of his reported helpers' own work do the peculiar graces of the purple passages of the *History* occur. The immortal descant on mortality with which the book closes, and which is one of the highest achievements of English prose, is not in the least like Jonson, not in the least like Selden, not in the least like any one of whose connection with Raleigh there is record. Donne might have written it; but there is not the smallest reason for supposing that he did, and many for being certain that he did not. Therefore, it is only fair to give Raleigh himself the credit for this and all other passages of the kind.—GEORGE SAINTSBURY, A *History of Elizabethan Literature*, 1887, p. 212–13

A great reservoir of facts, stated with all grace and dignity, but which, like a great many heavy, excellent books, is never read. The matter-of-fact young man remembers that Sir Walter Raleigh first brought potatoes and (possibly) tobacco into England; but forgets his ponderous *History*.—DONALD G. MITCHELL, *English Lands, Letters, and Kings (From Elizabeth to Anne)*, 1890, p. 13

SAMUEL DANIEL

c. 1562–1619

The son of a music master, Samuel Daniel was born in Taunton, Somerset, probably in 1562. He spent several years at Magdalen Hall, Oxford, but left without a degree. After a visit to the Continent, during which he worked for the English ambassador in Paris and traveled in Italy, Daniel returned to England and worked as a tutor and translator.

In 1592 his first collection of sonnets, entitled *Delia*, appeared along with *The Complaint of Rosamond*, an extended lyric poem. Several of these sonnets, which were inspired by the works of Tasso and Desportes, had been published previously as an appendix to the 1591 edition of Sidney's *Astrophel and Stella*. Among Daniel's other well-known poems are *Musophilus: Containing a Generall Defence of Learning* (1599) and "Ulisses and the Syren" which appeared in *Certain Small Poems* (1605). Daniel held various positions at court after the success of his masque, *The Vision of the Twelve Goddesses* (1604), written for Queen Anne. Other masques performed at court include *Thethys' Festival: or the Queenes Wake* (1610) and *Hymens' Triumph* (1615). Daniel also wrote several Senecan tragedies, such as *Tragedie of Cleopatra* (1594) and *Philotas* (1605).

In 1595 the first five books of his epic, *The Civile Warres*, were published. Eventually totaling eight books, this verse epic chronicled the events surrounding the Wars of the Roses. Daniel's *Defence of Ryme* (1603), in which he defended the fitness of the English language for rhymed verse, was written in response to Thomas Campion's *Observations in the Art of English Poesie*. Finally, between 1612 and 1618 Daniel published the *Collection of the History of England*, a lengthy prose work on English history up to the period dealt with in *The Civile Warres*.

Daniel, who began his career as a sonneteer and translator, successfully made the transition to the writing of masques, tragedies, and epics. He died in October, 1619, at his farm in Beckington, Somerset.

Personal

Samuel Daniel was a good honest man, had no children, bot no poet.—BEN JONSON, *Conversations with William Drummond*, 1619

He was a Servant in Ordinary to Queen Anne, who allowed him a fair Salary. As the Tortoise burieth himself all the Winter in the ground, so Mr. Daniel would lye hid at his Garden-house in Old-street, nigh London, for some months together (the more retiredly to enjoy the Company of the Muses); and then would appear in publick, to converse with his Friends, whereof Dr. Cowel and Mr. Camden were principal. Some tax him to smak of the Old Cask, as resenting of the Romish Religion; but they have a quicker Palate than I, who can make any such discovery. In his old age he turn'd Husbandman, and rented a Farm in Wiltshire nigh the Devises. I can give no account how he thrived thereupon; for, though he was well vers'd in Virgil, his Fellow Husbandman-Poet, yet there is more required to make a rich Farmer, than only to say his Georgicks by heart. . . . Besides, I suspect that Mr. Daniel's fancy was too fine and sublimated, to be wrought down to his private profit.

However, he had neither a bank of wealth, or lank of want; living in a competent condition. By Justina his wife he had no child; and I am unsatisfied both in the place and time of death; but collect the latter to be about the end of the Reign of King James.—THOMAS FULLER, *The History of the Worthies of England*, 1662

Thethy's Festival was a thing merely written in honour of the unfortunate CHARLES, when he was created Prince of Wales, *Hymen's Triumph* was also an occasional thing on the nuptials of lord ROXBOROUGH, and The *Vision of the Twelve Goddesses* was again complimentary, DANIEL having written it as an allegorical representation of the blessings of peace enjoyed under JAMES the first. So that it is plain he wrote his dramatic pieces in quality of poet laureat, and that he worked hard for his But of Sack.

This, indeed, is the worst trait in the character of DANIEL, for the subjects of his productions were little worthy of the verses bestowed upon them, and indeed, were we to take all we know of history, we should find upon a comparison that the worst vices of bad men have been often glossed over by good poets, while the best virtues of good men have passed unrecorded; and the reason is evident. Vice needs the ablest talents to defend it; virtue is its own advocate; and thus it is only that, by a collective review of various exertions, characters are accorded legitimate fame.

The other play of DANIEL, called *Philotas*, is said to have very nearly jostled him out of his feat as poet laureat on account of a report, supposed to have been connived at by JONSON who succeeded to that honourable post after him. This report was that DANIEL, in the character of PHILOTAS, had brought forward the unfortunate earl of ESSEX, a subject certainly of too tender a nature to touch on at that time, and the consequences became so serious that he was under the necessity of vindicating himself in an apology printed at the end of the play.

The fact of this report having been propagated there can be no doubt of, but the ground on which it is supposed that JONSON connived at it is not firm, for it is presumed upon under an idea that the play made its first appearance in 1606, which is the period admitted by every writer that I have looked into; but it has not the least probability to support it. I have no doubt the mistake has arisen from a supposition that DANIEL was only laureat to JAMES the first, whereas he succeeded to that situation at the death of SPENCER, four years before the death of ELIZABETH, during which time no doubt he brought out this play. Hence the predicament into which his enemies attempt to plunge him, and this speaks for itself; for what did JAMES care about the earl of ESSEX?

I do not, however, mean to say that this exculpates JONSON, whose envy was no doubt as tingling in the reign of ELIZABETH as in the reign of JAMES, and the hateful bent of whose private character needs not this trait to magnify its deformity. My intention is only to give an added proof how little dates are to be relied upon, and to rectify false *ipse dixits* by detecting them through circumstances. The fact upon this principle as to DANIEL's plays is, that *Philotas*, which is al-lowed on all hands to be his first, he wrote in the reign of ELIZABETH; and, having had a taste of that danger he was likely to run among his enemies at court, he deferred his other dramatic writings till the next reign; when, in order to keep on the safe side of the post, he went into the other extreme and quitted satire for adulation.—CHARLES DIBDIN, *A Complete History of the Stage*, 1795, Vol. 3, pp. 282–85

General

And there is a new shepherd late up sprong,
The which doth all afore him far surpass:
Appearing well in that well-tuned song,
Which late he sung unto a scornful Lass.
Yet doth his trembling Muse but lowly fly,
As daring not too rashly mount on height,
And doth her tender plumes as yet but try
In love's soft lays and looser thoughts' delight.
Then rouse thy feathers quickly, Daniel,
And to what course thou please thyself advance:
But most, me seems, thy accent will excell
In tragic plaints and passionate mischance.

> —EDMUND SPENSER, *Colin Clouts Come Home Again*, 1595

The sweetest song-man of all English Swains.—HENRY CHETTLE, *England's Mourning Garment*, 1603

Let other countries (sweet Cambridge) envie (yet admire) my Virgil, thy Petrarch, divine *Spenser*. And unlesse I erre (a thing easie in such simplicite) deluded by dearlie beloved *Delia*, and fortunatelie fortunate *Cleopatra*, Oxford thou maist extoll thy court-deare verse happie *Daniell*, whose sweete refined Muse, in contracted shape, were sufficient amongst men, to gaine pardon of the sinne to *Rosamond*, and euer-living praise to her loving *Delia*.—WILLIAM CLARKE, *Polimanteia*, 1595

The works of Samuel Daniel containe somewhat aflat, but yet withal a very pure and copious English, and words as warrantable as any man, and fitter perhaps for prose than measure.—EDMUND BOLTON, *Hypercritica*, 1624

Amongst these *Samuel Daniel*, whom if I
May spake of, but to sensure doe denie,
Onely have heard some wisemen him rehearse,
To be too much *Historian* in verse;
His rimes were smooth, his meeters well did close,
But yet his maner better fitted prose:

> —MICHAEL DRAYTON, "To My Most Dearely-Loved Friend Henry Reynolds Esquire, of Poets and Poesie," c. 1627

Mr. *Daniel's* Works are very various, and consist of History, Plays, and Poems; in all which he appears to me a Person of great Good-Sense, and unbiass'd Integrity; both Clear, and Concise in his Expression; rather too simple and void of Ornament, and not comparable in his Numbers either to *Fairfax* or *Spenser*; But, on the whole, highly worthy of Esteem and Reputation.—ELIZABETH COOPER, *The Muses Library*, 1737

Sound morality, prudential wisdom, and occasional touches of the pathetic, delivered in a style of then unequalled chastity and perspicuity, will be recognised throughout his work; but neither warmth, passion, nor sublimity, nor the most distant trace of enthusiasm can be found to animate the mass.—NATHAN DRAKE, *Shakspeare and His Times*, 1817, Vol. 1, p. 611

Daniel frequently wrote below his subject and his strength, but always in a strain of tender feeling, and in language as easy and natural as it is pure. For his diction alone he would deserve to be studied by all students or lovers of poetry, even if his works did not abound with passages of singular beauty. Thoughtful, grateful, right-minded and gentle-hearted, there is no poet in our language of whom it may be affirmed with more certainty, from his writings, that he was an amiable and wise and good man.—ROBERT SOUTHEY, *Select Works of the British Poets from Chaucer to Jonson*, 1831

Faithfully adhering to truth, which he does not suffer so much as an ornamental episode to interrupt, and equally studious to avoid the bolder figures of poetry, it is not surprising that Daniel should be little read. It is, indeed, certain that much Italian and Spanish poetry, even by those whose name has once stood rather high, depends chiefly upon merits which he abundantly possesses,—a smoothness of rhythm, and a lucid narration in simple language. But that which from the natural delight in sweet sound is enough to content the ear in the Southern tongues, will always seem bald and tame in our less harmonious verse. It is the chief praise of Daniel, and must have contributed to what popularity he enjoyed in his own age, that his English is eminently pure, free from affectation of archaism and from pedantic innovation, with very little that is now obsolete. Both in prose and in poetry, he is, as to language, among the best writers of his time, and wanted but a greater confidence in his own power, or, to speak less indulgently, a greater share of it, to sustain his correct taste, calm sense, and moral feeling.—HENRY HALLAM, *Introduction to the Literature of Europe*, 1837–39, Pt. 3, Ch. 5, Par. 43

Fuller says of ⟨Daniel⟩ that "he carried, in his Christian and surname, two holy prophets, his monitors, so to qualify his raptures that he abhorred all profaneness." Amiable in character, gentle in disposition, and with a genius meditative rather than energetic, he appears to have possessed that combination of qualities which makes men personally pleasing if it does not make them permanently famous. He was patronized both by Elizabeth and James, was the friend of Shakespeare and Camden, and was highly esteemed by the most accomplished women of his time. A most voluminous writer in prose and verse, he was distinguished in both for the purity, simplicity, and elegance of his diction. Browne calls him "the well-languaged Daniel." But if he avoided the pedantry and quaintness which were too apt to vitiate the style of the period, and wrote what might be called modern English, it has still been found that modern Englishmen cannot be coaxed into reading what is so lucidly written. His longest work, a versified History of the Civil Wars, dispassionate as a chronicle and unimpassioned as a poem, is now only read by those critics in whom the sense of duty is victorious over the disposition to doze. The best expressions of his pensive, tender, and thoughtful nature are his epistles and his sonnets. Among the epistles, that to the Countess of Cumberland is the best. It is a model for all adulatory addresses to women; indeed, a masterpiece of subtile compliment; for it assumes in its object a sympathy with whatever is noblest in sentiment, and an understanding of whatever is most elevated in thought. The sonnets, first published in 1592, in his thirtieth year, record the strength and the disappointment of a youthful passion. The lady, whom he addresses under the name of Delia, refused him, it is said, for a wealthier lover, and the pang of this baffled affection made him wretched for years, and sent him

> Haunting untrodden paths to wail apart.

Echo,—he tells us, while he was aiming to overcome the indifference of the maiden,—

> Echo, daughter of the air,
> 　Babbling guest of rocks and rills,
> Knows the name of my fierce fair,
> 　And sounds the accents of my ills.

Throughout the sonnets, the matchless perfection of this Delia is ever connected with her disdain of the poet who celebrates it:—

> Fair is my love, and cruel as she's fair;
> 　Her brow shades frowns, although her eyes are
> 　　sunny;
> Her smiles are lightning, though her pride despair;
> 　And her disdains are gall, her favors honey.
> A modest maid, decked with a blush of honor,
> 　Who treads along green paths of youth and love,
> The wonder of all eyes that gaze upon her,
> 　Sacred on earth, designed a saint above.

This picture of the "modest maid, decked with a blush of honor," is exquisite; but it is still a picture, and not a living presence. Shakespeare, touching the same beautiful object with his life-imparting imagination, suffuses at once the sense and soul with a feeling of the vital reality, when he describes the French princess as a "maiden rosed over with the virgin crimson of modesty."

The richest and most elaborately fanciful of these sonnets is that in which the poet calls upon his mistress to give back her perfections to the objects from which she derived them:—

> Restore thy tresses to the golden ore;
> 　Yield Cytherea's son those arcs of love;
> Bequeath the heavens the stars that I adore;
> 　And to the orient do thy pearls remove.
> Yield thy hand's pride unto the ivory white;
> 　To Arabian odors give thy breathing sweet;
> Restore thy blush unto Aurora bright;
> 　To Thetis give the honor of thy feet.
>
> Let Venus have thy graces, her resigned;
> 　And thy sweet voice give back unto the spheres;
> But yet restore thy fierce and cruel mind
> 　To Hyrcan tigers and to ruthless bears;
> Yield to the marble thy hard heart again;
> So shalt thou cease to plague and I to pain."

There is a fate in love. This man, who could not conquer the insensibility of one country girl, was the honored friend of the noblest and most celebrated woman of his age. Eventually, at the age of forty, he was married to a sister of John Florio, to whom his own sister, the Rosalind who jilted Spenser, is supposed to have been previously united.—EDWIN P. WHIPPLE, "Minor Elizabethan Poets," *Atlantic*, July 1868, pp. 27–28

Had Daniel lived in the present day, his destiny probably would have been to write scholarly and elegant articles in the magazines, ripe fruits of leisurely study, cultivated taste, and easy command of polite English. His was not one of the stormy irregular natures that laid the foundation and raised the structure of the English drama: the elements of his being were softly blended, and wrought together mildly and harmoniously. In the prologue to *Hymen's Triumph*, he declares that he has no rude antique sport to offer—

> But tender passions, motions soft and grave
> 　The still spectators must expect to have.

He wrote for Cynthia, and therefore his play—

> 　　　Must be gentle like to her
> Whose sweet affections mildly move and stir.

He might have said the same about all his poetry. He was no master of strong passions: he never felt them, and he could not paint them. Between his Cleopatra and Shakspeare's there is a wide gulf. But he is most exquisite and delicate in pencilling "tender passions, motions soft and grave."

Without being strikingly original, Daniel has a way and a vein of his own. He fills his mind with ideas and forms from extraneous sources, and with quietly operating plasticity reshapes them in accordance with the bent of his own modes of thought and feeling. He had not the Shakespearian lightning quickness in adaptation and extension; the process in him was more peaceable and easy. The diction of his poems is choice; the versification easy and flowing. He often puts things with felicitous terseness and vigour, and his words almost invariably come together happily and harmoniously.—WILLIAM MINTO, *Characteristics of English Poets*, 1874, pp. 250–51

The poetical value of Daniel may almost be summed up in two words—sweetness and dignity. He is decidedly wanting in strength, and, despite *Delia*, can hardly be said to have had a spark of passion. Even in his own day it was doubted whether he had not overweighted himself with his choice of historical subjects, though the epithet of "well-languaged," given to him at the time, evinces a real comprehension of one of his best claims to attention. No writer of the period has such a command of pure English, unadulterated by xenomania and unweakened by purism, as Daniel. Whatever unfavourable things have been said of him from time to time have been chiefly based on the fact that his chaste and correct style lacks the fiery quaintness, the irregular and audacious attraction of his contemporaries. Nor was he less a master of versification than of vocabulary. His *Defence of Rhyme* shows that he possessed the theory: all his poetical works show that he was a master of the practice. He rarely attempted and probably would not have excelled in the lighter lyrical measures. But in the grave music of the various elaborate stanzas in which the Elizabethan poets delighted, and of which the Spenserian, though the crown and flower, is only the most perfect, he was a great proficient, and his couplets and blank verse are not inferior. . . . Quiet, indeed, is the overmastering characteristic of Daniel. It was this no doubt which made him prefer the stately style of his Senecan tragedies, and the hardly more disturbed structure of pastoral comedies and tragi-comedies, like the *Queen's Arcadia* and *Hymen's Triumph*, to the boisterous revels of the stage proper in his time. He had something of the schoolmaster in his nature as well as in his history. Nothing is more agreeable to him than to moralise; not indeed in any dull or crabbed manner, but in a mellifluous and at the same time weighty fashion, of which very few other poets have the secret. It is perhaps by his scrupulous propriety, by his anxious decency (to use the word not in its modern and restricted sense, but in its proper meaning of the generally becoming), that Daniel brought upon himself the rather hard saying that he had a manner "better suiting prose."—GEORGE SAINTSBURY, *A History of Elizabethan Literature*, 1887, pp. 135–36

The almost unrelieved excision of all ornament and colour, the uniform stateliness, the lack of passion, which render Daniel admirable and sometimes even charming in a short poem, weary us in his long productions, and so invariably sententious is he that we are tempted to call him a Polonius among poets.—EDMUND GOSSE, *The Jacobean Poets*, 1894, pp. 13–14

A most accomplished and conscientious artist in verse, who had a genuine, but mild, poetic nature. The care he took to revise his work is evidence of his conscience as a workman, and the fact that his changes were commonly for the better is proof of his judgment. It is mainly the beauty of his English which will cause him to be read for ever among the rest.—DAVID HANNAY, *The Later Renaissance*, 1898, p. 215

Daniel seems to have been more deeply influenced by the Latin moralists and pastoralists than any of his contemporaries. The motive of almost all his work is ethical. He was the only considerable disciple of Seneca in England: his two tragedies are moral dialogues. The *Rosamond*, *Octavia*, and *The Civile Wars* are moralized narrative or romance; the Epistles are moral discourses on the uses of adversity, on equity, on the serenity of the virtuous and philosophic mind; *Hymen's Triumph* celebrates the beauty and the reward of faithfulness in love. Daniel has an easy, natural style, unadorned but untormented, with little imagery, singularly lucid and supple, eminently graceful in *Hymen's Triumph*, weighty and antithetical in the Epistles. He has no rapture and little emotion of any kind: at times he drops into diction that is completely prosaic; at times he rises to a grave eloquence that is almost majestic. There is nothing in Elizabethan literature finer in its way than a passage in his epistle to Margaret, Countess of Cumberland. He is speaking of the serenity of the wise and virtuous man—a favourite Elizabethan theme:

> He looks upon the mightiest monarch's wars
> But only as on stately robberies,
> Where evermore the fortune that prevails
> Must be the right; the ill-succeeding mars
> The fairest and the best-faced enterprise:
> Great pirate Pompey lesser pirates quails;
> Justice, he sees, as if seduced, still
> Conspires with power, whose cause must not be ill.
>
> . . .
>
> And whilst distraught Ambition compasses
> And is encompassed; whilst as craft deceives
> And is deceived; whilst man doth ransack man
> And builds on blood and rises by distress;
> And the inheritance of desolation leaves
> To great expecting hopes; he looks thereon
> As from the shore of peace with unwet eye
> And bears no venture in impiety.

This is Daniel at his best; but he is equally at his best in that very graceful and truly Arcadian poem *Hymen's Triumph*, in which he uses alike blank verse and rhyme with charm and distinction. Though his verse has little colour, it has great beauty of line, and though his imagination is not profound, few poets match him in sanity and lucidity, and in a plain gracefulness. The weakest of all his productions is the most ambitious of them in appearance, *The Civile Wars*. This is little more than a matter-of-fact versification of the chronicle.—THOMAS SECCOMBE, J. W. ALLEN, *The Age of Shakespeare*, 1903, pp. 53–54

Works

DELIA

Kisse Delia's hand for her sweet Prophets sake,
 Whose, not affected but well couched, teares
Have power, have worth a marble minde to shake;
 Whose fame no Iron-age or time out wears:
Then lay you down in Phillis lappe and sleepe,
Untill she weeping read, and reading weepe.
 —THOMAS LODGE, "Phillis," 1593

And thou, the sweet Museus of these times,
Pardon my rugged and unfiled rymes,

Whose scarce invention is too meane and base,
When Delias glorious Muse dooth come in place.
—MICHAEL DRAYTON, *Endimion and Phœbe*,
1594

As Parthenius Nicæus excellently sang the praises of Arete:
so Daniel hath divinely sonnetted the matchless beauty of Delia.—FRANCIS MERES, *Palladis Tamia*, 1598

The publication of Daniel's sonnets in 1592 is an epoch in the
history of the English Sonnet. This was the first body of sonnets written in what is sometimes called by pre-eminence the
English form—three independent quatrains closed in by a couplet. Daniel also set an example to Shakespeare in treating the
sonnet as a stanza, connecting several of them together as
consecutive parts of a larger expression. Apart from their form,
there is not very much interest in the sonnets to Delia. They
have all Daniel's smoothness and felicity of phrase, and are
pervaded by exceedingly sweet and soft sentiment. Though
they rouse no strong feelings, they may be dwelt upon by a
sympathetic reader with lively enjoyment. One of them, with
somewhat greater depth of feeling than most of the others, the
sonnet beginning—"Care-charmer Sleep, son of the sable
Night," is ranked among the best sonnets in the language. But
their most general interest is found in their relation to Shakespeare's sonnets, several of which seem to have been built up
from ideas suggested by the study of those to Delia.—WILLIAM
MINTO, *Characteristics of English Poets*, 1874, pp. 251–52

I do not suppose it is likely now that we shall ever know who
"Delia" was. But I for one recognize in these Sonnets a human
passion, and not mere "sportive wit" or "idle play." The grief
grows o'times monotonous and even grotesque, but ever and
anon there comes the genuine "cry" of a man's heart in suspen-
sive anguish. He is by no means a strong man—contrariwise
reveals a good deal of valetudinarian sentimentalism; yet is
there reality of "love," and not simply rhyme-craft.—ALEX-
ANDER B. GROSART, "Memorial-Introduction" to *The Complete Works of Samuel Daniel*, 1885, Vol. 1, p. xvii

THE COMPLAINT OF ROSAMOND

Some dul-headed diuines deeme it no more cunninge to write
an exquisit Poem, than to preach pure Caluin, or distill the
juice of a Commentary in a quarter sermon.

. . . You shall finde there goes more exquisite paines and
puritie of wit, to the writing of one such rare Poem as
Rosamond than to a hundred of your dunsticall Sermons.—
THOMAS NASHE, *Piers Penilesse his Supplication to the Divell*,
1592

As every one mourneth, when he heareth of the lamentable
plangors of Thracian Orpheus for his dearest Euridyce: so every
one passionateth, when he readeth the afflicted death of
Daniel's distressed *Rosamond*.—FRANCIS MERES, *Palladis
Tamia*, 1598

Samuel Daniel's *Complaint of Rosamond*, with its seven-line
stanza (1592), stood to *Lucrece* in even closer relation than
Lodge's *Scilla*, with its six-line stanza, to *Venus and Adonis*.
The pathetic accents of Shakespeare's heroine are those of
Daniel's heroine purified and glorified.—SIDNEY LEE, A *Life
of William Shakespeare*, 1898, p. 76

THE CIVIL WARS

Daniel wrote *Civill Warres* & yet hath not one batle in all his
Book.—BEN JONSON, *Conversations with William Drummond*, 1619

HISTORY OF ENGLAND

He was also a judicious Historian; witness his *Lives of our
English Kings, since the Conquest, until King Edward the
Third*; wherein he hath the happiness to reconcile brevity with
clearnesse, qualities of great distance in other Authours; a work
since commendably continued (but not with equal quicknesse
and judgment) by Mr. Trussell.—THOMAS FULLER, *The History of the Worthies of England*, 1662

Daniel's *History of England from the Conquest to the Reign of
Edward III.*, published in 1618, is deserving of some attention
on account of its language. It is written with a freedom from all
stiffness, and a purity of style which hardly any other work of so
early a date exhibits. These qualities are indeed so remarkable
that it would require a good deal of critical observation to
distinguish it even from writings of the reign of Anne; and
where it differs from them, (I speak only of the secondary class
of works, which have not much individuality of manner,) it is
by a more select idiom, and by an absence of the Gallicism or
vulgarity which are often found in that age. It is true that the
merits of Daniel are chiefly negative; he is never pedantic, or
antithetical, or low, as his contemporaries were apt to be; but
his periods are ill constructed, he has little vigour or elegance;
and it is only by observing how much pains he must have taken
to reject phrases which were growing obsolete, that we give him
credit for having done more than follow the common stream of
easy writing. A slight tinge of archaism, and a certain majesty
of expression, relatively to colloquial usage, were thought by
Bacon and Raleigh congenial to an elevated style; but Daniel, a
gentleman of the king's household, wrote as the court spoke,
and his facility would be pleasing if his sentences had a less
negligent structure. As an historian, he has recourse only to
common authorities; but his narration is fluent and perspicuous, with a regular vein of good sense, more the characteristic of his mind, both in verse and prose, than any
commanding vigour.—HENRY HALLAM, *Introduction to the
Literature of Europe*, 1837–39, Pt. 3, Ch. 7, Par. 33

As a branch of literature, English history in the new shape
which we have noted began in the work of the poet Daniel.
The chronicles of Stowe and Speed, who preceded him, are
simple records of the past, often copied almost literally from
the annals they used, and utterly without style or arrangement;
while Daniel inaccurate and superficial as he is, gave his story
a literary form, and embodied it in a pure and graceful prose—
JOHN RICHARD GREEN, A *Short History of the English People*,
1874, Ch. 7, Sec. 5

A. T. QUILLER-COUCH
"Samuel Daniel" (1894)
Adventures in Criticism
1895, pp. 50–60

The writings of Samuel Daniel and the circumstances of his
life are of course well enough known to all serious students
of English poetry. And, though I cannot speak on this point
with any certainty, I imagine that our younger singers hold to
the tradition of all their fathers, and that Daniel still

renidet in angulo

of their affections, as one who in his day did very much,
though quietly, to train the growth of English verse; and proved
himself, in everything he wrote, an artist to the bottom of his
conscience. As certainly as Spenser, he was a "poet's poet"
while he lived. A couple of pages might be filled almost off-
hand with the genuine compliments of his contemporaries,

and he will probably remain a "poet's poet" as long as poets write in English. But the average reader of culture—the person who is honestly moved by good poetry and goes from time to time to his bookshelves for an antidote to the common cares and trivialities of this life—seems to neglect Daniel almost utterly. I judge from the wretched insufficiency of his editions. It is very hard to obtain anything beyond the two small volumes published in 1718 (an imperfect collection), and a volume of selections edited by Mr. John Morris and published by a Bath bookseller in 1855; and even these are only to be picked up here and there. I find it significant, too, that in Mr. Palgrave's *Golden Treasury* Daniel is represented by one sonnet only, and that by no means his best. This neglect will appear the more singular to anyone who has observed how apt is the person whom I have called the "average reader of culture" to be drawn to the perusal of an author's works by some attractive idiosyncrasy in the author's private life or character. Lamb is a staring instance of this attraction. How we all love Lamb, to be sure! Though he rejected it and called out upon it, "gentle" remains Lamb's constant epithet. And, curiously enough, in the gentleness and dignified melancholy of his life, Daniel stands nearer to Lamb than any other English writer, with the possible exception of Scott. His circumstances were less gloomily picturesque. But I defy any feeling man to read the scanty narrative of Daniel's life and think of him thereafter without sympathy and respect.

He was born in 1562—Fuller says in Somersetshire, not far from Taunton; others say at Beckington, near Philip's Norton, or at Wilmington in Wiltshire. Anthony Wood tells us that he came "of a wealthy family;" Fuller that "his father was a master of music." Of his earlier years next to nothing is known; but in 1579 he was entered as a commoner at Magdalen Hall, Oxford, and left the university three years afterwards without taking a degree. His first book—a translation of Paola Giovio's treatise on Emblems—appeared in 1585, when he was about twenty-two. In 1590 or 1591 he was travelling in Italy, probably with a pupil, and no doubt busy with those studies that finally made him the first Italian scholar of his time. In 1592 he published his *Sonnets to Delia*, which at once made his reputation; in 1594 his *Complaint of Rosamond* and *Tragedy of Cleopatra*; and in 1595 four books of his *Civil Wars*. On Spenser's death, in 1599, Daniel is said to have succeeded to the office of poet-laureate.

> That wreath which, in Eliza's golden days,
> My master dear, divinist Spenser, wore;
> That which rewarded Drayton's learned lays,
> Which thoughtful Ben and gentle Daniel wore

But history traces the Laureateship, as an office, no further back than Jonson, and we need not follow Southey into the mists. It is certain, however, that Daniel was a favorite at Elizabeth's Court, and in some way partook of her bounty. In 1600 he was appointed tutor to the Lady Anne Clifford, a little girl of about eleven, daughter of Margaret, Countess of Cumberland; and his services were gratefully remembered by mother and daughter during his life and after. But Daniel seems to have tired of living in great houses as private tutor to the young. The next year, when presenting his works to Sir Thomas Egerton, he writes:—"Such hath been my misery that whilst I should have written the actions of men, I have been constrained to bide with children, and, contrary to mine own spirit, put out of that sense which nature had made my part."

Now there is but one answer to this—that a man of really strong spirit does not suffer himself to be "put out of that sense which nature had made my part." Daniel's words indicate the weakness that in the end made futile all his powers: they indicate a certain "donnish" timidity (if I may use the epithet), a certain distrust of his own genius. Such a timidity and such a distrust often accompany very exquisite faculties: indeed, they may be said to imply a certain exquisiteness of feeling. But they explain why, of the two contemporaries, the robust Ben Jonson is to-day a living figure in most men's conception of those times, while Samuel Daniel is rather a fleeting ghost. And his self-distrust was even then recognized as well as his exquisiteness. He is indeed "well-languaged Daniel," "sweet honey-dropping Daniel," "Rosamund's trumpeter, sweet as the nightingale," revered and admired by all his compeers. But the note of apprehension was also sounded, not only by an unknown contributor to that rare collection of epigrams, *Skialetheia, or the Shadow of Truth*.

> Daniel (as some hold) might mount, *if he list*;
> But others say he is a Lucanist

—but by no meaner a judge than Spenser himself, who wrote in his *Colin Clout's Come Home Again*:

> And there is a new shepherd late upsprung
> The which doth all afore him far surpass;
> Appearing well in that well-tunéd song
> Which late he sung unto a scornful lass.
> *Yet doth his trembling Muse but lowly fly,*
> *As daring not too rashly mount on height;*
> And doth her tender plumes as yet but try
> In love's soft lays, and looser thoughts delight.
> Then rouse thy feathers quickly, DANIEL,
> And to what course thou please thyself advance;
> But most, meseems, thy accent will excel
> In tragic plaints and passionate mischance.

Moreover, there is a significant passage in the famous *Return from Parnassus*, first acted at Cambridge during the Christmas of 1601:

> Sweet honey-dropping Daniel doth wage
> War with the proudest big Italian
> That melts his heart in sugar'd sonneting,
> *Only let him more sparingly make use*
> *Of others' wit and use his own the more.*

Now it has been often pointed out that considerable writers fall into two classes—(1) those who begin, having something to say, and are from the first rather occupied with their matter than with the manner of expressing it; and (2) those who begin with the love of expression and intent to be artists in words, *and come through expression to profound thought*. It is fashionable just now, for some reason or another, to account Class 1 as the more respectable; a judgment to which, considering that Shakespeare and Milton belonged undeniably to Class 2, I refuse to assent. The question, however, is not to be argued here. I have only to point out in this place that the early work of all poets in Class 2 is largely imitative. Virgil was imitative, Keats was imitative—to name but a couple of sufficiently striking examples. And Daniel, who belongs to this class, was also imitative. But for a poet of this class to reach the heights of song, there must come a time when out of imitation he forms a genuine style of his own, *and loses no mental fertility in the transformation*. This, if I may use the metaphor, is the *mauvais pas* in the ascent of Parnassus: and here Daniel broke down. He did indeed acquire a style of his own; but the effort exhausted him. He was no longer prolific; his ardor had gone: and his innate self-distrustfulness made him quick to recognize his sterility.

Soon after the accession of James I., Daniel, at the recommendation of his brother-in-law, John Florio, possibly furthered by the interest of the Earl of Pembroke, was given a post as gentleman extraordinary and groom of the privy chamber to Anne of Denmark; and a few months after was appointed to take the oversight of the plays and shows that were performed by the children of the Queen's revels, or children of the Chapel, as they were called under Elizabeth. He had thus a snug position at Court, and might have been happy, had it been another Court. But in nothing was the accession of James more apparent than in the almost instantaneous blasting of the taste, manners, and serious grace that had marked the Court of Elizabeth. The Court of James was a Court of bad taste, bad manners, and no grace whatever: and Daniel—"the remnant of another time," as he calls himself—looked wistfully back upon the days of Elizabeth.

> But whereas he came planted in the spring,
> And had the sun before him of respect;
> We, set in th' autumn, in the withering
> And sullen season of a cold defect,
> Must taste those sour distastes the times do bring
> Upon the fulness of a cloy'd neglect.
> Although the stronger constitutions shall
> Wear out th' infection of distemper'd days

And so he stood dejected, while the young men of "stronger constitutions" passed him by.

In this way it happened that Daniel, whom at the outset his contemporaries had praised with wide consent, and who never wrote a loose or unscholarly line, came to pen, in the dedicatory epistle prefixed to his tragedy of *Philotas*, these words—perhaps the most pathetic ever uttered by an artist upon his work:

> And therefore since I have outlived the date
> Of former grace, acceptance and delight.
> I would my lines, late born beyond the fate
> Of her spent line, had never come to light;
> So had I not been tax'd for wishing well,
> Nor now mistaken by the censuring Stage,
> Nor in my fame and reputation fell,
> Which I esteem more than what all the age
> Or the earth can give. *But years hath done this wrong,*
> *To make me write too much, and live too long.*

I said just now that Daniel had done much, though quietly, to train the growth of English verse. He not only stood up successfully for its natural development at a time when the clever but less largely informed Campion and others threatened it with fantastic changes. He probably did as much as Waller to introduce polish of line into our poetry. Turn to the famous *Ulysses and the Siren*, and read. Can anyone tell me of English verses that run more smoothly off the tongue, or with a more temperate grace?

> Well, well, Ulysses, then I see
> I shall not have thee here:
> And, therefore, I will come to thee,
> And take my fortune there.
> I must be won that cannot win,
> Yet lost were I not won;
> For beauty hath created been
> T'undo or be undone.

To speak familiarly, this is as easy as an old shoe. To speak yet more familiarly, it looks as if any fool could turn off lines like these. Let the fool try.

And yet to how many anthologies do we not turn in vain for "Ulysses and the Siren"; or for the exquisite spring song, beginning—

> Now each creature joys the other,
> Passing happy days and hours;

> One bird reports unto another
> In the fall of silver showers

—or for that lofty thing, the "Epistle to the Countess of Cumberland"?—which Wordsworth, who quoted it in his *Excursion*, declares to be "an admirable picture of the state of a wise man's mind in a time of public commotion." Certainly if ever a critic shall arise to deny poetry the virtue we so commonly claim for her, of fortifying men's souls against calamity, this noble Epistle will be all but the last post from which he will extrude her defenders.

JOHN ERSKINE
From "The Sonnet-Series"
The Elizabethan Lyric
1903, pp. 134–40

In . . . 1592, appeared Samuel Daniel's *Delia*,[1] which to the literary student must always suggest the two great sequences. It recalls *Astrophel and Stella*, because Delia is almost certainly Sidney's sister Mary, Countess of Pembroke; it is associated with Shakspere because it illustrates the first extended use of his sonnet-form. It is at first surprising that these sonnets show so little of Sidney's influence, but it is not hard to find the explanation. The Countess of Pembroke was Daniel's patroness, and out of gratitude he wished to celebrate her in his art. His love, to say the least, was disinterested, and never quite distinguishable from respectful friendship. Five sonnets of the first edition, the third, eighth, tenth, twelfth, and sixteenth, he afterward omitted, apparently because they were vehement in their declaration of passion. With the intention, then, of "eternizing" his lady in this distant manner, he could hardly use the burning art of Sidney; he could but imitate the most chivalrous phases of Petrarch's worship of Laura. Of course this meant simply to ignore the sincere note of *Astrophel*, and to return to the French models or to the subjective quality of Wyatt's love-plaints. This low temperature of the lyric passion is accompanied by a revival of old themes; for example, that of the lady's cruelty, Petrarch's familiar motive, on which fully half of the *Delia* sonnets are written. Sidney had escaped from the conventionality of this theme through the circumstances of his love, where honor dictated that he should not love at all; Stella thereby came almost to symbolize virtue, and Astrophel's love, in his own eyes, was terribly like desire, so that the repulses and final dismissal were not acts of cruelty, but triumphs of spiritual love. To offset this, however, the very conditions of Daniel's admiration for the Countess of Pembroke would persuade him to dwell on her intellectual and spiritual beauty rather than on physical charms, as Sidney had done. In one sonnet, the sixth, we might feel a suggestion of Platonic emphasis on the soul, often the motive of Spenser's love-poetry:—

> A modest maid, decked with a blush of honor,
> Whose feet do tread green paths of youth and love;
> The wonder of all eyes that look upon her,
> Sacred on earth, designed a saint above.[2]

There is no narrative element in *Delia*, nor any progression in the lover's moods. The poet sings praises of his lady, or laments her cruelty, or introduces decorative themes—perhaps after Sidney's example, but more probably in direct imitation of French poets. The best of these incidental themes, and the most familiar sonnet, is the one on sleep:—

> Care-charmer Sleep, son of the sable night.[3]

It has been pointed out that this is one of the favorite decorative themes of all the sonnet-series; evidently Sidney's sonnet is followed here.[4] The famous image of the rose from canto sixteen of the *Gerusalemme liberata*, afterwards entering our literature once for all in bk. iv, canto xii of the *Faerie Queene*, here serves a decorative purpose as translated in the thirty-sixth sonnet:—

> Look, Delia, how w' esteem the half-blown rose,
> The image of thy blush, and summer's honor.[5]

Daniel introduces from Italian poetry the "eternizing" theme—the promise to make his love immortal by his verse. The idea of the deathless quality of poetry has been seen in the Anglo-Saxon song *Widsith*, where praise is rendered to the patron "free in gifts, who would be raised among his friends to fame"; it is found also in Homer; but its most persistent expression is in the sonnet-sequences that follow Daniel. The fact that he introduced this theme, a favorite one later with Shakspere, is another link to bind him with the great poet.

The main reason for considering the two names together is that Daniel uses largely the English sonnet of three quatrains and a couplet. Critics have objected that the form was in use long before *Delia* was written, and that the knowledge of it was general. But Daniel first discovered its proper development, to which Shakspere added nothing—the gradual rise of emotion and thought to an epigrammatic climax in the last two lines, instead of the swell and fall of the Petrarchan stanza. In the ninth sonnet Daniel anticipates the very cadence of much of Shakspere, where he begins each quatrain and the couplet with a subordinate clause, and completes the sense in the last lines:—

> If this be love, to draw a weary breath,
> To paint on floods till the shore cry to th' air; .
> . . .
> If this be love, to war against my soul,
> Lie down to wail, rise up to sign and grieve,
> . . .
> If this be love, to clothe me with dark thoughts,
> Haunting untrodden paths to wail apart,
> . . .
> If this be love, to live a living death,
> Then do I love and draw this weary breath.[6]

Daniel, like Shakspere, frequently gives different versions of one theme. In that case he binds the sonnets together, either by making them grammatically dependent, as are sonnets six and seven, or more usually, by making the last line of each sonnet the first line of the next. A series on one theme thus bound together are sonnets thirty-six, thirty-seven, thirty-eight, thirty-nine, and forty. This method of concatenation has been observed already in the English lyric in the stanzas of Minot's poems, and perhaps should be referred ultimately to a similar stylistic device in Welsh poetry.

In several minor points Daniel recalls the lyrics of the miscellanies; as, to take an external trait, where he prefaces one sonnet by a title-introduction, which is necessary for understanding the poem: *Alluding to the Sparrow pursued by A Hawk, that flew into the Bosom of Zenocrates.*[7] In another sonnet he repeats the old thought—with more sincerity, no doubt, than most love-poets could—that his passion finds ample satisfaction in having aimed high.

> The mounting venture for a high delight
> Did make the honor of the fall the more.
> . . .
> And therefore, Delia, 'tis to me no blot
> To have attempted though attained thee not.[8] ·

Finally, two sonnets on going to Italy[9] recall the old lyric theme of travel. The resemblance is strengthened by the patriotic apostrophe to *Albion*, in which, by the way, such a small

thing as absence from Delia is quite forgotten in the more keenly felt absence from English shores.

In the fifty-fourth sonnet,—

> Like as the lute delights or else dislikes
> As is his art that plays upon the same,[10]

a musical instrument appears in the sonnets for the first time as an image of love and its moods. The habit persists into Shakspere's series, with the famliar picture in his hundred and twenty-eighth sonnet, of virginal-playing. It has been customary for scholars to collect such passages as this from Daniel, to prove an Elizabethan's familiarity with the music of his time; and as the lute is most often mentioned, the deduction is made that the instrument was in every one's hands. It may not be out of place, however, to notice that this and similar references to the lute are probably literary, in the same spirit in which sculptors carve Homer always with his lyre. The lute survives even in modern lyrics, perhaps because of its very melodious name, and possibly because our minds refuse to associate the poet's art with a familiar musical instrument, like the piano, for example, or the guitar. The difficulty was as great to the Elizabethans, who could not picture their poets seated at the virginal; the fact that they do imagine them with a lute in their hands, would seem to argue that the lute already was becoming a literary convention, and superseded as a practical instrument. It is a proof of Shakspere's power to find his image near at hand, that he uses the virginal, instead of the lute; but it is his mistress who plays, not the poet.

Notes

1. *Elizabethan Sonnet-Cycles*, Martha F. Crow, ii.
2. Ibid., p. 21.
3. Ibid., p. 66.
4. See *Mod. Lang. Notes*, iv. 8, 229, and v. 1, 11.
5. *Elizabethan Sonnet-Cycles*, ii. p. 51.
6. Ibid., p. 24.
7. No. xxviii, p. 43.
8. No. xxxii, p. 47.
9. Nos. xlix, p. 64, l, p. 65.
10. Ibid., p. 69.

W. J. COURTHOPE
From "Spenser's Successors: Samuel Daniel"
A *History of English Poetry*
1903, Volume 3, pp. 16–23

There is much illumination in the analogy suggested by Coleridge between the poetry of Wordsworth and that of Daniel, and the principle of composition adopted by both these poets is the secret alike of the virtues and the defects of their poetical styles. Both were idealists and philosophers in the first place, poets only in the second. Both were so strongly moved by the ardour of their thought, that they cared comparatively little to discriminate as to the best vehicle for its expression. And as each was accustomed, by the inclination of his genius, to write in verse, they frequently used this form of diction, even when the subject-matter of their conceptions was more akin to prose. But, on the other hand, as they were both always moved by a genuine enthusiasm, the weight and dignity of their thought seldom fails to penetrate through their prosaic modes of expression, and leaves in the imagination of the reader a sense of strength and character. The prime impulse in Wordsworth's poetry is the spirit of liberty characteristic of the first age of the French Revolution. Daniel's leading idea was the individual energy which was the most worthy feature of the pioneers of Humanism in Italy. This is strongly expressed in the two lines cited by Wordsworth in *The Excursion:*—

> Unless himself above himself he can
> Erect himself, how poor a thing is man!

His poetry is inspired by two constant ideals, which become more clearly defined after his Italian travels. In the midst of the decaying institutions of external chivalry, Daniel cherishes the idea, suggested to him by his studies of Castiglione, of a Court concentrating in itself all that is noble in the customs of the past, and furnishing to the nation a model of the refinement required by the present. And again, in the midst of the affectations of Court Euphuism, he kept steadily before his eyes the image of the true courtier, as he is presented in the pages of *Il Cortegiano*, the modern gentleman, complete in arts and letters as well as in arms, and assiduous in cultivating a pure and correct use of his native language.

But as Daniel is a poet of less energetic conception than Wordsworth, so is there also less of individuality in his style of metrical expression. In his early poems, at least, he is content to employ the forms consecrated by long usage, and to such an extent that his contemporaries reproached him for his timidity. Thus the author of *The Return from Parnassus*, while giving him high praise says:—

> Only let him more sparingly make use
> Of others' wit, and use his own the more,
> That well may scorn base imitation.[1]

Except for the grace and literary skill of passages resembling those which I have quoted, there is nothing individually characteristic in *Delia*; though the lifelong aim of the poet is already clearly indicated in the oblique criticism—not invidiously intended—on the archaic revivals recommended by the practice of Spenser:—

> Let others sing of knights and paladines
> In aged accents and untimely words;
> Paint shadows in imaginary lines,
> Which well the reach of their high wits records.[2]

The Complaint of Fair Rosamond, which follows the general lines of composition in *The Mirror for Magistrates*, and particularly the tragedy of *Shore's Wife* by Churchyard, is remarkable for little beyond the polished purity of its English.

In the superficial form of *The Civil Wars* the hand of the imitator was no less visible to Daniel's contemporaries. Mr. Grosart, the poet's biographer, seems indeed to be perplexed by the criticism of Guilpin—"others say that he's a Lucanist"—the meaning of which, however, is clear enough, in view of the fact that imitations of the *Pharsalia* may be noticed throughout *The Civil Wars*.[3]

Daniel only took hints from Lucan: the spirit in which he constructed his own epic was quite different from the air of deliberate and sustained rhetoric which animates the work of the clever Roman poet. He writes as at once a patriot and a moralist, with the purpose of pointing out in a worthy manner the successive steps by which the kingdom of England grew to its state of greatness and glory out of the disorders of past times. How closely the idea of poetry in his mind was associated with the idea of politics is shown by his eulogy of the English Constitution, in his animated *Defence of Rhyme:*—

> Let us go no further, but look upon the wonderful architecture of the State of England, and see whether they were deformed times that could give it such a form: where there is no one the least pillar of majesty but was set with the most profound judgment, and borne with the just conveniency of Prince and People; no Court of Justice but laid by the rule and

square of Nature, and the best of the best Commonwealths that ever were in the world: so strong and substantial as it hath stood against all the storms of factions, both of belief and ambition, which so powerfully beat upon it, and all the tempestuous alterations of humorous times whatsoever: being continually in all ages furnished with spirits fit to maintain the majesty of her own greatness, and to match in an equal concurrency all other kingdoms round about with whom it had to encounter.[4]

It was Daniel's ambition to make his native language worthy of the country whose Constitution he so much admired and loved:—

> O that the Ocean did not bound our stile
> Within these strict and narrow limits so,
> But that the melody of our sweet isle
> Might now be heard to Tyber, Arne, and Po,
> That they might know how far Thames doth outgo
> The music of declinéd Italy,
> And, listening to our songs another while,
> Might learn of thee their notes to purify.[5]

The thought that all his work is done with an eye to his noble ideal constantly sustains him:—

> But (Madam) this doth animate my mind,
> That yet I shall be read among the rest,
> And though I do not to perfection grow,
> Yet something shall I be, though not the best.[6]

And in another place:—

> I know I shall be read among the rest,
> So long as men speak English, and so long
> As verse and virtue shall be in request,
> Or grace to honest industry belong.[7]

Nevertheless, in spite of the lofty patriotism which inspires the poem, it must be admitted that Drayton's criticism on *The Civil Wars* was justified. Daniel was "too much historian in verse." Carried away by his patriotic enthusiasm, he did not reflect that his subject lacked the universal and world-wide interest of the *Pharsalia*, and that though the wars of Cæsar and Pompey might justify the use of the epic, the example could hardly warrant an English imitator of Lucan in adapting the style to events of such purely local significance as the political changes of Warwick, the King-maker, or the battles of Towton and St. Albans. In making himself the poetical chronicler of his country, Daniel did not do full justice to his genius: in such a subject "his manner better fitted prose."

His poetical ideals are exhibited to far more advantage in his Horatian Epistles and his didactic poems; and among these two are deserving of particular notice, namely, the admirable *Panegyric Congratulatorie*, addressed to James I. on his accession, and *Musophilus*, in which he throws into the form of a poetical dialogue Castiglione's views as to the importance of literature in refining the manners of a Court. No poem of the time illustrates more vividly than the former of these compositions the personal influence of an English monarch on the fortunes of the people. The general tendency of things in all countries was, as I have said, towards absolutism, and in the eyes of Daniel, James was an absolute monarch:—

> So that the weight of all seems to rely
> Wholly upon thine own discretion;
> Thy judgment now must only rectify
> This frame of power thy glory stands upon:
> From thee must come that thy posterity
> May joy this peace, and hold this union,
> For whilst all work for their own benefit,
> Thy only work must keep us all upright.

Daniel, like Bacon and almost all other political reasoners of that age, had come to the conclusion that the unsettlement of the times, caused by the anarchy of a dying feudalism, could only be righted by the firm central government of the Crown. He recalls, with skilful enthusiasm, the descent of James from Margaret Tudor, and dwells on the principle from which the reigning family derived its popular support, namely, the repression of feudalism by Henry VII.:—

> And as he laid the model of this frame,
> By which was built so strong a work of State,
> As all the powers of changes in the same,
> All that excess of a disordinate
> And lustful prince, and all that after came,
> Nor child, nor stranger, nor yet woman's fate,
> Could once disjoint in the couplements whereby
> It held together in just symmetry, etc.

Glancing for a moment at James's successful struggle with the feudal nobility of Scotland, Daniel concluded that the King would not attempt to alter the tradition of his immediate predecessors.[8] He assumed, unfortunately without warrant, that with his absolutism James would combine that knowledge of the character of the English people, which all the Tudor sovereigns possessed instinctively, but which no experience could impart to the Stuarts. Indeed, the poet himself shows that his own observation does not penetrate much below the surface of things. His mind is entirely occupied with the unsettlement of the times and the decay of manners; he says nothing of the difficulties arising out of the rupture of religious tradition, or of the despotic suppression by the Crown of the ancient liberties of the country. What he hopes to see is the Court leading the way back from the excesses of foreign affectation to the plain living and high thinking of the good old English times:—

> And bring us back unto ourselves again,
> Unto our ancient native modesty,
> From out these foreign sins we entertain,
> These loathsome surfeits, ugly gluttony;
> From this unmanly and this idle vein
> Of wanton and superfluous bravery;
> The wreck of gentry, spoil of nobleness,
> And square us by thy temperate soberness.

Daniel was in fact one of the now dwindling school of English Humanists, a convinced follower of More and Erasmus, in sympathy at once with Catholic tradition and with the rationalism of the Renaissance, and desirous of seeing the spirit of ancient art and literature accommodated to the genius of the English language. He embodied his ideal very nobly in *Musophilus*, a dialogue in verse between a courtier and a man of letters. The former (Philocosmus), depreciating the value of Humanism, points to the neglect of letters, and seeks to persuade his friend to content himself with making his way at Court:—

> And therefore leave the left and out-worn course
> Of unregarded ways, and labour how
> To fit the times with what is most in force:
> Be new with men's affections that are new:[9]
> Strive not to run an idle counter-course
> Out from the scent of humours men allow:
> For not discreetly to compose our parts

> Unto the form of men (which we must be),
> Is to put off ourselves and make our arts
> Rebels to nature and society;
> Whereby we come to bury our desarts
> In the obscure grave of singularity.

Virtue, Musophilus replies, is its own reward. Fashion does not endure. Knowledge alone is worth living for; and, with the true enthusiasm of a child of the Renaissance, he points out how men may extend their own spiritual life in the life of literature:—

> O blessèd Letters, that combine in one
> All ages past, and make one live with all!
> By you we do confer with who are gone,
> And the dead-living into council call;
> By you th' unborn shall have communion
> Of what we feel and what doth us befall.

Though Philocosmus still insists that action without culture is the more reasonable aim, he is moved by the eloquence of Musophilus to make an important admission:—

> Yet do I not dislike that in some wise
> Be sung the great heroical desarts
> Of brave renownèd spirits, whose exercise
> Of worthy deeds may call up others' hearts,
> And serve a model for posterities,
> To fashion them fit for like glorious parts;
> But so that all our spirits may tend thereto
> To make it not our grace to say but do.

In his reply Musophilus contends that art and letters are in themselves a species of action, though their value can only be measured by the "audience fit but few":—

> And for my part, if only one allow
> The care my labouring spirits take in this,
> He is to me a theatre large enow,
> And his applause only sufficient is:
> All my respect is bent but to his brow;
> That is my all; and all I am is his.
> And if some worthy spirits be pleasèd too,
> It shall more comfort breed, but not more will.
> But what if none? It cannot yet undo
> The love I bear unto this holy skill.
> This is the thing that I was born to do,
> This is my scene, this part must I fulfil.

Notes

1. *Return from Parnassus*, Act i. Sc. 2.
2. Sonnet lv.
3. Grosart's edition of Daniel's Works, Memorial-Introduction, p. xi. Compare, for example, *Civil Wars*, book i. stanzas 2, 3, with *Pharsalia*, lib. i. 8–66, and *Civil Wars*, book i, stanzas 109–118, with Pharsalia, lib. i. 523–583, and lib. ii. 16–66.
4. Daniel, *Defence of Ryme* (Works, Grosart's edition, vol. iv. p. 53).
5. Dedication of *Tragedy of Cleopatra*, to Countess of Pembroke. Grosart's edition, vol. iii. p. 26.
6. Ibid., vol. iii. p. 27.
7. Introductory Poem, "To the Reader." Grosart's edition, vol. i. p. 14.
8.   Thou wilt not alter the foundation
          Thy ancestors have laid of this estate.
                    (*Panegyric Congratulatorie.*)
9. The usual reading. I suspect Daniel, who was careful in his rhymes, wrote: "Be *now* with men's affections that are *now*": i.e. accommodate yourself to the needs of the present time.

THOMAS CAMPION

1567–1620

Thomas Campion was born on Ash Wednesday, February 12, 1567, in London. His father, a lawyer, as well as his mother died while he was still a child. Campion entered Peterhouse College, Cambridge, in 1581. He left in 1584 without a degree and entered Gray's Inn in 1586; although he was never called to the bar, he eventually obtained a medical degree in 1606.

Campion's first writings appeared in the appendix to Sidney's 1591 edition of *Astrophel and Stella*. In 1595 he published his own collection of Latin epigrams, *Poemata*. He is best known for his combination of lyric poetry with musical arrangements. His first *Book of Ayres* was published in 1601. Along with the musician Philip Rosseter, he composed scores to accompany his verses. In 1602 Campion published *Observations in the Art of English Poesie*, a literary treatise concerned with the theory of rhyme. He also wrote a technical music handbook, *A New Way of Making Four Parts in Counter-point*, which was reprinted throughout the seventeenth century.

Campion published the fourth and final *Book of Ayres* in 1617. He died on March 1, 1620, and was buried at St. Dunstan's, London.

"Ear-pleasing rhymes without art." Such is the description that Campion gives of his songs. "Ear-pleasing" they undoubtedly are; there are no sweeter lyrics in English poetry than are to be found in Campion's song-books. But "without art" they assuredly are not, for they are frequently models of artistic perfection. It must be admitted that there is inequality in Campion's work; that some of the poems are carelessly worded, others diffuse. But when criticism has said its last word in the way of disparagement, what a wealth of golden poetry is left! Turn where we will, images of beauty meet our eyes. There is nothing antiquated about these old songs; they are as fresh as if they had been written yesterday. Campion was certainly not "born out of his due time"; he came at just the right moment. Lodge and Nicholas Breton were less fortunate; they could not emancipate themselves, once for all, from the lumbering versification on which their youth had been fostered. Campion's poetry is sometimes thin, commonplace if you will, but it is never rude or heavy. "In these English airs," he writes in the address To the Reader before *Two Books of Airs*, "I have chiefly aimed to couple my words and notes lovingly together"; and he succeeded. His lyrics are always graceful and happy and unconstrained; never a jarring note; everywhere ease and simplicity. John Davies of Hereford (in the addresses To Worthy Persons appended to *The Scourge of Folly*, 1610–11) praised him in most felicitous language:—

> Never did lyrics' more than happy strains,
> Strained out of Art by Nature so with ease,
> So purely hit the moods and various veins
> Of Music and her hearers as do these.

The praise could hardly be bettered; for every reader must be struck by Campion's sureness of touch and by his variety. His devotional poetry is singularly excellent; but its worth has never been recognized. You may search your sacred anthologies and you will not meet a mention of Campion's name. But where will you find in these anthologies a poem that for spiritual fervour can compare with "Awake, awake! thou heavy sprite"? The achievements of our devotional poets are for the most part worthless, and our secular poets seem to lose their inspiration when they touch on sacred themes. All the more valuable, therefore, are these devotional poems of Campion. To fine religious exaltation he joined the true lyric faculty; and such a union is one of the rarest of literary phenomena. His sacred poems never offend against good taste. In richness of imagination the man who wrote "When thou must home to shades of

underground," and "Hark, all you ladies that do sleep," was at least the equal of Crashawe; but he never failed to exhibit in his sacred poetry that sobriety of judgment in which Crashawe was so painfully deficient.—A. H. BULLEN, "Introduction," *The Works of Thomas Campion*, 1889, pp. xv–xvii

One of Campion's acute friends observed of his "happy lyrics" that they were "strained out of art by nature so with ease." These words very well express the adroit and graceful distinction which marks his verse. His taste was at once classical and romantic. So classical was it, that for a while he was beguiled away from rhyme altogether, and gave the sanction of his delicate accomplishment to those who, like the earlier Areopagites, desired to do away with the ornament of rhyme, and to write pure English sapphics and alcaics. Fortunately, this erroneous judgment did not prevail, and Campion returned to those numbers in which he had so eminent a skill.

His knowledge of music and the exigencies of the airs to which he wrote, gave great variety and yet precision to his stanzaic forms and his rhyme-arrangements. In certain respects, he reminds us of Fletcher at his best, and as Fletcher was the younger man, it is probable that he wrote some of his lyrics under Campion's influence. But no other writer of the time arrived at anything approaching to Campion's throbbing melody in such pieces as that beginning—

> Follow your saint, follow with accents sweet,
> Haste your sad notes, fall at her flying feet,

or his quaint, extravagant grace, as in—

> I care not for these ladies,
>   That must be wooed and prayed:
> Give me kind Amaryllis,
>   The wanton country maid.
> Nature art disdaineth,
> Her beauty is her own;
>   Her when we court and kiss,
>   She cries "Forsooth, let go!"
> But when we come where comfort is,
>   She never will say "No!"

or his unexpected turns of metre, as in—

> All that you will hold watch with love,
> The fairy queen Proserpina
> Will make you fairer than Dione's dove;
> Roses red, lilies white,
>   And the clear damask hue

Shall on your cheeks alight;
Love will adorn you.

The songs of Campion are commonly of an airy, amatory kind, plaintive, fanciful, and sensuous. But not infrequently he strikes another key, and comes closer to the impassioned sincerity of Donne. The following song, from the first *Book of Airs*, is of a very high quality—

When thou must home to shades of underground,
And there arrived, a new admirèd guest,
The beauteous spirits do engirt thee round,
White Iopë, blithe Helen, and the rest,
To hear the stories of thy finished love,
From that smooth tongue whose music hell can move;

Then wilt thou speak of banqueting delights,
Of masques and revels which sweet youth did make,
Of tourneys and great challenges of kinghts,
And all those triumphs for thy beauty's sake;
When thou has told these honours done to thee,
Then tell, O tell, how thou didst murder me.

This may naturally be put by the side of "The Apparition" of Donne.

The four existing masques of Campion are skilful and gorgeous; they would be the best in English, if we could exclude the rich repertory of Ben Jonson. They give us an opportunity of judging that Campion would, had he chosen to do so, have excelled in the more elaborate kinds of poetry. His heroic verse, especially in the *Lords' Masque*, is full and stately, and deformed by none of those crabbed distortions of accentuation which many of his contemporaries affected. Campion's *Observations in the Art of English Poetry*, published in 1602, is a learned treatise on prosody, which has been unduly neglected. None of the experiments which it contains, however,—neither its "iambic dimetre," nor its "anacreontic licentiate—" are fit to compare with the author's more conventional rhymed verse.—EDMUND GOSSE, *The Jacobean Poets*, 1894, pp. 90–92

He wrote, and wrote well, in Latin as well as in English, but his importance for English literature is of a double character, and the halves are curiously opposed to each other. We have from him, in the first place, besides some masques, certain collections of verses for music, which contain much of the most exquisite rhymed poetry of the time; and, in the second place, a formal treatise intended to show, by precept and example, that English poetry ought to be unrhymed, and arranged on ancient quantitative models. It is not fair, though it has sometimes been done, to regard Campion as an apostle of the preposterous hexameters, etc., which deluded Harvey, and all but seduced Spenser. He had seen the unsuitableness of these to English (which as he acutely observed is rebel to dactyls); and though he made some Sapphics, his own attempts are chiefly in very cunningly balanced iambic and trochaic unrhymed measures, some of which—such as the most often quoted,

Rose-cheeked Laura, come—

are at least the equals, if not the superiors, of Collins's "Ode to Evening" in this unnatural kind of abstinence from the greatest charm of English verse. In his "airs," on the other hand, he allows himself the full liberty of our poetical Sion, and with the very happiest results, literally dozens of his lyrics being among the most delightful of their kind. In fact, the difficulty is to find in the *Four Books of Airs* anything that is bad—GEORGE SAINTSBURY, *A Short History of English Literature*, 1898, pp. 357–58

From the beginning of the century the new music and the lighter forms of lyrics are in the ascendency, and the madrigal is superseded largely by the airs. This second period of the song-books is for the literary student most important, because it includes the work of the greatest Elizabethan song-writer, Thomas Campion. In 1601 he collaborated with Philip Rossiter in the *Booke of Ayres* already noticed. Himself a musician as well as a poet, he composed half the music, and is supposed to have written all the words. From the musical standpoint the book is remarkable because the songs are for solo voices, with an accompaniment of lute, orpharian (a large kind of lute), and bass viol. From the literary standpoint, no other song-book can compare with this for the exquisite perfection of its lyrics. It is largely on Campion's verses that the general high opinion of Elizabethan song is founded, and it is largely from the dainty lilt of his poems that the age gets its reputation for light-hearted music. But no song writer is more independent of musical accompaniment than Campion; his lyrics have a sweetness of word-melody that could not be improved by any setting.—JOHN ERSKINE, *The Elizabethan Lyric*, 1903, pp. 230–31

Not only was he writing good verse at an early age—his first poem appearing when he was 24—but its appearance is all the more striking by its unlikeness to the poetry of the day, which with few exceptions was heavy and lumbering. Breton, Lodge, and the rest of the men on Campion's level, were not as yet emancipated from the trammels of laborious versification; but Campion's verse was from the beginning free and musical. This musical quality is indeed the one which distinguishes the whole of his poetry; it is undoubtedly connected with the practice of musical composition and due to a feeling for musical effect, to which, with his trained musical ear, he was peculiarly susceptible.

Among the earliest poems, and itself one of the freest and most charming, is 'Harke, all you ladies'. It will be noticed that this song has a somewhat curious scheme of dactyls and anapaests; the first three lines of each stanza follow the usual iambic or trochaic rhythm; but the final quatrain changes, its first two lines being anapaestic, the third dactylic, and the fourth an Adonic (except in the last stanza, where dactyls take the place of anapaests throughout). I am inclined to think that this poem foreshadows Campion's subsequent experiments in classical metres; while *Canto Secuñdo* in the same set most certainly does. These curious lines are an attempt at composition in an accentual version of the Latin First Asclepiad, the metre of Horace's 'Maecenas atavis edite regibus'; and the effect is certainly extraordinary. As far as the individual lines are concerned, the result is sometimes fairly melodious, sometimes almost doggerel; while an occasional deviation from the strict scheme may perhaps be put down to textual corruption. But it will be noticed that in such an accentual scheme the last accent must fall on the antepenultimate syllable; and unless the poet makes use of *versi sdruccioli* or antepenultimate rhymes (which he never does) the rhymes will be unaccented and almost unheard. This is, in fact, what actually happens; for the rhymes are submerged, except in so far as it is possible to get a slight secondary accent on the last: and it is quite easy to read the poem at least once without perceiving that it is actually rhymed. Perhaps, indeed, this may have marked a second stage in the poet's progress towards unrhymed verse, as involving the discovery that, in some forms of 'classical' prosody, rhyme became a negligible quantity. The further course of Campion's infection with the prevailing hostility to rhyme I shall discuss more fully in the next chapter: suffice it to say here that in the whole of his English works, excluding the examples in the

Obseruations, we only get one complete specimen of his 'classical' metres, the abominable Sapphics at the end of Part I of *A Booke of Ayres*. His musical and artistic sense was too strong for his neoterizing tendencies.

One other aspect of Campion's verse should be noticed, the extraordinary fluidity and lack of stability in his rhythms. This again is referable to the purpose of musical composition with which they were written. The marriage of music to Campion's verse was no casual or one-sided union; nor was music a mistress with whom his poetry dallied, while possessed of more serious interest. Words and music were born for each other, and in their wedding was consummated the only object of their existence. Hence, to-day, in the divorce resulting from the verdict of time that the poetry is worthy of immortality, while the music is not, we are guilty of treating the former to some extent as *in vacuo*, and apart from its usual environment. It would be exceedingly instructive if an account could be obtained from a good composer-poet of the mental processes necessary to the writing of both words and music for the same song. In many instances the nature of the air would suggest the rhythm of the verse; and conversely a half-phrase or casual line would suggest a musical theme; with the result that both words and music might have assumed some form before either had been fully worked out or committed to writing. This must have occurred in most of Campion's lyrics. On some occasions he even wrote words to music, thus reversing the usual practice; for we find two pairs of songs written to the same music, where one poem in each pair must have been written subsequently. And this close interdependence between his words and his music is the quality for which above all others he took chief credit, and received it from his contemporaries. He says himself: 'In these English Ayres I haue chiefely aymed to couple my Words and notes louingly together, which will be much for him to doe that hath not power over both'; from which it seems that the result proceeded not only from spontaneous causes, but also from conscious effort. Again, it is to this quality that Davies alludes in the lines already quoted:—

> Neuer did Lyricks more then happie *straines*
> (Straind out of *Arte* by *nature*, so with ease,)
> So purely hitt the *moods* and various *Vaines*
> Of *Musick* and her Hearers as do These.

While, however, the cause and object of these fluid rhythms was the musical setting, we are left with nothing of which to complain in their artificial separation. Campion's verse is always fresh and melodious, and agreeably varied with subtle cadences.

Campion was one of the last of the Euphuists. . . . This Euphuism was not, however, of the grosser variety, but of a refined and sublimated type; which upon ultimate analysis may be reduced merely to an unemphatic balance, or antithesis, in the structure of his sentences; a very rare illustration from

natural objects; and an occasional flavour of moral sentiment. But in many of his poems even this degree of Euphuism is totally absent, as, for example, in 'Turn back, you wanton flyer', 'Harke, all you ladies', 'If thou long'st so much to view', and several others.

Attention should also be drawn to the unlyrical quality of some of Campion's songs, which are in reality little monologue sketches; consisting, not of the lover's prayer or praise in the detached atmosphere of his contemplation, but in an actual scene of life, a dramatic dialogue where one voice is not heard. Instances will be found in 'Come, you pretty false eied wanton', 'Your fair lookes urge my desire', and a few others.

Campion's gift is mainly lyrical, and the value which his masques have for us is solely lyrical. He served no apprenticeship in dramatic construction; and where the practised hand of Ben Jonson knew just the necessary degree of coherence that a masque would admit of with advantage, Campion's plots strike me as either slightly invertebrate or slightly complicated; the best being his first, that for the marriage of Lord Hayes. But as to the poetical quality of these masques there can be no dissentient voice. They abound with the most perfect lyrical gems, while the whole web of verse is of a very high order of beauty.

His work supplies a link between two periods of different inspiration: he was acquainted with the veteran Sackville, Lord Dorset, with whose *Induction* came the first promise of light for English poetry; and, during his declining years, he was contemporary with John Donne, whose influence was already pervading the world of letters. Campion escaped that influence because his style was fixed in the earlier school. His fame, which was so deservedly great in his own time, was soon extinguished. This is entirely due to historical events, and their effect upon the ephemeral media in which he worked. The masque was at all times too expensive an entertainment to be produced by any but rich nobles and prosperous institutions; and with the establishment of the Commonwealth it disappeared, never to return. In the same way the Puritan ascendancy, with its hatred of music, especially secular music, slew the short-lived vogue of the songbooks: some hint of the trend of opinion towards distaste for the madrigal and madrigal poetry may be seen in the *Theatrum Poetarum* of Edward Phillips, Milton's nephew, who only refers to Campion on account of his mention by Camden, and expresses the opinion that he was 'a writer of no extraordinary fame'. As might have been expected, the only song that can be traced as having survived any considerable time is a sacred one, 'Neuer weather-beaten Saile,' rightly held up to admiration by Mr. Bullen as an example of rare lyrical beauty united with sincere religious fervour. This song occurs in a commonplace-book of 1707 in circumstances which suggest that it was still living at that date as a hymn.—PERCIVAL VIVIAN, "Introduction" to *The Works of Thomas Campion*, 1909, pp. lv–lviii

WILLIAM CAMDEN

1551–1623

William Camden, famous antiquarian and historian, was born on May 2, 1551, in London. Although his family was quite poor, Camden received an excellent early education at Christ's Hospital and St. Paul's School. Later he studied at Magdalen College, Broadgates Hall (later Pembroke College), and Christ Church College, all at Oxford. He was awarded a B.A. in 1573, and became a teacher at the Westminster School. In 1586 *Britannica*, the first topographical survey of England, was published. Noted for its scientific approach to history, as opposed to reliance on legends and myths, *Britannica* was published in Latin six times before an English translation, undertaken by Philemon Holland, was made available in 1610.

Camden continued teaching at Westminster, becoming headmaster in 1593. In 1597 he was appointed Clarenceux king of arms and received a generous stipend. In 1615 the first volume of his history of Elizabeth, *Annales rerum Anglicarum et Hibernicarum regnante Elizabetha*, was published. The second volume, which covered the period from 1589 to Elizabeth's death, was published posthumously in 1627. Camden helped found the English Society of Antiquarians and endowed the Camden chair of Ancient History at Oxford. He retired to Chislehurst, Kent, in 1618, and died there on November 9, 1623.

Personal

William Cambden was born *Anno* 1550 in old Baily, in the City of London. His Father, Sampson Cambden, was descended of honest parentage in Staffordshire; but by his Mothers side he was extracted from the worshipfull family of the Curwens in Cumberland.

He was brought up first in Christ-Church, then in Pauls School in London, and at fifteen years of age went to Magdalen Colledge in Oxford, and thence to Broadgates Hall, where he first made those short Latine Graces, which the Servitours still use. From hence he was removed, and made student of Christ Church, where he profited to such eminency, that he was preferred to be Master of Westminster School, a most famous seminarie of learning.

For whereas before, of the two grand Schools of England, one sent all her Foundation-scholars to Cambrdige, the other all to Oxford, the good Queen (as the Head equally favouring both Breasts of Learning and Religion) divided her Scholars here betwixt both Universities, which were enriched with many hopefull plants sent from hence, through Cambdens learning, diligence, and clemency. Sure none need pity the beating of that Scholar, who would not learn without it under so meek a Master.

His deserts call'd him hence to higher employments. The Queen first made him Richmond Herald, and then Clarenceaux King of Arms. We read how Dionysius first King of Sicily turn'd afterwards a Schoolmaster in his old age. Behold here Dionysius inverted, one that was a Schoolmaster in his youth become a King (of Arms) in his riper years, which place none ever did or shall discharge with more integrity. He was a most exact Antiquary, witnesse his worthy work, which is a comment on three kingdomes; and never was so large a text more briefly, so dark a text more plainly expounded. Yea what a fair garment hath been made out of the very shreds and Remains of the greater Work?

It is most worthy observation with what diligence he inquired after ancient places, making Hue and Crie after many a City which was run away, and by certain marks and tokens pursuing to find it; as by the situation on the Romane highwayes, by just distance from other ancient cities, by some affinity of name, by tradition of the inhabitants, by Romane coyns digged up, and by some appearance of ruines. A broken urn is a whole evidence, or an old gate still surviving, out of which the city is run out. Besides, commonly some new spruce town, not farre off, is grown out of the ashes thereof, which yet hath so much naturall affection, as dutifully to own those reverend ruines for her Mother.

By these and other means he arrived at admirable knowledge, and restored Britain to herself. And let none tax him for presumption in conjectures where the matter was doubtfull; for many probable conjectures have stricken the fire, out of which Truths candle hath been lighted afterwards. Besides, conjectures, like parcells of unknown ore, are sold but at low rates: If they prove some rich metall, the buyer is a great gainer; if base, no looser, for he payes for it accordingly.

His candour and sweet temper was highly to be commended, gratefully acknowledging those by whome he was assisted in the work (in such a case confession puts the difference betwixt stealing and borrowing) and surely so heavy a log needed more levers then one. He honourably mentioneth such as differ from him in opinion; not like those Antiquaries, who are so snarling one had as good dissent a mile as an hairs breadth from them.

Most of the English ancient Nobility and Gentry he hath unpartially observed. Some indeed object that he claws and flatters the Grandees of his own age, extolling some families rather great then ancient, making them to flow from a farre fountain because they had a great channell, especially if his private friends. But this cavil hath more of malice then truth: indeed 'tis pitty he should have a tongue, that hath not a word for a friend on just occasion; and justly might the stream of his commendations run broader, where meeting with a confluence of desert and friendship in the same party. For the main, his pen is sincere and unpartiall, and they who complain that Grantham steeple stands awry will not set a straiter by it.

Some say that in silencing many gentile families, he makes baulks of as good ground as any he ploweth up. But these again acquit him, when they consider that it is not onely difficult but impossible to anatomize the English Gentry so exactly, as to shew where every smallest vein thereof runs. Besides, many Houses, conceived to be by him omitted, are rather rightly placed by him, not where they live, but whence they came. Lastly, we may perceive that he prepared another work on purpose for the English Gentry.

I say nothing of his learned Annalls of Queen Elizabeth, industriously performed. His very enemies (if any) cannot but commend him. Sure he was as farre from loving Popery, as from hating Learning, though that aspersion be generall on Antiquaries; as if they could not honour hoary hairs, but presently themselves must doat.

His liberality to Learning is sufficiently witnessed in his Founding of an History-Professour in Oxford, to which he gave the mannour of Bexley in Kent, worth in present a hundred and fourty pounds, but (some years expired) foure hundred pounds *per Annum*, so that he merited that distich,

> Est tibi pro Tumulo, Cambdene, Britannia tota,
> Oxonium vivens est Epigramma tibi.

The Military part of his office he had no need to imploy, passing it most under a peaceable Prince. But now having lived many years in honour and esteem, death at last, even contrarie to *Jus Gentium*, kill'd this worthy Herald, so that it seems, Mortality, the Law of Nature, is above the Law of Arms. He died *Anno* 1623. the ninth of November, in the seventie fourth yeare of his age.—THOMAS FULLER, "The Life of Mʳ W. Cambden," *The Holy State and the Profane State*, 1642

He lies buried in the South cross-aisle of Westminster Abbey, his effigies ½ on an altar, with this inscription:—

> Qui fide antiqua et opera assidua
> Britannicam antiquitatem indagavit
> Simplicitatem innatam
> honestis studiis excoluit
> Animi solertiam candore illustravit
> Gulielmus Camdenius
> ab Elizabetha regina ad regis armorum
> (Clarentii titulo) dignitatem evocatus
> Hic
> Spe certa resurgendi in Christo
> S. E.
> Qui obiit anno Domini 1623, 9 Novembris,
> Aetatis suae 74:

in his hand a booke, on the leaves whereof is writt BRITANNIA.—JOHN AUBREY, "William Camden," *Brief Lives*, 1669–96

Camden appears to have been of a peculiarly happy temperament. His gentleness of disposition made and kept him many friends. He was active in body, of middle height, of a pleasant countenance, and as his portraits, taken when he was well advanced in life, present him, of a ruddy complexion. He was careless of ordinary personal distinction, and refused knighthood. "I never made suit to any man," he writes in his letter to Ussher in 1618 (*ep.* 195), "no, not to his majesty, but for a matter of course, incident to my place; neither, God be praised, I needed, having gathered a contented sufficiency by my long labours in the school." And again, his own words, "My life and my writings apologise for me" (*ep.* 194), might have been adopted as his motto. Among his intimate friends Smith enumerates Sir Robert Cotton, Bishop Godwin, Matthew Sutcliffe, Sir Henry Savile, Sir Henry Wotton, Archbishop Ussher, Sir Henry Bourghchier, Sir Henry Spelman, and John Selden. In addition, his printed correspondence connects him with Thomas Savile, who died early (1592), Degory Wheare, John Johnstone of St. Andrews, Sir William Beecher the diplomatist, and many other Englishmen; and Ortelius, James Gruter, the librarian of the Elector Palatine, the historian and statesman, Jaques de Thou, Casaubon, Peter Sweerts, Peiresc, Jean Hotman, once Leicester's secretary, and others.—E. MAUNDE THOMPSON, *Dictionary of National Biography*, 1886, Vol. 8, p. 283

General

> Cambden! the nourice of antiquitie
>   And lanterne unto late succeeding age,
> To see the light of simple veritie
>   Buried in ruinse, through the great outrage
>   Of her own people led with warlike rage:
> Cambden! though Time all moniments obscure,
> Yet thy just labours ever shall endure.
> —EDMUND SPENSER, *The Ruines of Time*, 1591

The rat is not so contemptible but he may help the lion, at a pinch, out of those nets wherein his strength is hampered; and the words of an inferior may often carry matter in them to admonish his superior of some important consideration; and surely, of what account soever I might have seemed to this learned man, yet, in respect to my profession and courteous offer, (I being an officer-of-arms, and he then but a schoolmaster), might well have vouchsafed the perusal of my notes. . . . His incongruity in his principles of heraldry—for which I challenge him!—for depriving some nobles of issue to succeed them, who had issue, of whom are descended many worthy families: denying barons and earls that were, and making barons and earls of others that were not; mistaking the son for the father, and the father for the son; affirming legitimate children to be illegitimate, and illegitimate to be legitimate; and framing incestuous and unnatural marriages, making the father to marry the son's wife, and the son his own mother. —RALPH BROOKE, *A Second Discoverie of Errours Published in the Much-Commended Brittannia* (c. 1625), 1723

The glory of this queen's reign, as well as her successor's, and the prince of our English antiquaries, was Mr. Camden, whose life has been written at large by Dr. Smith, Mr. Wood, and Dr. Gibson. So that I need not here mention any of its particulars. His *Britannia* is the book which chiefly respects the subject of this chapter; and may honestly be stiled the common sun, whereat our modern writers have all lighted their little torches.—WILLIAM NICOLSON, *The English Historical Library*, 1696–99, Ch. 1

Camden's *History of Queen Elizabeth* may be esteemed good composition, both for style and matter. It is written with simplicity of expression, very rare in that age, and with a regard to truth. It would not, perhaps, be too much to affirm, that it is among the best historical productions which have yet been composed by any Englishman. It is well known that the English have not much excelled in that kind of literature. —DAVID HUME, "Appendix" to "James I.," *History of England*, 1754–62

This English Pausanius, as he has been called, took unwearied pains to celebrate all that was worthy, valiant, and great in the annals of his country; and, at the same time he excited emulation in young minds, he formed them for great undertakings; for he was master of Westminster school, whence have issued so many divines, lawyers, warriors, and statesmen. His opinions were proudly looked up to, and his learning, his judgment, his universal knowledge, and the discharge of his professional duties, procured him the protection of his sovereign, the association of the great, and the admiration of the literari, who dignified him by the appellation of the great Camden. —CHARLES DIBDIN, *A Complete History of the Stage*, 1795, Vol. 3, p. 139

Camden possessed one of those strongly directed minds which early in life plan some vast labour, while their imagination and their industry feed on it for many successive years; and they shed the flower and sweetness of their lives in the preparation of a work which at its maturity excites the gratitude of their nation. His passion for our national antiquities discovered itself even in his school-days, grew up with him at the University; and, when afterwards engaged in his public duties as master at Westminster school, he there composed his *Britannia*, "at spare hours, and on festival days." To the perpetual care of his work, he voluntarily sacrificed all other views in life, and even drew himself away from domestic pleasures; for he refused marriage and preferments, which might interrupt his beloved studies! The work at length produced, received all the admiration due to so great an enterprise; and even foreigners, as the work was composed in the universal language of learning, could sympathise with Britons, when they contemplated the stupendous labour. Camden was honoured by the titles (for the very names of illustrious genius become such), of the Varro, the Strabo, and the Pausanias of Britain.—ISAAC DISRAELI, "Camden and Brooke," *Quarrels of Authors*, 1812–13

William Camden, now scarcely thought of except as an antiquary, was in truth a trained and ripe scholar, and an intelligent student of history. England has more reason to be proud of him than of many whose names are more familiar to our ears. The man who won the friendship of the president De Thou, and corresponded on equal terms with that eminent historian, as also with Casaubon and Lipsius abroad, and Usher and Spelman at home, must have possessed solid and extraordinary merits. . . . In 1604 he published his *Reliquiæ Britannicæ*, a treatise on the early inhabitants of Britain. In this work, undeterred by the sham array of authorities which had imposed upon Holinshed, he "blew away sixty British kings with one blast." Burleigh, the great statesman of the reign of Elizabeth, the Cavour of the sixteenth century, singled out Camden as the fittest man in all England to write the history of the first thirty years of the Queen's reign, and intrusted to him, for that purpose, a large mass of state papers. Eighteen years elapsed before Camden discharged the trust. At last, in 1615, his *History, or Annals of England during the Reign of Queen Elizabeth* made its appearance. . . . His history must be taken as a vindication, but in a more moderate tone than was then usual, of the Protestant policy of England since the accession of Elizabeth. Its value would be greater than it is, but for his almost uniform neglect to quote his authorities for the statements he makes. This fact, coupled to the discovery, in our own times, of many new and independent sources of information, to him unknown, has caused his labours to be much disregarded.—THOMAS ARNOLD, *Chaucer to Wordsworth*, 1868, pp. 125–26

As a rule, an author whose works have been originally composed in Latin, and subsequently rendered into English, cannot claim to be accounted an English author, unless the translation has been made by himself. We have had, nevertheless, to recognise exceptions to this rule in Mandeville and Sir Thomas More, and a third and hardly less important one must be made in the person of William Camden, whose *Britannia* and *Annals*, though written in Latin, are so intensely English in spirit that the question of language becomes of minor importance. There is, moreover, reason to believe that the translation of the former by Philemon Holland, though not Camden's own, was made under his direction. It is, at all events, certain that Camden's work as a topographer was more important than that which had gained an honourable place in literature for his predecessor Leland; and that he was the first English historian of contemporary events who rose above the grade of a chronicler. . . .

Of Camden's two chief works, the *Britannia* belongs to the class of monumental achievements which form great literary landmarks without being in themselves literature. Continuing the succession of Leland, it marks the definitive acceptance of antiquarianism as a branch of culture, while its own spirit is rather scientific than literary. The essence of literary grace is tasteful selection, but the topographer must be exhaustive. Pausanias probably provided but dry reading for his own age: if it be otherwise now, it is from the consciousness that so much of what he saw can never be seen again. The piety of Pausanias was piety in the strictest sense of the term: Camden treads in the vestiges, not of the gods, but of the historians. "My first and principal design," he says, "was to trace out and rescue from obscurity those places which had been mentioned by Cæsar, Tacitus, Ptolemy, Antoninus Augustus, the *Notitiæ Provinciarum*, and other ancient writers." He also confined himself to the most illustrious families, thus incurring the displeasure of upstarts. Altogether, he left so much untold that his translator, Gough, spent seven years in rendering and supplementing him, and nine more in seeing him through the press. Gough's additions are frequently more interesting than the text, but want the charm of Camden's stately diction, a legacy from the original Latin.

It has rarely happened that a book of worth, not lost or grievously mutilated, has failed of meet recognition from posterity. If there ever has been such a case, it has been that of Camden's second great work, the *Annals of Queen Elizabeth*. All circumstances might have seemed to conspire in its favour: the theme, which might confer the distinction of a national prose epic upon a book of less worth; the real merit of the execution; the very fact of its being a translation from the Latin, which brings the style nearer to that of our own day. England might have been thought the least likely of all nations to neglect a relation of one of the most glorious epochs of her history; or at least, had the mutations of taste brought about a temporary eclipse, Camden might have been expected to have shared in the great Elizabethan revival of the nineteenth century. On the contrary, there has been no edition of the Latin original since 1717, or of either of the English translations since a still earlier period. Few Englishmen know that the patient antiquary produced a book worthy to rank with Shakespeare's historical plays and Hakluyt's records of voyages as a true prose epic. Merely considered as an historian, Camden is far above mediocrity; his work, but for the excessive space accorded to the trial and execution of Mary Stuart, is well proportioned, and shows acquaintance with the best models; few annalists have so successfully avoided the annalist's habitual dryness. The merit, nevertheless, is rather moral than literary, consisting in the fine glow of patriotic feeling which throughout maintains the narrative at epical height, while the treatment of enemies is fair and courteous. The work has the inestimable advantage of being composed at a period neither too near to nor too remote from the transactions described; written under James, it is a retrospect taken when calm judgment had ceased to be obscured by contemporary passions. The execution is singularly even, there are few great passages, but there is the cumulative charm of the ceaseless and orderly procession of picturesque details, the glory of the times rather than of the author, whose skill is mainly conspicuous in the judicious marshalling of them, and in the skill with which Elizabeth, with more poetical than historical truth, is made throughout the dominant figure, the life and soul of every undertaking. One reason of the neglect of the work may be its character as a translation, although its adoption into the national literature proves that a foreign origin need be no insuperable bar. The existing versions, one of which is made from the French, are respectable rather than brilliant; a new translation, conformable to the best modern standard, would be an undertaking worthy of a scholar and a patriot.—RICH-ARD GARNETT, EDMUND GOSSE, *English Literature: An Illustrated Record*, 1904, Vol. 2, pp. 76–79

GILES AND PHINEAS FLETCHER

c. 1588–1623   1582–1650

Phineas Fletcher was born in Cranbrook, Kent, and baptized on April 8, 1582. His brother, Giles Fletcher the younger, was born in London sometime between 1585 and 1588. Both were poets after the style of Spenser, and both wrote most of their poetry while studying at Cambridge. The dramatist John Fletcher was their first cousin; their father, Giles Fletcher the elder, was a poet as well.

Phineas Fletcher received his early education at Eton, and in 1600 entered King's College, Cambridge, where he subsequently received a B.A. in 1604 and an M.A. in 1608. After leaving Cambridge he served as chaplain to Sir Henry Willoughby at Risley, Norfolk, from 1615 to 1621. He was then presented to the living of Hilgay in Norfolk, which he held until his death in 1650. The first public appearance of his work was the production of his play *Sicelides* while he was a student, though a printed edition of it was not published until 1631. His *Locustae vel Pietas Jesuitica*, an attack on the Jesuits, was published in four versions during the sixteen years he worked on it; the final version had appended to it his English paraphrase called *The Locusts or Apollyonists* (1627). In 1633 the majority of his poetry appeared together in *The Purple Island, or the Isle of Man, together with Piscatory Eclogues and other Poetical Miscellanies*. The *Piscatory Eclogues* are in form similar to the pastoral eclogues written by other poets of the time, the shepherds and shepherdesses being replaced with fisher-folk. *The Purple Island* is a long allegorical discourse detailing, first, the parts of the human anatomy; and thereafter the parts of the soul, with attendant virtues and vices. Other works appearing that year were *Elisa, or An Elegie upon the Unripe Decease of Sr Antonie Irby*, and *Sylva Poetica*, a group of Latin occasional pieces and pastorals published together with his father's *Literis Antiquæ Britanniæ*. Twenty years after Phineas Fletcher's death, a London bookseller obtained and published his personal reflections written for his family, under the title A *Fathers Testament* (1670).

Giles Fletcher was educated first at Westminster School and then accepted into Trinity College, Cambridge, where he eventually received a B.A. While there, his "Canto upon the Death of Eliza," an elegy for Elizabeth I, appeared in the collection *Sorrowe's Joy*, presented by the Cambridge scholars to James I in 1603. He probably left the university in 1610, the year of his father's death that also saw the publication of *Christ's Victory and Triumph in Heaven and Earth, Over and After Death*. A long allegory of Christ's mercy and intercession on behalf of mankind, *Christ's Victory and Triumph* was a notable influence in the later poetry of Milton, and it is the work for which Giles Fletcher is chiefly remembered. After 1610 Giles removed to the living of Alderton, an isolated village in the maritime region of Suffolk, where he remained until his early death in 1623.

Brittain's Ida, a long poem based on the legend of Venus and Anchises, was credited to Edmund Spenser when it was first published in 1628. However, subsequent scholarship assigns authorship to either Giles or Phineas Fletcher, Phineas being held slightly more probable than Giles to have written it. Possibly this was done by the author's consent, since at that time both Fletchers were beneficed clergymen and perhaps not eager to acknowledge a basically erotic poem as their work.

Personal

Grave Father of this Muse, thou deem'st too light
  To wear thy Name, 'cause of thy youthful Brain
It seems a sportful Child; resembling right,
  Thy witty Childhood, not thy graver Strain,
  Which now esteems these Works of Fancy vain:
Let not thy Child, thee living, Orphan be;
Who when thou'rt dead, will give a Life to thee.

How many barren Wits would gladly own,
  How few o'th' pregnantest own such another!
Thou Father art, yet blushest to be known;

And though 't may call the best of Muses Mother,
Yet thy severer Judgment would it smother.
O judge not *Thou*, let *Readers* judge thy Book:
Such *Cates* shou'd rather please the *Guest*, than *Cook*.
O! but thou fear'st 'twill stain the reverend Gown
  Thou wearest now; nay then fear not to show it:
For were't a Stain, 'twere Nature's, not thy own:
  For thou art poet-born; who know thee, know it:
  Thy Brother, Sire, thy very Name's a Poet.
Thy very Name will make this Poem take,
This very Poem else thy Name will make.

—W. BENLOWES, "To the Learned Author, *Son*

and *Brother* to two judicious Poets, himself the third, not second to either," *The Purple Island, or The Isle of Man,* 1633

Giles Fletcher was born in this city ⟨London⟩, son to Giles Fletcher, doctor in law, and ambassador into Russia; of whom formerly in Kent. From Westminster school he was chosen first scholar, then fellow of Trinity college in Cambridge: one equally beloved of the Muses and the Graces, having a sanctified wit; witness his worthy poem, intituled *Christ's Victory,* made by him being but bachelor of arts, discovering the piety of a saint, and divinity of a doctor. He afterward applied himself to school divinity (cross to the grain of his genius as some conceive), and attained to good skill therein. When he preached at St. Mary's, his prayer before his sermon usually consisted of one entire allegory, not driven, but led on, most proper in all particulars. He was at last (by exchange of his living) settled in Suffolk, which hath the best and worst air in England; best about Bury, and worst on the sea-side, where Master Fletcher was beneficed. His clownish and low-parted parishioners (having nothing but their shoes high about them) valued not their pastor according to his worth; which disposed him to Melancholy, and hastened his dissolution. I behold the life of this learned poet, like those half-verses in Virgil's Æneid, broken off in the middle, seeing he might have doubled his days according to the ordinary course of nature; whose death happened about the year 162 . . . He had another brother, Phineas Fletcher, fellow of King's college in Cambridge, and beneficed also in Norfolk; a most excellent poet, witness his "Purple Island," and several other pieces of great ingenuity. —THOMAS FULLER, *The History of the Worthies of England,* 1662

This learned person ⟨Phineas Fletcher⟩, Son and Brother to two ingenious Poets, himself the third, not second to either, was son to *Giles Fletcher,* Doctor in Law, and Embassadour from Queen *Elizabeth* to *Theodor Juanowick* Duke of *Muscovia;* who though a Tyranick Prince, whose will was his Law, yet setled with him very good Terms for our Merchants trading thither. He was also brother to two worthy Poets, *viz. George Fletcher,* the Author of a Poem, entituled, *Christs Victory and Triumph over and after Death;* and *Giles Fletcher,* who wrote a worthy Poem, entituled, *Christs Victory,* made by him being but Batchelor of Arts, discovering the piety of a Saint, and divinity of a Doctor. This our *Phineas Fletcher* was Fellow of *Kings Colledge* in *Cambridge,* and in Poetick fame exceeded his two Brothers, in that never enough to be celebrated Poem, entituled, *The Purple Island,* of which to give my Reader a taste (who perhaps hath never seen the Book) I shall here add two Stanza's of it.

> Thrice happy was the worlds first infancy,
> Nor knowing yet, nor curious ill to know:
> Joy without grief, love without jealousie:
> None felt hard labour, or the sweating Plough:
>   The willing earth brought tribute to her King:
>   *Bacchus* unborn lay hidden in the cling
> Of big swollen Grapes; their drink was every silver
>   spring.

And in another place, speaking of the vanity of ambitious Covetousness.

> Vain men, too fondly wise, who plough the Seas,
> With Dangerous pains another earth to find:
> Adding new Worlds to th' old, and scorning ease,
> The earths vast limits daily more unbind!
>   The aged World, though now it falling shows,
>   And hasts to set, yet still in dying grows,

Whole lives are spent to win, what one Deaths hour
  must lose.

Besides this *Purple Island,* he wrote divers *Piscatorie Eclogues, and other Poetical Miscelanies,* also a Piscatory Comedy called *Sicelides,* which was acted at *Kings-Colledge* in *Cambridge.*—WILLIAM WINSTANLEY, *The Lives of the Most Famous English Poets,* 1687, pp. 158–60

General

He that would learn *Theology,* must first study *Autology.* The Way to GOD is by ourselves: it is a blind and dirty Way; it hath many Windings, and is easy to be lost. This Poem will make thee understand that Way; and therefore my Desire is, thou mayst understand this Poem. Peruse it, as thou shouldst thyself, from thy first Sheet, to thy last. The first View, perchance, may run thy Judgment in Debt; the second will promise Payment; and the third will perform Promise. Thou shalt find here *Philosophy* and *Morality,* two curious Handmaids, dressing the King's Daughter, whose Garments smell of Myrrh and Cassia; and being wrought with Needle-Work and Gold, shall make thee take Pleasure in her Beauty. Here are no Blocks for the Purblind; no Snares for the Timorous; no Dangers for the Bold. I invite all Sorts to be Readers; all Readers to understand; and all who understand to be happy.—DANIEL FEATLY, "To the Reader," *The Purple Island, or The Isle of Man,* 1633

> Man's *Body's* like a *House:* his greater *Bones*
> Are the main *Timber:* and the lesser ones
> Are smaller *Splints:* his *Ribs* are *Laths,* daub'd o'er,
> Plaster'd with *Flesh* and *Blood:* his *Mouth's* the Door,
> His *Throat's* the narrow *Entry;* and his *Heart*
> Is the *Great Chamber,* full of curious Art:
> His *Midriff* is a large *Partition-wall*
> 'Twixt the *Great Chamber* and the *Spacious Hall:*
> His *Stomach* is the *Kitchen,* where the Meat
> Is often but half sod, for want of Heat:
> His *Spleen's* a *Vessel* Nature does allot
> To take the *Scum* that rises from the Pot:
> His *Lungs* are like the *Bellows* that respire
> In ev'ry *Office,* quick'ning ev'ry *Fire:*
> His *Nose* the Chimney is, whereby are vented
> Such *Fumes* as with the *Bellows* are augmented:
> His *Bowels* are the *Sink,* whose Part's to drain
> All noisome Filth, and keep the *Kitchen* clean:
> His *Eyes* are crystal *Windows,* clear and bright;
> Let in the Object, and let out the Sight.
> And as the *Timber* is, or great, or small,
> Or strong, or weak, 'tis apt to stand, or fall:
> Yet is the likeliest *Building* sometimes known
> To fall by obvious Chances; overthrown
> Ofttimes by *Tempests,* by the full-mouth'd *Blasts*
> Of Heav'n; sometimes by *Fire:* sometimes it wastes
> Through unadvis'd *Neglect:* put case, the Stuff
> Were Ruin-proof, by Nature strong enough
> To conquer Time, and Age; put case, it should
> Ne'er know an End, alas! our Leases would.
> What hast thou then, *proud Flesh and Blood,* to boast?
> Thy Days are evil, at best; but few, at most;
> But sad, at merriest; and but weak, at strongest;
> Unsure, at surest; and but short, at longest.
> —FRANCIS QUARLES, Untitled poem, *The
>   Purple Island, or The Isle of Man,* 1633

I Vow (sweet Stranger) if my lazy Quill
Had not been disobedient to fulfil
My quick desires, this Glory which is thine

Had but the Muses pleased, had been mine.
My *Genius* jumpt with thine; the very fame
Was our *Foundation:* in the very *Frame*
Thy Genius jumpt with mine; it got the Start
In nothing, but *Priority* and *Art.*
If (my ingenious Rival) these dull Times
Shou'd want the present Strength to prize thy Rhymes,
The time-instructed Children of the next
Shall fill thy Margin, and admire the Text;
Whose well-read Lines will teach them how to be
The happy Knowers of themselves, and thee.

> —FRANCIS QUARLES, "To the Ingenious
> Composer of this Poem, The *Spenser* of this
> Age," *The Purple Island, or The Isle of
> Man,* 1633

It has often been lamented by wise and good Men, that whilst such a Number of useless and pernicious Writings are daily issuing from the Press, so many valuable Authors of the last Century should continue to remain in Obscurity. No one appears to have been more sensible of this, than the late excellent Mr. JAMES HERVEY, Author of the *Meditations among the Tombs,* &c. by whom several scarce and useful Books were rescued from the Pit of Oblivion. In the *Letters* written to his Friends, we find mention made of this very Poem; which was put into his Hands a few Weeks before his Decease: with which he was so well pleased, that he intended revising it for the Press; and to add another Poem entitled *Christ's Victory and Triumph in Heaven and on Earth.* To this he says, he "was more particularly inclined, there being so few Scriptural Poems in our Language, wrote by Men of Genius." . . .

PHINEAS ⟨FLETCHER⟩ was educated at *King's College, Cambridge,* and beneficed at *Hilgay* in *Norfolk.* This Poem procured him the Title of *The* SPENSER *of the Age,* from his Cotemporaries; particularly by QUARLES, Author of the *Emblems,* &c. Some may consider this as paying him too high a Compliment; yet it is acknowledged by all, that in this Piece there is great Fertility of Invention, a glowing Imagination, a Display of much Learning, and a Vein of Piety. This Poem being allegorical, it may be necessary to say something concerning that Species of Writing. An Allegory is a figurative Speech, in which more is contained than what the literal Meaning conveys. Thus the *Roman* Commonwealth is addressed by *Horace* under the Picture of a Ship. The Fables of *Esop,* the Iliad and Odyssey of *Homer,* and the Æneid of *Virgil,* are all reckoned of this Kind. The Use of it is of very early Date, and both *Plato* and *Socrates,* who are considered as the wisest amongst the Heathens, recommended it. But what fully evinces its Excellence and Utility is the frequent Use made of it in the Scriptures, and by our blessed LORD himself.

We have several Examples of allegorical Writing in the English Language both in Prose and Verse: amongst the latter, the following Piece has been greatly admired by those into whose Hands it has fallen; and which many wished to see reprinted, being exceeding scarce, and seldom to be purchased at any Rate.

As the *Stanza* used by the Author (nearly as in SPENSER'S *Fairy Queen*) is very different from the Measure in which most modern Poetry is written, it may seem awkward at first to some Persons. This the Editor found to be the Case with some of his Acquaintance; but who, after reading a few Pages, acknowledged it became both familiar and pleasing. It is requested of the Reader, to peruse all the Pieces prefixed to the Poem; and pay particular Attention to the Notes as they occur in the II. III. IV. and V. Cantos, which contain a full Description of that wonderful Structure the human Body. As this Poem was writ-

ten near Two Hundred Years ago, the Reader will not be surprised, if he should meet with an obsolete Word; which as Mr. HERVEY, on a similar Occasion, beautifully remarked, "may be likened to a Hair adhering to a fine Suit of Velvet, or like a Mote dropped upon a Globe of Crystal." For which Blemishes, and the Deficiency of the Rhyme in a few Instances, no further Apology will be necessary. Respecting the Luxuriance of the Descriptions in some Parts, we hope for the Allowance of Candour and Benevolence.—"P. B.," "Preface to the New Edition" of *The Purple Island, or The Isle of Man,* 1783

They were both the disciples of Spenser, and, with his diction gently modernized, retained much of his melody and luxuriant expression. Giles, inferior as he is to Spenser and Milton, might be figured, in his happiest moments, as a link of connexion in our poetry between those congenial spirits, for he reminds us of both, and evidently gave hints to the latter in a poem on the same subject with *Paradise Regained.*

Giles's *Temptation and Victory of Christ* has a tone of enthusiasm peculiarly solemn. Phineas, with a livelier fancy, had a worse taste. He lavished on a bad subject the graces and ingenuity that would have made a fine poem on a good design. Through five cantos of his *Purple Island,* he tries to sweeten the language of anatomy by the flowers of poetry, and to support the wings of allegory by bodily instead of spiritual phenomena. Unfortunately in the remaining cantos he only quits the dissecting table to launch into the subtlety of the schools, and describes Intellect, the Prince of the Isle of Man, with his eight counsellors, Fancy, Memory, the Common Sense, and the five external Senses, as holding out in the Human Fortress against the Evil Powers that besiege it. . . .

But the conclusion of the *Purple Island* sinks into such absurdity and adulation, that we could gladly wish the poet back again to allegorizing the bladder and kidneys. In a contest about the eternal salvation of the human soul, the event is decided by King James the First (at that time a sinner upon earth) descending from heaven with his treatise on the Revelations under his arm, in the form of an angel, and preceding the Omnipotent, who puts the forces of the dragon to the rout.

These incongruous conceptions are clothed in harmony, and interspersed with beautiful thoughts: but natural sentiments and agreeable imagery will not incorporate with the shapeless features of such a design, they stand apart from it like things of a different element, and, when they occur, only expose its deformity. On the contrary, in the brother's poem of *Christ's Triumph,* its main effect, though somewhat sombrous, is not marred by such repulsive contrasts; its beauties, therefore, all tell in relieving tedium, and reconciling us to defects.—THOMAS CAMPBELL, *Specimens of the British Poets,* 1819

Giles and Phineas Fletcher were brothers, cousins of the dramatist, and both clergymen. Giles, who died in 1623, is the author of a poem entitled *Christ's Victory and Triumph in Heaven and Earth over and after Death,* which was published in a quarto volume in 1610. It is divided into four parts, and is written in stanzas somewhat like those of Spenser, only containing eight lines each instead of nine; both the Fletchers, indeed, were professed disciples and imitators of the great author of the *Fairy Queen.* Phineas, who survived till 1650, published in 1633, along with a small collection of *Piscatory Eclogues and other Poetical Miscellanies,* a long allegorical poem, entitled *The Purple Island,* in twelve books or cantos, written in a stanza of seven lines. The idea upon which this performance is founded is one of the most singular that ever took possession of the brain even of an allegorist: the *Purple*

Island is nothing else than the human body, and the poem is, in fact, for the greater part, a system of anatomy, nearly as minute in its details as if it were a scientific treatise, but wrapping up everything in a fantastic guise of double meaning, so as to produce a languid sing-song of laborious riddles which are mostly unintelligible without the very knowledge they make a pretence of conveying. After he has finished his anatomical course, the author takes up the subject of psychology, which he treats in the same luminous and interesting manner. Such a work as this has not claim to be considered a poem even of the same sort with the *Fairy Queen*. . . . *The Purple Island* is rather a production of the same species with Dr. Darwin's *Botanic Garden*; but, forced and false enough as Darwin's style is in many respects, it would be doing an injustice to his poem to compare it with Phineas Fletcher's, either in regard to the degree in which nature and propriety are violated in the principle and manner of the composition, or in regard to the spirit and general success of the execution. Of course, there is a good deal of ingenuity shown in Fletcher's poem; and it is not unimpregnated by poetic feeling, nor without some passages of considerable merit. But in many other parts it is quite grotesque; and, on the whole, it is fantastic, puerile, and wearisome. . . . It ought to be mentioned, however, to the honour of these two writers, that the works of both of them appear to have been studied by Milton, and that imitations of some passages in each are to be traced in his poetry.—GEORGE L. CRAIK, *Sketches of the History of Literature and Learning in England*, 1845, Vol. 4, pp. 13–15

Works

It is common, and indeed natural, with most people who are either averse to thinking for themselves, or are dissident of the rectitude of their own opinions, to adopt implicitly, and retain with zeal, the opinions of those who have acquired a character in the world for ingenuity or penetration. The name of PISCATORY ECLOGUE is perhaps unfavourable, from the severe treatment which Mr. Addison has been pleased to bestow on what was the first attempt in this particular species of composition, *viz.* the *Eclogues* of *Sannazarius*, which (with all deference to the opinion of so able a critic) whoever shall peruse, will, it is believed, be convinced that they hardly deserve such usage. Perhaps the truth was, that Mr. Addison, before *Sannazarius* came in his way, had laid down what he esteemed the essential requisites of pastoral, and was afterwards, in his review of the pastoral writers, necessarily obliged to praise or condemn according to these rules.—However, it were extremely easy to show that several of his requisites are so far from being essentially necessary, that many of the most esteemed pastorals can by no means be reduced to, or measured by their standard.

The pastoral state, according to his rules, is a state of the most perfect simplicity, innocence, and ease; in short, a golden age.—It is not to be denied, that in order to paint the pleasures of a pastoral life, we must bestow a tint of simplicity, and easy contentment; at the same time, nothing can be more fantastical than to depart entirely from nature, and describe a manner of life, which neither ever did, nor could possibly exist. An affectation of this kind in the writers of pastoral, is the reason why we are justly displeased with most of the modern pastorals, as well as with many of the ancient. But the compositions in this way of writing, which are universally admired, will be found to have departed far from this rule. The most esteemed *Eclogues* of Virgil admit often of polished, and even of refined sentiments: and it is with justice that we admire these, since it is well known, that the earliest ages, and the greatest simpli-

city of manners have produced compositions rich in sentiments the most exalted, as well as most beautiful. Many of Spenser's pastorals are so intolerably rude, (or simple, if one chooses to call them so), that they only excite ridicule: some there are extremely beautiful, but they are those only where he has kept nature in view, and forbore an over-affectation of simplicity.

Another rule of pastoral, according to this writer, and which indeed has a necessary dependence on his first requisite, is, that the smallest hint of misfortune or calamity should be entirely banished from such a state of ease and innocence. He will allow only a few slight anxieties, such as what a shepherd may feel on having his foot pricked with a thorn, breaking his crook, or losing a favourite lamb; because, says he, we must think that life extremely happy, where these are the greatest misfortunes.—But besides the disgusting sentiment of improbability which this system conveys, we must always judge according to our own feelings; and instead of sympathising with the unhappy shepherd who laments such piteous calamities, we must undoubtedly laugh at him.—The complaints of Virgil's Melibæus will affect every reader, because they are real, and come home to every man's concerns.

So much has been said on these, which Mr. Addison calls the requisites to pastoral, because it is presumed he has on them founded his criticism upon the *Eclogues* of *Sannazarius*. It is on these principles that he censures both TASSO and GUARINI, in the *Aminta* and *Pastor fido*; and had he seen a composition, the produce of the northern part of our island, and allowed a master-piece of the pastoral kind, it had probably been measured by the same standard, and, in that case, as certainly condemned.

The word *Pastoral* implies, that the characters are shepherds: *Eclogue* signifies, a select poem of any kind; but is generally applied to compositions of the like nature with pastorals; and so far as they have some characterising marks in common, they may be judged of by a common standard; but an allowance must always be made for the sentiments which are peculiar to the several characters. Thus we have seen Town-eclogues as well as Pastoral Eclogues, to both of which it would be ridiculous to apply the same standard of simplicity, &c.; each have their different merits, and are capable of their peculiar beauties.—Piscatory Eclogue forms a third species, and cannot be measured by the standard of either of the former. One rule is certain in all these compositions: Examine the characters, and according as they conform to nature, let the performance be judged.—While we set up a visionary standard, such as that of a perfect state of innocence and simplicity, we shall never find two persons who agree exactly in opinion of the same performance.

Were it necessary to say any thing in recommendation of Piscatory Eclogue, we might assert perhaps its advantages over Pastoral. The life of a fisherman admits often of scenes as delightful as those which the shepherd enjoys, and those scenes are much more varied. The nature of the occupation of the former gives rise to a greater variety of incidents, and those likewise more interesting, than that of the latter can furnish.— A subject often handled must become trite, and Piscatory Eclogue has the advantage over Pastoral in displaying a field less beaten and less frequented.—But FLETCHER'S *Eclogues* will speak for themselves, and sufficiently vindicate both the nature of the composition and their own peculiar merit.

These *Eclogues* have been but once printed, above 130 years ago, and they have met with a fate which I am sure they do not merit, being now almost unknown.—ALEXANDER FRASER TYTLER, LORD WOODHOUSELEE, "Of Pastoral and

Piscatory Eclogue," Introduction to *Piscatory Eclogues, With Other Poetical Miscellanies*, 1771, pp. i–vii

⟨T⟩he five first cantos of *The Purple Island* are almost entirely taken up with an explanation of the title; in the course of which the reader forgets the poet, and is sickened with the anatomist. Such minute attention to this part of the subject was a material error in judgment; for which, however, ample amends is made in what follows. Nor is Fletcher wholly undeserving of praise for the intelligibility with which he has struggled through his difficulties, for his uncommon command of words, and facility of metre. After describing the body, he proceeds to personify the passions and intellectual faculties. Here fatigued attention is not merely relieved, but fascinated and enraptured; and, notwithstanding his figures, in many instances, are too arbitrary and fantastic in their habiliments, often disproportioned and overdone, sometimes lost in a superfluity of glaring colours, and the several characters, in general, by no means sufficiently kept apart; yet, amid such a profusion of images, many are distinguished by a boldness of outline, a majesty of manner, a brilliancy of colouring, a distinctness and propriety of attribute, and an air of life, that we look for in vain in modern productions, and that rival, if not surpass, what we meet with of the kind even in Spenser, from whom our author caught his inspiration. After exerting his creative powers on this department of his subject, the virtues and better qualities of the heart, under their leader Eclecta, or Intellect, are attacked by the vices: a battle ensues, and the latter are vanquished, after a vigorous opposition, through the interference of an angel, who appears at the prayers of Eclecta. The poet here abruptly takes an opportunity of paying a fulsome and unpardonable compliment to James the First (canto xii, stanza 55); on that account, perhaps, the most unpalatable passage in the book. From Fletcher's dedication of this his poem, with his *Piscatory Eclogues* and *Miscellanies*, to his friend Edmund Benlowes, it seems, that they were written very early, as he calls them "raw essays of my very unripe years, and almost childhood." It is to his honour that Milton read and imitated him, as every attentive reader of both poets must soon discover. He is eminently intitled to a very high rank among our old English classics. . . . —Quarles, in his Verses prefixed to *The Purple Island*, hints, that he had a poem on a similar subject in agitation, but was prevented from pursuing it by finding it had got into other hands.—HENRY HEADLEY, *Select Beauties of Ancient English Poetry*, 1787, Vol. 1

An ardent admiration for Spenser inspired the genius of two young brothers, Phineas and Giles Fletcher. The first, very soon after the Queen's death, as some allusions to Lord Essex seem to denote, composed, though he did not so soon publish, a poem, entitled *The Purple Island*. By this strange name he expressed a subject more strange; it is a minute and elaborate account of the body and mind of man. Through five cantos the reader is regaled with nothing but allegorical anatomy, in the details of which Phineas seems tolerably skilled, evincing a great deal of ingenuity in diversifying his metaphors, and in presenting the delineation of his imaginary island with as much justice as possible to the allegory without obtruding it on the reader's view. In the sixth canto he rises to the intellectual and moral faculties of the soul, which occupy the rest of the poem. From its nature it is insuperably wearisome; yet his language is often very poetical, his versification harmonious, his invention fertile. But that perpetual monotony of allegorical persons, which sometimes displeases us even in Spenser, is seldom relieved in Fletcher; the understanding revolts at the confused crowd of inconceivable beings in a philo-

sophical poem; and the justness of analogy, which had given us some pleasure in the anatomical cantos, is lost in tedious descriptions of all possible moral qualities, each of them personified, which can never co-exist in the *Purple Island* of one individual.

Giles Fletcher, brother of Phineas, in *Christ's Victory and Triumph*, though his subject has not all the unity that might be desired, had a manifest superiority in its choice. Each uses a stanza of his own; Phineas one of seven lines, Giles one of eight. This poem was published in 1610. Each brother alludes to the work of the other, which must be owing to the alterations made by Phineas in his *Purple Island*, written probably the first, but not published, I believe, till 1633. Giles seems to have more vigour than his elder brother, but less sweetness, less smoothness, and more affectation in his style. This, indeed, is deformed by words neither English nor Latin, but simply barbarous, such as *elamping, eblazon, deprostrate, purpured, glitterand*, and many others. They both bear much resemblance to Spenser: Giles sometimes ventures to cope with him, even in celebrated passages, such as the description of the Cave of Despair. And he has had the honour, in turn, of being followed by Milton, especially in the first meeting of our Saviour with Satan in the *Paradise Regained*. Both of these brothers are deserving of much praise; they were endowed with minds eminently poetical, and not inferior in imagination to any of their contemporaries. But an injudicious taste, and an excessive fondness for a style which the public was rapidly abandoning, that of allegorical personification, prevented their powers from being effectively displayed.—HENRY HALLAM, *Introduction to the Literature of Europe*, 1837–39, Pt. 3, Ch. 5, Pars. 32–33

The *Purple Island* is an allegorical description, in twelve cantos, of the corporeal and intellectual functions of man. Its interest and effect have been greatly injured by a too minute investigation of anatomical facts; the first five cantos being little else than a lecture in rhyme, and productive more of disgust than any other sensation. In the residue of the poem, the bard bursts forth with unshackled splendour, and the passions and mental powers are personified with great brilliancy of imagination, and great warmth of colouring. Like his brother, however, he is defective in taste; the great charm of composition, simplicity, is too often lost amid the mazes of quaint conception and meretricious ornament. Yet are there passages interspersed through this allegory, of exquisite tenderness and sweetness, alike simple and correct in diction, chaste in creative power, and melodious in versification.

The *Piscatory Eclogues*, to novelty of scenery add many passages of genuine and delightful poetry, and the music of the verse is often highly gratifying to the ear; but many of the same faults which are discernible in these pieces, which we remarked in the *Purple Island*; pedantry and forced conceits occasionally intrude, and, though the poet has not injured the effect of his delineations by coarseness, or rusticity of expression, he has sometimes forgotten the simple elegance which should designate the pastoral muse.—NATHAN DRAKE, *Shakespeare and His Times*, 1817, Vol. 1, p. 623

The so-called *Piscatory Eclogues* of Phineas Fletcher differ from Spenserian pastorals only in this, that the occupations of Thyrsilis, Thelgon, Dorus, Thomalin, and the rest, are those of fishermen rather than shepherds. Otherwise the fiction is the same; and, following his simple fisher-lads down the Cam, or the Thames, or the Medway, or out at sea in their skiffs along the rocky coasts, the poet, just as in the other case, but with more of watery than of sylvan circumstance, expresses his own feelings and makes his own plaint.

About the sixth canto,—where the poet passes from technical anatomy and physiology into what may be called the psychology of his subject, and begins to enumerate and marshall the faculties, habits, and passions of man, each under a separate personification, with a view to the great battle of the virtuous powers of the list under their leader Eclecta, or Choice, against the vices,—then the genius of the poet, already more than indicated even in the former cantos, takes wing into a freer element, which it fills, in the remaining six cantos, with beauty and sublimity in ill-devised profusion. Some of the personifications, in the latter part of the *Purple Island*, are not surpassed in Spenser; and, on the whole, the poetry, though still wearisome from the unflagging strain of the abominable allegory, is richer than in his brother's shorter production, if not so serenely solemn.—DAVID MASSON, *The Life of John Milton*, 1859, Vol. 1, Ch. 6

Of all the strange poems in existence, surely this is the strangest. *The Purple Island* is man, whose body is anatomically described after the allegory of a city, which is then peopled with all the human faculties personified, each set in motion by itself. They say the anatomy is correct: the metaphysics are certainly good. The action of the poem is just another form of the *Holy War* of John Bunyan—all the good and bad powers fighting for the possession of the Purple Island. What renders the conception yet more amazing is the fact that the whole ponderous mass of anatomy and metaphysics, nearly as long as the *Paradise Lost*, is put as a song, in a succession of twelve cantos, in the mouth of a shepherd, who begins a canto every morning to the shepherds and shepherdesses of the neighbourhood, and finishes it by folding-time in the evening. And yet the poem is full of poetry. He triumphs over his difficulties partly by audacity, partly by seriousness, partly by the enchantment of song. But the poem will never be read through except by students of English literature. It is a whole; its members are well-fitted; it is full of beauties—in parts they swarm like fireflies; and *yet* it is not a good poem. It is like a well-shaped house, built of mud, and stuck full of precious stones. I do not care, in my limited space, to quote from it. Never was there a more incongruous dragon of allegory.—GEORGE MAC-DONALD, *England's Antiphon*, 1868, pp. 155–56

EDMUND GOSSE
From *The Jacobean Poets*
1894, pp. 137–49

It is now time to discuss those non-dramatic writers who remained throughout the Jacobean period entirely devoted to the Spenserian tradition. Among these Giles Fletcher the younger was the most original and brilliant. He was a scion of that great house of poets to whom our early literature owed so much. His father, Giles the elder, was the Russian traveller and the author of *Licia*; his elder brother, Phineas, wrote *The Purple Island*; his cousin was John Fletcher, the dramatist. The exact date of his birth is unknown, but circumstances point to 1585 as the probable year. The death of Queen Elizabeth gave him his first opportunity of appearing before the public, in a "Canto upon the Death of Eliza," which was printed at Cambridge in 1603. In many respects it is a remarkable little poem, especially as showing the lad to have been already intellectually and artistically adult. The form of stanza chosen is exactly what Giles selected afterwards for his epic; and what has never been used (with a doubtful exception to be presently mentioned) before or since by any one but himself. The relation to Spenser, too, whose followers in style the whole family of the Fletchers distinctly were, is just as determined and scarcely more excessive than in his *Christ's Victory*. All that can be said is that the "Canto" displays none of those sudden intense beauties that are a wonder and a delight in its author's finished style. . . .

Of all the works written in direct discipleship of Spenser, *Christ's Victory* is undoubtedly the most coherent and the best. Such prodigies as *Psyche* can only be reverenced far off; such masses of poetic concrete as *The Purple Island* were made to dip into and to quote from. *Christ's Victory* has the great advantage of being easy to read all through. In its style, again, we note a distinction between its author and the other learned and more or less admirable Spenserians; while their highest success was found in gaining for a little time that serene magnificence, without distinct elevation, which bore their model on upon so soft and so steady a wing, Giles Fletcher aimed at higher majesties of melody and imagination than Spenser attempted, and not unfrequently he reached a splendour of phrase for a parallel to which we search the *Faery Queen* in vain. At the same time, it must not, in all candour, be forgotten that he lived in an age of rapid poetic decadence, and that his beautiful fancies are sometimes obscured by an uncouth phraseology and a studied use of bizarre and tasteless imagery. These improprieties and extravagancies of form have, it cannot be denied, a certain whimsical charm of their own, like the romanesque ornaments of debased periods in Art, nor would it be necessary to dwell on them as a positive blemish, if their adoption in poetry had not so often been proved to be the inevitable precursor of decay. But these, after all is said, and their magnitude pressed to its full, are slight stains on a writer otherwise so royally robed in pure poetic purple.

Christ's Victory and Triumph is the first important religious poem in seventeenth-century English. The full title is *Christ's Victory and Triumph in Heaven and Earth, Over and After Death*, and it is divided into four books, characterized by these four divisions of the epical theme. The stanza in which it is written is the nine-lined one of Spenser, compressed into an octett by the omission of the seventh line, and so deprived of that fourth rhyme which is one of its greatest technical difficulties. When it is added that each book contains from sixty to eighty of these stanzas, it will be perceived on how moderate and reserved a scale the whole has been composed; and the treatment is sensibly rendered more impressive by this very reserve. "Christ's Victory in Heaven" begins with a long array of theological paradoxes in the favourite manner of the time, but expressed with exceptional dignity; we soon find ourselves taken up to heaven and made present at that precise moment of the past ages in which Mercy—

> Lift up the music of her voice, to bar
> Eternal Fate, lest it should quite erase
> That from the world which was the first world's
>   grace.

Justice, however, rises to oppose her, and on this impersonation Fletcher has poured out the richest treasures of his imagination. In a strain that recalls the ripest manner of Keats, the manner that is of *Hyperion* and the last sonnets, he cries—

> She was a Virgin of austere regard;
>   Not as the world esteems her, deaf and blind;
> But as the eagle that hath oft compared
>   Her eye with Heaven's, so, and more brightly
>   shined
>   Her lamping sight.

A little later on and we might persuade ourselves that it was Shelley speaking, and in *Adonaïs*—

> The winged lightning is her Mercury,
>   And round about her mighty thunders sound;
> Impatient of himself lies pining by
>   Pale Sickness with his kercher'd head upwound.

The argument of Justice being that mankind has sinned so grossly against its Maker that it is now beyond the pale of hope, Mercy rises to defend the fallen against so sweeping a denunciation. The description of her personality might have served Coleridge with a text for his favourite sermon on the difference between imagination and fancy. Great is the falling off from the simple grandeur of the picture of Justice; the charm here is more superficial, the language more affected. Mercy is robed in garments by herself embroidered with trees and towers, beasts, and all the wonders of the world. Above her head she wears a headdress of azure crape, held up by silver wire, in which golden stars are burning against a flood of milk-white linen; a diamond canopy hangs over her, supported by little dancing angels and by King David. After she has pleaded, Repentance rises, disconsolate and ill-favoured, with her hair full of ashes, whom Mercy pauses to comfort—

> Such when as Mercy her beheld from high,
>   In a dark valley, drowned with her own tears,
> One of her Graces she sent hastily,
>   Smiling Irene, that a garland wears
> Of gilded olive on her fairer hairs,
>   To crown the fainting soul's true sacrifice;
>   Whom when as sad Repentance coming spies,
> The holy desperado wiped her swollen eyes.

Mercy at once comforting Repentance and assuaging Justice, charges the worst of Man's fault upon the Devil, and celebrates Christ from his nativity. The book closes so, with a peroration that is sometimes strangely Miltonic, as in these lines—

> The angels carolled loud their song of praise,
>   The cursed oracles were stricken dumb,

which Milton simply transferred to his *Ode on the Morning of Christ's Nativity.*

The second part, "Christ's Victory on Earth," is inferior in purity of style to the preceding. It is much more overloaded with figurative language of a rococo kind, with a choice of imagery which sacrifices propriety to magnificence, and with that paradoxical kind of ornament which is called conceit. Mercy, in her coach, attended by a thousand loves, finds Christ in the wilderness, and sinks, unperceived, into His breast. He is then minutely described in pretty and even luxurious language, which resembles nothing so much as the jewelled pictures of Fra Lippo Lippi and Benozzo Gozzoli, full of flowers and tall plants, gems and rare raiment, and angels with brilliant wings, where all is sumptuous, but the face of the Madonna meaningless and vapid. So the description here of Christ, with his curly jet hair and his strawberry-cream complexion, is too pretty to be in keeping with the solemnity of the subject. . . . The most significant passage in the rest of this canto is the description of the garden and the court of Vain-Glory, in which Fletcher attempts the peculiar style of which Spenser is most admirably a master, and approaches with extraordinary success to the sumptuous and splendid richness of his original.

The two remaining cantos are not so easy to describe, though none the less beautiful. "Christ's Triumph over Death" is a philosophical disquisition on the various modes in which the universe was affected by the Triumph; there is now no action and little description. We read here of the crucifixion, with the shame of earth and the anger of heaven, where—

> The mazèd angels shook their fiery wings,
>   Ready to lighten vengeance from God's Throne,

and of Christ's earlier passion in the garden. The fourth canto, "Christ's Triumph after Death," is, in fact, an ecstatic hymn of the Resurrection, and the beatific vision of God in Paradise. The gorgeous and luminous style of Giles Fletcher here reaches its highest pitch, and we find ourselves reminded, though without imitation, of Dante's *Paradiso.* The joys of heaven and earth in redemption are celebrated with a splendour of language hardly to be met with elsewhere in the whole of Protestant religious literature. . . .

Between Giles Fletcher and his elder brother Phineas there existed the closest fraternal affection and intellectual sympathy, and we find repeated in the works of each identical fragments of expression. The difference between them simply consisted in that indefinable distinction between genius and talent. But while Giles is for ever startling us with such incomparably poetic phrases as "a globe of wingèd angels," "the laughing blooms of sallow," "wide-flaming primroses," or "the moon's burning horns," Phineas, who was not less accomplished, and who lived to be far more voluminous, never reaches this white heat of imagination. He is none the less a poet of remarkable force and variety, curiously individual, and worthy of close examination. Phineas Fletcher was born at Cranbrook early in 1582, the eldest son of Giles Fletcher the elder. He proceeded to Eton and to King's College, Cambridge, residing at the University from 1600 to 1616. During these years his poetry was mainly, if not entirely, written, although most of it first saw the light far later; in 1611 he took priest's orders. In 1621 Phineas was presented to the living of Hilgay in Norfolk, where he seems to have stayed till the Civil War. In 1670 we are told that he died "several years since;" many of his descendants are said to exist still in the parish of Hilgay.

None of Phineas Fletcher's books were published until after the reign of James I. But what was probably the latest of them, the *Locustes*, appeared in 1627, the "piscatory" play of *Sicelides* (written in 1614) in 1631, and the volume containing *The Purple Island, or the Isle of Man, together with Piscatory Eclogues and other Poetical Miscellanies*, in 1633. The volume called the *Locustes* contains the satire so named, which is in Latin verse, and a paraphrase or poem of like theme in English, composed in a nine-line stanza which closely resembles the Spenserian. This is called *The Apollyonists*, and it is a noble epic fragment on the Fall of the Rebel Angels, with the figure of Satan as that of the hero; a bitter attack on the Jesuits is introduced. Milton was not only well acquainted with the writings of Phineas Fletcher, but he paid to the *Apollyonists* the compliment of borrowing more from it than from any other work when he came to write his own *Paradise Lost. Sicelides* is a choral drama, principally in rhyme, with comic prose passages; the romantic story, laid in Sicily, mainly pieced together with reminiscences from Ovid's *Metamorphoses.* The *Piscatory Eclogues* and the miscellaneous poems are so obviously variants in the manner of Phineas Fletcher's longest and most famous work that we may pass on without further delay to a description of the latter.

Successive generations of poetic readers have been disappointed to find that *The Purple Island* is not some purpureal province of fairyland washed by "perilous seas forlorn," but the ruddy body of man, laced with veins of purple blood. The poem, in fact, is an allegory descriptive of the corporeal and moral qualities of a human being, carried out with extreme persistence, even where the imagery is most grotesque and inconvenient. From internal indications, we may gather that

The Purple Island was written early in Fletcher's Cambridge career, perhaps about 1605, while his brother was still at his side, and other ardent young spirits were stirring Phineas to literary emulation. When we recover from the first shock of the plan, we have to confess *The Purple Island* to be extremely ingenious, cleverly sustained, and adorned as tastefully as such an unseemly theme can be by the embroideries of imaginative writing. In mere cleverness, few English poems of the same length have excelled it, and its vivacity is sustained to the last stanza of the last canto.

The poet supposes himself seated in summer under the orchard walls of Cambridge, by the slow waters of "learned Chamus," in company with two pleasant friends. With them he discusses poetry, history, fate, and his own biography, till the first canto closes with the announcement that he proposes to sing the story of "the little Isle of Man, or Purple Island." At the opening of the second canto, Thirsil, for so he calls himself, is discovered at sunset on a gentle eminence with "a lovely crew of nymphs and shepherd boys" clustered around him, and to this audience he pipes his strange anatomical ditty, each successive canto, however grisly its theme, being presented to us in a recurrence of this delicate pastoral setting.

In canto two, we read of the foundation of the Purple Island, its rescue from decay, the marble congelation of its bones, the azure river-system of its veins and arteries, the rose-white wall of its skin, and all the quaint devices by which the poet idealizes its digestive system. The third canto, after so exquisite an opening as this—

> The morning fresh, dappling her horse with roses,
>   Vexed at the lingering shades, that long had left
>   her
> In Tithon's freezing arms, the light discloses,
>   And, chasing night, of rule and heaven bereft
>   her,
> The sun with gentle beams his rage disguises,
> And, like aspiring tyrants, temporises,
> Never to be endured, but when he falls or rises,

takes an immediate plunge into the liver and that "porphyry house" in which "the Isle's great Steward," the heart, dwells. With all the humours and exudations of the body Phineas Fletcher laboriously sports, with a plentiful show of such physiology as was then attainable. In canto four the heart again and the lungs are treated; in canto five the head, the face, and the organs which occur in it. After describing the tongue, the story of Eurydice is told, and the anatomical portion of the allegory is concluded.

It is a pity that the physiology presses in so early in the poem, for the most beautiful part is yet to come. With canto six, the intellectual and moral qualities pass under consideration, and in particular we are introduced to the will, as fair Voletta, and to that "royal damsel and faithful counsellor" Synteresis, the conscience. In cantos seven and eight, the vices are personified at great length and with remarkable vigour; in cantos nine and ten, the virtues are similarly introduced. Cantos eleven and twelve describe a sort of holy war in Man's members, and the battle between virtue and vice which revolutionizes the Purple Island. Such is the rough outline of a work which resembles none other in our language, and which is so curious and interesting in its workmanship as to forbid us to lament the extraordinary nature of the author's original plan. Having chosen a theme of unusual ugliness and aridity, Phineas Fletcher has contrived so to treat it as to produce a work of positive, though of course Alexandrine and fantastic beauty. . . .

The relation of Phineas Fletcher to Spenser is very close, but the former possesses a distinct individuality. He is enamoured to excess of the art of personification, and the allegorical figures he creates in so great abundance are distinct and coherent, with, as a rule, more of Sackville than of Spenser in the evolution of their types. In his eclogues he imitates Sannazaro, but not without a reminiscence of *The Shepherd's Calendar*. Nevertheless, Spenser is the very head and fount of his being, and the source of some of his worst mistakes, for so bound is Phineas to the Spenserian tradition that he clings to it even where it is manifestly unfitted to the subject he has in hand.

THOMAS LODGE

1558–1625

Thomas Lodge was born in Lincolnshire in 1558. His father, Sir Thomas Lodge, was the Lord Mayor of London. Lodge was educated at the Merchant Taylors' School, London, and Trinity College, Oxford. Lodge briefly studied law at Lincoln's Inn in 1578, but abandoned law for literature.

Lodge's first published work, *A Defence of Plays* (c. 1580), was written in response to a Puritan pamphlet written by Stephen Gosse, *School of Abuse*. Lodge then wrote *An Alarum against Usurers* (1584), depicting the dangers of money lenders. Lodge's first romance, *The Delectable Historie of Forborius and Priscilla*, appeared in 1584. *Scillaes Metamorphosis* was published in 1589, and reissued as *Glaucus and Scilla* in 1610. After writing these early romances, Lodge traveled on two expeditions, the first in 1588 to the islands of Terceras and the Canaries and the second in 1591 to South America. During the first voyage Lodge wrote his best-known romance, *Rosalynde: Euphues' Golden Legacies*, which later served as a source for Shakespeare's *As You Like It*. Lodge's other works include *Phillis* (1593), a cycle of amorous sonnets based on French and Italian models, *A Fry for Momus* (1595), a collection of verse satires and epistles styled after Horace, and *A Looking Glasse for London and England*, a drama written with Robert Greene.

Lodge studied medicine at Oxford, becoming a doctor in 1603. Lodge may have converted to Catholicism sometime around 1600 with his marriage to Joan Aldred, a suspected Catholic. They spent several years in exile on the Continent, returning to England around 1612. Lodge's later works include *The Famous and Memorable Workes of Josephus* (1602), *A Treatise on the Plague* (1603), and a translation of *The Workes, both Morall and Natural, of Lucius Annaeus Seneca* (1614). Lodge died of the plague during the fall of 1625.

Personal

Was descended from a family of his name living in Lincolnshire, but whether born there, is not ascertained. He made his first appearance at the university of Oxford about the year 1573, and was afterwards a scholar under the learned Mr. Edward Hobye of Trinity College; where, says Wood, making very early advances, his ingenuity began first to be observed, in several of his poetical compositions. After he had taken one degree in arts, and dedicated some time to reading the bards of antiquity, he gained some reputation in poetry, particularly of the satiric species; but being convinced how barren a foil poetry is, and how unlikely to yield a competent provision for its professors, he studied physic, for the improvement of which he went beyond sea, took the degree of Dr. of that faculty at Avignon, returned and was incorporated in the university in the latter end of Queen Elizabeth's reign: Afterwards settling in London, he practiced physic with great success, and was particularly encouraged by the Roman Catholics, of which persuasion it is said he was.

. . . This learned gentleman died in the year 1625, and had tributes paid to his memory by many of his cotemporary poets, who characterised him as a man of very considerable genius. Winstanley has preserved an amorous sonnet of his, which we shall here insert.

If I must die, O let me chuse my death:
Suck out my soul with kisses, cruel maid!
In thy breasts crystal balls, embalm my breath,
Dole it all out in sighs, when I am laid;
Thy lips on mine like cupping glasses clasp;
Let our tongues meet, and strive as they would sting:
Crush out my wind with one straight-girting grasp,
Stabs on my heart keep time while thou dost sing.
Thy eyes like fearing irons burn out mine;
In thy fair tresses stifle me outright:
Like Circe, change me to a loathsome swine,
So I may live for ever in thy sight.
  Into heaven's joys can none profoundly see,
  Except that first they meditate on thee.

When our author wishes to be changed into a loathsome swine, so he might dwell in sight of his mistress, he should have considered, that however agreeable the metamorphosis might be to him, it could not be so to her, to look upon such a loathsome object.—THEOPHILUS CIBBER, *The Lives of the Poets*, 1753, Vol. 1, pp. 164–66

General

To the Gentlemen Readers, Health. Gentlemen, after many of mine owne labours that you have courteouslie accepted, I present you with *Euphues shadowe*, in the behalfe of my absent friend, M. Thomas Lodge, who at his departure to sea upon a long voyage, was willing, as a generall farewell to all courteous Gentlemen, to leave this his worke to the view, which if you grace with your favours eyther as his affected meaning, or the worthe of the worke requires, not onely I for him shall rest yours, but what laboures his Sea studies affords, shall be, I dare promise, offered to your sight, to gratifie your courtesies, and his pen, as himselfe every waye yours for ever. Farewell.— ROBERT GREENE, "Preface" to *Euphues Shadow*, 1592

And thou, my Goldey, which in Sommer dayes
Has feasted us with merry roundelayes;

And, when my Muse scarce able was to flye,
Didst imp her wings with thy sweete Poesie.
  —MICHAEL DRAYTON, *Endimion and Phœbe*,
  1594

Lodge for his oare in every paper boate,
He that turns over *Galen* every day,
To sit and simper *Euphues* legacy.
  —UNSIGNED, *The Returne from Pernassus*, 1606,
  Act 1, Sc. 2

Lodge and Greene are the only imitators of Lyly who have atoned for affectation of style by any felicity of genius or invention.—JOHN DUNLOP, *The History of Fiction*, 1814

Thomas Lodge was Greene's senior in age, and greatly his superior in conduct. He had been a graduate of Oxford; next a player, though probably for a short time; was a member of Lincoln's Inn; and, finally, a successful physician of the name of Thomas Lodge is held to be identical with Lodge the poet. He was the author of a tragedy, *The Wounds of Civil War: lively set forth in the true Tragedies of Marius and Sylla*. He had become a writer for the stage before the real power of dramatic blank verse had been adequately conceived. His lines possess not the slightest approach to flexibility; they invariably consist of ten syllables, with a pause at the end of every line—"each alley like its brother;" the occasional use of the triplet is the only variety. Lodge's tragedy has the appearance of a most correct and laboured performance; and the result is that of insufferable tediousness. In conjunction with Greene he wrote *A Looking Glass for London*, one of the most extraordinary productions of that period of the stage, the character of which is evidently derived not from any desire of the writers to accommodate themselves to the taste of an unrefined audience, but from an utter deficiency of that common sense which could alone recommend their learning and their satire to the popular apprehension. For pedantry and absurdity *The Looking Glass for London* is unsurpassed. Lodge, as well as Greene, was a writer of little romances; and here he does not disdain the powers of nature and simplicity. The early writers for the stage, indeed, seem one and all to have considered that the language of the drama was conventional; that the expressions of real passion ought never there to find a place; that grief should discharge itself in long soliloquies, and anger explode in orations set forth upon the most approved forms of logic and rhetoric. There is some of this certainly in the prose romances of Greene and Lodge. Lovers make very long protestations, which are far more calculated to display their learning than their affection. This is the sin of most pastorals. But nature sometimes prevails, and we meet with a touching simplicity, which is the best evidence of real power. Lodge, as well as Greene, gave a fable to Shakspere.—CHARLES KNIGHT, *Studies of Shakspere*, 1849, p. 30

In considering Lodge's literary character, it may be remarked that he belongs to a class of writers, the Greenes, Lylys, Marlowes, and Peeles, displaying poetical and dramatic genius, not indeed of the highest order, but from the versatility of their talents, and the early period in which they flourished, as the precursors of our greater English dramatists, not likely to be soon forgotten.—DAVID LAING, "Introduction" to Sidney's *A Defence of Poetry*, 1853, p. lviii

Lodge's love-poems have an exquisite delicacy and grace: they breathe a tenderer and truer passion than we find in any of his contemporaries. His sonnets are more loose and straggling, slighter and less compactly built, than Constable's or Daniel's; but they have a wonderful charm of sweet fancy and unaffected tenderness. His themes are the usual praises of beauty and complaints of unkindness; but he contrives to impart to them a most unusual air of sincere devotion and graceful fervour. None of his rivals can equal the direct and earnest simplicity and grace of his adoration of Phyllis, and avowal of faith in her constancy. . . .

There is a seeming artlessness in Lodge's sonnets, a winning directness, that constitutes a great part of their charm. They seem to be uttered through a clear and pure medium straight from the heart: their tender fragrance and music come from the heart itself. If the poet's design was to assume a pastoral innocence and simplicity, he has eminently succeeded. There are many conceits in his sonnets, but they are expressed so simply and naturally that they take on the semblance of half-earnest beliefs. . . .

It may, however, be acknowledged that Lodge's nature was not specially fitted for the sonnet form of composition; he was not sufficiently patient and meditative to elaborate intricate stanzas. His lines have on them the dewy freshness of an impulsive gush,—a freshness off which the dew has not been brushed by the travail of thought; and the opening of his sonnets in many cases leads us to expect better things than we find as we proceed when the leading idea has been hammered out into a quatorzain. . . .

Lodge's *Fig for Momus* is often amusing, but the satire is not very pungent. He was much too good-natured a man to be a satirist: he was not capable even of smiling spite, much less of bitter derision.—WILLIAM MINTO, *Characteristics of English Poets*, 1874, pp. 198–202

All the sonnets in the *Phillis*, a work of the most tantalizing inequality, suffer more or less from Lodge's caprices of style; so that while only a necessary discretion is exercised in limiting the selection to a single sonnet, it has been too frequently at a sacrifice of beauties which one would fain pluck from their commonplace environment.—DAVID M. MAIN, *A Treasury of English Sonnets*, 1879, p. 260

Lodge, flushed from lyric bowers.
—ALGERNON CHARLES SWINBURNE, "The Many," 1882

Lodge, indeed, as it seems to me, was one of the not uncommon persons who can always do best with a model before them. He euphuised with better taste than Lyly, but in imitation of him; his tales in prose are more graceful than those of Greene, whom he copied; it at least seems likely that he out-Marlowed Marlowe in the rant of the *Looking-Glass for London*, and the stiffness of the *Wounds of Civil War*, and he chiefly polished Sidney in his sonnets and madrigals. It is not to be denied, however, that in three out of these four departments he gave us charming work.—GEORGE SAINTSBURY, *A History of Elizabethan Literature*, 1887, p. 109

Lodge was the least boisterous of the noisy group of learned wits who, with Greene and Marlowe at their head, invaded London from the universities during the close of Elizabeth's reign. He began to write as early as 1580, and was among the first who adopted the style invented by Lyly in his *Euphues*; but it was not until Greene had successfully composed several romances in this manner that Lodge came forward and surpassed both Greene and Lyly in his lovely fantastic pastoral of *Rosalynde*,

composed under a tropical sky, as the author sailed with Captain Clarke between the Canaries and the Azores. During the next ten years Lodge was very prolific, closing this part of his career with the *Margarite of America*, an Arcadian romance, so named because the poet was in Patagonia when he wrote it. By this time, or soon after, all the young men of genius with whom he had associated were dead, and Lodge retired from literary life, and settled down as a physician. He lived on almost to the birth of Dryden; but his place as a poet is among the immediate followers of Spenser and precursors of Shakespeare.

In some respects Lodge is superior to most of the lyrical poets of his time. He is certainly the best of the Euphuists, and no one rivalled him in the creation of a dreamy scene, 'out of space, out of time,' where the loves and jousts of an ideal chivalry could be pleasantly tempered by the tending of sheep. His romances, with their frequent interludes of fine verse, are delightful reading, although the action flags, and there is simply no attempt at characterisation. A very courtly and knightly spirit of morality perfumes the stately sentences, laden with learned allusion and flowing imagery; the lovers are devoted beyond belief, the knights are braver, the shepherds wiser, the nymphs more lovely and more flinty-hearted than tongue can tell; the courteous amorous couples file down the long arcades of the enchanted forest, and find the madrigal that Rosader or the hapless Arsinous has fastened to the balsam-tree, or else they gather round the alabaster tomb of one who died for love, and read the sonnet that his own hand has engraved there. This languid elegant literature was of great service in refining both the language and the manners of the people. There was something false no doubt in the excessive delicacy of the sentiment, something trivial in the balanced rhythm and polish of the style; but both were excessively pretty, and both made possible the pastoral and lyrical tenderness of the next half-century. Among all the Elizabethans, no one borrowed his inspiration more directly from the Italians than Lodge; he was fortunately unaware of the existence of Marini, but the influence of Sannazaro and of the school of Tasso is strongly marked in his writings.

As a satirist Lodge is weak and tame; as a dramatist he is wholly without skill; as a writer of romances we have seen that he is charming, but thoroughly artificial. It is by his lyrical poetry that he preserves a living place in literature. His best odes and madrigals rank with the finest work of that rich age. In short pieces of an erotic or contemplative character he throws aside all his habitual languor, and surprises the reader, who has been toiling somewhat wearily through the forest of Arden, by the brilliance and rapidity of his verse, by the *élan* of his passion, and by the bright turn of his fancy. In his best songs Lodge shows a command over the more sumptuous and splendid parts of language, that reminds the reader of Marlowe's gift in tragedy; and of all the Elizabethans Lodge is the one who most frequently recalls Shelley to mind. His passion in the *Rosalynde* has a little of the transcendental and ethereal character of the *Epipsychidion*, while now and again there are phrases so curiously like Shelley's own, that we are tempted to believe that the rare quartos of Lodge must have passed through the later poet's hands. One such example is the

> A Turtle sate upon a leafless tree,
> Mourning her absent fere,

with its curious resemblance to

> A widow bird sate mourning for her love
> Upon a wintry bough.

The sonnets of Lodge are gorgeous in language, but lax in construction; he did not understand the art of concentrating and sustaining his fancy in a sonnet; but the volume entitled *Phillis* contains many beautiful fragments and irregular pieces, tending more or less to the sonnet form. His epics of *Scilla's Metamorphosis* and *Elstred* are rambling pieces in the six-line stanza, produced rather in consequence of the success of *Venus and Adonis* than out of any genuine desire to tell a classical story. In each poem the action is neglected, and the tale, such as it is, is smothered under a shower of courtly, flowery fancies. A poem 'in commendation of a solitary life,' is one of Lodge's most admirable pieces, but is too long to be given here, and does not lend itself to quotation. He was a poet of fine genius, fervent, harmonious, and florid; but he was too sympathetic or not strong enough to resist the current of contemporary taste, running swiftly towards conceit.—EDMUND GOSSE, "Thomas Lodge," *The English Poets*, ed. Thomas Humphry Ward, 1880, Vol. 1, pp. 424–26

Of all Lodge's multifarious writings, his contributions to the drama form the least valuable portion. He has written excellent prose pamphlets. His versions of Seneca and Josephus have placed him beside North and Holland in the front rank of Elizabethan translators. His *Fig for Momus* gives him a prominent place among the fathers of English classical satire. He is the author of some of the most exquisitely graceful and musical lyrics to be found in our early poetry. His pastoral poems, and above all his *Scilla's Metamorphosis*, though of a beauty too luscious and florid to please a severe taste, are among the good things of their kind. On his delightful prose romance, *Rosalynde, or Euphues' Golden Legacy*, Shakspeare founded *As You Like It*, and it is doing Lodge no more than justice to say that we still turn with pleasure from the drama to the novel. But his powers, versatile though they were, were not such as qualified him to excel as a dramatist. His only extant play . . . is *The Wounds of Civil War*. It treats of the struggle between Marius and Sulla, and is based partly on Plutarch and partly on apocryphal matter, which is, for aught we know, Lodge's own invention. The plot is ill constructed, the characters, though by no means without individuality, are without interest, and the action, in spite of its studied variety, has all the effect of the most tiresome monotony. Historically, the work is interesting as a step towards Shakspeare's Roman plays. It is, perhaps, the first English drama inspired by Plutarch, and the first attempt to romanticise, in the technical sense of the term, Roman history. Thus the introduction of a clown, two comic scenes, in one of which a Gaul talks in a jargon of French and broken English, and a scene in which Marius makes a complaint to respondent Echo, link it with the Romance. The blank verse is easy and fluent, but very monotonous, and is studiously constructed on the model of the couplet.—JOHN CHURTON COLLINS, "The Predecessors of Shakspeare," *Essays and Studies*, 1895, pp. 177–79

Lodge has suffered the fate of all poets who have thought of their style before their subject. He had a graceful fancy, a fine taste, and a tuneful ear, but his mind was not possessed by any idea of universal interest. He was first inspired to write by the atmosphere of prevailing Euphuism; most of his compositions—plays, novels, histories, sonnets, and satires—are steeped in this fashionable manner. For many of the subjects he attempted he had no turn. His dramas are written with a heavy hand; his satires are of that general kind which awakens no fear, and therefore no interest. The sonnet had long ceased to yield any fresh store of conceits; and the only novelties that Lodge could introduce into it for the glorification of his Phillis were double rhymes and fresh mechanical combinations of sound. . . .

The themes with which his genius is most in sympathy are mythological or romantic love stories in which his fancy can wander freely, and make excursions at pleasure into lyric verse. He had something of Ovid's ingenious invention; and this shines particularly in *Scilla's Metamorphosis*, the first of a long line of subjects suggested to English poets by classical mythology. . . .

Lodge may also claim the honour of having inspired Shakespeare with *As You Like It*. In *Euphues' Golden Legacy*, the story is very gracefully told in prose interspersed with lyrics, as in Sidney's *Arcadia* and Greene's *Menaphon*. The songs have much beauty though of an artificial kind.—W. J. COURTHOPE, *A History of English Poetry*, 1897, Vol. 2, pp. 322–25

Works

ROSALYNDE

Placing Lodge's novel by the side of other productions of the same class, we cannot hesitate to declare it a very amusing and varied composition, full of agreeable and graceful invention (for we are aware of no foreign authority for any of the incidents), and with much natural force and simplicity in the style of the narrative. That it is here and there disfigured by the faults of the time, by forced conceits, by lowness of allusion and expression, and sometimes by inconsistency and want of decorum in the characters, cannot be denied. These are errors which the judgment and genius of Shakespeare taught him to avoid; but the admitted extent and nature of his general obligations to Lodge afford a high tribute to the excellence of that "original," which Steevens pronounced "worthless."—JOHN PAYNE COLLIER, "Introduction" to *Rosalynde*, *Shakespeare's Library*, 1843, Vol. 1

The last work of fiction of any importance which distinctly bears the impress of euphuism. . . . It is probably the only work of fiction of Elizabeth's time which could be read through at the present day without impatience.—BAYARD TUCKERMAN, *A History of English Prose Fiction*, 1882, p. 88

Lodge was a true poet, though his path was on the lower slopes of Parnassus, and his *Rosalynde* has much natural beauty that is in some sense heightened by the artifices of its style.—HENRY MORLEY, *English Writers*, 1893, Vol. 10, p. 61

If Sidney had no followers in the line of ideal fiction, he had at least a rival with the novel readers of the time in the person of Thomas Lodge. The latter's *Rosalind*, which appeared about the same time as the *Arcadia*, resembles the latter in its essence, being an attempt to fuse in one narrative the best features of the heroic and pastoral school of fiction. It is possible that Lodge may have received some useful hints from the efforts of Sidney, but at all events his story is more compact, more logical, and consequently more readable. Certain situations of the romances of chivalry are here repeated and the pastoral notion of the heroine's disguise in man's dress plays a prominent part in the plot.—F. M. WARREN, *A History of the Novel Previous to the Seventeenth Century*, 1895, p. 338

J. PAYNE COLLIER
"On Thomas Lodge and His Works"
The History of English Dramatic Poetry
1831, Volume 3, pp. 213–20

As a poet, Lodge is to be placed in a rank superior to Greene, and in some respects inferior to Kyd. Greene's love of natural beauty was overlaid by a mass of affectation and conceit, which rarely allowed it to appear, and to a certain degree he was imitated by Lodge, with whom he was intimate, and with whom he wrote one dramatic performance. The love of natural beauty in Lodge, however, breaks through the fanciful allusions and artificial ornaments with which he endeavoured to adapt himself to the taste of the time. It is not my business to investigate the character of Lodge's poetry beyond its connection with the stage, but a collection of his pastoral and lyrical pieces, published in 1819, contains many specimens of beautiful versification, elegant thoughts, and natural imagery. It is well known that Shakespeare took the story of his *As You Like It* from a novel by Lodge, first published in 1590 under the title of *Rosalynde*, and subsequently often reprinted. Of this production it may be said (and no higher praise can well be given to it), that our admiration of many portions of it will not be diminished by a comparison with the work of our great dramatist.[1]

Lodge is second to Kyd in vigour and boldness of conception, but as a drawer of character (so essential a part of dramatic poetry) he unquestionably has the advantage, a point that is fully exemplified by his historical play, called *The Wounds of Civil War, lively set forth in the true tragedies of Marius and Sylla.* We can hardly call it a work of genius, but unquestionably it required no common talent to produce it. The only edition of it was published in 1594, but it had then been some years upon the stage: Lodge commenced author about 1580, when he wrote a defence of theatrical performances, and had perhaps, at that early date, produced, or been concerned in some plays; but *The Wounds of Civil War* was not written until after 1586, as the greater part of it is in blank-verse. One circumstance, which may lead to the opinion that *The Wounds of Civil War* was not performed long after the appearance of Marlow's *Tamburlaine the Great*, is that it contains a scene imitated from, and intended to rival one in that most applauded production. It is in Act iii., where Sylla returns victor over Mithridates, and, seated in a triumphant car, is drawn upon the stage by Moors and captive Princes.

The characters of old Marius and of his younger rival are drawn in *The Wounds of Civil War* with great force, spirit, and distinctness, a task the more difficult, because they so strongly resembled each other in the great leading features of ambition and cruelty. Marius possesses, however, far more generosity and sterner courage than Sylla, who is impetuously tyrannical and wantonly severe; and the old Roman until his death, after his seventh consulship, absorbs the interest of the reader. Young Marius is also introduced, and is distinguished by his fortitude, his constancy, and his affection for his father. Antony is another prominent personage, and is represented gifted with irresistible eloquence, of which many not unfavourable specimens are inserted. There are two females, Cornelia and Fulvia, the wife and daughter of Sylla, the one remarkable for her matronly firmness, and the other for her youthful delicacy and tenderness, which however do not prevent her conducting herself with the resolution becoming a Roman maid. A Clown and various coarsely comic characters are employed in two scenes, in order to enliven and vary the performance. The plot of the piece (which may be seen reprinted in Vol. viii. of the last edition of *Dodsley's Old Plays*) is founded chiefly upon the lives of Marius and Sylla, in Plutarch, and the scene is changed, just as the necessities of the poet required, from Rome to Pontus, Minturnum and Numidia.[2]

The blank-verse of Lodge runs with even more monotony than is found in the dramatic pieces of his contemporaries Peele and Greene: he now and then inserts an additional syllable, for convenience rather than by design; but he seems studiously to avoid the use of trochees at the ends of his lines, as if he considered them a defect, and that the verse ought to close with an emphatic and accented syllable. Of this opinion there are several striking proofs in the play: in one scene, Sylla says to his flying army,

> Are you the wonder'd legions of the world,
> And will you fly these shadows of *resist*?

If Lodge had not thought that a trochee at the end of a line ought to be avoided, he would, of course, have written 're-sistance' instead of 'resist,' which is an awkward conversion of a verb into a substantive. Another instance of the use of the same word, for the same reason, occurs afterwards, when Lucretius says to Tuditanus of the resolute opposition of young Marius and his followers at Præneste,

> Their valour, Tuditanus, and *resist*,
> The manlike fight of younger Marius,
> Makes me amaz'd to see their miseries.

So far did Lodge carry this notion, that he rarely terminates a verse with a word of the same quantity as that which closes the last of the preceding lines. Some long speeches are in rhyme, and stanzas and couplets are numerous throughout, which tend to establish that it was an early performance after the first introduction of blank-verse upon the common stage. One point connected with the rhymes of this play merits observation: Lodge often uses triplets, a circumstance of rare occurrence in other dramatic poets preceding Shakespeare. The following, from one of the speeches of Antony, may be taken as a sufficient specimen of the smoothness of the versification of Lodge: it is addressed to Sylla, to dissuade him from executing the bold and sturdy Granius:—

> Aye, but the milder passions show the man;
> For as the leaf doth beautify the tree,
> The pleasant flowers bedeck the painted spring,
> Even so in men of greatest reach and power.
> A mild and piteous thought augments renown.
> Old Antony did never see, my lord,
> A swelling shower did continue long,
> A climbing tower that did not taste the wind,
> A wrathful man not wasted with repent.
> I speak of love, my Sylla, and of joy,
> To see how fortune lends a pleasant gale
> Unto the spreading sails of thy desires;
> And loving thee must counsel thee withal:
> For as, by cutting, fruitful vines increase,
> So faithful counsels work a prince's peace.

This passage, in the word 'repent' for repentance, affords another instance of the constraint Lodge put upon himself in order to preserve the weight at the conclusion of his lines. The whole scene which relates to the capture of Cornelia and Fulvia, their contempt of death, and their liberation from the fear of it by the magnanimity of Marius, is finely written, making allowance for the system to which Lodge subscribed.

The dramatic performance which Lodge produced in conjunction with Robert Greene, and which was first printed in 1594,[3] must, of course, have been written prior to September, 1592, when Greene died. The whole scope of it seems to be to counteract the prevalent puritanical notion, that dramatic amusements were antiscriptural and immoral. It applies the story of Nineveh to the City of London, the prophet Oseas being introduced as a speaker; and after every scene, in which some fresh crime or vice is pourtrayed, he warns the inhabitants of the metropolis, lest they also in the same manner incur the wrath of heaven. His speeches, with one exception, are in rhyme, and of these the subsequent will be as long a specimen as is necessary.

Iniquity seeks out companions still,
And mortal men are armed to do ill.
London, look on, this matter nips thee near;
Leave off thy riot pride and sumptuous cheer.
Spend less at board and spare not at the door,
But aid the infant and relieve the poor;
Else seeking mercy, being merciless,
Thou be adjudg'd to endless heaviness.

Adultery, incest, murder, bribery, usury, drunkenness, &c., with their evil consequences, are exhibited in turn; and in order to accomplish this object the most incongruous matter is introduced, giving the manners of London as those of Nineveh, and mixing up Rasni and his queen and concubines with the knaves, lawyers, usurers, and beggars of the metropolis. It however contains a severe satire and moral lecture, and the authors seem to have had no scruple in speaking out; but the censure is always general, and never could have had any particular application. Jonas 'cast out of the whale' upon the stage, laments over the state of Israel, and after Oseas has taken his departure, he too warns the inhabitants of Nineveh to repent. Rasni and his adherents accordingly put on sackcloth and ashes, and the face of things is entirely changed; for, instead of shouts and revellings, nothing but lamentations and prayers are heard on every side, and Nineveh, by the mouth of Jonas, is forgiven: he thus moralises in the conclusion—

Wend on in peace and prosecute this course,
You islanders, on whom the milder air
Doth sweetly breathe the balm of kind increase,
Whose lands are fattened with the dew of heaven,
And made more fruitful than Actean plains,
You, whom delicious pleasures dandle soft;
Whose eyes are blinded with security,
Unmask yourselves, cast error clean aside.

He then likens the crimes of London to those of Nineveh, and ends with the following extravagant compliment to Queen Elizabeth—

And think the prayers and virtues of thy Queen
Defer the plague which otherwise would fall.
Repent, oh London! lest for thine offence
Thy shepherd fail, whom mighty God preserve,

That she may bide the pillar of his church
Against the storms of Romish Antichrist.
The hand of mercy overshade her head,
And let all faithful subjects say, Amen.

This is scarcely more absurd than all the rest of the performance, which is wearisomely dull, although the authors have endeavoured to lighten the weight by the introduction of scenes of drunken buffoonery between a 'clown and his crew of ruffians,' and between the same clown and a person disguised as the devil, in order to frighten him, but who is detected and well beaten. There was no such marked difference between the styles of Greene and Lodge as to enable us to decide which part of the play was written by the one and which by the other.

Notes

1. It is supposed that Lodge was born about 1556, and that after having been a player, in 1584 he became a student of Lincoln's Inn, and subsequently (at what date is uncertain) a Doctor of Medicine: probably when he went on a voyage with Cavendish in 1592, it was in the capacity of surgeon to the expedition. In 1596, he published his *Fig for Momus*, consisting of Satires, Eclogues, and Epistles, all of which have various degrees of merit, and in some pieces it is of a high order, especially his Satires. Heywood, in his *Troja Britannica*, 1609, mentions Lodge as one of the famous physicians of the day; and he was living in 1616, as is proved by the following extract from the Register of the Privy Council of that year.

                                        Jany. 10, 1616
   A passe for Tho. Lodge, Doctor of Physic, and Henry Savell, gent., to travell into the Arch-duke's Country, to recover such debts as are due unto them there, taking with them two servants, and to returne agayne within five moneths.

   It seems likely, therefore, that Lodge acquired considerable property by his practice.
2. Dramatic properties are little observed: Plutarch represents that the assassin employed to kill Marius on this occasion was a Gaul, and accordingly Lodge makes him a Frenchman, speaking broken English and scraps of his own language. This person swears *Par le sang de Dieu*, Jesu, &c.; and Marius himself, 'By our Lady.' Towards the close, a clown talks in Rome of the *Paul's steeple of honour* as the highest point that can be attained.
3. A unique copy of this edition is among the many dramatic rarities of the Duke of Devonshire.

NICHOLAS BRETON

c. 1545–c. 1626

Nicholas Breton was born in London, probably around 1545. The stepson of the poet George Gascoigne, he was educated at Oriel College, Oxford. His early patrons were Sir Philip Sidney and the latter's sister Mary, Countess of Pembroke. Among his many verse and prose works, two volumes of pastoral lyrics, *Britton's Boure of Delights* (1591) and *The Passionate Shepheard* (1604), are best remembered. Breton's poetry is characterized by the use of pre-Spenserian metres such as the six-line or rhyme-royal stanza. Eight of his poems appeared with the works of Sidney, Spenser, Marlowe, and Ralegh in the 1600 collection *England's Helicon*.

Breton's prose descriptions of the months and hours, *Fantasticks* (c. 1604), anticipated the fashion of character books, and were modeled after the *Characters* of Theophrastus, which were translated into Latin in 1592. A later work, *The Good and the Badde* (1616), is a further essay in this didactic genre. Little is known about Breton's own life, although most of his work has survived and was reprinted by Alexander B. Grosart in 1879. He is believed to have died around 1626.

Thov, that wouldst finde the habit of true passion,
    And see a minde attir'd in perfect straines;

No twearing moodes, as gallants doe a fashion,
    In these pide times, only to shewe their braines,

Looke here on BRETONS Worke, the master print:
　Where, such perfections to the life doe rise;
If they seeme wry, to such as looke asquint,
　The fault's not in the object, but their eyes.

For, as one comming with a laterall viewe
Vnto a cunning piece wrought perspectiue,
Wants facultie to make a censure true;
　So with this Authors readers will it thriue:

Which, being eyed directly, I diuine
His proofe their praise, will meet, as in this line.

　　　　—BEN JONSON, *In Authorem prefacing Breton's*
　　　　　"Melancolike Humors," 1600, p. 5.

Nicholas Breton, a writer of pastoral, sonnets, canzons and madrigals, in which kind of writing he keeps company with several other contemporary æmulators of Spencer and Sir Philip Sidny, in a publist collection of selected odes of the chief pastoral sonnetteers, &c. of that age.—EDWARD PHILLIPS, *Theatrum Poetarum Anglicanorum*, 1675

His happiest vein is in little pastoral pieces. In addition to the long roll of his indifferent works which are enumerated in the "Biographia Poetica," the "Censura Literaria" imputes to him a novel of singular absurdity, in which the miseries of the heroine of the story are consummated by having her nose bit off by an aged and angry rival of her husband.—THOMAS CAMPBELL, *Specimens of the British Poets*, 1819

In contrast with the largeness and diffuseness of many of his contemporaries, I regard it as a merit in our Worthy that he took time to be brief and compact. One secret of this is—as I have noted—the concinnity of his style. There are few Elizabethan prose-writers—Bacon stands alone in his 'Essaies'— who so abounds in 'picked and packed words.' Our word 'fluent' has deteriorated in latter days; so as to express mere volubility; but in its etymological sense it is nicely descriptive of Breton's style. It 'flows' with crystal clearness and closeness all round the thought, fancy, metaphor, apophthegm, quip, saying, story, that the Author wishes to tell us. I would have called it 'sinuous' were it not that somehow again the hiss of the serpent is inevitably associated with the word. *Ad aperturam libri*, his 'Characters vpon Essaies' and 'Good and Badde,' it would be preposterous to compare with Bacon's for weight and intellectual richness, and an unnameable charm of phrasing. But putting them out of court, I know not where to find better English, more substantive thinking (within its own relatively modest limits), or more memorable portraiture, as with a stroke of the pen—comparable in a way with the pencilled *memoranda* of the great Art-Masters.
　. . . ⟨T⟩here is a singularly pleasing sunniness—edged like all light with shadow—in these books of Breton. His misfortunes, his 'indiscretions,' his hardships, his wrongs, his lonelinesses, his outliving of contemporaries, imparted no sourness to his spirit, no bitterness to his tongue, no misanthropy to his pen. He abides to the end,—with fits of melancholy interposed,—a cheery, whole-hearted, sweet-natured, loveable old fellow. I have already notified his last-published book *Fantasticks*. It is as strong, as buoyant, as finished, as any of all his numerous writings. I can think, therefore, of no other word so interpretative of the feeling excited by these revived books of Nicholas Breton as this of their 'Brightness.' You may look into almost any of them, and this 'brightness' will gleam upon you. You may be led as into some tree-shut-in 'solitary place;' but even there a ray of golden light will be shot through the boughy green gloom.
　. . . His 'Brightness' is as of sunlight in the silver rain and

the quivering dew, rather than of the blinding sky and sultry air. The explanation is that, whether from boyhood-associations with the paternal town-house, 'fair garden,' 'bechen lane,' and the 'farms' in Essex and Lincolnshire, or his friendships with the gentry of England (as shown in his Epistles-dedicatory, *e.g.* the Houghtons of Lancashire, the Dallisons, Cradocks, Conquests, and others . . .) he must have had an open eye and heart for Nature. His close observation of Nature—thus early—is extremely noticeable, and gives a 'freshness' to his books simply inestimable. . . .
　Even in his more ordinary Prose he delights to fetch his images from the country, *e.g.* in his 'Wonders worth the Hearing', 'she would looke as demurely as a Rabbet that had newly washed her face in a deawy morning'. Birds and flowers, lambs and rabbits, kine and horse, the grass, the odorous hay, the shooting or yellowing corn, orchards, hedgerows and rural lanes, chiming brooks and bosky nooks, sparkle of dew, the May sprays, the Autumnal reddened leaves, the Yule-log, cakes and nut-brown ale, the merry pranks and sports, the fireside stories, the pat proverb, the snatch of old-world song, proud memories of 'Queen Bess' and stout Harry before her— to name only these—carry the 'freshness' of inviolate nature through verse and prose alike. The lambs and 'rabbits at base' are almost as inevitable in Breton's landscape as the grey horse of Wouverman. Let *Fantasticks* be turned and returned to for deliciously 'fresh' description. Even in 'A Mad World' his little gentle favourites are introduced with such a yearning and wistfulness of preference as seems to me ineffably pathetic:—

'Oh to see in a faire morning, or a sunnie evening, the lambes and rabbets run at base, the birds billing, the fishes playing, and the flowers budding, who would not leave the drinking in an alehouse, the wrangling in a dicing-house, the lying in a market, and the cheating in a fayre; and thinke *that the brightnesse of a faire day doth put doune all the beauties of the world'.*

　. . . ⟨I⟩n his Prose, regarding the books broadly, his English is rich and pure. I have elsewhere accentuated its concinnity. I think now of its fine simpleness, unpretence, ease, continuousness. There is nothing of Horace's 'purple patchwork.' All is of the every-day speech: now of the 'gentle,' and now of the 'simple.' . . . Whether he is dashing off a 'Character,' or sketching a 'Portrait,' or filling in a 'Landscape,' or telling a 'Fire-side Chat,' or carrying on a 'Dialogue,' all is done with spontaneity and naturalness. When you examine details you find, doubtless, that there must have been 'pains' and 'art;' but the working is concealed, and only the work shown. For bright, I might say sparkling, pleasant, equally-sustained, and unmistakable English, I claim special praise for the Prose of Breton. Except in its orthography and occasional obsolete words (some of which might to advantage be revived) his English is as much Victorian as Elizabethan-Jacobean. But as a phraser, as a maker of short, sharp, pointed sentences, he has no successor or representative in our day. It were better if, for the platitudinarian rhetoric of our time, we had something of his brevity, compactness, sententiousness, finish.
　. . . I think that his life-time popularity alluded to in Beaumont and Fletcher, and elsewhere, was deserved, and was a *factor* in the formative elements of the grand Elizabethan and early Jacobean age. I think that while without that pronounced genius that compels our wonder and our submission, he had things in him that only genius owns. I make no 'great' claims for him. He was of the rank and file, not of the Leaders and 'mighty' Captains; but within his own lowly and homely and familiar sphere, he is worthy of our gratitude as of our praise,

and of our study as of our remembrance.—ALEXANDER B. GROSART, "Memorial-Introduction," *The Works of Nicholas Breton*, 1879, Vol. 1, pp. xli–lxxii

As a literary man Breton impresses us most by his versatility and his habitual refinement. He is a satirical, religious, romance, and pastoral writer in both prose and verse. But he wrote with exceptional facility, and as a consequence he wrote too much. His fertile fancy often led him into fantastic puerilities. It is in his pastoral lyrics that he is seen at his best. The pathos here is always sincere; the gaiety never falls into grossness, the melody is fresh and the style clear.—SIDNEY LEE, *Dictionary of National Biography*, 1886, Vol. 6, p. 276

If we could take as his the charming lullaby of "The Arbour of Amorous Devices" he would stand (if only as a kind of "single-speech") high as a poet. But I fear that Dr. Grosart's attribution of it to him is based on little external and refuted by all internal evidence. His best certain thing is the pretty "Phillida and Corydon" idyll, which may be found in *England's Helicon* or in Mr. Ward's *Poets*. But I own that I can never read this latter without thinking of two lines of Fulke Greville's in the same metre and on no very different theme—

> O'er enamelled meads they went,
> Quiet she, he passion-rent,

which are simply worth all the works of Breton's prose and verse, unless we count the "Lullaby," put together. In the *mots rayonnants*, the *mots de lumière*, he is sadly deficient. But his work (which is nearly as plentiful in verse as in prose) is, as has been said, very interesting to the literary student, because it shows better perhaps than anything else the style of literature which a man, disdaining to condescend to burlesque or bawdry, not gifted with any extraordinary talent, either at prose or verse, but possessed of a certain literary faculty, could then produce with a fair chance of being published and bought. It cannot be said that the result shows great daintiness in Breton's public. The verse, with an improvement in sweetness and fluency, is very much of the doggerel style which was prevalent before Spenser; and the prose, though showing considerable faculty, if not of invention, yet of adroit imitation of previously invented styles, is devoid of distinction and point. . . .

The pervading characteristics are Breton's invariable modesty, his pious, and, if I may be permitted to use the word, gentlemanly spirit, and a fashion of writing which, if not very pointed, picturesque, or epigrammatic, is clear, easy, and on the whole rather superior in observance of the laws of grammar and arrangement to the work of men of much greater note in his day.—GEORGE SAINTSBURY, *A History of Elizabethan Literature*, 1887, pp. 239–40

Nicholas Breton was an Elizabethan primitive, who went on publishing fresh volumes until after the death of James I., but without having modified the sixteenth-century character of his style. . . . Of these short productions "The Passionate Shepherd" is by far the best, and ranks very high among Breton's contributions to poetry. It is a collection of pastoral lyrics, in a variety of measures, very lightly, liquidly, and innocently thrown off, with no sense of intellectual effort and no great attention to style. Breton has a very pleasant acquaintance with nature. . . . Breton had the root of poetry in him, but he was no scholar, inartistic, and absolutely devoid of the gift of self-criticism.—EDMUND GOSSE, *The Jacobean Poets*, 1894, pp. 15–17

There is a naturalness, an easy flow, and gaiety, a tenderness and purity about Breton that ought to restore him to fame.—FELIX E. SCHELLING, *A Book of Elizabethan Lyrics*, 1895, p. 226

As fresh as Nash, as copious as Lodge, but endowed with a finer artistic feeling, and altogether captivating in his ready grace and buoyancy.—FREDERICK IVES CARPENTER, "Introduction" to *English Lyric Poetry 1500–1700*, 1897, p. xliii

Nicholas Breton, a writer of romances highly praised by his contemporaries, but now somewhat lacking in distinction. . . . Breton always inclined to the simple stanzas and long, narrative manner of the miscellanies. His lyrics are too diffuse.—JOHN ERSKINE, *The Elizabethan Lyric*, 1903, pp. 121–22

LANCELOT ANDREWES

1555–1626

Lancelot Andrewes was born in London in 1555. Educated at the Merchant Taylors' School and Pembroke Hall, Cambridge, he earned a B.A. in 1575, and was ordained a deacon in 1585. Andrewes also earned a bachelor of divinity in 1585. He was a leading Anglican minister, serving as bishop of Chicester, Ely, and Winchester. From 1619 to 1626 Andrewes was the dean of the Royal Chapel.

Andrewes was the author of numerous theological works, including various sermons collected and published at the request of Charles I. Most of Andrewes's works were devoted to criticizing Catholic dogma. Andrewes translated the *Pentateuch* for the Authorized Version of the Bible. *Private Devotions*, a translation of his own *Preces Privatae*, reveals his strict asceticism and deeply held religious beliefs. Andrewes died in 1626 and was buried in the Southwark Cathedral.

Lancelot Andrews, D.D. was born in this city ⟨London⟩, in Tower Street; his father being a seaman of good repute belonging to Trinity-house. He was bred scholar, fellow, and master of Pembroke Hall in Cambridge.

He was an inimitable preacher in his way; and such plagiaries who have stolen his sermons could never steal his preaching, and could make nothing of that whereof he made all things as he desired. Pious and pleasant bishop Felton (his contemporary and colleague) endeavoured in vain in his sermon to assimilate his style; and therefore said merrily of himself, "I had almost marred my own natural trot, by endeavouring to imitate his artificial amble." But I have spoken largely of this peerless prelate in my *Church History*. He died anno Domini 1626.—THOMAS FULLER, *The History of the Worthies of England*, 1662

Lancelot Andrewes, Lord Bishop of Winton, was borne in London; went to Schoole at Merchant Taylors schoole. Mr. Mulcaster was his schoolemaster, whose picture he hung in his Studie.

Old Mr. Sutton, a very learned man in those dayes, of Blandford St. Maries, Dorset, was his school fellow, and sayd that Lancelot Andrewes was a great long boy of 18 yeares old at least before he went to the University.

The Puritan faction did begin to increase in those dayes, and especially at Enamuel College. This party had a great mind to drawe in this learned young man, whom (if they could make theirs) they knew would be a great honour to them. They carried themselves outwardly with great sanctity and strictnesse. They preached up very strict keeping and observing the Lord's day: made, upon the matter, damnation to breake it, and that 'twas less Sin to kill a man. Yet these Hypocrites did bowle in a private green at their colledge every Sunday after Sermon; and one of the Colledge (a loving friend to Mr. L. Andrewes) to satisfie him, one time lent him the Key of a Private back dore to the bowling green, on a Sunday evening, which he opening, discovered these zealous Preachers with their Gownes off, earnest at play. But they were strangely surprised to see the entry of one that was not of the Brotherhood.

There was then at Cambridge a good fatt Alderman that was wont to sleep at Church, which the Alderman endeavoured to prevent but could not. Well! this was preached against as a signe of Reprobation. The good man was exceedingly troubled at it, and went to Andrewes his Chamber to be satisfied in point of Conscience. Mr. Andrewes told him, that it was an ill habit of Body, not of Mind, and that it was against his Will; advised him on Sundays to make a more sparing meale, and to mend it at Supper. The Alderman did so, but Sleepe comes on again for all that, and was preached at; comes againe to be resolved with Teares in his eies. Andrewes then told him he would have him make a good heartie meal as he was wont to doe, and presently take out his full sleep. He did so, came to St. Maries, where the Preacher was prepared with a Sermon to damne all who slept at Sermon, a certain signe of Reprobation. The good Alderman, having taken his full nap before, lookes on the Preacher all Sermon time, and spoyled the design. But I should have sayd that Andrewes was most extremely spoken against and preached against for offering to assoile or excuse a sleeper in sermon time. But he had learning and witt enough to defend himselfe.

His good learning quickly made him known in the University, and also to King James, who much valued him for it, and advanced him, and at last made him Bishop of Winchester: which Bishoprick he ordered with great Prudence as to government of the Parsons, preferring of ingeniose persons that were staked to poore livings and did *delitescere*. He made it his Enquiry to find out such men. Amongst severall others (whose names have escaped my memorie) Nicholas Fuller (he wrote *Critica Sacra*), Minister of Allington, neer Amesbury in Wilts, was one. The Bishop sent for him, and the poor man was afrayd and knew not what hurt he had donne. Makes him sitt downe to Dinner and, after the Desert, was brought in, in a dish, his Institution and Induction, or the donation of a Prebend; which was his way.

He dyed at Winchester house in Southwark, and lies buried in a Chapell at St. Mary Overies, where his Executors have erected (but I beleeve according to his Lordship's will, els they would not have layed out 1000 pounds) a sumptuose Monument for Him.

He had not that smooth way of Oratory, as now. It was a shrewd and severe animadversion of a Scotish Lord, who, when King James asked him how he liked Bp. A.'s sermon, said that he was learned, but he did play with his Text, as a Jack-an-apes does, who takes up a thing and tosses and playes with it, and then he takes up another, and playes a little with it. Here's a pretty thing, and there's a pretty thing!—JOHN AUBREY, "Lancelot Andrewes," *Brief Lives*, 1669–96

⟨Archbishop John Williams's⟩ Predecessors (whose Names and Actions are not forgotten) were Men of good Report. Two above all, because none were comparable to them, he cast in his Head to imitate, Abbat *Islip*, and Dr. *Andrews*. Dr. *Andrews* for advancing Learning in the School, Abbat *Islip* for his Cost expended upon the Fabric of the Minster, and the Dean's place. I dispose it so, to mention first what a Foster-Father he was to the Scholars, because himself proceeded to greater Designments by that Order. He had heard much what Pains Dr. *Andrews* did take both day and night to train up the Youth bred in the public School, chiefly the *Alumni* of the College so called. For more certain Information, he called me from *Cambridge* in the *May* before he was Installed, to the House of his dear Cousin Mr. *Elwis Winn* in *Chancery-Lane*, a Clerk of the Petty-Bag, a Man of the most general and gracious Acquaintance with all the great Ones of the Land that ever I knew. There he moved his Questions to me about the Discipline of Dr. *Andrews*. I told him how strict that excellent Man was, to charge our Masters, that they should give us Lessons out of none but the most Classical Authors; that he did often supply the Place both of Head School-master and Usher for the space of an whole week together, and gave us not an hour of Loitering-time from morning to night. How he caused our Exercises in Prose and Verse to be brought to him, to examine our Style and Proficiency. That he never walk'd to *Cheswick* for his Recreation, without a brace of this young Fry; and in that way-faring Leisure, had a singular dexterity to fill those narrow Vessels with a Funnel. And, which was the greatest burden of his Toil, sometimes thrice in a week, sometimes oftener, he sent for the uppermost Scholars to his Lodgings at night, and kept them with him from eight till eleven, unfolding to them the best Rudiments of the *Greek* Tongue, and the Elements of the *Hebrew* Grammar, and all this he did to Boys without any compulsion of Correction; nay, I never heard him utter so much as a word of Austerity among us. Alas! this is but an Ivy-Leaf crept into the Laurel of his Immortal Garland. This is that *Andrews*, the Ointment of whose Name is *sweeter then all Spices, Cant.* 4. 10. This is that celebrated Bishop of *Winton*, whose Learning King *James* admired above all his Chaplains; and that King, being of most excellent Parts himself, could the better discover what was Eminent in another. Indeed he was the most Apostolical and Primitive-like Divine, in my Opinion, that wore a Rochet in his Age; of a most venerable Gravity, and yet most sweet in all Commerce; the most Devout that ever I saw, when he appeared before God; of such a Growth in all kind of Learning, that very able Clerks were of a low Stature to him: *Colossus inter icunculas*; full of Alms and Charity; of which none knew but his Father in secret: A certain Patron to Scholars of Fame and Ability, and chiefly to those that never expected it. In the Pulpit an *Homer* among Preachers, and may fitly be set forth in *Quintilian's* Judgment of *Homer; Nonne humani ingenii modum excessit? Ut magni sit viri virtutes ejus non æmulatione (quod fieri non potest) sed intellectu sequi.* I am transported even as in a Rapture to make this Digression:

For who could come near the Shrine of such a Saint, and not offer up a few Grains of Glory upon it? Or how durst I omit it? For he was the first that planted me in my tender Studies, and water'd them continually with his Bounty. The occasion that brings in this, was the new Dean's addition to his Pattern, that looking into such a Mirror, he might keep up the Learning of that happy Plantation, that it might never hear worse, then as Mr. *Camden* testifies for it, *Felix eruditorum in Ecclesiam & Rempublicam proventus. Eliz.* p. 61. Fol. In his Zeal to this Work, as soon as he was possess'd of the Deanery, he was assiduous in the School, and miss'd not sometimes every week, if he were resident in the College, both to dictate Lectures to the several Classes, and to take account of them. The choicest Wits had never such Encouragement for Praise, and Reward. He was very Bountiful in both, and they went always together, scattering Money, as if it had been but Dung to manure their Industry. And seldom he did fail, no not when he kept the Great-Seal, to call forth some of them to stand before him at his Table, that in those intervals of best Opportunity he might have account of their Towardliness; which ripen'd them so fast, made them so Prompt and Ingenuous, that the number of the Promoted to the Universities, which swarm'd out of that Stock, was double for the most part to those that were Transplanted in the foregoing Elections.—JOHN HACKET, *Scrinia Reserata*, 1693, pp. 44–45

The sermons of Bishop Andrewes exemplify, very pertinently, the chief defects in style that have been attributed to the writers of his period; while to these they add other faults, incident to the effusions of a mind poor in fancy, coarse in taste, ingeniously rash in catching at trivial analogies, and constantly burying good thoughts under a heap of useless phrases. Yet, though they were corrupt models, and dangerous in proportion to the fame of the author, it is not surprising that they made the extraordinary impression they did. They contain, more than any other works of their kind and time, the unworked materials of oratory; and of oratory, too, belonging to the most severe and powerful class. There is something Demosthenic in the impatient vehemence, with which the pious bishop showers down his short, clumsy, harsh sentences; and the likeness becomes still more exact, when we hear him alternating stern and eager questions with sad or indignant answers. His Latin quotations, though incessant, are always brief: his field of erudite illustration is prudently confined; and his multiplied divisions and subdivisions, being quite agreeable to the growing fashion, may have helped to increase the respect of the hearers for the great strength and ingenuity of thought which the preacher so often showed. There is often much aptness in the parallels which it is his besetting fault to accumulate so thickly, and to overdraw so grotesquely; and an overpowering effect must sometimes have been produced by the dexterous boldness with which, anticipating an adverse opinion or feeling, he throws it back in the teeth of those who were likely to entertain it.—WILLIAM SPALDING, *The History of English Literature*, 1853, p. 219

The Church of England contains no name more truly venerable than that of this good prelate. For polish and suavity of manners he was excelled by no gentleman of the court; in piety, by no anchorite of better times and purer days. In the discharge of all the duties of religion, he so walked as to be an illustrious exemplar to his flock and to the church of God. James I. had so high an opinion of his abilities, that he employed him to answer Bellarmine's Treatise against his own Defence of the Right of Kings. He was also a favourite with Charles I. Casaubon, Cluverius, Vossius, Grotius, Peter du Moulin, Barclay, and Erpenius were among his corre-

spondents. Lord Clarendon regrets that he was not raised to the primacy on the death of Archbishop Bancroft. Thus respected in life, he was not less honoured at his death, by a Latin elegy from the author of *Paradise Lost.*—S. AUSTIN ALLIBONE, *A Critical Dictionary of English Literature*, 1854–58, Vol. 1, p. 61

He was, perhaps, the most learned of the English theologians of that learned time, and was besides a person of great vigor and acuteness of understanding; so that his death was regarded by scholars both at home and abroad as the extinction of the chief light of the English Church. Milton, then a youth of seventeen, bewailed the event in a Latin elegy, full of feeling and fancy; and even in a tract written many years afterwards, when his opinions had undergone a complete change, he admits that "Bishop Andrews of late years, and in these times the Primate of Armagh (Usher), for their learning are reputed the best able to say what may be said" in defence of episcopacy. Both the learning and ability of Andrews, indeed, are conspicuous in everything he has written; but his eloquence, nevertheless, is to a modern taste grotesque enough. In his more ambitious passages he is the very prince of verbal posture-masters,—if not the first in date, the first in extravagance, of the artificial, quibbling, syllable-tormenting school of our English pulpit rhetoricians; and he undoubtedly contributed more to spread the disease of that manner of writing than any other individual. Not only did his eminence in this line endear him to the royal tastes of Elizabeth and James; all men admired and strove to copy after him. Fuller declares that he was "an inimitable preacher in his way"; and then he tells us that "pious and pleasant Bishop Felton, his contemporary and colleague, endeavoured in vain in his sermons to assimilate his style, and therefore said merrily of himself, I had almost marred my own natural trot by endeavouring to imitate his artificial amble." Many a "natural trot" Andrews no doubt was the cause of spoiling in his day, and long after it. This bishop is further very notable, in the history of the English Church, as the first great asserter of those semi-popish notions touching doctrines, rites, and ecclesiastical government with which Laud afterwards blew up the establishment. Andrews, however, was a very different sort of person from Laud,—as superior to him in sense and policy as in learning and general strength and comprehensiveness of understanding. A well-known story that is told of him proves his moderation as much as his wit and readiness: when he and Dr. Neal, bishop of Durham, were one day standing behind the king's chair as he sat at dinner (it was the day on which James dissolved his third parliament, and the anecdote is related on the authority of Waller, the poet, who was present), his majesty, turning round, addressed the two prelates—My lords, cannot I take my subjects' money when I want it, without all this formality in parliament? "The bishop of Durham readily answered, God forbid, sir, but you should; you are the breath of our nostrils. Whereupon the king turned, and said to the bishop of Winchester, Well, my lord, what say you? Sir, replied the bishop, I have no skill to judge of parliamentary cases. The king answered, No put-offs, my lord, answer me presently. Then, sir, said he, I think it is lawful for you to take my brother Neal's money, for he offers it." Clarendon has expressed his belief that if Archbishop Bancroft had been succeeded in the see of Canterbury by Andrews, instead of Abbot, the infection of the Geneva fire would have been kept out, which could not afterwards be so easily expelled.— GEORGE L. CRAIK, *A Compendious History of English Literature and of the English Language*, 1861, Vol. 1, pp. 610–11

Each sermon of Bishop Andrewes might furnish a diffuse writer matter for an entire treatise. No one can read them without being fairly bewildered and astonished at the vast stores of thought and learning which are poured out almost recklessly before him. But with regard to manner the case is different. Bishop Andrewes's manner is in the highest degree peculiar. He tortures, twists, and twirls his subject about, so that one can hardly imagine that he could have been listened to with becoming gravity. Sometimes he indulges in puns and curious plays on words; sometimes by an extraordinary jumbling together of English, Latin, and Greek words, he produces the most curious effect; so that we are tempted to say that as these sermons are the richest and most copious in matter, so are they the worst in style and manner of any that have ever obtained a more than passing celebrity. We feel persuaded that the Bishop of Winchester must have been "followed" by many of the courtiers not for edification but for amusement; that his oddities must have furnished them with a stock of good stories, and that King James often enjoyed a hearty laugh over these congenial *facetiæ*. . . .

There are few more eminent names in our Church history than that of Bishop Andrewes. . . . For more than twenty years regarded as without question the leading divine of the Church of England.—GEORGE G. PERRY, *The History of the Church of England*, 1861–64, Vol. 1, pp. 54, 354–55

Lancelot Andrewes, the most devout and, at the same time, the most honest of the nascent High Church party of that period, lamented alike by Clarendon and by Milton, was Dean for five years. Under his care, probably in the Deanery, met the Westminster Committee of the Authorised Version of James I., to which was confided the translation of the Old Testament, from Genesis to Kings, and of the Epistles in the New. In him the close connection of the Abbey with the School reached its climax.—ARTHUR PENRHYN STANLEY, *Historical Memorials of Westminster Abbey*, 1867, p. 413

Andrewes was eminent in three capacities: (1) As a prelate. Few men have more happily combined the various qualities which contribute to make a great prelate than Andrewes. His principles were most distinct and definite, and from these principles he never swerved. He was a thorough English churchman, as far removed from Romanism on the one hand, as from puritanism on the other. He never interfered in public affairs, either as a privy councillor or in any other capacity, except when the spiritual interests of the church seemed to him to be at stake; and then, in spite of his constitutional modesty, he spoke out boldly and to the point. His learning was unequalled. From his childhood to his death he was an indefatigable student; his multifarious business as a public man was never allowed to interfere with his studies. He made a rule of not being interrupted, except for public or private prayer, before dinnertime (12 o'clock); when he was intruded upon, he would say "he was afraid he was no true scholar who came to see him before noon." The result was that he made himself master of fifteen languages, if not more, while his knowledge of patristic theology was quite unrivalled. . . .

(2) As a preacher, Andrewes was generally held to be the very "stella prædicantium," an "angel in the pulpit.". . .

(3) As a writer. Andrewes published but little in his lifetime, though his works now fill eight 8vo volumes in the *Library of Anglo-Catholic Theology*.—J. H. OVERTON, *Dictionary of National Biography*, 1885, Vol. 1, pp. 402–4

I must not, however, pass from this topic without some attempt to do justice to the signal benefit which Newman conferred by his admirable translation of Bishop Andrewes's *Private Devotions*. It was indeed an invaluable boon, for which all of us, but the clergy especially, cannot be too thankful. O! that he had clung to Bishop Andrewes as his guide not only *orandi*, but *credendi!*—CHARLES WORDSWORTH, *Annals of My Early Life, 1806–1846*, 1890, p. 345

Andrewes may be said with truth to have been one of the most learned and holy men by whom the Church has ever been ruled. His sermons—quaint, erudite, humorous, and spiritual—were the delight of his own age. His prayers have been constantly brought out in new editions and have been the companions of the piety of two centuries. His controversial writings laid the foundation of the Anglican position as it was expressed and defended by the divines of the rest of the century. The special characteristic of his work was its appeal to primitive antiquity and the resort for interpretation to the historical formularies of the undivided Church. The strength of the appeal which he made to the intelligence of his own and the next age lay in the fact that he spoke to the heart no less than to the head.—WILLIAM HOLDEN HUTTON, *Social England*, ed. H. D. Traill, 1895, Vol. 4, p. 25

His sermons on the Nativity and upon the Resurrection are amongst the finest of their kind in our pulpit literature. However overflowing they may be with learned illustrations, and of these there is no stint, they are conspicuous for their triumphant trust and their fervid piety. In his fourth sermon he speaks of the fulness of time and its fruits thus: "And so growing from grace to grace, finally from this fulness, we shall come to be partakers of another yet behind, to which we aspire. For all this but the fulness of *time*; but for that the fulness of *eternity*, when time shall be run out and his glass empty, *Et tempus non erit amplius*: which is at His next sending. For yet once more shall God send Him, and He come again. At which coming we shall then indeed receive the fulness of our redemption, not from the *Law* (that we have already), but from *corruption*, to which our bodies yet are subject; and receive the full fruition of the inheritance, whereto we are here but adopted. And then it will be perfect, complete, absolute fulness indeed, when we shall all be filled with the fulness of Him that filleth all in all. Not as here he is something (and but something) in every one; but then *omnia in omnibus*. And then the measure shall be so full, as it cannot enter into us, we cannot hold it; we must enter into it; *intra in gaudium Domini tui*. To this we aspire, and to this in the fulness appointed to every one of our times, Almighty God, bring us by Him and for His sake, that in this fulness of time was sent to work for us in His person; and work it in us by the operation of His blessed spirit." The eloquence of this passage is indisputable, and the tone of mysticism which pervades it springs from the deep conviction and the long hours of private communion of the preacher. The same spirit is observable in all of these sermons on the Nativity, and in many others. Andrewes spoke not so much what he believed as what he knew, and that is the secret of his success as a preacher. He made his hearers feel that he was closer to God than they, and they heard him and were satisfied. Only a man who is in part a mystic can do this; and only a mystic who is in part practical can produce a similar effect.

Throughout his sermons the attentive reader perceives a close adherence to the Articles, as drawn up under the auspices of Edward VI., and as revised by the theologians of Elizabeth. But his mind was too Catholic to be thereby prevented from seeing the good in the system of John Calvin, though he had an instinctive dislike of the Genevan method of Church government. As has been said, he took the view of the Eucharist, which is expounded in the Book of Common Prayer, and not the veiled Romanism of the doctrine of the modern Anglo-

Catholic, as he loves to call himself with a ludicrous deficiency of philological insight. It is not within the scope of this study to trace in detail the theology of this great prelate; those who wish to know what he believed, and why, will find his doctrine set forth clearly in his various sermons, a thoughtful perusal of which will amply repay the modern reader. His influence remains in all that is highest and best in the national Church, and it is to be regretted that more of those who profess to be his disciples do not read his works, in order to correct some of the Romanising crudities of their theological tendencies. Quite as strongly as Joseph Hall, the Puritan Bishop of Norwich, Andrewes would have maintained, and does in fact maintain, that there is no peace with Rome. Some of the older ceremonies he loved and practised; but he knew what he would have, and he would have been the last person in the land to have sent over a deputation to the Pope to humbly crave his gracious recognition of the validity of Anglican Orders. Let those who imagine that he had any leanings in this direction read his ten sermons on the Gunpowder Treason, and they will both derive much benefit from the sermons themselves, and learn that one of the greatest of the bishops of our history was convinced that the cleavage from the older Church at the time of the Reformation was an abiding cleavage, a gulf across which no bridge of compromise could by any means known to man be thrown.

In the midst of his mysticism Andrewes has many sermons of a distinctly practical type, which show how deeply he felt the need that every man should do his duty. He saw, on the one hand, corruption and license walking side by side through the vicious society of his day; while upon the other was the grim religious view of the Puritan. To him both of these pronounced extremes were repellent, though from very different reasons; for license he had no toleration whatever, and he never failed to rebuke its manifestations to the face, while he disliked the outward rigidity of Puritanism, which he regarded with feelings akin to distrust. He saw and respected the moral purity of the average Presbyterian, he noted the contrast between the foul language of the courtiers and the prim yet godly speech of the Puritan. But the system of the Presbytery he did not love; it seemed to him a needless unsettling of the primitive model, and he viewed with grave displeasure the so-called free prayer of its ministers. It therefore stands all the more conspicuously to his credit that he refrained from persecution, and in most cases even from repression. His broad mind and his kindly soul shrunk back with horror from propagating the Gospel by any such means as had cast an abiding and richly deserved odium upon the leaders of the Inquisition. He relied upon the surer methods of persuasion, and he bent all the powers of his commanding intellectual gifts upon this charitable aim. He argued, preached, prayed, and conferred; but he refused to put into force the authority, which was his by virtue of his position, except to reduce clamorous opponents to silence. That he did not succeed the Primacy of the English Church was a national misfortune as grave in its own kind as the later appointment of a narrow-minded man like Laud, who was lovable enough in private, but who was a theological Tartar in his public capacity.—ARTHUR W. FOX, "The Bishop: Lancelot Andrewes," *A Book of Bachelors*, 1899, pp. 153–55

RICHARD W. CHURCH
From "Lancelot Andrewes"
Masters in English Theology, ed. Alfred Barry
1877, pp. 101–8

It seems to me that the key to the influence which Andrewes had in his own day, and which recommended his theology, is to be found in his *Devotions*. For they show what was the true meaning and reach of his theology, how unspeakably real and deep he felt its language to be, and how naturally it allied itself and was interwoven with the highest frames of thought and feeling in a mind of wide range, and a soul of the keenest self-knowledge and the strongest sympathies. There are books which go deeper into the struggles, the questionings, the temptations, the discipline, the strange spiritual mysteries of the devout spirit. There are books which perhaps rise higher in the elevations of devotion. But nowhere do we see more so original and spontaneous a result of a man's habits of devotion; nowhere, that I know of, does the whole mind of the student, the divine, and the preacher, reflect itself in his prayers so simply and easily and harmoniously as in this book. His knowledge, his tastes, his systematic and methodical theology, the order and articles of his creed, translate themselves into the realities of worship. All his interests, all his customary views of God, of man, of nature, of his relations to his place and time—all that he has been reading about or employed upon, suggest themselves when he places himself in God's presence, and find their natural and fit expression in the beautifully applied words of Psalm or ancient Liturgy. Nothing can be more comprehensive and more complete in their proportions than his devotions for each day; nothing more tender and solemn; nothing more compressed and nervous than their language. The full order of prayer and all its parts is always there: the introductory contemplation, to sober, to elevate, to kindle; the confession, the profession of faith, the intercession, the praise and thanksgiving. There is equally there the consciousness of individual singleness, and the sense of great and wide corporate relations. His confessions show in severely restrained and precise language the infinite acknowledgment of unworthiness and want, and the infinite hope in God's mercy and love, in one who searched and judged himself with keen and unflinching truth. But he did not stop at himself, his sins and hopes. He also felt himself, even in private prayer, one of the great body of God's creation and God's Church. He reminded himself of it, as he did of the Object of his worship, in the profession of his faith. He acted on it in his detailed and minute intercessions. And then he surrendered himself to the impulses of exulting wonder and rejoicing at the greatness of his Christian lot. The poetical and imaginative side of his nature shows itself in the vivid pictures which he calls up, with a few condensed and powerful touches, of the glories of Nature, and the wonders of God's kingdom, its history, its manifold organisation. Thus, "the connection of every day," says . . . Dr. Mozley,[1] "with the great works which each day saw in the work of creation, converts the several days of the week into beautiful mementos of the fact that we and all that we see are God's creatures, as well as of the sanctity of the week itself as a division of time; and it evidences that character of mind in the writer which realises the facts of Scripture, sees mysteries in common things, and feels itself still living amid visible traces of a Divine dispensation. It is obvious how such a method gives the beauty of natural objects a place in his religion." The Apostles' Creed is no dry recital, but expands day after day into petitions and desires founded on its awful facts. And so again, "man, human society, his country, as an object of prayer, is not the mere human mass—a number of individuals, but man and man in certain relations to each other, high and low, rich and poor, king and subject, noble and dependent, all living together in the system of God's ordinance,". . . . "actual trades and states of life," definitely enumerated, as Homer enumerates names of men and places; not only "king and queen, parliament and judicature, army and police, commons and their leaders," but "farmers, graziers, fishers, merchants, traders, and mechanics, down to mean workmen and the poor." There is no class of men, no condition, no relation of life, no necessity or emergency of it, which does not at one time or another rise up before his memory, and claim his intercession: none for which he does not see a place in the order of God's world, and find a refuge under the shadow of His wing.

Into such devotions I think it would be impossible to translate the Puritan theology of the time. It is too narrow, too suspicious, too much enslaved to technical forms and language. The piercing and rapid energy of Andrewes' devotions, their ordinary severe conciseness, their nobleness and manliness, their felicitous adaptations, their free and varied range, the way in which they call up before the mind the whole of the living realities of God's creation and God's revelations, and, in the portion devoted to praise, their rhythmical flow and music, incorporating bursts of adoration and Eucharistic triumph for the Liturgies of St. James or St. Chrysostom, recalling the most ancient Greek hymns of the Church, the "Gloria in Excelsis" and the Evening Hymn, preserved at the end of the Alexandrian manuscript of the New Testament,[2]—all this is in the strongest contrast to anything that I know of in the private devotions of the time. It was the reflection, in private prayer, of the tone and language of the public Book of Common Prayer, its Psalms, and its Offices: it supplemented the public book, and carried on its spirit from the Church to the closet. And this was the counterpart of what Andrewes taught in the pulpit. To us it shows how real and deeply held his theology was; and it also explains that persuasiveness of conviction, which has as much to do as intellectual force and breadth, in making men listen to their teachers and accept their words. The reformed English Church had had its martyrs, statesmen, doctors, champions; in Andrewes it had a saint—not called so, not canonised, but one in whom men felt the irresistible charm of real holiness. It had some one in high place not only to admire, but to love. And churches need saints, as much as theologians and statesmen, and even martyrs.

In these ways, Andrewes marks a period and a step in the unfolding of the theology of the Reformed Church of England and in the practical course of the Reformation. Hooker had vindicated on its behalf the rights of Christian and religious *reason*, that reason which is a reflection of the mind of God. Andrewes vindicated on its behalf the rights of Christian *history*. Hooker had maintained the claims of reason, against a slavish bondage to narrow and arbitrary interpretations of the letter of Scripture. Andrewes claimed for the English Church its full interest and membership in the Church universal, from which Puritan and Romanist alike would cut off the island Church by a gulf as deep as the sea. The spirit of historical investigation had awoke in England as in the rest of Europe, against the passion for abstract and metaphysical argument which had marked and governed the earlier stages of the Reformation. It had converted Causaubon from Calvinism, and at the same time made him the most formidable critic of the magnificent, but unhistorical picture presented in the annals of Baronius. Widened knowledge had done as much for Andrewes and the men of his school, Field and Donne and Overall, may I not add, in this matter, Andrewes' close friend, Lord Bacon? History had enlarged their ideas of the Church universal. Its facts and concrete lessons and actual words had overborne the traditions and general assumptions in which the necessities of an age of religious war had educated them. They opened their eyes and saw that the prerogatives which the Puritans confined to an invisible Church, and which Rome confined to the obedience of the Pope, belonged to the universal historical Church, lasting on with varied fortunes through all the centuries from the days of Pentecost; on earth "the habitation of God through the spirit." Maintaining jealously and stoutly the inherent and indefeasible rights of the national Church of England, and resisting with uncompromising determination the tyranny which absorbed in a single hand the powers of the Catholic Church, they refused to forget, even in England, what God's Spirit had done in other portions of Christendom, perhaps far removed, perhaps for the time bitterly hostile. They learned to pray, as Andrewes did, "for the Catholic Church, its establishment and increase; for the Eastern, its deliverance and union; for the Western, its adjustment and peace; for the British, the supply of what is wanting in it, the strengthening of that which remains in it." They recognised the authority of its great and unquestionable decisions. They were willing to appeal to its authority, if it could be expressed legitimately. They introduced, even into controversy, at least to some extent, the habits of discrimination and respect. Their teaching shows how, after the first fever and excitement of the revolt against Roman usurpation had passed, the leaders of the English Church felt that much natural mistatement and exaggeration had to be qualified and corrected; it shows how anxious they were, in accordance with the declared policy of the Reformation, to keep hold on the undivided and less corrupted Church of the early centuries as their standard and guide: it shows how much they found in their increased acquaintance with it, to enrich, to enlarge, to invigorate, to give beauty, proportion and force to their theology.

Notes

1. *British Critic*, Jan. 1845, pp. 189–92.
2. Φῶς ἱλαρόν; translated in the *Lyra Apostolica*, No. 62.

SIR FRANCIS BACON

1561–1626

Francis Bacon, philosopher, statesman, and essayist, was born on January 22, 1561, at York House off the Strand, London. He was the youngest son of Sir Nicholas Bacon and Ann Cooke. Bacon studied at Trinity College from 1573 to 1575. Plagued by ill health and dissatisfaction with the Aristotelian philosophy, he left Cambridge and went to France, where he studied diplomacy until the death of his father in 1579. Bacon then entered Gray's Inn to study law, becoming a barrister in 1582. He entered Parliament in 1584, remaining a prominent member until 1614. Although he had served as sometime adviser to Elizabeth I, he fell out of favor with the Queen over his objections to a bill for royal subsidies towards expenses incurred in the war against Spain.

By 1591 Bacon had become, along with his brother Anthony, a friend and adviser to Robert Devereux, Earl of Essex, at that time a favorite of the Queen's. Essex recommended Bacon for a number of posts, including that of Solicitor General (given instead to Sir Edward Coke, a lawyer and one of Bacon's lifelong rivals), and gave Bacon a generous tract of land at Twickenham. Bacon in turn tried to protect the interests of the unstable Essex, but felt compelled to break with him after his abortive rebellion in early 1601. Bacon's tract denouncing Essex helped to secure the Earl's conviction for treason.

Having received no significant appointments during the reign of Elizabeth, Bacon did not begin to flourish until the succession of James I in 1603. At this time Bacon was knighted, and he became Solicitor General in 1607. In 1605 he published *The Advancement of Learning*, dedicated to the King, and married Alice Barnham in 1606. After Coke's dismissal in 1616, Bacon's career progressed rapidly, and he was appointed Lord Keeper in 1617, Lord Chancellor and Baron Verulam in 1618, and Viscount St. Albans in 1620–21. Bacon's advancement can be attributed to his dedication to both Parliament and the court, his own constant letters of self-recommendation, and his association with George Villiers (later the Duke of Buckingham), a favorite of the King's.

In 1621 Bacon's fortunes were suddenly reversed. Accused of accepting bribes from defendants who had cases pending, Bacon admitted the charge but claimed that the practice never influenced his decisions. He resigned from his position as Lord Chancellor, was found guilty, fined £40,000, and briefly imprisoned in the Tower of London. Disgraced, Bacon retired from public life. From 1621 until his death on April 9, 1626, he devoted much time to literary production.

In 1597 Bacon published his ten *Essayes*, the first "essays" in English; fifty-eight essays were published in 1625. These, along with *The Advancement of Learning* (1605), were written in English, although the latter was published in an expanded Latin version, *De Augmentis Scientiarum*, in 1623. Bacon's famous *Novum Organum* (literally "New Instrument") was published in Latin in 1620. This, along with the Latin version of *The Advancement of Learning* and the *Sylva Sylvarum; or A Natural History*, comprise a part of the *Instauratio Magna*, or great plan for a restoration of knowledge. In calling for a future of surer, more scientific knowledge founded upon empiricism and induction, Bacon wrote the *New Atlantis* (c. 1610), an unfinished account of an ideal commonwealth dominated by natural philosophers.

Aside from his philosophical writings, Bacon produced many legal and political works, as well as poems, apophthegms, translations of psalms into English, and a history of the reign of Henry VII.

Personal

She ⟨Queen Elizabeth⟩ did acknowledge you had a great wit and an excellent gift of speech, and much other good learning. But in the law she rather thought you could make *show* to the utmost of your knowledge than that you were *deep.*—EARL OF ESSEX, Letter to Francis Bacon, n.d.

I have found an alderman's daughter, a handsome maiden to my liking.—FRANCIS BACON, Letter to Sir Robert Cecil (May 1606)

Sir Francis Bacon was married yesterday to his young wench in Maribone Chapel. He was clad from top to toe in purple, and hath made himself and his wife such store of fine raiments of cloth of silver and gold that it draws deep into her portion. The dinner was kept at his father-in-law Sir John Packington's lodging, over against the Savoy, where his chief guests were the three knights, Cope, Hicks, and Beeston; and upon this conceit (as he said himself), that since he could not have my Lord of Salisbury in person, which he wished, he would have him at least in his representative body.—SIR DUDLEY CARLETON, Letter (May 11, 1606)

Haile, happie Genius of this antient pile!
How comes it all things so about thee smile?
The fire, the wine, the men, and in the midst
Thou stand'st, as if some mystery thou did'st!
Pardon, I read it in thy face, the day
For whose returnes, and many, all these pray:
And so doe I. This is the sixtieth year,
Since Bacon, and thy Lord, was borne and here;
Son to the grave, wise Keeper of the Seale,
Fame and foundation of the English weale:
What then his father was, that since is he,

Now with a title more to the degree.
England's High Chancellor! the destined heire
In his soft cradle to his father's chair;
Whose even thred the Fates spinne round and full,
Out of their choycest and their whitest woole.
'Tis a brave cause of joy; let it be knowne,—
For 'twere a narrow gladnesse, kept thine owne.
Give me a deep-crowned bowle, that I may sing,
In raysing him, the wysdome of my King.
—BEN JONSON, "Lord Bacons Birth-day," 1620

You found me of the Learned Counsel Extraordinary, without patent or fee—a kind of *individuum vagum*. You established me, and brought me into *Ordinary*. Soon after, you placed me *Solicitor*, where I served seven years. Then your majesty made me your *Attorney*, or *Procurator General*. Then *Privy Counselor*, while I was attorney—a kind of miracle of your favor that had not been in many ages. Thence *Keeper of your Seal*; and because that was a kind of planet and not fixed, *Chancellor*. And when your majesty could raise me no higher, it was your grace to illustrate me with beams of honor: first making me *Baron Verulam*, and now *Viscount St. Albans*. So this is the eighth rise or reach, a diapason in music, even a good number and accord for a close. And so I may without superstition be buried in St. Alban's habit or vestment.—FRANCIS BACON, Letter to King James I (1621)

The Chancellor being convicted of bribery, pretends, as if being weary of honour, he would resign his place, being much loaded with calumnies.—WILLIAM CAMDEN, *Annales Jacobi Regis*, 1603–23

There happened in my time one noble speaker, who was full of gravity in his speaking. His language (where he could spare or pass by a jest) was nobly censorious. No man ever spake more neatly, more pressly, more weightily, or suffered less emptiness, less idleness, in what he uttered. No member of his speech, but consisted of his own graces. His hearers could not cough, or look aside from him, without loss. He commanded where he spoke; and had his judges angry and pleased at his devotion. No man had their affections more in his power. The fear of every man that heard him was, lest he should make an end. . . . My conceit of his person was never increased toward him by his place, or honours: but I have and do reverence him, for the greatness that was only proper to himself, in that he seemed to me ever, by his work, one of the greatest men, and most worthy of admiration, that had been in many ages. In his adversity I ever prayed, that God would give him strength; for greatness he could not want. Neither could I condole in a word or syllabel for him, as knowing no accident could do harm to virtue, but rather help to make it manifest.—BEN JONSON, *Timber, or Discoveries*, 1641

His great spirit was brought low, and this humiliation might have raised him again, if his offences had not been so weighty as to keep him down. . . . He was a fit jewel to have beautified and adorned a flourishing kingdom, if his flaws had not disgraced the lustre that should have set him off.—ARTHUR WILSON, *The History of Great Britain; Being the Life and Reign of King James I*, 1653

None can character him to the life, save himself. He was in parts more than a man; who in any liberal profession might be whatsoever he would himself: a great honourer of ancient authors, yet a great deviser and practiser of new ways in learning: privy counsellor, as to king James, so to nature itself, diving into many of her abstruse mysteries. New conclusions he would dig out with mattocks of gold and silver; not caring what

his experience cost him, expending on the trials of nature all and more than he got by the trials at the bar; posterity being the better for his—though he the worse for his own—dear experiments. He and his servants had all in common; the men never wanting what their master had; and thus what came flowing in unto him was sent flying away from him, who, in giving of rewards, knew no bounds but the bottom of his own purse. Wherefore, when king James heard that he had given ten pounds to an under-keeper, by whom he had sent him a buck, the king said merrily, "I and he shall both die beggars;" which was condemnable prodigality in a subject. He lived many years after; and in his books will ever survive: in the reading whereof, modest men commend him in what they do—condemn themselves in what they do not—understand, as believing the fault in their own eyes, and not in the object.—THOMAS FULLER, *The Church History of Britain*, 1655

He was so excellent, so agreeable a speaker, that all who heard him were uneasy if he was interrupted, and sorry when he concluded. . . . Now this general knowledge he had in all things husbanded by his wit, and dignified by so majestical a carriage, he was known to own, struck such an awful reverence in those he questioned, that they durst not conceal the most intrinsic part of their mysteries from him, for fear of appearing ignorant or saucy: all of which rendered him no less necessary than admirable at the Council-table, where in reference to impositions, monopolies, &c., where the meanest manufactures were a usual argument; and, as I have heard, did in this baffle the Earl of Middlesex, that was born and bred a Citizen; yet without any great (if at all,) interrupting his other studies, as is not hard to be imagined of a quick apprehension, in which he was admirable.—FRANCIS OSBORNE, *Historical Memoires of the Reigns of Queen Elizabeth and King James*, 1658

Shortly after the king dissolved the Parliament, but never restored that matchless lord to his place, which made him then to wish the many years he had spent in state policy and law study had been solely devoted to true philosophy: for (said he) the one, at the best, doth but comprehend man's frailty in its greatest splendour; but the other the mysterious knowledge of all things created in the six days' work.—THOMAS BUSHELL, *Abridgment of the Lord Chancellor Bacon's Philosophical Theory in Mineral Prosecutions*, 1659

Sir Francis Bacon, knight, youngest son to Sir Nicholas Bacon, lord keeper, was born in York House, anno 1561; for, being demanded his age by Queen Elizabeth, he returned that he was two years younger than her majesty's reign. He was bred in Trinity College in Cambridge, and there first fell into a dislike of Aristotle's philosophy, as barren and jejune, enabling some to dispute, more to wrangle, few to find out truth, and none, if confining themselves to his principles.

Hence it was that afterwards he traded so largely in experiments; so that, as Socrates is said to be the first who stooped towering speculations into practical morality, Sir Francis was one of the first who reduced notional to real and scientifical philosophy.

He was afterwards bred in Gray's Inn in the study of our municipal law, attaining to great eminency, but no preferment therein, during the reign of Queen Elizabeth; imputable to the envy of a great person, who hindered his rising, for fear to be hindered by him if risen, and eclipsed in his own profession. Thus the strongest wing of merit cannot mount if a stronger weight of malice doth depress it. Yet was he even then favourite to a favourite, I mean the earl of Essex, and more true to him than the earl was to himself, for, finding him to prefer destructive before displeasing counsel, Sir Francis fairly forsook not his person (whom his pity attended to the grave) but practices; and herein was not the worse friend for being the better subject.

By King James he was made his solicitor, and afterwards his attorney (then privileged, contrary to custom, to sit a member *in Dom. Com.*) and at last lord chancellor of England. His abilities were a clear confutation of two vulgar errors, libels on learned men: first, that judgment, wit, fancy and memory cannot eminently be in conjunction in the same person; whereas our knight was a rich cabinet, filled with all four, besides a golden key to open it, elocution. Secondly, that he who is something in all, is nothing in any one art; whereas he was singular *in singulis*, and, being in-at-all, came off with credit.

Such who condemn him for pride, if in his place, with the fifth part of his parts, had been ten times prouder themselves. He had been a better master if he had been a worse, being too bountiful to his servants, and either too confident of their honesty, or too conniving at their falsehood. The story is told to his advantage, that he had two servants, one in all causes patron to the plaintiff, whom his charity presumed always injured, the other to the defendant, pitying him as compelled to law; but taking bribes of both, with this condition, to restore the money received if the cause went against them. Their lord, ignorant hereof, always did unpartial justice; whilst his men (making people pay for what was given them) by compact shared the money betwixt them, which cost their master the loss of his office.

Leading a private life, he much delighted to study in the shade of solitariness; and many useful discoveries in nature were made by him, so that he may be said to have left nothing to his executors, and all to his heirs, under which notion the learned of all ages may be beheld. His vast bounty to such who brought him presents from great persons occasioned his want afterwards, who, in rewarding them, so remembered that he had been lord chancellor, that he forgot that he was but the Lord Verulam.

He died, Anno Domini 1626, in the house of the earl of Arundel at Highgate, and was buried in Saint Michael's Church in Saint Alban's, Master Mutis his grateful servant erecting a monument for him. Since, I have read that his grave being occasionally opened, his skull (the relic of civil veneration) was by one King, a doctor of physic, made the object of scorn and contempt; but he who then derided the dead is since become the laughing-stock of the living.—THOMAS FULLER, *The History of the Worthies of England*, 1662

Methinks in this one man I do at once find enough occasion to admire the strength of human wit, and to bewail the weakness of a mortal condition; for is it not wonderful, that he who had run through all the degrees of that profession which usually takes up men's whole time, who had studied, and practised, and governed the Common Law, who had always lived in the crowd, and borne the greatest burden of civil business, should yet find leisure enough for these retired studies, to excel all those men who separate themselves for this very purpose? He was a man of strong, clear, powerful, imagination; his genius was searching and invincible, and of this I need give no other proof than his style itself; which, as, for the most part, it describes men's minds as well as pictures do their bodies, so it did his above all men living; the comparisons, fetched out of the way, and yet the most easy; in all, expressing a soul equally skilled in men and nature.—THOMAS SPRAT, *History of the Royal Society of London*, 1667

Pity it was he was not entertained with some liberal salary,

abstracted from all affairs, both of court and judicature, and furnished with sufficiency both of means and helps for the going on of his design; which, had it been, he might have given us such a body of Natural Philosophy, and made it so subservient to the public good, that neither Aristotle nor Theophrastus amongst the Ancients nor Paracelsus, or the rest of our latest chymists, would have been considerable.—PETER HEYLYN, *Cyprianus Anglicus: or, the Life and Death of Archbishop Laud*, 1668

Who can forbear to observe and lament the weakness and infirmity of human nature? To see a man so far exalted above the common level of his fellow-creatures, to sink so far below it; to see a man who, like Seneca, gave admirable rules for the conduct of life, and condemning the avaricious pursuit after riches, and, what is unlike Seneca, condemning them in his own person, and yet be defiled thereby.—ROBERT STEPHENS, "Introduction" to *Letters of Lord Bacon*, 1702

I was infinitely pleased to find among the works of this extraordinary man a prayer of his own composing, which, for the elevation of thought, and greatness of expression, seems rather the devotion of an angel than a man. . . . In this prayer, at the same time that we find him prostrating himself before the great mercy seat, and humbled under afflictions which at that time lay heavy upon him, we see him supported by the sense of his integrity, his zeal, his devotion, and his love to mankind; which give him a much higher figure in the minds of thinking men, than that greatness had done from which he was fallen.—JOSEPH ADDISON, *The Tatler*, No. 267, Dec. 23, 1710

> If Parts allure thee, think how Bacon shined,
> The wisest, brightest, meanest of mankind!
> —ALEXANDER POPE, *An Essay on Man*, 1734,
> Ep. IV, ll. 281–82

A man universally admired for the greatness of his genius, and beloved for the courteousness and humanity of his behaviour. He was the great ornament of his age and nation; and nought was wanting to render him the ornament of human nature itself, but that strength of mind which might check his intemperate desire of preferment, that could add nothing to his dignity, and might restrain his profuse inclination to expense, that could be requisite neither for his honour nor entertainment. His want of economy, and his indulgence to servants, had involved him in necessities; and, in order to supply his prodigality, he had been tempted to take bribes, by the title of presents, and that in a very open manner, from suitors in chancery. . . . The Lords insisted on a particular confession of all his corruptions. He acknowledged twenty-eight articles; and was sentenced to pay a fine of forty thousand pounds, to be imprisoned in the Tower during the King's pleasure, to be for ever incapable of any office, place, or employment, and never again to sit in Parliament, or come within the verge of the court. This dreadful sentence, dreadful to a man of nice sensibility to honour, he survived five years; and, being released in a little time from the Tower, his genius, yet unbroken, supported itself amidst involved circumstances and a depressed spirit, and shone out in literary productions, which have made his guilt or weaknesses be forgotten or overlooked by posterity.—DAVID HUME, *History of England*, 1754–62

The moral qualities of Bacon were not of a high order. We do not say that he was a bad man. He was not inhuman or tyrannical. He bore with meekness his high civil honours, and the far higher honours gained by his intellect. He was very seldom, if ever, provoked into treating any person with malignity and insolence. No man more readily held up the left cheek to those who had smitten the right. No man was more expert at the soft answer which turneth away wrath. He was never accused of intemperance in his pleasures. His even temper, his flowing courtesy, the general respectability of his demeanour, made a favourable impression on those who saw him in situations which do not severally try the principles. His faults were—we write it with pain—coldness of heart and meanness of spirit. He seems to have been incapable of feeling strong affection, of facing great dangers, of making great sacrifices.—THOMAS BABINGTON MACAULAY, "Lord Bacon," *Edinburgh Review,* 1837

He idolized state and magnificence in his own person; the brilliancy of his robes and the blaze of his equipage his imagination seemed to feed on; he loved to be gazed on in the streets, and to be wondered at in the cabinet: but, with this feminine weakness, this philosopher was still so philosophic as to scorn the least prudential care of his fortune; so that, while he was enamoured of wealth, he could not bring himself down to the love of money. Participating in the corruptions of the age, he was himself incorruptible: the Lord Chancellor never gave a partial or unjust sentence; and Rushworth has told us, that not one of his decrees was ever reversed. Such a man was not made to crouch and to fawn, to breathe the infection of a corrupted court, to make himself the scapegoat in the mysterious darkness of court-intrigues; but he was this man of wretchedness!—ISAAC DISRAELI, "Bacon," *Amenities of Literature,* 1841

Bacon and Pascal appear to be men naturally very similar in their temper and powers of mind. ⟨Bacon⟩, born in York House, Strand, of courtly parents, educated in court atmosphere, and replying, almost as soon as he could speak, to the queen asking how old he was—"Two years younger than Your Majesty's happy reign!"—has the world's meanness and cunning engrafted into his intellect, and remains smooth, serene, unenthusiastic, and in some degree base, even with all his sincere devotion and universal wisdom; bearing, to the end of life, the likeness of a marble palace in the street of a great city, fairly furnished within, and bright in wall and battlement, yet noisome in places about the foundations.—JOHN RUSKIN, *Modern Painters,* 1843–60, Pt. 5, Ch. 20

There is in this Lord Keeper an appetite, not to say a ravenousness, for earthly promotion and the envy of surrounding flunkies, which seems to me excessive. Thou knowest him, O reader: he is that stupendous Bacon who discovered the new way of discovering truth,—as has been very copiously explained for the last half century,—and so made men of us all. Undoubtedly a most hot seething, fermenting piece of Life with liquorish viper eyes; made of the finest elements, a beautiful kind of man, if you will; but of the earth, earthy; a certain seething, ever-fermenting prurience which prodigally burns up things:—very beautiful, but very clayey and terrene every thing of them;—not a great soul, which he seemed so near being, ah no!—THOMAS CARLYLE, *Historical Sketches of Notable Persons and Events in the Reigns of James I and Charles I,* 1844

The meanness of Bacon, spoken of in the bitterest line of one of the bitterest poets, contrasts so strangely with the elevation of Bacon's genius, that even they who cannot get rid of the impression left upon their minds by his conduct to Essex remain perplexed by the apparent enigma. . . . That much of Bacon's advice seems, in itself, intrinsically mean, we do not for a moment deny; but what we feel very strongly is, that until we

can place ourselves in the peculiar focus of his own familiar position, and of the personal relations of the great family of statesmen who then lived round the English throne, occupied by an able, crafty, and conceited—a vacillating and dangerous woman, whose word could and did decide the fate of any one or more of them, we cannot rightly judge the exact standard of Bacon's worldly wisdom.—BERNARD CRACROFT, *Essays, Political and Miscellaneous,* 1868

I am persuaded for my own part that, if he had died before Christmas 1620, his example and authority upon all questions of business, politics, administration, legislation, and morals, would have stood quite as high and been as much studied and quoted, and with quite as good reason, as it has upon questions purely intellectual. All his life he had been studying to know and to speak the truth; and I doubt whether there was ever any man whose evidence upon matters of fact may be more absolutely relied on, or who could more truly say with Kent, in *Lear,*—

> All my reports go with the modest truth;
> Nor more, nor clipp'd; but so.

. . . All the evidence shows that he was a very sensitive man, who felt acutely both kindness and unkindness, but that he was at the same time remarkably free from the ordinary defect of sensitive natures,—irritability and aptness to take offense. . . . Bacon's record is unusually full, and as his life presented to himself many doubtful problems for action, it has left to us many questionable actions for criticism; and among them not a few which he would not himself have repeated or attempted to justify. One thing, however, must be admitted to his advantage. Of the contemporaries whose opinion of him is known to us, those who saw him nearest in his private life give him the best character.—JAMES SPEDDING, *An Account of the Life and Times of Francis Bacon,* 1878, Vol. 2, pp. 521–654

He was anything rather than "mean." On the other hand, he was generous, open-hearted, affectionate, peculiarly sensitive to kindnesses, and equally forgetful of injuries. The epithet of "great," which has been so ungrudgingly accorded to him as a writer, might, without any singular impropriety, be applied to him also as a man. The story of his life, it must be confessed, is not altogether what the reader of his works would have desired, but the contrast has been so exaggerated as to amount to a serious and injurious misrepresentation.—THOMAS FOWLER, *Francis Bacon,* 1881, p. 28

The vast intellect of "high-browed Verulam" commands our respectful admiration, but it is icy and ungenial; we cannot bring ourselves to love the man, however much we may venerate the writer.—HENRY J. NICOLL, *Landmarks of English Literature,* 1882, p. 94

If James had been capable of appreciating Bacon's genius, the name of the prophet of natural science might have come down to us as great in politics as it is in philosophy. The defects in his character would hardly have been known, or, if they had been known, they would have been lost in the greatness of his achievements.—SAMUEL R. GARDINER, *History of England,* 1883, Vol. 1, p. 164

The life of Francis Bacon is one which it is a pain to write or to read. It is the life of a man endowed with as rare a combination of noble gifts as ever was bestowed on a human intellect; the life of one with whom the whole purpose of living and of every day's work was to do great things to enlighten and elevate his race, to enrich it with new powers, to lay up in store for all ages to come a source of blessings which should never fail or dry up;

it was the life of a man who had high thoughts of the ends and methods of law and government, and with whom the general and public good was regarded as the standard by which the use of public power was to be measured; the life of a man who had struggled hard and successfully for the measure of prosperity and opulence which makes work easy and gives a man room and force for carrying out his purposes. All his life long his first and never-sleeping passion was the romantic and splendid ambition after knowledge, for the conquest of nature and for the service of man; gathering up in himself the spirit and longings and efforts of all discoverers and inventors of the arts, as they are symbolised in the mythical Prometheus. He rose to the highest place and honour; and yet that place and honour were but the fringe and adornment of all that made him great. It is difficult to imagine a grander and more magnificent career; and his name ranks among the few chosen examples of human achievement. And yet it was not only an unhappy life; it was a poor life. . . . When he is a lawyer, he seems only a lawyer. If he had not been the author of the *Instauratio*, his life would not have looked very different from that of any other of the shrewd and supple lawyers who hung on to the Tudor and Stuart Courts, and who unscrupulously pushed their way to preferment. . . . Both in his philosophical thinking, and in the feelings of his mind in the various accidents and occasions of life, Bacon was a religious man, with a serious and genuine religion. . . . It is not too much to say that in temper, in honesty, in labour, in humility, in reverence, he was the most perfect example that the world had yet seen of the student of nature, the enthusiast for knowledge. That such a man was tempted and fell, and suffered the Nemesis of his fall, is an instance of the awful truth embodied in the tragedy of *Faust*. —RICHARD WILLIAM CHURCH, *Bacon*, 1884, pp. 1–225

What a great failure Bacon was, whenever he was tried! Poor Essex, hunted to death merely for "getting up a row," and Bacon sacrificing him without compunction, and without seeing that he was probably made a tool of, merely to serve his personal advantage! Then the poetical justice, as they call it,—very prosaic justice,—of his own destruction, by a bolt out of a clear sky, which an enemy was adroit enough to direct to his ruin. And poor Bacon with conscience enough to feel that he deserved it, but not spirit enough to make a fight. No, if Pope's fling was undeserved, as you say, it was because of the mean and ignoble set around him. Almost as pitiable and tragic in its way, pitiable in its true sense, was the upshot of Bacon's higher and nobler life, conceiving vaguely and laboring all his days over that which he was unable and incompetent to bring to the birth. His memory reaping a great reward of fame for a century or so, and then the conclusion reluctantly reached that nothing tangible in the advancement of Natural Science can be attributed to him. Altogether, what a solemn sermon! It might be preached from the pulpit of St. Paul's. —ASA GRAY, *Letters*, 1884, Vol. 2, p. 749

Probably in consenting to contribute to the destruction of his friend ⟨Essex⟩, Bacon was acting under, what must have seemed to him, considerable pressure. If he had refused the task assigned to him by the Crown, he must have given up all chance of the Queen's favour and with it all hope of promotion. Very inferior men have made as great, or greater, sacrifices; but Bacon was not the man to make such a sacrifice. . . . Bacon had a keen sense of the value of fortune, of the possibilities of a learned leisure, of the importance of his own colossal plans for the benefit of the human race; on the other hand he had a very dull sense of the claims of honour and friendship. Forced to choose between prosperity and friend-

ship, he preferred to be prosperous even at the cost of facilitating the ruin of a friend for whom ruin, in any case, was ultimately inevitable. . . . One of the strongest helps that a man can have in the time of trouble seems to have been denied to Bacon. No record in any letter or document hitherto has attested that his wife sympathised with his pursuits, or shared any of his aspirations. Her name is scarcely mentioned in his voluminous correspondence, except in a letter indicating that her convenience, as well as his own, required that York House should be retained. —EDWIN ABBOTT ABBOTT, *Francis Bacon: An Account of His Life and Works*, 1885, pp. 81–82, 308

Bacon, with his brilliant intellectual equipment and his consciousness of his great powers, is not to be set down as simply a bad man. But his heart was cold, and he had no greatness of soul. He was absorbed, to a quite unworthy degree, in the pursuit of worldly prosperity. Always deeply in debt, he coveted above everything fine houses and gardens, massive plate, great revenues, and, as essential preliminaries, high offices and employments, titles and distinctions, which he might well have left to men of meaner worth. He passed half his life in the character of an office-seeker, met with one humiliating refusal after another, and returned humble thanks for the gracious denial. Once and once only, in his early days in Parliament, did he display some independence and rectitude; but when he saw that it gave offence in the highest places, he repented as bitterly as though he had been guilty of a sin against all political morality, and besought her Majesty's forgiveness in terms that might have befitted a detected thief. —GEORGE BRANDES, *William Shakespeare: A Critical Study*, 1898, Vol. 1, p. 309

General

Crown of all modern authors. —GEORGE SANDYS, "Notes" to *Ovid's Metamorphosis*, 1621–26

Lewis Elzevir wrote me lately from Amsterdam, that he was designed to begin shortly an edition in *quarto*, of all the works of Lord Bacon; and he desired my advice and any assistance I could give him; to the end that, as far as possible, these works might come abroad with advantage, which have been long received with the kindest eulogies, and with the most attested applause of the learned world. —ISAAC GRUTER, Letter to William Rawley (1652), *Baconiana*, ed. Thomas Tenison, 1679

Who knows not how Herbary had been improved by Theophrastus, Dioscorides, the Arabians, and other Peripatetics? who can deny that Physic, in every part of it, was improved by Galen and others, before the Lord Bacon ever sucked? and what accessionals had not Chemistry received by the cultivation of the Aristotelians, before his House of Solomon was dreamed of? Let us, therefore, not be concluded by the aphorisms of this Lord. Let his *insulse adherents* buy some salt, and make use of more than one grain when they read him; and let us believe better of the ancients, than that their methods of science were so unfruitful. —HENRY STUBBE, "Preface" to *Lord Bacon's Relation of the Sweating-Sickness Examined*, 1671, p. 5

A man who, for the greatness of genius, and compass of knowledge, did honour to his age and country; I could almost say to human nature itself. He possessed at once all these extraordinary talents which were divided amongst the greatest authors of antiquity. He had the sound, distinct, comprehensive knowledge of Aristotle, with all the beautiful lights, graces, and embellishments of Cicero. One does not know which to admire most in his writings, the strength of reason, force of style, or brightness of imagination.—JOSEPH ADDISON, *The Tatler*, No. 267, Dec. 23, 1710

Lord Bacon was the greatest genius that England (or perhaps any country) ever produced.—ALEXANDER POPE (1734–36), cited in Joseph Spence, *Anecdotes, Observations and Characters of Books and Men*, ed. S. W. Singer, 1820

Allowing as much sense to Sir Philip ⟨Sidney⟩ as his warmest admirers can demand for him, surely this country has produced many men of far greater abilities, who have by no means met with a proportionate share of applause. It were a vain parade to name them—take Lord Bacon alone, who I believe of all our writers, except Newton, is most known to foreigners, and to whom Sir Philip was a puny child in genius.—HORACE WALPOLE, Letter to David Hume (July 15, 1758)

The great glory of literature in this island, during the reign of James, was Lord Bacon. . . . If we consider the variety of talents displayed by this man; as a public speaker, a man of business, a wit, a courtier, a companion, an author, a philosopher; he is justly the object of great admiration. If we consider him merely as an author and philosopher, the light in which we view him at present, though very estimable, he was yet inferior to his contemporary Galileo, perhaps even to Kepler. Bacon pointed out at a distance the road to true philosophy: Galileo both pointed it out to others, and made himself considerable advances in it. The Englishman was ignorant of geometry: the Florentine revived that science, excelled in it, and was the first that applied it, together with experiment, to natural philosophy. The former rejected, with the most positive disdain, the system of Copernicus; the latter fortified it with new proofs, derived both from reason and the senses. Bacon's style is stiff and rigid; his wit, though often brilliant, is also often unnatural and far-fetched; and he seems to be the original of those pointed smiles and long-spun allegories which so much distinguish the English authors; Galileo is a lively and agreeable, though somewhat a prolix writer. But Italy, not united in any single government, and perhaps satiated with that literary glory which it has possessed both in ancient and modern times, has too much neglected the renown which it has acquired by giving birth to so great a man. That national spirit which prevails among the English, and which forms their great happiness, is the cause why they bestow on all their eminent writers, and on Bacon among the rest, such praises and acclamations as may often appear partial and excessive.—DAVID HUME, *History of England*, 1754–62

Who is there, that, upon hearing this name, does not instantly recognise everything of genius the most profound, everything of literature the most extensive, everything of discovery the most penetrating, everything of observation on human life the most distinguishing and refined? All these must be instantly recognised, for they are all inseparably associated with the name of Lord Verulam.—EDMUND BURKE, "Speech on the Impeachment of Warren Hastings," May 28, 1794

If it be true that the compositions of Bacon are scarcely at all read in his native country, I could not devise a more effectual charm to revive a taste which ought never to have declined, than a just translation of the *Cogitata et visa*. When Hume denied this author the praise of eloquence, he must either have forgot that such a work issued from his pen; or that profound observations, clothed with enlarged sentiments and the images of a copious and exquisite fancy, will fully compensate the want of idiomatic purity, or a rhetorical structure of periods.—FRANCIS HORNER, *Journal, Memoirs and Correspondence*, 1801, Vol. 1, p. 168

That Shakespeare's appearance upon a soil so admirably prepared was neither marvellous nor accidental is evidenced even by the corresponding appearance of such a contemporary as Bacon. Scarcely can anything be said of Shakespeare's position generally with regard to mediæval poetry which does not also bear upon the position of the renovator Bacon with regard to mediæval philosophy. Neither knew nor mentioned the other, although Bacon was almost called upon to have done so in his remarks upon the theatre of his day. It may be presumed that Shakespeare liked Bacon but little, if he knew his writings and life, that he liked not his ostentation, which, without on the whole interfering with his modesty, recurred too often in many instances; that he liked not the fault-finding which his ill-health might have caused, nor the narrow-mindedness with which he pronounced the histrionic art to be infamous, although he allowed that the ancients regarded the drama as a school for virtue; nor the theoretic precepts of worldly wisdom which he gave forth; nor, lastly, the practical career which he lived. Before his mind, however, if he had fathomed it, he must have bent in reverence. For just as Shakespeare was an interpreter of the secrets of history and of human nature, Bacon was an interpreter of lifeless nature.—G. G. GERVINUS, *Shakespeare Commentaries*, 1845, tr. F. E. Bunnètt, p. 884

If I were asked to describe Bacon as briefly as I could, I should say that he was the liberator of the hands of knowledge. —LEIGH HUNT, *Table Talk*, 1851, p. 84

I refer to him, because I fancy that many have a notion of his books on the Interpretation of Nature as very valuable for scientific men, and his books on Morals and Politics as very wise for statesmen and men of the world, but not as friends. They form this notion because they suppose, that the more we know of Bacon himself, the less sympathy we should have with him. I should be sorry to hold this opinion, because I owe him immense gratitude; and I could not cherish it if I thought of him, even as the sagest of book-makers and not as a human being. I should be sorry to hold it, because if I did not find in him a man who deserved reverence and love, I should not feel either the indignation or the sorrow which I desire to feel for his misdoings.—FREDERICK DENISON MAURICE, "On the Friendship of Books" (1856), *The Friendship of Books and Other Lectures*, ed. Thomas Hughes, 1874, p. 11

What is true of Shakespeare is true of Bacon. Bacon thought in parables. Of the astounding versatility of his thought, of the universality of its reach, the subtlety of its discrimination, the practical Machiavellian omniscience of motive good and evil, it is difficult by words to convey any adequate idea. But the plasticity of his thought is always the humble servant of his omnipresent imagination. His intellect is always at the mercy of his fancy for a clothing. All his intellectual facts are wrapt in visions of beautiful illustration.—BERNARD CRACROFT, *Essays, Political and Miscellaneous*, 1868, Vol. 2, p. 218

Of Bacon, more than of any other writer, it may be said that "in the very dust of his writings there is gold."—FREDERIC WILLIAM FARRAR, *Families of Speech*, 1870

Read a page of Macaulay, and you exhaust the thought at a single perusal. Read a page of Bacon twenty times, and at each reading you will discover new meanings, unobserved before. That haze which the naked eye could not penetrate is found by the telescope to be a nebula, composed of innumerable distinct stars. The one writer informs, the other stimulates, the mind. The one enlightens, the other inspires. The first communicates facts and opinions; the second floods and surcharges you with mental life.—WILLIAM MATHEWS, *Getting On in the World,* 1872, p. 245

His utterances are not infrequently marked with a grandeur and solemnity of tone, a majesty of diction, which renders it impossible to forget, and difficult even to criticise them. . . . There is no author, unless it be Shakespeare, who is so easily remembered or so frequently quoted. . . . The terse and burning words, issuing, as it were, from the lips of an irresistible commander.—THOMAS FOWLER, *Francis Bacon,* 1881, p. 202

In the matter of diction he uses more obsolete words than either Hooker or Sidney, but he is immeasurably superior to them both in the perspicuity of his sentences which, though occasionally involved, as a rule allow us to see into his thoughts with great distinctness. The aphoristic style of his essays is worthy of all praise, and he may be considered the first English master of antithesis: it was perhaps his work in this direction which gave his peculiar bent to the literature of the early part of the 17th century.—C. R. L. FLETCHER, *The Development of English Prose Style,* 1881, p. 10

It is in Bacon's philosophy that the key to his political life is to be found. In its general conceptions, his statesmanship was admirable. The change which was to make religion thoughtful and tolerant, and the change which was to make England the home of peaceful industry and commercial activity, were ever present to his mind. He took no part in the wrangling disputations of contending theologians, and he turned a deaf ear to the interruptions of legal pedants.

No point of Bacon's political system has been so thoroughly discarded by later generations as that which deals with the relations between the Crown and the Houses of Parliament. Yet even here his mistake lay rather in the application of his principles than in the spirit by which they were animated. His hardest blows were directed against the error of which the French Constituent Assembly of 1789 has furnished the weightiest example; the error which regards the Executive Power and the Representative Body as capable, indeed, of treating with one another on a friendly footing, but as incapable of merging their distinct personalities in each other. It was thus that the Great Contract of 1610 was utterly distasteful to him. The King and the Lower House, he held, were not adverse parties to enter into bargains. They were members of the same commonwealth, each charged with its appropriate functions. It was not well that the King should redress grievances merely because he expected to receive something in return. It was not well that the Commons should vote supplies as the purchase-money of the redress of grievances. If the King wished to have obedient and liberal subjects, let him place himself at their head as one who knew how to lead them. Let the administration of justice be pure. Let the exercise of the prerogative be beneficent. Let Parliament be summoned frequently, to throw light upon the necessities of the country. If mutual confidence could be thus restored, everything would be gained.

In proclaiming this doctrine, Bacon showed that he had entered into the spirit of the future growth of the constitution as completely as he showed, in the *Novum Organum,* that he had entered into the spirit of the future growth of European science. That it is the business of the Government to rule, and that it is also the business of the Government to retain the confidence of the representatives of the people, are the principles which, taken together, distinguish the later English constitution from constitutions resting upon assemblies formed either after the model of the first French Empire or after the model of the Popular Assembly of Athens. Yet no man would have been more astonished than Bacon, if he had been told what changes would be required to realise the idea which he had so deeply at heart. Clinging to the old forms, he hoped against hope that James would yet win the confidence of the nation, and he shut his eyes to the defects in his character which rendered such a consummation impossible.

So far, indeed, is it from being true that the domestic policy of James must of necessity have been opposed to Bacon's views, that we have every reason to believe that in its main lines it was dictated, as far as it went, by Bacon himself. It was otherwise with James's foreign policy. For, though Bacon looked forward with hopefulness to the time when Europe should no longer be distracted by religious difficulties, he regarded Spain with the deepest distrust, and he cherished the belief that it was a national duty to prevent any further aggression of the Catholic Powers upon the Protestant States on the Continent. In this spirit he had prepared the draft of the proclamation which James had refused to use, and it was the expectation that this spirit would animate both King and Parliament which had raised his patriotic hopes more highly than they had been raised at any time since James had come to the throne.—SAMUEL R. GARDINER, *History of England,* 1883, Vol. 3, pp. 396–98

Imagination is a compound of intellectual power and feeling. The intellectual power may be great, but if it is not accompanied with feeling, it will not minister to feeling; or it will minister to many feelings by turns, and to none in particular. As far as the intellectual power of a poet goes, few men have excelled Bacon. He had a mind stored with imagery, able to produce various and vivid illustrations of whatever thought came before him; but these illustrations touched no deep feeling; they were fresh, original, racy, fanciful, picturesque, a play of the head that never touched the heart. The man was by nature cold; he had not the emotional depth or compass of an average Englishman. Perhaps his strongest feeling of an enlarged or generous description was for human progress, but it did not rise to passion; there was no fervour, no fury in it. Compare him with Shelley on the same subject, and you will see the difference between meagreness and intensity of feeling. What intellect can be, without strong feeling, we have in Bacon; what intellect is, with strong feeling, we have in Shelley. The feeling gives the tone to the thoughts; sets the intellect at work to find language having its own intensity, to pile up lofty and impressive circumstances; and then we have the poet, the orator, the thoughts that breathe, and the words that burn. Bacon wrote on many impressive themes—on Truth, on Love, on Religion, on Death, and on the Virtues in detail; he was always original, illustrative, fanciful; if intellectual means and resources could make a man feel in these things, he would have felt deeply; yet he never did.—ALEXANDER BAIN, *Practical Essays,* 1884, p. 16

Bacon's style varied almost as much as his handwriting; but it was influenced more by the subject-matter than by youth or old age. Few men have shown equal versatility in adapting their language to the slightest shade of circumstance and purpose. His style depended upon whether he was addressing a king, or a great nobleman, or a philosopher, or a friend; whether he was composing a State paper, pleading in a State trial, magnifying the Prerogative, extolling Truth, discussing studies, exhorting a judge, sending a New Year's present, or sounding a trumpet to prepare the way for the Kingdom of Man over Nature. It is a mistake to suppose that Bacon was never florid till he grew old. On the contrary, in the early *Devices,* written during his connection with Essex, he uses a rich exuberant style and poetic rhythm; but he prefers the rhetorical question of appeal to the complex period. On the other hand, in all his formal philosophical works, even in the *Advancement of Learning*, published as early as 1605, he uses the graver periodic structure, though often illustrated with rich metaphor. . . . In his estimation, literary style was a snare quite as often as a help. —EDWIN ABBOTT ABBOTT, *Francis Bacon: An Account of His Life and Works*, 1885, pp. 447–53

⟨A⟩fter his fall, in May 1621, Bacon wakened afresh to the importance of his native language. In a poignant letter to the King, who was to "plough him up and sow him with anything," he promised a harvest of writings in the vernacular. In 1605 he had already made a splendid contribution to criticism in his *Advancement of Learning*; otherwise, he had mainly issued his works in Ciceronian Latin. But in 1621 he finished his *History of Henry VII.*; in 1624 he was writing the *New Atlantis*; in 1625 the *Essays* (first issued in nucleus in 1597, and meagerly enlarged in 1612) were published in full, and the *Sylva Sylvarum* was completed. These works, with his public and private letters, combine to form the English writings of Bacon. They constitute a noble mass of work, but there is no question that the reputation of Bacon dwindles if we are forced to cut away his Latin books; he no longer seems to have taken the whole world of knowledge into his province. And in his English works, considered alone, we have to confess a certain poverty. He who thought it the first distemper of learning, that men should study words and not matter, is now in the singular condition of having outlived his matter, or, at least, a great part of it, while his words are as vivid as ever. We could now wish that he could have been persuaded to "hunt more after choiceness of the phrase, and the round and clear composition of the sentence, and the sweet falling of the clauses," qualities which he had the temerity to profess to despise.

Bacon described himself as "a bell-ringer, who is up first to call others to church." The *Advancement of Learning* was dictated by this enthusiasm. He would rise at cock-crowing to bid the whole world welcome to the intellectual feast. This is the first book in the English language which discusses the attitude of a mind seeking to consolidate and to arrange the stores of human knowledge. It was planned in two parts, the first to be a eulogy of the excellence of learning—its "proficience"—and the second to be a survey of the condition of the theme—its "advancement." Bacon had little leisure and less patience, and his zeal often outran his judgment in the act of composition. The *Advancement* is written, or finished at least, obviously in too great haste; the Second Book is sometimes almost slovenly, and the close of it leaves us nowhere. But the opening part, in which Bacon sums up first the discredits and then the dignity of learning, defending wisdom, and justifying it to its sons, remains one of the great performances of the seventeenth century. The matter of it is obsolete, human knowledge having progressed so far forwards and backwards since 1605; and something dry and unripe in Bacon's manner—which mellowed in later life—diminishes our pleasure in reading what is none the less a very noble work, and one intended to be the prologue to the author's vast edifice of philosophical inquiry. At this point, however, he unluckily determined to abandon English brick for Latin stone.

This futile disregard of his own language robs English literature of the greater part of its heritage in Bacon. He desired an immortality of readers, and fancied that to write in English would "play the bankrupt with books." Hence, even in his *Essays* we are conscious of a certain disdain. The man is not a

serious composer so much as a collector of maxims and observations; he keeps his note-book and a pencil ever at his side, and jots down what occurs to him. If it should prove valuable, he will turn it out of this ragged and parochial English into the statelier and more lasting vehicle of Latin. He has no time to think about style; he will scribble for you a whole book of apophthegms in a morning. The *Essays* themselves—his "recreations," as he carelessly called them—are often mere notations or headings for chapters imperfectly enlarged, in many cases merely to receive the impressions of a Machiavellian ingenuity. They are almost all too short; the longest, those on "Friendship" and "Gardens," being really the only ones in which the author gives himself space to turn round. As a constructor of the essay considered as a department of literary art, Bacon is not to be named within hail of Montaigne.

Bacon desired that prose should be clear, masculine, and apt, and these adjectives may generally be applied to what he wrote with any care in English. He was so picturesque a genius, and so abounding in intellectual vitality, that he secured the graces without aiming at them. His *Essays* hold a certain perennial charm, artless as they are in arrangement and construction; but the student of literature will find greater instruction in examining the more sustained and uplifted paragraphs of the *Advancement*, where he can conveniently parallel Bacon with Hooker, the only earlier prose-writer who can be compared with him. He will observe with interest that the diction of Bacon is somewhat more archaic than that of Hooker. —EDMUND GOSSE, *A Short History of Modern English Literature*, 1897, pp. 130–32

The central figure in prose of the entire Jacobean period is undoubtedly Francis Bacon. He holds this position a little in spite of himself; for it was his own opinion, apparently deliberate and persistent, that English was an untrustworthy makeshift, likely to play tricks to any book written in it, and that the only secure medium for posterity was Latin. And he also holds it in spite of the fact that he had more than reached middle life at the date of the King's accession, and that his one contribution of unquestioned importance to English literature, as distinguished from English science and philosophy, was first published long before that time. For the really characteristic editions of the *Essays*—those which are not shorthand bundles of aphorisms, but works of prose art—date much later, and the whole complexion of Bacon's mind and of his matured style has the cast of Jacobean thought and manner. . . .

It is at once true of Bacon that no man has a more distinct style than he has, and that no man's style is more characteristic of its age than his. It has, indeed, been attempted to show that he had more than one style; but this does not come to much more than saying that he wrote on a considerable number of different subjects, and that, like a reasonable man, he varied his expression to suit them. Always when he is most himself— in the *Essays* as well as in the *Advancement of Learning*, in the *Henry VII.* as well as in any other English work—we come sooner or later on certain manners which are almost unmistakable, and which, though in part possessed in common with other men of the time, are in part quite idiosyncratic. All Jacobean authors, and Bacon among them, interlard their English with scraps of Latin, and constantly endeavour to play in their English context on the Latin uses of words. All aim first of all at what is called pregnancy, and attain that pregnancy by a free indulgence in conceit. Few, despite the stateliness which they affect, have any objection to those "jests and clinches" which even Jonson seems to have thought of as interfering with the "noble censoriousness" of Bacon himself. In all a certain desultoriness of detail, illustration, and the like—as if the writer had so full a mind and commonplace-book that he could not help emptying both almost at random—is combined with a pretty close faculty of argument, derived from the still prevailing familiarity with scholastic logic.

But Bacon, in addition to these characteristics, which he shares with others, has plenty of his own. His sentences, indeed, do not attain to that extraordinary music which is seen in some of Brooke and Donne, which is not wanting in Burton, which is the glory of Sir Thomas Browne, the saving grace of Milton's best prose, and the almost over-lavished and sometimes frittered away charm of Jeremy Taylor. He had begun, as we see in the earliest form of the *Essays*, with a very curt, stenographic, sharply antithetic form; and though he suppled and relaxed this afterwards, he never quite attained the full, languorous grace of Donne or Browne. But he became gorgeous enough later, the glitter of his antithesis being saved from any tinsel or "snip-snap" effect by the fulness of his thought, and his main purport being by degrees set off with elaborate paraphernalia of ornament and imagery. In the successive version of the *Essays* we see the almost skeleton forms of the earliest filling out, taking on trappings, acquiring flesh and colour and complexion in the later, while in some of the latest, the well-known ones on Building and on Gardens especially, the singular interest in all sorts of minute material facts which distinguishes him comes in with a curiously happy effect. Both the pieces just mentioned are much more like description of scenery in the most elaborate romance than like ideal suggestions for practical carrying out, drawn up by a grave lawyer, statesman, and philosopher.

No point in Bacon's literary manner is more characteristic, both of his age and of himself, than his tendency to figure. Such a sentence as this in the *Advancement*, "Nay, further, in general and in sum, certain it is that *Veritas* and *Bonitas* differ but as the seal and the print; for truth points goodness; and they be but the clouds of error which descend in the storms of passions and perturbations,"—would show itself to any person of experience as almost certainly written between 1580 and 1660 in the first place, while in the second it would at least suggest itself to such a person as being most probably Bacon's. Although all the world in his day was searching for tropes and comparisons and conceits, the minds of few were so fertile as his; and it is not unworthy notice that even the apparently bold, even startling, change of metaphor from the "seal" to the "cloud" is in reality a much more legitimate change than it seems.

It will stand to reason that such a style is displayed to the best possible advantage by bold and richly-coloured surveys of science in general, like the *Advancement*, or by handlings of special points, like the *Essays*. Whether Bacon was really "deep," either in knowledge or in thought, has been disputed; but he was certainly one of the greatest rhetoricians, in the full and varied sense of rhetoric, that ever lived. His knowledge, deep or not, was very wide, ever ready to his hand for purposes more often perhaps of divagation than of penetration. His command of phrase was extraordinary. No one knows better than he either how to leave a single word to produce all its effect by using it in some slightly uncommon sense, and setting the wits at work to discern and adjust this; or how to unfold all manner of applications and connotations, to open all inlets of side-view and perspective. That he dazzles, amuses, half-delusively suggests, stimulates, provokes, lures on, much more than he proves, edifies, instructs, satisfies, is indeed perfectly true. But the one class of performances is at least as suitable for literary exhibition as the other, and Bacon goes through the exhibition

with a gusto and an effect which can hardly be too much admired. Fertile in debate as almost all his qualities have proved, there is at least one of them about which there can be little difference of opinion, and that is his intense literary faculty. It was entirely devoted to and displayed in prose—he wrote very little verse, and that little is nothing out of the way. But in prose rhetoric—in the use, that is to say, of language to dazzle and persuade, not to convince—he has few rivals and no superiors in English. His matter is sometimes not very great, and almost always seems better than it is, but this very fact is the greatest glory of his manner.—GEORGE SAINTSBURY, *A Short History of English Literature*, 1898, pp. 369–73

In Bacon's sentences we may often find remarkable condensation of thought in few words. One does not have to search for two grains of wheat hid in two bushels of chaff. . . . His work abounds in illustrations, analogies, and striking imagery. —REUBEN POST HALLECK, *History of English Literature*, 1900, pp. 124–25

Works

ESSAYS

Sir Francis Bacon hath set out new Essays, where, in a chapter of *Deformity*, the world takes notice that he paints out his little cousin ⟨Robert Cecil, Earl of Salisbury⟩ to the life.—NICHOLAS CHAMBERLAIN, Letter to Sir Dudley Carleton (Dec. 17, 1621), *Court and Times of James I*, ed. Thomas Birch, 1849, Vol. 1, p. 214

The virtue of these *Essays* is too well allowed to require any comment. Without the elegance of Addison, or the charming egotism of Montaigne, they have acquired the widest circulation: and if Bacon had written no more, they would have bequeathed his name undying to posterity. Burke preferred them to the rest of his writings, and Dr. Johnson observed that "their excellence and value consists in their being the observations of a strong mind operating upon life, and, in consequence, you will find there what you seldom find in other books."—EDMUND MALONE, *Life of Sir Joshua Reynolds*, 1794

No book contains a greater fund of useful knowledge, or displays a more intimate acquaintance with human life and manners. The style, however, is not pleasing; it is devoid of melody and simplicity, and the sentences are too short and antithetic.—NATHAN DRAKE, *Essays Illustrative of the* Tatler, Spectator, *and* Guardian, 1804, Vol. 2, p. 20

The small volume to which he has given the title of *Essays*, the best known and the most popular of all his works. It is one of those where the superiority of his genius appears to the greatest advantage; the novelty and depth of his reflections often receiving a strong relief from the triteness of the subject. It may be read from beginning to end in a few hours; and yet after the twentieth perusal one seldom fails to remark in it something overlooked before. This, indeed, is a characteristic of all Bacon's writings, and is only to be accounted for by the inexhaustible aliment they furnish to our own thoughts, and the sympathetic activity they impart to our torpid faculties. —DUGALD STEWART, "First Preliminary Dissertation," *Encyclopaedia Britannica*, 1815–21

The *Essays*, which are ten in number, abound with condensed thought and practical wisdom, neatly, pressly, and weightily stated, and, like all his early works, are simple, without imagery. They are written in his favourite style of aphorisms, although each essay is apparently a continued work; and without that love of antithesis and false glitter to which truth and justness of thought is frequently sacrificed by the writers of maxims.—BASIL MONTAGU, "The Life of Francis Bacon," *Bacon's Complete Works*, 1834, Vol. 1

The transcendent strength of Bacon's mind is visible in the whole tenor of these *Essays*, unequal as they must be from the very nature of such compositions. They are deeper and more discriminating than any earlier, or almost any later, work in the English language, full of recondite observation, long matured and carefully sifted. . . . Few books are more quoted; and, what is not always the case with such books, we may add, that few are more generally read. In this respect they lead the van of our prose literature: for no gentleman is ashamed of owning that he has not read the Elizabethan writers: but it would be somewhat derogatory to a man of the slightest claim to polite letters, were he unacquainted with the *Essays* of Bacon. It is, indeed, little worth while to read this or any other book for reputation's sake; but very few in our language so well repay the pains, or afford more nourishment to the thoughts.—HENRY HALLAM, *Introduction to the Literature of Europe*, 1837–39, Pt. 3, Ch. 4, Par. 34

Bacon's *Essays* are the portrait of an ambitious and profound calculator,—a great man of the vulgar sort. Of the upper world of man's being they speak few and faint words.—RALPH WALDO EMERSON, "Milton" (1838), *Works*, Riverside ed., Vol. 12, p. 152

Bacon's sentence bends beneath the weight of his thought, like a branch beneath the weight of its fruit. Bacon seems to have written his essays with Shakespeare's pen. . . . He writes like one on whom presses the weight of affairs, and he approaches a subject always on its serious side. He does not play with it fantastically. He lives amongst great ideas, as with great nobles, with whom he dare not be too familiar. In the tone of his mind there is ever something imperial. When he writes on building, he speaks of a palace with spacious entrances, and courts, and banqueting-halls; when he writes on gardens, he speaks of alleys and mounts, waste places and fountains, of a garden "which is indeed prince-like."—ALEXANDER SMITH, *Dreamthorp*, 1863, pp. 31–32

His *Essays* are not at all sceptical, like the French essays, from which he may have borrowed this appellation: they are thoroughly dogmatic. . . . They are extremely instructive for the internal relations of English society. They show wide observation and calm wisdom, and, like his philosophical works, are a treasure for the English nation, whose views of life have been built upon them.—LEOPOLD VON RANKE, *A History of England*, 1875, Vol. 1, p. 459

Whatever may be said of Bacon's capacity to be the prophet of science, there can be but one opinion of his genius for the office of practical philosopher and professor of worldly wisdom. Nowhere perhaps in all literature ancient or modern can we find any other book which can be compared with Bacon's *Essays* as a manual of that wisdom which consists of the knowledge, not of man but of men—their tendencies, passions, prejudices, weaknesses; nowhere at any rate a book in which the whole experience of a most sagacious observer of human life is reproduced in such brief compass, expressed in language so packed with meaning, yet so sparkling with wit and fancy, grave humour, picturesque metaphor, and felicitous illustration. The *Essays* betray no talent for abstract speculation. There is no attempt in them at the exhaustive analysis of principles. The movement of thought is analogical rather than logical. They consist, for the most part, of miscellaneous remarks on human conduct, on the motives, illusions, self-deceptions, jealousies, ambitions, failures, successes, of men in the various relations of life, of prudential maxims, hints for the dexterous management of individuals and classes, counsels for youth and age, for the married and single, for parents and children, suggestions for the attainment of success in life, and consolations for the lack of it—advices to all sorts of people, sometimes profound, always sagacious and sensible, set off by striking illustrations and apt historic allusions, and couched in a form of expression, quaint, pointed, picturesque, and in almost every sentence having the stamp of a strong and original nature upon it. Now this obviously is a kind of philosophy which is not to be learnt in lettered retirement, but only through much converse with the world. If Bacon had fled, as he often threatened to do, from the distractions of public life to the seclusion of a college cloister, or to the solitude of his study and gardens at Gorhambury, we might have gained more cumbrous treatises on scientific method, and a fuller elaboration of his vast yet impracticable scheme for the reorganization of human knowledge; but we should never have possessed the less pretentious but, in its own way, more genuine philosophy, the distilled essence of worldly wisdom and practical common sense which is preserved for us in the pages of the *Essays*.—JOHN CAIRD, "The Scientific Character of Bacon" (1880), *University Addresses*, 1898

In certain features they stand alone in this field of writing. There is nothing of the gay paradox of Montaigne, the sounding verbiage of Seneca, or the witty sophistry of Rochefoucauld. They express the "practical reason" of the English mind. Each sentence is beaten gold. One of his observations on men and manners is like a chalk outline by Michael Angelo. And as a model of English style, the *Essays* are unrivalled, although I think they have less of stately eloquence than the *Advancement of Learning*.—EMELYN W. WASHBURN, *Studies in Early English Literature*, 1884, p. 202

Less than seventy years after the death of Bacon his *Essays* were so completely forgotten that when extracts from them were discovered in the common-place book of a deceased lady of quality, they were supposed to be her own, were published and praised by people as clever as Congreve, went through several editions, and were not detected until within the present century.—EDMUND GOSSE, "Tennyson—and After," *Questions at Issue*, 1894, p. 190

THE ADVANCEMENT OF LEARNING

Neither the most liberal of the professions, nor even the wider field of politics and legislation, could supply to the genius of Bacon a sufficient sphere of activity; and turning aside for a short space from the career of worldly ambition, in which he had many competitors, to that in which he marched unrivalled and alone, he completed and gave to the world in 1605 his immortal work on the *Advancement of Learning*. . . . The experience of ages has shown, that he who assumes the character of a reformer in the art of reasoning, an expositor of the errors of the schools, soars above the region of popular applause only to excite the alarms, or encounter the hostility, of the learned; whose pride, whose prejudices and whose interests he offends or threatens. Thus, whilst a few inquisitive and enlightened spirits, such as Jonson and Wotton and Raleigh, hailed with delight and awe the discoveries of their great contemporary, born to establish an era in the progress of the human mind, the erudite disciples of ancient error busied themselves in depreciating and decrying what they would not or could not understand.—LUCY AIKIN, *Memoirs of the Court of King James the First*, 1822, Vol. 1, pp. 193–95

The work is dedicated to King James the First, and its introduction inspires a mingled sentiment of admiration of the boldness and grandeur of the design which it announces, and of heartache at the depth of degradation to which it sinks in the servile adulation with which it besmears the king. . . . The stupendous magnitude of this undertaking, the courtly cunning, ingenuity, and meanness of suggesting it to the King as if it was an enterprise of his own, the lofty consciousness of its sublimity, and the sly implied disclaimer of it as anything more on the part of the author than a mere speculative whim to be moulded into form and substance, are all deserving of profound meditation—of more than I can give. He proceeds then to enumerate and to refute the objections against learning—of divines, of politicians, as arising from the fortunes, manners, or studies of learned men. He discusses the diseases of learning—the peccant humors which have not only given impediment to the proficiency of learning, but have given occasion to the traducement thereof. And he closes the book with a copious and cheering exhibition of the dignity of learning—a theme upon which I follow him with delight. The style is a continuous and perpetual citation of classical and scriptural quotations. — JOHN QUINCY ADAMS, *Diary* (July 19, 1844), *Memoirs*, ed. Charles Francis Adams, Vol. 12, p. 72

Marked the first decisive appearance of the new philosophy. . . . He did not thoroughly understand the older philosophy which he attacked. His revolt from the waste of human intelligence which he conceived to be owing to the adoption of a false method of investigation blinded him to the real value of deduction as an instrument of discovery; and he was encouraged in his contempt for it as much by his own ignorance of mathematics as by the non-existence in his day of the great deductive sciences of physics and astronomy. Nor had he a more accurate prevision of the method of modern science. —JOHN RICHARD GREEN, *A Short History of the English People*, 1874, Ch. 9

NOVUM ORGANUM

I have received three copies of that work, wherewith your Lordship hath done a great and everlasting benefit to all the children of Nature, and to Nature herself in her utmost extent and latitude, who never before had so true an Interpreter, or so inward a Secretary of her Cabinet.—SIR HENRY WOTTON, Letter to Francis Bacon (1622), *Reliquiae Wottonianae*, 1651

He saw and taught his contemporaries and future ages, that reasoning is nothing worth, except as it is founded on facts. . . . Most valuable of all his works, and by him most highly valued. It is written in a plain unadorned style in aphorisms, invariably stated by him to be the proper style for philosophy, which, conscious of its own power, ought to go forth "naked and unarmed;" but, from the want of symmetry and ornament, from its abstruseness, from the novelty of its terms, and from the imperfect state in which it was published, it has, although the most valuable, hitherto been too much neglected; but it will not so continue. The time has arrived, or is fast approaching, when the pleasures of intellectual pursuit will have so deeply pervaded society, that they will, to a considerable extent, form the pleasures of our youth; and the lamentation in the "Advancement of Learning" will be diminished or pass away.—BASIL MONTAGU, "The Life of Francis Bacon," *Bacon's Complete Works*, 1834, Vol. 1

If Bacon constructed a method to which modern science owes its existence, we shall find its cultivators grateful for the gift, and offering the richest incense at the shrine of a benefactor whose generous labours conducted them to immortality. No such testimonies, however, are to be found. Nearly two hundred years have gone by, teeming with the richest fruits of human genius, and no grateful disciple has appeared to vindicate the rights of the alleged legislator of science. Even Newton, who was born and educated after the publication of the *Novum Organon*, never mentions the name of Bacon or his system; and the amiable and indefatigable Boyle treated him with the same disrespectful silence. When we are told, therefore, that Newton owed all his discoveries to the method of Bacon, nothing more can be meant than that he proceeded in that path of observation and experiment which had been so warmly recommended in the *Novum Organon*; but it ought to have been added, that the same method was practised by his predecessors; that Newton possessed no secret that was not used by Galileo and Copernicus; and that he would have enriched science with the same splendid discoveries if the name and the writings of Bacon had never been heard of.—SIR DAVID BREWSTER, *Memoirs of the Life, Writings, and Discoveries of Sir Isaac Newton*, 1855, Vol. 2, p. 402

There is no book which gives me such a sense of greatness; because the sayings are like keys which turn every way and *fit* whichever chamber of truth you want to turn into,—physical, mental, and moral science alike.—DORA GREENWELL (1860), cited in William Dorling, *Memoirs of Dora Greenwell*, 1885, p. 47

Bacon the magnificent might be fit to lay down the chart of all knowledge; Bacon the despised seems fitter to guide patient and foot-sore pilgrims through tangled roads, amidst dangers arising from their own presumption, into a region of light. And this is, at last, the true glory of the *Novum Organum*.—FREDERICK DENISON MAURICE, *Moral and Metaphysical Philosophy*, 1862, Vol. 2, p. 233

In spite however of his inadequate appreciation either of the old philosophy or the new, the almost unanimous voice of later ages has attributed, and justly attributed, to the *Novum Organum* a decisive influence on the development of modern science.—JOHN RICHARD GREEN, *A Short History of the English People*, 1874, Ch. 9

And now at last the *Novum Organum*, the fragmentary relic of that grand scheme for the restoration of the sciences which had floated before his youthful imagination in the days when he boasted that he had "taken all knowledge for his province," had passed through the press. For the reception with which it met, he cared but little: Coke might recommend him with a snarl to restore the justice and the laws of England before he meddled with the doctrines of the old philosophers; James might meet him with the silly jest that the book was like the peace of God, because it passed all understanding. It was for posterity that he worked, and for the judgment of posterity he was content to wait. . . . As a practical book addressed to practical men, it was as complete a failure as was the commercial policy of its writer. . . . That which gives to the author of the *Novum Organum* a place apart amongst "those who know," is, that being, as he was, far behind some of his contemporaries in scientific knowledge, and possessing scarcely any of the qualifications needed for scientific investigation, he was yet able, by a singular and intuitive prescience, to make the vision of the coming age his own, and not only to point out the course which would be taken by the stream even then springing into life, but to make his very errors and shortcomings replete with the highest spirit of that patient and toilsome progress from which he himself turned aside.—SAMUEL R. GARDINER, *History of England*, 1883, Vol. 3, pp. 394–95

HISTORY OF HENRY VII

But this good Work was the most effectually undertaken and compleated by the Incomparable Sir Francis Bacon, who has bravely surmounted all those difficulties, and pass'd over those Rocks and Shallows, against which he took such Pains to caution other less experienc'd Historians. He has perfectly put himself into King Henry's own Garb and Livery, giving as sprightly a View of the Secrets of his Council, as if himself had been President in it. Not trivial Passages, such as are below the Notice of a Statesman, are mix'd with his Sage Remarks: Nor is any thing of Weight or Moment slubber'd over with that careless Hast and Indifferency which is too common in other Writers. No Allowances are given to the Author's own Conjecture or Invention; where a little Pains and Consideration will serve to set the Matter in its proper and true Light. No Impertinent Digressions, nor fanciful Comments, distract his Readers: But the whole is written in such a Grave and Uniform Style, as becomes both the Subject and the Artificer.—WILLIAM NICOLSON, *The English Historical Library*, 1696–99

The only two pieces of history we have, in any respect to be compared with the ancient, are, the reign of Henry the Seventh by my lord Bacon, and the history of our civil wars in the last century by your noble ancestor my lord chancellor Clarendon.—HENRY ST. JOHN, VISCOUNT BOLINGBROKE, "Letter 6" (1735–38), *Letters on the Study and Use of History*, 1752

Sir Thomas More wrote the reign of Richard III with the inconsideration of a boy; Lord Bacon wrote an apology for a tyrant with as little regard for truth, as if nobody but a tyrant was ever to read it. The first weighed nothing he retailed; the second vended justice for wisdom, and was the more criminal of the two: for History only injures the individuals it blackens, but prejudices all mankind by palliating tyranny; and encourages it, by recommending it as policy.—HORACE WALPOLE, Letter to Robert Henry (March 28, 1783), *Correspondence*, ed. W. S. Lewis, Vol. 15, pp. 177–78

A work which, done under every advantage, would have been a rare specimen of skill, diligence, and spirit in the workman; but for which, begun as it was immediately after so tremendous an overthrow, and carried on in the middle of so many difficulties in the present and anxieties for the future, it would be hard to find a parallel. Though not one of his works which stand highest either in reputation or popularity with later times,—being neither generally read (an accident which it shares with most of the others) nor generally supposed to be of great value (in which it is more singular),—it has done its work more effectually perhaps than any of them. None of the histories which had been written before conveyed any idea either of the distinctive character of the man or the real business of his reign. Every history which has been written since has derived all its light from this, and followed its guidance in every question of importance; and the additional materials which come to light from time to time, and enable us to make many corrections in the history of the events, only serve to confirm and illustrate the truth of its interpretation of them.—JAMES SPEDDING, *An Account of the Life and Times of Francis Bacon*, 1878, Vol. 2, p. 542

The government of the first Tudor, though by no means one of the worst, was a government of usurpation. Its most efficient means of accomplishing its ends was the secret court of Star Chamber. This court kept no records, and was not responsible for its acts. Whatever was necessary for the firmer establishment of the new line was done probably without question and without scruple. Very little documentary evidence was left. But even what little existed in Bacon's time seems not to have been used by the historian. From the beginning to the end of his work, Bacon has given only one reference to an authority, and even that reference is so indefinite as almost to justify the suspicion that it was meant to mislead. The value of the history as a record of truth, therefore, rests solely upon the nature of the habits then prevailing in the investigation of knowledge, and on the character of the historian for veracity. Unfortunately, neither of these foundations is trustworthy. Bacon was not born till more than fifty years after the death of the king whose history he undertook to write. Three important and turbulent reigns had intervened. Bacon had every interest in giving to the facts, as he narrated them, a certain color. Unfortunately, we are debarred from believing that he would be overscrupulous in his searches after exact knowledge, even if exact knowledge were accessible. But it was not. It is therefore but simple truth to say that no court in any civilized community would accept of Bacon's testimony as a basis on which to build up any judicial decision whatever. Historical evidence, in order to be conclusive, must be of the same general nature as all other evidence. The conclusion to which we are brought is obvious. The book teaches us something of Bacon; it teaches us possibly something of the way in which Bacon regarded Henry VII.; it teaches us still more of the way in which Bacon desired his readers to regard his opinions of Henry VII.; but of Henry VII. himself, or of his reign, it teaches us very little indeed. —CHARLES KENDALL ADAMS, A *Manual of Historical Literature*, 1882, p. 8

Is a model of clear historical narration, not exactly picturesque, but never dull; and though not exactly erudite, yet by no means wanting in erudition, and exhibiting conclusions which, after two centuries and a half of record-grubbing, have not been seriously impugned or greatly altered by any modern historian. In this book, which was written late, Bacon had, of course, the advantage of his long previous training in the actual politics of a school not very greatly altered since the time he was describing, but this does not diminish the credit due to him for formal excellence.—GEORGE SAINTSBURY, A *History of Elizabethan Literature*, 1887, p. 209

PHILOSOPHY

You formerly wrote me, that you knew persons who were willing to labour for the advancement of the sciences, at the cost of all sorts of observations and experiments: now, if any one who is inclined this way, could be prevailed upon to undertake a history of the appearances of the heavenly bodies, to be drawn up according to the Verulamian method, without the admixture of hypothesis; such a work as this would prove of great utility, and would save me a great deal of trouble in the prosecution of my inquiries.—RENÉ DESCARTES, Letter to Father Mersenne (c. 1650)

The entire logic of Lord Verulam is directed toward physics in itself, and therefore toward the truth, or genuine knowledge of things. Moreover, it consists principally in forming clear ideas since he desires foremost that all preconceived notions be wiped out, and then that new notions, or ideas inferred from new experiments properly conducted, be formed. Likewise, it consists in expressing ideas clearly, since he desires that we construct axioms from individual cases duly examined through experimentation, not by flying off the handle directly up to the highest, or most general, axioms, but by proceeding gradually in an orderly manner through intermediate steps. It consists also in making clear deductions, but only universal statements from individual cases since that is done by a legitimate induction, and not individual truths from universals, since that is done by means of the syllogism, which he does not approve of. However, since the sinew and muscle of all reasoning actually lies in the syllogism, and not even induction proves anything except by the force of a syllogism because of the general proposition clearly implied [in inductive reasoning] according to which it is claimed that everything which can be enumerated individually has been enumerated, or that not one thing can be found which does not agree with the statement, the syllogism seems to be condemned quite without reason inasmuch as he can be convicted of using it whenever he reasons at all, even though he condemns it. Accordingly, he does not seem to have rejected the syllogism totally but merely the syllogism which is founded on statements that have not been sufficiently examined and adequately confirmed; therefore, before he explains the form or uses of the syllogism, he may be expected to have estimated to what extent general propositions subject to no exceptions may exist. Meanwhile, however, just this treatise on the syllogism is lacking, and so is any general treatment of method, although he perhaps intended to furnish some such treatment when he spoke about the partition of the sciences. I shall not try to justify all those words that may be considered a trifle too affected since the founder of a new system seems to have the right to use new words or words in a new way. —PIERRE GASSENDI, *Syntagma*, 1658, tr. Craig B. Brush

It is certain that Lord Bacon's way of experiment, as now prosecuted by sundry English gentlemen, affords more probabilities of glorious and profitable fruits, than the attempts of any other age or nation whatsoever. —GEORGE HAVERS, *Another Collection of Philosophical Conferences*, 1664

The Royal Society was a work well becoming the largeness of Bacon's wit to devise, and the greatness of Clarendon's prudence to establish. —THOMAS SPRAT, *History of the Royal Society of London*, 1667

> Bacon at last, a might man, arose, . . .
> And boldly undertook the injur'd pupil's cause.
> Bacon, like Moses, led us forth at last,
> The barren wilderness he pas'd;
>   Did on the very border stand
>   Of the bles'd promised land;
> And, from the mountain's top of his exalted wit,
>   Saw it himself, and shew'd us it.
>   —ABRAHAM COWLEY, "Ode to the Royal
>   Society," c. 1667

When our renowned Lord Bacon had demonstrated the methods for a perfect restoration of all parts of real knowledge, the success became on a sudden stupendous, and effective philosophy began to sparkle, and even to flow into beams of bright shining light all over the world. —HENRY OLDENBURG, "Preface" to *Philosophical Transactions of the Royal Society*, 1672

Though there was bred in Mr. Bacon so early a dislike of the Physiology of Aristotle, yet he did not despise him with that pride and haughtiness with which youth is wont to be puffed up. He has a just esteem of that great master of learning, greater than that which Aristotle expressed himself towards the philosophers that went before him; for he endeavoured (some say) to stifle all their labours, designing to himself an universal monarchy over opinions, as his patron Alexander did over men. Our hero owned what was excellent in him, but in his inquiries

into nature he proceeded not upon his principles. He began the work anew, and laid the foundation of philosophic theory in numerous experiments. —THOMAS TENISON, *Baconiana*, 1679

The late most wise Chancellor of England was the chief writer of our age, and carried as it were the standard that we might press forward, and make greater discoveries in Philosophic matters, than any of which hitherto our schools had rung. So that if in our time any great improvements have been made in Philosophy, there has been not a little owing to that great man. —SAMUEL PUFENDORF, *Spicilegium Controversiarum*, 1680

It was owing to the sagacity and freedom of Lord Bacon that men were then pretty well enabled both to make discoveries and to remove the impediments that had hitherto kept physics from being useful. —ROBERT BOYLE, *New Experiments and Observations Touching Cold*, 1683

By standing up against the Dogmatists, he emancipated and set free philosophy, which had long been a miserable captive, and which hath ever since made conquest in the territories of Nature. —JOHN EVELYN, *Numismata*, 1697

While poorly instructed or badly intentioned adversaries made open war on it, philosophy sought refuge, so to speak, in the works of a few great men. They had not the dangerous ambition of removing the blindfolds from their contemporaries' eyes; yet silently in the shadows they prepared from afar the light which gradually, by imperceptible degrees, would illuminate the world.

   The immortal Chancellor of England, Francis Bacon, ought to be placed at the head of these illustrious personages. His works, so justly esteemed (and more esteemed, indeed, than they are known), merit our reading even more than our praises. One would be tempted to regard him as the greatest, the most universal, and the most eloquent of the philosophers, considering his sound and broad views, the multitude of objects to which his mind turned itself, and the boldness of his style, which everywhere joined the most sublime images with the most rigorous precision. Born in the depths of the most profound night, Bacon was aware that philosophy did not yet exist, although many men doubtless flattered themselves that they excelled in it (for the cruder a century is, the more it believes itself to be educated in all that can be known). Therefore, he began by considering generally the various objects of all the natural sciences. He divided these sciences into different branches, of which he made the most exact enumeration that was possible for him. He examined what was already known concerning each of these objects and made the immense catalogue of what remained to be discovered. This is the aim of his admirable book *The Advancement of Learning*. In his *Novum Organum*, he perfects the views that he had presented in the first book, carries them further, and makes known the necessity of experimental physics, of which no one was yet aware. Hostile to systems, he conceives of philosophy as being only that part of our knowledge which should contribute to making us better or happier, thus apparently confining it within the limits of the science of useful things, and everywhere he recommends the study of Nature. His other writings were produced on the same pattern. Everything, even their titles, proclaims the man of genius, the mind that sees things in the large view. He collects facts, he compares experiments and points out a large number to be made; he invites scholars to study and perfect the arts, which he regards as the most exalted and most essential part of human science; he sets forth with a noble simplicity his

Conjectures and Thoughts on the different objects worthy of men's interest; and he would have been able to say, like that old man in Terence, that nothing which touches humanity was alien to him. Natural science, ethics, politics, economics, all seem to have been within the competence of that brilliant and profound mind. And we do not know which we ought to admire more, the riches he lavishes upon all the subjects he treats or the dignity with which he speaks of them. His writings can best be compared to those of Hippocrates on medicine; and they would be no less admired, nor less read, if the culture of the mind were as dear to mankind as the conservation of health. But in every area only the works of those who head a school of disciples make a brilliant impression. Bacon was not of that number, and the form of his philosophy prevented it; it was too wise to astonish anyone. Scholasticism, which continued to dominate, could not be overthrown except by bold and new opinions. And apparently circumstances are not such that a philosopher who is content to say to men: "Here is the little that you have learned, there is what remains for you to find," is destined to cause much stir among his contemporaries. If we did not know with what discretion, and with what superstition almost, one ought to judge a genius so sublime, we might even dare reproach Chancellor Bacon for having perhaps been too timid. He asserted that the scholastics had enervated science by their petty questions, and that the mind ought to sacrifice the study of general beings for that of individual objects; nonetheless, he seems to have shown a little too much caution or deference to the dominant taste of his century in his frequent use of the terms of the scholastics, sometimes even of scholastic principles, and in the use of divisions and subdivisions, fashionable in his time. After having burst so many irons, this great man was still held by certain chains which he could not, or dared not, break.—JEAN LE ROND D'ALEMBERT, *Preliminary Discourse to the Encyclopedia*, 1751, trs. Richard N. Schwab, Walter E. Rex

It has been frequently the subject of inquiry among philosophers, whether there be a first principle of human knowledge: some have supposed but one, some two, others more. Every man, I think, may by his own experience be sure of the truth of that principle on which this work is founded. Perhaps we shall even be convinced that the connexion of ideas is without comparison the simplest, the clearest, and even the most fruitful principle. At the very time when its influence was not observed, we were indebted to it for every improvement made by the human understanding.

Such were the reflexions I had made on method when I began to read my lord Bacon's works. I was afterwards as much pleased that my notions happened to coincide with this great man's on some particular points, as I was surprised that the Cartesians had borrowed nothing from him. No man was better acquainted with the cause of human error: for he perceived that there was an original defect in the framing of those ideas which are the workmanship of the mind; and consequently that to advance in the investigation of truth, new combinations are requisite. This is an advice he often repeats. But how was it possible for him to be heard? The public were so strongly prejudiced in favour of the school jargon, and of innate ideas, that they treated the regeneration of the human understanding as a chimerical project. The method proposed by his lordship was too perfect to produce a revolution; that of Descartes, by letting some errors continue, was sure of success. Farther, the English philosopher had such weighty employments as hindered him from putting his own theory in practice; consequently he was obliged to be satisfied with giving advice, which

must have made but a slight impression on superficial minds. Descartes, on the contrary, delivered himself up intirely to philosophic studies, and having a more lively and more fruitful imagination, in the room of former errors he sometimes introduced others of a more imposing nature, which contributed not a little to his reputation.—ETIENNE BONNOT DE CONDILLAC, *An Essay on the Origin of Human Knowledge*, 1756, tr. Thomas Nugent, Pt. 2, Sec. 2, Ch. 3

Never did two men, gifted with such genius, recommend paths of inquiry so widely different. Descartes aspired to deduce an explanation of the whole system of things by reasoning *a priori* upon assumed principles: Bacon, on the contrary, held that it was necessary to observe Nature thoroughly before attempting to explain her ways; that we must ascend to principles through the medium of facts; and that our conclusions must be warranted by what we observe. Descartes reasoned about the World, as if the laws which govern it had not yet been established, as if every thing were still to create. Bacon considered it as a vast edifice, which it was necessary to view in all directions, to explore through all its recesses and windings, before any conjecture even could be safely formed as to the principles of its construction, or the foundations on which it rests. Thus, the philosophy of Bacon, by recommending the careful observation of Nature, still continues to be followed, whilst that of Descartes, whose essence lay in hypothesis, has wholly disappeared.—JEAN SYLVAIN BAILLY, *Histoire de l'astronomie moderne*, 1775–85, Vol. 2, Bk. 4

The influence of Bacon's genius on the subsequent progress of physical discovery, has been seldom duly appreciated; by some writers almost entirely overlooked, and by others considered as the sole cause of the reformation in science which has since taken place. Of these two extremes, the latter certainly is the least wide of the truth; for, in the whole history of letters, no other individual can be mentioned, whose exertions have had so indisputable an effect in forwarding the intellectual progress of mankind. On the other hand, it must be acknowledged, that before the era when Bacon appeared, various philosophers in different parts of Europe had struck into the right path; and it may perhaps be doubted, whether any one important rule with respect to the true method of investigation be contained in his works, of which no hint can be traced in those of his predecessors. His great merit lay in concentrating their feeble and scattered lights; fixing the attention of philosophers on the distinguishing characteristics of true and of false science, by a felicity of illustration peculiar to himself, seconded by the commanding powers of a bold and figurative eloquence.—DUGALD STEWART, *Account of the Life and Writings of Thomas Reid*, 1802–3, Sec. 2

This mighty genius ranks as the father of modern physics, inasmuch as he brought back the spirit of investigation from the barren verbal subtleties of the schools to nature and experience: he made and completed many important discoveries himself, and seems to have had a dim and imperfect foresight of many others. Stimulated by his capacious and stirring intellect, experimental science extended her boundaries in every direction: intellectual culture, nay, the social organization of modern Europe generally, assumed a new shape and complexion.—FRIEDRICH SCHLEGEL, *Lectures on the History of Literature*, 1815, p. 286

Bacon's grand distinction, considered as an improver of physics, lies in this, that he was the first who clearly and fully pointed out the rules and safeguards of right reasoning in physical inquiries. Many other philosophers, both ancient and modern, had referred to observation and experiment in a cursory way, as furnishing the materials of physical knowledge; but no one, before him, had attempted to systematize the true method of discovery; or to prove that the *inductive*, is the *only* method by which the genuine office of philosophy can be exercised, and its genuine ends accomplished. It has sometimes been stated, that Galileo was, at least in an equal degree with Bacon, the father of the Inductive Logic; but it would be more correct to say, that his discoveries furnished some fortunate illustrations of its principles. To explain these principles was no object of his; nor does he manifest any great anxiety to recommend their adoption, with a view to the general improvement of science.—MACVEY NAPIER, "Lord Bacon" (1818), *Lord Bacon and Sir Walter Raleigh*, 1853, p. 14

The opinion so prevalent during the last thirty years, that Lord Bacon introduced the art of experimental inquiry on physical subjects, and that he devised and published a method of discovering scientific truth, called the method of induction, appears to me to be without foundation, and perfectly inconsistent with the history of science. This heresy, which I consider as most injurious to the progress of scientific inquiry, seems to have been first propagated by d'Alembert, and afterwards fostered in our University by Mr. Stewart and Mr. Playfair, three men of great talent, but not one of whom ever made a single discovery in physics. . . . It has been said, however, by the admirers of Bacon, that though a few philosophers knew the secret of making advances in science, yet the great body were ignorant of it, and that Paracelsus, Van Helmont, and many others, were guided in their inquiries by very inferior methods. . . . It seems quite clear that Bacon, who knew nothing either of Mathematics or Physics, conceived the ambitious design of establishing a general method of scientific inquiry. This method, which he has explained at great length, is neither more nor less than a crusade against Aristotle, with the words *experiment and observation* emblazoned on his banner. . . . The method given by Bacon is, independent of all this, quite useless, and in point of fact has never been used in any successful inquiry. A collection of facts, however skilfully they may be conjured with, can never yield general laws unless they contain that master-fact in which the discovery resides, or upon which the law mainly depends.—SIR DAVID BREWSTER, Letter (April 26, 1824), cited in Margaret Brewster, *The Home Life of Sir David Brewster*, 1869, pp. 128–30

Bacon has been likened to the prophet who from Mount Pisgah surveyed the Promised Land, but left it for others to take possession of. Of this happy image perhaps part of the felicity was not perceived by its author. For though Pisgah was a place of large prospect, yet still the Promised Land was a land of definite extent and known boundaries, and moreover it was certain that after no long time the chosen people would be in possession of it all. And this agrees with what Bacon promised to himself and to mankind from the instauration of the sciences. . . . In this respect, then, as in others, the hopes of Francis Bacon were not destined to be fulfilled. It is neither to the technical part of his method nor to the details of his view of the nature and progress of science that his great fame is justly owing. His merits are of another kind. They belong to the spirit rather than to the positive precepts of his philosophy.—ROBERT LESLIE ELLIS, "General Preface" to *Bacon's Philosophical Works*, 1857, Vol. 1, pp. 63–64

With the audacity of ignorance, he presumed to criticise what he did not understand, and, with a superb conceit, disparaged the great Copernicus. . . . The more closely we examine the writings of Lord Bacon, the more unworthy does he seem to have been of the great reputation which has been awarded to him. The popular delusion to which he owes so much originated at a time when the history of science was unknown. They who first brought him into notice knew nothing of the old school of Alexandria. This boasted founder of a new philosophy could not comprehend, and would not accept, the greatest of all scientific doctrines when it was plainly set before his eyes. It has been represented that the invention of the true method of physical science was an amusement of Bacon's hours of relaxation from the more laborious studies of law and duties of a court. His chief admirers have been persons of a literary turn, who have an idea that scientific discoveries are accomplished by a mechanico-mental operation. Bacon never produced any great practical results himself, no great physicist has ever made any use of his method. He has had the same to do with the development of modern science that the inventor of the orrery has had to do with the discovery of the mechanism of the world. . . . No man can invent an organon for writing tragedies and epic poems. . . . Few scientific pretenders have made more mistakes than Lord Bacon. He rejected the Copernican system, and spoke insolently of its great author; he undertook to criticise adversely Gilbert's treatise *De Magnete*; he was occupied in the condemnation of any investigation of final causes, while Harvey was deducing the circulation of the blood from Aquapendente's discovery of the valves in the veins; he was doubtful whether instruments were of any advantage, while Galileo was investigating the heavens with the telescope. Ignorant himself of every branch of mathematics, he presumed that they were useless in science, but a few years before Newton achieved by their aid his immortal discoveries. It is time that the sacred name of philosophy should be severed from its long connexion with that of one who was a pretender in science, a time-serving politician, an insidious lawyer, a corrupt judge, a treacherous friend, a bad man.—JOHN WILLIAM DRAPER, *History of the Intellectual Development of Europe*, 1864, Vol. 2, pp. 258–60

The actual and undeniable facts that when compared with the writings of the Italian natural philosophers those of Bacon breathe more of the modern spirit, and yet that he ignores the discoveries which have proved themselves to be most fruitful for subsequent times, and even their originators (Copernicus, Galileo, Gilbert, Harvey, and others), or at least is less able to appreciate them than the former,—that, further, in spite of his praise of natural science he has exerted on its development no influence worthy of the name—(facts which in recent times have led to such different verdicts on Bacon), can only be harmonised (but then easily harmonised) when we do not attribute to Bacon the position of the initiator of modern philosophy, but see in him the close of the philosophy of the Middle Ages. He has left behind him the standpoint from which natural science subjected itself to dogma and in which she contended against it. Therefore he stands higher and nearer to modern times. But this advance refers only to the relation of the doctrines of natural science to religion and the Church. . . . Measured by the standard of the Middle Ages Bacon appears modern, by that of modern times he appears mediæval. But to say this implies that his merit is no small one.—JOHANN EDWARD ERDMANN, *A History of Philosophy*, tr. Williston S. Hough, 1865–76, Vol. 1, pp. 682–83

He certainly never made utility the sole object of science, or at least never restricted utility to material advantages. He asserted in the noblest language the superiority of abstract truth to all the fruits of invention, and would never have called those speculations useless which form the intellectual character of an age. Yet, on the other hand, it must be acknowledged that the general tone of his writings, the extraordinary emphasis which he laid upon the value of experiments, and above all upon the bearing of his philosophy on material comforts, represents a tendency which was very naturally developed into the narrowest utilitarianism.—W. E. H. LECKY, *Spirit of Rationalism in Europe*, 1865, Vol. 1, Ch. 4, Pt. 1

The whole endeavor of Bacon in science is to attain the fact, and to ascend from particular facts to general. He turned away with utter dissatisfaction from the speculating *in vacuo* of the Middle Ages. His intellect demanded positive knowledge; he could not feed upon the wind. From the tradition of philosophy and from authority he reverted to nature. Between faith and reason Bacon set a great and impassable gulf. Theology is something too high for human intellect to discuss. Bacon is profoundly deferential to theology, because, as one cannot help suspecting, he was profoundly indifferent about it. The schoolmen for the service of faith had summoned human reason to their aid, and Reason, the ally, had in time proved a dangerous antagonist. Bacon, in the interest of science, dismissed faith to the unexceptionable province of supernatural truths. To him a dogma of theology was equally credible whether it possessed an appearance of reasonableness or appeared absurd. The total force of intellect he reserved for subjugating to the understanding the world of positive fact.—EDWARD DOWDEN, *Shakespere: A Critical Study of His Mind and Art*, 1875, p. 16

Certainly, more than any man of his time, Bacon seems to have realized that he was standing at the vestibule of a new age, and was charged with the mission of showing the insufficiency of the past and the bright hopes of the future.—OSCAR BROWNING, *An Introduction to the History of Educational Theories*, 1881

I get driven out of all patience by Spedding's special pleading for him. He seems to me to have done no *work*, to have shown no example of what he calls his method. But his imagination was his great faculty, and all that is most valuable in him is due to the prescient instinctive insight with which he looked on the possibilities of knowledge; the enthusiasm of a seer, not of a philosopher who had measured, and weighed, and compared, and done what Mozley calls the underground work of solid thinking. Galileo, as you say, and Pascal *did* what Bacon talked about without knowing how to do it, and they talked *after* they had touch of the realities of a hunt after physical truth. —RICHARD WILLIAM CHURCH, Letter to Asa Gray (1883), *Life and Letters of Dean Church*, 1894, p. 376

Was this not the very time when Bacon stood out before Europe the herald, if not the leader, of the great scientific movement of modern days, and to his own land set an example of sober practical thinking which the English mind has never since forgotten? If Hobbes, in the last years of Bacon's life, was gradually working his way through scholarly studies to the position of a philosophical thinker, under whose influence but Bacon's could the development proceed? From whom but the first of English modern philosophers should the second, being in actual contact with him, learn to think with the freedom of a modern, and the practical purpose of an Englishman? —GEORGE CROOM ROBERTSON, *Hobbes*, 1886, p. 18

No delusion is greater than the notion that method and industry can make up for lack of motherwit, either in science or in practical life; and it is strange that, with his knowledge of mankind, Bacon should have dreamed that his, or any other, "via inveniendi scientias" would "level men's wits" and leave

little scope for that inborn capacity which is called genius. As a matter of fact, Bacon's "via" has proved hopelessly impracticable; while the "anticipation of nature" by the invention of hypotheses based on incomplete inductions, which he specially condemns, has proved itself to be a most efficient, indeed an indispensable, instrument of scientific progress. Finally, that transcendental alchemy—the superinducement of new forms on matter—which Bacon declares to be the supreme aim of science, has been wholly ignored by those who have created the physical knowledge of the present day. Even the eloquent advocacy of the Chancellor brought no unmixed good to physical science. It was natural enough that the man who, in his better moments, took "all knowledge for his patrimony," but, in his worse, sold that birthright for the mess of pottage of Court favour and professional success, for pomp and show, should be led to attach an undue value to the practical advantages which he foresaw, as Roger Bacon and, indeed, Seneca had foreseen, long before his time, must follow in the train of the advancement of natural knowledge.—THOMAS HUMPHRY WARD, *The Reign of Queen Victoria*, 1887, Vol. 2, p. 325

Bacon is the *bête noire* and butt of Specialists, the modern Schoolmen, who resent his insufficient view of their little worlds. Mere politicians complain that he was neither a Whig nor a Tory: Mere theologians see that, with all his orthodox protestations, Religion was on the fringe of his system: Mere physicists, led by Harvey, who begins the attack in his dictum that he "wrote like a Lord Chancellor," dislike or distrust his metaphysics, and dwell, as Baron Liebig does, with acrimonious exclusiveness on his defects. Their comments are narrowly correct; but, like those of mere dryasdust philologists on the classics of literature, so one-sided as to be impertinent. The inaccuracies inevitable to universal views, must be conceded to the ingratitude of those prone to bite the hand that feeds them.—JOHN NICOL, *Francis Bacon: His Life and Philosophy*, 1889, p. 242

GEORGE CHAPMAN
Dedication to *The Georgicks of Hesiod*
1618

TO THE MOST NOBLE COMBINER OF LEARNING AND HONOUR,

SIR FRANCIS BACON, KNIGHT,

LORD HIGH CHANCELLOR OF ENGLAND, ETC.

Antient wisdom being so worthily eternized by the now-renewed instance of it in your Lordship; and this ancient Author, one of the most authentic for all wisdom crowned with justice and piety; to what sea owe these poor streams their tribute, but to your Lordship's ocean? The rather, since others of the like antiquity, in my Translation of Homer, teach these their way, and add comfort to their courses, by having received right cheerful countenance and approbation from your Lordship's most grave and honoured predecessor.

All judgments of this season (savouring anything the truth) preferring, to the wisdom of all other nations, these most wise, learned, and circularly-spoken Grecians. According to that of the poet:—

> *Graiis ingenium, Graiis dedit ore rotundo*
> *Musa loqui.*

And why may not this Roman eulogy of the *Graians* extend in praiseful intention (by way of prophetic poesy) to *Gray's-Inn* wits and orators? Or if the allusion (or petition of the principle) beg with too broad a licence in the general; yet serious truth, for the particular, may most worthily apply it to your Lordship's truly Greek inspiration, and absolutely Attic elocution. Whose all-acknowledged faculty hath banished flattery therein even from the Court; much more from my country and more-than-upland simplicity. Nor were those Greeks so circular in their elegant utterance, but their inward judgments and learnings were as round and solid; their solidity proved in their eternity; and their eternity propagated by love of all virtue and integrity;—that love being the only parent and argument of all truth, in any wisdom or learning; without which all is sophisticate and adulterate, howsoever painted and splinted with degrees and languages. Your Lordship's *Advancement of Learning*, then, well showing your love to it, and in it, being true to all true goodness, your learning, strengthening that love, must needs be solid and eternal. This *istōr phōs*, therefore, expressed in this Author, is used here as if prophesied by him then, now to take life in your Lordship, whose life is chief soul and essence to all knowledge and virtue; so few there are that live now combining honour and learning. This time resembling the terrible time whereof this poet prophesied; to which he desired he might not live, since not a Grace would then smile on any pious or worthy; all greatness much more gracing impostors than men truly desertful. The worse depraving the better; and that so frontlessly, that shame and justice should fly the earth for them. To shame which ignorant barbarism now emboldened, let your Lordship's learned humanity prove nothing the less gracious to Virtue for the community of Vice's graces; but shine much the more clear on her for those clouds that eclipse her; no lustre being so sun-like as that which passeth above all clouds unseen, over fields, turrets, and temples; and breaks out, in free beams on some humblest cottage. In whose like Jove himself hath been feasted; and wherein your Lordship may find more honour than in the fretted roofs of the mighty. To which honour, oftentimes, nothing more conduceth than noble acceptance of most humble presentments. On this nobility in your Lordship my prostrate humility relying, I rest ever submitted, in all simple and hearty vows,

Your Honour's most truly,
And freely devoted,
GEORGE CHAPMAN.

WILLIAM RAWLEY
"The Life of Bacon"
Resuscitatio
1657–61

Francis Bacon, the glory of his age and nation, the adorner and ornament of learning, was born in York House, or York Place, in the Strand, on the two and twentieth day of January, in the year of our Lord 1560 ⟨i.e. 1561⟩. His father was that famous counsellor to Queen Elizabeth, the second prop of the kingdom in his time, Sir Nicholas Bacon, knight, lord-keeper of the great seal of England; a lord of known prudence, sufficiency, moderation, and integrity. His mother was Anne, one of the daughters of Sir Anthony Cook; unto whom the erudition of King Edward the Sixth had been committed; a choice lady, and eminent for piety, virtue, and learning; being exquisitely skilled, for a woman, in the Greek and Latin tongues. These being the parents, you may easily imagine what the issue was like to be; having had whatsoever nature or breeding could put into him.

His first and childish years were not without some mark of eminency; at which time he was endued with that pregnancy and towardness of wit, as they were presages of that deep and universal apprehension which was manifest in him afterward; and caused him to be taken notice of by several persons of worth and place, and especially by the queen; who (as I have been informed) delighted much then to confer with him, and to prove him with questions; unto whom he delivered himself with that gravity and maturity above his years, that Her Majesty would often term him, *The young Lord-keeper*. Being asked by the queen *how old he was*, he answered with much discretion, being then but a boy, *That he was two years younger than Her Majesty's happy reign*; with which answer the queen was much taken.

At the ordinary years of ripeness for the university, or rather something earlier, he was sent by his father to Trinity College, in Cambridge, to be educated and bred under the tuition of Doctor John White-gift, then master of the college; afterwards the renowned archbishop of Canterbury; a prelate of the first magnitude for sanctity, learning, patience, and humility; under whom he was observed to have been more than an ordinary proficient in the several arts and sciences. Whilst he was commorant in the university, about sixteen years of age, (as his lordship hath been pleased to impart unto myself), he first fell into the dislike of the philosophy of Aristotle; not for the worthlessness of the author, to whom he would ever ascribe all high attributes, but for the unfruitfulness of the way; being a philosophy (as his lordship used to say) only strong for disputations and contentions, but barren of the production of works for the benefit of the life of man; in which mind he continued to his dying day.

After he had passed the circle of the liberal arts, his father thought fit to frame and mould him for the arts of state; and for that end sent him over into France with Sir Amyas Paulet then employed ambassador lieger into France; by whom he was after awhile held fit to be entrusted with some message or advertisement to the queen; which having performed with great approbation, he returned back into France again, with intention to continue for some years there. In his absence in France his father the lord-keeper died, having collected (as I have heard of knowing persons) a considerable sum of money, which he had separated, with intention to have made a competent purchase of land for the livelihood of this his youngest son (who was only unprovided for; and though he was the youngest in years, yet he was not the lowest in his father's affection); but the said purchase being unaccomplished at his father's death, there came no greater share to him than his single part and portion of the money dividable amongst five brethren; by which means he lived in some straits and necessities in his younger years. For as for that pleasant site and manor of Gorhambury, he came not to it till many years after, by the death of his dearest brother, Mr. Anthony Bacon, a gentleman equal to him in height of wit, though inferior to him in the endowments of learning and knowledge; unto whom he was most nearly conjoined in affection, they two being the sole male issue of a second *venter*.

Being returned from travel, he applied himself to the study of the common law, which he took upon him to be his profession; in which he obtained to great excellency, though he made that (as himself said) but as an accessary, and not his principal study. He wrote several tractates upon that subject: wherein, though some great masters of the law did out-go him in bulk, and particularities of cases, yet in the science of the grounds and mysteries of the law he was exceeded by none. In this way he was after awhile sworn of the queen's council learned, extraordinary; a grace (if I err not) scarce known before. He seated himself, for the commodity of his studies and practice, amongst the Honourable Society of Gray's-Inn, of which house he was a member; where he erected that elegant pile or structure commonly known by the name of *The Lord Bacon's Lodgings*, which he inhabited by turns the most part of his life (some few years only excepted) unto his dying day. In which house he carried himself with such sweetness, comity, and generosity, that he was much revered and beloved by the readers and gentlemen of the house.

Notwithstanding that he professed the law for his livelihood and subsistence, yet his heart and affection was more carried after the affairs and places of estate; for which, if the majesty royal then had been pleased, he was most fit. In his younger years he studied the service and fortunes (as they call them) of that noble but unfortunate earl, the Earl of Essex; unto whom he was, in a sort, a private and free counsellor, and gave him safe and honourable advice, till in the end the earl inclined too much to the violent and precipitate counsel of others his adherents and followers; which was his fate and ruin.

His birth and other capacities qualified him above others of his profession to have ordinary accesses at court, and to come frequently into the queen's eye, who would often grace him with private and free communication, not only about matters of his profession or business in law, but also about the arduous affairs of estate; from whom she received from time to time great satisfaction. Nevertheless, though she cheered him much with the bounty of her countenance, yet she never cheered him with the bounty of her hand; having never conferred upon him any ordinary place or means of honour or profit, save only one dry reversion of the Register's Office in the Star Chamber, worth about 1600*l. per annum*, for which he waited in expectation either fully or near twenty years; of which his lordship would say in Queen Elizabeth's time, *That it was like another man's ground buttalling upon his house, which might mend his prospect, but it did not fill his barn*; (nevertheless, in the time of King James it fell unto him); which might be imputed, not so much to Her Majesty's averseness and disaffection towards him, as to the arts and policy of a great statesman then, who laboured by all industrious and secret means to suppress and keep him down; lest, if he had risen, he might have obscured his glory.

But though he stood long at a stay in the days of his mistress Queen Elizabeth, yet after the change, and coming in of his new master King James, he made a great progress; by whom he was much comforted in places of trust, honour, and revenue. I have seen a letter of his lordship's to King James, wherein he makes acknowledgment, *That he was that master to him, that had raised and advanced him nine times; thrice in dignity, and six times in office*. His offices (as I conceive) were Counsel Learned Extraordinary to His Majesty, as he had been to Queen Elizabeth; King's Solicitor-General; His Majesty's Attorney-General; Counsellor of Estate, being yet but Attorney; Lord-Keeper of the Great Seal of England; lastly, Lord Chancellor; which two last places, though they be the same in authority and power, yet they differ in patent, height, and favour of the prince; since whose time none of his successors, until this present honourable lord ⟨Sir Edward Hyde⟩, did ever bear the title of Lord Chancellor. His dignities were first Knight, then Baron of Verulam; lastly, Viscount St. Alban; besides other good gifts and bounties of the hand which His Majesty gave him, both out of the Broad Seal and out of the Alienation Office, to the value in both of eighteen hundred pounds per annum; which, with his manor of Gorhambury, and other lands and possessions near thereunto adjoining, amounting to a third part more, he retained to his dying day.

Towards his rising years, not before, he entered into a married estate, and he took to wife Alice, one of the daughters and coheirs of Benedict Barnham, Esquire and Alderman of London; with whom he received a sufficiently ample and liberal portion in marriage. Children he had none; which, though they be the means to perpetuate our names after our deaths, yet he had other issues to perpetuate his name, the issues of his brain; in which he was ever happy and admired, as Jupiter was in the production of Pallas. Neither did the want of children detract from his good usage of his consort during the intermarriage, whom he prosecuted with much conjugal love and respect, with many rich gifts and endowments, besides a robe of honour which he invested her withal; which she wore unto her dying day, being twenty years and more after his death.

The last five years of his life, being withdrawn from civil affairs and from an active life, he employed wholly in contemplation and studies—a thing whereof his lordship would often speak during his active life, as if he affected to die in the shadow and not in the light; which also may be found in several passages of his works. In which time he composed the greatest part of his books and writings, both in English and Latin, which I will enumerate (as near as I can) in the just order wherein they were written:—*The History of the Reign of King Henry the Seventh*; *Abcedarium Naturæ*, or a Metaphysical piece which is lost; *Historia Ventorum*; *Historia Vitæ et Mortis*; *Historia Densi et Rari*, not yet printed; *Historia Gravis et Levis*, which is also lost; *a Discourse of a War with Spain*; *a Dialogue touching an Holy War*; *the Fable of the New Atlantis*; *a Preface to a Digest of the Laws of England*; *the beginning of the History of the Reign of King Henry the Eighth*; *De Augmentis Scientiarum*, or the Advancement of Learning, put into Latin, with several enrichments and enlargements; *Counsels Civil and Moral*, or his book of *Essays*, likewise enriched and enlarged; *the Conversion of certain Psalms into English Verse*; *the Translation into Latin of the History of King Henry the Seventh*, of the *Counsels Civil and Moral*, of the *Dialogue of the Holy War*, of the *Fable of the New Atlantis*, for the benefit of other nations; his revising of his book *De Sapientiâ Veterum*; *Inquisitio de Magnete*; *Topica Inquisitionis de Luce et Lumine*; both these not yet printed; lastly, *Sylva Sylvarum*, or *the Natural History*. These were the fruits and productions of his last five years. His lordship also designed, upon the motion and invitation of his late majesty, to have written the reign of King Henry the Eighth; but that work perished in the designation merely, God not lending him life to proceed farther upon it than only in one morning's work; whereof there is extant an *ex ungue leonem*, already printed in his lordship's *Miscellany Works*.

There is a commemoration due as well to his abilities and virtues as to the course of his life. Those abilities which commonly go single in other men, though of prime and observable parts, were all conjoined and met in him. Those are, *sharpness of wit, memory, judgment*, and *elocution*. For the former three his books do abundantly speak them; which with what sufficiency he wrote, let the world judge; but with what celerity he wrote them, I can best testify. But for the fourth, his *elocution*, I will only set down what I heard Sir Walter Raleigh once speak of him by way of comparison (whose judgment may well be trusted), *That the Earl of Salisbury was an excellent speaker, but no good penman; that the Earl of Northampton (the Lord Henry Howard) was an excellent penman, but no good speaker; but that Sir Franis Bacon was eminent in both.*

I have been induced to think, that if there were a beam of knowledge derived from God upon any man in these modern times, it was upon him. For though he was a great reader of books, yet he had not his knowledge from books, but from some grounds and notions from within himself; which, notwithstanding, he vented with great caution and circumspection. His book of *Instauratio Magna* (which in his own account was the chiefest of his works) was no slight imagination or fancy of his brain, but a settled and concocted notion, the production of many years' labour and travel. I myself have seen at the least twelve copies of the *Instauration*, revised year by year one after another, and every year altered and amended in the frame thereof, till at last it came to that model in which it was committed to the press; as many living creatures do lick their young ones, till they bring them to their strength of limbs.

In the composing of his books he did rather drive at a masculine and clear expression than at any fineness or affectation of phrases, and would often ask if the meaning were expressed plainly enough, as being one that accounted words to be but subservient or ministerial to matter, and not the principal. And if his style were polite, it was because he would do no otherwise. Neither was he given to any light conceits, or descanting upon words, but did ever purposely and industriously avoid them; for he held such things to be but digressions or diversions from the scope intended, and to derogate from the weight and dignity of the style.

He was no plodder upon books; though he read much, and that with great judgment, and rejection of impertinences incident to many authors; for he would ever interlace a moderate relaxation of his mind with his studies, as walking, or taking the air abroad in his coach, or some other befitting recreation; and yet he would lose no time, inasmuch as upon his first and immediate return he would fall to reading again, and so suffer no moment of time to slip from him without some present improvement.

His meals were refections of the ear as well as of the stomach, like the *Noctes Atticæ*, or *Convivia Deipnosophistarum*, wherein a man might be refreshed in his mind and understanding no less than in his body. And I have known some, of no mean parts, that have professed to make use of their note-books when they have risen from his table. In which conversations, and otherwise, he was no dashing man, as some men are, but ever a countenancer and fosterer of another man's parts. Neither was he one that would appropriate the speech wholly to himself, or delight to outvie others, but leave a liberty to the co-assessors to take their turns. Wherein he would draw a man on and allure him to speak upon such a subject, as wherein he was peculiarly skilful, and would delight to speak. And for himself, he contemned no man's observations, but would light his torch at every man's candle.

His opinions and assertions were for the most part binding, and not contradicted by any; rather like oracles than discourses; which may be imputed either to the well weighing of his sentence by the scales of truth and reason, or else to the reverence and estimation wherein he was commonly had, that no man would contest with him; so that there was no argumentation, or *pro* and *con* (as they term it), at his table: or if there chanced to be any, it was carried with much submission and moderation.

I have often observed, and so have other men of great account, that if he had occasion to repeat another man's words after him, he had an use and faculty to dress them in better vestments and apparel than they had before; so that the author should find his own speech much amended, and yet the substance of it still retained; as if it had been natural to him to use good forms, as Ovid spake of his faculty of versifying,

Et quod tentabam scribere, versus erat.

When his office called him, as he was of the king's coun-

cil learned, to charge any offenders, either in criminals or capitals, he was never of an insulting and domineering nature over them, but always tenderhearted, and carrying himself decently towards the parties (though it was his duty to charge them home), but yet as one that looked upon the *example* with the eye of severity, but upon the *person* with the eye of pity and compassion. And in civil business, as he was counsellor of estate, he had the best way of advising, not engaging his master in any precipitate or grievous courses, but in moderate and fair proceedings: the king whom he served giving him this testimony, *That he ever dealt in business* suavibus modis; *which was the way that was most according to his own heart.*

Neither was he in his time less gracious with the subject than with his sovereign. He was ever acceptable to the House of Commons when he was a member thereof. Being the king's attorney, and chosen to a place in parliament, he was allowed and dispensed with to sit in the House; which was not permitted to other attorneys.

And as he was a good servant to his master, being never in nineteen years' service (as himself averred) rebuked by the king for anything relating to His Majesty, so he was a good master to his servants, and rewarded their long attendance with good places freely when they fell into his power; which was the cause that so many young gentlemen of blood and quality sought to list themselves in his retinue. And if he were abused by any of them in their places, it was only the error of the goodness of his nature, but the badges of their indiscretions and intemperances.

This lord was religious: for though the world be apt to suspect and prejudge great wits and politics to have somewhat of the atheist, yet he was conversant with God, as appeareth by several passages throughout the whole current of his writings. Otherwise he should have crossed his own principles, which were, *That a little philosophy maketh men apt to forget God, as attributing too much to second causes; but depth of philosophy bringeth a man back to God again.* Now I am sure there is no man that will deny him, or account otherwise of him, but to have him been a deep philosopher. And not only so; but he was able *to render a reason of the hope which was in him,* which that writing of his of the *Confession of the Faith* doth abundantly testify. He repaired frequently, when his health would permit him, to the service of the church, to hear sermons, to the administration of the sacrament of the blessed body and blood of Christ; and died in the true faith, established in the church of England.

This is most true—he was free from malice, which (as he said himself) *he never bred nor fed.* He was no revenger of injuries; which if he had minded, he had both opportunity and place high enough to have done it. He was no heaver of men out of their places, as delighting in their ruin and undoing. He was no defamer of any man to his prince. One day, when a great statesman was newly dead, that had not been his friend, the king asked him, *What he thought of that lord which was gone?* he answered, *That he would never have made His Majesty's estate better, but he was sure he would have kept it from being worse;* which was the worst he would say of him: which I reckon not among his moral, but his Christian virtues.

His fame is greater and sounds louder in foreign parts abroad, than at home in his own nation; thereby verifying that divine sentence, *A prophet is not without honour, save in his own country, and in his own house.* Concerning which I will give you a taste only, out of a letter written from Italy (the storehouse of refined wits) to the late Earl of Devonshire, then the Lord Candish: *I will expect the new essays of my Lord Chancellor Bacon, as also his History, with a great deal of desire, and whatsoever else he shall compose: but in particular of his History I promise myself a thing perfect and singular, especially in Henry the Seventh, where he may exercise the talent of his divine understanding. This lord is more and more known, and his books here more and more delighted in; and those men that have more than ordinary knowledge in human affairs, esteem him one of the most capable spirits of this age; and he is truly such.* Now his fame doth not decrease with days since, but rather increase. Divers of his works have been anciently and yet lately translated into other tongues, both learned and modern, by foreign pens. Several persons of quality, during his lordship's life, crossed the seas on purpose to gain an opportunity of seeing him and discoursing with him; whereof one carried his lordship's picture from head to foot over with him into France, as a thing which he foresaw would be much desired there, that so they might enjoy the image of his person as well as the images of his brain, his books. Amongst the rest, Marquis Fiat, a French nobleman, who came ambassador into England, in the beginning of Queen Mary, wife to King Charles, was taken with an extraordinary desire of seeing him; for which he made way by a friend; and when he came to him, being then through weakness confined to his bed, the marquis saluted him with this high expression, *That his lordship had been ever to him like the angels; of whom he had often heard, and read much of them in books, but he never saw them.* After which they contracted an intimate acquaintance, and the marquis did so much revere him, that besides his frequent visits, they wrote letters one to the other, under the titles and appellations of father and son. As for his many salutations by letters from foreign worthies devoted to learning, I forbear to mention them, because that is a thing common to other men of learning or note, together with him.

But yet, in this matter of his fame, I speak in the comparative only, and not in the exclusive. For his reputation is great in his own nation also, especially amongst those that are of a more acute and sharper judgment; which I will exemplify but with two testimonies and no more. The former, when his *History of King Henry the Seventh* was to come forth, it was delivered to the old Lord Brook, to be perused by him; who, when he had dispatched it, returned it to the author with this eulogy, *Commend me to my lord, and bid him take care to get good paper and ink, for the work is incomparable.* The other shall be that of Doctor Samuel Collins, late provost of King's College in Cambridge, a man of no vulgar wit, who affirmed unto me, *That when he had read the book of the Advancement of Learning, he found himself in a case to begin his studies anew, and that he had lost all the time of his studying before.*

It hath been desired, that something should be signified touching his diet, and the regimen of his health, of which, in regard of his universal insight into nature, he may perhaps be to some an example. For his diet, it was rather a plentiful and liberal diet, as his stomach would bear it, than a restrained; which he also commended in his book of the *History of Life and Death.* In his younger years he was much given to the finer and lighter sort of meats, as of fowls, and such like; but afterward, when he grew more judicious, he preferred the stronger meats, such as the shambles afforded, as those meats which bred the more firm and substantial juices of the body, and less *dissipable;* upon which he would often make his meal, though he had other meats upon the table. You may be sure he would not neglect that himself, which he so much extolled in his writings, and that was the use of nitre; whereof he took in the quantity of about three grains in thin warm broth every morning, for thirty years together next before his death. And for physic, he did indeed live physically, but not miserably; for he

took only a maceration of rhubarb, infused into a draught of white wine and beer mingled together for the space of half an hour, once in six or seven days, immediately before his meal (whether dinner or supper), that it might dry the body less; which (as he said) did carry away frequently the grosser humours of the body, and not diminish or carry away any of the spirits, as sweating doth. And this was no grievous thing to take. As for other physic, in an ordinary way (whatsoever hath been vulgarly spoken) he took not. His receipt for the gout, which did constantly ease him of his pain within two hours, is already set down in the end of the *Natural History.*

It may seem the moon had some principal place in the figure of his nativity: for the moon was never in her passion, or eclipsed, but he was surprised with a sudden fit of fainting; and that, though he observed not nor took any previous knowledge of the eclipse thereof; and as soon as the eclipse ceased, he was restored to his former strength again.

He died on the ninth day of April in the year 1626, in the early morning of the day then celebrated for our Saviour's resurrection, in the sixty-sixth year of his age, at the Earl of Arundel's house in Highgate, near London, to which place he casually repaired about a week before; God so ordaining that he should die there of a gentle fever, accidentally accompanied with a great cold, whereby the defluxion of rheum fell so plentifully upon his breast, that he died by suffocation; and was buried in St. Michael's church at St. Albans; being the place designed for his burial by his last will and testament, both because the body of his mother was interred there, and because it was the only church then remaining within the precincts of old Verulam: where he hath a monument erected for him in white marble (by the care and gratitude of Sir Thomas Meautys, knight, formerly his lordship's secretary, afterwards clerk of the King's Honourable Privy Council under two kings); representing his full portraiture in the posture of studying, with an inscription composed by that accomplished gentleman and rare wit, Sir Henry Wotton.

FRANCISCUS BACON, BARO DE VERULAM,
S^t. ALBANI VIC^{mes},

SEU NOTIORIBUS TITULIS

SCIENTIARUM LUMEN FACUNDIÆ LEX

SIC SEDEBAT.

QUI POSTQUAM OMNIA NATURALIS SAPIENTIÆ

ET CIVILIS ARCANA EVOLVISSET

NATURÆ DECRETUM EXPLEVIT

COMPOSITA SOLVANTUR

AN. DNI M.DC.XXVI.

ÆTAT^s LXVI.

TANTI VIRI

MEM.

THOMAS MEAUTUS

SUPERSTITIS CULTOR

DEFUNCTI ADMIRATOR

H. P.

But howsoever his body was mortal, yet no doubt his memory and works will live, and will in all probability last as long as the world lasteth. In order to which I have endeavoured (after my poor ability) to do this honour to his lordship, by way of conducing to the same.

FRANÇOIS MARIE AROUET DE VOLTAIRE
"Letter 12: On Chancellor Bacon"
Letters on England (Lettres Philosophiques)
tr. Leonard Tancock
1734

Not long ago, in a distinguished company, they were discussing this time-honoured and frivolous question: who was the greatest man, Caesar, Alexander, Tamburlaine, Cromwell, etc.

Somebody answered that it was unquestionable Isaac Newton. He was right, for if true greatness consists in having received from heaven a powerful genius and in having used it to enlighten himself and others, a man such as Newton, the like of whom is scarcely to be found in ten centuries, is the truly great man, and these politicians and conquerors, in which no period has been lacking, are usually nothing more than illustrious criminals. It is to the man who rules over minds by the power of truth, not to those who enslave men by violence, it is to the man who understands the universe and not to those who disfigure it, that we owe our respect.

Since you ask me to tell you about the famous men England has given birth to, I shall begin with men like Bacon, Locke, Newton, etc. The generals and ministers will come in their turn.

I must begin with the famous Earl of Verulam, known in Europe by the name of Bacon, his family name. He was the son of the Lord Keeper of the Great Seal, and for a long time was Chancellor under King James I. Yet, amid the intrigues of Court and the preoccupations of his office, enough to absorb a man completely, he found time to be a great scientific thinker, a good historian and an elegant writer, and what is even more astonishing, he lived in an age when the art of good writing was hardly known, still less scientific thought. As is customary among men, he has been more respected since his death than in his lifetime. His enemies were at Court in London, his admirers in the whole of Europe.

When the Marquis d'Effiat conducted to England Princess Marie, daughter of Henry the Great, who was to marry the Prince of Wales, this minister went and paid a visit to Bacon who, being ill in bed, received him with the curtains drawn. 'You are like the angels,' said d'Effiat, 'one always hears about them, they are thought to be much superior to men, but one never has the consolation of seeing them.'

You know, Monsieur, how Bacon was accused of a crime ill befitting a philosopher, that of letting himself be corrupted by money, you know how he was condemned by the House of Lords to a fine of about 400,000 *livres* of our money, and to lose his rank as Chancellor and Peer.

Today the English so revere his memory that they are unwilling to admit that he may have been guilty. If you ask me what I think about it I will answer by borrowing a word I heard Lord Bolingbroke say. In his presence the conversation touched on the avarice of which the Duke of Marlborough was accused, and they gave examples of it and asked Lord Bolingbroke to bear witness because, having been his declared enemy, he could perhaps express an opinion without impropriety. 'He was such a great man,' was the answer, 'that I have forgotten his vices.'

So I will confine myself to telling you what earned for Chancellor Bacon the respect of Europe.

The best and most remarkable of his works is the one which is the least read today and the least useful: I refer to his *Novum Scientiarum Organum*. It is the scaffolding by means of which modern scientific thought has been built, and when that edifice had been raised, at least in part, the scaffolding ceased to be of any use.

Chancellor Bacon did not yet understand nature, but he knew and pointed out the roads leading to it. He had very early scorned what the Universities called Philosophy, and he did everything in his power to prevent these institutions, set up for the perfection of human reason, from continuing to spoil it with their *quiddities*, their *abhorrence of a vacuum*, their *substantial forms* and all the inappropriate expressions which not only ignorance made respectable, but which a ridiculous confusion with religion had made almost sacred.

He is the father of experimental philosophy. It is true that some amazing secrets had been discovered before his time. Men had invented the compass, printing, engraving, oil-painting, mirrors, the art of restoring to some extent sight to the aged by glasses, called spectacles, gunpowder, etc. Men had searched for, found and conquered a new world. Who would not have thought that these sublime discoveries had been made by the greatest scientists in times much more enlightened than ours? Not at all; it was in the age of the most mindless barbarism that these great changes were made on the earth. Chance alone produced almost all these inventions, and there is even every appearance that what may be called chance played a large part in the discovery of America—at all events it has always been believed that Christopher Columbus only undertook his voyage on the word of a captain who had been cast ashore by a storm on the Caribbean islands.

However that may be, men already knew how to get to the ends of the earth, how to destroy cities with an artificial thunder more terrible than the real thing, but they knew nothing about the circulation of the blood, the weight of the atmosphere, the laws of dynamics, the number of the planets, etc., and a man who upheld a thesis on the categories of Aristotle, on the universal *a parte rei* or some other such idiocy, was regarded as a prodigy.

The most wonderful and useful inventions are not those which do most honour to the human mind.

It is to a mechanical instinct, which exists in most men, that we owe all the skills, and not to a sound philosophy.

The discovery of fire, the art of making bread, of melting and forging metals, building houses, the invention of the shuttle, are of much more practical necessity than printing or the compass, yet these skills were invented by men still in a state of savagery.

Since then what prodigious use the Greeks and Romans have made of mechanical invention! Yet they thought in their time that the skies were of crystal and the stars were little lamps which sometimes fell down into the sea, and one of their great philosophers, after much research, had discovered that the heavenly bodies were pebbles that had come loose from the earth.

In a word, nobody before Chancellor Bacon had grasped experimental science, and of all the practical applications made since, scarcely one is not foreshadowed in his book. He had made several himself; he made a kind of pneumatic machine by means of which he guessed at the elasticity of the air, and he circled all round the discovery of its weight, indeed he almost had it, but the truth was seized upon by Torricelli. Not long afterwards experimental physics was suddenly taken up simultaneously in almost all parts of Europe. It was a hidden treasure the existence of which Bacon had suspected and which all the scientists, encouraged by his promise, strove to dig out.

But what has surprised me most has been to see in his book, in explicit terms, this new law of attraction for the invention of which Newton has the credit.

'We must try to discover,' says Bacon, 'whether there might not be a kind of magnetic force operating between the earth and things with weight, between the moon and the ocean, between the planets, etc.'

Elsewhere he says:

It must either be that heavy bodies are impelled towards the centre of the earth, or that they are mutually attracted by it, and in the latter case it is evident that the nearer these falling bodies get to the earth the more strongly they are attracted to each other. We must see whether the same clock with weights will go faster at the top of a mountain or at the bottom of a mine; it is probable, if the pull of the weights decreases on the mountain and increases in the mine, that the earth has a real attraction.

This precursor of science was also an elegant writer, a historian and a wit.

His *Essays* are very well thought of, but they are intended to instruct rather than to please, and being neither a satire on human nature like the *Maxims* of La Rouchefoucauld, nor a school for sceptics like Montaigne, they are less often read than those two ingenious books.

His *History of Henry VII* passed for a masterpiece, but I should be much mistaken if it could be compared with the work of our illustrious de Thou.

Speaking of the famous impostor Parkins, a Jew by birth, who so brazenly assumed the title of Richard IV, King of England, encouraged by the Duchess of Burgundy, and who laid claim to the crown of Henry VII, this is how Chancellor Bacon expresses himself:

At about this time, King Henry was haunted by evil spirits through the magic of the Duchess of Burgundy, who conjured up from the underworld the shade of Edward IV to torment King Henry. When the Duchess of Burgundy had instructed Parkins she began to deliberate about which region of the sky she would make the comet come from, and she resolved that it would burst forth first on the horizon of Ireland.

It seems to me that our wise de Thou does not go in for all this rigmarole that was formerly taken as inspired, but is nowadays rightly called mumbo-jumbo.

THOMAS BABINGTON MACAULAY
From "Lord Bacon" (1837)
Critical, Historical, and Miscellaneous Essays
1860, Volume 3, pp. 436–95

Two words form the key of the Baconian doctrine, Utility and Progress. The ancient philosophy disdained to be useful, and was content to be stationary. It dealt largely in theories of moral perfection, which were so sublime that they never could be more than theories; in attempts to solve insoluble enigmas; in exhortations to the attainment of unattainable frames of mind. It could not condescend to the humble office of ministering to the comfort of human beings. All the schools contemned that office as degrading; some censured it as immoral. Once indeed Posidonius, a distinguished writer of the age of Cicero and Cæsar, so far forgot himself as to enumerate, among the humbler blessings which mankind owed to philosophy, the discovery of the principle of the arch, and the introduction of the use of metals. This eulogy was considered as an affront, and was taken up with proper spirit. Seneca vehemently disclaims these insulting compliments.[1] Philosophy,

according to him, has nothing to do with teaching men to rear arched roofs over their heads. The true philosopher does not care whether he has an arched roof or any roof. Philosophy has nothing to do with teaching men the uses of metals. She teaches us to be independent of all material substances, of all mechanical contrivances. The wise man lives according to nature. Instead of attempting to add to the physical comforts of his species, he regrets that his lot was not cast in that golden age when the human race had no protection against the cold but the skins of wild beasts, no screen from the sun but a cavern. To impute to such a man any share in the invention or improvement of a plough, a ship, or a mill, is an insult. "In my own time," says Seneca, "there have been inventions of this sort, transparent windows, tubes for diffusing warmth equally through all parts of a building, short-hand, which has been carried to such a perfection that a writer can keep pace with the most rapid speaker. But the inventing of such things is drudgery for the lowest slaves; philosophy lies deeper. It is not her office to teach men how to use their hands. The object of her lessons is to form the soul. *Non est, inquam, instrumentorum ad usus necessarios opifex.*" If the *non* were left out, this last sentence would be no bad description of the Baconian philosophy, and would, indeed, very much resemble several expressions in the *Novum Organum.* "We shall next be told," exclaims Seneca, "that the first shoemaker was a philosopher." For our own part, if we are forced to make our choice between the first shoemaker, and the author of the three books *On Anger*, we pronounce for the shoemaker. It may be worse to be angry than to be wet. But shoes have kept millions from being wet; and we doubt whether Seneca ever kept any body from being angry. . . .

The spirit which appears in the passage of Seneca to which we have referred, tainted the whole body of the ancient philosophy from the time of Socrates downwards, and took possession of intellects with which that of Seneca cannot for a moment be compared. It pervades the dialogues of Plato. It may be distinctly traced in many parts of the works of Aristotle. Bacon has dropped hints, from which it may be inferred that, in his opinion, the prevalence of this feeling was in a great measure to be attributed to the influence of Socrates. Our great countryman evidently did not consider the revolution which Socrates effected in philosophy as a happy event, and constantly maintained that the earlier Greek speculators, Democritus in particular, were, on the whole, superior to their more celebrated successors.[2]

Assuredly if the tree which Socrates planted and Plato watered is to be judged of by its flowers and leaves, it is the noblest of trees. But if we take the homely test of Bacon, if we judge of the tree by its fruits, our opinion of it may perhaps be less favourable. When we sum up all the useful truths which we owe to that philosophy, to what do they amount? We find, indeed, abundant proofs that some of those who cultivated it were men of the first order of intellect. We find among their writings incomparable specimens both of dialectical and rhetorical art. We have no doubt that the ancient controversies were of use, in so far as they served to exercise the faculties of the disputants; for there is no controversy so idle that it may not be of use in this way. But, when we look for something more, for something which adds to the comforts or alleviates the calamities of the human race, we are forced to own ourselves disappointed. We are forced to say with Bacon that this celebrated philosophy ended in nothing but disputation, that it was neither a vineyard nor an olive-ground, but an intricate wood of briars and thistles, from which those who lost themselves in it brought back many scratches and no food.[3] . . .

At length the time arrived when the barren philosophy which had, during so many ages, employed the faculties of the ablest of men, was destined to fall. It had worn many shapes. It had mingled itself with many creeds. It had survived revolutions in which empires, religions, languages, races, had perished. Driven from its ancient haunts, it had taken sanctuary in that Church which it had persecuted, and had, like the daring fiends of the poet, placed its seat

next the seat of God,
And with its darkness dared affront his light.

Words, and more words, and nothing but words, had been all the fruit of all the toil of all the most renowned sages of sixty generations. But the days of this sterile exuberance were numbered.

Many causes predisposed the public mind to a change. The study of a great variety of ancient writers, though it did not give a right direction to philosophical research, did much towards destroying that blind reverence for authority which had prevailed when Aristotle ruled alone. The rise of the Florentine sect of Platonists, a sect to which belonged some of the finest minds of the fifteenth century, was not an unimportant event. The mere substitution of the Academic for the Peripatetic philosophy would indeed have done little good. But any thing was better than the old habit of unreasoning servility. It was something to have a choice of tyrants. "A spark of freedom," as Gibbon has justly remarked, "was produced by this collision of adverse servitude."

Other causes might be mentioned. But it is chiefly to the great reformation of religion that we owe the great reformation of philosophy. The alliance between the Schools and the Vatican had for ages been so close that those who threw off the dominion of the Vatican could not continue to recognise the authority of the Schools. Most of the chiefs of the schism treated the Peripatetic philosophy with contempt, and spoke of Aristotle as if Aristotle had been answerable for all the dogmas of Thomas Aquinas. "Nullo apud Lutheranos philosophiam esse in pretio," was a reproach which the defenders of the Church of Rome loudly repeated, and which many of the Protestant leaders considered as a compliment. Scarcely any text was more frequently cited by the reformers than that in which St. Paul cautions the Colossians not to let any man spoil them by philosophy. Luther, almost at the outset of his career, went so far as to declare that no man could be at once a proficient in the school of Aristotle and in that of Christ. Zwingle, Bucer, Peter Martyr, Calvin, held similar language. In some of the Scotch universities, the Aristotelian system was discarded for that of Ramus. Thus, before the birth of Bacon, the empire of the scholastic philosophy had been shaken to its foundations. There was in the intellectual world an anarchy resembling that which in the political world often follows the overthrow of an old and deeply rooted government. Antiquity, prescription, the sound of great names, had ceased to awe mankind. The dynasty which had reigned for ages was at an end; and the vacant throne was left to be struggled for by pretenders.

The first effect of this great revolution, was, as Bacon most justly observed,[4] to give for a time an undue importance to the mere graces of style. The new breed of scholars, the Aschams and Buchanans, nourished with the finest compositions of the Augustan age, regarded with loathing the dry, crabbed, and barbarous diction of respondents and opponents. They were far less studious about the matter of their writing than about the manner. They succeeded in reforming Latinity; but they never even aspired to effect a reform in philosophy.

At this time Bacon appeared. It is altogether incorrect to say, as has often been said, that he was the first man who rose up against the Aristotelian philosophy when in the height of its power. The authority of that philosophy had, as we have shown, received a fatal blow long before he was born. Several speculators, among whom Ramus is the best known, had recently attempted to form new sects. Bacon's own expressions about the state of public opinion in the time of Luther are clear and strong: "Accedebat," says he, "odium et contemptus, illis ipsis temporibus ortus erga Scholasticos." And again, "Scholasticorum doctrina despectui prorsus haberi cœpit tanquam aspera et barbara."[5] The part which Bacon played in this great change was the part, not of Robespierre, but of Bonaparte. The ancient order of things had been subverted. Some bigots still cherished with devoted loyalty the remembrance of the fallen monarchy and exerted themselves to effect a restoration. But the majority had no such feeling. Freed, yet not knowing how to use their freedom, they pursued no determinate course, and had found no leader capable of conducting them.

That leader at length arose. The philosophy which he taught was essentially new. It differed from that of the celebrated ancient teachers, not merely in method, but also in object. Its object was the good of mankind, in the sense in which the mass of mankind always have understood and always will understand the word good. "Meditor," said Bacon, "instaurationem philosophiæ ejusmodi quæ nihil inanis aut abstracti habeat, quæque vitæ humanæ conditiones in melius provehat."[6]

The difference between the philosophy of Bacon and that of his predecessors cannot, we think, be better illustrated than by comparing his views on some important subjects with those of Plato. We select Plato, because we conceive that he did more than any other person towards giving to the minds of speculative men that bent which they retained till they received from Bacon a new impulse in a diametrically opposite direction.

It is curious to observe how differently these great men estimated the value of every kind of knowledge. Take Arithmetic for example. Plato, after speaking slightly of the convenience of being able to reckon and compute in the ordinary transactions of life, passes to what he considers as a far more important advantage. The study of the properties of numbers, he tells us, habituates the mind to the contemplation of pure truth, and raises us above the material universe. He would have his disciples apply themselves to this study, not that they may be able to buy or sell, not that they may qualify themselves to be shopkeepers or travelling merchants, but that they may learn to withdraw their minds from the ever-shifting spectacle of this visible and tangible world, and to fix them on the immutable essences of things.[7]

Bacon, on the other hand, valued this branch of knowledge, only on account of its uses with reference to that visible and tangible world which Plato so much despised. He speaks with scorn of the mystical arithmetic of the later Platonists, and laments the propensity of mankind to employ, on mere matters of curiosity, powers the whole exertion of which is required for purposes of solid advantage. He advises arithmeticians to leave these trifles, and to employ themselves in framing convenient expressions, which may be of use in physical researches.[8]

The same reasons which led Plato to recommend the study of arithmetic led him to recommend also the study of mathematics. The vulgar crowd of geometricians, he says, will not understand him. They have practice always in view. They do not know that the real use of the science is to lead men to the knowledge of abstract, essential, eternal truth.[9] Indeed, if we are to believe Plutarch, Plato carried this feeling so far that he considered geometry as degraded by being applied to any purpose of vulgar utility. Archytas, it seems, had framed machines of extraordinary power on mathematical principles.[10] Plato remonstrated with his friend, and declared that this was to degrade a noble intellectual exercise into a low craft, fit only for carpenters and wheelwrights. The office of geometry, he said, was to discipline the mind, not to minister to the base wants of the body. His interference was successful; and from that time, according to Plutarch, the science of mechanics was considered as unworthy of the attention of a philosopher.

Archimedes in a later age imitated and surpassed Archytas. But even Archimedes was not free from the prevailing notion that geometry was degraded by being employed to produce any thing useful. It was with difficulty that he was induced to stoop from speculation to practice. He was half ashamed of those inventions which were the wonder of hostile nations, and always spoke of them slightingly as mere amusements, as trifles in which a mathematician might be suffered to relax his mind after intense application to the higher parts of his science.

The opinion of Bacon on this subject was diametrically opposed to that of the ancient philosophers. He valued geometry chiefly, if not solely, on account of those uses, which to Plato appeared so base. And it is remarkable that the longer Bacon lived the stronger this feeling became. When in 1605 he wrote the two books on the *Advancement of Learning*, he dwelt on the advantages which mankind derived from mixed mathematics; but he at the same time admitted that the beneficial effect produced by mathematical study on the intellect, though a collateral advantage, was "no less worthy than that which was principal and intended." But it is evident that his views underwent a change. When, near twenty years later, he published the *De Augmentis*, which is the Treatise on the *Advancement of Learning*, greatly expanded and carefully corrected, he made important alterations in the part which related to mathematics. He condemned with severity the high pretensions of the mathematicians, "delicias et fastum mathematicorum." Assuming the well-being of the human race to be the end of knowledge,[11] he pronounced that mathematical science could claim no higher rank than that of an appendage or an auxiliary to other sciences. Mathematical science, he says, is the handmaid of natural philosophy; she ought to demean herself as such; and he declares that he cannot conceive by what ill chance it has happened that she presumes to claim precedence over her mistress. He predicts—a prediction which would have made Plato shudder—that as more and more discoveries are made in physics, there will be more and more branches of mixed mathematics. Of that collateral advantage the value of which, twenty years before, he rated so highly, he says not one word. This omission cannot have been the effect of mere inadvertence. His own treatise was before him. From that treatise he deliberately expunged whatever was favourable to the study of pure mathematics, and inserted several keen reflections on the ardent votaries of that study. This fact, in our opinion, admits of only one explanation. Bacon's love of those pursuits which directly tend to improve the condition of mankind, and his jealousy of all pursuits merely curious, had grown upon him, and had, it may be, become immoderate. He was afraid of using any expression which might have the effect of inducing any man of talents to employ in speculations, useful only to the mind of the speculator, a single hour which might be employed in extending the empire of man over matter.[12] If Bacon erred here, we must acknowledge that we greatly prefer his error to the opposite error of Plato. We have no patience with a philosophy which, like those Roman matrons who swallowed abortives in order to preserve their shapes, takes pains to be barren for fear of being homely.

Let us pass to astronomy. This was one of the sciences which Plato exhorted his disciples to learn, but for reasons far removed from common habits of thinking. "Shall we set down astronomy," says Socrates, "among the subjects of study?"[13] "I think so," answers his young friend Glaucon: "to know something about the seasons, the months, and the years is of use for military purposes, as well as for agriculture and navigation." "It amuses me," says Socrates, "to see how afraid you are, lest the common herd of people should accuse you of recommending useless studies." He then proceeds, in that pure and magnificent diction which, as Cicero said, Jupiter would use if Jupiter spoke Greek, to explain that the use of astronomy is not to add to the vulgar comforts of life, but to assist in raising the mind to the contemplation of things which are to be perceived by the pure intellect alone. The knowledge of the actual motions of the heavenly bodies Socrates considers as of little value. The appearances which make the sky beautiful at night are, he tells us, like the figures which a geometrician draws on the sand, mere examples, mere helps to feeble minds. We must get beyond them; we must neglect them; we attain to an astronomy which is as independent of the actual stars as geometrical truth is independent of the lines of an ill-drawn diagram. This is, we imagine, very nearly, if not exactly, the astronomy which Bacon compared to the ox of Prometheus,[14] a sleek, well-shaped hide, stuffed with rubbish, goodly to look at, but containing nothing to eat. He complained that astronomy had, to its great injury, been separated from natural philosophy, of which it was one of the noblest provinces, and annexed to the domain of mathematics. The world stood in need, he said, of a very different astronomy, of a living astronomy,[15] of an astronomy which should set forth the nature, the motion, and the influences of the heavenly bodies, as they really are.[16]

On the greatest and most useful of all human inventions, the invention of alphabetical writing, Plato did not look with much complacency. He seems to have thought that the use of letters had operated on the human mind as the use of the go-cart in learning to walk, or of corks in learning to swim, is said to operate on the human body. It was a support which, in his opinion, soon became indispensable to those who used it, which made vigorous exertion first unnecessary and then impossible. The powers of the intellect would, he conceived, have been more fully developed without this delusive aid. Men would have been compelled to exercise the understanding and the memory, and, by deep and assiduous meditation, to make truth thoroughly their own. Now, on the contrary, much knowledge is traced on paper, but little is engraved in the soul. A man is certain that he can find information at a moment's notice when he wants it. He therefore suffers it to fade from his mind. Such a man cannot in strictness be said to know any thing. He has the show without the reality of wisdom. These opinions Plato has put into the mouth of an ancient king of Egypt.[17] But it is evident from the context that they were his own; and so they were understood to be by Quintilian.[18] Indeed they are in perfect accordance with the whole Platonic system.

Bacon's views, as may easily be supposed, were widely different.[19] The powers of the memory, he observes, without the help of writing, can do little towards the advancement of any useful sicence. He acknowledges that the memory may be disciplined to such a point as to be able to perform very extraordinary feats. But on such feats he sets little value. The habits of his mind, he tells us, are such that he is not disposed to rate highly any accomplishment, however rare, which is of no practical use to mankind. As to these prodigious achievements of the memory, he ranks them with the exhibitions of rope-dancers and tumblers. "The two performances," he says, "are of much the same sort. The one is an abuse of the powers of the body; the other is an abuse of the powers of the mind. Both may perhaps excite our wonder; but neither is entitled to our respect."

To Plato, the science of medicine appeared to be of very disputable advantage.[20] He did not indeed object to quick cures for acute disorders, or for injuries produced by accidents. But the art which resists the slow sap of a chronic disease, which repairs frames enervated by lust, swollen by gluttony, or inflamed by wine, which encourages sensuality by mitigating the natural punishment of the sensualist, and prolongs existence when the intellect has ceased to retain its entire energy, had no share of his esteem. A life protracted by medical skill he pronounced to be a long death. The existence of the art of medicine ought, he said, to be tolerated, so far as that art may serve to cure the occasional distempers of men whose constitutions are good. As to those who have bad constitutions, let them die; and the sooner the better. Such men are unfit for war, for magistracy, for the management of their domestic affairs, for severe study and speculation. If they engage in any vigorous mental exercise, they are troubled with giddiness and fulness of the head, all which they lay to the account of philosophy. The best thing that can happen to such wretches is to have done with life at once. He quotes mythical authority in support of this doctrine; and reminds his disciples that the practice of the sons of Æsculapius, as described by Homer, extended only to the cure of external injuries.

Far different was the philosophy of Bacon. Of all the sciences, that which he seems to have regarded with the greatest interest was the science which, in Plato's opinion, would not be tolerated in a well regulated community. To make men perfect was no part of Bacon's plan. His humble aim was to make imperfect men comfortable. The beneficence of his philosophy resembled the beneficence of the common Father, whose sun rises on the evil and the good, whose rain descends for the just and the unjust. In Plato's opinion man was made for philosophy; in Bacon's opinion philosophy was made for man; it was a means to an end; and that end was to increase the pleasures and to mitigate the pains of millions who are not and cannot be philosophers. That a valetudinarian who took great pleasure in being wheeled along his terrace, who relished his boiled chicken and his weak wine and water, and who enjoyed a hearty laugh over the Queen of Navarre's tales, should be treated as a *caput lupinum* because he could not read the *Timæus* without a headache, was a notion which the humane spirit of the English school of wisdom altogether rejected. Bacon would not have thought it beneath the dignity of a philosopher to contrive an improved garden chair for such a valetudinarian, to devise some way of rendering his medicines more palatable, to invent repasts which he might enjoy, and pillows on which he might sleep soundly; and this though there might not be the smallest hope that the mind of the poor invalid would ever rise to the contemplation of the ideal beautiful and the ideal good. As Plato had cited the religious legends of Greece to justify his contempt for the more recondite parts of the art of healing, Bacon vindicated the dignity of that art by appealing to the example of Christ, and reminded men that the great Physician of the soul did not disdain to be also the physician of the body.[21]

When we pass from the science of medicine to that of legislation, we find the same difference between the systems of these two great men. Plato, at the commencement of the *Dialogue on Laws*, lays it down as a fundamental principle that the end of legislation is to make men virtuous. It is unnecessary to point out the extravagant conclusions to which such a proposition leads. Bacon well knew to how great an extent the happiness of every society must depend on the virtue of its members; and he also knew what legislators can and what they cannot do for the purpose of promoting virtue. The view which he has given of the end of legislation, and of the principal means for the attainment of that end, has always seemed to us eminently happy, even among the many happy passages of the same kind with which his works abound. "Finis et scopus quem leges intueri atque ad quem jussiones et sanctiones suas dirigere debent, non alius est quam ut cives feliciter degant. Id fiet si pietate et religione recte instituti, moribus honesti, armis adversus hostes externos tuti, legum auxilio adversus seditiones et privatas injurias muniti, imperio et magistratibus obsequentes, copiis et opibus locupletes et florentes fuerint."[22] The end is the well-being of the people. The means are the imparting of moral and religious education; the providing of every thing necessary for defence against foreign enemies; the maintaining of internal order; the establishing of a judicial, financial, and commercial system, under which wealth may be rapidly accumulated and securely enjoyed.

Even with respect to the form in which laws ought to be drawn, there is a remarkable difference of opinion between the Greek and the Englishman. Plato thought a preamble essential; Bacon thought it mischievous. Each was consistent with himself. Plato, considering the moral improvement of the people as the end of legislation, justly inferred that a law which commanded and threatened, but which neither convinced the reason, nor touched the heart, must be a most imperfect law. He was not content with deterring from theft a man who still continued to be a thief at heart, with restraining a son who hated his mother from beating his mother. The only obedience on which he set much value was the obedience which an enlightened understanding yields to reason, and which a virtuous disposition yields to precepts of virtue. He really seems to have believed that, by prefixing to every law an eloquent and pathetic exhortation, he should, to a great extent, render penal enactments superfluous. Bacon entertained no such romantic hopes; and he well knew the practical inconveniences of the course which Plato recommended. "Neque nobis," says he, "prologi legum qui inepti olim habiti sunt, et leges introducunt disputantes non jubentes, utique placerent, si priscos mores ferre possemus. . . . Quantum fieri potest prologi evitentur, et lex incipiat a jussione."[23]

Each of the great men whom we have compared intended to illustrate his system by a philosophical romance; and each left his romance imperfect. Had Plato lived to finish the *Critias*, a comparison between that noble fiction and the new Atlantis would probably have furnished us with still more striking instances than any which we have given. It is amusing to think with what horror he would have seen such an institution as Solomon's House rising in his republic: with what vehemence he would have ordered the brewhouses, the perfume houses, and the dispensatories to be pulled down; and with what inexorable rigour he would have driven beyond the frontier all the Fellows of the College, Merchants of Light and Depredators, Lamps and Pioneers.

To sum up the whole, we should say that the aim of the Platonic philosophy was to exalt man into a god. The aim of the Baconian philosophy was to provide man with what he requires while he continues to be man. The aim of the Platonic philosophy was to raise us far above vulgar wants. The aim of the Baconian philosophy was to supply our vulgar wants. The former aim was noble; but the latter was attainable. Plato drew a good bow; but, like Acestes in Virgil, he aimed at the stars; and therefore, though there was no want of strength or skill, the shot was thrown away. His arrow was indeed followed by a track of dazzling radiance, but it struck nothing.

> Volans liquidis in nubibus arsit arundo
> Signavitque viam flammis, tenuisque recessit
> Consumpta in ventos.

Bacon fixed his eye on a mark which was placed on the earth, and within bow-shot, and hit it in the white. The philosophy of Plato began in words and ended in words, noble words indeed, words such as were to be expected from the finest of human intellects exercising boundless dominion over the finest of human languages. The philosophy of Bacon began in observations and ended in arts.

The boast of the ancient philosophers was that their doctrine formed the minds of men to a high degree of wisdom and virtue. This was indeed the only practical good which the most celebrated of those teachers even pretended to effect; and undoubtedly, if they had effected this, they would have deserved far higher praise than if they had discovered the most salutary medicines or constructed the most powerful machines. But the truth is that, in those very matters in which alone they professed to do any good to mankind, in those very matters for the sake of which they neglected all the vulgar interests of mankind, they did nothing, or worse than nothing. They promised what was impracticable; they despised what was practicable; they filled the world with long words and long beards; and they left it as wicked and as ignorant as they found it.

An acre in Middlesex is better than a principality in Utopia. The smallest actual good is better than the most magnificent promises of impossibilities. The wise man of the Stoics would, no doubt, be a grander object than a steam-engine. But there are steam-engines. And the wise man of the Stoics is yet to be born. A philosophy which should enable a man to feel perfectly happy while in agonies of pain would be better than a philosophy which assuages pain. But we know that there are remedies which will assuage pain; and we know that the ancient sages liked the toothache just as little as their neighbours. A philosophy which should extinguish cupidity would be better than a philosophy which should devise laws for the security of property. But it is possible to make laws which shall, to a very great extent, secure property. And we do not understand how any motives which the ancient philosophy furnished could extinguish cupidity. We know indeed that the philosophers were no better than other men. From the testimony of friends as well as of foes, from the confessions of Epictetus and Seneca, as well as from the sneers of Lucian and the fierce invectives of Juvenal, it is plain that these teachers of virtue had all the vices of their neighbours, with the additional vice of hypocrisy. Some people may think the object of the Baconian philosophy a low object, but they cannot deny that, high or low, it has been attained. They cannot deny that every year makes an addition to what Bacon called "fruit." . . .

Bacon has been accused of overrating the importance of those sciences which minister to the physical well-being of man, and of underrating the importance of moral philosophy; and it cannot be denied that persons who read the *Novum Organum* and the *De Augmentis*, without adverting to the circumstances under which those works were written, will find much that may seem to countenance the accusation. It is certain, however, that though in practice he often went very wrong, and though, as his historical work and his essays prove,

he did not hold, even in theory, very strict opinions on points of political morality, he was far too wise a man not to know how much our well-being depends on the regulation of our minds. The world for which he wished was not, as some people seem to imagine, a world of water-wheels, power-looms, steam-carriages, sensualists, and knaves. He would have been as ready as Zeno himself to maintain that no bodily comforts which could be devised by the skill and labour of a hundred generations would give happiness to a man whose mind was under the tyranny of licentious appetite, of envy, of hatred, or of fear. If he sometimes appeared to ascribe importance too exclusively to the arts which increase the outward comforts of our species, the reason is plain. Those arts had been most unduly depreciated. They had been represented as unworthy the attention of a man of liberal education. "Cogitavit," says Bacon of himself, "eam esse opinionem sive æstimationem humidam et damnosam, minui nempe majestatem mentis humanæ, si in experimentis et rebus particularibus, sensui subjectis, et in materia terminatis, diu ac multum versetur: præsertim cum hujusmodi res ad inquirendum laboriosæ ad meditandum ignobiles, ad discendum asperæ, ad practicam illiberales, numero infinitæ, et subtilitate pusillæ videri soleant, et ob hujusmodi conditiones, gloriæ artium minus sint accommodatæ."[24] This opinion seemed to him "omnia in familia humana turbasse." It had undoubtedly caused many arts which were of the greatest utility, and which were susceptible of the greatest improvements, to be neglected by speculators, and abandoned to joiners, masons, smiths, weavers, apothecaries. It was necessary to assert the dignity of those arts, to bring them prominently forward, to proclaim that, as they have a most serious effect on human happiness, they are not unworthy of the attention of the highest human intellects. Again, it was by illustrations drawn from these arts that Bacon could most easily illustrate his principles. It was by improvements effected in these arts that the soundness of his principles could be most speedily and decisively brought to the test, and made manifest to common understandings. He acted like a wise commander who thins every other part of his line to strengthen a point where the enemy is attacking with peculiar fury, and on the fate of which the event of the battle seems likely to depend. In the *Novum Organum*, however, he distinctly and most truly declares that his philosophy is no less a Moral than a Natural Philosophy, that, though his illustrations are drawn from physical science, the principles which those illustrations are intended to explain are just as applicable to ethical and political inquiries as to inquiries into the nature of heat and vegetation.[25]

He frequently treated of moral subjects; and he brought to those subjects that spirit which was the essence of his whole system. He has left us many admirable practicable observations on what he somewhat quaintly called the Georgics of the mind, on the mental culture which tends to produce good dispositions. Some persons, he said, might accuse him of spending labour on a matter so simple that his predecessors had passed it by with contempt. He desired such persons to remember that he had from the first announced the objects of his search to be not the splendid and the surprising, but the useful and the true, not the deluding dreams which go forth through the shining portal of ivory, but the humbler realities of the gate of horn.[26]

True to this principle, he indulged in no rants about the fitness of things, the all-sufficiency of virtue, and the dignity of human nature. He dealt not at all in resounding nothings, such as those with which Bolingbroke pretended to comfort himself in exile, and in which Cicero vainly sought consolation after the loss of Tullia. The casuistical subtilties which occupied the attention of the keenest spirits of his age had, it should seem, no attractions for him. The doctors whom Escobar afterwards compared to the four beasts and the four-and-twenty elders in the Apocalypse Bacon dismissed with most contemptuous brevity. "Inanes plerumque evadunt et futiles."[27] Nor did he ever meddle with those engimas which have puzzled hundreds of generations, and will puzzle hundreds more. He said nothing about the grounds of moral obligation, or the freedom of the human will. He had no inclination to employ himself in labours resembling those of the damned in the Grecian Tartarus, to spin for ever on the same wheel round the same pivot, to gape for ever after the same deluding clusters, to pour water for ever into the same bottomless buckets, to pace for ever to and fro on the same wearisome path after the same recoiling stone. He exhorted his disciples to prosecute researches of a very different description, to consider moral science as a practical science, a science of which the object was to cure the diseases and perturbations of the mind, and which could be improved only by a method analogous to that which has improved medicine and surgery. Moral philosophers ought, he said, to set themselves vigorously to work for the purpose of discovering what are the actual effects produced on the human character by particular modes of education, by the indulgence of particular habits, by the study of particular books, by society, by emulation, by imitation. Then we might hope to find out what mode of training was most likely to preserve and restore moral health.[28]

What he was as a natural philosopher and a moral philosopher, that he was also as a theologian. He was, we are convinced, a sincere believer in the divine authority of the Christian revelation. Nothing can be found in his writings, or in any other writings, more eloquent and pathetic than some passages which were apparently written under the influence of strong devotional feeling. He loved to dwell on the power of the Christian religion to effect much that the ancient philosophers could only promise. He loved to consider that religion as the bond of charity, the curb of evil passions, the consolation of the wretched, the support of the timid, the hope of the dying. But controversies on speculative points of theology seem to have engaged scarcely any portion of his attention. In what he wrote on Church Government he showed, as far as he dared, a tolerant and charitable spirit. He troubled himself not at all about Homoousians and Homoiousians, Monothelites and Nestorians. He lived in an age in which disputes on the most subtle points of divinity excited an intense interest throughout Europe, and nowhere more than in England. He was placed in the very thick of the conflict. He was in power at the time of the Synod of Dort, and must for months have been daily deafened with talk about election, reprobation, and final perseverance. Yet we do not remember a line in his works from which it can be inferred that he was either a Calvinist or an Arminian. While the world was resounding with the noise of a disputatious philosophy and a disputatious theology, the Baconian school, like Alworthy seated between Square and Thwackum, preserved a calm neutrality, half scornful, half benevolent, and, content with adding to the sum of practical good, left the war of words to those who liked it.

We have dwelt long on the end of the Baconian philosophy, because from this peculiarity all the other peculiarities of that philosophy necessarily arose. Indeed, scarcely any person who proposed to himself the same end with Bacon could fail to hit upon the same means.

The vulgar notion about Bacon we take to be this, that he invented a new method of arriving at truth, which method is called Induction, and that he detected some fallacy in the syllogistic reasoning which had been in vogue before his time. This notion is about as well founded as that of the people who, in the middle ages, imagined that Virgil was a great conjurer. Many who are far too well informed to talk such extravagant nonsense entertain what we think incorrect notions as to what Bacon really effected in this matter.

The inductive method has been practised ever since the beginning of the world by every human being. It is constantly practised by the most ignorant clown, by the most thoughtless schoolboy, by the very child at the breast. That method leads the clown to the conclusion that if he sows barley he shall not reap wheat. By that method the schoolboy learns that a cloudy day is the best for catching trout. The very infant, we imagine, is led by induction to expect milk from his mother or nurse, and none from his father.

Not only is it not true that Bacon invented the inductive method; but it is not true that he was the first person who correctly analysed that method and explained its uses. Aristotle had long before pointed out the absurdity of supposing that syllogistic reasoning could ever conduct men to the discovery of any new principle, had shown that such discoveries must be made by induction, and by induction alone, and had given the history of the inductive process, concisely indeed, but with great perspicuity and precision.

Again, we are not inclined to ascribe much practical value to that analysis of the inductive method which Bacon has given in the second book of the *Novum Organum*. It is indeed an elaborate and correct analysis. But it is an analysis of that which we are all doing from morning to night, and which we continue to do even in our dreams. A plain man finds his stomach out of order. He never heard Lord Bacon's name. But he proceeds in the strictest conformity with the rules laid down in the second book of the *Novum Organum*, and satisfies himself that minced pies have done the mischief. "I ate minced pies on Monday and Wednesday, and I was kept awake by indigestion all night." This is the *comparentia ad intellectum instantiarum convenientium*. "I did not eat any on Tuesday and Friday, and I was quite well." This is the *comparentia instantiarum in proximo quæ natura data privantur*. "I ate very sparingly of them on Sunday, and was very slightly indisposed in the evening. But on Christmas-day I almost dined on them, and was so ill that I was in great danger." This is the *comparentia instantiarum secundum magis et minus*. "It cannot have been the brandy which I took with them. For I have drunk brandy daily for years without being the worse for it." This is the *rejectio naturarum*. Our invalid then proceeds to what is termed by Bacon the *Vindemiatio*, and pronounces that minced pies do not agree with him.

We repeat that we dispute neither the ingenuity nor the accuracy of the theory contained in the second book of the *Novum Organum*; but we think that Bacon greatly overrated its utility. We conceive that the inductive process, like many other processes, is not likely to be better performed merely because men know how they perform it. William Tell would not have been one whit more likely to cleave the apple if he had known that his arrow would describe a parabola under the influence of the attraction of the earth. Captain Barclay would not have been more likely to walk a thousand miles in a thousand hours, if he had known the place and name of every muscle in his legs. Monsieur Jourdain probably did not pronounce D and F more correctly after he had been apprised that D is pronounced by touching the teeth with the end of the tongue, and F by putting the upper teeth on the lower lip. We cannot perceive that the study of Grammar makes the smallest difference in the speech of people who have always lived in good society. Not one Londoner in ten thousand can lay down the rules for the proper use of *will* and *shall*. Yet not one Londoner in a million ever misplaces his *will* and *shall*. Doctor Robertson could, undoubtedly, have written a luminous dissertation on the use of those words. Yet, even in his latest work, he sometimes misplaced them ludicrously. No man uses figures of speech with more propriety because he knows that one figure is called a metonymy and another a synecdoche. A drayman in a passion calls out, "You are a pretty fellow," without suspecting that he is uttering irony, and that irony is one of the four primary tropes. The old systems of rhetoric were never regarded by the most experienced and discerning judges as of any use for the purpose of forming an orator. "Ego hanc vim intelligo," said Cicero, "esse in præceptis omnibus, non ut ea secuti oratores eloquentiæ laudem sint adepti, sed quæ sua sponte homines eloquentes facerent, ea quosdam observasse, atque id egisse; sic esse non eloquentiam ex artificio, sed artificium ex eloquentia natum." We must own that we entertain the same opinion concerning the study of Logic which Cicero entertained concerning the study of Rhetoric. A man of sense syllogizes in *celarent* and *sesare* all day long without suspecting it; and, though he may not know what an *ignoratio elenchi* is, has no difficulty in exposing it whenever he falls in with it; which is likely to be as often as he falls in with a Reverend Master of Arts nourished on mode and figure in the cloisters of Oxford. Considered merely as an intellectual feat, the *Organum* of Aristotle can scarcely be admired too highly. But the more we compare individual with individual, school with school, nation with nation, generation with generation, the more do we lean to the opinion that the knowledge of the theory of logic has no tendency whatever to make men good reasoners.

What Aristotle did for the syllogistic process Bacon has, in the second book of the *Novum Organum*, done for the inductive process; that is to say, he has analysed it well. His rules are quite proper; but we do not need them, because they are drawn from our own constant practice.

But, though everybody is constantly performing the process described in the second book of the *Novum Organum*, some men perform it well and some perform it ill. Some are led by it to truth, and some to error. It led Franklin to discover the nature of lightning. It led thousands, who had less brains than Franklin, to believe in animal magnetism. But this was not because Franklin went through the process described by Bacon, and the dupes of Mesmer through a different process. The *comparentiæ* and *rejectiones* of which we have given examples will be found in the most unsound inductions. We have heard that an eminent judge of the last generation was in the habit of jocosely propounding after dinner a theory, that the cause of the prevalence of Jacobinism was the practice of bearing three names. He quoted on the one side Charles James Fox, Richard Brinsley Sheridan, John Horne Tooke, John Philpot Curran, Samuel Taylor Coleridge, Theobald Wolfe Tone. These were *instantiæ convenientes*. He then proceeded to cite instances *absentiæ in proximo*, William Pitt, John Scott, William Windham, Samuel Horsley, Henry Dundas, Edmund Burke. He might have gone on to instances *secundum magis et minus*. The practice of giving children three names has been for some time a growing practice, and Jacobinism has also been growing. The practice of giving children three names is more common in America than in England. In England we still have a King and a House of Lords; but the Americans are republicans. The *rejectiones* are obvious. Burke and Theobald Wolfe Tone are both Irishmen; therefore the being an Irishman is not the cause of Jacobinism. Horsley and Horne Tooke are both clergymen; therefore the being a clergyman is not the cause of Jacobinism. Fox and Windham were both educated at Oxford; therefore the being educated at Oxford is not the cause of Jacobinism. Pitt and Horne Tooke were both educated at Cambridge; therefore the being educated at Cambridge is not the cause of Jacobinism. In this way, our inductive philosopher arrives at what Bacon calls the Vintage, and pronounces that the having three names is the cause of Jacobinism.

Here is an induction corresponding with Bacon's analysis and ending in a monstrous absurdity. In what then does this induction differ from the induction which leads us to the conclusion that the presence of the sun is the cause of our having more light by day than by night? The difference evidently is not in the kind of instances, but in the number of instances; that is to say, the difference is not in that part of the process for which Bacon has given precise rules, but in a circumstance for which no precise rule can possibly be given. If the learned author of the theory about Jacobinism had enlarged either of his tables a little, his system would have been destroyed. The names of Tom Paine and William Wyndham Grenville would have been sufficient to do the work.

It appears to us, then, that the difference between a sound and unsound induction does not lie in this, that the author of the sound induction goes through the process analysed in the second book of the *Novum Organum*, and the author of the unsound induction through a different process. They both perform the same process. But one performs it foolishly or carelessly; the other performs it with patience, attention, sagacity, and judgment. Now precepts can do little towards making men patient and attentive, and still less towards making them sagacious and judicious. It is very well to tell men to be on their guard against prejudices, not to believe facts on slight evidence, not to be content with a scanty collection of facts, to put out of their minds the *idola* which Bacon has so finely described. But these rules are too general to be of much practical use. The question is, What is a prejudice? How long does the incredulity with which I hear a new theory propounded continue to be a wise and salutary incredulity? When does it become an *idolum specus*, the unreasonable pertinacity of a too sceptical mind? What is slight evidence? What collection of facts is scanty? Will ten instances do, or fifty, or a hundred? In how many months would the first human beings who settled on the shores of the ocean have been justified in believing that the moon had an influence on the tides? After how many experiments would Jenner have been justified in believing that he had discovered a safeguard against the small-pox? These are questions to which it would be most desirable to have a precise answer; but unhappily they are questions to which no precise answer can be returned.

We think then that it is possible to lay down accurate rules, as Bacon has done, for the performing of that part of the inductive process which all men perform alike; but that these rules, though accurate, are not wanted, because in truth they only tell us to do what we are all doing. We think that it is impossible to lay down any precise rule for the performing of that part of the inductive process which a great experimental philosopher performs in one way, and a superstitious old woman in another.

On this subject, we think, Bacon was in an error. He certainly attributed to his rules a value which did not belong to them. He went so far as to say, that, if his method of making discoveries were adopted, little would depend on the degree of force or acuteness of any intellect; that all minds would be reduced to one level, that his philosophy resembled a compass or a rule which equalises all hands, and enables the most unpractised person to draw a more correct circle or line than the best draughtsmen can produce without such aid.[29] This really seems to us as extravagant as it would have been in Lindley Murray to announce that everybody who should learn his *Grammar* would write as good English as Dryden, or in that very able writer, the Archbishop of Dublin, to promise that all the readers of his *Logic* would reason like Chillingworth, and that all the readers of his *Rhetoric* would speak like Burke. That Bacon was altogether mistaken as to this point will now hardly be disputed. His philosophy has flourished during two hundred years, and has produced none of this levelling. The interval between a man of talents and a dunce is as wide as ever; and is never more clearly discernible than when they engage in researches which require the constant use of induction.

It will be seen that we do not consider Bacon's ingenious analysis of the inductive method as a very useful performance. Bacon was not, as we have already said, the inventor of the inductive method. He was not even the person who first analysed the inductive method correctly, though he undoubtedly analysed it more minutely than any who preceded him. He was not the person who first showed that by the inductive method alone new truth could be discovered. But he was the person who first turned the minds of speculative men, long occupied in verbal disputes, to the discovery of new and useful truth; and, by doing so, he at once gave to the inductive method an importance and dignity which had never before belonged to it. He was not the maker of that road; he was not the discoverer of that road; he was not the person who first surveyed and mapped that road. But he was the person who first called the public attention to an inexhaustible mine of wealth, which had been utterly neglected, and which was accessible by that road alone. By doing so, he caused that road, which had previously been trodden only by peasants and higglers, to be frequented by a higher class of travellers.

That which was eminently his own in his system was the end which he proposed to himself. The end being given, the means, as it appears to us, could not well be mistaken. If others had aimed at the same object with Bacon, we hold it to be certain that they would have employed the same method with Bacon. It would have been hard to convince Seneca that the inventing of a safety-lamp was an employment worthy of a philosopher. It would have been hard to persuade Thomas Aquinas to descend from the making of syllogisms to the making of gunpowder. But Seneca would never have doubted for a moment that it was only by means of a series of experiments that a safety-lamp could be invented. Thomas Aquinas would never have thought that his *barbara* and *baralipton* would enable him to ascertain the proportion which charcoal ought to bear to saltpetre in a pound of gunpowder. Neither common sense nor Aristotle would have suffered him to fall into such an absurdity.

By stimulating men to the discovery of new truth, Bacon stimulated them to employ the inductive method, the only method, even the ancient philosophers and the schoolmen themselves being judges, by which new truth can be discovered. By stimulating men to the discovery of useful truth, he furnished them with a motive to perform the inductive process well and carefully. His predecessors had been, in his phrase, not interpreters, but anticipators of nature. They had been content with the first principles at which they had arrived by the most scanty and slovenly induction. And why was this? It was, we conceive, because their philosophy proposed to itself no practical end, because it was merely an exercise of the mind. A man who wants to contrive a new machine or a new medicine has a strong motive to observe accurately and pa-

tiently, and to try experiment after experiment. But a man who merely wants a theme for disputation or declamation has no such motive. He is therefore content with premises grounded on assumption, or on the most scanty and hasty induction. Thus, we conceive, the schoolmen acted. On their foolish premises they often argued with great ability; and as their object was "assensum subjugare, non res,"[30] to be victorious in controversy, not to be victorious over nature, they were consistent. For just as much logical skill could be shown in reasoning on false as on true premises. But the followers of the new philosophy, proposing to themselves the discovery of useful truth as their object, must have altogether failed of attaining that object if they had been content to build theories on superficial induction.

Bacon has remarked[31] that in ages when philosophy was stationary, the mechanical arts went on improving. Why was this? Evidently because the mechanic was not content with so careless a mode of induction as served the purpose of the philosopher. And why was the philosopher more easily satisfied than the mechanic? Evidently because the object of the mechanic was to mould things, whilst the object of the philosopher was only to mould words. Careful induction is not at all necessary to the making of a good syllogism. But it is indispensable to the making of a good shoe. Mechanics, therefore, have always been, as far as the range of their humble but useful callings extended, not anticipators but interpreters of nature. And when a philosophy arose, the object of which was to do on a large scale what the mechanic does on a small scale, to extend the power and to supply the wants of man, the truth of the premises, which logically is a matter altogether unimportant, became a matter of the highest importance; and the careless induction with which men of learning had previously been satisfied gave place, of necessity, to an induction far more accurate and satisfactory.

What Bacon did for inductive philosophy may, we think, be fairly stated thus. The objects of preceding speculators were objects which could be attained without careful induction. Those speculators, therefore, did not perform the inductive process carefully. Bacon stirred up men to pursue an object which could be attained only by induction, and by induction carefully performed; and consequently induction was more carefully performed. We do not think that the importance of what Bacon did for inductive philosophy has ever been overrated. But we think that the nature of his services is often mistaken, and was not fully understood even by himself. It was not by furnishing philosophers with rules for performing the inductive process well, but by furnishing them with a motive for performing it well, that he conferred so vast a benefit on society.

To give to the human mind a direction which it shall retain for ages is the rare prerogative of a few imperial spirits. It cannot, therefore, be uninteresting to inquire what was the moral and intellectual constitution which enabled Bacon to exercise so vast an influence on the world.

In the temper of Bacon,—we speak of Bacon the philosopher, not of Bacon the lawyer and politician,—there was a singular union of audacity and sobriety. The promises which he made to mankind might, to a superficial reader, seem to resemble the rants which a great dramatist has put into the mouth of an Oriental conqueror half-crazed by good fortune and by violent passions.

> He shall have chariots easier than air,
> Which I will have invented; and thyself
> That art the messenger shall ride before him,
> On a horse cut out of an entire diamond,

That shall be made to go with golden wheels,
I know not how yet.

But Bacon performed what he promised. In truth, Fletcher would not have dared to make Arbaces promise, in his wildest fits of excitement, the tithe of what the Baconian philosophy has performed.

The true philosophical temperament may, we think, be described in four words, much hope, little faith; a disposition to believe that any thing, however extraordinary, may be done; an indisposition to believe that any thing extraordinary has been done. In these points the constitution of Bacon's mind seems to us to have been absolutely perfect. He was at once the Mammon and the Surly of his friend Ben. Sir Epicure did not indulge in visions more magnificent and gigantic. Surly did not sift evidence with keener and more sagacious incredulity.

Closely connected with this peculiarity of Bacon's temper was a striking peculiarity of his understanding. With great minuteness of observation he had an amplitude of comprehension such as has never yet been vouchsafed to any other human being. The small fine mind of Labruyère had not a more delicate tact than the large intellect of Bacon. The *Essays* contain abundant proofs that no nice feature of character, no peculiarity in the ordering of a house, a garden, or a court-masque, could escape the notice of one whose mind was capable of taking in the whole world of knowledge. His understanding resembled the tent which the fairy Paribanou gave to Prince Ahmed. Fold it; and it seemed a toy for the hand of a lady. Spread it; and the armies of powerful Sultans might repose beneath its shade.

In keenness of observation he has been equalled, though perhaps never surpassed. But the largeness of his mind was all his own. The glance with which he surveyed the intellectual universe resembled that which the Archangel, from the golden threshold of heaven, darted down into the new creation.

Round he surveyed,—and well might, where he
  stood
So high above the circling canopy
Of night's extended shade,—from eastern point
Of Libra, to the fleecy star which bears
Andromeda far off Atlantic seas
Beyond the horizon.

His knowledge differed from that of other men, as a terrestrial globe differs from an Atlas which contains a different country on every leaf. The towns and roads of England, France, and Germany are better laid down in the Atlas than on the globe. But while we are looking at England we see nothing of France; and while we are looking at France we see nothing of Germany. We may go to the Atlas to learn the bearings and distances of York and Bristol, or of Dresden and Prague. But it is useless if we want to know the bearings and distances of France and Martinique, or of England and Canada. On the globe we shall not find all the market towns in our own neighbourhood; but we shall learn from it the comparative extent and the relative position of all the kingdoms of the earth. "I have taken," said Bacon, in a letter written when he was only thirty-one, to his uncle Lord Burleigh, "I have taken all knowledge to be my province." In any other young man, indeed in any other man, this would have been a ridiculous flight of presumption. There have been thousands of better mathematicians, astronomers, chemists, physicians, botanists, mineralogists, than Bacon. No man would go to Bacon's works to learn any particular science or art, any more than he would go to a twelve-inch globe in order to find his way from Kennington turnpike to Clapham Common. The art which Bacon taught was the art of inventing arts. The knowledge in which

Bacon excelled all men was a knowledge of the mutual relations of all departments of knowledge.

The mode in which he communicated his thoughts was peculiar to him. He had no touch of that disputatious temper which he often censured in his predecessors. He effected a vast intellectual revolution in opposition to a vast mass of prejudices; yet he never engaged in any controversy: nay, we cannot at present recollect, in all his philosophical works, a single passage of a controversial character. All those works might with propriety have been put into the form which he adopted in the work entitled *Cogitata et visa*: "Franciscus Baconus sic cogitavit." These are thoughts which have occurred to me: weigh them well: and take them or leave them.

Borgia said of the famous expedition of Charles the Eighth, that the French had conquered Italy, not with steel, but with chalk; for that the only exploit which they had found necessary for the purpose of taking military occupation of any place had been to mark the doors of the houses where they meant to quarter. Bacon often quoted this saying, and loved to apply it to the victories of his own intellect.[32] His philosophy, he said, came as a guest, not as an enemy. She found no difficulty in gaining admittance, without a contest, in every understanding fitted, by its structure and by its capacity, to receive her. In all this we think that he acted most judiciously; first, because, as he has himself remarked, the difference between his school and other schools was a difference so fundamental that there was hardly any common ground on which a controversial battle could be fought; and, secondly, because his mind, eminently observant, preëminently discursive and capacious, was, we conceive, neither formed by nature nor disciplined by habit for dialectical combat.

Though Bacon did not arm his philosophy with the weapons of logic, he adorned her profusely with all the richest decorations of rhetoric. His eloquence, though not untainted with the vicious taste of his age, would alone have entitled him to a high rank in literature. He had a wonderful talent for packing thought close, and rendering it portable. In wit, if by wit be meant the power of perceiving analogies between things which appear to have nothing in common, he never had an equal, not even Cowley, not even the author of *Hudibras*. Indeed, he possessed this faculty, or rather this faculty possessed him, to a morbid degree. When he abandoned himself to it without reserve, as he did in the *Sapientia Veterum*, and at the end of the second book of the *De Augmentis*, the feats which he performed were not merely admirable, but portentous, and almost shocking. On these occasions we marvel at him as clowns on a fair-day marvel at a juggler, and can hardly help thinking that the devil must be in him.

These, however, were freaks in which his ingenuity now and then wantoned, with scarcely any other object than to astonish and amuse. But it occasionally happened that, when he was engaged in grave and profound investigations, his wit obtained the mastery over all his other faculties, and led him into absurdities into which no dull man could possibly have fallen. We will give the most striking instance which at present occurs to us. In the third book of the *De Augmentis* he tells us that there are some principles which are not peculiar to one science, but are common to several. That part of philosophy which concerns itself with these principles is, in his nomenclature, designated as *philosophia prima*. He then proceeds to mention some of the principles with which this *philosophia prima* is conversant. One of them is this. An infectious disease is more likely to be communicated while it is in progress than when it has reached its height. This, says he, is true in medicine. It is also true in morals; for we see that the example of very abandoned men injures public morality less than the example of men in whom vice has not yet extinguished all good qualities. Again, he tells us that in music a discord ending in a concord is agreeable, and thus the same thing may be noted in the affections. Once more, he tells us, that in physics the energy with which a principle acts is often increased by the antiperistasis of its opposite; and that it is the same in the contests of factions. If the making of ingenious and sparkling similitudes like these be indeed the *philosophia prima*, we are quite sure that the greatest philosophical work of the nineteenth century is Mr. Moore's *Lalla Rookh*. The similitudes which we have cited are very happy similitudes. But that a man like Bacon should have taken them for more, that he should have thought the discovery of such resemblances as these an important part of philosophy, has always appeared to us one of the most singular facts in the history of letters.

The truth is that his mind was wonderfully quick in perceiving analogies of all sorts. But, like several eminent men whom we could name, both living and dead, he sometimes appeared strangely deficient in the power of distinguishing rational from fanciful analogies, analogies which are arguments from analogies which are mere illustrations, analogies like that which Bishop Butler so ably pointed out, between natural and revealed religion, from analogies like that which Addison discovered, between the series of Grecian gods carved by Phidias and the series of English kings painted by Kneller. This want of discrimination has led to many strange political speculations. Sir William Temple deduced a theory of government from the properties of the pyramid. Mr. Southey's whole system of finance is grounded on the phænomena of evaporation and rain. In theology, this perverted ingenuity has made still wilder work. From the time of Irenæus and Origen down to the present day, there has not been a single generation in which great divines have not been led into the most absurd expositions of Scripture, by mere incapacity to distinguish analogies proper, to use the scholastic phrase, from analogies metaphorical.[33] It is curious that Bacon has himself mentioned this very kind of delusion among the *idola specus*; and has mentioned in language which, we are inclined to think, shows that he knew himself to be subject to it. It is the vice, he tells us, of subtle minds to attach too much importance to slight distinctions; it is the vice, on the other hand, of high and discursive intellects to attach too much importance to slight resemblances; and he adds that, when this last propensity is indulged to excess, it leads men to catch at shadows instead of substances.[34]

Yet we cannot wish that Bacon's wit had been less luxuriant. For, to say nothing of the pleasure which it affords, it was in the vast majority of cases employed for the purpose of making obscure truth plain, of making repulsive truth attractive, of fixing in the mind forever truth which might otherwise have left but a transient impression.

The poetical faculty was powerful in Bacon's mind, but not, like his wit, so powerful as occasionally to usurp the place of his reason, and to tyrannize over the whole man. No imagination was ever at once so strong and so thoroughly subjugated. It never stirred but at a signal from good sense. It stopped at the first check from good sense. Yet, though disciplined to such obedience, it gave noble proofs of its vigour. In truth, much of Bacon's life was passed in a visionary world, amidst things as strange as any that are described in the *Arabian Tales*, or in those romances on which the curate and barber of Don Quixote's village performed so cruel an *auto-da-fé*, amidst buildings more sumptuous than the palace of Aladdin, fountains more wonderful than the golden water of Parizade, con-

veyances more rapid than the hippogryph of Ruggiero, arms more formidable than the lance of Astolfo, remedies more efficacious than the balsam of Fierabras. Yet in his magnificent day-dreams there was nothing wild, nothing but what sober reason sanctioned. He knew that all the secrets feigned by poets to have been written in the books of enchanters are worthless when compared with the mighty secrets which are really written in the book of nature, and which, with time and patience, will be read there. He knew that all the wonders wrought by all the talismans in fable were trifles when compared to the wonders which might reasonably be expected from the philosophy of fruit, and that, if his words sank deep into the minds of men, they would produce effects such as superstition had never ascribed to the incantations of Merlin and Michael Scot. It was here that he loved to let his imagination loose. He loved to picture to himself the world as it would be when his philosophy should, in his own noble phrase, "have enlarged the bounds of human empire."[35] We might refer to many instances. But we will content ourselves with the strongest, the description of the House of Solomon in the *New Atlantis*. By most of Bacon's contemporaries, and by some people of our time, this remarkable passage would, we doubt not, be considered as an ingenious rodomontade, a counterpart to the adventures of Sinbad or Baron Munchausen. The truth is, that there is not to be found in any human composition a passage more eminently distinguished by profound and serene wisdom. The boldness and originality of the fiction is far less wonderful than the nice discernment which carefully excluded from that long list of prodigies every thing that can be pronounced impossible, every thing that can be proved to lie beyond the mighty magic of induction and of time. Already some parts, and not the least startling parts, of this glorious prophecy have been accomplished, even according to the letter; and the whole, construed according to the spirit, is daily accomplishing all around us. . . .

Without any disparagement to the admirable treatise *De Augmentis*, we must say that, in our judgment, Bacon's greatest performance is the first book of the *Novum Organum*. All the peculiarities of his extraordinary mind are found there in the highest perfection. Many of the aphorisms, but particularly those in which he gives examples of the influence of the *idola*, show a nicety of observation that has never been surpassed. Every part of the book blazes with wit, but with wit which is employed only to illustrate and decorate truth. No book ever made so great a revolution in the mode of thinking, overthrew so many prejudices, introduced so many new opinions. Yet no book was ever written in a less contentious spirit. It truly conquers with chalk and not with steel. Proposition after proposition enters into the mind, is received not as an invader, but as a welcome friend, and though previously unknown, becomes at once domesticated. But what we most admire is the vast capacity of that intellect which, without effort, takes in at once all the domains of science, all the past, the present, and the future, all the errors of two thousand years, all the encouraging signs of the passing times, all the bright hopes of the coming age. Cowley, who was among the most ardent, and not among the least discerning followers of the new philosophy, has, in one of his finest poems, compared Bacon to Moses standing on Mount Pisgah. It is to Bacon, we think, as he appears in the first book of the *Novum Organum*, that the comparison applies with peculiar felicity. There we see the great Lawgiver looking round from his lonely elevation on an infinite expanse; behind him a wilderness of dreary sands and bitter waters, in which successive generations have sojourned, always moving, yet never advancing, reaping no harvest, and building no abiding city; before him a goodly land, a land of promise, a land flowing with milk and honey. While the multitude below saw only the flat sterile desert in which they had so long wandered, bounded on every side by a near horizon, or diversified only by some deceitful mirage, he was gazing from a far higher stand on a far lovelier country, following with his eye the long course of fertilising rivers, through ample pastures, and under the bridges of great capitals, measuring the distances of marts and havens, and portioning out all those wealthy regions from Dan to Beersheba.

It is painful to turn back from contemplating Bacon's philosophy to contemplate his life. Yet without so turning back it is impossible fairly to estimate his powers. He left the University at an earlier age than that at which most people repair thither. While yet a boy he was plunged into the midst of diplomatic business. Thence he passed to the study of a vast technical system of law, and worked his way up through a succession of laborious offices, to the highest post in his profession. In the mean time he took an active part in every Parliament; he was an adviser of the Crown: he paid court with the greatest assiduity and address to all whose favour was likely to be of use to him; he lived much in society; he noted the slightest peculiarities of character, and the slightest changes of fashion. Scarcely any man has led a more stirring life than that which Bacon led from sixteen to sixty. Scarcely any man has been better entitled to be called a thorough man of the world. The founding of a new philosophy, the imparting of a new direction to the mind of speculators, this was the amusement of his leisure, the work of hours occasionally stolen from the Woolsack and the Council Board. This consideration, while it increases the admiration with which we regard his intellect, increases also our regret that such an intellect should so often have been unworthily employed. He well knew the better course, and had, at one time, resolved to pursue it. "I confess," said he in a letter written when he was still young, "that I have as vast contemplative ends as I have moderate civil ends." Had his civil ends continued to be moderate, he would have been, not only the Moses, but the Joshua of philosophy. He would have fulfilled a large part of his own magnificent predictions. He would have led his followers, not only to the verge, but into the heart of the promised land. He would not merely have pointed out, but would have divided the spoil. Above all, he would have left, not only a great, but a spotless name. Mankind would then have been able to esteem their illustrious benefactor. We should not then be compelled to regard his character with mingled contempt and admiration, with mingled aversion and gratitude. We should not then regret that there should be so many proofs of the narrowness and self-ishness of a heart, the benevolence of which was yet large enough to take in all races and all ages. We should not then have to blush for the disingenuousness of the most devoted worshipper of speculative truth, for the servility of the boldest champion of intellectual freedom. We should not then have seen the same man at one time far in the van, at another time far in the rear of his generation. We should not then be forced to own that he who first treated legislation as a science was among the last Englishmen who used the rack, that he who first summoned philosophers to the great work of interpreting nature, was among the last Englishmen who sold justice. And we should conclude our survey of a life placidly, honourably, beneficently passed, "in industrious observations, grounded conclusions, and profitable inventions and discoveries,"[36] with feelings very different from those with which we now turn away from the checkered spectacle of so much glory and so much shame.

Notes

1. Seneca, *Epist.* 90.
2. *Novum Organum*, Lib. 1. Aph. 71, 79. *De Augmentis*, Lib. 3. Cap. 4. *De Principiis atque originibus. Cogitata et visa. Redargutio philosophiarum.*
3. *Novum Organum*, Lib. 1. Aph. 73.
4. *De Augmentis*, Lib. 1.
5. Both these passages are in the first book of the *De Augmentis*.
6. *Redargutio Philosophiarum.*
7. Plato's *Republic*, Book 7.
8. *De Augmentis*, Lib. 3. Cap. 6.
9. Plato's *Republic*, Book 7.
10. Plutarch, *Sympos.* viii. and *Life of Marcellus*. The machines of Archytas are also mentioned by Aulus Gellius and Diogenes Laertius.
11. Usui et commodis hominum consulimus.
12. Compare the passage relating to mathematics in the Second Book of the *Advancement of Learning*, with the *De Augmentis*, Lib. 3. Cap. 6.
13. Plato's *Republic*, Book 7.
14. *De Augmentis*, Lib. 3. Cap. 4.
15. Astronomia viva.
16. "Quae substantiam et motum et influxum coelestium, prout re vera sunt proponat." Compare this language with Plato's "*ta d'en tō ouranō iasomen.*"
17. Plato's *Phaedrus*.
18. Quinctilian, XI.
19. *De Augmentis*, Lib. 5. Cap. 5.
20. Plato's *Republic*, Book 3.
21. *De Augmentis*, Lib. 4. Cap. 2.
22. *De Augmentis*, Lib. 8. Cap. 3. Aph. 5.
23. *De Augmentis*, Lib. 8. Cap. 3. Aph. 69.
24. *Cogitata et visa*. The expression *opinio humida* may surprise a reader not accustomed to Bacon's style. The allusion is to the maxium of Heraclitus the obscure: "Dry light is the best." By dry light, Bacon understood the light of the intellect, not obscured by the mists of passion, interest, or prejudice.
25. *Novum Organum*, Lib. 1. Aph. 127.
26. *De Augmentis*, Lib. 7. Cap. 3.
27. Ib., Lib. 7. Cap. 2.
28. *De Augmentis*, Lib. 7. Cap. 3.
29. *Novum Organum*, Praef. and Lib. 1. Aph. 122.
30. *Novum Organum*, Lib. 1. Aph. 29.
31. *De Augmentis*, Lib. 1.
32. *Novum Organum*, Lib. 1. Aph. 35 and elsewhere.
33. See some interesting remarks on this subject in Bishop Berkeley's *Minute Philosopher*, Dialogue IV.
34. *Novum Organum*, Lib. 1. Aph. 55.
35. *New Atlantis*.
36. From a letter of Bacon to Lord Burleigh.

RICHARD WILLIAM CHURCH
"Bacon as a Writer"
Bacon
1884, pp. 209–27

Bacon's name belongs to letters as well as to philosophy. In his own day, whatever his contemporaries thought of his *Instauration of Knowledge*, he was in the first rank as a speaker and a writer. Sir Walter Raleigh, contrasting him with Salisbury, who could speak but not write, and Northampton, who could write but not speak, thought Bacon eminent both as a speaker and a writer. Ben Jonson, passing in review the more famous names of his own and the preceding age, from Sir Thomas More to Sir Philip Sidney, Hooker, Essex and Raleigh, places Bacon without a rival at the head of the company as the man who had "fulfilled all numbers," and "stood as the mark and *akmè* of our language." And he also records Bacon's power as a speaker. "No man," he says, "ever spoke more neatly, more pressly, or suffered less emptiness, less idle-ness, in what he uttered." . . . "His hearers could not cough or look aside from him without loss. He commanded when he spoke, and had his judges angry and pleased at his devotion . . . the fear of every man that heard him was that he should make an end." He notices one feature for which we are less prepared, though we know that the edge of Bacon's sarcastic tongue was felt and resented in James's Court. "His speech," says Ben Jonson, "was nobly censorious when he could *spare and pass by a jest.*" The unpopularity which certainly seems to have gathered round his name may have had something to do with this reputation.

Yet as an English writer Bacon did not expect to be re-membered, and he hardly cared to be. He wrote much in Latin, and his first care was to have his books put into a Latin dress. "For these modern languages," he wrote to Toby Mat-thew towards the close of his life, "will at one time or another play the bank-rowte with books, and since I have lost much time with this age, I would be glad if God would give me leave to recover it with posterity." He wanted to be read by the learned out of England, who were supposed to appreciate his philosophical ideas better than his own countrymen, and the only way to this was to have his books translated into the "general language." He sends Prince Charles the *Advancement* in its new Latin dress. "It is a book," he says, "that will live, and be a citizen of the world, as English books are not." And he fitted it for continental reading by carefully weeding it of all passages that might give offence to the censors at Rome or Paris. "I have been," he writes to the King, "mine own *Index Expurgatorius,* that it may be read in all places. For since my end of putting it in Latin was to have it read everywhere, it had been an absurd contradiction to free it in the language and to pen it up in the matter." Even the *Essays* and the *History of Henry VII.* he had put into Latin "by some good pens that do not forsake me." Among these translators are said to have been George Herbert and Hobbes, and on more doubtful authority, Ben Jonson and Selden. The *Essays* were also translated into Latin and Italian with Bacon's sanction.

Bacon's contemptuous and hopeless estimate of "these modern languages," forty years after Spenser had proclaimed and justified his faith in his own language, is only one of the proofs of the short-sightedness of the wisest and the limitations of the largest-minded. Perhaps we ought not to wonder at his silence about Shakespeare. It was the fashion, except among a set of clever but not always very reputable people, to think the stage, as it was, below the notice of scholars and statesmen; and Shakespeare took no trouble to save his works from neglect. Yet it is a curious defect in Bacon that he should not have been more alive to the powers and future of his own language. He early and all along was profoundly impressed with the contrast, which the scholarship of the age so abundantly presented, of words to things. He dwells in the *Advancement* on that "first distemper of learning, when men study words and not matter." He illustrates it at large from the reaction of the new learning and of the popular teaching of the Reformation against the utilitarian and unclassical terminology of the schoolmen; a reaction which soon grew to excess and made men "hunt more after choiceness of the phrase, and the round and clean com-position of the sentence and the sweet falling of the clauses," than after worth of subject, soundness of argument, "life of invention or depth of judgment." "I have represented this," he says, "in an example of late times, but it hath been and will be *secundum majus et minus* in all times;" and he likens this "vanity" to "Pygmalion's frenzy,"—"for to fall in love with words which are but the images of matter, is all one as to fall in

love with a picture." He was dissatisfied with the first attempt at translation into Latin of the *Advancement* by Dr. Playfer of Cambridge, because he "desired not so much neat and polite, as clear, masculine, and apt expression." Yet, with this hatred of circumlocution and prettiness, of the cloudy amplifications, and pompous flourishings, and "the flowing and watery vein," which the scholars of his time affected, it is strange that he should not have seen that the new ideas and widening thoughts of which he was the herald would want a much more elastic and more freely-working instrument than Latin could ever be-come. It is wonderful indeed what can be done with Latin. It was long after his day to be the language of the exact sciences. In his *History of the Winds,* which is full of his irrepressible fancy and picturesqueness, Bacon describes in clear and intel-ligible Latin the details of the rigging of a modern man-of-war, and the mode of sailing her. But such tasks impose a yoke, sometimes a rough one, on a language which has "taken its ply" in very different conditions, and of which the genius is that of indirect and circuitous expression, "full of majesty and circumstance." But it never, even in those days of scholarship, could lend itself to the frankness, the straightforwardness, the fullness and shades of suggestion and association, with which, in handling ideas of subtlety and difficulty, a writer would wish to speak to his reader, and which he could find only in his mother tongue. It might have been thought that with Bacon's contempt of form and ceremony in these matters, his con-sciousness of the powers of English in his hands might have led him to anticipate that a flexible, and rich, and strong language might create a literature, and that a literature, if worth study-ing, would be studied in its own language. But so great a change was beyond even his daring thoughts. To him, as to his age, the only safe language was the Latin. For familiar use English was well enough. But it could not be trusted; "it would play the bankrupt with books." And yet Galileo was writing in Italian as well as in Latin; only within twenty-five years later, Descartes was writing *De la Méthode,* and Pascal was writing in the same French in which he wrote the *Provincial Letters,* his *Nouvelles Expériences touchant le Vide,* and the controversial pamphlets which followed it; showing how in that interval of five-and-twenty years an instrument had been fashioned out of a modern language such as for lucid expression and clear rea-soning, Bacon had not yet dreamed of. From Bacon to Pascal is the change from the old scientific way of writing to the mod-ern; from a modern language as learned and used in the 16th century, to one learned in the 17th.

But the language of the age of Elizabeth was a rich and noble one, and it reached a high point in the hands of Bacon. In his hands it lent itself to many uses, and assumed many forms, and he valued it, not because he thought highly of its qualities as a language, but because it enabled him with least trouble "to speak as he would," in throwing off the abundant thoughts that rose within his mind, and in going through the variety of business which could not be done in Latin. But in all his writing it is the matter, the real thing that he wanted to say, which was uppermost. He cared how it was said, not for the sake of form or ornament, but because the force and clearness of what was said depended so much on how it was said. Of course, what he wanted to say varied indefinitely with the various occasions of his life. His business may merely be to write "a device" or panegyric for a pageant in the Queen's honour, or for the revels of Gray's Inn. But even these trifles are the result of real thought, and are full of ideas, ideas about the hopes of knowledge or about the policy of the State; and though, of course, they have plenty of the flourishes and quaint absurdities indispensable on such occasions, yet the "rhetorical affectation" is in the thing itself, and not in the way it is handled: he had an opportunity of saying some of the things which were to him of deep and perpetual interest, and he used it to say them, as forcibly, as strikingly, as attractively as he could. His manner of writing depends, not on a style, or a studied or acquired habit but on the nature of the task which he has in hand. Everywhere his matter is close to his words, and governs, animates, informs his words. No one in England before had so much as he had the power to say what he wanted to say, and exactly as he wanted to say it. No one was so little at the mercy of conventional language or customary rhetoric, except when he persuaded himself that he had to submit to those necessities of flattery, which cost him at last so dear.

The book by which English readers, from his own time to ours, have known him best, better than by the originality and the eloquence of the *Advancement*, or than by the political weight and historical imagination of the *History of Henry VII.*, is the first book which he published, the volume of *Essays*. It is an instance of his self-willed but most skilful use of the freedom and ease which the "modern language," which he despised, gave him. It is obvious that he might have expanded these "Counsels, moral and political," to the size which such essays used to swell to after his time. Many people would have thanked him for doing so; and some have thought it a good book on which to hang their own reflections and illustrations. But he saw how much could be done by leaving the beaten track of set treatise and discourse, and setting down unceremoniously the observations which he had made and the real rules which he had felt to be true, on various practical matters which come home to men's "business and bosoms." He was very fond of these moral and political generalisations, both of his own collecting and as found in writers who, he thought, had the right to make them, like the Latins of the Empire and the Italians and Spaniards of the Renaissance. But a mere string of maxims and quotations would have been a poor thing and not new; and he cast what he had to say into connected wholes. But nothing can be more loose than the structure of the essays. There is no art, no style, almost, except in a few, the political ones, no order: thoughts are put down and left unsupported, unproved, undeveloped. In the first form of the ten, which composed the first edition of 1597, they are more like notes of analysis or tables of contents; they are austere even to meagreness. But the general character continues in the enlarged and expanded ones of Bacon's later years. They are like chapters in Aristotle's *Ethics* and *Rhetoric* on virtues and characters; only Bacon's takes Aristotle's broad marking lines as drawn, and proceeds with the subtler and more refined observations of a much longer and wider experience. But these short papers say what they have to say without preface, and in literary undress, without a superfluous word, without the joints and bands of structure: they say it in brief, rapid sentences, which come down, sentence after sentence, like the strokes of a great hammer. No wonder that in their disdainful brevity they seem rugged and abrupt, "and do not seem to end, but fall." But with their truth and piercingness and delicacy of observation, their roughness gives a kind of flavour which no elaboration could give. It is none the less that their wisdom is of a somewhat cynical kind, fully alive to the slipperiness and self-deceits and faithlessness which are in the world and rather inclined to be amused at them. In some we can see distinct records of the writer's own experience: one contains the substance of a charge delivered to Judge Hutton on his appointment; another of them is a sketch drawn from life of a character which had crossed Bacon's path, and in the essay on *Seeming Wise* we can trace from the impatient notes put down in his *Commentarius Solu-*

tus, the picture of the man who stood in his way, the Attorney-General Hobart. Some of them are memorable oracular utterances not inadequate to the subject, on *Truth*, or *Death*, or *Unity*. Others reveal an utter incapacity to come near a subject, except as a strange external phenomena, like the essay on *Love*. There is a distinct tendency in them to the Italian school of political and moral wisdom, the wisdom of distrust and of reliance on indirect and roundabout ways. There is a group of them, "of *Delays*," "of *Cunning*," "of *Wisdom for a Man's Self*," "of *Despatch*," which show how vigilantly and to what purpose he had watched the treasurers and secretaries and intriguers of Elizabeth's and James's Courts; and there are curious self-revelations, as in the essay on *Friendship*. But there are also currents of better and larger feeling, such as those which show his own ideal of "*Great Place*," and what he felt of its dangers and duties. And mixed with the fantastic taste and conceits of the time, there is evidence in them of Bacon's keen delight in nature, in the beauty and scents of flowers, in the charm of open air life, as in the essay on *Gardens*, "The purest of human pleasures, the greatest refreshment to the spirits of man."

But he had another manner of writing for what he held to be his more serious work. In the philosophical and historical works there is no want of attention to the flow and order and ornament of composition. When we come to the *Advancement of Learning*, we come to a book which is one of the landmarks of what high thought and rich imagination have made of the English language. It is the first great book in English prose of secular interest; the first book which can claim a place beside the *Laws of Ecclesiastical Polity*. As regards its subject-matter, it has been partly thrown into the shade by the greatly enlarged and elaborate form in which it ultimately appeared, in a Latin dress, as the first portion of the scheme of the *Instauratio*, the *De Augmentis Scientiarum*. Bacon looked on it as a first effort, a kind of call-bell to awaken and attract the interest of others in the thoughts and hopes which so interested himself. But it contains some of his finest writing. In the *Essays* he writes as a looker-on at the game of human affairs, who, according to his frequent illustration, sees more of it than the gamesters themselves, and is able to give wiser and faithful counsel, not without a touch of kindly irony at the mistakes which he observes. In the *Advancement* he is the enthusiast for a great cause and a great hope, and all that he has of passion and power is enlisted in the effort to advance it. The *Advancement* is far from being a perfect book. As a survey of the actual state of knowledge in his day, of its deficiencies and what was wanted to supply them, it is not even up to the materials of the time. Even the improved *De Augmentis* is inadequate; and there is reason to think the *Advancement* was a hurried book, at least in the later part, and it is defective in arrangement and proportion of parts. Two of the great divisions of knowledge—history and poetry—are despatched in comparatively short chapters; while in the division on "Civil Knowledge," human knowledge as it respects society, he inserts a long essay, obviously complete in itself and clumsily thrust in here, on the ways of getting on in the world, the means by which a man may be "*Faber fortunæ suæ*"—the architect of his own success; too lively a picture to be pleasant of the arts with which he had become acquainted in the process of rising. The book, too, has the blemishes of its own time; its want of simplicity, its inevitable though very often amusing and curious pedantries. But the *Advancement* was the first of a long line of books which have attempted to teach English readers how to think of knowledge; to make it really and intelligently the interest, not of the school or the study or the laboratory only, but of society at large. It was a book with a purpose, new then, but of which we have seen the fulfilment. He wanted to impress on his generation, as a very practical matter, all that knowledge might do in wise hands, all that knowledge had lost by the faults and errors of men and the misfortunes of time, all that knowledge might be pushed to in all directions by faithful and patient industry and well-planned methods for the elevation and benefit of man in his highest capacities as well as in his humblest. And he further sought to teach them *how* to know; to make them understand that difficult achievement of self-knowledge, to know *what it is* to know; to give the first attempted chart to guide them among the shallows and rocks and whirlpools which beset the course and action of thought and inquiry; to reveal to them the "idols" which unconsciously haunt the minds of the strongest as well as the weakest, and interpose their delusions when we are least aware,—"the fallacies and false appearances inseparable from our nature and our condition of life." To induce men to believe not only that there was much to know that was not yet dreamed of, but that the way of knowing needed real and thorough improvement, that the knowing mind bore along with it all kinds of snares and disqualifications of which it is unconscious, and that it needed training quite as much as materials to work on, was the object of the *Advancement*. It was but a sketch; but it was a sketch so truly and forcibly drawn, that it made an impression which has never been weakened. To us its use and almost its interest is passed. But it is a book which we can never open without coming on some noble interpretation of the realities of nature or the mind; some unexpected discovery of that quick and keen eye which arrests us by its truth; some felicitous and unthought-of illustration, yet so natural as almost to be doomed to become a commonplace; some bright touch of his incorrigible imaginativeness, ever ready to force itself in amid the driest details of his argument.

The *Advancement* was only one shape out of many into which he cast his thoughts. Bacon was not easily satisfied with his work; even when he published he did so, not because he had brought his work to the desired point, but lest anything should happen to him and it should "perish." Easy and unstudied as his writing seems, it was, as we have seen, the result of unintermitted trouble and varied modes of working. He was quite as much a talker as a writer, and beat out his thoughts into shape in talking. In the essay on *Friendship* he describes the process with a vividness which tells of his own experience:

> But before you come to that [the faithful counsel that a man receiveth from his friend], certain it is that whosoever hath his mind fraught with many thoughts, his wits and understanding do clarify and break up in the communicating and discoursing with another. He tosseth his thoughts more easily; he marshalleth them more orderly; he seeth how they look when they are turned into words; finally, he waxeth wiser than himself, and that more by an hour's discourse than by a day's meditation. It was well said by Themistocles to the King of Persia, "That speech was like cloth of arras opened and put abroad, whereby the imagery doth appear in figure; whereas in thought, they lie in packs." Neither is this second fruit of friendship, in opening the understanding, restrained only to such friends as are able to give a man counsel. (They are, indeed, best.) But even without that, a man learneth of himself, and bringeth his own thoughts to light, and whetteth his wits against a stone which itself cuts not. In a word, a man were better to relate himself to a *statua* or a picture, than to suffer his thoughts to pass in smother.

Bacon . . . was a great maker of notes and note-books: he was careful not of the thought only but of the very words in which it presented itself; everything was collected that might turn out useful in his writing or speaking, down to alternative modes of beginning or connecting or ending a sentence. He watched over his intellectual appliances and resources much more strictly than over his money concerns. He never threw away and never forgot what could be turned to account. He was never afraid of repeating himself, if he thought he had something apt to say. He was never tired of re-casting and re-writing, from a mere fragment or preface to a finished paper. He has favourite images, favourite maxims, favourite texts, which he cannot do without. *"Da Fidei quæ sunt Fidei,"* comes in from his first book to his last. The illustrations which he gets from the myth of Scylla, from Atalanta's ball, from Borgia's saying about the French marking their lodgings with chalk, the saying that God takes delight, like the "innocent play of children," "to hide his works in order to have them found out," and to have kings as "his playfellows in that game," these, with many others, reappear, however varied the context, from the first to the last of his compositions. An edition of Bacon with marginal references and parallel passages would show a more persistent recurrence of characteristic illustrations and sentences than perhaps any other writer.

The *Advancement* was followed by attempts to give serious effect to its lesson. This was nearly all done in Latin. He did so, because in these works he spoke to a larger and, as he thought, more interested audience; the use of Latin marked the gravity of his subject as one that touched all mankind; and the majesty of Latin suited his taste and his thoughts. Bacon spoke, indeed, impressively on the necessity of entering into the realm of knowledge in the spirit of a little child. He dwelt on the paramount importance of beginning from the very bottom of the scale of fact, of understanding the commonplace things at our feet, so full of wonder and mystery and instruction, before venturing on theories. The sun is not polluted by shining on a dunghill, and no facts were too ignoble to be beneath the notice of the true student of nature. But his own genius was for the grandeur and pomp of general views. The practical details of experimental science were, except in partial instances, yet a great way off; and what there was, he either did not care about or really understand, and had no aptitude for handling. He knew enough to give reality to his argument; he knew, and insisted on it, that the labour of observation and experiment would have to be very heavy and quite indispensable. But his own business was with great principles and new truths; these were what had the real attraction for him; it was the magnificent thoughts and boundless hopes of the approaching "kingdom of man" which kindled his imagination and fired his ambition. "He writes philosophy," said Harvey, who had come to his own great discovery through patient and obscure experiments on frogs and monkeys, "he writes philosophy like a Lord Chancellor." And for this part of the work, the stateliness and dignity of the Latin corresponded to the proud claims which he made for his conception of the knowledge which was to be. English seemed to him too homely to express the hopes of the world, too unstable to be trusted with them. Latin was the language of command and law. His Latin, without enslaving itself to Ciceronian types, and with a free infusion of barbarous but most convenient words from the vast and ingenious terminology of the schoolmen, is singularly forcible and expressive. It is almost always easy and clear; it can be vague and general, and it can be very precise where precision is wanted. It can, on occasion, be magnificent, and its gravity is continually enlivened by the play upon it, as upon a background, of his picturesque and unexpected fancies. The exposition of his philosophical principles was attempted in two forms. He began in English. He began, in the shape of a personal account, a statement of a series of conclusions to which his thinking had brought him, which he called the "Clue of the Labyrinth," *Filum Labyrinthi.* But he laid this aside unfinished, and rewrote and completed it in Latin, with the title *Cogitata et visa.* It gains by being in Latin; as Mr. Spedding says, "it must certainly be reckoned among the most perfect of Bacon's productions." The personal form with each paragraph begins and ends. *"Franciscus Bacon sic cogitavit . . . itaque visum est ei,"* gives to it a special tone of serious conviction, and brings the interest of the subject more keenly to the reader. It has the same kind of personal interest, only more solemn and commanding, which there is in Descartes's *Discours de la Méthode.* In this form Bacon meant at first to publish. He sent it to his usual critics, Sir Thomas Bodley, Toby Matthew, and Bishop Andrewes. And he meant to follow it up with a practical exemplification of his method. But he changed his plan. He had more than once expressed his preference for the form of *aphorisms* over the argumentative and didactic continuity of a set discourse. He had, indeed, already twice begun a series of aphorisms on the true methods of interpreting nature, and directing the mind in the true path of knowledge, and had begun them with the same famous aphorism with which the *Novum Organum* opens. He now reverted to the form of the aphorism, and resolved to throw the materials of the *Cogitata et visa* into this shape. The result is the *Novum Organum.* It contains, with large additions, the substance of the treatise, but broken up and re-arranged in the new form of separate impersonal generalised observations. The points and assertions and issues which, in a continuous discourse, careful readers mark and careless ones miss, are one by one picked out and brought separately to the light. It begins with brief, oracular, unproved maxims and propositions, and goes on gradually into larger developments and explanations. The aphorisms are meant to strike, to awaken questions, to disturb prejudices, to let in light into a nest of unsuspected intellectual confusions and self-misunderstandings, to be the mottoes and watchwords of many a laborious and difficult inquiry. They form a connected and ordered chain, though the ties between each link are not given. In this way Bacon put forth his proclamation of war on all that then called itself science; his announcement that the whole work of solid knowledge must be begun afresh, and by a new, and, as he thought, infallible method. On this work Bacon concentrated all his care. It was twelve years in hand, and twelve times underwent his revision. "In the first book especially," says Mr. Ellis, "every word seems to have been carefully weighed; and it would be hard to omit or change anything without injuring the meaning which Bacon intended to convey." Severe as it is, it is instinct with enthusiasm, sometimes with passion. The Latin in which it is written answers to it; it has the conciseness, the breadth, the lordliness of a great piece of philosophical legislation.

The world has agreed to date from Bacon the systematic reform of natural philosophy, the beginning of an intelligent attempt, which has been crowned by such signal success, to place the investigation of nature on a solid foundation. On purely scientific grounds his title to this great honour may require considerable qualification. What one thing, it is asked, would not have been discovered in the age of Galileo and Harvey, if Bacon had never written? What one scientific discovery can be traced to him, or to the observance of his peculiar rules? It was something, indeed, to have conceived, as clearly as he conceived it, the large and comprehensive idea of what natural knowledge must be, and must rest upon, even if he were not able to realise his idea, and were mistaken in his practical methods of reform. But great ideas and great principles need their adequate interpreter, their *vates sacer,* if they are to influence the history of mankind. This was what Bacon was to science, to that great change in the thoughts and activity of men in relation to the world of nature around them: and this is his title to the great place assigned to him. He not only understood and felt what science might be, but he was able to make others—and it was no easy task beforehand, while the wonders of discovery were yet in the future—understand and feel it too. And he was able to do this because he was one of the most wonderful of thinkers and one of the greatest of writers. The disclosure, the interpretation, the development of that great intellectual revolution which was in the air, and which was practically carried forward in obscurity, day by day, by the fathers of modern astronomy and chemistry and physiology, had fallen to the task of a genius, second only to Shakespeare. He had the power to tell the story of what they were doing and were to do with a force of imaginative reason of which they were utterly incapable. He was able to justify their attempts and their hopes as they themselves could not. He was able to interest the world in the great prospects opening on it, but to which none but a few students had the key. The calculations of the astronomer, the investigations of the physician, were more or less a subject of talk, as curious or possibly useful employments. But that which bound them together in the unity of science, which gave them their meaning beyond themselves, which raised them to a higher level and gave them their real dignity among the pursuits of men, which forced all thinking men to see what new and unsuspected possibilities in the knowledge and in the condition of mankind were opened before them, was not Bacon's own attempts at science, not even his collections of facts and his rules of method, but that great idea of the reality and boundless worth of knowledge which Bacon's penetrating and sure intuition had discerned, and which had taken possession of his whole nature. The impulse which he gave to the progress of science came from his magnificent and varied exposition of this idea; from his series of grand and memorable generalisations on the habits and faults of the human mind—on the difficult and yet so obvious and so natural precautions necessary to guide it in the true and hopeful track. It came from the attractiveness, the enthusiasm, and the persuasiveness of the pleading; from the clear and forcible statements, the sustained eloquence, the generous hopes, the deep and earnest purpose of the *Advancement* and the *De Augmentis*; from the nobleness, the originality, the picturesqueness, the impressive and irresistible truth of the great aphorisms of the *Novum Organum.*

SIR JOHN DAVIES

1569–1626

John Davies was baptised on April 16, 1569, at the parish church in Tisbury, Wiltshire. Davies attended the Winchester School from 1580 to 1585, going on to study at Queen's College, Oxford. He left Oxford in 1587 and entered Middle Temple, London. Davies traveled on the Continent for several years and in 1595 he was called to the bar. In 1596 Davies published his first poetical work, *Orchestra*. Modeled after Spenser, this poem was written about the same time as his collaboration with Marlowe in *Epigrammes and Elegies of Ovid*. In 1599 Davies published *Hymnes of Astraea*, a collection of acrostics on the name Elizabeth, and *Nosce Teipsum*, a philosophical poem on the nature of man and the immortality of the soul. Davies's poetry, characterized by the use of irony and parody, was well received by his contemporaries.

Davies's literary output largely came to an end around 1600. In 1601 he was elected a member of Parliament and in 1603 he went to Ireland to serve as Solicitor-General. In 1606 he became Attorney-General of Ireland and in 1613 he was elected Speaker of the Lower House of the Irish Parliament. He returned to England in 1619 and again served in Parliament. Davies was among the founders of the Society of Antiquarians. In 1626 he was appointed Lord Chief Justice, but he died suddenly on December 7, 1626, before taking office.

Personal

Sir John Davis, the learned and well accomplisht father of a no less learned and accomplisht daughter, the present Countess Dowager of Huntington: his poem *Nosce Teipsum* (besides which and his *Orchestra*, publisht together with it, both the products of his younger years, I remember to have seen from the hands of the Countess, a judicious metaphrase of several of David's psalms) is said to have made him first known to Queen Elizabeth, and afterwards brought him in favor with King James, under whose auspices, addicting himself to the study of the Common Law of England, he was made the King's first Serjeant, and afterwards his Attorney General in Ireland.
—EDWARD PHILLIPS, *Theatrum Poetarum Anglicanorum*, 1675

Sir *John Davis* was the Son of a wealthy Tanner of *Chisgrove*, in the Parish of *Tysbury* in *Wiltshire*; and, at Fifteen Years of Age, enter'd a Commoner of *Queen's* College in *Oxford*; from whence, after several Years Residence, He remov'd to the *Middle-Temple*, to study the Law, tho', 'tis said, against his Inclination, and was call'd to the Bar: But having a Quarrel with one Mr. *Richard Martyn*, (afterwards Recorder of *London*) He bastinado'd him in the *Temple-Hall*, at Dinner-Time, in the Sight of the whole Society. For which Contempt He was forthwith expell'd, and retir'd, somewhat uneasy, to *Oxford*; where he, again, follow'd his Studies closely; but without resuming the Scholar's Gown, and compos'd the excellent Poem ⟨*Nosce Teipsum*⟩. After this, we find him honour'd with the Protection of *Thomas* Lord *Ellesmore*, Lord-Keeper of the Great Seal; and, not only restor'd to his Chambers in the *Temple*, but return'd a Member of Parliament, *Ann.* 1601. Upon the Death of the Queen, He, with several other Gentlemen, accompany'd the Lord *Hunsdon* into *Scotland*, to congratulate King *James* on his Accession to the Throne of *England*: And, being introduc'd to his *Majesty*, by Name, the King immediately inquir'd if he was *Nosce Teipsum*? (The Title of his first Poem!) and, being inform'd He was, most graciously embrac'd Him, and speedily made him his Sollicitor, and Attorney-General for *Ireland*. (It being a Mistake that he received those Preferments from Queen *Elizabeth*.) Beside which, He was one of the King's Serjeants in *England*; several Times an Assistant-Judge, and had the Honour of being Knighted by His Majesty, at *White-Hall*, An. 1607.—At length being ap-

pointed Lord Chief-Justice of the *King's-Bench*, He dy'd suddainly, before He could take Possession of that eminent Dignity; But left behind Him more valuable Witnesses of his Merit, than all the Titles that Heraldry can invent, or Monarchs bestow: The joint Applauses of *Cambden*, Sir *John Harington*, Ben *Johnson*, *Selden*, *Donn*, *Corbet*, &c! These are great, and unquestionable Authorities in Favour of this Author; and I shall only presume to add, That, in my humble Opinion, no Philosophical Writer, I have met with, ever explain'd their Ideas more clearly, or familiarly even in Prose; or any so beautifully or harmoniously in Verse. There is a peculiar Happiness in his Similies, being introduc'd to illustrate, more than adorn; which renders them as useful, as entertaining; and distinguishes his from those of every other Author.—But his Memory has already received the highest Compliments that can be paid to it. The late excellent Lord *Dorset* admir'd his Writings so much, that he recommended such of them as remain, to be republish'd by Mr. *Tate*; which was, accordingly done, under His Protection; and the World has justify'd his Lordship's Taste so effectually, that another Edition appear'd in the Year 1714. . . . 'Tis call'd there an *Introduction* to his Essay, on the *Nature*, and *Immortality of the Soul*: But, without Question, is the *Nosce Teipsum*, for which He was so highly caress'd by King *James*; as fully appears by the Contents of the Poem it self.—ELIZABETH COOPER, *The Muses Library*, 1737, pp. 331–33

General

Acute *John Davis*, I affect thy rymes,
That ierck in hidden charmes these looser times:
Thy plainer verse, thy vnaffected vaine,
Is grac'd with a faire (end and sooping traine).
    —UNSIGNED, *The Return from Pernassus*, 1606,
        Act 1, Sc. 2

Davies and *Wither*, by whose *Muses* power
A *naturall* day to me seemes but an houre,
And could I euer heare their learned layes,
Ages would turne to artificiall dayes.
    —WILLIAM BROWNE, *Britannia's Pastorals*,
        1613, Bk. 2, Song 2

The two works on which his fame as a poet rests are on the widely different themes of Dancing, and the Immortality of the Soul. The first is in the form of a dialogue between Penelope and one of her wooers, and most melodiously expresses "the antiquity and excellence of dancing." Only in the Elizabethan age could such a great effort of intellect, learning, and fancy have arisen from the trifling incident of asking a lady to dance. It was left unfinished; and, indeed, as it is the object of the wooer to prove to Penelope that dancing is the law of nature and life, the poem could only be brought to an end by the exhaustion of the writer's ingenuity in devising subtile analogies for the wooer and answers as subtile from Penelope, who aids

> The music of her tongue
> With the sweet speech of her alluring eyes.

To think logically from his premises was the necessity of Davies's mind. In the poem on Dancing the premises are fanciful; in the poem on the Immortality of the Soul the premises are real; but the reasoning in both is equally exact. It is usual among critics, even such critics as Hallam and Campbell, to decide that the imaginative power of the poem on the Immortality of the Soul consists in the illustration of the arguments rather than in the perception of the premises. But the truth would seem to be that the author exhibits his imagination more in his insight than in his imagery. The poetic excellence of the work comes from the power of clear, steady beholding of spiritual facts with the spiritual eye,—of beholding them so clearly that the task of stating, illustrating, and reasoning from them is performed with masterly ease. In truth, the great writers of the time *believed* in the soul's immortality, because they were conscious of having souls; the height of their thinking was due to the fact that the soul was always in the premises; and thought, with them, included imaginative vision as well as dialectic skill. From a lower order of minds than Shakespeare, Hooker, and Bacon, than Chapman, Sidney, and Davies, proceed the theories of materialism, for no thinking *from* the soul can deny the soul's *existence*. It is curious to observe the advantage which Davies holds over his materialistic opponents, through the circumstance that, while his logical understanding is as well furnished as theirs, it reposes on central ideas and deep experiences which they either want or ignore.—EDWIN P. WHIPPLE, *The Literature of the Age of Elizabeth*, 1869, pp. 238–40

We have to thank Dr Grosart for what is probably a quite complete edition of Sir John Davies's Poems. Besides *Nosce Teipsum*, the *Hymns to Astræa*, and other well-known works, he gives us some 200 pages of pieces 'either printed for the first time, or for the first time published among Davies's Poems.' These additions are more important for the sake of the completeness of the collection, than for their intrinsic merit. The metaphrase of some of the psalms, printed from a MS. in the possession of Dr David Laing, though superior to some other efforts of the same kind, is yet far from being a success. The work is executed with the editor's characteristic care and accuracy. A few misprints may have escaped him, as in ii. 30. ('He first taught him that keeps the monuments.') We do not know how he would read the second of these two lines:

> Brunns which deems himself a faire sweet youth,
> Is thirty-nine yeares of age at least;

Dyce reads:

> Is nine-and-thirty years of age at least

with a note, 'So MS., except that it has thirtieth, and we see no reason for altering or retaining the alteration of 'ranging' into 'raging' in the seventeenth Epig.:

> To thoughts of drinking, thriving, duelling, war,
> And borrowing money ranging in his mind.

But, so far as the collection and the text are concerned, Dr Grosart has done his work well.

Few will deny that it was work worth doing, and doing well. It is vain indeed to make definitions of poetry which would deprive any poet of his well-won title. Whatever may be said as to what poetry should be, the fact remains that the author of *Nosce Teipsum* is a poet. In the kingdom of poetry, as has been said, are many mansions, and undoubtedly one of these belongs to Sir John Davies, however we may describe it, however we may censure its style and arrangement. Far be from us any such critical or scholastic formulæ as would prevent us from all due appreciation of such refined, imaginative thought and subtle, finished workmanship, as mark the first notable philosophical poem of our literature.

The epigrams possess an interest of a very different kind, for Davies differed a good deal from himself, to speak in a Greek manner. Like Stephano's Monster, he had two voices. 'His forward voice' is heard when he discourses of the soul of man and the immortality thereof; 'his backward voice is to utter foul speeches and detract.' Dr Grosart, it seems, had 'compunctious visitings' as to republishing these latter utterances; but he had the good sense to resist them. Certainly he would have failed to do his duty had he not resisted them. And one must be careful not to judge in an exaggerated manner of what there is of grossness in these pieces. There are many worse ways of speaking than plain language. Words that are nauseous to our fine palates had once no bad taste for natures that were certainly as truly healthful and as genuinely refined as we can boast to be. Anyhow, the life pictures these epigrams give are much too precious to be lost or thrown aside. They bring the old Elizabethan London vividly before us, with all its rough humours, its wild wit, its boisterous vitality. They did not play at living, those Elizabethans, but lived hard, and fully and furiously. It was not their way to sip at the cup of enjoyment, they drank deep, and jested loudly, and laughed louder.— JOHN W. HALES, "Sir John Davies's Poems" (1876), *Folia Litteraria*, 1893, pp. 162–64

Sir John Davies belongs to that late Elizabethan circle of courtly poets which still gathered round the declining age of the great Queen with apparently as much personal devotion as the circle of Sidney and Spenser had gathered round her prime. His *Nosce Teipsum*, published in 1599, was dedicated

> To that clear majesty which in the North
> Doth like another sun in glory rise;

and the *Hymns to Astraea*, which appeared in the same year, may be ranked as one of the most readable and freely written expressions of that complex sentiment toward the Queen of which each considerable Elizabethan poet became in turn the mouthpiece. This later group is to be distinguished on the one hand from the earlier lyrical and pastoral school, and on the other from the great dramatic circle which crowds the foreground of this second period. Its production was reflective and philosophical, and only occasionally and subordinately either lyrical or dramatic. It testified to revolt against pastorals and love poetry, but no member of it was possessed of a sufficiently great or pliant genius to achieve any important triumph outside the older and well-worn fashions. Lord Brooke in point of power reigns supreme among these philosophers in verse, but Sir John Davies' *Nosce Teipsum* enjoyed a wider contemporary reputation than anything of Lord Brooke's, and has been far more frequently read since. It is a strange performance, and is to be admired rather for the measure of victory it obtains over unfavourable conditions, than for any absolute poetical merits. Some handbook of Christian philosophy seems to have fallen in the author's way during a year of retirement at Oxford,— possibly the *De Natura Hominis* of Nemesius, of which Wither published an English translation in 1636,—and the text suited a sobered mood, while it offered an opportunity for rehabilitating a reputation shaken by youthful folly and extravagance. Accordingly the *Nosce Teipsum* was produced, an 'oracle expounded in two Elegies—(1) of Human Knowledge; (2) of the Soul of Man and the Immortality thereof.' It is an exposition in the verse of *Gondibert* and the *Annus Mirabilis* of what Davies himself calls the 'received opinions,' the orthodox metaphysic of his time, and treats such topics as 'what the soul is;' 'that the soul is more than the Temperature of the Humors of the Body;' 'that the soul is created immediately by God;' 'the vegetative or Quickening power;' 'the power of sense, the Relations between wit and will,' &c. &c. All these interminable and tremendous subjects are indeed handled with admirable clearness and brevity. Where Lord Brooke would have wandered on to unmeasured length, thinking his way from cloud to clearness with laborious sincerity, Sir John Davies, a man of far inferior temper and morale, plays the artist with his inartistic material, clearly foresees his end, maps out his arguments and 'acclamations,' and infuses just so much imagination and so much eloquence as will carry the subject to the ears it is intended to reach. Hallam said of *Nosce Teipsum* that it scarcely contained a languid verse. It may be said of it with equal truth that it scarcely contains a verse of real energy, and that it shows not a spark of that genuine poetic gift which at rare intervals lightens the most heavy and formless of Lord Brooke's *Treatises*. Nothing in Davies' smoothly turned and occasionally eloquent introduction to his subject proper, 'The Elegy of Human Knowledge,' has the poetic flavour of such lines as these, which break the monotony of Lord Brooke's Treatise on the same subject:—

> The chief use then in man of that he knows,
> Is his painstaking for the good of all;
> Not fleshly weeping for our own-made woes,
> Not laughing from a melancholy gall,
> Not hating from a soul that overflows
> With bitterness, breathed out from inward thrall;
>   But sweetly rather to ease, to loose or bind,
>   As need requires, this frail fall'n human kind.

Expression of this high and tender quality is not to be looked for in *Nosce Teipsum*. The poem deals with an eternally poetic subject, the longings, griefs, and destiny of the soul, in such a way as to furnish one more illustration of the futility of 'philosophical poetry,'—of the manner in which the attempt to combine poetry and science extracts all pathos and all influence from the most pathetic and the most potent of themes. From this judgment we may perhaps exclude the passages, quoted below, which deserve to live when the rest of *Nosce Teipsum* is forgotten.

Orchestra was a poem of the author's youth, 'a sudden rash half-capreol of my wit,' as he calls it in the dedication. It is unfinished and immature in style, but there is considerable charm in its wandering fancifulness. The graceful and delicate verse beginning 'For lo, the sea that fleets about the land, will remind a reader of well-known lines in the *Ancient Mariner*. In one or two other passages Sir John Davies may be suggestively matched with modern poets. The resemblance of his 38th Epigram to Wordsworth's *Power of Music* has been already pointed out, and a verse of another modern poem,—

> We see all sights from pole to pole,
> And glance and nod and bustle by,

> And never once possess our soul
> Before we die,—

recalls a passage in the Elegy 'Of Human Knowledge':—

> We that acquaint ourselves with every Zone,
> And pass both Tropics, and behold the Poles,
> When we come home are to ourselves unknown,
> And unacquainted still with our own souls.
>   —MARY A. WARD, "Sir John Davies," *The English Poets*, ed. Thomas Humphry Ward, 1880, Vol. 1, pp. 548–50

His poetical work consists chiefly of three poems or collections of poems. These are *Nosce Teipsum*, or the immortality of the soul, in quatrains, and as light as the unsuitableness of the subject to verse will allow; a singularly clever collection of acrostics called *Astraea*, all making the name of Elizabetha Regina; and the *Orchestra*, or poem on dancing, which has made his fame. Founded as it is on a mere conceit—the reduction of all natural phenomena to a grave and regulated motion which the author calls dancing—it is one of the very best poems of the school of Spenser, and in harmony of metre (the seven-lined stanza) and grace of illustration is sometimes not too far behind Spenser himself.—GEORGE SAINTSBURY, *A History of Elizabethan Literature*, 1887, p. 294

Sir John Davies, whose philosophical poems were among the most original and beautiful literary productions of the close of Elizabeth's reign, was suddenly silenced by the admiration James I. conceived for his judgment in practical affairs, and was henceforth wholly absorbed in politics. But an examination of Davies' work, had we space for it here, would form no ill preparation for the study of several classes of Jacobean poetry. He was eminently a writer before his time. His extremely ingenious *Orchestra*, a poem on dancing, has much in it that suggests the Fletchers on one side and Donne on the other, while his more celebrated *magnum opus* of the *Nosce Teipsum* is the general precursor of all the school of metaphysical ingenuity and argumentative imagination. In Davies there is hardly a trace of those qualities which we have sought to distinguish as specially Elizabethan, and we have difficulty in obliging ourselves to remember that his poems were given to the public during the course of the sixteenth century. To the exquisite novelty and sweetness of his *Hymns of Astræa*, critical justice has never yet been done.—EDMUND GOSSE, *The Jacobean Poets*, 1894, pp. 8–9

Works

NOSCE TEIPSUM

Davies's *Nosce Teipsum* is an excellent poem, in opening the nature, faculties, and certain immortality of man's soul.— RICHARD BAXTER, "Prefatory Address" to *Poetical Fragments*, 1681

Davies carried abstract reasoning into verse with an acuteness and felicity which have seldom been equalled. His reasons, undoubtedly, with too much labour, formality, and subtlety, to afford uniform poetical pleasure. The generality of his stanzas exhibit hard arguments interwoven with the pliant materials of fancy, so closely, that we may compare them to a texture of cloth and metallic threads, which is cold and stiff, while it is spendidly curious. There is this difference, however, between Davies and the commonly styled metaphysical poets, that *he* argues like a hard thinker, and *they*, for the most part, like madmen. If we conquer the drier parts of Davies's poem, and bestow a little attention on thoughts which were meant, not to gratify the indolence, but to challenge the activity of the mind, we shall find in the entire essay fresh beauties at every perusal: for in the happier parts we come to logical truths so well illustrated by ingenious similes, that we know not whether to call the thoughts more poetically or philosophically just. The judgment and fancy are reconciled, and the imagery of the poem seems to start more vividly from the surrounding shades of abstraction.—THOMAS CAMPBELL, *An Essay on English Poetry*, 1819

Perhaps no language can produce a poem, extending to so great a length, of more condensation of thought, or in which fewer languid verses will be found. Yet, according to some definitions, the *Nosce Teipsum* is wholly unpoetical, inasmuch as it shows no passion and little fancy. If it reaches the heart at all, it is through the reason. But, since strong argument in terse and correct style fails not to give us pleasure in prose, it seems strange that it should lose its effect when it gains the aid of regular metre to gratify the ear and assist the memory. Lines there are in Davies which far outweigh much of the descriptive and imaginative poetry of the last two centuries, whether we estimate them by the pleasure they impart to us, or by the intellectual vigor they display.—HENRY HALLAM, *Introduction to the Literature of Europe*, 1837–39, Pt. 2, Ch. 5, Par. 70

Sir John Davies must have been about fifteen years younger than Sir Fulk Grevill. He was born in 1570, was bred a barrister, and rose to high position through the favour of James I.—gained, it is said, by the poem which the author called *Nosce Teipsum*, but which is generally entitled *On the Immortality of the Soul*, intending by *immortality* the spiritual nature of the soul, resulting in continuity of existence. It is a wonderful instance of what can be done for metaphysics in verse, and by means of imagination or poetic embodiment generally. Argumentation cannot of course naturally belong to the region of poetry, however well it may comport itself when there naturalized; and consequently, although there are most poetic no less than profound passages in the treatise, a light scruple arises whether its constituent matter can properly be called poetry. At all events, however, certain of the more prosaic measures and stanzas lend themselves readily, and with much favour, to some of the more complex of logical necessities. And it must be remembered that in human speech, as in the human mind, there are no absolute divisions: power shades off into feeling; and the driest logic may find the heroic couplet render it good service.

Sir John Davies's treatise is not only far more poetic in image and utterance than that of Lord Brooke, but is far more clear in argument and firm in expression as well. Here is a fine invocation:

> O Light, which mak'st the light which makes the day!
> Which sett'st the eye without, and mind within;
> Lighten my spirit with one clear heavenly ray,
> Which now to view itself doth first begin.
>
> Thou, like the sun, dost, with an equal ray,
> Into the palace and the cottage shine;
> And show'st the soul both to the clerk and lay,
> By the clear lamp of th' oracle divine.

He is puzzled enough to get the theology of his time into harmony with his philosophy, and I cannot say that he is always triumphant in the attempt; but here at least is good argument in justification of the freedom of man to sin.

> If by His word he had the current stayed
> Of Adam's will, which was by nature free,
> It had been one as if his word had said,
> "I will henceforth that Man no Man shall be."
>
> For what is Man without a moving mind,
> Which hath a judging wit, and choosing will?

> Now, if God's pow'r should her election bind,
> Her motions then would cease, and stand all still.
> So that if Man would be unvariable,
> He must be God, or like a rock or tree;
> For ev'n the perfect angels were not stable,
> But had a fall more desperate than we.

The poem contains much excellent argument in mental science as well as in religion and metaphysics; but with that department I have nothing to do.—GEORGE MACDONALD, "Lord Bacon and His Coevals," *England's Antiphon*, 1868, pp. 105–7

For the history of philosophy it is of great significance, as it enables the student to understand the psychology and philosophy which were current before the introduction of the philosophies of Descartes on the one hand and of Hobbes and Locke on the other. The versification is uncommonly successful. It may be regarded as a triumph of diction in the expression of subtle thought in concise and fluent verse. It is by no means free from the conceits which were current in all the versification of its time, but it is remarkable in the history of literature for the skill with which it conducts philosophical discussion in the forms, and with somewhat of the spirit of elevated poetry.—FRIEDRICH ÜBERWEG, *History of Philosophy*, tr. George S. Morris, 1874, Vol. 2, p. 352

With considerable appositeness of argument, and clearness of exposition, Sir John Davies sets forth his thoroughly spiritualistic psychology, and develops numerous considerations tending to establish the doctrine of the soul's immortality, all founded on the best philosophy the world had produced, and pervaded by an obvious breath of sincere and independent conviction; this, too, in spite of the apparent over-confidence (and very mediocre poetry) of the concluding stanza. . . .

The poem may stand as a document to prove what was the thoughtful faith of the best type of English gentlemen in his day.—GEORGE S. MORRIS, *British Thought and Thinkers*, 1880, pp. 67–68

ALEXANDER B. GROSART
From "Memorial-Introduction"
The Complete Poems of Sir John Davies
1876, pp. lix–lxxxix

I value *Nosce Teipsum* as a first thing for its *deep and original thinking*, i.e. for its *intellectual strength*—all the more remarkable that . . . he was only in his 28th–29th year when he composed it. Of its art I shall have somewhat to say anon: but regarding it as a *"philosophical poem"* and as a contribution to metaphysic, I place foremost the THOUGHT in it, as at once a characteristic and a merit (if merit be not too poor a word). DAVIES (along with FULKE GREVILLE, LORD BROOKE and DONNE) simply as Thinker on the profoundest problems of nature and human nature, seems to me to stand out pre-eminently, and in saying this, I regard it as sheer nonsense to exalt the workmanship at the expense of the material—to ask me to recognize in a bit of tin ingeniously and painstakingly etched into a kind of miracle of execution something co-equal with a solid bar of gold as it gleams i' the face of the sun in its purged and massive simpleness; or to put it unmetaphorically, I must pronounce judgment on the rank of a Poet *qua* a Poet fundamentally on the kind and quality of the thought on higher and deeper things that he puts into his verse and that he strikes out in others. Your mere artist-Poet is surely third-rate and must even go beneath the music-composer of to-day.

Nosce Teipsum as it was practically the earliest so it remains the most remarkable example of deep reflective-meditative thinking in verse in our language or in any language. The student of this great poem will very soon discover that within sometimes homeliest metaphors there is folded a long process of uncommon thought on the every-day facts of our mysterious existence. I call the thinking deep, because *Nosce Teipsum* reveals more than eyes that looked on the surface—reveals penetrative and bold descent to the roots of our being and reachings upward to the Highest. Your mere realistic word-painter of what he sees, is shallow beside a Poet who passes beneath the surface and circumstance and fetches up from sunless depths or down from radiant altitudes fact and facts—each contributory to that ultimate philosophy which while it shall accept every proved fact, will not rush off hysterically shouting "eureka," with ribald accusations of all that generations have held to be venerable and sustaining. I call the thinking original, for there is evidence everywhere in *Nosce Teipsum* that the penitent recluse of Oxford made his own self his study—as really if not as avowedly as Wordsworth.

I am aware in claiming originality for Davies that in that huge waste-basket of our Literature—Nichols' *Literary Illustrations* (Vol. IV. pp. 549–50) there is a letter from an Alexander Dalrymple, Esq., who is designated "the great hydrographer" to "Mr. Herbert" (the Bibliographer I opine) wherein he takes different ground. We must traverse his charge. He thus writes:—"Dear Sir, I have lately purchased the following old books" (he enumerates several). . . . "I have also got 'Wither's translation of Nemesius de Naturâ hominis' by which I find Sir John Davies's poem on the Immortality of the Soul is chiefly taken from Nemesius. . . . I have picked up a tract in 4to by Thomas Jenner, with some very good plates, the marginal notes of which seem to be what the heads of Tate's edition of Sir John Davies's are taken from."

Were this true it would utterly take from *Nosce Teipsum* the first characteristic and merit I claim for it—deep and original thought. But it is absolutely untrue, an utter delusion, as any one will find who takes the pains that I have done to read, either the original Nemesius, or what this sapient book-buyer mentions, Wither's translation. With my mind and memory full of *Nosce Teipsum* and the poem itself beside me, I have read and re-read every page, sentence and word of Nemesius and Wither (and there is a good deal of Wither in his translation: 1636) and I have not come upon a single metaphor or (as the old margin-notes called them) "similies," or even observation in *Nosce Teipsum* drawn from Nemesius or Wither. The only element in common is that necessarily Nemesius adduces and discusses the opinions of the Heathen Philosophers on the many matters handled by him, and Sir John Davies does the same with equal inevitableness. But to base a charge of plagiarism against *Nosce Teipsum* on this, is to reason on the connection between Tenterden Steeple and Goodwin Sands (if the well-worn folly be a permissible reference). The following is the title-page of the quaint old tome and as it is by no means scarce, any reader can cross-question our witness: "The Nature of Man. A learned and useful Tract written in Greek by Nemesius, surnamed the Philosopher; sometime Bishop of a City in Phœnecia, and one of the most ancient Fathers of the Church. Englyshed, and divided into Sections, with briefs of their principle contents by Geo. Wither. London: Printed by M. F. for Henry Taunton in St. Duncan's Churchyard in Fleetstreet. 1636." (12° 21 leaves and pp. 661.) Chronologically—Wither's translation was not published until 1636, while *Nosce Teipsum* was published in 1599; but Nemesius' own book no more than Wither's warrants any such pre-

posterous statements as this Alexander Dalrymple makes. Even in the treatment of the "opinions" of the Heathen Philosophers which come up in Nemesius, and in *Nosce Teipsum*, the latter while 'intermedling' with the same returns wholly distinct answers in refutation. The "opinions" themselves as being derived of necessity from the same sources are identical; but neither their statement nor refutation. Nemesius is ingenious and well-learned, but heavy and prosaic. Sir John Davies is light of touch and a light of poetic glory lies on the lamest "opinion." The "Father of the Church" goes forth to war with encumbering armour: the Poet naked and unarmed beyond the spear wherewith he 'pierces' everything, viz. human consciousness. Jenner's forgotten book had perhaps been read by Tate, but that concerns Tate not Sir John Davies. I pronounce it a hallucination to write "Sir John Davies' poem on the immortality of the Soul is chiefly taken from Nemesius." Not one line was taken from Nemesius. . . .

A second characteristic of *Nosce Teipsum* that calls for notice is its *perfection of workmanship* shown in the *mastery of an extremely difficult stanza*, as well as its solidity of material. Here unquestionably Sir John Davies far excels Lord Brooke and Donne, and later, Sir William Davenant in *Gondibert*. The two former are occasionally (it must be granted) semi-inarticulate, and the last is very often monotonous and trying. *Nosce Teipsum* is throughout articulate and unmistakeable, and never flags. You have a fear o' times that a metaphor will prove grotesque or mean: or a vein of thought pinch and go out from ore to bare limestone. But invariably an imaginative touch, or a colour-like epithet, or a thrill of emotion, lifts up the mean into a transfiguring atmosphere as of sun-set purples and crysolites, and gives to grotesquest gargoyles (as of cathedrals) a strange fitness. Then when a thought or illustration seems about to end, debasedly, another forward-carrying and ennobling, swiftly succeeds.

. . . Davies elected his measure and stanza with evidently entire spontaneity; and it is an odd reversal of the simple matter of fact to ascribe the 'artificial restraints' chosen, to an absence 'of a fiery and teeming imagination,' when, as all observation demonstrates, the more fiery and fecund the imagination of a Poet, the more exquisitely obedient is he to the subtlest and most intricate movements of his measure—just as the bluest-blooded race-horse is a law to itself whereas your stolid dray-cart or plough-drawer needs the "artificial restraints" of all kinds of gear, and the constraint of whip and blow and vociferation. I can well suppose that but for the *Fairy Queen* Sir John Davies might have chosen its stanza, but just as to-day *In Memoriam* has taken to itself its form and music to the exclusion of every other—though a very ancient English measure—so Spenser's immortal poem precluded *Nosce Teipsum* following in the same. I cannot admit "artificial restraints" in the sense of needed restraints or aid. There was the stanza, and the genius of Sir John Davies appropriated it—since Spenser's, in all worship, could not be taken—and, like a great Vine, clad its natural slenderness and poorness of build with wealth of bright green leafage and clustered fruitage. The nicety and daintiness of workmanship, the involute and nevertheless firmly-completed and manifested imagery of *Nosce Teipsum* wherewith this nicety and daintiness are wrought, place Sir John Davies artistically among the finest of our poets. . . .

These two characteristics, viz., (1) *deep and original thinking*, (2) *perfection of workmanship, or mastery of an extremely difficult stanza*—embrace that in *Nosce Teipsum*, regarded broadly, which I am anxious to have the Reader recognize and 'prove' for himself. Subsidiary to them is one other thing—not shared with many of our Poets and therefore demanding specific statement—viz. its *condensation through-out*. Hallam and Craik have called attention to this; and the student cannot fail to be struck with it. It is not simply that the stanzas are as so many rings of gold each complete in itself—much as Proverbs are—but that whether it be idea or opinion or metaphor there is no beating of it out, as though yards of gold-leaf or tin-foil were more valuable than the relatively small solid ore that has been so manipulated: or the common mistake of imagining that a pound of feathers is heavier than a pound of lead. From Dean Donne until now "comparisons are odious." Nevertheless when one recalls the attenuated thought and the blatant verbiage of not a few of our Poets, this resolute sifting out of everything extraneous is not less noticeable than commendable. It assures us that the Poet was conscious of his resources—of his unused wealth of thought and imagination and fancies. He who compacts his carbon into a Koh-i-noor has infinite supplies of it. Similarly a Poet who could and did so lavishly add great thought to great thought and vivid metaphor to vivid metaphor, and still go on adding in smallest possible compass, declares his intellect to be of the highest.

E. HERSHEY SNEATH
From "Biographical Sketch"
Philosophy in Poetry:
A *Study of Sir John Davies's Poem* Nosce Teipsum
1903, pp. 34–48

Davies was undoubtedly affected by the literary spirit of the age. Classical training and learning figured in his education. Like other poets of the Elizabethan period, he reveals in his poetry a familiarity with Latin and Greek authors. There are numerous allusions to classical mythology in his writings. Not a few of these are to be found in *Nosce Teipsum*. They also indicate some knowledge of classical history. The acquaintance of our poet with classical literature naturally raises the question whether, since *Nosce Teipsum* is really the first formally developed system of philosophy in English poetry, its author found a model among the Greek or Latin poets. It has been suggested that he found such a model in the *De Rerum Natura* of Lucretius. However, there does not seem to be any substantial evidence for such a suggestion. External evidence on this point would only indicate a possibility of a knowledge of Lucretius as a result of Davies's interest in philosophy and classical literature. But internal evidence certainly does not indicate that the poem of Lucretius was the model for *Nosce Teipsum*. The two poems are altogether unlike, both in form and content. So far as form is concerned, their metrical framework is entirely different. So far as content is concerned, they differ radically. The work of Lucretius is much more comprehensive than is the work of Davies. The former is a philosophy of all reality—of things as well as of minds; the latter is merely a philosophy of mind. The former is a materialistic philosophy; the latter is a spiritualistic philosophy. Furthermore, the materialism which Davies refutes in *Nosce Teipsum*, which regards the soul as corporeal, is not peculiar to Lucretius, but is common to Democritus, the Stoics, and Epicureans as well. Again, in Davies's elaborate consideration of the objections to the immortality of the soul, he does not consider any of the many objections urged by Lucretius[1] against the belief. Even the idea of writing a philosophical poem does not seem to have been suggested by the work of Lucretius. The most natural explanation of the origin of *Nosce Teipsum* is the one already hinted at in the account given in the biographical sketch. Davies's disbarment, with the humiliation and disgrace involved, led him to betake himself to serious introspection and reflection. He himself tells us what the results of his "affliction" were:—

> If ought can teach vs ought, *Afflictions* lookes,
> (Making vs looke into our selues so neere,)
> Teach vs to *know our selues* beyond all bookes,
> Or all the learned Schooles that euer were.
>
> This *mistresse* lately pluckt me by the eare,
> And many a golden lesson hath me taught;
> Hath made my *Senses* quicke, and Reason cleare,
> Reform'd my Will and rectifide my Thought.
>
> . . .
>
> She within *lists* my ranging minde hath brought,
> That now beyond my selfe I list not goe;
> My selfe am *center* of my circling thought,
> Onely *my selfe* I studie, learne, and know.

The conclusions born of such a soul-study Davies desired to communicate to others; and, being a poet, what more natural than that he should choose verse as the means of communication? The result was, a philosophical poem—*Nosce Teipsum*.

But what of Davies's relation to the spirit of his age so far as the philosophy and theology of his poem are concerned? To what extent was he influenced in his thinking by the philosophical and theological thought of his time? This question can best be answered in connection with a more general question; namely, What are the chief sources of Davies's philosophical indebtedness? Philosophical thinkers generally are influenced by their speculative environment and by preceding speculative thought. Davies is no exception to the rule. It is rather difficult to determine by specific external evidence to whom he is specially indebted. Internal evidence, however, seems to point to the influence of four thinkers,—Aristotle, Cicero, Nemesius, and Calvin.

In the first place, a careful comparison of Davies's poem with Aristotle's *De Anima* reveals Davies's acquaintance with this celebrated work of the great Greek philosopher. This is manifest in the similarity of their teachings on fundamental points, as, the reality of the soul, the nature of the soul, the soul's relation to the body, the rational soul's relation to sense, the powers of the soul, the activity of the soul, etc. These similarities of teaching will be more specifically pointed out in the course of our study, and they will be found sufficiently striking to remove any scepticism concerning the influence of the Stagyrite upon our poet's thinking. Of course external evidence would seem to indicate this also. Aristotle was a power in Scholastic thought, and the Renaissance and Protestant Reformation only led to a more *direct* study of his works. Despite the early antipathy of the theologians of the Reformation to Aristotle (as for example Luther and Melancthon), later they found it necessary to turn to him for aid in their reconstruction of theology. But they turned to the real Aristotle rather than to his Scholastic interpreters. So that Aristotle was influential in the speculative thought of the sixteenth century. And it was quite natural that Davies should seek help from this powerful mind in his study of the human soul.

In the second place, internal evidence strongly indicates the influence of Cicero upon the thinking of Davies. This is manifest in his argument for the reality of the soul; but more especially in his argument for its immortality. The greater portion of his reasoning on this subject is taken from Cicero's *Tusculan Disputations*. The arguments from universal assent, from contempt of death in righteous souls, the fear of death in wicked souls, the intimations of immortality manifest in the desire for posthumous fame, and in the care for posterity;—all of this, as we shall see later by careful comparison, is taken from the Roman philosopher.

In the third place, internal evidence points more or less conclusively to the influence of Nemesius upon Davies. Nemesius was one of the early Christian Fathers and Bishop of one of the cities in Phœnicia. He wrote a work in Greek on *The Nature of Man*. This work was translated into English by George Wither, the poet, and published in London, 1636. In Nichols's *Literary Illustrations*[2] there is a letter written by one Alexander Dalrymple to a Mr. Herbert in which, after stating that he had recently purchased some old books, he says: "I have also got 'Wither's translation of Nemesius de Naturâ hominis' by which I find Sir John Davies's poem on the Immortality of the Soul is chiefly taken from Nemesius. . . . I have picked up a tract in 4to by Thomas Jenner, with some very good plates, the marginal notes of which seem to be what the heads of Tate's edition of Sir John Davies's are taken from."[3]

To Dalrymple's accusation of plagiarism on the part of Davies Grosart takes vigorous exception. . . . As the view of Davies's indebtedness to Nemesius taken in this study differs materially from the view of Grosart, it is only fair that his view should be presented here in full. . . .

Now, undoubtedly Dalrymple was in error in accusing Davies of borrowing from Wither's translation of Nemesius's *De Natura Hominis*, for, as Grosart points out, *Nosce Teipsum* was published in 1599 and Wither's translation of Nemesius did not appear in print until 1636. He was also in error in making such a sweeping statement as "I find Sir John Davies's poem on the Immortality of the Soul is chiefly taken from Nemesius," for the contents of the two volumes vary greatly. In the first place, early in their works, both writers treat of the Fall of Man, and they differ in their conceptions of the consequences of the Fall. Nemesius conceives of these as moral; whereas Davies represents them as both moral and intellectual. In the second place, in his refutation of Materialism, Davies to a certain extent moves along lines of argument differing from those of Nemesius. In the third place, in their discussions of the reality of the soul, Davies presents an elaborate refutation of Sensationalism, whereas Nemesius is silent on this formidable theory. In the fourth place, Davies treats the question of the mode of the Soul's origin in relation to the body much more elaborately and after a different fashion than does Nemesius. They differ also in their conclusions on this question. Davies is a Creationist, whereas Nemesius believes in the doctrine of pre-existence. In the fifth place, there is a noticeable difference in their psychological analysis—in their analysis and division of mental powers or "faculties." Davies presents a different classification, and enumerates more "faculties" than does Nemesius. In the sixth place, there is a difference in their treatment of the subject of the soul's immortality. The treatment of Nemesius, for a work of such a character, is lamentably and inexcusably meagre; whereas Davies presents an elaborate discussion, involving numerous arguments for belief in immortality, also objections and replies, as well as misgivings and answers. In all of these fundamental, as well as in many minor respects, the two works differ so materially that an accusation of plagiarism is utterly unjust. Furthermore, Davies reveals such great obligations to other thinkers as to make an accusation of wholesale plagiarism from Nemesius, such as Dalrymple makes, absurd.

But while this may be said without fear of successful contradiction, a careful comparison of *Davies's Nosce Teipsum* with Nemesius's *De Natura Hominis* makes it impossible to agree with Grosart, that "Not one line was taken from Nemesius"; that "not one scintilla of obligation suggests itself to the Reader"; and that, with regard to "resemblances and suggestions," "there is not a jot or tittle of either." On the contrary, there are "resemblances and suggestions" of such a striking character as to indicate beyond reasonable doubt, that Davies was familiar with the Church Father's work, and was influenced by it to a considerable extent. These "resemblances and suggestions" will appear in our further study. They can hardly be accounted for on grounds of coincidence, or of dealing with the same question. They indicate rather, that Davies, like every intelligent author, in treating his subject, inquired into what his predecessors had said on the same subject; and that, in so doing, he found himself in accord with some of their views, and received valuable suggestions from them in forming still other views. They indicate, further, that Nemesius was one of the predecessors whom Davies had consulted with advantage.

Another thinker to whom our poet was indebted is Calvin. This is manifest in the more specifically theological portions of *Nosce Teipsum*, as in the discussion of the Fall of man in the first part of the poem; and the problem of original sin, in the second part. It was quite natural that, in seeking help on such subjects, he should turn to the works of a theologian whose influence was dominant in the Protestant theology of his country. A comparison of the theological portions of *Nosce Teipsum* with Calvin's *Institutes of the Christian Religion*, which will be made in the course of our interpretation of the poem, will indicate the extent of Davies's obligation to the Genevan theologian.

But although Davies was greatly indebted to these thinkers—Aristotle, Cicero, Nemesius, and Calvin—he reveals such a thorough grip on the problems of the philosophy of mind, and such a unique and clever way of dealing with them, as to make his philosophy and his philosophical poetry in a true sense *his* own.

Notes
1. *De Rerum Natura*, Lib. III.
2. Vol. IV. pp. 549–550.
3. Alexander B. Grosart, "Memorial-Introduction" to *The Complete Poems of John Davies* (1876), p. lxi.

JOHN FLETCHER

SAMUEL DANIEL

FRANCIS BEAUMONT

SIR WALTER RALEGH

MICHAEL DRAYTON

JOHN DONNE

SIR FRANCIS BACON

CYRIL TOURNEUR

c. 1575–1626

Little is known about the life of Cyril Tourneur. Scholars believe that he was born between 1570 and 1580, and there is no further record of him before the publication in 1600 of a long satirical poem, *The Transformed Metamorphosis*.

Tourneur is best known as a dramatist. *The Atheist's Tragedy* (1611) expresses Christian stoicism, while *The Revenger's Tragedy* (1607) deals with murder, seduction, and passionate revenge. Although later seventeenth-century booksellers attributed the anonymously published Jacobean masterpiece *The Revenger's Tragedy* to Tourneur, there now seems to be little evidence to support the assignment; it is widely held that Thomas Middleton actually wrote the play. Tourneur is known to have written another play, *The Nobleman*, which was performed in 1613 at court but is now lost. Tourneur also wrote several elegies, including "A Griefe on the Death of Prince Henry" (1613) and "A Funeral poem upon the Death of the Most Worthy and True Scholar, Sir Francis Vere" (1609). Tourneur was secretary to Vere, an English general in the Netherlands.

In 1625 Tourneur was serving as secretary to the council of war when an attack on Cadiz was undertaken. The expedition was led by Sir Robert Cecil, about whom Tourneur wrote *The Chronical of Robert Cecil, Earl of Salisbury*. The expedition failed and Tourneur was put off the ship, mortally ill, at Kinsale, Ireland, where he died on February 18, 1626.

Of the two extant plays known as his, *The Atheist's Tragedy, or The Honest Man's Revenge*, printed in 1611, was unmistakeably the earlier. The crudity of its versification, which abounds in 'light endings' to the lines, and has in fact a not very bearable kind of lilt, leaves no room for doubt on this score. A passage in the play suggests that it was written either during, or immediately after, the siege of Ostend (1601–4). As a whole, it is a work of striking originality; but this feature distinguishes rather the General conception and manner of the play than particular passages of high individual merit, of which but few remain to be added to those extracted—with his usual felicity of choice—by Charles Lamb. The story, which was probably made up from more sources than one, runs riot in some of its later turns, and is mixed up with a revolting underplot (turning on the amours of Levidulcia, which are represented with unspeakable grossness). The author, incapable or reckless of distinguishing between the terrible and the grotesque, sought to cap the horror of the midnight murder in the gravel-pit by a churchyard scene full of real and sham ghosts; and his atheist ends, when no longer master of his movements, by inflicting an accidental wound upon himself with the executioner's axe with which he was about to do to death the victims of his train of crimes. The exposition of the character of d'Amville, the ruthless villain of the play, is however impressive, and the connexion between his black emptiness of soul and the evil-doing to which he abandons himself is, though not very consecutively, kept in view down to his dying recantation. Marlowe might have imagined such a hero, who, when thunder and lightning terrify the accomplice of his nocturnal crime, arrogantly philosophises on the origin of these phenomena;—and who justifies incest by the general liberty allowed by nature to her creatures. But the progress of the action fails to heighten the effect of the character; we have supped too full with horrors before the play is more than half done to have much stomach left for all that is to follow of lust and death; and the atheist's catastrophe—the overthrow of his reason by the death of his younger son and the consequent collapse of his schemes,—is not presented with overwhelming force. Moreover, the moral which this tragedy attempts to teach—that vengeance should be left to Heaven—is hardly brought out as a principle of action, and the virtuous Charlemont and the sorely-tried Castabella, even when re-united they lie down to rest 'with either of them a Death's head for a pillow,' can hardly be regarded as interesting in themselves.

If *The Atheist's Tragedy* seems to carry us back to the period which gave rise to so many dramas on a theme cognate to that of *Hamlet*, there can be no doubt but that one of its most impressive passages was suggested by *Hamlet* itself. But in truth ample evidence may be found elsewhere of its author's familiarity with Shakspere's ideas or phraseology.

The Revenger's Tragedy, printed in 1607, had been uniformly assigned to Tourneur, until Mr. Fleay threw doubts on the correctness of the assumption. I cannot, however, consider this scepticism warranted. Undoubtedly, the distance is considerable between the style of this play and that of its predecessor; and although the reflexion of Shakspere is still constantly cast upon the troubled waters, the writer has acquired a power of condensed expression of his own which he owes to no example or model. The versification, again, differs essentially from that of *The Atheist's Tragedy*; the structure of the verse is strong, and its peculiar effect seems to me to gain from the frequent use of rime. One can only conclude that the order of sequence between the two plays according to the dates of publication known to us must be reversed, and that *The Revenger's Tragedy*, in its original form, was composed several years before its successor.

Unfortunately the plot of *The Revenger's Tragedy*, the source of which is unknown, is in its sewer-like windings one of the blackest and most polluting devised by the perverted imagination of an age prone to feed on the worst scandals of the Italian decadence. At the same time, an over-powering self-consistency pervades the picture of this nameless Italian court,—its old Duke, the 'parched lascar'; his heir Lussurioso, to whom every woman is a concubine at his beck and call; his 'step-Duchess' ready for adultery with her husband's bastard; her sons (a brood worse than Catharine de' Medici's), Ambitioso, Supervacuo, and a third (the perpetrator of the outrage that sets the action in motion) who alone goes by a colourless name (Junior); his reckless bastard Spurio; his obsequious judges, and his fawning nobles. Vindici, the hero of the drama, a figure suggested by *Hamlet* or *Hoffman*, and his brother Hippolito, come near to realising the ideal of a tragedy of revenge which is satirically propounded in a play of rather later date. The brothers do not indeed kill themselves, but they welcome death as a fitting termination to their performance of their self-appointed task. Horribly realistic on some of its effects, which but too successfully express the 'quaintness of malice' commended in Vindici by Hippolito, this play may be described as wholly devoid of relief. While we feel thankful that no comic effects are sought to be produced in this stifling atmosphere, we are inspired with no human sympathy even by the chaste Castiza, whose experiment upon the better elements in her mother's nature excites in us a pardonable fear that there is after all no difference between parent and child. The whole episode of the mother, tempted by the pretended persuasions of her son to sinful connivance with her daughter's shame, is against kind; and the climax of Vindici's vengeance reaches the *non plus ultra* of pruriency steeped in horrors. It has been thought possible to find in such a play 'the noblest ardour of moral emotion,' and 'the most fervent passion of eager and indignant sympathy with all that is best and abhorrence of all that is worst in women or in men.' Beyond dispute, however, it contains evidence of high tragic power, and of a gift of diction matching itself with extraordinary fitness to demands such as few if any of our dramatists have ever made upon their powers. Passages in this tragedy are illuminated by an imagery of singular distinctness as well as intensity. And if, as we are not prepared to doubt, *The Revenger's Tragedy* was Tourneur's work, it is with a sense of amazement that we turn from this solitary monument of his genius as a tragic poet of unmistakeable distinction—ADOLPHUS WILLIAM WARD, *A History of English Dramatic Poetry* (1875), 1899, Vol. 3, pp. 66–71

His two tragedies, *The Atheist's Tragedy* and *The Revenger's Tragedy*, have been rather variously judged. The concentration of gloomy and almost insane vigour in *The Revenger's Tragedy*, the splendid poetry of a few passages which have long ago found a home in the extract books, and the less separable but equally distinct poetic value of scattered lines and phrases, cannot escape any competent reader. But, at the same time, I find it almost impossible to say anything for either play as a whole, and here only I come a long way behind Mr. Swinburne in his admiration of our dramatists. The *Atheist's Tragedy* is an inextricable imbroglio of tragic and comic scenes and characters, in which it is hardly possible to see or follow any clue; while the low extravagance of all the comedy and the frantic rant of not a little of the tragedy combine to stifle the real pathos of some of the characters. *The Revenger's Tragedy* is on a distinctly higher level; the determination of Vindice to revenge his wrongs, and the noble and hapless figure of Castiza, could not have been presented as they are presented except by a man with a distinct strain of genius, both in conception and execution. But the effect, as a whole, is marred by a profusion of almost all the worst faults of the drama of the whole period from Peele to Davenant. The incoherence and improbability of the action, the reckless, inartistic, butcherly prodigality of blood and horrors, and the absence of any kind of redeeming interest of contrasting light to all the shade, though very characteristic of a class, and that no small one, of Elizabethan drama, cannot be said to be otherwise than characteristic of its faults.—GEORGE SAINTSBURY, *A History of Elizabethan Literature*, 1887, p. 285

Tourneur was a fierce and bitter spirit. The words in which he unpacked his heart are vitalised with passion. He felt so keenly that oftentimes his phrase is the offspring of the emotion, so terse and vigorous and apt, so vivid and so potent and eager, it appears. As an instance of this avidity of wrath and scorn find-

ing expression in words the fittest and most forcible, leaving the well-known scenes embalmed in Elia's praise, one might take the three or four single words in which Vindici (*The Revenger's Tragedy*), on as many several occasions, refers to the caresses of Spurio and the wanton Duchess. Each is of such amazing propriety, is so keenly discriminated, is so obviously the product of an imagination burning with rage and hate, that it strikes you like an affront: each is an incest taken in the fact and branded there and then. And this quality of verbal fitness, this power of so charging a phrase with energy and colour as to make it convey the emotion of the writer at the instant of inspiration, is perhaps the master quality of Tourneur's work.

They that would have it are many; they that achieve their desire are few. For in the minor artist the passionate—the elemental quality—is not often found: he being of his essence the ape or zany of his betters. Tourneur is not a great tragic. *The Atheist's Tragedy* is but grotesquely and extravagantly horrible; its personages are caricatures of passion; its comedy is inexpressibly sordid; its incidents are absurd when they are not simply abominable. But it is written in excellent dramatic verse and in a rich and brilliant diction, and it contains a number of pregnant epithets and ringing lines and violent phrases. And if you halve the blame and double the praise you will do something less than justice to that *Revenger's Tragedy* which is Tourneur's immortality. After all its companion is but a bastard of the loud, malignant, antic muse of Marston; the elegies are cold, elaborate, and very tedious; the *Transformed Metamorphosis* is better verse but harder reading than *Sordello* itself. But the *Revenger's Tragedy* has merit as a piece of art and therewith a rare interest as a window on the artist's mind. The effect is as of a volcanic landscape. An earthquake has passed, and among grisly shapes and blasted aspects here lurks and wanders the genius of ruin.—W. E. HENLEY, "Tourneur," *Views and Reviews*, 1890

JOHN CHURTON COLLINS
From "Introduction"
The Plays and Poems of Cyril Tourneur
1878, Volume 1, pp. xl–lvi

It would be needless to enter at length into an examination of the various attributes which constitute the commanding splendour of Tourneur's genius, for, unlike the coy and retiring merits of subtler artists, they lie in startling prominence on the surface; but it may be well to notice one or two interesting and distinctive features. He belonged to the school of Shakespeare. *The Atheist's Tragedy* is in its most pleasing and successful passages a study of the master's earlier style. In some cases he has modelled a whole speech with exquisite felicity, on his original, as in Castabella's appeal to D'Amville, in the fourth scene of the third act; sometimes he copies literal expressions, as in Castabella's prayer at Charlamont's tomb, in the first scene of the same act; at other times he clothes, in his own words, borrowed scenes and positions, as in the third scene of the fourth act, which is evidently a reminiscence of the churchyard scene in *Hamlet*. So subtly and exactly has he caught the ring, phrase, and trick of Shakespeare's style that it would sometimes be impossible to distinguish master from pupil. I would instance among many others:

> To guide your green improvidence of youth
> And make you ripe for your inheritance.
>
> (Act iii. sc. iv.)

> I'll be an instrument

To grace performance with dexteritie.
                    (Act i. sc. ii,)

    Be not displeas'd if on
The altar of his tomb I sacrifice
My teares. They are the jewels of my love
Dissolved into grief, and fall upon
His blasted Spring as April dew upon
A sweet young blossom shak'd before the time.
                    (Act iii. sc. i.)

    I am an emperor of a world,
This little world of man. My passions are
My subjects.
                    (Act iii. sc. iii.)

In the *Revenger's Tragedy* he catches much of his master's later form; he echoes often his terse and weighty phrase; he has borrowed epithets and touches, he has selected passages for parodying; he has taken types for characters—the younger brother, for instance, is a close copy of Claudio in *Measure for Measure*, as Vindici is possibly modelled on Hamlet—but there all resemblance ceases. At the point at which most imitators begin, he breaks off to tread his own lonely and independent path. To institute comparisons between inferior men who differ in degree only, but not in kind, is the legitimate exercise of perverted and harmless ingenuity; but to institute comparisons between men of original and distinctive features is always futile and usually misleading. Tourneur has been compared to Webster, as the *Revenger's Tragedy* has been compared to Hamlet, and the comparison, as usual, lies merely on the surface. He has, indeed, none of those elements in his genius which won for Webster Charles Hazlitt's and Lamb's appropriate and happy appellation of "the noble-minded;" he has none of Webster's breadth and insight, none of his instinctive sympathy with the great and the true, none of his searching, subtle pathos, none of that quick analogical instinct which loads *Vittoria Corombona* and the *Duchess of Malfi* with wide-ranging imagery, metaphor, and simile. Webster has humour, like that of Thucydides—a humour subdued and severe, peculiar and difficult to characterise, but seldom altogether absent. Tourneur has none, for what usurps its name is either a mocking irony, or, still more frequently, the gross and quaint expression of some foul passion stinging within. They were both cynics, but Webster's was the cynicism of a profoundly reflective intellect, the world-weariness and bitter impatience which comes upon a great, fearless, sensitive thinker who sees and feels all, but who cannot always interpret and who will not compromise. If Tourneur is to be compared with any of his contemporaries he may be compared appropriately with Marston, but the parallel, so far as it goes, is so obvious that it is not worth drawing.

Like Juvenal and Marston, he loves to satirise that he may secure for himself the luxury of prurient description. He did not hate men because he hated vice, but he hated vice because he hated men. It is very evident that he had received a classical training and possessed a knowledge probably of the Greek—certainly of the Latin—poets of such a kind that it is not likely to have been second-hand. This accomplishment he occasionally displays, like too many of his contemporaries, with unpleasant ostentation, though at other times it is employed with that apt felicity and unconscious readiness which can only be the result of assimilative thoroughness.

I am certainly inclined to suspect that he had some acquaintance with the Greek tragedians. That his purely sensual conception of the passion of love, however, in which he stands in unenviable solitude among his fellow-dramatists, does not

arise from any Hellenic bias, but springs purely from his own diseased and perverted consciousness, cannot, of course, be seriously doubted. It has, it is easy to see, narrowed and damaged his work.

It could hardly be expected, perhaps, that a poet whose instincts lie so entirely on the side of tragedy could possess any comic power, or aim at any comic effects. He has, however, unfortunately thought it necessary to do so, and appears, like Dryden, to have made a point of substituting indecency for wit, and mere filth for drollery. Apollo and Melpomene may have smiled on his tragic offspring, but his comedy is certainly the joint and vigorous progeny of Priapus and Cloacina. His attempts in this walk, indeed, are at their best only less contemptible than Harlowe and only less grotesque than Æschylus, though it must be confessed that the scene in the churchyard between Snuffe and Soquette in the *Atheist's Tragedy* will wring out a reluctant smile hardly to be extorted by the dreary ribaldry of Wagner in *Doctor Faustus*, or the nauseous babble of the nurse in the *Chöephoræ*. But the Muse of Tragedy has, after all, been a jealous goddess in the case of all her votaries save Shakespeare and Racine. The stage has seen two, and two only, who could unite the various and dissimilar powers necessary for the production of an *Othello* and a *Much Ado about Nothing*, of an *Athalie* and a *Les Plaideurs*.

To review briefly Tourneur's comic characters. Dandolo, who appears for a moment in the *Revenger's Tragedy*, is a despicable and blundering parody of Shakespeare's worst farce. Soquette, Fresco, etc., in the *Atheist's Tragedy*, are below contempt. Cataplasma would be intolerable even in the haunts over which she presides, and Sebastian's wit is as stale as his paramour's love. Languebeau Snuffe is his only attempt of any merit in this walk, but he is at best a vulgar caricature superfluously elaborated and impertinently introduced, a concession, doubtless, to the groundlings, who had, however, been taught to laugh at better things. But we can forgive the creator of Vindici any deficiency on this score as freely as we forgive anything to the creators of Orlando Friscobaldo and Sir Giles Over-reach.

It is not so easy, however, to overlook or excuse his pointed and superfluous allusions to certain nameless and detestable abominations to which his countrymen were for the most part strangers, and which our noble and manly literature has systematically passed over with the contemptuous silence they deserve. Marston may be forgiven, and something may be conceded to Churchill, though even satire should fly at something higher than carrion, and at nothing lower than humanity. But enough.

Eleven stanzas crown Sappho for ever peerless queen of the lyre strung by Erato; a few disjointed fragments sufficed to satisfy Goethe that in Menander perished the supreme genius of grace and symmetry; on five hundred and twenty lines rests unshaken the fame of Persius; and the composition of a single play enthrones Tourneur among the lords of English tragedy. Without being insensible to the splendid, impressive, and elaborate work of Beaumont and Ford, so minutely and eloquently interpreted to us by Mr. Swinburne's Essays, we must certainly rank together the *Duchess of Malfi*, *Vittoria Corombona*, and the *Revenger's Tragedy* as the noblest and worthiest of the many offerings laid by rapt disciples at the feet of their common master—Shakespeare. The play has many defects, no doubt; of some of them I have already spoken; with respect to others, they lie principally in the delineation of the subordinate characters, who want colour and complexity. Hippolito, for instance, is a mere shadow; Ambitioso and Supervacuo are simply what their names imply, they are not men so much as abstractions; they enact a set part, and reveal no capabilities for anything else. Castiza never appears except to assert or defend her chastity, a treasure much too cheap, and necessarily, to justify her wearisome eulogies. There is something unsatisfactory and unpleasantly rapid about the change in the character and position of the mother, though her repentance at the dagger's edge probably left her as base as it found her—but Tourneur should have marked it. The action of the play sometimes flags when it should hurry on, and sometimes hurries on when it might with advantage slacken its pace. But through this chaos of bleared, rapid, and uneven work spring into fierce and vivid light a series of scenes and positions unique in conception, brilliant and powerful in execution. The opening scene, with the torch-light flaring on the blood-stained, lust-rotted, hellish crew, as they pass over the stage, hearing not nor heeding the Revenger, the trial of the younger brother, the scene between the Duchess and Spurio, the scenes between Castiza and her mother, between Vindici, his mother, and sister, between the brothers and their mother, the murder of the Duke, the scene at the feast—some of these are of an excellence almost unapproachable; all of them may rank among the most graphic and impressive passages in the whole body of our drama. The character of Vindici in its appalling and unrelieved intensity, in its savage and devilish energy, bitter cynicism, and angry grandeur, is unrivalled among the creations of an age which abounds in similar portraits. The Duke, the Duchess, and the younger brother are all masterly sketches, vigorously conceived and admirably sustained. . . .

Tourneur's great defect as a dramatic poet is undoubtedly the narrowness of his range of vision—of his insight and sympathies—and this is evident in the sketchy and abstract nature of many of his subordinate characters. Even D'Amville, the hero of the *Atheist's Tragedy*, finely conceived, is very inadequately sustained, and fades at last into mere burlesque. His four principal female figures, Castabella, Castiza, Levidulcia, and Gratiana, differ merely in name, and what slight difference there is between them would seem to arise simply from the difference of the circumstances in which they are placed. They are even grouped similarly. Levidulcia and Gratiana, cast in the same mould, have pretty much the same character, and Castabella assumes the same attitude towards Levidulcia in the one play as Castiza assumes towards Gratiana in the other. None of his dramatis personæ are at all complex; they are either the personifications of certain attributes—tragic studies of tragic humours, as Ben Jonson's masterpieces are comic studies of comic humours—or they are abstractions, phantoms, failures. He has apparently noticed the former peculiarity himself, and been careful to mark it in the nomenclature adopted for his characters. It is curious also to observe that where his names are not thus allegorically coined they are almost without exception borrowed from contemporary dramas.

In closing our review of these works it is difficult to leave them without pausing for a moment over the memory of their author, who, with obvious but perhaps unconscious egotism, has evidently left in their strange and melancholy pages no inconsiderable fragments of his own strange and melancholy autobiography. Of his life among men, of his struggles and vicissitudes, not a trace, as we have seen, remains; but of that inner life, which is the soul of action, and is all that can interest or concern any one when the grave has closed over the actor, we cannot but feel that the veil has been uplifted, and that these two plays have other than mere literary fascination. Nothing, it is true, is so idle, so easy, and so presumptuous as to speculate and theorise on subjects like these; but here it is no officious recreation, but an imperative duty, with such lyric

intensity and passionate abandonment has a poet stamped on his writings the terrible traces of so much bitter experience, of so much suffering, cynicism, and despair. Never, indeed, with the single exception of Byron, has a dramatist, while preserving successfully a certain superficial and technical consistency in the delineation of subordinate characters altogether out of the range of his care, comprehension, and sympathy, so obviously and so defiantly interwoven and interpenetrated objective embodiment with an intense all-absorbing subjectivity. Dramatic more in form than spirit, in particular detail rather than in general conception, these two plays have the same dreary burden, the same melancholy moral, and in all the various speeches of their many actors rings out the same hollow laughter, or falters low the same hopeless pathos. One chord is struck and there are no variations; one tale is told and there are no episodes. But how deep and piercing is the note, how savage and significant the burden! It is the egotism of a powerful and distorted mind, which narrowed as it hardened and gained in intellectual vigour as it lost in sensuality and enthusiasm. It would seem that he united the not uncommon anomaly of a fiery and restless soul with a cold and logical intellect. Where such a perilous union, no longer mutually corrective, fails to secure in consistent purpose the principle of healthy and harmonious actions, or to find at all events a narcotic in the possession of humour, it must either work its own speedy destruction, or, tortured into morbid and irritable action, become the fruitful parent of "all monstrous, all abhorred things."

Nature, who had in many respects endowed him so richly, had altogether denied him this sense of humour, and consequently the balance and insight which humour is usually able to bestow. Hence, no doubt, the diseased, warped, and chaotic character of much of his work.

The incidents and struggles of his personal life probably differed little from those of two-thirds of his fellow-dramatists, among whom it would seem he had not received the recognition to which his genius certainly entitled him. All this operating on a man of his exceptional and peculiar temperament, of his sullen, unsocial and retiring disposition, would naturally make him what he appears to have been, so far at least as we can read his character from his writings. In the lonely laboratory of self he worked out his theory of the world-drama evolving round him, and flung his indignant transcript for all to read and some to understand—and a melancholy page it is. Man is not with him the creature of mixed motives, nor life the battleground between alternating light and darkness. It is the dreary stage on which Vindicis, Lussuriosos, Borachios, Soquettes, Cataplasmas, D'Amvilles, Snuffes, Levidulcias, Gratianas and Spurios are to sin their barren sins, or Castizas, Antonios, Montferrers, and Sebastians to drain the cup of their aimless and grotesque sufferings for the amusement of the mocking beholder and expectant hell. Like Marlowe, he hungers and thirsts after the sensuous, the defiant and the forbidden, but he has none of Marlowe's glory, grandeur and idealism. Like Webster, he loves to live among horrors till he has become "native and endowed unto that element;" but he moves not with the same firm tread through tangled labyrinths of gloom and wreck with "Look you, the stars shine still!" as creed at once and comment. Sin and misery, lust and cynicism, fixed their fangs deep in his splendid genius, marring and defacing his art, poisoning and paralysing the artist. But his life's work, such as it was, was complete and consistent, and it is not the province of criticism either to regret what is or to speculate about what might have been. That he perished prematurely while passing through a stage which is with most men of genius essentially transitory can scarcely be conjectured with any confidence, for crude and bitter as his philosophy of life may seem, its crudeness is not the crudeness of immaturity, or its bitterness the sort of bitterness which a wider experience would have been likely to sweeten.

ALGERNON CHARLES SWINBURNE
"Cyril Tourneur"
Nineteenth Century, March 1887, pp. 415–27

'They, shut up under their roofs, the prisoners of darkness, and fettered with the bonds of a long night, lay exiled, fugitives from the eternal providence. For while they supposed to lie hid in their secret sins, they were scattered under a dark veil of forgetfulness, being horribly astonished, and troubled with sights. . . . Sad visions appeared unto them with heavy countenances. No power of the fire might give them light: neither could the bright flames of the stars endure to lighten that horrible night. Only there appeared unto them a fire kindled of itself, very dreadful: for being much terrified, they thought the things which they saw to be worse than the sight they saw not. . . . The whole world shined with clear light, and none were hindered in their labour: over them only was spread an heavy night, an image of that darkness which should afterwards receive them: but yet were they unto themselves more grievous than the darkness.' In this wild world of fantastic retribution and prophetic terror the genius of a great English poet—if greatness may be attributed to a genius which holds absolute command in a strictly limited province of reflection and emotion—was born and lived and moved and had its being. The double mainspring of its energy is not difficult to define: its component parts are simply adoration of good and abhorrence of evil: all other sources of emotion were subordinate to these: love, hate, resentment, resignation, self-devotion, are but transitory agents on this lurid and stormy stage, which pass away and leave only the sombre fire of meditative indignation still burning among the ruins of shattered hopes and lives. More splendid success in pure dramatic dialogue has not been achieved by Shakespeare or by Webster, than by Cyril Tourneur in his moments of happiest invention or purest inspiration: but the intensity of his moral passion has broken the outline and marred the symmetry of his general design. And yet he was at all points a poet: there is an accent of indomitable self-reliance, a note of persistence and resistance more deep than any note of triumph, in the very cry of his passionate and implacable defection, which marks him as different in kind from the race of the great prosaic pessimists whose scorn and hatred of mankind found expression in the contemptuous and rancorous despondency of Swift or of Carlyle. The obsession of evil, the sensible prevalence of wickedness and falsehood, self-interest and stupidity, pressed heavily on his fierce and indignant imagination: yet not so heavily that mankind came to seem to him the 'damned race,' the hopeless horde of millions 'mostly fools' too foolish or too foul to be worth redemption, which excited the laughing contempt of Frederic the Great and the raging contempt of his biographer. On this point the editor to whom all lovers of high poetry were in some measure indebted for the first collection and reissue of his works has done much less than justice to the poet on whose text he can scarcely be said to have expended an adequate or even a tolerable amount of pains. A reader of his introduction who had never studied the text of his author might be forgiven if he should carry away the impression that Tourneur, as a serious or tragic poet, was little more than a better sort of Byron; a quack less impudent but not less transparent than the less inspired and more inflated ventriloquist of *Childe Harold's Pilgrimage*: whereas it is hardly too much to say that the earnest and fiery intensity of Tourneur's moral rhetoric is no less unmistakable than the blatant and flatulent ineptitude of Byron's.

It seems to me that Tourneur might say with the greatest of the Popes, 'I have loved justice, and hated iniquity: therefore I die in exile;' therefore, in other words, I am cast aside and left behind by readers who are too lazy, too soft and slow of spirit, too sleepily sensual and self-sufficient, to endure the fiery and purgatorial atmosphere of my work. But there are breaths from heaven as surely as there are blasts from hell in the tumultuous and electric air of it. The cynicism and egotism which the editor already mentioned has the confidence to attribute to him are rather the outer garments than the inner qualities of his genius: the few and simple lines in which his purer and nobler characters are rapidly but not roughly drawn suffice to give them all due relief and all requisite attraction. The virtuous victims of the murderous conspirator whose crimes and punishment are the groundwork of *The Atheist's Tragedy* have life and spirit enough to make them heartily interesting: and the mixed character of Sebastian, the high-hearted and gallant young libertine whose fearless frankness of generosity brushes aside and breaks away the best-laid schemes of his father, is as vividly and gracefully drawn as any of the same kind on the comic or the tragic stage.

In this earlier of the two plays extant which preserve the name of Cyril Tourneur the magnificent if grotesque extravagance of the design may perhaps be partly accounted for by the didactic or devotional aim of the designer. A more appalling scarecrow or scarebabe, as the contemporaries of his creator would have phrased it, was certainly never begotten by orthodoxy on horror than the figure of the portentous and prodigious criminal who here represents the practical results of indulgence in free thought. It is a fine proof of the author's naturally dramatic genius that this terrific successor of Vanini and precursor of Diderot should be other than a mere man of straw. Huge as is the wilful and deliberate exaggeration of his atrocity, there are scenes and passages in which his daring and indomitable craft is drawn with native skill as well as force of hand; in which it is no mere stage monster, but a genuine man, plausible and relentless, versatile and fearless, who comes before us now clothed in all the cajoleries of cunning, now exultant in all the nakedness of defiance. But indeed, although the construction of the verse and the composition of the play may both equally seem to bear witness of crude and impatient inexperience, there is no lack of life in any of the tragic or comic figures which play their part through these tempestuous five acts. Even so small a figure as the profligate Puritan parasite of the atheist who hires his hypocrisy to plead against itself is bright with touches of real rough humour. There is not much of this quality in Tourneur's work, and what there is of it is as bitter and as grim in feature and in flavour as might be expected of so fierce and passionate a moralist: but he knows well how to salt his invective with a due sprinkling of such sharply seasoned pleasantry as relieves the historic narrative of John Knox; whose 'merry'[1] account, for instance, of Cardinal Beaton's last night in this world has the very savour of Tourneur's tragic irony and implacable disgust in every vivid and relentless line of it.

The execution of this poem is singularly good and bad: there are passages of such metrical strength and sweetness as will hardly be found in the dramatic verse of any later English poet; and there are passages in which this poet's verse sinks wellnigh to the tragic level of a Killigrew's, a Shadwell's, or a Byron's. Such terminations as 'of,' 'to,' 'with,' 'in,' 'and,' 'my,' 'your,' preceding the substantive or the verb which opens the next verse, make us feel as though we were reading *Sardanapalus* or *The Two Foscari*—a sensation not easily to be endured. In a poet so far superior as Tourneur to the author of those abortions we must seek for an explanation of this perverse error in a transient and tentative theory of realism rather than in an incurable infirmity or obliquity of talent: for no quality is more remarkable in the execution of his masterpiece than his mastery of those metrical properties in which the style of this play is so generally deficient. Whether in dialogue or in monologue, *The Revenger's Tragedy* is so equally admirable for instinctive obedience to nature and imaginative magnificence of inspiration, so equally perfect in the passionate harmony of its verse and the inspired accuracy of its locution, that years of study and elaboration might have seemed necessary to bring about his inexpressible improvement in expression of yet more sombre and more fiery thought or feeling. There are gleams in *The Atheist's Tragedy* of that clear light in which the whole Shakespearean world lay shining, and here and there the bright flames of the stars do still endure to lighten the gloom of it by flashes or by fits; the gentle and noble young lovers, whose patient loyalty is at last rescued from the toils of crime to be crowned with happiness and honour, are painted, though rapidly and slightly, with equal firmness of hand and tenderness of touch; and there is some vigorous and lively humour in the lighter action of the comic scenes, however coarse and crude in handling: but there is no such relief to the terrors of the maturer work, whose sultrier darkness is visible only by the fire kindled of itself, very dreadful, which burns in the heart of the revenger whom it lights along his bloodstained way. Nor indeed is any relief wanted; the harmony of its fervent and stern emotion is as perfect, as sufficient, as sublime as the full rush and flow of its diction, the fiery majesty of its verse. There never was such a thunderstorm of a play: it quickens and exhilarates the sense of the reader as the sense of a healthy man or boy is quickened and exhilarated by the rolling music of a tempest and the leaping exultation of its flames. The strange and splendid genius which inspired it seems now not merely to feel that it does well to be angry, but to take such keen enjoyment in that feeling, to drink such deep delight from the inexhaustible wellsprings of its wrath, that rage and scorn and hatred assume something of the rapturous quality more naturally proper to faith and hope and love. There is not a breath of rant, not a pad of bombast, in the declamation which fills its dazzling scenes with fire; the language has no more perfect models of style than the finest of its more sustained and elevated passages. The verse is unlike any other man's in the solemn passion of its music: if it reminds us of Shakespeare's or of Webster's, it is simply by right of kinship and equality of power with the most vivid and sonorous verse that rings from the lips of Coriolanus or of Timon, of Brachiano or the duchess of Malfy; not by any servility of discipleship or reverberation of an imitative echo. It is so rich and full and supple, so happy in its freedom and so loyal in its instinct, that its veriest audacities and aberrations have an indefinable harmony of their own. Even if we admit that Tourneur is to Webster but as Webster is to Shakespeare, we must allow, by way of exception to this general rule of relative rank, that in his noblest hours of sustained inspiration he is at least the equal of the greater dramatist on the score of sublime and burning eloquence, poured forth in verse like the rushing of a mighty wind, with fitful breaks and pauses that do but enhance the majestic sweetness and perfection of its forward movement, the strenuous yet spontaneous energy of its triumphant ardour in advance.

To these magnificent qualities of poetry and passion no critic of the slightest note or the smallest pretention to poetic instinct has ever failed to do ample and cordial justice: but to the truthfulness and the power of Cyril Tourneur as a dramatic student and painter of human character, not only has such justice not generally been done, but grave injustice has been too generally shown. It is true that not all the agents in the evolution of his greater tragedy are equally or sufficiently realized and vivified as active and distinct figures: true, for instance, that the two elder sons of the duchess are little more than conventional outlines of such empty violence and futile ambition as might be inferred from the crude and puerile symbolism of their respective designations: but the third brother is a type no less living than revolting and no less dramatic than detestable: his ruffian cynicism and defiant brutality are in life and death alike original and consistent, whether they express themselves in curses or in jeers. The brother and accomplice of the hero in the accomplishment of his manifold revenge is seldom much more than a serviceable shadow: but there is a definite difference between their sister and the common type of virginal heroine who figures on the stage of almost every dramatist then writing; the author's profound and noble reverence for goodness gives at once precision and distinction to the outline and a glow of active life to the colour of this pure and straightforward study. The brilliant simplicity of tone which distinguishes the treatment of this character is less remarkable in the figure of the mother whose wickedness and weakness are so easily played upon and blown about by every gust of penitence or temptation; but there is the same lifelike vigour of touch in the smallest detail of the scenes between her children and herself. It has been objected that her ready avowal of weakness as common to all her sex is the undramatic epigram of a satirist, awkwardly ventriloquizing through the mechanism of a tragic puppet: but it is really quite in keeping with the woman's character to enlarge and extenuate the avowal of her own infamy and infirmity into a sententious reflection on womanhood in general. A similar objection has been raised against the apparent change of character implied in the confession made by the hero to the duke elect, at the close of the play, that he and his brother had murdered the old duke—'all for your grace's good,' and in the cry when arrested and sentenced to instant execution, 'Heart, was't not for your good, my lord?' But if this seems incompatible with the high sense of honour and of wrong which is the mainspring of Vindice's implacable self-devotion and savage unselfishness, the unscrupulous ferocity of the means through which his revenge is worked out may surely be supposed to have blunted the edge of his moral perception, distorted his natural instinct, and infected his nobler sympathies with some taint of contagious egotism and pessimistic obduracy of imagination. And the intensity of sympathy with which this crowning creation of the poet's severe and fiery genius is steadily developed and displayed should make any critic of reasonable modesty think more than twice or thrice before he assumes or admits the likelihood or the possibility of so gross an error or so grave a defect in the conception of so great an artist. For if the claim to such a title might be disputed in the case of a claimant who could show no better credentials than his authorship of *The Atheist's Tragedy*—and even in that far from faultless work of genius there are manifest and manifold signs, not merely of excellence, but of greatness—the claim of the man who could write *The Revenger's Tragedy* is questionable by no one who has any glimmering of insight or perception as to what qualities they are which confer upon a writer the indisputable title to a seat in the upper house of poets.

This master work of Cyril Tourneur, the most perfect and most terrible incarnation of the idea of retribution impersonate and concentrated revenge that ever haunted the dreams of a tragic poet or the vigils of a future tyrannicide, is a figure as original and as impossible to forget, for any one who has ever felt the savage fascination of its presence, as any of the humaner figures evoked and immortalized by Shakespeare. The rage of Swift, without his insanity and impurity, seems to utter in every word the healthier if no less consuming passion of a heart lacerated by indignation and envenomed by contempt as absolute, as relentless, and as inconsolable as his own. And in the very torrent of the man's meditative and solitary passion, a very Phlegethon of agony and fury and ravenous hunger after the achievement of a desperate expiation, comes the sudden touch of sarcasm which serves as a momentary breakwater to the raging tide of his reflections, and reveals the else unfathomable bitterness of a spiritual Marah that no plummet even of his own sinking can sound, and no infusion of less fiery sorrow or less venomous remembrance can sweeten. The mourner falls to scoffing, the justicer becomes a jester: the lover, with the skull of his murdered mistress in his hand, slides into such reflections on the influence of her living beauty as would beseem a sexless and malignant satirist of her sex. This power of self-abstraction from the individual self, this impersonal contemplation of a personal wrong, this contemptuous yet passionate scrutiny of the very emotions which rend the heart and inflame the spirit and poison the very blood of the thinker, is the special seal or sign of original inspiration which distinguishes the type most representative of Tourneur's genius, most significant of its peculiar bias and its peculiar force. Such a conception, clothed in mere prose or in merely passable verse, would be proof sufficient of the mental power which conceived it; when expressed in such verse as follows, it proves at once and preserves for ever the claim of the designer to a place among the immortals.

> Thou sallow picture of my poisoned love,
> My study's ornament, thou shell of death,
> Once the bright face of my betrothed lady,
> When life and beauty naturally filled out
> These ragged imperfections;
> When two heaven-pointed diamonds were set
> In these unsightly rings;—then 'twas a face
> So far beyond the artificial shine
> Of any woman's bought complexion
> That the uprightest man (if such there be,
> That sin but seven times a day) broke custom
> And made up eight with looking after her.

The very fall of the verse has a sort of fierce and savage pathos in the note of it; a cadence which comes nearer to the echo of such laughter as utters the cry of an anguish too deep for weeping and wailing, for curses or for prayers, than anything in dramatic poetry outside the part of Hamlet. It would be a conjecture not less plausible than futile, though perhaps not less futile than plausible, which should suggest that the influence of Shakespeare's Hamlet may be responsible for the creation of Tourneur's Vindice, and the influence of Tourneur's Vindice for the creation of Shakespeare's Timon. It is a certainty indisputable except by the blatant audacity of immedicable ignorance, that the only poet to whose manner and style the style and manner of Cyril Tourneur can reasonably be said to bear any considerable resemblance is William Shakespeare. The more curt and abrupt style of Webster is equally unlike the general style of either. And if, as his first editor observes, 'the parallel' between Tourneur and Marston, 'as far as it goes, is so obvious that it is not worth drawing,' it is no less certain that the divergence between the genius which created Andrugio and the genius which created Vindice is at least as

wide as the points of resemblance or affinity between them are vivid and distinct. While Marston's imaginative and tragic power was at its highest, his style was crude and quaint, turgid and eccentric; when he had cured and purified it,—perhaps, as Gifford suggests, in consequence of Ben Jonson's unmerciful but salutary ridicule—he approved himself a far abler writer of comedy or tragicomedy than before, but his right hand had forgotten its cunning as the hand of 'a tragic penman.' Now the improvement of Tourneur's style, an improvement amounting to little less than transfiguration, keeps time with his advance as a student of character and a tragic dramatist as distinguished from a tragic poet. The style of his earlier play has much of beauty, of facility, and of freshness: the style of his later play, I must repeat, is comparable only with Shakespeare's. In the superb and inexhaustible imprecations of Timon there is a quality which reminds us of Cyril Tourneur as delightfully as we are painfully reminded of John Marston in reading certain scenes and passages which disfigure and deface the magnificent but incomprehensible composition of *Troilus and Cressida*.

Of Tourneur's two elegies on the death of Sir Francis Vere and of Henry Prince of Wales, it may be said that they are about as good as Chapman's work of the same order: and it may be added that his first editor has shewn himself, to say the least, unreasonably and unaccountably virulent in his denunciation of what he assumes to be insincere and sycophantic in the elegiac expression of the poet's regret for a prince of such noble promise as the elder brother of Charles the First. The most earnest and fervent of republicans, if not wanting in common sense and common courtesy, would not dream of reflecting in terms of such unqualified severity on the lamentation of Lord Tennyson for the loss of Albert the Good: and the warmest admirer of that loudly lamented person will scarcely maintain that this loss was of such grave importance to England as the loss of a prince who might probably have preserved the country from the alternate oppression of prelates and of Puritans, from the social tyranny of a dictator and the political disgrace of the Restoration.

The existence of a comedy by the author of *The Revenger's Tragedy*, and of a comedy bearing the suggestive if not provocative title of *Laugh and Lie Down*, must always have seemed to the students of Lowndes one of the most curious and amusing pieces of information to be gathered from the *Bibliographer's Manual*; and it is with a sense of disappointment proportionate to this sense of curiosity that they will discover the non-existence of such a comedy, and the existence in its stead of a mere pamphlet in prose issued under that more than promising title: which yet, if attainable, ought surely to be reprinted, however dubious may be its claim to the honour of a great poet's authorship. In no case can it possibly be of less interest or value than the earliest extant publication of that poet—*The Transformed Metamorphosis*. Its first editor has given proof of very commendable perseverance and fairly creditable perspicacity in his devoted attempt at elucidation of this most astonishing and indescribable piece of work: but no interpretation of it can hope to be more certain or more trustworthy than any possible exposition of Blake's *Jerusalem* or the Apocalypse of St. John. All that can be said by a modest and judicious reader is that any one of these three effusions may unquestionably mean anything that anybody chooses to read into the text; that a Luther is as safe as a Loyola, that a Renan is no safer than a Cumming, from the chance of confutation as a less than plausible exponent of its possible significance: but that, however indisputable it may be that they were meant to mean something, not many human creatures who can be trusted to go abroad without a keeper will be likely to pretend to a positive understanding of what that significance may be. To me, the most remarkable point in Tourneur's problematic poem is the fact that this most monstrous example of senseless and barbarous jargon that ever disfigured English type should have been written—were it even for a wager—by one of the purest, simplest, most exquisite and most powerful writers in the language.

This extraordinary effusion is the single and certainly the sufficient tribute of a great poet, and a great master of the purest and the noblest English, to the most monstrous and preposterous taste or fashion of his time. As the product of an eccentric imbecile it would be no less curious than Stanihurst's Virgil: as the work of Cyril Tourneur it is indeed 'a miracle instead of wit.' For it cannot be too often repeated that in mere style, in commanding power and purity of language, in positive instinct of expression and direct eloquence of inspiration, the author of *The Revenger's Tragedy* stands alone in the next rank to Shakespeare. Many if not most of their contemporaries could compose a better play than he probably could conceive—a play with finer variation of incidents and daintier diversity of characters: not one of them, not even Webster himself, could pour forth poetry of such continuous force and flow. The fiery jet of his molten verse, the rush of its radiant and rhythmic lava, seems alone as inexhaustible as that of Shakespeare's. As a dramatist, his faults are doubtless as flagrant as his merits are manifest: as a writer, he is one of the very few poets who in their happiest moments are equally faultless and sublime. The tone of thought or of feeling which gives form and colour to this splendid poetic style is so essentially what modern criticism would define as that of a natural Hebraist, and so far from that of a Hellenist or Latinist of the Renaissance, that we recognize in this great poet one more of those Englishmen of genius on whom the direct or indirect influence of the Hebrew Bible has been actually as great as the influences of the country and the century in which they happened to be born. The single-hearted fury of unselfish and devoted indignation which animates every line of his satire is more akin to the spirit of Ezekiel or Isaiah than to the spirit of Juvenal or Persius: though the fierce literality of occasional detail, the prosaic accuracy of implacable and introspective abhorrence, may seem liker the hard Roman style of impeachment by photography than the great Hebrew method of denunciation by appeal. But the fusion of sarcastic realism with imaginative passion produces a compound of such peculiar and fiery flavour as we taste only from the tragic chalice of Tourneur or of Shakespeare. The bitterness which serves but as a sauce or spice to the meditative rhapsodies of Marston's heroes or of Webster's villains is the dominant quality of the meats and wines served up on the stage which echoes to the cry of Vindice or of Timon. But the figure of Tourneur's typic hero is as distinct in its difference from the Shakespearean figure which may possibly have suggested it as in its difference from the Shakespearean figure which it may not impossibly have suggested. There is perhaps too much play made with skulls and crossbones on the stage of Cyril Tourneur: he cannot apparently realize the fact that they are properties of which a thoughtful poet's use should be as temperate and occasional as Shakespeare's: but the graveyard meditations of Hamlet, perfect in dramatic tact and instinct, seem cool and common and shallow in sentiment when set beside the intensity of inspiration which animates the fitful and impetuous music of such passages as these.

> *Vindice:*   Here's an eye
>   Able to tempt a great man—to serve God;

> A pretty hanging lip, that has forgot now to
>   dissemble.
> Methinks this mouth should make a swearer
>   tremble,
> A drunkard clasp his teeth, and not undo 'em
> To suffer wet damnation to run through 'em.
> Here's a cheek keeps her colour let the wind go
>   whistle;
> Spout, rain, we fear thee not: be hot or cold,
> All's one with us; and is not he absurd,
> Whose fortunes are upon their faces set
> That fear no other God but wind and wet?
> *Hippolito:* Brother, y'ave spoke that right;
>   Is this the face that living shone so bright?
> *Vindice:* The very same.
>   And now methinks I could e'en chide myself
>   For doting on her beauty, though her death
>   Shall be revenged after no common action.
>   Does the silk-worm expend her yellow labours
>   For thee? for thee does she undo herself?
>   Are lordships sold to maintain ladyships
>   For the poor benefit of a bewitching minute?[2]
>   Why does yon fellow falsify high-ways
>   And put his life between the judge's lips,
>   To refine such a thing, keeps horse and men
>   To beat their valours for her?
>   Surely we're all mad people,[3] and they
>   Whom we think are, are not: we mistake those:
>   'Tis we are mad in sense, they but in clothes.
> *Hippolito:* 'Faith, and in clothes too we, give us our
>   due.
> *Vindice:* Does every proud and self-affecting dame
>   Camphire her face for this? and grieve her
>   Maker
>   In sinful baths of milk,—when many an infant
>   starves,
>   For her superfluous outside—all for this?

What follows is no whit less noble: but as much may be said of the whole part—and indeed of the whole play. Violent and extravagant as the mere action or circumstance may be or may appear, there is a trenchant straightforwardness of appeal in the simple and spontaneous magnificence of the language, a depth of insuppressible sincerity in the fervent and restless vibration of the thought, by which the hand and the brain and the heart of the workman are equally recognizable. But the crowning example of Cyril Tourneur's unique and incomparable genius is of course to be found in the scene which would assuredly be remembered, though every other line of the poet's writing were forgotten, by the influence of its passionate inspiration on the more tender but not less noble sympathies of Charles Lamb. Even the splendid exuberance of eulogy which attributes to the verse of Tourneur a more fiery quality, a more thrilling and piercing note of sublime and agonising indignation, than that which animates and inflames the address of Hamlet to a mother less impudent in infamy than Vindice's, cannot be considered excessive by any capable reader who will candidly and carefully compare the two scenes which suggested this comparison. To attempt the praise or the description of anything that has been praised or described by Lamb would usually be the veriest fatuity of presumption: and yet it is impossible to write of a poet whose greatness was first revealed to his countrymen by the greatest critic of dramatic poetry that ever lived and wrote, and not to echo his words of righteous judgment and inspired applause with more or less feebleness of reiteration. The startling and magical power of single verses, ineffaceable and ineradicable from the memory on which they have once impressed themselves, the consciousness in which they have once struck root, which distinguishes and denotes the peculiar style of Cyril Tourneur's tragic poetry, rises to its highest tidemark in this part of the play. Every other line, one might almost say, is an instance of it; and yet not a single line is undramatic, or deficient in the strictest and plainest dramatic propriety. It may be objected that men and women possessed by the excitement of emotions so desperate and so dreadful do not express them with such passionate precision of utterance: but, to borrow the saying of a later and more famous bearer of the name which Cyril sometimes spelt as Turner, 'don't they wish they could?' or rather, ought they not to wish it? What is said by the speakers is exactly what they might be expected to think, to feel, and to express with less incisive power and less impressive accuracy of ardent epigram or of strenuous appeal.[4]

There are among poets, as there are among prose writers, some whose peculiar power finds vent only in a broad and rushing stream of speech or song, triumphant by the general force and fullness of its volume, in which we no more think of looking for single lines or phrases that may be detached from the context and quoted for their separate effect than of selecting for peculiar admiration some special wave or individual ripple from the multitudinous magnificence of the torrent or the tide. There are others whose power is shown mainly in single strokes or flashes as of lightning or of swords. There are few indeed outside the pale of the very greatest who can display at will their natural genius in the keenest concentration or the fullest effusion of its powers. But among these fewer than few stands the author of *The Revenger's Tragedy*. The great scene of the temptation and the triumph of Castiza would alone be enough to give evidence, not adequate merely but ample, that such praise as this is no hyperbole of sympathetic enthusiasm, but simply the accurate expression of an indisputable fact. No lyrist, no satirist, could have excelled in fiery flow of rhetoric the copious and impetuous eloquence of the lines, at once luxurious and sardonic, cynical and seductive, in which Vindice pours forth the arguments and rolls out the promises of a professional pleader on behalf of aspiring self-interest and sensual self-indulgence: no dramatist that ever lived could have put more vital emotion into fewer words, more passionate reality into more perfect utterance, than Tourneur in the dialogue that follows them.

> *Mother*: Troth, he says true.
> *Castiza*:   False: I defy you both:
>   I have endured you with an ear of fire:
>   Your tongues have struck hot irons on my face.
>   Mother, come from that poisonous woman
>   there.
> *Mother*: Where?
> *Castiza*: Do you not see her? she's too inward then.

I could not count the lines which on reperusal of this great tragic poem I find apt for illustrative quotation, or suggestive of a tributary comment: but enough has already been cited to prove beyond all chance of cavil from any student worthy of the name that the place of Cyril Tourneur is not among minor poets, nor his genius of such a temper as naturally to attract the sympathy or arouse the enthusiasm of their admirers; that among the comrades or the disciples who to us may appear but as retainers or satellites of Shakespeare his rank is high and his credentials to that rank are clear. That an edition more carefully revised and annotated, with a text reduced to something more of coherence and intelligible arrangement, than has yet been vouchsafed to us, would suffice to place his name among theirs of whose eminence the very humblest of their educated countrymen are ashamed to seem ignorant, it would probably be presumptuous to assert. But if the noblest ardour of moral emotion, the most fervent passion of eager and indignant sympathy with all that is best and abhorrence of all that is worst in women or in men—if the most absolute and imperial command of all resources and conquest of all difficulties inherent in the most effective and the most various instrument ever yet devised for the poetry of the tragic drama—if the keenest insight and the sublimest impulse that can guide the perception and animate the expression of a poet whose line of work is naturally confined to the limits of moral or ethical tragedy—if all these qualities may be admitted to confer a right to remembrance and a claim to regard, there can be no fear and no danger of forgetfulness for the name of Cyril Tourneur.

Notes

1. 'These thingis we wreat mearelie.'—(*Works of John Knox*, vol. i. p. 180.)

2. This is not, I take it, one of the poet's irregular though not unmusical lines; the five short unemphatic syllables, rapidly run together in one slurring note of scorn, being not more than equivalent in metrical weight to three such as would take their places if the verse were thus altered—and impaired;
    For the poor price of one bewitching minute.

3. Perhaps we might venture here to read—'and only they.' In the next line, 'whom' for 'who' is probably the poet's own license or oversight.

4. It is, to say the least, singular to find in the most famous scene of a play so often reprinted and re-edited a word which certainly requires explanation passed over without remark from any one of the successive editors. When Gratiana, threatened by the daggers of her sons, exclaims—
    Are you so barbarous to set iron nipples
    Upon the breast that gave you suck?
Vindice retorts, in reply to her appeal—
            That breast
        Is turned to quarled poison.
    This last epithet is surely unusual enough to call for some attempt at interpretation. But none whatever has hitherto been offered. In the seventh line following from this one there is another textual difficulty. The edition now before me, Eld's of 1608, reads literally thus:—
    Vind. Ah is it possible, *Thou onely*, you powers on hie,
    That women should dissemble when they die.
Lamb was content to read,
        Ah, is it possible, you powers on high,
and so forth. Perhaps the two obviously corrupt words in italics may contain a clue to the right reading, and this may be it.
    Ah!
    Is't possible, you heavenly powers on high,
    That women should dissemble when they die?

WILLIAM ROWLEY

c. 1585–1626

Little is known about William Rowley's early life, except that he was probably born in 1585. He first appeared in London around 1607, working as an actor and playwright. From 1609 to 1617 he was with the Duke of York's Men, later to become Prince Charles's Company. He is known to have worked with the King's Company in 1623 and supposedly played the role of the fat clown in numerous stage productions.

Rowley's name appears in connection with over fifty plays. He collaborated with Dekker, Massinger, Webster, and others. His best-known collaborations were with Thomas Middleton and include *A Faire Quarrell* (c.1616), *The World Tost at Tennis* (1620), *The Changeling* (1622), and *The Spanish Gipsie* (1623). Among Rowley's other notable collaborative efforts are *The Witch of Edmonton* (1621), written with Dekker and Ford, and *A Cure for a Cuckold*, written with Webster. Rowley also is credited with having written four plays single-handedly, *Alls Lost by Lust; A New Wonder, a Woman Never Vext; a Shoo-maker a Gentleman;* and *A Match at Mid-night*, all published posthumously. Rowley also published a prose pamphlet, *A Search for Money* (1609), in which he satirizes London society. Rowley died in February 1626.

An Author that flourish'd in the Reign of King *Charles* the First; and was sometime a Member of *Pembroke* Hall in *Cambridge.* I can say nothing further of his Life or Country; but as to his Poetry, and his intimate Acquaintance with the prime Poets of that Age, I can speak at large. He was not only beloved by those Great Men, *Shakespear, Fletcher,* and *Johnson;* but likewise writ with the former, *The Birth of Merlin.* Besides what he joyned in writing with poets of the second Magnitude, as *Heywood, Middleton, Day* and *Webster;* as you may see under each of their Names; our Author has four Plays in print of his own Writing, of which take the following Account; viz.

All's lost by Lust, a Tragedy divers times acted by the Lady *Elizabeth's* Servants; and with great applause at the *Phœnix* in *Drury-Lane,* and printed 4o. *Lond.* 1633. This is a good old Play, and the Story it self may be read in the *Spanish* Histories: See *Mariana* Lib. 21, 22, 23. *Suritta's Annales, &c.* Lib. I. C. I. *Turquet,* L. 3. C. 30. As to *Margaretta's* Design'd Revenge on her Husband *Antonio,* read the *Unfortunate Lovers,* Novel the 3.

Match at Midnight, a plesant Comedy acted by the Children of the Revels; and printed 4o, *Lond.* 1633. The Plot of *Alexander Bloodhound's* being hid by *Jarvis* under the Widow's Bed, is founded on an old Story inserted in the *English Rogue,* part 4. Ch. 19.

Shoomaker's a Gentleman, a Comedy printed 4o. *Lond.* ——Not having this Play by me at present, I cannot inform my Reader where it was acted, or when printed. But this I know, that it has not many Years since been revived at the Theatre in *Dorset-Garden,* and been formerly acted abroad in the Country: and the Comical part of it, is an usual Entertainment at *Bartholomew* and *Southwarke* Fairs; it being a Copy to which all Stroling Companies lay claim to. The Play is founded on a stitcht Pamphlet in quarto, called *The History of the Gentle-Craft.* The Reader may find an Epilogue printed in *Duffet's* Poems, p. 60. writ for this Play, when 'twas revived.

New Wonder, a Woman never vext; a pleasant Comedy, sundry times acted, and printed 4o. *Lond.* 1632. That passage of the Widows finding her Wedding-Ring, which she dropp'd in crossing the *Thames,* in the Belly of a Fish which her Maid bought accidentally in the Market, is founded either upon the Story of *Polycrates* of *Samos,* as the Author may read at large in *Herodotus,* Lib. 3 *sive Thalia;* or upon the like Story related of one *Anderson* of Newcastle, by Doctor *Fuller,* in his *Worthies of* England.

I know of nothing else written by our Author, neither can I tell the time of his Death, and therefore I must leave it to Persons of better Information to acquaint the World, with more particulars of his Life, whilst I hasten to an Account of his Names sake.—GERARD LANGBAINE, *An Account of the English Dramatick Poets,* 1691

That a writer who was deemed a worthy assistant in such plays as *The Witch of Edmonton, The Thracian Wonder,* and *The Spanish Gipsey,* must have possessed no very inferior abilities, can admit of little doubt, and is confirmed indeed by his own exclusive compositions; for *A Match at Midnight,* and *All's Lost by Lust,* the former in the comic, and the latter in the tragic, department of his art, evince, in incident and humour, in character and in pathos, powers which repel the charge of mediocrity. Upon the whole, however, we consider him as ranking last in the roll of worthies who have thus far graced our pages.—NATHAN DRAKE, *Shakespeare and His Times,* 1817, Vol. 2, p. 570

Though his name is found in one instance affixed to a piece conjointly with Shakespeare's, he is generally classed only in the third rank of our dramatists. His Muse is evidently a plebeian nymph, and had not been educated in the school of the Graces. His most tolerable production is the *New Wonder, or a Woman Never Vext.* Its drafts of citizen life and manners have an air of reality and honest truth—the situations and characters are forcible, and the sentiments earnest and unaffected.—THOMAS CAMPBELL, *Specimens of the British Poets,* 1819

William Rowley, like certain other authors of merit in other departments or periods of our literature, seems to have cared but little for the kind of reputation which is made by the arts of *réclame.* No doubt there is justice in the demand:

> In full recompensacioun
> Of good worke, give us good renoun.

But William Rowley would seem to have been one of that minority among men of letters to whom, even before the days of journalism and its compensations, a personal literary reputation has always been more or less a matter of indifference. At all events, he cared little or nothing for the undivided empire of a title-page. With Middleton . . . he collaborated in the production of at least four extant pieces, in which the respective share of each author, if determinable at all, can hardly be pronounced upon with certainty, even where the test of versification comes to our aid. So far as this is concerned, there can be no doubt that there are to be distinguished in these joint plays (*The Spanish Gypsy, A Fair Quarrel,* and *The Changeling;* and the masque *The World Tost at Tennis*) two styles of blank verse, the one rough in form, and remarkably free in the use of unaccented syllables and the inversion of feet, and further marked by a relative paucity of feminine endings,—the other different in each of these respects, and at the same time closely resembling the verse ordinarily employed by Middleton. In Rowley's case, however, the evidence of plays written by him solely, though so far as I am acquanted with it, generally corroborative of the conclusion that in the above-named points his verse differed entirely from Middleton's, is at the best insufficient to identify the versification of so productive and accommodating a writer with anything like certainty. The argument therefore must rest in the main upon our knowledge of Middleton. William Rowley is likewise stated to have co-operated as a dramatist with Dekker, Thomas Heywood, Day, George Wilkins, Fletcher, Webster, and Massinger; although with regard to the last-named two authors modern criticism suggests important modifications of traditional statements. At all events, Langbaine's assertion that Shakespere was associated with William Rowley in the authorship of *The Birth of Merlin* may be summarily rejected. But a ready ear may at the same time be lent to the previous statement of the same chronicler that he was beloved by Shakspere, Fletcher, and Jonson, although no evidence is supplied in support of this pleasant tradition. . . .

Not more than four plays are known to have been printed purporting to have been written by William Rowley without the co-operation of another author. The first of these in date of publication is the comedy entitled *A New Wonder, a Woman Never Vexed* (printed 1632).

This comedy was evidently intended to appeal to the sympathies of the sort of audience for whom plays dealing with traditions of the City of London were as a rule, primarily at all events, designed. It is, however, a noteworthy play, which would of itself prove its author to have been a dramatist deficient neither in skill nor in power. A genuinely dramatic use is made in it of the story of Sir Stephen Foster, as told by Stow, Strype, and other authorities. This City worthy, after having been himself at one time a prisoner in Ludgate, was raised to wealth and honour (he was ultimately elected Lord Mayor) by marriage with a compassionate widow, with whose consent he afterwards became the benefactor of the prison where he had formerly been confined. Rowley has invented the character of the son, who against his father's wish assists his uncle in the season of his troubles, and afterwards succours his father himself when he has in his turn been overtaken by calamity. The character of the widow, whose persistent good fortune resembles the famous Herodotean episode of Polycrates (of which an English version appeared in 1627 in a tract called *Vox Piscis*), except in so far that her kindness disarms Nemesis, is likewise an original, though perhaps not a very striking, conception. The pathos is by no means deep, and the humour the reverse of refined; while the change in the disposition of the scapegrace uncle is too sudden to leave any moral impression. But the action as a whole is brisk, the tone healthy, and the writing vigorous.

In 1633 was printed William Rowley's tragedy of *All's Lost by Lust,* founded on a Spanish story called *The Unfortunate Lovers.* It was revived after the Restoration, when its performance was witnessed by Pepys under unfortunate circumstances, and again under the title of *The Conquest of Spain,* an adaptation attributed to Miss Pix, in 1705. In the same year as this

sanguinary tragedy was printed the comedy of *A Match at Midnight,* which both Mr. Fleay and Mr. Bullen consider to have been altered by Rowley from an original play by Middleton. It must in any case be described as an outrageous farce with an extremely curt moral. Its heroine is a pretended widow, whose pursuers are baffled after five acts of intolerable grossness, unredeemed even by the vivacity and humour which the piece undeniably displays. The Welshman Randall is one of the most amusing specimens of a favourite personage of Elisabethan comedy. Lasty, *A Shoomaker a Gentleman, with the Life and Death of the Cripple that stole the Weather-cock at Paules* (thus runs the full title of the entry in Stationers' Registers of this exposition of the arts and crafts of City life), was printed in 1638, but acted, as seems certain, by 1609). It is stated to be founded on the tract, printed in 1598, of *Crispin and Crispianus, or The History of the Gentle Craft.*

It would be worse than pretentious to insist upon the impression conveyed by two of the four plays noticed above, as if it could supply a basis for an opinion concerning William Rowley's distinctive qualities as a dramatist. . . . No doubt can be entertained either as to the flexibility of his genius, or as to the rare vigour which it infused into both his tragic and his comic work. In more than one play in which he had a hand we recognise a perception of theatrical effect that we feel strongly inclined to trace to his co-operation; for a gift of this kind, although it comes by nature, is only perfected by actual and prolonged experience of the stage. A performer—as we know him to have been occasionally—of low comedy parts was not likely as a writer to refine too nicely; but I imagine him to have possessed a sureness of touch which to a dramatist is more than delicacy of pathos or subtlety of wit. Can he, however, be supposed to have worked otherwise than with a brush at times as rough as it was always ready? But to what degree, in enhancing the effect, he occasionally marred the charm of other men's conceptions, and in what measure creations essentially due to his own genius were subjected to analogous treatment at the hands of his coadjutors, are questions which his system of authorship has, for better or for worse, made it impossible definitely to answer.—ADOLPHUS WILLIAM WARD, *A History of English Dramatic Literature* (1875), 1899, Vol. 2, pp. 540–45

The part taken by Rowley in ⟨*Fair Quarrel*⟩ is easy for any tiro in criticism to verify. The rough and crude genius of that perverse and powerful writer is not seen here by any means at its best. I cannot as yet lay claim to an exhaustive acquaintance with his works, but judging from what I have read of them I should say that his call was rather towards tragedy than towards comedy; that his mastery of severe and serious emotion was more genuine and more natural than his command of satirical or grotesque realism. The tragedy in which he has grappled with the subject afterwards so differently handled in the first and greatest of Landor's tragedies is to me of far more interest and value than such comedies as that which kindled the enthusiasm of a loyal Londoner in the civic sympathies of Lamb. Disfigured as it is towards the close by indulgence in mere horror and brutality after the fashion of Andronicus or Jeronimo, it has more beauty and power and pathos in its best scenes than a reader of his comedies—as far as I know them— would have expected. There are noticeable points of likeness— apart from the coincidence of subject—between this and Mr. Caldwell Roscoe's noble tragedy of *Violenzia.* But in the underplot of *A Fair Quarrel* Rowley's besetting faults of coarseness and quaintness, stiffness and roughness, are so flagrant and obtrusive that we cannot avoid a feeling of regret and irritation at such untimely and inharmonious evidence of his partnership with a poet of finer if not of sturdier genius. The same sense of discord and inequality will be aroused on comparison of the worse with the better parts of *The Old Law*. The clumsiness and dullness of the farcical interludes can hardly be paralleled in the rudest and hastiest scenes of Middleton's writing: while the sweet and noble dignity of the finer passages have the stamp of his ripest and tenderest genius on every line and in every cadence. But for sheer bewildering incongruity there is no play known to me which can be compared with *The Mayor of Queenborough*. Here again we find a note so dissonant and discordant in the lighter parts of the dramatic concert that we seem at once to recognize the harsher and hoarser instrument of Rowley. The farce is even more extravagantly and preposterously mistimed and misplaced than that which disfigures the play just mentioned: but I thoroughly agree with Mr. Bullen's high estimate of the power displayed and maintained throughout the tragic and poetic part of this drama; to which no previous critic has ever vouchsafed a word of due acknowledgement. The story is ugly and unnatural, but its repulsive effect is tranfigured or neutralized by the charm of tender or passionate poetry; and it must be admitted that the hideous villainy of Vortiger and Horsus affords an opening for subsequent scenic effects of striking and genuine tragical interest. . . .

In the last and the greatest work ⟨*The Honest Whore*⟩ which bears their united names—a work which should suffice to make either name immortal if immortality were other than an accidental attribute of genius—the very highest capacity of either poet is seen at its very best. There is more of mere poetry, more splendour of style and vehemence of verbal inspiration, in the work of other poets then writing for the stage: the two masterpieces of Webster are higher in tone at their highest, more imaginative and more fascinating in their expression of terrible or of piteous wrath: there are more superb harmonies, more glorious raptures of ardent and eloquent music, in the sometimes unsurpassed and unsurpassable poetic passion of Cyril Tourneur. But even Webster's men seem but splendid sketches, as Tourneur's seem but shadowy or fiery outlines, beside the perfect and living figure of De Flores. The man is so horribly human, so fearfully and wonderfully natural, in his single-hearted brutality of devotion, his absolute absorption of soul and body by one consuming force of passionately cynical desire, that we must go to Shakespeare for an equally original and an equally unquestionable revelation of indubitable truth. And in no play by Beaumont and Fletcher is the concord between the two partners more singularly complete in unity of spirit and of style than throughout the tragic part of this play. The underplot from which it most unluckily and absurdly derives its title is very stupid, rather coarse, and almost vulgar: but the two great parts of Beatrice and De Flores are equally consistent, coherent and sustained, in the scenes obviously written by Middleton and in the scenes obviously written by Rowley. The subordinate part taken by Middleton in Dekker's play of *The Honest Whore* is difficult to discern from the context or to verify by inner evidence: though some likeness to his realistic or photographic method may be admitted as perceptible in the admirable picture of Bellafront's morning reception at the opening of the second act of the first part. But here we may assert with fair confidence that the first and the last scenes of the play bear the indisputable sign-manual of William Rowley. His vigorous and vivid genius, his somewhat hard and curt directness of style and manner, his clear and trenchant power of straightforward presentation or exposition, may be traced in every line as plainly as the hand of Middleton must be recognized in the main part of the tragic

action intervening. To Rowley therefore must be assigned the very high credit of introducing and of dismissing with adequate and even triumphant effect the strangely original tragic figure which owes its fullest and finest development to the genius of Middleton. To both poets alike must unqualified and equal praise be given for the subtle simplicity of skill with which they make us appreciate the fatal and foreordained affinity between the ill-favoured, rough-mannered, broken-down gentleman, and the headstrong unscrupulous unobservant girl whose very abhorrence of him serves only to fling her down from her high station of haughty beauty into the very clutch of his ravenous and pitiless passion. Her cry of horror and astonishment at first perception of the price to be paid for a service she had thought to purchase with mere money is so wonderfully real in its artless and ingenuous sincerity that Shakespeare himself could hardly have bettered it:

> Why, 'tis impossible thou canst be so wicked,
> And shelter such a cunning cruelty,
> To make his death the murderer of my honour!

> —ALGERNON CHARLES SWINBURNE, "Thomas
> Middleton," *Nineteenth Century*, Jan. 1886,
> pp. 145–52

His gift in comedy can be . . . easily observed, and in particular *A New Wonder* is a typical instance of it. Even here, however, we feel that to be dogmatic would be to be rash, and that Rowley holds, in existing drama, such a subaltern position that it is very difficult to form an opinion with regard to his talent. He is a kitchen-maid rather than a cook, and it is impossible to be certain what share he has had in the preparation of any comic feast that is set before us. So far, however, as we are able to form an opinion, we are apt to consider that the influence of Rowley upon Middleton was an unwholesome one. Middleton was strangely compacted of gold and clay, of the highest gifts and of the lowest subterfuges of the playwright. In Rowley, all that was not clay was iron, and it is difficult to believe that he sympathized with or encouraged his friend's ethereal eccentricities. That Rowley had a hand in the underplot of several of Middleton's noblest productions does not alter our conviction that his own sentiments were rather brutal and squalid, and that he cared for little but to pander to the sensational instincts of the groundlings. The mutual attitude of these friends has been compared to that of Beaumont and Fletcher, but it is hard to think of Middleton in any other light than as a poet unequally yoked with one whose temper was essentially prosaic.—EDMUND GOSSE, *The Jacobean Poets*, 1894, pp. 130–31

A tradition handed down by Langbaine records that Rowley was beloved by those great men, Shakespeare, Fletcher, and Jonson; while his partnership in so many plays by a variety of writers has been regarded as proof of the amiability of his character. As a useful and safe collaborator he seems to have been only less in demand than Dekker. His hand is often difficult to identify, though his verse may generally be detected by its metrical harshness and irregularity. His style is disfigured by a monotonously extravagant emphasis, and he is sadly wanting in artistic form and refinement. He had, however, a rare vein of whimsical humour (cf. the episode of Gnotho in the *Old Law*, iii.1), and occasionally he shows an unexpected mastery of tragic pathos. Drake ranks him in the same class with Massinger, Middleton, Heywood, Ford, Dekker, and Webster, but puts him last in this category.—THOMAS SECCOMBE, *Dictionary of National Biography*, 1897, Vol. 49, p. 363

THOMAS MIDDLETON

c. 1580–1627

Thomas Middleton, the son of a bricklayer, was probably born in 1580 in London. After the death of his father, his mother remarried a grocer, Thomas Harvey, with whom Middleton was involved repeatedly in legal conflicts over his late father's estate. In 1598 Middleton entered Queen's College, Oxford, and it is believed he remained there for two years and left without a degree.

The *Wisdom of Solomon*, a verse rendering of the biblical story into English, was published in 1597. Middleton, however, is known mainly for his dramas. *The Mayor of Quinborough*, published after his death in 1661, may actually be Middleton's first play. Most of his other plays are satirical comedies of contemporary manners, including *Michaelmas Terme* (1607), *The Trick to Catch the Old One* (1607), *A Mad World, My Masters* (1608), and *A Chast Mayd in Cheape-Side* (c. 1613). Middleton often collaborated with other dramatists, especially William Rowley, Thomas Dekker, and John Webster. In 1608 a comedy written with Dekker, *The Roaring Girle*, was performed. With Rowley, Middleton wrote *The Changeling* (1622) which is considered, along with *Women Beware Women*, among his best tragedies. Middleton also wrote tragicomedies, including his collaboration with Rowley on *A Faire Quarrell* (c. 1615). Middleton was a prolific dramatist, having participated in the writing of dozens of dramas. Some critics have argued that he may even have written the well-known *Revenger's Tragedy*, and not Cyril Tourneur, as is generally thought.

Middleton received frequent commissions to write and produce the Lord Mayor's pageants and other civic entertainments. In 1620 he was appointed the city chronologer of London, a post he held until his death. One of Middleton's last plays, a political satire about relations between the Spanish and English crowns, entitled *A Game of Chesse* (1624), was eventually banned by the Privy Council for violating a law which prohibited the stage depiction of living monarchs. Two years after the difficulties surrounding *A Game of Chesse*, city officials again were irritated with Middleton over what they considered a poorly performed pageant that he had prepared.

Middleton died soon after, and was buried on July 4, 1627, in Newington Butts, Surrey.

Personal

Quicke are your wits, sharp your conceits,
　　Short, and more sweete your layes:
Quicke, but no wit, sharpe, no conceit,
　　Short, and lesse sweete, my praise.
　　—JOHN WEEVER, "Ad Ro: Allot, & Chr. Middleton," *Epigrammes in the Oldest Cut and Newest Fashion*, 1599

An Author of good Esteem in the Reign of King *Charles* the First. He was Contemporary with those Famous Poets *Johnson*, *Fletcher*, *Massinger* and *Rowley*, in whose Friendship he had a large Share; and tho' he came short of the two former in parts, yet like the *Ivy* by the Assistance of the *Oak*, (being joyn'd with them in several Plays) he clim'd up to some considerable height of Reputation. He joyn'd with *Fletcher* and *Johnson*, in a Play called *The Widow*, of which we have already spoken . . . in the Account of *Johnson*; and certainly most Men will allow, That he that was thought fit to be receiv'd into a *Triumvirate*, by two such Great Men, was no common Poet. He club'd with *Massinger* and *Rowley* in Writing the *Old Law*, as before I have remarked already. . . . He was likewise assisted by *Rowley* in three Plays, of which we shall presently give an Account; and in those Plays which he writ alone, there are several Comedies; as *Michaelmass-Term*, *Mayor of Quinborough*, &c which speak him a Dramatick Poet of the Second Rank.—GERARD LANGBAINE, *An Account of the English Dramatick Poets*, 1691

General

Middleton's style was not marked by any peculiar quality of his own, but was made up, in equal proportions, of the faults and excellences common to his contemporaries. In his *Women Beware Women*, there is a rich marrowy vein of internal sentiment, with fine occasional insight into human nature, and cool cutting irony of expression. He is lamentably deficient in the plot and denouement of the story. It is like the rough draught of a tragedy, with a number of fine things thrown in, and the best made use of first; but it tends to no fixed goal, and the interest decreases, instead of increasing, as we read on, for want of previous arrangment and an eye to the whole. We have fine studies of heads, a piece of richly-coloured drapery, 'a foot, an hand, an eye from Nature drawn, that's worth a history'; but the groups are ill disposed, nor are the figures proportioned to each other or the size of the canvas. The author's power is *in* the subject, not *over* it; or he is in possession of excellent materials, which he husbands very ill. This character, though it applies more particularly to Middleton, might be applied generally to the age. Shakspear alone seemed to stand over his work, and to do what he pleased with it. He saw to the end of what he was about, and with the same faculty of lending himself to the impulses of Nature and the impression of the moment, never forgot that he himself had a task to perform, nor the place which each figure ought to occupy in his general design.—The characters of Livia, of Bianca, of Leantio and his Mother, in the play of which I am speaking, are all admirably drawn. The art and malice of Livia shew equal want of principle and acquaintance with the world; and the scene in which she holds the mother in suspense, while she betrays the daughter into the power of the profligate Duke, is a masterpiece of dramatic skill. The proneness of Bianca to tread the primrose path of pleasure, after she has made the first false step, and her sudden transition from unblemished virtue to the most abandoned vice, in which she is notably seconded by her mother-in-law's ready submission to the temptations of wealth and power, form a true and striking picture. The first intimation of the intrigue that follows, is given in a way that is not a little remarkable for simplicity and acuteness. Bianca says,

Did not the Duke look up? Methought he saw us.

To which the more experienced mother answers,

> That's every one's conceit that sees a Duke.
> If he looks stedfastly, he looks straight at them,
> When he perhaps, good careful gentleman,
> Never minds any, but the look he casts
> Is at his own intentions, and his object
> Only the public good.

It turns out however, that he had been looking at them, and not 'at the public good.' The moral of this tragedy is rendered more impressive from the manly, independent character of Leantio in the first instance, and the manner in which he dwells, in a sort of doting abstraction, on his own comforts, in being possessed of a beautiful and faithful wife. . . .

The *Witch* of Middleton is his most remarkable performance; both on its own account, and from the use that Shakespear has made of some of the characters and speeches in his *Macbeth*. Though the employment which Middleton has given to Hecate and the rest, in thwarting the purposes and perplexing the business of familiar and domestic life, is not so grand or appalling as the more stupendous agency which Shakespear has assigned them, yet it is not easy to deny the merit of the first invention to Middleton, who has embodied the existing superstitions of the time, respecting that anomalous class of beings, with a high spirit of poetry, of the most grotesque and fanciful kind. The songs and incantations made use of are very nearly the same. The other parts of this play are not so good; and the solution of the principal difficulty, by Antonio's falling down a trap-door, most lame and impotent.—WILLIAM HAZLITT, *Lectures on the Dramatic Literature of the Age of Elizabeth*, 1820

Middleton partakes of the poetry and sweetness of Decker, but not to the same height: and he talks more at random. You hardly know what to make of the dialogue or stories of some of his plays. But he has more fancy; and there is one character of his (De Flores in the *Changeling*) which, for effect at once tragical, probable, and poetical, surpasses anything I know of in the drama of domestic life. Middleton has the honour of having furnished part of the witch poetry to *Macbeth*, and of being conjoined with it also in the powerful and beautiful music of Locke.—LEIGH HUNT, *Imagination and Fancy*, 1844

Middleton's rank among our dramatists has been the subject of dispute among the few critics who have hitherto bestowed much attention upon this unduly neglected author; but it is quite unnecessary to construct tables of precedence in surveying any period or department of literature. The modesty with which Middleton himself appears to have abstained from any endeavour to assert his claims to fame or eminence of any kind pleads in his favour, and it may be asserted without fear of objection that he possessed not a few among the many qualities which constitute a dramatist of the order next to the highest. In the works attributed to him which exhibit the nearest approach to tragic power he had the advantage of William Rowley's co-operation; and although it is impossible to determine in each case how much of the result obtained was due to the rough and ready force of his coadjutor and to his trained insight into the theatrical effect of both tragic and comic work, we may at all events conclude that the entire credit of these compositions cannot be attributed to Middleton. He certainly understood the secret of dramatic action, whether serious or comic in the nature of its interest; and upon the whole his plays are strikingly rapid in their movement. It was his usual practice to combine two plots into a single play; and this he ordinarily effected with much constructive skill, although he worked too hurriedly to attend to minor unevennesses, and here and there forgot in his haste to carry out fully the moral lesson which he intended to convey.

What, however, appears to me most notable in Middleton is the absence of effort, which, if combined with a generally true instinct of effect, is a sure sign of genuine artistic power. Something of this may be due to the circumstances of his breeding and training. Apart from the gross indecency which was a characteristic of his times rather than of his class, he writes with the light touch of a well-bred gentleman, and with a habitual grace wanting to the slovenly Dekker on the one hand, and to the pedantic Marston on the other. Both in tragic and in comic composition he was averse to anything like exaggeration, and it is quite possible that the tendency to self-restraint which had become second nature to him at times interfered with the theatrical effectiveness of his work, when unmixed with stimulants of coarser derivation. He seems far from desirous of exhibiting his accomplishments as a reader, although he must have been acquainted with various kinds of literature—thus it is pleasing to note his evident fondness for Chaucer. But while he writes with ease, and while as a rule his versification, which resembles Fletcher's, is fluent and his prose style perfectly natural, he cannot be said to show any lack of force, though it is not his way to seek effect from mere strength of phrase. From bombast he is upon the whole singularly free.

More than ordinarily successful in romantic comedy, at times even here very felicitous in his choice of subjects, he seems to exhibit his full powers when in contact with his native soil. His imagination seems to have been strong enough to penetrate into regions of abnormal passion and of impulses such as seem to swallow up the whole being of man; but, upon the whole, his comedies dealing with the national life of his own age seem most congenial to his gifts, while constituting as a whole the truest dramatic representation of the sphere within which they move. He is less intent upon reproducing strong and enduring types of the Jonsonian kind, than upon drawing faithful pictures of men and manners such as shall in an unlaboured manner bring home the straightforward lessons of morality and virtue which it is in the power of his comic muse to teach. In general, therefore, it is less easy for the reader of Middleton to recall particular characters from his dramas, than to bear witness to the admirable effect created by the *ensemble* of such comedies as *Michaelmas Term, A Trick to Catch the Old One*, or *A Mad World, My Masters*. If these plays may be taken as fair examples of the comedy of manners which the age enjoyed, and by enjoying acknowledged as true, the most notable significance of Middleton's works in our dramatic literature will become apparent. For his whole genius was free from any tendency to exaggeration, while of his moral aim there is no reason whatever to doubt. It may be questioned whether he was cast in a sufficiently strong mould to impress his age with the purpose which animated his satire; but there is no hollowness about his principles as to the conduct of life, and no unreality about his method of enforcing them. In brilliancy and, regarding his works as a whole, in depth of either pathos or humour he falls below many of his fellow-dramatists; but in lightness, vivacity, and sureness of touch it would be difficult—with one exception always—to name his superior.—ADOLPHUS WILLIAM WARD, *A History of English Dramatic Literature* (1875), 1899, Vol. 2, pp. 538–40

A wild moon riding high from cloud to cloud,
　　That sees and sees not, glimmering far beneath,
　　Hell's children revel along the shuddering heath
With dirge-like mirth and raiment like a shroud:

A worse fair face than witchcraft's, passion-proud,
  With brows blood-flecked behind their bridal wreath
  And lips that bade the assassin's sword find sheath
Deep in the heart whereto love's heart was vowed:
A game of close contentious crafts and creeds
  Played till white England bring black Spain to shame:
A son's bright sword and brighter soul, whose deeds
  High conscience lights for mother's love and fame:
Pure gipsy flowers, and poisonous courtly weeds:
  Such tokens and such trophies crown thy name.
       —ALGERNON CHARLES SWINBURNE, "Thomas
       Middleton," *Sonnets on English Dramatic
       Poets,* 1882

There are critics who station poets in order of merit as a school-master ranges his pupils in the classroom. This process I do not intend to adopt with Middleton. The test of a poet's real power ultimately resolves itself into the question whether he leaves a permanent impression on the mind of a capable reader. . . .

Middleton may be charged with extravagance and coarseness. True: but he could make the blood tingle; he could barb his words so that they pierce the heart through and through. If *The Changeling, Women Beware Women, The Spanish Gipsy,* and *A Fair Quarrel* do not justify Middleton's claims to be considered a great dramatist, I know not which of Shakespeare's followers is worthy of the title.—A. H. BULLEN, "Introduction" to *The Works of Thomas Middleton,* 1885, Vol. 1, pp. xcii–xciii

It has not been usual to put Thomas Middleton in the front rank among the dramatists immediately second to Shakespere; but I have myself no hesitation in doing so. If he is not such a poet as Webster, he is even a better, and certainly a more versatile, dramatist; and if his plays are inferior as plays to those of Fletcher and Massinger, he has a mastery of the very highest tragedy, which neither of them could attain. Except the best scenes of *The White Devil,* and *The Duchess of Malfi,* there is nothing out of Shakespere that can match the best scenes of *The Changeling;* while Middleton had a comic faculty, in which, to all appearance, Webster was entirely lacking. . . .

Middleton's acknowledged, or at least accepted, habit of collaboration in most of the work usually attributed to him, and the strong suspicion, if not more than suspicion, that he collaborated in other plays, afford endless opportunity for the exercise of a certain kind of criticism. By employing another kind we can discern quite sufficiently a strong individuality in the work that is certainly, in part or in whole, his; and we need not go farther. He seems to have had three different kinds of dramatic aptitude, in all of which he excelled. The larger number of his plays consist of examples of the rattling comedy of intrigue and manners, often openly representing London life as it was, sometimes transplanting what is an evident picture of home manners to some foreign scene apparently for no other object than to make it more attractive to the spectators. To any one at all acquainted with the Elizabethan drama their very titles speak them. These titles are *Blurt Master Constable, Michaelmas Term, A Trick to Catch the Old One, The Family of Love* [a sharp satire on the Puritans], *A Mad World, My Masters, No Wit No Help Like a Woman's, A Chaste Maid in Cheapside, Anything for a Quiet Life, More Dissemblers besides Women.* As with all the humour-comedies of the time, the incidents are not unfrequently very improbable, and the action is conducted with such intricacy and want of clearly indicated lines, that it is sometimes very difficult to follow. At the same time, Middleton has a faculty almost peculiar to himself of carrying, it might almost be said of hustling, the reader or

spectator along, so that he has no time to stop and consider defects. His characters are extremely human and lively, his dialogue seldom lags, his catastrophes, if not his plots, are often ingenious, and he is never heavy. The moral atmosphere of his plays is not very refined,—by which I do not at all mean merely that he indulges in loose situations and loose language. All the dramatists from Shakespere downwards do that; and Middleton is neither better nor worse than the average. But in striking contrast to Shakespere and to others, Middleton has no kind of poetical morality in the sense in which the term poetical justice is better known. He is not too careful that the rogues shall not have the best of it; he makes his most virtuous and his vilest characters hobnob together very contentedly; and he is, in short, though never brutal, like the post-Restoration school, never very delicate. The style, however, of these works of his did not easily admit of such delicacy, except in the infusion of a strong romantic element such as that which Shakespere almost always infuses. Middleton has hardly done it more than once—in the charming comedy of *The Spanish Gipsy,*—and the result there is so agreeable that the reader only wishes he had done it oftener.

Usually, however, when his thoughts took a turn of less levity than in these careless humorous studies of contemporary life, he devoted himself not to the higher comedy, but to tragedy of a very serious class, and when he did this an odd phenomenon generally manifested itself. In Middleton's idea of tragedy, as in that of most of the playwrights, and probably all the playgoers of his day, a comic underplot was a necessity; and, as we have seen, he was himself undoubtedly able enough to furnish such a plot. But either because he disliked mixing his tragic and comic veins, or for some unknown reason, he seems usually to have called in on such occasions the aid of Rowley, a vigorous writer of farce, who had sometimes been joined with him even in his comic work. Now, not only was Rowley little more than a farce writer, but he seems to have been either unable to make, or quite careless of making, his farce connect itself in any tolerable fashion with the tragedy of which it formed a nominal part. The result is seen in its most perfect imperfection in the two plays of *The Mayor of Queenborough* and *The Changeling,* both named from their comic features, and yet containing tragic scenes, the first of a very high order, the second of an order only overtopped by Shakespere at his best. The humours of the cobbler Mayor of Queenborough in the one case, of the lunatic asylum and the courting of its keeper's wife in the other, are such very mean things that they can scarcely be criticised. But the desperate love of Vortiger for Rowena in *The Mayor,* and the villainous plots against his chaste wife, Castiza, are real tragedy. Even these, however, fall far below the terrible loves, if loves they are to be called, of Beatrice-Joanna, the heroine of *The Changeling,* and her servant, instrument, and murderer, De Flores. The plot of the tragic part of this play is intricate and not wholly savoury. It is sufficient to say that Beatrice having enticed De Flores to murder a lover whom she does not love, that so she may marry a lover whom she does love, is suddenly met by the murderer's demand of her honour as the price of his services. She submits, and afterwards has to purchase fresh aid of murder from him by a continuance of her favours that she may escape detection by her husband. Thus, roughly described, the theme may look like the undigested horrors of *Lust's Dominion,* of *The Insatiate Countess,* and of *The Revenger's Tragedy.* It is, however, poles asunder from them. The girl, with her southern recklessness of anything but her immediate desires, and her southern indifference to deceiving the very man she loves, is sufficiently remarkable, as she stands out of the canvas. But De Flores,—

the broken gentleman, reduced to the position of a mere dependant, the libertine whose want of personal comeliness increases his mistress's contempt for him, the murderer double and treble dyed, as audacious as he is treacherous, and as cool and ready as he is fiery in passion,—is a study worthy to be classed at once with Iago, and inferior only to Iago in their class. The several touches with which these two characters and their situations are brought out are as Shakesperian as their conception, and the whole of that part of the play in which they figure is one of the most wonderful triumphs of English or of any drama. . . .

Two other remarkable plays of Middleton's fall with some differences under the same second division of his works. These are *The Witch* and *Women Beware Women*. Except for the inevitable and rather attractive comparison with *Macbeth*, *The Witch* is hardly interesting. It consists of three different sets of scenes most inartistically blended,—an awkward and ineffective variation on the story of Alboin, Rosmunda and the skull for a serious main plot, some clumsy and rather unsavoury comic or tragi-comic interludes, and the witch scenes. The two first are very nearly worthless; the third is intrinsically, though far below *Macbeth*, interesting enough and indirectly more interesting because of the questions which have been started, as to the indebtedness of the two poets to each other. The best opinion seems to be that Shakespere most certainly did not copy Middleton, nor (a strange fancy of some) did he collaborate with Middleton, and that the most probable thing is that both borrowed their names, and some details from Reginald Scot's *Discovery of Witchcraft*. *Women Beware Women* on the other hand is one of Middleton's finest works, inferior only to *The Changeling* in part, and far superior to it as a whole. The temptation of Bianca, the newly-married wife, by the duke's instrument, a cunning and shameless woman, is the title-theme, and in this part again Middleton's Shakesperian verisimilitude and certainty of touch appears. The end of the play is something marred by a slaughter more wholesale even than that of *Hamlet*, and by no means so well justified. Lastly, *A Fair Quarrel* must be mentioned, because of the very high praise which it has received from Lamb and others. This praise has been directed chiefly to the situation of the quarrel between Captain Ager and his friend, turning on a question (the point of family honour), finely but perhaps a little tediously argued. The comic scenes, however, which are probably Rowley's, are in his best vein of bustling swagger.—GEORGE SAINTSBURY, *A History of Elizabethan Literature*, 1887, pp. 266–73

The strength of Middleton lies, not in his rather gross and careless comedies, but in his romantic dramas, his singularly imaginative tragedies and tragi-comedies. Lamb, although he seems scarcely to have appreciated Middleton, speaks with extreme felicity of his "exquisiteness of moral sensibility, making one to gush out tears of delight." There is, unfortunately, too much of Middleton in existence; a single volume might be selected which would give readers an exceedingly high impression of his genius. He had no lyrical gift, and his verse, although it is enlivened by a singularly brilliant and unexpected diction, is not in itself of any great beauty. There is no better example of Middleton's work, to which a student can be recommended, than the serious part of *The Changeling*. Mr. Bullen has spoken of the great scene between De Flores and Beatrice as "unequalled outside Shakespeare's greatest tragedies," and the praise can hardly be held excessive. The plot of *The Changeling*, which turns on the stratagem of a girl who, being in love with one man, and affianced to a second, turns to a third to extricate her from her difficulty, is in the highest

degree curious and novel. But when De Flores has been persuaded to murder Alonzo, Beatrice is no nearer to Alsemero; for De Flores and his insolent conditions stand in her way. At length she has to confess Alonzo's murder to her lover, and the play ends, crudely, in a cluster of deaths. But nothing in Jacobean drama is finer than the desperate flutterings of Beatrice, or the monstrous determination of De Flores.

Another great play of Middleton's is *The Spanish Gipsy*, but this is of a far less gloomy type, although it opens with menacing gravity. The air lightens as the plot develops, and we assist at length at the denoûment of a graceful and peaceful comedy, drawn on the combined lines of two stories from Cervantes. Some writers have considered that the finest of Middleton's plays is the tragedy of *Women Beware Women*, but to admit this would be to excuse too much what we may call the ethical tastelessness of the age. The story of *Women Beware Women* is so excessively disagreeable, and the play closes in a manner so odious, that the reader's sympathy is hopelessly alienated. This radical fault may perhaps disturb, but can scarcely destroy our appreciation of the beauty and invention of the style. The scene between Livia and the widow may be by Middleton or by Rowley; the polish and elasticity of the verse may probably induce us to conjecture the former. We have yet to mention, in analyzing Middleton's masterpieces, the passages which he contributed to *A Fair Quarrel*. The duel scene in which Captain Agar fights with his friend the colonel to avenge his mother's honour is the best-known existing page of Middleton, for Charles Lamb drew especial attention to it in his *Specimens*. That it is Middleton's can scarcely be questioned; all competent critics will agree with Mr. Bullen when he says, "to such a height of moral dignity and artistic excellence Rowley never attained."

The early comedies of Middleton are curiously incoherent in form; scarcely one but contains passages of high romantic beauty. Later on, his comic talent became more assured and less fitful, but the plays lose the Elizabethan flavour of romance; passages of pure poetry become rarer and rarer in them. It is very difficult to obtain any satisfaction out of such incongruous work as, for instance, *More Dissemblers besides Women*. On the other hand, *A Game of Chess*, which gained for Middleton more money and notoriety than all of his other works put together, is a patriotic comedy of real delicacy and distinction, and of all Middleton's nontragic plays is probably the one which may be studied with most satisfaction by the modern reader. Popular as political scandal made this play, it is yet almost incredible that the receipts at its performance amounted to fifteen hundred pounds, but if half of this is true, it must have thrown a flush of real success over the close of Middleton's laborious life.—EDMUND GOSSE, *The Jacobean Poets*, 1894, pp. 126–29

ALGERNON CHARLES SWINBURNE
"Thomas Middleton"
Nineteenth Century, January 1886, pp. 138–53

If it be true, as we are told on high authority, that the greatest glory of England is her literature and the greatest glory of English literature is its poetry, it is not less true that the greatest glory of English poetry lies rather in its dramatic than its epic or its lyric triumphs. The name of Shakespeare is above the names even of Milton and Coleridge and Shelley: and the names of his comrades in art and their immediate successors are above all but the highest names in any other province of our song. There is such an overflowing life, such a superb exuberance of abounding and exulting strength, in the dramatic poetry of the half-century extending from 1590 to 1640, that all other epochs of English literature seem as it were but half awake and half alive by comparison with this generation of giants and of gods. There is more sap in this than in any other branch of the national bay-tree: it has an energy in fertility which reminds us rather of the forest than the garden or the park. It is true that the weeds and briars of the underwood are but too likely to embarrass and offend the feet of the rangers and the gardeners who trim the level flower-plots or preserve the domestic game of enclosed and ordered lowlands in the tamer demesnes of literature. The sun is strong and the wind sharp in the climate which reared the fellows and the followers of Shakespeare. The extreme inequality and roughness of the ground must also be taken into account when we are disposed, as I for one have often been disposed, to wonder beyond measure at the apathetic ignorance of average students in regard of the abundant treasure to be gathered from this widest and most fruitful province in the poetic empire of England. And yet, since Charles Lamb threw open its gates to all comers in the ninth year of the present century, it cannot but seem strange that comparatively so few should have availed themselves of the entry to so rich and royal an estate. The subsequent labours of Mr. Dyce made the rough ways plain and the devious paths straight for all serious and worthy students. And now again Mr. Bullen has taken up a task than which none more arduous and important, none worthier of thanks and praise, can be undertaken by any English scholar. In his beautiful and valuable edition of Marlowe there are but two points to which exception may be taken. It was, I think, a fault of omission to exclude the apocryphal play of *Lust's Dominion* from a place in the appendix: it was, I am certain, a fault of commission to admit instead of it the much bepuffed and very puffy rubbish of the late Mr. Horne. That clever, versatile, and energetic writer never went so far out of his depth, or floundered so pitifully in such perilous waters, as when he ventured to put verses of his own into the mouth of Christopher Marlowe. These errors we must all hope to see rectified in a second issue of the text: and meantime we can but welcome with all possible gratitude and applause the magnificent series of old plays by unknown writers which we owe to the keen research and the fine appreciation of Marlowe's latest editor. Of these I may find some future occasion to speak: my present business is with the admirable poet who has been promoted to the second place in Mr. Bullen's collection of the English dramatists.

The selection of Middleton for so distinguished a place of honour may probably not approve itself to the judgment of all experts in dramatic literature. Charles Lamb, as they will all remember, would have advised the editor 'to begin with the collected plays of Heywood:' which as yet, like the plays of Dekker, of Marston, and of Chapman, remain unedited in any serious or scholarly sense of the term. The existing reprints merely reproduce, without adequate elucidation or correction, the corrupt and chaotic text of the worst early editions: while Middleton has for upwards of half a century enjoyed the privilege denied to men who are usually accounted his equals if not his superiors in poetic if not in dramatic genius. Even for an editor of the ripest learning and the highest ability there is comparatively little to do where Mr. Dyce has been before him in the field. However, we must all give glad and grateful welcome to a new edition of a noble poet who has never yet received his full meed of praise and justice: though our gratitude and our gladness may be quickened and dilated by the proverbial sense of further favours to come.

The first word of modern tribute to the tragic genius of Thomas Middleton was not spoken by Charles Lamb. Four years before the appearance of the priceless volume which established his fame for ever among all true lovers of English poetry by copious excerpts from five of his most characteristic works, Walter Scott, in a note on the fifty-sixth stanza of the second fytte of the metrical romance of *Sir Tristrem*, had given a passing word of recognition to the 'horribly striking' power of 'some passages' in Middleton's masterpiece: which was first reprinted eleven years later, in the fourth volume of Dilke's Old Plays. Lamb, surprisingly enough, has given not a single extract from that noble tragedy: it was reserved for Leigh Hunt, when speaking of its author, to remark that 'there is one character of his (De Flores in *The Changeling*) which, for effect at once tragical, probable, and poetical, surpasses anything I know of in the drama of domestic life.' The praise is not a whit too high: the truth could not have been better said.

The play with which Mr. Bullen, altering the arrangment adopted by Mr. Dyce, opens his edition of Middleton, is a notable example of the best and the worst qualities which distinguish or disfigure the romantic comedy of the Shakespearean age. The rude and reckless composition, the rough intrusion of savourless farce, the bewildering combinations of incident and the far more bewildering fluctuations of character—all the inconsistences, incongruities, incoherences of the piece are forgotten when the reader remembers and reverts to the passages of exquisite and fascinating beauty which relieve and redeem the utmost errors of negligence and haste. To find anything more delightful, more satisfying in its pure and simple perfection of loveliness, we must turn to the very best examples of Shakespeare's youthful work. Nay, it must be allowed that in one or two of the master's earliest plays—in the *Two Gentlemen of Verona*, for instance—we shall find nothing comparable for charm and sincerity of sweet and passionate fancy with such enchanting verses as these.

> O happy persecution, I embrace thee
> With an unfettered soul! So sweet a thing
> It is to sigh upon the rack of love,
> Where each calamity is groaning witness
> Of the poor martyr's faith. I never heard
> Of any true affection, but 'twas nipt
> With care, that, like the caterpillar, eats
> The leaves off the spring's sweetest book, the rose.
> Love, bred on earth, is often nursed in hell:
> By rote it reads woe, ere it learn to spell.

Again: the 'secure tyrant, but unhappy lover,' whose prisoner and rival has thus expressed his triumphant resignation, is counselled by his friend to 'go laugh and lie down,' as not having slept for three nights; but answers, in words even more delicious than his supplanter's:

> Alas, how can I? he that truly loves
> Burns out the day in idle fantasies;
> And when the lamb bleating doth bid good night
> Unto the closing day, then tears begin
> To keep quick time unto the owl, whose voice
> Shrieks like the bellman in the lover's ears:
> Love's eye the jewel of sleep, O, seldom wears!
> The early lark is wakened from her bed,
> Being only by love's plaints disquieted;
> And, singing in the morning's ear, she weeps,
> Being deep in love, at lovers' broken sleeps:
> But say a golden slumber chance to tie
> With silken strings the cover of love's eye,
> Then dreams, magician-like, mocking present
> Pleasures, whose fading leaves more discontent.

Perfect in music, faultless in feeling, exquisite in refined simplicity of expression, this passage is hardly more beautiful and noble than one or two in the play which follows. *The Phœnix* is a quaint and homely compound of satirical realism in social studies with utopian invention in the figure of an ideal prince, himself a compound of Harun al-Rashid and 'Albert the Good,' who wanders through the play as a detective in disguise, and appears in his own person at the close to discharge in full the general and particular claims of justice and philanthropy. The whole work is slight and sketchy, primitive if not puerile in parts, but easy and amusing to read; the confidence reposed by the worthy monarch in noblemen of such unequivocal nomenclature as Lord Proditor, Lussurioso, and Infesto, is one of the signs that we are here still on the debatable borderland between the old Morality and the new Comedy—a province where incarnate vices and virtues are seen figuring and posturing in what can scarcely be called masquerade. But the two fine soliloquies of Phœnix on the corruption of the purity of law (Act i. scene iv.) and the profanation of the sanctity of marriage (Act ii. scene ii.) are somewhat riper and graver in style, with less admixture of rhyme and more variety of cadence, than the lovely verses above quoted. Milton's obligation to the latter passage is less direct than his earlier obligation to a later play of Middleton's, from which he transferred one of the most beautiful as well as most famous images in *Lycidas*: but his early and intimate acquaintance with Middleton had apparently (as Mr. Dyce seems to think[1]) left in the ear of the blind old poet a more or less distinct echo from the noble opening verses of the dramatist's address to 'reverend and honourable matrimony.'

In *Michaelmas Term* the realism of Middleton's comic style is no longer alloyed or flavoured with poetry or fancy. It is an excellent Hogarthian comedy, full of rapid and vivid incident, of pleasant or indignant humour. Its successor, *A Trick to Catch the Old One*, is by far the best play Middleton had yet written, and one of the best he ever wrote. The merit of this and his other good comedies does not indeed consist in any new or subtle study of character, any Shakespearean creation or Jonsonian invention of humours or of men: the spendthrifts and the misers, the courtesans and the dotards, are figures borrowed from the common stock of stage tradition: it is the vivid variety of incident and intrigue, the freshness and ease and vigour of the style, the clear straightforward energy and vivacity of the action, that the reader finds most praiseworthy in the best comic work of such ready writers as Middleton and Dekker. The dialogue has sometimes touches of real humour and flashes of genuine wit: but its readable and enjoyable quality is generally independent of these. Very witty writing may be very dreary reading, for want of natural animation and true dramatic movement: and in these qualities at least the rough and ready work of our old dramatists is seldom if ever deficient.

It is, however, but too probable that the reader's enjoyment may be crossed with a dash of exasperation when he finds a writer of real genius so reckless of fame and self-respect as the pressure of want or the weariness of overwork seems but too often and too naturally to have made too many of the great dramatic journeymen whose powers were half wasted or half worn out in the struggle for bare bread. No other excuse than this can be advanced for the demerit of Middleton's next comedy. Had the author wished to show how well and how ill he could write at his worst and at his best, he could have given no fairer proof than by the publication of the two plays issued under his name in the same year 1608. *The Family of Love* is in my judgment unquestionably and incomparably the worst of Middleton's plays: very coarse, very dull, altogether distasteful and ineffectual. As a religious satire it is so utterly pointless as to leave no impression of any definite folly or distinctive knav-

ery in the doctrine or the practice of the particular sect held up by name to ridicule: an obscure body of feather-headed fanatics, concerning whom we can only be certain that they were decent and inoffensive in comparison with the yelling Yahoos whom the scandalous and senseless license of our own day allows to run and roar about the country unmuzzled and unwhipped.

There is much more merit in the broad comedy of *Your Five Gallants*, a curious burlesque study of manners and morals not generally commendable for imitation. The ingenious and humorous invention which supplies a centre for the picture and a pivot for the action is most singularly identical with the device of a modern detective as recorded by the greatest English writer of his day. 'The Butcher's Story,' told to Dickens by the policeman who had played the part of the innocent young butcher, may be profitably compared by lovers of detective humour with the story of Fitsgrave—a 'thrice worthy' gentleman who under the disguise of a young gull fresh from college succeeds in circumventing and unmasking the five associated swindlers of variously villainous professions by whom a fair and amiable heiress is beleaguered and befooled. The play is somewhat crude and hasty in construction, but full of life and fun and grotesque variety of humorous event.

The first of Middleton's plays to attract notice from students of a later generation, *A Mad World, My Masters*, if not quite so thoroughly good a comedy as *A Trick to Catch the Old One*, must be allowed to contain the very best comic character ever drawn or sketched by the fertile and flowing pen of its author. The prodigal grandfather, Sir Bounteous Progress, is perhaps the most lifelike figure of a good-humoured and liberal old libertine that ever amused or scandalized a tolerant or intolerant reader. The chief incidents of the action are admirably humorous and ingenious: but the matrimonial part of the catastrophe is something more than repulsive, and the singular intervention of a real live succubus, less terrible in her seductions than her sister of the *Contes drolatiques*, can hardly seem happy or seasonable to a generation which knows not King James and his Demonology.

Of the two poets occasionally associated with Middleton in the composition of a play, Dekker seems usually to have taken in hand the greater part, and Rowley the lesser part, of the composite poem engendered by their joint efforts. The style of *The Roaring Girl* is full of Dekker's peculiar mannerisms: slipshod and straggling metre, incongruous touches or flashes of fanciful or lyrical expression, reckless and awkward inversions, irrational and irrepressible outbreaks of irregular and fitful rhyme. And with all these faults it is more unmistakably the style of a born poet than is the usual style of Middleton. Dekker would have taken a high place among the finest if not among the greatest of English poets if he had but had the sense of form—the instinct of composition. Whether it was modesty, indolence, indifference or incompetence, some drawback or shortcoming there was which so far impaired the quality of his strong and delicate genius that it is impossible for his most ardent and cordial admirer to say or think of his very best work that it really does him justice—that it adequately represents the fullness of his unquestionable powers. And yet it is certain that Lamb was not less right than usual when he said that Dekker 'had poetry enough for anything.' But he had not constructive power enough for the trade of a playwright—the trade in which he spent so many weary years of ill-requited labour. This comedy in which we first find him associated with Middleton is well written and well contrived, and fairly diverting—especially to an idle or an uncritical reader: though even such an one may suspect that the heroine here represented as a virginal virago must have been in fact rather like Dr. Johnson's fair friend Bet Flint; of whom the Great Lexicographer 'used to say that she was generally slut and drunkard; occasionally whore and thief' (Boswell, May 8, 1781). The parallel would have been more nearly complete if Moll Cutpurse 'had written her own Life in verse,' and brought it to Selden or Bishop Hall with a request that he would furnish her with a preface to it. But the seventeenth century was inadequate to so perfect a production of the kind; and we doubt not through the ages one increasing purpose runs, and the thoughts of girls are widened with the process of the suns.

The plays of Middleton are not so properly divisible into tragic and comic as into realistic and romantic—into plays of which the mainspring is essentially prosaic or photographic, and plays of which the mainspring is principally fanciful or poetical. Two only of the former class remain to be mentioned; *Anything for a Quiet Life*, and *A Chaste Maid in Cheapside*. There is very good stuff in the plot or groundwork of the former, but the workmanship is hardly worthy of the material. Mr. Bullen ingeniously and plausibly suggests the partnership of Shirley in this play: but the conception of the character in which he discerns a likeness to the touch of the lesser dramatist is happier and more original than such a comparison would indicate. The young stepmother whose affectation of selfish levity and grasping craft is really designed to cure her husband of his infatuation, and to reconcile him with the son who regards her as his worst enemy, is a figure equally novel, effective and attractive. The honest shopkeeper and his shrewish wife may remind us again of Dickens by their points of likeness to Mr. and Mrs. Snagsby; though the reformation of the mercer's jealous vixen is brought about by more humorous and less tragical means than the repentance of the law-stationer's 'little woman.' George the apprentice, through whose wit and energy this happy consummation becomes possible, is a very original and amusing example of the young Londoner of the period. But there is more humour, though very little chastity, in the *Chaste Maid*; a play of quite exceptional freedom and audacity, and certainly one of the drollest and liveliest that ever broke the bounds of propriety or shook the sides of merriment.

The opening of *More Dissemblers besides Women* is as full at once of comic and of romantic promise as the upshot of the whole is unsatisfactory—a most lame and impotent conclusion. But some of the dialogue is exquisite; full of flowing music and gentle grace, of ease and softness and fancy and spirit; and the part of a poetic or romantic Joseph Surface, as perfect in the praise of virtue as in the practice of vice, is one of Middleton's really fine and happy inventions. In the style of *The Widow* there is no less fluency and facility: it is throughout identical with that of Middleton's other comedies in metre; a style which has so many points in common with Fletcher's as to make the apocryphal attribution of a share in this comedy to the hand of the greater poet more plausible than many other ascriptions of the kind. I am inclined nevertheless to agree with Mr. Bullen's apparent opinion that the whole credit of this brilliant play may be reasonably assigned to Middleton; and especially with his remark that the only scene in which any resemblance to the manner of Ben Jonson can be traced by the most determined ingenuity of critical research is more like the work of a pupil than like a hasty sketch of the master's. There is no lack of energetic invention and beautiful versification in another comedy of adventure and intrigue, *No Wit, No Help like a Woman's*: the unpleasant or extravagant quality of certain incidents in the story is partially neutralized or modified by the unfailing charm of a style worthy of Fletcher himself in his ripest and sweetest stage of poetic comedy.

But high above all the works yet mentioned there stands and will stand conspicuous while noble emotion and noble verse have honour among English readers the pathetic and heroic play so memorably appreciated by Charles Lamb, *A Fair Quarrel*. It would be the vainest and emptiest impertinence to offer a word in echo of his priceless and imperishable praise. The delicate nobility of the central conception on which the hero's character depends for its full relief and development should be enough to efface all remembrance of any defect or default in moral taste, any shortcoming on the æsthetic side of ethics, which may be detected in any slighter or hastier example of the poet's invention. A man must be dull and slow of sympathies indeed who cannot respond in spirit to that bitter cry of chivalrous and manful agony at sense of the shadow of a mother's shame:—

> Quench, my spirit,
> And out with honour's flaming lights within thee!
> Be dark and dead to all respects of manhood!
> I never shall have use of valour more.

Middleton has no second hero like Captain Ager: but where is there another so thoroughly noble and lovable among all the characters of all the dramatists of his time but Shakespeare?

The part taken by Rowley in this play is easy for any tiro in criticism to verify. The rough and crude genius of that perverse and powerful writer is not seen here by any means at its best. I cannot as yet lay claim to an exhaustive acquantance with his works, but judging from what I have read of them I should say that his call was rather towards tragedy than towards comedy; that his mastery of severe and serious emotion was more genuine and more natural than his command of satirical or grotesque realism. The tragedy in which he has grappled with the subject afterwards so differently handled in the first and greatest of Landor's tragedies is to me of far more interest and value than such comedies as that which kindled the enthusiasm of a loyal Londoner in the civic sympathies of Lamb. Disfigured as it is towards the close by indulgence in mere horror and brutality after the fashion of Andronicus or Jeronimo, it has more beauty and power and pathos in its best scenes than a reader of his comedies—as far as I know them—would have expected. There are noticeable points of likeness—apart from the coincidence of subject—between this and Mr. Caldwell Roscoe's noble tragedy of *Violenzia*. But in the underplot of *A Fair Quarrel* Rowley's besetting faults of coarseness and quaintness, stiffness and roughness, are so flagrant and obtrusive that we cannot avoid a feeling of regret and irritation at such untimely and inharmonious evidence of his partnership with a poet of finer if not of sturdier genius. The same sense of discord and inequality will be aroused on comparison of the worse with the better parts of *The Old Law*. The clumsiness and dullness of the farcical interludes can hardly be paralleled in the rudest and hastiest scenes of Middleton's writing: while the sweet and noble dignity of the finer passages have the stamp of his ripest and tenderest genius on every line and in every cadence. But for sheer bewildering incongruity there is no play known to me which can be compared with *The Mayor of Queenborough*. Here again we find a note so dissonant and discordant in the lighter parts of the dramatic concert that we seem at once to recognize the harsher and hoarser instrument of Rowley. The farce is even more extravagantly and preposterously mistimed and misplaced than that which disfigures the play just mentioned: but I thoroughly agree with Mr. Bullen's high estimate of the power displayed and maintained throughout the tragic and poetic part of this drama; to which no previous critic has ever vouchsafed a word of due acknowledgement. The story is ugly and unnatural, but its repulsive effect is transfigured or neutralized by the charm of tender or passionate poetry; and it must be admitted that the hideous villany of Vortiger and Horsus affords an opening for subsequent scenic effects of striking and genuine tragical interest.

The difference between the genius of Middleton and the genius of Dekker could not be better illustrated than by comparison of their attempts at political and patriotic allegory. The lazy, slovenly, impatient genius of Dekker flashes out by fits and starts on the reader of the play in which he has expressed his English hatred of Spain and Popery, his English pride in the rout of the Armada, and his English gratitude for the part played by Queen Elizabeth in the crowning struggle of the time: but his most cordial admirer can hardly consider *The Whore of Babylon* a shining or satisfactory example of dramatic art. The play which brought Middleton into prison, and earned for the actors a sum so far beyond parallel as to have seemed incredible till the fullest evidence was procured, is one of the most complete and exquisite works of artistic ingenuity and dexterity that ever excited or offended, enraptured or scandalized an audience of friends or enemies: the only work of English poetry which may properly be called Aristophanic. It has the same depth of civic seriousness, the same earnest ardour and devotion to the old cause of the old country, the same solid fervour of enthusiasm and indignation, which animated the third great poet of Athens against the corruption of art by the sophistry of Euripides and the corruption of manhood by the sophistry of Socrates. The delicate skill of the workmanship can only be appreciated by careful and thorough study; but that the infusion of poetic fancy and feeling into the generally comic and satiric style is hardly unworthy of the comparison which I have ventured to challenge, I will take but one brief extract for evidence.

> Upon those lips, the sweet fresh buds of youth,
> The holy dew of prayer lies, like pearl
> Dropt from the opening eyelids of the morn
> Upon a bashful rose.

Here for once even 'that celestial thief' John Milton has impaired rather than improved the effect of the beautiful phrase borrowed from an earlier and inferior poet. His use of Middleton's exquisite image is not quite so apt—so perfectly picturesque and harmonious—as the use to which it was put by the inventor.

Nothing in the age of Shakespeare is so difficult for an Englishman of our own age to realize as the temper, the intelligence, the serious and refined elevation of an audience which was at once capable of enjoying and applauding the roughest and coarsest kinds of pleasantry, the rudest and crudest scenes of violence, and competent to appreciate the finest and the highest reaches of poetry, the subtlest and the most sustained allusions of ethical or political symbolism. The large and long popularity of an exquisite dramatic or academic allegory such as *Lingua*, which would seem to appeal only to readers of exceptional education, exceptional delicacy of perception, and exceptional quickness of wit, is hardly more remarkable than the popular success of a play requiring such keen constancy of attention, such vivid wakefulness and promptitude of apprehension, as this even more serious than fantastic work of Middleton's. The vulgarity and puerility of all modern attempts at any comparable effect need not be cited to throw into relief the essential finish, the impassioned intelligence, the high spiritual and literary level, of these crowded and brilliant and vehement five acts. Their extreme cleverness, their indefatigable ingenuity, would in any case have been remarkable: but their fullness of active and poetic life gives them an interest far

deeper and higher and more permanent than the mere sense of curiosity and wonder.

But if *A Game at Chess* is especially distinguished by its complete and thorough harmony of execution and design, the lack of any such artistic merit in another famous work of Middleton's is such as once more to excite that irritating sense of inequality, irregularity, inconstancy of genius and inconsequence of aim, which too often besets and bewilders the student of our early dramatists. There is poetry enough in *The Witch* to furnish forth a whole generation of poeticules: but the construction or composition of the play, the arrangement and evolution of event, the distinction or development of character, would do less than little credit to a boy of twelve; who at any rate would hardly have thought of patching up so ridiculous a reconciliation between intending murderers and intended victims as here exceeds in absurdity the chaotic combination of accident and error which disposes of inconvenient or superfluous underlings. But though neither Mr. Dyce nor Mr. Bullen has been at all excessive or unjust in his animadversions on these flagrant faults and follies, neither editor has given his author due credit for the excellence of style, of language and versification, which makes this play readable throughout with pleasure, if not always without impatience. Fletcher himself, the acknowledged master of the style here adopted by Middleton, has left no finer example of metrical fluency and melodious ease. The fashion of dialogue and composition is no doubt rather feminine than masculine: Marlowe and Jonson, Webster and Beaumont, Tourneur and Ford,—to cite none but the greatest of authorities in this kind—wrote a firmer if not a freer hand, struck a graver if not a sweeter note of verse: this rapid effluence of easy expression is liable to lapse into conventional efflux of facile improvisation: but such command of it as Middleton's is impossible to any but a genuine and a memorable poet.

As for the supposed obligations of Shakespeare to Middleton or Middleton to Shakespeare, the imaginary relations of *The Witch* to *Macbeth* or *Macbeth* to *The Witch*, I can only say that the investigation of this subject seems to me as profitable as a research into the natural history of snakes in Iceland. That the editors to whom we owe the miserably defaced and villainously garbled text which is all that has reached us of *Macbeth*, not content with the multilation of the greater poet, had recourse to the interpolation of a few superfluous and incongruous lines or fragments from the lyric portions of the lesser poet's work—that the players who mangled Shakespeare were the pilferers who plundered Middleton—must be obvious to all but those (if any such yet exist anywhere) who are capable of believing the unspeakably impudent assertion of those mendacious malefactors that they have left us a pure and perfect edition of Shakespeare. These passages are all thoroughly in keeping with the general tone of the lesser work: it would be tautology to add that they are no less utterly out of keeping with the general tone of the other. But in their own way nothing can be finer: they have a tragic liveliness in ghastliness, a grotesque animation of horror, which no other poet has ever conceived or conveyed to us. The difference between Michel Angelo and Goya, Tintoretto and Gustave Doré, does not quite efface the right of the minor artists to existence and remembrance.

The tragedy of *Women Beware Women*, whether or not it be accepted as the masterpiece of Middleton, is at least an excellent example of the facility and fluency and equable promptitude of style which all students will duly appreciate and applaud in the riper and completer work of this admirable poet. It is full to overflowing of noble eloquence, of inventive resource and suggestive effect, of rhetorical affluence and theatrical ability. The opening or exposition of the play is quite masterly: and the scene in which the forsaken husband is seduced into consolation by the temptress of his wife is worthy of all praise for the straightforward ingenuity and the serious delicacy by which the action is rendered credible and the situation endurable. But I fear that few or none will be found to disagree with my opinion that no such approbation or tolerance can be reasonably extended so as to cover or condone the offences of either the underplot or the upshot of the play. The one is repulsive beyond redemption by elegance of style, the other is preposterous beyond extenuation on the score of logic or poetical justice. Those who object on principle to solution by massacre must object in consistency to the conclusions of *Hamlet* and *King Lear*: nor are the results of Webster's tragic invention more questionable or less inevitable than the results of Shakespeare's: but the dragnet of murder which gathers in the characters at the close of this play is as promiscuous in its sweep as that cast by Cyril Tourneur over the internecine shoal of sharks who are hauled in and ripped open at the close of *The Revenger's Tragedy*. Had Middleton been content with the admirable subject of his main action, he might have given us a simple and unimpeachable masterpiece: and even as it is he has left us a noble and a memorable work. It is true that the irredeemable infamy of the leading characters degrades and deforms the nature of the interest excited: the good and gentle old mother whose affectionate simplicity is so gracefully and attractively painted passes out of the story and drops out of the list of actors just when some redeeming figure is most needed to assuage the dreariness of disgust with which we follow the fortunes of so meanly criminal a crew: and the splendid eloquence of the only other respectable person in the play is not of itself sufficient to make a living figure, rather than a mere mouthpiece for indignant emotion, of so subordinate and inactive a character as the Cardinal. The lower comedy of the play is identical in motive with that which defaces the master-work of Ford: more stupid and offensive it hardly could be. But the high comedy of the scene between Livia and the Widow is as fine as the best work in that kind left us by the best poets and humourists of the Shakespearean age; it is not indeed unworthy of the comparison with Chaucer's which it suggested to the all but impeccable judgment of Charles Lamb.

The lack of moral interest and sympathetic attraction in the characters and the story, which has been noted as the principal defect in the otherwise effective composition of *Women Beware Women*, is an objection which cannot be brought against the graceful tragicomedy of *The Spanish Gipsy*. Whatever is best in the tragic or in the romantic part of this play bears the stamp of Middleton's genius alike in the sentiment and the style. 'The code of modern morals,' to borrow a convenient phrase from Shelley, may hardly incline us to accept as plausible or as possible the repentance and the redemption of so brutal a ruffian as Roderigo: but the vivid beauty of the dialogue is equal to the vivid interest of the situation which makes the first act one of the most striking in any play of the time. The double action has some leading points in common with two of Fletcher's, which have nothing in common with each other: Merione in *The Queen of Corinth* is less interesting than Clara, but the vagabonds of *Beggars' Bush* are more amusing than Rowley's or Middleton's. The play is somewhat deficient in firmness or solidity of construction: it is, if such a phrase be permissible, one of those half-baked or underdone dishes of various and confused ingredients, in which the cook's or the baker's hurry has impaired the excellent materials of wholesome bread and savoury meat. The splendid slovens who served their audience with spiritual work in which the gods had

mixed 'so much of earth, so much of heaven, and such impetuous blood'—the generous and headlong purveyors who lavished on their daily provision of dramatic fare such wealth of fine material and such prodigality of superfluous grace—the foremost followers of Marlowe and of Shakespeare were too prone to follow the reckless example of the first rather than the severe example of the second. There is perhaps not one of them—and Middleton assuredly is not one—whom we can reasonably imagine capable of the patience and self-respect which induced Shakespeare to rewrite the triumphantly popular parts of Romeo, of Falstaff, and of Hamlet, with an eye to the literary perfection and permanence of work which in its first light outline had won the crowning suffrage of immediate or spectacular applause.

The rough and ready hand of Rowley may be traced, not indeed in the more high-toned passages, but in many of the most animated scenes of *The Spanish Gipsy*. In the most remarkable of the ten masques or interludes which appear among the collected works of Middleton the two names are again associated. To the freshness, liveliness, and spirited ingenuity of this little allegorical comedy Mr. Bullen has done ample justice in his excellent critical introduction. *The Inner-Temple Masque*, less elaborate than *The World Tost at Tennis*, shows no lack of homely humour and invention: and in the others there is as much waste of fine flowing verse and facile fancy as ever excited the rational regret of a modern reader at the reckless profusion of literary power which the great poets of the time were content to lavish on the decoration or exposition of an emphemeral pageant. Of Middleton's other minor works, apocryphal or genuine, I will only say that his authorship of *Microcynicon*—a dull and crabbed imitation of Marston's worst work as a satirist—seems to me utterly incredible. A lucid and melodious fluency of style is the mark of all his metrical writing: and this stupid piece of obscure and clumsy jargon could have been the work of no man endowed with more faculty of expression than informs or modulates the whine of an average pig. Nor is it rationally conceivable that the Thomas Middleton who soiled some reams of paper with what he was pleased to consider or to call a paraphrase of the *Wisdom of Solomon* can have had anything but a poet's name in common with a poet. This name is not like that of the great writer whose name is attached to *The Transformed Metamorphosis*: there can hardly have been two Cyril Tourneurs in the field, but there may well have been half a dozen Thomas Middletons. And Tourneur's abortive attempt at allegoric discourse is but a preposterous freak of prolonged eccentricity: this paraphrase is simply a tideless sea of limitless and inexhaustible drivel. There are three reasons—two of them considerable, but the third conclusive—for assigning to Middleton the two satirical tracts in the style of Nash, or rather of Dekker, which appeared in the same year with his initials subscribed to their prefatory addresses. Mr. Dyce thought they were written by the poet whose ready verse and realistic humour are both well represented in their text: Mr. Bullen agrees with Mr. Dyce in thinking that they are the work of Middleton. And Mr. Carew Hazlitt thinks that they are not.

No such absolute and final evidence as this can be adduced in favour or disfavour of the theory which would saddle the reputation of Middleton with the authorship of a dull and disjointed comedy, the work (it has hitherto been supposed) of the German substitute for Shakespeare. Middleton has no doubt left us more crude and shapeless plays than *The Puritan*; none, in my opinion,—excepting always his very worst authentic example of farce or satire, *The Family of Love*—so heavy and so empty and so feeble. If it must be assigned to any author of higher rank than the new Shakspere, I would suggest that it is much more like Rowley's than like Middleton's worst work. Of the best qualities which distinguish either of these writers as poet or as humourist, it has not the shadow or the glimmer of a vestige.

In the last and the greatest work which bears their united names—a work which should suffice to make either name immortal if immortality were other than an accidental attribute of genius—the very highest capacity of either poet is seen at its very best. There is more of mere poetry, more splendour of style and vehemence of verbal inspiration, in the work of other poets than writing for the stage: the two masterpieces of Webster are higher in tone at their highest, more imaginative and more fascinating in their expression of terrible or of piteous wrath: there are more superb harmonies, more glorious raptures of ardent and eloquent music, in the sometimes unsurpassed and unsurpassable poetic passion of Cyril Tourneur. But even Webster's men seem but splendid sketches, as Tourneur's seem but shadowy or fiery outlines, beside the perfect and living figure of De Flores. The man is so horribly human, so fearfully and wonderfully natural, in his single-hearted brutality of devotion, his absolute absorption of soul and body by one consuming force of passionately cynical desire, that we must go to Shakespeare for an equally original and an equally unquestionable revelation of indubitable truth. And in no play by Beaumont and Fletcher is the concord between the two partners more singularly complete in unity of spirit and of style than throughout the tragic part of this play. The underplot from which it most unluckily and absurdly derives its title is very stupid, rather coarse, and almost vulgar: but the two great parts of Beatrice and De Flores are equally consistent, coherent and sustained, in the scenes obviously written by Middleton and in the scenes obviously written by Rowley. The subordinate part taken by Middleton in Dekker's play of *The Honest Whore* is difficult to discern from the context or to verify by inner evidence: though some likeness to his realistic or photographic method may be admitted as perceptible in the admirable picture of Bellafront's morning reception at the opening of the second act of the first part. But here we may assert with fair confidence that the first and the last scenes of the play bear the indisputable sign-manual of William Rowley. His vigorous and vivid genius, his somewhat hard and curt directness of style and manner, his clear and trenchant power of straightforward presentation or exposition, may be traced in every line as plainly as the hand of Middleton must be recognized in the main part of the tragic action intervening. To Rowley therefore must be assigned the very high credit of introducing and of dismissing with adequate and even triumphant effect the strangely original tragic figure which owes its fullest and finest development to the genius of Middleton. To both poets alike must unqualified and equal praise be given for the subtle simplicity of skill with which they make us appreciate the fatal and foreordained affinity between the ill-favoured, rough-mannered, broken-down gentleman, and the headstrong unscrupulous unobservant girl whose very abhorrence of him serves only to fling her down from her high station of haughty beauty into the very clutch of his ravenous and pitiless passion. Her cry of horror and astonishment at first perception of the price to be paid for a service she had thought to purchase with mere money is so wonderfully real in its artless and ingenuous sincerity that Shakespeare himself could hardly have bettered it:

Why, 'tis impossible thou canst be so wicked,
And shelter such a cunning cruelty,
To make his death the murderer of my honour!

That note of incredulous amazement that the man whom

she has just instigated to the commission of murder 'can be so wicked' as to have served her ends for any end of his own beyond the pay of a professional assassin is a touch worthy of the greatest dramatist that ever lived. The perfect simplicity of expression is as notable as the perfect innocence of her surprise; the candid astonishment of a nature absolutely incapable of seeing more than one thing or holding more than one thought at a time. That she, the first criminal, should be honestly shocked as well as physically horrified by revelation of the real motive which impelled her accomplice into crime, gives a lurid streak of tragic humour to the lifelike interest of the scene; as the pure infusion of spontaneous poetry throughout redeems the whole work from the charge of vulgar subservience to a vulgar taste for the presentation or the contemplation of criminal horror. Instances of this happy and natural nobility of instinct abound in the casual expressions which give grace and animation always, but never any touch of rhetorical transgression or florid superfluity, to the brief and trenchant swordplay of the tragic dialogue.

That sigh would fain have utterance: take pity on't,
And lend it a free word; 'las, how it labours
For liberty! I hear the murmur yet
Beat at your bosom.

The wording of this passage is sufficient to attest the presence and approve the quality of a poet: the manner and the moment of its introduction would be enough to show the instinctive and inborn insight of a natural dramatist. As much may be said of the few words which give us a ghastly glimpse of supernatural terror:—

Ha! what art thou that tak'st away the light
Betwixt that star and me? I dread thee not:
'Twas but a mist of conscience.

But the real power and genius of the work cannot be shown by extracts—not even by such extracts as these. His friend and colleague Dekker shows to better advantage by the process of selection: hardly one of his plays leaves so strong and sweet an impression of its general and complete excellence as of separate scenes or passages of tender and delicate imagination or emotion beyond the reach of Middleton: but the tragic unity and completeness of conception which distinguish this masterpiece will be sought in vain among the less firm and solid figures of his less serious and profound invention. Had *The Changeling* not been preserved, we should not have known Middleton: as it is, we are more than justified in asserting that a critic who denies him a high place among the poets of England must be not merely ignorant of the qualities which involve a right or confer a claim to this position, but incapable of curing his ignorance by any process of study. The rough and rapid work which absorbed too much of this poet's time and toil seems almost incongruous with the impression made by the noble and thoughtful face, so full of gentle dignity and earnest composure, in which we recognise the graver and loftier genius of a man worthy to hold his own beside all but the greatest of his age. And that age was the age of Shakespeare.

Notes

1. Mr. Dyce would no doubt have altered his opinion had he lived to see the evidence adduced by the Director of the New Meltun Society that the real author of *A Game at Chess* was none other than John Milton himself: whose earliest poems had appeared the year before the publication of that anti-papal satire. This discovery is only less curious and precious than a later revelation which we must accept on the same authority, that *Comus* was written by Sir John Suckling, *Paradise Regained* by Lord Rochester, and *Samson Agonistes* by Elkanah Settle: while on the other hand it may be affirmed with no less confidence that Milton—who never would allow his

name to be spelt right on the title-page or under the dedication of any work published by him—owed his immunity from punishment

after the Restoration to the admitted fact that he was the real author of Dryden's *Astræa Redux.*

FULKE GREVILLE
Lord Brooke

1554–1628

Fulke Greville was born on October 3, 1554, at Beauchamp Court, Warwickshire. He entered the Shrewsbury School in 1564, on the same day as Sir Philip Sidney. Both men entered Jesus College, Cambridge, in 1568. Greville traveled with Sidney to Heidelberg in 1577 on a diplomatic mission for Elizabeth. A favorite of Elizabeth's, Greville held various positions under both Elizabeth and James I, including Secretary of the Principality of Wales (1583–1628), Treasurer of the Navy (1598–1604), and Chancellor of the Exchequer (1614–1621). Greville served as a member of Parliament and was created a peer in 1621.

Most of Greville's works, many of which had political themes, were not published during his lifetime. The notable exceptions are an elegy on Sidney, published in the miscellany *The Phoenix Nest* (1593), two poems which appeared in the 1600 edition of *England's Helicon*, and Greville's tragedy *Mustapha* (1609). His other works include another tragic drama, *Alaham*, a study of the life of Sidney, and *Caelica*, a collection of 109 short poems. Greville was a founding member of Gabriel Harvey's literary society Areopagus. On September 30, 1628, Greville died of stab wounds inflicted by a servant displeased with his master's will. Greville was buried at St. Mary's Church, Warwickshire.

Personal

He had the longest lease, and the smoothest time without rub, of any of her (Elizabeth's) Favorites. . . . He was a brave Gentleman, and honourably descended. . . . Neither illiterate; for . . . there are of his now extant, some fragments of his Poem, and of those times, which doe interest him in the Muses; and which shews, the Queen's election had ever a noble conduct, and its motions more of virtue and judgment, than of fancy.—SIR ROBERT NAUNTON, *Fragmenta Regalia*, c. 1630

Sir Fulke Grevil Knight, son to Sir Fulke Grevil the elder, of Becham Court in this county (Warwickshire). He was bred first in the university of Cambridge. He came to the court, backed with a full and fair estate; and queen Elizabeth loved such substantial courtiers as could plentifully subsist of themselves. He was a good scholar, loving much to employ (and sometimes to advance) learned men, to whom worthy bishop Overal chiefly owed his preferment, and Mr. Camden (by his own confession) tasted largely of his liberality.

His studies were most in poetry and history, as his works do witness. His style, conceived by some to be swelling, is allowed for lofty and full by others. King James created him baron Brook of Beauchamp Court, as descended from the sole daughter and heir of Edward Willoughby, the last lord Brook, in the reign of king Henry the Seventh.

His sad death, or murder rather, happened on this occasion. His discontented servant, conceiving his deserts not soon or well enough rewarded, wounded him mortally; and then (to save the law the labour) killed himself, verifying the observation, "that he may when he pleaseth be master of another man's life, who contemneth his own."

He lieth buried in Warwick church, under a monument of black and white marble, whereon he is styled "servant to queen Elizabeth, counsellor to king James, and friend to Sir Philip Sidney." Dying Semptember 30, 1628, without issue,

and unmarried, his barony, by virtue of entail in the patent, descended on his kinsman Robert Grevil lord Brook, father to the right honourable Robert lord Brook.—THOMAS FULLER, *The History of the Worthies of England*, 1662

(Sir William Davenant) was next a servant (as I remember, a Page also) to Sir Fulke Grevil, Lord Brookes, with whom he lived to his death, which was that a servant of his (that had long wayted on him, and his Lordship had often told him that he would doe something for him, but did not, but still putt him off with delayes) as he was trussing up his Lord's pointes comeing from Stoole (for then their breeches were fastned to the doubletts with points; then came in hookes and eies; which not to have fastened was in my boy-hood a great crime) stabbed him. This was at the same time that the Duke of Buckingham was stabbed by Felton, and the great noise and report of the Duke's, Sir William told me, quite drowned this of his Lord's, that 'twas scarce taken notice of. This Sir Fulke G. was a good witt, and had been a good Poet in his youth. He wrote a Poeme in folio which he printed not till he was old, and then (as Sir W. said) with too much judgement and refining, spoyled it, which was at first a delicate thing.—JOHN AUBREY, "Sir William Davenant," *Brief Lives*, 1669–96

Fulke Grevil, descended from an ancient and knightly fam. of his name living at Milcot in Warwickshire, and they from those of Cambden in Gloucestershire, was born in that county, an. 1554, being the same year wherein sir Philip Sidney received his first breath, did spend some time in the condition of a gent. commoner in this university, either before he went to Trin. coll. in Cambridge, or at his return thence, but in what house, unless in Ch. Ch. or Broadgate's, I cannot well tell, nor doth it matter much, seeing that he was more properly a Cambridge man (to which university he was a benefactor) than an Oxonian. After he had left the university he travelled, and at his return, being well accomplished, was introduced into the court by his uncle, Rob. Grevil a servant to Q. Elizabeth, where he was esteemed a most ingenious person, and had in favour by all such that were lovers of arts and sciences. At length obtaining an honourable office under the queen, he became one of her favourites, which he held for no short term, but had the longest lease of any, and the smoothest time without rub. In the beginning of 1588, he, among other persons of honour and quality, was actually created master of arts, which, I think, was the highest degree that was conferred upon him in this university. In 1603, he was made knight of the Bath at the coronation of K. Jam. I. and soon after obtained the grant of the ruinous castle of Warwick. In the 12th year of the said king's reign, being constituted under-treasurer and chancellor of the exchequer, he was made choice of for one of the king's privy-council. And meriting much for his faithful services in those employments, was, by letters patents, bearing date 9 Jan. 18. Jac. I. advanced to the dignity of a baron of this realm, by the title of lord Brook of Beauchamps-court. In Sept. 1621, he was made one of the gentlemen of the king's bedchamber; whereupon giving up his chancellorship of the exchequer, Rich. Weston (afterwards earl of Portland) succeeded him. He was always esteemed a brave gentleman and honourably descended, as being sprung from the family of Willoughby lord Brook, was favoured by qu. Elizabeth, and such that knew he had interest in the muses. His life was always single, and tho' he lived and died a constant courtier of the ladies, yet he prosecuted his studies in history and poetry; in which, consider him as a gentleman of noble birth and great estate, he was most excellent in his time. . . . At length our author, (who was counsellor state to Ch.I.) neglecting to reward one Haywood, who had spent the greatest and chiefest part of his time in his personal service, for which he expostulated the matter with his master, but was sharply rebuked for it; the said Haywood thereupon gave him a mortal stab on his back (they two being then only together) in his bedchamber in Brook house in Holbourn near London, of which wound he died 30 Sept. in sixteen hundred twenty and eight, aged 74. Which being done, the assassine discerning his own condition desperate, went into another room, and there having lock'd the door, murdered himself with his own sword. On the 27 of Oct. following he the said lord Brook was buried in a vault, situate on the north side of the collegiat church at Warwick, which formerly had been a chapter house belonging thereunto: wherein he had, in his life time, erected a fair tomb, with his epitaph thereon. '*Fulke Grevil, Servant to Queen Elizabeth, Counsellor to King James, and Friend to Sir Philip Sidney.*'—ANTHONY À WOOD, *Athenae Oxonienses*, 1691–1721

Sir Fulke Grevill, Lord Brooke, a man of much note in his time, but one of those admired wits who have lost much of their reputation in the eyes of posterity. A thousand accidents of birth, court-favour, or popularity, concur sometimes to gild a slender proportion of merit. After-ages, who look when those beams are withdrawn, wonder what attracted the eyes of the multitude.—HORACE WALPOLE, *A Catalogue of the Royal and Noble Authors of England, Scotland, and Ireland*, 1758

General

Swell proudly Numbers on words' windy seas
To raise this buskin-poet to the skies;
And fix him there among the Pleyades,
To light the Muse in gloomy tragedies.
Vpon Times scowling brow he hath indorc'd
A tragedy that shall that brow out-weare;
Wherein the Muse beyond the minde is forc'd

(In rarest raptures) to Arts highest spheare:
No line but reaches to the firmament
Of highest sense, from surest ground of wit.
No word but is like Phebus luculent;
Then all yeeld luster well-nere infinite:
So shine bright scænes till on the starry stage
The gods re-act you in their equipage.
—SIR JOHN DAVIES, "To the immortall memory and deserued honor of the Writer of the *Tragedy of Mustapha*, (as it is written, not printed) by Sir Fulk Grevill, Knight," *The Scourge of Folly*, 1611

The English poems of sir Walter Raleigh, of John Donne, of Hugh Holland, but especially of sir Foulk Grevile in his matchless *Mustapha*, are not easily to be mended.—EDMUND BOLTON, *Hypercritica*, 1624

The two tragedies of Lord Brooke might with more propriety have been termed political treatises than plays. Their author has strangely contrived to make passion, character and interest, of the highest order subservient to the expression of state dogmas and mysteries. He is nine parts Machiavel and Tacitus, for one part Sophocles or Seneca. In this writer's estimate of the faculties of his own mind, the understanding must have held a most tyrannical pre-eminence. Whether we look into his plays, or his most passionate love-poems, we shall find all frozen and made rigid with intellect. The finest movements of the human heart, the utmost grandeur of which the soul is capable, are essentially comprised in the actions and speeches of Cælica and Camena. Shakspeare, who seems to have had a peculiar delight in contemplating womanly perfection, whom for his many sweet images of female excellence all women are in an especial manner bound to love, has not raised the *idéal* of the female character higher than Lord Brooke in these two women has done. But it requires a study equivalent to the learning of a new language to understand their meaning when they speak. It is indeed hard to hit:

Much like thy riddle, Samson, in one day
Or seven though one should musing sit.

It is as if a being of pure intellect should take upon him to express the emotions of our sensitive natures. There would be all knowledge, but sympathetic expression would be wanting.—CHARLES LAMB, *Specimens of English Dramatic Poets*, 1808

Fulke Greville alone could go beyond him in gravity and mystery. The plays of the latter (*Mustapha* and *Alaham*) are abstruse as the mysteries of old, and his style inexplicable as the riddles of the Sphinx. As an instance of his love for the obscure, the marvellous, and impossible, he calls up 'the ghost of one of the old kings of Ormus,' as prologue to one of his tragedies; a very reverend and inscrutable personage, who, we may be sure, blabs no living secrets.—WILLIAM HAZLITT, *Lectures on the Dramatic Literature of the Age of Elizabeth*, 1820

The titles of Lord Brooke's poems, "A Treatise of Human Learning," "A Treatise of Monarchy," "A Treatise of Religion," "An Inquisition upon Fame and Honor," lead us to anticipate more of sense than fancy. In this we are not deceived: his mind was pregnant with deep reflection upon multifarious learning; but he struggles to give utterance to thoughts which he had not fully endowed with words, and amidst the shackles of rhyme and metre, which he had not learned to manage. Hence of all our poets he may be reckoned the most obscure; in aiming at condensation, he becomes elliptical beyond the bounds of the language; and his rhymes, being forced for the sake of sound, leave all meaning behind. Lord Brooke's poetry is chiefly worth notice as an indication of that thinking spirit upon political science which was to produce the riper speculations of Hobbes and Harrington and Locke.—HENRY HALLAM, *Introduction to the Literature of Europe,* 1837–39, Pt. 3, Ch. 5, Par. 35

"A Treatise on Religion," in which, if the reader do not find much of poetic form, he will find at least some grand spiritual philosophy, the stuff whereof all highest poetry is fashioned. It is one of the first poems in which the philosophy of religion, and not either its doctrine, feeling, or history, predominates. It is, as a whole, poor, chiefly from its being so loosely written. There are men, and men whose thoughts are of great worth, to whom it never seems to occur that they may utter very largely and convey very little; that what is clear to themselves is in their speech obscure as a late twilight. Their utterance is rarely articulate; their spiritual mouth talks with but half-movements of its lips; it does not model their thoughts into clear-cut shapes, such as the spiritual ear can distinguish as they enter it. Of such is Lord Brooke.—GEORGE MACDONALD, *England's Antiphon,* 1868, pp. 89–90

Charles Lamb, who never penned a more felicitously expressed criticism than his *envoi* to the extracts given by him from ⟨Greville's⟩ tragedies, observes that they 'might with more propriety have been termed political treatises than plays,' and that their author shows himself in them 'nine parts Machiavel and Tacitus, for one part Sophocles or Seneca.' Yet even as the tragedies stand, they fail to do full justice to the original design of the writer, who informs us that he had at first intended the 'treatises,' now printed separately and extending to much the same length as the tragedies themselves, to serve as choruses to the several acts of the latter, in addition no doubt to the choruses proper, for the most part tolerably lengthy in themselves, already appended to them. On the difficult style and the profundity of meaning which characterise the treatises there is no need for descanting here; but even in the tragedies as they stand, in the dialogue as well as in the purely didactic—they cannot be called lyric—excursuses, the language is extremely obscure. This is the result, not of ambiguity or vagueness of diction, but of a closeness as well as abstruseness of thought to which to all intents and purposes no reader will prove equal unless he approaches these so-called dramas as a student addresses himself to a set of long series of problems. It is this peculiarity of style—a peculiarity extending to almost everything that he has left behind him in verse—which must continue to leave Lord Brooke's tragedies unread except by a resolute few. Seneca and Euripides, whom he generally though not slavishly follows as his dramatic models, are not responsible for what is the reverse of a rhetorical, and only as it were incidentally a sententious, style. It should be added that there are to be found in these strange compositions not only characters as strongly conceived as they are subtly worked out, but situations full of awe and pathos; but everything, to recur to Lamb's inimitable phraseology, is 'frozen and made rigid with intellect.'

Both Lord Brooke's tragedies were first printed in the folio edition of his works, printed five years after his murder; but they were written in his younger days, and *Mustapha* is praised in some lines by John Davies of Hereford, printed probably in 1611. The earlier of the two tragedies (according to the arrangement in the folio) is simply entitled *Alaham,* and its scene is placed in Ormus, an island which, according to Langbaine, is situated at the entrance of the Persian Gulf. In a *Prologus* of overpowering gloom the Ghost of one of the old Kings of

Ormus ascends from the depths of Hades to announce that all the sins of his line are about to come home as curses to its last representatives, and analyses with terrible power of insight the characters of his doomed descendants. Then the plot begins slowly to work itself out. Urged on by his abandoned wife Hala, Alaham, the second son of the old King, brings about the deposition of his father, and puts out his eyes and those of the imbecile heir; in their desolation they are protected by the King's daughter—one of those characters in which the author seeks to embody his lofty conception of womanhood. She shares their cruel fate, which is in the last act narrated to Alaham by a Nuntius; filled with remorse and horror, he survives only long enough to include his adulterous wife as a murderess in the common doom of all that was his.

In *Mustapha* there is no change of style or of external form. The metre of the dialogue, too, is the same, viz. a mixture of rimed quatrains and couplets with occasional blank verse. The Choruses at the close of the acts consist of various groups, and their discourse is connected with the action only through the suggestion of thought by thought. But the action of *Mustapha,* which seems to have been derived from an episode of French romance, is on the whole less opaque than that of *Alaham.* The personages, too—Mustapha the high-minded heir to the throne, Rossa the scheming Sultana who seeks to effect his destruction so as to make possible the succession of her own son Zanger, and Camena his noble-hearted step-sister—appeal less remotely to human interest than the sepulchral dynasty of Ormus. The final speech of Rossa, whose own children have in life and in death rebelled against her ruthless ambition, plunges us once more into a metaphysical abyss. For her there is no mercy, for in her there is no trust; die she will not, for death ends pain; with the evil and the passion she bears away with her she will set 'all hearts, all times, all worlds on fire.'—ADOLPHUS WILLIAM WARD, *A History of English Dramatic Literature* (1875), 1899, Vol. 2, pp. 614–17

Lord Brooke was not universally popular, and a very savage contemporary epitaph on him has been preserved. But he had been the patron of the youthful Davenant, and has left not a little curious literary work, which has only been recently collected, and little of which saw the light in his own lifetime. Of his two singular plays, *Mustapha* and *Alaham* (closet-dramas having something in common with the Senecan model), *Mustapha* was printed in 1609; but it would seem piratically. His chief prose work, the *Life of Sidney,* was not printed till 1652. His chief work in verse, the singular *Poems of Monarchy* (ethical and political treatises), did not appear till eighteen years later, as well as the allied *Treatise on Religion.* But poems or tracts on human learning, on wars, and other things, as singularly inappropriate to verse, had appeared in 1633. This publication, a folio volume, also contained by far the most interesting part of his work, the so-called sonnet collection of *Cælica*—a medley, like many of those mentioned in this chapter, of lyrics and short poems of all lengths and metrical arrangements, but, unlike almost all of them, dealing with many subjects, and apparently addressed to more than one person. It is here, and almost here only, that the reader who has not a very great love for Elizabethan literature and some experience of it, can be recommended to seek confirmation of the estimate in which Greville was held by Charles Lamb, and of the very excusable and pious, though perhaps excessive, admiration of his editor Dr. Grosart. Even *Cælica* is very unlikely to find readers as a whole, owing to the strangely repellent character of Brooke's thought, which is intricate and obscure, and of his style, which is at any rate sometimes as harsh and eccentric as the theories of poetry which made him compose verse-treatises on politics. Nevertheless there is much nobility of thought and expression in him, and not unfrequent flashes of real poetry, while his very faults are characteristic.—GEORGE SAINTSBURY, A *History of Elizabethan Literature*, 1887, pp. 98–99

Brooke writes in his discursive memoir of Sidney with reference to his tragedies: "For my own part I found my creeping genius more fixed upon the images of life than the images of wit." This is a just criticism of all Brooke's literary work. To "elegancy of style" or "smoothness of verse" he rarely aspires. He is essentially a philosopher, cultivating "a close, mysterious, and sentenious way of writing," which is commonly more suitable to prose than poetry. His subjects are for the most part incapable of imaginative treatment. In his collection of love poems, which, though written in varied metres, he entitles sonnets, he seeks to express passionate love, and often with good lyrical effects; but the understanding seems as a rule to tyrannise over emotion, and all is "frozen and made rigid with intellect." Sidney's influence is very perceptible, and some of Brooke's stanzas harshly echo passages from *Astrophel and Stella*.—SIDNEY LEE, *Dictionary of National Biography*, 1890, Vol. 23, p. 162

EDMUND GOSSE
From *The Jacobean Poets*
1894, pp. 194–200

An isolated figure in the literature of the age is Fulke Greville, Lord Brooke, who was born earlier than any other writer included in the scope of this volume, but who composed the poetry of his which we possess, mainly, in all probability, in the reign of James I. Lord Brooke's verse is unsympathetic and unattractive, yet far too original and well-sustained to be overlooked. He is like one of those lakes, which exist here and there on the world's surface, which are connected with no other system of waters, and by no river contribute to the sea. Lord Brooke's abstruse and acrid poetry proceeded from nowhere and influenced no one. It is a solitary phenomenon in our literature, and the author a kind of marsupial in our poetical zoology. In the breadth of his sympathy for everything written between 1580 and 1630, Charles Lamb embraced Lord Brooke's strange poems and plays. It is not possible to improve on the verdict of this admirable critic; Lamb says of Lord Brooke:—"He is nine parts Machiavel and Tacitus, for one part Sophocles or Seneca. In this writer's estimation of the faculties of his own mind, the understanding must have held a most tyrannical pre-eminence. Whether we look into his plays, or his most passionate love-poems, we shall find all frozen and made rigid with intellect." It is quite incredible that Lord Brooke's poetry should ever become popular, but it deserves as much attention as can be given to work essentially so unexhilarating.

Fulke Greville was born at Beauchamp Court, in Warwickshire, in 1554. In November, 1564, he proceeded to Shrewsbury School, where was entered, on the same day, a boy named Philip Sidney, whose intimate friend and biographer he was destined to become. They were, however, separated after their school-life was over, for while Sidney went to Oxford, Greville became a fellow-commoner at Jesus College, Cambridge, in 1568. Later on, in the court of Elizabeth, he renewed his companionship with Sir Philip Sidney, and became intimate with Sir Edward Dyer. Sidney celebrates their enthusiastic affection in several well-known poems—

Welcome my two to me,

The number best beloved;
    Within my heart you be
In friendship unremoved;
Join hands and hearts, so let it be,
Make but one mind in bodies three.

While Dyer and Sidney, however, applied themselves early to poetry, and took part in the prosodical revolutions of the Areopagus, Greville seems to have refrained from verse, or else, what he wrote has not come down to us. At all events, his existing works appear to belong, in the main, to the post-Elizabethan period; the cycle of *Cælica*, which seems to date from the close of the sixteenth century, being excepted. He was a very scanty contributor to the Elizabethan miscellanies. His interests, in fact, seem to have been mainly political, and after the death of Sidney, Greville rose to high honours in the state. As early as 1576 he began to receive offices in Wales, and before he was thirty, he had been made secretary for the whole principality. In 1597 he was knighted. It has been supposed that his fortunes sustained some check at the accession of James I., but this must have been very temporary, for we find him confirmed for life in his Welsh office, and in 1614 raised to the position of Chancellor of the Exchequer. He was made a peer in 1620, but was never married. The young William Davenant was brought up in his service; and Lord Brooke was, indeed, throughout his career, though accused of extreme parsimony, the patron of poets and scholars. In September, 1628, in circumstances which have remained very obscure, Lord Brooke was murdered in his London house in Holborn, by a serving-man of the name of Haywood, who stabbed him in the back in his bed-chamber, and then committed suicide before he could be brought to justice.

Lord Brooke published nothing during his own lifetime, for the edition of his tragedy of *Mustapha*, which appeared in 1609, was almost certainly issued against his will. Five years after his death was printed, in a small folio, *Certain Learned and Elegant Works*, 1633, a collection which comprised the treatises *Of Human Learning*, *Upon Fame and Honour*, and *Of Wars*, the tragedies of *Alaham* and *Mustapha*, the lyrical cycle of a hundred and nine poems called *Cælica*, and some prose miscellanies. So late as 1670 appeared *The Remains of Fulk Greville, Lord Brooke*, being the *Treatises of Monarchy and Religion*. These two volumes contain, with very trifling exceptions, the entire poetical works of Lord Brooke, his famous prose life of Sir Philip Sidney being also posthumous. It is a vexed question when these works were written. The publisher of 1633 averred that "when he grew old he revised the poems and treatises he had wrote long before," but this is very vague. The collection called *Cælica* has something of an Elizabethan character; the rest seem undoubtedly, both by external and internal evidence, to belong to the seventeenth century. The *Treatise of Monarchy*, for instance, could not have been written till some years after the accession of James.

A great monotony of style marks the poetry of Lord Brooke. It is harsh and unsympathetic; the verse, which depends for life on its stateliness alone, sinks, between the purple passages, to a leaden dulness. The "treatises" are exceedingly difficult to read through. They all begin—and this is a very curious point—with an eloquent stanza or two, only to sink immediately into a jog-trot of prose in lengths. One or two critics have chosen to praise Lord Brooke with something like extravagance. It is true that he is full of ripe and solemn thought; it is not less true that he is always endeavouring to present to us noble views of character and conduct. As Phillips said, in his *Theatrum Poetarum* of 1675, Lord Brooke has "a close, mysterious, and sentenious way of writing." But, except here and there in the course of *Cælica*, he entirely forgets that the poet has to be an artist; he thinks of him purely as a teacher, and as a prophet. He does not shrink from such lines as—

Knowledge's next organ is imagination,

or from rhyming "heart" with "arts," and alternating "pain" and "gain" by "fame" and "frame." His dignity, his earnestness, his religious and moral sententiousness are unilluminated by colour, imagery, or melody. . . .

In his bold political speculations and his reflections on the effects of tyranny taken from ancient history and modern experience, he sometimes reminds us of Sir John Davies, but at a great distance.

His plays are what Lamb described them to be, frozen. He tells us that he wrote others, to which he intended his elaborate didactic "treatises" to serve as choruses; and in particular he burned with his own hand an *Antony and Cleopatra* which it would have been amusing to compare with Shakespeare's. The two we possess are, however, all that we can desire, and few have had the patience to read them. They are, in some measure, composed upon the Seneca model. *Alaham* opens with a long rhymed prologue of sonorous irregular stanza, spoken by the ghost of a murdered King of Ormuz, descriptive of hell. . . .

Some of these choruses, in a long broken metre, must, even then, have seemed exceedingly old-fashioned. *Mustapha* is an easier play to follow, and Mrs. Humphrey Ward has drawn attention to the almost Miltonic magnificence of the Chorus of Tartars at the end of the fifth act.

Vast superstition! glorious style of weakness!
Sprung from the deep disquiet of man's passion,
To desolation and dispair of nature!
The texts bring princes' titles into question;
Thy prophets set on work the sword of tyrants;
They manacle sweet Truth with their distinctions;
Let Virtue blood; teach cruelty for God's sake;
Fashioning one God, yet him of many fashions;
Like many-headed Error in their passions.

Mustapha has less rhyme introduced into it than *Alaham*, and has a somewhat more modern air. Human interest and the play of the emotions are entirely neglected in these curious wooden dramas.

GABRIEL HARVEY

c. 1545–1630

The son of a ropemaker, Gabriel Harvey was born at Saffron Walden, Essex, probably in 1545. He entered Christ's College, Cambridge, in 1566, and became a fellow of Pembroke Hall in 1570. In 1574 he was elected a professor of rhetoric and in 1578 he was chosen a fellow of Trinity Hall. Harvey left Cambridge after failing to become master of Trinity Hall; he eventually earned a law degree at Oxford in 1584.

Harvey was a friend to Edmund Spenser, to whom he offered frequent literary advice. Harvey appears in Spenser's *The Shepheardes Calendar* (1579) as Hobbinol. Harvey's own works include some satiric Latin poetry as well as *Rhetor* and *Ciceronianus*, two tracts on rhetorical theory. Harvey's *Foure Letters and Certaine Sonnets* (1592) involved him in a bitter literary quarrel with Robert Greene and Thomas Nashe. Harvey wrote two more satires aimed at Thomas Nashe, *Pierce's Supererogation* (1593) and *Trimming of Thomas Nashe* (1597). Eventually the Archbishop of Canterbury ordered the satires of both men burned in 1599. A formidable scholar and critic, Harvey unsuccessfully tried to introduce classical hexameter into English. His association with Spenser is captured in a series of highly polished letters that Harvey wrote to Spenser. Harvey is remembered for his severe criticism of *The Faerie Queene*. Harvey returned to Saffron Walden in 1598, and he resided there until his death on February 11, 1630.

Now I trust M. Haruey, that vpon sight of your speciall frends and fellow Poets doings, or els for enuie of so many vnworthy Quidams, which catch at the garlond, which to you alone is dewe, you will be perswaded to pluck out of the hateful darknesse, those so many excellent English poemes of yours, which lye hid, and bring them forth to eternall light. Trust me you doe both them great wrong, in depriuing them of the desired sonne, and also your selfe, in smoothering your deserued prayses, and all men generally, in withholding from them so diuine pleasures, which they might conceiue of your gallant English verses, as they haue already doen of your Latine Poemes, which in my opinion both for inuention and Elocution are very delicate, and superexcellent. And thus againe, I take my leaue of my good Mayster Haruey from my lodging at London thys 10. of Aprill. 1579.—E. K., "Dedicatory Epistle" to Spenser's *Shepherdes Calender*, 1579

Good Master G. I perceiue by your most curteous and frendly Letters your good will to be no lesse in deed, than I alwayes esteemed. In recompence wherof, think I beseech you, that I wil spare neither speech, nor wryting, nor aught else, whensoeuer, and wheresoeuer occasion shal be offred me: yea, I will not stay, till it be offred, but will seeke it, in al that possibly I may. And that you may perceiue how much your Counsel in al things preuaileth with me, and how altogither I am ruled and ouer-ruled thereby: I am now determined to alter mine owne former purpose, and to subscribe to your aduizement: being notwithstanding resolued stil, to abide your farther resolution. My principal doubts are these. First, I was minded for a while to haue intermitted the vttering of my writings: leaste by ouermuch cloying their noble eares, I should gather a contempt of my self, or else seeme rather for gaine and commoditie to doe it, for some sweetnesse that I haue already tasted. Then also me seemeth the work too base for his excellent Lordship, being made in Honour of a priuate Personage vnknowne, which of some yl-willers might be vpbraided, not to be so worthie, as you knowe she is: or the matter not so weightie, that it should be offred to so weightie a Personage: or the like. The selfe former Title stil liketh me well ynough, and your fine Addition no lesse. If these, and the like doubtes, maye be of importaunce in your seeming, to frustrate any parte of your aduice, I beeseeche you, without the leaste selfe loue of your own purpose, councell me for the beste: and the rather doe it faithfullye, and carefully, for that, in all things I attribute so muche to your iudgement, that I am euermore content to adnihilate mine owne determinations, in respecte thereof. And indeede for your selfe to, it sitteth with you now, to call your wits, and senses togither, (which are alwaies at call) when occasion is so fairely offered of Estimation and Preferment. For, whiles the yron is hote, it is good striking, and minds of Nobles varie, as their Estates. *Verùm ne quid durius.*

. . . I am, of late, more in loue wyth my Englishe Versifying, than with Ryming: whyche I should haue done long since, if I would then haue followed your councell. *Sed te solum iam tum suspicabar cum Aschamo sapere: nunc Aulam video egregios alere Poëtas Anglicos.* Maister *E. K.* hartily desireth to be commended vnto your Worshippe: of whome, what accompte he maketh, youre selfe shall hereafter perceiue, by hys paynefull and dutifull Verses of your selfe.

Thus muche was written at Westminister yesternight: but comming this morning, beeyng the sixteenth of October, to Mystresse *Kerkes*, to haue it deliuered to the Carrier, I receyued youre letter, sente me the laste weeke: whereby I perceiue you otherwhiles continue your old exercise of Versifying in English: whych glorie I had now thought shoulde haue bene onely ours heere at London, and the Court.

Truste me, your Verses I like passingly well, and enuye your hidden paines in this kinde, or rather maligne, and grudge at your selfe, that woulde not once imparte so muche to me. But once, or twice, you make a breache in Maister *Drants* Rules: *quod tamen condonabimus tanto Poëtae, tuaeque ipsius maximae in his rebus autoritati.* You shall see when we meete in London, (whiche, when it shall be, certifye vs) howe fast I haue followed after you, in that Course: beware, leaste in time I ouertake you. *Veruntamen te solùm sequar, (vt saepenumerò sum professus,) nunquam sanè assequar, dum viuam.*—ED-MUND SPENSER, Letter to Gabriel Harvey (c. 1579)

> Haruey, the happy aboue happiest men
> I read: that sitting like a Looker-on
> Of this worldes Stage, doest note with critique pen
> The sharpe dislikes of each condition:
> And as one carelesse of suspition,
> Ne fawnest for the fauour of the great:
> Ne fearest foolish reprehension
> Of faulty men, which daunger to thee threat.
> But freely doest, of what thee list, entreat,
> Like a great Lord of peerelesse liberty:
> Lifting the Good vp to high Honours seat,
> And the Euill damning euermore to dy.
> For Life, and Death is in thy doomefull writing:
> So thy renowme liues euer by endighting.
>
> —EDMUND SPENSER, "To the right worshipfull,
> my singular good frend, M. Gabriell Haruey,
> Doctor of the Lawes," 1586

This place haue I purposely reserued for one, who is not only, yet in my iudgement principally deserueth the tytle of the rightest English Poet, that euer I read: that is, the Author of the Sheepeheardes Kalender, intituled to the woorthy Gentleman Master *Phillip Sydney*, whether it was Master *Sp.* or what rare Scholer in Pembrooke Hall soeuer, because himself and his freendes, for what respect I knowe not, would not reueale it, I force not greatly to sette downe: sorry I am that I can not find none other with whom I might couple him in this *Catalogue*, in his rare gyft of Poetry: although one there is, though nowe long since, seriously occupied in grauer studies, (Master *Gabriell Haruey*) yet, as he was once his most special freende and fellow Poet, so because he hath taken such paynes, not onely in his Latin Poetry (for which he enioyed great commendations of the best both in iudgment and dignity in thys Realme) but also to reforme our English verse, and to beautify the fame with braue deuises, of which I thinke the cheefe lye hidde in hatefull obscurity: therefore wyll I aduenture to sette them together, as two of the rarest witts, and learnedst masters of Poetrie in England. Whose worthy and notable skyl in this faculty, I would wysh if their high dignities and serious businesses would permit, they would styll graunt to bee a furtheraunce to that reformed kinde of Poetry, which Master *Haruey* did once beginne to ratify: and surely in mine opinion, if hee had chosen some grauer matter, and handled but with halfe that skyll, which I knowe he could haue doone, and not powred it foorth at a venture, as a thinge between iest and earnest, it had taken greater effect then it did.—WILLIAM WEBBE, A *Discourse of English Poetrie*, 1586

A proverb it is, as stale as sea-biefe, save a thief from the gallows and hee'le be the first to shew thee the way to Saint Gilesesse. Harvey I manifestly saved from the knot under the eare: Verily, he had hanged him selfe had I gone forwards in my vengeance; but, I know not how, upon his prostrate intreatie, I was content to give him a short Psalme of mercy. Now, for reprieving him when he was ripe for execution, thus he requites me. Sixe and thirty sheets of mustard-pot paper since that hath he published against me. . . . Some few crummes of my booke hath he confuted: all the rest of his invention is nothing but an oxe with a pudding in his bellie. . . . Maister Lillie, poore deceasses Kit Marlow, reverent Doctor Perne, with a hundred other quiet senselesse carcasses before the Conquest departed, in the same worke he hath most notoriously and vilely dealt with; and, to conclude, he hath proved him selfe to be the only Gabriel Grave-digger under heaven.—THOMAS NASHE, *Christ's Teares over Jerusalem*, 1594

This person, who made a great noise in his time, was born at Saffron-walden in Essex; and tho' his father was a ropemaker as Thomas Nash, a great scoffer, and his antagonist, tells us, yet he had rich kindred and was nearly allied to Sir Thomas Smith, the great statesman in Queen Elizabeth's reign.—ANTHONY À WOOD, *Fasti Oxonienses*, 1691–1721

Of this writer, so well known in his time, the author of many respectable works, and of no inferior accomplishments in learning or talents, very imperfect accounts are to be found in any of our biographical compilations. He certainly deserves a place among the national records of his countrymen.—WILLIAM BELOE, "Gabriel Harvey," *Anecdotes of Literature and Scarce Books*, 1807, Vol. 2, p. 197

Harvey was a pedant, but pedantry was part of the erudition of an age when our national literature was passing from its infancy; he introduced hexameter verses into our language, and pompously laid claim to an invention which, designed for the reformation of English verse, was practised till it was found sufficiently ridiculous. His style was infected with his pedantic taste, and the hard outline of his satirical humour betrays the scholastic cynic, not the airy and fluent wit. He had, perhaps, the foibles of a man who was clearing himself from obscurity; he prided himself on his family alliances, while he fastidiously looked askaunce on the trade of his father, a rope-manufacturer. He was somewhat rich in his apparel, according to the rank in society he held; and, hungering after the notice of his friends, they fed him on soft sonnet and relishing dedication, till Harvey ventured to publish a collection of panegyrics on himself—and thus gravely stepped into a niche erected to Vanity. At length he and his two brothers, one a divine and the other a physician, became students of astronomy; but then an astronomer usually ended in an almanack maker, and above all, in an astrologer;—an avocation which tempted a man to become a prophet. Their "Sharpe and learned judgment on Earthquakes" drove the people out of their senses (says Wood); but when nothing happened of their predictions, the brothers received a severe castigation from those great enemies of prophets, the wits. The buffoon, Tarleton, celebrated for his extempore humour, jested on them at the theatre; Elderton, a drunken ballad-maker, "consumed his ale-crammed nose to nothing in bear-baiting them with bundles of ballads." One on the Earthquake commenced with "Quake! quake! quake!" They made the people laugh at their false terrors, or, as Nash humorously describes their fanciful panic, "when they sweated and were not a haire the worse."

. . . Unfortunately for the learned Harvey, his "critique pen," which is strange in so polished a mind and so curious a student, indulged a sharpness of invective which would have been peculiar to himself, had his adversary, Nash, not quite outdone him. Marsyas did not endure a more memorable flaying from the divinity of wit, than was inflicted on Harvey by Nash. He was ridiculed to his grave! Their pamphlets foamed against each other, till Nash, in his vehement invective, involved the whole generation of the Harveys, made one brother more ridiculous than the other, and even attainted the fair name of Gabriel's respectable sister. Gabriel, indeed, after the death of Robert Greene, the crony of Nash, sitting like a vampire on his grave, sucked blood from his corpse, in a memorable narrative of the debaucheries and miseries of this town-wit. I throw into the note the most awful satirical address I ever read. It became necessary to dry up the floodgates of these rival ink-horns, by an order of the Archbishop of Canterbury. The order is a remarkable fragment of our literary history, and is thus expressed; "that all Nashe's bookes and Dr. Harvey's bookes be taken wheresoever they may be found, and that none of the said bookes be ever printed hereafter."—ISAAC DISRAELI, "Literary Ridicule," *Calamities of Authors*, 1812

A dry hard student, full of caustic wit, but not lacking, when the humor took him, grace and tenderness. He hurled fierce, stinging words in profusion at any one with whom he chanced to be offended, but to all who pleased him he was a warm and helpful friend. His genius was wasted in his efforts to naturalize the hexameter and other classical metres in English, and of this idle attempt he claimed to be the originator.—H. R. FOX BOURNE, *A Memoir of Sir Philip Sidney*, 1862, p. 44

Harvey is a remarkable instance of the refining influence of classical studies. Amid the pedantic farrago of his omnisufficiency (to borrow one of his own words) we come suddenly upon passages whose gravity of sentiment, stateliness of movement, and purity of diction remind us of Landor. These lucid intervals in his overweening vanity explain and justify the friendship of Spenser. Yet the reiteration of emphasis with which he insists on all the world's knowing that Nash had called him an ass, probably gave Shakespeare the hint for one

of the most comic touches in the character of Dogberry. —JAMES RUSSELL LOWELL, "Spenser" (1875), *Prose Works*, Riverside ed., Vol. 4, p. 285

. . . Gabriel Harvey was a man who had influence on Spenser's ideas and purposes, and on the direction of his efforts. He was a classical scholar of much distinction in his day, well read in the Italian authors then so fashionable, and regarded as a high authority on questions of criticism and taste. Except to students of Elizabethan literary history, he has become an utterly obscure personage; and he has not usually been spoken of with much respect. He had the misfortune, later in life, to plunge violently into the scurrilous quarrels of the day, and as he was matched with wittier and more popular antagonists, he has come down to us as a foolish pretender, or at least as a dull and stupid scholar who knew little of the real value of the books he was always ready to quote, like the pedant of the comedies, or Shakespeare's schoolmaster Holofernes. Further, he was one who, with his classical learning, had little belief in the resources of his mother tongue, and he was one of the earliest and most confident supporters of a plan than fashionable, for reforming English verse, by casting away its natural habits and rhythms, and imposing on it the laws of the classical metres. In this he was not singular. The professed treatises of this time on poetry, of which there were several, assume the same theory, as the mode of "reforming" and duly elevating English verse. It was eagerly accepted by Philip Sidney and his Areopagus of wits at court, who busied themselves in devising rules of their own—improvements as they thought on those of the university men—for English hexameters and sapphics, or as they called it, artificial versifying. They regarded the comparative value of the native English rhythms and the classical metres, much as our ancestors of Addison's day regarded the comparison between Gothic and Palladian architecture. One, even if it sometimes had a certain romantic interest, was rude and coarse; the other was the perfection of polite art and good taste. Certainly in what remains of Gabriel Harvey's writing, there is much that seems to us vain and ridiculous enough; and it has been naturally surmised that he must have been a dangerous friend and counsellor to Spenser. But probably we are hard upon him. His writings, after all, are not much more affected and absurd in their outward fashion than most of the literary composition of the time; his verses are no worse than those of most of his neighbours; he was not above, but he was not below, the false tastes and clumsiness of his age; and the rage for "artificial versifying" was for the moment in the air. And it must be said, that though his enthusiasm for English hexameters is of a piece with the puritan use of Scripture texts in divinity and morals, yet there is no want of hard-headed shrewdness in his remarks; indeed, in his rules for the adaptation of English words and accents to classical metres, he shows clearness and good sense in apprehending the conditions of the problem, while Sidney and Spenser still appear confused and uncertain. But in spite of his pedantry, and though he had not, as we shall see, the eye to discern at first the genius of the *Faery Queen*, he has to us the interest of having been Spenser's first, and as far as we can see, to the last, dearest friend.—R. W. CHURCH, *Spenser* (1879), 1888, pp. 22–25

The names of Nash and Harvey are intertwined even more closely than those, of Greene and Lodge; but the conjunction is not a grasp of friendship but a grip of hatred—a wrestle, not an embrace. The fact of the quarrel has attracted rather disproportionate attention from the days of Issac Disraeli onwards; and its original cause is still extremely obscure and very unimportant. By some it is connected, causally as well as acciden-tally, with the Martin Marprelate business; by some with the fact that Harvey belonged to the inner Sidneian clique, Nash to the outer ring of professional journalists and Bohemians. It at any rate produced some remarkable varieties of the pamphlet, and demonstrated the keen interest which the world takes in the proceedings of any couple of literary men who choose to abuse and befoul one another. Harvey, though no mean scholar, was a poor writer, no match for Nash; and his chief answer to the latter, *Pierce's Supererogation*, is about as ram-bling, incoherent, and ineffective a combination of pedantry and insolence as need be wished for. It has some not unin-teresting, though usually very obscure, hints on literary mat-ters. Besides this, Harvey wrote letters to Spenser with their well-known criticism and recommendation of classical forms, and *Foure Letters Touching Robert Greene and Others: with the Trimming of Thomas Nash, Gentleman. . . .*

In Harvey, more perhaps than anywhere else in prose, appears the abusive exaggeration, not humorous or Rabelai-sian, but simply rancorous and dull, which mars so much Elizabethan work. In order not to fall into the same error ourselves, we must abstain from repeating the very strong lan-guage which has sometimes been applied to his treatment of dead men, and such dead men as Greene and Marlowe, for apparently no other fault than their being friends of his enemy Nash. It is sufficient to say that Harvey had all the worst traits of "Donnishness," with out having apparently any notion of that dignity which sometimes half excuses the Don. He was em-phatically of Mr. Carlyle's "acrid-quack" genus.—GEORGE SAINTSBURY, *A History of Elizabethan Literature*, 1887, pp. 230–32

HENRY MORLEY
"Spenser's 'Hobbinol'"
Fortnightly Review, March 1869, pp. 274–83

When, in 1579, their old comrade at Pembroke Hall, Edward Kirke, prefixed to Spenser's first venture in verse, *The Shepheardes' Calender*, a letter to Gabriel Harvey, as its unnamed author's "special friend and fellow-poet," he only told in prose what is shown by the Calender itself, where Harvey is enshrined as Spenser's Hobbinol. The difference is great between this Hobbinol as we may see him if we care to look for his true features, and the figure which stands for him in encyclopædias, in text-books, and in that lively account of the paper war between Harvey and Nash which most of us have read with natural enjoyment in Issac D'Israeli's *Calamities of Authors*. Hardly a definite fact has been stated, real or imagi-nary, which has not had a turn given to it unfavourable to the good name of this much misrepresented scholar. A vague con-cession that "the friend of Spenser and Sidney could hardly have been contemptible," is all that we have given us in *The Calamities of Authors* to qualify the finding of a portrait in the mere caricature produced by an unscrupulous wit, who had more genius but less worth than his antagonist, and who amused himself and the town with extravagant exaggeration of what he took to be the weaknesses of his opponent's character. Yet there is not one—actually not one—sharp point in the indictment against Gabriel Harvey which does not break at a touch when we look from the burlesque upon him to the man himself. He did not become a great man, or what he called "a megalander;" we may, if we will, class him with what is fossil or extinct in literature—its megatherium or dodo. But in his day he worked hard, aspired nobly, and left witness to his labour and his aspiration. Perhaps we do not care, for his own sake, to

read the evidence, but set him aside as one of the small mat-ters, if any there be, in which it is not worth while to be just. Then let him have the advantage of being not merely Gabriel Harvey, although to him that was something, but also Spenser's Hobbinol, which to us is more. He was, during some impor-tant years of Spenser's life, the poet's "long-approved and sin-gular good friend" and counsellor. The counsel was outgrown, but not the friendship. To our credence as well as Harvey's, Spenser has left what he once called "the eternal memory of our everlasting friendship, the inviolable memory of our un-spotted friendship, the sacred memory of our vowed friend-ship;" and it is a little due perhaps to Spenser that we should ascertain how much credit is due to the commentators who would have us think that he wrote in this way to a conceited pedant seven years older than himself.

Gabriel Harvey was the eldest of four sons of a ropemaker at Saffron Walden, a prosperous man who, when his boys were young, filled the chief offices of his native town, and spent his money freely on their education. Three of the boys were sent to the neighbouring University of Cambridge, and they all three became noticeable men. The son, of whom nothing is known, may have succeeded to his father's business. Of the three who took to scholarship, Gabriel became, while yet a young man, in or not long before the year 1576, a lecturer on Rhetoric at Cambridge, with Cicero for his guide, and large attendance at his lectures. The year usually given as the probable date of Gabriel Harvey's birth is 1545; and then, as the date of his death is known, it has to be added that he reached the age of ninety. It does not inevitably follow that because Gabriel Harvey was at Cambridge before Spenser, and had ceased to be an undergraduate when his friend first came to college, he was—as the young would count years—a much older man; although the presumption would be fair if there were not evi-dence to the contrary. But then the fact seems to have been overlooked that there is rather good evidence to the contrary. Harvey's Introductory Lecture upon meeting his class at Cambridge, in the year 1577, was published as his "Cicero-nianus," dedicated to William Lewin, who, in a letter prefixed to it, gives his own opinion upon the most eminent masters of eloquence, and speaks of his friend Harvey as *adhuc adoles-centem*; which he would hardly have done if Harvey had been thirty-two years old. No doubt the range of a man's years com-prehended under that term might have been taken by a Roman as from seventeen to thirty; Cicero called himself *adolescens* at the time of his consulship when his age was forty-four, but he speaks elsewhere of five-and-twenty as the term of adolescence, and that certainly answers so well to our own usage, that Harvey could scarcely have been spoken of as *adhuc adoles-centem* when he was thirty-two years old. It is more probable that his age did not exceed five or six-and-twenty, and that he had begun the public teaching of rhetoric in his university in the preceding year. For in the next year, 1578, his two first lectures were published as his *Rhetor*, and we find that, in referring modestly to the full attendance before him, while valuable teachers such as Byng and Dodington, whom he named with reverence, were lecturing to empty benches, he said that he ascribed the fulness of his class in the preceding year to students' love of novelty, but warned them that there was no more of that—"Harvey is old now, and leaves novelty to new professors." As the introductory lecture of the preceding year was upon the occasion of his again meeting his class, we may assume that he had begun to teach in 1576, when he was—*adhuc adolescens*—twenty-five years old, or a year younger. The known age of his brother John was thirteen or fourteen, and Richard could not have been very much older, for he also, when he went to Cambridge in 1575, as a pensioner of Pembroke Hall, found in his brother Gabriel a guide and tutor. Theere was at least one sister in the family, and there might have been several intermediate in age between Gabriel and Richard. At any rate, here is good reason for believing that Gabriel Harvey, instead of being a pedantic scholar seven and more years older than his friends Spenser and Sidney, a man who could give himself some airs of seniority in social intercourse with them, was a familiar friend, with no more difference of age than is consistent, in free fellowship of youth, with equal sharing of enthusiasms and exchange of thought. Spenser and Harvey at Cambridge were both of the same college, Pembroke Hall, and Spenser was in his last year, taking his degree of M.A., when Harvey began, if he had not sooner begun, lecturing on Rhetoric. As for Philip Sidney, Oxford was his university, and although he is commonly said to have gone for a few months to Cambridge at the age of fifteen or sixteen, there is no evidence that he did so. If we would know how the strong friendship between Harvey and Sidney first arose, we must understand more than we do of the relations between Harvey and Sidney's uncle Leicester, whom Gabriel, in his *Gratulationes Waldenses* incidentally, and also specially in the inscription of that part of it which is dedicated to him, distinguished as "his Lord;" and who, in July, 1578, when Queen Elizabeth paid her visit to Audley End, was about to send him into France and Italy.

In Harvey's *Walden Gratulations*, written to commemorate the visit of her Majesty to Audley End, the great house of his native town of Saffron Walden, two significant scraps of dialogue, are left upon record. An impetuous member of the University of Cambridge, there present by its representatives to pay honour to Queen Bess, stepped out of the ranks and knelt to her. The over-zealous gentleman was, let us say, about six-and-twenty years old, tall, keen of feature, swarthy, and black-haired. "Who is this man?" the Queen asked in her blunt way. "Who is this? Is it Leicester's man that we were speaking of?" And when told that it was, she said, "I'll not deny you my hand, Harvey." In a short Latin verse exercise appended to the first of the four books of his *Gratulations* upon the Queen's coming to Walden and Audley End, Gabriel Harvey gives that piece of dialogue. He adds another set of verses on another saying of the Queen's upon the same occasion. "Tell me," she said of him to Leicester, "is it settled that you send this man to Italy and France?" "It is," said he. "That's well," she replied; "for already he has an Italian face, and the look of a man; I should hardly have taken him to be an Englishman." In his lines upon this theme, we have Gabriel's own witness to the dusky hue, which scoffing Nash compared to rancid bacon. Harvey's service of Leicester, here so distinctly indicated, may have led to the establishment of that warm friendship for Leicester's nephew Sidney, which breathes out of another poem in the *Walden Gratulations*. It certainly enabled Harvey the more safely to counsel his friend Spenser, gone northward, to leave "those hills where harbrough nis to see," and resort to the dales with their rich shepherds and fruitful flocks. It may have been not as a poet only that Harvey sent Spenser to Leicester, though enough for Sidney that he was a poet of his own age who thought with him on the great religious questions of the day. The fact that it was Gabriel Harvey who sent Spenser to London, seems to connect this reference in 1578 to Leicester's purpose of sending Harvey abroad with the affectionate Latin hexameters addressed to his friend Harvey in October, 1579, by Edmund Spenser, then on the point of travelling into France; "dispatched by my lord, I go thither," Spenser said, in the postcript dated from Leicester House, "as

sent by him, and maintained (most what) of him; and there am to employ my time, my mind, to his honour's service." Through those two scraps of the Queen's talk recorded in the Walden Gratulations, we come perhaps a little nearer to the prose version of Hobbinol's advice that Colin should resort to the rich shepherds of the dales.

On the occasion of the Queen's coming to Audley End, Dr. Howland, the Vice-Chancellor of the University, had notified to Lord Burghley that he and the heads of colleges would there wait on her Majesty, and have ready some disputants upon two moral questions—one whether clemency or severity be more praiseworthy in a prince; the other, of Fortune and Fate; also that they would present a book, which was, in fact, a Greek Testament, bound in red velvet and gold. Burghley chose the debate on clemency and severity, and accepted the offer of the book, upon condition that it was not to be scented with spike, which her Majesty could not abide. There must be also some gloves and a few verses for Leicester, the Earl of Oxford, and Sir Christopher Hatton; Burghley himself wanted none. The University duly appeared by dignitaries in their gowns and hoods; the Queen arrived, hot and faint, from her journey, in July weather, and went indoors; but after due refreshments the debate took place, and lasted for three hours. Mr. Fleming, of King's College, argued for clemency; Byng, Master of Clare Hall, concluded; Harvey of Pembroke, Palmer, of John's, and Hawkings, of Peterhouse, opposed; Fletcher, of King's College, was moderator; but the Lord Treasurer, as Chancellor of the University, took on himself to interfere, and cut short all repetitions or long discourses by way of confutation with the dictum, "Loquor ut Cancellarius, disputa dialecticè." There is in the library of the British Museum an old copy of Quintilian, which once belonged to Gabriel Harvey, and has wide margins liberally besprinkled, in some places crammed, with notes in his firm and elegant handwriting. On the blank space at the end we find him fortifying himself for this conflict, using Quintilian as a whetstone to his wit, and inscribing over against references to sections on extempore speech, memory, pronunciation, audacity, and courage, and against all manner of diffidence and despair—"My notes against my disputation at Audley End, in the Court, before my Lord Treasurer, my Lord of Leicester, and in the Queen's hearing." He writes under this a sound reflection, founded on the popularity among Italians of the artificial style of Aretino: "Unico Aretino—in Italian, singular for rare and hyperbolical amplifications. He is a simple orator that cannot mount as high as the quality or quantity of his matter requireth. Vain and fantastical amplifications argue an idle brain. But when the very majesty and dignity of the matter itself will indeed bear out a stately and haughty style, there is no such trial of a gallant discourser and right orator. Always an especial regard to be had of decorum, as well for orators and all manner of parleys as in other actions." Is this the thought which animates fantastic pedantry? The notes here quoted are at the end of the book, before the fly-leaf, which is covered with citations from many authors, made, apparently, in view of the same occasion, and therefore before July, 1578. The rest of the notes, which are part Latin, part English, and the incessant light underlining of words as the whole book was read carefully, pen in hand, belong chiefly to the following year; for in a closing memorandum Harvey sets down that he had read the book through again from the beginning, in September, 1579, and compared it with Cicero ad Brutum and Ramus, meaning, no doubt, Ramus's "Brutinæ Quæstiones." The notes often illustrate pleasantly their writer's character, and give his estimate of the reputations of contemporary scholars. It is interesting, for example, to find him noting as "tria vividissima Britannorum ingenia," Chaucer, Sir Thomas More, and Bishop Jewell; to which he adds, as the next triad, "tres florentissimas indoles," Heywood, Sidney, and Spenser. "Qui quærit illustriorum Anglorum ingenia, inveniet obscuriora," from which censure he excepts; he says, a very few, and first of them Sir Thomas Smith, Ascham, Wilson, Digges, Blundeville, Hakluyt, "mea corcula"—my favourites.

But how little of a dry pedant young Gabriel Harvey was, we can learn without reference to MS. if we will only look into his three published lectures, delivered, as the custom was, in Latin. In his introductory lecture, upon returning to the University in 1577, he says, after the fashion of wit in his day, that during the vacation he had been breakfasting on Tully, dining on Cæsar, and supping on Virgil. He will not say with which viand he took nectar, with which wine, and with which beer, but will speak of the talk of the guests, which is the sweetest seasoning of banquets. He then characterises the style of different writers. A friend had said that it would be less wonderful that Duffield should leave his philosophy than Harvey the eloquence he loves and exalts *supra mundum, supra modum.* Philosophers, says Harvey, are not always prophets; and he proceeds at once emphatically to recant much that he had taught in the preceding year. He had followed those Italians—Bembo, Sadolet, Nizolius—who exalted above all things the Ciceronian style, and had detested men who were not absolute Cicero-worshippers, as Erasmus, More, and Budé. He had abused Politian and Pico della Mirandola. He cites his own old Ciceronian formulas for the beginnings of speeches and letters, speaks of the delight he had in big Roman capitals, as IVP. O. M. "I produce," he said, "my folly to make you wiser. I worshipped M.T. as the god of Latinity, and would rather have been a Ciceronian than a saint." But he had since fallen upon Jean Sambuc's *Ciceronianus.* It had made him think, and sent him to the study of the old masters of Latinity. From that he had gone to the *Ciceronianus* of Peter Ramus, and to that of Professor Freig, of Basle, and to a preface by Sturmius, of Strasburg, and he had learned now to look at the ground and roots of Ciceronian eloquence; to relish the independent thought in Pico, and Erasmus, and Politian; to look for the whole man in a writer as the source of style, and, still exalting Cicero, to attend first to the life and power of the man, and not to the mere surface polish of his language. Let every man, he says, learn to be, not a Roman, but a Frenchman, German, Briton, or Italian. That certainly is not the lecture of a pedant rigid in the forms to which he had been bred. And the manliness of scholarship grew upon Harvey. In one of the MS. notes made by him three years later on the margin of his Quintilian, a sentence of the text suggests to him that "Mr. Ascham, in his fine discourse of Imitation, is somewhat too precise and scrupulous for Tully only, on all points; we having such excellent and dainty choice in the Latin tongue, worthy to be regarded and resembled in fitting place," and then he cites, with a differently defining adjective to each, nearly a score of authors. On another page he notes that a man without Greek is half learned; as Ascham said in joke of Mr. Haddon, though he loved him dearly, that he fluttered on one wing.

Thus Gabriel Harvey won honour to himself at Cambridge while he was training his two younger brothers, Richard and John. Richard was a lively pupil, ready to turn Latin verse on any subject, and warmly attached to his brother. He had Gabriel's fervid spirit without his discretion. He passed through a course of medicine and philosophy to study for the Church, and held a vicarage at the time when his brother John, who had obtained a physician's degree from his University, died—twenty-nine years old—at Lynn, in Norfolk, where he had

been establishing himself in practice. Dr. John Harvey was a quiet, studious man, who wrote little books indicating healthy tastes and calm judgment. But the Rev. Richard was restless and impulsive. He plunged into the Marprelate controversy; he played prophet; he attacked the wits of the town as "piperly players and makebates;" and it was he who brought the wits down on himself, and provoked them, in the reckless fashion of the time, to scoff at all his family.

Then Gabriel's resentment of an insult diverted the enemy's fire, and it was he who had to bear the whole brunt of the battle. He had at that time left Cambridge; and having in 1585 obtained grace for a degree of D.C.L. at Oxford, was practising in London as an advocate in the Prerogative Court.

Gabriel Harvey was a man of quick parts and high character—ardent, impressible, with a keen interest in intellectual pursuits, and a critical appreciation not exceptional, but modified and bounded by the notions of his time and by the studies of the University. He stood for an influential class, and fairly represented it. We have always been told to believe, on the authority of Thomas Nash, that he was ashamed of his father, the rope-maker; and encyclopædists have it that he ostentatiously claimed kindred with Sir Thomas Smith, another Saffron Walden man, who had been, with Cheke, joint chief of the Greeks at Cambridge, and who died a Secretary of State in 1577. But his writings, and those of his brothers, show that Gabriel Harvey was warmly and openly attached to his family and to his native town. Evidently it was not in boast of worldly position, but as the most natural reply to a libel on the old man's character, that, in the course of the Nash controversy, Harvey made known that his father, twenty years before, held the chief offices in his town, and that he had spent a thousand pounds upon the education of his sons. These were the public evidences of his father's worth. Again, it is not true that Harvey showed eagerness to claim Sir Thomas Smith as one of his relations. The reverse is true. He avoided the boast. As a Cambridge scholar and a Saffron Walden man who had a reputation for his Latin verse, Gabriel Harvey followed an old custom in producing "Smithus, vel Musarum Lacrymæ," upon the death of a scholar who was one of the chief glories of his University, who also was of Saffron Walden, and to whom, he says, he had looked up as his model of life, studies, and character. It seems that there was a family connection: for in one of his later letters Harvey speaks very incidentally of Sir Thomas Smith's son as his cousin. But in this series of laments, or *Tears of the Muses*, they are the Muses who speak for themselves in their own character, and some of them exalt the scholar they mourn by naming him as of their kindred. When speaking in his own person, at the opening and close of his work, to Walter Mildmay and to Sir John Wood, Smith's nephew and late secretary, Harvey is far from claiming, as it seems he could have claimed, a family connection with the man whose memory deserved his honour.

Again, it has been said, in the pleasant book, *The Calamities of Authors*, that Gabriel Harvey's vanity caused him to publish a collection of panegyrics upon himself. Where is it? Can it be that the title of the four books of the *Gratulations of Walden*, a collection of laudatory Latin epigrams and poems upon Queen Elizabeth, Leicester, Burghley, and three other personages of the Court—the third of them, and dearest of all, Harvey's friend, Philip Sidney—can it be that this volume, produced in honour of the Queen's visit to Walden and Audley End, has been mistaken for a set of panegyrics on its editor? Or is such a description given to the nine pages of verses on the Harvey and Nash quarrel attached to the 229 pages of *Pierce's Supererogation?* This is the sort of attention and justice clever men get from posterity when they have once been well covered with abuse from which it is nobody's particular business to defend them, and when they have not achieved in their lives anything great enough to draw on them the general attention of their countrymen in after times.

On the authority of Nash, Gabriel Harvey and his brothers John and Richard, have been confounded in one common charge of a ridiculous addiction to astrology. Thoughtful men of their time believed in the influences of the stars, and our language attests the old strength and prevalence of such convictions. But of these Harveys, as before said, Richard alone was an enthusiastic student of astronomy; and it was against him and his *Astrological Discourse upon the great and notable Conjunction of the two Inferior Planets, Saturn and Jupiter, on the 28th of April, 1583,* that Nash, in a passage of *Pierce Penniless, his Supplication to the Devil,* levelled his abusive wit. Richard's unlucky astrological prediction was addressed at its close—"From my father's house in Walden . . . to my very good and most loving brother, Master Gabriel Harvey, at his chamber in Trinity Hall." Gabriel then held a fellowship of Trinity. That Gabriel Harvey, had he been at Walden, would have discouraged, as he had before discouraged, his younger brother's astrological enthusiasm, is evident from the opening of this treatise: "Good brother, I have in some part done my endeavour to satisfy your late request, wherein you advertise me either not so much to addict myself to the study and contemplation of judicial astrology, or else by some sensible and evident demonstration to make certain and infallible proof what general good I can do my country thereby, or what special fruit I can reap thereof myself." John Harvey, the other brother, published in 1588 A *Discoursive Problem concerning Prophecies; how far they are to be valued or credited, according to the surest Rules and Directions in Divinity, Philosophy, and other Learning*; but this was written for the purpose of confuting and condemning superstitious faith in traditions and pretended prophecies, and it especially undertook to examine and reject an old prophecy of terrible things which were to happen in 1588, though admitting that this year might see the prologue to serious events of which the five acts and the epilogue would in due time probably follow. One of Gabriel Harvey's letters, printed without his knowledge and against his wish, was set forth as containing "a short and sharp judgment on earthquakes." As the set of letters to which this belongs is known through Haslewood's reprint in 1815 of *Ancient Critical Essays,* and Haslewood left out the earthquake letter because the matter of it was foreign to his purpose, the world has assumed pretty generally, from its title only, that here Gabriel displayed his addiction to astrology. But the letter exactly accords with the spirit in which he had sought to abate Richard's astrological enthusiasm. It reports to Spenser talk of the night before over an earthquake of which the shock had just been felt; the earthquake of 1580, which set in motion the pens of Arthur Golding, Thomas Churchyard, and many others; and Harvey repeats the argument he had then held, that earthquakes proceed from natural causes, and that although doubtless it is in the power of God miraculously to produce them, it is not the business of man to treat them superstitiously. He speaks with supreme contempt of the crop of pamphlets and prophecies that the recent earthquake shock was likely to produce. In the same letter Harvey reported Cambridge news with a sharpness of censure which, when these private letters were printed without his knowledge, by an injudicious friend, made it his duty to apologise to the Cambridge authorities. In the course of the Nash quarrel, when a distorted version of this is cast up against him, he admits that he was then unduly irritated because he

had failed in his application for the office of Orator to the University.

That he was unduly irritated in the Nash quarrel is quite as true. Gabriel had just laid his brother John, the young physician, in the grave, when a gross attack on the whole family, provoked by his brother Richard, came into his hands. It consisted only of a few lines, which were afterwards expunged from the satire, Greene's *Quip for an Upstart Courtier,* in the text of which they had been interpolated. The copies which contained it were destroyed, and we do not know what the scoffs were which caused Gabriel to come to town, determined to proceed by law against the libeller. He found Greene dying miserably, and his judgment was so far overpowered by his anger, that he allowed himself to be urged into a written expression of it after Greene was dead. Yet there are earnest and generous thoughts blended with the words of wrath, and there is a pathetic strain of earnestness in the whole letter which contains Gabriel's reference to his dead brother, and record of his latest words to him: "Oh, brother, Christ is the best physician, and my only physician. Farewell, Galen—farewell human arts. There is nothing divine upon earth except the soul aspiring towards heaven."

I do not justify the temper of the Harvey and Nash quarrel, but I do protest against any continuance of the belief that students are reading literary history when they find in Isaac D'Israeli's *Calamities of Authors,* this quarrel made the basis of a misrepresentation of all facts in the life of a man whom Sidney and Spenser honoured as their friend—a misrepresentation which extends even to so trifling a detail as the suggestion that "it became necessary to dry up the floodgates of these rival ink-horns by an order of the Archbishop of Canterbury. The order is a remarkable fragment of our literary history, and is thus expressed: 'That all Nashe's bookes and Dr. Harvey's bookes be taken wheresoever they may be found, and that none of the said bookes be ever printed hereafter.'" It is, indeed, a remarkable fragment, for it is quoted with omission of the fact that this was not a condemnation special to Harvey and Nash, but part of a general excommunication of books by which, in the year 1599, Whitgift and Bancroft made themselves ridiculous. They ordered the burning of Marston's *Pygmalion,* of Marlowe's Ovid and of his Satires, of Hall's Satires, of the Epigrams of Davies and others, of the *Caltha Poetarum* besides Nash's and Harvey's books; and decreed that no satires or epigrams should be printed for the future. Indeed, says Warton, in that year "the Hall of the Stationers underwent as great a purgation as was carried on in Don Quixote's library." Had the *Calamities of Authors* been then in existence, probably that learned and entertaining book would also have gone to the fire; and one author at least would have been spared the additional calamity of being known to the world, less by what he said than by what Issac D'Israeli said of him.

ALEXANDER B. GROSART
From "Memorial-Introduction"
The Works of Gabriel Harvey
1884, Volume 1, pp. ix–xvi, xlviii–l

In his Preface to the *Letter-Book of Gabriel Harvey, A.D. 1573–80* (Camden Society, 1884), Mr. E. J. Long Scott, M.A., commences his little notice thus:

> Gabriel Harvey, the writer of the following Letter-Book, is better known to us than almost any other man among the literary characters who crowd the Elizabethan stage. His celebrated controversy with

Nashe (who raked up against him every circumstance in his life and writings in order to pour unlimited abuse and contempt upon his head) has furnished us with a vivid picture, not only of Harvey's manners and conversation, but even of his dress and physiognomy. (p. v)

This, while true in a way—that is, to the few who have mastered the "wordy war" between Nashe and Harvey—is exceptionally untrue regarded biographically. For of no contemporary of equal notoriety in men's mouths over so many years, do we know so little as of him. The Damascus blade of Thomas Nashe wounded him mortally. He was speedily forgotten—though he lived on to an unusual age; and no one seems to have cared to rescue his memory from its swift and inexorable oblivion. Even his academic course is obscure and dateless. We have had to wait for these long centuries to learn the chief facts of it contained in his (so-called) *Letter-Book*. Mr. Scott has not himself added one grain of new information, as he has not troubled himself so much as to bring together what of scanty record has hitherto been made. His one distinguishing service is to have reproduced so admirably a troublesome manuscript.

None of the Registers or Parish-Books of Saffron Walden now extant go so far back as the birth of Gabriel Harvey, nor is there any mention of the Harveys in any of the later local MSS. But it is known from other sources that he was born at Saffron Walden, in Essex, 'about 1545,' or some seven years before Spenser.[1] He was the eldest son, of a family of six children—four boys and two girls. As everybody knows who knows anything at all of the Harvey's, their father was a Ropemaker. If only his eldest son had been as satisfied with the paternal 'trade' as was that father himself, the unlucky victim of Nashe's scorpion-tongue and pen had been spared much misery and infamy. Even at this late day there remains a curious proof that so far from having been ashamed of his rope-making the elder Harvey proclaimed it—viz., in the town's museum there is preserved the most of a once fine fireplace from Harvey's house. Its entablature is in three (marble) compartments, after this fashion:—

ALIIS NON NOBIS
Ox, with pack, eating of thistles.
NOSTRI PLACENTE
NEC ALLIS NEC NOBIS
Three men making a rope.
[Broken out]
ALIIS ET NOBIS
Hive and bees at work.
LABOR

The middle compartment also contains all the adjuncts to a farmyard—somewhat mutilated—*e.g.*, the end of a house, a bullock or cow, yard with the head of a cow peeping out, a pig, poultry, bullock and corn, and (seemingly) flax or hemp (grown probably for the supply of his trade); also a plant of saffron, whilst on a tree hangs a satchel. From these designs it is to be inferred that Harvey senior carried on a Farm as well as his rope-making business. This is incidentally confirmed by Gabriel's assertion in the notorious matter of his sister Mercy's experiences that she "fetched home and milked the cows." But the main thing is—and all honour to him for it—the rope-making was held for honest labour and trade, not stigma, by the old man.[2] If—as is pretty certain—Gabriel supplied these Latin mottoes, he too must have originally acquiesced. Of course it was one thing thus to have a home-memorial of the family-occupation, and another to have it shouted from the housetop with flout and jeer and waggish drollery. Anthony à-Wood puts the thing as follows:

This person, who made a great noise in his time, was born at Saffron Walden, in Essex; and tho' his father was a ropemaker, as Thomas Nashe, a great scoffer and his antagonist, tells us, yet he had rich kindred, and was nearly allied to Sir Thomas Smith, the great statesman in Queen Elizabeth's reign. (*Fasti*, by Bliss, i. 230)

The Smith alliance is very doubtful, and certainly was not "near." But, as unquestionably, the Ropemaker was well-to-do and mindful of the educational interests of his sons (at least). It is to be remembered to his credit that he sent three sons to the University (of Cambridge), and spent on them a good thousand pounds, as Gabriel was ever forward to attest.

From the warmth—not to say exaggerate eulogy—of our Harvey's celebration of Sir Thomas Smith, of Audley End, Saffron Walden, it would appear that this once famous Knight had interested himself from the outset in his poetic celebrator. Gabriel must have been a clever boy, probably the proverbial 'clever boy' of the village school. We know nothing of his earlier training. He is found at Cambridge University before Edmund Spenser (who proceeded thither in 1565). "His first academical breeding," says Wood, "was in Christ College, Cambridge; where in a short time he made great proficiency, to the wonder and amazement of his tutor" (as before).

In 1573 he was tutor at Pembroke College. Later he was of Trinity Hall, being addressed by his brother Richard in his *Astrological Discourse*, in 1583, as his "verie good and most loving Brother . . . at his chambers in Trinitie Hall." He passed both degrees of B.A. and M.A. The following note to Wood's *Fasti* (i. 230–1) summarizes most of the preceding data—"Gabr. Harvey aulæ Pembr. socius prius, electus Nov. 3. 1570; dein socius aulæ Trin. electus, Dec. 18. 1578. Spe et opinione magister futurus sit magna de spe excidit" (Baker, MSS. coll., vol. vi., 104, Cole). The latter involved him in a protracted quarrel by the denial of a grace for it. His *Letter-Book* (as before) contains his correspondence on the weary and irksome matter with Dr. John Young, Master of Pembroke, etc. (pp. 1–54). He was the winner ultimately, and henceforward his "victorie" dated his letters to intimate friends. These letters are of the oddest and quaintest ever perpetrated by sane man on another. Their vocabulary is simply a wonder; their insistence of self-assertion a still greater wonder; and their tumultuous vituperation of 'enemies,' most wonderful of all. Sooth to say, combined with the Letters to Spenser (as "Immerito" and "Benevolo")—the actual takes down our ideal of Cambridge in Elizabethan days. Such narrownesses, bitternesses, and vulgarities of enmity among scholarly and dignified men humiliate one to-day. It is a relief to find Spenser uninvolved in the paltry contention—by quiet withdrawal.

According to his own statements he became renowned beyond all precedent (before 1576) as a Lecturer on Rhetoric, with Cicero for guide. Our after-quotations from his *Ciceronianus* and *Rhetor* will illustrate this. Many of the books of his Library—preserved in public and private libraries—go to show what an omnivorous and careful reader he was of all that he came across. Professor Morley, in his paper yclept "Hobbinol" (as onward), gives some interesting quotations from notes on his *Quintilian* in British Museum. It is doubtful, notwithstanding the references in the *Gratulations of Walden*, whether he ever really travelled in service of the State for Leicester—just as it is equally doubtful whether Spenser did. One incidental allusion by his brother Richard would seem to indicate intended but not executed journeying—*e.g.*, in the epistle-dedicatory of his *Astrological Discourse* to John, Bishop of London, in counting upon his acceptance thereof, he thus writes:

> If not for mine owne sake or the worthines of the thing itself, yet for Cambridge sake, and that es-peciall affection which you have always borne to-ward Vniuersitie men, and namely your singular curtesie toward my brother Gabriel, when he should have trauailed to Smalcaldie; which courtesie he doth often recognise.

"Afterwards," continues Anthony à-Wood, "he became fellow in Trinity Hall, and so excellent and learned an orator and poet, that books of these faculties were dedicated to him. . . . he was proctor of that University, and at elder years he applied his studies to astrology, wherein he became emi-nent, and wrote as 'tis said Almanacks much in esteem in the reign of Queen Elizabeth" (as before). His 'Almanacks' have not survived, save in association with his absurd brothers in the sarcastic pages of Nashe. His addiction to astrology is a measure of his *calibre*—whatever of miscellaneous learning he may have acquired. He was disappointed in a candidature for Orator of the University. He studied Civil Law, and in 1585 was ad-mitted at Oxford Doctor of Laws. He thereafter practised as an Advocate in the Prerogative Court of Canterbury.

There are two indubitable facts that check utter contempt toward Gabriel Harvey, and constrain us to conclude that, spite of his pedantry and conceit, shocking and dastardly malignity toward Robert Greene, and intellectual poverty, there must have been something above these in him: (*a*) That he was the "familiar" acquaintance of Sir Philip Sidney; (*b*) That for life he retained the friendship of Edmund Spenser. The latter's fine Sonnet from Dublin secures that his name can never perish. None the less do they remain simple matters-of-fact, that on the one hand he blackened the memory of "deade" Robert Greene, repelled the conciliatory advances of Thomas Nashe, and all through betrayed the most ludicrous self-conceit and over-estimate of himself.

As distinguished from his Latin productions, his English books in warfare with Greene and Nashe have a certain go in them, a certain vigour, a dexterous, apt-worded, wary fence, and (as already noted) an astounding vocabulary; but after all they are mere "Curiosities of Literature," and to be preserved and collected, as we have done, mainly as realistic pictures of the time, and for a background to the magnificent badinage and satire of our English Rabelais—Thomas Nashe,—and as completing the triumvirate—Greene, Nashe, and Harvey.

In strange and suggestive contrast with the "immature" death of his illustrous friend Edmund Spenser—Gabriel Harvey survived until February 7th, 1630 (buried at Saffron Walden Februrary 11th), in at least his eighty-fifth year. Not a single certain syllable is heard of him after Spenser's death (in 1599), albeit there is a floating tradition that the folios of 1607 and 1611 were published under his supervision (to their damage.) . . .

No Vindication of Gabriel Harvey is possible, by Professor Morley or anybody else, so long as these three things remain:—

1. *The Hexameter device*. None but a "fantastic pedant" could have insisted on experiment so nonsensical, and none but a man blinded by "vanity" could so have boasted of being the Inventor of Hexameter. The paper on "Hobbinol" is deftly dumb on the whole absurdity. With its mal-influence on Sidney and the hazard of losing the *Faery Queen* by it, we cannot allow it to be thus dropped.

2. *The malignant traducing of Robert Greene*. Whilst again and again iterating that he warred not with the dead, Harvey has worked into his *Foure Letters* every idle piece of gossip and every venomous accusation that his pestiferous in-dustry could ferret out. Professing never to have read Greene's books, he nevertheless piles up epithets of abuse upon them, and rancorous nicknames; and all in the worst style of cold-blooded sentence-spinning. My regard for Professor Morley will not allow me to characterize his verdict on those infamous *Foure Letters*; than which nothing viler, baser, more heartless, exists in our language; for Harvey makes not the slightest refer-ence to Greene's pathetic and passionate penitence.

3. *The rejection of Nashe's offer of reconciliation*. Whoso reads the epistle to the first edition of the *Tears* must recognise sincerity and characteristic generosity of forgiveness on the part of one to whom it could not be very easy to bring himself so to stoop. Equally self-evident is the truthfulness of Nashe's record as to how he was misled into such an overture of peace. This being so, it is impossible to acquit Harvey of measureless vin-dictiveness as of scarcely describable treachery. Nor less de-clarative of a pedant's "vanity" is his failure to recognise what an ass he had written himself down, and how incomparable was the intellectual force and ability of his young antagonist.

Take him all-in-all, Gabriel Harvey must abide a monu-mental example of how little "much learning" (granting that) does for CHARACTER; how possible it is to be a Scholar, and at the same time a Blockhead—mastered by, not mastering his acquisitions; how contemporary reputation often proves to be the toadyism of a clique; and how some men have the art or the un-art of putting their worst foot foremost. Gabriel Harvey one cannot admire, much less love. Associated with Sidney and Spenser indissolubly, we think of Sidney and Spenser, not of him, save by-the-bye. His learning was heavy, but not solid (much as a pound of feathers is of the same weight as a pound of lead, yet incompact); his 'rhetoric' magniloquent rather than eloquent; his verse fluent and smooth, but without inspiration; his temperament, vain, cantankerous, malignant; his long life a melancholy failure; his books a tomb, not a monument. I would not, however, leave the Friend of Edmund Spenser blamable and despised merely.

Therefore I add last of all.—It must never be forgotten that it was Gabriel Harvey who called "Colin Clout" from North-East Lancashire to London, and (practically) introduced him to Leicester and Sidney, and "affairs of State."[3]

Notes

1. Professor Henry Morley, in his paper on Harvey as "Hobbinol" (of which more in the sequel) seeks to make out that Harvey was of the same age with Spenser; but he is not successful. Throughout, the attitude of Harvey is of an elder addressing, not to say patronizing, a younger man. Besides, when Spenser matriculated at the Univer-sity, Harvey was already notable there. It has even been alleged that he was tutor to Spenser and Kirke.

2. I owe special thanks to Joseph Clarke, Esq., The Roos, Saffron Walden, for these details and after-information. Mr. Scott quotes from Glascock's *Records of St. Michael's Parish Church, Bishop's Stortford* (1882), this entry—"1579. Paid to Harvie of Walden for a rope for the [church] bell ij^s iij^d" (p. 59).

3. See new Life of Spenser before Works in ten vols (Vol. I., *frequenter*). It may be added that in Life of Greene, with Notes and Illustrations; in Notes and Illustrations to Nashe, and in Notes and Illustrations to Harvey, in Works, a good deal more of biographical-critical mate-rial will be found, including illustrative and elucidative *bits* from the Letter-Book (as before).

MICHAEL DRAYTON

1563–1631

Michael Drayton was born in 1563 at Hartshill, North Warwickshire. It is believed that he came from a family of well-to-do tradespeople, much like Shakespeare's family; it is not known, however, if Drayton had any formal education.

His first work, a volume of religious verse entitled *The Harmonie of the Church*, was published in 1591. Throughout his career Drayton was an admirer of Spenser, and Drayton's *The Shepheardes Garland* (1593) recalls the Spenserian tradition of eclogues. Most of Drayton's early work also shows the influence of his contemporary, Samuel Daniel. In 1594 Drayton first published *Ideas Mirrour*, a series of sonnets that eventually went through twelve editions in his lifetime, most containing extensive revisions and additions. With the poem *Piers Gaveston* (1593) Drayton began a series of historical poems, known as legend poems, which included *Matilda* (1594), *The Tragicall Legend of Robert, Duke of Normandie* (1596), *Mortimeriados* (1603; rewritten as *The Barrons Warres*), and *The Legend of Great Cromwell* (1607). Perhaps one of the most successful of his historical works is *Englands Heroicall Epistles* (1597). This collection of imaginary letters from heroic lovers featured twelve couples in the first edition, including Henry II and Fair Rosamund and King John and Matilda Fitzwater, and was modeled after Ovid's *Heroides*. About this time Drayton worked as a playwright for Philip Henslowe, collaborating with Munday, Dekker, Webster, Middleton, and others on several plays.

In 1604 *The Owle*, a satire, was published, followed in 1606 by the appearance of *Odes*. In the *Odes*, which were later revised and republished in 1619, Drayton used the Horatian model. In 1612 the first eighteen songs of his great topographical poem, *Poly-Olbion*, appeared. By 1622 twelve more songs were added to the original eighteen, completing the recounting of various local English legends and myths. In 1627 Drayton published *The Battaile of Agincourt*, which contained several major poems: "Nymphidia," a mock-heroic, and "The Quest of Cynthia" and "The Shepheardes Sirena," both pastorals.

Drayton's final work, *The Muses Elizium*, was published in 1630, along with the three *Divine Poems*, which tell the biblical stories of Moses, Noah, and David and Goliath. Drayton died in December 1631, and was buried in the north aisle of Westminster Abbey.

Personal

As *Aulus Persius Flaccus* is reported among al writers to be of an honest life and vpright conuersation: so *Michael Drayton* (*quem toties honoris & amoris causa nomino*) among schollers, souldiours, Poets, and all sorts of people, is held for a man of vertuous disposition, honest conuersation, and wel gouerned cariage, which is almost miraculous among good wits in these declining and corrupt times, when there is nothing but rogery in villanous man, & when cheating and craftines is counted the cleanest wit, and soundest wisedome.—FRANCIS MERES, *Palladis Tamia*, 1598

Drayton feared him, and he esteemed not of him.—BEN JONSON, *Conversations with William Drummond*, 1619

Michael Drayton, born in this county ⟨Warwickshire⟩ at Atherston, as appeareth in his poetical address thereunto:

My native country,
If there be virtue yet remaining in thy earth,
Or any good of thine thou breath'st into my birth,
Accept it as thine own, whilst now I sing of thee;
Of all thy later brood th' unworthiest though I be.

He was a pious poet, his conscience having always the command of his fancy; very temperate in his life, slow of speech, and inoffensive in company. He changed his laurel for a crown of glory, anno 1631; and is buried in Westminister abbey, near the south door, with this epitaph:

Do, pious marble, let thy readers know.
What they and what their children owe
To Drayton's name, whose sacred dust
We recommend unto thy trust.

Protect his memory, and preserve his story,
Remain a lasting monument of his glory:
And when thy ruins shall disclaim
To be the treasurer of his name;
His name that cannot fade, shall be
An everlasting monument to thee.

He was born within a few miles of William Shakespeare, his countryman and fellow poet; and buried within fewer paces of Jeffrey Chaucer and Edmund Spenser.—THOMAS FULLER, *The History of the Worthies of England*, 1662

General

And *Drayton*, whose wel-written Tragedies,
And sweete Epistles, soare thy fame to skies.
Thy learned Name, is æquall with the rest;
Whose stately Numbers are so well addrest.
—RICHARD BARNFIELD, "A Remembrance of Some English Poets," *Poems in Divers Humors*, 1598

As *Lucan* hath mournefully depainted the ciuil wars of *Pompey* & *Cæsar*: so hath *Daniel* the ciuill wars of Yorke and Lancaster; and *Drayton* the ciuill wars of *Edward* the second, and the Barons.

As *Virgil* doth imitate *Catullus* in yᵉ like matter of *Ariadne* for his story of Queen *Dido*: so *Michael Drayton* doth imitate *Ouid* in his *Englands Heroical Epistles*.

As *Sophocles* was called a Bee for the sweetness of his tongue: so in *Charles Fitz-Iefferies Drake*, *Drayton* is termed *Golden-mouth'd*, for the purity and pretiousnesse of his stile and phrase.

As *Accius, M. Attilius* and *Milithus* were called *Tragœdiographi*, because they writ Tragedies: so may wee truly terme *Michael Drayton Tragœdiographus*, for his passionate penning the downfals of valiant *Robert of Normandy*, chast *Matilda*, and great *Gaueston*.

As *Ioan. Honterus* in Latine verse writ 3. Bookes of Cosmography w' Geographicall tables: so *Michael Drayton* is now in penning in English verse a Poem called *Polu-olbion* Geographical and Hydrographicall of all the forests, woods, mountaines, fountaines, riuers, lakes, flouds, bathes and springs that be in England.—FRANCIS MERES, *Palladis Tamia*, 1598

The Peeres of heau'n kept a parliament,
And for Wittes-mirrour *Philip Sidney* sent,
To keepe another when they doe intend,
Twenite to one for *Drayton* they will send,
    Yet bade him leaue his learning, so it fled,
    And vow'd to liue with thee since he was dead.
            —JOHN WEEVER, "Ad Michaelem Drayton,"
                *Epigrammes in the Oldest Cut and Newest
                Fashion*, 1599

Draytons sweete muse is like a sanguine dy, Able to rauish the rash gazers eye. How euer he wants one true note of a Poet of our times, and that is this, hee cannot swagger it well in a Tauerne, nor dominere in a hot house.—UNSIGNED, *The Return from Pernassus*, 1606, Act 1, Scene 2

Our second *Ouid*, the most pleasing *Muse*
That heau'n did e're in mortals braine infuse,
All-loued *Draiton*, in soule-raping straines,
A genuine noat, of all the *Nimphish* traines
Began to tune; on it all eares were hung
As sometime *Dido's* on *Æneas* tongue.
            —WILLIAM BROWNE, *Britannia's Pastorals*,
                1616, Bk. 2, Song 2

Englands braue *Genius*, raise thy head; and see,
We have a *Muse* in this mortalitie
Of *Vertue* yet surviues; All met not Death,
When wee intoomb'd our deare *Elizabeth*.
Immortall *Sydney*, honoured *Colin Clout*,
Presaging what wee feele, went timely out.
Then why lives *Drayton*, when the *Times* refuse,
Both *Meanes* to live, and *Matter* for a *Muse*?
Onely without *Excuse* to leave us quite,
And tell us, Durst we act, he durst to write.
    Now, as the people of a famish'd *Towne*,
Receiving no *Supply*, seeke up and downe
For mouldy Corne, and Bones long cast aside,
Wherewith their hunger may bee satisfide:
(Small store now left) we are inforc'd to prie
And search the darke Leaues of Antiquitie
For some good *Name*, to raise our *Muse* againe,
In this her *Crisis*, whose harmonious straine
Was of such compasse, that no other Nation
Durst ever venture on a sole *Translation*;
Whilst our full language, Musicall, and hie,
Speakes as themselves their best of *Poesie*.
    Drayton, amongst the worthi'st of all those,
The glorious *Laurell*, or the *Cyprian Rose*
Have ever crown'd, doth claime in every *Lyne*,
An equall honor from the sacred *Nyne*:
For if old *Time* could like the restlesse Maine,
Roule himselfe backe into his Spring againe,
And on his wings beare this admired *Muse*,

For *Ovid, Virgil, Homer*, to peruse.
They would confesse, that never happier *Pen*,
Sung of his *Loues*, his *Countrey*, and the *Men*.
            —WILLIAM BROWNE, "To My Honor'd Friend
                Mr Drayton," *The Second Part, or Continu-
                ance of Poly-Olbion*, 1622

It hath beene question'd, MICHAEL, if I bee
A Friend at all; or, if at all, to thee:
Because, who make the question, haue not seene
Those ambling visits, passe in verse, betweene
Thy *Muse*, and mine, as they expect. 'Tis true:
You haue not writ to me, nor I to you;
And, though I now begin, 'tis not to rub
Hanch against Hanch, or raise a riming *Club*
About the towne: this reck'ning I will pay,
Without conferring symboles. This's my day.
    It was no Dreame! I was awake, and saw!
Lend me thy voyce, O FAME, that I may draw
Wonder to truth! and haue my Vision hoorld,
Hot from thy trumpet, round, about the world.
    I saw a Beauty from the Sea to rise,
That all Earth look'd on; and that earth, all Eyes!
It cast a beame as when the chear-full Sun
Is fayre got vp, and day some houres begun!
And fill'd an Orbe as circular, as heauen!
The Orbe was cut forth into Regions seauen.
And those so sweet, and well proportion'd parts,
As it had beene the circle of the Arts!
When, by thy bright *Ideas* standing by,
I found it pure, and perfect *Poësy*,
There read I, streight, thy learned *Legends* three,
Heard the soft ayres, between our Swaynes & thee,
Which made me thinke, the old *Theocritus*,
Or Rurall *Virgil* come, to pipe to vs!
But then, thy'epistolar *Heroick* Songs,
Their loues, their quarrels, iealousies, and wrongs,
Did all so strike me, as I cry'd, who can
With vs be call'd, the *Naso*, but this man?
And looking vp, I saw *Mineruas* fowle,
Pearch'd ouer head, the wise *Athenian* Owle:
I thought thee then our *Orpheus*, that wouldst try
Like him, to make the ayre, one volary:
And I had stil'd thee, *Orpheus*, but before
My lippes could forme the voyce, I heard that Rore,
And Rouze, the Marching of a mighty force,
Drums against Drums, the neighing of the Horse,
The Fights, the Cryes, and wondring at the Iarres
I saw, and read, it was thy *Barons Warres*!
O, how in those, dost thou instruct these times,
That Rebells actions, are but valiant crimes!
And caried, though with shoute, and noyse, confesse
A wild, and an authoriz'd wickednesse!
Sayst thou so, *Lucan*? But thou scornst to stay
Vnder one title. Thou hast made thy way
And flight about the Ile, well neare, by this,
In thy admired *Periégesis*,
Or vniuersall circumduction
Of all that reade thy *Poly-Olbyon*.
That reade it? that are rauish'd! such was I
With euery song, I sweare, and so would dye:
But that I heare, againe, thy Drum to beate
A better cause, and strike the brauest heate
That euer yet did fire the *English* blood!
Our right in *France*! if ritely vnderstood.

There, thou art *Homer!* Pray thee, vse the stile
Thou hast deseru'd: And let me reade the while
Thy Catalogue of Ships, exceeding his,
Thy list of aydes, and force, for so it is:
The Poets act! and for his Country's sake
Braue are the Musters, that the Muse will make.
And when he ships them where to vse their Armes,
How do his trumpets breath! What loud alarmes!
Looke, how we read the Spartans were inflam'd
With bold *Tyrtæus* verse, when thou art nam'd,
So shall our *English* Youth vrge on, and cry
An *Agincourt,* an *Agincourt,* or dye.
This booke! it is a *Catechisme* to fight,
And will be bought of euery Lord, and Knight,
That can but reade; who cannot, may in prose
Get broken peeces, and fight well by those.
The miseries of *Margaret* the Queene
Of tender eyes will more be wept, then seene:
I feele it by mine owne, that ouer flow,
And stop my sight, in euery line I goe.
But then refreshed, with thy *Fayerie Court,*
I looke on *Cynthia,* and *Sirenas* sport,
As, on two flowry Carpets, that did rise,
And with their grassie greene restor'd mine eyes.
Yet giue mee leaue, to wonder at the birth
Of thy strange *Moon-Calfe,* both thy straine of mirth,
And Gossip-got acquaintance, as, to vs
Thou hadst brought *Lapland,* or old *Cobalus,*
Empusa, Lamia, or some Monster, more
Then *Affricke* knew, or the full *Grecian* store!
I gratulate it to thee, and thy *Ends,*
To all thy vertuous, and well chosen Friends,
Onely my losse is, that I am not there:
And, till I worthy am to wish I were,
I call the world, that enuies mee, to see
If I can be a Friend, and Friend to thee.
　　　　—BEN JONSON, "The Vision of Ben. Ionson,
　　　　　on the Muses of His Friend M. Drayton,"
　　　　　The Battaile of Agincourt, 1627

Draiton is sweet and Smooth; though not exact
Perhaps, to stricter Eyes; yet he shall live
Beyond their Malice. To the Sceane, and Act,
Read Comicke Shakespeare; or if you would give
　　Praise to a Iust Desert, crowning the Stage
　　See Beaumont, once the honour of his Age.
　　　　—GEORGE DANIEL, "A Vindication of Poesie,"
　　　　　1647

Michael Drayton, contemporary of *Spenser* and *Sir Philip Sydney,* and for fame and renown in poetry not much inferior in his time to either: however he seems somewhat antiquated in the esteem of the more curious of these times, especially in his *Polyalbion;* the old-fashioned kind of verse whereof seems somewhat to diminish that respect which was formerly paid to the subject as being both pleasant and elaborate; and thereupon thought worthy to be commented upon by that once-walking library of our nation *Selden.* His *England's Heroical Epistles* are more generally liked; and to such as love the pretty chat of Nymphs and Shepherds his *Nymphals* and other things of that nature cannot be unpleasant.—EDWARD PHILLIPS, *Theatrum Poetarum Anglicanorum,* 1675

As we walked along to a particular part of the temple (Westminister Abbey), "There," says the gentleman, pointing with his finger, "that is the Poets' Corner; there you see the monuments of Shakespeare, and Milton, and Prior, and Drayton." "Drayton!" I replied, "I never heard of him before."
—OLIVER GOLDSMITH, *The Citizen of the World,* 1762, Letter 13

The excellent fable of the maddening rain I have found in Drayton's "Moon Calf," most miserably marred in the telling! vastly inferior to Benedict Fay's Latin exposition of it, and that is no great thing. *Vide* his Lucretian Poem on the Newtonian System. Never was a finer tale for a satire, or, rather, to conclude a long satirical poem of five or six hundred lines.
—SAMUEL TAYLOR COLERIDGE, *Anima Poetae: From the Unpublished Notebooks* (entry for 1805), ed. Ernest Hartley Coleridge, 1895, p. 130

The language of Drayton is free and perspicuous. With less depth of feeling than that which occasionally bursts from Cowley, he is a less excruciating hunter of conceits, and in harmony of expression is quite a contrast to Donne. A tinge of grace and romance pervades much of his poetry: and even his pastorals, which exhibit the most fantastic views of nature, sparkle with elegant imagery. . . . On a general survey, the mass of his poetry has no strength or sustaining spirit adequate to its bulk. There is a perpetual play of fancy on its surface; but the impulses of passion, and the guidance of judgment give it no strong movements nor consistent course. In scenery or in history he cannot command selected views, but meets them by chance as he travels over the track of detail. His great subjects have no interesting centre, no shade for uninteresting things. Not to speak of his dull passages, his description is generally lost in a flutter of whimsical touches. His muse has certainly no strength for extensive flights, though she sports in happy moments on a brilliant and graceful wing—THOMAS CAMPBELL, *Specimens of the British Poets,* 1819

Michael Drayton's *Poly-Olbion* is a work of great length and of unabated freshness and vigour in itself, though the monotony of the subject tires the reader. He describes each place with the accuracy of a topographer, and the enthusiasm of a poet, as if his Muse were the very *genius loci.* His *Heroical Epistles* are also excellent. He has a few lighter pieces, but none of exquisite beauty or grace. His mind is a rich marly soil that produces an abundant harvest, and repays the husbandman's toil, but few flaunting flowers, the garden's pride, grow in it, nor any poisonous weeds.—WILLIAM HAZLITT, *Lectures on the Dramatic Literature of the Age of Elizabeth,* 1820

Drayton wrote well in every metre which he attempted: but what he thus says of the Italian stanza may be more truly said of the English one invented by Spenser, and used by him in one of the noblest works of human genius. And he committed a great error when he fixed upon the Alexandrine as the measure in which to write his *Polyolbion;* for of all measures it is that which, in our language, admits the least variety.—ROBERT SOUTHEY, *The Life of Cowper,* 1835

Hail to thee, Michael! true, painstaking wight,
So various that 'tis hard to praise thee right;
For driest fact and finest faery fable
Employ'd thy genius indefatigable.
What bard more zealous of our England's glory,
More deeply versed in all her antique story,
Recorded feat, tradition quaint and hoary?
What muse like thine so patiently would plod
From shire to shire in pilgrim sandal shod,
Calling to life and voice, and conscious will,
The shifting streamlet and the sluggish hill?

Great genealogist of earth and water,
The very Plutarch of insensate matter.

— HARTLEY COLERIDGE, "Drayton," *Sketches of
English Poets*, 1849

The sentence which Hazlitt allots to Drayton is perhaps one of the most felicitous examples of short metaphorical criticism. 'His mind,' says the critic, 'is a rich marly soil that produces an abundant harvest and repays the husbandman's toil; but few flaunting flowers, the garden's pride, grow in it, nor any poisonous weeds.' Such figurative estimates must indeed always be in some respects unsatisfactory, yet in this there is but little of inadequacy. It is exceedingly uncommon for the reader to be transported by anything that he meets with in the author of the *Polyolbion*. Drayton's jewels five words long are of the rarest, and their sparkle when they do occur is not of the brightest or most enchanting lustre. But considering his enormous volume, he is a poet of surprisingly high merit. Although he has written some fifty or sixty thousand lines, the bulk of them on subjects not too favourable to poetical treatment, he has yet succeeded in giving to the whole an unmistakeably poetical flavour, and in maintaining that flavour throughout. The variety of his work, and at the same time the unfailing touch by which he lifts that work, not indeed into the highest regions of poetry, but far above its lower confines, are his most remarkable characteristics. The *Polyolbion*, the *Heroical Epistles*, the *Odes*, the *Ballad of Agincourt*, and the 'Nymphidia' are strikingly unlike each other in the qualities required for successful treatment of them, yet they are all successfully treated. It is something to have written the best war song in a language, its best fantastic poem, and its only topographical poem of real value. Adverse criticism may contend that the 'Nymphidia' and the *Polyolbion* were not worth the doing, but this is another matter altogether. That the *Ballad of Agincourt* was not worth the doing, no one who has any fondness for poetry or any appreciation of it will attempt to contend. In the lyric work of the *Odes*, scanty as it is, there is the same evidence of mastery and of what may be called thoroughness of workmanship. Exacting critics may indeed argue that Drayton has too much of the thoroughly accomplished and capable workman, and too little of the divinely gifted artist. It may be thought, too, that if he had written less and concentrated his efforts, the average merit of his work would have been higher. There is, at any rate, no doubt that the bulk of his productions, if it has not interfered with their value, has interfered with their popularity.

The Barons' Wars, which, according to some theories, should have been Drayton's best work, is perhaps his worst. The stanza, which he has chosen for good and well-expressed reasons, is an effective one, and the subject might have been made interesting. As a matter of fact it has but little interest. The somewhat 'kite-and-crow' character of the disturbance chronicled is not relieved by any vigorous portraiture either of Mortimer or of Edward or of the Queen. The first and last of these personages are much better handled in the *Heroical Epistles*. The level of these latter and of the *Legends* is decidedly high. Not merely do they contain isolated passages of great beauty, but the general interest of them is well sustained, and the characters of the writers subtly differenced. One great qualification which Drayton had as a writer of historical and geographical verse was his possession of what has been called, in the case of M. Victor Hugo, *la science des noms*. No one who has an ear can fail to recognise the felicity of the stanza in *Agincourt* which winds up with 'Ferrars and Fanhope,' and innumerable examples of the same kind occur elsewhere. Without this science indeed the *Polyolbion* would have been

merely an awkward gazetteer. As it is, the 'strange herculean task,' to borrow its author's description of it, has been very happily performed. It may safely be assumed that very few living Englishmen have read it through. But those who have will probably agree that there is a surprising interest in it, and that this interest is kept up by a very artful admixture of styles and subjects. Legends, fancy pieces such as that of the Marriage of Thame and Isis, with its unmatched floral description, accounts of rural sports and the like, ingeniously diversify the merely topographical narrative. Had the *Polyolbion* been its author's only work, Goldsmith's sneer would still have been most undeserved. But the variety of Drayton's performance is almost as remarkable as its bulk. . . . But to the foregoing remarks it may be added that Drayton was master of a very strong and at the same time musical decasyllabic line. His practice in Alexandrines and in complicated stanzas seems to have by no means injured his command of the ordinary heroic couplet. His series of Sonnets to Idea is perhaps his least successful work if we compare him with other men, just as *The Barons' Wars* is his worst performance if his own work only be considered. The 'Nymphidia' has received higher praise than any other of his poems, and its fantastic conception and graceful tripping metre deserve this praise well enough. The curious poems of *The Owl* and 'The Man in the Moon' show, if they show nothing else, his peculiar faculty of raising almost any subject to a certain poetical dignity by dint of skilful treatment. Lastly, his prose Prefaces deserve attention here, because many of them display the secret of his workmanlike skill. It is evident from them that Drayton was as far as possible from holding the false and foolish improvisation-theory of poetry, and they testify to a most careful study of his predecessors and contemporaries, and to deliberate practice in the use of the poet's tools of language and metre. — G. SAINTSBURY, "Michael Drayton," *The English Poets*, ed. Thomas Humphry Ward, 1880, Vol. 1, pp. 526–28

. . . Drayton, what with his artistic weaknesses, what with living till the bitter end, or after it, of a great patriotic age, and what with surviving into one of different poetical interests, left no school, exercised little authority, and soon barely remained in the educated mind as one of the secondary Elizabethans famous in their day. The reason for this neglect is to be found not merely in his over-production, in his acres of verbiage; there is also the character of his talent. He is too strong to be called an imitator; but he tried to absorb too much, he had a vast appetite for facts, and he was for ever exercising himself on models. Hence he seldom reacted enough upon the gathered masses of material, to present them perfectly in new and imposing forms. In his *opus magnum* he attempted so much, that it is hard to obtain popularity for its noble episodes. The successful *Epistles* were indeed a new kind, but not one of high or lasting value. His most original and impregnable verse is, I believe, to be found in his handful of *Odes*. There is little doubt about the fate of a poet of fitful executive talent, encumbered in all these ways.

But the change of poetical taste also unduly marred his fame. He, much more than Milton, who is often loosely so styled, was the last real Elizabethan. He sounded the great bugle-calls of the older generation; he sang of fervent chivalrous love, hope of immortal verse, passion for the land and its ancient things. In the middle of the seventeenth century, the themes, whether of Milton or of smaller men, were, as every one knows, quite different. The Caroline fragments which Drayton wrote in his later years were lost in the crowd of similar works. Hence he was forgotten for some things and overshadowed in others. There had been greater sonnetteers, greater poets dealing with our history. But take his whole range, travel with him over his ground, and he is seen to stand not quite among the authentic gods, hardly indeed among the mightier demi-gods, but as an athlete of commanding stature, and of power to lift, or nearly lift, weighty burdens; not without a sturdy dignified beauty of his own, and often a soft musical grace; speaking, too, now and then with something like the real divine accent. Alike for humanity and strength he ranks among the men of intellectual muscle, Jonson, Selden, Chapman: and he is one of those on whom the old enemy he so often challenged has wrought unmerited mischief.—OLIVER ELTON, *An Introduction to Michael Drayton*, 1895, pp. 52–53

During a life more prolonged than that of most of his contemporaries, he never ceased to write—feverishly, crudely, copiously, very rarely giving to his work that polish which it needed to make it durable. Of his lyrical vocation there could be no doubt; yet, if Daniel and Davys were prose-men who wrote poetry, Drayton was a prosaic poet. His masterpiece of topographical ingenuity, the *Poly-Olbion*, a huge British gazetteer in broken-backed twelve-syllable verse, is a portent of misplaced energy. In his earlier historical pieces Drayton more closely resembles Daniel, whom, however, he exceeds in his lyrics as much as he limps behind him in his attempts at gnomic verse. Drayton writes like a man, and a few of his odes are still read with fervour; but his general compositions, in spite of all their variety, abundance, and accomplishment, fail to interest us; a prosy flatness spoils his most ambitious efforts. He helps us to comprehend the change which was to come in sixty years, and through Cowley the prophesies of Dryden.—EDMUND GOSSE, *A Short History of Modern English Literature*, 1897, pp. 120–21

Works

POLY-OLBION

In publishing this Essay of my Poeme, there is this great disadvantage against me; that it commeth out at this time, when Verses are wholly deduc't to Chambers, and nothing esteem'd in this lunatique Age, but what is kept in Cabinets, and must only passe by Transcription; In such a season, when the Idle Humerous world must heare of nothing, that either savors of Antiquity, or may awake it to seeke after more, then dull and slothfull ignorance may easily reach unto: These, I say, make much against me; and especially in a Poeme, from any example, either of Ancient, or Modern, that have proved in this kind: whose unusuall tract may perhaps seeme difficult, to the female Sex; yea, and I feare, to some that think themselves not meanly learned, being not rightly inspired by the Muses: such I meane, as had rather read the fantasies of forraine inventions, then to see the Rarities and Historie of their owne Country delivered by a true native Muse. Then, whosoever thou be, possest with such stupidity and dulnesse, that, rather then thou wilt take paines to search into ancient and noble things, choosest to remaine in the thicke fogges and mists of ignorance, as neere the common Lay-stall of a Citie; refusing to walke forth into the *Tempe* and Feelds of the Muses, where through most delightfull Groves the Angellique harmony of Birds shall steale thee to the top of an easie hill, where in artificiall caves, cut out of the most naturall Rock, thou shalt see the ancient people of this Ile delivered thee in their lively images: from whose height thou mai'st behold both the old and later times, as in thy prospect, lying farre under thee; then convaying thee downe by a soule-pleasing Descent through delicate embroidered Meadowes, often veined with gentle glid-

ing Brooks; in which thou maist fully view the dainty Nymphes in their simple naked bewties, bathing them in Crystalline streames; which shall lead thee, to most pleasant Downes, where harmlesse Shepheards are, some exercising their pipes, some singing roundelaies, to their gazing flocks: If as, I say, thou hadst rather, (because it asks thy labour) remaine, where thou wert, then straine thy selfe to walke forth with the Muses; the fault proceeds from thy idlenesse, not from any want in my industrie. And to any that shall demand wherfore having promised this Poeme of the generall Iland so many yeeres, I now publish only this part of it; I plainly answere, that many times I had determined with my selfe, to have left it off, and have neglected my papers sometimes two yeeres together, finding the times since his Majesties happy comming in, to fall so heavily upon my distressed fortunes, after my zealous soule had labored so long in that, which with the general happinesse of the kingdom, seem'd not then impossible somewhat also to have advanced me. But I instantly saw all my long nourisht hopes even buried alive before my face: so uncertaine (in this world) be the ends of our cleerest endevors. And what ever is herein that tastes of a free spirit, I thankfully confesse it to proceed from the continuall bounty of my truly Noble friend Sir *Walter Aston*; which hath given me the best of those howres, whose leasure hath effected this which I now publish. Sundry other Songs I have also, though yet not so perfect that I dare commit them to publique censure; and the rest I determine to go forward with, God enabling me, may I find means to assist my endevour. Now Reader, for the further understanding of my Poeme, thou hast three especiall helps; First the Argument to direct thee still, where thou art, and through what Shires the Muse makes her journey, and what she chiefly handles in the Song thereto belonging. Next, the Map, lively delineating to thee, every Mountaine, Forrest, River, and Valley; expressing in their sundry postures; their loves, delights, and naturall situations. Then hast thou the Illustration of this learned Gentleman, my friend, to explaine ever hard matter of history, that, lying farre from the way of common reading, may (without question) seem difficult unto thee. Thus wishing thee thy hearts desire, and committing my Poeme to thy charitable censure, I take my leave.—MICHAEL DRAYTON, "To the General *Reader*," *Poly-Olbion*, 1613

That Michael Draytons Polyabion (if ⟨he⟩ had performed what he promised to write the deads of all ye worthies) had been excellent his long verses pleased him not.—BEN JONSON, *Conversations with William Drummond*, 1619

When I first undertooke this Poeme, or as some very skilfull in this kind, have pleased to tearme it, this Herculean labour. I was by some vertuous friends perswaded, that I should receive much comfort and incouragement therein; and for these Reasons: First, that it was a new, cleere way, never before gone by any; then, that it contained all the Delicacies, Delights, and Rarities of this renowned Isle, interwoven with the Histories of the Britanes, Saxons, Normans, and the later English: And further that there is scarcely any of the Nobilitie, or Gentry of this land, but that he is some way or other, by his Blood interressed therein. But it hath fallen out otherwise; for instead of that comfort, which my noble friends (from the freedome of their Spirits) proposed as my due, I have met with barbarous Ignorance, and base Detraction; such a cloud hath the Devill drawne over the Worlds Judgement, whose opinion is in few yeares fallen so farre below all Ballatry, that the Lethargy is incurable; nay some of the Stationers, that had the Selling of the first part of this Poeme, because it went not so fast away in the Sale, as some of their beastly and abominable Trash, (a shame both to our Language and Nation) have either de-spightfully left out, or at least carelessely neglected the Epistles to the Readers, and so have cousoned the Buyers with unperfected Bookes; which these that have undertaken the second Part, have beene forced to amend in the first, for the small number that are yet remaining in their hands. And some of our outlandish, unnaturall English, (I know not how otherwise to expresse them) stick not to say, that there is nothing in this Island worthy studying for, and take a great pride to bee ignorant in any thing thereof; for these, since they delight in their folly, I wish it may be hereditary from them to their posteritie, that their children may bee beg'd for Fooles to the fift Generation, untill it may be beyond the memory of man to know that there was ever any other of their Families: neither can this deterre mee from going on with Scotland, if Meanes and Time doe not hinder me, to performe as much as I have promised in my first Song:

> Till to the sleepy Maine, to *Thuly* I have gone,
> And seene the Frozen Isles, the cold *Deucalidon*,
> Amongst whose Iron Rocks, grim *Saturne* yet
>   remaines,
> Bound in those gloomy Caves with Adamantine
>   Chaines.

And as for those Cattell whereof I spake before, *Odi profanum vulgus & arceo*, of which I account them, bee they never so great, and so I leave them. To my friends, and the lovers of my Labors, I wish all happinesse.—MICHAEL DRAYTON, "To Any That Will Read It," *The Second Part, or Continuance of Poly-Olbion*, 1622

> Drayton, sweet ancient Bard, his Albion sung,
> With their own praise her echoing Valleys rung;
> His bounding Muse o'er ev'ry mountain rode,
> And ev'ry river warbled where he flow'd.

> —JAMES KIRKPATRICK, *The Sea-Piece*, 1750,
>   Canto 2

His *Poly-Olbion* is one of the most singular works this country has produced, and seems to me eminently original. The information contained in it is in general so acute, that he is quoted as an authority both by Hearne and Wood. His perpetual allusions to obsolete traditions, remote events, remarkable facts and personages, together with his curious genealogies of rivers, and his taste for natural history, have contributed to render his work very valuable to the antiquary.—HENRY HEADLEY, *Select Beauties of Ancient English Poetry*, 1787

He has treated the subject with such topographical and minute detail as to chain his poetry to the map; and he has unfortunately chosen a form of verse which, though agreeable when interspersed with other measures, is fatiguing in long continuance by itself: still it is impossible to read the poem without admiring the richness of his local associations, and the beauty and variety of the fabulous allusions which he scatters around him. Such, indeed is the profusion of romantic recollections in the *Poly-olbion*, that a poet of taste and selection might there find subjects of happy description, to which the author who suggested them had not the power of doing justice; for Drayton started so many remembrances, that he lost his inspiration in the effort of memory.—THOMAS CAMPBELL, *Specimens of the British Poets*, 1819

It is, indeed, one of the most learned and ingenious poems in the language, and unique in literature; being a treasure-house of topographic, antiquarian, and traditional lore, which the heavy versification alone was sufficient to sink into neglect, even if public taste had not changed since the age of garrulity

which it was written to instruct and entertain.—JAMES MONTGOMERY, *Lectures on General Literature, Poetry, &c.*, 1833

Drayton's *Polyolbion* is a poem of about 30,000 lines in length, written in Alexandrine couplets, a measure from its monotony, and perhaps from its frequency in doggerel ballads, not at all pleasing to the ear. It contains a topographical description of England, illustrated with a prodigality of historical and legendary erudition. Such a poem is essentially designed to instruct, and speaks to the understanding more than to the fancy. The powers displayed in it are, however, of a high cast. It has generally been a difficulty with poets to deal with a necessary enumeration of proper names. The catalogue of ships is not the most delightful part of the *Iliad*, and Ariosto never encountered such a roll of persons or places without sinking into the tamest insipidity. Virgil is splendidly beautiful upon similar occasions; but his decorative elegance could not be preserved, nor would continue to please, in a poem that kept up through a great length the effort to furnish instruction. The style of Drayton is sustained, with extraordinary ability, on an equable line, from which he seldom much deviates, neither brilliant nor prosaic; few or no passages could be marked as impressive, but few are languid or mean. The language is clear, strong, various, and sufficiently figurative; the stories and fictions interspersed, as well as the general spirit and liveliness, relieve the heaviness incident to topographical description. There is probably no poem of this kind in any other language, comparable together in extent and excellence to the *Polyolbion*; nor can any one read a portion of it without admiration for its learned and highly-gifted author. Yet, perhaps, no English poem, known as well by name, is so little known beyond its name; for while its immense length deters the common reader, it affords, as has just been hinted, no great harvest for selection, and would be judged very unfairly by partial extracts. It must be owned, also, that geography and antiquities may, in modern times, be taught better in prose than in verse; yet, whoever consults the *Polyolbion* for such objects, will probably be repaid by petty knowledge which he may not have found anywhere else.—HENRY HALLAM, *Introduction to the Literature of Europe*, 1837–39, Pt. 3, Ch. 5, Par. 44

The *Polyolbion* is nothing less than a versified gazetteer of England and Wales,—fortunately Scotland was not yet annexed, or the poem would have been even longer, and already it is the plesiosaurus of verse. Mountains, rivers, and even marshes are personified, to narrate historical episodes, or to give us geographical lectures. There are two fine verses in the seventh book, where, speaking of the cutting down some noble woods, he says,—

> Their trunks like aged folk now bare and naked stand,
> As for revenge to heaven each held a withered hand;

and there is a passage about the sea in the twentieth book that comes near being fine; but the far greater part is mere joiner-work. Consider the life of man, that we flee away as a shadow, that our days are as a post, and then think whether we can afford to honor such a draft upon our time as is implied in these thirty books all in alexandrines! Even the laborious Selden, who wrote annotations on it, sometimes more entertaining than the text, gave out at the end of the eighteenth book.—JAMES RUSSELL LOWELL, "Spenser" (1875), *Works*, Riverside ed., Vol. 4, pp. 279–80

THE BATTAILE OF AGINCOURT

Out of the strong came forth sweetness. Samson's riddle could hardly find a fitter answer than Elizabethan poetry. What in all the hives of the world is so sweet as Elizabethan lyric poetry? And what is it that distinguishes its sweetness from the sickly sweetness, say, of our recent æsthetic poetry? Simply that it was the sweetness hidden in the hearts of strong men—the infinite tenderness of heroes. What makes King Harry's wooing fill our eyes on the instant, when courtly wooers leave us cold? Because he had but just won Agincourt. How true was Lovelace's word. Our poets too often love honour less, and so they cloy our palates. Elizabethan sweetness is the sweetness of cold spring water; Elizabethan passion, as a modern writer expresses it, is 'noble strength on fire.' The Elizabethan poet wrote with his sword and breastplate hung above his desk. Like that 'belated Elizabethan,' old William Chamberlayne, he was ready at any moment to put down one and gird on the other:

> I must
> Let my pen rest awhile, and see the rust
> Scoured from my own sword.

It is that background of manhood which makes the love-poetry of Browning so uniquely sweet in latter-day poetry. It is the soldier's kiss the woman loves best, the embrace of the heroic spirit.

Lyrical sweetness, fertility of invention, richness of descriptive power, are Drayton's most characteristic qualities, but along with these he has the great style of an heroic time. He has, perhaps, little of the dramatic gift, as usually understood, though, as Mr. Symonds has admonished us, much of the so-called dramatic work of the Elizabethans is really lyrical. Besides, Drayton had one essential of the dramatic gift: he could at least make single figures live and move before us. Witness his description in the poem under notice of various incidents typical of all the ferment of preparation which followed Henry's declaration of war:

> In all men's mouthes now was no word but warre,
> As though no thing had any other name;
> And folke would aske of them arriv'd from farre,
> What forces were preparing whence they came?
> 'Gainst any bus'nesse 'twas a lawfull barre
> To say for France they were; and 'twas a shame
> For any man to take in hand to doe
> Ought, but something that did belong thereto. . . .
>
> Tents and Pavillions in the fields are pitcht
> (E'n full wrought up their Roomthynesse to try),
> Windowes, and Towers, with Ensignes are inricht,
> With ruffling Banners, that doe brave the sky,
> Wherewith the wearied Labourer, bewitcht
> To see them thus hang waving in his eye,
> His toylsome burthen from his back doth throwe,
> And bids them worke that will, to France hee'll
> goe.

Surely that labourer is still alive in Drayton's verse as when he threw his burden down with such infectious valour. Or, take this picture of the old veteran 'with teares of joy' recalling to his son the English valour at Cressy:

> And, Boy, quoth he, I have heard thy Grandsire say
> That once he did an English Archer see,
> Who, shooting at a French twelve score away,
> Quite through the body stuck him to a Tree.
> Upon their strengths a King his Crowne might lay:
> Such were the men of that brave age, quoth he,
> When with his Axe he at his Foe let drive,
> Murrian and scalpe downe to the teeth did rive.

One other picture, of noble touching farewells:

> There might a man have seene in ev'ry streete,
> The Father bidding farewell to his Sonne:
> Small children kneeling at their Father's feete:

> The Wife with her deare Husband ne'r had done:
> Brother, his Brother, with adieu to greete:
> One Friend to take leave of another runne:
> The Mayden with her best belov'd to part,
> Gave him her hand, who tooke away her heart.

Though thus excellent in parts, Dr. Garnett is, of course, right in saying that as a whole the *Battaile of Agincourt* has many faults of construction. Drayton seems to have exercised no selection upon his materials, but to have followed the chronicler almost slavishly from point to point: though, as Dr. Garnett adds, 'old Holinshed at his worst was no contemptible writer.' He has, too, observed no sense of proportion between the parts: he describes the siege of Harfleur with Pre-Raphaelite minuteness, but treats the battle itself with relatively much greater brevity, and his poem dies anything but proudly. Its ending gives one the impression that he had grown tired before he reached it. One characteristic sin against proportion is a long catalogue of the English ships, in which at least, said Ben Jonson, in somwhat doubtful complimentary verses (which we may further discount by Jonson's remark to Drummond, that 'Drayton feared him; and he esteemed not of him'), he had certainly surpassed Homer; and also a description of all the armorial banners carried by the battalions of the various counties. In themselves, these descriptions, however, are delightful; done as no poet but Drayton could have done them, alive with that untiring invention which, in the *Polyolbion*, was able to so remarkably vitalise the topography of forty counties. It is true too, as Dr. Garnett remarks in a most admirable introduction which leaves nothing to be said, that Drayton gives us no comprehensive view of the battle. 'He minutely describes a series of episodes, in themselves often highly picturesque, but we are no better able to view the conflict as a whole than if we ourselves had fought in the ranks.' So Jonson, though with less justice, spoke of Daniel, in his talks with Drummond. 'Daniel,' he said, 'wrott Civil Warres, and yett hath not one battle in all his book.' In the naturalism of some of Drayton's episodes we are disagreeably reminded of *La Débâcle*:

> One with a gleave neere cut off by the waste,
> Another runnes to ground with halfe a head:
> Another, stumbling, falleth in his flight,
> Wanting a legge, and on his face doth light.

And terribly grim is the description of the ferocious onslaught of the English:

> The dreadfull bellowing of whose strait-brac'd
> Drummes;
> To the French sounded like the dreadfull doome, . . .
> Whilst Scalps about like broken potsherds fly,
> And kill, kill, kill, the Conquering English cry.

Whatever deductions, however, we make from Drayton's poem, it remains an inspiring piece of work: and though the patriotism may seem perhaps at times a little strident to ears attuned to the philosophic pleading of the historical spirit, yet it is patriotism largely tempered by that chivalric admiration for the courage of a fallen foe, which was so noble a trait of glorious 'King Harry':

> Henry the fift, that man made out of fire,
> Th' Imperiall wreath placed on his Princely browe.

> —RICHARD LE GALLIENNE, "Michael Drayton:
> *The Battaile of Agincourt*" (1893), *Retrospective Reviews*, 1896, Vol. 2, pp. 50–54

ISAAC DISRAELI

"Drayton"

Amenities of Literature

1841

The *Poly-olbion* of DRAYTON is a stupendous work, "a strange Herculean toil," as the poet himself has said, and it was the elaborate production of many years. The patriotic bard fell a victim to its infelicitous but glorious conception; and posterity may discover a grandeur in this labour of love, which was unfelt by his contemporaries.

The *Poly-olbion* is a chorographical description of England and Wales; an amalgamation of antiquarianism, of topography, and of history; materials not the most ductile for the creations of poetry. This poem is said to have the accuracy of a road-book; and the poet has contributed some notices, which add to the topographic stores of CAMDEN; for this has our poet extorted an alms of commendation from such a niggardly antiquary as Bishop Nicholson, who confesses that this work affords "a much truer account of this kingdom than could be well expected from the pen of a poet."

The grand theme of this poet was his fatherland! The muse of Drayton passes by every town and tower; each tells some tale of ancient glory, or of some "worthy" who must never die. The local associations of legends and customs are animated by the personifications of mountains and rivers; and often, in some favourite scenery, he breaks forth with all the emotion of a true poet. The imaginative critic has described the excursions of our muse with responsive sympathy. "He has not," says Lamb, "left a rivulet so narrow that it may be stepped over without honourable mention, and has associated hills and streams with life and passion beyond the dreams of old mythology." But the journey is long, and the conveyance may be tedious; the reader, accustomed to the decasyllabic or heroic verse, soon finds himself breathless among the protracted and monotonous Alexandrines, unless he should relieve his ear from the incumbrance, by resting on the cæsura, and thus divide those extended lines by the alternate grace of a ballad-stanza. The artificial machinery of Drayton's personifications of mountains and rivers, though these may be often allowed the poet, yet they seem more particularly ludicrous, as they are crowded together on the maps prefixed to each county, where this arbitrary mythology, masculine and feminine, are to be seen standing by the heads of rivers, or at the entrances of towns.

This extraordinary poem remains without a parallel in the poetical annals of any people; and it may excite our curiosity to learn its origin. The genealogy of poetry is often suspicious; but I think we may derive the birth of the *Poly-olbion* from LELAND'S magnificent view of his designed work on *Britain*, and that hint expanded by the *Britannia* of CAMDEN, who inherited the mighty industry, without the poetical spirit of LELAND: DRAYTON embraced both.

It is a nice question to decide how far history may be admitted into poetry; like *Addison's Campaign*, the poem may end in a rhymed gazette. And in any other work of invention, a fiction, by too free an infusion of historical matter, can only produce that monster called "the Romance of History," a nonsensical contradiction in terms, for neither can be both; or that other seductive and dangerous association of real persons and fictitious incidents, the historical romance! It is remarkable that DRAYTON censures DANIEL, his brother poet, for being *too historical* in his *Civil Wars*, and thus transgressing the boundaries of history and poetry, of truth and invention. Of these just boundaries, however, he himself had no clear notion. Drayton in his *Baron's Wars* sunk into a grave chronicler; and in the *Poly-olbion*, we see his muse treading a labyrinth of geography, of history, and of topography!

The author of the *Poly-olbion* may truly be considered as the inventor of a class of poems peculiar to our country, and which, when I was young, were popular or fashionable. These are loco-descriptive poems. Such were Denham's *Cooper's Hill*,[1] and its numerous and, some, happy imitations. In these local descriptions some favoured spot in the landscape opens to the poet not only the charm of its natural appearance, but in the prospect lie scenes of the past. Imagination, like a telescope fixed on the spot, brings nearer to his eyes those associations which combine emotion with description; and the contracted spot, whence the bard scattered the hues of his fancy, is aggrandized by noble truths.

The first edition of the *Poly-olbion*, in 1613, consisted of eighteen "Songs," or cantos, and every one enriched by the notes and illustrations of the poet's friend, our great national antiquary, SELDEN, whose avarice of words in these recondite stories conceals almost as many facts as he affords phrases. This volume was ill received by the incurious readers of that age. Drayton had vainly imagined that the nobles and gentlemen of England would have felt a filial interest in the tale of their fathers, commemorated in these poetic annals, and an honourable pride in their domains here so graphically pictured. But no voice, save those of a few melodious brothers, cheered the lonely lyrist, who had sung on every mountain, and whose verse had flowed with every river. After a hopeless suspension of nine years, the querulous author sent forth the concluding volume to join its neglected brother. It appeared with a second edition of the first part, which is nothing more than the unsold copies of the first, to which the twelve additional "Songs" are attached, separately paged. These last come no longer enriched by the notes of Selden, or even embellished by those fanciful maps which the unfortunate poet now found too costly an ornament. Certain accidental marks of the printer betray the bibliographical secret, that the second edition was in reality but the first.[2] The preface to the second part is remarkable for its inscription, in no good humour,

To any that will read it!

There was yet no literary public to appeal to, to save the neglected work which the great SELDEN had deemed worthy of his studies: but there was, as the poet indignantly designates them, "a cattle, *odi profanum vulgus et arceo*, of which I account them, be they never so great." And "the cattle" conceived that there was nothing in this island worthy studying. We had not yet learned to esteem ourselves at a time when six editions of Camden's "Britannia," in the original Latin, were diffusing the greatness of England throughout Europe.

But though this poet devoted much of his life to this great antiquarian and topographic poem, he has essayed his powers in almost every species of poetry; fertility of subject, and fluency of execution, are his characteristics. He has written historical narratives too historical; heroic epistles hardly Ovidian; elegies on several occasions, or rather, domestic epistles, of a Horatian cast; pastorals, in which there is a freshness of imagery, breathing with the life of nature; and songs, and satire, and comedy. In comedy he had not been unsuccessful, but in satire he was considered more indignant than caustic. There is one species of poetry, rare among us, in which he has been eminently successful; his "Nymphidia, or Court of Faerie," is a model of the grotesque, those arabesques of poetry, those lusory effusions on chimerical objects. There are grave critics who would deny the poet the liberty allowed to the painter. The "Nymphidia" seems to have been ill understood by some modern critics. The poet has been censured for "neither imparting nor feeling that half-believing seriousness which enchants us in the wild and magical touches of Shakespeare;" but the poet designed an exquisitely ludicrous fiction. Drayton has, however, relieved the grotesque scenes, by rising into the higher strains of poetry, such as Gray might not have disdained.

It was the misfortune of Drayton not to have been a popular poet, which we may infer from his altercations with his booksellers, and from their frequent practice of prefixing new title pages, with fresher dates, to the first editions of his poems. That he was also in perpetual quarrel with his muse, appears by his frequent alteration of his poems. He often felt that curse of an infelicitous poet, that his diligence was more active than his creative power. Drayton was a poet of volume, but his genius was peculiar; from an unhappy facility in composition, in reaching excellence he too often declined into mediocrity. A modern reader may be struck by the purity and strength of his diction; his strong descriptive manner lays hold of the fancy; but he is always a poet of reason, and never of passion. He cannot be considered as a poet of mediocrity, who has written so much above that level; nor a poet who can rank among the highest class, who has often flattened his spirit by its redundance.

There was another cause, besides his quarrel with his muse, which threw a shade over the life of Drayton. He had been forward to greet James the First, on his accession to the throne of England, with a congratulatory ode; but for some cause, which has not been revealed, he tells us, "he suffered shipwreck by his forward pen." The king appears to have conceived a personal dislike to the bard, a circumstance not usual with James towards either poets or flatterers. It seems to arise from some state-matter, for Drayton tells us,

> I feare, as I do stabbing, this word, state.

According to Oldys, Drayton appears to have been an agent in the Scottish king's intercourse with his English friends; some unlucky incident probably occurred, which might have indisposed the monarch towards his humble friend. The unhappy result of his court to the new sovereign cast a sour and melancholy humour over his whole life; Drayton, in his "Elegy" to his brother-poet, Sandys, has perpetuated his story.

Notes

1. Dr. Johnson has ascribed the invention of local poetry to Denham, who, he thought, had "traced a new scheme of poetry, copied by Garth and Pope, after whose names little will be gained by an enumeration of smaller poets." Johnson and the critics of his day were wholly unacquainted with the Fathers of our poetry; nor is it true that we have not had loco-descriptive poems since Garth and Pope, which may rank with theirs.

2. Perhaps none of our poets have been more luckless in their editors than Drayton. He himself published a folio edition of his works in 1619; but some of his more interesting productions, now lying before me, are contained in a small volume, 1631—the year in which he died.

   A modern folio edition was published by Dodsley in 1748. The title-page assures us that this volume contains *all* his writings; while a later edition, in four volumes 8vo, 1753, pretends to supply the deficiencies of the former, which at length Dodsley had discovered, but it is awkwardly done by an *Appendix*, and is still deficient. The rapid demand for a new edition of Drayton between 1748 and 1753 bears a suspicious aspect. An intelligent bibliopolist, Mr. Rodd, informs me that this *octavo* edition is in fact the identical folio, only arranged to the octavo form by a contrivance, well known

among printers, at the time of printing the folio. The separation of the additional poems in the Appendix confirms this suggestion.

Of the *Poly-olbion*, the edition called the second, of 1622, has fetched an excessive price; while the first, considered incomplete, may be procured at a very moderate price. The possessor of the first edition, however, enjoys the whole treasure of Selden's lore. Mr. Southey, in his *Specimens of Our Ancient Poets*, has reprinted the entire *Poly-olbion* with his usual judgment; but, unhappily, the rich stores of Selden the publishers probably deemed superfluous. Drayton is worthy of a complete edition of his works.

EDMUND GOSSE
From *The Jacobean Poets*
1894, pp. 93–101

It is impossible to yield to Drayton the position in this volume which his pretensions demand, since a very important portion of his work lies entirely outside our scope. His career is divided into two distinct halves, and the former of these, as purely Elizabethan, calls for no detailed consideration here. Michael Drayton was born near Atherstone, in Warwickshire, in 1563. He came up to town while still a young man, and in the last decade of Elizabeth produced divine poems, sonnets in the fashion of the hour, pastorals, and, above all, certain epical studies in historical poetry, which were akin in nature to those produced during so long a period, and in such diverse manners, by the versifiers of the *Mirror for Magistrates*. He was forty years of age when James I. came to the throne, and was already one of the most prominent poets of the age.

Drayton's earliest act in the new reign was an unfortunate one. He hastened to be the first welcomer in the field, and hurried out "A Gratulatory Poem to King James." His zeal, however, went beyond his discretion; he was told that he should have waited until the mourning for the queen was over, and the new king refused to patronize him. Henceforth, a petulant note is discernible in Drayton's writings, the note of disappointment and disillusion. He was exceedingly active, however, and brought out, in quick succession, fresh and greatly revised editions of his old historical poems, *The Baron's Wars*, and *England's Heroical Epistles*. A new didactic and religious piece, *Moses in a Map of his Miracles*, 1604, added little to his reputation; but the *Owl*, of the same year, is a lengthy and important composition in the heroic couplet. The writer feigns, in the mediæval manner, that he fell asleep under a tree on a May morning, and heard all the birds talking in human speech. The opening of the poem is of a Chaucerian prettiness. Among those birds who speak—

> The little Redbreast teacheth charity,

but the Linnet and the Titmouse presently twit the Owl on his silence, and the fiercer birds fall upon him with beak and claw. They would kill him, did not the Falcon protect him, and the Eagle come swooping down to see what is the matter. Then the Owl speaks. He has looked through the windows of the Eagle's court, and seen all the evil that is done there. At last the Eagle, having listened to the Owl's long satire, flies away, and the Owl is applauded and comforted. This curious satirical fable has passages of great merit; among them is this pathetic episode of the Crane:—

> Lo, in a valley peopled thick with trees,
> Where the soft day continual evening sees,
> Where, in the moist and melancholy shade,
> The grass grows rank, but yields a bitter blade,
> I found a poor Crane sitting all alone,
> That from his breast sent many a throbbing groan;
> Grov'lling he lay, that sometime stood upright;

Maimed of his joints in many a doubtful fight;
His ashy coat that bore a gloss so fair,
So often kiss'd of the enamour'd air,
Worn all to rags, and fretted so with rust,
That with his feet he trod it in the dust;
And wanting strength to bear him to the springs,
The spiders wove their webs e'en in his wings.

Probably in 1606, Drayton issued one of the most charming of his books, *Poems Lyric and Pastoral*, consisting of odes,
eclogues, and a curious romance called "The Man in the
Moon." The Odes doubtless belong to his youth; they are
particularly happy in their varied versification, of which two
brief specimens may suffice. This stanza exemplifies the "Ode
on the New Year"—

Give her the Eoan brightness,
Wing'd with that subtle lightness,
    That doth transpierce the air;
The roses of the morning,
The rising heaven adorning,
    To mesh with flames of hair.

and this the "Ode to his Valentine"—

Muse, bid the morn awake,
Sad winter now declines,
Each bird doth choose a make,
This day's Saint Valentine's.
For that good bishop's sake,
Get up and let us see,
What beauty it shall be,
That fortune us assigns.

These are fresh and lively, without any strong grip on
thought. By far the best of the odes, however, is the noble
Battle of Agincourt, which is Drayton's greatest claim to the
recognition of posterity, and the most spirited of all his lyrics.

In a bold preface to his *Eclogues*, Drayton promises something new; but these pastorals are not to be distinguished from
Elizabethan work of the same kind, except by the fine lyrics
which are introduced in the course of them. Of these the best is
the very remarkable birthday ode to Beta in the third eclogue—

Stay, Thames, to hear my song, thou great and
        famous flood,
Beta alone the phœnix is of all thy watery brood,
        The queen of virgins only she,
        The king of floods allotting thee
Of all the rest, be joyful thou to see this happy day,
Thy Beta now alone shall be the subject of thy lay.
With dainty and delightsome strains of dapper
        virelays,
Come, lovely shepherds, sit by me, to tell our Beta's
        praise;
        And let us sing so high a verse
        Her sovereign virtues to rehearse,
That little birds shall silent sit to hear us shepherds
        sing,
Whilst rivers backwards bend their course, and flow
        up to their spring.
Range all thy swans, fair Thames, together on a rank,
And place them each in their degree upon thy
        winding bank,
        And let them set together all,
        Time keeping with the waters' fall,
And crave the tuneful nightingale to help them with
        her lay,
The ouzel and the throstle-cock, chief music of our
        May.

Sound loud your trumpets then from London's loft-
        iest towers
To beat the stormy tempests back, and calm the
        raging showers,
        Set the cornet with the flute,
        The orpharion to the lute,
Tuning the tabor and the pipe to the sweet violins,
And mock the thunder in the air with our loud
        clarions.

For the rest, these pieces present a vague but pretty impression of nymphs singing and dancing in the flowery meadows around a middle-aged swain who deplores to them his
want of material success and courtly recognition.

Passing, for the moment, the *Poly-Olbion*, we come in
1627 to a miscellaneous volume, consisting of seven independent poetical works not before given to the public. Of these
two, *The Battle of Agincourt* (not to be confounded with the
ode) and "The Miseries of Queen Margaret," are fragments of
that epic in *ottava rima* which Drayton was always projecting
and never completed. "Nimphidia, or the Court of Fairy," is a
fantastic little romance, perhaps closer to being a masterpiece
than any other which Drayton composed, dealing with the
loves of Pigwiggin and Queen Mab in a style of the most airy
fancy. "The Moon-Calf" is as clumsy as its predecessor is elegant and exquisite; this is a kind of coarse satirical fable in the
heroic couplet. "The Quest of Cinthia" is a long ballad, so
smooth, and it must be confessed, so conventional, that it
might almost have been written a century and a half later. "The
Shepherd's Sirena" is a lyric pastoral of much lightness and
charm, and the volume closes with some *Elegies* of various
merit.

At least as early as 1598, as we learn from Francies Meres,
Drayton had designed a heroic and patriotic poem of great
extent. It was to celebrate the kingdom of Great Britain with
the exactitude of Camden, but with the addition of every species of imaginative ornament. At length, in 1613, a folio appeared, entitled *Poly-Olbion*, "a chorographical description of
tracts, rivers, mountains, forests, and other parts of this renowned isle." This original instalment contained eighteen
"Songs" or cantos, and was enriched by copious notes from the
pen of John Selden, and a map to each "song." *Poly-Olbion*
was reissued in 1622, with twelve new cantos, but Selden
contributed no more notes.

As the poet says, the composition of *Poly-Olbion* was "a
Herculean toil," and it was one which scarcely rewarded the
author. He had a great difficulty in finding a publisher for the
complete work, and he told the sympathetic Drummond—
"my dear sweet Drummond"—that the booksellers were "a
company of base knaves." The work is written in a couplet of
twelve-syllable iambic lines, in imitation of the French Alexandrine, but with an unfailing cœsura after the third foot,
which becomes very tiresome to the ear.

As an example of the method of the poem, may be selected the passage in which Drayton describes the habits of the
aboriginal beaver of South Wales—

More famous long agone than for the salmons' leap,
For beavers Tivy was, in her strong banks that bred,
Which else no other brook in Britain nourishèd;
Where Nature, in the shape of this now-perish'd
        beast,
His property did seem to have wondrously expressed;
Being bodied like a boat, with such a mighty tail
As serv'd him for a bridge, a helm, or for a sail,
When kind did him command the architect to play,

That his strong castle built of branchèd twigs and
    clay;
Which, set upon the deep, but yet not fixèd there,
He easily could remove as it he pleas'd to steer
To this side or to that; the workmanship so rare,
His stuff wherewith to build, first being to prepare,
A foraging he goes, to groves or bushes nigh,
And with his teeth cuts down his timber; which laid
    by,
He turns him on his back,—his belly laid abroad,—
When with what he hath got, the others do him load,
Till lastly, by the weight, his burden he hath found;
Then with his mighty tail his carriage having bound
As carters do with ropes, in his sharp teeth he gript
Some stronger stick, from which the lesser branches
    stript,
He takes it in the midst; at both the ends, the rest
Hard holding with their fangs, unto the labour prest,
Going backward, tow'rds their home their laded
    carriage led,
From whom those first here born were taught the
    useful sled.

At the same time, it must be confessed that the entire
originality of the poem, its sustained vivacity, variety and accuracy, and its unlikeness to any other work of the age, give an
indubitable interest to *Poly-Olbion*, which will always be referred to with pleasure, though seldom followed from "the
utmost end of Cornwall's furrowing beak," to the fall of Esk
and Eden into the Western Sands.

The confidence of Drayton in his own divine mission is
sublime and pathetic. However unlucky he may be, he invariably takes the attitude of a poet of unquestioned eminence. In
his "Man in the Moon," the shepherds give Rowland (Drayton's accepted pseudonym) the office of their spokesman, because he was—

By general voice, in times that then was grown,
So excellent, that scarce there had been known,
Him that excell'd in piping or in song.

His popularity might account for, yet scarcely excuse this
attitude; but, in spite of this egotism, Drayton is a writer who
commands our respect. He is manly and direct, and his virile
style has the charm of what is well-performed in an easy and
straightforward manner. He had studied the earlier poets to
good effect. His critical knowledge of literature was considerable, and his acquaintance with natural objects exceptionally
wide. His vocabulary is rich and uncommon; he has a pleasing
preference for technical and rustic words. His variety, his ambition, his excellent versification claim our respect and admiration; but Drayton's weak point is that he fails to interest his
reader. All is good, but little is superlatively entertaining. His
most perfect poem was introduced by him, without any special
attention being drawn to it, in what is supposed to be the sixth
edition of his *Poems*, the folio of 1619. It is the following
touching and passionate sonnet:—

Since there's no help, come let us kiss and part,—
Nay, I have done, you get no more of me;
And I am glad, yea glad with all my heart,
That thus so cleanly I myself can free.
Shake hands for ever, cancel all our vows,
And when we meet at any time again,
Be it not seen in either of our brows,
That we one jot of former love retain.

Now at the last gasp of love's latest breath,
When, his pulse failing, passion speechless lies,
When, faith is kneeling by his bed of death,
And innocence is closing up his eyes,—
—Now if thou wouldst, when all have given him
    over,
From death to life thou mightst him yet recover!

Drayton continued to write and to publish verses after the
death of James I., and did not until the 23rd of December,
1631, as his monument in Poet's Corner has it, "exchange his
laurel for a crown of glory." Ben Jonson, who had not appreciated Drayton in his lifetime, is said to have composed the
epitaph graven in letters of gold beneath his bust in Westminister Abbey.

JOHN DONNE

1572–1631

John Donne was born in London in 1572. His father was a well-to-do merchant; his mother,
Elizabeth, came from an illustrious, staunchly Roman Catholic family whose members included
Donne's grandfather, John Heywood, and Sir Thomas More. In 1576 Donne's father died, and
shortly thereafter Elizabeth Donne married Dr. John Symmons, a widowed physician. Two years
after Symmons's death in 1588, Elizabeth married Richard Rainsford.

In 1584 Donne and his brother Henry were sent up to Hart Hall, Oxford; Donne probably
spent three years there, possibly followed by a year at Cambridge. Because he could not, as a Roman
Catholic, take the oaths affirming the Act of Supremacy and the Thirty-nine Articles, he did not
receive a degree from either institution. From 1589 to 1591 he appears to have traveled on the
Continent; he returned to England to study law, entering Thavies Inn in 1591 and Lincoln's Inn in
1592. His career at law was interrupted by his participation in expeditions under Essex and Ralegh
in Cadiz (1596) and the Azores (1597). On his return to England in 1597, he became secretary to
Sir Thomas Egerton, the Lord Keeper.

In 1601 Donne took a step which was to change his life radically. In December of that year he
secretly married Ann More, his employer's niece. When he confessed the marriage to his wife's
father in February 1602, he was dismissed from his post and imprisoned. After the validity of the
marriage was upheld in April in the Court of Audiences, he and his wife moved to Surrey to live

with Ann's relatives. Although he tried repeatedly to find employment—in the Queen's household, the Virginia Company, and in government service—his marriage blocked all possibility of advancement; in a bitter moment, he wrote "John Donne, Ann Donne, Un-done."

Marrying Ann More was one of the crucial decisions Donne made which determined the course of his life; the other was to convert to Anglicanism and enter the priesthood. He had been writing anti-Roman Catholic pamphlets since 1606, and had been urged to take orders as early as 1607. Pleading unworthiness, he declined to do so at that time, but was eventually ordained deacon and priest in 1615. From then on, in addition to serving in various chaplaincies and parishes, he began to acquire a reputation as a subtle and eloquent preacher. He was heard frequently at Court and Lincoln's Inn, and also abroad. In 1621 he was appointed Dean of St. Paul's, and shortly thereafter began hearing cases as a judge in the Court of Delegates. Although he was considered for a bishopric in 1630, he died Dean of St. Paul's in 1631 and was buried in that cathedral.

Few of the poems for which Donne is best known today were published in his lifetime: the *Anniversaries* were published together in 1612, several of the *Songs and Sonnets* appeared in collections, and many of the sermons were published immediately after their delivery, but the bulk of the *Songs and Sonnets* and the divine poems were simply passed around in manuscript amongst Donne's friends. The first printed collection of his poetry appeared in 1633; *LXXX Sermons* was published in 1640.

Personal

JOHANNES DONNE,
Sac. Theol. Profess.
Poet Varia Studia, Quibus Ab Annis
Tenerrimis Fideliter, Nec Infeliciter
Incubuit;
Instinctu Et Impulsu Sp. Sancti, Monitu
Et Hortatu
Regis Jacobi, Ordines Sacros Amplexus,
Anno Sui Jesu, MDCXIV. Et Suæ Ætatis
XLII.
Decanatu Hujus Ecclesiæ Indutus,
XXVII. Novembris, MDCXXI
Exutus Morte Ultimo Die Martii,
MDCXXXI.
Hic Licet In Occiduo Cinere, Aspicit Eum
Cujus Nomen Est Oriens.
—Inscription on Monument

To have liv'd eminent, in a degree
Beyond our lofty'st flights, that is, like thee
Or t'have had too much merit, is not safe;
For such excesses find no Epitaph.
At common graves we have Poetick eyes
Can melt themselves in easy Elegies. . . .
But at Thine, Poem or Inscription
(Rich soul of wit, and language,) we have none;
Indeed, a silence does that tomb befit,
Where is no Herald left to blazon it.
    —HENRY KING, "Upon the death of my ever de-
    sired friend Doctor Donne Dean of Pauls,"
    c. 1631

He was of Stature moderately tall, of a strait and equally-proportioned body, to which all his words and actions gave an unexpressible addition of Comeliness.

The melancholy and pleasant humor, were in him so contempered, that each gave advantage to the other, and made his Company one of the delights of Mankind.

His fancy was unimitably high, equalled only by his great wit; both being made useful by a commanding judgment.

His aspect was chearful, and such, as gave a silent testimony of a clear knowing soul, and of a Conscience at peace with it self.

His melting eye, shewed that he had a soft heart, full of noble compassion; of too brave a soul to offer injuries, and too much a Christian not to pardon them in others.

He did much contemplate (especially after he entred into his Sacred Calling) the *mercies* of Almighty God, the *immortality of the Soul*, and the *joyes of Heaven*; and would often say, in a kind of sacred extasie—*Blessed be God that he is God only, and divinely like himself.*

He was by nature highly passionate, but more apt to reluct at the excesses of it. A great lover of the offices of humanity, and of so merciful a spirit, that *he never beheld the miseries of Mankind without pity and relief.*

He was earnest and unwearied in the search of knowledge; with which, his vigorous soul is now satisfied, and employed in a continual praise of that God that first breathed it into his active body; that body, which once was a *Temple of the Holy Ghost* and is now become a small quantity of *Christian dust:*

But I shall see it reanimated.—SIR HENRY WOTTON, cited in Izaak Walton, *The Life of Dr. John Donne*, 1640

Mr. John Dunne, who leaving Oxford, lived at the Innes of Court, not dissolute, but very neat; a great Visitor of Ladies, a great frequenter of Playes, a great writer of conceited Verses; until such times as King James taking notice of the pregnancy of his Wit, was a means that he betook him to the study of Divinity, and thereupon proceeding Doctor, was made Dean of Pauls; and became so rare a Preacher, that he was not only commended, but even admired by all who heard him.—SIR RICHARD BAKER, *A Chronicle of the Kings of England*, 1641

The life of Donne is more interesting than his poetry. —THOMAS CAMPBELL, *Specimens of the British Poets*, 1819

Dr. Donne, once so celebrated as a writer, now so neglected, is more interesting for his matrimonial history, and for one little poem addressed to his wife, than for all his learned, metaphysical, and theological productions.—ANNA BROWNELL JAMESON, *The Loves of the Poets*, 1829, Vol. 2, p. 94

The knowledge of Donne's immense learning, the subtlety and capacity of his intellect, the intense depth and wide scope of his thought, the charm of his conversation, the sadness of his life, gave a vivid meaning and interest to his poems . . . circulated among his acquaintants, which at this distance of time we cannot reach without a certain effort of imagination. . . . Dr. Donne is one of the most interesting personalities among our men of letters. The superficial facts of his life are so incongruous as to be an irresistible provocation to inquiry. What are we to make of the fact that the founder of a licentious school of erotic poetry, a man acknowledged to be the greatest wit in a licentious Court, with an early bias in matters of religion towards Roman Catholicism, entered the Church of

England when he was past middle age and is now numbered among its greatest divines? Was he a convert like St. Augustine, or an indifferent worldling like Talleyrand? Superficial appearances are rather in favour of the later supposition. —WILLIAM MINTO, "John Donne," *Nineteenth Century*, May 1880, p. 849

Against the wall of the south choir aisle in the Cathedral of St. Paul is a monument which very few of the thousands who visit the church daily observe, or have an opportunity of observing, but which, once seen, is not easily forgotten. It is the long, gaunt, upright figure of a man, wrapped close in a shroud, which is knotted at the head and feet, and leaves only the face exposed—a face wan, worn, almost ghastly, with eyes closed as in death. This figure is executed in white marble, and stands on an urn of the same, as if it had just arisen therefrom. The whole is placed in a black niche, which, by its contrast, enhances the death-like paleness of the shrouded figure. Above the canopy is an inscription recording that the man whose effigy stands beneath, though his ashes are mingled with western dust, looks towards Him whose name is the Orient. . . . It was not such a memorial as Donne's surviving friends might think suitable to commemorate the deceased, but it was the very monument which Donne himself designed as a true emblem of his past life and his future hopes.—J. B. LIGHTFOOT, *Historical Essays*, 1895, pp. 221–23

His graceful person, vivacity of conversation, and many accomplishments secured for him the *entrée* at the houses of the nobility and a recognised position among the celebrities of Queen Elizabeth's court. He was conspicuous as a young man of fortune who spent his money freely, and mixed on equal terms with the courtiers, and probably had the character of being richer than he was. . . . The young man, among his other gifts, had the great advantage of being able to do with very little sleep. He could read all night and be gay and wakeful and alert all day. He threw himself into the amusements and frivolities of the court with all the glee of youth, but never so as to interfere with his duties. The favourite of fortune, he was too the favourite of the fortunate—the envy of some, he was the darling of more. Those of his contemporaries who knew him intimately speak of him at all times as if there was none like him; the charm of his person and manners were irresistible. He must have had much love to give, or he could never had so much bestowed upon him.—AUGUSTUS JESSOPP, *John Donne, Sometime Dean of St. Paul's*, 1897, pp. 13–18

History presents us with no instance of a man of letters more obviously led up to by the experience and character of his ancestors than was John Donne. As we have him revealed to us, he is what a genealogist might wish him to be. Every salient feature in his mind and temperament is foreshadowed by the general trend of his family, or by the idiosyncrasy of some individual member of it. . . . The greatest preacher of his age. . . . No one, in the history of English literature, as it seems to me, is so difficult to realise, so impossible to measure, in the vast curves of his extraordinary and contradictory features. Of his life, of his experiences, of his opinions, we know more now than it has been vouchsafed to us to know of any other of the great Elizabethan and Jacobean galaxy of writers, and yet how little we fathom his contradictions, how little we can account for his impulses and his limitations. Even those of us who have for years made his least adventures the subject of close and eager investigation must admit at last that he eludes us. He was not the crystal-hearted saint that Walton adored and exalted. He was not the crafty and redoubtable courtier whom the recusants suspected. He was not the prophet of the intri-

cacies of fleshly feeling whom the young poets looked up to and worshipped. He was none of these, or all of these, or more. What was he? It is impossible to say, for, with all his superficial expansion, his secret died with him. We are tempted to declare that of all great men he is the one of whom least is essentially known. Is not this, perhaps, the secret of his perennial fascination?—EDMUND GOSSE, *The Life and Letters of John Donne*, 1899, Vol. 1, pp. 3–11, Vol. 2, p. 290

Works

SERMONS

A preacher in earnest; weeping sometimes for his auditory, sometimes with them; always preaching to himself, like an angel from a cloud, but in none; carrying some, as St. Paul was, to heaven in holy raptures; and enticing others by a sacred art and courtship to amend their lives: here picturing a Vice so as to make it ugly to those that practised it; and a Virtue so as to make it beloved, even by those who loved it not; and all this with a most particular grace and an unexpressible addition of comeliness.—IZAAK WALTON, *The Life of Dr. John Donne*, 1640

The sermons of Donne have sometimes been praised in late times. They are undoubtedly the productions of a very ingenious and a very learned man; and two folio volumes by such a person may be expected to supply favorable specimens. In their general character, they will not appear, I think, much worthy of being rescued from oblivion. The subtilty of Donne, and his fondness for such inconclusive reasoning as a subtle disputant is apt to fall into, runs through all of these sermons at which I have looked. His learning he seems to have perverted in order to cull every impertinence of the fathers and schoolmen, their remote analogies, their strained allegories, their technical distinctions; and to these he has added much of a similar kind from his own fanciful understanding.—HENRY HALLAM, *Introduction to the Literature of Europe*, 1837–39, Pt. 3, Ch. 2, Par. 70

Donne's published sermons are in form nearly as grotesque as his poems, though they are characterized by profounder qualities of heart and mind. It was his misfortune to know thoroughly the works of fourteen hundred writers, most of them necessarily worthless; and he could not help displaying his erudition in his discourses. Of what is now called taste he was absolutely destitute. His sermons are a curious mosaic of quaintness, quotation, wisdom, puerility, subtilty, and ecstasy. The pedant and the seer possess him by turns, and in reading no other divine are our transitions from yawning to rapture so swift and unexpected. He has passages of transcendent merit, passages which evince a spiritual vision so piercing, and a feeling of divine things so intense, that for the time we seem to be communing with a religious genius of the most exalted and exalting order; but soon he involves us in a maze of quotations and references, and our minds are hustled by what Hallam calls "the rabble of bad authors" that this saint and sage has always at his skirts, even when he ascends to the highest heaven of contemplation.—EDWIN P. WHIPPLE, *The Literature of the Age of Elizabeth*, 1869, p. 237

In Donne's sermons, an intellectual epicure not too fastidious to read sermons will find a delicious feast. Whether these sermons can be taken as patterns by the modern preacher is another affair. It will not be contended that any congregation is equal to the effort of following his subtleties. In short, as exercises in abstract subtlety, fanciful ingenuity, and scholarship, the sermons are admirable. Judged by the first rule of popular exposition, the style is bad—a bewildering maze to the ordinary reader, much more to the ordinary hearer.—WILLIAM MINTO, *Manual of English Prose Literature*, 1872, p. 253

POETRY

One thing more I must tell you; but so softly, that I am loth to hear myself: and so softly, that if that good lady were in the room, with you and this letter, she might not hear. It is, that I am brought to a necessity of printing my poems, and addressing them to my Lord Chamberlain. This I mean to do forthwith: not for much public view, but at mine own cost, a few copies. I apprehend some incongruities in the resolution; and I know what I shall suffer from many interpretations; but I am at an end, of much considering that; and, if I were as startling in that kind, as I ever was, yet in this particular, I am under an unescapable necessity, as I shall let you perceive when I see you. By this occasion I am made a rhapsodist of mine own rags, and that cost me more diligence, to seek them, than it did to make them. This made me ask to borrow that old book of you, which it will be too late to see, for that use, when I see you; for I must do this as a valediction to the world, before I take orders. But this is it, I am to ask you: whether you ever made any such use of the letter in verse, *à notre comtesse chez vous*, as that I may not put it in, amongst the rest to persons of that rank; for I desire it very much, that something should bear her name in the book, and I would be just to my written words to my Lord Harrington to write nothing after that. I pray tell me as soon as you can, if I be at liberty to insert that: for if you have by any occasion applied any pieces to it, I see not, that it will be discerned, when it appears in the whole piece. Though this be a little matter, I would be sorry not to have an account of it, within as little after New Year's-tide, as you could.—JOHN DONNE, Letter to Sir Henry Goodyere ⟨Dec. 20, 1614⟩, *The Works of John Donne*, ed. Henry Alford, 1839, Vol. 6, p. 367

> Donne, the delight of PHOEBUS and each *Muse*,
>   Who, to thy one, all other braines refuse;
> Whose every work of thy most earely wit,
>   Came forth example, and remaines so, yet:
> Longer aknowing than most wits do, live,
>   And which no affection praise enough can give!
> To it, thy language, letters, arts, best life,
>   Which might with half, mankind maintayne a strife.
> All which I meant to praise, and, yet I would;
>   But leave, because I cannot as I should!
>   —BEN JONSON, "To John Donne," 1616

That Done's Anniversarie was profane and full of blasphemies: that he told Mr. Done, if it had been written of the Virgin Marie it had been something; to which he answered, that he described the Idea of a Woman, and not as she was. That Done, for not keeping of accent, deserved hanging. . . . He esteemeth John Done the first poet in the world in some things: his verses of the "Lost Chaine" he heth by heart; and that passage of the "Calme," *That dust and feathers doe not stirr, all was so quiet.* Affirmeth Done to have written all his best pieces ere he was 25 years old.—BEN JONSON, *Conversations with William Drummond*, 1619

> The Muses garden, with pedantique weedes
> O're-spread, was purg'd by thee, the lazie seeds
> Of servile imitation throwne away,
> And fresh invention planted; thou didst pay
> The debts of our penurious banquerout age:
> . . . whatsoever wrong
> By ours was done the Greeke or Latine tongue,
> Thou hast redeem'd, and Opened as a Mine

> Of rich and pregnant fancie . . .
>   to the awe of thy imperious wit
> Our troublesome language bends, made only fit,
> With her tough thick-rib'd hoopes, to gird about
> Thy Gyant fancie
>   —THOMAS CAREW, "An Elegie upon the death
>   of Doctor *Donne*, Deane of Pauls" c. 1631

>   all the softnesses,
> The Shadow, Light, the Ayre, & Life of Love;
> The Sharpnes of all Witt; ev'n bitternes
> Makes Satire Sweet; all wit did soe emprove,
>   'Twas flamed in him, 'Twas but warm upon
>   His Embers; He was more; & yet is Donne
>   —GEORGE DANIEL, "A Vindication of Poesie,"
>   1647

Wou'd not *Donn's* Satires, which abound with so much Wit, appear more Charming, if he had taken care of his Words, and of his Numbers? But he follow'd *Horace* so very close, that of necessity he must fall with him: And I may safely say it of this present Age, That if we are not so great Wits as *Donn*, yet, certainly, we are better Poets.—JOHN DRYDEN, *Discourse concerning the Original and Progress of Satire*, 1693

If it be true that the purport of poetry should be to please, no author has written with such utter neglect of the rule. It is scarce possible for a human ear to endure the dissonance and discord of his couplets, and even when his thoughts are clothed in the melody of Pope, they appear to me hardly worth the decoration.—NATHAN DRAKE, *Literary Hours*, 1798, No. 28

Nothing could have made Donne a poet, unless as great a change had been worked in the internal structure of his ears, as was wrought in elongating those of Midas.—ROBERT SOUTHEY, *Specimens of the Later English Poets*, 1807, Vol. 1, p. xxiv

Donne had not music enough to render his broken rhyming couplets sufferable, and neither his wit, nor his pointed satire, were sufficient to rescue him from that neglect which his uncouth and rugged versification speedily superinduced.—HENRY KIRKE WHITE, "Melancholy Hours," *Remains*, 1807, Vol. 2

Since Dryden, the metre of our poets leads to the sense; in our elder and more genuine bards, the sense, including the passion, leads to the metre. Read even Donne's satires as he meant them to be read, and as the sense and passion demand, and you will find in the lines a manly harmony.—SAMUEL TAYLOR COLERIDGE, "Notes on Beaumont and Fletcher" (1818), *Literary Remains*, ed. Henry Nelson Coleridge, 1836, Vol. 2, pp. 291–92

Donne was the "best good-natured man, with the worst natured Muse." A romantic and uxorious lover, he addresses the object of his real tenderness with ideas that outrage decorum. He begins his own epithalamium with most indelicate invocation to his bride. His ruggedness and whim are almost proverbially known. Yet there is a beauty of thought which at intervals rises from his chaotic imagination, like the form of Venus smiling on the waters.—THOMAS CAMPBELL, *An Essay on English Poetry*, 1819

Donne is the most inharmonious of our versifiers, if he can be said to have deserved such a name by lines too rugged to seem metre. Of his earlier poems, many are very licentious; the later are chiefly devout. Few are good for much; the conceits have not even the merit of being intelligible: it would perhaps be difficult to select three passages that we should care to read again.—HENRY HALLAM, *Introduction to the Literature of Europe*, 1837–39, Pt. 3, Ch. 5, Par. 39

Having a dumb angel, and knowing more noble poetry than he articulates.—ELIZABETH BARRETT BROWNING, *The Book of Poets* (1842), *Life, Letters and Essays of Elizabeth Barrett Browning*, 1863, Vol. 2, p. 50

> Of stubborn thoughts a garland thought to twine;
> To his fair maid brought cabalistic posies,
> And sung quaint ditties of metempsychosis;
> 'Twists iron pokers into true love-knots',
> Coining hard words, not found in polyglots.
> —HARTLEY COLERIDGE, "Donne," *Sketches of the English Poets*, 1849

Donne, altogether, gives us the impression of a great genius ruined by a false system. He is a charioteer run away with by his own pampered steeds. He begins generally well, but long ere the close, quibbles, conceits, and the temptation of shewing off recondite learning, prove too strong for him, and he who commenced following a serene star, ends pursuing a will-o'-wisp into a bottomless morass. Compare, for instance, the ingenious nonsense which abounds in the middle and the close of his "Progress of the Soul" with the dark, but magnificent stanzas which are the first in the poem. In no writings in the language is there more spilt treasure—a more lavish loss of beautiful, original, and striking things than in the poems of Donne.—GEORGE GILFILLAN, *Specimens with Memoirs of the Less-Known British Poets*, 1860, Vol. 1, p. 203

On a superficial inspection, Donne's verses look like so many riddles. They seem to be written upon the principle of making the meaning as difficult to be found out as possible,—of using all the resources of language, not to express thought, but to conceal it. Nothing is said in a direct, natural manner; conceit follows conceit without intermission; the most remote analogies, the most farfetched images, the most unexpected turns, one after another, surprise and often puzzle the understanding; while things of the most opposite kinds—the harsh and the harmonious, the graceful and the grotesque, the grave and the gay, the pious and the profane—meet and mingle in the strangest of dances. But, running through all this bewilderment, a deeper insight detects not only a vein of the most exuberant wit, but often the sunniest and most delicate fancy, and the truest tenderness and depth of feeling.—GEORGE L. CRAIK, *A Compendious History of English Literature and of the English Language*, 1861, Vol. 1, p. 579

There is indeed much in Donne, in the unfolding of his moral and spiritual life, which often reminds us of St. Augustine. I do not mean that, noteworthy as on many accounts he was, and in the language of Carew, one of his contemporaries,

> A king who ruled as he thought fit
> The universal monarchy of wit.

he at all approached in intellectual or spiritual stature to the great Doctor of the Western Church. But still there was in Donne the same tumultuous youth, the same final deliverance from them; and then the same passionate and personal grasp of the central truths of Christianity, linking itself as this did with all that he had suffered, and all that he had sinned, and all through which by God's grace he had victoriously struggled. — RICHARD CHENEVIX TRENCH, *A Household Book of English Poetry*, 1868, p. 403

With vast learning, with subtle and penetrating intellect, with a fancy singularly fruitful and ingenious, he still contrived to disconnect, more or less, his learning from what was worth

learning, his intellect from what was reasonable, his fancy from what was beautiful. His poems, or rather his metrical problems, are obscure in thought, rugged in versification, and full of conceits which are intended to surprise rather than to please; but they still exhibit a power of intellect, both analytical and analogical, competent at once to separate the minutest and connect the remotest ideas. This power, while it might not have given his poems grace, sweetness, freshness, and melody, would still, if properly directed, have made them valuable for their thoughts; but in the case of Donne it is perverted to the production of what is *bizarre* or unnatural, and his muse is thus as hostile to use as to beauty. The intention is, not to idealize what is true, but to display the writer's skill and wit in giving a show of reason to what is false. The effect of this on the moral character of Donne was pernicious. A subtile intellectual scepticism, which weakened will, divorced thought from action and literature from life, and made existence a puzzle and a dream, resulted from this perversion of his intellect. He found that he could wittily justify what was vicious as well as what was unnatural; and his amatory poems, accordingly, are characterized by a cold, hard, labored, intellectualized sensuality, worse than the worst impurity of his contemporaries, because it has no excuse of passion for its violations of decency.—EDWIN P. WHIPPLE, *The Literature of the Age of Elizabeth*, 1869, p. 231

A pungent satirist, of terrible crudeness, a powerful poet, of a precise and intense imagination, who still preserves something of the energy and thrill of the original inspiration. But he deliberately abuses all these gifts, and succeeds with great difficulty in concocting a piece of nonsense. . . . Twenty times while reading him we rub our brow, and ask with astonishment, how a man could so have tormented and contorted himself, strained his style, refined on his refinement, hit upon such absurd comparisons?—HIPPOLYTE TAINE, *History of English Literature*, 1871, tr. H. Van Laun, Vol. 1, Bk. 2, Ch. 1, pp. 203–4

His reputation as a poet, great in his own day, low during the latter part of the seventeenth and the whole of the eighteenth centuries, has latterly revived. In its days of abasement, critics spoke of his harsh and rugged versification, and his leaving nature for conceit. It seems to be now acknowledged that, amidst much bad taste, there is much real poetry, and that of a high order, in Donne.—ROBERT CHAMBERS, *Cyclopædia of English Literature*, 3rd ed. by Robert Carruthers, 1876

> Better and truer verse none ever wrote . . .
> Than thou, revered and magisterial Donne!
> —ROBERT BROWNING, *The Two Poets of Croisic*, 1877

We find little to admire, and nothing to love. We see that farfetched similes, extravagant metaphors, are not here occasional blemishes, but the substance. He should have given us simple images, simply expressed; for he loved and suffered much: but fashion was stronger than nature.—ALFRED H. WELSH, *Development of English Literature and Language*, 1882, Vol. 1, p. 413

Donne's poems were first collected in 1633: they cover an extraordinary range in subject, and are throughout marked with a strange originality almost equally fascinating and repellent. It is possible that his familiarity with Italian and Spanish literatures, both at that time deeply coloured by fantastic and far-fetched thought, may have in some degree influenced him in that direction. His poems were probably written mainly during youth. There is a strange solemn passionate earnestness about them, a quality which underlies the fanciful "conceits" of all his work.—FRANCIS T. PALGRAVE, *The Treasury of Sacred Song*, 1889, p. 333, Note

In him the Jacobean spirit, as opposed to the Elizabethan, is paramount. His were the first poems which protested, in their form alike and their tendency, against the pastoral sweetness of the Spenserians. Something new in English literature begins in Donne, something which proceeded, under his potent influence, to colour poetry for nearly a hundred years. The exact mode in which that influence was immediately distributed is unknown to us, or very dimly perceived. To know more about it is one of the great desiderata of literary history. The imitation of Donne's style begins so early, and becomes so general, that several critics have taken for granted that there must have been editions of his writings which have disappeared. . . . The style of Donne, like a very odd perfume, was found to cling to every one who touched it, and we observe the remarkable phenomenon of poems which had not passed through a printer's hands exercising the influence of a body of accepted classical work. In estimating the poetry of the Jacobean age, therefore, there is no writer who demands more careful study than this enigmatical and subterranean master, this veiled Isis whose utterances outweigh the oracles of all the visible gods.—ED-MUND GOSSE, *The Jacobean Poets*, 1894, pp. 47–48

After he had taken holy orders Donne seldom threw his passions into verse; even his "Divine Poems" are, with few exceptions, of early date; the poet in Donne did not cease to exist, but his ardour, his imagination, his delight in what is strange and wonderful, his tenderness, his tears, his smiles, his erudition, his intellectual ingenuities, were all placed at the service of one whose desire was that he might die in the pulpit, or if not die, that he might take his death in the pulpit, a desire which was in fact fulfilled. . . . Donne as a poet is certainly difficult of access. . . . He sometimes wrote best, or thought he wrote best, when his themes were wholly of the imagination. Still it is evident that Donne, the student, the recluse, the speculator on recondite problems, was also a man who adventured in pursuit of violent delights which had violent ends. . . . In whatever sunny garden, and at whatever banquet Donne sits, he discerns in air the dark Scythesman of that great picture attributed to Orcagna. An entire section of his poetry is assigned to death.—EDWARD DOWDEN, *New Studies in Literature*, 1895, pp. 90–91, 107–17

"The Will of John Donne" is probably the wittiest and the bitterest lyric in our language. Donne's love passages and their record in verse were over before the author was of age. His wit then turned into metaphysical sermon-writing and theological polemics, and his bitterness into a despairing austerity. — OSWALD CRAWFURD, *Lyrical Verse from Elizabeth to Victoria*, 1896, p. 426

Donne is a thoroughly original spirit and a great innovator; he is thoughtful, indirect, and strange; he nurses his fancies, lives with them, and broods over them so much that they are still modern in all their distinction and ardour, in spite of the strangeness of their apparel—a strangeness no greater perhaps than that of some modern poets, like Browning, as the apparel of their verse will appear two hundred years hence. Ingenuity, allusiveness, the evocation of remote images and of analogies that startle the mind into a more than half acquiescence, phantoms of deep thoughts, and emotions half-sophisticated and wholly intense: these things mark the poetry of Donne. His lyric is original and taking, but it lacks simple thoughts; it does not sing. It is ascetic and sometimes austere; the sense of sin,

the staple of contemporary tragedy, enters the lyric with Donne. He is all for terseness and meaning; and his versification accords with his thought and is equally elliptical. —FREDERIC IVES CARPENTER, "Introduction" to *English Lyric Poetry, 1500–1700*, 1897, p. lviii

One of the most enigmatical and debated, alternately one of the most attractive and most repellent, figures in English literature.—DAVID HANNAY, *The Later Renaissance*, 1898, p. 220

Was the mind of the dialectician, of the intellectual adventurer; he is a poet almost by accident, or at least for reasons with which art in the abstract has but little to do. He writes verse, first of all, because he has observed keenly, and because it pleases the pride of his intellect to satirise the pretensions of humanity. Then it is the flesh which speaks in his verse, the curiosity of woman, which he has explored in the same spirit of adventure; then passion, making a slave of him for love's sake, and turning at last to the slave's hatred; finally, religion, taken up with the same intellectual interest, the same subtle indifference, and, in its turn, passing also into passionate reality. A few poems are inspired in him by what he has seen in remote countries; some are marriage songs and funeral elegies, written for friendship or for money. But he writes nothing "out of his own head," as we say; nothing lightly, or, it would seem, easily; nothing for the song's sake. He speaks, in a letter, of "descending to print anything in verse"; and it is certain that he was never completely absorbed by his own poetry, or at all careful to measure his achievements against those of others. He took his own poems very seriously, he worked upon them with the whole force of his intellect; but to himself, even before he became a divine, he was something more than a poet. Poetry was but one means of expressing the many-sided activity of his mind and temperament. Prose was another, preaching another; travel and contact with great events and persons scarcely less important to him, in the building up of himself.—ARTHUR SYMONS, "John Donne," *Fortnightly Review*, Nov. 1, 1899, p. 735

In one way he has partly become obsolete because he belonged so completely to the dying epoch. The scholasticism in which his mind was steeped was to become hateful and then contemptible to the rising philosophy; the literature which he had assimilated went to the dust-heaps; preachers condescended to drop their doctorial robes; downright common-sense came in with Tillotson and South in the next generation; and not only the learning but the congenial habit of thought became unintelligible. Donne's poetical creed went the same way, and if Pope and Parnell perceived that there was some genuine ore in his verses and tried to beat it into the coinage of their own day, they only spoilt it in trying to polish it. But on the other side, Donne's depth of feeling, whether tortured into short lyrics or expanding into voluble rhetoric, has a charm which perhaps gains a new charm from modern sentimentalists. His morbid or "neurotic" constitution has a real affinity for latter-day pessimists. If they talk philosophy where he had to be content with scholastic theology the substance is pretty much the same. He has the characteristic love for getting pungency at any price; for dwelling upon the horrible till we cannot say whether it attracts or repels him; and can love the "intense" and supersublimated as much as if he were skilled in all the latest æsthetic canons. —SIR LESLIE STEPHEN, "John Donne," *National Review*, Dec. 1899, p. 613

John Donne is of interest to the student of literature chiefly because of the influence which he exerted on the poetry of the age. His verse teems with forced comparisons and analogies between things remarkable for their dissimilarity. An obscure likeness and a worthless conceit were as important to him as was the problem of existence to Hamlet.—Reuben Post Halleck, *History of English Literature*, 1900, p. 186

WILLIAM HAZLITT
From "On Cowley, Butler, Suckling, etc."
Lectures on the English Comic Writers
1818

Donne, who was considerably before Cowley, is without his fancy, but was more recondite in his logic, and rigid in his descriptions. He is hence led, particularly in his satires, to tell disagreeable truths in as disagreeable a way as possible, or to convey a pleasing and affecting thought (of which there are many to be found in his other writings) by the harshest means, and with the most painful effort. His Muse suffers continual pangs and throes. His thoughts are delivered by the Cæsarean operation. The sentiments, profound and tender as they often are, are stifled in the expression; and 'heaved pantingly forth,' are 'buried quick again' under the ruins and rubbish of analytical distinctions. It is like poetry waking from a trance: with an eye bent idly on the outward world, and half-forgotten feelings crowding about the heart; with vivid impressions, dim notions, and disjointed words. The following may serve as instances of beautiful or impassioned reflections losing themselves in obscure and difficult applications. He has some lines to a Blossom, which begin thus:

> Little think'st thou, poor flow'r,
> Whom I have watched six or seven days,
> And seen thy birth, and seen what every hour
> Gave to thy growth, thee to this height to raise,
> And now dost laugh and triumph on this bough.
>   Little think'st thou
> That it will freeze anon, and that I shall
> To-morrow find thee fall'n, or not at all.

This simple and delicate description is only introduced as a foundation for an elaborate metaphysical conceit as a parallel to it, in the next stanza.

> Little think'st thou (poor heart
> That labour'st yet to nestle thee,
> And think'st by hovering here to get a part
> In a forbidden or forbidding tree,
> And hop'st her stiffness by long siege to bow:)
>   Little think'st thou,
> That thou to-morrow, ere the sun doth wake,
> Must with this sun and me a journey take.

This is but a lame and impotent conclusion from so delightful a beginning.—He thus notices the circumstance of his wearing his late wife's hair about his arm, in a little poem which is called the Funeral.

> Whoever comes to shroud me, do not harm
>   Nor question much
> That subtle wreath of hair, about mine arm;
> The mystery, the sign you must not touch.

The scholastic reason he gives quite dissolves the charm of tender and touching grace in the sentiment itself—

> For 'tis my outward soul,
> Viceroy to that, which unto heaven being gone,
>   Will leave this to control,
> And keep these limbs, her provinces, from
>   dissolution.

Again, the following lines, the title of which is Love's Deity,

are highly characteristic of this author's manner, in which the thoughts are inlaid in a costly but imperfect mosaic-work.

> *I long to talk with some old lover's ghost,*
> *Who died before the God of Love was born:*
> I cannot think that he, who then lov'd most,
> Sunk so low, as to love one which did scorn.
> But since this God produc'd a destiny,
> And that vice-nature, custom, lets it be;
> I must love her that loves not me.

The stanza in the Epithalamion on a Count Palatine of the Rhine, has been often quoted against him, and is an almost irresistible illustration of the extravagances to which this kind of writing, which turns upon a pivot of words and possible allusions, is liable. Speaking of the bride and bridegroom he says, by way of serious compliment—

> Here lies a she-Sun, and a he-Moon there,
> She gives the best light to his sphere;
> Or each is both and all, and so
> They unto one another nothing owe.

His love-verses and epistles to his friends give the most favourable idea of Donne. His satires are too clerical. He shews, if I may so speak, too much disgust, and, at the same time, too much contempt for vice. His dogmatical invectives hardly redeem the nauseousness of his descriptions, and compromise the imagination of his readers more than they assist their reason. The satirist does not write with the same authority as the divine, and should use his poetical privileges more sparingly. 'To the pure all things are pure,' is a maxim which a man like Dr. Donne may be justified in applying to himself; but he might have recollected that it could not be construed to extend to the generality of his readers, *without benefit of clergy.*

J. SPENCE (?)
"Donne's Poems"
Retrospective Review, 1823, pp. 31–35

Theobald, in his egregious preface to Shakspeare, calls Donne's Poems "nothing but a continued heap of riddles."—We shall presently shew that he knew as little about Donne as he himself has shewn that he knew about Shakspeare. If *he* could have written such "riddles," or even expounded them, Pope might have put him into the *Dunciad* in vain.

Donne was contemporary with Shakspeare, and was not unworthy to be so. He may fairly be placed, in point of talent, at the head of the minor poets of that day. Imbued, to saturation, with all the learning of his age—with a most active and piercing intellect—an imagination, if not grasping and comprehensive, most subtle and far-darting—a fancy rich, vivid, picturesque, and, at the same time, highly *fantastical*,—if we may so apply the term—a mode of expression singularly terse, simple, and condensed—an exquisite ear for the melody of versification— and a wit, admirable as well for its caustic severity as its playful quickness; all he wanted to make him an accomplished poet of the second order was, sensibility and taste: and both of these he possessed in a certain degree; but neither in a sufficient degree to keep them from yielding to the circumstances in which he was placed. His sensibility was by nature strong, but sluggish and deep-seated. It required to be roused and awakened by the imagination, before it would act; and this process seldom failed to communicate to the action which it created, an appearance of affectation (for it was nothing more than the appearance), which is more destructive to the effect of sentimental poetry than any thing else. We do not mind the images and illustrations of a sentiment being recondite and far-fetched; and, indeed, this has frequently a good effect; but if the sentiment itself has any appearance of being so, we doubt the truth of it immediately; and if we doubt its truth, we are disposed to give it any reception rather than a sympathetic one. The scholastic habits of Donne's intellect also, without weakening his sensibility, contributed greatly to deform and denaturalize its outward manifestations. It was not the fashion of his time for a scholar and a poet to express himself as other people would; for if he had done so, what advantage would he or the world have derived from his poetry or his scholarship? Accordingly, however intense a feeling might be, or however noble a thought, it was to be heightened and illustrated, in the expression of it, by clustering about it a host of images and associations (congruous or not, as it might happen), which memory or imagination, assisted by the most quick-eyed wit, or the most subtle ingenuity, could in any way contrive to link to it: thus pressing the original thought or sentiment to death, and hiding even the form of it, beneath a profusion of superfluous dress. This was the crying fault of all the minor poets of the Elizabethan age; and of Donne more than of any other: though *his* thoughts and feelings would, generally speaking, bear this treatment better than those of any of his rivals in the same class. These persons never acted avowedly, (though they sometimes did unconsciously) on the principle that an idea or a sentiment may be poetical *per se*; for they had no notion whatever of the fact. They considered that *man* was the creator of poetry, not Nature; and that any thing might be made poetical, by connecting it, in a certain manner, with something else. A thought or a feeling was, to them, not a thing *to express*, but a theme to write *variations* upon—a nucleus, about which other thoughts and feelings were to be made to crystallize. A star was not bright to *their* eyes till it had been set in a constellation; a rose was not sweet till it had been gathered into a bouquet, and its hue and odour contrasted and blended with a thousand others. In fact, they had little simplicity of feeling, and still less of taste. They did not know the real and intrinsic value of any object, whether moral or physical; but only in what manner it might be connected with any other object, so as to be made subservient to their particular views at the moment. They saw at once how far it was available *to them*, but nothing whatever of the impression it was calculated to make for itself.

We are speaking, now, of a particular class or school of poets of that day; for they differed as much from all others, and were as much allied by a general resemblance of style among themselves, as the Della Cruscan school in our own day. Indeed, in some particulars, there is no slight resemblance between the two styles; inasmuch, as both are purely artificial, and are dependent for their effect on a particular *manner* of treating their subject: at least, their intended effect is dependent on this—for the school to which Donne belongs often delights us in the highest degree, not in consequence of this manner, but in spite of it. There is also this other grand difference in favour of the latter,—that, whereas the Della Cruscans tried to make things poetical by means of *words* alone, *they* did it by means of thoughts and images;—the one considered poetry to consist in a certain mode of expression; the other, in a certain mode of seeing, thinking, and feeling. This is nearly all the difference between them; but this is a vast difference indeed: for the one supposes the necessity of, and in fact uses, a vast fund of thoughts and images; while the other can execute all its purposes nearly as well without any of these. In short, the one kind of writing requires very considerable talent to produce it, and its results are very often highly poetical; whereas the other

requires no talent at all, and can in no case produce poetry, but very frequently covers and conceals it where it is.

But it is not at present our intention to go into a general discussion of that particular school of poetry to which Donne belongs; but merely to bring to light some of the exquisite beauties which have hitherto lain concealed from the present age, among the learned as well as unlearned lumber which he has so unaccountably mixed up with them. We say unaccountably—for it is impossible to give a reasonable account of any poetical theory, the perpetual results of which are the most pure and perfect beauties of every kind—of thought, of sentiment, of imagery, of expression, and of versification—lying in immediate contact with the basest deformities, equally of every kind; each given forth alternately in almost equal proportions, and in the most unconscious manner on the part of the writer as to either being entitled to the preference; and indeed without one's being able to discover that he saw any difference between them, even in kind.

Before doing this, however, it may be well to let the reader know what was thought of Donne in his own day, lest he should suppose that we are introducing him to a person little known at that time, or lightly valued.

If a prophet has little honour in his own time and country, the same can seldom be said of a poet; though *he*, too, is in some sort a prophet. The day in which Donne lived was the most poetical the world ever knew, and yet there can be little doubt, from the evidence of the fugitive literature of the time, that Donne was, upon the whole, more highly esteemed than any other of his contemporaries. We do not, however, mean to attribute all his fame to his published poetry. He was undoubtedly a very extraordinary person in many other respects. He possessed vast knowledge and erudition, and was highly distinguished for the eloquence of his public preaching. But the greater part of the admiration bestowed on him, was avowedly directed to the poetical writings. . . .

It is remarkable that the writer, of whom this could be said by persons of repute, (whether truly or not is no matter) in an age which produced Shakspeare and the elder dramatists—besides Spenser, Syndey, Herbert, Raleigh, and a host of minor names—should so long have remained unknown in an after age, one of the distinguishing boasts of which is, that it has revived a knowledge of, and a love for its great predecessor, at the same time that it has almost rivalled it.

In pieces that can be read with unmingled pleasure, and admired as perfect wholes, the poetry of Donne is almost entirely deficient. This may serve, in some degree, to account for the total neglect which has so long attended him. Almost every beauty we meet with, goes hand in hand with some striking deformity, of one kind or another; and the effect of this is, at first, so completely *irritating* to the imagination, as well as to the taste, that, after we have experienced it a few times, we hastily determine to be without the one, rather than purchase it at the price of the other. But the reader who is disposed, by these remarks, and the extracts that will accompany them, to a perusal of the whole of this poet's works, may be assured that this unpleasant effect will very soon wear off, and he will soon find great amusement and great exercise for his *thinking* faculties, (if nothing else) even in the objectionable parts of Donne; for he is always, when indulging in his very worst vein, filled to overflowing with thoughts, and materials for engendering thought.

The following short pieces are beautiful exceptions to the remark made just above, as to the mixed character of this poet's writings. The first is a farewell from a lover to his mistress, on leaving her for a time. For clearness and smoothness of construction, and a passionate sweetness and softness in the music of the versification, it might have been written in the present day, and may satisfy the ear of the most fastidious of modern readers; and for thought, sentiment, and imagery, it might *not* have been written in the present day;—for, much as we hold in honour our living poets, we doubt if any one among them is capable of it. In fact, it is one of those pieces which immediately strike us as being purely and exclusively attributable to the writer of them—which satisfy us, that, *but for him*, we never could have become possessed of them—which bear a mark that we cannot very well expound, even to ourselves, but which we know no one could have placed on them but him; and this, by-the-bye, is one of the most unequivocal criterions of a true poet. Perhaps the piece itself will explain better what we mean, than any thing we could say of it.

As virtuous men pass mildly away

The simile of the compasses, notwithstanding its quaintness, is more perfect in its kind, and more beautiful, than any thing we are acquainted with. Perhaps the above is the only poem we could extract, that is not disfigured by *any* of the characteristic faults of Donne. Several of them have, however, very few. The following is one of these. It has an air of serious gaiety about it, as if it had been composed in the very bosom of bliss. The versification too, is perfect. It is called, "The Good-Morrow."

I wonder by my troth, what thou and I
Did till we lov'd

The following, though not entirely without the faults of his style, is exceedingly graceful and elegant:

THE DREAM
Dear love, for nothing less than thee

What follows is extremely solemn and fine, and scarcely at all disfigured by the author's characteristic faults:

THE APPARITION
When by thy scorn, O murderess, I am dead

The next specimens that we shall give of this singular writer will be taken from among those of his poems which unite, in a nearly equal proportion, his characteristic faults and beauties; and which may be considered as scarcely less worthy of attention than the foregoing, partly on account of that very union of opposite qualities, but chiefly on account of their remarkable fullness of thought and imagery; in which, indeed, his very worst pieces abound to overflowing.

Notwithstanding the extravagance, as well as the ingenuity, which characterize the two following pieces, there is an air of sincerity about them, which renders their general effect impressive, and even solemn; to say nothing of their individual beauties, both of thought and expression.

THE ANNIVERSARY
All kings, and all their favourites

LOVE'S GROWTH
I scarce believe my love to be so pure

The reader will not fail to observe the occasional obscurities which arise out of the extreme condensation of expression in the foregoing pieces, and in most of those which follow. These passages may always be unravelled by a little attention, and they seldom fail to repay the trouble bestowed upon them. But they must be regarded as unequivocal faults nevertheless.

The following is, doubtless, "high-fantastical," in the last degree; but it is fine notwithstanding, and an evidence of something more than mere ingenuity.

Let me pour forth

The feelings which dictated such poetry as this, (for it is poetry, and nothing but real feelings *could* dictate it,) must have pierced deeper than the surface of both the heart and the imagination. In fact, they wanted nothing but to have been excited under more favourable circumstances, to have made them well-springs of the richest poetry uttering itself in the rarest words.

For clearness of expression, melody of versification, and a certain wayward simplicity of thought peculiarly appropriate to such compositions as these, the most successful of our modern lyrists might envy the following trifle:

THE MESSAGE
Send home my long stray'd eyes to me

Perhaps the two short pieces which follow, include all the characteristics of Donne's style—beauties as well as faults.

A LECTURE [UPON THE SHADOW]
Stand still, and I will read to thee

THE EXPIRATION
So, so,—break off this last lamenting kiss

The following piece, entitled "The Funeral," is fantastical and far-fetched to be sure; but it is very fine nevertheless. The comparison of the nerves and the braid of hair, and anticipating similar effects from each, could never have entered the thoughts of any one but Donne; still less could any one have made it *tell* as he has done. The piece is altogether an admirable and most interesting example of his style.

Whoever comes to shroud me, do not harm

As a specimen of Donne's infinite fullness of meaning, take a little poem, called "The Will"; almost every line of which would furnish matter for a whole treatise in modern times.

Before I sigh my last gasp, let me breathe

The following (particularly the first stanza) seems to us to express even more than it is intended to express; which is very rarely the case with the productions of this writer. The love expressed by it is a love for the passion excited, rather than for the object exciting it; it is a love that lives by "*chewing the cud of sweet and bitter fancy*," rather than by hungering after fresh food—that broods, like the stock dove, over its own voice, and listens for no other—that is all sufficient to itself, and (like virtue) its own reward.

I never stooped as low as they

What follows is in a different style, and it offers a singular specimen of the perverse ingenuity with which Donne sometimes bandies a thought about (like a shuttle-cock) from one hand to the other, only to let it fall to the ground at last.

THE PROHIBITION
Take heed of loving me

The following, in common with many other whole pieces and detached thoughts of this writer, has been imitated by other love-poets in proportion as it has not been read.

SONG
Go and catch a falling star

The following is to the same purpose, but more imbued with the writer's subtlety of thought and far-fetched ingenuity of illustration.

WOMAN'S CONSTANCY
Now thou hast loved me one whole day

The whole of the foregoing extracts are taken from the first department of Donne's poetry—the Love-verses. The only others that we shall choose from these, will be a few specimens of the truth and beauty that are frequently to be met with in Donne, in the shape of detached thoughts, images, &c. Nothing was every more exquisitely felt or expressed, than this opening stanza of a little poem, entitled "The Blossom."

> Little thinkest thou, poor flower

The admirer of Wordsworth's style of language and versification will see, at once, that it is, at its best, nothing more than a *return* to this.

How beautiful is the following bit of description!

> When I behold a stream, which from the spring
> Doth with doubtful melodious murmuring,
> Or in a speechless slumber calmly ride
> Her wedded channel's bosom, and there chide,
> And bend her brows, and swell, if any bough
> Do but stoop down to kiss her utmost brow, &c.

The following is exquisite in its way. It is part of an epithalamion.

> —and night is come; and yet we see
> Formalities retarding thee.
> What mean these ladies, which (as though
> They were to take a clock to pieces) go
> So nicely about the bride?
> A *bride, before a good-night could be said,*
> *Should vanish from her cloathes into her bed,*
> *As souls from bodies steal, and are not spy'd.*

The simile of the clock is an example (not an offensive one) of Donne's peculiar mode of illustration. He scarcely writes a stanza without some ingenious simile of this kind.

The two first lines of the following are very solemn and far-thoughted. There is nothing of the kind in poetry superior to them. I add the lines which succeed them, merely to shew the manner in which the thought is applied.

> I long to talk with some old lover's ghost
> Who died before the God of Love was born

Of Donne's other poems, the Funeral Elegies, Epistles, Satires, and what he calls his "Divine Poems," particularly the last named, we have little to say in the way of general praise, and but few extracts to offer. We shall, however, notice and illustrate each class briefly, in order that the reader may have a fair impression of the whole body of this writer's poetical works.

The Epistles of Donne we like less than any of his other poems, always excepting the religious ones. Not that they are without his usual proportion of subtle thinking, felicitous illustration, and skilful versification; but they are disfigured by more than his usual obscurity—by a harshness of style, that is to be found in few of his other poems, except the satires—by an extravagance of hyperbole in the way of compliment, that often amounts to the ridiculous—and by an evident want of sincerity, that is worse than all. To whomever they are addressed, all are couched in the same style of expression, and reach the same pitch of praise. Every one of his correspondents is, without exception, "wisest, virtuousest, discreetest, best." It is as if his letters had been composed at leisure, and kept ready *cut and dried* till wanted.

Though it will not exactly bear quotation, perhaps the most poetical, as well as the most characteristic of the Epistles is the imaginary one (the only one of that description) from Sappho to Philaenis.

The following is finely thought and happily expressed. It is part of an Epistle to Sir Henry Wotton.

> Be then thine own home, and in thyself dwell;
> Inn anywhere, continuance maketh hell.
> And seeing the snail, which everywhere doth roam,

> Carrying his own house still, still is at home,
> Follow (for he is easy paced) this snail,
> Be thine own palace, or the world's thy goal.
> And in the world's sea, do not like cork sleep
> Upon the water's face; nor in the deep
> Sink like a lead without a line: but as
> Fishes glide, leaving no print where they pass,
> Nor making sound, so closely thy course go,
> Let men dispute, whether thou breathe, or no.

We can afford no other extract from the Epistles, although many most curious ones might be found; but pass on to the Funeral Elegies. All Donne's poems, even his best, with one or two exceptions, are laboured in the highest degree; and the Funeral Elegies are still more so than any of the others. They have all the faults of his style, and this one above all. Still they abound in passages of great force, depth, and beauty; but none of them will bear extracting entire—at least, none which are properly included in this class. But there is one poem printed among these, which we shall extract the greater portion of, and which the reader will find to be written in a somewhat different style from that of almost all the others that we have quoted. There is a solemn and sincere earnestness about it, which will cause it to be read with great interest, even by those who may not be capable of appreciating, in detail, the rich and pompous flow of the verse, and the fine harmony of its music; the elegant simplicity of the language; and the extreme beauty of some of the thoughts and images.

The poem seems to have been addressed to his mistress, on the occasion of his taking leave of her, after her having offered to attend him on his journey in the disguise of a page. It is headed strangely enough.

ELEGY ON HIS MISTRESS
By our first strange and fatal interview

It only remains to speak of Donne's Satires; for his Divine Poems must be left to speak for themselves. General readers are probably acquainted with Donne chiefly as a writer of satires; and, in this character, they know him only through the medium of Pope; which is equivalent to knowing Homer only through the same medium. The brilliant and refined modern attempted to give his readers an idea of Donne, by changing his roughness into smoothness, and polishing down his force into point. In fact, he altered Donne into Pope—which was a mere impertinence. Each is admirable in his way—quite enough so to make it impossible to change either, with advantage, into a likeness of any other.

Donne's Satires are as rough and rugged as the unhewn stones that have just been blasted from their native quarry; and they must have come upon the readers at whom they were levelled, with the force and effect of the same stones flung from the hand of a giant. The following detached character is the only specimen we have left ourselves room to give of them. It strikes us as being nearly the perfection of this kind of writing.

> Therefore I suffered this; towards me did run
> A thing more strange than on Nile's slime the sun
> E'er bred, or all which into Noah's Ark came:
> A thing, which would have posed Adam to name:
> Stranger than seven antiquaries' studies,
> Than Afric's monsters, Guiana's rarities,
> Stranger than strangers; one, who for a Dane,
> In the Danes' Massacre had sure been slain,
> If he had lived then; and without help dies,
> When next the 'prentices 'gainst strangers rise.
> One, whom the watch at noon lets scarce go by,
> One, to whom, the examining Justice sure would
>   cry,

'Sir, by your priesthood tell me what you are.'
His clothes were strange, though coarse; and black,
    though bare;
Sleeveless his jerkin was, and it had been
Velvet, but 'twas now (so much ground was seen)
Become tufftaffaty; and our children shall
See it plain rash awhile, then naught at all.
This thing hath travelled, and saith, speaks all
    tongues
And only knoweth what to all states belongs,
Made of th' accents, and best phrase of all these,
He speaks one language; if strange meats displease,
Art can deceive, or hunger force my taste,
But pedant's motley tongue, soldier's bombast,
Mountebank's drugtongue, nor the terms of law
Are strong enough perparatives, to draw
Me to bear this, yet I must be content
With his tongue: in his tongue, called compliment:
. . .
He names me, and comes to me; I whisper, 'God!
How have I sinned, that thy wrath's furious rod,
This fellow, chooseth me?' He sayeth, 'Sir,
I love your judgement; whom do you prefer,
For the best linguist?' And I sillily
Said, that I thought Calepine's Dictionary;
'Nay but of men, most sweet Sir'. Beza then,
Some Jesuits, and two reverend men
Of our two Academies, I named. There
He stopped me, and said; 'Nay, your Apostles were
Good pretty linguists, and so Panurge was;
Yet a poor gentleman, all these may pass
By travail.' Then, as if he would have sold
His tongue, he praised it, and such wonders told
That I was fain to say, 'If you had lived, Sir,
Time enough to have been interpreter
To Babel's bricklayers, sure the Tower had stood.'
He adds, 'If of Court life you knew the good,
You would leave loneness.' I said, 'Not alone
My loneness is; but Spartan's fashion,
To teach by painting drunkards, doth not last
Now; Aretine's pictures have made few chaste;
No more can princes' Courts, though there be few
Better pictures of vice, teach me virtue';
He, like to a high stretched lute string squeaked, 'O
    Sir,
'Tis sweet to talk of kings.' 'At Westminster,'
Said I, 'the man that keeps the Abbey tombs,
And for his price doth with whoever comes,
Of all our Harrys, and our Edwards talk,
From king to king and all their kin can walk:
Your ears shall hear naught, but kings; your eyes
    meet
Kings only; The way to it, is King Street.'
He smacked, and cried, 'He's base, mechanic,
    coarse,
So are all your Englishmen in their discourse.
Are not your Frenchmen neat?' 'Mine? as you see,
I have but one Frenchman, look, he follows me.'
'Certes they are neatly clothed. I of this mind am,
Your only wearing is your grogaram.'
'Not so Sir, I have more.' Under this pitch
He would not fly; I chaffed him; but as itch
Scratched into smart, and as blunt iron ground
Into an edge, hurts worse: so, I (fool) found,
Crossing hurt me; to fit my sullenness,
He to another key his style doth dress,
And asks, 'What news?' I tell him of new plays.
He takes my hand, and as a still, which stays
A semi-breve 'twixt each drop, he niggardly,

As loth to enrich me, so tells many a lie,
More than ten Holinsheds, or Halls, or Stows,
Of trivial household trash he knows; he knows
When the Queen frowned, or smiled, and he knows
    what
A subtle statesman may gather of that;
He knows who loves; whom; and who by poison
Hastes to an office's reversion;
He knows who hath sold his land, and now doth beg
A licence, old iron, boots, shoes, and egg-
Shells to transport; shortly boys shall not play
At span-counter, or blow-point, but they pay
Toll to some courtier; and wiser than all us,
He knows what lady is not painted; thus

We had intended to close this paper with a few examples of the most glaring faults of Donne's style; but the reader will probably think that we have made better use of our space. We have endeavoured to describe those faults, and the causes of them; and not a few of them—or of those parts which should perhaps be regarded as *characteristics*, rather than absolute faults—will be found among the extracts now given. Those who wish for more may find them in almost every page of the writer's works. They may find the most far-fetched and fantastical allusions and illustrations brought to bear upon the thought or feeling in question, sometimes by the most quick-eyed and subtle ingenuity, but oftener in a manner altogether forced and arbitrary; turns of thought that are utterly at variance with the sentiment and with each other; philosophical and scholastic differences and distinctions, that no sentiment could have suggested, and that nothing but *searching for* could have found; and, above all, paradoxical plays of words, antitheses of thought and expression, and purposed involutions of phrase, that nothing but the most painful attention can untwist. All this they may find, and more. But, in the midst of all, they not only may, but must find an unceasing activity and an overflowing fullness of mind, which seem never to fail or flag, and which would more than half redeem the worst faults (of mere style) that could be allied to them.

JOHN ALFRED LANGFORD
From "An Evening with Donne"
Working Man's Friend, December 1850, pp. 18–21

Among the many glories of English literature, not the least is her possession of so long a list of truly religious poets. In this, the highest order of poetry, we have names unsurpassed by those of any nation, or of any time. Setting aside the matchless glory of Milton, we have the quaint song of the pious old George Herbert; the epigrammatic force of the "Night Thoughts" of Young; the genial, warm-hearted homeliness of the strains of Cowper; the childlike lyrics of the ever-loved Watts; the smooth, stream-like flow of Montgomery; the soul-raising thought of the nature-loving Wordsworth; and not to mention others of high and lofty fame, whose works the world will not willingly let die, we have him with whom we propose to spend the present evening—the old, antiquated, and venerable DONNE.

Dr. Johnson has offered some very curious reasons why religious poetry has not been successful in attaining a very high state of excellence. We venture to opine that in this respect the Doctor has committed himself, by giving a verdict which posterity will not confirm. We could select from our religious writers passages unequalled, in all that constitutes high poetry, by any equal number of passages from the greatest bards who have not especially devoted their talents to religion, such as Byron and Shelley, for instance. It is curious to think that the Doctor should fall into such a mistake; and it is still more curious to think of the numbers who have since re-echoed the opinion, considering that all the facts are against them. Why, the greatest of every land, and of every faith, are the religious ones, whether we look at the sublime old Hebrew bards, with "the fires of Sinai, and the thunders of the Lord!" or at the poets of classic Greece, or at their numerous successors, who have drawn their inspiration from the Christian faith, the fact is the same. Well has a modern poet said,

> The high and holy works, mid lesser lays,
> Stand up like churches among village cots:
> And it is joy to think that in every age,
> However much the world was wrong therein,
> The greatest works of mind or hand have been
> Done unto God. So may they ever be!
> It shows the strength of wish we have to be great,
> And the sublime humility of might.
> —*Festus.*

But now to Donne. He was born in London in the year 1573. His parents were of the Roman Catholic faith, but their son, convinced of the truth of Protestantism, early declared himself a proselyte to the doctrines of the Reformation. He studied, and successfully, at both the Universities, and became, as one of the critics well observes, "completely *saturated* with the learning of his times." His works are rather voluminous, filling six goodly sized volumes, and consist of satires, ejaculations, occasional poems, elegies, and devotional pieces.

There is a class of poets known as the metaphysical. Of these Donne is perhaps the first in point of time, though some give "rare old Ben," the precedence. Their chief characteristic is their intellectualism. Forsaking the pure and genial naturalness of the Elizabethan poets, they seek by strange and far-fetched allusions, similes, and figures, to clothe a simple thought in party-coloured garments; and to offer it to the reader in as many varied aspects as the most violent twistings and torturings of this brave English language would allow. Extremely learned, in whatever was considered learning in their day, they ransacked all their store in the search for refined, *recherché*, and difficult analogies. Physics, metaphysics, scholastic literature, were made to bear tribute to their love of "the blue-eyed maid" chimera. "The metaphysical poets," says Dr. Johnson, "were men of learning; and to show their whole endeavour, but, unluckily, resolving to show it in rhyme, instead of writing poetry, they only wrote verses, and very often such verses as stood the trial of the finger better than of the ear, for the modulation was so imperfect, that they were only found to be verses by counting the syllables." Such is sure to be the case, when men sit down to put thoughts into verse, instead of waiting till the divine afflatus compels them to utter their feelings, which necessarily take the form of song; as different a thing from verse as light is from darkness. Goethe has well said in one of those world-famous *Xenien* of his,

> What many sing and say,
> Must still by us be borne!
> Ye worthy—great and small—
> Tired you sing yourselves and lorn;
> And yet let no one tune his lay
> Except for what he has to say.

But of these poets, if we except Cowley, Donne holds the highest place. He had much wit, in which gift Dryden confesses himself and his contemporaries to be inferior. He had, as we have seen, a vast erudition, some fancy and elegance, together with strong piety. These combined must surely make a poet of no ordinary power. His satires are strong, vigorous, and masculine. Compared with Pope his verses would certainly want smoothness, but Pope himself would have been a much greater poet, had he possessed some of the wholesome roughness, and known that amidst a profusion of sweets that a bitter is often welcome and good. It is true that Donne is very capricious about the place of accent; but few readers would have to count the fingers to tell whether it were verse or no. Certain we are, if much of his writing be not verse, there is much of it that is poetry. Take the following lines on the "Last Night of the Year":—

> This twilight of two years, not past nor next,
>   Some emblem is of me, or I of this,
> Who meteor-like, of stuff and form perplext,
>   Whose what and where in disputation is,
>   If I should call me anything, should miss.
> I sum the years and me, and find me not,
>   Debtor to th' old, nor creditor to th' new.
> That cannot say, my thanks I have forgot,
>   Nor trust I this with hopes, and yet scarce
>   true
>   This bravery is, since these times showed me
>   you.

The critic we have quoted above as saying that Donne was saturated with all the learning of his times, also says of him "That he was endowed with a most active and piercing intellect—an imagination, if not grasping and comprehensive, most subtle and far-darting—a fancy rich, vivid, and picturesque—and a wit admirable as well for its caustic severity as for its playful quickness." This is particularly applicable to his satires, which are the precursors of Dryden and Pope's. It would be useless to select from these, as it is but by examination of them as a whole that their force, their truthfulness, and their caustic severity and playful quickness can be felt. To take a passage from any at all adapted to the limits of this paper, in order to show their quality, would be about as wise as the man who having a house to sell, carried a brick with him as a specimen. We may say of them, what can be said of but few satires, that they possess more than a temporary interest, and may be read with profit and advantage at the present time.

The following piece illustrates pretty well the best and worst qualities of Donne.

> As virtuous men pass mildly away,
>   And whisper to their souls, to go,
> Whilst some of their sad friends do say,
>   The breath goes now, and some say, no:
> So let us melt, and make no noise,
>   No tear-floods, nor sigh-tempests move,
> 'Twere profanation of our joys
>   To tell the laity our love.
> Moving of th' earth brings harms and fears,
>   Men reckon what it did and meant,
> But trepidation of the spheres,
>   Though greater far, is innocent.
> Dull sublunary lovers' love
>   (Whose soul is sense) cannot admit
> Absence, because it doth remove
>   Those things which elemented it.
> But we by a love, so much refined,
>   That our selves know not what it is,
> Inter-assured of the mind,
>   Care less, eyes, lips, and hands to miss.
> Our two souls therefore, which are one,
>   Though I must go, endure not yet

A breach, but an expansion,
Like gold to aery thinness beat.
If they be two, they are two so
As stiff twin compasses are two,
Thy soul the fixed foot, makes no show
To move, but doth, if th'other do.
And though it in the centre sit,
Yet when the other far doth roam,
It leans, and hearkens after it,
And grows erect, as that comes home.
Such wilt thou be to me, who must
Like th' other foot, obliquely run;
Thy firmness makes my circle just,
And makes me end, where I begun.

A strange analogy this; but yet not so absurd as at first reading it may appear. It is true it may need reading over more than once clearly to seize its hidden meaning; but what then, shall we turn aside from every one "who does not wear his heart upon his sleeve for daws to peck at"?

One more extract, and we bid our poet good night. It is on the littleness of temporal existence, compared with the great, solemn eternity beyond. The lines are quaint, but their spirit fine.

Think in how poor a prison thou didst lie
After, enabled but to suck and cry.
Think, when 'twas grown to most, 'twas a poor inn,
A province packed up in two yards of skin,
And that usurped or threatened with the rage
Of sicknesses, or their true mother, age.
But think that death hath now enfranchised thee,
Thou hast thy expansion now, and liberty;
Think that a rusty piece, discharged, is flown
In pieces, and the bullet is his own,
And freely flies; this to thy soul allow,
Think thy shell broke, think thy soul hatched but
now.

GEORGE MACDONALD
From "Dr. Donne: His Mode and Style"
England's Antiphon
1868, pp. 114–24

He ⟨Donne⟩ is represented by Dr. Johnson as one of the chief examples of that school of poets called by himself the *metaphysical*, an epithet which, as a definition, is almost false. True it is that Donne and his followers were always ready to deal with metaphysical subjects, but it was from their mode, and not their subjects, that Dr. Johnson classed them. What this mode was we shall see presently, for I shall be justified in setting forth its strangeness, even absurdity, by the fact that Dr. Donne was the dear friend of George Herbert, and had much to do with the formation of his poetic habits. Just twenty years older than Herbert, and the valued and intimate friend of his mother, Donne was in precisely that relation of age and circumstance to influence the other in the highest degree.

The central thought of Dr. Donne is nearly sure to be just: the subordinate thoughts by means of which he unfolds it are often grotesque, and so wildly associated as to remind one of the lawlessness of a dream, wherein mere suggestion without choice or fitness rules the sequence. As some of the writers of whom I have last spoken would play with words, Dr. Donne would sport with ideas, and with the visual images or embodiments of them. Certainly in his case much knowledge reveals itself in the association of his ideas, and great facility in the management and utterance of them. True likewise, he says nothing unrelated to the main idea of the poem; but not the less certainly does the whole resemble the speech of a child of active imagination, to whom judgment as to the character of his suggestions is impossible, his taste being equally gratified with a lovely image and a brilliant absurdity: a butterfly and a shining potsherd are to him similarly desirable. Whatever wild thing starts from the thicket of thought, all is worthy game to the hunting intellect of Dr. Donne, and is followed without question of tone, keeping, or harmony. In his play with words, Sir Philip Sidney kept good heed that even that should serve the end in view; in his play with ideas, Dr. John Donne, so far from serving the end, sometimes obscures it almost hopelessly: the hart escapes while he follows the squirrels and weasels and bats. It is not surprising that, their author being so inartistic with regard to their object, his verses themselves should be harsh and unmusical beyond the worst that one would imagine fit to be called verse. He enjoys the unenviable distinction of having no rival in ruggedness of metric movement and associated sounds. This is clearly the result of indifference; an indifference, however, which grows very strange to us when we find that he *can* write a lovely verse and even an exquisite stanza.

Greatly for its own sake, partly for the sake of illustration, I quote a poem containing at once his best and his worst, the result being such an incongruity that we wonder whether it might not be called his best *and* his worst, because we cannot determine which. He calls it *Hymn to God, my God, in my Sickness.* The first stanza is worthy of George Herbert in his best mood.

Since I am coming to that holy room,
Where with the choir of saints for evermore
I shall be made thy music, as I come
I tune the instrument here at the door,
And what I must do then, think here before.

To recognize its beauty, leaving aside the depth and truth of the phrase, "Where I shall be made thy music," we must recall the custom of those days to send out for "a noise of musicians." Hence he imagines that he has been summoned as one of a band already gone in to play before the king of "The High Countries:" he is now at the door, where he is listening to catch the tone, that he may have his instrument tuned and ready before he enters. But with what a jar the next stanza breaks on heart, mind, and ear!

Whilst my physicians by their love are grown
Cosmographers, and I their map, who lie
Flat on this bed, that by them may be shown
That this is my south-west discovery,
Per fretum febris—by these straits to die;—

Here, in the midst of comparing himself to a map, and his physicians to cosmographers consulting the map, he changes without warning into a navigator whom they are trying to follow upon the map as he passes through certain straits— namely, those of the fever—towards his south-west discovery, Death. Grotesque as this is, the absurdity deepens in the end of the next stanza by a return to the former idea. He is alternately a map and a man sailing on the map of himself. But the first half of the stanza is lovely: my reader must remember that the region of the West was at that time the Land of Promise to England.

I joy that in these straits I see my West;
For though those currents yield return to
none,
What shall my West hurt me? As west and east
In all flat maps (and I am one) are one,
So death doth touch the resurrection.

It is hardly worth while, except for the strangeness of the phenomenon, to spend any time in elucidating this. Once more a map, he is that of the two hemispheres, in which the east of the one touches the west of the other. Could anything be much more unmusical than the line, "In all flat maps (and I am one) are one"? But the next stanza is worse.

> Is the Pacific sea my home? Or are
>   The eastern riches? Is Jerusalem?
> Anvan, and Magellan, and Gibraltar?
>   All straits, and none but straits are ways to
>   them,
>   Whether where Japhet dwelt, or Cham, or
>   Sem.

The meaning of the stanza is this: there is no earthly home: all these places are only straits that lead home, just as they themselves cannot be reached but through straits.

Let my reader now forget all but the first stanza, and take it along with the following, the last two:

> We think that Paradise and Calvary,
>   Christ's cross and Adam's tree, stood in one
>   place:
> Look, Lord, and find both Adams met in me;
>   As the first Adam's sweat surrounds my face,
>   May the last Adam's blood my soul embrace.
>
> So, in his purple wrapped, receive me, Lord;
>   By these his thorns give me his other crown;
> And as to others' souls I preached thy word,
>   Be this my text, my sermon to mine own:
>   *Therefore, that he may raise, the Lord throws
>   down.*

Surely these are very fine, especially the middle verse of the former and the first verse of the latter stanza. The three stanzas together make us lovingly regret that Dr. Donne should have ridden his Pegasus over quarry and housetop, instead of teaching him his paces.

The next I quote is artistic throughout. Perhaps the fact, of which we are informed by Izaak Walton, "that he caused it to be set to a grave and solemn tune, and to be often sung to the organ by the choristers of St. Paul's church in his own hearing, especially at the evening service," may have something to do with its degree of perfection. There is no sign of his usual haste about it. It is even elaborately rhymed after Norman fashion, the rhymes in each stanza being consonant with the rhymes in every stanza.

A HYMN TO GOD THE FATHER.

> Wilt thou forgive that sin where I begun,
>   Which was my sin, though it were done before?
> Wilt thou forgive that sin, through which I run,
>   And do run still, though still I do deplore?—
>   When thou hast done, thou hast not done;
>   For I have more.
> Wilt thou forgive that sin which I have won
>   Others to sin, and made my sins their door?
> Wilt thou forgive that sin which I did shun
>   A year or two, but wallowed in a score?—
>   When thou hast done, thou hast not done;
>   For I have more.
> I have a sin of fear, that when I've spun
>   My last thread, I shall perish on the shore;
> But swear by thyself, that at my death thy Son
>   Shall shine, as he shines now and heretofore;
>   And having done that, thou hast done:
>   I fear no more.

In those days even a pun might be a serious thing: witness the play in the last stanza on the words *son* and *sun*—not a

mere pun, for the Son of the Father is the Sun of Righteousness: he is Life *and* Light.

What the Doctor himself says concerning the hymn, appears to me not only interesting but of practical value. He "did occasionally say to a friend, 'The words of this hymn have restored to me the same thoughts of joy that possessed my soul in my sickness, when I composed it.'" What a help it would be to many, if in their more gloomy times they would but recall the visions of truth they had, and were assured of, in better moments!

Here is a somewhat strange hymn, which yet possesses, rightly understood, a real grandeur:

A HYMN TO CHRIST

At the Author's last going into Germany.[1]

> In what torn ship soever I embark,
> That ship shall be my emblem of thy ark;
> What sea soever swallow me, that flood
> Shall be to me an emblem of thy blood.
> Though thou with clouds of anger do disguise
> Thy face, yet through that mask I know those eyes,
>   Which, though they turn away sometimes—
>   They never will despise.
>
> I sacrifice this island unto thee,
> And all whom I love here and who love me:
> When I have put this flood 'twixt them and me,
> Put thou thy blood betwixt my sins and thee.
> As the tree's sap doth seek the root below
> In winter, in my winter[2] now I go
>   Where none but thee, the eternal root
>   Of true love, I may know.
>
> Nor thou, nor thy religion, dost control
> The amorousness of an harmonious soul;
> But thou wouldst have that love thyself: as thou
> Art jealous, Lord, so I am jealous now.
> Thou lov'st not, till from loving more thou free
> My soul: who ever gives, takes liberty:
>   Oh, if thou car'st not whom I love,
>   Alas, thou lov'st not me!
>
> Seal then this bill of my divorce to all
> On whom those fainter beams of love did fall;
> Marry those loves, which in youth scattered be
> On face, wit, hopes, (false mistresses), to thee.
> Churches are best for prayer that have least light:
> To see God only, I go out of sight;
>   And, to 'scape stormy days, I choose
>   An everlasting night.

To do justice to this poem, the reader must take some trouble to enter into the poet's mood.

It is in a measure distressing that, while I grant with all my heart the claim of his "Muse's white sincerity," the taste in—I do not say *of*—some of his best poems should be such that I will not present them.

Out of twenty-three *Holy Sonnets*, every one of which, I should almost say, possesses something remarkable, I choose three. Rhymed after the true Petrarchian fashion, their rhythm is often as bad as it can be to be called rhythm at all. Yet these are very fine.

> Thou hast made me, and shall thy work decay?
>   Repair me now, for now mine end doth haste;
>   I run to death, and death meets me as fast,
> And all my pleasures are like yesterday.
> I dare not move my dim eyes any way,
>   Despair behind, and death before doth cast
>   Such terror; and my feeble flesh doth waste
> By sin in it, which it towards hell doth weigh.

Only thou art above, and when towards thee
    By thy leave I can look, I rise again;
But our old subtle foe so tempteth me,
    That not one hour myself I can sustain:
Thy grace may wing me to prevent his art,
And thou like adamant draw mine iron heart.

If faithful souls be alike glorified
    As angels, then my father's soul doth see,
    And adds this even to full felicity,
That valiantly I hell's wide mouth o'erstride:
But if our minds to these souls be descried
    By circumstances and by signs that be
    Apparent in us—not immediately—
How shall my mind's white truth by them be tried?
    They see idolatrous lovers weep and mourn,
And, style blasphemous, conjurors to call
On Jesu's name, and pharisaical
    Dissemblers feign devotiön. Then turn,
O pensive soul, to God; for he knows best
Thy grief, for he put it into my breast.

Death, be not proud, though some have callèd thee
    Mighty and dreadful, for thou art not so;
    For those whom thou think'st thou dost
      overthrow,
Die not, poor Death; nor yet canst thou kill me.
From rest and sleep, which but thy picture be,
    Much pleasure, then from thee much more
      must flow;
    And soonest our best men with thee do go,
Rest of their bones, and soul's delivery!
    Thou'rt slave to fate, chance, kings, and
      desperate men,
And dost with poison, war, and sickness dwell;
And poppy or charms can make us sleep as well,
    And better than thy stroke. Why swell'st thou
      then?
One short sleep past, we wake eternally,
And death shall be no more: Death, thou shalt die.

In a poem called *The Cross*, full of fantastic conceits, we find the following remarkable lines, embodying the profoundest truth.

    As perchance carvers do not faces make,
    But that away, which hid them there, do take:
    Let crosses so take what hid Christ in thee,
    And be his image, or not his, but he.

One more, and we shall take our leave of Dr. Donne. It is called a fragment; but it seems to me complete. It will serve as a specimen of his best and at the same time of his most characteristic mode of presenting fine thoughts grotesquely attired.

RESURRECTION

Sleep, sleep, old sun; thou canst not have
    re-past
As yet the wound thou took'st on Friday last.
Sleep then, and rest: the world may bear thy stay;
A better sun rose before thee to-day;
Who, not content to enlighten all that dwell
On the earth's face as thou, enlightened hell,
And made the dark fires languish in that vale,
As at thy presence here our fires grow pale;
Whose body, having walked on earth and now
Hastening to heaven, would, that he might allow
Himself unto all stations and fill all,
For these three days become a mineral.
He was all gold when he lay down, but rose
All tincture; and doth not alone dispose

Leaden and iron wills to good, but is
Of power to make even sinful flesh like his.
Had one of those, whose credulous piety
Thought that a soul one might discern and see
Go from a body, at this sepulchre been,
And issuing from the sheet this body seen,
He would have justly thought this body a soul,
If not of any man, yet of the whole.

What a strange mode of saying that he is our head, the captain of our salvation, the perfect humanity in which our life is hid! Yet it has its dignity. When one has got over the oddity of these last six lines, the figure contained in them shows itself almost grand.

As an individual specimen of the grotesque form holding a fine sense, regard for a moment the words,

    He was all gold when he lay down, but rose
    All tincture;

which means, that, entirely good when he died, he was something yet greater when he rose, for he had gained the power of making others good: the *tincture* intended here was a substance whose touch would turn the basest metal into gold.

Through his poems are scattered many fine passages; but not even his large influence on the better poets who followed is sufficient to justify our listening to him longer now.

Notes

1. He was sent by James I. to assist an embassy to the Elector Palatine, who had married his daughter Elizabeth.
2. He has lately lost his wife, for whom he had a rare love.

EDMUND GOSSE
"John Donne"
The Jacobean Poets
1894, pp. 51–67

The poems of Donne were not published until after his death. The first edition, the quarto of 1633, is very inaccurate and ill-arranged; the octavos of 1635 and 1639 are much fuller and more exact. Donne, however, still lacks a competent editor. We have no direct knowledge of the poet's own wish as to the arrangement of his poems, nor any safe conjecture as to the date of more than a few pieces. The best lyrics, however, appear to belong to the first decade of James I.'s reign, if they are not even of earlier composition. There seems to be no doubt that the *Satires*, an imperfect manuscript of which bears the date 1593, are wholly Elizabethan. These are seven in number, and belong to the same general category as those of Hall, Lodge, and Guilpin. Neither in date nor in style do they belong to the period treated of in this volume, and it is therefore not necessary to dwell on them at great length here. They are brilliant and picturesque beyond any of their particular compeers, even beyond the best of Hall's satires. But they have the terrible faults which marked all our Elizabethan satirists, a crabbed violence alike of manner and matter, a fierce voluble conventionality, a tortured and often absolutely licentious and erroneous conception of the use of language. The fourth is, doubtless, the best written, and may be taken as the best essay in this class of poetry existing in English literature before the middle-life of Dryden; its attraction for Pope is well known.

"The Progress of the Soul," as named by its author "Poema Satyricon," takes its natural place after the satires, but is conjectured to have been written not earlier than 1610. De Quincey, with unwonted warmth, declared that "massy diamonds compose the very substance of this poem, thoughts and descriptions which have the fervent and gloomy sublimity of Ezekiel or Æschylus." It is written in a variant of the Spenserian stanza, and is a hyperbolical history of the development of the human soul, extended to more than five hundred lines, and not ended, but abruptly closed. It is one of the most difficult of Donne's writings, and started a kind of psychological poetry of which, as the century progressed, many more examples were seen, none, perhaps, of a wholly felicitous character. It has the poet's characteristics, however, to the full. The verse marches with a virile tread, the epithets are daring, the thoughts always curious and occasionally sublime, the imagination odd and scholastic, with recurring gleams of passion.

Here is a fragment of this strange production—

Into an embryon fish our soul is thrown,
And in due time thrown out again, and grown
To such vastness, as if, unmanacled
From Greece, Morea were, and that, by some
Earthquake unrooted, loose Morea swum,
Or seas from Afric's body had severèd
And torn the hopeful promontory's head;
This fish would seem these, and, when all hopes fail,
A great ship overset, or without sail
    Hulling, might (when this was a whelp) be like
      this whale.

At every stroke his brazen fins do take
More circles in the broken sea they make
Then cannons' voices, when the air they tear;
His ribs are pillars, and his high-arch'd roof,
Of bark that blunts best steel, is thunder-proof;
Swim in him, swallow'd dolphins, without fear,
And feel no sides, as if his vast womb were
Some inland sea, and ever as he went
He spouted rivers up, as if he meant
    To join our seas with seas above the
      firmament.

. . .

Now drinks he up seas, and he eats up flocks;
He jostles islands and he shakes firm rocks;
Now in a roomful house this soul doth float,
And like a prince she sends her faculties
To all her limbs, distant as provinces.
The Sun hath twenty times both crab and goat
Parchèd, since first launch'd forth this living boat;
'Tis greatest now and to destruction
Nearest; there's no pause at perfection,
    Greatness a period hath, but hath no station.

Far less extraordinary are the Epistles, which form a large section of Donne's poetical works. All through life he was wont to address letters, chiefly in the heroic couplet, to the most intimate of his friends. These epistles are conceived in a lighter vein than his other writings, and have less of his characteristic vehemence. The earliest, however, "The Storm," which he addressed from the Azores, possesses his Elizabethan mannerism; it is crudely picturesque and licentious, essentially unpoetical. "The Calm," which is the parallel piece, is far better, and partly deserves Ben Jonson's high commendation of it to Drummond. The epistle to Sir Henry Goodyer is noticeable for the dignified and stately manner in which the four-line stanza, afterwards adopted by Gray for his *Elegy*, is employed; this poem is exceedingly like the early pieces written by Dryden some fifty years later. The school of the Restoration is plainly foreshadowed in it.

Many of these epistles are stuffed hard with thoughts, but poetry is rarely to be found in them; the style is not lucid, the construction is desperately parenthetical. It is not often that the weary reader is rewarded by such a polished piece of versifica-

tion as is presented by this passage about love in the "Letter to the Countess of Huntingdon."

It is not love that sueth, or doth contend;
Love either conquers, or but meets a friend.
Man's better part consists of purer fire,
And finds itself allowed, ere it desire.
Love is wise here, keeps home, gives reason sway,
And journeys not till it find summer-way.
A weather-beaten lover, but once known,
Is sport for every girl to practise on.
Who strives, through woman's scorns, woman to
    know,
Is lost, and seeks his shadow to outgo;
It must be sickness, after one disdain,
Though he be called aloud, to look again;
Let others sin and grieve; one cunning slight
Shall freeze my love to crystal in a night.
I can love first, and, if I win, love still,
And cannot be removed, unless she will;
It is her fault if I unsure remain;
She only can untie, I bind again;
The honesties of love with ease I do,
But am no porter for a tedious woe.

Most of these epistles are New Year's greetings, and many are addressed to the noble and devout ladies with whom he held spiritual converse in advancing years. The poet superbly aggrandizes the moral qualities of these women, paying to their souls the court that younger and flightier cavaliers reserved for the physical beauty of their daughters.

The Epithalamia of Donne form that section of his work in which, alone, he seems to follow in due succession after Spenser. These marriage-songs are elegant and glowing, though not without the harshness which Donne could not for any length of time forego. That composed for the wedding of Frederick Count Palatine and the Lady Elizabeth, in 1613, is perhaps the most popular of all Donne's writings, and opens with a delicious vivacity.

Hail, Bishop Valentine, whose day this is!
    All the air is thy diocese,
    And all the chirping choristers
And other birds are thy parishioners;
    Thou marryest every year
The lyric lark and the grave whispering dove,
The sparrow that neglects his life for love,
The household bird with the red stomacher;
Thou mak'st the blackbird speed as soon
As doth the goldfinch or the halcyon;
The husband cock looks out, and straight is sped,
And meets his wife, which brings her feather-bed.
This day more cheerfully than ever shine,—
This day, which might enflame thyself, old
    Valentine.

The ode within the rather stiff setting of the Allophanes and Idios eclogue is scarcely less felicitous.

The miscellaneous secular poems of Donne are generically classed under the heading of "Elegies." We have here some of the most extraordinary aberrations of fancy, some of the wildest contrasts of character and style, to be observed in literature. They are mainly Ovidian or Tibullan studies of the progress of the passion of love, written by one who proclaims himself an ardent, but no longer an illusioned lover,—hot, still, but violent and scandalous. The youth of the author is disclosed in them, but it is not the callous youth of first inexperience. He is already a past master in the subtle sophistry of love, and knows by rote "the mystic language of the eye and hand." Weary with the beauty of spring and summer, he has learned to find fascination in an autumnal face. The voluptuous character of these elegies has scandalized successive critics. Several of them, to be plain, were indeed too outspoken for the poet's own, or for any decent age. Throughout it is seldom so much what the unbridled lover says, as his utter intemperance in saying it, that surprises, especially in one who, by the time the poems were given to the public, had come to be regarded as the holiest of men. Even saints, however, were coarse in the age of James, and the most beautiful of all Donne's elegies, the exquisite "Refusal to Allow His Young Wife to Accompany Him Abroad as a Page," which belongs to his mature life and treats of a very creditable passion, is marred by almost inconceivable offences against good taste.

Another section of Donne's poems is composed of funeral elegies or requiems, in which he allowed the sombre part of his fancy to run riot. In these curious entombments we read nothing that seems personal or pathetic, but much about "the magnetic force" of the deceased, her spiritual anatomy, and her soul's "meridians and parallels." Amid these pedantries, we light now and then upon extraordinary bursts of poetic observation, as when the eminence of the spirit of Mistress Drury reminds the poet of a vision, seen years before in sailing past the Canaries, and he cries out—

Doth not a Teneriffe or higher hill,
Rise so high like a rock, that one might think
The floating moon would shipwreck there, and sink,

or as when one of his trances comes upon him, and he sighs—

when thou know'st this,
Thou know'st how wan a ghost this our world is.

These lovely sudden bursts of pure poetry are more frequent in the "Funeral Elegies" than in any section of Donne's poetry which we have mentioned, and approach those, to be presently noted, in the Lyrics. The spirit of this strange writer loved to dwell on the majestic and gorgeous aspects of death, to wave his torch within the charnel-house and to show that its walls are set with jewels.

This may be taken as an example of his obscure mortuary imagination—

As men of China, after an age's stay,
Do take up porcelain where they buried clay,
So at this grave, her limbeck (which refines
The diamonds, rubies, sapphires, pearls and mines
Of which this flesh was), her soul shall inspire
Flesh of such stuff, as God, when his last fire
Annuls this world, to recompense it, shall
Make and name them the elixir of this All.
They say, the sea, when it gains, loseth too,
If carnal Death (the younger brother) do
Usurp the body; our soul, which subject is
To the elder Death, by sin, is freed by this;
They perish both, when they attempt the just,
For graves our trophies are, and both death's dust.

The presence of the emblems of mortality rouses Donne to an unusual intellectual ecstasy. The latest of these elegies is dated 1625, and shows that the poet retained his art in this kind of writing to the very end of his career, adding polish to his style, without any perceptible falling off in power.

A large number of "Holy Sonnets," which Izaak Walton thought had perished, were published in 1669, and several remain still unprinted. They are more properly quatorzains than sonnets, more correct in form than the usual English sonnet of the age—for the octett is properly arranged and rhymed—but closing in the sestett with a couplet. These sonnets are very interesting from the light they throw on Donne's prolonged sympathy with the Roman Church, over which his

biographers have been wont to slur. All these "Holy Sonnets" probably belong to 1617, or the period immediately following the death of Donne's wife. In the light of certain examples in the possession of the present writer, which have not yet appeared in print, they seem to confirm Walton's remark that though Donne inquired early in life into the differences between Protestantism and Catholicism, yet that he lived until the death of his wife without religion.

A pathetic sonnet from the Westmoreland manuscript, here printed for the first time, shows the effect of that bereavement upon him—

Since she whom I loved hath paid her last debt,
    To Nature, and to hers and my good is dead,
    And her soul early into heaven vanished.—
Wholly on heavenly things my mind is set.
Here the admiring her my mind did whet
    To seek thee, God; so streams do show their
        head,
    But tho' I have found thee, and thou my thirst
        has fed,
A holy thirsty dropsy melts me yet.
But why should I beg more love, when as thou
    Does woo my soul for hers, off'ring all thine:
And dost not only fear lest I allow
    My love to Saints and Angels, things divine,
But in thy tender jealousy dost doubt
Lest this World, Flesh, yea Devil put thee out?

The sonnet on the Blessed Virgin Mary, however, has probably been attributed to Donne by error; the more likely name of Constable has been suggested as that of its author. In his other divine poems, also, the Roman element is often very strong, and the theology of a cast which is far removed from that of Puritanism. In the very curious piece called "The Cross," he seems to confess to the use of a material crucifix, and in "A Litany" he distinctly recommends prayer to the Virgin Mary,

That she-cherubim which unlocked Paradise.

All these are matters which must be left to the future biographers of Donne, but which are worthy of their closest attention in developing the intricate anomalies of his character.

We have now, by a process of exhaustion, arrived at what is the most interesting of the sections of Donne's poetry, his amatory lyrics. These are about seventy in number, and so far as the scanty evidence can be depended upon, belong to various periods from his twentieth to his thirty-fifth year. The series, as we now hold it, begins with the gross and offensive piece of extravagance called, "The Flea," but is followed by "The Good-Morrow," which strikes a very different note. As a rule, these poems are extremely personal, confidential, and vivid; the stamp of life is on them. None the less, while confessing with extraordinary frankness and clearness the passion of the writer, they are so reserved in detail, so immersed and engulphed in secrecy, that no definite conjecture can be hazarded as to the person, or persons, or the class of persons, to whom they were addressed. One or two were evidently inspired by Donne's wife, others most emphatically were not, and in their lawless, though not gross, sensuality, remind us of the still more outspoken "Elegies." In spite of the alembicated verbiage, the tortuousness and artificiality of the thought, sincerity burns in every stanza, and the most exquisite images lie side by side with monstrous conceits and ugly pedantries.

A peculiarity of the lyrics is that scarcely two of the seventy are written in the same verse-form. Donne evidently laid himself out to invent elaborate and farfetched metres. He was imitated in this down to the Restoration, when all metrical effects tended to merge in the heroic couplet. But of the innumerable form-inventions of Donne and of his disciples scarcely one has been adopted into the language, although more than one, by their elegance and melody, deserve to be resumed.

This exemplifies one of the prettiest of his stanza-forms—

> If thou be'st born to strange sights,
>   Things invisible to see,
> Ride ten thousand days and nights,
>   Till age snow white hairs on thee;
> Thou, when thou return'st, wilt tell me
> All strange wonders that befell thee,
>   And swear
>   Nowhere
> Lives a woman true and fair.
>
> If thou find'st one, let me know;
>   Such a pilgrimage were sweet.
> Yet do not,—I would not go
>   Though at next door we might meet,
> Though she were true when you met her,
> And last till you write your letter,
>   Yet she
>   Will be
> False, ere I come, with two or three.

It now remains to examine this body of poetry in general terms, and, first of all, it is necessary to make some remarks with regard to Donne's whole system of prosody. The terms "irregular," "unintelligible," and "viciously rugged," are commonly used in describing it, and it seems even to be supposed by some critics that Donne did not know how to scan. This last supposition may be rejected at once; what there was to know about poetry was known to Donne. But it seems certain that he intentionally introduced a revolution into English versification. It was doubtless as a rebellion against the smooth and somewhat nerveless iambic flow of Spenser and the earliest contemporaries of Shakespeare, that Donne invented his violent mode of breaking up the line into quick and slow beats. The best critic of his own generation, Ben Jonson, hated the innovation, and told Drummond "that Donne, for not keeping of accent, deserved hanging." It is difficult to stem a current of censure which has set without intermission since the very days of Donne itself, but I may be permitted to point out what I imagine was the poet's own view of the matter.

He found, as I have said, the verse of his youth, say of 1590, exceedingly mellifluous, sinuous, and inclining to flaccidity. A five-syllabled iambic line of Spenser or of Daniel trots along with the gentlest amble of inevitable shorts and longs. It seems to have vexed the ear of Donne by its tendency to feebleness, and it doubtless appeared to him that the very gifted writers who immediately preceded him had carried the softness of it as far as it would go. He desired new and more varied effects. To see what he aimed at doing, we have, I believe, to turn to what has been attempted in our own time, by Mr. Robert Bridges, in some of his early experiments, and by the Symbolists in France. The iambic rhymed line of Donne has audacities such as are permitted to his blank verse by Milton, and although the felicities are rare in the older poet, instead of being almost incessant, as in the later, Donne at his best is not less melodious than Milton. When he writes—

> Blasted with sighs and surrounded with tears,

we must not dismiss this as not being iambic verse at all, nor,—much less,—attempt to read it—

> Blastéd with síghs, and surróundéd with teárs,

but recognize in it the poet's attempt to identify the beat of his verse with his bewildered and dejected condition, reading it somewhat in this notation:—

> Blasted | with sighs || and surrounded | with tears.

The violence of Donne's transposition of accent is most curiously to be observed in his earliest satires, and in some of his later poems is almost entirely absent. Doubtless his theory became modified with advancing years. No poet is more difficult to read aloud. Such a passage as the following may excusably defy a novice:

> No token of worth but Queen's man and fine
> Living barrels of beef and flagons of wine.
> I shook like a spied spy. Preachers which are
> Seas of wit and arts, you can then dare
> Drown the sins of this place, for, for me,
> Which am but a scant brook, it enough shall be
> To wash the stains away.

But treat the five-foot verse not as a fixed and unalterable sequence of cadences, but as a norm around which a musician weaves his variations, and the riddle is soon read—

> No token | of worth | but Queen's | man | and fine
> Living | barrels of | beef and | flagons of | wine.
> I shook | like a spied | spy. | Preachers | which are
> Seas | of wit | and arts, | you can then | dare
> Drown | the sins | of this place, | for, | for me,
> Which am | but a scant | brook, | it enough | shall be
> To wash | the stains | away.

The poetry of Donne possesses in no small degree that "unusual and indefinable witchery" which Dr. Jessopp has noted as characteristic of the man himself. But our enjoyment of it is marred by the violence of the writer, by his want of what seems to us to be good taste, and by a quality which has been overlooked by those who have written about him, but which seems to provide the key to the mystery of his position. Donne was, I would venture to suggest, by far the most modern and contemporaneous of the writers of his time. He rejected all the classical tags and imagery of the Elizabethans, he borrowed nothing from French or Italian tradition. He arrived at an excess of actuality in style, and it was because he struck them as so novel and so completely in touch with his own age that his immediate coevals were so much fascinated with him. His poems are full of images taken from the life and habits of the time. Where earlier poets had summoned the myths of Greece to adorn their verse, Donne weaves in, instead, the false zoology, the crude physics and philosophy, of his own fermenting epoch. The poem called "Love's Exchange," is worthy of careful examination in this respect. Each stanza is crowded with conceits, each one of which is taken from the practical or professional life of the moment in which the poet wrote. This extreme modernness, however, is one potent source of our lack of sympathy with the poetry so inspired. In the long run, it is the broader suggestion, the wider if more conventional range of classic imagery, which may hope to hold without fatigue the interest of successive generations.

For us the charm of Donne continues to rest in his occasional felicities, his burst of melodious passion. If his song were not so tantalizingly fragmentary, we should call him the unquestioned nightingale of the Jacobean choir. No other poet of that time, few poets of any time, have equalled the concentrated passion, the delicate, long-drawn musical effects, the bold and ecstatic rapture of Donne at his best. In such a poem as "The Dream," he realizes the very paroxysm of amatory song. In his own generation, no one approached the purity of his cascades of ringing monosyllables, his

> For God's sake, hold your tongue and let me love,

or,

> I long to talk with some old lover's ghost
> Who died before the God of Love was born,

or,

> Oh more than moon,
> Draw not thy seas to drown me in thy sphere.

or,

> A bracelet of bright hair about the bone.

In these and similar passages, of which a not very slender florilegium might be gathered from his voluminous productions, Donne reminds us that Ben Jonson esteemed him "the first poet in the world in some things." But this quality of passionate music is not the only one discernible, nor often to be discerned. The more obvious characteristic was summed up by Coleridge in a droll quatrain—

> With Donne, whose Muse on dromedary trots,
> Wreathe iron pokers into true-love-knots;
> Rhyme's sturdy cripple, Fancy's maze and clue,
> Wit's forge and fire-blast, Meaning's press and screw.

In the use of these ingenuities, which it was once the fashion to call "metaphysical," Donne shows an amazing pertinacity. He is never daunted by the feeling that his wit is exercised "on subjects where we have no right to expect it," and where it is impossible for us to relish it. He pushes on with relentless logic,—sometimes, indeed, past chains of images that are lovely and appropriate; but, oftener, through briars and lianas that rend his garments and trip up his feet. He is not affected by the ruggedness of his road, nor by our unwillingness to follow him. He stumbles doggedly on until he has reached his singular goal. In all this intellectual obstinacy he has a certain kinship to Browning, but his obscurity is more dense. It is to be hoped that the contemporary maligned him who reported Donne to have written one of his elegies in an intentional obscureness, but that he delighted in putting his readers out of their depth can scarcely be doubted. It is against this lurid background, which in itself and unrelieved would possess a very slight attraction to modern readers, that the electrical flashes of Donne's lyrical intuition make their appearance, almost blinding us by their brilliancy, and fading into the dark tissue of conceits before we have time to appreciate them.

The prominence here given to Donne will be challenged by no one who considers what his influence was on the poetical taste of the time. It is true that among his immediate contemporaries the following of Spenser did not absolutely cease at once. But if a study on the poets of Charles I. were to succeed the present volume, the name of Donne would have to be constantly prominent. On almost everything nondramatic published in the succeeding generation, from Crashaw to Davenant, from Carew to Cowley, the stamp of Donne is set. Dryden owed not a little to him, although, as time went on, he purged himself more and more fully of the taint of metaphysical conceit. So late as 1692, in the preface to *Eleanora*, Dryden still held up Donne as "the greatest wit, though not the best poet of our nation." His poems were among the few nondramatic works of the Jacobean period which continued to be read and reprinted in the age of Anne, and Pope both borrowed from and imitated Donne.

So far as we trace this far-sweeping influence exercised on the poets of a hundred years, we have difficulty in applauding its effects. The empassioned sincerity, the intuitions, the clarion note of Donne were individual to himself and could not be transmitted. It was far otherwise with the jargon of "metaphysical" wit, the trick of strained and inappropriate imagery. These could be adopted by almost any clever person, and were, in fact, employed with fluent effect by people in whom the poetical quality was of the slightest. Writers like Mildmay Fane, Earl of Westmoreland, or like Owen Feltham (in his

verse), show what it was that Donne's seed produced when it fell upon stony ground.

FELIX E. SCHELLING
From "Introduction"
A Book of Elizabethan Lyrics
1895, pp. xxi–lxix

The most important poetical influence of this decade ⟨1590–1600⟩ is that of that grave and marvelous man, Dr. John Donne. I would respectfully invite the attention of those who still persist with Dr. Johnson in regarding this great poet as the founder of a certain "Metaphysical School of Poetry,"[1] a man all but contemporary with Cowley, and a writer harsh, obscure, and incomprehensible in his diction, first to an examination of facts which are within the reach of all, and, secondly, to an honest study of his works. Ben Jonson told Drummond[2] that "Donne's best poems were written before he was twenty-five years old," *i.e.*, before 1598, and Francis Davison, apparently when collecting material for his *Poetical Rhapsody* in 1600, includes in a memorandum of "M.S.S. to get," certain poems of Donne.[3] The Carews, Crashaws, and Cowleys begin at least thirty years later, and, be their imitations of Donne's characteristics what they may, Donne himself is an Elizabethan in the strictest possible acceptation of that term, and far in fact as in time from the representative of a degenerate and false taste. It is somewhat disconcerting to find an author whom, like Savage Landor in our own century, the critic cannot glibly classify as the founder of a school or the product of a perfectly obvious series of literary influences. Donne is a man of this difficult type. For, just as Shakespeare touched life and man at all points, and, absorbing the light of his time, gave it forth a hundredfold, so Donne, withdrawn almost wholly from the influences affecting his contemporaries, shone and glowed with a strange light all his own.

Few lyrical poets have ever rivaled Donne in contemporary popularity. Mr. Edmund Gosse has recently given a reason for this, which seems worthy of attention, while by no means explaining everything. "Donne was, I would venture to suggest, by far the most modern and contemporaneous of the writers of his time. . . . He arrived at an excess of actuality of style, and it was because he struck them as so novel, and so completely in touch with his age, that his immediate coevals were so much fascinated with him."[4] A much bequoted passage of the *Conversations with Drummond* informs us that Ben Jonson "esteemeth Donne the first poet in the world in some things."[5] An analysis of these "some things," which space here forbids, will, I think, show them to depend, to a large degree, upon that deeper element of the modern lyric, poetic insight; the power which, proceeding by means of the clash of ideas familiar with ideas remote, flashes light and meaning into what has hitherto appeared mere commonplace. This, mainly, though with much else, is the positive originality of Donne. A quality no less remarkable is to be found in what may be called his negative originality, by which I mean that trait which caused Donne absolutely to give over the current mannerisms of his time; to write neither in the usual Italian manner, nor in borrowed lyrical forms; indeed, to be at times wantonly careless of mere expression, and, above all, to throw away every trace of the conventional classic imagery and mannerisms which infected and conventionalized the poetry of so many of his contemporaries. It seems to me that no one, excepting Shakespeare, with Sidney, Greville, and Jonson in lesser measure, has done so much to develop intellectualized emotion in the

Elizabethan lyric as John Donne. But Donne is the last poet to demand a proselyting zeal of his devotees, and all those who have learned to love his witching personality will agree to the charming sentiment of his faithful adorer, Izaak Walton, when he says: "Though I must omit to mention divers persons, . . . friends of Sir Henry Wotton; yet I must not omit to mention of a love that was there begun betwixt him and Dr. Donne, some-time Dean of Saint Paul's; a man of whose abilities I shall forbear to say anything, because he who is of this nation, and pretends to learning or ingenuity, and is ignorant of Dr. Donne, deserves not to know him."[6]

But in the great age of Elizabeth, miracles were not the monopoly of the immortals. Strenuous Titans, such as those that wrought poetical cosmos out of the chaos of *Barons' Wars* or *Civil Wars*, out of disquisitions on statecraft and ponderous imitations of Senecan rhetoric, could also work dainty marvels in song. The lyrics of that most interesting and "difficult" of poets, Fulke Greville, have already been noticed, and are the more remarkable in their frequent grace of fancy, uncommon wit, originality, and real music of expression in that they are the sister products of the obscure and intricate musings and the often eccentric didacticism of *Mustapha* and *Alaham*. Of Daniel, a conscientious artist as he was a sensible theorist in verse, we might expect less masterly restraint; whilst Donne displayed the daring of an individualism that enabled him, while his poems were yet in manuscript, to exercise upon his contemporaries the effect of an accepted classic.

The story of Shakespeare's gradual enfranchisement from the trammels of imitation and the adherence to ephemeral rules of art has been often told, and is as true of his work, considered metrically, as from any other point of view. With increasing grasp of mind came increasing power and abandon in style and versification; and this applies to the incidental lyrics of his plays (as far as the data enables us to judge), as it applies to the sweep and cadence of his blank verse.[7]

On the other hand, Jonson, despite his unusual versatility in the invention and practice of new and successful lyrical forms, displays the conservative temper throughout, in avoiding mixed meters, stanzas of irregular structure or of differing lengths, and in such small matters as his careful indication of elision where the syllable exceeds the strict number demanded by the verse-scheme. Many of Jonson's utterances, too, attest his detestation of license (*e.g.*, "that Donne, for not keeping of accent, deserved hanging"); his esteem of the formal element in literature (*e.g.*, "that Shakespeare wanted art"); or his dislike to innovation.[8] Towards the close of his life, Jonson grew increasingly fond of the decasyllabic rimed couplet, the meter which was to become the maid of all work in the next generation. This meter it was that he defended in theory against the heresies of Campion and Daniel,[9] and it was in this meter that he wrote, at times with a regularity of accent and antithetical form that reminds us of the great hand of Dryden in the next age.[10] Jonson's tightening of the reins of regularity in the couplet and in lyric forms—in which latter, despite his inspiration, Herrick followed his master with loving observance of the law—is greatly in contrast with the course of dramatic blank verse, which, beginning in the legitimate freedom of Shakespeare, descended, through the looseness of Fletcher and Massinger, to the license of Davenant and Crowne.

By far the most independent lyrical metrist of this age was John Donne, who has been, it seems to me, quite as much misunderstood on this side as on the side of his eccentricities of thought and expression. In a recent chapter on Donne, in several other respects far from satisfactory, Mr. Edmund Gosse has treated this particular topic very justly. Speaking of Donne's

"system of prosody," he says: "The terms 'irregular,' 'unintelligible' and 'viciously rugged,' are commonly used in describing it, and it seems even to be supposed by some critics that Donne did not know how to scan. This last supposition may be rejected at once; what there was to know about poetry was known to Donne. But it seems certain that he intentionally introduced a revolution into English versification. It was doubtless a rebellion against the smooth and somewhat nervous iambic flow of Spenser and the earliest contemporaries of Shakespeare, that Donne invented his violent mode of breaking up the line into quick and slow beats." Mr. Gosse finds this innovation the result of a desire for "new and more varied effects," adding: "The iambic rimed line of Donne has audacities such as are permitted to his blank verse by Milton, and although the felicities are rare in the older poet instead of being almost incessant, as in the later, Donne at his best is not less melodious than Milton."[11] We need not be detained by the query, whether it was not the strange personality of the poet rather than any unusual desire for "new and more varied effects" which produced a result so unusual. It is certain, that for inventive variety, fitness, and success, the lyrical stanzas of Donne are surpassed by scarcely any Elizabethan poet. In short, Donne seems to have applied to the lyric the freedom of the best dramatic verse of his age, and stood as the exponent of novelty and individualism in form precisely as Jonson stood for classic conservatism.

We have thus seen how in form as well as in thought the governing influence upon the English Elizabethan lyric was the influence of Italy, the Italy of the Renaissance; how, organically considered, there was a steady advance towards greater variety of measure and inventiveness in stanzaic form, and a general growth of taste in such matters as alliteration, the distribution of pauses, and the management of rime. As might be expected, the analogies of certain forms of verse to certain forms of thought were far less rigidly preserved in the English literature of this day than in that of Italy; and there is scarcely a form of English verse, of which it can be said that it was restricted to a given species of poetry. Spenser less completely than Sidney is the exponent of the Italianate school of poetry in England; for in Sidney is to be found not only its pastoral presentation, but the sonnet sequence and the madrigal, both long to remain the favorite utterance of contemporary lyrists. But even if Sidney was the representative of the Italianate school, the lyric took almost at once in his hands, and in those of Spenser and Shakespeare, the characteristics of a genuine vernacular utterance which it afterwards maintained, adapting itself in the minutiæ of style and versification as in the character of thought and theme. The Italian influence, although completely assimilated especially among dramatists like Dekker, Fletcher, and Beaumont, and in Browne and the later poetry of Drayton, still continued dominant in poets such as Davison, Drummond, and the writers of madrigals; but failed, as the classic influence too failed, to reach Donne. It was here that the new classic influence arose with Ben Jonson, an assimilated classicism—as far as possible removed from the imitative classicism of Harvey and Spenser in the days of the Areopagus; and it was this spirit that came finally to prevail—not that of Donne which substituted one kind of radicalism for another;—it was this spirit of conservative nicety of style and regularity of versification that led on through Herrick and Sandys to the classicism of Dryden and Pope.

Notes

1. *Lives of the English Poets*, ed. Tauchnitz, I,11.
2. *Conversations*, Shakespeare Society, p. 8.

3. *Poetical Rhapsody*, ed. Nicolas, p. xlv.
4. Edmund Gosse, *The Jacobean Poets*, 1894, p. 64.
5. *Conversations*, as above, p. 8.
6. *Life of Wotton, Lives*, etc., Amer. ed., 1846, p. 136.
7. There is a wide step in versification between *Silvia* or the *Song* from the *Merchant of Venice*, and the free cadenced songs of the *Tempest*.
8. See *Jonson's Conversations, Sh. Soc. Pub.*, p. 3.
9. See, especially, the opening passage of the *Conversations* concerning his Epic, "all in couplets, for he detesteth all other rimes. Said he had written a Discourse of Poesie, both against Campion and Daniel, . . . where he proves couplets to be the bravest sort of verse, especially when they are broken like hexameters," i.e., exhibit a strong medial caesura.
10. See, especially, the later epistles and occasional verses, such as the *Epigrams* to the Lord Treasurer of England, *To my Muse*, etc.
11. *The Jacobean Poets*, p. 61 f.

J. B. LIGHTFOOT
"Donne, the Poet-Preacher"
Historical Essays
1896, pp. 232–45

As a layman he had been notably a poet; as a clergyman he was before all things a preacher. He had remarkable gifts as an orator, and he used them well. Henceforward preaching was the main business of his life. After he had preached a sermon, "he never gave his eyes rest," we are told, "till he had chosen out a new text, and that night cast his sermon into a form, and his text into divisions, and the next day he took himself to consult the fathers, and so commit his meditations to his memory, which was excellent."[1] On the Saturday he gave himself an entire holiday, so as to refresh body and mind, "that he might be enabled to do the work of the day following not faintly, but with courage and cheerfulness." When first ordained he shunned preaching before town congregations. He would retire to some country church with a single friend, and so try his wings. His first sermon was preached in the quiet village of Paddington. But his fame grew rapidly; and he soon took his rank as the most powerful preacher of his day in the English Church. Others envied him and murmured, says an admirer, that, having been called to the vineyard late in the day, he received his penny with the first.[2]

More than a hundred and fifty of his sermons are published. Some of them were preached at Lincoln's Inn, where he held the Lectureship; others at St. Dunstan's-in-the-West, of which church he was vicar; others at Whitehall, in his turn as Royal Chaplain, or before the Court on special occasions; others, and these the most numerous, at St. Paul's. Of this last class a few were delivered at the Cross, by special appointment, but the majority within the Cathedral, when year after year, according to the rule which is still in force at St. Paul's, he preached as Dean at the great festivals of the Church—Christmas and Easter and Whitsunday—or when he expounded the Psalms assigned to his prebendal stall, or on various incidental occasions.

An eminent successor of Donne, the late Dean Milman, finds it difficult to "imagine, when he surveys the massy folios of Donne's sermons—each sermon spreads out over many pages—a vast congregation in the Cathedral or at Paul's Cross listening not only with patience, but with absorbed interest, with unflagging attention, even with delight and rapture, to those interminable disquisitions. . . ." "It is astonishing to us," he adds, "that he should hold a London congregation enthralled, unwearied, unsatiated."[3]

And yet I do not think that the secret of his domination is far to seek.

Fervet immensusque ruit.

There is throughout an energy, a glow, an impetuosity, a force as of a torrent, which must have swept his hearers onward despite themselves. This rapidity of movement is his characteristic feature. There are faults in abundance, but there is no flagging from beginning to end. Even the least manageable subjects yield to his untiring energy. Thus he occupies himself largely with the minute interpretation of scriptural passages. This exegesis is very difficult of treatment before a large and miscellaneous congregation. But with Donne it is always interesting. It may be subtle, wire-drawn, fanciful at times, but it is keen, eager, lively, never pedantic or dull. So, again, his sermons abound in quotations from the fathers; and this burden of patristic reference would have crushed any common man. But here the quotations are epigrammatic in themselves; they are tersely rendered, they are vigorously applied, and the reader is never wearied by them. Donne is, I think, the most animated of the great Anglican preachers.

I select two or three examples out of hundreds which might be chosen, as exhibiting this eagerness of style, lit up by the genius of a poet, and heated by the zeal of an evangelist. Hear this, for instance:—

"God's house is the house of prayer. It is His court of requests. There he receives petitions; there He gives orders upon them. And you come to God in His house as though you came to keep Him company, to sit down and talk with Him half an hour; or you come as ambassadors, covered in His presence, as though ye came from as great a prince as He. You meet below, and there make your bargains for biting, for devouring usury, and then you come up hither to prayers, and so make God your broker. You rob and spoil and eat His people as bread by extortion and bribery, and deceitful weights and measures, and deluding oaths in buying and selling, and then come hither, and so make God your receiver, and His house a den of thieves. . . . As if the Son of God were but the son of some lord that had been your schoolfellow in your youth, and so you continue a boldness to him ever after; so because you have been brought up with Christ from your cradle, and catechised in His name, His name becomes reverend unto you; and *sanctum et terribile*, holy and reverend, holy and terrible, should His name be.". . .[4]

Listen to such words as I have read; and to complete the effect summon up in imagination the appearance and manner of the preacher. Recall him as he is seen in the portrait attributed to Vandyck—the keen, importuning "melting eye,"[5] the thin, worn features, the poetic cast of expression, half pensive, half gracious. Add to this the sweet tones of his voice and the "speaking action,"[6] which is described by eye-witnesses as more eloquent than the words of others, and you will cease to wonder at the thraldom in which he held his audience. "A preacher in earnest," writes Walton, "weeping sometimes *for* his auditory, sometimes *with* them; always preaching to himself; like an angel *from* a cloud but *in* none; carrying some, as St. Paul was, to heaven in holy raptures and enticing others by a sacred art and courtship to amend their lives; here picturing a vice so as to make it ugly to those who practised it, and a virtue so as to make it beloved even by those that loved it not. . . ."[7] Indeed we cannot doubt that he himself was alive to that feeling which he ascribes to the "blessed fathers" when preaching, "a holy delight to be heard and to be heard with delight."[8]

Donne's sermons are not faultless models of pulpit oratory. From this point of view they cannot be studied as the sermons of the great French preachers may be studied. Under the circumstances this was almost an impossibility. Preaching his hour's sermon once or twice weekly, he had not time to arrange and rearrange, to prune, to polish, to elaborate. As it is, we marvel at the profusion of learning, the richness of ideas and imagery, the abundance in all kinds, poured out by a preacher who thus lived, as it were, from hand to mouth.

Moreover, the taste of the age for fantastic imagery, for subtle disquisition, for affectations of language and of thought, exercised a fascination over him. Yet even here he is elevated above himself and his time by his subject. There is still far too much of that conceit of language, of that subtlety of association, of that "sport with ideas," which has been condemned in his verse compositions; but, compared with his poems, his sermons are freedom and simplicity itself. And, whenever his theme rises, he rises too; and then in the giant strength of an earnest conviction he bursts these green withes which a fantastic age has bound about him, as the thread of tow snaps at the touch of fire. Nothing can be more direct or more real than his eager impetuous eloquence, when he speaks of God, of redemption, of heaven, of the sinfulness of human sin, of the bountifulness of Divine Love.

At such moments he is quite the most modern of our older Anglican divines. He speaks directly to our time, because he speaks to all times. If it be the special aim of the preacher to convince of sin and of righteousness and of judgment, then Donne deserves to be reckoned the first of our classic preachers. We may find elsewhere more skilful arrangement, more careful oratory, more accurate exegesis, more profuse illustration; but here is the light which flashes and the fire which burns.

Donne's learning was enormous; and yet his sermons probably owe more to his knowledge of men than to his knowledge of books. The penitent is too apt to shrink into the recluse. Donne never yielded to this temptation. He himself thus rebukes the mistaken extravagance of penitence: "When men have lived long from God, they never think they come near enough to Him, except they go beyond Him."[9] No contrition was more intense than his; but he did not think to prove its reality by cutting himself off from the former interests and associations of his life. He had been a man of the world before; and he did not cease to be a man in the world now. "Beloved"—he says this term "beloved" is his favourite mode of address—"Beloved, salvation itself being so often presented to us in the names of glory and of joy, we cannot think that the way to that glory is a sordid life affected here, an obscure, a beggarly, a negligent abandoning of all ways of preferment or riches or estimation in this world, for the glory of heaven shines down, in those beams hither. . . . As God loves a cheerful giver, so He loves a cheerful taker that takes hold of His mercies and His comforts with a cheerful heart."[10] This healthy, vigorous good sense is the more admirable in Donne, because it is wedded to an intense and passionate devotion.

I wish that time would allow me to multiply examples of his lively imagination flashing out in practical maxims and lighting up the common things of life; as, for instance, where he pictures the general sense of insecurity on the death of Elizabeth: "Every one of you in the city were running up and down like ants with their eggs bigger than themselves, every man with his bags, to seek where to hide them safely."[11] Or where he enforces the necessity of watchfulness against minor temptations: "As men that rob houses thrust in a child at the window, and he opens greater doors for them, so lesser sins make way for greater."[12] Or when he describes the little effect of preaching on the heartless listener: "He hears but the logic or the rhetoric or the ethic or the poetry of the sermon, but the

sermon of the sermon he hears not."[13] Of such pithy sayings Donne's sermons are an inexhaustible storehouse, in which I would gladly linger; but I must hasten on to speak of one other feature before drawing to a close. Irony is a powerful instrument in the preacher's hands, if he knows how to wield it; otherwise it were better left alone. The irony of Donne is piercing. Hear the withering scorn which he pours on those who think to condone sinful living by a posthumous bequest: "We hide our sins in His house by hypocrisy all our lives, and we hide them at our deaths, perchance, with an hospital. And truly we had need do so; when we have impoverished God in His children by our extortions, and wounded Him and lamed Him in them by our oppressions, we had need to provide God an hospital."[14] Or hear this again, on the criticism of sermons: "Because God calls preaching foolishness, you take God at His word and think preaching a thing under you. Hence it is that you take so much liberty in censuring and comparing preacher and preacher."[15] And lastly, observe the profound pathos and awe which are veiled under the apparent recklessness of these daring words: "At how cheap a price was Christ tumbled up and down in this world! It does almost take off our pious scorn of the low price at which Judas sold Him, to consider that His Father sold Him to the world for nothing."[16]

For preaching Donne lived; and in preaching he died. He rose from a sick-bed and came to London to take his customary sermon at Whitehall on the first Friday in Lent. Those who saw him in the pulpit, says Walton quaintly, must "have asked that question in Ezekiel, 'Do these bones live?'" The sermon was felt to be the swan's dying strain. Death was written in his wan and wasted features, and spoke through his faint and hollow voice.

The subject was in harmony with the circumstances. He took as his text[17] the passage in the Psalms, "Unto God the Lord belong the issues of death." His hearers said at the time that "Dr. Donne had preached his own funeral sermon."

The sermon was published. It betrays in part a diminution of his wonted fire and animation. We seem to see the preacher struggling painfully with his malady. But yet it is remarkable. The theme and the circumstances alike invest it with a peculiar solemnity; and there are flashes of the poet-preacher still.

"This whole world," he says, "is but a universal churchyard, but one common grave: and the life and motion that the greatest persons have in it is but as the shaking of buried bodies in their graves by an earthquake."[18]

"The worm is spread under thee, and the worm covers thee. *There* is the mats and carpet that lie under, and *there* is the state and the canopy that hangs over the greatest of the sons of men."[19]

"The tree lies as it falls, it is true, but yet it is not the last stroke that fells the tree, nor the last word nor the last gasp that qualifies the man."[20]

Hear now the closing words, and you will not be at a loss to conceive the profound impression which they must have left on his hearers, as the dying utterance of a dying man:—

"There we leave you in that blessed dependency, to hang upon Him that hangs upon the Cross. There bathe in His tears, there suck at His wounds, and lie down in peace in His grave, till He vouchsafes you a resurrection and an ascension into that kingdom which He hath purchased for you with the inestimable price of His incorruptible blood. Amen."

Amen it was. He had prayed that he might die in the pulpit, or (if not this) that he might die of the pulpit; and his prayer was granted. From this sickness he never recovered; the effort hastened his dissolution; and, after lingering on a few weeks, he died on the last day of March 1631.

This study of Donne as a preacher will be fitly closed with the last stanza from his poem entitled, "Hymn to God, my God, in my sickness," which sums up the broad lesson of his life and teaching:—

> So in *His* purple wrapped, receive me, Lord;
> By these *His* thorns give me His other crown;
> And as to others' souls I preached Thy Word,
> Be this my text, my sermon to mine own:
> Therefore, *that He may raise, the Lord throws*
>   *down.*[21]

Notes

1. Walton's *Life*, p. 119.
2. Elegy by Mr. R. B., attached to *Poems* by John Donne (1669), p. 393.
3. *Annals of St. Paul's Cathedral*, p. 328.
4. *Works*, vol. iii. p. 217 sq.
5. Walton's *Life*, p. 150.
6. Elegy by Mr. Mayne, attached to *Poems* by John Donne (1669), p. 387.
7. *Life*, p. 69.
8. *Works*, vol. i. p. 98.
9. *Works*, vol. ii. p. 31.
10. *Works*, vol. ii. p. 142.
11. Ibid. vol. vi. p. 137.
12. Ibid. vol. ii. p. 556.
13. Ibid. vol. i. p. 72.
14. Ibid. vol. ii. p. 555.
15. Ibid. vol. ii. p. 219.
16. Ibid. vol. i. p. 61.
17. *Life*, p. 135 sq.
18. *Works*, vol. vi. p. 283.
19. Ibid. p. 288.
20. Ibid. p. 290.
21. *Poems*, vol. ii. p. 340.

EDMUND GOSSE
From *The Life and Letters of John Donne*
1899, Vol. 1, pp. 263–69, Vol. 2, pp. 329–44

Divine Poems

The Divine Poems of Donne offer considerable difficulty to his biographer. A few of them already are, or can approximately be, dated, but the majority are subject to conjecture founded upon internal evidence. They are of two orders; there are hymns and spiritual poems of Donne's which, however rugged their form, breathe a fervid spirit of faith and a genuine humility. In others the intellectual element outweighs the religious. These verses are rather extremely ingenious exercises in metrical theology than bursts of impulsive piety. It may be broadly suggested that the latter belong to the second, and the former to the third or final, division of Donne's career. That is to say, the more metaphysical pieces are the outcome of the years when religious inquiry formed one of his prominent studies, but when no exclusive call had summoned him to the ministry. In form all the sacred poetry of Donne suffers from his determination to introduce Spanish effects into English prosody, and Spanish ingenuities into the expression of English thought. If Donne's early hymns and litanies do not move us, it is largely due to the fact that they did not move himself. They are frigid, they are stiffened with legal and medical phraseology, the heart of a sinner saved does not beat beneath their "cross and correct concupiscence of wit."

An excess of ingenuity is peculiarly fatal to the unction of religious poetry. Unless it is spontaneous, unless it palpitates with ecstasy or moans with aspiration, unless it is the outpouring of a contrite spirit, it leaves upon the listener a sense of painful artificiality. The dogmatic verses of Donne do not escape from this disability. We admit their cleverness, and are sure that it is misplaced. The solemn mystery of Christ's three days' sojourn in the tomb is not, for instance, illuminated when Donne speaks of Him as one

> Whose body, having walk'd on earth, and now
> Hasting to heaven, would—that He might allow
> Himself unto all stations and fill all—
> For those three days become a mineral.
> He was all gold when He lay down, but rose
> All tincture, and doth not alone dispose
> Leaden and iron wills to good, but is
> Of power to make e'en sinful flesh like His.

Here Donne's intellectual arrogance stood him in evil stead. He would not continue and intensify the tradition of such gentle Catholic singers of the Elizabethan age as Southwell and Constable; the hymns of Wither he had probably never seen, and would have despised; he shows not the slightest sign of having read the noblest religious poem written between the *Vision of Piers Plowman* and *Paradise Lost*, that *Christ's Victory and Triumph* which Giles Fletcher published just when Donne was moving into Drury House in 1610. He had doubtless read, without advantage to his style, Sylvester's popular version of the *Divine Weeks and Works*. But he disdained all that was purely English. His sympathy with Elizabethan verse, good or bad, was a negative quality, and we can scarcely trace that he allowed himself to be even conscious of the existence of Spenser or Shakespeare. Among his English contemporaries he admired but one poet, Ben Jonson, and to him he was attracted by the very qualities which we now recognise as being anti-Elizabethan. Hence, in the history of literature, the sacred poetry of Donne is interesting mainly for its resolute independence of all existing English types, and for its effect in starting a new and efficient school of religious verse in which many of the disciples far exceeded the master. Donne prophesied, while those poets were not born or were but children, of George Herbert, of Crashaw, of the Vaughans, of Herrick in the *Noble Numbers*, of Cowley in the *Davideis*; and when we come to consider his posthumous glory we shall have to return to his crabbed and litigious early sacred poetry.

Of Donne's spiritual poems the most important, if we omit the two cycles of "Holy Sonnets," which belong to a later period, is that which he called "A Litany." He composed it in his bed, during his tedious illness at Mitcham in 1609, and he sent it to Sir Henry Goodyer with a learned note on the Litaneia, or public form of chanted prayer to God, and on its use in the Primitive Church. His own specimen is composed in a curious measure of his invention, in grave lines with an odd singing break in the middle of each stanza, an artifice from which, it is only fair to say, he rarely extracts so much charm as we might reasonably expect. The "Litany" is burdened with ingenuity. From a dogmatic point of view it shows Donne still imperfectly divorced from the tenets of Rome. He still proclaims the efficacy of the Virgin Mary's prayers to God the Father for souls on earth. Donne, who was much occupied at this time with the principle of martyrdom, dedicates these stanzas to the martyrs and confessors—

> And since Thou so desirously
> Didst long to die, that long before thou could'st
>   And long since Thou no more could'st die,
> Thou in thy scatter'd mystic body would'st
>   In Abel die; and ever since
>   In Thine; let their blood come
> To beg for us a discreet patience

Of death, or of worse life; for O, to some
Not to be martyrs is a martyrdom.
    Therefore with thee triumpheth there
    A virgin squadron of white cónfessors,
        Whose bloods betroth'd, not married, were,
Tender'd, not taken, by those ravishers.
      They know, and pray that we may know,
      In every Christian
Hourly tempestuous persecutions grow;
Temptations martyr us alive; a man
Is to himself a Diocletian.

The ingenious darkness of Donne's poetical expression never went further or achieved a richer gloom than it does in some of his Sacred Poems. The "Litany" is certainly not for use by the poor of the flock. The intellectual dangers so strangely petitioned against in the following stanza do not certainly afflict many humble-minded Christians, although they were real enough to Donne—

    That learning, Thine ambassador,
    From Thine allegiänce we never tempt;
      That beauty, paradise's flower,—
    For physic made,—from poison be exempt;
      That wit—born apt high good to do—
        By dwelling lazily
On Nature's nothing be not nothing too;
That our affections kill us not, nor die;
Hear us, weak echoes, O Thou Ear and Eye.

One more stanza may be given from this highly metaphysical poem, in which a considerable flower of beauty is choked by the weeds of pedantry and misplaced intelligence—

    From being anxious, or secure,
    Dead clods of sadness, or light squibs of mirth,
      From thinking that great courts immure
    All, or no happiness, or that this earth
      Is only for our prison fram'd;
      Or that Thou'rt covetous
To them whom Thou lovest, or that they are maim'd
From reaching this world's sweet who seek Thee
      thus,
With all Thy might, Good Lord, deliver us.

A poem which we can exactly date is that written for Good Friday 1613. Donne had been staying at Polesworth, in Warwickshire, with Sir Henry Goodyer, and he set forth on horseback to visit Magdalen Herbert and her son, Sir Edward, at Montgomery Castle. Six years earlier he had sent to this beloved lady "holy hymns and sonnets," of which but one survives, the quatorzain beginning—

    Her of your name, whose fair inheritance
      Bethina was, and jointure Magdalo.

He now, looking forward to the joys of high spiritual converse with these elected friends, sends to him whom he leaves at Polesworth a meditation on the day. He is more direct and less tortured than usual—

      I am carried towards the west,
This day, when my soul's form bows to the East;
There I should see a Sun by rising set,
And by that setting endless day beget;
But that Christ on His cross did rise and fall,
Sin had eternally benighted all.
Yet dare I almost be glad, I do not see
That spectacle of too much weight for me;
Who sees God's face, that is self-life, must die,—
What a death were it then to see God die!

That is impressive, and comparatively simple; but a spasm of his disease of style catches him, and he proceeds—

It made His own lieutenant, Nature, shrink,
It made His footstool crack, and the sun wink.
Could I behold those hands, which span the poles
And tune all spheres at once, pierced with those holes?
Could I behold that endless height, which is
Zenith to us and our antipodes,
Humbled below us?

Nothing could be more odious; yet, such was the taste of the day that, no doubt, when he read these verses that evening in Montgomery Castle, the noble Herberts were not merely astonished, but charmed and edified.

We may confidently attribute "The Cross" to the Mitcham period. It shows Donne still more indignant at the obstinacy of political recusants than convinced with regard to the dogmas which separate Rome from the Reformed Churches. He writes here precisely as any fervent Italian or Spanish monk might do—

From me no pulpit, nor misgrounded law,
Nor scandal taken, shall this cross withdraw,

and he rejoices to see its emblem in every manifestation of natural force—

Look down, thou spiest out crosses in small things;
Look up, thou seest birds rais'd on cross'd wings;
All the globe's frame, and spheres, is nothing else
But the meridian's crossing parallels.

In composing these early sacred poems, although he was at the very time fighting with Morton for the Anglicans, he could not but look back to Rome as the real arbiter, and he had no warmer excuse to make for his odes and litanies than that the Roman Church herself need not call them defective.

It is to be observed that the early and amatory writings of Donne contain no single example of the sonnet, and that with the exception of one or two unimportant epistles in the quatorzain form, all his work in this class is to be found among his divine poems. He disdained the softness and vagueness of the Petrarchists, and had no ambition to compete with Drayton or Daniel in their addresses to a dimly-outlined Idea or Delia. The form he ultimately adopted for his sonnets is neither purely Italian, nor purely Elizabethan. He had not Milton's courage in recurring to the splendid fulness of the sonnet of Petrarch, but he eschewed the laxity of the English writers of his age; and though we have to regret that he adopted the final couplet, his octett is of perfect arrangement, and boasts but two rhymes. It is strange that he did not perceive how much his sonnets lose in grandeur by this concession to triviality in the sestett. It is part, however, of Donne's irremediable imperfection as an artist, that he has produced much noble poetry in his divine sonnets, and yet not one sonnet that can be considered faultless.

The style of this section of his poetry is extremely characteristic of himself and of certain exotic influences of his time. When he was in Italy, he must have been familiar with Tansillo and Molza, the polished Petrarchists of the age, who celebrated love and religion with an equal refinement. But he is not more touched by their manner of writing than by that of Spenser. Underneath the graceful accomplishment of the Cinque Cento, however, there ran hidden the vehement stream of speculative philosophic style, rugged and bold, and it was this which attracted Donne. With Galileo we know that he had a close sympathy. Did he dip with curiosity into the forbidden writings of Galileo's fellow-martyr, Giordano Bruno? We know not; yet here at least was an Italian with whom Donne had not a little fellowship in the construction of his mind. He had still more with that of a Dominican monk who was more exactly his contemporary, and of whose misfortunes he cannot fail to have heard. The Sonnets of Campanella have more kinship with "La Corona" and the Ecclesiastical Sonnets of Donne than with any other English writings. Yet neither poet can well have read the work of the other, and it is even a stretch of probability to hope that Donne may have seen the obscure volume of Campanella's poems which the German, Tobias Adami, published in 1622. The similarity is accidental, and is founded upon a certain double sympathy with the obscurity and with the heterodoxy of the strange Italian pantheists of the age. Had Donne been born south of the Alps, his work might probably have taken a less tormented form than it actually adopted, but his body would almost certainly have been tortured with Campanella's, if by a happy fate it escaped the stake with Vanini's. . . .

The Influence of Donne

In examining the remarkable wide and deep, though almost entirely malign, influence of Donne upon the poetry of this country, it is necessary first of all to dwell on the complete intellectual isolation of his youth and middle age. The Elizabethan poets were, as a rule, a sociable and sympathetic body of men. They acted and interacted upon one another with vivacity; they met at frequent intervals to encourage themselves in the art they exercised and to read each other's verses. The habit which sprang up of contributing strings of complimentary effusions to accompany the published efforts of a friend was symptomatic of the gregarious tendency of the age. So, even, were the fierce feuds and noisy, rather than envenomed, encounters which periodically thrilled the poetic world. It was not hatred, so much, or even jealousy, which inspired these famous battles, as the inevitability that in a society, the atoms of which hustled about so rapidly in the immediate neighbourhood of the rest, collisions should occasionally occur. In the last years of Elizabeth and the first years of James, London swarmed with poets and poeticules, and each of these was, more or less, in personal relation with the others.

Herein lies the first peculiarity of Donne. After the juvenile concession to the taste of the hour, implied in his *Satires* of 1593 and onward, he gave no further hostages to the fashion. Nor do we find that he paid any attention to the leaders of literature whom it was inevitable that he should meet at Court or in the taverns. At no period even of his youth does he seem to have been impressed by the fame of his English compeers, to have felt admiration or even curiosity in their work. One is left with the impression that Donne would not have turned to see Edmund Spenser go by, nor have passed into an inner room at the Mermaid to listen to the talk of Shakespeare. His was the scornful indifference of the innovator, the temperament of the man born to inaugurate a new order of taste. . . .

It is a curious fact that Jonson alone, of those who in the first half of the seventeenth century discussed the characteristics of Donne's style, commented on the peculiarities of his metre. This would seem to have filled even his fondest disciples with horror, and it is much to be doubted whether they understood the principle upon which he worked. On this point, successive critics have agreed in finding Donne an unpardonable sinner. It seems even to be supposed by some writers that the curious condition of his early verse is due to ignorance, and that Donne did not know how to scan. As to this, I can but repeat, what I have said before,[2] that what there was to know about prosody was, we may be sure, perfectly known by Donne. But it is evident that he intentionally essayed to introduce a revolution into English versification. One of the main objections he took to the verse of his youth was that it was so mellifluous, sinuous, and soft. A five-syllabled iambic line of Spenser or of Daniel trots along with the gentlest amble of

inevitable shorts and longs. Donne thought that the line should be broken up into successive quick and slow beats. The conventional line vexed his ear with its insipidity, and it doubtless appeared to him that his great predecessors had never completely shaken off a timidity and monotony which had come down to them from Surrey and Gascoigne. It is possible that he wished to improve on the rhymed verse of Spenser, as Shakespeare had improved on the blank verse of Sackville.

The curious ruggedness of the *Satires* and *Elegies* becomes comprehensible only when we adopt some such theory I have suggested. Part of Donne's iconoclasm consisted in his scorn of the flaccid beat of the verse of the sonneteers. He desired greatly to develop the orchestral possibilities of English verse, and I have remarked that the irregular lyrics of Mr. Robert Bridges and the endless experiments of the Symbolists in France are likely to be far more fruitful to us in trying to understand Donne's object, than any conventional repetition of the accepted rules of prosody. The iambic rhymed line of Donne has audacities such as are permitted to his blank verse by Milton; and although the felicities are rare in the older poet, instead of being almost incessant as in the younger, Donne at his best is not less melodious than Milton. One of his most famous traps for the ear, is the opening line of "Twickenham Garden," which the ordinary reader is ever tempted to dismiss as not being iambic verse at all. We have to recognise in it the poet's attempt to identify the beat of his verse with his bewildered and dejected state, reading it somewhat in this notation:—

Blásted | with sighs || and | surroúnded | with teárs.

It is almost certain that this intrepid shifting about at will of the accent is a symptom of youth in the poem, that we can almost, that is to say, approximately, date any given piece of his by the degree in which this prosodical violence is sustained.[3] After middle-life, Donne dropped the experiment more and more completely, having found, no doubt, that his closest friends were by no means certain to comprehend what he meant by the rapid changes of the instrument; nor, in reading to themselves, could produce the effect which he had intended. These variations of cadence, then, must be looked upon as a peculiarity not essential to Donne's style, nor persistent in it, but as a studied eccentricity of his youth. At his very best, as in

> I long to talk with some old lover's ghost,
>   Who died before the God of Love was born,

or as in

> A naked, thinking heart, that makes no show,
>   Is to a woman but a kind of ghost,

there is no trace of this "not keeping of accent," which puzzled and enraged Ben Jonson.

His conscious isolation, no doubt, made Donne hesitate to press his poetry upon his own generation. He found its flavour, the strong herbal perfume of it, not agreeable in the nostrils of the latest Elizabethans. Neither the verse, nor the imagination, nor the attitude of soul were what people in 1600 were ready to welcome, or even to apprehend. We can imagine Donne rather wistfully saying—

> Ho io appreso quel che, s'io ridico,
>   A molti fia savor di forte agrume,[4]

and this may have been a main reason why he refrained from publication. He kept his rosemary and his marjoram, his rough odorous herbs, to himself. . . .

What these young poets ⟨who emulated Donne between 1620 and 1650⟩ saw in Donne, and what attracted them so passionately to him, was the concentration of his intellectual personality. He broke through the tradition; he began as if poetry had never been written before; he, as Carew says—

open'd us a mine
Of rich and pregnant fancy.

He banished the gods and goddesses from his verse, not a
Roundhead fiercer than he in his scorn of "those old idols." He
wiped away "the wrong" which the English language in its neo-
pagan raptures had "done the Greek or Latin tongue." His
gigantic fancy put such a strain upon the resources of the
English language, that its "tough, thick-ribb'd hoops" almost
burst beneath the pressure. The earlier Elizabethan writers had
been "libertines in poetry"; Donne recalled them to law and
order. This is how Carew describes the extraordinary emotion
caused by the first reading of Donne's poems—

the flame
Of thy brave soul, that shot such heat and light
As burned our earth and made our darkness bright,
Committed holy rapes upon the will,
Did through the eye the melting heart distil,
And the deep knowledge of dark truths did teach.

Once again, Donne has

open'd us a mine
Of rich and pregnant fancy, drawn a line
Of masculine expression . . .
Thou shalt yield no precedence, but of time,—

that is to say, the ancient poets have no advantage of originality
over thee, save the purely accidental one of having been born
in an earlier age.

When we turn to Donne's poems, but in particular to his
lyrics, and endeavour to find out what it was which excited
these raptures of appreciation, we are at first unable to accept
the seventeenth-century point of vision. Nothing is more difficult than to be certain that we value in the old poets what their
contemporaries valued. Those pieces of Shakespeare which are
on every tongue to-day, and excite our unbounded admiration,
are not alluded to by any of his contemporaries. We have no
evidence that a single friend of Milton saw what we all see in
the central part of "L'Allegro" or in "At a Solemn Music."
What contemporary criticism found in Herrick was "a pretty
flowery and pastoral gale of fancy, in a vernal prospect of some
hill, cave, rock, or fountain." We ask ourselves, in despair,
what can the people who wrote such words have seen in
"Gather the Rosebuds While Ye May," or in "Bid Me to Live"?
In the same way, we have the greatest difficulty in constraining
ourselves to regard Donne's verse from the point of view and in
the light of its early, enthusiastic readers of 1620.

Perhaps we cannot do better than read over again an entirely typical poem, written towards the middle of his career, and
illustrating, without extravagance, the very peculiarities which
Donne's disciples admired. For this purpose, "Twickenham
Garden" may serve as well as any:—

Blasted with sighs, and surrounded with tears,
Hither I come to seek the spring,
And at mine eyes, and at mine ears,
Receive such balms as else cure every thing.
But O! self-traitor, I do bring
The spider Love, which transubstantiates all,
And can convert manna to gall;
And that this place may thoroughly be thought
True paradise, I have the serpent brought.
'Twere wholesomer for me that winter did
Benight the glory of this place,
And that a grave frost did forbid
These trees to laugh and mock me to my face;
But that I may not this disgrace
Endure, nor yet leave loving, Love, let me
Some senseless piece of this place be;

Make me a mandrake, so I may grow here,
Or a stone fountain weeping out my year.
Hither with crystal phials, lovers, come,
And take my tears, which are love's wine,
And try your mistress' tears at home,
For all are false, that taste not just like mine.
Alas! hearts do not in eyes shine,
Nor can you more judge woman's thoughts by tears
Than, by her shadow, what she wears.
O perverse sex, where none is true but she
Who's therefore true, because her truth kills me.

If we compare this with an analogous piece of ordinary
Elizabethan or early Jacobean poetry, we observe, first of all,
that it is tightly packed with thought. As to the value of the
thought, opinions may differ, but of the subtlety, the variety,
and the abundance of mental movement in this piece there can
be no question. The Elizabethan poet had held a mirror up to
nature; Donne (the illustration is almost his own) shivered the
glass, and preserved a reflection from every several fragment.
This redundancy of intellectual suggestion was one of Donne's
principal innovations.

In the second place, we notice an absence of all conventional or historical ornament. There is no mention here of
"cruel Amaryllis," or "great Pan," or "the wanton shears of
Destiny." A rigid adherence to topics and to objects familiar to
the non-poetical reader of the moment is strictly observed.
This, as I suppose, was another of the main sources of Donne's
fascination; he was, in a totally new and unprecedented sense,
a realist. In this he revolted with success against all the procedure of the Renaissance, and is, in his turbid and unskilful
way, the forerunner of modern Naturalism in English poetry.
This is an aspect of his influence which has been strangely
overlooked, and, no doubt, for this reason, that what was realistic in the reign of James I. seems utterly old-fangled and
antiquarian in that of Victoria; so that the poetry of Donne,
instead of striking us—as it did his contemporaries—as
amazingly fresh and new in its illustrations, strikes us as unspeakably moth-eaten and decrepid. In this poem of
"Twickenham Hill" there is even an innovation in naming,
topographically, a place by its existing, modern name; and this
prepares us for all the allusions to habits, superstitions, rites,
occasions of the moment which occur to the rapid brain of the
author.

If the poems of Donne are examined, we shall find that it
is only on the rarest occasions that he draws his imagery from
mythology or romantic history. He has no interest in Greek or
Latin legend. He neither translates nor paraphrases the poets of
antiquity. For the conventional elements of beauty, as it was
understood in that age, for roses, that is to say, and shepherds,
lutes, zephyrs, "Thetis' crystal floods," and "flower-enamelled
meadows," Donne has a perfect contempt. He endeavours to
extract intellectual beauty from purely subjective sources, by
the concentration of intensity and passion upon modern
thought. Accordingly, he draws his illustrations, not from as-
phodel or from the moon, but from the humdrum professional
employments of his own age, from chemistry, medicine, law,
mechanics, astrology, religious ritual, daily human business of
every sort. The decency of reticence between lovers reminds
him of a sacerdotal mystery, and he cries—

'Twere profanation of our joys
To tell the laity our love.

Love is a spider dropped into the luscious chalice of life and
"transubstantiating" it to poison. The sun is no more Phœbus, or
the golden-haired son of Hyperion, but a pedantic lackey,

whose duty is to "tell court-huntsmen that the king will ride."
If the poet abuses his mistress for her want of faith, he does it in
the language of an attorney, and his curses are "annexed in
schedules" to the document. A woman's tear, on which her
lover's tear falls, is like a round ball, on which a skilled workman paints the countries of the world.

From the days of Dr. Johnson downwards, the nature of
these images has been not a little misunderstood. They have
two characteristics, which have been unduly identified—they
are sometimes realistic, and they are sometimes inappropriate.
To us to-day they are almost all grotesque, because they are
fetched from a scheme of things now utterly obsolete; but we
must endeavour to recollect that such phrases as—

> no chemic yet the elixir got
> But glorifies his pregnant pot,
> If by the way to him befall
> Some odoriferous thing, or medicinal,

or,

> As he that sees a star fall, runs apace,
> And finds a jelly in the place,

phrases which now call for a commentary, and disturb our
appreciation of the poet's fancy, were references to the science
or half-science of the Jacobean age as modern and "topical" as
allusions to the Röntgen rays would be today.

. . . We must, at length, give to Donne such credit as is
due to complete originality in working out and forcing upon
English taste a style in which affectation and wilful obscurity
took a part so prominent that by ordinary readers no other
qualities are nowadays perceived.

Notes

1. If, as I think likely, this was written about 1595, the "clime" was
   probably France, and "the king" Henry IV., a mighty hunter, our
   ally, and very popular in England. But there is no need to press a
   poet to this extremity of exact allusion.
2. *The Jacobean Poets*, 1894, pp. 60–63; from which a few lines are
   here reproduced.
3. In the interesting notes scribbled in 1811 by Coleridge, in Lamb's
   copy of Donne's *Poems*, S.T.C. remarks on the judicious use
   Donne makes of the anapaest in iambic measures where he wishes,
   in the eagerness of haste, to confirm or to exaggerate emotion. This
   valuable copy is now in the possession of Mr. W. H. Arnold, of New
   York.
4. *Paradiso*, xvii. 116, 117.

W. J. COURTHOPE

From "The School of Metaphysical Wit: John Donne"
A History of English Poetry
1903, Volume 3, pp. 147–68

Beyond the sphere of theological allegory, in which the
traditions of the schools were still preserved, lay the region
of pure thought; and here the contradiction between mediæval
and modern ideas furnished ample materials for the exercise of
"wit." Assailed at once by the forces of the new faith, the new
science, and the growing spirit of civic liberty, the ancient
fabric of Catholicism and Feudalism fell more and more into
ruin, but the innovating philosophy was yet far from having
established a system of order and authority. The reasoning of
Copernicus and Galileo shook men's belief in the truth of the
Ptolemaic astronomy: the discoveries of Columbus extended
their ideas of the terrestrial globe: the study of Greek and
Hebrew literature in the original disturbed the symmetrical
methods of scholastic logic: the investigations of the Arabian
chemists produced havoc in the realm of encyclopædic science. Still, the old learning had rooted itself too firmly in the
convictions of society to be easily abandoned, and the first
effect of the collision between the opposing principles was to
propagate a feeling of philosophic doubt. In the sphere of reason a new kind of Pyrrhonism sprang up, which expressed itself
in Montaigne's motto, *Que sçay je?* and this disposition of
mind naturally exerted another kind of influence on the men
of creative imagination. In active life the confusion of the times
was the opportunity of the buccaneer and the soldier of fortune, who hoped to advance themselves by their swords; and
like these, many poets, in their ideal representations of Nature,
seized upon the rich materials of the old and ruined philosophy
to decorate the structures which they built out of their lawless
fancy. On such foundations rose the school of metaphysical
wit, of which the earliest and most remarkable example is
furnished in the poetry of John Donne. . . .

The character of Donne's poetry reflects very exactly the
changes in his life and opinions. Most of his compositions in
verse are said to have been written while he was still a young
man. To this class belong his *Satires*, his *Songs and Sonnets*,
his *Elegies*, and *The Progress of the Soul*. A graver and more
philosophic period follows, in which were produced most of
the *Verse Epistles*, his *Epicedes and Obsequies*, and *The Anatomy of the World*; while the *Divine Poems* and the paraphrase of
the *Lamentations of Jeremiah* are the work of the time when he
was about to be, or had been, ordained.

Ben Jonson said to Drummond, speaking of *The Progress
of the Soul*: "Of this he (Donne) never wrote but one sheet, and
now, since he was made Doctor, repenteth highly, and seeketh
to destroy all his poems." The thing is probable enough.
Donne was educated as a Roman Catholic. His love-poems are
those of a man who has assimilated, with thorough appreciation, all the learning and intellectual methods of the schoolmen—their fine distinctions, their subtle refinement, their
metaphysical renderings of the text of Scripture. We know that,
at some uncertain date, he abandoned the Roman Catholic
faith, but his scholastic education had grounded in his mind a
doctrine which, to the close of his life, continued to lie at the
root of all his convictions, and to give form and colour to his
poetical style, namely, the belief in the indestructible character
of the soul. He constantly alludes to the old theory of the
schoolmen respecting the triple nature of the soul, as in the
lines:—

> We first have souls of growth and sense; and those,
> When our last soul, our soul immortal, came,
> Were swallowed into it, and have no name.[1]

In the middle period of his life, when his opinions were becoming more settled and religious, he writes of this individual
soul:—

> Our soul, whose country's heaven, and God her
>   father,
>   Into this world, corruption's sink, is sent;
> Yet so much in her travel she doth gather,
>   That she returns home wiser than she went.[2]

This mixture of strong religious instinct and philosophic
scepticism appears in its simplest form in his third *Satire*,
which we know to have been among the earliest of his works.
What interest is there, the poet asks, which can compare with
religion? Why, then, are men prepared to risk their lives for the
smallest material stake—money, adventure, honour—while at
the same time they give no thought to their spiritual foes—the
world, the flesh, and the devil?—

> Flesh itself's death; and joys which flesh can taste
> Thou lovest; and thy fair goodly soul, which doth
> Give this flesh power to taste joy, thou dost loathe.

But then he goes on: "Seek true religion, O where?" Some, he says, seek her in the ancient, decayed authority of Rome; others in the sullen Protestantism of Geneva; some put up with Erastianism; others abhor all forms of religion, just because all cannot be good; others, on the contrary, think all are equally good. He concludes:—

> Doubt wisely; in strange way
> To stand inquiring right, is not to stray;
> To sleep or run wrong is. On a huge hill,
> Cragged and steep, Truth stands, and he that will
> Reach her, about must and about must go,
> And what th' hill's suddenness resists win so.
> Yet strive so, that before age, death's twilight,
> Thy soul rest, for none can work in that night.

On this principle he himself seems to have proceeded. Certain it is that, in his poem called *The Progress of the Soul*, he had reached a stage of contemplative scepticism. To this composition, which bears the following title and date: "Infinitati sacrum, 16 August 1601. Metempsychosis. Poema Satyricon," is prefixed a highly characteristic epistle, in which the author says:—

> I forbid no reprehender, but him that like the Trent Council forbids not books but authors, damning whatever such a name hath or shall write. None writes so ill, that he gives not something exemplary to follow or fly. Now when I begin this book I have no purpose to come into any man's debt; how my stock will hold out I know not; perchance waste, perchance increase in use. If I do borrow anything of antiquity, besides that I make account that I pay it with as much and as good, you shall still find me to acknowledge it, and to thank not only him that hath digged out treasure for me, but that hath lighted me a candle to the place, all which I will bid you remember (for I will have no such readers as I can teach) is, that the Pythagorean doctrine doth not only carry one soul from man to man, nor man to beast, but indifferently to plants also; and therefore you must not grudge to find the same soul in an Emperor, in a Posthorse, and in a Macaron, since no unreadiness in the soul, but an indisposition in the organs, works this.

In the poem itself Donne feigns that the soul, which moves all things—plants and beasts, as well as men—entered into the world by the plucking of an apple from the Tree of Life. The subtle and searching analysis of the poet's imagination may be illustrated by the following stanza:—

> For the great soul which here amongst us now
> Doth dwell, and moves that hand, and tongue, and
>   brow,
> Which, as the moon the sea, moves us; to hear
> Whose story with long patience you will long,
> —For 'tis the crown and last strain of my song—
> This soul to whom Luther and Mahomet were
> Prisons of flesh; this soul which oft did tear
> And mend the wracks of th' Empire, and late Rome,
> And lived when every great change did come,
>   Had first in Paradise a low but fatal room.

By the woman eating the apple, corruption passed by transmission through the whole race of mankind; and Donne's "wit" settles on each detail of the metaphysical conception, thus:—

> Prince of the orchard, fair as dawning morn,
> Fenced with the law, and ripe as soon as born,
> That apple grew, which this soul did enlive,
> Till the then climbing serpent, that now creeps
> For that offence, for which all mankind weeps,

> Took it, and to her whom the first man did wive
> —Whom and her race only forbiddings drive—
> He gave it, she to her husband; both did eat:
> So perished the eaters and the meat;
>   And we—for treason taints the blood—thence
>   die and sweat.
> Man all at once was thus by woman slain,
> And one by one we're here slain o'er again
> By them. The mother poisoned the well-head,
> The daughters here corrupt us, rivulets;
> No smallness scapes, no greatness breaks their nets;
> She thrust us out, and by them we are led
> Astray, from turning to whence we are fled.
> Were prisoners judges, 'twould seem rigorous:
> She sinned, we bear; part of our pain is thus
>   To love them whose fault to this painful love
>   yoked us.
> So fast in us did this corruption grow,
> That now we dare ask why we should be so.
> Would God—disputes the curious rebel—make
> A law, and would not have it kept? Or can
> His creature's will cross His? Of every man
> For one will God (and be just) vengeance take?
> Who sinned? 'twas not forbidden to the snake,
> Nor her, who was not then made; nor is't writ
> That Adam cropp'd, or knew, the apple; yet
>   The worm, and he, and she, and we endure
>   for it.

The apple once plucked, the soul flies from the Tree through the aperture, and enters successively into a plant (the mandrake), the egg of a bird (sparrow, symbol of lechery), a fish, a sea-osprey, a whale, a mouse, an elephant, a wolf, an ape, and a woman. All these are described, with various allegorical and satirical reflections by the way upon the manners and morals of mankind, especially at Court. The poem has no conclusion. Ben Jonson told Drummond: "The conceit of Done's transformation or Metempsychōsis was that he sought the soul of that apple which Eve pulled, and thereafter made it the soul of a bitch, then of a she-wolf, and so of a woman: his general purpose was to have brought in all the bodies of the heretics from the soul of Cain, and at last left it in the body of Calvin." Though this description of the poem is inaccurate in detail, it may well be that Donne originally designed some satiric stroke against Calvin; for his conclusion is steeped in the merest Pyrrhonism:—

> Whoe'er thou beest that read'st this sullen writ,
> Which just so much courts thee as thou dost it,
> Let me arrest thy thoughts; wonder with me,
> Why ploughing, building, ruling, and the rest
> Or most of these arts, whence our lives are blest,
> By cursed Caïn's race invented be,
> And blest Seth vex'd us with astronomy.
> There's nothing simply good or ill alone;
> Of every quality Comparison
> The only measure is, and judge, Opinion.

Here we have plainly the utterance of a sceptic in religion, who, having thrown off the forms of authoritative belief, indulges his imagination with a reconstruction of the ruins of Pythagorean and Rabbinical philosophy. Many allusions to natural history and theological dogma are scattered through Donne's *Songs and Sonnets*, and all are couched in the same reckless spirit.

And as Donne was at this stage a sceptic in religion, so was he a revolutionist in love. We have seen that, for many centuries, the law of chivalrous love had been rigorously defined. The Provençal poets and the female presidents of the *Cours d'Amours* had revised and extended the ancient canons of the art as expounded by Ovid; and, while they tacitly recognised the physical basis of the passion, they disguised it by the elaborate character of the imaginative superstructure they raised upon it. In the delicacy of their observation, the nicety of their distinctions, and the keenness of their logic, they rivalled the theological science of the schoolmen; and by allying the phenomena of love with the loftier virtues of constancy, patience, loyalty, and self-surrender, they so spiritualised the former that, under the *régime* of chivalry—to use the words of Burke,—"vice itself lost half its evil by losing all its grossness."[3]

This fine Platonic edifice is ruthlessly demolished in the poetry of Donne. To him love, in its infinite variety and inconsistency, represented the principle of perpetual flux in Nature. At the same time, his imagination was stimulated by the multitude of paradoxes and metaphors which were suggested to him by the varying aspects of the passion. He pushed to extremes the scholastic analysis and conventional symbolism of the Provençals; but he applied them within the sphere of vulgar *bourgeois* intrigue, as may be inferred from the following characteristic lines:—

> Nature's lay idiot, I taught thee to love,
> And in that sophistry, O! thou dost prove
> Too subtle; fool, thou didst not understand
> The mystic language of the eye nor hand;
> Nor couldst thou judge the difference of the air
> Of sighs, and say, "This lies, this sounds despair";
> Nor by th' eye's water cast a malady,
> Desperately hot, or changing feverously.
> I had not taught thee then the alphabet
> Of flowers, how they, devisefully being set
> And bound up, might, with speechless secrecy,
> Deliver errands mutely and mutually.
> Remember since all thy words used to be
> To every suitor, "Ay, if my friends agree";
> Since household charms thy husband's name to
>   teach,
> Were all the love-tricks that thy wit could reach;
> And since an hour's discourse could scarce have
>   made
> An answer in thee, and that ill-arrayed
> In broken proverbs and short sentences.[4]

The law of love in the *Cours d'Amours* required unfailing constancy in both lovers: in the philosophy of Donne this law is contrary to Nature, and is therefore heresy:—

> Venus heard me sigh this song,
> And by love's sweetest part, variety, she swore
> She heard not this till now; it should be so no more.
> She went, examined, and returned ere long,
> And said, "Alas! some two or three
> Poor heretics in love there be,
> Which think to 'stablish dangerous constancy.
> But I have told them, 'Since you will be true,
> You shall be true to them who're false to you.'"[5]

Over and over again he insists on the essential falsehood and fickleness of women. He asks, for instance, "where lives a woman true and fair," and proceeds:—

> If thou find'st one let me know;
>   Such a pilgrimage were sweet.
> Yet do not, I would not go,
>   Though at next door we might meet.
> Though she were true when you met her,
> And last till you write your letter,
>   Yet she
>   Will be
> False, ere I come, to two or three.[6]

This is the spirit of Ariosto's story of Giocondo. But Donne goes further, and cynically erects this observed habit of fickleness into a rule for constant, but discriminating, change:—

> By Nature, which gave it, this liberty
> Thou lovest, but O! canst thou love it and me?
> Likeness glues love; and if that thou so do,
> To make us like and love, must I change too?
> More than thy hate I hate it; rather let me
> Allow her change, then change as oft as she;
> And so not teach, but force, my opinion
> To love not any one, nor every one.
> To live in one land is captivity,
> To run all countries a wild roguery.
> Waters stink soon, if in one place they bide,
> And in that vast sea are more putrified;
> But when they kiss one bank, and leaving this
> Never look back, but the next bank do kiss,
> There are they purest; change is the nursery
> Of music, joy, life, and eternity.[7]

From this spirit of cynical lawlessness he was perhaps reclaimed by genuine love. To his wife he seems to have been devotedly attached, and in the poems written after his marriage in 1601 we find a complete change of sentiment and style. The old underlying conviction of the indestructible nature of the soul and of the corruption of the material world remains, but it is now made the starting-point for a graver philosophy of conduct. The *Verse Letters* written to the Countesses of Bedford, Huntingdon, and Salisbury, though all are couched in a vein of metaphysical compliment, are decorous in tone; in *The Anatomy of the World* Donne seems to have intended to embody his serious thoughts about the meaning and duties of human life. Whether there was any real ground for the hyperbolical praise with which he exalts the memory of Elizabeth Drury, we have no means of knowing. It is said, indeed, that she was betrothed to Henry, Prince of Wales; but Ben Jonson probably expressed a general opinion when he said to Drummond that "Done's 'Anniversarie' was profane and full of blasphemies: that he told Mr. Done, if it had been written of the Virgin Marie it had been something; to which he answered that it described the Idea of a Woman, and not as she was."

Viewed literally, *The Anatomy of the World* fully deserves the sentence passed upon it by Jonson. The poet asserts that after the death of Elizabeth Drury the whole mortal universe lost its vitality; that nothing but the shadow of life remained in it; that the disorder in the constitution of things, the decay and weakness of mankind, and the failure of the influence of the heavenly bodies, are all due to her removal from the earthly sphere. It is no wonder that such absurdities should have provoked matter-of-fact criticism. They are, however, not of the essence of the composition. "I hear from England," writes Donne in Paris to a correspondent with the initials Sir G. F., "of many censures of my book of Mrs. Drury; if any of these censures do but pardon me my descent in printing anything in verse (which if they do they are more charitable than myself; for I do not pardon myself, but confess that I did it against my conscience, that is against my own opinion, that I should not have done so), I doubt not that they will soon give over that other part of the indictment, which is that I have said so much; for nobody can imagine that I, who never saw her, could have purpose in that, than that when I had received so very good testimony of her worthiness, and was gone down to print verses, it became me to say, not what I was sure was just truth, but the best that I could conceive; for that would have been a new weakness in me to have praised anybody in printed verse, that had not been capable of the best verse that I could give."

The true character of *The Anatomy of the World* is indicated in the respective titles of the two Anniversaries. That of the first runs: "Wherein, *by occasion of the untimely death of Mistress Elizabeth Drury*, the frailty and decay of this whole world is represented." The subject of the second is defined thus: "Wherein, *by occasion of the religious death of Mistress Elizabeth Drury*, the incommodities of the soul in this life, and her exaltation in the next, are contemplated." In other words, the early death and religious character of Elizabeth Drury are merely the text justifying an elaborate exposition of Donne's philosophy of life. The girl stood to Donne, for his poetical purpose, in the same relation as Beatrice stood to Dante in the *Vita Nuova* and the *Divine Comedy*, being the incarnate symbol of the spiritual perfection—the Idea of Woman, as he put it to Ben Jonson—which he sought to express. When he says that her death was the cause of all the imperfections of the material world, he intended, in the first place, to pay a hyperbolical compliment to the daughter of his patron, and in the second, to express the theological doctrine of the corruption of Nature after the fall of man from his original state of perfection.

On the whole, it seems to me probable that the publication of *The Anatomy of the World* was part of a deliberate literary design on Donne's part. His affected depreciation of verse-writing is not to be taken seriously. His views of life were changing with his years: he was anxious for either secular or sacred employment: he regretted the evidences of a dissipated past which existed in his youthful poems: he hoped to attain the object of his ambition by giving public proof of the present gravity of his mind, and by securing the special favour of the most influential patrons of literature, such as the famous ladies of the Court, to whom so many of his *Verse Letters* are addressed. He writes to a correspondent in 1614: "This made me ask to borrow that old book" (*i.e.* an MS. collection of his poems), "which it will be too late to see, for that use, when I see you: for I must do this as a valediction to the world before I take orders. But this it is I am to ask of you: whether you ever made any such use of the letter in verse *à nostre comtesse chez vous*, as that I may put it in among the rest to persons of rank; for I desire it very much that something should bear her name in the book, and I would be just to my written words to my Lord Harrington, to write nothing after that." To Lady Bedford herself he writes, in a *Verse Letter*, perhaps the one above referred to:—

> So whether my hymns you admit or choose,
> In me you've hallowèd a pagan muse,
> And denizened a stranger who, mistaught
> By blamers of the times they've marred, hath sought
> Virtues in corners, which now bravely do
> Shine in the world's best part, or all it,—you.

As to the poems being a "valediction to the world," Donne kept his promise. His letter to Sir H. Goodyere was written within a year of his taking orders, and henceforth all his publications in prose and verse were of a religious and theological cast. The last period of his poetical genius contains the *Divine Poems*, comprising meditations on the various mysteries of the Christian faith, a version of Tremellius' *Lamentations of Jeremiah*, written after the death of his much-loved wife, and other religious topics. As John Chudleigh, one of his panegyrists, said in the edition of his poems published after his death in 1650:—

> Long since this task of tears from you was due,
> Long since, O poets, he did die to you,
> Or left you dead, when wit and he took flight
> On divine wings, and soared out of your sight.

In close friendship with George Herbert and other divines of the period, he helped during the remainder of his life to swell the volume of Anglican ascetic thought which, under the direction of Laud, formed, in the reign of Charles I., the counterbalancing force to the movement of iconoclastic Puritanism.

But though his view of life and his object in art were thus completely altered, his poetical method remained consistently the same. As his admirer, Chudleigh, again remarks:—

> He kept his loves, but not his objects: Wit
> He did not banish, but transplanted it;
> Taught it his place and use, and brought it home
> To piety which it doth best become;
> He showed us how for sins we ought to sigh,
> And how to sing Christ's epithalamy.

How just this criticism is may be seen from Donne's *Hymn to Christ at the Author's last going into Germany:*—

> Nor Thou, nor Thy religion, dost control
> The amorousness of an harmonious soul;
> But Thou wouldst have that love Thyself; as Thou
> Art jealous, Lord, so am I jealous now;
> Thou lovest not, till from loving more Thou free
> My soul; whoever gives takes liberty;
>   Oh, if Thou carest not whom I love,
>   Alas! Thou lovest not me.
> Seal then this bill of my divorce to all
> On whom those fainter beams of love did fall;
> Marry those loves, which in youth scattered be
> On fame, wit, hopes—false mistresses—to Thee.
> Churches are best for prayer that have least light;
> To see God only I go out of sight;
>   And to escape stormy days, I choose
>   An everlasting night.

Here we have precisely the same kind of paradoxical logic, the same subtlety of thought and imagery, as we find in the *Elegy on Change*, and though the imagination is now fixed on an unchangeable object, it plays round it precisely in the same way. The essence of Donne's wit is abstraction. Whether he is writing on the theme of sacred or profane love, his method lies in separating the perceptions of the soul from the entanglements of sense, and after isolating a thought, a passion, or a quality, in the world of pure ideas, to make it visible to the fancy by means of metaphorical images and scholastic allusions. The most characteristic specimens of his wit are to be found in his *Songs and Sonnets*, where he is dealing with the metaphysics of love, for here his imagination is at liberty to move whithersoever it chooses; and the extraordinary ingenuity with which he masters and reduces to epigrammatic form the most minute distinctions of thought, as well as the facility with which he combines contrary ideas and images, are well exemplified in a poem called *The Primrose Hill:*—

> Upon this Primrose Hill,
>   Where, if heaven would distil
> A shower of rain, each several drop might go
> To his own primrose, and grow manna so;
> And where their form and their infinity
>   Make a terrestrial galaxy,
>   As the small stars do in the sky,
> I walk to find a true-love, and I see
> That 'tis not a mere woman that is she,
> But must or more or less than woman be.[8]
>
>   Yet know I not which flower
>   I wish, a six or four:
> For should my true love less than woman be,
> She were scarce anything; and then should she
> Be more than woman, she would get above
>   All thought of sex, and think to move
>   My heart to study her, and not to love.

Both these were monsters; since there must reside
Falsehood in woman, I could more abide
She were by art than nature falsified.

  Live, primrose, then, and thrive
  With thy true number five;
And, woman, whom this flower doth represent,
With this mysterious number be content;
Ten is the farthest number; if half ten
  Belongs unto each woman, then
  Each woman may take half us men:
Or—if this will not serve their turn—since all
Numbers are odd or even, and they fall
First into five, women may take us all.[9]

But for the purposes of great and true art the flight of metaphysical wit soon reveals the limitations of its powers. Sceptic as he was, Donne never formed any organic idea of Nature as a whole, and his sole aim, as a poet, was to associate the isolated details of his accumulations of learning with paradoxes and conceits, which are of no permanent value. For example, he was acquainted with the Copernican theory, but he is only interested in it as far as it helps to supply him with a poetical illustration:—

As new philosophy arrests the sun,
And bids the passive earth about it run,
So we have dulled our mind; it hath no ends,
Only the body's busy, and pretends.[10]

The theory that the earth was gradually approaching the sun suggests to him the following reflection:—

If the world's age and death be argued well
  By the sun's fall, which now towards earth
   doth bend,
Then we might fear that virtue, since she fell
  So low as woman, should be near her end.

But he at once corrects this conclusion into an extravagant compliment:—

But she's not stooped but raised; exiled by men,
  She fled to heaven, that's heavenly things,
   that's you.[11]

The general scepticism, produced in his mind by the collision between the new philosophy and the old theology, is forcibly expressed in his first Anniversary:—

The new philosophy calls all in doubt;
The element of fire is quite put out;
The sun is lost, and th' earth, and no man's wit
Can well direct him where to look for it.
And freely men confess that the world's spent,
When in the planets and the firmament
They seek so many new; they see that this
Is crumbled out again to his atomies.
'Tis all in pieces, all coherence gone,
All just supply and all relation.
Prince, subject, father, son, are things forgot,
For every man alone thinks he hath got
To be a phœnix, and that there can be
None of that kind of which he is, but he.[12]

The conclusion at which he finally arrived was the one to which all such souls, who have in them the element of religion, must be brought:—

In this low form, poor soul, what wilt thou do?
When wilt thou shake off this pedantry
Of being taught by sense and fantasy?
Thou look'st through spectacles; small things seem
  great
Below; but up into thy watch-tower get,
And see all things despoiled of fallacies;

Thou shalt not peep through lattices of eyes,
Nor hear through labyrinths of ears, nor learn
By circuit or collections to discern.
In heaven thou straight know'st all concerning it,
And what concerns it not shalt straight forget.

But before he arrives at this intelligible goal, his soul, wandering through an infinite maze of metaphysical ideas, has made shift to embody its transitory perceptions in the forms of poetical art; and, while he is engaged in a business which he acknowledges to be vain, he delights in involving himself and his readers in inextricable labyrinths of paradox. One of his favourite ideas is that Love is Death, and this thought he divides and subdivides by means of an endless variety of images. Thus he finds an opportunity of associating it with the reflections aroused by the shortest day, sacred to St. Lucy. All Nature, he says, seems to have shrivelled into nothing:—

The world's whole sap is sunk;
The general balm th' hydroptic earth hath drunk,
Whither, as to the bed's feet, life is shrunk,
Dead and interr'd; yet all these seem to laugh,
Compared to me, who am their epitaph.

He then calls on all lovers to come and study him as a "very dead thing,"

For whom Love wrought new alchemy;
  For his art did express
A quintessence even from nothingness,
From dull privations, and lean emptiness;
He ruin'd me, and I am rebegot
Of absence, darkness, death—things which are not.

He goes on to intensify the idea of annihilation, by saying that he is "the grave of all that's nothing"; that he is

  Of the first nothing the elixir grown;

nay, he is something less than nothing:

If I an ordinary nothing were,
As shadow, a light and body must be here,
But I am none.[13]

In a poem called *The Paradox* he indulges in still more intricate logic on the same subject:—

No lover saith I love, nor any other
  Can judge a perfect lover;
He thinks that else none can nor will agree
  That any loves but he:
I cannot say I loved, for who can say
  He was killed yesterday?
Love with excess of heat, more young than old,
  Death kills with too much cold.
We die but once, and who loved best did die,
  He that saith twice did lie;
For though he seem to move and stir awhile,
  He doth the sense beguile.
Such life is like the light which bideth yet,
  When the life's light is set,
Or like the heat which fire in solid matter
  Leaves behind two hours after.
Once I loved and died; and am now become
  Mine epitaph and tomb;
Here dead men speak their last, and so do I;
  Love slain, lo! here I lie.

This perpetual endeavour to push poetical conception beyond the limits of sense and Nature produced its necessary effect on the character of Donne's metrical expression. When he seeks to embody a comparatively simple and natural thought, he can write with admirable harmony, as in the following lines, describing love in the Golden Age:—

What pretty innocence in those days moved!
Man ignorantly walked by her he loved;
Both sigh'd and interchang'd a speaking eye;
Both trembled and were sick; both knew not why.
That natural fearfulness, that struck man dumb,
Might well—those times considered—man become.
As all discoverers, whose first essay
Finds but the place, after, the nearest way,
So passion is to woman's love, about,
Nay, farther off, than when we first set out.
It is not love that sueth or doth contend;
Love either conquers or but meets a friend;
Man's better part consists of purer fire,
And finds itself allowed ere it desire.[14]

Here, too, is an excellent compliment in a *Verse Letter* to the Countess of Salisbury, grounded on the idea that chivalrous love is a liberal education:—

So, though I'm born without those eyes to live,
Which Fortune, who hath none herself, doth give,
Which are fit means to see bright courts and you,
Yet, may I see you thus, as now I do:
I shall by that all goodness have discern'd,
And, though I burn my library, be learn'd.

His whole philosophy of life, in his early days, is condensed in the following couplet:—

Be then thine own home, and in thyself dwell;
Inn anywhere: continuance maketh hell.[15]

And he is most vivid in the presentation of abstract ideas, as in the famous lines:—

Her pure and eloquent blood
Spoke in her cheeks, and so distinctly wrought
That one might almost say her body thought.[16]

The abrupt and forcible openings of his poems often strike a key-note of thought which promises completeness of treatment, but his metaphysical wit and his love of endless distinctions generally cause the composition to end nowhere. He begins a poem called *Love's Deity* thus:—

I long to talk with some old lover's ghost,
Who died before the God of Love was born.

The object of the discourse is to be the mystery why love should be forced from one lover where there is no return from the other. This is a subject of universal interest, and the poet, on the assumption that Love, after being made into a deity, has abused his power, conducts a striking thought, by means of an appropriate image, to an intelligible conclusion:—

O were we wakened by this tyranny
To ungod this child again, it could not be
I should love her who loves not me.

But such straight forward logic would not have suited the super-subtle character of Donne's intellect; and he proceeds to invert his reasoning, and to close his poem with a stanza of pure paradox, leaving the mind without that sense of repose which art requires:—

Rebel and atheist, why murmur I,
As though I felt the worst that love could do?
Love may make me leave loving, or might try
A deeper plague, to make her love me too;
Which, since she loves before, I'm loth to see.
Falsehood is worse than hate; and that must be,
If she whom I love should love me.

Where he thinks simply the reader perceives that his thoughts are really common enough. He begins a *Verse Letter* to Sir H. Goodyere on his favourite subject of the necessity of change:—

Who makes the last a pattern for next year,

Turns no new leaf, but still the same thing
reads;
Seen things he sees again, heard things doth hear,
And makes his life but like a pair of beads.

This has the simplicity and directness of Sir John Davies in his *Nosce Teipsum*. But we soon come to a quatrain in which the poet is anxious to show his wit:—

To be a stranger hath that benefit,
We can beginnings, but not habits choke.
Go—whither? hence. You get, if you forget;
New faults, till they prescribe to us, are
smoke.

We certainly do *not* get anything by the mere negative act of forgetting; and nobody could gather from the last line that the meaning was, "new faults, till they become our masters, are *merely* smoke." Eagerness for novelty and paradox leads the poet to obscurity of expression; and the reader is justly incensed when he finds that the labour required to arrive at the meaning, hidden behind involved syntax and unmeasured verse, has been expended in vain. Ben Jonson does not express this feeling too strongly when he says, "That Done for not keeping of accent deserved hanging." It is superfluous to justify this verdict by examples. The reader, in the numerous extracts I have given from Donne's poems, will have observed for himself how deliberately he seeks to attract attention to the extravagance of his thought, by the difficulty of his grammatical constructions, and by the dislocation of his accents.

All these things must be taken into account in deciding the place to be assigned to this acute and powerful intellect in the history of English poetry. Donne's qualities were essentially those of his age. His influence on his contemporaries and on the generation that succeeded him was great. They had all been educated under the same scholastic conditions as himself; they were all in touch with his theological starting-point, and set a value on the subtlety of his metaphysical distinctions. In Dryden's time, when the prestige of "wit," still represented by the genius of Cowley, was weakening before the poetical school which aimed first at correctness of expression, men continued to speak with reverence of Donne's genius. But as the philosophy of Bacon, Newton, and Locke gradually established itself, the traditions of the schoolmen fell into discredit, so that, in the days of Johnson and Burke, the practice of the metaphysical wits had come to be regarded in the light of an obsolete curiosity. The revival of mediæval sentiment, which has coloured English taste during the last three generations, has naturally awakened fresh interest in the poems of Donne, and there is perhaps in our own day a tendency to exaggerate his merits. "If Donne," writes a learned and judicious critic, "cannot receive the praise due to the accomplished poetical artist, he has that not perhaps higher, but certainly rarer, of the inspired poetical creator."[17] Poetical creation implies that organic conception of Nature, and that insight into universal human emotions, which make the classical poets of the world—Homer and Dante, and Chaucer and Milton; and to this universality of thought, as I have endeavoured to show, Donne has no claim. Nor can he be reckoned among the poets who, by their sense of harmony and proportion, have helped to carry forward the refinement of our language from one social stage to another. The praise which Johnson bestows upon his learning adds little to his fame, for the science contained in his verse is mostly derived from those encyclopædic sources of knowledge which, even in his own time, were being recognised as the fountains of "Vulgar Error." On the other hand, to those who see in poetry a mirror of the national life, and who desire to amplify and enrich their own imagination by a sympathetic study of the spiritual existence of their ancestors, the work of Donne will always be profoundly interesting. No more lively or characteristic representative can be found of the thought of an age when the traditions of the ancient faith met in full encounter with the forces of the new philosophy. The shock of that collision is far from having spent its effect, even in our own day; and he who examines historically the movements of imagination will find in Donne's subtle analysis and refined paradoxes much that helps to throw light on the contradictions of human nature.

Notes

1. *Verse Letter* to the Countess of Bedford.
2. *Verse Letter* to Sir H. Goodyere.
3. *Reflections on the French Revolution.*
4. Elegy vii.
5. *The Indifferent.*
6. Song, "Go and catch a falling star."
7. Elegy iii.
8. The conceit of the poem turns on the two facts that the normally constituted primrose has five segments in its corolla, and that the token of true love among the country folk of Donne's time was the exceptional primrose, with either four or six segments.
9. The argument in this stanza is drawn from the science of numbers. Five being half of ten, the farthest number (i.e. the first double number, and the basis of the whole metric system), women may claim to represent half of what is in human nature; or, if this be not enough for their ambition, then (numbers being either odd or even, and falling first into five, i.e. 2 + 3) since five is woman's number, women may have the whole of human nature given over to them.
10. *Verse Letter* to Countess of Bedford.
11. *Verse Letter* to Countess of Huntingdon.
12. *Anatomy of the World*, first Anniversary, 205–218.
13. A *Nocturnal upon St. Lucy's Day.*
14. *Verse Letter* to the Countess of Huntingdon.
15. *Verse Letter* to Sir H. Wotton.
16. *Anatomy of the World*, second Anniversary, 244–246.
17. Professor Saintsbury, *Preface to Poems of John Donne.* Edited by E. K. Chambers.

THOMAS DEKKER

c.1572–1632

Thomas Dekker is first mentioned as a dramatist in Philip Henslowe's *Diary* under the entry dated January 8, 1598. His first known play, *Old Fortunatus*, and what was to become his best-known comedy, *The Shoemaker's Holiday*, were staged in 1599. In 1604 Dekker began his long and fortunate collaboration with Thomas Middleton, with whom he wrote *The Honest Whore* and, several years later, *The Roaring Girl*. Dekker also appears to have collaborated with Webster on *Westward Hoe* (1604) and with Rowley and Ford on *Northward Hoe* (1605). All in all, Dekker is thought to have had a hand in the composition of forty-four plays.

Dekker is also known as the author of numerous pamphlets. One of the most noteworthy is *The Guls Hornebooke* (1609), which portrays a day in the life of a young Jacobean dandy. His depiction of London in a plague year in *The Wonderfull Yeare* (1603) has been compared with the social "realism" of Defoe. Other prose works include *The Seven Deadly Sins of London* (1606) and *A Rod for Runawayes* (1625).

Dekker marshaled his satiric talents in a vitriolic battle of wits with Ben Jonson, who referred to him in the *Poetaster* as a mere "dresser of plays." Dekker responded in kind, probably enlisting the aid of the satirist John Marston, with *Satiromastix, or the Untrussing of the Humorous Poet*, performed in 1601 and printed in 1602.

In addition to his endeavors in the areas of comedy, pamphleteering, and satire, Dekker possessed a considerable lyric gift. His poetry was frequently anthologized during his lifetime.

Dekker's finances, always precarious, took a turn for the worse during the latter part of his life. Dekker in all probability died destitute, and was buried at St. James Parish, Clerkenwell, on August 25, 1632.

Personal

Sharpham, Day, Dicker were all Rogues.—BEN JONSON, *Conversations with William Drummond*, 1619

Out of the depths of darkling life where sin
  Laughs piteously that sorrow should not know
  Her own ill name, nor woe be counted woe;
Where hate and craft and lust make drearier din
Than sounds through dreams that grief holds revel in;
  What charm of joy-bells ringing, streams that flow,
  Winds that blow healing in each note they blow,
Is this that the outer darkness hears begin?
O sweetest heart of all thy time save one,
Star seen for love's sake nearest to the sun,

Hung lamplike o'er a dense and doleful city,
Not Shakespeare's very spirit, howe'er more great,
Than thine toward man was more compassionate,
  Nor gave Christ praise from lips more sweet with pity.
—ALGERNON CHARLES SWINBURNE, "Thomas Decker," *Sonnets on English Dramatic Poets*, 1882

More than ordinarily tantalizing and disappointing has been the outcome of prolonged and earnest search in all likely sources and by all likely helpers for light on the long-dimmed story of Thomas Dekker. It is no new experience to such Worker as myself in Elizabethan-Jacobean literary-biographical fields. None the less is it trying to find one who demonstrably was in many men's mouths, and was noticeably and continuously a popular writer, so utterly overlooked by those from whom loving memories might have been counted on: e. g., associated intimately as he was with the Playwrights of his period, from Ben Jonson to Massinger and Ford, and George Wilkins, it seems inexplicable that not one of all their superabundant productions yields a single distinct personal reference.—ALEXANDER B. GROSART, "Memorial-Introduction" to *The Non-Dramatic Works of Thomas Dekker*, 1886, Vol. 5, p. ix

In Henslowe's Diary, among the curious items which Alleyn's fellow manager in the Fortune and other theatres set down concerning his transactions in the plays of the time, the name of a certain "Mr. Dickers," will be found under date 8th of January, 1597. In this way, the adventure of Thomas Dekker into the precarious field of dramatic authorship is first recorded for us. The entry refers to some twenty shillings "lent unto Thomas Dowton" to buy a book of Dekker's, no doubt the MS. of some play written by him, the name of which, however, is not given. A week later, a second entry notes again a disbursement, this time of four pounds, also for a book of his "called Fayeton" (Phaeton), possibly a further part of the same work. The third entry referring to him is ominous: "Lent unto the companey, the 4 of febreary 1598, to disecharge Mr. Dicker owt of the cownter in the powltrey, the some of fortie shillings. I saye dd to Thomas Dowton. . . . .xxxxˢ." In the sorry indication of these three entries, showing first the promising emergence of the young playwright, and then immediately the coming of disaster upon him, and his being lodged for debt in "the Counter in the Poultry," we have at once the key to Dekker's career. Dekker, perhaps the most original and most striking figure among the lesser known men of that brilliant array which follows Marlowe, is at the same time one of the most unfortunate in his life and its artistic outcome, judged by the standard of his own genius. It was as if Fortune, to take a figure from his own play, having first presented him with the gift which, as a poet of the time, he most desired,—the playwright's great opportunity, then turned upon him, and said,—

But now go dwell with cares, and quickly die.

If, however, he lived with cares, he laughed at them, and he was too strong to let them kill him outright. But, nevertheless, there they were; they never perhaps quite upset that undaunted good-humour of his, but they defeated him as an artist, they allied themselves insidiously with his own natural weaknesses to defeat the consummation of a really great poetic faculty.—ERNEST RHYS, "Thomas Dekker," *The Best Plays of the Old Dramatists: Thomas Dekker*, ed. Ernest Rhys, 1887, pp. vii–viii

General

Quick Anti-Horace.—HENRY CHETTLE, *England's Mourning Garment*, 1603

Why, sir, sayd I, there is a booke called *Greenes Ghost haunts Conycatchers*; another called *Legerdemaine*, and *The Blacke Dog of Newgate*, but the most wittiest, elegantest and eloquentest peece (Master Dekkers, the true heire of Appolo composed) called *The Bell-man of London*, have already set foorth the vices of the time so vively, that it is unpossible the Anchor of any other mans braine can sound the sea of a more deepe and dreadful mischeefe.—WILLIAM FENNOR, *The Compter's Commonwealth*, 1617

Thomas Decker, a high-flier in wit, even against *Ben. Johnson* himself in his Comedy called *The Untrussing of the Humourous Poet*: besides which he wrote many others, as *the Wonder of a Kingdom;—The Honest Whore*, in two Parts; *Fortunatus;—The Whore of Babylon;—If this ben't a good play, the Devil's in't.*—EDWARD PHILLIPS, *Theatrum Poetarum Anglicanorum*, 1675

A Poet that liv'd in the Reign of King *James* the First, and was Contemporary with that admirable *Laureat*, Mr. *Benjamin Johnson*. He was more famous for the contention he had with him for the Bays, than for any great Reputation he had gain'd by his own Writings. Yet even in that Age, he wanted not his Admirers, nor his Friends amongst the Poets: in which number I reckon the Ingenious Mr. *Richard Brome*; who always stil'd him by the Title of *Father*. He clubb'd with *Webster* in writing Three Plays; and with *Rowley* and *Ford* in another: and I think I may venture to say, that these Plays as far exceed those of his own Brain, as a platted Whip-cord exceeds a single Thread in strength. Of those which he writ alone, I know none of much Esteem, except *The Untrussing the Humourous Poet*, and that chiefly on account of the Subject of it, which was the Witty *Ben Johnson*. He has had a Hand in Twelve Plays, Eight whereof were of his own Writing.—GERALD LANGBAINE, *An Account of the English Dramtick Poets*, 1691

Upon the whole, Decker cannot be ranked with Chapman and Heywood, and it is very probable that he could not have been half so well respected as he was, had not the envy of Jonson, who had he possessed an atom of good sense would have smiled and passed by him, lifted him into a consequence, not only fancied by himself but credited by the world.—CHARLES DIBDIN, *A Complete History of the Stage*, 1795, Vol. 3, p. 260

I take Webster and Decker to have been the two greatest of the Shakspeare men, for unstudied genius, next after Beaumont and Fletcher; and in some respects they surpassed them. Beaumont and Fletcher have no such terror as Webster, nor any such piece of hearty, good, affecting human clay, as Decker's "Old Signior Orlando Friscobaldo." Is there any such man even in Shakspeare?—any such exaltation of that most delightful of all things, *bonhomie*? Webster sometimes overdoes his terror; nay, often. He not only riots, he debauches in it; and Decker, full of heart and delicacy as he is, and qualified to teach refinement to the refined, condescends to an astounding coarseness. Beaumont and Fletcher's good company saved them from that, in words. In spirit they are full of it. But Decker never mixes up (at least not as far as I can remember) any such revolting and impossible contradictions in the same character as they do. Neither does he bring a doubt on his virtues by exaggerating them. He believes heartily in what he does believe, and you love him in consequence. It was he that wrote that character, the piety of which has been pronounced equal to its boldness:—

> The best of men
> That e'er wore earth about him was a sufferer;
> A soft, meek, patient, humble, tranquil spirit;
> The first true gentleman that ever breath'd.

His universal sympathy enabled him to strike out that audacious and happy simile, "untameable as *flies*," which Homer would have admired, though it is fit to make poetasters shudder. The poetaster, had Decker offered to make him a present of it, would have been afraid of being taken for a fly himself. Images are either grand in themselves, or for the thought and feeling that accompany them. This has all the greatness of Nature's "equal eye." You may see how truly Decker felt it to be of this kind, by the company in which he has placed it; and there is a consummation of propriety in its wildness, for he is speaking of lunatics:—

There are of madmen, as there are of tame,
All humour'd not alike. We have here some
So apish and fantastic, will play with a feather;
And though 'twould grieve a soul to see God's image
So blemish'd and defaced, yet do they act
Such antic and such pretty lunacies,
That, spite of sorrow, they will make you smile.
Others again we have *like hungry lions,*
Fierce as wild bulls, untameable as flies.
—LEIGH HUNT, *Imagination and Fancy,* 1844

Though his lyrical gifts were of a rare quality, though he was master of a vigorous if not elevated rhetoric, and though his natural humour, which shows itself at its height already in his earliest extant comedy, seems to have been constantly fed by lively observation, he produced no one dramatic work of a high order. It is in scattered scenes and passages rather than in the working out of characters or plots that he displays elements of real tragic power; for at times his pathos is singularly sudden and direct. A fuller measure of success he commands only within a limited sphere. Inside of this, although the grossness of his realism makes it impossible for a more refined age to dwell with unalloyed pleasure on his pictures of contemporary life, the unaffected healthiness of his spirit and the vigour of his comic genius are beyond dispute. What can I see, asks the son of Fortunatus, in mine own country? You may see, answers his interlocutor, 'things enough, for what can you see abroad that is not at home? The same Sun calls you up in the morning, and the same man in the Moon lights you to bed at night, our fields are as green as theirs in summer, and their frosts will nip us in winter. Our birds sing as sweetly and our women are as fair.' And though Dekker seems to prefer to dwell on aspects of his native land different from these, yet there is a healthy endeavour in him to take human nature at least as he finds it, and to reproduce his impressions and tell his truths with simple directness rather than seek for artificial effects by attempting flights beyond his range. He is as homely in his moral teaching as he is downright in his exemplification of vice; but there is in him no affectation of being more than he is. His plays are among the most characteristic monuments of the ways of thought and feeling belonging to his age; and while generally rude in form,—alternating between prose, blank-verse, and rime (to which last he seems very prone),—they are for the most part full of genuine dramatic life, strong in their drawing of character, and spirited if uneven in their execution. A life of hard rubs with fortune well accords with a genius of rough but not unkindly vigour; and though much that Dekker has written may remain outside the range of what most of us can bring ourselves to enjoy, we shall gladly accord to him the recognition due to a writer possessed of a manly spirit and a genuine though limited dramatic power, as well as of a choice gift of song.—ADOLPHUS WILLIAM WARD, *A History of English Dramatic Literature* (1875), 1899, Vol. 2, pp. 471–72

Dekker had several qualities which made him a desirable coadjutor in play-writing. He was a master of the craft of the stage. A man of quick sympathies, unconquerable buoyancy of spirit, infinite readiness and resource, he had lived among the people who filled the theatres, and took a genuine delight in moving them by the exhibition of common joys and sorrows. His whole heart went with his audience, and, though he had not the loftiness of aim of his greatest contemporaries, none of them had a finer dramatic instinct. He knew London as well as Dickens, and had something of the same affection for its oddities and its outcasts. The humour which lights up its miseries, the sunshine which plays over its tears, the simple virtues of the poor and unfortunate, patience, forgiveness, mirthfulness,

were the favourite themes of this tender-hearted dramatist. His plays are full of life and movement, of pathos that is never maudlin and humour that is never harsh. Vice always gets the worst of it, hardness of heart above all never goes unpunished, but relenting leniency always comes in to keep retribution within gentle bounds. Virtue is always triumphant, but it is discovered in the most fantastic shapes and the least conventional habiliments. It needs some charity to tolerate such heroes and heroines as Simon Eyre, the mad shoemaker, Candido, the patient citizen, Orlando Friscobaldo, Bellafronta, and other types of strangely disguised goodness, but the dramatist's own love for them, with all their absurd eccentricities, is infectious. He laughs at them heartily, and carries us with him in his humour, but he knows how to change the key and soften laughter into tenderness.

Dekker's verse is naturally graceful and copious, keeping unforced pace with the abundance of matter supplied by his fertile invention. He was not a careful writer. He probably 'never blotted a line,' and one cannot read his plays without wishing that he had 'blotted a thousand.' His intellect had not the intense chemical energy of Shakespeare's, through which no thought could pass unchanged; and he did not strain after originality as some of his great compeers did, Webster, Jonson, Ford, and Chapman. He poured out in an easy stream whatever came readiest, and his best passages do not run far without being marred by some poor commonplace, tumbled out as it entered the mint, without any new stamp impressed upon it. It is in his songs, interspersed at too rare intervals through his plays, that Dekker appears at his best. He had the most exquisite gift of song. Few of his contemporaries had a harder life, but all the miscellaneous drudgery through which he had to toil for a precarious livelihood failed to destroy his elasticity and spirits, and his songs rise from the earth like bird-songs, clear, fresh, spontaneous. There is genuine lyrical rapture in the notes. Like most town-bred poets, he had a passion for the country, and his fancy is never more happy than when dwelling on rustic delights.—WILLIAM MINTO, "Thomas Dekker," *The English Poets*, ed. Thomas Humphry Ward, 1880, Vol. 2, pp. 55–56

A hundred years ago Thomas Dekker was probably little more than a name to all but professed students of Elizabethan literature, and he waited longer than any of his fellows for due recognition by presentation of his work in a complete form. It is not fifteen years since his plays were collected; it is scarcely as many months since his prose works had the same honour. Yet, since attention was directed to Dekker in any way, the best authorities have been unanimous in his praise. Lamb's famous outburst of enthusiasm, that he had "poetry enough for anything," has been soberly endorsed by two full generations of the best judges, and whatever differences of detail there may be as to his work, it is becoming more and more the received, and correctly-received opinion, that, as his collaborator Webster came nearest to Shakespere in universalising certain types in the severer tragedy, so Dekker has the same honour on the gently pathetic side. Yet this great honour is done to one of the most shadowy personalities in literature. We have four goodly volumes of his plays and five of his other works: yet of Thomas Dekker, the man, we know absolutely less than of any one of his shadowy fellows. We do not know when he was born, when he died, what he did other than writing in the certainly long space between the two unknown dates. In 1637 he was by his own words a man of threescore, which, as it has been justly remarked, may mean anything between fifty-five and seventy. He was in circumstances a complete contrast to his fellow-victim in Jonson's satire, Marston. Marston was apparently a gentleman born and bred, well connected, well educated, possessed of some property, able to make testamentary dispositions, and probably in the latter part of his life, when Dekker was still toiling at journalism of various kinds, a beneficed clergyman in country retirement. Dekker was, it is to be feared, what the arrogance of certain members of the literary profession has called, and calls, a gutter-journalist—a man who had no regular preparation for the literary career, and who never produced anything but hand-to-mouth work. Jonson went so far as to say that he was a "rogue;" but Ben, though certainly not a rogue, was himself not to be trusted when he spoke of people that he did not like; and if there was any but innocent roguery in Dekker he has contrived to leave exactly the opposite impression stamped on every piece of his work. And it is particularly interesting to note, that constantly as he wrote in collaboration, one invariable tone, and that the same as is to be found in his undoubtedly independent work, appears alike in plays signed with him by persons so different as Middleton and Webster, as Chettle and Ford. When this is the case, the inference is certain, according to the strictest rules of logic. We can define Dekker's idiosyncrasy almost more certainly than if he had never written a line except under his own name. That idiosyncrasy consists, first, of an exquisite lyrical faculty, which, in the songs given in all collections of extracts, equals, or almost equals, that of Shakespere; secondly, of a faculty for poetical comedy, for the comedy which transcends and plays with, rather than grasps and exposes, the vices and follies of men; thirdly, for a touch of pathos again to be evened only to Shakespere's; and lastly, for a knack of representing women's nature, for which, except in the master of all, we may look in vain throughout the plentiful dramatic literature of the period, though touches of it appear in Greene's Margaret of Fressingfield, in Heywood, in Middleton, and in some of the anonymous plays which have been fathered indifferently, and with indifferent hopelessness of identification, on some of the greatest of names of the period, on some of the meanest, and on an equal number of those that are neither great nor mean.—GEORGE SAINTSBURY, A *History of Elizabethan Literature*, 1887, pp. 199–201

Works

OLD FORTUNATUS

The humour of a frantic lover, in the scene where Orleans to his friend Galloway defends the passion with which himself, being a prisoner in the English king's court, is enamoured to frenzy of the king's daughter Agripyna, is done to the life. Orleans is as passionate an inamorato as any which Shakespeare ever drew. He is just such another adept in Love's reasons. The sober people of the world are with him

A swarm of fools
Crowding together to be counted wise.

He talks "pure Biron and Romeo," he is almost as poetical as they, quite as philosophical, only a little madder. After all, Love's secretaries are a reason unto themselves. We have gone retrograde to the noble heresy, since the days when Sidney proselyted our nation to this mixed health and disease; the kindliest symptom, yet the most alarming crisis in the ticklish state of youth; the nourisher and the destroyer of hopeful wits; the mother of twin births, wisdom and folly, valour and weakness; the servitude above freedom; the gentle mind's religion; the liberal superstition—CHARLES LAMB, *Specimens of English Dramatic Poets*, 1808

Olde Fortunatus is of course founded in subject on the old tale, to which it would be hazardous to assign an exclusively Teu-

tonic source, and which at all events derived contributions from the literature or life of nearly every European country. The first known version of the story is the German *Volksbuch* of 1509, in which however many Romance elements are traceable. It was repeatedly reprinted or reproduced in other languages during the sixteenth century, about the middle of which (1533) Hans Sachs published his *tragedia* on the subject. An organic connexion manifestly exists between the theme of Fortunatus and that of Faust; so that in *Olde Fortunatus* Dekker was at work on material cognate to that with which, though in an already dramatised shape, he was brought into contact when set to provide 'additions' to Marlowe's *Doctor Faustus*. Yet, so far as general treatment is concerned, Dekker's play is even ruder than Marlowe's, with which it has no pretence to compare either in tragic interest or in passages of supreme poetic beauty. There can be no doubt that the play as we have it represents an enlargement of the *Fortunatus* mentioned without the author's name by Henslowe as *The First Part of Fortunatus* in 1596 into *The Whole History of Olde Fortunatus*, mentioned by him with Dekker's name, and printed, in 1600. Ushered in by a prologue, abounding in the sturdiest sort of flattery to 'Eliza' (then in her sixty-eighth year) 'flourishing like May,' the play opens, after an introductory speech by its hero, with an allegorical speech adorned by many historical allusions. Fortunatus having fixed his choice upon the gift of wealth, is accordingly endowed with the wonderful purse. He then begins a series of travels, in the course of which he robs the unwary Grand Turk of the wonderful hat; but his riches cannot save him from a miserable death. The lesson of his fate has however been lost upon his son Andelocia, with whose marvellous adventures—leading to an end even more wretched than that of his sire—the remainder of the play is occupied. The construction of this drama is necessarily lax; the wild defiance of the unities of time and place accords well with the nature of the subject; but as the author seems so strongly impressed by the moral of his story, he ought not to have allowed the virtuous and the vicious son of Fortunatus to come alike to grief. Among the minor characters may be noticed the honest servingman Shadow, the clown of the piece, and the 'frantic lover' Orleans, the drawing of which latter character Lamb has much overpraised. Altogether this romantic comedy attracts by a singular vigour and freshness; but its principal charm lies in the appropriately *naïf* treatment of its simple, not to say child-like, theme.—ADOLPHUS WILLIAM WARD, *A History of English Dramatic Literature* (1875), 1899, Vol. 2, pp. 457–59

THE HONEST WHORE

This simple picture of Honour and Shame (in *The Honest Whore*), contrasted without violence, and expressed without immodesty, is worth all the *strong lines* against the Harlot's Profession, with which both Parts of this play are offensively crowded. A Satyrist is always to be suspected, who, to make vice odious, dwells upon all its acts and minutest circumstances with a sort of relish and retrospective gust. But so near are the boundaries of panegyric and invective, that a worn-out Sinner is sometimes found to make the best Declaimer against Sin. The same high-seasoned descriptions which in his unregenerate state served to inflame his appetites, in his new province of a Moralist will serve him (a little turned) to expose the enormity of those appetites in other men. No one will doubt, who reads Marston's Satires, that the Author in some part of his life must have been something more than a theorist in vice. Have we never heard of an old preacher in the pulpit display such an insight into the mystery of ungodliness, as made us wonder with reason how a good man came by it?

When Cervantes with such proficiency of fondness dwells upon the Don's library, who sees not that he has been a great reader of books of Knight Errantry? perhaps was at some time of his life in danger of falling into those very extravagances which he ridicules so happily in his Hero?—CHARLES LAMB, *Specimens of English Dramatic Poets*, 1808

. . . ⟨O⟩ld honest Deckar's Signior Orlando Friscobaldo I shall never forget! I became only of late acquainted with this last-mentioned worthy character; but the bargain between us is, I trust, for life. We sometimes regret that we had not sooner met with characters like these, that seem to raise, revive, and give a new zest to our being. Vain the complaint! We should never have known their value, if we had not known them always: they are old, very old acquaintance, or we should not recognise them at first sight. We only find in books what is already written within 'the red-leaved tables of our hearts.' The pregnant materials are there; 'the pangs, the internal pangs are ready; and poor humanity's afflicted will struggling in vain with ruthless destiny.' But the reading of fine poetry may indeed open the bleeding wounds, or pour balm and consolation into them, or sometimes even close them up for ever! . . .

The rest of the character is answerable to the beginning. The execution is, throughout, as exact as the conception is new and masterly. There is the least colour possible used; the pencil drags; the canvas is almost seen through: but then, what precision of outline, what truth and purity of tone, what firmness of hand, what marking of character! The words and answers all along are so true and pertinent, that we seem to see the gestures, and to hear the tone with which they are accompanied. So when Orlando, disguised, says to his daughter, 'You'll forgive me,' and she replies, 'I am not marble, I forgive you;' or again, when she introduces him to her husband, saying simply, 'It is my father,' there needs no stage-direction to supply the relenting tones of voice or cordial frankness of manner with which these words are spoken. It is as if there were some fine art to chisel thought, and to embody the inmost movements of the mind in every-day actions and familiar speech. It has been asked,

> Oh! who can paint a sun-beam to the blind,
> Or make him feel a shadow with his mind?

But this difficulty is here in a manner overcome. Simplicity and extravagance of style, homeliness and quaintness, tragedy and comedy, interchangeably set their hands and seals to this admirable production. We find the simplicity of prose with the graces of poetry. The stalk grows out of the ground; but the flowers spread their flaunting leaves in the air. The mixture of levity in the chief character bespeaks the bitterness from which it seeks relief; it is the idle echo of fixed despair, jealous of observation or pity. The sarcasm quivers on the lip, while the tear stands congealed on the eye-lid. This 'tough senior,' this impracticable old gentleman softens into a little child; this choke-pear melts in the mouth like marmalade. In spite of his resolute professions of misanthropy, he watches over his daughter with kindly solicitude; plays the careful housewife; broods over her lifeless hopes; nurses the decay of her husband's fortune, as he had supported her tottering infancy; saves the high-flying Matheo from the gallows more than once, and is twice a father to them. The story has all the romance of private life, all the pathos of bearing up against silent grief, all the tenderness of concealed affection:—there is much sorrow patiently borne, and then comes peace. Bellafront, in the two parts of this play taken together, is a most interesting character. It is an extreme, and I am afraid almost an ideal case. She gives the play its title, turns out a true penitent, that is, a practical

one, and is the model of an exemplary wife. She seems intended to establish the converse of the position, that *a reformed rake makes the best husband*, the only difficulty in proving which, is, I suppose, to meet with the character. The change of her relative position, with regard to Hippolito, who, in the first part, in the sanguine enthusiasm of youthful generosity, has reclaimed her from vice, and in the second part, his own faith and love of virtue having been impaired with the progress of years, tries in vain to lure her back again to her former follies, has an effect the most striking and beautiful. The pleadings on both sides, for and against female faith and constancy, are managed with great polemical skill, assisted by the grace and vividness of poetical illustration. As an instance of the manner in which Bellafront speaks of the miseries of her former situation, 'and she has felt them knowingly,' I might give the lines in which she contrasts the different regard shewn to the modest or the abandoned of her sex.

> I cannot, seeing she's woven of such bad stuff,
> Set colours on a harlot bad enough.
> Nothing did make me when I lov'd them best,
> To loath them more than this: when in the street
> A fair, young, modest damsel, I did meet;
> She seem'd to all a dove, when I pass'd by,
> And I to all a raven: every eye
> That followed her, went with a bashful glance;
> At me each bold and jeering countenance
> Darted forth scorn: to her, as if she had been
> Some tower unvanquished, would they all vail;
> 'Gainst me swoln rumour hoisted every sail.
> She crown'd with reverend praises, pass'd by them;
> I, though with face mask'd, could not 'scape the hem;
> For, as if heav'n had set strange marks on whores,
> Because they should be pointing-stocks to man,
> Drest up in civilest shape, a courtesan,
> Let her walk saint-like, noteless, and unknown,
> Yet she's betray'd by some trick of her own.

Perhaps this sort of appeal to matter of fact and popular opinion, is more convincing than the scholastic subtleties of the Lady in Comus. The manner too, in which Infelice, the wife of Hippolito, is made acquainted with her husband's infidelity, is finely dramatic; and in the scene where she convicts him of his injustice by taxing herself with incontinence first, and then turning his most galling reproaches to her into unbraidings against his own conduct, she acquits herself with infinite spirit and address. The contrivance, by which, in the first part, after being supposed dead, she is restored to life, and married to Hippolito, though perhaps a little far-fetched, is affecting and romantic. There is uncommon beauty in the Duke her father's description of her sudden illness. In reply to Infelice's declaration on reviving, 'I'm well,' he says,

> Thou wert not so e'en now. Sickness' pale hand
> Laid hold on thee, ev'n in the deadst of feasting:
> And when a cup, crown'd with thy lover's health,
> Had touch'd thy lips, a sensible cold dew
> Stood on thy cheeks, as if that death had wept
> To see such beauty altered.

Candido, the good-natured man of this play, is a character of inconceivable quaintness and simplicity. His patience and good-humour cannot be disturbed by any thing. The idea (for it is nothing but an idea) is a droll one, and is well supported. He is not only resigned to injuries, but 'turns them,' as Falstaff says of diseases, 'into commodities.' He is a patient Grizzel out of petticoats, or a Petruchio reversed. He is as determined upon winking at affronts, and keeping out of scrapes at all events, as the hero of the Taming of a Shrew is bent upon picking quarrels out of straws, and signalizing his manhood without the smallest provocation to do so. The sudden turn of the character of Candido, on his second marriage, is, however, as amusing as it is unexpected.

Matheo, 'the high-flying' husband of Bellafront, is a masterly portrait, done with equal ease and effect. He is a person almost without virtue or vice, that is, he is in strictness without any moral principle at all. He has no malice against others, and no concern for himself. He is gay, profligate, and unfeeling, governed entirely by the impulse of the moment, and utterly reckless of consequences. His exclamation, when he gets a new suit of velvet, or a lucky run on the dice, 'do we not fly high,' is an answer to all arguments. Punishment or advice has no more effect upon him, than upon the moth that flies into the candle. He is only to be left to his fate. Orlando saves him from it, as we do the moth, by snatching it out of the flame, throwing it out of the window, and shutting down the casement upon it! —WILLIAM HAZLITT, *Lectures on the Dramatic Literature of the Age of Elizabeth*, 1820

The best of his plays is probably one in which he allied himself with Middleton in 1604, a second part appearing several years later. In this occurs the famous passage about patience, which has been universally attributed to Dekker—

> Patience! why, 'tis the soul of peace:
> Of all the virtues, 'tis nearest kin to heaven;
> It makes men look like gods. The best of men
> That e'er wore earth about him was a sufferer,
> A soft, meek, patient, humble, tranquil spirit;
> The first true gentleman that every breathed.

The delicately humorous character of Orlando Friscobaldo is an example of work excellently done in a class rarely attempted by Dekker, who is unrivalled in short pathetic scenes, has a tenderness that is all his own, combines with a sweet fancy a rare lyrical gift, but is excessively unequal as a craftsman, and mars some of his finest efforts by his impatience, his incoherence, and his carelessness. It is difficult to understand how it can be possible that the author of the detestable stuff called *If it be not good, the Devil is in it*, could have turned away to contribute to Massinger's *Virgin Martyr* the exquisite episode between the heroine and the angel. This extravagant inequality, ever recurring, creates the standing difficulty about the literary position of Dekker.—EDMUND GOSSE, *The Jacobean Poets*, 1894, pp. 21–22

ALGERNON CHARLES SWINBURNE
"Thomas Dekker"
Nineteenth Century, January 1887, pp. 81–103

Of all English poets, if not of all poets on record, Dekker is perhaps the most difficult to classify. The grace and delicacy, the sweetness and spontaneity of his genius are not more obvious and undeniable than the many defects which impair and the crowning deficiency which degrades it. As long, but so long only, as a man retains some due degree of self-respect and respect for the art he serves or the business he follows, it matters less for his fame in the future than for his prosperity in the present whether he retains or discards any vestige of respect for any other obligation in the world. François Villon, compared with whom all other reckless and disreputable men of genius seem patterns of austere decency and elevated regularity of life, was as conscientious and self-respectful an artist as a Virgil or a Tennyson: he is not a great poet only, but one of the most blameless, the most perfect, the most faultless among his fel-

lows in the first class of writers for all time. If not in that class, yet high in the class immediately beneath it, the world would long since have agreed to enrol the name of Thomas Dekker, had he not wanted that one gift which next to genius is the most indispensable for all aspirants to a station among the masters of creative literature. For he was by nature at once a singer and a maker: he had the gift of native music and the birthright of inborn invention. His song was often sweet as honey; his fancy sometimes as rich and subtle, his imagination as delicate and strong, as that of the very greatest among dramatists or poets. For gentle grace of inspiration and vivid force of realism he is eclipsed at his very best by Shakespeare's self alone. No such combination or alternation of such admirable powers is discernible in any of his otherwise more splendid or sublime compeers. And in one gift, the divine gift of tenderness, he comes nearer to Shakespeare and stands higher above others than in any other quality of kindred genius.

And with all these gifts, if the vulgar verdict of his own day and of later days be not less valid than vulgar, he was a failure. There is a pathetic undertone of patience and resignation not unqualified by manly though submissive regret, which recurs now and then, or seems to recur, in the personal accent of his subdued and dignified appeal to the casual reader, suggestive of a sense that the higher triumphs of art, the brighter prosperities of achievement, were not reserved for him; and yet not unsuggestive of a consciousness that, if this be so, it is not so through want of the primal and essential qualities of a poet. For, as Lamb says, 'Dekker had poetry enough for anything;' at all events, for anything which can be accomplished by a poet endowed in the highest degree with the gifts of graceful and melodious fancy, tender and cordial humour, vivid and pathetic realism, a spontaneous refinement and an exquisite simplicity of expression. With the one great gift of seriousness, of noble ambition, of self-confidence rooted in self-respect, he must have won an indisputable instead of a questionable place among the immortal writers of his age. But this gift had been so absolutely withheld from him by nature or withdrawn from him by circumstance that he has left us not one single work altogether worthy of the powers now revealed and now eclipsed, now suddenly radiant and now utterly extinct, in the various and voluminous array of his writings. Although his earlier plays are in every way superior to his later, there is evidence even in the best of them of the author's infirmity of hand. From the first he shows himself idly or perversely or impotently prone to loosen his hold on character and story alike before his plot can be duly carried out or his conceptions adequately developed. His 'pleasant Comedie of The Gentle Craft,' first printed three years before the death of Queen Elizabeth, is one of his brightest and most coherent pieces of work, graceful and lively throughout, if rather thin-spun and slight of structure: but the more serious and romantic part of the action is more slightly handled than the broad light comedy of the mad and merry Lord Mayor Simon Eyre, a figure in the main original and humorous enough, but somewhat over persistent in ostentation and repetition of jocose catchwords after the fashion of mine host of the Garter; a type which Shakespeare knew better than to repeat, but of which his inferiors seem to have been enamoured beyond all reason. In this fresh and pleasant little play there are few or no signs of the author's higher poetic abilities: the style is pure and sweet, simple and spontaneous, without any hint of a quality not required by the subject: but in the other play of Dekker's which bears the same date as this one his finest and rarest gifts of imagination and emotion, feeling and fancy, colour and melody, are as apparent as his ingrained faults of levity and laziness. The famous passage in which Webster couples together the names of 'Mr. Shakespeare, Mr. Dekker, and Mr. Heywood,' seems explicable when we compare the style of *Old Fortunatus* with the style of *A Midsummer Night's Dream*. Dekker had as much of the peculiar sweetness, the gentle fancy, the simple melody of Shakespeare in his woodland dress, as Heywood of the homely and noble realism, the heartiness and humour, the sturdy sympathy and the joyful pride of Shakespeare in his most English mood of patriotic and historic loyalty. Not that these qualities are wanting in the work of Dekker: he was an ardent and a combative patriot, ever ready to take up the cudgels in prose or rhyme for England and her yeomen against Popery and the world: but it is rather the man than the poet who speaks on these occasions: his singing faculty does not apply itself so naturally to such work as to the wild wood-notes of passion and fancy and pathos which in his happiest moments, even when they remind us of Shakespeare's, provoke no sense of unworthiness or inequality in comparison with these. It is not with the most popular and famous names of his age that the sovereign name of Shakespeare is most properly or most profitably to be compared. His genius has really far less in common with that of Jonson or of Fletcher than with that of Webster or of Dekker. To the last-named poet even Lamb was for once less than just when he said of the 'frantic Lover' in *Old Fortunatus* that 'he talks pure Biron and Romeo; he is almost as poetical as they.' The word 'almost' should be supplanted by the word 'fully'; and the criticism would then be no less adequate than apt. Sidney himself might have applauded the verses which clothe with living music a passion as fervent and as fiery a fancy as his own. Not even in the rapturous melodies of that matchless series of songs and sonnets which glorify the inseparable names of Astrophel and Stella will the fascinated student find a passage more enchanting than this.

> Thou art a traitor to that white and red
>   Which sitting on her cheeks (being Cupid's
>   throne)
> Is my heart's sovereign: O, when she is dead,
>   This wonder, Beauty, shall be found in none.
> Now Agripyne's not mine, I vow to be
> In love with nothing but deformity.
> O fair Deformity, I muse all eyes
> Are not enamoured of thee: thou didst never
> Murder men's hearts, or let them pine like wax,
> Melting against the sun of thy disdain;[1]
> Thou art a faithful nurse to Chastity;
> Thy beauty is not like to Agripyne's,
> For cares, and age, and sickness, hers deface,
> But thine's eternal: O Deformity,
> Thy fairness is not like to Agripyne's,
> For, dead, her beauty will no beauty have,
> But thy face looks most lovely in the grave.

Shakespeare has nothing more exquisite in expression of passionate fancy, more earnest in emotion, more spontaneous in simplicity, more perfect in romantic inspiration. But the poet's besetting sin of laxity, his want of seriousness and steadiness, his idle, shambling, shifty way of writing, had power even then, in the very prime of his promise, to impede his progress and impair his chance of winning the race which he had set himself—and yet which he had hardly set himself—to run. And if these things were done in the green tree, it was only too obvious what would be done in the dry; it must have been clear that this golden-tongued and gentle-hearted poet had not strength of spirit or fervour of ambition enough to put conscience into his work and resolution into his fancies. But even from such headlong recklessness as he had already displayed no

reader could have anticipated so singular a defiance of all form and order, all coherence and proportion, as is exhibited in his *Satiromastix*. The controversial part of the play is so utterly alien from the romantic part that it is impossible to regard them as component factors of the same original plot. It seems to me unquestionable that Dekker must have conceived the design, and probable that he must have begun the composition, of a serious play on the subject of William Rufus and Sir Walter Tyrrel, before the appearance of Ben Jonson's *Poetaster* impelled or instigated him to some immediate attempt at rejoinder; and that being in a feverish hurry to retort the blow inflicted on him by a heavier hand than his own he devised— perhaps between jest and earnest—the preposterously incoherent plan of piecing out his farcical and satirical design by patching and stitching it into his unfinished scheme of tragedy. It may be assumed, and it is much to be hoped, that there never existed another poet capable of imagining—much less of perpetrating—an incongruity so monstrous and so perverse. The explanation so happily suggested by a modern critic that William Rufus is meant for Shakespeare, and that 'Lyly is Sir Vaughan ap Rees,' wants only a little further development, on the principle of analogy, to commend itself to every scholar. It is equally obvious that the low-bred and foul-mouthed ruffian Captain Tucca must be meant for Sir Philip Sidney; the vulgar idiot Asinius Bubo for Lord Bacon; the half-witted underling Peter Flash for Sir Walter Raleigh; and the immaculate Celestina, who escapes by stratagem and force of virtue from the villainous designs of Shakespeare, for the lady long since indicated by the perspicacity of a Chalmers as the object of that lawless and desperate passion which found utterance in the sonnets of her unprincipled admirer—Queen Elizabeth. As a previous suggestion of my own, to the effect that George Peele was probably the real author of *Romeo and Juliet*, has had the singular good fortune to be not merely adopted but appropriated—in serious earnest—by a contemporary student, without—as far as I am aware—a syllable of acknowledgment, I cannot but anticipate a similar acceptance in similar quarters for the modest effort at interpretation now submitted to the judgment of the ingenuous reader.

Gifford is not too severe on the palpable incongruities of Dekker's preposterous medley: but his impeachment of Dekker as a more virulent and intemperate controversialist than Jonson is not less preposterous than the structure of this play. The nobly gentle and manly verses in which the less fortunate and distinguished poet disclaims and refutes the imputation of envy or malevolence excited by the favour enjoyed by his rival in high quarters should have sufficed, in common justice, to protect him from such a charge. There is not a word in Jonson's satire expressive of anything but savage and unqualified scorn for his humbler antagonist: and the tribute paid by that antagonist to his genius, the appeal to his better nature which concludes the torrent of recrimination, would have won some word of honourable recognition from any but the most unscrupulous and ungenerous of partisans. That Dekker was unable to hold his own against Jonson when it came to sheer hard hitting—that on the ground or platform of personal satire he was as a light weight pitted against a heavy weight—is of course too plain, from the very first round, to require any further demonstration. But it is not less plain that in delicacy and simplicity and sweetness of inspiration the poet who could write the scene in which the bride takes poison (as she believes) from the hand of her father, in presence of her bridegroom, as a refuge from the passion of the king, was as far above Jonson as Jonson was above him in the robuster qualities of intellect or genius. This most lovely scene, for pathos tempered with fancy and for passion distilled in melody, is comparable only with higher work, of rarer composition and poetry more pure, than Jonson's: it is a very treasure-house of verses like jewels, bright as tears and sweet as flowers. When Dekker writes like this, then truly we seem to see his right hand in the left hand of Shakespeare.

To find the names of Ben Jonson and Thomas Dekker amicably associated in the composition of a joint poem or pageant within the space of a year from the publication of so violent a retort by the latter to so vehement an attack by the former must amuse if it does not astonish the reader least capable of surprise at the boyish readiness to quarrel and the boyish readiness to shake hands which would seem to be implied in so startling a change of relations. In all the huge, costly, wearisome, barbaric and pedantic ceremonial which welcomed into London the Solomon of Scotland, the exhausted student who attempts to follow the ponderous elaboration of report drawn up by these reconciled enemies will remark the solid and sedate merit of Jonson's best couplets with less pleasure than he will receive from the quaint sweetness of Dekker's lyric notes. Admirable as are many of Ben Jonson's songs for their finish of style and fullness of matter, it is impossible for those who know what is or should be the special aim or the distinctive quality of lyric verse to place him in the first class—much less, in the front rank—of lyric poets. He is at his best a good way ahead of such song-writers as Byron: but Dekker at his best belongs to the order of such song-writers as Blake or Shelley. Perhaps the very finest example of his flawless and delicate simplicity of excellence in this field of work may be the well-known song in honour of honest poverty and in praise of honest labour which so gracefully introduces the heroine of a play published in this same year of the accession of James—*Patient Grissel*; a romantic tragicomedy so attractive for its sweetness and lightness of tone and touch that no reader will question the judgment or condemn the daring of the poets who ventured upon ground where Chaucer had gone before them with such gentle stateliness of step and such winning tenderness of gesture. His deepest note of pathos they have not even attempted to reproduce: but in freshness and straightforwardness, in frankness and simplicity of treatment, the dramatic version is not generally unworthy to be compared with the narrative which it follows afar off.[2] Chettle and Haughton, the associates of Dekker in this enterprise, had each of them something of their colleague's finer qualities; but the best scenes in the play remind me rather of Dekker's best early work than of *Robert Earl of Huntington* or of *Englishmen for my Money*. So much has been said of the evil influence of Italian example upon English character in the age of Elizabeth, and so much has been made of such confessions or imputations as distinguish the clamorous and malevolent penitence of Robert Greene, that it is more than agreeable to find at least one dramatic poet of the time who has the manliness to enter a frank and contemptuous protest against this habit of malignant self-excuse.

'Italy,' says an honest gentleman in this comedy to a lying and impudent gull, 'Italy infects you not, but your own diseased spirits. Italy? Out, you froth, you scum! because your soul is mud, and that you have breathed in Italy, you'll say Italy has defiled you: away, you boar: thou wilt wallow in mire in the sweetest country in the world.'

There are many traces of moral or spiritual weakness and infirmity in the writings of Dekker and the scattered records or indications of his unprosperous though not unlaborious career: but there are manifest and manifold signs of an honest and earnest regard for justice and fair dealing, as well as of an inexhaustible compassion for suffering, an indestructible persistency of pity, which found characteristic expression in the most celebrated of his plays. There is a great gulf between it and the first of Victor Hugo's tragedies: yet the instinct of either poet is the same, as surely as their common motive is the redemption of a fallen woman by the influence of twin-born love and shame. Of all Dekker's works, *The Honest Whore* comes nearest to some reasonable degree of unity and harmony in conception and construction: his besetting vice of reckless and sluttish incoherence has here done less than usual to deform the proportions and deface the impression of his design. Indeed, the connection of the two serious plots in the first part is a rare example of dexterous and happy simplicity in composition: the comic underplot of the patient man and shrewish wife is more loosely attached by a slighter thread of relation to these two main stories, but is so amusing in its light and facile play of inventive merriment and harmless mischief as to need no further excuse. Such an excuse, however, might otherwise be found in the plea that it gives occasion for the most beautiful, the most serious, and the most famous passage in all the writings of its author. The first scene of this first part has always appeared to me one of the most effective and impressive on our stage: the interruption of the mock funeral by the one true mourner whose passion it was intended to deceive into despair is so striking as a mere incident or theatrical device that the noble and simple style in which the graver part of the dialogue is written can be no more than worthy of the subject: whereas in other plays of Dekker's the style is too often beneath the merit of the subject, and the subject as often below the value of the style. The subsequent revival of Infelice from her trance is represented with such vivid and delicate power that the scene, short and simple as it is, is one of the most fascinating in any play of the period. In none of these higher and finer parts of the poem can I trace the touch of any other hand than the principal author's: but the shop-keeping scenes of the underplot have at least as much of Middleton's usual quality as of Dekker's; homely and rough-cast as they are, there is a certain finish or thoroughness about them which is more like the careful realism of the former than the slovenly naturalism of the latter. The coarse commonplaces of the sermon on prostitution by which Bellafront is so readily and surprisingly reclaimed into respectability give sufficient and superfluous proof that Dekker had nothing of the severe and fiery inspiration which makes a great satirist or a great preacher: but when we pass again into a sweeter air than that of the boudoir or the pulpit, it is the unmistakable note of Dekker's most fervent and tender mood of melody which enchants us in such verses as these, spoken by a lover musing on the portrait of a mistress whose coffin has been borne before him to the semblance of a grave.

> Of all the roses grafted on her cheeks,
> Of all the graces dancing in her eyes,
> Of all the music set upon her tongue,
> Of all that was past woman's excellence
> In her white bosom, look, a painted board
> Circumscribes all!

Is there any other literature, we are tempted to ask ourselves, in which the writer of these lines, and of many as sweet and perfect in their inspired simplicity as these, would be rated no higher among his countrymen than Thomas Dekker?

From the indisputable fact of Middleton's partnership in this play Mr. Dyce was induced to assume the very questionable inference of his partnership in the sequel which was licensed for acting five years later. To me this second part seems so thoroughly of one piece and one pattern, so apparently the result of one man's invention and composition, that without more positive evidence I should hesitate to assign a share in it to any colleague of the poet under whose name it first appeared. There are far fewer scenes or passages in this than in the preceding play which suggest or present themselves for quotation or selection: the tender and splendid and pensive touches of pathetic or imaginative poetry which we find in the first part, we shall be disappointed if we seek in the second: its incomparable claim on our attention is the fact that it contains the single character in all the voluminous and miscellaneous works of Dekker which gives its creator an indisputable right to a place of perpetual honour among the imaginative humourists of England—and therefore among the memorable artists and creative workmen of the world. Apart from their claim to remembrance as poets and dramatists of more or less artistic and executive capacity, Dekker and Middleton are each of them worthy to be remembered as the inventor or discoverer of a wholly original, interesting, and natural type of character, as essentially inimitable as it is undeniably unimitated: the savage humour and cynic passion of De Flores, the genial passion and tender humour of Orlando Friscobaldo, are equally lifelike in the truthfulness and completeness of their distinct and vivid presentation. The merit of the play in which the character last named is a leading figure consists mainly or almost wholly in the presentation of the three principal persons: the reclaimed harlot, now the faithful and patient wife of her first seducer; the broken-down, ruffianly, light-hearted and light-headed libertine who has married her; and the devoted old father who watches in the disguise of a servant over the changes of her fortune, the sufferings, risks, and temptations which try the purity of her penitence and confirm the fortitude of her constancy. Of these three characters I cannot but think that any dramatist who ever lived might have felt that he had reason to be proud. It is strange that Charles Lamb, to whom of all critics and all men the pathetic and humorous charm of the old man's personality might most confidently have been expected most cordially to appeal, should have left to Hazlitt and Leigh Hunt the honour of doing justice to so beautiful a creation—the crowning evidence to the greatness of Dekker's gifts, his power of moral imagination and his delicacy of dramatic execution. From the first to the last word of his part the quaint sweet humour of the character is sustained with an instinctive skill which would do honour to a far more careful and a far more famous artist than Dekker. The words with which he receives the false news of his fallen daughter's death; 'Dead? my last and best peace go with her!'—those which he murmurs to himself on seeing her again after seventeen years of estrangement; 'The mother's own face, I ha' not forgot that'—prepare the way for the admirable final scene in which his mask of anger drops off, and his ostentation of obduracy relaxes into tenderness and tears. 'Dost thou beg for him, thou precious man's meat, thou? has he not beaten thee, kicked thee, trod on thee? and dost thou fawn on him like his spaniel? has he not pawned thee to thy petticoat, sold thee to thy smock, made ye leap at a crust? yet wouldst have me save him?—What, dost thou hold him? let go his hand: if thou dost not forsake him, a father's everlasting blessing fall upon both your heads!' The fusion of humour with pathos into perfection of exquisite accuracy in expression which must be recognized at once and remembered for ever by any competent reader of this scene is the highest quality of Dekker as a writer of prose, and is here displayed at its highest: the more poetic or romantic quality of his genius had already begun to fade out when this second part of his finest poem was written. Hazlitt has praised the originality, dexterity, and vivacity of the effect produced by the stratagem which Infelice

employs for the humiliation of her husband, when by accusing herself of imaginary infidelity under the most incredibly degrading conditions she entraps him into gratuitous fury and turns the tables on him by the production of evidence against himself; and the scene is no doubt theatrically effective: but the grace and delicacy of the character are sacrificed to this comparatively unworthy consideration: the pure, high-minded, noble-hearted lady, whose loyal and passionate affection was so simply and so attractively displayed in the first part of her story, is so lamentably humiliated by the cunning and daring immodesty of such a device that we hardly feel it so revolting an incongruity as it should have been to see this princess enjoying, in common with her father and her husband, the spectacle of imprisoned harlots on penitential parade in the Bridewell of Milan; a thoroughly Hogarthian scene in the grim and vivid realism of its tragicomic humour.

But if the poetic and realistic merits of these two plays make us understand why Webster should have coupled its author with the author of *Twelfth Night* and *The Merry Wives of Windsor*, the demerits of the two plays next published under his single name are so grave, so gross, so manifold, that the writer seems unworthy to be coupled as a dramatist with a journeyman poet so far superior to him in honest thoroughness and smoothness of workmanship as, even at his very hastiest and crudest, was Thomas Heywood. In style and versification the patriotic and anti-Catholic drama which bears the Protestant and apocalyptic title of *The Whore of Babylon* is still, upon the whole, very tolerably spirited and fluent, with gleams of fugitive poetry and glimpses of animated action; but the construction is ponderous and puerile, the declamation vacuous and vehement. An Æschylus alone could have given us, in a tragedy on the subject of the Salamis of England, a fit companion to the *Persœ*; which, as Shakespeare let the chance pass by him, remains alone for ever in the incomparable glory of its triumphant and sublime perfection. Marlowe perhaps might have made something of it, though the task would have taxed his energies to the utmost, and overtasked the utmost of his skill; Dekker could make nothing. The empress of Babylon is but a poor slipshod ragged prostitute in the hands of this poetic beadle: 'non ragioniam di lei, ma guarda e passa.'

Of the three plays in which Dekker took part with Webster, the two plays in which he took part with Ford, and the second play in which he took part with Middleton, I have spoken respectively in my several essays on those other three poets. The next play which bears his name alone was published five years later than the political or historical sketch or study which we have just dismissed; and which, compared with it, is a tolerable if not a creditable piece of work. It is difficult to abstain from intemperate language in speaking of such a dramatic abortion as that which bears the grotesque and puerile inscription, *If this be not a good Play, the Devil is in it*. A worse has seldom discredited the name of any man with a spark of genius in him. Dryden's delectable tragedy of *Amboyna*, Lee's remarkable tragicomedy of *Gloriana*, Pope's elegant comedy of *Three Hours after Marriage*, are scarcely more unworthy of their authors, more futile or more flaccid or more audacious in their headlong and unabashed incompetence. Charity would suggest that it must have been written against time in a debtor's prison, under the influence of such liquor as Catherina Bountinall or Doll Tearsheet would have flung at the tapster's head with an accompaniment of such language as those eloquent and high-spirited ladies, under less offensive provocation, were wont to lavish on the officials of an oppressive law. I have read a good deal of bad verse, but anything like the metre of this play I have never come across in all the range of that excruciating experience. The rare and faint indications that the writer was or had been an humourist and a poet serve only to bring into fuller relief the reckless and shameless incompetence of the general workmanship.[3]

This supernatural and 'superlunatical' attempt at serious farce or farcical morality marks the nadir of Dekker's ability as a dramatist. The diabolic part of the tragicomic business is distinctly inferior to the parallel or similar scenes in the much older play of *Grim the Collier of Croydon*, which is perhaps more likely to have been the writer's immediate model than the original story by Machiavelli. The two remaining plays now extant which bear the single name of Dekker give no sign of his highest powers, but are tolerable examples of journeyman's work in the field of romantic or fanciful comedy. *Match me in London* is the better play of the two, very fairly constructed after its simple fashion, and reasonably well written in a smooth and unambitious style: *The Wonder of a Kingdom* is a light, slight, rough piece of work, in its contrasts of character as crude and boyish as any of the old moralities, and in its action as mere a dance of puppets: but it shows at least that Dekker had regained the faculty of writing decent verse on occasion. The fine passage quoted by Scott in *The Antiquary*, and taken by his editors to be a forgery of his own, will be familiar to many myriads of readers who are never likely to look it up in the original context. Of two masques called *Britannia's Honour* and *London's Tempe* it must suffice to say that the former contains a notable specimen of cockney or canine French which may serve to relieve the conscientious reader's weariness, and the latter a comic song of blacksmiths at work which may pass muster at a pinch as a tolerably quaint and lively piece of rough and ready fancy. But Jonson for the court and Middleton for the city were far better craftsmen in this line than ever was Dekker at his best.

Two plays remain for notice in which the part taken by Dekker would be, I venture to think, unmistakable, even if no external evidence were extant of his partnership in either. As it is, we know that in the winter which saw the close of the sixteenth century he was engaged with the author of *The Parliament of Bees* and the author of *Englishmen for My Money* in the production of a play called *The Spanish Moor's Tragedy*. More than half a century afterwards, a tragedy in which a Spanish Moor is the principal and indeed the only considerable agent was published, and attributed—of all poets in the world—to Christopher Marlowe, by a knavish and ignorant bookseller of the period. That *Lust's Dominion, or the Lascivious Queen*, was partly founded on a pamphlet published after Marlowe's death was not a consideration sufficient to offer any impediment to this imposture. That the hand which in the year of this play's appearance on the stage gave *Old Fortunatus* to the world of readers was the hand to which we owe the finer scenes or passages of *Lust's Dominion*, the whole of the opening scene bears such apparent witness as requires no evidence to support and would require very conclusive evidence to confute it. The sweet spontaneous luxury of the lines in which the queen strives to seduce her paramour out of sullenness has the very ring of Dekker's melody: the rough and reckless rattle of the abrupt rhymes intended to express a sudden vehemence of change and energy; the constant repetition or reiteration of interjections and ejaculations which are evidently supposed to give an air of passionate realism and tragic nature to the jingling and jerky dialogue; many little mannerisms too trivial to specify and too obvious to mistake; the occasional spirit and beauty, the frequent crudity and harshness, of the impetuous and uncertain style; the faults no less than the merits, the merits as plainly as the faults, attest the presence of his fitful

and wilful genius with all the defects of its qualities and all the weakness of its strength. The chaotic extravagance of collapse which serves by way of catastrophe to bring the action headlong to a close is not more puerile in the violence of its debility than the conclusions of other plays by Dekker; conclusions which might plausibly appear, to a malcontent or rather to a lenient reader, the improvisations of inebriety. There is but one character which stands out in anything of lifelike relief; for the queen and her paramour are but the usual diabolic puppets of the contemporary tragic stage: but there is something of lifeblood in the part of the honest and hot-headed young prince. This too is very like Dekker, whose idle and impatient energy could seldom if ever sustain a diffused or divided interest, but except when working hopelessly and heartlessly against time was likely to fix on some special point, and give life at least to some single figure.

There is nothing incongruous in his appearance as a playwright in partnership with Middleton or with Chettle, with Haughton or with Day; but a stranger association than that of Massinger's name with Dekker's it would not be easy to conceive. Could either poet have lent the other something of his own best quality; could Massinger have caught from Dekker the freshness and spontaneity of his poetic inspiration, and Dekker have learnt of Massinger the conscientious excellence and studious self-respect of his dramatic workmanship; the result must have been one of the noblest and completest masterpieces of the English stage. As it is, the famous and beautiful play which we owe to the alliance of their powers is a proverbial example of incongruous contrasts and combinations. The opening and the closing scenes were very properly and very fortunately consigned to the charge of the younger and sedater poet: so that, whatever discrepancy may disturb the intervening acts, the grave and sober harmonies of a temperate and serious artist begin and end the concert in perfect correspondence of consummate execution. 'The first act of the Virgin Martyr,' said Coleridge, 'is as fine an act as I remember in any play.' And certainly it would be impossible to find one in which the business of the scene is more skilfully and smoothly opened, with more happiness of arrangment, more dignity and dexterity of touch. But most lovers of poetry would give it all, and a dozen such triumphs of scenical and rhetorical composition, for the brief dialogue in the second act between the heroine and her attendant angel. Its simplicity is so childlike, its inspiration so pure in instinct and its expression so perfect in taste, its utterance and its abstinence, its effusion and its reserve, are so far beyond praise or question or any comment but thanksgiving, that these forty-two lines, homely and humble in manner as they are if compared with the refined rhetoric and the scrupulous culture of Massinger, would suffice to keep the name of Dekker sweet and safe for ever among the most memorable if not among the most pre-eminent of his kindred and his age. The four scenes of rough and rank buffoonery which deface this act and the two following have given very reasonable offence to critics from whom they have provoked very unreasonable reflections. That they represent the coarser side of the genius whose finer aspect is shown in the sweetest passages of the poem has never been disputed by any one capable of learning the rudiments or the accidence of literary criticism. An admirable novelist and poet who had the misfortune to mistake himself for a theologian and a critic was unlucky enough to assert that he knew not on what ground these brutal buffooneries had been assigned to their unmistakable author: in other words, to acknowledge his ignorance of the first elements of the subject on which it pleased him to write in a tone of critical and spiritual authority. Not even when his unwary and unscrupulous audacity of self-confidence impelled Charles Kingsley to challenge John Henry Newman to the duel of which the upshot left him gasping so piteously on the ground selected for their tournament—not even then did the author of *Hypatia* display such a daring and immedicable capacity of misrepresentation based on misconception as when this most ingenuously disingenuous of all controversialists avowed himself 'aware of no canons of internal criticism which would enable us to decide as boldly as Mr. Gifford does that all the indecency is Dekker's and all the poetry Massinger's.' Now the words of Gifford's note on the dialogue of which I have already spoken, between the saint and the angel, are these. 'What follows is exquisitely beautiful. . . . I am persuaded that this also was written by Dekker.' And seeing that no mortal critic but Kingsley ever dreamed of such absurdity as Kingsley rushes forward to refute, his controversial capacity will probably be regarded by all serious students of poetry or criticism as measurable by the level of his capacity for accurate report of fact or accurate citation of evidence.

There are times when we are tempted to denounce the Muse of Dekker as the most shiftless and shameless of slovens or of sluts; but when we consider the quantity of work which she managed to struggle or shuffle through with such occasionally admirable and memorable results, we are once more inclined to reclaim for her a place of honour among her more generally respectable or reputable sisters. I am loth to believe what I see no reason to suppose, that she was responsible for the dismal drivel of a poem on the fall of Jerusalem, which is assigned, on the surely dangerous ground of initials subscribed under the dedication, to a writer who had the misfortune to share these initials with Thomas Deloney. The ballad-writing hack may have been capable of sinking so far below the level of a penny ballad as to perpetrate this monstrous outrage on human patience and on English verse; but the most conclusive evidence would be necessary to persuade a jury of competent readers that a poet must be found guilty of its authorship. And we know that a pamphlet or novelette of Deloney's called *Thomas of Reading, or the Six Worthy Yeomen of the West*, was ascribed to Dekker until the actual author was discovered. Dr. Grosart, to whom we owe the first collected edition of Dekker's pamphlets, says in the introduction to the fifth of his beautiful volumes that he should have doubted the responsibility of Dekker for this poem had he not been detected as the author of another religious book. But this latter is a book of the finest and rarest quality—one of its author's most unquestionable claims to immortality in the affection and admiration of all but the most unworthy readers; and *Canaan's Calamity* is one of the worst metrical samples extant of religious rubbish. As far as such inferential evidence can be allowed to attest anything, the fact of Dekker's having written one of the most beautiful and simple of religious books in prose tends surely rather to disprove than to prove his authorship of one of the feeblest and most pretentious of semi-sacred rhapsodies in verse.

Among his numerous pamphlets, satirical or declamatory, on the manners of his time and the observations of his experience, one alone stands out as distinct from the rest by right of such astonishing superiority in merit of style and interest of matter that I prefer to reserve it for separate and final consideration. But it would require more time and labour than I can afford to give an adequate account of so many effusions or improvisations as served for fuel to boil the scanty and precarious pot of his uncertain and uncomfortable sustenance. 'The Wonderful Year' of the death of Elizabeth, the accession of James, and the devastation of London by pestilence, supplied him with matter enough for one of his quaintest and

liveliest tracts: in which the historical part has no quality so valuable or remarkable as the grotesque mixture of horror and humour in the anecdotes appended 'like a merry epilogue to a dull play, of purpose to shorten the lives of long winter's nights that lie watching in the dark for us,' with touches of rude and vivid pleasantry not unworthy to remind us, I dare not say of the Decameron, but at least of the *Cent Nouvelles Nouvelles*. In *The Seven Deadly Sins of London*—one of the milder but less brilliant 'Latterday Pamphlets' of a gentler if no less excitable Carlyle—there are touches of earnest eloquence as well as many quaint and fitful illustrations of social history; but there is less of humorous vigour and straightforward realism than in the preceding tract. And yet there are good things to be gathered out of this effusive and vehement lay sermon: this sentence for example is worth recollection:—'He is not slothful that is only lazy, that only wastes his good hours and his silver in luxury and licentious ease:—no, he is the true slothful man, that does no good.' And there is genuine insight as well as honesty and courage in his remonstrance with the self-love and appeal against the self-deceit of his countrymen, so prone to cry out on the cruelty of others, on the bloodthirstiness of Frenchmen and Spaniards, and to overlook the heavy-headed brutality of their own habitual indifference and neglect. Although the cruelty of penal laws be now abrogated, yet the condition of the poorest among us is assuredly not such that we can read without a sense of their present veracity the last words of this sentence:—'Thou set'st up posts to whip them when they are alive: set up an hospital to comfort them being sick, or purchase ground for them to dwell in when they be well, *and that is, when they be dead.*' The next of Dekker's tracts is more of a mere imitation than any of his others: the influence of a more famous pamphleteer and satirist, Tom Nash, is here not only manifest as that of a model, but has taken such possession of his disciple that he is hardly more than a somewhat servile copyist; not without a touch of his master's more serious eloquence, but with less than little of his peculiar energy and humour. That rushing wind of satire, that storm of resonant invective, that inexhaustible volubility of contempt, which rages through the controversial writings of the lesser poet, has sunk to a comparative whisper; the roar of his Homeric or Rabelaisian laughter to a somewhat forced and artificial chuckle. This *News from Hell, Brought by the Devil's Carrier*, and containing *The Devil's Answer to Pierce Penniless*, might have miscarried by the way without much more loss than that of such an additional proof as we could have been content to spare of Dekker's incompetence to deal with a subject which he was curiously fond of handling in earnest and in jest. He seems indeed to have fancied himself, if not something of a Dante, something at least of a Quevedo; but his terrors are merely tedious, and his painted devils would not terrify a babe. In this tract, however, there are now and then some fugitive felicities of expression; and this is more than can be said for either the play or the poem in which he has gone, with feebler if not more uneasy steps than Milton's Satan, over the same ground of burning marl. There is some spirit in the prodigal's denunciation of his miserly father: but the best thing in the pamphlet is the description of the soul of a hero bound for paradise, whose name is given only in the revised and enlarged edition which appeared a year later under the title of A *Knight's Conjuring; done in earnest; discovered in jest.* The narrative of 'William Eps his death' is a fine example of that fiery sympathy with soldiers which flows in so many pages of Dekker's verse, and flashes out by fits through the murky confusion of his worst and most formless plays; but the introduction of this hero is as fine a passage of prose as he has left us.

The foremost of them was a personage of so composed a presence, that Nature and Fortune had done him wrong, if they had not made him a soldier. *In his countenance there was a kind of indignation, fighting with a kind of exalted joy*, which by his very gesture were apparently decipherable; for he was jocund, that his soul went out of him in so glorious a triumph; but disdainfully angry, that she wrought her enlargement through no more dangers: yet were there bleeding witnesses enow on his breast, which testified, he did not yield till he was conquered, and was not conquered, till there was left nothing of a man in him to be overcome.

That the poet's loyalty and devotion were at least as ardent when offered by his gratitude to sailors as to soldiers we may see by this description of 'The Seaman' in his next work:—

A progress doth he take from realm to realm,
With goodly water-pageants borne before him;
The safety of the land sits at his helm,
No danger here can touch, but what runs o'er him:
But being in heaven's eye still, it doth restore him
To livelier spirits; to meet death with ease,
If thou wouldst know thy maker, search the seas.[4]

These homely but hearty lines occur in a small and mainly metrical tract bearing a title so quaint that I am tempted to transcribe it at length:—'The Double PP. A Papist in Arms. Bearing Ten several Shields. Encountered by the Protestant. At Ten several Weapons. A Jesuit Marching before them. Comìnùs and Emìnùs.' There are a few other vigorous and pointed verses in this little patriotic impromptu, but the greater part of it is merely curious and eccentric doggrel.

The next of Dekker's tracts or pamphlets was the comparatively well-known *Gull's Horn-Book*. This brilliant and vivid little satire is so rich in simple humour, and in life-like photography taken by the sunlight of an honest and kindly nature, that it stands second only to the author's masterpiece in prose—*The Bachelor's Banquet*, which has waited so much longer for even the limited recognition implied by a private reprint. There are so many witty or sensible or humorous or grotesque excerpts to be selected from this pamphlet—and not from the parts borrowed or copied from a foreign satire on the habits of slovenly Hollanders—that I take the first which comes under my notice on reopening the book; a study which sets before us in fascinating relief the professional poeticule of a period in which as yet clubs, coteries, and newspapers were not—or at the worst were nothing to speak of.

If you be a Poet, and come into the Ordinary, (though it can be no great glory to be an ordinary Poet) order yourself thus. Observe no man, doff not cap to that Gentleman today at dinner, to whom, not two nights since, you were beholden for a supper; but, after a turn or two in the room, take occasion (pulling out your gloves) to have some Epigram, or Satire, or Sonnet fastened in one of them, that may (as it were unwittingly[5] to you) offer itself to the Gentlemen: they will presently desire it: but, without much conjuration from them, and a pretty kind of counterfeit lothness in yourself, do not read it; and, though it be none of your own, swear you made it.

This coupling of injunction and prohibition is worthy of Shakespeare or of Sterne.

Marry, if you chance to get into your hands any witty thing of another man's, that is somewhat better, I would counsel you then, if demand be made who composed it, you may say: ''Faith, a learned Gen-

tleman, a very worthy friend.' And this seeming to lay it on another man will be counted either modesty in you, or a sign that you are not ambitious of praise, *or else that you dare not take it upon you, for fear of the sharpness it carries with it.*

The modern poetaster by profession knows a trick worth any two of these: but it is curious to observe the community of baseness, and the comparative innocence of awkwardness and inexperience, which at once connote the species and denote the specimens of the later and the earlier animalcule.

The 'Jests to make you merry,' which in Dr. Grosart's edition are placed after *The Gull's Horn-Book*, though dated two years earlier, will hardly give so much entertainment to any probable reader in our own time as 'The Misery of a Prison, and a Prisoner,' will give him pain to read of in the closing pages of the same pamphlet, when he remembers how long—at the lowest computation—its author had endured the loathsome and hideous misery which he has described with such bitter and pathetic intensity and persistency in detail. Well may Dr. Grosart say that 'it shocks us today, though so far off, to think of 1598 to 1616 onwards covering so sorrowful and humiliating trials for so finely touched a spirit as was Dekkers'; but I think as well as hope that there is no sort of evidence to that surely rather improbable as well as deplorable effect. It may be 'possible,' but it is barely possible, that some 'seven years' continuous imprisonment' is the explanation of an ambiguous phrase which is now incapable of any certain solution, and capable of many an interpretation far less deplorable than this. But in this professedly comic pamphlet there are passages as tragic, if not as powerful, as any in the immortal pages of *Pickwick* and *Little Dorrit* which deal with a later but a too similar phase of prison discipline and tradition.

The thing that complained was a man:—'Thy days have gone over thee like the dreams of a fool, thy nights like the watchings of a madman.—Oh sacred liberty! with how little devotion do men come into thy temples, when they cannot bestow upon thee too much honour! Thy embracements are more delicate than those of a young bride with her love, and to be divorced from thee is half to be damned! For what else is a prison but the very next door to hell? It is a man's grave, wherein he walks alive: it is a sea wherein he is always shipwrackt: it is a lodging built out of the world: it is a wilderness where all that wander up and down grow wild, and all that come into it are devoured.'

In Dekker's next pamphlet, his 'Dream,' there are perhaps half-a-dozen tolerably smooth and vigorous couplets immersed among many more vacuous and vehement in the intensity of their impotence than any reader and admirer of his more happily inspired verse could be expected to believe without evidence adduced. Of imagination, faith, or fancy, the ugly futility of this infernal vision has not—unless I have sought more than once for it in vain—a single saving trace or compensating shadow.

Two years after he had tried his hand at an imitation of Nash, Dekker issued the first of the pamphlets in which he attempted to take up the succession of Robert Greene as a picaresque writer, or purveyor of guidebooks through the realms of rascaldom. *The Bellman of London*, or Rogue's Hornbook, begins with a very graceful and fanciful description of the quiet beauty and seclusion of a country retreat in which the author had sought refuge from the turmoil and forgetfulness of the vices of the city; and whence he was driven back upon London by disgust at the discovery of villainy as elaborate

and roguery as abject in the beggars and thieves of the country
as the most squalid recesses of metropolitan vice or crime could
supply. The narrative of this accidental discovery is very lively
and spirited in its straightforward simplicity: and the subsequent revelations of rascality are sometimes humorous as well
curious: but the demand for such literature must have been
singularly persistent to evoke a sequel to his book next year—
Lantern and Candle-light, or the Bellman's Second Night-Walk;
in which Dekker continues his account of vagrant and villainous society, its lawless laws and its unmannerly manners;
and gives the reader some vivid studies, interspersed with facile
rhetoric and interlarded with indignant declamation, of the
tricks of horsedealers and the shifts of gipsies—or 'moon-men'
as he calls them; a race which he regarded with a mixture of
angry perplexity and passionate disgust. A *Strange Horse-Race*
between various virtues and vices gives occasion for the display
of some allegoric ingenuity and much indefatigable but fatiguing pertinacity in the exposure of the more exalted swindlers of
the age—the crafty bankrupts who anticipated the era of the
Merdles described by Dickens, but who can hardly have done
much immediate injury to a capitalist of the rank of Dekker.
Here too there are glimpses of inventive spirit and humorous
ingenuity; but the insufferable iteration of jocose demonology
and infernal burlesque might tempt the most patient and the
most curious of readers to devote the author, with imprecations
or invocations as elaborate as his own, to the spiritual potentate
whose 'last will and testament' is transcribed into the text of this
pamphlet.

In *The Dead Term* such a reader will find himself more or
less relieved by the return of his author to a more terrene and
realistic sort of allegory. This recriminatory dialogue between
the London and the Westminister of 1608 is now and then
rather flatulent in its reciprocity of rhetoric, but is enlivened by
an occasional breath of genuine eloquence, and redeemed by
touches of historic or social interest. The title and motto of the
next year's pamphlet—*Work for Armourers, or The Peace Is
Broken.—God help the Poor, the rich can shift*—were presumably designed to attract the casual reader, by what would now
be called a sensational device, to consideration of the social
question between rich and poor—or, as he puts it, between the
rival queens, Poverty and Money. The forces on either side are
drawn out and arrayed with pathetic ingenuity, and the result is
indicated with a quaint and grim effect of humorous if indignant resignation. *The Raven's Almanack* of the same year,
though portentous in its menace of plague, famine, and civil
war, is less noticeable for its moral and religious declamation
than for its rather amusing than edifying anecdotes; which, it
must be admitted, in their mixture of jocular sensuality with
somewhat ferocious humour, rather remind us of King Louis
the Eleventh than of that royal novelist's Italian models or
precursors. A *Rod for Runaways* is the title of a tract which
must have somewhat perplexed the readers who came to it for
practical counsel or suggestion, seeing that the very title-page
calls their attention to the fact that, 'if they look back, they may
behold many fearful judgments of God, sundry ways pronounced upon this city, and on several persons, both flying
from it, and staying in it.' What the medical gentleman to
whom this tract was dedicated may have thought of the author's
logic and theology, we can only conjecture. But even in this
little pamphlet there are anecdotes and details which would
repay the notice of a social historian as curious in his research
and as studious in his condescension as Macaulay.

A prayerbook written or compiled by a poet of Dekker's
rank in Dekker's age would have some interest for the reader of
a later generation even if it had not the literary charm which

distinguishes the little volume of devotions now reprinted from
a single and an imperfect copy. We cannot be too grateful for
the good fortune and the generous care to which we are indebted for this revelation of a work of genius so curious and so
delightful that the most fanatical of atheists or agnostics, the
hardest and the driest of philosophers, might be moved and
fascinated by the exquisite simplicity of its beauty. Hardly even
in those almost incomparable collects which Macaulay so aptly
compared with the sonnets of Milton shall we find sentences or
passages more perfect in their union of literary grace with ardent sincerity than here. Quaint as are several of the prayers in
the professional particulars of their respective appeals, this
quaintness has nothing of irreverence or incongruity: and the
subtle simplicity of cadence in the rhythmic movement of the
style is so nearly impeccable that we are perplexed to understand how so exquisite an ear as Dekker's at its best can have
been tolerant of such discord or capable of such collapse as so
often disappoints or shocks us in the hastier and cruder passages
of his faltering and fluctuating verse. The prayer for a soldier
going to battle and his thanksgiving after victory are as noble in
the dignity of their devotion as the prayers for a woman in
travail and 'for them that visit the sick' are delicate and earnest
in their tenderness. The prayer for a prisoner is too beautiful to
stand in need of the additional and pathetic interest which it
derives from the fact of its author's repeated experience of the
misery it expresses with such piteous yet such manful resignation. The style of these faultlessly simple devotions is almost
grotesquely set off by the relief of a comparison with the bloated
bombast and flatulent pedantry of a prayer by the late Queen
Elizabeth which Dekker has transcribed into his text—it is
hardly possible to suppose, without perception of the contrast
between its hideous jargon and the refined purity of his own
melodious English. The prayer for the Council is singularly
noble in the eloquence of its patriotism: the prayer for the
country is simply magnificent in the austere music of its fervent
cadences: the prayer in time of civil war is so passionate in its
cry for deliverance from all danger of the miseries then or lately
afflicting the continent that it might well have been put up by a
loyal patriot in the very heat of the great war which Dekker
might have lived to see break out in his own country. The
prayer for the evening is so beautiful as to double our regret for
the deplorable mutilation which has deprived us of all but the
opening of the morning prayer.[6] The feathers fallen from the
wings of these 'Four Birds of Noah's Ark' would be worth more
to the literary ornithologist than whole flocks of such 'tame
villatic fowl' as people the ordinary coops and hen-roosts of
devotional literature.

One work only of Dekker's too often overtasked and
heavy-laden genius remains to be noticed; it is one which gives
him a high place for ever among English humourists. No
sooner has the reader run his eye over the first three or four
pages than he feels himself, with delight and astonishment, in
the company of a writer whose genius is akin at once to Goldsmith's and to Thackeray's; a writer whose style is so pure and
vigorous, so lucid and straightforward, that we seem to have
already entered upon the best age of English prose. Had Mr.
Matthew Arnold, instead of digging in Chapman for preposterous barbarisms and eccentricities of pedantry, chanced to
light upon this little treatise; or had he condescended to glance
over Daniel's compact and admirable *Defence of Rhyme*; he
would have found in writers of the despised Shakespearean
epoch much more than a foretaste of those excellent qualities
which he imagines to have been first imported into our literature by writers of the age of Dryden. The dialogue of the very
first couple introduced with such skilful simplicity of presenta-

tion at the opening of Dekker's pamphlet is worthy of Sterne: the visit of the gossip or kinswoman in the second chapter is worthy of Molière; and the humours of the monthly nurse in the third are worthy of Dickens. The lamentations of the lady for the decay of her health and beauty in consequence of her obsequious husband's alleged neglect—'no more like the woman I was than an apple is like an oyster;' the description of the poor man making her broth with his own hands, jeered at by the maids and trampled underfoot by Mrs. Gamp; the preparations for the christening supper and the preliminary feast of scandal; are full of such bright and rich humour as to recall even the creator of Dogberry and Mrs. Quickly. It is of Shakespeare again that we are reminded in the next chapter, by the description of the equipage to which the husband of 'a woman that hath a charge of children' is reduced when he has to ride to the assizes in sorrier plight than Petruchio rode in to his wedding; the details remind us also of Balzac in the minute and grotesque intensity of their industrious realism: but the scene on his return reminds us rather of Thackeray at the best of his bitterest mood—the terrible painter of Mrs. Mackenzie and Mrs. General Baynes. 'The humour of a woman that marries her inferior by birth' deals with more serious matters in a style not unworthy of Boccaccio; and no comedy of the time—Shakespeare's always expected—has a scene in it of richer and more original humour than brightens the narrative which relates the woes of the husband who invites his friends to dinner and finds everything under lock and key. Hardly in any of Dekker's plays is the comic dialogue so masterly as here—so vivid and so vigorous in its lifelike ease and spontaneity. But there is not one of the fifteen chapters, devoted each to the description of some fresh 'humour,' which would not deserve, did space and time allow of it, a separate note of commentary. The book is simply one of the very finest examples of humorous literature, touched now and then with serious and even tragic effect, that can be found in any language; it is generally and comparatively remarkable for its freedom from all real coarseness or brutality, though the inevitable change of manners between Shakespeare's time and our own may make some passages or episodes seem now and then somewhat over particular in plain-speaking or detail. But a healthier, manlier, more thoroughly goodnatured and good-humoured book was never written; nor one in which the author's real and respectful regard for womanhood was more perceptible through the veil of a satire more pure from bitterness and more honest in design.

The list of works over which we have now glanced is surely not inconsiderable: and yet the surviving productions of Dekker's genius or necessity are but part of the labours of his life. If he wanted—as undoubtedly he would seem to have wanted—that 'infinite capacity for taking pains' which Carlyle professed to regard as the synonym of genius, he was at least not deficient in that rough and ready diligence which is habitually in harness, and cheerfully or resignedly prepared for the day's work. The names of his lost plays—all generally suggestive of some true dramatic interest, now graver and now lighter—are too numerous to transcribe: but one at least of them must excite unspeakable amazement as well as indiscreet curiosity in every reader of Ariosto or La Fontaine who comes in the course of the catalogue upon such a title as *Jocondo and Astolfo*. How on earth the famous story of Giocondo could possibly be adapted for representation on the public stage of Shakespearean London is a mystery which the execrable cook of the execrable Warburton has left for ever insoluble and inconceivable: for to

that female fiend, the object of Sir Walter Scott's antiquarian imprecations, we owe, unless my memory misguides me, the loss of this among other irredeemable treasures.

To do justice upon the faults of this poet is easy for any sciolist: to do justice to his merits is less easy for the most competent scholar and the most appreciative critic. In despite of his rare occasional spurts or outbreaks of self-assertion or of satire, he seems to stand before us as a man of gentle, modest, shiftless and careless nature, irritable and placable, eager and unsteady, full of excitable kindliness and deficient in strenuous principle; loving the art which he professionally followed, and enjoying the work which he occasionally neglected. There is no unpoetic note in his best poetry such as there is too often—nay, too constantly—in the severer work and the stronger genius of Ben Jonson. What he might have done under happier auspices, or with a tougher fibre of resolution and perseverance in his character, it is waste of time and thought for his most sympathetic and compassionate admirers to assume or to conjecture: what he has done, with all its shortcomings and infirmities, is enough to secure for him a distinct and honourable place among the humourists and the poets of his country.

Notes

1. As even Lamb allowed the meaningless and immetrical word 'destiny' to stand at the end of this line in place of the obviously right reading, it is not wonderful that all later editors of this passage should hitherto have done so.
2. I may here suggest a slight emendation in the text of the spirited and graceful scene with which this play opens. The original reads:

   > So fares it with coy dames, who, great with scorn,
   > Shew the care-pinèd hearts that sue to them.

   The word *Shew* is an obvious misprint—but more probably, I venture to think, for the word *Shun* than for the word *Fly*, which is substituted by Mr. Collier and accepted by Dr. Grosart.
3. As I have given elsewhere a sample of Dekker at his best, I give here a sample taken at random from the opening of this unhappy play.

   > Hie thee to Naples, Rufman; thou shalt find
   > A prince there newly crowned, aptly inclined
   > To any bendings: lest his youthful brows
   > Reach at stars only, weigh down his loftiest boughs
   > With leaden plummets, poison his best thoughts with taste
   > Of things most sensual: if the heart once waste,
   > The body feels consumption: good or bad kings
   > Breed subjects like them: clear streams flow from clear springs.
   > Turn therefore Naples to a puddle: with a civil
   > Much promising face, and well oiled, play the court devil.

   The vigorous melody of these 'masculine numbers' is not more remarkable for its virile force and honied fluency than is the lighter dialogue of the play for such brilliant wit or lambent humour as flashes out in pleasantries like this.

   > *King:* What are you, and whence come you?
   > *Rufman:*   From Helvetia.
   > *Spendola:* What hell says he?
   > *Jovinelli:* Peace; you shall know hot hell (*sic*) time enough.

   'I hope here be proofs' that my strictures on the worst work of a poet whose best work I treasure so heartily, and whose best qualities I rate so highly, are rather too sparing than too severe.
4. The italics are here the author's.
5. The text before me (Dr. Grosart's) reads 'armittingly.' The emendation is obvious.
6. A noticeable instance of the use of a common word in the original and obsolete sense of its derivation may be cited from the unfortunately truncated and scanty fragment of a prayer for the court:—'O Lord, be thou a husband' (house-band) 'to that great household of our King.'

GEORGE HERBERT

1593–1633

George Herbert was born at Montgomery Castle in Wales on April 3, 1593. As his father died when he was very young, his mother was the dominant influence of his early years. A very devout woman, Magdalen Herbert was also interested in literature; among her acquaintances was Donne, whose verse epistle "To Mrs M. H." was addressed to her. George Herbert's older brother, Edward Lord Herbert of Cherbury, is recognized as a minor poet in his own right.

Herbert left Wales for London in 1605 to attend the Westminster School. In 1613 he received a B.A. from Trinity College, Cambridge, followed in 1616 by an M.A. He remained at Cambridge after taking his degree, becoming a Reader in Rhetoric in 1618. The devout humility evident in much of his poetry was a mature development, for in his early years Herbert was very ambitious and dreamed of a successful career at Court. It was probably with this end in mind that he applied for the prestigious office of Public Orator of the University, a position to which he was appointed in 1620. Although he remained as Public orator until 1627, he also served as a Member of Parliament in 1624–25. It was not until he had relinquished his hopes of a Court career that he entered the clergy, an unusual step for a well-born man of his time. Ordained deacon in 1626, he was installed as Rector of Bemerton in 1630 and ordained priest later that year. He married Jane Danvers in 1629.

While Herbert had written and published Latin verse throughout his Cambridge years, the body of poetry for which he is chiefly celebrated was produced during the three short years at Bemerton before his death. *The Temple*, a collection of devotional poems, appeared in 1633, and a prose work, *A Priest to the Temple* (or *The Countrey Parson*), was published in the *Remains* of 1652. George Herbert died on March 1, 1633, and was buried at Bemerton.

Personal

A Sheafe of Snakes used heretofore to be
My Seal, The Crest of our poore Family.
Adopted in Gods Family, and so
Our old Coat lost, unto new armes I go.
The Crosse (my seal at Baptism) spred below,
Does, by that form, into an Anchor grow.
Crosses grow Anchors; Bear, as thou shouldst do
Thy Crossse, and that Crosse grows an Anchor too.
But he that makes our Crosses Anchors thus,
Is Christ, who there is crucifi'd for us.
Yet may I, with this, my first Serpents hold,
God gives new blessings, and yet leaves the old;
The Serpent, may, as wise, my pattern be;
My poison, as he feeds on dust, that's me.
And as he rounds the Earth to murder sure,
My death he is, but on the Crosse, my cure.
Crucifie nature then, and then implore
All Grace from him, crucified there before;
When all is Crosse, and that Crosse Anchor grown,
This Seal's a Catechism, not a Seal alone.
Under that little Seal great gifts I send,
〈Wishes,〉 and prayers, pawns, and fruits of a friend.
And may that Saint which rides in our great Seal,
To you, who bear his name, great bounties deal.
—JOHN DONNE, "To Mʳ *George Herbert*, with one of my Seals, of the Anchor and Christ" (Eng. trans.), c. 1615

The dedication of this work 〈*The Temple*〉 having been made by the Authour to the Divine Majestic onely, how should we now presume to interest any mortall man in the patronage of it! Much lesse think we it meet to seek recommendation of the Muses for that which himself was confident to have been inspired by a diviner breath then flows from Helicon. The world, therefore, shall receive it in that naked simplicitie with which he left it, without any addition either of support or ornament more then is included in itself. We leave it free and unforestalled to every man's judgement, and to the benefit that he shall finde by perusall. Onely, for the clearing of some passages, we have thought it not unfit to make the common Reader privie to some few particularities of the condition and disposition of the Person.

Being nobly born, and as eminently endued with gifts of the minde, and having by industrie and happy education perfected them to that great height of excellencie, whereof his fellowship of Trinitie Colledge in Cambridge, and his Oratorship in the Universitie, together with that knowledge which the King's Court had taken of him, could make relation farre above ordinarie. Quitting both his deserts and all the opportunities that he had for worldly preferment, he betook himself to the Sanctuarie and Temple of God, choosing rather to serve at God's altar then to seek the honour of State-employments. As for those inward enforcements to this course (for outward there was none), which many of these ensuing verses bear witnesse of, they detract not from the freedome, but adde to the honour of this resolution in him. As God had enabled him, so he accounted him meet not onely to be called, but to be compelled to this service: wherein his faithfull discharge was such as may make him justly a companion to the primitive saints, and a pattern or more for the Age he lived in.

To testifie his independencie upon all others, and to quicken his diligence in this kinde, he used in his ordinarie speech, when he made mention of the blessed name of our Lord and Saviour Jesus Christ, to adde 'My Master.'

Next God, he loved that which God himself hath magnified above all things, that is, his Word: so as he hath been heard to make solemne protestation, that he would not part with one leaf thereof for the whole world, if it were offered him in exchange.

His obedience and conformitie to the Church and the discipline thereof was singularly remarkable: though he abounded in private devotions, yet went he every morning and evening with his familie to the Church; and by his example, exhortations, and encouragements drew the greater part of his parishioners to accompanie him dayly in the public celebration of Divine Service.

As for worldly matters, his love and esteem to them was so little, as no man can more ambitiously seek then he did earnestly endeavour the resignation of an ecclesiastical dignitie, which he was possessour of. But God permitted not the accomplishment of this desire, having ordained him his instrument for re-edifying of the Church belonging thereunto, that had layen ruinated almost twenty years. The reparation whereof, having been uneffectually attempted by publick collections, was in the end by his own and some few others' private free-will offerings successfully effected. With the remembrance whereof, as of an especial good work, when a friend went about to comfort him on his death-bed, he made answer, 'It is a good work, if it be sprinkled with the bloud of Christ:' otherwise then in this respect he could finde nothing to glorie or comfort himself with, neither in this nor in any other thing.

And these are but a few of many that might be said, which we have chosen to premise as a glance to some parts of the ensuing book, and for an example to the Reader.

We conclude all with his own motto, with which he used to conclude all things that might seem to tend any way to his own honour,

Lesse than the least of God's mercies.

—NICHOLAS FERRAR, "The Printers to the Reader," *The Temple*, 1633

My brother George was so excellent a scholar, that he was made the public orator of the University of Cambridge; some of whose English works are extant; which, though they be rare in their kind, yet are far short of expressing those perfections he had in the Greek and Latin tongue, and all divine and human literature: his life was most holy and exemplary; insomuch, that about Salisbury, where he lived, beneficed for many years, he was little less than sainted. He was not exempt from passion and choler, being infirmities to which all our race is subject, but that excepted, without reproach in his actions.—EDWARD LORD HERBERT, *The Life of Edward Lord Herbert of Cherbury,* 1643

George Herbert was born at Montgomery castle, younger brother to Edward lord Herbert . . . ; bred fellow of Trinity College in Cambridge, and orator of the university, where he made a speech no less learned than the occasion was welcome, of the return of prince Charles out of Spain.

He was none of the nobles of Tekoa, who, at the building of Jerusalem, "put not their necks to the work of the Lord;" but, waving worldly preferment, chose serving at God's altar before state-employment. So pious his life, that, as he was a copy of primitive, he might be a pattern of sanctity to posterity. To testify his independency on all others, he never mentioned the name of Jesus Christ, but with this addition, "My Master." Next God the Word, he loved the Word of God; being heard often to protest, "That he would not part with one leaf thereof for the whole world."

Remarkable his conformity to Church discipline, whereby he drew the greater part of his parishioners to accompany him daily in the public celebration of Divine service. Yet had he (because not desiring) no higher preferment than the benefice of Bemerton nigh Salisbury (where he built a fair house for his successor); and the prebend of Leighton (founded in the cathedral of Lincoln) where he built a fair church, with the assistance of some few friends' free offerings. When a friend on

his deathbed went about to comfort him with the remembrance thereof, as an especial good work, he returned, "it is a good work, if sprinkled with the blood of Christ." But his "Church" (that inimitable piece of poetry) may out-last this in structure. His death happened anno Domini 163 . . .
—THOMAS FULLER, *The History of the Worthies of England,* 1662

In Brecknockshire, about 3 miles from Brecknock, is a village called Penkelly, where is a little Castle. It is an ancient Seate of the Herberts. Mr. Herbert, of this place, came, by the mother's side, of Wgan. The Lord Cherbery's ancestor came by the second venter, who was a Miller's daughter. The greatest part of the estate was settled on the issue by the 2d venter, viz. Montgomery castle, and Aberystwith. Upon this Match with the Miller's daughter are to this day recited, or sung, by the Welsh, verses to this sence:—*O God! Woe is me miserable, my father was Miller, and my mother a Milleresse, and I am now a Ladie.*

In a Buriall-place in the Church at Montgomery (belonging to the Castle) is a great freestone monument of Richard Herbert, Esq. (father to the learned Lord Herbert of Cherbery, and Mr. George Herbert, who wrote the Sacred Poëms) where are the effigies of him and Magdalene his wife, who afterwards was married to Sir John Danvers of Wilts, and lies interred at Chelsey church but without any monument. Dr. Donne, Dean of St. Paul's, preached her funerall sermon, to which are annexed severall verses, Latin and Greeke, by Mr. George Herbert, in Memorie of Her. She was buryed, as appears by the sermon, July 1, 1627.

Mr George Herbert was kinsman (remote) and Chapelaine to Philip, Earl of Pembroke and Montgomery, and Lord Chamberlayn. His Lordship gave him a Benefice at Bemmarton (between Wilton and Salisbury) a pittifull little chappell of Ease to Foughelston. The old house was very ruinous. Here he built a very handsome howse for the Minister, of Brick, and made a good garden and walkes. He lyes in the Chancell, under no large, nor yet very good, marble grave-stone, without any Inscription.

In the Chancell are many apt sentences of the Scripture. At his Wive's Seate, *My life is hid with Christ in God* (he hath verses on this Text in his Poëms). Above, in a little windowe-blinded, with a Veile (ill painted) *Thou art my hideing place.*

He maried Jane, the third daughter of Charles Danvers, of Bayntun, in com. Wilts, Esq. but had no issue by her. He was a very fine complexion and consumptive. His mariage, I suppose, hastened his death. My kinswoman was a handsome *bona roba* and ingeniose.

When he was first married he lived a yeare or better at Dantesey house. H. Allen, of Dantesey, was well acquainted with him, who has told me that he had a very good hand on the Lute, and that he sett his own Lyricks or sacred poems.

Scripsit:—Sacred Poems, called *The Church,* printed, Cambridge, 1633; a Booke entituled *The Country Parson,* not printed till about 1650, 8vo. He also writt a folio in Latin, which because the parson of Hineham could not read, his widowe (then wife to Sir Robert Cooke) condemned to the uses of good houswifry. (This account I had from Mr. Arnold Cooke, one of Sir Robert Cooke's sonnes, whom I desired to ask his mother-in-lawe for Mr. G. Herbert's MSS.)

He was buryed (according to his owne desire) with the singing service for the buriall of dead, by the singing men of Sarum. Francis Sambroke (attorney) then assisted as a Chorister boy; my uncle, Thomas Danvers, was at the Funerall.

'Tis an honour to the place, to have had the heavenly and

ingeniose contemplation of this good man, who was pious even
to prophesie; e.g.

> Religion now on tip-toe stands,
> Ready to goe to the American strands.
> —JOHN AUBREY, "George Herbert," *Brief Lives*,
> 1669–96

Mr. *Herbert's* Reputation is so firmly and so justly establish'd
among all Persons of *Piety* and *Ingenuity*, his Sense so good,
and most of his Poetry so fine, that those who Censure him will
be in more danger of having their Judgments question'd, than
such as with good reason Admire him. Nor can the Time he
writ in, when Poetry was not near so refin'd as 'tis now, be justly
objected against him, so as to make his Works of small or no
Value, any more than the *oddness* or *flatness* of some Expressions and Phrases, since something of these are to be found
in other Compositions that have yet appear'd in our Language;
and besides this, they were probably many of 'em made to
Tunes. Mr. *Herbert* being so great a Musitian, which every one
knows will often weaken the Sense. For *The Synagogue*, all
know 'tis none of his, tho' there are many fine Thoughts, and
not a few good Lines in't, carrying all thro' in an Air and Spirit
of great *Sense*, *Piety* and *Devotion*, much more Valuable than
all the foolish Wit that has so often directed the world at so dear
a Rate.—JOHN DUNTON, *Athenian Mercury*, Jan. 6, 1694

> Seraphic Singer! where's the fire
> That did these lines and lays inspire?
> B'ing dropt from heav'n, it scorn'd to dwell
> Long upon earth, and near to hell!
> The heart it purg'd, it did consume,
> Exhal'd the sacrifice in fume,
> And with it mounted, as of old
> The angel, in the smoke enroll'd;
> Return'd in haste, like thine own *Star*,
> Pleas'd with its prize, to native sphere.
> But blest perfume, that here I find,
> The sacrifice has left behind!
> Strange! how each fellow-saint's surpris'd
> To see himself anatomiz'd!
> The *Sion's* mourner breathes thy strains,
> Sighs thee, and in thy notes complains;
> Amaz'd, and yet refresh'd to see
> His wounds, drawn to the life, in thee!
> The warrior, just resolv'd to quit
> The field, and all the toils of it,
> Returns with vigour, will renew
> The fight, with victory in view;
> He stabbs his foes, and conquers harms,
> With spear, and nails, and *Herbert's* arms.
> The racer, almost out of breath,
> Marching through shades and vale of death.
> Recruits, when he to thee is come,
> And sighs for heav'n, and sings thy *Home;*
> The tempted soul, whose thoughts are whirl'd,
> About th' inchantments of the world,
> Can o'er the snares and scandals skip.
> Born up by *Frailty*, and the *Quip;*
> The victor has reward paid down,
> Has earnest here of life and crown;
> The conscious priest is well releas'd
> Of pain and fear, in *Aaron* drest;
> The preaching envoy can proclaim
> His pleasure in his *Master's* name;
> A name, that like the grace in him,
> Sends life and ease to ev'ry limb;

> Rich magazine of health! where's found
> Specific balm for ev'ry wound!
> Hail rev'rend bard! hail thou, th' elected shrine
> Of the great Sp'rit, and Shecinah divine!
> Who may speak thee! or aim at thy renown,
> In lines less venerable than thy own!
> Silent we must admire! upon no head
> Has, since thy flight, been half thy unction shed.
> What wit and grace thy lyric strains command!
> Hail, great apostle of the muses land!
> Scarce can I pardon the great *Cowley's* claim,
> He seems t' usurp the glories of thy fame;
> 'Tis *Herbert's* charms must chase (whate'er he boasts)
> The fiends and idols from poetic coasts;
> The *Mistress* the *Anacreontic* lays,
> More demons will, and more disorders raise,
> Than his fam'd hero's lyre, in modern play,
> Or tun'd by Cowley's self, I fear, can lay;
> 'Tis *Herbert's* notes must un-inchant the ear,
> Make the deaf adder, and th' old serpent hear.
>   Soon had religion, with a gracious smile,
> Vouchsaf'd to visit this selected isle;
> The *British* emp'ror first her liv'ry wore,
> And sacred cross with *Roman* eagles bore;
> The sev'ral states, at last, her empire own,
> And swear allegiance to her rightful throne;
> Only the muses lands abjure her sway,
> They heathen still, and unconverted lay,
> Loth was the prince of darkness to resign
> Such fertiliz'd dominions, and so fine,
> *Herbert* arose! and sounds the trumpet there,
> He makes the muses land the seat of war,
> The forts he takes, the squadrons does pursue,
> And with rich spoils erects a *Temple* too;
> A structure, that shall roofs of gold survive,
> Shall *Solomonic* and *Mosaic* work out-live,
> Shall stay to see the universal fire.
> And only, with the temple of the world, expire.
>   Strange, the late bard should his devotion rear
> At *Synagogue* when, lo! the *Temple's* near!
> Such sacrilege it were of old, t' espouse
> The wandring tent, before the wondrous house;
> The house, in which a southern queen might be
> A sacrifice to art and ecstasie.
> Poor poets thus ingeniously can prove
> Their sacred zeal misguided as their love!
>   Go forth, saint-bard! exert thy conqu'ring hand!
> Set up thy Temple through the muses land!
> Down with the stage, its wanton scenes cashier,
> And all the demons wont to revel there!
> Great *Pan* must dy, his oracles be dumb,
> Where'er thy temple and its flames shall come;
> Convert the *Muses*, teach them how to be
> Ambitious of the *Graces* companie;
> Purge *Helicon*, and make *Parnassus* still
> To send his vicious streams to *Sion's* hill!
> Thence banish all th' unhallow'd, tuneful men,
> From *Homer*, down to the phantastic *Ben!*
> Baptize the future poets, and infuse
> A sacred flame in all belov'd by muse!
> Teach them the efforts of great *Shiloh's* love,
> The anthems, and the melodies above!
> Tell them what matter, and what theam's in store,
> For sacred past'ral, and divine amour;
> *Shiloh* himself would condescend so low,

To be a shepherd, and a bridegroom too.
What myst'ries in church militant there to,
Teach them to look, and soar, and sing like thee.
Here poesy's high birth, and glory shine,
'Tis here, that it, like other grace, we see
From glory differs only in degree!
    Whilst to thy temple proselytes repair,
And offer, and inflame devotion there.
Whilst, on its pillars deep inscrib'd, thy name
Stands consecrated to immortal fame,
Do thou enjoy the rich resolves of *Love*,
The pleasures, the society above!
No more thou'lt tune thy lute unto a strain
That may with thee all day complain;
No more shall sense of ill, and *Griefs* of time
Dis-tune thy viol, and disturb thy rhyme;
No more shall *Sion's* wrongs and sorrows sharp,
Upon the willows hang thy trembling harp;
The wish'd-for sight, the dear perfection's gain'd
The *Longing*, and the *Search*, have now obtain'd;
On Sion's mount, join thou the blisful throng,
That here were skill'd in sacred love and song;
Consort with *Heman*, *Asaph*, and the rest,
Akin to thee, in Temple-service blest;
Who all rejoyce thy lov'd access to see,
And ply their harps, no doubt, to welcome thee;
Music and Love triumph! and *Herbert's* lyre,
Serenely sounds amidst th' harmonious quire!
There still, on *Love* in his own person, gaze,
Drink in the beams flow from his radiant face,
Still to thy harp chant forth th' immortal verse
Does *Love's* exploits in foreign land rehearse,
Move him to hasten his return below,
That church, now mil'tant, may triumphant grow,
And all thy pros'lyte-bands may mount, and see
The Temple there, and all the scenes of joy, with thee.
              —JOHN REYNOLDS, "To the Memory of the Di-
                  vine Mr. Herbert," A *View of Death*, 1725, pp.
                  110–18

"Life," it has been said, "is a Poem." This is true, probably, of the life of the human race as a whole, if we could see its beginning and end, as well as its middle. But it is not true of all lives. It is only a life here and there, which equals the dignity and aspires to the completeness of a genuine and great Poem. Most lives are fragmentary, even when they are not foul—they disappoint, even when they do not disgust—they are volumes without a preface, an index, or a moral. It is delightful to turn from such apologies for life to the rare but real lives which God-gifted men, like Milton or Herbert, have been enabled to spend even on this dark and melancholy foot-breadth for immortal spirits, called the earth.

    We class Milton and Herbert together, for this, among other reasons, that in both, the life and the poems were thoroughly correspondent and commensurate with each other. Milton lived the *Paradise Lost* and the *Paradise Regained*, as well as wrote them. Herbert was, as well as built, *The Temple*. Not only did the intellectual archetype of its structure exist in his mind, but he had been able, in a great measure, to realise it in life, before expressing it in poetry. His piety was of a more evangelical cast than Milton's—his purity was tenderer and lovelier—he had more of the Christian, and less of the Jew. Milton ranks with the austere and sin-denouncing prophets of ancient Israel—Herbert reminds us of that "disciple whom Jesus loved."—GEORGE GILFILLAN, "On the Life and Poetical

Works of George Herbert," *The Poetical Works of George Herbert*, 1854, pp. v–vi

General

⟨Herbert's⟩ holy *life* and *verse* gained many pious *Converts*, (of whom I am the least) and gave the first check to a most flourishing and admired *wit* of his time. After him followed diverse,—*Sed non passibus æquis*; they had more of *fashion*, then *force*: and the *reason* of their so vast *distance* from him, besides differing *spirits* and *qualifications* (for his *measure* was eminent) I suspect to be, because they aimed more at *verse*, then *perfection*; as may be easily gathered by their frequent *impressions*, and numerous *pages*: Hence sprang those wide, those weak, and lean *conceptions*, which in the most inclinable *Reader* will scarce give any nourishment or help to *devotion*; for not flowing from a true, practick piety, it was impossible they should effect those things abroad, which they never had acquaintance with at home; being onely the productions of a common spirit, and the obvious ebullitions of that light humor, which takes the pen in hand, out of no other consideration, then to be seen in print. It is true indeed, that to give up our thoughts to pious *Themes* and *Contemplations* (if it be done for pieties sake) is a great *step* towards *perfection*; because it will *refine*, and *dispose* to devotion and sanctity. And further, it will *procure* for us (so easily communicable is that *loving spirit*) some small *prelibation* of those heavenly *refreshments*, which descend but seldom, and then very sparingly, upon *men* of an ordinary or indifferent *holyness*; but he that desires to excel in this kinde of *Hagiography*, or holy writing, must strive (by all means) for *perfection* and true *holyness*, that a *door may be opened to him in heaven*, Rev. 4. 1. and then he will be able to write (with *Hierotheus* and holy *Herbert*) A *true Hymn*.
—HENRY VAUGHAN, "Preface" to *Silex Scintillans* (1654), 1655

George Herbert, a younger brother of the noble family of *Herberts of Montgomery*, whose florid wit, obliging humour in conversation, fluent eloquence, and great proficience in the Arts gained him that reputation at Oxford, where he spent his more youthful age, that he was chosen University Orator. At last, taking upon him Holy Orders, not without special encouragement from the King, who took notice of his parts, he was made parson of *Bemerton* near Salisbury. In this state his affection to poetry being converted to serious and divine subjects, produced those so generally known and approved poems, entitled *The Temple*.—EDWARD PHILLIPS, *Theatrum Poetarum Anglicanorum*, 1675

But I must confess, after all, that, next the Scripture Poems, there are none so savoury to me as Mr. George Herbert's and Mr. George Sandys'. I know that Cowley and others far exceed Herbert in wit and accurate composure; but as Seneca takes with me above all his contemporaries, because he speaketh things by words, feelingly and seriously, like a man that is past jest; so Herbert speaks to God like one that really believeth a God, and whose business in the world is most with God. Heart-work and Heaven-work make up his books.—RICHARD BAXTER, "Prefatory Address" to *Poetical Fragments*, 1681

Mr. Herbert's *Poems* have met with so general and deserv'd Acceptance, that they have undergone Eleven Impressions near Twenty Years ago: He hath obtain'd by way of Eminency, the Name of *Our Divine Poet*, and his Verses have been frequently quoted in Sermons and other Discourses; yet, I fear, few of them have been Sung since his Death, the Tunes not being at the Command of ordinary Readers.

This attempt therefore, (such as it is) is to bring so many of them as I well could, which I judg'd suited to the Capacity and Devotion of Private Christians, into the *Common Metre* to be Sung in their Closets or Families: The like I have done as to some of the New Testament Hymns in Dr. *Woodford's Paraphrase*: To all which I have added one *Ode* in the same Measures in which I had it, because I think it was never Printed, and I thought it Pity, it should be lost in a Private Hand. I hope I shall not be counted a *Plagiary*, seeing I claim nothing here as my own, but what they allow me, *viz.* a Liberty to Sing and use their Hymns, which I was no more able to do in their *Metre* and *Tunes*, than I was able to compose them as they did.

Nor will this hinder *their* use of the Lyrick Measures of *Herbert* and others, who are enabled to do it by their skill in Musick, which they ought to look upon as a Talent to be accounted for. How much more fit is *Herbert's Temple* to be set to the Lute, than *Cowley's Mistress*! It is hard that no one can be taught Musick, but in such wanton Songs as fill the Hearts of many Learners with Lust and Vanity all their Days. Why should it be thought a greater Prophaning of Spiritual Songs to use them in a Musick School, than it is of the New Testament, to teach Children to spell; yet what Christian would not rather have his Child taught to read in a Bible than in a Play-Book? Especially, when they who learn Musick are generally more apt to receive Impressions from the Matter of the Song, than Children are from the Books in which they first learn to Spell. My attempt hath been easie, only to alter the measures of some Hymns, keeping strictly to the Sence of the Author; but how noble an undertaking were it, if any one could and would rescue the high flights, and lofty strains found in the most Celebrated poets, from their sacrilegious Applications to *Carnal Love*, and restore them to the *Divine Love*! When the Devil drew off the Nations from the True God, He caus'd the same Institutions with which God was honoured, to be used in the Idol Service, *Temple, Priests, Sacrifices*, &c. and amongst the rest *Psalmody*: And it is strange, that when we have so long been emerg'd out of Heathenism, that such a Remnant of it should be amongst us, wherein the most devotional Part of Religion doth consist.

Almost all Phrases and Expressions of Worship due only to God, are continu'd in these artificial Composures in the Heathenish use of them, even from the *inspirations* that they invoke in their beginning, to the *Raptures, Flames, Adorations*, &c. That they pretend to in the Progress: Nor are these meer empty Names with them, but their Hearts are more feverently carried out in the musical life of them, than they would be if their Knees were bow'd to *Baal* and *Astaroth*: Few Holy Souls are more affected with the praise's of a Redeemer, than they are of the wanton Object that they profess to adore. Oh for some to write *Parodies*, by which Name I find one Poem in *Herbert* call'd, which begins, *Souls Joy, where art thou gone*, and was, I doubt not, a light Lovesong turn'd into a Spiritual Hymn. παρῳδία, *Est quum alterius Poetæ Versus in aliud Argumentum transferuntur*. I do not find it hath been made a Matter of scruple to turn the Temples built for Idols into Churches: And as to this Case, it is to be consider'd, that the Musick and Poetry was an excellent Gift of God, which ought to have been us'd for Him; and that their high strains of Love, Joy, &c. Suit none but the adorable Saviour; and all their most warm and affecting Expressions are stollen from the Churches Adoration of Christ; and who can doubt but the Church may take her own, wherever she finds it, whether in an Idolatrous Mass-Book or Prophane Love-Song? It was a noble Resolution of him that said,

I'll Consecrate my *Magdalene* to Thee—

The *Eyes, Mouth, Hair*, which had been abus'd to Lust and Vanity were us'd to *Wash, Kiss, Wipe* the Feet of a Saviour: May Men and Angels Praise him for ever and ever! Amen.
—UNSIGNED, "Preface" to *Select Hymns Taken out of Mr. Herbert's Temple*, 1697

Another poet in that age was George Herbert, the author of the *Temple* a little book of Divine songs and poems which ought to be on the shelf of every lover of religion and poetry. It is a book which is apt to repel the reader on his first acquaintance. It is written in the quaint epigrammatic style which was for a short time in vogue in England, a style chiefly marked by the elaborate decomposition to which every object is subjected. The writer is not content with the obvious properties of natural objects but delights in discovering abstruser relations between them and the subject of his thought. This both by Cowley and Donne is pushed to affectation. By Herbert it is used with greater temperance and to such excellent ends that it is easily forgiven if indeed it do not come to be loved.

It has been justly said of Herbert that if his thought is often recondite and far fetched yet the language is always simple and chaste. I should cite Herbert as a striking example of the power of exalted thought to melt and bend language to its fit expression. Language is an organ on which men play with unequal skill and each man with different skill at different hours. The man who stammers when he is afraid or when he is indifferent, will be fluent when he is angry, and eloquent when his intellect is active. Some writers are of that frigid temperament that their sentences always seem to be made with grammar and dictionary. To such the easy structure of prose is laborious, and metre and rhyme, and especially any difficult metre is an insurmountable bar to the expression of their meaning. Of these Byron says,

Prose poets like blank verse
Good workmen never quarrel with their tools.

Those on the contrary who were born to write, have a self-enkindling power of thought which never knows this obstruction but find words so rapidly that they seem coeval with the thought. And in general according to the elevation of the soul will be the power over language and lively thoughts will break out into spritely verse. No metre so difficult but will be tractable so that you only raise the temperature of the thought.

"For my part," says Montaigne, "I hold and Socrates is positive in it, that whoever has in his mind a lively and clear imagination, he will express it well enough in one kind or another and though he were dumb by signs." . . .

What Herbert most excels in is in exciting that feeling which we call the moral sublime. The highest affections are touched by his muse. I know nothing finer than the turn with which his poem on affliction concludes. After complaining to his maker as if too much suffering had been put upon him he threatens that he will quit God's service for the world's:

Well, I will change the service and go seek
    Some other master out
Ah, my dear God, though I be clean forgot
Let me not love thee if I love thee not.

Herbert's Poems are the breathings of a devout soul reading the riddle of the world with a poet's eye but with a saint's affections. Here poetry is turned to its noblest use. The sentiments are so exalted, the thought so wise, the piety so sincere that we cannot read this book without joy that our nature is capable of such emotions and criticism is silent in the exercise of higher faculties. —RALPH WALDO EMERSON, "Ben Jonson, Herrick, Herbert, Wotton" (c. 1835), *The Early Lectures of*

Ralph Waldo Emerson, eds. Stephen E. Whicher, Robert E. Spiller, 1959, Vol. 1, pp. 349–53

Now the imagination of George Herbert is just as vigourous ⟨as Bunyan's⟩, and his communings with God as immediate, but they are the imagination & the communings of a well bridled & disciplined mind, and therefore though he feels himself to have sold Christ over & over again for definite pieces of silver, for pleasures or promises of this world, he repents and does penance for such actual sin—he does not plague himself about a singing in his ears. There is as much difference between the writings & feelings of the two men as between the high bred, keen, severe, thoughtful countenance of the one—and the fat, vacant, vulgar, boy's *face* of the other. Both are equally Christians, equally taught of God, but taught through different channels, Herbert through his brains, Bunyan through his liver.—JOHN RUSKIN, Letter to Margaret Cock Ruskin (April 13, 1845)

I have been more and more struck on rethinking and re-reading with the singular differences between Bunyan & Herbert. Bunyan humble & contrite enough, but always dwelling painfully & exclusively on the relations of the deity to his own little self—not contemplating God as the God of all the earth, nor loving him as such, nor so occupied with the consideration of his attributes as to forget himself in an extended gratitude, but always looking to his own interests & his own state—loving or fearing or doubting, just as *he* happened to fancy God was dealing with him. Herbert on the contrary, full of faith & love, regardless of himself, outpouring his affection in all circumstances & at all times, and never *fearing*, though often weeping. Hear him speaking of such changes of feeling as Bunyan complains of:

> Whether I fly with angels, fall with dust,
> Thy hands made both, & I am there.
> Thy power & love, my love & trust
> Make one place everywhere.

> —JOHN RUSKIN, Letter to Margaret Cock Ruskin (April 20, 1845)

Herbert is the psalmist dear to all who love religious poetry with exquisite refinement of thought. So much piety was never married to so much wit. Herbert identifies himself with Jewish genius, as Michael Angelo did when carving or painting prophets and patriarchs, not merely old men in robes and beards, but with the sanctity and the character of the Pentateuch and the prophecy conspicuous in them. His wit and his piety are genuine, and are sure to make a lifelong friend of a good reader.— RALPH WALDO EMERSON, "Preface" to *Parnassus*, 1875, p. vi

The sacred poetry of Sandys was the dignified amusement of the evening of a successful life, whose morn had been spent in eastern travel and in colonial enterprise, without a trace of the internal struggles which form the staple of the poetry of Herbert. *The Temple* is the enigmatical history of a difficult resignation; it is full of the author's baffled ambition and his distress, now at the want of a sphere for his energies, now at the fluctuations of spirit, the ebb and flow of intellectual activity, natural to a temperament as frail as it was eager. There is something a little feverish and disproportioned in his passionate heart-searchings. . . . The flower of his poetry seems to belong to the two years of acute crisis which preceded his installation at Bemerton or to the Indian summer of content when he imagined that his failure as a courtier was a prelude to his success in the higher character of a country parson. The well-known poem on Sunday, which he sang to his lute so near the end, and the quaint poem on the ideal priest, which we extract, may

date from Bemerton. The Quip and The Collar may date from the years of crisis. Still, much, like the poems on Employment, of which we insert a specimen, dates from the years of hopeful ambition. There are no traces of consecration or defeat in the 'Church Porch,' where Herbert, like a precocious Polonius, frames a rule of life for himself and other pious courtiers. Herbert, who had thought much of national destiny, and decided that religion and true prosperity were to take flight for America, considered that England was 'full of sin, but most of sloth.'—G. A. SIMCOX, "Sandys, Herbert, Crashaw, Vaughan," *The English Poets*, ed. Thomas Humphry Ward, 1880, Vol. 2, pp. 193–94

Herbert's poetry, though smacking of the country, is not that of one intoxicated by the beauty of external nature; it is always the poetry of reflection and of reading. George Herbert was emphatically a scholar and a gentleman. The amusement of his leisure was to write fluent Greek and Latin as well as English verse. He was fastidious to an extreme both in his personal tastes and in his dress; he held himself aloof from the common herd of students at Cambridge, and shrank from coarseness and impurity in every shape. In point of date he belongs almost to the Renaissance; yet how different his tone! *The Temple* was published, posthumously, in 1633; Milton's *Comus*, in which the foul myth of Comus and the stores of classical fable and allusion are transfused into a drama of almost heavenly purity, appeared in 1638. Scarcely later, Jeremy Taylor was writing his *Holy Living and Dying*, in the notes to which, in strange contrast to the objects of his text, he cites obscene passages from Martial and Juvenal and Ovid; and the Discourse on a Christian's Death is illustrated by a tale worthy of Boccaccio or of the Heptameron. Yet in the poems of Herbert, a scholar equal to these, scarcely one classical allusion is to be found. Barnabas Oley, indeed, says: "He that reads Mr. Herbert's poems attendingly shall find the excellence of Scripture Divinity and choice passages of the Fathers bound up in metre." This is partly true, especially as to the Scripture; but Herbert's poetry is not Biblical as is Bunyan's allegory; and none of it recals the Fathers, as Isaac Barrow, for instance, in the style, if not in the matter, of his sermons, reminds us of St. Chrysostom. It is to another literature that we must look for much that is peculiar to George Herbert; and this will not only account for many of his faults, but will explain by what side of his character this scholar and gentleman was attracted to country life, and could find contentment in the talk and ways of villagers.

The writings to which we allude are those of the moralists of the silver age or later, pagans of the decline, or, at best, but demi-Christians, whose works seem to us so trite and dull, but on which our forefathers, unspoiled by excitement, and not yet exigent in literary style, ruminated with a quiet delight such as we seldom feel. It is from the writings of these authors in many cases that they formed the proverbs which they esteemed as the highest axioms of practical wisdom, and which George Herbert has treasured so fondly in his *Jacula Prudentum*. The chief of these writers were perhaps Seneca, Plutarch, Boethius, but, above all, the little Pseudo-Cato. Cato's *Distichs de Moribus* are now almost wholly forgotten, yet of this book more than fifty editions were published before the end of the fifteenth century; Caxton printed it in 1483. Erasmus edited it and enriched it with a copious commentary. A copy before us, edited by N. Baily (London, 1757), almost on the Hamiltonian system, and reproducing the comments of Erasmus, shows how long it kept its ground as a schoolbook. A polyglot edition, with translations into five languages appeared in Amsterdam in 1769. It was paraphrased or imitated in nearly every idiom of

Southern Europe, and it became almost the Bible of the peasant, reflecting, as these paraphrases do, with wonderful accuracy the better, but still harsh and intensely narrow, side of peasant character. No book has been more diversely judged. Cervantes intentionally misquotes it in the Prologo to *Don Quixote.* Sancho Panza has it often in his mouth, but dubs the author "Cato el zonzorino romano," the Roman dullard. Dibdin says, "Dulness can hardly be heavier than are the pages of its text." Yet if we compare the structure of "The Church Porch," the best sustained of all Herbert's poems, with imitations of the lesser Cato, we can hardly doubt that we have here the key to much that distinguishes him so widely from other classical scholars of his age. Compare, e.g., Herbert's first verse with that of the Béarnais imitation and with the opening lines of books iii. and iv. of the *Distichs,* and we cannot hesitate about the relationship.

> Thou whose sweet youth and early hopes inhance
> Thy rate and price, and mark thee for a treasure;
> Hearken unto a Verser, who may chance
> Rhyme thee to good, and make a bait of pleasure,
>   A verse may find him, who a sermon flies
>   And turn delight into a sacrifice.

> Hoc quicumque voles carmen cognoscere, Lector,
> Haec precepta feres, quae sunt gratissima vitae,
> Instrue praeceptis animum, nec discere cesses:
> Nam sine doctrina vita est quasi mortis imago.
> Commoda multa feres; sin autem sprevaris illyd,
> Non me scriptorem, sed te neglereris ipse.

>   Si bos sabé quaüque petit passatye
> Per te maintiene en tout temps san et net
> Escoute, amic, lou petit Catounet,
> Qué pots, dab eth, ha toun apprentissatye.
>
>   (*Lou Catounet Gascoun,*
>   G. Ader [Tolose, 1611])

The thoughts run on in exactly parallel lines. "The Church Porch" gives only rules for conduct; we are not yet in *The Temple,* we catch only from a distance the sweetness of its mystic melody, and are not yet moved to full ecstasy. Even there, as Mr. Shorthouse observes, Herbert cannot sustain his flights; and this comes, we think, from the favourite studies above alluded to, from his habit of thinking in proverbs and sentences. Who but one steeped to the lips in such literature could conclude the exquisite poem on "Vertue" thus?—

> Onely a sweet and vertuous soul,
> Like season'd timber, never gives;
> But though the whole world turn to coal,
>   Then chiefly lives.

It would take too long to discuss here how far Herbert was acquainted with Spanish and Italian literature, and his undoubted relationship to them as a poet. (His friend Ferrar translated Valdesso.) Many of his worst conceits and vices of form come thence. This we must leave to those who have access to richer libraries. That, in common with every schoolboy of that age, he knew his *Cato,* cannot be doubted; and that it, more than either Homer or Virgil influenced his English verse is also, we believe, a fact.—WENTWORTH WEBSTER, *Academy,* July 8, 1882, pp. 22–23

Herbert . . . is the type of the maker of conceits. Full of delicate ingenuity, he applies the tortured methods of Donne to spiritual experience, gaining more lucidity than his master at the expense of a good deal of intensity. But Herbert also, in his own field, was a courtier, like the lyrists of the Flesh, and he is close to Suckling and the other Royalists in the essential temper of his style. He was himself a leader to certain religious writers

of the next generation, whose place is at the close of this chapter.

The *Temple* is by far the best-known book of verses of the whole school, and it deserves, if hardly that pre-eminence, yet all its popularity. Herbert has an extraordinary tenderness, and it is his singular privilege to have been able to clothe the common aspirations, fears, and needs of the religious mind in language more truly poetical than any other Englishman. He is often extravagant, but rarely dull or flat; his greatest fault lay in an excessive pseudo-psychological ingenuity, which was a snare to all these lyrists, and in a tasteless delight in metrical innovations, often as ugly as they were unprecedented. He sank to writing in the shape of wings and pillars and altars.
—EDMUND GOSSE, *A Short History of Modern English Literature,* 1897, p. 147

An infinitely more popular poet than Crashaw, and certainly a more equable, though at the best of both Crashaw towers over him, was George Herbert, a member of the noble Norman-Welsh family of that name, and brother of Lord Herbert of Cherbury. He was born at Montgomery Castle on 13th April 1593, went to Cambridge, became Fellow of Trinity in 1615, and Public Orator four years later, at the early age of twenty-six. He held the place for eight years with great distinction, though he was charged with the fault of haughtiness, and seems to have looked forward to a political career. But something led him to the course of saintly life as a country clergyman, latterly at Bemerton, near Salisbury, which he pursued for six years, till his early death in 1632. His verse (almost entirely included in the well-known collection called *The Temple,* which made Crashaw call his *Steps to the Temple*) was not published till after his death, but very soon after, for though the date of the first edition is 1633, there are undated copies which seem to have been distributed in the previous year. *The Temple* consists of 160 pieces, arranged partly with a fancy of reference to the structural arrangement of a church, beginning with "The Porch"; partly under the heads of the great festivals and services; often under quite fantastic titles, "The Quip," "The Pulley," and so forth. There is no prevailing metre—couplets, stanzas, and regular and irregular lyrical forms being chosen as may best suit the poet's purpose, while occasionally he will even condescend, as in "Easter Wings," to that device of adjusting his verse lengths to artificial patterns which excited almost more horror than ridicule in the eighteenth century.

And the note of fantasy is at least as much present in idea and in diction, though Herbert seldom pushes either to very extravagant lengths. In the "Church Porch," which is a string of ethical and religious maxims, this fantasy does not often pass beyond the almost proverbial imagery to which we are accustomed in such connections. But in the more abstract and doctrinal poems Herbert gives himself a much wider range, and ransacks art and nature for quaint similes, sometimes worked out in the fashion of the emblem-poetry then so popular. The Game of Bowls; the real or fancied properties of the orange tree; the Palace of the World, with Wisdom sweeping away its cobwebs, Pleasure adorning it with balconies, Sin splitting the walls with stealthy fig-tree growth, Grace shoring them, and Death throwing them down; the imaginary peculiarities of the crocodile and elephant—Herbert presses all these and a myriad more into his service. Yet the unaffected piety, and perhaps still more the perfect charity, of his tone, his abstinence from anything like strife and crying, the heavenly peace that pervades him, have made his work tolerated by many who are not as a rule very tolerant of conceits.

As a poet he is certainly not the equal of either Crashaw or Vaughan, and in his own quiet fashion has in the present century been equalled by Keble and surpassed by Miss Christina Rossetti. He very seldom transports: the throb of response to the highest and happiest thoughts and expressions of the poets is very uncommon in reading him; his is an equable merit, a soothing and heathful pleasure, rather than the dazzling excellence, the contagious rapture of the great ones. But he can never be mentioned with contempt by any one who loves poetry, and he undoubtedly holds a high place among those who have attempted the exceedingly difficult task of sacred verse. If his successes are never so great as those of some others, it is hardly too much to say that he never fails with the maddening failure too common in religious poets, and this is in itself a great thing.—GEORGE SAINTSBURY, *A Short History of English Literature*, 1898, pp. 414–16

Works

Haile Sacred Architect
Thou doest a glorious Temple raise
    stil ecchoinge his praise.
who taught thy genius thus to florish it
with curious gravings of a Peircinge witt.
    Statelye thy Pillers bee,
Westwards the Crosse, the Quier, and
    thine Alter Eastward stande,
where Is most Catholique Conformitie
with out a nose-twange spoylinge harmonie.
    Resolve to Sinne noe more,
from hence a penitent sigh, and groane
    cann flintye heartes unstone;
and blowe them to their happy porte heaven's doore.
where Herberts Angell's flowen away before.
        —JOHN POLWHELE, "On Mr. Herberts Devine
          Poeme *The Church*," c. 1633

What Church is this? Christs Church. Who builds it?
Mr. *George Herbert*. Who assisted it?
Many assisted: who, I may not say,
So much contention might arise that way.
If I say Grace gave all, Wit straight doth thwart,
And sayes all that is there is mine: but Art
Denies and sayes ther's nothing there but's mine:
Nor can I easily the right define.
Divide: say, Grace the matter gave, and Wit
Did polish it, Art measured and made fit
Each severall piece, and fram'd it all together.
No, by no means: this may not please them neither.
None's well contented with a part alone,
When each doth challenge all to be his owne:
The matter, the expressions, and the measures,
Are eqyally Arts, Wits, and Graces treasures.
Then he that would impartially dicusse
This doubtfull question, must answer thus:
In building of this temple Mr. *Herbert*
Is equally all Grace, all Wit, all Art.
    Roman and *Grecian* Muses all give way:
    One *English* Poem darkens all your day.
        —CHRISTOPHER HARVEY, "The Synagogue,"
          1640

Know you faire, on what you looke?
Divinest love lyes in this booke:
Expecting fire from your eyes,
To kindle this his sacrifice.
When your hands unty these strings,
Thinke you have an Angell by th' wings.

One that gladly will bee nigh,
To wait upon each morning sigh.
To flutter in the balmy aire,
Of your well perfumed prayer.
These white plumes of his heele lend you,
Which every day to heaven will send you:
To take acquaintance of the spheare,
And all the smooth faced kindred there.
    And though *Herberts* name doe owe
    These devotions, fairest; know
    That while I lay them on the shrine
    Of your white hand, they are mine.
        —RICHARD CRASHAW, "On Mr. G. *Herberts*
          Booke Intituled *The Temple or Sacred Poems,*
          Sent to a Gentlewoman," *Steps to the Temple,*
          1646

    Lord! yet how dull am I?
      When I would flye!
Up to the Region, of thy Glories where
    Onlie true formes appeare;
My long brail'd Pineons, (clumsye, and unapt)
      I cannot Spread;
    I am all dullnes; I was Shap't
Only to flutter, in the lower Shrubbs
    Of Earth-borne-follies. Out alas!
      When I would treade
A higher Step, ten thousand, thousand Rubbs
      Prevent my Pace.
This Glorious Larke; with humble Honour. I
      Admire and praise;
      But when I raise
My Selfe, I fall asham'd, to see him flye:
The Royall Prophet, in his Extasie,
      First trod this path;
Hee followes neare; (I will not Say, how nigh)
    In flight, as well as faith.
Let me asham'd creepe backe into my Shell;
    And humbly Listen to his Layes:
Tis prejudice, what I intended Praise;
As where they fall soe Lowe, all Words are Still.
    Our Untun'd Liricks, onlie fitt
      To Sing, our Selfe-borne-Cares,
    Dare not, of Him. Or had wee Witt,
      Where might wee find out Ears
Worthy his Character? if wee may bring
      Our Accent to his Name?
This Stand, of Lirick's, Hee the utmost Fame
Has gain'd; and now they vaile, to heare Him Sing
Horace in voice; and Casimire in winge.
        —GEORGE DANIEL, "An Ode upon the Incom-
          parable Liricke Poesie Written by Mr George
          Herbert, Intituled, *The Temple*," 1648

I

So long had Poetry possessed been
By Pagans, that a Right in her they claim'd,

  Pleaded Prescription for their Sin,
And Laws they made, and Arguments they fram'd,
Nor thought it Wit, if God therein was nam'd:
The true GOD; for of false ones they had store,
  Whom Devils we may better call,
  And ev'ry thing they deifi'd,
And to a Stone, Arise and help they cri'd.
  And Woman-kind they fell before;

Ev'n Woman-kind, which caus'd at first their Fall,
Were almost the sole Subject of their pen,
And the chief Deities ador'd by fond and sottish Men.

II

    Herbert at last arose,
    Herbert inspir'd with holy Zeal,
Their Arguments he solv'd, their Laws he did repeal,
    And Spight of all th'enraged Foes
That with their utmost Malice did oppose,
He rescu'd the poor Captive, Poetry,
Whole her vile Masters had before decreed
All her immortal Spirit to employ
    In painting out the Lip or Eye
Of some fantastick Dame, whose Pride Incentives did not
    need.
This mighty *Herbert* could not brook;
It griev'd his pious Soul to see
    The best and noblest Gift,
    That God to Man has left,
Abus'd to serve vile Lust, and sordid Flattery:
So, glorious Arms in her Defence he took;
And when with great Success he'd set her free,
He rais'd her fancy on a stronger Wing,
Taught her of God above, and Things Divine to sing.

III

Th' infernal Powers that held her fast before
And great Advantage of their Pris'ner made,
    And drove of Souls a gainful Trade,
    Began to mutiny and roar.
So when *Demetrius* and his Partners view'd
Their Goddess, and with her, their dearer Gains to fall,
They draw together a confus'd Multitude,
    And into th' Theater they crowd,
And great *Diana*, great, they loudly call.
    Up into th' Air their Voices flie,
    Some one thing, some another crie,
    And most of them they know not why.
They crie aloud, 'till the Earth ring again,
    Aloud they crie; but all in vain.
Diana down must go; They can no more
Their sinking Idol help, than she could them before.
Down she must go with all her Pomp and Train:
The glorious Gospel-Sun her horned Pride doth stain,
No more to be renew'd, but ever in the Wane;
And Poetry, now grown Divine above must ever reign.

IV

    A Mon'ment of this Victory
Our *David*, our Sweet Psalmist, rais'd on high,
When he this Giant under foot did tread,
And with Verse, his own Sword, cut off the Monster's Head.
For as a Sling and Heav'n-directed Stone
Laid flat the *Gathite* Champion, who alone
Made Thousands tremble, while he proudly stood
Bidding Defiance to the Hosts of God:
So fell th' infernal Pow'rs before the Face
Of mighty *Herbert*, who upon the Place
    A Temple built, that does outdo
    Both *Solomon's*, and Herod's too,
And all the Temples of the Gods by far;
So costly the Materials, and the Workmanship so rare
A Temple built, as God did once ordain
    Without the Saw's harsh Noise
Or the untuneful Hammer's Voice,

But built with sacred Musick's sweetest strain,
Like *Theban* Walls of old, as witty Poets feign.

V

Hail, heav'nly Bard, to whom great LOVE has giv'n
    (His mighty Kindness to express)
To bear his Three mysterious Offices;
Prophet, and Priest on Earth thou wast, and now a King in
    Heav'n.
    There thou dost reign, and there
    Thy Bus'ness is the same 'twas here,
And thine old Songs thou singest o'er agen:
    The Angels and the Heav'nly Quire
    Gaze on thee, and admire
To hear such Anthems from an earthly Lyre,
Their own Hymns almost equall'd by an human Pen.
    We foolish Poets hope in vain
    Our Works Eternity shall gain;
    But sure those Poems needs must die
    Whose Theme is but Mortality.
Thy wiser and more noble Muse
    The best, the only way did chuse
To grow Immortal: For what Chance can wrong,
    What Teeth of Time devour that Song
Which to a Heav'nly Tune is set for glorifi'd Saints to use?
O may some Portion of thy Spirit on me
(Thy poor Admirer) light, whose Breast
By wretched mortal Loves hath been too long
    possest!
When, Oh! when will the joyful Day arise
    That rescu'd from these Vanities,
    These painted Follies I shall be,
If not an inspir'd Poet, yet an holy Priest like thee.

> —DANIEL BAKER, "On Mr. George Herbert's Sacred Poems, called, *The Temple*," *Poems upon Several Occasions*, 1697, pp. 83–89

The Countrey Parson is full from end to end of a sweet reasonableness, which has proved very attractive to a Church that makes much of the duty of private judgement. Herbert does not lay down the law, he is content to convince and persuade; and so he is careful to give reasons for what counsel he has to offer. For example, he defends the use of the Fathers and Commentators in the interpretation of Scripture against those who rely solely on the Inner Light, by the analogy of commerce: "As one country doth not bear all things, that there may be commerce, so neither hath God opened or will open all to one, that there may be a traffick in knowledge" (ch. IV.). He defends casuistry by the analogy of the shepherd's knowledge of poisonous grasses, and by the common sense question, How without it can you tell what is covetousness or gluttony (ch. XXVI.), or detraction (ch. XXXVII.)? He censures the "crumbling" of a text in preaching by the pithy saying that the "words apart are not Scripture, but a dictionary" (ch. VII.). Moreover the counsel he offers is in itself reasonable; while in points of principle he is inflexible, he is careful not to bind upon the backs of either clergy or laity burdens that will prove too heavy for them. A very good example of his moderation is offered by the chapter on Fasting. He begins by laying it down that fasting is obligatory, and admits that by authority fasting is to take a particular form, namely, abstinence from flesh; but he points out that this is after all only a particular application of a general rule, and an application which "came from hot Countreys . . . where flesh can be better spared"; and that therefore for most students, for the "sickly" as well as the "sick," fasting "should consist in eating less, or what is less pleasing, than in eating fish." Perhaps occasionally he carries the tendency to philosophise a little far, as when he finds a reason in the nature of things for the parson's keeping pigs and poultry (ch. X.). Perhaps occasionally also he elaborates what, even to country parsons, is pretty obvious; as when he gives three rules for ascertaining when one has had enough dinner (ch. XXVI.); but if this is to be considered a defect, it is a defect of his quality, a quality very necessary to the successful country parson, the disposition to descend to particulars, and think nothing so obvious as to be not worth saying. A good example may be found in chapter XXXII. where he imagines a gallant asking a parson who has been preaching against idleness "if he shall mend shoes, or what he shall do?" For answer he proceeds to detail the duties of country gentlemen, married and single, heirs and younger brothers, bidding the Member of Parliament "not be only a morning-man, but at Committees also," &c.

Inevitably the lapse of time has antiquated some things. It is no longer necessary for the parson to be the physician of his parish, or to choose his wife for her skill in poulticing (ch. XXIII.). There is probably only one living preacher who needs the advice about not exceeding his hour (ch. VII.), and it would be hardly possible now for anyone, without loss of simplicity, to introduce the apostrophes which Herbert recommends, or to read the prayers with dramatic gesture. Again, the advice on almsgiving will hardly approve itself to the best current opinion. Doubtless, if Herbert had been spared to a longer ministry at Bemerton he would have discovered that what he called "giving like a priest," i.e. using alms as a reward for Church attendance and knowledge of the Catechism, tended to foster hypocrisy. Again, the disappearance of discipline has robbed the parson of much of his authority. There is a good deal in *The Countrey Parson* about "exacting" this and that, "rebuking" various sorts of delinquents, and "presenting" them if they prove incorrigible. The country parson of to-day cannot "present," cannot "exact," and must confine even his "rebukes" to the infant school. Perhaps, too, a country parson here and there will turn with interest to the chapter headed "The Parson's Library," only to read with dismay "The Countrey Parsons library is a holy life." For Herbert expects his parson to have done his reading before entering upon his benefice. Here, again, a longer time at Bemerton might have convinced Herbert that even a country parson required fresher reading than his own common-place books; that in fact, as Bacon says, "distilled books are flashy things." One may have a shrewd suspicion that Milton had his eye on Herbert's fifth chapter when he wrote the famous invective in *Areopagitica* against the parson's "topic folio":

> It is no new thing never heard of before, for a *parochiall* Minister, who has his reward, and is at his Hercules pillars in a warm benefice, to be easily inclinable, if he have nothing else that may rouse up his studies, to finish his circuit in an English Concordance and a *topic folio*, the gatherings and savings of a sober graduatship, a *Harmony* and a *Catena*, treading the constant round of certain common doctrinall heads, attended with their uses, motives, marks and means, out of which as out of an alphabet or sol fa by forming and transforming, joyning and disjoyning variously, a little book-craft, and two hours meditation, might furnish him unspeakably to the performance of more than a weekly charge of sermoning.

But each country parson on reading Herbert's treatise will make his own exceptions, and *exceptis excipiendis* it is to-day what Izaak Walton called it, "a book so full of plain, prudent,

and useful rules, that that country parson that can spare 12d. and yet wants it, is scarce excusable": because it will "both direct him what he ought to do, and convince him for not having done it."—H. C. BEECHING, "Introduction" to *George Herbert's* Country Parson, 1898, pp. xxxviii–xlv

BARNABUS OLEY (?)
From "A Prefatory View of the Life of Mr Geo. Herbert"
Herbert's Remains
1652

This Authour, Mr. G. HERBERT, was extracted out of a Generous, *Noble*, and Ancient Family: His Father was RICHARD HERBERT of *Blache-hall*, in *Mountgomery*, Esq; descended from the *Great Sir* RICHARD HERBERT in *Edward* the Fourth's time; and so his Relation to the Noble Family of that Name, well known. His Mother was Daughter of Sir *Richard Newport* of *Arcoll*, who doubtlesse was a pious daughter, she was so good and godly a mother; She had ten children, *Job's* number, and *Job's* distinction, seven sons; for whose education she went and dwelt in the University, to recompence the losse of their Father, in giving them two Mothers. And this great care of her, this good son of hers studied to improve and requite, as is seen in those many Latin and Greek Verses, the Obsequious *Parentalia*, he made and printed in her memory: which though they be good, very good, yet (to speak freely even of this man I so much honour) they be dull or dead in comparison of his *Temple Poems*. And no marvel; To write those, he made his ink with water of *Helicon*, but these inspirations propheticall were distilled from above: In those are weake motions of Nature, in these Raptures of Grace. In those be writ Flesh and Blood: A fraile earthly Woman, though a MOTHER, but in these he praysed his Heavenly FATHER, the God of Men and Angels, and the Lord Jesus Christ *His Master*; for so (to quicken himself in Duties, and to cut off all depending on man, whose breath is in his nostrils) hee used ordinarily to call our *Saviour*.

I forget not where I left him: He did thrive so well there, that he was first chosen fellow of the Colledge, and afterward Oratour of the Universitie. The Memorials of him left in the Orators Book, shew how he discharged the Place: and himself intimates, *Church*. That whereas his Birth and Spirit prompted him to Martiall Atchievements, *The way that takes the Town*; and not to sit simpering over a Book; *God did often melt his spirit*, and entice him with Academick Honor, to be content to wear, and *wrap up himselfe in a gown*, so long, till he durst not put it off, nor retire to any other calling. However, probably he might, I have heard (as other Orators) have had a Secretary of States place.

But the good man like a genuine son of *Levi* (I had like to have said *Melchisedeck*) balked all secular wayes, saw neither father, nor mother, childe nor Brother, birth nor friends (save in Christ Jesus) chose the Lord for his portion, and his service for employment. And he knew full well what he did when he received Holy orders, as appears by every page in this Book and by the Poems call'd *Priesthood*, and *Aaron*: And by this unparalell'd *vigilancy* which he used over his Parrish, which made him (sayes that modest Authour of the *Epistle* before his Poems, N. F. who know him well) A Peer to the primitive *Saints, and more than a pattern to his own age.*

Besides his Parsonage, he had also a Prebend in the Church of *Lincoln*; which I think (because he lived far from, and so could not attend the duty of that place,) he would faine have resigned to Master *Ferrer*, and often earnestly sued to him to discharge him of it, but Master *F.* wholly refused, and diverted or directed his charity (as I take it) to the re-edifying of the ruined Church of *Leighton*, where the corps of the Prebend lay. So that the Church of *England* owes to him (besides what good may come by this Book, towards the repair of us Churchmen in point of morals,) the reparation of a *Church-materiall*, and erection of that costly piece (of Mosaick or Solomonick work,) *the Temple*; which flourishes and stands inviolate, when our other Magnificences are desolate, and despised.

These things I have said are high; but yet there is one thing which I admire above all the rest: The right managing of the *Fraternall duty of reproof* is (me thinks) one of the most difficult offices of Christian Prudence. O Lord! what is then *the Ministeriall*? To do it as wee should, is likely to anger a whole world of waspes, to set fire on the earth. This, I have conjectured, was that which made many holy men leave the world, and live in wildernesses; which, by the way, was not counted by Ancients, an act of Perfection, but of Cowardise and poor spiritednesse: of Flight to shade and shelter, not of Fight in dust and blood, and heat of the day. This Authour had not only got the courage to do this, but the Art of doing this aright.

There was not a man in his way (be he of what Ranke hee would) *that spoke awry* (in order to God) *but he wip'd his mouth with a modest, grave and Christian reproof*: This was heriocall; Adequate to that Royall Law, Thou shalt in any case reprove thy Brother, and not suffer sin upon him. And that he did this, I have heard from true Reporters, and thou mayst see he had learned it himselfe, else he never had taught it us, as hee does in divers passages of this Book.

His singular Dexterity in sweetning this Art, thou mayst see in the Garb and phrase of his writing. Like a wise Masterbuilder, he has set about a forme of Speech, transferred it in a Figure, as if he was all the while learning from another man's mouth or pen, and not teaching any. And whereas we all of us deserved the sharpnesse of Reproofe, ἔλεγχε ἀποτόμως, He saith, *He does this, and he does that*; whereas, poor men, we did no such thing. This dart of his, thus dipped, pierces the soul.

There is another thing (some will call it a Paradox) which I learned from Him (and *Mr. Ferrer*) in the *Managery* of their most cordiall and *Christian Friendship*. That this may be maintained in vigour and height without the Ceremonies of Visits and Complements; yea, without any Trade of secular courtesies, meerly in order to spirituall Edification of one another in love. I know they loved each other most entirely, and their very souls cleaved together most intimately, and drove a large stock of Christian Intelligence together long before their deaths: yet saw they not each other in many years, I think, scarce ever, but as Members of one Universitie, in their whole lives. . . .

It would swell this Preface too much to set down the severall excelencies of our Authour: His *consciencious expence of Time*, which he even measured by the *pulse*, that *native watch* God has set in every of us. His eminent *Temperance*, and *Frugality*, (the two best Purveiors for his Liberality and Beneficence,) his private *Fastings*, his *mortification of the body*, his extemporary exercises thereof, at the sight or visit of a *Charnell House*, where every Bone, before the day, rises up in judgement against fleshly lust and pride: at the *stroke of a passing bell*, when ancient charity used (said he) to run to Church, and assist the dying Christian with prayers and tears (for sure that was the ground of that custome;) and at all occasions he could lay hold of possibly, which he sought with the diligence that others shun and shift them. Besides his carefull, (not scrupulous) observation of *appointed Fasts*, *Lents*, and *Embers*:

The neglect and defect of this last, he said, had such influx on the children which the Fathers of the Church did beget at such times, as malignant Stars are said to have over naturall Productions; Children of such Parents, as be Fasting and Prayers, being like *Isaak*, and *Jacob*, and *Samuel*; most likely to become Children of the Promise, Wrastlers with God, and fittest to wear a linnen *Ephod*. And with this *Fasting* he imp'd his prayers both private and publick: His private must be left to God, who saw them in secret; his publick were *Morning and Evening Sacrifice* of the *Church Liturgie*, which he used with consciencious devotion, not of Custome, but serious Judgement; Knowing, 1. That the Sophism used to make people hate them, was a solid reason to make men of understanding love them; Namely, because taken out of the Masse Book: Taken out, but as gold from drosse, the precious from the vile. The wise Reformers knew *Rome* would cry *Shism*, schism, and therefore they kept all they could lawfully keep, being loth to give offence; as our blessed Saviour, being loth to offend the *Jews* at the great Reformation, kept divers old Elements, and made them new Sacraments and Services, as their frequent Washings he turned into one Baptisme; some service of the Passeover into the Lord's Supper. 2. That *the homelinesse and coursenesse*, which also was objected, was a great commendation. The Lambes poor of the Flock are forty, for one grounded Christian: proportionable must be the care of the Church to provide milk; that is, plain and easie nourishment for them: and so had our Church done, hoping that stronger Christians, as they abounded in Gifts, so they had such a store of the grace of Charity, as for their weak Brethren's sakes to be content therewith.

He thought also that a set Liturgy was of great use in respect of those without, whether erring Christians, or unbelieving men. That when we had used our best arguments against their errours or unbeliefe, we might shew them a Form wherein we did, and desired they would serve Almighty God with us: That we might be able to say, *This is our Church, Here would we land you*. Thus we believe, *see the Creed. Thus we pray, baptize, catechise, celebrate the Eucharist, Marry, Bury,* Intreat the sick, &c.

These, besides Unity, and other accessary benefits, he thought grounds sufficient to bear him out in this practise: wherein he ended his life, calling for the Church Prayers a while before his death, saying, *None to them, none to them* at once both commending them, and his soul to God in them, immediately before his dissolution, as some *Martyrs* did, *Mr. Hullier* by name, Vicar of *Babram*, burnt to death in *Cambridge*; who having the *Common-Prayer Book* in his hand, in stead of a Censor, and using the prayers as incense, offered up himselfe as a whole Burnt Sacrifice to God; with whom the very Book it selfe suffered Martyrdome, when fallen out of his consumed hands, it was by the Executioners thrown into the fire and burnt as an Hereticall Book.

He was moreover so great a Lover of *Church-Musick*, That he usually called it *Heaven upon earth*, and attended it a few days before his death. But above all, his chief delight was in the *Holy Scripture*, One leafe whereof he professed he would not part with, though he might have the whole world in Exchange. That was his *wisdome, his comfort, his joy*, out of that he took his Motto; LESSE THEN THE LEAST OF ALL GOD'S MERCIES. In that he found the substance, Christ, and in Christ Remission of sins, yea, in his blood he placed the goodnesse of his good works. *It is a good Work*, (said he of Building a Church,) *if it be sprinkled with the Blood of Christ*.

This high esteem of the *Word of life*, as it wrought in himselfe a wondrous expression of high Reverence, when ever he either read it himselfe, or heard others read it, so it made him *equally wonder, that those which pretended such extraordinary love to Christ Jesus, as many did,* could possibly give such leave and liberty to themselves as to hear that word that shall judge us at the last day, *without any the least expression* of that *holy feare* and *trembling,* which they ought to charge upon their souls in private, and in publick, to imprint upon others.

Thus have I with my foul hands soiled this (and the other) fair piece, and worn out thy patience: yet have I not so much as with one dash of a pensill, offered to describe that person of his, which afforded so unusuall a Contesseration of Elegancies, and set of Rarities to the Beholder; nor said I any thing of his Personall Relation, as an *Husband,* to a loving, and *vertuous Lady;* as a Kinsman, Master, &c. yet will I not silence his spirituall love and care of Servants: Teaching Masters this duty, To allow their Servants, daily time, wherein to pray privately, and to enjoyne them to do it: holding this for true generally, *That publick prayer alone to such persons, is no prayer at all.*

I have given thee onely these lineaments of his mind, and thou mayest fully serve thy selfe of this Book, in what vertue of his thy soul longeth after. *His* practice it was, and *His Character* it is, *His* as *Authour,* and *His* as *Object:* yet, Lo, the humility of this gracious man! He had small esteem of this Book, and but very little of his Poems. Though God had magnified him with extraordinary Gifts, yet said he, *God has broken into my Study, and taken off my chariot wheels, I have nothing worthy of God.* And even this lowlinesse in his own eyes, doth more advance their worth, and his vertues.

I have done, when I have besought the R. Fathers, some Cathedrall, Ecclesiasticall, and Academicall men, (which Ranks the modest Authour meddles not with,) to draw *Idæa's* for their severall Orders respectively. (Why should Papists (as *Timpius*) be more carefull or painfull in this kind then we?) If it do no other good, yet it help on in the way of *Repentance,* by discovery of former mistakes or neglects; which is the greatest, if not the onely Good that can probably be hoped for, out of this Tract: which being writ nigh *twenty years since,* will be lesse subject to misconstruction. The Good Lord prosper it according to the pious intent of the Authour, and hearty wishes of the Prefacer; who confesses himselfe unworthy *to carry out the Dung of Gods Sacrifices.*

IZAAK WALTON
From *The Life of Mr. George Herbert*
1670

George Herbert was born the third day of April, in the year of our redemption 1593. The place of his birth was near to the town of Montgomery, and in that castle that did then bear the name of that town and county. That castle was then a place of state and strength, and had been successively happy in the family of the Herberts, who had long possessed it, and, with it, a plentiful estate, and hearts as liberal to their poor neighbours; a family, that hath been blessed with men of remarkable wisdom, and a willingness to serve their country, and, indeed, to do good to all mankind; for which they are eminent. But alas! this family did in the late rebellion suffer extremely in their estates; and the heirs of that castle saw it laid level with that earth that was too good to bury those wretches that were the cause of it.

The father of our George was Richard Herbert, the son of Edward Herbert, Knight, the son of Richard Herbert, Knight, the son of the famous Sir Richard Herbert of Colebrook, in the county of Monmouth, Banneret, who was the youngest brother of that memorable William Herbert, Earl of Pembroke, that lived in the reign of our King Edward the Fourth.

His mother was Magdalen Newport, the youngest daughter of Sir Richard, and sister to Sir Francis Newport, of High Arkall, in the county of Salop, Knight, and grandfather of Francis Lord Newport, now Comptroller of his Majesty's Household; a family that for their loyalty have suffered much in their estates, and seen the ruin of that excellent structure, where their ancestors have long lived, and been memorable for their hospitality.

This mother of George Herbert (of whose person, and wisdom, and virtue, I intend to give a true account in a seasonable place) was the happy mother of seven sons, and three daughters, which, she would often say, was Job's number, and Job's distribution; and as often bless God, that they were neither defective in their shapes or in their reason; and very often reprove them that did not praise God for so great a blessing. . . .

George Herbert spent much of his childhood in a sweet content under the eye and care of his prudent mother, and the tuition of a chaplain or tutor to him and two of his brothers, in her own family (for she was then a widow), where he continued till about the age of twelve years; and being at that time well instructed in the rules of grammar, he was not long after commended to the care of Dr. Neale, who was then Dean of Westminster, and by him to the care of Mr. Ireland, who was then chief master of that school; where the beauties of his pretty behaviour and wit shined and became so eminent and lovely in this his innocent age, that he seemed to be marked out for piety, and to become the care of Heaven, and of a particular good angel to guard and guide him. And thus he continued in that school, till he came to be perfect in the learned languages, and especially in the Greek tongue, in which he after proved an excellent critic.

About the age of fifteen (he being then a king's scholar) he was elected out of that school for Trinity College in Cambridge, to which place he was transplanted about the year of 1608; and his prudent mother, well knowing that he might easily lose or lessen that virtue and innocence, which her advice and example had planted in his mind, did therefore procure the generous and liberal Dr. Nevil, who was then Dean of Canterbury, and Master of that College, to take him into his particular care, and provide him a tutor; which he did most gladly undertake; for he knew the excellences of his mother, and how to value such a friendship.

This was the method of his education, till he was settled in Cambridge, where we will leave him in his study, till I have paid my promised account of his excellent mother, and I will endeavour to make it short.

I have told her birth, her marriage, and the number of her children, and have given some short account of them; I shall next tell the reader, that her husband died when our George was about the age of four years: I am next to tell that she continued twelve years a widow; that she then married happily to a noble gentleman, the brother and heir of the Lord Danvers, Earl of Danby, who did highly value both her person and the most excellent endowments of her mind.

In this time of her widowhood, she being desirous to give Edward, her eldest son, such advantages of learning and other education as might suit his birth and fortune, and thereby make him the more fit for the service of his country, did at his being of a fit age remove from Montgomery Castle with him, and some of her younger sons, to Oxford; and having entered Edward into Queen's College, and provided him a fit tutor, she commended him to his care; yet she continued there with him, and still kept him in a moderate awe of herself, and so much under her own eye, as to see and converse with him daily: but she managed this power over him without any such rigid sourness, as might make her company a torment to her child, but with such a sweetness and compliance with the recreations and pleasures of youth, as did incline him willingly to spend much of his time in the company of his dear and careful mother; which was to her great content: for she would often say, "that, as our bodies take a nourishment suitable to the meat on which we feed, so our souls do as insensibly take in vice by the example or conversation with wicked company;" and would therefore as often say, "that ignorance of vice was the best preservation of virtue; and that the very knowledge of wickedness was as tinder to inflame and kindle sin, and to keep it burning." For these reasons she endeared him to her own company, and continued with him in Oxford four years; in which time her great and harmless wit, her cheerful gravity, and her obliging behaviour, gained her an acquaintance and friendship with most of any eminent worth or learning that were at that time in or near that university; and particularly with Mr. John Donne, who then came accidentally to that place in this time of her being there. It was that John Donne who was after Dr. Donne, and Dean of St. Paul's, London; and he, at his leaving Oxford, writ and left there, in verse, a character of the beauties of her body and mind. Of the first he says,

No spring nor summer beauty hath such grace,
As I have seen in an autumnal face.

Of the latter he says,

In all her words to every hearer fit,
You may at revels, or at council sit.

The rest of her character may be read in his printed poems, in that elegy which bears the name of "The Autumnal Beatuy." For both he and she were then past the meridian of man's life.

This amity, begun at this time and place, was not an amity that polluted their souls; but an amity made up of a chain of suitable inclinations and virtues; an amity like that of St. Chrysostom's to his dear and virtuous Olympias, whom, in his letters, he calls his Saint; or an amity, indeed, more like that of St. Hierom to his Paula, whose affection to her was such, that he turned poet in his old age, and then made her epitaph; wishing all his body were turned into tongues, that he might declare her just praises to posterity. And this amity betwixt her and Mr. Donne was begun in a happy time for him, he being then near to the fortieth year of his age (which was some years before he entered into sacred orders); a time when his necessities needed a daily supply for the support of his wife, seven children, and a family. And in this time she proved one of his most bountiful benefactors; and he as grateful an acknowledger of it. . . .

I need not declare that he was a strict student, because, that he was so, there will be many testimonies in the future part of his life. I shall therefore only tell, that he was made Bachelor of Arts in the year 1611; Major Fellow of the College, March 15, 1615: and that in that year he was also made Master of Arts, he being then in the twenty-second year of his age; during all which time, all, or the greatest diversion from his study, was the practice of music, in which he became a great master; and of which he would say, "that it did relieve his drooping spirits, compose his distracted thoughts, and raised his weary soul so far above the earth, that it gave him an earnest of the joys of heaven before he possessed them." And it may be noted, that from his first entrance into the college, the generous Dr. Nevil was a cherisher of his studies, and such a lover of his person, his behaviour, and the excellent endowments of his mind, that

he took him often into his own company, by which he confirmed his native gentleness; and, if during this time he expressed any error, it was that he kept himself too much retired, and at too great a distance with all his inferiors; and his clothes seemed to prove, that he put too great a value on his parts and parentage.

This may be some account of his disposition and of the employment of his time, till he was Master of Arts, which was Anno 1615; and in the year 1619 he was chosen Orator for the university. His two precedent Orators were Sir Robert Nanton and Sir Francis Nethersole: the first was not long after made Secretary of State; and Sir Francis, not very long after his being Orator, was made Secretary to the Lady Elizabeth, Queen of Bohemia. In this place of Orator, our George Herbert continued eight years, and managed it with as becoming and grave a gayety as any had ever before or since his time. For, "he had acquired great learning, and was blessed with a high fancy, a civil and sharp wit, and with a natural elegance, both of his behaviour, his tongue, and his pen." Of all which, there might be very many particular evidences, but I will limit myself to the mention of but three.

And the first notable occasion of showing his fitness for this employment of Orator was manifested in a letter to King James, upon the occasion of his sending that university his book, called *Basilicon Doron*; and their Orator was to acknowledge this great honor, and return their gratitude to his Majesty for such a condescension, at the close of which letter he writ,

Quid Vaticanam Bodleianamque objicis, hospes!
Unicus est nobis bibliotheca liber.

This letter was writ in such excellent Latin, was so full of conceits, and all the expressions so suited to the genius of the King, that he inquired the Orator's name, and then asked William Earl of Pembroke, if he knew him; whose answer was, "that he knew him very well, and that he was his kinsman; but he loved him more for his learning and virtue, than for that he was of his name and family." At which answer, the King smiled, and asked the Earl leave, "that he might love him too; for he took him to be the jewel of that university."

The next occasion he had and took to show his great abilities was with them, to show also his great affection to that church in which he received his baptism, and of which he professed himself a member; and the occasion was this. There was one Andrew Melvin, a minister of the Scotch Church, and rector of St. Andrews, who, by a long and constant converse with a discontented part of that clergy which opposed Episcopacy, became at last to be a chief leader of that faction; and had proudly appeared to be so to King James, when he was but king of that nation, who the second year after his coronation in England, convened a part of the bishops and other learned divines of his church, to attend him at Hampton Court, in order to a friendly conference with some dissenting brethren, both of this, and the Church of Scotland: of which Scotch party, Andrew Melvin was one; and he being a man of learning, and inclined to satirical poetry, had scattered many malicious bitter verses against our liturgy, our ceremonies, and our church government; which were by some of that party so magnified for the wit, that they were therefore brought into Westminster School, where Mr. George Herbert then, and often after, made such answers to them, and such reflection on him and his kirk, as might unbeguile any man that was not too deeply pre-engaged in such a quarrel.

. . . ⟨A⟩bout this time King James came very often to hunt at Newmarket and Royston, and was almost as often invited to Cambridge, where his entertainment was comedies suited to his pleasant humor; and where Mr. George Herbert was to welcome him with gratulations and the applauses of an Orator, which he always performed so well, that he still grew more into the King's favor, insomuch that he had a particular appointment to attend his Majesty at Royston; where, after a discourse with him, his Majesty declared to his kinsman, the Earl of Pembroke, "that he found the orator's learning and wisdom much above his age or wit." The year following, the King appointed to end his progress at Cambridge, and to stay there certain days; at which time he was attended by the great secretary of nature and all learning, Sir Francis Bacon (Lord Verulam), and by the ever memorable and learned Dr. Andrews, Bishop of Winchester, both which did at that time begin a desired friendship with our orator. Upon whom, the first put such a value on his judgment, that he usually desired his approbation before he would expose any of his books to be printed, and thought him so worthy of his friendship, that having translated many of the prophet David's Psalms into English verse, he made George Herbert his patron, by a public dedication of them to him, as the best judge of divine poetry. And for the learned bishop, it is observable, that at that time there fell to be a modest debate betwixt them two about predestination and sanctity of life; of both which the orator did, not long after, send the Bishop some safe and useful aphorisms, in a long letter, written in Greek; which letter was so remarkable for the language and reason of it, that after the reading it, the Bishop put it into his bosom, and did often show it to many scholars, both of this and foreign nations; but did always return it back to the place where he first lodged it, and continued it so near his heart till the last day of his life.

To these, I might add the long and entire friendship betwixt him and Sir Henry Wotton, and Dr. Donne, but I have promised to contract myself, and shall therefore only add one testimony to what is also mentioned in the Life of Dr. Donne; namely, that a little before his death, he caused many seals to be made, and in them to be engraven the figure of Christ crucified on an anchor (the emblem of hope), and of which Dr. Donne would often say, "Crux mihi anchora." These seals he gave or sent to most of those friends on which he put a value; and, at Mr. Herbert's death, these verses were found wrapt up with that seal which was by the Doctor given to him:

> When my dear friend could write no more,
> He gave this seal, and so gave o'er.
> When winds and waves rise highest, I am sure,
> *This* anchor keeps my faith, *that* me secure.

At this time of being Orator, he had learnt to understand the Italian, Spanish, and French tongues very perfectly; hoping, that as his predecessors, so he might in time attain the place of a secretary of state, he being at that time very high in the King's favor; and not meanly valued and loved by the most eminent and most powerful of the court nobility. This, and the love of a court conversation, mixed with a laudable ambition to be something more than he then was, drew him often from Cambridge to attend the King, wheresoever the court was, who then gave him a sinecure, which fell into his Majesty's disposal, I think, by the death of the Bishop of St. Asaph. It was the same, that Queen Elizabeth had formerly given to her favorite Sir Philip Sidney; and valued to be worth a hundred and twenty pounds per annum. With this, and his annuity, and the advantage of his college, and of his oratorship, he enjoyed his genteel humor for clothes and court-like company, and seldom looked towards Cambridge, unless the King were there, but then he never failed; and, at other times, left the manage of

his Orator's place to his learned friend Mr. Herbert Thorndike, who is now prebendary of Westminster.

I may not omit to tell, that he had often designed to leave the university, and decline all study, which, he thought, did impair his health; for he had a body apt to a consumption, and to fevers, and other infirmities, which he judged were increased by his studies; for he would often say, "he had too thoughtful a wit: a wit, like a penknife in too narrow a sheath, too sharp for his body." But his mother would by no means allow him to leave the university, or to travel; and though he inclined very much to both, yet he would by no means satisfy his own desires at so dear a rate, as to prove an undutiful son to so affectionate a mother; but did always submit to her wisdom. . . .

In this time of Mr. Herbert's attendance and expectation of some good occasion to remove from Cambridge to court, God, in whom there is an unseen chain of causes, did, in a short time, put an end to the lives of two of his most obliging and most powerful friends, Lodowick Duke of Richmond, and James Marquis of Hamilton; and not long after him, King James died also, and with them, all Mr. Herbert's court hopes: so that he presently betook himself to a retreat from London, to a friend in Kent, where he lived very privately, and was such a lover of solitariness, as was judged to impair his health more than his study had done. In this time of retirement, he had many conflicts with himself, whether he should return to the painted pleasures of a court-life, or betake himself to a study of divinity, and enter into sacred orders? (to which his dear mother had often persuaded him.)—These were such conflicts, as they only can know, that have endured them; for ambitious desires, and the outward glory of this world, are not easily laid aside; but, at last, God inclined him to put on a resolution to serve at his altar.

He did, at his return to London, acquaint a court friend with his resolution to enter into sacred orders, who persuaded him to alter it, as too mean an employment, and too much below his birth, and the excellent abilities and endowments of his mind. To whom he replied, "It hath been formerly judged that the domestic servants of the King of heaven should be of the noblest families on earth: and though the iniquity of the late times have made clergymen meanly valued, and the sacred name of priest contemptible; yet I will labor to make it honorable, by consecrating all my learning, and all my poor abilities, to advance the glory of that God that gave them; knowing that I can never do too much for Him that hath done so much for me, as to make me a Christian. And I will labor to be like my Saviour, by making humility lovely in the eyes of all men, and by following the merciful and meek example of my dear Jesus."

This was then his resolution, and the God of constancy, who intended him for a great example of virtue, continued him in it; for within that year he was made deacon, but the day when, or by whom, I cannot learn: but that he was about that time made deacon is most certain; for I find by the records of Lincoln, that he was made Prebendary of Layton Ecclesia, in the diocese of Lincoln, July 15, 1626; and that this prebend was given him by John, then Lord Bishop of that see. And now he had a fit occasion to show that piety and bounty that was derived from his generous mother, and his other memorable ancestors, and the occasion was this. . . .

About the year 1629, and the 34th of his age, Mr. Herbert was seized with a sharp quotidian ague, and thought to remove it by the change of air; to which end, he went to Woodford in Essex, but thither more chiefly to enjoy the company of his beloved brother Sir Henry Herbert, and other friends then of that family. In his house he remained about twelve months, and there became his own physician, and cured himself of his ague, by forbearing drink, and not eating any meat, no not mutton, nor a hen, or pigeon, unless they were salted; and by such a constant diet he removed his ague, but with inconveniences that were worse; for he brought upon himself a disposition to rheums and other weaknesses, and a supposed consumption. And it is to be noted, that in the sharpest of his extreme fits he would often say, "Lord, abate my great affliction, or increase my patience; but, Lord, I repine not; I am dumb, Lord, before thee, because thou doest it." By which, and a sanctified submission to the will of God, he showed he was inclinable to bear the sweet yoke of Christian discipline, both then and in the latter part of his life, of which there will be many true testimonies.

And now his care was to recover from his consumption by a change from Woodford into such an air as was most proper to that end. And his remove was to Dauntsey in Wiltshire, a noble house, which stands in a choice air; the owner of it then was the Lord Danvers Earl of Danby, who loved Mr. Herbert so very much, that he allowed him such an apartment in it as might best suit with his accommodation and liking. And in this place, by a spare diet, declining all perplexing studies, moderate exercise, and a cheerful conversation, his heath was apparently improved to a good degree of strength and cheerfulness: and then he declared his resolution, both to marry, and to enter into the sacred orders of priesthood. These had long been the desires of his mother and his other relations; but she lived not to see either, for she died in the year 1627. And though he was disobedient to her about Layton Church, yet, in conformity to her will, he kept his Orator's place till after her death, and then presently declined it; and the more willingly, that he might be succeeded by his friend Robert Creighton, who now is Dr. Creighton, and the worthy Bishop of Wells.

I shall now proceed to his marriage; in order to which, it will be convenient that I first give the reader a short view of his person, and then an account of his wife, and of some circumstances concerning both.

He was, for his person, of a stature inclining towards tallness; his body was very straight; and so far from being cumbered with too much flesh, that he was lean to an extremity. His aspect was cheerful, and his speech and motion did both declare him a gentleman; for they were all so meek and obliging, that they purchased love and respect from all that knew him.

These, and his other visible virtues, begot him much love from a gentleman, of a noble fortune, and a near kinsman to his friend the Earl of Danby; namely, from Mr. Charles Danvers of Bainton, in the county of Wilts, Esq.; this Mr. Danvers, having known him long and familiarly, did so much affect him, that he often and publicly declared a desire that Mr. Herbert would marry any of his nine daughters (for he had so many); but rather his daughter Jane than any other, because Jane was his beloved daughter. And he had often said the same to Mr. Herbert himself; and that if he could like her for a wife, and she him for a husband, Jane should have a double blessing; and Mr. Danvers had so often said the like to Jane, and so much commended Mr. Herbert to her, that Jane became so much a Platonic, as to fall in love with Mr. Herbert unseen.

This was a fair preparation for a marriage; but alas, her father died before Mr. Herbert's retirement to Dauntsey; yet some friends to both parties procured their meeting; at which time a mutual affection entered into both their hearts, as a conqueror enters into a surprised city, and love having got such possession governed, and made there such laws and resolutions as neither party was able to resist; insomuch that she changed her name to Herbert the third day after this first interview.

This haste might in others be thought a love-phrenzy, or worse; but it was not, for they had wooed so like princes, as to have select proxies; such as were true friends to both parties; such as well understood Mr. Herbert's and her temper of mind, and also their estates, so well before this interview, that the suddenness was justifiable by the strictest rules of prudence; and the more because it proved so happy to both parties: for the Eternal Lover of mankind made them happy in each other's mutual and equal affections and compliance; indeed so happy, that there never was any opposition betwixt them, unless it were a contest which most incline to a compliance with the other's desires. And though this begot, and continued in them, such a mutual love, and joy, and content, as was no way defective; yet this mutual content, and love, and joy did receive a daily augmentation, by such daily obligingness to each other, as still added such new affluences to the former fullness of these divine souls, as was only improvable in heaven, where they now enjoy it.

About three months after his marriage, Dr. Curle, who was then Rector of Bemerton in Wiltshire, was made Bishop of Bath and Wells, and not long after translated to Winchester; and by that means the presentation of a clerk to Bemerton did not fall to the Earl of Pembroke (who was the undoubted patron of it) but to the King, by reason of Dr. Curle's advancement. But Philip, then Earl of Pembroke (for William was lately dead), requested the King to bestow it upon his kinsman George Herbert; and the King said, "Most willingly to Mr. Herbert, if it be worth his acceptance." And the Earl as willingly and suddenly sent it him without seeking. But though Mr. Herbert had formerly put on a resolution for the clergy; yet, at receiving this presentation, the apprehension of the last great account, that he was to make for the cure of so many souls, made him fast and pray often, and consider for not less than a month; in which time he had some resolutions to decline both the priesthood and that living. And in this time of considering, "he endured," as he would often say, "such spiritual conflicts as none can think, but only those that have endured them."

In the midst of those conflicts, his old and dear friend Mr. Arthur Woodnot took a journey to salute him at Bainton (where he then was with his wife's friends and relations), and was joyful to be an eye-witness of his health and happy marriage. And after they had rejoiced together some few days, they took a journey to Wilton, the famous seat of the Earls of Pembroke; at which time the King, the Earl, and the whole Court were there, or at Salisbury, which is near to it. And at this time Mr. Herbert presented his thanks to the Earl, for his presentation to Bemerton, but had not yet resolved to accept it, and told him the reason why; but that night the Earl acquainted Dr. Laud, then Bishop of London, and after Archbishop of Canterbury, with his kinsman's irresolution. And the Bishop did the next day so convince Mr. Herbert, that the refusal of it was a sin, that a tailor was sent for to come speedily from Salisbury to Wilton, to take measure, and made him canonical clothes against next day; which the tailor did. And Mr. Herbert, being so habited, went with his presentation to the learned Dr. Davenant, who was then Bishop of Salisbury, and he gave him institution immediately (for Mr. Herbert had been made deacon some years before); and he was also the same day (which was April 26, 1630) inducted into the good, and more pleasant than healthful, parsonage of Bemerton; which is a mile from Salisbury.

I have now brought them to the parsonage of Bemerton,

and to the thirty-sixth year of his age, and must stop here, and bespeak the reader to prepare for an almost incredible story of the great sanctity of the short remainder of his holy life; a life so full of charity, humility, and all Christian virtues, that it deserves the eloquence of St. Chrysostom to commend and declare it! A life, that if it were related by a pen like his, there would then be no need for this age to look back into times past for the examples of primitive piety; for they might be all found in the life of George Herbert. But now, alas! who is fit to undertake it? I confess I am not; and am not pleased with myself that I must; and profess myself amazed, when I consider how few of the clergy lived like him then, and how many live so unlike him now. But it becomes not me to censure: my design is rather to assure the reader, that I have used very great diligence to inform myself, that I might inform him of the truth of what follows; and though I cannot adorn it with eloquence, yet I will do it with sincerity.

When at his induction he was shut into Bemerton church, being left there alone to toll the bell (as the law requires him), he stayed so much longer than an ordinary time before he returned to those friends that stayed expecting him at the church door, that his friend Mr. Woodnot looked in at the church window, and saw him lie prostrate on the ground before the altar: at which time and place (as he after told Mr. Woodnot) he set some rules to himself, for the future manage of his life; and then and there made a vow to labor to keep them. . . .

Doubtless Mr. Herbert had considered and given rules to himself for his Christian carriage both to God and man, before he entered into holy orders. And it is not unlike, but that he renewed those resolutions at his prostration before the holy altar, at his induction into the church of Bemerton; and as yet he was but a deacon, and therefore longed for the next Ember-week, that he might be ordained priest, and made capable of administering both the sacraments. At which time the Rev. Dr. Humphrey Henchman, now Lord Bishop of London (who does not mention him but with some veneration for his life and excellent learning), tells me, "he laid his hand on Mr. Herbert's head, and alas! within less than three years, lent his shoulder to carry his dear friend to his grave."

And that Mr. Herbert might the better preserve those holy rules which such a priest, as he intended to be, ought to observe; and that time might not insensibly blot them out of his memory, but that the next year might show him his variations from this year's resolutions; he, therefore, did set down his rules, then resolved upon, in that order as the world now sees them printed in a little book called *The Country Parson*; in which some of his rules are:

> The Parson's knowledge.
> The Parson on Sundays.
> The Parson praying.
> The Parson preaching.
> The Parson's charity.
> The Parson comforting the sick.
> The Parson arguing.
> The Parson condescending.
> The Parson in his journey.
> The Parson in his mirth.
> The Parson with his churchwardens.
> The Parson blessing the people.

And his behaviour toward God and man may be said to be a practical comment on these and the other holy rules set down in that useful book; a book so full of plain, prudent, and useful rules, that that country parson, that can spare twelve pence, and yet wants it, is scarce excusable; because it will both direct

him what he ought to do, and convince him for not having done it.

At the death of Mr. Herbert, this book fell into the hands of his friend Mr. Woodnot; and he commended it into the trusty hands of Mr. Barnabas Oley, who published it with a most conscientious and excellent Preface; from which I have had some of those truths, that are related in this Life of Mr. Herbert. The text for his first sermon was taken out of Solomon's Proverbs, and the words were, "Keep thy heart with all diligence." In which first sermon he gave his parishioners many necessary, holy, safe rules for the discharge of a good conscience both to God and man; and delivered his sermon after a most florid manner, both with great learning and eloquence; but, at the close of this sermon, told them, "that should not be his constant way of preaching; for since Almighty God does not intend to lead men to heaven by hard questions, he would not therefore fill their heads with unnecessary notions; but that, for their sakes, his language and his expressions should be more plain and practical in his future sermons." And he then made it his humble request, "that they would be constant to the afternoon's service and catechizing;" and showed them convincing reasons why he desired it; and his obliging example and persuasions brought them to a willing conformity to his desires. . . .

His chiefest recreation was music, in which heavenly art he was a most excellent master, and did himself compose many divine hymns and anthems, which he set and sung to his lute or viol. And though he was a lover of retiredness, yet his love to music was such, that he went usually twice every week, on certain appointed days, to the cathedral church in Salisbury; and at his return would say, "that his time spent in prayer, and cathedral music, elevated his soul, and was his heaven upon earth." But before his return thence to Bemerton, he would usually sing and play his part at an appointed private music meeting; and, to justify this practice, he would often say, "Religion does not banish mirth, but only moderates and sets rules to it." . . .

And he was most happy in his wife's unforced compliance with his acts of charity, whom he made his almoner, and paid constantly into her hand a tenth penny of what money he received for tithe, and gave her power to dispose that to the poor of his parish, and with it a power to dispose a tenth part of the corn that came yearly into his barn: which trust she did most faithfully perform, and would often offer to him an account of her stewardship, and as often beg an enlargement of his bounty; for she rejoiced in the employment: and this was usually laid out by her in blankets and shoes for some such poor people, as she knew to stand in most need of them. This as to her charity. And for his own, he set no limits to it; nor did ever turn his face from any that he saw in want, but would relieve them, especially his poor neighbours; to the meanest of whose houses he would go and inform himself of their wants, and relieve them cheerfully if they were in distress; and would always praise God, as much for being willing, as for being able to do it. And when he was advised by a friend to be more frugal, because he might have children, his answer was, "he would not see the danger of want so far off; but, being the Scripture does so commend charity, as to tell us, that charity is the top of Christian virtues, the covering of sins, the fulfilling of the law, the life of faith; and that charity hath a promise of the blessings of this life, and of a reward in that life which is to come; being these and more excellent things are in Scripture spoken of thee, O Charity! and that being all my tithes and church-dues are a deodate from thee, O my God, make me, O my God, so far to trust thy promise, as to return them back to thee; and by thy grace I will do so, in distributing them to any of thy poor members that are in distress, or do but bear the image of Jesus, my Master. Sir," said he to his friend, "my wife hath a competent maintenance secured her after my death, and therefore as this is my prayer, so this my resolution shall, by God's grace, be unalterable."

This may be some account of the excellencies of the active part of his life; and thus he continued, till a consumption so weakened him, as to confine him to his house, or to the chapel, which does almost join to it; in which he continued to read prayers constantly twice every day, though he were very weak: in one of which times of his reading his wife observed him to read in pain, and told him so, and that it wasted his spirits, and weakened him; and he confessed it did, but said, "his life could not be better spent, than in the service of his Master Jesus, who had done and suffered so much for him. "But," said he, "I will not be wilful; for though my spirit be willing, yet I find my flesh is weak; and therefore Mr. Bostock shall be appointed to read prayers for me to-morrow, and I will now be only a hearer of them, till this mortal shall put on immortality." And Mr. Bostock did the next day undertake and continue this happy employment, till Mr. Herbert's death. This Mr. Bostock was a learned and virtuous man, an old friend Mr. Herbert's, and then his curate to the church of Fulston, which is a mile from Bemerton, to which church Bemerton is but a chapel of ease. And this Mr. Bostock did also constantly supply the church service for Mr. Herbert in that chapel, when the music meeting at Salisbury caused his absence from it.

About one month before his death, his friend Mr. Ferrar (for an account of whom I am by promise indebted to the reader, and intend to make him sudden payment) hearing of Mr. Herbert's sickness, sent Mr. Edmund Duncon (who is now Rector of Fryer Barnet, in the county of Middlesex) from his house of Gidden Hall, which is near to Huntingdon, to see Mr. Herbert, and to assure him, he wanted not his daily prayers for his recovery; and Mr. Duncon was to return back to Gidden, with an account of Mr. Herbert's condition. Mr. Duncon found him weak, and at that time lying on his bed, or on a pallet; but at his seeing Mr. Duncon, he raised himself vigorously, saluted him, and with some earnestness inquired the health of his brother Ferrar; of which Mr. Duncon satisfied him; and after some discourse of Mr. Ferrar's holy life, and the manner of his constant serving God, he said to Mr. Duncon, "Sir, I see by your habit that you are a priest, and I desire you to pray with me;" which being granted, Mr. Duncon asked him, "What prayers?" to which Mr. Herbert's answer was, "O, sir, the prayers of my mother, the Church of England; no other prayers are equal to them! but at this time, I beg of you to pray only the Litany, for I am weak and faint;" and Mr. Duncon did so. After which, and some other discourse of Mr. Ferrar, Mrs. Herbert provided Mr. Duncon a plain supper and a clean lodging, and he betook himself to rest. This Mr. Duncon tells me; and tells me, that at this first view of Mr. Herbert he saw majesty and humility so reconciled in his looks and behaviour, as begot in him an awful reverence for his person; and says, "his discourse was so pious, and his motion so gentle and meek, that after almost forty years yet they remain still fresh in his memory."

The next moring, Mr. Duncon left him, and betook himself to a journey to Bath, but with a promise to return back to him within five days, and he did so. . . .

. . . (He) found Mr. Herbert much weaker than he left him: and, therefore, their discourse could not be long; but at Mr. Duncon's parting with him, Mr. Herbert spoke to this purpose: "Sir, I pray give my brother Ferrar an account of the decaying condition of my body, and tell him I beg him to continue his daily prayers for me; and let him know, that I have considered, that God only is what he would be; and that I am, by his grace, become now so like him, as to be pleased with what pleaseth him; and tell him, that I do not repine, but am pleased with my want of health; and tell him my heart is fixed on that place where true joy is only to be found; and that I long to be there, and do wait for my appointed change with hope and patience." Having said this, he did, with so sweet a humility as seemed to exalt him, bow down to Mr. Duncon, and with a thoughtful and contented look, say to him, "Sir, I pray deliver this little book to my dear brother Ferrar, and tell him, he shall find in it a picture of the many spiritual conflicts that have passed betwixt God and my soul, before I could subject mine to the will of Jesus, my Master in whose service I have now found perfect freedom; desire him to read it; and then, if he can think it may turn to the advantage of any dejected poor soul, let it be made public; if not, let him burn it; for I and it are less than the least of God's mercies." Thus meanly did this humble man think of this excellent book, which now bears the name of *The Temple; or, Sacred Poems and Private Ejaculations*; of which Mr. Ferrar would say, "there was in it the picture of a divine soul in every page; and that the whole book was such a harmony of holy passions, as would enrich the world with pleasure and piety." And it appears to have done so; for there have been more than twenty thousand of them sold since the first impression.

And this ought to be noted, that when Mr. Ferrar sent this book to Cambridge to be licensed for the press, the Vice-Chancellor would by no means allow the two so much noted verses,

> Religion stands a tip-toe in our land,
> Ready to pass to the American strand,

to be printed; and Mr. Ferrar would by no means allow the book to be printed and want them; but after some time, and some arguments for and against their being made public, the Vice-Chancellor said, "I knew Mr. Herbert well, and know that he had many heavenly speculations, and was a divine poet; but I hope the world will not take him to be an inspired prophet, and therefore I license the whole book." So that it came to be printed without the diminution or addition of a syllable, since it was delivered into the hands of Mr. Duncon, save only that Mr. Ferrar hath added that excellent preface that is printed before it.

At the time of Mr. Duncon's leaving Mr. Herbert (which was about three weeks before his death), his old and dear friend Mr. Woodnot came from London to Bemerton, and never left him till he had seen him draw his last breath, and closed his eyes on his death-bed. In this time of his decay he was often visited and prayed for by all the clergy that lived near to him, especially by his friends the Bishop and Prebendaries of the cathedral church in Salisbury; but by none more devoutly than his wife, his three nieces (then a part of his family), and Mr. Woodnot, who were the sad witnesses of his daily decay; to whom he would often speak to this purpose: "I now look back upon the pleasures of my life past, and see the content I have taken in beauty, in wit, and music, and pleasant conversation, are now all past by me like a dream or as a shadow that returns not, and are now all become dead to me, or I to them; and I see that as my father and generation hath done before me, so I also shall now suddenly (with Job) make my bed also in the dark; and I praise God I am prepared for it; and I praise him, that I am not to learn patience, now I stand in such need of it; and that I have practised mortification, and endeavoured to die daily, that I might not die eternally; and my hope is, that I shall shortly leave this valley of tears, and be free from all fevers and pain; and, which will be a more happy condition, I shall be free from sin, and all the temptations and anxieties that attend it; and this being past, I shall dwell in the New Jerusalem; dwell there with men made perfect; dwell where these eyes shall see my Master and Saviour, Jesus; and with him see my dear mother, and all my relations and friends. But I must die or not come to that happy place: and this is my content, that I am going daily towards it; and that every day which I have lived hath taken a part of my appointed time from me; and that I shall live the less time, for having lived this and the day past."—These, and the like expressions, which he uttered often, may be said to be his enjoyment of heaven before he enjoyed it. The Sunday before his death, he rose suddenly from his bed or couch, called for one of his instruments, took it into his hand, and said,

> My God, my God,
> My music shall find thee,
>   And every string
> Shall have his attribute to sing.

And having tuned it, he played and sung:

> The Sundays of man's life,
> Threaded together on time's string,
> Make bracelets to adorn the wife
> Of the eternal, glorious King:
> On Sundays heaven's door stands ope;
> Blessings are plentiful and rife,
>   More plentiful than hope.

Thus he sung on earth such hymns and anthems as the angels, and he, and Mr. Ferrar, now sing in heaven.

Thus he continued meditating, and praying, and rejoicing, till the day of his death; and on that day said to Mr. Woodnot, "My dear friend, I am sorry I have nothing to present to my merciful God but sin and misery; but the first is pardoned; and a few hours will now put a period to the latter; for I shall suddenly go hence and be no more seen." Upon which expression, Mr. Woodnot took occasion to remember him of the reëdifying Layton Church, and his many acts of mercy; to which he made answer, saying, "They be good works, if they be sprinkled with the blood of Christ, and not otherwise." After this discourse he became more restless, and his soul seemed to be weary of her earthly tabernacle; and this uneasiness became so visible, that his wife, his three nieces, and Mr. Woodnot stood constantly about his bed, beholding him with sorrow and an unwillingness to lose the sight of him, whom they could not hope to see much longer. As they stood thus beholding him, his wife observed him to breathe faintly, and with much trouble; and observed him to fall into a sudden agony, which so surprised her, that she fell into a sudden passion, and required of him to know how he did; to which his answer was, "that he had passed a conflict with his last enemy, and had overcome him by the merits of his Master, Jesus." After which answer he looked up and saw his wife and nieces weeping to an extremity, and charged them, "if they loved him, to withdraw into the next room, and there pray every one alone for him; for nothing but their lamentations could make his death uncomfortable." To which request their sighs and tears would not suffer them to make any reply, but they yielded him a sad obedience, leaving only with him Mr. Woodnot and Mr. Bostock. Immediately after they had left him, he said to Mr. Bostock, "Pray, sir, open that door, then look into that cabinet, in which you may easily find my last will, and give it into my

hand:" which being done, Mr. Herbert delivered it into the hand of Mr. Woodnot, and said, "My old friend, I here deliver you my last will, in which you find that I have made you my sole executor for the good of my wife and nieces; and I desire you to show kindness to them, as they shall need it. I do not desire you to be just, for I know you will be so for your own sake; but I charge you, by the religion of our friendship, to be careful of them." And having obtained Mr. Woodnot's promise to be so, he said, "I am now ready to die." After which words he said, "Lord, forsake me not, now my strength faileth me; but grant me mercy for the merits of my Jesus. And now, Lord,—Lord, now receive my soul." And with those words he breathed forth his divine soul, without any apparent disturbance, Mr. Woodnot and Mr. Bostock attending his last breath, and closing his eyes.

Thus he lived, and thus he died like a saint, unspotted of the world, full of alms-deeds, full of humility, and all the examples of a virtuous life; which I cannot conclude better, than with this borrowed observation:

> All must to their cold graves;
> But the religious actions of the just
> Smell sweet in death, and blossom in the dust.

Mr. George Herbert's have done so to this, and will doubtless do so to succeeding generations. I have but this to say more of him, that if Andrew Melvin died before him, then George Herbert died without an enemy. I wish (if God shall be so pleased) that I may be so happy as to die like him.

GEORGE MACDONALD
From "George Herbert"
England's Antiphon
1868, pp. 174–93

In George Herbert there is poetry enough and to spare: it is the household bread of his being. If I begin with that which first in the nature of things ought to be demanded of a poet, namely, Truth, Revelation—George Herbert offers us measure pressed down and running over. But let me speak first of that which first in time or order of appearance we demand of a poet, namely music. For inasmuch as verse is for the ear, not for the eye, we demand a good hearing first. Let no one undervalue it. The heart of poetry is indeed truth, but its garments are music, and the garments come first in the process of revelation. The music of a poem is its meaning in sound as distinguished from word—its meaning in solution, as it were, uncrystallized by articulation. The music goes before the fuller revelation, preparing its way. The sound of a verse is the harbinger of the truth contained therein. If it be a right poem, this will be true. Herein Herbert excels. It will be found impossible to separate the music of his words from the music of the thought which takes shape in their sound.

> I got me flowers to strow thy way,
>   I got me boughs off many a tree;
> But thou wast up by break of day,
>   And brought'st thy sweets along with thee.

And the gift it enwraps at once and reveals is, I have said, truth of the deepest. Hear this song of divine service. In every song he sings a spiritual fact will be found its fundamental life, although I may quote this or that merely to illustrate some peculiarity of mode. . . .

With a conscience tender as a child's, almost diseased in its tenderness, and a heart loving as a woman's, his intellect is none the less powerful. Its movements are as the sword-play of an alert, poised, well-knit, strong-wristed fencer with the rapier, in which the skill impresses one more than the force, while without the force the skill would be valueless, even hurtful, to its possessor. There is a graceful humour with it occasionally, even in his most serious poems adding much to their charm. . . .

No writer before him has shown such a love to God, such a childlike confidence in him. The love is like the love of those whose verses came first in my volume. But the nation had learned to think more, and new difficulties had consequently arisen. These, again, had to be undermined by deeper thought, and the discovery of yet deeper truth had been the reward. Hence, the love itself, if it had not strengthened, had at least grown deeper. And George Herbert had had difficulty enough in himself; for, born of high family, by nature fitted to shine in that society where elegance of mind, person, carriage, and utterance is most appreciated, and having indeed enjoyed something of the life of a courtier, he had forsaken all in obedience to the voice of his higher nature. Hence the struggle between his tastes and his duties would come and come again, augmented probably by such austere notions as every conscientious man must entertain in proportion to his inability to find God in that in which he might find him. From this inability, inseparable in its varying degrees from the very nature of growth, springs all the asceticism of good men, whose love to God will be the greater as their growing insight reveals him in his world, and their growing faith approaches to the giving of thanks in everything.

When we have discovered the truth that whatsoever is not of faith is sin, they way to meet it is not to forsake the human law, but so to obey it as to thank God for it. To leave the world and go into the desert is not thus to give thanks: it may have been the only way for this or that man, in his blameless blindness, to take. The divine mind of George Herbert, however, was in the main bent upon discovering God everywhere. . . .

Coming now to speak of his art, let me say something first about his use of homeliest imagery for highest thought. This, I think, is in itself enough to class him with the highest *kind* of poets. If my reader will refer to "The Elixir," he will see an instance in the third stanza, "You may look at the glass, or at the sky:" "You may regard your action only, or that action as the will of God." Again, let him listen to the pathos and simplicity of this one stanza, from a poem he calls "The Flower." He has been in trouble; his times have been evil; he has felt a spiritual old age creeping upon him; but he is once more awake.

> And now in age[1] I bud again;
> After so many deaths I live and write;
> I once more smell the dew and rain,
> And relish versing. O my only light,
>   It cannot be
>   That I am he
> On whom thy tempests fell all night!

Again:

> Some may dream merrily, but when they wake
> They dress themselves and come to thee.

 . . . Born in 1593, notwithstanding his exquisite art, he could not escape being influenced by the faulty tendencies of his age, borne in upon his youth by the example of his mother's friend, Dr. Donne. A man must be a giant like Shakspere or Milton to cast off his age's faults. Indeed no man has more of the "quips and cranks and wanton wiles" of the poetic spirit of his time than George Herbert, but with this difference from the rest of Dr. Donne's school, that such is the indwelling potency that it causes even these to shine with a radiance such that we wish them still to burn and not be consumed. His muse is seldom other than graceful, even when her motions are grotesque, and he is always a gentleman, which cannot be said of his master. We could not bear to part with his most fantastic oddities, they are so interpenetrated with his genius as well as his art.

In relation to the use he makes of these faulty forms, and to show that even herein he has exercised a refraining judgment, though indeed fancying he has quite discarded in only somewhat reforming it, I recommend the study of two poems, each of which he calls "Jordan," though why I have not yet with certainty discovered. . . .

There can hardly be a doubt that his tendency to unnatural forms was encouraged by the increase of respect to symbol and ceremony shown at this period by some of the external powers of the church—Bishop Laud in particular. Had all, however, who delight in symbols, a power, like George Herbert's, of setting even within the horn-lanterns of the more arbitrary of them, such a light of poetry and devotion that their dull sides vanish in its piercing shine, and we forget the symbol utterly in the truth which it cannot obscure, then indeed our part would be to take and be thankful. But there never has been even a living true symbol which the dulness of those who will see the truth only in the symbol has not degraded into the very cockatrice-egg of sectarianism. The symbol is by such always more or less idolized, and the light within more or less patronized. If the truth, for the sake of which all symbols exist, were indeed the delight of those who claim it, the sectarianism of the church would vanish. But men on all sides call that *the truth* which is but its form or outward sign—material or verbal, true or arbitrary, it matters not which—and hence come strifes and divisions.

Although George Herbert, however, could thus illumine all with his divine inspiration, we cannot help wondering whether, if he had betaken himself yet more to vital and less to half artificial symbols, the change would not have been a breaking of the pitcher and an outshining of the lamp. For a symbol may remind us of the truth, and at the same time obscure it—present it, and dull its effect. It is the temple of nature and not the temple of the church, the things made by the hands of God and not the things made by the hands of man, that afford the truest symbols of truth.

I am anxious to be understood. The chief symbol of our faith, *the Cross*, it may be said, is not one of these natural symbols. I answer—No; but neither is it an arbitrary symbol. It is not a symbol of *a truth* at all, but of *a fact*, of the infinitely grandest fact in the universe, which is itself the outcome and symbol of the grandest Truth. *The Cross* is an historical *sign*, not properly *a symbol*, except through the facts it reminds us of. On the other hand, *baptism* and the *eucharist* are symbols of the loftiest and profoundest kind, true to nature and all its meanings, as well as to the facts of which they remind us. They are in themselves symbols of the truths involved in the facts they commemorate.

Of Nature's symbols George Herbert has made large use; but he would have been yet a greater poet if he had made a larger use of them still. Then at least we might have got rid of such oddities as the stanzas for steps up to the church-door, the first at the bottom of the page; of the lines shaped into ugly altar-form; and of the absurd Easter wings, made of ever lengthening lines. This would not have been much, I confess, nor the gain by their loss great; but not to mention the larger supply of images graceful with the grace of God, who when he had made them said they were good, it would have led to the further purification of his taste, perhaps even to the casting out of all that could untimely move our mirth; until possibly (for illustration), instead of this lovely stanza, he would have given us even a lovelier:

> Listen, sweet dove, unto my song,
>   And spread thy golden wings on me;
> Hatching my tender heart so long,
>   Till it get wing, and fly away with thee.

The stanza is indeed lovely, and true and tender and clever as well; yet who can help smiling at the notion of the incubation of the heart-egg, although what the poet means is so good that the smile almost vanishes in a sigh?

There is no doubt that the works of man's hands will also afford many true symbols; but I do think that, in proportion as a man gives himself to those instead of studying Truth's wardrobe of forms in nature, so will he decline from the high calling of the poet. George Herbert was too great to be himself much injured by the narrowness of the field whence he gathered his symbols; but his song will be the worse for it in the ears of all but those who, having lost sight of or having never beheld the oneness of the God whose creation exists in virtue of his redemption, feel safer in a low-browed crypt than under "the high embowed roof."

When the desire after system or order degenerates from a need into a passion, or ruling idea, it closes, as may be seen in many women who are especial housekeepers, like an unyielding skin over the mind, to the death of all development from impulse and aspiration. The same thing holds in the church: anxiety about order and system will kill the life. This did not go near to being the result with George Herbert: his life was hid with Christ in God; but the influence of his *profession*, as distinguished from his work, was hurtful to his calling as a poet. He of all men would scorn to claim social rank for spiritual service; he of all men would not commit the blunder of supposing that prayer and praise are that service of God: they are *prayer* and *praise*, not *service*; he knew that God can be served only through loving ministration to his sons and daughters, all needy of commonest human help: but, as the most devout of clergymen will be the readiest to confess, there is even a danger to their souls in the unvarying recurrence of the outward obligations of their service; and, in like manner, the poet will fare ill if the conventions from which the holiest system is not free send him soaring with sealed eyes. George Herbert's were but a little blinded thus; yet something, we must allow, his poetry was injured by his profession. All that I say on this point, however, so far from diminishing his praise, adds thereto, setting forth only that he was such a poet as might have been greater yet, had the divine gift had free course. But again I rebuke myself and say, "Thank God for George Herbert." . . .

It will be observed how much George Herbert goes beyond all that have preceded him, in the expression of feeling as it flows from individual conditions, in the analysis of his own moods, in the logic of worship, if I may say so. His utterance is not merely of personal love and grief, but of the peculiar love and grief in the heart of George Herbert. There may be disease in such a mind; but, if there be, it is a disease that will burn itself out. Such disease is, for men constituted like him, the only path to health. By health I mean that simple regard to the truth, to the will of God, which will turn away a man's eyes from his own conditions, and leave God free to work his perfection in him—free, that is, of the interference of the man's self-consciousness and anxiety. To this perfection St. Paul had come when he no longer cried out against the body of his death, no more judged his own self, but left all to the Father, caring only to do his will. It was enough to him then that God

should judge him, for his will is the one good thing securing all good things. Amongst the keener delights of the life which is at the door, I look for the face of George Herbert, with whom to talk humbly would be in bliss a higher bliss.

Notes

1. He was but thirty-nine when he died.

SAMUEL R. GARDINER
From *History of England*
1883, Volume 7, pp. 265–69

George Herbert had much in common with Ferrar; but he never could have arrived at this perfect quiescence of spirit. A younger brother of that Edward Herbert who had been created by Charles Lord Herbert of Cherbury, he was fired, at an early age, with an ambition to rise in the service of the State. At Westminster and Cambridge he was noted for industry and intelligence, wrote lines, like so many others, to the memory of Prince Henry, and flashed before the University as the author of a series of Latin poems in defence of the ceremonies of the Church against Andrew Melville. If the reader misses in these sarcastic poems any manifestation of high spiritual devotion, they need not, on that account, be set down as a mere offering upon the altar of courtiership. Herbert was a ceremonialist by nature. The outward sign was to him more than to most men the expression of the inward fact. His religion fed itself upon that which he could handle and see, and that quaintness which strict criticism reprehends in his poetry, was the effect of his irresistible tendency to detect a hidden meaning in the most unexpected objects of sense.

In these Cambridge days Herbert's mind was distracted between two different aims, which yet appeared to him to be but one. Marked out by his character for a peaceful devotional life, and absolutely unfitted for the turmoil of political controversy, his youthful spirits were too buoyant to allow him to acknowledge at once his inability to play a stirring part in the world. One day he was writing religious poetry. Another day he was canvassing for preferment, and he contrived to persuade himself that preferment would enable him to help on the cause of religion better than writing poetry. In 1619 he succeeded Nethersole as Public Orator of the University. The position delighted him as giving him precedence next to the doctors, 'and such like gaynesses, which will please a young man well.' On the other hand, he reminded himself that progress in the study of divinity was still to be his main object. "This dignity," he wrote, "hath no such earthiness in it but it may very well be joined with heaven; or if it had to others, yet to me it should not, for aught I yet know."

Herbert's efforts after worldly distinction ended in failure. He had good friends at Court. Hamilton, Lennox, and James himself loved him well; but he was too honest to sink to the lower arts of a courtier's life, and he had not the practical abilities of a statesman. The oration with which he welcomed Charles on his return from Spain was an evidence of the sincerity with which he could not help accompanying flatteries neither more nor less absurd than those which flowed unmitigated from the pens of so many of his contemporaries. It was no secret that the Prince had come back bent upon war. Herbert disliked war, and he could not refrain from the maladroit compliment of commending Charles for going to Madrid in search of peace. All that he could bring himself to say was that, as war was sometimes necessary, he would be content to believe any war to be necessary to which James should give his consent. If Herbert bowed down it was not to the Prince whom it was his interest to captivate, but to the peaceful King who had maintained the ceremonies of the Church against their assailants.

A change came over Herbert's life. His three patrons—Hamilton, Lennox, and James—died. From Charles, rushing headlong into war, the lover of peace had no favour to expect. His health, always feeble, broke down. In this time of depression he formed a resolution to take orders, to become, as he said, one of 'the domestic servants of the King of heaven.' The clerical office was not in those days held in very high esteem. A friend dissuaded him from entering upon 'too mean an employment, and too much below his birth and the excellent abilities and endowments of his mind.' "Though the iniquity of the late times," he answered, "have made clergymen meanly valued, and the sacred name of priest contemptible, yet I will labour to make it honourable, by consecrating all my learning and all my poor abilities to advance the glory of that God that gave them, and I will labour to be like my Saviour by making humility lovely in the eyes of all men, and by following the merciful and meek example of my dear Jesus."

Nevertheless, Herbert hesitated long. He was still a layman when Williams presented him to the prebend of Leighton Ecclesia in the diocese of Lincoln. The church was in ruins, and Herbert signalised his connection with it by collecting money from his wealthy friends for its repair. As in Cosin's church at Brancepeth and Ferrar's at Little Gidding, the reading-desk and the pulpit were placed side by side, and both were made of the same height, in order that it might appear that 'they should neither have a precedency or priority of the other; but that prayer and preaching, being equally useful, might agree like brethren and have an equal honour and estimation.'

Four years after his acceptance of preferment in the Church, Herbert was still a layman. In 1630, at the request of the head of his family, the new Earl of Pembroke, he was presented by the King to the Rectory of Fugglestone and Bemerton, two hamlets lying between Salisbury and Wilton. Stories were afterwards told of his reluctance to undertake a duty which he held to be too high for his powers, and it is said that he only gave an unwilling consent on Laud's representation 'that the refusal of it was a sin.' It was doubtless at this time that he received ordination, either from Laud, or from Davenant his diocesan.[1]

The charm of Herbert's life at Bemerton lies in the harmony which had arisen between the discordant elements of his Cambridge life. The love of action, which was wanting in Ferrar, is still there. "A pastor," he declares, "is the deputy of Christ for reducing of man to the obedience of God." But it has blended with a quiet meditative devotion, and out of this soil spring the tenderest blossoms of poetic feeling. His own life was a daily sacrifice, but it was a sacrifice, made not by the avoidance, but by the pursuance of work. For him the sacraments and observances of the Church had a fellowship with the myriad-sided sacrament of nature. As the bee hummed and the tree sent forth its branches, they conveyed to his pure and observant mind the inward and spiritual grace which was to him a comfort and a strength. The things of nature formed a standing protest against idleness. "Every gift of ability," he said, "is a talent to be accounted for." There was to be no more crucifying of the flesh for its own sake, no turning of the back upon the world as evil. His sermons were filled with homely illustrations, and he took good care to explain to his parishioners the meaning of the prayers which they used. His own life was the best sermon. His predecessor had lived sixteen or twenty miles

off, and had left the church in need of repair, whilst the parsonage-house was in ruins. The congregation was that of an ordinary country parish, long untaught and untended, and accustomed to regard their rector as a mere grasper of tithe corn. The change produced by Herbert's presence was magical. Wherever he turned he gathered love and reverence round him, and when his bell tolled for prayers the hardworked labourer, weary with the toils of the day, would let his plough rest for a moment, and breathe a prayer to heaven before resuming his labour.

The dominant note of Herbert's poetry is the eagerness for action, mingled with a sense of its insufficiency. The disease which wasted his body filled him with the consciousness of weakness, and he welcomed death as the awakening to a higher life. Sometimes the sadness overpowers the joy, as in those pathetic lines:—

> Life is a business, not good cheer,
>   Ever in wars,
> The sun still shineth there or here;
>   Whereas the stars
> Watch an advantage to appear.
> Oh that I were an orange tree,
>   That busy plant!
> Then should I ever laden be,
>   And never want
> Some fruit for him that dressed me.
> But we are still too young or old;
>   The man is gone
> Before we do our wares unfold;
>   So we freeze on,
> Until the grave increase our cold.

To Herbert the life of the orange tree was the best; the life of strenuous restfulness which brings forth fruit without effort. He lived less than three years at Bemerton. When he died he left behind him a name which will never perish in England.

Notes

1. Walton's well-known story that the Court was at Wilton, and that the tailor was sent for from Salisbury to provide a clerical dress, is certainly untrue. The Court was at Whitehall, and the presentation, printed from the Patent Rolls in *Rymer* (xix. 258), is dated from Westminster. It also describes Herbert simply as a master of arts. The omission of the usual *Clericus* shows that he was still a layman at this time.

EDWARD DOWDEN
From "Anglo-Catholic Poets: Herbert, Vaughan"
Puritan and Anglican
1901, pp. 97–111

The poetry of the Anglican communion is most happily represented by two books—George Herbert's *The Temple* and Keble's *The Christian Year*. Each was the fruit or the foretaste of an Anglican revival. But Keble's collection of poems—designed to exhibit "the soothing tendency in the Prayer Book"—had more of a deliberate purpose and plan than that of Herbert. Many of Keble's pieces are poetical studies of themes, delicately touched with personal feeling, but rather meditative than possessed by lyrical passion. Herbert's best poems are lyrical cries, taken up by the intelligence and daintily arranged as if for the viol or the lute. The vitality of what he wrote is attested by the witness of two centuries, the seventeenth and the nineteenth. During the eighteenth century—the *sœculum rationalisticum*—his light shone dimly through a cloud.

The great event of Herbert's life was undoubtedly his turning from a mundane career to the humble duties and the quiet gladness of a country parson's lot. As a child, Walton tells us, "the beauties of his pretty behaviour and wit shined and became so eminent and lovely . . . that he seemed to be marked out for piety, and to become the care of Heaven, and of a particular good angel to guide and guard him." His classical scholarship at the age of twenty-five justified his appointment as public orator at Cambridge; he was skilled in Italian, Spanish, French, and hoped at one time that he might attain to the position of a Secretary of State. He kept himself at a distance from his inferiors, valued his parts and his distinguished parentage, and enjoyed his "gentle humour for clothes and court-like company." We learn with some satisfaction from his brother, Lord Herbert of Cherbury, that he was not exempt from passion and choler, the infirmities of his race; meekness that is grafted on ardour of temperament is something far removed from tameness.

A time came when Herbert began to doubt of the world and its coloured gifts:

> I shake my head, and all the thoughts and ends,
> Which my fierce youth did bandy, fall and flow
> Like leaves about me.

In the poem named "The Pilgrim," he appears as a traveller whose eyes are set upon a distant hill; passing the dangers of the way and its meadows of flowery temptation, he comes to the wild of passion, which some call the wold—

> A wasted place but sometimes rich.

At length the hill where lie his heart and hope is attained; alas! when the brow has been reached, all that the pilgrim finds is a brackish pool of tears; his true goal lies yet onward, only to be come at by the way of death; yet even so, wary but courageous, he resolves to pursue his brave adventure.

It is an allegory of Herbert's spiritual life. We may rest assured that the worst dangers of the wild of passion were unknown to his experience; his heart was never concentrated in one evil desire, but it had been scattered and squandered amid mundane attractions which afterwards seemed to him, in comparison with joys that he had found, mere dust or dross. He needed some coherence, some controlling unity, some centre of activity, some central rest in his spirit; and he found there, no overmastering evil perhaps, but a crowd of pestering idle wishes and shallow cares—"quarries of piled vanities," "thousands of toys," "bubbles of foam," "balls of wind," "balls of wild-fire":

> Chases in arras, gilded emptiness,
> Shadows well mounted, dreams in a career.

How far is man, he exclaims, from power and from settled peace! He is "some twenty several men at least each several hour." Herbert did not feel like Bunyan's Christian that he was crushed by a burden, a doomed and terrified inhabitant of the City of Destruction; he resembled rather Bunyan's other pilgrim who quitted Vanity Fair to seek abiding joys in the Celestial city.

He longed for constancy—a confirmed will—and he longed for true rest. He, the friend of Bacon, had known the ways of learning—

> what the stars conspire,
> What willing nature speaks, what forced by fire,
> Both the old discoveries, and the new found seas,
> The stock and surplus, cause and history.

He, a courtier, high in the King's favour and not meanly valued by the most eminent and powerful of the great lords, had known the ways of honour:

> what maintains
> The quick returns of courtesy and wit,
> In vies of favours whether party gains,
> When glory swells the heart.

He had known the ways of pleasure:

> What mirth and music mean; what love and wit
> Have done these twenty hundred years, and more.

And the distractions of knowledge and honour and pleasure seemed only to make an idle noise of thoughts within his heart. "Man," he cries, "is out of order hurled,

> Parcelled out to all the world."

He desired to escape from idle anarchy of the will, and to enter into the Divine order, which gives to all things their set forms, making sweet walks and bowers where the wild woods had been. He would fain be a link of God's great chain; a piping reed, if no more, in God's great concert; a flower, however lowly, in God's garden; a tree giving either fruit or shade—

> at least some bird would trust
> Her household to me, and I should be just.

How should constancy be attained amid vicissitude? And where is the dwelling-place of Peace?

He felt the dignity as well as the poverty of man, and knew that such dignity is wronged by entering as an atom into a vain whirl of dust. Man is in truth a stately palace built for God; a noble piece of symmetry; a harmony made to bear a part with the whole of the Divine creation—

> For head and foot hath private amity,
> And both with moons and tides.

Man is a master attended by the winds and the fountains, by stars and sun, by night and day. And yet he is a palace in decay; a tree that bears no fruit; a dissonance in nature; a master who wields no true authority, but squanders his wealth as a spendthrift. Since the world has grown old it seems as if life had become more difficult and the Divine Presence were less near. In the former days, when God lodged with Lot, struggled with Jacob, advised with Abraham, He might be encountered at any moment, suddenly on the right hand or the left:

> One might have sought and found Thee presently
> At some fair oak, or bush, or cave, or well:
> Is my God this way? No, they would reply,
> He is to Sinai gone, as we heard tell:
> List, ye may hear great Aaron's bell.

Yet, with such a sigh as this for the primitive age of wonder and direct intercourse with heaven, Herbert felt or came to feel that the secluded Deity is not far from every one of us, that in Him we live, and move, and have our being:

> Thou art in small things great, nor small in any:
> Thy even praise can neither rise nor fall.
> Thou art in all things one, in each thing many:
> For Thou art infinite in one and all.

> Tempests are calm to Thee; they know Thy hand,
> And hold it fast, as children do their father's,
> Which cry and follow. Thou hast made poor sand
> Check the proud sea, ev'n when it swells and
> gathers.

And thus the age of wonder is perpetually present.

In the City of Destruction by one who is oppressed beneath his awful burden God is thought of at first as the angry judge. Herbert thinks of God rather as a loving strategist, who lures His children to Himself by finer bribes than Vanity Fair can offer. He is like the mother who would not startle her infant when it was crawling on the edge of the precipice, but silently displayed her bosom and won the straggler back. We are beset by temptations to piety more than by temptations to sin. Dawn arises, and with it comes a sunbeam by which the soul may climb to heaven:

> I cannot ope mine eyes,
> 　But thou art ready there to catch
> My morning soul and sacrifice;
> 　Then we must needs for that day make a match.

Evening descends, and night shows no less love than the day; if day was the gale, evening is the harbour; if day was the garden, evening is the grove. Joy should lead us Godwards, and if joy fail, then there is grief; even weariness should toss us to God's breast. On every side our heart is enticed to its true happiness; millions of surprises waylay us; and the sound of glory is for ever ringing in our ears. The springtide of gladness, when

> Our days were strawed with flowers and happiness,
> 　There was no month but May,

is followed by the mercies of affliction—

> Thus thin and lean without a fence or friend
> I was blown through by every storm and wind.

And gladness and sorrow are alike parts of the Divine art by which souls are captured for their own good.

But the way to constancy and to content is through humility and obedience. Wits may enter into contest, and inscribe their rival posies on the pane: let our posy be the words, "Less than the least of all thy mercies." More than the other enthroned Virtues, Humility, who sits the lowest, is wise; let us till our own ground; let us roost and nestle under God's tent, not gadding abroad at the call of wandering thoughts and passions:

> Who cannot on his own bed sweetly sleep
> Can on another's hardly rest.

Let us know how to possess our secret, and harbour the flame within us as safely as the fire is hidden in the flint. Whether the world rides by him or lags behind, the honest man will constantly ride his sure and even trot; if trials come, he neither seeks nor shuns, but calmly abides them; his words and works are all of a piece, and all are clear and straight; if he has to deal with those who are governed by passion, he allows for that and keeps his steadfast course.

Constancy and content attained through humility and obedience—these substantial gains Herbert must needs choose rather than the various toys men chaffer for in the world's fair; and so the courtier of King James was transformed into the rector of Bemerton. He viewed deliberately the two methods of life, the two regiments, God's and the world's—

> Thine clad with simpleness and sad events,
> 　The other fine,
> Full of glory and gay weeds,
> Brave language, braver deeds—

and after certain scruples of conscience had been overcome with the aid of counsel from Laud, the issue was decided. What it meant for Herbert we can but inadequately conceive. "When at his induction," writes Walton, "he was shut into Bemerton church, being left there alone to toll the bell, as the law requires him, he stayed so much longer than an ordinary time before he returned to his friends, that stayed expecting him at the church door, that his friend Mr. Woodnot looked in at the church window, and saw him lie prostrate on the ground before the altar; at which time and place, as he after told Mr. Woodnot, he set some rules to himself for the future manage of his life, and then and there made a vow to labour to keep them."

To become part of a great and Divine Order, to regulate his life by rules, to perform a round of duties exactly, reverently, gracefully, gladly, and at the same time to express in song the tides, the fluctuations, the incursions, the ebb and flow of the spirit, made up the life of George Herbert. He could not wholly shape his course by rule. Still the passionate temperament of his race remained with him; but his ardour was in great measure regulated, and served before all else to quicken his fidelity in duty and to prevent his observance of forms from sinking into formalism. Still he was subject to swift alternations of mood:

> How should I praise Thee, Lord! how should my
> 　rhymes
> 　Gladly engrave Thy love in steel,
> If what my soul doth feel sometimes
> 　My soul might ever feel!
> Although there were some forty heavens, or more,
> 　Sometimes I peer above them all;
> Sometimes I hardly reach a score,
> 　Sometimes to hell I fall.
> O rack me not to such a vast extent.

In the poem entitled "Misery," Herbert reviews the infirmities and follies of the race of men; at the close, by a sudden return upon himself, he gives the whole a personal application. What is man, wavering on the billows of the world and flung upon the sands or rocky shelves? What is he but "a sick tossed vessel"

> 　　—dashing on each thing;
> Nay, his own shelf:
> My God, I mean myself.

Yet beneath all fluctuations of mood now lay steadfastness; beneath all restlessness of desire lay a deep content.

He knew that he was a tiny wheel or cog in the divine machinery, a machinery which had its pulse and movement in the spirit. A lover of beauty, he carried his sense of beauty into his realisation of a sacred order. He still could smell the dew and rain and relish versing. What are the songs that celebrate with ingenious praise a girdle or a glove but "dust blown by wit"? All his inventions he would seriously lay upon the altar. He had nobler beauties to sing than the red and white of a woman's cheek or the trammels of golden hair. He could wittily play with fancies and twist his metaphors, if the mood took him; for God does not disdain the pretty, pious sports of His children. He could spread his Easter wings, or build his visible altar of verse, upon the page, or labour his devout anagram, or tangle his wreath of rhymes; it was the fashion of the day, and why should not fashion itself be sanctified? But he could also be plain and bid farewell to sweet phrases, curled metaphors, trim inventions, honey of roses, winding stairs of subtle meaning:—

> Shepherds are honest people; let them sing:
> Riddle who list for me, and pull for prime:
> I envy no man's nightingale or spring.

And in truth Herbert's range as a poet was considerable. He could wind himself into the daintiest conceits. He could be gravely majestic:—

> 　This heap of dust,
> To which the blast of death's incessant motion,
> Fed with the exhalation of our crimes,
> 　Drives all at last.

He could write in a strain of genuine simplicity:—

> Teach me, my God and King,
> 　In all things Thee to see,
> And what I do in any thing,
> 　To do it as for Thee.

And whatever was within him, ornament or simplicity, seriousness or innocent play, belonged to God and to God's Church.

To God's Church, for that was part of the Divine order, through which he had been delivered from the anarchy of the world, and it was a part beautiful to his heart's desire. In all visible things he was pleased by comeliness. His gentle humour for clothes did not disappear on the morning when, forsaking his sword and silk, he summoned a tailor to come speedily from Salisbury to Wilton to take measure and made him canonical garments against next day, "which," adds Walton, to satisfy the reader's expectant sympathy, "the tailor did." But Herbert, we know, frail and graceful as he was, would not scruple to put off his canonical coat at need to help a poor man with a poorer horse that was fallen under his load, and never did the country parson, "which used to be so trim and clean," look happier than when he came soiled and discomposed into the company of his musical friends at Salisbury. He had now, however, a wider field than his own person on which to expend his decorative skill. He was already the re-edifier of the parish church at Layton Ecclesia, "being for the workmanship a costly mosaic, for the form an exact cross, and for the decency and beauty," his biographer assures us, "the most remarkable parish church that this nation affords." He proceeded forthwith to repair the chancel at Bemerton, and to rebuild in great part the parsonage, inscribing it to his successor in words which exhorted him to be good to the poor, that so the builder's labour should not be lost.

Herbert's feeling for order and beauty was satisfied by that middle way between splendour and plainness which he found in the Anglican Church:—

> The mean thy praise and glory is,
> And long may be.

The title given to his poems, perhaps by his friend Nicholas Ferrar, *The Temple*, sound somewhat too stately; as far as they are concerned with the public ordinances of religion "The Parish Church" would have been sufficient. Herbert's imagination was not spacious or rich enough to move at ease amid the noble pomps of ritual; these would have oppressed rather than borne upwards his spiritual aspirations. He needed grace and refinement as incentives, and he needed for repose some chastened order made sensible. The parish music of voices accompanied with viol and flute sufficed to lift him above all temporal cares:—

> Now I in you without a body move,
> Rising and falling with your wings:
> We both together sweetly live and love,
> Yet say sometimes *God help poor Kings*.

He loved to moralise the simple accessories of worship or of the place of prayer into dainty meanings—the checkered stones of the floor signify humility and patience, the stains of the marble are the stains of sin, the storied windows, in which colour and light combine to show forth sacred things, are the holy preachers; even the lock and key must yield a moral. The rites of the Church have for their character a spiritual power clothed in the beauty of simplicity. Baptism is the little gate and narrow way through which we enter into the realm of divine order; it reminds us that the childlike spirit should still be ours, for "childhood is health." In the Holy Communion Christ conveys Himself to the faithful "not in rich furniture or fine array" but by the way of nourishment and strength. The habit of the Christian priesthood is "a severe attire"; God makes vessels of lowly matter meet for high uses. The splendour of the true Aarons is now only for the inward eye:

> Holiness on the head,
> Light and perfections on the breast,
> Harmonious bells below raising the dead,
> To lead them unto life and rest.
> Thus are true Aarons drest.

From Walton's detailed account of the instruction given by Herbert to his parishioners we learn that the central thought of the teacher with respect to the whole service of the Church was that it is a reasonable service, and therefore acceptable to God.

A certain beautiful method and order is imparted to the religious emotions, which are too apt to run wild, by the progress of the Christian year. At Christmas the soul of the singer arrays itself in the garments of the shepherds, and leads its flock of thoughts to spiritual pastures. Lent is a "dear feast" rather than a season of fasting; if Christ fasted, we should follow and, though far behind His forty days of entire abstinence, we may meet Him in His own way:

> Perhaps my God, though He be far before
> May turn, and take me by the hand.

At Easter we taste the joy of the sun's early light and perfume, and are met by a deeper joy:

> I got me flowers to straw thy way;
> I got me boughs off many a tree;
> But thou wast up by break of day,
> And brought'st thy sweets along with thee.

On Whitsunday we pray that the Dove may spread his golden wings above our hearts. On Trinity Sunday we translate the mystery into renewed faith and hope and charity. There is no Sunday of all the year that does not pull and turn us round from wordly cares, to look on One whom if we were not very dull we should look on constantly:

> On Sunday heaven's gate stands ope;
> Blessings are plentiful and rife,
> More plentiful than hope.

To the Virgin mother Herbert is dutifully reverent and presents her with the toy of an anagram on her name. To her and to all angels and saints he is very courteous; reluctantly declining the dulia and hyperdulia because these are not bidden, he dares not go beyond the divine command, which they also gladly observe—

> Where His pleasure no injunction lays,
> ('Tis your own case) ye never move a wing.

Such self-denying apology on her singer's part must surely gratify the blessed Maid more than any fervours of misdirected homage.

Curious questions, which create divisions in religion, are set aside by Herbert's piety. "Love God, and love your neighbour. Watch and pray. Do as ye would be done unto"—these are the Gordian knots of religion, and they need no severing nor untying. Astronomers invent their epicycles to save a theory of the spheres; in divinity we may burn the ingenious epicycles of the theologians. The Holy Scriptures are a book of stars that lights us to eternal bliss. After entire self-confession to God, how lucid all things have grown! And there is the wisdom of prayer, concerning which Herbert has said perhaps his deepest word. The sonnet on Prayer is one of piled-up metaphors, as if no imagery were sufficient to express its sweetness and its strength; prayer is God's breath in man, a plummet, an engine against the Almighty, a tower, a tune, a bird of paradise; but in the last word of the sonnet all metaphor is dropped, and prayer is felt like the deep and satisfying and inexpressible discovery of Saint John as he lay on the divine comrade's breast; prayer is

Church-bells beyond the stars heard, the soul's blood,
    The land of spices; something understood.

"Something understood," which it is impossible to utter in words, and to which no imagery corresponds.

The last word of Herbert is neither of death nor doomsday, of judgment nor heaven; it is the poem named "Love." By Love the soul, "guilty of dust and sin," is welcomed to the feast; but the poor guest is embarrassed by a sense of unworthiness—

I, the unkind, ungrateful? Ah, my dear,
    I cannot look on thee.
Love took my hand, and smiling did reply,
    Who made the eyes but I.
Truth, Lord, but I have marr'd them: let my shame
    Go where it doth deserve.
And know you not, says Love, who bore the blame?
    My dear, then I will serve.
You must sit down, says Love, and taste my meat:
    So I did sit and eat.

Exquisite courtesy to the close, the courtesy of heaven meeting the humble fears and affectionate desires of earth. The last delicacy of Love, the strategist.

PAUL ELMER MORE
From "George Herbert"
Shelburne Essays: Fourth Series
1906, pp. 89–98

The dominant tone in Herbert is one of quiet joy and peace. From the very doubts and hesitations that beset him he wrung a submissive victory, as may be read in that most characteristic of his poem, "The Pulley":

When God at first made man,
Having a glasse of blessings standing by,
    Let us (said he) poure on him all we can.
Let the world's riches, which dispersed lie,
    Contract into a span.

    So strength first made a way,
Then beautie flow'd, then wisdome, honour, pleasure,
    When almost all was out, God made a stay,
Perceiving that alone of all his treasure
    Rest in the bottome lay.

    For if I should (said he)
Bestow this jewell also on my creature,
He should adore my gifts instead of me,
And rest in Nature, not the God of Nature.
    So both should losers be.

    Yet let him keep the rest,
But keep them with repining restlessness.
    Let him be rich and wearie, that at least,
If goodnesse leade him not, yet wearinesse
    May tosse him to my breast.

Will you pardon me a fancy? As often as I read these stanzas the picture rises before me of the Salisbury fields. It is an afternoon of the early autumn, when the grey sunlight shimmers in the air and scarcely touches the earth, brooding over all things with a kind of transient peace. A country parson, after a day of music in the cathedral and at the house of a friend, is walking homeward. In his heart is the quiet afterglow of rapture, not unlike the subdued light upon the meadows, and he knows that both are but for a little while. Memory is awake as she is apt to be in the trail of exaltation, and he recalls the earlier scenes of his life—the peculiar consecration of his youth, the half-hearted ambitions of the scholar and courtier,

the invisible guidance that had brought him at last to the sheltered haven whereto he was even now returning. Providence and the world had dealt kindly with him as with few others, yet one thing was still lacking—he had not found rest. He was aware, keenly aware, that this moment of perfect calm lay between an hour of enthusiasm and an hour of dejection. He was not like some he knew who laid violent hands on the kingdom of peace; he must suffer his moods. And then came the recollection of the Greek Hesiod whom he had studied at Cambridge, and of the story of Pandora. The quaint contrast of that myth with the certainty of his own faith teased him into reflection. Hope, indeed, the new dispensation had released from the box and had poured out blessings instead of ills; but one thing still remained shut up—*rest in the bottom lay*. And straightway he began to remould the Greek fable to his own experience.

All this is consonant with the tone which in the beginning he adopted as the lyric poet of divine love and which remained with him in his Bemerton study:

Why do I languish thus, drooping and dull,
    As if I were all earth?
O give me quicknesse, that I may with mirth
    Praise thee brim-full!

The wanton lover in a curious strain
    Can praise his fairest fair,
And with quaint metaphors her curled hair
    Curl o're again.

Thou art my lovelinesse, my life, my light,
    Beautie alone to me.
Thy bloudy death and underserv'd makes thee
    Pure red and white.
. . .
Where are my lines then? My approaches? Views?
    Where are my window-songs?
Lovers are still pretending, and ev'n wrongs
    Sharpen their Muse.
. . .
Lord, cleare thy gift, that with a constant wit
    I may but look towards thee.
Look onely; for to *love* thee, who can be,
    What angel fit?

To some this peculiarly individual note in religion, this anxiety over his personal beatitude, will be a stumbling-block. "For the most part," says Professor Palmer in disdain, "he is concerned with the small needs of his own soul." It is like a taunt thrown ungraciously at the ideals of a great and serious age. My dear sir, even to-day in the face of our magnified concerns, are the needs of a man's soul so small that we dare speak of them with contempt? I am not holding a brief from the human soul. Let it be, if you choose, a mere name for certain hopes and fears which separate from the world and project themselves into eternity; but let us recognise the fact that those hopes and fears have been of tremendous force in the past, and are still worthy of reverence. It is one of the glories of Herbert's age that it introduced into poetry that quick and tremulous sense of the individual soul. Religion came to those men with the shock of a sudden and strange reality, and we who read the report of their experience are ourselves stirred, willingly or rebelliously, to unused emotions. Do you know, in fact, what most of all is lacking in the devotional poetry of recent times? It is just this direct personal appeal. Take, for example, the better stanzas of Keble's "Whitsunday":

So, when the Spirit of our God
    Came down His flock to find,
A voice from Heaven was heard abroad,
    A rushing, mighty wind.

Nor doth the outward ear alone
    At that high warning start;
Conscience gives back the appalling tone;
    'Tis echoed in the heart.

It fills the Church of God; it fills
    The sinful world around;
Only in stubborn hearts and wills
    No place for it is found.

That is Keble's version of the coming of the Holy Ghost at
Pentecost; set it beside a single stanza of Herbert's poem of the
same name:

Listen, sweet Dove, unto my song
    And spread thy golden wings in me;
Hatching my tender heart so long,
    Till it get wing and flie away with thee.

Is the advantage all in favour of the modern faith? Or rather, is
not the response to the descending spirit in Keble dulled by the
intrusion of foreign interests, by the sense that he is writing for
the Church and imparting a moral lesson, whereas in Herbert
you feel the ecstatic uplift that springs from the immediate
contact of the poet's imagination with its object? Religion has
changed from the soul's intimate discovery of beatitude to the
dull convention of sermons. "He speaks of God like a man that
really believeth in God," said Baxter of Herbert; is this altogether a small matter?

Nor is it quite true that his personal concern with religion
is a selfish withdrawal from men or that "any notion of dedicating himself to their welfare is foreign to him." Such a statement would have been unintelligible to Herbert's
contemporaries; it forgets the sacramental nature of the
priesthood as it was then conceived. His days, indeed, were
given to the humblest duties and charities, yet to his friends it
would have seemed that the example of so saintly a life was a
still more perfect beneficence than any ministrations of the
body. Such, too, was the more difficult ideal that Herbert set
before himself:

Holinesse on the head,
    Light and perfections on the breast,
Harmonious bells below, raising the dead
    To lead them unto life and rest;
        Thus are true Aarons drest.

And, beyond the mere force of example, it was supposed that
worship in itself was an excellent thing, and that some grace
was poured out upon the people through the daily intercessions
of their priest:

Of all the creatures both in sea and land
    Onely to Man thou hast made known thy wayes,
And put the penne alone into his hand,
    And made him Secretarie of thy praise.

Beasts fain would sing; birds dittie to their notes;
    Trees would be tuning on their native lute
To thy renown; but all their hands and throats
    Are brought to Man, while they are lame and
        mute.

Man is the world's high Priest. He doth present
    The sacrifice for all; while they below
Unto the service mutter an assent,
    Such as springs use that fall and windes that blow.
. . .

Wherefore, most sacred Spirit, I here present
    For me and all my fellows praise to thee.
And just it is that I should pay the rent,
    Because the benefit accrues to me.

And it was in this sense that elsewhere he likened the priest to a
window in the temple wall, "a brittle crazy glass," through
which, nevertheless, the light fell upon the people stained with
holy images. His poems he called *window-songs*. Certainly to
Walton the concern "with the small needs of his own soul" did
not appear to be an abuse of precious talents. Says the Life:
"And there, by that inward devotion which he testified constantly by an humble behaviour and visible adoration, he, like
Joshua, brought not only his own household thus to serve the
Lord, but brought most of his parishioners, and many gentlemen in the neighbourhood, constantly to make a part of his
congregation twice a day. And some of the meaner sort of his
parish did so love and reverence Mr. Herbert that they would
let their plough rest when Mr. Herbert's saints-bell rung to
prayers, that they might also offer their devotions to God with
him; and would then return back to their plough. And his most
holy life was such that it begot such reverence to God, and to
him, that they thought themselves the happier when they carried Mr. Herbert's blessing back with them to their labour."
. . .

Just before the end Herbert gave to a friend who was
visiting him a manuscript book, bidding him deliver it to Nicholas Ferrar to be made public or burned as that gentleman
thought good. It was, as he described it, a picture of the many
spiritual conflicts that had passed betwixt God and his soul,
being the small volume of verse which was the labour and the
fruit of his life. There is much to censure critically in the work,
much that is frigid and fantastic; but at its best the note is rare
and penetrating, with the tinkling purity of a silver sacring bell.
Many have loved the book as a companion of the closet, and
many still cherish it for its human comfort; all of us may profit
from its pages if we can learn from them to wind ourselves out
of the vicious fallacy of the present, and to make our own some
part of Herbert's intimacy with divine things.

SIR EDWARD COKE

1552–1634

Edward Coke was born at Mileham, Norfolk, in 1552. The son of a lawyer, he attended the Norwich Free School and then entered Trinity College, Cambridge, in 1567. Coke went on to study at the Inner Temple, London, in 1571. Coke was Attorney-General under Elizabeth and chief justice of the Common Pleas and King's Bench under James I. A prolific legal author, Coke was the archrival of Sir Francis Bacon. This famous legal debate pitted Coke and common law versus Bacon and royal prerogative. Coke's *Reports*, issued in eleven volumes between 1610 and 1615, provide case law studies of various legal questions. The four volumes of his *Institutes* (1628–44) explain and defend common law rules with numerous references to Roman civil law. The first part of the *Institutes* comments on Sir Thomas Littleton's *Tenures* (c. 1475). Coke also is largely responsible for the legend of Magna Carta.

Coke was dismissed by the King in 1616 after a series of quarrels with the Court of Chancery. He spent most of his later years writing and defending English common law. He died on September 3, 1634, at his family estate, Stoke Poges. He was buried at Tittleshall Church, Norfolk.

Sir Edward Coke, Knight, son of Robert Coke, esquire, and of Winefred Knightly his wife, was born at Mileham, in this county ⟨Norfolk⟩; bred, when ten years of age, at Norwich school, and thence removed to Trinity College in Cambridge. After four years' continuance there, he was admitted into Clifford's Inn, London, and the year following entered a student of the municipal law in the Inner Temple. Such his proficiency therein, that at the end of six years (exceeding early in that strict age) he was called to the bar, and soon after for three years chosen reader in Lyon's Inn. Here his learned lectures so spread forth his fame, that crowds of clients sued to him for his counsel, and his own suit was the sooner granted, when tendering his affections, in order to marriage, unto Briget daughter and coheir of John Paston, esquire.

She was afterwards his incomparable wife; whose portion, moderately estimated, *viis et modis*, amounted unto thirty thousand pounds, her virtues not falling under valuation; and she enriched her husband with ten children.

Then began preferment to press upon him; the city of Norwich choosing him recorder, the county of Norfolk their knight to parliament, the queen her speaker therein, as also successively her solicitor and attorney. King James honoured him with knighthood, and made him chief justice, first of the Common Pleas, then of the King's Bench. Thus, beginning on a good bottom left him by his father, marrying a wife of extraordinary wealth, having at the first great and gainful practice, afterwards many and profitable offices, being provident to choose good pennyworths in purchases, leading a thrifty life, living to a great age, during flourishing and peaceable times (born as much after the persecution under queen Mary, as dying before our civil wars), no wonder if he advanced a fair estate, so that all his sons might seem elder brethren, by the large possessions left unto them.

Some falsely character him a back-friend to the church and clergy, being a grand benefactor to the church of Norwich, who gratefully, under their public seal, honoured him with the ensuing testimony:

"Edwardus Coke, Armiger, sæpius et in multis difficillimis negotiis ecclesiæ nostræ auxiliatus est, et nuper eandem contra Templorum Helluones, qui dominia, maneria, et hæreditamenta nostra devorare sub titulo obscuro (*Concelatum* dicunt) sponte suâ nobis inciis, et sine mercede ullâ, legitimè tutatus est; atque eandem suam nostri defensionem, in perpetuam tantæ rei memoriam, quam posterorum (si opus fuerit), magnâ cum industriâ et scriptis redegit, et nostræ ecclesiæ donavit."

As for the many benefices in his own patronage, he freely gave them to worthy men; being wont to say, in his law-language, that he would have church-livings pass by livery and seisen, not bargain and sale.

Five sorts of people he used to fore-design to misery and poverty; chemists, monopolizers, councillors, promoters, and rhyming poets. For three things he would give God solemn thanks; that he never gave his body to physic, nor his heart to cruelty, nor his hand to corruption. In three things he did much applaud his own success; in his fair fortune with his wife, in his happy study of the laws, and in his free coming by all his offices, *nec prece, nec pretio*; neither begging nor bribing for preferment.

His parts were admirable: he had a deep judgment, faithful memory, active fancy; and the jewel of his mind was put into a fair case, a beautiful body, with a comely countenance; a case which he did wipe and keep clean, delighting in good clothes, well worn; and being wont to say, "that the outward neatness of our bodies might be a monitor of purity to our souls."

In his pleadings, discourse, and judgments, he declined all circumlocutions, usually saying, "The matter lies in a little room." In all places, callings, and jurisdictions, he commended modesty and sobriety within their boundaries, saying, "If a river swells beyond its banks, it loseth its own channel."

If any adverse party crossed him, he would patiently reply, "If another punisheth me, I will not punish myself." In the highest term of business, he made vacation to himself at his table; and would never be persuaded privately to retract what he had publicly adjudged, professing, he was a judge in a court and not in a chamber. He was wont to say, "No wise man would do that in prosperity, whereof he should repent in adversity." He gave for his motto, "Prudens qui patiens;" and his practice was accordingly, especially after he fell into the disfavour of King James.

The cause hereof the reader may find in our English chronicles, whilst we behold how he employed himself when retired to a private life, when he did *frui suo infortunio*, and improved his loss to his advantage. He triumphed in his own innocency, that he had done nothing illegally, calling to mind the motto which he gave in his rings when made serjeant, "Lex est tutissima cassis," (the law is the safest helmet.)

And now he had leisure to peruse what formerly he had written, even thirty books, with his own hand; most pleasing himself with a manual, which he called his "Vade mecum," from whence, at one view, he took a prospect of his life passed, having noted therein most remarkables. His most learned and laborious works on the laws will last to be admired by the judicious posterity whilst Fame hath a trumpet left her, and any breath to blow therein. His judgment lately passed for an oracle in law; and if, since, the credit therof hath causelessly been questioned, the wonder is not great. If the prophet himself, living in an incredulous age, found cause to complain, "Who hath believed our report?" it need not seem strange, that our licentious times have afforded some to shake the authenticalness of the "reports" of any earthly judge.

He constantly had prayers said in his own house, and charitably relieved the poor with his constant alms. The foundation of Sutton's hospital (when indeed but a foundation) had been ruined before it was raised, and crushed by some courtiers in the hatching thereof, had not his great care preserved the same. The free-school at Thetford was supported in its being by his assistance; and he founded a school, on his own cost, at Godwick in this county.

It must not be forgotten, that Dr. Whitgift (afterwards archbishop of Canterbury) was his tutor, who sent unto his pupil when the queen's attorney, a fair New Testament, with this message: "He had now studied common law enough, let him hereafter study the law of God."

Let me add to this, that when he was under a cloud at court, and ousted of his judge's place, the lands belonging to the church of Norwich, which formerly he had so industriously recovered and settled thereon, were again called into question, being begged by a peer, who shall pass nameless. Sir Edward desired him to desist, telling him, that otherwise he would put on his gown and cap, and come into Westminster-hall once again, and plead there in any court in justification of what he had done. He died at Stoke Poges in Buckinghamshire, on Wednesday the 3d of September, being the 83rd year of his age, whose last words were, "Thy kingdom come, Thy will be done."—THOMAS FULLER, *The History of the Worthies of England*, 1662

Sir Edward Coke—that great oracle of our law.—EDMUND BURKE, *Reflections on the Revolution in France*, 1790

This great lawyer, perhaps, set the example of that style of railing and invective in the courts, which the egotism and craven insolence of some of our lawyers include in their practice at the bar. It may be useful to bring to recollection Coke's vituperative style in the following dialogue, so beautiful in its contrast with that of the great victim before him! The attorney-general had not sufficient evidence to bring the obscure conspiracy home to Rawleigh, with which, I believe, however, he had cautiously tampered. But Coke well knew that James the First had reason to dislike the hero of his age who was early engaged against the Scottish interests, and betrayed by the ambidexterous policy of Cecil. Coke struck at Rawleigh as a sacrifice to his own political ambition, as we have seen he afterwards immolated his daughter; but his personal hatred was now sharpened by the fine genius and elegant literature of the man; faculties and acquisitions the lawyer so heartily contemned! Coke had observed, "I know with whom I deal; for we have to deal to-day with a MAN OF WIT."

Coke: Thou art the most vile and execrable traytor that ever lived.
Rawleigh: You speak indiscreetly, barbarously, and uncivilly.

Coke: I want words sufficient to express thy viperous treason.
Rawleigh: I think you want words indeed, for you have spoken one thing half-a-dozen times.
Coke: Thou art an odious fellow; thy name is hateful to all the realm of England for thy pride.
Rawleigh: It will go near to prove a measuring cast between you and me, Mr. Attorney.
Coke: Well, I will now make it appear to the world that there never lived a viler viper upon the face of the earth than thou. Thou art a monster; thou hast an English face, but a Spanish heart. Thou viper! for I *thou* thee, thou traitor! Have I angered you?

Rawleigh replied, what his dauntless conduct proved—"I am in no case to be angry."

Coke had used the same style with the unhappy favourite of Elizabeth, the Earl of Essex. It was usual with him; the bitterness was in his own heart as much as in his words; and Lord Bacon has left among his memorandums one entitled, "Of the abuse I received of Mr. Attorney-General publicly in the Exchequer." A specimen will complete our model of his forensic oratory. Coke exclaimed—"Mr. Bacon, if you have any tooth against me, pluck it out; for it will do you more hurt than all the teeth in your head will do you good." Bacon replied—"The less you speak of your own greatness, the more I will think of it." Coke replied—"I think scorn to stand upon terms of greatness towards you, who are less than little, less than the least." Coke was exhibited on the stage for his ill usage of Rawleigh, as was suggested by Theobald in a note on *Twelfth Night*. This style of railing was long the privilege of the lawyers; it was revived by Judge Jeffreys; but the bench of judges in the reign of William and Anne taught a due respect even to criminals, who were not supposed to be guilty till they were convicted.

When Coke once was himself in disgrace, his high spirit sunk, without a particle of magnanimity to dignify the fall; his big words, and his "tyrannical courses," when he could no longer exult that "he was upon his wings again," sunk with him as he presented himself on his knees to the counciltable. Among other assumptions, he had styled himself "Lord Chief-Justice of England," when it was declared that this title was his own invention, since he was no more than of the King's Bench. His disgrace was a thunderbolt, which overthrew the haughty lawyer to the roots. When the *supersedeas* was carried to him by Sir George Coppin, that gentleman was surprised, on presenting it, to see that lofty "spirit shrunk into a very narrow room, for Coke received it with dejection and tears." The writer from whose letter I have copied these words adds, *O tremor et suspiria non cadunt in fortem et constantem.* The same writer incloses a punning distich: the name of our lord chief-justice was in his day very provocative of the pun, both in Latin and English; Cicero, indeed, had pre-occupied the miserable trifle.

Jus condire Cocus potuit; sed condere jura
Non potuit; potuit condere jura Cocus.

Six years afterwards, Coke was sent to the Tower, and then they punned against him in English. An unpublished letter of the day has this curious anecdote:—The room in which he was lodged in the Tower had formerly been a kitchen; on his entrance, the Lord chief-justice read upon the door, "This room wants a Cook!" They twitched the lion in the toils which held him. Shenstone had some reason in thanking Heaven that his name was not susceptible of a pun. This time, however, Coke was "on his wings;" for when Lord Arundel was sent by the king to the prisoner, to inform him that he would be allowed "Eight of the best learned in the law to advise him for his cause," our great lawyer thanked the king, "but he knew himself to be accounted to have as much skill in the law as any man in England, and therefore needed no such help, nor feared to be judged by the law."—Isaac Disraeli, "Of Coke's Style, and His Conduct," *Curiosities of Literature*, 1791–1824

The equitable jurisdiction, as it is called, of the court of chancery appears to have been derived from that extensive judicial power which, in early times, the king's ordinary council had exercised. The chancellor, as one of the highest officers of state, took a great share in the council's business; and when it was not sitting, he had a court of his own, with jurisdiction in many important matters, out of which process to compel appearance of parties might at any time emanate. It is not unlikely therefore that redress, in matters beyond the legal province of the chancellor, was occasionally given through the paramount authority of this court. We find the council and the chancery named together in many remonstrances of the commons against this interference with private rights, from the time of Richard II to that of Henry VI. It was probably in the former reign that the chancellor began to establish systematically his peculiar restraining jurisdiction. This originated in the practice of feoffments to uses, by which the feoffee, who had legal seisin of the land, stood bound by private engagement to suffer another, called the cestui que use, to enjoy its use and possession. Such fiduciary estates were well known to the Roman jurists, but inconsistent with the feudal genius of our law. The courts of justice gave no redress, if the feoffee to uses violated his trust by detaining the land. To remedy this, an ecclesiastical chancellor devised the writ of subpœna, compelling him to answer upon oath as to his trust. It was evidently necessary also to restrain him from proceeding, as he might do, to obtain possession; and this gave rise to injunctions, that is, prohibitions to sue at law, the violation of which was punishable by imprisonment as a contempt of court. Other instances of breach of trust occurred in personal contracts, and cases also wherein, without any trust, there was a wrong committed beyond the competence of the courts of law to redress; to all which the process of subpœna was made applicable. This extension of a novel jurisdiction was partly owing to a fundamental principle of our common law, that a defendant cannot be examined; so that, if no witness or written instrument could be produced to prove a demand, the plaintiff was wholly debarred of justice: but in a still greater degree to a strange narrowness and scrupulosity of the judges, who, fearful of quitting the letter of their precedents, even with the clearest analogies to guide them, repelled so many just suits, and set up rules of so much hardship, that men were thankful to embrace the relief held out by a tribunal acting in a more rational spirit. This error the common lawyers began to discover in time to resume a great part of their jurisdiction in matters of contract, which would otherwise have escaped from them. They made too an apparently successful effort to recover their exclusive authority over real property, by obtaining a statute for turning uses into possession; that is, for annihilating the fictitious estate of the feoffee to uses, and vesting the legal as well as equitable possession in the cestui que use. But this victory, if I may use such an expression (since it would have freed them, in a most important point, from the chancellor's control), they threw away by one of those timid and narrow constructions which had already turned so much to their prejudice; and they permitted trust estates, by the introduction of a few more words into a conveyance, to maintain their ground, contradistinguished from

the legal seisin, under the protection and guarantee, as before, of the courts of equity.

The particular limits of this equitable jurisdiction were as yet exceedingly indefinite. The chancellors were generally prone to extend them; and being at the same time ministers of state in a government of very arbitrary temper, regarded too little that course of precedent by which the other judges held themselves too strictly bound. The cases reckoned cognizable in chancery grew silently more and more numerous; but with little overt opposition from the courts of law till the time of sir Edward Coke. That great master of the common law was inspired not only with the jealousy of this irregular and encroaching jurisdiction which most lawyers seem to have felt, but with a tenaciousness of his own dignity, and a personal enmity towards Egerton, who held the great seal. It happened that an action was tried before him, the precise circumstances of which do not appear, wherein the plaintiff lost the verdict in consequence of one of his witnesses being artfully kept away. He had recourse to the court of chancery, filing a bill against the defendant to make him answer upon oath, which he refused to do, and was committed for contempt. Indictments were upon this preferred, at Coke's instigation, against the parties who had filed the bill in chancery, their council and solicitors, for suing in another court after judgment obtained at law; which was alleged to be contrary to the statute of præmunire. But the grand jury, though pressed, as is said, by one of the judges, threw out these indictments. The king, already incensed with Coke, and stimulated by Bacon, thought this too great an insult upon his chancellor to be passed over. He first directed Bacon and others to search for precedents of cases where relief had been given in chancery after judgment at law. They reported that there was a series of such precedents from the time of Henry VIII.: and some where the chancellor had entertained suits even after execution. The attorney-general was directed to prosecute in the star-chamber those who had preferred the indictments; and as Coke had not been ostensibly implicated in the business, the king contented himself with making an order in the council-book, declaring the chancellor not to have exceeded his jurisdiction.

The chief-justice almost at the same time gave another provocation, which exposed him more directly to the court's resentment. A cause happened to be argued in the court of king's bench, wherein the validity of a particular grant of a benefice to a bishop to be held in commendam, that is, along with his bishopric, came into question; and the council at the bar, besides the special points of the case, had disputed the king's general prerogative of making such a grant. The king, on receiving information of this, signified to the chief-justice, through the attorney-general, that he would not have the court proceed to judgment till he had spoken with them. Coke requested that similar letters might be written to the judges of all the courts. This having been done, they assembled, and, by a letter subscribed with all their hands, certified his majesty that they were bound by their oaths not to regard any letters that might come to them contrary to law, but to do the law notwithstanding; that they held with one consent the attorney-general's letter to be contrary to law, and such as they could not yield to, and that they had proceeded according to their oath to argue the cause.

The king, who was then at Newmarket, returned answer that he would not suffer his prerogative to be wounded, under pretext of the interest of private persons; that it had already been more boldly dealt with in Westminster Hall than in the reigns of preceding princes, which popular and unlawful liberty he would no longer endure; that their oath not to delay justice was not meant to prejudice the king's prerogative; concluding that out of his absolute power and authority royal he commanded them to forbear meddling any further in the cause till they should hear his pleasure from his own mouth. Upon his return to London the twelve judges appeared as culprits in the council-chamber. The king set forth their misdemeanors, both in substance and in the tone of their letter. He observed that the judges ought to check those advocates who presume to argue against his prerogative; that the popular lawyers had been the men, ever since his accession, who had trodden in all parliaments upon it, though the law could never be respected if the king were not reverenced; that he had a double prerogative—whereof the one was ordinary, and had relation to his private interest, which might be and was every day disputed in Westminster Hall; the other was of a higher nature, referring to his supreme and imperial power and sovereignty, which ought not to be disputed or handled in vulgar argument; but that of late the courts of common law are grown so vast and transcendent, as they did both meddle with the king's prerogative, and had encroached upon all other courts of justice. He commented on the form of the letter, as highly indecent; certifying him merely what they had done, instead of submitting to his princely judgment what they should do.

After this harangue the judges fell upon their knees, and acknowledged their error as to the form of the letter. But Coke entered on a defence of a substance, maintaining the delay required to be against the law and their oaths. The king required the chancellor and attorney-general to deliver their opinions; which, as may be supposed, were diametrically opposite to those of the chief-justice. These being heard, the following question was put to the judges: Whether, if at any time, in a case depending before the judges, his majesty conceived it to concern him either in power or profit, and thereupon required to consult with them, and that they should stay proceedings in the mean time, they ought not to stay accordingly? They all, except the chief-justice, declared that they would do so, and acknowledged it to be their duty; Hobart, chief-justice of the common-pleas, adding that he would ever trust the justice of his majesty's commandment. But Coke only answered that, when the case should arise, he would do what should be fit for a judge to do. The king dismissed them all with a command to keep the limits of their several courts, and not to suffer his prerogative to be wounded; for he well knew the true and ancient common law to be the most favorable to kings of any law in the world, to which law he advised them to apply their studies.

The behavior of the judges in this inglorious contention was such as to deprive them of every shadow of that confidence which ought to be reposed in their integrity. Hobart, Doddridge, and several more, were men of much consideration for learning; and their authority in ordinary matters of law is still held high. But, having been induced by a sense of duty, or through the ascendency that Coke had acquired over them, to make a show of withstanding the court, they behaved like cowardly rebels who surrender at the first discharge of cannon; and prostituted their integrity and their fame, through dread of losing their offices, or rather, perhaps, of incurring the unmerciful and ruinous penalties of the star-chamber.

The government had nothing to fear from such recreants; but Coke was suspended from his office, and not long afterwards dismissed. Having, however, fortunately in this respect, married his daughter to a brother of the duke of Buckingham, he was restored in about three years to the privy council, where his great experience in business rendered him useful; and had

the satisfaction of voting for an enormous fine on his enemy the earl of Suffolk, late high-treasurer, convicted in the star-chamber of embezzlement. In the parliament of 1621, and still more conspicuously in that of 1628, he became, not without some honorable inconsistency of doctrine as well as practice, the strenuous asserter of liberty on the principles of those ancient laws, which no one was admitted to know so well as himself; redeeming, in an intrepid and patriotic old age, the faults which we cannot avoid perceiving in his earlier life. —HENRY HALLAM, *The Constitutional History of England,* 1827, Ch. 6

Pedant, bigot, and brute as he was, he had qualities which bore a strong, though a very disagreeable resemblance to some of the highest virtues which a public man can possess. He was an exception to a maxim which we believe to be generally true, that those who trample on the helpless are disposed to cringe to the powerful. He behaved with gross rudeness to his juniors at the bar, and with execrable cruelty to prisoners on trial for their lives. But he stood up manfully against the King and the King's favourites. No man of that age appeared to so little advantage when he was opposed to an inferior, and was in the wrong. But, on the other hand, it is but fair to admit that no man of that age made so creditable a figure when he was opposed to a superior, and happened to be in the right. On such occasions, his half-suppressed insolence and his impracticable obstinacy had a respectable and interesting appearance, when compared with the abject servility of the bar and of the bench.—THOMAS BABINGTON MACAULAY, "Lord Bacon" (1837), *Critical, Historical, and Miscellaneous Essays,* 1860, Vol. 3, pp. 389–90

Coke also has a place in literature. His reports are, even at the present day, known without his name simply as *The Reports,* and his *Institutes* is one of the most learned works which this age produced. It is rather a collection provided with notes, but is instructive and suggestive from the variety of and the contrast of its contents. Coke traced the English laws to the remotest antiquity; he considered them as the common production of the wisest men of earlier ages, and at the same time as the great inheritance of the English people, and its best protection against every kind of tyranny, spiritual or temporal. Even the old Norman French, in which they were to a great extent composed, he would not part with, for a peculiar meaning attached itself, in his view, to every word.

On the other hand Bacon as Attorney-General formed the plan of comprising the common law in a code, by which a limit should be set to the caprice of the judges, and the private citizen be better assured of his rights. He thought of revising the Statute-Book, and wished to erase everything useless, to remove difficulties, and to bring what was contradictory into harmony.

Bacon's purpose coincided with the idea of a general system of legislation entertained by the King: he would have preferred the Roman law to the statute law of England. Coke was a man devoted to the letter of the law, and was inclined to offer that resistance to the sovereign which was implied in a strict adherence to the law as it was. In the conflict that arose the judges, influenced by his example, appealed to the laws as they were laid down, according to the verbal meaning of which they thought themselves bound to decide. Bacon maintained that the Judges' oath was meant to include obedience to the King also, to whom application must be made in every matter affecting his prerogative. This is probably what Queen Elizabeth also thought, and it was the decided opinion of King James. He made the man who cherished similar views his Lord Chancellor, and dismissed Coke from his service. Bacon when in office was responsible for a catastrophe which, as we shall see, not only ruined himself, but reacted upon the monarchy. The English, contemporaries and posterity alike, have taken the side of Coke.—LEOPOLD VON RANKE, *History of England*, 1875, Vol. 1, pp. 454–55

With Coke—the victim, it was said at the time, of "pride, prohibitions, præmunire, and prerogative"—no one who has read the trials of Raleigh, or noted how the vaunted champion of national rights veered in his view of them according to the place he happened to hold, can have any personal sympathy. A pedant and a boor, the assertion of his own undignified dignity, rather than any larger motive, determined his attitude. On the other hand, it must be admitted that he was sometimes in the right, and that his attempt to make his court an *imperium in imperio* foreran the assertion of the important principle that law has a place in the realm altogether apart from politics.—JOHN NICOL, *Francis Bacon: His Life and Philosophy*, 1888, p. 140

GEORGE CHAPMAN

c. 1559–1634

George Chapman was born near Hitchin, Hertfordshire, probably in 1559. He may have attended Oxford and Cambridge sometime before 1585, and probably served with the English army in the Netherlands during the late 1580s. From 1603 to 1612 Chapman was a Server-in-Ordinary to Prince Henry.

Best known for the first English translation of Homer's complete works, Chapman was also a poet and dramatist. Among his poetry collections are *The Shadow of Night* (1594), *Ovids Banquet of Sence* (1595), *The Tears of Peace* (1609), and *Andromeda Liberata* (1614). Chapman's poetry displays Platonic tendencies; some scholars believe that he may be the rival poet mentioned in Shakespeare's sonnets. Chapman's most successful dramas were two tragedies based on contemporary French history, *Bussy D'Ambois* (1607) and *The Revenge of Bussy D'Ambois* (1613). *The Blind Beggar of Alexandria* (1598), *A Humourous Day's Mirth* (1599), *All Fools* (1605), and *May Day* (1611) are among Chapman's many comedies. *Eastward Hoe* (1604), a comedy written with Jonson and Marston, landed Chapman in jail because of derogatory comments about the Scots.

In 1611 Chapman published a rhymed, fourteen-syllable translation of the *Iliad*, followed by a rhymed, ten-syllable translation of the *Odyssey* in 1616. Chapman included translations of the Homeric hymns and epigrams in *The Crown of All Homer's Works* (1624). He also translated several of Petrarch's sonnets (1612), as well as Hesiod's *Works and Days*, which he retitled *Georgicks* (1618). Chapman died on May 12, 1634, and was buried at St. Giles-in-the-Field.

Personal

Tis true, that *Chapmans* reverend ashes must
Lye rudely mingled with the vulgar dust,
Cause carefull heyers the wealthy onely have;
To build a glorious trouble o're the grave.
Yet doe I not despaire, some one may be
So seriously devout to Poesie
As to translate his reliques, and finde roome
In the warme Church, to build him up a tombe.
　　　　—WILLIAM HABINGTON, "To my honoured
　　　　　Friend and Kinsman, R. St., Esquire,"
　　　　　Castara, 1635

George Chapman, a person much famed in his time for the excellency of his muse, and for the great repute he obtained for his admirable translations, and advance of the English stage by his dramatic writings, was born in the year 1557, but of what family, unless of that, sometimes of Stone-castle (of which they were owners) in Kent, I cannot tell. In 1574, or thereabouts, he being well grounded in school-learning, was sent to the university, but whether first to this of Oxon, or that of Cambridge, is to me unknown: Sure I am that he spent some time in Oxon, where he was observed to be most excellent in the Lat. and Greek tongues, but not in logic or philosophy, and therefore I presume that that was the reason why he took no degree here. Afterwards he setled in the metropolis, and became much ad- mired by Edm. Spencer, Sam. Daniel, Will. Shakspeare, Christop. Marlowe, &c. by all whose writings, as also by those of sir Phil. Sydney, Will. Warner, and of those of our author Chapman, the English tongue was exceedingly enriched, and made quite another thing than what 'twas before. He was much countenanced in his virtuous and elaborate studies by sir Tho. Walsingham knight, who always had a constant friendship for him, as also by his toward and worthy son Tho. Walsingham esq; whom Chapman lov'd from his birth. He was also re- spected and patroniz'd by prince Henry, and by sir Rob. Carr E. of Somerset, but the first being untimely snatch'd away, and the other as untimely laid aside, his hopes of future advance were frustrated. However, if I am not mistaken, he was a sworn servant either to K. James I. or his royal consort queen Anne; through all whose time he was highly valued, but not so much as Ben. Johnson, who then, as in part of the reign of K. Ch. I. carried all before him. He (Chapman) was a person of most reverend aspect, religious and temperate, qualities rarely meet- ing in a poet, and was so highly esteemed by the clergy and academians, that some of them have said, that 'as Musæus, who wrote the Lives of Hero and Leander, had two excellent scholars Thamarus and Hercules, so had he in England (in the latter end of qu. Elizab.) two excellent imitators of him in the same argument and subject, viz. Christop. Marlow and George Chapman;' which last, whose name stands upon record for one of the famous drammatists of his time.—ANTHONY À WOOD, *Athenae Oxonienses*, 1691–1721

A Gentleman of no mean Repute for his Poetical Writings and Versions, amongst the Wits of the Age wherein he liv'd, *to wit*, in the later part of the Reign of Queen *Elizabeth*, and that of King *James*. I can give him no greater Commendation, than that he was so intimate with the famous *Johnson*, as to engage in a Triumvirate with Him, and *Marston* in a Play called *Eastward-Hoe*: a Favour which the haughty *Ben* could seldome be perswaded to. I might add to this, that he was so much valued in his time, by the Gentlemen of the *Middle-Temple* and *Lincoln's-Inn*, that when those two Honourable Societies agreed to Present Their Majesties with a Masque at *Whitehall*, on the joyful Occasion of the Marriage between the Princess *Elizabeth*, only Daughter to King *James* the First, and *Frederick* the Fifth of that Name, Count *Palatine* of the *Rhine*, and afterwards King of *Bohemia*: they chose Mr. *Chapman* for their Poet, to suit Language to the Occasion, and Mr. *Inigo Jones* for their Ingineer, to order the Machines, and Decoration of the Scenes.

He has writ many Dramatick Pieces, to the number of Eighteen: besides several other Poems and Translations: of all which his Tragedy of *Bussy d'Amboise* has the Preference. I know not how Mr. *Dryden* came to be so possest with Indignation against this Play, as to resolve to burn One annually to the Memory of *Ben Johnson*: but I know very well that there are some who allow it a just Commendation; and others that since have taken the liberty to promise a solemn annual Sacrifice of *The Hind and Panther*, to the Memory of Mr. *Quarles*, and *John Bunyan*: so that should this last Humour continue, *The Hind and Panther* would grow as scarce, as this Old Tragedy is at present.—GERARD LANGBAINE, *An Account of the English Dramatick Poets*, 1691

General

Detraction is the sworne friend to ignorance: For mine owne part I have ever truly cherisht my good opinion of other mens worthy Labours, especially of that full and haightned stile of maister *Chapman*.—JOHN WEBSTER, "To the Reader," *The White Devil*, 1612

> Then in a straine beyond an Oaten Quill
> The learned Shepherd of faire *Hitching* hill
> Sung the heroicke deeds of *Greece* and *Troy*,
> In lines so worthy life, that I imploy
> My Reed in vaine to ouertake his fame.
> All praiseful tongues doe wait vpon that name.
> —WILLIAM BROWNE, *Britannia's Pastorals*,
> 1613, Book 2, Song 2

George Chapman, a poetical writer flourishing in the reigns of Queen Elizabeth and King James, in that repute for his *Translations* both *of Homer* and *Hesiod*, and what he wrote of his own proper genius, that he is thought not the meanest of English Poets of that time; as his *Blind Beggar of Alexandria;—All Fools;—The Gentleman-Usher;—May-Day;—The Widow's Tears;—Monsieur d'Olive;—A Day's Mirth;—Eastward-hoe*; Comedies;—*Bussy d'Amboys;—Cæsar and Pompey*; Tragedies.—EDWARD PHILLIPS, *Theatrum Poetarum Anglicanorum*, 1675

In spite of the force and originality of English dramatic poetry in the age of Shakespeare, the poetical character of the time had much in common with the Alexandrian epoch in Greek literary history. At Alexandria, when the creative genius of Greece was almost spent, literature became pedantic and obscure. Poets desired to show their learning, their knowledge of the details of mythology, their acquaintance with the more fantastic theories of contemporary science. The same faults mark the poetry of the Elizabethan age, and few writers were more culpably Alexandrian than George Chapman. The spirit of Callimachus or of Lycophron seems at times to have come upon him, as the *lutin* was supposed to whisper ideas extraordinarily good or evil, to Corneille. When under the influence of this possession, Chapman displayed the very qualities and unconsciously translated the language of Callimachus. He vowed that he detested popularity, and all that can please 'the commune reader.' He inveighed against the 'invidious detractor' who became a spectre that dogged him in every enterprise. He hid his meaning in a mist of verbiage, within a labyrinth of conceits, and himself said, only too truly, about the 'sweet Leander' of Marlowe,

> I in floods of ink
> Must drown thy graces.

It is scarcely necessary to justify these remarks by illustrations from Chapman's works. Every reader of the poems and the prefaces finds barbarism, churlish temper, and pedantry in profusion. In spite of unpopularity, Chapman 'rested as resolute as Seneca, satisfying himself if but a few, if one, or if none like' his verses.

Why then is Chapman, as it were in his own despite, a poet still worthy of the regard of lovers of poetry? The answer is partly to be found in his courageous and ardent spirit, a spirit bitterly at odds with life, but still true to its own nobility, still capable, in happier moments, of divining life's real significance, and of asserting lofty truths in pregnant words. In his poems we find him moving from an exaggerated pessimism, a pessimism worthy of a Romanticist of 1830, to more dignified acquiescence in human destiny. *The Shadow of Night*, his earliest work, expresses, not without affectation and exaggeration, his blackest mood. Chaos seems better to him than creation, the undivided rest of the void is a happier thing than the crowded distractions of life. Night, which confuses all in shadow and rest, is his Goddess,

> That eagle-like doth with her starry wings,
> Beat in the fowls and beasts to Somnus' lodgings,
> And haughty Day to the infernal deep,
> Proclaiming silence, study, ease, and sleep.

As for day,

> In hell thus let her sit, and never rise,
> Till morns leave blushing at her cruelties.

In a work published almost immediately after *The Shadow of Night*, in *Ovid's Banquet of Sense*, Chapman 'consecrates his strange poems to those searching spirits whom learning hath made noble.' Nothing can well be more pedantic than the conception of the *Banquet of Sense*. Ovid watches Julia at her bath, and his gratification is described in a singular combination of poetical and psychological conceits. Yet in this poem, the redeeming qualities of Chapman and the soothing influence of that anodyne which most availed him in his contest with life, are already evident. *Learning* is already beginning to soothe his spirit with its spell. To *Learning*, as we shall see, he ascribed all the excellences which a modern critic assigns to culture. Learning, in a wide and non-natural sense, is his stay, support, and comfort. In the *Banquet of Sense*, too, he shows that patriotic pride in England, that enjoyment of her beauty, which dignify the *Carmen Epicum, de Guiana*, and appear strangely enough in the sequel of *Hero and Leander*. There are exquisite lines in the *Banquet of Sense*, like these, for example, which suggest one of Giorgione's glowing figures:—

> *She lay at length like an immortal soul,*
> *At endless rest in blest Elysium.*

But Chapman's interest in natural science breaks in unseasonably—

> Betwixt mine eye and object, certain lines
> Move in the figure of a pyramis,
> Whose chapter in mine eyes gray apple shines,
> The base within my sacred object is;
> —singular reflections of a lover by his lady's
> bower!

Chapman could not well have done a rasher thing than 'suppose himself executor to the unhappily deceased author of' *Hero and Leander*. A poet naturally didactic, Chapman dwelt on the impropriety of Leander's conduct, and confronted him with the indignant goddess of Ceremony. In a passage which ought to interest modern investigators of Ceremonial Government, the poet makes 'all the hearts of deities' hurry to Ceremony's feet:—

> She led Religion, all her body was
> Clear and transparent as the purest glass;
> Devotion, Order, State, and Reverence,
> Her shadows were; Society, Memory;
> All which her sight made live, her absence die.

The allegory is philosophical enough, but strangely out of place. The poem contains at least one image worthy of Marlowe—

> His most kind sister all his secrets knew,
> *And to her, singing like a shower, he flew.*

This too, of Hero, might have been written by the master of verse:—

> Her fresh heat blood cast figures in her eyes,
> And she supposed she saw in Neptune's skies
> How her star wander'd, washed in smarting brine,
> For her love's sake, that with immortal wine
> Should be embathed, and swim in more heart's-ease,
> Than there was water in the Sestian seas.

It is in *The Tears of Peace* (1609), an allegory addressed to Chapman's patron, the short-lived Henry, Prince of Wales, that the poet does his best to set forth his theory of life and morality. He 'sat to it,' he says, to his 'criticism of life,' and he was guided in his thoughts by his good genius, Homer. Inspired by Homer, he rises above himself, his peevishness, his controversies, his angry contempt of popular opinion, and he beholds the beauty of renunciation, and acquiesces in a lofty stoicism:—

> Free suffering for the truth makes sorrow sing,
> And mourning far more sweet than banquetting.

He comforts himself with the belief that Learning, rightly understood, is the remedy against discontent and restlessnesss:—

> For Learning's truth makes all life's vain war cease.

It is Learning that

> Turns blood to soul, and makes both one calm man.

By Learning man reaches a deep knowledge of himself, and of his relations to the world, and 'Learning the art is of good life':—

> *Let all men judge, who is it can deny*
> *That the rich crown of old Humanity*
> *Is still your birthright? and was ne'er let down*
> *From heaven for rule of beasts' lives, but your own?*

These noble words still answer the feverish debates of the day, for, whatever our descent,

> Still, at the worst, we are the sons of men!

In this persuasion, Chapman can consecrate his life to his work, can cast behind him fear and doubt,

> This glass of air, broken with less than breath,
> This slave bound face to face to death till death.

His work was that which the spirit of Homer put upon him, in the green fields of Hitchin.

> There did shine,
> A beam of Homer's freër soul in mine,

he says, and by virtue of that beam, and of his devotion to Homer, George Chapman still lives. When he had completed his translations he could say,

> The work that I was born to do, is done.

Learning and work had been his staff through life, and had won him immortality. But for his *Homer*, Chapman would only be remembered by professional students. His occasional inspired lines would not win for him many readers. But his translations of the Iliad and Odyssey are masterpieces, and cannot die.

Chapman's theory of translation allowed him great latitude. He conceived it to be 'a pedantical and absurd affectation to turn his author word for word,' and maintained that a translator, allowing for the different genius of the Greek and English tongues, 'must adorn' his original 'with words, and such a style and form of oration, as are most apt for the language into which they are converted.' This is an unlucky theory, for Chapman's idea of 'the style and form of oration most apt for' English poetry was remote indeed from the simplicity of Homer. The more he admired Homer, the more Chapman felt bound to dress him up in the height of rhetorical conceit. He excused himself by the argument, that we have not the epics as Homer imagined them, that 'the books were not set together by Homer.' He probably imagined that, if Homer had had his own way with his own works, he would have produced something much more in the Chapman manner, and he kindly added, ever and anon, a turn which he fancied Homer would approve. The English reader must be on his guard against this custom of Chapman's, and must remember, too, that the translator's erudition was exceedingly fantastic. Thus Chapman derives the difficult word ἀλφηστής from the letter ἄλφα, the first in the Greek alphabet, and decides that the men whom Homer calls ἀλφησταί, are what modern slang calls 'A 1 men.' Again, he names the Phoenician who seduced the nurse of Eumaeus, 'a great-wench-net-layer,' a word derived by him from πολυπαίπαλος, thus, 'παλεύω, *pertraho in retia, et* παῖς, *puella.*' He is full of these strange philological theories, and he boldly lets them loose in his translations. Chapman has another great fault, allied indeed to a great excellence. In his speed, in the rapidity of the movement of his lines, he is Homeric. The last twelve books of the *Iliad* were struck out at a white heat, in fifteen weeks. Chapman was carried away by the current of the Homeric verse, and this is his great saving merit. Homer inspires him, however uncouth his utterance, as Apollo inspired the Pythoness. He 'speaks out loud and bold,' but not clear. In the heat of his hurry, Chapman flies at any rhyme to end his line, and then his rhyme has to be tagged on by the introduction of some utterly un-Homeric mode of expression. Thus, in Chapman, the majestic purity of Homer is tormented, the bright and equable speed of the river of verse leaps brawling over rocks and down narrow ravines. What can be more like Chapman, and less like Homer, than these lines in the description of the storm,

> How all the tops he bottoms with the deeps,
> And in the bottoms all the tops he steeps?

Here the Greek only says 'Zeus hath troubled the deep.' It is thus that Chapman 'adorns his original.' Faults of this kind are perhaps more frequent in the *Iliad* than in the *Odyssey*. Coleridge's taste was in harmony with general opinion when he preferred the latter version, with its manageable metre, to the ruder strain of the *Iliad*, of which the verse is capable of degenerating into an amble, or dropping into a trot. The crudities, the inappropriate quaintnesses of Chapman's *Homer*, are visible enough, when we read only a page or two, here and there, in the work. Neither Homer, nor any version of Homer, should be studied piece-meal. 'He must not be read,' as Chapman truly says, 'for a few lines with leaves turned over capriciously in dismembered fractions, but throughout; the whole drift, weight, and height of his works set before the apprehensive eyes of his judge.' Thus read, the blots on Chapman's *Homer* almost disappear, and you see 'the massive and majestic memorial, where for all the flaws and roughnesses of the weather-beaten work the great workmen of days unborn would gather to give honour to his name.'—ANDREW LANG, "George Chapman," *The English Poets*, ed. Thomas Humphry Ward, 1880, Vol. 1, pp. 510–15

High priest of Homer, not elect in vain,
    Deep trumpets blow before thee, shawms behind
    Mix music with the rolling wheels that wind
Slow through the labouring triumph of thy train:
Fierce history, molten in thy forging brain,
    Takes form and fire and fashion from thy mind,
    Tormented and transmuted out of kind:
But howsoe'er thou shift thy strenuous strain,
Like Tailor smooth, like Fisher swollen, and now
    Grim Yarrington scarce bloodier marked than
        thou,
    Then bluff as Mayne's or broad-mouthed Barry's
        glee;
Proud still with hoar predominance of brow
And beard like foam swept off the broad blown sea,
Where'er thou go, men's reverence goes with thee.
        —ALGERNON CHARLES SWINBURNE, "George
        Chapman," *Sonnets on English Dramatic
        Poets*, 1882

A name which it is natural to think of in conjunction with Jonson's is that of George Chapman, who resembled him in the austerity of his judgment, in his devotion to the classics, and in his distinguished attitude to letters. But while Jonson was a noble dramatist and a very bad translator, Chapman was one of the best translators that England has ever produced, and, if I may venture to state a personal conviction, a dramatist whose merits were exceedingly scanty. This latter opinion is one which it may perhaps seem foolhardy to express, for Lamb, who first drew attention to his plays, has praised them exuberantly, and Mr. Swinburne has done Chapman the honour of dedicating to a study of his works a considerable volume, to which all careful readers must be recommended. That no injustice should be done here to this poet, I will at once record the fact that Lamb has said, "Of all the English playwriters, Chapman perhaps approaches nearest to Shakespeare in the descriptive and didactic, in passages which are less purely dramatic." It is rash to differ from Lamb, but I am bound in mere sincerity to admit that I find nothing even remotely Shakespearian in plays that seem bombastic, loose, and incoherent to the last extreme, and in which the errors of the primitive Elizabethans, due mainly to inexperience, are complacently repeated and continued through the noblest years of perfected art, in which Shakespeare, Jonson, and Fletcher held the stage. Chapman was an admirable and sometimes even a great poet, but it is hard to admit that he was ever a tolerable playwright.

George Chapman was born at Hitchin about 1559, and was therefore past middle life when James I. ascended the throne of England. He was educated at Oxford, but we know absolutely nothing about his occupations until he was nearly forty years of age. In the last years of Elizabeth he came to London, and was engaged in dramatic work from about 1595 to 1608. We know of eight or nine plays produced before the death of the queen, five of which have survived. His Jacobean dramas are *Monsieur d'Olive*, published in 1606, but acted earlier; *Bussy d'Ambois*, printed 1607; *Eastward Hoe!* of which mention has been already made, in which Chapman collaborated in 1605, with Jonson and Marston; *The Widow's Tears*, acted about the same time, but not published until 1612; *The Revenge of Bussy d'Ambois*, (printed in 1613, but acted much earlier;) *Byron's Conspiracy* and *Byron's Tragedy*, each of 1608. As late as 1631, there was published a tragedy of *Cæsar and Pompey*, evidently an old rejected play of Chapman's youth. With these exceptions, and those of two tragic fragments which Shirley found, completed and published in the next age, all Chapman's dramatic work may be safely consigned to the age of Elizabeth.

Webster commended Chapman more highly than any of his contemporaries, or, at least, in enumerating them mentioned his name first, and expressed his warm appreciation of "that full and heightened style" in which he considered Chapman's tragedies to be written. Such praise, from such a man, may not lightly be passed over; yet Chapman's last and most friendly apologist finds himself forced to admit that "the height indeed is somewhat giddy, and the fulness too often tends or threatens to dilate into tumidity." Of the four French tragedies, *Bussy d'Ambois* is undoubtedly the most interesting, being full of soliloquies and declamatory passages that have a true ring of epic poetry about them, and being at least as nearly allied to a play as the essentially undramatic mind of Chapman could make it. Of the comedies two are certainly readable: *Monsieur d'Olive*, a whirligig of fashionable humours and base love, is undoubtedly put together with a good deal of spirit and some humour, and *May Day*, a "coil to make wit and women friends," is a still madder piece of extravagance.

But even these prose plays, certainly the most coherent and amusing evidences of Chapman's talent as a dramatist, are in no sense thoroughly satisfactory. The estimate of women throughout is base to the last degree; no dramatist of the period satirizes the other sex with such malignant and persistent sarcasm as Chapman. It is a point that seriously militates against any claim he may put forward to greatness, since perhaps nothing displays the inherent littleness of an imaginative writer more than the petulance or affected indignation with which he presumes to regard the world of woman. The whole series of Chapman's comedies and tragedies contains, so far as I know, not one woman whose chastity is superior to temptation, whose wit is adaptable to other purposes than those of greedy or amatory intrigue, or whose disposition presents any of those features of sweetness and fidelity which it is the delight of a high-minded poet to dwell upon and to extol, and which most of the Elizabethans and Jacobeans, however base their fancy might take leave to be, never neglected to value.

At the opening of his dramatic career under Elizabeth, Chapman had published some strange and obscure poems which it is not our place to speak of here. But when he ceased to write plays, he turned his attention to poetry again. He dedicated to Prince Henry, in 1609, *The Tears of Peace*, and to the memory of the same "most dear and heroical patron," his *Epicedium* in 1612. "Eugenia," an elegy on William, Lord Russell, appeared in 1614, and *Andromeda Liberata*, an epithalamium on the scandalous nuptials of Robert Carr and Frances, Lady Essex, in the same year. As late as the summer of 1633 Chapman wrote, but did not conclude, an "Invocation against Ben Jonson." All these were composed in the heroic couplet. Of these poems *The Tears of Peace* is by far the most valuable, although "Eugenia" contains some highly wrought description of natural phenomena.

Here is a rising storm out of the latter poem—

> Heaven's drooping face was dress'd
> In gloomy thunderstocks; earth, seas, arrayed
> In all presage of storm; the bitterns played
> And met in flocks; the herons set clamours gone
> That rattled up air's triple region;
> The cormorants to dry land did address,
> And cried away all fowls that used the seas;
> The wanton swallows jerked the standing springs,
> Met in dull lakes, and flew so close, their wings
> Shaved the top waters; frogs croaked; the swart crow
> Measured the sea-sands, with pace passing slow,
> And often soused her ominous heat of blood
> Quite over head and shoulders in the flood,
> Still scolding at the rain's so slow access;
> The trumpet-throated, the Naupliades,
> Their clangours threw about, and summoned up
> All clouds to crown imperious tempest's cup.

In all, as Mr. Swinburne has said, "the allegory is clouded and confounded by all manner of perversities and obscurities, the verse hoarse and stiff, the style dense and convulsive, inaccurate and violent," with occasional lucid intervals of exquisite harmony, which affect the senses strangely in the midst of balderdash so raucous and uncouth.

It is, however, pre-eminently as a translator that Chapman takes high rank among the English poets. In 1598 he had published two small quartos, *Seven Books of the Iliads of Homer* and *The Shield of Achilles*, both dedicated to the Earl of Essex. In 1600 he completed Marlowe's exquisite *Hero and Leander*, keeping much closer to the text of Musæus. Prince Henry was among those who read and admired the Homer fragments, and he commanded Chapman to complete his translation. Accordingly, in 1609, in folio, appeared *Homer, Prince of Poets*, a version of the first twelve books of the *Iliad*. This was identical with the text of 1598, but with five books added. The entire *Iliad* was not published until 1611. In 1612, Chapman issued the *Penetential Psalms* of Petrarch. He returned, in spite of Prince Henry's death, to the translation of Homer, and published the first twelve books of the *Odyssey* in 1614, and the remainder of that epic in the next year. The *Iliad* and *Odyssey* appeared in one volume in 1616, and Chapman completed his version of Homer with the *Batrachomyomachia* printed, without a date, probably in 1622. Meanwhile, Chapman had been busy with Hesiod, and published a version of the *Georgics*, now extremely rare, in 1618; the *Just Reproof of a Roman Smell-feast*, translated from Juvenal, appeared in 1629. His violent quarrel with Jonson is, unfortunately, the latest fact which has been preserved about him; he died soon after, and was buried in London, at St. Giles-in-the-Fields, on the 12th of May, 1634.

The noble and famous sonnet written by Keats in a copy of Chapman's *Homer* is a witness to all time of the merit of that translation. Busy as Chapman was in many fields of literature, it is by Homer that he lives and will continue to live. He threw such an incomparable fire and gusto into the long, wave-like couplets of his *Iliad*, that poet after poet has been borne upon them into a new world of imagination.

Here is an example from the fifteenth book—

> Then on the ships all Troy,
> Like raw-flesh-nourish'd lions rushed, and knew they
> did employ
> Their powers to perfect Jove's high will; who still
> their spirits enflamed,

> And quench'd the Grecians'; one renown'd, the
> other often sham'd.
> For Hector's glory still he stood, and even went about
> To make him cast the fleet such fire, as never should
> go out;
> Heard Thetis foul petitión, and wish'd in any wise
> The splendour of the burning ships might satiate his
> eyes.
> From him yet the repulse was then to be on Troy
> conferr'd,
> The honour of it given the Greeks; which thinking
> on, he stirr'd
> With such addition of his spirit, the spirit Hector
> bore
> To burn the fleet, that of itself was hot enough
> before.
> But now he far'd like Mars himself, so brandishing
> his lance
> As, through the deep shades of a wood, a raging fire
> should glance,
> Held up to all eyes by a hill; about his lips a foam
> Stood as when th' ocean is enrag'd, his eyes were
> overcome
> With fervour, and resembled flames, set off by his
> dark brows
> And from his temples his bright helm abhorrèd light-
> nings throws.

Chapman "speaks out loud and bold," and the ancient world of Homer, with all its romantic purity and freshness, lies spread at our feet. It has often been noted with amazement that Chapman, whose original poems are perverse and cloudy to the last degree, should have been able so to clarify his style, and so to appreciate the lucidity of his original, as to write a translation of Homer which a boy may read with pleasure. The *Odyssey* of Chapman, which, like the *Hymns*, is in heroic couplet, has never been such a general favourite as the *Iliad*, where the rolling fourteen syllable line carried with it much of the melody and the movement of the Greek hexameter. His success, even here, is irregular and uncertain; sometimes he sinks into platitude or rushes into doggerel; sometimes he is outrageously false to his original and careless of the text. But, on the whole, no later verse-translator of Homer,—and translators have been myriad—has surpassed Chapman, and his *Iliad* remains one of the ornaments of our literature, and one of the principal poetical glories of the Jacobean age.—EDMUND GOSSE, *The Jacobean Poets*, 1894, pp. 39–46

Works

HERO AND LEANDER

In Chapman's continuation, as in everything that Chapman wrote, there are fine passages in abundance; but the reader is wearied by tedious digressions, dull moralising, and violent conceits. There are couplets in the "Tale of Teras" (Fifth Sestiad) that for purity of colour and perfection of form are hardly excelled by anything in the first two sestiads; such passages, however, are few.—A. H. BULLEN, "Introduction" to *The Works of Christopher Marlowe*, 1884, Vol. 1, p. lii

Marlowe died before he had completed ⟨*Hero and Leander*⟩; it was finished by George Chapman, and no stronger proof of the greatness of Marlowe's genius can be furnished than the contrast between the work of the two men. Chapman did not write without inspiration; but whereas Marlowe's style—as the above splendid passage shows—is all flame, his successor's, even in his most brilliant moments, is half smoke. He is smothered by his Euphuism; witness the following powerful and characteristic lines, describing the apparition of the angry Venus:—

All were in heaven, now they with Hero were:
But Venus' looks brought wrath and urgèd fear.
Her robe was scarlet; black her head's attire;
And through her naked breast shin'd streams of fire,
As when the rarefièd air is driven
In flashing streams, and opes the darken'd heaven.
In her white hands a wreath of yew she bore;
And breaking th' icy wreath sweet Hero wore,
She forc'd about her brows her wreath of yew,
And said, "Now, minion, to thy fate be true,
Though not to me; endure what this portends:
Begin where lightness will, in shame it ends.
Love makes thee cunning; thou art current now,
By being counterfeit: thy broken vow
Deceit with her pied garters must rejoin,
And with her stamp thou countenances must coin:
Coyness and pure deceits, for purities;
And still a maid wilt seem in cozened eyes,
And have an antic face to laugh within,
While thy smooth looks make men digest thy sin.
But since thy lips (least thought forsworn) forswore,
Be never virgin's vow worth trusting more."

In these two passages the reader will observe with what magnificent ease Marlowe masters thought, while Chapman seems to struggle with it; the consequence is that the verse of the former is harmonious and flowing, but that of the latter often labours heavily. Conceit itself—and he has plenty of it—seems to sit lightly on Marlowe; for example:—

So lovely-fair was Hero, Venus nun,
As Nature wept, thinking she was undone,
Because she took more from her than she left,
And of such wondrous beauty her bereft:
Therefore in sign her treasure suffered wrack,
Since Hero's time hath half the world been black.

A touch of humour redeems this extravagance; but when a conceit of Chapman's gets hold of the bit there is no holding it. Witness the passage describing Leander after swimming back from Sestos:—

His most kind sister all his secrets knew,
And to her, singing like a shower, he flew,
Sprinkling the earth that to their tombs took in,
Streams dead for love to leave his ivory skin;
Which yet a snowy foam did leave above,
As soul to the dead water that did love.
And from thence did the first white roses spring,
(For love is sweet and fair in everything),
And all the sweeten'd shore as he did go,
Was crown'd with odorous roses white as snow.

Even in the reflective passages, which are congenial to Chapman's style, Marlowe maintains his superiority:—

It lies not in our power to love or hate,
For will in us is overrul'd by fate.
When two are stript, long ere the course begin,
We wish that one should lose the other win,
And one especially do we affect,
Of two gold ingots, like in each respect:
The reason no man knows; let it suffice,
What we behold is censur'd by our eyes.
When both deliberate, the love is slight:
Who ever lov'd that lov'd not at first sight?

The following is the opening of the Third Sestiad, where Chapman takes up his predecessor's tale:—

New light gives new directions, fortunes new,
To fashion our endeavours that ensue.
More harsh, at least more hard, more grave and high,

Our subject runs, and our stern Muse must fly.
Love's edge is taken off, and that light flame,
Those thoughts, joys, longings, that before became
High inexperienc'd blood, and maid's sharp plights,
Must now grow staid, and censure the delights,
That, being enjoy'd, ask judgment; now we praise,
As having parted: evenings crown the days.

What distinguishes Marlowe from all other narrative or dramatic poets of his time, is a certain elemental simplicity and greatness of conception. He rises equally above the affectations of archaism and of novel conceit. Some of his contemporaries are distracted in their endeavour to conceive ideal action by means of the images of an extinct chivalry; others are perplexed by the intrusion into their religious creed of the images of an extinct polytheism. Marlowe fixes his imagination steadily on those elements of human nature which remain the same in all places and all ages. He ignores the traditions of chivalry and the moral restraints of religion. By so doing he gains energy for his ideas of human nature, but he at the same time renders them narrow and contracted, because the ethical principles of chivalry and Christianity have become part of the human conscience. Want of moral instinct and of Catholic sympathy prevents Marlowe from attaining, either as a dramatic or an epic poet, the supreme position which might have been his, had the force of his genius been tempered by those qualities. Compared with *Troilus and Criseyde*, his *Hero and Leander* lacks dramatic interest, variety, and relief. It never reaches the depths of pathos which Virgil sounds in the Fourth *Æneid*, nor the heights of spiritual feeling of which Spenser has given us examples in the *Faery Queen*. Fortune favoured him in obliging him to leave his poem a splendid fragment; and Chapman's comparative failure did him a further service, by suggesting what might have been accomplished had *Hero and Leander* been completed by the same hand that began it. In truth, however, there is little to lead us to suppose that Marlowe would have done much better than his successor. His poetic impulse had exhausted itself in a picture of youthful passion; and the poverty of invention, shown in the passage describing Leander swimming the Hellespont, makes it probable that the poet would have failed to bring the story to an adequately tragic conclusion.—W. J. COURTHOPE, A *History of English Poetry*, 1897, Vol. 2, pp. 326–30

TRANSLATION OF HESIOD

Whose worke could this be, *Chapman*, to refine
Olde *Hesiods* Ore, and giue it vs; but thine,
Who hadst before wrought in rich *Homers* Mine?

What treasure has thou brought vs! and what store
Still, still, dost thou arriue with, at our shore,
To make thy honour, and our wealth the more!

If all the vulgar Tongues, that speake this day,
Were askt of thy Discoueries; They must say,
To the Greeke coast thine onely knew the way.

Such Passage hast thou found, such Returnes made,
As, now, of all men, it is call'd thy Trade:
And who make thither else, rob, or inuade.

—BEN JONSON, "To my worthy and Honour'd
Friend, Mʳ George Chapman, on his Translation of Hesiods Workes, & Dayes," 1618

TRANSLATIONS OF HOMER

But yet now notwithstanding all this which I haue heere deliu-ered in the defence of Ryme, I am not so farre in loue with mine owne mysterie, or will seeme so froward, as to bee against the reformation, and the better setling these measures of ours. Wherein there be many things, I could wish were more certaine and better ordered, though my selfe dare not take vpon me to be a teacher therein, hauing so much neede to learne of others. And I must confesse, that to mine owne eare, those continuall cadences of couplets vsed in long and continued Poemes, are very tyresome, and vnpleasing, by reason that still, me thinks, they runne on with a sound of one nature, and a kinde of certaintie which stuffs the delight rather then intertaines it. But yet notwithstanding, I must not out of mine owne daintinesse, condemne this kinde of writing, which peraduenture to another may seeme most delightfull, and many worthy compositions we see to haue passed with commendation in that kinde. Besides, me thinkes sometimes, to beguile the eare, with a running out, and passing ouer the Ryme, as no bound to stay vs in the line where the violence of the matter will breake thorow, is rather gracefull then otherwise. Wherein I finde my *Homer-Lucan*, as if he gloried to seeme to haue no bounds, albeit hee were confined within his measures, to be in my conceipt most happy. For so thereby, they who care not for Verse or Ryme, may passe it ouer without taking notice thereof, and please themselues with a well-measured Prose.—SAMUEL DANIEL, *A Defence of Ryme*, 1603

> Others againe here lived in my dayes,
> That have of us deserved no lesse praise
> For their translations, then the daintiest wit
> That on *Parnassus* thinks, he highst doth sit,
> And for a chaire may mongst the Muses call,
> As the most curious maker of them all;
> As reverent *Chapman*, who hath brought to us,
> *Musæus, Homer*, and *Hesiodus*
> Out of the Greeke; and by his skill hath reard
> Them to that height, and to our tongue endear'd,
> That were those Poets at this day alive,
> To see their bookes thus with us to survive,
> They would think, having neglected them so long,
> They had bin written in the *English* tongue.
>
> —MICHAEL DRAYTON, "To My Most Dearely-
> Loved Friend Henery Reynolds Esquire, of
> Poets and Poesie," c. 1627

Upon the whole, I must confess my self utterly incapable of doing justice to *Homer*. I attempt him in no other Hope but that which one may entertain without much Vanity, of giving a more tolerable Copy of him than any entire Translation in Verse has yet done. We have only those of *Chapman, Hobbes*, and *Ogilby*. *Chapman* has taken the Advantage of an immeasurable Length of Verse, notwithstanding which there is scarce any Paraphrase more loose and rambling than his. He has frequent Interpolations of four or six Lines, and I remember one in the Thirteenth Book of the *Odysseis, ver*. 312. where he has spun twenty Verses out of two. He is often mistaken in so bold a manner, that one might think he deviated on purpose, if he did not in other Places of his Notes insist so much upon Verbal Trifles. He appears to have had a strong Affectation of extracting new Meanings out of his Author, insomuch as to promise in his Rhyming Preface, a Poem of the Mysteries he had revealed in *Homer*; and perhaps he endeavoured to strain the obvious Sense to this End. His Expression is involved in Fustian, a Fault for which he was remarkable in his Original Writings, as in the Tragedy of *Bussy d'Amboise*, &c. In a word, the Nature of the Man may account for his whole Performance; for he appears from his Preface and Remarks to have been of an arrogant Turn, and an Enthusiast in Poetry. His own Boast of having finish'd half the *Iliad* in less than fifteen Weeks, shews with what Negligence his Version was performed. But

that which is to be allowed him, and which very much contributed to cover his Defects, is a daring fiery Spirit that animates his Translation, which is something like what one might imagine *Homer* himself would have writ before he arriv'd to Years of Discretion.—ALEXANDER POPE, "Preface" to *The Iliad of Homer*, 1715

He has by no means represented the dignity or the simplicity of Homer. He is sometimes paraphrastic and redundant, but more frequently retrenches or impoverishes what he could not feel and express. In the meantime, he labours with the inconvenience of an aukward, inharmonious, and unheroic measure, imposed by custom, but disgustful to modern ears. Yet he is not always without strength or spirit. He has enriched our languages with many compound epithets, so much in the manner of Homer, such as the *silver-footed* Thetis, the *silver-throned* Juno, the *triple-feathered* helme, the *high-walled* Thebes, the *faire-haired* boy, the *silver-flowing* floods, the *hugely-peopled* towns, the Grecians *navy-bound*, the *strong-winged* lance, and many more which might be collected. Dryden reports, that Waller never could read Chapman's Homer without a degree of transport. Pope is of opinion, that Chapman covers his defects "by a daring fiery spirit that animates his translation, which is something like what one might imagine Homer himself to have writ before he arrived to years of discretion." But his fire is too frequently darkened, by that sort of fustian which now disfigured the diction of our tragedy. —THOMAS WARTON, *The History of English Poetry*, 1778–81, Sec. 59

Chapman I have sent in order that you might read the *Odyssey*; the *Iliad* is fine, but less equal in the translation, as well as less interesting in itself. What is stupidly said of Shakspeare, is really true and appropriate of Chapman; mighty faults counterpoised by mighty beauties. Excepting his quaint epithets which he affects to render literally from the Greek, a language above all others blest in the happy marriage of sweet words, and which in our language are mere printer's compound epithets— such as quaffed divine *joy-in-the-heart-of-man-infusing* wine, (the undermarked is to be one word, because one sweet mellifluous word expresses it in Homer);—excepting this, it has no look, no air, of a translation. It is as truly an original poem as the *Faery Queene*;—it will give you small idea of Homer, though a far truer one than Pope's epigrams, or Cowper's cumbersome most anti-Homeric Miltonism. For Chapman writes and feels as a poet,—as Homer might have written had he lived in England in the reign of Queen Elizabeth. In short, it is an exquisite poem, in spite of its frequent and perverse quaintnesses and harshnesses, which are, however, amply repaid by almost unexampled sweetness and beauty of language, all over spirit and feeling. In the main it is an English heroic poem, the tale of which is borrowed from the Greek. The dedication to the *Iliad* is a noble copy of verses, especially those sublime lines beginning,—

> O! 'tis wondrous much
> (Though nothing prisde) that the right vertuous
>   touch
> Of a well written soule, to vertue moves.
> Nor haue we soules to purpose, if their loves
> Of fitting objects be not so inflam'd.
> How much then, were this kingdome's maine soule
>   maim'd,
> To want this great inflamer of all powers
> That move in humane soules! All realmes but yours,
> Are honor'd with him; and hold blest that state
> That have his workes to reade and contemplate.
> In which, humanitie to her height is raisde;

Which all the world (yet, none enough) hath praisde.
Seas, earth, and heaven, he did in verse comprize;
Out sung the Muses, and did equalise
Their king Apollo; being so farre from cause
Of princes light thoughts, that their gravest lawes
May finde stuffe to be fashioned by his lines.
Through all the pompe of kingdomes still he shines
And graceth all his gracers. Then let lie
Your lutes, and viols, and more loftily
Make the heroiques of your Homer sung,
To drums and trumpets set his Angels tongue:
And with the princely sports of haukes you use,
Behold the kingly flight of his high Muse:
And see how like the Phœnix she renues
Her age, and starrie feathers in your sunne;
Thousands of yeares attending; everie one
Blowing the holy fire, and throwing in
Their seasons, kingdomes, nations that have bin
Subverted in them; lawes, religions, all
Offerd to change, and greedie funerall;
Yet still your Homer lasting, living, raigning.—

and likewise the 1st, the 11th, and last but one, of the prefatory sonnets to the *Odyssey*. Could I have foreseen any other speedy opportunity, I should have begged your acceptance of the volume in a somewhat handsomer coat; but as it is, it will better represent the sender,—to quote from myself—

A man disherited, in form and face,
By nature and mishap, of outward grace.

Chapman in his moral heroic verse, as in this dedication and the prefatory sonnets to his Odyssey, stands above Ben Jonson; there is more dignity, more lustre, and equal strength; but not midway quite between him and the sonnets of Milton. I do not know whether I give him the higher praise, in that he reminds me of Ben Jonson with a sense of his superior excellence, or that he brings Milton to memory notwithstanding his inferiority. His moral poems are not quite out of books like Jonson's, nor yet do the sentiments so wholly grow up out of his own natural habit and grandeur of thought, as in Milton. The sentiments have been attracted to him by a natural affinity of his intellect, and so combined;—but Jonson has taken them by individual and successive acts of choice.

And this and the preceding is well felt and vigorously, though harshly, expressed, respecting sublime poetry *in genere*; but in reading Homer I look about me, and ask how does all this apply here. For surely never was there plainer writing; there are a thousand charms of sun and moonbeam, ripple, and wave, and stormy billow, but all on the surface. Had Chapman read Proclus and Porphyry?—and did he really believe them,—or even that they believed themselves? They felt the immense power of a Bible, a Shaster, a Koran. There was none in Greece or Rome, and they tried therefore by subtle allegorical accommodations to conjure the poem of Homer in to the βιβλίον θεοπαράδοτον of Greek faith.

Chapman's identification of his fate with Homer's, and his complete forgetfulness of the distinction between Christianity and idolatry, under the general feeling of some religion, is very interesting. It is amusing to observe, how familiar Chapman's fancy has become with Homer, his life and its circumstances, though the very existence of any such individual, at least with regard to the *Iliad* and the *Hymns*, is more than problematic. N. B. The rude engraving in the page was designed by no vulgar hand. It is full of spirit and passion.

I am so dull, that neither in the original nor in any translation could I ever find any wit or wise purpose in this poem. The whole humour seems to lie in the names. The frogs and mice are not frogs or mice, but men, and yet they do nothing

that conveys any satire. In the Greek there is much beauty of language, but the joke is very flat. This is always the case in rude ages;—their serious vein is inimitable,—their comic low and low indeed. The psychological cause is easily stated, and copiously exemplifiable.—SAMUEL TAYLOR COLERIDGE, "Notes on Chapman's Homer" (1807), *Literary Remains*, ed. Henry Nelson Coleridge, 1836, Vol. 1, pp. 259–63

Of all the English Play-writers, Chapman perhaps approaches nearest to Shakspeare in the descriptive and didactic, in passages which are less purely dramatic. Dramatic Imitation was not his talent. He could not go out of himself, as Shakspeare could shift at pleasure, to inform and animate other existences, but in himself he had an eye to perceive and a soul to embrace all forms. He would have made a great Epic Poet, if indeed he has not abundantly shown himself to be one; for his Homer is not so properly a Translation as the Stories of Achilles and Ulysses re-written. The earnestness and passion which he has put into every part of these poems would be incredible to a reader of mere modern translations. His almost Greek zeal for the honour of his heroes is only paralleled by that fierce spirit of Hebrew bigotry, with which Milton, as if personating one of the Zealots of the old law, clothed himself when he sat down to paint the acts of Sampson against the Uncircumcised. The great obstacle to Chapman's Translations being read is their unconquerable quaintness. He pours out in the same breath the most just and natural and the most violent and forced expressions. He seems to grasp whatever words come first to hand during the impetus of inspiration, as if all other must be inadequate to the divine meaning. But passion (the all in all in Poetry) is everywhere present, raising the low, dignifying the mean, and putting sense into the absurd. He makes his readers glow, weep, tremble, take any affection which he pleases, be moved by words or in spite of them, be disgusted and overcome their disgust. I have often thought that the vulgar misconception of Shakspeare, as of a wild irregular genius "in whom great faults are compensated by great beauties," would be really true, applied to Chapman. But there is no scale by which to balance such disproportionate subjects as the faults and beauties of a great genius. To set off the former with any fairness against the latter, the pain which they give us should be in some proportion to the pleasure which we receive from the other. As these transport us to the highest heaven, those should steep us in agonies infernal.—CHARLES LAMB, *Specimens of English Dramatic Poets*, 1808

Much have I travelled in the realms of gold,
    And many goodly states and kingdoms seen;
    Round many western islands have I been
Which bards in fealty to Apollo hold.
Oft of one wide expanse had I been told
    That deep-browed Homer ruled as his demesne;
    Yet did I never breathe its pure serene
Till I heard Chapman speak out loud and bold:
Then felt I like some watcher of the skies
    When a new planet swims into his ken;
Or like stout Cortez when with eagle eyes
    He stared at the Pacific—and all his men
Looked at each other with a wild surmise—
    Silent, upon a peak in Darien.
        —JOHN KEATS, "On First Looking into Chapman's Homer," 1816

Chapman's style is not artificial and literary like Pope's nor his movement elaborate and self-retarding like the Miltonic movement of Cowper. He is plain-spoken, fresh, vigorous, and, to a certain degree, rapid; and all these are Homeric qualities. I cannot say that I think the movement of his fourteen-syllable line, which has been so much commended, Homeric; but on this point I shall have more to say by and by, when I come to speak of Mr. Newman's metrical exploits. But it is not distinctly anti-Homeric, like the movement of Milton's blank verse; and it has a rapidity of its own. Chapman's diction, too, is generally good, that is, appropriate to Homer; above all, the syntactical character of his style is appropriate. With these merits, what prevents his translation from being a satisfactory version of Homer? Is it merely the want of literal faithfulness to his original, imposed upon him, it is said, by the exigences of rhyme? Has this celebrated version, which has so many advantages, no other and deeper defect than that? Its author is a poet, and a poet, too, of the Elizabethan age; the golden age of English literature as it is called, and on the whole truly called; for, whatever be the defects of Elizabethan literature (and they are great), we have no development of our literature to compare with it for vigour and richness. This age, too, showed what it could do in translating, by producing a master-piece, its version of the Bible.

Chapman's translation has often been praised as eminently Homeric. Keats's fine sonnet in its honour every one knows; but Keats could not read the original, and therefore could not really judge the translation. Coleridge, in praising Chapman's version, says at the same time, 'It will give you small idea of Homer.' But the grave authority of Mr. Hallam pronounces this translation to be 'often exceedingly Homeric;' and its latest editor boldly declares that by what, with a deplorable style, he calls 'his own innative Homeric genius,' Chapman 'has thoroughly identified himself with Homer;' and that 'we pardon him even for his digressions, for they are such as we feel Homer himself would have written.'

I confess that I can never read twenty lines of Chapman's version without recurring to Bentley's cry, 'This is not Homer!' and that from a deeper cause than any unfaithfulness occasioned by the fetters of rhyme.

I said that there were four things which eminently distinguished Homer, and with a sense of which Homer's translator should penetrate himself as fully as possible. One of these four things was, the plainness and directness of Homer's ideas. I have just been speaking of the plainness and directness of his style; but the plainness and directness of the contents of his style, of his ideas themselves, is not less remarkable. But as eminently as Homer is plain, so eminently is the Elizabethan literature in general, and Chapman in particular, fanciful. Steeped in humours and fantasticality up to its very lips, the Elizabethan age, newly arrived at the free use of the human faculties after their long term of bondage, and delighting to exercise them freely, suffers from its own extravagance in this first exercise of them, can hardly bring itself to see an object quietly or to describe it temperately. Happily, in the translation of the Bible, the sacred character of their original inspired the translators with such respect that they did not dare to give the rein to their own fancies in dealing with it. But, in dealing with works of profane literature, in dealing with poetical works above all, which highly stimulated them, one may say that the minds of the Elizabethan translators were *too* active; that they could not forbear importing so much of their own, and this of a most peculiar and Elizabethan character, into their original, that they effaced the character of the original itself.

Take merely the opening pages to Chapman's translation, the introductory verses, and the dedications. You will find:—

> An Anagram of the name of our Dread Prince,
> My most gracious and sacred Mæcenas,
> Henry, Prince of Wales,
> Our Sunn, Heyr, Peace, Life,—

Henry, son of James the First, to whom the work is dedicated. Then comes an address,

> To the sacred Fountain of Princes,
> Sole Empress of Beauty and Virtue, Anne, Queen of
> England, etc.

All the Middle Age, with its grotesqueness, its conceits, its irrationality, is still in these opening pages; they by themselves are sufficient to indicate to us what a gulf divides Chapman from the 'clearest-souled' of poets, from Homer; almost as great a gulf as that which divides him from Voltaire. Pope has been sneered at for saying that Chapman writes 'somewhat as one might imagine Homer himself to have written before he arrived at years of discretion.' But the remark is excellent: Homer expresses himself like a man of adult reason, Chapman like a man whose reason has not yet cleared itself. For instance, if Homer had had to say of a poet, that he hoped his merit was now about to be fully established in the opinion of good judges, he was as incapable of saying this as Chapman says it,— 'Though truth in her very nakedness sits in so deep a pit, that from Gades to Aurora, and Ganges, few eyes can sound her, I hope yet those few here will so discover and confirm her that, the date being out of her darkness in this morning of our poet, he shall now gird his temples with the sun,'—I say, Homer was as incapable of saying this in that manner, as Voltaire himself would have been. Homer, indeed, has actually an affinity with Voltaire in the unrivalled clearness and straightforwardness of his thinking; in the way in which he keeps to one thought at a time, and puts that thought forth in its complete natural plainness, instead of being led away from it by some fancy striking him in connection with it, and being beguiled to wander off with this fancy till his original thought, in its natural reality, knows him no more. What could better show us how gifted a race was this Greek race? The same member of it has not only the power of profoundly touching that natural heart of humanity which it is Voltaire's weakness that he cannot reach, but can also address the understanding with all Voltaire's admirable simplicity and rationality.

My limits will not allow me to do more than shortly illustrate, from Chapman's version of the *Iliad*, what I mean when I speak of this vital difference between Homer and an Elizabethan poet in the quality of their thought; between the plain simplicity of the thought of the one, and the curious complexity of the thought of the other. As in Pope's case, I carefully abstain from choosing passages for the express purpose of making Chapman appear ridiculous; Chapman, like Pope, merits in himself all respect, though he too, like Pope, fails to render Homer.

In that tonic speech of Sarpedon, of which I have said so much, Homer, you may remember, has:—

> εἰ μὲν γὰρ, πόλεμον περὶ τόνδε φυγόντε,
> αἰεὶ δὴ μέλλοιμεν ἀγήρω τ' ἀθανάτω τε
> ἔσσεσθ',—

> if indeed, but once *this* battle avoided,
> We were for ever to live without growing old and
> immortal.

Chapman cannot be satisfied with this, but must add a fancy to it:—

> if keeping back
> Would keep back age from us, and death, and *that*
> we might not wrack
> In this life's human sea at all;

and so on. Again; in another passage which I have before quoted, where Zeus says to the horses of Peleus,

τί σφῶϊ δόμεν Πηλῆϊ ἄνακτι
θνητῷ; ὑμεῖς δ' ἐστὸν ἀγήρω τ' ἀθανάτω τε·

Why gave we you to royal Peleus, to a mortal? but ye
are without old age, and immortal.

Chapman sophisticates this into:—

Why gave we you t' a mortal king, when immortality
And *incapacity of age so dignifies your states?*

Again; in the speech of Achilles to his horses, where Achilles,
according to Homer, says simply, 'Take heed that ye bring your
master safe back to the host of the Danaans, in some other sort
than the last time, when the battle is ended,' Chapman sophisticates this into:—

*When with blood, for this day's fast observed, revenge
shall yield*
Our heart satiety, bring us off.

In Hector's famous speech, again, at his parting from An-
dromache, Homer makes him say: 'Nor does my own heart so
bid me' (to keep safe behind the walls), 'since I have learned to
be staunch always, and to fight among the foremost of the
Trojans, busy on behalf of my father's great glory, and my own.'
In Chapman's hands this becomes:—

The spirit I first did breathe
Did never teach me that; much less, since the
contempt of death
Was settled in me, *and my mind knew what a worthy
was,*
*Whose office is to lead in fight, and give no danger
pass*
*Without improvement. In this fire must Hector's trial
shine:*
*Here must his country, father, friends, be in him made
divine.*

You see how ingeniously Homer's plain thought is *tormented,*
as the French would say, here. Homer goes on: 'For well I
know this in my mind and in my heart, the day will be, when
sacred Troy shall perish:'—

ἔσσεται ἦμαρ, ὅτ' ἄν ποτ' ὀλώλῃ Ἴλιος ἱρή.

Chapman makes this:—

And such a *stormy* day shall come, in mind and soul
I know,
When sacred Troy *shall shed her towers, for tears of
overthrow.*

I might go on for ever, but I could not give you a better
illustration than this last, of what I mean by saying that the
Elizabethan poet fails to render Homer because he cannot
forbear to interpose a play of thought between his object and its
expression. Chapman translates his object into Elizabethan, as
Pope translates it into the Augustan of Queen Anne; both convey it to us through a medium. Homer, on the other hand, sees
his object and conveys it to us immediately.

And yet, in spite of this perfect plainness and directness of
Homer's style, in spite of this perfect plainness and directness
of his ideas, he is eminently *noble*; he works as entirely in the
grand style, he is as grandiose, as Phidias, or Dante, or
Michael Angelo. This is what makes his translators despair. 'To
give relief,' says Cowper, 'to prosaic subjects' (such as dressing,
eating, drinking, harnessing, travelling, going to bed), that is to
treat such subjects nobly, in the grand style, 'without seeming
unseasonably tumid, is extremely difficult.' It *is* difficult, but
Homer has done it. Homer is precisely the incomparable poet
he is, because he has done it. His translator must not be tumid,
must not be artificial, must not be literary; true: but then also
he must not be commonplace, must not be ignoble. I have
shown you how translators of Homer fail by wanting rapidity,

by wanting simplicity of style, by wanting plainness of thought:
in a second lecture I will show you how a translator fails by
wanting nobility.—MATTHEW ARNOLD, *On Translating Homer,* 1861

It is difficult to say whether on the whole Chapman's reputation as a dramatist has gained or lost from his renown as the
poetic translator of Homer. In his own day the glory reflecting
from what such of his contemporaries as pretended to taste and
judgment accounted the highest kind of poetical achievement,
although as it would seem failing to secure him against neglect,
raised his literary reputation to a height unattained perhaps by
any of his fellow-dramatists except Jonson. Nowadays, while
few writers are wont to excel equally in species of composition
so widely apart from one another as those essayed by Chapman, there are on the other hand not many critics ready to
acknowledge varied excellence in the same writer, even where
it exists; for criticism is not less under the influence of its times
than productive art. It neither, however, follows that Chapman
was eminent as a dramatist because he was eminent as an epic
translator, nor that he was incapable of greatness in one branch
of the poetic art because he was so distinguished in another. In
such a case a candid judgment will be especially on its guard to

Avoid extremes, and shun the fault of such
Who still are pleas'd too little or too much;

and perhaps the time has arrived for judging Chapman fairly as
a dramatist, now that something like a definite balance may be
said to have been established between the merits and the shortcomings of his translation of Homer. . . .

On the qualities of Chapman's *Homer,* which can never
be deprived of the place which it conquered for itself in our
poetic literature, this is not the place to enlarge. It was not only,
as Mr. Swinburne expresses it, 'the sovereign labour of his life';
but it bears from first to last the impress of a genius worthy even
of the great task which the English poet set himself and carried
through with indomitable devotion. As a translation proper it
inevitably suffered from the influence of later schools of poetry,
as well as from its own undeniable defects in the way of scholarly accuracy. But the neglect which befell Chapman's *Homer*
by reason of the success of the version by Pope and his coadjutors, produced the reaction in its favour represented by
Charles Lamb, Coleridge and Keats. They judged it, again to
quote Mr. Swinburne, by the standard of original work rather
than of pure translation,—not that this latter is the criterion by
which 'Pope's Homer' itself can claim to stand or fall. Of more
recent critics, none worthy of the name has refused to Chapman's *Homer* the praise due to its vigour and passion, qualities
without which Homer can never be fitly reproduced. But it is
equally true that Chapman's style has characteristics which are
partly proper to himself, partly shared by him with the literary
age to which he belonged; and that these characteristics are
entirely foreign to other Homeric qualities,—above all to those
of simplicity and directness. It should not be overlooked, in
connexion with what will be observed below as to the versification of Chapman, that the metre of his *Homer* is not blank-
verse, but in the case of the *Iliad* a rimed fourteen-syllable
metre, with seven accents, and in the case of the *Odyssey,*
rimed ten-syllable couplets.—ADOLPHUS WILLIAM WARD, A
History of English Dramatic Poetry (1875), 1899, Vol. 2, pp.
408–11

Plays

I have sometimes wonder'd, in the reading, what was become
of those glaring Colours which amaz'd me in *Bussy Damboys*
upon the Theatre: but when I had taken up what I suppos'd, a

fallen star, I found I had been cozen'd with a Jelly: nothing but a cold dull mass, which glitter'd no longer than it was shooting: A dwarfish thought dress'd up in gigantick words, repetition in aboundance, looseness of expression, and gross Hyperboles; the Sense of one line expanded prodigiously into ten: and, to sum up all, uncorrect English, and a hideous mingle of false Poetry and true Nonsense; or, at best, a scantling of wit which lay gasping for life and groaning beneath a Heap of Rubbish. A famous modern Poet us'd to sacrifice every year a *Statius* to *Virgil's* Manes: and I have Indignation enough to burn a *D'amboys* annually, to the memory of *Johnson*. But now, My Lord, I am sensible, perhaps too late, that I have gone too far: for I remember some verses of my own *Maximin* and *Almanzor*, which cry, Vengeance upon me for their Extravagance, and which I wish heartily in the same fire with *Statius* and *Chapman*: All I can say for those passages, which are I hope not many, is, that I knew they were bad enough to please, even when I writ them. —JOHN DRYDEN, Dedicatory Epistle to *The Spanish Fryar*, 1681

Next to Marston, I must put Chapman, whose name is better known as the translator of Homer than as a dramatic writer. He is, like Marston, a philosophic observer, a didactic reasoner: but he has both more gravity in his tragic style, and more levity in his comic vein. (His *Bussy d'Ambois*, though not without interest or some fancy, is rather a collection of apophthegms or pointed sayings in the form of a dialogue, than a poem or a tragedy.) In his verses the oracles have not ceased. Every other line is an axiom in morals—a libel on mankind, if truth is a libel. He is too stately for a wit, in his serious writings—too formal for a poet. *Bussy d'Ambois* is founded on a French plot and French manners. The character, from which it derives its name, is arrogant and ostentatious to an unheard-of degree, but full of nobleness and lofty spirit. His pride and unmeasured pretensions alone take away from his real merit; and by the quarrels and intrigues in which they involve him, bring about the catastrophe, which has considerable grandeur and imposing effect, in the manner of Seneca. Our author aims at the highest things in poetry, and tries in vain, wanting imagination and passion, to fill up the epic moulds of tragedy with sense and reason alone, so that he often runs into bombast and turgidity—is extravagant and pedantic at one and the same time. From the nature of the plot, which turns upon a love intrigue, much of the philosophy of this piece relates to the character of the sex. Milton says,

The way of women's will is hard to hit.

But old Chapman professes to have found the clue to it, and winds his uncouth way through all the labyrinth of love. Its deepest recesses 'hide nothing from his view.' The close intrigues of court policy, the subtle workings of the human soul, move before him like a sea dark, deep, and glittering with wrinkles for the smile of beauty. —WILLIAM HAZLITT, *Lectures on the Dramatic Literature of the Age of Elizabeth*, 1820

Although destitute of a knowledge of dramatic effect neither in the tragic nor in the comic branch of the playwright's art, it would almost seem as if Chapman had lacked the power, when working alone, of fully developing a character by means of dramatic action; certainly none of the comedies or tragedies written by him alone are as stage-plays comparable to *Eastward Hoe* and *Chabot* respectively. But though falling short of this power, he is happy in the invention of character in both tragedy and comedy,—in the latter more particularly, as his Monsieur d'Olive would alone suffice to prove.

The length of time over which his known years of activity as a dramatist extend would lead one *a priori* to expect a change, or changes, in style to be observable in the course of his labours. His tragedies, however, on the whole exhibit the same characteristics of manner, though these are most marked in the *Bussy d'Ambois* plays—themselves, it will be remembered, not the products of their author's youth. Of the two tragedies posthumously printed as his, the one (*Revenge for Honour*) stands on a far higher level than the other (*Alphonsus*). Among his comedies the earliest are certainly the least advanced.

The influence of the epical form of composition to which Chapman had become habituated is indisputably observable in his dramas. He loves to narrate at full length; thus we find him in three of his plays resorting to the classical expedient of a 'Nuntius' or Messenger, and in others he lingers with evident pleasure over passages of a narrative kind. But this influence is not so marked as might be expected; and both in tragedy and in comedy he shows a strong sense of the importance of situation, although to the expediency of a progressive conduct of the action he is not always sufficiently alive. In style he is too fond of indulging a tendency to rhetoric, which, in the earlier of his tragedies in particular, at times degenerates into bombast; but the instances of this in his plays remain after all the exception and not the rule. Of humour as well as wit he must be allowed to have possessed a real though not a very fertile vein.

But the strength of Chapman lies in particular passages rather than in his plays as a whole. With the exception of Shakspere ('always except Plato,' says the Duke of Savoy in *Byron's Conspiracy*), he has no superior or equal among our Elisabethan dramatists in the beauty of individual passages. This beauty is not solely one of form, nor is the pleasure derived from it merely due to the admiration excited by Chapman's poetic inventiveness, ranging over a wide field in the choice of similes and settling on its choice with wonderful felicitousness. Like Shakspere, he is able at times to reveal by these sudden flashes of poetic power depths of true feeling as well as of true wisdom. His observation is strikingly original as well as apt, and there is often something proverbial or gnomic about these passages, in which the physical as well as the moral world is called into play, and of which (if there be any profit in anthologies) it would be well worth while to attempt a complete list. He is particularly effective in his touches concerning the nature of women, whose sex he seems to have studied rather than loved—for he has hardly drawn a single female character of note (unless it be Tamyra), and those which he has drawn are for the most part examples of frailty rather than of purity. But his wisdom rises to its greatest dignity in connexion with a theme on which he must have thought deeply as well as keenly, and which rises far above the mere transitory feeling of the day on political topics. Again and again, this poet returns to his conception of true freedom as contained within the fulfilment of duty and obedience to law, while in lawlessness, whether in the despot or in the rebel, he finds a sin against the enduring principle of Order.

Chapman's style is unmistakeably influenced by his classical learning; but he cannot be pronounced pedantically fond of displaying it. With the exception of *Alphonsus*, his plays, though abounding in classical allusions, are not, either throughout or in parts, overlaid by them; he is too genuine a scholar to quote with complacency even out of season. His references to Homer are of course very numerous, and it would certainly have made a perceptible difference in Chapman's dramatic dialogue, had the concatenation of negatives suggested by the speculative Clermont stopped this particular source of illustrations. Other classical writers, however, are used as almost equally familiar authorities, after a fashion very different from the superficial show of classical learning in which so many of our earlier dramatists were wont to indulge. Yet although Chapman was manifestly a diligent student of historical as well as poetic literature, although he was to a certainty in the habit of reading French memoir-history, and probably well acquainted with the German tongue, his learning cannot in any case have extended over so wide a range as that of Ben Jonson, whose wonderful mental appetite absorbed almost every kind of material.

Finally, after the quotations incidentally given, it will be needless to speak at length of the extreme beauty of Chapman's versification. Some of his earlier plays show traces of at least one mannerism which he seems afterwards to have avoided— *viz.* the repetition of a closing word in several lines near to one another; while in what, if his, was probably one of his last plays (*Revenge for Honour*) the excessive use of feminine endings is characteristic of a school which he assuredly did not contribute to found. But, in general, Chapman's line holds the mean between the dissolved sweetness of Beaumont and Fletcher and the self-contained strength displayed by Marlowe in his earliest works; and in certain nobilities of versification, as in a lordly use of the matter which informs poetic style, Chapman perhaps more nearly resembles Shakspere, of whose achievements he was so manifestly cognisant, than can be asserted of any of their common contemporaries.—ADOLPHUS WILLIAM WARD, *A History of English Dramatic Literature* (1875), 1899, Vol. 2, pp. 447–50

The only complete edition of Chapman's works dates from our own days, and its three volumes correspond to a real division of subject. Although, in common with all these writers, Chapman has had much uncertain and some improbable work fathered on him, his certain dramas supply one of the most interesting studies in our period. As usual with every one except Shakespere and (it is a fair reason for the relatively disproportionate estimate of these so long held) Beaumont and Fletcher, they are extremely unequal. Not a certain work of Chapman is void of interest. The famous *Eastward Ho!* (one of the liveliest comedies of the period dealing with London life) was the work of three great writers, and it is not easy to distribute its collaboration. That it is not swamped with "humours" may prove that Jonson's learned sock was put on by others. That it is neither grossly indecent nor extravagantly sanguinary, shows that Marston had not the chief hand in it, and so we are left to Chapman. What he could do is not shown in the list of his own certain plays till *All Fools*. *The Blind Beggar of Alexandria* and *An Humorous Day's Mirth* partake of that singular promiscuousness—that heaping together of scenes without order or connection—which we have noticed in the first dramatic period, not to mention that the way in which the characters speak of themselves, not as "I" but by their names in the third person, is also unmistakable. But *All Fools* is a much more noteworthy piece, and though Mr. Swinburne may have praised it rather highly, it would certainly take place in a collection of the score best comedies of the time not written by Shakespere. *The Gentleman Usher* and *Monsieur d'Olive* belong to the same school of humorous, not too pedantic comedy, and then we come to the strange series of Chapman's French tragedies, *Bussy d'Ambois*, *The Revenge of Bussy d'Ambois*, *Byron's Conspiracy*, *The Tragedy of Charles, Duke of Byron*, and *The Tragedy of Philip Chabot, Admiral of France*. These singular plays stand by themselves. Whether the strong influence which Marlowe exercised on Chapman led the later poet (who it must be remembered was not the younger) to continue *The Massacre of Paris*, or what other cause begat them, cannot now be asserted or even guessed without lost labour. A famous criticism of Dryden's attests his attention to them, but does not, perhaps, to those who have studied Dryden deeply, quite express the influence which Chapman had on the leader of post-Restoration tragedy. As plays, the whole five are models of what plays should not be; in parts, they are models of what plays should be. Then Chapman returned to the humour-comedy and produced two capital specimens of it in *May-Day* and *The Widow's Tears*. *Alphonsus, Emperor of Germany*, which contains long passages of German, and *Revenge for Honour*, two tragedies which were not published till long after Chapman's death, are to my mind very dubiously his. Mr. Swinburne, in dealing with them, availed himself of the hypothesis of a mellowing, but at the same time weakening of power by age. It may be so, and I have not the slightest intention of pronouncing decidedly on the subject. They bear to my mind much more mark of the decadent period of Charles I., when the secret of blank verse was for a time lost, and when even men who had lived in personal friendship with their great predecessors lapsed into the slipshod stuff that we find in Davenant, in his followers, and among them even in the earlier plays of Dryden. It is, of course, true that this loosening and slackening of the standard betrays itself even before the death of Chapman, which happened in 1634. But I cannot believe that the author of *Bussy d'Ambois* (where the verse is rude enough but never lax) and the contemporary or elder of Shakespere, Marlowe, and all the great race, could ever have been guilty of the slovenliness which, throughout, marks *Revenge for Honour*.—GEORGE SAINTSBURY, *A History of Elizabethan Literature*, 1887, pp. 186–88

JOHN WEBSTER

c. 1570–c. 1634

Little is known of the life of John Webster. In a preface to his Lord Mayor's show for 1624, *Monuments of Honor*, Webster describes himself "born free" of the Merchant Taylor's Company, the son of another freeman, John Webster. A John Webster was a member of the English Comedians under Robert Brown, in the service of the German count Maurice of Hesse-Kessel in 1595, and another John Webster entered the Middle Temple in 1598 or still another John Webster, "clothworker," who died in September, 1625. Certainly, John Webster the playwright was dead by 1634, as in that year he was referred to in the past tense by a contemporary.

John Webster collaborated on plays with leading dramatists, including Dekker, Middleton, Drayton, Ford and perhaps Massinger, Chettle, Chapman, Heywood, and Rowley. Many of these plays, or rumored plays are lost. However, some eight plays are extant. In 1604, Webster wrote the introduction to Marston's *The Malcontent*. Collaborating chiefly with Thomas Dekker, Webster contributed to *The Famous History of Sir Thomas Wyatt* (with Dekker, published 1607) and wrote *Northward Hoe* and *Westward Hoe*, also with Dekker (both published in 1607). Plays which are attributed to Webster by most include *Appius and Virginia* (published in 1654), *A Cure for a Cuckold* (published 1661), *The Devil's Law-Case* (published 1623). It seems certain that Webster wrote *Monuments of Honour* (1624), a City pageant, as well as some non-dramatic verse, including an elegy on the death of Henry, Prince of Wales, titled *A Monumental Columne* (1613). In addition, Webster contributed prefatory verses to Munday's translation of *Palmerin of England* (1602), Harrison's *Arches of Triumph* (1604), and Heywood's *Apology for Actors* (1612).

Webster's fame rests chiefly on two plays which he himself wrote: *The White Devil: Or the Tragedy of Paolo Giordana Ursini, Duke of Brachiano, with the Life and Death of Vittoria Corombona the famous Venetian Curtizan* (first produced in 1608) known to most audiences simply as *The White Devil*, and *The Duchess of Malfi*, first produced between 1608 and 1614. These plays, particularly *The Duchess of Malfi*, are examples of the villain play, a type that developed out of the earlier revenge tragedy. In them, dark imagery and naturalistic (albeit brooding and violent) characters predominate over the interests of plot development, affording an atmosphere which combines scathing satire with a sense of overwhelming despair.

General

But hist! with him, crabbed Websterio,
The playwright-cartwright (whether either!). Ho!
No further. Look as you'd be looked into;
Sit as ye would be read. Lord! who would know him?
Was ever man so mangled with a poem?
See how he draws his mouth awry of late,
How he scrubs, wrings his wrists, scratches his pate.
A midwife, help! By his brain's coitus
Some centaur strange, some huge Bucephalus,
Or Pallas, sure, engendered in his brain,
Strike Vulcan, with thy hammer once again.
This is the critic that of all the rest
I'd not have view me, yet I fear him least.
Here's not a word cursively I have writ
But he'll industriously examine it,
And in some twelve months hence, or thereabout,
Set in a shameful sheet my errors out.
But what care I? It will be so obscure
That none shall understand him I am sure.
—HENRY FITZJEFFREY, "Notes from
Blackfriars," *Certain Elegies by Sundry
Excellent Wits*, 1617

Webster the next, though not so much of note
Nor's name attended with such noise and crowd,
Yet by the Nine and by Apollo's vote,
Whose groves of bay are for his head allowed—
Most sacred spirit (some may say I dote),
Of thy three noble tragedies be as proud
As great voluminous Jonson; thou shalt be
Read longer and with more applause than he.
—SAMUEL SHEPPARD, "The Fairy King," 1651

An Author that liv'd in the Reign of King *James* the First: and was in those Days accounted an Excellent Poet. He joyn'd with *Decker*, *Marston*, and *Rowley*, in several Plays; and was likewise Author of others, which have even in our Age gain'd Applause. . . . Mr. *Philips* has committed a great Mistake, in ascribing several Plays to our Author, and his Associate Mr. *Decker*; One of which belong to another Writer, whose Name is annexed, and the rest are Anonymous.—GERARD LANGBAINE, *An Account of the English Dramatick Poets*, 1691

In his pictures of wretchedness and despair, he has introduced touches of expression which curdle the very blood with terror, and make the hair stand erect. Of this, the death of The Dutchesse of Malfy, with all its preparatory horrors, is a most distinguishing proof. The fifth act of his *Vittoria Corombona* shows, also, with what occasional skill he could imbibe the imagination of Shakspeare, particularly where its features seem to breathe a more than earthly wildness.—NATHAN DRAKE, *Shakspere and His Times*, 1817, Vol. 2, p. 565

Some single scenes are to be found in ⟨Webster's⟩ works, inferior in power of passion to nothing in the whole range of the drama. He was a man of a truly original genius, and seems to have felt strong pleasure in the strange and fantastic horrors that rose up from the dark abyss of his imagination. The vices and the crimes which he delights to paint, all partake of an extravagance which, nevertheless, makes them impressive and terrible, and in the retribution and the punishment there is a character of corresponding wildness. But our sympathies, suddenly awakened, are allowed as suddenly to subside. There is nothing of what Wordsworth calls "a mighty stream of tendency" in the events of his dramas, nor, in our opinion, is there a single character that clearly and boldly stands out before us, like a picture.—JOHN WILSON (as "H.M."), *Blackwood's Edinburgh Magazine*, March 1818, pp. 657–58

Webster has a gloomy force of imagination, not unmixed with the beautiful and pathetic. But it is "beauty in the lap of horror:" he caricatures the shapes of terror, and his Pegasus is like a nightmare.—THOMAS CAMPBELL, *An Essay on English Poetry*, 1819

His *White Devil* and *Dutchess of Malfi*, upon the whole, perhaps, come the nearest to Shakspeare of any thing we have upon record: the only drawback to them, the only shade of imputation that can be thrown upon them, "by which they lose some colour," is, that they are too like Shakspeare, and often direct imitations of him, both in general conception and individual expression.—WILLIAM HAZLITT, *Lectures on the Dramatic Literature of the Age of Elizabeth*, 1820

John Webster, a mighty and funereal genius, is the next author we shall mention. We can compare his mind to nothing so well as to some old Gothic cathedral, with its arches soaring heavenward, but carved with monsters and angels, with saints and fiends, in grotesque confusion. Gleams of sunlight fall here and there, it is true, through the huge window, but they are coloured with the sombre dies of painted glass, bearing records of human pride and human nothingness, and they fall in long slanting columns, twinkling silently with motes and dusty splendour, upon the tombs of the mighty; lighting dimly up now the armour of a recumbent Templar or the ruff of some dead beauty, and now feebly losing themselves amid the ragged coffins and scutcheons in the vaults below. His fancy was wild and powerful, but gloomy and monstrous, dwelling ever on the vanities of earthly glory, on the nothingness of pomp, not without many terrible hints at the emptiness of our trust, and many bold questionings of human hopes of a hereafter.—THOMAS B. SHAW, *Outlines of English Literature*, 1847, p. 130

Webster's most famous works are *The Duchess of Malfy* and *Vittoria Corombona*, but we are strongly inclined to call *The Devil's Law-Case* his best play. The two former are in a great measure answerable for the "spasmodic" school of poets, since the extravagances of a man of genius are as sure of imitation as the equable self-possession of his higher moments is incapable of it. Webster had, no doubt, the primal requisite of a poet, imagination, but in him it was truly untamed, and Aristotle's admirable distinction between the *Horrible* and the *Terrible* in tragedy was never better illustrated and confirmed than in the *Duchess* and *Vittoria*. His nature had something of the sleuth-hound quality in it, and a plot, to keep his mind eager on the trail, must be sprinkled with fresh blood at every turn. . . . He has not the condensing power of Shakespeare, who squeezed meaning into a phrase with an hydraulic press, but he could carve a cherry-stone with any of the *concettisti*, and abounds in imaginative quaintnesses that are worthy of Donne, and epigrammatic tersenesses that reminds us of Fuller. Nor is he wanting in poetic phrases of the purest crystallization.—JAMES RUSSELL LOWELL, "Library of Old Authors" (1858–64), *Prose Works*, Vol. 1, pp. 279–81

Webster was one of those writers whose genius consists in the expression of special moods, and who, outside of those moods, cannot force their creative faculties into vigorous action. His mind by instinctive sentiment was directed to the contemplation of the darker aspects of life. He brooded over crime and misery until his imagination was enveloped in their atmosphere, found a fearful joy in probing their sources and tracing their consequences, became strangely familiar with their physiognomy and psychology, and felt a shuddering sympathy with their "deep groans and terrible ghastly looks." There was hardly a remote corner of the soul, which hid a feeling capable of giving mental pain, into which this artist in agony had not curiously peered. . . . He is such a spendthrift of his stimulants, and accumulates horror on horror, and crime on crime, with such fatal facility, that he would render the mind callous to his terrors, were it not that what is acted is still less than what is suggested, and that the souls of his characters are greater than their sufferings or more terrible than their deeds. The crimes and the criminals belong to Italy as it was in the sixteenth century, when poisoning and assassination were almost in the fashion; the feelings with which they are regarded are English; and the result of the combination is to make the poisoners and assassins more fiendishly malignant in spirit than they actually were. . . .

Of all the contemporaries of Shakespeare, Webster is the most Shakespearian. His genius was not only influenced by its contact with one side of Shakespeare's many-sided mind, but the tragedies . . . abound in expressions and situations either suggested by or directly copied from the tragedies of him he took for his model. . . . —EDWIN P. WHIPPLE, *The Literature of the Age of Elizabeth*, 1869, pp. 139–41

In passing onward to John Webster, we come into the presence of a poet to whom a foremost place has been rarely denied among the later writers of the great age of our drama, and in whom it is impossible not to recognise a genius of commanding originality, though apparently of not very versatile powers. It is most unfortunate that but few plays should have been preserved of which he was the sole author; for it is in these that his most distinctive gifts stand forth with incomparably the greatest clearness, and, as is pointed out by the most adequate of his modern critics, he seems, like Shakspere and Jonson, to have preferred to work alone.

. . . Webster loves to accumulate the favourite furniture of theatrical terror—murders and executions, the dagger and the pistol, the cord and the coffin, together with skulls and ghosts, and whatever horrors attend or are suggested by the central horror of them all. Herein he is not exceptional among the Elisabethans, of whom, from Kyd to Tourneur, so many were alike addicted to the employment of the whole apparatus of death. What is distinctive in Webster, is in the first place the extraordinary intensity of his imagination in this sphere of ideas, and again the elaborateness of his workmanship, which enabled him to surpass—it may fairly be said—all our old dramatists in a field which a large proportion were at all times ready to cultivate. As for later endeavours in our literature to rival this familiarity with death and its ghastly associations, they have rarely escaped the danger of artificiality or succeeded in stimulating the imaginative powers of any generation but their own. Among all these poets of the grave and its terrors we meet with but few whose very soul seems, like Webster's, a denizen of the gloom by which their creations are overspread.

But Webster's most powerful plays and scenes are characterised by something besides their effective appeal to the emotion of terror. He has a true insight into human nature, and is capable of exhibiting the operation of powerful influences upon it with marvellous directness. He is aware that men and women will lay open the inmost recesses of their souls in moments of deep or sudden agitation; he has learnt that on such occasions unexpected contrasts—an impulse of genuine compassion in an assassin, a movement of true dignity in a harlot—are wont to offer themselves to the surprised observer; he is acquainted with the fury and the bitterness, the goad and the after-sting of passion, and with the broken vocabulary of grief. All these he knows and understands, and is able to reproduce, not continually or wearisomely, but with that unerring recognition of supremely fitting occasions which is one of the highest, as it is beyond all doubt one of the rarest, gifts of true dramatic genius.

. . . What Webster in general reproduces with inimitable force, is a succession of situations of overpowering effect; in construction he is far from strong, and in characterisation he only exceptionally passes beyond the range of ordinary types. There seems little moral purpose at work in his most imposing efforts; and his imagination, instead of dwelling by preference on the associations of the law-court and the charnel-house, would have had to sustain itself on nutriment more diverse and more spiritual, in order to wing his mighty genius to freer and loftier flights.—ADOLPHUS WILLIAM WARD, *A History of English Dramatic Literature* (1875), 1899, Vol. 3, pp. 51–65

Thunder: the flesh quails, and the soul bows down.
    Night: east, west, south, and northward, very night.
    Star upon struggling star strives into sight,
Star after shuddering star the deep storms drown.
The very throne of night, her very crown,
        A man lays hand on, and usurps her right.
        Song from the highest of heaven's imperious height

Shoots, as a fire to smite some towering town.
Rage, anguish, harrowing fear, heart-crazing crime,
Make monstrous all the murderous face of Time
    Shown in the spheral orbit of a glass
Revolving. Earth cries out from all her graves,
Frail, on frail rafts, across wide-wallowing waves,
    Shapes here and there of child and mother pass.
        —ALGERNON CHARLES SWINBURNE, "John
        Webster," *Sonnets on English Dramatic Poets,*
        1882

John Webster excelled in the delineation of strange and fantastic horrors. He was pre-eminently the dramatist of Death. But his works abound in passages of surprising tenderness and beauty. The vices and crimes which he delighted to paint have, notwithstanding their extravagance, an appearance of terrible reality; and he had the wonderful faculty of surmising and looking into the inmost thoughts and springs of action in the human mind. He was an artist of the highest type.—JAMES BALDWIN, "English Poetry," *English Literature and Literary Criticism,* 1882, p. 238

Of *Appius and Virginia* the best thing to be said is to borrow Sainte-Beuve's happy description of Molière's *Don Garcie de Navarre,* and to call it an *essai pale et noble.* Webster is sometimes very close to Shakespere; but to read *Appius and Virginia,* and then to read *Julius Cæsar* or *Coriolanus,* is to appreciate, in perhaps the most striking way possible, the universality which all good judges from Dryden downwards have recognised in the prince of literature. Webster, though he was evidently a good scholar, and even makes some parade of scholarship, was a Romantic to the core, and was all abroad in these classical measures. *The Devil's Law Case* sins in the opposite way, being hopelessly undigested, destitute of any central interest, and, despite fine passages, a mere "salmagundi." There remain the two famous plays of *The White Devil* or *Vittoria Corombona* and *The Duchess of Malfi*—plays which have not, I think, been acted since their author's days, and of which the earlier and, to my judgment, better was not a success even then, but which the judgment of three generations has placed at the very head of all their class, and which contain magnificent poetry.—GEORGE SAINTSBURY, *A History of Elizabethan Literature,* 1887, p. 274

Webster, as man and artist, never descends to Tourneur's level. He selects his two great subjects from Italian story, deriving thence the pith and marrow of veracity. These subjects he treats carefully and conscientiously, according to his own conception of the dreadful depths in human nature revealed to us by sixteenth century Italy. He does not use the vulgar machinery of revenge and ghosts in order to evolve an action. In so far as this goes, he may even be said to have advanced a step beyond *Hamlet* in the evolution of the Tragedy of Blood. His dramatic issues are worked out, without much alteration, from the matter given in the two Italian tales he used. Only he claims the right to view human fates and fortunes with despair, to paint a broad black background for his figures, to detach them sharply in sinister or pathetic relief, and to leave us at the last without a prospect over hopeful things. "One great Charybdis swallows all," said the Greek Simonides; and this motto might be chosen for the work of Shakespeare's greatest pupil in the art of tragedy. Yet Webster never fails to touch our hearts, and makes us remember a riper utterance upon the piteousness of man's ephemeral existence:—

    Sunt lacrimæ rerum, et mentem mortalia tangunt.

It is just this power of blending tenderness and pity with the exhibition of acute moral anguish by which Webster is so superior to Tourneur as a dramatist.

    . . . No dramatist showed more consummate ability in heightening terrific effects, in laying bare the inner mysteries of crime, remorse, and pain combined to make men miserable. He seems to have had a natural bias toward the dreadful stuff with which he deals so powerfully. He was drawn to comprehend and reproduce abnormal elements of spiritual anguish. The materials with which he builds are sought for in the ruined places of abandoned lives, in the agonies of madness and despair, in the sarcasms of reckless atheism, in slow tortures, griefs beyond endurance, the tempests of sin-haunted conscience, the spasms of fratricidal bloodshed, the deaths of frantic hope-deserted criminals. He is often melodramatic in the means employed to bring these psychological elements of tragedy home to our imagination. He makes free use of poisoned engines, daggers, pistols, disguised murderers, masques, and nightmares. Yet his firm grasp upon the essential qualities of diseased and guilty human nature, his profound pity for the innocent who suffer shipwreck in the storm of evil passions not their own, save him, even at his gloomiest and wildest, from the unrealities and extravagances into which less potent artists—Tourneur, for example—blundered.—JOHN ADDINGTON SYMONDS, "Introduction" to *Webster and Tourneur,* 1888, pp. xi–xxii

There are, indeed, wondrous flashes of dramatic power; by whiles, too, there are refreshing openings-out to the light or sinlessness of common day—a lifting of thought and consciousness up from the great welter of crime and crime's entanglements; but there is little brightness, sparse sunshine, rare panoply of green or blooming things; even the flowers are put to sad offices, and

                do cover
The friendless bodies of unburied men.

When a man's flower culture gets reduced to such narrow margin as this it does not carry exhilarating odors with it. — DONALD G. MITCHELL, *English Lands, Letters, and Kings (From Elizabeth to Anne),* 1890, p. 90

On one point . . . with great diffidence, the present writer must confess that he cannot agree with those great authorities, Lamb and Mr. Swinburne, who have asserted, in their admiration for Webster, that he was always skilful in the introduction of horror. In his own mind, as a poet, Webster doubtless was aware of the procession of a majestic and solemn spectacle, but when he endeavours to present that conception on the boards of the theatre, his "terrors want dignity, his affrightments want decorum." The horrible dumb shows of *The Duchess of Malfy*—the strangled children, the chorus of maniacs, the murder of Cariola, as she bites and scratches, the scuffling and stabbing in the fifth act, are, it appears to me—with all deference to the eminent critics, who have applauded them—blots on what is notwithstanding a truly noble poem, and what, with more reserve in this respect, would have been one of the first tragedies of the world.

    Similar characteristics present themselves to us in *The White Devil,* but in a much rougher form. The sketchiness of this play, which is not divided into acts and scenes, and progresses with unaccountable gaps in the story, and perfunctory makeshifts of dumb show, has been the wonder of critics. But Webster was particularly interested in his own work as a romantic rather than a theatrical poet, and it must be remembered that after a long apprenticeship in collaboration, *The White Devil* was his first independent play. It reads as though the writer had put in only what interested him, and had left the rest for a coadjutor, who did not happen to present himself, to fill up. The central figure of Vittoria, the subtle, masterful, and exquisite she-devil, is filled up very minutely and vividly in the otherwise hastily painted canvas; and in the trial-scene, which is perhaps the most perfectly sustained which Webster has left us, we are so much captivated by the beauty and ingenuity of the murderess that, as Lamb says in a famous passage, we are ready to expect that "all the court will rise and make proffer to defend her in spite of the utmost conviction of her guilt." The fascination of Vittoria, like an exquisite poisonous perfume, pervades the play, and Brachiano strikes a note, which is the central one of the romance, when he says to her—

> Thou hast led me like a heathen sacrifice,
> With music and with fatal yokes of flowers,
> To my eternal ruin.

The White Devil is not less full than the *Duchess of Malfy* of short lines and phrases full of a surprising melody. In the fabrication of these jewels, Webster is surpassed only by Shakespeare.—EDMUND GOSSE, *The Jacobean Poets*, 1894, pp. 168–70

Nothing so much as a close and careful study of his imagery can bring home to one the extraordinary originality and power of Webster in his particular sphere. Webster worked consciously, deliberately, and with a thorough command of his materials. His pages are strewn with tropes, and, in spite of their profusion, such is the keenness of his marvelous "analogical instinct" and the dramatic force of his imagination that scarcely ever do they seem forced or out of keeping. Language here seems to reach the extreme of ruthless and biting intensity. There is scarcely any faded imagery, and there are very few conventional tags; everything stands out in sharp lines, as if etched. The characteristic fault of Webster's imagery, the defect of his peculiar quality, is that he errs if anything on the side of the bizarre, or even of the grotesque. This criticism could be enforced by many citations. . . . The acrid nature of Webster's genius is everywhere felt in his pungent use of similitudes. The sardonic character of Flamineo in *The White Devil* is heightened by the irony of his incessant similes. So in *The Duchess of Malfi* Antonio's rather colorless virtues are artfully depicted through his fondness for sententious comparisons.—FREDERIC IVES CARPENTER, *Metaphor and Simile in the Minor Elizabethan Drama*, 1895, pp. 75–77

Works

THE WHITE DEVIL
(VITTORIA COROMBONA)

To those who report I was a long time in finishing this tragedy, I confess I do not write with a goose-quill winged with two feathers; and, if they will needs make it my fault, I must answer them with that of Euripides to Alcestides, a tragick writer: Alcestides objecting that Euripides had onely in three daies composed three verses, whereas himself had written three hundredth; Thou telst truthe (quoth he), but heres the difference, thine shall onely be read for three daies, whereas mine shall continue three ages.—JOHN WEBSTER, "Preface" to *The White Devil*, 1612

⟨*The White Devil*⟩ is so disjointed in its action,—the incidents are so capricious and so involved,—and there is, throughout, such a mixture of the horrible and the absurd—the comic and the tragic—the pathetic and the ludicrous,—that we find it impossible, within our narrow limits, to give any thing like a complete and consistent analysis of it. . . .

There is great power in this drama, and even much fine

poetry,—but, on the whole, it shocks rather than agitates, and the passion is rather painful than tragical. There are, in truth, some scenes that altogether revolt and disgust,—and mean, abandoned, and unprincipled characters occupy too much of our attention throughout the action of the play. There is but little imagination breathed over the passions of the prime agents, who exhibit themselves in the bare deformity of evil,—and scene follows scene of shameless profligacy, unredeemed either by great intellectual energy, or occasional burstings of moral sensibilities. The character of Vittoria Corombona, on which the chief interest of the drama depends, is sketched with great spirit and freedom,—but though true enough to nature, and startling by her beauty and her wickedness, we feel that she is not fit to be the chief personage of tragedy, which ought ever to deal only with great passions, and with great events. There is, however, a sort of fascination about this "White Devil of Venice," which accompanies her to the fatal end of her career,—and something like admiration towards her is awakened by the dauntless intrepidity of her death.—JOHN WILSON (as "H.M."), *Blackwood's Edinburgh Magazine*, Aug. 1818, pp. 556–62

Of the two plays of Webster in which his tragic genius has produced its most potent effects, *The White Devil, or The Tragedy of Paulo Giordano Vrsini, Duke of Brachiano, with the Life and Death of Vittoria Corombona, the famous Venetian Curtizan*, first printed in 1612 and perhaps acted 1607–8, is the earlier. Although I cannot agree with those who regard this tragedy as the masterpiece of its author, it is beyond all doubt a most remarkable work. Its plot as well as its characters appears to have been borrowed directly from an Italian source, inasmuch as the history of the Duke of Brachiano and his two wives, of whom the second bore the name of Vittoria Accorambuoni and was the widow of the nephew of Cardinal Montalto, afterwards Pope Sixtus V, does not appear to have been reproduced in any English or French version.

This extraordinary tragedy, whose finest scenes and passages have, in the judgment of Mr. Swinburne, been never surpassed or equalled except by Shakspere 'in the crowning qualities of tragic or dramatic poetry,' must be described as at once highly elaborated and essentially imperfect. In the address *To the Reader* already referred to, Webster confesses with conscious pride that this play was the fruit of protracted labour; but his efforts appear to have been directed rather to accumulating and elaborating effective touches of detail than to producing a well-proportioned whole. The catastrophe seems to lag too far after the climax; and in spite of the mighty impression created by the genius of the author, it is difficult to resist a sense of weariness in the progress of the later part of the action. But a yet more serious defect appears to me to attach to *Vittoria Corombona*. The personages of this tragedy—above all that of the heroine—are conceived with the most striking original power and carried out with unerring consistency; but we crave—and crave in vain—some relief to the almost sickening combination of awe and loathing created by such characters and motives as this drama presents.

The character of Vittoria herself—the White Devil—is not easily to be put into words. Hot passion covering itself by an assumption of cool outward self-control and of contemptuous superiority to the ordinary fears or scruples of women,—this is a conception which we instinctively feel to be true to nature— to nature, that is, in one of her abnormal moods. In the first scene in which Vittoria appears she reveals the deadliness of her passionate resolution, when relating to her paramour the dream which is to urge him on to the murder of his duchess and her own husband. The ghastliness of the imagery of the vision is indescribably effective, together with the horrible scornfulness of the closing phrase:

> When to my rescue there arose, methought,
> A whirlwind, which let fall a massy arm
> From that strong plant;
> And both were struck dead by that sacred yew,
> *In that base shallow grave that was their due.*

The scene in which Vittoria is tried for the murder of her husband has attracted the comment of several critics—among others of Charles Lamb, who strangely enough speaks of her 'innocence-resembling boldness.' Dyce demurs to this view, which appears to me utterly erroneous, and destructive of the consistency which the character throughout maintains. Not 'sweetness' and 'loveliness' but a species of strange fascination, such as is only too often exercised by heartless pride, seems to pervade the figure and the speech of the defiant sinner who refuses to withdraw an inch from the position which she has assumed, and meets her judges with a front of withering scorn. Almost equally effective are the burst of passion with which she turns upon the jealous Brachiano, and the gradual subsiding of her wrath, as of a fire, under his caresses. The terrible energy of the last act is almost unparalleled; but the character of Vittoria remains true to itself, except perhaps in the last—rather trivial—reflexion with which she dies.

The remaining characters of the tragedy are drawn with varying degrees of force; but they all seem to stand forth as real human figures under the lurid glare of a storm-laden sky: nor is it easy to analyse the impression created by so dense a mixture of unwholesome humours, wild passions, and fearful sorrows. The total effect is unspeakably ghastly—though in one of the most elaborately terrible scenes the intention becomes too obvious, and 'several forms of distraction' exhibited by the mad Cornelia strike one as in some degree conventional, as they are to some extent plagiarised.

It must however be observed that in this play, as in *The Duchess of Malfi*, Webster creates some of his most powerful effects by single touches—flashes of genius which seem to light up of a sudden a wide horizon of emotions. It is in these flashes, so vivid as to illumine the dullest perception, so subtle as to search the closest heart, that Webster alone among our dramatists can be said at times to equal Shakspere. —ADOLPHUS WILLIAM WARD, *A History of English Dramatic Literature* (1875), 1899, Vol. 3, pp. 56–59

One of the most glorious works of the period. Vittoria is perfect throughout, and in the justly-lauded trial scene she has no superior on any stage. Brachiano is a thoroughly life-like portrait of the man who is completely besotted with an evil woman. Flamineo I have spoken of, and not favourably; yet in literature, if not in life, he is a triumph; and above all the absorbing tragic interest of the play, which it is impossible to take up without finishing, has to be counted in. But the real charm of *The White Devil* is the wholly miraculous poetry in phrases and short passages which it contains. Vittoria's dream of the yew-tree, almost all the speeches of the unfortunate Isabella, and most of her rival's, have this merit. But the most wonderful flashes of poetry are put in the mouth of the scoundrel Flamineo, where they have a singular effect. —GEORGE SAINTSBURY, *A History of Elizabethan Literature*, 1887, p. 275

In 1612 John Webster stood revealed to the then somewhat narrow world of readers as a tragic poet and dramatist of the very foremost rank in the very highest class. *The White Devil*, also known as *Vittoria Corombona*, is a tragedy based on events then comparatively recent—on a chronicle of crime and re-tribution in which the leading circumstances were altered and adapted with the most delicate art and the most consummate judgment from the incompleteness of incomposite reality to the requisites of the stage of Shakespeare. By him alone among English poets have the finest scenes and passages of this tragedy been ever surpassed or equalled in the crowning qualities of tragic or dramatic poetry—in pathos and passion, in subtlety and strength, in harmonious variety of art and infallible fidelity to nature.—ALGERNON CHARLES SWINBURNE, *Studies in Prose and Poetry*, 1894, p. 50

THE DUCHESS OF MALFI

> Crown him a poet, whom nor Rome nor Greece
> Transcend in all their's for a masterpiece;
> In which, whiles words and matter change, and men
> Act one another, he, from whose clear pen,
> They all took life, to memory hath lent
> A lasting fame to raise his monument.
> —JOHN FORD, "To the Reader of the Author, and
> His *Dutchess of Malfi*," 1623

> I never saw thy Duchess till the day
> That she was lively bodied in thy play:
> How'er she answer'd her low-rated love
> Her brother's anger did so fatal prove,
> Yet my opinion is, she might speak more,
> But never in her life so well before.
> —WILLIAM ROWLEY, "To His Friend, Mr. John
> Webster, Upon His *Dutchess of Malfi*," 1623

All the several parts of the dreadful apparatus with which the death of the Duchess is ushered in, the waxen images which counterfeit death, the wild masque of madmen, the tombmaker, the bellman, the living person's dirge, the mortification by degrees,—are not more remote from the conceptions of ordinary vengeance, than the strange character of suffering which they seem to bring upon their victim is out of the imagination of ordinary poets. As they are not like inflictions of this life, so her language seems not of this world. She has lived among horrors till she is become "native and endowed unto that element." She speaks the dialect of despair; her tongue has a smatch of Tartarus and the souls in bale. To move a horror skilfully, to touch a soul to the quick, to lay upon fear as much as it can bear, to wean and weary a life till it is ready to drop, and then step in with mortal instruments to take its last forfeit: this only a Webster can do. Inferior geniuses may "upon horror's head horrors accumulate" but they cannot do this. They mistake quantity for quality; they "terrify babes with painted devils;" but they know not how a soul is to be moved. Their terrors want dignity, their affrightments are without decorum.—CHARLES LAMB, *Specimens of English Dramatic Poets*, 1808

The *Duchess of Malfy* is not, in my judgment, quite so spirited or effectual a performance as the *White Devil*. But it is distinguished by the same kind of beauties, clad in the same terrors. I do not know but the occasional strokes of passion are even profounder and more Shakespearian; but the story is more laboured, and the horror is accumulated to an overpowering and insupportable height. However appalling to the imagination and finely done, the scenes of the madhouse to which the *Duchess* is condemned with a view to unsettle her reason, and the interview between her and her brother, where he gives her the supposed dead hand of her husband, exceed, to my thinking, the just bounds of poetry and of tragedy. At least, the merit is of a kind, which, however great, we wish to be rare.

—WILLIAM HAZLITT, *Lectures on the Dramatic Literature of the Age of Elizabeth*, 1820

The Duchess of Malfy abounds more in the terrible than *The White Devil*. It turns on the mortal offence which the lady gives to her two proud brothers, Ferdinand, Duke of Calabria, and a cardinal, by indulging in a generous, though infatuated passion, for Antonio, her steward. This passion, a subject always most difficult to treat, is managed in this case with infinite delicacy; and, in a situation of great peril for the author, she condescends, without being degraded, and declares the affection with which her dependant has inspired her, without losing anything of dignity and respect.—ABRAHAM MILLS, *The Literature and the Literary Men of Great Britain and Ireland*, 1851, Vol. 1, p. 345

APPIUS AND VIRGINIA

In *Appius and Virginia*, printed in 1654, probably after its author's death, we may consider ourselves justified in recognising a work of his later manhood, if not of his old age. The theme is indeed one which might readily be supposed to have commended itself to Webster's love of the terrible; but he has treated it without adding fresh effects of his own invention to those which he found ready to his hand. Yet the play has genuine power; and were it not that the action seems to continue too long after the death of Virginia, this tragedy might be described as one of the most commendable efforts of its class. The evenness, however, of its execution, and the absence (except in the central situation) of any passages of a peculiarly striking or startling character, exclude *Appius and Virginia* from the brief list of Webster's most characteristic productions.—ADOLPHUS WILLIAM WARD, *A History of English Dramatic Literature* (1875), 1899, Vol. 3, p. 62

. . . ⟨W⟩ithout a study of his Roman play, justice can hardly be done to the scope and breadth of Webster's genius. Of *Appius and Virginia* Mr. Dyce observed with excellent judgment: "this drama is so remarkable for its simplicity, its deep pathos, it unobtrusive beauties, its singleness of plot, and the easy, unimpeded march of its story, that perhaps there are readers who will prefer it to any other of our author's productions." Webster, who was a Latin scholar, probably studied the fable in Livy; but its outlines were familiar to English people through Painter's "Palace of Pleasure." He has drawn the mutinous camp before Algidum, the discontented city ruled by a licentious noble, the stern virtues of Icilius and Virginius, and the innocent girlhood of Virginia with a quiet mastery and self-restraint which prove that the violent contrasts of his Italian plays were calculated for a peculiar effect of romance. When treating a classical subject, he aimed at classical severity of form. The chief interest of the drama centres in Appius. This character suited Webster's vein. He delighted in the delineation of a bold, imperious tyrant, marching through crimes to the attainment of his lawless ends, yet never wholly despicable. He also loved to analyse the subtleties of a deep-brained intriguer, changing from open force to covert guile, fawning and trampling on the objects of his hate by turns, assuming the tone of diplomacy and the truculence of autocratic will at pleasure, on one occasion making the worse appear the better cause by rhetoric, on another espousing evil with reckless cynicism. The variations of such a character are presented with force and lucidity in *Appius*. Yet the whole play lacks those sudden flashes of illuminative beauty, those profound and searching glimpses into the bottomless abyss of human misery, which render Webster's two Italian tragedies unique. He seems to have been writing under self-imposed limitations, in order to obtain a certain desired effect—much

in the same way as Ford did when he composed the irreproachable but somewhat chilling history of *Perkin Warbeck*.—JOHN ADDINGTON SYMONDS, "Introduction" to *Webster and Tourneur*, 1888, pp. xvii–xix

Appius and Virginia differs largely from the other plays in diction and figure. It is more rhetorical and declamatory, it contains fewer striking and original similitudes; and with a sort of dramatic propriety its language is more latinized and conventional. The attempt is obviously in another vein than the Italianate tragedies of *The White Devil* and *The Duchess of Malfi*.—FREDERIC IVES CARPENTER, *Metaphor and Simile in the Minor Elizabethan Drama*, 1895, p. 80

CHARLES KINGSLEY
From "Plays and Puritans" (1859)
Plays and Puritans and Other Historical Essays
1889, pp. 50–56

The whole story of 'Vittoria Corrombona' is one of sin and horror. The subject-matter of the play is altogether made up of the fiercest and the basest passions. But the play is not a study of those passions from which we may gain a great insight into human nature. There is no trace—nor is there, again, in the *Duchess of Malfi*—of that development of human souls for good or evil which is Shakspeare's especial power—the power which, far more than any accidental 'beauties,' makes his plays, to this day, the delight alike of the simple and the wise, while his contemporaries are all but forgotten. The highest aim of dramatic art is to exhibit the development of the human soul; to construct dramas in which the conclusion shall depend, not on the events, but on the characters; and in which the characters shall not be mere embodiments of a certain passion, or a certain 'humour': but persons, each unlike all others; each having a destiny of his own by virtue of his own peculiarities, and of his own will; and each proceeding toward that destiny as he shall conquer, or yield to, circumstances; unfolding his own strength and weakness before the eyes of the audience; and that in such a way that, after his first introduction, they should be able (in proportion to their knowledge of human nature) to predict his conduct under those circumstances. This is indeed 'high art': but we find no more of it in Webster than in the rest. His characters, be they old or young, come on the stage ready-made, full grown, and stereotyped; and therefore, in general, they are not characters at all, but mere passions or humours in human form. Now and then he essays to draw a character: but it is analytically, by description, not synthetically and dramatically, by letting the man exhibit himself in action; and in the *Duchess of Malfi* he falls into the great mistake of telling, by Antonio's mouth, more about the Duke and the Cardinal than he afterwards makes them act. Very different is Shakspeare's method of giving, at the outset, some single delicate hint about his personages which will serve as a clue to their whole future conduct; thus 'showing the whole in each part,' and stamping each man with a personality, to a degree which no other dramatist has ever approached.

But the truth is, the study of human nature is not Webster's aim. He has to arouse terror and pity, not thought, and he does it in his own way, by blood and fury, madmen and screech-owls, not without a rugged power. There are scenes of his, certainly, like that of Vittoria's trial, which have been praised for their delineation of character: but it is one thing to solve the problem, which Shakspeare has so handled in *Lear, Othello*, and *Richard the Third*,—'Given a mixed character, to show how he may become criminal,' and to solve Webster's

'Given a ready-made criminal, to show how he commits his crimes.' To us the knowledge of character shown in Vittoria's trial scene is not an insight into Vittoria's essential heart and brain, but a general acquaintance with the conduct of all bold bad women when brought to bay. Poor Elia, who knew the world from books, and human nature principally from his own loving and gentle heart, talks of Vittoria's 'innocence-resembling boldness'[1]—and 'seeming to see that matchless beauty of her face, which inspires such gay confidence in her,' and so forth.

Perfectly just and true, not of Vittoria merely, but of the average of bad young women in the presence of a police magistrate: yet amounting in all merely to this, that the strength of Webster's confest master-scene lies simply in intimate acquaintance with vicious nature in general. We will say no more on this matter, save to ask, *Cui bono?* Was the art of which this was the highest manifestation likely to be of much use to mankind, much less able to excuse its palpably disgusting and injurious accompaniments?

The *Duchess of Malfi* is certainly in a purer and loftier strain: but in spite of the praise which has been lavished on her, we must take the liberty to doubt whether the poor Duchess is a 'person' at all. General goodness and beauty, intense though pure affection for a man below her in rank, and a will to carry out her purpose at all hazards, are not enough to distinguish her from thousands of other women: but Webster has no such purpose. What he was thinking and writing of was not truth, but effect; not the Duchess, but her story; not her brothers, but their rage; not Antonio, her major-domo and husband, but his good and bad fortunes; and thus he has made Antonio merely insipid, the brothers merely unnatural, and the Duchess (in the critical moment of the play) merely forward. That curious scene, in which she acquaints Antonio with her love for him and makes him marry her, is, on the whole, painful. Webster himself seems to have felt that it was so; and, dreading lest he had gone too far, to have tried to redeem the Duchess at the end by making her break down in two exquisite lines of loving shame: but he has utterly forgotten to explain or justify her love by giving to Antonio (as Shakspeare would probably have done) such strong specialties of character as would compel, and therefore excuse, his mistress's affection. He has plenty of time to do this in the first scenes,—time which he wastes on irrelevant matter; and all that we gather from them is that Antonio is a worthy and thoughtful person. If he gives promise of being more, he utterly disappoints that promise afterwards. In the scene in which the Duchess tells her love, he is far smaller, rather than greater, than the Antonio of the opening scene: though (as there) altogether passive. He hears his mistress's declaration just as any other respectable youth might; is exceedingly astonished, and a good deal frightened; has to be talked out of his fears till one naturally expects a revulsion on the Duchess's part into something like scorn or shame (which might have given a good opportunity for calling out sudden strength in Antonio): but so busy is Webster with his business of drawing mere blind love, that he leaves Antonio to be a mere puppet, whose worthiness we are to believe in only from the Duchess's assurance to him that he is the perfection of all that a man should be; which, as all lovers are of the same opinion the day before the wedding, is not of much importance.

Neither in his subsequent misfortunes does Antonio make the least struggle to prove himself worthy of his mistress's affection. He is very resigned and loving, and so forth. To win renown by great deeds, and so prove his wife in the right to her brothers and all the world, never crosses his imagination. His highest aim (and that only at last) is slavishly to entreat pardon

from his brothers-in-law for the mere offence of marrying their sister; and he dies by an improbable accident, the same pious and respectable insipidity which he has lived,—'*ne valant pas la peine qui se donne pour lui.*' The prison-scenes between the Duchess and her tormentors are painful enough, if to give pain be a dramatic virtue; and she appears in them really noble; and might have appeared far more so, had Webster taken half as much pains with her as he has with the madmen, ruffians, ghosts, and screech-owls in which his heart really delights. The only character really worked out so as to live and grow under his hand is Bosola, who, of course, is the villain of the piece, and being a rough fabric, is easily manufactured with rough tools. Still, Webster has his wonderful touches here and there—

> *Cariola:* Hence, villains, tyrants, murderers! Alas!
>   What will you do with my lady? Call for help!
> *Duchess:* To whom? to our next neighbours? they are mad folk.
>   Farewell, Cariola.
>   I pray thee look thou giv'st my little boy
>   Some syrup for his cold; and let the girl
>   Say her prayers ere she sleep.—Now, what you please;
>   What death?

And so the play ends, as does *Vittoria Corrombona*, with half a dozen murders *coram populo*, howls, despair, bedlam, and the shambles; putting the reader marvellously in mind of that well-known old book of the same era, *Reynolds's God's Revenge*, in which, with all due pious horror and bombastic sermonising, the national appetite for abominations is duly fed with some fifty unreadable Spanish histories, French histories, Italian histories, and so forth, one or two of which, of course, are known to have furnished subjects for the playwrights of the day.

Notes

1. C. Lamb, *Specimens of English Dramatic Poets*, p. 229. From which specimens, be it remembered, he has had to expunge not only all the comic scenes, but generally the greater part of the plot itself, to make the book at all tolerable.

ALGERNON CHARLES SWINBURNE
"John Webster" (1886)
The Age of Shakespeare
1908, pp. 15–59

There were many poets in the age of Shakespeare who make us think, as we read them, that the characters in their plays could not have spoken more beautifully, more powerfully, more effectively, under the circumstances imagined for the occasion of their utterance: there are only two who make us feel that the words assigned to the creatures of their genius are the very words they must have said, the only words they could have said, the actual words they assuredly did say. Mere literary power, mere poetic beauty, mere charm of passionate or pathetic fancy, we find in varying degrees dispersed among them all alike; but the crowning gift of imagination, the power to make us realise that thus and not otherwise it was, that thus and not otherwise it must have been, was given—except by exceptional fits and starts—to none of the poets of their time but only to Shakespeare and to Webster.

Webster, it may be said, was but as it were a limb of Shakespeare: but that limb, it might be replied, was the right arm. 'The kingly-crownèd head, the vigilant eye,' whose empire of thought and whose reach of vision no other man's faculty has ever been found competent to match, are Shakespeare's alone for ever: but the force of hand, the fire of heart, the fervour of pity, the sympathy of passion, not poetic or theatric merely, but actual and immediate, are qualities in which the lesser poet is not less certainly or less unmistakably pre-eminent than the greater. And there is no third to be set beside them: not even if we turn from their contemporaries to Shelley himself. All that Beatrice says in *The Cenci* is beautiful and conceivable and admirable: but unless we except her exquisite last words—and even they are more beautiful than inevitable—we shall hardly find what we find in *King Lear* and *The White Devil*, *Othello* and *The Duchess of Malfy*; the tone of convincing reality; the note, as a critic of our own day might call it, of certitude.

There are poets—in our own age, as in all past ages—from whose best work it might be difficult to choose at a glance some verse sufficient to establish their claim—great as their claim may be—to be remembered for ever; and who yet may be worthy of remembrance among all but the highest. Webster is not one of these: though his fame assuredly does not depend upon the merit of a casual passage here or there, it would be easy to select from any one of his representative plays such examples of the highest, the purest, the most perfect power, as can be found only in the works of the greatest among poets. There is not, as far as my studies have ever extended, a third English poet to whom these words might rationally be attributed by the conjecture of a competent reader.

> We cease to grieve, cease to be fortune's slaves,
> Nay, cease to die, by dying.

There is a depth of severe sense in them, a height of heroic scorn, or a dignity of quiet cynicism, which can scarcely be paralleled in the bitterest or the fiercest effusions of John Marston or Cyril Tourneur or Jonathan Swift. Nay, were they not put into the mouth of a criminal cynic, they would not seem unworthy of Epictetus. There is nothing so grand in the part of Edmund; the one figure in Shakespeare whose aim in life, whose centre of character, is one with the view or the instinct of Webster's two typical villains. Some touches in the part of Flamineo suggest, if not a conscious imitation, an unconscious reminiscence of that prototype: but the essential and radical originality of Webster's genius is shown in the difference of accent with which the same savage and sarcastic philosophy of self-interest finds expression through the snarl and sneer of his ambitious cynic. Monsters as they may seem of unnatural egotism and unallayed ferocity, the one who dies penitent, though his repentance be as sudden if not as suspicious as any ever wrought by miraculous conversion, dies as thoroughly in character as the one who takes leave of life in a passion of scorn and defiant irony which hardly passes off at last into a mood of mocking and triumphant resignation. There is a cross of heroism in almost all Webster's characters which preserves the worst of them from such hatefulness as disgusts us in certain of Fletcher's or of Ford's: they have in them some salt of manhood, some savour of venturesome and humorous resolution, which reminds us of the heroic age in which the genius that begot them was born and reared—the age of Richard Grenville and Francis Drake, Philip Sidney and William Shakespeare.

The earliest play of Webster's now surviving—if a work so piteously mutilated and defaced can properly be said to survive—is a curious example of the combined freedom and realism with which recent or even contemporary history was habitually treated on the stage during the last years of the reign of Queen Elizabeth. The noblest poem known to me of this peculiar kind is the play of *Sir Thomas More*, first printed by Mr. Dyce in 1844 for the Shakespeare Society: the worst must almost certainly be that 'Chronicle History of Thomas Lord Cromwell' which the infallible verdict of German intuition has discovered to be 'not only unquestionably Shakespeare's, but worthy to be classed among his best and maturest works.' About midway between these two I should be inclined to rank *The Famous History of Sir Thomas Wyatt*, a mangled and deformed abridgment of a tragedy by Dekker and Webster on the story of Lady Jane Grey. In this tragedy, as in the two comedies due to the collaboration of the same poets, it appears to me more than probable that Dekker took decidedly the greater part. The shambling and slipshod metre, which seems now and then to hit by mere chance on some pure and tender note of simple and exquisite melody—the lazy vivacity and impulsive inconsequence of style—the fitful sort of slovenly inspiration, with interludes of absolute and headlong collapse—are qualities by which a very novice in the study of dramatic form may recognise the reckless and unmistakable presence of Dekker. The curt and grim precision of Webster's tone, his terse and pungent force of compressed rhetoric, will be found equally difficult to trace in any of these three plays. *Northward Ho*, a clever, coarse, and vigorous study of the realistic sort, has not a note of poetry in it, but is more coherent, more sensibly conceived and more ably constructed, than the rambling history of Wyatt or the hybrid amalgam of prosaic and romantic elements in the compound comedy of *Westward Ho*. All that is of any great value in this amorphous and incongruous product of inventive impatience and impetuous idleness can be as distinctly traced to the hand of Dekker as the crowning glories of *The Two Noble Kinsmen* can be traced to the hand of Shakespeare. Any poet, even of his time, might have been proud of these verses, but the accent of them is unmistakable as that of Dekker.

> Go, let music
> Charm with her excellent voice an awful silence
> Through all this building, that her sphery soul
> May, on the wings of air, in thousand forms
> Invisibly fly, yet be enjoyed.

This delicate fluency and distilled refinement of expression ought properly, one would say, to have belonged to a poet of such careful and self-respectful genius as Tennyson's: whereas in the very next speech of the same speaker we stumble over such a phrase as that which closes the following sentence:—

> We feed, wear rich attires, and strive to cleave
> The stars with marble towers, fight battles, spend
> Our blood to buy us names, *and, in iron hold,*
> *Will we eat roots, to imprison fugitive gold.*

Which he who can parse, let him scan, and he who can scan, let him construe. It is alike incredible and certain that the writer of such exquisite and blameless verse as that in which the finer scenes of *Old Fortunatus* and *The Honest Whore* are so smoothly and simply and naturally written should have been capable of writing whole plays in this headlong and halting fashion, as helpless and graceless as the action of a spavined horse, or a cripple who should attempt to run.

It is difficult to say what part of these plays should be assigned to Webster. Their rough realistic humour, with its tone of somewhat coarse-grained good-nature, strikes the habitual note of Dekker's comic style: there is nothing of the fierce and scornful intensity, the ardour of passionate and compressed contempt, which distinguishes the savagely humorous satire of Webster and of Marston, and makes it hopeless to determine by intrinsic evidence how little or how much was added by Webster in the second edition to the original text of Marston's

Malcontent: unless—which appears to me not unreasonable—we assume that the printer of that edition lied or blundered after the manner of his contemporary kind in attributing on the title-page—as apparently he meant to attribute—any share in the additional scenes or speeches to the original author of the play. In any case, the passages thus added to that grimmest and most sombre of tragicomedies are in such exact keeping with the previous text that the keenest scent of the veriest blood-hound among critics could not detect a shade of difference in the savour.

The text of either comedy is generally very fair—as free from corruption as could reasonably be expected. The text of *Sir Thomas Wyatt* is corrupt as well as mutilated. Even in Mr. Dyce's second edition I have noted, not without astonishment, the following flagrant errors left still to glare on us from the distorted and disfigured page. In the sixth scene a single speech of Arundel's contains two of the most palpably preposterous:—

> The obligation wherein we all stood bound
>
> .   .   .
>
> Cannot be concealed without great reproach
> To us and to our issue.

We should of course read 'cancelled' for 'concealed': the sense of the context and the exigence of the verse cry alike aloud for the correction. In the sixteenth line from this we come upon an equally obvious error:—

> Advice in this I hold it better far,
> To keep the course we run, than, seeking change,
> Hazard our lives, our honours, and the realm.

It seems hardly credible to those who are aware how much they owe to the excellent scholarship and editorial faculty of Mr. Dyce, that he should have allowed such a misprint as 'heirs' for 'honours' to stand in this last unlucky line. Again, in the next scene, when the popular leader Captain Brett attempts to reassure the country folk who are startled at the sight of his insurgent array, he is made to utter (in reply to the exclamation, 'What's here? soldiers!') the perfectly fatuous phrase, 'Fear not good speech.' Of course—once more—we should read, 'Fear not, good people'; a correction which rectifies the metre as well as the sense.

The play attributed to Webster and Rowley by a publisher of the next generation has been carefully and delicately analysed by a critic of our own time, who naturally finds it easy to distinguish the finer from the homelier part of the compound weft, and to assign what is rough and crude to the inferior, what is interesting and graceful to the superior poet. The authority of the rogue Kirkman may be likened to the outline or profile of Mr. Mantalini's early loves: it is either no authority at all, or at best it is a 'demd' authority. The same swindler who assigned to Webster and Rowley the authorship of *A Cure for a Cuckold* assigned to Shakespeare and Rowley the authorship of an infinitely inferior play—a play of which German sagacity has discovered that 'none of Rowley's other works are equal to this.' Assuredly they are not—in utter stolidity of platitude and absolute impotence of drivel. Rowley was a vigorous artist in comedy and an original master of tragedy: he may have written the lighter or broader parts of the play which rather unluckily took its name from these, and Webster may have written the more serious or sentimental parts: but there is not the slightest shadow of a reason to suppose it. An obviously apocryphal abortion of the same date, attributed to the same poets by the same knave, has long since been struck off the roll of Webster's works.

The few occasional poems of this great poet are worth study by those who are capable of feeling interest in the comparison of slighter with sublimer things, and the detection in minor works of the same style, here revealed by fitful hints in casual phrases, as that which animates and distinguishes even a work so insufficient and incompetent as Webster's 'trage-comœdy' of *The Devil's Law-case*. The noble and impressive extracts from this most incoherent and chaotic of all plays which must be familiar to all students of Charles Lamb are but patches of imperial purple sewn on with the roughest of needles to a garment of the raggedest and coarsest kind of literary serge. Hardly any praise can be too high for their dignity and beauty, their lofty loyalty and simplicity of chivalrous manhood or their deep sincerity of cynic meditation and self-contemptuous mournfulness: and the reader who turns from these magnificent samples to the complete play must expect to find yet another and a yet unknown masterpiece of English tragedy. He will find a crowning example of the famous theorem, that 'the plot is of no use except to bring in the fine things.' The plot is in this instance absurd to a degree so far beyond the most preposterous conception of confused and distracting extravagance that the reader's attention may at times be withdrawn from the all but unqualified ugliness of its ethical tone or tendency. Two of Webster's favourite types, the meditative murderer or philosophic ruffian, and the impulsive impostor who is liable to collapse into the likeness of a passionate penitent, will remind the reader how much better they appear in tragedies which are carried through to their natural tragic end. But here, where the story is admirably opened and the characters as skilfully introduced, the strong interest thus excited at starting is scattered or broken or trifled away before the action is half-way through: and at its close the awkward violence or irregularity of moral and scenical effect comes to a crowning crisis in the general and mutual condonation of unnatural perjury and attempted murder with which the victims and the criminals agree to hush up all grudges, shake hands all round, and live happy ever after. There is at least one point of somewhat repulsive resemblance between the story of this play and that of Fletcher's 'Fair Maid of the Inn': but Fletcher's play, with none of the tragic touches or interludes of superb and sombre poetry which relieve the incoherence of Webster's, is better laid out and constructed, more amusing if not more interesting and more intelligent if not more imaginative.

A far more creditable and workmanlike piece of work, though glorified by no flashes of such sudden and singular beauty, is the tragedy of *Appius and Virginia*. The almost infinite superiority of Webster to Fletcher as a poet of pure tragedy and a painter of masculine character is in this play as obvious as the inferiority in construction and conduct of romantic story displayed in his attempt at a tragicomedy. From the evidence of style I should judge this play to have been written at an earlier date than *The Devil's Law-case*: it is, I repeat, far better composed; better, perhaps, than any other play of the author's: but it has none of his more distinctive qualities; intensity of idea, concentration of utterance, pungency of expression and ardour of pathos. It is written with noble and equable power of hand, with force and purity and fluency of apt and simple eloquence: there is nothing in it unworthy of the writer: but it is the only one of his unassisted works in which we do not find that especial note of tragic style, concise and pointed and tipped as it were with fire, which usually makes it impossible for the dullest reader to mistake the peculiar presence, the original tone or accent, of John Webster. If the epithet unique had not such a tang of German affectation in it, it would be perhaps the aptest of all adjectives to denote the genius or define the manner of this great poet. But in this tragedy, though whatever is said is well said and whatever is done well done, we miss that sense of positive and inevitable conviction, that instant and profound perception or impression as of immediate and indisputable truth, which is burnt in upon us as we read the more Websterian scenes of Webster's writing. We feel, in short, that thus it may have been: not, as I observed at the opening of these notes, that thus it must have been. The poem does him no discredit; nay, it does him additional honour, as an evidence of powers more various and many-sided than we should otherwise have known or supposed in him. Indeed, the figure of Virginius is one of the finest types of soldierly and fatherly heroism ever presented on the stage: there is equal force of dramatic effect, equal fervour of eloquent passion, in the scene of his pleading before the senate on behalf of the claims of his suffering and struggling fellow-soldiers, and in the scene of his return to the camp after the immolation of his daughter. The mere theatric effect of this latter scene is at once so triumphant and so dignified, so noble in its presentation and so passionate in its restraint, that we feel the high justice and sound reason of the instinct which inspired the poet to prolong the action of his play so far beyond the sacrifice of his heroine. A comparison of Webster's Virginius with any of Fletcher's wordy warriors will suffice to show how much nearer to Shakespeare than to Fletcher stands Webster as a tragic or a serious dramatist. Coleridge, not always just to Fletcher, was not unjust in his remark 'what strange self-trumpeters and tongue-bullies all the brave soldiers of Beaumont and Fletcher are'; and again almost immediately—'all B. and F.'s generals are pugilists, or cudgel-fighters, that boast of their bottom and of the "claret" they have shed.' There is nothing of this in Virginius; Shakespeare himself has not represented with a more lofty fidelity, in the person of Coriolanus or of Brutus, 'the high Roman fashion' of austere and heroic self-respect. In the other leading or dominant figure of this tragedy there is certainly discernible a genuine and thoughtful originality or freshness of conception; but perhaps there is also recognisable a certain inconsistency of touch. It was well thought of to mingle some alloy of goodness with the wickedness of Appius Claudius, to represent the treacherous and lecherous decemvir as neither kindless nor remorseless, but capable of penitence and courage in his last hour. But Shakespeare, I cannot but think, would have prepared us with more care and more dexterity for the revelation of some such redeeming quality in a character which in the act immediately preceding Webster has represented as utterly heartless and shameless, brutal in its hypocrisy and impudent in its brutality.

If the works already discussed were their author's only claims to remembrance and honour, they might not suffice to place him on a higher level among our tragic poets than that occupied by Marston and Dekker and Middleton on the one hand, by Fletcher and Massinger and Shirley on the other. *Antonio and Mellida*, *Old Fortunatus*, or *The Changeling*— *The Maid's Tragedy*, *The Duke of Milan*, or *The Traitor*— would suffice to counterweigh (if not, in some cases, to outbalance) the merit of the best among these: the fitful and futile inspiration of *The Devil's Law-case*, and the stately but subdued inspiration of *Appius and Virginia*. That his place was with no subordinate poet—that his station is at Shakespeare's right hand—the evidence supplied by his two great tragedies is disputable by no one who has an inkling of the qualities which confer a right to be named in the same day with the greatest writer of all time.

Æschylus is above all things the poet of righteousness. 'But in any wise, I say unto thee, revere thou the altar of righteousness': this is the crowning admonition of his doctrine, as its crowning prospect is the reconciliation or atonement of the principle of retribution with the principle of redemption, of the powers of the mystery of darkness with the coeternal forces of the spirit of wisdom, of the lord of inspiration and of light. The doctrine of Shakespeare, where it is not vaguer, is darker in its implication of injustice, in its acceptance of accident, than the impression of the doctrine of Æschylus. Fate, irreversible and inscrutable, is the only force of which we feel the impact, of which we trace the sign, in the upshot of *Othello* or *King Lear*. The last step into the darkness remained to be taken by 'the most tragic' of all English poets. With Shakespeare—and assuredly not with Æschylus—righteousness itself seems subject and subordinate to the masterdom of fate: but fate itself, in the tragic world of Webster, seems merely the servant or the synonym of chance. The two chief agents in his two great tragedies pass away—the phrase was, perhaps, unconsciously repeated—'in a mist': perplexed, indomitable, defiant of hope and fear; bitter and sceptical and bloody in penitence or impenitence alike. And the mist which encompasses the departing spirits of these moody and mocking men of blood seems equally to involve the lives of their chastisers and their victims. Blind accident and blundering mishap—'such a mistake,' says one of the criminals, 'as I have often seen in a play'—are the steersmen of their fortunes and the doomsmen of their deeds. The effect of this method or the result of this view, whether adopted for dramatic objects or ingrained in the writer's temperament, is equally fit for pure tragedy and unfit for any form of drama not purely tragic in evolution and event. In *The Devil's Law-case* it is offensive, because the upshot is incongruous and insufficient: in *The White Devil* and *The Duchess of Malfy* it is admirable, because the results are adequate and coherent. But in all these three plays alike, and in these three plays only, the peculiar tone of Webster's genius, the peculiar force of his imagination, is distinct and absolute in its fullness of effect. The author of *Appius and Virginia* would have earned an honourable and enduring place in the history of English letters as a worthy member—one among many—of a great school in poetry, a deserving representative of a great epoch in literature: but the author of these three plays has a solitary station, an indisputable distinction of his own. The greatest poets of all time are not more mutually independent than this one—a lesser poet only than those greatest—is essentially independent of them all.

The first quality which all readers recognise, and which may strike a superficial reader as the exclusive or excessive note of his genius and his work, is of course his command of terror. Except in Æschylus, in Dante, and in Shakespeare, I at least know not where to seek for passages which in sheer force of tragic and noble horror—to the vulgar shock of ignoble or brutal horror he never condescends to submit his reader or subdue his inspiration—may be set against the subtlest, the deepest, the sublimest passages of Webster. Other gifts he had as great in themselves, as precious and as necessary to the poet: but on this side he is incomparable and unique. Neither Marlowe nor Shakespeare had so fine, so accurate, so infallible a sense of the delicate line of demarcation which divides the impressive and the terrible from the horrible and the loathsome—Victor Hugo and Honoré de Balzac from Eugène Sue and Émile Zola. On his theatre we find no presentation of old men with their beards torn off and their eyes gouged out, of young men imprisoned in reeking cesspools and impaled with red-hot spits. Again and again his passionate and daring genius attains the utmost limit and rounds the final goal of tragedy; never once does it break the bounds of pure poetic instinct. If ever for a moment it may seem to graze that goal too closely, to brush too sharply by those bounds, the very next moment finds it clear of any such risk and remote from any such temptation as sometimes entrapped or seduced the foremost of its forerunners in the field. And yet this is the field in which its paces are most superbly shown. No name among all the names of great poets will recur so soon as Webster's to the reader who knows what it signifies, as he reads or repeats the verses in which a greater than this great poet—a greater than all since Shakespeare—has expressed the latent mystery of terror which lurks in all the highest poetry or beauty, and distinguishes it inexplicably and inevitably from all that is but a little lower than the highest.

> Les aigles sur les bords du Gange et du Caÿstre
>   Sont effrayants;
> Rien de grand qui ne soit confusément sinistre;
>   Les noirs pæans,
> Les psaumes, la chanson monstrueuse du mage
>   Ezéchiel,
> Font devant notre œil fixe errer la vague image
>   D'un affreux ciel.
> L'empyrée est l'abîme, on y plonge, on y reste
>   Avec terreur.
> Car planer, c'est trembler; si l'azur est céleste,
>   C'est par l'horreur.
> L'épouvante est au fond des choses les plus belles;
>   Les bleus vallons
> Font parfois reculer d'effroi les fauves ailes
>   Des aquilons.

And even in comedy as in tragedy, in prosaic even as in prophetic inspiration, in imitative as in imaginative works of genius, the sovereign of modern poets has detected the same touch of terror wherever the deepest note possible has been struck, the fullest sense possible of genuine and peculiar power conveyed to the student of lyric or dramatic, epic or elegiac masters.

> De là tant de beautés difformes dans leurs œuvres;
>   Le vers charmant
> Est par la torsion subite des couleuvres
>   Pris brusquement;
> A de certains moments toutes les jeunes flores
>   Dans la forêt
> Ont peur, et sur le front des blanches métaphores
>   L'ombre apparaît;
> C'est qu'Horace ou Virgile ont vu soudain le spectre
>   Noir se dresser;
> C'est que là-bas, derrière Amaryllis, Électre
>   Vient de passer.

Nor was it the Electra of Sophocles, the calm and impassive accomplice of an untroubled and unhesitating matricide, who showed herself ever in passing to the intent and serious vision of Webster. By those candid and sensible judges to whom the praise of Marlowe seems to imply a reflection on the fame of Shakespeare, I may be accused—and by such critics I am content to be accused—of a fatuous design to set Webster beside Sophocles, or Sophocles—for aught I know—beneath Webster, if I venture to indicate the superiority in truth of natural passion— and, I must add, of moral instinct—which distinguishes the modern from the ancient. It is not, it never will be, and it never can have been natural for noble and civilised creatures to accept with spontaneous complacency, to discharge with unforced equanimity, such offices or such duties as weigh so lightly on the spirit of the Sophoclean Orestes that the slaughter of a mother seems to be a less serious undertaking for his unreluctant hand than the subsequent execution of her paramour. The immeasurable superiority of Æschylus to

his successors in this quality of instinctive righteousness—if a word long vulgarised by theology may yet be used in its just and natural sense—is shared no less by Webster than by Shakespeare. The grave and deep truth of natural impulse is never ignored by these poets when dealing either with innocent or with criminal passion: but it surely is now and then ignored by the artistic quietism of Sophocles—as surely as it is outraged and degraded by the vulgar theatricalities of Euripides. Thomas Campbell was amused and scandalised by the fact that Webster (as he is pleased to express it) modestly compares himself to the playwright last mentioned; being apparently of opinion that *Hippolytus* and *Medea* may be reckoned equal or superior, as works of tragic art or examples of ethical elevation, to *The White Devil* and *The Duchess of Malfy*; and being no less apparently ignorant, and incapable of understanding, that as there is no poet morally nobler than Webster so is there no poet ignobler in the moral sense than Euripides: while as a dramatic artist—an artist in character, action, and emotion—the degenerate tragedian of Athens, compared to the second tragic dramatist of England, is as a mutilated monkey to a well-made man. No better test of critical faculty could be required by the most exacting scrutiny of probation than is afforded by the critic's professed or professional estimate of those great poets whose names are not consecrated—or desecrated—by the conventional applause, the factitious adoration, of a tribunal whose judgments are dictated by obsequious superstition and unanimous incompetence. When certain critics inform a listening world that they do not admire Marlowe and Webster—they admire Shakespeare and Milton, we know at once that it is not the genius of Shakespeare—it is the reputation of Shakespeare that they admire. It is not the man that they bow down to: it is the bust that they crouch down before. They would worship Shirley as soon as Shakespeare—Glover as soon as Milton—Byron as soon as Shelley—Ponsard as soon as Hugo—Longfellow as soon as Tennyson—if the tablet were as showily emblazoned, the inscription as pretentiously engraved.

The nobility of spirit and motive which is so distinguishing a mark of Webster's instinctive genius or natural disposition of mind is proved by his treatment of facts placed on record by contemporary annalists in the tragic story of Vittoria Accorambuoni, Duchess of Bracciano. That story would have been suggestive, if not tempting, to any dramatic poet: and almost any poet but Shakespeare or Webster would have been content to accept the characters and circumstances as they stood nakedly on record, and adapt them to the contemporary stage of England with such dexterity and intelligence as he might be able to command. But, as Shakespeare took the savage legend of Hamlet, the brutal story of Othello, and raised them from the respective levels of the Heimskringla and the Newgate Calendar to the very highest 'heaven of invention,' so has Webster transmuted the impressive but repulsive record of villainies and atrocities, in which he discovered the motive for a magnificent poem, into the majestic and pathetic masterpiece which is one of the most triumphant and the most memorable achievements of English poetry. If, in his play, as in the legal or historic account of the affair, the whole family of the heroine had appeared unanimous and eager in complicity with her sins and competition for a share in the profits of her dishonour, the tragedy might still have been as effective as it is now from the theatrical or sensational point of view; it might have thrilled the reader's nerves as keenly, have excited and stimulated his curiosity, have whetted and satiated his appetite for transient emotion, as thoroughly and triumphantly as now. But it would have been merely a criminal melodrama, compiled by the labour and vivified by the talent of an able theatrical journeyman. The one great follower of Shakespeare—'haud passibus æquis' at all points; 'longo sed proximo intervallo'—has recognised, with Shakespearean accuracy and delicacy and elevation of instinct, the necessity of ennobling and transfiguring his characters if their story was to be made acceptable to the sympathies of any but an idle or an ignoble audience. And he has done so after the very manner and in the very spirit of Shakespeare. The noble creatures of his invention give to the story that dignity and variety of interest without which the most powerful romance or drama can be but an example of vigorous vulgarity. The upright and high-minded mother and brother of the shameless Flamineo and the shame-stricken Vittoria refresh and purify the tragic atmosphere of the poem by the passing presence of their virtues. The shallow and fiery nature of the fair White Devil herself is a notable example of the difference so accurately distinguished by Charlotte Brontë between an impressionable and an impressible character. Ambition, self-interest, passion, remorse and hardihood alternate and contend in her impetuous and wayward spirit. The one distinct and trustworthy quality which may always be reckoned on is the indomitable courage underlying her easily irritable emotions. Her bearing at the trial for her husband's murder is as dexterous and dauntless as the demeanour of Mary Stuart before her judges. To Charles Lamb it seemed 'an innocence-resembling boldness'; to Mr. Dyce and Canon Kingsley the innocence displayed in Lamb's estimate seemed almost ludicrous in its misconception of Webster's text. I should hesitate to agree with them that he has never once made his accused heroine speak in the natural key of innocence unjustly impeached: Mary's pleading for her life is not at all points incompatible in tone with the innocence which it certainly fails to establish—except in minds already made up to accept any plea as valid which may plausibly or possibly be advanced on her behalf; and the arguments advanced by Vittoria are not more evasive and equivocal, in face of the patent and flagrant prepossession of her judges, than those put forward by the Queen of Scots. It is impossible not to wonder whether the poet had not in his mind the actual tragedy which had taken place just twenty-five years before the publication of this play: if not, the coincidence is something more than singular. The fierce profligacy and savage egotism of Brachiano have a certain energy and activity in the display and the development of their motives and effects which suggest rather such a character as Bothwell's than such a character as that of the bloated and stolid sensualist who stands or grovels before us in the historic record of his life. As presented by Webster, he is doubtless an execrable ruffian: as presented by history, he would be intolerable by any but such readers or spectators as those on whom the figments or the photographs of self-styled naturalism produce other than emetic emotions. Here again the noble instinct of the English poet has rectified the æsthetic unseemliness of an ignoble reality. This 'Brachiano' is a far more living figure than the porcine paramour of the historic Accorambuoni. I am not prepared to maintain that in one scene too much has not been sacrificed to immediate vehemence of effect. The devotion of the discarded wife, who to shelter her Antony from the vengeance of Octavius assumes the mask of raging jealousy, thus taking upon herself the blame and responsibility of their final separation, is expressed with such consummate and artistic simplicity of power that on a first reading the genius of the dramatist may well blind us to the violent unlikelihood of the action. But this very extravagance of self-sacrifice may be thought by some to add a crowning touch of pathos to the unsurpassable beauty of the scene in which her child, after the murder of his mother,

relates her past sufferings to his uncle. Those to whom the great name of Webster represents merely an artist in horrors, a ruffian of genius, may be recommended to study every line and syllable of this brief dialogue.

    Francisco: How now, my noble cousin? what, in
      black?
    Giovanni: Yes, uncle, I was taught to imitate you
      In virtue, and you [?now] must imitate me
      In colours of your garments. My sweet mother
      Is—
    Francisco: How! where?
    Giovanni: Is there; no, yonder: indeed, sir, I'll not
      tell you,
      For I shall make you weep.
    Francisco: Is dead?
    Giovanni: Do not blame me now, I did not tell
      you so.
    Lodovico: She's dead, my lord.
    Francisco: Dead!
    Monticelso: Blest lady, thou art now above thy
      woes!
. . . .
    Giovanni: What do the dead do, uncle? do they
      eat,
      Hear music, go a hunting, and be merry,
      As we that live?
    Francisco: No, coz; they sleep.
    Giovanni: Lord, Lord, that I were dead!
      I have not slept these six nights.—When do
      they wake?
    Francisco: When God shall please.
    Giovanni: Good God, let her sleep ever!
      For I have known her wake an hundred nights
      When all the pillow where she laid her head
      Was brine-wet with her tears. I am to complain
      to you, sir;
      I'll tell you how they have used her now she's
      dead:
      They wrapped her in a cruel fold of lead,
      And would not let me kiss her.
    Francisco: Thou didst love her.
    Giovanni: I have often heard her say she gave me
      suck,
      And it should seem by that she dearly loved me,
      Since princes seldom do it.
    Francisco: O, all of my poor sister that remains!—
      Take him away, for God's sake!

I must admit that I do not see how Shakespeare could have improved upon that. It seems to me that in any one of even his greatest tragedies this scene would have been remarkable among its most beautiful and perfect passages; nor, upon the whole, do I remember a third English poet who could be imagined capable of having written it. And it affords, I think, very clear and sufficient evidence that Webster could not have handled so pathetic and suggestive a subject as the execution of Lady Jane Grey and her young husband in a style so thin and feeble, so shallow in expression of pathos and so empty of suggestion or of passion, as that in which it is presented at the close of *Sir Thomas Wyatt*.

There is a perfect harmony of contrast between this and the death-scene of the boy's father: the agony of the murdered murderer is as superb in effect of terror as the sorrow of his son is exquisite in effect of pathos. Again we are reminded of Shakespeare, by no touch of imitation but simply by a note of kinship in genius and in style, at the cry of Brachiano under the first sharp workings of the poison:

        O thou strong heart!

There's such a covenant 'tween the world and it,
They're loth to break.

Another stroke well worthy of Shakespeare is the redeeming touch of grace in this brutal and cold-blooded ruffian which gives him in his agony a thought of tender care for the accomplice of his atrocities:

Do not kiss me, for I shall poison thee.

Few instances of Webster's genius are so well known as the brief but magnificent passage which follows; yet it may not be impertinent to cite it once again.

Brachiano: O thou soft natural death, that art joint twin
    To sweetest slumber! no rough-bearded comet
    Stares on thy mild departure; the dull owl
    Beats not against thy casement; the hoarse wolf
    Scents not thy carrion; pity winds thy corpse,
    Whilst horror waits on princes.
Vittoria: I am lost for ever.
Brachiano: How miserable a thing it is to die
    'Mongst women howling!—What are those?
Flamineo: Franciscans:
    They have brought the extreme unction.
Brachiano: On pain of death, let no man name
    death to me;
    It is a word [? most] infinitely terrible.

The very tremor of moral and physical abjection from nervous defiance into prostrate fear which seems to pant and bluster and quail and subside in the natural cadence of these lines would suffice to prove the greatness of the artist who could express it with such terrible perfection: but when we compare it, by collation of the two scenes, with the deep simplicity of tenderness, the childlike accuracy of innocent emotion, in the passage previously cited, it seems to me that we must admit, as an unquestionable truth, that in the deepest and highest and purest qualities of tragic poetry Webster stands nearer to Shakespeare than any other English poet stands to Webster; and so much nearer as to be a good second; while it is at least questionable whether even Shelley can reasonably be accepted as a good third. Not one among the predecessors, contemporaries, or successors of Shakespeare and Webster has given proof of this double faculty—this coequal mastery of terror and pity, undiscoloured and undistorted, but vivified and glorified, by the splendour of immediate and infallible imagination. The most grovelling realism could scarcely be so impudent in stupidity as to pretend an aim at more perfect presentation of truth: the most fervent fancy, the most sensitive taste, could hardly dream of a desire for more exquisite expression of natural passion in a form of utterance more naturally exalted and refined.

In all the vast and voluminous records of critical error there can be discovered no falsehood more foolish or more flagrant than the vulgar tradition which represents this high-souled and gentle-hearted poet as one morbidly fascinated by a fantastic attraction towards the 'violent delights' of horror and the nervous or sensational excitements of criminal detail; nor can there be conceived a more perverse or futile misapprehension than that which represents John Webster as one whose instinct led him by some obscure and oblique propensity to darken the darkness of southern crime or vice by an infusion of northern seriousness, of introspective cynicism and reflective intensity in wrongdoing, into the easy levity and infantile simplicity of spontaneous wickedness which distinguished the moral and social corruption of renascent Italy. Proof enough of this has already been adduced to make any protestation or appeal against such an estimate as preposterous in its super-

fluity as the misconception just mentioned is preposterous in its perversity. The great if not incomparable power displayed in Webster's delineation of such criminals as Flamineo and Bosola—Bonapartes in the bud, Napoleons in a nutshell, Cæsars who have missed their Rubicon and collapse into the likeness of a Catiline—is a sign rather of his noble English loathing for the traditions associated with such names as Cæsar and Medici and Borgia, Catiline and Iscariot and Napoleon, than of any sympathetic interest in such incarnations of historic crime. Flamineo especially, the ardent pimp, the enthusiastic pandar, who prostitutes his sister and assassinates his brother with such earnest and single-hearted devotion to his own straightforward self-interest, has in him a sublime fervour of rascality which recalls rather the man of Brumaire and of Waterloo than the man of December and of Sedan. He has something too of Napoleon's ruffianly good-humour—the frankness of a thieves' kitchen or an imperial court, when the last thin figleaf of pretence has been plucked off and crumpled up and flung away. We can imagine him pinching his favourites by the ear and dictating memorials of mendacity with the self-possession of a self-made monarch. As it is, we see him only in the stage of parasite and pimp—more like the hired husband of a cast-off Creole than the resplendent rogue who fascinated even history for a time by the clamour and glitter of his triumphs. But the fellow is unmistakably an emperor in the egg—so dauntless and frontless in the very abjection of his villainy that we feel him to have been defrauded by mischance of the only two destinations appropriate for the close of his career—a gibbet or a throne.

This imperial quality of ultimate perfection in egotism and crowning complacency in crime is wanting to his brother in atrocity, the most notable villain who figures on the stage of Webster's latest masterpiece. Bosola is not quite a possible Bonaparte; he is not even on a level with the bloody hirelings who execute the orders of tyranny and treason with the perfunctory atrocity of Anicetus or Saint-Arnaud. There is not, or I am much mistaken, a touch of imaginative poetry in the part of Flamineo: his passion, excitable on occasion and vehement enough, is as prosaic in its homely and cynical eloquence as the most fervent emotions of a Napoleon or an Iago when warmed or goaded into elocution. The one is a human snake, the other is a human wolf. Webster could not with equal propriety have put into the mouth of Flamineo such magnificent lyric poetry as seems to fall naturally, however suddenly and strangely, from the bitter and bloodthirsty tongue of Bosola. To him, as to the baffled and incoherent ruffian Romelio in the contemporary play of *The Devil's Law-case*, his creator has assigned the utterance of such verse as can only be compared to that uttered by Cornelia over the body of her murdered son in the tragedy to which I have just given so feeble and inadequate a word of tribute. In his command and in his use of the metre first made fashionable by the graceful improvisations of Greene, Webster seems to me as original and as peculiar as in his grasp and manipulation of character and event. All other poets, Shakespeare no less than Barnfield and Milton no less than Wither, have used this lyric instrument for none but gentle or gracious ends: Webster has breathed into it the power to express a sublimer and a profounder tone of emotion; he has given it the cadence and the colour of tragedy; he has touched and transfigured its note of meditative music into a chord of passionate austerity and prophetic awe. This was the key in which all previous poets had played upon the metre which Webster was to put to so deeply different an use.

Walking in a valley greene,

Spred with Flora summer queene:
Where shee heaping all hir graces,
Niggard seem'd in other places:
Spring it was, and here did spring
All that nature forth can bring.
(*Tullies Loue*, p. 53, ed. 1589.)

Nights were short, and daies were long;
Blossoms on the Hauthorns hung:
Philomele (Night-Musiques King)
Tolde the comming of the spring.
(Grosart's Barnfield [1876], p. 97.)

On a day (alack the day!)
Love, whose month is ever May,
Spied a blossom passing fair
Playing in the wanton air.
(*Love's Labour's Lost*, Act iv.
Sc. iii.)

And now let us hear Webster.

Hearke, now every thing is still,
The Scritch-Owle, and the whistler shrill,
Call upon our Dame, aloud,
And bid her quickly don her shrowd:
Much you had of Land and rent,
Your length in clay's now competent.
A long war disturb'd your minde,
Here your perfect peace is sign'd.
Of what is 't, fooles make such vaine keeping?
Sin their conception, their birth, weeping:
Their life, a generall mist of error,
Their death, a hideous storme of terror.
Strew your haire with powders sweete:
Don cleane linnen, bath[e] your feete,
And (the foule feend more to checke)
A crucifixe let blesse your necke:
'Tis now full tide 'tweene night and day,
End your groane, and come away.
(*The Tragedy of the Dutchesse of Malfy*: 1623:
sig. K, K 2.)

The toll of the funereal rhythm, the heavy chime of the solemn and simple verse, the mournful menace and the brooding presage of its note, are but the covering, as it were, or the outer expression, of the tragic significance which deepens and quickens and kindles to its close. Æschylus and Dante have never excelled, nor perhaps have Sophocles and Shakespeare ever equalled in impression of terrible effect, the fancy of bidding a live woman array herself in the raiment of the grave, and do for her own living body the offices done for a corpse by the ministers attendant on the dead.

The murderous humourist whose cynical inspiration gives life to these deadly lines is at first sight a less plausible, but on second thoughts may perhaps seem no less possible a character than Flamineo. Pure and simple ambition of the Napoleonic order is the motive which impels into infamy the aspiring parasite of Brachiano: a savage melancholy inflames the baffled greed of Bosola to a pitch of wickedness not unqualified by relenting touches of profitless remorse, which come always either too early or too late to bear any serviceable fruit of compassion or redemption. There is no deeper or more Shakespearean stroke of tragic humour in all Webster's writings than that conveyed in the scornful and acute reply—almost too acute perhaps for the character—of Bosola's remorseless patron to the remonstrance or appeal of his instrument against the insatiable excess and persistence of his cruelty: 'Thy pity is nothing akin to thee.' He has more in common with Romelio in *The Devil's Law-case*, an assassin who misses his aim and flounders into penitence much as that discomfortable drama

misses its point and stumbles into vacuity: and whose unsatisfactory figure looks either like a crude and unsuccessful study for that of Bosola, or a disproportioned and emasculated copy from it. But to him too Webster has given the fitful force of fancy or inspiration which finds expression in such sudden snatches of funereal verse as this:

How then can any monument say
'Here rest these bones till the last day,'
When Time, swift both of foot and feather,
May bear them the sexton kens not whither?
What care I, then, though my last sleep
Be in the desert or the deep,
No lamp nor taper, day and night,
To give my charnel chargeable light?
I have there like quantity of ground,
And at the last day I shall be found.

The villainous laxity of versification which deforms the grim and sardonic beauty of these occasionally rough and halting lines is perceptible here and there in *The Duchess of Malfy*, but comes to its head in *The Devil's Law-case*. It cannot, I fear, be denied that Webster was the first to relax those natural bonds of noble metre 'whose service is perfect freedom'—as Shakespeare found it, and combined with perfect loyalty to its law the most perfect liberty of living and sublime and spontaneous and accurate expression. I can only conjecture that this greatest of the Shakespeareans was misguided out of his natural line of writing as exemplified and perfected in the tragedy of Vittoria, and lured into this cross and crooked byway of immetrical experiment, by the temptation of some theory or crotchet on the score of what is now called naturalism or realism; which, if there were any real or natural weight in the reasoning that seeks to support it, would of course do away, and of course ought to do away, with dramatic poetry altogether: for if it is certain that real persons do not actually converse in good metre, it is happily no less certain that they do not actually converse in bad metre. In the hands of so great a tragic poet as Webster a peculiar and impressive effect may now and then be produced by this anomalous and illegitimate way of writing; it certainly suits well with the thoughtful and fantastic truculence of Bosola's reflections on death and dissolution and decay—his 'talk fit for a charnel,' which halts and hovers between things hideous and things sublime. But it is a step on the downward way that leads to the negation or the confusion of all distinctions between poetry and prose; a result to which it would be grievous to think that the example of Shakespeare's greatest contemporary should in any way appear to conduce.

The doctrine or the motive of chance (whichever we may prefer to call it) is seen in its fullest workings and felt in its furthest bearings by the student of Webster's masterpiece. The fifth act of *The Duchess of Malfy* has been assailed on the very ground which it should have been evident to a thoughtful and capable reader that the writer must have intended to take up— on the ground that the whole upshot of the story is dominated by sheer chance, arranged by mere error, and guided by pure accident. No formal scheme or religious principle of retribution would have been so strangely or so thoroughly in keeping with the whole scheme and principle of the tragedy. After the overwhelming terrors and the overpowering beauties of that unique and marvellous fourth act, in which the genius of this poet spreads its fullest and its darkest wing for the longest and the strongest of its flights, it could not but be that the subsequent action and passion of the drama should appear by comparison unimpressive or ineffectual; but all the effect or impression possible of attainment under the inevitable burden of this difficulty is achieved by natural and simple and straightforward means. If Webster has not made the part of Antonio dramatically striking and attractive—as he probably found it impossible to do—he has at least bestowed on the fugitive and unconscious widower of his murdered heroine a pensive and manly grace of deliberate resignation which is not without pathetic as well as poetical effect. In the beautiful and well-known scene where the echo from his wife's unknown and new-made grave seems to respond to his meditative mockery and forewarn him of his impending death, Webster has given such reality and seriousness to an old commonplace of contemporary fancy or previous fashion in poetry that we are fain to forget the fantastic side of the conception and see only the tragic aspect of its meaning. A weightier objection than any which can be brought against the conduct of the play might be suggested to the minds of some readers—and these, perhaps, not too exacting or too captious readers—by the sudden vehemence of transformation which in the great preceding act seems to fall like fire from heaven upon the two chief criminals who figure on the stage of murder. It seems rather a miraculous retribution, a judicial violation of the laws of nature, than a reasonably credible consequence or evolution of those laws, which strikes Ferdinand with madness and Bosola with repentance. But the whole atmosphere of the action is so charged with thunder that this double and simultaneous shock of moral electricity rather thrills us with admiration and faith than chills us with repulsion or distrust. The passionate intensity and moral ardour of imagination which we feel to vibrate and penetrate through every turn and every phrase of the dialogue would suffice to enforce upon our belief a more nearly incredible revolution of nature or revulsion of the soul.

It is so difficult for even the very greatest poets to give any vivid force of living interest to a figure of passive endurance that perhaps the only instance of perfect triumph over this difficulty is to be found in the character of Desdemona. Shakespeare alone could have made her as interesting as Imogen or Cordelia; though these have so much to do and dare, and she after her first appearance has simply to suffer: even Webster could not give such individual vigour of characteristic life to the figure of his martyr as to the figure of his criminal heroine. Her courage and sweetness, her delicacy and sincerity, her patience and her passion, are painted with equal power and tenderness of touch: yet she hardly stands before us as distinct from others of her half angelic sisterhood as does the White Devil from the fellowship of her comrades in perdition. But if, as we may assuredly assume, it was on the twenty-third 'nouell' of William Painter's *Palace of Pleasure* that Webster's crowning masterpiece was founded, the poet's moral and spiritual power of transfiguration is here even more admirable than in the previous case of his other and wellnigh coequally consummate poem. The narrative degrades and brutalises the widowed heroine's affection for her second husband to the actual level of the vile conception which the poet attributes and confines to the foul imagination of her envious and murderous brothers. Here again, and finally and supremely here, the purifying and exalting power of Webster's noble and magnanimous imagination is gloriously unmistakable by all and any who have eyes to read and hearts to recognise.

For it is only with Shakespeare that Webster can ever be compared in any way to his disadvantage as a tragic poet: above all others of his country he stands indisputably supreme. The place of Marlowe indeed is higher among our poets by right of his primacy as a founder and a pioneer: but of course his work has not—as of course it could not have—that plenitude and perfection of dramatic power in construction and dramatic subtlety in detail which the tragedies of Webster share in so large a measure with the tragedies of Shakespeare. Marston, the poet with whom he has most in common, might almost be said to stand in the same relation to Webster as Webster to Shakespeare. In single lines and phrases, in a few detached passages and a very few distinguishable scenes, he is worthy to be compared with the greater poet; he suddenly rises and dilates to the stature and the strength of a model whom usually he can but follow afar off. Marston, as a tragic poet, is not quite what Webster would be if his fame depended simply on such scenes as those in which the noble mother of Vittoria breaks off her daughter's first interview with Brachiano—spares, and commends to God's forgiveness, the son who has murdered his brother before her eyes—and lastly appears 'in several forms of distraction,' 'grown a very old woman in two hours,' and singing that most pathetic and imaginative of all funereal invocations which the finest critic of all time so justly and so delicately compared to the watery dirge of Ariel. There is less refinement, less exaltation and perfection of feeling, less tenderness of emotion and less nobility of passion, but hardly less force and fervour, less weighty and sonorous ardour of expression, in the very best and loftiest passages of Marston: but his genius is more uncertain, more fitful and intermittent, less harmonious, coherent, and trustworthy than Webster's. And Webster, notwithstanding an occasional outbreak into Aristophanic license of momentary sarcasm through the sardonic lips of such a cynical ruffian as Ferdinand or Flamineo, is without exception the cleanliest, as Marston is beyond comparison the coarsest writer of his time. In this as in other matters of possible comparison that 'vessel of deathless wrath,' the implacable and inconsolable poet of sympathy half maddened into rage and aspiration goaded backwards to despair—it should be needless to add the name of Cyril Tourneur—stands midway between these two more conspicuous figures of their age. But neither the father and master of poetic pessimists, the splendid and sombre creator of Vindice and his victims, nor any other third whom our admiration may discern among all the greatest of their fellows, can be compared with Webster on terms more nearly equal than those on which Webster stands in relation to the sovereign of them all.

GEORGE HERBERT

GEORGE CHAPMAN

SIR EDWARD COKE

THOMAS RANDOLPH

THOMAS CAREW

SIR HENRY WOTTON

BEN JONSON

JOHN MARSTON

1576–1634

John Marston was born at Wardington, Oxfordshire, and was baptized on October 7, 1576. He entered Brasenose College, Oxford, in 1592, and received a B.A. in 1594. He read at Middle Temple, London, in 1595, but probably never practiced law. In 1598 Marston published two volumes of satirical verses, *Metamorphosis of Pygmalion's Image* and *Scourge of Villainie*. In 1599 Marston began a ten-year association with London's various dramatic companies, including Paul's Boys and the Queen's Revels. His first play, *Histrio-Mastix* (1599), began a feud with fellow playwrights Joseph Hall and Ben Jonson. Marston's 1600 play *What You Will* also satirized Jonson. Jonson responded by attacking Marston in *Every Man out of His Humour* (1599), *Cynthia's Revels* (1600), and *Poetaster* (1601). Having seemingly settled their differences, Marston wrote commendatory verses to Jonson's *Sejanus* (1603). In 1605 Marston and Jonson, along with Chapman, collaborated on *Eastward Hoe*.

Marston's other dramas include the dark and morose *Antonio and Mellida* (1599) and its sequel, *Antonio's Revenge* (1599). Perhaps Marston's most successful plays are *The Malcontent* (1604) and *The Dutch Courtezean* (1605). These plays were followed by *The Tragedy of Sophonisba* (1606) and *The Insatiate Countess* (c. 1608). In 1609 Marston gave up writing and became an ordained minister. He served as rector of Christchurch, Hampshire, from 1616 to 1631. Marston died on June 25, 1634, in Aldermanbury, London, and was buried next to his father at Middle Temple.

Personal

⟨Jonson⟩ had many quarrels with Marston, beat him, and took his pistol from him, wrote his *Poetaster* on him; the beginning of them were that Marston represented him in the stage. —BEN JONSON, *Conversations with William Drummond*, 1619

John Marston, a Tragic and Comic writer, not of the meanest rank among our English dramatics. His Comedies are *The Dutch Curtesan*; *The Fawn*; *What You Will*: his Tragedies *Antonio and Melida*:—*The Insatiate Countess*, besides *The Male-content*, a Tragi-comedy; *The Faithful Shepherd*, a pastoral. —EDWARD PHILLIPS, *Theatrum Poetarum Anglicanorum*, 1675

John Marston, a gentleman that wrote divers things of great ingenuity in the latter end of the reign of qu. Elizabeth, and beginning of K. James I. did receive his academical education, as it seems, in Oxford, but in what house, unless in C.C. coll. I cannot justly tell you. One Joh. Marston, son of a father of both his names of the city of Coventry, esq; became either a commoner or gent. com. of Brasennose coll. in 1591, and in the beginning of Feb. 1593, he was admitted bach. of arts, as the eldest son of an esq; and soon after compleating that degree by determination, he went his way, and improv'd his learning in other faculties. This person dying on the 25th of June, an. 1634, was buried by his father (sometimes a counsellor of the Middle-Temple) in the church belonging to the Temple in the suburb of London, under the stone which hath written on it *Oblivioni sacrum*, as I have told you in the *Athene et Fasti Oxon*, under the year 1608. Another Joh. Marston I find to have been a student in Corp. Ch. coll. who was admitted bach. of arts 23 Feb. 1592, but in what county he was born, I cannot yet find, because (1) That he was not matriculated, (2) That he was not scholar of that house, or fellow; in the admissions of both which, their counties of nativity are constantly registred. This last of C.C. coll. who seems to be John Marston, the poet, whom we are farther to mention, (who dying before 1633, in which year most of his works were published by Will. Shakespeare, and therefore cannot be that Marston of Brasennose coll. who died in 1634, as before 'tis told you) and has

been taken by some of that house to be the same, was not inferior to any in writing of comedies and tragedies, especially if you consider the time when they were penn'd; and perhaps equal to some who lived 20 years after his time. —ANTHONY À WOOD, *Athenae Oxonienses*, 1691–1721

General

When *Fuscus* first had taught his Muse to scold,
He gloried in her rugged vaine so much,
That euery one came to him, heare her should,
First *Victor*, then *Cinna*, nor did he grutch
To let both players, and artificers,
Deale with his darling, as if confident,
None of all these he did repute for Lechers,
Or thought her face would all such lusts preuent:
    But how can be a bawdes surname refuse,
    Who to all sorts thus prostitutes his Muse?
        —EVERARD GUILPIN, "Of Fuscus," *Skialetheia*, 1598

Marston, thy Muse enharbours *Horace* vaine,
Then some *Augustus* giue thee *Horace* merit,
And thine embuskin'd *Iohnson* doth retaine
So rich a stile, and wondrous gallant spirit;
That if to praise your Muses I desired,
My Muse would muse. Such wittes must be
    admired.
      —JOHN WEEVER, "Ad I.: Marston, & Ben: Iohnson," *Epigrammes in the Oldest Cut and Newest Fashion*, 1599

Methinks he is a ruffian in his style;
Withouten bands' or garters' ornament,
He quaffs a cup of Frenchmen's helicon,
Then royster doyster in his oily terms,
Cuts, thrusts, and foins at whomsoe'er he meets,
And shews about Ram-alley meditations.
   · · ·

Aye, there is one that backs a paper steed
And manageth a pen knife gallantly;
Strikes his poinado at a button's breadth,

Brings the great battering-ram of terms to towns,
And at first volley of his cannon shot
Batters the walls of the old fusty world.
—UNSIGNED, *The Return from Pernassus*, 1606,
Act 1, Sc. 2

It is Marston's misfortune, that he can never keep clear of the impurities of the brothel. His stream of poetry, if sometimes bright and unpolluted, almost always betrays a muddy bottom. The satirist who too freely indulges himself in the display of that licentiousness which he means to proscribe, absolutely defeats his own design. He inflames those passions which he professes to suppress, gratifies the depravations of a prurient curiosity, and seduces innocent minds to an acquaintance with ideas which they might never have known.—THOMAS WARTON, *The History of English Poetry*, 1778–81, Sec. 65

MARSTON, who wrote in all but eight plays, produced six of them after the death of ELIZABETH. The *Insatiate Countess*, performed in 1604, is one of them, and contains under feigned titles the history of JOAN, the first queen of JERUSALEM, NAPLES, and SICILY, whose story had been pretty well handled before, both for the stage and as a novel. The reader will remember that BERENGER DE PARASOLS was poisoned for making free with this lady's character, and this queen is intended by ANNE, duchess of ULME, in GOD'S revenge against adultery. Very little is known as to the real merit of this play.

The *Malcontent*, produced in 1604. This is the play which MARSTON, as we have seen, dedicated with such warmth to JONSON, with whom he had afterwards so severe a quarrel. Some of MARSTON'S enemies endeavoured to induce a general belief that this piece was intended as a satire on particular characters, which invidious report JONSON is supposed secretly to have seconded, and the probability is that this gave rise to the dispute which made the breach between these authors. There does not appear, however, the smallest ground for this imputation; for by several writers, but particularly LANGBAINE, we are assured the *Malcontent* was a fair, manly, general satire; besides, we are capable of ascertaining this ourselves, and so far we must vouch in favour of the author, whose piece certainly goes to the times both then and now; but this does not preclude the possibility that particular persons sat for their portraits, for satire was certainly the vein of MARSTON, and it is impossible to be critically satirical without fitting the cap somewhere.

The *Dutch Curtizan*. This comedy is full of the intrigue of those times, and must certainly have had success, for The *Revenge, or a Match in Newgate*, which was attributed to BETTERTON, and which possesses a great deal of whim and pleasantry, though in other respects it is a strange excentric thing, in nothing more than an alteration of MARSTON'S play which was again wrought into a farce that at one time greatly succeeded, under the title of The *Vintner Tricked*.

Parisitaster, or the Fawn, performed in 1606, is taken partly from The *Decameron* of BOCCACE, and partly from *Ovid*. It has particular merit, but is not so good a play as any other of the productions of MARSTON.

The *Wonder of Women; or Sophonisha*, produced in 1606. This play is rather imitated than copied from history, for the author himself says that he has not laboured in it to tye himself to relate every thing as a historian, but to enlarge every thing as a poet.

What You Will, a comedy, was brought out in 1607. This piece, which did but little itself, has provided materials for other dramatic productions since. It appears to be taken from PLAUTUS, but the equivoque of mistaking one person for another cannot properly be said to belong to any particular author; it has been used in all times, and by all writers; and so the circumstances vary it may be considered always a novelty.

MARSTON having consulted regularity and correctness in the conduct of his plays, and besides having written them naturally, and both with humour and pathos, must rank before DECKER, and essentially, upon a par with CHAPMAN and HEYWOOD, especially when we are told that his poems rendered him still more celebrated than his plays. Being, however, a severe satirist, his cotemporaries were not willing to allow him his due portion of praise, and posterity cannot properly judge of his whole merit. What we know of him, however, ranks him very respectfully as a writer.—CHARLES DIBDIN, *A Complete History of the Stage*, 1795, Vol. 3, pp. 260–63

This writer was the antagonist of Jonson in the drama, and the rival of Bishop Hall in satire, though confessedly inferior to them both in their respective walks of poetry. While none of his biographers seem to know anything about him, Mr. Gifford (in his *Memoirs of Ben Jonson*) conceives that Wood has unconsciously noticed him as a gentleman of Coventry, who married Mary, the daughter of the Rev. W. Wilkes, chaplain to King James, and rector of St. Martin, in Wiltshire. According to this notice, our poet died at London in 1634, and was buried in the church belonging to the Temple. These particulars agree with what Jonson said to Drummond respecting this dramatic opponent of his, in his conversation at Hawthornden, viz. that Marston wrote his father-in-law's preachings, and his father-in-law Marston's comedies. Marston's comedies are somewhat dull; and it is not difficult to conceive a witty sermon of those days, when puns were scattered from the pulpit, to have been as lively as an indifferent comedy. Marston is the Crispinus of Jonson's *Poetaster*, where he is treated somewhat less contemptuously than his companion Demetrius (Dekker); an allusion is even made to the respectability of his birth. Both he and Dekker were afterwards reconciled to Jonson; but Marston's reconcilement, though he dedicated his *Malcontent* to his propitiated enemy, seems to have been subject to relapses.
—THOMAS CAMPBELL, *An Essay on English Poetry*, 1819

. . . of all the dramatists of the time, the most disagreeable in disposition, though by no means the least powerful in mind, was John Marston. The time of his birth is not known; his name is entangled in contemporary records with that of another John Marston; and we may be sure that his mischief-loving spirit would have been delighted could he have anticipated that the antiquaries, a century after his death, would be driven to despair by the difficulty of discriminating one from the other. It is more than probable, however, that he was the John Marston who was of a respectable family in Shropshire, who took his bachelor's degree at Oxford in 1592, and who was afterwards married to a daughter of a chaplain of James the First. Whatever may have been Marston's antecedents, they were such as to gratify his tastes as a cynical observer of the crimes and follies of men,—an observer whose hatred of evil sprang from no love of good, but to whom the sight of depravity and baseness was welcome, inasmuch as it afforded him the occasion to indulge his own scorn and pride. His ambition was to be the English Juvenal; and it must be conceded that he had the true Iago-like disposition "to spy out abuses." Accordingly, in 1598, he published a series of venomous satires called *The Scourge of Villanie*, rough in versification, condensed in thought, tainted in matter, evincing a cankered more than a caustic spirit, and producing an effect at once indecent and inhuman. To prove that this scourging of villany, which would have put Mephistopheles to the blush, was inspired by no respect for virtue, he soon followed it up with a poem so licentious that, before it was circulated to any extent, it was suppressed by order of Archbishop Whitgift, and nearly all the copies destroyed. A writer could not be thus dishonored without being brought prominently into notice, and old Henslowe, the manager, was after him at once to secure his libellous ability for the Rose. Accordingly, we learn from Henslowe's diary, under date of September 28, 1599, that he had lent to William Borne, "to lend unto John Mastone," "the new po-ete," "the sum of forty shillings," in earnest of some work not named. There is an undated letter of Marston to Henslowe, written probably in reference to this matter, which is characteristic in its disdainfully confident tone. Thus it runs:—

Mr. Henslowe, at the Rose on the Bankside.

If you like my playe of Columbus, it is verie well, and you shall give me noe more than twentie poundes for it, but If nott, lett me have it by the Bearer againe, as I know the kinges men will freelie give me as much for it, and the profitts of the third daye moreover.

Soe I rest yours,

John Marston.

He seems not to have been popular among the band of dramatists he now joined, and it is probable that his insulting manners were not sustained by corresponding courage. Ben Jonson had many quarrels with him, both literary and personal, and mentions one occasion on which he beat him and took away his pistol. His temper was Italian, rather than English, and one would conceive of him as quicker with the stiletto than the fist. His connection with the stage ceased, in 1613, after he had produced a number of dramas, of which nine have been preserved. He died about twenty years afterwards, in 1634, seemingly in comfortable circumstances.

Marston's plays, whether comedies or tragedies, all bear the mark of his bitter and misanthropic spirit,—a spirit that seemed cursed by the companionship of its own thoughts, and forced them out through a well-grounded fear that they would fester if left within. His comedies of *The Malcontent*, *The Fawn*, and *What You Will*, have no genuine mirth, though an abundance of scornful wit,—of wit which, in his own words, "stings, blisters, galls off the skin, with the acrimony of its sharp quickness." The baser its objects, the brighter its gleam. It is stimulated by the desire to give pain, rather than the wish to communicate pleasure. Marston is not without sprightliness, but his sprightliness is never the sprightliness of the kid, though it is sometimes that of the hyena, and sometimes that of the polecat. In his *Malcontent* he probably drew a flattering likeness of his inner self: yet the most compassionate reader of the play would experience little pity in seeing the *Malcontent* hanged. So much, indeed, of Marston's satire is directed at depravity, that Ben Jonson used to say that "Marston wrote his father-in-law's preachings, and his father-in-law his comedies." It is to be hoped, however, that the spirit of the chaplain's tirades against sins was not, like his son-in-law's, worse than the sins themselves.

If Marston's comic vein is thus, to use one of Dekkar's phrases, that of "a thorny-toothed rascal," it may be supposed that his tragic is a still fiercer libel on humanity. His tragedies, indeed, though not without a gloomy power, are extravagant and horrible in conception and conduct. Even when he copies, he makes the thing his own by caricaturing it. Thus the plot of *Antonio's Revenge* is plainly taken from *Hamlet*, but it is *Hamlet* passed through Marston's intellect and imagination, and so debased as to look original. Still, the intellect in Marston's tragedies strikes the reader as forcible in itself, and as

capable of achieving excellence, if it could only be divorced from the bad disposition and deformed conscience which direct its exercise. He has fancy, and he frequently stutters into imagination; but the imp that controls his heart corrupts his taste and taints his sense of beauty, and the result is that he has a malicious satisfaction in deliberately choosing words whose uncouthness finds no extenuation in their expressiveness, and in forging elaborate metaphors which disgust rather than delight.—Edwin P. Whipple, *The Literature of the Age of Elizabeth*, 1869, pp. 125–29

It was his misfortune by his earliest tragedy not only to have furnished an opportunity for merited ridicule to his chief adversary among writers for the Elisabethan stage, but also to have lent colour to the charges brought by his foremost rival in a different form of satire against that stage at large. The blood and thunder which in Marston's *Antonio and Mellida* recall Marlowe and Kyd are enveloped in a bombast of terms as 'astounding' as theirs; and in his two remaining tragedies, though he has learnt to moderate the extravagance of his phraseology, his imagination seems still intent upon themes belonging to the reign of the morally grotesque. He is equally ambitious in comedy; for both *The Malcontent* and *The Fawn* aim at an unusual degree of originality in the conception of their main characters and situations; but in the former—in which Marston's work had the advantage of Webster's additions—he can only be said to have achieved a partial success, and in the latter he has from a literary point of view fallen short of it altogether. He is happier in a less ambitious kind of comedy, of which *The Dutch Courtesan* is in many respects a most praiseworthy example; while with regard to *Eastward Hoe* it is impossible to say in what degree the credit of this admirable play is attributable to him, and in what to Chapman. The literary satire of *What You Will* and of the plays in which Marston's co-operation seems traceable is necessarily in part obscure, but it cannot be held to rise above the level—no high one in itself—of his *Satyres* proper.

Either Marston was painfully aware of the limits of his powers, or the warning example in a contrary direction furnished by his adversary Jonson determined him to adopt a deprecatory attitude towards the public. But the iteration with which he assures the spectators of his 'constant modesty,' of his 'modest diffidence and selfe-mistrust,' and of his freedom from self-admiration, and confesses the 'slightness' of his productions, will affect some minds more disagreeably than the self-assertion of Ben Jonson. There is something of the molluscous Crispinus of the *Poetaster* in these appeals to a magnanimous public; and it is difficult not to interpret them as signs that Marston felt himself unable to command success without these conciliatory flourishes. A further symptom of the same self-distrust is his unmistakeable addiction to the practice of borrowing—a habit which in literature as well as in other spheres is more easily acquired than shaken off. Shakspere in particular shines through the seams of most of Marston's plays. His literary ambition was manifestly very great; and opposition vexed him to the quick. But though his ambition was sustained by many acquirements, and by the powers of occasional pathos and fluent humour, while at times he could rise to poetic beauty of expression, yet there is a false ring about most of his efforts, and a want of sustained force in nearly all. He sought to excel in various dramatic species, but can hardly be said to have reached excellence unless in the depiction of the abnormal excesses of contemporary manners; and even here he fails in concentration of effect. Thus I remain in doubt whether on the whole he deserves to be ranked among the great dramatists, with whose names his own is habitually associated, as having like them adorned our dramatic literature with creations of original genius.—ADOLPHUS WILLIAM WARD, *A History of English Dramatic Literature* (1875), 1899, Vol. 2, pp. 491–93

WILLIAM HAZLITT
From *Lectures on the Dramatic Literature of the Age of Elizabeth*

1820

Marston is a writer of great merit, who rose to tragedy from the ground of comedy, and whose *forte* was not sympathy, either with the stronger or softer emotions, but an impatient scorn and bitter indignation against the vices and follies of men, which vented itself either in comic irony or in lofty invective. He was properly a satirist. He was not a favourite with his contemporaries, nor they with him. He was first on terms of great intimacy, and afterwards at open war, with Ben Jonson; and he is most unfairly criticised in *The Return from Parnassus*, under the name of Monsieur Kinsayder, as a mere libeller and buffoon. Writers in their life-time do all they can to degrade and vilify one another, and expect posterity to have a very tender care of their reputations! The writers of this age, in general, cannot however be reproached with this infirmity. The number of plays that they wrote in conjunction, is a proof of the contrary; and a circumstance no less curious, as to the division of intellectual labour, than the cordial union of sentiment it implied. Unlike most poets, the love of their art surmounted their hatred of one another. Genius was not become a vile and vulgar pretence, and they respected in others what they knew to be true inspiration in themselves. They courted the applause of the multitude, but came to one another for judgment and assistance. When we see these writers working together on the same admirable productions, year after year, as was the case with Beaumont and Fletcher, Middleton and Rowley, with Chapman, Deckar, and Jonson, it reminds one of Aristo's eloquent apostrophe to the Spirit of Ancient Chivalry, when he has seated his rival knights, Renaldo and Ferraw, on the same horse.

> Oh ancient knights of true and noble heart,
> They rivals were, one faith they liv'd not under;
> Besides, they felt their bodies shrewdly smart
> Of blows late given, and yet (behold a wonder)
> Thro' thick and thin, suspicion set apart,
> Like friends they ride, and parted not asunder,
> Until the horse with double spurring drived
> Unto a way parted in two, arrived.[1]

Marston's *Antonio and Mellida* is a tragedy of considerable force and pathos; but in the most critical parts, the author frequently breaks off or flags without any apparent reason but want of interest in his subject; and farther, the best and most affecting situations and bursts of feeling are too evidently imitations of Shakespear. Thus the unexpected meeting between Andrugio and Lucio, in the beginning of the third act, is a direct counterpart of that between Lear and Kent, only much weakened: and the interview between Antonio and Mellida has a strong resemblance to the still more affecting one between Lear and Cordelia, and is most wantonly disfigured by the sudden introduction of half a page of Italian rhymes, which gives the whole an air of burlesque. The conversation of Lucio and Andrugio, again, after his defeat seems to invite, but will not bear a comparison with Richard the Second's remonstrance with his courtiers, who offered him consolation in his misfor-

tunes; and no one can be at a loss to trace the allusion to Romeo's conduct on being apprized of his banishment, in the termination of the following speech.

> *Antonio*: Each man takes hence life, but no man death:
> He's a good fellow, and keeps open house:
> A thousand thousand ways lead to his gate,
> To his wide-mouthed porch: when niggard life
> Hath but one little, little wicket through.
> We wring ourselves into this wretched world
> To pule and weep, exclaim, to curse and rail,
> To fret and ban the fates, *to strike the earth
> As I do now.* Antonio, curse thy birth,
> And die.

The following short passage might be quoted as one of exquisite beauty and originality—

> As having clasp'd a rose
> Within my palm, the rose being ta'en away,
> My hand retains a little breath of sweet;
> So may man's trunk, his spirit slipp'd away,
> Hold still a faint perfume of his sweet guest.
> (Act IV. Scene 1.)

The character of Felice in this play is an admirable satirical accompaniment, and is the favourite character of this author (in all probability his own), that of a shrewd, contemplative cynic, and sarcastic spectator in the drama of human life. It runs through all his plays, is shared by Quadratus and Lampatho in *What You Will* (it is into the mouth of the last of these that he has put that fine invective against the uses of philosophy, in the account of himself and his spaniel, 'who still slept while he baus'd leaves, tossed o'er the dunces, por'd on the old print'), and is at its height in the Fawn and Malevole, in his *Parasitaster* and *Malcontent*. These two comedies are his *chef d'œuvres*. The character of the Duke Hercules of Ferrara, disguised as the Parasite, in the first of these, is well sustained throughout, with great sense, dignity, and spirit. He is a wise censurer of men and things, and rails at the world with charitable bitterness. He may put in a claim to a sort of family likeness to the Duke, in *Measure for Measure*: only the latter descends from his elevation to watch in secret over serious crimes; the other is only a spy on private follies. There is something in this cast of character (at least in comedy—perhaps it neutralizes the tone and interest in tragedy), that finds a wonderful reciprocity in the breast of the reader or audience. It forms a kind of middle term or point of union between the busy actors in the scene and the indifferent byestander, insinuates the plot, and suggests a number of good wholesome reflections, for the sagacity and honesty of which we do not fail to take credit to ourselves. We are let into its confidence, and have a perfect reliance on its sincerity. Our sympathy with it is without any drawback; for it has no part to perform itself, and 'is nothing, if not critical.' It is a sure card to play. We may doubt the motives of heroic actions, or differ about the just limits and extreme workings of the passions; but the professed misanthrope is a character that no one need feel any scruples in trusting, since the dislike of folly and knavery in the abstract is common to knaves and fools with the wise and honest! Besides the instructive moral vein of Hercules as the Fawn or Parasitaster, which contains a world of excellent matter, most aptly and wittily delivered; there are two other characters perfectly hit off, Gonzago the old prince of Urbino, and Granuffo, one of his lords in waiting. The loquacious, good-humoured, undisguised vanity of the one is excellently relieved by the silent gravity of the other. The wit of this last character (Granuffo) consists in his not speaking a word through the whole play; he never contradicts what is said, and only assents by implication.

He is a most infallible courtier, and follows the prince like his shadow, who thus graces his pretensions.

. . . Marston's style was by no means more guarded than that of his contemporaries. He was also much more of a free-thinker than Marlowe, and there is a frequent, and not unfavourable allusion in his works, to later sceptical opinions.—In the play of the *Malcontent* we meet with an occasional mixture of comic gaiety, to relieve the more serious and painful business of the scene, as in the easy loquacious effrontery of the old *intriguante* Marquerella, and in the ludicrous facility with which the idle courtiers avoid or seek the notice of Male-vole, as he is in or out of favour; but the general tone and import of the piece is severe and moral. The plot is somewhat too intricate and too often changed (like the shifting of a scene), so as to break and fritter away the interest at the end; but the part of Aurelia, the Duchess of Pietro Jacomo, a dissolute and proud-spirited woman, is the highest strain of Marston's pen. The scene in particular, in which she receives and exults in the supposed news of her husband's death, is nearly unequalled in boldness of conception and in the unrestrained force of passion, taking away not only the consciousness of guilt, but overcoming the sense of shame.

Notes
1. Sir John Harrington's translation.

GEORGE SAINTSBURY
From A *History of Elizabethan Literature*
1887, pp. 153–55, 195–99

John Marston, who out-Halled ⟨Joseph⟩ Hall in all his literary misdeeds, was, it would appear, a member of a good Shropshire family which had passed into Warwickshire. He was educated at Coventry School, and at Brasenose College, Oxford, and passed early into London literary society, where he involved himself in the inextricable and not much worth extricating quarrels which have left their mark in Jonson's and Dekker's plays. In the first decade of the seventeenth century he wrote several remarkable plays, of much greater literary merit than the work now to be criticised. Then he took orders, was presented to the living of Christchurch, and, like others of his time, seems to have forsworn literature as an unholy thing. He died in 1634. Here we are concerned only with two youthful works of his—*Pigmalion's Image* and some Satires in 1598, followed in the same year by a sequel, entitled *The Scourge of Villainy*. In these works he called himself "W. Kinsayder," a pen-name for which various explanations have been given. It is characteristic and rather comical that, while both the earlier Satires and *The Scourge* denounce lewd verse most full-mouthedly, *Pigmalion's Image* is a poem in the *Venus and Adonis* style which is certainly not inferior to its fellows in luscious descriptions. It was, in fact, with the *Satires* and much similar work, formally condemned and burnt in 1599. Both in Hall and in Marston industrious commentators have striven hard to identify the personages of the satire with famous living writers, and there may be a chance that some at least of their identifications (as of Marston's Tubrio with Marlowe) are correct. But the exaggeration and insincerity, the deliberate "society-journalism" (to adopt a detestable phrase for a corresponding thing of our own days), which characterise all this class of writing make the identifications of but little interest. In every age there are writers who delight in representing that age as the very worst of the history of the world, and in ransacking literature and imagination for accusations against their fellows.

The sedate philosopher partly brings and partly draws the conviction that one time is very like another. Marston, however, has fooled himself and his readers to the very top of his and their bent; and even Churchill, restrained by a more critical atmosphere, has not come quite near his confused and only half-intelligible jumble of indictments for indecent practices and crude philosophy of the moral and metaphysical kind. A vigorous line or phrase occasionally redeems the chaos of rant, fustian, indecency, ill-nature, and muddled thought.

> Ambitious Gorgons, wide-mouth'd Lamians,
> Shape-changing Proteans, damn'd Briarians,
> Is Minos dead, is Radamanth asleep,
> That ye thus dare unto Jove's palace creep?
> What, hath Ramnusia spent her knotted whip,
> That ye dare strive on Hebe's cup to sip?
> Ye know Apollo's quiver is not spent,
> But can abate your daring hardiment.
> Python is slain, yet his accursed race
> Dare look divine Astrea in the face;
> Chaos return and with confusion
> Involve the world with strange disunion;
> For Pluto sits in that adorèd chair
> Which doth belong unto Minerva's heir.
> O hecatombs! O catastrophe!
> From Midas' pomp to Irus' beggary!
> Prometheus, who celestial fire
> Did steal from heaven, therewith to inspire
> Our earthly bodies with a sense-ful mind,
> Whereby we might the depth of nature find,
> Is ding'd to hell, and vulture eats his heart
> Which did such deep philosophy impart
> To mortal men.

The contrast of this so-called satire, and the really satiric touches of Marston's own plays, when he was not cramped by the affectations of the style, is very curious. . . .

With regard to Marston (of whose little-known personality something has been said in connection with his satires) I find myself somewhat unable to agree with the generality of critics, who seem to me to have been rather taken in by his blood-and-thunder work, his transpontine declamation against tyrants, and his affectation of a gloomy or furious scorn against mankind. The uncouthness, as well as the suspicion of insincerity, which we noted in his satirical work, extend, as it seems to me, also to his dramas; and if we class him as a worker in horrors with Marlowe earlier, and with Webster and Ford later, the chief result will be to show his extreme inferiority to them. He is even below Tourneur in this respect, while, like Tourneur, he is exposed to the charge of utterly neglecting congruity and proportion. With him we relapse not merely from the luminous perfection of Shakespere, from the sane order of work which was continued through Fletcher, and the best of Fletcher's followers, but from the more artificial unity of Jonson, back into the chaotic extravagances of the First Period. Marston, like the rest, is fond of laughing at *Jeronimo*, but his own tragic construction and some of his own tragic scenes are hardly less bombastic, and scarcely at all less promiscuous than the tangled horrors of that famous melodrama. Marston, it is true, has lucid intervals—even many of them. Hazlitt has succeeded in quoting many beautiful passages, one of which was curiously echoed in the next age by Nat. Lee, in whom, indeed, there was a strong vein of Elizabethan melodrama. The sarcasm on philosophical study in *What You Will* is one of the very best things of its own kind in the range of English drama,—light, sustained, not too long nor too short, in fact, thoroughly "hit off."

Delight my spaniel slept, whilst I baused leaves,
Tossed o'er the dunces, pored on the old print
Of titled words, and still my spaniel slept.
Whilst I wasted lamp oil, bated my flesh,
Shrunk up my veins, and still my spaniel slept,
And still I held converse with Zabarell,
Aquinas, Scotus, and the musty saws
Of antique Donate: still my spaniel slept.
Still on went I: first *an sit anima,*
Then, an' 'twere mortal. O hold, hold!
At that they are at brain buffets, fell by the ears,
Amain [pell-mell] together—still my spaniel slept.
Then whether 'twere corporeal, local, fixed,
Ex traduce; but whether't had free will
Or no, hot philosophers
Stood banding factions all so strongly propped,
I staggered, knew not which was firmer part;
But thought, quoted, read, observed and pried,
Stuffed noting-books, and still my spaniel slept.
At length he waked and yawned, and by yon sky
For aught I know, he knew as much as I.

There is real pathos in *Antonio and Mellida*, and real satire in *Parasitaster* and *The Malcontent*. Hazlitt (who had a very high opinion of Marston) admits that the remarkable inequalities of this last piece "seem to show want of interest in the subject." This is an odd explanation, but I suspect it is really only an anticipation in more favourable words of my own theory, that Marston's tragic and satiric moods were not really sincere; that he was a clever man who found a fashion of satire and a fashion of blood-and-thunder tragedy prevailing, and threw himself into both without much or any heart in the matter. This is supported by the curious fact that almost all his plays (at least those extant) were produced within a very few years, 1602–1605, though he lived thirty years after the latter date, and more than twenty after his last dated appearances in literature, *The Insatiate Countess*, and *Eastward Ho!* That he was an ill-tempered person with considerable talents, who succeeded, at any rate for a time, in mistaking his ill-temper for *sæva indignatio*, and his talents for genius, is not, I think, too harsh a description of Marston. In the hotbed of the literary influences of the time, these conditions of his produced some remarkable fruit. But when my friend Professor Minto attributes to him "amazing and almost Titanic energy," mentions "life" several times over as one of the chief characteristics of his personages (I should say that they had as much life as violently-moved marionettes), and discovers "amiable and admirable characters" among them, I am compelled not, of course, to be positive that my own very different estimate is right, but to wonder at the singularly different way in which the same things strike different persons, who are not as a rule likely to look at them from very different points of view.

Marston's plays, however, are both powerful enough and famous enough to call for a somewhat more detailed notice. *Antonio and Mellida*, the earliest and if not the best as a whole, that which contains the finest scenes and fragments, is in two parts—the second being more properly called *The Revenge of Antonio*. The revenge itself is of the exaggerated character which was so popular with the Elizabethan dramatists, but in which (except in the famous Cornwall and Gloucester scene in *Lear*) Shakespere never indulged after his earliest days. The wicked tyrant's tongue is torn out, his murdered son's body is thrown down before him, and then the conspirators, standing round, gibe, curse, and rant at him for a couple of pages before they plunge their swords into his body. This goodly conclusion is led up to by a sufficient quantity of antecedent and casual crimes, together with much not very excellent fooling by a court gull, Balurdo, who might be compared with Shakespere's fools of the same kind, with very great advantage, by those who do not appreciate the latter. The beautiful descriptive and reflective passages which, in Lamb's *Extracts*, gave the play its reputation, chiefly occur towards the beginning, and this is the best of them:—

> *And.*: Why man, I never was a Prince till now.
> 'Tis not the bared pate, the bended knees,
> Gilt tipstaves, Tyrian purple, chairs of state,
> Troops of pied butterflies, that flutter still
> In greatness summer, that confirm a prince:
> 'Tis not the unsavoury breath of multitudes,
> Shouting and clapping, with confusèd din;
> That makes a prince. No, Lucio, he's a king,
> A true right king, that dares do aught save wrong,
> Fears nothing mortal, but to be unjust,
> Who is not blown up with the flattering puffs
> Of spungy sycophants: who stands unmov'd
> Despite the jostling of opinion:
> Who can enjoy himself, maugre the throng
> That strive to press his quiet out of him:
> Who sits upon Jove's footstool as I do
> Adoring, not affecting majesty:
> Whose brow is wreathèd with the silver crown
> Of clear content: this, Lucio, is a king,
> And of this empire, every man's possessed
> That's worth his soul.

Sophonisba, which followed, is much less rambling, but as bloody and extravagant. The scene where the witch Erichtho plays Succubus to Syphax, instead of the heroine, and in her form, has touches which partly, but not wholly, redeem its extravagance, and the end is dignified and good. *What You Will*, a comedy of intrigue, is necessarily free from Marston's worst faults, and here the admirable passage quoted above occurs. But the main plot—which turns not only on the courtship, by a mere fribble, of a lady whose husband is supposed to be dead, and who has very complacently forgotten all about him, but on a ridiculous plot to foist a pretender off as the dead husband itself—is simply absurd. The lack of probability, which is the curse of the minor Elizabethan drama, hardly anywhere appears more glaringly. *Parasitaster*, or *The Fawn*, a satirical comedy, is much better, but the jealous hatred of *The Dutch Courtesan* is again not made probable. Then came Marston's completest work in drama, *The Malcontent*, an anticipation, after Elizabethan fashion, of *Le Misanthrope* and *The Plain Dealer*. Though not free from Marston's two chief vices of coarseness and exaggerated cynicism, it is a play of great merit, and much the best thing he has done, though the reconciliation, at the end, of such a husband and such a wife as Piero and Aurelia, between whom there is a chasm of adultery and murder, again lacks verisimilitude. It is to be observed that both in *The Fawn* and *The Malcontent* there are disguised dukes—a fact not testifying any very great originality, even in borrowing. Of *Eastward Ho!* we have already spoken, and it is by no means certain that *The Insatiate Countess* is Marston's. His reputation would not lose much were it not. A *fabliau*-like underplot of the machinations of two light-o'-love citizens' wives against their husbands is not unamusing, but the main story of the Countess Isabella, a modern Messalina (except that she adds cruelty to the vices of Messalina) who alternately courts lovers and induces their successors to assassinate them, is in the worst style of the whole time—the tragedy of lust that is not dignified by the slightest passion, and of murder that is not excused by the slightest poetry of motive or treatment. Though the writing is not of the lowest order, it might have been composed by any one of some thirty or forty writers. It was actually attributed at the time to William Barksted, a minor poet of some power, and I am inclined to think it not Marston's, though my own estimate of him is, as will have been seen, not so high as some other estimates. It is because those estimates appear to me unduly high that I have rather accentuated the expression of my own lower one. For the last three-quarters of a century the language of hyperbole has been but too common about our dramatists, and I have known more than one case in which the extravagant praise bestowed upon them has, when students have come to the works themselves, had a very disastrous effect of disappointment. It is, therefore, all the more necessary to be candid in criticism where criticism seems to be required.

ALGERNON CHARLES SWINBURNE
From "John Marston"
Nineteenth Century, October 1888, pp. 531–47

If justice has never been done, either in his own day or in any after age, to a poet of real genius and original powers, it will generally be presumed, with more or less fairness or unfairness, that this is in great part his own fault. Some perversity or obliquity will be suspected, even if no positive infirmity or deformity can be detected, in his intelligence or in his temperament: some taint or some flaw will be assumed to affect and to vitiate his creative instinct or his spiritual reason. And in the case of John Marston, the friend and foe of Ben Jonson, the fierce and foul-mouthed satirist, the ambitious and overweening tragedian, the scornful and passionate humourist, it is easy for the shallowest and least appreciative reader to perceive the nature and to estimate the weight of such drawbacks or impediments as have so long and so seriously interfered with the due recognition of an independent and remarkable poet. The praise and the blame, the admiration and the distaste excited by his works, are equally just, but are seemingly incompatible: the epithets most exactly appropriate to the style of one scene, one page, one speech in a scene or one passage in a speech, are most ludicrously inapplicable to the next. An anthology of such noble and beautiful excerpts might be collected from his plays, that the reader who should make his first acquaintance with this poet through the deceptive means of so flattering an introduction would be justified in supposing that he had fallen in with a tragic dramatist of the very highest order—with a new candidate for a station in the very foremost rank of English poets. And if the evil star which seems generally to have presided over the literary fortunes of John Marston should misguide the student, on first opening a volume of his works, into some such arid or miry tract of wilderness as too frequently deforms the face of his uneven and irregular demesne, the inevitable sense of disappointment and repulsion which must immediately ensue will too probably discourage a casual explorer from any renewal of his research.

Two of the epithets which Ben Jonson, in his elaborate attack on Marston, selected for ridicule as characteristically grotesque instances of affected and infelicitous innovation—but which nevertheless have taken root in the language, and practically justified their adoption—describe as happily as any that could be chosen to describe the better and the worse quality of his early tragic and satiric style. These words are 'strenuous' and 'clumsy.' It is perpetually, indefatigably, and fatiguingly strenuous; it is too often vehemently, emphatically, and laboriously clumsy. But at its best, when the clumsy and ponderous incompetence of expression which disfigures it is supplanted by a strenuous felicity of ardent and triumphant aspiration, it has notes and touches in the compass of its course not unworthy of Webster or Tourneur or even Shakespeare

himself. Its occasionally exquisite delicacy is as remarkable as its more frequent excess of coarseness, awkwardness, or violent and elaborate extravagance. No sooner has he said anything especially beautiful, pathetic, or sublime, than the evil genius must needs take his turn, exact as it were the forfeit of his bond, impel the poet into some sheer perversity, deface the flow and form of the verse with some preposterous crudity or flatulence of phrase which would discredit the most incapable or the most fantastic novice. And the worst of it all is that he limps or stumbles with either foot alternately. At one moment he exaggerates the license of artificial rhetoric, the strain and swell of the most high-flown and hyperbolical poetic diction; at the next, he falls flat upon the naked level of insignificant or offensive realism.

These are no slight charges; and it is impossible for any just or sober judgment to acquit John Marston of the impeachment conveyed in them. The answer to them is practical and simple: it is that his merits are great enough to outweigh and overshadow them all. Even if his claim to remembrance were merely dependent on the value of single passages, this would suffice to secure him his place of honour in the train of Shakespeare. If his most ambitious efforts at portraiture of character are often faulty at once in colour and in outline, some of his slighter sketches have a freshness and tenderness of beauty which may well atone for the gravest of his certainly not infrequent offences. The sweet constancy and gentle fortitude of a Beatrice and a Mellida remain in the memory more clearly, leave a more lifelike impression of truth on the reader's mind, than the light-headed profligacy and passionate instability of such brainless bloodthirsty wantons as Franceschina and Isabella. In fact, the better characters in Marston's plays are better drawn, less conventional, more vivid and more human than those of the baser sort. Whatever of moral credit may be due to a dramatist who paints virtue better than vice, and has a happier hand at a hero's likeness than at a villain's, must unquestionably be assigned to the author of *Antonio and Mellida*. Piero, the tyrant and traitor, is little more than a mere stage property: like Mendoza in *The Malcontent* and Syphax in *Sophonisba*, he would be a portentous ruffian if he had a little more life in him; he has to do the deeds and express the emotions of a most bloody and crafty miscreant; but it is only now and then that we catch the accent of a real man in his tones of cajolery or menace, dissimulation or triumph. Andrugio, the venerable and heroic victim of his craft and cruelty, is a figure not less living and actual than stately and impressive: the changes of mood from meditation to passion, from resignation to revolt, from tenderness to resolution, which mark the development of the character with the process of the action, though painted rather broadly than subtly and with more of vigour than of care, show just such power of hand and sincerity of instinct as we fail to find in the hot and glaring colours of his rival's monotonous ruffianism. Again, in *The Wonder of Women*, the majestic figures of Massinissa, Gelosso, and Sophonisba stand out in clearer relief than the traitors of the senate, the lecherous malignity of Syphax, or the monstrous profile of the sorceress Erichtho. In this laboured and ambitious tragedy, as in the two parts of *Antonio and Mellida*, we see the poet at his best—and also at his worst. A vehement and resolute desire to give weight to every line and emphasis to every phrase has too often misled him into such brakes and jungles of crabbed and convulsive bombast, of stiff and tortuous exuberance, that the reader in struggling through some of the scenes and speeches feels as though he were compelled to push his way through a cactus hedge: the hot and heavy blossoms of rhetoric blaze and glare out of a thickset fence of jagged barbarisms and exotic monstrosities of metaphor. The straining and sputtering declamation of narrative and oratory scarcely succeeds in expressing through a dozen quaint and far-fetched words or phrases what two or three of the simplest would easily and amply have sufficed to convey. But when the poet is content to deliver his message like a man of this world, we discover with mingled satisfaction, astonishment, and irritation, that he can write when he pleases in a style of the purest and noblest simplicity; that he can make his characters converse in a language worthy of Sophocles when he does not prefer to make them stutter in a dialect worthy of Lycophron. And in the tragedy of *Sophonisba* the display of this happy capacity is happily reserved for the crowning scene of the poem. It would be difficult to find anywhere a more preposterous or disjointed piece of jargon than the speech of Asdrubal at the close of the second act.

> Brook open scorn, faint powers!—
> Make good the camp!—No, fly!—yes, what?—wild
>   rage!—
> To be a prosperous villain! yet some heat, some hold;
> But to burn temples, and yet freeze, O cold!
> Give me some health; now your blood sinks: thus
>   deeds
> I'll nourished rot: without Jove nought succeeds.

And yet this passage occurs in a poem which contains such a passage as the following.

> And now with undismayed resolve behold,
> To save you—you—for honour and just faith
> Are most true gods, which we should much adore—
> With even disdainful vigour I give up
> An abhorred life!—You have been good to me,
> And I do thank thee, heaven. O my stars,
> I bless your goodness, that with breast unstained,
> Faith pure, a virgin wife, tried to my glory,
> I die, of female faith the long-lived story;
> Secure from bondage and all servile harms,
> But more, most happy in my husband's arms.

. . . The laboured eccentricity of style which signalises and disfigures the three chief tragedies or tragic poems of Marston is tempered and subdued to a soberer tone of taste and a more rational choice of expression in his less ambitious and less unequal works. It is almost impossible to imagine any insertion or addition from the hand of Webster which would not be at once obvious to any reader in the text of *Sophonisba* or in either part of *Antonio and Mellida*. Their fierce and irregular magnificence, their feverish and strenuous intemperance of rhetoric, would have been too glaringly in contrast with the sublime purity of the greater poet's thought and style. In the tragicomedy of *The Malcontent*, published two years later than the former and two years earlier than the latter of these poems, if the tone of feeling is but little changed or softened, the language is duly clarified and simplified. 'The Malcontent, (augmented) by Marston, with the additions written by John Webster,' is as coherent, as harmonious, as much of a piece throughout, as was the text of the play in its earlier state. Not all the conscientious art and skill of Webster could have given this uniformity to a work in which the original design and execution had been less in keeping with the bent of his own genius and the accent of his natural style. Sad and stern, not unhopeful or unloving, the spirit of this poem is more in harmony with that of Webster's later tragedies than with that of Marston's previous plays; its accent is sardonic rather than pessimistic, ironical rather than despondent. The plot is neither well conceived nor well constructed; the catastrophe is little less than absurd, especially from the ethical or moral point of view;

the characters are thinly sketched, the situations at once forced and conventional; there are few sorrier or stranger figures in serious fiction than is that of the penitent usurper when he takes to his arms his repentant wife, together with one of her two paramours, in a sudden rapture of forgiving affection; the part which gives the play its name is the only one drawn with any firmness of outline, unless we except that of the malignant and distempered old parasite; but there is a certain interest in the awkward evolution of the story, and there are scenes and passages of singular power and beauty which would suffice to redeem the whole work from condemnation or oblivion, even though it had not the saving salt in it of an earnest and evident sincerity. The brooding anger, the resentful resignation, the impatient spirit of endurance, the bitter passion of disdain, which animate the utterance and direct the action of the hero, are something more than dramatically appropriate; it is as obvious that these are the mainsprings of the poet's own ambitious and dissatisfied intelligence, sullen in its reluctant submission and ardent in its implacable appeal, as that his earlier undramatic satires were the tumultuous and turbid ebullitions of a mood as morbid, as restless, and as honest. Coarse, rough, and fierce as those satires are, inferior alike to Hall's in finish of verse and to Donne's in weight of matter, it seems to me that Dr. Grosart, their first careful and critical editor, is right in claiming for them equal if not superior credit on the score of earnestness. The crude ferocity of their invective has about it a savour of honesty which atones for many defects of literary taste and executive art; and after a more thorough study than such rude and unattractive work seems at first to require or to deserve, the moral and intellectual impression of the whole will not improbably be far more favourable than one resulting from a cursory survey or derived from a casual selection of excerpts. They bring little or no support to a very dubious imputation which has been cast upon their author; the charge of having been concerned in a miserably malignant and stupid attempt at satire under the form of a formless and worthless drama called *Histriomastix*;[1] though his partnership in another anonymous play—a semi-romantic semi-satirical comedy called *Jack Drum's Entertainment*—is very much more plausibly supportable by comparison of special phrases as well as of general style with sundry mannerisms as well as with the habitual turn of speech in Marston's acknowledged comedies. There is a certain incomposite and indigested vigour in the language of this play which makes the attribution of a principal share in its authorship neither utterly discreditable to Marston nor absolutely improbable in itself; and the satire aimed at Ben Jonson, if not especially relevant to the main action, is at all events less incongruous and preposterous in its relation to the rest of the work than the satirical or controversial part of Dekker's *Satiromastix*. But on the whole, if this play be Marston's, it seems to me the rudest and the poorest he has left us, except perhaps the comedy of *What You Will*; in which several excellent and suggestive situations are made less of than they should have been, and a good deal of promising comic invention is wasted for want of a little more care and a little more conscience in cultivation of material and composition of parts. The satirical references to Jonson are more pointed and effective in this comedy than in either of the two plays last mentioned; but its best claim to remembrance is to be sought in the admirable soliloquy which relates the seven years' experience of the student and his spaniel. Marston is too often heaviest when he would and should be lightest, owing apparently to a certain infusion of contempt for light comedy as something rather beneath him, not wholly worthy of his austere and ambitious capacity. The parliament of pages in this play is a diverting interlude of farce, though a mere irrelevance and impediment to the action; but the boys are less amusing than their compeers in the anonymous comedy of *Sir Giles Goosecap*, first published in the year preceding: a work of genuine humour and invention, excellent in style if somewhat infirm in construction, for a reprint of which we are indebted to the previous care of Marston's present editor. Far be it from me to intrude on the barren and boggy province of hypothetical interpretation and controversial commentary; but I may observe in passing that the original of Simplicius Faber in *What You Will* must surely have been the same hanger-on or sycophant of Ben Jonson's who was caricatured by Dekker in his *Satiromastix* under the name of Asinius Bubo. The gross assurance of self-complacent duncery, the apish arrogance and imitative dogmatism of reflected self-importance and authority at second hand, are presented in either case with such identity of tone and colouring that we can hardly imagine the satire to have been equally applicable to two contemporary satellites of the same imperious and masterful egoist.

That the same noble poet and high-souled humourist was not responsible for the offence given to Caledonian majesty in the comedy of *Eastward Ho*, the authentic word of Jonson would be sufficient evidence; but I am inclined to think it a matter of almost certain likelihood—if not of almost absolute proof—that Chapman was as innocent as Jonson of a jest for which Marston must be held responsible—though scarcely, I should imagine, blamable at the present day by the most rabid of Scottish provincialists. In the last scene of *The Malcontent* a court lady says to an infamous old hanger-on of the court—'And is not Signor St. Andrew a gallant fellow now?' to which the old hag replies—'Honour and he agree as well together as a satin suit and wollen stockings.' The famous passage in the comedy which appeared a year later must have been far less offensive to the most nervous patriotism than this; and the impunity of so gross an insult, so obviously and obtrusively offered, to the new knightships and lordships of King James's venal chivalry and parasitic nobility, may naturally have encouraged the satirist to repeat his stroke next year—and must have astounded his retrospection, when he found himself in prison, and under threat of worse than imprisonment, together with his unoffending associates in an admirable and inoffensive comedy. It is impossible to suppose that he would not have come forward to assume the responsibility of his own words—as it is impossible to imagine that Jonson or Chapman would have given up his accomplice to save himself. But the law of the day would probably have held them all responsible alike.

In the same year as *Eastward Ho* appeared the best and completest piece of work which we owe to the single hand of Marston. A more brilliant and amusing play than *The Dutch Courtesan*, better composed, better constructed, and better written, it would be difficult to discover among the best comic and romantic works of its incomparable period. The slippery and sanguinary strumpet who gives its name to the play is sketched with such admirable force and freedom of hand as to suggest the existence of an actual model who may unconsciously have sat for the part under the scrutiny of eyes as keen and merciless as ever took notes for a savagely veracious caricature—or for an unscrupulously moral exposure. The jargon in which her emotions are expressed is as Shakespearean in its breadth and persistency as that of Dr. Caius or Captain Fluellen; but the reality of those emotions is worthy of a less farcical vehicle for the expression of such natural craft and passion. The sisters, Beatrice and Crispinella, seem at first too evidently imitated from the characters of Aurelia and Phœnixella in the earliest surviving comedy of Ben Jonson; but the

'comedy daughter,' as Dickens (or Skimpole) would have expressed it, is even more coarsely and roughly drawn than in the early sketch of the more famous dramatist. On the other hand, it must be allowed—though it may not be recognised without a certain sense of surprise—that the nobler and purer type of womanhood or girlhood which we owe to the hand of Marston is far above comparison with any which has been accomplished or achieved by the studious and vehement elaboration of Ben Jonson's. The servility of subservience which that great dramatist exacts from his typically virtuous women—from the abject and anæmic wife of a Corvino or a Fitzdottrel—is a quality which could not coexist with the noble and loving humility of Marston's Beatrice. The admirable scene in which she is brought face to face with the impudent pretentions of the woman who asserts herself to have been preferred by the betrothed lover of the expectant bride is as pathetic and impressive as it is lifelike and original; and even in the excess of gentleness and modesty which prompts the words—'I will love you the better; I cannot hate what he affected'—there is nothing less noble or less womanly than in the subsequent reply to the harlot's repeated taunts and inventions of insult. 'He did not ill not to love me, but sure he did not well to mock me: gentle minds will pity, though they cannot love; yet peace and my love sleep with him.' The powerful soliloquy which closes the scene expresses no more than the natural emotion of the man who has received so lovely a revelation of his future bride's invincible and single-hearted love.

> Cannot that woman's evil, jealousy,
> Despite disgrace, nay, which is worse, contempt,
> Once stir thy faith?

Coarse as is often the language of Marston's plays and satires, the man was not coarse-minded—not gross of spirit nor base of nature—who could paint so delicately and simply a figure so beautiful in the tenderness of its purity.

The farcical underplot of this play is worthy of Molière in his broader mood of farce. Hardly any Jourdain or Pourceaugnac, any Georges Dandin or Comtesse d'Escarbagnas of them all, undergoes a more grotesque experience or plays a more ludicrous part than is devised for Mr. and Mrs. Mulligrub by the ingenuity of the indefatigable Cocledemoy—a figure worthy to stand beside any of the tribe of Marscarille as *fourbum imperator*. The animation and variety of inventive humour which keep the reader's laughing attention awake and amused throughout these adventurous scenes of incident and intrigue are not more admirable than the simplicity and clearness of evolution or composition which recall and rival the classic masterpieces of Latin and French comedy. There is perhaps equal fertility of humour, but there certainly is not equal harmony of structure, in the play which Marston published next year—*Parasitaster, or The Fawn*; a name probably suggested by that of Ben Jonson's *Poetaster*, in which the author had himself been the subject of a greater man's rage and ridicule. The wealth and the waste of power displayed and paraded in this comedy are equally admirable and lamentable; for the brilliant effect of its various episodes and interludes is not more obvious than the eclipse of the central interest, the collapse of the serious design, which results from the agglomeration of secondary figures and the alternations of perpetual byplay. Three or four better plays might have been made out of the materials here hurled and huddled together into one. The Isabelle of Molière is not more amusing or more delightful in her audacity of resource, in her combination of loyalty with duplicity, innocence with intrigue, than the daring and single-hearted young heroine of this play; but the *École des maris* is not encumbered with such a crowd of minor interests and characters, of subordinate humours and complications, as the reader of Marston's comedy finds interposed and intruded between his attention and the main point of interest. He would fain see more of Dulcimel and Tiberio, the ingenious and enterprising princess, the ingenuous and responsive prince; he is willing to see as much as is shown him of their fathers, the masquerading philosopher and the self-complacent dupe; Granuffo, the patrician prototype of Captain John Bunsby, may take a seat in the chambers of his memory beside the commander of the *Cautious Clara*; the humours of a jealous foul-minded fool and a somewhat audaciously virtuous wife may divert him by the inventive and vigorous exposure of their various revolutions and results; but the final impression is one of admiring disappointment and possibly ungrateful regret that so much energetic satire and so much valuable time should have been spent on the somewhat nauseous follies of 'sickly knights' and 'vicious braggarts,' that the really admirable and attractive parts of the design are cramped and crowded out of room for the due development of their just and requisite proportions.

A more eccentric, uneven, and incomposite piece of work than *The Insatiate Countess* it would be difficult to find in English or in other literature. The opening scene is picturesque and impressive; the closing scene of the serious part is noble and pathetic; but the intervening action is of a kind which too often aims at the tragic and hits the burlesque. The incessant inconstancy of passion which hurries the fantastic heroine through such a miscellaneous multitude of improvised intrigues is rather a comic than a tragic motive for the conduct of a play; and the farcical rapidity with which the puppets revolve makes it impossible for the most susceptible credulity to take any real interest or feel any real belief in the perpetual rotation of their feverish moods and motives, their irrational doings and sufferings. The humour of the underplot constantly verges on horseplay, and is certainly neither delicate nor profound; but there is matter enough for mirth in it to make the reader duly grateful for the patient care and admirable insight which Mr. Bullen has brought to bear upon the really formidable if apparently trivial task of reducing the chaotic corruption and confusion of the text to reasonable form and comprehensible order. William Barkstead, a narrative poet of real merit, and an early minister at the shrine of Shakespeare, has been credited with the authorship of this play: I am inclined to agree with the suggestion of its latest editor—its first editor in any serious sense of the word—that both he and Marston may have had a hand in it. His *Myrrha* belongs to the same rather morbid class of poems as Shakespeare's *Venus and Adonis* and Marston's *Pygmalion's Image*. Of the three, Shakespeare's is not more certainly the finest in occasional touches of picturesque poetry than it is incomparably the most offensive to good taste and natural instinct on the score of style and treatment. Marlowe's *Hero and Leander* can only be classed with these elaborate studies of sensual aberration or excess by those 'who can see no difference between Titian and French photographs.' (I take leave, for once in a way, to quote from a private letter—long since addressed to the present commentator by the most illustrious of writers on art.)

. . . His rank is high in his own regiment; and the colonel of that regiment is Ben Jonson. At first sight he may seem rather to belong to that brighter and more famous one which has Webster among its captains, Dekker among its lieutenants, Heywood among its privates and Shakespeare at its head. Nor did he by any means follow the banner of Jonson with such automatic fidelity as that imperious martinet of genius was wont to exact from those who came to be 'sealed of the tribe of Ben.' A rigid critic—a critic who should push rigidity to the verge of injustice—might say that he was one of those recruits in literature whose misfortune it is to fall between two stools—to halt between two courses. It is certain that he never thoroughly mastered either the cavalry drill of Shakespeare or the infantry drill of Jonson. But it is no less certain that the few finest passages which attest the power and the purity of his genius as a poet are above comparison with any such examples of tragic poetry as can be attributed with certainty or with plausibility to the hand which has left us no acknowledged works in that line except *Sejanus His Fall* and *Catiline His Conspiracy*. It is superfluous to add that *Volpone* was an achievement only less far out of his reach than *Hamlet*. But this is not to say or to imply that he does not deserve an honourable place among English poets. His savage and unblushing violence or vehemence of satire has no taint of gloating or morbid prurience in the turbid flow of its fitful and furious rhetoric. The restless rage of his invective is as far as human utterance can find itself from the cynical infidelity of an Iago. Of him we may say with more rational confidence what was said of that more potent and more truculent satirist:

> An honest man he is, and hates the slime
> That sticks on filthy deeds.

We may wish that he had not been so much given to trampling and stamping on that slime as to evoke such malodorous exhalations as infect the lower and shallower reaches of the river down which he proceeds to steer us with so strenuous a hand. But it is in a spirit of healthy disgust, not of hankering delight, that he insists on calling the indignant attention of his readers to the baser and fouler elements of natural or social man as displayed in the vicious exuberance or eccentricity of affectation or of self-indulgence. His real interest and his real sympathies are reserved for the purer and nobler types of womanhood and manhood. In his first extant tragedy, crude and fierce and coarse and awkward as is the general treatment of character and story, the sketch of Mellida is genuinely beautiful in its pathetic and subdued simplicity; though certainly no such tender and gentle figure was ever enchased in a stranger or less attractive setting. There is an odd mixture of care and carelessness in the composition of his plays which is exemplified by the fact that another personage in the first part of the same dramatic poem was announced to reappear in the second part as a more important and elaborate figure; but this second part opens with the appearance of his assassin, red-handed from the murder: and the two parts were published in the same year. And indeed, except in *Parasitaster* and *The Dutch Courtesan*, a general defect in his unassisted plays is the headlong confusion of plot, the helterskelter violence of incident, which would hardly have been looked for in the work of a professional and practised hand. *What You Will* is modestly described as 'a slight-writ play:' but slight and slovenly are not the same thing; nor is simplicity the equivalent of incoherence. Marston is apt to be heaviest when he aims at being lightest; not, like Ben Jonson, through a laborious and punctilious excess of conscience which is unwilling to let slip any chance of effect, to let pass any detail of presentation; but rather, we are tempted to suspect, through a sardonic sense of scorn for the perfunctory task on which his ambitious and impatient hand is for the time employed. Now and then, however—or perhaps it would be more accurate to say once or twice—a gayer note is struck with a ligher touch than usual: as for instance in the excellent parody of Lyly put into the mouth of an idiot in the first scene of the fifth act of the first part of *Antonio and Mellida*. 'You know, the stone called *lapis*, the nearer it comes to the fire, the hotter it is; and the bird which the geometricians call *avis*, the further it is from the earth, the nearer it is to the heaven; and love, the nigher it is to the flame, the more remote (there's a word, remote!) the more remote it is from the frost.' Shakespeare and Scott have condescended to caricature the style or the manner of the inventor of euphuism: I cannot think their burlesque of his elaborate and sententious triviality so happy, so humorous, or so exact as this. But it is not on his capacity as a satirist or humourist, it is on his occasionally triumphant success as a serious or tragic poet, that the fame of Marston rests assuredly established. His intermittent power to rid himself for awhile of his besetting faults, and to acquire or assume for a moment the very excellences most incompatible with these, is as extraordinary for the completeness as for the transitory nature of its successful effects. The brief fourth act of *Antonio and Mellida* is the most astonishing and bewildering production of belated human genius that ever distracted or discomfited a student. Verses more delicately beautiful followed by verses more simply majestic than these have rarely if ever given assurance of eternity to the fame of any but a great master in song.

> Conceit you me: as having clasped a rose
> Within my palm, the rose being ta'en away,
> My hand retains a little breath of sweet,
> So may man's trunk, his spirit slipped away,
> Hold still a faint perfume of his sweet guest.
> 'Tis so: for when discursive powers fly out,
> And roam in progress through the bounds of heaven,
> The soul itself gallops along with them
> As chieftain of this wingèd troop of thought,
> Whilst the dull lodge of spirit standeth waste
> Until the soul return.

Then follows a passage of sheer gibberish; then a dialogue of the noblest and most dramatic eloquence; then a chaotic alternation of sense and nonsense, bad Italian and mixed English, abject farce and dignified rhetoric, spirited simplicity and bombastic jargon. It would be more and less than just to take this act as a sample or a symbol of the author's usual way of work; but I cannot imagine that a parallel to it, for evil and for good, could be found in the works of any other writer.

The Muse of this poet is no maiden of such pure and august beauty as enthralls us with admiration of Webster's; she has not the gipsy brightness and vagrant charms of Dekker's, her wild soft glance, and flashing smiles and fading traces of tears; she is no giddy girl, but a strong woman with fine irregular features, large and luminous eyes, broad intelligent forehead, eyebrows so thick and close together that detraction might call her beetle-browed, powerful mouth and chin, fine contralto voice (with an occasional stammer), expression alternately repellent and attractive, but always striking and sincere. No one has ever found her lovely; but there are times when she has a fascination of her own which fairer and more famous singers might envy her; and the friends she makes are as sure to be constant as she, for all her occasional roughness and coarseness, is sure to be loyal in the main to the nobler instincts of her kind and the loftier traditions of her sisterhood.

Notes

1. This abortion of letters is such a very mooncalf, begotten by malice on idiocy, that no human creature above the intellectual level of its author will ever dream of attempting to decipher the insignificant significance which may possibly—though improbably—be latent under the opaque veil of its inarticulate virulence.

EDWARD FAIRFAX

c. 1575–1635

Edward Fairfax, the illegitimate son of Sir Thomas Fairfax of Denton, was born in Leeds around 1575. He may have attended Clare Hall, Cambridge, and is known to have been a favorite of his father's. Fairfax's translation of Tasso's *Gerusalemme liberata*, entitled *Godfrey of Bulloigne or the Recoverie of Jerusalem* (1600), is noted for its accuracy and poetic creativity. Fairfax was also the author of twelve eclogues, of which only two survive. An elegy written upon the death of James I was published in the 1848 collection *The Fairfax Correspondence*. Fairfax narrated the events surrounding his family's contact with witchcraft in *Daemonologia*. In this chronicle Fairfax describes the trial against the witches accused by Fairfax's daughters of trying to possess them. Fairfax died at Newhall, his family house in Fewston, Yorkshire, on January 27, 1635.

One of the most judicious, elegant, and haply in his time, most approved of English Translatours, both for his choice of so worthily extoll'd a heroic poet as Torquato Tasso; as for the exactness of his version, in which he is judg'd by some to have approved himself no less a poet than in what he hath written of his own genius.—EDWARD PHILLIPS, *Theatrum Poetarum Anglicanorum*, 1675

Milton has acknowledg'd to me, that *Spencer* was his Original; and many besides my self have heard our famous *Waller* own, that he deriv'd the Harmony of his Numbers from the *Godfrey of Bulloign*, which was turn'd into *English* by Mr. *Fairfax*. —JOHN DRYDEN, "Preface" to *Fables*, 1700

Edward Fairfax, Esq; a gentleman of so much Merit, that he eminently deserves to be rank'd among the First of our *English*

Writers; yet has He hitherto been treated with so much Neglect, to say no Worse, That no one Author has afforded us a tolerable Sketch of his Life; or given Themselves even the Trouble to make the slightest Enquiry after Him.—*Philips* so far overlooks him, that he was forc'd to crowd him into his Supplement, and his Transcriber *Winstanly*, does, in a Manner, the same, by postponing him till after the Earl of *Rochester*. Sir *Thomas Pope Blunt* makes no mention of him at all: And Mr. *Jacob* informs us he wrote in the Reign of King *Charles* the *First*; tho' He dedicates his Translation of *Tasso* to Queen *Elizabeth*: Indeed all that name him, do him the Justice to allow he was an accomplish'd Genius; but then 'tis in so cool, and careless a Manner, as plainly indicates they were very little acquainted with the Merit they prais'd.—'Twas impossible for the great Mr. *Dryden* to be so insensible; and, accordingly we find him introducing *Spenser*, and *Fairfax*, almost on the Level, as the leading Authors of their Times; nay tacitly yielding the Palm in Point of Musick to the last; by asserting, That *Waller* confess'd He ow'd the Harmony of his Numbers to the *Godfrey* of *Bulloign*, of *Fairfax*.—In Fact, this Gentleman is the only Writer down to *D'Avenant*, that needs no Apology to be made for him, on Account of the Age he lived in.—His Diction being, generally speaking, so pure, so elegant, and full of Graces, and the Turn of his Lines so perfectly Melodious, that I hardly believe the Original *Italian*, has greatly the Advantage in either: Nor could any Author, in my Opinion, be justify'd for attempting *Tasso* anew, as long as his Translation can be read.

Mr. *Fairfax* was natural Son of Sir *Thomas Fairfax* of *Denton*, and natural Brother to Sir *Thomas Fairfax*, the first who was created Baron of *Cameron*. His younger Brother was Knighted; and slain at the memorable Siege of *Ostend*, 1601. of which Place he was some Time Governor.

Whom he marry'd, is not on Record; or in what Circumstances he liv'd; But 'tis to be presum'd, his Father took Care to support him in a Manner suitable to his own Quality, and his Son's Merit. He being always stil'd *E. Fairfax*, Esq; of *New-Hall* in *Fuystone*, in the Forest of *Knaseborough*:—The Year he dy'd in, is likewise uncertain; and the last we hear of him, is, that He was living in 1631: which argu'd that he was then pretty well advanc'd in Years; and, as I suppose, gave occasion to the many Mistakes that have been made, as to the Time he wrote in.

His eldest Son was *William* a very learned, but splenetick Man; who was a Kind of a Tutor; or rather an intimate Friend to Mr. *Stanley*, who publish'd the *Lives of the Philosophers*; The greatest Part of the Work, as well as the Notes on *Euripides* truly belonging to Mr. *W. Fairfax*; tho' his Modesty, and Friendship declin'd the Reputation.

Mr. *Fairfax*, the Father, beside the Translation of *Godfrey of Bulloigne*, wrote the History of *Edward* the *Black Prince*, and certain witty Eclogues, which are yet in Manuscript, tho' by the Indulgence of the Family (from whom I had likewise the Honour of these Memoirs) I am permitted to oblige the World with a Specimen of their Beauties: A Favour that I am proud to say will, in one Sense however, make this Collection compleat, since it was impossible it should be so without. He wrote also a Book call'd *Dæmonologie*, in which, tho' the Story is particular, He shows a great deal of ancient Reading and Knowledge: It is still a MS. and, in the Beginning, He gives this Character of Himself.

"I am in Religion, neither a fantastick Puritan, nor superstitious Papist, but so settled in Conscience that I have the sure Ground of God's Word to warrant all I believe, and the commendable Ordinances of our *English* Church to approve all I practise: In which Course I live a faithful Christian and an Obedient, and so teach my Family."—ELIZABETH COOPER, *The Muses Library*, 1737, pp. 342–44

Fairfax has translated Tasso with an elegance and ease, and at the same time with an exactness, which, for that age, are surprising.—DAVID HUME, *History of England*, 1754–62

I question whether any late attempt to naturalize the beautiful epic of Tasso can be considered as superior, either in energy or fidelity, to this old but admirable version. In many places the diction of Fairfax is peculiarly pleasing; and he greatly excels in transfusing the rural imagery of his author, and which sometimes receives even improvement from his colouring.
—NATHAN DRAKE, *Literary Hours*, 1798, No. 28

His translation of the Jerusalem was published when he was a young man, was inscribed to Queen Elizabeth, and forms one of the glories of her reign.—THOMAS CAMPBELL, *Specimens of the British Poets*, 1819

Fairfax's Tasso has been more praised, and is better known. Campbell has called it, in rather strong terms, "one of the glories of Elizabeth's reign." It is not the first version of the Jerusalem, one very literal and prosaic having been made by Carew in 1594. That of Fairfax, if it does not represent the grace of its original, and deviates also too much from its sense, is by no means deficient in spirit and vigour. It has been considered as one of the earliest works, in which the obsolete English, which had not been laid aside in the days of Sackville, and which Spenser affected to preserve, gave way to a style not much differing, at least in point of single words and phrases, from that of the present age. But this praise is equally due to Daniel, to Drayton, and to others of the later Elizabethan poets. The translation of Ariosto by Sir John Harrington, in 1591, is much inferior.—HENRY HALLAM, *Introduction to the Literature of Europe*, 1837–39, Pt. 2, Ch. 5, Par. 74

HENRY MORLEY
From *English Writers*
1893, Volume 10, pp. 458–63

Edward Fairfax, of Newhall, in the parish of Faiston, Yorkshire, was of a Yorkshire family and married to a Yorkshire woman. He was born at Leeds. His father was Sir Thomas Fairfax, of Denton and Nun Appleton and Bilborough, in Yorkshire, whose eldest son, born at Bilborough, was Thomas, first Lord Fairfax of Cameron in the Scottish peerage. Thomas was born in 1560, and lived to the age of eighty; but there is no record of the birth-date of his brother Edward, who died five years before him. Edward was very serviceable to his eldest brother, for he lived a studious life upon his own little estate near by, as one of the family (though his legitimacy has been doubted), and had looked after the education of his brother's children. He had also the charge of his brother's affairs while Thomas was much away on diplomatic and military service in the reign of Queen Elizabeth. It was not till after the accession of James I. that Thomas, first Lord Fairfax, settled down at Denton, where he gave attention to the breeding of his horses and carefully defined the duties of his servants.

Edward Fairfax married a sister of Walter Laycock, of Copmanthorpe, in Yorkshire, and had several children of his own. His translation of Tasso was his chief work. It was first published in 1600, towards the end of the reign of Elizabeth, and dedicated to the queen. It was valued greatly by King James, who gave it a first place in English poetry. It is said to have solaced Charles I. in his confinement, and Dryden records that he and others had heard Waller say that he "derived the harmony of his numbers from *Godfrey of Bulloigne*."

Edward Fairfax wrote also twelve eclogues, of which two or three have been printed and the rest are lost. He died in 1635, and was buried at Faiston on the twenty-seventh of January. His wife survived him thirteen years. . . .

Fairfax, in his translation of the first five cantos, shows now and then that he has read Carew's translation; but on the whole, here, as throughout, he takes his own way, and writes like an English poet of his day, according to the fashion of his day, but with addition of the clearest evidence of his delight in Spenser. Many a phrase and image used in the elaboration of his stanzas has been suggested to Fairfax by his study of *The Faerie Queene*, which was a new poem while he wrote—its first three books published in 1590, its next three in 1596; Fairfax's

Godfrey of Bulloigne in 1600. He translates, indeed, stanza for stanza, so that the numbering of his stanzas corresponds with that of the original. But, like Harington in his *Orlando*, he gives in his own way the sense of each stanza, or what he takes it to be, when he is doubtful, or goes, unconscious of error, more or less astray as to the meaning of a sentence. Spenser had planned his great poem in early life to be a spiritual allegory, with a poem of knights, ladies, and enchantments, that was to have outward resemblance to the *Orlando* of Ariosto; only it was to be "in sage and solemn tunes,"

> Of turneys and of trophies hung,
> Of forests and enchantments drear,
> Where more is meant than meets the ear.

While Spenser was planning and beginning to write, Tasso's *Godfrey*, called afterwards *Jerusalem Delivered*, came, as a new poem, into his hands. His pleasure in it was declared by touches of paraphrase and imitations in his verse. Of a beautiful song in the gardens of Armida he gave a poet's translation in the last canto of his second book, where the description of the gardens of Acrasia owed many a touch to recollections of Tasso. In such passages Fairfax translated with Spenser in his mind.

Fairfax's worst blunders, or seeming blunders, in translation do little damage to the spirit of his text. Thus, in canto iii. stanza 32, the commonest inflexion of a familiar verb, *volgere*, "to turn," which, of course, he knew, and, here as elsewhere, has translated rightly, slips through his eye into his mind the name of a great river, and we have this version of the lines—

> Tàl gran tauro talor ne l'ampio agone,
> *Se volge il corno* ai cani ond' è seguito,
> S'arretran essi; e s'a fuggir si pone,
> Ciascun ritorna a seguitarlo ardito.

> As the swift ure, by *Volga's* rolling flood,
> Chased through the plains the mastiff curs toforn,
> Flies to the succour of some neighbour wood,
> And often *turns against his* dreadful *horn*
> Against the dogs imbrued in sweat and blood,
> That bite not till the beast to flight return.

Here there is no blunder at all. *Se volge il corno* is translated; the image is correctly given, although part is amplified and part condensed. We only find that the word *volge* suggested to Fairfax his addition of the river. In and after Elizabeth's time river names were much used as ornaments of verse.

The English of Fairfax's *Godfrey* has, in pronunciation and vocabulary, some ring of the north. Fairfax interspersed old words in his translation to grace an antique tale, for the same reason that caused Spenser to use them in *The Faerie Queene*; he had also, in this respect, by imitation and by likeness of experience—for Spenser's family was also of the north of England—a Spenserian vocabulary. He often uses the prefix "y" for the old "ge" in past participles, as "yclept," "ypraised." Sometimes he adds the "n" of the infinitive where it had been dropped by the usage of his time—"Two barons bold approachen gan the place;" "Do thou permit the chosen ten to gone." He has old plurals in "n," "eyne," "fone," "treen."

Sometimes he drops, sometimes retains, the "n" of a past participle, writing "know" for "known," "bounden" for "bound." Very commonly he takes the old indicative-present of the verb "to be," using "been" for "are." Now and then he drops the sign of a weak verb ending in "t."

As translator, according to the fashion of his day in England, Fairfax turns many a direct and simple sentence of his original into metaphor or simile, interweaves mythological and scriptural allusions, or finds emphasis in a homely English proverb, as "A stick to beat the dog he long had sought," or "Doubtless the county thought his bread well baken."

With all this, Fairfax found that the vowel-endings on Italian add many syllables that lengthen the expression of a thought while making it more musical. Chaucer translated eight lines into seven. Fairfax, by the compactness of his style, was led to devices of expansion as well as of addition. He set up triplets of words where Tasso had but one, and sometimes gave an air of condensed energy to a line that was in fact one bold expansion by a string of words.[1]

Iteration is part of a speaker's art, because the spoken word has wings, and may not always be caught as it is uttered. In our Church Service its use is recognised by frequent doublings of nouns and verbs, as when we "acknowledge and confess our manifold sins and iniquities;" and the form of writing is not ill-suited to a poem that one may imagine planned for recitation. Fairfax uses it to excess, but there is so much robust vigour in his way of suiting to his own time and country the contents of each successive stanza, and his own music is so clear and tuneful, that his translation still holds high place in our literature among the books "that so did please Eliza and our James," and have not lost their pleasantness by lapse of time.

Notes

1. When Tasso simply wrote (xiv. 1)—

> E i venticelli dibattendo l'ali
> Lusingavano il sonno de' mortali,

Fairfax translated—

> And sweet-breathed Zephyr on his spreading wings,
> Sleep, ease, repose, rest, peace, and quiet brings.

When Tasso wrote—

> China poi, disse, e gli additò la terra,
> Gli occhi a ciò che quel globo ultimo serra,

Fairfax, having used up the rest of the matter of the stanza in five lines, and having three to fill, translated—

> Then bend thine eyes on yonder earth and mould,
> All in that mass, that globe and compass see,
> Land, sea, spring, fountain, man, beast, grass, and tree.

And as an example of the frequent triplets in Fairfax, which became a favourite device, we may take the translation of Tasso's—

> Ben sono in parte altr' uom da quel ch'io fui;
> Ch' or da lui pendo, e mi rivolgo a lui.

> Thus hath he changed my thoughts, my heart, my will,
> And rules mine art, my knowledge, and my skill.

RICHARD CORBETT

1582–1635

Richard Corbett was born in Ewell, Surrey, in 1582. The son of a gardener, Corbett attended the Westminster School, London, and entered Broadgates Hall, now Pembroke College, Oxford, in 1598. In 1599 he moved to Christ Church, Oxford, beginning a thirty-year association with that college. He earned a B.A. in 1602, an M.A. in 1605, and a B.D. in 1617. Corbett took holy orders in 1613 and held various preferments. He was Chaplain to James I and Dean of Christ Church, Oxford. Eventually he became bishop of Oxford in 1628, later holding the office of bishop at Norwich in 1632.

Corbett's poetry circulated widely during his lifetime in manuscript. In 1647 the first collection of his verse, *Certain Elegant Poems*, was published by John Donne the younger. The following year a second collection, *Poetica Stromata; or, A Collection of Sundry Pieces*, appeared. Corbett's longest poem, "Iter Boreale," celebrated a journey through the Midlands. Another of Corbett's well-known poems, "The Faeryes Farewell," actually was meant to be sung as a ballad. Corbett died on July 28, 1635, and was buried in the Norwich Cathedral.

Richard Corbet, D.D., was the son of Vincent Corbet, who was a Gardner at Twicknam. He was a Westminster scholar; old Parson Bussey, of Alscott in Warwickshire, went to schoole with him. He would say that he was a very handsome man, but something apt to abuse, and a Coward.

He was a Student of Christ Church in Oxford. He was very facetious, and a good Fellowe. One time, he and some of his acquaintance being merry at Fryar Bacon's study (where was good liquor sold) they were drinking on the Leads of the house, and one of the scholars was a sleepe, and had a paire of goode silke stockings on. Dr. Corbet (then M.A. if not B.D.) gott a paire of Cizers and cutt them full of little Holes, but when the other awaked, and perceived how and by whom he was abused, he did chastise him, and made him pay for them.

After he was Doctor of Divinity, he sang Ballads at the Crosse at Abingdon on a market-day. He and some of his Camerades were at the Taverne by the Crosse (which, by the way, was then the finest of England; I remember it when I was a Freshman; it was admirable curious Gothique Architecture, and fine Figures in the niches; 'twas one of those built by King Edward I for his Queen). The Ballad-singer complayned he had no custome; he could not putt-off his Ballads. The jolly Dr. putts-off his Gowne, and putts-on the Ballad-singer's Leathern jacket, and being a handsome man, and had a rare full Voice, he presently vended a great many, and had a great Audience.

He was made Deane of Christ Church. He had good Interest with great men, as you may find in his Poems, and with the then great Favourite, the Duke of Bucks. His excellent Witt was lettres of recommendation to him. I have forgott the story, but at the same time that Dr. Fell thought to have carried it, Dr. Corbett putt a pretty trick on, to lett him take a journey on purpose to London for it, when he had already the Graunt of it. His Poems are pure naturall Witt, delightfull and easie.

He preached a Sermon before the King at Woodstock (I suppose King James) and no doubt with a very good grace; but it happened that he was out, on which occasion there were made these verses:

> A reverend Deane,
> With his Ruffe starch't cleane,
>   Did preach before the King:
> In his Band-string was spied
> A Ring that was tyed,
>   Was not that a pritty thing?

> The Ring without doubt
> Was the thing putt him out,
>   So oft hee forgot what was next;
> For all that were there,
> On my conscience dare sweare
>   That he handled it more than his Text.

His conversation was extreme pleasant. Dr. Stubbins was one of his Cronies; he was a jolly fatt Dr. and a very good house-keeper; parson in Oxfordshire. As Dr. Corbet and he were riding in Lob Lane in wett weather ('tis an extraordinary deepe, dirty lane) the coach fell; and Dr. Corbet sayd that Dr. Stubbins was up to the elbowes in mud, he was up to the elbowes in Stubbins.

He was made Bishop of Oxford, and I have heard that he had an admirable, grave and venerable aspect.

One time, as he was Confirming, the country-people pressing in to see the Ceremonie, sayd he, *Beare off there, or I'le confirm yee with my Staffe*. Another time, being to lay his hand on the head of a man very bald, he turns to his chaplaine, Lushington, and sayd, *Some Dust, Lushington*, (to keepe his hand from slipping). There was a man with a great venerable Beard: sayd the Bishop, *You, behind the Beard*.

His Chaplain, Dr. Lushington, was a very learned and ingeniose man, and they loved one another. The Bishop sometimes would take the key of the wine-cellar, and he and his Chaplaine would goe and lock themselves in and be merry. Then first he layes downe his Episcopall hat—*There lyes the Doctor.* Then he putts off his gowne—*There lyes the Bishop.* Then 'twas, *Here's to thee, Corbet*, and *Here's to thee, Lushington.*

He married Alice Hutton, whom 'twas sayd he bigott. She was a very beautifull woman, and so was her mother. He had a son that went to schoole at Westminster, with Ned Bagshawe: a very handsome youth, but he is run out of all, and goes begging up and downe to Gentlemen.

His Antagonist, Dr. Price the Anniversarist, was made Deane of Hereford. Dr. Watts, Canon of that church, told me that this Deane was a mighty Pontificall proud man, and that one time when they went in Procession about the Cathedral church, he would not doe it the usually way in his surplice, hood, etc., on foot, but rode on a mare thus habited, with the Common prayer booke in his hand, reading. A stone horse happend to breake loose, and smelt the mare, and ran and leapt her, and held the Deverend Deane all the time so hard in his

Embraces, that he could not gett off till the horse had done his bussinesse. But he would never ride in procession afterwards.

The last words he sayd were, *Good night, Lushington.* —JOHN AUBREY, "Richard Corbet," *Brief Lives*, 1669–96

Richard Corbet was born of a genteel family at Ewel in Surrey, son of

> Vincent Corbet farther known
> By Poynter's name, than by his own.

And after he had spent some years in Westminster school, was sent to Broadgate's hall in Lent-term 1597–8, aged 15, and in the year after was made student of Ch. Ch. In 1605, he proceeded M. of A. being then esteemed one of the most celebrated wits in the university, as his poems, jests, romantic fancies and exploits, which he made and perform'd extempore, shew'd. Afterwards entring into holy orders, he became a most quaint preacher and therefore much followed by ingenious men. At length being made one of the chaplains to his maj. K. Jam. I. (who highly valued him for his fine fancy and preaching) he was by his favour promoted to the deanery of Ch. Ch. in Oxon. an. 1620, being then D. of D. senior student of that house, vicar of Cassington near to Woodstock in Oxfordshire, and prebendary of Bedminster Secunda in the church of Sarun. At length upon the translation of Dr. Howson to the see of Durham; he "by the interest of the earl of Dorset (to make way for his deserving chaplain, Dr. Duppa to be dean of that church) obtain'd" the king's letters to be elected bishop of Oxon, 30 July 1629, and was afterwards consecrated at Lambeth 19 Octob. and installed in his chair 3 Nov. following. Upon the translation of Dr. White to Ely, he was elected bishop of Norwich 7 Apr. 1632, and had restitution of the temporalities belonging thereunto, made to him on the 12 of May the same year. —ANTHONY À WOOD, *Athenae Oxonienses*, 1691–1721

The anecdotes of this facetious bishop, quoted by Headley from the Aubrey MSS., would fill several pages of a jest-book. It is more to his honour to be told, that though entirely hostile in his principles to the Puritans, he frequently softened, with his humane and characteristic pleasantry, the furious orders against them which Laud enjoined him to execute. —THOMAS CAMPBELL, *Specimens of the British Poets*, 1819

His reputation for facetiousness and good fellowship had begun while he was yet a student of Christ Church, Oxford, and had accompanied him through his clerical career. It was said that, after he was Doctor of Divinity, he had, in a freak, put on a ballad-singer's jacket, and sold off his stock of ballads for him at the market-cross of Abingdon. Riding once in a coach, in a very dirty lane, in wet weather, with a Dr. Stubbins, who was "one of his cronies and a jolly fat doctor," he had a breakdown, the results of which he described by saying that, on recovering his senses, he found Stubbins up to the elbows in mud, and himself up to the elbows in Stubbins. "One time, as he was confirming, the country people pressing in to see the ceremony, said he, 'Bear off there, or I'll confirm ye with my staff.' Another time, being to lay his hand on the head of a man very bald, he turns to his chaplain and said, 'Some dust, Lushington,' *i.e.* to keep his hand from slipping. This chaplain, Dr. Lushington, was a very learned, ingenious man, and they loved one another. The bishop would sometimes take the key of the wine-cellar, and he and his chaplain would go and lock themselves in, and be merry; then first he lays down his hood, 'There lies the doctor;' then he puts off his gown, 'There lies the bishop:' then 'twas, 'Here's to thee, Corbet;' 'Here's to thee, Lushington.'" These stories, whether true of the bishop

or only fathered upon him, are in the exact spirit of the specimens of his verse that remain—written some of them as early as 1610, but others after he was bishop. His ballad entitled "The Fairies' Farewell" has some fancy as well as liveliness in it.

> At morning and at evening both
> You merry were and glad;
> So little care of sleep or sloth
> These pretty ladies had.
> When Tom came home from labour,
> Or Ciss to milking rose,
> Then merrily, merrily went their tabour,
> And nimbly went their toes.
>
> Witness those rings and roundelays
> Of theirs which yet remain,
> Were footed in Queen Mary's days
> On many a grassy plain:
> But since, of late, Elizabeth,
> And, later, James came in,
> They never danced on any heath,
> As when the time hath bin.
>
> By which we note the fairies
> Were of the old profession;
> Their songs were Ave-Maries,
> Their dances were procession.
> But now, alas! they all are dead,
> Or gone beyond the seas,
> Or farther for Religion fled,
> Or else they take their ease.

He loses no opportunity of having a good-humoured slap at the Puritans. Thus:—

> In the house of pure Emanuel
> I had my education,
> Where my friends surmise
> I dazzled my eyes
> With the light of Revelation.
> Boldly I preach, hate a cross, hate a surplice,
> Mitres, copes, and rotchets;
> Come hear me pray, nine times a day,
> And fill your heads with crotchets.

This is from a ballad expressly satirical of the Puritans; but throughout Corbet's poems there are allusions, such as afterwards became more frequent, to "zealous brothers from the Blackfriars," their long sermons, the upturned whites of their eyes, and their nasal utterance. Nature had put nothing of the Puritan into the jolly bishop's constitution; but neither had she qualified him to be a persecutor. He died in 1635, leaving a son, Vincent, then a mere child, whom Aubrey afterwards knew as a handsome youth, going about "begging of gentlemen" after having spent all he had. It was not till 1647 that Corbet's scraps of verse were published collectively. Unlike most of the collections of the period, they are readable still from beginning to end. —DAVID MASSON, *The Life of John Milton*, 1859, Vol. 1, Ch. 6

One of the most remarkable among the clerical poets of this earlier half of the seventeenth century was Dr. Richard Corbet. . . . Corbet's poetry is a mixture of alternation of gravity and drollery. But it is the subject or occasion, rather than the style or manner, that makes the difference; he never rises to anything higher than wit; and he is as witty in his elegies as in his ballads. As that ingredient, however, is not so suitable for the former as for the latter, his graver performances are worth very little. Nor is his merriment of a high order; when it is most elaborate it is strained and fantastic, and when more natural it is apt to run into buffoonery. But much of his verse, indeed, is merely prose in rhyme, and very indifferent rhyme for the most part.—GEORGE L. CRAIK, A *Compendious History of English Literature and of the English Language*, 1861, Vol. 2, p. 21

Coleridge, in one of his most eccentric moods, wished that the poems of Corbet (he was Bishop, first of Oxford and then of Norwich, and died in 1635) might be published for modern delectation, and expressed himself sure that they would be popular. For myself I should be very glad indeed to have written, and am glad to read the book; but I doubt the popularity. Corbet's work is of that peculiar class which is usually, though not always, due to "university wits," and which only appeals to people with a considerable appreciation of humour, and a large stock of general information. It is always occasional in character, and rarely succeeds so well as when the treatment is one of distinct *persiflage.* Thus the elegy on Donne is infinitely

inferior to Carew's, and the mortuary epitaph on Arabella Stuart is, for such a subject and from the pen of a man of great talent, extraordinarily feeble. His critics have been much disturbed by a certainly very ungallant epistle to a certain Mistress Mallet, "An unhandsome woman who made love to him," but, as they seem partly to have perceived, it is almost certain that the thing is a mere Horatian reminiscence. On the other hand, the burlesque epistle to Lord Mordaunt on his journey to the North is great fun, and the "Journey into France," though, to borrow one of its own jokes, rather "strong," is as good. The "Exhortation to Mr. John Hammond," a ferocious satire on the Puritans, distinguishes itself from almost all precedent work of the kind by the force and directness of its attack, which almost anticipates Dryden.—GEORGE SAINTSBURY, A *History of Elizabethan Literature*, 1887, p. 383

THOMAS RANDOLPH

1605–1635

Thomas Randolph was baptized on June 15, 1605, at Newnham-cum-Badby, near Daventry, Northamptonshire. He attended the Westminster School, London, as a King's Scholar, and matriculated at Trinity College, Cambridge, in 1624. He earned a B.A. in 1628, and a M.A. in 1632. Randolph was also a fellow of Trinity College.

Beginning in 1628 Randolph made frequent trips to London. He associated with other young admirers of Ben Jonson in the so-called "Tribe of Ben." Two dramatic sketches were published in 1630, *The Conceited Peddlar* and *Artistippus; or, The Joviall Philosopher.* Randolph also wrote several full-length dramas, including *Amyntas* (1630), *The Muse's Looking-Glasse* (1630), *The Jealous Lover* (1632), and *Hey for Honesty, Down with Knavery,* adapted from an Aristophanes play and printed in 1651. Randolph's noted poetic efforts include "An Ode to Master Anthony Stafford," "An Eglogue to Mr Johnson," and another eclogue included in *Annalia Dubrensia,* a verse collection celebrating Captain Dover's Cotswold Games. Randolph led an increasingly dissipated life, which supposedly precipitated his early death. He was buried on March 17, 1635, in Blatherwick Church, Northamptonshire.

Thomas Randolph, one of the most pregnant young wits of his time, flourishing in the University of Cambridge: the quick conceit and clear poetic fancy discovered in his extant poems, seemed to promise something extraordinary from him, had not his indulgence to the too liberal converse with the multitude of his applauders drawn him to such an immoderate way of living, as, in all probability, shortened his days. Besides his two Comedies, *Amintas,* and *the Muses Looking-Glass,* and the Interlude *Aristippus* printed with his other works, there are attributed to him, a comedy called *Hey for Honesty, and Down for Knavery;* and *The Jealous Lovers,* a tragedy.—EDWARD PHILLIPS, *Theatrum Poetarum Anglicanorum,* 1675

⟨Randolph⟩ was born at Newnham near to Daintry in Northamptonshire, 15 June 1605, son of William Randolphe of Hams near to Lewis in Sussex (steward to Edw. lord Zouch) by Elizabeth his wife, daughter of Tho. Smith of Newnham before-mention'd, educated in Westminster school, and went thence (being one of the king's scholars) to Trinity coll. in Cambridge 1623, of which he became fellow. Afterwards he commenced master of arts, in which degree he was incorporated at Oxon, became famous for his ingenuity, an adopted son of Ben. Johnson, and accounted one of the most pregnant wits of his age; the quickness of which was first discovered when he was about 9 or 10 years old, at which time, he wrote the

History of the Incarnation of our Saviour, in verse, which is at this day preserved in MS. under his own hand writing. When he arrived to man's estate, and perhaps before, he wrote (1) *Poems.* (2) *The Muses Looking-glass,* a comedy, (3) *Amyntas or the impossible dowry,* a pastoral, (4) *Aristippus, or the jovial Philosopher,* &c. trag. presented in a private shew, (5) *The conceited Pedler,* presented in a strange shew. Lond. 1630, qu. (6) *Jealous Lovers,* tr. com. (7) *Hey for honesty, down with knavery,* com. translated out of Aristophanes his *Plutus:* Augmented and published by F.J. Lond. 1651, qu. All which, except the last, were gathered together, and printed in one vol. by the care of his brother Rob. Randolphe student of Ch. Ch. in Oxon, being then commended to the world by divers poets of the said university. Several other things of the like nature, were expected from the said young poet Tho. Randolphe, but by indulging himself too much with the liberal conversation of his admirers (a thing incident to poets) brought him untimely to his end, in the house of Will. Stafford of Blatherwyke in Northamptonshire, esq. (having spent some time in that of his father at Little Houghton in the said county in his delightful studies) whereupon his body being buried in an isle, joining to the church at that place (among those of the Staffords) on the 17th day of March, an. 1634, had soon after a monument of white marble, wreathed about with laurel, erected over his grave, at the charge of sir Christopher (afterwards lord) Hatton of Kirby. The inscription on which, in Lat. and Engl. ver. was made by the poet's friend Pet. Hausted of Cambridge.—AN-THONY À WOOD, *Athenae Oxonienses*, 1691–1721

He flourisht in the Reign of King *Charles* the First; and was Born at *Houghton*, in *Northamptonshire*; from whence he was sent for Education to *Westminster* School; and thence was remov'd to *Cambridge*, where he became Fellow of *Trinity* Colledge in that University. He was accounted one of the most pregnant Wits of his Time; and was not only admir'd by the Wits of *Cambridge*, but likewise belov'd and valu'd by the Poets, and Men of the Town in that Age. His Gay Humour, and Readiness at Repartee, begat *Ben. Johnson's* Love to that Degree, that he Adopted him his Son: on which Account Mr. *Randolph* writ a Gratulatory Poem to him, which is printed, these Lines being part of the Copy:

> When my Muse upon obedient knees
> Asks not a Father's Blessing, let her leese
> The Fame of this Adoption; 'tis a Curse
> I wish her cause I cannot think a worse.

. . . I know not when our Author died; tho' I presume he liv'd to no great Age, being too much addicted to the Principles of his Predecessor *Aristippus*, Pleasure, and Contempt of Wealth.

My Readers are not to expect any Discoveries of Thefts, for this Author had no occasion to practice Plagiary, having so large a Fond of Wit of his own, that he needed not to borrow from others; and therefore I may justly say, with a Friend of his,

> With what an Extasie shall we behold
> This Book? which is no Ghost of any old
> Worm-eaten Author: here's no Jest, or Hint,
> But had his Head both for its Oar, and Mint.
> Wer't not for some Translations none could know
> Whether he had e're look'd in Book or no.

Of this Nature, are not only his several Versions, as the Second *Epod* of *Horace*, several Pieces out of *Claudian*, &c. but likewise a Dramatick Piece from *Aristophanes*, called in the Original Πλοῦτος, but by our Translator,

Hey for Honesty, Down with Knavery; a pleasant Comedy, printed 4o *Lond.* 1651. This Play was first translated by our Author; and afterwards augmented and published by *F.J.* I shall not pretend to determine, whether this Translation, or that published in octavo be better; but leave it to those more vers'd in the Original than I pretend to. Permit me therefore to conclude all with the following Lines, writ by One of St. *John's*, in Memory of our Author.

> Immortal *Ben* is dead, and as that Ball
> On *Ida* toss'd, so is his Crown, by all
> The Infantry of Wit. Vain Priests! That Chair
> Is only fit for his true Son and Heir.
> Reach here thy Laurel: *Randolph*, 'tis thy praise:
> Thy naked Skull shall well become the *Bays*.
> See, *Daphne* courts thy Ghost: and spite of Fate,
> Thy *Poems* shall be 'Poet *Laureate*.
> —GERARD LANGBAINE, *An Account of the English Dramatick Poets*, 1691

His wit and learning endeared him to Ben Jonson, who owned him, like Cartwright, as his adopted son in the Muses. Unhappily he followed the taste of Ben not only at the pen, but at the bottle; and he closed his life in poverty, at the age of twenty-nine,—a date lamentably premature, when we consider the promises of his genius. His wit and humour are very conspicuous in the Puritan characters, whom he supposes the spectators of his scenes in the *Muse's Looking-Glass*. Throughout the rest of that drama (though it is on the whole his best

performance) he unfortunately prescribed to himself too hard and confined a system of dramatic effect.—THOMAS CAMPBELL, *Specimens of the British Poets*, 1819

Randolph has a good deal of fancy, and his verse flows very melodiously; but his poetry has in general a bookish and borrowed air. Much of it is on subjects of love and gallantry; but the love is chiefly of the head, or, at most, of the senses,—the gallantry, it is easy to see, that merely of a fellow of a college and a reader of Ovid.—GEORGE L. CRAIK, *A Compendious History of English Literature and of the English Language*, 1861, Vol. 2, p. 20

It seems probable that in the premature death of Randolph, English literature underwent a very heavy loss. He died unexpectedly when he was only twenty-nine, leaving behind him a mass of writing at once very imperfect and very promising. The patronage of Ben Jonson, it would seem, rather than any very special bias to the stage, led him to undertake dramatic composition, and though he left six plays behind him, it is by no means certain that he would have ended as a dramatist. His knowledge of stage requirements is very small indeed; it would be impossible to revive any of his pieces on the modern boards on account of the essential uncouthness of the movement, the length of the soliloquies, and the thinnness of the plot. His three best dramas are distinguished by a vigorous directness and buoyancy of language, and by frequent passages of admirable rhetorical quality, but they are hardly plays at all, in the ordinary sense. His master-piece, *The Muses' Looking Glass*, is a moral essay in a series of dialogues, happily set in a framework of comedy; the *Jealous Lovers* is full, indeed, of ridiculous stratagems and brisk humorous transitions, but it has no sanity of plot; while *Amyntas* is a beautiful holiday dream, aery and picturesque, and ringing with peals of faery laughter, but not a play that any mortal company of actors could rehearse. Intellect and imagination Randolph possessed in full measure, but as he does not seem to have been born to excel in play-writing or in song-writing, and as he died too early to set his own mark on literature, we are left to speculate down what groove such brilliant and energetic gifts as his would finally have proceeded. Had he lived longer his massive intelligence might have made him a dangerous rival or a master to Dryden, and as he shows no inclination towards the French manner of poetry, he might have delayed or altogether warded off the influx of the classical taste. He showed no precocity of genius; he was gradually gathering his singing-robes about him, having already studied much, yet having still much to learn. There is no poet whose works so tempt the critic to ask, 'what was the next step in his development?' He died just too soon to impress his name on history.

Besides his dramas, Randolph conposed a considerable number of lyrics and occasional poems. Of these the beautiful "Ode to Master Anthony Stafford to hasten him into the country" is the best. In this he is more free and graceful in his Latinism than usual. He was a deep student of the Roman poets, and most of his non-dramatic pieces are exercises, performed in a hard though stately style, after Ovid, Martial and Claudian. It cannot be said that these have much charm, except to the technical student of poetry, who observes, with interest, the zeal and energy with which Randolph prepared himself for triumphs which were never to be executed. In pastoral poetry he had attained more ease than in any other, and some of his idyls are excellently performed. The glowing verses entitled "A Pastoral Courtship" remind the reader of the twenty-seventh idyl of Theocritus, on which they were probably modelled. The "Cotswold Eclogue," which originally appeared in a very curious book entitled *Annalia Dubrensia*, 1636, is one of the best pastorals which we possess in English. But in reviewing the fragments of the work of Randolph, the critic is ever confronted by the imperfection of his growing talent, the insufficiency of what exists to account for the personal weight that Randolph carried in his lifetime, and for the intense regret felt at his early death. Had he lived he might have bridged over, with a strong popular poetry, the abyss between the old romantic and the new didactic school, for he had a little of the spirit of each. As it is, he holds a better place in English literature than Dryden, or Gray, or Massinger would have held had they died before they were thirty.—EDMUND GOSSE, "Thomas Randolph," *The English Poets*, ed. Thomas Humphry Ward, 1880, Vol. 2, pp. 219–20

> Sons born of many a loyal Muse to Ben,
>   All true-begotten, warm with wine or ale,
>   Bright from the broad light of its presence, hail!
> Prince Randolph, nighest his throne of all his men,
> Being highest in spirit and heart who hailed him
>   then
>   King, nor might other spread so blithe a sail.
>   —ALGERNON CHARLES SWINBURNE, "The Tribe
>   of Benjamin," *Sonnets on English Dramatic
>   Poets*, 1882

Thomas Randolph, the most gifted (according to general estimate rather than to specific performance) of the Tribe of Ben, was a much younger man than Shirley, though he died more than thirty years earlier. Randolph was born near Daventry in 1605, his father being a gentleman, and Lord Zouch's steward. He was educated at Westminster, and at Trinity College, Cambridge, of which he became a fellow, and he was also incorporated at Oxford. His life is supposed to have been merry, and was certainly short, for he died, of what disease is not known, in his thirtieth year. He left, however, no inconsiderable literary results; and if his dramas are not quite so relatively good as his poems (there is certainly none of them which is in its own kind the equal of the fine answer to Ben Jonson's threat to leave the stage and the Ode to Anthony Stafford), still they are interesting and show a strong intellect and great literary facility. The two earliest, *Aristippus* and *The Conceited Pedlar*, the first a slight dramatic sketch, the second a monologue, are eminent examples of the class of university, not to say of undergraduate, wit; but far stronger and fuller of

promise than most specimens of that class. *The Jealous Lovers*, a play with classical nomenclature, and at first seeming to aim at the Terentian model, drifts off into something like the Jonsonian humour-comedy, of which it gives some good studies, but hardly a complete example. Much better are *The Muses' Looking-Glass* and *Amyntas*, in which Randolph's academic schemes and names do not hide his vivid and fertile imagination. *The Muses' Looking-Glass*, a play vindicating the claim of the drama in general to the title, is a kind of morality, but a morality carried off with infinite spirit, which excuses the frigid nature of the abstractions presented in it, and not seldom rises to the height of real comedy. The scene between Colax and Dyscolus, the professional flatterer and the professional snarler, is really excellent: and others equally good might be picked out. Of the two I am inclined to think that this play shows more natural genius in the writer for its style, than the pretty pastoral of *Amyntas*, which has sometimes been preferred to it. The same penchant for comedy appears in *Down with Knavery*, a very free and lively adaptation of the *Plutus* of Aristophanes. There is no doubt that Randolph's work gives the impression of considerable power. At the same time it is fair to remember that the author's life was one very conducive to precocity, inasmuch as he underwent at once the three stimulating influences of an elaborate literary education, of endowed leisure to devote himself to what literary occupations he pleased, and of the emulation caused by literary society. Jonson's friendship seems to have acted as a forcing-house on the literary faculties of his friends, and it is quite as possible that, if Randolph had lived, he would have become a steady-going soaker or a diligent but not originally productive scholar, as that he would have produced anything of high substantive and permanent value. It is true that many great writers had not at his age done such good work; but then it must be remembered that they had also produced little or nothing in point of bulk. It may be plausibly argued that, good as what Randolph's first thirty years gave is, it ought to have been better still if it was ever going to be of the best. But these excursions into possibilities are not very profitable, and the chief excuse for indulging in them is that Randolph's critics and editors have generally done the same, and have as a rule perhaps pursued the indulgence in a rather too enthusiastic and sanguine spirit. What is not disputable at all is the example given by Randolph of the powerful influence of Ben on his "tribe."—GEORGE SAINTSBURY, *A History of Elizabethan Literature*, 1887, pp. 413–15

BEN JONSON

c. 1573–1637

Ben Jonson, dramatist, poet and critic, was probably born in Westminster, near London, the posthumous son of a clergyman. Jonson himself claimed to be of Scottish ancestry. He attended a school in St. Martin's Lane, then the Westminster School, where the kindness of the headmaster, the antiquary William Camden, later inspired Jonson to dedicate plays to him. His mother remarried a bricklayer, to whom Jonson was apprenticed after graduating from the Westminster School. Little is known of the next five years, except that Jonson volunteered for military service in Flanders, and married in 1594.

By 1597, Jonson was a member of Philip Henslowe's company, serving as an actor and as a playwright. That year, Jonson was arrested, along with the author and others, for acting in Nashe's *Isle of Dogs*. During these early years with Henslowe, Jonson collaborated with Dekker, Marston, Chapman, Chettle and others. In 1598 he was arrested again, this time for killing the actor Gabriel

Spenser. Jonson escaped capital punishment by pleading "benefit of clergy," based on his ability to read the Bible in Latin, although his thumb was branded. While in prison, Jonson became a Roman Catholic, a faith he was to hold for twelve years. Also in 1598, Jonson's play *Every Man in his Humour* was produced, followed by *Every Man Out of his Humour* (1599), *Cynthia's Revels, or The Fountain of Self-love* (1600) and *Poetaster, or The Arraignment* (1601), the latter of which lampooned Marston and Dekker and contributed to the "war of the theatres." One of the two extant classical tragedies Jonson wrote, *Sejanus, His Fall* (1603), included Shakespeare in its cast. Shakespeare was to remain a close colleague. Jonson's next play, *Eastward Hoe* (1604), was written in collaboration with Marston and Chapman, which led to a brief imprisonment for all three, because of allegedly treasonous statements regarding the Scots.

The subsequent period constitutes Jonson's most successful one, in which he wrote the comedies *Volpone, or The Fox* (1606), *Epicoene, or The Silent Woman* (1609), *The Alchemist* (1610) and *Bartholomew Fair* (1614). During this time, Jonson also wrote his second tragedy, *Catiline, His Conspiracy* (1611). His later plays, which include *The Devil is an Asse* (1616), *The Staple of News* (1625), *The New Inne* (1629), and others, were not widely admired, and were later labelled by Dryden "mere dotages."

In 1605, Jonson's quasi-drama *The Masque of Blackness* was presented to the court of James I, and with it Jonson embarked on a fairly lengthy career of court entertainment. In all, Jonson was to write over twenty-five masques, including *Hymenaei* (1606), commemorating the marriage of the Earl of Essex and Francis Howard, *The Masque of the Queens* (1609), in which Jonson introduces the "antimasque," and numerous others. These masques were generally staged—and upstaged—by the architect and designer Inigo Jones, with whom Jonson engaged in fierce rivalry. During these years, Jonson also spent a year in Europe acting as tutor to Sir Walter Raleigh's son (1612–13) and travelled to Scotland (1618–19), making what became a famous visit to William Drummond of Hawthornden, who kept a detailed record of their conversation. He was honored by the city of Edinburgh and claimed to have received honorary degrees from both Oxford and Cambridge, although records survive of the Oxford induction only. In 1621, James I offered him a knighthood, which he did not take; he was relatively secure in a small pension he received from the king. In 1623 Jonson's personal library was burned in a fire, an event commemorated in his poem "An Execration upon Vulcan."

After the death of James I in 1625, Jonson was not asked to write masques for the new court of Charles I until 1628. Meanwhile, he served as official Chronologer of London in 1628, until he suffered from a stroke in that same year. Although weakened, Jonson continued to lead the life of a London wit, acting as unofficial Poet Laureate (receiving the pay, although not the title, of the position). Widely admired in his time, Jonson headed a generation of authors known as "the tribe of Ben," and held court first in the Mermaid Tavern, then in the Devil. After Jonson's death, a collection of elegies from thirty-three admirers, *Jonsonus Virbius* (1638), was published.

Jonson's own poems, most of which adhered to classical forms, were collected in *Epigrams* and *The Forrest* (both 1616), as well as *Underwoods* (1640). The best known of Jonson's prose works remains *Timber; or Discourses made upon Men and Matters*, a series of notes and essays on life and letters (1640). Jonson's only pastoral, *The Sad Shepherd*, was left unfinished. The first folio edition of his works was published in 1616; a second, in 1640. The playwright died on August 6, 1637, and is buried in Westminster Abbey, under the inscription "O rare Ben Jonson."

Personal

His Grandfather came from Carlisle, and, he thought, from Anandale to it: he served King Henry 8, and was a gentleman. His Father losed all his estate under Queen Marie, having been cast in prisson and forfaitted; at last turn'd Minister: so he was a minister's son. He himself was posthumous born, a moneth after his father's decease; brought up poorly, putt to school by a friend (his master Cambden): after taken from it, and put to ane other craft (*I think was to be a wright or bricklayer*), which he could not endure; then went he to the Low Countries: but returning soone he betook himself to his wonted studies. In his service in the Low Countries, he had, in the face of both the campes, killed ane enemie and taken *opima spolia* from him; and since his comming to England, being appealed to the fields, he had killed his adversarie, which had hurt him in the arme, and whose sword was 10 inches longer than his; for the which he was emprissoned, and almost at the gallowes. Then took he his religion by trust, of a priest who visited him in prisson. Thereafter he was 12 yeares a Papist.

He was Master of Arts in both the Universities, by their favour, not his studie.

He maried a wyfe who was a shrew, yet honest: 5 yeers he had not bedded with her, but remayned with my Lord Aulbanie.

In the tyme of his close imprisonment, under Queen Elizabeth, his judges could get nothing of him to all their demands but I and No. They placed two damn'd villains to catch advantage of him, with him, but he was advertised by his keeper: of the Spies he hath ane epigrame.

When the King came in England at that tyme the pest was in London, he being in the country at Sir Robert Cotton's house with old Cambden, he saw in a vision his eldest sone, then a child and at London, appear unto him with the mark of a bloodie crosse on his forehead, as if it had been cutted with a suord, at which amazed he prayed unto God, and in the morning he came to Mr. Cambden's chamber to tell him; who persuaded him it was but ane apprehension of his fantasie, at which he should not be disjected: in the mean tyme comes there letters from his wife of the death of that boy in the plague. He appeared to him (he said) of a manlie shape, and of that grouth that he thinks he shall be at the resurrection.

He was delated by Sir James Murray to the King, for writting something against the Scots, in a play Eastward Hoe, and voluntarily imprissonned himself with Chapman and Marston, who had written it amongst them. The report was, that they should then [have] had their ears cut and noses. After their delivery, he banqueted all his friends; there was Camden, Selden, and others: at the midst of the feast his old Mother dranke to him, and shew him a paper which she had (if the sentence had taken execution) to have mixed in the prisson among his drinke, which was full of lustie strong poison, and that she was no churle, she told, she minded first to have drunk of it herself.

He had many quarrells with Marston, beat him, and took his pistol from him, wrote his Poetaster on him; the beginning of them were, that Marston represented him in the stage, in his youth given to venerie. He thought the use of a maide nothing in comparison to the wantoness of a wyfe, and would never have ane other mistress. He said two accidents strange befell him: one, that a man made his own wyfe to court him, whom he enjoyed two yeares ere he knew of it, and one day finding them by chance, was passingly delighted with it: ane other, lay divers tymes with a woman, who shew him all that he wished, except the last act, which she would never agree unto.

S. W. Raulighe sent him governour with his Son, anno 1613, to France. This youth being knavishly inclyned, among other pastimes (as the setting of the favour of damosells on a cwdpiece), caused him to be drunken, and dead drunk, so that he knew not wher he was, therafter laid him on a carr, which he made to be drawen by pioners through the streets, at every corner showing his governour stretched out, and telling them, that was a more lively image of the Crucifix then any they had: at which sport young Raughlie's mother delyghted much (saying, his father young was so inclyned), though the Father abhorred it.

He can set horoscopes, but trusts not in them. He with the consent of a friend cousened a lady, with whom he had made ane appointment to meet ane old Astrologer, in the suburbs, which she keeped; and it was himself disguysed in a longe gowne and a whyte beard at the light of dimm burning candles, up in a little cabinet reached unto by a ledder.

Every first day of the new year he had 20 lb. sent him from the Earl of Pembrok to buy bookes.

After he was reconciled with the Church, and left of to be a recusant, at his first communion, in token of true reconciliation, he drank out all the full cup of wyne.

Being at the end of my Lord Salisburie's table with Inigo Jones, and demanded by my Lord, Why he was not glad? My Lord, said he, yow promised I should dine with yow, bot I doe not, for he had none of his meate; he esteemed only that his meate which was of his own dish.

He heth consumed a whole night in lying looking to his great toe, about which he hath seen Tartars and Turks, Romans and Carthaginians, feight in his imagination.

Northampton was his mortall enimie for beating, on a St. George's day, one of his attenders: He was called before the Councell for his Sejanus, and accused both of poperie and treason by him.

Sundry tymes he hath devoured his bookes, i.[e.] *sold them all for necessity.*

He heth a minde to be a churchman, and so he might have favour to make one sermon to the King, he careth not what therafter should befall him: for he would not flatter though he saw Death.

At his hither comming, Sʳ Francis Bacon said to him, He loved not to sie Poesy goe on other feet than poeticall Dactylus and Spondaeus. . . .

He is a great lover and praiser of himself; a contemner and scorner of others; given rather to losse a friend than a jest;

jealous of every word and action of those about him (especiallie after drink, which is one of the elements in which he liveth); a dissembler of ill parts which raigne in him, a bragger of some good that he wanteth; thinketh nothing well bot what either he himself or some of his friends and countrymen hath said or done; he is passionatelie kynde and angry; careless either to gaine or keep; vindicative, but, if he be well answered, at himself.

For any religion, as being versed in both. Interpreteth best sayings and deeds often to the worst. Oppressed with fantasie, which hath ever mastered his reason, a generall disease in many Poets. His inventions are smooth and easie; but above all he excelleth in a Translation.—BEN JONSON, *Conversations with William Drummond,* 1619

> A session was held the other day,
> And Apollo himself was at it, they say,
> The laurel that had been so long reserv'd,
> Was now to be given to him best deserv'd.
>   And
>
> Therefore the wits of the town came thither,
> 'Twas strange to see how they flocked together.
> Each strongly confident of his own way,
> Thought to gain the laurel away that day.
>
> . . . .
> The first that broke silence was good old Ben,
> Prepared before with canary wine,
> And he told them plainly he deserved the bays,
> For his were called works, where others were but plays.
>   And
> Bid them remember how he had purg'd the stage
> Of errors, that had lasted many an age,
> And he hoped they did not think the *Silent Woman,*
> The *Fox* and the *Alchemist,* outdone by no man.
>
> Apollo stopt him there, and bade him not go on,
> 'Twas merit, he said, and not presumption
> Must carry't, at which Ben turned about.
> And in great choler offer'd to go out:
>   But
>
> Those that were there thought it not fit
> To discontent so ancient a wit;
> And therefore Apollo call'd him back again,
> And made him mine host of his own New Inn.
>   —SIR JOHN SUCKLING, "The Wits," 1637

Though I cannot with all my industrious inquiry find him in his cradle, I can fetch him from his long coats. When a little child, he lived in Harts-horn-lane near Charing-cross, where his Mother married a Bricklayer for her second husband. . . . He help'd in the building of the new structure of Lincoln's Inn, when, having a trowell in his hand, he had a book in his pocket. Some gentlemen, pitying that his parts should be buried under the rubbish of so mean a calling, did by their bounty manumise him freely to follow his own ingenious inclinations. Indeed his parts were not so ready to run of themselves, as able to answer the spur; so that it may be truly said of him, that he had an elaborate wit wrought out by his own industry. He would sit silent in learned company, and suck in (besides wine) their several humors into his observation. What was ore in others, he was able to refine to himself. . . .

Many were the wit-combates betwixt ⟨Shakespeare⟩ and *Ben Johnson*; which two I behold like a Spanish Great Gallion and an English man-of-War: Master *Johnson* (like the former) was built far higher in Learning; Solid, but Slow in his performances. *Shakespear,* with the English man-of-War, lesser in bulk, but lighter in sailing, could turn with all tides, tack about, and take advantage of all winds, by the quickness of his Wit and invention.—THOMAS FULLER, *The History of the Worthies of England*, 1662

His mother, after his father's death, maried a Bricklayer; and 'tis generally said that he wrought sometime with his father-in-lawe (and particularly on the Garden-wall of Lincoln's Inne next to Chancery Lane) and that a Knight, a Bencher, walking thro', and hearing him repeate some Greeke verses out of Homer, discoursing with him and finding him to have a Witt extraordinary, gave him some Exhibition to maintaine him at Trinity College in Cambridge.

Then he went into the Lowe-countreys, and spent some time (not very long) in the armie, not to disgrace, as you may find in his *Epigrammes*.

Then he came over into England, and acted and wrote, but both ill, at the Green Curtaine, a kind of Nursery or obscure Play-house, somewhere in the Suburbes (I thinke towards Shoreditch or Clarkenwell). . . .

Then he undertooke again to write a Playe, and did hitt it admirably well, viz. *Every Man* . . . , which was his first good one. . . .

He was (or rather had been) of a clear and faire skin; his habit was very plaine. I have heard Mr. Lacy, the Player, say that he was wont to weare a coate like a coachman's coate, with slitts under the arme-pitts. He would many times exceed in drinke (Canarie was his beloved liquor) then he would tumble home to bed, and, when he had thoroughly perspired, then to studie. I have seen his studyeing chaire, which was of strawe, such as olde woemen used, and as Aulus Gellius is drawen in. . . .

He lies buryed in the north aisle in the path of square stone (the rest is Lozenge) opposite to the Scutcheon of Robertus de Ros, with this Inscription only on him, in a pavement square of blew marble, about 14 inches square,

O RARE BENN JOHNSON

which was donne at the charge of Jack Young, afterwards knighted, who, walking there when the grave was covering, gave the fellow eighteen pence to cutt it.—JOHN AUBREY, "Ben Johnson," *Brief Lives*, 1669–96

Jonson hath been often represented as of an envious, arrogant, overbearing temper, and insolent and haughty in his converse; but these ungracious drawings were the performance of his enemies; who certainly were not solicitous to give a flattering likeness of the original. But considering the provocations he received, with the mean and contemptible talents of those who opposed him, what we condemn as vanity or conceit, might be only the exertions of conscious and insulted merit. . . . In his studies Jonson was laborious and indefatigable: his reading was copious and extensive; his memory so tenacious and strong that, when turned of forty, he could have repeated all that he ever wrote: his judgment was accurate and solid; and often consulted by those who knew him well, in branches of very curious learning, and far remote from the flowery paths loved and frequented by the muses.—PETER WHALLEY, "Life of Jonson," *Jonson's Works*, 1756, p. lv

How Decker's hearers must have appreciated every allusion to the arrogant Ben the Poet; with the fierce mouth and small beard; his face marked with small pox; his hollow cheeks; his speaking through his nose; his sour face when he reads his own songs; his stamping on the stage as if he was treading mortar. The audience all knew Master Jonson had once killed a man in a duel, and had left brick-making to make rails; they knew he took months writing a play, and that he despised the opinion of

his audience, and they laughed accordingly.—GEORGE WALTER THORNBURY, *Shakspere's England*, 1856, Vol. 2, p. 13

This man, Ben Jonson, commonly stands next to Shakespeare in a consideration of the dramatic literature of the age of Elizabeth; and certainly if the "thousand-souled" Shakespeare may be said to represent mankind, Ben as unmistakably stands for English-kind. He is "Saxon" England in epitome,—John Bull passing from a name into a man,—a proud, strong, tough, solid, domineering individual, whose intellect and personality cannot be severed, even in thought, from his body and personal appearance. Ben's mind, indeed, was rooted in Ben's character; and his character took symbolic form in his physical frame. He seemed built up, mentally as well as bodily, out of beef and sack, mutton and Canary; or, to say the least, was a joint product of the English mind and the English larder, of the fat as well as the thought of the land, of the soil as well as the soul of England. The moment we attempt to estimate his eminence as a dramatist, he disturbs the equanimity of our judgment by tumbling head-foremost into the imagination as a big, bluff, burly, and quarrelsome man, with "a mountain belly and a rocky face." He is a very pleasant boon companion as long as we make our idea of his importance agree with his own; but the instant we attempt to dissect his intellectual pretensions, the living animal becomes a dangerous subject,—his countenance flames, his great hands double up, his thick lips begin to twitch with impending invective, and, while the critic's impression of him is thus all the more vivid, he is checked in its expression by a very natural fear of the consequences. There is no safety but in taking this rowdy leviathan of letters at his own valuation; and the relation of critics towards him is as perilous as that of the jurymen towards the Irish advocate, who had an unpleasant habit of sending them the challenge of the duellist whenever they brought in a verdict against any of his clients. There is, in fact, such a vast animal force in old Ben's self-assertion, that he bullies posterity as he bullied his contemporaries; and, while we admit his claim to rank next to Shakespeare among the dramatists of his age, we beg our readers to understand that we do it under intimidation.—EDWIN P. WHIPPLE, *The Literature of the Age of Elizabeth*, 1869, p. 85

Jonson's person was not built on the classical type of graceful or dignified symmetry: he had the large and rugged dimensions of a strong Borderland river, swollen by a sedentary life into huge corpulence. Although in his later days he jested at his own "mountain belly and his rocky face," he probably bore his unwieldy figure with a more athletic carriage than his namesake the lexicographer. Bodily as well as mentally he belonged to the race of Anak. His position among his contemporaries was very much what Samuel Johnson's might have been had he been contradicted, and fought against by independent rivals, jealous and resentful of his dictatorial manner. Ben Jonson's large and irascible personality could not have failed to command respect; but his rivals had too much respect for themselves to give way absolutely to his authority. They refused to be as grasshoppers in his sight. We should do wrong, however, to suppose that this disturbed the giant's peace of mind. —WILLIAM MINTO, *Characteristics of English Poets*, 1874, p. 338

Besides being a born critic, Jonson was possessed of both a generous heart and a robust intellect; and there is a ludicrous incongruity with the transparent nature of the man in the supposition that it was poisoned by a malignant hatred of Shakspere and his fame. The difference between the two poets was indeed extremely great, and reflects itself in almost everything left to us from their respective hands. But it is not a whit less absurd to look upon Jonson and Shakspere as the heads of opposite schools or tendencies in literature, than to suppose the one writer to have personally regarded the other with a jealous feeling of rivalry. . . . Ben Jonson was a genuine scholar, whose chief pride was his library, afterwards destroyed by a fire which inflicted an irreparable loss upon our literature. His love of reading must have been insatiable; of his book-learning numberless illustrations are furnished by his plays, in one of which he bears testimony to it with pardonable self-sufficiency. But to the canary-sack must be ascribed part of the boastfulness which made him tell Drummond that "he was better versed, and knew more in Greek and Latin, than all the Poets in England, and"—here Drummond appears to have imperfectly understood the author of the "English Grammar"—"quintessence their brains."—ADOLPHUS WILLIAM WARD, *A History of English Dramatic Literature* (1875), 1899, Vol. 2, pp. 297–314

A man of extreme convivial and decidedly undomestic turn, he was accessible to everyone at the taverns he frequented, and besides the group of "Sons," which is famous, and included all the more noted men of letters of the second half of our period, he seems to have had a wide circle of *protégés* and clients extending, as later traditions more or less dimly indicate, all over the kingdom. This semi-Falstaffian gift of tavern-kingship, however, could not have availed of itself to give Jonson the postion he held. But his more solid claims to literary respect were usually great. Although it is very doubtful whether he belonged to either University in any but an honorary capacity, scholars of the strictest academic sufficiency like Selden, Farnaby, and others, admitted his scholarship; he was the honoured friend of Raleigh and Bacon; and it is impossible for any reader, himself possessing the slightest tincture of classical learning, not to recognise in every work of Jonson's—be it play, poem, or prose—the presence of reading which never obscured, though it sometimes stiffened and hardened, the creative faculties of the author.—GEORGE SAINTSBURY, *Social England*, ed. H. D. Traill, 1895, Vol. 4, p. 113

According to the local tradition, he asked the King (Charles I.) to grant him a favour. "What is it?" said the King.—"Give me eighteen inches of square ground." "Where?" asked the King.—"In Westminster Abbey." This is one explanation given of the story that he was buried standing upright. Another is that it was in view to his readiness for the Resurrection. . . . This stone ⟨covering his grave⟩ was taken up when, in 1821, the Nave was repaved, and was brought back from the stoneyard of the clerk of the works, in the time of Dean Buckland, by whose order it was fitted into its present place in the north wall of the Nave. Meanwhile, the original spot had been marked by a small triangular lozenge, with a copy of the old inscription. When, in 1849, Sir Robert Wilson was buried close by, the loose sand of Jonson's grave (to use the expression of the clerk of the works who superintended the operation) "rippled in like a quicksand," and the clerk "saw the two leg-bones of Jonson, fixed bolt upright in the sand, as though the body had been buried in the upright position; and the skull came rolling down among the sand, from a position above the leg-bones, to the bottom of the newly-made grave. There was still hair upon it, and it was of a red colour." It was seen once more on the digging of John Hunter's grave; and "it had still traces of red hair upon it. The world long wondered that he should lie buried from the rest of the poets and want a tomb." This monument, in fact, was to have been erected by subscription soon after his death, but was delayed by the breaking-out of the Civil War. The present medallion in Poets' Corner was set up in the middle of the last century by "a person of quality, whose name was desired to be concealed." By a mistake of the sculptor, the buttons were set on the left side of the coat. Hence this epigram—

> O rare Ben Jonson—what a turncoat grown!
> Thou ne'er wast such, till clad in stone:
> Then let not this disturb thy sprite,
> Another age shall set thy buttons right.
> —ARTHUR PENRHYN STANLEY, *Historical Memorials of Westminster Abbey*, 1896, pp. 288–89

He was strong and massive in body, racy and coarse, full of self-esteem, and combative instincts, saturated with the conviction of the scholar's high rank and the poet's exalted vocation, full of contempt for ignorance, frivolity, and lowness, classic in his tastes, with a bent towards careful structure and leisurely development of thought in all that he wrote, and yet a true poet in so far as he was not only irregular in his life and quite incapable of saving any of the money he now and then earned, but was, moreover, subject to hallucinations: once saw Carthaginians and Romans fighting on his great toe, and, on another occasion, had a vision of his son with a bloody cross on his brow, which was supposed to forbode his death. . . . With all his weaknesses, however, he was a sturdy, energetic, and high-minded man, a commanding, independent, and very comprehensive intelligence, and from 1598, when he makes his first appearance on Shakespeare's horizon, throughout the rest of his life, he was, so far as we can see, the man of all his contemporaries whose name was oftenest mentioned along with Shakespeare's. . . . Though his society may have been somewhat fatiguing, it must nevertheless have been both instructive and stimulating to Shakespeare, since Ben was greatly his superior in historical and linguistic knowledge, while as a poet he pursued a totally different ideal.—GEORGE BRANDES, *William Shakespeare, A Critical Study*, 1898, Vol. 1, pp. 385–88

General

Our English Horace.—CHETTLE HENRY, *England's Mourning Garment*, 1603

> Johnson whose full of merit to reherse
> Too copious is to be confinde in verse;
> Yet therein only fittest to be known,
> Could any write a line which he might owne.
> One, so judicious; so well knowing; and
> A man whose least worth is to understand;
> One so exact in all he doth preferre
> To able censure; for the *Theater*
> Not *Seneca* transcends his worth of praise;
> Who writes him well shall well deserve the *Bayes*.
> —WILLIAM BROWNE, *Britannia's Pastorals*, 1613, Bk. 2, Song 2

If I should declare mine own rudeness rudely, I should then confess, that I never tasted English more to my liking, nor more smart, and put to the height of use in poetry, than in that vital, judicious, and most practicable language of Benjamin Jonson's poems.—EDMUND BOLTON, *Hypercritica*, 1624

> He better loves Ben Jonson's book of plays,
> But that therein of wit he finds such plenty
> That he scarce understands a jest of twenty.
> —FRANCIS LENTON, "The Young Gallant's Whirligig," 1629

What are his faults (O Envy!) that you speake
English at Court, the learned Stage acts Greeke?
That Latine Hee reduc'd, and could command
That which your *Shakespeare* scarce could understand?
　　　—H. RAMSAY, "Upon the Death of Benjamin
　　　　　Jonson," 1638

And now, since Jonson's gone, we well may say,
The stage hath seen her glory and decay.
Whose judgment was't refined it? or who
Gave laws, by which hereafter all must go,
But solid Jonson? from whose full strong quill,
Each line did like a diamond drop distil,
Though hard, yet clear.
　　　—OWEN FELTHAM, "To the Memory of Immor-
　　　　　tal Ben," 1638

Had this been for some meaner poet's herse,
I might have then observ'd the laws of verse:
But here they fail, nor can I hope to express
In numbers, what the world grants numberless:
Such are the truths, we ought to speak of thee,
Thou great refiner of our poesy,
Who turn'st to gold that which before was lead;
Then with that pure elixir rais'd the dead!
Nine sisters who (for all the poets lies),
Had been deem'd mortal, did not Jonson rise,
And with celestial sparks (not stoln) revive
Those who could erst keep winged fame alive:
'Twas he that found (plac'd) in the seat of wit,
Dull grinning ignorance, and banish'd it;
He on the prostituted stage appears
To make men hear not by their eyes, but ears;
Who painted virtues, that each one might know,
And point the man, that did such treasure owe:
So that who could in Jonson's lines be high,
Needed not honors, or a riband buy;
But vice he only shewed us in a glass,
Which by reflection of those rays that pass,
Retains the figure lively, set before.
And that withdrawn, reflects at us no more;
So, he observ'd the like decorum, when
He whipt the vices, and yet spar'd the men:
When heretofore, the Vice's only note,
And sign from virtue was his party-coat;
When devils were the last men on the stage,
And pray'd for plenty, and the present age.
　　　Nor was our English language only bound
To thank him, for he Latin Horace found
(Who so inspired Rome, with his lyric song)
Translated in the macaronic tongue;
Cloth'd in such rags, as one might safely vow,
That his Mæcenas would not own him now:
On him he took this pity, as to clothe
In words, and such expression, as for both,
There's none but judgeth the exchange will come
To twenty more, than when he sold at Rome.
Since then, he made our language pure and good,
And us to speak, but what we understood,
We owe this praise to him, that should we join
To pay him, he were paid but with the coin
Himself hath minted, which we know by this,
That no words pass for current now, but his.
And though he in a blinder age could change
Faults to perfections, yet 'twas far more strange
To see (however times and fashions frame)

His wit and language still remain the same
In all men's mouths; grave preachers did it use
As golden pills, by which they might infuse
Their heavenly physic; ministers of state
Their grave dispatches in his language wrate;
Ladies made curt'sies in them, courtiers, legs,
Physicians bills;—perhaps, some pedant begs
He may not use it, for he hears 'tis such,
As in few words a man may utter much.
Could I have spoken in his language too,
I had not said so much, as now I do,
To whose clear memory I this tribute send,
Who dead's my Wonder, living was my Friend.
　　　—SIR JOHN BEAUMONT, "To the Memory of him
　　　　　who can never be Forgotten, Master Benjamin
　　　　　Jonson," 1638

To compare our English Dramatick Poets together (without taxing them) *Shakespear* excelled in a natural Vein, *Fletcher* in Wit, and *Johnson* in Gravity and ponderousness of Style; whose onely fault was, he was too elaborate; and had he mixt less erudition with his Playes, they had been more pleasant and delightful than they are. Comparing him with *Shakespear*, you shall see the difference betwixt Nature and Art; and with *Fletcher*, the difference between Wit and Judgement: Wit being an exuberant thing, like *Nilus*, never more commendable then when it overflowes; but Judgement a stayed and reposed thing, always containing it self within its bounds and limits.—RICHARD FLECKNOE, *A Short Discourse of the English Stage*, c. 1660–64

He was paramount in the Dramatique part of Poetry, and taught the Stage an exact conformity to the laws of Comedians. His Comedies were above the Volge (which are only tickled with downright obscenity), and took not so well at the first stroke as at the rebound, when beheld the second time; yea they will endure reading, and that with due commendation, so long as either ingenuity or learning are fashionable in our Nation. If his later be not so spriteful and vigorous as his first pieces, all that are old will, and all that desire to be old should, excuse him therein.—THOMAS FULLER, *The History of the Worthies of England*, 1662

. . . Ben Jonson is to be admired for many excellencies; and can be taxed with fewer failings than any English poet. I know I have been accused as an enemy of his writings; but without any other reason, than that I do not admire him blindly, and without looking into his imperfections. For why should there be any *ipse dixit* in our poetry, any more than there is in our philosophy? I admire and applaud him where I ought: Those, who do more, do but value themselves in their admiration of him; and, by telling you they extol Ben Jonson's way, would insinuate to you that they can practise it. For my part, I declare that I want judgment to imitate him; and should think it a great impudence in myself to attempt it. To make men appear pleasantly ridiculous on the stage, was, as I have said, his talent; and in this he needed not the acumen of wit but that of judgment. For the characters and representations of folly are only the effects of observation; and observation is an effect of judgment. Some ingenious men, for whom I have a particular esteem, have thought I have much injured Ben Jonson, when I have not allowed his wit to be extraordinary: But they confound the notion of what is witty, with what is pleasant. That Ben Jonson's plays were pleasant, he must want reason who denies: But that pleasantness was not properly wit, or the sharpness of conceit; but the natural imitation of folly: Which I confess to be excellent in its kind, but not to be of that kind which they pretend. . . .—JOHN DRYDEN, "Preface" to *An Evening's Love, or the Mock Astrologer*, 1671

I cannot be of their Opinion, who think he wanted Wit: I am sure, if he did, he was so far from being the most faultless, that he was the most faulty Poet of his Time. But it may be answered, that his Writings were correct, though he wanted Fire; but I think flat and dull Things are as incorrect, and shew as little Judgment in the Author, nay less, than sprightly and mettled Nonsense does. But I think he had more true Wit than any of his Contemporaries: that other Men had sometimes Things, that seem'd more Fiery than his, was because they were placed with so many sordid and mean Things about them, that they made a greater Show. . . .

Nor can I think, to the writing of his Humours (which were not only the Follies, but the Vices and Subtilties of Men) that Wit was not required, but Judgment; where, by the way, they speak as if Judgment were a less thing than Wit. But certainly it was meant otherwise by Nature, who subjected Wit to the Government of Judgment, which is the noblest Faculty of the Mind. Fancy rough-draws, but Judgment smooths and finishes: nay, Judgment does not comprehend Wit; for no Man can have that, who has not Wit. In Fancy Mad-men equal, if not excell, all others; and one may as well say, that one of those Mad-men is as good a Man, as temperate a Wise-man, as that one of the very fanciful Plays (admir'd most by Women) can be so good a Play, as one of *Johnson's* Correct and Well-govern'd Comedies.

The Reason given by some, why *Johnson* needed not Wit in writing Humour, is, because Humour is the effect of Observation, and Observation the effect of Judgment; but Observation is as much Necessary in all other Plays, as in Comedies of Humour. . . .

The most Excellent *Johnson* put Wit into the Mouths of the meanest of his People, and, which is infinitely Difficult, made it proper for 'em. And I once heard a Person of the greatest Wit and Judgment of the Age say, That *Bartholomew-Fair*, (which consists most of low Persons) is one of the wittiest Plays in the World. If there be no Wit required, in the rendring Folly ridiculous, or Vice odious, we must accuse *Juvenal*, the best Satyrist and wittiest Man of all the *Latin* Writers, for want of it.—THOMAS SHADWELL, "Preface" to *The Humorists*, 1671

Benjamin Johnson, the most learned, judicious and correct, generally so accounted, of our *English* Comedians, and the more to be admired for being so, for that neither the height of natural parts, for he was no *Shakespear*, nor the cost of Extraordinary Education; for he is reported but a Bricklayers Son, but his own proper Industry and Addiction to Books advanc't him to this perfection: In three of his Comedies, namely the *Fox*, *Alchymist* and *Silent Woman*, he may be compared, in the Judgment of Learned Men, for Decorum, Language, and well Humouring of the Parts, as well with the chief of the Ancient Greec and Latin Comedians as the prime of Modern *Italians*, who have been judg'd the best of *Europe* for a happy Vein in Comedies, nor is his *Bartholomew-Fair* much short of them; as for his other Comedies *Cinthia's Revells*, *Poetaster*, and the rest, let the name of *Ben Johnson* protect them against whoever shall think fit to be severe in censure against them: The Truth is, his Tragedies *Sejanus* and *Catiline* seem to have in them more of an artificial and inflate than of a pathetical and naturally Tragic height: In the rest of his Poetry, for he is not wholly Dramatic, as his Underwoods, Epigrams, &c. he is sometimes bold and strenuous, sometimes Magisterial, sometimes Lepid and full enough of conceit, and sometimes a Man as other

Men are.—EDWARD PHILLIPS, *Theatrum Poetarum Anglicanorum*, 1675

Men of the quickest apprehensions, and aptest Geniuses to anything they undertake, do not always prove the greatest Masters in it. For there is more Patience and Flegme required in those that attaine to any Degree of Perfection, then is commonly found in the Temper of active, and ready wits, that soone tire and will not hold out; as the swiftest Race-horse will not perform a longe Jorney so well as a sturdy dull Jade. Hence it is that Virgil who wanted much of that Natural easines of wit that Ovid had, did nevertheless with hard Labour and long Study in the end, arrive at a higher perfection then the other with all his Dexterity of wit, but less Industry could attaine to: The same we may observe of Johnson, and Shakespeare. *For he that is able to thinke long and study well*, will be sure to finde out better things then another man can hit upon suddenly, though of more quick and ready Parts, *which is commonly but chance, and the other Art and Judgment.*—SAMUEL BUTLER, *Characters and Passages from Note-books*, c. 1680

To come lastly to *Ben Johnson*, who (as Mr. *Dryden* affirms) has borrow'd more from the Ancients than any: I crave leave to say in his behalf, that our late *Laureat* ⟨Dryden⟩ has far outdone him in Thefts, proportionable to his Writings: and therefore he is guilty of the highest Arrogance, to accuse another of a Crime, for which he is most of all men liable to be arraign'd.

Quis tulerit Gracchos de seditione querentes?

I must further alledge that Mr. *Johnson* in borrowing from the Ancients, has only follow'd the Pattern of the great Men of former Ages, *Homer*, *Virgil*, *Ovid*, *Horace*, *Plautus*, *Terence*, *Seneca*, &c. all which have imitated the Example of the industrious Bee, which sucks Honey from all sorts of Flowers, and lays it up in a general Repository. 'Twould be *actum agere* to repeat what is known to all Learned Men; that there was an *Illiad* written before that of *Homer*, which *Aristotle* mentions; and from which . . . *Homer* is supposed to have borrow'd his Design. . . . I could enumerate more Instances, but these are sufficient Precedents to excuse Mr. *Johnson*.

Permit me to say farther in his behalf, That if in imitation of these illustrious Examples, and Models of Antiquity, he has borrow'd from them, as they from each other; yet that he attempted, and as some think, happily succeeded in his Endeavours of Surpassing them: insomuch that a certain Person of Quality makes a Question, "Whether any of the Wit of the Latine Poets be more Terse and Eloquent in their Tongue, than this Great and Learned Poet appears in ours."

Whether Mr. *Dryden*, who has likewise succeeded to admiration in this way, or Mr. *Johnson* have most improv'd, and best advanc'd what they have borrow'd from the Ancients, I shall leave to the decision of the abler Criticks: only this I must say, in behalf of the later, that he has no ways endeavour'd to conceal what he has borrow'd, as the former has generally done. Nay, in his Play called *Sejanus* he has printed in the Margent throughout, the places from whence he borrow'd: the same he has practic'd in several of his Masques, (as the Reader may find in his Works;) a Pattern, which Mr. *Dryden* would have done well to have copied, and had thereby sav'd me the trouble of the following Annotations.

There is this difference between the Proceedings of these Poets, that Mr. *Johnson* has by Mr. *Dryden's* Confession *Design'd his Plots himself*; whereas I know not any One Play, whose Plot may be said to be the Product of Mr. *Dryden's* own Brain. When Mr. *Johnson* borrow'd, 'twas from the Treasury of the Ancients, which is so far from any diminution of his

Worth, that I think it is to his Honor; at least-wise I am sure he is justified by his Son *Carthwright*, in the following Lines:

What tho' thy searching Muse did rake the dust . . .

Give me leave to say a word, or two, in Defence of Mr. *Johnson's* way of Wit, which Mr. *Dryden* calls *Clenches*.

There have been few great Poets which have not propos'd some Eminent Author for their Pattern. . . . Mr. *Johnson* propos'd *Plautus* for his Model, and not only borrow'd from him, but imitated his way of Wit in English. There are none who have read him, but are acquainted with his way of playing with Words. . . . Nor might this be the sole Reason for Mr. *Johnson's* Imitation, for possibly 'twas his Compliance with the Age that induc'd him to this way of writing, it being then as Mr. *Dryden* observes the Mode of Wit, the Vice of the Age, and not *Ben Johnson's*: and besides Mr. *Dryden's* taxing Sir *Philip Sidney* for playing with his Words, I may add that I find it practis'd by several Dramatick Poets, who were Mr. *Johnson's* Cotemporaries. . . .

As to his Reflections on this Triumvirate in general: I might easily prove, that his Improprieties in Grammar, are equal to theirs: and that He himself has been guilty of Solecisms in Speech, and Flaws in Sence, as well as *Shakespear, Fletcher*, and *Johnson*.—GERARD LANGBAINE, *An Account of the English Dramatick Poets*, 1691

Sometimes *Personal Defects are misrepresented for Humours*.

I mean, sometimes Characters are barbarously exposed on the Stage, ridiculing Natural Deformities, Casual Defects in the Senses, and Infirmities of Age. . . . But much need not be said upon this Head to any body, especially to you, who, in one of your Letters to me concerning Mr. *Johnson's Fox*, have justly excepted against this Immoral part of *Ridicule* in *Corbaccio's* Character; and there I must agree with you to blame him whom otherwise I cannot enough admire for his great Mastery of true Humour in Comedy. . . .

The Character of *Morose* in the *Silent Woman* I take to be a Character of Humour. And I choose to instance this Character to you from many others of the same Author, because I know it has been Condemn'd by many as Unnatural and Farce: And you have your self hinted some dislike of it for the same Reason, in a Letter to me concerning some of *Johnson's* Plays.

Let us suppose *Morose* to be a Man Naturally Splenetick and Melancholly; is there any thing more offensive to one of such a Disposition than Noise and Clamour? Let any Man that has the Spleen . . . be Judge. . . . Well, but *Morose*, you will say, is so Extravagant, he cannot bear any Discourse or Conversation above a Whisper. Why, It is his excess of this Humour that makes him become Ridiculous, and qualifies his Character for Comedy. If the Poet had given him but a Moderate proportion of that Humour, 'tis odds but half the Audience would have sided with the Character and have Condemn'd the Author for Exposing a Humour, which was neither Remarkable nor Ridiculous. Besides, the distance of the Stage requires the Figure represented to be something larger than the Life; and sure a Picture may have Features larger in Proportion, and yet be very like the Original. . . .

The Character of Sir *John Daw* in the same Play is a Character of Affectation. He every where discovers an Affectation of Learning, when he is not only Conscious to himself, but the Audience also plainly perceives that he is Ignorant. . . .

The Character of *Cob* in *Every Man in his Humour* and most of the under Characters in *Bartholomew-Fair* discover only a Singularity of Manners, appropriated to the several Educations and Professions of the Persons represented. They are

not Humours but Habits contracted by Custom.—WILLIAM CONGREVE, "Mr. Congreve to Mr. Dennis, Concerning Humour in Comedy," *Letters upon Several Occasions*, 1696, pp. 80–96

Too nicely Jonson knew the critic's part;
Nature in him was almost lost in art.
—WILLIAM COLLINS, "An Epistle: Addrest to Sir Thomas Hanmer on his Edition of Shakespear's Works," 1743

Ben Johnson has *Humour* in his *Characters*, drawn with the most masterly Skill and Judgement; In Accuracy, Depth, Propriety, and Truth, he has no *Superior* or *Equal* amongst *Ancients* or *Moderns*; But the *Characters* he exhibits are of a *satirical*, and *deceitful*, or of a *peevish*, or *despicable* Species; as *Volpone, Subtle, Morose*, and *Abel Drugger*; In all of which there is something very justly to be *hated* or *despised*; And you feel the same Sentiments of *dislike* for every other *Character* of *Johnson's*; so that after you have been *gratify'd* with their *Detection* and *Punishment*, you are quite tired and disgusted with their Company. . . .

Johnson in his COMIC Scenes has expos'd and ridicul'd *Folly* and *Vice*; *Shakespear* has usher'd in *Joy, Frolic*, and *Happiness*.—The *Alchymist, Volpone*, and *Silent Woman* of Johnson, are most exquisite *Satires*. The *comic* Entertainments of *Shakespear* are the highest Compositions of *Raillery, Wit*, and *Humour*. *Johnson* conveys some Lesson in every Character. *Shakespear* some new Species of Foible and Oddity. The one pointed his Satire with masterly Skill; the other was inimitable in touching the Strings of Delight. With *Johnson* you are confin'd and instructed, with *Shakespear* unbent and dissolv'd in Joy. *Johnson* excellently concerts his Plots, and all his Characters unite in the one Design. *Shakespear* is superior to such Aid or Restraint; His Characters continually sallying from one independent Scene to another, and charming you in each with fresh Wit and Humour.

It may be further remark'd, that *Johnson* by pursuing the most useful Intention of *Comedy*, is in Justice oblig'd to *hunt down* and *demolish* his own *Characters*. Upon this Plan he must necessarily expose them to your *Hatred*, and of course can never bring out an amiable Person. His *Subtle*, and *Face* are detected at last, and become mean and despicable. Sir *Epicure Mammon* is properly trick'd, and goes off ridiculous and detestable. The *Puritan Elders* suffer for their Lust of Money, and are quite nauseous and abominable; And his *Morose* meets with a severe Punishment, after having sufficiently tired you with his Peevishness.—But *Shakespear*, with happier Insight, always supports his Characters in your *Favour*. His Justice *Shallow* withdraws before he is tedious; The *French* Doctor, and *Welch* Parson, go off in full Vigour and Spirit; Ancient *Pistoll* indeed is scurvily treated; however, he keeps up his Spirits; and continues to threaten to do well, that you are still desirous of his Company; and it is impossible to be tir'd or dull with the gay unfading Evergreen *Falstaff*.

But in remarking upon the Characters of *Johnson*, it would be unjust to pass *Abel Drugger* without notice; This is a little, mean, sneaking, sordid Citizen, hearkening to a Couple of Sharpers, who promise to make him rich; they can scarcely prevail upon him to resign the least Tittle he possesses, though he is assur'd, it is in order to get more; and your Diversion arises, from seeing him *wrung* between *Greediness* to *get* Money, and *Reluctance* to *part* with any for that Purpose. His Covetousness continually prompts him to follow the Conjurer, and puts him at the same Time upon endeavouring to stop his Fees. All the while he is excellently managed, and spirited on by *Face*. However, this Character upon the whole is *mean* and *despicable*, without any of that free spiritous jocund Humour abounding in *Shakespear*. But having been strangely exhibited upon the Theatre, a few Years ago, with odd Grimaces and extravagant Gestures, it has been raised into more Attention than it justly deserved; It is however to be acknowledg'd, that *Abel* has no Hatred, Malice, or Immorality, nor any assuming Arrogance, Pertness or Peevishness; And his eager Desire of getting and saving Money, by Methods he thinks lawful, are excusable in a Person of his Business; He is therefore not odious or detestable, but harmless and inoffensive in private Life; and from thence, correspondent with the Rule already laid down, he is the most capable of any of *Johnson's* Characters, of being a Favourite on the Theatre.

It appears, that in Imagination, Invention, Jollity, and gay Humour, *Johnson* had little *Power*; But *Shakespear* unlimited Dominion. The first was cautious and strict, not daring to sally beyond the Bounds of Regularity. The other bold and impetuous, rejoicing like a Giant to run his Course, through all the Mountains and Wilds of Nature and Fancy.

It requires an almost painful Attention to mark the Propriety and Accuracy of *Johnson*, and your Satisfaction arises from Reflection and Comparison; But the Fire and Invention of *Shakespear* in an instant are shot into your Soul, and enlighten and chear the most indolent Mind with their own Spirit and Lustre.—Upon the whole, *Johnson's* Compositions are like finished Cabinets, where every Part is wrought up with the most excellent Skill and Exactness;—*Shakespear's* like magnificent Castles, not perfectly finished or regular, but adorn'd with such bold and magnificent Designs, as at once delight and astonish you with their Beauty and Grandeur.—CORBYN MORRIS, *An Essay towards Fixing the True Standards of Wit, Humour, Raillery, Satire, and Ridicule*, 1744, pp. 29–36

Then Jonson came, instructed from the school,
To please in method, and invent by rule;
His studious patience and laborious art,
By regular approach assail'd the heart:
Cold approbation gave the lingering bays,
For those, who durst not censure, scarce could praise.
A mortal born, he met the general doom,
But left, like Egypt's kings, a lasting tomb.
        —SAMUEL JOHNSON, "Prologue, spoken by Mr.
        Garrick at the opening of the Theatre Royal,
        Drury Lane," 1747

Jonson possessed all the learning which was wanting to Shakspeare, and wanted all the genius of which the other was possessed. Both of them were equally deficient in taste and elegance, in harmony and correctness. A servile copyist of the ancients, Jonson translated into bad English the beautiful passages of the Greek and Roman authors, without accommodating them to the manners of his age and country. His merit has been totally eclipsed by that of Shakspeare, whose rude genius prevailed over the rude art of his contemporary.—DAVID HUME, *History of England*, 1754–62

Jonson, in the serious drama, is as much an imitator as Shakespeare is an original. He was very learned, as Samson was very strong, to his own hurt: blind to the nature of tragedy, he pulled down all antiquity on his head, and buried himself under it; we see nothing of Jonson, nor indeed of his admired (but also murdered) ancients; for what shone in the historian is a cloud on the poet; and *Catiline* might have been a good play, if Sallust had never written.

Who knows whether Shakespeare might not have thought less, if he had read more? Who knows, if he might not have

laboured under the load of Jonson's learning, as Enceladus under Etna?—EDWARD YOUNG, *Conjectures on Original Composition*, 1759

> The book of man he read with nicest art,
> And ransack'd all the secrets of the heart;
> Exerted penetration's utmost force,
> And traced each passion to its proper source;
> Then, strongly mark'd, in liveliest colours drew
> And brought each foible forth to public view:
> The coxcomb felt a lash in every word,
> And fools, hung out, their brother fools deterr'd.
> His comic humour kept the world in awe,
> And laughter frighten'd Folly more than Law.
>   —CHARLES CHURCHILL, *The Rosciad*, 1761

He was as defective in tragedy, as he was excellent in comedy; and that excellence is confined to a few of his works. In Shakspeare, we see the force of genius; in Jonson, the power of industry. He is frequently deficient in the harmony, and sometimes even in the measure, of his verses. What appears to be facility in his compositions is generally the effect of uncommon labour.—JAMES GRANGER, *Biographical History of England*, 1769–1824, Vol. 2, p. 125

Jonson gave an early example of metaphysical poetry; indeed, it was the natural resource of a mind amply stored with learning, gifted with a tenacious memory and the power of constant labour, but to which was denied that vivid perception of what is naturally beautiful, and that happiness of expression, which at once conveys to the reader the idea of the poet. . . . In reading Shakspeare, we often meet passages so congenial to our nature and feelings, that, beautiful as they are, we can hardly help wondering they did not occur to ourselves; in studying Jonson, we have often to marvel how his conceptions could have occurred to any human being. The one is like an ancient statue, the beauty of which, springing from the exactness of proportion, does not always strike at first sight, but rises upon us as we bestow time in considering it; the other is the representation of a monster, which is at first only surprising, and ludicrous or disgusting ever after.—SIR WALTER SCOTT, *Life of John Dryden*, 1805

He endeavoured to form an exact estimate of what he had on every occasion to perform; hence he succeeded best in that species of the drama which makes the principal demand on the understanding and with little call on the imagination and feeling,—the comedy of character. He introduced nothing into his works which critical dissection should not be able to extract again, as his confidence in it was such, that he conceived it exhausted everything which pleases and charms us in poetry. He was not aware that in the chemical retort of the critic what is most valuable, the volatile living spirit of a poem, evaporates. His pieces are in general deficient in soul, in that nameless something which never ceases to attract and enchant us even because it is indefinable. In the lyrical pieces, his Masques, we feel the want of a certain mental music of imagery and intonation, which the most accurate observation of difficult measures cannot give. He is everywhere deficient in those excellencies which, unsought, flow from the poet's pen, and which no artist who purposely hunts for them can ever hope to find. We must not quarrel with him, however, for entertaining a high opinion of his own works, since whatever merits they have he owed, like acquired moral properties, altogether to himself. The production of them was attended with labour, and unfortunately it is also a labour to read them. They resemble solid and regular edifices, before which, however, the clumsy scaffolding still remains, to interrupt and prevent us from viewing the architecture with ease and receiving from it a harmonious impression.—AUGUSTUS WILLIAM SCHLEGEL, *Lectures on Dramatic Art and Literature*, tr. John Black, 1809

Ben Jonson is original; he is, indeed, the only one of the great dramatists of that day who was not either directly produced, or very greatly modified, by Shakspere. In truth, he differs from our great master in everything—in form and in substance—and betrays no tokens of his proximity. He is not original in the same way as Shakspere is original; but after a fashion of his own, Ben Jonson is most truly original. . . . Ben Jonson exhibits a sterling English diction, and he has with great skill contrived varieties of construction; but his style is rarely sweet or harmonious, in consequence of his labour at point and strength being so evident. In all his works, in verse or prose, there is an extraordinary opulence of thought; but it is the produce of an amassing power in the author, and not of a growth from within. Indeed a large proportion of Ben Jonson's thoughts may be traced to classic or obscure modern writers, by those who are learned and curious enough to follow the steps of this robust, surly, and observing dramatist.—SAMUEL TAYLOR COLERIDGE, "Lecture VII: Ben Jonson, Beaumont and Fletcher, and Massinger" (1818), *Literary Remains*, 1836, ed. Henry Nelson Coleridge, Vol. 1, p. 92

In the regular drama he certainly holds up no romantic mirror to nature. His object was to exhibit human characters at once strongly comic and severely and instructively true; to nourish the understanding, while he feasted the sense of ridicule. He is more anxious for verisimilitude than even for comic effect. He understood the humors and peculiarities of his species scientifically, and brought them forward in their greatest contrasts and subtlest modifications. If Shakspeare carelessly scattered illusion, Jonson skillfully prepared it. This is speaking of Jonson in his happiest manner. There is a great deal of harsh and sour fruit in his miscellaneous poetry. It is acknowledged that in the drama he frequently overlabours his delineation of character, and wastes it tediously upon uninteresting humours and peculiarities. He is a moral painter, who delights overmuch to show his knowledge of moral anatomy.— THOMAS CAMPBELL, *An Essay on English Poetry*, 1819

I do not think that his Poetical merits are yet properly appreciated. I cannot consent that the palm of humour alone shall be given to him; while in wit, feeling, pathos, and Poetical diction, he is to be sunk fathoms below Fletcher and Massinger. In the last particular, I think that he excels them both, and, indeed, all his contemporaries, excepting Shakspeare. —HENRY NEELE, *Lectures on English Poetry*, 1828

Ben Jonson was a man of the *new* age, and the *new* direction of mind; he was that half of Shakspeare which reached forward into the future, but in a more eminent degree. His chief strength was in the very excess of his one-sidedness. With the immense force of his intellectual, reflective, and critical powers, he knocked down everything in his own way—but overthrew the good together with the bad. His first principle was, to have definite palpable reasons for everything: he wished at every point *to know* what ought to be done or left undone. The clearness of the reflecting *consciousness* was the standard to which he referred everything; but of that immediate creative faculty of fancy and feeling which is properly artistic, he possessed scarcely a germ. On this account the other half of Shakspeare's character, which, like the whole of the English national theatre, belonged to the romantic middle ages, was to him hateful, inconceivable, and worthless.—HERMANN ULRICI, *Shakspeare's Dramatic Art*, 1839, pp. 81–82

Jonson's intense observation was microscopical when turned to the minute evolutions of society, while his diversified learning at all times bore him into a nobler sphere of comprehension. This taste for reality, and this fullness of knowledge on whatever theme he chose, had a reciprocal action; and the one could not go without the other. Our poet doggedly set to "a humour" through its slightest anomalies, and, in the pride of his comic art, expanded his prototype. Yet this was but half the labor which he loved: his mind was stored with the most burdensome knowledge; and to the scholar the various erudition which he had so diligently acquired threw a more permanent light over those transient scenes which the painter of manners had so carefully copied.—ISAAC DISRAELI, "The 'Humours' of Jonson," *Amenities of Literature*, 1841

O rare Ben Jonson, let us have thy songs, rounded each with a spherical thought, and the lyrics from thy masques alive with learned fantasy, and thine epigrams keen and quaint, and thy noble epitaphs, under which the dead seem stirring! . . . At Jonson's name we stop perforce, and do salutation in the dust to the impress of that "learned sock." He was a learned man, as everybody knows; and as everybody does not believe, not the worse for his learning. His material, brought laboriously from East and West, is wrapt in a flame of his own. If the elasticity and abandonment of Shakespeare and of certain of Shakespeare's brothers, are not found in his writings, the reason of the defects need not be sought out in his readings. His genius, high and verdant as it grew, yet belonged to the hard woods: it was lance-wood rather than bow-wood—a genius rather noble than graceful—eloquent, with a certain severity and emphasis of enunciation.—ELIZABETH BARRETT BROWNING, *The Book of the Poets*, 1842

With this basis of sound English sense, Jonson has fancy, humor, satire, learning, a large knowledge of men and motives, and a remarkable command of language, sportive, scornful, fanciful, and impassioned. One of the fixed facts in English literature, he is too strongly rooted ever to be upset. He stands out from all his contemporaries, original, peculiar, leaning on none for aid, and to be tried by his own merits alone. Had his imagination been as sensitive as that of many of his contemporaries, or his self-love less, he would probably have fallen into their conscious or unconscious imitation of Shakespeare; but, as it was, he remained satisfied with himself to the last, delving in his own mine.—EDWIN P. WHIPPLE, "Old English Dramatists" (1846), *Essays and Reviews*, 1848, Vol. 2, p. 26

Shakespeare had permanently near him one envious person, Ben Jonson, an indifferent comic poet, whose *début* he assisted.—VICTOR HUGO, *William Shakespeare*, tr. A. Baillot, 1864, p. 23

Ben Jonson has been regarded as the first person who has done much in settling the "*grammar* of the English language." This merit is duly awarded to him, and Pope gives him the credit of having brought critical learning into vogue; also of having instructed both actors and spectators in what was the proper province of the dramatic Muse. His prose style, however, is a transcript of his laborious and painstaking mind, ostentatiously correct, and frequently forcible, with commonly a satisfactory felicity of epithet; but his sentences never appear to be extemporaneous, but always studied, and as being one result of the primæval curse, for he seems to have produced both his thoughts and his language "by the sweat of his brow." —CHARLES COWDEN CLARKE, "On the Comic Writers of England," *Gentleman's Magazine*, May 1871, p. 633

Ben Jonson had a mind of immense force and pertinacious

grasp; but nothing could be wider of the truth than the notion maintained with such ferocity by Gifford, that he was the father of regular comedy, the pioneer of severe and correct taste. Jonson's domineering scholarship must not be taken for more than it was worth: it was a large and gratifying possession in itself, but he would probably have written better plays and more poetry without it. It is a sad application of the mathematical method to the history of our literature to argue that the most learned playwright of his time superseded the rude efforts of such untaught mother-wits as Shakespeare with compositions based on classical models. What Jonson really did was to work out his own ideas of comedy and tragedy, and he expressly claimed the right to do so. The most scrupulous adherence to the unity of time, and the most rigid exclusion of tragic elements from comedy, do not make a play classical. Ben Jonson conformed to these externals; but there was not a more violently unclassical spirit than his among all the writers for the stage in that generation.—WILLIAM MINTO, *Characteristics of English Poets*, 1874, p. 337

To the modern reader, Ben Jonson's plays have lost their old attraction; but his occasional poems are full of heroic thought, and his songs are among the best in the language.— RALPH WALDO EMERSON, "Preface" to *Parnassus*, 1875, p. 6

By literary comedies, I mean comedies of classic inspiration, drawn chiefly from Menander and the Greek New Comedy through Terence; or else comedies of the poet's personal conception, that have had no model in life, and are humorous exaggerations, happy or otherwise. These are the Comedies of Ben Jonson, Massinger, and Fletcher. Massinger's Justice Greedy we can all of us refer to as a type, 'with fat capon lined' that has been and will be; and he would be comic, as Panurge is comic, but only a Rabelais could set him moving with real animation. Probably Justice Greedy would be comic to the audience of a country booth and to some of our friends. If we have lost our youthful relish for the presentation of characters put together to fit a type, we find it hard to put together the mechanism of a civil smile at his enumeration of his dishes. Something of the same is to be said of Bobadil, swearing 'by the foot of Pharaoh'; with a reservation, for he is made to move faster, and to act. The comic of Jonson is a scholar's excogitation of the comic; that of Massinger a moralist's.—GEORGE MEREDITH, "On the Idea of Comedy and of the Uses of the Comic Spirit" (1877), *Miscellaneous Prose*, 1910, pp. 10–11

> Broad-absed, broad-fronted, bounteous, multiform,
> With many a valley impleached with ivy and vine,
> Wherein the springs of all the streams run wine,
> And many a crag full-faced against the storm,
> The mountain where thy Muse's feet made warm
> Those lawns that revelled with her dance divine,
> Shines yet with fire as it was wont to shine
> From tossing torches round the dance aswarm.
> Nor less, high-stationed on the gray grave heights,
> High-thoughted seers with heaven's heart-kindling lights
> Hold converse: and the herd of meaner things
> Knows or by fiery scourge or fiery shaft
> When wrath on thy broad brows has risen, and laughed,
> Darkening thy soul with shadow of thunderous wings.
> —ALGERNON CHARLES SWINBURNE, "Ben Jonson," *Sonnets on English Dramatic Poets*, 1882

Ben Jonson stands at the head of that school of dramatists who take for their *Dramatis Personæ* not individuals but conventional types, and who somewhat ignore the complexities of human nature. No argument is wanted to show that

Shakspere's method of truly holding the mirror up to nature is the higher, the greater, and the truer method, but Jonson has ancient tradition in favour of his view of the dramatic art. . . . Seldom departs from the strict tradition: his cowardly braggarts are most inveterate cowards and braggarts, his knaves most arrant knaves, his fools have no redeeming touch of good sense, and his misers are grasping and avaricious beyond all human precedent and possibility. Nevertheless, the magnificent genius of the man—chiefly a literary genius—takes the reader's judgment by storm; and if the reader's, how much more would the hearer be captivated by the broad persistent humor of Bobadill and the mordant cynicism of Mosca and Volpone!—OSWALD CRAWFURD, *English Comic Dramatists*, 1883, p. 12

The more I read of the literary history of those days the more impressed I am by the predominance of Ben Jonson;—a great, careless, hard-living, hard-drinking, not ill-natured literary monarch. His strength is evidenced by the deference shown him—by his versatility; now some musical masque sparkling with little dainty bits which a sentimental miss might copy in her album or chant in her boudoir; and this, matched or followed by some labored drama full of classic knowledge, full of largest wordcraft, snapping with fire-crackers of wit, loaded with ponderous nuggets of strong sense, and the whole capped and booted with prologue and epilogue where poetic graces shine through proudest averments of indifference—of scorn of applause—of audacious self-sufficiency.—DONALD G. MITCHELL, *English Lands, Letters, and Kings (From Elizabeth to Anne)*, 1890, p. 26

He repels his admirers, he holds readers at arm's length. He is the least sympathetic of all the great English poets, and to appreciate him the rarest of literary tastes is required,—an appetite for dry intellectual beauty, for austerity of thought, for poetry that is logical, and hard, and lusty. Yet he did a mighty work for the English language. At a time when it threatened to sink into mere prettiness or oddity, and to substitute what was non-essential for what was definite and durable, Jonson threw his massive learning and logic into the scale, and forbade Jacobean poetry to kick the beam. He was rewarded by the passionate devotion of a tribe of wits and scholars; he made a deep mark on our literature for several generations subsequent to his own, and he enjoys the perennial respect of all close students of poetry.—EDMUND GOSSE, *The Jacobean Poets*, 1894, pp. 37–38

Jonson, whose splendid scorn took to itself lyric wings in the two great Odes to Himself, sang high and aloof for a while, then the frenzy caught him, and he flung away his lyre to gird himself for deeds of mischief among nameless and noteless antagonists. . . . He lost the calm of his temper and the clearness of his singing voice, he degraded his magnanimity by allowing it to engage in street-brawls, and he endangered the sanctuary of the inviolable soul.—WALTER RALEIGH, *Style*, 1897, pp. 68–71

It was Jonson who first revealed to the age the literary possibilities of the masque, and lesser men were not slow to follow in the path which he had marked out. Had it not been for Jonson, it is hardly too much to say that the masque would today be the exclusive property of the Court chronicler and the antiquarian, and of no more significance to literature than a tilting match or a Christmas gambol.—HERBERT ARTHUR EVANS, "Introduction" to *English Masques*, 1897, p. xi

Works

EVERY MAN IN HIS HUMOUR

In . . . low characters of vice and folly, lay the excellency of ⟨Jonson,⟩ that inimitable writer; who, when at any time he aimed at wit in the stricter sense, that is, sharpness of conceit, was forced either to borrow from the ancients, as to my knowledge he did very much from Plautus; or, when he trusted himself alone, often fell into meanness of expression. Nay, he was not free from the lowest and most grovelling kind of wit, which we call clenches, of which *Every Man in his Humour* is infinitely full; and, which is worse, the wittiest persons in the drama speak them.—JOHN DRYDEN, "Defence of the Epilogue," *The Conquest of Granada*, 1671

Every Man in his Humour is founded on such follies and passions as are perpetually incident to, and connected with, man's nature; such as do not depend upon local custom or change of fashion; and, for that reason, will bid fair to last as long as many of our old comedies. The language of Jonson is very peculiar; in perspicuity and elegance he is inferior to Beaumont and Fletcher, and very unlike the masculine dialogue of Massinger. It is almost needless to observe that he comes far short of the variety, strength, and natural flow, of Shakspeare. To avoid the common idiom, he plunges into stiff, quaint, and harsh, phraseology: he has borrowed more words, from the Latin tongue, than all the other authors of his time. However, the style of this play, as well as that of *The Alchemist* and *Silent Woman*, is more disentangled and free from foreign auxiliaries than the greatest part of his works. Most of the characters are truly dramatic.—THOMAS DAVIES, *Dramatic Miscellanies*, 1783, Vol. 2, p. 53

Every Man in his Humour is perhaps the earliest of European domestic comedies that deserves to be remembered; for even the Mandragora of Machiavel shrinks to a mere farce in comparison. A much greater master of comic powers than Jonson was indeed his contemporary, and, as he perhaps fancied, his rival; but, for some reason Shakspeare had never yet drawn his story from the domestic life of his countrymen. Jonson avoided the common defect of the Italian and Spanish theatre, the sacrifice of all other dramatic objects to one only, a rapid and amusing succession of incidents: his plot is slight and of no great complexity; but his excellence is to be found in the variety of his characters, and in their individuality, very clearly defined, with little extravagance.—HENRY HALLAM, *Introduction to the Literature of Europe*, 1837–39, Pt. 2, Ch. 6, Par. 53

EVERY MAN OUT OF HIS HUMOUR

If the reader would see the extravagance of building dramatic manners on abstract ideas, in its full light, he needs only turn to B. Johnson's *Every Man out of his Humour*; which under the name of a *play of character* is in fact, an unnatural, and, as the painters call it, *hard* delination of a group of simply existing passions, wholly chimerical, and unlike to anything we observe in the commerce of real life. Yet this comedy has always had its admirers. And *Randolph* in particular, was so taken with the design, that he seems to have formed his *muse's looking-glass* in express imitation of it.—RICHARD HURD, *A Dissertation on the Several Provinces of the Drama*, 1757, Vol. 1, p. 266

He is above everything a satirist of vice: he hates it, and he lashes it with a whip of scorpions. Listen to Asper—clearly Jonson himself—in the introduction to *Every Man Out of His Humour*. It is very scathing; but it is very splendid. As a mere question, of language, how nervous it is, how like the very best and strongest utterings of our own time! Contempt is the most

frequent note; but sometimes it swells to defiance, and becomes gratuitously, recklessly insulting.—T. E. BROWNE, "Ben Jonson," *The New Review*, May 1896, p. 522

THE POETASTER

This Roman play ⟨*The Poetaster*⟩ seems written to confute those enemies of Ben in his own days and ours, who have said that he made a pedantical use of his learning. He has here revived the whole Court of Augustus, by a learned spell. We are admitted to the society of the illustrious dead. Virgil, Horace, Ovid, Tibullus, converse in our own tongue more finely and poetically than they were used to express themselves in their native Latin. Nothing can be imagined more elegant, refined, and court-like, than the scenes between this Louis the Fourteenth of antiquity and his literati. The whole essence and secret of that kind of intercourse is contained therein. The economical liberality by which greatness, seeming to waive some part of its prerogative, takes care to lose none of the essentials; the prudential liberties of an inferior, which flatter by commanded boldness and soothe with complimentary sincerity. These, and a thousand beautiful passages from his *New Inn*, his *Cynthia's Revels*, and from those numerous court-masques and entertainments which he was in the daily habit of furnishing, might be adduced to show the poetical fancy and elegance of mind of the supposed rugged old bard.—CHARLES LAMB, *Specimens of English Dramatic Poets*, 1808

Poetaster is Jonson's acknowledged reply to the numerous attacks that had been made upon him during a period of three years. . . . So far as Jonson was concerned "The War of the Theatres" was ended, although peace was not declared. —JOSIAH H. PENNIMAN, *The War of the Theatres*, 1897, p. 118

SEJANUS

Act I.—
> *Arruntius:* The name Tiberius,
> I hope, will keep, howe'er he hath foregone
> The dignity and power.
> *Silius:* Sure, while he lives.
> *Arr.:* And dead, it comes to Drusus. Should he fail,
> To the brave issue of Germanicus;
> And they are three: too many (ha?) for him
> To have a plot upon?
> *Sil.:* I do not know
> The heart of his designs; but, sure, their face
> Looks farther than the present.
> *Arr.:* By the gods,
> If I could guess he had but such a thought,
> My sword should cleave him down . . .

The anachronic mixture in this Arruntius of the Roman republican, to whom Tiberius must have appeared as much a tyrant as Sejanus, with his James-and-Charles-the-First zeal for legitimacy of descent in this passage, is amusing. Of our great names Milton was, I think, the first who could properly be called a republican. My recollections of Buchanan's works are too faint to enable me to judge whether the historian is not a fair exception.

> Act ii. Speech of Sejanus:
> Adultery! it is the lightest ill
> I will commit. A race of wicked acts
> Shall flow out of my anger, and o'erspread
> The world's wide face, which no posterity
> Shall e'er approve, nor yet keep silent . . .

The more we reflect and examine, examine and reflect, the more astonished shall we be at the immense superiority of

Shakespeare over his contemporaries;—and yet what contemporaries!—giant minds indeed! Think of Jonson's erudition, and the force of learned authority in that age; and yet, in no genuine part of Shakespeare's works is there to be found such an absurd rant and ventriloquism as this, and too, too many other passages ferruminated by Jonson from Seneca's tragedies, and the writings of the later Romans. I call it ventriloquism, because Sejanus is a puppet, out of which the poet makes his own voice appear to come.

Act v. Scene of the sacrifice to Fortune.

This scene is unspeakably irrational. To believe, and yet to scoff at, a present miracle is little less than impossible. Sejanus should have been made to suspect priestcraft and a secret conspiracy against him.—SAMUEL TAYLOR COLERIDGE, "Notes on Ben Jonson" (1818), *Literary Remains*, 1836, ed. Henry Nelson Coleridge, Vol. 2, p. 274

In 1603, he produced his weighty tragedy of *Sejanus*, at Shakespeare's theatre, The Globe,—Shakespeare himself acting one of the inferior parts. Think of Shakespeare laboriously committing to memory the blank verse of Jonson! Though *Sejanus* failed of theatrical success, its wealth of knowledge and solid thought made it the best of all answers to his opponents. It was as if they had questioned his capacity to build a ship, and he had confuted them with a man-of-war.—EDWIN P. WHIPPLE, *The Literature of the Age of Elizabeth*, 1859, p. 102

⟨*Sejanus* was⟩ not very successful, but it succeeded better after he had recast it in part and made it all his own. It was printed in 1605, and the small criticisms of a pedantic age Ben Jonson forestalled by footnotes citing the authority for all that he had worked into harmonious and very noble play. Because the footnotes were there, and looked erudite, the superficial thing to do was to pronounce the play pedantic. But it is not pedantic. Jonson was no pedant. He had carried on for himself the education received at Westminster School, was a good scholar, delighted in his studies, and accumulated a large library, which, in or about the year 1622, was burnt. But he was true poet and true artist.—HENRY MORLEY, W. HALL GRIFFIN, *English Writers*, 1895, Vol. 11, p. 219

VOLPONE, OR THE FOX

> . . .the art which thou alone
> Hast taught our tongue, the rules of time, of place,
> And other rites, delivered with the grace
> Of comic style, which only, is far more
> Than any English stage hath known before.
> —FRANCIS BEAUMONT, "To My Dear Friend,
> Master Ben Jonson, upon his *Fox*," c. 1607

In the comedy of *The Fox*, there is not much to be censured, except the language, which is so pedantic and struck so full of Latinity, that few, except the learned, can perfectly understand it. "Jonson," says Dr. Young, "brought all the antients upon his head: by studying to speak like a Roman, he forgot the language of his country."—THOMAS DAVIES, *Dramatic Miscellanies*, 1783, Vol. 2, p. 97

This admirable, indeed, but yet more wonderful than admirable, play is, from the fertility and vigour of invention, character, language, and sentiment, the strongest proof how impossible it is to keep up any pleasurable interest in a tale, in which there is no goodness of heart in any of the prominent characters. After the third act, this play becomes not a dead, but a painful, weight on the feelings. *Zeluco* is an instance of the same truth. Bonario and Celia should have been made in some way or other principals in the plot; which they might have been, and the objects of interest, without having been

made characters. In novels, the person in whose fate you are most interested, is often the least marked character of the whole. If it were possible to lessen the paramountcy of Volpone himself, a most delightful comedy might be produced, by making Celia the ward or niece of Corvino, instead of his wife, and Bonario her lover.—SAMUEL TAYLOR COLERIDGE, "Notes on Ben Jonson" (1818), *Literary Remains*, 1836, ed. Henry Nelson Coleridge, Vol. 2, p. 276

The revolting aspects of life exhibited in ⟩*Volpone*⟩ are likely to prevent full justice being rendered its merits by most modern readers. Yet it long retained its hold over the national stage, while—which is less to be wondered at—the central character continued for generations to express to the popular mind the incarnation of a most loathsome variety of the vast *genus* hypocrite. Everybody knows how, at a critical stage of events in the reign of Queen Anne, Dr. Sacheverell in his notorious sermon pointed an attack upon the Whig leaders as representatives of revolution principles, by alluding to the Lord Treasurer Godolphin under the nickname of the Old Fox or Volpone.—ADOLPHUS WILLIAM WARD, *A History of English Dramatic Literature* (1875), 1899, Vol. 2, p. 363

EPICOENE, OR THE SILENT WOMAN

When his play of a *Silent Woman* was first acted, ther was found verses after on the stage against him, concluding that that play was well named the *Silent Woman*, ther was never one man to say Plaudite to it.—BEN JONSON, *Conversations with William Drummond*, 1619

⟨*Epicoene*⟩ is to my feelings the most entertaining of old Ben's comedies, and more than any other, would admit of being brought out anew, if under the management of a judicious and stage-understanding play-wright; and an actor, who had studied Morose, might make his fortune.—SAMUEL TAYLOR COLERIDGE, "Notes on Ben Jonson" (1818), *Literary Remains*, 1836, ed. Henry Nelson Coleridge, Vol. 2, p. 277

The plot is a distasteful one to my own feelings: it is coarse in design, coarse in its improbability, and, in short, is a direct contradiction of the author's own theory as to that which should characterise *legitimate* comedy; for the play of *Epicene* is little better than a hoydening farce. The character of Morose himself is certainly well sustained, although in it an extreme case is put throughout; and enormous demands are made upon the credulity of the audience that such a man could be supposed to exist at all, with so morbid a sensitiveness to noise as to poison his whole existence.—CHARLES COWDEN CLARKE, "On the Comic Writers of England," *Gentleman's Magazine*, May 1871, p. 643

THE ALCHEMIST

> To say, this comedy pleased long ago,
> Is not enough to make it past you now.
> Yet, gentlemen, your ancestors had wit;
> When few men censured, and when fewer writ.
> And Jonson, of those few the best, chose this,
> As the best model of his masterpiece.
> Subtle was got by our Albumazar,
> That Alchymist by this Astrologer;
> Here he was fashion'd, and we may suppose
> He liked the fashion well, who wore the clothes.
> But Ben made nobly his what he did mould;
> What was another's lead becomes his gold:
> Like an unrighteous conqueror he reigns,
> Yet rules that well, which he unjustly gains.
> —JOHN DRYDEN, "Prologue," *Albumazar*, 1668

This comedy, which was laudably written to ridicule a prevailing folly, must, no doubt, have been greatly successful originally, since we have seen it very much followed and admired during the time Garrick ornamented the stage. His incomparable performance, however, of Abel Drugger was a considerable drawback from the proper reputation of the author, and in great measure the cause of the successs of the play; at the same time it must be confessed that the best acting can do nothing without good materials, with which certainly the *Alchymist* abounds. —CHARLES DIBDIN, A *Complete History of the Stage*, 1795, Vol. 3, p. 295

The judgment is perfectly overwhelmed by the torment of images, words, and book-knowledge, with which Epicure Mammon (Act 2, Scene 2) confounds and stunts his incredulous hearer. They come pouring out like the successive falls of Nilus. They "doubly redouble strokes upon the foe." Description outstrides proof. We are made to believe effects before we have testimony for their causes. If there is no one image which attains the height of the sublime, yet the confluence and assemblage of them all produces a result equal to the grandest poetry. The huge Xerxean army contervails against single Achilles. Epicure Mammon is the most determined offspring of its author. It has the whole "matter and copy of the father—eye, nose, lip, the trick of his frown." It is just such a swaggerer as contemporaries have described old Ben to be. Meercraft, Bobadil, the Host of the New Inn, have all his image and superscription. But Mammon is arrogant pretension personified. Sir Samson Legend, in "Love for Love," is such another lying, overbearing character, but he does not come up to Epicure Mammon. What a "towering bravery" there is in his sensuality! he affects no pleasure under a Sultan. It is as if "Egypt with Assyria strove in luxury."—CHARLES LAMB, *Specimens of English Dramatic Poets*, 1808

⟨*The Alchemist*⟩ remains, in spite of its proved unfittedness for the stage, and its antiquated interests, one of the most splendid compositions written by an English hand. Lamb, with unerring instinct, hit upon the central jewel of the whole splendid fabric when he selected for special praise the long scene in Subtle's house, where Epicure Mammon boasts what rare things he will do when he obtains the philosopher's stone. Here Jonson, running and leaping under the tremendous weight of his own equipment, perfectly overwhelms the judgment "by the torrent of images, words, and book-knowledge with which Mammon confounds and stuns" us.—EDMUND GOSSE, *The Jacobean Poets*, 1894, p. 28

CATILINE

> With strenuous, sinewy words that Catiline swells,
> I reckon it not among men—miracles.
> How could that poem well a vigour lack,
> When each line oft cost Ben a cup of sack.
> —R. BARON, *Pocula Castalia*, 1650, p. 113

Catiline is only less interesting than *Sejanus*, because it presents no such difficult problem of characterisation as Tiberius. Within the limits of his subject, however, Jonson has fully availed himself of his opportunities. Each of the characters, notably those of the conspirators, stands out distinctly from the rest; perhaps in his effort to draw distinctly, the dramatist has, after his manner, rather overdrawn the humours, thereby impairing the humanity, of his personages,—the visionary imbecility of Lentulus, the braggadocio of Cethegus, the savage ferocity of Catiline. On the other hand, the oratorical expansiveness of Cicero is delicately, though copiously illustrated; the danger is avoided of rendering him ridiculous, although both

his love of speech and his respect for his own achievements are allowed ample expression. Of Cæsar and of Cato enough is hardly made; the key to the double-handed policy of the former is not clearly revealed, while the latter appears too generally as the mere echo of Cicero. The female characters of the play are drawn with a humour nothing less than exuberant.—ADOLPHUS WILLIAM WARD, A *History of English Dramatic Literature* (1875), 1899, Vol. 2, p. 341

BARTHOLOMEW FAIR

In *Bartholomew Fair*, or the lowest kind of comedy, that degree of heightening is used, which is proper to set off that subject: It is true the author was not there to go out of prose, as he does in his higher arguments of comedy, *The Fox* and *Alchemist*; yet he does so raise his matter in that prose, as to render it delightful; which he could never had performed, had he only said or done those very things, that are daily spoken or practised in the fair: for then the fair itself would be as full of pleasure to an ingenious person as the play, which we manifestly see it is not. But he hath made an excellent lazar of it; the copy is of price, though the original be vile. You see in *Catiline* and *Sejanus* where the argument is great, he sometimes ascends to verse, which shows he thought it not unnatural in serious plays; and had his genius been as proper for rhyme as it was for honour, or had the age in which he lived attained to as much knowledge in verse as ours, it is probable he would have adorned those subjects with that kind of writing.—JOHN DRYDEN, A *Defence of an Essay of Dramatic Poesy*, 1668

This strange play, out of which might be framed the humour of half a dozen farces, is fuller, perhaps, of comic characters than any thing that ever appeared on the stage. We are given to understand that Jonson wrote it purposely to ridicule the age in which he lived, for the prevalent preference given to low wit, instead of polished and refined writing. If this was his motive he has outwitted himself, for there is more nature in *Bartholomew Fair* than in any one of his other works; but yet, being as it is, crammed full of extraneous and heterogeneous incidents, he has as much overshot the mark as he had come short of it in his *Catiline*, which this play was written purposely to defend; that tragedy having nothing interesting in it, on account of its dullness and declamation; and this comedy, on account of its wildness and extravagance. —CHARLES DIBDIN, A *Complete History of the Stage*, 1795, Vol. 3, p. 297

Absolutely original, so far as is known, in both conception and construction, it abounds with the most direct kind of satire and with the broadest fun.—ADOLPHUS WILLIAM WARD, A *History of English Dramatic Literature* (1875), 1899, Vol. 2, p. 37

There is no dramatic work in English at all comparable in its own kind with this brilliant and bewildering presentment of a comic turmoil, and, by a curious chance, it is exactly here, where it might be expected that the dramatist would be peculiarly tempted to subordinate all attempt at character-painting to the mere embodiment of humours, that one of Ben Jonson's few really living and breathing creatures is found in the person of the Puritan, Rabbi Zeal-of-the Land.—EDMUND GOSSE, *The Jacobean Poets*, 1894, p. 32

THE SAD SHEPHERD

Fletcher's pastoral, blasted as it is in some parts by fire not from heaven, is still a green and leafy wilderness of poetical beauty; Jonson's, deformed also by some brutality more elaborate than anything of the same sort in Fletcher, is at the best but a trim garden, and, had it been ever so happily finished, would have been nothing more.—GEORGE L. CRAIK, A *Compendious*

History of English Literature and of the English Language,
1861, Vol. 1, p. 605

A very charming fragment; so sweet and gentle, that it stands
alone in conspicuous beauty amidst the rough and stalwart
productions of his dramatic Muse. —CHARLES COWDEN
CLARKE, "On the Comic Writers of England," *Gentleman's
Magazine,* May 1871, p. 649

The *Sad Shepherd* is not quite complete; but, though not without a few blots and stains, it contains some of Jonson's finest
poetry. The shepherdess Amie is such a sweet creation that one
is indignant at the dramatist for the vulgar and wholly superfluous immodesty of one of her expressions in her first confession of unrest: to the pure all things are pure, but it exposes the
simple shepherdess to unnecessary ridicule from the ordinary
reader. One is surprised to find such sympathy with simple
innocence in rare but rough Ben—all the more that the *Sad
Shepherd* was written in his later years, when he was exacer-
bated by failure and poverty. —WILLIAM MINTO, *Characteristics of English Poets,* 1874, p. 343

JOHN DRYDEN
From *An Essay of Dramatick Poesie*
1668

As for *Johnson,* to whose Character I am now arriv'd, if we
look upon him while he was himself, (for his last Playes
were but his dotages) I think him the most learned and judicious Writer which any Theater ever had. He was a most severe
Judge of himself as well as others. One cannot say he wanted
wit, but rather that he was frugal of it. In his works you find
little to retrench or alter. Wit and Language, and Humour also
in some measure we had before him; but something of Art was
wanting to the *Drama* till he came. He manag'd his strength to
more advantage then any who preceded him. You seldome find
him making Love in any of his Scenes, or endeavouring to
move the Passions; his genius was too sullen and saturnine to
do it gracefully, especially when he knew he came after those
who had performed both to such an height. Humour was his
proper Sphere, and in that he delighted most to represent Mechanick people. He was deeply conversant in the Ancients,
both *Greek* and *Latine,* and he borrow'd boldly from them:
there is scarce a Poet or Historian among the *Roman* Authours
of those times whom he has not translated in *Sejanus* and
Catiline. But he has done his Robberies so openly, that one
may see he fears not to be taxed by any Law. He invades
Authours like a Monarch, and what would be theft in other
Poets, is onely victory in him. With the spoils of these Writers
he so represents old *Rome* to us, in its Rites, Ceremonies and
Customs, that if one of their Poets had written either of his
Tragedies, we had seen less of it then in him. If there was any
fault in his Language, 'twas that he weav'd it too closely and
laboriously, in his Comedies especially: perhaps too, he did a
little too much Romanize our Tongue, leaving the words
which he translated almost as much *Latine* as he found them:
wherein though he learnedly followed their language, he did
not enough comply with the Idiom of ours. If I would compare
him with *Shakespeare,* I must acknowledge him the more correct Poet, but *Shakespeare* the greater wit. *Shakespeare* was the
Homer, or Father of our Dramatick Poets; *Johnson* was the
Virgil, the pattern of elaborate writing; I admire him, but I love
Shakespeare. To conclude of him, as he has given us the most
correct Playes, so in the precepts which he has laid down in his
Discoveries, we have as many and profitable Rules for perfecting the Stage as any wherewith the *French* can furnish us.

Having thus spoken of the Authour, I proceed to the examination of his Comedy, *The Silent Woman.*

Examen of the Silent Woman

To begin first with the length of the Action, it is so far
from exceeding the compass of a Natural day, that it takes not
up an Artificial one. 'Tis all included in the limits of three
hours and an half, which is no more than is requir'd for the
presentment on the Stage. A beauty perhaps not much observ'd; if it had, we should not have look'd on the *Spanish*
Translation of *Five Hours* with so much wonder. The Scene of
it is laid in *London;* the latitude of place is almost as little as you
can imagine: for it lies all within the compass of two Houses,
and after the first Act, in one. The continuity of Scenes is
observ'd more than in any of our Playes, except his own *Fox*
and *Alchymist.* They are not broken above twice or thrice at
most in the whole Comedy, and in the two best of *Corneille's*
Playes, the *Cid* and *Cinna,* they are interrupted once. The
action of the Play is intirely one; the end or aim of which is the
setling *Morose's* Estate on *Dauphine.* The Intrigue of it is the
greatest and most noble of any pure unmix'd Comedy in any
Language: you see in it many persons of various characters and
humours, and all delightful: As first, *Morose,* or an old Man, to
whom all noise but his own talking is offensive. Some who
would be thought Criticks, say this humour of his is forc'd: but
to remove that objection, we may consider him first to be
naturally of a delicate hearing, as many are to whom all sharp
sounds are unpleasant; and secondly, we may attribute much of
it to the peevishness of his Age, or the wayward authority of an
old man in his own house, where he may make himself
obeyed; and to this the Poet seems to allude in his name *Morose.* Beside this, I am assur'd from divers persons, that *Ben.
Johnson* was actually acquainted with such a man, one altogether as ridiculous as he is here represented. Others say it is
not enough to find one man of such an humour; it must be
common to more, and the more common the more natural. To
prove this, they instance in the best of Comical Characters,
Falstaffe: There are many men resembling him; Old, Fat,
Merry, Cowardly, Drunken, Amorous, Vain, and Lying: But to
convince these people, I need but tell them, that humour is the
ridiculous extravagance of conversation, wherein one man differs from all others. If then it be common, or communicated to
many, how differs it from other mens? or what indeed causes it
to be ridiculous so much as the singularity of it? As for
Falstaffe, he is not properly one humour, but a Miscellany of
Humours or Images, drawn from so many several men; that
wherein he is singular is his wit, or those things he says,
præter expectatum, unexpected by the Audience; his quick
evasions when you imagine him surpriz'd, which as they are
extreamly diverting of themselves, so receive a great addition
from his person; for the very sight of such an unwieldy old
debauch'd fellow is a Comedy alone. And here having a place
so proper for it I cannot but enlarge somewhat upon this subject of humour into which I am fallen. The Ancients had little
of it in their Comedies; for the *to geloin* of the old Comedy, of
which *Aristophanes* was chief, was not so much to imitate a
man, as to make the people laugh at some odd conceit, which
had commonly somewhat of unnatural or obscene in it. Thus
when you see *Socrates* brought upon the Stage, you are not to
imagine him made ridiculous by the imitation of his actions,
but rather by making him perform something very unlike himself: something so childish and absurd, as by comparing it with
the gravity of the true *Socrates,* makes a ridiculous object for
the Spectators. In their new Comedy which succeeded, the
Poets sought indeed to express the *emos* as in their Tragedies the
pathos of Mankind. But this *emos* contain'd only the general

Characters of men and manners; as old men, Lovers, Servingmen, Courtizans, Parasites, and such other persons as we see in their Comedies; all which they made alike: that is, one old man or Father; one Lover, one Courtizan so like another, as if the first of them had begot the rest of every sort: *Ex homine hunc natum dicas*. The same custome they observ'd likewise in their Tragedies. As for the *French*, though they have the word *humeur* among them, yet they have small use of it in their Comedies, or Farces; they being but ill imitations of the *ridiculum*, or that which stirr'd up laughter in the old Comedy. But among the *English* 'tis otherwise: where by humour is meant some extravagant habit, passion, or affection; particular (as I said before) to some one person: by the oddness of which, he is immediately distinguish'd from the rest of men; which being lively and naturally represented, most frequently begets that malicious pleasure in the Audience which is testified by laughter: as all things which are deviations from customes are ever the aptest to produce it: though by the way this laughter is onely accidental, as the person represented is Fantastick or Bizarre; but pleasure is essential to it, as the imitation of what is natural. The description of these humours, drawn from the knowledge and observation of particular persons, was the peculiar genius and talent of *Ben. Johnson*; To whose Play I now return.

Besides *Morose*, there are at least 9 or 10 different Characters and humours in the *Silent Woman*, all which persons have several concernments of their own, yet are all us'd by the Poet, to the conducting of the main design to perfection. I shall not waste time in commending the writing of this Play, but I will give you my opinion, that there is more wit and acuteness of Fancy in it then in any of *Ben. Johnson's*. Besides that, he has here describ'd the conversation of Gentlemen in the persons of *True-Wit*, and his Friends, with more gayety, ayre and freedom, then in the rest of his Comedies. For the contrivance of the Plot 'tis extream elaborate, and yet withal easie; for the *lysis*, or untying of it, 'tis so admirable, that when it is done, no one of the Audience would think the Poet could have miss'd it; and yet it was conceald so much before the last Scene, that any other way would sooner have enter'd into your thoughts. But I dare not take upon me to commend the Fabrick of it, because it is altogether so full of Art, that I must unravel every Scene in it to commend it as I ought. And this excellent contrivance is still the more to be admir'd, because 'tis Comedy where the persons are onely of common rank, and their business private, not elevated by passions or high concernments as in serious Playes. Here every one is a proper Judge of all he sees; nothing is represented but that with which he daily converses: so that by consequence all faults lie open to discovery, and few are pardonable. 'Tis this which *Horace* has judiciously observ'd:

> Creditur ex medio quia res arcessit habere
> Sudoris minimum, sed habet Comedia tanto
> Plus oneris, quanto veniæ minus.——

But our Poet, who was not ignorant of these difficulties, has made use of all advantages; as he who designes a large leap takes his rise from the highest ground. One of these advantages is that which *Corneille* has laid down as the greatest which can arrive to any Poem, and which he himself could never compass above thrice in all this Playes, *viz.* the making choice of some signal and long-expected day, whereon the action of the Play is to depend. This day was that design'd by *Dauphine* for the setling of his Uncles Estate upon him; which to compass he contrives to marry him: that the marriage had been plotted by him long beforehand is made evident by what he tells *True-Wit*

in the second Act, that in one moment he had destroy'd what he had been raising many months.

There is another artifice of the Poet, which I cannot here omit, because by the frequent practice of it in his Comedies, he has left it to us almost as a Rule, that is, when he has any Character or humour wherein he would show a *Coup de Maistre*, or his highest skill; he recommends it to your observation by a pleasant description of it before the person first appears. Thus, in *Bartholomew Fair* he gives you the Pictures of *Numps* and *Cokes*, and in this those of *Daw*, *Lafoole*, *Morose*, and the *Collegiate Ladies*; all which you hear describ'd before you see them. So that before they come upon the Stage you have a longing expectation of them, which prepares you to receive them favourably; and when they are there, even from their first appearance you are so far acquainted with them, that nothing of their humour is lost to you.

I will observe yet one thing further of this admirable Plot; the business of it rises in every Act. The second is greater then the first; the third then the second, and so forward to the fifth. There too you see, till the very last Scene, new difficulties arising to obstruct the action of the Play; and when the Audience is brought into despair that the business can naturally be effected, then, and not before, the discovery is made. But that the Poet might entertain you with more variety all this while, he reserves some new Characters to show you, which he opens not till the second and third Act. In the second, *Morose*, *Daw*, the *Barber* and *Otter*; in the third the *Collegiat Ladies*: All which he moves afterwards in by-walks, or under-Plots, as diversions to the main design, least it should grow tedious, though they are still naturally joyn'd with it, and somewhere or other subservient to it. Thus, like a skilful Chest-player, by little and little he draws out his men, and makes his pawns of use to his greater persons.

If this Comedy, and some others of his, were translated into *French* Prose (which would now be no wonder to them, since *Moliere* has lately given them Playes out of Verse which have not displeas'd them) I believe the controversie would soon be decided betwixt the two Nations, even making them the Judges. But we need not call our Hero's to our ayde; Be it spoken to the honour of the *English*, our Nation can never want in any Age such who are able to dispute the Empire of Wit with any people in the Universe. And though the fury of a Civil War, and Power, for twenty years together, abandon'd to a barbarous race of men, Enemies of all good Learning, had buried the Muses under the ruines of Monarchy; yet with the restoration of our happiness, we see reviv'd Poesie lifting up its head, & already shaking off the rubbish which lay so heavy on it. We have seen since His Majesties return, many Dramatick Poems which yield not to those of any forreign Nation, and which deserve all Lawrels but the *English*. I will set aside Flattery and Envy: it cannot be deny'd but we have had some little blemish either in the Plot or writing of all those Playes which have been made within these seven years: (and perhaps there is no Nation in the world so quick to discern them, or so difficult to pardon them, as ours:) yet if we can perswade our selves to use the candour of that Poet, who (though the most severe of Criticks) has left us this caution by which to moderate our censures;

> Ubi plura nitent in carmine non ego paucis
> offendar maculis.

If in consideration of their many and great beauties, we can wink at some slight, and little imperfections; if we, I say, can be thus equal to our selves, I ask no favour from the *French*. And if I do not venture upon any particular judgment of our late Playes, 'tis out of the consideration which an Ancient Writer gives me; *Vivorum, ut magna admiratio ita censura difficilis*: betwixt the extreams of admiration and malice, 'tis hard to judge uprightly of the living. Onely I think it may be permitted me to say, that as it is no less'ning to us to yield to some Playes, and those not many of our own Nation in the last Age, so can it be no addition to pronounce of our present Poets that they have far surpass'd all the Ancients, and the Modern Writers of other Countreys.

WILLIAM HAZLITT

From *Lectures on the Dramatic Literature of the Age of Elizabeth*
1820

Lecture 4
On Beaumont and Fletcher, Ben Jonson, Ford, and Massinger

B en Jonson's serious productions are, in my opinion, superior to his comic ones. What he does, is the result of strong sense and painful industry; but sense and industry agree better with the grave and severe, than with the light and gay productions of the muse. "His plays were works," as some one said of them, "while others' works were plays." The observation had less of compliment than of truth in it. He may be said to mine his way into a subject, like a mole, and throws up a prodigious quantity of matter on the surface, so that the richer the soil in which he labours, the less dross and rubbish we have. His fault is, that he sets himself too much to his subject, and cannot let go his hold of an idea, after the insisting on it becomes tiresome or painful to others. But his tenaciousness of what is grand and lofty, is more praiseworthy than his delight in what is low and disagreeable. His pedantry accords better with didactic pomp than with illiterate and vulgar gabble; his learning, engrafted on romantic tradition or classical history, looks like genius.

> Miraturque novas frondes et non sua poma.

He was equal, by an effort, to the highest things, and took the same, and even more successful pains to grovel to the lowest. He raised himself up or let himself down to the level of his subject, by ponderous machinery. By dint of application, and a certain strength of nerve, he could do justice to Tacitus and Sallust no less than to mine host of the New Inn. His tragedy of *The Fall of Sejanus*, in particular, is an admirable piece of ancient mosaic. The principal character gives one the idea of a lofty column of solid granite, nodding to its base from its pernicious height, and dashed in pieces by a breath of air, a word of its creator—feared, not pitied, scorned, unwept, and forgotten. The depth of knowledge and gravity of expression sustain one another throughout: the poet has worked out the historian's outline, so that the vices and passions, the ambition and servility of public men, in the heated and poisoned atmosphere of a luxurious and despotic court, were never described in fuller or more glowing colours. I am half afraid to give any extracts, lest they should be tortured into an application to other times and characters than those referred to by the poet. Some of the sounds, indeed, may bear (for what I know) an awkward construction: some of the objects may look double to squint-eyed suspicion. But that is not my fault. It only proves that the characters of prophet and poet are implied in each other; that he who describes human nature well once, describes it for good and all, as it was, is, and, I begin to fear, will ever be. Truth always was, and must always remain, a libel to the tyrant and the slave. Thus Satrius Secundus and Pinnarius Natta, two public informers in those days, are described as

Two of Sejanus' blood-hounds, whom he breeds
    With human flesh, to bay at citizens.

But Rufus, another of the same well-bred gang, debating the point of his own character with two senators whom he has entrapped, boldly asserts, in a more courtly strain,

. . . To be a spy on traitors
        Is honourable vigilance.

This sentiment of the respectability of the employment of a government spy, which had slept in Tacitus for near two thousand years, has not been without its modern patrons. The effects of such "honourable vigilance" are very finely exposed in the following high-spirited dialogue between Lepidus and Arruntius, two noble Romans, who loved their country, but were not unfashionable enough to confound their country with its oppressors, and the extinguishers of its liberty.

Arr.: What are thy arts (good patriot, teach them
        me)
    That have preserv'd thy hairs to this white dye,
    And kept so reverend and so dear a head
    Safe on his comely shoulders?
Lep.: Arts, Arruntius!
    None but the plain and passive fortitude
    To suffer and be silent; never stretch
    These arms against the torrent; live at home
    With my own thoughts and innocence about
        me,
    Not tempting the wolves' jaws: these are my arts.
Arr.: I would begin to study 'em, if I thought
    They would secure me. May I pray to Jove
    In secret, and be safe? ay, or aloud?
    With open wishes? so I do not mention
    Tiberius or Sejanus! Yes, I must,
    If I speak out. 'Tis hard, that. May I think,
    And not be rack'd? What danger is't to dream?
    Talk in one's sleep, or cough? Who knows the
        law?
    May I shake my head without a comment? Say
    It rains, or it holds up, and not be thrown
    Upon the Gemonies? These now are things
    Whereon men's fortunes, yea, their fate depends;
    Nothing hath privilege 'gainst the violent ear.
    No place, no day, no hour (we see) is free
    (Not our religious and most sacred times)
    From some one kind of cruelty; all matter,
    Nay, all occasion pleaseth. Madman's rage,
    The idleness of drunkards, women's nothing,
    Jesters' simplicity, all, all is good
    That can be catch'd at.

'Tis a pretty picture; and the duplicates of it, though multiplied without end, are seldom out of request.

The following portrait of a prince besieged by flatterers (taken from *Tiberius*) has unrivalled force and beauty, with historic truth:

                . . . If this man
    Had but a mind allied unto his words,
    How blest a fate were it to us, and Rome?
    Men are deceived, who think there can be thrall
    Under a virtuous prince. Wish'd liberty
    Ne'er lovelier looks than under such a crown.
    But when his grace is merely but lip-good,
    And that, no longer than he airs himself
    Abroad in public, there to seem to shun
    The strokes and stripes of flatterers, which within
    Are lechery unto him, and so feed
    His brutish sense with their afflicting sound,
    As (dead to virtue) he permits himself
    Be carried like a pitcher by the ears

To every act of vice; this is a case
Deserves our fear, and doth presage the nigh
And close approach of bloody tyranny.
Flattery is midwife unto princes' rage:
And nothing sooner doth help forth a tyrant
Than that, and whisperers' grace, that have the time,
The place, the power, to make all men offenders!

The only part of this play in which Ben Jonson has completely forgotten himself (or rather seems not to have done so) is in the conversations between Livia and Eudemus, about a wash for her face, here called a *fucus*, to appear before Sejanus. *Catiline's Conspiracy* does not furnish by any means an equal number of striking passages, and is spun out to an excessive length with Cicero's artificial and affected orations against Catiline, and in praise of himself. His apologies for his own eloquence, and declarations that in all his art he uses no art at all, put one in mind of Polonius's circuitous way of coming to the point. Both these tragedies, it might be observed, are constructed on the exact principles of a French historical picture, where every head and figure is borrowed from the antique; but, somehow, the precious materials of old Roman history and character are better preserved in Jonson's page than on David's canvas.

Two of the most poetical passages in Ben Jonson are the description of Echo in *Cynthia's Revels*, and the fine comparison of the mind to a temple, in the 'New Inn;' a play which, on the whole, however, I can read with no patience. . . .

Lecture 6
On Miscellaneous Poems; F. Beaumont,
P. Fletcher, Drayton, Daniel, etc.;
Sir P. Sidney's Arcadia, *and other works*

. . . Ben Jonson's detached poetry I like much, as indeed I do all about him, except when he degraded himself by "the laborious foolery" of some of his farcical characters, which he could not deal with sportively, and only made stupid and pedantic. I have been blamed for what I have said, more than once, in disparagement of Ben Jonson's comic humour; but I think he was himself aware of his infirmity, and has (not improbably) alluded to it in the following speech of Crites in *Cynthia's Revels:*

Oh, how despised and base a thing is man,
If he not strive to erect his groveling thoughts
Above the strain of flesh! But how more cheap,
When even his best and understanding part
(The crown and strength of all his faculties)
Floats like a dead-drown'd body, on the stream
Of vulgar humour, mix'd with common'st dregs:
I suffer for their guilt now; and my soul
(Like one that looks on ill-affected eyes)
Is hurt with mere intention on their follies.
Why will I view them then? my sense might ask me:
Or is't a rarity or some new object
That strains my strict observance to this point:
But such is the perverseness of our nature,
That if we once but fancy levity,
(How antic and ridiculous soever
It suit with us) yet will our muffled thought
Chuse rather not to see it than avoid it . . .

Ben Jonson had self-knowledge and self-reflection enough to apply this to himself. His tenaciousness on the score of critical objections does not prove that he was not conscious of them himself, but the contrary. The greatest egotists are those whom it is impossible to offend, because they are wholly and incurably blind to their own defects; or if they could be made to see them, would instantly convert them into so many beauty-spots and ornamental graces. Ben Jonson's fugitive and lighter pieces are not devoid of the characteristic merits of that class of composition; but still often in the happiest of them, there is a specific gravity in the author's pen, that sinks him to the bottom of his subject, though buoyed up for a time with art and painted plumes, and produces a strange mixture of the mechanical and fanciful, of poetry and prose, in his songs and odes. For instance, one of his most airy effusions is the 'Triumph of his Mistress:' yet there are some lines in it that seem inserted almost by way of burlesque. It is, however, well worth repeating.

See the chariot at hand here of love
Wherin my lady rideth!
Each that draws it is a swan or a dove;
And well the car love guideth!
As she goes all hearts do duty
Unto her beauty:
And enamour'd, do wish so they might
But enjoy such a sight,
That they still were to run by her side,
Through swords, through seas, whither she would
ride.
Do but look on her eyes, they do light
All that love's world compriseth!
Do but look on her hair, it is bright
As love's star when it riseth!
Do but mark, her forehead's smoother
Than words that soothe her:
And from her arch'd brows, such a grace
Sheds itself through the face,
As alone their triumphs to the life
All the gain, all the good of the elements' strife.

Have you seen but a bright lily grow,
Before rude hands have touch'd it?
Ha' you mark'd but the fall of the snow
Before the soil hath smutch'd it?
Ha' yu felt *the wool of beaver?*
Or swan's down ever?
Or have smelt o' the bud o' the briar?
Or *the nard in the fire?*
Or have tasted the bag of the bee?
Oh, so white! Oh, so soft! Oh, so sweet is she!

His 'Discourse with Cupid,' which follows, is infinitely delicate and *piquant*, and without one single blemish. It is a perfect "nest of spicery."

Noblest Charis, you that are
Both my fortune and my star!
And do govern more my blood,
Than the various moon the flood!
Hear, what late discourse of you,
Love and I have had; and true.
'Mongst my Muses finding me,
Where he chanc'd your name to see
Set, and to this softer strain;
'Sure,' said he, 'If I have brain,
This here sung can be no other,
By description, but my mother!
So hath Homer prais'd her hair;
So Anacreon drawn the air
Of her face, and made to rise,
Just about her sparkling eyes,
Both her brows bent like my bow.
By her looks I do her know,
Which you call my shafts. And see!
Such my mother's blushes be,
As the bath your verse discloses

In her cheeks, of milk and roses;
Such as oft I wanton in.
And, above her even chin,
Have you plac'd the bank of kisses,
Where you say, men gather blisses,
Ripen'd with a breath more sweet,
Than when flowers and west-winds meet,
Nay, her white and polish'd neck,
With the lace that doth it deck,
Is my mother's! hearts of slain
Lovers, made into a chain!
And between each rising breast
Lies the valley, call'd my nest,
Where I sit and proyne my wings
After flight; and put new stings
To my shafts! Her very name
With my mother's is the same.'—
'I confess all,' I replied,
'And the glass hangs by her side,
And the girdle 'bout her waist,
All is Venus: save unchaste.
But, alas! thou seest the least
Of her good, who is the best
Of her sex; but could'st thou, Love,
Call to mind the forms that strove
For the apple, and those three
Make in one, the same were she.
For this beauty yet doth hide
Something more than thou hast spied.
Outward grace weak love beguiles:
She is Venus when she smiles,
But she's Juno when she walks,
And Minerva when she talks.'

In one of the songs in *Cynthia's Revels*, we find, amidst some very pleasing imagery, the origin of a celebrated line in modern poetry—

Drip, drip, drip, drip, drip . . .

This has not even the merit of originality, which is hard upon it. Ben Jonson had said two hundred years before,

Oh, I could still
(Like melting snow upon some craggy hill)
Drop, drop, drop, drop,
Since nature's pride is now a wither'd daffodil.

His 'Ode to the Memory of Sir Lucius Cary and Sir H. Morrison' has been much admired, but I cannot but think it one of his most fantastical and perverse performances.

I cannot, for instance, reconcile myself to such stanzas as these:

Of which we priests and poets say
Such truths as we expect for happy men,
And there he lives with memory; and Ben

The Stand.

Jonson, who sung this of him, ere he went
Himself to rest,
Or taste a part of that full joy he meant
To have exprest,
In this bright asterism;
Where it were friendship's schism
(Were not his Lucius long with us to tarry)
To separate these twi-
Lights, the Dioscuri;
And keep the one half from his Harry.
But fate doth so alternate the design,
While that in Heaven, this light on earth doth shine.

This seems as if because he cannot without difficulty write smoothly, he becomes rough and crabbed in a spirit of de-

fiance, like those persons who cannot behave well in company, and affect rudeness to show their contempt for the opinions of others.

His *Epistles* are particularly good, equally full of strong sense and sound feeling. They show that he was not without friends, whom he esteemed, and by whom he was deservedly esteemed in return. The controversy started about his character is an idle one, carried on in the mere spirit of contradiction, as if he were either made up entirely of gall, or dipped in "the milk of human kindness." There is no necessity or ground to suppose either. He was no doubt a sturdy, plain-spoken, honest, well-disposed man, inclining more to the severe than the amiable side of things; but his good qualities, learning, talents, and convivial habits preponderated over his defects of temper or manners; and in a course of friendship some difference of character, even a little roughness or acidity, may relish to the palate; and olives may be served up with effect as well as sweetmeats. Ben Jonson, even by his quarrels and jealousies, does not seem to have been curst with the last and damning disqualification for friendship,—heartless indifference. He was also what is understood by a *good fellow*, fond of good cheer and good company: and the first step for others to enjoy your society, is for you to enjoy theirs. If any one can do without the world, it is certain that the world can do quite as well without him. His 'Verses Inviting a Friend to Supper' give us as familiar an idea of his private habits and character, as his 'Epistle to Michael Drayton,' that to Selden, &c.; his 'Lines to the Memory of Shakspeare,' and his noble prose 'Eulogy on Lord Bacon,' in his disgrace, do a favourable one.

ALGERNON CHARLES SWINBURNE
From A *Study of Ben Jonson*
1889, pp. 9–89

There is nothing accidental in the work of Ben Jonson: no casual inspiration, no fortuitous impulse, ever guides or misguides his genius aright or astray. And this crowning and damning defect of a tedious and intolerable realism was even exceptionally wilful and premeditated. There is little if anything of it in the earliest comedy admitted into the magnificent edition which was compiled and published by himself in the year of the death of Shakespeare. And the humours of a still earlier comedy attributed to his hand, and printed apparently without his sanction just seven years before, are not worked out with such wearisome patience nor exhibited with such scientific persistency as afterwards distinguished the anatomical lecturer on vice and folly whose ideal of comic art was a combination of sarcasm and sermon in alternately epigrammatic and declamatory dialogue. I am by no means disposed to question the authenticity of this play, an excellent example of romantic comedy dashed with farce and flavoured with poetry: but, as far as I am aware, no notice has yet been taken of a noticeable coincidence between the manner or the circumstances of its publication and that of a spurious play which had nine years previously been attributed to Shakespeare. Some copies only of *The Case is Altered* bear on the title-page the name of Jonson, as some copies only of *Sir John Oldcastle* bear on the title-page the name of Shakespeare. In the earlier case, there can of course be no reasonable doubt that Shakespeare on his side, or the four actual authors of the gallimaufry on theirs, or perhaps all five together in the common though diverse interest of their respective credits, must have interfered to put a stop to the piratical profits of a lying and thieving publisher by compelling him to cancel the impudently mendacious title-page which imputed to Shakespeare the authorship of a play announced in its very prologue as the work of a writer or writers whose intention was to counteract the false impression given by Shakespeare's caricature, and to represent Prince Hal's old lad of the castle in his proper character of hero and martyr. In the later case, there can be little if any doubt that Jonson, then at the height of his fame and influence, must have taken measures to preclude the circulation under his name of a play which he would not or could not honestly acknowledge. So far, then, as external evidence goes, there is no ground whatever for a decision as to whether *The Case is Altered* may be wholly or partially or not at all assignable to the hand of Jonson. My own conviction is that he certainly had a hand in it, and was not improbably its sole author: but that on the other hand it may not impossibly be one of the compound works on which he was engaged as a dramatic apprentice with other and less energetic playwrights in the dim back workshop of the slave-dealer and slave-driver whose diary records the grinding toil and the scanty wages of his lean and laborious bondsmen. Justice, at least since the days of Gifford, has generally been done to the bright and pleasant quality of this equally romantic and classical comedy; in which the passionate humour of the miser is handled with more freshness and freedom than we find in most of Jonson's later studies, while the figure of his putative daughter has more of grace and interest than he usually vouchsafed to be at the pains of bestowing on his official heroines. It is to be regretted, it is even to be deplored, that the influence of Plautus on the style and the method of Jonson was not more permanent and more profound. Had he been but content to follow his first impulse, to work after his earliest model—had he happily preferred those 'Plautinos et numeros et sales' for which his courtly friend Horace expressed so courtily a contempt to the heavier numbers and the more laborious humours which he set himself to elaborate and to cultivate instead, we might not have had to applaud a more wonderful and admirable result, we should unquestionably have enjoyed a harvest more spontaneous and more gracious, more generous and more delightful. Something of the charm of Fletcher, his sweet straightforward fluency and instinctive lightness of touch, would have tempered the severity and solidity of his deliberate satire and his heavy-handed realism.

And the noble work of comic art which followed on this first attempt gave even fuller evidence in its earlier than its later form of the author's capacity for poetic as well as realistic success. The defence of poetry which appears only in the first edition of *Every Man in his Humour* is worth all Sidney's and all Shelley's treatises thrown together. A stern and austere devotion to the principle which prohibits all indulgence in poetry, precludes all exuberance of expression, and immolates on the altar of accuracy all eloquence, all passion, and all inspiration incompatible with direct and prosaic reproduction of probable or plausible dialogue, induced its author to cancel this noble and majestic rhapsody; and in so doing gave fair and full forewarning of the danger which was to beset this too rigid and conscientious artist through the whole of his magnificent career. But in all other points the process of transformation to which its author saw fit to subject this comedy was unquestionably a process of improvement. Transplanted from the imaginary or fantastic Italy in which at first they lived and moved and had their being to the actual and immediate atmosphere of contemporary London, the characters gain even more in lifelike and interesting veracity or verisimilitude than in familiar attraction and homely association. Not only do we feel that we know them better, but we perceive that they are actually more real and cognisable creatures than they were under their former conditions of dramatic existence. But it must be with regret as well as with wonder that we find ourselves constrained to recognize the indisputable truth that this first acknowledged work of so great a writer is as certainly his best as it certainly is not his greatest. Never again did his genius, his industry, his conscience and his taste unite in the triumphant presentation of a work so faultless, so satisfactory, so absolute in achievement and so free from blemish or defect. The only three others among all his plays which are not unworthy to be ranked beside it are in many ways more wonderful, more splendid, more incomparable with any other product of human intelligence or genius: but neither *The Fox*, *The Alchemist*, nor *The Staple of News*, is altogether so blameless and flawless a piece of work; so free from anything that might as well or better be dispensed with, so simply and thoroughly compact and complete in workmanship and in result. Molière himself has no character more exquisitely and spontaneously successful in presentation and evolution than the immortal and inimitable Bobadil: and even Bobadil is not unworthily surrounded and supported by the many other graver or lighter characters of this magnificent and perfect comedy.

It is difficult to attempt an estimate of the next endeavours or enterprises of Ben Jonson without incurring either the risk of impatient and uncritical injustice, if rein be given to the natural irritation and vexation of a disappointed and bewildered reader, or the no less imminent risk of one-sided and one-eyed partiality, if the superb literary quality, the elaborate intellectual excellence, of these undramatic if not inartistic satires in dialogue be duly taken into account. From their author's point of view, they are worthy of all the applause he claimed for them; and to say this is to say much; but if the author's point of view was radically wrong, was fundamentally unsound, we can but be divided between condemnation and applause, admiration and regret. No student of our glorious language, no lover of our glorious literature, can leave these miscalled comedies unread without foregoing an experience which he should be reluctant to forego: but no reader who has any sense or any conception of comic art or of dramatic harmony will be surprised to find that the author's experience of their reception on the stage should have driven him by steady gradations of fury and consecutive degrees of arrogance into a state of mind and a style of work which must have seemed even to his well-wishers most unpromising for his future and final triumph. Little if anything can be added to the excellent critical remarks of Gifford on *Every Man out of his Humour*, *Cynthia's Revels*, and *Poetaster, or his Arraignment*. The first of these magnificent mistakes would be enough to ensure immortality to the genius of the poet capable of so superb and elaborate an error. The fervour and intensity of the verse which expresses his loftier mood of intolerant indignation, the studious and implacable versatility of scorn which animates the expression of his disgust at the viler or crueller examples of social villainy then open to his contemptuous or furious observation, though they certainly cannot suffice to make a play, suffice to make a living and imperishable work of the dramatic satire which passes so rapidly from one phase to another of folly, fraud, or vice. And if it were not an inadmissible theory that the action or the structure of a play might be utterly disjointed and dislocated in order to ensure the complete presentation or development, the alternate exhibition or exposure, of each figure in the revolving gallery of a satirical series, we could hardly fear that our admiration of the component parts which fail to compose a coherent or harmonious work of art could possibly carry us too far into extravagance of applause. The noble rage which inspires the overture is not more absolute or perfect than the majestic structure of the verse: and the best comic or realistic scenes of the ensuing play are worthy to be compared—though it may not be altogether to their advantage—with the similar work of the greatest succeeding artists in narrative or dramatic satire. Too much of the studious humour, too much of the versatile and laborious realism, displayed in the conduct and evolution of this satirical drama, may have been lavished and misused in the reproduction of ephemeral affectations and accidental forms of folly: but whenever the dramatic satirist, on purpose or by accident, strikes home to some deeper and more durable subject of satire, we feel the presence and the power of a poet and a thinker whose genius was not born to deal merely with ephemeral or casual matters. The small patrician fop and his smaller plebeian ape, though even now not undiverting figures, are inevitably less diverting to us, as they must have been even to the next generation from Jonson's, than to the audience for whom they were created: but the humour of the scene in which the highly intelligent and intellectual lady, who regards herself as the pattern at once of social culture and of personal refinement, is duped and disgraced by an equally simple and ingenious trick played off on her overweening and contemptuous vanity, might have been applauded by Shakespeare or by Vanbrugh, approved by Congreve or Molière. Here, among too many sketches of a kind which can lay claim to no merit beyond that of an unlovely photograph, we find a really humorous conception embodied in a really amusing type of vanity and folly; and are all the more astonished to find a writer capable of such excellence and such error as every competent reader must recognize in the conception and execution of this rather admirable than delightful play. For Molière himself could hardly have improved on the scene in which a lady who is confident of her intuitive capacity to distinguish a gentleman from a pretender with no claim to that title is confronted with a vulgar clown, whose introducers have assured her that he is a high-bred gentleman masquerading for a wager under that repulsive likeness. She wonders that they can have imagined her so obtuse, so ignorant, so insensible to the difference between gentleman and clown: she finds that he plays his part as a boor very badly and transparently; and on discovering that he is in fact the boor she would not recognize, is driven to vanish in a passion of disgust. This is good comedy: but we can hardly say as much for the scene in which a speculator who has been trading on the starvation or destitution of his neighbours and tenants is driven to hang himself in despair at the tidings of a better market for the poor, is cut down by the hands of peasants who have not recognized him, and on hearing their loudly expressed regrets for this act of inadvertent philanthropy becomes at once a beneficent and penitent philanthropist. Extravagant and exceptional as is this instance of Jonson's capacity for dramatic error—for the sacrifice at once of comic art and of common sense on the altar of moral or satirical purpose, it is but an extreme example of the result to which his theory must have carried his genius, gagged and handcuffed and drugged and blindfolded, had not his genius been too strong even for the force and the persistence of his theory. No reader and no spectator of his next comedy can have been inclined to believe or encouraged in believing that it was. The famous final verse of the epilogue to *Cynthia's Revels* can hardly sound otherwise to modern ears than as an expression of blustering diffidence—of blatant self-distrust. That any audience should have sat out the five undramatic acts of this 'dramatic satire' is as inconceivable as that any reader, however exasperated and exhausted by its voluminous perversities, should fail to do justice to its literary merits; to the vigour and purity of its English, to the masculine refinement and the classic straightforwardness of its general style. There is an exquisite song in it, and there are

passages—nay, there are scenes—of excellent prose: but the intolerable elaboration of pretentious dullness and ostentatious ineptitude for which the author claims not merely the tolerance or the condonation which gratitude or charity might accord to the misuse or abuse of genius, but the acclamation due to its exercise and the applause demanded by its triumph—the heavy-headed perversity which ignores all the duties and reclaims all the privileges of a dramatic poet—the Cyclopean ponderosity of perseverance which hammers through scene after scene at the task of ridicule by anatomy of tedious and preposterous futilities—all these too conscientious outrages offered to the very principle of comedy, of poetry, or of drama, make us wonder that we have no record of a retort from the exhausted audience—if haply there were any auditors left—to the dogged defiance of the epilogue:

> By God 'tis good, and if you like 't you may.
> —By God 'tis bad, and worse than tongue can say.

For the most noticeable point in this studiously wayward and laboriously erratic design is that the principle of composition is as conspicuous by its absence as the breath of inspiration: that the artist, the scholar, the disciple, the student of classic models, is as indiscoverable as the spontaneous humourist or poet. The wildest, the roughest, the crudest offspring of literary impulse working blindly on the passionate elements of excitable ignorance was never more formless, more incoherent, more defective in structure, than this voluminous abortion of deliberate intelligence and conscientious culture.

There is a curious monotony in the variety—if there be not rather a curious variety in the monotony—of character and of style which makes it even more difficult to resume the study of *Cynthia's Revels* when once broken off than even to read through its burdensome and bulky five acts at a sitting; but the reader who lays siege to it with a sufficient supply of patience will find that the latter is the surer if not the only way to appreciate the genuine literary value of its better portions. Most of the figures presented are less than sketches and little more than outlines of inexpert and intolerant caricature: but the 'half-saved' or (as Carlyle has it) 'insalvable' coxcomb and parasite Asotus, who puts himself under the tuition of Amorphus and the patronage of Anaides, is a creature with something of real comic life in him. By what process of induction or deduction the wisdom of critical interpreters should have discerned in the figure of his patron, a fashionable ruffler and ruffian, the likeness of Thomas Dekker, a humble, hard-working, and highly-gifted hack of letters, may be explicable by those who can explain how the character of Hedon, a courtly and voluptuous coxcomb, can have been designed to cast ridicule on John Marston, a rude and rough-hewn man of genius, the fellow-craftsman of Ben Jonson as satirist and as playwright. But such absurdities of misapplication and misconstruction, once set afloat on the Lethean waters of stagnating tradition, will float for ever by grace of the very rottenness which prevents them from sinking. Ignorance assumes and idleness repeats what sciolism ends by accepting as a truth no less indisputable than undisputed. To any rational and careful student it must be obvious that until the publication of Jonson's *Poetaster* we cannot trace, I do not say with any certainty of evidence, but with any plausibility of conjecture, the identity of the principal persons attacked or derided by the satirist. And to identify the originals of such figures as Clove and Orange in *Every Man out of his Humour* can hardly, as Carlyle might have expressed it, be matter of serious interest to any son of Adam. But the famous polemical comedy which appeared a year later than the appearance of *Cynthia's Revels* bore evidence about it, unmistakable by reader or spectator, alike to the general design of the poet and to the particular direction of his personalities. Jonson of course asserted and of course believed that he had undergone gross and incessant provocation for years past from the 'petulant' onslaughts of Marston and Dekker: but what were his grounds for this assertion and this belief we have no means whatever of deciding—we have no ground whatever for conjecture. What we cannot but perceive is the possibly more important fact that indignation and ingenuity, pugnacity and self-esteem, combined to produce and succeeded in producing an incomparably better comedy than the author's last and a considerably better composition than the author's penultimate attempt. Even the 'apologetical dialogue' appended for the benefit of the reader, fierce and arrogant as it seems to us in its bellicose ambition and its quarrelsome self-assertion, is less violent and overweening in its tone than the furious eloquence of the prelude to *Every Man out of his Humour*. The purity of passion, the sincerity of emotion, which inspires and inflames that singular and splendid substitute for an ordinary prologue, never found again an expression so fervent and so full in the many and various appeals of its author to his audience, immediate or imaginary, against the malevolence of enemies or of critics. But in this Augustan satire his rage and scorn are tempered and adapted to something of dramatic purpose; their expression is more coherent, if not less truculent,—their effect is more harmonious, if not more genuine,—than in the two preceding plays.

There is much in the work of Ben Jonson which may seem strange and perplexing to the most devout and rapturous admirer of his genius: there is nothing so singular, so quaint, so inexplicable, as his selection of Horace for a sponsor or a patron saint. The affinity between Virgil and Tennyson, between Shelley and Lucretius, is patent and palpable: but when Jonson assumes the mask of Horace we can only wonder what would have been the sensation on Olympus if Pluto had suddenly proposed to play the part of Cupid, or if Vulcan had obligingly offered to run on the errands of Mercury. This eccentricity of egoism is only less remarkable than the mixture of care and recklessness in the composition of a play which presents us at its opening with an apparent hero in the person, not of Horace, but of Ovid; and after following his fortunes through four-fifths of the action, drops him into exile at the close of the fourth act, and proceeds with the business of the fifth as though no such figure had ever taken part in the conduct of the play. Shakespeare, who in Jonson's opinion 'wanted art,' assuredly never showed himself so insensible to the natural rules of art as his censor has shown himself here. Apart from the incoherence of construction which was perhaps inevitable in such a complication of serious with satirical design, there is more of artistic merit in this composite work of art than in any play produced by its author since the memorable date of *Every Man in his Humour*. The character of Captain Pantilius Tucca, which seems to have brought down on its creator such a boiling shower-bath or torrent of professional indignation from quarters in which his own distinguished service as a soldier and a representative champion of English military hardihood would seem to have been unaccountably if not scandalously forgotten, is beyond comparison the brightest and the best of his inventions since the date of the creation of Bobadil. But the decrease in humanity of humour, in cordial and genial sympathy or tolerance of imagination, which marks the advance of his genius towards its culmination of scenical and satirical success in *The Alchemist* must be obvious at this stage of his work to those who will compare the delightful cowardice and the inoffensive pretention of Bobadil with the blatant vulgarity

and the flagrant rascality of Tucca.

In the memorable year which brought into England her first king of Scottish birth, and made inevitable the future conflict between the revolutionary principle of monarchy by divine right and the conservative principle of self-government by deputy for the commonweal of England, the first great writer who thought fit to throw in his lot with the advocates of the royalist revolution produced on the boards a tragedy of which the moral, despite his conscious or unconscious efforts to disguise or to distort it, is as thoroughly republican and as tragically satirical of despotism as is that of Shakespeare's *Julius Cæsar*. It would be well for the fame of Jonson if the parallel could be carried further: but, although *Sejanus his Fall* may not have received on its appearance the credit or the homage due to the serious and solid merit of its composition and its execution, it must be granted that the author has once more fallen into the excusable but nevertheless unpardonable error of the too studious and industrious Martha. He was careful and troubled about many things absolutely superfluous and supererogatory; matters of no value or concern whatever for the purpose or the import of a dramatic poem: but the one thing needful, the very condition of poetic life and dramatic interest, he utterly and persistently overlooked. Tiberius, the central character of the action—for the eponymous hero or protagonist of the play is but a crude study of covetous and lecherous ambition,—has not life enough in the presentation of him to inform the part with interest. No praise—of the sort which is due to such labours—can be too high for the strenuous and fervid conscience which inspires every line of the laborious delineation: the recorded words of the tyrant are wrought into the text, his traditional characteristics are welded into the action, with a patient and earnest fidelity which demands applause no less than recognition: but when we turn from this elaborate statue—from this exquisitely articulated skeleton— to the living figure of Octavius or of Antony, we feel and understand more than ever that Shakespeare 'hath chosen the good part, which shall not be taken away from him.'

Coleridge has very justly animadverted on 'the anachronic mixture' of Anglican or Caledonian royalism with the conservatism of an old Roman republican in the character of Arruntius: but we may trace something of the same incongruous combination in the character of a poet who was at once the sturdiest in aggressive eagerness of self-assertion, and the most copious in courtly effusion of panegyric, among all the distinguished writers of his day. The power of his verse and the purity of his English are nowhere more remarkable than in his two Roman tragedies: on the other hand, his great fault or defect as a dramatist is nowhere more perceptible. This general if not universal infirmity is one which never seems to have occurred to him, careful and studious though he was always of his own powers and performances, as anything of a fault at all. It is one indeed which no writer afflicted with it could reasonably be expected to recognize or to repair. Of all purely negative faults, all sins of intellectual omission, it is perhaps the most serious and the most irremediable. It is want of sympathy; a lack of cordial interest, not in his own work or in his own genius,—no one will assert that Jonson was deficient on that score,—but in the individual persons, the men and women represented on the stage. He took so much interest in the creations that he had none left for the creatures of his intellect or art. This fault is not more obvious in the works of his disciples Cartwright and Randolph than in the works of their master. The whole interest is concentrated on the intellectual composition and the intellectual development of the characters and the scheme. Love and hatred, sympathy and antipathy, are superseded and supplanted by pure scientific curiosity: the clear glow of serious or humorous emotion is replaced by the dry light of analytical investigation. *Si vis me flere*—the proverb is something musty. Neither can we laugh heartily or long where all chance of sympathy or cordiality is absolutely inconceivable. The loving laughter which salutes the names of Dogberry and Touchstone, Mrs. Quickly and Falstaff, is never evoked by the most gorgeous opulence of humour, the most glorious audacity of intrigue, which dazzles and delights our understanding in the parts of Sir Epicure Mammon, Rabbi Zeal-of-the-Land Busy, Morose and Fitzdottrel and Mosca: even Bobadil, the most comically attractive of all cowards and braggarts on record, has no such hold on our regard as many a knave and many a fool of Shakespeare's comic progeny. The triumph of 'Don Face' over his confederates, though we may not be so virtuous as to grudge it him, puts something of a strain upon our conscience if it is heartily to be applauded and enjoyed. One figure, indeed, among all the multitude of Jonson's invention, is so magnificent in the spiritual stature of his wickedness, in the still dilating verge and expanding proportion of his energies, that admiration in this single case may possibly if not properly overflow into something of intellectual if not moral sympathy. The genius and the courage of Volpone, his sublimity of cynic scorn and his intensity of contemptuous enjoyment,—his limitless capacity for pleasure and his dauntless contemplation of his crimes,—make of this superb sinner a figure which we can hardly realize without some sense of imperious fascination. His views of humanity are those of Swift and of Carlyle: but in him their fruit is not bitterness of sorrow and anger, but rapture of satisfaction and of scorn. His English kinsman, Sir Epicure Mammon, for all his wealth of sensual imagination and voluptuous eloquence, for all his living play of humour and glowing force of faith, is essentially but a poor creature when set beside the great Venetian. Had the study of Tiberius been informed and vivified by something of the same fervour, the tragedy of *Sejanus* might have had in it some heat of more than merely literary life. But this lesser excellence, the merit of vigorous and vigilant devotion or application to a high and serious object of literary labour, is apparent in every scene of the tragedy. That the subject is one absolutely devoid of all but historical and literary interest—that not one of these scenes can excite for one instant the least tough, the least phantom, the least shadow of pity or terror—would apparently have seemed to its author no argument against its claim to greatness as a tragic poem. But if it could be admitted, as it will never be by any unperverted judgment, that this eternal canon of tragic art, the law which defines terror and pity as its only proper objects, the alpha and omega of its aim and its design, may ever be disregarded or ignored, we should likewise have to admit that Jonson had in this instance achieved a success as notable as we must otherwise consider his failure. For the accusation of weakness in moral design, of feeble or unnatural treatment of character, cannot with any show of justice be brought against him. Coleridge, whose judgment on a question of ethics will scarcely be allowed to carry as much weight as his authority on matters of imagination, objects with some vehemence to the incredible inconsistency of Sejanus in appealing for a sign to the divinity whose altar he proceeds to overthrow, whose power he proceeds to defy, on the appearance of an unfavourable presage. This doubtless is not the conduct of a strong man or a rational thinker: but the great minister of Tiberius is never for an instant throughout the whole course of the action represented as a man of any genuine strength or any solid intelligence. He is shown to us as merely a cunning, daring, unscrupulous and imperious upstart, whose

greed and craft, impudence and audacity, intoxicate while they incite and undermine while they uplift him.

The year which witnessed the appearance of *Sejanus* on the stage—acclaimed by Chapman at greater length if not with greater fervour than by any other of Jonson's friends or satellites—witnessed also the first appearance of its author in a character which undoubtedly gave free play to some of his most remarkable abilities, but which unquestionably diverted and distorted and absorbed his genius as a dramatist and his talent as a poet after a fashion which no capable student can contemplate without admiration or consider without regret. The few readers whose patient energy and conscientious curiosity may have led them to traverse—a pilgrimage more painful than Dante's or than Bunyan's—the entire record of the 'Entertainment' which escorted and delayed, at so many successive stations, the progress through London and Westminster of the long-suffering son of Mary Queen of Scots, will probably agree that of the two poetic dialogues or eclogues contributed by Jonson to the metrical part of the ceremony, the dialogue of the Genius and the Flamen is better than that of the Genius and Thamesis; more smooth, more vigorous, and more original. The subsequent prophecy of Electra is at all points unlike the prophecies of a Cassandra: there is something doubly tragic in the irony of chance which put into the mouth of Agamemnon's daughter a prophecy of good fortune to the royal house of Stuart on its first entrance into the capital and ascension to the throne of England. The subsequent *Panegyre* is justly praised by Gifford for its manly and dignified style of official compliment—courtliness untainted by servility: but the style is rather that of fine prose, sedately and sedulously measured and modulated, than that of even ceremonial poetry.

In the same energetic year of his literary life the Laureate produced one of his best minor works—*The Satyr*, a little lyric drama so bright and light and sweet in fancy and in finish of execution that we cannot grudge the expenditure of time and genius on so slight a subject. *The Penates*, which appeared in the following year, gave evidence again of the strong and lively fancy which was to be but too often exercised in the same field of ingenious and pliant invention. The metre is well conceived and gracefully arranged, worthy indeed of nobler words than those which it clothes with light and pleasant melody. The octosyllabics, it will be observed by metrical students, are certainly good, but decidedly not faultless: the burlesque part sustained by Pan is equally dexterous and brilliant in execution.

In 1605 the singular and magnificent coalition of powers which served to build up the composite genius of Jonson displayed in a single masterpiece the consummate and crowning result of its marvellous energies. No other of even his very greatest works is at once so admirable and so enjoyable. The construction or composition of *The Alchemist* is perhaps more wonderful in the perfection and combination of cumulative detail, in triumphant simplicity of process and impeccable felicity of result: but there is in *Volpone* a touch of something like imagination, a savour of something like romance, which gives a higher tone to the style and a deeper interest to the action. The chief agents are indeed what Mr. Carlyle would have called 'unspeakably unexemplary mortals': but the serious fervour and passionate intensity of their resolute and resourceful wickedness give somewhat of a lurid and distorted dignity to the display of their doings and sufferings, which is wanting to the less gigantic and heroic villainies of Subtle, Dol, and Face. The absolutely unqualified and unrelieved rascality of every agent in the later comedy—unless an exception should be made in favour of the unfortunate though enterprising Surly—

is another note of inferiority; a mark of comparative baseness in the dramatic metal. In *Volpone* the tone of villainy and the tone of virtue are alike higher. Celia is a harmless lady, if a too submissive consort; Bonario is an honourable gentleman, if too dutiful a son. The Puritan and shopkeeping scoundrels who are swindled by Face and plundered by Lovewit are viler if less villainous figures than the rapacious victims of Volpone.

As to the respective rank or comparative excellence of these two triumphant and transcendent masterpieces, the critic who should take upon himself to pass sentence or pronounce judgment would in my opinion display more audacity than discretion. The steadfast and imperturbable skill of hand which has woven so many threads of incident, so many shades of character, so many changes of intrigue, into so perfect and superb a pattern of incomparable art as dazzles and delights the reader of *The Alchemist* is unquestionably unique—above comparison with any later or earlier example of kindred genius in the whole range of comedy, if not in the whole world of fiction. The manifold harmony of inventive combination and imaginative contrast—the multitudinous unity of various and concordant effects—the complexity and the simplicity of action and impression, which hardly allow the reader's mind to hesitate between enjoyment and astonishment, laughter and wonder, admiration and diversion—all the distinctive qualities which the alchemic cunning of the poet has fused together in the crucible of dramatic satire for the production of a flawless work of art, have given us the most perfect model of imaginative realism and satirical comedy that the world has ever seen; the most wonderful work of its kind that can ever be run upon the same lines. Nor is it possible to resist a certain sense of immoral sympathy and humorous congratulation, more keen than any Scapin or Mascarille can awake in the mind of a virtuous reader, when Face dismisses Surly with a promise to bring him word to his lodging if he can hear of 'that Face' whom Surly has sworn to mark for his if ever he meets him. From the date of Plautus to the date of Sheridan it would surely be difficult to find in any comedy a touch of glorious impudence which might reasonably be set against this. And the whole part is so full of brilliant and effective and harmonious touches or strokes of character or of humour that even this crowning instance of serene inspiration in the line of superhuman audacity seems merely right and simply natural.

And yet, even while possessed and overmastered by the sense of the incomparable energy, the impeccable skill, and the indefatigable craftsmanship, which combined and conspired together to produce this æsthetically blameless masterpiece, the reader whose instinct requires something more than merely intellectual or æsthetic satisfaction must recognize even here the quality which distinguishes the genius of Ben Jonson from that of the very greatest imaginative humourists—Aristophanes or Rabelais, Shakespeare or Sterne, Vanbrugh or Dickens, Congreve or Thackeray. Each of these was evidently capable of falling in love with his own fancy—of rejoicing in his own imaginative humour as a swimmer in the waves he plays with: but this buoyant and passionate rapture was controlled by an instinctive sense which forbade them to strike out too far or follow the tide too long. However quaint or queer, however typical or exceptional, the figure presented may be—Olivia's or Tristram Shandy's uncle Toby, Sir John Brute or Mr. Peggotty, Lady Wishfort or Lady Kew,—we recognize and accept them as lifelike and actual intimates whose acquaintance has been made for life. Sir Sampson Legend might undoubtedly find himself as much out of place in the drawing-room of the Countess Dowager of Kew as did Sir Wilful Witwoud, on a memorable occasion, in the saloon of his aunt Lady Wishfort:

Captain Toby Shandy could hardly have been expected to tolerate the Rabelaisian effervescences of Sir Toby Belch: and Vanbrugh's typical ruffians of rank have little apparently in common with Dickens's representative heroes of the poor. But in all these immortal figures there is the lifeblood of eternal life which can only be infused by the sympathetic faith of the creator in his creature—the breath which animates every word, even if the word be not the very best word that might have been found, with the vital impulse of infallible imagination. But it is difficult to believe that Ben Jonson can have believed, even with some half sympathetic and half sardonic belief, in all the leading figures of his invention. Scorn and indignation are but too often the motives or the mainsprings of his comic art; and when dramatic poetry can exist on the sterile and fiery diet of scorn and indignation, we may hope to find life sustained in happiness and health on a diet of aperients and emetics. The one great modern master of analytic art is somewhat humaner than Jonson in the application of his scientific method to the purpose of dramatic satire. The study of Sludge is finer and subtler by far than the study of Subtle: though undoubtedly it is, in consequence of that very perfection and sublimation of exhaustive analysis, less available for any but a monodramatic purpose. No excuse, no plea, no pretext beyond the fact of esurience and the sense of ability, is suggested for the villainy of Subtle, Dol, and Face. But if we were to see what might possibly be said in extenuation of their rogueries, to hear what might possibly be pleaded in explanation or condonation of their lives, the comedy would fall through and go to pieces: the dramatic effect would collapse and be dissolved. And to this great, single, æsthetic end of art the consummate and conscientious artist who created these immortal figures was content to subdue or to sacrifice all other and subordinate considerations. Coleridge, as no reader will probably need to be reminded, 'thought the *Œdipus Tyrannus*, *The Alchemist*, and *Tom Jones*; the three most perfect plots ever planned.' With the warmest admiration and appreciation of Fielding's noble and immortal masterpiece, I cannot think it at all worthy of comparison, for blameless ingenuity of composition and absolute impeccability of design, with the greatest of tragic and the greatest of comic triumphs in construction ever accomplished by the most consummate and the most conscientious among ancient and modern artists. And when we remember that this perfection of triumphant art is exhibited, not on the scale of an ordinary comedy, whether classic or romantic, comprising a few definite types and a few impressive situations, but on a scale of invention so vast and so various as to comprise in the course of a single play as many characters and as many incidents, all perfectly adjusted and naturally developed out of each other, as would amply suffice for the entire dramatic furniture, for the entire poetic equipment, of a great dramatic poet, we feel that Gifford's expression, a 'prodigy of human intellect,' is equally applicable to *The Fox* and to *The Alchemist*, and is not a whit too strong a term for either. Nor can I admit, as I cannot discern, the blemish or imperfection which others have alleged that they descry in the composition of *Volpone*—the unlikelihood of the device by which retribution is brought down in the fifth act on the criminals who were left at the close of the fourth act in impregnable security and triumph. So far from regarding the comic Nemesis or rather Ate which infatuates and impels Volpone to his doom as a sacrifice of art to morality, an immolation of probability and consistency on the altar of poetic justice, I admire as a master-stroke of character the haughty audacity of caprice which produces or evolves his ruin out of his own hardihood and insolence of exulting and daring enjoyment. For there is something throughout of the lion as well as of the fox in this original and incomparable figure. I know not where to find a third instance of catastrophe comparable with that of either *The Fox* or *The Alchemist* in the whole range of the highest comedy; whether for completeness, for propriety, for interest, for ingenious felicity of event or for perfect combination and exposition of all the leading characters at once in supreme simplicity, unity, and fullness of culminating effect.

And only in the author's two great farces shall we find so vast a range and variety of characters. The foolish and famous couplet of doggrel rhyme which brackets *The Silent Woman* with *The Fox* and *The Alchemist* is liable to prejudice the reader against a work which if compared with those marvellous masterpieces must needs seem to lose its natural rights to notice, to forfeit its actual claim on our rational admiration. Its proper place is not with these, but beside its fellow example of exuberant, elaborate, and deliberately farcical realism—*Bartholomew Fair*. And the two are not less wonderful in their own way, less triumphant on their own lines, than those two crowning examples of comedy. Farcical in construction and in action, they belong to the province of the higher form of art by virtue of their leading characters. Morose indeed, as a victimized monomaniac, is rather a figure of farce than of comedy: Captain Otter and his termagant are characters of comedy rather broad than high: but the collegiate ladies, in their matchless mixture of pretention and profligacy, hypocrisy and pedantry, recall rather the comedies than the farces of Molière by the elaborate and vivid precision of portraiture which presents them in such perfect finish, with such vigour and veracity of effect. Again, if *Bartholomew Fair* is mere farce in many of its minor characters and in some of its grosser episodes and details, the immortal figure of Rabbi Busy belongs to the highest order of comedy. In that absolute and complete incarnation of Puritanism full justice is done to the merits while full justice is done upon the demerits of the barbarian sect from whose inherited and infectious tyranny this nation is as yet but imperfectly delivered. Brother Zeal-of-the-Land is no vulgar impostor, no mere religious quacksalver of such a kind as supplies the common food for satire, the common fuel of ridicule: he is a hypocrite of the earnest kind, an Ironside among civilians; and the very abstinence of his creator from Hudibrastic misrepresentation and caricature makes the satire more thoroughly effective than all that Butler's exuberance of wit and prodigality of intellect could accomplish. The snuffling glutton who begins by exciting our laughter ends by displaying a comic perversity of stoicism in the stocks which is at least more respectable if not less laughable than the complacency of Justice Overdo, the fatuity of poor Cokes, the humble jocosity of a Littlewit, or the intemperate devotion of a Waspe. Hypocrisy streaked with sincerity, greed with a cross of earnestness and craft with a dash of fortitude, combine to make of the Rabbi at once the funniest, the fairest, and the faithfullest study ever taken of a less despicable than detestable type of fanatic.

Not only was the genius of Jonson too great, but his character was too radically noble for a realist or naturalist of the meaner sort. It is only in the minor parts of his gigantic work, only in its insignificant or superfluous components or details, that we find a tedious insistence on wearisome or offensive topics of inartistic satire or ineffectual display. Nor is it upon the ignoble sides of character that this great satiric dramatist prefers to concentrate his attention. As even in the most terrible masterpieces of Balzac, it is not the wickedness of the vicious or criminal agents, it is their energy of intellect, their dauntless versatility of daring, their invincible fertility of resource, for which our interest is claimed or by which our

admiration is aroused. In Face as in Subtle, in Volpone as in Mosca, the qualities which delight us are virtues misapplied: it is not their cunning, their avarice, or their lust, it is their courage, their genius, and their wit in which we take no ignoble or irrational pleasure. And indeed it would be strange and incongruous if a great satirist who was also a great poet had erred so grossly as not to aim at this result, or had fallen so grievously short of his aim as not to vindicate the dignity of his design. The same year in which the stage first echoed the majestic accents of Volpone's opening speech was distinguished by the appearance of the *Masque of Blackness*: a work eminent even among its author's in splendour of fancy, invention, and flowing eloquence. Its companion or counterpart, the *Masque of Beauty*, a poem even more notable for these qualities than its precursor, did not appear till three years later. Its brilliant and picturesque variations on the previous theme afford a perfect example of poetic as distinct from prosaic ingenuity.

Between the dates of these two masques, which were first printed and published together, three other entertainments had employed the energetic genius of the Laureate on the double task of scenical invention and literary decoration. The first occasion was that famous visit of King Christian and his hard-drinking Danes which is patriotically supposed to have done so much harm to the proverbially sober and abstemious nation whose temperance is so vividly depicted by the enthusiastic cordiality of Iago. The *Entertainment of Two Kings at Theobalds* opens well, with two vigorous and sonorous couplets of welcome: but the Latin verses are hardly worthy of Gifford's too fervid commendation. The mock marriage of the boyish Earl of Essex and the girl afterwards known to ill fame as Countess of Somerset gave occasion of which Jonson availed himself to the full for massive display of antiquarian magnificence and indefatigable prodigality of inexhaustible detail. The epithalamium of these quasi-nuptials is fine—when it is not coarse (we cannot away, for instance, with the comparison, in serious poetry, of kisses to—cockles!): but the exuberant enthusiasm of Gifford for 'this chaste and beautiful gem' is liable to provoke in the reader's mind a comparison 'with the divine original': and among the very few poets who could sustain a comparison with Catullus no man capable of learning the merest rudiments of poetry will affirm that Ben Jonson can be ranked. His verses are smooth and strong, 'well-torned and true-filed': but the matchless magic, the impeccable inspiration, the grace, the music, the simple and spontaneous perfection of the Latin poem, he could pretend neither to rival nor to reproduce. 'What was my part,' says Jonson in a note, 'the faults here, as well as the virtues, must speak.' These are the concluding words of a most generous and cordial tribute to the merits of the mechanist or stage-carpenter, the musician, and the dancing-master—Inigo Jones, Alfonso Ferrabosco, and Thomas Giles—who were employed on the composition of this magnificent if ill-omened pageant: and they may very reasonably be applied to the two translations from Catullus which the poet—certainly no prophet on this particular occasion—thought fit to introduce into the ceremonial verse of the masques held on the first and second nights of these star-crossed festivities. The faults and the virtues, the vigour of phrase and the accuracy of rendering, the stiffness of expression and the slowness of movement, are unmistakably characteristic of the workman. But in the second night's masque it must be noted that the original verse is distinctly better than the translated stanzas: the dispute of Truth and Opinion is a singularly spirited and vigorous example of amœbæan allegory. In the next year's *Entertainment* of the king and queen at Theobalds, then ceded by its owner to the king, the happy simplicity of invention and arrangement is worthily seconded or supported by the grave and dignified music of the elegiac verse which welcomes the coming and speeds the parting master. Next year *The Masque of Beauty* and the masque at Lord Haddington's marriage, each containing some of Jonson's finest and most flowing verse, bore equal witness to the energy and to the elasticity of his genius for apt and varied invention. The amœbæan stanzas in the later of these two masques have more freedom of movement and spontaneity of music than will perhaps be found in any other poem of equal length from the same indefatigable hand. The fourth of these stanzas is simply magnificent: the loveliness of the next is impaired by that anatomical particularity which too often defaces the serious verse of Jonson with grotesque if not gross deformity of detail. No other poet, except possibly one of his spiritual sons, too surely 'sealed of the tribe of Ben,' would have introduced 'liver' and 'lights' into a sweet and graceful effusion of lyric fancy, good alike in form and sound; a commendation not always nor indeed very frequently deserved by the verse of its author. The variations in the burden of 'Hymen's war' are singularly delicate and happy.

The next was a memorable year in the literary life of Ben Jonson: it witnessed the appearance both of the magnificent *Masque of Queens* and of the famous comedy or farce of *The Silent Woman*. The marvellously vivid and dexterous application of marvellous learning and labour which distinguishes the most splendid of all masques as one of the typically splendid monuments or trophies of English literature has apparently eclipsed, in the appreciation of the general student, that equally admirable fervour of commanding fancy which informs the whole design and gives life to every detail. The interlude of the witches is so royally lavish in its wealth and variety of fertile and lively horror that on a first reading the student may probably do less than justice to the lofty and temperate eloquence of the noble verse and the noble prose which follow.

Of *The Silent Woman* it is not easy to say anything new and true. Its merits are salient and superb: the combination of parts and the accumulation of incidents are so skilfully arranged and so powerfully designed that the result is in its own way incomparable—or comparable only with other works of the master's hand while yet in the fullness of its cunning and the freshness of its strength. But a play of this kind must inevitably challenge a comparison, in the judgment of modern readers, between its author and Molière: and Jonson can hardly, on the whole, sustain that most perilous comparison. It is true that there is matter enough in Jonson's play to have furnished forth two or three of Molière's: and that on that ground—on the score of industrious intelligence and laborious versatility of humour—*The Silent Woman* is as superior to the *Misanthrope* and the *Bourgeois Gentilhomme* as to *Twelfth Night* and *Much Ado about Nothing*. But even when most dazzled by the splendour of studied wit and the felicity of deliberate humour which may even yet explain the extraordinary popularity or reputation of this most imperial and elaborate of all farces, we feel that the author could no more have rivalled the author of *Twelfth Night* than he could have rivalled the author of *Othello*. The Nemesis of the satirist is upon him: he cannot be simply at ease: he cannot be happy in his work without some undertone of sarcasm, some afterthought of allusion, aimed at matters which Molière would have reserved for a slighter style of satire, and which Shakespeare would scarcely have condescended to recognise as possible objects of even momentary attention. His wit is wonderful—admirable, laughable, laudable—it is not in the fullest and the deepest sense delightful. It is radically cruel, contemptuous, intolerant:

the sneer of the superior person—Dauphine or Clerimont—is always ready to pass into a snarl: there is something in this great classic writer of the bull-baiting or bear-baiting brutality of his age. We put down *The Fox* or *The Alchemist* with a sense of wondering admiration, hardly affected by the impression of some occasional superfluity or excess: we lay aside *The Silent Woman*, not indeed without grateful recollection of much cordial enjoyment, but with distinct if reluctant conviction that the generous table at which we have been so prodigally entertained was more than a little crowded and overloaded with multifarious if savoury encumbrance of dishes. And if, as was Gifford's opinion, Shakespeare took a hint from the mock duellists in this comedy for the mock duellists in *Twelfth Night*, how wonderfully has he improved on his model! The broad rude humour of Jonson's practical joke is boyishly brutal in the horseplay of its violence: the sweet bright fun of Shakespeare's is in perfect keeping with the purer air of the sunnier climate it thrives in. The divine good-nature, the godlike good-humour of Shakespeare can never be quite perfectly appreciated till we compare his playfulness or his merriment with other men's. Even that of Aristophanes seems to smack of the barbarian beside it.

I cannot but fear that to thorough-going Jonsonians my remarks on the great comedy in which Dryden found the highest perfection of dramatic art on record may seem inadequate if not inappreciative. But to do it anything like justice would take up more space than I can spare: it would indeed, like most of Jonson's other successful plays, demand a separate study of some length and elaboration. The high comedy of the collegiate ladies, the low comedy of Captain and Mrs. Otter, the braggart knights and the Latinist barber, are all as masterly as the versions of Ovid's elegiacs into prose dialogue are tedious in their ingenuity and profitless in their skill. As to the chief character—who must evidently have been a native of Ecclefechan—he is as superior to the *malade imaginaire*, or to any of the Sganarelles of Molière, as is Molière himself to Jonson in lightness of spontaneous movement and easy grace of inspiration. And this is perhaps the only play of Jonson's which will keep the reader or spectator for whole scenes together in an inward riot or an open passion of subdued or unrepressed laughter.

The speeches at Prince Henry's Barriers, written by the Laureate for the occasion of the heir apparent's investiture as Prince of Wales, are noticeable for their fine and dexterous fusion of legend with history in eloquent and weighty verse. But the *Masque of Oberon*, presented the day before the tournament in which the prince bore himself so gallantly as to excite 'the great wonder of the beholders,' is memorable for a quality far higher than this: it is unsurpassed if not unequalled by any other work of its author for brightness and lightness and grace of fancy, for lyric movement and happy simplicity of expression.

Such work, however, was but the byplay in which the genius of this indefatigable poet found its natural relaxation during the year which gave to the world for all time a gift so munificent as that of *The Alchemist*. This 'unequalled play,' as it was called by contemporary admirers, was not miscalled by their enthusiasm; it is in some respects unparalleled among all the existing masterpieces of comedy. No student worthy of the name who may agree with me in preferring *The Fox* to *The Alchemist* will wish to enforce his preference upon others. Such perfection of plot, with such multiplicity of characters—such ingenuity of incident, with such harmony of construction—can be matched, we may surely venture to say, nowhere in the whole vast range of comic invention—nowhere in the whole wide world of dramatic fiction. If the interest is less poignant than in *Volpone*, the fun less continuous than in *The Silent Woman*, the action less simple and spontaneous than that of *Every Man in his Humour*, the vein of comedy is even richer than in any of these other masterpieces. The great Sir Epicure is enough in himself to immortalize the glory of the great artist who conceived and achieved a design so fresh, so daring, so colossal in its humour as that of this magnificent character. And there are at least nine others in the play as perfect in drawing, as vivid in outline, as living in every limb and every feature, as even his whose poetic stature overtops them all. The deathless three confederates, Kastrill and Surly, Dapper and Drugger, the too perennial Puritans whose villainous whine of purity and hypocrisy has its living echoes even now—not a figure among them could have been carved or coloured by any other hand.

Nor is the list even yet complete of Jonson's poetic work during this truly wonderful year of his literary life. At Christmas he produced 'the Queen's Majesty's masque' of *Love freed from Ignorance and Folly*; a little dramatic poem composed in his lightest and softest vein of fancy, brilliant and melodious throughout. The mighty and majestic Poet Laureate would hardly, I fear, have accepted with benignity the tribute of a compliment to the effect that his use of the sweet and simple heptasyllabic metre was worthy of Richard Barnfield or George Wither: but it is certain that in purity and fluency of music his verse can seldom be compared, as here it justly may, with the clear flutelike notes of *Cynthia* and *The Shepherd's Hunting*. An absurd misprint in the last line but three has afflicted all Jonson's editors with unaccountable perplexity. 'Then, then, angry music sound,' sings the chorus at the close of a song in honour of 'gentle Love and Beauty.' It is inconceivable that no one should yet have discovered the obvious solution of so slight but unfortunate an error in the type as the substitution of 'angry' for 'airy.'

The tragedy of *Catiline his Conspiracy* gave evidence in the following year that the author of *Sejanus* could do better, but could not do much better, on the same rigid lines of rhetorical and studious work which he had followed in the earlier play. Fine as is the opening of this too laborious tragedy, the stately verse has less of dramatic movement than of such as might be proper—if such a thing could be—for epic satire cast into the form of dialogue. Catiline is so mere a monster of ravenous malignity and irrational atrocity that he simply impresses us as an irresponsible though criminal lunatic: and there is something so preposterous, so abnormal, in the conduct and language of all concerned in his conspiracy, that nothing attributed to them seems either rationally credible or logically incredible. Coleridge, in his notes on the first act of this play, expresses his conviction that one passage must surely have fallen into the wrong place—such action at such a moment being impossible for any human creature. But the whole atmosphere is unreal, the whole action unnatural: no one thing said or done is less unlike the truth of life than any other: the writing is immeasurably better than the style of the ranting tragedian Seneca, but the treatment of character is hardly more serious as a study of humanity than his. In fact, what we find here is exactly what we find in the least successful of Jonson's comedies: a study, not of humanity, but of humours. The bloody humour of Cethegus, the braggart humour of Curius, the sluggish humour of Lentulus, the swaggering humour of Catiline himself—a huffcap hero as ever mouthed and strutted out his hour on the stage—all these alike fall under the famous definition of his favourite phrase which the poet had given twelve years before in the induction to the second of his ac-

knowledged comedies. And a tragedy of humours is hardly less than a monster in nature—or rather in that art which 'itself is nature.' Otherwise the second act must be pronounced excellent: the humours of the rival harlots, the masculine ambition of Sempronia, the caprices and cajoleries of Fulvia, are drawn with Jonson's most self-conscious care and skill. But the part of Cicero is burden enough to stifle any play: and some even of the finest passages, such as the much-praised description of the dying Catiline, fine though they be, are not good in the stricter sense of the word; the rhetorical sublimity of their diction comes most perilously near the verge of bombast. Altogether, the play is another magnificent mistake: and each time we open or close it we find it more difficult to believe that the additions made by its author some ten years before to *The Spanish Tragedy* can possibly have been those printed in the later issues of that famous play.[1] Their subtle and spontaneous notes of nature, their profound and searching pathos, their strange and thrilling tone of reality, the beauty and the terror and the truth of every touch, are the signs of a great, a very great tragic poet: and it is all but unimaginable that such an one could have been, but a year or so afterwards, the author of *Sejanus*—and again, eight years later, the author of *Catiline*. There is fine occasional writing in each, but it is not dramatic: and there is good dramatic work in each, but it is not tragic.

For two years after the appearance of *Catiline* there is an interval of silence and inaction in the literary life of its author; an intermission of labour which we cannot pretend to explain in the case of this Herculean workman, who seems usually to have taken an austere and strenuous delight in the employment and exhibition of his colossal energies. His next work is one of which it seems all but impossible for criticism to speak with neither more nor less than justice. Gifford himself, the most devoted of editors and of partisans, to whom all serious students of Jonson owe a tribute of gratitude and respect, seems to have wavered in his judgment on this point to a quite unaccountable degree. In his memoirs of Ben Jonson *Bartholomew Fair* is described as 'a popular piece, but chiefly remarkable for the obloquy to which it has given birth.' In his final note on the play, he expresses an opinion that it has 'not unjustly' been considered as 'nearly on a level with those exquisite dramas, *The Fox* and *The Alchemist*.' Who shall decide when not only do doctors disagree, but the most self-confident of doctors in criticism disagrees with himself to so singular an extent? The dainty palate of Leigh Hunt was naturally nauseated by the undoubtedly greasy flavour of the dramatic viands here served up in such prodigality of profusion: and it must be confessed that some of the meat is too high and some of the sauces are too rank for any but a very strong digestion. But those who turn away from the table in sheer disgust at the coarseness of the fare will lose the enjoyment of some of the richest and strongest humour, some of the most brilliant and varied realism, that ever claimed the attention or excited the admiration of the study or the stage. That 'superlunatical hypocrite,' the immortal and only too immortal Rabbi Busy, towers above the minor characters of the play as the execrable fanaticism which he typifies and embodies was destined to tower above reason and humanity, charity and common sense, in its future influence on the social life of England. But in sheer force and fidelity of presentation this wonderful study from nature can hardly be said to exceed the others which surround and set it off; the dotard Littlewit, the booby Cokes, the petulant fidelity and pig-headed self-confidence of Waspe, the various humours and more various villainies of the multitudinous and riotous subordinates; above all, that enterprising and intelligent champion of social purity, the conscientious and clear-sighted Justice Adam

Overdo. When all is said that can reasonably be said against the too accurate reproduction and the too voluminous exposition of vulgar and vicious nature in this enormous and multitudinous pageant—too serious in its satire and too various in its movement for a farce, too farcical in its incidents and too violent in its horseplay for a comedy—the delightful humour of its finer scenes, the wonderful vigour and veracity of the whole, the unsurpassed ingenuity and dexterity of the composition, the energy, harmony, and versatility of the action, must be admitted to ensure its place for ever among the minor and coarser masterpieces of comic art.

. . . 1616, though to us more mournfully memorable for the timeless death of Shakespeare, is also for the student of Ben Jonson a date of exceptional importance and interest. The production of two masques and a comedy in verse, with the publication of the magnificent first edition of his collected plays and poems, must have kept his name more continuously if not more vividly before the world than in any preceding year of his literary life. The masque of *The Golden Age Restored*, presented on New Year's Night and again on Twelfth Night, is equally ingenious and equally spirited in its happy simplicity of construction and in the vigorous fluency of its versification; which is generally smooth, and in the lyrical dialogue from after the first dance to the close may fairly be called sweet; an epithet very seldom applicable to the solid and polished verse of Jonson. And if *The Devil is an Ass* cannot be ranked among the crowning masterpieces of its author, it is not because the play shows any sign of decadence in literary power or in humorous invention: the writing is admirable, the wealth of comic matter is only too copious, the characters are as firm in outline and as rich in colour as any but the most triumphant examples of his satirical or sympathetic skill in finished delineation and demarcation of humours. On the other hand, it is of all Ben Jonson's comedies since the date of *Cynthia's Revels* the most obsolete in subject of satire, the most temporary in its allusions and applications: the want of fusion or even connection (except of the most mechanical or casual kind) between the various parts of its structure and the alternate topics of its ridicule makes the action more difficult to follow than that of many more complicated plots: and, finally, the admixture of serious sentiment and noble emotion is not so skilfully managed as to evade the imputation of incongruity. Nevertheless, there are touches in the dialogue between Lady Tailbush and Lady Eitherside in the first scene of the fourth act which are worthy of Molière himself, and suggestive of the method and the genius to which we owe the immortal enjoyment derived from the society of Cathos and Madelon—I should say, Polixène and Aminte, of Célimène and Arsinoé, and of Philaminte and Bélise. The third scene of the same act is so nobly written that the reader may feel half inclined to condone or to forget the previous humiliation of the too compliant heroine—her servile and undignified submission to the infamous imbecility of her husband—in admiration of the noble and natural eloquence with which the poet has here endowed her. But this husband, comical as are the scenes in which he develops and dilates from the part of a dupe to the part of an impostor, is a figure almost too loathsome to be ludicrous—or at least, however ludicrous, to be fit for the leading part in a comedy of ethics as well as of manners. And the prodigality of elaboration lavished on such a multitude of subordinate characters, at the expense of all continuous interest and to the sacrifice of all dramatic harmony, may tempt the reader to apostrophize the poet in his own words:

> You are so covetous still to embrace
> More than you can, that you lose all.

Yet a word of parting praise must be given to Satan: a small part as far as extent goes, but a splendid example of high comic imagination after the order of Aristophanes, admirably relieved by the low comedy of the asinine Pug and the voluble doggrel of the antiquated Vice.

. . . ⟨T⟩he year 1625 is memorable to the students and admirers of Ben Jonson for the appearance of a work worth almost all his masques together; a work in which the author of *The Fox* and *The Alchemist* once more reasserted his claim to a seat which no other poet and no other dramatist could dispute. The last complete and finished masterpiece of his genius is the splendid comedy of *The Staple of News*. This, rather than *The Silent Woman*, is the play which should be considered as the third—or perhaps we should say the fourth—of the crowning works which represent the consummate and incomparable powers of its author. No man can know anything worth knowing of Ben Jonson who has not studied and digested the text of *Every Man in his Humour*, *The Fox*, *The Alchemist*, and *The Staple of News*: but any man who has may be said to know him well. To a cursory or an incompetent reader it may appear at first sight that the damning fault of *The Devil is an Ass* is also the fault of this later comedy: that we have here again an infelicitous and an incongruous combination of realistic satire with Aristophanic allegory, and that the harmony of the different parts, the unity of the composite action, which a pupil of Aristophanes should at least have striven to attain—or, if he could not, at least to imitate and to respect—can here be considered as conspicuous only by their absence. But no careful and candid critic will retain such an impression after due study has been given to the third poetic comedy which reveals to us the genius of Jonson, not merely as a realistic artist in prose or a master of magnificent farce, but as a great comic poet. The scheme of his last preceding comedy had been vitiated by a want of coherence between the actual and the allegorical, the fantastic and the literal point of view; and the result was confusion without fusion of parts: here, on the other hand, we have fusion without confusion between the dramatic allegory suggested by Aristophanes, the admirably fresh and living presentation of the three Pennyboys, and the prophetic satire of the newsmarket or Stock Exchange of journalism. The competent reader will be divided between surprise at the possibility and delight in the perfection of the success achieved by a poet who has actually endowed with sufficiency of comic life and humorous reality a whole group of symbolic personifications; from the magnificent Infanta herself, Aurelia Clara Pecunia, most gracious and generous yet most sensitive and discreet of imperial damsels, even down to little 'blushet' Rose Wax the chambermaid. Her young suitor is at least as good a picture of a generous light-headed prodigal as ever was shown on any stage: as much of a man as Charles Surface, and very much more of a gentleman. The miserly uncle, though very well drawn, is less exceptionally well drawn: but Pennyboy Canter, the disguised father, is equally delightful from the moment of his entrance with an extempore carol of salutation on his lips to those in which he appears to rescue the misused Infanta from the neglectful favourite of her choice, and reappears at the close of the play to rescue his son, redeem his brother, and scatter the community of jeerers: to whose humour Gifford is somewhat less than just when he compares it with 'the *vapouring* in *Bartholomew Fair*': for it is neither coarse nor tedious, and takes up but very little space; and that not unamusingly. As for the great scene of the Staple, it is one of the most masterly in ancient or modern comedy of the typical or satirical kind. The central 'Office' here opened, to the great offence (it should seem) of 'most of the spectators'—a fact which, as Gifford justly remarks, 'argues very little for the good sense of the audience,'—may be regarded by a modern student as representing the narrow little nest in which was laid the modest little egg of modern journalism—that bird of many notes and many feathers, now so like an eagle and now so like a vulture: now soaring as a falcon or sailing as a pigeon over continents and battle-fields, now grovelling and groping as a dunghill kite, with its beak in a very middenstead of falsehood and of filth. The vast range of Ben Jonson's interest and observation is here as manifest as the wide scope and infinite variety of his humour. Science and warfare, Spinoza and Galileo, come alike within reach of its notice, and serve alike for the material of its merriment. The invention of torpedos is anticipated by two centuries and a half; while in the assiduity of the newsmongers who traffic in eavesdropping detail we acknowledge a resemblance to that estimable race of tradesmen known to Parisian accuracy as interwieveurs. And the lunacy of apocalyptic interpreters or prophets is gibbeted side by side with the fanatical ignorance of missionary enthusiasm, with impostures of professional quackery and speculations in personal libel. Certainly, if ever Ben deserved the prophetic title of Vates, it was in this last magnificent work of his maturest genius. Never had his style or his verse been riper or richer, more vigorous or more pure. And even the interludes in which we hear the commentary and gather the verdict of 'these ridiculous gossips' (as their creator calls them) 'who tattle between the acts' are incomparably superior to his earlier efforts or excursions in the same field of humorous invention. The intrusive commentators on *Every Man out of his Humour*, for instance, are mere nullities—the awkward and abortive issue of unconscious uneasiness and inartistic egoism. But Expectation, Mirth, Tattle, and Censure, are genuine and living sketches of natural and amusing figures: and their dialogues, for appropriate and spirited simplicity, are worthy of comparison with even those of a similar nature which we owe not more to the genius than to the assailants of Molière.

In 1625 Ben Jonson had brought out his last great comedy: in 1626 he brought out the last of his finer sort of masques. The little so-called *Masque of Owls*, which precedes it in the table of contents, is (as Gifford points out) no masque at all: it is a quaint effusion of doggrel dashed with wit and streaked with satire. But in *The Fortunate Isles, and their Union*, the humour and the verse are alike excellent: the jest on Plato's ideas would have delighted Landor, and the wish of Merefool to 'see a Brahman or a Gymnosophist' is worthy of a modern believer in esoteric Buddhism. Few if any of the masques have in them lyrics of smoother and clearer flow; and the construction is no less graceful than ingenious. The next reappearance of the poet, after a silence during three years of broken or breaking health, was so memorably unfortunate in its issue that the name and the fate of a play which was only too naturally and deservedly hooted off the stage are probably familiar to many who know nothing of the masterpiece which had last preceded it. Ever since Lamb gathered some excerpts from the more high-toned and elaborate passages of *The New Inn, or The Light Heart*, and commended in them 'the poetical fancy and elegance of mind of the supposed rugged old bard,' it has been the fashion to do justice if not something more than justice to the literary qualities of this play; which no doubt contains much vigorous and some graceful writing, and may now and then amuse a tolerant reader by its accumulating and culminating absurdities of action and catastrophe, character and event. But that the work shows portentous signs of mental decay, or at all events of temporary collapse in judgment and in sense, can be questioned by no sane reader of so much as the

argument. To rank any preceding play of Jonson's among those dismissed by Dryden as his 'dotages' would be to attribute to Dryden a verdict displaying the veriest imbecility of impudence: but to *The New Inn* that rough and somewhat brutal phrase is on the whole but too plausibly applicable.

At the beginning of the next year Jonson came forward in his official capacity as court poet or laureate, and produced 'the Queen's Masque,' *Love's Triumph through Callipolis*, and again, at Shrovetide, 'the King's Masque,' *Chloridia*. A few good verses, faint echoes of a former song, redeem the first of these from the condemnation of compassion or contempt: and there is still some evidence in its composition of conscientious energy and of capacity not yet reduced from the stage of decadence to the stage of collapse. But the hymn which begins fairly enough with imitation of an earlier and nobler strain of verse at once subsides into commonplace, and closes in doggrel which would have disgraced a Sylvester or a Quarles. It is impossible to read *Chloridia* without a regretful reflection on the lapse of time which prevented it from being a beautiful and typical instance of the author's lyric power: but, however inferior it may be to what he would have made of so beautiful a subject in the freshness and fullness of his inventive and fanciful genius, it is still ingenious and effective after a fashion; and the first song is so genuinely graceful and simple as to remind us of Wordsworth in his more pedestrian but not uninspired moods or measures of lyrical or elegiac verse.

The higher genius of Ben Jonson as a comic poet was yet once more to show itself in one brilliant flash of parting splendour before its approaching sunset. No other of his works would seem to have met with such all but universal neglect as *The Magnetic Lady*; I do not remember to have ever seen it quoted or referred to, except once by Dryden, who in his *Essay of Dramatic Poesy* cites from it an example of narrative substituted for action, 'where one comes out from dinner, and relates the quarrels and disorders of it, to save the undecent appearance of them on the stage, and to abbreviate the story.' And yet any competent spectator of its opening scenes must have felt a keen satisfaction at the apparent revival of the comic power and renewal of the dramatic instinct so lamentably enfeebled and eclipsed on the last occasion of a new play from the same hand. The first act is full of brilliant satirical description and humorous analysis of humours: the commentator Compass, to whom we owe these masterly summaries of character, is an excellent counterpart of that 'reasonable man' who so constantly reappears on the stage of Molière to correct with his ridicule or control by his influence the extravagant or erratic tendencies of his associates. Very few examples of Jonson's grave and deliberate humour are finer than the ironical counsel given by Compass to the courtly fop whom he dissuades from challenging the soldier who has insulted him, on the ground that the soldier

> has killed so many
> As it is ten to one his turn is next:
> You never fought with any, less, slew any;
> And therefore have the [fairer] hopes before you.

The rest of the speech, with all that follows to the close of the scene, is no less ripe and rich in sedate and ingenious irony. There is no less admirable humour in the previous discourse of the usurer in praise of wealth—especially as being the only real test of a man's character:

> For, be he rich, he straight with evidence knows
> Whether he have any compassion
> Or inclination unto virtue, or no:
> Where the poor knave erroneously believes

If he were rich he would build churches, or
Do such mad things.

Most of the characters are naturally and vigorously drawn in outline or in profile: Dame Polish is a figure well worthy the cordial and lavish commendation of Gifford: and the action is not only original and ingenious, but during the first four acts at any rate harmonious and amusing. The fifth act seems to me somewhat weaker; but the interludes are full of spirit, good humour, and good sense.

A *Tale of a Tub*, which appeared in the following year, is a singular sample of farce elaborated and exalted into comedy. This rustic study, though 'not liked' by the king and queen when acted before them at court, has very real merits in a homely way. The list of characters looks unpromising, and reminds us to regret that the old poet could not be induced to profit by Feltham's very just and reasonable animadversions on 'all your jests so nominal'; which deface this play no less than *The New Inn*, and repel the most tolerant reader by their formal and laborious puerility. But the action opens brightly and briskly: the dispute about 'Zin Valentine' is only less good in its way than one of George Eliot's exquisite minor touches—Mr. Dempster's derivation of the word Presbyterian from one Jack Presbyter of historic infamy: the young squire's careful and testy 'man and governor' is no unworthy younger brother of Numps in *Bartholomew Fair*: and the rustic heroine, a figure sketched with rough realistic humour, is hardly less than delightful when she remarks, after witnessing the arrest of her intended bridegroom on a charge of highway robbery, 'He might have married one first, and have been hanged after, if he had had a mind to 't;' a reflection worthy of Congreve or Vanbrugh, Miss Hoyden or Miss Prue. But Jonson had never laid to heart the wisdom expressed in the admirable proverb—'Qui trop embrasse mal étreint;' the simple subject of the play and the homely motive of the action are overlaid and overloaded by the multiplicity of minor characters and episodical superfluities, and the upshot of all the poet's really ingenious contrivances is pointless as well as farcical and flat as well as trivial. But there is certainly no sign of dotage in any work of Ben Jonson's produced before or after the lamentable date of *The New Inn*. The author apologizes for the homely and rustic quality of his uncourtly play; but if it be a failure, it is not on account of its plebeian humility, but through the writer's want of any real sympathy with his characters, any hearty relish of his subject: because throughout the whole conduct of a complicated intrigue he shows himself ungenially observant and contemptuously studious of his models: because the qualities most needed for such work, transparent lucidity and straightforward simplicity of exposition, are not to be found in these last comedies: because, for instance, as much attention is needed to appreciate the ingenious process of 'humours reconciled' in *The Magnetic Lady*, or to follow the no less ingenious evolution of boorish rivalries and clownish intrigues in the play just noticed, as to follow the action and appreciate the design of *The Fox* or *The Alchemist*.

The masque of this year, *Love's Welcome at Welbeck*, is a thing of very slight pretentions, but not unsuccessful or undiverting after its homely fashion. In the next year's companion masque, *Love's Welcome at Bolsover*, the verse, though not wanting in grace or ease, is less remarkable than the rough personal satire on Inigo Jones; who, it may be observed, is as ready with a quotation from Chaucer as Goody Polish in *The Magnetic Lady* or Lovel in *The New Inn*.

Of this great dramatist's other than dramatic work in poetry or in prose this is not the place to speak: and his two posthumous fragments of dramatic poetry, interesting and characteristic as they are, can hardly affect for the better or for the worse our estimate of his powers. Had *Mortimer his Fall* been completed, we should undoubtedly have had a third example of rhetorical drama, careful, conscientious, energetic, impassive and impressive; worthy to stand beside the author's two Roman tragedies: and Mortimer might have confronted and outfaced Sejanus and Catiline in sonorous audacity of rhythmic self-assertion and triumphant ostentation of magnificent vacuity. In *The Sad Shepherd* we find the faults and the merits of his best and his worst masques so blended and confounded that we cannot but perceive the injurious effect on the Laureate's genius or instinct of intelligence produced by the habit of conventional invention which the writing of verse to order and the arrangement of effects for a pageant had now made inevitable and incurable. A masque including an antimasque, in which the serious part is relieved and set off by the introduction of parody or burlesque, was a form of art or artificial fashion in which incongruity was a merit; the grosser the burlesque, the broader the parody, the greater was the success and the more effective was the result: but in a dramatic attempt of higher pretention than such as might be looked for in the literary groundwork or raw material for a pageant, this intrusion of incongruous contrast is a pure barbarism—a positive solecism in composition. The collocation of such names and such figures as those of Æglamour and Earine with such others as Much and Maudlin, Scathlock and Scarlet, is no whit less preposterous or less ridiculous, less inartistic or less irritating, than the conjunction in Dekker's *Satiromastix* of Peter Flash and Sir Quintilian, Sir Adam Prickshaft and Sir Vaughan ap Rees, with Crispinus and Demetrius, Asinius and Horace: and the offence is graver, more inexcusable and more inexplicable, in a work of pure fancy or imagination, than in a work of poetic invention crossed and chequered with controversial satire. Yet Gifford, who can hardly find words or occasions sufficient to express his sense of Dekker's 'inconceivable folly,' or his contempt for 'a plot that can scarcely be equalled in absurdity by the worst of the plays which Dekker was ever employed to "dress,"' has not a syllable of reprehension for the portentous incongruities of this mature and elaborate poem. On the other hand, even Gifford's editorial enthusiasm could not overestimate the ingenious excellence of construction, the masterly harmony of composition, which every reader of the argument must have observed with such admiration as can but intensify his regret that scarcely half of the projected poem has come down to us. No work of Ben Jonson's is more amusing and agreeable to read, as none is more nobly graceful in expression or more excellent in simplicity of style.

The immense influence of this great writer on his own generation is not more evident or more memorable than is the refraction or reverberation of that influence on the next. This 'sovereign sway and masterdom,' this overpowering preponderance of reputation, could not but be and could not but pass away. No giant had ever the divine versatility of a Shakespeare: but of all the giant brood none ever showed so much diversity of power as Jonson. In no single work has he displayed such masterly variety of style as has Byron in his two great poems, *Don Juan* and *The Vision of Judgment*: the results of his attempts at mixture or fusion of poetry with farce will stand exposed in all their deformity and discrepancy if we set them beside the triumphant results of Shakespeare's. That faultless felicity of divine caprice which harmonizes into such absolute congruity all the outwardly incompatible elements of such works as *Twelfth Night* and *The Tempest*, the *Winter's Tale* and *A Midsummer Night's Dream*, is perhaps of all Shakespeare's incomparable gifts the one most utterly beyond reach of other poets. But when we consider the various faculties and powers of Jonson's genius and intelligence, when we examine severally the divers forces and capacities enjoyed and exercised by this giant workman in the performance of his work, we are amazed into admiration only less in its degree than we feel for the greatest among poets. It is not admiration of the same kind: there is less in it of love and worship than we give to the gods of song; but it is with deep reverence and with glowing gratitude that we salute in this Titan of the English stage 'il maestro di color che sanno.'

Notes

1. No student will need to be reminded of what is apparently unknown to some writers who have thought fit to offer an opinion on this subject—that different additions were made at different dates, and by different hands, to certain popular plays of the time. The original *Faustus* of Marlowe was altered and re-altered, at least three times, by three if not more purveyors of interpolated and incongruous matter: and even that superb masterpiece would hardly seem to have rivalled the popularity of Kyd's tragedy—a popularity by no means unmerited.

ELISABETH WOODBRIDGE
From *Studies in Jonson's Comedy*
1898, pp. 28–79

Chapter 3
Character Treatment in Jonson's Typical Comedy

Accepting . . . Jonson's work as of the judicial type, consider in detail his treatment of character. And first, it does not do to rest upon his own assertions with regard to his writing. For, with the best intentions, one seldom tells the exact truth about oneself, and though what a man says of himself is always significant and worth regarding, it is often to be taken as indirectly indicative of his real nature and purpose rather than as directly descriptive of them. Jonson, moreover, was sometimes singularly infelicitous in speaking of himself, and the mere culling from prologue and epilogue of all the lines in which he expresses his dramatic theory will not give quite an adequate conception of his actual work. Especially is this true of his comedies, where his artistic sense sometimes led him to depart as a playwright from some of his theories as a thinker. It was not that his utterances were insincere, but that his theory was not quite complete enough to cover all of his practice.

This method of collecting his statements and adding them together to stand for his art is perhaps responsible for the assumption generally made that Jonson's comedies always enforce a moral lesson. This is simply not true, although he himself does with great emphasis and entire sincerity assert that the duty of the comedian is to punish vice. Thus here:

> But with an armed and resolved hand,
> I'll strip the ragged follies of the time
> Naked as at their birth . . . .
> . . . . and with a whip of steel,
> Print wounding lashes in their iron-ribs.
> . . . . my strict hand
> Was made to seize on vice, and with a gripe
> Squeeze out the humor of such spongy souls,
> As lick up every idle vanity.[1]

This is well enough for a part of his work. It applies to *Volpone*; it applies also to *The Poetaster* and to *Cynthia's Revels*, though not in the same sense, for the genuine morality of *Volpone* is as diverse as possible from the pharisaic, egotistic superiority of the last two plays. It applies also to Jonson's two tragedies, and to parts of his other comedies. On the other hand, the moral of *The Alchemist* or of *Bartholomew Fair*

would be hard to find. For Jonson did indeed teach and scourge, but not always did his teaching inculcate morality or his scourging lash the scoundrel as such. On the whole, his efforts are directed quite as much against intellectual weakness as against moral, and he preached quite as emphatically from the text "don't be a fool" as from the text "don't be a knave," while if we except his tragedies, the weight of emphasis is rather on the first than on the second. Run rapidly through the important plays with this in view:

In *Every Man in His Humour* there are a number of rogues and a few honest men, but the line of division is drawn, not on a basis of honesty, but on a basis of wit. The three witty rogues, Wellbred, Young Knowell, and Brainworm, are successful in discomfiting not only the other rogues, but also the honest men, and Brainworm is at the end pardoned for his offenses because he has shown such ability in committing them. Such a play can scarcely be called moral, though no one would call it immoral either, unless it were some zealot such as Zeal-of-the-land Busy. If it teaches anything, it teaches that it is convenient to have a quick brain, a ready tongue, and an elastic conscience.

In *Every Man out of His Humour* the tone is more severe, and the author, speaking through Macilente, does indeed lash vice as well as folly. Every person is in turn exposed and censured, but the moral tone is spoiled by the fact that Macilente himself, through whose malignant activity these exposures are brought about, is left untouched. He is rather the most disagreeable scoundrel of them all, yet he goes free, and leaves the stage at the end licking his chops over the discomfiture he has occasioned.

In *Cynthia's Revels* and *The Poetaster* the pharisaic tone already alluded to may be called moral, but it seems more truly immoral than the most direct praise of vice could be.

Sejanus and *Volpone*, which follow, may be taken together, though one is called tragedy and one comedy. In these the tone, for the first and almost the last time, is that of a firm and strenuous morality. Both plays show stupendous vice bringing upon itself its own ruin—a negative kind of morality, to be sure, but genuine and consistent.

In *Epicoene*, however, we have pure farce, without a trace of moral tone, and all the better for its freedom from it, and in *The Alchemist* we have the very apotheosis of roguery. Three people conspire to cheat the world. Their success is complete and they outwit the vicious, the hypocritical, the simple; but they also bring about the discomfiture of the only honest man in the play. When at last they are brought to bay, one of the three saves himself by deserting the other two, and purchases his master's forgiveness by making over to him their ill-gotten gains.

Finally, in the coarse but good-natured laughter of *Bartholomew Fair*, even the fools are let off easily, while the knaves find the mad, merry rascality of the fair a very Elysium. One might go on through the rest of the plays, but the great ones end here, and the rest would not furnish anything new.

Jonson's comedy, then, is judicial but not always moral, that is, it always subjects its persons to a judgment according to some standard, but this standard is quite as apt to be an intellectual one as a moral one. Among those which apply an intellectual standard, *The Alchemist* and *Bartholomew Fair* are preëminent; among those which apply the moral standard, *Volpone* stands alone among the comedies, but in this as in other respects it may be classed with the tragedies *Sejanus* and *Catiline*.

Thus far we have been considering the general tone and purpose of the comedies in their treatment of character. The next question is as to the method of treatment. Satire, Moulton remarks, may accomplish its end in one of two ways; "the one declares a thing ridiculous, the other exhibits it in a ridiculous disguise. Reducing the two to their lowest terms, in the one you call a man a fool, in the other you disguise yourself in his likeness and then play the fool"—he illustrates by citing the *Saturday Review* and *Punch*, "the first alleges folly, the latter presents it."[2]

In the case of the dramatist, one would suppose that only the second method would be employed. As a matter of fact the temptation to "allege" folly as well to "present" it is usually too great to be resisted. Even Molière sometimes has a wise Dorine or a Cléante to explain or expose the follies of the other characters, while Jonson almost always has some such character to stand, as it were, with pointer in hand, as demonstrator of the action. Once one begins to watch for this feature it is really remarkable how constant it is. Sometimes there is one demonstrator for the entire play, sometimes there are several who take turns. Thus, in *Every Man out of His Humour* Macilente is demonstrator in chief; for the scenes where he is absent, Carlo Buffone acts as understudy.[3] In *Cynthia's Revels*, Crites holds the pointer;[4] in *The Poetaster*, it is Horace; in *The Silent Woman*, it is any one of the three friends: Truewit, Dauphine, or Clerimont; in *Volpone*, it is, for the main action, Mosca and Volpone themselves, who both egg on their victims and comment on their folly, while for the subinterest of Sir Politick Would-be, the demonstrator or showman is Peregrine. Even Jonson's tragedy is not free from this peculiarity, for in *Sejanus* the function of Arruntius in the play is only as a commenter on the other characters.

Such an expedient seems essentially undramatic. When used to excess, as Jonson often used it, it is so. To be constantly explaining the nature of the characters implies either that the dramatist does not trust the cogency of his presentation, or that he does not trust the perceptive powers of the audience. The latter alternative is in Jonson's case not unlikely, but it is also true that, save when he was at his very best, his genius was more expository than dramatic; his mind was more akin to Bacon's than to Shakespeare's, and it was possibly a little easier for him to explain in crisp phrase exactly how a man was a fool, than for him to give the man free scope to act according to his folly.[5] Some of the best things in his dramas are found in these non-dramatic lapses. In *Every Man out of His Humour*, for instance, in the scene where the scented courtier, Fastidious Brisk, meets the court lady, Saviolina, Macilente stands by watching, and one of his comments is worth all the rest of the scene put together. Fastidious, knowing the lady is about to enter, says, "A kind of affectionate reverence strikes me with a cold shivering, methinks." Macilente mutters sardonically: "I like such tempers well, as stand before their mistresses with fear and trembling; and before their Maker, like impudent mountains!"[6]

When the practise is not carried to excess, however; it is not out of place, but is entirely consistent with the spirit of this kind of comedy. For, as will more clearly appear in the discussion of plots, the characters in any such play may always be divided into two groups, a large group of victims, a small group of victimizers or intriguers who control events and search out ways to "gull" the victims. Such being the case, it is quite natural that they should at the same time laugh at and discuss their folly. Thus in *Volpone*, the comments of Mosca and his master on the stupid greed of the legacy-hunters are dramatically proper, whereas those of Peregrine on Sir Politick are doubtful. In *Epicoene* the gleeful asides of the three young men as they work up the two fools, Daw and La-Foole, are as legiti-

mate as are the whispered gibes of Sir Toby, Sir Andrew and Maria as they watch Malvolio from their ambush.

In his treatment of character, there are two dangers liable to beset the satiric dramatist. His material being human infirmity, his tone judicial and didactic, his temper a little superior if not scornful, he is apt to do one of two things:—if he is not broad-minded enough and impersonal enough he will be too particular, and fall into personal invective; if he has not a firm grasp of the concrete or artistic he will be too general, and will trench upon allegory.

The tendency toward personalities is easy to comprehend. It characterized the beginnings of comedy, and Aristophanes boldly and deliberately gave way to it. Menander appears to have broken away from it,—partly probably for political reasons,—and the Roman comedy is to some extent free from it, but it has always been one of the pitfalls of satire. Jonson certainly fell into it in two plays, *Cynthia's Revels* and *The Poetaster*, and probably in some parts of many of his other plays, and though he is vehement in defending himself from the charge of personality, his very defences, like his repeated assertions that he was above feeling the abuse of his enemies, do not leave upon us quite the impression he intended. Yet if this was his besetting sin, he knew it for a fault, knew that

> poet never credit gain'd
> By writing truths, but things, like truths, well feign'd.[7]

And doubtless he was often enough misunderstood and wilfully misinterpreted. There were plenty of "small fry" about town, ready to "make a libel which he meant a play,"[8] and he has us heartily on his side when he scores the "State-decypherer, or politick picklock of the scene," who is "so solemnly ridiculous as to search out, who was meant by the gingerbread-woman, who by the hobby-horse man, who by the costard-monger, nay, who by their wares. Or that will pretend to affirm on his own inspired ignorance, what Mirror of Magistrate is meant by the justice, what great lady by the pig-woman, what concealed statesman by the seller of mouse-traps, and so of the rest."[9]

Compare with this an interesting parallel in Molière:

Et voilà de quoi j'ouïs l'autre jour se plaindre Molière, parlant à des personnes qui le chargeoient de même chose que vous. Il disoit que rien ne lui donnoit du déplaisir comme d'être accusé de regarder quelqu'un dans les portraits qu'il fait; que son dessein est de peindre les moeurs sans vouloir toucher aux personnes . . . . et que si quelque-chose étoit capable de le dégoûter de faire des comédies, c'étoit les ressemblances qu'on y vouloit toujours trouver, etc.[10]

While, for an agreement which was perhaps even deliberately verbal, note Congreve's:

Others there are, whose malice we'd prevent:
Such, who watch plays, with scurrilous intent
To mark out who by characters are meant:
And though no perfect likeness they can trace,
Yet each pretends to know the copied face.
These, with false glosses, feed their own ill-nature,
And turn to libel what was meant a satire.[11]

The opposite tendency, that towards allegory, is a natural result of the comic point of view. For since the comedian regards defects, oddities of character, he is usually led to the study of temperaments in their extreme development, and his treatment is necessarily bound to emphasize the eccentricities in the temperament, leaving the rest of the personality somewhat shadowy. Indeed, it was a part of Jonson's theory that if eccentricity is anything more than external, it will effect the entire personality. To any such case he applies the term "humour," defining the term thus:

> As when some one peculiar quality
> Doth so possess a man, that it doth draw
> All his affects, his spirits, and his powers,
> In their confluctions, all to run one way,
> This may be truly said to be a humor.[12]

The theory is psychologically perfectly sound, but it, as well as Jonson's practice, has met with rather harsh treatment at the hands of critics. Thus Hazlitt:

> His imagination fastens instinctively on some one mark or sign by which he designates the individual, and never lets it go, for fear of not meeting with any other means to express himself by. A cant phrase, an odd gesture, an old-fashioned regimental uniform, a wooden leg, a tobacco-box, or a hacked sword, are the standing topics by which he embodies his characters to the imagination.[13]

Such a statement simply showed that Hazlitt entirely missed the point of Jonson's work. Curiously enough, too, his criticism may be answered out of Jonson's own mouth, if we simply go on quoting the passage from *Every Man out of His Humour* begun above. The speaker, Asper, who represents Jonson, continues—give ear, Hazlitt—

> But that a rook, by wearing a pyed feather,
> The cable hatband, or the three piled ruff,
> A yard of shoe-tye, or the Switzer's knot
> On his French garters, should affect a humor!
> O, it is more than most ridiculous.[14]

In other words, Jonson emphasizes the fact that it is inner and spiritual eccentricity with which he has to do, not accidents of external appearance.

Coleridge's censure touches him nearer, because it involves a truth, being scarcely more than a burlesque restatement of the above lines:

> Jonson's [characters] are either a man with a huge wen, having a circulation of its own, and which we might conceive amputated, and the patient thereby losing all his character; or they are mere wens themselves instead of men—wens personified, or with eyes, nose, and mouth cut out, mandrake fashion.[15]

Under the fantastic figure, Coleridge does here touch upon a real danger which besets all such writing—the danger of emphasizing a single odd trait to such an extent that the individual is lost sight of, or—which amounts to nearly the same thing—choosing as a subject for treatment some odd trait which is of so narrow a reach that it does not mold the rest of the character, but rather obscures it, and has the force of monomania, or "obsession." This is in fact a fault which Jonson's inferior work shows. Thus, the plot of *The Silent Woman* is based on a single characteristic of Morose, his hatred of noise. The play is, however, pure farce throughout, and as such the character of Morose is legitimate enough. If the play needed defense, however, the argument Gifford has chosen, if it were true, is the right one. He says:

> Both Upton and Whalley have mistaken the character of Morose, they suppose it to be a dislike of noise; whereas this is an accidental quality altogether dependent upon the master-passion, or 'humour,' a most inveterate and odious self-love.[16]

Even an admirer of Jonson may not quite agree with Gifford in this instance, but it is usually true that of Jonson's mature work Coleridge's criticism does not hold. In his three greatest plays, *The Alchemist, Volpone,* and *Bartholomew Fair,* he never passes the bounds of the dramatic. *Bartholomew Fair* is the most concretely realistic piece of portraiture he ever did, *Volpone* deals more with generalized types, while *The Alchemist* stands between the two, but all keep within artistic limits.

In his less great work, however, the tendency to personification of single qualities is very clear. In *The Magnetic Lady,* for example, Lady Loadstone's powers of attraction are continually alluded to, though with no apparent reason unless it be perhaps the sound of her name, and at the end she is married to Captain Ironside, presumably because magnet attracts iron. In *The Staple of News* the symbolism is more than verbal, but is puzzlingly capricious. Pecunia is apparently an ordinary young lady, but occasionally she is made to stand for money or wealth taken allegorically, and though young Pennyboy assures us that "she kisses like a mortal creature" the reader is never quite clear in his mind as to whether she is a girl or a money-bag.[17]

These are extreme cases, but it would be possible to choose out characters from the plays so as to make a series illustrating steps in the process all the way from vivid artistic portraiture like that of the Puritan zealot in *Bartholomew Fair* to personification like that of Lady Pecunia, with her attendant maids, Mortgage, Statute, Band and Wax, and her gentleman-usher, Broker. Finally, it is interesting to note that the lapses into personification occur more frequently in his late plays, as his powers waned, while his over-personal invective appears to have come early, before he was inclined to control his resentments.

Another objection, most comprehensive of all, is made to comedy of the class to which Jonson's belongs. It is of Molière's plays, but it might as well be of Jonson's, that Freytag says:

> The highest dramatic life is lacking to them—the processes of coming into being, the growth of character. We prefer to recognize on the stage how one *becomes* a miser, rather than how he *is* one.[18]

But this ⟨is⟩ an indictment, not of Molière's or Jonson's comedy, but of all comedy. What we must look for in Jonson's comedies, as in Molière's, is a study not of character development but of characters which are already formed, or which are treated as if they were already formed. For, "how a man becomes a miser" is not a comic but a tragic spectacle. The essentially tragic in Browning's *A Soul's Tragedy* is the spectacle of Chiappino's degeneration; but a comedian might take up Chiappino where Browning left him, and make him the hero of a comedy like *Tartuffe.* He could not take the period of his life that Browning takes—the period of his "becoming" and treat it deeply or truly, without making it tragic.[19] Again, the history of Lydgate in *Middlemarch,* is, as it stands, a "soul's tragedy"; but the final Lydgate, the conventional, prosperous physician, specialist in gout, would furnish good material for the satiro-comic artist. And Tartuffe himself—would it have been comic to watch how he *became* Tartuffe? It is indeed true, as Hegel suggests, that to preserve the comic in a comedy we must drop the curtain in time. But it is perhaps equally true that we must, at its beginning, not raise the curtain too soon.

Of Jonson's five great plays the earliest has been called, perhaps rightly, his most perfect.[20] *Bartholomew Fair* is certainly the most recklessly, riotously funny, while *The Alchemist* and *Volpone* contend for the position of the greatest. *The Alchemist,* is, indeed, structurally the most marvelous of plays, but there are some readers at least with whom no comedy leaves the impression that *Volpone* does,—an impression comparable in intensity with that made by a tragedy, though the effect here is mainly intellectual rather than emotional. It is the effect of the double character, Volpone-Mosca, which impresses us with a kind of hugeness, a diabolical fertility of power almost too great for comedy, and one cannot help wishing that Jonson had honored these two with opponents as worthy of their genius as those Shakespeare gave Iago.

Finally, to say that Jonson does not appeal to the imagination[21] is to forget Volpone, and Sir Epicure Mammon. What is true, is, that he appeals wholly to the intellect. Any one who expects to be emotionally touched will be disappointed, but if one is satisfied with the stimulus that comes of contact with a master mind, he will not seek in vain. Indeed one sometimes feels that, in coming from the sunny hedonism of some among the Elizabethans, there is a kind of pleasure, bracing while it chills, in getting into touch with this man, who stands apart from the rest, among them and not of them, whose "light" had not their "sweetness" and whose savage judgments never grew thoroughly humane, yet who had the nobleness that comes of power and sincerity and seriousness. . . .

Chapter 5
Jonson's Romantic Comedy

That Jonson had ever written any but satiric humor-comedy is hard to realize, for we are accustomed to thinking of him as one whose powers, like those of his own humor-ridden creations, "ran all one way." And indeed, the mature Jonson is singularly unvarying in point of view and in practice. We might apply to him Aurelia's mocking reproach to her sister:

What, true-stitch, sister! Both your sides alike![22]

But unvarying as he seems, Jonson had his romantic period. A few years younger than Shakespeare, he was still doing hackwork of the stage, recasting old plays, and acting, while the elder poet was producing his early comedies—*Love's Labour's Lost, The Comedy of Errors, The Two Gentlemen of Verona, A Midsummer Night's Dream*, and *The Merchant of Venice*. It is difficult to suppose that Jonson should have been uninfluenced by this wonderful series of plays, even if we imagine him, according to the conventional picture, with his eyes glued to the page of Plautus and Terence and Seneca. Of such influence we find few traces in his typical work and his expressed theory, but that it was for a time strong, parts of some of his plays and the whole of one give evidence.

This one is *The Case Is Altered*, produced apparently at the end of 1598, a few months after *Every Man in His Humour*. So different is this from his usual work, that it has been questioned whether the play really is Jonson's. The earliest printed form known to us is a quarto of 1609, of which some copies give Jonson's name, others do not, and we may take our choice of two hypotheses: either Jonson's name was unwarrantably inserted by the printers, and taken out of some copies by the writer's own orders: or it was printed without credit to him, and his name afterwards inserted.[23] Thus far no other evidence is forthcoming. Gifford and Cunningham both accept the play as Jonson's, as do all his critics, except C. H. Herford who, in his introduction to the 'Mermaid' edition of Jonson, writes: "The same year [1599!] probably produced a fourth [play], still extant, in which it seems equally clear that Jonson wrote a part, and that he did not write the whole—*The Case Is Altered*."[24] Mr. Herford gives no hint of his reasons either for dating the play a year later, or for denying its accepted authorship. The "part" written by Jonson is, we presume, Valentine's satirical description of the "Utopian" (English) stage, the hit at Anthony Munday, and the Jaques incident. But this last, which is unquestionably Jonson's, is so intimately bound in with the Rachel-plot that to accept it as Jonson's almost

involves accepting work as unlike his usual manner as any in the play.

Assuming, then, that the play is Jonson's, we have the interesting case of a purely "Romantic" comedy written by the greatest of the opposed school. It might almost be interpolated into the series of Shakespeare's comedies just mentioned—it would certainly be no more puzzling there than is *All's Well that Ends Well* in a later group. Structurally it is far above *Love's Labour's Lost*, though it has nothing so masterly as the great exposure scene of that play. If we had to place the play we should put it about with *The Two Gentlemen of Verona*, when Shakespeare's comedy was passing out of its stage of farce and situation, into its distinctive early form.

It may be worth while to pause a moment over these early plays. *Love's Labour's Lost* consists of one situation, the exposure of the four "forsworn" youths,—a scene worked out with a cleanness of stroke worthy of Molière. Indeed the motive of the play and its attitude strongly suggest Molière. Armado might be a study of a humor, and the catastrophe, where the four gentlemen are by the loving discipline of their ladies brought 'out of their humours' is Jonsonesque. Biron's recantation:

Taffeta phrases, silken terms precise,
I do forswear them, and I here protest,
. . .
Henceforth my wooing mind shall be express'd
In russet yeas and honest Kersey noes.[25]

finds a parallel—somewhat extravagant, indeed—in the litany of the reformed revellers in *Cynthia's Revels*:

From Spanish shrugs, French faces, smirks, irpes,
and all affected humors,
Good Mercury defend us, etc.[26]

The Comedy of Errors, largely farcical, adds nothing, except perhaps a firmer grasp of the laws of structure and plot. But in *The Two Gentlemen of Verona* the note of "Romantic Comedy" is clear. The interwoven love-plots give the delicate but firm setting, while Launce with his foil and victim Speed, serve as the most good natured of burlesques on the lofty raptures of the lovers.

The likeness between this play and *The Case Is Altered* is rather interesting. In part it can be reduced to details, in part it is a case of "atmosphere," or of the writer's attitude. One of the most striking points is the fact that the humor is the same. Onion and Juniper are, to be sure, not so bright as Launce and Speed, their humor is at once less funny and more coarse— there is no surer way of appreciating Shakespeare's delicate-mindedness than to compare his humorous scenes with those of his contemporaries—but it is the same in kind, it is the comedy of sympathy. We laugh at Juniper, "sweet youth, whose tongue has a happy turn when he sleeps," and at Onion, the ardent lover of Rachel, but we are fond of the fellows, and our laugh is very different from that provoked by "Master Stephen," or by any of the rest of the "gulls" and fools of Jonson's world. Moreover, the use of the comic element is somewhat the same in both. In *The Two Gentlemen of Verona*, following immediately on the farewell of Julia and Proteus, comes Launce's version of his own heartrending parting from his family—depicted the more graphically with the aid of his slippers and his stony-hearted dog. Again, hard upon Valentine, steeped in "endless dolor" at his banishment from Silvia, comes Launce again with the announcement that he too is in love:

He lives not now that knows me to be in love; yet I am in love; but a team of horse shall not pluck that from me; nor who 'tis I love; and yet 'tis a woman; but what woman I will not tell myself; and yet 'tis a milkmaid.[27]

The parody in *The Case Is Altered* is not so consistent nor so pointed, yet we can hardly miss the kindly satire implied in Onion's wooing of Rachel, even though it is separated by a whole act from the ardent pursuit of her by the various gentlemen of rank.

> *Onion*: O brave! she's yonder: O terrible!
>   she's gone.
> *Juniper*: Yea, so nimble in your dilemmas, and
>   your hyperboles! *Hey my love! O my love!* at
>   the first sight, by the mass.
> *Onion*: O how she scudded! O sweet scud, how
>   she tripped! O delicate trip and go![28]

In the serious parts of the play the intermingling of jest and earnest suggests Shakespeare. The two young girls, introducing themselves through Aurelia's mock-solemn announcement:

> Room for a case of matrons, colored black.

enter the scene almost like another Rosalind and Celia—at least they might have been first studies for them. Paulo, the ardent young lover, and Angelo, his faithless friend, remind us of Valentine and Proteus; indeed in V, 3 the exposure of Angelo's treachery by his friend and their instantaneous reconciliation is a situation identical with the conclusion of *The Two Gentlemen of Verona*.

Only the character of Jaques is out of keeping with the rest. He is distinctly Jonsonesque,[29] and in his addresses to his gold we feel the power of the author of *Volpone*, though even here there is a reminiscence of Shakespeare in his cry:

> "Thou hast made away my child, thou hast my gold:
> . . .
> The thief is gone, my gold's gone, Rachel's gone."[30]

Another point is the presence of sub-plots, or at least sub-interests. It is hard to decide what we can call the principal plot, but perhaps the Camillo-Gasper interest may serve as well as any. Besides this, we have: (1) the interests centering directly about Rachel, Paulo's love and Angelo's treachery being the central issues, while the infatuation of Ferneze, of Christophero and of Onion (!) are side interests; (2) the interest centering round Jaques, his gold, and his secret; this shades into (3) the Juniper and Onion interests, while (4) Aurelia and Chamont form a very slight fourth interest. All these threads are dexterously interwoven to a loose but fairly even tissue,—too even, perhaps, for the lack of a predominating group of characters is a fault.[31]

Finally, it will be noted that the comic element is found not in any of the more important plots, but in the under-issues or asides. This is a trait of the "Romantic" comedy; in Jonson's typical plays, the comic element is bound up with—is contained in—the main action.

The play, then, is distinctly romantic, and if we accept it as Jonson's it acquires peculiar significance as an indication of the kind of work he might have done in this field if he had chosen it for his mature activity.[32] That it was possibly written after his first play in his later manner need not be a difficulty.[33] With a poet who worked as consciously and deliberately as Jonson it would have been quite possible to write a play in the accepted manner, even while he was in the act of breaking away from that manner.[34]

It is interesting to note that in this, his one "Romantic" comedy, Jonson follows the Roman comedians more closely than anywhere else. In the Jaques incidents the *Aulularia* was

his model, in the Camillo-Gasper plot he was adapting from the *Captivi*. This would seem to bear out what was said in a preceding chapter as to the romantic possibilities of the Roman plots. The fact that Jonson so easily gave to his material the treatment needed to make these possibilities actual, is, moreover, an indication of his native power in other fields than those wherein he chose to excel. For this play, while not without faults, has in its manner a lightness of touch, in its humor a humaneness that is not equalled in the early work—scarcely in the mature work—of any contemporary save Shakespeare. That he turned aside to follow other courses we must, in the case of so conscious and conscientious an artist, attribute to deliberate choice; and in making an estimate of him we ought not to ignore, as critics have sometimes done, these two of his works wherein he showed other powers than those which he ordinarily allowed free play. Lightly to set aside *The Case Is Altered* and *The Sad Shepherd* as exceptions which need not be considered "in making up the main account" is only to justify the poet's slurs on "the world's coarse thumb and finger." Exceptional they are, but not accidental or unimportant.

Perhaps Jonson was right in choosing as he did, since in the work which he made characteristically his own he had no equal, whereas in the realms that he abandoned he would have had one superior. Yet the lover of Jonson cannot but find something pathetic in this self-imposed narrowing of his mighty powers,—cannot but wish that in determining the direction of his artistic genius, in pruning its growth, he had been a little less severe, less ruthless.

Notes

1. Induction, *Every Man out of His Humour*, *Works*, II, 12, 18.
2. Moulton, *The Ancient Classical Drama*, p. 256.
3. Cf. infra, pp. 58–60.
4. Mercury & Cupid are assistant-demonstrators; cf. infra, p. 83.
5. Extreme instances of this are *Every Man out of His Humour* and *Cynthia's Revels*. Cf. infra, pp. 57–60, 82, 83.
6. *Every Man out of His Humour*, Act III, Sc. 3; *Works*, II, 118.
7. Prologue, *The Silent Woman*; *Works*, III, 332.
8. Ibid. Cf. also in the Dedicatory Letter to *Volpone*: "I know that nothing can be so innocently writ or carried, but may be made obnoxious to construction," etc. *Works*, III, 158.
9. Induction, *Bartholomew Fair*; *Works*, IV, 353.
10. Moliere: *L'Impromptu de Versailles: Oeuvres*, III, 413.
11. Congreve: Epilogue, *The Way of the World*.
12. Induction, *Every Man out of His Humour*; *Works*, II, 16.
13. Hazlitt: *English Comic Writers*, 77.
14. Ibid., p. 17.
15. Coleridge: *Literary Remains*, II, 279.
16. Gifford's note, *The Silent Woman*, III, 399.
17. Cf. infra, pp. 90–92.
18. Freytag: *Technique of the Drama*, pp. 250–251.
19. Cf. Supra, pp. 17, 18. Note, however, that the process of reasoning does not imply any assertion that the converse is true; namely, that tragedy *must* involve character development. Few great tragedies have such a basis.
20. Swinburne: *A Study of Ben Jonson*, pp. 3, 14.
21. Aronstein: *Ben Jonson's Theorie des Lustspiels*; Anglia, XVII, 477.
22. *The Case Is Altered*, Act II. Sc. 3; *Works*, VI, 331.
23. Cf. Fleay: *A Chronicle of the English Drama*; I, 357–358.
24. Herford: Introduction to *The Best Plays of Ben Jonson*, p. xxv.
25. *Love's Labour's Lost*, V, 2.
26. Palinode, *Cynthia's Revels*, V, 3; *Works*, III, 337, 359.
27. *The Two Gentlemen of Verona*, III, 1.
28. *The Case Is Altered*, IV, 4; *Works*, VI, 364.
29. That he was modeled on Plautus is only another indication of this—such work was characteristic of Jonson.
30. *The Case Is Altered*, V, 1; *Works* VI, 380.
31. Nor is the texture without flaw; the two characters, Balladino and Francisco Colonia, are hangers-on in the play. The first was

evidently inserted as a "local hit." The presence of the second seems unmotived.

32. *The New Inn* is sometimes called a romantic comedy, and with a degree of reason . . . On the other hand, the romantic fragment, *The Sad Shepherd*, ought to be classed with Theocritus and Spenser, as romantic pastoral, rather than with romantic comedy.

33. Koeppel, however, thinks it was his first work. Cf. his *Quellen-Studien zu den Dramen Ben Jonson's, John Marston's und Beaumont's und Fletcher's*, pp. 1, 19.

34. The hit at Anthony Munday, Act I, sc. 1, may, indeed, be also a comment on some of the criticism to which the new play, *Every Man in His Humour*, must certainly have given rise.

SIR HENRY WOTTON

1568–1639

Henry Wotton was born on March 30, 1568, at Boughton Malherbe, Kent. He received his early education at the Winchester School and entered New College, Oxford, in 1584. He moved to Queen's College in 1585, and eventually was awarded a B.A. in 1588. Wotton spent the next seven years on the Continent. When he returned to England in 1595 he read briefly at Middle Temple, London, and then served as secretary to the Earl of Essex. After Essex's abortive rebellion in 1601, Wotton fled to Italy where he worked on a secret diplomatic mission. He again returned to England in 1603, and was knighted for his service to James I. From 1604 to 1624 he was intermittently the ambassador to Venice. He served on additional diplomatic missions to France, The Hague, and Vienna. Wotton was a member of Parliament and was ordained a deacon in 1627. In 1624 he became provost of Eton College, a position he held until his death.

Wotton's literary fame rests on several poems, the most famous of which, "You Meaner Beauties of the Night," was written for Elizabeth of Bohemia. Other notable poems are "Character of a Happy Life" and "On His Mistress, the Queen of Bohemia." Wotton's many years in Italy visibly influenced his thinking about art and architecture in his 1624 book, *The Elements of Architecture*. During his Eton years Wotton began A *Philosophical Survey of Education*. This humane theoretical tract was never completed. Wotton's writings were collected in 1651 by Izaak Walton in *Reliquiae Wottonianae*. Walton prefixed his *Life of Wotton* to this collection of his friend's poems, letters, and miscellaneous writings. Wotton also is remembered for his friendships with John Donne and Ben Jonson. Wotton died in December 1639 at Eton.

Personal

After those reverend papers, whose soule is
  Our good and great Kings lov'd hand and fear'd name,
By which to you he derives much of his,
  And (how he may) makes you almost the same,
A Taper of his Torch, a copie writ
  From his Originall, and a faire beame
Of the same warme, and dazeling Sun, though it
  Must in another Sphere his vertue streame:

After those learned papers which your hand
  Hath stor'd with notes of use and pleasure too,
From which rich treasury you may command
  Fit matter whether you will write, or doe:

After those loving papers, where friends send
  With glad griefe, to your sea-ward steps, farewel,
Which thicken on you now, as prayers ascend
  To heaven in troupes at'a good mans passing bell:

Admit this honest paper, and allow
  It such an audience as your selfe would aske;
What you must say at Venice this meanes now,
  And hath for nature, what you have for taske:

To sweare much love, not to be chang'd before
  Honour alone will to your fortune fit;
Nor shall I then honour your fortune, more
  Then I have done your honour wanting it.

But 'tis an easier load (though both oppresse)

To want, then governe greatnesse, for wee are
In that, our owne and onely businesse,
  In this, wee must for others vices care;
'Tis therefore well your spirits now are plac'd
  In their last Furnace, in activity;
Which fits them (Schooles and Courts and Warres o'rpast)
  To touch and test in any best degree.

For mee, (if there be such a thing as I)
  Fortune (if there be such a thing as shee)
Spies that I beare so well her tyranny,
  That she thinks nothing else so fit for mee;
But though she part us, to heare my oft prayers
  For your increase, God is as neere mee here;
And to send you what I shall begge, his staires
  In length and ease are alike every where.
    —JOHN DONNE, "To Sir Henry Wotton, at His
      Going Ambassador to Venice," c. 1604

What shall we say, since *silent* now is *He*
Who when he *Spoke*, all things would *Silent* be?
Who had so many *Languages* in store,
That onely *Fame* shall speak of him in *More*.
Whom *England* now no more return'd must see.
He's gone to *Heav'n* on his *Fourth Embassie*.
On earth he travell'd often; not to say
H'had been abroad, or pass loose *Time* away.
In whatsoever *Land* he chanc'd to come,
He read the *Men* and *Manners*, bringing home

Their *Wisdom*, *Learning*, and their *Pietie*,
As if he went *to Conquer*, not *to See*.
So well he understood the most and best
Of *Tongues* that *Babel* sent into the *West*,
Spoke them so truly, that he had (you'd swear)
Not only *Liv'd*, but *been Born* every where.
Justly each *Nations* Speech to him was known,
Who for the *World* was made, not *us* alone.
Nor ought the *Language* of that Man be less
Who in his Breast had *all things* to *express*.
We say that *Learning's* endless, and blame Fate
For not allowing Life a longer date.
He did the utmost *Bounds* of *Knowledge* find,
He found them not so large as was his *Mind*.
But, like the brave *Pellæan Youth*, did mone
Because that *Art* had no more *worlds* then *One*.
And when he saw that he through all had past,
He *dy'd*, lest he should *Idle* grow at last.
—ABRAHAM COWLEY, "On the Death of Sir
Henry Wootton," 1639

Henry Wotton, a person singularly accomplish'd, son of Tho. Wotton, esq; by his second wife Elizabeth, daughter of sir Will. Finch of the Mote in St. Martin's parish in the county of Kent, but the widow of one Morton of the same county esq; was born at Bocton hall in Kent 30 March 1568, educated in grammar learning in Wykeham's school near to Winchester, and thence in the beginning of 1584, he was transplanted to New coll. where living in the condition of a gent. com. had his chamber in Hart hall adjoyning, and to his chamber-fellow there Rich. Baker his countryman, afterwards a knight and a noted writer. But continuing there not long, he went to Queen's coll. where, by the benefit of a good tutor and severe discipline there practised, he became well vers'd in logic and philosophy; and for a diversion now and then, he wrote a tragedy for the private use of that house called *Tancredo*. On the 8 June 1588, he, as a member of Qu. coll. did supplicate the venerable congregation of regents that he might be admitted to the reading of any of the books of the logick of Aristotle, that is to be admitted to the degree of bach. of arts: which desire of his was granted conditionally that he should determine in the Lent following; but whether he was admitted, or did determine, or took any other degree, it doth not appear in any of the university registers, which I have exactly searched, and the more for this reason, because the author of his life (Izaak Walton) saith, that at 19 years of age he proceeded master of arts, and at that time did read three Lat. lectures *De Ocello*; which being learned, caused a friendship between him and Alberic. Gentilis, who thereupon ever after called him 'Henrice mi Ocelle.' The said author also saith, that the university treasury was rob'd by townsmen and poor scholars, of which such light was given by a letter written to Hen. Wotton from his father in Kent, occasioned by a dream relating to that matter, that the felons were thereupon discovered and apprehended, &c. But upon my search into the university registers, records, accompts, &c. from 1584, to 1589, in which time our author Wotton was resident in Oxon, I find no such robbery committed. To pass by other mistakes in the said life, especially as to time, which are not proper to set down in this place, I shall go forward. After our author had left Oxon, he betook himself to travel into France, Germany, and Italy; and having spent about 9 years in those places, he returned into England, and became secretary to Robert earl of Essex, with whom continuing till towards his fall, he left England once more, and retiring to Florence, became so noted to the great duke of Tuscany, that he was by him privately dispatched away with letters to James 6. K. of

Scots, under the name of Octavio Baldi, to advise him of a design to take away his life. Which message being welcome to that K. he was by him (when made K. of England) honoured with the degree of knighthood, sent thrice ambassador to the repub. of Venice, once to the states of the united Provinces, twice to Charles Emanuel duke of Savoy, once to the united princes of Upper Germany in the convention at Heylbrune, also to the archduke Leopold, to the duke of Wittenbergh, to the imperial cities of Strasburgh and Ulme, as also to the emperor Ferdinando the second. On the 15 July 1619, he returned from his embassy at Venice with a vain hope of obtaining the office of secretary of state, but missing his design, I cannot yet tell to the contrary but that he was sent to Venice again. Sure 'tis, that about 1623 he had the provostship of Eton coll. conferr'd upon him, which he kept to his dying day, being all the reward he had for the great services he had done the crown of England.—ANTHONY À WOOD, *Athenae Oxonienses*, 1691–1721

It appears to have been the peculiar privilege of sir Henry Wotton, and may be regarded by posterity as the most conclusive evidence of his merits, to have secured to himself through life, and amid all the vicissitudes of his fortune, the affection, the esteem and the cooperation of the master-spirits of the age in which he flourished.—LUCY AIKIN, *Memoirs of the Court of King James the First*, 1822, Vol. 1, p. 124

General

Though he was justly esteemed an elegant scholar, and an able critic, his works abound with exotic idioms; nor has he escaped censure for his pedantry. But it should be considered that he wrote in an age, when, to write like a pedant, was to write like a gentleman; or, to speak more properly, like a king.—JAMES GRANGER, *Biographical History of England*, 1769–1824

The poetry of Wotton, though chiefly written for the amusement of his leisure, and through the excitement of casual circumstances, possesses the invaluable attractions of energy, simplicity, and the most touching morality; it comes warm from the heart, and whether employed on an amatory or didactic subject, makes its appropriate impression with an air of sincerity which never fails to delight.—NATHAN DRAKE, *Shakspeare and His Times*, 1817, Vol. 1, p. 672

Amid so many desultory occupations and pleasures, he had not time to accomplish all that was expected of him in the way of original authorship. On accepting the Provostship of Eton, he had indulged in the hope of being able to write a Life of Luther, which he had long had in view, and in which he meant to involve a history of the German Reformation; but King Charles had persuaded him to abandon this design and think rather of a history of England. All that he had done towards this work consisted of but a few fragments; and his literary reputation depended, therefore, on two controversial letters or pamphlets published by him when he was ambassador at Venice, on a little treatise entitled *The Elements of Architecture* which he had published in 1624, on a few short poems of a moral or meditative character which had got about separately and were known to be his, and on several brief Essays, also unpublished, but known to his friends. The Poems, the Essays, and a selection of his private letters were published after his death as the *Reliquiæ Wottonianæ*. The Poems are in a graceful, thoughtful spirit, with a trace in them of the style of his friend Donne. The Essays are mostly on historical or political topics—a Panegyric on Charles I., a Character of William the Conqueror, a Parallel between the character of the Earl of

Essex and that of the Duke of Buckingham, &c.; but one of them is a brief tract "On Education, or Moral Architecture," containing hints derived from his experience as Provost of Eton School. The Panegyric on Charles is in a strain of the most reverent loyalty, and he particularly applauds Charles's policy for the suppression of controversies in the Church. *"Disputandi pruritus est ecclesiarum scabies"* ("The itch of disputing is the leprosy of Churches") was one of his favourite aphorisms. He was himself a man of liberal views, keeping a middle way between Calvinism and Arminianism, though deferring to the policy of Laud as that of the established power of the State. All in all, he deserved his reputation as one of the most accomplished and benevolent old gentlemen of his time; and it is pleasant yet to look at his portrait, representing him seated in his furred and embroidered gown, as Provost of Eton, leaning against a table, his head resting on his left hand, and his wise kind face looking straight towards you, as if listening so courteously.—DAVID MASSON, *The Life of John Milton*, 1859, Vol. 1, pp. 492–93

Of poetry he wrote but little; but of that little two pieces at least have obtained a permanent place in English literature, his 'Character of a Happy Life,' written probably circ. 1614; and the lines, 'On His Mistress the Queen of Bohemia,' circ. 1620. Of the apophthegm 'the style is of the man,' it would be difficult to find better illustrations. As in a mirror, they reflect the high refined nature of one who, living in the world, and a master of its ways and courtesies, was yet never of it—was never a worldling.—JOHN W. HALES, "Sir Henry Wotton," *The English Poets*, ed. Thomas Humphry Ward, 1880, Vol. 2, p. 108

The roll of our notable prose writers, like that of our poets of genius, would be incomplete without the name of Sir Henry Wotton, which is illuminated by something beyond the afterglow of the great age to which, both by his nurture and by his sympathies, he belonged. For he represents more distinctly perhaps than any other of his contemporaries the militant Protestantism which counted for so much in the whole life of their age. Like Bacon, he formed part of the younger generation which passed from the service of the great Queen into that of her successor. Had it been morally possible for James I. to allow their counsels to determine permanently the balance of his judgment, European history might have taken a different course. But this by the way. What concerns us is the type which in Wotton is so cherished by Englishmen. Advanced Protestants in their religious views (for to call them Puritans would be a misnomer), these heroes of an unheroic age were, it must be confessed, unhampered by too nice a scrupulosity in their methods of political conduct, and well fitted to co-operate with the statesmen who enjoyed the confidence of Henry IV., or contributed despatches to the Chancery of militant Calvinism in the Empire. Wotton, before he became a diplomatist himself and wrote despatches which lie outside our present range, and of which, for the rest, but few seem to have been preserved, took occasion to put forth a manifesto of his opinions which is certainly not lacking in plainness. In his later days he advised a young aspirant in his profession always to tell the truth, more especially since nobody would ever believe it to be such. But the spirit of *The State of Christendom*, written shortly before the death of Queen Elizabeth, and the largest and most important of Wotton's extant prose writings, is that of a self-confident aggressiveness without *arrière-pensées*. It opens with a plain statement that in the weary days of the author's foreign exile there had occurred to him, among other possible ways of bringing about his return, the notion of "murdering

some notable traitor to his prince and country"; but that on second thoughts he had not carried out the scheme, as likely to entail upon him both danger and disquietude. In the body of the essay he argues very audaciously, and at the same time very subtly, in defence of such disputable acts as the execution of Mary Queen of Scots and the murder of the Duke of Guise, but he is not less prepared to show cause why King Philip of Spain should be lawfully excommunicated and deposed, and dealt with accordingly. An argument conducted in this practical fashion may serve to show that revolutions, such as were attempted in the state of Western Christendom alike by the Calvinist propaganda and by the Catholic reaction, are not made with rose-water; but no refinements of style could render it pleasant reading, and to these indeed it makes no pretence. With this treatise should be compared Wotton's youthful letters to Lord Ford from Germany, which breathe the same defiant spirit. . . . His chief attempt in the field of natural science, for which he always retained a keen interest, was in Latin, and the work of his Oxford days; but his treatise on *The Elements of Architecture* is in the vernacular, and to the full as readable as any modern pamphlet on house-decoration. More ambitious in design, but, like nine-tenths of his writings, only fragmentary in execution, is the *Survey of Education; or, Moral Architecture*, which consists of aphorisms and a preface, the latter interesting as seeking to place education on its true, *i.e.* psychological, basis. The historical pieces are similarly unfinished, unless we should except the not very profound quasi-Plutarchian parallel between Essex and Buckingham, and the servile panegyric "to" Charles I. This king loved epigrams, and Wotton the making of them—witness his famous definition of an ambassador, as sent to 'lie abroad,' on behalf of his country—a witticism, wickedly published by Scioppius several years after date. The panegyric contains a more academic saying of which its author wished mention to be made in his epitaph, thus "Englished" by Izaak Walton:

> Here lies the first author of this sentence:
> "The itch of disputation will prove the scab of
> Churches."
> Inquire his name elsewhere.

We might well wish that he had, among his many designs, carried out that of a Life of Luther, with a history of the German Reformation; for nobody better knew how to correlate a great man and his times, and he had in him both enthusiasm and humour enough to understand the genius of the great Reformer. Wotton's own religious meditations have nothing specially characteristic in them, but they breathe the fervent piety which lends their deepest charm to his later letters, and which reveals itself even in the chance expressions of . . . his letters to Sir Edmund Bacon,—to my mind next to the *Poems* the pleasantest part of the *Reliquiæ Wottonianæ*. It is necessary to turn to this varied collection from Izaak Walton's delightful but imperfectly balanced *Life*, which presents to us the Provost of Eton in his cloistered retirement—a solitude of study and prayer—rather than the enthusiastic "servant" of Elizabeth of Bohemia, the eager friend of Father Paul, the courtier, the politician, and the wit. And to those who are not content with a mere glance at Wotton's prose, fragmentary as it is, most passages of his *Remains* will I think suggest a combination of characteristics rare in the style even of a highly cultivated writer, unless he is at the same time a man of convictions rooted in principle and matured by experience.—A. W. WARD, "Sir Henry Wotton," *English Prose*, ed. Henry Craik, 1893, Vol. 2, pp. 75–77

IZAAK WALTON
From *Life of Sir Henry Wotton*
1640

He was a great lover of his neighbours, and a bountiful entertainer of them very often at his table, where his meat was choice, and his discourse better.

He was a constant cherisher of all those youths in that school, in whom he found either a constant diligence, or a genius that prompted them to learning; for whose encouragement he was—beside many other things of necessity and beauty—at the charge of setting up in it two rows of pillars, on which he caused to be choicely drawn the pictures of divers of the most famous Greek and Latin historians, poets, and orators; persuading them not to neglect rhetoric, because 'Almighty God has left mankind affections to be wrought upon.' And he would often say, 'That none despised eloquence, but such dull souls as were not capable of it.' He would also often make choice of some observations out of those historians and poets; and would never leave the school without dropping some choice Greek or Latin apophthegm or sentence, that might be worthy of a room in the memory of a growing scholar.

He was pleased constantly to breed up one or more hopeful youths, which he picked out of the school, and took into his own domestic care, and to attend him at his meals; out of whose discourse and behaviour he gathered observations for the better completing of his intended work of education: of which, by his still striving to make the whole better, he lived to leave but part to posterity.

He was a great enemy to wrangling disputes of religion; concerning which I shall say a little, both to testify that, and to show the readiness of his wit.

Having at his being in Rome made acquaintance with a pleasant priest, who invited him one evening to hear their vesper music at church; the priest seeing Sir Henry stand obscurely in a corner, sends to him by a boy of the choir this question, writ on a small piece of paper; 'Where was your religion to be found before Luther?' To which question Sir Henry presently underwrit, 'My religion was to be found then, where yours is not to be found now, in the written Word of God.'

The next vesper, Sir Henry went purposely to the same church, and sent one of the choir boys with this question to his honest, pleasant friend, the priest: 'Do you believe all those many thousands of poor Christians were damned, that were excommunicated because the Pope and the Duke of Venice could not agree about their temporal power—even those poor Christians that knew not why they quarrelled? Speak your conscience.' To which he underwrit in French, 'Monsieur, excusez-moi.'

To one that asked him, 'Whether a Papist may be saved?' he replied, 'You may be saved without knowing that. Look to yourself.'

To another, whose earnestness exceeded his knowledge, and was still railing against the Papists, he gave this advice: 'Pray, sir, forbear till you have studied the points better; for the wise Italians have this proverb: "He that understands amiss concludes worse." And take heed of thinking, the farther you go from the Church of Rome, the nearer you are to God.'

And to another that spake indiscreet and bitter words against Arminius, I heard him reply to this purpose:

'In my travel towards Venice, as I passed through Germany, I rested almost a year at Leyden, where I entered into an acquaintance with Arminius,—then the Professor of Divinity in that university,—a man much talked of in this age, which is made up of opposition and controversy. And indeed, if I mistake not Arminius in his expressions,—as so weak a brain as mine is may easily do,—then I know I differ from him in some points; yet I profess my judgment of him to be, that he was a man of most rare learning, and I knew him to be of a most strict life, and of a most meek spirit. And that he was so mild appears by his proposals to our Master Perkins of Cambridge, from whose book, *Of the Order and Causes of Salvation*—which first was writ in Latin—Arminius took the occasion of writing some queries to him concerning the consequents of his doctrine; intending them, 'tis said, to come privately to Mr. Perkins' own hands, and to receive from him a like private and a like loving answer. But Mr. Perkins died before those queries came to him, and 'tis thought Arminius meant them to die with him; for though he lived long after, I have heard he forbore to publish them: but since his death his sons did not. And 'tis pity, if God had been so pleased, that Mr. Perkins did not live to see, consider, and answer those proposals himself; for he was also of a most meek spirit, and of great and sanctified learning. And though, since their deaths, many of high parts and piety have undertaken to clear the controversy; yet for the most part they have rather satisfied themselves, than convinced the dissenting party. And, doubtless, many middle-witted men, which yet may mean well, many scholars that are in the highest form for learning, which yet may preach well, men that are but preachers, and shall never know, till they come to heaven, where the questions stick betwixt Arminius and the Church of England,—if there be any,—will yet in this world be tampering with, and thereby perplexing the controversy, and do therefore justly fall under the rebuke of St. Jude, for being busybodies, and for meddling with things they understand not.'

And here it offers itself—I think not unfitly, to tell the reader, that a friend of Sir Henry Wotton's being designed for the employment of an ambassador, came to Eton, and requested from him some experimental rules for his prudent and safe carriage in his negotiations; to whom he smilingly gave this for an infallible aphorism: 'That, to be in safety himself, and serviceable to his country, he should always, and upon all occasions, speak the truth,—it seems a State paradox—for, says Sir Henry Wotton, you shall never be believed; and by this means your truth will secure yourself, if you shall ever be called to any account; and it will also put your adversaries—who will still hunt counter—to a loss in all their disquisitions and undertakings.' . . .

Sir Henry Wotton had proposed to himself, before he entered into his collegiate life, to write the Life of Martin Luther, and in it the History of the Reformation, as it was carried on in Germany: for the doing of which he had many advantages by his several embassies into those parts, and his interest in the several princes of the Empire; by whose means he had access to the records of all the Hans Towns, and the knowledge of many secret passages that fell not under common view; and in these he had made a happy progress, as was well known to his worthy friend Dr. Duppa, the late Reverend Bishop of Salisbury. But in the midst of this design, his late Majesty King Charles the First, that knew the value of Sir Henry Wotton's pen, did, by a persuasive loving violence—to which may be added a promise of £500 a year—force him to lay Luther aside, and betake himself to write the History of England; in which he proceeded to write some short characters of a few kings, as a foundation upon which he meant to build; but, for the present, meant to be more large in the story of Henry the Sixth, the founder of that college in which he then enjoyed all the worldly happiness of his present being. But Sir

Henry died in the midst of this undertaking, and the footsteps of his labours are not recoverable by a more than common diligence.

This is some account both of his inclination and the employment of his time in the college, where he seemed to have his youth renewed by a continual conversation with that learned society, and a daily recourse of other friends of choicest breeding and parts; by which that great blessing of a cheerful heart was still maintained; he being always free, even to the last of his days, from that peevishness which usually attends age.

And yet his mirth was sometimes damped by the remembrance of divers old debts, partly contracted in his foreign employments, for which his just arrears due from the King would have made satisfaction: but being still delayed with court promises, and finding some decays of health, he did, about two years before his death, out of a Christian desire that none should be a loser by him, make his last will; concerning which a doubt still remains, namely, whether it discovered more holy wit or conscionable policy. But there is no doubt but that his chief design was a Christian endeavour that his debts might be satisfied. . . .

The next thing wherewith I shall acquaint the reader is, that he went usually once a year, if not oftener, to that beloved Bocton Hall, where he would say, 'He found a cure for all cares, by the cheerful company, which he called the living furniture of that place: and a restoration of his strength, by the connaturalness of that which he called his genial air.'

He yearly went also to Oxford. But the summer before his death he changed that for a journey to Winchester College, to which school he was first removed from Bocton. And as he returned from Winchester towards Eton College, said to a friend, his companion in that journey: 'How useful was that advice of a holy monk, who persuaded his friend to perform his customary devotions in a constant place, because in that place we usually meet with those very thoughts which possessed us at our last being there! And I find it thus far experimentally true, that at my now being in that school, and seeing that very place where I sat when I was a boy, occasioned me to remember those very thoughts of my youth which then possessed me: sweet thoughts indeed, that promised my growing years numerous pleasures, without mixtures of cares: and those to be enjoyed, when time—which I therefore thought slow-paced—had changed my youth into manhood. But age and experience have taught me that those were but empty hopes; for I have always found it true, as my Saviour did foretell, "Sufficient for the day is the evil thereof." Nevertheless, I saw there a succession of boys using the same recreations, and, questionless, possessed with the same thoughts that then possessed me. Thus one generation succeeds another, both in their lives, recreations, hopes, fears, and death.'

After his return from Winchester to Eton, which was about five months before his death, he became much more retired and contemplative: in which time he was often visited by Mr. John Hales,—learned Mr. John Hales,—then a fellow of that college, to whom upon an occasion he spake to this purpose: 'I have, in my passage to my grave, met with most of those joys of which a discursive soul is capable; and been entertained with more inferior pleasures than the sons of men are usually made partakers of: nevertheless, in this voyage I have not always floated on the calm sea of content; but have often met with cross winds and storms, and with many troubles of mind and temptations to evil. And yet, though I have been, and am a man compassed about with human frailties, Almighty God hath by his grace prevented me from making shipwreck of faith and a good conscience, the thought of which is now the joy of my heart, and I most humbly praise him for it: and I humbly acknowledge that it was not myself, but he that hath kept me to this great age, and let him take the glory of his great mercy.—And, my dear friend, I now see that I draw near my harbour of death; that harbour that will secure me from all the future storms and waves of this restless world; and I praise God I am willing to leave it, and expect a better; that world wherein dwelleth righteousness; and I long for it!'

These and the like expressions were then uttered by him at the beginning of a feverish distemper, at which time he was also troubled with an asthma, or short spitting: but after less than twenty fits, by the help of familiar physic and a spare diet, this fever abated, yet so as to leave him much weaker than it found him; and his asthma seemed also to be overcome in a good degree by his forbearing tobacco, which, as many thoughtful men do, he also had taken somewhat immoderately. This was his then present condition, and thus he continued till about the end of October, 1639, which was about a month before his death, at which time he again fell into a fever, which though he seemed to recover, yet these still left him so weak, that they, and those other common infirmities that accompany age, were wont to visit him like civil friends, and after some short time to leave him,—came now both oftener and with more violence, and at last took up their constant habitation with him, still weakening his body and abating his cheerfulness; of both which he grew more sensible, and did the oftener retire into his study, and there made many papers that had passed his pen, both in the days of his youth and in the busy part of his life, useless, by a fire made there to that purpose. These, and several unusual expressions to his servants and friends, seemed to foretell that the day of his death drew near; for which he seemed to those many friends that observed him to be well prepared, and to be both patient and free from all fear, as several of his letters writ on this his last sick-bed may testify. And thus he continued till about the beginning of December following, at which time he was seized more violently with a quotidian fever; in the tenth fit of which fever, his better part, that part of Sir Henry Wotton which could not die, put off mortality with as much content and cheerfulness as human frailty is capable of, being then in great tranquillity of mind, and in perfect peace with God and man.

And thus the circle of Sir Henry Wotton's life—that circle which began at Bocton, and in the circumference thereof did first touch at Winchester School, then at Oxford, and after upon so many remarkable parts and passages in Christendom—that circle of his life was by death thus closed up and completed, in the seventy and second year of his age, at Eton College; where, according to his will, he now lies buried, with his motto on a plain gravestone over him: dying worthy of his name and family, worthy of the love and favour of so many princes, and persons of eminent wisdom and learning, worthy of the trust committed unto him, for the service of his prince and country.

And all readers are requested to believe that he was worthy of a more worthy pen, to have preserved his memory and commended his merits to the imitation of posterity.

FOSTER WATSON
From "Sir Henry Wotton: Gentleman and
Schoolmaster"
Gentleman's Magazine, March 1892, pp. 283–89

IV. Sir Henry Wotton as Schoolmaster

Mr. Thomas Murray, Provost of Eton College, the successor of the famous Sir Henry Savile, died in 1623. Sir Henry Wotton, by sheer dint of influence, amongst a number of competitors, secured the post. Indeed, it was lucky for him that he succeeded in obtaining it, for, to all account, his finances were in a most unsatisfactory state. We are told that he had to borrow money from his good friend, Mr. Nicholas Pey, to pay his expenses of removal. It is quite clear that Wotton took the Provostship as a means of livelihood, and not from any love of the pedagogic profession.

Teachers nowadays recognise the advisability, most, indeed, the necessity of adequate training for the work of, at any rate, a head master. It would be interesting to consider how far a large, wide, varied experience of human affairs by a large-minded and large-hearted man may practically more than compensate for the lack of special training. To suggest this I am afraid may seem rank heresy. But the fact is, we must admit, that we have had so seldom the opportunity of observing a thoroughly able man, with an active varied experience, set himself to the work of teaching, that we can hardly judge *a priori* what the result would be.

Moreover, in the case we are now considering, teaching, in the specialised sense in which we employ the term, scarcely can be said to have been stuff of the intellectual conscience. In the words of the good Jeremy Taylor, himself a schoolmaster, education leads a man to build and adorn his house "with advantages and ornaments of learning, upon the foundation of piety."

We may judge from such words that the ideal of a schoolmaster in those days was not that of the most methodic instiller of knowledge, but, as it is surely in all times, the most efficient man in influencing the whole character of pupils, of which the intellect forms an important part. Now in this work of influence on character, undoubtedly, Sir Henry Wotton was not inexperienced. It may be objected that his experience had reference to men only, and that men and boys are so widely different that experience in the one cannot be read off into terms of the other. Perhaps so, generally speaking, but the case of Sir Henry Wotton tends to show that this is not an impossibility. Wotton, in short, gives the impression of being a man whose resources (except, indeed, his financial resources) were never exhausted. He shows power in action, and what is quite as necessary, power in repose. He can act vigorously, and he can sit still, smoke his pipe, and forget there is a schoolroom only the other side of his study-door. *Voilà*, a model for some latter-day masters.

Now for his methods of teaching. Do not laugh at them. Remember he flourished 250 years ago. I give Izaac Walton's words, thankful such (must I call them unscientific?) methods can be spoken of so pleasantly:

He was a constant cherisher of all those youths in that school in whom he found either a constant diligence or a genius that prompted them to learning.

To-day the youngest pupil-teacher could tell him that he was only thinking of the "interesting" cases, and that he was neglecting the dull boys. Next, however, to our joy, we hear of something that looks uncommonly like an object-lesson.

He was (besides many other things of necessity and beauty) at the charge of setting up in it (the school) two rows of pillars, on which he caused to be choicely drawn the pictures of divers of the most famous Greek and Latin historians, poets, and orators: persuading them not to neglect rhetoric, because "Almighty God has left mankind affections to be wrought upon." And he would often say, "that none despised eloquence but such dull souls as were not capable of it." He would also often make choice of some observations out of those historians and poets, and would never leave the school without dropping some choice Greek or Latin apothegm or sentence that might be worthy of a room in the memory of a growing scholar.

Surely a pleasing picture! One too that should make us feel that essential as is the study of methods for us to-day, yet such study only goes a short way to make the teacher; beyond and above that is the personal influence which attracts, and which by its own graciousness unconsciously refines and draws those around into imitation. Wotton had, we allow, no knowledge of method, but he had the *otium cum dignitate*, and, above all, he had a passionate love of goodness and a restful content, which when joined with great powers of mind, fascinates young and old alike. In the life of the Hon. Robert Boyle, the well-known philosopher, we are told that he (Boyle) was "bred up at Eton College, whose provost at that time was Sir Henry Wotton, a person that was not only a fine gentleman himself, but very well skilled in the art of making others so."

To return to Izaak Walton.

Sir Henry "was pleased constantly to breed up one or more hopeful youths, which he picked out of the school and took into his own domestic care, and to attend him at his meals; out of whose discourse and behaviour he gathered observations for the *better completing of his intended book of education: of which, by his still striving to make the whole better, he lived to leave but part to posterity.*"

Now I have dwelt, it may be thought, with unnecessary emphasis on Sir Henry Wotton's ignorance of the study of methods. I was obliged to do so, because the idea of a man between fifty and sixty, ignorant of the science of education, holding a prominent educational post, to us is ludicrous. But I must therefore the more earnestly call attention to the passage I have just quoted. It is an instance of a man, over 250 years ago, without scientific training, deliberately setting about to consider for himself the psychological basis of education. Nor is that all. We have seen that to our notions Wotton was in some respects behindhand. Now I fear we have to see that he is in advance of some of us. How many of us practically observe and note down for useful purposes of reference and general direction that which goes on day by day in our contact with boys? How many head masters take hopeful boys and, at their own expense, "breed them up," so as to more closely see the conditions and possibilities of sound education? How many of us, with our vaunted interest in the science of education, study and make observations, and are able to quote our "cases," as do our professional fellows, the lawyer and the doctor?

Yet this is precisely what we find Sir Henry Wotton doing. The energetic and successful diplomatist, the graceful and refined courtier, the astute man of the world, if you will, the tasteful, tuneful poet, and the contented lover of the angle, is not only the most enterprising schoolmaster of his time (and that without training), but he is also an investigator of the principles of psychology on inductive lines, in exactly the way that our leaders would have us, in the nineteenth century, to go. Mark, too, his desire of thoroughness and his reluctance to rush into print. "Of which, by his still striving to make the whole better, he lived to leave but part to posterity."

His educational work, therefore, is unfortunately only a fragment. It is entitled "A Philosophical Survey of Education: or Moral Architecture." There is, as is usual with the age of Elizabeth and the early Stuarts, an Epistle Dedicatory to the Sovereign. Wotton early explains that education, though conversant with children, is not merely a domestic affair, but has a direct relation to the Commonwealth, and quotes the instances of the ancients to prove that it belongs to the domain of politics.

The heads under which he divides his work are:

    I. There must proceed a way how to discern the natural capacities and inclinations of children.
    II. Next, the culture and furnishment of the mind.
    III. The moulding of behaviour and decent forms.
    IV. The tempering of affections.
    V. The quickening and exciting of observations and practical judgments.
    VI. Timely instilling of conscientious principles and seeds of religion.

Sir Henry Wotton only completed his treatment of the first head, touching the study of natural capabilities and inclinations.

He urges that the teacher must search for "signatures of hopefulness" or "characters," whereby may timely be descried what the child will prove in probability.

"Characters" are either (1) impressed on the outward person, like stamps of Nature, or (2) taken from some emergent art of his mind.

As examples of "characters" impressed on the outer person he takes (a) the child's colour or complexion; (b) the structure and conformation of limbs; (c) "spirituous resultance" from the other two, which makes the countenance.

All these are matters of observation, and can be noted and reduced to empirical principles. For instance, it is easy to distinguish two classes of complexions—(a) a palish clearness (the sign of an even, phlegmatic humour); (b) a pure sanguine melancholic tincture.

As to the outward frame and fabric, Wotton draws attention to the importance of observing carefully the shape and size of the head and the quickness of the eye. As to the former he says: "It must needs be a silent character of hope, when there is good store of roomage and receipt where the powers (of mind) are stowed: as commonly we may think husbanding men to foresee their own plenty who prepare beforehand large barns and granaries." Yet Wotton candidly acknowledges that Thucydides is reported to have been "taper-headed," "as many of the Genoesers are at this day in common observation, who yet are a people of singular sagacity." Further, he cites as an instance against his own view, Il Donato Testolina, yet on the whole, he argues, in spite of instances to the contrary, the head he wishes in a child should be "great and round."

The eye, he considers, betrays in a manner the whole state of the mind, and "letteth out all our fancies and passions as it were by a window." He would therefore have in the eye of the child that is to excel a "settled vivacity." Once more, however, he candidly avows, "I have known a number of dull-sighted, very sharp-witted men."

With marked sagacity, however, Wotton insists that our judgments of children must be taken from what he well terms "the total resultance."

He then gives examples of "the more solid and conclusive characters," which start out of children when they are them-

selves least aware of them. He quotes Seneca and Angelus Politianus as saying:

1. *Tantum ingenii, quantum iræ.* (The child will have as much wit as he has waywardness.) Wotton is disposed to think this a sometimes fallacious "signature."

2. Quintilian says: *Tantum ingenii quantum memoriæ.* This maxim has a stronger consequence of hope, not only because it is important as showing a good retention, but also, as Wotton acutely points out, it is an infallible argument of *good attention!*

3. Parents should mark whether their children be naturally *apt to imitate.*

Besides these points, Sir Henry Wotton invites the attention of those who have the care of children to the following matters:

1. Note the witty excuses of children.

2. The kind of jests or pleasant incidents with which he is most taken in others.

3. Note especially the child at his play, or, as Wotton calls it, his "pretty pastime."

4. Note, not only articulate speech, but also the child's smiles and frowns, especially when they lighten or cloud the whole form in a moment.

5. Note his dreams.

So far of capacities.

As to inclinations, Sir Henry Wotton names two as examples of what should be noted:

1. Does the child love solitude and silence? He likes him not to do so.

2. When alone, does he sit still and do nothing? "If so, I like him worse. There is commonly but a little distance in time between doing of nothing and doing of ill."

In all this there is a downright, thorough-going attempt to an empirical child psychology. We know, of course, that the merest tyro in psychology would pronounce that much of Sir Henry Wotton's psychology is poor stuff; and much of it is simply empirical observation in physiognomy. But we could with equal cogency point out that many a boy in a fifth form could now do mathematics which Sir Isaac Newton never, in his palmiest days, attempted. Yet all our boys have not yet learned how to become Sir Isaac Newtons. So with Sir Henry Wotton. His ideas of studying complexions, and thence discovering "humours," are somewhat curious to the modern mind. His judgment of character and ability by the appearance is apt to be met by Shakespeare's

There is no art to read the mind's construction in the face.

Admitting all these and other limitations to the acceptance of Sir Henry Wotton's pedagogy, it has to be remembered that the essential value of Sir Henry's work is not in what he observed merely, so much as in the fact that he thought children worthy of observation. To an age which has received the impress of the genius of Froebel and his missionaries, this is part of our common-sense. It is in the air; moreover, it is not far above our heads. Hence, if we ever open our educational eyes at all, we see it writ large wherever we go. But to Wotton's age it was a paradox. We must never forget that *learning* was looked upon as the be-all and the end-all of education. Now *learning* never could be a possession of the young child; hence, educationally speaking, the child was uninteresting. It was the Scaligers, the Casaubons, the scholars, who invited the attention and aroused the envy of the schoolmasters. The little children were not scholars; experience showed that in ninety-nine cases out of a hundred they never became learned. Hence there was no satisfaction to be got out of them.

I hope, however, I have made clear the fact that Sir Henry Wotton was interested in those boys who personally came under his care, and that he was profoundly convinced of the importance of a careful study of the temperaments and dispositions of children with a view to training and developing them.

There is one aspect I cannot refrain from alluding to and even emphasizing. In Sir Henry's observations there are included natural capacities and inclinations, the culture and furnishing of the mind, behaviour and carriage, affections, observing powers, and practical judgments and the culture of religion. It is not too much to say that our boasted "liberal education" breaks down before such an analysis. To-day we lay stress on intellectual acquirements, and on those almost entirely. I am not now raising the question as to our wisdom or otherwise in so doing, I only point out that Sir Henry Wotton is wider and in some respects higher in his general outlook. The width and height of his observations are at least suggestive for us even to-day.

The truth is, that a man like Wotton, who knew the highways of life in so many directions, saw, with the clearness borne in upon him from experiences accumulating on every side, that life is more than learning, and that education is in its narrow sense preparation for life, and in its broad sense it is life itself. Such a man, deeply rooted in all the activities of the time, in the court, in the country, at home and abroad; well-read as to the past, a part of the present, hopeful of the future; unfettered by tradition, and without any knowledge of rules-of-the-thumb maxims of teaching, could not but throw light on the specialistic profession which he took up. He is the type of the successful all-round man, trying his hand at the education of boys. That one of the most distinguished diplomatists in his latter days should undertake the control of a school and the study of pedagogics, is an experiment little likely in our days or in the future to be repeated. If, therefore, the attempt, from the side of the accomplished gentleman, to become a schoolmaster has become impossible from the specialisation which now characterizes or is destined apparently to characterize teaching, it only remains for the schoolmasters to know their own work thoroughly, and to endeavour to approach Sir Henry Wotton by their grace of bearing, their culture, not only of learning, but of arts, of actions, of conversation, and of piety. He is accurately described as Sir Henry Wotton, Gentleman and Schoolmaster. Schoolmasters have before them still the desirability of the same combination. The circumstances of the age may demand the reversal of the order. Now it is schoolmaster and gentleman. The combination is essential for high work, and no example would more pointedly illustrate this than that of Sir Henry Wotton.

PHILIP MASSINGER

1583–c. 1639

Philip Massinger was baptized November 24, 1583, at St. Thomas's in Salisbury, Wiltshire. His father, Arthur Massinger, was a gentleman attached to the service of the Earl of Pembroke, filling among other duties the role of Pembroke's solicitor. He also served three terms as a Member of Parliament. In 1602 Philip Massinger matriculated at St. Alban's Hall, Oxford, and spent several years there but did not receive a degree. He then presumably settled in London, though nothing is definitely known of his further life until 1613. That year he was in debtor's prison, in company with fellow-playwrights Robert Daborne and Nathan Field, and was collaborating on hackwork dramas for the theatrical agent Philip Henslowe.

During the next decade he collaborated on many plays with Field, Daborne, Tourneur, Dekker, and repeatedly with John Fletcher, with whom he wrote *The False One* (c. 1620), *The Beggars' Bush* (1622), and *The Elder Brother* (c. 1625). His name first appeared on a title page in 1623 with the publication of *The Virgin Martir*, a collaboration with Thomas Dekker, and later that same year he was licensed as sole author of *The Duke of Millaine*, a play that bears some resemblance to *Othello*. Some scholars have suggested that Shakespeare's collaborator on *Henry VIII* and *The Two Noble Kinsmen* was actually Massinger rather than John Fletcher.

Other notable plays include *The Bond-Man* (1624), *The Roman Actor* (1626), and *The Great Duke of Florence* (c. 1627), but his two most popular works are *A New Way to Pay Old Debts* (c. 1621), based on Thomas Middleton's *A Trick to Catch the Old One*, and *The City-Madam* (c. 1632), which resembles *Eastward Hoe* by Chapman, Jonson, and Marston. These two plays continued to be produced into the twentieth century. In 1630 his *Believe as You List* was censored for its anti-Spanish sentiments, but Massinger eventually changed its setting from modern Spain and Portugal to Asia and classical Rome, and the play was performed in 1631.

He remained impoverished throughout his life, a typical circumstance of dramatists of his age. According to an elegy written by Sir Aston Cokayne in 1658, Massinger died in March of either 1639 or 1640, and was interred at St. Saviour's, Southwark, together with his collaborator John Fletcher.

Personal

Buried, Philip Massinger, a stranger.—PARISH REGISTER, Church of St. Saviour's, March 20, 1640

This day I searched the register of St. Saviour's, Southwark, by the playhouse then there, vulgo St. Mary's Overy's; and find Philip Massinger buryed March 18th, 1639. I am enformed at the place where he dyed, which was by the Bankes side neer the then playhouse, that he was buryed about the middle of the Bullhead-churchyard—i. e. that churchyard (for there are four) which is next the Bullhead taverne, from whence it has its denomination. He dyed about the 66th yeare of his age: went to bed well, and dyed suddenly—but not of the plague.—JOHN AUBREY, "Philip Massinger," *Brief Lives*, 1669–96

Of his private life literally nothing can be said to be known, except that his dedications bespeak incessant distress and dependence, while the recommendatory poems prefixed to his plays address him with attributes of virtue, which are seldom lavished with flattery or falsehood on those who are poor. . . . Of all his admirers only Sir Aston Cokayne dedicated a line to his memory. Even posterity did him long injustice: Rowe, who had discovered his merits in the depth of their neglect, forbore to be his editor, in the hopes of concealing his plagiarism from the *Fatal Dowry*; and he seemed on the eve of oblivion, when Dodsley's reprint of our old plays brought him faintly into that light of reputation, which has been made perfectly distinct by Mr. Gifford's edition of his works.—THOMAS CAMPBELL, *Specimens of the British Poets*, 1819

General

Massinger had not the higher requisites of his art in anything like the degree in which they were possessed by Ford, Webster, Tourneur, Heywood, and others. He never shakes or disturbs the mind with grief. He is read with composure and placid delight. He wrote with that equability of all the passions, which made his English style the purest and most free from violent metaphors and harsh constructions, of any of the dramatists who were his contemporaries.—CHARLES LAMB, *Specimens of English Dramatic Poets*, 1808

Massinger, like Fletcher, pursued the path in which Shakspeare had preceded him with such imperishable glory; but he wants the tenderness and wit of the former, and that splendour of imagination and that dominion over the passions, which characterise the latter. He has, however, qualities of his own, sufficiently great and attractive, to gift him with the envied lot of being contemplated, in union with these two bards, as one of the chief pillars and supporters of the *Romantic drama*. He exhibits, in the first place, a perfectibility, both in diction and versification, of which we have, in dramatic poesy at least, no corresponding example. There is a transparency and perspicuity in the texture of his composition, a sweetness, harmony, and ductility, together with a blended strength and ease in the structure of his metre, which, in his best performances, delight, and never satiate the ear. To this, in some degree technical merit, must be added a spirit of commanding *eloquence*, a dignity and force of thought, which, while they approach the precincts of sublimity, and indicate great depth and clearness of intellect, show, by the nervous elegance of language in which they are clothed, a combination and comprehension of talent of very unfrequent occurrence. —NATHAN DRAKE, *Shakspere and His Times*, 1817, Vol. 2, p. 561

Massinger makes an impression by hardness and repulsiveness of manner. In the intellectual processes which he delights to describe, 'reason panders will:' he fixes arbitrarily on some object which there is no motive to pursue, or every motive combined against it, and then by screwing up his heroes or heroines to the deliberate and blind accomplishment of this, thinks to arrive at 'the true pathos and sublime of human life.' That is not the way. He seldom touches the heart or kindles the fancy. It is in vain to hope to excite much sympathy with convulsive efforts of the will, or intricate contrivances of the understanding, to obtain that which is better left alone, and

where the interest arises principally from the conflict between the absurdity of the passion and the obstinacy with which it is persisted in. For the most part, his villains are a sort of *lusus naturæ*; his impassioned characters are like drunkards or madmen. Their conduct is extreme and outrageous, their motives unaccountable and weak; their misfortunes are without necessity, and their crimes without temptation, to ordinary apprehensions. I do not say that this is invariably the case in all Massinger's scenes, but I think it will be found that a principle of playing at cross-purposes is the ruling passion throughout most of them.—WILLIAM HAZLITT, *Lectures on the Dramatic Literature of the Age of Elizabeth*, 1820

There can be no doubt that Massinger admired and studied Shakspeare. In the haste of composition, his mind turned up many thoughts and phrases of the elder writer, in a more or less perfect state of preservation, but he was neither a plagiarist nor an imitator. His style, conduct, characterization, and metre, are perfectly distinct. No serious dramatist of the age owed Shakspeare so little. . . .

Massinger's excellence—a great and beautiful excellence it is—was in the expression of virtue, in its probation, its strife, its victory. He could not, like Shakspeare, invest the perverted will with the terrors of a magnificent intellect, or bestow the cestus of poetry on simple unconscious loveliness.—HARTLEY COLERIDGE, "Introduction" to *The Dramatic Works of Massinger and Ford*, 1840, pp. xlviii–liv

Massinger's account of Theophilus's conversion, will, we fear, make those who know any thing of that great crisis of the human spirit, suspect that Massinger's experience thereof was but small: the fact which is most interesting is, the *Virgin Martyr* is one of the foulest plays known. Every pains has been taken to prove that the indecent scenes in the play were not written by Massinger, but by Dekker; on what grounds we know not. If Dekker assisted Massinger in the play, as he is said to have done, we are aware of no cannons of internal criticism, which will enable us to decide, as boldly as Mr. Gifford does, that all the indecency is Dekker's, and all the poetry Massinger's. He confesses (as indeed he is forced to do) that "Massinger himself is not free from dialogues of low wit and buffoonery;" and then, after calling the scenes in question "detestable ribaldry," "a loathsome sorterkin, engendered of filth and dulness," recommends them to the reader's supreme scorn and contempt,—with which feelings the reader will doubtless regard them; but will also, if he be a thinking man, draw from them the following conclusions: that even if they be Dekker's, (of which there is no proof,) Massinger was forced, in order to the success of his play, to pander to the public taste, by allowing Dekker to interpolate these villainies; that the play which, above all others of the seventeenth century, contains the most supra-lunar rosepink of piety, devotion, and purity, also contains the stupidest abominations of any extant play; and lastly, that those who reprinted it for its rosepink piety and purity, as a sample of the Christianity of that past golden age of High-churchmanship had to leave out about one third of the play, for fear of becoming amenable to the laws against abominable publications.—CHARLES KINGSLEY, *Plays and Puritans*, 1859, pp. 99–100

Massinger possessed a large though not especially poetic mind, and a temperament equable rather than energetic. He lacked strong passions, vivid conceptions, creative imagination. In reading him we feel that the exulting, vigorous life of the drama of the age has begun to decay. But though he has been excelled by obscurer writers in special qualities of genius, he still attaches us by the harmony of his powers, and the uniformity of his excellence. The plot, style, and characters of one of his dramas all conduce to a common interest. His plays, indeed, are novels in dialogue. They rarely thrill, startle, or kindle us, but, as Lamb says, "are read with composure and placid delight."

. . . Massinger's style, though it does not evince a single great quality of the poet, has always charmed English readers by its dignity, flexibility, elegance, clearness, and ease. His metre and rhythm Coleridge pronounces incomparably good. Still his verse, with all its merits, is smooth rather than melodious; the thoughts are not born in music, but mechanically set to a tune; and even its majestic flow is frequently purchased at the expense of dramatic closeness to character and passion. —EDWIN P. WHIPPLE, *The Literature of the Age of Elizabeth*, 1869, pp. 181–82

The reader who peruses Massinger can hardly fail to be charmed with the force and chaste elegance of his language, happily yet sparingly enriched with choice classical allusions, and none of his contemporaries knew so well the art of developing his plot in such a way as to surprise and delight the spectator, while meting out strict poetical justice to all. His declamatory speeches are very fine models of their kind; and some of his characters, especially his females, are elaborated with great care. Massinger's style and versification are strongly marked with his own peculiar manner; yet so little is that manner known, even to professed scholars, that in most of the current manuals and books of "specimens," a scene from *The Virgin Martyr*, undoubtedly written by Decker, is given as an example of his brother poet's composition!—JAMES HAIN FRISWELL, *Essays on English Writers*, 1869, p. 160

Massinger had less original force than any of the other great dramatists. He was eminently a cultivated dramatist, a man of broad, liberal, adaptive mind, fluent and versatile, with just conceptions of dramatic effect, and the power of giving copious expression to his conceptions without straining or dislocating effort. Yet he was much too strong and vigorous to be a mere imitator. His nature was not such as to fight against the influence of his great predecessors: his mind opened itself genially to their work, and absorbed their materials and their methods; but he did not simply reproduce them—they decomposed, so to speak, in his mind, and lay there ready to be laid hold of and embodied in new organisms. So far he resembled Shakespeare, in that he had good sense enough not to harass himself in straining after little novelties: his judgment was broad and manly. But he was far from resembling Shakespeare in swiftness and originality of imagination: his muse was comparatively tame and even-paced. The common remark that his diction is singularly free from archaisms shows us one aspect of the soundness of his taste, and bears testimony, at the same time, to his want of eccentricity and original force. He was the Gray of his generation—greater than Gray, inasmuch as his generation was greater than Gray's—a man of large, open, fertile, and versatile mind. . . .

Gifford entertained the notion that Massinger must have turned Roman Catholic when he was at Oxford. The notion is based upon the use that Massinger makes of a Roman Catholic legend in *The Virgin Martyr*, and the fair character that he gives to a Jesuit priest in *The Renegado*. One wants proof more relative: this only proves that Massinger was able to treat Roman Catholics with dramatic impartiality. Coleridge's notion about Massinger's democratic leanings is equally questionable. Massinger, indeed, makes one of his characters sigh for the happy times when lords were styled fathers of families. He

makes another say that princes do well to cherish goodness where they find it, for—

> They being men and not gods, Contarino,
> They can give wealth and titles, but not virtues.

He makes Timoleon administer a sharp rebuke to the men of Syracuse for corruption prevailing in high places, and rate them soundly for preferring golden dross to liberty.

In the same play (*The Bondman*), he takes an evident pleasure in representing the indignities put upon high-fed madams by their insurgent slaves: and in *The City Madam* he ridicules with much zest the pretensions of upstart wealth. But all these things are as consistent with a benevolent paternal Toryism as with Whiggery, and are to be looked upon as indications simply of the dramatist's range of sympathies, and not of any discontent on his part with the established framework of government or society.

Hartley Coleridge, in his rambling and racy introduction to Massinger and Ford, commits himself to the extraordinary statement that Massinger had no humour. "Massinger would have been the dullest of jokers, if Ford had not contrived to be still duller." I have already remarked on the severity and ungeniality of Ford's character; but there is nothing connected with Massinger to imply that he bore the least resemblance to Ford in this point. On the contrary, all Massinger's characteristics are those of a widely sympathetic man, with a genial propensity to laughter. He has written several very obscene passages, such as the courtship of Asotus by Corisca in *The Bondman*, but they are all pervaded by genuine humour; and a countless number of his scenes, such as that between Wellborn and Marrall in *A New Way to Pay Old Debts*, are irresistibly laughable. It may perhaps be said with justice that there is often a certain serious motive underlying Massinger's humour, which connects itself with the earnestness of his distressed life; but humour he undoubtedly had, and that of the most ebullient and irrepressible sort.

One fancies indeed, but it may be the result of our knowledge of his painful life, that there is a certain sad didactic running through all Massinger's work. The *Duke of Milan*, by far his greatest drama, has not the satisfying close of Shakespeare's tragedies. It preaches directly the moral deducible from *Romeo and Juliet*, that violent delights have violent ends; but whereas we do not vex ourselves with vain wishes that Romeo and Juliet had been united in happy marriage, we are at the death of Sforza and Marcelia disconcerted by the feeling that their fate ought to have been, and easily might have been, different. And in his other tragedies we are haunted at the close by a similar uneasiness: the purgation of the mind by pity and terror is not effected—the tumult that they raise is not tranquillised. All tragedies, of course, are susceptible of a didactic interpretation; but those in which the didactic has a sharp edge, affect us in quite a different way from those in which it is vaguely present as part of a grand and overwhelming impression; and Massinger's conclusions have a sharp edge. Again, his romantic tragi-comedies, and even his comedies, have also a serious tinge, apart from the natural interest of the development of the story. They do not directly preach at us, but the colour of the subject-matter suggests that the dramatist was not wholly free-minded and studious only of dramatic and scenic impressions. —WILLIAM MINTO, *Characteristics of English Poets*, 1874, pp. 363–65

I was so enchanted with these plays of Massinger's, but more especially with the one called *The Maid of Honor*, that I never rested till I had obtained from the management its revival on the stage. The part of Camiola is the only one that I ever selected for myself. *The Maid of Honor* succeeded on its first representation, but failed to attract audiences. Though less defective than most of the contemporaneous dramatic compositions, the play was still too deficient in interest to retain the favor of the public. The character of Camiola is extremely noble and striking, but that of her lover so unworthy of her that the interest she excites personally fails to inspire one with sympathy for her passion for him. The piece in this respect has a sort of moral incoherency, which appears to me, indeed, not an infrequent defect in the compositions of these great dramatic pre-Shakespearites.—FRANCES ANN KEMBLE, *Records of a Girlhood*, 1878, p. 255

He had a high, a varied, and a fertile imagination. He had, and was the last to have, an extensive and versatile command of blank verse, never perhaps reaching the most perfect mastery of Marlowe or of Shakespere, but singularly free from monotony, and often both harmonious and dignified. He could deal, and deal well, with a large range of subjects; and if he never ascends to the height of a De Flores or a Bellafront, he never descends to the depths in which both Middleton and Dekker too often complacently wallow. Unless we are to count by mere flashes, he must, I think, rank after Shakespere, Fletcher, and Jonson among his fellows; and this I say, honestly avowing that I have nothing like the enthusiasm for him that I have for Webster, or for Dekker, or for Middleton. We may no doubt allow too much for bulk of work, for sustained excellence at a certain level, and for general competence as against momentary excellence. But we may also allow far too little; and this has perhaps been the general tendency of later criticism in regard to Massinger. It is unfortunate that he never succeeded in making as perfect a single expression of his tragic ability as he did of his comic, for the former was, I incline to think, the higher of the two. But many of his plays are lost, and many of those which remain come near to such excellence. It is by no means impossible that Massinger may have lost incomparably by the misdeeds of the constantly execrated, but never to be execrated enough, minion of that careless herald.—GEORGE SAINTSBURY, *A History of Elizabethan Literature*, 1887, p. 401

ARTHUR SYMONS
From "Introduction"
Philip Massinger
1889, pp. xiii–xxxii

When Massinger came to London, the English drama, as I have said, was at its height. But before he had begun any dramatic work of importance the turning-point had been reached, and the period of descent or degeneration begun. Elizabethan had given place to Stuart England, and with the dynasty the whole spirit of the nation was changing. Fletcher and Massinger together represent this period: Fletcher by painting with dashing brilliance the light bright showy superficial aristocratic life of wild and graceful wantonness; Massinger by limning with a graver and a firmer brush, in darker tints and more thoughtful outlines, the shadier side of the same impressive and unsatisfactory existence. The indications of lessening vitality and strength, of departing simplicity, of growing extravagance and affectation which mark the period of transition, reappear in the drama of Massinger, as in that of Shirley, and sever it, by a wide and visible gulf, from the drama which we properly name Elizabethan. Massinger is the late twilight of the long and splendid day of which Marlowe was the dawn.

The characteristics of any poet's genius are seen clearly in his versification. Massinger's verse is facile, vigorous, grave, in the main correct; but without delicacy or rarity, without splendour or strength of melody; the verse of a man who can write easily, and who is not always too careful to remember that he is writing poetry. Owing no doubt partly to the facility with which he wrote, Massinger often has imperfectly accentuated lines, such as:—

They did expect to be chain'd to the oar.

Coleridge has remarked on the very slight degree in which Massinger's verse is distinguished from prose; and no one can read a page of any of his plays without being struck with it. It is not merely that a large proportion of the lines run on and overlap their neighbours; this is only the visible sign of a radical peculiarity. The *pitch* of Massinger's verse is somewhat lower than the proper pitch of poetry; somewhat too near the common pitch of prose. Shakespeare, indeed, in his latest period extended the rhythm of verse to its loosest and freest limits; but not merely did he never pass beyond the invisible and unmistakeable boundary, he retained the true intonation of poetry as completely as in his straitest periods of metrical restraint.

Massinger set himself to follow in the steps of Shakespeare; and he succeeded in catching with admirable skill much of the easy flow and conversational facility at which he aimed. "His English style," says Lamb, "is the purest and most free from violent metaphors and harsh constructions, of any of the dramatists who were his contemporaries." But this "pure and free" style obtains its freedom and purity at a heavy cost: or let us say rather, the style possesses a certain degree of these two qualities because of the absence of certain others. Shakespeare's freest verse is the most full of episodical beauties and magical lines. But it is a singular thing that in the whole of Massinger's extant works there are scarcely a dozen lines of such intrinsic and unmistakeable beauty that we are forced to pause and brood on them with the true epicure's relish. It is singular, I repeat—especially singular in a writer distinguished not only by fluency but by dignity and true eloquence—that so few, so very few, of his lines can stand by themselves, on their own merits. It would be useless to look in the Massinger part of *The Virgin Martyr* for any lines like these—

> I could weary stars,
> And force the wakeful moon to lose her eyes,
> By my late watching.

It would be equally useless to search from end to end of his plays. Easy flowing lines, vigorous lines, eloquent and persuasive lines, we could find in plenty; but nowhere a line in which colour and music make a magical delight of golden concords. Not quite so difficult, but still very hard indeed, would it be to find any single lines of that rare and weighty sort which may be said to resemble the jar in the *Arabian Nights* into which Solomon had packed the genie. Had Massinger wished to represent Vittoria Accoramboni before her judges, he would have written for her a thoroughly eloquent, admirable and telling oration; but he could never have fashioned her speech into the biting dagger with which Webster drives home the splendid blows of her imperial scorn. That one line of infinite meaning—

> Cover her face; mine eyes dazzle; she died young—

spoken by Ferdinand in *The Duchess of Malfy* over the corpse of his murdered sister, has no parallel in Massinger, who would probably have begun a long and elaborate piece of rhetoric with—

> Stay, I feel
> A sudden alteration.

If we carry these considerations further, we shall see that the mental characteristics of Massinger correspond with the evidences of them in his versification. The ease and facility shown in the handling of metre are manifested equally in the plot and conduct of the plays. Massinger thoroughly understood the art of the playwright. No one perhaps, after Shakespeare, proved himself so constantly capable of constructing an orderly play and working it steadily out. His openings are as a rule admirable; thoroughly effective, explanatory and preparatory. How well, for instance, the first scene of *The Duke of Milan* prepares us, by a certain uneasiness or anxiety in its trembling pitch of happiness, for the events which are to follow. It is not always possible to say as much for his conclusions. Ingenuity, certainly, and considerable constructive skill, are usually manifested more or less; and in not a few instances (as in that delightful play *The Great Duke of Florence*, or in *Believe as You List*, a very powerful work) the conclusion is altogether right and satisfying. But in many instances Massinger's very endeavour to wind off his play in the neatest manner, without any tangles or frayed edges, spoils the proper artistic effect. His persistent aversion to a tragic end, even where a virtual tragedy demands it; his invincible determination to make things come to a fortunate conclusion, even if the action has to be huddled up or squashed together in consequence; in a word, his concession to the popular taste, no matter at what cost, not unfrequently distorts the conclusion of plays up to this point well conducted.

Massinger's treatment of character follows in some respects, while it seems in others to contradict, his treatment of versification and of construction. Where Massinger most conclusively fails is in a right understanding and a right representation of human nature; in the power to conceive passion and bring its speech and action vividly and accurately before us. His theory of human nature is apparently that of the puppet-player: he is aware of violent but not of consistent action, of change but not of development. No dramatist talks so much of virtue and vice, but he has no conception of either except in the abstract; and he sees nothing strange that a virtuous woman should on a sudden cry out—

Chastity,
Thou only art a name, and I renounce thee!

or that a fanatical Mohammedan should embrace Christianity on being told that the Prophet was a juggler, and taught birds to feed in his ear. His motto might be—

We are all the balls of time, tossed to and fro;

for his conception of life is that of a game of wild and inconsequent haphazard. It is true that he rewards his good people and punishes the bad with the most scrupulous care; but the good or bad person at the end of a play is not always the good or bad person of the beginning. Massinger's outlook is by no means vague or sceptical on religion[1] or on morals; he is moralist before all things, and the copy-book tags neatly pinned on to the conclusion of each play are only a somewhat clumsy exhibition of a real conviction and conscientiousness. But his morality is nerveless, and aimless in its general effect; or it translates itself, oddly enough, into a co-partner of confusion, a disturbing and distracting element of mischief.

Notwithstanding all we may say of Massinger's facility, it is evident that we have in him no mere improvisator, or contentedly hasty and superficial person. He was an earnest thinker, a thoughtful politician, a careful observer of the manners and men of his time, and, to the extent of his capacity, an eager student of human nature; but, for all that, his position is that of a foreigner travelling through a country of whose language he knows but a few words or sentences. He observes with keenness, he infers with acumen; but when he proceeds to take the last step—the final touch which transmutes recorded observation into vital fact—he finds (or, at least, we find) that his strength is exhausted, his limit reached. He observes, for instance, that the characters and motives of men are in general mixed; and especially, and in a special degree, those of men of a certain class, and in certain positions. But when we look at the personages whom he presents before us as mixed characters, we perceive that they are not so in themselves, but are mixed in the making. "We do not forbid an artist in fiction," says Mr. Swinburne in speaking of Charles Reade, "to set before us strange instances of inconsistency and eccentricity in conduct; but we do require of the artist that he should make us feel such aberrations to be as clearly inevitable as they are confessedly exceptional." Now this is just what Massinger does not do; it is just here that he comes short of success as a dramatic artist. In Calderón's figure, we see his men dancing to the rhythm of a music which we cannot hear: nothing is visible to us but the grotesque contortions and fantastic motions of the dancer.

Where Massinger fails is in the power of identifying himself with his characters, at least in their moments of profound passion or strenuous action. At his best (or almost his best, for of course there are exceptions) he succeeds on the one hand in representing the gentler and secondary passions and emotions; on the other, in describing the action of the primary passions very accurately and admirably, but, as it were, in the third person, and from the outside. As Mr. Leslie Stephen says with reference to a fine speech of Sir Giles Overreach in *A New Way to Pay Old Debts*, "Read 'he' for 'I,' and 'his' for 'my,' and it is an admirable bit of denunciation of a character probably intended as a copy from real life.[2] His characters seldom quite speak out; they have almost always about them a sort of rhetorical self-consciousness. The language of pure passion is unknown to them; they can only strive to counterfeit its dialect. In handling a situation of tragic passion, in developing a character subject to the shocks of an antagonistic Fate, Massinger manifests a singular lack of vital force, a singular failure in the realising imagination. He mistakes extravagance for strength, eloquence for conviction, feverishness for vitality. Take, for instance, the jealousy of Theodosius in *The Emperor of the East*. His conduct and language are altogether unreasoning and unreasonable, the extravagances of a weak and unballasted nature, depicted by one who can only thus conceive of strong passions. His sudden and overmastering jealousy at sight of the apple given by Eudocia to Paulinus is without probability; and Eudocia's lie when charged with it is without reason. It is almost too cruel in this connection to think of Desdemona's handkerchief; of the admirable and inevitable logic of the means by which Othello's mind is not so much imbued with suspicion as convinced. "All this pother for an apple!" as some sensible person in the play observes. Again, in *The Unnatural Combat*, compare for a moment Malefort's careful bombast, which leaves us cold and incredulous before an impossible and uninteresting monster of wickedness, with the biting and flaming words of Francesco Cenci, before which we shudder as at the fiery breath of the pit. Almost all Massinger's villains, notwithstanding the fearful language which they are in the habit of employing, fail to convince us of their particular wickedness; most of his tried and triumphant heroes fail to convince us of their vitality of virtue. Massinger's conception of evil is surprisingly naïve: he is frightened, completely taken in, by the big words and blustering looks of these bold bad men. He paints them with an inky brush, he tells us how bad, how very bad they are, and he sets them denouncing themselves and their wickedness with a beautiful tenderness of conscience. The blackness of evil and the contrasted whiteness of virtue are alike lost on us, and the good moral with them; for we are unable to believe in the existence of any such beings. It is the same with those exhibitions of tempted virtue of which Massinger is so fond. I do not allude at present to cases of actual martyrdom or persecution, such as those of Dorothea or Antiochus; but to situations of a more complex nature, such as that of Mathias with Honoria, or Bertoldo with Aurelia, in which we are expected to behold the conflict in the soul of virtue enthroned and vice assailant. The fault is that of inadequate realisation of the true bearing of the situation; inadequate representation of the conflict which is very properly assumed to be going on. Massinger is like a man who knows that the dial-hand of the clock will describe a certain circle, passing from point to point of significant figures; but instead of winding up the clock, and setting it going of itself, he can only move round the hand on the outside. To use another figure, his characters oscillate rather than advance, their conversions are without saving effect on their souls, their falls have no damnation. They are alike outside themselves, and they talk of "my lust," "my virtue," as of detached and portable conveniences.

When we drop to a lower level than that of pure tragedy, when we turn to characters who are grave or mild or melancholy or unfortunate rather than passionate, intense and flexible, we find that Massinger is more in his element. "Grave and great-hearted," as Mr. Swinburne styles him, he could bring before us with sympathetic skill, characters whose predominant bent is towards a melancholy and great-hearted gravity, a calm and eloquent dignity, a self-sacrificing nobility of service, or lofty endurance of inevitable wrong. Massinger's favourite play was *The Roman Actor:* "I ever held it," he says in his dedication, "the most perfect birth of my Minerva." It is impossible to say quite that; but it is certainly representative of some among the noble qualities of its writer, while it shows very clearly the defects of these qualities. What it represents is scarcely human nature; but actions and single passions writ large for the halls of kings. A certain cold loftiness, stately indeed, but not attained without some freezing of vital heat, informs it. Paris, the actor, is rather a grave and stately shadow than a breathing man; but the idealisation is nobly conceived; and both actor and tyrant, Paris and Domitian, are in their way impressive figures made manifest, not concealed, in rhetorical prolusions really appropriate to their time and character. Another classical play, the less-known *Believe as You List*, contains a figure in which I think we have the very best work of which Massinger was capable. The character of the deposed and exiled king Antiochus has a true heroism and kingliness about it; his language, a passionate and haughty dignity at times almost Marlowesque. The quiet constancy and undaunted and uncomplaining endurance of the utmost ills of Fate, which mark the character and the utterance of the Asian Emperor, raise the poetry of the play to a height but seldom attained by the pedestrian Pegasus of Massinger. As Antiochus is the most impressive of his heroes, so Flaminius is one of the most really human and consistent of his villains. The end of the play is natural, powerful and significant beyond that of any other; so natural, powerful and significant, that we may feel quite sure it was received with doubtful satisfaction by the audience above whose head and against whose taste the poet had for once elected to write.

In one or two striking portraits (those for example of the ironical old courtier Eubulus in *The Picture*, the old soldier Archidamus in *The Bondman*, or the faithful friend Romont in *The Fatal Dowry*), Massinger has shown his appreciation of honest worth and sober fidelity, qualities not of a showy kind, the recognition and representation of which do him honour. In *The Bashful Lover* and *The Maid of Honour* he has represented with special sympathy two phases of reverential and modest love. Hortensio, of the former, is a sort of pale Quixote; a knight-errant a little cracked or crazed; very sincere, and a trifle given to uttering vague and useless professions of hyperbolical humility and devotion. There is a certain febrile nobleness, a showy chivalry, about him; but we are conscious of something "got-up" and over-conscious in the exhibition. Adorni, the rejected lover in *The Maid of Honour*, is a truly noble and pathetic figure; altogether without the specious eloquence and petted despair of Hortensio, but thoroughly human and rationally self-sacrificing. His duet with Camiola at the close of the third act is one of the very finest scenes in Massinger's works—that passage, I mean, where the woman he loves despatches him to the rescue of the man on whom her own heart is set. "You will do this?" she says; and he answers, "Faithfully, madam"—and then to himself aside, "but not live long after." A touch of this sort is sufficiently rare in Massinger.

While I am speaking of *The Maid of Honour*, I may take the opportunity of referring to the character of Camiola herself,—incomparably the finest portrait of a woman ever achieved by the poet. Camiola—"that small but ravishing substance," as, with a rare and infrequent touch of delicate characterization, she is somewhere called,—is, notwithstanding a few flaws in her delineation, a thoroughly delightful and admirable creature; full of bright strength and noble constancy, of womanly heart and right manly spirit and wit. Her bearing in the scene, to a part of which I just alluded, is admirable throughout; not admirable alone, but exquisite, are her quick "Never think more then" to the servant; her outcry about the "petty sum" of the ransom; and especially the words of "perfect moan" which fall from her when she learns the hopeless estate of her lover, imprisoned by his enemy, abandoned by his King:—

> Possible! pray you, stand off.
> If I do not mutter treason to myself,
> My heart will break; and yet I will not curse him;
> He is my King. The news you have delivered
> Makes me weary of your company; we'll salute
> When we meet next. I'll bring you to the door.
> Nay, pray you, no more compliments.

When she learns of the treachery of the lover for whom she has done so much, her wondering sorrowful "O Bertoldo!" is worth a world of rhetoric. It is she who utters the most famous phrase in Massinger, the fearless indictment of the court doctrine of the divinity of kings. "With your leave," she says to the King of Sicily,—

> With your leave, I must not kneel, sir,
> While I reply to this: but thus rise up
> In my defence, and tell you, as a man.
> (*Since, when you are unjust, the deity,*
> *Which you may challenge as a king, parts from you*)
> 'Twas never read in holy writ, or moral,
> That subjects on their loyalty were obliged
> To love their sovereign's vices.

Her speech in answer to Bertoldo's hollow protestations of penitence,—the "Pray you, rise"—is full of exquisite genius and subtle beauty of spirit.

Unfortunately all Massinger's women are not of the stamp of Camiola. Lidia, indeed, in *The Great Duke of Florence*, is a good sweet modest girl; Cleora in *The Bondman* would like to be so; Bellisant in *The Parliament of Love* is a brilliant dashing creature; Margaret in *A New Way to Pay Old Debts* is an emphatically nice shrewd pleasant woman, and Matilda in *The Bashful Lover* a commonplace decent young person, without a thread or shade of distinction. But Massinger's general conception of women, and the greater number of his portraits of them, are alike debased and detestable. His bad women are incredible monsters of preposterous vice; his good women are brittle and tainted. They breathe the air of courts, and the air is poisoned. Themselves the vilest, they walk through a violent and unnaturally vicious world of depraved imagination, greedy of pleasure and rhetorical of desire. They are shamefacedly shameless; offensive and without passion; importunate and insatiable Potiphar's wives. "Pleasure's their heaven," affirms somebody; and their pleasure is without bit or bridle, without rule or direction. Massinger's favourite situation is that of a queen or princess violently and heedlessly enamoured of a man—apparently a common man, though he generally turns out to be a duke in disguise—whom she has never seen five minutes before. Over and over again is this wretched farce gone through; always without passion, sincerity or strength; always flatly, coldly, ridiculously. I am afraid Massinger thought his Donusas, Coriscas, Domitias, Aurelias, Honorias and Beaumelles brilliant and fascinating flowers of evil, sisters of Cleopatra and Semiramis, magnificently wicked women. In reality they never attain to the level of a Delilah. They are vulgar-minded to the core; weak and without stability; mere animals if they are not mere puppets. The stain of sensuality or the smutch of vulgarity is upon even the virtuous. Marcelia, in *The Duke of Milan*, supposedly a woman of spotless virtue, utters language full of covert licence; for Massinger seems to see virtue in women mainly as a sort of conscious and painful restraint. Eudocia, in *The Emperor of the East*, an injured innocent wife, betrays an unconscious vulgarity of mind which is enough to withdraw our sympathy from a fairly well-deserving object. The curious thing is, not so much that the same pen could draw Camiola and Corisca, but that the same pen could draw Camiola and Marcelia.

Massinger's main field is the Romantic Drama. He attempted, indeed, Tragedy, Comedy and History; but both tragedy and history assume in his hands a romantic cast, while his two great comedies verge constantly upon tragedy. Of his two most distinct and most distinguished tragedies, *The Duke of Milan* and *The Fatal Dowry*, the former is a powerful and impressive work, rising in parts to his highest level; the latter, despite its conventional reputation, which it owes partly to Rowe's effective plagiarisation in *The Fair Penitent*, an inadequate and unsatisfactory production. Two or three passages[3] in the latter part of *The Fatal Dowry* have the true accent of nature; but even these are marred by the base alloy with which they are mingled. But *The Duke of Milan*, despite much that is inadequate and even absurd in its handling, rises again and again to something of passion and of insight. The character and the circumstances of Sforza have been often compared with those of Othello: they are still more similar, I should venture to think, to those of Griffith Gaunt; and they have the damning fault of the latter in that the jealousy and its consequences are not made to seem quite inevitable. Sforza is an example, albeit perhaps the most favourable one, of that inconsequential oscillation of nature to which I have already referred as characteristic of most of Massinger's prominent characters. But his capacity for sudden and extreme changes of disposition, and his violent and unhinged passion, are represented with more dramatic power, with more force and naturalness, than it is at all usual to find in Massinger; who has here contrived to give a frequent effect of fineness to the frenzies and delusions of his hero. If Sforza is after all but a second-rate Othello, Marcelia is

certainly a very shrewish Desdemona, and Francisco a palpably poor Iago.[4]

In tragi-comedy, the romantic drama pure and simple, we may take *The Great Duke of Florence* as the most exquisite example. In this, the most purely delightful play, I think, ever written by Massinger,—a play which we read, to use Lamb's expression, "with composure and placid delight"—we see the sweetest and most delicate side of Massinger's genius: a country pleasantness and freshness, a masquerading genial gravity, altogether charming and attractive. The plot is admirably woven, and how prettily brought about to a happy conclusion, with its good humour, forgiveness, and friendship all round! There is something almost of Shakespeare's charm in people and events; in these princes and courtiers without ceremony and without vice, uttering pretty sentiments prettily, and playing elegantly at life; in these simple lovers, with their dainty easy trials and crosses on the way to happiness; in the villain who does no real harm, and whom nobody can hate. *The Guardian*, a late play, very fine and flexible in its rhythm, and very brisk in its action, has some exquisite country feeling, together with three or four of the most abominable characters and much of the vilest language in Massinger. One character at least, Darazzo, the male of Juliet's nurse, is really, though offensive enough in all conscience, very heartily and graphically depicted. A *Very Woman*, again, by Massinger and Fletcher,[5] has much that is pleasant and delightful; some of it very sweet and right, with some that is rank enough. I have spoken already of *The Maid of Honour*, or it might be mentioned here as a play uniting (somewhat as in *Measure for Measure*, which it partly resembles) the lighter and graver qualities of tragedy and comedy under the form of the romantic drama.

Massinger's lack of humour did not prevent him from writing comedy, nor yet from achieving signal success therein. *A New Way to Pay Old Debts* is the most memorable of his plays; but, though it is styled a comedy, it is certainly not for laughter that we turn to it. *A New Way* and *The City Madam* belong to the Comedy of Manners; satirical transcripts of contemporary life, somewhat after the style of Terence or Plautus. All Massinger's plays are distinguished by an earnest and corrective tone on contemporary politics and current fashions; and it is no wonder that he succeeded in a species of play devoted wholly to the exhibition and satirisation of the follies and vanities of the day. His constant touch on manners, even in romantic plays with classical or eastern localities, is peculiar, and suggests a certain preoccupation with the subject, possibly due to early associations at Wilton House, possibly to mere personal bent or circumstances. Remembering the letter of 1614, we may be allowed to fancy a personal applicability in the frequent denunciations of usurers and delineations of the misery of poor debtors. But besides this, I think that Massinger, being no great spirit, winged, and having force to enter into the deep and secret chambers of the soul, found his place to be in a censorship of society, and was right in concerning himself with what he could do so well. His professedly comic types, even Justice Greedy, are mere exaggerations, solitary traits frozen into the semblance of men; without really comic effect. But in the conduct of these two plays; in the episodical illuminations of London and provincial life; in the wealth of observation and satire which they exhibit, Massinger has left us work of permanent value; and in the character of Sir Giles Overreach he has made his single contribution to the gallery of permanent illustrations of human nature—a portrait to be spoken of with Grandet and with Harpagon.

Massinger is the product of his period, and he reflects faithfully the temper of court and society under the first

Charles. Much that we have to regret in him was due to the misfortune of his coming just when he did, at the ebb of a spent wave; but the best that he had was all his own. Serious, a thinker, a moralist; gifted with an instinct for nobility and a sympathy in whatever is generous and self-sacrificing; a practical student of history and an honest satirist of social abuses; he was at the same time an admirable story-teller, and a master of dramatic construction. But his grave and varied genius was lacking in the two primary requirements of the dramatist—imagination and grip. He has no real mastery over the passions, and his eloquence does not appeal to the heart. He interests us strongly; but he has no power to overwhelm or carry us away. The whole man is seen in the portrait by which we know him: in the contrast and contradiction of that singular face which attracts, yet always at the last look fails to satisfy us, with its melancholy and thoughtful grace, tempered always and marred by the weakness and the want which we can scarcely analyse, nor by any means overlook.

Notes

1. *The Renegado* is a treatise on Christian evidence, *The Virgin-Martyr* a chronicle of Christian martyrdom, *The Maid of Honour* concludes with a taking of the veil.
2. *Hours in a Library: Massinger.*
3. Found chiefly in the last scene of the fourth act; from "If this be to me, rise," to "That to be merciful should be a sin," and again in the few words following on the death of Beaumelle; with a passage or two in the fifth act.
4. There is one touch, however, in the temptings of Francisco which is really almost worthy of Iago:—

   She's yet guilty
   Only in her intent!

5. Fletcher's slave-market scene in Act III. is a piece of admirable merriment; singularly realistic and inventive.

EDMUND GOSSE
From *The Jacobean Poets*
1894, pp. 202–17

Nothing exemplifies more curiously the rapidity of development in poetical literature at the opening of the seventeenth century than the fact that the same brief reign which saw the last perfection placed on the edifice of Elizabethan drama saw also the products of the pen of Massinger. For, however much we may respect the activity of this remarkable man, however warmly we may acknowledge the power of his invention, the skill and energy with which he composed, and however agreeable his plays may appear to us if we compare them with what succeeded them in a single generation, there can be no question that the decline in the essential parts of poetry from Webster or Tourneur, to go no further back, to Massinger is very abrupt. Mr. Leslie Stephen has noted in this playwright "a certain hectic flush, symptomatic of approaching decay," and we may even go further and discover in him a leaden pallor, the sign of decreasing vitality. The "hectic flush" seems to me to belong more properly to his immediate successors, who do not come within the scope of this volume, to Ford, with his morbid sensibility, and to Shirley, with his mechanical ornament, than to Massinger, where the decline chiefly shows itself in the negation of qualities, the absence of what is brilliant, eccentric, and passionate. The sentimental and rhetorical drama of Massinger has its excellent points, but it is dominated by the feeling that the burning summer of poetry is over, and that a russet season is letting us down gently towards the dull uniformity of winter. Interesting and specious as Massinger is, we cannot avoid the impression that he is preparing us for that dramatic destitution which was to accompany the Commonwealth.

So much of Massinger's work appeared in the reign of Charles I., that he may perhaps be considered as scarcely Jacobean. But when we bear in mind the long apprenticeship he served with Fletcher and others, and if we regard, not the published dates of his principal plays, but the years in which they must reasonably be supposed to have been acted, we come to think of Massinger as not merely unalienably Jacobean, but as the leading poet of the close of James's reign. He was born at Salisbury, and was baptized at St. James's on the 24th of November, 1583, being thus nineteen years younger than Shakespeare and ten years than Ben Jonson. His father, whose name was Arthur, "happily spent many years, and died a servant" to the family of the Herberts, but he was "*generosus,*" and much respected by the heads of the clan which he thus "served" in delicate matters of business. It has been supposed that Sir Philip Sidney was the god-father of the poet, and that the boy became page to the Countess of Pembroke, but these are matters of mere conjecture. That he was brought up in or near Wilton, and was familiar with the stately occupants of that great house, may, at all events, be taken for certain.

On the 14th of May, 1602, Philip Massinger was entered as a commoner of St. Alban's Hall, Oxford. Wood gives us the impression that the Earl of Pembroke was disappointed in the lad, who "gave his mind more to poetry and romances for about four years and more, than to logic and philosophy, which he ought to have done, as he was patronized to that end." Langbaine, a poorer witness, denies this, saying that he was industrious, and that his father alone supported his charges. But he took no degree when he left Oxford in 1606, abruptly, owing either to his father's death or to the withdrawal of the Herbert patronage. Gifford supposed that Massinger had lost favour by becoming a Roman Catholic; the fact is in itself not certain, but it is made highly probable by the tone of several of his compositions. Wood says that on reaching London, Massinger, "being sufficiently famed for several specimens of wit, betook himself to writing plays." The "specimens of wit" have not come down to us, and we are unable to trace, for many years, the plays he wrote. But there is reason to believe that he lived in extreme poverty, and that his literary labours were for a long time restricted to partnership with luckier playwrights and to the re-modelling of old, discarded dramas of the Elizabethan age.

There exist signs that in 1613 Massinger was employed in writing plays with Fletcher and Field, and a little later with Daborne also. The earliest work in which his hand can certainly be traced is *The Fatal Dowry,* which he wrote in conjunction with Field about 1619. The *Very Woman* was performed at Court in 1621. But we possess the names of seven plays, all of which came into Warburton's hands, and were burned by his egregious cook—three tragedies, three comedies, and one tragi-comedy. All these, it seems probable, were written by Massinger without help from any author, before 1620. In thirteen or fourteen of Fletcher's plays, too, he had a hand or at least a main finger. Of all this large section of his work it is obvious that no criticism can be attempted, for all must be conjecture. Of his remodelling of plays, *The Virgin Martyr* is the one clearly defined example, and in this instance it cannot be said that Massinger shines as a poet by comparison with Dekker. All this time, he was probably very poor. When he was forty years of age, we find him piteously begging to be relieved by a loan of five pounds.

The earliest play which is known to survive in which Massinger was not assisted by any other poet is *The Duke of*

Milan, which was published, with a dedication to Lady Catherine Stanhope, in 1623, but probably acted about three years earlier. This marked the starting-point of a period during which Massinger broke away, we cannot guess for what reason, from the bondage of working under Fletcher, and determined, already rather late in life, to show that he could carry through a play unaided. Perhaps his next experiment was *The Maid of Honour*, although that was not published until 1632. A *New Way to Pay Old Debts* (printed 1632) could not have preceded, and yet must soon have followed the scandal about Sir Giles Mompesson in 1620. To the same period has been ascribed *The Unnatural Combat*. There may then have been a pause in Massinger's activity, or he returned to his work of collaboration with Fletcher; but four important dramas seem to belong to the closing years of the life of James I. These are *The Bondman*, published in 1624, *The Renegado*, *The Parliament of Love*, and *The Great Duke of Florence*. If those are correct who believe all these plays to have been produced on the boards before 1625, the question of the propriety of considering Massinger as a Jacobean poet is settled. He thought that he continued to improve, and that *The Roman Actor* was "the most perfect birth of my Minerva." But the truth is that we should be admirably acquainted with all his qualities and his defects if his career had closed with that of James I. As a matter of fact, he continued to live on until the 17th of March, 1638, when he was found dead in the morning in his house on the Bankside. His body was buried next day in St. Saviour's, Southwark, in the grave already occupied by the dust of John Fletcher. His later plays included *The Picture*, *The City Madam*, *Believe as you List*, *The Emperor of the East*, and *The Bashful Lover*.

The comparison has been made between Massinger and such earlier poets as Webster. This is a parallel which, from our present standpoint, militates strongly against the first-named writer. For, if the truth be told, Massinger is scarcely a poet, except in the sense in which that word may be used of any man who writes seriously in dramatic form. What we delight in in the earlier Elizabethans, the splendid bursts of imaginative insight, the wild freaks of diction, the sudden sheet-lightning of poetry illuminating for an instant dark places of the soul, all this is absent in Massinger. He is uniform and humdrum; he has no lyrical passages; his very versification, as various critics have observed, is scarcely to be distinguished from prose, and often would not seem metrical if it were printed along the page. Intensity is not within his reach, and even in the aims of composition we distinguish between the joyous instinctive lyricism of the Elizabethans, which attained to beauty without much design, and this deliberate and unimpassioned work, so plain and easy and workmanlike. It is very natural, especially for a young reader, to fling Massinger to the other end of the room, and to refuse him all attention.

This is unphilosophical and ungenerous. If we shift our standpoint a little, there is much in the author of *The Renegado* which demands our respect and insures our enjoyment. If he be less brilliant than these fiery poets, if his pictures of life do not penetrate us as theirs do, he has merits of construction which were unknown to them. The long practice which he had in prentice work was none of it thrown away upon him. It made him, when once he gained confidence to write alone, an admirable artificer of plays. He is the Scribe of the seventeenth century. He knows all the tricks by which curiosity is awakened, sustained, and gratified. He composes, as few indeed of his collaborators seem to have done, not for the study so much as for the stage. He perceived, we cannot doubt, certain faults in that noble dramatic literature of Fletcher's with which he was so long identified. He perceived Fletcher's care-

less exaggeration and his light ideal. It was Massinger who recalled English drama to sobriety and gravity.

The absence of bloody violence in his plays must strike every reader, and at the same time the tendency to introduce religious and moral reflections. The intellectual force of Massinger was extolled by Hazlitt, and not unjustly, but it was largely exercised in smoothing out and regulating his conceptions. The consequence is that Massinger tends to the sentimental and the rhetorical, and that description takes the place of passion. His characters too often say, in their own persons, what it should have been left for others to say of them. Variety of interest is secured, but sometimes at the sacrifice of evolution, and the personages act, not as human creatures must, but as theatrical puppets should. His humour possesses the same fault as his seriousness, that it is not intense. Without agreeing with Hartley Coleridge, who said that Massinger would be the worst of all dull jokers, if Ford had not contrived to be still duller, it must be admitted that the humour of Massinger is seldom successful unless when it is lambent and suffused, when, that is to say, it tinctures a scene rather than illuminates a phrase. In short, Massinger depends upon his broad effects, whether in comedy or tragedy, and must not be looked to for jewels ten words long. His songs have been the scoff of criticism; they really are among the worst ever written. He was, in short, as cannot be too often repeated, essentially unlyrical, yet his plays have great merits. They can always be read with ease, for they seem written with decorum; as Charles Lamb said, they are characterized by "that equability of all the passions, which made his English style the purest and most free from violent metaphors and harsh constructions, of any of the dramatists who were his contemporaries."

Further insight into the qualities of Massinger's work may perhaps be gained by a more detailed examination of one or two of his dramas. By general consent, the best written and the most characteristic of his tragedies is *The Duke of Milan*, the most solid and brilliant of his comedies *A New Way to Pay Old Debts*. In the former of these plays, Sforza, the Duke, is newly married to Marcelia, whom he loves with a frantic and almost maniacal uxoriousness. His delight in the Duchess is felt to be ridiculous and odious in its excess by his mother Isabella and his sister Mariana, who are, however, kept at bay by Francisco, a nobleman married to Mariana, and the Duke's especial favourite. Forced by the approach of the Emperor Charles to go forth to meet and avert his conquering army, Sforza tears himself from Marcelia, but not until he has wrung from Francisco, whom he leaves as regent, an oath that if his death should be reported, Francisco shall instantly kill Marcelia, whom Sforza cannot bear to think of as surviving him. During the Duke's absence, Francisco dishonourably makes love to the Duchess, and, to prejudice her against her husband, divulges this monstrous plan. Sforza comes back safe and sound, but observes at once the natural coldness of Marcelia, who does not appreciate having thus been doomed to execution. The play closes in violent and ferocious confusion; but that was the taste of the time. It is clearly constructed, the plot is lucidity itself, and the first act, as is usual with Massinger, is admirably devised to put the spectator in possession of all the necessary facts.

When, however, we come to reflect upon the conduct of this plausible drama, we find much which calls for unfavourable comment. There has been a great deal of bustle and show, and an interesting spectacle, but no play of genuine character. If, as has been conjectured, it was Massinger's intention deliberately to emulate Shakespeare in *Othello*, his failure is almost ludicrous. The figures are strongly contrasted, and they play at cross-purposes; did they not do so, the tragedy would come to a stand-still; their inconsistencies are the springs of the movement. Hazlitt and others have found great fault with the conception of Sforza, as being irrelevant and violent. It is not needful, however, to go so far as this in censure. It may surely be admitted that Sforza is a credible type of the neuropathic Italian despot. His agitation in the first act is true and vivid; his moods are those of a man on the verge of madness, but they do not cross that verge.

He reaches the highest pitch of hysterical agitation in the fine scene in the fifth act, where the dead body of Marcelia is brought across the stage—

> Carefully, I beseech you:
> The gentlest touch; and then think
> What I shall suffer. O you earthly gods,
> You second natures, that from your great master,
> Who join'd the limbs of torn Hippolytus
> And drew upon himself the Thunderer's envy,
> Are taught those hidden secrets that restore
> To life death-wounded men! You have a patient
> On whom to express the excellence of art
> Will bind even Heaven your debtor, tho' it pleases
> To make your hands the organs of the work
> The saints will smile to look on, and good angels
> Clap their celestial wings to give it plaudits.
> How pale and worn she looks! O, pardon me,
> That I presume (dyed o'er with bloody guilt,
> Which makes me, I confess, far, far unworthy),
> To touch this snow-white hand. How cold it is!
> This once was Cupid's firebrand, and still
> 'Tis so to me. How slow her pulses beat too!
> Yet in this temper she is all perfection,
> And mistress of a heat so full of sweetness,
> The blood of virgins in their pride of youth
> Are balls of snow or ice compar'd unto her.

The real fault of *The Duke of Milan* is not the unnaturalness of Sforza, but the fact that the dramatist has limited his attention to him. The remoteness of the Duke's passions, his nervous eccentricities, should have forced Massinger to keep all the characters at a low and quiet pitch, so to contrast the neurosis of Sforza with their normal condition. But all the other characters are no less frenzied than he is, without his excuses. The abrupt wooing of Francisco, who is a mere shadow of Iago, in the second act, is utterly untrue; his equally abrupt repentance, in the third act, is not less extraordinary, and is introduced for no other reason than that Marcelia should know Sforza's plan for her being killed in case he does not return alive. If we turn to the female characters, they are not more natural; the mother and sister of the Duke are vulgar scolds, Marcelia herself utterly ugly and absurd. Everything is extreme and yet weak; the characters are made of india-rubber, and the dramatist presses them down or pulls them out as he sees fit. His study of Sforza is carefully executed, and has passages of great suavity and charm—such as his meeting with the Emperor Charles—but to the evolution of this single character the entire play is sacrificed.

This speech of Sforza, when introduced to the Emperor Charles, is one of the best things in the play—

> If example
> Of my fidelity to the French, whose honours,
> Titles, and glories, are now mixed with yours,
> As brooks, devoured by rivers, lose their names,
> Has power to invite you to make him a friend,
> That hath given evident proof he knows to love,
> And to be thankful: this my crown, now yours,
> You may restore me, and in me instruct

> These brave commanders, should your fortune change,
> Which now I wish not, what they may expect
> From noble enemies for being faithful.
> The charges of the war I will defray,
> And what you may, not without hazard, force,
> Bring freely to you; I'll prevent the cries
> Of murder'd infants and of ravish'd maids,
> Which in a city sack'd, call on Heaven's justice,
> And stop the course of glorious victories:
> And when I know the captains and the soldiers,
> That have in the lost battle done best service,
> And are to be rewarded, I myself,
> According to their quality and merits,
> Will see them largely recompens'd.—I have said,
> And now expect the sentence.

When we turn from this tragedy to the comedy of *A New Way to Pay Old Debts*, we are struck by similar characteristics, modified, however, by the fact that this is a much stronger and more vivid play than *The Duke of Milan*. At the outset we are interested to find ourselves on a scene so frankly English and modern. Massinger had much of the spirit of the journalist, and it has been pointed out by Mr. Gardiner and others that he was constantly engaged in referring to events of passing politics. Here he was inspired by a sensational case which had but recently engaged the notice of the courts of law, and the comedy palpitates with topical allusions. The plot of the play is clear and interesting. Sir Giles Overreach, a self-made man, by alternately wheedling and bullying the lax gentry of the country-side, has ruined them all, and rules the whole neighbourhood. In particular, he has so cleverly played on the illusions and the vices of young Wellborn, the squire, that he has stripped him of everything, and the generous Wellborn has to appear among his late tenants in rags. Overreach has no son, but one daughter, and his design is to marry her to Lord Lovell, the local grandee, and so finally secure his own position in the county. He is overtricked, however, by a rich and eccentric widow, Lady Allworth, who patronizes Wellborn, the prodigal, and marries Lord Lovell herself. The intrigue of the last act, in which Wellborn constrains Overreach to give him the money with which he pays his old debts, gives name to the play, but is somewhat obscurely managed. Notwithstanding this, however, *A New Way to Pay Old Debts* is the example of the entire Elizabethan and Jacobean drama outside Shakespeare which has longest held its place on the modern stage.

As is customary with Massinger, the first act is singularly skilful. The story told in sarcasm to Wellborn by Tapwell, the rascally innkeeper, is exactly what we need to put us in possession of the facts. Wellborn's condition, character, and prospects are placed before us in absolute clearness, our sympathies are engaged, and the little mystery of his whisper to the lady, at the close of the act, is left dark so as to freshen and carry on our curiosity. In the second act, we begin to appreciate the force and cunning of Sir Giles Overreach, in whose wickedness there is something colossal that impresses the imagination. The third act sustains this impression and even increases it, but after this the threads become, not exactly entangled, but twisted, and the illusion of nature is gradually lost. In *A New Way to Pay Old Debts* that unhappy forcible-feebleness of Massinger's is not so strikingly prominent as elsewhere, yet we see something of it in Marall's crude and abrupt temptation of Wellborn to commit some crime and so put an end to his miseries. A certain Justice Greedy pervades the piece, a magistrate who is always raging for his food. Some critics have thought his gluttonies very diverting, but Massinger borrowed them directly from Beaumont and Fletcher, and they are too incessant not to become fatiguing. The charm of this play, after all, consists in its realistic picture of English country life in 1620, and in its curious portrait of the great savage parvenu, eater of widows and orphans, a huge machine for unscrupulous avarice and tyranny. In Sir Giles Overreach, Massinger approaches more nearly than anywhere else to a dramatic creation of the first order.

Little would be gained by examining with the like minuteness the rest of Massinger's dramas. For so brief a sketch as we must here confine ourselves to, it is enough to say that in the main they present the same characteristics. This playwright commonly shows a capacity for depicting courtly and gentle persons, engaged in pleasant converse amongst themselves. For suavity and refinement of this kind, *The Grand Duke of Florence* is remarkable. Lamb has praised *The Picture* for "good sense, rational fondness, and chastened feeling;" this is true of its execution, but hardly of its repulsive central idea. On the whole, Massinger may be commended for the prominence and the dignity which he readily assigns to women; but in attempting to show them independent, he not unfrequently paints them exceedingly coarse and hard. His political bias was towards a kind of oligarchic liberalism; Coleridge describes him as "a decided Whig." Sometimes he indulged this tendency in politics by satirizing the ladies of a less aristocratic walk of life than he usually affected, and *The City Madam* is a lively example of his gifts in this direction. The diction of the dramatist is particularly rich in the last-named play, and Massinger has not written better verse than this from Luke's soliloquy in the third act—

> Thou dumb magician [*taking out a key*] that without
>   a charm
> Didst make my entrance easy, to possess
> What wise men wish and toil for! Hermes' Moly,
> Sibylla's golden bough, the great elixir
> Imagin'd only by the alchymist,
> Compar'd with thee are shadows,—thou the
>   substance,
> And guardian of felicity! No marvel
> My brother made thy place of rest his bosom,
> Thou being the keeper of his heart, a mistress

To be hugg'd ever! In bye-corners of
This sacred room, silver in bags, heap'd up
Like billets saw'd and ready for the fire,
Unworthy to hold fellowship with bright gold
That flow'd about the room, conceal'd itself.
There needs no artificial light; the splendour
Makes a perpetual day there, night and darkness
By that still-burning lamp for ever banished!
But when, guided by that, my eyes had made
Discovery of the caskets, and they opened,
Each sparkling diamond from itself shot forth
A pyramid of flames, and in the roof
Fix'd it a glorious star, and made the place
Heaven's abstract or epitome! Rubies, sapphires,
And ropes of orient pearl, these seen, I could not
But look on with contempt.

When the directly Gallic fashion of the Restoration had gone out, the dramatists had turned once more to their Jacobean predecessors, Massinger came back into favour. His example had much to do in forming the style of such sentimental tragic writers as Rowe and Lillo, and again, a century later, his influence was paramount on Talfourd and Sheridan Knowles. He has always been easy to imitate, and it may be said that until Lamb began to show quite clearly what the old English drama really was, most readers vaguely took their impression of it from the pages of Massinger. He was succeeded, it is true, by several younger playwrights, particularly by Ford, Shirley, and Brome; but each of these—all poets whose works lie outside the scope of the present volume—returned closer than he did to the tradition of their fathers. Massinger is, really, though not technically and literally, the last of the great men. In him we have all the characteristics of the school in their final decay, before they dissolved and were dispersed. At the same time, it must never be forgotten that we do not know what he may have been capable of in his youth, and that he was nearly forty, and therefore possibly beyond his poetic prime, before he wrote the earliest play which has come down to us. If Warburton's miserable cook had not burned *Minerva's Sacrifice* and *The Italian Nightpiece*, we might, possibly, put Massinger on a higher level; but criticism can make no conjectures, and we must place the worthy and industrious playwright where we find him.

ROBERT BURTON

1577–1640

Robert Burton was born on February 8, 1577, at Lindley Hall, Leicestershire. Burton received his early education at the Free School at Sutton Coldfield and at the Nuneaton Grammar School. He entered Brasenose College, Oxford, in 1593, and was elected a student in Christ Church College in 1599. Burton took his bachelor of divinity in 1614, and in 1616 subsequently became vicar of St. Thomas' Church, Oxford. He later held preferments in Lincolnshire and Leicestershire.

Burton's earliest work is the Latin verse comedy, *Philosophaster* (1606). Burton later revised the play and it was staged in 1617 by students at Christ Church. Burton is, however, best remembered for his lengthy treatise entitled *The Anatomy of Melancholy*. An unusual work that combined medical, psychological, and philosophical analyses with humor, satire, philological excursuses, and political theory, it was first published in 1621. *The Anatomy of Melancholy* underwent four revisions during Burton's lifetime. Often described as a storehouse of eclectic and eccentric knowledge, Burton's masterpiece has won the admiration of various writers, including Samuel Johnson, Laurence Sterne, and Charles Lamb.

Burton spent the last days of his life at Oxford, where he died on January 25, 1640.

Personal

Robert Burton, his ⟨William Burton's⟩ younger brother, born Feb. 8, 1575, aferwards student of Christ's Church Oxon, and bachelor of divinity. He wrote an excellent book (commonly called "Democritus Junior,") of *The Anatomy of Melancholy* (none to the native, to describe a country), wherein he hath piled up variety of much excellent learning. On whose tomb is this epitaph:

> Paucis notus, paucioribus ignotus;
> Hic jacet Democritus junior,
> Cui vitam pariter et mortem
> Dedit Melancholia.

Scarce any book of philology in our land hath in so short a time passed so many impressions. He died rector of Segrave (presented by his patron George Lord Berkeley) in this country, about 1636.—THOMAS FULLER, *The History of the Worthies of England*, 1662

Robert Burton, known otherwise to scholars by the name of Democritus Junior, younger brother to Will. Burton, whom I shall mention under the year 1645, was born of an ancient and genteel family at Lindley, in Leicestershire, 8 Feb. 1576, and therefore in the titles of several of his choice books which he gave to the public library, he added to his sirname Lindliacus Leycestrensis. He was educated in grammar learning in the free-school of Sutton-Colfield in Warwickshire, whence he was sent to Brasennose coll. in the long vacation, an. 1593, where he made a considerable progress in logic and philosophy in the condition of a commoner. In 1599, he was elected student of Ch. Ch. and for form sake, tho' he wanted not a tutor, he was put under the tuition of Dr. John Bancroft, afterwards bishop of Oxon. In 1614, he was admitted to the reading of the sentences, and on the 29 Nov. 1616, he had the vicaridge of St. Thomas's parish in the west suburb of Oxon conferr'd on him by the dean and canons of Ch. Church, (to the parishioners whereof, he always gave the sacrament in wafers) which, with the rectory of Segrave in Leicestershire, given to him some years after by George lord Berkeley, he kept with much ado to his dying day. He was an exact mathematician, a curious calculator of nativities, a general read scholar, a thro' pac'd philologist, and one that understood the surveying of lands well. As he was by many accounted a severe student, a devourer of authors, a melancholy and humorous person; so by others, who knew him well, a person of great honesty, plain dealing and charity. I have heard some of the antients of Ch. Ch. often say that his company was very merry, facete and juvenile, and no man in his time did surpass him for his ready and dextrous interlarding his common discourses among them with verses from the poets or sentences from classical authors. Which being then all the fashion in the university, made his company more acceptable. He hath written,

The Anatomy of Melancholy.—First printed in qu. and afterwards several times in fol. an. 1624, 1632, 38, and 1652, &c. to the great profit of the bookseller, who got an estate by it. 'Tis a book so full of variety of reading, that gentlemen who have lost their time and are put to a push for invention, may furnish themselves with matter for common or scholastical discourse and writing. Several authors have unmercifully stolen matter from the said book without any acknowledgment, particularly one Will. Greenwood, in his book entit. *A Description of the Passion of Love, &c.* Lond. 1657. oct. Who, as others of the like humour do, sometimes takes his quotations without the least mention of Democritus Junior. He the said R. Burton paid his last debt to nature, in his chamber in Ch. Ch. at, or very near the time, which he had some years before

foretold from the calculation of his own nativity. Which being exact, several of the students did not forbear to whisper among themselves, that rather than there should be a mistake in the calculation, he sent up his soul to heaven thro' a slip about his neck. His body was afterwards with due solemnity buried near that of Dr. Rob. Weston, in the north isle which joyns next to the choir of the cath. of Ch. Church, on the 27 of January in sixteen hundred thirty and nine. Over his grave was soon after erected a comely monument on the upper pillar of the said isle, with his bust painted to the life: On the right hand of which, is the calculation of his nativity, and under the bust this inscription made by himself; all put up by the care of William Burton his brother. 'Paucis notus paucioribus ignotus, hic jacet Democritus junior, cui vitam dedit, & mortem Melancholia. Obiit viii. Id. Jan. A. C. MD CXXXIX.' He left behind him a very choice library of books, many of which he bequeathed to that of Bodley, and a hundred pounds to buy five pounds yearly for the supplying of Ch. Ch. library with books.—ANTHONY À WOOD, *Athenae Oxonienses*, 1691–1721

Mr. Burton was one of the most facetious and pleasant companions of that age, but his conversation was very innocent. It was the way then to mix a great deal of Latin in discoursing, at which he was wonderfull ready, (in the manner his book is wrote,) which is now looked upon as pedantry. Ant. à Wood was a great admirer of Mr. Burton, and of the books he bequeathed to the Bodleian library, a great many of which were little historicall diverting pamphlets, now grown wonderfull scarce, which Mr. Burton used to divert himself with, as he did with other little merry books, of which there are many in his benefaction, one of which is *The History of Tom Thumb.* —THOMAS HEARNE, *Reliquiae Hearnianae*, Jan. 28, 1733/4

Works

THE ANATOMY OF MELANCHOLY

Burton's *Anatomy of Melancholy*, he said, was the only book that ever took him out of bed two hours sooner than he wished to rise.—JAMES BOSWELL, *Life of Johnson*, 1791

I don't know whether you ever dipt into Burton's Anatomy. His manner is to shroud and carry off his feelings under a cloud of learned words. He has written but one Poem, which is prefix'd to his Anatomy, and called *The Abstract of Melancholy*. Most likely you have seen it. It is in the last edition of the Elegant Extracts. It begins: 'When I go musing all alone, Thinking of divers things foredone.'—So that I have collected my imitation rather from his prose Book, than any Poetry.

I call it

> A Conceipt of Diabolical Possession
>
> By myself walking,
> To myself talking,
> While as I ruminate
> On my untoward fate,
> Scarcely seem I
> Alone sufficiently;
> Black thoughts continually
> Crowding my privacy,
> They come unbidden.
> Like foes at a wedding,
> Thrusting their faces
> In better guests' places,
> Peevish and malcontent
> Clownish impertinents,
> Dashing the merriments;—
> So in like fashion

Dim cogitations
Follow & haunt me,
Striving to daunt me,
In my heart festering,
In my ears whispering,
'Thy friends are treacherous,
Thy foes are dangerous,
Thy dreams ominous'
Fierce Anthropophagi,
Spectra, Diaboli,
What scared Saint Anthony,
Shapes undefined,
With my fears twined,
Hobgoblin, Lemures,
Dreams of antipodes,
Night-riding Incubi,
Troubling the fantasy,
All dim illusions,
Causing confusions,
Figments heretical,
Scruples fantastical
Doubts diabolical,
Abaddon vexeth me,
Mahu perplexeth me,
Lucifer teareth me, . . .
Jesu Mariae, libera nos ab
his tentationibus, orat, implorat,
R. Burton Peccator.
—CHARLES LAMB, Letter to Thomas Manning
      (April 1800)

It is a commonplace that in the most absurd error there may generally be discovered, if not some considerable ground or background of truth, yet some fragment of explanation. There is such an explanation for the absurd craze which has induced its monomaniacs to include Robert Burton's work among those, dating from the last quarter of the sixteenth century and the first of the seventeenth, which they father upon Francis Bacon, or a secret society headed by him. To no one possessing one grain of critical power of separation could the work of Shakespeare, of Bacon, and of Burton seem to come from the same hand. But each stands apart from all his other contemporaries in a certain combination, different in each, of universality of comprehension, with intense individuality of expression. Burton's form of this combination of gifts lay in the union of almost universal reading with the application of that reading to the setting forth and illustration of a peculiar temperament of mind—the temperament which is expressed by writers as ancient as the Preacher, and as modern as Schopenhauer. To dwell on the way in which, as far as matter goes, he deals with the subject of Melancholy would be here impossible. It is sufficient to say that he had read almost everything—classical, mediaeval, and modern, theology, science (as science then went), law, history, poetry. He will quote Ovid one moment and Chaucer the next, a schoolman on this page, and—rarest of all quotations to be found in his own contemporaries—a contemporary playwright on that. The whole is cast into the form of a scientific investigation of the causes, symptoms, varieties, and cure of what he calls Melancholy. But as the manner of his age was (though no one else shows it in quite such perfection) the investigation passes into, or is continually accompanied by, an endless chain of citation from his innumerable authors. Nor is the fashion of this citation less peculiar than its abundance. For the most part the borrowed passages are not given singly to support and illustrate single sentences or

paragraphs of the author's own. They run on into endless series with each other, or are twisted in alternate strands with Burton's own writing. Sometimes his sentences read as if a string of references in a footnote had by some inadvertence cropped up in the text; often as if the clauses were written in shorthand—notes for the author's own use in future extension or selection. Now he will give the original of his version, or a paraphrase in a note; now he will quote his author in Latin or another tongue, and follow this up with a sort of half-gloss, half-version in English. To a careless reader, or to one quite out of sympathy with Burton's own mood, the method may seem either a cumbrous conglomeration, due to lack of taste, skill, and energy, or the lost labour of elaborate eccentricity. Not so to any one who takes the trouble to master Burton's own introduction, or who starts in harmony with the spirit of the book. If the *Anatomy of Melancholy* be regarded as mere outpouring of commonplace books, with a pretext of unity in purpose and subject, it is no great thing. To be understood it must be regarded as at once the exhibition of a temperament, and the discussion of a case.

Burton occupied rather more than twenty years, from the time of his election to a position of learned ease, in shaping his book for its first appearance in 1621: he spent rather less than another twenty in refashioning and perfecting the work. Frequently as it has been reprinted, no attempt has ever yet been made to execute a critical edition, indicating the variations which were thus introduced by him on the four occasions when reissues were called for in his own lifetime. These alterations and additions are very numerous and very considerable, and the author not unfrequently draws attention to them in the text. But he has never, in making them, broken through the singular unity and control of treatment which the book shows. As far as the *minutiæ* of style are concerned, Burton's characteristics are well marked, and not very numerous. His method of quotation obliges him of necessity to immense sentences, or rather clause-heaps. But it is noteworthy that when he intermits citation and narrates or argues in his own person he is less, not more, given than his contemporaries to the long sentence, and frequently has a distinctly terse and crisp arrangement of the members of his paragraph. Of definite mannerisms he chiefly affects apposition, the omission of conjunctions and connecting words of all kinds, and a very curious and characteristic use of the demonstrative he and its cases, which covers with him a range of senses from "that well-known person" to "anybody."

These details of form, however, though adding to the fantastic personality of the book, are as nothing compared to the idiosyncrasies of its matter and spirit. Apt as Burton is to digress—indeed he has a formal defence of the practice—and enormous as is the range of his digression, he has contrived to make all this huge congeries of material subservient to his purpose of illustrating a new "vanity of vanities," of combining, as it were, in one book the knowledge of Solomon, and his reflections on the futility of the things known and the knowing of them. Rigidly precise in appearance as is the scheme he lays out, its sweep and ramifications are so great and intricate that hardly anything introduced by him can be said to be absolutely irrelevant. He contrives to see all things in Melancholy, and yet to make his treatment of them anything but melancholic. Indeed with all his plunges in the *balneum diaboli*, all his love for quaint out-of-the-way knowledge, there is in Burton a strong vein of plain commonsense which is sometimes almost prosaic, in the transferred and uncomplimentary sense, and which emerges now and then, especially in his long and famous discourse of Love-melancholy. His own verse translations, too, are such mere doggrel for the most part that one almost suspects a trick and deliberation. But there are few things, indeed, that deserve censure in Burton, the perpetual refuge and delight of scholarly English readers, an unmatched storehouse of learning, and one not easily matched for wisdom, a writer who, by force of genius, has turned into an organic whole the hugest and most apparently heterogeneous stock of materials that ever an architect of letters set himself to build withal.—GEORGE SAINTSBURY, "Robert Burton," *English Prose*, ed. Henry Craik, 1893, Vol. 2, pp. 115–18

Robert Burton, a clergyman and university recluse, who passed his life in libraries, and dabbled in all the sciences, as learned as Rabelais, having an inexhaustible and overflowing memory; unequal, moreover, gifted with enthusiasm, and spasmodically gay, but as a rule sad and morose, to the extent of confessing in his epitaph that melancholy made up his life and his death; in the first place original, liking his own common sense, and one of the earliest models of that singular English mood which, withdrawing man within himself, develops in him, at one time imagination, at another scrupulosity, at another oddity, and makes of him, according to circumstances, a poet, an eccentric, a humorist, a madman, or a puritan. He read on for thirty years, put an encyclopædia into his head, and now, to amuse and relieve himself, takes a folio of blank paper. Twenty lines of a poet, a dozen lines of a treatise on agriculture, a folio page of heraldry, a description of rare fishes, a paragraph of a sermon on patience, the record of the fever fits of hypochondria, the history of the particle *that*, a scrap of metaphysics,—this is what passes through his brain in a quarter of an hour: it is a carnival of ideas and phrases, Greek, Latin, German, French, Italian, philosophical, geometrical, medical, poetical, astrological, musical, pedagogic, heaped one on the other; an enormous medley, a prodigious mass of jumbled quotations, jostling thoughts, with the vivacity and the transport of a feast of unreason. . . .

He is never-ending; words, phrases, overflow, are heaped up, overlap each other, and flow on, carrying the reader along, deafened, stunned, half-drowned, unable to touch ground in the deluge. Burton is inexhaustible. There are no ideas which he does not iterate under fifty forms: when he has exhausted his own, he pours out upon us other men's—the classics, the rarest authors, known only by savants—authors rarer still, known only to the learned; he borrows from all. Underneath these deep caverns of erudition and science, there is one blacker and more unknown than all the others, filled with forgotten authors, with crackjaw names, Besler of Nuremberg, Adricomius, Linschoten, Brocarde, Bredenbachius. Amidst all these antediluvian monsters, bristling with Latin terminations, he is at his ease; he sports with them, laughs, skips from one to the other, drives them all abreast. He is like old Proteus, the sturdy rover, who in one hour, with his team of hippopotami, makes the circuit of the ocean.

What subject does he take? Melancholy, his own individual mood; and he takes it like a schoolman. None of St. Thomas Aquinas' treatises is more regularly constructed than his. This torrent of erudition flows in geometrically planned channels, turning off at right angles without deviating by a line. At the head of every part you will find a synoptical and analytical table, with hyphens, brackets, each division begetting its subdivisions, each subdivision its sections, each section its subsections: of the malady in general, of melancholy in particular, of its nature, its seat, its varieties, causes, symptoms, prognosis; of its cure by permissible means, by forbidden means, by dietetic means, by pharmaceutical means. After the

scholastic process, he descends from the general to the particular, and disposes each emotion and idea in its labelled case. In this framework, supplied by the middle-age, he heaps up the whole, like a man of the Renaissance,—the literary description of passions and the medical description of madness, details of the hospital with a satire on human follies, physiological treatises side by side with personal confidences, the recipes of the apothecary with moral counsels, remarks on love with the history of evacuations. The discrimination of ideas has not yet been effected; doctor and poet, man of letters and savant, he is all at once; for want of dams, ideas pour like different liquids into the same vat, with strange spluttering and bubbling, with an unsavoury smell and odd effect. But the vat is full, and from this admixture are produced potent compounds which no preceding age has known.—HIPPOLYTE TAINE, *History of English Literature*, tr. H. Van Laun, 1871, Vol. 1, Book 2, pp. 336–42

UNSIGNED
"Burton's *Anatomy of Melancholy*"
Cornhill Magazine, April 1880, pp. 475–90

Dr. Johnson is not generally supposed to have erred as a critic on the side of excessive approbation. And yet he managed to bestow upon one book the most forcible eulogium ever uttered. Burton's *Anatomy of Melancholy* was, he said, the only book which ever took him out of bed two hours sooner than he intended. The compliment is always reproduced when Burton's book is mentioned. Second-hand booksellers judiciously quote it in their catalogues to stimulate the appetite of their customers. Every lover of books has been induced to prolong his evening sitting, sometimes to prolong it till daylight, by the charms of a fascinating author; but the most voracious of literary gluttons seldom breaks his morning slumbers under such an impulse. And when we add that it was Johnson who was thus beguiled, Johnson whose whole life was a continuous remorse for inability to rise early, when we see that Burton must have done for once what could be done neither by strong religious principles, nor by a morbidly keen conscience, nor by the pressure of stern necessity, and what the united energies of Boswell and the Thrales and the whole of the Club would have failed in securing, we must admit that the performance borders on the incredible. Doubtless it was the youthful Johnson whose slumbers he disturbed; and it was after the scanty fare of Lichfield, not the solid festivities of the "Mitre" or the "Turk's Head." With all deductions, we are still in presence of a "great fact." Many a young student must have turned with avidity to the promised treat, and a good many have probably retreated in disappointment. For, at first sight, the reader becomes aware of the curious mildness of another phrase of Johnson's; the book, he said, is "perhaps overloaded with quotations." That is rather like saying that Pickwick may "perhaps" be regarded as aiming at fun; that there is possibly a dash of humour in Charles Lamb; or that Pope may be accused of a tendency to satire. The *Anatomy* is all but made up of quotations; it is, as the author expressly says, a "cento collected from others;" a vast heterogeneous mass of miscellaneous reading; the contents of a commonplace book kept by a reader of boundless curiosity who has ranged over the whole field of learning then accessible, from the classical authors down through the fathers and the scholastic philosophers of the Middle Ages, to the grammarians, philosophers, physiologists and novelists of the Renaissance, and who has dipped into the most fashionable playbooks, poems, and essays of the day—Montaigne, Bacon, Spenser, Drayton, and even Ben Jonson and Shakspeare.[1] It is a patchwork stuck together with scissors and paste, a queer amorphous mass, in spite of its ostensible plan, where we are half-baffled and half-attracted by references to strange authors who delighted in masquerading with Latin terminations to their names. We have heard more or less of some of them, of Bodinus and Paracelsus, or Cardan, or Erasmus; but who, we wonder, was Rlasis the Arabian, or Skenkius, or Poggius, or Fuchsius, or Busbequius[2]—a name which has no doubt a peculiar flavour of pleasant quaintness? Such names carry with them a faint association of the days of high-built and ponderous pedantry; we catch a passing glimpse of some ancient doctor damning another for his theory of the irregular verbs, or settling the theory of the enclitic δξ, or conducting tremendous disputations in the schools with all the ponderous apparatus of the old syllogistic artillery. Yet it is possible to have too much of Busbequius; and, after dipping into the book, in search of that spirit and power which he is said (still by Johnson) to display when writing from his own mind, it is well if we do not give up the chase in despair, and decide that it is hardly worth cracking so vast a shell of effete pedantry to come at so small a kernel of sound sense.

It is well, I say; for after all there is a real charm in the old gentleman. Certainly the *Anatomy* is not a book to be read through; it would have no place in the short list of literary masterpieces which the intelligent reader is supposed to absorb into his mental structure. It is a book for odds and ends of time, and to be read only at appropriate seasons; not, perhaps, in a railway carriage or by the seaside, or in any place where the roaring wheels of our social machinery make themselves too plainly heard. It is rather a book to be taken up in a quiet library, by accident, not of malice prepense, and, in spite of Johnson, rather in the last hour of the night than at morning. When you are tired of blue-books or scientific wrangling or metaphysical hair-splitting; when you have turned to the last book from the circulating library only to discover that novel-writing is a forgotten art; that poetry has become a frivolous echo of sounding verbiage; that the smartest magazine article is a mere pert gabble of commonplace—jaundiced views which sometimes suggest themselves on such occasions—it may be pleasant to soothe yourself by entering this old museum of musty antiquities, and to feel as though you were entering a forgotten chamber where the skeletons of seventeenth-century spiders are still poised upon undisturbed cobwebs. The phantoms of Busbequius and his fellows may then have substantiality enough to hold converse with you for a time, and you gradually perceive that old Burton himself probably once filled an academical costume with a genuine structure of flesh and bone. Carefully as he retires behind his moth-eaten folios, there are moments when he drops his disguise, and you can depict the quaint smile of the humorous observer of men and manners, and believe that he had in his days a genuine share of the pathetic side of human folly. Nobody, it is true, is more provokingly shy. It is the shyness of the genuine old-fashioned scholar, who is half-ashamed of possessing tissues not made out of an ancient parchment. You ask him for an opinion, and he throws a dozen authorities at your head and effects his escape into an ingenious digression; he balances himself in curious equilibrium between the ranks of opposing doctors, and only lets slip at intervals an oblique intimation that he is inclined to think that one of them is a donkey. In all this he is certainly as different as possible from the ordinary humourist. He requires an interpreter, and must be cross-examined to make him yield up his real meaning; and yet, under all his concealments, he has a certain vein of shrewd humour which may at least serve

to excite such a portion of that faculty as we may ourselves happen to possess.

Burton, in his opening address to the reader, sets forth his claims to the title of Democritus junior; and he tells at length the legend of the laughing philosopher; how the citizens of Abdera took him to be mad by reason of his excessive perception of the ludicrous, and brought the weeping Hippocrates to cure him of his folly; how Hippocrates found him sitting on the ground cutting up beasts to find out the causes of melancholy; and how, when Hippocrates tried to point out that reasonable citizens employed themselves upon business or pleasure instead of dissection, Democritus answered every argument by peals of laughter and demonstrations of the utter absurdity of all the ordinary activities of man. So clearly did Democritus preach upon the old text, Vanity of Vanities, that Hippocrates departed with the fullest conviction of his sanity. Burton proposes to continue the discourse of Democritus. Never, he says, was there so much food for laughter as now; for now, "as Salisburiensis says in his time, *totus mundus histrionem agit*, the whole world plays the fool; we have a new theatre, a new scene, a new comedy of errors, a new company of personate actors; *Volupiæ sacræ* (as Calcagnius willingly feigns in his *Apologius*) are celebrated all the world over, when all the actors were madmen or fools, and every hour changed habits, or took that which came next." The world is a farce; princes are mad; great men are mad; philosophers and scholars are mad, and so are those who scorn them. "Methinks," he says, "most men are fools," if we may apply the judicious tests given by Æneas Sylvius. "Nevisanus, the lawyer, holds it for an axiom, most women are fools; Seneca, men, be they old or young; who doubts it, youth is mad as Elius in Tully, *stulti adolescentuli*; old age little better, *deliri senes*." And, after running through as many classes as he can think of, Burton confesses that he is himself as foolish and as mad as any one. We are tolerably familiar with the theory, "All the world is a stage," and the players are "mostly fools." Satirists and poets and moralists and essayists have set the same sentiment to different times; and it is the special function of the humourist to give fresh edge to the ancient doctrine. Burton has certainly chosen a thesis which affords ample room for the widest illustration; and we have only to ask how he acquits himself of his task.

And here we perceive that he begins to shrink a little. Some people, he says, will think his performance "too fantastical, too light and comical for a divine;" and he replies that he is only speaking an assumed part, and collecting the opinions of others. "'Tis not I, but they that say it." You must blame Nevisanus and Calcagnius for the startling theory just expounded, not the Rev. Richard Burton, student of Christ Church, and Rector of Segrave. He trembles at his own audacity, and retires behind his mask. And, as he carries out this principle only too systematically, he is a humourist only by proxy. He does not let us see what he feels himself; he is not a mere buffoon, for we are not sure that he has no serious meaning; but he does not rise to be a daring humourist, for he is afraid ever to laugh out. We often fail to discover whether he is slily laughing in his sleeve or advancing some preposterous doctrine in honest reverence for the authority upon which it rests; whether his elaborate pedantry is really part of himself or a mere mask which he knows to be really grotesque. We follow Montaigne with the sense that we are talking to a man of vigorous intellect, who reads books as they ought to be read by a full-grown thinker; who treats them as an equal or a superior; and quotes them to illustrate his own thoughts, not as providing unalterable moulds to which his thoughts are bound to conform. But that is just the point which Burton leaves doubtful. Is he really half in fun when he quotes a dozen learned men to prove that disease or poverty may be a cause of melancholy; or is he distinctly aware that the learned men are indulging in ludicrous platitudes; or perhaps simply turning out his commonplace book to show his learning?

That is the curious problem which haunts us through the whole performance. The man was no doubt a puzzle to his contemporaries, as he remains for us. The view which they took of him is typified in the two or three anecdotes which do duty for his biography, doubtless more or less apocryphal, as such anecdotes invariably are, and yet perhaps as significant of the truth as the most authentic narratives. Burton, as Wood tells us, was very "facete, merry, and juvenile" amongst his college companions, and no man could surpass him (as we may easily believe) at interlarding his discourse with appropriate quotations, according to the fashion of the time. He meant, it is said, to cure himself of a tendency to melancholy by compiling the *Anatomy*; but melancholy increased his weakness so much that at last he could only relieve himself by listening to the ribaldry of the Oxford bargees, an amusement which "rarely failed to throw him into a violent fit of laughter." Burton, no doubt, had the true humourist's termperament; a disposition to melancholy underlay his perception of the ludicrous, and this disposition might be fostered by a sedentary life and advancing years, till, tired of hunting for literary curiosities, he returned to the coarse brutalities of waterside buffoonery, as the sated epicure ends by finding the highest relish in simple beans and bacon. He died, we are told, at the exact time which he had foretold upon astrological grounds, and the students whispered that he had taken the necessary steps to secure the fulfilment of his own prediction. Certainly such a practical bull carried to a tragic conclusion, confirming the truth of astrology by a chance which really showed it to be false, and that at the cost of his own life, was a most fitting end for a thoroughgoing humourist. There would be a charm about setting such a trap for future dabblers in eccentric logical quibbles. In the *Anatomy*, Burton delivers his own views upon astrology with delightful ambiguity. If, he says, Sextus Empiricus, Picus Mirandula, Sextus ab Heminga, or others, have persuaded any man that the signs in the heavens have no more virtue than the signs over a shop or an inn, the sceptic may be referred to Bellantius, Pirovânus, Marascallerus, or Goclenius, who, let us hope, will give him satisfaction. Meanwhile, his own view is that the stars do not compel but incline, and incline so gently that a wise man may resist them. This charmingly elastic hypothesis is enough to allow your true humourist to reconcile his love of the marvellous with the occasional promptings of common sense. Burton, indeed, might have found authorities enough in his own day to make a genuine belief in astrology respectable. But downright belief was hardly in his way. The question for him was not the truth or falsehood of a doctrine, but the facility which it afforded for dallying with grotesque fancies. Living in the intellectual twilight, when the fantastic shapes of old superstition and mythical philosophy blended strangely with the growth of really scientific hypotheses, he could ramble at will through the stores of obsolete learning, picking up here and there whatever passage suited the fanciful faculty which had displaced his reason. To a genuine reasoner, or a man of independent common sense, there is a broad distinction between a proof and an illustration; between adducing evidence for a fact, and merely quoting some anecdote or phrase which expresses the opinion of a predecessor. He has beliefs of his own, and applies an independent test to other men's statements. But with Burton the distinction disappears, and we can therefore never quite settle whether he is a pedant

in earnest or in sport, or in a mood strangely composed of the two.

In the eighteenth century Burton fell into the hands of one who, whatever his faults, must be reckoned amongst the very greatest of literary artists. No man had a more acute sense than Sterne of the possibilities of transmuting unpromising material into refined ore. He used Burton in a way which savours, to say the least, of plagiarism. We could at least have wished for some passing allusion to the poor old author whose stores he was using so freely. Had the thief acknowledged his debts in the most cursory way, no one could have objected, even on moral grounds, to the admirable transformation of Burton into the elder Shandy. The extent of Sterne's obligations was revealed in Ferriar's *Illustrations*, but one case will be sufficient to exhibit the nature of the procedure. Burton, in one of his chapters (it is the fifth number of the third section of the second partition, being part of a "consolatory digression containing remedies to all discontents and passions of the mind"), goes through the good old series of reflections upon the death of friends. We know them all, alas! too well, and in new dresses they still do duty on occasions of administering "vacant chaff." "'Tis an inevitable chance," says Burton, "the first statute in Magna Charta, an everlasting Act of Parliament, all must die," and Sterne puts the phrase without alteration into Mr. Shandy's mouth. "Is it not much better not to hunger at all than to eat; not to thirst, than to drink to satisfy thirst; not to be cold, than to put on clothes to drive away cold?" asks Burton, translating from Lucian, and anticipating some modern pessimists; and Sterne appropriates not merely the venerable sophistry, but the words of his author. But the general style of Burton is most happily ridiculed, and the keynote of the sentiment struck in the opening passage:—

> 'Tis either Plato, or Plutarch, or Seneca, or Xenophon, or Epictetus, or Theophrastus, or Lucian, or some one, perhaps, of later date—either Cardan, or Budæus, or Petrarch, or Stella—or possibly it may be some divine or father of the Church, St. Austin, or St. Cyprian, or Bernard, who affirms that it is an irresistible and natural passion to weep for the loss of our friends or children—and Seneca (I'm positive) tells us somewhere that such griefs evacuate themselves best by that particular channel. And accordingly we find that David wept for his son Absalom, Adrian for his Antinous, Niobe for her children, and Apollodorus and Crito shed tears for Socrates before his death.

The passage gives virtually Sterne's criticism of Burton. It shows the point of view from which he had contemplated his victim, poring over the old folio, then a neglected curiosity, and chuckling to himself over curiosities so seldom disturbed as to permit him a sense of personal proprietorship. He just takes a characteristic passage from Burton, accentuates slightly the ludicrous side of his manner, and turns him out as an exquisite portrait of the ideal pedant. The art is inimitable, though possibly in the passage just quoted, Sterne is just a trifle too anxious to show that he is laughing with his reader, and so suggests the question whether Burton did not see the joke himself. My impression would be that, in spite of his elaborate mask of pedantry, Burton was at bottom quite conscious of the comic aspect of his preaching, and would have appreciated *Tristram Shandy* as well as any of its readers. After all, though the Oxford don of those days was nourished on great masses of obsolete scholasticism, there must have been sharp fellows enough in the common rooms, where Burton displayed his "merry and facete" wit, to understand the humour of serving up the tritest commonplaces with this portentous sauce of learned authority. When James was king, even humour loved to masquerade in quaint scholastic forms, and wit to resolve itself into queer logical quibbling.

The whole scheme of the book strikes us, in fact, as a semi-humorous affectation of elaborate system. Burton professes to "anatomise this humour of melancholy," melancholy being a name used with most convenient vagueness. From one point of view it is the general sense for human folly; it includes those who are "metaphorically mad, who are stupid, angry, drunken, sulky, sottish, proud, vain-glorious, ridiculous, beastly, peevish, obstinate, extravagant, dry, doting, dull, desperate, hare-brained," and so forth. More properly, it seems, it is a disease so common "in this crazed age of ours, that scarce one in a thousand is free from it, and that splenetical, hypochondriacal wind especially, which proceeds from the spleen and short ribs." Every age, indeed, seems to have the same pride in claiming a monopoly of hypochondria as was instituted by the excellent Mrs. Pullet in her array of bottles. But also it seems that melancholy may have pretty much its modern significance, as in the charming verses which are supposed to have given a hint to Milton:—

> When I go musing all alone,
> Thinking of diverse things foreknown;
> When I build castles in the air,
> Void of sorrow and void of fear;
> Pleasing myself with phantasms sweet,
> Methinks the time runs very fleet.
>   All my joys to this are folly,
>   Nought so sweet as melancholy.
>
> When I lay waking all alone,
> Recounting what I have ill done;
> My thoughts on me then tyrannise,
> Fear and sorrow me surprise,
> Whether I tarry still or go,
> Methinks the time moves very slow.
>   All my griefs to this are jolly,
>   Nought so bad as melancholy.

Melancholy is here a name for the ambiguous mood in which we hold the lessons of sweet silent thought. But, again, we drop to the most physiological, and, as we should now call it, materialistic view. Melancholy is "black choler," as its name imports; and we are treated to the definitions of the whole series of physicians, the question having been agitated by Galen, Avicenna, Valesius, Montanus, Cappivaccius, Bright, Fiennes, and others, with a variety of results anything but encouraging to the patient. We cannot but sympathise with the excellent Trincavellius, who, being demanded what he thought of a certain melancholy young man, "ingenuously confessed that he was indeed melancholy, but he knew not to what kind to reduce it." Trincavellius, indeed, being consulted on another occasion along with Fallopius and Francanzanus, each of these three famous doctors gave a different opinion—an unprecedented and startling phenomenon!

Undaunted, however, by this want of agreement, or rather encouraged by the boundless field of conjecture which it opened, Burton constructs a vast and systematic scheme of analysis, a network so comprehensive, with its judicious divisions and subdivisions, partitions and members, and sections and subsections, that the fish must indeed be strange which cannot be somewhere entangled in his toils. The causes of melancholy range from the highest of all causes, down through magicians, witches, the stars, old age, sickness, poverty, sorrow, and affright, to special peculiarities of diet, such as the consumption of "dried, soused, indurate fish, as ling, fumados,

red herring, sprats, stock-fish, haberdine, poorjohn, all shell-fish;" and even in detail we are generally left in a painful attitude of doubt. "Mesarius commends salmon, which Bruerimus contradicts," and who is to decide between Mesarius and Bruerimus? The physiology, indeed, which forms so large a part of the book is a very amusing illustration of the chaotic state of medical theory, which gave so many openings for the satirists of the period, and which has so happily been succeeded by perfect unanimity. Johnson was not improbably attracted to the *Anatomy* by the title, which promised to give him some hints in his life-long struggle with disease. If so, he must indeed have been edified. The general tone of the decisions of the physicians of the period is excellently given by the controversy as to hellebore. This drug fell out of its old repute, it appears, owing to the authority of Mesue and some other Arabians; and it is "still oppugned to this day by Crato and some junior physicians." Their reasons are briefly that Aristotle and Alexander Aphrodiseus called it a poison, whilst Constantine the Emperor, in his 'Graponics,' attributes no other virtue to it than to kill mice and rats, flies and mouldwarps." The most prominent argument, however, is that, according to Nicholas Leonicus, Solon, when "besieging I know not what city," poisoned the springs with hellebore, and so weakened the inhabitants that they could not bear arms. Recent writers, however, especially Paracelsus and Matthiolus, have restored the reputation of the injured drug. For so venerable and classical a medicine, it was perhaps natural to go back to the records of Solon's siege of "I know not what city." Indeed, another statement may remind us that, even in the reign of experimental philosophy, the effects of familiar drugs is not always established beyond possibility of dispute. "Tobacco," exclaims Burton, "divine, rare, and superexcellent tobacco, which goes far beyond all panaceas, potable gold and philosopher's stones, a sovereign remedy to all diseases. A good vomit, I confess, a virtuous herb, if it be well qualified, opportunely taken, and medicinally used; but, as it is commonly abused by most men, who take it as tinkers do ale, 'tis a plague, a mischief, a violent purger of goods, lands, health, hellish, devilish, and damned tobacco, the ruin and overthrow of body and soul." The controversy, as many contemporary allusions testify, was as keen at that time as it is at the present day. Bobadil, we may remember, professed to have lived for twenty-one weeks on the fumes of this simple, whilst Justice Overdo entreats all men to avoid "the creeping venom of this subtle serpent."

Burton, to do him justice, does not fail to insinuate a sly hit or two at his physicians, under due shelter of learned names. "Common experience," he points out, shows that those "live freest from all manner of infirmities that make least use of apothecaries' physic;" though apothecaries might possibly argue that he is here inverting cause and effect. But he goes further: "The devil himself was the first inventor of medicine," he argues; "for Apollo invented it, and what was Apollo but the devil?" He points out with more cogent logic the discord of the doctors of his day, and remarks: "This art is wholly conjectural, if it be an art, uncertain, imperfect, and got by killing of men; they are a kind of butchers, leeches, menslayers, chirurgeons and apothecaries especially, that are indeed the physicians' hangmen and common executioners, though, to say truth, the physicians themselves come not far behind, for, according to that facete epigram of Maximilianus Urentius" (which, in Burton's phrase, I here voluntarily pretermit), "what's the difference?" And, though Burton's scepticism is judiciously tempered by a consideration which has restrained many of his fellow-satirists—namely, that when he is ill he will probably want a physician himself—he significantly prefaces his selections from the "infinite variety of medicines which he finds in every pharmacopœia" by the warning that they should be used "very moderately and advisedly," and only when diet will not answer the purpose. The scepticism, indeed, was never pushed to any excess. He was slightly scandalised, he tells us, when he saw his mother apply a spider in a nutshell wrapped in silk for the cure of a sufferer from ague; but, on finding the very same remedy prescribed by Dioscorides, Matthiolus, and Alderovandus, he began to "have a better opinion of it," and decides wisely with Renodæus that such amulets are "not altogether to be rejected."

Burton's collection of the prescriptions of the day is a curious illustration of the time in which the most virtuous and benevolent men went about bleeding fever-struck patients to death, flogging others out of madness, and with equal confidence administering spiders in nutshells—and all from the best possible motives. Yet it is perhaps the least amusing part of the matter forced into an elaborate framework, which, as I have said, is contrived with a view to including the most heterogeneous stores of learning. One could wish that he had not bothered himself with any ostensible method, and had avowedly presented himself as a mere rambler, diverging hither and thither in obedience to any accidental association. Southey's *Doctor*, the last book of any note which may be regarded as in some degree belonging to the same class, is so far more judiciously constructed, though Southey perhaps falls into the contrary error of forcibly contorting the natural flow of his thought into an appearance of more arbitrary digressiveness than really belongs to him. A deliberate resolution to be funny and fanciful is perhaps more annoying than a forced appearance of methodical order. And there is certainly something characteristic in this thoroughgoing affectation which seems to be a part of the very nature of the old pedant. He cannot get rid of his academical costume even when he is disposed for a game of "high jinks." He discusses the philosophy of love-melancholy with all the airs of an anatomical demonstrator, and, if there is just a sly twinkle in his eye, he never permits himself such a smile as would be inconsistent with his views of professorial dignity. He proves with his usual array of imposing authorities that men often fall in love with beautiful women; and reminds us that "Achilles was moved in the midst of a battle by fair Briseis; Ajax by Tecmessa; Judith captivated that great captain Holofernes; Delilah, Samson; Rosamond, Henry the Second; Roxalana, Solyman the Magnificent, &c."; and we dimly wonder whether this comprehensive "&c." could even have included the excellent Burton himself. There is perhaps no class of men which is more apt to pride itself upon a knowledge of the world than the University don of modern times. A Fellow of a college resents the traditional estimate which would make of him a mere smoke-dried bachelor, ignorant, in virtue of his position, of the ordinary play of human passion. But old Burton accepts and prides himself upon his character of learned recluse. He has looked at the world, perhaps, more closely than he allows. He has been further from his common-room than merely to the bridge end to hear the ribaldry of the bargees. But he thinks it necessary to defend himself for discoursing upon love by more than his usual affectation of learned authority. "It is part of my treatise," he says roundly, "and I must and will perform my task," though in a spirit becoming a grave divine. And certainly no fair reader will complain that he has shown undue levity even in this department, where an access of gravity borders most closely upon the ludicrous.

To get a little closer to Burton himself, to catch a glimpse of the real man behind the elaborate mask, we naturally turn to the chapters in which his personal experience is forced to come nearer to the surface. "Democritus junior," the professional laugher at all human folly, might be expected to show his bitterness when he treats of his own craft. Beyond a doubt study is a cause of melancholy, and indeed, as Lavinius Lemmius assures us, the commonest of all causes. The theme should be a fruitful one, and, indeed, we find some touches of genuine feeling. It must be admitted, however, that Burton has a decidedly matter-of-fact and prosaic mode of regarding the subject. The most obvious reason, he tells us, of the melancholy of students is their ill-health. They alone, of all men, as Marsilius Ficinus observes, habitually neglect their tools. A painter washes his brushes, a smith looks to his anvil, a huntsman takes care of his hawks and hounds, and a musician of his lute; but a scholar never thinks of attending properly to his brains. Moreover, Saturn and Mercury, the patrons of learning, are both of them dry planets, so that the brains of their subjects become withered, and the animal spirits, used up for contemplation, do not keep the other organs properly employed. Whence it follows that bald students are commonly troubled with "gouts, catarrhs, rheums, cachexia, bradiopepsia," and a long list of other diseases due to "overmuch sitting," exceeding even those which beset a famous lady at Diss in Norfolk. A modern writer of Burton's meditative turn would despise this physiological cause; he would call his "bradiopepsia" Welt-Schmerz, and elaborate a philosophical pessimism, proving conclusively that a man's disposition to melancholy must be proportioned to the depth of his knowledge of the general system of things. Burton, in his old-fashioned way, considers melancholy to be at bottom a disease, and frequently due to direct Satanic agency; and therefore, though he certainly considers that the Evil One plays a very conspicuous part in human affairs, he cannot properly pride himself upon his melancholy as a proof of intellectual and moral superiority. We must not complain of him for not anticipating a modern discovery.

He speaks, however, feelingly of the folly of intellectual labour. Do not scholars labour like Thebet Benchorat, who spent forty years in finding out the motion of the eighth sphere, till they become "dizzards," and are scoffed at by gallants for not knowing how to manage a hack, salute a gentlewoman, carve at table, and make cringes and congés, "as every common swasher can do?" The greatest scholars are generally fools in all worldly matters, such as Paglarensis, who thought that his farmer must be a cheat for reporting that his sow had eleven pigs and his mare only one foal. This test of the imbecility of scholars was one upon which Hazlitt has dwelt in some vigorous essays, and which has doubtless come home more or less to many an honest senior wrangler, who has discovered that his mathematics did not enable him to tie his neckcloth after the latest model. But the man who could seriously whine over such a distress would be showing a deficiency of self-respect only too much in Hazlitt's vein. If here and there, in this polished age, a scholar is a bit of a clown, it is generally from puerile conceit, and his incapacity for business means only that he has admirers enough ready to do his dirty work. Burton has a much more serious ground for lamentation. Scholars, he says, are generally enforced to "want, poverty, and beggary." He quotes a passage from Virgil (applied by Johnson to precisely the same purpose) enumerating the terrible forms which surround the gates of hell—grief, care, labour, fear, hunger, and poverty—and observes that they are the familiar attendants of the scholar. His best chance was to keep a school, or turn lecturer or curate, for which he might receive "falconer's wages," ten pounds a year and his food, so long as he pleased the parish or his parson; or he might become chaplain in a gentleman's family, marry an old housekeeper or chambermaid, and be settled in a small living—the natural aspiration of a poor clergyman for a century later, according to the satirists and pamphleteers. The scholar, again, might get into a great man's family, and live, at the cost of gross flattery, as a worthless parasite; or, seeing the worthlessness of the higher learning, might take to one of the "bread studies"—and become a lawyer, to struggle against successful pettifoggers—or a physician, to find that in every village there were "so many mountebanks, empirics, quacksalvers, paracelsians," and others, that he could scarcely find a patient. The "grasping patrons," who plunder the Church for their own base purposes, are at the roots of the evil. It is useless to denounce them; they care not so long as they have money. 'Dea Moneta, Queen Money," the almighty dollar, was even then, it seems, the "goddess we adore." We need not wonder then that patrons were a "base, profane, epicurean, hypocritical rout." "So cold is my charity, so defective in this behalf, that I shall never think better of them, than that they are rotten at core, their bones are full of epicurean hypocrisy and atheistical marrow, they are worse than heathens." And then Burton proceeds to lament over the contempt for learning characteristic of his time, and, of course, of his time alone. Gentlemen thought it unworthy of them: merchants might study arithmetic, spectacle-makers optics, and "landleapers" geography—a rich man had no need of such knowledge. In that base utilitarian age men only thought of practical advantages; in "former times"— a very comprehensive period—the highest were scholars themselves, and loved scholars. "Evax, that Arabian prince," was "a most expert jeweller and exquisite philosopher;" Alexander sent Xenophanes fifty talents, because he was poor; and "Archelaus, that Macedonian king, would not willingly sup without Euripides (amongst the rest, he drank to him at supper one night, and gave him a cup of gold for his pains)." Those days are gone; though we still have our Cæsar, commonly called James I., "our amulet, our sun, our sole comfort and refuge; . . . a famous scholar himself, and the sole patron, pillar, and sustainer of learning:" to which, in later editions, it had to be added that James had left a worthy successor. But, after making his reverence to the King's majesty, and to certain rather hypothetical exceptions to the general ignorance of the gentry, Burton returns to his lamentations. Our modern nobles are abandoned to field-sports, gaming, and drinking; they need nothing but some romance, playbook, or pamphlet, and know only a few scraps of French and Italian picked up in a foreign journey. And yet such must be the patrons! and those will thrive who please them best. "If the patron be precise, so must the clerk be; if he be papistical, his clerk must be so too, or be turned out. These"—parasites and time-servers, to wit—"are those clerks which serve the turn, whilst, in the meantime, we, that are University men, like so many hide-bound calves in a pasture, tarry out our time, wither away as a flower ungathered in a garden, and are never used; or as so many candles, illuminate ourselves alone, obscuring one another's light, and are not discerned here at all—the least of which, translated to a dark room, or to some country benefice where it might shine apart, would give a fair light, and be seen over all."

"We that are University men!" It is pleasant to notice the touch of college pride which breaks out in this little reference. The University indeed was not quite immaculate, but Burton judiciously veils his suggestions for its reform in learned language; it was not for one of the "candles" to develop any doubt as to the brilliancy of his associated luminaries. We have the good old don—the genuine believer in the universities as the sole sources of pure light in a feebly appreciative country— who used to flourish till very recent times, and has perhaps not been utterly abolished even by the profane intrusion of reforming commissioners. But it is more curious to remark how easy it would be to rewrite all this lamentation so as to make it an apparent echo of modern jeremiads. When, in speaking of political disorders, Burton illustrates his case by "those goodly provinces in Asia Minor which govern under the burden of a Turkish government; and those vast kingdoms of Muscovia, Russia, under a tyrannizing duke," we fancy that he might have been looking at an article in yesterday's paper; and the complaints to which we have just been listening, require little more alteration. We know how nervous disorders (we do not now call them melancholy) are specially characteristic of the present age; how many of them may be traced to the excessive stimulation of youthful intellects in the period of academical study; how all professions are filled to repletion, and how many years a young man has to wait before he can get a brief or a patient; how little the spirit of genuine research is encouraged, and how, in consequence, young men take to those studies which are likely to bring immediate results in the shape of pounds, shillings, and pence; how ill patronage is distributed, and what a number of excellent clergymen are forced to keep up an excellent appearance on totally inadequate stipends; how, if patrons are no longer so conspicuous in our democratic age, a man is still tempted to seek for preferment by flattering the ignorant prejudices of the many, and prostituting his talents to the base acts of popularity-hunting; and how "in former times" these evils never existed; how people really believed what they said; sold what they professed to sell; revered their rulers; and lived sound, healthy lives, free from hysteria, humbug, and money-worship. In every age the last new prophet of the doctrine of deterioration is convinced of the startling novelty and unimpeachable truth of his teaching. The explanation is probably the obvious one hinted by an old writer, who remarks that, as he grows older, he is constantly inclined to fancy that the world must be getting worse. If not, why should he be less cheerful?

In this chapter Burton speaks more from his own mind, and gives us a stronger dose of pessimism than is his wont. Yet even here he does not quite come up to the modern standard, or, indeed, to that of some of his contemporaries. The evils upon which he dwells are too specific and contingent. He hardly seems to regard the melancholy of the scholar as due to an imperfection in human nature itself, but rather as something which might conceivably be removed by a virtuous prince and a judicious minister. He is thoroughly roused to anger by the baseness of patrons and the general misapplication of church property, but scarcely rises above the tone of a sturdy conservative of the common-room grumbling over the slowness of patronage and the growth of Puritanism. He does not rise to the sphere of thought in which the many political squabblings of the day appear as petty interludes in the vast drama of human history. The melancholy of the scholar does not suggest to him the lofty intellectual melancholy represented, for example, by Faust. Here and there, indeed, we have hints of the futility of all philosophy; celebrated authors have exploded school divinity, we are told, as a "vast ocean of obs and sols—a labyrinth of intricable questions, unprofitable contentions;" but he is scarcely sensible of that weariness of soul which comes over the profounder thinker, awed by the contemplation of the stupendous waste of the noblest human faculties, of the vast energy of intellect that has been dissipated in turning the everlasting metaphysical treadmill. He is more of a Wagner than a Faust. He does not tremble at the comparison between his narrow limits of human life and the illimitable series of problems to be solved, where each new answer only serves to

suggest new and more perplexing questions; nor is he frightened by the many names of men greater and wiser than himself
which are now mere labels to some exploded theory, nor disgusted with the empty verbiage presented to him by the most
pretentious teachers for solid truth; nor tempted to become a
charlatan himself in sheer bitterness of spirit, or to plunge into
sensual pleasure as the only substantial good in losing himself
in the stupendous labyrinths of sophistry and mutual contradiction misnamed philosophy. At a time when the keenest
thinkers were bracing themselves for a fresh departure in inquiry, a man of powerful as well as learned mind might have
given utterance to some such feeling in surveying the huge
wilderness of bygone speculation. Placed between the dead and
the living, a rising and an expiring school of thought, he might
have meditated on the vanity of human wisdom, or have delighted, like Sir Thomas Browne, to reflect, amidst the jarring
din of controversy, upon the mysterious depths in which all
philosophy must so speedily lose itself.

But Burton was really an honest University don, who had
rambled over many fields of learning, but had not really troubled himself to be profound and cynical. He rejoiced in "that
famous library, renewed by Sir Thomas Bodley"—not because
it suggested any reflections, inspiring or humiliating, as to the
past history of the mind—but rather because it suggested a
boundless potentiality of rambling amongst antiquarian curiosities. He was, according to his own account, a thoroughgoing
gossip. He delighted to hear "new news every day," "rumours of
plagues, fires, thefts, murders, inundations, massacres, meteors, comets, spectrums, prodigies, apparitions; of towns taken,
cities besieged, in France, Germany, Turkey, Persia, Poland,
&c.," as much as if he had lived at the present day, and gone to
the Union to read his *Times* and *Telegraph*. He heard of
"plenty, pride, perplexities and cares, simplicity and villany;
subtlety, knavery, candour, and integrity, mutually mixed and
offering themselves;" whilst he rubbed on *privus privatus*—left
to a solitary life and his own private discontents, and sometimes justified by the precedents of Diogenes and Democritus,
walking abroad to make a few observations, sarcastic, humorous, petulant, or indignant. His literary curiosity was pretty
much the counterpart of this kind of interest in the outside
world. It was not that of a philosopher or poet, but of a man
with insatiable appetite for every kind of printed matter, and
with enough pungency of feeling to give an occasional flavour
to his pages, and enable him to sustain fairly the character of
Democritus junior, when he happened to remember it; but yet
sufficient force to digest all his masses of knowledge, and satu-
rate them with a dominant sentiment. He forgets that he is
bound to be a satirist, and contents himself with tumbling out
his stores of queer information without any pretence at illustrating any doctrines, melancholy or consolatory. Especially
in those famous digressions concerning "the nature of devils"
and "of air," he exhibits his curiosities with as grave a face as if
he were displaying the most precious intellectual wares. The
stories which he relates must have tickled his fancy, for some
reason or other; but he leaves us to guess whether he is a
believer or a sceptic, amused or awestruck, or idly curious. We
hear how Cardan's father conjured up seven devils, on August
13, 1491, in Greek apparel, about forty years of age, some
ruddy and some pale, who assured him that they lived about
seven or eight hundred years; how, according to the schoolmen, there are nine kinds of bad spirits, the names of whose
princes are given; though Gregorius Holsanus, who is followed
by Marsilius Ficinus, makes only seven kinds, corresponding
to the seven planets; the angels being placed above and the
devils beneath the moon—an unlucky arrangement, one

would say, for human beings! how the sublunary devils may be
divided into six kinds, including water-nymphs, three of which
appeared to Macbeth and Banquo, "two Scotch lords," and
fairies which "are sometimes seen by old women and children;" whilst Paracelsus "reckons up many places in Germany
where they do usually walk in little coats, some two feet long;"
others, it seems, sat by the wayside to make men's horses stumble, rejoicing heartily if the rider swears; "with many such
pretty feats."

He gives his notes upon geography with just as much
gravity as his remarks upon the natural history of devils. "What
greater pleasure can there be," he asks, "than to view these
elaborate maps of Ortelius, Mercator, &c.?" He is curious about
the variation of the compass, recently discovered by Gilbert, and
wishes to find the source of the Nile, and to see "that great bird
ruck which can carry an elephant," and the Arabian phœnix; he
wants to know the depth of the atmosphere, and to determine
whether the peak of Teneriffe is 50 miles high, as Patricius holds,
or only 9, as Snellius demonstrates; he is curious about the shells
discovered on hill-tops, and the trees in bays, and also about the
ship which was dug out of a mountain near Berne (in the year
1460), with 48 human bodies in it, from a mine fifty fathoms
deep; and then he plunges into questions about the geography of
the infernal regions, Ribeira holding that there is a "natural and
local fire in the centre of the earth 200 Italian miles in diameter;"
whilst Lessius thinks that the diameter can only be one Dutch
mile, because he demonstrates that the space will hold
800,000,000,000 of damned bodies, "which will abundantly
suffice." Then he returns to more accessible questions, and asks
why places under the same latitude are not equally hot; why it
rains stones, frogs, mice, and rats; what is the nature of meteors;
what is the use of the moon; what is the true theory of the earth's
motion, "now so much in question;" and whether the stars are
inhabited. He seems to regard these last questions as insoluble,
laughing at the presumption and hopeless discord of astronomers, and wonders that they are somehow mixed up with the
eternal problem about the origin of evil. "But hoo!" exlaims the
worthy Burton, "I am now gone quite out of sight. I am almost
giddy with roaming about; I could have ranged further yet, but I
am an infant and not able to dive into those profundities and
sound those depths; not able to understand, much less to discuss.
I leave the contemplation of these things to stronger wits, that
have better ability and happier leisure to wade into such philosophical mysteries."

Wandering through this quaint museum we come here
and there upon familiar anecdotes; upon an early form of smart
sayings which have been given to the wits of successive generations; or queer illustrations of ancient forms of speculation.
Reading Burton's anecdote of two palm-trees which languished
till they grew high enough to see one another at a distance, we
may remember the two trees in Heine's familiar poem; and on
the next page we find the story from which Keats took his
Lamia; and not far off is a remark which Coleridge turned into
a well known epigram, pointing out that the devil, when he
robbed Job of all his goods, judiciously omitted to take his wife.
Just below is an anecdote which Thackeray has somewhere
quoted about the amazement of the wild Irish when they saw
the splendours of Henry the Second's court, and their foolish
desire to become English forthwith; "who but English! but
when they had now submitted themselves and lost their former
liberty, they began to rebel some of them, others repent of what
they had done, when it was too late." For one who delights in
literary coincidences, in tracing the forms in which anecdotes
present themselves in various ages, and observing how the old
materials are being constantly refashioned to suit the taste of

the present day, there is an ample hunting ground in Burton's curious miscellany; and we come to have a liking for the old gentleman even though we may admit that for the less curious reader it is better to take advantage of Sterne's spectacles and contemplate Burton as reflected in the elder Shandy.

Notes

1. Shakspeare is noticed at least twice; in a reference to Benedick and Beatrice in the Comedy, and a quotation from *Venus and Adonis*.
2. Busbecq, or Busbequius, was in fact a distinguished diplomatist in the sixteenth century; he went to Constantinople and wrote travels, and, according to the *Biographie Universelle*, was the first to introduce the lilac from Turkey. There is a full article about him in Bayle. Possibly his name has a scholastic flavour to us from a vague association with the famous Dr. Busby.

OLIVER WENDELL HOLMES
From "Pillow-Smoothing Authors"
Atlantic, April 1883, pp. 457–64

In passing a shop where books of every grade of cheapness are exposed I came upon an old edition of Burton's *Anatomy of Melancholy*. I always pity a fine old volume which has fallen into poor company, and sometimes buy it, even if I do not want it, that it may find itself once more among its peers. But in this case I was very glad to obtain a good copy of a good edition of a famous book at a reasonable and not an insulting price; for I remember being ashamed, once, when I picked up some Alduses at the cost of so many obsolete spelling-books. The prize which I carried home with me was a folio in the original binding, with the engraved title and in perfect preservation, the eighth edition, "corrected and augmented by the author," the date 1676. I had never thoroughly read Burton, and I knew enough of the book to think it was worth reading as well as dipping into, as most readers have done. So I took it for my mental night-cap, and read in it for the last quarter or half hour before going to bed, until I had finished it, which slow process took up a year or more, allowing for all interruptions. I made notes of such things as particularly struck me,—brief references, rather, to them,—in pencil, at the end of the volume. It is with these I propose to entertain the reader, using them somewhat as a clergyman uses his text, which furnishes him a pretext that will stretch like an india-rubber band to hold whatever he chooses to have it.

The first edition of the *Anatomy of Melancholy* was published in 1624, the year after the first folio edition of the Plays of Shakespeare, the Poems having been long before the public. Burton quotes a passage from *Venus and Adonis*, referring to its author "Shakespeare" in the margin, and calling him in the text "an elegant poet of our time." I note a certain number of coincidences, which look as if Burton was familiarly acquainted with the Plays. Falstaff "lards the lean earth as he walks along." The scribblers, whom Burton found so numerous even in his day, "lard their lean books with the fat of others' works." John of Gaunt says of himself,—

> My oil-dried lamp and time-bewasted light
> Shall be extinct with age and endless night.

and Burton says of life that it "is in the end dryed up by old age, and extinguished by death for want of matter, as a Lamp for defect of oyl to maintain it." Burton tells the Christopher Sly story from two old authors, but makes no allusion to Shakespeare's use of it.

> Non omnem molitor quæ fluit unda videt.

"The miller sees not all the water that goes by his mill," says Burton.

> What, man! more water glideth by the mill
> Than wots the miller of,

says Demetrius, in *Titus Andronicus*. Burton speaks of "Benedict and Betteris in the Comedy," with the marginal reference "Shakspeare." The name "Betteris" can hardly be a misspelling, but is probably a popular form of the Italian appellative.

Of the more or less curious words used by Burton, the following particularly attracted my attention. I will give them, or some of them, in their connection:—

"Of 15,000 *proletaries* slain in a battel, scarce fifteen are recorded in history, or one alone, the General perhaps."

"A good, honest, painful man many times hath a shrew to his wife, a sickly, dishonest, slothful, foolish, careless woman to his mate, a proud peevish *flurt*," and worse, if possible. The word which a generation ago meant a kind of half courtship between young people, is now applied to the more or less questionable relations of married persons tired of their own firesides.

He speaks of some demons, devils, or genii who as far excel men in worth as a man excels the meanest worm, "though some of them are inferior to those of their own rank in worth as the *black guard* in a Prince's Court."

Speaking of the excesses into which one who is fond of praise is liable to be led by his vanity, he says, after telling how one compares himself to Hercules or Samson, another to Tully or Demosthenes, another to Homer or Virgil,—

> He is mad, mad, mad, no *whoe* with him.

Certain "epicureal tenents" are "most accurately *ventilated* by Jo. Sylvaticus, a late Writer and Physitian of Millan."

On the same page is the well-known passage, "The Turks have a drink called *Coffa* (for they use no wine), so named of a berry as black as soot, and as bitter (like that black drink which was in use among the Lacedæmonians, and perhaps the same), which they still sip of, and sup as warm as they can suffer."

Burton must have been a bachelor, for if he had been a married man he would never have dared talk of women as he did.

"Take heed of your wives' flattering speeches over night, and *curtain sermons* in the morning."

His vocabulary of satire abounds with happy expressions. "*Theologasters*" is credited to him, and what can be more descriptive than his expression "*collapsed ladies*"?

"*Bayards*," gapers, "stupid, ignorant, blind" creatures, "*dummerers*," impostors feigning dumbness, "Abraham men" pretending blindness, are no longer heard of; but when we hear that Jodocus Damhoderius "hath some notable examples of such counterfeit *Cranks*," we find that a word only recently come into common use is an old one recalled from the rich phraseology of the Elizabethan period. Burton recommends "*cowcumbers*" to such as are of too ardent a temperament. Tobacco he spells as we do, but speaks of it in a way that reminds us at once of Charles Lamb's often-quoted Farewell to the great vegetable, which it probably suggested:—

"*Tobacco*, divine, rare, superexcellent *Tobacco*, which goes far beyond all their panaceas, potable gold and Philosophers stones, a soveraign remedy to all diseases. A vertuous herb, if it be well qualified, opportunely taken, and medicinally used, but as it is commonly abused by most men, which take it as Tinkers do Ale, 't is a plague, a mischief, a violent purger of goods, land, health, hellish, devilish and damned *Tobacco*, the ruine and overthrow of body and soul."

Burton makes great fun of the foolish old questions of the schoolmen and pedants, such as "*ovum prius extiterit an gallina*,"—whether the egg or the hen came first into being. He is a good Protestant, and very bitter at times against the "Papists," but I cannot help suspecting his own orthodoxy. One is reminded of the more recent "Genesis and Geology" battles in reading such sentences as this: "But to avoid these Paradoxes of the earth's motion (which the Church of *Rome* hath lately condemned as heretical) our latter mathematicians have rolled all the stones that may be stirred: and to solve all appearances and objections, have invented new hypotheses and fabricated new systems of the World, out of their own Dedalean heads;" or, as we should say, projected them out of their own inner consciousness. You may find here the mill of conscience that grinds the souls of sinners, as expressed by "those *Ægyptians* in their *Hieroglyphics*," and the saying "*quod ideo credendum quod incredibile*",—it is to be believed because it is incredible,—from Tertullian. One is surprised in reading this book, more than any other that I am acquainted with, to find how much of the new corn comes out of the old fields. The quarrel between science and that which calls itself religion was the same, essentially, in the days of Burton and those older authors whom he quotes that it is now.

"Others freely speak, mutter and would persuade the world (as *Marinus Marcenus* complains) that our modern Divines are too severe and rigid against Mathematicians; ignorant and peevish in not admitting their true demonstrations and certain observations, that they tyrannize over art, science, and all philosophy in suppressing their labors (saith *Pomponatius*), forbidding them to write, to speak a truth, all to maintain their superstition, and for their profits sake. As for those places of Scripture which oppugn it, they will have spoken *ad captum vulgi*, and if rightly understood, and favorably interpreted, not at all against it." We find the same old difficulties, and the same subterfuges to escape from them that we have seen and still see in our own day. Doctrines which we have always thought of as belonging to our own theology are traced to other and remote sources. Plato learned in Egypt that the devils quarrelled with Jupiter, and were driven by him down to hell. Others of our generally accepted beliefs he claims as of heathen parentage. "Twas for a politique end, and to this purpose the old Poets feigned those *Elysian* fields, their *Æacus*, *Minos*, and *Rhadamantus*, their infernal judges, and those *Stygian* lakes, fiery *Phlegeton's*, *Pluto's* Kingdom, and variety of torments after death. Those that had done well went to the *Elysian* fields, but evil doers to *Cocytus* and to that burning lake of Hell with fire and brimstone forever to be tormented."

"Old Probabilities" was anticipated by Lucian's Jupiter, who, as Burton says, spent much of the year, among other occupations, in "telling the hours when it should rain, how much snow should fall in such a place, which way the wind should stand in Greece, which way in Africk."

Never was there such a pawn-shop for poets to borrow from as the *Anatomy of Melancholy*. Byron knew this well, and tells the world as much. His own

> Mountains interposed
> Make enemies of nations who had else,
> Like kindred drops, been mingled into one,

may have been suggested by the *fluvio vel monte distincti sunt dissimiles*, which Burton gives without assigning its authorship. Herrick's beautiful

> Gather ye rose buds while ye may,
> Old Time is still a-flying,

finds its original more nearly in the lines Burton quotes from Ausonius than in the verse from the Wisdom of Solomon, from which it has been thought to have been borrowed:—

> Collige virgo rosas dum flos novus et nova pubes
> Et memor esto ævum sic properare tuum.

"Where God hath a Temple the Devil will have a Chappel," familiarly known in the couplet of Defoe, and referred by Mr. Bartlett to the *Jacula Prudentum*, is found here also.

> Qui jacet in terra non habet unde cadat,

says Burton.

> He that is down needs fear no fall,

says Bunyan.

> He that is down can fall no lower,

says Butler, in *Hudibras*.

"To be prepared for war is one of the most effectual means of preserving peace." So spoke George Washington.

"The Commonwealth of Venice in their Armory have this inscription, Happy is that City which in time of peace thinks of war. *Felix civitas quæ tempore pacis de bello cogitat.*" So says Burton.

> Qui desiderat pacem præparet bellum

is referred, in *Familiar Quotations*, to Vegetius, a Roman writer on military affairs, of the fourth century.

I read Mr. Emerson's complaint, in his first Phi Beta Kappa oration, that "the state of society is one in which the members have suffered amputation from the trunk, and strut about so many walking monsters,—a good finger, a neck, a stomach, an elbow, but never a man." Compare this with Burton's passage from Scaliger: "*Nequaquam nos homines sumus, sed partes hominis, ex omnibus aliquid fieri potest, idque non magnum; ex singulis fere nihil.*"

We have been in the habit of thinking that "liquor or fight" was a form of courtesy peculiar to our Western civilization. But we may learn from Burton that our German ancestors were before us in this social custom: "*How they love a man that will be drunk, crown him and honour him for it*, hate him that will not pledge him, stab him, kill him: A most intolerable offence, and not to be forgiven. *He is a mortal enemy that will not drink with him*, as *Munster* relates of the *Saxons*." We all remember Byron's writing under the inspiration of gin. His familiarity with Burton may have supplied him with the suggestion, for Burton tells us that "our Poets drink sack to improve their inventions." We are surprised, in reading the old author, to come upon ideas and practices which we thought belonged especially to our own time:—

"Such occult notes, Stenography, Polygraphy, *Nuncius animatus*, or *magnetical telling of their minds*, which Cabeus the Jesuit, by the way, counts fabulous and false."

If Burton had not been an irreclaimable bachelor, he would never have dared to make an onslaught like the following upon the female sex:—

"To this intent they *crush in their feet and bodies*, hurt and crucifie themselves, sometimes in lax clothes, one hundred yards I think in a gown, a sleeve, and sometimes again so close, *ut nudos exprimant artus*. Now long tails and trains, and then short, up, down, high, low, thick, thin, etc. Now little or no bands, then as big as cart-wheels; now loose bodies, then great fardingals and close girt," etc.

The trailing dresses which delicate ladies wore but a very few years ago, through our slovenly streets, were always an object of aversion to men, and seriously lowered the sex in their eyes. Nobody, however, seems to have taken the offense so much to heart as Sir David Lyndsay,—the old Scotch minstrel whom Sir Walter Scott speaks of as

> Sir David Lyndsay of the mount,
> Lord Lyon king at arms.

Before the disagreeable fashion threatens us again, let us hope that our ladies will read the old poet's "Supplication in Contemption of *Side Tails*;" for this is the name he gave to the

bedraggled finery with which showy women swept the sidewalks in his day, as they have done in ours,—*side* tails meaning
only *long* dresses,

> Whilk through the dust and dubs trails
> Three quarters lang behind their heels—
> Wherever they go it may be seen
> How kirk and causay they soop clean—
> In summer when the streets dries
> They raise the dust aboon the skies;
> Nane may gae near them at their ease
> Without they cover mouth and neese.

Sir David uses some harder words than these about the
garments

> Whilk over the mires and middings trails,

and ends with a couplet doubtless very severe, but which fortunately few of us can interpret:—

> Quoth Lindsay in contempt of the side tails
> That duddrons and duntibours through the dubs
> trails.

One can never be sure, in reading Burton, that he will not
find his own thoughts, his own sayings in prose or verse,
anticipated.

"So that affliction is a School or Academy, wherein the
best Scholars are prepared to the commencements of the
deity."

> Till dawns the great commencement day on every
> land and sea
> And *expectantur* all mankind to take their last
> degree.

It was a coincidence, and not a borrowing, for I had never read
Burton when I wrote those lines. I do not believe there is any
living author who will not find that he is represented in his
predecessors, if he will hunt for himself in Burton. Even the
external conditions of the residence of myself and my immediate neighbors are described as if he had just left us; for the
dwellers in this range of houses on one side "see the ships,
boats and passengers go by, out of their windows," and on the
other look out into a "thoroughfare street to behold a continual
concourse, a promiscuous rout, coming and going,"—which
conditions he considered as "excellent good" for the infirmity
of which he was treating, or professing to treat, while he discoursed about everything.

What a passion many now famous in other pursuits have
had for poetry, and what longings for the power to express
themselves in harmonious numbers! Blackstone and Murray,
John Quincy Adams and Joseph Story, at once occur to our
memory. It was said that at one time every member of the
existing British cabinet had published his volume of verse.
Every one remembers the story of Wolfe and Gray's *Elegy*. But
I confess I was a little surprised to find a famous old scholar
bewitched to such an extent as Burton represents him: "*Julius
Scaliger* was so much affected with Poetry that he brake out
into a pathetical protestation, he had rather be the author of
twelve Verses in *Lucan* or such an Ode in *Horace* (Lib. 3, Ode
9) than Emperour of *Germany*." A charming little quarrel it is
between Horace and Lydia, but one would hardly have expected such a juvenile outburst from a gray-beard old scholiast
like Julius Cæsar Scaliger.

From page to page we get striking and life-like portraits of
notable men of olden time. Here is a charming one of a great
Dutch scholar and critic:—

"*Heinsius*, the keeper of the Library at *Leiden* in *Holland*,
was mewed up in it all the year long; and that which to thy

thinking should have bred a loathing, caused in him a greater
liking.

"'*I no sooner* (saith he) *come into the Library, but I bolt the
door to me, excluding lust, ambition, avarice, and all such
vices, whose nurse is idleness, their mother Ignorance, and Melancholy herself, and in the very lap of eternity, amongst so many
divine souls, I take my seat, with so lofty a spirit and sweet
content, that I pity all our great ones, and rich men that know
not this happiness.*'"

And take as a background to this delightful picture the
dreadful glimpse which this brief passage gives us: "*Servetus*
the heretick that suffered in *Geneva*, when he was brought to the
stake, and saw the executioner come with fire in his hand,
*homo viso igne tam horrendum exclamavit, ut universum popu-
lum perterre facerit*, roared so loud that he terrified the
people."

We are often surprised at finding there are good reasons
for practices which seem to us quite singular, and even absurd.
I remember the first time I wandered in the streets of an old
European city,—Rouen,—I felt as if I was at the bottom of a
deep crevice, looking up at a narrow ribbon of blue sky. I read
in Burton, "In hot Countreys they make the streets of their
Cities very narrow. *Monpelier*, the habitation and University of
Physitians, is so built, with high houses, narrow streets to divert
the suns scalding rayes, which *Tacitus* commends," etc.

There is but one street at the West End of our City,
Boston,—the new part of it,—which one can walk through in
the middle of a hot summer day without danger of a sun-stroke:
that is Boylston Street. The front yards of all the others are so
wide that the sidewalks are in full sunshine, while this is a
shady refuge for the unfortunate prisoner *intra muros*.

I once amused myself with calculating how many grains
of sand there would be in our earth if it was made of them. It
was only necessary to see how many grains it took to make a
line of an inch in length, and this number, if I recollect, was
about a hundred, which gives a million to the cubic inch, and
so on; and although one might miss a few grains in calculating
the number of cubic feet in the oblate spheroid upon which we
dwell, it was easy to come near enough for all practical purposes. But Burton reminds me that I was only doing what
Archimedes had done before me.

He is severely satirical in speaking of the corrupt practices
and the quarrels of doctors. He accuses them of taking all
manner of advantage of their privileged intimacy. "*Paracelsus
did that in Physick which Luther did in Divinity.*" "*A drunken
rogue he was, a base fellow, a Magician, he had the Devil for his
master, Devils his familiar companions, and what he did, was
done by the help of the Devil.*" "Thus they contend and rail,
and every Mart [*sic*] write Books *pro* and *con* and *adhuc sub
judice lis est*; let them agree as they will, I proceed."

Not less sharp is he in commenting upon the practices of
another profession: "Now as for Monks, Confessors and
Friers—under colour of visitation, auricular confession, comfort and penance, they have free egress and regress, and corrupt
God knows how many."

"Mutual admiration" alliances are not the invention of
this century, for Burton speaks of "mutual offices," "praise and
dispraise of each other," "*mulus mulum scabit*," one mule
scratches another. In that very amusing book, which has much
in it that sounds like Dickens, with a great deal that is its own,
the Reverend Jonathan Jubb is busy writing the *Life and Times
of Rummins*, while Rummins is equally busy writing the *Life
and Times of the Reverend Jonathan Jubb*.

I have said that Burton must have been a bachelor, and so
he must have been; and the gentle sex will exclaim that he was

a hard-hearted old wretch, too, for he says, "As much pity is to be taken of a woman weeping as of Goose going barefoot."

Perhaps some wives with irritable husbands may like to hear the advice contained in his story of the honest woman "who, hearing one of her gossips by chance complain of her husband's impatience, told her an excellent remedy for it, and gave her withal a glass of water, which when he brauled she should hold still in her mouth, and that *toties quoties*, as often as he chid." This had such a good effect that the woman wished to know what she had mingled in her prescription, when her adviser "told her in brief what it was, *Fair Water* and no more: for it was not the water but her silence which performed the cure. Let every froward woman imitate this example, and be quiet within doors," and so on, giving his advice to the poor scolded woman as if she was to blame, and not the *brauling* husband! I am afraid the Cochituate will not be largely drawn upon by our matrons whose lords take their constitutional exercise in finding fault with their ladies.

I cannot be answerable for Burton's advice to women, but he gives some most sensible and kindly counsel to those who are abused by others, the substance of which is, Keep your temper and hold your tongue, but illustrated, amplified, made palpable and interesting by the large drapery of quotations in which it is robed, according to his habitual way of expanding and glorifying a maxim. "*Deesse robur arguit dicacitas*," or, as Dr. Johnson might have translated it, Verbosity indicates imbecility. Burton quotes the Latin phrase, and then pours out a flood of words to illustrate it.

That great modern naturalist, so well remembered, and so dear to many of us, used to remind me of the ancient observer and philosopher whom he admired, and in many points resembled.

"How much did *Aristotle* and Ptolomy spend? *Unius regni precium*, they say, more than a king's ransom; how many crowns *per annum*, to perfect arts, the one about his History of Creatures, the other on his *Almagest*." These are the words of Burton.

"How much," I once said to Agassiz, "would you really want for your Museum, if you could get it?"

"Ten millions!" was his immediate, robust, magnificent answer. "Ah!" I thought to myself, "what a pity there is not an Alexander for this Aristotle!" My wish came nearer fulfilment in after years than I could have dreamed at that time of its ever coming.

Even the puns and quibbles we have thought our own we are startled to find in these pages of Burton, which take, not the bread out of our mouths, perhaps, but at least the Attic salt which was the seasoning of our discourse. When we find him asking "What's matrimony but a matter of money?" we cannot help feeling that more jesting glideth through the lips than wots Joe Miller of, or even my good friend Mr. Punch, whom I have never thanked as I ought to have done for the pretty compliment he paid me some time ago.

And now let any somnolent reader who has tried on my night-cap wake himself up, and take down excellent Mr. Allibone's great Dictionary of Authors and turn to *Burton*. He will find what a high estimate was placed upon the work I have been getting my scant *spicilegium* out of for his entertainment. It was greatly esteemed by Johnson, by Sterne, who showed his regard by helping himself to his pleasantry and pathos, and by various other less generally known writers. Byron says that if the reader has patience to go through the *Anatomy of Melancholy* "he will be more improved for literary conversation than by the perusal of any twenty other works with which I am acquainted."

I did not read it to equip myself for "literary conversation," but to predispose myself to somnolence; and if, as I hope, this article shall prove as effective in bringing about that result for the reader as the book was for myself, it will have fully answered my tamest expectations.

EDWARD W. ADAMS
"Robert Burton and *The Anatomy of Melancholy*"
Gentleman's Magazine, July 1896, pp. 46–53

What De Quincey said of Charles Lamb might with even greater force be applied to Burton, viz. that he "ranks amongst writers whose works are destined to be for ever unpopular, and yet for ever interesting; interesting, moreover, by means of those very qualities which guarantee their non-popularity."

The qualities which militate against our author's popularity are: firstly, the inordinate length of his work; secondly, his habit of interpolating thousands of quotations from the classical authors at every conceivable and inconceivable opportunity; while a third disadvantage under which Burton labours is his fantastic discontinuity of thought. He has no hesitation whatever in branching out into long and irrelevant digressions at the smallest provocation; and although he makes a great show of treating his subject methodically and systematically with all his parade of "Partitions," "Sections," "Members," "Subsections," &c., yet a more veritable literary fantasia it would not be easy to find. With regard to his predilection for quotation, it seems as though the man were perpetually on the look-out for openings to utilise his classic lore. The consequence is that about half his work is practically written in a foreign language, and one feels sure that Sir Thomas Browne must have had his eye upon Burton when he complains in the introduction to *Vulgar Errors* that we shall soon have to learn Latin in order to understand English if certain writers persisted in their course! These extracts, dotted about on every page and almost in every line, give a hybrid look to the whole work, and make up an appearance which has been facetiously described as "literary small-pox." All these characteristics taken together make the perusal of the *Anatomy of Melancholy* a labour not to be lightly undertaken. Life is short, but Burton's *Anatomy of Melancholy* is very long. We are of opinion that (as Macaulay once said of the *Faerie Queene*) no one with a heart less stout than that of a commentator would ever get to the last page. Yet it is on account of these very qualities—the quaintness, the store of appropriate and apt quotation, the original unoriginality of the work, the unexpected and altogether delightful digressions, the strange excesses into which the writer allows himself to be led—it is on account of all these that the perusal of the *Anatomy* becomes if indeed a labour yet a most pleasant and diverting one.

The work at the time of its appearance proved so successful that eight editions were exhausted in a very short time, and, as Wood tells us, it proved so remunerative to the bookseller that he "got an estate by it." We are not, however, informed whether the venture was equally profitable to the author. A significant silence is preserved upon this point. But then we must remember that in those days Sir Walter Besant and the Society of Authors were not. Even now lovers of the little-read grand old authors—the Brownes, Burtons, Fullers, &c., those musty "old folios" beloved of Coleridge—find recreation and delight in the magnificent "cento" of "Democritus Junior." Charles Lamb never wrote a sentence which I should feel more inclined to endorse than this: "You cannot make a *pet* book of an author whom everybody reads." Sir Thomas Browne and Robert Burton fill the *rôle* par excellence of "pet authors." For one reason, they are but little read; for another, they reveal themselves so frankly and ingenuously to their reader, they lay bare before him their greatnesses and their weaknesses, their sublimities and their trivialities; no reserve is maintained between them and their audience—they give rein equally to their whims and caprices as to their sublimest thoughts and speculations. What Montaigne said of his *Essais* they might have said of their pieces: "I am my *Religio Medici*," or "I am my *Anatomy of Melancholy*."

It is to be expected that so rich a mine of quotation as is the work we are discussing would not be left unworked by writers desiring a cheap reputation for wide reading and erudition. Consequently we find that Burton's volume has been unmercifully rifled of its riches both borrowed and original. His biographer, Wood, points out one Will Greenwood as a notorious offender in this respect; and to mention a better known name, readers of Sterne's *Tristram Shandy* will not have failed to notice many tricks and turns of expression as well as whole sentences which have been copied from the *Anatomy*. Ludicrously enough one finds, on comparing the two volumes, that the very passage in which Sterne complains: "Shall we for ever make new books, as apothecaries make new mixtures, by pouring out of one vessel into another?" has been stolen from Burton. It is very comical to hear one plagiarist rebuking a fellow offender with a sentence which he has himself appropriated from another work! In one place Laurence Sterne facetiously declares: "I believe, in my conscience, I intercept many a thought which heaven intended for another man!" He only forgot to add, that when unable to intercept these thoughts in their passage, he hesitated not to remedy the failure by appropriation at a later stage.

But here it is necessary, as an introduction to a brief analysis of his work, to give a short sketch of Burton's career.

On the 8th day of February in the year 1576 at Lindley, in Leicestershire, Robert Burton made his acquaintance with what Mr. Shandy has been pleased to term "this scurvy and disastrous world of ours." His parents, according to Anthony à Wood, belonged to an ancient and "gentile" family of the county. Young Democritus received his early education at the Free School of Sutton Coldfield and at Nuneaton, which latter also abounds in memories of George Eliot. His school life appears to have passed in uneventful monotony, which was, however, frequently (but not altogether pleasantly) broken by periodical stimulations of his "muscular integument," administered by preceptors who, like those of Herr Diogenes Teufelsdröckh, held the view that the faculties of the human soul could only be thus reached, which castigations, however, the unfortunate victim seems to have relished as little as did the famous author of the Philosophy of Clothes. The foundations of his knowledge having been thus soundly laid in the above highly orthodox manner, he was, in 1593, entered as a commoner at Brasenose College, Oxford, at the time of the Long Vacation. He here made considerable progress in mathematics, classics, and divinity, and in due time graduated as "Batchellor of Divinity." He seems to have been a great favourite among his college contemporaries, his company being, we are told, "very merry, facete, and juvenile, and no man in his time did surpass him for his ready and dextrous interlarding his common discourses with verses from the poets and classical authors," a practice, however, which must have made his society very objectionable to an ordinary person. But the Universities being at that period mainly made up of a set of pedants, among whom the flash and glitter of learning were more valued than

sound scholarship, he acquired no little reputation. This habit of indiscriminate quotation thus early indulged in became with him a second nature, and constitutes at once the charm and the drawback of his literary efforts. In 1599 he was elected student of Christ Church, and for form's sake, though we read "he wanted not a tutor," he was placed under the tuition of a Dr. John Bancroft. Notwithstanding his apparently humorous and jovial disposition, he was subject from an early period of his life to profound fits of depression and melancholy, which grew with his growth until, in the hope of obtaining relief, he set about the composition of that work which has made him famous. His object was not, however, attained; and we find that his self-imposed task was but the means of increasing his malady, until we learn from Grainger that nothing could make him laugh "but going to a bridge and hearing the ribaldry of the bargemen, which rarely failed to throw him into a violent fit of laughter." In 1614 he was admitted to the reading of the sentences, and two years later was presented with the vicarage of St. Thomas, in the west suburb of Oxon, by the Dean and Canons of Christ Church. Some years afterwards he also received the rectory of Segrave, in Leicestershire, at the hands of George, Lord Berkeley. His ecclesiastical affairs, however, do not appear to have gone very smoothly with him, he being unfortunate (as we gather from his work) in some of his patrons, who seem to have had a very clear perception of the evils of riches, and determined that Robert should not be tempted to stray from the "funambulatory track and narrow path of goodness" (as Sir T. Browne would call it) on that account, thus conserving at one and the same time both *their* pockets and *his* morals.

In 1624 appeared the first edition, in quarto, of the *Anatomy of Melancholy*, which was so well received that six editions were required in the author's lifetime.

The remaining years of Burton's life were spent by him in preparing successive editions of his volume, and in indiscriminate and voracious devouring the books in the Bodleian Library. He died in his chambers at Christ Church, Oxford, in 1639, it is said, at or very near the time he had foretold from a calculation of his own nativity—for Burton added the study of astrology to his other labours. As in the case of Jerome Cardan, narrated by Bayle, there were not wanting those who hinted that, rather than his prediction should prove false, he took the only way open to him to make sure that it would be fulfilled. But no doubt this was a cruel calumny. It may indeed have been that his melancholy overstepped the limit that separated it from madness, and being thus bereft of the restraining force of reason, he took his own life. If so, the touching words with which he closes his section on Suicides receive a new and pathetic interest, and an almost prophetic significance, but no one who has perused these paragraphs could doubt for a moment but that he would not wilfully cut short his existence for the sake of the poor beggarly distinction of having proved a true prophet of his own end.

Thus died Robert Burton in the sixty-third year of his age, leaving behind him as his monument that work concerning which a few words will now be said.

Although it would be a waste of ingenuity to criticise seriously as a scientific treatise on the subject of melancholy such a literary extravaganza as is presented to us under the name of "Democritus Junior,"[1] yet having, as Hallam expresses it, "a style not by any means devoid of point and terseness, and writing with much good sense and observation of men as well as books, and having the skill of choosing his quotations from their rareness, oddity, and amusing character, without losing sight of their pertinence to the subject," he has produced a work which might well be termed a "vast storehouse of entertainment and singular learning." The book is divided into three parts, and is preceded by a long introduction, which is a powerful satire. In this portion he indulges in that favourite dream of social reformers, an ideal commonwealth. But it must be admitted that Burton's sketch of an ideal community is remarkably free from the wild impracticable fancies which are generally characteristic of these attempts to remodel society. He displays a most rare faculty for taking things as they are, and making the best of them, and a willingness to accept the present state of affairs as a basis from which to evolve a scheme of government as nearly perfect as may be. Like Solon, he frames his laws not to suit a perfect, although entirely visionary Golden Age, but with a view to meeting the existing temper of the community as he understands it. Certainly Burton would not have been included in Francis Bacon's humorous stricture: "As for the philosophers, they make imaginary laws for imaginary commonwealths, and their discourses are as the stars which give little light because they are so high."

Coming to the treatise proper, the first part treats of the Causes, Symptoms, and Prognostics of Melancholy; the second part of the Cure of Melancholy; and the third part is reserved for a special discussion of Love and Religious Melancholies.

Melancholy, according to Burton, has an objective existence, and may be composed of a material or an immaterial essence, or it may be a compound of both. In the two former cases the melancholy is simple, but in the latter it is compound. Material melancholy is one of the humours of the body, such as blood, pituita, serum, &c. The causes of this disease he fetches from the heavens above, the earth beneath, and the waters under the earth. And this statement is literally true. Probably no one ever had so fine and rare a collection of causes as Burton. In gathering them in he displays all the eagerness and enthusiasm of the collector, but none of the judicial balancing and weighing of the scientist. Among the causes we find mentioned: the Planets, Stars, the Devil, Witches, Magicians, Parents, Anger, Love, and Old Age, which is a cause for the reason that it is "cold and dry, and of the same quality as Melancholy." Another cause, which he cites out of Montaltus, is this: "The efficient cause of Melancholy is a hot and dry, not a cold and dry distemperature, as some hold, from the heat of the grain roasting the blood."

A propos of causes, we may as well give what he sets down as the cause of laughter. "laughter proceeds from an abundance of pleasant vapours which, proceeding from the heart, tickle the midriff, because it is transverse and full of nerves, by which titillation the sense being moved, and the arteries distended or pulled, the spirits from thence move, and possess the sides, veins, countenance, and eyes." Tears, the reader may be interested to know, proceed from "the heating of a moist brain."

But now let us see how he proposes to cure this distressing malady of melancholy. Now, if his collection of *causes* was extraordinary, what shall we say of that of his *cures*? Here are some of them: "Cauteries and hot irons," he says, "are to be used in the suture of the crown, and the seared or ulcerated place suffered to run a good while. 'Tis *not amiss* to bore the skull with an instrument to let out the fuliginous vapours." His patient, however, might perhaps think otherwise. This is a cure for head melancholy. Here is another even more barbarous: "Sallus. Salvianus . . . because this humour hardly yields to other physic, would have the leg cauterised—on the left leg, below the knee—and the head bored in two or three places." His reader is inclined to think that even if this malady did not yield readily to physic, there was no need to take so savage a revenge on the patient. He then goes on with inimitable *sang*

froid to relate (as an incentive to this desperate remedy, "how a melancholy man at Rome, that by no remedies could be healed, when by chance was wounded in the head, and his skull broken, he was *excellently cured*." And again: "Another, to the admiration of the beholders, 'breaking his head with a fall from on high, was instantly cured of his dotage.'" To those afflicted with love melancholy, he tells of a high rock in Greece, whence, if lovers precipitated themselves, they would be completely cured of their affliction. No doubt such a cure would be very complete and permanent, and we should think that the patient would be very unlikely to have any relapses after such treatment. It is reassuring to be able to state, however, that there is no evidence to show that Burton ever practically carried out his treatment either on himself or on others, unless, indeed, we like to infer that the strange reports which circulated as to the manner of his death were garbled accounts of the results of one of these operations, which our author had attempted to perform on himself in the hope of a cure.

A peculiarity about Burton's cures is that each individual remedy is more sure, more certain, and more valuable than any which come before or after. This or that remedy alone will most certainly cure where all others fail; it alone of itself will suffice, needing no combination with any other; its effect is marvellous—and so on. The fact is, that when our author once gets fairly launched on the sea of vigorous rhetoric, he gets carried away by his own eloquent fervour, and says a good deal more than he means, or would feel inclined in calmer moments to endorse. He throws himself with all his impetuous and eccentric energy into the topic upon which at the moment he happens to be discoursing, and in his own peculiar fashion thoroughly exhausts it; and not sufficiently considering the relation which that particular division of his subject upon which he is for the time engaged will bear to some other division, when it behoves him to treat of that portion he has practically to unsay much that he has said. One may be sure that if he throws his influence into one scale of the balance the opposite one will kick the beam. And this criticism applies to Burton's treatment of many other matters besides the cure for melancholy.

Owing to Burton's habit of tumbling out pell-mell the results of his researches among the erudite authors, one theory or rule of practice being piled upon another, with which it harmonises about as well as oil with water, the task of extracting any practical or useful advice from his volume would destroy a strong man. Yet, whenever this curious man chooses to write from his own knowledge and observation, there is, as Johnson remarks, no little force in what he says, which makes one the more regret that he was so fond of using his Commonplace Book. His graphic and picturesque description of the varying states of feeling in a melancholy man is a case in point, and must have evidently been written from his own experience. And notwithstanding the absurdity and inapplicability of much of his counsel, which naturally results from the importation into his book of a vast mass of crude, undigested, and often conflicting material, yet whenever he has been bold enough to stand on his own legs, and give us something of his own, he displays no small amount of shrewdness and good sense.

But it is in his consolatory chapters that Burton's true worth shines forth, and compels our admiration. He is here no longer the disappointed, churlish cynic, nor does he in these pages, as he often seems to do elsewhere, exhibit a longing, Paracelsus-like,[2] to save mankind, while he yet tramples on it, but, throwing off his ill-fitting disguise, shows himself the good honest fellow he really is—a comforter of the distressed, a sympathiser with the afflicted, a compassionate friend, a true, staunch champion of the oppressed and sorrowful. And here I will leave the consideration of his work with the conviction that, notwithstanding its many faults, oddities, and extravagancies, yet its peculiar literary merits, and the genuine sympathy for the unfortunate therein disclosed, will ever secure for it a place among those works which will last as long as the English language shall endure.

Notes

1. The *nom de plume* assumed by Burton on the title-page of his book.
2. *See* Browning's *Paracelsus*.

GAMALIEL BRADFORD, JR.
From "An Odd Sort of Popular Book"
Atlantic, April 1904, pp. 548–54

Multiplicity of editions does not make a book a classic. Otherwise Worcester's Dictionary and Mrs. Lincoln's Cook-Book might almost rival Shakespeare. Nevertheless, when a work which has little but its literary quality to recommend it achieves sudden and permanent popularity, it is safe to assume that there is something about it which will repay curious consideration. As to the popularity of *The Anatomy of Melancholy* there can be no dispute. "Scarce any book of philology in our land hath, in so short a time, passed through so many editions," says old Fuller; though why "philology"? The first of these editions appeared in 1621. It was followed by four others during the few years preceding the author's death in 1640. Three more editions were published at different times in the seventeenth century. The eighteenth century was apparently contented to read Burton in the folios; but the book was reprinted in the year 1800, and since then it has been issued in various forms at least as many as forty times, though never as yet with what might be called thorough editing.

Quantity of approval is in this case well supported by quality. Milton showed his admiration, as usual, by imitation. Sterne conveyed passage after passage almost bodily into *Tristram Shandy*. Southey's odd book, *The Doctor*, follows Burton closely in manner and often in matter. Dr. Johnson said that *The Anatomy of Melancholy* was the only book that ever took him out of bed two hours sooner than he wished to rise; large commendation surely, and I have never found any other, even of the most devout Burtonians, quite ready to echo it. Lamb was a reader, adorer, and imitator; Keats, the first two, at any rate. Finally, Mr. Saintsbury assures us that "for reading either continuous or desultory, either grave or gay, at all times of life and in all moods of temper, there are few authors who stand the test of practice so well as the author of *The Anatomy of Melancholy*." For all that, I would not advise the general reader to buy a copy in too great haste. He will, perhaps, find it easier to read about the book than to read it. . . .

Far more than most great writers . . . Burton left the reflection of his life and character in his work, and *The Anatomy of Melancholy* may be called one of the most intensely personal books that were ever written. To be sure, the author does not constantly and directly refer to himself and his own affairs. Nevertheless, the impress of his spirit is felt on every page.

Several of the biographical facts above mentioned are derived from casual remarks dropped here and there throughout the book. Of his mother, Mistress Dorothy Burton, he says that she had "excellent skill in chirurgery, sore eyes, aches, etc.," and that she had "done many famous and good cures upon diverse poor folks that were otherwise destitute of help." He gives us a reminiscence of his boyhood: "They think no slavery in the world (as once I did myself) like to that of a grammar scholar." He speaks with a grain of bitterness of a younger brother's lot: "I do much respect and honor true gentry and nobility; I was born of worshipful parents myself, in an ancient family; but I am a younger brother, it concerns me not."

He gives us many glimpses of his lonely scholar's life. In his youth he was ambitious: "I was once so mad to bussell abroad and seek about for preferment, tyre myself, and trouble all my friends." But the world is cold, friendship formal and touches not the heart: "I have had some such noble friends, acquaintance, and scholars, but most part they and I parted as we met; they gave me as much as I requested and that was—." His habits are those of the recluse and ascetic: "I am a bachelor myself and lead a monastic life in a college." "I am *aquæ potor*, drink no wine at all." Yet he loves the sweet of nature too, if the bitter thirst of knowledge would permit: "No man ever took more delight in springs, woods, groves, gardens, walks, fishponds, rivers, etc." Force of circumstance, lack of opportunity, younger brotherhood, timidity, have kept him secluded within the walls of great libraries, have piled huge dusty tomes on the human beating of his heart. "I have lived a silent, sedentary, solitary, private life in the University, as long almost as Xenocrates in Athens, to learn wisdom as he did, penned up most part in my study." Yet if the Fates had willed otherwise, the man would have been consenting. Let us note right here that this is the whole charm of Burton and his great book. It is no dry treatise of a gray-haired pedant, thumbing contentedly forever dull volumes of mouldy tradition. For all its quaint garb and thorny aspect, it is a great human document, the work of a man whose bodily life was passed in his study, but whose senses were all keenly, pantingly alert to catch the motion of the wide world beyond. Beauty—he adores beauty. "This amazing, confounding, admirable beauty; 't is nature's crown, gold, and glory." Love—Oh, how he could have loved! "I confess I am but a novice, a contemplator only," he writes of it; "Yet *homo sum*, I am a man, and not altogether inexpert in this subject." Like Flaubert, he doubtless leaned forth from his study window on many a moonlit night, and heard a company of revelers with merry song and pleasant jest, and caught the dim flutter of a white gown, and found all his books and learning mere dust beside the laughter and the passion of the world.

And so he grew melancholy, as often happens in such cases. When a man gets these fits on him, he may either rush out into active life for the sake of contrast, he may marry, or go into politics, or do something even more rash and criminal; or he may cut his throat; or he may write a book. On the whole, the last method is the most to be recommended. Burton adopted it; and, with homœopathic ingenuity, he wrote a book on melancholy itself. "I write against melancholy, by being busy, to avoid melancholy. . . . Shall I say, my mistress melancholy, my Egeria, or my evil genius?"

The loose and literary sense in which Burton uses the word melancholy is characteristic of the tone of his book. Without really attempting any precise definition, or, rather, having confused the reader with a multitude of definitions taken from all the authors under the sun, he proceeds to include every form of nervous depression, from a mere temporary fit of the blues to acute or chronic mania and insanity. At the same time, being a man of a logical and systematic turn of mind, he imposes on others, and perhaps on himself, with a great show of formal and scientific treatment. The work is mapped out into divisions, partitions, sections, members, subsections, arranged in as awful order of deduction as Euclid or the Ethics of Spinoza. But let no one be alarmed. This is pure matter of form. The author speaks of what he likes, when he likes. Occasionally he takes the pains to recognize that he is digressing, as in the delicious chapters entitled "A Digression of Spirits," "A Digression of Air." And then, with a sign, he tries to call himself back to the work in hand. "But my melancholy spaniels quest, my game is sprung, and I must suddenly come down and follow." The game leads him into strange places, however. The vast and checkered meadow of the human heart is his hunting-ground. Melancholy is the skeleton in the closet, always popping out at odd times and in unexpected corners; but he keeps it wreathed with bright flowers, and made sweet with strange and subtle savors, and brilliant and sparkling with jewels of quaint wit and wandering fancy. Nevertheless, when he does discuss his subject itself, he has bits of sound common sense, useful to-day and always, like his recommendation of "the three Salernitan Doctors, D. Merryman, D. Diet, and D. Quiet, which cure all diseases."

Some one may object that this saying is quoted and not Burton's own invention. Certainly, Burton is the greatest quoter in literature, far surpassing even Montaigne. His mind was full of the thoughts of others, and he poured them forth together with his own in inextricable mixture. He was a man drenched, drowned in learning, not learning of the quick, smart, practical, modern type, which enables its possessor to give interviews on the inhabitants of Mars and testify on poisons at a murder trial, but mediæval learning, drowsy, strange, unprofitable, and altogether lovely. In the discussion of these melancholy matters all preceding literature is laid under contribution, not only the classics, but countless writers of the Middle Ages, doubtless respectable in their own day and possibly in Burton's, but now so dead that the reader stares and gasps at them and wonders whether his author is not inventing references, like the Oracle in the Innocents Abroad. Melanelius, Ruffus, Aëtius describe melancholy "to be a bad and pievish disease." Hercules de Saxonia approves this opinion, as do Fuchsius, Arnoldus, Guianerius, and others—not unnaturally. Paulus takes a different view, and Halyabbas still another. Aretæus calls it "a perpetual anguish of the soul, fastened on one thing, without an ague." In this brilliant but hazy statement the absence of ague is at least a comfort. It is disquieting, indeed, to find that "this definition of his Merrialis taxeth;" but we are reassured by the solid support of Ælianus Montaltus. And so on.

Pure pedantry, you will say. Well, yes. It would be, if Burton were not saved from the extreme of pedantry by a touch of humor, which makes you somehow feel that he does not take all this quite seriously himself. Yet it is very hard for him to look at anything except through the eyes of some remote authority. We have heard him speak of his mother's excellent cures. It seems that one of her favorite remedies was "an amulet of a spider in a nutshell lapped in silk," super-sovereign for the ague. Burton finds it hard to swallow this; it was "most absurd and ridiculous; for what has a spider to do with a fever?" Ah, but one day "rambling amongst authors (as often I do) I found this very medicine in Dioscorides, approved by Matthiolus, repeated by Aldrovandus. . . . I began to have a better opinion of it, and to give more credit to amulets." I can see from here Mistress Dorothy Burton's lovely scorn at being confirmed by Dioscorides. What did she care for Dioscorides? Did she not have the recipe from her great-aunt, and has she not proved it a dozen times herself?

This trick of constant quoting has led some shallow people to set Burton down as a mere quoter and nothing else. There could be no greater mistake. It is the activity and independence of his own mind which make him so eager to watch and compare the minds of others; and while he profited by their think-

ing, he was abundantly able to do his own, as every page of his book shows. One need ask no better specimen, of strong, shrewd, satirical reflection than the sketch of a Utopian commonwealth in the introduction which purports to be by Democritus Junior; and of many other passages we may say the same.

Nor was our author lacking in deep, human sympathy, although his solitary life and keen intellect disposed him to be a trifle cynical. The celebrated bit with the refrain "Ride on!"— so brilliantly imitated by Sterne—shows a pitiful appreciation of sorrow and misery, which, indeed, are abundantly recognized everywhere in the *Anatomy*.

But perhaps the most characteristic illustration of Burton's intense appetite for humanity is his frequent reference to common daily life and manners. M. Anatole France tells us that the author of *The Imitation* must certainly have been a man of the world before he betook himself to his lonely cell and pious meditation. If Burton never was a man of the world, he would certainly have liked to be one. He peers out from behind the bars of his cells and catches every possible glimpse of the curious things which are shut away from him. Shreds of fashion, hints of frivolity, quips of courtiers, the flash of swords and glittering of jewels,—he will find a place for them. Woman fascinates him especially,—that singular creature who apparently cares nothing for books and study, laughs, weeps, scolds, caresses, without any reasonable cause whatever. Certainly no philosopher should take any notice of her,—yet they all do. And he exhausts himself in cunning heaps of observation, vain interrogations of mysterious boudoirs: "Why do they make such glorious shows with their scarfs, feathers, fans, masks, furs, laces, tiffanies, ruffs, falls, calls, cuffs, damasks, velvets, tinsel, cloth of gold, silver, tissue? With colors of heavens, stars, planets; the strength of metals, stones, odors, flowers, birds, beasts, fishes, and whatsoever Africk, Asia, America, sea, land, art and industry of man can afford? why do they use such novelty of inventions; such new-fangled tires; and spend such inestimable sums on them? . . . Why is it but, as a daynet catcheth larks, to make young men stoop unto them?" And old philosophers also, he might have added.

I have taken this passage from the section on Love Melancholy; for Burton devotes a large portion of his work to that delightful subject. He feels it necessary to make some apology for entering upon it. Some persons will think it hardly becoming in so grave, reverend, and dignified a gentleman,—a clergyman too. But he has good authors on his side: "I excuse myself with Peter Godefridus, Valleriola, Ficinus, Languis, Cadmus Milesius, who writ fourteen books of love." Surely, he would be very critical who should ask more than this.

The apology once made, with what gusto he sets forth, how he luxuriates in golden tidbits from love's delicate revels! "A little soft hand, pretty little mouth, small, fine, long fingers, 't is that which Apollo did admire in Daphne." "Of all eyes (by the way) black are most amiable, enticing, and fair." "Oh, that pretty tone, her divine and lovely looks, her everything lovely, sweet, amiable, and pretty, pretty, pretty." Is it not the mere ecstasy of amorous frenzy? Again, he gives us a very banquet, a rosy wreath of old, simple English names, a perfect old-fashioned garden: "Modest Matilda, pretty, pleasing Peg, sweet, singing Susan, mincing, merry Moll, dainty dancing Doll, neat Nancy, jolly Jone, nimble Nell, kissing Kate, bouncing Bess with black eyes, fair Phillis, with fine white hands, fiddling Frank, tall Tib, slender Sib, etc." Do you not hear their merry laughter, as he heard it in his dim study, a dream of fair faces and bright forms twisting, and turning, and flashing back and forth under the harvest moon?

Yet, after all, love is a tyrant and a traitor, a meteor rushing with blind fury among the placid orbs of life. What is a man to make of these wild contrasts and tragical transitions? At one moment the lover seems to be on the pinnacle of felicity, "his soul sowced, imparadised, imprisoned in his lady; he can do nothing, think of nothing but her; she is his cynosure, Hesperus, and Vesper, his morning and evening star, his goddess, his mistress, his life, his soul, his everything; dreaming, waking, she is always in his mouth; his heart, eyes, ears, and all his thoughts are full of her." But then something goes wrong and the note is altogether changed. "When this young gallant is crossed in his love, he laments, and cries, and roars downright. 'The virgin's gone and I am gone, she's gone, she's gone, and what shall I do? Where shall I find her? whom shall I ask? what will become of me? I am weary of this life, sick, mad, and desperate.'"

It becomes the sage, then, to be clear of these toys. If he is to write about Love Melancholy, let him cure it. Let him hold up a warning to the unwary. What is the use of days and nights spent in toiling over learned authors, if the young and foolish are not to have the benefit of one's experience? If only the young and foolish would profit! If only the unwary would beware! Still we must do our part. Let us remind them that beauty fades. It is a rather well-known fact, but youth is so prone to forget it. "Suppose thou beholdest her in a frosty morning, in cold weather, in some passion or perturbation of mind, weeping, chafing, etc., riveled and ill-favored to behold. . . . Let her use all helps art and nature can yield; be like her, and her, and whom thou wilt, or all these in one; a little sickness, a fever, small-pox, wound, scar, loss of an eye or limb, a violent passion, mars all in an instant, disfigures all." Then let us exalt the charms of a bachelor's life. It has its weak points, as I feel, writing here alone in the dust and chill, with nothing but books about me, no prattle of children, no merry chatter of busy women. But what then? It is quieter, after all. "Consider how contentedly, quietly, neatly, plentifully, sweetly, and how merrily he lives! He hath no man to care for but himself, none to please, no charge, none to control him, is tied to no residence, no cure to serve, may go and come when, whither, live where he will, his own master, and do what he list himself." Nevertheless, it all sounds a little hollow, and as I sit here in the winter midnight with my old pipe, I wonder if it might not have been otherwise.

I have made my quotations with very little skill, if the ingenious reader does not by this time feel that Burton was in his way a great master of style. His skill and power as a writer, more than anything else, show that he was not a mere pedant or Dryasdust. It is true, he himself disclaims any such futile preoccupation. He has not "amended the style, which now flows remissly, as it was first conceived." His book is "writ with as small deliberation as I do ordinarily speak, without all affectation of big words, fustian phrases, jingling terms." But the facts belie him, and one shudders to think what must have been his idea of the big words he does not use. A careful collation of the first edition of the *Anatomy* with the last published in the author's lifetime not only shows a great number of additions and alterations, but proves conclusively that these changes were made, in many cases, with a view to style and to style only. Take a single instance. In the first edition Burton wrote: "If it be so that the earth is a moon, then are we all lunatic within." Later he amplified this as follows, with obvious gain in the beauty of the phrase: "If it be so that the earth is a moon, then are we also giddy, vertiginous, and lunatic within this sublunary maze." Amended, I think, but oh, for the "big words, fustian phrases, jingling terms"!

Yes, Burton was a master of style. He could bend language to his ends and do as he willed with it. If he is often rough, harsh, wanton in expression, it is simply because like Donne, he chose to be so. Does he wish to tell a plain story? Who can do it more lightly, simply, briefly? "An ass and a mule went laden over a brook, the one with salt, the other with wool; the mule's pack was wet by chance; the salt melted, his burden the lighter; and he thereby much eased. He told the ass, who, thinking to speed as well, wet his pack likewise at the next water; but it was much the heavier, he quite tired."

Does he wish to paint the foul and horrible? I know of nothing in Swift or Zola more replete with the luxury of hideousness than the unquotable description of the defects which infatuated love will overlook,—a description which Keats tells a correspondent he would give his favorite leg to have written. Here, as in so many passages I have quoted, Burton piles up epithet after epithet, till it seems as if the dictionary would be exhausted,—a trick which, by the bye, he may have caught from Rabelais, and which would become very monotonous, if it were not applied with such wonderful variety and fertility.

Then, at his will, the magician can turn with ease from the bitter to the sweet. When he touches love or beauty, all his ruggedness is gone. His words become full of grace, of suave, vague richness, of delicacy, of mystery, as in the phrase which Southey quotes in *The Doctor*: "For peregrination charms our senses with such unspeakable and sweet variety that some count him unhappy that never traveled, a kind of prisoner, and pity his case, that from his cradle to his old age beholds the same still; still, still the same, the same." Or, to take a more elaborate picture, see this, which might be a Tintoretto or a Spenser: "Witty Lucian, in that pathetical love-passage or pleasant description of Jupiter's stealing of Europe and swimming from Phœnicia to Crete, makes the sea calm, the winds hush, Neptune and Amphitrite riding in their chariot to break the waves before them, the Tritons dancing round about with every one a torch; the sea-nymphs, half-naked, keeping time on dophins' backs and singing Hymenæus; Cupid nimbly tripping on the top of the waters; and Venus herself coming after in a shell, strawing roses and flowers on their heads."

I have dwelt thus long on Burton's style because it is absolutely characteristic, and because it proves by its eminent artistic qualities that he was not simply a compiler and quoter, but a thinking and feeling man, a strong, shrewd, passionate temperament, gazing with intense interest out of his scholastic windows at the strange and moving spectacle of life. In his fullness and abundance he, more than any other English author, recalls Montaigne, whom he quotes so frequently: he has less fluidity, more conventional prejudice, but also more sincerity, more robust moral force. Again, he in a certain sense resembles a greater than Montaigne, his own greatest contemporary, Shakespeare, whom he also quotes enough to show that he knew and loved his writings, at any rate, if not himself. Shakespeare's work is like a glorious piece of tapestry, a world of rich and splendid hues, woven into a thousand shapes of curious life. Burton's is like the reverse side of the same: all the bewildering wealth of color, but rough, crude, misshapen, undigested.

One of the characteristic oddities of Burton's style is his perpetual use of the phrase *etc*. When his quick and fluent pen has heaped together all the nouns or adjectives in heaven and in earth, and in the waters under the earth, he completes the picture with the vast, vague gesture of an *etc*. Take an often-quoted passage in the introduction, in which he describes his own life as an observer and contemplator: "Now come tidings of weddings, maskings, mummeries, entertainments, jubilees, embassies, tilts and tournaments, trophies, triumphs, revels, sports, plays; then again, as in a new-shifted scene, treasons, cheating tricks, robberies, enormous villanies in all kinds, funerals, burials, death of princes, new discoveries, expeditions, now comical, then tragical matters; to-day we hear of new lords and officers created, to-morrow of some great men deposed, again of fresh honors conferred; one is let loose, another imprisoned; one purchaseth, another breaketh; he thrives, his neighbor turns bankrupt; now plenty, then again dearth and famine; one runs, another rides, wrangles, laughs, weeps, etc."

So we may sum up *The Anatomy of Melancholy* in an *etc.* The general tone of the book, with its infinite multiplicity, reminds one of nothing more than of the quaint blending of mirth, mystery, and spiritual awe so deliciously expressed in Stevenson's baby couplet,—

> The world is so full of a number of things,
> I'm sure we should all be as happy as kings.

Only Burton would have laid a mischievous and melancholy emphasis on should.

JOHN FORD

1586–c. 1640

John Ford was baptized on April 17, 1586, in Ilsington, Devonshire. He attended Exeter College, Oxford, from 1601 to 1602; in 1602 he entered Middle Temple, London, to study law. In 1605 he was expelled for failure to pay his bill. He was readmitted in 1608, and is believed to have left again in 1617, never having practiced his profession.

Ford is best known for his dramas; however, his earliest works were mostly non-dramatic verses and prose pamphlets. The funeral elegy *Fame's Memorial* (1606) was written upon the death of Charles Blount, Earl of Devonshire. *Honour Triumphant; or, The Peers' Challenge* (1606) is a prose work depicting a discussion among four gallants about ethical paradoxes. Ford's first dramatic endeavor was his collaboration with Thomas Dekker on *The Witch of Edmonton*, a story based on Elizabeth Sawyer's execution in 1621 for witchcraft. The earliest extant play that Ford wrote himself is the romantic *Lover's Melancholy* (1621). Ford's most notable plays include *The Broken Heart* (1633), *Love's Sacrifice* (1637), *'Tis Pitty Shees a Whore* (1633), *Perkin Warbeck: A Strange Truth* (1634), and *The Ladies Triall* (1638).

Ford probably retired from London to Devonshire in 1638. The last record we have of him is in 1639. Scholars assume that he died shortly thereafter.

Personal

A Gentleman of the *Middle-Temple*, who liv'd in the Reign of King *Charles* the First: Who was a Well-wisher to the Muses, and a Friend and Acquaintance of most of the Poets of his Time.—GERARD LANGBAINE, *An Account of the English Dramatick Poets*, 1691

Of his social habits there little can be told with certainty. There is sufficient, however, to show that he lived, if not familiarly, yet friendlily, with the dramatic writers of his day, and neither provoked nor felt personal enmities. He speaks, indeed, of opposition; but this is merely the language of the stage; opposition is experienced by every dramatic writer worth criticism, and has nothing in common with ordinary hostility. In truth, with the exception of an allusion to the "voluminous" and rancorous Prynne, nothing can be more general than his complaints. Yet Ford looked not much to the brighter side of life; he could, like Jaques, "suck melancholy out of a song as a weasel sucks eggs;" but he was unable, like this wonderful creation of our great poet, to extract mirth from it. When he touched a lighter string, the tones, though pleasingly modulated, were still sedate; and it must, I think, be admitted that his poetry is rather that of a placid and serene than of a happy mind: he was in truth, an amiable ascetic amidst a busy world.—WILLIAM GIFFORD, "Introduction" to *Dramatic Works of John Ford*, 1827

General

The author has not much of the oratorical stateliness and imposing flow of Massinger; nor a great deal of the smooth and flexible diction, the wandering fancy, and romantic sweetness of Beaumont and Fletcher; and yet he comes nearer to these qualities than to any of the distinguishing characteristics of Jonson or Shakespeare. He excels most in representing the pride and gallantry, and high-toned honour of youth, and the enchanting softness, or the mild and graceful magnanimity of female character. There is a certain melancholy air about his most striking representations; and, in the tender and afflicting pathetic, he appears to us occasionally to be second only to him who has never yet had an equal. The greater part of every play, however, is bad; and there is not one which does not contain faults sufficient to justify the derision even of those who are incapable of comprehending its contrasted beauties. The diction we think for the most part beautiful, and worthy of the inspired age which produced it.—FRANCIS LORD JEFFREY (1811), *Contributions to the* Edinburgh Review, 1844, Vol. 2, p. 301

Ford possesses nothing of the energy and majesty of Massinger, and but little of the playful gaiety and picturesque fancy of Fletcher, yet scarcely Shakspeare himself has exceeded him in the excitement of pathetic emotion. Of this, his two Tragedies of *'Tis Pitty She's a Whore*, and the *Broken Heart*, bear the most overpowering testimony. Though too much loaded in their fable with a wildness and horror often felt as repulsive, they are noble specimens of dramatic genius; and who that has a heart to feel, or an eye to weep, can, in the first of these productions, view even the unhallowed loves of Giovanni and Annabella; or in the second, the hapless and unmerited fates of Calantha and

Penthea, with a cheek unbathed in tears!—NATHAN DRAKE, *Shakspeare and His Times*, 1817, Vol. 2, p. 563

Ford is not so great a favourite with me as with some others, from whose judgment I dissent with diffidence. It has been lamented that the play of his which has been most admired (*'Tis Pity She's a Whore*) had not a less exceptionable subject. I do not know, but I suspect that the exceptionableness of the subject is that which constitutes the chief merit of the play. The repulsiveness of the story is what gives it its critical interest; for it is a studiously prosaic statement of facts, and naked declaration of passions. It was not the least of Shakespear's praise, that he never tampered with unfair subjects. His genius was above it; his taste kept aloof from it. I do not deny the power of simple painting and polished style in this tragedy in general, and of a great deal more in some few of the scenes, particularly in the quarrel between Annabella and her husband, which is wrought up to a pitch of demoniac scorn and phrensy with consummate art and knowledge; but I do not find much other power in the author (generally speaking) than that of playing with edged tools, and knowing the use of poisoned weapons. And what confirms me in this opinion is the comparative inefficiency of his other plays. Except the last scene of the Broken Heart (which I think extravagant—others may think it sublime, and be right) they are merely exercises of style and effusions of wire-drawn sentiment. Where they have not the sting of illicit passion, they are quite pointless, and seem painted on gauze, or spun of cobwebs. The affected brevity and division of some of the lines into hemistichs, &c. so as to make in one case a mathematical stair-case of the words and answers given to different speakers, is an instance of frigid and ridiculous pedantry. An artificial elaborateness is the general characteristic of Ford's style. In this respect his plays resemble Miss Baillie's more than any others I am acquainted with, and are quite distinct from the exuberance and unstudied force which characterised his immediate predecessors. There is too much of scholastic subtlety, an innate perversity of understanding or predominance of will, which either seeks the irritation of inadmissible subjects, or to stimulate its own faculties by taking the most barren, and making something out of nothing, in a spirit of contradiction. He does not *draw along with* the reader: he does not work upon our sympathy, but on our antipathy of our indifference; and there is as little of the social or gregarious principle in his productions as there appears to have been in his personal habits, if we are to believe Sir John Suckling, who says of him in the Sessions of the Poets—

> In the dumps John Ford alone by himself sat
> With folded arms and melancholy hat.
>
> —WILLIAM HAZLITT, *Lectures on the Dramatic Literature of the Age of Elizabeth*, 1820

I know few things more difficult to account for than the deep and lasting impression made by the more tragic portions of Ford's poetry. Whence does it derive that resistless power which all confess, of afflicting, I had almost said harassing, the better feelings? It is not from any peculiar beauty of language,—for in this he is equalled by his contemporaries, and by some of them surpassed; nor is it from any classical or mythological allusions happily recollected and skilfully applied,—for of these he seldom avails himself: it is not from any picturesque views presented to the mind,—for of imaginative poetry he has little or nothing; he cannot conjure up a succession of images, whether grave or gay, to flit across the fancy or play in the eye. Yet it is hardly possible to peruse his passionate scenes without the most painful interest, the most heart-thrilling delight. This can only arise—at least I can conceive nothing else adequate to

the excitement of such sensations—from the overwhelming efficacy of intense thought devoted to the embodying of conceptions adapted to the awful situations in which he has, imperceptibly and with matchless felicity, placed his principal characters.—WILLIAM GIFFORD, "Introduction" to *Dramatic Works of John Ford*, 1827

At a considerable distance below Massinger we may place his contemporary, John Ford. In the choice of tragic subjects from obscure fictions which have to us the charm of entire novelty, they resemble each other; but in the conduct of their fable, in the delination of their characters, each of these poets has his distinguishing excellencies. 'I know,' says Gifford, 'few things more difficult to account for than the deep and lasting impression made by the more tragic portions of Ford's poetry.' He succeeds, however, pretty well in accounting for it; the situations are awfully interesting, the distress intense, the thoughts and language becoming the expression of deep sorrow. Ford, with none of the moral beauty and elevation of Massinger, has, in a much higher degree, the power over tears; we sympathise even with his vicious characters, with Giovanni and Annabella and Bianca. Love, and love in guilt or sorrow, is almost exclusively the emotion he portrays; no heroic passion, no sober dignity, will be found in his tragedies. But he conducts his stories well and without confusion; his scenes are often highly wrought and effective; his characters, with no striking novelty, are well supported; he is seldom extravagant or regardless of probability. *The Broken Heart* has generally been reckoned his finest tragedy; and if the last act had been better prepared, by bringing the love of Calantha for Ithocles more fully before the reader in the earlier part of the play, there would be very few passages of deeper pathos in our dramatic literature. 'The style of Ford,' it is said by Gifford, 'is altogether original and his own. Without the majestic march which distinguishes the poetry of Massinger, and with little or none of that light and playful humour which characterises the dialogue of Fletcher, or even of Shirley, he is yet elegant, and easy, and harmonious; and though rarely sublime, yet sufficiently elevated for the most pathetic tones of that passion on whose romantic energies he chiefly delighted to dwell.' Yet he censures afterwards Ford's affectation of uncouth phrases, and perplexity of language. Of comic ability this writer does not display one particle. Nothing can be meaner than those portions of his dramas which, in compliance with the prescribed rules of that age, he devotes to the dialogue of servants or buffoons.—HENRY HALLAM, *Introduction to the Literature of Europe*, 1837–39, Pt. 3, Ch. 6, Par. 97

It would be unfair . . . to conclude that he delighted in the contemplation of vice and misery as vice and misery. He delighted in the sensation of intellectual power, he found himself strong in the imagination of crime and of agony; his moral sense was gratified by indignation at the dark possibilities of sin, by compassion for rare extremes of suffering. He abhorred vice—he admired virtue; but ordinary vice or modern virtue were, to him, as light wine to a dram drinker. His genius was a telescope, ill-adapted for neighbouring objects, but powerful to bring within the sphere of vision, what nature has wisely placed at an unsociable distance. Passion must be incestuous or adulterous; grief must be something more than martyrdom, before he could make them big enough to be seen. Unquestionably he displayed great *power* in these horrors, which was all he desired; but had he been "of the first order of poets," he would have found and displayed superior power in "familiar matter of to-day," in failings to which all are liable, virtues which all may practise, and sorrows for which all may be the better.

—HARTLEY COLERIDGE, "Introduction" to *The Dramatic Works of Massinger and Ford*, 1840, p. lviii

As in the case of Clarendon, almost absolutely contradictory opinions have been delivered, by critics of great authority, about John Ford. In one of the most famous outburst of his generous and enthusiastic estimate of the Elizabethan period, Lamb has pronounced Ford to be of the first order of poets. Mr Swinburne, while bringing not a few limitations to this tremendous eulogy, has on the whole supported it in one of the most brilliant of prose essays; and critics as a rule have bowed to Lamb's verdict. On the other hand, Hazlitt (who is "gey ill to differ with" when there are, as here, no extra-literary considerations to reckon) has traversed that verdict in one of the most damaging utterances of commonsense, yet not commonplace, criticism anywhere to be found, asking bluntly and pointedly whether the exceptionableness of the subject is not what constitutes the merit of Ford's greatest play, pronouncing the famous last scene of *The Broken Heart* extravagant, and fixing on "a certain perversity of spirit" in Ford generally. It is pretty clear that Hartley Coleridge (who might be paralleled in our own day as a critic, who seldom went wrong except through ignorance, though he had a sublime indifference as to the ignorance that sometimes led him wrong) was of no different opinion. It is not easy to settle such a quarrel. But I had the good fortune to read Ford before I had read anything except Hartley Coleridge's rather enigmatic verdict about him, and in the course of five-and-twenty years I have read him often again. The resulting opinion may not be exceptionally valuable, but it has at least stood the test of frequent re-reading of the original, and of reading of the main authorities among the commentators.

John Ford, like Fletcher and Beaumont, but unlike almost all others of his class, was a person not compelled by need to write tragedies,—comedies of any comic merit he could never have written, were they his neck verse at Hairibee. His father was a man of good family and position at Ilsington in Devon. His mother was of the well-known west-country house of the Pophams. He was born two years before the Armada, and three years after Massinger. He has no university record, but was a member of the Middle Temple, and takes at least some pains to assure us that he never wrote for money. Nevertheless, for the best part of thirty years he was a playwright, and he is frequently found collaborating with Dekker, the neediest if nearly the most gifted gutter-playwright of the time. Once he worked with Webster in a play (*The Murder of the Son upon the Mother*) which must have given the fullest possible opportunity to the appetite of both for horrors. Once he, Rowley, and Dekker combined to produce the strange masterpiece (for a masterpiece it is in its own undisciplined way) of the *Witch of Edmonton*, where the obvious signs of a play hastily cobbled up to meet a popular demand do not obscure the talents of the cobblers. It must be confessed that there is much less of Ford than of Rowley and Dekker in the piece, except perhaps its comparative regularity and the quite unreasonable and unintelligible bloodiness of the murder of Susan. In *The Sun's Darling*, due to Ford and Dekker, the numerous and charming lyrics are pretty certainly Dekker's; though we could pronounce on this point with more confidence if we had the two lost plays, *The Fairy Knight* and *The Bristowe Merchant*, in which the same collaborators are known to have been engaged. *The Fancies, Chaste and Noble*, and *The Lady's Trial* which we have, and which are known to be Ford's only, are but third-rate work by common consent, and *Love's Sacrifice* has excited still stronger opinions of condemnation from persons favourable to

Ford. This leaves us practically four plays upon which to base our estimate—*'Tis Pity She's a Whore*, *The Lover's Melancholy*, *The Broken Heart*, and *Perkin Warbeck*. The last-named I shall take the liberty of dismissing summarily with the same borrowed description as Webster's *Appius and Virginia*. Hartley Coleridge, perhaps willing to make up if he could for a general distaste for Ford, volunteered the strange judgment that it is the best specimen of the historic drama to be found out of Shakespere; and Hazlitt says nothing savage about it. I shall say nothing more, savage or otherwise. *The Lover's Melancholy* has been to almost all its critics a kind of lute-case for the very pretty version of Strada's fancy about the nightingale, which Crashaw did better; otherwise it is naught. We are, therefore, left with *'Tis Pity She's a Whore*, and *The Broken Heart*. For myself, in respect to the first, after repeated readings and very careful weighings of what has been said, I come back to my first opinion—to wit, that the Annabella and Giovanni scenes, with all their perversity, all their availing themselves of what Hazlitt, with his unerring instinct, called "unfair attractions," are among the very best things of their kind. Of what may be thought unfair in them I shall speak a little later; but allowing for this, the sheer effects of passion—the "All for love and the world well lost," the shutting out, not instinctively or stupidly, but deliberately, and with full knowledge, of all other considerations except the dictates of desire—have never been so rendered in English except in *Romeo and Juliet* and *Antony and Cleopatra*. The comparison of course brings out Ford's weakness, not merely in execution, but in design; not merely in accomplishment, but in the choice of means for accomplishment. Shakespere had no need of the *haut goût* of incest, of the unnatural horrors of the heart on the dagger. But Ford had; and he in a way (I do not say fully) justified his use of these means. . . .

Ford—an Elizabethan in the strict sense for nearly twenty years—did not suffer from the decay which, as noted above, set in in regard to versification and language among the men of his own later day. He has not the natural trick of verse and phrase which stamps his greatest contemporaries unmistakably, and even such lesser ones as his collaborator, Dekker, with a hardly mistakable mark; but his verse is nervous, well proportioned, well delivered, and at its best a noble medium. He was by general consent utterly incapable of humour, and his low-comedy scenes are among the most loathsome in the English theatre. His lyrics are not equal to Shakespere's or Fletcher's, Dekker's or Shirley's, but they are better than Massinger's. Although he frequently condescended to the Fletcherian license of the redundant syllable, he never seems to have dropped (as Fletcher did sometimes, or at least allowed his collaborators to drop) floundering into the Serbonian bog of stuff that is neither verse nor prose. He showed indeed (and Mr. Swinburne, with his usual insight, has noticed it, though perhaps he has laid rather too much stress on it) a tendency towards a severe rule-and-line form both of tragic scheme and of tragic versification, which may be taken to correspond in a certain fashion (though Mr. Swinburne does not notice this) to the "correctness" in ordinary poetry of Waller and his followers. Yet he shows no sign of wishing to discard either the admixture of comedy with tragedy (save in *The Broken Heart*, which is perhaps a crucial instance), or blank verse, or the freedom of the English stage in regard to the unities. In short, Ford was a person distinctly deficient in initiative and planning genius, but endowed with a great executive faculty. He wanted guidance in all the greater lines of his art, and he had it not; the result being that he produced unwholesome and undecided work, only saved by the unmistakable presence of poetical faculty. I do not think that Webster could ever have done anything better than he did: I think that if Ford had been born twenty years earlier he might have been second to Shakespere, and at any rate the equal of Ben Jonson and of Fletcher. But the flagging genius of the time made its imprint on his own genius, which was of the second order, not the first.—GEORGE SAINTSBURY, A *History of Elizabethan Literature*, 1887, pp. 401–9

What Ford especially imitated from Greene was the art of writing romantic tales with plenty of adventures, unexpected meetings and discoveries, much love, and improbabilities enough to enchant Elizabethan readers and sell the book up to any number of editions. In this he rivalled his model very successfully, and his romances were among the most popular of the time of Shakespeare. The number of their editions was extraordinary, and they were renewed at almost regular intervals up to the eighteenth century; there was a far greater demand for them than for any play of Shakespeare. Besides imitating Greene, who obviously revealed to him the success to be won by writing romantic tales, he imitated at the same time the Italians and the Spaniards, introducing into his romances a licentiousness quite unknown to Greene, but well known to Boccaccio, and heroic adventures similar to those his friend Anthony Munday was just then putting into English. These last were to be the chief delight of novel-readers in the seventeenth century, and did more than anything for the great popularity of Ford's novels during that period.—J. J. JUSSERAND, "Lyly's Legatees," *The English Novel in the Time of Shakespeare*, 1890, p. 193

In the delineation of the strongest human passions—love, grief, revenge—Ford is without a peer among the later Elizabethan dramatists. He seeks, in own words, to

> Sing out a lamentable tale of things,
> Done long ago, and ill done; and when sighs
> Are wearied, piece up what remains behind
> With weeping eyes and hearts that bleed to death.

He has no dramatic reserve, and shrinks from no touch of horror that can add intensity to the situation. It is in this that his want of due restraint betrays itself. A sane and healthy mind revolts instinctively from such scenes as that in which the reaking heart of Annabella is borne into the banquet-hall on the dagger of Giovanni; they awaken neither pity nor indignation, nor that purifying rest in accomplished purpose, which is the highest end of tragedy. We are first stunned, then repelled, by the morbid fatalism of his greatest tragedies; they are like the hospital-museums where human deformities and distortions are catalogued and exhibited, and from which we long to escape into the fresh air and sunshine.—J. HOWARD B. MASTERMAN, *The Age of Milton*, 1897, p. 83

Last of all, in a final brief blaze of the sinking embers, we encounter John Ford, perhaps as genuine a tragic poet as any one of his forerunners, Shakespeare alone excepted, reverting for a moment to the old splendid diction, the haughty disregard of convention, the contempt for ethical restrictions. And so the brief and magnificent school of English drama, begun by Marlowe scarcely more than a generation before, having blazed and crackled like a forest fire fed with resinous branches, sinks almost in a moment, and lingers only as a heap of white ash and glowing charcoal.—EDMUND GOSSE, *A Short History of Modern English Literature*, 1897, p. 138

Works

'TIS PITY SHE'S A WHORE

. . . ⟨T⟩hence to Salsbury Court play-house, where was acted the first time *Tis pitty shee's a Whore*—a simple play and ill acted; only, it was my fortune to sit by a most pretty and most ingenious lady, which pleased me much.—SAMUEL PEPYS, *Diary*, Sept. 9, 1661

⟨T⟩he writing . . . is in many parts, strong and poetical, for nothing can be more revolting than the subject; and, therefore, the warmer and more glowing pictures of love are worked up, the more reprehensible is the author, because the deeper is the wound given to honour, and to decorum.

"But," say the critics, "the title bears out the author, and the catastrophe is so shocking that that all those who may be inclined to practise such monstrous crimes, will be warned by it." Nothing can be more false than such argument. No warning, no catastrophe can deter such wretches as are here described; and, as to the title, Is ANNABELLA merely a strumpet? No; she is the strumpet of her brother. And is she to be pitied for that? Such reasoning is equally monstrous, ridiculous, and supererogate, and of course reprehensible; for it is not the province of a dramatic writer to seek for monsters, and to record prodigies; is it his duty to reprobate such vices as are commonly known, and often practised, in which catalogue, for the honour of human nature, incest without a motive has no place; but if it had, it ought to be introduced as a deed of darkness which could not be pleaded for or argued on, even by the wretches themselves, therefore, all we can say in favour of FORD, is, to wish he had employed his beautiful writing to a more laudable purpose.—CHARLES DIBDIN, A *Complete History of the Stage*, 1795, Vol. 3, pp. 279–80

Ford was of the first order of poets. He sought for sublimity, not by parcels, in metaphors or visible images, but directly where she has her full residence in the heart of man; in the actions and sufferings of the greatest minds. There is a grandeur of the soul above mountains, seas, and the elements. Even in the poor perverted reason of Giovanni and Annabella, in the play which stands at the head of the modern collection of the works of this author, we discern traces of that fiery particle, which, in the irregular starting from out the road of beaten action, discovers something of a right line even in obliquity, and shows hints of an improvable greatness in the lowest descents and degradations of our nature—CHARLES LAMB, *Specimens of English Dramatic Poets*, 1808

Never has genius more miserably misused its gifts. If, as the title of 'Tis Pity She's a Whore implies, this tragedy be intended to awaken a feeling akin to sympathy, or bordering upon it, on behalf of the heroine of its story of incest, the endeavour, so far as I can judge, fails in achieving the purpose insinuated. In truth, the dramatist's desire is to leave an impression far other and more perilous than that of a mere feeling of compassion for a fair sinner;—his purpose is to persuade us that passion is irresistible. But his efforts are vain, and so too is the sophistry of those who seek to explain away their chief force; for while recognising their charm, the soul revolts against the fatalism which, in spite of the Friar's preaching and Annabella's repentance, the sum-total of the action of this drama implies.—ADOLPHUS WILLIAM WARD, A *History of English Dramatic Literature* (1875), 1899, Vol. 3, p. 78

This man who conceived the horrors of the Italian Renaissance in the spirit in which they were committed is Ford. In his great play ⟨'Tis Pity She's a Whore⟩ he has caught the very tone of the Italian Renaissance: the abominableness of the play consisting not in the coarse slaughter scenes added merely to please the cockpit of an English theatre, but the superficial innocence of tone; in its making evil lose its appearance of evil, even as it did to the men of the Renaissance. Giovanni and Annabella make love as if they were Romeo and Juliet: there is scarcely any struggle, and no remorse; they weep and pay compliments and sigh and melt in true Aminta style. There is in the love of the brother and sister neither the ferocious heat of tragic lust, nor the awful shudder of unnatural evil; they are lukewarm, neither good nor bad. Their abominable love is in their eyes a mere weakness of the flesh; there is no sense of revolt against man and nature and God; they are neither dragged on by irresistible demoniac force nor held back by the grip of conscience; they slip and slide, even like Francesca and Paolo. They pay each other sweet and mawkish compliments. The ferocious lust of Francesco Cenci is moral compared with the way in which the "trim youth" Giovanni praises Annabella's beauty; the blushing, bride-like way in which Annabella, "white in her soul," acknowledges her long love. The atrociousness of all this is, that if you strike out a word or two the scene may be read with perfect moral satisfaction, with the impression that this is really "sacred love." For in these scenes Ford wrote with a sweetness and innocence truly diabolical, not a shiver of horror passing through him—serene, unconscious; handling the filthy without sense of its being unclean, to the extent, the incredible extent, of making Giovanni and Annabella swear on their mother's ashes eternal fidelity in incest: horror of horrors, to which no Walpurgis Night abomination could ever approach, this taking as witness of the unutterable, not an obscene Beelzebub with abominable words and rites, but the very holiest of holies. If ever Englishman approached the temper of the Italian Renaissance, it was not Tourneur, nor Shelley with his cleansing hell fires of tragic horror, but this sweet and gentle Ford. If ever an artistic picture approached the reality of such a man as Gianpaolo Baglioni, the incestuous murderer whom the Frolliere chronicler, enthusiastic like Matarazzo, admires, for "his most beautiful person, his benign and amiable manner and lordly bearing," it is certainly not the elaborately villainous Francesco Cenci of Shelley, boasting like another Satan of his enormous wickedness, exhausting in his picture of himself the rhetoric of horror, committing his final enormity merely to complete the crown of atrocities in which he glories; it is no such tragic impossibility of moral hideousness as this; it is the Giovanni of Ford, the pearl of virtuous and studious youths, the spotless, the brave, who, after a moment's reasoning, tramples on a vulgar prejudice—"Shall a peevish sound, a customary form from man to man, of brother and of sister, be a bar 'twixt my eternal happiness and me?" who sins with a clear conscience, defies the world, and dies, bravely, proudly, the "sacred name" of Annabella on his lips, like a chivalrous hero. The pious, pure Germany of Luther will give the world the tragic type of the science-damned Faustus; the devout and savage Spain of Loyola will give the tragic type of Don Juan damned for mockery of man and of death and of heaven; the Puritan England of Milton will give the most sublimely tragic type of all, the awful figure of him who says, "Evil, be thou my good." What tragic type can this evil Italy of Renaissance give to the world? None: or at most this miserable, morbid, compassionated Giovanni; whom Ford would have us admire, and whom we can only dispise.—VERNON LEE (Violet Paget), *Euphorion*, 1884, Vol. 1, pp. 99–102

The work of Ford's, which his admirers now call his masterpiece, is not, however, the *Broken Heart*, but the play with the disagreeable title and the still more disagreeable subject. The crime of incest was the not infrequent theme of the great tragic poets of antiquity, but they at least are guiltless of the charge of throwing over it a sentimental glamour such as pervades this production of Ford's. *'Tis Pity She's a Whore* is certainly a work of accomplished literary skill, but its very air of artistic finish enhances its moral repulsiveness; for Ford, unlike most of his Elizabethan brethren, was ever a deliberate, cool, calculating literary workman, and while he is weaving this story of abnormal passion and investing it with all the grace and charm at his command, it is manifest that he is nowise carried away by the imaginative contemplation of it himself, but is all the while curiously studying the monstrous growth of his own diseased fancy in a cold anatomical fashion that rouses our moral repugnance in direct proportion as it excites our æsthetic admiration. He is always the craftsman, possessing a faculty of self-criticism rare among his compeers of that age. He has no fine frenzies, but a soberly disposed modern reader will hardly quarrel with him on that score, for frenzies, fine and otherwise, are quite plentiful enough in the works of Ford's contemporaries to be readily spared in his own. Unlike much of theirs, his verse is clean-cut and compact, but without special force or nerve, and entirely wanting in felicity and magic. Neither passages nor lines live in the reader's recollection. Regarding his human delineations, Mr Swinburne says that Ford 'was rather a sculptor of character than a painter,' and this looks like an admirable critical distinction until we perceive that it is only a cleverly illusory way of saying, what is the plain truth, that Ford's *dramatis personæ* are discriminated in a very broad, general, elementary fashion, without subtlety of portraiture, without moral *nuances.*—WILLIAM WATSON, "Some Literary Idolatries," *Essays in Criticism*, 1893, pp. 9–11

THE BROKEN HEART

I do not know where to find, in any play, a catastrophe so grand, so solemn, and so surprising as in this. . . . What a noble thing is the soul in its strengths and its weaknesses! Who would be less weak than Calantha? Who can be so strong? The expression of this transcendent scene almost bears us in imagination to Calvary and the Cross; and we seem to perceive some analogy between the scenical sufferings which we are here contemplating, and the real agonies of that final completion to which we dare no more than hint a reference. —CHARLES LAMB, *Specimens of English Dramatic Poets*, 1808

In the preface to *The Broken Heart* the names of the *dramatis personae* are explained as being 'fitted to their qualities,' and from this one might carelessly rush to the conclusion that the strangeness of Ford's characters is due to their being extravagant personifications of single attributes, and not types of real men and women. But his art was much too profound, his mastery of thought and emotion much too living for any such mechanical superficiality. His creations are not inanimate figures; the pulse of life beats in them. The secret of their strangeness seems to lie in a certain intensity and concentration of nature, a hardness and strength of fibre which will not relax where once it has taken hold. The kinship of passion to insanity is strongly suggested by Ford's plays. We seem to have before us men and women with a fixed delusion on some one point, impressed upon them not by the force of overmastering circumstances, but by some vicious warp in their own nature.—WILLIAM MINTO, "John Ford," *The English Poets*, ed. Thomas Humphry Ward, 1880, Vol. 2, pp. 60–61

The perverse absurdity of a man like Orgilus letting Penthea die by the most horrible of deaths must be set aside: his vengeance (the primary absurdity granted), is exactly and wholly in character. But if anything could be decisive against Ford being "of the first order of poets," even of dramatic poets, it would be the total lack of interest in the characters of Calantha and Ithocles. Fate-disappointed love seems (no doubt from something in his own history) to have had a singular attraction for Lamb; and the glorification, or, as it were, apotheosis of it in

Calantha must have appealed to him in one of those curious and illegitimate ways which every critic knows. But the mere introduction of Bassanes would show that Ford is not of the first order of poets. He is a purely contemptible character, neither sublimed by passion of jealousy, nor kept whole by salt of comic exposition; a mischievous poisonous idiot who ought to have had his brains knocked out, and whose brains would assuredly have been knocked out, by any Orgilus of real life. He is absolutely unequal to the place of central personage, and causer of the harms, of a romantic tragedy such as *The Broken Heart*.

I have said "by any Orgilus of real life," but Ford has little to do with real life; and it is in this fact that the insufficiency of his claim to rank among the first order of poets lies. He was, it is evident, a man of the greatest talent, even of great genius, who, coming at the end of a long literary movement, exemplified the defects of its decadence. I could compare him, if there was here any space for such a comparison, to Baudelaire or Flaubert with some profit; except that he never had Baudelaire's perfect sense of art, and that he does not seem, like Flaubert, to have laid in, before melancholy marked him for her own, a sufficient stock of living types to save him from the charge of being a mere study-student. There is no Frédéric, no M. Homais, in his repertory. Every Giovanni—even Orgilus, his two masterpieces, are, if not exactly things of shreds and patches, at any rate artificial persons, young men who have known more of books than of life, and who persevere in their eccentric courses with almost more than a half knowledge that they are eccentric. Annabella is incomplete, though there is nothing, except her love, unnatural in her. The strokes which draw her are separate imaginations of a learned draughtsman, not fresh transcripts from the living model. Penthea and Calantha are wholly artificial; a live Penthea would never have thought of such a fantastic martyrdom, unless she had been insane or suffering from green-sickness, and a live Calantha would have behaved in a perfectly different fashion, or if she had behaved in the same, would have been quit for her temporary aberration. We see (or at least I think I see) in Ford exactly the signs which are so familiar to us in our own day, and which repeat themselves regularly at the end of all periods of distinct literary creativeness—the signs of *excentricité voulue*. The author imagines that "all is said" in the ordinary way, and that he must go to the ends of the earth to fetch something extraordinary. If he is strong enough, as Ford was, he fetches it, and it *is* something extraordinary, and we owe him, with all his extravagance, respect and honour for his labour. But we can never put him on the level of the men who, keeping within ordinary limits, achieve masterpieces there.—GEORGE SAINTSBURY, *A History of Elizabethan Literature*, 1887, pp. 407–8

LOVE'S SACRIFICE

Vnto this Altar, rich with thy owne spice,
I bring one graine, to thy *Loves Sacrifice*:
And boast to see thy flames ascending, while
Perfumes enrich our Ayre from thy sweet Pile.
Looke here THOV that hast *malice* to the Stage,
And *Impudence* enough for the whole Age;
Voluminously-Ignorant! be vext
To read this Tragedy, and thy owne be next.
—JAMES SHIRLEY, "To my friend Mr IOHN FORD," c. 1633

Thou cheat'st us *Ford*, mak'st one seeme two by Art.
What is *Loves Sacrifice*, but *the broken Heart*?
—RICHARD CRASHAW, "Upon *Ford's* two Tragedyes," *The Delights of the Muses*, 1646

Its theme is a tissue of passion and revenge, into which too many coarse threads are allowed to enter. . . . The dramatist has drawn so wavering a line between sin and self-restraint, guilt and innocence, that he may be suspected of having wished to leave unsettled the "problem" which he proposes. If so, he stands from every point of view self-condemned. The bye-plot of the play is utterly revolting, and in the character of d'Avolos, and the passages in which he excites the jealousy of the Duke against Fernando, Ford has most palpably copied Iago.—ADOLPHUS WILLIAM WARD, *A History of English Dramatic Literature* (1875), 1899, Vol. 3, p. 82

PERKIN WARBECK

It is indeed the best specimen of the historic drama to be found out of Shakspeare; and, as a compact consecutive representation of a portion of English history, excels *King John* or the two Parts of *Henry IV*. It has as much unity as the dramatic history admits or requires; a clearly defined catastrophe, to which every incident contributes, and every scene advances. Ford showed great judgment in selecting a manageable episode of history, instead of a reign or a "life and death," which no one but Shakspeare could ever make practicable.—HARTLEY COLERIDGE, "Introduction" to *The Dramatic Works of Massinger and Ford*, 1840, p. lviii

As the last attempt at historical drama it suffers by contrast with the masterpieces of Shakespeare, but its merits are considerable, and entirely different from those of Ford's other works. The tragedy is founded on Bacon's *Life of Henry the Seventh*, and the character of the monarch is developed with skill and discretion. The play, interesting, dignified and occasionally humorous, seems to indicate that Ford's genius was capable of a wider range than his prevailing melancholy allowed. We doubt, indeed, whether more to wonder that he should have written one such play, or that, having written one, he should have written no more.—J. HOWARD B. MASTERMAN, *The Age of Milton*, 1897, p. 82

ALGERNON CHARLES SWINBURNE
From "John Ford"
Essays and Studies
1875, pp. 276–313

Whenever the name of the poet Ford comes back to us, it comes back splendid with the light of another man's genius. The fiery panegyric of Charles Lamb is as an aureole behind it. That high-pitched note of critical and spiritual enthusiasm exalts even to disturbance our own sense of admiration; possibly, too, even to some after injustice of reaction in the rebound of mind. Certainly, on the one hand, we see that the spirit of the critic has been kindled to excess by contact and apprehension of the poet's; as certainly, on the other hand, we see the necessary excellence of that which could so affect and so attach the spirit of another man, and of such another man as Lamb. And the pure excess of admiration for things indeed admirable, of delight in things indeed delightful, is itself also a delightful and admirable thing when expressed to such purpose by such men.

And this poet is doubtless a man worthy of note and admiring remembrance. He stands apart among his fellows, without master or follower; he has learnt little from Shakespeare or Marlowe, Jonson or Fletcher. . . . (The poetry of Ford) might rather be likened to a mountain lake shut in by solitary highlands, without visible outlet or inlet, seen fitlier by starlight than by sunlight; much such an one as the Lac de

Gaube above Cauterets, steel-blue and sombre, with a strange attraction for the swimmer in its cold smooth reticence and breathless calm. For nothing is more noticeable in this poet than the passionless reason and equable tone of style with which in his greatest works he treats of the deepest and most fiery passions, the quiet eye with which he searches out the darkest issues of emotion, the quiet hand with which he notes them down. At all times his verse is even and regular, accurate and composed; never specially flexible or melodious, always admirable for precision, vigour, and purity. . . .

The fame of Ford hangs mainly upon two great tragedies, which happily are strong enough in structure to support a durable reputation. Two others among his plays are indeed excellent, and worthy of a long life of honor; but among the mighty throng of poets then at work a leading place could hardly have been granted to the author only of *The Lover's Melancholy* and *Perkin Warbeck*. To the author of '*Tis Pity She's a Whore* and *The Broken Heart* it cannot be refused.

It is somewhat unfortunate that the very title of Ford's masterpiece should sound so strangely in the ears of a generation "whose ears are the chastest part about them." For of these great twin tragedies the first-born is on the whole the greater. The subtleties and varieties of individual character do not usually lie well within the reach of Ford's handling; but in the part of Giovanni we find more of this power than elsewhere. Here the poet has put forth all his strength; the figure of his protagonist stands out complete and clear. There is more ease and life in it than in his other sculptures; though here as always Ford is rather a sculptor of character than a painter. But the completeness, the consistency of design is here all the worthier of remark, that we too often find this the most needful quality for a dramatist wanting in him as in other great writers of his time.

. . . In Ford's best work we are usually conscious of a studious arrangement of emotion and expression, a steady inductive process of feeling as of thought, answering to the orderly measure of the verse. That swift and fiery glance which flashes at once from all depths to all heights of the human spirit, that intuition of an indefinable and infallible instinct which at a touch makes dark things clear and brings distant things close, is not a gift of his; perhaps Webster alone of English poets can be said to share it in some measure with Shakespeare. Bosola and Flamineo, Vittoria Corombona and the Duchess of Malfi, even Romelio and Leonora in that disjointed and chaotic play *The Devil's Law-case*, good characters and bad alike, all have this mark upon them of their maker's swift and subtle genius; this sudden surprise of the soul in its remoter hiding-places at its most secret work. In a few words that startle as with a blow and lighten as with a flame, the naked natural spirit is revealed, bare to the roots of life. And this power Ford also has shown here at least; witness the passionate subtlety and truth of this passage, the deepest and keenest of his writing, as when taken with the context it will assuredly appear:—

> *Annabella:* Be not deceived, my brother;
> This banquet is an harbinger of death
> To you and me; assure yourself it is,
> And be prepared to welcome it.
> *Giovanni:*   Well, then:
> The schoolmen teach that all this globe of earth
> Shall be consumed to ashes in a minute.
> *Ann.:* So I have read too.
> *Gio.:*   But 'twere somewhat
>   strange
> To see the waters burn; could I believe

> This might be true, I could believe as well
> There might be hell or heaven.
> *Ann.:*   That's most certain.
> *Gio.:* A dream, a dream! else in this other world
>   We should know one another.
> *Ann.:*   So we shall.
> *Gio.:*   Have you heard so?

All the horror of this wonderful scene is tempered into beauty by the grace and glow of tenderness which so suffuses it as to verify the vaunt of Giovanni—

>   If ever after-times should hear
> Of our fast-knit affections, though perhaps
> The laws of conscience and of civil use
> May justly blame us, yet when they but know
> Our loves, that love will wipe away that rigour
> Which would in other incests be abhorred.
> Give me your hand; how sweetly life doth run
> In these well-coloured veins! how constantly
> These palms do promise health! but I could chide
> With nature for this cunning flattery—
> Kiss me again—forgive me.

The soft and fervent colour of Ford's style, the smooth and finished measure of his verse, never fail him throughout the nobler parts of this tragedy; but here as elsewhere we sometimes find, instead of these, a certain hardness of tone peculiar to him. The ferocious nakedness of reciprocal invective in the scene where Soranzo discovers the pregnancy of Annabella has no parallel in the works of his great compeers. M. Taine has translated the opening passages of that scene in the division of his history of English literature which treats of our great dramatists. He has done full justice to the force and audacity of Ford's realism, which indeed he seems to rate higher than the depth and pathos, the sweet and subtle imagination, of other poets, if not than the more tender and gracious passages of Ford himself. He has dwelt, it appears to me, with especial care and favour upon three men of high genius, in all of whom this quality or this defect is conspicuous, of hardness too often deepening into brutality. A better and keener estimate of Ford, of Dryden, and of Swift can hardly be found than M. Taine's. Their vigorous and positive genius has an evident attraction for his critical spirit, which enjoys and understands the tangible and definable forces of mind, handles the hard outline, relishes the rough savour of the actual side of things with which strength of intellect rather than strength of imagination has to deal. As with Swift and Dryden among their fellows, so with Ford among his, the first great quality that strikes a student is the force of grasp, the precision of design, the positive and resolute touch with which all things are set down. A dramatic poet of Ford's high quality cannot of course be wanting in beauty and tenderness, in delicacy and elevation, unknown to men whose mightiest gift was that of noble satire, though the genius so applied were as deep and wide and keen, the spirit so put to service as swift and strong and splendid, as that of the two great men just mentioned. Not only the lovely lines above cited, but the very names of Calantha and Penthea, bear witness at once in our memory to the grace and charm of their poet's work at its best. The excess of tragic effect in his scenes, his delight in "fierce extremes" and volcanic eruptions of character and event, have in the eyes of some critics obscured the milder side of his genius. They are not without excuse. No one who has studied Ford throughout with the care he demands and deserves can fail to feel the want of that sweet and spontaneous fluency which belongs to the men of Shakespeare's school—that bird-like note of passionate music which vibrates in their verse to every breath of joy or sorrow. There is something too much now and then of rule and line, something indeed of hard limitation and apparent rigidity of method. I say this merely by comparison; set against the dramatists of any later school, he will appear as natural and instinctive a singer as any bird of the Shakespearian choir. But of pure imagination, of absolute poetry as distinguished from intellectual force and dramatic ability, no writer of his age except Massinger has less. Yet they are both poets of a high class, dramatists of all but the highest. They both impress us with a belief in their painstaking method of work, in the care and conscience with which their scenes were wrought out. Neither Ford nor Massinger could have ventured to indulge in the slippery style and shambling license which we pardon in Decker for the sake of his lyric note and the childlike delicacy of his pathos, his tenderness of colour and his passionate fancy; nor could they have dared the risk of letting their plays drift loose and shift for themselves at large, making the best that might be made of such rough and unhewn plots as Cyril Tourneur's, Middleton's, or Chapman's—sustained and quickened by the unquenchable and burning fire, the bitter ardour and angry beauty of Tourneur's verse, the grace and force of Middleton's fluent and exuberant invention, the weight of thought and grave resonance of Chapman's gnomic lines. They could not afford to let their work run wild; they were bound not to write after the erratic fashion of their time. All the work of Massinger, all the serious work of Ford, is the work of an artist who respects alike himself, his art, and the reader or spectator who may come to study it. There is scarcely another dramatic poet of their time for whom as much can be said. On the other hand, there is scarcely another dramatic poet of their time who had not more than they had of those "raptures" which "were all air and fire," of "that fine madness which rightly should possess a poet's brain." The just and noble eulogy of Drayton, though appropriate above all to the father of English tragedy, is applicable also more or less to the successors of Marlowe, as well as to the master of the "mighty line" himself. To Ford it is less appropriate; to Massinger it is not applicable at all. This is said out of no disrespect or ingratitude to that admirable dramatist, whose graver and lighter studies are alike full of interest and liberal of enjoyment; but the highest touch of imagination, the supreme rapture and passion of poetry, he has not felt, and therefore he cannot make us feel. . . .

The tragic genius of Ford takes a softer tone and more tender colour in *The Broken Heart* than in any of his other plays; except now and then in the part of Bassanes, there are no traces of the ferocity and brutality which mark in the tragedy preceding it such characters as Soranzo, Vasques, and Grimaldi. But here too there is something of Ford's severity, a certain rigid and elaborate precision of work, unlike the sweet seeming instinctiveness, the noble facility of manner and apparent impulse of gracious or majestic speech, which imbues and informs the very highest dramatic style; the quality which Marlowe and Shakespeare bequeathed to their successors, which kept fresh the verse of Beaumont and Fletcher despite its overmuch easiness and exuberance of mannerism, which gave life to the roughest outlines of Webster, Decker, Tourneur, which even Marston and Chapman, with all their faults of crudity and pedantry, showed when they had to rise to the height of any great and tragic argument. The same rigidity is noticeable to some extent in the characters: the marble majesty of Calantha is indeed noble and proper, and gives force and edge to the lofty passion of the catastrophe; but in Penthea too there is something over hard and severe; we find a vein of harshness and bitterness in her angry grief which Shakespeare or indeed Webster would have tempered and sweetened. In the

faultless and most exquisite scene where she commits to the princess her legacies of "three poor jewels," this bitterness disappears, and the sentiment is as delicate and just as the expression; while the gracious gentleness of Calantha gives a fresh charm of warmth and sympathy to her stately presence and office in the story. The quality of pity here made manifest in her brings her own after suffering within reach of our pity. Again, in the previous interview of Ithocles with Penthea, and above all in her delirious dying talk, there is real and noble pathos, though hardly of the most subtle and heart-piercing kind; and in the parts of Ithocles and Orgilus there is a height and dignity which ennoble alike the slayer and the slain. None could give this quality better than Ford: this, the most complete and equal of his works, is full of it throughout.

From the "high-tuned poem," as he justly calls it, which he had here put forth in evidence of his higher and purer part of power, the fall, or collapse rather, in his next work was singular enough. I trust that I shall not be liable to any charge of Puritan prudery though I avow that this play of *Love's Sacrifice* is to me intolerable. In the literal and genuine sense of the word, it is utterly indecent, unseemly and unfit for handling. The conception is essentially foul because it is essentially false; and in the sight of art nothing is so foul as falsehood. The incestuous indulgence of Giovanni and Annabella is not improper for tragic treatment; the obscene abstinence of Fernando and Bianca is wholly improper. There is a coarseness of moral fibre in the whole work which is almost without parallel among our old poets. More than enough has been said of their verbal and spiritual license; but nowhere else, as far as I know, shall we find within the large limits of our early drama such a figure as Ford's Bianca set up for admiration as a pure and noble type of woman. For once, to my own wonder and regret, I find myself at one with the venomous moralist Gifford on a question of morals, when he observes of "that most innocent lady" that "she is, in fact, a gross and profligate adulteress, and her ridiculous reservations, while they mark her lubricity, only enhance her shame." The worst is, that we get no moment of relief throughout from the obtrusion of the very vilest elements that go to make up nature and deform it. No height or grandeur of evil is here to glorify, no aspiration or tenderness of afterthought is here to allay, the imbecile baseness, the paltry villainies and idiocies, of the "treacherous, lecherous, kindless" reptiles that crawl in and out before our loathing eyes. The language of course is in the main elaborate, pure, and forcible; the verse often admirable for its stately strength; but beyond this we can find nothing to plead in extenuation of uncleanness and absurdity. The only apparent aim of the quasi-comic interludes is to prove the possibility of producing something even more hateful than the tragic parts. The indecency of Ford's farcical underplots is an offence above all things to art. How it may seem from the preacher's point of view is no present concern of ours; perhaps he might find it by comparison harmless and powerless, as assuredly it can attract or allure the intellect or the senses of no creature above the level of apes and swine; but in the artist's eyes it is unsufferable and damnable. Without spirit, without humour, without grace, it encumbers the scene as with dried and congealed filth. In the face of much exquisite work of painter and sculptor, poet and humourist, which is anything but conventionally decent, we cannot allow that art must needs "lean to virtue's side," and lend her voice or hand to swell the verdict or prop the pulpit of judge or moralist; but two things she cannot away with; by the very law of her life, by the very condition of her being, she is bound to reject whatever is brutal, whatever is prurient; Swift cannot bend her to the worship of Cloacina, Moore cannot teach her the lisp and leer of his toad-faced Cupids. Great men may sin by mad violence and brutality, like that fierce world-satirist who stood out with lacerated heart against all bitterest infliction and "envious wrath of man or God," a Titan blasted by the fires but not beaten by the strokes of heaven; but small men only can teach their tongues the tittering accent of a vicious valet, the wriggling prurience of such lackey's literature as is handed round on a salver to the patrons of drawing-room rhymesters and ante-chamber witlings. Ford was a poet, and a poet of high mark; he could not therefore, even in a meaner age, have learnt the whimper or the smirk of sentimental or jocose prurience; he could never have submitted to ignoble handling the sweet or bitter emotions and passions of sense or spirit; all torture and all rapture of the flesh or of the soul he would always have treated with the frank and serious freedom of the artist, never with the bragging and simpering petulance of the social poetaster and parasitic plagiarist; but the other inadmissible thing he has too often admitted within the precinct of his work. The dull brutality of his lame and laborious farce is a fault quite unlike the faults of his fellows; his cold and dry manner makes his buffoonery at once rancid and insipid; while the "bluff beastliness" of Jonson's plebeian part, the overflowing and boyish wantonness of Fletcher, the foul-mouthed fidelity of Decker's transcripts from the low life of his period, even the rank breadth of Marston's shameless satire, may admit of excuse in the sight of art, the pointless and spiritless licence of Ford's attempts at comedy can be neither honourably excused nor reasonably explained. Of Shakespeare alone we can be sure that no touch is wrong, no tone too broad, no colour too high for the noble and necessary purposes of his art; but of his followers, if excuse be needed for their errors and excesses, the most may plead in palliation either the height of spirits and buoyancy of blood, or the passion of a fierce sincerity, or the force and flavour of strong comic genius, or the relief given by contrast to the high pure beauty of the main work; all alike may plead the freedom of the time, the freshness of young life and energy of the dawn, working as they did when the art was new-born, too strong a child of earth and heaven and too joyous to keep always a guard on its ways and words, to walk always within bounds and speak always within compass. But Ford is no poetic priest or spiritual witness against evil, whose lips have been touched with the live coal of sacred satire, and set on fire of angry prophecy; the wrath and scorn of Jonson, the rage of Tourneur and the bitterness of Marston, find in him no echo of response; and of the bright sweet flow and force of life which feed as from a springing fountain the joyful genius of Beaumont and Fletcher, of the gladness and grace of that wild light Muse who sings "as if she would never grow old," whether her song be of men's joy or sorrow, he has nothing to show in excuse of worse faults than theirs; with him

> The heyday in the blood is tame, it's humble,
> And waits upon the judgment.

Massinger has been accused of the same dull and deliberate license of speech; but Massinger, though poor in verbal wit, had a strong and grave humour, an occasional breadth and warmth of comic invention, which redeems his defects or offences. Harley Coleridge, in his notice of the two poets, says that Massinger would have been the dullest of all bad jokers, had not Ford contrived to be still duller. But Massinger, if not buoyant and brilliant as Fletcher, or rich with the spiritual wealth and strong with the gigantic thews of Jonson, has his own place of honour in pure as well as mixed comedy; Belgarde, Justice Greedy, Borachia, and others, are worthy to stand, in their lower line of humour, below the higher level of

such studies as Overreach and Luke; whereas, if Ford's lighter characters are ever inoffensive for a moment, it is all that can be said of them, and more than could be hoped. The strength and intensity of his genius require a tragic soil to flourish in, an air of tragedy to breathe; its lightning is keenest where the night of emotion and event is darkest in which it moves and works. In romantic drama or mixed comedy it shines still at times with a lambent grace and temperance of light; but outside the limit of serious thought and feeling it is quenched at once, and leaves but an unsavoury fume behind. Even in those higher latitudes the moral air is not always of the clearest; the sanctity of Giovanni's confessor, for example, has something of the compliant quality of Bianca's virtue; it sits so loosely and easily on him that, fresh from the confession of Annabella's incest, he assists in plighting her hand to Soranzo, and passing off on the bridegroom as immaculate a woman whom he knows to be with child by her brother; and this immediately after that most noble scene in which the terror and splendour of his rebuke has bowed to the very dust before him the fair face and the ruined soul of his penitent. After this we cannot quite agree with Macaulay that Ford has in this play "assigned a highly creditable part to the friar;" but certainly he has the most creditable part there is to play; and as certainly he was designed on the whole for a type of sincere and holy charity. The jarring and startling effect of such moral discords weakens the poet's hold on the reader by the shock they give to his faith and sympathy. Beaumont and Fletcher have sinned heavily in the same way; and the result is that several of their virtuous characters are more really and more justly offensive to the natural sense, more unsavoury to the spiritual taste, than any wantonness of words or extravagance of action can make their representative figures of vice.

In the gallery of Ford's work, as in the gallery of Webster's, there is one which seems designed as a sample of regular and classic form, a sedate study after a given model. Ford's *Perkin Warbeck* holds the same place on his stage as *Appius and Virginia* does on Webster's. In both plays there is a perfect unity of action, a perfect straightforwardness of design; all is clear, orderly, direct to the point; there is no outgrowth or overgrowth of fancy, there are no byways of poetry to divert the single progress of the story. By the side of *The Duchess of Malfi* or *The Broken Heart* they look rigid and bare. Both are noble works; Webster's has of course the more ardour and vehemence of power, Ford's has perhaps the more completeness of stage effect and careful composition. The firmness and fidelity of hand with which his leading characters are drawn could only be shown by a dissection of the whole play scene by scene. The simple and lofty purity of conception, the exact and delicate accuracy of execution, are alike unimpaired by any slip or flaw of judgment or of feeling. The heroic sincerity of Warbeck, his high courtesy and constancy, his frank gratitude and chivalrous confidence, give worthy proof of Ford's ability to design a figure of stainless and exalted presence; the sad strong faith of his wife, the pure and daring devotion of the lover who has lost her, the petulant and pathetic pride of her father, all melted at last into stately sympathy and approval of her truth in extremity of trial; and, more than all these, the noble mutual recognition and regard of Warbeck and Dalyell in the time of final test; are qualities which raise this drama to the highest place among its compeers for moral tone and effect. The two kings are faithful and forcible studies; the smooth resolute equanimity and self-reliant craft of the first Tudor sets off the shallow chivalry and passionate unstable energy of the man of Flodden. The insolent violence of constraint put upon Huntley in the disposal of his daughter's hand is of a piece with the almost brutal tone of contempt assumed towards Warbeck, when he begins to weary of supporting the weaker cause for the mere sake of magnanimous display and irritable self-assertion. His ultimate dismissal of the star-crossed pretender is "perfect Stuart" in its bland abnegation of faith and the lofty courtliness of manner with which engagements are flung over and pledges waved aside; whether intentionally or not, Ford has touched off to the life the family habit of repudiation, the hereditary faculty of finding the most honourable way to do the most dishourable things. Nor is the other type of royalty less excellently real and vivid; the mixture of warmth and ceremony in Katherine's reception by Henry throws into fresh and final relief the implacable placidity of infliction with which he marks her husband for utmost ignominy of suffering.

Of imaginative beauty and poetic passion this play has nothing; but for noble and equable design of character it stands at the head of Ford's works. There is no clearer example in our literature of the truth of the axiom repeated by Mr. Arnold from the teaching of the supreme Greek masters, that "all depends upon the subject." There are perhaps more beautiful lines in *Love's Sacrifice* than in *Perkin Warbeck*; yet the former play is utterly abortive and repulsive, a monument of discomfiture and discredit, as the latter of noble aim and noble success. It is the one high sample of historic drama produced between the age of Shakespeare and our own; the one intervening link—a link of solid and durable metal—which connects the first and the latest labours in that line of English poetry; the one triumphant attempt to sustain and transmit the tradition of that great tragic school founded by Marlowe, perfected by Shakespeare, revived by the author of *Philip van Artevelde*. The central figure of Ford's work is not indeed equal in stature of spirit and strength of handling to the central figure of Sir Henry Taylor's; there is a broader power, a larger truth, in the character of Artevelde than in the character of Warbeck; but the high qualities of interest based on firm and noble grounds, of just sentiment and vital dignity, of weight, force, and exaltation of thought, shown rather in dramatic expansion and development of lofty character by lofty method than in scenes and passages detachable from the context as samples of reflection and expression—these are in great measure common to both poets. Ford, again, has the more tender and skilful hand at drawing a woman; his heroines make by far the warmer and sharper impression on us; this on the whole is generally his strongest point, as it is perhaps the other's weakest; while, though we may not think his female studies up to the mark of his male portraits, there is certainly no English dramatist since Shakespeare who can be matched as a student of men, comparable for strong apprehension and large heroic grasp of masculine character, with the painter of Comnenus, of Artevelde, and of Dunstan.

. . . No poet is less forgettable than Ford; none fastens (as it were) the fangs of his genius and his will more deeply in your memory. You cannot shake hands with him and pass by; you cannot fall in with him and out again at pleasure; if he touch you once he takes you, and what he takes he keeps his hold of; his work becomes part of your thought and parcel of your spiritual furniture for ever; he signs himself upon you as with a seal of deliberate and decisive power. His force is never the force of accident; the casual divinity of beauty which falls as though direct from heaven upon stray lines and phrases of some poets falls never by any such heavenly chance on his; his strength of impulse is matched by his strength of will; he never works more by instinct than by resolution; he knows what he would have and what he will do, and gains his end and does his work with full conscience of purpose and insistence of design. By the might of a great will seconded by the force of a great hand he won the place he holds against all odds of rivalry in a race of rival giants. In that gallery of monumental men and mighty memories, among or above the fellows of his godlike craft, the high figure of Ford stands steadily erect; his name is ineffaceable from the scroll of our great writers; it is one of the loftier landmarks of English poetry.

THOMAS CAREW

c. 1594–c. 1640

Thomas Carew was born in West Wickham, Kent, probably in 1594 or 1595. His father, Sir Thomas, was a master in Chancery. Carew entered Merton College, Oxford, in 1608, and received a B.A. in 1611. He read law at Middle Temple, London, during 1612 and went to Venice as the secretary to the British ambassador Sir Dudley Carleton in 1613. In 1616 Carew accompanied Carleton to The Hague, where he remained for only a short time; in 1619 he was at the French court with Edward Herbert of Cherbury.

Carew was one of the Cavalier poets at the court of Charles I; a poetic disciple of Jonson, he was also influenced by the Italian Baroque poet Giambattista Marino, and based several of his own poems on the latter's lyrics. In 1630 Carew became a Gentleman of Charles I's Privy Chamber. He wrote the masque *Coelum Britannicum*, which was performed at Whitehall, with stage settings by Inigo Jones, on Shrove Tuesday of 1634. One of his most famous poems, "An Elegie upon the Death of the Dean of Pauls, Dr John Donne," was published in 1633. The longest of his lyrics is the licentious *The Rapture*.

Carew is believed to have died in 1640. His *Poems* were published shortly after his death.

Personal

Thomas Carew was a younger brother of a good family, and of excellent parts, and had spent many years of his youth in France and Italy; and returning from travel, followed the court; which the modesty of that time disposed men to do some time, before they pretended to be of it; and he was very much esteemed by the most eminent persons in the court, and well looked upon by the king himself, some years before he could obtain to be sewer to the king; and when the king conferred that honour upon him, it was not without the regret even of the whole Scotch nation, which united themselves in recommending another gentleman to the place: of so great value were those relations held in that age, when majesty was beheld with the reverence it ought to be. He was a person of a pleasant and facetious wit, and made many poems, (especially in the amorous way,) which for the sharpness of the fancy, and the elegancy of the language in which that fancy was spread, were at least equal, if not superior to any of that time: but his glory was, that after fifty years of his life, spent with less severity or exactness than it ought to have been, he died with the greatest remorse for that license, and with the greatest manifestation of Christianity that his best friends could desire.—EDWARD HYDE, EARL OF CLARENDON, *The Life of Edward Earl of Clarendon*, c. 1668

Then was told this by Mr. Anthony Faringdon, and have heard it discourst by others, that Mr. Thomas Cary, a poet of note, and a great libertine in his life and talke, and one that had in his youth bein acquainted with Mr. Ha., sent for Mr. Hales to come to him in a dangerous fit of sickness, and desired his advice and absolution, which Mr. Hales, upon a promise of amendment, gave him, (this was I think in the country). But Mr. Cary came to London, fell to his old company, and into a more visible scandalous life, and especially in his discourse, and be (being?) taken very sick, that which proved his last, and being much trowbled in mind, procured Mr. Ha. to come to him in this his sickness and agony of minde, desyring earnestly, after a confession of many of his sins, to have his prayers and his absolution. Mr. Ha. told him he shoold have his prayers, but woold by noe meanes give him then either the sacrament or absolution.—IZAAK WALTON, MSS. Collections for the Life of John Hales, c. 1683

Thomas Carew, one of the famed poets of his time for the charming sweetness of his lyric odes and amorous sonnets, was younger brother to sir Matthew Carew a great royalist in the time of the puritanical rebellion, and both of the family of the Carews of Glocestershire, but descended, as I presume, from the ancient family of their name in Devonshire, had his academical education in Corp. Ch. coll. as those that knew him have informed me, yet he occurs not matriculated as a member of that house, or that he took a scholastical degree. Afterwards improving his parts by travelling and conversation with ingenious men in the metropolis, he became reckon'd among the chiefest of his time for delicacy of wit and poetic fancy. About which time being taken into the royal court for his most admirable ingenuity, was made a gentleman of the privy chamber, and sewer in ordinary to King Ch. I. who always esteemed him to the last one of the most celebrated wits in his court, and therefore by him as highly valued, so afterwards grieved at his untimely death.—ANTHONY À WOOD, *Athenae Oxonienses*, 1691–1721

General

Tom Carew was next, but he had a fault
That would not well stand with a Laureat;
His Muse was hard bound, and th'issue of's brain
Was seldom brought forth but with trouble and pain.
　　　　　And
All that were present there did agree,
A Laureats Muse should be easie and free;
Yet sure 'twas not that, but 'twas thought that his
　　　　　Grace

Consider'd he was well he had a Cup-bearers place.
　　—SIR JOHN SUCKLING, "The Wits," 1637

The want of boldness and expansion in Carew's thoughts and subjects, excludes him from rivalship with *great* poetical names; nor is it difficult, even within the narrow pale of his works, to discover some faults of affectation, and of still more objectionable indelicacy. But among the poets who have walked in the same limited path, he is pre-eminently beautiful, and deservedly ranks among the earliest of those who gave a cultivated grace to our lyrical strains. His slowness in composition was evidently that sort of care in the poet, which saves trouble to his reader. His poems have touches of elegance and refinement, which their trifling subjects could not have yielded without a delicate and deliberate exercise of the fancy; and he unites the point and polish of later times with many of the genial and warm tints of the elder muse. Like Waller, he is by no means free from conceit; and one regrets to find him addressing the surgeon bleeding Celia, in order to tell him that the blood which he draws proceeds not from the fair one's arm, but from the lover's heart. But of such frigid thoughts he is more sparing than Waller; and his conceptions, compared to that poet's, are like fruits of a richer flavour, that have been cultured with the same assiduity.—THOMAS CAMPBELL, *Specimens of the British Poets*, 1819

More of a poet than Corbet, and accounted the prince of the amorous versifiers of his day, was Thomas Carew, of the Carews of Gloucestershire, born about 1589, and now, in his forty-fourth year, Gentleman of the Privy Chamber and Sewer in Ordinary to King Charles, who "always esteemed him," says Wood, "one of the most celebrated wits in his court." He was "much respected, if not adored by the poets of his time, especially Ben Jonson;" and, according to Oldys, his verses, especially such as were set to music by Henry Lawes and other composers, were more in request in aristocratic society between 1630 and 1640 than those of any other poet. It is easy, in reading them yet, or his masque of *Coelum Britannicum*, written in 1633, and performed at Whitehall by the king in person and some of the chief nobility, to see the reason of this popularity. There is a light French spirit in his love poems, a grace and even a tenderness of sentiment, and a lucid softness of style, that make them peculiarly pleasing, and that, even when he becomes licentious, help to save him. He has an elegy on Donne's death, from which we gather his extraordinary veneration for that poet. He has also verses of strong compliment to Ben Jonson and his style. But, though there is evident sincerity in his praises of these poets, and in several of his pieces he writes in their strain, Spenser and Shakespeare seem to have been his favourites for private reading, and he seems to have formed his style partly from them and partly from the light artificial French poets with whom he had become acquainted in his travels. This is in Carew's characteristic vein:—

He that loves a rosy cheek,
　　Or a coral lip admires,
Or from star-like eyes doth seek
　　Fuel to maintain his fires,—
As old Time makes those decay,
So his flames must waste away.

But a smooth and stedfast mind,
　　Gentle thoughts and calm desires,
Hearts with equal love combined,
　　Kindle never-dying fires.
Where these are not, I despise
Lovely cheeks or lips or eyes.

These and some hundred pieces, chiefly of the same graceful

artificial cast of lyric, were published collectively as Carew's poems in 1640. The author had died in the preceding year, regretting, according to Clarendon, that his life had not been better spent.—DAVID MASSON, *The Life of John Milton*, 1859, Vol. 1, Ch. 6

Two or three writers had anticipated Carew in the name which he has chosen for his mistress. In 1594, William Percy printed *Sonnets to the fairest Coelia*; Sir David Murray of Gorthy celebrated the same unknown goddess in 1611; and about 1625 William Browne, the Devonshire poet, composed fourteen stanzas similarly superscribed. The Sonnets of Percy and Murray are scarcely worth discussion; some of Browne's are excellent both in matter and manner; but on the whole Carew may certainly be allowed to excel in purity and perspicuity of diction, in exquisite happiness and elegance of sentiment, in the harmony of his numbers, in a certain charming finish of style, and in peculiar freedom from affectation, pedantry, and false taste.

It is to be regretted that here and there (but very occasionally) are to be found exceptionable descriptions or allusions, which place Carew in this respect at a disadvantage in comparison with the politer Waller; but the licentiousness of Carew's muse proceeds from an unpruned luxuriance of fancy and a tolerated freedom of expression; and although it outrages modern ideas of decorum, it is not either prurient or nauseous, like many of the obscenities in Herrick's *Hesperides*.

The writings of Carew abound with conceits, but, unlike the conceits of some of his less noted contemporaries, they generally reconcile themselves to us by good taste in the treatment and delicacy of execution.—WILLIAM CAREW HAZLITT, "Some Account of Thomas Carew," *The Poems of Thomas Carew*, 1870, pp. xlvii–xlviii

Among the Royalist lyrists of the seventeenth century Carew takes a foremost place. In genius he is surpassed by Herrick only, and in age he is the first of that gallant band of cavalier song-writers of whom Rochester is the last. Born in the flush of the Elizabethan summer, when the whole garden of English poetry was ablaze with blossom, he lived to hand down to his followers a tradition of perfume and dainty form, that vivified the autumn of the century with a little Martin's summer of his own. The lyrists of the school of Carew preserved something of the brave Shakespearean tradition when the dramatists of the school of Shirley had completely lost it, and the transition from romanticism to classicism was more gently made in this order of writing than in any other. It is the special glory of Carew that he formularised the practice of writing courtly amorous poetry. Strains very similar to his own had appeared in the works of older poets, as in *The Forest* of Ben Jonson and in the plays of Fletcher, but always casually; it was Carew who seized this floating improvisation, and made an art of it. As there were Anacreontic poets before Anacreon, so there were octosyllabic addresses to Julia or Celia before Carew; yet we grant to him the praise of the invention, since he gave his best work, and not, as others had done, his lightest to it.

In his elegiac lines on Donne, Carew joins the chorus of eulogy with more than customary earnestness, and claims for that great man the title of king among the English poets. Yet no one of Donne's contemporaries was less injuriously affected by the presence of that most crabbed and eccentric genius than Carew, whose sweet and mellow Muse neither rises into the dangerous heights nor falls into the terrible pitfalls haunted by her audacious sister. A certain tendency to conceit was the sin not of one school but of the age, and Carew's trivialities have

none of the vehemence or intellectual perversity of Donne's. In company with Herrick, this thoroughly sensual poet draws his pet conceit from the art of the kitchen, and offends us mostly by being reminded of his dinner as he walks abroad;—

> No more the frost
> Candies the grass, or casts an icy cream
> Upon the silver lake or crystal stream,

are phrases that justly excite our ridicule, but they are far removed from the heavy machinery of symbolism with which Donne, and a whole host of imitators after him, sought to involve their simplest fancies in sublimity. Carew was far too indolent to trouble himself with the rhetoric of the schools or to speculate upon the conduct of the mind. He loved wine, and roses, and fair florid women, to whom he could indite joyous or pensive poems about their beauty, adoring it while it lasted, regretting it when it faded. He has not the same intimate love of detail as Herrick; we miss in his poems those realistic touches that give such wonderful freshness to the verses of the younger poet; nor does he indulge in the same amiable pedantry. But the habit of the two men's minds was very similar; both were pagans and given up to an innocent hedonism; neither was concerned with much beyond the eternal commonplaces of bodily existence, the attraction of beauty, the mutability of life, the brevity and sweetness of enjoyment. In the hands of the disciples the strings of the lyre became tenser, the garlands less luxuriant, and when we read Sedley and Rochester we find little trace left of Herrick and Carew save the brisk, elegant versification, and the courtly turn of compliment.

It is unfortunate that Carew was never persuaded to attempt a long poem. His masque of *Coelum Brittannicum*, which was undertaken in company with Inigo Jones to grace a royal visit, has the customary faults of pieces of this kind. It is abstract in interest, fragmentary in form, and the separate passages of verse have little charm of fancy. The best poem of Carew, *The Rapture*, is also the longest, yet does not reach the length of two hundred lines. Unhappily its beauties are presented to us with so much enthusiasm and with so little reticence, that no adequate citation from it can be laid before the general reader. But it gives the student a finer impression of Carew's powers than he would gain from any other piece, and betrays narrative and descriptive qualities that would have risked nothing in competition with Browne or with Giles Fletcher. It is, of course, by his lyrics alone that Carew is known to the ordinary reader of poetry. His songs are extremely mellifluous and well-balanced; he has an unusual art of sustaining his flight through an entire lyric, so that his poems are not strings of more or less pretty stanzas, but organic structures. It is in this that he excels Habington, Lovelace, and even Suckling, whose separate stanzas are often as graceful as his, but who rarely succeed in maintaining the same elegance of language throughout. It would seem that this admirable instinct for form led Carew to compose with great care, and to polish his verses assiduously. Sir John Suckling upbraids him with the 'trouble and pain' with which his muse brought forth children, and hazards the criticism that a laureate poet should be easy and free. We can only wish that Suckling himself had been a more conscientious artist, and a less free and easy rhymester; but the remark is interesting as showing us the stumbling-block on which the later Cavalier lyrists fell. They were such fine gentlemen that they disdained to cultivate their art and live laborious days, and we suffer as we search here and there for gems of spontaneous song amid the rubbish-heap that their carelessness has bequeathed us. To Carew, as to Webster before him, the impertinence of his contemporaries can have mattered little in comparison with the satisfaction he must have felt in his work as an artist.

The claim of Carew to a place among the artificers of our language must not be overlooked. In his hands English verse took a smooth and flexible character that had neither the splendours nor the discords of the great Elizabethan school, but formed an admirable medium for gentle thought and florid reverie. The praise that Voltaire gave to Waller might be transferred to Carew if it were not that to give such praise to any one writer is uncritical. But Waller might never have written, and the development of English verse would be still unbroken, whereas Carew is a necessary link between the Elizabethans and Prior. He represents the main stream of one of the great rivers of poetic influence proceeding from Ben Jonson, and he contrived to do so much because he remained so close to that master and yet in his particular vein excelled him. He is sometimes strangely modern. Such verses as those beginning—

As Celia rested in the shade
With Cleon by her side,

have all the character of the eighteenth century. Carew is thus a transitional figure. He holds Shakspeare with one hand and Congreve with the other, and leads us down the hill of the seventeenth century by a path more flowery and of easier incline than any of his compeers. Yet we must never forget, in considering his historical position, that his chief merit lies, after all, in his fresh colouring and sincere and tender passion.—EDMUND GOSSE, "Thomas Carew," *The English Poets*, ed. Thomas Humphry Ward, 1880, Vol. 2, pp. 111–14

Indissolubly connected with Herrick in age, in character, and in the singularly unjust criticism which has at various times been bestowed on him, is Thomas Carew. He was a slightly older man than Herrick, having been born in the year after the Armada; but he died nearly forty years before the author of the *Hesperides*, and nearly ten before the *Hesperides* themselves were published, while his own poems were never collected till after his own death. He was of a Gloucestershire branch of the famous Devonshire family of Carew, Cary, or Cruwys, was educated at Corpus Christi College, Oxford, travelled, followed the Court, was a disciple of Ben Jonson, and a member of the learned and accomplished society of Clarendon's earlier days, obtained a place in the household of Charles I., is said by his friend Hyde to have turned to devotion after a somewhat libertine life, and died in 1639, before the evil days of triumphant Puritanism, *felix opportunitate mortis.* He wrote little, and the scantiness of his production, together with the supposed pains it cost him, is ridiculed in Suckling's doggerel "Sessions of the Poets." But this reproach (which Carew shares with Gray, and with not a few others of the most admirable names in literature), unjust as it is, is less unjust than the general tone of criticism on Carew since. The *locus classicus* of depreciation both in regard to him and to Herrick is to be found, as might be expected, in one of the greatest, and one of the most wilfully capricious and untrustworthy of English critics, in Hazlitt. I am sorry to say that there can be little hesitation in setting down the extraordinary misjudgment of the passage in question (it occurs in the sixth Lecture on Elizabethan Literature), in part, at least, to the fact that Herrick, Carew, and Crashaw, who are summarily damned in it, were Royalists. If there were any doubt about the matter, it would be settled by the encomium bestowed in the very same passage on Marvell, who is, no doubt, as Hazlitt says, a true poet, but who as a poet is not worthy to untie the shoe strings of the authors of "The Litany," *The Rapture,* and "The Flaming Heart." Hazlitt, then, while on his way to tell us that Herrick's two best

pieces are some trivial anacreontics about Cupid and the Bees—things hackneyed through a dozen literatures, and with no recommendation but a borrowed prettiness—while about, I say, to deny Herrick the spirit of love or wine, and in the same breath with the dismissal of Crashaw as a "hectic enthusiast," informs us that Carew was "an elegant Court trifler," and describes his style as a "frequent mixture of the superficial and commonplace, with far-fetched and improbable conceits."

What Carew really is, and what he may be peremptorily declared to be in opposition even to such a critic as Hazlitt, is something quite different. He is one of the most perfect masters of lyrical form in English poetry. He possesses a command of the overlapped heroic couplet, which for sweep and rush of rhythm cannot be surpassed anywhere. He has, perhaps in a greater degree than any poet of that time of conceits, the knack of modulating the extravagances of fancy by the control of reason, so that he never falls into the unbelievableness of Donne, or Crashaw, or Cleveland. He had a delicacy, when he chose to be delicate, which is quintessential, and a vigour which is thoroughly manly. Best of all, perhaps, he had the intelligence and the self-restraint to make all his poems wholes, and not mere congeries of verses. There is always, both in the scheme of his meaning and the scheme of his metre, a definite plan of rise and fall, a concerted effect. That these great merits were accompanied by not inconsiderable defects is true. Carew lacks the dewy freshness, the unstudied grace of Herrick. He is even more frankly and uncontrolledly sensual, and has paid the usual and inevitable penalty that his best poem, *The Rapture,* is, for the most part, unquotable, while another, if he carried out its principles in this present year of grace, would run him the risk of imprisonment with hard labour. His largest attempt—the masque called *Cœlum Britannicum*—is heavy. His smaller poems, beautiful as they are, suffer somewhat from want of variety of subject. There is just so much truth in Suckling's impertinence that the reader of Carew sometimes catches himself repeating the lines of Carew's master, "Still to be neat, still to be drest," not indeed in full agreement with them, but not in exact disagreement. One misses the "wild civility" of Herrick. This acknowledgment, I trust, will save me from any charge of overvaluing Carew.

A man might, however, be easily tempted to overvalue him, who observes his beauties, and who sees how, preserving the force, the poetic spell, of the time, he was yet able, without in the least descending to the correctness of Waller and his followers, to introduce into his work something also preserving it from the weaknesses and inequalities which deface that of almost all his contemporaries, and which, as we shall see, make much of the dramatic and poetical work of 1630–1660 a chaos of slipshod deformity to any one who has the sense of poetical form. It is an unwearying delight to read and re-read the second of his poems, the "Persuasions to Love," addressed to a certain A. L. That the sentiment is common enough matters little; the commonest things in poetry are always the best. But the delicate interchange of the catalectic and acatalectic dimeter, the wonderful plays and changes of cadence, the opening, as it were, of fresh stops at the beginning of each new paragraph of the verse, so that the music acquires a new colour, the felicity of the several phrases, the cunning heightening of the passion as the poet comes to "Oh! love me then, and now begin it," and the dying fall of the close, make up to me, at least, most charming pastime. It is not the same kind of pleasure, no doubt, as that given by such an outburst as Crashaw's, to be mentioned presently, or by such pieces as the great soliloquies of Shakespere. Any one may say, if he likes to use words which are question-begging, when not strictly meaningless, that it is not such a "high" kind. But it is a kind, and in that kind perfect.—GEORGE SAINTSBURY, A *History of Elizabethan Literature*, 1887, pp. 359–62

It was Carew, indeed, who first sounded these "courtly amorous strains" thoughout the English land; who first taught his fellow-poets that to sing of love was not the occasional pastime, but the serious occupation of their lives. Yet what an easy, indolent suitor he is! What lazy raptures over Celia's eyes and lips! What finely poised compliments, delicate as rose leaves, and well fitted for the inconstant beauty who listened, with faint blushes and transient interest, to the song!—AGNES REPPLIER, "English Love-Songs," *Points of View*, 1891, p. 36

Carew would seem to have been the victim of a conspiracy of silence. His case is precisely the antithesis of Waller's. Waller has enjoyed considerably more fame than he deserved, Carew considerably less. As a poet he has been consistently belittled or ignored, as a man maligned. It has been considered sufficient to dismiss him in the same breath with Phineas Fletcher, Habington, Cleveland, and Suckling, as a 'Marinist,' an affected trifler, one of that school of fantastic euphuistic poets which flourished at the court of Charles I. To this injustice has been added that of regarding him as a licentious voluptuary, exclusively a maker of indecent song. At best he has been classed with one-poem poets like Suckling and Lovelace, whose collected works are merely so much oyster-shell enclosing those two famous pearls, the 'Ballad of a Wedding' and 'To Althea from Prison.' Nor has more recent criticism brought much compensation to Carew. Early in the century the forgotten critic Headley, and Nathan Drake, author of that delightful *mélange*, the *Literary Hours*,—a critic who had a love for our 'old poets' rare in his day, and whose judgments upon them are singularly sound as well as sympathetic—both complained of this injustice to Carew. 'To say of Carew that he is superior to Waller,' wrote Drake, 'is saying nothing; for if every line of Waller were lost I know not that poetry would have much to lament.' And wrote Headley, 'Waller is too exclusively considered as the first man who brought versification to anything like its present standard. Carew's pretensions to the same merit are seldom sufficiently either considered or allowed.' Yet Mr. Gosse, who is not wont 'to pour forgetfulness upon the dead,' in his exhaustive consideration of Waller's share in the history of the couplet, does not consider Carew's claims worth mentioning, and prefers instead to draw attention to 'the agonies and contortions' of one of his least successful poems, an elegy on the King of Sweden, which, after all, is no more agonised or contorted than poems on such themes were apt sometimes to be, even in the hands of that arch-eulogist and toady Waller himself. Archbishop Trench and Mr. Saintsbury, so far as I have noted, are the only latter-day critics who have given its due to what Mr. Saintsbury calls 'the miraculous art of Carew.' For, instead of Carew's poetry being characteristically euphuistic, licentious, trivial, and sporadic, the exact opposite is the truth. It is true that he has his concetti, like the other poets of his day, but they are relatively to the whole of his verse but a small proportion. His most famous poem, *The Rapture*, is certainly as frank an utterance of amorous passion as any in the language, but its very frankness is its virtue; as Mr. Ebsworth well says, it is 'not a tenth part so vicious as are the sickly sentimental pruriencies and pruderies of our *fin de siècle* poets.' The humour of its almost Rabelaisian hyperbole keeps it healthy; it is lusty, but not lascivious, and I agree with Mr. Ebsworth (who, being a clergyman, may be trusted to look after our souls in the matter) that 'no one need feel injury or disgust' in the reading of it. And over and above the merry wickedness

of it, what truly 'miraculous art'! But though, doubtless owing to its subject, A *Rapture* is the best known of Carew's poems, its theme is not by any means specially characteristic of its writer. A much graver, more dignified, mood is more frequent with him, as in lofty 'Counsel to his Mistress' on the transitoriness of

> Beauty's flower,
> Which will away, and doth together
> Both bud and fade, both blow and wither;

and on the wisdom of gathering roses while she may, not with every chance flatterer, but with the true lover who will 'love for an age, not for a day,' for

> When beauty, youth, and all sweets leave her,
> Love may return, but lovers never.

If one had to select one poem as representative of Carew it would not be *The Rapture*, or such fancies as 'The Hue and Cry,' but rather the lovely lyric 'Disdain Returned,' which is well rid of its doubtfully authentic third verse:

> He that loves a rosy cheek,
>   Or a coral lip admires,
> Or, from star-like eyes, doth seek
>   Fuel to maintain his fires;
> As old Time makes these decay,
> So his flames must waste away.
>
> But a smooth and steadfast mind,
>   Gentle thoughts and calm desires,
> Hearts with equal love combined,
>   Kindle never-dying fires.
> Where these are not, I despise
> Lovely cheeks, or lips, or eyes.

Of course this is a familiar lyric in anthologies, but it is curious that, well known as it is, it has not sufficed to keep green the memory of Carew as his one lyric keeps that of Lovelace, or 'Go, lovely rose,' that of Waller. It seems the more unfair, because Carew is not, as many of his contemporaries were, a one-poem poet. With a very slight deduction, his volume is good throughout. There are few pages on which one is not struck by something fine. Carew was an artist as well as a poet. If he in some slight degree misses the gay, artless charm of Suckling, he has a more serious attractiveness. There is a richness and dignity, likewise an intellectual force, in his verse which lifts him to the rank of a serious poet, and makes one regret that, with such natural gifts and artistic acquirements, he did not devote himself to poetry more continuously and of set purpose. For, to a considerable degree, he shared with Waller the gift of the stately line, and his verse has that body and glamour in which for the most part Waller's is deficient. There was indeed a drop of the ruddy Elizabethan blood in Carew. We recognise it in the poignancy of such lines as these:

> Thus parting, never more to touch,
>   To let eternal absence in;

in the vividness of:

> The sacred hand of bright Eternity;

in the sensuous beauty of:

> Naked for gold their sacred bodies show;

(both lines from his stately Masque) or this of the nightingale:

> She winters and keeps warm her note—

which reminds us that some of the Elizabethan love of nature yet lingered on in Carew.

It is interesting to remark incidentally that Burns once adapted a song of Carew's—the song beginning:

> Ask me why I send you here
> This firstling of the infant year?

and I may here point out a curious parallel between his famous image of 'the guinea stamp' and these lines of Carew:

> To lead or brass, or some such bad
> Metal, a Prince's stamp may add
> That value which it never had;
> But to the pure refined Ore
> The stamp of Kings imparts no more
> Worth, than the metal held before.

As Burns knew one poem of Carew's it seems unlikely that he did not know this also. And here is a seventeenth-century motto for nineteenth century Socialism:

> For mark how few there are that share the world.
> —RICHARD LE GALLIENNE, "Thomas Carew"
> (1894), *Retrospective Reviews*, 1896, Vol. 2,
> pp. 76–80

SIR JOHN SUCKLING
1609–1642

John Suckling was born in Whitton, Middlesex, and was baptized in the church of St. Mary the Virgin on February 10, 1609. He entered Trinity College, Cambridge, in 1623, but left in 1626 without taking a degree and entered Gray's Inn, London. With the death of his father in 1627, Suckling inherited his large family estates and gave up his law studies; after several years of travel on the Continent, he returned to England in 1630 and was knighted by Charles I. He was briefly in the service of the English ambassador to Gustavus Adolphus in Germany, but returned in 1632 to become a court poet.

In 1637 Suckling produced his controversial play *Aglaura*. The tragic fifth act was not well received, and it was replaced with a comic ending; this version was then performed at Court in 1638. Other plays include the comedy *The Goblins* (1638) and *The Discontented Colonell* (1640), later expanded and republished in 1646 under the title *Brennoralt*. *Brennoralt* was inspired by the poet's experiences during the Scottish campaigns of 1639–40. Suckling is best known, however, for his lyrics, many of which were set to music. He was a great admirer of Donne, and in 1637 he published a series of satiric verses titled *The Wits* (or *A Sessions of the Poets*). Most of his poems were published posthumously in *Fragmenta Aurea* (1646). This collection also contained plays, several political and religious tracts, and personal letters.

Suckling served as a member of Parliament in 1640. The following year he helped to engineer the Army Plot, a scheme designed to win command of the army for the king. The plot was discovered and Suckling had to flee to France, where it is thought he died in 1642, probably by taking poison.

Personal

Suckling next was call'd, but did not appear,
And strait one whisperd *Apollo* in's ear,
That of all men living he cared not for't,
He loved not the Muses so well as his sport;
    And
Prized black eyes, or a lucky hit
At bowls, above all the Trophies of wit;
But *Apollo* was angry, and publiquely said
'Twere fit that a fine were set on his head.
    —SIR JOHN SUCKLING, "The Wits," 1637

Suckling, whose numbers could invite
Alike to wonder and delight;
And with new spirit did inspire
The Thespian scene and Delphic lyre:
Is thus express'd in either part
Above the humble reach of art.
Drawn by the pencil, here you find
His form—by his own pen, his mind.
    —THOMAS STANLEY, Lines beneath Marshall's
    Portrait, 1646

I have heard Mris. Bond say that Sir John's father was but a dull fellow (her husband Mr. Thomas Bond knew him) the witt came by the mother.

By 18 he had well travelled France and Italie, and part of Germany, and (I thinke also) of Spaine.

He returned to England an extraordinary accomplished Gent., grew famous at Court for his readie sparkling witt; which was envyed, and he was (Sir William Davenant sayd) the Bull that was bayted. He was incomparably readie at repartying, and his Witt most sparkling when most sett-upon and provoked.

He was the greatest gallant of his time, and the greatest Gamester, both for Bowling and Cards, so that no Shopkeeper would trust him for 6d, as today, for instance, he might by winning, be worth 200 pounds, and the next day he might not be worth half so much, or perhaps sometimes be *minus nihilo*. He was one of the best Bowlers of his time in England. He played at Cards rarely well, and did use to practise by himselfe a-bed, and there studied how the best way of managing the cards could be. His Sisters would come to the Peccadillo-bowling-green, crying for feare he should loose all their Portions.

Sir John Suckling invented the game of Cribbidge. He sent his Cards to all Gameing places in the countrey, which were marked with private markes of his; he gott twenty thousand pounds by this way.

Sir William Davenant (who was his intimate friend and loved him intirely) would say that Sir John, when he was at his lowest ebbe in gameing, I meane when unfortunate, then would make himselfe most glorious in apparell, and sayd that it exalted his spirits, and that he had then best Luck when he was most gallant, and his Spirits were highest.

Sir William would say that he did not much care for a

Lord's converse, for they were in those dayes damnably Proud and arrogant, and the French would say that *My Lord d'Angleterre look't comme un Mastif-dog.* But now the age is more refined, and much by the example of his gracious Majestie who is the Patterne of Courtesie.

There happened, unluckily, a difference between Sir John Suckling and Sir John Digby (brother to Sir Kenelme) about a Mistresse or Gameing, I have now forgott. Sir John was but a slight timberd man, and of midling stature; Sir John Digby was a proper person of great strength and courage answerable, and yielded to be the best swordsman of his time. Sir John, with two or three of his party, assaults Sir John Digby goeing into a Play-house. Sir J. D. had only his Lacquey with him, but Sir J. D. flew on them like a Tigre, and made them run. 'Twas pitty that this accident brought the blemish of Cowardise to such an ingeniose young Sparke. Sir J. D. was such a Hero that there were very few but he would have served in like manner.

Mr. Snowdon tells me that after Sir John's unluckie rencounter, or Quarrel with Sir John Digby, wherin he was baffled, 'twas strange to see the envie and ill-nature of people to trample, and Scoffe at, and deject one in disgrace; inhumane as well as unchristian. The Lady Moray had made an entertainment for severall persons of quality at Ashley, in Surrey, near Chertsey, whereat Mr. Snowdon then was. There was the Countess of Middlesexe, whom Sir John had highly courted, and had spent on her, and in treating her, some thousands of pounds. At this entertainment she could not forbeare, but was so severe and ingrate as to upbraid Sir John of his late received Baffle; and some other Ladys had their flirts. The Lady Moray (who invited them) seeing Sir John out of Countenance, for whose worth she alwaies had a respect: Well, sayd shee, I am a merry Wench, and will never forsake an old friend in disgrace, so come, sitt downe by me, Sir John (said she) and seated him on her right hand, and countenanced him. This raysed Sir John's dejected spirites that he threw his Reparties about the Table with so much sparklingnesse and Gentilenes of Witt, to the admiration of them all.

When the Expedition was into Scotland, Sir John Suckling, at his owne chardge raysed a Troope of 100 very handsome young proper men, whom he clad in white doubletts and scarlett breeches, and scarlet Coates, hatts, and feathers, well horsed and armed. They say 'twas one of the finest sights in those days. But Sir John Menis made a Lampoon of it:—

> The Ladies opened the Windows to see,
> So fine and goodly a sight-a . . . etc.

I thinke the Lampoon sayes he made an inglorious chardge against the Scotts.

He was of middle stature and slight strength, brisque round eie, reddish fac't, and red nose (ill liver) his head not very big, his hayre a kind of sand colour, hs beard turned-up naturally, so that he had a briske and gracefull looke. He died a Batchelour.

He made a magnificent entertainment in London for a great number of Ladies of Quality, all beauties and young, which cost him many hundreds of poundes, where were all the rarities that this part of the world could afford, and the last service of all was Silk Stockings and Garters, and I thinke also Gloves.

Anno Domini 1637, Sir John Suckling, William Davenant, Poet Laureate (not then knighted) and Jack Young, came to Bathe. Sir John came like a young Prince for all manner of Equipage and convenience, and Sir W. Davenant told me that he had a Cart-load of Bookes carried down; and 'twas there at Bath, that he writt the little Tract in his Booke about Socinian-

ism. 'Twas as pleasant a journey as ever men had; in the height of a long Peace and luxury, and in the Venison Season. The second night they lay at Marlborough, and walking on the delicate fine downes at the Backside of the Towne, whilest supper was making ready, the maydes were drying of cloathes on the bushes. Jack Young had espied a very pretty young Girle, and had got her consent for an assignation, which was about midnight, which they happened to overheare on the other side of the hedge, and were resolved to frustrate his designe. They were wont every night to play at Cards after supper a good while: but Jack Young pretended wearinesse, etc., and must needes goe to Bed, not to be perswaded by any meanes to the contrary. They had their landlady at supper with them; said they to her, Observe this poor Gentleman, how he yawnes: now is his mad fit comeing upon him. We beseech you that you make fast his doores, and gett somebody to watch and looke to him, for about midnight he will fall to be most outragious. Gett the Hostler, or some strong fellow, to stay-up, and we will well content him, for he is our worthy friend, and a very honest Gent., only, perhaps, twice in a yeare he falls into these fitts.

Jack Young slept not, but was ready to goe out as the clocke struck to the houre of appointment, and then going to open the Dore he was disappointed, knocks, bounces, stampes, calls *Tapster! Chamberlayne! Hostler!* sweares and curses dreadfully; nobody would come to him. Sir John and W. Davenant were expectant all this time, and ready to dye with laughter. I know not how, he happened to get open the Dore, and was comeing downe the stayres. The Hostler, a huge lusty fellow, fell upon him, and held him, and cryed, Good Sir, take God in your mind, you shall not goe out to destroy yourself. J. Young struggled and strived, insomuch that at last he was quite spent and dispirited, and was faine to goe to bed to rest himselfe.

In the morning the Landlady of the House came to see how he did, and brought him a Cawdle; Oh, Sir, sayd she, You had a heavy fitt last night; pray, Sir, be pleased to take some of this to comfort your heart. Jack Young thought the woman had been mad, and being exceedingly vexed, flirted the porrenger of Cawdle in her face. The next day his Camerades told him all the plott, how they crosse-bitt him. That night they went to Bronham House, Sir Edward Baynton's (then a noble seate, since burnt in the Civill Warres) where they were nobly entertained severall dayes. From thence, they went to West Kington to Parson Davenant, Sir William's eldest brother, where they stayd a weeke—mirth, witt and good cheer flowing. From thence to Bath, six or seven miles.

My Ladye Southcott, whose husband hanged himselfe, was Sir John Suckling's sister. At her house in Bishopsgate-Street, London, is an originall of her brother Sir John of Sir Anthony van-Dyke, all at length, leaning against a rock, with a play-booke, contemplating. It is a piece of great value.

When his *Aglaura* was put on, he bought all the Cloathes himselfe, which were very rich; no tinsell, all the lace pure gold and silver, which cost him . . . I have now forgott. He had some scaenes to it, which in those dayes were only used at Masques.

He went into France, where after sometime, being come to the bottome of his Found, reflecting on the miserable and despicable condition he should be reduced to, having nothing left to maintaine him, he (having a convenience for that purpose, lyeing at an apothecarie's house in Paris) tooke poyson, which killed him miserably with vomiting. He was buryed in the Protestants Churchyard. This was (to the best of my remembrance) 1646.

His Picture, which is like him, before his Poemes, says

that he was about 28 years old when he dyed.—JOHN AUBREY, "Sir John Suckling," *Brief Lives*, 1669–96

Sir John Suckling was an immoral man, as well as debauched. The story of the French cards was told me by the late Duke of Buckingham; and he had it from old Lady Dorset herself. That lady took a very odd pride in boasting of her familiarities with Sir John Suckling. She is the Mistress and Goddess in his poems; and several of those pieces were given by herself to the printer. This the Duke of Buckingham used to give as one instance of the fondness she had to let the world know how well they were acquainted.—ALEXANDER POPE (1728–30), cited in Joseph Spence, *Anecdotes, Observations and Characters of Books and Men*, ed. S. W. Singer, 1820

Sir John Suckling, a poet of great vivacity, and some elegance, was one of the finest gentemen of his time.—JAMES GRANGER, *Biographical History of England*, 1769–1824

He comes among a herd of scented fops with careless natural grace, and an odour of morning flowers upon him. You know not which would have been most delighted with his compliments, the dairy maid or the duchess. He was thrown too early upon a town life; otherwise a serious passion for some estimable woman, which (to judge from his graver poetry) he was very capable of entertaining, might have been the salvation of him. As it was, he died early, and, it is said, not happily; but this may have been the report of envy or party-spirit; for he was a great loyalist. It is probable, however, that he excelled less as a partizan than as a poet and a man of fashion. He is said to have given a supper to the ladies of his acquaintance, the last course of which consisted of millinery and trinkets. The great Nelson's mother was a Suckling of the same stock, in Norfolk.—LEIGH HUNT, *Wit and Humour*, 1846

General

While *Sucklins* name is in the forehead of this Booke, these *Poems* can want no preparation: It had been a prejudice to Posterity they should have slept longer, and an injury to his own ashes. They that convers'd with him alive, and truly, (under which notion I comprehend only knowing Gentlemen, his soule being transcendent, and incommunicable to others, but by reflection) will honour these posthume Idæa's of their friend: And if any have liv'd in so much darknesse, as not to have knowne so great an Ornament of our Age, by looking upon these Remaines with Civility and Understanding, they may timely yet repent, and be forgiven.

In this Age of Paper-prostitutions, a man may buy the reputation of some Authors into the price of their Volume; but know, the Name that leadeth into this Elysium, is sacred to *Art* and *Honour*, and no man that is not excellent in both, is qualified a *Competent Judge*: For when Knowledge is allowed, yet Education in the Censure of a Gentleman, requires as many descents, as goes to make one; And he that is bold upon his unequall Stock, to traduce this Name, or Learning, will deserve to be condemned againe into Ignorance his Originall sinne, and dye in it.

But I keep backe the Ingenuous Reader, by my unworthy Preface: The gate is open, and thy soule invited to a Garden of ravishing variety: admire his wit, that created these for thy delight, while I withdraw into a shade, and contemplate who must follow.—HUMPHREY MOSELEY, "To the Reader," *Fragmenta Aurea*, 1646

⟨*Aglaura* is⟩ full of flowers, but rather stuck in than growing there.—RICHARD FLECKNOE, *A Short Discourse on the English Stage*, 1664

His poems are clear, sprightly, and natural,—his plays well-humoured and taking,—his letters fragrant and sparkling. —DAVID LLOYD, *Memoirs of Excellent Personages*, 1668

Sir John Suckling is acknowledged to have left far behind him all former writers of song in gayety and ease: it is not equally clear that he has ever since been surpassed. His poetry aims at no higher praise: he shows no sentiment or imagination, either because he had them not, or because he did not require either in the style he chose. Perhaps the Italians may have poetry in that style equal to Suckling's; I do not know that they have, nor do I believe that there is any in French: that there is none in Latin I am convinced.—HENRY HALLAM, *Introduction to the Literature of Europe*, 1837–39, Pt. 3, Ch. 5, Par. 56

For one who now reads anything of Carew there are twenty who know by heart some verses of his friend and brother-courtier, Sir John Suckling. His ballad upon a wedding, with the necessary omission of a verse or two, is in all our books of poetic extracts.—DAVID MASSON, *The Life of John Milton*, 1859, Vol. 1, Ch. 6

With Carew, Suckling, and Herrick, prettiness takes the place of the beautiful. That which strikes them is no longer the general features of things; and they no longer try to express the inner character of what they describe. They no longer possess that liberal conception, that instinctive penetration, by which we sympathise with objects, and grow capable of creating them anew. They no longer boast of that overflow of emotions, that excess of ideas and images, which compelled a man to relieve himself by words, to act externally, to represent freely and boldly the interior drama which made his whole body and heart tremble. They are rather wits of the court, cavaliers of fashion, who wish to show off their imagination and style. In their hands love becomes gallantry; they write songs, fugitive pieces, compliments to the ladies. There are no more upwellings from the heart. They write eloquent phrases in order to be applauded, and flattering exaggerations in order to please. The divine faces, the serious or profound looks, the virgin or impassioned expressions which burst forth at every step in the early poets, have disappeared; here we see nothing but agreeable countenances, painted in agreeable verses. Blackguardism is not far off; we meet with it already in Suckling, and crudity to boot, and prosaic epicurism; their sentiment is expressed before long, in such a phrase as: "Let us amuse ourselves, and a fig for the rest." The only objects they can still paint, are little graceful things, a kiss, a May-day festivity, a dewy primrose, a daffodil, a marriage morning, a bee. Herrick and Suckling especially produce little exquisite poems, delicate, ever pleasant or agreeable, like those attributed to Anacreon, or those which abound in the *Anthology*. In fact, here, as at the Grecian period alluded to, we are in the decline of paganism; energy departs, the reign of the agreeable begins.—HIPPOLYTE TAINE, *History of English Literature*, tr. H. Van Laun, 1871, Vol. 1, p. 201

Suckling—strange as it may appear to those who only know his career as a poet—wrote a brief religious treatise, entitled 'An Account of Religion by Reason.' There is little of thought or genuine argument in the treatise. It is the work of an elegant *littérateur* handling a subject which he knows imperfectly, and only from the outside. But the mere fact is a testimony to the theological excitement which then everywhere pervaded society, and indicates the desire there must have been in many minds, besides those whose writings and speculations have come to the surface, to examine the subject of religion rationally. Suckling avows that he feared the charge of Socinianism in his undertaking. Then, as in later times, this charge was recklessly applied to all who thought for themselves in religion; or, in other words, who did not take a side with either theological extreme. "Every man," he says, "that offers to give an account of religion by reason is suspected to have none at all;" yet he has "made no scruple to run that hazard—not knowing why a man should not use the best weapon his Creator hath given him for his defence." The treatise itself, if only a meagre and imperfect sketch of the great subjects which it touches—the Trinity, Incarnation, Passion, and Resurrection of our Lord—is substantially orthodox. God is declared "to be one, and but one; it being gross to imagine two omnipotents, for then neither would be so. Yet since this good is perfectly good, and perfect goodness cannot be without perfect love; nor perfect love without communication, nor to an unequal or created—for then it must be inordinate; we include a second coeternal though begotten; nor are these contrary, though they seem to be so." Thus theologised the gay Suckling at Bath, in the year 1637; and although the points of contact betwixt him and Falkland must have been superficial rather than real, we can imagine them not only contending for the "laurel," as depicted in the well-known verses—a contention in which our poet would have had no chance with him—but also trying their strength in religious argument during those stirring years.—JOHN TULLOCH, "Lord Falkland—A Moderate and Liberal Church," *Rational Theology and Christian Philosophy in England in the Seventeenth Century*, 1872, Vol. 1, pp. 112–13

It is impossible to consider the poems of Suckling without regard to his career. No English poet has lived a life so public, so adventurous and so full of vicissitude as his. Nothing short of an irresistible bias toward the art of poetry could have induced so busy and so fortunate a man to write in verse at all. Beautiful and vigorous in body, educated in all the accomplishments that grace a gentleman, endowed from earliest youth with the prestige of a soldier and a popular courtier, his enormous wealth enabled him to indulge every whim that a fondness for what was splendid or eccentric in dress, architecture and pageantry could devise. Such a life could present no void which literary ambition could fill, and Suckling's scorn for poetic fame was well known to his contemporaries. At the age of nineteen he went away to the continent, and wandered through France, Italy, Germany and Spain for four years, seeking adventure. He offered his sword to the King of Sweden, fought in command of a troop in front of Glogau and of Magdeburg, performed astounding feats of prowess in Silesia, and returned before the battle of Lützen simply because his imperious fancy began to find the great war a tedious pastime. He proceeded to London, and lived for six years in a style of such gorgeous profusion that at last he contrived to cripple one of the amplest fortunes of that age. He retired for a while, ostentatiously enough, into a literary seclusion at Bath, taking the obsequious Davenant with him as a sort of amanuensis. During this brief time, no doubt, his tragedies were composed. The King, however, fretted for his return, and he emerged as the leader of the Royalist party in its earliest troubles. After the crisis, Suckling fled to France, and thence to Spain; at Madrid he fell into the clutches of the Inquisition, and underwent horrible tortures. He escaped to Paris, with a mind probably unstrung by these torments, for he poisoned himself in his thirty-fourth year. Such was the career of a man whose light verses, carelessly thrown off and half forgotten, have outlived the pomp and public glitter of his famous adventures, by which he now seems to us rather dwarfed and injured than exalted.

Written under such circumstances, and preserved in a fragmentary state by friends, it would be surprising if the poems of Suckling presented any great finish or completeness. In point of fact, they display to us but the ruins of his genius. A ballad of wonderful brightness and sweetness, half-a-dozen songs full of the most aery and courtly grace, these alone of all he has left behind him are in any sense worthy of their author's splendid fame. His contemporaries, and the men of the next generation, remembering his shining qualities of personal presence, his wit, his fluent fancy and, perhaps, many fine poems that we shall never see, spoke of him as an epoch-making writer, in terms that we reserve for Herrick, of whom they never speak. His name still lives in the popular ear, as the names of poets far greater than he will never live. His figure takes a place in poetic literature which the student fresh from his pages is apt to consider unduly high, and which his 'golden fragments' scarcely seem to justify. But the instinct of the people, in this as in so many other cases, is probably right, and though the imperfections of his poems may cloud it, there is no doubt that his genius existed. It shows itself even more in his disciples than in himself; his manner of writing affected the course of English literature, and showed its strength less in his own lyrics, than in the fact that for the next fifty years no one could write a good love-song without more or less reminding the reader of Suckling. To the very end of the century 'natural, easy Suckling' was the type of literary elegance to the Millamants and Lady Froths of fashion.

His existing works consist of a slender collection of lyrical and complimentary poems, and of four plays, one of them incomplete. Suckling, who had a creditable adoration for Shakespeare, inherited none of his dramatic genius. A worse playwright is scarcely to be found, even in that miserable period, among the Gomersalls, Lowers, and Killigrews. *Aglaura*, a monster of tedious pageantry, was arranged with a tragic and a comic ending, according to choice: but this was not so unique as has been supposed, for we find the same silly contrivance in Howard's *Vestal Virgin* and in the *Pandora* of Sir William Killigrew.

The only drama of Suckling's which is at all readable is *Brennoralt*, which is incoherent enough, but does contain some fine tragic writing. The only real merit of these plays however consists in the beautiful songs they harbour.

The lyrical pieces of Suckling's which were collected under the title of *Fragmenta Aurea* present considerable difficulty to the critic. Never was a volume of poems so unequal in merit presented to the public. Side by side with songs that will be enjoyed as long as the English language exists, we find stanzas which it is impossible either to scan or to construe, and which would disgrace the Poet's Corner of a provincial newspaper. The famous 'Session of the Poets,' one of those pieces which were most admired in the age that saw its production, is full of laxities of style that fairly astonish the modern reader. Such a stanza, for instance, as that dedicated to Jonson, limps and waddles along with a strangely gouty gait:—

The first that broke silence was good old Ben.
Prepared before with Canary wine,
And he told them plainly he deserved the bays,
For his were called works, while others were but
    plays.

In the case of other poems, in which we find awkward and confused passages, we may suppose that Suckling left the verse confused or incomplete, and that the text suffers from inartistic revision, but 'The Session of the Poets' is one of the few pieces published in his life-time, and we are therefore inclined to suppose that he was but little affected by errors of style that are palpable to us. When, however, he is at his best, he throws off all awkwardness and obscurity; his versification becomes liquid and nimble, and in one instance, the famous 'Ballad upon a Wedding,' he has contrived to keep up his tone of airy vivacity through twenty-two incomparable verses. But as a rule his lyric flights are brief. His songs owe their special charm to their gallantry and impudence, their manly ardour and their frivolous audacity. The temper expressed in 'Why so pale and wan, fond lover?' was in sympathy with the age, and gave a delight which seems to us extravagant; Suckling's admiration for Shakespeare not preventing him from being one of the chief heralds of the poetry of the Restoration. He sings like a royalist gentleman; he leaves the weaving of conceits to learned contemporaries, such as Cowley and Lovelace; he inaugurates a simpler, most straightforward expression of inflamed fancy and amorous discontent. This is in his songs only; in his moral pieces, such as that beginning

> My dearest rival, lest our love
> Should with eccentric motion move,

he is as quaint and conceited, if not so ingenious, as the best of the poets once called Metaphysical. His great praise is his manliness: after all the rhymesters who for a century had been sonneting their mistress' eyebrow, and avowing the most abject deference, the attitude of Suckling strutting with his impudent smiling face through the galaxy of ladies, struck the contemporary mind as refreshing, and a new fashion in gallantry set in. What had been good sense in Suckling, soon however became effrontery in Sedley, and cynicism in Congreve, and the base sensual feast to which the poets of the Restoration sat down we feel to have been a sorry exchange for the Arcadian diet of the Elizabethans. Even here also there was some brisk music of a gallantry not wholly base, and for this we have to thank Suckling and his sprightly mood.—EDMUND GOSSE, "Sir John Suckling," *The English Poets*, ed. Thomas Humphry Ward, 1880, Vol. 2, pp. 170–173

> The blithest throat that ever carrolled love
> In music made of morning's merriest heart,
> Glad Suckling stumbled from his seat above,
> And reeled on slippery roads of alien art.
> —ALGERNON CHARLES SWINBURNE, "James
> Shirley," *Sonnets on English Dramatic Poets*,
> 1882

In the garden of Suckling's verse, side by side with rare blossoms of delightful fragrance, grew unsightly and noisome weeds. Of course they were affected by their surroundings and by the unnatural light of his court and his time; but some of his writings outrage the taste or morality of to-day. He is, however, although not as widely read or known as he should be, one of the immortals in literature, and had he written nothing but "A Ballad upon a Wedding" and the song beginning "Why so pale and wan, fond lover," he would have earned his immortality. Their simplicity, grace, and wit are unmatched and are peculiarly his own. Their flavor is most rare: it delights at once, and is never forgotten. The path which Suckling's verse takes never scales sublime heights, but runs through fields where music and laughter are heard, where beauty is seen, and where there are occasional stormy days. His imagination never awes, nor does his feeling stir us deeply; but his fancy pleases us, his wit and gayety provoke a smile, and his careless ease and grace charm us.—FREDERICK A. STOKES, "Preface" to *The Poems of Sir John Suckling*, 1886, p. xiii

True, he is often careless in the bad sense as well as in the good, though the doggerel of the "Sessions" and some other pieces is

probably intentional. But in his own vein, that of coxcombry that is not quite cynical, and is quite intelligent, he is marvellously happy. The famous song in *Aglaura*, the Allegro to Lovelace's Penseroso, "Why so pale and wan, fond lover?" is scarcely better than "Tis now since I sat down before That foolish fort a heart," or "Out upon it! I have loved Three whole days together." Nor in more serious veins is the author to be slighted, as in "The Dance;" while as for the "Ballad on a Wedding," the best parts of this are by common consent incomparable. Side by side by these are to be found, as in Lovelace, pieces that will not even scan, and, as *not* in Lovelace (who is not seldom loose but never nasty), pieces of a dull and disgusting obscenity, which unluckily helped, if they did not set, the worst fashion of the time, and were echoed in miscellanies, song books, and even the works of the less scrupulous authors of individual repute, for a couple of generations. But we do not go to Suckling for these; we go to him for his easy grace, his agreeable impudence, his scandalous mock-disloyalty (for it is only mock-disloyalty after all) to the "Lord of Terrible Aspect," whom all his elder contemporaries worshipped so piously. Suckling's inconstancy and Lovelace's constancy may or may not be equally poetical,—there is some reason for thinking that the lover of Althea was actually driven to something like despair by the loss of his mistress. But that matters to us very little. The songs remain, and remain yet unsurpassed, as the most perfect celebrations, in one case of chivalrous devotion, in the other of the coxcomb side of gallantry, that literature contains or is likely ever to contain. —GEORGE SAINTSBURY, *A History of Elizabethan Literature*, 1887, p. 376

I admire Suckling's graceful audacity. It is luckier to do a little thing surpassingly well than a larger thing indifferently so. —FREDERICK LOCKER-LAMPSON, *My Confidences*, 1896, p. 181

ALFRED SUCKLING
From "Memoirs of the Life of Sir John Suckling"
Selections from the Works of Sir John Suckling
1836, pp. 53–61

As a writer, Sir John Suckling will command admiration, so long as a taste for whatever is delicate and natural in poetry shall remain. His works are the production of a genius truly poetic and original: his language is animated and forcible; his versification, for the age, smooth and flowing; the structure of his stanzas is simple, and occasionally novel, founded apparently, in some instances, on Italian models. In descriptions of feminine grace and beauty he is peculiarly happy; and in his prose compositions, is clear, nervous, and sparkling.

If we bring his poems to the test of comparison with succeeding writers, notwithstanding the continued progress of elegant literature since his day, the result will prove that in the lighter species of poetry he remains unrivalled. Had his name been unknown in any other department of literature, or unconnected with any historical associations, his ballads and songs alone would render his fame imperishable.[1] In applying metaphysics to poetry, a style of writing very fashionable in his day, but to which he has rarely, though occasionally, stooped, he has employed his conceptions with considerable ingenuity, nor has he allowed his ideas to overstep the limits of propriety. In the following stanza, taken from his "Love's World," these remarks will be found, I think, to apply with justness; nor can very strong objections be made to the comparisons employed in the remaining verses.

The sea's my mind, which calm would be,
Were it from winds, my passions, free;
But, out alas! no sea, I find,
Is troubled like a lover's mind.
    With it rocks and shallows be,
    Despair and fond credulity.

But, least the writer's judgment should be considered as warped by prepossession in his favour, a few testimonies of others, better qualified than himself to appreciate the merits of composition, are adduced.

"The grace and elegance of his songs and ballads," says Mr. Ellis, "are inimitable."

"They have a pretty touch," says Phillips, "of a gentle spirit, and seem to savour more of the grape than lamp." And Mr. Lloyd, in his *Memoirs, &c.* has the following discriminative remarks. "His poems are clean, sprightly, and natural—his discourses full and convincing—his plays well humoured and taking—his letters fragrant and sparkling."

A writer in the *British Critic* observes, that, "if these models had been more frequently and more happily copied, the French would not have been unrivalled in light poetry." Lockier, Dean of Peterborough, says, "considering the manner of writing then in fashion, the purity of Sir John Suckling's style is quite surprising."

In his prose compositions, Suckling has been equally admired; his letters are full of wit, spirit, and gallantry, and have been rarely surpassed. His "Account of Religion by Reason," and his letter to Mr. Jermyn, prove his ability to reason with closeness and compose with nervous elegance.

He fails most as a dramatist, though Phillips says his plays continued to draw audience to the theatres in his days. They did not, however, long retain popularity; nor is this surprising, for the genius of Suckling no where appears to so little advantage as in his plays: besides bearing very evident marks of crudity in the plans, and hurry in the execution, they are marred by the recurrence of trifling incidents, which distract the attention from the developement of the main catastrophe, and fritter it into littleness and poverty of effect. They are deficient, moreover, in that sweetness of versification and originality of thought, which elsewhere distinguish his compositions; and the gleams of fire and intellect, which occasionally warm us in their perusal, are obscured too frequently by tedious pages of prolix declamation.

His plays are but four—of these, the *Sad One* is an unfinished tragedy, which, if completed in the style of the four acts left us by the author, could scarcely have entertained an audience at any time. The compilers of the *Biographia Dramatica*, however, consider it as showing the hand of a master; yet it possesses, in the opinion of the writer, a complicated machinery, great plotting, and much bloodshed; smoke, in fact, but no fire: violent death in the very opening scene is afterwards repeated without sufficient reason. The scenes too are abrupt, and the language poor. The best lines, as might be expected from Suckling's known talents that way, are contained in the little song sung by Florelio's page, in the fourth act—

Hast thou seen the down i' th' air
When wanton blasts have toss'd it? &c.

As usual, Suckling is most successful in his descriptions of feminine grace: describing Francelia's beauty, he says—

She has an eye, round as a globe,
And black as jet; so full of majesty and life,
That when it most denies, it most invites.
Her lips are gently swell'd unto
Some blushing cherry, that hath newly tasted
The dew from heaven.

In the fourth act, Signor Multicarni and his assistants are introduced, for no other purpose, it would appear, than as vehicles for a stroke of satire against lawyers. After appropriating to certain performers their several parts, he exclaims—

But who shall act the honest lawyer?
Tis a hard part that!

The simile of comparing Clairmont's counsel to

Smith's water flung upon coals
    Which more inflames,

is original, I believe, though not elegant.

Aglaura was, I fancy, Suckling's favorite play; and it is so contrived that, by adopting either of two fifth acts, it can be represented as a tragedy or a comedy. The splendour with which it was first brought out, has been noticed in a former page. It is certainly better conceived, and written with more spirit than the *Sad One*; though, as a tragedy, is scarcely less bloody. But scenes of theatrical horror were witnessed in those days with greater delight than in our own; and Shakspeare's bloodiest exhibitions in *Hamlet* or *Macbeth*, were then regarded with more than mere complacency. Suckling is, therefore, so far defensible—for he wrote in accordance with the taste of his age. The plan of *Aglaura*, however, is not only very similar to that of the *Sad One*, but it contains many ideas and entire sentences which occur in the latter; though *Aglaura*, it is to be remembered, was the original play.

Like Shakspeare, Sir John is very fond of concluding his scenes with couplets. When acted as a tragedy, this piece should not have been protracted after the death of Aglaura. Like the *Sad One*, it contains many lines descriptive of feminine charms; a subject on which Sir John seems ever willing to dwell.

Lips
Perfum'd by breath, sweet as the bean's first blossom.

In the opening scene of the first act, and in the first scene of the fourth act, are ideas, which Suckling's familiarity with courts had probably suggested.

We are envy's mark, and court-eyes carry far.

Court friendship
Is like a cable, that in storms is ever cut.

In the fourth act is a fine dialogue between Semanthe and Iolas.

Semanthe: Believe me, Iolas, the honest swain,
    That from the brow of some steep cliff, far off
    Beholds a ship labouring in vain against
    The boisterous and unruly elements, ne'er had
    Less power, or more desire, to help, than I.
    At every sigh I die; and every look
    Does move: and, any passion you will have,
    But love, I have in store! I will be angry,
    Quarrel with destiny, and with myself,
    That it is no better; be melancholy;
    And though my own disasters well might plead
    To be in chief; yours only shall have place.
    I'll pity! and, if that's too low, I'll grieve
    (As for my sins) I cannot give you ease.
    All this I'll do! and this, I hope, will prove,
    'Tis greater torment not to love, than love. (*Exit.*)
Iolas: So perishing sailors pray to storms,
    And, so they hear again: so, men
    With death about them, look on physicians that
    Have given them o'er! and, so they turn away.
    Two fixed stars, that keep a constant distance,
    And, by laws made with themselves, must know
    No motion eccentric, may meet as soon as we.
    The anger, that the foolish sea doth show,

When it does brave it out, and roar against
A stubborn rock, that still denies it passage,
Is not so vain, and fruitless as my prayers.

The address of Orbella to the corpse of Ariaspes, is full of pathos and sensibility, and not unworthy of Shakspeare himself.

Sleep—sleep for ever! and, forgotten too:
All but thy ills; which, may succeeding time
Remember, as the seaman does his marks,
To know what to avoid. May, at thy name,
All good men start, and bad too: may it prove
Infection to the air; that people dying on't,
May help to curse thee for me.
(This to ZIRIFF; then turning to the body of Ariaspes)—
Could I but call *thee* back as easily now;
But, that's a subject for our tears, not hopes!
There is no piecing tulips to their stalks,
When they are once divorc'd by a rude hand;
All we can do, is to preserve in water
A little life, and give, by courteous art,
What scanted nature wants commission for:
That thou shal't have: for, to thy memory,
Such tribute of moist sorrow I will pay;
And that, so purified by love, that on thy grave,
Nothing shall grow, but violets and primroses.

The plan of *Aglaura* has been followed by Sir Robert Howard in his *Vestal Virgin*—while Pope has, without acknowledgment, transferred Suckling's ideas, in several instances, from these plays to his own poetry.[2]

The vivacity of Suckling's mind promised better success from his attempts in comedy: yet *The Goblins*, it must be confessed, possesses little merit. The idea of the play is evidently borrowed from Shakspeare; and the same arguments may be advanced in defence of the machinery adopted in it, as have been so powerfully adduced by Dr. Johnson, in support of Shakspeare's employment of witches in *Macbeth*. A belief in the agency of witchcraft was still an universal notion in Suckling's time—nay, it had been rendered a fashionable illusion, by the publication of King James's work on demonology. The curious expression which occurs in this play—

The Sedgly curse upon thee,
And the great fiend ride through thee
Booted and spurr'd, with a scythe on his neck,

is explained in Ray's *Proverbs*, where we are told that it is a Staffordshire saying.

In the second song in the third act is an extraordinary line—

The prince of darkness is a gentleman.

The Lady Juliana Barnes uses an expression very similar—

Jesus was a gentleman.

Dodsley has published *The Goblins*, with copious notes, in his collection of old plays.

Brennoralt, I consider Suckling's best play: and it might, with little alteration, be adapted to modern taste. The dialogue is more lively, and the plot less complicated and bloody, than in his other tragedies. It abounds in allusions to the existing state of public affairs, and has been thought to point in some places to his own situation.

When he says, the court is

A most eternal place of low affronts,
And then, as low submissions,

the conduct and humiliation of Digby were, probably, in the author's recollection.

In the beginning of the third act he introduces the king in conversation with Brennoralt, and his counsellors; which affords an opportunity of discussing the subjects then in agitation between Charles and the Scots. The passage is too long to be repeated in this place, particularly as it will be found in the body of this volume: but it is worthy of an attentive perusal. The play contains many excellent strokes. There is a strong satire, in the first scene, on men whose lives have been spent uselessly to society.

Formal beards,
Men, who have no other proof of their
Long life; but, that they are old!

Villanor's idea in the first scene of the fourth act has been copied by Moore in his earlier poems.

Look babies again in our eyes.

Brennoralt's reflections on the king's gifts and honours are touchingly expressed.

A princely gift, but, Sir, it comes too late!
Like sunbeams on the blasted blossoms, do
Your favours fall.

Suckling has not scrupled to introduce, without any acknowledgment, several entire lines of Shakspeare,—and is also convicted of having borrowed largely from Balzac's *Letters*.

Brennoralt was first published under the title of the *Discontented Colonel*, in 1639, as a satire on the Scottish malcontents.

Sucking has also appeared before us on two occasions as a translator; and notwithstanding the just objections of Dr. Johnson[3] to the style of literal translation pursued during the early part of the seventeenth century, Sir John's version of the little French ode, beginning

A quoy servent d'artifices,

forms a marked and happy exception to the general usage—it unites much freedom and grace with very great fidelity to the original, and leaves us to regret that more of the light ballads and odes of our neighbours had not engaged his attention.

Notes

1. His lyric poems were set to music by Mr. Henry Lanyer, gentleman of the king's chapel and one of his Majesty's private musicians.—*Harl. MSS.*

2.   But, as when an authentic watch is shown,
          Each man winds up, and rectifies his own,
          So in our very judgments.
                    (Epilogue to *Aglaura*.)
          'Tis with our judgments as our watches, none
          Go just alike, yet each believes his own.
                    (Pope's *Essay on Criticism*.)
          High Characters, cries one, and he would see
          Things that ne'er were, nor are, nor e'er will be.
                    (Epilogue to *The Goblins*.)
          Whoever thinks a faultless piece to see,
          Thinks what ne'er was, nor is, nor e'er shall be."
                    (Pope's *Essay on Criticism*.)

3. *Idler*, No. 69.

GEORGE BARNETT SMITH
From "Sir John Suckling"
Gentleman's Magazine, October 1878, pp. 418–39

A brief career, marked occasionally by brilliant, but still more frequently by melancholy and erratic episodes, is associated with the author of the "Ballad upon a Wedding." This exquisite poem finds a place in every collection of lyric verse, yet of its writer comparatively little is known. Anticipating the wits and courtiers of the Restoration, we find their idiosyncrasies prefigured in Suckling: like them, he wore his life and his heart upon his sleeve; like them, he spent his substance upon gorgeous apparel and riotous living, while the thunderbolts of a nation's anger were being forged; and like many of the minions of Charles II., he ended a life of extremes by a violent and miserable death. But there was a touch of true chivalry in Suckling's nature absent from those later men, whom Macaulay describes as possessing "foreheads of bronze, hearts like the nether millstone, and tongues set on fire of hell." Suckling fought creditably in the field during the Thirty Years' War. Moreover, by his counsels, he did all that was possible to check the drifting tide of events which ultimately alienated Charles I. from the great body of his people. A letter now extant, written by the poet to his friend Jermyn (afterwards Earl of St. Alban's), is distinguished for its wise political judgment, and its remarkable foresight. To this letter some subsequent references will be made. It is, however, as a poet that Suckling chiefly deserves to be, and will continue to be, remembered. In the course of a chequered existence he had many moments of true inspiration. Recklessness and debauchery could not utterly eradicate the gleams of genius, and in his happiest effusions he touches a point of excellence far beyond the reach of a Sedley or a Rochester. . . .

The character of Suckling had to a large extent manifested itself at the time of his father's death in 1627. The brilliant youth, then nearly nineteen, had been admitted to Court, had already mingled in its gaieties, and had become infected by its spirit. How this fact impressed a grave and careful man like the father, may be inferred from the circumstance that by his will the latter debarred his heir from entering upon full possession of the family estates until he had attained his twenty-fifth year. Suckling had already become the devotee of pleasure, and was one of her most ardent worshippers. He had a natural aptitude towards the frivolities which distinguished the bulk of the frequenters of the Court, and possessed as well many attractions of person and manner. The gilded butterfly life which was even now a characteristic of fashionable society exactly suited Suckling's temperament and disposition. . . .

Suckling not only speedily took a high place in the favour of the Court, but he even strove to emulate Royalty itself in the magnificence of the entertainments he provided both at his country seat at Whitton and at his town residence. One of these entertainments appears to have outshone all the rest, and to have cost many thousands of pounds—an immense sum two centuries ago. Having regaled his guests, we are told, in a sumptuous fashion—every court lady of youth and beauty was present—he provided a last course of silk stockings, garters, and gloves. This act gratified his desire for gallantry and his partiality for the *bizarre* and the extraordinary at the same time. He does not appear to have passed his calmer moments in feelings of regret over fortune squandered and health undermined, but rather to have devoted them to the composition of letters to the reigning beauties of the period. Having entered upon the seductive path, he found the descent very easy; any spare moments he had while attending upon the Court he devoted to play, and it is stated that on one occasion his sisters came to the Piccadilly bowling-green, "crying for the feare he should lose all their portions." Cards and bowls became his infatuation, and the knowledge of his pursuits soon spread over the whole town; so much so, says a contemporary writer, "that no shopkeeper would trust him for a sixpence; as to-day, for instance, he might, by winning, be worth £200; the next day, he might not be worth half so much, or perhaps, *minus nihil.*"

. . . While it is true that Suckling is devoid of imagination—in the higher sense of that word—it is a little unjust to deny him the presence of sentiment. But when a writer cannot be a great dramatist, it is something to be a true lyric poet, and this distinction Suckling rightfully enjoys. There is no finer poem of its kind than the "Ballad upon a Wedding," while many of the shorter pieces of this writer will compare favourably with the lyrics of Herrick and Waller. Many poets have written lyrics with ease and freedom; but Suckling cut cameos, and some of them are almost worthy of standing alone. . . .

The later poets of the Restoration failed to attain ⟨his⟩ nimble grace, and crisp, sharp expression. Their diamonds were not so clearly and beautifully cut, though in substance they enjoyed the same power of fancy and conceit. In this lighter species of poetry, where elegance and a sparkling fancy are the chief constituent elements, Suckling has had few rivals. His versification is occasionally halting and defective, but on the whole his compositions are remarkable specimens of delicacy of structure, ingenious conceptions, and graceful and harmonious verse. As in the case of many other authors, so with the present writer, it is not always his best lyrics which are the most popular. His stanzas headed "The Invocation" are rarely mentioned amongst the most favourable specimens of his art, and yet it may be doubted whether he has left behind him any more worthy of remembrance:—

> Ye juster powers of love and fate,
>   Give me the reason why
>   A lover cross'd,
>   And all hopes lost,
>   May not have leave to die.
>
> It is but just, and love needs must
>   Confess it is his part,
>   When he does spy
>   One wounded lie,
>   To pierce the other's heart.
>
> But yet if he so cruel be
>   To have one breast to hate;
>   If I must live,
>   And thus survive,
>   How far more cruel's fate!
>
> In this same state I find too late
>   I am: and here's the grief:
>   Cupid can cure,
>   Death heal, I'm sure,
>   Yet neither sends relief.
>
> To live, or die, beg only I,
>   Just Powers! some end me give;
>   And traitor-like,
>   Thus force me not
>   Without a heart to live.

The construction of such lines as the above, with the quick recurring rhymes—setting aside all question of idea at the root of the poem—is a very difficult achievement; yet it is one which Suckling frequently accomplishes with ease.

The most celebrated of all poems by Suckling, however, is the "Ballad upon a Wedding," and upon the whole it well deserves the preëminence. In no other example has the poet given such a charming description of female beauty. The lines are exquisitely turned, and Suckling surpasses himself in his dainty conceits. . . .

Of Suckling's four plays, sprinkled as they are with fine passages, we are not able to speak so highly. The poet was, in the first place, unequal to a great or extended conception; and in the second, lacked the power, which distinguishes the true dramatist, of giving breadth of treatment to such conceptions as he had. *Aglaura* is said to have been the poet's favourite drama. It was produced before the Court under circumstances of much magnificence, but it must yield the palm in almost every intrinsic respect to its successor. The former is a tragi-comedy; it may be represented as tragedy or comedy, by adopting one of two fifth acts. Whether the phrase commonly current, and which describes Satan as a gentleman, originated with Suckling or not, cannot now be traced; but he certainly has in one of his plays the words "The Prince of Darkness is a Gentleman." *Aglaura* is studded with beautiful lines, and now and then there is even a sustained passage, but on the whole we are obliged to confess that the drama is stilted and unnatural. There is a good deal of love in the play, though in this respect the characters seem modelled after those of Suckling's time, and betray a singular aptitude for effecting rapid transfer of their affections. We have a king in love with Aglaura, and a prince in love with Aglaura; we have a queen at first mistress to Ziriff, Captain of the Guard, but subsequently enamoured of Ariaspes, brother to the king; then there is Iolas, a Lord of the Council, a pretended friend of the prince, but really a traitor, in love with Semanthe, while the latter indulges a Platonic affection for Ziriff; there is also Aglaura herself, in love with the prince, but named mistress to the king; Orithie, in love with the prince; and two young lords, Orsames and Philan, who are anti-Platonic. It will thus be seen that the drama is most unconscionably full of warring love-elements, sufficient to gratify the most exacting taste in this respect. . . .

It has been remarked that Suckling modelled both his style and his dramatic compositions upon Shakespeare. The criticism is not very accurate, for, if this be the case, Suckling has not produced that sincerest kind of flattery, an excellent imitation. Placed beside Shakespeare, indeed, his efforts are as moonlight unto sunlight. He lacks strength, and has only in place of it the humours of a man of society, touched with the poetic temperament. If he had eschewed the more ambitious *role* of the dramatist, and adhered to his love songs, he might have left behind him a still finer legacy than that which he has bequeathed to posterity.

We have glanced at Suckling's *Aglaura*, but his *Brennoralt* is generally regarded as his best dramatic work. The scene of the play is laid in Poland, but the Lithuanians are intended for the Scotch. The play originally appeared with the title of *The Discontented Colonel*, and Suckling chose it as the medium for satirising the Scotch rebels. One prominent character in this drama is Iphigene, a young Palatine lady, "who has been brought up as a man, and whose love doings and sayings are more according to circumstance than propriety." Steele greatly admired a passage describing the love of Brennoralt and Francelia, and compared the delineation of the latter with one of Eve in Milton's *Paradise Lost*. The lines of Suckling run:—

> Her face is like the milky way i' th' sky,
> A meeting of gentle lights without name.
> Heav'ns! shall this fresh ornament
> Of the world, this precious love-lines,
> Pass with other common things
> Amongst the wastes of time? What pity 'twere.

The versification of *Brennoralt* is almost as crude and halting as that of *Aglaura*,—though, as a whole, the former must take precedence for its superior dramatic qualities. Yet the lyrics in *Aglaura* are far superior to those found in the later drama. Suckling's comedy of *The Goblins* need not detain us. The idea of the play is evidently borrowed from Shakespeare; and the same arguments may be adduced in defence of the machinery adopted in it as have been so powerfully adduced by Dr. Johnson in support of Shakespeare's employment of witches in *Macbeth*. When it is remembered that so sagacious a man as

Sir Matthew Hale believed in witchcraft, we can scarcely wonder that there was a prevalent belief in it in Suckling's time, especially amongst the lower classes. The comedy in which Suckling avails himself of this belief is not noticeable for wit or brilliancy. A very short tragedy, entitled "The Sad One," completes the list of the poet's dramatic works. It is concerned with civil troubles in Sicily. There is a considerable amount of fighting and "running through" with deadly weapons, but the literary vigour of the author is by no means commensurate with the military vigour of the characters.

Suckling is most successful, as we have remarked, in his lyrics; but a word of appreciation and admiration is due as regards his prose writings. All his sprightliness of fancy seems to be called into requisition in many of his letters, which are able, shrewd, and full of worldly wisdom. It is also in these that he shows the extent of his erudition. His discourse entitled "An Account of Religion by Reason," inscribed to the Earl of Dorset, exhibits a good controversial faculty, together with strong powers of reasoning. Suckling is very learned upon his subject, and traces the progress of faith from the earliest times. In one portion of this essay is to be found a simile which, upwards of a century later, was improved upon and expanded by Paley. By way of showing the excellence and the dignity of Suckling's prose, we will extract the following passage, not as expressing belief in its conclusions or otherwise. Suckling is arguing upon the subject of the Trinity:—

> The head of a spring is not a head, but in respect of the spring; for if something flowed not from it, it were no original; nor the spring a spring, if it did not flow from something; nor the stream a stream, but in respect of both: now all these three are but one water; and though one is not the other, yet they can hardly be considered one without the other. Now, though I know this is so far from a demonstration, that it is but an imperfect instance—perfect being impossible of infinite by finite things—yet there is a resemblance great enough to let us see the possibility. And, here, the eye of reason needed no more the spectacles of faith than for these things, of which we make sympathy the cause, as in the loadstone; or antipathy, of which every man almost gives instances from his own nature. Nor is it there so great a wonder that we should be ignorant; for this is distant and removed from sense; these near and subject to it; and it were stranger for me to conclude that God did not work *ad extra*, thus one and distinct within himself, because I cannot conceive how begotten, how proceeding, than if a clown should say the hand of a watch did not move, because he could not give an account of the wheel within. So far is it from being unreasonable because I do not understand it, that it would be unreasonable I should: for why should a created substance comprehend an uncreated? a circumscribed and limited an uncircumscribed and unlimited? And this I observe in those great lovers and lords of reason, quoted by the fathers, Zoroaster, Trismegistus, Plato, Numenius, Plotinus, Proclus, Aurelius, and Avicen; that when they spoke of this mystery of the Trinity—of which all write something, and some almost as plainly as Christians themselves—that they discussed it not as they did other things, but delivered themselves as oracles, which they had received themselves without dispute.

The feverish life of Suckling never fulfilled its true issues. Expatriated and disgraced, his sun went down in a foreign land, ere almost it had reached its meridian. He possessed, however, a true and exquisite genius, as his lyrical outpourings abundantly testify. The vicious habits he contracted in early life almost paralysed his talents, except on rare and special occasions, when the brilliancy of his genius forced its way through the clouds of sorrow and humiliation. He remains to us chiefly a name, though there is indicated the outline of a master of lyric verse but little below the first rank. He never carried his

genius to such perfection as did Herrick, but he has individual stanzas and poems which are equal to anything that Herrick, Wither, or Waller ever achieved. To the allurements of a court at first brilliant and trifling, then sensual and devilish, we owe in great measure the failure of Suckling's life, and the extinction of his fine genius. But, when all deductions have been made, there still remains substantial reasons for classing the poet honourably amongst the distinguished men of his age.

WILLIAM BROWNE

1591–c. 1643

William Browne was born in 1591, in Tavistock, Devon. He was educated at the Tavistock Grammar School and Exeter College, Oxford. He left Oxford without taking a degree around 1600. He read law at Clifford's Inn and Inner Temple, London. He returned to Oxford in 1624 as tutor to Robert Dormer, Earl of Carnarvon.

Browne's first printed poem was an elegy written upon the death of Prince Henry in 1613. The first book of his narrative poem, *Britannia's Pastorals*, appeared in 1613. Book II was published in 1616, and the third book remained in manuscript until its publication in 1852. In 1614 Browne published the seven eclogues comprising *Shepherd's Pipe*, written with the assistance of his friend George Wither. Along with Drayton and Wither, Browne considered himself the poetic heir to Spenser. Browne even included a eulogy to Spenser at the end of the first song of Book II of *Britannia's Pastorals*. In 1614 Browne produced *The Inner Temple Masque*. Browne's works were collected by W. C. Hazlitt in 1868. Browne is thought to have died around 1643.

Personal

William Browne, son of Tho. Br. of Tavystock in Devonsh. gent. was born there, spent some time among the muses in Exeter coll. after K. Jam. I came to the crown; whence retiring to the Inner Temple, without any degree conferr'd upon him, became famed there for his poetry, especially after he had published,

Britannia's Pastorals—Esteemed then, by judicious persons, to be written in a sublime strain, and for subject amorous and very pleasing. The first part of it was printed at Lond. 1613. fol. and then usher'd into the world with several copies of verses made by his learned acquaintance, as by Joh. Selden, Mich. Drayton, Christoph. Brook, &c. The second part, or book, was printed at Lond. 1616. fol. and then commended to the world by various copies made by John Glanvill, (whom I shall mention elsewhere, for his sufficiencies in the common law,) Joh. Davies of Hereford, George Withers of Linc. Inn, Ben. Johnson, Thom. Wenman of the Inner Temple, &c. which last I take to be the same, that had been fellow of Bal. coll. and public orator of this university. These two books, or parts, in fol. were also printed in two vol. in oct. (1625.) which I have not yet seen. Our author Browne hath also written a poem entit.

The Shepard's Pipe; in 7 Eclogues. Lond. 1614. oct. The fourth eclogue is dedicated to Mr. Tho. Manwood, (who died about that time) son of sir Pet. Manwood, and the fifth to his ingenious friend Mr. Christoph. Brook, mentioned elsewhere in this work.

Elegy on the never enough bewailed, &c. Prince Henry. Lond. 1613. qu. and other poems, as 'tis probable, but such I have not yet seen. However the reader is to know, that as he had honoured his country with his elegant and sweet pastorals, so was he expected, and also intreated a little farther, to grace

it, by drawing out the line of his poetic ancestors, beginning in Josephus Iscanius, and ending in himself; but whether ever published, having been all or mostly written, as 'twas said, I know not. In the beginning of the year 1624 he retired to Exeter coll. again, being then about 34 years of age, and was tutor or gov. to Rob. Dormer of that house, the same who was afterwards earl of Caernarvon, and killed in Newbury fight, 20 Sept. 1643. In the same year he was actually created master of arts, . . . and after he had left the coll. with his pupil, he became a retainer to the Pembrochian family, was beloved by that generous count, William E. of Pembroke, and got wealth and purchased an estate, which is all I know of him hitherto, only that as he had a little body, so a great mind. In my searches I find that one Will. Browne of Ottery S. Mary in Devon. died in the winter time of 1645. whether the same with the poet, I am hitherto ignorant. After the time of the said poet, appeared another person of both his names, author of two common law-books, written in English, entit. *Formulæ bene placitandi*, and of *Modus intrandi Placita generalia*, and of other things pertaining to that faculty.—ANTHONY À WOOD, *Athenae Oxonienses*, 1691–1721

General

It appears to us, that sufficient justice has not, since the era of Milton, been paid to his talents; for, though it be true, as Mr. Headley has observed, that puerilities, forced allusions, and conceits, have frequently debased his materials; yet are these amply atoned for by some of the highest excellencies of his art; by an imagination ardent and fertile, and sometimes sublime; by a vivid personification of passion; by a minute and truly faithful delineation of rural scenery; by a peculiar vein of tenderness which runs through the whole of his pastorals, and by a versification uncommonly varied and melodious. With these are combined a species of romantic extravagancy which sometimes heightens, but more frequently degrades, the effect of his pictures. Had he exhibited greater judgment in the selection of his imagery, and greater simplicity in his style, his claim on posterity had been valid, had been general and undisputed. —NATHAN DRAKE, *Shakspeare and His Times*, 1817, Vol. 1, p. 605

His facility of rhyming and command of harmonious expression are very great; and, within their proper sphere, his invention and fancy are also extremely active and fertile. His strength, however, lies chiefly in description, not the thing for which poetry or language is best fitted, and a species of writing which cannot be carried on long without becoming tiresome; he is also an elegant didactic declaimer; but of passion, or indeed of any breath of actual living humanity, his poetry has almost none. This, no doubt, was the cause of the neglect into which after a short time it was allowed to drop; and this limited quality of his genius may also very probably have been the reason why he so soon ceased to write and publish.—GEORGE L. CRAIK, *A Compendious History of English Literature and of the English Language*, 1861, Vol. 2, p. 55

He will never again be popular as he was unquestionably in his lifetime; but he will, I think, be always read by poets and students of poetry. The task of reading his works is not wholly pleasurable. If he charms us on one page, he wearies us on another; if he delights us one moment with a genuine bit of nature, in the next he is involved in the subtleties of allegory, and becomes unreadable if not unintelligible. When at his best his poetry is like a breath of sweet country air, or the scent of newly mown grass. His similes, drawn from what we are wont to call common objects, are often singularly happy; he gives us fresh draughts from nature, and his verse is frequently marked by an Arcadian simplicity, contrasting pleasurably with the classical conceits and forced allusions over which, in other portions, the reader is doomed to groan.—JOHN DENNIS, *Heroes of Literature*, 1883, p. 95

Browne was evidently a man of very wide literary sympathy, which saved him from falling into the mere groove of the Fletchers. He was a personal friend and an enthusiastic devotee of Jonson, Drayton, Chapman. He was a student of Chaucer and Occleve. He was the dear friend and associate of a poet more gifted but more unequal than himself, George Wither. All this various literary cultivation had the advantage of keeping him from being a mere mocking-bird, though it did not quite provide him with any prevailing or wholly original pipe of his own. *Britannia's Pastorals* (the third book of which remained in MS. for more than two centuries) is a narrative but extremely desultory poem, in fluent and somewhat loose couplets, diversified with lyrics full of local colour, and extremely pleasant to read, though hopelessly difficult to analyse in any short space, or indeed in any space at all. Browne seems to have meandered on exactly as the fancy took him; and his ardent love for the country, his really artistic though somewhat unchastened gift of poetical description and presentment enabled him to go on just as he pleased . . .

The Shepherd's Pipe, his other considerable work, is in parts reminiscent of Chaucer, in parts of Spenser, but always characterised by the free and unshackled movement which is Browne's great charm; and the same characteristics appear in the few minor poems attributed to him. Browne has been compared to Keats, who read and loved him, and there are certainly not a few points of resemblance. Of Keat's higher or more restrained excellences, such as appear in the finest passages of *St. Agnes' Eve*, and *Hyperion*, in the "Ode to a Gre-

cian Urn," and such minor pieces as "In a Drear-Nighted December," Browne had nothing. At the same time it is fair to say that there is in him no trace of the mawkish silliness which (blasphemy as the assertion may seem to some adorers of Keats) disfigures occasionally the work of that great poet. But Browne, like Keats, had that kind of love of Nature which is really the love of a lover, not a mere artist, or a mere man of science, or a mere preacher; and he had, like Keats, a wonderful gift of expression of his love. When he tried other themes he was not generally successful, but his success, such as it is, is great; and, close student of poetry as Browne has been admitted to be, it must be added that, like Keats, who was also a close student in his way, he never smells of the lamp. It is evident that he would at any time and in any circumstances have sung, and that his studies have only to some extent coloured and conditioned the manner of his singing. Nor is he ever prosaic, a praise which certainly cannot be accorded to some men of far greater repute, and perhaps of occasionally higher gifts both in his own time and others. The rarest notes of Apollo he has not, but he is never driven, as the poet and friend of his—to whom we next come—was often driven, to the words of Mercury, and of a Mercury destitute of *talaria* and *caduceus* alike, when he thought that he was echoing the Delphian lyre. This special poetic gift was not very common at the time; and though that time produced better poets than Browne, it is worth noting in him. He may never reach the highest poetry, but he is always a poet.—GEORGE SAINTSBURY, *A History of Elizabethan Literature*, 1887, pp. 299–302

The very high praise awarded by some critics to the poetry of Browne is somewhat unaccountable. To compare him with Keats, as has been done, is quite preposterous. In his work we have a return to the pure Elizabethan manner, loose and fluid versification, and ingenuous pursuit of simple beauty. But the early freshness of the pastoral poets is gone, and the archaic words, introduced in imitation of Spenser, have lost their illusion. Browne is happiest in single lines, such as—

An uncouth place fit for an uncouth mind,

or,

Shrill as a thrush upon a morn of May,

but these beauties are infrequent. His genuine love of natural scenery and phenomena gives charm to his occasional episodes, and his poems have a species of local propriety; they suggest his early haunts, the Tavy brawling down from Dartmoor between its rocks and wooded glens, the ancient borough of Tavistock, the "sandy Plim," and, farther away, the Channel with its "sea-binding chains." Vaguely, and at intervals, this Devonshire scenery is revealed to us for a moment by a turn in Browne's conventional poetry.

A sort of story runs through the long, unfinished poem in heroic couplet called *Britannia's Pastorals*, but it is exceedingly difficult to seize. The first book was published in 1613, the same year that saw the issue of the *Poly-Olbion*, but Browne sings of "dear Britannia" in a mode diametrically opposed to that of his friend Drayton. There is neither geography, nor antiquity, nor, in spite of a flourish about

The snow-white cliffs of fertile Albion,

even patriotism. It is simply a very vague and mawkish tale of semi-supernatural love-making in south-western Devonshire. There is one Marina, who, loving Celandine, but doubtful of the direction of his passion, determines on suicide in the Tavy. She flings herself in, and a young shepherd takes her out again. The story moves at a snail's pace, amid unrestrained long-winded dialogue. Marina, still despairing, flings herself into a well or pool, and the first canto closes. The God of the pool saves her, and he and a nymph, his sister, converse, at extreme length, in octosyllabics. Marina casually drinks of a magic spring, and has the good fortune to forget Celandine. But a wicked shepherd carries her off in a boat. It is hardly necessary to follow the thread of narrative further, for Browne was absolutely devoid of all epic or dramatic talent. His maids and shepherds have none of the sweet plausibility which enlivens the long recitals of Spenser. They outrage all canons of common sense. When a distracted mother wants to know if a man has seen her lost child, she makes the inquiry in nineteen lines of deliberate poetry. An air of silliness broods over the whole conception. Marina meets a lovely shepherd, whose snowy buskins display a still silkier leg, and she asks of him her way to the marish; he misunderstands her to say "marriage," and tells her that the way is through love; she misunderstands him to refer to some village so entitled, and the languid comedy of errors winds on through pages.

The best of the poem consists in its close and pretty pictures of country scenes. At his best, Browne is a sort of Bewick, and provides us with vignettes of the squirrel at play, a group of wrens, truant schoolboys, or a country girl,

> When she upon her breast, love's sweet repose,
> Doth bring the Queen of Flowers, the English Rose.

But these happy "bits" are set in a terrible waste of what is not prose, but poetry and water, foolish babbling about altars and anagrams, long lists of blooms and trees and birds, scarcely characterized at all, soft rhyming verse meandering about in a vaguely pretty fashion to no obvious purpose. On the first book of *Britannia's Pastorals* the stamp of extreme youth is visible clearly enough; but the second book, which belongs to Browne's manhood, and the two cantos of the third, which probably date from his advanced age, show little more skill in the evolution of a story, or power in making the parts of a poem mutually cohere.

The seven eclogues of the *Shepherd's Pipe* which are Browne's (for this was a composite work in which Brooke, Wither, and Davies of Hereford joined) are designed closely in the manner of Spenser, in lyrical measures of great variety and not a little sweetness. The fourth, on the death of Philarete, is the finest, and is supposed to have influenced Milton in the composition of *Lycidas*; for this is an elegy, rather than an eclogue, and a very melodious specimen of its class. It may be interesting to note, as showing the especial attraction felt by Milton to all the poets of this Spenserian school, that in Mr. Huth's library there exists a copy of Browne copiously annotated in the hand of his great successor. The *Inner Temple Masque*, which was prepared for performance about 1617, opens with this Song of the Sirens, the most perfect of Browne's poems—

> Steer hither, steer your wingèd pines,
>   All beaten mariners!
> Here lie love's undiscovered mines,
>   A prey to passengers,—
> Perfumes far sweeter than the best
> Which make the Phœnix' urn and nest;
>   Fear not your ships,
> Nor any to oppose you save our lips;
>   But come on shore,
> Where no joy dies till love hath gotten more.
> For swelling waves, our panting breasts,
>   Where never storms arise,
> Exchange; and be awhile our guests,
>   For stars gaze in our eyes;
> The compass Love shall hourly sing,

> And as he goes about the ring,
>   We will not miss
> To tell each point he nameth with a kiss;
>   Then come on shore,
> Where no joy dies till love hath gotten more.

The masque, a slight and picturesque affair, deals with the story of Circe and Ulysses. Among the miscellaneous poems of Browne, now appears the celebrated epitaph on the Countess Dowager of Pembroke, long attributed to Ben Jonson—

> Underneath this sable hearse
> Lies the subject of all verse,
> Sidney's sister, Pembroke's mother;
> Death, ere thou hast slain another
> Fair and learn'd and good as she,
> Time shall throw a dart at thee,

but the manner does not recall that of Browne, and the authorship of this pathetic trifle must still be held dubious.
—EDMUND GOSSE, *The Jacobean Poets*, 1894, pp. 152–56

It has been objected to the author of *Britannia's Pastorals* that their perusal sends you to sleep. It had been subtler criticism, as well as more amiable, to observe that you can wake up again and, starting anew at the precise point where you dropped off, continue the perusal with as much pleasure as ever, neither ashamed of your somnolence nor imputing it as a fault to the poet. For William Browne is perhaps the easiest figure in our literature. He lived easily, he wrote easily, and no doubt he died easily. He no more expected to be read through at a sitting than he tried to write all the story of Marina at a sitting. He took up his pen and composed: when he felt tired he went off to bed, like a sensible man: and when you are tired of reading he expects you to be sensible and do the same.

. . . He learned his art, as he confesses, from Spenser and Sidney; and he took it over ready-made, with all the conventions and pastoral stock-in-trade—swains languishing for hard-hearted nymphs, nymphs languishing for hard-hearted swains; sheep-cotes, rustic dances, junketings, anadems, and true-love knots; monsters invented for the perpetual menace of chastity; chastity undergoing the most surprising perils, but always saved in the nick of time, if not by an opportune shepherd, then by an equally opportune river-god or earthquake; episodes innumerable, branching off from the main stem of the narrative at the most critical point, and luxuriating in endless ramifications. Beauty, eluding unwelcome embraces, is never too hotly pressed to dally with an engaging simile or choose the most agreeable words for depicting her tribulation. Why indeed should she hurry? It is all a polite and pleasant make-believe; and when Marina and Doridon are tired, they stand aside and watch the side couples, Fida and Remond, and get their breath again for the next figure. As for the finish of the tale, there is no finish. The narrator will stop when he is tired; just then and no sooner. What became of Marina after Triton rolled away the stone and released her from the Cave of Famine? I am sure I don't know. I have followed her adventures up to that point (though I should be very sorry to attempt a *précis* of them without the book) through some 370 pages of verse. Does this mean that I am greatly interested in her? Not in the least. I am quite content to hear no more about her. Let us have the lamentations of Celadyne for a change—though "for a change" is much too strong an expression. The author is quite able to invent more adventures for Marina, if he chooses to, by the hour together. If he does not choose to, well and good.
—A. T. QUILLER-COUCH, "William Browne" (1894), *Adventures in Criticism*, 1896, pp. 59–63

(Browne) either wanted power to condense, or did injustice to a pretty talent by fluency "long drawn out," by want of taste and of proportion. His natural descriptions are apt to be in the old catalogue fashion; as if determined to outdo Chaucer or Spenser, he gives twenty-six lines to enumerate the trees in an imagined forest. Yet amongst his wearisome shepherd tales we have occasional glimpses of true landscape. — FRANCIS TURNER PALGRAVE, *Landscape in Poetry*, 1896, p. 152

Works

BRITANNIA'S PASTORALS

This *Plant* is knotlesse that puts forth these leaues,
Vpon whose Branches I his praise doe sing:
Fruitfull the Ground, whose verdure it receiues
From fertile Nature, and the learned *Spring*.
In zeale to Good; knowne, but vnpractiz'd Ill,
Chast in his thoughts, though in his youthfull *Prime*,
He writes of Past'rall Loue, with Nectar'd Quill,
And offers vp his first Fruits vnto Time.
Receiue them (*Time*) and in thy Border place them
Among thy various Flowers of Poesie;
No *Enuy* blast, nor *Ignorance* deface them,
But keepe them fresh in fairest Memorie!
　　And, when from *Daphne's tree* he plucks more *Baies*,
　　His *Shepheards Pipe* may chant more heau'nly laies.
　　　　—CHRISTOPHER BROOKE, "To His Friend the
　　　　　　Author upon His Poem," *Britannia's Pastorals*,
　　　　　　1613

Drive forth thy Flocke, young Pastor, to that Plaine,
Where our old Shepheards wont their flocks to feed;
To those cleare walkes, where many a skilfull Swaine
To'ards the calme ev'ning, tun'd his pleasant Reede.
Those, to the *Muses* once so sacred, Downes,
As no rude foote might there presume to stand:
(Now made the way of the unworthiest Clownes,
Dig'd and plow'd up with each unhallowed hand)
If possible thou canst, redeeme those places,
Where, by the brim of many a silver Spring,
The learned Maydens, and delightfull Graces
Often have sate to heare our Shepheards sing:
Where on those *Pines* the neighb'ring Groves among,
(Now utterly neglected in these dayes)
Our Garlands, Pipes, and Cornamutes were hong
The monuments of our deserved praise.
So may thy Sheepe like, so thy Lambes increase,
And from the Wolfe feede ever safe and free!
So maist thou thrive, among the learned prease,
As thou, young Shepheard, art belov'd of mee!
　　　　—MICHAEL DRAYTON, "To His Friend the
　　　　　　Author," *Britannia's Pastorals*, 1613

So much a Stranger my *Seuerer Muse*
Is not to Loue-straines, or a Shepwards Reed,
But that She knowes some Rites of *Phœbus* dues,
Of *Pan*, of *Pallas*, and hir Sisters meed.
Reade and Commend She durst these tun'd essaies
Of *Him that loues her* (She hath euer found
Hir studies as one peece.) Next She prayes
His Readers be with *Rose* and *Myrtle* crown'd!
No *Willow* touch them! As His * *Baies* are free
From wrong of Bolts, so may their Chaplets bee.
　　　　—JOHN SELDEN, "Commendatory Verses,"
　　　　　　Britannia's Pastorals, 1613

Pipe on, sweet *Swaine*, till Ioy, in Blisse, sleepe waking;
Hermes, it seemes, to thee, of all the *Swaines*,
Hath lent his *Pipe* and *Art*: For thou art making

With sweet *Notes* (noted) *Heau'n* of *Hils* and *Plaines!*
Nay, if as thou beginst, thou dost hold on,
The totall *Earth* thine *Arcadie* will bee;
And *Neptunes Monarchy* thy *Helicon*:
So, all in both will make a *God* of thee.
To whom they will exhibit *Sacrifice*
Of richest *Loue* and *Praise*; and enuious *Swaines*
(Charm'd with thine *Accents*) shall thy *Notes* agnize
To reach aboue great *Pans* in all thy *Straines*.
Then, ply this *Veyne*: for, it may well containe
The richest *Morals* vnder poorest *Shroud*;
And sith in thee the *Past'rall spirit* doth raigne,
On such *Wits-Treasures* let it fit abrood:
Till it hath hatch'd such *Numbers* as may buy
The rarest *Fame* that e're enriched *Ayre*;
Or fann'd the Way faire, to ÆTERNITY,
To which vnfoil'd, thy *Glory* shall repaire!
Where (with the *Gods* that in faire *Starres* doe dwell,
When thou shalt, blazing, in a *Starre* abide)
Thou shalt be stil'd the *Shepherds-Starre*, to tell
Them many *Mysteries*; and be their *Guide*.
　　Thus, doe I spurre thee on with sharpest *praise*,
　　To vse thy *Gifts* of *Nature*, and of *Skill*,
　　To double-gilde *Apollos Browes*, and *Bayes*,
　　Yet make great NATVRE *Arts* true *Sou'raigne* still.
　　So, *Fame* shall euer say, to thy renowne,
　　The *Shepherds-Star*, or bright'st in *Skie*, is *Browne*!
　　　　—JOHN DAVIES, "To My *Browne*, yet Brightest
　　　　　　Swaine That Woons, or Haunts or Hill or
　　　　　　Plaine," *Britainnia's Pastorals*, *Second Book*,
　　　　　　1616

Some men, of Bookes or Freinds not speaking right,
　　May hurt them more with praise, then Foes with spight.
But I haue seene thy worke, and I know thee:
　　And, if thou list thy self, what thou canst bee.
For, though but early in these pathes thou tread,
　　I find thee write most worthy to be read.
It must be thine owne iudgment, yet, that sends
　　This thy worke forth: that iudgment mine commends.
And, where the most reade bookes, on *Authors* fames,
　　Or, like our Money-Brokers, take vp names
On credit, and are cossen'd; see, that thou
　　By offring not more sureties, then inow,
Hold thyne owne worth vnbroke: which is so good
　　Vpon th'*Exchange* of *Letters*, as I wou'd
More of our writers would like thee, not swell
　　With the *how much* they set forth, but th'*how well*.
　　　　—BEN JONSON, "To My Truly-Belov'd Friend,
　　　　　　Mr. Browne: on His *Pastorals*," *Britannia's
　　　　　　Pastorals*, *Second Book*, 1616

Tis knowne I scorne to flatter (or commend)
What merits not applause though in my *Friend*:
Which by my censure should now more appeare,
Were *this* not full as *good* as thou art *deare*:
But since thou couldst not (erring) make it so,
That I might my impartiall humour show
By finding fault; Nor one of these friends tell
How to shew loue so ill, that I as well
Might paint out mine: I feele an enuious touch,
And tell thee *Swaine*: that at thy fame I grutch,
Wishing the Art that makes this *Poeme* shine,
And this thy Worke (wert not thou wronged) mine.
For when Detraction shal forgotten be,
This will continue to eternize thee;

And if hereafter any busie wit
Should, wronging thy conceit, miscensure it,
Though seeming learn'd or wise: here he shall see,
Tis prais'd by wiser and more learn'd then hee.
　　　　—GEORGE WITHER, "To The Authour,"
　　　　　Britannia's Pastorals, Second Book, 1616

Many inferior faculties are yet left, wherein our Devon hath displaied her abilities as well as in the former, as in Philosophers, Historians, Oratours and Poets, the blazoning of whom to the life, especially the last, I had rather leave to my worthy friend Mr. W. Browne, who, as hee hath already honoured his countrie in his elegant and sweet *Pastoralls*, so questionles will easily be intreated a little farther to grace it by drawing out the line of his Poeticke Auncesters, beginning in Josephus Iscanus and ending in himselfe.—NATHANAEL CARPENTER, *Geography Delineated Forth in Two Bookes*, 1625

In Brown's *Pastorals*, notwithstanding the weakness and prolixity of his general plan, there are repeated examples of single lines and passages of extreme beauty and delicacy, both of sentiment and description, such as the following Picture of Night.

　　　Clamour grew dumb, unheard was shepherd's song,
　　　And silence girt the woods: no warbling tongue
　　　Talk'd to the echo; Satyrs broke their dance,
　　　And all the upper world lay in a trance,
　　　Only the curled streams soft chidings kept;
　　　And little gales that from the green leaf swept
　　　Dry summer's dust, in fearful whisp'rings stirr'd,
　　　As loth to waken any singing bird.

Poetical beauties of this sort are scattered, not sparingly, over the green lap of nature through almost every page of our author's writings. His description of the squirrel hunted by mischievous boys, of the flowers stuck in the windows like the hues of the rainbow, and innumerable others might be quoted.—WILLIAM HAZLITT, *Lectures on the Dramatic Literature of the Age of Elizabeth*, 1820

His *Britannia's Pastorals* appear to have been much read then by persons of fine taste; nor could persons of the same class find now, among the books of that time, a more pleasant book of the kind for a day or two of peculiar leisure. The plan of the book is that of a story of shepherds and shepherdesses, with allegorical personages introduced into their society, wandering in quest of their loves and adventures, through scenes of English rural nature; but the narrative is throughout subordinate to the descriptions for which it gives occasion. A rich and sweet, and yet varied sensuousness, characterizes these descriptions. . . . The mood is generally calm and quiet, like that of a painter of actual scenery; there is generally the faintest possible breath of human interest; but now and then the sensuous takes the hue of the ideal, and the strain rises in vigor. In the course of the poem Spenser is several times acknowledged as the poet whose genius the author venerates most. The influence of other poets may, however, be traced, and especially that of Du Bartas.
—DAVID MASSON, *The Life of John Milton*, 1859, Vol. 1, pp. 414–15

────────

W. T. ARNOLD
"William Browne"
The English Poets, ed. Thomas Humphry Ward
1880, Volume 2, pp. 65–70

Browne was fortunate in his friends. His life at the Inner Temple brought him into contact not only with his inti-

mate friend Wither and Charles Brooke, but also with such a man as Selden, who wrote commendatory verses to the first book of his *Pastorals*. He was too, apparently, one of that knot of brilliant young men who called themselves the 'sons' of Ben Jonson, and there are some interesting verses, of warm yet not extravagant praise, prefixed by Ben Jonson to the second book of the same poem. With Drayton he appears to have been on cordial and intimate terms. Some verses by Browne are prefixed to the second edition of the *Polyolbion*, and some of the most charming commendatory verses that were ever written were penned by Drayton in honour of *Britannia's Pastorals*. Chapman too 'the learned Shepherd of fair Hitching Hill,' was, as more than one indication sufficiently proves, intimate with our poet, and Browne was not only familiar with his friend's *Iliad* and *Odyssey*, but also, we may be very sure, knew well that golden book of poetry, the *Hero and Leander*. With such contemporary influences, and with the fullest knowledge of and reverence for such of his predecessors as Sidney and Spenser, Browne had every advantage given to his genius, and every help to enable him to float in the full and central stream of poetic tradition.

　Browne was apparently a diligent student of our early poetry. In his *Shepherd's Pipe* he gives in full a long story from Occleve, a poet about whom probably, at the time he wrote, no one but himself knew anything whatever. He also, though he nowhere refers to him by name, had undoubtedly studied Chaucer to some purpose. The following passage—

　　　As when some malefactor judged to die
　　　For his offence, his execution nigh,
　　　Casteth his sight on states unlike to his
　　　And weighs his ill by other's happiness,

reveals its origin at once to anyone familiar with the *Knightes Tale*. The description of the Cave of Famine, again, is transparently studied from Chaucer's description of the temple of Mars; though Browne's poverty in what the critics of the last century called 'invention' makes him compare ill with his prototype in passages of this kind. Still more familiar to Browne than the *Canterbury Tales* were Shakspeare's plays and poems. Reminiscences of Shakspeare might easily be pointed out in his heroic verse, and a still closer study is apparent in certain of the songs scattered about his *Britannia's Pastorals*. The two poets, however, to whom Browne owed most, and whose praises he has most gratefully recorded are Spenser and Sidney. The influence of the former's *Aeglogues* as well as of the *Faerie Queene* upon Browne's style and manner is very perceptible. For Sidney he had that enthusiastic and affectionate reverence which was commonly felt by all the poets of that time for the poet and the author of the *Defence of Poesie*. The passages on Spenser and Sidney are, besides their literary interest, of poetic value in themselves, and will therefore be found among the following selections. Between Browne and Wither there existed a very intimate friendship, and in Wither's youth their work ran to a certain extent upon the same lines. The hand of the author of the *Shepherd's Hunting* can apparently be traced in several passages of the *Shepherd's Pipe*, and in his own poems Wither speaks in the most affectionate and respectful terms of the 'singer of the Western main.'

　Of Browne's possible relation to Milton it is unnecessary to speak at length. Milton certainly had read Browne's poems and read them carefully, and it is interesting to compare the *Inner Temple Masque* with *Comus* and the elegies contained in the *Pastorals* and the *Shepherd's Pipe* with 'Lycidas'. The little song entitled the 'Charme' in the former poem bears a strong likeness, as Warton has pointed out, to a well-known passage in *Comus*, and the general design of the two poems is similar enough to excite attention. But while it is right to think of Milton as a friendly reader of our poet, it would be a mistake to ascribe to Browne any great share in his poetic development. What is certain is that both poets felt and showed in their different ways the combined and contending influences of classical and Puritan feeling. Browne is at once a pagan and a Protestant.

There is another English poet of a later day with whom Browne may fairly be brought into some sort of comparison. That poet is Keats[1]. It is unnecessary to say that Browne is a poet of a quite different and lower rank; but he is like Keats in being before all things an artist, he has the same intense pleasure in a fine line or a fine phrase for its own sake, and he further resembles Keats in possessing very little pure constructive or narrative power. One thinks of Keats passing a fine phrase over his mental palate with an almost sensual pleasure; 'I look upon fine phrases like a lover,' he himself says in one passage; and in a lesser degree one can fancy much the same of Browne. There is one passage which is here quoted, the value of which depends almost wholly on the masterly use of proper names. Their beauty of sound and delicate appropriateness to the place they occupy in the line—alliteration and such like expedients being freely employed—help out the historical and literary associations which make such names as Coos or Cilicia in themselves poetical. So in what may be called a 'colour-passage,' a rare control of the resources of our tongue and a rare feeling for and discrimination in shades of colour go to make up a description of real beauty and power. Browne is something of a literary epicure, and however feeble or disconnected may be his narrative of events, he rarely gives us a line which has not been tried and allowed by a taste far more delicate than common. It is consistent with this that he should be a warm defender of poetry.

> 'Tis not the rancour of a cankered heart
> That can debase the excellence of art,

he says in one passage; and how easily one might fancy Keats, transplanted to the age of James I, the author of these most characteristic lines:—

> In lieu of hounds that make the wooded hills
> Talk in a thousand voices to the rills,
> *I like the pleasing cadence of a line,*
> *Struck by the consort of the sacred Nine.*

Browne's natural tendency is to be copious and glowing in description, and his warm fancy is always tending to run away with him. He wants to be luscious and sweet. So he appeals to the 'blessed Muses';—

> Dwell on my lines, and, till the last sand fall,
> Run hand in hand with my weak pastoral;
> Cause every coupling cadence flow in blisses,
> And fill the world with envy of such kisses.
> Make all the rarest beauties of our clime,
> That deign a sweet look on my younger rhyme,
> To linger on each line's enticing graces
> As on their lover's lips and chaste embraces.

But with all this he feels strongly the force of the flowing Puritan tide, and spoils his poetry here and there, as Keats never does, by his resolution to improve the occasion. Browne is a staunch Protestant, and uses plain language about nuns and nunneries, Spain and Rome. All this does his poetry no good. We can imagine him passionate and powerful enough if he had lived a generation earlier. As it is, one has the feeling in reading him that he is living between two worlds of poetry without vital hold on either. His is neither the ardent muse of the young Shakspeare, nor the pure august muse of the great Puritan poet who was to follow him.

The rare qualities of Browne's work cannot blind us to the fact that he is almost destitute of constructive or narrative power. As a narrative poem *Britannia's Pastorals* is deplorable. The reader is perpetually passing from the woes of one fair one to those of another, and has great difficulty in making it clear to himself at any given time whether he is reading about Marina or Idya or Celia. The third book ends without any particular conclusion, and there is no reason why Browne should not have gone on in the same strain for half a dozen books more. On the other hand, as pastoral poetry, the work is not without peculiar excellences. It is true that the attempts to keep up the pastoral illusion are sometimes of a desperate character,—as for instance when the poet addresses his readers as 'swaines,'—but Browne's very accurate knowledge of his native county, and his loving enthusiasm for it, give his work a special value, and stamp much of it with the character of a direct personal impression. The allusions to Devonshire are innumerable. Browne had a peculiar love for his native streams, and the waters of his own Tavy are ever murmuring musically through his song. Just as Wordsworth said that he had made thousands of verses as he strolled by his beloved Rotha, so Browne speaks of

> Tavy's voiceful stream, to whom I owe
> More strains than from my pipe can ever flow.

The little tributary Walla has inspired some of his most charming lines. He abounds in old local words like *Berry* and *trend*, and he calls the Tavy trout

> The *shoats* with whom is Tavy frought.

He is enthusiastic about the Devonshire heroes. His knowledge of the country is inbred, and he reveals himself as passing, like Wordsworth, a 'dedicated' youth:—

> Nor could I wish those golden hours unspent
> Wherein my fancy led me to the woods,
> And tuned soft lays of rural merriment,
> Of shepherd's love, and never-resting floods.

We owe to this knowledge and love of the country those pictures of the shepherd wending his early way to his day's work, of the shepherd boy sitting alone on the fell top and piping as he watches his sheep,—a charming mixture, the whole passage, of literal fact and classical reminiscence;—of the country maid straying through the fields to make her nosegay, of the boys searching the woods for bird's eggs or hunting the squirrel from tree to tree. It is in such pictures that the reader of *Britannia's Pastorals* finds his chief pleasure. Browne cannot be said to have victoriously overcome the inherent difficulties of pastoral poetry, but his genuine delight in country sights and sounds makes him less unreal than any other English poet—if we except perhaps Ramsay,—who has tried this form of composition. He, again like Wordsworth, must be read in selections, if he is to be read with unmixed enjoyment; but in his best passages—and they are not few—he will send to the listener wafts of pure and delightful music as the young figure steps across the moors,

> δοχμιᾶν διὰ κλιτύων
> ποιμνίτας ὑμεναίους
> συρίζων.

Notes

1. Keats prefixes a quotation from *Britannia's Pastorals* to his own *Epistles.*

A. H. BULLEN
From "Introduction"
The Poems of William Browne, ed. Gordon Goodwin
1893, Volume 1, pp. xxvii–xxxiv

The bulk of William Browne's poetry was composed in youth and early manhood. He states that the First Book of *Britannia's Pastorals* was written before he had reached his twentieth year:—

> O how, methinks, the imps of Mneme bring
> Dews of invention from the sacred spring!
> Here could I spend that spring of poesy
> Which not twice ten suns have bestow'd on me.

The story of the *Pastorals*, if story there be, is naught; it would be a hopeless task to attempt to give an intelligible summary of the adventures of Celand, Marina, and the others. But the dallying diffuseness of the poem constitutes no small part of its charm. Horace Walpole threw out the suggestion that somebody should issue a series of "Lounging Books"—books that one can take up, without fatigue, at odd moments. I fear that his nice critical judgment would not have included William Browne in the series; but to the lovers of our old poets *Britannia's Pastorals* will always be a favourite lounging book. They know that, at whatever page they open, they have not far to travel before they find entertainment. In the Third Song of the Second Book there is a description of a delightful grove, perfumed with "odoriferous buds and herbs of price," where fruits hang in gallant clusters from the trees, and birds tune their notes to the music of running water; so fair a pleasaunce

> that you are fain
> Where last you walk'd to turn and walk again.

A generous reader might apply that description to Browne's poetry; he might urge that the breezes which blew down those leafy alleys and over those trim parterres were not more grateful than the fragrance exhaled from the *Pastorals*, that the brooks and birds babble and twitter in the printed page not less blithely than in that western Paradise.

What so pleasant as to read of May-games, true-love knots, and shepherds piping in the shade? of pixies and fairy-circles? of rustic bridals and junketings? of angling, hunting the squirrel, nut-gathering? Of such-like subjects William Browne treats, singing like the shepherd in the *Arcadia* as though he would never grow old. He was a happy poet. It was his good fortune to grow up among wholesome surroundings, whose gracious influences sank into his spirit. He loved the hills and dales round Tavistock, and lovingly described them in his verse. Frequently he indulges in descriptions of sunrise and sunset; they leave no vivid impression, but charm the reader by their quiet beauty. It cannot be denied that his fondness for simple, homely images sometimes led him into sheer fatuity;[1] and candid admirers must also admit that, despite his study of simplicity, he could not refrain from hunting (as the manner was) after far-fetched outrageous conceits.

Browne had nothing of that restless energy which inspired the old dramatists; he was all for pastoral contentment. Assuredly he was not a great poet, but he was a true poet, and a modest. In the Fourth Song of the Second Book he tells of the pleasure that he took in writing his poetry, and manfully declares that his free-born Muse shall never stoop to servile flattery. He cultivated poetry for its own sake, and not for what it might bring of advantage or reward:—

> In this case I, as oft as I will choose,
> Hug sweet content by my retired Muse,

> And in a study find as much to please
> As others in the greatest palaces.

Sidney and Spenser, whom he regarded as his masters, he held in highest veneration. Among his friends were Ben Jonson, Chapman ("the learned shepherd of fair Hitchin hill"), "well-languaged Daniel," Christopher Brooke, John Davies of Hereford, and Wither. In the Second Song of the Second Book he passes these poets in review, and eulogizes each in turn. The praise that he bestowed on contemporary poets was by them amply repaid; and with poets of a later age Browne has found favour. In Mr. Huth's library is preserved a copy of the folio edition of *Britannia's Pastorals*, containing MS. annotations stated to be in the handwriting of Milton (who may possibly have taken some hints for *Comus* from Browne's *Inner Temple Masque*). Henry Vaughan, in his praises of the river Usk, borrowed from the Second Song of the First Book of the *Pastorals*. Keats, who chose a motto from the *Pastorals* for one of his early poems, was much under Browne's influence at the beginning of his glorious career, but quickly passed to regions of fancy far removed from the ken of the earlier poet. Mrs. Browning did not omit to introduce Browne in her *Vision of the Poets*.

Browne was not only a poet, but a scholar and antiquary,—the friend of Selden. At the beginning of the *Pastorals* he refers (in a marginal note) to an MS. copy of William of Malmesbury "in the hands of my learned friend M. Selden." In *The Shepherd's Pipe* he printed from MS. a poem of Hoccleve, and announced "As this shall please, I may be drawn to publish the rest of his works, being all perfect in my hands." Seemingly the public of those days had no anxiety to see Hoccleve's works collected: the project fell through. A curious passage occurs in Nathaniel Carpenter's[2] *Geography Delineated Forth in Two Bookes*, 1625 (pp. 263–4):—"Many inferiour faculties are yet left, wherein our Devon hath displaied her abilities as well as in the former, as in Philosophers, Historians, Oratours and Poets, the blazoning of whom to the life, especially the last, I had rather leave to my worthy friend Mr. W. Browne, who, as hee hath already honoured his countrie in his elegant and sweet *Pastoralls*, so questionles will easily bee intreated a little farther to grace it by drawing out the line of his Poeticke Auncesters, beginning in Josephus Iscanus and ending in himselfe." Probably Carpenter threw out this suggestion at a venture, for there is no evidence to show that Browne had any intention of collecting materials for Lives of the Poets of Devonshire.[3]

The Two Books of *Pastorals*, the Eclogues in *The Shepherd's Pipe*, and some contributions to the 1614 edition of *England's Helicon*, contain all the poetry that Browne published. He left in MS. a Third Book of *Pastorals*, the *Inner Temple Masque*, and some miscellaneous poems. Among the miscellaneous pieces are the excellent bacchanalian song "Now that the spring hath filled our veins,"[4] and the famous ballad "Lydford Journey." Browne lived in an age of song-writing, and at times he could sing with the best. Some charming songs, notably "Shall I tell you whom I love?" and "Venus by Adonis' side," are scattered through the *Pastorals*, and there are good lyrical passages in the *Masque*.

In 1647 appeared a translation from the French of M. Le Roy, Sieur de Gomberville,—*The History of Polexander. Done into English by William Browne, Gent. For the Right Honourable Philip, Earle of Pembroke and Montgomery, &c.* London, printed by Tho: Harper for Thomas Walkley, fol. It is to be noted that Walkley was the publisher of the 1620 edition of *The Shepherd's Pipe*. The translation (a holiday task of slender interest) was issued without dedication or preface. Probably the translator may be identified with the author of the *Pastorals*, for we hear of no other William Browne who was connected with the Pembroke family. A copy of the French original is in the library at Wilton, but not of the English translation.

Whether his be the translation or not, the poet was dead when *Polexander* appeared. His early years were passed in the delightful town of Tavistock; he spent much time at Wilton, the home of the Herberts; and he died in, or near, Dorking. Tavistock,—Wilton,—Dorking. Surely few poets have had a more tranquil journey to the Elysian Fields.

Notes

1. No excuse can be offered for such a passage as the following (Book I, Song 3):—

> As when some boy trying the somersault,
> Stands on his head, and feet, as he did lie
> To kick against earth's spangled canopy;

> When seeing that his heels are of such weight,
> That he cannot obtain their purpos'd height,
> Leaves any more to strive; and thus doth say,
> What now I cannot do, another day
> May well effect: it cannot be denied
> I show'd a will to act, because I tried.

2. Carpenter was a fellow of Exeter College. He dedicated his *Geography* to William, Earl of Pembroke.
3. Anthony à Wood and others, garbling Carpenter's words, have represented that Browne was engaged on a History of English Poetry.
4. It was popular in the xviith century, though no early printed copy is extant. In *Poor Robin's Almanac*, 1699, it is mentioned as a well-known song:—"Now [June] is the time when Farmers shear their Sheep . . . and yet for all this, the old Song is in force still, and ever will be.

> Shear Sheep that have 'em cry we still."

WILLIAM CARTWRIGHT

1611–1643

William Cartwright was born at Northway, near Tewkesbury, Gloucestershire, in 1611. The son of a well-to-do family that had fallen on hard times, Cartwright received his early education at the Cirencester Free School. He later attended the Westminster School, London, as a King's Scholar. In 1628 he entered Christ Church, Oxford, and in 1632 he earned a B.A.

Cartwright remained at Oxford, writing and working toward the M.A. he eventually received in 1635. His first play, written around 1634, was the comedy *The Ordinary*. Two tragicomedies date from 1635, *The Lady-Errant* and *The Siege; or, Love's Convert*. Cartwright's dramatic masterpiece, *The Royall Slave*, was performed before Charles I during a visit to Oxford in 1636. In 1651 a posthumous collection of Cartwright's works, titled *Comedies, Tragi-Comedies, with Other Poems*, was printed.

Around 1638 Cartwright abandoned his literary efforts and took holy orders. He was a frequent preacher at Oxford, and one sermon, *An Off-spring of Mercy, Issuing out of the Womb of Cruelty*, survives today. In 1642 Cartwright became a Reader in Metaphysic at Oxford. The same year he also was appointed to the Council of War and in 1643 he became a Junior Proctor at Oxford. Cartwright died suddenly on November 29, 1643. He was buried in the south aisle of Christ Church Cathedral, Oxford.

Personal

Glocestershire is famous for the birth of William Cartwright at a place called Northway neer Tewksbury. Were he alive now he would be sixty-one. (This I have from his brother, who lives not far from me, and from his sisters whom I called upon in Glocestershire at Leckhampton. His sister Howes was 57 yeares old the 10 March last: her brother William was 4 yeares older.)

His father was a gentleman of 300 pounds per annum. He kept his Inne at Cirencester, but a year or therabout, where he declined and lost by it too. He had by his wife 100 pounds per annum, in Wiltshire, an impropriation, which his son has now (but having many children, lives not handsomely and haz lost his Learning: he was by the second wife, whose estate this was).

He writt a Treatise of Metaphysique, as also Sermons, particularly the Sermon that by the King's command he preached at His return from Edge-hill fight.

William Cartwright was buried in the south aisle in Christ Church, Oxon. Pitty 'tis so famous a Bard should lye without an Inscription.

'Tis not to be forgott that King Charles 1st dropt a teare at the newes of his death.—JOHN AUBREY, "William Cartwright," *Brief Lives*, 1669–96

William Cartwright the most noted poet, orator and philosopher of his time, was born at North-way near Tewksbury in Glocestershire in Sept. 1611. (9 Jac. 1.) and baptized there on the 26th day of the same month. His father Will. Cartwright was once a gentleman of a fair estate, but running out of it, I know not how, was forced to keep a common inn in Cirencester in the same county, where living in a middle condition, caused this his son, of great hopes, to be educated under Mr. Will. Topp master of the free-school there. But so great a progress did he make in a short time, that by the advice of friends, his father got him to be sped a king's-scholar at Westminster; where compleating his former learning to a miracle under Mr. Lambert Osbaldeston, was elected student of Ch. Ch. in 1628, put under the tuition of Jerumael Terrent, went through the classes of logic and philosophy with an unwearied industry, took the degrees in arts (that of master being compleated in 1635) holy orders, and became the most florid and seraphical preacher in the university. He was another Tully and Virgil, as being most excellent for oratory and poetry, in which faculties, as also in the Greek tongue, he was so full and absolute, that those that best knew him, knew not in which he most excelled. So admirably well vers'd also was he in metaphysics, that when he was reader of them in the university, the exposition of them was never better performed than by him and his predecessor Tho. Barlow of Qu. coll. His preaching also was so graceful, and profound withal, that none of his time or age went beyond him. So that if the wits read his poems, divines his sermons, and philosophers his lectures on Aristotle's metaphysics, they would scarce believe that he died at a little above thirty years of age. But that which is most remarkable, is that these his high parts and abilities were accompanied with so much candour and sweetness, that they made him equally beloved and admired of all persons, especially those of the gown and court, who esteemed also his life a fair copy of practic piety, a rare example of heroic worth, and in whom arts, learning, and language made up the true complement of perfection.

. . . Cartwright, who had the succentor's place in the church of Salisbury conferr'd on him by bishop Duppa, in the month of Octob. 1642, . . . was untimely snatch'd away by a malignant fever call'd the camp-disease, that raged in Oxon. (he being then one of the proctors of the university) to the great grief of all learned and virtuous men, and to the resentment of the K. and Qu. then there (who very anxiously enquired of his health in the time of his sickness) on the 29th of November in sixteen hundred forty and three, and was buried on the first day of December, towards the upper end of the south isle joyning to the choir of the cathedral of Christ Church. —ANTHONY À WOOD, *Athenae Oxonienses*, 1691–1721

A Person as Eminent for Loyalty and Learning, (his years consider'd) as any this Age has produc'd. One, whose Character has been written by several Pens; and therefore has afforded me, (who fetch my knowledge from Books, more than verbal Information) the larger subject to expatiate on.

The Place of this Author's Nativity, the time, and his Father's Name, are differently represented by those Authors that have mention'd him. Mr. *Lloyd* says that he was the Son of *Thomas Carthwright* of *Burford* in *Oxford-shire*, and Born *Aug.* 16. in the year 1615. Mr. *Wood* says that he was the Son of *William Carthwright*, and Born at *Northway* near *Tewskbury* in *Gloucester-shire*, in *Sept.* 1611. and Christned the 26th day of the same Month. That his Father had dissipated a fair Inheritance, he knew not how, and as his last Refuge turn'd Innkeeper at *Cirencester*. This Account contradicts the Publisher of his Poems, who says that he Died at Thirty. But however uncertain the place and time of his Birth be; certain it is, that he was bred a King's-Scholar under the Reverend and Learned Dr. *Oldbaston*: and in the year 1631 was chose Student of *Christ-Church* College in *Oxford*, and plac'd under the care of Mr. *Terrent*. He took his several Degrees, of Bachelor and Master of Arts, and afterwards was chosen by the House as Proctor, and admitted as Junior to Mr. *Wake* of *Magdalen* College by the University, the Twelfth of *April* 1643. and the same year, *viz.* on the 29th of *November*, he Died of a Malignant Feaver, which then raign'd, and was that year Fatal to others of his Contemporaries, as Mr. *Masters* of *New-College*, Mr. *Diggs* of *All-Souls*, and others both Men of the Gown and Sword. He was Buried the first of *December* in the *South-Isle*, being lamented not only by all good and learned Men, but even by majesty it self: the King and Queen having anxiously enquir'd after him all the time of his Sickness, and shewed themselves much afflicted at his Death. On the Ninth of *December* Mr. *Maplet* of the same House, was chose to supply his Place the remaining part of the year.

He was extreamly remarkable both for his outward, and inward Endowments; his Body being as handsome as his Soul. He was an expert Linguist, understanding not only Greek and Latine, but French and Italian, as perfectly as his Mother-tongue. He was an excellent Orator, and yet an admirable Poet, a Quality which *Cicero* with all his pains could not attain to. Nor was *Aristotle* less known to him than *Cicero* and *Virgil*: and those who heard his Metaphysical Lectures, gave him the Preference to all his Predecessors, the present Bishop of *Lincoln* excepted. His Sermons were as much admired as his other Composures, and One fitly applied to our Author, that Saying of *Aristotle* concerning *Æschron* the Poet, that *He could not tell what Æschron could not do*.

In a word he was of so sweet a disposition, and so replete with all Virtues, that he was beloved by all Learned Men that knew him, and admired by all Strangers: and to close all with the Character the Reverend and Pious Dr. *Fell* (sometime Bishop of *Oxford*) gave of him, Carthwright *was the utmost Man could come to.* —GERARD LANGBAINE, *An Account of the English Dramatick Poets*, 1691

William Cartwright not only wrote some of the best poems and plays of his time, and preached some of the best sermons, but as reader of metaphysics in his University he earned special praise. King Charles wore black on the day of his funeral, and fifty wits and poets of the time supplied their tributary verses to the volume, first published in 1651, of *Comedies, Tragi-Comedies, with other Poems, by Mr. William Cartwright, late Student of Christ Church in Oxford, and Proctor of the University. The Airs and Songs set by Mr. Henry Lawes.* There is in this book a touching portrait of young Cartwright, evidently a true likeness, with two rows of books over his head, and his elbow upon the open volume of Aristotle's metaphysics. He rests on his hand a young head, in which the full under-lip and downy beard are harmonized to a face made spiritual by intensity of thought. Cartwright died, in his thirty-second year, of a camp fever that killed many in Oxford. —HENRY MORLEY, "Introduction" to *The King and the Commons*, 1868, p. viii

General

I did but *see* thee! and how *vain* it is
To *vex* thee for it with *remonstrances*,
Though *things* in fashion, let those *judge*, who sit
Their *twelve-pence* out, to *clap* their *hands* at *wit*;
I fear to *sin* thus *near* thee; for (*great Saint!*)
'Tis known, *true beauty* hath no need of *paint*.
  Yet, since a *label* fixed to thy fair *hearse*
Is all the *mode*, and *tears* put into *verse*
Can teach *posterity* our present *grief*
And their own *loss*, but never give *relief*;
I'll tell them (and a *truth* which needs no *pass*,)
That *wit* in *Cartwright* at her *zenith* was,
Arts, *fancy*, language, all *convened* in thee,
With those *grand miracles* which *deify*
The old world's *writings*, kept yet from the *fire*,
Because they *force* these worst times to *admire*.
Thy matchless *genius*, in all thou didst write,
Like the *sun*, wrought with such *staid heat*, and *light*,
That not a *line* (to the most *critic* he)
Offends with *flashes*, or *obscurity*.
  When thou the *wild* of *humours* track'st, thy *pen*
So imitates that *motley stock* in men,
As if thou hadst in all their *bosoms* been,
And seen those *leopards* that lurk within.
The amorous *youth* steals from thy *courtly page*
His *vowed address*, the *soldier* his *brave rage*;
And those *soft beauteous readers* whose *looks* can
Make some men *poets*, and make any man
A *lover*, when thy *Slave* but *seems* to die,

Turn all his *mourners,* and melt at the *eye.*
Thus, thou thy *thoughts* hast *dressed* in such a *strain*
As doth not only *speak,* but *rule* and reign,
Nor are those *bodies* they assumed, *dark clouds,*
Or a *thick bark,* but *clear, transparent shrouds,*
Which who *looks* on, the *rays* so strongly beat
They'll *brush* and *warm* him with a *quickening heat,*
So *souls* shine at the *eyes,* and *pearls* display
Through the *loose-crystal-streams* a *glance of day.*
But what's all this unto a *Royal test?*
Thou art the *man,* whom great *Charles* so expressed!
Then let the *crowd* refrain their *needless hum,*
When *thunder* speaks, then *squibs* and *winds* are *dumb.*
　　—HENRY VAUGHAN, "Upon the Poems and Plays
　　　　of the Ever Memorable Mr William Cart-
　　　　wright," 1651

To have the same person cast his net and catch souls as well in the pulpit as on the stage! . . . A miracle of industry and wit, sitting sixteen hours a day at all manner of knowledge, an excellent preacher in whom hallowed fancies and reason grew visions and holy passions, raptures and extasies, and all this at thirty years of age!—DAVID LLOYD, *Memoirs of Excellent Personages,* 1668

To speak of his Poetry, there needs no other Character of it in general, then that the ablest Judge of Poetry at that time, I mean *Ben Jonson,* said with some Passion, *My Son* Cartwright *writes all like a Man.*

He writ Four Plays besides other Poems, all which were printed together in octavo, *Lond.* 1651. accompanied with above Fifty Copies of Verses writ by the most eminent Wits of the University, every One being desirous to appear in the Number of his Friends, and to give a publick Testimony to the world of the Value they had for his Memory.

Ordinary, a Comedy: I know not where this Play was acted, but I remember part of the second Scene of the first Act, between the Widow *Pot-luck, Slicer,* and *Hear-say,* is transcrib'd by the Composer of *Wits Interpreter,* in his Love-Dialogues, under the Title of the *Old Widow.* pag. 81.

Lady Errant, a Tragi-Comedy, of which I can give no Account where acted, only that it is esteem'd by some a good Comedy.

Royal Slave, a Tragi-Comedy; presented to the King and Queen by the Students of *Christ Church* in *Oxford,* Aug. 30. 1636. Presented since to both Their Majesties at *Hampton-Court* by the King's Servants. This Play gave such Content to Their Majesties, and the whole Court, as well for the stately Scenes, the Richness of the *Persian* Habits, the excellency of the Songs, (which were set by that admirable Composer, Mr. *Henry Lawes,* Servant to his Majesty King *Charles* the First, in his publick and private Musick:) as for the noble Stile of the Play it self, and the ready Address and graceful Carriage of the Actors (amongst which Dr. *Busby,* the famous Master of *Westminster* School approv'd himself a second *Roscius*); that they unanimously acknowledged that it did exceed all things of that Nature which they had ever seen. The Queen in particular so much admired it, that in *November* following, she sent for the Habits and Scenes to *Hampton-Court:* she being desirous to see her own Servants represent the same Play, (whose profession it was) that she might the better judge of the several Performances, and to whom the Preference was due. The Sentence was universally given by all the Spectators in favour of the *Gown:* tho' nothing was wanting on Mr. *Carthwright's* side, to inform the Players as well as the Scholars, in what belong'd to the Action and Delivery of each Part.

Siege, or *Love's Convert,* a Tragi-Comedy; where acted I know not, but 'tis dedicated by the Author to King *Charles* the First, by an Epistle in Verse. The Story of *Misander,* and *Leucatia,* is founded on *that* of *Pausanias* and *Cleonice,* in *Plutarch's* Life of *Cymon.* The junction which the Rich Widow *Pyle* laid upon her Lovers is borrow'd from *Boccace's Novels.* Day 9th, *Nov.* 1.

Amongst his Poems, there are several concerning the Dramatick Poets and their Writings, which must not be forgot: as those two copies which he writ on Mr. *Thomas Killegrew's* Plays, *The Prisoner,* and *Claracilla;* Two Copies on *Fletcher,* and One in Memory of *Ben Johnson,* which are so Excellent that the Publisher of Mr. *Carthwright's* Poems speaks as in a Rapture in the Preface; *viz.* 'What had *Ben* said, had he read his own Eternity in that lasting Elegy given him by our Author.'

Besides these Poems, our Author has extant other Pieces on different Subjects, as a *Sermon,* printed *Lond.* 1652. and a Book which I never saw, but is mentioned by Mr. *Wood* (ᵍ) under this Title; *Dies in Mense Novembri maxime notabiles Coronam nempe & familiam regiam spectantes.* Lond. 1671.—GERARD LANGBAINE, *An Account of the English Dramatick Poets,* 1691

In noticing the catalogue of poets ranged under the title of "Amatory and Miscellaneous," it is impossible not to be struck with the mutability of popular applause. Cowley and Cartwright were the favourites of their times, were considered as the first of poets, celebrated by their literary contemporaries in loud and repeated panegyrics, and their names familiar in every class of society. What is now their fate? To be utterly neglected, and, except to those who justly think it necessary to be intimate with every stage of our literature, nearly unknown. Have they deserved this? Let the patient reader wade through their numerous works, and he will probably answer, Yes.
—NATHAN DRAKE, *Literary Hours,* 1798, No. 28

The specific gravity of the poems, so to speak, is far greater than that of any of his contemporaries; everywhere is thought, fancy, force, varied learning. He is never weak or dull; though he fails often enough, is often enough wrong-headed, fantastical, affected, and has never laid bare the deeper arteries of humanity, for good or for evil. Neither is he altogether an original thinker; as one would expect he has over-read himself; but then he has done so to good purpose. If he imitates, he generally equals. The table of fare in *The Ordinary* smacks of Rabelais or Aristophanes, but then it is worthy of either; and if one cannot help suspecting that, *The Ordinary* never would have been written had not Ben Jonson written *The Alchemist,* one confesses that Ben Jonson need not have been ashamed to have written the play himself: although the plot, as all Cartwright's are, is somewhat confused and inconsequent. . . .

The *Royal Slave,* too, is a gallant play, righthearted and lofty from beginning to end, though enacted in an impossible court-cloud world akin to that in which the classic heroes and heroines of Corneille and Racine call each other Monsieur and Madame. . . . The *Royal Slave* seems to have been considered, both by the Court and by his contemporaries, his masterpiece. And justly so. . . .

The songs are excellent, as are all Cartwright's; for grace, simplicity, and sweetness, equal to any (save Shakspeare's) which the seventeenth century produced: but, curiously enough, his lyric faculty seems to have exhausted itself in these half-dozen songs. His minor poems are utterly worthless, out-Cowleying Cowley in frigid and fantastic conceits; and his various addresses to the king and queen are as bombastic, and stupid, and artificial, as any thing which disgraced the reigns of Charles II. or his brother.—CHARLES KINGSLEY, "Plays and Puritans" (1859), *Plays and Puritans and other Historical Essays*, 1873

Cartwright, whom his academical and literary contemporaries regarded as a phenomenon, is to us chiefly interesting as a type. If it be allowable to regard as extravagant the tendencies represented by him in both his life and his poetry, he may justly be remembered as a sufficiently prominent title among English poets—that of the typically extravagant Oxford resident of his period. He was a most enthusiastic royalist in the most royalist city and community of the kingdom; and, in a sense, he died a martyr to his political sentiment. In an age of 'florid and seraphical preachers,' this designation was attached distinctively to the youthful succentor of Salisbury Cathedral and junior proctor of the University. It is therefore but natural that among the panegyrical poets of an age given to panegyric, Cartwright's efforts in this direction should have remained unsurpassed. His muse devoted herself with that unshrinking courtliness which has often characterised our old Universities to singing the praises of the King, the Queen, their 'fourth child,' their 'sixth child,' and all the royal family, as occasion might demand, invite or suggest. When 'our happy Charles' recovered from the terrible epidemic of his times, Cartwright, in the first of the poems given here, was at hand with an exercise of flattery, which in its central conceit was afterwards imitated, but hardly equalled, by the youthful Dryden. Other events belonging to the sphere of the Court chronicler prompted longer and loftier strains: returns from journeys across the border or abroad, marriages, and above all occasions sacred to Lucina, the favourite deity, and indeed the safest inspiration, of panegyrical poets. In default of these, there were the deaths of noblemen and noblewomen, and the advents of promising Vice-Chancellors to be sung, or the merits of brother dramatists past or present, a Fletcher or a Killigrew, to be extolled, and there was the living 'Father of Poets,' Ben Jonson, to be venerated *coram publico* by his pious son.

And yet Ben Jonson himself, among whose foibles it was not to overpraise even friends and followers, was not in error when he proclaimed of 'his son Cartwright' that he 'wrote all like a man.' Cartwright, though his study of Horace and Martial had failed to teach him the grace of simplicity, was a sure and a ripe scholar; and he moves among classical illustrations and allusions with an almost alarming ease. His conceits, fetched from far and near, and jostling one another in their superabundance, mark him out as a genuine member of the Fantastic School of poets. In his lines "To the Memory of Ben Jonson," he blames his fellow-playwrights,

> who into one piece do
> Throw all that they can say, and their friends too,
> Pumping themselves for one term's noise so dry
> As if they made their wills in poetry.

Among non-dramatic poets at all events, Cartwright is as amenable to this very charge of too visible effort as any other member of the school to which he belongs.

Of the higher imaginative power and tenderer grace to be found in some of the members of that school Cartwright has but few traces. But he possessed a real rhetorical inventiveness, and an extraordinary felicity of expression. These gifts he was able to display on occasions of the most opposite and diverse character, great and small, public and private,—from the occurrence of an unexampled frost to the publication of a treatise on the art of vaulting. Yet even with a panegyrical poet of the Fantastic School the relations between his theme and his own tastes and sentiments are of the highest importance. In ingenuity Cartwright can hardly be said to have elsewhere surpassed the longest of the three following pieces congenial to himself in its subject, though elaborately singular in treatment. For it may safely be asserted that this Ordination poem achieves its object of being altogether unique, without being altogether inappropriate. On the other hand, there could be no more common theme for elegiac verse than a premature death; but the lines on an occasion of the kind here reprinted are out of the common, though by no means unpleasing. Whether, had Cartwright lived beyond early manhood, he would have fulfilled or exceeded the promise of his youth, it is useless to enquire. He was more genuinely successful as a writer of occasional lyrics and elegies than as a dramatist. Perhaps the seriousness of the epoch at the opening of which he died might have turned his efforts to religious poetry, in which the Fantastic School of English poetry achieved its noblest results, and to which this academical preacher's and poet's mind must have had a natural bias. What he actually accomplished in this direction was but little, though not altogether unworthy of being associated with the music of Milton's friend and favourite composer.—A. W. WARD, "William Cartwright," *The English Poets*, ed. Thomas Humphry Ward, 1880, Vol. 2, pp. 227–29

GEORGE SANDYS

1578–1644

George Sandys was born on March 2, 1578, at Bishopthorpe, near York, Yorkshire. He was the youngest son of Edwin Sandys, the Archbishop of York. Sandys entered St. Mary's Hall, Oxford, in 1589, and may have moved to Corpus Christi College shortly thereafter. There is, however, no record of his taking a degree at Oxford. He read law at Middle Temple, London, beginning in 1596. In 1610 Sandys traveled to Italy, Turkey, Egypt, and Palestine, in an effort to escape the litigation surrounding the failure of his first marriage. Upon his return to England he published *Relation of a Journey* (1615). This account of his travels to the East was extremely popular, going through nine reprints in the seventeenth century.

Sandys began his verse translation of Ovid's *Metamorphoses* shortly before his departure for Virginia in 1621. He remained in America until 1626 as treasurer of the Virginia Company. A complete translation of the *Metamorphoses* was published upon his return in 1626. In 1632 a revised edition with a translation of Book I of the *Aeneid* was printed. Sandys's *Paraphrase upon the Psalmes of David* (1636) appeared in a folio edition with music by Henry Lawes in 1638. A verse translation of Grotius's tragedy *Christus Patiens* was published in 1640 as *Christ's Passion, a Tragedie*. Sandys's paraphrase of *The Song of Solomon* was published in 1641. He was buried at Boxley Abbey, Kent, on March 7, 1644.

Personal

When that Arabian bird, the phœnix dies,
Who on her pile of spices bedrid lies,
And does t'herselfe a sacrifice become
Making her graue an altar, and a wombe,
T'inclose her pregnant dust, she can redeem
Those ruines she herselfe has made, and teem
With a new phœnix: but now Sandys is gone,
And melted to a dissolution
I'th furnace of a feaver, can his vrne
An equall fire, or interest returne
For those remains it keeps? Alas, we here
Are wholly beggar'd; for his sepulcher
Is like some thrifty steward, put in trust
To take account of every grain of dust
That moulders from the fabrick of his clay;
But when the generall fire, which the last day
Shall sparkle with, shall a new flame inspire
Into his vrne, and that poetick fire
Which was so long an inmate to his brest,
Shall be call'd forth from out that marble chest,
Where it now lies rak'd up amongst the dust,
And embers of his clay: and when that rust
That choakes it up, shall be dispers'd, the light
Of this infranchis'd flame shall shine so bright
Amidst our horison, 'twill seem to be
The constellation of all poetrie.
Tell me not then, that piramids disband,
And drop to dust; that Time's ungentle hand
Has crush'd into an undigested masse,
And heap of ruines, obelisques of brasse;
That our perfidious tombs (as loath to say
We once had life and being too) decay;
And that those flowers of beauty which do grow
In ladies cheeks, amidst a bed of snow,
Are wither'd on their stalk; or that one gust
Of a bleake ague can resolve to dust
Those hands which did a globe and scepter hold,
Or that that head which wore a crowne of gold,
May be wrap'd up within a shroud of lead,
Neglected, and forgot, since Sandys is dead;
Within whose brest Wit's empire seem'd to be,
And in whose braine a mine of poetrie:
For who'l not now confesse, that Time's that moth
Which frets into all art, and nature both;
Since he who seem'd within his active brain
So much of salt and verdure to contain,
He might haue ever been preserv'd, is gone,
And shrunk away into corruption:
But these excursions their conception owe
To passion, or from our wild phansies flow;
All that we now do is to returne
Some flowers of poesie unto his vrne,
Which being burnt in his own funerall flame,
Wee'l offer up as incense to his name,
Which yet by sent and colour will be known
T'haue sprung from him, and t'haue been first his own.
And if these flowers cannot so perfume

His name, but that 'twill (mauger these) consume,
Our tears strew'd on it, will repeale that fate,
And in his wither'd fame, new life create;
As when the treasures of the spring are crop'd
And by untimely martyrdom unlop'd,
From off their stalke, we can their death repreive,
And a new life by water to them give:
So now when Sandys like the spring's flowry birth,
By Death's rude sithe is mowed from off the earth,
And throwne into a grave, to wither there
Into a heap of ashes, though no teare
Can piece his dust together, we may weep
A bath of tears, in which we yet may steep
His memorie, which will (like Æson) when
'Tis thus manur'd, grow fresh and young agen;
And being thus embalm'd, a relique be
To be ador'd by all posteritie.
—THOMAS PHILLPOT, "On the Death of Mr. George Sandys," *Poems*, 1646

George Sandys, youngest Son of Edwin Sandys Arch-bishop of York, was born at Bishop's Thorp in this County (Yorkshire). He proved a most accomplished Gentleman, and an observant *Travailer*, who went as far as the *Sepulchre* at *Jerusalem*; and hath spared other men's paines in going thither, by bringing the *Holy Land* home to them; so lively is his Description thereof, with his passage thither, and return thence.

He most elegantly translated *Ovid's Metamorphoses* into English verse; so that, as the soul of Aristotle was said to have transmigrated into Thomas Aquinas (because rendring his sense so naturally), Ovid's genius may seem to have passed into Master Sandys. He was a servant, but no slave, to his subject; well knowing that a Translatour is a person in *Free Custody*; *Custody*, being bound to give the true sense of the Author he translated; *Free*, left at liberty to cloath it in his own expression.

Nor can that in any degree by applyed to Master Sandys, which one rather bitterly then falsly chargeth on an Author, whose name I leave to the Reader's conjecture:

We know thou dost well
    as a Translatour,
But where things require
    a genius and a fire,
Not kindled before by others pains,
    as often thou hast wanted brains.

Indeed some men are better *Nurses* then *Mothers* of a Poem; good onely to feed and foster the Fancies of others; whereas Master Sandys was altogether as dexterous at *inventing* as *translating*; and his own Poems as spritefull, vigorous, and masculine. He lived to be a very aged man, whom I saw in the Savoy, anno 1641, having a youthfull soul in a decayed body; and I believe he dyed soon after.—THOMAS FULLER, *The History of the Worthies of England*, 1662

I happened to speake with his niece, my lady Wyat, at whose howse, viz. at Boxley abbey, he dyed. She saies he told her a little before he dyed that he was about 63.

He lies buried in the chancel neer the dore on the south side, but without any remembrance or stone—which is pitty so sweet a swan should lye so ingloriously.

He had something in divinity ready for the presse, which my lady lost in the warres—the title of it shee does not remember.—JOHN AUBREY, "George Sandys," *Brief Lives*, 1669–96

George Sandys, a younger son of Edwin archb. of York, was born at Bishops Thorpe in that county, and as a member of S. Mary's hall was matriculated in the university in the beginning of Dec. 1589, and in that of his age eleven, at which time Henry his elder brother was remitted into the said matricula, but both, as I conceive, received their tuition in Corp. Ch. coll. How long George tarried there, or whether he took a degree, it appears not. In the month of Aug. 1610 he began a long journey, and after he had travelled thro' several parts of Europe, visited divers cities (particularly Constantinople) and countries under the Turkish empire, as Greece, Egypt, and the Holy Land. Afterwards he took a view of the remote parts of Italy, and the islands adjoyning. That being done he went to Rome, the antiquities and glories of which place were in four days time shew'd unto him by Nich. Fitzherbert sometimes an Oxford student, who, as I have before told you, ended his days in 1612. Thence our author went to Venice (from whence he first set out) and so to England.

. . . The author upon his return in 1612 or after, being improved in several respects by this his large journey, became an accomplish'd gent. as being master of several languages, of a fluent and ready discourse and excellent comportment. He had also naturally a poetical fancy, and a zealous inclination to all human learning, which made his company desir'd, and acceptable to most virtuous men and scholars of his time.

. . . ⟨Sandys⟩ being then or lately one of the gent. of the privy chamber to K. Ch. I. gave way to fate in the house of his niece the lady Margaret Wyat (dau. of sir Sam. Sandys and widow of sir Francis Wyat kt. grandson to sir Tho. Wyat beheaded in queen Mary's reign) called Boxley abbey in Kent, in the beginning of March in sixteen hundred forty and three, and was buried in the chancel of the parish church there, near to the door, on the south side, but hath no remembrance at all over his grave, nor any thing at that place, only this which stands in the common register belonging to the said church. 'Georgius Sandys poetarum Anglorum sui sæculi facile princeps, sepultus fuit Martii 7 stilo Anglic. an. dom. 1643.'—ANTHONY À WOOD, *Athenae Oxonienses*, 1691–1721

General

A Gentleman who flourish'd in the Reign of King *Charles* the Martyr; if one may so say, of a Person, who sympathiz'd so deeply with his Prince and Country in their misfortunes. He was Son to his Grace *Edwin*, Arch-bish. of *York*: and was born in the Year 1577 at *Bishops-Thorp*, in the same County, being his Father's youngest Child. He was sent to the University that memorable Year 1588. being then eleven Years of Age; and was enter'd of St. *Mary* Hall in *Oxford*. How long he stay'd, I know not: but in the Year 1610. memorable for the Murder of that Great Hero *Henry* the Fourth of *France*, by that Villain *Ravaillac*, he began his Travels thro' *France, Italy, Turky, Ægypt, Palestine*, &c. an Account of which you may read in his *Travels*, printed Fol. *Lond*. 1658. But 'tis not on this Account, but his Poetry, that he is here mentioned; and therefore I shall hasten to speak of his Writings in that kind, and first of that excellent Piece of Dramatick Poetry, which he has left us; and chiefly in this Account challenges a particular place; *viz.*

Christ's Passion, a Tragedy, with Annotations, printed 8o. *Lond*. 1640. and dedicated to King *Charles* the First. This Play is translated from the *Latin* Original writ by *Hugo Grotius*.

This Subject was handled before in *Greek*, by that Venerable Person, *Apollinarius* of *Laodicea*, Bishop of *Hierapolis*; and after him by *Gregory Nazianzen*: tho' this of *Hugo Grotius*, (in our Author's Opinion) transcends all on this Argument. As to the Translator, I doubt not but he will be allow'd an Excellent Artist, by Learned Judges; and as he has follow'd *Horace*'s Advice of Avoiding a servile Translation,

> Nec verbum verbo curabis reddere fidus
> Interpres:

So he comes so near the Sence of the Author, that nothing is lost, no Spirits evaporate in the decanting of it into *English*; and if there be any Sediment, it is left behind. This Book was reprinted with Figures, 8o. *Lond*. 1688.

Nor are his other Translations less valu'd, especially *Ovid's Metamorphosis*, printed with Cuts, Fol. *Oxon*. 1632. This Translation was so much esteem'd in former times, that I find two old Copies of Verses, speaking in praise of our Author. In the first, called A *Censure of the Poets*, are these Lines:

> Then dainty *Sands*, that hath to *English* done
> Smooth-sliding *Ovid*, and hath made him One,
> With so much sweetness, and unusual Grace,
> As tho' the neatness of the *English* Pace
> Should tell your setting *Latin*, that it came
> But slowly after, as though stiff or lame.

The other on the *Time Poets*, says thus,

> *Sands* Metamorphos'd so into another,
> We know not *Sands*, and *Ovid* from each other.

To this I may add the Translation of the first Book of *Virgil's Æneis*; by which Specimen, we may see how much he has excell'd Mr. *Ogilby*. For his other Divine Pieces, as his *Paraphrase on the Psalms, Job, Ecclesiastes, Lamentations of Jeremiah*, &c. I have heard them much admired by Devout and Ingenious Persons, and I believe very deservingly.—GERARD LANGBAINE, *An Account of the English Dramatick Poets*, 1691

Belon . . . gives a good description of the Propontis, but contents himself with the vague expression of one day and one night's sail. When Sandys . . . talks of 150 furlongs in length as well as breadth, we can only suppose some mistake of the press in the text of that judicious traveller.—EDWARD GIBBON, *The History of the Decline and Fall of the Roman Empire*, 1776–78, Ch. 17, note

Sandys wrote before Waller and Denham as well as the average versifiers who came after Dryden. His classical translations are not equal to his scriptural paraphrases, and if he had finished the *Æneid* Dryden would have left it alone. Like Dryden he did his best work late: he was fifty-nine when he published the Psalms. It does not do to compare Sandys with the authorised version of the Bible. Wherever the original is peculiarly striking he is disappointing: he gives his reader no such compensation for his temerity as Sternhold's version of the Theophany in the 18th Psalm or the close of the 24th, or as Watts's equally well-known paraphrase of the 90th. Even Tate and Brady at their best, as in the 139th Psalm, come very near to Sandys' highest level; but he is much more equable; he never subsides, like Sternhold and Hopkins, into doggerel; he never subsides, like Tate and Brady, into diffuse platitudes. He always grasps the meaning for himself; he seems to work, if not always from the Hebrew, from an ancient version, and he sometimes exhibits a really masterly power of condensation, as in the 119th and the 159th Psalms. Apart from the strictly relative praise due to the versification, the paraphrase on Job is appallingly tame.—G. A. SIMCOX, "Sandys, Herbert, Crashaw, Vaughan," *The*

English Poets, ed. Thomas Humphry Ward, 1880, Vol. 2, pp. 192–93

In 1620, when Waller was but fourteen, "the learned and ingenious Mr. Sandys" had written lines which, if we modernize the spelling, we might easily pass off upon the unwary reader as Pope's heroics. And in spite of Pope's obligations to the large genius of Dryden, it is to his early delight in Sandys's translation of the *Metamorphoses* that owed that ease and harmony of numbers which was his from first to last.—DUNCAN C. TOVEY, "Edmund Waller," *Reviews and Essays in English Literature*, 1897, pp. 89–90

Works

OVID'S METAMORPHOSIS

Your Gracious acceptance of the first fruits of my Trauels, when You were our Hope, as now our Happinesse; hath actuated both Will and Power to the finishing of this Peece: being limn'd by that vnperfect light, which was snatcht from the houres of night and repose. For the day was not mine, but dedicated to the seruice of your Great Father, and your Selfe: which, had it proued as fortunate as faithfull, in me, and others more worthy; we had hoped, ere many yeares had turned about, to haue presented you with a rich and wel-peopled Kingdome; from whence now, with my selfe, I onely bring this Composure:

Inter victrices Hederam tibi serpere Laurus.

It needeth more then a single denization, being a double Stranger: Sprung from the Stocke of the ancient Romanes; but bred in the New-World, of the rudenesse whereof it cannot but participate; especially hauing Warres and Tumults to bring it to light, in stead of the Muses. But how euer vnperfect, Your fauour is able to supply; and to make it worthy of life, if you iudge it not vnworthy of your Royall Patronage. To this haue I added, as the Mind to the Body, the History and Philosophicall sense of the Fables (with the shadow of either in Picture) which I humbly offer at the same Altar, that they may, as the rest of my labours, receiue their estimation from so great an Authority. Long may you liue to bee, as you are, the delight and Glorie of your People: and slowly, yet surely, exchange your mortal Diadem for an immortal.—GEORGE SANDYS, Dedication to Charles I, *Ovid's Metamorphosis*, 1626

> Then dainty *Sands* that hath to *English* done,
> Smooth sliding *Ovid*, and hath made him run
> With so much sweetnesse and unusuall grace,
> As though the neatnesse of the *English* pace,
> Should tell the Jetting *Lattine* that it came
> But slowly after, as though stiffe and lame.
>
> —MICHAEL DRAYTON, "To My Most Dearely-Loved Friend Henery Reynolds Esquire, of Poets and Poesie," c. 1627

'Twas a wonderfull helpe to my phansie, my reading of Ovid's *Metamorphy* in English by Sandys, which made me understand the Latin the better.—JOHN AUBREY, "John Aubrey," *Brief Lives*, 1669–96

Mr. *Chapman* in his Translation of *Homer*, professes to have done it somewhat paraphrastically; and that on set purpose; his Opinion being, that a good Poet is to be Translated in that manner. I remember not the Reason which he gives for it: But I suppose it is, for fear of omitting any of his Excellencies: sure I am, that if it be a Fault, 'tis much more pardonable, than that

of those, who run into the other extream, of a litteral, and close Translation, where the Poet is confin'd so streightly to his Author's Words, that he wants elbow-room, to express his Elegancies. He leaves him obscure; he leaves him Prose, where he found him Verse. And no better than thus has *Ovid* been serv'd by the so much admir'd *Sandys*. This is at least the Idea which I have remaining of his Translation; for I never Read him since I was a Boy. They who take him upon Content, from the Praises which their Fathers gave him; may inform their Judgment by Reading him again: And see, (if they understand the Original) what is become of *Ovid*'s Poetry, in his Version; whether it be not all, or the greatest part of it evaporated. But this proceeded from the wrong Judgment of the Age in which he Liv'd: They neither knew good Verse, nor lov'd it; they were Scholars 'tis true, but they were Pedants. And for a just Reward of their Pedantick pains, all their Translations want to be Translated, into *English*.—JOHN DRYDEN, Dedication to *Examen Poeticum*, 1693

⟨Sandys's⟩ rendering of Ovid's *Metamorphoses* has chiefly preserved his name in literary circles. A writer in *Wits Recreations* (1640) congratulated Ovid on "the sumptous bravery of that rich attire" in which Sandys had clad the Latin poet's work. He followed his text closely, and managed to compress his rendering into the same number of lines as the original—a feat involving some injury to the poetic quality and intelligibility of the English. But Sandys possessed exceptional metrical dexterity, and the refinement with which he handled the couplet entitles him to a place beside Denham and Waller. In a larger measure than either of them, he probably helped to develop the capacity of heroic rhyme. He was almost the first writer to vary the cæsura efficiently, and, by adroitly balancing one couplet against another, he anticipated some of the effects which Dryden and Pope brought to perfection. Both Dryden and Pope read Sandys's Ovid in boyhood.—SIDNEY LEE, *Dictionary of National Biography*, 1897, Vol. 50, p. 292

DIVINE POEMS AND PSALMS

I press not to the quire, nor dare I greet
The holy place with my unhallow'd feet:
My unwash'd Muse pollutes not things divine,
Nor mingles her profaner notes with thine:
Here, humbly at the porch, she listening stays,
And with glad ears sucks in thy sacred lays.
So devout penitents of old were wont,
Some without door and some beneath the font,
To stand and hear the Church's liturgies,
Yet not assist the solemn exercise.
Sufficeth her, that she a lay-place gain,
To trim thy vestments, or but bear thy train:
Though nor in tune nor wing she reach thy lark,
Her lyric feet may dance before the ark.
Who knows, but that her wandering eyes, that run
Now hunting glowworms, may adore the sun?
A pure flame may, shot by Almighty Power
Into my breast, the earthly flame devour:
My eyes in penitential dew may steep
That brine which they for sensual love did weep:
So (though 'gainst Nature's course) fire may be quench'd
With fire, and water be with water drench'd.
Perhaps my restless soul, tir'd with pursuit
Of mortal beauty, seeking, without fruit,
Contentment there, which hath not, when enjoy'd,
Quench'd all her thirst, nor satisfied, though cloy'd;

Weary of her vain search below, above,
In the first fair, may find th'immortal love.
Prompted by thy example, then, no more
In moulds of clay will I my God adore,
But tear those idols from my heart, and write
What His Blest Spirit, not fond love, shall indite.
Then I no more shall court the verdant bay,
But the dry leafless trunk on Golgotha;
And rather strive to gain from thence one thorn,
Than all the flourishing wreaths by laureates worn.
    —THOMAS CAREW, "To My Worthy Friend Mr.
     George Sandys," 1638

Such is the verse thou writ'st, that who reads thine
Can never be content to suffer mine;
Such is the verse I write, that, reading mine,
I hardly can believe I have read thine;
And wonder that, their excellence once known,
I nor correct nor yet conceal mine own.
Yet though I danger fear than censure less,
Nor apprehend a breach like to a press,
Thy merits, now the second time, inflame
To sacrifice the remnant of my shame.
Nor yet (as first) alone, but join'd with those
Who make the loftiest verse seem humblest prose.
Thus did our Master, to His praise, desire,
That babes should with philosophers conspire;
And infants their hosannas should unite
With the so famous Areopagite.
Perhaps my style, too, is for praise most fit;
Those shew their judgment least who shew their wit,
And are suspected, lest their subtler aim
Be rather to attain than to give fame.
Perhaps whilst I my earth do interpose
Betwixt thy sun and them, I may aid those
Who have but feebler eyes and weaker sight,
To bear thy beams, and to support thy light:
So thy eclipse, by neighbouring darkness made,
Were no injurious but a useful shade.
Howe'er I finish here, my Muse her days
Ends in expressing thy deservéd praise;
Whose fate in this seems fortunately cast,
To have so just an action for her last.
And since there are who have been taught that death
Inspireth prophecy, expelling breath,
I hope, when these foretell what happy gains
Posterity shall reap from these thy pains;
Nor yet from these alone, but how thy pen,
Earth-like, shall yearly give new gifts to men;
And thou fresh praise, and we fresh good receive
(For he who thus can write can never leave)
How time in them shall never force a breach,
But they shall always live and always teach,
That the sole likelihood which these present
Will from the more-rais'd souls command assent;
And the so taught will not belief refuse
To the last accents of a dying Muse.
    —LORD FALKLAND, Untitled poem, 1638

Others translate, but you the beams collect
Of your inspiréd authors, and reflect
Those heavenly rays with new and strong effect.
Yet human language only can restore
What human language had impair'd before,
And, when that once is done, can give no more.
Sir, I forbear to add to what is said,

Lest to your burnish'd gold I bring my lead,
And with what is immortal mix the dead.
    —SIDNEY GODOLPHIN, "To My Very Much
     Honoured Friend Mr. George Sandys, upon
     His Paraphrase on the Poetical Parts of the
     Bible," 1638

How bold a work attempts that pen
Which would enrich our vulgar tongue,
With the high raptures of those men
Who here with the same spirit sung,
   Wherewith they now assist the quire
   Of angels, who their songs admire!
Whatever those inspiréd souls
Were urgéd to express, did shake
The agéd deep, and both the poles:
Their numerous thunder could awake
   Dull earth, which doth with heaven consent
   To all they wrought, and all they meant.
Say, sacred bard, what could bestow
Courage on thee to soar so high?
Tell me, brave friend, what help'd thee so
To shake off all mortality?
   To light this torch thou hast climb'd higher
   Than he who stole celestial fire.
    —EDMUND WALLER, "To His Worthy Friend
     Mr. George Sandys, on His Sacred Poems,"
    1638

When Sir Philip Sidney was about twenty-three years old, George Sandys was born; and about fifty years after Sidney's early death, Sandys' version of the Psalms was published. It is difficult to believe that so brief a period separated the versions of the two men. Sidney's rhymes are for the most part rough and halting, while Sandys' verse, masculine and careful in construction, glides smoothly along and delights the ear with its music.—JOHN DENNIS, *Heroes of Literature*, 1883, p. 83

MICHAEL DRAYTON
"To Master George Sandys
Treasurer for the English Colony in Virginia"
1621

Friend, if you thinke my Papers may supplie
  You, with some strange omitted Noveltie,
Which others Letters yet have left untould,
You take me off, before I can take hould
Of you at all; I put not thus to Sea,
For two monthes Voyage to *Virginia*,
With news which now, a little something here,
But will be nothing ere it can come there.
  I feare, as I doe Stabbing; this word, State,
I dare not speake of the *Palatinate*,
Although some men make it their hourely theame,
And talke what's done in *Austria*, and in *Beame*,
I may not so; what *Spinola* intends,
Nor with his *Dutch*, which way Prince *Maurice* bends;
To other men, although these things be free,
Yet (GEORGE) they must be misteries to mee.
  I scarce dare praise a vertuous friend that's dead,
Lest for my lines he should be censured;
It was my hap before all other men
To suffer shipwrack by my forward pen:
When King JAMES entred; at which joyfull time
I taught his title to this Ile in rime:
And to my part did all the Muses win,

With high-pitch *Pæans* to applaud him in:
When cowardise had tyed up every tongue,
And all stood silent, yet for him I sung;
And when before by danger I was dar'd,
I kick'd her from me, nor a jot I spar'd.
Yet had not my cleere spirit in Fortunes scorne,
Me above earth and her afflictions borne;
He next my God on whom I built my trust,
Had left me troden lower then the dust:
But let this passe; in the extreamest ill,
Apollo's brood must be couragious still,
Let Pies, and Dawes, sit dumb before their death,
Onely the Swan sings at the parting breath.

And (worthy GEORGE) by industry and use,
Let's see what lines *Virginia* will produce;
Goe on with OVID, as you have begunne,
With the first five Bookes; let your numbers run
Glib as the former, so shall it live long,
And doe much honour to the *English* tongue:
Intice the Muses thither to repaire,
Intreat them gently, trayne them to that ayre,
For they from hence may thither hap to fly,
T'wards the sad time which but to fast doth hie,
For Poesie is followed with such spight,
By groveling drones that never raught her height,
That she must hence, she may no longer staye:
The driery fates prefixed have the day,
Of her departure, which is now come on,
And they command her straight wayes to be gon;
That bestiall heard so hotly her pursue,
And to her succour, there be very few,
Nay none at all, her wrongs that will redresse,
But she must wander in the wildernesse,
Like to the woman, which that holy JOHN
Beheld in *Pathmos* in his vision.

As th' *English* now, so did the stiff-neckt *Jewes*,
Their noble Prophets utterly refuse,
And of those men such poore opinions had,
They counted *Esay* and *Ezechiel* mad;
When *Jeremy* his Lamentations writ,
They thought the Wizard quite out of his wit,
Such sots they were, as worthily to ly,
Lock't in the chaines of their captivity,
Knowledge hath still her Eddy in her Flow,
So it hath beene, and it will still be so.

That famous *Greece* where learning flowrisht most,
Hath of her muses long since left to boast,
Th'unletter'd *Turke*, and rude *Barbarian* trades,
Where HOMER sang his lofty *Iliads*;
And this vaste volume of the world hath taught,
Much may to passe in little time be brought.

As if to *Symptoms* we may credit give,
This very time, wherein we two now live,
Shall in the compasse, wound the Muses more,
Then all the old *English* ignorance before;
Base Balatry is so belov'd and sought,
And those brave numbers are put by for naught,
Which rarely read, were able to awake,
Bodyes from graves, and to the ground to shake
The wandring clouds, and to our men at armes,
'Gainst pikes and muskets were most powerfull charmes.
That, but I know, insuing ages shall,
Raise her againe, who now is in her fall;
And out of dust reduce our scattered rimes,
Th'rejected jewels of these slothfull times,

Who with the Muses would mispend an hower,
But let blind Gothish Barbarisme devoure
These feverous Dogdays, blest by no record,
But to be everlastingly abhord.

If you vouchsafe rescription, stuffe your quill
With naturall bountyes, and impart your skill,
In the description of the place, that I,
May become learned in the soyle thereby;
Of noble *Wyats* health, and let me heare,
The Governour; and how our people there,
Increase and labour, what supplyes are sent,
Which I confesse shall give me much content;
But you may save your labour if you please,
To write to me ought of your Savages.
As savage slaves be in great *Britaine* here,
As any one that you can shew me there.
And though for this, Ile say I doe not thirst,
Yet I should like it well to be the first,
Whose numbers hence into *Virginia* flew,
So (noble *Sandis*) for this time adue.

HENRY KING
"To My Much Honoured Friend Mr. George Sandys"
1638

It is, sir, a confess'd intrusion here,
That I before your labours do appear;
Which no loud herald need, that may proclaim,
Or seek acceptance, but the author's fame.
Much less that should this happy work commend,
Whose subject is its license, and doth send
It to the world to be receiv'd and read,
Far as the glorious beams of truth are spread.
Nor let it be imagin'd that I look
Only with custom's eye upon your book;
Or in this service that 'twas my intent
T''exclude your person from your argument.
I shall profess, much of the love I owe
Doth from the root of our extraction grow.
To which though I can little contribute,
Yet with a natural joy I must impute
To our tribe's honour what by you is done,
Worthy the title of a prelate's son.
And scarcely have two brothers farther borne
A father's name, or with more value worn
Their own, than two of you; whose pens and feet
Have made the distant points of heav'n to meet:
He by exact discoveries of the West,
Yourself by painful travels in the East.
Some more like you would powerfully confute
Th' opposers of priests' marriage by the fruit;
And (since 'tis known, for all their strait-vow'd life,
They like the sex in any style but wife)
Cause them to change their cloister for that state
Which keeps men chaste by vows legitimate.
Nor shame to father their relations,
Or under nephews' names disguise their sons.
This child of yours, born without spurious blot,
And fairly midwiv'd as it was begot,
Doth so much of the parent's goodness wear,
You may be proud to own it for your heir.
Whose choice acquits you from the common sin
Of such who finish worse than they begin.
You mend upon yourself, and your last strain

Does of your first the start in judgment gain.
Since, what in curious travel was begun,
You here conclude in a devotion,
Where in delightful raptures we descry,
As in a map, Sion's chorography;
Laid out in so direct and smooth a line,
Men need not go about through Palestine.
Who seek Christ here will the strait road prefer,
As nearer much than by the Sepulchre.
    For not a limb grows here but is a path
Which in God's city the blest centre hath,
And doth so sweetly on each passion strike,
The most fantastic taste will somewhat like.
To the unquiet soul Job still from hence
Speaks in th' example of his patience.
The mortified may hear the Wise King preach,
When his repentance made him fit to teach.
Here are choice hymns and carols for the glad,
And melancholy dirges for the sad.
Last, David (as he could his art transfer)
Speaks like himself by an interpreter.
Your Muse rekindled hath the Prophet's fire,
And tun'd the strings of his neglected lyre,
Making the note and ditty so agree,
They now become a perfect harmony.
    I must confess I have long wish'd to see
The Psalms reduc'd to this conformity;
Grieving the songs of Sion should be sung
In phrase not diff'ring from a barbarous tongue,
As if, by custom warranted, we may
Sing that to God we would be loth to say.
Far be it from my purpose to upbraid
Their honest meaning, who first offer made
That book in metre to compile, which you
Have mended in the form and built anew.
And it was well, considering the time
Which scarcely could distinguish verse and rhyme:
But now the language, like the Church, hath won
More lustre since the Reformation;
None can condemn the wish, or labour spent,

Good matter in good words to represent.
    Yet in this jealous age some such there be
So (without cause) afraid of novelty,
They would by no means (had they power to choose)
An old ill custom for a better lose.
Men who a rustic plainness so affect,
They think God servéd best by their neglect;
Holding the cause would be profan'd by it,
Were they at charge of learning or of wit,
And therefore bluntly, what comes next, they bring
Coarse and ill-studied stuff for offering;
Which, like th' old Tabernacle's covering, are
Made up of badger's skins and of goat's hair.
But these are paradoxes they must use,
Their sloth and bolder ignorance to excuse.
Who would not laugh at one will naked go,
'Cause in old hangings Truth is pictur'd so?
Though plainness be reputed Honour's note,
They mantles add to beautify the coat.
So that a curious unaffected dress
Adds much unto the body's comeliness;
And wheresoe'er the subject's best, the sense
Is better'd by the speaker's eloquence.
    But, sir, to you I will not trophy raise
From other men's detraction or dispraise.
That jewel never had inherent worth,
Which ask'd such foils as these to set it forth.
If any quarrel your attempt or style,
Forgive them; their own folly they revile.
Since 'gainst themselves their factious envy shall
Confess this work of yours canonical.
    Nor may you fear the poet's common lot,
Read and commended, and then quite forgot.
The brazen mines and marble rocks shall waste,
When your foundation will unshaken last.

'Tis Fame's best pay, that you your labours see
By their immortal subject crownéd be.
For ne'er was author in oblivion hid,
Who firm'd his name on such a pyramid.

FRANCIS QUARLES

1592–1644

Born near Romford, Essex, Francis Quarles was baptised on May 8, 1592. Quarles attended Christ's College, Cambridge, probably receiving a B.A. in 1608. Subsequently he read law at Lincoln's Inn, London. Quarles was cup-bearer to Princess Elizabeth, traveling abroad with her upon her marriage to Frederick, Elector of Palatine, in 1613. Quarles later lived in Ireland from around 1620 to 1630. He served as private secretary to James Ussher, bishop of Meath and archbishop of Armagh. In 1639 Quarles was appointed Chronologer of the City of London, a post he held until his death five years later.

Quarles's earliest literary endeavor was the 1620 paraphrase of the book of Jonah, titled *Feast for Wormes*. Quarles's best-remembered works are two collections of poetry highlighted by numerous woodcuts, *Emblemes* (1635) and *Hieroglyphikes* (1638). Quarles also wrote an Arcadian romance, *Argalus and Parthenia* (1629), a collection of aphorisms, *Enchiridion* (1640), as well as several political pamphlets. Shortly before Quarles's death, the Puritans sequestered his property and destroyed several of his manuscripts because of pamphlets he had written in support of Charles I. Quarles died in London on September 8, 1644.

Francis Quarles, Esquire, son to James Quarles, Esquire, was born at Stewards, in the Parish of Rumford, in this County 〈Essex〉, where his son (as I am informed) hath an estate in expectancy. He was bred in Cambridge; and, going over into

Ireland, became Secretary to the Reverend James Usher, Archbishop of Armagh. He was a most excellent Poet; and had a mind byassed to devotion. Had he been contemporary with Plato (that great back-friend to Poets), he would not onely have allowed him to live, but advanced him to an office in his *Common-wealth*.

Some Poets, if debarr'd profaness, wantoness, and satyricalness (that they may neither abuse God, themselves, nor their neighbours), have their tongues cut out in effect. Others onely trade in *wit at the second hand*, being all for translations, nothing for invention. Our Quarles was free from the faults of the first, as if he had drank of *Jordan* instead of *Helicon*, and slept on *Mount Olivet* for his *Parnassus*; and was happy in his own invention. His *visible Poetry* (I mean his *Emblems*) is excellent, catching therein the eye and fancy at one draught, so that he hath *out-Alciated* therein, in some men's judgement. His Verses on Job are done to the life, so that the Reader may see his sores, and through them the anguish of his soul.

The troubles of Ireland, where his losses were great, forced his return hither, bearing his crosses with great patience; so that (according to the advice of Saint Hierome) "verba vertebat in opera;" and practised the Job he had described, dying about the year 1643.—THOMAS FULLER, *The History of the Worthies of England*, 1662

Francis Quarles, the darling of our plebeian judgements; that is, such as have ingenuity enough to delight in poetry, but are not sufficiently instructed to make a right choice and distinction. His *Emblems*, being a Copy from *Hermannus Hugo's* original; his *Version of Job* into English verse; his *Feast of Worms*; or *history of Jonas*, and other divine poems, have been ever, and still are, in wonderful veneration among the vulgar; and no less his *Argalus and Parthenia*, a history taken out of Sir Philip Sydney's *Arcadia*. There hath also been acted a Comedy of his, called *The Virgin Widow*.—EDWARD PHILLIPS, *Theatrum Poetarum Anglicanorum*, 1675

Tinnit, inane est, with the picture of one ringing on the globe with his finger, is the best thing I have the luck to remember in that great Poet Quarles.—ALEXANDER POPE, Letter to Francis Atterbury (March 19, 1721/2)

> Here lay poor Fletcher's half-eat scenes, and here
> The Frippery of crucify'd Moliere;
> There hapless Shakespear, yet of Tibbald sore,
> Wish'd he had blotted for himself before.
> The rest on Out-side merit but presume,
> Or serve (like other Fools) to fill a room;
> Such with their shelves as due proportion hold,
> Or their fond Parents drest in red and gold;
> Or where the pictures for the page attone,
> And Quarles is sav'd by Beauties not his own.
> —ALEXANDER POPE, *The Dunciad* (1728), 1742,
> Bk. 1, ll. 131–40

> The Hero William, and the Martyr Charles,
> One knighted Blackmore, and one pension'd Quarles.
> —ALEXANDER POPE, *Imitations of Horace*,
> 1737, Ep. II.i.386–87

Milton was forced to wait till the world had done admiring Quarles.—HORACE WALPOLE, Letter to George Montagu (Aug. 25, 1757)

Examples of bad writing might no doubt be produced, on almost any occasion, from Quarles and Blackmore; but as no body reads their works, no body is liable to be misled by them.—JAMES BEATTIE, *An Essay on Poetry and Music*, 1776

The charitable criticism of the present age has done justice to Quarles, in contrasting his merits with his acknowledged deformities. . . . A considerable resemblance to Young may be traced in the blended strength and extravagance, and ill-assorted wit and devotion of Quarles. Like Young, he wrote vigorous prose—witness his *Enchiridion*. In the parallel, however, it is due to the purity of Young to acknowledge, that he never was guilty of such indecency as that which disgraces the *Argalus and Parthenia* of our pious author.—THOMAS CAMPBELL, *Specimens of the British Poets*, 1819

I have been reading lately what of Quarles's poetry I could get. He was a contemporary of Herbert, and a kindred spirit. I think you would like him. It is rare to find one who was so much of a poet and so little of an artist. He wrote long poems, almost epics for length, about Jonah, Esther, Job, Samson, and Solomon, interspersed with meditations after a quite original plan,—Shepherd's Oracles, Comedies, Romancies, Fancies, and Meditations,—the quintessence of meditation—and Enchiridions of Meditation all divine,—and what he calls his Morning Muse; besides prose works as curious as the rest. He was an unwearied Christian, and a reformer of some old school withal. Hopelessly quaint, as if he lived all alone and knew nobody but his wife, who appears to have reverenced him. He never doubts his genius; it is only he and his God in all the world. He uses language sometimes as greatly as Shakespeare; and though there is not much straight grain in him, there is plenty of tough, crooked timber. In an age when Herbert is revived, Quarles surely ought not to be forgotten.—HENRY DAVID THOREAU, Letter to Mrs. Emerson (Oct. 16, 1843)

As a poet he has been somewhat hardly dealt with; having been judged more by the evidence of his conceits, absurdities, and false taste, than by his striking and original images, his noble and manly thoughts, and the exceeding fertility of his language. It is not surprising that posterity has failed to reverse the unjust judgment passed upon him by his contemporaries. . . . No writer is either more affected or more obscure. It is only by raking that we can gather the gold; yet it is such as will reward the seeker who has courage to undertake the search. His sagacity and good sense are unquestionable, and occasionally there is a rich outbreak of fancy; while at times he startles us by compressing, as it were, a volume into a single line.—SAMUEL CARTER HALL, *Book of Gems*, 1848

Among the poets of the prevailing Calvinism might be reckoned Wither, whose Hymns of the Church and other devotional lyrics have recently been disinterred from the mass of his writings, and presented as specimens of pure and simple English. So far as Wither is theological, he is Calvinistic. As a theological poet, however, he was not so popular, it would seem, as Francis Quarles; in whom, not withstanding that his subsequent political connexions were with the Royalists and not with the Puritans, we also recognise a mode of thought essentially puritanical. In 1632 Quarles was forty years of age. An Essex man by birth, and educated at Cambridge and at Milton's own college there, he had studied law at Lincoln's Inn, had been in the service of the Queen of Bohemia abroad, and had also been some time in Ireland as private secretary to Archbishop Usher. In 1620 he had published his first poem, *The History of Jonah, or a Feast for Worms*, being a paraphrase of the story of Jonah, with interspersed meditations, in the common heroic couplet; and this had been followed by other publications of a similar character—the story of *Esther*, in 1621; *Job Militant*, in 1624; *Sion's Sonnets* (a paraphrase of Solomon's Song, in eight-line stanzas), and *Sion's Elegies* (a paraphrase of the Lamentations of the Prophet Jeremiah), both in 1625; in the same year an *Alphabet of Elegies*, on the death of Dr. Aylmer, Archdeacon of London; in 1631 the *History of Samson*, &c. The popularity of Quarles was to be immensely increased by subsequent publications, more especially by his well-known *Emblems*, the first edition of which appeared in 1635; but already he was near being what his *Emblems* made him during the rest of that century, and he has not yet wholly ceased to be—"the darling of our plebian judgments." Personally, he seems to have been a man of sufficiently shrewd and comfortable habits. He was occupied in business; he held in succession several snug situations; and when he died, at the age of fifty-two, he left eighteen children. But in his poems all is gloomy, terrible, and miserable. In one of his *Emblems*, illustrating the text, "O wretched man that I am, who shall deliver me from the body of this death?" the design is that of a man literally enclosed within the ribs of a skeleton, through which he gazes wofully, as through imprisoning bars. This is a type of his poetry. His most frequent meditation is as follows:—

> Why, what are men but quickened lumps of earth,
> A feast for worms, a bubble full of breath,
> A looking-glass for grief, a flash, a minute,
> A painted tomb with putrefaction in it,
> A map of death, a burthen of a song,
> A winter's dust, a worm of five feet long;
> Begot in sin, in darkness nourished, born
> In sorrow, naked, shiftless, and forlorn!
> His first voice heard is crying for relief:
> Alas! he comes into a world of grief.
> His age is sinful and his youth is vain;
> His life's a punishment, his death's a pain;
> His life's an hour of joy, a world of sorrow;
> His death's a winter-night that finds no morrow.

Again,

> O what a crocodilian world is this,
> Composed of treacheries and ensnaring smiles!

Through this miserable life man is hunted by the terrors of the law, and Justice is present with her iron flail! One can see how, illustrating, as he did, thoughts of this order and doctrines still more peculiarly Calvinistic with a coarse, yet not unlearned vigour, and in a style which, though stern and abrupt, wanted neither poetic embellishment nor a quaint seasoning of conceits, Quarles should have become a favourite in Calvinistic households. To the serious citizen, to the ancient severe widow, to all downcast in the world, and seeing Dives with envy, nay, to Dives himself occasionally contemplating the world's vanity, or writhing with pain in his purple, the poetry of Quarles was not only poetry, but strong theological food.—DAVID MASSON, *The Life of John Milton*, 1859, Vol. 1, pp. 449–50

Like Byrom in the next century, like not a few poets in the Middle Ages, Quarles was a kind of journalist to whom the vehicle of verse came more easily than the vehicle of prose, and the dangers of that state of things are well known. . . . All Quarles's work is journey-work, but it is only fair to note the frequent wealth of fancy, the occasional felicity of expression, which illustrate this wilderness. I should not like to be challenged to produce twenty good lines of his in verse or prose written consecutively, yet it might be a still more dangerous challenge to produce any journalist in verse or prose of the present day who has written so much, and in whom the occasional flashes—the signs of poetical power in the individual and of what may be called poetical atmosphere in his "surroundings"—are more frequent.—GEORGE SAINTSBURY, *A History of Elizabethan Literature*, 1887, p. 378

GEORGE GILFILLAN
From "The Life and Poetry of Francis Quarles"
The Poetical Works of Richard Crashaw; and Quarles' Emblems
1857, pp. 183–97

The words, "a minor poet," are often very deceptive in their application. Sometimes they describe one who is in reality no poet at all, but whose name, in some dull and mediocre age, has been permitted, either through the carelessness of critics, or the influence of fashion, or the praise of a popular author, or by sheer personal impudence, or by the influence of wealth, or by accident, to creep into the list of poetical writers. Such are justly entitled to the damaging title of "minor poets;" and few will refuse this name to Pomfret, Yalden, Duke, Sprat, and others who tarnish the pages of Johnson's *Lives*, or to Mason, Hayley, and others in later times, who stand a little higher in the scale. But there is another class to whom the name, "minor poet," is altogether misapplied, who are, in reality, men of high genius, but who either have been cut off in the bud of their promise, or have written little, or who have been obscured by the lustre of contemporary orbs of transcendant brightness. Thus Ford, Webster, Dekker, and many others, as dramatists, were drowned in the glory of Shakspeare, and not resuscitated for two centuries after his and their death. And yet how great some of them now appear beside the dramatic writers of our age! And so between the two sovereign stars of Spenser and Milton there sparkled out a cluster of noble luminaries, such as Crashaw, Herbert, William Browne, Quarles, the two Fletchers, and others, who possessed in some points a striking similitude to the poets of the *Faery Queen* and of the *Paradise Lost*, particularly in moral and spiritual tone, and in serious sublimity of imagination, although, partly from inferiority in size to the others, and partly because crowded too closely amongst themselves, they were rather long in gaining a reputation commensurate with their genius. We have already spoken of some of the general characteristics of this school, and now proceed to record the life, and examine the writings of one who, next to George Herbert, has been the most popular of them all—Francis Quarles; whose little book of *Emblems* early found its way, and to some extent still maintains its place in the cottages of the peasantry, and has made many a visitant to poor men's huts adopt Coleridge's language, and say over little old crumbling copies of the quaint and pleasing poem, "This is true fame." From the character of Quarles' poetry one could scarcely have expected him to have been a man engaged in the bustle of active life, but rather an imaginative recluse. He lived long before the age when the banns between business and poetry have been proclaimed, and when no man has ventured to forbid them,—when genius of the truest kind has been found now compounding jalaps, and now writing sonnets; at one time unpacking muslins, and at another inditing melodious songs; now making up a basket of Portugal onions, and anon behymning all the orbs of heaven; and, antithesis still bolder, now mingling in the storm and strife of political controversy, and again daguerreotyping the private and social life of the time in poetic fiction. But even in the sixteenth century we find that a few were able to harmonise the active and the contemplative life, and prominent among these was the author of the *Emblems*. . . .

The *Emblems* are dedicated to Quarles' friend, Edward Benlowes. This was a gentleman of fortune and family in Essex, who, although not a great poet himself, and satirised for his abortive efforts by Butler, was the generous patron of poets, and to whom Phineas Fletcher, as well as Quarles, was indebted, dedicating to him, in acknowledgment of his munificence, that remarkable poem, *The Purple Island*. It is sad to think that Benlowes, too, ere he came to die, required patronage, and ended his life in poverty and sorrow.

To the *Emblems* succeeded the *Hieroglyphics*. These were inscribed to Mary, Countess of Dorset, who had been the friend of Drayton, and who became Quarles' active and powerful ally. They were not so popular as the former, although studded with the same curious fancies, and radiant with pictorial illustrations nearly as fantastic. The odd and grotesque, as well as the sublime, should be husbanded. Two *Tristram Shandys* would not have been tolerated by the public, and one hybrid of noble moral lessons and wretched prints, seems, like the *Emblems*, to have been deemed sufficient. . . .

Besides the poems we have enumerated in the course of the Life, he wrote also "The School of the Heart," an Elegy on a friend of his, Dr Wilson (rendered solemn by the fact that two hours before Wilson's death, Quarles sat by his side at the table of Sir Julius Cæsar, Master of the Rolls)—*Solomon's Recantation*, being a Paraphrase of Ecclesiastes—*The Virgin Widow*, a comedy, (the name of which play the author of *Philip von Artevelde* has borrowed, and appended to a very different dramatic production)—*The Shepherd's Oracles*, and a number of smaller pieces, published by old Thomas Fuller, in his Abel Redivivus. One of these little poems, on the martyrdom of Ridley, has some striking lines, such as—

> Rome thundered Death, but Ridley's dauntless eye
> *Stared in Death's face*, and scorned Death standing by.

Our readers will remember the coincidence between the above lines and those in a celebrated modern poem on Montrose:—

> Well they knew the hero's soul
> Was *face* to *face* with Death.

It is said that Quarles was engaged at one time on an elaborate poem describing the life of Christ, but no trace of it now exists. . . .

In the *Emblems*, as well as in his other poems, quaintnesses are common enough, but are not quite so frequent or so elaborately odd as in Donne, Crashaw, or Herbert. Quarles has, on the whole, a sterner and a more masculine genius, and his taste sins rather in exaggerations than in conceits. The oddity of his volume lies more in its prints than in its poetry. He has been compared by Campbell to Young of the *Night Thoughts*, for his blending of strength and extravagance, but Young, although possessed of a far richer imagination, and a more brilliant rhetoric than Quarles, is, considering his age, much more fantastic and falsely ingenious. But there is a deeper similitude between them than what is merely artistic: they are both intensely pervaded by the Christian spirit—they both see, and shew in verse, terribly true and mournfully emphatic, the vanity of earthly things, the fading fashion of this world, the madness of ambition, the folly of avarice, the disease of pride, the inability of even Nature to fill and satisfy the heart, and the strong argument deducible from such facts in favour of a future state of existence. To Bunyan, too, Quarles bears a considerable resemblance in the objective character of his genius. Quarles wrote up to, and beyond Herman Hugo's prints. And Bunyan always seems to be writing to illustrations, not, indeed, suspended in his study, but strongly inscribed on his imagination. He is copying from models and portraits, from landscapes and faces, which are all but visible to his eye, and which stand out so vividly on the external page to us, because, on the inner canvass, they had before so deeply imprinted

themselves on him. Who can doubt, for instance, when after awaking for a brief time from his dream, in the first part of the "Pilgrim," he says, "I dreamed again, and beheld the same two pilgrims going down the mountains toward the city," that he had a "vision" of his own, and that while he wrote the words, his eye brightened as if he saw his two heroes suddenly reappearing and pursuing their immortal journey? Macaulay attributes to all men of highest genius a certain "unsoundness of mind,"—he might, with greater accuracy, have called it a certain preternatural lustre of vision, through which, at favoured seasons, the things unseen supplant the things seen, the distant overtops the near, and the present retires before the future. In modern times, Quarles, Bunyan, Swedenborg, Blake, and Shelley have principally exhibited this faculty—a faculty which, in some of them, such as Swedenborg, Blake, and Shelley, bordered on the brink of madness, but which, in all of them, is closely connected with the finest workings and results of their genius. The poet is the truest and most far-seeing of clairvoyants, although, when like the sleep-walker he awakes, he sometimes finds himself looking over the verge of a precipice.

We have just alluded to the gloomy view Quarles, as well as Young, has taken of the present world. Goethe, in his *Autobiography*, complains of the English writers generally, as guilty of exaggerating the evils of the earth, and as loving to sing of skulls, churchyards, death and hell, and contrasts this with what he thinks the truer and gayer tendencies of the continental genius. We forget if Goethe assigns any reason for this tendency; but it probably may be traced to the greater depth with which the Protestant religion had ploughed itself into the British mind, during both the 18th and 17th centuries. Catholicism, as a religion of ceremony, tends rather to hide from the view of its votaries the mysteries of existence; the skeleton, Death, is dyed and disguised by extreme unction—purgatory becomes a screen shading the unquenchable fire—and the dread agony of the Passion is set to music and modified by the splendours of the mass. Hence, as we saw in the Life of Crashaw, the poetry inspired by Popery is sensuous, elevated, rapturous. In Germany, during Goethe's earlier days, Protestantism was, in the belief of men of genius, fast yielding to the power of modern infidelity; whereas in Britain, our poets were our true preachers, and were expressing the more serious and sublime aspects of our faith. Probably they erred in omitting to do justice to the lovelier aspects of Christianity; but the power of their protests against the vices of their very wicked period, their pictures of moral depravity, the solemn step with which they tread the aisles of death, and the reverent yet daring glimpses which they take into the darkness of the unseen world, all served to impress the popular mind with awe of the subject, and to pave the way for the brighter pages of Montgomery, Heber, Trench, Keble, and the Lake poets which came in the next age. We, for our part, prefer the chiaroscuro of Quarles, Young, Foster, and Cowper, to the false clearness and unhealthy glitter with which Goethe and some other writers seek to conceal the sad conditions of being—a clearness and a glare which are apt to react into a gloom far heavier than that of the Christian thinker. The light of the German thought may be compared to that of a tropical day—very splendid and cheering—but producing, ere it close, lassitude and bilious gloom; while that of English sacred poetry is the light of a shadowed autumn evening—clouds covering the sky, save where here sunbeams, like ravishing smiles, steal through and fall upon favoured spots, and there furrows of glory strike athwart the sea of vapour, and yonder a yellow rim in the east proclaims that the full moon is about to rise. The great question, of course, is which of the two views is the more approximately *true*; but suppose Goethe's the correct one, then let those who entertain similar notions rejoice in their own smiles, and walk in the "sparks of their own kindling," but seek not to disturb the darker moods of those who think that "man walketh in a vain show, and disquieteth himself in vain," that death, evil, sin, and hell, are dire realities, and that but for a revelation and the hopes of a future state of being, nature is a magnificent mute, the world a riddle, life a failure, and man a hybrid as monstrous and inscrutable as the sphinx; nor let them seek, besides, to intermeddle with the strange and sublime joys which mingle with these moods, even as autumn lights WILL seam and brighten autumn shadows, and which at times more than compensate for the surrounding gloom. Indeed, Quarles, Young, Cowper, Pollok, and the rest, seem sometimes deliberately to pile up and deepen the darkness, that the golden point of the Cross, and the zodiacal light of the future, may be relieved into greater brilliance and shine forth in fuller display.

Let us hear Quarles' notion of this world expressed in his poetry:—

> Fond earth! proportion not my seeming love
>   To my long stay; let not my thoughts deceive thee;
> *Thou art my prison*—and my home's above;
>   My life's a preparation but to leave thee;
>   Like one *that seeks a door*, I walk about thee;
> With thee I cannot live: I cannot live without thee
> The world's a lab'rinth, whose anfractuous ways
>   Are all composed of rubs and crook'd meanders—
> No resting here: he's hurried back that stays
>   A thought, and he that goes unguided wanders.
> Her way is dark, her path untrod, uneven;
> So hard's the way from earth, so hard's the way to
>   heaven.

We have heard of the prince who, confined and starved in a dungeon, was fed by grains of barley dropping down on him from a granary above. This is the view which Quarles, and which the Bible uniformly gives of the present condition of man. He is a dethroned and fallen king—he is chained in a dungeon—but from above, from the granary of heaven, he receives a secret supply of celestial food, and, like his Master, has "meat to eat which the world knoweth not of." Like the coursers of Achilles, he is fed on the golden barley of the gods; and magnificent as is his earthly environment, his dungeon-dwelling, with its mountain-walls, its flowery carpet, its rock foundations, its roof painted with sun, moon, and stars, and dyed in blue—it is a dungeon still, and often he fancies that there *are others confined with him there*, and when he hears the sigh of the midnight wind, it reminds him of the wail of a spirit who has lost his way to God; and when he listens to the moan of midnight rivers, he imagines that, like that fairy page in poetry, they are crying, in the name of the world, "Lost! Lost! Lost!"—a cry to which his own soul, feeling its misery and loneliness, would utter a sad echo, were it not that in the gospel of Christ he hears a counter, and a joyful voice, "Found! Found! Found!" Here, accordingly, is the conclusion of Quarles' whole matter:—

> Great God, *Thou* art the flowing spring of light,
>   Enrich mine eyes with Thy refulgent ray;
> Thou art my path, direct my steps aright,
>   I have no other light, no other way;
> I'll trust my God, and Him alone pursue,
> His law shall be my path, His heavenly light my
>   clue.

Besides the qualities we have chiefly ascribed to this poet, namely, grandeur and deep-hearted Christian earnestness, he has some minor but interesting qualities. He possesses a style, manly, nervous, generally clear, and more modern than that of almost any poet in his age. He has a keen discrimination of human nature, a copious supply of apt and bold imagery, and adds to this, extensive reading, particularly in the ancient fathers of the Church. Being a layman, too, his piety and zeal tell much better in favour of Christianity than had he been a minister; and Quarles ranks with Grotius, Addison, Pascal, Johnson, Coleridge, and Isaac Taylor, as one of the eminent "lay brothers" in the Christian Church, whose testimony is above all challenge, and whose talents lift their religion above all contempt.

The popularity of the *Emblems* is a suggestive thought. It is an argument, subordinate indeed, but of considerable weight, in favour of the evangelical form of our religion, that many popular books in the English language have been imbued with its spirit. Think of *The Pilgrim's Progress, Robinson Crusoe,* Hervey's *Meditations,* Young, Cowper, and Quarles; and in our times of Pollok's *Course of Time,* M'Cheyne's *Memoirs,* and Vicars' *Life.* We know that there is a *per contra* to this argument, and that some may plead, on the other hand, the popularity of *Don Juan,* Paine's *Works,* and the infamous novels of the Anglo-French school. It ought, however, to be remembered, that while the authors of the latter class flatter the prejudices, passions, and evils of the world, the former unsparingly denounce them. In loving the latter, the world is only "loving" its own; in loving the former, or at least bearing with them, it is receiving the missives of a power who wars with, and is to destroy the world. The paradox comes to a point when we think of the popularity of the Bible. Yet it is a sad reflection, that while these books are read, circulated, praised, they are not obeyed; and that the Bible is hitherto not the law to, but a true and glorious libel on, the world—not its rule, but its condemnation. And if this be the case with it, how much more with such reflections of it as Quarles' *Emblems*? Still *valeat quantum valere potest.* And we commend it to our readers as one of those precious productions, in which we know not whether more to admire the strength or the consecration of their author's genius.

ALEXANDER B. GROSART
From "Memorial-Introduction"
*The Complete Works in Prose and Verse
of Francis Quarles*
1880, Volume 1, pp. xxv–xxviii, lxiv–lxv

I. The Poems

Broadly regarded, I have no doubt that what mainly repels your merely literary critic to-day,—the pervading piety of these Poems,—was the attraction of them to high and humbler in the outset and onward. With the exception of *Argalus and Parthenia* and his *Elegies* (in part) and minor poems, his main poetical work was religious. Then 'fair lady' and 'knight' and noble, and 'the people' at large, were not ashamed or afraid to hold in reverence and affection the Bible and its Gospel, or to live under the influence of 'the powers of the world to come,' as conscious of day-by-day moving forward into the everlasting. Hence apart—as we shall find by-and-by—from their real poetic faculty and cunning touch and music, the *aroma* of their sanctity, the honey-comb-like richness of their Bible facts and phrasing, 'familiar in their mouths as household words,' and their guiding, nurturing, quickening godliness, laid hold, and kept hold, of head and heart and conscience. I would therefore re-accentuate my dedicatory-sonnet's words to any Reader of mine who may chance to come to the Works of Quarles with a foregone and oblique conclusion:—

In Times Old
THE WISEST, NOBLEST welcomed thy quaint ways
O' putting things in prose and verse.

I abate not by one jot my condemnation of your 'slant-browed fools' who would not have men read Francis Quarles. Whoever will with insistence of patience master these three massive tomes will never regret it—will, in my judgment, find he has reward for any strenuousness of resolve not to surcease until all is read. He will have many marked places to be returned upon. Emphatically he will not be perplexed over the unquestioned 'popularity' of the books on their first issue, and across as renowned a century-and-a-half as our England owns.

But with all this absoluteness of claim for Quarles, I am free to admit that there are DEFECTS in these Poems that go far to explain the dimming of their fame. *In limine* he is without TASTE. The word is scarcely what I would choose ordinarily; but it will suffice to put my finger on *the* repelling element that any reader of this Poet has to overcome. You can scarcely ever be sure of him. You come on a 'thing of beauty' in the fancy of it, in the vividness of it, in the epithetic colouring of it, in the charm of it every way; but lo! in the heart of the rose a slug nuzzles and taints. Or you are held by the spell of some magnificent image, a great, strong, passionate conception; and within a line of it you have no commonplace merely but bathos. . . . I name it now and here that the Reader may be prepared for aggravating alternations, and that he may not suppose the Editor to be an indiscriminate blindfold admirer. But taking this lack of TASTE and its concomitants into account, I nevertheless affirm of Francis Quarles that he is a Maker, with a soul of imagination and music in him. If I may be permitted to change the metaphor, the marble is of Carrara, albeit there are veins and stains in it that 'spoil' its absolute perfection in all too many cases.

One other general observation I would make on these Poems, on one side of it a merit (if the word be not too lukewarm) and another side a fault. I mean his 'moralising' of well-nigh everything. The old Divines were wont to speak of 'improving' public events and deaths and other lights and shadows of circumstance in wider or narrower spheres. Very effective and fitted to thrill human breasts at this hour are many of the Sermons that so 'improved' occurrences. Donne and Richard Sibbes may be taken as representatives. I do not therefore in the abstract, or in relation to the thing by itself, condemn such 'moralising.' But there is 'moralising' *and* 'moralising,' and I must confess that in these Poems the vacuity of thought is not atoned for by their applications to the circumstances of the day. His piety I value, his inevitable aspiration under the stir of Scriptural themes and words I find myself lifted up by. But over and over he says and says, not because he has something to say, but in order to say something. This was almost unavoidable by the fact that to a considerable extent he gives a 'Periphrase'—as his word is—of Holy Scripture. The wine of the divine Word is watered down to 'wershness' (*Scoticè*), and the appended 'improvements' which I have in my thought partake pretty often of the same character. And yet—as I have also indicated—if there be fault there is also merit. Not unseldom, if the Reader persevere, he will discover that after the most meagre and unsatisfying 'Periphrase' there is substantive thinking, unaffected emotion and memorableness of wording in the succeeding 'Meditations' or 'Reflections.' I would single out his *Historie of Samson*—one of the rarest of his books in its original form—as an exemplification of the finer side of his 'moralising.' In study-

ing it I have been arrested and 'held' by things mint-marked of genius.

Summarily—and again venturing a new metaphor—in the Poems of Quarles the Reader will find in the most golden grain (as in our corn-fields) pestiferous and inodorous weeds, not to say the full measure of chaff. But there *is* a harvest of 'golden grain' to be gathered, and many a bloom touched of the daisy's red, rather than of the poppy's papal scarlet, and fragrances and dewinesses correspondent with the odours and the freshness of the 'rath primrose' and the sense-taking honeysuckle on the hedgerow, or the sprays of 'the May,' ay, and ever and anon as it were, an up-springing lark palpitating under the 'inspiration' of its song. Finally—these Poems must be read with allowance; and so I clinch my appeal from Horace (A. P. ll. 351–3):—

> Verum ubi plura nitent in carmine, non ego paucis
> Offendar maculis, quas aut incuria fudit,
> Aut humana parum cavit natura.

III. The Prose

. . . Headley in his *Selections* has remarked of the *Enchyridion*—'If this little piece had been written at Athens, or Rome, its author would have been classed among the wise men of his country.' No one who has really 'studied' the brief Essays and Meditations of the book named, and its companions—for all are of the same type, save the controversial tractates—but must have been struck with the amount and variety of their thought. I do not for a moment claim for them the weight of the inimitable graciousness of Bacon's *Essays*; but putting these aside as unique and simply not comparable with any others, I know not where to look for so much well-weighed SENSE; and sense in my opinion is only a synonym of 'wisdom.' Dr. Dibdin, in his usual foolish and hasty fashion, traces a resemblance between *Enchyridion* and the (so-called) *Essays* of Sir William Cornwallis, the first edition of which appeared in 1601–2; but there is no resemblance whatever. Cornwallis is diffuse, Quarles is compact; the earlier is commonplace, the later original; the one has simply read, the other has 'pondered;' the knight is pretentious and empty, the commoner is modest and full; in fine, the *Essays* are righteously forgotten, while *Enchyridion* and *Judgement and Mercy* are as *quick* and suggestive to-day as of old—keeping an undisputed companionship with Fuller's *Good Thoughts in Bad Times* and associates.

It may be that I shall be condemned by your superfine Critics for it, but I must avow my liking of antithesis and word-play. Consequently I estimate the Prose of Francis Quarles at the high rate I do because of its antithesis and quaint playing on words. From Plutarch onward, the freshest and most direct Thinkers have possessed and used this power. To me antithesis is as the facets to the diamond. A thought may be great, deep, strong, or beautiful; but if ill-worded or over-worded it misses even your meditative deliberate reader. Let it be put antithetically, and it flashes forth its message as the diamond its immaculate light. Similarly with word-play, where it is well done. It is as the flight or whir of the humming bird, that alone reveals the metallic or jewelled exquisiteness of neck, crest, wing. The recurrence of the word, in the change and inter-change of the antithetic thought, compels attention, and things are impressed in the memory that otherwise had either not been noticed at all, or evanescently. These three characteristics of the Prose of Quarles: (*a*) Sense—common-sense, if you will, or wisdom or wiseness; (*b*.) Antithesis; (*c*.) Word-play, distinguish him from all contemporary writers of Prose known to me. You have no grandeurs, no 'thunderings or lightnings, or earthquake,' no passion, no pomp and splendour of imagination, no bearing-down power; but from first to last you feel yourself to be in the society of a grave, somewhat stately, reflective and communicative 'old English gentleman,' who has seen a good deal and pondered a good deal, not without apprehension of the awfulness and mystery and tragicalness of this life and world of ours, neither forgetful of the eternities that ensphere the fragmentariness and failure, the conquering evil and mastering pain, of our hither-side existence. As in his Poems, the '*goodness*' of the man comes out in manifold quiet and simple ways. He has his prejudices, his infirmities, his spectacles across his nose, in looking on some men and things, his dislikes, his innocent assumptions; and his Writings—Prose and Verse alike—reflect and exemplify these. But in the aggregate, this Prose is manly, healthy, inflexible, and o'times infinitely pathetic, with a pathos born of real emotion and pitifulness, and desire to be a Barnabas, even while walking in the footsteps of the Boanerges in stout witness against wrong and pride and cruelty and lying.

I would only notice another characteristic—the APHORISTIC form of many of the 'Thoughts,' 'Meditations,' 'Reflections.' Quarles was a well-read man in books and men, and he delights in working in 'wise saws and modern instances.' He has ready proverb, fitting adage, pat sentence, effective formula, allusive fact. But over and above these—and not including his patristic readings and gleanings, put at the end of his paragraphs—he has a felicitous way of so tersely expressing a given thought, opinion or principle, that it stands out before you as a maxim, or axiom. That's what I intended by the aphoristic form of much of his Prose. . . . I would assure the Reader, who does not know the Prose of Quarles, that a very slight acquaintance will satisfy that you have the bullion of thought, not gold-leaf tinsel, you have substantive not ghostly talk, you have self-originated not traditional discussion, and experience not fiction, and all in good firm homely English. Turning to *Enchyridion* and *Judgement and Mercy* is to assure (passing) oblivion of the hurry and falsities and vanity and show of the present, and redemption of the past. With these rare old tomes open before one in the sequestered stillness of one's study, or under the tree-shadows of one's garden, we are carried back again to the 'Days of old,' and can realize how true is George MacDonald's delicious bit of word-music, with which I end my say on the Prose of Quarles:—

> Days of old,
> Ye are not dead, though gone from me;
> Ye are not cold,
> But like the summer-birds gone o'er the sea.
> The sun brings back the swallows fast,
> O'er the sea:
> When thou comest at the last,
> The days of old come back to me.

VI. The Man and His Place in Our Literature

. . . My observations on the 'Poems' and 'Prose' I so arranged as very much to anticipate the final estimate, while the succeeding sections present materials for it, independent on what I have got to add. It is not much. The Reader, if at all sympathetic, must have had two things made clear: (*a.*) That in Francis Quarles as a Prose Writer we have an Essayist and Moralist of fine powers and characteristics. We may not agree with all his 'Observations' on men and things. I shall immediately have further to dissent absolutely from certain of his verdicts. But regarding these as accidents, and sprung of the evil inheritance of his 'Royalism,' substantively his Prose is charm-

ing reading, and suggestive, intellectually and ethically. When 'pondered' I always find his antitheses to be antitheses of thought and not mere words, and so reminding of Plutarch's *Parallels*. He thought deeply. He felt passionately. He uttered himself unmistakably. He had a seeing eye. He had a 'hearing' ear. He was a whole-hearted man.

Then it has been made clear, (*b.*) That your sneerer and scorner of Quarles as a Poet—in some vague uncertain fashion catching up the half-remembered *spite* of Pope's *Dunciad*—is neither more nor less than a block-head, to be put out of court in any judgments upon our elder literature. With deductions in various kinds and degrees, with admitted uncertainty of what he will say next, with concession of vile taste in the most unexpected places, it is nevertheless not to be borne for a moment from any one that in the Poet of the *Emblems* and *Argalus and Parthenia* and the examples I have adduced—mere 'gleanings' of a golden harvest—we are not to acknowledge a true Singer. He had a 'soul of music' in him. He had brain, imagination, fervid temperament, a unique inspiration, and often and often exquisiteness of utterance. His rhyme and rhythm, his nervous strength and harmony, his general integrity of workmanship, will bear comparison with far higher lauded names in my deliberate judgment, let who will gainsay.

The 'Man,' as an actor in the events and circumstances of a momentous epoch, had . . . the 'courage of his opinions,' and all his 'opinions' were convictions. He stood pathetically and gallantly true to his 'Royalism,' to his 'anointed' King. It seems probable that he was 'with the king' in Oxford, and so that he wrote 'the Loyal Convert' under the spell of the 'royal' presence. Be this as it may, he is out-and-out 'for the King.' He 'lost' I fear all his possessions as well as his Manuscripts—worth, I do not doubt, all the other losses put together—and he were a poor creature who should withhold the meed of his admiration for allegiance so unselfish and unswerving, and for sacrifices so direct and personal and continuous. All this I would assert and recall without grudge. But in the interests of historic veracity and righteousness, we must take every opportunity of protesting against a 'Royalism' and personal adherence to a sovereign (irrespective of *who* and *what* that sovereign was, and did, and did not) that were opposed to 'Loyalty' to the Nation and to the national interests as against the individual 'royal' interests, real or alleged. In the measure that Francis Quarles held fast to his conscience-ruled principles, I honour, revere him. In the measure that he discredited like conscience-ruled principles of the noblest men and women England has had, who stood for Country and not merely for King, and who could see naught of 'anointed,' of truthful or trustful, of noble or even capable, in Charles I. (not to say Charles II.) and contrariwise saw in him a false, 'tricky,' treacherous, superstitious rather than pious, favourite-governed, weak and criminal ruler—I must as emphatically condemn him. That's all I feel called on to pronounce here. But as a corollary, it were to be recreant to what I hold dearest and most sacred, not to similarly protest against Quarles's hard, harsh, historically mendacious and libellous flouts and gibes and sneers on the Puritans, and other (so-called) Heretics and Schismatics. In the *Shepheard's Oracles* I might select a score of texts whereupon to 'preach' many a sermon of retort and remonstrance. I would deny myself the irksome task. If in the *Shepheard's Oracles* and elsewhere, he is not quite so savage as Dr. Joseph Beaumont, he certainly would have sympathised really with Sydney Smith when (*jocularly*) he said to a Puseyite, 'that he was so weak he did not think he could even stick a knife into a Dissenter.' Nonconformity or Dissent, early or of the living present, has nothing to fear in any judicial and candid comparison of its work *for* the Master, and blessing and success in that work *by* the Master, with any of the (so-called) National or Established Churches. Such bigotry and assumption and sectarianism and ignorance, as the like of Quarles showed, and as modern Churchmen unhappily affect and effect (disastrously), suggest anachronism to-day; nay more, it is fully time surely that fellow-Christians recognised a 'brother' in every one outside or under their own section of the Church Universal, of whom it may be said, however imperfectly, 'Like unto Christ.' He by His Holy Spirit is not 'ashamed' of the lowliest conventicle. As matter of actual and benignant fact and observation and experience, He 'converts' and 'sanctifies' and builds up men and women everywhere, who as 'looking' to Him have been 'drawn' and 'won' to Him, whether under Conformity or Nonconformity. This being so, how deplorable, how measurelessly evil, that down the long ages men shall insist on their Shibboleth and Sibboleth as the only divine watchword!

At this late day, Francis Quarles is to be regarded not for what was accident and infirmity and of circumstance, but as he looks out upon us from his wise and delightful *Essays* and as a 'sweet Singer' in the grand Antiphone of the comparatively small band of our Sacred Poets. Thus lifted above intervening 'mists,' he appears,—as in truth and not mere phrase,—one of the Worthies of England, and secured of an abiding place in our literature and in men's hearts. Across the more than two hundred years since he 'fell asleep,' I greet him as exemplar, in the Laureate's great word-portraiture, of

> The grand old name of gentleman
> Defamed by every charlatan,
> And soil'd with all ignoble use.

WILLIAM CHILLINGWORTH

1602–1644

The son of a well-to-do Oxford family and godson of William Laud, William Chillingworth was born in 1602. He attended grammar school in Oxford and in 1618 entered Trinity College, Oxford. He became a fellow of Trinity in 1628, but refused to take holy orders because of his philosophical differences with Laudian religious theory. In 1630 Chillingworth openly embraced Catholicism, residing with Jesuits at the College of Douai. He returned to Oxford in 1631, and three years later announced his return to the Protestant fold.

Chillingworth was the author of numerous religious tracts. The most famous of these, *The Religion of Protestants a Safe Way to Salvation* (1637), argues for free inquiry and the necessity of personal conviction. Chillingworth's claim that the honest pursuit of truth could not be condemned angered both Catholics and Puritans. In 1638 Chillingworth accepted a preferment at Salisbury and in 1640 he became master of Wigston's Hospital in Leicestershire. At the outbreak of the Civil War Chillingworth joined the Royalist forces. He fought at the siege of Gloucester, falling ill at Arundel Castle. Chillingworth died shortly thereafter on January 30, 1644, in Chichester. He was buried in the Chichester Cathedral.

Personal

William Chillingworth was born in the city of Oxford; so that, by the benefit of his birth, he fell from the lap of his mother into the arms of the Muses. He was bred in Trinity College in this university; an acute and subtil disputant, but unsettled in judgment, which made him go beyond the seas, and in some sort was conciled to the church of Rome: but whether because he found not the respect he expected (which some shrewdly suggest), or because his conscience could not close with all the Romish corruptions (which more charitably believe), he returned into England; and, in testimony of his true conversion, wrote a book entituled, *The Religion of Protestants a safe way to Salvation*, against Mr. Knot the Jesuit: I will not say, "Malo nodo malus quærendus est cuneus," but affirm no person better qualified than this author, with all necessary accomplishments to encounter a Jesuit. It is commonly reported that Dr. Prideaux compared his book to a lamprey; fit for food, if the venomous string were taken out of the back thereof: a passage, in my opinion, inconsistent with the doctor's approbation, prefixed in the beginning of his book. This William Chillingworth was taken prisoner by the parliament forces at Arundel castle, and not surprised and slain in his studies, as Archimedes at the sacking of Syracuse (as some have given it out); but was safely conducted to Chichester, where, notwithstanding, hard usage hastened his dissolution—THOMAS FULLER, *The History of the Worthies of England*, 1662

Mr. Chillingworth was of a stature little superior to Mr. Hales, (and it was an age in which there were many great and wonderful men of that size,) and a man of so great a subtilty of understanding, and so rare a temper in debate, that, as it was impossible to provoke him into any passion, so it was very difficult to keep a man's self from being a little discomposed by his sharpness and quickness of argument, and instances, in which he had a rare facility, and a great advantage over all the men I ever knew. He had spent all his younger time in disputation, and had arrived to so great a mastery, as he was inferior to no man in those skirmishes: but he had, with his notable perfection in this exercise, contracted such an irresolution and habit of doubting, that by degrees he grew confident of nothing, and a sceptic, at least, in the greatest mysteries of faith.

This made him, from first wavering in religion, and indulging to scruples, to reconcile himself too soon and too easily to the church of Rome; and carrying still his own inquisitiveness about him, without any resignation to their authority, (which is the only temper can make that church sure of its proselytes,) having made a journey to St. Omer's, purely to perfect his conversion by the conversation of those who had the greatest name, he found as little satisfaction there; and returned with as much haste from them; with a belief, that an entire exemption from error was neither inherent in nor necessary to any church: which occasioned that war, which was carried on by the Jesuits with so great asperity and reproaches against him, and in which he defended himself by such an admirable eloquence of language, and clear and incomparable power of reason, that he not only made them appear unequal adversaries, but carried the war into their own quarters; and made the pope's infallibility to be as much shaken, and declined by their own doctors, (and as great an acrimony amongst themselves upon that subject,) and to be at least as much doubted, as in the schools of the reformed or protestant; and forced them since to defend and maintain those unhappy controversies in religion, with arms and weapons of another nature than were used or known in the church of Rome when Bellarmine died; and which probably will in time undermine the very foundation that supports it.

Such a levity, and propensity to change, is commonly attended with great infirmities in, and no less reproach and prejudice to the person; but the sincerity of his heart was so conspicuous, and without the least temptation of any corrupt end; and the innocence and candour of his nature so evident, and without any perverseness; that all who knew him clearly discerned, that all those restless motions and fluctuations proceeded only from the warmth and jealousy of his own thoughts, in a too nice inquisition for truth. Neither the books of the adversary, nor any of their persons, though he was acquainted with the best of both, had ever made great impression upon him; all his doubts grew out of himself, when he assisted his scruples with all the strength of his own reason, and was then too hard for himself; but finding as little quiet and repose in those victories, he quickly recovered, by a new appeal to his own judgment; so that he was, in truth, upon the matter, in all his sallies and retreats, his own convert; though he was not so totally divested of all thoughts of this world, but that when he was ready for it, he admitted some great and considerable churchmen to be sharers with him in his public conversion.

Whilst he was in perplexity, or rather some passionate disinclination to the religion he had been educated in, he had the misfortune to have much acquaintance with one Mr. Lugar, a minister of that church; a man of a competency of learning in those points most controverted with the Romanists, but of no acute parts of wit or judgment; and wrought so far upon him, by weakening and enervating those arguments, by which he found he was governed, (as he had all the logic, and all the rhetoric, that was necessary to persuade very powerfully men of the greatest talents,) that the poor man, not able to live long in doubt, too hastily deserted his own church, and betook himself to the Roman: nor could all the arguments and reasons of Mr. Chillingworth make him pause in the expedition he was using, or reduce him from that church after he had given himself to it; but he had always a great animosity against him, for having (as he said) unkindly betrayed him, and carried him into another religion, and there left him. So unfit are some constitutions to be troubled with doubts after they are once fixed.

He did really believe all war to be unlawful; and did not think that the parliament (whose proceedings he perfectly abhorred) did in truth intend to involve the nation in a civil war, till after the battle of Edge-hill; and then he thought any expedient or stratagem that was like to put a speedy end to it, to be the most commendable: and so having too mathematically conceived an engine, that should move so lightly as to be a breastwork in all encounters and assaults in the field, he carried it, to make the experiment, into that part of his majesty's army, which was only in that winter season in the field, under the command of the lord Hopton, in Hampshire, upon the borders of Sussex; where he was shut up in the castle of Arundel; which was forced, after a short, sharp siege, to yield for want of victual; and poor Mr. Chillingworth with it, falling into the rebels' hands; and being most barbarously treated by them, especially by that clergy which followed them; and being broken with sickness, contracted by the ill accommodation, and want of meat and fire during the siege, which was in a terrible season of frost and snow, he died shortly after in prison. He was a man of excellent parts, and of a cheerful disposition; void of all kind of vice, and endued with many notable virtues; of a very public heart, and an indefatigable desire to do good; his only unhappiness proceeded from his sleeping too little, and thinking too much; which sometimes threw him into violent fevers.—EDWARD HYDE, EARL OF CLARENDON, *The Life of Edward Earl of Clarendon*, c. 1668

William Chillingworth, D.D., was borne in Oxford. His father was a Brewer.

About anno 1630, he was acquainted with one who drew him and some other scholars over to Doway, where he was not so well entertained as he thought he merited for his great Disputative Witt. They made him the porter (which was to trye his temper, and exercise his obedience) so he stole over and came to Trinity College again, where he was fellowe.

William Laud, A.B.C., was his Godfather and great friend. He sent his Grace weekly intelligence of what passed in the University. Sir William Davenant (poet laureat) told me that notwithstanding this Doctor's great Reason, he was guilty of the detestable Crime of Treacherie. Dr. Gill, Filius Dris. Gill (Schoolmaster of Paules-schoole) and Chillingworth held weekely intelligence one with another for some yeares, wherein they used to nibble at states-matters. Dr. Gill in one of his letters calles King James and his sonne, *the old foole and the young one*, which letter Chillingworth communicates to W. Laud, A. B. Cant. The poore young Dr. Gill was seised, and a terrible storme pointed towards him, which, by the eloquent intercession and advocation of Edward, Earle of Dorset, together with the Teares of the poore old Doctor, his father, and supplications on his knees to his Majestie, were blowne-over. I am sorry so great a witt should have such a *naeve*.

He was a little man, blackish haire, of a Saturnine complexion. He never swore to all the points of the Church of England.

The Lord Falkland and he had such extraordinary clear reasons, that they were wont to say at Oxon that if the great Turke were to be converted by naturall reason, these two were the persons to convert him.

When Doctor Kettle (the president of Trin. Coll. Oxon.) dyed, which was in anno 1643, Dr. Chillingworth was Competitor for the Presidentship, with Dr. Hannibal Potter and Dr. Roberts. Dr. Han. Potter had been formerly Chaplain to the Bishop of Winton, who was so much Dr. Potter's friend, that though (as Will Hawes haz told me) Dr. Potter was not lawfully elected, upon referring themselves to their visitor (Bishop of Winton), the Bishop (Curle) ordered Dr. Potter possession; and let the fellowes gett him out if they could. This was shortly after the Lord Falkland was slaine, who had he lived, Dr. Chillingworth assured Will. Hawes, no man should have carried it against him: and that he was so extremely discomposed and wept bitterly for the losse of his deare Friend, yet notwithstanding he doubted not to have an astergance for it.

My tutor, W. Browne, haz told me, that Dr. Chillingworth studied not much, but when he did, he did much in a little time. He much delighted in Sextus Empeiricus. He did walke much in the College grove, and there contemplate, and meet with some *cod's-head* or other, and dispute with him and baffle him. He thus prepared himselfe before-hand. I thinke it was an Epidemick evill of that time, which I thinke is growne out of fashion, as unmannerly and boyish. He was the readiest and nimblest Disputant of his time in the university, perhaps none haz equalled him since.

I have heard Mr. Thomas Hobbes, Malmsb. (who knew him) say, that he was like a lusty fighting fellow that did drive his enimies before him, but would often give his owne party smart back-blowes.

He lies buried in the south side of the Cloysters at Chichester, where he dyed of the *morbus castrensis . . .* after the taking of Arundel castle by the Parliament: wherin he was very much blamed by the King's soldiers for his Advice in military affaires there, and they curst *that little Priest* and imputed the Losse of the Castle to his advice. In his sicknesse he was inhumanely treated by Dr. Cheynell, who, when he was to be buryed, threw his booke into the grave with him, saying, *Rott with the rotten; let the dead bury the dead.*—JOHN AUBREY, "William Chillingworth," *Brief Lives,* 1669–96

William Chillingworth, son of Will. Chillingworth citizen (afterwards mayor) of Oxford, was born in S. Martin's parish there, in a little house on the north side of the conduit at Quatervois, in Octob. 1602, and on the last of that month received baptism there. After he had been educated in grammar learning under Edw. Sylvester a noted Latinist and Grecian, (who taught privately in All-saints parish) or in the free-school joyning to Magd. coll. or in both, he became scholar of Trin. coll. under the tuition of Mr. Rob. Skinner, on the second of June 1618, being then about two years standing in the university, and going thro' with ease the classes of logic and philosophy, was admitted M. of A. in the latter end of 1623, and fellow of the said coll. 10 June 1628. He was then observed to be no drudge at his study, but being a man of great parts would do much in a little time when he settled to it. He would often walk in the college grove and contemplate, but when he met with any scholar there, he would enter into discourse, and dispute with him, purposely to facilitate and make the way of wrangling common with him; which was a fashion used in those days, especially among the disputing theologists, or among those that set themselves apart purposely for divinity. But upon the change of the times, occasion'd by the puritan, that way forsooth was accounted boyish and pedagogical, to the detriment, in some respects, of learning. About the same time being much unsettled in his thoughts, he became acquainted with one who went by the name of Joh. Fisher a learned Jesuit and sophistical disputant, who was often conversant in these parts. At length, by his persuasions, and the satisfaction of some doubts which he could not find among our great men at home, he went to the Jesuits coll. at S. Omers, forsook his religion, and by these motives following, which he left among them under his own hand, became a Rom. Catholic, 'First because perpetual visible profession which could never be wanting to the religion of Christ, nor any part of it, is apparently wanting to Protestant religion; so far as concerns the points in contestation. (2.) Because Luther and his followers, separating from the church of Rome, separated also from all churches, pure or impure, true or untrue, then being in the world: upon which ground I conclude that either God's promises did fail of performance, if there were then no church in the

world, which held all things necessary and nothing repugnant to salvation; or else that Luther and his sectaries, separating from all churches then in the world and so from the true, if there were any true, were damnable schismaticks. (3.) Because if any credit might be given to as creditable records as any are extant, the doctrine of Catholics hath been frequently confirmed, and the opposite doctrine of Protestants confounded with supernatural and divine miracles. (4.) Because many points of Protestant doctrine are the damned opinions of heretics, condemned by the primitive church. (5.) Because the prophecies of the Old Test. touching the conversion of kings and nations to the true religion of Christ, have been accomplished in, and by, the Catholic Rom. religion, and the professors of it. (6.) Because the doctrine of the church of Rome is conformable, and the doctrine of the Protestants contrary, to the doctrine of the fathers of the primitive church, even by the confession of Protestants themselves; I mean those fathers, who lived within the compass of the first 600 years; to whom protestants themselves do very frequently and confidently appeal. (7.) Because the first pretended reformers had neither extraordinary commission from God, nor ordinary mission from the church, to preach Protestant doctrine. (8.) Because Luther, to preach against the mass (which contains the most material points now in controversy) was persuaded by reasons suggested to him by the devil himself, disputing with him. So himself professeth in his book *De Missa privata,* that all men might take heed of following him, who professeth himself to follow the devil. (9.) Because the Protestant cause is now, and hath been from the beginning, maintained with gross falsifications and calumnies; whereof their prime controversy writers are notoriously and in high degree guilty. (10.) Because by denying all humane authority, either of pope, or councils, or church, to determine controversies of faith, they have abolished all possible means of suppressing heresy, or restoring unity to the church.' These were his motives, as my author tells me, who adds, that, 'they were so strong, that he (Chillingworth) could never since frame his mind to Protestancy: And the profession of Catholic religion not suiting with his desires and designs, he fell upon Socinianism, that is no religion, &c. To these motives, which are owned and reprinted by Mr. Chillingworth, he made an answer three years or better before the first edition of his book called, *The Religion of Protestants,* &c. came out. Which answer was not published for two reasons, one, because the motives were never public, until the author of *The Direction to N. N.* made them so. The other, because he was loth to proclaim to all the world so much weakness as he shew'd, in suffering himself to be abused by such silly sophisms. All which proceeded upon mistakes and false suppositions, which unadvisedly he took for granted, as 'twill quickly appear when the motives with his respective answers made to them and printed, shall be impartially weighed in the ballance against each other. Tho' Mr. Chillingworth embraced Protestantism very sincerely, as it seems, when he wrote his book of *The Religion of Protestants,* &c. yet notwithstanding not long before, and I think then also, he refused to subscribe the 39 articles, and so consequently did not desert the religion of Rome out of desire of preferment, or for temporal ends (which the author of *The Direction to N. N.* objected to him) by reason that this his refusal did incapacitate him for all places of benefit in England, a previous subscription of the said 39 articles being the only common door that here leads to any such. This refusal was grounded on his scrupling the truth only of one or two propositions contained in them; and these his small doubts too were afterwards fully satisfied and removed before his advancement in the church, otherwise he could not have conscientiously subscribed the 39 articles, which is indispensibly required of all persons upon any ecclesiastical promotion. But to return: so it was, that he finding not that satisfaction from the Jesuits concerning various points of religion, or (as some say) not that respect which he expected (for the common report among his contemporaries in Trin. coll. was, that the Jesuits to try his temper, and exercise his obedience, did put him upon servile duties far below him) he left them in the year 1631, returned to the church of England (tho' the presbyterians said not, but that he was always a papist in his heart, or, as we now say, in masquerade) and was kindly received by his godfather Dr. Laud then B. of London. So that fixing himself for a time in his beloved Oxford, he did, in testimony of his reconcilement, make a recantation, and afterwards wrote a book against the papists, as I shall anon tell you. For which his service he was rewarded with the chancellorship of the church of Salisbury, upon the promotion of Dr. Br. Duppa to the see of Chichester, in the month of July 1638, and about the same time with the mastership of Wygstan's hospital in the antient borough of Leicester: Both which, and perhaps other preferments, he kept to his dying day. He was a most noted philosopher and orator, and without doubt a poet also, otherwise sir Joh. Suckling would not have brought him into his poem, called *The Session of Poets*; and had such an admirable faculty in reclaiming schismatics, and confuting papists, that none in his time went beyond him. He had also very great skill in mathematics, and his aid and counsel was often used in making fortifications for the king's garrisons, especially those of the city of Gloucester, and Arundell castle in Sussex. . . . He was a subtle and quick disputant, and would several times put the king's professor to a push. Hobbes of Malmsbury would often say, that he was like a lusty fighting fellow, that did drive his enemies before him, but would often give his own party smart back-blows. And 'twas the current opinion in this university, that he and Lucius lord Falkland had such extraordinary clear reason, that if the great turk or devil were to be converted, they were able to do it. . . . He was a man of little stature, but of great soul; which if times had been serene, and life spared, might have done incomparable service to the church of England.

. . . It must be now known, that in the beginning of the civil dissentions, our author Chillingworth suffer'd much for the king's cause, and being forced to go from place to place for succour, as opportunity served, went at length to Arundell castle in Sussex, where he was in quality of an engineer in that garrison. At length the castle coming into the hands of the parliamentarian forces, on the sixth day of January 1643, he was by the endeavours of Mr. Franc. Cheynell (about that time rector of Petworth) made to sir Will. Waller the prime governor of those forces, conveyed to Chichester, and there lodged in the bishop's house, because that he, being very sick, could not go to London with the prisoners taken in the said castle. In the said house he remained to his dying day, and tho' civilly used, yet he was much troubled with the impertinent discourses and disputes of the said Cheynell, which the loyal party of that city looked upon as a shortning of our author's days. He gave way to fate on the 24th of January (or thereabouts) in sixteen hundred forty and three, and the next day his body being brought into the cath. church accompanied by the said royal party, was certain service said, but not common prayer according to the defunct's desire.—ANTHONY À WOOD, *Athenae Oxonienses*, 1691–1721

General

Besides perspicuity, there must be also right reasoning, without which perspicuity serves but to expose the speaker. And for attaining of this, I should propose the constant reading of Chillingworth, who, by his example, will teach both perspicuity and the way of right reasoning, better than any book that I know, and therefore will deserve to be read upon that account over and over again, not to say any thing of his argument.—JOHN LOCKE, "Some Thoughts concerning Reading and Study for a Gentleman," c. 1704

While Charles the First governed England, and was himself governed by a Catholic queen, it cannot be denied that the missionaries of Rome laboured with impunity and success in the Court, the country, and even the universities. One of his sheep,

> Whom the grim wolf, with privy paw
> Daily devours apace, and nothing said,

is Mr William Chillingworth, Master of Arts, and fellow of Trinity College, who, at the ripe age of twenty-eight years, was persuaded to elope from Oxford to the English seminary of Douay in Flanders. Some disputes with Fisher, a subtle Jesuit, might first awaken him from the prejudices of education, but he yielded to his own victorious argument 'That there must be somewhere an infallible judge, and that the Church of Rome is the only Christian society, which either does or can pretend to that character.' After a short trial of a few months Mr Chillingworth was again tormented by religious scruples; he returned home, resumed his studies, unravelled his mistakes, and delivered his mind from the yoke of authority and superstition. His new creed was built on the principle that the Bible is our sole judge, and private reason our sole interpreter: and he ably maintains this principle in the *Religion of a Protestant*, a book (1634) which, after startling the doctors of Oxford, is still esteemed the most solid defence of the Reformation. The learning, the virtue, the recent merits of the author entitled him to fair preferment, but the slave had now broken his fetters, and the more he weighed, the less was he disposed to subscribe the thirty-nine articles of the Church of England. In a private letter he declares, with all the energy of language, that he could not subscribe them, without subscribing his own damnation, and that if ever he should depart from this immoveable resolution, he would allow his friends to think him a madman or an atheist. As the letter is without a date, we cannot ascertain the number of weeks or months that elapsed between this passionate abhorrence, and the Salisbury Register which is still extant. '*Ego Gulielmus Chillingworth . . . omnibus hisce articulis et singulis in iisdem contentis, volens et ex animo subscribo, et consensum meum iisdem praebeo. 20 die Julii 1638.*' But alas! the chancellor and prebendary of Sarum soon deviated from his own subscription; as he more deeply scrutinized the article of the Trinity, neither Scripture nor the primitive fathers could long uphold his orthodox belief, 'and he could not but confess, that the doctrine of Arius is either a truth, or at least no damnable heresy'. From this middle region of the air, the descent of his reason would naturally rest on the firmer ground of the Socinians: and if we may credit a doubtful story and the popular opinion, his anxious enquiries at last subsided in philosophic indifference. So conspicuous however were the candour of his nature and the innocence of his heart, that this apparent levity did not affect the reputation of Chillingworth. His frequent changes proceeded from too nice an inquisition into truth. His doubts grew out of himself, he assisted them with all the strength of his reason: he was then too hard for himself; but finding as little quiet and repose in those victories, he quickly recovered by a new appeal to his own judgement; so that in all his sallies and retreats, he was, in fact, his own convert. —EDWARD GIBBON, *Memoirs of My Life*, 1792–93

Chillingworth had not the reputation of great scholarship. He was rather an incomparable debater. The picture of him walking in Trinity Gardens looking for some one to argue with shows the habit of the man. Yet he never argued merely to secure a triumph over an adversary. His temporary conversion to Roman Catholicism proves his earnestness. Yet it may fairly be said that this single translation of theory into practice sufficed him. He did not again face the practical issues of his speculations. Though he arrived at a rationalism that was inconsistent with the idea of a Church, he signed the Articles, as a basis of peace and union, with a subscription which satisfied Laud. Rationalism and toleration were Chillingworth's guiding principles. He recognised the voice of God spoken in Scripture as the only authority in religion, and he allowed the free right of individual reason to interpret the Bible. The final appeal to the Bible separated him from the Anglicans of Laud's school on the one hand; and on the other his latitudinarianism roused the bitter hatred of Cheynell and his Puritan friends. *The Religion of Protestants* was a contribution to a controversy between Edward Knott, a Jesuit, and Dr. Potter, Provost of Queen's College, Oxford. Knott opened with a book styled *Charity mistaken, with the want whereof Catholics are unjustly charged for affirming, as they do with grief, that Protestancie, unrepented, destroys Salvation.* Potter retorted with a volume styled *Want of Charity justly charged on all such Romanists as dare (without truth and modesty) affirm that Protestancie destroyeth Salvation.* It was to the Jesuit's second assault, a pamphlet headed *Mercy and Truth or Charity maintained by Catholics,* that Chillingworth set himself to reply in his *Religion of Protestants.* This work is a model of elaborate and close reasoning. Indeed, its elaborateness and closeness stagger the modern student, who is not accustomed to find a matter so taken from the root up. Chillingworth aimed at perfect balance and absolute fairness. He fought his adversary preface by preface, and chapter by chapter, and placed every argument he had to meet before the reader in full and in front of his own answer to it. It is necessary, therefore, to penetrate a dense mass of minor ideas and issues, mainly irrelevant, before reaching the heart of the matter. Yet Chillingworth never relaxes hold of his chief argumentation, never loses sight of the real end which he has in view, and which is not so much to put down the arrogance of Rome and defend the dignity of the Church of England, as to assert the right of free inquiry, and the necessity for personal conviction. The desideratum of both disputants was an infallible means of determining religious truth. Knott maintained that the source of certitude was the Roman Catholic Church. Chillingworth on the other hand, held that the Bible, and the Bible only, was the religion of Protestants. That, of course, is the common doctrine of Protestantism. It is valid only so long as there is general agreement as to the interpretation of the Bible. Chillingworth's contribution to theology is this gloss upon it, that the great principles of religion, as contained in Scripture, are too plain to be mistaken—they are embraced in the Apostle's Creed; Christians may safely differ upon those matters of speculation which divide the sects. For a plain workaday rule he lays it down that "nothing is necessary to be believed but what is plainly revealed." Scripture tested, save in fundamentals, by the free open mind—the "right reason" he called it—was for Chillingworth the sole source of religious certainty. He bowed to no authority, save the universal tradition which was the common warrant for belief in the Bible.

Reason must rule—it being, indeed, a plain improbability for any man to submit his reason but to reason. Chillingworth's argumentative clearness was regarded by Locke as a model. His style is, indeed, admirably suited at once to the matter and to the form of his work. He commands a considerable vocabulary, and although his sentences are often loosely constructed, he writes, when he is at his best, with point and carefully chosen phrase. His rhetorical weapons are retort and homely illustration. His manner of building up an argument is, indeed, worthy of Locke's encomium. If he desires to deal a specially heavy blow he reduces his reasoning to a formal syllogism, and crushes his opponent with it. He has a keen scent for a fallacy, and exposes one when he finds it with trenchant humour. He never condescends to quibbling, but all throughout an argument maintains a dignity which, more than anything else, gave him his strength in debate. It was a mind of no common order that could give unity to a work constructed on such a plan as *The Religion of Protestants.* Even in the graces of composition, Chillingworth excels his contemporaries. The flexibility and pointedness of his style are virtues as great as the richness and power of Hooker's and Bacon's, and, for his purpose, of greater value. The heat of debate sometimes hurries him into undue vehemence, but he never loses his temper. His other works are not important. These are nine sermons, a series of tracts entitled *Additional Discourses,* and a fragment called *The Apostolic Institution of Episcopacy demonstrated,* in which he maintains that Episcopacy is not repugnant to the government settled in and for the Church by the Epistles.—W. WALLACE, "William Chillingworth," *English Prose,* ed. Henry Craik, 1894, Vol. 2, pp. 259–61

Works

THE RELIGION OF PROTESTANTS

The celebrated work by Chillingworth on the *Religion of Protestants,* is generally admitted to be the best defence which the Reformers have been able to make against the church of Rome. It was published in 1637, and the position of the author would induce us to look for the fullest display of bigotry that was consistent with the spirit of his time. Chillingworth had recently abandoned the creed which he now came forward to attack; and he, therefore, might be expected to have that natural inclination to dogmatize with which apostasy is usually accompanied. Besides this, he was the godson and the intimate friend of Laud, whose memory is still loathed, as the meanest, the most cruel, and the most narrow-minded man who ever sat on the episcopal bench. He was, moreover, a fellow of Oxford, and was a constant resident at that ancient university, which has always been esteemed as the refuge of superstition, and which has preserved to our own day its unenviable fame. If we turn now to the work that was written under these auspices, we can scarcely believe that it was produced in the same generation, and in the same country, where, only twenty-six years before, two men had been publicly burned because they advocated opinions different to those of the established church. It is, indeed, a most remarkable proof of the prodigious energy of that great movement which was now going on, that its pressure should be felt under circumstances the most hostile to it which can possibly be conceived; and that a friend of Laud, and a fellow of Oxford, should, in a grave theological treatise, lay down principles utterly subversive of that theological spirit which for many centuries had enslaved the whole of Europe.

In this great work, all authority in matters of religion is openly set at defiance. Hooker, indeed, had appealed from the jurisdiction of the Fathers to the jurisdiction of reason; he had, however, been careful to add, that the reason of individuals ought to bow before that of the church, as we find it expressed in great Councils, and in the general voice of ecclesiastical tradition. But Chillingworth would hear of none of these things. He would admit of no reservations which tended to limit the sacred right of private judgment. He not only went far beyond Hooker in neglecting the Fathers, but he even ventured to despise the Councils. Although the sole object of his work was to decide on the conflicting claims of the two greatest sects into which the Christian church has broken, he never quotes as authorities the Councils of that very church respecting which the disputes were agitated. His strong and subtle intellect, penetrating the depths of the subject, despised that sort of controversy which had long busied the minds of men. In discussing the points upon which the Catholics and Protestants were at issue, he does not inquire whether the doctrines in question met the approval of the early church, but he asks if they are in accordance with human reason; and he does not hesitate to say that, however true they may be, no man is bound to believe them if he finds that they are repugnant to the dictates of his own understanding. Nor will he consent that faith should supply the absence of authority. Even this favorite principle of theologians is by Chillingworth made to yield to the supremacy of the human reason. Reason, he says, gives us knowledge; while faith only gives us belief, which is a part of knowledge, and is, therefore, inferior to it. It is by reason, and not by faith, that we must discriminate in religious matters; and it is by reason alone that we can distinguish truth from falsehood. Finally, he solemnly reminds his readers, that in religious matters no one ought to be expected to draw strong conclusions from imperfect premises, or to credit improbable statements upon scanty evidence; still less, he says, was it ever intended that men should so prostitute their reason, as to believe with infallible faith that which they are unable to prove with infallible arguments.—HENRY THOMAS BUCKLE, *History of Civilization in England*, 1857, Vol. 1, pp. 251–53

In his main argument that 'nothing is necessary to be believed but what is plainly revealed' Chillingworth did little more than put in a clearer and more logical form, with all its excrescences stripped away, the contention of Laud in the conference with Fisher. That which marks the pre-eminence of the younger writer is his clear sense of the subordination of intellectual conviction to moral effort. If men, he says, 'suffer themselves neither to be betrayed into their errors, nor kept in them by any sin of their will; if they do their best endeavour to free themselves from all errors, and yet fail of it through human frailty, so well am I persuaded of the goodness of God, that if in me alone should meet a confluence of all such errors of all the Protestants of the world that were thus qualified, I should not be so much afraid of them all as I should be to ask pardon for them.'

In these words, not in the counter-dogmatism of the Puritan zealot, lay the true answer to the claim to infallibility which was so ostentatiously flaunted before the world by the Roman missionaries. It was the old doctrine of Sir Thomas More and the men of the new learning coming to the surface once more, under happier auspices. It breathed the very spirit of mutual regard for zeal and earnestness in the midst of intellectual differences. It became men, Chillingworth held, to be very careful how they set up the creatures of their own imaginations as if they were the veriest certainties of Divine revelation. "This presumptuous imposing of the sense of men upon the general words of God," he writes, "and laying them upon men's consciences together, under the equal penalty of death

and damnation; this vain conceit that we can speak of the things of God better than in the words of God; this deifying our own interpretations and tyrannous enforcing them upon others; this restraining of the Word of God from that latitude and generality, and the understandings of men from that liberty wherein Christ and the Apostles left them—is and hath been the only fountain of all the schisms of the Church, and that which makes them immortal; the common incendiary of Christendom, and that which tears into pieces, not the coat, but the bowels and members of Christ. . . . Take away these walls of separation, and all will quickly be one. Take away this persecuting, burning, cursing, damning of men for not subscribing to the words of men as the words of God; require of Christians only to believe Christ, and to call no man master, but Him only; let those leave claiming infallibility that have no title to it, and let them that in their words disclaim it disclaim it also in their actions." "Christians," he says again, "must be taught to set a higher value upon those high points of faith and obedience wherein they agree than upon those matters of less moment wherein they differ, and understand that agreement in those ought to be more effectual to join them in one communion than their difference in other things of less moment to divide them. When I say in one communion, I mean in a common profession of those articles wherein all consent—a joint worship of God, after such a way as all esteem lawful, and a mutual performance of all those works of charity which Christians owe one to another."

It is not given to any one man, even if he be a Chillingworth, to make out with complete fulness the remedies needed for the evils of his age. Dogmatism, too, has its functions to perform in the work of the world. The vain belief in the possession of all truth is higher and more ennobling than the disbelief that truth exists at all; and it is impossible to deny that to the mass of Chillingworth's contemporaries the suspension of judgment, which was to him the ultimate result of a keen and earnest search after truth, would seem to be the very negation of the existence of truth itself. Even calmer judgments might well doubt whether Chillingworth's notion of a 'joint worship of God after such a way as all esteem lawful' was feasible, or whether, even if it proved feasible, it was at all desirable. Chillingworth's mind was too purely intellectual to enable him to understand how any given ritual could either raise admiration or provoke hostility. He cared much whether a proposition was true or not. He had but a languid interest in forms of prayer. In his reply to Knott's last pamphlet he took up the defence of the recent changes. "What," he said, "if out of fear that too much simplicity and nakedness in the public service of God may beget in the ordinary sort of men a dull and stupid irreverence, and out of hope that the outward state and glory of it, being well-disposed and wisely moderated, may engender, quicken, increase, and nourish the inward reverence, respect, and devotion which is due unto God's sovereign majesty and power; what if, out of a persuasion and desire that Papists may be won over to us the sooner by the removing of this scandal out of their way, and out of a holy jealousy that the weaker sort of Protestants might be the easier seduced to them by the magnificence and pomp of their Church service, in case it were not removed—I say, what if, out of these considerations, the governors of our Church, more of late than formerly, have set themselves to adorn and beautify the places where God's honour dwells, and to make them as heaven-like as they can with earthly ornaments?" There is something contemptuous in such a defence as this. Above all, there is no acknowledgment by Chillingworth of the fact that moral influence may spread abroad from men who are very wrong-headed and very positive. The toleration which cheerfully grants free liberty to those who differ irreconcilably from us is the complement of the tolerance which seeks out by preference the points in which others agree with us rather than those in which they differ. The

latter was Chillingworth's contribution to the peace of the Church and nation; for the former we must look elsewhere. —SAMUEL R. GARDINER, *History of England*, 1883, Vol. 8, pp. 262–64

WILLIAM LAUD

1573–1645

William Laud was born on October 7, 1573, in Reading. The only son of a clothier, he attended the free school in Reading before entering St. John's College, Oxford, in 1589. He graduated with a bachelor's degree in 1594, a master's in 1598, and a doctorate in 1608. In 1601 he took holy orders. During the 1620s he was named to a number of bishoprics: St. David's in 1621, Bath and Wells in 1626, and London in 1628. Finally, in 1633, he was made Archbishop of Canterbury. In addition to his enormous ecclesiastical power, his secular influence was considerable. He became Chancellor of Oxford in 1630, and from the time of his consecration as Archbishop until the meeting of the Long Parliament, wielded authority almost equal to that of a present-day Prime Minister.

Laud is chiefly remembered, however, for his formative influence on the English Church. Although he is considered the first outstanding figure in the Anglo-Catholic tradition, Laud took pains to steer a course between Roman Catholicism and Puritanism. His critique of the former is best presented in his Controversy with Fisher, a dispute which took place in 1621. Yet while he explicitly rejected many Roman Catholic doctrines and practices, his love of liturgy and ritual did not endear him to the Puritans. They were even more outraged by his contention that the Church of Rome was a true branch of the Church, however corrupt its dogma and polity. Through the 1630s Laud's relations with the Puritans deteriorated and when the Long Parliament convened it impeached him on charges of high treason as one of its first acts. In 1641 he was incarcerated in the Tower, where he remained until he stood trial in 1644. In 1645 he was condemned and beheaded.

With the exception of a few of his sermons published in 1641, the majority of Laud's works first appeared in a collected edition published from 1695 to 1700.

It is true the roughness of his uncourtly nature sent most men discontented from him, yet would he often (of himself) find ways and means to sweeten many of them again when they least looked for it. —SIR EDWARD DEARING, "Preface" to *Speeches in Matters of Religion*, 1642

My very pockets searched; my Diary, my very Prayer-book taken from me, and after used against me; and that in some cases not to prove but to make a charge. Yet I am thus far glad, even for this sad accident. For by my Diary your Lordships have seen the passages of my life; and by my Prayer-book the greatest secrets between God and my soul; so that you may be sure you have me at the very bottom: yet, blessed by God, no disloyalty is found in the one, no Popery in the other. —WILLIAM LAUD, Speech before the House of Lords, 1645

A man vigilant enough, of an active or rather of a restless mind, more ambitious to undertake than politic to carry on, of a disposition too fierce and cruel for his coat which notwithstanding he was so far from concealing in a subtle way that he increased the envy of it by insolence. He had few vulgar and private vices, as being neither taxed of covetousness, intemperance nor incontinence, and, in a word, a man not altogether so bad in his personal character as unfit for the state of England. —THOMAS MAY, *History of the Long Parliament*, 1647

Of apprehension he was quick and sudden, of a very sociable wit and a pleasant humour; and one that knew as well how to put off the gravity of his place and person when he saw occasion, as any man living; accessible enough at all times, but

when he was tired out with multiplicity and vexation of business, which some, who did not understand him, ascribed unto the natural ruggedness of his disposition . . . constant not only to the public prayers in his chapel, but to his private devotions in his closet. —PETER HEYLYN, *Cyprianus Anglicus: or, the Life and Death of Archibishop Laud*, 1644

Thus died and was buried the king's and Church's martyr, a man of such integrity, learning, devotion and courage, as had he lived in the primitive times, would have given him another name: whom tho' the cheated multitude were taught to misconceive (for those honoured him most who best knew him) yet impartial posterity will know how to value him, when they hear the rebels sentenced him on the same day they voted down the liturgy of the Church of England. —ANTHONY À WOOD, *Athenae Oxonienses*, 1691–1721

A man of such admirable judgment and learning, that he knew what danger the nation was in, and whence it proceeded, and did declare, that if they would take his advise, he could heal all breaches; which the fanaticks (or *puritans*, as Joyner calls them) well perceiving, they dispatched him as soon as possible; which when they had done, they used these words,

> All praise and glory to the Lord,
> And *Laud* unto the devil.
> —THOMAS HEARNE, *Reliquiae Hearnianae*,
> Nov. 17, 1705

The very enemies of the unfortunate archbishop admitted that he was learned and pious, attentive to his duties and unexceptionable in his morals: on the other hand his friends could not deny that he was hasty and vindictive, positive in his opinions, and inexorable in his enmities. To excuse his participation in the arbitrary measures of the council, and his concurrence in the severe decrees of the star-chamber, he alleged that he was only one among many; and that it was cruel to visit on the head of a single victim the common faults of the whole board. But it was replied, with great appearance of truth that "though only one, he was the chief;" that his authority and influence swayed the opinions both of his sovereign and his colleagues; and that he must not expect to escape the just reward of his crimes, because he had possessed the ingenuity to make others his associates in guilt. Yet I am of opinion that it was religious, and not political rancour, which led him to the block. Could the zealots have forgiven his conduct as archbishop, he might have lingered out the remainder of his life in the tower. There was, however, little difference in this respect between them and their victim. Both were equally obstinate, equally infallible, equally intolerant.—JOHN LINGARD, A *History of England*, 1819, Vol. 10, Ch. 2

> Prejudged by foes determined not to spare,
> An old weak Man for vengeance thrown aside,
> Laud, "in the painful art of dying" tried,
> (Like a poor bird entangled in a snare
> Whose heart still flutters, though his wings forbear
> To stir in useless struggle) hath relied
> On hope that conscious innocence supplied,
> And in his prison breathes celestial air.
> Why tarries then thy chariot? Wherefore stay,
> O Death! the ensanguined yet triumphant wheels,
> Which thou prepar'st, full often, to convey
> (What time a State with madding faction reels)
> The Saint or Patriot to the world that heals
> All wounds, all perturbations doth allay?
> —WILLIAM WORDSWORTH, "Laud" (1821),
> *Ecclesiastical Sonnets*, 1822

The friend of Strafford, archbishop Laud, with less worldly passions, and a more disinterested ardour, brought into the council the same feelings, the same designs. Austere in his conduct, simple in his life, power, whether he served it or himself wielded it, inspired in his mind a fanatical devotion. To prescribe and to punish, this was in his eyes to establish order, and order ever seemed to him justice. His activity was indefatigable, but narrow in its views, violent, and harsh. Alike incapable of conciliating opposing interests, and of respecting rights, he rushed, with head down and eyes closed, at once against liberties and abuses; opposing to the latter his rigid probity, to the former his furious hate, he was as abrupt and uncompromising with the courtiers as with the citizens; seeking no man's friendship, anticipating and able to bear no resistance, persuaded, in short, that power is all-sufficient in pure hands; and constantly the prey of some fixed idea, which ruled him with all the violence of passion, and all the authority of duty—FRANÇOIS PIERRE GUILLAUME GUIZOT, *History of the English Revolution of 1640* (1826), 1844, p. 39

For the individual, indeed, we entertain a more unmitigated contempt than for any other character in our history. The fondness with which a portion of the church regards his memory, can be compared only to that perversity of affection which sometimes lead a mother to select the monster or the idiot of the family as the object of her especial favour. . . . The severest punishment which the two Houses could have inflicted on him would have been to set him at liberty, and send him to Oxford. There he might have stayed, tortured by his own dia-

bolical temper, hungering for Puritans to pillory and mangle, plaguing the Cavaliers, for want of somebody else to plague, with his peevishness and absurdity, performing grimaces and antics in the cathedral, continuing that incomparable diary, which we never see without forgetting the vices of his heart in the abject imbecility of his intellect; minuting down his dreams, counting the drops of blood which fell from his nose, watching the direction of the salt, and listening for the note of the screech-owl! Contemptuous mercy was the only vengeance which it became the Parliament to take on such a ridiculous old bigot.—THOMAS BABINGTON MACAULAY, "Hallam's Constitutional History" (1828), *Critical, Historical, and Miscellaneous Essays*, 1860, Vol. 2, pp. 492–94

Cast in a mould of proportions that are much above our own, and of stature akin to the elder days of the Church.—JOHN HENRY NEWMAN, "Preface" to *The Autobiography of Dr. William Laud*, 1839

Laud seems to have been an imitator, or follower, of Bishop Andrewes: and in some particulars the resemblance holds. The seven sermons contained few doctrinal allusions, with the exception of an important discussion on the future state of the Jews in Sermon I.; and they are chiefly remarkable as expositions *ad populum* of Laud's high views of the regal office. Thus they show him as a statesman more than a theologian, and their value is rather in relation to the political than to the ecclesiastical or controversial history of the Caroline era. Public, and especially State, occasions, almost necessitate a stiff and artificial manner, as well as a confined range of thought; and it is much to be regretted that none of the many Sermons Laud preached in the ordinary course of his ministry have been preserved. That he was a theologian, and had read extensively and accurately, is proved both by his "Conference" and "Defence." That he was a frequent preacher his Diary abundantly testifies: and that his religion was eminently deep and earnest, we know from his published Devotions, as well as from his patient endurance of persecution and suffering. But neither as a divine, nor in other respects, must his character be altogether measured by these Sermons.—WILLIAM SCOTT, "Preface to Sermons," *The Works of William Laud*, 1847, Vol. 1, p. vii

Whose memory is still loathed, as the meanest, the most cruel, and the most narrow-minded man who ever sat on the episcopal bench.—HENRY THOMAS BUCKLE, *History of Civilization in England*, 1857, Vol. 1, p. 251

Laud, largely as he figures in the social history of his period, is a less figure in our ordinary literary histories than Herrick, who would have licked his shoe.—DAVID MASSON, *The Life of John Milton*, 1859, Vol. 1, Ch. 6

The "Conference with Fisher" is marked throughout by a reasonableness and masculine good sense which might not be expected by those who know Laud only through the partisan pages of certain popular historians. Laud was learned, but he was no mere "bookman," to use a word of his own; and in this controversy he does not suffer from being a man of the world, accustomed to observe, to consider, and to judge the facts of life and history. But, it seems to me, the chief interest that now attaches to the "Conference," is the light that it throws on the general attitude of mind, and particular beliefs, of the most prominent high-churchman of his day.— JOHN DOWDEN, *Outlines of the History of the Theological Literature of the Church of England*, 1897

———

C. M. SIMPKINSON
"The Devotional Life"
Life and Times of William Laud
1894, pp. 283–91

It will probably have occurred to the reader to ask how it was that Laud was able to set himself such severe limits in his use of power, refused even to think of organising a permanent military force, and did not, while he was able, strike terror into his enemies by such tremendous punishments as those which overwhelmed the opponents of Richelieu in France, or even of Strafford in Ireland. This self-restraint remains inexplicable until we turn to the pages of that book of devotions of which it will be remembered Prynne barbarously deprived him in the Tower. Here we find the secret of his life, and are enabled to look into the deepest recesses of the man's heart.

Writers who have glanced cursorily over Laud's remains in compiling the history of the times have been content to set him down as a ceremonialist, full of vulgar superstitions. They have contrasted his merely external religion with the heart-felt religion of the greater Puritans. But superstitious ceremonialists do not leave the impression Laud has left on the religious life of a great people. Undoubtedly this student of the Bible attached some importance to the visions of the night; now and again he sets down in his *Diary* an account of dreams—some which he notes came true; others which startled him as confirming the accusations of his enemies; others again which strangely harmonised with his predominant anxieties at the moment.[1] Nor could this man as a lover of antiquity help being sometimes impressed in periods of difficulty and danger by omens; the fall of his picture at Lambeth on the eve of the Long Parliament seemed to him to coincide appallingly with his own anticipations of evil.[2] These were the superstitions (if we must call them so) of the thoughtful men of his own day; they differ from the superstitions of the nineteenth century, which will in their turn move the laughter of equally superstitious ages to come; they are distinctly marked off from that astrological superstition which tainted many of the leaders of the Long Parliament, such as Hollis and Stapleton and Whitelock, and even had some influence upon Bishop Williams;[3] and it must be remembered that Laud entirely refused to believe in witchcraft.[4] Nor can a man who notes these for possible warnings sent from on high be fairly accused of superstition, when, as in the case of the archbishop, he never allows them to sway him from what he believes to be the path of duty.

As to ceremonialism, he was convinced, we have seen, that grand and dignified worship helped human souls to realise the grandeur and dignity of God. Outward show he abhorred, except at the service and in the house of God; he rebuked all splendour in clerical apparel and himself set the example of peculiarly simple and inexpensive dress.[5] But he saw how careless men were of religion, and he knew by the experience of his own busy life how hard it was not to forget God in the hurry and bustle of affairs.[6]

To keep his own soul conscious of his dependence upon God, he made a habit of private prayer seven times every day. For this purpose he compiled a short service, differing with each day of the week. These rapid devotions were almost entirely personal; he humbled himself in them before his Maker, and entreated to be guarded against his unknown sins and against the failings which he had already detected. Having these written with his own hand in a small book which he carried in his pocket, he was able, wherever he might be, to recollect himself seven times a day in the presence of God. By putting them into writing he ensured immediate concentration. Gathering them from many saints of the past and adding to them devotions composed by himself, he ensured sufficient variety to lay his whole heart bare to God.

It was by this practice of continual prayer that he was able to check mere selfish ambition, to humble his pride, to keep his mind fixed on high aims, and finally to endure with patience the trials of his later life. To be seven times a day quite alone with God was the safeguard of his soul; "a man who so often made up his accounts with his Maker could not go very far astray".[7]

But besides these short private prayers at fixed times which, with those of his own model Bishop Andrewes, became the model of devotion to many of the great saints of the Restoration, he regularly attended the public prayers of the Church; and further spent a considerable time every day in intercession for others. His regular devotions, varied no doubt as to their time by the press of business, included special prayers for (1) the Catholic Church and unity, (2) the particular part of it to which he belonged, (3) the king, the royal family and the officers of the State, (4) his relations and friends, (5) his servants, to whom he was always devotedly attached, and who repaid him with the most unstinted affection, (6) the sick throughout the Church of Christ, (7) all mankind and especially his own personal enemies; for he was constantly on the watch to subdue personal rancour against the libellers of his character. These chief private devotions of the day were commenced with a general confession of sin, a thanksgiving and a prayer for usefulness, and concluded with a self-surrender of his life into the hands of God.

He added to them from time to time special prayers which he felt to be necessary. Now all his affairs were going so prosperously that he dreaded pride; now sickness or adversity was injuring or seemed to be injuring his usefulness. Again his hasty temper and quick, passionate utterance were getting the better of him at a time of ill-health or special difficulty. Then he saw his flock perishing from some all too frequent outbreak of the plague; or there was war in England or a time of dearth.

It was his custom also to offer special intercession to God for the poor, so little thought of in those days by haughty nobles and despotic gentry, by wealthy merchants and manufacturers: "O Lord, when thou makest inquisition for blood, remember and forget not the complaint of the poor".

Certain days were observed as fast days for his own sins and the sins of the people; some of them general fast days of the Church; two days on which he himself had grievously sinned and brought discredit upon the Church of God, St. Stephen's Day and the 28th of July.

Other days in like manner were observed each year as days of thanksgiving, such as the day of recovery from a serious accident, and the day on which he scarcely escaped from the fire at St. John's College. On the 11th of April and the 24th of November, on which his father and mother had died, he added special prayers for a happy reunion with them in heaven. The reception of the Holy Communion was commemorated also with carefully composed thanksgivings; for how could he thank God enough for the benefits He had done to his soul?

As the shadows of life close round him the prayers become naturally more and more pathetic. Old age is advancing and he has had so little time for the great work allotted to him. The king's ministers are flying abroad from the wrath of the Long Parliament, and he fears that he too may be driven from the England which he has loved so intensely. Then he is carried to prison and he must ask with insistence for that Divine patience which has always been so difficult to his fiery temper and clear intellect. He feels his complete innocence of the charges brought against him; but he has foreseen years ago that his opponents would be satisfied with nothing but his death; he would wish, and God alone can help him to do it, that he may answer the scurrilous accusations of his enemies with none of those bitter scathing retorts which from his keen understanding rose so naturally and so easily to his lips. The message of condemnation finds him prepared to spend the last hours of his life in prayer for his own safe transition through death into life, and for the many who are in like case.

Probably we owe this beautiful collection of devotions to the hostility of Prynne. That unforgiving enemy had picked out sentences here and there and published them abroad with comments to stir indignation against his victim. Laud, who, with all his humility, knew how important a part his personal character must play in the future of the Church, was most anxious that it should be well understood that he had died fearlessly, and in the orthodox faith of the Catholic Church as established in England, and therefore allowed his chaplains to give the book to the public.

The larger part of the devotions was published as early as 1650, and was warmly welcomed by a people who lay under the tyranny of the small remnant of a Parliament elected ten years before, and of the Westminster Assembly of Divines. Many who were widows and desolate; many who were imprisoned or doomed to grinding poverty; many who were longing for devotional guidance, away from the controversial preaching and still more controversial praying of the times, into the very presence of God Himself, welcomed this collection of prayers, and found therein a comfort until better days. After the Restoration, the book of devotions passed through a great number of editions.

No one who has studied with care the devotions[8] and the *Diary* of William Laud can doubt that his religion was personal, deep and strong; that his sympathies were wide and his ideals high; that the ceremonial which he advocated was dear to him only so far as it stimulated a more intimate knowledge and love of God; and that his personal sanctity must have played a notable part in the events of his disturbed and difficult life.

The last words of a book which has tried not to conceal his faults, nor the mistakes by which he imperilled English liberty, while it showed his real greatness and sincerity, shall be taken from the closing phrases of his will, made on the 13th of January, 1644.

"Thus I forgive all the world and heartily desire forgiveness of God and the world; and so again commend and commit my soul into the hands of God the Father who gave it, in the merits and mercies of my blessed Saviour Jesus Christ who redeemed it, and in the peace and comfort of the Holy Ghost who blessed it; and in the truth and unity of this Holy Catholic Church, and in the Communion of the Church of England, as it yet stands established by law.

"I most willingly leave the world, being weary at the very heart of the enmities of it, and of my own sins, many and great, and of the grievous distractions of the Church of Christ almost in all parts of Christendom."

Notes

1. *Diary*, 14th December, 1623; 30th January, 3rd July, 21st August, 4th and 26th September, 1625; 21st December, 1626; 5th, 14th and 16th January, 9th February, 8th and 27th March, 7th July, 1627; 31st January, 1628; 6th June, 12th July, 1633; 26th October, 1635; 3rd August, 14th October, 20th November, 24th December, 1636; 12th February, 1639; 24th January, 1640; 2nd November, 1642;

10th March, 1643, seems to be the only passages; most of them, it will be noted, occur in periods, and generally at times of ill-health.
2. *Diary*, 27th October, 1640.
3. See Lilly's *Autobiography*.
4. At his instigation the king delivered witches in Lancashire in 1633.
5. In this he was a striking contrast to his rival Bishop Williams (Stanley, *Westminster Abbey*).
6. See Salmonet, ii. 216, on the value of the English love of Christmas.
7. Lloyd's *Memoirs of those who Suffered*, 231.
8. *E.g.*, 25th January, 1624; 30th January, 1625. "Sunday night, my dream of my blessed Lord and Saviour Jesus Christ. One of the most comfortable passages that ever I had in my life" (19th August, 1636).

WILLIAM HOLDEN HUTTON
From "Theology, and Attitude towards Rome"
William Laud
1895, pp. 139–52

Laud's reputation, good or ill, as an ecclesiastical statesman has almost entirely obscured his fame as a theologian. His sermons are almost unknown even to students of the seventeenth-century pulpit, and his Controversy with Fisher is rarely, if ever, referred to by modern controversialists who contend over the same field and not infrequently, though perhaps unconsciously, use the same weapons.

Two hundred years ago men thought differently. The sermons were reprinted even in the dark days of the suppression of the Church,[1] and the Conference, republished four times in the seventeenth century, became the authoritative statement of the position of Anglicanism in opposition to the Roman claims. Charles I. made an analysis of it with his own hands, and, as his last gift to his daughter Elizabeth, put it side by side with Andrewes's *Sermons* and Hooker's *Ecclesiastical Polity*.

For the oblivion into which Laud's pulpit discourses have fallen many reasons might be assigned. They are probably not even typical of his style. He was a constant, and, from the demand, apparently an admired preacher. He preached as willingly and as often in little country churches as in London or at Court. But he seems to have intentionally avoided all ostentation and as far as possible all record of his pulpit ministry. Not until comparatively late in his career did he notice in his Diary even his most important discourses; and he never suffered any of his sermons to be printed except by direct royal command. In his will he left the publication entirely in the hands of his executors. Thus, during his lifetime, only six of his sermons were published: all of them were preached on public occasions, and issued by order of James I. or Charles I. One other sermon, preached on March 27, 1631, on the anniversary of the royal accession, was printed without his correction or revision, after his death. We have thus to form our judgment of Laud as a preacher on seven only of his sermons, and those all of an "official" or "occasional" nature. There are few preachers who would wish to be judged by this test.

The first point that strikes a reader of the sermons is that they were modelled on those of Bishop Andrewes. Chamberlain, writing to Carleton of the first of these discourses, says, "Herewithal I send you a sermon of Dr. Laud's, because it is after the manner of the Bishop of Winchester's preaching." There can be no doubt that Laud admired and reverenced Andrewes more than any other Churchman of his day. He refers to him constantly in his writings, and in his defence during his trial, and as to an authority beyond appeal. Again and again he declares that he followed him and him only. "All that I used was according to the copy of the late Reverend

Bishop of Winchester." "Nor did I follow the *Pontifical*, but a copy of learned and reverend Bishop Andrewes," and the like. In his Diary he thus recorded his death: "Episcopus Winton. meritissimus, lumen orbis Christiani, mortuus est."

Andrewes was admittedly the greatest preacher of the day, and it is in keeping with the assimilative and receptive tone of Laud's mind that he should have thus consciously modelled himself on the preacher whose theology he so completely accepted. No imitation has the freshness of the original, but it must be admitted, I think, that Laud was more successful than Bishop Felton, who "had almost marred" his "own natural trot by endeavouring to imitate his artificial amble." His aim, then, was completeness rather than connection. His sermon was directly upon the text selected. He would not pass to application till he had thoroughly dissected and probed to the uttermost the passage he had selected to dwell upon. He sought too, if he did not always achieve, a clearness of direct statement: he had noted this as a merit when he first issued the sermons of his exemplar to the world. His illustrations are drawn from the Fathers and schoolmen, not often from the reformers, except Calvin, whom it may be conjectured he had read originally to confute him. His mental attitude is conservative, and yet touched with a certain sharp and unconventional freedom. Like all the preachers of the day, he does not disdain the assistance of humour and irony and of illustration of a very homely sort. Where he did not succeed in at all approaching his model was in pathos or imagination: yet here we may remind ourselves of the very limited field which is covered by the discourses we possess. We do not know how he preached of the Incarnation, the Divine Ministry, the Passion.

The original characteristics of his sermons appear to be two. They illustrate both the tendency of his mind and his view of the questions of the time. He refers again and again to the lessons, or the psalms, of the day. It was the providential ordering of God through the fixed worship and ceremonial of the Church which appealed to him from the first, and increasingly, with a solemn and overmastering force. God taught through rules which past ages had laid down, not independently of them. So the daily lessons and psalms spoke to him with a distinct message, a special teaching, for the day. It was so when he was charged with treason and stayed waiting till the evening before he was taken to the Tower. "I went to evening prayer in my chapel. The psalms of the day (ninety-three and ninety-four) gave me great comfort. God make me worthy of it and fit to receive it." So in his sermon before the Parliament of 1628, he draws teaching from the first lesson at Evening Prayer, and then ends with S. Paul's prayer and benediction. "It is the prayer of this day, for it is the second lesson at evening service."

The other characteristic is his appeal to history, seen in his fondness for historical allusion or illustration. Preaching on March 17, on Unity, he is reminded that on "this day Julius Cæsar overthrew Sextus Pompeius. . . . and this very day too Frederick II. entered Jerusalem, and recovered whatsoever Saladin had taken from the Christians. But I must tell you these emperors and their forces were great keepers of unity." Like all the writers of the time, he has an insatiate fondness for quotation: in this same sermon he quotes Lucan, Cæsar, Cassiodorus, Tacitus, Seneca, S. Leo, S. Augustine, S. Basil, S. Gregory, S. Chrysostom, S. Bernard, S. Thomas Aquinas, Calvin, Bucer, and many more; but in the case of the Greek Fathers he generally used Latin versions, and his quotations are seldom exact, indeed they are many of them rather of the nature of references. The sermon on Unity is typical of his method. It was designed for a practical object—to bring the Commons at the opening of the Parliament of 1628 to see the

weakness that was caused to the State by divisions. It was a familiar thought with him. Jerusalem, he said in his first sermon before King James, "stands not here for the city and the State only, as many of the ancient name the city only, nor for the Temple and the Church only; but jointly for both. For both: therefore when you sit down to consult, you must not forget the Church; and when we kneel down to pray, we must not forget the State: both are but one Jerusalem."[2] His third sermon chose the same subject—"Jerusalem is built as a city that is at unity in itself." Unhappily it was easier to urge than to influence.

Few then as are the sermons of Laud which we possess, they serve in a measure to explain the nature of his power over Churchmen. They express his mind—decided, clear, forgetful of self, fixed on great ends, and believing that the policy which he set forth was based on right, on precedent, and on the direction of God in history. . . .

In the ⟨Controversy with Fisher⟩ Laud was under two disadvantages. He had little if any knowledge of the previous discussions, and no information of the ground which he was himself to contest, nor so much as twenty-four hours to prepare himself. And, secondly, he was hampered—it is the greatest disadvantage of English controversialists since the Reformation—by the unauthorized publications of Protestant divines, claiming to speak for the English Church. The clearness and accuracy of his mind nevertheless served him in good stead, and he was able to steer clear of the dangers that beset him.

The leading lines of his work bear considerable resemblance to those taken by the divines of to-day. The position of the Greek Church,[3] "a true Church in the main substance, to and at this day, though erroneous perhaps in some points," was a strong argument against the exclusive claims of Rome. "I dare not deny them to be a true Church," he said, and on the *Filioque* controversy he spoke with true theological judgment.

The infallibility of the Church also was a point of strongest contention: and Laud would not allow infallibility to any particular or local church. The particular Church of Rome has erred, and cannot be infallible. To this point he returns again and again. Rome is "a true Church, I grant,"[4] but not *the* true Church. The whole Church cannot err,[5] but parts can err and have erred. Salvation, surely, is open to Romanists, but "not as they are Romanists but as they are Christians; that is, as they believe the Creed and hold the foundation Christ Himself, not as they associate themselves wittingly and knowingly to the gross superstitions of the Romish Church."[6] Yet to say this is not to deny the privilege of the Church. "For we confess as well as you, that out of the Catholic Church of Christ there is no salvation. But what do you mean by 'out of the Church'? Sure, out of the Roman Church. Why, the Roman Church and the Church of England are but two distinct members of that Catholic Church which is spread over the face of the earth. Therefore, Rome is not the house where the Church dwells; but Rome itself, as well as other particular Churches, dwells in this great universal house."[7]

It is Christ Who is the foundation of the Universal Church: and Peter's Rock "is not S. Peter's person, either only or properly, but the faith which he professed. And to this, besides the evidence which is in text and truth, the Fathers come in with very full consent."[8]

The work of the Reformation and the deeds of the reformers were, then as now, confused by controversialists for purposes of attack on the English Church. Laud's answer is dignified and complete. "Reformation, especially in cases of religion, is so difficult a work, and subject to so many pretensions, that it is almost impossible but the reformers should step too far, or fall too short, in some smaller things or other;

which, in regard of the far greater benefit coming by the Reformation itself, may well be passed over and borne withal. But if there have been any wilful and gross errors, not so much in opinion as in fact, sacrilege too often pretending to reform superstition, that is the crime of the reformers, not of the Reformation; and they are long since gone to God to answer it, to Whom I leave them."[9]

Careful though he is to reject the errors of the reformers, Laud does not reject the name of Protestant. He rather explains its meaning and its historical and Catholic usage. "The Protestants did not get that name by protesting against the Church of Rome, but by protesting, and that when nothing else would serve, against her errors and superstitions. Do you but remove them from the Church of Rome, and our Protestation is ended, and the separation too. Nor is Protestation itself such an unheard-of thing in the very heart of religion. For the sacraments both of the Old and New Testaments are called by your own school 'visible signs protesting the faith.' Now if the sacraments be *protestantia*, 'signs protesting,' why may not men also, and without all offence, be called Protestants, since by receiving the true sacraments and by refusing them which are corrupted, they do but protest the sincerity of their faith against the doctrinal corruption which hath invaded the great Sacrament of the Eucharist, and other parts of religion? Especially, since they are men which must protest their faith by these visible signs and sacraments."[10]

Yet Protestant though he be, Laud by no means departs from Catholic doctrine. "For the Church of England nothing is more plain than that it believes and teaches the true and real presence of Christ in the Eucharist[11]; unless A. C. can make a Body no Body, and Blood no Blood—as perhaps he can by transubstantiation, as well as bread no bread, and wine no wine. And the Church of England is Protestant too."[12] He brings Ridley as a witness. "Both you and I," he said to his Roman opponent, "agree herein: that in the Sacrament is the very true and natural Body and Blood of Christ, even that which was born of the Virgin Mary, which ascended into heaven, which sitteth on the right hand of God the Father, which shall come from thence to judge the quick and the dead; only we differ *in modo*, 'in the way and manner of being': we confess all one thing to be in the Sacrament, and dissent in the manner of being there. I (being fully by God's word thereunto persuaded) confess Christ's natural Body to be in the Sacrament [indeed] by spirit and grace, &c. You make a grosser kind of being, enclosing a natural [a lively and a moving] Body under the shape and form of bread and wine."[13] Nor is he less precise or less judicious on the doctrine of the Eucharistic sacrifice. "At and in the Eucharist we offer up to God three sacrifices: one by the priest only, that is the commemorative sacrifice of Christ's death; . . . another by the priest and people jointly, and that is the sacrifice of praise and thanksgiving; . . . the third, by every particular man for himself only, and that is the sacrifice of every man's body and soul to serve Him in both all the rest of his life."[14] In the same style he speaks of the authority of scripture and of general councils, condemns private judgment and the Romish doctrine of purgatory, and ends by a repeated denial of the Pope's infallibility.[15]

So far we find Laud a stalwart assertor of the position of the English Church as firm in adherence to the Catholic doctrine. Of equal interest, and calculated to win an even wider respect and agreement, is his decisive claim for breadth and tolerance. The Church of England, in his assertion, is strong and Catholic because she utters no anathemas where Christ has not uttered them. "She comes far short of the Church of Rome's severity, whose anathemas are not only for thirty-nine articles, but for very many more, above one hundred in matter of doctrine, and that in many points as far remote from the foundation; though, to the far greater rack of men's consciences, they must all be made fundamental, if the Church have once determined them: whereas the Church of England never declared that every one of her articles are fundamental in the faith. For it is one thing to say, No one of them is superstitious or erroneous; and quite another to say, Every one of them is fundamental, and that in every part of it, to all men's belief. Besides, the Church of England prescribes only for her own children, and by those articles provides but for her own peaceable consent in those doctrines of truth. But the Church of Rome severely imposes her doctrine upon the whole world, under the pain of damnation."[16]

For himself, as for the National Church, he says that it is impossible to set bounds to the Divine compassion. "Nor will I ever take upon me to express that tenet or opinion, the denial of the foundation only excepted, which may shut any Christian, even the meanest, out of heaven."

These were bold words, or so they seem to us who draw our knowledge of seventeenth-century theology from the bitter controversialists of Rome and Geneva. The "ever-memorable John Hales," says Clarendon, "would often say that he would renounce the religion of the Church of England to-morrow if it obliged him to believe that any other Christian should be damned." Chillingworth and Falkland were with him; and William Laud, disciplinarian and Catholic though he was, was of the company.

Notes
1. An edition was published in 1651.
2. *Works*, i. 5, 6.
3. Ibid., ii. 25.
4. Ibid., ii. 143.
5. Ibid., ii. 155–8.
6. Ibid., ii. 333.
7. Ibid., ii. 346.
8. Ibid., ii. 257.
9. Ibid., ii. 173–4.
10. Ibid., ii. 152.
11. He adds a note quoting the English Liturgy.
12. The rest of the passage is not relevant to my point here. It may be argued that as he declares Calvin to have believed in a Real Presence, he admits English agreement with him. But he nowhere says this; and if he had meant it he would have said it.
13. *Works*, ii. 330. From these and many other passages it is clear that Mr. Simpkinson, *Life of Laud*, p. 129, is in error when he implies that Laud did not teach the Presence of Christ in the consecrated elements.
14. Ibid., ii. 340–41.
15. It should be observed, that the author of *Laud's Labyrinth* asserts that "Catholic faith (in this particular) only obliges us to maintain that the Pope is infallible when he defines with a general council" (p. 143).
16. *Works*, i. p. 60.

WILLIAM DRUMMOND

FRANCIS QUARLES

WILLIAM LAUD

SIR JOHN SUCKLING

THOMAS FULLER

RICHARD LOVELACE

JOSEPH HALL

EDWARD LORD HERBERT

1583–1648

Edward Herbert, son of a prominent Welsh family, was born on March 3, 1583, at Eyton-on-Severn, Shropshire. The elder brother of the poet George Herbert, Edward Herbert attended University College, Oxford, from 1596 to 1599. From 1619 to 1624 he served as English Ambassador to France. Upon his return to England he published *De Veritate* (1624), a philosophical treatise on the principles of natural religion and truth. Herbert felt unrewarded for his service of the crown and wrote a defense of Buckingham's actions during the Isle of Rhé incident, *The Expedition to the Isle of Rhé* (1629), hoping to obtain the favor of Charles I. Eventually he became a member of the Council of War in 1632. He began to work on his history of Henry VIII during the 1630s. Modeled after Bacon's portrait of Henry VII, *The Life and Raigne of King Henry the Eighth* was published posthumously in 1649.

The first edition of his poems, published by his son in 1665, includes the well-known "Elegy over a Tomb" and "An Ode upon a Question Moved, Whether Love Should Continue for Ever." After attending Charles I on his 1639–40 Scottish expedition, Herbert returned to Montgomery Castle. Eventually forced to surrender his home to the Parliamentary forces in 1644, Herbert spent his final days in London, living on a small stipend provided by Parliament. In 1645 he published *De Causis Errorum* and *De Religione Laici*, two supplements to his earlier *De Veritate*; these tracts have won for him the reputation of being the first systematic English Deist.

During the 1640s Herbert wrote his autobiography, covering his life up to 1624. The manuscript was not published until 1764, when it was edited by Horace Walpole. Herbert died on August 20, 1648 and was buried in St. Giles-in-the-Fields, London.

Personal

Edward Herbert, son of Richard Herbert, Esquire, and Susan Newport his wife, was born at Montgomery castle in this county ⟨Montgomeryshire⟩; knighted by king James, who sent him over ambassador into France. Afterwards king Charles the First created him Baron of Castle Island in Ireland, and some years after Baron of Cherbury in this county. He was a most excellent artist and rare linguist, studied both in books and men, and himself the author of two works most remarkable, viz. "A Treatise of Truth," written in French, so highly prized beyond the seas, that (as I am told) it is extant at this day with great honour in the Pope's Vatican.

He married the daughter and sole heir of Sir William Herbert of St. Julian's in Monmouthshire, with whom he had a large inheritance both in England and Ireland. He died in August, anno Domini 1648; and was buried in St. Giles's in the Fields, London, having designed a fair monument, of his own invention, to be set up for him in the church of Montgomery, according to the model following:

"Upon the ground a hath-pace of fourteen foot square, on the midst of which is placed a Dorrick column, with its rights of pedestal, basis, and capital, fifteen foot in height; on the capital of the columne is mounted an urn with an heart flamboul supported by two angels. The foot of this columne is attended with four angeles placed on pedestals at each corner of the said hath-pace, two having torches reversed, extinguishing the motto of Mortality; the other two holding up palmes, the emblems of Victory."

This monument hath not hitherto been (by what obstruction I list not to inquire) and I fear will not be finished; which hath invited me the rather to this description, that it might be erected in paper when it was intended in marble.—THOMAS FULLER, *The History of the Worthies of England*, 1662

I have seen him severall times with Sir John Danvers; he was a black man.

The Castle of Montgomery was a most Romancy seate: It stood upon a high Promontory, the north side 30 + feete high. From hence is a most delightsome prospect, 4 severall wayes. Southwards, without the Castle, is Prim-rose-hill: vide Donne's Poem:—

> Upon this Prim-rose-hill,
> Where, if Heaven would distill
> A Showre of raine, each severall drop might goe
> To his owne Prim-rose, and grow Manna so;
> And where their forme, and their infinitie
> Make a terrestiall Galaxie,
> As the small starres doe in the Skie:

In this pleasant Solitude did this noble Lord enjoy his Muse.

This stately Castle was demolished since the late Warres at the Chardge of the Countrey.

Mr. Fludd tells me he had constantly prayers twice a day in his howse, and Sundayes would have his Chaplayne, Dr. Coote (a Cambridge scholar and a learned) read one of Smyth's Sermons.

James Usher, Lord Primate of Ireland, was sent for by him, when in his death-bed, and he would have received the sacrament. He sayd indifferently of it that *if there was good in any-thing 'twas in that,* or *if it did no good 'twould doe no hurt.* The Primate refused it, for which many blamed him. He then turned his head to the other side and expired very serenely.
—JOHN AUBREY, "Edward Herbert: Lord Herbert of Cherbury," *Brief Lives*, 1669–96

He was a Person well studied in the Arts and Languages, a good Philosopher and Historian, and understood Men as well as Books, as it evidently appears in his Writings. . . . He surrendered up his last breath in his House in Queenstreet near London in sixteen hundred forty and eight, and was buried in the Chancel of S. Giles's Church in the Fields. Over his Grave, which is under the South Wall, was laid a flat Marble Stone with this Inscription engraven thereon, *Heic inhumatur corpus Edwardi Herbert, Equitis Balnei, Baronis de Cherbury &c Castle Island, auctoris libri cui titulus est* De veritate.

Reddor ut herbœ; vicesimo die Augusti anno Domini, 1648. —ANTHONY À WOOD, *Athenae Oxonienses,* 1691–1721

Lord Edward Herbert was one of the handsomest men of his day, of a beauty alike stately, chivalric and intellectual. His person and features were cultivated by all the disciplines of a time when courtly graces were not insignificant, because a monarch mind informed the court, nor warlike customs, rude or mechanical, for individual nature had free play in the field, except as restrained by the laws of courtesy and honor. The steel glove became his hand, and the spur his heel; neither can we fancy him out of his place, for any place he would have made his own. But all this grace and dignity of the man of the world was in him subordinated to that of the man, for in his eye, and in the brooding sense of all his countenance, was felt the life of one who, while he deemed that his present honour lay in playing well the part assigned him by destiny, never forgot that it was but a part, and fed steadily his forces on that within that passes show.—S. MARGARET FULLER, *Papers on Literature and Art,* 1846

General

His lordship seems to have been one of the first that formed Deism into a System, and asserted the sufficiency, universality, and absolute perfection of natural religion, with a view to discard all extraordinary revelation, as useless and needless. He seems to assume to himself the glory of having accomplished it with great labour, and a diligent inspection into all religions; and applauds himself for it, as happier than any *Archimedes.* This universal religion he reduceth to five articles, which he frequently mentioneth in all his works. 1. That there is one supreme God. 2. That he is chiefly to be worshipped. 3. That piety and virtue is the principal part of his worship. 4. That we must repent of our sins; and if we do so, God will pardon them. 5. That there are rewards for good men, and punishments for bad men, in a future state; or, as he sometimes expresseth it, both here and hereafter. These he represents as common notices inscribed by God on the minds of all men, and undertakes to shew that they were universally acknowledged in all nations, ages, and religions. . . .

One would be apt to think by what this noble writer here offers, that he must have a very favourable opinion of Christianity as contained in the holy scriptures; since he represents it as the great design of all its doctrines, and even of the rites and sacraments there injoined, to establish those great principles in which he makes religion properly to consist. Accordingly he expressly declares in the above-mentioned treatise, that it was far from his intention to do harm to *the best religion,* as he there calls Christianity, or the true faith, but rather to establish both.

But I am sorry that I am obliged to say, that notwithstanding these fair professions, his Lordship on all occasions insinuateth prejudices against all revealed religion, as absolutely uncertain, and of little or no use. He inveigheth promiscuously, as many others have done since, against all pretences to revelation, without making a distinction between the false and the true. He often speaks to the disadvantage of *particular* religion, which is a name he bestoweth upon the Christian religion, and any revelation that is not actually known and promulgated to the whole world. And he representeth it as containing doctrines, which disgust some men against all religion, and therefore is for recommending what he calls the universal religion, as the best way to prevent mens having no religion at all.

. . . I would observe that the principal design of his treatise *de Religione Laici* seems to be to shew, that the people can never attain to any satisfaction as to the truth and certainty of any particular revelation, and therefore must rest in the five articles agreed to by all religions. This particularly is the intention of his fourth and fifth queries in the appendix to that treatise. In his fourth query he supposes, that the things which are added to those common principles from the doctrines of faith are uncertain in their original; and that though God be true, the *Laics* can never be certain that what is pretended to be a revelation from God is indeed a true revelation from God. In his fifth query he urgeth, that supposing the originals to be true, yet they are uncertain in their explications. To this purpose he takes notice of the multiplicity of sects among Christians; and that the *Laics* can never be sufficiently sure of the meaning of the revelation concerning which there are so many controversies; that in order to arrive at any certainty in these matters, it would be necessary either to *learn all languages, to read all the celebrated writers, and to consult all those learned men that have not written,* a method which is manifestly absurd and impracticable; or else to have recourse to a *supreme judge of controversies* appointed by common consent.

It is an observation that will undoubtedly occur to you on this occasion, that his Lordship here maketh use precisely of the same way of talking, to shew that the *Laics* can have no certainty about any revelation at all, which the writers of the *Romish* Church have frequently urged to shew the necessity the people are under to rely intirely upon the authority of the Church or *Pope,* because of the difficulties or the impossibility of their coming to any certainty in the way of examination or private judgment. But if the *Laity* cannot be certain of revealed religion, because of the controversies that have been raised about the articles of it, for the same reason it may be said, that they can arrive at no certainty with respect to his Lordship's catholic universal religion: for though he representeth men as universally agreed in the five articles, in which he makes that religion to consist, it is undeniable that there have been great controversies about them . . .

From this general view of Lord *Herbert*'s Scheme, it sufficiently appears that his design was to overturn all revealed, or, as he calls it, particular religion, and to establish that natural and universal religion, the clearness and perfection of which he so much extols, in its room, as that which alone ought to be acknowledged and embraced as true and divine.—JOHN LELAND, *A View of the Principal Deistical Writers,* 1757, Vol. 1, pp. 3–7

Too much space may seem to have been bestowed on a writer who cannot be ranked high among metaphysicians. But Lord Herbert was not only a distinguished name, but may claim the priority among those philosophers in England. If his treatise *De Veritate* is not, as an entire work, very successful, or founded always upon principles which have stood the test of severe reflection, it is still a monument of an original, independent thinker, without rhapsodies of imagination, without pedantic technicalities, and, above all, bearing witness to a sincere love of the truth he sought to apprehend. The ambitious expectation that the real essences of things might be discovered, if it were truly his, as Gassendi seems to suppose, could not be warranted by any thing, at least, within the knowledge of that age. But, from some expressions of Herbert, I should infer that he did not think our faculties competent to solve the whole problem of *quiddity,* as the logicians called it, or the real nature of any thing, at least, objectively without us. He is, indeed, so obscure, that I will not vouch for his entire consistency. It has been an additional motive to say as much as

I have done concerning Lord Herbert, that I know not where any account of his treatise *De Veritate* will be found. Brucker is strangely silent about this writer, and Buhle has merely adverted to the letter of Gassendi. Descartes has spoken of Lord Herbert's book with much respect, though several of their leading principles were far from the same.—HENRY HALLAM, *Introduction to the Literature of Europe*, 1837–39, Pt. 3, Ch. 3, Par. 28

His celebrated treatise *De Veritate, prout distinguitur a Revelatione, a Verisimili, a Possibili et a Falso*,—a book, as he says himself, "so different from anything which had been written before," that he had not dared to publish it, till, in answer to his prayers, he had received a supernatural sign from heaven. He had circulated copies of the book among the continental thinkers, "without suffering it to be divulged to others;" but, satisfied with the result, he was now preparing a second edition to be published in London. When this edition appeared (1633,) it bore the "imprimatur" of Laud's domestic chaplain, stating that nothing had been found in it "contrary to good morals or the truth of the Faith." It is the custom now, however, to regard the book as the first English Deistical treatise, and the author as the first English Deist. It may be doubted whether this judgment is, in any respect, correct; nay, whether, if the conspicuous heads of that day were carefully counted, there might not be found among them one or two whose speculations passed the bounds of any form of Theism whatever. —DAVID MASSON, *The Life of John Milton*, 1859, Vol. 1, Ch. 6

With Lord Herbert appeared a systematic deism.—HIPPOLYTE TAINE, *History of English Literature*, tr. H. Van Laun, 1871, Vol. 1, p. 207

His literary activity was various and considerable. His greatest work—a treatise which has been rashly called the foundation of English deism, but which rather expresses the vague and not wholly unorthodox doubt expressed earlier by Montaigne, and by contemporaries of Herbert's own, such as La Mothe le Vayer—was written in Latin, and has never been translated into English. He was an English verse writer of some merit, though inferior to his brother. His ambitious and academic *History of Henry VIII.* is a regular and not unsuccessful effort in English prose, prompted no doubt by the thorough-going courtiership which ranks with his vanity and want of stability on the most unfavourable aspect of Herbert's character. But posterity has agreed to take him as an English writer chiefly on the strength of the Autobiography, which remained in manuscript for a century and more, and was published by Horace Walpole, rather against the will of Lord Powis, its possessor and its author's representative. It is difficult to say that Lord Powis was wrong, especially considering that Herbert never published these memoirs, and seems to have written them as much as anything else for his own private satisfaction. It may be doubted whether there is any more astounding monument of coxcombry in literature. Herbert is sometimes cited as a model of a modern knight-errant, of an Amadis born too late. Certainly, according to his own account, all women loved and all men feared him; but for the former fact we have nothing but his own authority, and in regard to the latter we have counter evidence which renders it exceedingly doubtful. He was, according to his own account, a desperate duellist. But even by this account his duels had a curious habit of being interrupted in the immortal phrase of Mr. Winkle by "several police constables;" while in regard to actual war the exploits of his youth seem not to have been great, and those of his age were wholly discredita-

ble, inasmuch as being by profession an ardent Royalist, he took the first opportunity to make, without striking a blow, a profitable composition with the Parliament. Nevertheless, despite the drawbacks of subject-matter, the autobiography is a very interesting piece of English prose. The narrative style, for all its coxcombry and its insistence on petty details, has a singular vivacity; the constructions, though sometimes incorrect ("the edict was so severe as they who transgressed were to lose their heads"), are never merely slovenly; and the writer displays an art, very uncommon in his time, in the alternation of short and long sentences and the general adjustment of the paragraph. Here and there, too, there are passages of more elevated style which give reason for regretting that the *De Veritate* was not written in English. It is very much to be feared that the chief reason for its being written in Latin was a desire on the author's part to escape awkward consequences by an appearance of catering for philosophers and the learned only. It must be admitted that neither of the two great free-thinking Royalists, Hobbes and Herbert, is a wholly pleasant character; but it may be at least said for the commoner (it cannot be said for the peer) that he was constant to his principles, and that if somewhat careful of his skin, he never seems to have been tempted to barter his conscience for it as Herbert did. —GEORGE SAINTSBURY, *A History of Elizabethan Literature*, 1887, pp. 138–40

Herbert is best known to modern readers by his autobiography. Childlike vanity is the chief characteristic of the narrative. He represents himself mainly as a gay Lothario, the hero of innumerable duels, whose handsome face and world-wide reputation as a soldier gained for him the passionate adoration of all the ladies of his acquaintance and the respect of all men of distinction. He enters into minute details about his person and habits. He declares that he grew in height when nearly forty years old, that he had a pulse in his head, that he never felt cold in his life, and that he took to tobacco in his later years with good effect on his health. But Herbert's veracity even on such points is disputable; his accounts of his literary friends and his mother are very incomplete, his dates are conflicting, and he does himself an injustice by omitting almost all mention of his serious studies, which give him an important place in the history of English philosophy and poetry. He only shows the serious side of his character in a long digression on education in the early part of his memoirs, where he recommends a year's reading in philosophy and six months' study of logic, although "I am confident," he adds, "a man may have quickly more than he needs of these arts." Botany he praises as "a fine study," and "worthy of a gentleman," and he has some sensible remarks on moral and physical training. At the end of his autobiography he states that he had written a work on truth, which he had shown to two great scholars, Tilenus and Grotius, who had exhorted him to print it, and that a miraculous sign to the same effect had been vouchsafed to him from heaven in answer to a prayer. . . .

As a poet he was a disciple of Donne, and excelled his master in obscurity and ruggedness. Ben Jonson was impressed by his "obscureness." His satires are very poor, but some of his lyrics have the true poetic ring, and at times suggest Herrick. He often employs the metre which was brought to perfection by Tennyson in *In Memoriam*. His Latin verses are scholarly, and chiefly deal with philosophic subjects.—SIDNEY LEE, *Dictionary of National Biography*, 1891, Vol. 27, pp. 178–80

The philosophical works of Lord Herbert of Cherbury are written in Latin: his English prose works are his *History of King Henry VIII.* and his own *Life*. In neither of these latter is it possible to find much excellence of rhetoric. The *History* was intended to challenge comparison with Bacon's *Henry VII.*, but all the labour of its author failed to secure for it anything like the spring and liveliness of Bacon's narrative. The *Autobiography* cannot be called tedious or heavy, but the author's manner is uncertain, and there is a provoking discrepancy between the arrogant valour of the sentiments, and the ill-cut phrases and loose construction of the language. In a mere philosopher this negligence might pass.

The *Autobiography* was edited by Horace Walpole in a spirit of mischief. "I was resolved the world should not think I admired it seriously, though there are really fine passages in it, and good sense too. I drew up an equivocal preface in which you will discover my opinion." This "equivocal preface" states the contrast which first attracted Walpole, and which still brings readers to the book: the contrast between the philosophical solemnity of the author and his inexpugnable self-confidence in respect of gallantry and the point of honour. This is what preserves his name—not the mere stories of his adventures, though they are good, nor any skill in writing; not his metaphysics nor his religious advice; but the impression of his singular character.

In that character there was no flaw: it was incapable of any suspicion of itself, and being proof against that danger it was proof against all other weakness. His metaphysical system and his moral and religious arguments are the expansion and the evolution of his individual consciousness of rectitude. From the beginning to the end of his life he is anxious to make all the world of the same mind as himself; from the beginning to the end he is vexed rather than surprised at the dulness and unreadiness of all the world in face of this opportunity of enlightenment. He explained to the regent of the English College at Rome his tolerance of errors in religion; on his deathbed he explained to Archbishop Ussher his reasonable, tolerant, and infinitesimal desire for the last rites of the Church, and among his latest thoughts must have been one of forgiveness for Ussher, who refused the request of a gentleman so free from prejudices. More interesting than most passages in his *Life of Henry VIII.* is the speech introduced by him in the report of the parliament of 1529, where a nameless orator is put up to expound the doctrines of the *Religio Laici* and *De Veritate*:—

> Each nation may be permitted the beliefe of any pious miracle that conduceth to God's glory; without that on this occasion we need to scandalize or offend each other. The common truths in religion formerly mentioned, being firmer bonds of unity, than that anything emergent out of traditions (whether written or unwritten) should dissolve them. Let us therefore establish and fix those catholike or universall notions. They will not hinder us to believe whatsoever else is faithfully taught upon the authority of the Church. So that whether the Eastern, Western, Northern, or Southern teachers, etc., and particularly whether my Lord of Rochester, Luther, Eccius, Zuinglius, Erasmus, Melancthon, etc., be in the right, wee laiques may so build upon these catholike and infallible grounds of religion, as whatsoever superstructures of faith be rais'd, these foundations yet may support them.

The historian does not report King Henry's opinion about this tolerant reasoner: the ghostly orator escapes.

The Life of Lord Herbert is full of adventures and of encounters with great personages. The adventures are well told; there is seldom anything very striking in the descriptions of people. King Louis XIII. and the fair maid of an inn are de-

scribed more particularly than the rest: the writer has little to say of Casaubon or Grotius, of Henry IV. or Queen Margaret. Spinola, though there is not much about him, is represented as a soldier and a gallant gentleman, whom Herbert offered to follow "if ever he did lead an army against the infidels." The fortunes and the ideas of Herbert are generally sufficient for him: he is not much interested in other people. The story comes to an end in 1624; the writer did not go on to tell of his difficulty in understanding what the civil war of England was all about, and of the inconvenience which it caused him. —W. P. KER, "Lord Herbert of Cherbury," *English Prose*, ed. Henry Craik, 1893, Vol. 2, pp. 175–77

Works

THE LIFE AND RAIGNE OF
KING HENRY THE EIGHTH

Above all, Edward, Lord Herbert, of Cherbury, may be truly said to have written the life and reign of King Henry the Eight; having acquitted himself with the like reputation as the Lord-Chancellor Bacon gained by that of Henry the Seventh. For, in the politic and martial part of this honourable author has been admirably particular and exact, from the best records that were extant; though, as to the ecclesiastical, he seems to have looked upon it as a thing out of his province, and an undertaking more proper for men of another profession.—WILLIAM NICOLSON, *The English Historical Library*, 1696–99

Lord Herbert stands in the first rank of the public ministers, historians, and philosophers of his age. It is hard to say whether his person, his understanding, or his courage, was the most extraordinary; as the fair, the learned, and the brave, held him in equal admiration. But the same man was wise and capricious; redressed wrongs and quarrelled for punctilios; hated bigotry in religion, and was himself a bigot to philosophy. He exposed himself to such dangers, as other men of courage would have carefully declined; and called in question the fundamentals of religion which none had the hardiness to dispute beside himself—JAMES GRANGER, *Biographical History of England*, 1769–1824

POEMS

The world has long done justice to Lord Herbert's famous treatise *De Veritate*, to his admirable *Life of Henry VIII*, to his singularly interesting Autobiography; but no one has yet been found to vindicate his claim to a place among English poets. His poems first appeared in a little volume which was published in 1665, nearly eighteen years after his death; and, as we gather from the preface, were collected by Henry Herbert, uncle to the second Lord Herbert of Cherbury, to whom they are dedicated. They consist of Sonnets, Epitaphs, Satires, Madrigals, and Odes in various measures. Herbert is, like his more distinguished brother, a disciple of the Metaphysical School, though his poems, unlike those of George, are not of a religious character. With much of that extravagance which deforms the lyric poetry of his contemporaries, Lord Herbert has in a large measure grace, sweetness, and originality. He never lacks vigour and freshness. His place is, with all his faults, beside Donne and Cowley. His versification is indeed as a rule far superior to theirs. It is uniformly musical, and his music is often at once delicate and subtle. Though he did not invent the metre, he certainly discovered the melody of that stanza with which Tennyson's great poem has familiarised us, and he has as certainly anticipated some of its most beautiful effects. He is never likely to hold the same place among English poets as his brother, but we do not hesitate to say that no collection of representative English poets should be considered complete which does not contain the poetical works of Lord Herbert of Cherbury.—JOHN CHURTON COLLINS, "Lord Herbert of Cherbury," *The English Poets*, ed. Thomas Humphry Ward, 1880, Vol. 2, p. 188

I have no wish to rob Oblivion of its legitimate prey. Some of Lord Herbert's poems are, I freely admit, not worth resuscitation, but many of them, or portions at least of many of them, seem to me authentic poetry. In almost all of them we find originality and vigour, however fantastic the conception, however rough the execution. But were their merits even less than they are, no cultivated man could regard them with indifference. The name of their writer would be a sufficient passport to indulgent attention. . . . In my estimate of Lord Herbert's poems I have hitherto stood alone. . . . It is strange that in his *Autobiography* Lord Herbert makes no mention of his Poems, the existence of which seems not to have been suspected by any of his distinguished contemporaries. They were evidently jotted down in moments of leisure, as occasion offered. Some of them were the work of his youth, some of his middle age; the last was written four years before his death. . . . But Herbert's greatest metrical triumph is that he was the first to discover the harmony of that stanza with which the most celebrated poet of our own day has familiarised us. The glory of having invented it belongs indeed to another, but the glory of having passed it almost perfect into Mr. Tennyson's hands belongs unquestionably to Herbert. And it is due also to Herbert to say that he not only revealed its sweetness and beauty, but that he anticipated some of its most exquisite effects and variations. . . . The Latin poems of Herbert are scarcely likely to find favour in the eyes of modern scholars. Their diction is, as a rule, involved and obscure; they teem with forced and unclassical expressions. His hendecasyllabics are intolerably harsh, and violate almost every metrical canon. His Elegiacs are not more successful; indeed, the only tolerable copy among the poemata are the verses on a Dial, for the epigrams are below contempt.—JOHN CHURTON COLLINS, "Introduction" to *The Poems of Lord Herbert of Cherbury*, 1881, pp. xviii–xxxiii

AUTOBIOGRAPHY

Being written when Lord Herbert was past sixty, the work was probably never completed. The spelling is in general given as in the MS. but some obvious mistakes it was necessary to correct, and a few notes have been added, to point out the most remarkable persons mentioned in the text. The style is remarkably good for that age, which coming between the nervous and expressive manliness of the preceding century, and the purity of the present standard, partook of neither. His lordship's observations are new and acute, some very shrewd; his discourse on the Reformation very wise. . . . Nothing is more marked than the air of veracity or persuasion which runs through the whole narrative. If he makes us wonder, and wonder makes us doubt, the charm of his ingenuous integrity dispels our hesitation. The whole relation throws singular light on the manners of the age, though the gleams are transient.—HORACE WALPOLE, "Advertisement," *Autobiography of Edward Lord Herbert of Cherbury*, 1764

In many passages the autobiography of Lord Herbert is of a style so charming, and of a manner and matter so singularly characteristic of his order, age, and nation, that one might easily believe it written by some skilful student of the period, with a tacit modern consciousness of the wonderful artistic success of the study. As you read, you cannot help thinking now and then that Thackeray himself could not have done it better, if he had been minded to portray a gentleman of the first James's time. Yet this picture, so frank, so boldly colored, so full of the very life of a young English noble, is one of the most remarkable instances of self-portraiture in any language, in the absence of that consciousness which the momentarily bewildered sense attributes to it; its great value to the reader of our day is, that the author sits to himself as unconstrainedly as if posterity should never come to look over his shoulder, and all his attitudes and expressions are those of natural ease. A rare sincerity marks the whole memoir, and gives it the grace of an antique simplicity.—WILLIAM DEAN HOWELLS, *Life of Lord Herbert of Cherbury*, 1877, p. 1

JOHN HENEAGE JESSE
From Memoirs of the Court of England during the Reign of the Stuarts
1839–57, Volume 2, pp. 75–89

The life of Lord Herbert of Cherbury, written by himself, is one of the most curious works of the kind that has ever issued from the press. Who can read without delight a narrative, and such a narrative, too, of the private foibles and most secret thoughts of the soldier, the statesman, the wit, and the philosopher? That he was truth itself is undoubted; and if his vanity sometimes occasions a smile, we must bear in mind the peculiar features of the period in which he lived. We must remember that chivalry was not then extinct, and that the smiles of beauty and the honours of battle were considered as indispensable in conferring not only reputation, but respect. Gifted by nature with wit, beauty, and talent, and possessing courage almost amounting to a fault, can we wonder that, in a martial and romantic age, Lord Herbert should have engaged the hearts of women, almost as universally as he won for himself the respect of men? If he speaks somewhat ostentatiously of his own merits, at least with equal candour he lays open to us his faults. . . .

There were many contradictions in Lord Herbert's character. "The same man," observes Granger, "was wise and capricious; redressed wrongs, and quarrelled for punctilios; hated bigotry in religion, and was himself a bigot to philosophy. He exposed himself to such dangers as other men of courage would have carefully declined, and called in question the fundamentals of a religion which none had the hardiness to dispute besides himself." His famous philosophical work, *De Veritate*, was expressly written against revealed religion. With the publication of this work is connected an extraordinary instance of human vanity and human inconsistency. The same man, whose time and talents had been employed in arguing against the possible existence of miracles, was, nevertheless, ready to believe that the divine intentions were communicated miraculously to himself; in a word, he who discredited a revelation, which comprehended the happiness of the whole human race, was, notwithstanding, fully convinced that a miracle was wrought in his own person, and that a preternatural agency was employed to watch over himself and his own insignificant pursuits. "Being," he says, "in my chamber, one fair day in the summer, my casement being opened toward the south, the sun shining clear, and no wind stirring, I took my book, *De Veritate*, in my hand, and kneeling on my knees, devoutly said these words: 'Oh, thou Eternal God, Author of the light which now shines upon me, and Giver of all inward illuminations, I do beseech thee, of thy infinite goodness, to pardon a greater request than a sinner ought to make. I am not satisfied enough whether I shall publish this book, *De Veritate*; if it be for thy glory, I beseech thee give me some sign from heaven; if not, I shall suppress it.'

"I had no sooner spoken these words, but a loud, though yet gentle noise came from the heavens (for it was like nothing on earth), which did so comfort and cheer me that I took my petition as granted, and that I had the sign I demanded, whereupon, also, I resolved to print my book. This (how strange soever it may seem) I profess before the eternal God is true; neither am I any way superstitiously deceived herein, since I did not only clearly hear the noise, but in the serenest sky that ever I saw, being without all cloud, did to my thinking see the place from whence it came."

Lord Herbert was at least a conscientious deist. According to Aubrey, twice a day he had prayers in his house, and on Sundays a sermon was preached by his chaplain.

In his last illness, when he knew himself to be dying, he expressed a wish that Archbishop Usher might be sent for. When it was proposed to him to receive the sacrament, he said indifferently, that if there was good in anything it was in that, and at all events it could do him no harm. Under the circumstances the primate refused to administer it, for which he was afterward much blamed. Lord Herbert died serenely. Shortly before he breathed his last, he inquired the hour, and on receiving a reply, "An hour hence," he said, "I shall depart." He then turned his face to the opposite side, and shortly afterward expired.

His death took place in his house in Queen Street, St.

Giles's in the Fields, in 1648. In his will, he gave directions that a white horse, to which he was much attached, should be carefully fed and attended to during its life. He also bequeathed a large collection of books to Jesus College, Oxford. On the 5th of August, 1648, he was buried in the chancel of St. Giles's Church in the Fields. "As a soldier," says Horace Walpole, "he won the esteem of those great captains, the Prince of Orange and the Constable de Montmorency; as a knight, his chivalry was drawn from the purest founts of the *Faerie Queene*. Had he been ambitious, the beauty of his person would have carried him as far as any gentle knight can aspire to go. As a public minister, he supported the dignity of his country, even when its prince disgraced it; and that he was qualified to write its annals as well as to ennoble them, the history I have mentioned proves, and must make us lament that he did not complete, or that we have lost, the account he purposed to give of his embassy. These busy scenes were blended with, and terminated by, meditation and philosophic inquiries. Strip each period of its excesses and errors, and it will not be easy to trace out or dispose the life of a man of quality into a succession of employments which would better become him. Valour and military activity in youth; business of state in middle age; contemplation and labours for the information of posterity in the calmer scenes of closing life." Such is the outline of Lord Herbert's character, as sketched by another. He has himself completed the picture by his own curious delineation of his private thoughts and secret motives for action, forming, if not the most perfect, at least one of the most remarkable characters in the gallery of human portraits.

WILLIAM DRUMMOND

1585–1649

William Drummond was born on December 13, 1585, at Hawthornden, near Edinburgh. Descended from Scottish gentry, Drummond attended Edinburgh High School before entering the University of Edinburgh. He graduated with an M.A. in 1605, and afterwards studied law in France for several years. With the death of his father in 1610 Drummond returned to Hawthornden, where he resided for the next forty years.

Drummond's earliest poetic work, *Tears on the Death of Moeliades*, was written upon the death of Prince Henry in 1613. Drummond's fiancé, Mary Cunningham of Barns, died on the eve of their wedding in 1615. Shortly thereafter Drummond published *Poems, Amorous, Funereall, Divine, Pastorall, in Sonnets, Songs, Sextains, Madrigals* (1616). Drummond's poetry is noted for its similarity to Italian and French models. His collection of religious verse, *Flowres of Sion* (1633), contained two well-known poems, "Saint John Baptist" and "For the Magdalene." *The Cypresse Grove*, a prose meditation on death, accompanied these verses. Drummond's *History of Scotland 1423–1524* was printed posthumously in 1685. His other works include a verse collection and a play prepared for separate royal visits to Edinburgh, *Forth Feasting* (1617), and *The Entertainment* (1633).

Drummond was a friend to Ben Jonson and Michael Drayton, recording his discussions with Jonson in a book titled *Conversations* (recorded in 1619; first published 1842). Drummond was a reclusive scholar, remembered also for his sixteen patents of military and scientific instruments. He died at Hawthornden on December 4, 1649.

Personal

And my deare *Drummond* to whom much I owe
For his much love, and proud I was to know,
His poesie, for which two worthy men
I *Menstry* still shall love, and Hauthorne-den.

—MICHAEL DRAYTON, "To My Most Dearely-Loved Friend Henery Reynolds Esquire, of Poets and Poesie," c. 1627

I have no doubt that Drummond, a valetudinarian and "minor poet," was thoroughly borne down by the superior powers, physical and mental, of Jonson, and heartily glad when he saw the last of his somewhat boisterous and somewhat arrogant guest. The picture drawn by one who thus felt himself "sat upon" at every turn was not likely to be a flattering one, and yet there is nothing in the *Conversations* to lead us to expect that the portrait given at the end of them would be composed almost entirely of shadows. But may we not suppose that on the 24th of January, 1619, on his way to Leith, Jonson may have passed the night at Hawthornden, and full of the idea of returning home, and warmed with the generous liquors, for the abundance and quality of which

The heart of Scotland, Britain's other eye

has always been famous, have forgotten that he was at the table of a prim Scotch laird, and dreaming himself already in the Apollo or at the Mermaid, given vent to each feeling as it rose, whether vanity, scorn, contempt, ridicule, mistrust, boasting, love of country and friends, passionate kindness, regardlessness of money and gain, eagerness to conquer, and readiness to own himself vanquished. Had Drummond waited till time and distance had mellowed his feelings, he would, I am persuaded, have employed some such terms as I have here one by one carefully softened down from the harsher-sounding synonymes actually recorded.—WILLIAM GIFFORD, *The Works of Ben Jonson*, 1816, Vol. 9, p. 416

He loved a beautiful girl of the noble family of Cunningham, who is the Lesbia of his poetry. After a fervent courtship, he succeeded in securing her affections; but she died, "in the fresh April of her years," and when their marriage-day had been fixed. Drummond has left us a most charming picture of his mistress; of her modesty, her retiring sweetness, her accomplishments, and her tenderness for him. . . .

He travelled for eight years, seeking, in change of place and scene, some solace for his wounded peace. There was a kind of constancy even in Drummond's inconstancy; for meeting many years afterwards with an amiable girl, who bore the most striking resemblance to his lost mistress, he loved her for that very resemblance, and married her. Her name was Margaret Logan.—ANNA BROWNELL JAMESON, *Memoirs of the Loves of the Poets*, 1829, Vol. 1, pp. 267–69

Drummond was evidently a man of superior talents and accomplishments. We are informed that he was familiarly acquainted with the best Greek and Latin authors: his long residence on the Continent afforded him an excellent opportunity of acquiring a knowledge of the living languages: and he is said to have spoken French, Italian, and Spanish as fluently as his native tongue. To his graver qualifications he added no mean proficiency in music; and he occasionally sought a relaxation of his studies by playing on the lute, "which he did to admiration." He seems to have devoted a considerable portion of his time to the invention or improvement of various instruments and machines, applicable to various purposes of peace or war. They are curiously enumerated, to the extent of sixteen, in a patent which he obtained in the year 1627, and which secured to him the sole right and property within the kingdom of Scotland for the space of twenty-one years.—DAVID IRVING, *The History of Scotish Poetry*, ed. John Aitken Carlyle, 1861, pp. 540–41

The church and churchyard of Lasswade are on a height overlooking the village, and about two miles and a half from Hawthornden. The present church was built about a hundred years ago; but, in a portion of the well-kept churchyard, railed in separately from the rest, as more select and important, there is the fragmentary outline of the smaller old church, with some

of the sepulchral monuments that belonged to it. Drummond's own aisle, abutting from one part of the ruined wall, is still perfect, a small arched space of stone-work, with a roofing of strong stone slabs, and a grating of iron for door-way. Within that small arched space Drummond's ashes certainly lie, though there is no inscription to mark the precise spot as distinct from the graves of some of his latest descendants who are also buried there, and to one of whom there is a commemorative tablet. The small arched aisle itself is his monument, and it is a sufficient one. There could hardly be a more peaceful rustic burying-ground than that in which it stands, the church and the manse close to it on the height, with only steep descending lanes from them to Lasswade village and to the road leading from Lasswade to Edinburgh.—DAVID MASSON, *Drummond of Hawthornden*, 1873, p. 456

He was a man of varied culture, and his writings in poetry and prose were widely read. He was the foremost of that band of men which broke the tradition that Scottish literature ought to be written in the Scottish national tongue, and which strove to express their thoughts in the language which had served the purposes of Shakspeare and Jonson, and was one day to serve the purposes of Scott and Campbell. He was withal an upright and honest man, craving for philosophic and literary culture rather than for Calvinistic orthodoxy, and fearing the inquisitive meddling of the Presbyterian clergy who would be sure to bear hard upon one of his tastes and opinions. He was one who, like Patrick Forbes, had formed part of that wave of liberal reaction, which, through the blunders of James and Charles, had already spent its force.—SAMUEL R. GARDINER, *History of England*, 1883, Vol. 7, p. 295–96

If Drummond, as he sat under his sycamore-tree that memorable afternoon, watching Jonson's approach, did not cry, "Welcome, welcome, royal Ben," and if Jonson did not reply on the instant, "Thank'e, thank'e, Hawthornden," as tradition has ever since asserted, there can be no question that the welcome was a right royal one. Jonson might not have been so free with his thanks and his speech, however, if he had known that his "Hawthornden" was to become, at his expense, the inventor of interviewing.—LAWRENCE HUTTON, *Literary Landmarks of Edinburgh*, 1891, p. 17

General

⟨Jonson's⟩ censure of my verses was that they were all good especiallie my Epitaph of the Prince, save that they smelled too much of ye schooles and were not after the fancie of ye time for a child says he may writte after the fashion of ye Greeks & latine verses in running. yett that he wished to please the King. that piece of Forth-Feasting had been his owne.—WILLIAM DRUMMOND, *Notes on Ben Jonson's Conversations*, 1619

To say that these Poems are the effects of a genius the most polite and verdant that ever the Scottish nation produced, although it be a commendation not to be rejected (for it is well known that that country hath afforded many rare and admirable wits), yet it is not the highest that may be given him; for, should I affirm that neither Tasso, nor Guarini, nor any of the most neat and refined spirits of Italy, nor even the choicest of our English Poets, can challenge to themselves any advantage above him, it could not be judged any attribute superior to what he deserves, nor shall I think it any arrogance to maintain that among all the several fancies that in these times have exercised the most nice and curious judgments there hath not come forth anything that deserves to be welcomed into the world with greater estimation and applause.—EDWARD PHIL-

LIPS, "Preface" to *Poems by that most famous Wit, William Drummond of Hawthornden*, 1656

The earliest piece of *Waller* is that to the King on his navy, in 1625. The piece, in which Sir John *Denham's* greatest force lies, *Cooper's Hill*, was not written till 1640. The harmony of *Drummond*, therefore, at a time when those, who are usually called the first introducers of a smooth and polished versification, had not yet begun to write, is an honor to him, that should never be forgotten. Nor is his excellence half enough praised, or acknowledged.

Drummond and Petrarca had this in common, that each lamented, first the cruelty, and then the loss of his mistress: so that their *Sonnets* are alike naturally divided into two parts; those before, and those after their several mistresses deaths. It may justly be doubted that, among all the sonneteers in the English language, any one is to be preferred to *Drummond*. He has shewn, in some of these compositions, nearly the spirit of *Petrarca* himself.—PHILIP LE NEVE, *Cursory Remarks on Some of the Ancient English Poets, Particularly Milton*, 1789, pp. 49–50

It is not easy to determine, whether a dead language, in which men had been initiated, and of which the purest models had been studied, from their earliest years, or a foreign dialect which the tongue was unable to pronounce, and to the purity and precision of which the mind was unaccustomed, imposed the severest constraint upon original genius. Yet at a time when the rugged numbers of Donne and Johnson prevailed in poetry, Drummond of Hawthornden gave the first specimen of a rich and melodious versification, and discovered a vein of tender, unaffected sentiment which succeeding poets have not disdained to imitate. His taste was formed in the Italian school; and he preceded Denham and Waller in the refinement of our numbers; though his poetry, like theirs, is neither always equal, nor always correct.—MALCOLM LAING, *The History of Scotland*, 1800–04, Vol. 3, p. 476

The Scottish Court of James the Sixth, in the midst of pedantry, scholastic jargon, and polemic theology, produced several poets by no means devoid of genius. Some possessed quaintness of wit, some easy versification, and some the power of affecting the emotions of the heart; but the various talents of the poets were seldom concentrated in the same person. The rays of poetical light were refracted and divided among several poets. In Drummond alone were they united, and displayed the solar radiance of fancy.—JOHN LEYDEN, *Scottish Descriptive Poems*, 1803, p. 254

The elegance of Drummond's sonnets, and the humour of his Scotch and Latin macaronics, have been at least sufficiently praised: but when Milton had been described as essentially obliged to him, the compliment to his genius is stretched too far. A modern writer, who edited the works of Drummond, has affirmed, that, "perhaps," if we had had no Drummond, we should not have seen the finer delicacies of Milton's *Comus*, "Lycidas," "L'Allegro," and "Il Penseroso." "Perhaps" is an excellent leading-string for weak assertions. One or two epithets of Drummond may be recognised in Milton, though not in the minor poems already mentioned. It is difficult to apply any precise idea to the tautology of "fine delicacies;" but whatever the editor of Drummond meant by it, he may be assured that there is no debt on the part of Milton to the poet of Hawthornden, which the former could be the least improverished by returning. Phillips, the nephew of Milton, edited and extolled Drummond, and pronounced him equal to Tasso himself. It has been inferred from some passages of the *Theatrum Poetarum*, that Milton had dictated several critical opinions in that performance; and it has been taken for granted that Phillips's high opinion of Drummond was imbibed from the author of *Paradise Lost*. But the parallel between Drummond and Tasso surely could not have been drawn by Milton. Phillips had a turn for poetry, and in many of his critical opinions in the *Theatrum Poetarum*, shewed a taste that could not be well attributed to his uncle—in none more than in this exaggerated comparison of a smoother sonnetteer to a mighty poet. It is equally improbable that he imbibed this absurdity from Milton, as that he caught from him his admiration of Drummond's prose compositions and arbitrary principles.—THOMAS CAMPBELL, *Specimens of the British Poets*, 1819

And Mr. Drummond was a genius? I expect his singing will differ a little from that of the old Iliad Homerides,—merging direct with fiery veracity towards the fact, melting into music by the very truth and fire of it. Alas, yes, from the Greek Homerides, from the Norse Skalds, from the English or Scotch ballad-singer, from all men that ever at any time sang truly. The true singer hurries direct—towards the fact, intent on that alone, melts into music by the very fire of his veracity. Drummond's genius one would say is that of an accomplished Upholsterer rather. Different from Homer's—as a pair of the costliest slashed puff-breeches, stuffed broader than a bushel with nothing in them, may differ from a pair of Grecian Hippolytus' limbs with nothing superfluous on them, but good Mr. Drummond is a type of his age. His monstrous unveracious puff-breeches ovation is the emblem of so much other unveracity.—THOMAS CARLYLE, *Historical Sketches of Noble Persons and Events in the Reigns of James I and Charles I*, 1844

Through the greater part of his verse we hear a certain muffled tone of the sweetest, like the music that ever threatens to break out clear from the brook, from the pines, from the rain-shower, —never does break out clear, but remains a suggested, etherially vanishing tone. His is a *voix voilée*, or veiled voice of song.—GEORGE MACDONALD, *England's Antiphon*, 1868, p. 146

Scotland, underneath all her apparent unanimity for the Covenant during the last two years, and her exultation in the new Presbyterian order of things, yet contained, as may be readily guessed, a good deal of lurking or diffused *Drummondism*. That was not the name by which it was known at the time; it was called Malignancy by the Covenanters, and Loyalty and the like by its professors; but *Drummondism* is the best name for us, and we are quite entitled to introduce it into the language of this portion of Scottish History. For, though Drummond was only a private man, no one had expressed, or was capable of expressing, so eloquently and energetically as he had done, in his "Irene" and subsequent tracts, the very essence of all the antipathy to the established order of things existing anywhere among his countrymen. These tracts were, in fact, the best unpublished manifestoes, if such a phrase may pass, of the scattered, diffused, and suppressed discontent. All the disaffected in Scotland were virtual Drummondists. So far as words went, Drummond was their universal representative. —DAVID MASSON, *Drummond of Hawthornden*, 1873, p. 342

The interest of Drummond lies chiefly, for a modern reader, in the circumstances of his life. He is one of the earliest instances in our literature of the man of letters pure and simple; of the man who writes neither for his bread, like the great dramatists his contemporaries, nor to adorn the leisure moments of an active life, like Chaucer and Sir Philip Sidney, but who, when his fortune allows him to choose his career, elects to write for the sake of writing. It is true he travelled, both as a very young man and later; he corresponded regularly with his Scottish friends at the courts of James and Charles, especially with Sir William Alexander Earl of Stirling, the poet and statesman; he took part in such royal festivities as a rare chance might bring to Edinburgh; he keenly felt and sharply criticised the course of public affairs; but for all this his centre and his home was the beautiful house on the bank of the Esk, into the solitudes of which even the din of Bishops' Wars could scarcely penetrate. Other poets are known by their names alone; we talk of Jonson and Herrick, of Dryden and Addison; but Drummond is for all time Drummond of Hawthornden. . . .

Drummond is a literary and even learned poet. With Alexander, he deliberately preferred to write English, as it was spoken in England, rather than his native Scotch. His wealth and his leisure enabled him to surround himself with books; he was familiar with both ancient and modern literature. An interesting gift of his to the newly founded University of Edinburgh has preserved for us a selection of the very volumes that he read; English poetry and prose, including works of Bacon and Selden, of Drayton and Donne, of Ben Jonson and Shakespeare; Latin, French, Italian volumes in great numbers. Moreover, among the *excerpta* from his papers which Mr. Laing printed we find exact lists of the books that he read from period to period, the year's task sometimes extending to forty or fifty separate writers, some of them of the dimensions of Knox's *History of the Reformation*, and Sidney's *Arcadia*, and Lyly's *Euphues*, and Rabelais, and *Amadis de Gaule*. Like every other cultivated man of his day, he had read Marini; and his copy of Montaigne is extant. His favourite forms of verse are the sonnet, of the Shakespearian rather than the true Italian type, and a short song or madrigal, combining the six-syllabled and the ten-syllabled lines in a very happy way; but he also uses other metres, such as the heroic couplet, and now and then ventures upon a difficult foreign experiment, as in his two Sextains and his one attempt in *terza rima*. The matter of his verse is described by himself on the title-page of his first miscellaneous volume of Poems—'Amorous, Funerall, Divine, Pastorall'—the Pastoral being of little account, and the Funeral neither better nor worse than the average of their class. What are really interesting in the poetry that he published during his life are the sonnets and songs directly inspired by Mary Cunningham—sonnets and songs that ring true, and contrast with the cold conventionality of such poems as the 'Aurora' of Drummond's friend Lord Stirling—and the grave *Flowers of Sion*. Among the posthumous poems also are some that are noticeable; one or two genuine cries of anguish at what the author thought to be the evil of the times, and a few hymns (such as the 'hymns for the week,' following the order of the days of Creation) fit to rank with many of those that have become classical.

Good as are some of the love-sonnets and madrigals, Drummond is best where he is most serious. His deepest interests are metaphysical and religious; he is for ever taking refuge from the ills of the present in meditations on Death, Eternity, the Christian Doctrine. The Universe, 'this All' as he calls it,—that conception of the earth with its concentric spheres which belonged to the older astronomy,—is an idea on which he dwells in almost monotonous fashion. The finest of all his writings, the prose tract called *The Cypresse Grove*, is a discourse upon Death, reminding us, as Mr. Masson well says, of the best work of Sir Thomas Browne; the most striking of his poems are certainly those where, as in the sonnet 'For the Baptist,' he presents in his own rich language the severer portions of the Christian history, or the inexhaustible theme of the shortness and the mystery of life. What saves him from becoming wearisome is partly the nobility of his verse at its best, its stateliness and sonorous music; partly his evident sincerity, and his emancipation, speaking generally, from the evil influences that were creeping in to corrupt English poetry at that time. His conceits, where he indulges in them, are bad indeed; the sun to him is

> Goldsmith of all the stars, with silver bright
> Who moon enamels, Apelles of the flowers;

the waves that toss the boat that holds his love have their ready explanation:—

> And yet huge waves arise; the cause is this,
> That ocean strives with Forth the boat to kiss.

But these are the accidents of his poetry, and his theory and practice are better learnt from such words as those he sent at an uncertain date to Dr. Arthur Johnston, a writer of Latin verse well known in his day. 'Poesy,' he says, 'subsisteth by herself, and after one demeanour and continuance her beauty appeareth to all ages. In vain have some men of late, transformers of everything, consulted upon her reformation, and endeavoured to abstract her to metaphysical ideas and scholastical quiddities, denuding her of her own habits, and those ornaments with which she hath amused the world some thousand years. Poesy is not a thing that is yet in the finding and search, or which may be otherwise found out.' Such is the mature view of Drummond; the view of a man who has read the best that the poets of all ages have made, has enjoyed it, has assimilated it, and will not allow himself to be drawn away from the main current by the fashion of the day. It is difficult to withhold admiration from a poet who in the first half of the seventeenth century had studied Marini and yet kept himself for the most part free from conceits; and, if we turn from his poetry to his life, it is difficult to withhold sympathy from a man whose private happiness was ruined by a fatal blow, and whose public hopes were wasted in witnessing the steady upward progress of a cause which he regarded with abhorrence.—THOMAS HUMPHRY WARD, "William Drummond of Hawthornden," *The English Poets*, ed. Thomas Humphry Ward, 1880, Vol. 2, pp. 24–27

Drummond belonged to the class of artistic or cultivated poets, to that which is made by literature rather than born of spontaneous creation. In the earliest of his sonnets, Drummond admits as much:—"I first began to read, then loved to write." But among poets of this studious and literary kind, he ranks very high indeed. He possesses style, distinction, a practised and regulated skill, in a degree denied to many of his more spontaneously gifted fellows. It would be a grave error, in any estimate of Jacobean poetry, to underrate this admirable poetic artist. . . .

His sonnets, a form in which he is peculiarly successful, approach more nearly to perfection of rhyme-structure than any of those of his contemporaries, except perhaps Donne's; but he is rarely able to resist the tempting error of the final couplet. One or two long and glowing odes of great merit he styles "songs." This first collection of his poems contains many lyrics that are admirable, and few that are without dignity and skill. He uses flowers and pure colours like a Tuscan painter, and strikes us as most fantastic when he essays to write in dispraise of beauty, since no poet of his time is so resolute a worshipper of physical loveliness as he is. In Drummond's voluptuous and gorgeous verse there is no trace of the Elizabethan *naïveté* or dramatic passion. It is the deliberate poetry of an accomplished scholar-artist.

As he grew older, Drummond became pious, but without

changing his style. His *Flowers of Sion* of 1623 are gnomic or moral, and not by any means exclusively religious. . . .

What are most remarkable, from the point of view of style, among these divine poems, are certain canzonets in which there is found such a sensuous ardour and fiery perfume as were not to be met with again in English religious verse until the days of Crashaw. In "Hymn to the Passion" we have one of the earliest, if not the very earliest, lengthy exercise in *terza rima* in our language, a *tour de force* carried out with surprising ease. More spirited is the ode on the "Resurrection," and it might be difficult to overpraise, in its own elaborate and glittering manner, the ode called "An Hymn of the Ascension." . . .

What Drummond says is never so important as the way in which he says it, and it would be as absurd to look for any spiritual fervour or record of deep experience in these *Flowers of Sion* as it would be to suppose them in any way disingenuous. The spangled style was the cassock which best suited the sincere but sensuous piety of this poetical preacher. To the *Flowers of Sion* was appended *The Cypress Grove*, a prose treatise to edification, containing some few sonnets, not the author's best.—EDMUND GOSSE, *The Jacobean Poets*, 1894, pp. 101–6

With one exception the Scottish poets of mark of the Jacobean period were something more than simple men of letters. Courtiers, statesmen, or, as in the case of the later Montrose, soldiers, the main interests of their lives lay in the world of action, and poetry was with them either the solace of hours of retirement or the outcome of experience gained in active life. William Drummond, alone of them all, can be said to have lived a life devoted to the art of poetry. To this circumstance may possibly, to some extent, be attributed the fact that of all the Scottish poets of that time he, without question, holds the highest place. . . .

Drummond's poetry, though it is limited in range, was certainly the finest English poetry of its time. . . . The chief characteristics of Drummond's verse are its lustrous beauty and its melodious sweetness. For these qualities it has been termed Spenserian, but Spenser was not its model. . . . If he appears to lack vigour and originality, as has sometimes been said, that lack is more than atoned for by the wonderful sensuous richness and perfection of his work. His genius, it is true, seems to have been unfitted for the production of any long-sustained composition, but so also, later, was the genius of Robert Burns, and it may well be doubted whether the yard-measure serves as any very valuable criterion of poetic merits.—GEORGE EYRE-TODD, *Scottish Poetry of the Seventeenth Century*, 1895, pp. 139, 151–52

The imagination of Drummond aspires to Spenser's rich standard of association and contrast: he has a refined poetic sensuousness and delight in objective imagery; his sentiment is romantic, melancholy, and musical; but the new subjective and meditative emotion which pervades his verse, and a slight involuntary tendency to the new conceits and metaphysical quiddities mark him also as one of the new age.—FREDERIC IVES CARPENTER, "Introduction" to *English Lyric Poetry, 1500–1700*, 1897, p. liii

Works

SONNETS

Without ostentatious praise (which is always to be suspected) it is but truth to observe that many of his sonnets, those more especially which are divested of Italian conceits, resemble the best Greek epigrams in their best taste, in that exquisite delicacy of sentiment, and simplicity of expression, for which our language has no single term, but which is known to all classical readers by the word αφετεια. It is in vain we lament the fate of many of our poets, who have undeservedly fallen victims to a premature oblivion, when the finished productions of this man are little known, and still less read.—HENRY HEADLEY, *Select Beauties of Ancient English Poetry*, 1787

The name of Drummond of Hawthornden is in a manner entwined in cypher with that of Ben Jonson. He has not done himself or Jonson any credit by his account of their conversation; but his Sonnets are in the highest degree elegant, harmonious, and striking. It appears to me that they are more in the manner of Petrarch than any others that we have, with a certain intenseness in the sentiment, an occasional glitter of thought, and uniform terseness of expression.—WILLIAM HAZLITT, *Lectures on the Dramatic Literature of the Age of Elizabeth*, 1820

As a poet in the broadest sense of the word, Drummond of Hawthornden ranks far below Spenser; but in the 'sonnet's scanty plot' he rules as of right divine, and even the lord of the world of faery must stand uncovered before him. There is not the same weight of matter in his sonnets that there is in the irregular sonnets of Shakspeare, nor is there the same penetrative vigour of language; but there are qualities equally precious if not equally impressive—exquisite keenness of sensibility, attested by peculiar delicacy of touch; imaginative vision and notable power of rendering it; native spontaneousness happily allied with fine mastery of the secrets of metre and melody; and the rare art—carried to perfection in the sonnets of Mr Rossetti—of making his verse the expression, not of crude passion, which, as Edgar Poe pointed out, is not genuine poetic material, but rather the reflection of passion in the still deeps of imaginative reverie. In Drummond's sonnet work, we certainly miss one characteristic which is almost a constant note of high genius, the magnificent recklessness which takes no thought of finite limitations, but boldly essays the impossible. He knew what he could do and what he could not do, and the outcome of this knowledge is a pervading equality of craftsmanship. Though almost all his sonnets are beautiful, there is not one of such overmastering beauty that it storms the citadel of the soul and takes the memory captive. We feel, and cannot help feeling, that when Drummond had exhausted his expressional possibilities, he had still a store of the raw material of poetry which remained unworked and unworkable, and he therefore remains for ever what Dr George MacDonald, with fine insight, calls him—'a *voix voilée*, or veiled voice of song.'—JAMES ASHCROFT NOBLE, *The Sonnet in England*, 1880, pp. 22–23

Drummond said that Drayton seemed rather to love his muse than his mistress, judging by his many artificial similes, which showed the quality of his mind, but not the depth of his passion. Perhaps Drummond alone of the poets of his period, excepting Shakspeare only, had just license to write so, for what he says with truth of Drayton might with equal appropriateness have been urged against all his other contemporaries save one. A wanton desire to revel in petty conceits at any sacrifice of naturalness and to all but total disregard of fundamental emotional prompting (which had the damaging effect of drawing off attention from the subject of a poem and centring it upon the poet) was of course the besetting weakness of the Elizabethan sonnet-writers. In Shakspeare's case the many felicitous thoughts felicitously expressed, in the poems spoken in his own person, are always subordinated to a mastering passion, which often leaves the mind too much exhausted by the emotional tension to be at once capable of realising the full splendour of the poetic medium. And Drummond also was free from excess of the kind that marred contemporaries possessed of more vital impulse; for much that reality of absorbing passion did for Shakspeare in preserving him from the artificial expression of affected suffering, time itself acting healingly on a great sorrow did for him. After the early book in which he told the story of his life's one loss, Drummond seemed to sit above the need of that languishing craving for love-experience which was the will-o'-the-wisp which led his contemporaries into one knows not what quagmires of poetic mockery. Drummond's sonnets are wholly devoid of those excellences of conception and phrase which, where they exist in the best of his brother poets, seem to be delved out of the full depth of a deep nature, but they are distinguished by a healthful seriousness and enlarged view of life and its operative relationships, such as must have come to him equally from his patient submission to untoward circumstance, and from the distance at which he stood removed from the irritating atmosphere of small rivalries, which in London narrowed the sympathies of men so much above him in original gift as Ben Jonson.—HALL CAINE, "Notes" to *Sonnets of Three Centuries*, 1882, pp. 277–78

THE HISTORY OF SCOTLAND

Had there been nothing extant of him but his *History of Scotland*, consider but the language, how florid and ornate it is, consider the order and the prudent conduct of the story, and you will rank him in the number of the best writers, and compare him even with Thuanus himself.—EDWARD PHILLIPS, "Preface" to *Poems by that most famous Wit, William Drummond of Hawthornden*, 1656

To take what came to hand in any easily accessible form—the mere first tea-leaves, let us say, that had already yielded three or four infusions calling themselves Histories; to get from these, by his art as a stylist, yet another weak dilution, which he could tinge with his doctrine of kingly prerogative; thus, in the guise of a new History, to inculcate the same Drummondism in politics which he had expounded more openly in his pamphlets: such was Drummond's method, and such his purpose. Even the literary ability shown in the execution of the task is not great. There is nothing graphic in the book; you are in a haze as you read; you cannot, except at a point or two, discern a group of faces, or see things happening.—DAVID MASSON, *Drummond of Hawthornden*, 1873, p. 470

THEOPHILUS CIBBER
From "The Life of William Drummond of Hawthornden Esq"
The Lives of the Poets
1753, Volume 1, pp. 302–12

This gentleman was a native of Scotland, and a poet of no inconsiderable rank. We had at first some doubt whether he fell within our design, as being no Englishman, but upon observing that Mr. Langbain has given a place to the earl of Stirling, a man of much inferior note; and that our author, though a Scotchman, wrote extremely pure and elegant English, and his life, that is fruitful of a great many incidents, without further apology, it is here presented to the readers.

He was born the 13th of November, 1585; his father was Sir John Drummond of Hawthornden, who was Gentleman Usher to King James VI. but did not enjoy that place long,

being in three months after he was raised to his new dignity, taken away by death.[1] The family of Drummond in the arcle of antiquity is inferior to none in Scotland, where that kind of distinction is very much regarded.

The first years of our author's youth were spent at the high school at Edinburgh, where the early promises of that extraordinary genius, which afterwards appeared in him, became very conspicuous. He was in due time sent to the university of Edinburgh, where after the ordinary stay, he was made Master of Arts. When his course at the university was finished, he did not, like the greatest part of giddy students, give over reading, and vainly imagine they have a sufficient stock of learning: he had too much sense thus to deceive himself; he knew that an education at the university is but the ground-work of knowledge, and that unless a man digests what he has there learned, and endeavours to produce it into life with advantage, so many years attendance were but entirely thrown away. Being convinced of this truth, he continued to read the best authors of antiquity, whom he not only retained in his memory, but so digested, that he became quite master of them, and able to make such observations on their genius and writings, as fully shewed that his judgment had been sufficiently exercised in reading them.

In the year 1600 his father sent him into France, he being then only twenty-one years old. He studied at Bourges the civil law, with great diligence and applause, and was master not only of the dictates of the professors, but made also his own observations on them, which occasioned the learned president Lockhart to observe, that if Mr. Drummond had followed the practice, he might have made the best figure of any lawyer in his time; but like all other men of wit, he saw more charms in Euripides, Sophocles, Seneca, and others the illustrious ancients, than in the dry wranglings of the law; as there have been often instances of poets, and men of genius being educated to the law, so here it may not be amiss to observe, that we remember not to have met with one amongst them who continued in that profession, a circumstance not much in its favour, and is a kind of proof, that the professors of it are generally composed of men who are capable of application, but without genius. Mr. Drummond having, as we have already observed, a sovereign contempt for the law, applied himself to the sublimer studies of poetry and history, in both which he became very eminent.

Having relinquished all thoughts of the bar, or appearing in public, he retired to his pleasant seat at Hawthornden, and there, by reading the Greek and Latin authors, enriched the world with the product of his solitary hours. After he had recovered a very dangerous fit of sickness, he wrote his *Cypress Grove*, a piece of excellent prose, both for the fineness of the stile, and the sublimity and piety of the sentiments: In which he represents the vanity and instability of human affairs; teaches a due contempt of the world; proposes consolations against the fear of death, and gives us a view of eternal happiness. Much about this time he wrote the *Flowers of Sion* in verse. Though the numbers in which these poems are wrote are not now very fashionable, yet the harmony is excellent, and during the reign of King James and Charles I. we have met with no poet who seems to have had a better ear, or felt more intimately the passion he describes. The writer of his life already mentioned, observes, that notwithstanding his close retirement, love stole upon him, and entirely subdued his heart. He needed not to have assigned retirement as a reason why it should seem strange that love grew upon him, for retirement in its own nature is the very parent of love. When a man converses with but few ladies, he is apt to fall in love with her who charms him most; whereas were his attention dissipated, and his affections bewildered by variety, he would be preserved from love by not being able to fix them; which is one reason why we always find people in the country have more enthusiastic notions of love, than those who move in the hurry of life. This beautiful young lady, with whom Mr. Drummond was enamoured, was daughter of Mr. Cunningham of Barnes, of an ancient and honourable family. He made his addresses to her in the true spirit of gallantry, and as he was a gentleman who had seen the world, and consequently was accomplished in the elegancies of life, he was not long in exciting proper returns of passion; he gained her affections, and when the day of the marriage was appointed, and all things ready for its solemnization, she was seized with a fever, and snatched from him, when his imagination had figured those scenes of rapture which naturally fill the mind of a bridegroom. As our author was a poet, he no doubt was capable of forming still a greater ideal feast, than a man of ordinary genius, and as his mistress was, as Rowe expresses it, 'more than painting can express, or youthful poets fancy when they love,' those who have felt that delicate passion, may be able in some measure to judge of the severity of distress into which our poetical bridegroom was now plunged: After the fervours of sorrow had in some measure subsided, he expressed his grief for her in several letters and poems, and with more passion and sincerity celebrated his dead mistress, than others praise their living ones. This extraordinary shock occasioned by the young lady's death, on whom he doated with such excessive fondness, so affected his spirits, that in order as much as possible to endeavour to forget her, he quitted his retirement, and resided eight years at Paris and Rome; he travelled through Germany, France and Italy, where he visited all the famous universities, conversed with the learned men, and made an excellent collection of the best ancient Greek, and of the modern Spanish, French, and Italian books. Mr. Drummond, though a scholar and a man of genius, did not think it beneath him to improve himself in those gay accomplishments which are so peculiar to the French, and which never fail to set off wit and parts to the best advantage. He studied music, and is reported to have possessed the genteel accomplishment of dancing, to no inconsiderable degree.

After a long stay of eight years abroad, he returned again to his native country, where a civil war was ready to break out. He then found that as he could be of no service by his action, he might at least by his retirement, and during the confusion, he went to the seat of his Brother-in-law, Sir John Scott, of Scots, Tarvat, a man of learning and good sense. In this interval it is supposed he wrote his *History of the Five James's, successively Kings of Scotland*, which is so excellent a work, whether we consider the exact conduct of the story, the judicious reflections, and the fine language, that no Historian either of the English or Scotch nation (the lord Clarendon excepted) has shewn a happier talent for that species of writings, which tho' it does not demand the highest genius; yet is as difficult to attain, as any other kind of literary excellence. This work was received in England with as much applause, as if it had been written by a countryman of their own, and about English affairs. It was first published six or seven years after the author's death, with a preface, or introduction by Mr. Hall of Grays-Inn, who, tho' not much disposed to think favourably of the Scotch nation, has yet done justice to Mr. Drummond; for his manner of writing, says he,

> though he treats of things that are rather many than great, and rather troublesome than glorious; yet he

has brought so much of the main together, as it may be modestly said, none of that nation has done before him, and for his way of handling it, he has sufficiently made it appear, how conversant he was with the writings of venerable antiquity, and how generously he has emulated them by a happy imitation, for the purity of that language is much above the dialect he wrote in; his descriptions lively and full, his narrations clear and pertinent, his orations eloquent, and fit for the persons who speak, and his reflections solid and mature, so that it cannot be expected that these leaves can be turned over without as much pleasure as profit, especially meeting with so many glories, and trophies of our ancestors.

. . . In the short notes which Mr. Drummond has left behind him in his own life, he says, that he was the first in the island that ever celebrated a dead mistress; his poems consist chiefly of Love-Verses, Madigrals, Epigrams, Epitaphs, &c. they were highly esteemed by his contemporaries both for the wit and learning that shone in them. Edward Philips, Milton's nephew, writes a preface to them, and observes, 'that his poems are the effects of genius, the most polite and verdant that ever the Scots nation produced, and says, that if he should affirm, that neither Tasso, Guarini, or any of the most neat and refined spirits of Italy, nor even the choicest of our English poets can challenge any advantage above him, it could not be judged any attribute superior to what he deserves; and for his history he says, had there been nothing else extant of his writings, consider but the language how florid and ornate it is; consider the order and prudent conduct of the story, and you will rank him in the number of the best writers, and compare him even with Thuanus himself: Neither is he less happy in his verse than prose, for here are all those graces met together, that conduce any thing towards the making up a compleat and perfect poet, a decent and becoming majesty, a brave and admirable heighth, and a wit flowing.' Thus far the testimony of Mr. Philips.

In order to divert himself and his friends; he wrote a small poem which he called "Polemio-Middinia"; 'tis a sort of Macronic poetry, in which the Scots words are put in Latin terminations. In Queen Anne's time it was reprinted at Oxford, with a preface concerning Macronic poetry. It has been often reprinted in Scotland, where it is thought a very humorous performance. . . .

In the time of the public troubles, Mr. Drummond, besides composing his history, wrote several tracts against the measures of the covenanters, and those engaged in the opposition of Charles I. In a piece of his called "Irene," he harangues the King, nobility, gentry, clergy and commons, about their mutual mistakes, jealousies and fears; he lays before them the dismal consequences of a civil war, from indisputable arguments, and the histories of past times. The great marquis of Montrose writ a letter to him, desiring him to print this "Irene," as the best means to quiet the minds of the distracted people; he likewise sent him a protection, dated August, 1645, immediately after the battle of Kylsyth, with another letter, in which he highly commends Mr. Drummond's learning and loyalty. Besides this work of "Irene," he wrote the "Load Star," and an "Address to the Noblemen, Barons, Gentlemen, &c." who leagued themselves for the defence of the liberties and religion of Scotland, the whole purport of which is, to calm the disturbed minds of the populace, to reason the better sort into loyalty, and to check the growing evils which he saw would be the consequence of their behaviour. . . . He had great intimacy and correspondence with the two famous English poets, Michael Drayton, and Ben Johnson, the latter of whom travelled from London on foot, to see him at his seat at Hawthornden. During the time Ben remained with Mr. Drummond, they often held conversation about poetry and poets, and Mr. Drummond has preserved the heads of what passed between them; and as part of it is very curious, and serves to illustrate the character of Johnson, we have inserted it in his life: though it perhaps was not altogether fair in Mr. Drummond, to commit to writing things that passed over a bottle, and which perhaps were needlessly advanced. It is certain some of the particulars which Mr. Drummond has preserved, are not much in Ben's favour, and as few people are so wise as not to speak imprudently sometimes, so it is not the part of a man, who invites another to his table, to expose what may there drop inadvertently; but as Mr. Drummond had only made memorandums, perhaps with no resolution to publish them, he may stand acquitted of part of this charge. It is reported of our author that he was very smart, and witty in his repartees, and had a most excellent talent at extempore versifying, above any poet of his time. . . . As our author was a great cavalier, and addicted to the King's party, he was forced by the reformers to send men to the army which fought against the King, and his estate lying in three different counties, he had not occasion to send one entire man, but halves, and quarters, and such like fractions, that is, the money levied upon him as his share, did not amount to the maintaining one man, but perhaps half as much, and so on through the several counties, where his estates lay; upon this he wrote the following verses to the King.

> Of all these forces, rais'd against the King,
> 'Tis my strange hap not one whole man to bring,
> From diverse parishes, yet diverse men,
> But all in halves, and quarters: great king then,
> In halves, and quarters, if they come, 'gainst thee,
> In halves and quarters send them back to me.

Being reputed a malignant, he was extremely harrassed by the prevailing party, and for his verses and discourses frequently summoned before their circular tables. In the short account of his life written by himself, he says, 'that he never endeavoured to advance his fortune, or increase such things as were left him by his parents, as he foresaw the uncertainty and shortness of life, and thought this world's advantages not worth struggling for.' The year 1649, remarkable for the beheading of Charles I. put likewise a period to the life of our author: Upon hearing the dismal news that his Sovereign's blood was shed on a scaffold, he was so overwhelmed with grief, and being worn down with study, he could not overcome the shock, and though we find not that he ever was in arms for the King, yet he may be said, in some sense, to have fallen a sacrifice to his loyalty. He was a man of fine natural endowments, which were cultivated by reading and travelling; he spoke the Italian, Spanish, and French languages as well as his mother tongue; he was a judicious and great historian, a delicate poet, a master of polite erudition, a loyal subject, a friend to his country, and to sum up all, a pious christian.

Notes

1. The reader will please to observe, that I have taken the most material part, of this account of Mr. Drummond, from a life of him prefixed to a 4to Edition printed at Edinburgh, 1711.

W. S. M'CORMICK
"William Drummond"
English Prose, ed. Henry Craik
1893, Volume 2, pp. 191–95

A *Cypress Grove* is a remarkable, and in some respects unique, example of sonorous poetic prose. Detached passages of similar eloquence are to be found in the prose of Drummond's contemporaries and immediate successors; none of them has maintained the same height of imaginative contemplation throughout a piece of equal length. A *Cypress Grove* is the first original work in which an English writer has deliberately set himself to make prose do service for poetry. It is a dignified "Meditation upon Death," tinged with melancholy; and the whole has unity of tone and conception. Opening with a picture of his fears as "in the quiet solitariness of the night" he thinks "on the last of human terrors," the author reflects upon the necessity and universality of death; upon the vexations, disasters, indignities, and meanness of life—where beauty, greatness, knowledge, are but vanity, "on so small a round as is this earth, and bounded with so short a course of time"; where to die young is to leave the feast before satiety; where fame is defeated by oblivion. Then, from these purely mundane views, he breaks into a train of idealistic thoughts which are put into the form of an apostrophe to his soul. Having at last fallen asleep, he sees in a dream the vision of a lost friend who reveals to him the meaning of death and the joys of eternity. A *Cypress Grove* is, therefore, not a series of "dispersed meditations," as Bacon defines his "Essay"; nor is its argument intended as a chain of connected reasoning. The meditation is imaginatively conceived; it is presented as the expression of an individual mood, rising to a natural climax, and placed in an artistic setting.

This essential character of the work has been neglected by some of its critics. It has been objected that its argument is one-sided; that the author has not given a more wholesome and bracing view of life as the scene of joyous and passionate endeavour. This is no doubt true; yet the objection is beside the mark. For it applies an alien standard to what is not an essay, but a reverie. It blames what is practically a poem on resignation to death for not depicting the joys of life. One might as reasonably complain that Milton had not mingled the moods of "L'Allegro" and "Il Penseroso." The critic is not called upon to refute poetical reflections by formal logic. His true criterion is congruity. And it is part of the success of A *Cypress Grove* that no dissonant note mars its pensive melancholy.

The most characteristic qualities of Drummond's style are wealth of imagery, variety of sentence-structure, and rhythmic flow. His metaphors are apt and pregnant; he uses similes less frequently than the writers of his age, and seldom draws them out beyond a line. The antithesis of some of the apophthegms which break the continuity of his periods is not over-strained. Two cases of word-play occur, but they are venial. The composition, though carefully elaborated, is seldom laboured or overcharged with ornament; and his ear is rarely, if ever, betrayed into a preference of sound to sense. The even pitch of subdued eloquence at which the style is maintained would prove monotonous but for the ever-changing and contrasting formation of the sentences. This skilful variation of construction, by diversifying the length and cadence of the clauses, gives to the pages of A *Cypress Grove* the peculiar charm of richly modulated music.

Drummond's idealistic bent is seen in the recurrence of certain ideas—at times of phrases and allusions. The pettiness of earthly life is a constant refrain. The earth is "a mote of dust encircled by a pond"; another time, "an anthill, and men as many pismires and grasshoppers." Again, "This globe of the earth, which seemeth huge to us, in respect of the universe and compared with that wide pavilion of heaven, is less than little, of no sensible quantity, and but as a point." He returns more than once to the image of the Ptolemaic cosmos for his conception of "the All."

On a theme so common among the Elizabethan writers, it is not strange that Drummond's treatment should occasionally echo theirs. In the Platonic apostrophe to his soul one is reminded of Spenser's Hymn to Beauty, and his stanzas on Mutability. Passages here and there seem to be paraphrases or expansions of the monologues of Hamlet and of Prospero. There is even at times a similarity of phrase, as in "The goodly fabric of this world," "This fair and admirable frame," "The rank weeds in this garden of the world," and in the recurring comparisons of the world to a stage, of life to a dream, and of death to sleep. Drummond was, as his library shows, a diligent reader of the English literature of his time; yet these parallels may be accidental. But the exact reproduction of some of Bacon's phrases in his Essay on Death proves that this at least had been closely studied. In the following—"So do little *children fear to go in the dark, and their fear is increased with tales*"; "Death nor painful is, nor evil, except *in contemplation of the cause*"—the parts italicised are transcripts of the words in Bacon's two opening sentences. When Drummond speaks of death as "being of itself as indifferent as birth," and of "the marble colours of obsequies, weeping and funeral pomp," adding "much more ghastliness unto it than otherwise it hath," he paraphrases Bacon more loosely. But Bacon's sentence (in the 1612 edition), "*There is no passion* in the mind of man *so weak*, but *masters* the fear of death," is copied as literally as Drummond's context will allow. It must not be supposed, however, that these coincidences detract from the originality of *A Cypress Grove*. The contrast between Drummond's and Bacon's works has been already emphasised.

Mr. Masson's comparison of *A Cypress Grove* with *Hydriotaphia* has been repeated by later critics. Beyond the similarity of subject there is little or nothing upon which to base it. No resemblance is traceable between the learning and wit of Sir Thomas Browne's reflections on ancient burial rites, and the poetic melancholy of Drummond. Had Browne read *A Cypress Grove* he might have applied to the author words from his *Urn-Burial*: "Many are too early old"; "Pious spirits who pass their days in raptures of futurity, make little more of this world than the world that was before it." The idealistic creed common to both writers affords some parallels of thought among the concluding pages of the *Religio Medici*. But the healthy zest in life of the busy physician is a contrast to the relaxing introspection of the recluse of Hawthornden; and their styles, where it is possible to compare them, reflect the difference between their characters.

A Cypress Grove was written under the inspiration of affliction and depression, when, as we learn from a letter to Sir William Alexander, "The loss of friends had estranged him from himself," and after he had

Twice been at the doors of death,
And twice found shut those gates which ever mourn.

It was published with his "Flowers of Zion," its counterpart in verse. We have no previous prose of his except some notes and letters, and his later writings are disappointing. The *History of the Five Jameses*, much the longest of his works, is a dull and commonplace chronicle, of no historical and small literary

value. His *Irene* and Σκιαμαχία contain some trenchant pages; but, with the rest of his tracts, their main interest consists in their revelation of Drummond's attitude during the political and ecclesiastical troubles through which he lived. He longed, like the saner spirits of his time, for tolerance and peace; and, though a royalist, he did not scruple on occasion to criticise the policy of Charles.

Though Drummond's life, except for a few short intervals, was spent in Scotland, his work belongs properly to English literature. The pure Scots dialect had in his time almost fallen out of literary use. Even Knox's prose is anglicised, and the Union of the Crowns had completed what the Reformation had begun. Drummond's friend, Sir William Alexander, with the other Scottish poets who had followed James to his English court, had taken English models for their verses. But Drummond may be regarded as the earliest prose writer in Scotland who uses English as a mother-tongue; for James, even in his later work, occasionally falls back on a northern word or idiom. As in his sonnets he attaches himself to the school of Spenser, so his prose has its place alongside that of Sidney, Raleigh, and Bacon. He was the one star in the "Σκοτία Scotorum" of his age: a late survival of the Scottish renaissance which had already disappeared before the reforming zeal of presbyteries.

HUGH WALKER
From "Poets of the XVIIth Century"
Three Centuries of Scottish Literature
1893, Volume 1, pp. 148–60

Neither the atmosphere of a court nor the life of homeless adventure is favourable to poetry; and one or other was the lot of most of the Scotchmen who cultivated the art in the early part of the seventeenth century. There was however one exception, one man whose happier star preserved him from the evils of both, and gave him just those surroundings which best suited his genius. William Drummond was the son of a Lothian laird of good position. He was born 13th December, 1585, and educated at the High School and University of Edinburgh, where he graduated in 1605. Soon afterwards he went abroad to study law; but in 1609 he was in Scotland once more; and the death of his father in the following year, making Drummond master of a competency, banished from his mind all thoughts of seriously prosecuting an uncongenial study. He retired to Hawthornden, the domain for ever associated with his name and memory, the "classic Hawthornden" and "caverned Hawthornden" of later poetry, the haunt of the modern tourist attracted thither partly by Drummond, partly by Scott, partly by the natural beauty which charmed both. The place might have been made by the gods for a poet of Drummond's meditative, romantic temperament. He felt that it suited him, and he lived there for many years a retired life whose most exciting incidents were the composition and publication of his various works. The leisure which this retirement gave him prompted Drummond to those voluminous jottings which have in many points proved so interesting to modern inquirers. Among the rest are a catalogue of his library soon after the death of his father, and various lists of the books actually read by the owner of the library between the years 1606–14. They are worthy of notice for the light they throw upon Drummond's mind and habits. The books marked as read number in all 220, including much poetry, both English and French. The contents of his library in 1610 were 267 Latin books, 35 Greek, 11 Hebrew, 61 Italian, 8 Spanish, 120 French, 50 English—a very good collection for a country gentleman of the seventeenth century, and one the linguistic proportions of which are useful to remind us how much a library of two or three centuries ago differed from a modern one.[1]

For two years Drummond seems to have read and vaguely meditated without visible result. He would probably have continued to do so longer but for the death of Prince Henry in 1612, an event which set almost every Scottish pen scribbling, and a good many English to boot. *Teares for the Death of Mœliades*, the earliest published of Drummond's works, appeared in 1613. It is a piece of about two hundred lines, of little interest or value in itself, but graceful and full of promise. It brought the author into poetic contact with Sir William Alexander, whose piece on the same subject appeared the year before. Drummond shows himself from the outset the better poet of the two; but the fame of Alexander, who was senior both as man and as author, was so much better established that when, in 1614, the pair met at Menstrie, Drummond felt himself honoured by the regard of his fellow-poet. It is to the credit of Alexander that he generously recognised the power of the younger man. The two men became fast friends, kept up a literary correspondence, and wrote sonnets and other poetic compliments to one another under the names of Damon and Alexis.

A more important event in Drummond's life, the most important perhaps of all for literature, was his meeting with a daughter of Cunningham of Barns, which seems to have taken place about this time. He fell in love with the lady, wooed and won her; the marriage day was fixed, but before it came she died of a fever. Drummond's genuine and deep affection for her and the tragic close of their love had a profound effect upon his poetry. It strengthened and confirmed the melancholy which, implanted by nature, had been nourished by the quietude of Hawthornden. It fed his mystic idealism; it gave him, both during the lady's life and after she was dead, a real subject for his muse; and thus it did much to save him from that tendency to conceits which was creeping like a canker into English poetry. This passion is the source of nearly all the poet's next publication, the *Poems: Amorous, Funerall, Divine, Pastorall*, etc., which was issued in 1616. These poems are Drummond's most valuable contribution to literature. The series of pieces commemorating his love is divided into two parts, one prior, the other subsequent to her death. Together they contain most of what is truly excellent in the author's poetry; only occasionally in later years did he rise as high. His favourite measure, and that in which he was most successful, was the sonnet, not always constructed on the strict Italian model, but generally approximating to it, and showing more regard for its rules and spirit than most of the English sonnets loosely so called of the age of Elizabeth. The best of Drummond's pieces entitle him to a place in the first rank of English sonneteers; and it is to be wondered that he has not, in virtue of these exquisite poems, taken a higher place in the rolls of literature. A few specimens will give the best idea of the grace and harmonious beauty of Drummond's verse. The first embodies a conception never long absent from his mind, and here prettily turned to account to celebrate his love:—

That learned Grecian, who did so excel
In knowledge passing sense, that he is nam'd
Of all the after-worlds divine, doth tell,
That at the time when first our souls are fram'd,
Ere in these mansions blind they come to dwell,
They live bright rays of that eternal light,
And others see, know, love, in heaven's great height,
Not toil'd with aught to reason doth rebel.
Most true it is, for straight at the first sight

My mind me told, that in some other place
It elsewhere saw the idea of that face,
And lov'd a love of heavenly pure delight;
    No wonder now I feel so fair a flame,
    Sith I her lov'd ere on this earth she came.

It is however in the second part, where he laments the death of his mistress, that Drummond is at his best. There are perhaps no sonnets in it which can be pronounced decisively superior to one or two in the former part, but it contains a much greater proportion of excellent work. The poet generally chooses to approach the subject of his love indirectly, but the following is expressly devoted to it:—

Sweet soul, which in the April of thy years
So to enrich the heaven mad'st poor this round,
And now with golden rays of glory crown'd
Most blest abid'st above the sphere of spheres;
If heavenly laws, alas! have not thee bound
From looking to this globe that all upbears,
If ruth and pity there above be found,
O deign to lend a look unto those tears.
Do not disdain, dear ghost, this sacrifice,
And though I raise not pillars to thy praise,
Mine offerings take; let this for me suffice,
My heart a living pyramid I raise;
    And whilst kings' tombs with laurels flourish
        green
    Thine shall with myrtle and these flowers be
        seen.

This again illustrates Drummond's feeling for nature and the manner in which he wove it in with the idea of his love:—

Sweet Spring, thou turn'st with all thy goodly train,
Thy head with flames, thy mantle bright with flowers;
The zephyrs curl the green locks of the plain,
The clouds for joy in pearls weep down their show'rs.
Thou turn'st, sweet youth, but, ah! my pleasant hours
And happy days with thee come not again;
The sad memorials only of my pain
Do with thee turn, which turn my sweet in sours.
Thou art the same which still thou wast before,
Delicious, wanton, amiable, fair;
But she, whose breath embalm'd thy wholesome air,
Is gone; nor gold, nor gems, her can restore.
    Neglected virtue, seasons go and come,
    While thine forgot lie closed in a tomb.

But though Drummond is happiest in the sonnet, he can manage other measures with effect. The following song reads like Herrick at his best, though it is more serious than Herrick generally is:—

O Pan, Pan, winter is fallen in our May,
Turn'd is in night our day;
Forsake thy pipe, a sceptre take to thee,
Thy locks disgarland, thou black Jove shalt be.
Thy flocks do leave the meads,
And, loathing three-leav'd grass, hold up their heads;
The streams not glide now with a gentle roar,
Nor birds sing as before;
Hills stand with clouds, like mourners, veil'd in black,
And owls on cabin roofs foretel our wrack.
    That zephyr every year
So soon was heard to sigh in forests here,
It was for her; that wrapt in gowns of green,
Meads were so early seen,
That in the saddest months oft sung the merles,
It was for her; for her trees dropt forth pearls.
    That proud and stately courts
Did envy those our shades, and calm resorts,

It was for her; and she is gone, O woe!
Woods cut again do grow,
Bud doth the rose and daisy, winter done,
But we, once dead, no more do see the sun.

In his later poetry Drummond is on the whole less successful. The *Flowers of Sion*, published in 1623 along with the *Cypresse Grove*, contains indeed some fine pieces, one of which, the sonnet "For the Baptist," may be quoted as illustrating a side of the poet's mind and work which is barely represented in the earlier poems:—

The last and greatest herald of heaven's King,
Girt with rough skins, hies to the deserts wild,
Among that savage brood the woods forth bring,
Which he than man more harmless found and mild:
His food was locusts, and what young doth spring,
With honey that from virgin hives distill'd;
Parch'd body, hollow eyes, some uncouth thing
Made him appear long since from earth exil'd.
There burst he forth: 'All ye, whose hopes rely
On God, with me amidst these deserts mourn;
Repent, repent, and from old errors turn.'
Who listen'd to his voice, obey'd his cry?
Only the echoes which he made relent,
Rung from their marble caves, 'Repent, Repent!'

As a rule however the ideas of the later poems are but repetitions of those contained in the earlier, a fact which points to the conclusion that Drummond's powers, though exquisite, were narrow in their range. This criticism is essentially true of the fine "Hymn of the Ascension": it is still more true of the "Hymn of the Fairest Fair," a characteristic poem embodying its author's philosophy of the universe. For the rest, Drummond's poems include a collection of epigrams and madrigals, some clear, some coarse, few remarkable; a number of miscellaneous pieces, some of which are interesting for their bearing on contemporary literature; and a collection of posthumous poems, many of them relating to the politics of his time, but otherwise of little value. There is also ascribed to Drummond the curious and amusing macaronic poem, *Polemo-Middinia*, to which his name was first attached in the edition published at Oxford in 1691 under the editorship of Gibson, subsequently Bishop of London. The first edition known, which was published at Edinburgh in 1584, was anonymous; and there is no evidence except tradition to connect Drummond with a composition utterly foreign to his usual tone and habit of mind.

Meanwhile the fame of Drummond was steadily growing and his reputation becoming established as the first man of letters in Scotland. The visit of James to his ancient kingdom in 1617 gave the poet a fresh opportunity of playing the courtier, and the result of his labours was the poem, *Forth Feasting*. It is startling to find the pacific, not to say cowardly sovereign described as the "Mars-daunting King"; but if the adulation is gross, it is no worse than that of others in Drummond's generation and the preceding one. The poets at that time seem to have differed chiefly, not in independence, but in the degrees of ingenuity with which their flattery was bestowed; and in this respect Drummond stands high. None of the poems composed upon the occasion of this visit can rival *Forth Feasting*. Its rhymed decasyllabic lines are smooth, polished, and pointed to a degree which at times almost anticipates Pope. The whole is skilful and full of fancy, and the close is really eloquent.

Towards the close of 1618, or in the beginning of 1619, occurred that visit from Ben Jonson which has given rise to endless controversy with regard to Drummond's character. The admirers of Jonson accuse the Scottish poet of playing the spy upon and traducing the great dramatist who was his guest and

who opened his heart in the confidence of friendship. It cannot be denied that the character at the end of the conversations is ungenerously drawn, but the conversations themselves are sufficiently innocent. There is no evidence, nor likelihood, that they were meant for publication; nor were they published till long after the writer's death. It is no doubt an uncomfortable reflection for great men that their most confidential and least considered remarks may be set down in a permanent record; and perhaps it would be wiser on the part of the listener to think that he has no right to take notes of conversations. But he who does so is not necessarily a traitor. The bitterness of Drummond's own remarks on Jonson is probably due to the angularities of that rough and massive character fretting a disposition retired, delicate, and somewhat finical. Silence would have been in better taste; but to take private notes and to add, perhaps in a moment of pique, an estimate of character, is not a grave offence. Gifford, in his zeal for Jonson, exaggerated the fault of Drummond.

Shortly after the publication of the *Flowers of Sion* the life of Drummond seems to have undergone a change. Little is known about him until in 1626 we find him unexpectedly amongst inventors; and, being a man of peace, he must needs contrive instruments of war. In 1627 he obtained a patent for the construction of a variety of military engines, and appears to have given much attention to these projects. The poetic *Paraeneticon* which he wrote for Sir Thomas Kellie's military treatise, *Pallas Armata*, shows that his interest in such matters was not limited to his own devices. In 1632 he married. A political paper written in the same year on the subject of the earldom of Stratherne, and some pieces in verse occasioned by the visit of Charles I. to Scotland in 1633, seemed to hold out some faint promise of a return to literary interests. The disturbances, however, which arose shortly after this visit proved an effectual and permanent barrier to Drummond's converse with the muses. He continued indeed to write occasional verses, but never afterwards gave his whole mind to poetry, and never produced anything quite worthy of his earlier promise. He wrote mostly in prose and upon politics, in the interest of the royalist party. Among these prose works is an ambitious and high-flown essay entitled "Irene," described on the title-page as "a remonstrance for concord, amity, and love, amongst his Majesty's subjects." A more sustained work is the *History of the Lives and Reigns of the Five James's*. It was finished about 1644, but not published till eleven years later. Drummond wrote nothing more of moment, and died in 1649.

The prose of Drummond does not fall within the subject of this essay; and all that he wrote in those years of turmoil may be passed over wthout criticism. There is however an earlier essay, which, though prose in form, has so much of the spirit of poetry that it ought to be mentioned here. This is the *Cypresse Grove*, already mentioned as having been published along with the *Flowers of Sion*. In this, unquestionably the most perfect specimen of Drummond's prose, the author happily follows the bent of his own mind, unburdened by any practical purpose. It is an essay on death, written in the spirit of Plato and ending in a dream corresponding to the Platonic myth. A number of particular hints are borrowed from Bacon's essay on Death; one passage may be traced to Ben Jonson's well-known lines, "It is not growing like a tree"; and others to other writers of the time. But Drummond has made the thoughts his own, and has woven them into a prose style often beautiful, and at its highest quite equal to the best of his poetry. The essay however as a whole is uneven. The language is at times laboured to a degree almost painful, the imagery is frequently overwrought, and sometimes degenerates into conceits. The following passage is a specimen of Drummond at his best:—

"If on the great Theatre of this Earth amongst the numberless Number of men, *To dy* were only proper to thee and thine, then undoubtedly thou hadst reason to repine at so severe and partial a Law: But since it is a Necessity, from which never any Age by-past hath been exempted, and unto which they which be, and so many as are to come, are thralled (no Consequent of Life being more common and familiar), why shouldst thou with unprofitable and nought-availing Stubbornness, oppose so inevitable and necessary a Condition? This is the High-way of Mortality and our general Home: Behold what millions have trod it before thee, what Multitudes shall after thee, with them which at that same Instant run. In so universal a Calamity (if Death be one) private Complaints cannot be heard: With so many Royal Palaces, it is no loss to see thy poor Cabin burn. Shall the Heavens stay their ever-rolling wheels (for what is the motion of them but the motion of a swift and ever-whirling wheel, which twineth forth, and again uprolleth our Life) and hold still Time to prolong thy miserable Days, as if the highest of their Working were to do Homage unto thee? Thy Death is a Pace of the Order of this *All*, a Part of the Life of this World; for while the World is the World, some Creatures must dy, and others take life."

This piece strengthens the impression derived from a study of the poems, that while Drummond was to a rare degree perfect within his own limits, his range was narrow. It is further evident that there was a certain effeminacy about his mind which made him largely the creature of circumstance. The conditions of his life were long favourable to his genius; and even in his later days the distractions under which he personally suffered would not have checked the productiveness of a robuster genius; for he was not, like Milton, a participant in the stormy events of the time. But Drummond was a hot-house plant, and even a slight breath of untempered air shrivelled him up. Probably however there is little to regret in the fact that his best poetry was all written before he was thirty. It may be doubted whether he could have done much more than repeat what he had already said. There would have been under other conditions more sonnets, sweet, musical, and melancholy, perhaps more essays on themes of mysticism; but there would have been no great poem. For a short flight Drummond can scarcely be surpassed, but his wing soon tires. His most felicitous strokes are often single lines; as in the epithets of spring in one of the sonnets already quoted, "Delicious, wanton, amiable, fair"; or, from another sonnet, "The stately comeliness of forests old." Such lines combine artistic skill with truth of description.

It is worthy of remark that both these specimens of Drummond's happiest art have reference to external nature. Whether it was due to his long retirement at Hawthornden or not may be hard to say, but the fact is certain that he had a truer, more sensitive, and more catholic taste in regard to natural scenes than any of his contemporaries, English or Scotch. Professor Veitch has remarked that he was the first to find beauty in one of the most beautiful of natural objects, a snow-clad mountain. And while he did not shrink from aspects of nature associated with ideas of cold and physical discomfort, he revelled in those which call up more pleasant reminiscences. Probably his references to nature would be regarded by some critics as artificial. But they are artificial only in the sense of being the work of a painstaking artist, who does not permit his art to degenerate into artifice or to interfere with truth.

Notes

1. These details are taken from Professor Masson's *Life of Drummond*.

JOHN WINTHROP

1588–1649

John Winthrop was born on January 12, 1588, at Edwardston, Suffolk. From 1600 to 1605 he studied at Trinity College, Cambridge, without earning a degree. Before leaving England Winthrop was a lawyer and served as chief justice and lord of Groton Manor. He set sail for the New World aboard the *Arbella* on March 22, 1630. As one of the charter members of the self-governing Massachusetts Bay Colony, Winthrop was the settlement's first governor. He wrote several pamphlets supporting strict adherence to Puritan laws in response to Sir Henry Vane's call for toleration for Anne Hutchinson. Winthrop was involved in various political intrigues, including the formation in 1643 of the New England Confederation.

Winthrop's literary fame derives from the diaries he kept from 1630 to 1649. The first volumes of his journal were published by Noah Webster in 1790, and the complete *History of New England 1630–1649* was published in 1826. Winthrop's miscellaneous writings were published by the Massachusetts Historical Society in a five-volume set, *The Winthrop Papers* (1929–47). Winthrop was also a collaborator on *The Humble Request of . . . the Company late gone for New England*, a tract in support of Puritanism written aboard the *Arbella* just before its departure. Married four times, Winthrop was the father of John Winthrop the younger, who later served as governor of Connecticut. Winthrop died on March 26, 1649, and was buried in the King's Chapel graveyard, Boston.

The Massachusetts Company proper, with their charter, had not left their final anchorage at the Cowes, near the Isle of Wight, in 1630, before the governor of that colony—John Winthrop—had made the first entry in a journal or history, which he continued from day to day, and from year to year, until his death in 1648–9. That work, too, remained in perishable manuscript for a century and a half. The original was in three volumes; the first two of which were printed, for the first time, at Hartford, in 1790, from an inaccurate copy, which had been commenced by Governor Trumbull, with a preface and dedication by the great lexicographer, Noah Webster, who subsequently confessed that he had never even read the original manuscript. It remained for one whom we now recognize, since the death of our veteran Quincy, as the venerable senior member of our Society, and its former President,—John Savage,—to decipher and annotate and edit the whole; for lo! in 1816, the third volume, of which nothing had been seen or heard for more than sixty years, turned up in the tower of the Old South Meeting-house! The Rev. Thomas Prince, the pastor of that church, who kept his library in that tower, and is known to have had all three of the volumes in 1755, died without returning this third volume to the family of the author, from whom I have the best reason to think they were all borrowed. And so in 1825–6, one hundred and ninety-five years after that first entry, on that Easter Monday, while the *Arbella* was "riding at the Cowes," these annals of the first nineteen years of the Massachusetts colony were published in a correct and complete form. But as if to illustrate the risks to which they had been so long exposed, and to signalize the perils they had so providentially escaped, one of the original volumes was destroyed by a memorable fire in Court Street, before Mr. Savage had finished the laborious corrections and annotations to which he had devoted himself.—ROBERT C. WINTHROP, "Massachusetts and Its Early History" (1869), *Addresses and Speeches on Various Occasions*, 1852–86, Vol. 3

Winthrop was an intelligent man, and familiar with some part of the English literature of his day; thus he called George Wither "our modern spirit of poetry"; and he did not do discredit to the general spirit of intelligence which pervaded the Puritan movement. His letters—even those of affection—were written in a somewhat stately style, and abounded in religious allusions and Biblical quotations. The literary style of the leading settlers of New England, it may be said here, was materially indebted to their familiarity with the grandeur and poetry of the Bible. They were well acquainted with the Geneva version, and the King James' translation had recently appeared. The letters of the Puritans almost seemed like copies of the New Testament epistles, so full were they of counsels, prayers, and benedictions.

The work bearing the somewhat ambitious title of *The History of New England* is only one of those diaries which were common in the seventeenth century. Winthrop's theme was of lasting importance, and his treatment of it was, of course, intelligent. His spirit was, on the whole, just and tolerant, special praise belonging to his accounts of his difficulties with rivals in office and influence. The record begins "Anno Domini, 1630, March 29, Monday," the day after Easter: "Riding at the Cowes, near the Isle of Wight, in the Arbella, a ship of three hundred and fifty tons, whereof Capt. Peter Milborne was master, being manned with fifty-two seamen, and twenty-eight pieces of ordnance, (the wind coming to the N. by W. the evening before,) in the morning there came aboard us Mr. Cradock, the late governour, and the masters of his two ships, Capt. John Lowe, master of the Ambrose, and Mr. Nicholas Hurlston, master of the Jewel, and Mr. Thomas Beecher, master of the Talbot, (which three ships rode then by us,—the Charles, the Mayflower, the William and Francis, the Hopewell, the Whale, the Success, and the Trial being still at Hampton and not ready when, upon conference, it was agreed, that (in regard it was uncertain when the rest of the fleet would be ready) these four ships should consort together; the Arbella to be admiral, the Talbot vice-admiral, the Ambrose rear-admiral, and the Jewel a captain; and accordingly, articles of consortship were drawn between the said captains and masters; whereupon Mr. Cradock took leave of us, and our captain gave him a farewell with four or five shot." Thus minutely—though

usually in more graceful English than this—Winthrop carries his chronicle to November 11, 1648, a little more than four months before his death. The work, as has already been said, is a diary, not properly a history; and it includes whatever would naturally be entered in the diary of a public man in a little state: meteorological accounts during the ocean voyage; the appearance of Massachusetts on landing; descriptions of notable deeds and days, religious and political; losses and gains of the colonists; accidents and peculiar experiences; trials, executions, and minor punishments; ecclesiastical and doctrinal discussions, etc. The governor's half-superstitious belief in "special providences" appears quite frequently, and the diary closes with the story of the drowning of a child in a well in a cellar, on a Sunday evening, while the parents were visiting a neighbor. On the previous evening, too, the father had "wrought an hour within night," so that the Sabbath was broken on any theory. "The father, freely in the open congregation, did acknowledge it the righteous hand of God for his profaning his holy day against the checks of his own conscience." Just before this is an account of the drowning of two children while their parents were at the lecture [sermon]. "The parents had no more sons, and confessed they had been too indulgent toward him, and had set their hearts over much upon him." . . .

The character of Winthrop somewhat resembled that of Washington: both were discreetly aristocratic, ruled wisely and conservatively, and benefited the state more than sensational or radical minds could have done. Both were unjustly accused of showing an unduly monarchical spirit, but both triumphed, and were afterward held in affectionate veneration. Winthrop—mild, firm, politic, brave—was well entitled to his election, September 7, 1643, to that almost prophetic office, President of the United Colonies of New England.—CHARLES F. RICHARDSON, *American Literature 1607–1885*, 1887, Vol. 1, pp. 91–97

His public statues in Boston and in the National Capital present him with the Holy Bible in one hand and the Charter of Massachusetts in the other. No emblematic expression could be more true. Without question he was primarily a man of religion. To himself the main purport of the work he wrought was religious. In his eyes Massachusetts was ever, before all things else, a Church. The State was for the sake of the Church, incident and subordinate to it. And this probably is the reason why he so quietly accepted and adjusted himself to changes in the interior civil polity of the commonwealth that were adverse to his judgment. They concerned the secondary interest. While in his political principles he was liberal in that large sense in which Puritanism was liberal, in his practical view of government, as between aristocracy and democracy he inclined to the former. Yet his temper was such as to make him a potent mediator between the aristocratic and democratic elements that were ever in conflict around him. By the moderating influence of his self-control, humility, disinterestedness, patriotism, the strife of rival parties was again and again so restrained as to save the State from serious detriment. In this respect he was a prototype of Abraham Lincoln. The particular service with which, above all his contemporaries, he stands identified is that of the defence of the Charter. Which is to say that he was the preeminent representative in the Massachusetts colony of the idea of independent self-government.—JOSEPH HOPKINS TWITCHELL, *John Winthrop*, 1891, p. 232

As Bradford is the historian of the Plymouth Colony, so Winthrop is the chronicler of Massachusetts Bay. He was the first governor of the Plantation, and from 1643 until his death he was governor of the united Colonies of Massachusetts.

The first entries in Winthrop's journal were made on shipboard during the long two months' voyage to New England in 1630, and the entries were continued from time to time until their author's death.

These journals, by the most prominent men in the two colonies, naturally invite comparison. Bradford's work is without doubt the better of the two. It is readable, and its literary style is excellent. Winthrop's history is dull and often unreadable. It has more historical value than Bradford's, simply because the Colony of Massachusetts Bay became of more importance than the Plymouth Plantation. Winthrop delights in recording miracles, apparitions, and monstrosities. He dwells on the darker side of Puritanism, while Bradford constantly aims to display its brighter phases.

Winthrop's history has proved a rich mine for later writers. Hawthorne probably conceived of his *Scarlet Letter* while perusing its pages. He found in it the story of "Endicott and the Red Cross," and "The Maypole of Merry Mount." Whittier's "John Underhill" and many of Longfellow's *New England Tragedies* were founded on facts obtained from this old diary.
—FRED LEWIS PATTEE, A *History of American Literature*, 1896, pp. 30–31

COTTON MATHER

From "Nehemias Americanus: The Life of
John Winthrop, Esq., Governour of
the Massachuset Colony"
Magnalia Christi Americana
1702

Let Greece boast of her patient Lycurgus, the lawgiver, by whom diligence, temperance, fortitude and wit were made the fashions of a therefore long-lasting and renowned commonwealth: let Rome tell of her devout Numa, the lawgiver, by whom the most famous commonwealth saw peace triumphing over extinguished war and cruel plunders; and murders giving place to the more mollifying exercises of his religion. Our New-England shall tell and boast of her WINTHROP, a lawgiver as patient as Lycurgus, but not admitting any of his criminal disorders; as devout as Numa, but not liable to any of *his* heathenish madnesses; a governour in whom the excellencies of Christianity made a most improving addition unto the virtues, wherein even without *those* he would have made a *parallel* for the great men of Greece, or of Rome, which the pen of a Plutarch has eternized.

A stock of *heroes* by right should afford nothing but what is *heroical*; and nothing but an extream degeneracy would make any thing less to be expected from a stock of Winthrops. Mr. Adam Winthrop, the son of a worthy gentleman wearing the same name, was himself a worthy, a discreet, and a learned gentleman, particularly eminent for skill in the law, nor without remark for love to the gospel, under the reign of King Henry VIII., and brother to a memorable favourer of the reformed religion in the days of Queen Mary, into whose hands the famous martyr Philpot committed his papers, which afterwards made no inconsiderable part of our *martyr-books*. This Mr. Adam Winthrop had a son of the same name also, and of the same endowments and imployments with his father; and this third Adam Winthrop was the father of that renowned John Winthrop, who was the father of New-England, and the founder of *a colony*, which, upon many accounts, like *him* that founded it, may challenge the first place among the English glories of America. Our JOHN WINTHROP, thus born at the

mansion-house of his ancestors, at Groton in Suffolk, on June 12, 1587, enjoyed afterwards an agreeable education. But though he would rather have devoted himself unto the study of Mr. John Calvin, than of Sir Edward Cook; nevertheless, the accomplishments of a lawyer were those wherewith Heaven made his chief opportunities to be serviceable.

Being made, at the unusually early age of *eighteen*, a justice of peace, his virtues began to fall under a more general observation; and he not only so bound himself to the behaviour of a Christian, as to become exemplary for a conformity to the laws of Christianity in his own conversation, but also discovered a more than ordinary measure of those qualities which adorn an officer of humane society. His justice was impartial, and used the ballance to weigh not the *cash*, but the *case* of those who were before him: *prosopolatria* he reckoned as bad as *idolatria*: his wisdom did exquisitely temper things according to the *art of governing*, which is a business of more contrivance than the *seven arts* of the schools; *oyer* still went before *terminer* in all his administrations: his courage made him *dare to do right*, and fitted him to stand among the lions that have sometimes been the supporters of the throne: all which virtues he rendred the more illustrious, by emblazoning them with the constant liberality and hospitality of a gentleman. This made him the *terror* of the wicked, and the *delight* of the sober, the *envy* of the many, but the *hope* of those who had any hopeful design in hand for the common good of the nation and the interests of religion.

Accordingly when the noble design of carrying a colony of chosen people into an American wilderness, was by some eminent persons undertaken, *this* eminent person was, by the consent of all, chosen for the Moses, who must be the leader of so great an undertaking: and indeed nothing but a *Mosaic spirit* could have carried him through the temptations, to which either his farewel to his own land, or his travel in a strange land, must needs expose a gentleman of his education. Wherefore having sold a fair estate of six or seven hundred a year, he transported himself with the effects of it into New-England in the year 1630, where he spent it upon the service of a famous plantation, founded and formed for the seat of the most *reformed Christianity*: and continued there, conflicting with temptations of all sorts, as many years as the *nodes* of the *moon* take to dispatch a revolution. Those persons were never concerned in a new plantation, who know not that the unavoidable difficulties of such a thing will call for all the prudence and patience of a mortal man to encounter therewithal; and they must be very insensible of the influence, which the *just wrath* of Heaven has permitted the *devils* to have upon this world, if they do not think that the difficulties of a new plantation, devoted unto the evangelical worship of our Lord Jesus Christ, must be yet more than ordinary. How prudently, how patiently, and with how much resignation to our Lord Jesus Christ, our brave Winthrop waded through these difficulties, let posterity consider with admiration. And know, that as the picture of this their governour was, after his death, hung up with honour in the State-house of his country, so the wisdom, courage, and holy zeal of his life, were an example well-worthy to be copied by all that shall succeed him in government.

Were he now to be considered only as a Christian, we might therein propose him as greatly imitable. He was a very religious man; and as he strictly kept his *heart*, so he kept his *house*, under the laws of piety; there he was every day constant in holy duties, both morning and evening, and on the Lord's days, and lectures; though he wrote not after the preacher, yet such was his attention, and such his retention in hearing, that he repeated unto his family the sermons which he had heard in the congregation. But it is chiefly as a governour that he is now to be considered. Being the governour over the considerablest part of New-England, he maintained the figure and honour of his place with the spirit of a true gentleman; but yet with such obliging condescention to the circumstances of the colony, that when a certain troublesome and malicious calumniator, well known in those times, printed his libellous nick-names upon the chief persons here, the worst nick-name he could find for the governour was *John Temper-well*; and when the calumnies of that ill man caused the Arch-bishop to summon one Mr. Cleaves before the King, in hopes to get some accusation from him against the country, Mr. Cleaves gave such an account of the governour's laudable carriage in all respects, and the serious devotion wherewith prayers were both publickly and privately made for his Majesty, that the King expressed himself most highly *pleased* therewithal, only *sorry* that so worthy a person should be no better accommodated than with the hardships of America. He was, indeed, a governour, who had most exactly studied that book, which, pretending to teach politicks, did only contain *three leaves*, and but *one word* in each of those leaves, which word was, MODERATION. Hence, though he were a zealous enemy to all vice, yet his practice was according to his judgment thus expressed: "In the infancy of plantations, justice should be administered with more lenity than in a settled state; because people are more apt then to transgress; partly out of ignorance of new laws and orders, partly out of oppression of business, and other straits. *Lento Gradu* was the old rule; and if the strings of a new instrument be wound up unto their heighth, they will quickly crack." But when some leading and learned men took offence at his conduct in this matter, and upon a conference gave it in as their opinion, "That a stricter discipline was to be used in the beginning of a plantation, than after its being with more age established and confirmed," the governour being readier to see *his own* errors than *other men's*, professed his purpose to endeavour their satisfaction with less of *lenity* in his administrations. At that conference there were drawn up several other articles to be observed between the governour and the rest of the magistrates, which were of this import: "That the magistrates, as far as might be, should aforehand ripen their consultations, to produce that unanimity in their publick votes, which might make them liker to the voice of God; that if differences fell out among them in their publick meetings, they should speak only to the case, without any reflection, with all due modesty, and but by way of question; or desire the deferring of the cause to further time; and after sentence to imitate privately no dislike; that they should be more familiar, friendly and open unto each other, and more frequent in their visitations, and not any way expose each other's infirmities, but seek the honour of each other, and all the Court; that one magistrate shall not cross the proceedings of another, without first advising with him; and that they should in all their appearances abroad, be so circumstanced as to prevent all contempt of authority; and that they should support and strengthen all under officers. All of which articles were observed by no man more than by the governour himself.

But whilst he thus did, as our New-English Nehemiah, the part of a *ruler* in managing the public affairs of our American Jerusalem, when there were Tobijahs and Sanballats enough to vex him, and give him the experiment of Luther's observation, *Omnis qui regit est tanquam signum, in quod omnia jacula, Satan et Mundus dirigunt*, he made himself still an exacter *parallel* unto that governour of Israel, by doing the part of a neighbour among the distressed people of the new plantation. To teach them the frugality necessary for those times, he abridged himself of a thousand comfortable things,

which he had allowed himself elsewhere: his *habit* was not that *soft raiment*, which would have been disagreeable to a wilderness; his table was not covered with the superfluities that would have invited unto sensualities: water was commonly his own drink, though he gave wine to others. But at the same time his liberality unto the needy was even beyond measure generous; and therein he was continually causing "the blessing of him that was ready to perish to come upon him, and the heart of the widow and the orphan to sing for joy:" but none more than those of deceased Ministers, whom he always treated with a very singular compassion; among the instances whereof we still enjoy with us the worthy and now aged son of that reverend Higginson, whose death left his family in a wide world soon after his arrival here, publickly acknowledging the charitable Winthrop for his *foster-father*. It was oftentimes no small trial unto his faith, to think how a table for the people should be furnished when they first came into the wilderness! and for very many of the people his own good works were needful, and accordingly employed for the answering of his faith. Indeed, for a while the governour was the Joseph, unto whom the whole body of the people repaired when their corn failed them; and he continued relieving of them with his open-handed bounties, as long as he had any stock to do it with; and a lively *faith* to *see* the return of the "bread after many days," and not starve in the days that were to pass till that return should be seen, carried him chearfully through those expences.

Once it was observable that, on February 5, 1630, when he was distributing the last handful of the meal in the barrel unto a poor man distressed by the "wolf at the door," at that instant they spied a ship arrived at the harbour's mouth, laden with provisions for them all. Yea, the governour sometimes made his own *private purse* to be the *publick*: not by *sucking* into it, but by *squeezing* out of it; for when the publick treasure had nothing in it, he did himself defray the charges of the publick. And having learned that lesson of our Lord, "that it is better to give than to receive," he did, at the general court, when he was a third time chosen governour, make a speech unto this purpose: "That he had received gratuities from divers towns, which he accepted with much comfort and content; and he had likewise received civilities from particular persons, which he could not refuse without incivility in himself: nevertheless he took them with a trembling heart, in regard of God's word, and the conscience of his own infirmities; and therefore he desired them that they would not hereafter take it ill if he refused such presents for the time to come." 'Twas his custom also to send some of his family upon errands unto the houses of the poor, about their *meal time*, on purpose to *spy* whether they *wanted*; and if it were found that they wanted, he would make *that* the opportunity of sending supplies unto them. And there was one passage of his charity that was perhaps a little unusual: in an hard and long winter, when wood was very scarce at Boston, a man gave him a private information that a needy person in the neighbourhood stole wood sometimes from *his* pile; whereupon the governour in a seeming anger did reply, "Does he so? I'll take a course with him; go, call that man to me; I'll warrant you I'll cure him of stealing." When the man came, the governour considering that if he had stolen, it was more out of necessity than disposition, said unto him, "Friend, it is a severe winter, and I doubt you are but meanly provided for wood; wherefore I would have you supply your self at my wood-pile till this cold season be over." And he then merrily asked his friends, "Whether he had not effectually cured this man of stealing his wood?"

One would have imagined that so good a man could have had no enemies, if we had not had a daily and woful experience to convince us that goodness it self will make enemies. It is a wonderful speech of Plato, (in one of his books, *De Republica*,) "For the trial of true vertue, 'tis necessary that a good man μηδὲν ἀδικῶν δόζαν ἔχει τῶν μεγιστήν ἀδικίας: Though he do no unjust thing, should suffer the infamy of the greatest injustice." The governour had by his unspotted integrity procured himself a great reputation among the people; and then the crime of popularity was laid unto his charge by such, who were willing to deliver him from the danger of having *all men speak well of him*. Yea, there were persons eminent both for figure and for number, unto whom it was almost *essential* to *dislike* every thing that came from *him*; and yet *he* always maintained an amicable correspondence with them; as believing that they acted according to their judgment and conscience, or that their eyes were held by some temptation in the worst of all their oppositions. Indeed, his right works were so many, that they exposed him unto the envy of his neighbours; and of such *power* was that *envy*, that sometimes he could not *stand before it*; but it was by *not standing* that he most effectually *withstood* it all. Great attempts were sometimes made among the freemen to get him left out from his place in the government upon little pretences, lest by the too frequent choice of one man, the government should cease to be by *choice*; and with a particular aim at him, sermons were preached at the anniversary Court of election, to disswade the freemen from chusing one man twice together. This was the reward of his *extraordinary serviceableness!* But when these attempts *did* succeed, as they sometimes did, his profound humility appeared in that equality of mind, wherewith he applied himself chearfully to serve the country in whatever station their votes had allotted for him. And one year when the votes came to be numbered, there were found six less for Mr. Winthrop than for another gentleman who then stood in competition: but several other persons regularly tendring their votes before the election was published, were, upon a very frivolous objection, refused by some of the magistrates that were afraid lest the election should at last fall upon Mr. Winthrop: which, though it was well perceived, yet such was the self-denial of this patriot, that he would not permit any notice to be taken of the injury. But these trials were nothing in comparison of those harsher and harder treats, which he sometimes had from the frowardness of not a few in the days of their paroxisms; and from the faction of some against him, not much unlike that of the Piazzi in Florence against the family of the Medices: all of which he at last conquered by conforming to the famous Judge's motto, *Prudens qui Patiens*. The oracles of God have said, "Envy is rottenness to the bones;" and Gulielmus Parisiensis applies it unto rulers, who are as it were the *bones* of the societies which they belong unto: "Envy," says he, "is often found among them, and it is rottenness unto them." Our Winthrop encountered this *envy* from others, but conquered it, by being free from it himself. . . .

In the year 1632, the governour, with his pastor, Mr. Wilson, and some other gentleman, to settle a good understanding between the two colonies, travelled as far as Plym-

outh, more than forty miles, through an howling wilderness, no better accommodated in those early days than the princes that in Solomon's time saw "servants on horseback," or than *genus* and *species* in the old epigram, "going on foot." The difficulty of the *walk*, was abundantly compensated by the honourable, *first* reception, and *then* dismission, which they found from the rulers of Plymouth; and by the good correspondence thus established between the new colonies, who were like the floating bottels wearing this motto: *Si Collidimur Frangimur*. But there were at this time in Plymouth two ministers, leavened so far with the humours of the rigid separation, that they insisted vehemently upon the unlawfulness of calling any unregenerate man by the name of "good-man such an one," until by their indiscreet urging of this whimsey, the place began to be disquieted. The wiser people being troubled at these trifles, they took the opportunity of Governour Winthrop's being there, to have the thing publickly propounded in the congregation; who in answer thereunto, distinguished between a *theological* and a *moral* goodness; adding, that when Juries were first used in England, it was usual for the crier, after the names of persons fit for that service were called over, to bid them all, "Attend, good men and true;" whence it grew to be a *civil custom* in the English nation, for neighbours living by one another, to call one another "good man such an one;" and it was pity now to make a stir about a civil custom, so innocently introduced. And that speech of Mr. Winthrop's put a lasting stop to the little, idle, whimsical conceits, then beginning to grow obstreperous. Nevertheless, there was one civil custom used in (and in few *but*) the English nation, which this gentleman did endeavour to abolish in this country; and that was, *the usage of drinking to one another*. For although by drinking to one another, no more is meant than an act of courtesie, when one going to drink, does invite another to do so too, for the same ends with himself; nevertheless the governour (not altogether unlike to Cleomenes, of whom 'tis reported by Plutarch, ἀηοντί οὐδεὶς ποτήριον προσέφερε, *Nolenti poculum nunquam præbuit*,) considered the *impertinency* and *insignificancy* of this usage, as to any of *those ends* that are usually pretended for it; and that indeed it ordinarily served for *no ends* at all, but only to provoke persons unto *unseasonable* and perhaps *unreasonable* drinking, and at last produce that abominable *health-drinking*, which the fathers of old so severely rebuked in the Pagans, and which the Papists themselves do condemn, when their casuists pronounce it, *Peccatum mortale, provocare ad Æquales Calices, et Nefas Respondere*. Wherefore in his own most hospitable house he left it off; not out of any silly or stingy fancy, but meerly that by his *example* a greater temperance, with liberty of drinking, might be recommended, and sundry inconveniences in drinking avoided; and his example accordingly began to be much followed by the sober people in this country, as it now also begins among persons of the highest rank in the English nation it self; until an order of court came to be made against that ceremony in drinking, and then, the *old wont* violently returned, with a *Nitimur in Veititum*.

RICHARD CRASHAW

c. 1612-1649

Richard Crashaw was born in London, probably in 1612. His father, William Crashaw, was a Puritan divine noted for his adamant opposition to Roman Catholicism. Crashaw attended the Charterhouse in London, and entered Pembroke Hall, Cambridge, in 1631. In 1634 he received a B.A. and published a collection of Latin epigrams; the following year he became a Fellow of Peterhouse, Cambridge, which was at that time a bastion of Laudian High Churchmanship. Whether he took orders at this time is not certain, but he seems to have held some sort of official post at Little St. Mary's in Cambridge. Fervently devout, he is said to have spent long nights in vigil there, and was a frequent visitor at the community of Little Gidding. In 1643, however, a Parliamentary Commission visited Cambridge and, disapproving of its Laudian leanings, stripped Little St. Mary's and the Peterhouse Chapel. Crashaw fled to the Continent.

His movements over the next few years are uncertain; he spent some time in Leyden and probably returned briefly to Oxford. By 1646 he was living in Paris and had converted to Roman Catholicism. During his stay in Paris he was introduced to Queen Henrietta Maria by Abraham Cowley, an old Cambridge friend. At Henrietta's urging Crashaw left for Rome, carrying her recommendation to Cardinal Palotto. Despite his status as a royal protégé, however, Crashaw languished unnoticed in Rome until 1649, when he was appointed to a post at the Cathedral of Loreto. He died shortly after his arrival in Loreto, on August 21, 1649.

Crashaw's reputation rests chiefly on *Steps to the Temple*, a collection of devotional poems which he published in 1646. A revised edition of *Steps to the Temple* was published in 1648 as *The Delights of the Muses*. The final edition of this collection, entitled *Carmen Deo Nostro*, was published posthumously in Paris in 1652.

Personal

Poet and *Saint*! to thee alone are given
    The two most sacred *Names* of *Earth* and *Heaven*.
The hard and rarest *Union* which can be
Next that of *Godhead* with *Humanitie*. . . .
    Thy spotless *Muse*, like *Mary*, did contain
The boundless *Godhead*; she did well disdain
That her *eternal Verse* employ'd should be
On a less subject then *Eternitie*; . . .
    Pardon, my *Mother Church*, if I consent
That *Angels* led him when from thee he went,
For even in *Error* sure no *Danger* is
When joyn'd with so much *Piety* as His.
Ah, mighty *God*, with shame I speak't, and grief,
Ah that our greatest *Faults* were in *Belief*!
And our weak *Reason* were ev'en weaker yet,
Rather then thus our *Wills* too strong for it.
His *Faith* perhaps in some nice *Tenents* might
Be wrong; his *Life*, I'm sure, was *in the right*.
And I my self a *Catholick* will be,
So far at least, great *Saint*, to *Pray* to thee. . . .
Lo here I beg (I whom thou once didst prove
So humble to *Esteem*, so Good to *Love*)
Not that thy *Spirit* might on me *Doubled* be,
I ask but *Half* thy mighty *Spirit* for Me.
And when my *Muse* soars with so strong a *Wing*,
'Twill learn of things *Divine*, and first of *Thee* to sing.
        —ABRAHAM COWLEY, "On the Death of Mr.
        Crashaw," 1650

If Crashaw was not generally popular, and if his detractors malignantly defamed him as a "small poet," a "slip of the times," and as a "peevish, silly seeker, who glided away from his principles in a poetical vein of fancy and an impertinent curiosity," he enjoyed, on the other hand, the praise of some applauded men, and a general "sweet savour" of renown in his day and generation. He is said to have been a universal scholar—versed in the Hebrew, Greek, Latin, Spanish, and Italian languages—to have made the Grecian and Roman poets his study—and to have possessed, besides, the accomplishments of music, drawing, engraving, and painting. In his habits, too, he was temperate to severity; indeed, had he not been so, his poetry would have sunk from a panegyric on God into a bitter, unintentional satire on himself.—GEORGE GILFILLAN, "The Life and Poetry of Richard Crashaw," *The Poetical Works of Richard Crashaw*, 1857, p. vii

General

Learned Reader,
The Authors friend, will not usurpe much upon thy eye: This in onely for those, whom the name of our Divine Poet hath not yet siezed into admiration, I dare undertake, that what *Jamblicus* (in vita *Pythagoræ*) affirmeth of his Master, at his Contemplations, these Poems can, *viz*. They shal lift thee Reader, some yards above the ground: and, as in *Pythagoras* Schoole, every temper was first tuned into a height by severall proportions of *Musick*; and spiritualiz'd for one of his weighty Lectures; So maist thou take a Poem hence, and tune thy soule by it, into a heavenly pitch; and thus refined and borne up upon the wings of meditation. In these Poems thou maist talke freely of God, and of that other state.

Here's *Herbert's* second, but equall, who hath retriv'd Poetry of late, and return'd it up to its Primitive use; Let it bound back to heaven gates, whence it came. Think yee, St. *Augustine* would have steyned his graver Learning with a booke of Poetry, had he fancied their dearest end to be the vanity of Love-Sonnets, and Epithalamiums? No, no, he thought with this, our Poet, that every foot in a high-borne verse, might helpe to measure the soule into that better world: *Divine Poetry*;

I dare hold it, in position against *Suarez* on the subject, to be the Language of the Angels; it is the Quintessence of Phantasie and discourse center'd in Heaven; 'tis the very Outgoings of the soule; 'tis what alone our Author is able to tell you, and that in his owne verse.

It were prophane but to mention here in the Preface those under-headed Poets, Retainers to seven shares and a halfe; Madrigall fellowes, wholse onely businesse in verse, is to rime a poore six-penny soule, a Subburd sinner into hell;—May such arrogant pretenders to Poetry vanish, with their prodigious issue of tumorous heats and flashes of their adulterate braines, and for ever after, may this our Poet fill up the better roome of man. Oh! when the generall arraignment of Poets shall be, to give an accompt of their higher soules, with what a triumphant brow, shall our divine Poet sit above, and looke downe upon poore *Homer, Virgil, Horace, Claudian?* &c. who had amomgst them the ill lucke to talke out a great part of their gallant Genius, upon Bees, Dung, froggs, and Gnats, &c. and not as himselfe here, upon Scriptures, divine Graces, Martyrs and Angels.

Reader, we stile his Sacred Poems, *Stepps to the Temple,* and aptly, for in the Temple of God, under his wing, he led his life in St. *Maries* Church neere St. *Peters* Colledge: There he lodged under *Tertullian's* roofe of Angels: There he made his nest more gladly than *David's* Swallow neere the house of God: where like a primitive Saint, he offered more prayers in the night, then others usually offer in the day; There, he penned these Poems, *Stepps* for happy soules to climbe heaven by.

And those other of his pieces intituled, *The Delights of the Muses,* (though of a more humane mixture) are as sweet as they are innocent.

The praises that follow are but few of many that might be conferr'd on him, hee was excellent in five Languages (besides his Mother tongue) *vid.* Hebrew, Greek, Latine, Italian, Spanish, the two last whereof hee had little helpe in, they were of his owne acquisition.

Amongst his other accomplishments in Accademick (as well pious as harmlesse arts) hee made his skill in Poetry, Musicke, Drawing, Limming, graving, (exercises of his curious invention and sudden fancy) to bee but his subservient recreations for vacant houres, not the grand businesse of his soule.

To the former Qualifications I might adde that which would crowne them all, his rare moderation in diet (almost Lessian temperance) hee never created a Muse out of distempers, nor with our Canary scribblers cast any strange mists of surfets before the Intelectuall beames of his mind or memory, the latter of which, hee was so much a master of, that hee had there under locke and key in readinesse, the richest treasures of the best Greeke and Latine Poets, some of which Authors hee had more at his command by heart, then others that onely read their workes, to retaine little, and understand lesse.

Enough Reader, I intend not a volume of praises, larger then his booke, nor need I longer transport thee to thinke over his vast perfections, I will conclude all that I have impartially writ of this Learned young Gent. (now dead to us) as hee himselfe doth, with the last line of his Poem upon Bishop *Andrews* Picture his Sermons

> *Verto paginas.*
> —*Look on his following leaves, and see him breath.*
> —UNSIGNED, "The Preface to the Reader," *The Delights of the Muses,* 1648

It seems that my late mention of *Crashaw,* and my quotation from him, has mov'd your curiosity. I therefore send you the whole Author, who has held a place among my other books of this nature for some years; in which time having read him twice or thrice, I find him one of those whose works may just deserve reading. I take this Poet to have writ like a Gentleman, that is, at leisure hours, and more to keep out of idleness, than to establish a reputation: so that nothing regular or just can be expected from him. All that regards Design, Form, Fable, (which is the Soul of Poetry) all that concerns exactness, or consent of parts, (which is the Body) will probably be wanting; only pretty conceptions, fine metaphors, glitt'ring expressions, and something of a neat cast of Verse, (which are properly the dress, gems, or loose ornaments of Poetry) may be found in these verses.—ALEXANDER POPE, Letter to Henry Cromwell (Dec. 17, 1710)

Crashawe possessed the requisites of a genuine poet, enthusiasm and sublimity; but he never undertook any grand or original work. His choice of Marino, a poet abounding in concetti, was injudicious; and though his translation has several passages which challenge admiration, yet as a whole it is far from pleasing. Many of his images are disgusting and absurdly gigantic, and tend rather to call up ludicrous than terrible ideas. —NATHAN DRAKE, *Literary Hours,* 1798, No. 28

Crashaw formed his style on the most quaint and conceited school of Italian poetry, that of Marino; and there is a prevalent harshness and strained expression in his verses; but there are also many touches of beauty and solemnity, and the strength of his thoughts sometimes appears even in their distortion. —THOMAS CAMPBELL, *Specimens of the British Poets,* 1819

Crashaw was a hectic enthusiast in religion and in poetry, and erroneous in both.—WILLIAM HAZLITT, *Lectures on the Dramatic Literature of the Age of Elizabeth,* 1820

These verses were ever present to my mind whilst writing the second part of "Christabel"; if indeed, by some subtle process of the mind, they did not suggest the first thought of the whole poem.—SAMUEL TAYLOR COLERIDGE, cited in Thomas Allsop, *Letters, Conversations and Recollections of S. T. Coleridge,* 1836, p. 606

I can only mention to you Quarles, a great favorite with my uncle Southey, and Crashaw, whose sacred poetry I think more truly poetical than any other, except Milton and Dante. I asked Mr. Wordsworth what he thought of it, and whether he did not admire it; to which he responded very warmly. My father, I recollect, admired Crashaw; but then neither Quarles nor Crashaw would be much liked by the modern general reader. They would be thought queer and extravagant.—SARA COLERIDGE, Letter to Mrs. Richard Townsend (Sept. 1847), *Memoir and Letters,* 1873, pp. 320–21

Had Milton, before leaving Christ's College, become acquainted with the younger versifier of Pembroke, and read his "Music's Duel," his "Elegies on the Death of Mr. Herrys," and such other pieces of verse, original or translated, as he then had to show, he would have found in them a sensuous beauty of style and sweetness of rhythm quite to his taste.

. . . On the whole, there was a richer vein of poetical genius in Crashaw than in Herbert. . . . Apart from the modified intellectual assent expressly accorded by Donne, by Ferrar, and by others, to some of the Catholic doctrines which Crashaw seems to have made his spiritual diet, we trace a more occult effect of the same influence in a rhetorical peculiarity common to many of the writers of this theological school. We cannot define the peculiarity better than by saying that it consists in a certain flowing effeminacy of expression, a certain languid sensualism of fancy, or, to be still more particular, an almost cloying use of the words, "sweet," "dear," and their cognates, in reference to all kinds of objects.—DAVID MASSON, *The Life of John Milton,* 1859, Vol. 1, Ch. 6

As a poet, his works have ever been appreciated by those most qualified to decide upon their sterling beauties, and have suggested to others (too frequently without acknowledgment) some of their finest imageries. In every volume of any pretensions to taste, designed to offer specimens of English poetry, extracts are to be found; yet, with the exception of being partially, and by no means accurately, printed in the bulky and inconvenient collections of Chalmers and Anderson, it is somewhat remarkable that, in an age when familiarity with our Old English Authors is so eagerly sought, a full reprint should have been deferred till now.—WILLIAM B. TURNBULL, "Preliminary Observations," *Complete Works of Richard Crashaw,* 1858, p. x

Having said so much on this subject, I fear I cannot point out as much in detail as I would wish, a very striking peculiarity in Crashaw's lyrical poems which seems deserving of special attention. I refer to the extraordinary resemblance both in structure, sentiment, and occasionally in expression, which many passages (that are comparatively less spoiled than others by the prevailing bad taste of Crashaw's time) bear to the lyrics of that first of England's *poet*-lyrists,—I of course mean Shelley. Strange as it may appear, there are many things in common between them. They both, at great personal sacrifices, and with equal disinterestedness, embraced what they conceived to be the truth. Fortunately, in Crashaw's case, Truth and Faith were synonymous; unhappily with Shelley the Abnegation of Faith seemed to be of more importance than the reception of any tangible or intelligible substitute. Both were persecuted, neglected, and misunderstood; and both terminated their brief lives, at about the same age, on opposite shores of the same beautiful country, whither even at that early period "The Swans of Albion" had begun to resort, there perchance in a moment of peace to sing one immortal death-song, and so die.—D. F. M'CARTHY, "Crashaw and Shelley," *Notes and Queries,* June 5, 1858, p. 419

He is perhaps, after Donne, the greatest of these religious poets of the early part of the seventeenth century. He belongs in manner to the same school with Donne and Herrick, and in his lighter pieces he has much of their lyrical sweetness and delicacy; but there is often a force and even occasionally what may be called a grandeur of imagination in his more solemn poetry which Herrick never either reaches or aspires to. —GEORGE L. CRAIK, *A Compendious History of English Literature and of the English Language,* 1861, Vol. 2, p. 20

If Richard Crashaw, a poet who, by reason of his entire devotion to his faith and his absolute purity, belongs to this group ⟨Southwell, Habington, Crashaw⟩, had written nothing except the final of "The Flaming Heart," he would deserve more fame than at present distinguishes his name. "The Flaming Heart," marred as it is by those exasperating conceits which Crashaw never seemed tired of indulging in, is full of the intense fervor which the subject—"the picture of the seraphical Saint Teresa, as she is usually expressed with seraphim beside her"—would naturally suggest to a religious and poetic mind. After what Mr. Simcox very justly calls "an atrocious and prolonged conceit," ⟨*The English Poets*⟩ this poem beautifully closes:

> O thou undaunted daughter of desires!
> By all thy dower of lights and fires;
> By all the eagle in thee, all the dove;
> By all thy lives and deaths of love;
> By thy large draughts of intellectual day,

> And by thy thirsts of love more large than they;
> By all thy brim-fill'd bowls of fierce desire,
> By thy last morning's draught of liquid fire,
> By the full kingdom of that final kiss
> That seized thy parting soul and sealed thee His;
> By all the heav'n thou hast in him,
> (Fair sister of the seraphim!)
> By all of him we have in thee,
> Leave nothing of myself in me.
> Let me so read thy life that I
> Unto all life of mine may die.

The mystical fire which lights this poem is a characteristic of all Crashaw's religious verses. "Intellectual day" is a favorite expression of his; "the brim-fill'd bowls of fierce desire" is one of those lowering conceits that occur so jarringly in Habington's poetry and that are intolerably frequent in Crashaw. Born about 1615, he began to write at a time when a poem lacking in quaint conceits was scarcely a poem, and his verse, delicate, tender, original, and singularly fluent in diction, lost much strength from this circumstance and from his habit of diluting a thought or a line until all its force was lost. No poet since his time has been given so greatly to dilution and repetition, except Swinburne. In the famous "Wishes," written to a mythical mistress,

> Whoe'er she be,
> That not impossible she
> That shall command my heart and me,

he plays with one idea, fantastically twisting it and repeating it until the reader grows weary.

In 1646, four years before his death, Richard Crashaw published "Steps to the Temple." Reading it, one may well exclaim, with Cowley:

> Poet and saint to thee alone are given,
> The two most sacred names in earth and heaven!

It glows with an impetuous devotion which is like the rush of a fiery chariot. It carries the soul upward, although an occasional earthly conceit clogs its ascending rush. And yet it is evident that the devotion of the poet was so genuine that he did not think of his mode of expression. He tore out the words that came nearest to him, in order to build a visible thought. Pope did not hesitate to borrow the finest passages in "Eloise and Abelard" from Crashaw, and there are many lines in Crashaw's poems which unite the perfect finish of Pope to a spontaneity and poetic warmth which the "great classic" never attained.

Crashaw was born in an "intellectual day" tempered by a dim religious light. His father, like Habington's, was an author, a preacher in the Temple Church, London, near which the poet was born. He took his degree at Cambridge. He entered the Anglican Church as a minister. But his views were not orthodox; he was expelled from his living, and soon after he became a Catholic. From his poems it is plain that Crashaw was always a Catholic at heart. He entered the church as one who, having lived in a half-forgotten place in dreams, enters it without surprise. Crashaw went to court, but gained no preferment. The "not impossible she" whose courtly opposites suggested the portrait never "materialized" herself. He became a priest, and died in 1650, canon of Loretto—an office which he obtained, it is said, through the influence of the exiled Queen Henrietta Maria. Crashaw's poems are better known than Habington's, though, with the exception of "Wishes," which, like Herrick's "To Daffodils," is quoted in almost every reader, and the lovely poem beginning,

> Lo! here a little volume but large book,
> (Fear it not, sweet,

It is no hypocrite,)
Much larger in itself than in its look,

they are read only in odd lines or striking couplets. Crashaw had the softened fire of Southwell with the placid sweetness of Habington. He possessed a wider range than either of them; the fact that he was at his best in paraphrases shows that he did not own the force and power which Habington had in less degree than Southwell, or that his fluency of diction and copiousness of imagery easily led him to ornament the work of others rather than to carve out his own. As he stands, any country—even that which boasts of a Shakspere—may be proud to claim him. For the fame of our three Catholic poets it is unfortunate that they wrote in the great shade of Shakspere; but in the presence of great intellectual giants they are by no means dwarfs. Flawless as men, unique and genuine as poets, they cannot die as long as the world honors goodness and that divine spark which men call poetry. They were Catholic; true alike to their faith and their inspiration; faithful, and, being faithful, pure as poets or men are seldom pure.—MAURICE F. EGAN, "Three Catholic Poets," *Catholic World*, Oct. 1880, pp. 138-40

Crashaw is full of diffuseness and repetition; in the "Wishes for his Mistress" he puts in every fantastic way possible the hope that she will not paint; often the variations are so insignificant that he can hardly have read the poem through before sending it to press. . . . He spins the 23rd psalm into three dozen couplets. The Stabat Mater is very far from being the severest of mediæval hymns, but there is no appropriateness in Crashaw's own title for his paraphrase "A Pathetical descant on the devout Plain Song of the Church," as though he were a pianist performing variations upon a classical air. He extemporises at ease in his rooms at Peterhouse, then the ritualistic college of Cambridge. Like Herbert he was a piece of a courtier, but he did not go to court to seek his fortune, he found nothing there but materials for a sketch of the supposed mistress who never disturbed his pious vigils.—G. A. SIMCOX, "Sandys, Herbert, Crashaw, Vaughan," *The English Poets*, ed. Thomas Humphry Ward, 1880, Vol. 2, pp. 195–96

Crashaw's verse is marked by some of the highest qualities of poetry. He has strong affinities to two of our great nineteenth-century poets; he has the rich imagination and sensuousness of Keats, and the subtlety of thought and exquisite lyrical flow of Shelley. Crashaw is essentially a sacred poet, and, compared with George Herbert, is his superior, judged from the purely poetic standpoint. Herbert is, in a limited degree, a popular poet; Crashaw is not, and has never been so. One of the reasons for this is (probably) the taste for artificial poetry of the school of Waller, Dryden, Pope, &c., during the seventeenth and eighteenth centuries. The fact of his being a Catholic would also deter many readers from studying his works; but, poetical thought now being wider, and religious intolerance almost a thing of the past, it may be hoped that Crashaw will soon receive the recognition which is his due.—J. R. TUTIN, "Preface" to *Poems of Richard Crashaw*, 1887, p. viii

Crashaw's sacred poems breathe a passionate fervour of devotion, which finds its outlet in imagery of a richness seldom surpassed in our language. . . . Diffuseness and intricate conceit, which at times become grotesque, are the defects of Crashaw's poetry. His metrical effects, often magnificent, are very unequal. He has little of the simple tenderness of Herbert, whom he admired, and to whom he acknowledged his indebtedness.—SIDNEY LEE, *Dictionary of National Biography*, 1888, Vol. 13, pp. 35–36

Crashaw represents sensuous Mysticism. . . . Like Quarles, (though not to the same degree), he quits the ideal point of view, the high Platonic aether. We cannot say of him, as has been said of that "Son of Light," Origen, the great founder of Christian Mysticism, that he "is never betrayed into the imagery of earthly passion used by the monastic writers," and which also marked the style of the Italian Marino, from whose "Herod" Crashaw has left a brilliant paraphrase. Yet this mode of feeling has its place; it also demands and deserves its compartment in a Sacred Anthology. Crashaw's work in poetry, as a whole, is incomplete and irregular; Pope, whilst praising him, was correct in recognizing that he was an amateur rather than an artist. It was the same with Marvell:—neither, one would say, did justice to his fine natural gift. But Crashaw has a charm so unique, an imagination so nimble and subtle, phrases of such sweet and passionate felicity, that readers who . . . turn to his little book, will find themselves surprised and delighted, in proportion to their sympathetic sense of Poetry, when touched to its rarer and finer issues.—FRANCIS TURNER PALGRAVE, *The Treasury of Sacred Song*, 1889, p. 342, Note

Crashaw is remarkable among poets for the extraordinary inequality of his work. It is impossible to open a page of his poems without being rewarded by some charming novelty of metre or language, some sudden turn of expression of melodious cadence of rhythm. But the music flags, and the moment or inspiration passes, and Crashaw sinks to earth, the child of Marini and Gongora, the weaver of trivial conceits and over-elaborate fancies. It is this inequality that has made his poetry less read than it deserves to be. Poets of as widely different schools as Pope, Coleridge, and Shelley—have each acknowledged their indebtedness to him; and Mr. Swinburne has in our own day restored some of his lyrical measures to English verse.—J. HOWARD B. MASTERMAN, *The Age of Milton*, 1897

Crashaw is in poetry as in religion an emotional ritualist; a rich and sensuous pathos characterizes his diction and his rhythms, and redeems from tastelessness conceits over-subtle and symbolical, and marked by all the extravagance of the rococo vein.—FREDERIC IVES CARPENTER, "Introduction" to *English Lyric Poetry, 1500-1700*, 1897, p. lix

His age gave the preference to Cowley, in whose odes there is unlimited ostentation of dominating ardour without the reality, the result being mere capricious and unmeaning dislocation of form. Too much of the like is there in Crashaw; but every now and again he ascends into real fervour, such as makes metre and diction plastic to its own shaping spirit of inevitable rightness. This is the eminent praise of Crashaw, that he marks an epoch, a turn of the tide in English lyric, though the crest of the tide was not to come till long after, though—like all first innovators—he not only suffered present neglect, but has been overshadowed by those who came a century after him. He is fraught with suggestion—infinite suggestion. More than one poet has drawn much from him, yet much remains to be drawn. But it is not only for poets he exists. Those who read for enjoyment can find in him abundant delight, if they will be content (as they are content with Wordsworth) to grope through his plenteous infelicity. He is no poet of the human and household emotions; he has not pathos, or warm love, or any of the qualities which come home to the natural kindly race of men. But how fecund is his brilliant imagery, rapturous ethereality. He has, at his best, an extraordinary cunning of diction, cleaving like gold-leaf to its object. In such a poem as "The Musician and the Nightingale" the marvel of diction becomes even too conscious; in the moment of wondering at the miracle, we feel that the miracle is too researched: it is the feat of an amazing gymnast in words rather than of an unpremeditating angel. Yet this poem is an extraordinary verbal achievement, and there are numerous other examples in which the miracle seems as unconscious as admirable.—FRANCIS THOMPSON, "Excursions in Criticism," *Academy*, Nov. 20, 1897, p. 427

A more ardent temperament than either Herbert's or Vaughan's, a more soaring and glowing lyrical genius, belonged to Richard Crashaw (1613–1649). The son of a Puritan preacher who denounced the Pope as Antichrist, Crashaw at Cambridge came under the influence of that powerful wave of reaction of which the Laudian movement was only a symptom. His artistic temperament felt the charm of church music and architecture, and his ardent disposition responded, like the Dutch Vondel's, to the Catholic glorification of love as well as faith, the devotion to Christ and the Virgin of the martyr and the saint. He read Italian and Spanish, and was infected by the taste for what one might call the religious confectionery of which Marino's poems are full. His *Epigrammata Sacra* (1634) elaborate with great cleverness and point tender and pious conceits. Of his English poems, the secular *Delights of the Muses* (1648) include experiments in conceit and metrical effect such as *Love's Duel* and *Wishes*, and eulogies in the highly abstract style of Donne's, with less of thought and more of sentiment. But his most characteristic and individual work is the religious poetry contained in the *Steps to the Temple* (1646) written before, and the *Carmen Deo Nostro* (1652) published in Paris after his ardent nature and the failure of Laud's endeavour had driven him to seek shelter in the bosom of the Roman Church, poems on all the favourite subjects of Catholic devotion—the Name of Christ, the Virgin, Mary Magdalene weeping, martyrs, saints, and festivals.

Crashaw's style may have been influenced by Marino as well as Donne. His conceits are frequently of the physical and luscious character, to which the Italian tended always, the English poet never. He translated the first canto of the *Strage degli Innocenti*, frequently intensifying the imaginative effect, at other times making the conceit more pointed and witty, occasionally going further in the direction of confectionery even than Marino. The latter does not describe hell as a "shop of woes," nor say that the Wise Men went—

Westward to find the world's true Orient

nor would Marino, I think, speak of the Magdalen's tears as flowing upward to become the cream upon the Milky Way. Marino's early and purer style in religious poetry is better represented by Drummond's sacred sonnets.

But if Crashaw's taste in conceits is at times worse than Marino's, his lyrical inspiration is stronger, his spiritual ecstasies more ardent. There is more of Vondel than Marino in the atmosphere of his religious poetry. The northern temperament vibrates with a fuller music. His hymn, *On the Glorious Assumption*, is written in the same exalted strain as Vondel's dedication of the *Brieven der Heilige Maeghden*, but Vondel's style is simpler and more masculine. Crashaw's fire is too often coloured—"happy fireworks" is the epithet he applies to his beloved Saint Theresa's writings—but its glow is unmistakable, and occasionally, as in the closing lines of *The Flaming Heart*, it is purified by its own ardour.—HERBERT J. C. GRIERSON, "English Poetry," *The First Half of the Seventeenth Century*, 1906, pp. 169-71

GEORGE GILFILLAN
From "The Life and Poetry of Richard Crashaw"
Poetical Works of Richard Crashaw
1857, pp. viii–xviii

From the beginning of his being, Crashaw was a Catholic; and in saying so, we deem that we have stated at once the source of his poetic weakness and strength, as well as that of all men of genius similarly situated. Roman Catholicism, in our judgment, is not Christianity; but, by dwelling in its neighbourhood, and trying to mimic its marvellous results, it has imbibed a portion of its spirit, and bears nearly that relation to it which Judaism would have done, had it been contemporaneous with, instead of prior to the Christian scheme. Besides, the admixture of fiction, the amount of ceremony, the quantity to be *supposed*, to be implicitly believed, to be loved without reason, and admitted without proof,—all this renders Popery favourable to the exercise of the poetic imagination; while, on the other hand, the false and useless mystery, the tame subjection it requires of soul and heart and intellect, its "proud limitary spirit," the routine of idle monotonous rite,— stamp a certain vulgarity upon it, against which the wings of lofty genius have to struggle, and often to struggle in vain. In Crashaw, the struggle is generally successful. He looks at Popery, not as Dryden does, through the cold medium of the intellect, but through the burning haze of the imagination. His spirit is generally that of a true Christian poet, although considerably perverted by a false and bad form of the religion. In soaring imagination, in gorgeous language, in ardent enthusiasm, and in ecstasy of lyrical movement, Crashaw very much resembles Shelley, and may be called indeed the Christian Shelley.

> His raptures are,
> All air and fire.

His verse is pervaded everywhere by that fine madness, characteristic of the higher order of bards.

There can, we think, be little doubt that a great deal of Popish, and not a little of Protestant piety, is animalism inverted and transfigured. The saying of Pope about lust, "through certain strainers well-refined," becoming "gentle love," admits of another application. Desire, thrown into a new channel, becomes devotion—devotion sincere and strong, although assuming a spurious and exaggerated form. Hence in some writers, the same epithets are applied to the Saviour and to God, which in others are used to the objects of earthly tenderness, and we are disgusted with a profusion of "sweet Saviour," "dear lovely Jesus," &c. In the writings of the mystics, in the poems for instance of Madame Guion, you see a temperament of the warmest kind turned into the channel of a high-soaring and rather superstitious piety. Conceive of Anacreon converted, and beginning to sing of celestial love, in the same numbers with which he had previously chanted the praises of women and wine! Nay, we need not make any such supposition. Moore—the modern Anacreon—has written Hebrew melodies, in which you find something of the same lusciousness of tone as in Tom Little's poems; the *nature* coming out irresistibly in both. We are far from questioning the sincerity of these writers, and far from denying that they are better employed when singing of Divine things, than when fanning the flames of earthly passion; but we should ever be ready, while reading their strains, to *subtract* a good deal on account of their temperament. Such writers too frequently become mawkish, and loathsomely sweet, and thus at once repel the tasteful and gratify the profane. Croly says, somewhere, "our religion is a *manly* religion," but we would not refer those who wished a proof of this to the love-sick and sentimental class in question, who seem to prefer Solomon's Song to every other book of the Bible, and without the excuse of oriental day, discover all the languor and voluptuousness of the oriental bosom. There is, too, considerable danger of a reaction on their part—that the fire, after turning up its crest for a season toward heaven, should sink into its old furnace again, and that then their "last state should be worse than the first."

These remarks apply in some measure to Crashaw, although the strength of his genius in a measure counteracts the impression. Yet, often you hear the language of earthly instead of celestial love, and discover a certain swooning, languishing voluptuousness of feeling, as when in his lines on Teresa, he says:

> Oh, what delight when she shall stand,
> And teach *thy lips Heaven* with her hand,
> On which thou now may'st to thy wishes
> Heap up thy *consecrated kisses*.
> What joy shall seize thy soul when she,
> Bending her blessed eyes on thee,
> Those second smiles of Heaven, shall dart
> Her mild rays through thy *melting* heart.

More offensive are the following lines on "The Wounds of our Crucified Lord:"

> O thou, that on this foot hast laid,
>   Many a kiss, and many a tear,
> Now thou shalt have all repaid,
>   Whatsoe'er thy charges were.
> This foot hath got a mouth and lips,
>   To pay the *sweet sum of thy kisses*;
> To pay thy tears, an eye that weeps,
>   Instead of tears, such gems as this is.

We may remark, in passing, how different and how far superior is Milton's language in reference to women to that of the Crashaw school! How respectful, dignified, admiring, yet modest and delicate, all Milton's allusions to female beauty! How different from the tone of languishment, the everlasting talk about "sighs," and "kisses," and "bosoms," found in some parts of our poet! Milton seems as much struck with woman's resemblance to, as with her difference from man, and regards her as a fainter stamp of the same Divine image—fainter but more exquisitely finished: her smile that of man, dying away in a dimple of loveliness, the lovelier for the dissolution; her eye his, less, but seeming sometimes larger from the tenderness with which it is filled; her brow his, in minia-desire, and shedding a mild steadfast moonlight on the whole picture and scheme of things;—all this, and much more than all this, to be found in Roman Catholicism, is calculated to please the fancy or delight the taste, or to rouse and rivet the imagination. All this Milton, as well as Crashaw, understood and felt; but he had the intellectual strength and moral hardihood to resist their fascination. He entered the splendid Catholic temple, and he did not refuse his admiration, he bathed his brow in the "dim religious light," he praised the pictures, he was ravished with the music, but he did not remain to worship; he turned away in sorrow and in anger, saying, "It is iniquity, even the solemn meeting: your new moons and your appointed feasts my soul hateth: they are a trouble unto me; I am weary to bear them." Crashaw, on the other hand, seems, without a struggle, to have yielded to the soft seductions of the system, and was soon sighingly but luxuriously lost.

He is a strong man, but no Milton—nay, rather a strong man unnerved by perfumes and lulled with unhealthy opiates—who writes the following lines "in a prayer-book:"

> Am'rous languishments, luminous trances,
>   Sights which are not seen with eyes,
> Spiritual and soul-piercing glances,
>   Whose pure and subtle lightning flies
> Home to the heart, and sets the house on fire,
> And melts it down in sweet desire,
>   Yet doth not stay
> To ask the windows' leave to pass that way.
> Delicious deaths, soft exhalations
> Of soul! dear, and divine annihilations!
>   A thousand unknown rites
>   Of joys, and rarefied delights;
> An hundred thousand loves and graces,
>   And many a mystic thing,
>   Which the divine embraces
> Of th' dear spouse of spirits with them will bring.

If our readers will turn to Shelley, and read his "Lines addressed to the noble and unfortunate Lady Emilia V—," they will find extremes meeting, and that the sceptical Shelley, and the Roman Catholic Crashaw, write, the one of earthly, nay, illicit love, and the other of spiritual communion, in language marvellously similar both in beauty and extravagance. These two poets resembled each other in the weakness that was bound up with their strength. Their fault was an excess of the emotional—a morbid excitability and enthusiasm, which in Shelley, and probably in Crashaw too, sprung from a scrofulous habit and a consumptive tendency. Shelley's conception of love, however, is in general purer and more ideal than that of the other poet.

Crashaw's volume is a small one, and yet small as it is, it contains a good deal of that quaint and tricky conceit, which Johnson has called, by a signal misnomer, "metaphysic." Crashaw, at least, has never mingled metaphysics with his poetry, although here and there he is as fantastic as Donne or Cowley, or any of the class. For instance, he writes thus on the text—"And he answered them nothing:"

> O mighty Nothing! unto thee,
> Nothing, we owe all things that be;
> God spake once when he all things made,
> He saved all when he nothing said.
> The world was made by Nothing then;
> 'Tis made by Nothing now again.

Johnson valued himself on his brief but vigorous account of the "Metaphysical Poets," in his *Life of Cowley*. We think, however, with all deference to his high critical authority, that not only has he used the word "metaphysical" in an arbitrary and inapposite sense, but that he has besides confounded wit with perverted ingenuity, and very much under-rated the genius of the men. He calls them, after Dryden, "wits, not poets," but if wit is almost always held to signify a *sudden perception of analogies more or less recondite*, along with a TENDENCY *to the ludicrous*, then these writers have very little of the quality indeed. They see and shew remote analogies, but the analogies are too remote or too grave to excite any laughable emotion. Coming from far—coming as captives—and coming violently chained together in pairs, they produce rather wonder, tinctured with melancholy, than that vivid delight which creates smiles, if it does not explode into laughter. Sometimes, indeed, the conceits produce a ridiculous effect, but this arises rather from their absurdity than their wit. Who can laugh, however, at such lines as these describing God harmonising the chaos?

> Water and air he for the *Tenor* chose,
> Earth made the *Base*—the *Treble* flame arose.

But apart from their perverted ingenuity, their straining after effect, their profusion of small and often crooked points, and their desire to shew their learning, these writers had undoubtedly high imagination. Cowley, in his poetry and in his prose, has given undeniable evidences of a genius at once versatile, elegant, and powerful—nay, we venture to uphold the great poetical merit of some of the lines Johnson quotes from him to condemn—of the following for example:

> His bloody eyes he *hurls* round; his sharp paws
> Tear up the ground—then runs he wild about,
> Lashing his angry tail, and roaring out;
> Beasts creep into their dens, and tremble there.
> Trees, though no wind is stirring, shake for fear;
> Silence and horror fill the place around,
> *Echo itself dares scarce repeat the sound.*

These are bold metaphors, but they are not conceits. We feel them to rise naturally out of, and exactly to measure the majesty of the theme, not like conceits, to be *arbitrarily embossed* upon the shield of a subject, without any regard to its size, proportions, or general effect. We are happy to find De Quincy coinciding in part with our opinion of Johnson's criticism. Let us hear him speaking with a special reference to Donne: "Dr Johnson inconsiderately calls him and Cowley, &c., metaphysical poets, but rhetorical would have been a more accurate designation. In saying that, however, we revert to the original use of the word rhetoric, as laying the principal stress upon the management of the thoughts, and only a secondary one upon the ornaments of style. Few writers have shewn a more extraordinary compass of powers than Donne, for he combined the last sublimation of dialectical subtlety and address with the most impassioned majesty. Many diamonds compose the very substance of his poem on the Metempsychosis, thoughts and descriptions which have the fervent and gloomy sublimity of Ezekiel or Eschylus, whilst a diamond dust of rhetorical brilliance is strewed over the whole of his occasional verses and his prose. No criticism was ever more unhappy than that of Dr Johnson, which denounces all this artificial display as so much perversion of taste. There cannot be a falser thought than this, for upon that principle a whole class of compositions might be vicious by conforming to its own ideal. The artifice and machinery of rhetoric furnishes in its degree as legitimate a basis for intellectual pleasure as any other—that the pleasure is of an inferior order can no more attain the idea or model of the composition, than it can impeach the excellence of an epigram that it is not a tragedy. Every species of composition is to be tried by its own laws."

Here it will be noticed that De Quincy takes somewhat different ground from what we would take in reply to Johnson. He seems to think that Johnson principally objected to the *manner* of these writers, and he argues, very justly, that as professed rhetoricians they had a right to use the artifices of rhetoric, and none the less that they wrote in metre; and he might have maintained, besides, that finding a peculiar mode of writing in fashion, they were quite as justifiable in using it, IF they did not caricature it, as in wearing the bag, sword, and ruffles of their day. But Johnson, besides, denied that these men were poets; he objected to the *matter* as well as the manner of their song; and here we join issue with him, nay, are ready to admit that they were often rhetorically faulty, even by their own standard, if it be granted that they possessed a real and sublime poetic genius. That De Quincy agrees with us in this belief, we are certain, but it was his part to defend them upon another and a lower basis of assault. The most powerful passage in Johnson's account of the Metaphysical Poets is that in which he denies their claims to sublimity. He says with great eloquence—"The sublime was not within their reach—they never attempted that comprehension and expanse of mind,

which at once filled the whole mind, and of which the first effect is sudden astonishment, and the second rational admiration. Sublimity is produced by aggregation, and littleness by dispersion. Great thoughts are always general, and consist in positions not limited by exceptions, and in descriptions not descending to minuteness. It is with great propriety that subtlety, which in its original import means exility of particles, is taken, in its metaphorical meaning, for nicety of distinction. Those writers who lay on the watch for novelty could have little hope of greatness; for great things cannot have escaped former observation. Their attempts were always analytic; they broke every image into fragments, and could no more represent, by their slender conceits and laboured particularities, the prospects of nature or the scenes of life, than he who dissects a sunbeam with a prism can exhibit the wide effulgence of a summer's noon."

In these remarks there is much truth as well as splendour; but Dr Johnson seems to forget that with all the elaborate pettiness of much in their writings—Cowley in portions of his "Davideis;" Donne in his "Metempsychosis;" Crashaw in his "Sospetto d'Herode;" Quarles in a few of his "Emblems;" and Herbert in certain parts of his *Temple*, have, perhaps *in spite of* their own system, attained a rare grandeur of thought and language. He might have remembered, too, that in prose Jeremy Taylor and Sir Thomas Browne, who both sinned in over-subtlety and subdivision of thinking, and were "Metaphysical Prose Poets," have both produced passages surpassed by nothing, even in Milton, for sublimity of imagination. He says "Great things cannot have escaped former observation;" but surely, although all men in all ages have seen the sun, the ocean, the earth, and the stars, new aspects of them are often presenting themselves to the poetic eye: all men in all ages have seen the sun, but did all men from the beginning see him eclipsed at noonday in May 1836? all men have seen the stars, but have all looked through a Rossian telescope at the Moon, Mars, or Saturn? The truth is, Dr Johnson had great sympathy with the broad—the materially sublime and the colossally great; but, from a defect in eyesight and in mind, had little or none with either the beautiful or the subtle, and did not perceive the exquisite effects which a minute use of the knowledge of both these often produces. Of the great passages of Milton he had much admiration, but could not understand such lines as—

> Many a winding bout
> Of linked sweetness long drawn out,—

as what a poet calls it—"a charming embodiment of thin air and sound in something palpable, tangible, malleable;" nor that other wondrous line of "imaginative incarnation"—

> Rose like a steam of rich, distill'd perfumes;

nor would he have, we fear, admired Crashaw's "Music's Duel," which, altogether, we think, is not only his finest effort, but accomplishes with magical ease one of the most difficult of poetic tasks, and seems almost higher than nature. Like an Arabian sorcerer, the soul of the poet leaps back and forward, from the musician to the bird, entering into the very heart, and living in the very voice of each. Let our readers read the whole, and they will agree with us that they have read the most deliciously-true and incredibly-sustained piece of poetry in probably the whole compass of the language.

Just think of this; could Shakspeare have surpassed it?—

> Her supple breast thrills out
> Sharp airs, and *staggers in a warbling doubt*
> Of dallying sweetness, hovers o'er her skill,
> And *folds in wav'd notes with a trembling bill*

The *pliant series of her slipp'ry song*;
Then starts she suddenly into a throng
Of short, thick sobs,

We may close by strongly recommending to our readers the "Sospetto d'Herode," that fine transfusion of Crashaw's—a poem from which Milton, in his "Hymn on the Nativity," has derived a good deal; and by expressing the peculiar satisfaction with which we present the public with a handsome edition of the too little known productions of this exquisite poet.

GEORGE MACDONALD
From "Crashaw and Marvell"
England's Antiphon
1868, pp. 238–46

I come now to one of the loveliest of our angel-birds, Richard Crashaw. Indeed he was like a bird in more senses than one; for he belongs to that class of men who seem hardly ever to get foot-hold of this world, but are ever floating in the upper air of it.

What I said of a peculiar Æolian word-music in William Drummond applies with equal truth to Crashaw; while of our own poets, somehow or other, he reminds me of Shelley, in the silvery shine and bell-like melody both of his verse and his imagery; and in one of his poems, *Music's Duel*, the fineness of his phrase reminds me of Keats. But I must not forget that it is only with his sacred, his best poems too, that I am now concerned.

The date of his birth is not known with certainty, but it is judged about 1616, the year of Shakspere's death. He was the son of a Protestant clergyman zealous even to controversy. By a not unnatural reaction Crashaw, by that time, it is said, a popular preacher, when expelled from Oxford in 1644 by the Puritan Parliament because of his refusal to sign their Covenant, became a Roman Catholic. He died about the age of thirty-four, a canon of the Church of Loretto. There is much in his verses of that sentimentalism which, I have already said in speaking of Southwell, is rife in modern Catholic poetry. I will give from Crashaw a specimen of the kind of it. Avoiding a more sacred object, one stanza from a poem of thirty-one, most musical, and full of lovely speech concerning the tears of Mary Magdalen, will suit my purpose.

Hail, sister springs,
Parents of silver-footed rills!
Ever-bubbling things!
Thawing crystal! Snowy hills,
Still spending, never spent!—I mean
Thy fair eyes, sweet Magdalene!

The poem is called *The Weeper*, and is radiant of delicate fancy. But surely such tones are not worthy of fitting moth-like about the holy sorrow of a repentant woman! Fantastically beautiful, they but play with her grief. Sorrow herself would put her shoes off her feet in approaching the weeping Magdalene. They make much of her indeed, but they show her little reverence. There is in them, notwithstanding their fervour of amorous words, a coldness like that which dwells in the ghostly beauty of icicles shining in the moon.

But I almost reproach myself for introducing Crashaw thus. I had to point out the fact, and now having done with it, I could heartily wish I had room to expatiate on his loveliness even in such poems as *The Weeper*.

His *Divine Epigrams* are not the most beautiful, but they are to me the most valuable of his verses, inasmuch as they make us feel afresh the truth which he sets forth anew. In them

some of the facts of our Lord's life and teaching look out upon us as from clear windows of the past. As epigrams, too, they are excellent—pointed as a lance.

UPON THE SEPULCHRE OF OUR LORD
Here, where our Lord once laid his head,
Now the grave lies buriëd.

THE WIDOW'S MITES
Two mites, two drops, yet all her house and land,
Fall from a steady heart, though trembling hand;
The other's wanton wealth foams high and brave:
The other cast away—she only gave.

ON THE PRODIGAL
Tell me, bright boy! tell me, my golden lad!
Whither away so frolic? Why so glad?
What! *all* thy wealth in council? *all* thy state?
Are husks so dear? Troth, 'tis a mighty rate!

I value the following as a lovely parable. Mary is not contented: to see the place is little comfort. The church itself, with all its memories of the Lord, the gospel-story, and all theory about him, is but his tomb until we find himself.

COME, SEE THE PLACE WHERE THE LORD LAY
Show me himself, himself, bright sir! Oh show
Which way my poor tears to himself may go.
Were it enough to show the place, and say,
"Look, Mary; here see where thy Lord once lay;"
Then could I show these arms of mine, and say,
"Look, Mary; here see where thy Lord once lay."

From one of eight lines, on the Mother Mary looking on her child in her lap, I take the last two, complete in themselves, and I think best alone.

This new guest to her eyes new laws hath given:
'Twas once *look up*, 'tis now *look down to heaven*.

And there is perhaps his best.

TWO WENT UP INTO THE TEMPLE TO PRAY
Two went to pray? Oh rather say,
One went to brag, the other to pray.

One stands up close, and treads on high,
Where the other dares not lend his eye.

One nearer to God's altar trod;
The other to the altar's God.

This appears to me perfect. Here is the true relation between the forms and the end of religion. The priesthood, the altar and all its ceremonies, must vanish from between the sinner and his God. When the priest forgets his mediation of a servant, his duty of a door-keeper to the temple of truth, and takes upon him the office of an intercessor, he stands between man and God, and is a Satan, an adversary. Artistically considered, the poem could hardly be improved.

Here is another containing a similar lesson.

I AM NOT WORTHY THAT THOU SHOULDST COME UNDER MY ROOF
Thy God was making haste into thy roof;
Thy humble faith and fear keeps him aloof.
He'll be thy guest: because he may not be,
He'll come—into thy house? No; into thee.

The following is a world-wide intercession for them that know not what they do. Of those that reject the truth, who can be said ever to have *truly* seen it? A man must be good to see truth. It is a thought suggested by our Lord's words, not an irreverent opposition to the truth of *them*.

BUT NOW THEY HAVE SEEN AND HATED
Seen? and yet *hated thee?* They did not see—

They saw thee not, that saw and hated thee!
No, no; they saw thee not, O Life! O Love!
Who saw aught in thee that their hate could move.

We must not be too ready to quarrel with every oddity: an oddity will sometimes just give the start to an outbreak of song. The strangeness of the following hymn rises almost into grandeur.

EASTER DAY.
Rise, heir of fresh eternity,
From thy virgin-tomb;
Rise, mighty man of wonders, and thy world with
thee;
Thy tomb, the universal East—
Nature's new womb;
Thy tomb—fair Immortality's perfuméd nest.
Of all the glories make noon gay
This is the morn;
This rock buds forth the fountain of the streams of
day;
In joy's white annals lives this hour,
When life was born,
No cloud-scowl on his radiant lids, no tempest-
lower.
Life, by this light's nativity,
All creatures have;
Death only by this day's just doom is forced to die.
Nor is death forced; for, may he lie
Throned in thy grave,
Death will on this condition be content to die.

When we come, in the writings of one who has revealed masterdom, upon any passage that seems commonplace, or any figure that suggests nothing true, the part of wisdom is to brood over that point; for the probability is that the barrenness lies in us, two factors being necessary for the result of sight— the thing to be seen and the eye to see it. No doubt the expression may be inadequate, but if we can compensate the deficiency by adding more vision, so much the better for us.

In the second stanza there is a strange combination of images: the rock buds; and buds a fountain; the fountain is light. But the images are so much one at the root, that they slide gracefully into each other, and there is no confusion or incongruity: the result is an inclined plane of development.

I now come to the most musical and most graceful, therefore most lyrical, of his poems. I have left out just three stanzas, because of the sentimentalism of which I have spoken: I would have left out more if I could have done so without spoiling the symmetry of the poem. My reader must be friendly enough to one who is so friendly to him, to let his peculiarities pass unquestioned—amongst the rest his conceits, as well as the trifling discord that the shepherds should be called, after the classical fashion—ill agreeing, from its associations, with Christian song—Tityrus and Thyrsis.

A HYMN OF THE NATIVITY SUNG BY THE SHEPHERDS.

Chorus: Come, we shepherds, whose blest sight
Hath met love's noon in nature's night;
Come, lift we up our loftier song,
And wake the sun that lies too long.
To all our world of well-stolen[1] joy
He slept, and dreamed of no such thing,
While we found out heaven's fairer eye,
And kissed the cradle of our king:
Tell him he rises now too late
To show us aught worth looking at.
Tell him we now can show him more
Than he e'er showed to mortal sight—

Than he himself e'er saw before,
Which to be seen needs not his light:
Tell him, Tityrus, where thou hast been;
Tell him, Thyrsis, what thou hast seen.
Tityrus: Gloomy night embraced the place
Where the noble infant lay:
The babe looked up and showed his face:
In spite of darkness it was day.
It was thy day, sweet, and did rise
Not from the east, but from thy eyes.
Chorus: It was thy day, sweet, &c.
Thyrsis: Winter chid aloud, and sent
The angry north to wage his wars:
The north forgot his fierce intent,
And left perfumes instead of scars.
By those sweet eyes' persuasive powers,
Where he meant frosts, he scattered flowers.
Chorus: By those sweet eyes', &c.
Both: We saw thee in thy balmy nest,
Young dawn of our eternal day;
We saw thine eyes break from the east,
And chase the trembling shades away.
We saw thee, and we blessed the sight;
We saw thee by thine own sweet light.
Chorus: We saw thee, &c.
Tityrus: "Poor world," said I, "what wilt thou do
To entertain this starry stranger?
Is this the best thou canst bestow—
A cold and not too cleanly manger?
Contend, the powers of heaven and earth,
To fit a bed for this huge birth."
Chorus: Contend, the powers, &c.
Thyrsis: "Proud world," said I, "cease your contest,
And let the mighty babe alone:
The phœnix builds the phœnix' nest—
Love's architecture is his own.
The babe, whose birth embraves this morn,
Made his own bed ere he was born."
Chorus: The babe, whose birth, &c.
Tityrus: I saw the curl'd drops, soft and slow,
Come hovering o'er the place's head,
Offering their whitest sheets of snow
To furnish the fair infant's bed:
"Forbear," said I; "be not too bold:
Your fleece is white, but 'tis too cold."
Chorus: "Forbear," said I, &c.
Thyrsis: I saw the obsequious seraphim
Their rosy fleece of fire bestow;
For well they now can spare their wings,
Since heaven itself lies here below.
"Well done," said I; "but are you sure
Your down, so warm, will pass for pure?"
Chorus: "Well done," said I, &c.
       . . .
Full Chorus: Welcome all wonders in one sight!
Eternity shut in a span!
Summer in winter! day in night!
Heaven in earth, and God in man!
Great little one, whose all-embracing birth
Lifts earth to heaven, stoops heaven to earth!
       . . .
Welcome—though not to those gay flies
Gilded i' th' beams of earthly kings—
Slippery souls in smiling eyes—
But to poor shepherds, homespun things,

Whose wealth's their flocks, whose wit's to be
Well read in their simplicity.

Yet when young April's husband showers
   Shall bless the fruitful Maia's bed,
We'll bring the firstborn of her flowers
   To kiss thy feet, and crown thy head:
To thee, dear Lamb! whose love must keep
The shepherds while they feed their sheep.

To thee, meek Majesty, soft king
   Of simple graces and sweet loves,
Each of us his lamb will bring,
   Each his pair of silver doves.
At last, in fire of thy fair eyes,
Ourselves become our own best sacrifice.

A splendid line to end with! too good for the preceding
one. All temples and altars, all priesthoods and prayers, must
vanish in this one and only sacrifice. Exquisite, however, as the
poem is, we cannot help wishing it looked less heathenish. Its
decorations are certainly meretricious.

Notes

1. How unpleasant conceit can become. The joy of seeing the Saviour
was *stolen* because they gained it in the absence of the sun!

ALEXANDER B. GROSART

From "Essay on the Life and Poetry of Crashaw"
Complete Works of Richard Crashaw
1873, Volume 2, pp. lxii–lxxv

Four things appear to me to call for examination, in order
to give the essentials of Crashaw as a Poet, and to gather
his main characteristics: (*a*) Imaginative-sensuousness; (*b*) Subtlety of emotion; (*c*) Epigrams; (*d*) Translations and (briefly)
Latin and Greek Poetry. I would say a little on each.

(*a*) *Imaginative-sensuousness.* Like 'charity' for 'love,' the
word 'sensuous' has deteriorated in our day. It is, I fear, more
than in sound and root confused with 'sensual,' in its base
application. I use it as Milton did, in the well-known passage
when he defined Poetry to be 'simple, *sensuous*, and passionate;' and I qualify 'sensuousness' with 'imaginative,' that I may
express our Poet's peculiar gift of looking at everything with a
full, open, penetrative eye, yet through his imagination; his
imagination not being as spectacles (coloured) astride the nose,
but as a light of white glory all over his intellect and entire
faculties. Only Wordsworth and Shelley, and recently Rossetti
and Jean Ingelow, are comparable with him in this. You can
scarcely err in opening on any page in your out-look for it. The
very first poem, 'The Weeper,' is lustrous with it. For example,
what a grand reach of 'imaginative' comprehensiveness have
we so early as in the second stanza, where from the swimming
eyes of his 'Magdalene' he was, as it were, swept upward to the
broad transfigured sky in its wild ever-varying beauty of the
glittering silver rain!

Heauns thy fair eyes be;
   Heauens of ever-falling starres.
'Tis seed-time still with thee;
   And starres thou sow'st whose haruest dares
Promise the Earth to counter-shine
Whateuer makes heaun's forehead fine.

How grandly vague is that 'counter-shine *whatever*,' as it leads
upwards to the 'forehead'—superb, awful, Godcrowned—of
the 'heauns'! Of the same in kind, but unutterably sweet and
dainty also in its exquisiteness, is stanza vii.:

The deaw no more will weap
The primrose's pale cheek to deck:

The deaw no more will sleep
   Nuzzel'd in the lily's neck:
Much rather would it be thy tear,
   And leaue them both to tremble there.

Wordsworth's vision of the 'flashing daffodils' is not finer than
this. A merely realistic Poet (as John Clare or Bloomfield)
would never have used the glorious singular, 'thy tear,' with its
marvellous suggestiveness of the multitudinous dew regarding
itself as outweighed in everything by one 'tear' of such eyes.
Every stanza gives a text for commentary; and the rapid,
crowding questions and replies of the Tears culminate in the
splendid homage to the Saviour in the conclusion, touched
with a gentle scorn:

We goe not to seek
   The darlings of Aurora's bed,
   The rose's modest cheek,
   Nor the violet's humble head,
Though the feild's eyes too Weepers be,
Because they want such teares as we.
   Much lesse mean to trace
   The fortune of inferior gemmes,
   Preferr'd to some proud face,
   Or pertch't vpon fear'd diadems:
*Crown'd heads are toyes. We goe to meet
A worthy object, our Lord's feet.*

'Feet' at highest; mark the humbleness, and the fitness too.
Even more truly than of Donne (in Arthur Wilson's 'Elegy')
may it be said of Crashaw, here and elsewhere, thou 'Couldst
give both life and sense unto a flower,'—faint prelude of
Wordsworth's 'meanest flower.'

Dr. Macdonald (in *Antiphon*) is perplexingly unsympathetic, or, if I may dare to say it, wooden, in his criticism on
'The Weeper;' for while he characterises it generally as 'radiant
of delicate fancy,' he goes on: 'but surely such tones are not
worthy of flitting moth-like about the holy sorrow of a repentant woman! Fantastically beautiful, they but play with her
grief. Sorrow herself would put her shoes off her feet in approaching the weeping Magdalene. They make much of her
indeed, but they show her little reverence. There is in them,
notwithstanding their fervour of amorous words, a coldness,
like that which dwells in the ghostly beauty of icicles shining in
the moon' (p. 239). Fundamentally blundering is all this: for
the Critic ought to have marked how the Poet's 'shoes' are put
off his feet in approaching the weeping Magdalene; but that *she*
is approached as far-back in the Past or in a Present wherein her
tears have been 'wiped away,' so that the poem is dedicate not
so much to The Weeper as to her Tears, as things of beauty and
pricelessness. Mary, 'blessed among women,' is remembered
all through; and just as with her Divine Son we must 'sorrow'
in the vision of His sorrows, we yet have the remembrance that
they are all done, 'finished;' and thus we can expatiate on them
not with grief so much as joy. The prolongation of 'The
Weeper' is no 'moth-like flitting about the holy sorrow of a
repentant woman,' but the never-to-be-satisfied rapture over
the evidence of a 'godly sorrow' that has worked to repentance,
and in its reward given loveliness and consecration to the tears
shed. The moon 'shining on icicles' is the antithesis of the
truth. Thus is it throughout, as in the backgrounds of the great
Portrait-painters as distinguished from Land-scapists and Sea-
scapists and Sky-scapists—Crashaw inevitably works out his
thoughts through something he has looked at as transfigured by
his imagination, so that you find his most mystical thinking
and feeling framed (so to say) with images drawn from Nature.
That he did look not at but into Nature, let 'On a foule Morning, being then to take a Journey,' and 'To the Morning; Satis-

faction for Sleepe,' bear witness. In these there are penetrative 'looks' that Wordsworth never has surpassed, and a richness almost Shakesperean. Milton must have studied them keenly. There is this characteristic also in the 'sensuousness' of Crashaw, that while the Painter glorifies the ignoble and the coarse (as Hobbima's Asses and red-cloaked Old Women) in introducing it into a scene of Wood, or Wayside, or Sea-shore, his outward images and symbolism are worthy in themselves, and stainless as worthy (passing exceptions only establishing the rule). His epithets are never superfluous, and are, even to surprising nicety, true. Thus he calls Egypt '*white* Egypt' (vol. i. p. 81); and occurring as this does 'In the glorious Epiphanie of ovr Lord God,' we are reminded again how the youthful Milton must have had this extraordinary composition in his recollection when he composed his immortal Ode.[1] Similarly we have '*hir'd* mist' (vol. i. p. 84); '*pretious* losse' (ib.); '*fair-ey'd* fallacy of Day' (ib. p. 85); '*black* but faithfull perspectiue of Thee' (ib. p. 86); '*abasèd* liddes' (ib. p. 88); '*gratious* robbery' (ib. p. 156); 'thirsts of loue' (ib.); '*timerous* light of starres' (ib. p. 172); '*rebellious* eye of Sorrow' (ib. p. 112); and so in hundreds of parallels. Take this from 'To the Name above every Name' (ib. p. 60):

> O come away . . .
> O, see the weary liddes of wakefull Hope—
> Love's eastern windowes—all wide ope
>   With curtains drawn,
> To catch the day-break of Thy dawn.
> O, dawn at last, long-lookt-for Day,
> Take thine own wings, and come away.

Comparing Cowley's and Crashaw's 'Hope,' Coleridge thus pronounces on them: 'Crashaw seems in his poems to have given the first ebullience of his imagination, unshapen into form, or much of what we now term sweetness. In the poem Hope, by way of question and answer, his superiority to Cowley is self-evident;' and he continues, 'In that on the Name of Jesus, equally so; but his lines on St. Teresa are the finest.' 'Where he does combine richness of thought and diction, nothing can excel, as in the lines you so much admire,

> Since 'tis not to be had at home
>   . . .
> She'l to the Moores and martyrdom.[2]

And then as never-to-be-forgotten 'glory' of the Hymn to Teresa, he adds: 'these verses were ever present to my mind whilst writing the second part of Christabel; if indeed, by some subtle process of the mind, they did not suggest the first thought of the whole poem' (*Letters and Conversations*, 1836, i. 196). Coleridge makes another critical remark which it may be worth while to adduce and perhaps qualify. 'Poetry as regards small Poets may be said to be, in a certain sense, conventional in its accidents and in its illustrations. Thus [even] Crashaw uses an image "as sugar melts in tea away;" which although *proper then* and *true now*, was in bad taste at that time equally with the present. In Shakespeare, in Chaucer, there was nothing of this' (as before). The great Critic forgot that 'sugar' and 'tea' were not vulgarised by familiarity when Crashaw wrote, that the wonder and romance of their gift from the East still lay around them, and that their use was select, not common. Thus later I explain Milton's homeliness of allusion, as in the word 'breakfast,' and 'fell to,' and the like; words and places and things that have long been not prosaic simply, but demeaned and for ever unpoetised. I am not at all careful to defend the 'sugar' and 'tea' metaphor; but it, I think, belongs also to his imaginative-sensuousness, whereby orient awfulness almost, magnified and dignified it to him.

Moreover the canon in *Antiphon* is sound: 'When we come, in the writings of one who has revealed masterdom, upon any passage that seems commonplace, or any figure that suggests nothing true, the part of wisdom is to brood over that point; for the probability is that the barrenness lies in us, two factors being necessary for the result of sight—the thing to be seen, and the eye to see it. No doubt the expression may be inadequate; but if we can compensate the deficiency by adding more vision, so much the better for us' (p. 243).

I thank Dr. George Macdonald[3] (in *Antiphon*) for his quaint opening words on our Crashaw, and forgive him, for their sake, his blind reading of 'The Weeper.' 'I come now to one of the loveliest of our angel-birds, Richard Crashaw. Indeed, he was a bird in more senses than one; for he belongs to that class of men who seem hardly ever to get foot-hold of this world, but are ever floating in the upper air of it' (p. 238). True, and yet not wholly; or rather, if our Poet ascends to 'the upper air,' and sings there with all the divineness of the skylark, like the skylark his eyes fail not to over-watch the nest among the grain beneath, nor his wings to be folded over it at the shut of eve. Infinitely more, then, is to be found in Crashaw than Pope (in his Letter to his friend Henry Cromwell) found: 'I take this poet to have writ like a gentleman; that is, at leisure hours, and more to keep out of idleness than to establish a reputation: so that nothing regular or just can be expected of him. All that regards design, form, fable (which is the soul of poetry), all that concerns exactness, or consent of parts (which is the body), will probably be wanting; only pretty conceptions, fine metaphors, glittering expressions, and something of a neat cast of verse (which are properly the dress, gems, or loose ornaments of poetry), may be found in these verses.' Nay verily, the form is often exquisite; but 'neat' and 'pretty conceptions' applied to such verse is as 'pretty' applied to Niagara—so full, strong, deep, thought-laden is it. I have no wish to charge plagiarism on Pope from Crashaw, as Peregrine Phillips did (see onward); but neither is the contemptuous as ignorant answer by a metaphor of Hayley to be received. The two minds were essentially different: Pope was talented, and used his talents to the utmost; Crashaw had absolute as unique genius.[4]

(*b*) *Subtlety of emotion.* Dr. Donne, in a memorable passage, with daring originality, sings of Mrs. Drury rapturously:

> Her pure and eloquent soul
> Spoke in her cheeks, and so distinctly wrought,
> That one might almost say her body thought.

I have much the same conception of Crashaw's thinking. It was so emotional as almost always to tremble into feeling. Bare intellect, 'pure' (= naked) thought, you rarely come on in his Poems. The thought issues forth from (in old-fashioned phrase) the heart, and its subtlety is something unearthly even to awfulness. Let the reader give hours to the study of the composition entitled 'In the glorious Epiphanie of ovr Lord God, a Hymn svng as by the three Kings,' and 'In the holy Nativity of ovr Lord God.' Their depth combined with elevation, their grandeur softening into loveliness, their power with pathos, their awe bursting into rapture, their graciousness and lyrical music, their variety and yet unity, will grow in their study. As always, there is a solid substratum of original thought in them; and the thinking, as so often in Crashaw, is surcharged with emotion. If the thought may be likened to fire, the praise, the rapture, the yearning may be likened to flame leaping up from it. Granted that, as in fire and flame, there are coruscations and jets of smoke, yet is the smoke that 'smoak' of which Chudleigh in his 'Elegy for Donne' sings:

> Incense of love's and fancie's *holy smoak*;

or, rather, that 'smoke' which filled the House to the vision of Isaiah (vi. 4). The hymn 'To the admirable Sainte Teresa,' and the 'Apologie' for it, and related 'Flaming Heart,' and 'In the glorious Assvmption of our Blessed Lady,' are of the same type. Take this from the 'Flaming Heart' (vol. i. p. 155):

> Leaue her . . . the flaming heart:
> Leaue her that, and thou shalt leaue her
> Not one loose shaft, but Loue's whole quiver.
> *For in Loue's feild was neuer found*
> *A nobler weapon than a wovnd.*
> Loue's passiues are his actiu'st part,
> The wounded is the wounding heart.
>
> . . .
>
> Liue here, great heart; and loue and dy and kill,
> And bleed and wound; and yeild and conquer still.

His homage to the Virgin is put into words that pass the bounds which we Protestants set to the 'blessed among women' in her great renown, and even while a Protestant Crashaw fell into what we must regard as the strange as inexplicable forgetfulness that it is The *Man*, not The Child, who is our ever-living High-Priest 'within the veil,' and that not in His mother's bosom, but on the Throne of sculptured light, is His place. Still, you recognise that the homage to the Virgin-mother is to the Divine Son through her, and through her in fine if also mistaken humility. 'Mary' is the Muse of Crashaw; the Lord Jesus his 'Lord' and hers. I would have the reader spend willing time, in slowly, meditatively reading the whole of our Poet's sacred Verse, to note how the thinking thus thrills into feeling, and feeling into rapture—the rapture of adoration. It is miraculous how he finds words wherewith to utter his most subtle and vanishing emotion. Sometimes there is a daintiness and antique richness of wording that you can scarcely equal out of the highest of our Poets, or only in them. Some of his images from Nature are scarcely found anywhere else. For example, take this very difficult one of ice, in the 'Verse-Letter to the Countess of Denbigh' (vol. i. p. 298, ll. 21–26), 'persuading' her no longer to be the victim of her doubts:

> So, when the Year takes cold, we see
> Poor waters *their own prisoners be*;
> *Fetter'd and lock'd-up fast they lie*
> *In a cold self-captivity.*
> Th' astonish'd Nymphs their Floud's strange fate deplore,
> To find themselves their own severer shoar.

Young is striking in his use of the ice-metaphor:

> in Passion's flame
> Hearts melt; but *melt like ice, soon harder froze.*
> (Night-Thoughts, N. ii. l. 522–3.)

But how strangely original is the earlier Poet in so cunningly working it into the very matter of his persuasion! Our quotation from Young recalls that in the 'Night-Thoughts' there are evident reminiscences of Crashaw: *e.g.*

> Midnight veil'd his face:
> Not such as this, not such as Nature makes;
> A midnight Nature shudder'd to behold;
> A midnight new; a dread eclipse, without
> Opposing spheres, from her Creator's frown.
> (Night iv. ll. 246–250.)

So in 'Gilt was Hell's gloom' (N. vii. l. 1041), and in this portrait of Satan:

> Like meteors in a stormy sky, how roll
> His baleful eyes!
> (N. ix. ll. 280–1.)

and

> the fiery gulf,
> That flaming bound of wrath omnipotent;
> (Ib. ll. 473–4)

and

> Banners streaming as the comet's blaze;
> (Ib. l. 323)

and

> Which makes a hell of hell,
> (Ib. l. 340)

we have the impress and inspiration of our Poet.

How infinitely soft and tender and Shakesperean is the 'Epitaph vpon a yovng Married Covple dead and bvryed together' (with its now restored lines), thus!—

> Peace, good Reader, doe not weep;
> Peace, the louers are asleep.
> They, sweet turtles, folded ly
> In the last knott that Loue could ty.
> And though they ly as they were dead,
> Their pillow stone, their sheetes of lead
> (Pillow hard, and sheetes not warm),
> Loue made the bed; they'l take no harm:
> Let them sleep; let them sleep on,
> Till this stormy night be gone,
> And the æternall morrow dawn;
> Then . . . .
> (vol. i. pp. 230–1.)

The hush, the tranquil stillness of a church-aisle, within which 'sleep' old recumbent figures, comes over one in reading these most pathetically beautiful words. Of the whole poem, Dodd in his 'Epigrammatists' (as onward) remarks, 'after reading this Epitaph, all others on the same subject must suffer by comparison. Yet there is much to be admired in the following by Bishop Hall, on Sir Edward and Lady Lewkenor. It is translated from the Latin by the Bishop's descendant and editor, the Rev. Peter Hall (Bp. Hall's Works, 1837–9, xii. 331):

> In bonds of love united, man and wife,
> Long, yet too short, they spent a happy life;
> United still, too soon, however late,
> Both man and wife receiv'd the stroke of fate:
> And now in glory clad, enraptur'd pair,
> The same bright cup, the same sweet draught they share.
> Thus, first and last, a married couple see,
> In life, in death, in immortality.

There is much beauty also in an anonymous epitaph in the 'Festoon' 143, 'On a Man and his Wife:'

> Here sleep, whom neither life nor love,
> Nor friendship's strictest tie,
> Could in such close embrace as thou,
> Their faithful grave, ally;
> Preserve them, each dissolv'd in each,
> For bands of love divine,
> For union only more complete,
> Thou faithful grave, than thine.
> (p. 253.)

His 'Wishes to his (supposed) Mistresse' has things in it vivid and subtle as anything in Shelley at his best; and I affirm this deliberately. His little snatch on 'Easter Day,' with some peculiarities, culminates in a grandeur Milton might bow before. The version of 'Dies Irae' is wonderfully severe and solemn and intense. Roscommon undoubtedly knew it. And so we might go on endlessly. His melody—with exceptional discords—is as the music of a Master, not mere versification. Once read receptively, and the words haunt almost awfully, and, I must again use the word, unearthily. Summarily—as in our claim for Vaughan, as against the preposterous traditional assertions of his indebtedness to Herbert poetically, while really it was for spiritual benefits he was obligated—we cannot for an instant rank George Herbert as a Poet with Crashaw. Their piety is alike, or the 'Priest' of Bemerton is more definite, and clear of the 'fine mist' of mysticism of the recluse of 'Little St. Mary's;' but only very rarely have you in *The Temple* that light of genius which shines as a very Shekinah-glory in the *Steps to the Temple*. These 'Steps' have been spoken of as 'Steps' designed to lead into Herbert's *Temple*, whereas they were 'Steps' to the 'Temple' or Church of the Living God. Crashaw 'sang' sweetly and generously of Herbert (vol. i. pp. 139–140); but the two Poets are profoundly distinct and independent. Clement Barksdale, probably, must bear the blame of foolishly subordinating Crashaw to Herbert, in his Lines in 'Nympha Libethris' (1651):

HERBERT AND CRASHAW

When unto Herbert's Temple I ascend
By Crashaw's Steps, I do resolve to mend
My lighter verse, and my low notes to raise,
And in high accent sing my Maker's praise.
Meanwhile these sacred poems in my sight
I place, that I may learn to write.

Notes

1. The 'Epiphanie' has some of the grandest things of Crashaw, and things so original in the thought and wording as not easily to be paralleled in other Poets: *e.g.* '*Dread* Sweet' (l. 236), and the superb 'Something a *brighter shadow*, Sweet, of thee' (l. 250). The most Crashaw-like of early 'Epiphany' or Christmas Hymns is that of Bishop Jeremy Taylor, from which I take these lines:

Awake, my soul, and come away!
Put on thy best array;
Least if thou longer stay,
Thou lose some minitts of so blest a day,
Goe run,
And bid good-morrow to the sun;
Welcome his safe return
To Capricorn;
And that great Morne
Wherein a God was borne,
Whose story none can tell,
But He whose every word's a miracle.

(Our ed. of Bp. Taylor's *Poems*, pp. 22–3.)

En Passant, since our edition of Bishop Taylor's *Poems* was issued we have discovered that a 'Christmas Anthem or Carol by T.P.,' which appeared in James Clifford's 'Divine Services and Anthems' (1663), is Bishop Taylor's Hymn. This we learn from *The Musical Times*, Feb. 1st, 1871, in a paper on Clifford's book. Criticising the words as by an unknown T. P.—ignorant that he was really criticising Bp. Jeremy Taylor—the (I suppose) learned Writer thus appreciatively writes of the grand Hymn and these passionate yearning words: 'Who, for instance, could seriously sing in church such stuff as the following Christmas Anthem or Carol, by T. P.? which Mr. William Childe (not yet made Doctor) had set to music.' Ahem! And so on, in stone-eyed, stone-eared stupidity.—Of modern celebrations I name as worthy of higher recognition than it has received the following 'Hymn to the Week above every Week,' by Thomas II. Gill; Lon., Mudie, 1844 (pp. 24). There is no little of the rich quaint matter and manner of our elder Singers in this fine Poem.

2. Cf. vol. i. p. 143.

3. Like Macaulay in his *History of England* (1st edition), Dr. Macdonald by an oversight speaks of Crashaw as 'expelled from *Oxford*,' instead of Cambridge (cf. our vol. i. p. 32).

4. The Letter of Pope to Mr. Henry Cromwell is in all the editions of his Correspondence. Willmott (as before) also gives it *in extenso*. Of 'The Weeper' Pope says: 'To confirm what I have said, you need but look into his first poem of 'The Weeper,' where the 2d, 4th, 6th, 14th, 21st stanzas are as sublimely dull as the 7th, 8th, 9th, 16th, 17th, 20th, and 23d stanzas of the same copy are soft and pleasing. And if these last want anything, it is an easier and more unaffected expression. The remaining thoughts in that poem might have been spared, being either but repetitions, or very trivial and mean. And by this example one may guess at all the rest to be like this; a mixture of tender gentle thoughts and suitable expressions, of forced and inextricable conceits, and of needless fillers-up of the rest,' &c. &c. 'Sweet' is the loftiest epithet Pope uses for Crashaw, and that in the knowledge of the 'Suspicion of Herod.' In 'The Weeper' he passes some of the very finest things. In his 'Abelard and Eloisa' he incorporates felicities from Crashaw's 'Alexias' within inverted commas; but elsewhere is not very careful to mark indebtedness.

EDMUND GOSSE
From "Richard Crashaw" (1882/1913)
Seventeenth Century Studies
1913, Volume 1, pp. 157–82

No sketch of the English literature of the middle of the seventeenth century can pretend to be complete if it does not tell us something of that serried throng of poets militant who gave in their allegiance to Laud, and became ornaments and then martyrs of the High Church party. Their piety was much more articulate and objective than that which had inspired the hymn-writers and various divine songsters of an earlier age; an element of political conviction, of anger and apprehension, gave ardour and tension to their song. They were conservative and passive, but not oblivious to the tendencies of the time, and the gathering flood of Puritanism forced them, to use an image that they would not themselves have disdained, to climb on to the very altar-step of ritualism, or even in extreme instances to take wing for the mystic heights of Rome itself.

It is from such extreme instances as the latter that we learn to gauge their emotion and their desperation, and it is therefore Crashaw rather than Herbert whom we select for the consideration of a typical specimen of the High Church poets. Nor is it only the hysterical intensity of Crashaw's convictions which marks him out for our present purpose; his position in history, his manhood spent in the last years of the reign of "Thorough," and in the very forefront of the crisis, give him a greater claim upon us than Herbert, who died before Laud succeeded to the Primacy, or Vaughan, who was still a boy when Strafford was executed. There are many other points of view from which Crashaw is of special interest; his works present the only important contribution to English literature made by a pronounced Catholic, embodying Catholic doctrine, during the whole of the seventeenth century, while as a poet, although extremely unequal, he rises, at his best, to a mounting fervour which is quite electrical, and hardly rivalled in its kind before or since. . . .

Crashaw's English poems were first published in 1646, soon after his arrival in Paris. He was at that time in his thirty-fourth year, and the volume contains his best and most mature as well as his crudest pieces. It is, indeed, a collection of juvenile and manly verses thrown together with scarcely a hint of arrangement, the uncriticised labour of fifteen years. The title is *Steps to the Temple, Sacred Poems, with other delights of the Muses*. The sacred poems are so styled by his anonymous editor because they are "steps for happy souls to climb heaven by;" the *Delights of the Muses* are entirely secular, and the two divisions of the book, therefore, reverse the order of Herrick's similarly edited *Hesperides* and *Noble Numbers*. The *Steps to the Temple* are distinguished at once from the collection with which it is most natural to compare them, the *Temple* of Herbert, to which their title refers with a characteristic touch of modesty, by the fact that they are not poems of experience, but of ecstasy—not of meditation, but of devotion. Herbert, and with him most of the sacred poets of the age, are autobiographical; they analyse their emotions, they take themselves to task, they record their struggles, their defeats, their consolation.

But if the azure cherubim of introspection are the dominant muses of English sacred verse, the flame-coloured seraph of worship reigns in that of Crashaw. He has made himself familiar with all the amorous phraseology of the Catholic metaphysicians; he has read the passionate canticles of St. John of the Cross, the books of the Carmelite nun, St. Teresa, and all the other rosy and fiery contributions to ecclesiastical literature laid by Spain at the feet of the Pope during the closing decades of the sixteenth century. The virginal courage and ardour of St. Teresa inspire Crashaw with his loveliest and most faultless verses. We need not share nor even sympathise with the sentiment of such lines as these to acknowledge that they belong to the highest order of lyric writing:

> Thou art Love's victim, and must die
> A death more mystical and high;
> Into Love's arms thou shalt let fall
> A still-surviving funeral.
> His is the dart must make thy death,
> Whose stroke will taste thy hallowed breath—
> A dart thrice dipped in that rich flame
> Which writes thy spouse's radiant name
> Upon the roof of heaven, where aye
> It shines and with a sovereign ray
> Beats bright upon the burning faces
> Of souls which in that name's sweet graces
> Find everlasting smiles. So rare,
> So spiritual, pure, and fair,
> Must be the immortal instrument
> Upon whose choice point shall be spent
> A life so loved; and that there be
> Fit executioners for thee,
> The fairest first-born sons of fire,
> Blest seraphim, shall leave their choir,
> And turn Love's soldiers, upon thee
> To exercise their archery.

Nor in the poem from which these lines are quoted does this melodious rapture flag during nearly two hundred verses. But such a sustained flight is rare, as in the similar poem of "The Flaming Heart," also addressed to St. Teresa, where, after a long prelude of frigid and tuneless conceits, it is only at the very close that the poet suddenly strikes upon this golden chord of ecstasy:

> Let all thy scattered shafts of light, that play
> Among the leaves of thy large books of day,
> Combined against this breast at once break in,
> And take away from me myself and sin;
> This gracious robbery shall thy bounty be,
> And my best fortunes such fair spoils of me.
> O thou undaunted daughter of desires!
>   By all thy dower of lights and fires,
>   By all the eagle in thee, all the dove,
>   By all thy lives and deaths of love.
>   By thy large draughts of intellectual day,
> And by thy thirsts of love more large than they,
> By all thy brim-filled bowls of fierce desire,
> By thy last morning's draught of liquid fire,
> By the full kingdom of that final kiss

> That seized thy parting soul and sealed thee His;
> By all the heaven thou hast in Him,
> Fair sister of the seraphim!
> By all of thine we have in thee—
> Leave nothing of myself in me;
> Let me so read thy life that I
> Unto all life of mine may die.

If Crashaw had left us nothing more than these two fragments, we should be able to distinguish him by them among English poets. He is the solitary representative of the poetry of Catholic psychology which England possessed until our own days; and Germany has one no less unique in Friedrich Spe. I do not know that any critic has compared Spe and Crashaw, but they throw lights upon the genius of one another which may seasonably detain us for a while. The great Catholic poet of Germany during the seventeenth century was born in 1591. Like Crashaw, he was set in motion by the Spanish Mystics; like him, he stood on the verge of a great poetical revolution without being in the least affected by it. To Waller and to Opitz, with their new dry systems of precise prosody, Crashaw and Spe owed nothing; they were purely romantic and emotional in style. Spe was born a Catholic, spent all his life among the Jesuits, and died, worn out with good works and immortalised by an heroic struggle against the system of persecution for witchcraft, in the hospital of Trèves in 1635, just when Crashaw was becoming enthralled by the delicious mysteries of Little Gidding. Both of them wrote Jesuit eclogues. In Spe the shepherd winds his five best roses into a garland for the infant Jesus; in Crashaw he entertains the "starry stranger" with conceits about his diamond eyes and the red leaves of his lips. In each poet there is an hysterical delight in blood and in the details of martyrdom, in each a shrill and frantic falsetto that jars on the modern ear, in each a sweetness of diction and purity of fancy that redeem a hundred faults.[1] The poems of Spe, entitled *Trutz-Nachtigal*, were first printed in 1649, the year that Crashaw died.

The chief distinction between Spe and Crashaw is, in the first place, that Crashaw is by far the greater and more varied of the two as regards poetical gifts, and, secondly, that while Spe was inspired by the national *Volkslied*, and introduced its effects into his song, Crashaw was an adept in every refinement of metrical structure which had been invented by the poet-artists of England, Spain, and Italy. The progress of our poetical literature in the seventeenth century will never be thoroughly explained until some competent scholar shall examine the influence of Spanish poetry upon our own. This influence seems to be particularly strong in the case of Donne, and in the next generation in that of Crashaw. I am not sufficiently familiar with Spanish poetry to give an opinion on this subject which is of much value; but as I write I have open before me the works of Gongora, and I find in the general disposition of his *Octavas Sacras* and in the style of his *Canciones* resemblances to the staves introduced to us by Crashaw which can scarcely be accidental.

Mr. Shorthouse reminds me that Ferrar was much in Spain; we know that Crashaw "was excellent in Italian and Spanish," and we are thus led on to consider the more obvious debt which he owed to the contemporary poetry of Italy. One of the largest pieces of work which he undertook was the translation of the first canto of the *Strage degli Innocenti*, or *Massacre of the Innocents*, a famous poem by the Neapolitan Cavaliere Marini, who had died in 1625. Crashaw has thrown a great deal of dignity and fancy into this version, which, however, outdoes the original in ingenious illustration, as the true Marinists, such as Achillini, outdid Marini in their conceited sonnets. Crashaw, in fact, is a genuine Marinist, the happiest specimen which we possess in English, for he preserves a high level of fantastic foppery, and seldom, at his worst, sinks to those crude animal imagings—illustrations from food, for instance—which occasionally make such writers as Habington and Carew not merely ridiculous but repulsive.

In criticising with severity the piece on Mary Magdalene which stands in the forefront of Crashaw's poems, and bears the title of "The Weeper," I have the misfortune to find myself at variance with most of his admirers. I cannot, however, avoid the conviction that the obtrusion of this eccentric piece on the threshold of his shrine has driven away from it many a would-be worshipper. If language be ever liable to abuse in the hands of a clever poet, it is surely outraged here. Every extravagant and inappropriate image is dragged to do service to this small idea—namely, that the Magdalen is for ever weeping. Her eyes, therefore, are sister springs, parents of rills, thawing crystal, hills of snow, heavens of ever-falling stars, eternal breakfasts for brisk cherubs, sweating boughs of balsam, nests of milky doves, a voluntary mint of silver, and Heaven knows how many more incongruous objects, from one to another of which the labouring fancy flits in despair and bewilderment. In this poem all is resigned to ingenuity; we are not moved or softened, we are merely startled, and the irritated reader is at last appeased for the fatigues he has endured by a frank guffaw, when he sees the poet, at his wits' end for a simile, plunge into the abyss of absurdity, and style the eyes of the Magdalen

> Two walking baths, two weeping motions,
> Portable and compendious oceans.

These are the worst lines in Crashaw. They are perhaps the worst in all English poetry, but they must not be omitted here, since they indicate to us the principal danger to which not he only but most of his compeers were liable. It was from the tendency to call a pair of eyes "portable and compendious oceans" that Waller and Dryden, after both of them stumbling on the same stone in their youth, finally delivered us. It is useless to linger with indulgence over the stanzas of a poem like "The Weeper," simply because many of the images are in themselves pretty. The system upon which these juvenile pieces of Crashaw are written is in itself indefensible, and is founded upon what Mr. Matthew Arnold calls an "incurable defect of style."

Crashaw, however, possesses style, or he would not deserve the eminent place he holds among our poets. The ode in praise of Teresa, written while the author was still among the Protestants, and therefore probably about 1642, has already been cited here. It is an exquisite composition, full of real vision, music of the most delicate order, and imagery which, although very profuse and ornate, is always subordinated to the moral meaning and to the progress of the poem. The "Shepherd's Hymn," too, is truly ingenious and graceful, with its pretty pastoral tenderness. "On Mr. G. Herbert's Book sent to a Gentleman" evidently belongs to the St. Teresa period, and contains the same charm. The lyrical epistle persuading the Countess of Denbigh to join the Roman communion contains extraordinary felicities, and seems throbbing with tenderness and passion. We have already drawn attention to the splendid close of "The Flaming Heart." There is perhaps no other of the sacred poems in the volume of 1646 which can be commended in its entirety. Hardly one but contains felicities; the dullest is brightened by such flashes of genius as—

> Lo, how the thirsty lands

> Gasp for the golden showers with long-stretch'd
> hands!

But the poems are hard, dull, and laborious, the exercises of a saint indeed, but untouched by inspiration, human or divine. We have to return to the incomparable "Hymn to St. Teresa" to remind ourselves of what heights this poet was capable.

There can be very little doubt that Crashaw regarded the second section of his book, the secular *Delights of the Muses*, as far inferior in value and importance to the *Steps to the Temple*. That is not, however, a view in which the modern reader can coincide, and it is rather the ingenuity of his human poems than the passion of his divine which has given him a prominent place among poets. The *Delights* open with the celebrated piece called the "Muse's Duel," paraphrased from the Latin of Strada. As one frequently sees a reference to the "Latin poet Strada," it may be worth while to remark that Famianus Strada was not a poet at all, but a lecturer in the Jesuit colleges. He belonged to Crashaw's own age, having been born in 1572, and dying in the year of the English poet's death, 1649. The piece on the rivalry of the musician and the nightingale was published first at Rome in 1617, in a volume of *Prolusiones* on rhetoric and poetry, and occurs in the sixth lecture of the second course on poetic style. The Jesuit rhetorician has been trying to familiarise his pupils with the style of the great classic poets by reciting to them passages in imitation of Ovid, Lucretius, Lucan, and the rest, and at last he comes to Claudian. This, he says, is an imitation of the style of Claudian, and so he gives us the lines which have become so famous. That a single fragment in a school-book should suddenly take root and blossom in European literature, when all else that its voluminous author wrote and said was promptly forgotten, is very curious, but not unprecedented.

In England the first person who adopted or adapted Strada's exercise was John Ford, in his play of *The Lover's Melancholy*, in 1629. Dr. Grosart found another early version among the Lansdowne MSS., and Ambrose Phillips a century later essayed it. There are numerous references to it in other literatures than ours, and in the present age M. François Coppée has introduced it with charming effect into his pretty comedy of *Le Luthier de Crémone*. Thus the schoolmaster's task, set as a guide to the manner of Claudian, has achieved, by an odd irony of fortune, a far more general and lasting success than any of the actual verses of that elegant writer. With regard to the comparative merits of Ford's version, which is in blank verse, and of Crashaw's, which is in rhyme, a confident opinion has generally been expressed in favour of the particular poet under consideration at the moment; nor is Lamb himself superior to this amiable partiality. He denies that Crashaw's version "can at all compare for harmony and grace with this blank verse of Ford's." But my own view coincides much rather with that of Mr. Swinburne, who says that "between the two beautiful versions of Strada's pretty fable by Ford and Crashaw, there will always be a diversity of judgment among readers; some must naturally prefer the tender fluency and limpid sweetness of Ford, others the dazzling intricacy and affluence in refinements, the supple and cunning implication, the choiceness and subtlety of Crashaw." Mr. Shorthouse, on the other hand, suggests to me that "Crashaw's poem is surely so much more full and elaborate, that it must be acknowledged to be the more important effort." There can be no doubt that it presents us with the most brilliant and unique attempt which has been made in our language to express the very quality and variety of musical notation in words. It may be added that the only reference made by Crashaw in any part of his writings to any of the dramatists his contemporaries is found in a couplet addressed to Ford:

> Thou cheat'st us, Ford, mak'st one seem two by art;
> What is *love's sacrifice* but *the broken heart?*

After "Music's Duel," the best-known poem of Crashaw's is his "Wishes to his Supposed Mistress," a piece in forty-two stanzas, which Mr. Palgrave reduced to twenty-one in his *Golden Treasury.* He neglected to mention the "sweet theft," and accordingly most readers know the poem only as he reduced and rearranged it. The act was bold, perhaps, but I think that it was judicious. As Crashaw left it, the poem extends beyond the limits of a lyric, tediously repeats its sentiments and gains neither in force nor charm by its extreme length. In Mr. Palgrave's selection it challenges comparison with the loveliest and most original pieces of the century. It never, I think, rises to the thrilling tenderness which Donne is capable of on similar occasions. Crashaw never pants out a line and a half which leave us faint and throbbing, as if the heart of humanity itself had been revealed to us for a moment; with all his flying colour and lambent flame, Crashaw is not Donne. But the "Wishes" is more than a charming, it is a fascinating poem, the pure dream of the visionary poet, who liked to reflect that he too might marry if he would, and choose a godly bride. He calls upon her—

> Whoe'er she be
> That not impossible She
> That shall command my heart and me;
>
> Where'er she lie
> Locked up from mortal eye
> In shady leaves of destiny—

to receive the embassy of his wishes, bound to instruct her in that higher beauty of the spirit which his soul demands—

> Something more than
> Taffata or tissue can,
> Or rampant feather, or rich fan.

But what he requires is not spiritual adornment alone; he will have her courteous and accomplished in the world's ways also, the possessor of

> Sydneian showers
> Of sweet discourse, whose powers
> Can crown old Winter's head with flowers;

and finally,

> Life, that dares send
> A challenge to his end,
> And when it comes say, 'Welcome, friend.'
>
> I wish her store
> Of worth may leave her poor
> Of wishes; and I wish—no more.

The same refined and tender spirit animates the "Epitaph upon Husband and Wife, who died and were buried together." The lovely rambling verses of "To the Morning, in satisfaction for Sleep," are perhaps more in the early manner of Keats than any other English lines. In some of those sacred poems which we have lately been considering, he reminds us no less vividly of Shelley, and there are not a few passages of Crashaw which it would require a very quick ear to distinguish from Mr. Swinburne. We may safely conjecture that the latter poet's "Song in Season" was written in deliberate rivalry of that song of Crashaw's which runs—

> O deliver
> Love his quiver;
> From thine eyes he shoots his arrows,
> Where Apollo

> Cannot follow,
> Feathered with his mother's sparrows.

But perhaps the sweetest and most modern of all Crashaw's secular lyrics is that entitled *Love's Horoscope.* The phraseology of the black art was never used with so sweet and picturesque an ingenuity, and the piece contains some of the most delicately musical cadences to be found in the poetry of the age:

> Thou know'st a face in whose each look
> Beauty lays ope Love's fortune-book,
> On whose fair revolutions wait
> The obsequious motions of Love's fate.
> Ah! my heart! her eyes and she
> Have taught thee new astrology.
> Howe'er Love's native hours were set,
> Whatever starry synod met,
> 'Tis in the mercy of her eye
> If poor Love shall live or die.

It is probable from internal and from external evidence also that all these secular poems belong to Crashaw's early years at Cambridge. The pretty lines "On Two Green Apricocks sent to Cowley by Sir Crashaw" evidently date from 1633; the various elegies and poems of compliment can be traced to years ranging from 1631 to 1634. It is doubtful whether the "Wishes" themselves are at all later than this. Even regarding him as a finished poet ten years before the publication of his book, however, he comes late in the list of seventeenth century lyrists, and has no claims to be considered as an innovator. He owed all the basis of his style, as has been already hinted, to Donne and to Ben Jonson. His originality was one of treatment and technique; he forged a more rapid and brilliant short line than any of his predecessors had done, and for brief intervals and along sudden paths of his own he carried English prosody to a higher refinement, a more glittering felicity, than it had ever achieved. Thus, in spite of his conceits and his romantic colouring, he points the way for Pope, who did not disdain to borrow from him freely.

It is unfortunate that Crashaw is so unequal as to be positively delusive; he baffles analysis by his uncertain hold upon style, and in spite of his charm and his genius is perhaps most interesting to us because of the faults he shares with purely modern poets. It would scarcely be unjust to say that Crashaw was the first real poet who allowed himself to use a splendid phrase when a simple one would have better expressed his meaning; and in an age when all but the best poetry was apt to be obscure, crabbed, and rugged, he introduces a new fault, that of being visionary and diffuse, with a deliberate intention not only, as the others did, to deck Nature out in false ornament, but to represent her actual condition as being something more "starry" and "seraphical" than it really is. His style has hectic beauties that delight us, but evade us also, and colours that fade as promptly as the scarlet and the amber in a sunset sky. We can describe him best in negatives; his is not so warm and real as Herrick, nor so drily intellectual as the other hymnists, nor coldly and respectably virile like Cowley. To use an odd simile of Shelley's, he sells us gin when the other poets offer us legs of mutton, or at all events baskets of bread and vegetables. . . .

Too often it is with regret, or with a grudged esteem, that we hail newly-discovered works by standard authors. The best writing generally takes care of itself, and is remembered and preserved, whatever may be lost. The first sprightly running is commonly the best, and editors scarcely earn our thanks by troubling the lees for us. For once we have an exception before us. The pamphlet of newly-discovered poems by Crashaw which Dr. Grosart forwarded to his subscribers in 1888 contains some things which, even in the congested condition of our national literature, are never likely to be obscured again. The British Museum bought from a bookseller, who had picked it up as an odd lot at Sotheby's or Puttick & Simpson's, a MS. volume of Crashaw's poems, indubitably, as would appear, in his own, previously untraced, handwriting. Dr. Grosart gives us an example of the latter in facsimile, selecting the page which contains the well-known epigram on "The Water being made Wine."

We turn at once to the poems which are entirely new. Here is one apparently intended to form the dedication to a gift-volume of the poet's *Steps to the Temple*:

> At the ivory tribunal of your hand,
> Fair one, these tender leaves do trembling stand,
> Knowing 'tis in the doom of your sweet eye
> Whether the Muse they clothe shall live or die;
> Live she or die to Fame, each leaf you meet
> Is her life's wing, or else her winding-sheet.

We could swear this was Crashaw if we picked it up anonymous on Pitcairn's Island. Moreover, something very like the second couplet is to be found already in *Love's Horoscope*:

> 'Tis in the mercy of her eye
> If poor Love shall live or die.

It is very pretty. But this, a nameless lyric, is more than pretty; it is exquisite, and in Crashaw's most transcendental manner:

> Though now 'tis neither May nor June,
> And nightingales are out of tune,
> Yet in these leaves, fair One, there lies
> (Sworn servant to your sweetest eyes)
> A nightingale, who, may she spread
> In your white bosom her chaste bed,
> Spite of all the maiden snow
> Those pure untrodden paths can show,
> You straight shall see her wake and rise,
> Taking fresh life from your fair eyes,
> And with claspt wings proclaim a spring,
> Where Love and she shall sit and sing;
> For lodged so near your sweetest throat
> What nightingale can lose her note?
> Nor let her kindred birds complain
> Because she breaks the year's old reign;
> For let them know she's none of those
> Hedge-quiristers whose music owes
> Only such strains as serve to keep
> Sad shades, and sing dull night asleep.
> No, she's a priestess of that grove,
> The holy chapel of chaste love,
> Your virgin bosom. Then whate'er
> Poor laws divide the public year,
> Whose revolutions wait upon
> The wild turns of the wanton sun,
> Be you the Lady of Love's year,
> Where your eyes shine his suns appear,
> There all the year is Love's long Spring,
>   There all the year
> Love's nightingales shall sit and sing.

The break in the penultimate verse is a charming addition to the melody, and I am very much mistaken if this lyric does not take its place among the best of Charles I.'s reign.

The remainder of the new poems are religious, and they are not in Crashaw's very finest manner. "To Pontius, Washing his Blood-stained Hands," is a typical example of the monstrous chains of conceits which these most unequal poets were at any moment liable to produce. The face of Pilate was originally a nymph—

> The daughter of a fair and well-famed fountain
> As ever silver-tipped the side of shady mountain,—

(in itself a charming image); this nymph has suffered the fate of Philomela from this new Tereus, the hand of Pilate, and "appears nothing but tears." A paraphrase of Grotius gives us a first version of the well-known verse on the Eucharist:

> The water blushed and started into wine.

We trace the great Crashaw of the fiery surprises but seldom in this long, tame, and somewhat crabbed poem; but he asserts himself in a few such phrases as this:

> Before the infant shrine
> Of my weak feet, the Persian Magi lay,
> And left their mithra for my star;

and this, which well describes the condition of Crashaw's muse:

> A sweet inebriated ecstasy.

The new readings of old poems which the MS. gives are neither, it would seem, very numerous nor very important. "The Weeper" is such a distressing, indeed such a humiliating poem, that we receive a new stanza of it with indifference; we may note one novelty,—this string of preposterous conceits on the tears of the Magdalen must in future close with a conceit that swallows up all the rest:

> Of such fair floods as this
> Heaven the crystal ocean is.

Dr. Grosart takes this opportunity of recording an interesting little discovery. Crashaw's important Latin poem "Bulla" is found to have made its first appearance in a very rare Cambridge volume, the *Crepundia Siliana* of Heynsius, in 1646, two years after the poet's ejection from his Fellowship. It appeared the same year in the *Delights of the Muses*, with a considerable number of variations of the text. It is a pity that Crashaw did not write "Bulla" in English, for it is full of the characteristics of his style.

Notes

1. As an illustration of almost all these qualities, and as a specimen of Spe's metrical gifts, I give one stanza from the *Trutz-Nachtigal*:

> Aus der Seiten
> Lan sich leiten
>   Rote Strahlen wie Korall;
> Aus der Seiten
> Lan sich leiten
>   Weisse Wässer wie Krystal!
> O du reines,
> Hübsch und feines
>   Bächlein von Korall und Glas,
> Nit noch weiche,
> Nit entschleiche,
>   O Rubin und Perlengass!

GEORGE SAINTSBURY
From "Caroline Poetry"
A History of Elizabethan Literature
1887, pp. 364–69

The third of this great trio of poets ⟨Carew, Herrick and Crashaw⟩, and with them the most remarkable of our whole group, was Richard Crashaw. He completes Carew and Herrick both in his qualities and (if a kind of bull may be permitted) in his defects, after a fashion almost unexampled elsewhere and supremely interesting. Hardly any one of the three could have appeared at any other time, and not one but is distinguished from the others in the most marked way. Herrick, despite his sometimes rather obtrusive learning, is emphatically the natural man. He does not show much sign of the influence of good society, his merits as well as his faults have a singular unpersonal and, if I may so say, *terræfilian* connotation. Carew is a gentleman before all; but a rather profane gentleman. Crashaw is religious everywhere. Again, Herrick and Carew, despite their strong savour of the fashion of the time, are eminently critics as well as poets. Carew has not let one piece critically unworthy of him pass his censorship: Herrick (if we exclude the filthy and foolish epigrams into which he was led by corrupt following of Ben) has been equally careful. These two bards may have trouble with the *censor morum*,—the *censor literarum* they can brave with perfect confidence. It is otherwise with Crashaw. That he never, as far as can be seen, edited the bulk of his work for press at all matters little or nothing. But there is not in his work the slightest sign of the exercise of any critical faculty before, during, or after production. His masterpiece, one of the most astonishing things in English or any other literature, comes without warning at the end of "The Flaming Heart." For page after page the poet has been poorly playing on some trifling conceits suggested by the picture of Saint Theresa and a seraph. First he thinks the painter ought to have changed the attributes; then he doubts whether a lesser change will not do; and always he treats his subject in a vein of grovelling and grotesque conceit which the boy Dryden in the stage of his elegy on Lord Hastings would have disdained. And then in a moment, in the twinkling of an eye, without warning of any sort, the metre changes, the poet's inspiration catches fire, and there rushes up into the heaven of poetry this marvellous rocket of song:

> Live in these conquering leaves: live all the same;
> And walk through all tongues one triumphant flame;
> Live here, great heart; and love, and die, and kill;
> And bleed, and wound, and yield, and conquer still.
> Let this immortal life where'er it comes
> Walk in a crowd of loves and martyrdoms.
> Let mystic deaths wait on't; and wise souls be
> The love-slain witnesses of this life of thee.
> O sweet incendiary! show here thy art,
> Upon this carcase of a hard cold heart;
> Let all thy scatter'd shafts of light, that play
> Among the leaves of thy large books of day,
> Combin'd against this breast at once break in,
> And take away from me myself and sin;
> This gracious robbery shall thy bounty be
> And my best fortunes such fair spoils of me.
> O thou undaunted daughter of desires!
> By all thy pow'r of lights and fires;
> By all the eagle in thee, all the dove;
> By all thy lives and deaths of love;
> By thy large draughts of intellectual day;
> And by thy thirsts of love more large than they;
> By all thy brim-fill'd bowls of fierce desire;
> By thy last morning's draught of liquid fire;
> By the full kingdom of that final kiss
> That 'sayed thy parting soul, and seal'd thee his;
> By all the heavens thou hast in him,
> (Fair sister of the seraphim)
> By all of him we have in thee;
> Leave nothing of myself in me.
> Let me so read thy life, that I
> Unto all life of mine may die.

The contrast is perhaps unique as regards the dead col-

ourlessness of the beginning, and the splendid colour of the end. But contrasts like it occur all over Crashaw's work. . . .

Our chief subject . . . is the English poems proper, sacred and profane. In almost all of these there is noticeable an extraordinary inequality, the same in kind, if not in degree, as that on which we have commented in the case of "The Flaming Heart." Crashaw is never quite so great as there; but he is often quite as small. His exasperating lack of self-criticism has sometimes led selectors to make a cento out of his poems—notably in the case of the exceedingly pretty "Wishes to His Unknown Mistress," beginning, "Whoe'er she be, That not impossible she, That shall command my heart and me"—a poem, let it be added, which excuses this dubious process much less than most, inasmuch as nothing in it is positively bad, though it is rather too long. Here is the opening, preceded by a piece from another poem, "A Hymn to Saint Theresa":

> Those rare works, where thou shalt leave writ
> Love's noble history, with wit
> Taught thee by none but him, while here
> They feed our souls, shall clothe thine there.
> Each heavenly word by whose hid flame
> Our hard hearts shall strike fire, the same
> Shall flourish on thy brows and be
> Both fire to us and flame to thee:
> Whose light shall live bright, in thy face
> By glory, in our hearts by grace.
>
> Thou shalt look round about, and see
> Thousands of crown'd souls throng to be
> Themselves thy crown, sons of thy vows:
> The virgin births with which thy spouse
> Made fruitful thy fair soul; go now
> And with them all about thee, bow
> To Him, 'Put on' (He'll say) 'put on,
> My rosy love, that thy rich zone,
> Sparkling with the sacred flames,
> Of thousand souls whose happy names
> Heaven heaps upon thy score, thy bright
> Life brought them first to kiss the light
> That kindled them to stars.' And so
> Thou with the Lamb thy Lord shall go,
> And whereso'er He sets His white
> Steps, walk with Him those ways of light.
> Which who in death would live to see
> Must learn in life to die like thee."
>
> Whoe'er she be,
> That not impossible she,
> That shall command my heart and me;
>
> Where'er she lie,
> Lock'd up from mortal eye,
> In shady leaves of destiny;
>
> Till that ripe birth
> Of studied Fate stand forth,
> And teach her fair steps to our earth:
>
> Till that divine
> Idea take a shrine
> Of crystal flesh, through which to shine:
>
> Meet you her, my wishes
> Bespeak her to my blisses,
> And be ye call'd, my absent kisses.

The first hymn to Saint Theresa, to which "The Flaming Heart" is a kind of appendix, was written when Crashaw was still an Anglican (for which he did not fail, later, to make a characteristic and very pretty, though quite unnecessary, apology). It has no passage quite up to the Invocation—Epiphonema, to give it the technical term—of the later poem. But it is, on the contrary, good almost throughout, and is, for uniform exaltation, far the best of Crashaw's poems. Yet such uniform exaltation must be seldom sought in him. It is in his little bursts, such as that in the stanza beginning, "O mother turtle dove," that his charm consists. Often, as in verse after verse of "The Weeper," it has an unearthly delicacy and witchery which only Blake, in a few snatches, has ever equalled; while at other times the poet seems to invent, in the most casual and unthinking fashion, new metrical effects and new jewelries of diction which the greatest lyric poets since— Coleridge, Shelley, Lord Tennyson, Mr. Swinburne—have rather deliberately imitated than spontaneously recovered. Yet to all this charm there is no small drawback. The very maddest and most methodless of the "Metaphysicals" cannot touch Crashaw in his tasteless use of conceits. When he, in "The Weeper" just above referred to, calls the tears of Magdalene "Wat'ry brothers," and "Simpering sons of those fair eyes," and when, in the most intolerable of all the poet's excesses, the same eyes are called "Two waking baths, two weeping motions, Portable and compendious oceans," which follow our Lord about the hills of Galilee, it is almost difficult to know whether to feel most contempt or indignation for a man who could so write. It is fair to say that there are various readings and omissions in the different editions which affect both these passages. Yet the offence is that Crashaw should ever have written them at all. Amends, however, are sure to be made before the reader has read much farther. Crashaw's longest poems—a version of Marini's *Sospetto d'Herode*, and one of the rather overpraised "Lover and Nightingale" story of Strada—are not his best; the metre in which both are written, though the poet manages it well, lacks the extraordinary charm of his lyric measures. It does not appear that the "Not impossible she" ever made her appearance, and probably for a full half of his short life Crashaw burnt only with religious fire. But no Englishman has expressed that fire as he has, and none in his expression of any sentiment, sacred and profane, has dropped such notes of ethereal music. At his best he is far above singing, at his worst he is below a very childish prattle. But even then he is never coarse, never offensive, not very often actually dull; and everywhere he makes amends by flowers of the divinest poetry.

FRANCIS THOMPSON
From "Excursions in Criticism: VI.—Crashaw"
Academy, November 20, 1897, pp. 427–28

Strange are both the commissions and omissions of this day, in which an uncritical zeal for the poets of the sixteenth and seventeenth centuries has stimulated reprint upon reprint. It seems to be enough for editorial zeal that a poet should have been born in one of those privileged centuries; and he shall find republication. Not alone Campion and other minor lyrists of merit, but even a wielder of frigid conceits like Henry Constable finds his editor—nay, is issued with all the pomp of sumptuous decorative *ensemble*. Yet, while editors search among the dross of these ages for poets to revive, they neglect the gold. Else how comes it that while Henry Vaughan finds reprint, his worthy yokefellow, Crashaw, is passed by? How comes it that Cowley is inaccessible yet to modern readers? Eminent modern poets have singled Crashaw as a man of genius and a source of inspiration. Coleridge declared that Crashaw's "Hymn to St. Teresa" was present to his mind while he was writing the second part of "Christabel"; "if, indeed, by some subtle process of the mind, they did not suggest the first thought of the whole

poem." The influence of Crashaw is to be traced in the "Unknown Eros": notably and conspicuously in the "Sponsa Dei."
. . .

Lyric poetry is a very inclusive term. It includes Milton and Herrick, Burns and Shelley, "Tintern Abbey" and "The Grecian Urn," the odes of Coventry Patmore and the songs of Tennyson. But its highest form—that which is to other lyric forms what the epic is to the narrative poem or the ballad—is the form typically represented by the ode. This order of lyric may again be divided into such lyrics as are distinguished by stately structure, and such as are distinguished by ardorous abandonment. In the former kind ardour *may* be present, though under the continual curb of the structure; and this is the highest species of the lyric. In the latter kind the ardour is naked and predominant: it is to the former kind what the flight of the skylark is to the flight of the eagle. The conspicuous first appearance of the former kind in English poetry was the monumental *Epithalamion* of Spenser. Ardour cannot, as a rule, be predicated of Spenser; but *there* is ardour of the most ethereal impulse, equipoised throughout with the most imperial and imperious structure. For the development of the latter kind English poetry had to await the poet of *Prometheus Unbound*. But its first, almost unnoticed and unperfected appearance, was in the work of Richard Crashaw. His age gave the preference to Cowley, in whose odes there is unlimited ostentation of dominating ardour without the reality, the result being mere capricious and unmeaning dislocation of form. Too much of the like is there in Crashaw; but every now and again he ascends into real fervour, such as makes metre and diction plastic to its own shaping spirit of inevitable rightness. This is the eminent praise of Crashaw, that he marks an epoch, a turn of the tide in English lyric, though the crest of the tide was not to come till long after, though—like all first innovators—he not only suffered present neglect, but has been overshadowed by those who came a century after him.

He is fraught with suggestion—infinite suggestion. More than one poet has drawn much from him, yet much remains to be drawn. But it is not only for poets he exists. Those who read for enjoyment can find in him abundant delight, if they will be content (as they are content with Wordsworth) to grope through his plenteous infelicity. He is no poet of the human and household emotions; he has not pathos, or warm love, or any of the qualities which come home to the natural kindly race of men. But how fecund is his brilliant imagery, rapturous ethereality. He has, at his best, an extraordinary cunning of diction, cleaving like gold-leaf to its object. In such a poem as "The Musician and the Nightingale" (not in this volume included) the marvel of diction becomes even too conscious; in the moment of wondering at the miracle, we feel that the miracle is too researched: it is the feat of an amazing gymnast in words rather than of an unpremeditating angel. Yet this poem is an extraordinary verbal achievement, and there are numerous other examples in which the miracle seems as unconscious as admirable.

For an example of his sacred poems, take the "Nativity," which has less deforming conceit than most. Very different from Milton's great Ode, which followed it, yet it has its own characteristic beauty. The shepherds sing it turn by turn—as thus:

> Gloomy night embraced the place
>   Where the noble Infant lay.
> The Babe looked up and showed His face;
>   In spite of darkness, it was day.
> It was Thy day, Sweet! and did rise,
>   Not from the East, but from Thine eyes.

Here is seen one note of Crashaw—the human and lover-like tenderness which informs his sacred poems, differentiating them from the conventional style of English sacred poetry, with its solemn aloofness from celestial things.

> I saw the curled drops, soft and slow
>   Come hovering o'er the place's head;
> Offering their whitest sheets of snow
>   To furnish the fair Infant's bed:
> Forbear, said I,; be not too bold,
>   Your fleece is white, but 'tis too cold.
>
> I saw the obsequious Seraphim
>   Their rosy fleece of fire bestow,
> For well they now can spare their wing,
>   Since heaven itself lies here below.
> Well done, said I; but are you sure
>   Your down so warm will pass for pure?

In the second stanza is shown the fire of his fancy; in "The curled drops," &c., the happiness of his diction. In "The Weeper" (a poem on the Magdalen), amid stanzas of the most frigid conceit, are others of the loveliest art in conception and expression:

> The dew no more will weep
>   The primrose's pale cheek to deck:
> The dew no more will sleep
>   Nuzzled in the Lily's neck;
> Much rather would it be thy tear,
> And leave them both to tremble here.
>
>   . . .
>
> Not in the Evening's eyes
>   When they red with weeping are
> For the Sun that dies,
>   Sits Sorrow with a face so fair.
> Nowhere but here did ever meet
> Sweetness so sad, sadness so sweet.

Two more alien poets could not be conceived than Crashaw and Browning. Yet in the last couplet of these most exquisite stanzas we have a direct coincidence with Browning's line—

> Its sad in sweet, its sweet in sad.

In the "Hymn to St. Teresa" are to be found the most beautiful delicacies of language and metre. Listen to this (*apropos* of Teresa's childish attempt to run away and become a martyr among the Moors):

> She never undertook to know
> What Death with Love should have to do;
> Nor has she e'er yet understood
> Why to show love she should shed blood;
> Yet though she cannot tell you why,
> She can love, and she can die.

Among the poems not contained in this volume ⟨J.R. Tutin, *Poems of Richard Crashaw*, 1905⟩, the wonderfully dainty "Wishes to a Supposed Mistress" shows what Crashaw might have been as an amative poet:

> Whoe'er she be,
>   That not impossible She,
>   That shall command my heart and me;
> Where'er she lie,
>   Shut up from mortal eye
>   In shady leaves of Destiny.

And so on through a series of unequal but often lovely stanzas. So, too, does "Love's Horoscope." His epitaphs are among the sweetest and most artistic even of that age, so cunning in such kind of verse. For instance, that on a young gentleman:

> Eyes are vocal, tears have tongues,

And there be words not made with lungs—
> Sententious showers; O let them fall!
> Their cadence is rhetorical!

But, to come back to the poems contained in Mr. Tutin's book, with what finer example can I end than the close of "The Flaming Heart," Crashaw's second hymn to St. Teresa?—

> Oh, thou undaunted daughter of desires!
> By all thy dower of lights and fires;
> By all the eagle in thee, all the dove;
> By all thy lives and deaths of love;
> By thy large draughts of intellectual day,
> And by thy thirsts of love more large than they;
> By all thy brim-filled bowls of fierce desire,
> By thy last morning's draught of liquid fire;
> By the full kingdom of that final kiss,
> That seized thy parting soul, and sealed thee His;
> By all the Heaven thou hast in Him
> (Fair Sister of the seraphim!)
> By all of Him we have in thee;
> Leave nothing of myself in me.
> Let me so read thy life, that I
> Unto all life of mine may die.

It has all the ardour and brave-soaring transport of the highest lyrical inspiration.

FELIX E. SCHELLING
From "Introduction"
A Book of Seventeenth Century Lyrics
1899, pp. xxx–xxxiii, li–liii

It is an error to regard the Caroline conceit as wholly referable to Donne's irresponsible use of figure. It is neither so limited and abstract in the range of phenomena chosen for figurative illustration, so unconcerned with the recognition of the outward world, nor so completely referable to the intellectualization of emotion. Let us take a typical passage of Donne:

> But, O, alas! so long, so far
>   Our bodies why do we forbear?
> They are ours, though not we; we are
>   The intelligences, they the spheres;
> We owe them thanks, because they thus
>   Did us to us at first convey,
> Yielded their senses' force to us,
>   Nor are dross to us but alloy.
> On man heaven's influence works not so,
>   But that it first imprints the air;
> For soul into the soul may flow
> Though it to body first repair.[1]

This passage is subtle, almost dialectic. A keen, sinuous, reasoning mind is playing with its powers. Except for the implied personification of the body regarded apart from the soul, the language is free from figure; there is no confusion of thought. There is the distinctively Donnian employment of ideas derived from physical and speculative science: the body is the 'sphere' or superficies which includes within it the soul, a term of the old astro-philosophy; the body is not 'dross' but an 'alloy,' alchemical terms; the 'influence' of heaven is the use of that word in an astrological sense, meaning "the radiation of power from the stars in certain positions or collections affecting human actions and destinies"; and lastly, the phrase "imprints the air" involves an idea of the old philosophy, by which "sensuous perception is explained by effluxes of atoms from the things perceived whereby images are produced ('imprinted') which strike our senses." Donne subtly transfers this purely physical conception to the transference of divine influences.[2]

On the other hand, take this, the one flagging stanza of Crashaw's otherwise noble "Hymn of the Nativity." The Virgin is spoken of, and represented with the Child, who is addressed by the poet:

> She sings thy tears asleep, and dips
> 　　Her kisses in thy weeping eye;
> She spreads the red leaves of thy lips,
> 　　That in their buds yet blushing lie.
> She 'gainst those mother diamonds tries
> The points of her young eagle's eyes.[3]

This difficult passage may perhaps be thus explained: the Virgin sings to her babe until, falling asleep, his tears cease to flow. "And dips her kisses in thy weeping eye," she kisses lightly his eyes, suffused with tears. Here the lightness of the kiss and the over-brimming fullness of the eyes suggest the hyperbole and the implied metaphor, which likens the kiss to something lightly dipped into a stream. "She spreads the red leaves of thy lips," i.e., kisses the child's lips, which lie lightly apart in infantile sleep, and which are like *rosebuds* in their color and in their childish undevelopment. "Mother diamonds" are the eyes of the Virgin, bright as diamonds and resembling those of the child. "Points" are the rays or beams of the eye, which, according to the old physics, passed, in vision, from one eye to another. Lastly, the eyes of the child are likened to those of a young eagle, and the Virgin tests them against her own as the mother eagle is supposed to test her nestling's eyes against the sun.

Leaving out the figure involved in 'points,' which is Donnian and probably wholly due to the fashion set by him, this passage of Crashaw is inspired, not by the intellect, which clears and distinguishes objects, but by passion, which blends and confuses them. The language is one mass of involved and tangled figure, in which similarity suggests similarity in objects contemplated and intensely visualized—not in abstractions incapable of visualization. Donne fetches his images from the byways of mediæval science and metaphysic and intellectualizes them in the process. Crashaw derives his imagery from the impetus of his feelings and from an intense visualization of the outer world, which causes him to revel in light, color, motion, and space. He at times confuses his images in a pregnancy of thought that involves a partial obscuration of the thing to be figured. These two methods are at the very poles from each other, and incapable of derivation, the one from the other. But if the difficulties of Donne are largely due to subtlety of thought, and those of Crashaw to impetus of feeling, the figures of the lesser poets may often be referred to a striving after original effect, an ingenious pursuit of similitudes in things repugnant, that amounts to a notorious vice of style. The books are full of illustrations of this false taste, and it is easy to find them in the verse of Quarles, Cartwright, Crashaw, Lovelace, and Davenant; even in Carew, Herbert, and Vaughan. . . .

In 1646 appeared *Steps to the Temple*, with a few secular poems under the sub-title, *The Delights of the Muses*, by Richard Crashaw. The *Steps* was so named in modest reference and relation to Herbert's *Temple*, which was Crashaw's immediate inspiration. Crashaw while a student at Cambridge came under influences which, considering the difference in the two ages, are not incomparable to the Oxford or Tractarian Movement of our own century. In the fervent and pious life of Nicholas Ferrar, into whose hands we have already seen the dying Herbert confiding his poetry, Crashaw found much to emulate and admire. Ferrar, notable in science, and a successful man of affairs, forsook the world and formed, with his kinfolk about him, a small religious community at Little Giddings in Hunt-

ingdonshire, where he sought to lead a spiritual life in accord with the principles of the Anglican Church. Predisposed as was Crashaw to that intense and sensuous visualization of spiritual emotion which has characterized the saints and fathers of the Roman Church in many ages, in the life of Saint Theresa the poet found his ideal and his hope. His artistic temperament had led him early "to denounce those who disassociate art from religious worship"; the charity and benignity of his temper caused him equally to oppose those who made an attack upon the papacy an article of faith. It is easy to see how this attitude, under the spiritual influence of such men as Herbert, Robert Shelford, and Ferrar, should gradually have led Crashaw, with the help of some added political impetus, over to the old faith. This impetus came in the form of the parliamentary act by which it was provided that all monuments of superstition be removed from the churches and that the fellows of the universities be required to take the oath of the Solemn League and Covenant. On the enforcement of this act against Peterhouse, Crashaw's own college, and the consequent desecration of its beautiful chapel, Crashaw indignantly refused the League and Covenant, and was expelled from his fellowship. Before long he withdrew to Paris, where he met Cowley. Crashaw died in Italy a few years later, a priest of the Church of Rome. The picture of Cowley, the fair-minded, meditative Epicurean, befriending the young enthusiast, when both were in exile, is pleasant to dwell upon.

The relation of Crashaw to Herbert, save for his discipleship, which changed very little Crashaw's distinctive traits, is much that of Herrick and Carew. Herbert and Crashaw were both good scholars; Herbert knew the world and put it aside as vanity; Crashaw could never have been of the world; his was a nature alien to it, and yet there is a greater warmth in Crashaw than in Herbert. Crashaw turns the passions of earth to worship and identifies the spiritual and the material in his devotion; Herbert has the Puritan spirit within him, which is troubled in the contemplation of earthly vanities, and struggles to rise above and beyond them. It is the antithesis of Protestantism and Roman Catholicism, an antithesis which we can understand better if we can bring ourselves to sympathize with each than if we seek to throw ourselves into an attitude of attack or defense of either.

In matter of poetic style, too, despite his quips and conceits, and despite the fact that with him, as with many devotional poets, execution waits upon the thought and often comes limpingly after, Herbert is far more self-restrained, and his poetry of more uniform workmanship and excellence. But if Herbert has never fallen into Crashaw's extravagances, he is equally incapable of his inspired, rhapsodic flights. Herbert felt the beauties of this visible world and has some delicate touches of appreciation, as where he says:

> I wish I were a tree
> 　For sure then I should grow
> To fruit or shade; at least some bird would trust
> Her household to me, and I should be just.[4]

Crashaw knows less of the concrete objects of the world, but is a creature of light and atmosphere, and revels in color and the gorgeousness thereof. Crashaw often rhapsodizes without bridle, and is open at times to grave criticism on the score of taste. It is for these shortcomings that he has been, time out of mind, the stock example of the dreadful things into which the ill-regulated poetical fancy may fall. The "sister baths" and "portable oceans" of *Magdalene* are easily ridiculed, but it is almost as easy, while ridiculing these distortions of fancy, to forget the luminousness and radiance, the uncommon imaginative power and volatility of mind—if I may venture the term—of this devout Shelley of the reign of Charles I.

Notes

1. "The Ecstasy," ed. 1650, p. 43.
2. See Ueberweg's *History of Philosophy*, I, 71.
3. See Felix Schelling, *A Book of Seventeenth Century Lyrics*, 1899, p. 113.
4. Herbert, ed. Grosart, p. 40.

H. C. BEECHING
From "Introduction"
Poems of Richard Crashaw, ed. J. R. Tutin
1905, pp. xxxvi–lv

The most interesting feature of ⟨*Steps to the Temple*⟩ . . . is the dedicatory poem to the Countess of Denbigh "against irresolution in religion" and still more interesting is the fact that a revised and enlarged version of this exists in a single copy in the British Museum, bearing the imprint "London," but with no publisher's name, and with a manuscript note in a contemporary hand, marking the date of publication as 23 Sext. (*i.e.* August) 1653. It may have been that Crashaw revised the poem after leaving Paris, and sent his corrected MS. to the Countess or to Cowley, without sending a copy to his editor; or it may have been that Car mislaid the revised copy, and recovered it too late for publication in the volume. But it is idle to conjecture. Turnbull noted the existence of this second version, but it was not reprinted until Dr Grosart included it in his private issue (1874). . . . It is in Crashaw's happiest vein. The suggestion that the lady addressed is sure to come over to the writer's side by-and-bye, and so is guilty now of the sin of delay, is a sufficiently subtle weapon in controversy; but how poetically subtle is the expression Crashaw gives it:

Who grants at last, a great while tried,—
And did his best,—to have denied.

Having assumed that Rome is her destined haven, he chides her for not emulating the urgency of all natural things, which, as Bacon says, "move violently to their place." But the climax of the poem is the ironical suggestion of reasons for man's reluctance to be saved, passing into a passionate enunciation of the great Christian dogma of the love which prompted the Incarnation.

All things swear friends to Fair and Good,
Yea suitours; man alone is woo'd,
Tediously woo'd and hardly won,
Only not slow to be undone.
As if the bargain had been driven
So hardly betwixt Earth and Heaven;
Our God would thrive too fast, and be
Too much a gainer by't, should we
Our purchas'd selves too soon bestow.
On Him, who has not lov'd us so.
When love of us called Him to see
If we'd vouchsafe His company,
He left His father's court, and came
Lightly as a lambent flame,
Leaping upon the hills, to be
The humble king of you and me.

I know nothing in devotional poetry finer than this. The best known of the religious poems is the "Hymn to St. Teresa," which has been praised by every critic—by Coleridge amongst the number; and praise can hardly be too high for it. From first to last the inspiration does not flag, but passes with sure success from the tender humour and pathos in which the child's ardour

for martyrdom is told, to the ecstatic picture of the mystical martrydom that does await her, followed by the calm bliss of the beatific vision. This poem is succeeded by an Apology for its being written "when the author was among the Protestants," but Protestantism is not referred to in it. Rather it is an apology to Englishmen for praising a Spaniard, and to Spaniards for writing in English. In the second edition (1648), the Apology embraces both the Hymn and a poem called "The Flaming Heart," which was added to that volume and needs more than all the apology that can be made for it. For seventy lines the writer discourses with a pitiful want of taste upon a picture of Saint Teresa, "with a seraphim beside her," to the general effect that the saint is the better seraph of the two. But in the edition of 1652 twenty-four lines are added, which have nothing to do with the picture, but are a passionate invocation of the saint herself. The first eight of these seem to have been written in order to connect the new with the old, but they barely serve their purpose; for the purple passage beginning, "O thou undaunted daughter of desires," is as far superior to them as they are to the old poem. In fact, these glowing verses may well be recognised as the highest achievement of the Muse of religious ecstasy.[1]

The most ambitious of the religious poems, and the one which the poet himself probably ranked highest, for with it he opened his final selection, is the hymn "To the Name above every Name"— an appeal to all the voices of Nature and Art to join with him in the great celebration. It is full of good things. The passages about music are especially beautiful:

O you, my soul's most certain wings,
Complaining pipes and prattling strings;
Bring all the store
Of sweets you have, and murmur that you have no
more.

And a little below wood and stringed instruments are described as

Such
As sigh with supple wind
Or answer artful touch.

Again how noble is the opening of the final invocation (ll. 114–133), and the passage towards the close about the martyrs, beginning, "O that it were as it was wont to be" (l. 190). But with all its merits, the poem cannot, as a whole, be reckoned a success. It is too fluent; there are repetitions both as to sentiments and phrases—*e.g.* the word *nest* occurs no fewer than five times and always as a rhyme; and there is not enough substance in the thought to bear being spun into two hundred and forty verses. Moreover, Crashaw indulges himself now and then in a "conceit" which leaves the modern reader gasping (*e.g.* ll. 132–5). To be successful he needed a subject less vague in definition, and a metre constraining to conciseness. One cannot help wishing that Crashaw had been born a few years earlier, so that at Cambridge he might have formed a friendship with Milton instead of with Cowley. He would have been attracted, we cannot doubt, to "the Lady of Christ's"; and Milton's jealous care that the word, the phrase, the paragraph should be as perfect as choice could make them, would have been invaluable to Crashaw, if he could have learned it. There might also have been some reciprocal influence in matters of temperament which was as sorely needed. But *dis aliter visum*, and we could not have afforded the loss of Cowley's noble elegy on the "Martyr and Saint," even at the price of "Lycidas" purged of its venomous onslaught on the clergy.

"Charitas Nimia" is one of the few religious poems of Crashaw in which no critic could wish for an excision; it is perhaps also the only one that shows any influence of George

Herbert. The Hymns upon Christmas and Epiphany, which in form resemble one another, are of curiously different merit. One might have anticipated that such a subject as the visit of the Magi would have set Crashaw's imagination on fire, but it did not do so. The poem is turgid and full of dull "conceits." The Christmas poem, on the contrary, is as full of happy expressions and ideas, such as the line about the snow, the description of courtiers as "slippery souls in smiling eyes," and the stanza on the Mother and Child. Many of the religious poems are elaborate versions of the old Church hymns, best perhaps described in the poet's own phrase as "a descant upon plain song." Nothing could be more unlike the simple directness of the Latin than Crashaw's flamboyant paraphrases; at the same time it must be admitted that he always keeps to his subject and in his wildest excursion never loses the key. The most admired of these has been the "Dies Iræ"; the closest version is the *Laudes Sion Salvatorem*, which nevertheless succeeds in breathing poetry into a piece of mediæval scholasticism; the most elaborate is the *Office of the Holy Crosse*. To show Crashaw's method, it will be sufficient to put one stanza of his by a stanza of the original. The hymn in the Office for the third hour runs:

> *Crucifige* clamitant hora tertiarum:
> Illusus induitur veste purpurarum:
> Caput ejus pungitur corona spinarum:
> Crucem portat humeris ad locum pœnarum.

This becomes in Crashaw's rendering:

> The third hour's deafened with the cry
> Of *Crucify Him, crucify.*
> So goes the vote (nor ask them why!)
> 'Live Barabas, and let God die.'
> But there is wit in wrath, and they will try
> A 'Hail' more cruel than their 'crucify.'
> For while in sport He wears a spiteful crown,
> The serious showers along His decent face run sadly
> 　　down.

The antiphons in the Office deserve particular notice; in the original they are, of course, in prose. Among the translations are included characteristic versions of two Psalms. No one but Crashaw would have rendered "He leadeth me in the paths of righteousness," etc., by

> He expounds the weary wonder
> Of my giddy steps, and under
> Spreads a path, clear as day,
> Where no churlish rub says *nay*
> To my joy-conducted feet,
> Whilst they gladly go to meet
> Grace and Peace to learn new lays
> Tun'd to my great Shepherd's praise.

The longest of all the translations is the *Suspicion of Herod*, a canto of sixty-six stanzas done, with Crashaw's usual licence, out of the Italian of Marini. As a piece of writing it is excellent, the stanza with its triple rhyme is well managed, and there are not a few passages which for dignity of style recall Milton, who had undoubtedly profited by its perusal. Take, for example, this verse from the speech of Satan:

> He has my heaven (what would He more?) whose
> 　　bright
> And radiant sceptre this bold hand should bear:
> And for the never-fading fields of light,
> My fair inheritance, he confines me here
> To this dark house of shades, horror, and night,
> To draw a long-liv'd death, where all my cheer
> 　　Is the solemnity my sorrow wears
> 　　That mankind's torment waits upon my tears.

Among the religious poems are usually included two about which a word must be added—the amœbean stanzas upon Hope between Crashaw and Cowley, and "The Weeper." Coleridge, referring to the former in a letter to a friend, remarks that "Crashaw's superiority to Cowley is self-evident." I must confess, temerarious as it is to differ from Coleridge on a point of literary criticism, that even though I am at the moment holding a brief for Crashaw the superiority seems to me altogether on the other side. There is undoubtedly great cleverness in the way Cowley's points are taken up one by one and turned against him; but there is nothing in Crashaw's verse that finds a lodging in the memory, as do Cowley's fine lines about the cloud:

> Thin empty cloud which th' eye deceives
> With shapes that our own fancy gives.
> A cloud which gilt and painted now appears
> But must drop presently in tears;

or these in the last stanza:

> Brother of Fear, more gaily clad,
> The merrier fool o' th' two, yet quite as mad.
> Sire of repentance, child of fond desire
> That blow'st the chymick's and the lover's fire
> 　　Still leading them insensibly on
> 　　With the strong witchcraft of anon.

"The Weeper" is the poem that in most editions opens the *Steps to the Temple*, and it has proved a stumblingblock to many would-be worshippers; amongst others, to that very appreciative critic Mr Edmund Gosse, who in an essay included in his *Seventeenth Century Studies* speaks of it as "distressing" and "humiliating" and "a string of preposterous conceits." Undoubtedly it is a poem that requires us at the outset not to be entirely out of sympathy with our author's subject. If we start by calling the theme "a very small" one, we shall inevitably be more and more provoked as the poem draws out its length. But it is the first duty of a critic to renounce prejudice, and one would imagine that in reading the works of a Roman Catholic poet for æsthetic purposes it might be pardonable to abate something from the rigour of our Protestantism. It may be granted that there are stanzas in the poem—most of them added in the second edition—which ought never to have been written, and need not be read; such as the 4th to 6th, 19th to 22nd, 27th, and 29th.[2] But when these nine stanzas have been excised from the thirty-three, there remains a poem which, if its topic be once allowed—it is a rosary of devotion to St Mary Magdalene—should give nothing but delight to the lover of poetry. To begin with, the stanza is admirably fashioned for a "rosary" (by which I mean a string of stanzas the thought in each of which is complete in itself), because it opens with a shortened trochaic[3] line, which emphasises each new beginning, and concludes in a couplet which emphasises the close. The only other poem in English that for a similar contemplative effect can be compared with it, is Rossetti's "Staff and Scrip," but in that case the separate roundness of each stanza is not so completely an advantage, as the poem tells a continuous tale. It will be observed how much variety of rhythm Crashaw obtains within each stanza, without violating the metre, by merely shifting the pause.

> Th' dew no more will weep
> 　　The primrose's pale cheek to deck:
> Th' dew no more will sleep
> 　　Nuzzel'd in the lily's neck;
> Much rather would it be thy tear,
> And leave them both to tremble here
> Not the soft gold which

Steals from the amber-weeping tree,
Makes sorrow half so rich
    As the drops distill'd from thee,
Sorrow's best jewels lie in these
Caskets, of which heaven keeps the keys.

Not in th' Evening's eyes
    When they red with weeping are
For the sun that dies,
    Sits sorrow with a face so fair,
Nowhere but here did ever meet
Sweetness so sad, sadness so sweet.

But, says Mr. Gosse, these are "preposterous conceits." What is a "conceit?" How does it differ from the legitimate poetical image, the offspring of that imaginative power which illuminates one object by the light reflected on it from another? According to Dr Johnson, the difference is that the latter, though not obvious, is upon its first production acknowledged to be just, whereas, in the case of conceits, "the reader, far from wondering that he missed them, wonders more frequently by what perverseness of industry they were ever found." This distinction, stated in the straightforward commonsense manner of the great eighteenth-century critic, seems to be a true one, and indeed seems to be the grain of truth at the bottom of the more pretentious distinction between the images of the "fancy" and the "imagination," of which Coleridge, and after him Ruskin, have made so much. Accordingly we may expect to find that, although the greater the poet is, the more natural and satisfying will be the general run of his images, yet even among those of the greatest poets some will strike us by their cleverness rather than their truth, and even in times when the rage for novelty is paramount, some will charm by their truth as much as their novelty. The seventeenth-century writers, coming in the ebb of the great Elizabethan wave, were certainly tempted to depend too much upon ingenuity, too little upon the freshness of natural suggestion; and Cowley's writings afforded Dr Johnson an inexhaustible storehouse of the wrong sort of "wit"; but then Cowley is no less full of metaphors that are as just as they are striking. The lines quoted above are an instance. And so it is with Crashaw. It cannot be denied that when the bright heaven of invention is overcast, he can be beyond measure dull and tedious with his hackneyed conceits of "nests" and "fires" and "eyes," but what ample amends he makes by-and-by whether in single epithets like the *weary* lids of Hope" or in such splendid images as that in the Description of a Religious House, "still rolling a round sphere of still returning pain." Our modern taste may be jarred by the arrogance of poets who set out with the deliberate intention of saying as many fine things as they can upon Hope or a Saint's tears, instead of "waiting for the spark from heaven to fall"; but for all that we have no right to condemn the result *en bloc*: we must take each several trope upon its merits. Of course it is never the mere intellectual element in the figure that constitutes the poetry, apart from the emotion that has suggested it, or at any rate prompted the search for it, and it is the intellectual element that is predominant in the Caroline poets, but Crashaw's verses do not lack passion. And besides all this, there is the actual writing; and those who refuse to find the conceits other than ingenious, and the passion other than preposterous, cannot be deaf to the exquisite music of the verse.

There's no need at all
That the balsam-sweating bough
    So coyly should let fall
    Her med'cinable tears; for now
Nature hath learnt to extract a dew
More sovereign and sweet from you.

Yet let the poor drops weep—
Weeping is the ease of woe—
    Softly let them creep,
    Sad that they are vanquisht so,
They, though to others no relief,
Balsam may be for their own grief.

Golden though he be,
Golden Tagus murmurs though;
    Were his way by thee,
    Content and quiet he would go,
So much more rich would he esteem
Thy silver, than his golden stream.

Well does the May, that lies
Smiling in thy cheeks, confess
    The April in thine eyes;
    Mutual sweetness they express.
No April ere lent kinder showers
Nor May returned more faithful flowers.

To pass now from the *Steps to the Temple* to the "other delights of the Muses," Crashaw's temperament was so eminently devotional that it is not surprising to find but few of his secular pieces of any high merit. The best, and the best known through its inclusion in the *Golden Treasury* (though in a too curtailed form, and from an inferior text) is the "Wishes to his (supposed) Mistress," a poem written in an original and effective metre of three lines of four, six, and eight syllables. It is full of fine thoughts and phrases, some in Crashaw's own superlative manner, as when he speaks of "tresses"

Whose native ray
Can tame the wanton day
Of gems that in their bright shades play.

Each ruby there
Or pearl, that dare appear
Be its own blush, be its own tear;

Others in a direct style of high and simple dignity, that might belong to any of the greater masters; as when he wishes for his mistress

Whate'er delight
Can make day's forehead bright
Or give down to the wings of night.

Days that need borrow
No part of their good morrow
From a fore-spent night of sorrow.

Life that dares send
A challenge to his end,
And when it comes, say, 'Welcome, friend.'

The version of Strada's contest between the lutanist and the nightingale, called "Music's duel," is rather a *tour de force* than a very successful or pleasing poem, inasmuch as vocabulary, though necessary to poetry, is not so necessary as feeling. The reader is amazed more than he is delighted. But an amazing poem it is, and the merit is Crashaw's; for though the story and the plan of the poem are taken from Strada, most of the description of the nightingale's song is Crashaw's own. To even describe the description would task a poet. Mr Swinburne speaks of "its dazzling intricacy and affluence in refinements, its supple and cunning implications, its choiceness and subtlety." But it must be confessed that a part, as often with Crashaw, would have been more than the whole. The "Epitaph on a young Married Couple" is written in the octosyllables that hardly any seventeenth-century poet could handle without some success, and Crashaw is always happy in them.

Peace, good reader, do not weep.
Peace, the lovers are asleep.

They, sweet turtles, folded lie
In the last knot that love could tie.
And though they lie as they were dead,
Their pillow stone, their sheets of lead,
(Pillow hard, and sheets not warm)
Love made the bed; they'll take no harm.

"Love's Horoscope," in octosyllabic stanzas, is an even finer piece of writing, curiously perfect in its balanced structure, and the astrological idea is fully worked out, but without over-elaboration. A "song out of the Italian," in a metre copied by Mr Swinburne, equally fantastic in idea, is equally perfect in execution. The decasyllabic poems are not so completely successful, though occasionally they admit of effects in Crashaw's peculiar style, as in the close of "Satisfaction for Sleep":

Why threatst thou so?
Why dost thou shake thy leaden sceptre? Go
Bestow thy poppy upon wakeful Woe,
Sickness, and Sorrow, whose pale lids ne'er know
Thy downy finger; dwell upon their eyes,
Shut in their tears, shut out their miseries.

The history of the development of the heroic couplet is too large a subject to discuss at the end of an Introduction. It happens, however, that Pope in one of his letters to Henry Cromwell has given a criticism upon Crashaw, interesting in itself and for the light it throws upon the eighteenth-century standards of taste. The following extract gives the substance of the criticism

I take this poet to have writ like a gentleman, that is at leisure hours, and more to keep out of idleness than to establish a reputation; so that nothing regular or just can be expected from him. All that regards design, form, fable (which is the soul of poetry), all that concerns exactness, or consent of parts (which is the body) will probably be wanting; only pretty conceptions, fine metaphors, glittering expressions, and something of a neat cast of verse (which are properly the dress, gems, or loose ornaments of poetry) may be found in these verses. . . . To speak of his numbers is a little difficult, they are so various and irregular, and mostly Pindarick: 'tis evident his heroic verse (the best example of which is his 'Music's Duel') is carelessly made up; but one may imagine, from what it now is, that had he taken more care, it had been musical and pleasing enough, not extremely majestic, but sweet. And the time considered, of his writing, he was (even as incorrect as he is) none of the worse versificators.[4]

There is justice in some of these strictures. Crashaw was certainly wanting in the architectonics of poetry, and never attempted an epic or a drama. As certainly he was given to vain repetitions. But he had imagination and he had passion, neither of which qualities has a place in Mr Pope's Anatomy of Poetry. But to speak only of the heroic couplet; let the reader turn to Crashaw's "Description of a Religious House," and then to Pope's "Eloisa and Abelard" and say whether he can fail to adjudge the meed to Crashaw.[5] Pope's couplet, excellent for satiric verse and epigram, is too frail a vehicle for passion. The recurring cæsura in the third foot, often followed by a conjunction or preposition, and the inevitable epithet in every line make a thin and artificial instrument which soon disgusts. Crashaw's verses have far greater variety and far greater robustness, and his epithets, while perhaps they are over-plentiful, all add something to the conception.

Another poet who headed the reaction from the school of

Pope agrees with him generally both in his praise and blame of Crashaw. "Crashaw," says Coleridge, "seems in his poems to have given the first ebullience of his imagination, unshapen into form, or much of what we now term sweetness." He goes on to say that certain verses from the Hymn to St Teresa (ll. 43–64) "were ever present to my mind whilst writing the second part of Christabel; if, indeed by some subtle process of the mind they did not suggest the first thought of the whole poem." The student who turns to the second part of Christabel will be puzzled to trace any direct influence of Crashaw upon the poem. Coleridge's versification, with its abundance of extra syllables is jerky by comparison, and suggests hasty workmanship far more than Crashaw's. But perhaps Coleridge is referring to that portion of the second part of Christabel which was never written.[6] Coleridge, however, sometimes recalls Crashaw by the richness of his lines, as Shelley does by his smooth and limpid flow; but at his best Crashaw has more radiance than either.

There is a further respect in which Crashaw and Coleridge are alike: they both belong to that body of poets between whose best and worst there seems no recognisable relation. At worst they are both singularly flat and unprofitable and sometimes ludicrous; at best their verse supplies a meaning to the term commonly used of poets, the word "inspiration"; it suggests a theory that the poet is only a medium for supernatural powers to play upon, an Æolian harp for the spirit which blows as it lists; for their best writing seems as far as possible removed from any result that Art alone could compass. Jonson tells us that "a good poet's made as well as born," and in reading Jonson, and indeed in reading his greater disciple Milton, we assent to the theory, for the conscious artist reveals himself in every line. But when we turn to Crashaw we revert to the older theory of the poet as a paradisal creature, "born not made," a "winged and holy being,"[7] whose poems are not the work of man, but divine, and though we may readily admit that Prospero would be a more useful member of human society than Ariel, we cannot but regard Ariel with the more wonder for his gift of ethereal music. But besides this inexplicable charm of music, when inspired, Crashaw was gifted with the fervour of a devout enthusiast; and so it comes about that although he has occasionally fine poetry which is not religious, and too often ardent religious verse which is not poetry, yet his most exalted verse is that in which both influences meet. Then the whole man is sublimed and becomes, "all air and fire."

Notes

1. Crashaw's critics usually speak as if the concluding lines of "The Flaming Heart" had formed part of the original poem. Thus Mr Saintsbury: "And then in a moment, in the twinkling of an eye, without warning of any sort, the metre changes, the poet's inspiration catches fire, and there rushes up into the heaven of poetry this marvellous rocket of song" (*Elizabethan Literature*, p. 365).
2. The numeration follows the 1652 edition adopted in J.R. Tutin, *Poems of Richard Crashaw*, 1905.
3. That the effect of the line is meant to be generally trochaic seems certain from the fact that it is so in most of the early stanzas which fix the mould of the metre; also the twelfth stanza opens "There's no need at all," where otherwise it would have been as simple to write "There is no need at all." Even in the lines having six syllables, which are the majority, it will be observed that the dissyllabic words are trochees.
4. Correspondence, Croker and Elwin, vi. 116. The letter contains also a fairly just criticism of "The Weeper."
5. Pope in this psuedo-Gothic poem borrows a verse from Crashaw's "Description," which, alas, will not fit its new context:

How happy is the blameless vestal's lot,
The world forgetting, by the world forgot:

Eternal sunshine of the spotless mind!
Each pray'r accepted and each wish resign'd
Labour and rest that equal periods keep,
'Obedient slumbers that can wake and weep.'
                                            (ll. 201–12)

It is plain that if labour and rest keep equal periods, the slumbers must be such as do *not* wake and weep. But it is easy to sympathise with Pope's admiration for Crashaw's line. In its own place it is admirable:

A hasty portion of prescribed sleep;
Obedient slumbers, that can wake and weep,
And sing, and sigh, and work, and sleep again;
Still rolling a round sphere of still-returning pain.

6. *Letters, Conversations, and Recollections of Samuel Taylor Coleridge*, 1836. Coleridge repeatedly spoke of the poem as containing 1400 lines, but the editions know only of less than half this number. See note to Dykes Compbell's edition, p. 602.
7. Plato, *Ion*, 534.

THOMAS HEYWOOD

c. 1573–1641

Thomas Heywood was born in Lincolnshire, probably in 1573. He possibly attended Cambridge for several years before settling in London around 1593. A prolific dramatist known for his studies of domestic life, Heywood may have been involved in the writing of over 220 plays, of which 35 still survive.

Heywood's first published work was a verse imitation of Ovid, *Oenone and Paris* (1594). By 1596 Heywood was working for London theatrical agent Philip Henslowe. Among Heywood's early plays are *The Four Prentices of London* (c. 1600), *A Woman Kilde with Kindnesse* (1603), his two-part history of England, *If You Know Not Me, You Know Nobody*, *The Rape of Lucrece* (1608), based on an incident in Roman history from Livy, and *The Fair Maid of the West* (c. 1610). Around 1611 Heywood began his five part history of Greek mythology with *The Golden Age*. *The Silver Age* (1612), *The Brazen Age* (1613), and *The Iron Age* (1613), written in two parts, completed the series. Heywood succeeded Thomas Dekker as the writer of mayoral pageants for the City of London in 1631. Among the many masques and pageants Heywood wrote, *Love's Mistress; or, The Queen's Masque* (1634), is well remembered. Heywood's later works include *The English Traveller* (1627) and his revival of Marlowe's *The Jew of Malta* (1632), to which he appended a prologue and an epilogue, and a collaboration with Richard Brome, *The Late Lancashire Witches* (1634).

Aside from his many plays, Heywood also is known for his prose works, including *An Apology for Actors* (1612), and *Nine Books of Various History concerning Women* (1624), later published as *The General History of Women* in 1657. Heywood also published two translations: Ovid's *De Arte Amandi; or, The Art of Love* and Sallust's *The Two Most Worthy and Notable Histories of Catiline and Jugurtha*. Heywood was buried on August 16, 1641, at the Church of St. James, Clerkenwell.

Personal

An Author that liv'd in the Time of Queen *Elizabeth*, and the Reign of King *James* the First. Tho' he were but an Actor, as is manifest by Mr. *Kirkman's* Testimony, and apparent from a Piece writ by him, call'd *The Actors Vindication*; yet his Plays were in those Days accounted of the Second-Rate. He was the most Voluminous Writer that ever handled Dramatick Poetry in our Language; and I know none but the Famous *Spaniard*, *Lopez de Vega*, that can vye with him; if at least we give Credit to his own Attestation, in the Preface to One of his Plays; 'This Tragi-comedy (as he says) being One reserv'd amongst two Hundred and Twenty, in which I have had either an entire Hand, or at the least a main Finger. Of this Number we have, that I know of, but Five and Twenty entire Plays remaining: the Reason of which the Author gives us in the same Epistle. 'True it is, that my Plays are not exposed unto the world in Volumes, to bear the Title of *Works*, (as others) one Reason is, That many of them by shifting and change of Companies, have been negligently lost, Others of them are still retained in the Hands of some Actors, who think it against their peculiar profit to have them come in Print; and a third, That it was never any great Ambition in me to be Voluminously read.

These seem to me, to be more plausible Reasons than what Mr. *Winstanley* gives for their Miscarriage; 'Tis said, that

he not only acted himself almost every day, but also wrote each day a Sheet; and that he might loose no time, many of his Plays were compos'd in the Tavern, on the back-side of Tavern Bills; which may be the occasion that so many of them be lost. Certainly the Tavern Bills were very large, or Mr. *Winstanley* must think his Readers Credulity of the same extent with his own; who would subscribe to the belief of so ridiculous a Story. This Report Mr. *Winstanley* partly borrows from Mr. *Kirkman's* Advertisement at the End of his Catalogue, and as Stories lose nothing in the carriage, Mr. *Winstanley* had added the Contrivance of making use of Tavern Bills to save Paper. But tho' many of these Plays being written loosely in Taverns as Mr. *Kirkman* observes, might occasion their being so mean; yet it did not in probability much contribute to their loss, as Mr. *Winstanley* would have it.

To do our Author justice, I cannot allow that his Plays are so mean as Mr. *Kirkman* has represented them: for he was a general Scholar, and an indifferent Linguist, as his several Translations from *Lucian*, *Erasmus*, *Textor*, *Beza*, *Buchanan*, and other Latine and Italian *Authors*, sufficiently manifest. Nay, further in several of his Plays he has borrow'd many Ornaments from the Ancients; as more particularly in his Plays call'd *The Ages*, he has intersperst several Things, borrow'd from *Homer*, *Virgil*, *Ovid*, *Seneca*, *Plautus*, &c. which extreamly set them off. What Opinion the Wits of the last Age had of him may appear from the following Verses, extracted from a Copy of the Poets of those Times: *viz.*

> The squibbing *Middleton,* and *Heywood* Sage,
> Th' Apologetick *Atlas* of the Stage;
> Well of the *Golden Age,* he could entreat,
> But little of the *Mettal,* he could get;
> Threescore sweet Babes he fashion'd at a Lump,
> For he was Christen'd in *Parnassus* Pump;
> The Muses Gossip to *Aurora's* Bed,
> And ever since that time his Face was Red.

—GERARD LANGBAINE, *An Account of the English Dramatick Poets,* 1691

General

Thomas Heywood . . . who like his cotemporaries, Hardy in France, and Lopez de Vega in Spain, seems to have derived all his merit from the number instead of the quality of his dramatic works, demands some mention here, though no more than two of his plays, at least that we know of, appeared during the life of Elizabeth.

This man, by some of the biographers, has been greatly extolled as a writer without any great appearance, however, of either truth or justice; for the prodigious quantity he wrote, for which he ransacked the ancients without mercy, whatever might have been his real merit had he taken time to correct and polish his works, rendered it impossible for him to turn any thing out of hand likely to secure him a solid reputation; and thus we have a list of twenty-four pieces, out of two hundred and twenty which he himself says he either wrote or was concerned in, little more known at this moment than by their titles.

Heywood was certainly a good classical scholar, and as an actor he was pretty celebrated. Indeed the pursuing this occupation, and his being perpetually in company, for we are ridiculously told that he wrote his plays upon the backs of tavern bills, must have left him but little opportunity to complete the difficult task of writing plays, especially such an immense number as are attributed to him.—CHARLES DIBDIN, *A Complete History of the Stage,* 1795, Vol. 3, pp. 105–6

If I were to be consulted as to a Reprint of our Old English Dramatists, I should advise to begin with the collected Plays of Heywood. He was a fellow Actor, and fellow Dramatist, with Shakspeare. He possessed not the imagination of the latter; but in all those qualities which gained for Shakspeare the attribute of *gentle,* he was not inferior to him. Generosity, courtesy, temperance in the depths of passion; sweetness, in a word, and gentleness; Christianism; and true hearty Anglicism of feelings, shaping that Christianism; shine throughout his beautiful writings in a manner more conspicuous than in those of Shakspeare, but only more conspicuous, inasmuch as in Heywood these qualities are primary, in the other subordinate to poetry. I love them both equally, but Shakspeare has most of my wonder. Heywood should be known to his countrymen, as he deserves. His plots are almost invariably English. I am sometimes jealous, that Shakspeare laid so few of his scenes at home. . . .

Heywood is a sort of *prose* Shakspeare. His scenes are to the full as natural and affecting. But we miss *the Poet,* that which in Shakspeare always appears out and above the surface of *the nature.* Heywood's characters, his Country Gentlemen, etc., are exactly what we see (but of the best kind of what we see) in life. Shakspeare makes us believe, while we are among his lovely creations, that they are nothing but what we are familiar with, as in dreams new things seem old: but we awake,

and sigh for the difference.—CHARLES LAMB, *Specimens of English Dramatic Poets,* 1808

He possesses considerable power of interesting the affections, by placing his plain and familiar characters in affecting situations. The worst of him is, that his commonplace sentiments and plain incidents fall not only beneath the ideal beauty of art, but are often more fatiguing than what we meet with in the ordinary and unselected circumstances of life. When he has hit upon those occasions where the passions should obviously rise with accumulated expression, he lingers on through the scene with a dull and level indifference. The term artlessness may be applied to Heywood in two very opposite senses. His pathos is often artless in the better meaning of the word, because its objects are true to life, and their feelings naturally expressed. But he betrays still more frequently an artlessness, or we should rather call it, a want of art, in deficiency of contrivance.
—THOMAS CAMPBELL, *Specimens of the British Poets,* 1819

Heywood I shall mention next, as a direct contrast to Marlowe in everything but the smoothness of his verse. As Marlowe's imagination glows like a furnace, Heywood's is a gentle, lambent flame that purifies without consuming. His manner is simplicity itself. There is nothing supernatural, nothing startling, or terrific. He makes use of the commonest circumstances of every-day life, and of the easiest tempers, to shew the workings, or rather the inefficacy of the passions, the *vis inertiæ* of tragedy. His incidents strike from their very familiarity, and the distresses he paints invite our sympathy, from the calmness and resignation with which they are borne. The pathos might be deemed purer from its having no mixture of turbulence or vindictiveness in it; and in proportion as the sufferers are made to deserve a better fate. In the midst of the most untoward reverses and cutting injuries, good-nature and good sense keep their accustomed sway. He describes men's errors with tenderness, and their duties only with zeal, and the heightenings of a poetic fancy. His style is equally natural, simple, and unconstrained. The dialogue (bating the verse), is such as might be uttered in ordinary conversation. It is beautiful prose put into heroic measure. It is not so much that he uses the common English idiom for everything (for that I think the most poetical and impassioned of our elder dramatists do equally), but the simplicity of the characters, and the equable flow of the sentiments do not require or suffer it to be warped from the tone of level speaking, by figurative expressions, or hyperbolical allusions. A few scattered exceptions occur now and then, where the hectic flush of passion forces them from the lips, and they are not the worse for being rare. Thus, in the play called *A Woman Killed with Kindness,* Wendoll, when reproached by Mrs. Frankford with his obligations to her husband, interrupts her hastily, by saying

> Oh speak no more!
> For more than this I know, and have recorded
> Within the *red-leaved table* of my heart.

And further on, Frankford, when doubting his wife's fidelity, says, with less feeling indeed, but with much elegance of fancy,

> Cold drops of sweat sit dangling on my hairs,
> Like morning dew upon the golden flow'rs.

So also, when returning to his house at midnight to make the fatal discovery, he exclaims,

> Astonishment,
> Fear, and amazement beat upon my heart,
> Even as a madman beats upon a drum.

It is the reality of things present to their imaginations, that makes these writers so fine, so bold, and yet so true in what they describe. Nature lies open to them like a book, and was not to them 'invisible, or dimly seen' through a veil of words and filmy abstractions. Such poetical ornaments are however to be met with at considerable intervals in this play, and do not disturb the calm serenity and domestic simplicity of the author's style. The conclusion of Wendoll's declaration of love to Mrs. Frankford may serve as an illustration of its general merits, both as to thought and diction.

> Fair, and of all beloved, I was not fearful
> Bluntly to give my life into your hand,
> And at one hazard, all my earthly means.
> Go, tell your husband: he will turn me off,
> And I am then undone. I care not, I;
> 'Twas for your sake. Perchance in rage he'll kill me;
> I care not; 'twas for you. Say I incur
> The general name of villain thro' the world,
> Of traitor to my friend: I care not, I;
> Poverty, shame, death, scandal, and reproach,
> For you I'll hazard all: why what care I?
> For you I love, and for your love I'll die.

The affecting remonstrance of Frankford to his wife, and her repentant agony at parting with him, are already before the public, in Mr. Lamb's *Specimens*. The winding up of this play is rather awkwardly managed, and the moral is, according to established usage, equivocal. It required only Frankford's reconciliation to his wife, as well as his forgiveness of her, for the highest breach of matrimonial duty, to have made a Woman Killed with Kindness a complete anticipation of the Stranger. Heywood, however, was in that respect but half a Kotzebue!—The view here given of country manners is truly edifying. As in the higher walk of tragedy we see the manners and moral sentiments of kings and nobles of former times, here we have the feuds and amiable qualities of country 'squires and their relatives; and such as were the rulers, such were their subjects. The frequent quarrels and ferocious habits of private life are well exposed in the fatal rencounter between Sir Francis Acton and Sir Charles Mountford about a hawking match, in the ruin and rancorous persecution of the latter in consequence, and in the hard, unfeeling, cold-blooded treatment he receives in his distress from his own relations, and from a fellow of the name of Shafton. After reading the sketch of this last character, who is introduced as a mere ordinary personage, the representative of a class, without any preface or apology, no one can doubt the credibility of that of Sir Giles Over-reach, who is professedly held up (I should think almost unjustly) as a prodigy of grasping and hardened selfishness. The influence of philosophy and prevalence of abstract reasoning, if it has done nothing for our poetry, has done, I should hope, something for our manners. The callous declaration of one of these unconscionable churls,

> This is no world in which to pity men,

might have been taken as a motto for the good old times in general, and with a very few reservations, if Heywood has not grossly libelled them.—Heywood's plots have little of artifice or regularity of design to recommend them. He writes on carelessly, as it happens, and trusts to Nature, and a certain happy tranquillity of spirit, for gaining the favour of the audience. He is said, besides attending to his duties as an actor, to have composed regularly a sheet a day. This may account in some measure for the unembarrassed facility of his style. His own account makes the number of his writings for the stage, or those in which he had a main hand, upwards of 200. In fact, I do not wonder at any quantity that an author is said to have written; for the more a man writes, the more he can write.
—WILLIAM HAZLITT, *Lectures on the Dramatic Literature of the Age of Elizabeth*, 1820

Heywood's best plays evince large observation, considerable dramatic skill, a sweet and humane spirit, and an easy command of language. His style, indeed, is singularly simple, pure, clear, and straightforward; but it conveys the impression of a mind so diffused as almost to be characterless, and incapable of flashing its thoughts through the images of imaginative passion. He is more prosaic, closer to ordinary life and character, than his contemporaries. Two of his plays, and the best of them all, A *Woman Killed with Kindness*, and *The English Traveller*, are thoroughly domestic dramas, the first, and not the worst, of their class. The plot of *The English Traveller* is specially good; and in reading few works of fiction do we receive a greater shock of surprise than in Geraldine's discovery of the infidelity of Wincott's wife, whom he loves with a Platonic devotion. It is as unanticipated as the discovery, in Jonson's *Silent Woman*, that Epicœne is no woman at all, while at the same time it has less the appearance of artifice, and is more the result of natural causes.—EDWIN P. WHIPPLE, *The Literature of the Age of Elizabeth*, 1869, pp. 122–23

> Tom, if they loved thee best who called thee Tom,
>   What else may all men call thee, seeing thus bright
>   Even yet the laughing and the weeping light
> That still thy kind old eyes are kindled from?
> Small care was thine to assail and overcome
>   Time and his child Oblivion: yet of right
>   Thy name has part with names of lordlier might
> For English love and homely sense of home,
> Whose fragrance keeps thy small sweet bayleaf young
>   And gives it place aloft among thy peers
>   Whence many a wreath once higher strong Time has
>   hurled:
> And this thy praise is sweet on Shakespeare's tongue—
>   'O good old man, how well in thee appears
>   The constant service of the antique world!'
>   —ALGERNON CHARLES SWINBURNE, "Thomas
>   Heywood," *Sonnets on English Dramatic
>   Poets*, 1882

What Heywood has in common with Shakespere, though his prosaic rather than poetic treatment brings it out in a much less brilliant way, is his sympathy with ordinary and domestic character, his aversion from the fantastic vices which many of his fellows were prone to attribute to their characters, his humanity, his kindness. The reckless tragedy of blood and massacre, the reckless comedy of revelry and intrigue, were always repulsive to him, as far as we can judge from the comparatively scanty remnant of the hundreds of plays in which he boasted that he had had a hand, if not a chief hand. Besides these plays (he confesses to authorship or collaboration in two hundred and twenty) he was a voluminous writer in prose and verse, though I do not myself pretend to much knowledge of his nondramatic work. Its most interesting part would have been a *Lives of the Poets*, which we know that he intended, and which could hardly have failed to give much information about his famous contemporaries. As it is, his most remarkable and best-known work, not contained in one of his dramas, is the curious and constantly quoted passage half complaining that all the chief dramatists of his day were known by abbreviations of their names, but characteristically and good-humouredly ending with the license—

> I hold he loves me best who calls me Tom.

We have unfortunately no knowledge which enables us to call him many names except such as are derived from critical examination of his works. Little except the facts that he was a

Lincolnshire man and a Fellow of Peterhouse is recorded of his personal history. His masterpiece, *The Woman Killed with Kindness* (in which a deceived husband, coming to the knowledge of his shame, drives his rival to repentance, and his wife to repentance and death, by his charity), is not wholly admirable. Shakespere would have felt, more fully than Heywood, the danger of presenting his hero as something of a wittol without sufficient passion of religion or affection to justify his tolerance. But the pathos is so great, the sense of "the pity of it" is so simply and unaffectedly rendered, that it is impossible not to rank Heywood very high. . . .

In the great number of other pieces attributed to him, written in all the popular styles, except the two above referred to, merits and defects are mixed up in a very curious fashion. Never sinking to the lowest depth of the Elizabethan playwright, including some great ones, Heywood never rises to anything like the highest height. His chronicle plays are very weak, showing no grasp of heroic character, and a most lamentable slovenliness of rhythm. Few things are more curious than to contrast with *Henry VI.* (to which some critics will allow little of Shakespere's work) and *Richard III.* the two parts of *Edward IV.*, in which Heywood, after a manner, fills the gap. There are good lines here and there, and touching traits; but the whole, as a whole, is quite ludicrously bad, and "written to the gallery," the City gallery, in the most innocent fashion. *If You Know Not Me You Know Nobody*, or *The Troubles of Queen Elizabeth*, also in two parts, has the same curious innocence, the same prosaic character, but hardly as many redeeming flashes. Its first part deals with Elizabeth's real "troubles," in her sister's days; its second with the Armada period and the founding of the Royal Exchange. For Heywood, unlike most of the dramatists, was always true to the City, even to the eccentric extent of making, in *The Four Prentices of London*, Godfrey of Bouillon and his brethren members of the prentice-brotherhood. His classical and allegorical pieces, such as *The Golden Age* and its fellows, are most tedious and not at all brief. The four of them (*The Iron Age* has two parts) occupy a whole volume of the reprint, or more than four hundred closely printed pages; and their clumsy dramatisation of Ovid's *Metamorphoses*, with any other classical learning that Heywood could think of thrust in, presents (together with various minor pieces of a somewhat similar kind) as striking a contrast with *Troilus and Cressida*, as *Edward IV.* does with *Henry VI.* His spectacles and pageants, chiefly in honour of London (*London's Jus Honorarium*, with other metaphorical Latin titles of the same description) are heavy, the weakness of his versification being especially felt in such pieces. His strength lies in the domestic and contemporary drama, where his pathos had free play, unrestrained by the necessity of trying to make it rise to chivalrous or heroic height, and where his keen observation of his fellow-men made him true to mankind in general, at the same time that he gave a vivid picture of contemporary manners. Of this class of his plays *A Woman Killed with Kindness* is undoubtedly the chief, but it has not a few companions, and those in a sufficiently wide and varied class of subject. *The Fair Maid of the Exchange* is, perhaps, not now found to be so very delectable and full of mirth as it is asserted to be on its title-page, because it is full of that improbability and neglect of verisimilitude which has been noted as the curse of the minor Elizabethan drama. The "Cripple of Fenchurch," the real hero of the piece, is a very unlikely cripple; the heroines chop and change their affections in the most surprising manner; and the characters generally indulge in that curious self-description and soliloquising in dialogue which is never found in Shakespere, and is found everywhere

else. But it is still a lively picture of contemporary manners. We should be sorry to lose *The Fair Maid of the West* with its picture of Devonshire sailors, foreign merchants, kings of Fez, Bashaws of various parts, Italian dukes, and what not. The two parts make anything but a good play, but they are decidedly interesting, and their tone supports Mr. Bullen's conjecture that we owe to Heywood the, in parts, admirable play of *Dick of Devonshire*, a dramatisation of the quarter-staff feats in Spain of Richard Peake of Tavistock. *The English Traveller* may rank with *A Woman Killed with Kindness* as Heywood's best plays (there is, indeed, a certain community of subject between them), but *A Maidenhead Well Lost*, and *The Witches of Lancashire*, are not far behind it; nor is *A Challenge for Beauty*. We can hardly say so much for *Love's Mistress*, which dramatises the story of *Cupid and Psyche*, or for *The Wise Woman of Hogsdon* (Hoxton), a play rather of Middleton's type. But in *The Royal King and Loyal Subject*, and in *Fortune by Land and Sea*, the author shows again the sympathy with chivalrous character and adventure which (if he never can be said to be fully up to its level in the matter of poetic expression) was evidently a favourite and constant motive with him. In short, Heywood, even at his worst, is a writer whom it is impossible not to like. His very considerable talent, though it stopped short of genius, was united with a pleasant and genial temper, and little as we know of his life, his dedications and prefaces make us better acquainted with his personality than we are with that of much more famous men.—GEORGE SAINTSBURY, *A History of Elizabethan Literature*, 1887, pp. 280–84

The remarks of Charles Lamb on Heywood are well known. "Heywood," says Elia, "is a sort of prose Shakespeare. His scenes are to the full as natural and affecting. But we miss *the Poet*, that which in Shakespeare always appears out and above the surface of *the nature.*" Given thus in its amplification, the criticism, if still a little too enthusiastic, is sound and intelligible. But to speak casually of Heywood as a "prose Shakespeare" is to offer a stumbling-block to the feet of inexperienced readers. It needs the imagination of a Lamb to divine the one aspect in which it is possible to read Shakespeare into Heywood. He is curiously lacking in that distinction of temper which was so frequent in his age. In studying most of the great men of that time, we are forced in some measure to lift ourselves into their altitudes in order to enjoy their qualities. The humours of Ben Jonson, the funereal silences of Webster, the frenzies of Middleton, the romantic intoxication of Fletcher—these are conditions of the imagination with which our modern life is little in sympathy, and to throw ourselves cordially into them we must resolutely forget the habits of thought which chequer our modern daily life. It is not so with what is most characteristic in Heywood. No effort is needed to make the spirit in sympathy with him. This mild and genial nature knew nothing of the subtle mysteries of human experience, and satisfied himself with presenting before us such simple and realistic pictures as shall move us to quiet laughter and passing tears. As a history of domestic sorrow, nobly borne by the wronged, and bitterly atoned by the wrong-doer, without heroic circumstances and without high-flown phrases, *A Woman Killed with Kindness* remains unexcelled, perhaps unequalled, in our poetical literature. It is the most highly finished of the dramas of Heywood, and the only one which has been put on the stage within recent times. It was first published in 1607.

When Heywood came to write *The English Traveller* he was more under the influence of Ben Jonson than of Shakespeare. His language has here lost its simple and straightforward character; it is full of quips and catches, and the dialogue is studded with conceited oaths. The plot of this play is founded on that of the *Mostellaria* of Plautus, and the really affecting scenes of it deal with the unselfish love of an old gentleman, recently wedded to a young wife, for one of the fine young men that become so familiar to readers of Heywood. He trusts the youth with his house, wealth, and wife, secure in his known honour; but sorrow is brought on all the characters by the heartless intrigues of a friend whom the young man introduces into his old host's house. This play is full of clever and picturesque passages, and there is in particular one describing a riotous party of drinking men, which is perhaps the most spirited page of Heywood's writing. The Shakespearian qualities of sweetness and gentleness which Charles Lamb has claimed for this author are pleasantly exemplified in *The Challenge for Beauty*, a Spanish story of the love of Petrocella for a noble English captive, Montferrers, and in the romantic tragedy of *Fortune by Land and Sea*. . . .

Heywood was not one of those poets on whom the gaze of all critics turns, as to a star whose beams lend themselves to infinite analysis; it is easy enough to divide the clear rays in his one pencil of light. He is a poet who will never, in future, want his friends, but who will scarcely claim one lover. It is not possible to be enthusiastic over the memory of a gossip so cheerful, garrulous, and superficial as this haunter of the Strand and the Exchange. He has a thousand entertaining things to tell us about the shops and the shop-girls; about the handsome young gallants, and the shocking way in which they waste their money; about the affectations of citizen fathers, and the tempers of citizen mothers. He is the most confirmed button-holer of our poetical acquaintance; and if he were only a little more monotonous, he would be universally voted a bore. Somehow or other, he has a little group of listeners always round him; it is not easy to drag one's self away till his stories are finished. His voice trembles as he tells us the strangest, saddest tale of how this or that poor girl came to shame and sorrow—of how such a noble gentleman, whom we must have often seen in the streets, lost all his estate, and died in want; and though there is nothing new in what he tells us, and though he hurries with characteristic timidity over every embarrassing or painful detail, we cannot help paying his loquacity the tribute of our laughter and our tears.—EDMUND GOSSE, *The Jacobean Poets*, 1894, pp. 119–22

In 1851 Collier reprinted two plays by Thomas Heywood under the general title *If You Know Not Me, You Know No Bodie*. The first part has the subtitle, *or The Troubles of Queene Elizabeth*, the second, the added words: "*With the building of the Royall Exchange and the famous Victory of Queen Elizabeth: Anno 1588.*" The original dates of publication were 1605 and the year following, and the popularity of both plays was such that five subsequent editions of the first part appeared and three of the second, the last bearing date 1633. Despite all these reprintings the first play is fragmentary if not corrupt. It was printed (according to a prologue which the author wrote for its revival at the Cockpit at a date unknown) from a stolen stenographic report. And the assurance of this prologue that "the Author now to vindicate that wrong hath tooke the paines, upright upon its feete to teach it walke" does not seem to have been fulfilled. The second part is in better condition and has probably come down to us substantially as it was presented. Both plays appear to be founded on a pamphlet of Heywood's later published as *Englands Elizabeth*, 1631.

The first part of *If You Know Not Me* opens at the period in the reign of Queen Mary at which the play of *Sir Thomas Wyatt* ends. Wyatt and Lady Jane Grey have suffered execu-

tion, and Mary, sure of her crown, is preparing to meet Prince Philip who is reported "safely arrived and landed at Southampton." From this point onward the one consistent theme is the persecution to which the Princess Elizabeth was subjected by the jealousy of her sister and the incessant machinations of Gardiner, Bishop of Winchester: her trials, imprisonments and the petty hardships to which she was exposed at the hands of overzealous servants of the queen. Mary is thrown as much as possible into the background and her religious persecutions are not so much as mentioned. Elizabeth's maidenly demeanor, her virtue, her steadfastness in refusing to plead guilty before Winchester and thus submit to the false charges of unloyalty, the sorrow of her household, the affection which she inspired in common folk and in the very guard set to watch her prison—these are the themes which are expanded and illustrated in a series of dramatized anecdotes, eked out by dumb shows depicting matter such as the departure of Philip, and Mary's consequent despair, the funeral of Winchester and the coronation of Elizabeth. The following brief scene is one of the series of little sketches which joined together go to make up this loosely knit play. It serves in its place as one of several like devices by which Heywood produces what we should call the historical atmosphere.

> *Enter the Englishman and Spaniard.*
>
> *Spa.*: The wall, the wall.
> *Eng.*: Sblood. Spaniard, you get no wall here, vnless you would haue your head and the wall knockt together.
> *Spa.*: Signor Cavalero Danglatero, I must haue the wall.
> *Eng.*: I doe protest, hadst thou not enforst it, I had not regarded it; but since you will needs haue the wall, Ile take thepains to thrust you into the kennel.
> *Spa.*: Oh, base Cavalero, my sword and poynard, well-tried in Toledo, shall giue thee the imbrocado.
> *Eng.*: Marry, and welcome, sir. Come on.
>
> *They fight: he hurts the Spaniard.*
>
> *Spa.*: Holo, Holo! Thou hast given me the canvissado.
> *Eng.*: Come, sir; will you any more?
> *Spa.*: Signor Cavalero, look behind thee. A blade of Toledo is drawne against thee.
>
> *He lookes backe: he [the Spaniard] kills him.*

At this moment Philip of Spain enters and, horrified at the baseness of the deed, protests that the great Turk's empire shall not redeem his cowardly follower from a felon's death; and he forthwith orders him to execution. Indeed throughout the play Philip is represented in a remarkably favorable light, as a just and courteous gentleman, zealous to bring about a reconciliation of the royal sisters and in the end successful.

The second part of *If You Know Not Me* is made up of a comedy of London merchant life and a few sketchy and unsatisfactory historical scenes; the proportion of the two elements is four-fifths comedy and one-fifth "history." The actual hero of this play is Sir Thomas Gresham, who it will be remembered was glorified at a much earlier date in the Latin play, *Byrsa Basilica*. In the English play Gresham figures not only in his capacity of a typical London merchant but in his famous rôle of founder of the Royal Exchange. Indeed this renowned structure, of which the Elizabethans were never weary of boasting, rises before the mind's eye in the play from its foundations to the grasshopper, the sign of the Greshams, which adorned the pinnacle. This drama is an excellent, if somewhat rambling, specimen of its class; and is of peculiar interest for the reason that it stands between the biographical drama on the one hand and the comedies of London life with their pictures of purely fictitious events on the other, and in this respect belongs with the earlier merchant scenes of *Cromwell* and the first act of *Sir Thomas Stukeley*. The historical parts of 2 *If You Know Not Me* sketch in outline Parry's attempt on the queen's life, the deliberations of the Duke of Medina and his council before the sailing of the Spanish fleet, the queen's review of her troops at Tilbury and a purely epic account—and that a very bald one—of the defeat of the Armada. The play ends with the royal reception of Sir Francis Drake, and Sir Martin Frobisher who present their captured Spanish standards to the queen and talk very prosily about their victory. With due allowance for an imperfect text in the first part, not obscuring, however, the readiness of diction and cleverness of dramatic device which is found even in the inferior work of Heywood, the historical parts of these dramas might have been written in 1590. In view of the possibilities of the subject and the abilities of such a dramatist as Heywood is at his best, it is impossible not to deplore the throwing away of so unusual an opportunity.—FELIX E. SCHELLING, "The Biographical Chronicle Play," *The English Chronicle Play*, 1902, pp. 234–38

ADOLPHUS WILLIAM WARD
From "The Later Elisabethans"
A History of English Dramatic Literature (1875)
1899, Volume 2, pp. 585–89

It would grieve me to seem unjust towards a writer to whom I have long felt very specially attracted—and this by no means only because of a pious although perhaps more or less apocryphal bond. Yet the highest praise which it seems right to bestow upon Thomas Heywood is that which was happily expressed by Tieck when he described him as 'the model of a light and rapid talent[1].' Carried, it may be, by fortune or by choice from the tranquil court of Peterhouse to a very different scene of intellectual effort, he worked during a long and laborious life with an energy in itself deserving of respect, and manifestly also with a facility attesting no ordinary natural endowment. His creative power was, however, of that secondary order which is content with accommodating itself to conditions imposed by the prevailing tastes of the day. It may be merely his 'prentice hand that he tried on a dramatic reproduction of chronicles and popular story-books; but though even here the simplicity of his workmanship was due to a natural directness of touch by no means to be confounded with rudeness of hand, he cannot be said to have done much to revive a species which though still locally popular was already doomed to decay. When at a later date he endeavoured to treat dramatically the oft-told tales of classical history and legend, he proved deficient in the poetical *afflatus* which had entitled earlier dramatists to vindicate to themselves the use of such materials. On the other hand, he had caught the contagion of that spirit of adventure by land, and more especially by sea, which was like the inspiration of a tenth Muse to so many of our Elisabethans; and he contrived—though in truth there was little of contrivance in the process—to interfuse it with the homely pathos which was perhaps his most distinctive literary gift. Happily for his fame, a taste had formed, or was forming, itself for the treatment on the stage of incidents of private life—events of which the interest came home to domestic experience, crimes which disturbed the peace of families rather than of nations, sorrows such as their

common humanity enables gentle and simple alike to understand. In the works in which he dealt with subjects of this description his tact and skill as a playwright were enhanced by the pathetic power with which he was signally endowed. Thus—whether by 'accident' or not, it is idle to enquire—he produced among a mass of plays such masterpieces as *A Woman Killed with Kindness* and *The English Traveller*. Of humour he had his share—or he would have been no master of pathos; but he cannot be said to have excelled in humorous characterisation; there is as a rule little individuality in his comic figures at large, and his clowns, although good examples of their kind, are made to order. Indeed, the inferior sort of wit—which of all writers dramatists most readily acquire as a literary accomplishment—his practised inventiveness displays with the utmost abundance; of all the Elisabethan playwrights he is one of the most unwearied, and to my mind one of the most intolerable punsters. In outward form he is nearly as Protean as in choice of subject and of treatment; his earlier plays more especially abound with rimes; in general, fluent verse and easy prose are freely intermixed. But—apart from the pathetic force of particular passages and scenes, and a straightforward naturalness which lends an irresistible charm to a writer as it does to a friend in real life—his strength lies in a dramatic insight which goes far towards the making of a master of the playwright's art, while it has undoubtedly been possessed by some not entitled to rank as dramatic poets.

He thoroughly understood what is meant by an effective—an irresistible—dramatic situation; and upon the invention and preparation of such he concentrated his powers with the sureness of a modern French dramatist intent upon his *scène à faire*. The climax of *A Royal King and a Loyal Subject*, the discovery and sentence in *A Woman Killed with Kindness*, and the final concatenation and *dénouement* of *The Wise Woman of Hogsdon* would make the fortune of a play in any period of the stage. Heywood, with all his *naïveté*, is an author the study of whom cannot be too strongly recommended to writers for the theatre.

While, then, the sterling merits of Thomas Heywood are such as to leave stingless the contemptuous taunts of the Restoration satirists[2], Charles Lamb's famous description of him as 'a prose Shakspere' must not tempt us to overestimate the sum of his powers as a dramatist. With a later interpreter of this kindly and witty saying[3], we may hold it warranted in two respects. The moral purity of Heywood, as compared with other dramatists of his age, recalls that of his greatest contemporary, serenely resting like his on trust in the Divinity which is wiser than ourselves. And the 'natural repose'—or the measure of it—which we recognise amidst all the stir and bustle of Heywood's plays, is refreshing to any one who turns to them from the uncomfortable heat or the artificial spasms of so many of his contemporaries; and it is in harmony with the innate modesty of the man who claimed no inspiration for his Muse but the human life by which she was surrounded. His 'dull and earthy Muse' he humbly calls her in the Prologue to his most famous play; and he well knew that to him was denied that gift of irradiating human things by the celestial light of genius which belongs only to a great poet. Yet even as a prose Shakspere—a writer who shared or approached some of the qualities of the master without being able to aspire to that supreme gift—Heywood lacked the most indispensable of these very qualities. This was the power of characterisation, without which all resemblances to the genius of Shakspere as a dramatist must remain merely superficial. Of truth and depth of feeling Heywood gives many proofs; but it lies beyond his power to create living individualities, representatives in

THE NEW MOULTON'S LIBRARY

nature's own never-ending variety of the everlasting types of human character. Even in his best plays it is the situations rather than the characters developed by them which engage our attention. A Shakspere—even a prose Shakspere—would have formed the erring wife and the loyal vassal into figures which we should have remembered for their own sake, human beings of whom we might have said, 'Thus, and not otherwise, they must have acted.' Of such an achievement Heywood falls something short; and Charles Lamb's famous description of him must after all be dismissed as essentially misleading—which indeed such epigrammatic labellings not unfrequently are[4].

Rapidity without carelessness of composition; effectiveness in construction, except for his usual habit of leaving mainplot and bye-plot to come together as best they may, if indeed they are to be united at all; tenderness of feeling and vivacity of touch; together with an entire absence of affectation, and consequently a refreshing freedom from sham pathos and false sentiment: these seem to me Thomas Heywood's most distinguishing characteristics as a dramatist.

As a man, it is not too much to say that there is evidence enough for concluding that he must have resembled Shakspere in that quality which is the most loveable, although not the most constant, accompaniment of merit and success. He worked zealously in the profession, for which in argument he broke so vigorous a lance, and in the conjunct branch of authorship, but 'with great modesty, and small noise[5]'; he was in truth, so far as external as well as internal evidence goes, one of the most modest of our dramatists—perhaps of our poets—in his estimate of himself. Faithful in his own person to the service of the stage during a period of great length, including both the height of its national importance and the beginning of its visible decline and degradation, he might with a good conscience indite his apology for his brethren and himself; since we may confidently assume that there was little in his life, as there is certainly nothing in his works, so far as they have come down to us, for which he needed to blush.

Notes

1. *Shakespeare's Vorschule*, vol. i, *Vorrede*, p. xl.
2. Dryden in his *Mac Flecknoe* laughs at Heywood, Shirley, and Ogilby promiscuously as 'neglected authors,' 'martyrs of pies,' &c.; and Oldham follows suit, if he had not led the way, with a similar jumble of names:

    Quarles, Chapman, Heywood, hither had applause,
    And Wild and Ogilby in former days.
                    (*A Satire Dissuading from Poetry.*)

3. See an article in the *Edinburgh Review* for April, 1841, entitled 'Beaumont and Fletcher and Their Contemporaries,' cited in the 'Introductory Memoir' in Pearson's reprint, p. xxx.
4. For instance, the description of Crabbe as 'Pope in worsted stockings.' Crabbe is not deficient in polish, but he now and then wants point, and never leaves a sting behind him.
5. Address 'To the Reader' prefixed to *The Fair Maid of the West*.

ALGERNON CHARLES SWINBURNE
"The Romantic and Contemporary Plays of Thomas Heywood"
Nineteenth Century, September 1895, pp. 397–410

I

The eleven plays already considered in my essay[1] on Heywood's Historical and Classical Plays make up the two divisions of Heywood's work which with all their great and real merit have least in them of those peculiar qualities most distinctive and representative of his genius: those qualities of which when we think of him we think first, and which on summing up his character as a poet we most naturally associate with his name. As a historical or mythological playwright, working on material derived from classic legends or from English annals, he shows signs now and then, as occasion offers, of the sweet-tempered manliness, the noble kindliness, which won the heart of Lamb: something too there is in these plays of his pathos, and something of his humour: but if this were all we had of him we should know comparatively little of what we now most prize in him. Of this we find most in the plays dealing with English life in his own day: but there is more of it in his romantic tragicomedies than in his chronicle histories or his legendary compilations and variations on the antique. The famous and delicious burlesque of Beaumont and Fletcher cannot often be forgotten but need not always be remembered in reading *The Four Prentices of London*. Externally the most extravagant and grotesque of dramatic poems, this eccentric tragicomedy of chivalrous adventure is full of poetic as well as fantastic interest. There is really something of discrimination in the roughly and readily sketched characters of the four crusading brothers: the youngest especially is a lifelike model of restless and reckless gallantry as it appears when incarnate in a hot-headed English boy; unlike even in its likeness to the same type as embodied in a French youngster such as the immortal d'Artagnan. Justice has been done by Lamb, and consequently as well as subsequently by later criticism, to the occasionally fine poetry which breaks out by flashes in this Quixotic romance of the City, with its seriocomic ideal of crusading counter-jumpers: but it has never to my knowledge been observed that in the scene 'where they toss their pikes so,' which aroused the special enthusiasm of the worthy fellow-citizen whose own prentice was to bear the knightly ensign of the Burning Pestle, Heywood, the future object of Dryden's ignorant and pointless insult, anticipated with absolute exactitude the style of Dryden's own tragic blusterers when most busily bandying tennis balls of ranting rhyme in mutual challenge and reciprocal retort of amœbæan epigram.[2]

It is a pity that Heywood's civic or professional devotion to the service of the metropolis should ever have been worse employed than in the transfiguration of the idealised prentice: it is a greater pity that we cannot exchange all Heywood's extant masques for any one of the two hundred plays or so now missing in which, as he tells us, he 'had either an entire hand, or at the least a main finger.' The literary department of a Lord Mayor's show can hardly be considered as belonging to literature, even when a poet's time and trouble were misemployed in compiling the descriptive prose and the declamatory verse contributed to the ceremony. Not indeed that it was a poet who devoted so much toil and goodwill to celebration or elucidation of the laborious projects and objects both by water and land which then distinguished or deformed the sundry triumphs, pageants, and shows on which Messrs. Christmas Brothers and their most ingenious parent were employed in a more honourable capacity than the subordinate function of versifier or showman—an office combining the parts and the duties of the immortal Mrs. Jarley and her laureate Mr. Shum. Lexicographers might pick out of the text some rare if not unique Latinisms or barbarisms such as 'prestigion' and 'strage': but except for the purpose of such 'harmless drudges' and perhaps of an occasional hunter after samples of the bathetic which might have rewarded the attention of Arbuthnot or Pope, the text of these pageants must be as barren and even to them it would presumably be as tedious a subject of study as the lucubrations of the very dullest English moralist or American humourist; a course of reading digestible only by such constitutions as could survive and assimilate a diet of Martin Tupper or Mark Twain. And yet even in the very homeliest doggrel of Heywood's or Shakespeare's time there is something comparatively not contemptible; the English, when not alloyed by fantastic or pedantic experiment, has a simple historic purity and dignity of its own; the dulness is not so dreary as the dulness of mediæval prosers, the commonplace is not so vulgar as the commonplace of more modern scribes.

The Trial of Chivalry is a less extravagant example of homely romantic drama than *The Four Prentices of London*. We owe to Mr. Bullen the rediscovery of this play, and to Mr. Fleay the determination and verification of its authorship. In style and in spirit it is perfect Heywood: simple and noble in emotion and conception, primitive and straightforward in construction and expression; inartistic but not ineffectual; humble and facile, but not futile or prosaic. It is a rather more rational and natural piece of work than might have been expected from its author when equipped after the heroic fashion of Mallory or Froissart: its date is more or less indistinctly indicated by occasional rhymes and peculiar conventionalities of diction: and if Heywood in the panoply of a knight-errant may now and then suggest to his reader the figure of Sancho Panza in his master's armour, his pedestrian romance is so genuine, his modest ambition so high-spirited and high-minded, that it would be juster and more critical to compare him with Don Quixote masquerading in the accoutrements of his esquire. Dick Bowyer, whose life and death are mendaciously announced on the catchpenny title-page, and who (like Tiny Tim in *A Christmas Carol*) "does *not* die," is a rather rough, thin, and faint sketch of the bluff British soldier of fortune who appears and reappears to better advantage in other plays of Heywood and his fellows. That this must be classed among the earlier if not the earliest of his works we may infer from the primitive simplicity of a stage direction which recalls another in a play printed five years before. In the second scene of the third act of *The Trial of Chivalry* we read as follows:—'Enter Forester, missing the other taken away, speaks anything, and exit.' In the penultimate scene of the second part of *King Edward IV* we find this even quainter direction, which has been quoted before now as an instance of the stage conditions or habits of the time:— 'Jockie is led to whipping over the stage, speaking some words, but of no importance.'

A further and deeper debt of thanks is due to Mr. Bullen for the recovery of *The Captives, or The Lost Recovered*, after the lapse of nearly three centuries. The singularly prophetic sub-title of this classic and romantic tragicomedy has been justified at so late a date by the beneficence of chance, in favourable conjunction with the happy devotion and fortunate research of a thorough and a thoroughly able student, as to awaken in all fellow-lovers of dramatic poetry a sense of hopeful wonder with regard to the almost illimitable possibilities of yet further and yet greater treasure to be discovered and recovered from the keeping of 'dust and damned oblivion.' Meantime we may be heartily thankful for the recovery of an excellent piece of work, written throughout with the easy mastery of serious or humorous verse, the graceful pliancy of style and the skilful simplicity of composition, which might have been expected from a mature work of Heywood's: though the execution of it would now and then have suggested an earlier date. The clown, it may be noticed, is the same who always reappears to do the necessary comicalities in Heywood's plays; if hardly 'a fellow of infinite jest,' yet an amusing one in his homely way; though one would have thought that on the

homeliest London stage of 1624 the taste for antiphonal improvisation of doggrel must have passed into the limbo of obsolete simplicities. The main plot is very well managed, as with Plautus once more for a model might properly have been expected; the rather ferociously farcical underplot must surely have been borrowed from some *fabliau*. The story has been done into doggrel by George Colman the younger: but that cleanly and pure-minded censor of the press would hardly have licensed for the stage a play which would have required, if the stage-carpenter had been then in existence, the production of a scene which would have anticipated what Gautier so plausibly plumed himself upon as a novelty in stage effect—imagined for the closing scene of his imaginary tragedy of *Heliogabalus*.

There are touches of pathetic interest and romantic invention in *A Maidenhead Well Lost*: two or three of the leading characters are prettily sketched if not carefully finished, and the style is a graceful compromise between unambitious poetry and mildly spirited prose: but it is hardly to be classed among Heywood's best work of the kind: it has no scenes of such fervid and noble interest, such vivid and keen emotion, as distinguish *A Challenge for Beauty*: and for all its simple grace of writing and ingenuous ingenuity of plot it may not improbably be best remembered by the average modern reader as remarkable for the most amusing and astonishing example on record of anything but 'inexplicable' dumb show—to be paralleled only and hardly by a similar interlude of no less elaborate arrangement and significant eccentricity in the sole dramatic venture of Henri de Latouche—*La Reine d'Espagne*.

Little favour has been shown by modern critics and even by modern editors to *The Royal King and the Loyal Subject*: and the author himself, in committing it to the tardy test of publication, offered a quaint and frank apology for its old-fashioned if not obsolete style of composition and versification. Yet I cannot but think that Hallam was right and Dyce was wrong in his estimate of a play which does not challenge and need not shrink from comparison with Fletcher's more elaborate, rhetorical, elegant and pretentious tragicomedy of *The Loyal Subject*; that the somewhat eccentric devotion of Heywood's hero is not more slavish or foolish than the obsequious submission of Fletcher's; and that even if we may not be allowed to make allowance for the primitive straightforwardness or take delight in the masculine simplicity of the elder poet, we must claim leave to object that there is more essential servility of spirit, more preposterous prostration of manhood, in the Russian ideal of Fletcher than in the English ideal of Heywood. The humour is as simple as is the appeal to emotion or sympathetic interest in this primitive tragicomedy; but the comic satire on worldly venality and versatility is as genuine and honest as the serious exposition of character is straightforward and sincere.

The best of Heywood's romantic plays is the most graceful and beautiful, in detached scenes and passages, of all his extant works. The combination of the two plots—they can hardly be described as plot and underplot—is so dexterously happy that it would do the highest credit to a more famous and ambitious artist: the rival heroes are so really noble and attractive that we are agreeably compelled to condone whatever seems extravagant or preposterous in their relations or their conduct: there is a breath of Quixotism in the air which justifies and ennobles it. The heroines are sketched with natural grace and spirit: it is the more to be regretted that their bearing in the last act should have less of delicacy or modesty than of ingenious audacity in contrivances for striking and daring stage effect; a fault as grave in æsthetics as in ethics, and one rather to have been expected from Fletcher than from Heywood. But the general grace and the occasional pathos of the writing may fairly be set against the gravest fault that can justly be found with so characteristic and so charming a work of Heywood's genius at its happiest and brightest as A *Challenge for Beauty*.

II

The line of demarcation between realism and romance is sometimes as difficult to determine in the work of Heywood as in the character of his time: the genius of England, the spirit of Englishmen, in the age of Shakespeare, had so much of the practical in its romance and so much of the romantic in its practice that the beautiful dramatic poem in which the English heroes Manhurst and Montferrers play their parts so nobly beside their noble Spanish compeers in chivalry ought perhaps to have been classed rather among the studies of contemporary life on which their author's fame must principally and finally depend than among those which have been defined as belonging to the romantic division of his work. There is much the same fusion of interests, as there is much the same mixture of styles, in the conduct of a play for which we have once more to tender our thanks to the living benefactor at once of Heywood and of his admirers. That Mr. Bullen was well advised in putting forward a claim for Heywood as the recognisable author of a play which twelve years ago had never seen the light is as evident as that his estimate of the fine English quality which induced this recognition was justified by all rules of moral evidence. There can be less than little doubt that *Dick of Devonshire* is one of the two hundred and twenty in which Heywood had 'a main finger'—though not, I should say, by any means 'an entire hand.' The metre is not always up to his homely but decent mark: though in many of the scenes it is worthy of his best plays for smoothness, fluency, and happy simplicity of effect. Dick Pike is a better study of the bluff and tough English hero than Dick Bowyer in *The Trial of Chivalry*: and the same chivalrous sympathy with the chivalrous spirit and tradition of a foreign and a hostile nation which delights us in A *Challenge for Beauty* pervades and vivifies this long-lost and long-forgotten play. The partial sacrifice of ethical propriety or moral consistency to the actual or conventional exigences of the stage is rather more startling than usual: a fratricidal ravisher and slanderer could hardly have expected even from theatrical tolerance the monstrous lenity of pardon and dismissal with a prospect of being happy though married. The hand of Heywood is more recognisable in the presentation of a clown who may fairly be called identical with all his others, and in the noble answer of the criminal's brother to their father's very natural question, 'Why dost thou take his part so?'

> Because no drop of honour falls from him
> But I bleed with it.

This high-souled simplicity of instinct is as traceable in the earlier as in the later of Heywood's extant works: he is English of the English in his quiet, frank, spontaneous expression, when suppression is no longer either possible or proper, of all noble and gentle and natural emotion. His passion and his pathos, his loyalty and his chivalry, are always so unobtrusive that their modesty may sometimes run the risk of eclipse before the glory of more splendid poets and more conspicuous patriots: but they are true and trustworthy as Shakespeare's or Milton's or Wordsworth's or Tennyson's or Browning's.

It was many a year before Dick Pike had earned the honour of commemoration by his hand or by any other poet's that Heywood had won his spurs as the champion presenter—if I may be allowed to revive the word—of his humbler and homelier countrymen under the light of a no less noble than simple realism. *The Fair Maid of the Exchange* is a notable example of what I believe is professionally or theatrically called a one-part piece. Adapting Dr. Johnson's curiously unjust and inept remark on Shakespeare's *King Henry VIII.*—the play in which, according to the principles or tenets of the new criticism which walks or staggers by the new light of a new scholarship, 'the new Shakspere' may or must have been assisted by Flitcher, (why not also by Meddletun, Messenger, and a few other *novi homines*?) we may say, and it may be said this time with some show of reason, that the genius of the author limps in and limps out with the Cripple. Most of the other characters and various episodical incidents of the incomposite story are alike, if I may revive a good and expressive phrase of the period, hastily and unskilfully slubbered up: Bowdler is a poor secondhand and thirdrate example of the Jonsonian gull; and the transfer of Moll's regard from him to his friend is both childishly conceived and childishly contrived. On the whole, a secondrate play, with one or two firstrate scenes and passages to which Lamb has done perhaps no more than justice by the characteristic and eloquent cordiality of his commendations. Its date may be probably determined as early among the earliest of its author's by the occurrence in mid dialogue of a sestet in the popular metre of *Venus and Adonis*, with archaic inequality in the lengths of the second and fourth rhyming words: a notable note of metrical or immetrical antiquity in style. The self-willed if high-minded Phyllis Flower has something in her of Heywood's later heroines, Bess Bridges of Plymouth and Luce the goldsmith's daughter, but is hardly as interesting or attractive as either.

Much less than this can be said for the heroines, if heroines they can in any sense be called, of the two plays by which Heywood is best known as a tragic and a comic painter of contemporary life among his countrymen. It is certainly not owing to any exceptional power of painting or happiness in handling feminine character that the first place among his surviving works has been generally and rationally assigned to A *Woman Killed with Kindness*. The fame of this famous realistic tragedy is due to the perfect fitness of the main subject for treatment in the manner of which Heywood was in his day and remains to the present day beyond all comparison the greatest and the most admirable master. It is not that the interest is either naturally greater, or greater by force and felicity of genius in the dramatist, than that of other and far inferior plays. It is not that the action is more artistically managed: it is not that curiosity or sympathy is aroused or sustained with any particular skill. Such a play as *Fatal Curiosity* is as truthfully lifelike and more tragically exciting: it is in mere moral power and charm, with just a touch of truer and purer poetry pervading and colouring and flavouring and quickening the whole, that the work of a Heywood approves itself as beyond the reach or the ambition of a Lillo. One figure among many remains impressed on his reader's memory once for all: the play is full of incident, perhaps over full of actors, excellently well written and passably well composed; but it lives, it survives and overtops its fellows, by grace of the character of its hero. The underplot, whether æsthetically or historically considered, is not more singular than extravagant and unpleasant to natural taste as well as to social instinct: the other agents in the main plot are little more than sketches—sometimes deplorably out of drawing: Anne is never really alive till on her deathbed, and her paramour is never alive—in his temptation, his transgression, or his impenitence—at all. The whole play, as far as we remember or care to remember it, is Frankford: he suffices to make it a noble poem and a memorable play.

The hero of *The English Traveller*, however worthy to stand beside him as a typical sample of English manhood at its noblest and gentlest, cannot be said to occupy so predominant a place in the conduct of the action or the memory of the reader. The comic Plautine underplot—Plautus always brought good luck to Heywood—is so incomparably preferable to the ugly and unnatural though striking and original under-plot of *A Woman Killed with Kindness* as wellnigh to counterbalance the comparative lack of interest, plausibility and propriety in the main action. The seduction of Mrs. Frankford is so roughly slurred over that it is hard to see how, if she could not resist a first whisper of temptation, she can ever have been the loyal wife and mother whose fall we are expected to deplore: but the seduction of Mrs. Wincott, or rather her transformation from the likeness of a loyal and high-minded lady to the likeness of an impudent and hypocritical harlot, is neither explained nor explicable in the case of a woman who dies of a sudden shock of shame and penitence. Her paramour is only not quite so shapeless and shadowy a scoundrel as the betrayer of Frankford: but Heywood is no great hand at a villain: his nobly simple conception and grasp and development of character will here be recognised only in the quiet and perfect portraiture of the two grand old gentlemen and the gallant unselfish youth whom no more subtle or elaborate draughtsman could have set before us in clearer or fuller outline, with more attractive and actual charm of feature and expression.

The Fair Maid of the West is one of Heywood's most characteristic works, and one of his most delightful plays. Inartistic as this sort of dramatic poem may seem to the lovers of theatrical composition and sensational arrangement, of emotional calculations and premeditated shocks, it has a place of its own, and a place of honour, among the incomparably various forms of noble and serious drama which English poets of the Shakespearean age conceived, created, and left as models impossible to reproduce or to rival in any generation of poets or readers, actors or spectators, after the decadent forces of English genius in its own most natural and representative form of popular and creative activity had finally shrivelled up and shuddered into everlasting inanition under the withering blast of Puritanism. Before that blight had fallen upon the country of Shakespeare, the variety and fertility of dramatic form and dramatic energy which distinguished the typical imagination or invention of his countrymen can only be appreciated or conceived by students of what yet is left us of the treasure bequeathed by the fellows and the followers of Shakespeare. Every other man who could speak or write at all was a lyric poet, a singer of beautiful songs, in the generation before Shakespeare's: every other such man in Shakespeare's was a dramatic poet above or beyond all comparison with any later claimant of the title among Shakespeare's countrymen. One peculiarly and characteristically English type of drama which then flourished here and there among more ambitious if not more interesting forms or varieties, and faded for ever with the close of the age of Shakespeare, was the curious and delightful kind of play dealing with records or fictions of contemporary adventure. The veriest failures in this line have surely something of national and historical interest; telling us as they do of the achievements or in any case of the aspirations and the ideals, the familiar traditions and ambitions and admirations, of our simplest and noblest forefathers. Even such a play as that in which the adventures of the Shirleys were hurried and huddled into inadequate and incoherent presentation as *The Travels of Three English Brothers*, however justly it may offend or dissatisfy the literary critic, can hardly be without attraction for the lover of his country: curiosity may be disappointed of its

hope, yet patriotism may find matter for its sympathy. And if so much may be said on behalf of a poetic and dramatic failure, this and far more than this may be claimed on behalf of such plays as *The Fair Maid of the West* and *Fortune by Land and Sea*. Of these the first is certainly the better play: I should myself be inclined to rank it among Heywood's very best. He never wrote anything brighter, sprightlier, livelier or fuller of life and energy: more amusing in episodical incident or byplay, more interesting and attractive in the structure or the progress of the main story. No modern heroine with so strong a dash of the Amazon—so decided a cross of the male in her—was ever so noble, credible, and lovable as Bess Bridges: and Plymouth ought really to do itself the honour of erecting a memorial to her poet. An amusing instance of Heywood's incomparable good nature and sweetness of temper in dealing with the creatures of his genius—incomparable I call it, because in Shakespeare the same beautiful quality is more duly tempered and toned down to more rational compliance with the demands of reason and probability, whether natural or dramatic—is here to be recognised in the redemption of a cowardly bully, and his conversion from a lying ruffian into a loyal and worthy sort of fellow. The same gallant spirit of sympathy with all noble homeliness of character, whether displayed in joyful search of adventure or in manful endurance of suffering and wrong, informs the less excellently harmonious and well-built play which bears the truly and happily English title of *Fortune by Land and Sea*. It has less romantic interest than the later adventures of the valiant Bess and her Spencer with the amorous king of Fez and his equally erratic consort; not to mention the no less susceptible Italians among whom their lot is subsequently cast: but it is a model of natural and noble simplicity, of homely and lively variety. There is perhaps more of the roughness and crudity of style and treatment which might be expected from Rowley than of the humaner and easier touch of Heywood in the conduct of the action: the curious vehemence and primitive brutality of social or domestic tyranny may recall the use of the same dramatic motives by George Wilkins in *The Miseries of Enforced Marriage*: but the mixture or fusion of tender and sustained emotion with the national passion for enterprise and adventure is pleasantly and peculiarly characteristic of Heywood.

In *The Wise Woman of Hogsdon* the dramatic ability of Heywood, as distinct from his more poetic and pathetic faculty, shews itself at its best and brightest. There are not many much better examples of the sort of play usually defined as a comedy of intrigue, but more properly definable as a comedy of action. The special risk to which a purveyor of this kind of ware must naturally be exposed is the tempting danger of sacrificing propriety and consistency of character to effective and impressive suggestions or developments of situation or event; the inclination to think more of what is to happen than of the persons it must happen to—the characters to be actively or passively affected by the concurrence or the evolution of circumstances. Only to the very greatest of narrative or dramatic artists in creation and composition can this perilous possibility be all but utterly unknown. Poets of the city no less than poets of the court, the homely Heywood as well as the fashionable Fletcher, tripped and fell now and then over this awkward stone of stumbling—a very rock of offence to readers of a more exacting temper or a more fastidious generation than the respective audiences of patrician and plebeian London in the age of Shakespeare. The leading young man of this comedy now under notice is represented as 'a wild-headed gentleman,' and revealed as an abject ruffian of unredeemed and irredeemable rascality. As much and even more may be said of the execrable wretch who fills a similar part in an admirably written play published thirty-six years earlier and verified for the first time as Heywood's by the keen research and indefatigable intuition of Mr. Fleay. The parallel passages cited by him from the broadly farcical underplots are more than suggestive, even if they be not proof positive, of identity in authorship: but the identity in atrocity of the two hideous figures who play the two leading parts must reluctantly be admitted as more serious evidence. The abuse of innocent foreign words or syllables by comparison or confusion with indecent native ones is a simple and school-boylike sort of jest for which Master Heywood, if impeached as even more deserving of the birch than any boy on his stage, might have pleaded the example of the captain of the school, and protested that his humble audacities, if no less indecorous, were funnier and less forced than Master Shakespeare's. As for the other member of Webster's famous triad, I fear that the most indulgent sentence passed on Master Dekker, if sent up for punishment on the charge of bad language and impudence, could hardly in justice be less than Orbilian or Draconic. But he was apparently if not assuredly almost as incapable as Shakespeare of presenting the most infamous of murderers as an erring but pardonable transgressor, not unfit to be received back with open arms by the wife he has attempted, after a series of the most hideous and dastardly outrages, to dispatch by poison. The excuse for Heywood is simply that in his day as in Chaucer's the orthodox ideal of a married heroine was still none other than Patient Grizel: Shakespeare alone had got beyond it.

The earlier of these two plays, 'a pleasant' if somewhat sensational 'comedy entitled *How to Choose a Good Wife from a Bad,*' is written for the most part in Heywood's most graceful and poetical vein of verse, with beautiful simplicity, purity, and fluency of natural and musical style. In none of his plays is the mixture or rather the fusion of realism with romance more simply happy and harmonious: the rescue of the injured wife by a faithful lover from the tomb in which, like Juliet, she has been laid while under the soporific influence of a supposed poison could hardly have been better or more beautifully treated by any but the very greatest among Heywood's fellow-poets. There is no merit of this kind in the later play: but from the dramatic if not even from the ethical point of view it is on the whole a riper and more rational sort of work. The culmination of accumulating evidence by which the rascal hero is ultimately overwhelmed and put to shame, driven from lie to lie and reduced from retractation to retractation as witness after witness starts up against him from every successive corner of the witch's dwelling, is as masterly in management of stage effect as any contrivance of the kind in any later and more famous comedy: nor can I remember a more spirited and vivid opening to any play than the quarrelling scene among the gamblers with which this one breaks out at once into lifelike action, full of present interest and promise of more to come. The second scene, in which the fair sempstress appears at work in her father's shop, recalls and indeed repeats the introduction of the heroine in an earlier play: but here again the author's touch is firmer and his simplicity more masculine than before. This coincidence is at least as significant as that between the two samples of flogging-block doggrel collated for comparison by Mr. Fleay: it is indeed a suggestive though superfluous confirmation of Heywood's strangely questioned but surely unquestionable claim to the authorship of *The Fair Maid of the Exchange.* A curious allusion to a more famous play of the author's is the characteristic remark of the young ruffian Chartley, 'Well, I see you choleric hasty men are the kindest when all is done. Here's such wetting of handkerchers! he weeps to think

of his wife, she weeps to see her father cry! Peace, fool, we shall else have thee claim kindred of the woman killed with kindness.' And in the fourth and last scene of the fourth act the same scoundrel is permitted to talk Shakespeare:—'I'll go, although the devil and mischance look big.'

Poetical justice may cry out against the dramatic lenity which could tolerate or prescribe for the sake of a comfortable close to this comedy the triumphant escape of a villainous old impostor and baby-farmer from the condign punishment due to her misdeeds; but the severest of criminal judges if not of professional witch-finders might be satisfied by the justice or injustice done upon 'the late Lancashire Witches' in the bright and vigorous tragicomedy which, as we learn from Mr. Fleay, so unwarrantably and uncharitably (despite a disclaimer in the epilogue) anticipated the verdict of their judges against the defenceless victims of terrified prepossession and murderous perjury. But at this time of day the mere poetical reader or dramatic student need not concern himself, while reading a brilliant and delightful play, with the soundness or unsoundness of its moral and historical foundations. There may have been a boy so really and so utterly possessed by the devil who seems now and then to enter into young creatures of human form and be-monster them as to amuse himself by denouncing helpless and harmless women to the most horrible of deaths on the most horrible of charges: that hideous passing fact does not affect or impair the charming and lasting truth of Heywood's unsurpassable study, the very model of a gallant and lifelike English lad, all compact of fearlessness and fun, audacity and loyalty, so perfectly realised and rendered in this quaint and fascinating play. The admixture of what a modern boy would call cheek and chaff with the equally steadfast and venturesome resolution of the indomitable young scapegrace is so natural as to make the supernatural escapades in which it involves him quite plausible for the time to a reader of the right sort: even as (to compare this small masterpiece with a great one) such a reader, while studying the marvellous text of Meinhold, is no more sceptical than is their chronicler as to the sorceries of Sidonia von Bork. And however condemnable or blameworthy the authors of *The Witches of Lancashire* may appear to a modern reader or a modern magistrate or jurist for their dramatic assumption or presumption in begging the question against the unconvicted defendants whom they describe in the prologue as 'those witches the fat jailor brought to town,' they can hardly have been either wishful or able to influence the course of justice towards criminals of whose evident guilt they were evidently convinced. Shadwell's later play of the same name, though not wanting in such rough realistic humour and coarse-grained homespun interest as we expect in the comic produce of his hard and heavy hand, makes happily no attempt to emulate the really noble touches of poetry and pathos with which Heywood has thrown out into relief the more serious aspect of the supposed crime of witchcraft in its influence or refraction upon the honour and happiness of innocent persons. Og was naturally more in his place and more in his element as the second 'fat jailer' of Lancashire witches than as the second English dramatic poet of Psyche: he has come closer than his precursors, closer indeed than could have been thought possible, to actual presentation of the most bestial and abominable details of demonolatry recorded by the chroniclers of witchcraft: and in such scenes as are rather transcribed than adapted from such narratives he has imitated his professed master and model, Ben Jonson, by appending to his text, with the most minute and meticulous care, all requisite or more than requisite references to his original authorities. The allied poets who had preceded him were content to handle the matter more easily and lightly, with a quaint apology for having nothing of more interest to offer than 'an argument so thin, persons so low,' that they could only hope their play might 'pass pardoned, though not praised.' Brome's original vein of broad humour and farcical fancy is recognisable enough in the presentation of the bewitched household where the children rule their parents and are ruled by their servants; a situation which may have suggested the still more amusing development of the same fantastic motive in his admirable comedy of *The Antipodes*. There is a noticeable reference to *Macbeth* in the objurgations lavished by the daughter upon the mother under the influence of a revolutionary spell: 'Is this a fit habit for a handsome young gentlewoman's mother? as I hope to be a lady, you look like one o' the Scottish wayward sisters.' The still more broadly comic interlude of the bewitched rustic bridegroom and his loudly reclamatory bride is no less humorously sustained and carried through. Altogether, for an avowedly hasty and occasional piece of work, this tragicomedy is very creditably characteristic of both its associated authors.

How small a fraction of Heywood's actual work is comprised in these twenty-six plays we cannot even conjecturally compute: we only know that they amount to less than an eighth part of the plays written wholly or mainly by his indefatigable hand, and that they are altogether outweighed in volume, though decidedly not in value, by the existing mass of his undramatic work. We know also, if we have eyes to see, that the very hastiest and slightest of them does credit to the author, and that the best of them are to be counted among the genuine and imperishable treasures of English literature. Such amazing fecundity and such astonishing industry would be memorable even in a far inferior writer: but, though I certainly cannot pretend to anything like an exhaustive or even an adequate acquaintance with all or any of his folios, I can at least affirm that they contain enough delightfully readable matter to establish a more than creditable reputation. His prose, if never to be called masterly, may generally be called good and pure: its occasional pedantries and pretentions are rather signs of the century than faults of the author: and he can tell a story, especially a short story, as well if not better than many a better-known writer. I fear, however, that it is not the poetical quality of his undramatic verse which can ever be said to make it worth reading: it is, as far as I know, of the very homeliest homespun ever turned out by the very humblest of workmen. His poetry, it would be pretty safe to wager, must be looked for exclusively in his plays: but there, if not remarkable for depth or height of imagination or of passion, it will be found memorable for unsurpassed excellence of unpretentious elevation in treatment of character. The unity (or, to borrow from Coleridge a barbaric word, the triunity) of noble and gentle and simple in the finest quality of the English character at its best—of the English character as revealed in our Sidneys and Nelsons and Collingwoods and Franklins—is almost as apparent in the best scenes of his best plays as in the lives of our chosen and best beloved heroes: and this, I venture to believe, would have been rightly regarded by Thomas Heywood as a more desirable and valuable success than the achievement of a noisier triumph, or the attainment of a more conspicuous place among the poets of his country.

Notes

1. See *Nineteenth Century* for April 1895.
2. Compare this with any similar sample of heroic dialogue in *Tyrannic Love* or *The Conquest of Granada*:

   'Rapier and pike, is that thy honoured play?
   Look down, ye Gods, this combat to survey.'
   'Rapier and pike this combat shall decide:
   Gods, angels, men, shall see me tame thy pride.'
   'I'll teach thee: thou shalt like my zany be,
   And feign to do my cunning after me.'

   This will remind the reader not so much of the *Rehearsal* as of Butler's infinitely superior parody in the heroic dialogue of Cat and Puss.

JOHN SELDEN

1584–1654

John Selden was born at Salvington, near West Tarring, Sussex, on December 16, 1584. The son of a yeoman, Selden received his early education at the Chichester Free School. In 1600 he entered Hart Hall, Oxford, but left without taking a degree in 1602. He read law at Clifford's Inn until 1604, when he moved to the Inner Temple. Selden was called to the bar in 1612, beginning a long public career. Throughout Charles I's reign Selden was an active member of Parliament, often criticizing the Crown but steering clear of the Puritans.

Selden was the author of numerous legal works. His *History of Tythes* (1618) so offended clergymen that it was suppressed by the Privy Council. Other legal works include *Mare Clausum* (1635), which rebutted Hugo Grotius's claim that sovereignty could not be exercised over the seas, and the old English law book *Fleta* (1647), to which Selden appended an important study of the origins of English law. In 1617 Selden published the first of his Oriental studies, *De Diis Syris Syntagmata*, a book on Middle Eastern polytheism.

Selden was a friend of Jonson and was admired by Milton. He wrote notes to the first eighteen cantos of Drayton's *Poly-Olbion*, as well as commendatory verses in Greek, Latin, and English to William Browne's *Britannia's Pastorals*. Selden's best known work was not published until 1689. *Table-Talk*, a collection of Selden's utterances compiled by his secretary, Richard Milward, covers his thoughts about politics, religion, and literature during the last twenty years of his life. Selden died on November 30, 1654, and was buried in the Inner Temple Church, London.

Personal

Mr. Selden was a person whom no character can flatter, or transmit in any expressions equal to his merit and virtue. He was of so stupendous learning in all kinds and in all languages, (as may appear in his excellent and transcendent writings,) that a man would have thought he had been entirely conversant amongst books, and had never spent an hour but in reading and writing; yet his humanity, courtesy, and affability was such, that he would have been thought to have been bred in the best courts, but that his good nature, charity, and delight in doing good, and in communicating all he knew, exceeded that breeding. His style in all his writings seems harsh and sometimes obscure; which is not wholly to be imputed to the abstruse subjects of which he commonly treated, out of the paths trod by other men; but to a little undervaluing the beauty of a style, and too much propensity to the language of antiquity: but in his conversation he was the most clear discourser, and had the best faculty of making hard things easy, and presenting them to the understanding, of any man that hath been known. Mr. Hyde was wont to say, that he valued himself upon nothing more than upon having had Mr. Selden's acquaintance from the time he was very young; and held it with great delight as long as they were suffered to continue together in London; and he was very much troubled always when he heard him blamed, censured, and reproached, for staying in London, and in the parliament, after they were in rebellion, and in the worst times, which his age obliged him to do; and how wicked soever the actions were which were every day done, he was confident he had not given his consent to them; but would have hindered them if he could with his own safety, to which he was always enough indulgent. If he had some infirmities with other men, they were weighed down with wonderful and prodigious abilities and excellencies in the other scale.—EDWARD HYDE, EARL OF CLARENDON, *The Life of Edward Earl of Clarendon*, c. 1668

His father was a yeomanly man, of about fourty pounds per annum, and played well on the violin, in which he tooke delight, and at Christmas time, to please him selfe and his neighbours, he would play to them as they danced.

He was of Hart-hall in Oxon, and Sir Giles Mompesson told me that he was then of that house, and that he was a long scabby-pold boy, but a good student.

Thence he came to the Inner-Temple. He was quickly taken notice of for his learning, and was Sollicitor and Steward to the Earle of Kent, whose Countesse, being an ingeniose woman and loving men, would let him lye with her, and her husband knew it. After the Earle's death he maried her. He did lye with Mris. Williamson (one of my Lady's woemen) a lusty bouncing woman, who robbed him on his death-bed. I remember in 1646, or 1647, they did talk also of my Lady's Shee Blackamore.

I remember my Sadler (who wrought many years to that Family) told me that Mr. Selden had got more by his Prick then he had done by his practise. He was no eminent practiser at Barre.

He never owned the mariage with the Countesse of Kent till after her death, upon some Lawe-account.

He kept a plentifull Table, and was never without learned company: he was temperate in eating and drinking. He had a slight stuffe, or silke, kind of false carpet, to cast over the table where he read and his papers lay, when a stranger came-in, so that he needed not to displace his bookes or papers.

His treatise that Tythes were not *jure divino* drew a great deale of Envy upon him from the Clergie. W. Laud, Arch-bishop of Canterbury, made him make his Recantation before the High Commission Court. After, he would never forgive the Bishops, but did still in his writings levell them with Presbyterie.

After he had got a *dulce ocium* he chiefly addicted him-selfe to his more ingeniose studies and Records. He was one of the Assembly of Divines and was like a Thorne in their sides: he was wont to mock the Assembly-men about their little gilt Bibles, and would baffle and vexe them sadly: sayd he, *I doe consider the original*: for he was able to runne them all downe with his Greeke and Antiquities.

He was very tall, I guesse about 6 foot high, sharp ovall face, head not very big, long nose inclining to one side, full popping Eie (gray). He was a Poet.

In his younger yeares he affected obscurity of style, which, after, he quite left off, and wrote perspicuously. 'Twill be granted that he was one of the greatest Critiques of his time.

Mr. J. Selden writt a 4to booke called *Tabletalke*; which will not endure the Test of the Presse.

Sir Robert Cotton (the great Antiquary, that collected the Library) was his great Friend, whose son Sir Thomas Cotton was obnoxious to the Parliament and skulked in the Countrey. Mr. Selden had the Key and command of the Library, and preserved it, being then a Parliament-man.

He intended to have given his owne Library to the University of Oxford, but received disobligation from them, for that they would not lend him some MSS.; wherfore by his Will he left it to the disposall of his Executors (viz. Lord Chiefe Justice Hales, Lord Chief Justice Vaughan, Rowland Jukes, and his flatterer) who gave it to the Bodleian Library, at Oxon.

He would tell his intimate friends, Sir Bennet Hoskyns, etc., that he had no body to make his heire, excepte, it were a Milke-mayd: and that such people did not know what to doe with a great estate. (Bishop Grostest, of Lincoln, told his brother, who asked him to make him a grate man; Brother, said he, if your Plough is Broken, I'le pay the mending of it; or if an Oxe is dead, I'le pay for another: but a Plough-man I found you, and a Plough-man I'le leave you.)

He dyed of a Dropsey; he had his Funerall Scutcheons all ready moneths before he dyed. When he was neer death, the Minister was comeing to him to assoile him: Mr. Hobbes happened then to be there, sayd he, What, will you that have wrote like a man, now dye like a woman? So the Minister was not let in.

Mr. Johnson, Minister of the Temple, buryed him, the Directory way, where, amongst other things, he quoted the sayeing of a learned man (he did not name him) that *when a learned man dies, there dyes a great deale of learning with him*, and that *if Learning could have kept a man alive our Brother had not dyed*.—JOHN AUBREY, "John Selden," *Brief Lives*, 1669–96

> So fell the sacred Sybill, when of old
> Inspir'd with more than mortal breast could hold,
> The gazing multitude stood doubtful by
> Whether to call it Death or Extasie:
> She silent lies, and now the Nations find
> No Oracles but the Leaves she left behind.
>
>   Monarch of Time and Arts, who travell'dst o'er
> New worlds of knowledge, undescried before,
> And hast on everlasting columns writ,
> The utmost bounds of Learning and of Wit.
> Had'st thou been more like us, or we like thee,
> We might add something to thy memory.
> Now thy own Tongues must speak thee, and thy praise

Be from those Monuments thyself did'st raise;
And all those Titles thou did'st once display,
Must yield thee Titles greater far than they.

    Time which had wings till now, and was not known
To have a Being but by being gone,
You did arrest his motion, and have lent
A way to make him fixt and permanent;
Whilst by your labours Ages past appear,
And all at once we view a Plato's year.

    Actions and Fables were retriev'd by you,
All that was done, and what was not done too.
Which in your breast did comprehended lye
As in the bosom of Eternity;
You purg'd Records and Authors from their rust,
And sifted Pearls out of Rabbinick dust.
By you the Syrian Gods do live and grow
To be Immortal, since you made them so.
Inscriptions, Medals, Statues look fresh still,
Taking new brass and marble from your quill;
Which so unravels time, that now we do
Live our own Age, and our Forefathers' too,
And thus enlarg'd, by your discoveries, can
Make that an ell, which Nature made a span.

    If then we judge, that to preserve the State
Of things, is every moment to create,
The World's thus half your creature, whilst it stands
Rescued to memory by your learned Hands.
And unto you, now fearless of decay,
Times past owe more than Times to come can pay.

    How might you claim your Country's just applause,
When you stood square and upright as your cause
In doubtful times, nor ever would forego
Fair Truth and Right, whose bounds you best did know.

    You in the Tower did stand another Tower,
Firm to yourself and us, whilst jealous power
Your very soul imprison'd, that no thought
By books might enter, nor by pen get out;
And stripp'd of all besides, left you confined
To the one volume of your own vast Mind;
There Virtue and strict Honor past the guard,
Your only friends that could not be debarr'd;
And dwelt in your retirement; arm'd with these
You stood forth more than Admiral of our Seas;
Your Hands enclosed the Wat'ry Plains, and thus
Was no less Fence to them, than they to us;
Teaching our Ships to conquer, while each fight
Is but a Comment on those books you write.

    No foul disgraces, nor the worst of things
Made you like him (whose Anger Homer sings)
Slack in your Country's Quarrel, who adore,
Their Champion now, their Martyr heretofore:
Still with yourself contending, whether you
Could bravelier suffer, or could bravelier do.
We ask not now for Ancestors, nor care
Tho' *Selden* do no kindred boast, nor Heir,
Such worth best stands alone, and joys to be
To th' self at once both Founder and Posterity.
As when old Nilus who with bounteous flows
Waters an hundred Nations as he goes,
Scattering rich Harvests keep his Sacred Head
Amongst the Clouds still undiscovered.

    Be it now thy Oxford's Pride, that having gone
Through East and West, no Art, nor Tongue unknown;

Laden with Spoils thou hang'st thy Arms up here,
But set'st thy great Example every where.

    Thus when thy Monument shall itself lie dead,
And thy own Epitaph no more be read,
When all thy Statues shall be worn out so,
That even Selden should not Selden know;
Ages to come shall in thy Virtue share:
He that dies well makes all the world his Heir.
      —RICHARD BATHURST, "On the Death of the
        Learned Mr. John Selden," *Examen Poeticum*,
        ed. John Dryden, 1693

He was the first and greatest of the "Trimmers" who enlisted during this stormy century so large a contingent of our nation's strength. As long as personal sovereignty menaced the traditional privileges of Englishmen he was distinctly popular in sympathy, and even stood a certain amount of persecution in the popular cause. When that cause had got the upper hand and began to presume, Selden drew back. He was an Oxford man; but the greatest Cambridge poet of our time has exactly summarised Selden's idea, without probably thinking of Selden, in the well-known lines about

      Freedom slowly broadening down
      From precedent to precedent.

He was thus very horrible to "high-fliers" and men in a hurry on either side; and indeed to the present day there is a certain cold-bloodedness about him. He had the lawyer's—especially the English lawyer's—dislike of ecclesiasticism; he had the scholar's dislike of democracy. He was almost a great man; but he was not in the least a hero.—GEORGE SAINTSBURY, *Social England*, ed. H. D. Traill, 1895, Vol. 4, p. 98

General

I know to whom I write. Here, I am sure,
Though I am short, I cannot be obscure:
Lesse shall I for the Art or dressing care,
Truth, and the Graces best, when naked are.
Your Booke, my *Selden*, I have read, and much
Was trusted, that you thought my judgement such
To ask it: though in most of workes it be
A pennance, where a man may not be free,
Rather then Office, when it doth or may
Chance that the Friends affection proves Allay
Unto the Censure. Yours all need doth flie
Of this so vitious Humanitie.
Then which there is not unto Studie'a more
Pernitious enemie; we see, before
A many'of bookes, even good judgements wound
Themselves through favouring what is there not found:
But I on yours farre otherwise shall doe,
Not flie the Crime, but the Suspition too:
Though I confesse (as every Muse hath err'd,
And mine not least) I have too oft preferr'd
Men past their termes, and prais'd some names too much,
But 'twas with purpose to have made them such.
Since, being deceiv'd, I turne a sharper eye
Upon my selfe, and aske to whom? and why?
And what I write? and vexe it many dayes
Before men get a verse: much lesse a Praise;
So that my Reader is assur'd, I now
Meane what I speake: and still will keepe that Vow.
Stand forth my Object, then, you that have beene
Ever at home: yet, have all Countries seene:
And like a Compasse keeping one foot still

Upon your Center, doe your Circle fill
Of generall knowledge; watch'd men, manners too,
Heard what times past have said, seene what ours doe:
Which Grace shall I make love to first? your skill,
Or faith in things? or is't your wealth and will
T(o)'instruct and teach? or your unweary'd paine
Of Gathering? Bountie' in pouring out againe?
What fables have you vext! what truth redeem'd!
Antiquities search'd! Opinions dis-esteem'd!
Impostures branded! and Authorities urg'd!
What blots and errours, have you watch'd and purg'd
Records, and Authors of! how rectified
Times, manners, customes! Innovations spide!
Sought out the Fountaines, Sources, Creekes, paths, wayes,
And noted the beginnings and decayes!
Where is that nominall marke, or reall rite,
Forme, Art or Ensigne, that hath scap'd your sight?
How are Traditions there examin'd: how
Conjectures retriv'd! And a Storie now
And then of times (besides the bare Conduct
Of what it tells us) weav'd in to instruct!
I wonder'd at the richnesse, but am lost,
To see the workmanship so'(e)xceed the cost!
To marke the excellent seas'ning of your Stile!
And manly elocution, not one while
With horrour rough, then rioting with wit!
But to the Subject, still the Colours fit
In sharpnesse of all Search, wisdome of Choise,
Newnesse of Sense, Antiquitie of voyce!
    I yeeld, I yeeld, the matter of your praise
Flowes in upon me, and I cannot raise
A banke against it. Nothing but the round
Large claspe of Nature, such a wit can bound.
Monarch in Letters! 'Mongst thy Titles showne
Of others honours, thus, enjoy thine owne.
I first salute thee so; and gratulate,
With that thy Stile, thy keeping of thy State,
In offering this thy worke to no great Name,
That would, perhaps, have prais'd, and thank'd the same,
But nought beyond. He thou hast given it to,
Thy learned Chamber-fellow, knowes to doe
It true respects. He will not only love,
Embrace, and cherish; but he can approve
And estimate thy Paines; as having wrought
In the same Mines of knowledge; and thence brought
Humanitie enough to be a friend,
And strength to be a Champion, and defend
Thy gift 'gainst envie. O how I doe count
Among my commings in, and see it mount,
The Gaine of your two friendships! *Hayward* and
Selden! two Names that so much understand!
On whom I could take up, and ne're abuse
The Credit, what would furnish a tenth Muse!
But here's no time, nor place, my wealth to tell,
You both are modest. So am I. Farewell.
        —BEN JONSON, "An Epistle to Master John Sel-
        den" (1614), *Under-Wood*, 1640

Whereof what better witnes can ye expect I should produce,
then one of your own now sitting in Parlament, the chief of
learned men reputed in this Land, Mr. *Selden*, whose volume
of naturall & national laws proves, not only be great autorities
brought together, but by exquisite reasons and theorems almost
mathematically demonstrative, that all opinions, yea errors,
known, read, and collated, are of main service & assistance

toward the speedy attainment of what is truest. —JOHN
MILTON, *Areopagitica*, 1644

The famous Dr. Pocock assisted Mr. Selden very much, as
Selden himself is pleased to acknowledge in several places,
particularly in his edition of Eutychius' *Origines Ecclesiæ Alex-*
andrinæ, which Origines is only a small inconsiderable fragment of Eutychius' *Annales* that Pocock himself afterwards
published in Arabic and Latin. Indeed Selden, notwithstanding his great pretences, had but little skill in Arabic, and he
made use of others' help in that, as in many other things. His
design of printing these Annals was purely out of his hatred to
episcopacy. His Commentary upon them, which is large, is a
mere rhapsody, learned indeed and full of reading, but generally like his other performances injudicious. His efforts against
episcopacy are but weak, and yet he did what he was able.
—THOMAS HEARNE, *Reliquiae Hearnianae*, Jan. 24, 1727

It is by his conversation rather than by his writings that Selden
claims a place in this series. Most of his learned treatises were
written in Latin, and the few that are in English can hardly be
regarded as specimens of English prose. Documents and records in all languages form the body of his works. Selden does
little more than arrange and cement them together. This
method of writing history has evident advantages, but they are
not of a literary character. In the *Titles of Honour* there is not
one page of consecutive English. The passage quoted below—
where for once he tells a legend in his own words instead of
quoting the original—is the longest uninterrupted piece of
English in *The History of Tithes*, with the exception of the
preface. Selden contents himself with quoting his authorities;
for his aim in all his works is an exposition of facts, and he
allows them to speak for themselves.

    There is no reason to doubt Millward's statement in his
dedication of the *Table-Talk* to Selden's friends, that "the sense
and notion here is wholly his (Selden's), and most of the
words." "You will quickly perceive them to be his," he adds,
"by the familiar illustrations wherewith they are set off, and in
which way you know he was so happy, that, with a marvellous
delight to those that heard him, he would presently convey the
highest points of religion, and the most important affairs of
state, to an ordinary apprehension." And this appeal is sustained by the evidence of Clarendon—which might serve for a
description of the *Table-Talk*—that "in his conversation he was
the most clear discourser, and had the best faculty of making
hard things easy, and of presenting them to the understanding
of any man that hath been known." The ordinary reader, ignorant of the circumstances which from time to time gave occasion to the *Table-Talk*, must miss the full significance of much
that is contained in it. Even an apophthegm or anecdote loses
half its flavour apart from context and circumstances; and Mill-
ward, though he desires his readers to "carry along with them
the *When* and the *Why* many of these things were spoken"
gives them no help. The detached notes, taken at different
times over a period of twenty years, are classified under headings according to subject. It would have been better, since there
was no attempt to edit them, had they been left in chronological sequence. "We can no more know," says Selden, in one of
these *obiter dicta*, "what a minister said in his sermon by two or
three words picked out of it, than we can tell what tune a
musician played last upon the lute by two or three single
notes." In some degree the same applies to these fragments of
conversation. Yet, if put together as a whole, the reader may
trace in them, as in a broken mirror, some reflection of Selden's personality. A greater part of them forms a commentary
on the exciting events and problems of his time—prerogative,

divine right, episcopacy, parliament, etc. His statements are naturally less restrained here than in his more public utterances, and serve as a key to his political position during the years in which he acted as the bulwark of the constitution and arbiter of the rights of king and of commons. His favourite text, "All is as the State pleases," gives the central principle of his political philosophy. He considers that the rights and authority of King, Church, and Commons alike take their origin from, and are subject to, "the laws of the kingdom," of which he takes the purely empirical view of a practical lawyer. Selden adds to his marvellous range of learning a wide experience of life and keen analytic powers. His usual method of exposition is to reduce the subject at issue to its simplest form, and to illustrate it by homely analogy. Take, as an example, this on "Consecrated Places." "All things are God's already; we can give him no right, by consecrating any, that he had not before, only we set it apart to his service. Just as a gardener brings his lord and master a basket of apricots and presents them, his lord thanks him, perhaps gives him something for his pains, and yet the apricots were as much his lord's before as now." For refutation he frequently uses the *reductio ad absurdum*, as in the following: "If we once come to leave that outloose, as to pretend conscience against law, who knows what inconvenience may follow? For thus, suppose an Anabaptist comes and takes my horse. I sue him; he tells me he did according to his conscience; his conscience tells him all things are common amongst the saints, what is mine is his; therefore you do ill to make such a law, 'If any man takes another's horse he shall be hanged.' What can I say to this man? He does according to his conscience." Selden's judgments, though occasionally betraying his dislikes, are given without acerbity or passion. He speaks with the quiet assurance of a man who knows his facts, and discusses the issues which were so deeply moving his contemporaries with the calmness of a retrospective historian. His advice in practical affairs now and then recalls the worldly wisdom of Bacon's *Essays*. "In a troubled state," he says in one passage, "we must do as in foul weather upon the Thames, not think to cut directly through, so the boat may be quickly full of water, but rise and fall as the waves do, give as much as conveniently we can." And in another place he says: "'Tis not juggling that is to be blamed, but much juggling; for the world cannot be governed without it." His humour is characteristic. At times it takes the form of epigram, as in the following: "They talk (but blasphemously enough) that the Holy Ghost is president of their general councils, when the truth is, the odd man is still [always] the Holy Ghost." At others, it suggests a ludicrous parallel. "Doctor Prideaux, in his lectures, several days used arguments to prove predestination; at last he tells his auditory they are damned that do not believe it; doing herein just like schoolboys, when one of them has got an apple, or something the rest have a mind to, they use all the arguments they can to get some of it from him. *I gave you some t'other day; you shall have some with me another time.* When they cannot prevail, they tell him he's a jackanapes, a rogue, and a rascal." Selden has the limitations of one whose feet are always planted firmly on solid earth. He is a guide, a critic; not a leader, an inspirer. As he is untouched by the fanaticisms, he is incapable of the fine enthusiasms of his day. His remarks on poetry show no powers of literary appreciation. Clarendon justly remarked upon his "undervaluing of style." In his writings his sentences are usually ponderous, and often involved— a striking contrast to the homeliness and lucidity of his conversations, which, however, show also carelessness as to form. Yet in both there is an entire absence of pedantry. Selden estimated knowledge at its true value. "No man," he says, "is the wiser

for his learning; it may administer matter to work in, or objects to work upon; but wit and wisdom are born with a man." It is matter for regret that one who was pre-eminent in his age for both learning and wisdom should have devoted himself so exclusively to the pursuit of the former as to leave us nothing of the latter except a few fragments collected after his death by his secretary.—W. S. M'CORMICK, "John Selden," *English Prose*, ed. Henry Craik, 1893, Vol. 2, pp. 165–68

It is, indeed, with ecclesiastical rather than with religious subjects that Selden concerns himself. He was an Erastian of the deepest dye. His opinions, expressed with a frankness that did not suit the times, brought him into trouble in the time of King James. He published a *History of Tythes*, in which, without expressly denying the divine right of ecclesiastical persons to the possession of them, he made it plain that he set no value on it. With the fear of the Court of High Commission before his eyes he made a retraction, so ingeniously worded however, that, in the author's mind at least, it retracted nothing. He acknowledged his error in publishing, not in arguing, as he did, though it must be confessed that his language, at first sight at least, looks like a recantation. Selden, however, always maintained that he acknowledged his argument to be inopportune only. All contentions for the *jus divinum* found in him a decided antagonist. He ridiculed the idea that Bishops possessed it, though he has no hesitation in saying that "Bishops do stand best with Monarchy," and that, on the whole, the episcopal government of the Church is the most convenient. Anyhow, he thought, it was better to keep it than to change it. "They that would pull down the Bishops and erect a new way of government, do as he that pulls down an old house, and builds another of another fashion. There is a great deal ado, and a great deal of trouble; the old rubbish must be carried away, and new materials must be brought; workmen must be provided; and perhaps the old one would have served as well." This kind of language did not please, as may be supposed, either the friends or the enemies of Episcopacy. For the *jus divinum* of Presbyters Selden had no more regard than he had for that of Bishops. He is very scornful of the demeanour of the Westminster Assembly when, challenged to produce proofs of their claim to spiritual power, they demanded time for their reply. "Their asking time to answer them [the queries put by Parliament] was a satire upon themselves. . . . They do just as you have seen a fellow do at a tavern reckoning; when he should come to pay his share, he puts his hands into his pockets, and keeps a-grabling and a-fumbling and shaking, at last he tells you he has left his money at home." Nor did Selden please the Independents much better than he pleased their rivals, Episcopalian or Presbyterian. "The lecture in Black-friars, performed by officers of the Army, tradesmen, and ministers, is as if a great man should make a feast, and he would have his cook dress one dish, and his coachman another, his porter a third," &c. The only divine right in which Selden believed was of a man doing his own business. A soldier preaching was as intolerable to him as a layman pleading or judging. He had, indeed, a high standard for the education of the clergy. For preaching they must read Augustine, Ambrose, Chrysostom, both the Gregories, Tertullian, Clement of Alexandria, and Epiphanius,—"which last," he remarks, "have more learning in them than all the rest." For Church history they were to read Baronius and the Magdeburg Centuriators, and judge between the two. "Without school divinity, a divine knows nothing logically: nor will he be able to satisfy a rational man out of the pulpit." Finally, "The study of the casuists must follow the study of the schoolmen." This is a large programme, and yet Selden seems to think that it was not altogether over the heads of the class for whom it was intended. He writes:—"All confess there never was a more learned clergy." They could scarcely have been the ignorant boors whom Macaulay describes.

One of the few abstract questions with which we find Selden dealing is the ultimate sanction of morality. "I cannot fancy to myself," he writes, "what the law of Nature means but the law of God. How should I know I ought not to steal, I ought not to commit adultery, unless somebody had told me so?. . . . Whence comes the restraint? From a higher power; nothing else can bind." Selden's general attitude of mind on this subject makes this decided expression of the necessity of a Divine Sanction peculiarly valuable. This sanction, it must be understood, he did not find in conscience, of which indeed he manifestly thinks very little; a scrupulous conscience is like a shying horse, he thinks, and "generally to pretend conscience against law is dangerous," though he allows that there may be cases. The divine sanction which he wanted for morals was a revealed sanction.

The *jus divinum* of Kings did not fare better with him than that of Bishops and Presbyters. "A King is a thing men have made for their own sakes, for quietness' sake. Just as in a family one man is appointed to buy the meat." And again, "there is no species of Kings." Nevertheless, he clearly held kingship to be a convenient thing. He had stood firm against Royal usurpations, and suffered for his principles. He gave his services as a lawyer in drawing up the Protestation of 1621 (made against the doctrine that the rights of Parliament depended on a Royal grant), and suffered five weeks' imprisonment in consequence. In 1629, again, "Tertio Caroli," as he says more than once in his *Table-Talk*, he was committed to the Tower, in company with Denzil Holles, Elliot, and others. He was kept there for eight months, transferred to the King's Bench prison, but allowed the liberty of the rules. He was kept in some sort of confinement for two years. But the triumph of the Parliament did not bring him satisfaction. He saw in it the possibility of as great a tyranny as that from which England had been delivered. "The Parliament men are as great princes as any in the world, when whatever they please is privilege of Parliament. . . . The Senate at Venice are not so much as our Parliament, nor have they that power over the people." One remark under this heading has a curiously close application to present circumstances. "The Parliament party do not play fair-play in sitting up till two of the morning to vote something they have a mind to." Of Cromwell Selden makes no mention. Indeed, the names of contemporaries very seldom occur, though allusions are frequent. The common-sense view that Selden took of tithes might be extended with advantage to many well-meaning people who talk very wildly on that subject. Occasions of modern application are, indeed, not unfrequent. The loose way that has grown up of regarding contracts, for instance, would not have found a supporter in Selden. "Let them look to the making of bargains," he answers to an objection that by keeping a contract certain persons would lose all. "If I sell my lands, and when I have done, one comes and tells me I have nothing else to keep me, I and my wife and children must starve, if I part with my land: must I not therefore let them have my land that bought it and paid for it?"

But little of Selden's own personality comes out in this *Table-Talk*, and that little is seldom pleasing. He illustrates his remarks now and then with unnecessary coarseness. The good qualities with which Whitelock and others credit him—generosity, greatness of soul, and so forth—do not appear. As far as we know, he was not married, though Aubrey declares that he

was secretly married to the Countess of Kent. Of women he speaks with but scant respect. "'Tis reason a man that will have a wife should be at the charge of all her trinkets, and pay all the scores she sets on him. He that will keep a monkey, 'tis fit he should pay for the glasses she breaks." And again, "Marriage is a desperate thing. The frogs in Æsop were extreme wise; they had an extreme mind to some water, but they would not leap into the well, because they could not get out again."
—UNSIGNED, "Selden's *Table-Talk*," *Spectator*, Oct. 14, 1893, p. 489

Works

TITLES OF HONOUR

J. Selden liveth on his owne, is the Law book of the Judges of England, the bravest man in all languages; his booke *Titles of Honour*, written to his chamber-fellow Heyward.—BEN JONSON, *Conversations with William Drummond*, 1619

As to what concerns our nobility and gentry, all that come within either of those lists, will allow that Mr. Selden's *Titles of Honour* ought first to be well perused, for the gaining of a general notion of the distinction of degrees, from an emperor, down to a country gentleman.—WILLIAM NICOLSON, *The English Historical Library*, 1696–99

Selden's *Titles of Honour* a gentleman should not be without.—JOHN LOCKE, "Some Thoughts concerning Reading and Study for a Gentleman," c. 1704

DE DIIS SYRIIS

For the enumeration of the Syrian and Arabian deities, it may be observed that Milton has comprised in one hundred and thirty very beautiful lines the two large and learned syntagmas which Selden had composed on that abstruse subject.—EDWARD GIBBON, *The History of the Decline and Fall of the Roman Empire*, 1776–78, Ch. 15, Note

This was Selden's celebrated work, which placed him at once in the rank of the first scholars of the age. The primary purpose was to treat on the false gods mentioned in the Old Testament, but with which he joined an inquiry into the Syrian idolatry in general, and an occasional illustration of the ancient Theology of the other Heathen nations.—JOHN AIKIN, *The Lives of John Selden, Esq., and Archbishop Usher*, 1812

TABLE TALK

Were you not Executors to that Person, who (while he liv'd) was the Glory of the Nation, yet I am Confident any thing of his would find Acceptance with you; and truly the Sense and Notion here is wholly his, and most of the Words. I had the opportunity to hear his Discourse twenty Years together; and lest all those Excellent things that usually fell from him might be lost, some of them from time to time I faithfully committed to Writing, which here digested into this Method, I humbly present to your Hands. You will quickly perceive them to be his by the familiar Illustrations wherewith they are set off, and in which way you know he was so happy, that, with a marvellous delight to those that heard him, he would presently convey the highest Points of Religion, and the most important Affairs of State, to an ordinary apprehension.

In reading be pleased to distinguish Times, and in your Fancy carry along with you, the *When* and the *Why* many of these things were spoken; this will give them the more Life, and the smarter Relish.—RICHARD MILWARD, Dedication to Sir Matthew Hale et al., *Table Talk*, 1689

There is more weighty bullion sense in this book than I ever found in the same number of pages of any uninspired writer. . . . O! to have been with Selden over his glass of wine, making every accident an outlet and a vehicle of wisdom.
—SAMUEL TAYLOR COLERIDGE, "Notes on Selden's *Table Talk*," *Literary Remains*, ed. Henry Nelson Coleridge, 1836, Vol. 2, pp. 361–62

The thoughts of Sir Walter Raleigh on moral prudence are few, but precious. And some of the bright sallies of Selden recorded in his *Table Talk* are of the same description, though the book is too miscellaneous to fall under any single head of classification. The editor of this very short and small volume, which gives, perhaps, a more exalted notion of Selden's natural talents than any of his learned writings, requests the reader to distinguish times, and 'in his fancy to carry along with him the when and the why many of these things were spoken.' This intimation accounts for the different spirit in which he may seem to combat the follies of the prelates at one time, and of the presbyterians or fanatics at another. These sayings are not always, apparently, well reported; some seem to have been misunderstood, and in others the limiting clauses to have been forgotten. But on the whole they are full of vigour, raciness, and a kind of scorn of the half-learned, far less rude, but more cutting than that of Scaliger. It has been said that the *Table Talk* of Selden is worth all the Ana of the Continent. In this I should be disposed to concur; but they are not exactly works of the same class.—HENRY HALLAM, *Introduction to the Literature of Europe*, 1837–39, Pt. 3, Ch. 4, Par. 37

His homely, familiar manner, has its attractions as well for the scholar as for the common reader; pregnant as are his sentences with his great good sense, rare learning, bringing abstruse subjects home to the affairs of life in a style at once perspicuous and agreeable.—A. BRONSON ALCOTT, *Concord Days*, 1869, p. 249

HERBERT PAUL
From "The Autocrat of the Dinner Table"
Nineteenth Century, April 1900, pp. 624–36

The twenty years of John Selden's life began with the England of the great Queen, and ended with the England of the great Protector. Mark Pattison regarded him, not without reason, as a typical Englishman. He was never out of England, but, as Ben Jonson said of him, though he stayed at home, he knew the world. His learning was prodigious, even for a learned age, and yet he was conspicuously practical, even in the practical art of politics. He was one of the few lawyers who attained great eminence in the House of Commons, and one of the few statesmen who ever held their own in an assembly of divines. His published writings, except the *History of Tythes*, are dead, and even the *History of Tythes* is only consulted by professional students. He wrote a style which can never have been read with pleasure, and can scarcely now be read at all. *Stilus optimus magister dicendi*, says Crassus in the *De Oratore* —'The pen is the best master of speech.'[1] It was so with Cicero, it was so with Burke, it was so in our own day with Macaulay. But in Selden's case it was far otherwise. His pen had to be taken away from him before his mind could flow clearly and easily through natural channels. He lived, of course, long before the days of Parliamentary reporting. But by the general consent of his contemporaries he was one of the most powerful and effective debaters in Parliament. So, among others, says Clarendon, an unsparing critic of his books, and

himself a consummate master of all the rich resources of our English tongue. Selden's speeches have perished, like Strafford's, and Eliot's, and Pym's. The happy accident which has preserved his *Table Talk* enables us to see for ourselves the immeasurable superiority of his spoken to his written word. Scarcely any book in the English language has a value so utterly disproportionate to its size. The duodecimo edition of 1847 can be carried comfortably in the pocket. The larger and more elaborate volume, brought out by the late Mr. Harvey Reynolds in 1892, contains only two hundred pages. These pages show us how an accomplished man, famous for his conversation, entertained his company more than two hundred and fifty years ago. The knowledge is priceless, and would be so even if the publication of the book thirty-four years after Selden's death had led to no direct result. But it is impossible to read Selden's witty aphorisms and brilliant illustrations without perceiving how much the great talker of the eighteenth century was indebted to the great talker of the seventeenth. It is no disparagement of a strong man's original force to say that Samuel Johnson derived his colloquial manner from John Selden.

If Selden had lived in ordinary times, his career would have been uneventful, for he was neither adventurous nor ambitious. Civil troubles forced him into prominence, and when he was compelled to take an active part in public affairs he showed that he was no time-server, but a man of principle. He had the intellectual honesty which is to some men what morality or enthusiasm is to others. He would not make a fool of himself by saying what he knew to be untrue. In deference to King James he expressed regret for having argued that tithes were not payable by divine law. To retract the argument, to acknowledge himself in the wrong, he absolutely refused. Selden belonged to the middle class, which in this country more than in any other answers Aristotle's description, and acts as the bulwark of the State. He was a native of Sussex, and received his early education at the free school of Chichester. From Chichester he went to Oxford, with which for the remainder of his life he was destined to be connected. He matriculated at Hart Hall, and it is curious that this great scholar, who represented the University throughout the Long Parliament, took no degree. He was called to the Bar at the Inner Temple, and, so far as he adopted any profession, he adopted the profession of the law. But his heart was in study, and in the larger affairs of State. Two views of the law of England have come down to us from the seventeenth century. To Sir Edward Coke it was the perfection of human reason, to Oliver Cromwell it was a tortuous and ungodly jumble. Selden was too much of an antiquary to agree with Cromwell, and too much of a philosopher to agree with Coke. He must very soon have mastered whatever the law-books of those days could teach him, and in legal learning he had no superior at the Bar or on the bench. He was a conveyancer, and had a large amount of chamber practice. But he is said to have appeared in court only when his vast knowledge was required by some case of unusual character and special importance. He became, when he was quite a young man, steward to Henry Grey, ninth Earl of Kent, and his close connection with that family only ended with the death of the Countess, three years before his own. One consequence of this appointment was that he spent his vacations at Wrest, in Bedfordshire, then Lord Kent's, and now Lord Cowper's. Another was, that after the Earl's death he came to live at Lady Kent's house, The Carmelites, in Whitefriars, where he kept his splendid library and his choice collection of Greek Marbles. If he was ever married at all, he was privately married to Lady Kent. Sir Edward Fry, from whose admirable article in the *Dictionary of National Biography* I have taken the facts of

Selden's life, does not believe the story of the marriage. In any case, there was no scandal, which is creditable to the somewhat censorious society of the time.

Like Lord Mansfield, who in his youth 'drank champagne with the wits,' Selden enjoyed the best of good company from the first. He was the friend of Ben Jonson, of Camden the famous author of *Britannia*, and of Sir Robert Cotton the antiquary, at whose house in Palace Yard he read and studied. His *History of Tythes* from the days of Melchisedec appeared in 1617, and he soon discovered that England was not a free country. For denying what was called the *jure divinoship* of the clerical tenth he was haled before the High Commission, and apologised lest worse should happen to him. He did not follow the example of Galileo by retracting as error what he believed to be truth, but he submitted to the jurisdiction. The incident is thoroughly characteristic. Selden had a profound contempt for 'the great vulgar and the small.' He did not care two straws what the High Commission thought about a matter of which they knew nothing. He knew the difference between his own real learning and the sham learning of King James. But he sincerely respected law and order. His mind was not naturally speculative, like the mind of his illustrious friend Thomas Hobbes, but practical and historical. If the Commissioners chose to talk nonsense, that was their affair. He submitted to their authority without prejudice to his contempt for their understandings. Nor was he cast (few men are) in the heroic mould. When it was his duty to express an opinion, he never shrank from expressing it because it was dangerous or unpopular. But to go to prison for a theory of tithes he regarded as absurd, and as the times grew more turbulent he may have thought that the supply of martyrs was likely to exceed the demand. He was not, however, timid like Hobbes. He braved the wrath of King Charles by acting as a manager in the impeachment of Buckingham, and risked the vengeance of a Parliamentary majority by opposing the impeachment of Strafford. Nor did he always escape the penalty of his boldness. In 1629 he was committed to the Tower with Eliot, Hobbes, and six other Members of Parliament. He was shifted from prison to prison, and was not finally released till 1631. But it is a curious fact, as Sir Edward Fry points out, that he bore no malice against the King. He must have been a man of singularly even temper, cold but placable, never carried out of his way by enthusiasm or resentment or the passion for notoriety which has been the motive of so many otherwise inexplicable acts. . . .

Selden's *Table Talk* covers the last twenty years of his life, from 1634 to 1654. It is probable that during most of that time he resided under Lady Kent's roof, occupying his own sumptuous apartments in her large and beautiful house near the Temple and the river. Though himself a man temperate in all things, he was extremely hospitable, was famous for his good dinners, and loved to entertain. His guests had better entertainment than food and wine, for there have been few such brilliant talkers as Selden. The crabbed English, and the still more crabbed Latin, of his books present a strange contrast to the racy vernacular of his delightful conversation. A shrewd, cynical, sarcastic, but not unkindly observer of men and things, he always went straight to the heart of his subject, and his command of humorous illustration was scarcely surpassed by Swift. I cannot help thinking that Mr. Reynolds was too severe upon his indecency. There are perhaps half a dozen passages which a delicate taste might censure. But we have no reason to suppose that they were uttered in the presence of women, and they are purity itself when compared with the habitual converse of the succeeding age. Of his alleged impiety

there is no trace, though he handled ecclesiastical subjects with a homely freedom. From the superstitions of his time he was absolutely exempt, and nothing can be more exquisite than his own account of the way in which by means of an amulet he cast out sham devils from a self-tormented friend. His secretary, Richard Milward, to whom we are indebted for these flashes of a master mind, observes that the origin of the sayings will be proved to all Selden's acquaintance by 'the familiar illustrations wherewith they are set off.'

One of the most justly famous occurs under the heading of 'Bishops.' Selden's habitual tolerance broke down at Bishops. He had no use for them, and even went so far as to deny that they were a separate order in the Church. One can easily imagine how a man like Selden must have been irritated by the fussy, domineering arrogance of the man whom Carlyle profanely calls W. Cant. The Long Parliament never did a more foolish thing than when they made a martyr of that mean and cruel pedant.

'The Bishops,' says Selden, 'were too hasty, else with a discreet slowness they might have had what they aimed at. The old story of the fellow that told the gentleman he might get to such a place if he did not ride too fast would have fitted their turn.'

And not their turn only. The apologue should be hung up, framed and glazed, in every public office, from the Colonial Office downwards. That is the best of Selden. He always sticks to the point, and yet he throws out pregnant hints for general application to human affairs. *Festina lente* looks like a frigid paradox, though it is not so. The story of the fellow that told the gentleman is 'the wisdom of many, and the wit of one.'

Selden's mind was essentially political—even more political than legal. He was under the influence of Hobbes, though his ideal of constitutional monarchy was entirely opposed to Hobbes's absolute doctrines. Selden was certainly no democrat. He believed in the natural supremacy of the leisurely and educated classes, and he probably held that, as Bishop Horsley put it, more than a century later, the mass of the people had nothing to do with the laws except to obey them. Of Parliamentary freedom he was a devotee, but to the notion of self-government in its widest sense he was a stranger. Like a good Erastian, he desired the retention of the Bishops in the House of Lords, and stoutly maintained against all comers that they sat there by as good a right as the hereditary peers. 'To take away Bishops' votes,' he said, 'is but the beginning to take them away; for then they can be of no longer use to the King or State. 'Tis but like the little wimble to let in the greater auger.' It is amusing to find our old friend, the thin end of the wedge, in this early and rudimentary form. Selden's conception of a Bishop was rather like that of Lord Westbury, who said in the Judicial Committee, of Bishops Gray and Colenso, 'Both these ecclesiastical personages are creatures of the law.' For apostolical succession he did not care a rap. A Bishop not a Lord of Parliament was to him no Bishop at all, which of course implied that he had no faith in Episcopacy as a divine or even as a human institution. As a matter of historical fact he was right, and he lived to see it; for in 1646, by ordinance of Parliament, the 'name, title, style and dignity of Archbishop and Bishop were wholly taken away.' It is true that there are now Bishops, suffragans and others, who have no seats in the House of Lords, and that the Bishop of Sodor and Man never had a vote. But they are exceptions, and, in the true meaning of the Latin proverb, the existence of exceptions proves the existence of a rule. On another occasion Selden declared his own views with a dogmatic severity unusual in him. 'They are equally mad,' he exclaimed, 'who say Bishops are so *jure divino* that they must be continued, and they who say they are so anti-Christian that they must be put away. All is as the State likes.' It would have been a strong thing to affirm that all Roman Catholics and all Presbyterians were mad, or even unreasonable, which is what Selden meant. But he was a staunch Church of England man, regarding the Church as part of the Constitution, and he spoke as an ecclesiastical lawyer.

The popular theology of his time was by no means to Selden's taste, and that is no doubt why he was accused of irreligion. He suffered in that as in other respects for being in advance of his age. He belonged as a theologian rather to the nineteenth century than to the seventeenth, and would have found himself in perfect agreement with Thirlwall or Stanley. His contrast between Christianity and Mahommedanism is curiously modern.

> The Turks tell their people of a heaven where there is a sensible pleasure, but of a hell where they shall suffer they do not know what. The Christians quite invert this order. They tell us of a hell where we shall feel sensible pain, but of a heaven where we shall enjoy we cannot tell what.

Neither Milton nor Bunyan can be said altogether to have escaped the application of this caustic criticism. Selden had what the French call the positive spirit, which is sensible of its own limitations, and will not go beyond them. The imagination of his time, especially the Puritan imagination, ran riot in the wildest fancies of future woe for the enemies of the saints, and Selden, though a man of high character, must have been conscious that he was no saint. He was one of those who would rather live up to a comparatively low standard than fall short of a comparatively high one. He must have secretly sympathised with the young man in the parable who went away sorrowful because he had great possessions. He took the Englishman's love of compromise into religion as well as into politics, and with the whole force of his nature he hated extremes. There are traces in his *Table Talk* of the Baconian temper, the grave, dignified, philosophic calm with which an intellect, unclouded by passion or prejudice, contemplates the wild surging of ignorant enthusiasm in its desperate efforts to find truth where there is no road.

'The laws of the Church are most favourable to the Church, because they were the Church's own making; as the heralds are the best gentlemen, because they make their own pedigree.' This is an invaluable text for the Erastian in all times. It is also a perfect specimen of Selden's best manner. There is not a word too much in it; it condenses a whole theory into a couple of sentences, of which one is fact and the other illustration. In a formal treatise it would have to be expanded or to be followed by a formal essay. In talk it is just as it should be. Selden had a singular gift of conversational completeness. He could sum up and dismiss a subject in a phrase which adhered to the memory while memory remained. Perhaps the talker who most resembled him in this particular was Talleyrand. The Duke of Wellington was once asked whether he considered Talleyrand to be good company. He replied that in the ordinary sense of the term he was not. 'He would often,' added the Duke, 'sit silent for hours. But once or twice in an evening he would say something which you could not forget as long as you lived.' I cannot recall the Duke's exact words, but such, I am sure, is the substance of them. We do not know how large a share Selden took in the talk at his own dinner table. Probably it was much larger than Talleyrand's, and we only have scattered fragments of it in Mr. Milward's record. But we have quite enough to show us of what sort it was. It did not burst out in a torrent, like Johnson's, or flow in a rich volume like

Coleridge's. Johnson owed much to Selden, but his own natural eloquence swept away all barriers. Selden kept his temper, and was not easily moved to sympathy or to indignation. He must have been, I think, a good listener, not because he was patient of contradiction or ready to be convinced, but because he wished to have the last word. When he said a thing it was to be so. His natural dignity and acquired learning gave him a legitimate advantage of which he must have been fully aware.

Having compared Convocation with a court leet, Selden, like a good Protestant, turned his guns upon the General Councils of the Church of Rome. 'They talk (but blasphemously enough) that the Holy Ghost is President of their General Councils, when the truth is, the odd man is still the Holy Ghost.' By the odd man he meant of course the majority. The charge of blasphemy might perhaps be retorted, though I think without reason, by those against whom it was directed. Selden, in common with many men whose religion lies altogether below the surface, was disgusted by its unseasonable intrusion. It affronted his sense of reverence as much as it irritated his intellect to hear men say that an issue would be determined by inspiration when they knew that it would be determined by numbers. But it is true of this as of almost all his wise and pithy sayings, that they have an application far wider than that which he originally gave them. There is not much outward resemblance between a Council of the Church and a political convention in the United States. But a belief in the infallibility of the odd man is a political as well as a theological superstition. Those who support representative and democratic government merely as the fairest and most convenient method yet discovered for carrying out the will of a free people are beyond the reach of Selden's sarcasm. Yet it may be useful even for them to be reminded that the rule of majorities is an arrangement, not a principle, and that truth must often be on the losing side. Selden had too much of Horace's contempt for the unholy mob, who, after all, may be presumed to know their own minds and understand their own business. He did not always remember, though he knew, that there might be men as learned as himself without a hundredth part of his practical sagacity, and that, on the other hand, shrewd mother-wit is a safer guide through life than learning. A Conservative will not get much good out of Selden, who will only strengthen him in his prejudices. But as a cooling medium for enthusiastic democrats I venture to recommend the *Table Talk*.

It would be interesting to know what Selden thought of James the First. He often quotes that highly educated monarch, with whom he argued about the divine right of tithes and other matters. The right divine of kings to govern wrong was His Majesty's favourite tenet, and he believed also in the divine right of Episcopacy, because, as he tersely said, 'No Bishop, no King.' Indeed, James's notion of his own attributes and of the sacrosanctity of the system which made him possible left little scope for the Governor of the Universe. Selden had old scores to pay off against the King, and he laughed at him after his death in a characteristic fashion by telling an anecdote. Henry the Fourth of France was killed, observes Selden, according to some, for his apostasy; according to others, for his debauchery. 'No,' says King James (who could not abide fighting), 'he was killed for permitting duels in his kingdom.' 'Commonly,' adds the table talker, 'we say judgment falls upon a man for something in him we cannot abide.' That is the secular and mundane version of the moral drawn for all time in the Gospels from the fall of the Tower of Siloam. In a homelier vein is 'Old friends are best. King James used to call for his old shoes; they were easiest for his feet.' That is all. Selden did not often elaborate, if we may trust, as surely we can trust, his constant friend and companion, Mr. Milward. He had not the fault of our English nation that when they have a good thing they make it too common. The worst and most tiresome talkers are those who worry a subject to death. Selden threw out a hint, sometimes shot a Parthian arrow, and passed on. He knew better than to deliver in conversation an essay on friendship. Everyone feels the comfort of old shoes. Selden was too fond of his old shoes, too worldly a sage, too fond of peace and wealth. As he grew bolder he became more and more impressed with the sinfulness of being uncomfortable. I can hear the impassioned moralist declaim against the low view of friendship which Selden's apophthegm implies. It was not intended to be exhaustive, but to be suggestive. It was table talk.

'No man,' says Selden, 'is the wiser for his learning.' He had a right to this paradox, and, as in all paradoxes worthy of the name there is some truth in it. But it is difficult to conceive Selden apart from his learning, or to suppose that the inexhaustible wealth of illustration with which it supplied him did not suggest new ideas, besides enriching and adorning the old. Yet, on the other hand, we may say with confidence that Selden's wisdom is often most manifest in the homeliest images. Like Bacon he took a low view of marriage, and he had little respect for the minds of women. The frogs in Æsop, he tells us, were exceeding wise, because they would not venture themselves into the well, although they longed to drink. That is rather a cheap form of cynicism, and below Selden's powers. On the other hand, nothing can be better than his example of the old truth that we measure the excellency of other men by some excellency we conceive to be in ourselves. 'Nash, a poet, poor enough (as poets used to be), seeing an alderman with his gold chain, upon his great horse, by way of scorn, said to one of his companions, "Do you see yon fellow, how goodly, how big he looks? Why, that fellow cannot make a blank verse."' Selden goes on to preach a little sermon against what is or was called Anthropomorphism, the only answer to which is that if we do not think of God in human terms we cannot think of Him at all. We know too well from daily experience that blank verse of a sort can be made by anyone, and we have had not only Aldermen but Lord Mayors who could ride to hounds. After Tennyson poverty can no longer be safely predicated of poets, and Ben Jonson, the admiring friend of Selden, was in easy circumstances. But poor Nash and irrelevant contempt are as perennial as human nature itself. I confess that I have far more respect for Nash than I should have if he had envied the Alderman his great horse and his gold chain. He at least respected himself, and a blank verse of Shakespeare's or Milton's is worth all the gold chains in the world.

Others of Selden's contemporaries were illogical besides poor Nash. Selden was an attentive critic of sermons, which he did not always hear with humble submission. 'Preachers,' says he, 'will bring anything into a text. The young Masters of Arts preached against non-residence in the University; whereupon the Heads made an order that no man should meddle with anything but what was in the text. The next day one preached upon these words, *Abraham* begat *Isaac;* when he had gone a good way, at last he observed that Abraham was resident, for if he had been non-resident he could never have begot Isaac; and so fell foul upon the non-residents.' Queen Elizabeth was a stickler for relevancy in sermons. She loved to tune the pulpits, and her famous 'Stick to your text, Mr. Dean,' is historical. It is not perhaps unnatural that the clergy, having to connect their thoughts with a verse of scripture, which after all is limited, should sometimes be in sore straits. 'Hear the Church' was very tempting, and to leave out the condition as easy as lying. Archbishop Whately's pungent comment, 'I should like to hear that young man preach on "Hang all the law and the prophets,"' was quite in Selden's vein. I suspect that Selden, like many laymen, would have liked to preach himself, and that when he attended the Westminster Assembly the pent-up energies of years broke out in a flood which astonished the divines. 'For a man of the world,' said Burke, in reference to religious questions—'for a man of the world, I have thought of these things.' Selden had thought, and read, and written on many ecclesiastical subjects. He was not to be taught by parsons, who were, as he reminded them, only 'persons' differently spelt. Mr. Reynolds has pointed out that he contradicted himself about their learning, which in one place he extols and in another denies. But substantially he agreed with Clarendon that they had bad judgment, and were unsafe guides in mundane affairs. Selden practised his own theories. One great merit of his talk is that it always goes straight to the point. His stories, like Lincoln's, are always told for a purpose, and never because he had a story to tell. Abraham Lincoln was probably the best storyteller known to fame. There may have been mute, inglorious Lincolns who equalled him in that respect, if in no other way. But of Lincoln it was said, and of Lincoln only could it be said, that he illustrated by a story every argument he used, that he invented every story he told, and that he never told the same story twice. Selden's stories were not invented. He had a wonderful memory, upon which he freely drew, but he never dragged his anecdotes in by the head and ears, nor did he dilute them or spin them out. They are short, pithy, pointed, easy to remember, and impossible to misunderstand. The man who is determined to tell his favourite story or the last story he has heard, whether there be a legitimate opening for it or not, destroys conversation, and ought to be destroyed himself. There should be a heavy social penalty for the use of the phrase 'By the way, that reminds me.' If a story does not explain itself, if its connection with the subject is not at once seen, both it and its narrator are social solecisms. Soli is their native town, although they never heard of it.

The most profound and searching of all Selden's utterances is partly characteristic of his age, but far more characteristic of him. 'Aye or no never answered any question. The not distinguishing where things should be distinguished, and the not confounding where things should be confounded, is the cause of all the mistakes in the world.' One would give a good deal to know the precise occasion on which this deep and subtle remark was made. The when and the why, as Mr. Milward justly observes in his dedication to the Executors, give these sentences the more life and the smarter relish. Unfortunately he did not supply the want, and to guess is futile. All we know is that a 'doubt' of some kind had been 'propounded.' It may have been whether monarchy was the best form of government, or whether a subject was justified in resisting his sovereign, or whether faith without works was more salutary than works without faith. But tantalising as our ignorance is, we can fall back upon the general truth of the apophthegm. There are questions which answer themselves, because they are questions only in form. Where there is a real dispute, aye or no raises more difficulties than it solves. It is easy to lay down universal propositions. The difficulty arises when we come to apply them. Selden lived in stirring times, full of action and speculation, when erroneous opinions might at any moment lead to some blunder which was worse than a crime. The impartial historian, if such a superhuman being were possible, could not acquit either the Court or the Parliament of serious and even fatal errors. They were both always answering aye or no to every question, until Charles lost his crown and his head because he would be a despot or nothing, and Cromwell, the vindicator of national rights, had to rule England without a Parliament by military force. They both confounded things which ought to be distinguished, and distinguished things which ought to be confounded. In an age of political philosophy the voice of the philosopher was unheeded.

It is, I am afraid, arguable that Selden was a lukewarm patriot. No man more thoroughly enjoyed that pleasure of looking down upon the errors of the vulgar which Lucretius has so magnificently described. Not that he had any ill-will to either party. He bore no malice, he harboured no feeling fiercer than contempt.

Non quia vexari quemquam est jucunda voluptas,
Sed quibus ipse malis careas quia cernere suave est.

There is a tradition, not authentic, that at the close of Selden's life he wished he had been a justice of the peace, and in that humble way useful to his neighbours. He would certainly have been the wisest justice on the banks of Trent, or Thames. Such wishes are not to be taken seriously. But Selden might have had a great career as a sagacious statesman, guiding the counsels and moderating the zeal of the Parliamentary party. He deliberately turned from what became in his eyes a vulgar broil. The 'great refusal' has never been made with more dignity. Selden retained the respect of his old colleagues, and his funeral in the Temple Church was attended by the judges of the land. He died, as he had lived, plain John Selden, while his intellectual inferiors filled high offices of State. He wanted a quiet life; he got it, and he paid for it. He has painted the situation in a quaint allegory:

Wise men say nothing in dangerous times. The lion, you know, called the sheep to ask her if his breath smelt; she said aye; he bit off her head for a fool. He called a wolf and asked him; he said no; he tore him in pieces for a flatterer. At last he called the fox and asked him. Truly he had got a cold and could not smell.

Selden's cold was chronic. During the period of these conversations the last civil war in England (except Monmouth's trumpery rebellion) was waged, Charles the First was executed, Oliver Cromwell became Protector of the realm. But to none of these events is there the smallest allusion in the talk of Selden's table. Such silence in private is amazing, and of course we do not know how much the secretary suppressed.

But one can imagine that Selden, having definitively abandoned public life, would not care for such a pale simulacrum of it as talking politics with his friends. He had filled a great place, and there is nothing less dignified than a partial retirement; or it may be that men of very different opinions came to his house, and that to content them all he adopted a cleanlier shift than Sir Robert Walpole's by talking of universal truths. Posterity would be ungrateful to quarrel with the result. Except Bacon's Essays there is hardly so rich a treasure-house of worldly wisdom in the English language as Selden's *Table Talk*. Some of it, indeed, is thoroughly Baconian, as 'Wit and wisdom differ; wit is upon the sudden turn, wisdom is in bringing about ends.' But most of it is entirely his own, the mature thought of a princely intellect equally at home in the book of the world and in the world of books. Johnson compared it with French collections of *ana*, such as the *Menagiana*, but it is intensely and characteristically English. Although he asks, 'Is there not enough to meddle withal upon the stage, or in love, or at the table, but religion?' religion was seldom out of his thoughts. He considered it as a statesman, not as a pietist, but he recognised its all-pervading influence on human affairs. An Erastian of the Erastians he was no materialist, like his friend Hobbes. He was indeed a typical Church of England man, as far removed from Geneva as from Rome. He did not shrink from the free handling of sacred subjects, and there was an element of brutality in some of his sledge-hammer attacks on current superstition. But if he had been the scoffing sceptic that some in fear of his learning dubbed him, so saintly a man as Sir Matthew Hale could not have called him a resolved, serious Christian. Coleridge complained of the lack of poetry in Selden, and this complaint is just. He was too much under the influence of reason, he had little or no imagination, and he underrated the force of sentiment, religious or otherwise. The ridiculous aspect of things struck him so forcibly that it sometimes blinded him to their graver significance. Every man has his limitations, and these were his. But those who know best what good talk is will be the readiest to admire the incomparable excellence of Selden's.

Notes

1. The exact words are *Stilus optimus et præstantissimus dicendi effector et magister*. They have the air in the dialogue of a familiar quotation, but I cannot indicate their original source.

WILLIAM HABINGTON

1605–1654

William Habington was born at Hindlip Hall, Worcestershire, on November 4, 1605. His father Thomas, a Catholic, was imprisoned for his involvement in the Gunpowder Plot. Habington was educated at St. Omer's and in Paris. Around 1633 Habington married Lucy Herbert, youngest daughter of the first baron Powis. His collection of love poems, *Castara* (1634), contains many sonnets in praise of his wife. In 1635 Habington reissued *Castara*, this time under his name and with several added elegies on his friend George Talbot. Habington again revised *Castara* in 1640, adding several sacred poems.

Habington was an ardent Royalist, although for the most part his political activities were limited to Hindlip Hall. In 1640 he produced a tragicomedy, *The Queene of Arragon*, which was staged successfully before Charles and Henrietta Maria. Habington's other works include *Observations upon Historie* (1641) and the completion of his father's *Historie of Edward the Fourth* (1640). He was a friend of James Shirley and William Davenant, and was a great admirer of Ben Jonson. Habington died on November 30, 1654, and was buried at the Hindlip parish church.

Personal

William Habington . . . was born at Hendlip, on the fourth (some say the fifth) day of November 1605, educated in S. Omers and Paris; in the first of which he was earnestly invited to take upon him the habit of the Jesuits, but by excuses got free and left them. After his return from Paris, being then at man's estate, he was instructed at home in matters of history by his father, and became an accomplish'd gentleman. He hath written and published (1) *Poems*, Lond. 1635, in oct. sec. edit. under the title of *Castara*. They are divided into three parts, under a different title suitable to their subject. The first, which was written when he was a suiter to his wife, (the humane goddess that inspired him, viz. Lucia daughter of Will. lord Powis) is usher'd in, by a character writ in prose, of a mistress. The second, are copies writ to her after marriage, by the character of a wife: after which is a character of a friend, before several funeral elegies. The third part consists of divine poems, some of which are paraphrases on several texts out of Job and the book of Psalms; before which is the portraict of a holy man. (2) *Queen of Arragon*, a trag. com. which play he communicating to Philip earl of Pembroke l. chamberlain of the houshold to K. Charles I. he caused it to be acted at court, and afterwards to be publish'd against the author's will. (3) *Observations upon History.* Lond. 1641. oct. (4) *History of Edward the fourth, King of England.* Lond. 1640. in a thin fol. written and published at the desire of K. Charles I. being then by many esteemed to have a stile sufficiently florid, and better becoming a poetical, than historical, subject. This person Will. Habington, who did run with the times, and was not unknown to Oliver the usurper, died on the 30th of November 1654, and was buried in the vault before-mentioned by the bodies of his father and grand-father. The MSS which he (and his father) left behind, are in the hands of his son Thomas, and might be made useful for the public, if in others.—ANTHONY À WOOD, *Athenae Oxonienses*, 1691–1721

> And when I'm lost in death's cold night,
> Who will remember now I write?

So wrote William Habington, nearly two centuries and a half ago, foreboding, perhaps, the neglect which was so soon to settle on his name. His was not a genius of that robust and cheerful temper which calmly forestalls the verdict of posterity and usurps immortality as its birthright, the royal purple of the sovereigns of song. His premonition, if such it were, had speedy fulfilment. So popular during his lifetime that no less than three editions of his poems were called for in the short space of five years, he seems, upon his death, to have dropped out of notice as quietly and quickly as a pebble tossed into a stream. So far as we can learn, not even a single buble of elegy—and a prodigious quantity of such "airy nothings" the drowning poets of his day were wont to set afloat, to show for a little where they had sunk in the Lethean river—marked his exit.—D. A. CASSERLY, "A Catholic Poet of the Seventeenth Century," *American Catholic Quarterly Review*, Oct. 1877, p. 614

General

William Habington, the author of Poems which came forth above twenty years since under the title of *Castara*, the feigned name, no doubt, of that human Goddess that inspired them; but better known by his History of *The Reign of King the fourth*; in which also he hath a style sufficiently florid; and perhaps better becoming a poetical than historical subject. In respect of his Poems, however they are now almost forgotten, he may be rank'd in my opinion with those that deserve neither the highest nor the lowest seat in the Theatre of Fame.—EDWARD PHILLIPS, *Theatrum Poetarum Anglicanorum*, 1675

There is no very ardent sensibility in his lyrics, but they denote a mind of elegant and chaste sentiments. He is free as any of the minor poets of his age from the impurities which were then considered as wit. He is indeed rather ostentatiously platonic, but his love language is far from being so elaborate as the complimentary gallantry of the preceding age. A respectable gravity of thought, and succinct fluency of expression, are observable in the poems of his later life.—THOMAS CAMPBELL, *Specimens of the British Poets*, 1819

Habington proclaims it to be his purpose to teach the world a new strain in poetry. Speaking in his preface ⟨to *Castara*⟩ of most love poets as "heathens, who can give no nobler testimony of twenty years' employment than some loose copies of lust happily expressed," he hopes that, "if the innocency of a chaste muse shall be more acceptable and weigh heavier in the balance of esteem," he may drive those rivals out of the field. The poems, accordingly, are poems first of virtuous aristocratic wooing, and then of satisfied conjugal affection; and occasion is taken throughout to expound the author's idea of the character and behaviour proper in woman, and of her just relations to the other sex. A kind of sweet, modest punctiliosity is the virtue he strives to paint and inculcate in his ideal woman. Thus, in his prose character of "A Mistress," prefixed to the first portion of his poems: "She is deaf to the whispers of love, and even in the marriage-hour can break off without the least suspicion of scandal to the former liberty of her carriage. She avoids a too near conversation with man, and, like the Parthian, overcomes by flight. . . . She never arrived to so much familiarity with man as to know the diminutive of his name and call him by it, and she can show a competent favour without yielding her hand to his gripe." . . .

In his poems descriptive of the wifely virtues, the same strain is continued with the due variation. Modest obedience to the husband is the chief of these virtues. "She is inquisitive only of new ways to please him, and her wit sails by no other compass than that of his direction. She looks upon him as conjurers upon the circle, beyond which there is nothing but death and hell; and in him she believes paradise circumscribed. His virtues are her wonder and imitation, and his errors her credulity thinks no more frailty than makes him descend to the title of man." And so in his appended set of meditative or religious poems, in which he describes the feelings of a good man in matters higher than the matrimonial. "Catholic faith," he says, "is the foundation on which he erects religion, knowing it a ruinous madness to build in the air of a private spirit or on the sands of any new schism. His impiety is not so bold to bring Divinity down to the mistake of Reason, or to deny those mysteries his apprehension reacheth not. His obedience moves still by the direction of the magistrate; and, should conscience inform him that the demand is unjust, he judgeth it nevertheless high treason by rebellion to make good his tenets." From these sentences it will be seen that Habington, in this particular portion of his poems, takes a place among the religious poets of the time, beside Donne and Herbert, with about as much difference as might be supposed to arise from the mode of thought of a loyal English Catholic, as compared with that of two Anglican churchmen. In these poems he rises above his pedantry and frigidity, and even seems to leave poor Castara behind, as, though still perfect enough in her way, only an impediment in the higher ecstasies of his private contemplations. Thus in his poem "*Cogitabo pro peccato meo*," after passing in review all the stages of his past life, his love and his literature included, as but time trifled away, he concludes,—

> But now, my soul, prepare
> To ponder what and where we are:
> How frail is life, how vain a breath
> Opinion, how uncertain death;
> How only a poor stone shall bear
> Witness that once we were:
> How a shrill trumpet shall
> Us to the bar as traitors call.
> Then shall we see too late that pride
> Hath hope with flattery belied;
> And that the mighty in command
> Pale cowards there must stand.

In Habington's poetry, more easily than in any other poetry of the period of the same virtuous aim and tendency, there may be detected (and perhaps his Jesuit training had something to do with it) a characteristic which nevertheless exists in almost all the poets with whom we have associated him. It may be described as consisting in an inordinately particular recognition of the fact of sex. These words are used to distinguish between what they are here meant to signify and that apparently identical but really different perception which pervades the poetry of all ages, and without which history would be full of fallacy and philosophy itself imperfect—the perception of love as an influence in all human affairs, of the perpetual working at all points of human society of Aphrodite's white hand. Quite different was the mental habit of which we speak. It was rather a fascination of the mind round the radical fact of sex, a limitation of the mental activity within the range of the immediate suggestions of that fact, a diffusion of it, and of deductions from it, through all kinds of considerations. There may be noted, for example, in most of the writers under view, a strained attention to the fact, as if all morality depended on continual reference to it; a vigilance of it as of the only tree of the knowledge of good and evil within the whole circle of the garden wherein men now walk. The word sin, in their language, almost invariably means but one class of those actions which are included in a larger and manlier definition. Hence, in some of them, a view of human duty negative and special rather than positive or broad. Even the saintly Herbert is not free from this narrowness, and Ferrar's very notion of the best means towards a blessed life may be referred to some such cause. But it is worse when, as is the case with some of them, they will not, with all their alarm respecting the fact, take the obvious precaution of getting out of its vicinity. With some of them it is as if, in walking round and round this one charmed tree, and avoiding every other part of the garden in their anxiety to mark it well, they divided their business between warnings not to eat of the fruit and praises of its deliciousness when licit.—DAVID MASSON, *The Life of John Milton*, 1859, Vol. 1, Ch. 6

His religion is a further reason why to Catholic readers he should be better known than he is. Habington is, in all respects, a Catholic poet, not only like Lodge, a Catholic, who chanced to be a poet, or like Pope, a poet who chanced to be a Catholic, but rather like Aubrey de Vere, one in whom faith and genius are so interfused and blended that he seems to be a poet because he is a Catholic, and a Catholic because he is a poet. In a man of Habington's nature, his religion is not a social form or a sentimental fancy, but a deep and pervading influence in his life and work.—D. A. CASSERLY, "A Catholic Poet of the Seventeenth Century," *American Catholic Quarterly Review*, Oct. 1877, p. 618

Works

CASTARA

The Presse hath gathered into one, what fancie had scattered in many loose papers. To write this, love stole some houres from businesse, and my more serious study. For though Poetry may challenge if not priority, yet equality with the best Sciences, both for antiquity and worth; I never set so high a rate upon it, as to give my selfe entirely up to its devotion. It hath too much ayre, and (if without offence to our next transmarine neighbour,) wantons too much according to the French garbe. And when it is wholly imployed in the soft straines of love, his soule who entertaines it, loseth much of that strength which should confirme him man. The nerves of judgement are weakned most by its dalliance, and when woman, (I meane onely as she is externally faire) is the supreme object of wit, we soone degenerate into effeminacy. For the religion of fancie declines into a mad superstition, when it adores that Idoll which is not secure from age and sicknesse. Of such heathens, our times afford us a pittyed multitude, who can give no nobler testimony of twenty yeares imployment, then some loose coppies of lust happily exprest. Yet these the common people of wit blow up with their breath of praise, and honour with the Sacred name of Poets: To which as I beleeve they can never have any just claime, so shall I not dare by this essay to lay any title, since more sweate and oyle he must spend, who shall arrogate so excellent an attribute. Yet if the innocency of a chaste Muse shall bee more acceptable, and weigh heavier in the ballance of esteeme, than a fame, begot in adultery of study; I doubt I shall leave them no hope of competition. For how unhappie soever I may be in the elocution, I am sure the Theame is worthy enough. In all those flames in which I burnt, I never felt a wanton heate; nor was my invention ever sinister from the straite way of chastity. And when love builds upon that rocke, it may safely contemne the battery of the waves, and threatnings of the wind. Since time, that makes a mockery of the firmest structures shall it selfe be ruinated, before that be demolisht. Thus was the foundation layd. And though my eye in its survey, was satisfied, even to curiosity, yet did not my search rest there. The Alabaster, Ivory, Porphir, Iet, that lent an admirable beauty to the outward building, entertained me with but a halfe pleasure, since they stood there onely to make sport for ruine. But when my soule grew acquainted with the owner of that mansion; I found that Oratory was dombe when it began to speak her, and wonder (which must necessarily seize the best at that time) a lethargie, that dulled too much the faculties of the minde, onely fit to busie themselves in discoursing her perfections, Wisdome, I encounter'd there, that could not spend it selfe since it affected silence, attentive onely to instructions, as if all her sences had beene contracted into hearing: Innocencie, so not vitiated by conversation with the world, that the subtile witted of her sex, would have tearm'd it ignorance: Wit, which seated it selfe most in the apprehension, and if not inforc't by good manners, would scarce have gain'd the name of affability. Modesty, so timorous, that it represented a besieg'd Citty, standing watchfully upon her guard, strongest in the loyalty to her Prince. In a word, all those vertues which should restore woman to her primitive state of beauty, fully adorn'd her. But I shall be censur'd, in labouring to come nigh the truth, guilty of an indiscreet Rhetoricke. However such I fancied her, for to say shee is, or was such, were to play the Merchant, and boast too much the value of a Iewell I possesse, but have no minde to part with. And though I appeare to strive against the streame of best wits, in erecting the selfe same Altar, both to chastity and love; I will for once adventure to doe well, without a president.

Nor if my rigid friend question superciliously the setting forth of these Poems, will I excuse my selfe (though justly perhaps I might) that importunity prevail'd, and cleere judgements advis'd: This onely I dare say, that if they are not strangled with envie of the present, they may happily live in the not dislike of future times. For then partiality ceaseth, and vertue is without the idolatry of her clients, esteemed worthy honour. Nothing new is free from detraction, and when Princes alter customes even heavie to the subject, best ordinances are interpreted innovations. Had I slept in the silence of my acquaintance, and affected no study beyond that which the chase or field allowes, Poetry had then beene no scandall upon me, and the love of learning no suspition of ill husbandry. But what malice, begot in the Country upon ignorance, or in the City upon Criticisme, shall prepare against me, I am armed to endure. For as the face of vertue lookes faire without the adultery of Art, so fame needes no ayde from rumour to strengthen her selfe. If these lines want that courtship, (I will not say flattery) which insinuates it selfe into the favour of great men, best; they partake of my modesty: If Satyre to win applause with the envious multitude; they expresse my content, which maliceth none, the fruition of that, they esteeme happie. And if not too indulgent to what is my owne; I thinke even these verses will have that proportion in the worlds opinion, that heaven hath allotted me in fortune; not so high, as to be wondred at, nor so low as to be contemned.—WILLIAM HABINGTON, "The Author," *Castara*, 1634

Not in the silence of content and store
Of private sweets ought thy Muse charme no more
Then thy *Castara's* eare. 'Twere wrong such gold
Should not like Mines, (poore nam'd to this) behold
It selfe a publike joy. Who her restraine,
Make a close prisoner of a Soveraigne.
Inlarge her then to triumph. While we see
Such worth in beauty, such desert in thee,
Such mutuall flames between you both, as show
How chastity, though yce, like love can glow,
Yet stand a Virgin: How that full content
By vertue is to soules united, lent,
Which proves all wealth is poore, all honours are
But empty titles, highest power but care,
That quits not cost. Yet Heaven to Vertue kind,
Hath given you plenty to suffice a minde
That knowes but temper. For beyond your state
May be a prouder, not a happier Fate.
I Write not this in hope t'incroach on fame,
Or adde a greater lustre to your name.
Bright in it selfe enough. We two are knowne
To th' World, as to our selves, to be but one
In blood as study: And my carefull love
Did never action worth my name, approve,
Which serv'd not thee. Nor did we ere contend,
But who should be best patterne of a friend.
Who read thee, praise thy fancie, and admire
Thee burning with so high and pure a fire,
As reaches heaven it selfe. But I who know
Thy soule religious to her ends, where grow
No sinnes by art or custome, boldly can
Stile thee more than good Poet, a good man.
Then let thy temples shake off vulgar bayes,
Th' hast built an Altar which enshrines thy praise:
And to the faith of after time commends
Yee the best paire of lovers, us of friends.

    —GEORGE TALBOT, "To His Best Friend and

Kinsman *William Habington*, Esquire," *Castara*, 1634

They possess much elegance, much poetical fancy; and are almost everywhere tinged with a deep moral cast, which ought to have made their fame permanent. Indeed I cannot easily account for the neglect of them.—SAMUEL EGERTON BRYDGES, *Censura Literaria*, 1805–09

The poetry of Habington is that of a pure and amiable mind, turned to versification by the custom of the age, during a real passion for a lady of birth and virtue, the Castara whom he afterwards married; but it displays no great original power, nor is it by any means exempt from the ordinary blemishes of hyperbolical compliment and far-fetched imagery.—HENRY HALLAM, *Introduction to the Literature of Europe*, 1837–39, Pt. 2, Ch. 5, Par. 55

It is upon *Castara* that his fame rests. To tell the truth it is, though, as has been said, an estimable, yet a rather irritating work. That Habington was a true lover every line of it shows; that he had a strong infusion of the abundant poetical inspiration then abroad is shown by line after line, though hardly by poem after poem, among its pieces. His series of poems on the death of his friend Talbot is full of beauty. His religion is sincere, fervent, and often finely expressed; though he never rose to Herbert's pure devotion, or to Crashaw's flaming poetry. There are also traces of humour in his work, and an "Encomium on Sack," which shows that he was a "good felawe."

    . . . But *Castara* is a real instance of what some foreign critics very unjustly charge on English literature as a whole—a foolish and almost canting prudery. The poet dins the chastity of his mistress into his readers' heads until the readers in self-defence are driven to say, "Sir, did any one doubt it?" He protests the freedom of his own passion from any admixture of fleshly influence, till half a suspicion of hypocrisy and more than half a feeling of contempt force themselves on the hearer. A relentless critic might connect these unpleasant features with the uncharitable and more than orthodox bigotry of his religious poems. Yet Habington, besides contributing much agreeable verse to the literature of the period, is invaluable as showing the counterside to Milton, the Catholic Puritanism which is no doubt inherent in the English nature, and which, had it not been for the Reformation, would probably have transformed Catholicism in a very strange fashion.—GEORGE SAINTSBURY, *A History of Elizabethan Literature*, 1887, pp. 380–82

William Habbington, who sings to us with such monotonous sweetness of Castara's innocent joys, surpasses Lodge alike in the charm of his descriptions and in the extravagance of his follies. In reading him we are sharply reminded of Klopstock's warning, that "a man should speak of his wife as seldom and with as much modesty as of himself;" for Habbington, who glories in the fairness and the chastity of his spouse, becomes unduly boastful now and then in vaunting these perfections to the world. He, at least, being safely married to Castara, feels none of that haunting insecurity which disturbs his fellow-poets.

All her vows religious be,
And her love she vows to me,

he says complacently, and then stops to assure us in plain prose that she is "so unvitiated by conversation with the world that the subtle-minded of her sex would deem it ignorance." Even to her husband-lover she is "thrifty of a kiss," and in the marble coldness and purity of her breast his glowing roses find a chilly sepulchre. Cupid, perishing, it would seem, from a mere description of her merits, or, as Habbington singularly expresses it,—

> But if you, when this you hear,
> Fall down murdered through your ear,

is, by way of compensation, decently interred in the dimpled cheek which has so often been his lurking-place. Lilies and roses and violets exhale their odors around him, a beauteous sheet of lawn is drawn up over his cold little body, and all who see the "perfumed hearse"—presumably the dimple—envy the dead god, blest in his repose. This is as bad in its way as Lovelace's famous lines on "Ellinda's Glove," where that modest article of dress is compelled to represent in turn a snow-white farm with five tenements, whose fair mistress has deserted them, an ermine cabinet too small and delicate for any occupant but its own, and a fiddle-case without its fine-tuned instrument.—AGNES REPPLIER, "English Love-Songs," *Points of View*, 1891, pp. 50–51

W. T. ARNOLD
"William Habington"
The English Poets, ed. Thomas Humphry Ward
1880, Volume 2, pp. 158–62

The centre alike of Habington's life and of his poetry is the lady whom he has sung under the fanciful name of Castara. She was Lucy, daughter of William, Lord Powis, rather above her lover in rank and wealth, as his own verses plainly show, but, as is not less obvious, at no time indifferent to his courtship. What obstacles were interposed by her parents and relatives yielded to their mutual constancy, and Habington was allowed to carry off his bride to his country-house at Hindlip, in Worcestershire, a house which, as he tells her,

> doth not want extent
> Of roome, (though not magnificent)
> To give free welcome to content.

There they seem to have lived a happy equable life together. Habington devotes as many of his poems to his wife, as to his mistress, and in them reaches a higher level of poetic accomplishment than he elsewhere attains. It is pleasant to contemplate the happy course of this pure and honourable affection, and it is impossible not to feel a kind of liking for so constant a wooer, so good a friend, and so upright a man. We must not complain if, like Evelyn, Habington seems to have gone through the Civil War without taking a decided part one way or the other. The man was no hero, nor born to shine in public life. What political sympathies his writings reveal were strongly Royalist; he himself came of an old Catholic stock, and was educated at St. Omer; and we may be sure that as far as he took any side at all, he took part against those whom he would regard as rebels and schismatics. Habington—as revealed to us by his own verses—was something of a dreamer, something of an ascetic, something even of a bigot. His was just the sort of life and character which could live through, as not of them, the din and turmoil and passion of those stirring years. He was not of those who are great among the sons of men; nevertheless the interest that his work arouses is likely rather to increase than diminish, for though narrow in scope it is intense in feeling, and though in parts feeble and one-sided, it is as a whole made vital by the impress of a distinct and original personality.

It is not altogether easy to gather from Habington's poems in what relation he stood to previous or contemporary singers. The one indubitable fact is his devotion to Sidney, a sentiment he shares in common with all the poets of that time, on whom the Astrophel and Stella sonnets made the most marked impression. Of his few references to other poets the first occurs in a poetical account of his own youthful years, which he gives in 'The Holy Man':—

> Grown elder I admired
> Our poets, as from Heaven inspired,
> What obelisks decreed I fit
> For Spenser's art and Sydney's wit!
> But waxing sober, soon I found
> Fame but an idle sound.

Another mention of Sidney occurs in a sonnet commemorating Ovid's Corinna and Petrarch's Laura—

> while our famous Thames
> Doth whisper Sidney's Stella to her streams.

There are also two passing mentions of Drayton and Spenser, and an interesting allusion to 'Chapman's reverend ashes' lying 'rudely mingled in the vulgar dust.' There are no allusions to such poets as Herbert, whose genius was in some respects akin to his own, but this is easily explained by the difference between the two men's religious opinions.

Castara is divided into three, by some editors into four parts. There are at any rate four distinct themes—the Mistress, the Wife, the Friend, and the Holy Man. It is by his love verses that Habington is best known, though some of his most powerful and deeply-felt work is to be found in the other sections. A feature which strikes the reader of these verses is their almost exaggerated purity of tone. Habington is never tired of assuring us of the chastity of his affection, and the reader wearies of the monotony of assertions which might very well be taken for granted. In one passage he says scornfully of other poets—

> You who are earth and cannot rise
> Above your sense,
> Boasting the envied wealth which lies
> Bright in your mistress' lips or eyes,
> Betray a pitied eloquence.

It is only fair however to say that, all deductions made, Habington's love poems are often sweet and tunable enough, and show real warmth of feeling and delicacy of sentiment. The verses on his friend and kinsman Talbot, a nephew of the Earl of Shrewsbury, who died young, also contain some fine passages; but more characteristic and less agreeable features of the writer's mind come out in 'The Holy Man.' There are some exceedingly powerful and sombre verses in this collection, but the tone of them is more than Catholic; in parts is revealed an almost Calvinistic relentlessness of bigotry. Habington speaks, as in duty bound, as a good Catholic, and assumes that the Holy Man is necessarily of his own creed. 'Catholique faith is the foundation on which he erects religion; knowing it a ruinous madnesse to build in the ayre of a private spirit or on the sands of any new schisme.' This is as it should be; one admires him for his sturdy maintenance of unpopular opinions; but it is not easy equally to sympathise with his description of his God, who 'without passion didst provide to punish treason racks and death in hell,' and who

> when he as your judge appears
> In vain you'll tremble and lament,
> And hope to soften him with teares,
> To no advantage penitent.

But gloomy as his theology may be, it is yet the natural outcome of that intense and narrow spirit, and some of the lines in this section have a searching penetrating power such as is not often found in Herbert or other religious poets more widely famous. Habington is terribly in earnest; he has forgotten his love for his mistress and his friend; as he draws on in life the ascetic element which betrayed itself in him from the first, gains in strength, he throws this life scornfully behind him, and his thoughts fasten themselves more and more exclusively upon death and immortality.

From a purely literary point of view, Habington only rarely reaches high water mark in poetry. There are no glaring faults in his verse, and few conceits. The mass of his work is fluent, ingenious, tolerable poetry. It does not often attain to the inner music which can only proceed from a born singer, or to the flawless expression of a noble thought. Perfect literary tact Habington does not possess; he will follow up a fine stanza with a lame and halting one, apparently without sense of the incongruity. It takes a strong *furor poeticus* to uplift him wholly, and keep him at a high level throughout an entire poem, however short. He excels greatly sometimes in single lines or couplets. He now and then surprises us with expressions like 'the weeping magic of my verse'; or so sonorous a line as

> and keep
> *Strayed honour in the true magnificke way;*

or a delicious commencement of a poem which falls off as it proceeds, such as

> Where sleepes the north wind when the south
>   inspires
> Life in the spring, and gathers into quires
> The scattered nightingales;

or a strange and impressive thought like that comparison of virtue, which, lost to the world by his friend Talbot's death, only lives still in some solitary hermit's cell—

> So 'mid the ice of the far northern sea
> A star about the arctic circle may
> Than ours yield clearer light, yet that but shall
> Serve at the frozen pilot's funeral.

It is quite consistent with this that the couplets which terminate a poem are with him sometimes extraordinarily vigorous and happy. In more than one case this final line or couplet constitutes the entire value of the poem. Take this, for instance:—

> And thus there will be left no bird to sing
> Farewell to the waters, welcome to the spring;

or this—

> All her vows religious be
> And her love she vows to me;

or this—

> But virtuous love is one sweet endless fire;

or this—

> The bad man's death is horror; but the just
> Keeps something of his glory in his dust.

But his inadequate sense of poetic form does not allow him often to attain to a perfect whole. He is too fond of awkward elisions, and endeavours to force more into a line than it will fairly hold. His sonnets, one or two of which rank among the best efforts, are formally speaking, not sonnets at all, but strings of seven rhyming couplets. He does not sufficiently know, he has not sufficiently laboured at, the technical business of his art. 'Quoi qu'on en puisse dire, la poésie est un art qui s'apprend, qui a ses méthodes, ses formules, ses arcanes, son contre-point et son travail harmonique. L'inspiration doit trouver sous ses mains un clavier parfaitement juste, auquel ne manque aucune corde.' Habington is one of the many English poets whose imperfect realisation of this aspect of the truth has left their achievement inferior to their talent.

MAURICE FRANCIS EGAN
From "Three Catholic Poets"
Catholic World, October 1880, pp. 132–38

William Habington, who was born in 1605, has been strangely neglected by Catholics and the public in general. The pathos of Southwell's death did much toward keeping his fame alive; but it is difficult to understand why, when Crashaw is remembered, Habington is almost forgotten. In those wonderful *mélanges* of literature compounded "for the use of schools and colleges" it is difficult to find mention of him, and well did he write in "The Holy Man":

> Grown older I admired
> Our poets as from heaven inspired;
> What obelisks decreed I fit
> For Spenser's art and Sydney's wit!
> But waxing sober soon I found
> Fame but an idle sound.

It is not surprising that we, who have left the name of a real Catholic poet, George Miles, fade away, and to whom the Catholic Canadian, Louis Fréchette, is only an unknown name, should not delve into volumes of forgotten law for Habington's poems; it is surprising that at this time, when the resurrecting of musty poets has become a mania, that so little has been done for one who, if not a born singer, was yet so near the divine voice as to catch some exquisite echoes. He was pre-eminently the poet of conjugal love, as Southwell was the poet of the higher love. His song is always of two pure hearts feeling hope and fear, to whom the fever of passion is unknown. Habington came of a good Catholic family, which is a distinction in a country where the good families had been so willing to barter faith for fortune. The stanchness of his blood was proved by the way his ancestors had kept the faith. His uncle, Edward Habington, having been implicated in Babington's famous conspiracy to rescue the Queen of Scots, was hanged, drawn, and quartered at St. Giles in the Fields. As usual, there was a Protestant minister at the scaffold, who urged him to be of a lively faith. He answered that he believed steadfastly in the Catholic faith. The minister feared that he deceived himself, and asked what he meant. "I mean," he answered, "that faith and religion which is holden in almost all Christendom, except here in England." After this, much to the disgust of the reverend gentleman, he would answer no question, but prayed to himself in Latin. In his dying speech he "cast out threats and terrors of the blood that was ere long to be shed in England." The poet's father, Thomas Habington, was also implicated in the same conspiracy. He escaped probably because the people were becoming tired of the shedding of the blood of some of the noblest men in England. It was not hard for the public to sympathize with generous youths who, as if to return to the days of chivalry, had risked their lives in behalf of a beautiful and unfortunate queen. The people at heart were not entirely devoted to the daughter of Anne Boleyn, and the wily politicians around her throne knew when it was prudent to stop the shedding of blood. Hence Thomas Habington escaped the fate of his brother. He went to prison, however, and when he was released Mary Stuart had bidden farewell to earth and gone, let us hope, to a land happier than even "le plaisant pays de France." He retired to his ancestral manor, Hendlip, where he led a life of lettered leisure, producing several works of local topography and a translation of the epistle of Geldus à Britain. He suffered a second imprisonment for suspected implication in the Gunpowder Plot. That he sheltered the Jesuits, Father Garnett and Father Oldcorne, afterwards most unjustly hanged, at Hendlip, was the only evidence against him. James is said always to have been partial to the partisans of his mother, and it is possible that Thomas Habington's connection with the Babington plot may have worked in favor of his release. His brother-in-law, Lord Monteagle, interceded in his behalf, and after his escape a second time he betook himself to the company of his children and books.

Of his son, the poet, little is known, except his love-story. He was educated at St. Omer and at Paris. Returning to England with the down just sprouting on his lip, he fell in love. The lady of his thoughts was Lucy Herbert, the daughter of Lord Powis. Habington was a gentleman of small estate and the bearer of a name that of late had not been on the winning side. Lord Powis felt that the niece of Northumberland and the granddaughter of an earl might look for a more splendid suitor. But Lucy—the incomparable *Castara* of Habington's poem— looked with favor on the poet. The course of true love did not run smooth, but its variations were rather the ripples of an April shower than the waves of an autumn storm. Following the fashion, young Habington wooed his lady-love in verse. It does not take much to excite turmoil in a poet's soul, and Habington's troubles must have been mild indeed, since they did not excite anything but the most proper and gentlemanlike protest:

> Parents' laws must bear no weight
> When they happiness prevent,
> And our sea is not so strait
> But it room has for content.

This is about the most violent sentiment he utters. Lord Powis belonged to the Catholic branch of the Herberts, and the stanchness of the Habington faith must have had some effect in softening his opposition. He was not a very cruel parent, and the fact that Habington had a small estate neutralized his demerit, in a father's eyes, of occasionally dropping into poetry. In all his raptures of Castara's sighs, glances, eyebrows, and bosom Habington never loses a certain consciousness of "deportment." He is never tired of protesting that the bent of his love is honorable and his purpose marriage—an iteration that the occasion does seem to require. But if his verse was somewhat mannered—and even the spiritual Southwell did not escape the conceits of his time—his sentiment is always honest, manly, and pure. His thoughts did not wander from his wife, the wonderful Castara. Next to religion she was the lodestar of his thoughts. He was married at the age of twenty-eight, and the years of his life afterwards kept the peaceful and happy promise of his wedding-day. . . .

He was friendly with all the great literary men of the time. There is a tradition that he was not absent from those feasts of reason and flows of sack in which Jonson, Massinger, and the jolly crew of the famous old inns indulged; with him all things were enjoyed in moderation. Tranquil, serene, surrounded by his children and supported by a firm faith, of which "The Holy Man," the fourth part of *Castara*, is an evidence, he ended a happy and peaceful life in 1654.

He had not been unaccustomed to the pomp of that court in which Charles I. and Henrietta Maria reigned, in which Waller sang and Vandyke painted, and in his volume of poems (republished by Arber in 1870) the most celebrated names of the epoch appear in dedications. His tragi-comedy of *The Queene of Arragon* was acted in 1640 at Whitehall. The favor of the court did not disturb him, nor did the Civil War draw him from his seclusion. He was not a man to act except under strong impulse, and it is probable that neither the Cavaliers nor the Roundheads wholly had his sympathy.

Castara is divided into four parts, "The Mistress," "The Wife," "The Friend," and "The Holy Man." It speaks well for the unpoetical constancy of Habington that Castara as the wife is even more beloved than Castara the mistress. The muse did not say imperatively to him, as she did to a later and very different bard,[1] "Poëte, prends ton luth." Indeed, one cannot help suspecting that he often took up his lute because he had nothing else to do. From lack of perception Habington is often uneven. That perfect art that welds all parts into simplicity was unknown to him or to most of the Elizabethan poets. He startles the reader with vivid lines which are like the bright scarlet of the salt-marsh's bushes among the tawny hues of autumn. He cares little for the technical part of his art. His sonnet to "Castara in a Trance," although very fine, lacks the dignity of the sonnets of Milton, which he must have known. To those scornful critics who assert that the sonnet at its best is only fourteen jingling lines, it will be an interesting comparison with any one of Dante's or with Wordsworth's "The World Is Too Much with Us."

> Forsake me not so soon; Castara, stay,
> And as I break the prison of my clay
> I'll fill the canvas with my expiring breath,
> And sail with thee o'er the vast main of Death.
> Some cherubim thus, as we pass, shall play:
> 'Go, happy twins of love!' The courteous sea
> Shall smooth her wrinkled brow; the winds shall
> sleep,
> Or only whisper music to the deep;
> Every ungentle rock shall melt away,
> The sirens sing to please, not to betray;
> The indulgent sky shall smile; each starry choir
> Contend which shall afford the brighter fire;
>   While Love, the pilot, steers his course so even,
>   Ne'er to cast anchor till we reach to Heaven.

. . . Habington's worst faults are those of taste. They go no deeper. *Castara*, as a whole, is a noble poem that deserves to live. Probably in no other poet's works—if we except Tennyson—has a higher, yet not superhuman, idea of womanhood been given. The most exceptional and beautiful characteristic of the three truly Catholic poets, Southwell, Habington, and Crashaw, is their spotless purity of word and thought. Faith and purity go hand-in-hand. If *Castara* were studied in this age it might almost make chastity fashionable among men. This virtue of Sir Galahad was not common in Habington's time, and it has always required much courage in a man of the world to proclaim that he possesses a quality which is generally regarded as the crowning attribute of womanhood. To this poet, who dared to dedicate, in a licentious age, his work to the woman who was to him as the church to Christ, we owe honor; it was his Catholic faith and practice that made him so noble among the men of his time. Habington ought to be studied by all young Catholics. Americans have inherited his poems along with that language which was forced on the ancestors of some of us, but which is none the less our own. His faults of *technique*, so glaringly apparent in this day of almost perfect *technique* in poetry, offer lessons in themselves. No man can read *Castara* without feeling better and purer; and of how many poets can this be said? Since Pope taught the critics to place execution above conception Habington has found no place. It remains for the rising generation of young Catholics who read and think to give him a niche that will not be unworthy of the poet of that chaste love which was born from Christianity.

Notes

1. De Musset, "Nuit de mai."

JOSEPH HALL

1574–1656

Joseph Hall was born in Ashby-de-la-Zouch, Leicestershire, on July 1, 1574. He attended grammar school in Ashby and entered Emmanuel College, Cambridge, in 1589. He received a B.A. in 1592, an M.A. in 1596, and a B.D. in 1603. Hall was a fellow of Emmanuel College and took holy orders in 1600. While at Cambridge Hall wrote his verse satires *Virgidemiae*, published in 1597 and 1598. Hall's prose satire *Mundus Alter et Idem* (1605) was translated by John Healey and printed as *The Discovery of a New World* (1609). Hall is credited with having written the first Juvenalian satires in English. Another of Hall's literary works, *Characters of Vertues and Vices* (1608), contained prose sketches modelled on Theophrastus. The short character portraits were intended to have educational and moral value.

Hall left Cambridge in 1601 to become rector at Hawstead, Suffolk. He remained there until 1607, when he was appointed rector of Waltham Holy Cross. A favorite of James I, he was made Prince Henry's chaplain in 1608. Later Hall served as dean of Worcester, bishop of Exeter (1627–41), and bishop of Norwich. Hall also attended the 1618 Synod of Dort as James I's delegate. Hall was the author of devotional works, religious tracts, and sermons, including *Meditations and Vowes* (1605) and *Episcopacy by Divine Right* (1641). This last tract imbroiled him in a war of pamphlets with Milton. Hall was imprisoned in the Tower in 1642 for protesting the exclusion of bishops from Parliament. Although he was soon released, he was deprived of his bishopric. In 1648 he retired to a farm in Higham, Norfolk, where he died on September 8, 1656. Hall was buried in the parish churchyard at Higham.

Personal

Joseph Hall was born at Ashby de la Zouch in this County ⟨Leicestershire⟩, where his Father, under the Earl of Huntington, was Governour or Bayly of the Town. So soon almost as Emanuel Colledge was admitted into Cambridge, he was admitted into that Colledge, within few years after the first foundation thereof. He passed all his degrees with great applause. First, noted in the University, for his ingenuous maintaining (be it *Truth*, or *Paradox*) that *Mundus senescit*, "The World groweth old." Yet, in some sort, his position confuteth his position, the wit and quickness whereof did argue an increase rather than a decay of parts in this latter age.

He was first beneficed by Sir Robert Drury at Halsted in Suffolk; and thence removed by Edward Lord Denny (afterward Earl of Norwich) to Waltham Abbey in Essex. Here I must pay the Tribute of my gratitude to his memory, as building upon his foundation, beholding myself as his Great-grandchild in that place, three degrees from him in succession: but, oh! how many from him in ability! His little Catechisme hath done great good in that populous parish; and I could wish that Ordinance more generally used all over England.

Being Doctor of Divinity, he was sent over by King James to the Synod of Dort, whence only indisposition of body forced him to return before the rest of his Colleagues. He was preferred, first Dean of Worcester, then Bishop of Exeter, then Bishop of Norwich, then Bishop of no place; surviving to see his sacred function buried before his eyes. He may be said to have dyed with his pen in his hand, whose *Writing* and *Living* expired together. He was commonly called our *English Seneca*, for the purenesse, plainesse, and fulnesse of his style. Not unhappy at *Controversies*, more happy at *Comments*, very good in his *Characters*, better in his *Sermons*, best of all in his *Meditations*. Nor will it be amiss to transcribe the following passage out of his Will:

In the name of God, Amen. I Joseph Hall, D.D. not worthy to be called Bishop of Norwich, &c. First, I bequeath my soul, &c. My body I leave to be in-terred, without any funeral pomp, at the discretion of my Executors; with this only monition, that I do not hold God's House a meet repository for the dead bodies of the greatest Saints.

He dyed September the 8th, anno Domini 1656; and was buried at Hyhem near Norwich.—THOMAS FULLER, *The History of the Worthies of England*, 1662

Hall's part in that revival of the spirit of the Renaissance in an ecclesiastical form which has been conveniently, but improperly, stamped with the name of Laud, deserved more genial treatment. That intellectually it, and not Puritanism, inspired the progressive movement of the age can be doubted by no one who impartially considers the history of the century as a whole. That those who were under its influence ruined their own cause, at least temporarily, by endeavouring to force a system on those who were unwilling to receive it, is equally beyond dispute. . . .

Hall's part in the progress is particularly interesting, for, unlike Laud, who seems to have entered on active life ready furnished with a whole stock of opinions, he developed from year to year. We can thus, so to speak, watch him growing. The influence of the age worked upon him as well as in him, and he moved on imperceptibly—*ohne Hast, aber ohne Rast*. He is thus, more than any other man of his time, the personification of a great intellectual and spiritual movement. A character of which this could be said would hardly be one of great intellectual force; and, in fact, there is no trace in him of any individual opposition to the ideas floating in the circles in which he moved. His ecclesiastical opinions were the same as those of Laud; he had the same reverence for authority, and the same notion of the position of the king in the constitution. There is nothing to show that he was capable of contributing a single useful thought to avert the dangers which threatened his party and his country.

Hall's highest qualities, in truth, were moral rather than intellectual. Whatever doctrine he held, he did not push it to extremes; and, whatever order he enforced, he not only tried persuasion first, but he had the knack of persuading persuasively. If he had been Archbishop of Canterbury instead of Laud, he would have maintained much the same principles as Laud did, but he would have caused far less irritation.—SAMUEL R. GARDINER, *Academy*, April 17, 1886, p. 267

General

As *Horace, Lucilius, Iuuenall, Persius & Lucullus* are the best for Satyre among the Latines: so with vs in the same faculty these are chiefe, *Piers Plowman, Lodge, Hall* of Imanuel Colledge in Cambridge.—FRANCIS MERES, *Palladis Tamia*, 1598

Joseph Hall, bishop of Exon, etc.: he was a keeper's son in Norfolke (I thinke, neer Norwich).—From old Mr. Theophilus Woodenoth.

He wrote most of his fine discourses at Worcester, when he was deane there.—From Mr. Francis Potter, who went to schole there.

Monsieur Balzac exceedingly admired him and often quotes him: vide Balzac's *Apologie.*—JOHN AUBREY, "Joseph Hall," *Brief Lives*, 1669–96

In naming Hall, indeed, we name a prince and chief among our English divines—equally good at all weapons, equally surpassing in every department of theology. . . . The highest tribute to the merits of Bishop Hall's writings is their great and unceasing popularity with the unlearned and poor. Side by side with the writings of Bunyan and Defoe, portions of them are to be found on many a cottage shelf; and the pious contemplations of the witty and eloquent bishop have gladdened and strengthened many a soul in sickness, sorrow, and pain. Do we seek the cause of this? It will be found in the fact that Joseph Hall had not only earnest, practical piety, great learning, great zeal, but also the invaluable gift of genuine wit and humour. Resembling Bishop Andrewes in the raciness, point, and piquancy of his imaginings, he far surpassed him in his power of expressing, in nervous and telling words, the products of his brain. His style is eminently happy, effective, graphic, and genuine. His mind was stored with learning. He had studied men and things under many circumstances, in various lands. His power of illustration is inexhaustible; his wit always fresh and telling; his knowledge of Scripture profound; his sense of the wants, dangers, and difficulties of men deep and practical; his charity and loving spirit abundant. With these qualifications he could scarcely fail of addressing himself effectively to men. And he shone in all subjects. His satires are the best imitations of the Juvenalian vein which we possess; his letters some of the most charming specimens of earnestness, without dulness.—GEORGE G. PERRY, *History of the Church of England*, 1861, Vol. 1, p. 629

Hall writes with skill and with spirit. It can scarcely be said of him: *Facit indignatio versum*. He finds a pleasure in imitating, and in some sort reproducing, his Latin models; and this is rather his inspiration than any moral fervour. And the chief value of his work is its vigorous picture of Elizabethan ways and manners. Whatever the old comedy did for Athens in the way of illustrating the old Athenian life, that satire did for Rome, and with inferior, but yet no mean force, Hall did for Elizabethan London. It is no contemptible service to have helped to keep alive for us an age so fascinating, so glorious, so momentous. Whoever would picture to himself the very town in the midst of which Shakespeare moved, its lights and shadows, its whims and phantasies and follies—"a mad world, my masters"—see "the very age and body of the time, his form and presence," and learn what were its daily thoughts, interests, cares, credulities, passions—will find truly valuable aid in

Hall's satires.—JOHN W. HALES, "Bishop Hall," *Antiquary*, Nov. 1881, p. 190

Joseph Hall's father was the agent and representative of the Earl of Huntingdon, and was thus in a position to secure for his son some patronage of the kind to which so many notable men of the time in Church and State were indebted for their University training. But Hall seems to have been most influenced by the character of his mother, whose portrait, which her son has painted in a few striking lines, gives us the impression of greater force than attractiveness. She emulated the famous women of antiquity in her sanctity, which had more than a tincture of puritanic gloom in its composition. Much of each day was spent in private devotion: "whence," says her son, "she would still come forth, with a countenance of undesembled mortification." Other symptoms which he describes as proof of her indubitable piety, savour strongly of hypochondria; but gloomy as she must have made her surroundings, she undoubtedly retained a strong hold upon the reverence and affection of her son, and to her he doubtless owed that early puritanic leaning, which subsequent experience curbed, but did not altogether eradicate.

From a home where the chief impression was one of sincere but gloomy and melancholy piety, Hall passed to the University of Cambridge, where he evidently acquired a position such as would nowadays be gained by one who secured the highest honours of the Schools. He was one of the teaching staff of his college; and his literary reputation, as the author of the *Satires*, must have given him some position and notoriety, although in his own reminiscences we hear nothing of these early efforts. His later years were occupied with other fights, carried on with very different weapons; and as the *Satires* were cast up as a reproach to him by Milton in the Smectymnuus controversy, Hall found it neither convenient nor congenial to recall these youthful poems. Criticism of the *Satires* does not fall within the scope of the present notice; but they have much interest for any one who would appreciate Hall's later prose work. They are not only remarkable as the productions of a youth who was little past his majority (they were published in 1597), but they also link Hall with the literature of a previous generation. His compeers then were the last of the Elizabethan dramatists; the chief object of his admiration was Spenser. In language the *Satires* are artificially archaic: and the tone that pervades them has very little in common with the spirit of his later work. But they brought a freedom and a vigour to his prose style which it never lost, and the practice which they gave him in his early years not only added force and liveliness to his later controversial style, but also gave to his religious writings the quick movement, the variety and the lavish illustration, which are their chief characteristics.

Hall thus combined some elements which are rarely found in combination. Educated amongst puritanic influences and under the shadow of a religion that regarded each individual accident as brought about by the special intervention of providence; passing from this to the classical influences of the University, and finding his models in antiquity; thrusting himself as a youth into the literary struggles of the day—he brought to his later work as a divine some unique qualities. His earliest religious writings are devout and earnest, but they borrow their illustrations largely from secular sources; they have no strongly marked dogmatic features, and their language has a freedom and a force that are peculiar. Hating the Romanists he was nevertheless most conspicuously the opponent of the sects that accused the Church of England of Romanist inclination. During a great part of his life, Hall strove to maintain a position which had much to commend it, which was inspired by right-minded charity, which had entirely good objects, but which inevitably exposed him to misconstruction, involved him in disputes with his ecclesiastical superiors, and necessarily gave to his writing, in spite of its force and freedom, something of incompleteness in point of logic. He strove to maintain a middle course. He talked much of the evils of uncharitable judgment. He deprecated division, except upon what he deemed to be fundamentals, forgetting that the most complete cleavage between man and man must necessarily arise from differences as to what is, and what is not, fundamental. Undoubtedly this gives to his religious writings something of platitude, which is not saved by the freedom and force of his literary touch. There is a want of conviction, which no earnestness can quite supply. Yet side by side with this, there is the self-satisfaction which comes from the puritanical tenet, that all his life is ordered for him by providence, and that the misfortunes which befall an opponent are the contrivance of divine power. He preaches on the one hand the duty of charity, and on the other the evils of laxity, from a standpoint which is none the less narrow because it is midway between two extremes. "If," he says, "men be allowed a latitude of opinions in some unnecessary verities, it may not be endured that in matter of religion every man should think what he lists, and utter what he thinks, and defend what he utters, and publish what he defends, and gather disciples to what he publisheth. This liberty, or rather licentiousness, would be the bane of any church." He forgets that men cannot be brought to agree as to what are "verities," but yet "unnecessary"; and that no utterance such as this brings us, for practical purposes, one whit nearer to agreement.

No wonder that he was suspected by such a man as Laud; no wonder that he writes as an outsider, and that his devotional writings often reflect the pagan moralist. In the end, fate was too strong for him: and when the flood-gates were opened, he speaks like a man, overwhelmed and confounded by the fierceness of controversies, the logical importance of which he never rightly appreciated. Yet at times, baffled as he is between authority and private judgment, he hits the mark with unerring accuracy, as a student of human nature. "The Romanists," he says "are all for blind obedience: the Romanists therefore go away with peace, without truth; ours, under pretence of striving for some truths, abandon peace."

Besides his devotional writings we have from Hall some treatises on casuistry. Such treatises have never thriven in England. They do not appeal to a wide audience, and are therefore scarcely literature in the proper sense. Hall's casuistical writings lack the subtlety of the Romanist casuists, and they have none of his own special characteristics. They have none of the free and almost reckless vigour of his controversial writing; little of the variety of illustration of his devotional treatises; and only now and then, as when he covertly attacks Milton, in dealing with the question of divorce, do they show any of the vigour which we associate with his pen.

His most striking prose works are those of devotion and of Scriptural exegesis, which are often wordy, but always free and flowing in point of composition. They bear the impress of pulpit oratory, in which, as he tells us himself, he followed the practice of composing the whole sermon beforehand, but delivering it from memory and not from a manuscript. "Never," he says, "durst I climb into the pulpit to preach any sermon, whereof I had not before, in my poor and plain fashion, penned every word in the same order, wherein I *hoped* to deliver it; although in the expression I listed not to be a slave to syllables."—H. CRAIK, "Bishop Hall," *English Prose*, ed. Henry Craik, 1893, Vol. 2, pp. 133–36.

Works

SATIRES

In the following Section I must foretell ye, Readers, the doings will be rough and dangerous, the bating of a *Satir*. And if the work seeme more triviall or boistrous then for this discourse, let the Remonstrant thank the folly of this confuter, who could not let a private word passe, but he must make all this blaze of it. I had said that because the Remonstrant was so much offended with those who were tart against the Prelats, sure he lov'd toothlesse Satirs, which I took were as improper as a toothed Sleekstone. This Champion from behind the Arras cries out that those toothlesse Satyrs were of the Remonstrants making; and armes himselfe here tooth and naile and *horne*, to boot, to supply the want of teeth, or rather of gumms in the Satirs. And for an onset tels me that the simily of a Sleekstone *shewes I can be as bold with a Prelat as familiar with a Laundresse*. But does it not argue rather the lascivious promptnesse of his own fancy, who from the harmelesse mention of a Sleekstone could neigh out the remembrance of his old conversation among the *Viraginian* trollops? For me, if he move me, I shall claime his owne oath, the oath *Ex officio* against any Priest or Prelat in the kingdome to have ever as much hated such pranks as the best and chastest of them all. That exception which I made against toothlesse Satirs the Confuter hopes I had from the *Satirist*, but is farre deceav'd: neither had I ever read the hobbling *distick* which he means. For this good hap I had from a carefull education to be inur'd and season'd betimes with the best and elegantest authors of the learned tongues, and thereto brought an eare that could measure a just cadence, and scan without articulating; rather nice and humorous in what was tolerable, then patient to read every drawling versifier. Whence lighting upon this title of *toothlesse Satirs*, I will not conceale ye what I thought, Readers, that sure this must be some sucking Satir, who might have done better to have us'd his corall, and made an end of breeding, ere he took upon him to weild a Satirs whip. But when I heard him talk of *scouring the rusted swords of elvish Knights*, doe not blame me, if I chang'd my thought, and concluded him some desperate Cutler. But why *his scornefull muse could never abide with tragick shoos her ankles for to hide*, the pace of the verse told me that her maukin knuckles were never shapen to that royall buskin. And turning by chance to the sixth Satyr of his Second book I was confirm'd; where having begun loftily *in heavens universall Alphabet* he fals downe to that wretched poorenesse and frigidity as to talke of *Bridge street in heav'n, and the Ostler of heav'n*, and there wanting other matter to catch him a heat, (for certaine he was in the frozen *Zone* miserably benumm'd) with thoughts lower then any Beadle betakes him to whip the signe posts of *Cambridge* Alehouses, the ordinary subject of freshmens tales, and in a straine as pittifull. Which for him who would be counted *the first English Satyr*, to abase himselfe to, who might have learnt better among the Latin, and Italian Satyrists, and in our own tongue from the *vision and Creed of Pierce plowman*, besides others before him, manifested a presumptuous undertaking with weak, and unexamin'd shoulders. For a Satyr as it was borne out of a *Tragedy*, so ought to resemble his parentage, to strike high, and adventure dangerously at the most eminent vices among the greatest persons, and not to creepe into every blinde Taphouse that fears a Constable more then a Satyr. But that such a Poem should be toothlesse I still affirme it to be a bull, taking away the essence of that which it calls it selfe. For if it bite neither the persons nor the vices, how is it a Satyr, and if it bite either, how is it toothlesse, so that toothlesse Satyrs are as much as if he had said toothlesse teeth. What we should do therefore with this learned Comment upon *teeth* and *horns* which hath brought this confutant into his *Pedantick* kingdome of *Cornucopia*, to reward him for glossing upon *hornes* even to the *Hebrew root*, I know not unlesse we should commend him to be Lecturer in East-cheap upon S. *Lukes* day, when they send their tribute to that famous hav'n by Detford. But we are not like to scape him so. For now the worme of *Criticisme* works in him, he will tell us the derivation of *German rutters, of meat, and of ink*, which doubtlesse rightly apply'd with some gall in it may prove good to heale this tetter of *Pedagoguisme* that bespreads him, with such a *tenasmus* of originating, that if he be an Arminian and deny originall sinne, all the *etymologies* of his book shall witnesse that his brain is not meanly tainted with that infection. —JOHN MILTON, *An Apology for Smectymnuus*, 1641

Bishop *Hall* was born in 1574, and, publishing ⟨his⟩ Satires twenty-three Years after, was, as he himself asserts, in the Prologue, the first Satyrist in the *English* Language:

> In the first Adventure with fool-hardy Might
> To tread the Steps of perilous Despight;
> I first adventure, follow me who list,
> And be the second *English* Satyrist.

And if we consider the Difficulty of introducing so nice a Poem as Satire into a Nation, we must allow it required the Assistance of no common and ordinary Genius. The *Italians* had their *Ariosto*, and the *French* their *Regnier*, who might have served him as Models for Imitation; but he copies after the Antients, and chiefly *Juvenal* and *Persius*; tho' he wants not many Strokes of Elegance and Delicacy, which shew him perfectly acquainted with the manner of *Horace*. Among the several Discouragements which attended his Attempt in that kind, he mentions one peculiar to the Language and Nature of the *English* Versification, which would appear in the Translation of one of *Persius*'s Satires: "The Difficulty and Dissonance whereof, says he, shall make good my Assertion; besides the plain Experience thereof in the Satires of *Ariosto*; save which, and one base *French* Satire, I could never attain the View of any for my Direction." Yet we may pay him almost the same Compliment which was given of old to *Homer* and *Archilochus*: For the Improvements which have been made by succeeding Poets, bear no manner of Proportion to the Distance of Time between him and them. The Verses of Bishop *Hall* are in general extremely musical and flowing, and are greatly preferable to Dr. *Donne*'s, as being of a much smoother Cadence; neither shall we find him deficient, if compared with his Successor, in Point of Thought and Wit; and to exceed him with respect to his Characters, which are more numerous, and wrought up with greater Art and Strength of Colouring. Many of his Lines would do Honour to the most ingenious of our modern Poets; and some of them have thought it worth their Labour to imitate him, especially Mr. *Oldham*. Bishop *Hall* was not only our first Satirist, but was the first who brought epistolary Writing to the View of the Public; which was common in that Age to other Parts of *Europe*, but not practised in *England*, till he published his own Epistles. It may be proper to take Notice, that the *Virgidemiarum* are not printed with his other Writings; and that all Account of them is omitted by him, thro' his extreme Modesty, in the Specialties of his Life, prefixed to the 3d Vol. of his Works in Folio. —PETER WHALLEY, *An Enquiry into the Learning of Shakespeare*, 1748, pp. 41–42

Have you seen Bishop Hall's Satires, call'd Virgidemiæ, republish'd lately. They are full of spirit & poetry; as much of the first, as Dʳ Donne, & far more of the latter. —THOMAS GRAY, Letter to Thomas Wharton (Dec. 19, 1752)

These satires are marked with a classical precision, to which English poetry had yet rarely attained. They are replete with animation of style and sentiment. The indignation of the satirist is always the result of good sense. Nor are the thorns of severe invective unmixed with the flowers of pure poetry. The characters are delineated in strong and lively colouring, and their discriminations are touched with the masterly traces of genuine humour. The versification is equally energetic and elegant, and the fabric of the couplets approaches to the modern standard. It is no inconsiderable proof of a genius predominating over the general taste of an age when every preacher was a punster, to have written verses, where laughter was to be raised, and the reader to be entertained with sallies of pleasantry, without quibbles and conceits. His chief fault is obscurity, arising from a remote phraseology, constrained combinations, unfamiliar allusions, elleiptical apostrophes, and abruptness of expression. Perhaps some will think, that his manner betrays too much of the laborious exactness and pedantic anxiety of the scholar and the student. Ariosto in Italian, and Regnier in French, were now almost the only modern writers of satire: and I believe there had been an English translation of Ariosto's satires. But Hall's acknowledged patterns are Juvenal and Persius, not without some touches of the urbanity of Horace. His parodies of these poets, or rather his adaptations of antient to modern manners, a mode of imitation not unhappily practised by Oldham, Rochester, and Pope, discover great facility and dexterity of invention. The moral gravity and the censorial declamation of Juvenal, he frequently enlivens with a train of more refined reflection, or adorns with a novelty and variety of images. —THOMAS WARTON, *The History of English Poetry*, 1778–81, Sec. 62

In his *Satires*, which were published at the age of twenty-three, he discovered not only the early vigour of his own genious, but the powers and pliability of his native tongue. Unfortunately, perhaps unconsciously, he caught, from studying Juvenal and Persius as his models, an elliptical manner and an antique allusion, which cast obscurity over his otherwise spirited and amusing traits of English manners; though the satirist himself was so far from anticipating this objection, that he formally apologizes for *"too much stooping to the low reach of the vulgar."* But in many instances he redeems the antiquity of his allusions by their ingenious adaptation to modern manners; and this is but a small part of his praise; for in the point and volubility, and vigour of Hall's numbers, we might frequently imagine ourselves perusing Dryden. —THOMAS CAMPBELL, *Specimens of the British Poets*, 1819

The man whom our literary historians have agreed to consider the father of English satire, in the modern form in which it has been practised by Dryden, Pope, and others, as distinct from the older form exemplified in *Piers Ploughman*, Skelton, and the like, was still alive in 1632, at the age of fifty-eight (exactly Ben Jonson's age), but with four-and-twenty years of his eventful life yet before him. This was Joseph Hall, already known to us as Bishop of Exeter since 1627. It was now about thirty-five years since Hall, then a youth of three-and-twenty, and fresh from Cambridge, had published in two portions (1597 and 1598) his six books of satires—the first three books entitled *Toothless Satires*, and the last three *Biting Satires*. In the opening lines of the first book he had distinctly announced himself as the beginner of a new form of literature:—

> I first adventure, with foolhardy might,
> To tread the steps of perilous despite;
> I first adventure, follow me who list,
> And be the second English satirist.

On inquiry it is found that Donne might have the better claim to absolute priority, *his* satires having been written by 1594. But Hall's were first published; they were written without knowledge of Donne's; and they were after a more orderly type of satire. The first book of the *Toothless Satires* was directed against the faults, literary and other, of the poets of the age; the second treated of academical abuses; the third of public manners and morality, which also form the matter of the *Biting Satires*. The author's acknowledged models are Juvenal and Persius; and he professes that it was to their nervous and crabbed style of poetry, rather than to the imitation of Virgil and Spenser, that his genius inclined him.

> Rather had I, albe in careless rhymes,
> Check the misordered world and lawless times.

What Hall's satires did towards "checking the misordered world" may not have been much; but, as compositions of the satirical order, they have kept a place in our literature. Interesting still on historical grounds for their references to contemporary manners, they are admired for their direct energy of expression, their robust though somewhat harsh tone of feeling, and, above all, the wonderfully modern appearance of their metrical structure. Thus, on modern luxury:—

> Time was, and that was termed the time of gold,
> When world and time were young that now are old,
> When quiet Saturn swayed the mace of lead,
> And pride was yet unborn and yet unbred;
> Time was that, while the autumn fall did last,
> Our hungry sires gaped for the falling mast;—
> Could no unhusked acorn leave the tree
> But there was challenge made whose it might be.
> . . .
>
> They naked went, or clad in ruder hide,
> Or home-spun russet, void of foreign pride;
> But thou canst mask in garish gawdery,
> To suit a fool's far-fetchèd livery—
> A French head joined to neck Italian,
> Thy thighs from Germany and breast from Spain;
> An Englishman in none, a fool in all,
> Many in one, and one in several.
> Then men were men; but now the greater part
> Beasts are in life and women are in heart.

Thus had Hall written when Spenser was alive, and Shakespeare and his coevals were in the height of their dramatic fame; and in virtue of such verses had he been named by Meres, in his list of the English literary celebrities of 1598, as a promising English Persius. In the long intervening period of his life, however,—though retaining something of the hard style of intellect shown in his satires,—he had advanced into other occupations, rising step by step in the Church to the prelacy, and writing those numerous and various prose works, under which the recollection of his satires had been all but buried, so that his name was no longer the English Persius, but the English Seneca.—DAVID MASSON, *The Life of John Milton*, 1859, Vol. 1, Ch. 6

As a satirist, if we reject the claim of Gascoigne to precedence, he was the earliest that English literature can boast. In his own words,

> I first adventure: follow me who list,
> And be the second English satirist.

He had two qualifications for his chosen task,—penetrating observation and unshrinking courage. The follies and vices, the manners, prejudices, delusions, and crimes of his time, form the materials of his satires; and these he lashes, or laughs at, according as the subject-matter provokes his indignation or

his contempt. "Sith," he says in his Preface, "faults loathe nothing more than the light, and men love nothing more than their faults," it follows that, "what with the nature of the faults and the faults of the persons," it is impossible "that so violent an appeachment should be quietly brooked." But to those who are offended he vouchsafes but this curt and cutting defence of his plain-speaking: "Art thou guilty? Complain not, thou art not wronged. Art thou guiltless? Complain not, thou art not touched." These satires, however, striking as they are for their compactness of language and vigor of characterization, convey but an inadequate idea of the depth, devoutness, and largeness of soul displayed in Hall's theological writings. His Meditations, especially, have been read by thousands who never heard of him as a tart and caustic wit. But the one characteristic of sententiousness marks equally the sarcasm of the youthful satirist and the raptures of the aged saint.—EDWIN P. WHIPPLE, *The Literature of the Age of Elizabeth*, 1869, pp. 242–43

His Satires belong to his early Cambridge days, and to the last decade of the sixteenth century. They have on the whole been rather overpraised, though the variety of their matter and the abundance of reference to interesting social traits of the time to some extent redeem them. The worst point about them, as already noted, is the stale and commonplace impertinence with which their author, unlike the best breed of young poets and men of letters, attempts to satirise his literary betters; while they are to some extent at any rate tarred with the other two brushes of corrupt imitation of the ancients, and of sham moral indignation. Indeed the want of sincerity—the evidence of the literary exercise—injures Hall's satirical work in different ways throughout. We do not, as we read him, in the least believe in his attitude of Hebrew prophet crossed with Roman satirist, and the occasional presence of a vigorous couplet or a lively metaphor hardly redeems this disbelief. Nevertheless, Hall is here as always a literary artist—a writer who took some trouble with his writings.—GEORGE SAINTSBURY, *A History of Elizabethan Literature*, 1887, pp. 152–53

MUNDUS ALTER ET IDEM

Mundus Alter et Idem . . . is a witty and ingenious Invention of a Learned Prelate, writ by him in his younger days (but well enough becoming the austerity of the gravest Head), in which he distinguisheth the Vices, Passions, Humours, and ill Affections most commonly incident to mankind into several Provinces; gives us the Character of each, as in the descriptions of a Country, People, and chief Cities of it, and sets them forth unto the Eye in such lively Colours, that the Vitious man may see therein his own Deformities, and the well-minded man his own Imperfections. The Scene of this Design is laid by the Reverend Author in this *Terra Australis*; the *Decorum* happily preserved in the whole Discovery; the style acutely clear, in the invention singular.—PETER HEYLYN, *Cosmography*, 1652, Bk. 4

With Hall's satires should be ranked his *Mundus Alter et Idem*, an ingenious satirical fiction in prose, where, under a pretended description of the Terra Australis, he forms a pleasant invective against the characteristic vices of various nations, and is remarkably severe on the Church of Rome. This piece was written about the year 1600, before he had quitted the classics for the fathers, and published some years afterwards against his consent.—THOMAS WARTON, *The History of English Poetry*, 1778–81, Sec. 64

Despite Hallam's remark that "not much of the Satire has any especial relation to England," "Mercurius Britannicus" needed not to have left England or to have gone far beyond the walls of London for examples of the manners he has described in *Mundus Alter et Idem*. The names of persons and places are easily identified. Ram Alley, a notorious passage leading to the Temple, Petticoat Lane, the Fleet Prison, the feasting at Guildhall, drinking at the taverns, and other incidents are thinly disguised. There is also a humorous reference to tobacco and the habit of smoking (so much abhorred by James I.) as having been introduced by one Topia Waralladorem, an ungodly fellow of this country, who had been taught to smoke by an Indian devil. This can refer only to the people's favourite, Raleigh, lodged in the Tower since December 16, 1603. The author tells the story of a poor man who is drugged and carried away in his sleep to wake up in a palace of pleasure and delight, and afterwards carried out again, a story older than Boccaccio. Although "Mercurius Britannicus" wanders through the newly discovered "Terra Australis," "Nova Guinea," and the "Psittacorum Regio," with their imaginary cities, rivers, and mountains, underlying the whole is the London of Elizabeth and James I. The same Alsatia is reflected in the *Mundus* as was long afterwards discovered to us by Scott in the *Fortunes of Nigel*.

In the state of "Crapulia" the inhabitants are given over to eating and drinking; their laws are against fasting, and cooks, bakers, tavern-keepers, the well-fed, greedy, and jolly only are eligible for citizenship, the highest offices being reserved for such as have attained a certain "rotundity." In "Viraginia" the government is by the women. Here as in Erasmus, later on in Neville, and in our own time, in Trevelyan, the ladies have their assembly or parliament. In the *Mundus Alter* the women's parliament is perpetual, so that what is voted to-day may be repealed to-morrow. "Moronia" is the country of fools, and "Lavernia" that of thieves, cutpurses, and rogues. The work of a scholar, it is also that of a scholar whose acquaintance with continental speech was very considerable, as there are scattered over its pages nearly two hundred proper names of persons, places, and things of which thirty-nine are Spanish, thirty-five Latin, twenty-nine Italian, twenty-eight Greek, twenty-eight French, fifteen German, six English, and one Hebrew.—EDWARD A. PETHERICK, "*Mundus Alter et Idem*," *Gentleman's Magazine*, July 1896, p. 71

JOHN HALES

1584–1656

John Hales was born in Bath on April 19, 1584. After attending the Bath Grammar School, Hales entered Corpus Christi College, Oxford, in 1597. He graduated with a B.A. in 1603, and in 1605 was made a fellow of Merton College. In 1609 Hales received an M.A. and became a lecturer in Greek. Later, in 1613, he obtained a fellowship at Eton. Hales accompanied Sir Dudley Carleton, as his chaplain, to Holland in 1616. Two years later Hales returned to attend the Synod of Dort. During the Dort Synod Hales took a strong dislike to Calvinism, a sentiment which augmented his previous bias against the Church of Rome. A moderate and tolerant preacher, Hales returned to his Eton fellowship in 1619.

In 1639 Hales was appointed canon of Windsor. Hales's *Schisms and Schismaticks* (1642) reveals his tolerant attitude towards religious diversity and his reliance on the Scriptures as the source of truth. During the Commonwealth Hales lost his Windsor preferment and his Eton fellowship. He was forced to sell his prized collection of books in order to maintain himself. Hales died on May 19, 1656, at Eton. Three years later John Pearson published *The Golden Remains of the Ever-Memorable Mr John Hales* (1659). This selection of sermons, letters, and fragmentary thoughts was followed by the publication of a complete edition of Hales's writings in 1765.

Personal

Hales set by himself most gravely did smile
To see them about nothing keep such a coil;
Apollo had spied him, but knowing his mind
Past by, and call'd *Faulkland* that sate just behind.
  —SIR JOHN SUCKLING, "The Wits," 1637

Mr. John Hales had been Greek professor in the university of Oxford; and had borne all the labour of that excellent edition and impression of St. Chrysostom's Works, set out by sir Harry Savile; who was then warden of Merton college, when the other was fellow of that house. He was chaplain in the house with sir Dudley Carleton, ambassador at the Hague in Holland, at the time when the synod of Dort was held, and so had liberty to be present at the consultations in that assembly; and hath left the best memorial behind him, of the ignorance, and passion, and animosity, and injustice of that convention; of which he often made very pleasant relations; though at that time it received too much countenance from England. Being a person of the greatest eminency for learning, and other abilities, from which he might have promised himself any preferment in the church, he withdrew himself from all pursuits of that kind into a private fellowship in the college of Eton, where his friend sir Harry Savile was provost; where he lived amongst his books, and the most separated from the world of any man then living: though he was not in the least degree inclined to melancholy, but, on the contrary, of a very open and pleasant conversation; and therefore was very well pleased with the resort of his friends to him, who were such as he had chosen, and in whose company he delighted, and for whose sake he would sometimes, once in a year, resort to London, only to enjoy their cheerful conversation.

He would never take any cure of souls; and was so great a contemner of money, that he was wont to say, that his fellowship, and the bursar's place, (which, for the good of the college, he held many years,) was worth him fifty pounds a year more than he could spend; and yet, besides his being very charitable to all poor people, even to liberality, he had made a greater and better collection of books, than were to be found in any other private library that I have seen; as he had sure read more, and carried more about him in his excellent memory, than any man I ever knew, my lord Falkland only excepted, who I think sided him. He had, whether from his natural temper and constitution, or from his long retirement from all crowds, or from his profound judgment and discerning spirit, contracted some opinions which were not received, nor by him published, except in private discourses; and then rather upon occasion of dispute, than of positive opinion: and he would often say, his opinions he was sure did him no harm, but he was far from being confident that they might not do others harm who entertained them, and might entertain other results from them than he did; and therefore he was very reserved in communicating what he thought himself in those points, in which he differed from what was received.

Nothing troubled him more than the brawls which were grown from religion; and he therefore exceedingly detested the tyranny of the church of Rome; more for their imposing uncharitably upon the consciences of other men, than for the errors in their own opinions: and would often say, that he would renounce the religion of the church of England tomorrow, if it obliged him to believe that any other Christians should be damned; and that nobody would conclude another man to be damned, who did not wish him so. No man more strict and severe to himself; to other men so charitable as to their opinions, that he thought that other men were more in fault for their carriage towards them, than the men themselves were who erred; and he thought that pride and passion, more than conscience, were the cause of all separation from each other's communion; and he frequently said, that that only kept the world from agreeing upon such a liturgy, as might bring them into one communion; all doctrinal points, upon which men differed in their opinions, being to have no place in any liturgy. Upon an occasional discourse with a friend, of the frequent and uncharitable reproaches of heretic and schismatic, too lightly thrown at each other, amongst men who differ in their judgment, he writ a little discourse of schism, contained in less than two sheets of paper; which being transmitted from friend to friend in writing, was at last, without any malice, brought to the view of the archbishop of Canterbury, Dr. Laud, who was a very rigid surveyor of all things which never so little bordered upon schism; and thought the church could not be too vigilant against, and jealous of, such incursions.

He sent for Mr. Hales, whom, when they had both lived in the university of Oxford, he had known well; and told him, that he had in truth believed him to be long since dead; and chid him very kindly for having never come to him, having been of his old acquaintance: then asked him, whether he had lately written a short discourse of schism, and whether he was of that opinion which that discourse implied. He told him that he had, for the satisfaction of a private friend, (who was not of his mind,) a year or two before, writ such a small tract, without any imagination that it would be communicated; and that he believed it did not contain any thing that was not agreeable to the judgment of the primitive fathers: upon which, the archbishop debated with him upon some expressions of Irenæus, and the most ancient fathers; and concluded with saying, that the time was very apt to set new doctrines on foot, of which the wits of the age were too susceptible; and that there could not be too much care taken to preserve the peace and unity of the church; and from thence asked him of his condition, and whether he wanted any thing: and the other answering, that he

had enough, and wanted or desired no addition, so dismissed him with great courtesy; and shortly after sent for him again, when there was a prebendary of Windsor fallen, and told him, the king had given him the preferment, because it lay so convenient to his fellowship of Eton; which (though indeed the most convenient preferment that could be thought of for him) the archbishop could not without great difficulty persuade him to accept, and he did accept it rather to please him than himself; because he really believed he had enough before. He was one of the least men in the kingdom; and one of the greatest scholars in Europe.—EDWARD HYDE, EARL OF CLARENDON, *The Life of Edward Earl of Clarendon*, c. 1668

Went to School, at Bath (as I take it). Fellow of Merton Colledge: afterwards fellow of Eaton College.

He was a generall Scolar, and I beleeve a good poet: for Sir John Suckling brings him into the *Session of the Poets*:

Little Hales all the time did nothing but smile,
To see them, about nothing, keepe such a coile.

When the Court was at Windsor, the learned Courtiers much delighted in his company, and were wont to grace him with their company.

Mr. Hales was the common Godfather there, and 'twas pretty to see, as he walked to Windsor, how his Godchildren fell on their Knees. When he was Bursar, he still gave away all his Groates for the Acquittances to his Godchildren; and by that time he came to Windsor bridge, he would have never a Groate left.

He had a noble Librarie of bookes, and those judicially chosen, which cost him not lesse then 2500 pounds; and which he sold to Cornelius Bee, Bookeseller, in Little Britaine (as I take it, for 1000 pounds) which was his maintenance after he was ejected out of his Fellowship at Eaton-College. Mris. Powney told me that she was much against the sale of 'em, because she knew it was his Life and joy. He had then only reserved some few for his private use, to wind-up his last dayes withall.

I have heard his nephew, Mr. Sloper, say, that he much loved to read Stephanus, who was a Familist, I thinke that first wrote of that Sect of the Familie of Love: he was mightily taken with it, and was wont to say that sometime or other those fine Notions would take in the world. He was one of the first Socinians in England, I think the first.

The Ladie Salter (neer Eaton) was very kind to him after his Sequestration; he was very welcome to her Ladyship and spent much of his time there: (from her Nephew.)

He lodged (after his Sequestration) at Mris. Powney's house, a widowe-woman, in Eaton, opposite to the church-yard, adjoyning to the Christopher Inne southwards. She is a very good woman and of a gratefull spirit. She told me that when she was maried, Mr. Hales was very bountifull to them in setting them up to live in the world. She was very gratefull to him and respectfull to him: a woman primitively good, and deserves to be remembered. She has been handsome: a good understanding, and cleanlie. I wish I had her Christian name.

She has a handsome darke old-fashioned howse. The hall, after the old fashion, above the wainscot, painted cloath, with godly sentences out of the Psalmes, etc., according to the pious custome of old times; a convenient garden and orchard.

'Tis the howse where I sawe him, a prettie little man, sanguine, of a cheerfull countenance, very gentile, and courteous; I was recieved by him with much humanity: he was in a kind of violet-colourd cloath Gowne, with buttons and loopes (he wore not a black gowne) and was reading Thomas à Kempis; it was within a yeare before he deceased. He loved Canarie; but moderately, to refresh his spirits.

He had a bountifull mind. I remember in 1647, a little after the Visitation, when Thomas Mariett, Esq., Mr. William Radford, and Mr. Edward Wood (all of Trinity College) had a frolique from Oxon to London, on foot, having never been there before; they happened to take Windsore in their way, made their addresse to this good Gentleman, being then Fellow. Mr. Edward Wood was the Spookes-man, remonstrated that they were Oxon Scholars: he treated them well, and putt into Mr. Wood's hands Ten shillings.

This Mris. Powney assures me that the poor were more relievable (that is to say) that he recieved more kindnesse from them than from the Rich. That that I putt downe of my Lady Salter is false. She had him to her house indeed, but 'twas to teach her sonne, who was such a blockhead he could not read well.

He might have been restored to his Fellowship again, but he would not accept the offer. He was not at all Covetous, and desired only to leave X pounds to bury him.

He lies buried in the Church yard at Eaton, under an altar monument of Black marble, erected at the sole chardge of Mr. Curwyn, with a too long Epitaph. He was no Kiff, or Kin to him.—JOHN AUBREY, "John Hales," *Brief Lives*, 1669–96

John Hales a younger son of Joh. Hales, (steward to the family of the Horners in Somersetshire) eldest son of Edw. Hales of Highchurch in the said county, son of Jo. Hales of the same place, son of Rich. Hales, by his wife the daughter of Beauchamp; was born in the parish of S. James within the city of Bath and educated in grammar learning there. At 13 years of age he was sent to the university in the beginning of the year 1597, and was for some time a scholar of Corp. Ch. coll. At length the prodigious pregnancy of his parts being discovered by the hedge-beaters of sir Hen. Savile, he was encouraged by them to stand for a fellowship of Merton coll. Whereupon an election being appointed and made in 1605 (3 Jac. 1.) and all the candidates sifted and examined to the utmost, he was the first that was chosen. In which election, as he shew'd himself a person of learning above his age and standing, so thro' the whole course of his bachellorship there was never any one in the then memory of man (so I have been informed by certain seniors of that coll. at my first coming thereunto) that ever went beyond him for subtle disputations in philosophy, for his eloquent declamations and orations; as also for his exact knowledge in the Greek tongue, evidently demonstrated afterwards, not only when he read the Greek lecture in that coll. but also the public lecture of that tongue in the schools. His profound learning and natural endowments, (not that I shall take notice of his affability, sweetness of nature and complaisance, which seldom accompany hard students and critics) made him beloved of all good men, particularly to Savile before-mentioned, who found him, tho' young, serviceable in his edition of S. Chrysostom's works, and therefore often mention'd with honour by that noted Grecian Andrew Downes, Greek professor of Cambridge. Afterwards he was made fellow of Eaton coll. partly, if I mistake not, by the help of Savile, and partly by sir Dudley Carleton, with whom he went, in the quality of chaplain, when he was sent ambassador to the United Provinces, at what time the synod of Dort was celebrated, Jan. 1618, where our author Hales did good service in several respects, so far as his capacity did permit him. From that time till about the year 1638, no great matters occur memorable of him, only his acquaintance with Will. Chillingworth, whom he assisted in his great work, as I shall anon tell you, which made him to be noted among the learned, especially for certain opinions that were not thought fit to be by him entertained. In that year, I say, Dr. Laud archb. of Canterbury, who had received cognisance of his great worth, did send for him to Lambeth, sifted, and ferreted him about from one hole to another, in certain matters of religion that he partly then, but more in his younger days, maintained: And finding him an absolute master of learning, made him, upon his complyance, one of his chaplains, and procured a canonry of Windsor for him, installed therein 27 of June 1639, which, with his fellowship, was all that this most incomparable person, whom I may justly stile a walking library, enjoy'd. He was a man highly esteemed by learned men beyond, and within, the seas, from whom he seldom fail'd to receive letters every week, wherein his judgment was desir'd as to several points of learning. He was a very hard student to the last, and a great faster, it being his constant custom to fast from Thursday dinner to Saturday: and tho' a person of wonderful knowledge, yet he was so modest, as to be patiently contented to hear the disputes of persons at table, and those of small abilities, without interposing or speaking a word, till desir'd. As for his justness and uprightness in his dealings, all that knew, have avouched him to be incomparable: For when he was bursar of his coll. and had received bad money, he would lay it aside, and put good of his own in the room of it to pay to others. Insomuch that sometimes he has thrown into the river 20 and 30*l.* at a time. All which he hath stood to, to the loss of himself, rather than others of the society should be endamaged. After the civil war began, occasion'd by the iniquity of the restless presbyterians, he was turn'd out of all, and into his fellowship was thrust by the authority of parliament, one Penwarden, who being afterwards touch'd in conscience for the wrong he had done so worthy a person by eating his bread, went and voluntarily would have resign'd up the place again to him, but Mr. Hales refused, telling him, that the parliament having put him out, he was resolved never to be put in again by them. As for his canonry of Windsor, it lay void till his majesty's restoration, an. 1660, and then 'twas bestowed on Anth. Hawles D.D. sometimes of Queen's coll. in Oxon. At length he, being reduced to necessity, was forced to sell the best part of his most admirable library (which cost him 2500*l.*) to Cornelius Bee of London bookseller, for 700*l.* only as I have been informed by persons of unquestionable veracity. 'Tis true that one of the Sedleian family of Kent did invite him to live in his family, with an allowance of 100*l.* per an. the keeping of two horses and a servant's diet, but he being wedded to a retir'd and studious life, refused to accept of that generous offer; yet about that time he accepted of a quarter of that salary, with his diet, in the family of one madam Salter (sister, if I mistake not, to Dr. Duppa bishop of Sarum) who lived near Eaton, purposely that he should instruct her son Will. Salter; but he being blockish, Hales could do nothing upon him. Afterwards a declaration issuing out, prohibiting all persons from harbouring malignants, that is royalists, he left that family, notwithstanding the lady desired him to the contrary, telling him, that she would undergo all danger that might ensue by harbouring him, and retiring to Eaton, he took up his quarters and sojourned in an house next to the Christopher Inn, belonging then to Hannah the widow of John Dickenson, (a servant from his youth to our author Hales) and afterwards the wife and widow of one Sim. Powney; which Hannah was very careful of, and respectful to, him, as having formerly at her marriage received of his bounty. Other persons of the loyal party, would have exhibited to, had they not been equal sharers in affliction with, him, and therefore it was that he died in an obscure condition, much pitied by many then in being, but by more in the next generation, particularly by such (which you'll say is a wonder) that were no friends to the church of England, who did reckon it not one of the least ignominies of that age, that so eminent a person of the church of England (as Hales was) should have been by the iniquity of the times reduced to those necessities under which he lived, &c. And whereas he had been heard to say in his former days that he thought he should never die a martyr, yet he was known to live a confessor, and died little less than a martyr for the doctrine and discipline of the church of England. The publisher of his *Remains* doth tell us, that 'He was a man of as great sharpness, quickness, and stability of wit, as ever this, or perhaps any, nation bred. His industry did strive, if it were possible, to equal the largeness of his capacity. Proportionable to his reading was his meditation, which furnished him with a judgment beyond the vulgar reach of man. So that he really was a most prodigious example of an acute and piercing wit, of a vast and illimited knowledge, of a severe and profound judgment,' &c. He tells us also, that he was true and just in his secular transactions, and charitable beyond example, and as a Christian, none was ever more acquainted with the nature of the Gospel, because none more studious of the knowledge of it than he. That he was solicited to write, and thereby to teach the world, but would resolve against it; yet did not hide his talent, being so communicative that his chamber was a church, and his chair a pulpit, and was as communicative of his knowledge, as the celestial bodies of their light and influences. . . . Those that remember and were well acquainted with Mr. Hales, have said, that he had the most ingenious countenance that ever they saw, that it was sanguine, chearful, and full of air: also that his stature was little and well proportion'd, and his motion quick and nimble. And they have verily supposed, that had not extremities contributed to the shortning of his days, nature would have afforded him life till he had been 90 years old or more.—Anthony à Wood, *Athenae Oxonienses*, 1691–1721

He was a man of an inveterately companionable disposition. He disliked being alone, except for study—in congenial company a sympathetic talker; once a year for a short time he used to resort to London for the polite conversation which he so much enjoyed, and when the Court was at Windsor he was greatly in request, being not only a good talker, but a better listener, as his biographer says; not only divines and scholars resorting to the rooms of this *bibliotheca ambulans*, as Provost Wotton called him, but courtiers, sprightly wits, and gay sparks from the castle. This it was that earned him his soubriquet. He was familiar with, or corresponded with, all the ablest men of the day, counting as he did, Davenant, Suckling, Ben Jonson, and Lord Falkland, and all that brilliant circle, among his intimate friends. . . .

He was one of those great men who have a genuine dislike of publicity. He could not be induced to publish anything in his lifetime except a Latin funeral oration—not that it mattered, as one of his contemporaries hinted, "for he was so communicative that his chair was a pulpit and his chamber a church." In fact it became so much a matter of habit that his friends should propound questions on which he should discourse, that he is recorded to have made a laughing refusal; "he sets up tops," he said, in his allusive way "and I am to whip them for him." But it is plain that he had a genuine contempt for his own written style: he says that on the one side he errs by being "overfamiliar and subrustic;" on the other as "sour and satyrical." He evidently had the ironical quality in great perfection; his writings and recorded conversation abound in quaint little unexpected turns and capricious illustrations; he had one of those figurative minds that love to express one idea in the terms of another, and see unexpected and felicitous connections. His sermons are strange compositions; they straggle on through page after page of thickly printed octavos, "he being a great preacher according to the taste of those times," says an antique critic of them, going on to object that they keep the reader in a "continued twitter throughout." He must have been very light of heart who could have "twittered" continuously through the good hour that the very shortest of them must have taken to deliver. Quotations from Homer, mystically interpreted, strange mythological stories, well worn classical jests; perhaps the sense of humour was as different among the men of that era from ours as their sense of theology undoubtedly was—more discursive if not deeper!

It has struck more than one writer about John Hales, that the following is a curious trait: he was a remarkably good man of business: he was bursar of Eton for many years, and his precise, formal signature may still be seen in the audit books, and it is told of him that he was accustomed to throw into the river at the bottom of the college garden any base or counterfeit coin that he chanced to receive on behalf of the college, paying the loss out of his own pocket.

Pure-minded, simple-hearted little man, reading Thomas-à-Kempis in his violet gown; poor, degraded, but not dishonoured; what a strong, grave protest your quiet, exiled life, self-contained and serious, is, against the crude follies, the boisterous energies of the revolution seething and mantling all about you! the clear-sighted soul can adopt no party cries, swears allegiance to no frantic school; enlightened, at the mercy of no tendency or prejudice, it resigns all that gave dignity to blessed quiet, and takes the peace without the pomp; with unobtrusive, unpretentious hopes and prospects shattered in the general wreck, the true life-philosopher still finds his treasures in the old books, the eternal thoughts and the kindly offices of retired life. This is a gentle figure that Eton's sons may well be glad to connect with her single street, her gliding waters and her immemorial groves; though as yet the reverence of antiquity sate lightly upon her, though she was not yet in the forefront of the loud educational world, yet in her sequestered peace there was a cloistral stateliness that she somewhat misses now. Not that we grudge her the glory of a nobler mission, a wider field of action, a more extended influence, in days when the race and battle are more than ever for the fleet and strong. But we lament over the nooks that the ancient years so jealously guarded and fenced about from the world and its incisive voice, where among some indolence and some luxury and much littleness the storage of great forces was accomplished, and the tones of a sacred voice not rarely heard. Ah! it is an ideal that this century has lost the knack of sympathising with! Perhaps she is but creating the necessity for its imperious recall.—A. C. Benson, "The Ever-Memorable John Hales," *Essays*, 1896, pp. 12–18

General

The genial recluse, with his prodigious memory and his keen, rapier-like thrust of argument, was the most loving and tender-hearted of men. In his Eton fellowship he found himself at home under the provostship of the large-minded Sir Henry Wotton. His views of life and religion were in the main identical with those of Chillingworth, but he approached the subject from the other side. In Chillingworth the logical faculty was supreme. In Hales it was at the service of a singularly gentle and affectionate heart. Hence he began where Chillingworth left off. He did not argue himself into the belief that the intention to go wrong, and not the failure itself, was culpable. He rather made it the starting-point of his reasoning. "He would often say that he would renounce the religion of the Church of England to-morrow if it obliged him to believe that any other Christian should be damned, and that nobody would conclude another man to be damned that did not wish him so." "Every Christian," he wrote, "may err that will; for if we might not err wilfully, then there would be no heresy, heresy being nothing else but wilful error. For if we account mistakes befalling us through human frailties to be heresies, then it will follow that every man since the Apostles' times was an heretic." Hence he could take but little interest in Chillingworth's search after fundamental truths. That men should err was, in his eyes, a necessity of their nature. The venerable names of the Fathers of the ancient Church, the imposing solemnity of ecclesiastical councils, conferred no exemption from the universal law. "If truth and goodness," he wrote, "go by universality and multitude, what mean then the prophets and holy men of God everywhere in the Scripture so frequently, so bitterly to complain of the small number of good men careful of God and truth? Neither is the complaint proper to Scripture; it is the common complaint of all that have left any records of antiquity behind them. Could wishing do any good, I could wish well to this kind of proof; but it shall never go so well with mankind that the most shall be the best. The best that I can say of argument and reason drawn from universality in multitude is this: such reason may perchance serve to excuse an error, but it can never serve to warrant a truth."

Yet, for all this, the investigation of truth was the highest work of man. The words of the Apostle, "Be not deceived," were spoken not only to the wise and learned, but 'to everyone, of whatever sex, of whatever rank or degree and place soever, from him that studies in his library to him that sweats at the plough-tail.' But the command is not obeyed by those who content themselves with storing their memories with opinions learned by rote. He that would not be deceived must not only know 'what it is that is commanded,' must not therefore take his duties on trust from a Church claiming to be infallible, or from a venerated preacher, but must also know 'wherefore— that is, upon what authority, upon what reason.' At last the new thought which was to form the modern world had reached its full and clear expression.

Like Chillingworth, Hales too had his dream of Utopian harmony of worship. "Were liturgies and public forms of service so framed," he argued, "as that they admitted not of particular and private fancies, but contained only such things as in which all Christians do agree, schisms in opinion were utterly vanished. For consider of all the liturgies that are or ever have been, and remove from them whatsoever is scandalous to any party, and leave nothing but what all agree on, and the event shall be that the public service and honour of God shall no ways suffer; whereas to load our public forms with the private fancies upon which we differ is the most sovereign way to perpetuate schism unto the world's end. Prayer, confession, thanksgiving, reading of Scripture, exposition of Scripture, administration of sacraments in the plainest and simplest manner, were matter enough to furnish out a sufficient liturgy, though nothing else of private opinion, or of church pomp, of garments, of prescribed gestures, of imagery, of music, of matter concerning the dead, of many superfluities which creep into churches under the name of order and decency, did interpose itself."—SAMUEL R. GARDINER, *History of England*, 1883, Vol. 8, pp. 265–67

Among the English rationalists of the seventeenth century, the "ever memorable" John Hales of Eton is in a manner over-

shadowed by the greater figure which Falkland makes in history; his memory suffers, in comparison even with Chillingworth's, in consequence of his extreme reticence. Yet in strict temporal sequence, Hales precedes both in the line of spiritual descent from Colet, Cranmer, and Hooker. And he yields to neither—who, though much younger men, predeceased him—in scholarship, or in clearness of mental vision. The materials for an estimate of Hales are, indeed, scanty. He himself published nothing but his funeral oration on Sir Thomas Bodley. His *Works* in three volumes, which Lord Hailes edited in 1765, contain, besides merely occasional tracts, including the famous *On Schism and Schismaticks*, sermons, and his letters from the Synod of Dort. Still, even if not a line of his had survived we should be obliged to accept the testimony offered as to his exceptional scholarship by Clarendon, Bishop Pearson, Andrew Marvell, Dr. Heylin, and Bishop Stillingfleet. Anthony Wood styles him "a walking library." In the brief passage which may be styled his *apologia* he wrote, "The pursuit of truth hath been my only care, ever since I understood the meaning of the word. For this I have forsaken all hopes, all desires, all friends which might bias me, and hinder me from driving right at what I aimed." Clarendon furnished the complement of his character in words which he gives out to be Hales's own:—"His opinions, he was sure, did him no harm, but he was far from being confident that they might not do others harm who entertained them, and might entertain other results from them than he did. There is then no mystery about the lifelong seclusion and reticence of 'one of the clearest heads and best prepared hearts of Christendom.'" It is easy enough to discern the genesis of his quiescent temper, if not of his thirst for truth in his early experience of theological controversy at Dort. Hales began his report of the proceedings with a strong Calvinistic bias, and though he could never quite cast off his prejudices against the (Arminian) Remonstrants his tone was in the later letters distinctly modified. Yet he left the Synod—as he had entered it, a Calvinist. Though he professed to "bid Calvin good night," he did not, as the late Principal Tulloch puts it, "say good morning to Arminius." He came away from Dort disgusted with the violence of the dogmatic disputations he had listened to, and convinced that truth could not be compressed into creed or system. He went straight into residence at Eton, and, for seventeen years he, of his own freewill, gave no writing to the world. Two Latin treatises, dated respectively 1628 and 1633, which have been attributed to him, but without warrant, are worthy of notice because they provide the ground for the untrue charge of Socinianism brought against him, chiefly by Anthony Wood. The tract *On Schism and Schismaticks* appears to have been written about 1636, most probably for the benefit of Chillingworth, whose *Religion of Protestants* appeared in the following year. It was little more than a brief categorical statement of what he had long been in the habit of maintaining in conversation—that it was only pride and passion which kept Christendom from agreeing upon such a liturgy as might bring the world into one communion. "Why may I not go," he asked, "if occasion require, into an Arian church, so there be no Arianism expressed in their liturgy?" Schisms, he held, had crept into the Church by one of three ways, upon matter of fact, upon matter of opinion, or upon a point of ambition. The kernel of the tract was the contention "that in cases of separation among Christians those who would impose burdens on others, and enforce an unnecessary conformity, were really responsible for the schism, and that episcopal ambition had been the great cause of frequent, continuous, and bloody schisms." But Hales's clearness of mental sight and rational thoroughness are really nowhere so manifest as in the posthumously published tract *On the Sacrament of the Lord's Supper*. He assailed Protestants as well as Catholics for holding that the words of consecration were anything but "a mere trope." Turning to the question whether the Church might err in fundamentals, he poured contempt on the doctrine of the Infallibility of Councils. "It was never heard," he said, "in any profession that the conclusion of truth went by plurality of voices, the Christian profession only excepted; and I have often mused how it comes to pass that the way which in all other sciences is not able to warrant the poorest conclusion, should be thought sufficient to give authority to conclusions in divinity, the supremest empress of sciences." Hales is most distinctively modern, perhaps, in his sermon *Of Enquiry and Private Judgment in Religion*. Infallibility was, he argued, not a favour peculiar to any one man; all must have it. A man must know not only what he has to believe, but why he has to believe. Hales's literary style is, in the main, the reflection of his lucid manner of thinking. When he argues, he goes straight to the point, and, barring a certain looseness in the construction of his sentences, he is a master of exposition. His illustrations, though copious, never weary the reader, being always the natural overflow of a mind well stocked with learning, and not a mere display of pedantry. There runs through his writings a thin thread of humour characteristic of the man—himself in earnest, but scorning the earnestness about non-essentials which he discovers in others.—W. WALLACE, "John Hales," *English Prose*, ed. Henry Craik, 1893, Vol. 2, pp. 183–85

JOHN TULLOCH
From "John Hales of Eton:
Religion and Dogmatic Orthodoxy"
*Rational Theology and Christian Philosophy
in England in the Seventeenth Century*
1872, Volume 1, pp. 221–37, 259–60

The value of Hales's writings consists not in any elaborate treatment of theological questions, but in the singular spirit of enlightenment, and calm, penetrating, comprehensive wisdom which pervade them. They contain no special treatise to which subsequent ages have appealed as a model of theological exposition or argument. They are only tracts, sermons, or letters; and the sermons are neither rich with the jewelled eloquence of a Jeremy Taylor, nor weighty with the solid reasoning and systematic power of a Barrow. But there is in all our author's writings exactly that which so many theological writings want, the light of a bright, open-eyed, candid intelligence, which sees frequently far beyond the range of the most powerful systematic intellect straight to the truth—"an acute and piercing wit," a wise, calm, and "profound judgment." A great reader and student, versed in a various and even (according to Bishop Pearson) a "universal" erudition, he is yet entirely free from the pedantry of learning, a rare attainment for his age. His accumulated knowledge of books and systems never encumbers him. He never, or rarely, uses it as materials of exposition, or stuff for dilating and parading arguments in themselves worthless, after the prevailing fashion. But all his knowledge has become an enriching basis of his own thought, and raises him above "the vulgar reach of man" to see for himself clearly and widely. It has entered into the very life of his quick and genial intellect, and contributes to the wealth of his meditative insight, and his tolerant, comprehensive, and sweetly-tempered genius. The simplicity and breadth of his religious

thought are astonishing for his time. He goes to the heart of controversies, and distinguishes with a delicate and summary skill the essential from the accidental in religion as in other things.

Hales's works may be said to be of two classes—miscellaneous tracts and pieces, such as mostly fill the first of the three volumes to which we have adverted; and sermons, which compose the greater part of the two remaining volumes. About the half of the third volume is occupied by his *Letters from the Synod of Dort*. These letters, of course, with the exception of his "Oratio Funebris" on the founder of the Bodleian Library, are the earliest of all his writings. As to the others, it is impossible to fix their relative chronological position. We have already given our reasons for believing that the most significant of his undated tracts—that on the Lord's Supper—belongs to about the same period as his tract on Schism; and most of his sermons probably belong to the same or a still earlier period, although not collected, nor with a single exception[1] published, till long afterwards. There is no evidence of his writing anything after the commencement of the troubles in which he and his friends were so directly involved; and no trace in the volumes of allusion to subsequent events, or the special controversies which they called forth.

It is impossible, therefore, and unnecessary, to attempt any further arrangement of his writings. His favourite ideas are scattered here and there through them all—now simplified and popularly illustrated in a sermon, and now urged with more brevity, sharpness, and incision in a tract. We shall accordingly draw our quotations from them as may suit our purpose, and endeavour to present his ideas under some sequence of thought or subject rather than in any order of growth or time.

1. The first aspect of his teaching which deserves attention is his clear exposition of the principle more or less underlying all his thought—that theological or dogmatic differences are not really religious differences, and should not break the unity of common faith and worship. All theological opinion implies certain human additions to the religious element—certain "conceits of men," which in their very nature provoke and admit of diversity of criticism; but this diversity is no ground of religious separation. There is no reason why men of very differing opinions in such matters should not worship together. The "liberty of judging," which Hales took to himself, he not only extended to all, but he felt that such liberty was an inherent Christian right, which it was the business of the Church not only to tolerate, but, so to speak, to educate and find room for. It was not difference of opinion which the Church had to fear, but the hardness and perversity of will which turned such difference into a cause of unchristian estrangement. Truth and error were, after all, each man's own responsibility, and even those who fell into error might be nearer the truth in spirit than those who professed to hold it. "He thought," says Clarendon, "that other men were more in fault for their carriage towards them than the men themselves were who erred; and he thought that pride and passion, more than conscience, were the cause of all separation from each other's communion, and he frequently said that that only kept the world from agreeing upon such a liturgy as might bring them into one communion." This is the key-note of a great deal of his writing.

"It is not the variety of opinions," he says in one of his sermons, "but our own perverse wills, who think it meet that all should be conceited as ourselves are, which hath so inconvenienced the Church. Were we not so ready to anathematise each other, where we concur not in opinion, we might in hearts be united, though in our tongues we were divided, and that with singular profit to all sides. It is 'the unity of the Spirit in the bond of peace' (Eph. iv. 3), and not identity of conceit, which the Holy Ghost requires at the hands of Christians."[2] . . .

This mode of thought is now sufficiently familiar. But it was far from familiar in Hales's time, and it may be inferred from his letters that it had only gradually grown up in his mind as the fruit of much reflection and experience of religious controversy. His spiritual insight, his sense, moderation, and candid deference to facts, had borne him out of the current of religious partisanship, and opened up to him a higher vision than was common to his contemporaries. His mind was evidently in continual quest of truth. He did not take up his opinions and then no more trouble himself to examine them. He was continually going deeper in search of principles, and mastering them with a clearer sight, so as to recognise their true meaning and bearing, and the modifications which they undergo. A healthy modesty, and constantly penetrating and subtle delicacy in consequence, mark his conclusions. He is reverential in the highest sense, and yet keenly original. He is reserved, and yet he speaks out his mind in the face of what he must have known to be cherished prejudices. . . .

It is sufficiently obvious that, quiet and unobtrusive as Hales's life may have been, he was a man of marked influence upon a few higher minds. Personally he had no ambition, and apparently but little activity. He kept aloof from the fierce practical controversies of his time. It was his nature to do so—to brood and meditate on the principles underlying religious controversy, rather than to take any active part in it. His intellectual refinement—his sympathies with the Past—his love of the concrete, and tolerance of the historical results to which Christian usage and opinion had gradually grown in England—made him incline to the Royalist party, with which he ultimately threw in his lot, and whose misfortunes he shared. In no circumstances can he be conceived a Puritan. Those instincts of political liberty which were the highest and most aggressive element of Puritanism, if not uncongenial, could only have feebly influenced him, while his ideas of religious freedom were plainly of a more thorough and comprehensive—in a word, of a more rational—character than Puritanism has ever shown itself capable of attaining. The importance attached by the Puritan party to minute matters, details of worship, or special interpretations of doctrine, were scarcely intelligible to a mind like his. Their dogmatic handling of Scripture, their love of formal theory and abstruse logic, openly repelled him. Like his friend Falkland, therefore, he stands significantly aside from both extremes. He is a Churchman without narrowness; a friend of authority, who must yet have hated in his heart and deeply felt the folly of Laud's tyranny. In freedom of thought and clearness of faith, he greatly excels the mere professional divine of any age. He is evangelical without dogmatism, and preaches grace without despising philosophy. At once conservative in feeling, and liberal in opinion, he hates all extremes, as of the nature of falsehood, and a prolific source of wrong. He is the representative—the next after Hooker—of that catholicity yet rationality of Christian sentiment which has been the peculiar glory of the Church of England.

Notes
1. The Sermon *Of Duels*, which he preached while resident at the Hague.
2. Hales's *Works* (1765), ii. 94.

WILLIAM BRADFORD

1590–1657

William Bradford was born in Austerfield, Yorkshire, and was baptised on March 19, 1590. His father, a prosperous yeoman, died in 1591. His mother died six years later, leaving Bradford in the care of relatives. Bradford probably received some education at the grammar school in Austerfield. At an early age Bradford became involved in the religious fervor surrounding radical Puritan sects. In 1609 he emigrated to Amsterdam with the Scrooge Separatists, who moved to Leyden before departing for the New World in 1620. Upon the arrival of the *Mayflower* in Provincetown Harbor, Bradford's first wife, Dorothy Mays, drowned in the waters near the ship. In 1623 Bradford married a widow, Alice Carpenter, by whom he had three children. He was elected governor of the Plymouth Colony in 1621, a post he held for thirty one-year terms before his retirement in 1656.

Bradford's literary fame derives from his *History of Plimmoth Plantation*, which he began in 1630 and completed in 1651. This history of New England's earliest settlement was lost in 1776, probably taken from a private library by a departing British soldier. In 1855 the manuscript resurfaced in the Fulham Palace Library, London, and was published by the Massachusetts Historical Society the following year. Along with Edward Winslow's diary, Bradford's journal was published in *Mourt's Relation* (1622), a chronicle of life during his first months in the New World. Two of his *Dialogues* survive today. These *Dialogues* recount discussions between young settlers born in America and the founding fathers born in Europe. Bradford died in Plymouth on May 9, 1657.

Governor Bradford's reputation as an author is decidedly of a posthumous character. He left a MS. history, in a folio volume of 270 pages, of the Plymouth colony, from the formation of their church in 1602 to 1647. It furnished the material for Morton's Memorial, was used by Prince and Governor Hutchinson in the preparation of their histories, and deposited, with the collection of papers of the former, in the library of the Old South Church, in Boston. During the desecration of this edifice as a riding-school by the British in the Revolutionary war, the MS. disappeared. A copy of a portion closing with the year 1620, in the handwriting of Nathaniel Morton, was discovered by the Rev. Alexander Young in the library of the First Church, at Plymouth, and printed in his *Chronicles of the Pilgrim Fathers of the Colony of Plymouth*, in 1841. A "letter-book," in which Bradford preserved copies of his correspondence, met with a similar fate, a portion only having been rescued from a grocer's shop in Halifax, and published in the Collections of the Massachusetts Historical Society, in 1794, vol. iii. of the first series of Collections, with a fragment of a poem on New England. These, with two other specimens of a few lines each, first published by the same Society in 1838, form, with the exception of some slight controversial pieces, the whole of his literary productions.—EVART A. DUYCKINCK, GEORGE L. DUYCKINCK, *Cyclopædia of American Literature*, 1855, Vol. 1, p. 35

Though not enjoying special educational advantages in early life, Bradford possessed more literary culture than was common among those of similar occupation to himself. He had some knowledge of Latin and Greek, and knew sufficient Hebrew to enable him to "see with his own eyes the ancient oracles of God in their native beauty." He was also well read in history and philosophy, and an adept in the theological discussion peculiar to the time. He employed much of his leisure in literary composition.—T. F. HENDERSON, *Dictionary of National Biography*, 1886, Vol. 6, p. 163

Bradford was a forerunner of literature, not a historian. He stands not as an early Palfrey or Bancroft, but ranks with the useful company of annalists, diarists, and autobiographers, few of whom have equalled him in strength of character and fidelity of purpose. He was the first Pilgrim writer in America, the first recorder of doings in New England, and a story-teller of considerable power, as well as of absolute truthfulness in matters of fact.—CHARLES F. RICHARDSON, *American Literature 1607–1885*, 1887, Vol. 1, p. 75

COTTON MATHER

From "Galeacius Secundus: The Life of William Bradford, Esq., Governour of Plymouth Colony"
Magnalia Christi Americana
1702

William Bradford . . . was born *Anno* 1588, in an obscure village called Ansterfield, where the people were as unacquainted with the Bible, as the Jews do seem to have been with *part* of it in the days of Josiah; a most ignorant and licentious *people*, and *like unto their priest*. Here, and in some other places, he had a comfortable inheritance left him of his honest parents, who died while he was yet a child, and cast him on the education, first of his grand parents, and then of his uncles, who devoted him, like his ancestors, unto the affairs of husbandry. Soon a long sickness kept him, as he would afterwards thankfully say, from the *vanities of youth*, and made him the fitter for what he was afterwards to undergo. When he was about a dozen years old, the reading of the Scriptures began to cause great impressions upon him; and those impressions were much assisted and improved, when he came to enjoy Mr. Richard Clifton's illuminating ministry, not far from his abode; he was then also further befriended, by being brought into the company and fellowship of such as were then called professors; though the young man that brought him into it did after become a prophane and wicked *apostate*. Nor could the wrath of his uncles, nor the scoff of his neighbours, now turned upon

him, as one of the *Puritans*, divert him from his pious inclinations.

At last, beholding how fearfully the evangelical and apostolical *church-form*, whereinto the churches of the primitive times were cast by the good spirit of God, had been *deformed* by the apostacy of the succeeding times; and what little progress the Reformation had yet made in many parts of Christendom towards its recovery, he set himself by reading, by discourse, by prayer, to learn whether it was not his duty to withdraw from the communion of the parish-assemblies, and engage with some society of the faithful, that should keep close unto the *written word* of God, as the *rule* of their worship. And after many distresses of mind concerning it, he took up a very deliberate and understanding resolution, of doing so; which resolution he chearfully prosecuted, although the provoked rage of his friends tried all the ways imaginable to reclaim him from it, unto all of whom his answer was:

> Were I like to endanger my life, or consume my estate by any ungodly courses, your counsels to me were very seasonable; but you know that I have been diligent and provident in my calling, and not only desirous to augment what I have, but also to enjoy it in your company; to part from which will be as great a cross as can befal me. Nevertheless, to keep a good conscience, and walk in such a way as God has prescribed in his Word, is a thing which I must prefer before you all, and above life it self. Wherefore, since 'tis for a good cause that I am like to suffer the disasters which you lay before me, you have no cause to be either angry with me, or sorry for me; yea, I am not only willing to part with every thing that is dear to me in this world for this cause, but I am also thankful that God has given me an heart to do, and will accept me so to suffer for him.

Some lamented him, some derided him, *all* disswaded him: nevertheless, the more they did it, the more fixed he was in his purpose, to seek the ordinances of the gospel, where they should be dispensed with most of the *commanded purity*; and the sudden deaths of the chief relations which thus lay at him, quickly after convinced him what a folly it had been to have quitted his profession, in expectation of any satisfaction from them. So to Holland he attempted a removal.

Having with a great company of Christians hired a ship to transport them for Holland, the master perfidiously betrayed them into hands of those persecutors, who rifled and ransacked their goods, and clapped their persons into prison at Boston, where they lay for a month together. But Mr. Bradford being a young man of about eighteen, was dismissed sooner than the rest, so that within a while he had opportunity with some others to get over to Zealand, through *perils*, both by *land* and *sea* not inconsiderable; where he was not long ashore ere a viper seized on his hand—that is, an officer—who carried him unto the magistrates, unto whom an envious passenger had accused him as having *fled* out of England. When the magistrates understood the true cause of his coming thither, they were well satisfied with him; and so he repaired joyfully unto his brethren at Amsterdam, where the difficulties to which he afterwards stooped in learning and serving of a Frenchman at the working of silks, were abundantly compensated by the delight wherewith he sat under the shadow of our Lord, in his purely dispensed ordinances. At the end of two years, he did, being of age to do it, convert his estate in England into money; but setting up for himself, he found some of his designs by the *providence* of God frowned upon, which he judged a *correction* bestowed by God upon him for certain decays of *internal piety*, whereinto he had fallen; the consumption of his *estate* he thought came to prevent a consumption in his *virtue*. But after he had resided in Holland about half a score years, he was one of those who bore a part in that hazardous and generous enterprise of removing into New-England, with part of the English church at Leyden, where, at their first landing, his dearest consort accidentally falling overboard, was drowned in the harbour; and the rest of his days were spent in the services, and temptations, of that American wilderness.

Here was Mr. Bradford, in the year 1621, unanimously chosen the governour of the plantation: the difficulties whereof were such, that if he had not been a person of more than ordinary piety, wisdom and courage, he must have sunk under them. He had, with a laudable industry, been laying up a treasure of experiences, and he had now occasion to use it: indeed, nothing but an *experienced* man could have been suitable to the necessities of the people. The potent nations of the Indians, into whose country they were come, would have cut them off, if the blessing of God upon *his* conduct had not quelled them; and if his prudence, justice and moderation had not over-ruled them, they had been ruined by their own distempers. One specimen of his demeanour is to this day particularly spoken of. A company of young fellows that were newly arrived, were very unwilling to comply with the governour's order for working abroad on the publick account; and therefore on Christmas-day, when he had called upon them, they excused themselves, with a pretence that it was against their conscience to *work* such a day. The governour gave them no answer, only that he would spare them till they were better informed; but by and by he found them all at *play* in the streets sporting themselves with various diversions; whereupon commanding the instruments of their games to be taken from them, he effectually gave them to understand, *"That it was against his conscience that they should play whilst others were at work*: and that if they had any devotion to the day, they should show it at home in the exercises of religion, and not in the streets with pastime and frolicks;"* and this gentle reproof put a final stop to all such disorders for the future.

For two years together after the beginning of the colony, whereof he was now governour, the poor people had a great experiment of "man's not living by bread alone;" for when they were left all together without one morsel of bread for many months one after another, still the good providence of God relieved them, and supplied them, and this for the most part out of the *sea*. In this low condition of affairs, there was no little exercise for the prudence and patience of the governour, who chearfully bore his part in all: and, that industry might not flag, he quickly set himself to settle *propriety* among the new-planters; foreseeing that while the whole country laboured upon a common stock, the husbandry and business of the plantation could not flourish, as Plato and others long since dreamed that it would, if a *community* were established. Certainly, if the spirit which dwelt in the old puritans, had not inspired these new-planters, they had sunk under the burden of these difficulties; but our Bradford had a double portion of that spirit.

The plantation was quickly thrown into a storm that almost overwhelmed it, by the unhappy actions of a minister sent over from England by the adventurers concerned for the plantation; but by the blessing of Heaven on the conduct of the governour, they weathered out that storm. Only the adventurers hereupon breaking to pieces, threw up all their concernments with the infant-colony; whereof they gave this as one reason, "That the planters dissembled with his Majesty and their friends in their petition wherein they declared for a

church-discipline, agreeing with the French and others of the reforming churches in Europe." Whereas, 'twas now urged, that they had admitted into their communion a person who at his admission utterly renounced the Churches of England, (which person, by the way, was *that* very man who had made the complaints against them,) and therefore, though they denied the *name* of Brownists, yet they were the thing. In answer, the very words written by the governour were these:

> Whereas you tax us with dissembling about the *French discipline*, you do us wrong, for we both hold and practice the *discipline* of the French and other Reformed Churches (as they have published the same in the *Harmony of Confessions*) according to our means, in effect and substance. But whereas you would tie us up to the *French discipline* in every circumstance, you derogate from the *liberty* we have in Christ Jesus. The Apostle Paul would have none to *follow him* in any thing, but wherein he *follows* Christ; much less ought any Christian or church in the world to do it. The French may err, we may err, and other churches may err, and doubtless do in many *circumstances*. That honour therefore belongs only to the *infallible Word of God*, and *pure Testament of Christ*, to be propounded and followed as the only rule and pattern for direction herein to all churches and Christians. And it is too great arrogancy for any man or church to think that he or they have so sounded the Word of God unto the bottom, as precisely to set down the church's discipline without error in substance or circumstance, that no other without blame may digress or differ in any thing from the same. And it is not difficult to shew that the Reformed Churches differ in many *circumstances* among themselves.

By which words it appears how far he was free from that rigid spirit of separation, which broke to pieces the Separatists themselves in the Low Countries, unto the great scandal of the reforming churches. He was indeed a person of a well-tempered spirit, or else it had been scarce possible for him to have kept the affairs of Plymouth in so good a temper for thirty-seven years together; in every one of which he was chosen their governour, except the three years wherein Mr. Winslow, and the two years wherein Mr. Prince, at the choice of the people, took a turn with him.

The leader of a people in a wilderness had need to be a Moses; and if a Moses had not led the people of Plymouth Colony, when this worthy person was their governour, the people had never with so much unanimity and importunity still called him to lead them. Among many instances thereof, let this one piece of self-denial be told for a memorial of him, wheresoever this History shall be considered: The Patent of the Colony was taken in his name, running in these terms: "To William Bradford, his heirs, associates, and assigns." But when the number of the freemen was much increased, and many new townships erected, the General Court there desired of Mr. Bradford, that he would make a surrender of the same into their hands, which he willingly and presently assented unto, and confirmed it according to their desire by his hand and seal, reserving no more for himself than was his proportion, with others, by agreement. But as he found the providence of Heaven many ways recompensing his many acts of self-denial, so he gave this testimony to the faithfulness of the divine promises: "That he had forsaken friends, houses and lands for the sake of the gospel, and the Lord gave them him again." Here he prospered in his estate; and besides a worthy son which he had by a former wife, he had also two sons and a daughter by another, whom he married in this land.

He was a person for study as well as action; and hence, notwithstanding the difficulties through which he passed in his youth, he attained unto a notable skill in languages: the Dutch tongue was become almost as vernacular to him as the English; the French tongue he could also manage; the Latin and the Greek he had mastered; but the Hebrew he most of all studied, "Because," he said, "he would see with his own eyes the ancient oracles of God in their native beauty." He was also well skilled in History, in Antiquity, and in Philosophy; and for Theology he became so versed in it, that he was an irrefragable disputant against the *errors*, especially those of Anabaptism, which with trouble he saw rising in his colony; wherefore he wrote some significant things for the confutation of those errors. But the *crown* of all was his holy, prayerful, watchful, and fruitful walk with God, wherein he was very exemplary.

At length he fell into an indisposition of body, which rendered him unhealthy for a whole winter; and as the spring advanced, his health yet more declined; yet he felt himself not what he counted sick, till one day; in the night after which, the God of heaven so filled his mind with ineffable consolations, that he seemed little short of Paul, rapt up unto the unutterable entertainments of Paradise. The next morning he told his friends, "That the good Spirit of God had given him a pledge of his happiness in another world, and the first-fruits of his eternal glory;" and on the day following he died, May 9, 1657, in the 69th year of his age—lamented by all the colonies of New-England, as a common blessing and father to them all.

O miki si Similis Contingat Clausula Vitæ!

Plato's brief description of a governour, is all that I will now leave as his character, in an EPITAPH.

Νομεὺς Τροφός ἀγελής ἀνθρωπίνης

MEN are but FLOCKS: BRADFORD beheld their need,
And long did them at once both rule and feed.

RICHARD LOVELACE

1618–c. 1657

The son of a wealthy Kentish knight, Richard Lovelace was born in Woolwich, Kent, or perhaps Holland, in 1618. He attended the Charterhouse School, London, before entering Gloucester Hall, Oxford, in 1634. He was awarded an honorary M.A. in 1636, and briefly studied at Cambridge in 1637. During these years Lovelace wrote a lost comedy, *The Scholar*, in addition to numerous lyrics. Lovelace was a true courtier and an ardent Royalist. While he was fighting in the Bishops' Wars in Scotland (1639–40) Lovelace wrote a tragedy, *The Soldier*, which also has been lost.

In 1642 Lovelace was imprisoned for his presentation of the Kentish Petition before the Long Parliament. He was released and is believed to have gone to the Continent to fight with the French Army against the Spanish. He was wounded at Dunkirk in 1646 and returned to England in 1648. He was jailed upon his arrival and remained in Peterhouse prison until 1649. During this second incarceration Lovelace prepared his volume of verses *Lucasta: Epodes, Odes, Sonnets, Songs, etc.* Included in this 1649 publication were the famous poems "To Althea from Prison" and "To Lucasta on Going to Wars." Lovelace depleted his vast estates for the King's cause and is thought to have spent his last years living in poverty in Gunpowder Alley, London. He probably died in 1657. The following year his brother published a collection of Lovelace's works, *Lucasta: Posthume Poems*.

Personal

I can compare no Man so like this Colonel *Lovelace* as Sir *Philip Sidney*, of which latter it is said by one in an Epitaph made of him,

Nor is it fit that more I should acquaint,
Lest Men adore in one
A Scholar, Souldier, Lover, and a Saint.

As for their parallel, they were both of noble Parentage, Sir *Philip*'s Father being Lord Deputy of *Ireland*, and President of *Wales*; our Colonel of a Vicount's name and Family; Scholars none can deny them both: The one Celebrated his Mistress under the bright name of *Stella*, the other the Lady Regent of his Affections, under the Banner of *Lucasta*, both of them endued with transcendent Sparks of Poetick Fire, and both of them exposing their Lives to the extreamest hazard of doubtful War; both of them such Soldiers as is expressed by the Poet.

Undaunted Spirits, that encounter those
Sad dangers, we to Fancy scarce propose.

To conclude, Mr. *Lovelace's* Poems did, do, and still will live in good Esteem with all knowing true Lovers of Ingenuity.—WILLIAM WINSTANLEY, *The Lives of the Most Famous English Poets*, 1686, p. 170

Richard Lovelace, Esq.; he was a most beautifull Gentleman.

Obiit in a Cellar in Long Acre, a little before the Restauration of his Majestie. Mr. Edmund Wyld, etc., have made collections for him, and given him money. George Petty, Haberdasher, in Fleet Street, carried xxs. to him every Monday morning from Sir John Many and Charles Cotton, Esq., for many moneths, but was never repayd.

One of the handsomest men in England. He was an extraordinary handsome Man, but prowd. He wrote a Poem called *Lucasta*.—JOHN AUBREY, "Richard Lovelace," *Brief Lives*, 1669–96

Richard Lovelace . . . became a gent. commoner of Glocester hall in the beginning of the year 1634, and in that of his age 16, being then accounted the most amiable and beautiful person that ever eye beheld, a person also of innate modesty, virtue and courtly deportment, which made him then, but especially after, when he retired to the great city, much admired and adored by the female sex. In 1636, when the King and Queen were for some days entertained at Oxon, he was, at the request of a great Lady belonging to the Queen, made to the Archb. of Cant. then Chancellor of the University, actually created, among other persons of quality, Master of Arts, tho' but of two years standing; at which time his conversation being made public, and consequently his ingenuity and generous soul discovered, he became as much admired by the male, as before by the female, sex. . . .

He died in a very mean lodging in Gun-powder Alley near Shoe-lane, and was buried at the West-end of the Church of S. Bride alias Bridget in London, near to the body of his kinsman Will. Lovelace of Greys-Inn Esq; in sixteen hundred fifty and eight, having before been accounted by all those that well knew him, to have been a person well vers'd in the Greek and Lat. poets, in music whether practical or theoretical, instrumental or vocal, and in other things befitting a gentleman—ANTHONY À WOOD, *Athenae Oxonienses*, 1691–1721

Aubrey says that Lovelace's death took place in a cellar in Long Acre, and adds: "Mr. Edm. Wylde, etc., had made a collection for him and given him money." But Aubrey's authority is not valued against Wood's. He is to be read like a proper gossip, whose accounts we may pretty safely reject or believe as it suits other testimony.—LEIGH HUNT, *The Town*, 1848, p. 101

Faults and virtues, Richard Lovelace, as a man and as a writer, may be taken as an impersonation of the cavalier of the civil wars, with much to charm the reader, and still more to captivate the fair.—MARY RUSSELL MITFORD, *Recollections of a Literary Life*, 1851, p. 295

We see the gallant cavalier in the happy moods when he was true to his natural feelings, and wrote as men with any power at all always write when unfettered by a system, unprejudiced by a theory. In prison his poetry was freer than when he himself was at liberty. The fetters on his body seemed not only not to chain his mind, but to leave it more elastic and buoyant to roam in the fairy-land of love and poetry. What would have overcome less self-reliant and heroic men, and bound them down until they became equal to the degrading circumstances which oppressed them, only raised the poet and made him what men, strong and heroic men always are, superior to those circumstances—their lord and master. . . .

When in the stone walls of his cell he lifts up his voice and sings in honour of love, of constancy, of loyalty and truth, he strikes a chord so true, so national and so universal, that we cheerfully lend him our ear; willingly give ourselves up to the delight of his verse; and yield him our warmest praise. A more generous, chivalrous, and noble-hearted man than Richard Lovelace never made a prison famous, or glorified a dungeon by the power of song.—JOHN ALFRED WAGNER, *Prison Books and Their Authors*, 1861, pp. 212–13

There is no reason to suppose that Richard Lovelace, the poet of Bethersden, was ever married.

He played an active part in the stormy drama of the great English Rebellion, his natural extravagance and unswerving loyalty, at a period when loyalty was more expensive than extravagance, must have brought him at an early period into serious pecuniary difficulties, and for a part of his brief career he was probably, like his father, a soldier of fortune. When not actually in military service he was either plotting or in prison, and his romantic life closed in obscurity and wretchedness.

In the short period of his Court life he was apparently a great favourite with women; we have the assurance of Wood that he was the handsomest man of his time; and to the exterior graces of his person were united a cultivated and brilliant mind, a refined courtesy of manner, and a disposition at once gentle and heroic. Lucasta and Althea are the subjects of his amorous verses; a third, Amarantha, seems to have been another name for Lucasta, to whom we may conclude, from the evidence of the poems themselves, that he was actually betrothed. The seeds of future domestic happiness were therefore sown, and in a happier time might have borne rich fruit to the unhappy poet. As it is, there is no evidence forthcoming to contradict the story preserved by Wood, and which has been already referred to, except the fact that the posthumous poems of Richard Lovelace contain no reference to Lucasta's broken troth.— ARTHUR EDWARD WAITE, "Richard Lovelace," *Gentleman's Magazine*, Nov. 1884, p. 474

> True love's own talisman, which here
> Shakespeare and Sidney failed to teach,
> A steel-and-velvet Cavalier
> Gave to our Saxon speech:
>> Chief miracle of theme and touch
>> That upstart enviers adore:
>> *I could not love thee, dear, so much,*
>> *Loved I not Honour more.*
>
> . . .
>
> 'T was virtue's breath inflamed your lyre,
> Heroic from the heart it ran;
> Nor for the shedding of such fire
> Lives since a manlier man.
>
> And till your strophe sweet and bold
> So lovely aye, so lonely long,
> Love's self outdo, dear Lovelace! hold
> The pinnacles of song.
>
> —LOUISE IMOGEN GUINEY, "A Footnote to a Famous Lyric," *A Roadside Harp*, 1893, pp. 39–40

General

> Sir,
> Our times are much degenerate from those,
> Which your sweet Muse, which your fair fortune chose;
> And as complexions alter with the climes,
> Our wits have drawne th' infection of our times.
> That candid age no other way could tell
> To be ingenious, but by speaking well.
> Who best could prayse, had then the greatest prayse;
> 'Twas more esteem'd to give then wear the bayes.
> Modest ambition studi'd only then
> To honour not her selfe, but worthy men.
> These vertues now are banisht out of towne,
> Our Civill Wars have lost the civicke crowne.
> He highest builds, who with most art destroys,
> And against others fame his owne employs.
> I see the envious caterpillar sit
> On the faire blossome of each growing wit.
>   The ayre's already tainted with the swarms
> Of insects, which against you rise in arms.
> Word-peckers, paper-rats, book-scorpions,
> Of wit corrupted the unfashion'd sons.
> The barbed censurers begin to looke
> Like the grim Consistory on thy booke;
> And on each line cast a reforming eye
> Severer then the yong presbytery.
> Till, when in vaine they have thee all perus'd,

You shall for being faultless be accus'd.
Some reading your Lucasta will alledge
You wrong'd in her the Houses priviledge
Some that you under sequestration are,
Because you write when going to the Warre;
And one the book prohibits, because Kent
Their first Petition by the Authour sent.

But when the beauteous ladies came to know,
That their deare Lovelace was endanger'd so:
Lovelace, that thaw'd the most congealed brest,
He who lov'd best, and them defended best,
Whose hand so rudely grasps the steely brand,
Whose hand so gently melts the ladies hand,
They all in mutiny, though yet undrest,
Sally'd, and would in his defence contest.
And one, the loveliest that was yet e're seen,
Thinking that I too of the rout had been,
Mine eyes invaded with a female spight
(She knew what pain 't would be to lose that sight.)
O no, mistake not, I reply'd: for I
In your defence, or in his cause, would dy.
But he, secure of glory and of time,
Above their envy or mine aid doth clime,
Him valianst men and fairest nymphs approve,
His booke in them finds judgement, with you, love.

> —ANDREW MARVELL, "To His Noble Friend,
> Mr. Richard Lovelace, upon his Poems,"
> *Lucasta*, 1649

His pieces, which are light and easy, had been models in their way, were their simplicity but equal to their spirit: they were the offspring of gallantry and amusement, and, as such, are not to be reduced to the test of serious criticism. This we may infer from the verses signed F. Lenton, prefixed to his book:

> Thus if they *careless* draughts are call'd the best,
> What would thy lines have been, hadst thou *profess'd*
> That faculty (infus'd) of poetry?

> —HENRY HEADLEY, *Select Beauties of Ancient English Poetry*, 1787

Richard Lovelace, a truly elegant poet of the last century, who is less remembered, deserves a better fate. Kent has the honour of his birth and residence; his family were eminent there; but the accounts given of it by Hasted, in his History, are so broken, scattered, and inaccurate, that it requires some time to understand them. . . . Sir William Lovelace . . . obtained a seat at Woolwich by marrying Anne, daughter and heir of Sir William Barnes, of that place (by Dorothy, daughter of Sir Peter Manwood, of St. Stephen's, near Canterbury, son of Sir Roger, Chief Baron of the Exchequer). By her Sir William was father of Col. Richard Lovelace, the poet, of Bethersden, and of Hever, in the parish of Kingsdowne, near Wrotham (Hast. I. 287, 288). He was born in 1618, and educated at the Charter-house, and at Oxford. His polished manners, and the uncommon beauty of his person, set off by a graceful diffidence, rendered him at this time the delight of the women. And in 1636 (two years afterwards), when the King and Queen came to Oxford, being, amongst other persons of quality, created Master of Arts, he had an opportunity, by wider conversation, of displaying his genius and his heart, and became as great a favourite of the male sex as he already was of the female. From the University, he attended with great splendour the Court, and became a soldier under the Lord Goring. "After the pacification at Berwick, he retired," says Wood, "to his native country, and took possession of his estates at Lovelaceplace, in Bethersden, at Canterbury, Chart, Holden, &c. worth at least

500*l per annum*; about which time he was made choice of by the whole body of the county of Kent at an assize, to deliver the *Kentish Petition* to the House of Commons, for the restoring the King to his rights, and for settling the government, &c. For which piece of service he was committed to the Gate-house at Westminster, where he made the celebrated song, called, "Stone Walls do not a Prison make," &c. (Wood's *Ath.* II. 227). . . .

After three or four months imprisonment, he had his liberty upon bail of 40,000*l*. Not to stir out of the lines of communication without a pass from the Speaker. But during this confinement he lived beyond the income of his estate, to keep up the credit and reputation of the King's cause, by furnishing men with horses and arms, and by relieving ingenious men in want, whether scholars, musicians, or soldiers. He furnished also his two brothers, Col. Francis Lovelace and Capt. William Lovelace (afterwards slain at Carmarthen) with money for the King's cause, and his other brother, Dudley Posthumus Lovelace, he supported in Holland to study tactics and fortification in the school of war. —"CLIFFORDIENSIS," *Gentleman's Magazine*, Dec. 1791, pp. 1094–95

After the rendition of Oxford garrison in 1646, he formed a regiment for the service of the French King, was Colonel of it, and wounded at Dunkirk, and in 1648, returning to England, he was, with his brother Dudley-Posthumus, then a captain under him, committed a prisoner to Peter-house in London, and he prepared his first vol. of Poems, entituled, *Lucasta*, (consisting of Epodes, Odes, Sonnets, Songs, &c. London, 1649) for the press. . . . The volume was intituled *Lucasta*, in honour of his mistress, Lucy Sacheverel, (quasi *Lux casta*) who, however, on a strong report that Lovelace was dead of his wound at Dunkirk, soon after married. Such titles to poems were the fashion of the day . . . —"CLIFFORDIENSIS," *Gentleman's Magazine*, Feb. 1792, p. 99

In ⟨("Armantha")⟩, though too often very quaint, and sometimes even ridiculous, there is a frequent display of a very elegant and fertile fancy, and of a rhythm, in which, though they, whose ears are not thoroughly habituated to the poetical writers of those days, will be more disgusted with it, there is still no inconsiderable harmony. . . .

In preparing such elegant verses . . . for the press did Lovelace soothe himself in his confinement! After the murder of Charles I. he was set at liberty, and, according to *Wood's* words, "having by that time consumed all his estate, grew very melancholy (which brought him at length into a consumption), became very poor in body and purse, was the object of charity, went in ragged cloaths (whereas, when he was in his glory, he wore cloth of gold and silver), and mostly lodged in obscure and dirty places, more befitting the worst of beggars, and poorest of servants, &c." What an instance of the cruel necessities of the times! I have read few things more truly affecting than this picture of the degradation of the elegant mind and manners of Lovelace. Yet *Hasted* does not believe this report of his poverty, because several of his estates descended to his daughter and heir, married into the illustrious family of COKE of Norfolk. But this reason by no means invalidates the story, since the estates might be entailed, and his own life in them sold, or sequestered, and afterwards restored, &c.—"CLIFFORDIENSIS," *Gentleman's Magazine*, April 1792, pp. 320–21

Lest the history of the life and poems of Lovelace (which was continued in your Magazine for April) be totally forgot amidst a variety of other avocations, and the contest for admission of the

crowded materials of your incomparable publication, I send you the character given of him by Philips, in his *Theatrum Poetarum*, p. 160; a critick, whose opinions are of considerable value, as they are supposed to have had the sanction of his uncle Milton. "Richard Lovelace," says he, "an approved both souldier, gentleman, and lover, and a fair pretender to the title of poet; a souldier, having commanded a regiment in the late king's army; a gentleman of a Viscount's [He should have said *Baron's*—Baron Lovelace, of Hurley] name and family; a lover militant under the banner of Lucasta, the lady regent under a poetical name of his poetical endeavours; and as to the last of his qualifications, besides the acute and not unpleasant stile of his verses, a man may discern therein sometimes those sparks of poetic fire, which, had they been the main design, and not parergon, in some work of heroic argument, might happily have blazed out into the perfection of sublime poetry."
—"CLIFFORDIENSIS," *Gentleman's Magazine*, July 1792, pp. 604–5

I fear I shall tire your readers with my account of *Lovelace*; but, having begun it, I cannot let it go imperfect; and, besides, have perhaps some faint hopes that (through the channel of your publication, which is so much attended to) this elegant poet may be brought to the recollection of the Editors of the *Biographica Britannica*, from the first edition of which he seems to be unfairly excluded. A second volume of *Lucasta*, containing his posthumous poems, was published by his brother, Dudley Posthumus Lovelace in 1659, London, printed by William Godbid, for Clement Darby. . . .

I cannot say much for the judgement of this well-meaning brother, who could select from the poet's papers what appear the refuse of his Common-place book. But, in the volume published by himself, there is, though much carelessness, a poetical spirit truly elegant.—"CLIFFORDIENSIS," *Gentleman's Magazine*, No. 1792, pp. 971–72

Lovelace is chiefly known by a single song: his other poetry is much inferior; and indeed it may be generally remarked, that the flowers of our early verse, both in the Elizabethan and the subsequent age, have been well culled by good taste and a friendly spirit of selection. We must not judge of them very favorably, by the extracts of Headley or Ellis.—HENRY HAL-LAM, *Introduction to the Literature of Europe*, 1837–39, Pt. 3, Ch. 5, Par. 56

Three short pieces of Lovelace's have lived, and deserved to live: "To Lucasta from Prison," "To Lucasta on going to the Wars," and "The Grasshopper." They are graceful, airy, and nicely finished. The last especially is a charming poem, delicate in expression, and full of quaint fancy, which only in the latter half is strained to conceit. As the verses of a gentleman they are among the best, though not of a very high order as poetry. He is to be classed with the *lucky* authors who, without great powers, have written one or two pieces so facile in thought and fortunate in phrase as to be carried lightly in the memory, poems in which analysis finds little, but which are charming in their frail completeness. This faculty of hitting on the precise *lilt* of thought and measure that shall catch the universal ear and sing themselves in everybody's memory, is a rare gift. We have heard many ingenious persons try to explain the *cling* of such a poem as "The Burial of Sir John Moore," and the result of all seemed to be, that there were certain verses that were good, not because of their goodness, but because one could not forget them. They have the great merit of being portable, and we have to carry so much luggage through life, that we should be thankful for what will pack easily and take up no room.

All that Lovelace wrote beside these three poems is utterly worthless, mere chaff from the threshing of his wits. Take out the four pages on which they are printed, and we have two hundred and eighty-nine left of the sorriest stuff that ever spoiled paper. The poems are obscure, without anything in them to reward perseverance, dull without being moral, and full of conceits so far-fetched that we could wish the author no worse fate than to carry them back to where they came from. We are no enemies to what are commonly called conceits, but authors bear them, as heralds say, with a difference. And a terrible difference it is! With men like Earle, Donne, Fuller, Butler, Marvell, and even Quarles, conceit means wit; they would carve the merest cherry-stone of thought in the quaintest and delicatest fashion. But with duller and more painful writers, such as Gascoyne, Marston, Felltham, and a score of others, even with cleverer ones like Waller, Crashawe, and Suckling, where they insisted on being fine, their wit is conceit. Difficulty without success is perhaps the least tolerable kind of writing. Mere stupidity is a natural failing; we skip and pardon. But the other is Dulness in a domino, that travesties its familiar figure, and lures us only to disappoint.—JAMES RUS-SELL LOWELL, *North American Review*, July 1864, pp. 310–11

Party feeling did not blind Wither or Marvell to the genius of Lovelace. A living poet had the living fellowship of his competitors, a dead poet their praise.—HENRY MORLEY, "Introduction" to *The King and the Commons*, 1868, p. vii

It may safely be said that of all the Royalist lyrists Lovelace has been overestimated the most, as Carew has been the most neglected. The reason of this is not hard to find. Carew was a poet of great art and study, whose pieces reach a high but comparatively uniform standard, while Lovelace was an improvisatore who wrote two of the best songs in the language by accident, and whose other work is of much inferior quality. A more slovenly poet than Lovelace it would be difficult to find; his verses have reached us in the condition of unrevised proofs sent out by a careless compositor; but it is plain that not to the printer only is due the lax and irregular form of the poems. It did not always occur to Lovelace to find a rhyme, or to persist in a measure, and his ear seems to have been singularly defective. To these technical faults he added a radical tastelessness of fancy, and an excess of the tendency of all his contemporaries to dwell on the surroundings of a subject rather than on the subject itself. His verses on 'Ellinda's Glove' must have been remarkable even in an age of *concetti*. The poet commences by calling the glove a snowy farm with five tenements; he has visited there to pay his daily rents to the white mistress of the farm, who has gone into the meadows to gather flowers and hearts. He then changes his image, and calls the glove an ermine cabinet, whose alabaster lady will soon come home, since any other tenant would eject himself, by finding the rooms too narrow to contain him. The poet, therefore, leaves his rent, five kisses, at the door, observing, with another change of figure, that though the lute is too high for him, yet, like a servant, he is allowed to fiddle with the case. Such trivialities as these were brought into fashion by the wayward genius of Donne, and continued in vogue long enough to betray the youth of Dryden. In Lovelace we find the fashion in its most insipid extravagance.

Yet there are high qualities in the verses of Lovelace, though he rarely allows us to see them unalloyed. His language has an heroic ring about it; he employs fine epithets and gallant phrases, two at least of which have secured the popular ear, and become part of our common speech. 'Going to the Wars,' his best poem, contains no line or part of a line that could by any possibility be improved; 'To Althea' is less perfect, but belongs to a higher order of poetry. The first and fourth stanzas of this exquisite lyric would do honour to the most illustrious name, and form one of the treasures of our literature. It is surprising that a poet so obscure could for once be so crystalline, and that the weaver of gossamer conceits could contrive to be so tenderly sincere. The romantic circumstances under which Lovelace wrote these lines have given to them a popular charm. The imprisonment under which he was suffering was brought upon him in the unselfish performance of duty. He had been chosen by the whole body of the county of Kent to deliver the Kentish petition to the House of Commons; the result was, doubtless, what he expected, the petition being burned by the Common Hangman, and he himself, on the 30th of April, 1642, thrown into the Gatehouse Prison.

The romantic career of Lovelace must be taken into consideration when we blame the defects of his poems. He was born to wealth and station, he was generously educated, and he became a favourite with the royal family while he was but a youth. During the brief period of his prosperity he lived the life of a spoiled child. He was the handsomest man of his generation, he was addressed under the name of Adonis, and he spent his time in reading Greek poetry, in playing and singing, and in feats of arms. His manners were, we are told 'incomparably graceful.' Yet, born into that iron age, his career closed in the most tragic way. It being reported that he was killed, his betrothed married another man; and after wasting all his substance in the recklessness of despair, this darling of the Graces died in extreme want, and in a cellar. A life of only forty years spent in such vicissitudes gave little opportunity for that retirement from the world which scholarship and art require. His hasty verses were thrown off at a heat, and the genius in them is often rather a spark than a steady flame. In the curious verses entitled 'The Grasshopper,' . . . we seem to possess an instance of his hurried and jejune mode of composition. He commences by addressing the grasshopper, in lines of unusual dignity and pregnancy, but he presently forgets this, and, without any sign of transition, recommences 'Thou best of men and friends,' this time plainly addressing the friend, Charles Cotton, to whom the ode was sent. It is difficult to believe that he ever himself read over his lines, for it could not fail to occur to him, had he done so, that the same object could not be spoken to as 'Poor verdant fool' and as 'Thou best of men and friends.' But when we consider with what nonchalance the lyrical poets of the seventeenth century composed and then neglected their effusions, the surprising thing is not that these have reached us in so inaccurate and fragmentary a form, but that they have reached us at all.—EDMUND GOSSE, "Richard Lovelace," *The English Poets*, ed. Thomas Humphry Ward, 1880, Vol. 2, pp. 181–83

It is not quite true that Lovelace left nothing worth reading but the two immortal songs, "To Lucasta on going to the Wars" and "To Althea from Prison;" and it is only fair to say that the corrupt condition of his text is evidently due, at least in part, to incompetent printing and the absence of revision. "The Grasshopper" is almost worthy of the two better-known pieces, and there are others not far below it. But on the whole any one who knows those two (and who does not?) may neglect Lovelace with safety.—GEORGE SAINTSBURY, *A History of Elizabethan Literature*, 1887, pp. 375–76

As a poet Lovelace is known almost exclusively by his best lyrics. Popularly his name is more familiar than those of his contemporaries, Carew, Suckling, Randolph, and Waller, who are at most points his superiors. This is due partially, no doubt,

to the fact that his poems not being very accessible except in anthologies, few have courted disappointment by perusing his minor pieces. . . .

Whether Lovelace is a mere reckless improvisatore, or the most fastidious of the concettists, may be open to argument, but it is tolerably certain that to the majority of readers his minor lyrics will remain as poetry unintelligible. If none of his song-writing contemporaries, with the possible exception of Wither, could have surpassed the exquisite "Tell me not (sweet) I am unkind," few could have written short pieces so inelegant or so vapid as some of the *Posthume Poems*. On a surer foundation than the permananence of his poetry rests the chivalrous repute in which his life has been held. The Adonis of the court, "the handsomest man of his time," he rejected a courtier's career for the profession of arms, and his heroism, rather than his rhyme, challenged the oft-quoted comparison with Sir Philip Sidney.—THOMAS SECCOMBE, *Dictionary of National Biography*, 1893, Vol. 34, p. 171

Among cavalier poets, Lovelace would occupy a very unimportant position if he had not been the author of two lyrics which have deservedly secured a permanent place in English poetry. "To Lucasta on going to the Wars," and "To Althea from Prison," are not, it is true, his only verses of any value, but they are so much better than the rest of his poetry, that, in comparison, it may almost be neglected. . . .

Much of Lovelace's verse is almost hopelessly obscure, but it is hard to say whether this obscurity is due to overelaboration, or to want of care. The earlier editions abound in printer's errors, which it is now impossible to correct.

His two masterpieces, already referred to, are familiar to all readers of poetry. Of his other poems, the ode on *The Grasshopper*, addressed to Mr. Charles Cotton, is perhaps the best, and is not unworthy to take a place beside Cowley's exquisite effusion on the same theme.—J. HOWARD B. MASTERMAN, *The Age of Milton*, 1897, pp. 97–99

Lovelace is associated in the mind of the average reader with two poems. He was the author of that famous song "To Althea from prison," and of that almost equally famous song "To Lucasta; going to the Warres." Incidentally these verses embalm the celebrated phrases:

> Stone Walls doe not a Prison make,
> Nor I'ron bars a Cage.

and

> I could not love thee (Deare) so much,
> Lov'd I not Honour more.

These sentiments enshrine Lovelace in the public esteem; but it may be doubted if he is otherwise known. The handsome, dashing captain who bearded the Parliament with a loyal petition and was committed to the Tower, the ragged spendthrift who died prematurely at forty "in a very mean lodging in Gunpowder Alley," are not sufficiently or justly remembered. Lovelace's very name has an air of gallantry, and it is ill to recall how, according to Aubrey's version, "obiit in a cellar in Long Acre." The soldier, who was also a poet, took a wound before Dunkirk, was reported dead, and returned to find his ladylove married to another. This Lucy, who was inconstant to his memory, he idealised; she became "lux casta;" and his poems, indited from a second prison at thirty, are inscribed "Lucasta."

It is said that Lovelace is inferior in respect of melody to Herrick, of wit to Suckling, and of fancy to others of his age. Mr. Carew Hazlitt has pronounced Withers to be superior, and declared "Shall I wasting in despair" to be a finer poem than

"To Althea." But to tell the truth, it is an ungrateful task to compare these Caroline lyrists. There was an outburst of pretty song. If not so definitely as in the glorious Elizabethan days, England was still a nest of singing birds. And Lovelace fitted into his place becomingly. He had not Herrick's coarseness; he lacked also Herrick's exuberant fancy. But he had more depth in him than his contemporaries; he presented more sides. Not only Catullus was his master. Curious echoes unexpectedly ring in his verses. Would Herrick have been able to write that handsome and sustained pastoral, "Amarantha," with its vague Miltonic stirrings?

> Far hence all *Iberian* smells,
> Hot Amulets, Pomander spells;
> Fragrant Gales, cool Ay'r, the fresh,
> And naturall Odour of her Flesh,
> Proclaim her sweet from th' Wombe as Morne.
> Those colour'd things were made not borne,
> Which fixt within their narrow straits,
> Do looke like their own counterfeyts.
> So like the Provance Rose she walkt,
> Flowered with Blush, with Verdure stalkt.

Is there not something of "L'Allegro" in this? There is a tenderness underlying his sprightliest pieces which we miss in Suckling or Herrick. Recall the song to "Lucasta weeping."

> *Lucasta* wept, and still the bright
> Inamour'd God of Day,
> With his soft Handkercher of Light
> Kist the wet Pearles away.

It is artificial, it is on a conventional model; it is keyed to a sentimental standard. But it has a softness and simplicity which attract us. It must be remembered, moreover, that the fashion of that day had "standardised" the treatment of certain sentiments and emotions. You approached your mistress in a conventional manner, as had the *trouvères* some centuries before. Yet what mistress would not be approached in such lines as these?

> Like to the Sent'nel Stars, I watch all Night;
> For still the grand round of your Light,
>   And glorious Breast
>   Awake's in me an East:
> Nor will my rolling Eyes ere know a West.

He is as playful as you will, but that was exacted of him. He deals with Lucasta's gloves, her muff, her patches, in all frivolous seriousness. He begs Amarantha, "sweet and faire, Ah brade no more than shining haire." There is where you may take him on Herrick's ground, if you will, and contrast the two. Herrick desires more musically "a sweet disorder in the dresse." Lovelace asks that his lady should "dishevell her haire." But Herrick could never have done better than:

> Doe not then winde up that light
> In Ribands, and o're-cloud in Night,
>   Like the Sun in's early ray;
> But share your head and scatter day.
>   See 'tis broke!

It is prettily done, and is a pleasant conceit. And Herrick could not have written:

> From the dire Monument of thy black roome,
> Wher now that vestal flame thou dost intombe,
> As in the inmost Cell of all Earths Wombe.
>
> Sacred Lucasta like the pow'rfull ray
> Of Heavenly Truth passe this Cimmerian way,
> Whilst all the Standards of your beames display.
>
> Arise and climbe our whitest highest Hill;

> There your sad thoughts with joy and wonder fill,
> And see Seas calme as Earth, Earth as your Will

Lovelace was capable of dignified flights; he had a certain odic quality of verse, which passed into his lyrics. Saving for a little uncouthness of melody, to which he was subject, the first verse of this song is perfect.

> In mine own Monument I lye,
>   And in my Self am buried;
> Sure the quick Lightning of her Eye
>   Melted my Soul ith' Scabberd dead;
> And now like some pale ghost I walk,
> And with anothers Spirit talk.
>
> Nor can her beams a heat convey
>   That may my frozen bosome warm,
> Unless her Smiles have pow'r, as they
>   That a cross charm can countercharm;
> But this is such a pleasing pain,
> I'm loth to be alive again.

The fact is that Lovelace had really a serious mind. He was earnest in his politics, in his soldiering, in his affections; and he was compelled to write light amative verse. Nowhere do you find him breaking out into the wantonness of his contemporaries. That explains the fine note which characterises both the poems to Lucasta on going to the wars, and to Althea, which has rendered them immortal. I do not suggest for a moment that Lovelace's temperament was puritanical. On the contrary, he had the wine of life in all his arteries. But he scarcely approached life with the outlook of most of his contemporaries. One of his most striking and original poems shows this divergence. It has almost a modern note; and might suggest to some minds in a fanciful moment the sentimental cynicism of Thackeray's verse. It is one of the two poems, designated "A Loose Saraband":

> Nay, prethee, Dear, draw nigher,
>   Yet closer, nigher yet;
> Here is a double Fire,
>   A dry one and a wet:
> True lasting Heavenly Fuel
> Puts out the Vestal jewel,
> When once we twining marry
> Mad Love with wilde Canary.
>
> Off with that crowned Venice
>   'Till all the House doth flame,
> Wee'l quench it straight in Rhenish,
>   Or what we must not name:
> Milk lightning still asswageth,
> So when our fury rageth,
> As th' only means to cross it,
> Wee'l drown it in Love's posset.
>
>   . . .
>
> Now tell me, thou fair Cripple,
>   That dumb canst scarcely see
> Th' almightinesse of Tipple,
>   And th' ods 'twixt thee and thee:
> What of Elizium's missing?
> Still Drinking and still Kissing;
> Adoring plump *October*;
> Lord! what is Man and Sober?

Of course Thackeray would not have expressed such sentiments, but Byron would, and Henley has. It is a melancholy thought that Lovelace should have died so untimely and in such straits. Some of his best numbers were included in the posthumous volume which his brother published to his memory. Lovelace was a good brother, and appears to have been a

lovable man. I think he is a better poet than is generally supposed; and had he lived he might have been better still.—M. W.,

"A Literary Causerie: Richard Lovelace," *Academy*, May 20,
1905, pp. 542–43

JOHN CLEVELAND

1613–1658

John Cleveland was baptized on June 20, 1613, in Loughborough, Leicestershire, where his father
was a rural clergyman and grammar school assistant. As a boy Cleveland studied with but seems to
have been uninfluenced by the Rev. Richard Vines, who later became a prominent Presbyterian
leader. In 1627 Cleveland was admitted as a lesser pensioner at Christ's College, Cambridge,
beginning a successful academic career. As an undergraduate in 1629 he was chosen to deliver the
Latin address of welcome to the Chancellor of the University, and it was probably during this period
that he was made "Father" of the Cambridge revels. He received a B.A. in 1631 and an M.A. in
1635, and became a fellow of St. John's College and then Rhetoric Reader there in 1634 and 1635.
Cleveland was a university wit, and the only blot on his university record was his authorship of
"How the Commencement Grows New," sung at Sidney College on commencement night in 1636,
which he publicly retracted a month later. Other notable poems written during this period include
"On Princess Elizabeth," the elegies on Edward King, "A Dialogue between Two Zealots, upon the
&c. in the Oath," and "To P. Rupert" (also titled "Rupertismus").

Cleveland's sentiments were with the Royalist faction, and upon the outbreak of the Civil War
he left Parliamentarian Cambridge, joining the King's camp at Oxford in the early 1640s. There he
wrote his famous "The Rebell Scot," a stinging poetic satire on the Scots Conenanter's invasion of
England, and also *The Character of a London-Diurnall* (1644), an anti-Parliamentarian prose
pamphlet. He was appointed Judge Advocate at Newark in May 1645, a post he held until the
surrender of King Charles I in May 1646. Nothing is known about the next ten years of his life,
though it has been suggested that he may at times have been in London, working on the pro-
Royalist "mercuries," or early newspapers, that had sprung up there. In 1655 he was arrested in
Norwich on rather insubstantial charges and imprisoned at Yarmouth for some three months. His
petition for release was granted by Cromwell, and he removed to Gray's Inn in London, where he
died if an intermittent fever on April 29, 1658.

Cleveland is considered to be one of the "metaphysical poets," and his poems are packed with
allusions, puns, and extravagantly fantastical conceits; many are satirical. His work was greatly
admired during his lifetime, and more than two dozen editions were issued in the years between
1647 and 1687. These were published without his permission—a common practice among publishers in that day—and incorporated both numerous errors and revisions not made by the author,
and also a quantity of poems by other writers which were misleadingly attributed to Cleveland. In a
posthumous edition,—*Clievelandi Vindiciae*, published in 1677—two of his former pupils attempted to compile a corrected version of his works, but the canon of his poetry remains somewhat
problematical.

John Cleveland was born in this county ⟨Leicestershire⟩ at
Hinckley (where his father was vicar), and bred therein under
Mr. Richard Vines his schoolmaster. He was afterwards scholar
of Christ's, then fellow St. John's, in Cambridge; and during
the late civil wars was much conversant in the garrison of
Newark, where, as I am informed, he had the place of advocate
general.

A general artist, pure Latinist, exquisite orator, and
(which was his master-piece) eminent poet. His epithets were
pregnant with metaphors, carrying in them a difficult plainness, difficult at the hearing, plain at the considering thereof.
His lofty fancy may seem to stride from the top of one mountain to the top of another, so making to itself a constant level
and champain of continued elevations.

Such who have *Clevelandized*, endeavouring to imitate

his masculine style, could never go beyond the hermophrodite,
still betraying the weaker sex in their deficient conceits. Some
distinguish between the vein and strain of poetry, making the
former to flow with facility, the latter pressed with pains, and
forced with industry. Master Cleveland's poems do partake of
both, and are not to be the less valued by the reader, because
most studied by the writer thereof. As for his anagram "JOHN
CLEVELAND," (Heliconean Dew), the difficult trifle, I confess,
is rather well endeavoured than exactly performed. He died on
Thursday morning the 29th of April 1658, at his chamber in
Grey's Inn, from whence his body was brought to Hunsdon
House, and on Saturday, being May-day, was buried at College
Hill Church, Mr. John Pearson, his good friend, preaching his
funeral sermon. He rendered this reason why he cautiously
declined all commending of the party deceased, because such

praising of him would not be adequate to any expectation in that auditory, seeing such who knew him not, would suspect it far above, whilst such who were acquainted with him did know it much beneath, his due desert. The self-same consideration shall put a period to my pen in his present character; only this I will add, that never so eminent a poet was interred with fewer (if any remarkable) elegies upon him.

I read in an excellent author, how one Johannes Passerativus, professor of the Latin tongue in the university of Paris, being no bad poet (but morose and conceited of himself) forbade by his dying words, under an imprecation, "that his hearse should be burthened with bad funeral verses;" whereupon out of fear to offend his ghost, very few verses were made upon him. Too much the modesty and charity of Mr. Cleveland, by any such injunction to obstruct his friends expressing their affection to his memory. Be it rather imputed to the royal party, at that juncture of time generally in restraint, so that their fancies may seem in some sort to sympathise with the confining of their persons, and both in due season may be enlarged.

Of such verses as came to my hand these were not the worst, made by my good friend since deceased.

> Ye Muses, do not me deny,
> I ever was your votary;
> And tell me, seeing you do deign
> T'inspire and feed the hungry brain,
> With what choice cates, with what choice fare
> Ye Cleveland's fancy still repair?
> Fond man, say they, who dost thou question thus?
> Ask rather with what nectar he feeds us.

But I am informed, that there is a book intended by the poets of our age, in the honour of his memory, who was so eminent a member of their society.—THOMAS FULLER, *The History of the Worthies of England*, 1662

John Cleveland was a fellow of St. John's Colledge in Cambridge, where he was more taken notice of for his being an eminent Disputant, then a good Poet. Being turned out of his Fellowship for a malignant he came to Oxford, where the King's Army was, and was much caressed by them. After the King was beaten out of the field, he came to London, and retired in Grayes Inne. He, and Sam Butler, &c. of Grayes Inne, had a Clubb every night.

In my fathers time, they had a Clubb (*fustis*) at the schooldore: and when they desired leave *exeundi foras* (two went together still) they carried the Clubbe. I have heard that this was used in my time in Country-schooles before the Warres. When Monkes or Fryars goe out of their Convent, they always are licensed by couples; to be witnesses of one anothers actions or behaviour. We use now the word Clubbe for a Sodality at a Taverne or Drinking-house.—JOHN AUBREY, "Samuel Butler," *Brief Lives*, 1669–96

This year ⟨1637⟩, among several Cambridge men that were incorporated mast. of arts, must not be forgotten John Cleaveland the poet, not that it appears so in the public register, but from the relation of a certain person who was then a master of this university.—This Mr. Cleaveland, who was the vicar's son of a market-town called Hinkley in Leicestershire, was born there, and in the same town received his grammatical education under one Mr. Rich. Vines a zealous puritan; where obtaining a perfection in Lat. and Greek learning was sent to Christ's coll. in Cambridge; and in short time proving an exquisite orator and pure Latinist, was prefer'd to a fellowship of S. John's coll. in the said university; and as the delight and

ornament of that house he continued there, about nine years, and from his oratory became an eminent poet. At length upon the eruption of the civil war, he was the first champion that appeared in verse for the king's cause against the presbyterians; for which, and his signal loyalty, he was ejected thence. Whereupon retiring to Oxon, the king's head quarter, lived there for a time, and was much venerated and respected not only by the great men of the court, but by the then wits remaining among the affrighted and distressed muses, for his high panegyrics and smart satyrs. From Oxon he went to Newark upon Trent, where he was so highly valued by all, especially by the then most loyal and generous sir Rich. Willis baronet, the governor of that garrison for his majesty, that he was made judge advocate, and continued there till the surrender thereof for the use of the parliament, shewing himself a prudent judge for the king and a faithful advocate for the country. Afterwards being imprison'd at Yarmouth, where he continued in a lingring condition, and with little hopes of relief, drew up an address to Oliver Cromwell written in such towring language and so much gallant reason, that upon the perusal of, he was so much melted down with it, that he forthwith ordered his release. Afterwards he retired to London, where finding a generous Mecænas setled in Greys inn in Holborn and became much admired, if not adored, by all generous loyalists and ingenious men. He hath written (1) *Poems*. Lond. in oct. there again, with additions, 1651, oct. and several times after. (2) *Characters*. (3) *Orations*. (4) *Epistles*, &c. Several times also printed. At length an intermitting feaver seizing him, brought him to his grave in the church of St. Michael Royal, commonly called College-hill-church within the city of London, on the first day of May 1658. Soon after were published several elegies on him, particularly that entit. *Upon the most ingenious and incomparable Musophilist of his Time Mr. John Cleaveland. A living Memorial of his most devotional Brother and cordial Mourner*, printed at London on the broad side of a sheet of paper, an. 1658. 'Twas written by his brother Phil. Cleaveland, who tells us there that the said John Cleaveland died 28 Apr. 1658. I have another elegy lying by me entit. *An Elegy upon the Death of the most excellent Poet Mr. John Cleaveland*. printed also on one side of a sheet of paper, in May 1658. It was written by Francis Vaux a servitor of Queen's coll. in Oxon, of about 3 years standing, the same who printed A *Poem in Praise of Typography*; which is all I know of him, as having taken no degree in this university. "There is also printed *Clevelandi Vindiciæ, or Cleveland's genuine Poems, Orations, Epistles, &c. purged from many false and spurious ones which had usurp'd his Name, and from innumerable Errors and Corruptions in the true*, &c. Lond. (Quære, this must be a false date) 1617, oct. before which is a little account of his life, wherein 'tis said that Tho. Thurman perform'd the office of burial, and Dr. Pearson afterwards B. of Chester preached his funeral sermon."—ANTHONY À WOOD, *Fasti Oxonienses*, 1691–1721

Cleveland is commonly regarded as a mere dealer in satire and invective, and as having no higher qualities than a somewhat rude force and vehemence. His prevailing fault is a straining after vigor and concentration of expression; and few of his pieces are free from a good deal of obscurity, harshness, or other disfigurement, occasioned by this habit or tendency, working in association with an alert, ingenious, and fertile fancy, a neglect of and apparently a contempt for neatness of finish, and the turn for quaintness and quibbling characteristic of the school to which he belongs—for Cleveland must be considered as essentially one of the old wit poets. Most of his poems seem to have been thrown off in haste, and never to have been afterwards corrected or revised. There are, however, among them some that are not without vivacity and sprightliness; and others of his more solemn verses have all the dignity that might be expected from his prose letter to Cromwell.—GEORGE L. CRAIK, *A Compendious History of English Literature and of the English Language*, 1861, Vol. 2, pp. 33–36

John Cleveland, Cleavland, or Clieveland, for his name appears in various forms, was for ten years fellow and tutor at St. John's College, Cambridge, where he won for himself a high reputation for learning and wit. 'He was,' says Fuller, 'a general artist, an eminent poet. His epithets were pregnant with metaphors, carrying in them a difficult plainness, difficult at the hearing, plain at the considering thereof. His lofty fancy may seem to stride from the top of one mountain to the top of another, so making to itself a constant level and champion of continued elevation.' Cleveland distinguished himself by vehemently opposing Cromwell's election as member for Cambridge in 1640, and on the outbreak of war fled to the King at Oxford, and became the chief poetical champion of the royalist cause. His earliest and most effective satire, *The Rebel Scot*, was the cavaliers' reply to Pym's treaty with the Scots in 1643. Stray lines are familiar still:

> Had Cain been Scot, God would have changed his
>   doom,
> Nor forc'd him wander, but confin'd him home.
> Like Jews they spread, and as infection fly,
> As if the devil had ubiquity.

Or again:

> A Scot, when from the gallows-tree got loose,
> Drops into Styx and turns a Solan-goose.

The Scots' Apostasy followed in the same vein of coarse satire, and as the political struggle developed, Cleveland's 'satiric rage' fell successively on the assembly and the Parliament, the Puritan divines, and the Protector:

> Æsop's proud ass veil'd in a lion's skin
> An outward saint lin'd with a devil within . . .
> He is a counterfeited piece, that shows,
> Charles his effigies with a copper nose.
> In fine, he's one we must Protector call,
> From whom the King of Kings protect us all!

When Cleveland was imprisoned at Yarmouth in 1655, as a 'person of great ability, and so able to do the greater disservice,' Cromwell, with unusual magnanimity, answered the poet's manly and outspoken petition by giving prompt order for his release. His last years were passed in London, where royalist wits, fallen on evil days, had formed a literary club in faint imitation of the more prosperous assemblies at the 'Apollo.' Here his closest friend was Butler, whose *Hudibras* was in no slight degree modelled on the work of the older satirist. Besides his numerous satires, Cleveland wrote several fulsome panegyrics on Prince Rupert, Laud, and other leaders of the royalist party. More notable than these are his non-political verses. Though disfigured often by extravagant conceits, and not unfrequently by grossness, they are melodious and polished effusions, comparatively free from the careless disregard of metre and rhyme that spoils much of the work of Cartwright, Suckling, and other Caroline poets. Sometimes Cleveland's verse has a very modern ring:

> Mystical grammar of amorous glances,
> Feeling of pulses, the physic of love;
> Rhetorical courtings and musical dances,
> Numb'ring of kisses arithmetic prove.
> Eyes like Astronomy,

> Straight-limb'd geometry,
> In her heart's ingeny
> Our wits are sharp and keen, etc.

This is a favourable specimen of rhythmic consistency, but in such metres Cleveland is venturing on an unexplored country; he soon returns to the octosyllabic couplet, and making this an effective instrument for satire, he appears as the precursor of Dryden.—J. HOWARD B. MASTERMAN, *The Age of Milton*, 1897, pp. 139–41

CLINTON SCOLLARD
"A Forgotten Poet:
A Glance at the Life and Poetry of John Cleveland"
Dial, May 1, 1893, pp. 268–70

In the history of English Literature there is no poet, among those once held in high repute, over whose work the "mantle of forgetfulness" has fallen more completely than over that of John Cleveland. To the ordinary reader of poetry, Cleveland is wholly unknown; to the student, he is little more than a name. Yet he was one who bore a vital part in the literary, political, and social life of his age. During the Cromwellian wars he was the most popular English bard, and at the time Milton with difficulty found a publisher for *Paradise Lost*, Cleveland's poems were in eager and constant demand.

Though the perusal of Cleveland's work is likely to afford but little pleasure, there are reasons why he should not fall into utter oblivion. He was one of those men in whom lay the possibilities of more than ordinary, if not of great, achievement. The spirit of the age into which he was born was adverse to the development of his finest powers. He saw dimly,—never clearly,—that the poetic tide was setting toward wrong channels, yet he had not the force to stem it. Had kindlier influences been brought to bear upon his life, had peace instead of turmoil surrounded him in his mature years, he might have made a strong resistance to the growing flood, though he never could more than slightly have diverted it, so irresistible was its impetus.

Poetry at the beginning of the reign of Charles I. had taken on the affectations of the school of the Neapolitan, Marini, and there soon began to be a slow but sure movement toward that precision and starched stiffness of form which culminated with Pope in the next century. The license and unrestrained freedom of the Elizabethans had already come into disrepute; nature was more and more being regarded from a false and wholly perverted standpoint; the "metaphysical" had made its appearance as an element in poetics; and, on the whole, the condition of English literature bore a strong resemblance to the unsettled condition of English politics. A fondness for conceits, for far-fetched similes, was leading the poets to the maddest hyperbole. Such was the prevailing literary atmosphere when John Cleveland, having been born at Loughborough, in Leicestershire, on June 20, 1613, and schooled at Hinckley under a celebrated Presbyterian clergyman, Richard Vines, went to Cambridge, and was there admitted as a student to Christ's College in the year 1627.

The spirit of the Italian, Marini, was strong at this period both at Oxford and Cambridge, and Cleveland is said to have outdone the most devoted disciples of this school. He obtained his degree in 1631 as a member of Christ's College, but in 1634 was made a fellow of St. John's, where he passed the remaining years of his university life.

The first direct record that we have of Cleveland's active interest in national affairs is an account of his strenuous but vain attempt to prevent the election of Oliver Cromwell as member of Parliament for Cambridge. This was in 1640, and at this time Cleveland, with extraordinary foresight, is said to have prophesied the fatal events that were to follow. Oxford had honored Cleveland with the degree of Master of Arts in 1637, and thither the poet retired when the royal forces began to be unsuccessful in the eastern counties. He was received with marks of great favor, for just before this he had begun discharging the arrows of his satire which rankled like thorns in the sides of the Covenanters. It was probably while at Oxford that he composed *The Rebel Scott*, the most noted of his satirical poems.

In 1645, the poet was made Judge Advocate of the garrison at Newark under the governor, Sir Richard Willis. Here he performed his duties with much skill and diplomacy, while he continued to harass the enemies of Charles with stinging ridicule from his pen. When, in 1646, Newark, the last royal stronghold, surrendered, in accordance with the wishes of the King, Cleveland was allowed to go free. We now lose trace of him for nine years. That he lived with royalist friends during this period is probable, for he was entirely without means of support. He was not altogether idle, however, for he composed at least two elegies upon King Charles. It must have been during these years, too, and when he felt the weight of adversity and poverty, that he addressed the following lines to a patron:

> I have a suit to you that you would be
> So kind as send another *suit* to me.

We next hear of Cleveland in 1655, when he was seized and thrown into Yarmouth prison. It was while he was confined at Yarmouth that he addressed his noted petition to Cromwell,—a petition couched in direct and logical terms, and showing a fine courage and manliness. The poet's frankness and fearless spirit had its effect upon Cromwell, and he gave orders for Cleveland's release,—a most generous act on the Protector's part, be it confessed, for the man he was setting free had lampooned him without mercy.

Cleveland now found in London a benevolent patron. This worthy Mæcenas appears to have been the poet's fellow townsman, the counsellor Oneby. The sun of prosperity having again risen, Cleveland took chambers at Gray's Inn, and became a prominent member of a club of royalists to which *Hudibras* Butler is said to have belonged. Then, as the pathway of life was daily growing brighter, he was attacked by an epidemic fever, and died on the 29th of April, 1658. It is recorded that his friends gave him "a splendid funeral," and poets vied with one another in singing his praises both in English and in Latin. He was buried in the Church of St. Michael Royal, which was swept away by the deluge of fire that purged London in 1666.

It was as a satirist that Cleveland was best known and most highly esteemed during his lifetime, and it is as a satirist that he will retain what slight hold he has upon fame. Yet, as was at the outset stated, he saw possibilities in other directions. His first ventures into the realm of poesy betrayed a most extravagant species of Marinism, and this tendency to exaggerate was always one of his most marked characteristics. He was often wont to goad a simile to death. In his "Fuscara, or the Bee Errant," full as it is of single lines of great beauty, fancy runs completely mad, and so too in "The Sense's Festival." The best example of his efforts in the vein of the cavalier bards is a poem "Upon Phyllis Walking in the Morning before Sunrise." In this he shows a freshness and charm that remind one of Herrick. Here is an excerpt:

> The wingèd choristers began
> To chirp their matins, and the fan
> Of whistling winds like organs played,
> Until their voluntaries made
> The wakened earth in odors rise
> To be her morning sacrifice.
> The flowers, called from out their beds,
> Start and raise up their drowsy heads;
> And he that for their color seeks
> May see it vaulting to her cheeks,
> Where roses mix; no civil war
> Divides her York and Lancaster.

It is difficult to quote with entirety from Cleveland. He is rarely sustained, and not infrequently offends against the canons of good taste. The song entitled "On Black Eyes," however, is quite as happy as some pieces by his contemporaries to be found in anthologies of to-day.

> In faith 'tis true I am in love;
>   'Tis your black eyes have made me so;
> My resolutions they remove,
>   And former niceness overthrow.
>
> Those glowing charcoals set on fire
>   A heart that former flames did shun,
> Who, heretic unto desire,
>   Now's judged to suffer martyrdom.
>
> But, Beauty, since it is thy fate
>   At distance thus to wound so sure,
> Thy virtues I will imitate,
>   And see if distance prove a cure.
>
> Then farewell mistress, farewell love,
>   Those lately entertained desires
> Wise men can from that plague remove;
>   Farewell black eyes and farewell fires.

The most extravagant of Cleveland's poems are two entitled "For Sleep" and "Against Sleep." In these he outdoes Crashaw in the use of hyperbole. One moment sleep is "grief's antidote," "soul's charter," "bodie's writ of ease," "reason's reprieve," "life's serenest shore," "a smooth-faced death," and "the firm cement of unraveled hours": the next it is "joy's lethargy," "the sense's curfew," "night's winter," "an unexplored chaos," "the unfathomed gulf of time," and other things equally doleful.

Passing from all this folly, we find that Cleveland was probably the first English poet to make deliberate use of the dactyl and anapest,—that is, if we do not take into account the pre-Chaucerian rhymesters. Here was his opportunity of winning for himself a permanent place in literature; and had he not been turned aside by force of circumstances, those ear-catching measures that have so delighted latter-day readers and poets might have been given to the language more than a century earlier. In some of Cleveland's political pieces is heard the trip of the anapest, and also in a rollicking poem reminiscent of the poet's early Cambridge days. In a fantastic, impetuous lyric, "Mark Antony," the dactyls go madly chasing one another. In form this is the precise counterpart of Scott's famous song in the *Lady of the Lake*,—

> Row, vassals, row for the pride of the highlands.

May it not be possible that Scott, poring over an unearthed copy of Cleveland's poems (almost as little known in Scott's time as now), came upon and was fascinated by the stanza in which the whimsical poem is cast, and adopted it for his own uses?

The confusion, the spite, the bitterness of civil war, turned Cleveland's thoughts and energies towards those whom he considered the worst foes of the State,—the growing, the successful party that opposed the King. He quitted his experiments with anapests and dactyls, and began dealing strong blows with iambics. He was the first poet to champion the royal cause, and from the beginning of the conflict until the surrender of the garrison at Newark he was untiring in his spirited attacks. He made himself very repugnant to the Covenanters, for we hear him spoken of by one of that body as "that grand malignant of Cambridge." As a satirist Cleveland has much of the virility of Donne. He uses to the best advantage his powers of exaggeration, and even the tough Puritans winced under his lash of ridicule. He is at his best in *The Rebel Scott*. In this scourging fashion he begins:

> How! Providence! and yet a Scottish crew!
> Then Madam Nature wears black patches too.

In another poem he urges Prince Rupert on with vehement lines; he raises an ironical "Hue and Cry after Sir John Presbyter"; he shows burning indignation in the "King's Disguise"; and bursts forth in bitter vituperation in verses upon Cromwell.

From these satires of Cleveland Butler drew his inspiration for *Hudibras*, one of the most remarkable satirical poems in the language, neglected though it is by modern readers; while Andrew Marvell and even Dryden felt their influence.

In the character of Cleveland there is much to admire. He was steadfast in his principles when such men as Waller cringed and vacillated; he entered into the thick of the conflict with arm and pen while Cowley and Davenant fled to the French court, serving the cause far away from the actual scenes of struggle and distress. In a ponderous tome, *The History and Antiquities of Leicestershire*, compiled when an "s" still had an "f"-ish look, there is a portrait of the poet taken from a painting by the artist Fuller. The face is strong and noble, set in a frame of long waving hair. In one hand is a scroll upon which is inscribed *The Rebel Scott*, and encircling the portrait are these lines,—

> This, this is he, who, in poetic rage,
> With scorpions lashed the madness of the age.

SIR THOMAS URQUHART

1611–1660

Thomas Urquhart, the oldest son of Scottish gentry, was born in Cromarty in 1611. He entered King's College, Aberdeen, but apparently never took a degree. During the early 1630s he traveled to France, Spain, and Italy before returning home to settle financial problems with his father's estate. In 1639 Urquhart fought with the Scottish Royalists against the Covenanters at Turriff. Urquhart was later knighted for his efforts in 1641. The following year Urquhart published his *Epigrams: Divine and Moral*. He appears to have left immediately after its publication and remained on the Continent during the Civil War.

Urquhart was with Prince Charles at the battle of Worcester. His manuscripts were destroyed by Cromwell's forces and he was imprisoned in Windsor Castle. Upon his release Urquhart published his translation of the first two books of Rabelais's *Gargantua and Pantagruel* in 1653. His translation of the third book was published posthumously by P. A. Motteux in 1693. Motteux translated the remaining books in 1694. Although Urquhart perhaps is best known as a translator, he was the author of numerous other works. His survey of Scotland and its great historical figures, *The Jewel* (1652), contains an account of the Scottish scholar James Crichton. In addition to this account, titled *The Admirable Crichtoun*, Urquhart published numerous treatises with strange Greek names. *Trissotetras* (1645) deals with mathematics, while *Logopandecteision* (1653) theorizes about a universal language. In the *Pantochronochanon* (1652) Urquhart traces his own family's genealogy. Urquhart is believed to have died abroad in 1660. Legend has it that he died in a fit of laughter induced by news of the Restoration.

We believe, that the expectation of posthumous fame which commonly animates the secret breast of the author, and which the poet sometimes boldly anticipates in his verses, was never more egregiously disappointed than in the case of Sir Thomas Urquhart, of Cromartie, Knight. In the opinion of his contemporaries, he must have been accounted a remarkable man; his works possess a considerable portion of a wild and irregular talent, and, if we may be allowed to gather from his remaining writings the estimation in which he held them and himself, very different, indeed, ought to have been the treatment of posterity. . . .

His translation of Rabelais is accounted by the best judges to be the most perfect version of any author whatever—which is no mean praise, when we call to mind the obscurity, singularity, and difficulty of the original, in despite of which he has managed to transfuse the spirit of his author with undiminished force and vigour. . . .

The style of Sir Thomas is of so singular a kind, he possesses such a copious fund of sesquipedalian eloquence, and stalks along his subject with such a rapid and gigantic stride, that we can ensure our readers a certain portion of amusement, at least; and from the curious subject of one of the extracts, perhaps some share of information.—H. SOUTHERN, "Sir Thomas Urquhart's *Jewel*," *Retrospective Review*, 1822, pp. 177–79

He was unquestionably an extraordinary man. There occur in some characters anomalies so striking, that, on their first appearance, they surprise even the most practised in the study of human nature. By a careful process of analysis, however, we may arrive, in most instances, at what may be regarded as the simple elements which compose them, and see the mystery explained. But it is not thus with the character of Sir Thomas. Anomaly seems to have formed its very basis, and the more we analyse the more inexplicable it appears. It exhibits traits so opposite, and apparently so discordant, that the circumstance of their amazing contrariety renders him as decidedly an original as the Caliban of Shakspere.

His inventive powers seem to have been of a high order. The new chemical vocabulary, with all its philosophical ingenuity, is constructed on principles exactly similar to those which he divulged more than a hundred years prior to its invention, in the preface to his *Universal Language*. By what process could it be anticipated that the judgment which had enabled him to fix upon these principles, should have suffered him to urge in favour of that language the facility it afforded in the making of anagrams! . . . It is remarked of the Greek language by Monboddo—that, "were there nothing else to convince him of its being a work of philosophers and grammarians, its dual number would of itself be sufficient; for, as certainly as the principles of body are the point, the line, and the surface, the principles of number are the monad and the duad, though philosophers only are aware of the fact." His Lordship, in even this—one of the most refined of his speculations—was anticipated by Sir Thomas. He, too, regarded the duad, "not as number, but as a step towards number—as a medium between multitude and unity;" and he has therefore assigned the dual its proper place in his *Universal Language*. And is it not strikingly anomalous, that, with all this learning, he should not only have failed to detect the silly fictions of the old chroniclers, but that he himself should have attempted to impose on the world with fictions equally extravagant! We find him, at one time, seriously pleading with the English Parliament that he had a claim, as the undoubted head and representative of the family of Japhet, to be released from the Tower. We see him at another producing solid and powerful arguments to prove that a union of the two kingdoms would be productive of beneficial effects to both. When we look at his literary character in one of its phases, and see how unconsciously he lays himself open to ridicule, we wonder how a writer of such general ingenuity should be so totally devoid of that sense of the incongruous which constitutes the perception of wit. But, viewing him in another, we find that he is a person of exquisite humour, and the most successful of all the translators of Rabelais. We are struck in some of his narratives (his narrative of the death of Crichton, for instance) by a style of description so gorgeously imaginative, that it seems to partake in no slight degree of the grandeur and elevation of epic poetry. We turn over a few of the pages in which these occur, and find some of the meanest things in the language. And his moral character seems to have been equally anomalous. He would sooner have died in prison than have concealed, by a single falsehood, the respect which he entertained for the exiled Prince, at the very time when he was fabricating a thousand for the honour of his family. Must we not regard him as a kind of intellectual monster—a sort of moral centaur! His character is wonderful, not in any of its single parts, but in its incongruity as a whole. The horse is formed like other animals of the same species, and the man much like other men; but it is truly marvellous to find them united.—HUGH MILLER, *Scenes and Legends of the North of Scotland*, 1834, pp. 102–4

Sir Thomas Urquhart is one of those personages—proportionally rather numerous during the seventeenth century, and certainly more numerous then than at any other time—who seem to be characters of fiction strayed into the world of fact. That Sir Walter Scott, who must have known all about him, did not put him into one of his books is chiefly to be taken as a proof of Scott's shrewd judgment, for Urquhart was complete already as presented by himself. Indeed Sir Walter may be said

to have decomposed him: and flashes of Urquhart appear in Dugald Dalgetty, in the Baron of Bradwardine, in King James, and elsewhere. That is to say, Sir Thomas was an exaggeratedly typical example of a certain class of Scottish gentleman of his time—learned to pedantry, original to the verge of madness, proud as a peacock, brave and faithful as steel. The extracts which follow will show him better than any description in short space can do, though not so well, perhaps, as a very large number of scraps sifted and arranged from his extraordinary works. His most famous, and perhaps his best single passage is his long account of the Admirable Crichton, who seems to represent his own ideal—an account on which most subsequent writers who have depicted that half-mythical personage have drawn. . . . The shorter sketch of Dr. Seaton . . . and the introduction to one of the books of *Logopandecteision* will probably suffice to exhibit, as well as can be done, the strange jumble of his matter, the lawless freedom of his vocabulary, and the way in which any subject, even the most remote, is brought somehow or other round to the interests and fortunes of the Urquhart family in general, and to those of "C. P." in particular. It may be suspected that Urquhart, like some others whose naturally fantastic brains were superheated by those troublous times, was not entirely sane. But his learning, or at least his reading, was thoroughly genuine: the *Trissotetras* is not unworthy of a countryman and contemporary of Napier, and the *Logopandecteision* in the midst of its exuberant oddities displays acuteness enough. In language Urquhart is merely an extreme example of the deliberately extravagant quaintness which characterised his time, but it must be admitted that he is one of the most extreme, and that it would be nearly impossible to go beyond him. How far the study of Rabelais, and perhaps of other French writers of the same school encouraged his natural tendencies, and how far these tendencies inclined him to the study of Rabelais, are questions which in the absence of data it is not very profitable to discuss. But he is certainly one of our greatest translators, despite the liberties which he sometimes takes with his text.—GEORGE SAINTSBURY, "Sir Thomas Urquhart," *English Prose*, ed. Henry Craik, 1893, Vol. 2, pp. 305–6

Despite its obvious extravagance, Urquhart's *Jewel* has not only many graphic and humorous touches, but much truth of observation; while its inimitable quaintness justifies its title in the eyes of lovers of recondite literature. . . . The same year (1653) saw the appearance of Urquhart's admirable translation of the first book of Rabelais—"one of the most perfect transfusions of an author from one language into another that ever man accomplished." In point of style Urquhart was Rabelais incarnate, and in his employment of the verbal resources, whether of science and pseudo-science or slang, he almost surpassed Rabelais himself. As for his mistakes, they are truly "condoned by their magnificence." He often met the difficulty of finding the exact equivalent of a French word by emptying all the synonyms given by Cotgrave into his version; thus on one occasion a list of thirteen synonyms in Rabelais is expanded by the inventive Urquhart into thirty-six. Some of the chapters are in this way almost doubled in length. . . .

Urquhart was a Scottish euphuist, with a brain at least as fertile and inventive as that of the Marquis of Worcester (many of whose hundred projects he anticipated). His sketch of a universal language exhibits rare ingenuity, learning, and critical acumen. Hugh Miller pointed out that the modern chemical vocabulary, with all its philosophical ingenuity, is constructed on principles exactly similar to those which Urquhart divulged more than a hundred years prior to its invention in the preface to his *Universal Language*. His fantastic and eccentric diction, which accurately reflects his personality, obscures in much of his writing his learning and his alertness of intellect. Urquhart's singularities of mind and style found, however, their affinity in Rabelais, and conspired to make his translation of the great French classic a universally acknowledged "monument of literary genius."—THOMAS SECCOMBE, *Dictionary of National Biography*, 1899, Vol. 58, pp. 48–49

CHARLES WHIBLEY
From "Sir Thomas Urquhart"
New Review, July 1897, pp. 29–38

He was not new to authorship; as early as 1641, the year of his knighthood, he had dedicated a volume of Epigrams to the Marquis of Hamilton. But this slender volume gives not the slightest promise of talent. Its stanzas are indistinguished and indistinguishable. There is no reason why any one should have written them, but, on the other hand, there is no reason why any one should not. They express the usual commonplaces: the inevitableness of death and the worth of endeavour. A mildly Horatian sentiment is dressed up in the tattered rags of Shakespearianism, and the surprise is that the author, whose prose is restrained by no consideration of sound or sense, should have deemed it worth while to print so tame a collection of exercises. Four years later came *The Trissotretras: or a Most Exquisite Table for Resolving all Manner of Triangles*, in which the greatness of Urquhart is already foreshadowed. This work, "published for the benefit of those that are mathematically affected," is reputed unintelligible even to professors of mathematics, but it is prefaced by a dedication "to my deare and loving mother," and a eulogy of that "brave spark," Lord Napier of Merchiston, which are composed in the true vein. However, it was not until after defeat had stimulated invention that Urquhart came into the full and free possession of his amazing style. The Ἐκσκυβάλαυρον, *or the Discovery of a Most Exquisite Jewel*, and the *Logopandecteision, or an Introduction to the Universal Language*, have not their counterpart in any literature. Though the one serves "to frontal a vindication of the honour of Scotland," though the other was contrived "for the utilitie of all pregnant and ingenious spirits," the glorification of Sir Thomas Urquhart is the object of both. The author discusses history and theology, philosophy and politics, and all the sciences are but a cloak to his own excellencies. Sir Thomas Urquhart is a captive; the world stands idle upon its axis; the sun declines to rise and set; liberate Sir Thomas and the universe will resume its functions; darkness will usurp the light at the proper season; and the brilliance of day will succeed to the sullen obscurity of night. But in one respect his modesty conquered his ambition of notoriety, and he pretends to keep the secret of authorship inviolate. His Ἐκσκυβάλαυρον is written with the definite aim of eulogising Scotland and of restoring the great and good Sir Thomas to his own kingdom. And who wrote it? From internal evidence it is plainly disinterested, for Sir Thomas is ever belauded in the third person. As the famous pedigree, that illustrious Παντοχρονοκάνον, which gives the Knight of Cromarty Deucalion for an ancestor, was rescued from the battlefield and thereafter printed by a "surprising honest and civil officer of Colonel Pride's regiment," and prefaced by an unknown and mysterious G. P., so the vindication of Scotland and Sir Thomas might have been composed by a partial stranger. The object is frankly confessed: "He is the only man for whom the book is intended," the mere scope whereof is the furtherance of his weal and the credit of his country. Again, he describes himself as "the author whose muse I honour, and the strains of whose pen to imitate is my

greatest ambition." And then, weary of mystification, he boasts, with an engaging frankness, "that it mentioneth Sir Thomas Urquhart in the third person, which seldom is done by any author in a treatise of his own penning!"

But, in truth, it was his constant fancy to cover reality with a shield of romance, and to conceal his purpose with perpetual digression. And thus, having designed a lofty panegyric of himself and his country, he breaks off, in the *Precious Jewel*, into a brief description of his Universal Language. But he reveals no more than shall whet the public appetite, since he desires to sell his invention for the wealth and leisure which should justly be his. The secret of learning which he claims to have discovered will, says he, abridge the labour of scholars by two years out of five, a benefit which cannot be estimated at less than ten thousand pounds a year. Nor does he make appeal to the generosity of Parliament. If only the Lord Protector will restore to him the inheritance which the "cochlimatory wasps" of the Presbytery have torn from him, he is ready to devote his whole life to the cause of learning, and to the manifest embellishment of the Scottish nation. But the Lord Protector was not tempted to interfere, and Sir Thomas's language remains a vague and summary sketch.

The praise of Scotland, on the other hand, is neither summary nor vague. No literature in the world can show such another piece of boastfulness; and, despite its elaborate decoration, it is an historical treatise of enduring value. Sir Thomas himself had witnessed the supremacy of his countrymen both in the schools and in the tourney. He had seen the discomfiture of their opponents in all the capitals of Europe, and himself had carried off a dozen trophies. None, then, was better qualified to sing the praise of the ever-admired Bothwell, or to applaud the prowess of Francis Sinclair, the valiant bastard of Caithness, who conquered a gallant nobleman of High Germany in the presence of the Emperor and all his Court. But the supreme hero of all time in Urquhart's eye was Crichton, *Scotus Admirabilis*, the matchless and noble-hearted warrior, the irresistible lover, the miracle of eloquence. If Sir Thomas failed to force his Universal Language upon the world's acceptance, he invented that which was far more wonderful—the Admirable Crichton. A single episode, let drop by hazard into the *Precious Jewel*, not only conferred legitimate glory upon a renowned adventurer, but fixed for all time the type of perfection. Crichton's achievement at the Duke of Mantua's Court; the glorious victory of wit snatched from the thrice-renowned University of Paris; his brilliant appearance in a buff suit, "more like a favourite of Mars than one of the Muses," at the Louvre, where, in presence of some Princes of the Court and great ladies who came to behold his gallantry, he carried away the ring fifteen times on end, and broke as many lances as the "Saracen"—these are related in a very gust of enthusiasm, and with a breathless torrent of strange, high-sounding words. And then, to prove that bombast was not the only note upon his lyre, he describes with a veritable pathos the death of Crichton at the hands of the Prince whose Court he had freed of a monster. The amplitude of his vocabulary merely quickens the narrative and intensifies the emotion. When Crichton falls, you can but echo the frenzied lament of the Princess who, "rending her garments and tearing her hair, like one of the Graces possessed with a Fury, spoke thus:—'O villains! what have you done? You vipers of men! that have thus basely slain the valiant Crichton, the sword of his own sex and the buckler of ours, the glory of the age, and restorer of the lost honour of the Court of Mantua! O Crichton, Crichton!'"

Such is the sum of Sir Thomas Urquhart's original achievement, and the style in which his treatises are composed falls not an inch below his ingenious fancy. Like many another Scot, like Hawthornden, like Thomson, like Robert Louis Stevenson, he wrote English as a foreign tongue, which he had acquired after painful effort. You cannot read a page without being convinced that English was not to him the language of common speech, but a strange instrument, which at the touch of a master should yield a lofty sounding music. The tongue which he wrote was as remote from his native Scots as Greek or Latin, and he decorated it with a curious elaboration, which proves that he recognised the difference between literature and conversation. There is, perhaps, a touch of pedantry in his scrupulous avoidance of Scottish words. A diligent search has revealed but one—"spate"—and the avoidance is the more remarkable because he had no aversion from slang and the proverbs of the street. But the Flytings—those masterpieces of amœbean scurrility, which, doubtless, he knew well, and which encouraged his habit of stringing synonyms—exerted no more than a general influence upon him, and this influence is more noticeable in his *Rabelais* than in his original treatises. His vocabulary is vast and various; he pilfered from a dozen languages and all the sciences that he might enlarge it; nor does he ever hesitate to invent such words as are lacking to his purpose. He frankly avows his detestation of what is common or obvious. Where others would employ a paraphrase he is quick to invent so new a term as *scripturiency* or *nixurience*. "Preface" being without significance he prefers (after Mathurin Régnier) "epistle liminary," and in the use of such strange compounds as "accresce" he is ingenious as the decadents of ten years ago. Moreover, he defends his practice in a passage, which will serve as a plea for a free vocabulary:—"That which makes this disease (the paucity of words) the more incurable is that, when an exuberant spirit would to any high researched conceit adapt a peculiar word of his own coining, he is branded with incivility, if he apologise not for his boldness with a *quod ita dixerim, parcant Ciceronianæ manes, ignoscat Demosthenis genius*, and other such phrases, acknowledging his fault of making use of words never uttered by others, or at least by such as were most renowned for eloquence." And he assuredly asks no pardon from the shade of Cicero, but straightway declares that the Indians "were very temulencious symposiasts," and presently proceeds to denounce the mean as "clusterfists," or to reproach the Presbyterians with their "blinkerd minds."

His style, again, was curiously shaped by his study of science and mathematical metaphors are found on every page. Thus he describes the effect of Crichton's apparition:—"The affections of the beholders, like so many several diameters drawn from the circumference of their various intents, did all encounter in the point of his perfection." On the other hand, no artifice is too familiar, if his mood be flippant. "How now, peascods on it!" he cries when he has forgotten a name, or he will confuse a piece of new-fangled science with the slang of the minute. Moreover he has a constant care for the rhythm of his prose; he wrote with his ear as well as with his brain, and knew well how to set his periods to music. Where the poor apostle of simplicity at any price would write "back-gate," Sir Thomas prefers "some secret angiport and dark postern-door"; and the advantage both for sound and expression is on the side of Sir Thomas. Of course he is apt to forget proportion, or, in his own simile, to put such a "porch upon a cottage as better befits a cathedral." Yet he would be punctilious in his adaptation of words to thoughts. The conclusion of the *Precious Jewel*, the most complicated rhapsody in English prose, is nothing else than an apology for its simple reticence. "I might," he confesses, "have enlarged this discourse with a choice variety of phrase, and made it overflow the field of the

reader's understanding, with an inundation of greater eloquence. . . . I could have introduced, in case of obscurity, synonymal, exargastick, and palilogetick elucidations; for sweetness of phrase, antimetathetick commutations of epithets." But he quenched his ardour; he "adhibited to the embellishment of his tractate" none of these tropes or figures, because "the matter was more prevalent with him than the superficial formality of a quaint discourse." In such wise does he formulate his theory of the relation of sound to sense, and if you did not recognise the sincerity of his humour, you might believe that for once he was laughing at his reader's innocence.

Never once in all his works does he mention Rabelais, though in his astounding genealogy as in his extravagant diction, he pays him the compliment of imitation. Yet it is to his translation of Gargantua and Pantagruel the Urquhart owes his immortality, and surely no man better deserves the wreath of undying fame. His masterpiece shares the honour with our own Authorised Version of being the finest translation ever made from one language into another. The English lacks none of the abounding life and gaiety, which make the original a perpetual joy. In fact, it is not a translation at all: had Rabelais been a Briton, it is precisely in these terms that he would have written his golden book. It might have been composed afresh, as was the original, "in eating and drinking." The very spirit of Rabelais breathes again in this perfect version, which, without the dimmest appearance of effort, echoes the very rhythm of the French, and for all its ingenuity of phrase and proverb, resolutely respects the duty of interpretation. But failure was impossible from the beginning: once in the history of the world a master of language found the task for which his genius was eminently adapted. In point of style, Urquhart was Rabelais reincarnate. If Master Alcofribas handled a vocabulary of surpassing richness, Sir Thomas, the most travelled man of his age, had stored his memory with the pearls of five languages. Science and slang were the hobbies of each, and both Scot and Frenchman were as quick to find their metaphors in the gutter as to gather them after thoughtful research in the solemn treatises of the Middle Ages. But above all, in his treatment of slang Urquhart shows his supremacy. His courage was as great as his knowledge, and, bookish as he was, he must have kept his ears alert to the quick impressions of the street. The puritan who, finding not enough immorality in life to glut his censure, invests simple blameless words with the virtues and vices which they connote, has wreaked his idle fury on the dead Sir Thomas, and more than once has dragged his masterpiece into the dock. But the masterpiece remains to defy the puritan as it defies the critic, and it is no less assured of eternity than its magnificent original. To belaud its perfection is to confess its blemishes, yet its blemishes lean ever to the side of excellence. Though Urquhart crept into the very skin of Rabelais, at times the skin sits a little tightly upon him. He outdoes even Rabelais in extravagance, thereby achieving what might have seemed a plain impossibility. When the master exhausts every corner of human knowledge or of human life in a list of synonyms, Urquhart is always ready to increase the number from the limitless depths of his own research. One list of thirteen he has expanded to thirty-six; another famous chapter he has doubled in length; and yet every line bears the true impress of Rabelais. Again, at times he is apt to explain rather than to interpret; but his explanation is so rigidly within the boundaries of the original that not even the pedant can find heart to protest. And as for his mistakes, they are condoned by their magnificence, and if now and then he says what Rabelais did not, you wonder which has the better of it, the original or the version.

Like most great works, Urquhart's translation had its forerunner, and its forerunner was Randle Cotgrave's superb dictionary (here is the style and title of the first edition:—*A Dictionarie of the French and English Tongues*. Compiled by Randle Cotgrave. London. Printed by Adam Islip. Anno 1611) without which the *Rabelais* might never have been accomplished. It is the common superstition of the schools that the use of a dictionary is fatal to the acquisition of a full and free vocabulary. Yet here is Urquhart, whose eccentric vocabulary has never been surpassed, working with a dictionary at his elbow. Now, Cotgrave's "bundle of words," as his modesty styles it, contains such fagots as never before were gathered by mortal man. No wonder his French colleague declares that he had read books of kind and in every dialect; nor is it strange that, writing at the very beginning of the seventeenth century, he should have made a generous use of Rabelais. But he was one of those to whom words are living, breathing things, with colour and character of their own, and his dictionary may still be read with the rapidity and excitement of a romance. In his love of synonyms he rivalled Urquhart; like Urquhart he would never content himself with one word when twenty were available. A famous naturalist, he helped the translator at the point wherein his weakness was most palpably confessed, and the names of strange birds and beasts may easily be traced to their authentic source. Cotgrave, moreover, packs into his book—this "verball creature," and indeed it is "a creature," a living thing—all the folk-lore and superstitions of his age; and here again he was a sure guide to the footsteps of Urquhart, who followed him even in his errors. To quote a single example: "Friar John of the Funnels," is at least as celebrated as "Frère Jean des Entommeures," and you wonder where Urquhart found his false translation, until you consult the page of Cotgrave, which refers you from Entommeures to Entonnoir, which being interpreted is a funnel. And thus it is that in English Friar John takes the title, which he will never lose, not from the "cuttings" or "carvings," but from the funnels. Of Cotgrave himself we know nothing save that he dedicated his dictionary to "The Right Honourable, and my very good Lord and Maister, Sir William Cecil, Knight, Lord Burghley, and sonne and heire apparent unto the Earle of Exeter." But never in any enterprise were three masters so admirably matched as these three: Rabelais, Cotgrave, and Urquhart. And who shall say which of the three within his limits was the greatest?

Urquhart translated Rabelais, and, had they been of the same century, Rabelais would have flouted the hero who gave him a second life. For as in style Urquhart was the last of the Elizabethans, so in science he resumed the fallacies of the Middle Ages. He regarded with a childish reverence the many problems at which Rabelais laughed from the comfortable depths of his easy chair. And there is a delightful irony in the truth that this perfect translator was in his own original essays nothing else than Rabelais stripped of humour. He would discuss the interminable stupidities of the schoolmen with a grave face and ceaseless ingenuity. He had no interest in aught save the unattainable. To square the circle and perfect the Universal Language were the least of his enterprises. And so we touch the tragedy of his life. He was like the man he met at Venice: "who believed he was Sovereign of the whole Adriatic Sea, and sole owner of all the ships that came from the Levant." His madness—for it was nothing less—inspired him with the confidence that all things were possible to his genius. He was Don Quixote with a yet wilder courage. "I do promise," he says somewhere, "shortly to display before the world ware of greater value than ever from the East Indies was brought in ships to Europe"; and straightway he pictures himself another Andromeda chained to the rock of hard usage and exposed to the

merciless dragon usury, beseeching "the sovereign authority of the country, like another Perseus mounted on the winged Pegasus of respect to the weal and honour thereof, to relieve me by their power from the eminent danger of the jaws of so wild a monster." But despite his madness, he was in many respects wise beyond the wisdom of his generation. When all the world was resolute in the persecution of witches he looked upon witchcraft with a sensible scepticism worthy of Reginald Scot. He would leave all men free to speculate in theology, for, says he, every one, if he be sincere, will confess that he has his own religion. Even in his discourse upon the Universal Language there is many a generalisation, which, being set forth many years after by Lord Monboddo and others, was deemed a marvel of intelligence. In politics, above all, he was inspired to a noble patriotism. He insisted with all his eloquence upon the closer union of England and Scotland. He would have compelled the general use of the title of Great Britain, and he pleaded that Scots should find the equal privileges in London which had long since been granted them by the city of Paris. Withal his character was gay, sanguine, and honourable. So honest a gentleman was he that he would never change an opinion for the sake of profit, and he persisted in his just condemnation of the Kirk and Parliament, even when he was suing his enemies for their consideration. Of his amiability and courage there is no doubt. With characteristic candour he declared that he had never coveted the goods of any man; he had never violated the trust reposed in him; he had never given ground to the enemy before the day of Worcester. That he is surnamed Parresiastes, or Free of Speech, is his favourite boast, for he loves ever to be open-hearted and of an explicit discourse. What wonder is it, then, in the triumph of traitors and covenants, that he should have been condemned to lifelong misfortune?

He left no school, and only one imitator: the Earl of Worcester, hapless and ingenious as himself. This nobleman echoed the career of Urquhart perforce, and echoed of set purpose his language and research. He, too, met ruin in Worcester field; he, too, spent his eloquence in the hopeless demand for liberty, a favour which he too would have repaid by discoveries no less marvellous than the New Language. Freedom for him meant the discovery of the steam-engine and a revolution in the art of war, and he pleaded for freedom in the very terms used by Urquhart. He too lost his notes,[1] and the title of the treatise which he was not permitted to publish, and which he also valued at many thousands of pounds, might have been composed by the author of the *Precious Jewel*.

Thus a single generation produced two men, whose eccentric genius and unmerited misfortune gives them a place apart in the history of the world. Urquhart's misery is the more acute for the greater height of his aspiration. His life was marred by broken ambitions and made by one surpassing masterpiece. His manifold schemes of progress and of scholarship died with the brain which they inhabited. The Italian artificers and French professors whom he bade to Cromarty never obeyed his invitation; the castle, which stood upon the South Suter, was so fiercely demolished that the place of its foundation is left unmarked. The vulgar reputation of Hugh Miller has persuaded the town whereof Urquhart was sheriff to forget that it was the birthplace of a great man. But the translation of Rabelais remains, and that will only die with the death of Pantagruel himself.

Notes

1. "A Century of the Names and Scantlings of such Inventions as at present I can call to mind to have tried and perfected (my former notes being lost)," with much more to the same purpose.

THOMAS FULLER

1608–1661

Thomas Fuller was born on June 19, 1608, at Aldwincle St. Peter's, Northamptonshire, where his father served as rector. In 1621 Fuller entered Queen's College, Cambridge. His uncle, John Davenant, was president of the college and helped guide Fuller's university career. Fuller graduated with a B.A. in 1624, an M.A. in 1628, and a B.D. in 1635. His early preferments included posts at Netherbury, Salisbury, and at Broadwindsor, Dorsetshire. An excellent preacher and noted scholar, Fuller's earliest published work was a collection of verse dating from 1631, *David's Hainous Sinne*.

Fuller is best known for his histories. His *History of the Holy Warre* (1639) gives a fascinating and witty account of the Crusades. Fuller was the preacher at the Chapel Royal at Savoy from 1641 to 1643. During his tenure there he published *The Holy State and the Profane State* (1641). Forced to flee to Oxford, Fuller became chaplain to the Royalist commander, Sir Ralph Hopton. During the Civil War years Fuller wrote *Good Thoughts in Bad Times* (1645), *Good Thoughts in Worse Times* (1647), and *Andronicus, or the Unfortunate Politician* (1646), a satire directed against Cromwell. During the Commonwealth Fuller's moderate views allowed him to hold several preferments; they were, however, generally less important posts. In 1650 he published *A Pisgah-Sight of Palestine*, and in 1655 two more histories appeared, *The Church History of Britain: From the Birth of Christ to 1648* and *History of the University of Cambridge*. With the Restoration Fuller recovered his post at Savoy and became chaplain in extraordinary to the king. His final work, *The History of the Worthies of England*, was published posthumously in 1662, still unfinished. Fuller died in Covent Garden of fever on August 16, 1661. He was buried at Cranford.

Personal

I met with Dr. Tho. Fuller and took him to the Dogg, where he tells me of his last and great book that is coming out: that is, his history of all the families of England—and could tell me more of my owne then I knew myself. And also to what perfection he hath now brought the art of memory; that he did lately to four eminently great Schollars dictate together in Latin upon different Subjects of their proposing, faster then they were able to write, till they were tired.

And by the way, in discourse tells me that the best way of beginning a sentence, if a man should be out and forget his last sentence (which he never was), that then his last refuge is to begin with an *Utcunque*.—SAMUEL PEPYS, *Diary*, Jan. 22, 1660/1

Thomas Fuller, D.D., borne at Orwincle in Northamptonshire. His father was minister there, and married . . . one of the sisters of John Davenant, bishop of Sarum,—From Dr. Edward Davenant.

He was a boy of a pregnant witt, and when the bishop and his father were discoursing, he would be by and hearken, and now and then putt in, and sometimes beyond expectation, or his yeares.

He was of a middle stature; strong sett; curled haire; a very working head, in so much that, walking and meditating before dinner, he would eate-up a penny loafe, not knowing that he did it. His naturall memorie was very great, to which he had added the *art of memorie*: he would repeate to you forwards and backwards all the signes from Ludgate to Charing-crosse.

He was fellow of Sydney College in Cambridge, where he wrote his *Divine Poemes*. He was first minister of Broad Windsor in Dorset, and prebendary of the church of Sarum. He was sequestred, being a royalist, and was afterwards minister of Waltham Abbey, and preacher of the Savoy, where he died, and is buried.

He was a pleasant facetious person, and a *bonus socius*.

Scripsit *Holy Warre*; *Holy State*; *Pisgah Sight*; *England's Worthies*; severall Sermons, among others, a funerall sermon on Henry Danvers, esq., the eldest son of Sir John Danvers, (and only [son] by his second wife, Dantesey), brother to Henry earl of Danby, preached at Lavington in Wilts 1654: obiit 19⁰ Novembr.

He was minister of Waltham Crosse in Essex, and also of the Savoy in the Strand, where he dyed (and lies buryed) not long after the restauracion of his majestie.—JOHN AUBREY, "Thomas Fuller," *Brief Lives*, 1669–96

General

His writings are very facetious, and (where he is careful) judicious. His *Pisgah Sight* is the exactest; his *Holy War and State*, the wittiest; his *Church History*, the unhappiest,—written in such a time when he could not do the truth right with safety, nor wrong it with honour; and his *Worthies*, not finished at his death, the most imperfect. As for his other works, he that shall but read FULLER'S name unto them will not think them otherwise but worthy of that praise and respect which the whole nation afforded unto the author.—WILLIAM WINSTANLEY, *England's Worthies*, 1660

The writings of Fuller are usually designated by the title of quaint, and with sufficient reason; for such was his natural bias to conceits, that I doubt not upon most occasions it would have been going out of his way to have expressed himself out of them. But his wit is not always a *lumen siccum*, a dry faculty of surprising; on the contrary, his conceits are oftentimes deeply steeped in human feeling and passion. Above all, his way of telling a story, for its eager liveliness, and the perpetual running commentary of the narrator happily blended with the narration, is perhaps unequalled.—CHARLES LAMB, "Specimens from the Writings of Fuller, the Church Historian," 1811

Next to Shakspeare, I am not certain whether Thomas Fuller, beyond all other writers, does not excite in me the sense and emotion of the marvellous;—the degree in which any given faculty or combination of faculties is possessed and manifested, so far surpassing what one would have thought possible in a single mind, as to give one's admiration the flavour and quality of wonder! Wit was the stuff and substance of Fuller's intellect. It was the element, the earthen base, the material which he worked in, and this very circumstance has defrauded him of his due praise for the practical wisdom of the thoughts, for the beauty and variety of the truths, into which he shaped the stuff. Fuller was incomparably the most sensible, the least prejudiced, great man of an age that boasted a galaxy of great men. He is a very voluminous writer, and yet in all his numerous volumes on so many different subjects, it is scarcely too much to say, that you will hardly find a page in which some one sentence out of every three does not deserve to be quoted for itself—as motto or as maxim. God bless thee, dear old man! may I meet with thee!—which is tantamount to—may I go to heaven!—SAMUEL TAYLOR COLERIDGE, "Fuller's Church History" (1829), *Literary Remains*, ed. Henry Nelson Coleridge, 1836, Vol. 2, pp. 389–90

Of all forms of wit, Fuller affects that of the satirist least. Though he can be caustic, and sometimes is so, he does not often indulge the propensity; and when he does, it is without bitterness—a sly irony, a good-humoured gibe, at which even its object could hardly have helped laughing, is all he ventures upon. Perhaps there is no mental quality whatever, which so much depends on the temperament and moral habitudes of the individual, as this of wit; so much so indeed, that they will often wholly determine its character. We are inclined to think, that he who is master of any one species of wit, might make himself no mean proficient in all; and whether it shall have the quality of waspish spleen, or grave banter, or broad and laughing humour, depends far more on moral than on intellectual causes. Imagine Fuller's wit in a man of melancholic temperament, querulous disposition, sickly health, morbid sensibility, and irritable vanity—and we should have a satirist whose malignity would repel, still more than his wit would attract. As it is, we enjoy his sallies without any drawback, even when they are a little satirical; so innocent, so childlike, so free from malice, are they. He was, we know, of a joyous temperament and boundless good-nature; endowed with that happy buoyancy of spirit, which, next to religion itself, is the most precious possession of man; and which is second only to religion, in enabling us to bear with ease the trials and burdens of humanity. In Fuller, both conspired to render him habitually lighthearted. With such a temperament, added to unfeigned piety and unfeigned benevolence; with a heart open to all innocent pleasures, and purged from the 'leaven of malice and uncharitableness,' it was as natural that he should be full of mirth, as it is for the grashopper to chirp, or the bee to hum, or the birds to warble, in the spring breeze and the bright sunshine. His very physiognomy was an index to his natural character. As described by his contemporaries, he had light flaxen hair, bright, blue, and laughing eyes, a frank and open visage. Such a face was a sort of guarantee, that the wit with which he was endowed could not be employed for any purpose inconsistent with constitutional good-nature. Accordingly, never was mirth more devoid of malice than his; unseasonable and in excess it doubtless often is, but this is all that can be charged upon it. His gibes are so pleasant, so tinctured by an overflowing *bonhommie*, that we doubt whether the very subjects of them could forbear laughing in sympathy, though at their own expense. Equally assured we are, that, as he never uttered a joke on another with any malice, so he was quite ready to laugh when any joke was uttered upon himself. Never dreaming of ill-will to his neighbour, and equally unsuspicious of any towards himself, it must have been a bitter joke indeed in which he could not join. It is rarely that a professed joker relishes wit

when directed against himself; and the manner in which he receives it may usually be taken as an infallible indication of his temper. He well knows the difference between laughing at another, and being laughed at himself. Fuller was not one of that *irritabile genus*, who wonder that any should be offended at their innocent pleasantry; and yet can never find any pleasantry innocent but their own! There is a story told, which, though not true, *ought* to have been true, and which, if not denied by Fuller, would have been supposed to authenticate itself. It is said that he once 'caught a Tartar' in a certain Mr Sparrowhawk, of whom he asked, 'What was the difference between an owl and a sparrowhawk?' The reply was, that 'an owl was *fuller* in the head, and *fuller* in the face, and *fuller* all over!' We believe that if the retort had been really uttered, it would have been received by the object of it, not with that curious expression of face so common on such occasions, in which constrained mirth struggles with mortified vanity, and simulated laughter vainly strives to cover real annoyance, but with a peal of hearty gratulation. As the temperament of Fuller was most cheerful, and a pledge for the innocence of his wit, so he jested by what may be called a necessity of his nature—on all subjects, at all times, under all circumstances. Wit, in one or other of its multitudinous shapes, was sure to be the attire of his thoughts and feelings. With the kindest heart in the world, he could not recite even a calamitous story without investing it with a tinge of the ludicrous. It would seem as if a jest were the natural expression of all emotion; and that he is no more to be wondered at for mingling his condolence and his lamentations with merriment, than are other men for accompanying them with tears and sighs. An epitaph in his hand would have been a sort of epigram, not free from grotesque humour; and his ordinary pulpit discourses must, we are convinced, have often contained passages which severely tried the gravity of his audience. . . .

So exuberant is Fuller's wit, that, as his very melancholy is mirthful, so his very wisdom wears motley. But it is wisdom notwithstanding; nor are there many authors, in whom we shall find so much solid sense and practical sagacity, in spite of the grotesque disguise in which they masque themselves. Nothing can be more true than the remark . . . from Coleridge, that Fuller's wit has defrauded him of some of the praise of wisdom which is his due. There was nothing, however, of the reality, whatever there might be of the appearance of profane, or inhuman levity, in his mode of dealing with sacred or serious subjects. His was the natural expression of much hilarity conjoined with much wit. He would have been mirthful, whether he had had much wit or not; having also much wit, his mirth expressed itself in the forms most natural to him. He spoke only as he felt; and though we may think that another mode of speech would have been more proper, and better adapted to the ordinary feelings of mankind under the circumstances, we cannot consent to rank the *facetiæ* of Fuller on grave subjects, with the profane heartless witicisms of those with whom nothing is sacred, and who speak lightly because they feel lightly. His whole life, and even his whole writings, prove him to have been possessed of genuine veneration for all that is divine, and genuine sympathy with all that is human.—HENRY ROGERS, "Life and Writings of Thomas Fuller," *Edinburgh Review*, Jan. 1842, pp. 340–44

The *locus classicus* of English criticism respecting Fuller has long been, and no doubt will long be, Coleridge's marginal note, beginning "Wit was the stuff and substance of Fuller's intellect." It is not easy to speak or think too highly of the genius of Coleridge; but it is much easier to overvalue separate *obiter dicta* of his, especially *dicta* of the critical character. For he was as little given to co-ordinate and check his thoughts as to take any other sort of intellectual trouble, and the very genius which made him so often clothe those thoughts in memorable form, makes it necessary to be doubly careful in mistaking the form for the "stuff and substance." His *dictum* on Fuller, however, has so far received general acceptance from competent persons that probably few critics would refuse to bracket Fuller with Sydney Smith as the wittiest of Englishmen. . . . One of his latest editors, Dr. Jessopp, who has also made the comparison with Sydney Smith, has taken occasion, with all due apologies, to tone down, albeit carefully and without any direct antagonism or depreciation, the lofty eulogies which Coleridge and Lamb had bestowed on the author of the *Worthies of England*. It must have been an ungrateful, but was to some extent a necessary task. For excessive laudation has this drawback, that it constantly creates revulsion in readers who, not quite adjusted to the point of view, endeavour to take it at the bidding of their betters and fail. Such a result would be specially lamentable in Fuller's case, because he is, taken rightly and enjoyed rightly, one of the most delectable of English authors. But it is very likely to happen when such a reader as has just been glanced at goes from extracts and specimens, still more from critical laudations, to his complete works. His two great contemporaries and analogues, Burton and Browne, have nothing to fear from any such process; Fuller perhaps has, and it may possibly be due to a sort of feeling of this that, though he has never wanted for fervent admirers, they seem always rather to have shrunk from paying him the greatest and the most necessary, if the most trying, honour that can be paid to an author by issuing a complete edition of his works. There are many curious contradictions in Fuller's character, both personal and literary, and it is not impossible that the presence of them communicates to his personality and his literature the almost unmatched piquancy which both possess, and which have never failed to attract fit persons. A Puritan Cavalier (Dr. Jessopp calls him a Puritan, and though I should hardly go so far myself, there is no doubt that Fuller leaned far more to the extreme Protestant side than most of his comrades in loyalty), a man of the sincerest and most unaffected piety, who never could resist a joke, an early member of the exact or antiquarian school of historians, who was certainly not a very profound or wide scholar, and who constantly laid himself open to the animadversions of others by his defects in scholarship—Fuller is a most appetising bundle of contradictions. But his contradictions undoubtedly sometimes disgust; and perhaps even some almost insatiable lovers of "the humour of it" may occasionally think that he carries the humour of it too far.

It is however his positive rather than his negative side with which we have chiefly to do. From this side Fuller may be described as having had an extraordinary loyalty to and affection for his native country, which led him to acquire the mass of information laid up in his *Church History* and *Worthies*; a sincere, though not a very erudite theology; and the above-mentioned wit, which, being the ruling characteristic of his nature, showed itself at all times and in all places. Its direct and immediate effects, if not always exactly suitable to time and place, are always delightful. The memorable anthology in quintessence of Fullerisms which Charles Lamb has collected might be very largely increased, and indeed the work of Dr. Jessopp, to which reference has been made, does so increase it. But though, as has been hinted, the reading of the great mass of Fuller's work may induce a certain occasional revulsion, it may be doubted whether the full virtue of the Fullerian wit is perceptible till such reading has been undertaken. Only then can

the mild wisdom, which hardly ever fails of mildness unless the Roman Catholic Church is concerned, be fully appreciated, and the vivid wit which accompanies it be fully comprehended. The singular fertility in conjoining strange societies of thought, which has generally been considered the essence of wit, is present everywhere, and always delightful. The imagination—or fancy, rather—which supplies Fuller with these conjunctions is not poetical, as it was in his nearer contemporary, Browne; it is not erudite and all-compelling, as in the case of his somewhat older contemporary, Burton. It is a little desultory, a very little "Philistine," sometimes a little childish but it is always and everywhere delightful, and sometimes strangely stimulative and informing.

The indirect literary effects of this peculiarity of Fuller's on his style are noteworthy. For it can hardly be doubted that Fuller's essential quality of thought, the quaint and perpetual bubbling up within him of odd jests, comparisons, and what not, had a good deal to do with his comparative freedom from the besetting sin of his time—the sin of long, complicated, overweighted sentences. Although a parenthesis or an additional clause will sometimes suffice for such spirts and fireworks of jest as those in which Fuller, be the subject sacred or profane, be the form of his utterance sermon, essay, history, or what not, must needs indulge, it will not always suffice for them; and there are many reasons for putting the jest in a sentence by itself, and so leaving the most serious part of the narrative or argument ostensibly uninterrupted. However this may be, it is certain that Fuller, his quaintness excepted, is one of the least antique or obsolete of mid seventeenth-century writers. That he is one of the most agreeable and also one of the most instructive is the unanimous verdict of competent critics; and if some of those critics dwell most on their sense of pleasure, and others most on the limitations which they perceive in the giver of it, that is not a very serious difference. But it is impossible not to express regret at the absence of a really complete edition of his works. Comparatively few people may have noticed how great is the effect of diversity in mechanical presentment of books on the mind of the reader, but he must be an unusually critical mind who brings exactly the same faculties of appreciation to a seventeenth-century folio, to one of the stately quartos of the close of the eighteenth and the beginning of this, to a bookseller's octavo of the early Victorian period, and to batches of reprints of all shapes and sizes since. There ought to be a complete Fuller; and in any country but England there would long since have been one.—GEORGE SAINTSBURY, "Thomas Fuller," *English Prose*, ed. Henry Craik, 1893, Vol. 2, pp. 374–76

And among these agreeable purveyors of amusement, civilisers of that over-serious age, must not be omitted Thomas Fuller, indignant as he might have been at being classed with persons so frivolous. His activity between 1639, when he published the *Holy War*, and 1661, when he died, was prodigious. Without endorsing the extravagant praise of Coleridge, we must acknowledge that the wit of Fuller was amazing, if he produced too many examples of it in forms a little too desultory for modern taste. He was all compact of intellectual vivacity, and his active fancy helped him to a thousand images as his pen rattled along. In such writers we see the age of the journalist approaching, although as yet the newspaper, as we understand it, was not invented. Fuller would have made a superb leader-writer, and Howell an ideal special correspondent. There was little in either of them of the solemnity of the age they lived in, except the long-windedness of their sentences. In them we see English literature eager to be freed from the last fetters of the

Renaissance.—EDMUND GOSSE, *A Short History of Modern English Literature*, 1897, pp. 152–53

LESLIE STEPHEN
From "Thomas Fuller"
Cornhill Magazine, January 1872, pp. 33–41

For one reason or another Fuller has become a kind of privileged pet amongst those traders in literary curiosities whose favourite hunting-ground is amongst the great writers of the seventeenth century. He is the spoilt child of criticsm whose most audacious revolts against the respectable laws of taste have an irresistible claim. Some of their eulogies rather tax our credulity. Coleridge almost ventures the assertion that, next to Shakspeare, Fuller, beyond all other writers, "excites in him the sense and emotion of the marvellous—the degree in which any given faculty, or combination of faculties, is possessed and manifested so far surpassing what one would have thought possible in a single mind, as to give one's admiration the flavour and quality of wonder." A recent writer, labouring to give some notion of Fuller's extraordinary fertility of illustration, declares that, in this respect, Burke and Jeremy Taylor are his only rivals. The comparison, even when narrowed to this point, requires so many qualifications before it can be made to hold water that we need not consider its merits. Such analogies, to say the truth, are at best a dangerous game. Fuller is too obstinately original to allow us to find any tolerably homogeneous writer against whom he could be fairly measured. If, however, we were driven to discover some parallel, it would be better to seek in rather lower regions; the wit which detects innumerable points of unsuspected resemblance at contrast throughout earth and heaven seems to differ in essence, as well as in degree, from the splendid imaginations which lay all knowledge under contribution. The peculiarity of Fuller's illustrations is, that the two things compared are as unlike as possible, whilst precisely the reverse is true of the greatest imaginative writers. Their metaphors cast light into dark places; Fuller's, as a general rule, strike out a brilliant spark, which only flashes upon you a deceitful gleam of resemblance. With all due love of Fuller, it is easier to detect a humbler resemblance with our modern clerical humourist—Sydney Smith. Their writings, indeed, are as different as the tastes of their periods. But, if we imagine the worthy canon transported to the seventeenth century, and encouraged to give the reins to his comic fancy, we imagine that he could have rivalled his great predecessor. His popular sayings have something of the Fuller flavour. The proposal to take off his flesh and sit in his bones is a good specimen of the extravagant conceit; and, for a shrewd quibble, Fuller would have delighted in the recommendation to the Aldermen to lay their heads in order to make a wooden pavement. The wit was in both cases planted in a sound substratum of sound common sense, and in both cases united with a healthy temperament which prevented it from turning sour, and prompted innocent fun rather than bitterness. The pugnacious element indeed was developed to infinitely greater excess in Smith, and the Edinburgh Reviewer, if immersed in the civil wars, would hardly have lived out his days without some close acquaintance with the gaol and the pillory.

Not to pursue the parallel too far, it may, perhaps, be safely said that, if Fuller and Sydney Smith could have exchanged centuries, each would have adopted some of the most striking peculiarities of the other's manner. Of the two, we should say that Fuller was the most felicitously placed. The age in which he lived was prepared to fool him to the top of his bent; instead of cramping his energies by literary proprieties, it fairly threw the reins on his neck, and left him to plunge and rear and throw up his heels as he pleased. Indeed, it stimulated rather than permitted his freaks of fancy. A man with so much quicksilver in his blood would have been comic even if placed in a modern pulpit, and swathed in sevenfold respectability. But at that day no whim, however preposterous, no quibble, however childish, no allusion, however far-fetched, was forbidden to him. Wide, indeed, as was the licence granted to him, he succeeded in astonishing his contemporaries. His antagonist Heylin reproaches him for the "merry tales and scraps of trencher-jests," which would be fitter as a supplement to the *Hundred Merry Tales* than as part of a Church history. Fuller is scandalized at this charge, and declares that, if his accuser will produce "the most light and ludicrous story in all the book, he will match it with equal levities in the gravest authors extant." Though Fuller might have been hard put to it to maintain his challenge, his apparent unconsciousness of impropriety is characteristic. The most ordinary form of Fuller's wit is a singular compromise between jest and earnest. One reader might regard as said in all seriousness what would strike another as outrageously grotesque. One cannot but suspect that Fuller sometimes said good things with genuine unconsciousness of their wit, and even that some of his good things have become good since his death. The explanation is simple. The quaintness of Fuller and some of his contemporaries is a peculiar literary species, which may be described as a hybrid between pedantry and wit. The secret of much of his facetiousness is that he forces the formal phraseology of the expiring school to play strange antics for the amusement of the new. Sometimes he uses it with so grave a face that we almost take him for a genuine pedant, and sometimes with so broad a grin that he almost sinks to buffoonery. Something of the same thing may be observed at the present day. A youth fresh from the universities will, at times, ornament his conversation with strange metaphors derived from his studies. Such a youth, for example, has been heard to describe heaven as a sphere in which the holiness varies inversely as the radius. Take him seriously, and he is a pedant, or, in modern language, a prig. Credit him with a perception of his own absurdity, and we have one of the quaint formulæ in which Fuller's soul delighted. The secret here is the use of technical language in a totally inappropriate sphere, and in one shape or another Fuller performs infinite variations upon this trick. Here, for example, is a freak of language adapted for the atmosphere of the schools. David, he says, formed a practical syllogism, of which the major was a lion, the minor was a bear, and the practical conclusion that he could kill Goliah. The true scholar, he tells us, is provided with all manner of offensive and defensive weapons, as "syllogisms, long swords; enthymemes, short daggers; dilemmas, two-edged swords that cut on both sides; sorites, chain-shot; and for the defensive, distinctions, which are shields; retractions, which are targets with a pike in the midst of them, both to defend and oppose." A pleasure, which we find it hard to understand, was taken in flourishing all the instruments in this armoury. Wonderful were the word-tournaments in which our ancestors delighted. Fuller tells us of the charming entertainment provided for Queen Elizabeth on her last visit to Oxford. It was disputed, "whether it be lawful to dissemble in matters of religion?" One of the opponents, he says, "endeavoured to prove the affirmative by his own example, who then did what was lawful, and yet he dissembled in speaking against the truth—the Queen being well pleased at the wittiness of the argument." It is quite in harmony with this vein of wittiness when Fuller fills pages with such quibbles as this: "Malice is angry with him (the good judge) because she cannot be angry with him." Or, again, Fuller's outrageous puns are not unfrequently puns of pure wantonness—mere purposeless freaks of language; but they pass by imperceptible degrees into serious philological statements. *"Templum,"* he says, gravely, "quasi *tectum amplum,* a large covered space;" Minden, he declares, means *mine-thine,* because the town had two founders; "malignant" may be derived either from "malis ignis," bad fire, or *"malum-lignum,"* bad wood; bonfire, however, a word which he can seldom mention without a pun, is not, in his opinion, derived from *bone*-fire, as carrying a reference to the "burning of martyrs, first fashionable in England in the reign of King Henry IV." It was held in those days that any two words which could be tortured into any resemblance of sound and meaning were necessarily related. In other words, etymology was simply punning; and Fuller differs only from the genuine pedant in so far as he evidently rejoices in proportion to the utterly outrageous nature of the suggestion.

Punning, however, is, in this sense, merely one branch of a more general method. There are puns, if one may say so, in substance as well as in words; and these strange derivations of words bear to modern philology the same relation that such allegories as Bacon expounded in his book on the wisdom of the ancients bear to the new science of comparative mythology. Any meaning which can be twisted out of words or out of ancient legends, when put on the rack of a boundless ingenuity, is assumed to be the explanation of their origin. Take any text in the Bible, for example, without the slightest regard to its history or its position, and assume that it is not only true, but that any inference drawn from it, or any symbolical meaning that can be fitted to it is equally certain, and you have a boundless field for ingenuity. Every sermon and treatise of those days teems with ingenious applications which may remind us of the celebrated argument of the "angelical doctor" who deduced the necessity of implicit faith from the words "the oxen were ploughing and the oxen feeding beside them." It is here, above all, that Fuller finds the widest field for the exercise of his marvellous faculty of discovering unsuspected analogies. Even his ingenuity could scarcely surpass the performances of many grave divines. He quotes, for example, as an authority against toleration, the text, "Thou shalt not plough with an ox and an ass." His own meditations are full of such remarks as this: "Can one commit one sin more, and but one sin more? Unclean creatures went by couples into the ark." He is far too much pleased with this quaint parallel to care for the utter irrelevancy of the remark. Rather, the irrelevancy is the reason why he loves it. He gives his theory in an anecdote of a certain preacher, whom he much commends for extracting all manner of fruitful lessons from this rather unpromising text: "Am not I thine ass, upon which thou hast ridden ever since I was thine unto this day?" "How fruitful," he exclaims, "are the seeming barren places of Scripture!" or, indeed, of any other work, if only you are permitted to deduce from it any conclusion which the most fertile imagination can hang on to it by means of the most arbitrary associations.

The peculiarity, then, of Fuller, is not that he makes far-fetched quotations, or that his logical gambols are of the most unaccountable nature. So far he is merely adopting a recognized method in which half the preachers and writers of his time might be his rivals. His merit is that his most fantastic caprices are always witty. Nothing is more wearisome than this incessant straining of the invention in the hands of an essentially dull writer; the jokes of such a man are always missing fire. Fuller's instinct is infallible; he touches his queer fancies

so lightly that you are never disgusted; if for a moment he seems to be serious, he is instantly off upon some outrageous conceit which would extort laughter from a bishop at a funeral. The same love of strange conceits was equally prevalent amongst the poets whom Dr. Johnson chose to call the metaphysical school, probably because the doctor held—with what justice need not be inquired—that metaphysics is merely a name for verbal juggling. In poetry the effect is simply vexatious. The warmest admirers of George Herbert—who is now probably the best known poet of the school—have been profoundly annoyed when he descends from his loftier strain to the wretched quibbles which mar it so cruelly—when he devotes a poem to a wretched, if not profane, pun about "I ease you," and crams into fourteen lines more than a score of quaint similitudes for prayer, each more far-fetched than its predecessor; or when he spoils a fine stanza by its last two lines after this fashion:—

> For us the winds do blow,
> The earth doth rest, heaven move and water flow;
>   Nothing we see but means our good
>   As our delight or as our measure;
>   *The whole is either our cupboard of food,*
>   Or *cabinet of pleasure.*

In Fuller's lively prose, the quaintness would be an additional charm: in Herbert's solemn devotion it is the fly in the pot of ointment. Or take one of Cowley's often-quoted absurdities. "I saw," he says in the *Davideis*—

> I saw him fling the stone as if he meant
> At once his murder and his monument.

This, as a bit of serious eloquence, is hopelessly absurd; but it is one of Fuller's pet jokes, and his variations are always amusing; as where he speaks of "Aphek, whose walls falling down, gave both death and gravestones to 27,000 of Benhadad's soldiers;" or, to quote a rather similar grotesque, observes of the amiable habit of Elizabethan sailors, who threw negroes into the sea, "the murder is not so soon drowned as the men." The good captain, he adds, "counts the image of God as nevertheless his image cut in ebony as if done in ivory." . . .

It is comparatively rare . . . for Fuller to rise to the borders of that lofty region of eloquence where Sir Thomas Browne treads like a native. In fact, he is little given to soaring, and distinctly prefers the earth to the clouds; his wisdom is such as comes from excellent good sense, without any great profundity of thought; his piety is that of a cheerful and admirably expressive person who has never sounded the depths of despair or risen to ecstatic rapture; and his wit owes its charm to its being obviously the spontaneous outburst of a nature of irrepressible buoyancy and childlike frivolity of amusement. Whatever emotion is excited in his breast, it seems to stir him to the same outward expression: any fuel will support his flame; if in a merry mood, he jests to express, and if solemn, he jests, as we must suppose, to hide them. Answering an assailant, in a passage full of real feeling, he indulges himself with this outrageous pun. "As for other stains and spots in my soul, I hope (be it spoken without the least verbal reflection) that He who is the Fuller's soap (Malachi iii. 2) will scour them forth with His merit." It is amusing to see Fuller's compunction constraining him to call attention to his pun by disavowing it. On the same principle, he is careful to tell us that we ought not to indulge in such unreasonable jokes as that of a dying man who was asked by the priest preparing to administer extreme unction, where were his feet, and replied "at the end of my legs." We are quite sure, notwithstanding, that Fuller himself, when *in extremis,* would have been unable to resist such a quibble. One other specimen of this rather questionable tendency may be enough. When Drake's ships were in great danger Fuller tells us that the crews received the Holy Communion, "dining on Christ in the sacrament, expecting no other than to sup with him in heaven." This illustrates the further peculiarity that Fuller's wit runs riot whenever he has a tragedy to relate. A perfect shower of puns, quibbles, absurd analogies, and quaint quotations is his mode of testifying sympathy, as well as every other passion. He laments, for example, the hard fate of Ridley and Hooper; but he is unable to refrain from noticing the odd result that, as their legs were burnt before their bodies, "their upper parts were but confessors, whilst their lower parts were martyrs." Even when describing the massacre of the babes at Bethlehem, a certain sense of the ludicrous blends with his pathos. "One mother," he says, "stood amazed, as if she had lost her son and senses together; another bleeds out sorrow in her eyes to prevent festering in her heart;" and yet, as he concludes, "their mourning going several ways, all must meet in one common misery, whilst the souls of these children are charitably conceived by the primitive Church all marched to heaven, as the *infantry of the noble army of martyrs.*" Perhaps the most grotesque of all these queer outbreaks is in Fuller's account of an accident which happened to a Roman Catholic congregation at Blackfriars in 1623. The sermon, he says, "began to incline to the middle, the day to the end thereof, when, on a sudden, the floor fell down whereon they were assembled. It gave no charitable warning groan beforehand, but cracked, brake, and fell, all in an instant. Many were killed, more bruised, all frighted. Sad sight to behold, the flesh and blood of different persons mingled together, and the brains of one on the head of another! One lacked a leg, another an arm; a third nothing but breath, stifled in the ruins." Impute not this comic vein, as Fuller would put it, to want of kindliness, or even to want of sympathy with Roman Catholics, irresistibly ludicrous as the circumstances appeared to him, and tempting as was the coincidence suggested by the occurrence of the accident on the 5th of November. Fuller cites the Tower of Siloam, and says that the death of these sufferers was "the object of pity" (though also, it would seem, of no little amusement) to all wise and good persons; and, indeed—to pause for one moment in my remarks—I could find it in my heart to commend Fuller's style to the attentive consideration of those masters of descriptive language in whose mouths a man is always an individual and fire a devouring element. How much more lively would have been the descriptions of the burning of Chicago, or the fighting in Paris, if our sense of propriety were a little less exacting! The narratives, treated in Fuller's style, would have bristled with Scriptural quotations—for the most part utterly inappropriate—and with puns, good only by reason of their inconceivable badness. Strange parallels and contrasts would have been drawn between the fate of Chicago and of Sodom and Gomorrah; and the sieges of Paris and Jerusalem would prove to have had unsuspected points of resemblance. Even the fate of the sufferers would have afforded matter for quibbling, if not for

downright fun. The difficulty of choosing between roasting and boiling would have suggested absurd comments in the case of Chicago, and the terrors of Paris would have been carefully paralleled with the Massacre of the Innocents. Alas! we have lost the *naïveté* which excuses such eccentricities; we cannot laugh without being cynical; and, though I have seen very amiable people fairly upset in private by the comic aspect of a murder or a bad accident, it is perfectly clear that no living writer could convince us of the warmth of his sympathies at the very time that he was playing the queerest of literary pranks. In his reflections Fuller tells us of an ape which carried a child to the top of a house, much to the horror of the family watching from below, till the ape, tired out with his tricks, laid the child gently back in the cradle. In Fuller's allegory, the child represents true religion, and the ape the wild fanaticism of his time. We might allegorize the same story by putting Fuller's wit for the ape, and his genuine kindliness for the child. We, the lookers-on, are always trembling; but this wit never changes playfulness for spite.

The same unmistakable peculiarities run through all Fuller's writings. Each page, as it were, bears his signature. They may be divided roughly into the antiquarian and the didactic. The *Church History* and the *Worthies*—his chief performances in the first department—are interesting (for our present purpose) chiefly as displaying the art in which Charles Lamb declares him to be unrivalled—that of telling a story. His "eager liveliness, and the perpetual running comment of the narrator, happily blended with the narration," are doubtless delightful. Perhaps it should be added that the anecdote must be a short one. Adopting Gray's comparison of a grand poetical style to the flight of an eagle, we must compare Fuller's to the pretty though rapid flight of some small bird. Or—for quaint illustrations are surely lawful in such a case—he reminds us of that amiable creature, the ratel, in the Zoological Gardens, who, with untiring regularity, used to take half-a-dozen lively steps at a round trot and then throw a somersault. Fuller cuts up his so-called history into short anecdotes, and in each of them generally springs two or three jokes upon us, which explode as unexpectedly as a cracker in a drawing-room. For example, he gives a short notice of an English pope, Adrian IV., in the *Worthies.* He gets through it with the seriousness of a steady-going antiquarian—excepting of course a pun or two—till he reaches the poor pope's death. Then we have this genuine bit of humour. Adrian "held his place four years, eight months, and twenty-eight days, and Anno 1158, as he was drinking, was choaked with a fly, which *in the large territory of St. Peter's patrimony had no place but his throat to get into.* But since a fly stopt his breath, fear shall stop my breath, not to make uncharitable conclusions from such casualties." The *Worthies* reminds us of a pithy biographical dictionary, where some humourist has illustrated every article by a quaint caricature; when to these anecdotes we add his queer collection of proverbs, his odd description of the various counties, and the miscellaneous bits of information that crop up at intervals, the *Worthies* is perhaps one of his most amusing books.

KATHERINE PHILIPS

1631–1664

Katherine Philips was born on January 1, 1631, in London. The daughter of a wealthy London merchant, John Fowler, Philips's early education consisted of lessons given to her by a cousin, Mrs. Blacket. At age eight she was sent to the then fashionable boarding school at Hackney. In 1647 she married James Philips of Cardigan and thereafter divided her time between London and Wales.

Philips was probably the first English woman poet to have her works published. She used the pseudonym Orinda, which her friends expanded to "the matchless Orinda." She was in a literary circle that included Vaughan, Cowley, and Jeremy Taylor. Her earliest verses were prefixed to Henry Vaughan's *Poems* (1651). In 1663 she traveled to Ireland where her translation of Corneille's *Pompée* was staged at the Smock-Alley Theatre. Her first play was so successful that she undertook a translation of a second Corneille play, *Horace*. She never finished her translation. In 1664 an unauthorized version of her poetry was published. Shortly thereafter Philips died of smallpox on June 22, 1664. She was buried in the Church of St. Benet Sherehog, London. A collection of her verses was published in 1667 under the supervision of her friend Sir Charles Cotterel. In 1705 *Letters of Orinda to Poliarchus* (a pseudonym for Cotterel) was published.

We allow'd You Beauty, and we did submit
    To all the Tyrannies of it;
Ah! Cruel Sex, will you depose us too in Wit?
    Orinda do's in that too raign,
Do's Man behind her in Proud Triumph draw,
And Cancel great Apollo's Salick Law.
    We our old Title plead in vain,
Man may be Head, but Woman's now the Brain.
    Verse was Love's fire-arms heretofore,
    In Beautie's Camp it was not known,
Too many Armes besides that Conquerour bore:
    'Twas the great Canon we brought down
    T''assault a stubborn Town;
Orinda first did a bold sally make,
    Our strongest Quarter take,
    And so successful prov'd, that she
Turn'd upon Love himself his own Artillery.
Women as if the Body were their Whole,
    Did that, and not the Soul
    Transmit to their Posterity;
    If in it sometime they conceiv'd,
    Th' abortive Issue never liv'd.
'Twere Shame and pitty, Orinda, if in thee
A Spirit so rich, so noble, and so high
    Should unmanur'd, or barren lye.
But thou industriously hast sow'd and till'd
    The fair, and fruitful field;
And 'tis a strange Increase, that it does yield.
    As when the happy Gods above
    Meet altogether at a feast,
    A secret Joy unspeakably does move,
In their great Mother Cybele's contented breast:
    With no less pleasure thou methinks shouldst see,
    This thy no less Immortal Progenie.
    And in their Birth thou no one touch dost find
    Of th' ancient Curse to Woman-kind;
    Thou bring'st not forth with pain;
It neither Travel is, nor Labour of the brain,
    So easily they from thee come,
    And there is so much room
In th' exhausted and unfathom'd Womb;
That like the Holland Countess thou may'st bear
A Child for ev'ry Day of all the fertil Year.
    Thou dost my wonder, would'st my envy raise,

If to be prais'd I lov'd more than to praise;
    Where-e'er I see an excellence,
I must admire to see thy well-knit sense,
Thy numbers gentle, and thy Fancies high:
Those as thy fore-head smooth, these sparkling as
    thine eye.
    'Tis solid, and 'tis manly all,
    Or rather 'tis Angelical;
    For as in Angels, we
    Do in thy Verses see
    Both improv'd Sexes eminently meet;
They are than Man more strong, and more than
    Woman sweet.

    They talk of Nine, I know not who,
Female Chimera's that o'er Poets reign,
    I ne'r could find that fancy true,
But have invok'd them oft I'm sure in vain:
They talk of Sappho, but alass, the shame!
Ill manners soil the lustre of her Fame:
Orinda's inward virtue is so bright,
That like a Lanthorn's fair-inclosed Light,
It through the paper shines where she does write.
Honour and Friendship, and the Generous scorn
    Of things, for which we were not born,
(Things that can only by a fond Disease,
Like that of Girles, our vicious Stomachs please)
Are the instructive Subjects of her pen,
    And as the Roman Victory
Taught our rude Land, Arts and Civility,
At once she overcomes, enslaves, and betters Men.

But Rome, with all her Arts, could ne're inspire,
    A Female Breast with such a Fire.
    The warlike Amazonian train,
Who in Elysium now do peacefull reign,
And wit's mild Empire before Arms prefer,
Hope 'twill be setled in their sex by her.
Merlin the Seer, (and sure he would not ly,
    In such a sacred Company,)
    Does Prophecies of Learn'd Orinda show,
Which he had darkly spoke so long ago.
Ev'n Boadicia's angry Ghost,
    Forgets her own misfortune, and disgrace,
    And to her injur'd Daughters now does boast,

That Rome's o'recome at last, by a woman of her
  Race.
    —ABRAHAM COWLEY, "On *Orinda's* Poems,"
    1663

She was very religiously devoted when she was young; prayed
by herself an hower together, and tooke Sermons verbatim
when she was but 10 yeares old. (At the age of nine yeares,
Thomas Randolph wrot the History of our Saviour's Incarnation in English verse, which his brother John haz to shew
under his owne handwriting—never printed, kept as a Raritie.)

She was when a Child much against the Bishops, and
prayd to God to take them to him, but afterwards was reconciled to them. Prayed aloud, as the hypocriticall fashion then
was, and was overheared.

From her cosen Blacket, who lived with her from her
swadling cloutes to eight, and taught her to read:—when a
child she was mighty apt to learne, and she assures me that she
had read the Bible thorough before she was full four yeares old;
she could have sayd I know not how many places of Scripture
and chapters. She was a frequent Hearer of Sermons; had an
excellent Memory and could have brought away a sermon in
her memory. Very good-natured; not at all high-minded; pretty
fatt; not tall; read pumpled face; wrote out Verses in Innes, or
Mottos in windowes, in her table-booke.

Mr. J. Oxenbridge, her uncle, is now Prisoner in the Fleet
on her account for a Dept of her husband, bound for him 28
yeares since.—JOHN AUBREY, "Katherine Philips," *Brief Lives,*
1669–96

   soft Orinda, whose bright shining Name
Stands next great Sappho's in the Ranks of Fame.
    —JOHN OLDHAM, "A Pastoral on the Death of
    the Earl of Rochester," 1681

A Lady of that admirable Merit, and Reputation, that her
Memory will be honour'd of all Men, that are Favourers of
Poetry. One, who not only has equall'd all that is reported of
the Poetesses of Antiquity, the *Lesbian Sapho*, and the Roman
Sulpitia, but whose Merit has justly found her Admirers,
amongst the greatest Poets of our Age: and though I will not
presume to compare our Poets with *Martial*, who writ in praise
of *Sulpitia*, or *Horace*, *Ausonius*, and *Sydonius*, who commended *Sapho*, least I offend their Modesty who are still living:
yet I will be so far bold as to assert, that the Earls of *Orrery*, and
Roscommon, the Incomparable *Cowley*, and the Ingenious
Flatman, with others (amongst whom I must not forget my
much respected Countryman *James Tyrrel* Esq;) would not
have employ'd their Pens in praise of the Excellent *Orinda*,
had she not justly deserv'd their Elogies, and possibly more
than those Ladies of Antiquity. . . .

The Occasion of our mention of this Excellent Person in
this place, is on the Account of two Dramatick Pieces, which
she has translated from the *French* of Monsieur *Corneille*; and
that with such exquisite Art and Judgment, that the Copies of
each seem to transcend the Original.

Horace, a Tragedy; which I suppose was left imperfect by
the untimely Death of the Authress; and the fifth Act was
afterwards supply'd by Sir *John Denham*. This Play was acted at
Court, by Persons of Quality; the Duke of *Monmouth* speaking
the Prologue. . . .

Pompey, a Tragedy, which I have seen acted with great
applause, at the Duke's Theatre; and at the End was acted that
Farce printed in the fifth Act of *The Play-house to be Let*. This
Play was translated at the Request of the Earl of *Orrery*, and

published in Obedience to the Commands of the Right Honourable the Countess of *Corse*; to whom it is dedicated. . . .

Both these Plays with the rest of her Poems, are printed in
one Volume in Fol. *Lond.* 1678. This Lady to the Regret of all
the *Beau Monde* in general, died of the *Smallpox*, on the 22ᵈ.
of *June* 1664. being but One and Thirty Years of Age, having
not left any of her Sex, her Equal in *Poetry*.—GERARD LANG-
BAINE, *An Account of the English Dramatick Poets*, 1691

She was author of several poems, which are more to be admired for propriety and beauty of thought, than for harmony of
versification, in which she was generally deficient.—JAMES
GRANGER, *Biographical History of England*, 1769–1824

The world, and especially our England, has, within the last
thirty years been vexed and teazed by a set of Devils, whom I
detest so much that I almost hunger after an acherontic promotion to a Torturer, purposely for their accommodation. These
Devils are a set of Women, who having taken a snack or
Luncheon of Literary scraps, set themselves up for towers of
Babel in Languages Sapphos in Poetry—Euclids in Geometry—and everything in nothing. Among such the name of
Montague has been preeminent. The thing has made a very
uncomfortable impression on me.—I had longed for some real
feminine Modesty in these things, and was therefore gladdened
in the extreme on opening the other day one of Bayley's
Books—a Book of Poetry written by one beautiful Mʳˢ Philips,
a friend of Jeremy Taylor's, and called "the matchless Orinda"—You must have heard of her, and most likely read her
Poetry—I wish you have not, that I may have the pleasure of
treating you with a few stanzas—I do it at a venture. . . .

In other of her Poems there is a most delicate fancy of the
Fletcher kind.—JOHN KEATS, Letter to John Hamilton Reynolds (Sept. 21, 1817)

Some of the verses of Katherine Phillips, . . . have an easy
though antithetical style, like the lighter ones of Cowley, or the
verses of Sheffield and his French contemporaries.—LEIGH
HUNT, "Specimens of British Poetesses," *Men, Women, and
Books*, 1847

It was not until the second half of the seventeenth century that
women began to be considered competent to undertake literature as a profession. In the crowded galaxy of Elizabethan and
Jacobean poets there is no female star even of the seventh
magnitude. But with the Restoration, the wives and daughters,
who had learned during the years of exile to act in political and
diplomatic intrigue with independence and skill, took upon
themselves to write independently too, and the last forty years
of the century are crowded with the names of "celebrated scribbling women." Among all these the Matchless Orinda takes the
foremost place—not exactly by merit, for Aphra Behn surpassed her in genius, Margaret, Duchess of Newcastle, in versatility, and Catherine Trotter in professional zeal; but by the
moral eminence which she attained through her elevated public career, and which she sealed by her tragical death. When
the seventeenth century thought of a poetess, it naturally
thought of Orinda; her figure overtopped those of her literary
sisters; she was more dignified, more regal in her attitude to the
public, than they were; and, in fine, she presents us with the
best type we possess of the woman of letters in the seventeenth
century.

. . . I suppose she may fairly be considered as dead to the
British public. If I venture to revive her here, it is not that I
greatly admire her verses, or consider her in the true sense to
have been a poet, for even the praise from Keats seems to me
exaggerated; but it is because of the personal charm of her

character, the interest of her career, and its importance as a chapter in the literary history of the Restoration. Nor was she, like so many of her contemporaries, an absurd, or preposterous, or unclean writer: her muse was uniformly pure and reasonable; her influence, which was very great, was exercised wholly in favour of what was beautiful and good; and if she failed, it is rather by the same accident by which so many poets of less intelligence have unexpectedly succeeded. . . .

There are few collections of seventeenth century verse so personal as the poems of Orinda. Her aspirations and sentimentalities, her perplexities and quarrels, her little journeys and her business troubles, all are reflected in her verse as a mirror. She goes from Tenby to Bristol by sea in September 1652, and she gives Lucasia an account of the uneventful voyage in verse:—

> But what most pleased my mind upon the way,
> Was the ships' posture that in harbour lay ;
> Which to a rocky grove so close were fixed
> That the trees' branches with the tackling mixed,—
> One would have thought it was, as then it stood,
> A growing navy or a floating wood.

These are verses for which we have lost all taste, but they were quite as good as those by which Waller was then making himself famous, and in the same modern manner. These and others were handed about from one friend to another till they reached London, and gained the enthusiastic poetess literary and artistic friends. Among these latter were Henry Lawes, the great musician, and Samuel Cooper, the finest miniature painter of the day, to both of whom she has inscribed flowing copies of verses, informed by her familiar stately wit.

But the subject that chiefly inspired her was the excellence of her female friends, and in treating this theme she really invented a new species of literature. She is the first sentimental writer in the English language, and she possesses to the full those qualities which came into fashion a century and a half later in the person of such authors as Letitia Landon. Orinda communes with the stars and the mountains, and is deeply exercised about her own soul. She is all smiles, tears, and sensibility. She asks herself if her affection has been slighted, she swears eternal troth, she yearns for confidences, she fancies that she is "dying for a little love." With Antenor, her husband, she keeps up all the time a prosaic, humdrum happiness, looking after his affairs, anxious about his health, rather patronisingly affectionate and wifely; but her poetical heart is elsewhere, and her leisure moments are given up to romantic vows with Rosania and Lucasia, and correspondence about the human heart with the noble Silvander. The whole society, one cannot help feeling, was entirely created and kept alive by the sensibility of Orinda, and nothing but her unremitting efforts could have sustained its component parts at the proper heights of sympathy. Mrs. Philips, in fact, had come to the conclusion that, as she put it, "Men exclude women from friendship's vast capacity," and she was determined, in spite of the difficulties in her path, to produce some shining specimens of female friendship. The seventeenth century was quite astonished, and looked on with respectful admiration, while the good Orinda laboured away, undeterred by the irritating circumstances that her *sociétaires* would get married at the very moment when they seemed approaching perfection, and that after marriage they were much more difficult for her to manage.—EDMUND GOSSE, "The Matchless Orinda" (1881), *Seventeenth Century Studies* (1883), 1913, pp. 229–36

⟨H⟩er two translations of *Pompée* and *Horace* are proofs of good judgment, taste, and real talent such as no one need be ashamed to leave behind him. The conscientious, well-trained literary worker is everywhere apparent, and the poet of undoubted talent shows herself if not on every page at least at crucial points.

This is the first rhymed version of a French tragedy made in English, and the ability with which Mrs. Philips handles the heroic couplet gives to the English a much closer resemblance to the French than blank verse can ever do. It would be difficult to think of Mrs. Philips's using blank verse in any work of this kind, for she seems to have imbued herself with the spirit of the original so thoroughly that the rhyme, an essential element in the French, would have come inevitably to her lips in translating. She was from the first a copious writer, much given to inditing extremely affectionate poems to her women friends, and her long practice in rhyming laments for her beloved Lucasia stands her in good stead in rendering the swelling Cornellian Alexandrines.

Any passage chosen at random will show the conscientious fidelity of Orinda to her text; and passages chosen with only a little care will show that higher fidelity to the spirit of the original and success in reproducing it which make her the best of Restoration translators, and perhaps the best who ever translated French tragedy. (Act IV. Scene 4.)

> Oh, truly Roman heart
> And worthy Him of whom you were a part,
> His Soul which sees from its exalted State
> How I endeavor to revenge his Fate
> Forgets his hate and is become so kind
> To save my life by what he left behind.
> Whatever Treason could to Pompey do
> Yet he doth still subsist and act in you
> And prompts you to a thing so brave that he
> May vanquish me in generosity.

There could scarcely be a translation more faithful. In one of her letters to Poliarchus Mrs. Philips sets up for herself the following ideal of Translation: "I think a Translation ought not to be us'd as Musicians do a ground with all the liberty of Descant, but as Painters when they copy." This is an ideal of fidelity which she has successfully realized in almost every instance. In the passage just quoted there is only one line where the translator has deviated in the slightest from a word-for-word rendering of Corneille, and yet she has reproduced his ten lines in ten of her own.—DOROTHEA FRANCES CANFIELD, "The Matchless Orinda," *Corneille and Racine in England*, 1904, pp. 41–43

ERIC S. ROBERTSON
From *English Poetesses*
1883, pp. 1–5

I remember to have conceived a humble affection for the "Matchless Orinda," England's first professed poetess, at a very early age. In the dusty recesses of an Edinburgh book-shop I had been burrowing through a rarely-visited accumulation of old folios, and came upon three treasures side by side: a perfect copy of the first complete *Faery Queen*, the original *Arcadia*, and *Poems by Mrs. Katherine Philips, the Matchless Orinda, to which is added Monsieur Corneille's Pompey and Horace, Tragedies, with several other Translations out of the French.* London: 1667.

Such was the title of a goodly volume in excellent preservation, adorned by a portrait of the author, and inscribed with many notes in various characters of handwriting. These notes gave the volume a dignity that Rivière's stateliest binding could not have bestowed upon it. I recollect that the first entry eulogised the poetess in ludicrously unstinted terms, and ended with the trite quotation beginning "Nec Jovis ira, nec ignis, nec ferrum poterit." But other inscriptions proved that the work had been handed down from one possessor to another as a thing to be cherished and reverenced, and the repeated occurrence of one name—Bonner—marked it as an heirloom of some bookish family. This pedigree made me covet the volume; and no doubt it would now be on one of my shelves but for the still greater attractions displayed by the folio Spenser at the same time. Even the Spenser alone was more than my fortunes at the moment could command, for its price was two guineas, certainly little enough for such a volume. There was talk with the bookseller about a premium of five shillings to be paid if the book were reserved till I returned to claim it in a few days; and in a few days, accordingly, my two guineas made me possessor of the *Faery Queen*, the worthy vendor, in the end, declining all advance on the original price. It was then that I indulged myself with another peep at the "matchless Orinda," still longing to possess and love what so many reverent hands had fondled. At this time, indeed, Katherine Philips was but a name to me, yet the living pen-scratches of these dead admirers seemed to give her a worth in my eyes beyond the public fame she had won as the friend of Jeremy Taylor and Cowley. From the testimony of these unpretending and obscure followers, I then and there grew to a conviction that there must be something very lovable in her, much as one makes sure of a woman's goodness of heart when her servants are overheard to praise her. A short time afterwards I took occasion to inquire if the book was still unbought, but my hopes of ultimately being able to cherish its declining years were dispelled. It had been advertised by catalogue, and written for by a London gentleman. This is the only first folio of "Orinda" I have ever seen. Copies of the edition are scarce now.

Whatever the judgment of to-day may be upon the writings of Katherine Philips, nobody can doubt that in her age she deserved her wonderful reputation. Her wit and her beauty were sought in the Court of Charles the Second, but she contented herself with a quiet country life in Wales. She was intimate with the most brilliant spirits of the times, and commanded their admiration, without once lowering the dignity of her womanhood by participation in the looseness of morals prevalent among them. She was well read in general literature,—quite beyond the average of women of her time, her acquaintance with the Bible being not the least noticeable feature of her condition. She exhibited a remarkable interest in politics, and was not afraid to make her political opinions known. She was the first Englishwoman who ever wrote much verse that people talked about, yet so modest was she that she would not consent that any of it should be published during her lifetime. Before she was thirty she was a great power in the literature of the day. Cowley, Dryden, Sir John Denham, and others felt, regarding her, as, later, Sir Richard Steele felt regarding another, that to love her had been a liberal education. At the age of thirty-three, when she died, she was giving every promise of developing into such a factor in English society as Madame Rambouillet had been in France. One of her poems, indeed, indicates that she had actually inaugurated an association which we may presume to have borne resemblance to the *coterie* of the *Precieuses*. Not a breath of scandal had ever touched her. Not a line had ever left her pen that she need have blushed for. Her end fulfilled the wish expressed in her own lines:

> So that, in various accidents,
> I conscience may, and honour, keep,

> I with that ease and innocence
> Shall die, as infants go to sleep.

In short, she shines to us as she shone for those who surrounded her, a sweet woman in a corrupt society.

All this can be said of Katherine Philips, while yet we may confess that her poetry is not very interesting to the modern reader. It is affected. There is little heart-beating to be felt in it. Even to the extent of sickly prudery, she eschews the romance of love as a theme, and versifies platonically on the delights of friendship, generally friendship between one woman and another. Some of her strongest thinking is expended on political poems which have lost all savour now; and stilted use of stale classical metaphor is abundant. If her acquaintance, Mrs. Owen, goes to sea, verses are written encharging her to the care of a sufficiently respectable Triton. His Majesty crossing from France must be addressed in an epistle comparing him to Arion on a dolphin. And so on. These faults are easily pointed to: but there yet remains a great deal of worth in Katherine Philips's verse.

Two things have to be borne in mind when we judge her. In the first place, we have to recollect the recognition she deserves as being the first Englishwoman with sufficient imagination (and confidence in it) to adopt pliant verse as the habitual vehicle for her thinking, in defiance of the almost vested right in it which male writers had till then preserved. Her courage may be compared to that of a woman who should make herself as skilful with the rapier as a man. Over form of verse Orinda exhibits as much command as any author of her time. And, as our first poetess, she at any rate should obtain rank relatively as high as that which we accord to Cædmon, our first poet.

In the second place, we have to give attention to the fact that for her, as for all other writers of the period, French influence was supreme. It was largely woman's influence, too, that the French thus gave us at this time. The affected delicacy of the *Précieuses* was teaching us how to be very proper in our ways of speech. They did not exactly recommend us the proverbial "prunes and prisms," but they certainly preached prudery and precision beyond all things. It is scarcely to be wondered at that, amid the general looseness both of morality and of literary form that had been bred by the Restoration, a pure-minded woman of talent like Orinda should have clung to the new French doctrines as a means of elevating the literary taste of her country. Thus we find that her whole influence is cast into the scale of the French system of classical formality, as against the very rough and ready style of the Restoration. The classicality of her imagery and her themes is thus accounted for. She completely adopts the Rambouillet system of nomenclature. Her husband and her friends Sir Edward Deering and Mrs. Owen and Mrs. Montague are not to be thought of by names with such commonplace associations. They are always addressed, accordingly, as Palæmon and Silvander, and Lucasia, and Rosania. So with all others with whom the poetess had occasion to come in contact. She herself is Orinda,— Katherine Philips no more. This was strictly in accord with the dictation of the French lady-precisians. They fenced their personalities round with these fantastic names, pretty much as they were fencing their bodies round with those swelling hoops that robbed them of any semblance to the commonplace appearance of Eve.

There is no doubt that what we borrowed of all this from the French did us much more good than harm. It sobered and clarified the blood of our literature, which had been exhibiting what we might call a gouty tendency. In so far, then, as Katherine Philips propagated the French purism, she may be thanked for her influence on our language, through the many authors who read her, and through the extraordinary influence that she undoubtedly exercised in private. Thus the coldness and rigidity which repel us as readers of her work are themselves seen to be, in some degree, tokens of a boon conferred by her upon English letters, when considered duly.

SIR KENELM DIGBY

1603–1665

Kenelm Digby was born as Gayhurst, Buckinghamshire, on July 11, 1603. Despite his father's execution for involvement in the Gunpowder Plot of 1605, the Digby estates were not sequestered, and no prejudice was attached to Kenelm Digby's later career on his father's account. From 1618 to 1620 he was a student at Gloucester Hall, Oxford, though he never took a degree. After leaving school he traveled to Spain where he met Prince Charles; later, in 1623, Charles knighted Digby and made him a gentleman of the bedchamber. After a long and idiosyncratic courtship, Sir Kenelm Digby married Venetia Stanley in 1625. She was a celebrated beauty of the day to whom a certain amount of controversy and unsubstantiated gossip had become attached; many years later Digby wrote his *Private Memoirs*, sometimes called *Loose Fantasies* (1827), partly in vindication of her reputation.

In 1628 Digby led a successful privateering expedition, engaging the French and Venetian fleets in Scanderoon Harbor. After his return to England he professed himself a Protestant; despite his father's political affiliations Digby had been raised a Catholic. But then in 1636 he returned to Catholicism, and in 1638 wrote his *Conference with a Lady about Choice of Religion*. During this time he was in service to the Queen, a change made in the wake of his wife's unexpected death in 1633.

He was briefly imprisoned, 1642–43, on account of his political conspiracies, and after his release lived in exile in Paris. Both during and after his imprisonment he engaged in philosophical and scientific studies, writing *Of the Immortality of Man's Soule* and *Of the Nature of Bodies*, both published in 1644, and replying to Thomas Browne in his *Observations upon* Religio Medici (1643). For this last work he was praised in some quarters, while elsewhere he was attacked along with Browne, and also attacked by Browne's defenders.

Digby returned to England in 1654, was sent back to the Continent to work on behalf of Oliver Cromwell, and then after the Restoration took up residence in England again, becoming Chancellor to Queen Henrietta Maria. His other works include *Sir Kenelm Digby's Closet Opened*, a compendium of recipes, household hints, and brewing instructions; *Sympathetic Powder*, on the uses of a healing preparation Digby had used extensively; and various scientific treatises, among them *On the Cure of Wounds* (1658) and *A Discourse concerning the Vegtation of Plants* (1660). A founding member of the Royal Society, Kenelm Digby is credited with having discovered the role of oxygen in plant respiration. He died in London on June 11, 1665, and was buried in Christ Church at Newgate.

Tho', happy *Muse*, thou know my *Digby* well,
    Yet read him in these lines: He doth excell
In honour, courtesie, and all the parts
    Court can call hers, or Man could call his Arts.
Hee's prudent, valiant, just, and temperate;
    In him all vertue is beheld in State:
And he is built like some imperiall roome
    For that to dwell in, and be still at home.
His brest is a brave Palace, a broad Street,
    Where all heroique ample thoughts doe meet.
Where Nature such a large survey hath ta'en,
    As other soules, to his, dwell in a Lane.
    —BEN JONSON, "An Epigram, To my MVSE, the Lady *Digby*, on her Husband, Sir KENELME DIGBY," *The Vnder-wood*, c. 1635

But it troubles mee like the fall of Phaeton, that Monsieur le Chevalier, ⟨Digby⟩—who passes both for a wit and a judgment, should attempt to reyne the horses of the sunne, and *Schioppir* on ⟨to fire upon⟩ *Religio Medici*; I wish hee had thought on the motto of that noble family, ⟨the Duke of Dorset⟩ whence hee

tooke that employment, *aut nunquam tentes aut perfice*, or that hee had animadverted better, or had beene *aliud agendo*, then soe *nihil agendo* on that piece, sure then he would have crost himselfe, blest him for that undertaking, and gone to bed rather then to have sitt up soe late to soe little purpose, and lose his sleepe, unles hee intended to make an opiate for his readers. —HENRY BATES, Letter to Sir Thomas Browne (August 28, 1647)

Sir Kenelme Digby was held to be the most accomplished Cavalier of his time. He went to Glocester Hall in Oxon, anno 1618. The learned Mr. Thomas Allen (then of that house) was wont to say that he was the *Mirandula* of his age.

He was such a goodly handsome person, gigantique and great voice, and had so gracefull Elocution and noble addresse, etc., that had he been drop't out of the Clowdes in any part of the World, he would have made himself respected. But the Jesuites spake spitefully, and sayd 'twas true, *but then he must not stay there above six weekes*. He was Envoyé from Henrietta Maria (then Queen-mother) to the Pope, where at first he was mightily admired; but after some time he grew high, and Hectored with his Holinesse, and gave him the Lye. The pope sayd he was mad.

Tempore Caroli I^{mi} he received the Sacrament in the Chapell at Whitehall, and professed the Protestant Religion, which gave great scandal to the Roman Catholiques; but afterwards *he looked back.*

In the Times of Confusion, the Bishop of Winchester's Lodging in Southwark, being a large Pile of Building, was made a Prison for the Royalists; and here Sir Kenelm Digby wrote his Book *of Bodies*, and diverted himself in Chymistry, and used to make artificial precious Stones, as Rubies, Emeralds, &c. out of Flint, as Sir Francis Dodington, Prisoner with him at the same Time, told me.

. . . Digby, that renowned Knight, great Linguist, and Magazen of Arts, was born and died on the Eleventh of June, and also fought fortunately at Scanderoon the same day. Hear his Epitaph, composed by Mr. Farrer:

> Under this Stone the Matchless Digby lies,
> Digby the Great, the Valiant, and the Wise:
> This Age's Wonder, for his Noble Parts;
> Skill'd in six Tongues, and learn'd in all the Arts.
> Born on the day he died, th' Eleventh of June,
> On which he bravely fought at Scanderoon.
> 'Tis rare that one and self-same day should be
> His day of Birth, of Death, of Victory.
> —JOHN AUBREY, "Sir Kenelm Digby," *Brief Lives*, 1669–96

His knowledge, though various and extensive, appeared to be greater than it really was; as he had all the powers of elocution and address to recommend it. He knew how to shine in a circle of ladies, or philosophers; and was as much attended to when he spoke on the most trivial subjects, as when he spoke on the most important. He was remarkably robust, and of a very uncommon size, but moved with peculiar grace and dignity. Though he applied himself to experiment, he was sometimes hypothetical in his philosophy; and there are instances of his being very bold and paradoxical in his conjectures: hence he was called the "Pliny of his age for lying."—JAMES GRANGER, *Biographical History of England*, 1769–1824

⟨T⟩he explanation which he has given of his motive for writing ⟨his memoirs⟩, and his wish that it might never be read by others, is, perhaps, the most interesting part of his lucubrations. He commences with expressing a hope, that if by accident the MS. should ever fall into any person's hands but his own, "this last scrawl may beg pardon for the rest." His object in composing the Memoir appears to have been to preserve his virtue; for, having been separated from his fleet by a storm which forced him into an island, which he calls Milo, where he remained to repair his ship, he was invited on shore by the chief persons of the place; and his host, to divert him from the retirement which he courted, obligingly offered to interest some ladies on his behalf, "who, in all ages, have been known to be no niggards of their favours," and which might, he says, have been willingly accepted by an individual in his situation, had he not had his thoughts filled with the remembrance of so divine a creature as his ⟨wife⟩ Venetia. To avoid, therefore, giving offence by a refusal, he pretended to have many dispatches to write; but, as his facility in composition was always very great, he observes, he soon finished his letters, and then resolved to commit to paper such events in his life as related to the fair object of his contemplation. He then "gives warning before hand, that no man hath reason to lose any time in perusing so trivial a discourse of a young and unstayed head,

which was, at the first, begun only for my own recreation, and then continued, and since preserved only for my own private content;" and concludes by requesting some friendly hand to convert "these blotted sheets into a clear flame," should they survive him, "which funeral fire will be welcome obsequies to my departed soul; who, till then, will be in continual fear that the world may have occasion to renew the memory of my indiscretion, and condemn me then as much for want of judgment in writing, as formerly it hath done for too deep passion in my actions." That the MS. was not destroyed, is fortunate for those who are gratified by perusing the description which genius gives of itself, as well as for Digby's memory, as it contains many facts highly creditable to his character, and tends, in some degree, to redeem that of his wife; whilst much light is thrown by it upon the early part of his career. As a piece of autobiography it is, perhaps, one of the most extraordinary which is extant, and every line bears striking evidence of the peculiar temper and still more singular opinions of the writer.

The MS. which is called by Digby *Loose Fantasies*, is in his own hand, and contains proof of having been frequently and most carefully revised.—SIR NICHOLAS HARRY NICOLAS, "Introduction" to *The Private Memoirs of Sir Kenelm Digby, Gentleman of the Bedchamber to King Charles the First, Written by Himself*, 1827, pp. xlii–xlv

One of the most attractive figures visible on that imaginary line where the eve of chivalry and the dawn of science unite to form a mysterious yet beautiful twilight, is that of Sir Kenelm Digby. To our imagination he represents the knight of old before the characteristics of that romantic style of manhood were diffused in the complex developments of modern society, and the philosopher of the epoch when fancy and superstition held sway over the domain of the exact sciences. Bravery, devotion to the sex, and a thirst for glory, nobleness of disposition and grace of manner, traditional qualities of the genuine cavalier, signalized Sir Kenelm, not less than an ardent love of knowledge, a habitude of speculation, and literary accomplishment; but his courage and his gallantry partook of the poetic enthusiasm of the days of Bayard, and his opinions and researches were something akin to those of the alchemists. High birth and a handsome person gave emphasis to these traits; and we have complete and authentic memorials whereby he is distinctly reproduced to our minds. These, however, do not consist of those elaborate treatises which, doubtless, cost him severe application; his views of the nature of corporeal and spiritual laws are quite obsolete,—learned and ingenious, perhaps, but not of present significance.

. . . Educated a Protestant, he early commenced those travels abroad then deemed essential to a gentleman; and the first inkling of scientific zeal and public spirit appears in the recipe he brought home (which soon became famous), for making a "sympathetic powder," by applying which to anything that had received the blood of the wounded, instant relief was thought to be afforded, even if the patient was not present. This idea was never abandoned; it was one of the results of the occult studies then in vogue; and the "sympathetic powder" is as intimately associated with Sir Kenelm Digby's name, as tar-water with Bishop Berkeley's.—HENRY T. TUCKERMAN, "The Modern Knight," *Essays, Biographical and Critical*, 1857, pp. 75–77

Digby was a notorious pervert, having been educated a Protestant, although his father was a Catholic, and suffered for his share in the Gunpowder Plot. His perversion took place in France about 1635; and from this time he appears to have made himself conspicuous in the French capital for his constant intrigues with the Jesuits, and parade of his new "persuasion, to the prejudice of the English Church." . . . The fact seems to be that, with striking superficial qualities and an imposing air of ability, Sir Kenelm Digby was a man distinguished more by a certain restless liveliness of nature than by any higher attributes of head or heart.—JOHN TULLOCH, "Lord Falkland—A Moderate and Liberal Church," *Rational Theology and Christian Philosophy in England in the Seventeenth Century*, 1872, Vol. 1, pp. 107–8

Amongst the many strange personalities of the 17th century, there are few whose character it is more difficult to gauge than that of Kenelm Digby. He played his part as courtier, man of fashion, romancer, critic, soldier, virtuoso, and philosopher; and although he was distinguished in each, there was no sphere in which some suspicion of charlatanism did not attach to him. It is indeed difficult to avoid the conclusion that an element of madness entered into his composition, or at least that his versatility was united to an abnormal eccentricity, which, if it partly relieves him of the worst charges, yet explains how small his influence was in any single sphere of activity. His vanity was prodigious, and is naturally most conspicuous where his writings (as is frequently the case) relate to his own actions.

His *Private Memoirs*, first printed from his MS. in 1827, give us an account of his life down to 1628; and the larger part is occupied with a singular history of his early love and marriage with Venetia Stanley. The story is told as a romance under assumed names, and it is impossible to tell what part of it is true and what part pure romancing. In style it is inflated and turgid, and exhibits all the absurd magniloquence of diction characteristic of the romances of the day, with a strange perversity in its moralisings which is peculiar to Digby himself. Besides this we have some shorter narratives; one entitled *Sir Kenelm Digby's Honour Maintained*, in which his prowess in resenting an insult to his king by single combat is set forth; and another, the journal of his privateering expedition, which is simple and direct narrative. In 1643, he printed his *Observations on* Religio Medici, written in feverish haste, and with something of captious criticism of Browne's work; in 1644, his *Observations* on an obscure passage in Spenser's Fairie Queene; and in the same year his chief philosophical work, *On the Nature of Bodies, and the Nature of Man's Soul*.

Some of his most marked peculiarities are best exhibited by the contrast between Browne and himself, which appears in his *Observations on* Religio Medici. In Browne's mysticism the imagination is always stronger than the ingenuity, and the breadth of a generous and liberal sympathy is more conspicuous than any definiteness of formal belief. But Digby is always straining after a system; and he evidently wrote the criticism under the influence of the philosophical theory which he sets forth more elaborately in the longer treatise on the *Nature of Bodies and the Nature of Man's Soul*. What attracts us most in Browne is his keen perception of the bearing of religious belief upon the faculties of man; he never obtrudes any dogmatism, but he steers his way through the labyrinth of creeds, with a calm and steady equipoise which never loses its courteous dignity. Digby, with far less of philosophic calm, is much more of the schoolman; without attacking any religious dogma, he yet pursues, with greater pertinacity, a sort of rationalistic system. He will not subscribe to Browne's gentle contempt for the impotence of human reason, but would fain base religion upon the foundations of reason. The germ of freethinking was there; and it is difficult to avoid the belief that Swift, whose writings are full of reminiscences both in Browne and of Digby, found in Digby's sprightly philosophising a type of the mental complacency against which he directed his satire.

His more elaborate philosophical work begins by tracing the operations of physical nature, and through them, explains the action of instinct in animals. He distinguishes sharply between these instincts (the result, as he maintains, solely of physical causes), and the operations of the human intellect, even when these approach most nearly to the semblance of the instincts in animals. From this distinction he argues that there must be some basis for these operations which is not physical; that this basis is the sole foundation for a belief in the existence of the soul; and enunciates in a somewhat different form, the thesis *Cogito ergo sum*. And because this basis is not physical and is not therefore subject to physical laws, it must be immortal. The theory is open to assault at many points; but it is worked out with much care and ingenuity; and by the very care and accuracy of his argument, Digby's style becomes clear, exact, and forcible. He has not the boldness or the mastery of language which invents new expressions or clothes new thoughts in words. But he writes with the polished ease and grace which in his carriage and his manner so vividly impressed all his contemporaries, even when they were compelled to admit his total want of veracity. He has the confidence, and, at the same time, the breadth of view, acquired by converse with every phase of life. His prose has not the quaint turns, and the sympathetic subtlety of Browne's; but . . . he can rise occasionally to very lofty heights of dignity and eloquence. With all this, however, there is a pervading impression of artificiality, as of one whose character was above all things theatrical; and of superficial confidence, as of one to whom philosophical lucubrations were only a phase of eccentric and ill-balanced restlessness.—HENRY CRAIK, "Sir Kenelm Digby," *English Prose*, ed. Henry Craik, 1893, Vol. 2, pp. 291–93

It was in his prison at Winchester House that Sir Kenelm wrote his "*Observations upon* Religio Medici *occasionally written by* Sir Kenelme Digby Knt."

In the form of a letter to Edward, Earl of Dorset, Sir Kenelm "digested these observations during the night between 22nd and 23rd December, 1642". "In this work," says Dr. Johnson in his *Life of Browne*, "though mingled with some positions fabulous and uncertain, there are acute remarks, just censures, and profound speculations; yet its principal claim to admiration is, that it was written in twenty-four hours of which part was spent in procuring Browne's book and part in reading it."

While at Winchester House Sir Kenelm also wrote his *Observations on the twenty-second stanza in the ninth canto of the second book of Spencer's* Faerie Queen, as a letter to his friend Sir Edward Stradling, who had accompanied him in his expedition to the Mediterranean.

⟨John Aubrey, in *Letters Written by Eminent Persons*⟩ states that while "a prisoner for the King at Winchester House," Sir Kenelm "practised chymistry, and wrote a booke of Bodies and Soule". Very likely he may have done so; but the dedication to his son, Kenelm, with which it opens, is dated "*Paris the last of August 1644*". In this bulky treatise, 429 pages are devoted to the body and 144 to the soul. The volume forms the most pretentious of the author's books, although, to his biographers, his *Private Memoirs* and his *Voyage to the Mediteranean* are infinitely more interesting. *The Nature of Bodies* is full of curiosities. . . .

On the philosophical treatise on *The Soul*, I am very ill-qualified to give an opinion; I therefore asked a very able critic of such matters to read the book and report on it. He writes that it is of some interest because it dated before the philosophical speculations of Hobbes, Cudworth, Locke and Berkeley, but that it is of little intrinsic value. That which is true in it is not new, and that which is new in it is not true.—THOMAS LONGUEVILLE, *The Life of Sir Kenelm Digby, by one of his Descendants*, 1896, pp. 256–59

⟨Digby's⟩ friendship with Descartes, Hobbes and other leaders of the new philosophy invested his erratic speculations with an importance that they little deserved. Though he was in close intercourse with the chief men of science of the time, his writings are a singular medley of Aristotelian Philosophy, Astrology, Alchemy, and absurd superstitions. His romantic courtship of Venetia Stanley—the history of which is recorded in his *Private Memoirs*, published in 1827—his successful privateering expedition in 1627, and the various confidential missions in which he was engaged on behalf of the Queen, and

subsequently in the service of the Protector, all serve to perpetuate the memory of one of the most picturesque and eccentric characters of the period. His two most important works—*Of Bodies*, and *Of the Immortality of Man's Soul*—were published in Paris in 1644, and owe much to the influence of Thomas White, a Roman Catholic philosopher with whom Digby lived for some time. Cowley, in dedicating to Sir Kenelm Digby his Pastoral Comedy, *Love's Riddle*, in 1638, writes:

> Learning by right of conquest is your own,
> And every liberal art your captive grown;

Evelyn, on the other hand, writing after the Restoration, describes him as an 'errant mountebank.'—J. HOWARD B. MASTERMAN, *The Age of Milton*, 1897, pp. 236–37

JAMES SHIRLEY

1596–1666

James Shirley was born in September 1596 in London. He entered the Merchant Taylors' School in 1608 and studied there until his admittance to St. John's College, Oxford, in 1612. According to Dr. Laud, Master of St. John's and later Archbishop of Canterbury, Shirley remained at Oxford for less than a year. Subsequently he attended St. Catharine's College, Cambridge, receiving a B.A. in 1617. In the same year he was ordained and accepted a preferment near St. Albans. It seems likely that Shirley then converted to Catholicism and was thus forced to leave his clerical post. He taught at the Edward VI Grammar School in St. Albans for several years before settling in London in 1625 to work as a playwright for Queen Henrietta's company. Shirley's masque, *The Triumph of Peace*, was successfully performed before the King and Queen in 1634.

Shirley wrote over forty dramas, most of which survive today. Among his best-known tragedies are *The Maides Revenge* (1626), *The Traytor* (1631), *Loves Crueltie* (1631), *The Politician* (1639), and *The Cardinall* (1641). Shirley's comedies include *Changes; or, Love in a Maze* (1632), *Hide Parke* (1632), *The Gamester* (1633), *The Coronation* (1635), *The Lady of Pleasure* (1635), *The Imposture* (1640), and *The Sisters* (1642). From 1636 to 1640 Shirley worked at Ogilby's Theater, Dublin, while London theatres were closed because of the plague. During the Civil War Shirley followed his patron, the Earl of Newcastle, until the Royalist defeat. He then taught during the Commonwealth and wrote several grammar books. Around 1650 he wrote *The Contention of Ajax and Ulysses for the Armor of Achilles*, a short dramatic piece based on Ovid's *Metamorphoses*.

Shirley died as a result of the Great Fire of 1666. He was buried on October 29 at St. Giles-in-the-Fields, London.

Personal

James, thou and I did spend some precious yeeres
At Katherine-Hall; since when, we some times feele
In our poetick braines, (as plaine appeares)
A whirling tricke, then caught from Katherine's wheele.

> —THOMAS BANCROFT, *Two Bookes of Epigrammes*, 1639

He was educated at St. John's College, in Oxford, where he was taken great notice of by Dr. Laud, then president of that house. He entered into holy orders; though he was much discouraged from it, by his friend the president, on account of a large mole on his left cheek; and was some time a parish priest in Hertfordshire. He afterward turned Roman Catholic, and kept a school at St. Alban's, but soon grew tired of that employment, and going to London commenced poet. He wrote no less than thirty dramatic pieces, some of which were acted with great applause. In the Interregnum, he was necessitated to return to his former profession of schoolmaster; in which he became eminent and wrote several grammatical books for the

use of his scholars.—JAMES GRANGER, *Biographical History of England*, 1769–1824

General

In the play of *The Ball* written by Shirley and acted by the Queen's players there were divers personated so naturally both of lords and others in the Court that I took it ill and would have forbidden the play but that Beeston promised many things which I found fault withall should be left out, and that he would not suffer it to be done by the poet any more, who deserves to be punished: and the first who offends in this kind of poets or players shall be sure of public punishment.—SIR HENRY HERBERT, *Master of the Revels Office Book*, Nov. 18, 1632

> Sh—— alone, of all my Sons, is he
> Who stands confirm'd in full stupidity.
> The rest to some faint meaning make pretence,
> But Sh—— never deviates into sense.
> Some Beams of Wit on other souls may fall,
> Strike through and make a lucid intervall;

But *Sh*——'s genuine night admits no ray,
His rising Fogs prevail upon the Day:
Besides his goodly Fabrick fills the eye,
And seems design'd for thoughtless Majesty:
Thoughtless as Monarch Oakes, that shade the plain,
And, spread in solemn state, supinely reign.
Heywood and *Shirley* were but Types of thee,
Thou last great Prophet of Tautology:
Even I, a dunce of more renown than they,
Was sent before but to prepare thy way.

     —JOHN DRYDEN, *Mac Flecknoe*, 1682

⟨Shirley⟩ was the Chief of the Second-rate Poets: and by some has been thought even equal to *Fletcher* himself. . . .

I need not take pains to shew his Intimacy, not only with the Poets of his Time; but even the Value and Admiration that Persons of the first Rank had for him; since the Verses before severall of his Works, and his Epistles Dedicatory sufficiently shew it. He has writ severall *Dramatick Pieces*, to the Number of 37, which are in print: besides others which are in Manuscript.—GERARD LANGBAINE, *An Account of the English Dramatick Poets*, 1691

Think, ye fain scribbling tribe of Shirley's fate,
You that write farce, and you that farce translate;
Shirley, the scandal of the ancient stage
Shirley, the very Durfey of his age;
Think how he lies in Ducklane shops forlorn,
And never mention'd but with utmost scorn:
Think that the end of all your boasted skill,
As I presume to prophecy it will
Justly,—for many of you write as ill.

     —ROBERT GOULD, "The Play House: A Satire,"
1709

Shirley claims a place amongst the worthies of this period, not so much for any transcendent talent in himself, as that he was the last of a great race, all of whom spoke nearly the same language, and had a set of moral feelings and notions in common. A new language, and quite a new turn of tragic and comic interest, came in with the Restoration.—CHARLES LAMB, *Specimens of English Dramatic Poets*, 1808

Shirley was the last of our good old dramatists. When his works shall be given to the public they will undoubtedly enrich our popular literature. His language sparkles with the most exquisite images. Keeping some occasional pruriencies apart, the fault of his age rather than of himself, he speaks the most polished and refined dialect of the stage; and even some of his over-heightened scenes of voluptuousness are meant, though with a very mistaken judgment, to inculcate morality. I consider his genius, indeed, as rather brilliant and elegant than strong or lofty. His tragedies are defective in fire, grandeur, and passion; and we must *select* his comedies to have any favourable idea of his humour. His finest poetry comes forth in situations rather more familiar than tragedy and more grave than comedy, which I should call sentimental comedy, if the name were not associated with ideas of modern insipidity. That he was capable, however, of pure and excellent comedy will be felt by those who have yet in reserve the amusement of reading his *Gamester*, *Hyde Park*, and *Lady of Pleasure*. In the first and last of these there is a subtle ingenuity in producing comic effect and surprise, which might be termed Attic, if it did not surpass anything that is left us in Athenian comedy.

I shall leave to others the more special enumeration of his faults, only observing, that the airy touches of his expression, the delicacy of his sentiments, and the beauty of his similes, are often found where the poet survives the dramatist, and where he has not the power to transfuse life and strong individuality through the numerous characters of his voluminous drama. His style, to use a line of his own, is "studded like a frosty night with stars;" and a severe critic might say that the stars often shine when the atmosphere is rather too frosty. In other words, there is more beauty of fancy than strength of feeling in his works. From this remark, however, a defender of his fame might justly appeal to exceptions in many of his pieces. From a general impression of his works I should not paint his Muse with the haughty form and features of inspiration, but with a countenance, in its happy moments, arch, lovely, and interesting, both in smiles and in tears; crowned with flowers, and not unindebted to ornament, but wearing the drapery and chaplet with a claim to them from natural beauty.

The contempt which Dryden expresses for Shirley might surprise us, if it were not recollected that he lived in a degenerate age of dramatic taste, and that his critical sentences were neither infallible nor immutable. He at one time undervalued Otway, though he lived to alter his opinion.—THOMAS CAMPBELL, *An Essay on English Poetry*, 1819

Although it will not, perhaps, be disputed by those who know any thing of his works, that Shirley has succeeded better in the serious than in the lighter department of the stage, it cannot, on the other hand, be denied, that he sometimes places ludicrous characters in irresistibly comic situations: and here it may be observed, that, as he terms Ben Jonson his "acknowledged master," he follows him, particularly in his earlier efforts, in the general cast of his personages—that is to say, he deals very much in the display of what were then called *humours*, or the representation of individual peculiarities, which may or may not extend to a class. Of this *The Example* (1637) may be taken as an instance; and as this stile of writing seems to have prevailed with him less afterwards, I am led by it, and other circumstances, to infer that that comedy was one of his youthful productions: the names of some of the persons introduced into *The Example* inform the reader at once of the nature of their characters: thus, Sir Solitary Plot is always smelling out an imaginary trick to impose upon him, while his servant, Dormant, is fast asleep when he ought to be most vigilant: and in the same play we have Lord Fitzavarice, Mr. Confident Rapture, Oldrat, Vainman, and Lord Fitzamorous.

There are very few of our author's absolute comedies that have not some serious persons and scenes in them, and that of which we are now speaking has a few excellent interviews in which Sir Walter Peregrine and Bellamia are concerned, in whose characters is involved much of the interest of the piece. Indeed, in such as these, Shirley always succeeded best; and, in inserting into his tragedies interludes of coarse humour, he complied with the habit and expectation of the age, rather than followed his own uninfluenced inclination.—"K. Q. X." (John Payne Collier?), "On the Character and Writings of James Shirley," *London Magazine*, May 1820, p. 527

Shirley's facility in composition is proved by the number of his plays; and doubtless they would have swelled into an ampler catalogue, had not the anti-poetic spirit of Puritanism suppressed the stage, while the vigour of his genius was yet unimpaired. No single writer, among the early English dramatists, with the exception of Shakespeare, has bequeathed so many regular five-act pieces to posterity. . . .

His fine moral feeling rejected those unhallowed themes, on which some of his contemporaries boldly ventured; he offends us by no glowing pictures of incestuous love. His writings are soiled, in a certain degree, by gross and immodest allusions;

but whoever is conversant with our ancient drama will admit that the Muse of Shirley is comparatively chaste. . . .

He abounds in brilliant thoughts, in noble and majestic sentiments, yet exhibits little of profound reflexion. His imagination seldom takes a lofty flight: he loves to crowd his dramas with events of romantic beauty; but he shews no fondness for the ideal world, its ghosts, and magic wonders. —ALEXANDER DYCE, "Introduction" to *Dramatic Works and Poems of James Shirley*, 1833, Vol. 1, pp. lxiii–lxv

If the character of Shirley's genius is less marked, he has escaped the mannerism of many of his predecessors; if there is no one qualification of the dramatist in which he is pre-eminent in the great school to which he belongs, yet he combines more than most, except the very first writers; and it is impossible not to admire the variety and versatility with which he ranges, if with a less vigorous and decided, yet with an easy and graceful step, through every province of the drama; rarely perhaps exciting any violent or profound emotion, yet rarely failing to awaken and keep alive the curiosity, to amuse and delight the imagination. For, after all, it is the life and activity of Shirley's mind, the fertility of his invention, which is the most extraordinary point in his poetic character. Among all the plays, which nearly fill the volumes before us, there are few in which the interest, however often strange and improbable, is not sustained to the end; few, in which we do not find scenes or speeches of easy and unlaboured beauty, which could only be poured forth in such profusion by a true poet.

As a tragic writer, Shirley betrays, perhaps with least disguise, that he is the last of his school. He seems to write for an audience accustomed to sup full of horrors. There is a prodigality of crime, a profuse pouring forth of blood, not altogether in the coarse and *King Cambyses* manner of the older school, but still crowded together, as if nothing less than such strong stimulants would produce any effect; as if the poet were under the necessity of working up to an established standard of terror—to equal, if not to surpass, the awful scenes which were in full possession of the public imagination. —UNSIGNED, *Quarterly Review*, April 1833, p. 15

Shirley is a dramatic writer much inferior to those who have been mentioned, but has acquired some degree of reputation, or at least notoriety of name, in consequence of the new edition of his plays. These are between twenty and thirty in number; some of them, however, written in conjunction with his fellow dramatists. A few of these are tragedies, a few are comedies drawn from English manners; but in the greater part we find the favourite style of that age, the characters foreign and of elevated rank, the interest serious, but not always of buskined dignity, the catastrophe fortunate; all, in short, that has gone under the vague appellation of tragic-comedy. Shirley has no originality, no force in conceiving or delineating character, little of pathos, and less, perhaps, of wit; his dramas produce no deep impression in reading, and of course can leave none in the memory. But his mind was poetical, his better characters, especially females, express pure thoughts in pure language; he is never tumid or affected and seldom obscure; the incidents succeed rapidly, the personages are numerous, and there is a general animation in the scenes, which causes us to read him with some pleasure. No very good play, nor, possibly, any very good scene could be found in Shirley; but he has many lines of considerable beauty. Among his comedies *The Gamesters* may be reckoned the best. Charles I. is said to have declared that it was "the best play he had seen these seven years;" and it has even been added that the story was of his royal suggestion. It certainly deserves praise both for lan-

guage and construction of the plot, and it has the advantage of exposing vice to ridicule; but the ladies of that court, the fair forms whom Vandyke has immortalised, must have been very different indeed from their posterity, as in truth I believe they were, if they could sit it through. *The Ball*, and also some more among the comedies of Shirley are so far remarkable and worthy of being read, that they bear witness to a more polished elegance of manners, and a more free intercourse in the higher class, than we find in the comedies of the preceding reign. A queen from France, and that queen Henrietta Maria, was better fitted to give this tone than Anne of Denmark. But it is not from Shirley's pictures that we can draw the most favourable notions of the morals of that age. —HENRY HALLAM, *Introduction to the Literature of Europe*, 1837–39, Pt. 3, Ch. 6, Par. 98

Shirley was essentially an imitative not an original genius. His claim to a place among the great poets of his age rests solely upon his wonderful manipulative dexterity, his power of assimilating and reshaping the creations of his great predecessors. Towards the close of a grand period, perhaps even while its leading spirits are in full creative swing, two distinct tendencies manifest themselves. Men of independent mind separate themselves from the main current, and cast about for fields which the masters have left unoccupied. Men of more pliant and docile intellect follow humbly in the footsteps of the masters, and seize freely upon the wealth which they have accumulated. Shirley belonged to the latter class. He did not try to invent new types, or to say what had not been said before; but stored his mind with the thoughts and the imagery of his predecessors, and reproduced them with joyous facility. We may admire the fluency, the elegance, and the force of Shirley's verse, the ease and naturalness of his dramatic situations, but the attentive reader of his predecessors is never called upon to admire anything new. Fletcher was his chief model and exemplar, but he laid them all freely under contribution. The chief critical pleasure in reading him is the pleasure of memory. —WILLIAM MINTO, "James Shirley," *The English Poets*, ed. Thomas Humphry Ward, 1880, Vol. 2, p. 215

> The dusk of day's decline was hard on dark
>   When evening trembled round thy glowworm
>   lamp
>   That shone across her shades and dewy damp,
> A small clear beacon whose benignant spark
> Was gracious yet for loiterers' eyes to mark,
>   Though changed the watchword of our English
>   camp
>   Since the outposts rang round Marlowe's lion
>   ramp,
> When thy steed's pace went ambling round Hyde
>   Park
>
>   —ALGERNON CHARLES SWINBURNE, "James
>   Shirley," *Sonnets on Early English Drama-
>   tists*, 1882

Shirley was neither a very great nor a very strong man; and without originals to follow, it is probable that he would have done nothing. But with Fletcher and Jonson before him he was able to strike out a certain line of half-humorous, half-romantic drama, and to follow it with curious equality through his long list of plays, hardly one of which is very much better than any other, hardly one of which falls below a very respectable standard. He has few or no single scenes or passages of such high and sustained excellence as to be specially quotable; and there is throughout him an indefinable flavour as of study of his elders and betters, an appearance as of a highly competent and gifted pupil in a school, not as of a master and leader in a movement. The palm is perhaps generally and rightly assigned to *The Lady of Pleasure*, 1635, a play bearing some faint resemblances to Massinger's *City Madam*, and Fletcher's *Noble Gentleman* (Shirley is known to have finished one or two plays of Fletcher's), and in its turn the original, or at least the forerunner of a long line of late seventeenth and eighteenth century plays on the extravagance and haughtiness and caprice of fine ladies. Shirley indeed was much acted after the Restoration, and exhibits, though on the better side, the transition of the older into the newer school very well. Of his tragedies *The Traitor* has the general suffrage, and perhaps justly. One of Shirley's most characteristic habits was that not of exactly adapting an old play, but of writing a new one on similar lines accommodated to the taste of his own day. He constantly did this with Fletcher, and once in *The Cardinal* he was rash enough to endeavour to improve upon Webster. His excuse may have been that he was evidently in close contact with the last survivors of the great school, for besides his work with or on Fletcher, he collaborated with Chapman in the tragedy of *Chabot* and the comedy of *The Ball*—the latter said to be one of the earliest *loci* for the use of the word in the sense of an entertainment. His versification profited by this personal or literary familiarity. It is occasionally lax, and sins especially by the redundant syllable or syllables, and by the ugly break between auxiliary verbs and their complements, prepositions and their nouns, and so forth. But it never falls into the mere shapelessness which was so common with his immediate and younger contemporaries. Although, as has been said, long passages of high sustained poetry are not easily producible from him, two short extracts from *The Traitor* will show his style favourably, but not too favourably. Amidea, the heroine, declares her intention—

> To have my name
> Stand in the ivory register of virgins,
> When I am dead. Before one factious thought
> Should lurk within me to betray my fame
> To such a blot, my hands shall mutiny
> And boldly with a poniard teach my heart
> To weep out a repentance.

And this of her brother Florio's is better still—

> Let me look upon my sister now:
> Still she retains her beauty,
> Death has been kind to leave her all this sweetness.
> Thus in a morning have I oft saluted
> My sister in her chamber: sat upon
> Her bed and talked of many harmless passages.
> *But now 'tis night, and a long night with her:*
> *I shall ne'er see these curtains drawn again*
> *Until we meet in heaven.*

Here the touch, a little weakened it may be, but still the touch of the great age, is perceptible, especially in the last lines, where the metaphor of the "curtains," common enough in itself for eyelids, derives freshness and appositeness from the previous mention of the bed. But Shirley is not often at this high tragic level. His supposed first play, *Love Tricks*, though it appeared nearly forty years before the Restoration, has a curious touch of post-Restoration comedy in its lively, extravagant, easy farce. Sometimes, as in *The Witty Fair One*, he fell in with the growing habit of writing a play mainly in prose, but dropping into verse here and there, though he was quite as ready to write, as in *The Wedding*, a play in verse with a little prose. Once he dramatised the *Arcadia* bodily and by name. At another time he would write a downright interlude like the *Contention for Honour and Riches*, or a thinly-veiled morality like *Honoria and Mammon*. He was a proficient at masques. *The Grateful Servant*, *The Royal Master*, *The Duke's Mistress*, *The Doubtful Heir*, *The Constant Maid*, *The Humorous Courtier*, are plays whose very titles speak them, though the first is much the best. *The Changes* or *Love in a Maze* was slightly borrowed from by Dryden in *The Maiden Queen*, and *Hyde Park*, a very lively piece, set a fashion of direct comedy of manners which was largely followed, while *The Brothers* and *The Gamester* are other good examples of different styles. Generally Shirley seems to have been a man of amiable character, and the worst thing on record about him is his very ungenerous gibing dedication of *The Bird in a Cage* to Prynne, then in prison, for his well-known attack on the stage, a piece of retaliation which, if the enemy had not been "down," would have been fair enough.

Perhaps Shirley's comedy deserves as a whole to be better spoken of than his tragedy. It is a later variety of the same kind of comedy which we noted as written so largely by Middleton,—a comedy of mingled manners, intrigue, and humours, improved a good deal in coherence and in stage management, but destitute of the greater and more romantic touches which emerge from the chaos of the earlier style. Nearly all the writers whom I shall now proceed to mention practised this comedy, some better, some worse; but no one with quite such success as Shirley at his best, and no one with anything like his industry, versatility, and generally high level of accomplishment. It should perhaps be said that the above-mentioned song, the one piece of Shirley's generally known, is not from one of his more characteristic pieces, but from *The Contention of Ajax and Ulysses*, a work of quite the author's latest days.—GEORGE SAINTSBURY, *A History of Elizabethan Literature*, 1887, pp. 410–13

Shirley is in complete contrast with Ford in that he neither sought for overstrained and unnatural situations as a stimulus for his tragedy, nor allowed his comedy to degenerate into coarse buffoonery. Writing at the close of an extraordinarily prolific dramatic period, and at a time when the works of the great dramatists of that period were being made accessible in collected form, he drew freely from them for characters, situations, and ideas. But though there is little originality in his dramas, he shews great dexterity in the management of his material, and a facility of poetic expression which is pleasing until it grows monotonous. The plots of many of his plays are ingenious and interesting, and, as in the case of Massinger, a healthy moral tone underlies his occasional grossness.

Shirley's masques are of considerable literary value, and the few lyrics he wrote show him to be a lyric poet of no mean power.—J. HOWARD B. MASTERMAN, *The Age of Milton*, 1897, p. 87

G. BURNETT SMITH
From "Shirley"
Gentleman's Magazine, May 1880, pp. 603–10

In *The Lady of Pleasure* we find a comedy of an altogether superior order, and one rich in those surprises which are the life of the comic dramatist's art. Campbell was not far wrong in asserting that in this and one other comedy by Shirley "there is a subtle ingenuity in producing comic effect and surprise which might be termed Attic, if it did not surpass anything that is left us in Athenian comedy." The story—relating the means by which a wealthy lady, who had quitted a country life to plunge into the dissipations of the metropolis, is drawn from the vortex of pleasure—is not unknown both in French and

Spanish comedy; but it has probably never been treated with more brilliancy and vivacity than it is here by Shirley. We can give no fair idea of the liveliness of this comedy of manners by brief quotations, and shall therefore refrain from extracting what could not be described as its best passages, for the reason that the play must be regarded as a whole; the character of Aretina, Lady Bornwell, with her disgust of country life, and her desire for the pleasures of the town, is admirably drawn. In *The Royal Master*, the dramatist again adventures to southern climes for his inspiration. The King of Naples, who furnishes the title to the play, has a favourite, one Montalto, a hypocritical villain, who aspires to the hand of his sister Theodosia. She is already, however, betrothed to the Duke of Florence. The latter is induced to believe that Theodosia and Montalto are secretly pledged to each other, and another maiden is thrown in his way who makes a deep impression upon him. A good deal of melodramatic business ensues, but finally Montalto's plot is exposed, and poetic justice prevails. The play abounds in short passages like the following, which show Shirley at his best as poet and dramatist:—

> What a brave armour is
> An innocent soul! How like a rock it bids
> Defiance to a storm against whose ribs
> The insolent waves but dash themselves in pieces,
> And fall and hide their heads in passionate foam!
> How would a guilty person tremble now,
> Look pale, and, with his eyes chained to the ground,
> Betray his fear of justice!

The poet is frequently most felicitous in his personification of the passions. Montalto charges Theodosia with wearing "a smiling summer in her brow, yet frost within her heart." Upon the tragedy of *The Duke's Mistress*, the tragi-comedy of *The Doubtful Heir*, and the comedies of *The Constant Maid* and *The Humorous Courtier*, we do not propose to dwell, for, while they are not without merit, they do not express with force their author's dramatic genius. Some mention, however, should be made of *St. Patrick for Ireland*, perhaps Shirley's most extraordinary effort—extraordinary, that is, as a hopeless medley of religion, tradition, and buffoonery. This intermeddling with the supernatural, whether it was the author's intention to produce such an effect or not, is certainly the reverse of impressive to the mind of the reader. Archimagus, the chief priest of the false gods, becoming aware of the advent of St. Patrick, informs King Leogarius that he will be destroyed by the infernal powers. A long conflict ensues between the Saint and Archimagus, during which the former shows himself to be possessed of miraculous powers. The chief priest is in the end discomfited, and sinks into the earth with curses; while the King, convinced by many extraordinary events, accepts St. Patrick. The drama is left incomplete, Shirley contemplating a second part, which was never undertaken. For this he deserves the thanks of posterity, who will be unable to discover any valid reason why he ever undertook the first. One effect of the play is assuredly to bring into contempt the system of belief in the magic power of relics so prevalent in the Romish Church. The comedy of *The Gentleman of Venice* is concerned with the fortunes of Giovanni, supposed son of a gardener, but in reality the son of a duke. He had been changed at his birth. Giovanni is a youth of noble sentiments, and there are many entertaining and elevating passages between him and Bellaura, the Duke's niece. They contract a mutual affection even during Giovanni's mean conditon. There is a second plot of almost equal interest. *The Politician* does not, as its name might imply, deal with the common schemer in politics, but with the Court conspirator. He is in this case one Gotharus, who, as

Shirley describes him to us, is active to serve his pleasures and ambition. He is a great favourite of the Queen of Norway, who has been advanced to the royal condition through his artifices. The hero himself is of an easy and credulous disposition— ready to be deceived by any specious courtier. There are other characters in the piece furnishing the minor lights and shades, but the chief interest centres in Gotharus, who, after a career famed for treacheries and bloody deeds, at length meets with his just doom. *The Imposture*, a comedy which the dramatist himself said "may march in the first rank of his compositions," has not won this high favour from the critics, although it is not destitute either of dramatic skill or humour. Shirley's assessment of the value of this comedy, nevertheless, may on the whole be taken as another indication that poets frequently misjudge their own labours. But with regard to the tragedy of *The Cardinal*—also regarded by the author with special feelings of satisfaction and admiration—there is a general consensus of opinion that it deserves equality with his best work. It would be futile for us to quarrel with this estimate, yet for ourselves we regard *The Traitor* as possessing more of the real dignity and grandeur of true tragedy. The characters in *The Cardinal* act as if oppressed with some chronic fever of the brain, and in the Cardinal and Rosaura we do not find the majestic "passion and the nobility" to be found in Sciarrha and Amidea. Mr. Dyce says: "There can be little doubt that while composing this tragedy Shirley kept his eye on Webster's *Duchess of Malfi*: the former, indeed, contains no scenes or passages which can be pointed out as plagiarisms from the latter, yet the general resemblance between the two dramas could scarcely have been accidental. Though *The Cardinal* is not characterised by the dark terrors, the profound pathos, and the intense passion of *The Duchess of Malfi*, it is a very powerful and affecting play, and less offensive to correct taste than its sublimer prototype." The leading motives of Shirley's tragedy are easily indicated. We have the powerful cardinal, and his nephew Columbo, to whom the Duchess Rosaura is obliged to plight her troth— although she is in love with the Count d'Alvarez. Columbo having been despatched to the wars, the Duchess obtains from him by stratagem a letter releasing her from her vows. But now the bloody work of the drama begins. Columbo having been murdered, Alvarez is slain in his turn by Hernando, who has been instigated by the Duchess in her mad desire for vengeance, and to whom she has promised her hand as the reward of his work. We know not why petty ends are so frequently assigned to the heads of the Romish Church in their intrigues, but this tragedy of Shirley might surely have had some more lofty leading *motif* than the determination of the Cardinal to marry his nephew with the Duchess. It dwarfs the tragedy of its grandeur, and seems too small an aim to be the basis of so much ambition, intrigue, and bloodshed. The end of the tragedy, however, is extraordinary and ingenious. The Cardinal, hopelessly defeated in his schemes, and wounded as he believes mortally by Hernando, confesses his crimes before the king and his attendants and professes the utmost contrition for them. Amongst other things he confesses that he had mingled a slow but sure poison with the food last partaken of by the Duchess, and he now offers her some powder dissolved in wine as a sovereign antidote thereto. To convince her of the truth of what he is saying he first drinks of the mixture, whereupon the Duchess follows his example, though a courtier remarks the while, "Strange he should have a good thing in readiness!" As soon as the Duchess has taken the draught, which, of course, is deadly poison, the Cardinal cannot conceal his delight, which breaks forth in extravagant manifestations; but these suffer a bitter revulsion when he discovers that after all he himself need not have taken poison, as his wounds were not mortal. This is a splendid example of "the biter bit." The whole tragedy, if scarcely equal to Shakespeare's and Webster's finest work, can compare favourably with any tragic compositions beneath theirs. As for *The Traitor*, it might fairly challenge still higher praise. . . .

The name of Shirley . . . suggests one reflection *àpropos* to the whole galaxy of Elizabethan dramatists. Regarding them now for a moment not as writers of tragedy and comedy, but as lyric poets, where shall we find amongst modern writers such exquisite tenderness, such dainty conceits, and such musical numbers? Who has equalled the songs of Shakespeare and Jonson, and the lyrics and madrigals of their brother dramatists? Such writing seems to be a lost art amongst the moderns, who have substituted to a very large extent artificiality for nature and precision for music. To Shirley must be awarded the distinction of having written stanzas equal to anything produced by the dramatists of his time, and stanzas worthy of Wither and Suckling's best vein. Take this gem, from a scene in *The Imposture*, where the nuns are discovered singing:—

> O fly, my soul! what hangs upon
>   Thy drooping wings,
>   And weighs them down,
> With love of gaudy mortal things?
> The sun is now i' the east; each shade
>   As he doth rise,
>   Is shorter made,
> That earth may lessen to our eyes:
> Oh, be not careless, then, and play
>   Until the star of peace
> Hide all his beams in dark recess;
> Poor pilgrims needs must lose their way,
> When all the shadows do increase.

In a totally distinct but inimitable vein, here is the poet's reply to one who objected that his mistress was old:—

> Tell me not Time hath play'd the thief
> Upon her beauty; my belief
> Might have been mock'd, and I had been
> An heretic, if I had not seen;
> My mistress is still fair to me,
> And now I all those graces see
> That did adorn her virgin brow;
> Her eye hath the same flame in't now,
> To kill or save; the chemist's fire
> Equally burns; so my desire;
> Not any rosebud less within
> Her cheek, the same snow on her chin;
> Her voice, that heavenly music bears,
> First charm'd my soul, and in my ears
> Did leave it trembling; her lips are
> The self-same lovely twins they were:
> After so many years I miss
> No flower in all my paradise.
>   Time, I despise thy rage and thee;
>   Thieves do not always thrive, I see.

Again, where was character ever more epigrammatically summed up than that of the notorious Duke of Buckingham in the following stanza? Buckingham, the brilliant courtier, was stabbed by Felton, in 1628, in the thirty-sixth year of his age.

> Here lies the best and worst of fate,
> Two kings' delight, the people's hate,
> The courtier's star, the kingdom's eye,
> A man to draw an angel by,
>   Fear's despiser, Villiers' glory,
>   The great man's volume, all Time's story.

But the one lyrical composition by Shirley which will ensure him immortality, when everything else he has written may have faded into nothingness, occurs in his *Ajax and Ulysses*. It is stated that King Charles II. used often to have this solemn dirge sung to him; and that on the "recital of it Oliver Cromwell was seized with great terror and agitation of mind." The former incident need not be questioned, but we are not astonished to learn that the latter is unauthenticated. Cromwell, who never trembled before kings, was scarcely made of the stuff to be affrighted at the recitation of verses, however grand and sonorous they might be. Nevertheless, there cannot possibly be found in the whole range of poetry stanzas more noble or more striking than these, which conclude with the couplet referred to at the outset of this article:—

> The glories of our blood and state
>   Are shadows, not substantial things;
> There is no armour against fate;
>   Death lays his icy hand on kings:
>   Sceptre and crown
>   Must tumble down,
> And in the dust be equal made
> With the poor crooked scythe and spade.
>
> Some men with swords may reap the field,
>   And plant fresh laurels where they kill;
> But their strong nerves at last must yield;
>   They tame but one another still:
>   Early or late,
>   They stoop to fate,
> And must give up their murmuring breath,
> When they, pale captives, creep to death.
>
> The garlands wither on your brow,
>   Then boast no more your mighty deeds;
> Upon Death's purple altar now,
>   See, where the victor-victim bleeds:
>   Your heads must come
>   To the cold tomb:
> Only the actions of the just
> Smell sweet, and blossom in the dust.

For a single conception such as this, one would exchange a bushel of tragedies, comedies, interludes, and the like.

It is an essay from which we shrink, to speak with confident exactness upon the powers and merits of Shirley. A prose introduction on the subject of Poetry, which he wrote to the collected works of Beaumont and Fletcher, makes us regret that he did not devote himself more to this form of expression, in which he manifested something of the pictorial power of Jeremy Taylor and the stateliness of Bacon. With regard to his position as a dramatist, critical opinions differ. We have seen the high eulogium passed upon him by Wood, and Langbaine described him as "one of such incomparable parts that he was the chief of the second-rate poets; and by some he has been thought even equal to Fletcher himself." Campbell and Dyce had a high opinion of his talents, but Hallam says: "Shirley has no originality, no force in conceiving or delineating character, little of pathos and less perhaps of wit; his dramas produce no deep impression in the reading, and of course can leave none on the memory. But his mind was poetical; his better characters, especially females, express pure thoughts in pure language; he is never timid or affected, and very seldom obscure; the incidents succeed rapidly, the personages are numerous, and there is a general animation in the scenes which causes us to read him with some pleasure." The former part of this judgment, with all deference, would really seem to point to a perfunctory reading of Shirley on the part of Hallam, and it cannot altogether command assent. While most of the dramas of the Elizabethan writers owe their conceptions and chief incidents to the novelists, Shirley is almost free from this charge, which is sufficient of itself to prove that he had very considerable originality. Indeed, his fertility in invention is rather striking than otherwise. His writings, moreover, contain much of pathos, fervour, and tenderness; scene after scene could be cited of a moving nature; so that here also Hallam's dictum can scarcely be accepted as sound and just.

A critic writing some fifty years ago did more justice to Shirley's genius in the passage immediately ensuing, though this judgment also cannot be said to be exhaustive or wholly satisfactory. Premising that Shirley's poetic character is by no means so strongly marked as that of most of his predecessors, and that the distinctive peculiarities of genius were pre-occupied, the writer went on to say: "When Shirley came on the stage he might seem to succeed to a mine of which the wealth had been completely exhausted—a land, of which every nook and corner had been explored and cultivated to its utmost height of productiveness. Every source from which dramatic invention had drawn its materials might seem dried up. The history of every country had been dramatised—every distinguished personage in ancient or modern times had appeared on the stage—even the novelists of Italy were well-nigh run to their dregs; human nature itself might almost appear to have been worked out—every shade and modification of character had been variously combined, every incident placed in every possible light. Yet under all these disadvantages Shirley is an original writer; though he perpetually works up materials of the same kind as those of his predecessors, yet his forms are new; though we are constantly reminded of the earlier writers, particularly of Fletcher, his plays are far from servile copies; the manner of composition is the same; yet his lights and shadows are so infinitely varied that the impression is entirely different. Even his style is his own: far inferior in force, in variety, in richness to his master's, it has an ease, a grace, sometimes an elegance, essentially his own. As softened and more delicately pencilled outlines of characters with which we are familiar meet us again in the volumes of Shirley—so his poetry is full of the same images; yet, passing, as it were, through the clear and pellucid medium of his mind, they appear as if they were the new-born creations of his own fancy." With much of this a close reader of Shirley will agree. Yet he will at the same time feel that, though the writer is evidently animated by a desire to do justice to the poet, he might have been less measured in his praise of his originality.

The truth is that too much has been made of the charge that Shirley is but the follower and closer imitator of his immediate predecessors. We do not see why his laurels in tragedy should be regarded as being filched from Webster, or his laurels in comedy from Fletcher. Had he written precisely contemporaneously with them his fame would now have been greater. He suffered by comparison with those who had already enraptured the world by their dazzling lustre, and he was charged with having lit the flame of his own genius at their shrine. Literary judgments have been subjected to revision from the earliest ages of the world until now; and it may be that with a future generation the dramatic talents of Shirley will stand much higher than they do at present. His fine lyrical faculty is already universally acknowledged, whereas for upwards of a century it met with little recognition; and his position in the realm of dramatic art may yet come to be equally assured. He is no unworthy companion of the men who filled with noble music "the spacious times of great Elizabeth."

ALGERNON CHARLES SWINBURNE
From "James Shirley"
Fortnightly Review, April 1890, pp. 461–78

If ever the time-honoured French fashion of republishing the select works of an author in place of a complete edition might reasonably find favour in the eyes of an English student, it certainly might in the case of Shirley. A considerable section or division of the six goodly volumes which contain the first collection ever made of his multitudinous works is taken up by such vapid and colourless sketches, such mere shadows or phantoms of invertebrate and bloodless fancy, as leave no trace behind on the memory but a sense of tedious vanity and unprofitable promptitude of apparently copious but actually sterile invention. Very possibly he never wrote anything quite so bad, so insolently faulty, and so impudently preposterous, as the very worst improvisations of his master Fletcher; but even such otherwise unqualified rubbish as *The Sea Voyage* or *The Nice Valour* has the one qualifying merit, the one extenuating circumstance, of being readable—not without irritation, indignation, and astonishment, but at all events without stupefying fatigue and insuperable somnolence. Too many of Shirley's plays may be read or skimmed without exciting any more active or stimulating emotions than these. Royal Masters, Duke's Mistresses, Constant Maids, Young Admirals, Balls, Coronations, and Humorous Courtiers pass before the reader's half-closed eyes in a long thin stream of indistinguishable figures and immemorable events. They never, as far as he can observe or can remember, sink below a certain modest level of passable craftsmanship and humble merit; but they never rise into palpable distinction or cohere into substantial form. The worst that can be said of them is not that they are wanting in merits or abounding in faults, but that they do not exist; they have absolutely no principle of life, no reason for being, no germ of vitality whatever. It would be something if even they were bad; it would be something if even they were dull; but they are not bad, they are nothing; they are not dull, they are null. You read them, and feel next day as if you had read nothing. The leading articles of last week's journals have left as much mark on your memory, as much impression on your mind. Perhaps you can hardly tell—they may be rather good of their kind than bad; but their kind has no right to propagate, no reason to produce. Once or twice the writer may remind you of Jonson—with all the sap squeezed out of him, or of Fletcher—with all his grace evaporated; but as a rule they are simply wearisome and conventional, anæmic and invertebrate. Even those who loathe the Puritans with a loathing equal to that of Butler may admit, as one at least of their number is ready to do, that if the advent of those brainless and brutish devil-worshippers had cut off nothing better worth keeping than the average of Shirley's supply for the London stage, literature and art and poetry would have had no very heavy charge to bring against their deadliest and most desperate enemies.

On the other hand, it would be unjust to undervalue the merit of the work which seventy years since found its first articulate admirer in Campbell, and has lately found a no less cordial than capable advocate in Mr. Gosse. Nor will any one deny the claim of Shirley to the neutral credit of such negative commendation as may be due to a writer alike incapable of the faults and of the excellences which distinguish or disfigure the work of greater men. In Defoe's phrase, "he can't commit their crimes;" it would task a stronger genius than his to do so. But then the question with regard to a poet's claims is not a question of abstinence, but of achievement; he must be judged by consideration of what he has accomplished, not of what he has avoided. Virtue which depends on incompetence to sin can hardly be commended for withstanding temptation. "J'admire Scipion, soit," says Victor Hugo; "j'admire moins Origène."

Abstinence, however, is not Shirley's only virtue; if it were, he would now be sleeping with Tate and Home, Cumberland and Jephson, Talfourd and Sheridan Knowles. There are very remarkable and admirable exceptions to the general mediocrity of his level, conventional, unambitious, and languid work. The terrible sarcasm which lashed him into oblivion for a century and a half may possibly, if not justifiably, have been provoked by the revival of his first play, a year after the author's death: a resurrection which may not unnaturally have been regarded by Dryden—it must assuredly be regarded by modern students—as an example of the survival of the unfittest. That *Love Tricks, or the School of Complement* (in modern English, of accomplishments) should have been reissued on the stage forty-two years after its first appearance is so unaccountable a fact, that it may be allowed to account for the contempt with which the Laureate of the Restoration referred to the memory of Shirley fifteen years later. This first attempt of its author is a feebly preposterous and impotently imitative abortion, and the product of secondhand humour and secondrate sentiment: but though always absurd it is not always dull; there are one or two redeeming touches which indicate or suggest a latent or dormant capacity for better things. There is a pleasant anticipation of modern progress on the social lines of French democracy in the first scene, when an amorous elder on the eve of marriage reflects and resolves thus manfully: "I will get but one child, and that shall be a boy, lest having too many children I undo my heir, and my goods be divided." That a royalist playwright of retrogressive and reactionary England should thus early have foreseen and forecast the future of "the great nation," under the practical and exemplary influence of the most advanced and enlightened children of its unspeakably sublime revolution, may perhaps be no less edifying than amusing to readers not inoculated with incurable Gallomania.

The absurd fancy of representing an old man under the delusion that his youth had been restored to him can only be excelled in preposterous and irritating inanity of impotent invention by the ineffable notion of introducing a young libertine, in the heyday of impudent vigour and rampant recklessness, whom a virtuous young woman, assisted by acquaintances of such virtue as will ignore blows and kicks administered by the subject of the experiment, succeeds in persuading that he is dead. How such impudent and insufferable nonsense can ever have crawled on to the stage or crept into print it is difficult to understand. *The Witty Fair One* is wofully witless stuff—inane, incoherent, incomposite, impossible, and dull. A pretty piece of smooth and smirking verse, which might have passed unobserved among far nobler passages in almost any play of Dekker's or Middleton's or Marston's, attracted the attention of a critic who did not think overmuch of Shakespeare to a somewhat vapid and flaccid play of Shirley's: I doubt if the reader whom this quotation may induce or impel to peruse *The Brothers* will bless the memory of the critic who suggested such an enterprise. "They did not think," says one of the actors in the last scene, "to find this pale society of ghosts;" which shows that he had not had time to keep company with his fellow phantoms, the other and latter ghosts of their romantic or sentimental invention. A paler or more featureless "society" it would be difficult to find.

But when Shirley was not astray on the track of his adored Fletcher, limping and wheezing and hobbling behind that splendid if not always reliable racer, he could run better than

might have been expected by a spectator of his performances in a field reserved for steeds of finer blood and higher mettle. I can by no means agree with Mr. Dyce that the happiest efforts of his genius will perhaps be found in the tragic portions of these variegated dramas, his romantic or tragicomic studies in the school of Fletcher rather than Beaumont. Such a tragedy as *The Traitor*, such a comedy as *The Example*, may defy comparison with the best of these hybrid and imitative creatures of overworked invention and fatigued or enfeebled fancy. Even *The Maid's Revenge*, for which his very editors have hardly a good word, is a failure which makes us feel that it ought to have been a success; crude, rude, coarse, and rough as it is, there is more suggestion if not more presentation of natural passion and dramatic life in it than in a later play, so much better polished and composed, so much more equable and elaborate, as *The Cardinal*. But the fiendish atrocity of Catalina is a flight beyond the gentle capacity of Shirley: his pinion flags in the attempt, and his voice cracks in the effort to express such murderous and perfidious passions. A very fine tragedy might have been made out of the story: but when we think what Middleton and Rowley would have given us, had they happily chanced to undertake it, we cannot be thankful enough that the story of Beatrice and De Fleres fell into the right hands, and was treated by artists who could make at once the most and the best of it, as they would have made, and Shirley could not make, of the story of Antonio and Berinthia. . . .

The bright light comedy of *Hyde Park* is the second really good play of its kind on the long list of Shirley's works. In vigour of style and force of interest it is notably inferior to *The Wedding*: its tone is altogether more modern, more remote from tragicomedy, less serious and less ambitious; but it belongs unmistakeably to a period of transition. It is a quasi-poetic or semi-poetic piece of work, and so far belongs or aims at belonging to the same class as *The Spanish Curate*, or *The Guardian*—not to say, as *Twelfth Night* or *Much Ado about Nothing*. It aims also at a transient sort of realism, a photographic representation of the fancies or the follies of the hour, its passing affectations or extravagances of the drawing-room or the race-course, which anticipates in some degree the enterprise, if not the superb and perfect mastery in that line, of such artists as Congreve and Vanbrugh. The versatility and flexibility of talent required and displayed in such an attempt, admitting it to be fairly and moderately successful, may reasonably challenge our praise; but Mistress Carol, though bright and pleasant enough, is as far beneath the level of Millamant as beneath the level of Viola. Between the sunset of Fletcher and the sunrise of Etherege the moonlight of Shirley's more modest and subdued genius serves well enough to display him as a successor of the poetic or romantic dramatist whose fancy walks hand in hand with humour, and a precursor of the prosaic or realistic playwright whose cynical humour has swallowed up sentiment and fancy as a stork might swallow a frog; but this moonlit or starlit period of transition is noticeable rather for its refraction of the past than its anticipation of the coming day. The characters in such comedies as this of Shirley's seem to be playing at reality as shadows might play at being substantial, as ghosts might play at being alive, as children do play at being "grown up;" and this at least is a charge which can no more be brought against the ruffians and strumpets of Wycherley's or Shadwell's invention than against the noble men or women of Shakespeare's or of Webster's. The return of the shipwrecked husband to his supposed widow is borrowed from Marston's *What You Will*; and though Shirley's comedy is far more neatly and reasonably constructed, far more satisfactory to an æsthetic or intelligent judge of composition, it has nothing of such intellectual force or such literary merit as must be recognised here and there in the rougher and more vigorous work of the elder and greater though ruder and faultier poet. Marston, with all his shortcomings, is one of Jonson's if not of Shakespeare's men-at-arms; Shirley, with all his merits, is but one of Fletcher's body-guard.

There is some honest fun, though there is no great matter, in the little satirical comedy of *The Ball*: the sham traveller is a more original and amusing figure than a copy of Ben Jonson's rather ponderous Puntarvolo could have been; and even after all his precursors the braggart and beaten coward contrives to have some amusing and original touches of baseness and comicality about him, which may make us tolerate the reappearance of an almost worn-out and wearisome type of farce. The ladies and their lovers are so lamentably shadowy and shapeless that a modern reader has no difficulty in understanding the curious admission of the poet in a later and better and less reticent play that he had been "bribed to a modest admission of their antic gambols." Had he rejected the bribe, supposing it to have ever been offered, a less decorous and a less vacuous comedy might have been better worth our reading: but possibly, if not probably, the assertion or imputation may be merely part of the character to whom it is assigned. Shirley, however, must have all due credit for this fresh stripe of satire applied to the same idiotic affectation which he had lashed with as wholesome and cordial a stroke of contempt just four years earlier, in a passage already quoted. "You must encourage strangers, while you live; it is the character of our nation, we are famous for dejecting our own countrymen." Shirley's next play, *The Young Admiral*, is amusing enough for a lazy and consequently a tolerant reader to take up and put down with as much satisfaction as he might hope to derive from a novel obviously and exclusively intended for railway reading; it is not at all discreditable, and now and then promises—and breaks its promise—to be seriously interesting as well as tolerably entertaining; the hero and heroine are a very creditable couple of ultimately triumphant victims, the kings and knaves, bullies and fools, play their parts very decently and endurably. On the whole, we may say of this and indeed most of Shirley's plays that it admirably anticipates and agreeably realises Mrs. John Knightley's immortal receipt for "nice smooth gruel—thin, but not too thin."

The one thing memorable about this anæmic and invertebrate play is the fact that it had the dishonour to be commended for its decency and propriety by the mean puritan who then dishonoured even the discreditable post of dramatic censor. A censor of a far different kind has made of Shirley's next play the central point of his impeachment, the crowning witness in favour of his plea for puritans against playwrights, for William Prynne against William Shakespeare. A better point could not have been made; a better witness could not have been cited. It would be worse than useless for a lover of poetry and a hater of puritanism to undertake the defence of the admirably constructed and excellently written tragicomedy which Charles I. set Shirley to write on a subject supplied by the royal and kindly patron. The subject is excellent in its way, and suggestive of even better and stronger dramatic effects than Shirley has made out of it; but the utter vileness, the abject and atrocious treachery of the two mean tricksters and traffickers in women who play the leading parts in this comedy, cannot reasonably be condoned on consideration of the brilliant and striking situations which are brought about by the villainy of these gilded and varnished rascals. Fletcher was not a severe moralist; he is usually considered by modern critics to have sometimes broken the bounds of good taste and artistic tact in

his pictures of headlong youth and light-hearted passion: but not one of his Rubilios, Valentines, or Pinieros, can be imagined capable of such baseness as would disgrace a professional pander. *The Gamester* is a very clever, very powerful, and very amusing play: but Wycherley's *Plain Dealer*, though doubtless more impudent in its indecency, is certainly less immoral in its consummation. Fletcher in his own way, like Congreve in his, has always at least the graceless grace of high-bred wantonness; Shirley is nothing if not moral; or rather he is ruffianly and repulsive. . . .

If the treatment of character and passion had been equal to the development of interest and the management of the story, the vigorous and well-built tragedy of *The Cardinal* might have been what its author avowedly thought it, the flower of his flock; it is indeed a model of composition, simple and lucid and thoroughly well sustained in its progress towards a catastrophe remarkable for tragic originality and power of invention; with no confusion or encumbrance of episodes, no change or fluctuation of interest, no breach or defect of symmetry. But the story is more interesting than the actors; and the points of resemblance between this play and *The Duchess of Malfy* are consequently as noticeable as the points of resemblance between Macedon and Monmouth. There is a wicked cardinal in each, and the principal victim of his crimes is an innocent duchess. The very spirited and amusing comedy of *The Sisters* is only not one of Shirley's very best; *The Country Captain*, discovered and reissued by Mr. Bullen, is indisputably one of them. The traditional attribution of this brilliant play to the Duke of Newcastle will hardly persuade any competent reader that it is not mainly if not altogether the work of Shirley; though the burlesque picture of the trained bands may possibly be assigned to the professional hand of the martial and equestrian duke. The parody of Donne's most elaborately eccentric style in the verses ascribed to a fashionable poetaster seems curiously out of date in a generation of writers equally incapable of emulating the peculiar merits and of copying the peculiar mannerisms of the great poet who is to the Cowleys and Clevelands of Shirley's day as a giant to pigmies who cannot even mimic his gait; for the strong uneven stride of his verse is no more like the mincing amble of Cowley's than Wordsworth is like Moore. The attack on monopolists does credit to the independence and courage of the assailant; but it is unfortunate that a figure of mere farce should so much as recall what it does not pretend to compete with, the most famous character on the stage of Massinger. The humour is throughout as much stronger as it is coarser than usual with Shirley: the more high-flown parts are more than fair examples of his fluent and flowery style of rhetoric—not glaringly artificial, but suggestive rather of perfumery than of natural perfume. Some parts of the action, like some parts of the dialogue, are exceptionally daring in the license if not the licentiousness of their freedom; but the upshot is more satisfactory to the moral and intellectual taste or judgment of a critical reader than is that of *The Lady of Pleasure*—the only other play of Shirley's which can be compared with it for sheer brilliance and vivacity of movement and of style. *The Court Secret*, of apparently later date, is a thin dry cobweb of a play, with a few tender and graceful touches here and there which hardly serve to lighten or relieve the empty complications and confusions of its tedious and conventional story. But there are signs even here that the writer's invention, though now a spur-galled and broken-winded jade, was once a racer of some mettle. It is agreeable to reflect that the condensed satire of the following brief description is inapplicable to any politician of our own day.

Why, there's
A statesman that can side with every faction;
And yet most subtly can untwist himself
When he hath wrought the business up to danger!
He lives within a labyrinth.

There are some "pretty little tiny kickshaws" among Shirley's poems. His *Good Night* is a curious anticipation of Shelley's, though less graceful and serious in expression; but it would be flattery to honour his elegies with the qualification of mediocrity; and his *Narcissus* must surely be the very feeblest and faintest copy among all the innumerable imitations of Shakespeare's too popular first poem. *The Triumph of Beauty* is poor meagre stuff; the interlude of *Cupid and Death* is livelier and not ungraceful, though much beneath what it might have been. *The Contention of Ajax and Ulysses* is a very fair piece of work, more solid in versification than usual, though wanting alike in the stately grace of Ovid and the sprightly facility of Heywood; but memorable only as containing the one universally popular and famous poem of so fertile a writer as Shirley. This celebrated dirge or monody is no doubt a noble poem, but it has also been a very lucky one. There is many a yet finer lyric of the same age and kind which has had but two or three readers where Shirley's lament has had a thousand. His last work, the allegorical comedy of *Honoria and Mammon*, is not merely a recast or expansion of a twenty-six years older work, but a great improvement on that clever and bright little interlude. Shirley's wit, style, and humour are all at their best in the curious and ingenious drama with which he took a final farewell of the stage. It is amusing to find in his last as in his first play a touch of satire which would have been even more timely and appropriate in a satirist of our own generation. "I'll——build a bridge," says one of Lady Mammon's suitors, "from Dover cliff to Calais." "A drawbridge?" asks a countryman; and another observes, with due reticence,

This may be done; but I am of opinion
We shall not live to see it.

Amen to that: but the loyal and sensible old poet is surely deserving of serious praise and credit for his contemptuously imaginative anticipation of the most monstrous project ever hatched—except perhaps its fellow folly, a submarine instead of an aerial conspiracy against the beneficence of nature.

The works of Shirley fall naturally into three categories or classes: those in the first class are very good, those in the second class are very fair, those in the third class are very poor. *The Traitor, The Example, The Lady of Pleasure*, and *The Country Captain*, belong beyond all question to the first class: *The Wedding, Hyde Park, The Gamester*, and *The Cardinal*, stand high in the second. If these, with perhaps two or three more, were all we had of Shirley, it would be simply impossible to see the point or understand the meaning of Dryden's bitter sneer at his "tautology." But to the patient reader of all his plays the truth of the imputation will be as evident as the cruelty of the insult. The general charge of repetition, monotony, wearisome reiteration of similar types and similar effects, can hardly be disputed or denied. Of Heywood, whom Dryden in his headlong ignorance and his headstrong arrogance chose or chanced to bracket with Shirley as a subject for indiscriminate satire, this cannot either truthfully or plausibly be affirmed. He has always something to say, even though it be said in the homeliest of bald and prosy styles: Shirley at his worst has really nothing to say whatever. But the demerits of his duller and unhappier hours would hardly be remembered by the admirers of his better work if he had never been overpraised by such critics as depreciate or ignore his betters. The "poet-critic" who ignores the existence of Tourneur and dismisses Webster with a sneer expatiates with exuberance of unction on the attractions and fascinations of Shirley; and this enthusiasm on the part of Campbell inclines us to remember—if ever it were possible we should forget—that a breath of Cyril Tourneur's fiery passion would suffice to blast the fairest fruits of Shirley's garden into dust and ashes, and a glance from the eye of John Webster to strike its chirping and twittering birds into breathless and cowering silence. When we turn to such poets as these we can hardly see or hear or remember Shirley as a singer or a creator at all; but it is as unjust and ungracious to insist on the inferiority in kind which is established by such a comparison, as it would be preposterous and absurd to question it. The place of James Shirley among English poets is naturally unpretentious and modest: it is indisputably authentic and secure.

GEORGE WITHER

1588–1667

George Wither was born at Bentworth, Hampshire, on June 11, 1588. From 1604 to 1606 Wither was enrolled at Magdalen College, Oxford. By 1610 he was residing in London and writing poetry. His 1613 verse collection on the occasion of Princess Elizabeth's marriage, *Epithalamia; or, Nuptial Poems*, was well received. Later that same year his *Abuses Stript and Whipt; or, Satyricall Essays* landed him in prison at Marshalsea. In 1615 he published five pastorals in *The Shepherd's Hunting*, a continuation of his work written with William Browne, *Shepherd's Pipe*. *Fidelia*, a poetical epistle from a faithful nymph to an inconstant lover, also appeared in 1615. *Wither's Motto: Nec Habeo. Nec Careo. Nec Curo* (1621), landed him in Newgate prison. Wither's other verse works include a long panegyric titled *Faire-Virtue, the Mistresse of Phil'Arete* (1622), and a collection of his better-known poems, *Juvenilia* (1622).

During the early 1620s Wither became an open Puritan supporter. He served as a captain of horse in the First Bishops' War of 1639, and he later sold his estate to raise a regiment in 1642. He was Governor of Farnham Castle in 1642, and Major-General of the forces in Surrey in 1643. Under the Commonwealth Wither served as Justice of the Peace for Hampshire, Surrey, and Essex (1642–58). Among his many religious verse works are *Hymns and Songs of the Church* (1623),

Britains Remembrancer (1628), and *Heleluiah or Britains Second Remembrancer* (1641). One prose work, *The Scholars Purgatory* (c. 1625), is also noteworthy.

Wither lost his property and positions during the Restoration. He also spent about three years in Newgate prison. Wither died on May 2, 1667, and was buried in the Savoy Church in the Strand.

Personal

In the time of the Civill-warres, George Withers, the Poet, begged Sir John Denham's Estate at Egham of the Parliament, in whose cause he was a Captaine of Horse. It happened that G. W. was taken prisoner, and was in danger of his Life, having written severely against the King, &c. Sir John Denham went to the King, and desired his Majestie not to hang him, for that *whilest G. W. lived, he should not be the worst Poet in England.*
—JOHN AUBREY, "Sir John Denham," *Brief Lives,* 1669–96

George Wither, son of George Wither, the first son by a second venter, of the house of Wither of Manydowne near to Wotton S. Laurence in Hampshire, was born at Bentworth near to Alton in the said county, on the eleventh day of June 1588, (30 Eliz.) educated in gram. learning under the noted schoolmaster of those parts called Joh. Greaves of Colemore, sent to Magd. coll. in the year 1604 or thereabouts, where being put under the tuition of Joh. Warner, (afterwards bish. of Roch.) whom, if I mistake not, he serv'd, made some proficiency with much ado in academical learning; but his geny being addicted to things more trivial, was taken home after he had spent about three years in the said house, and thence sent to one of the inns of chancery in London, and afterwards to Lincolns inn, to obtain knowledge in the municipal law. But still his geny hanging after things more smooth and delightful, he did, at length, make himself known to the world (after he had taken several rambles therein) by certain specimens of poetry; which being dispersed in several hands, became shortly after a public author, and much admired by some in that age for his quick advancement in that faculty. But so it was, that he shewing himself too busy and satyrical in his *Abuses stript and whipt,* was committed prisoner to the Marshalsea, where continuing several months, was then more cried up, especially by the puritannical party, for his profuse pouring forth of English rhime, and more afterwards by the vulgar sort of people for his prophetical poetry, in regard that many things were fancied by them to come to pass, which he pretended to predict. In 1639 he was a captain of horse in the expedition against the Scots, and quarter-master gen. of the regiment wherein he was captain, viz. of that regiment of, or next under, the earl of Arundel, general of the forces in the said expedition. But this our author, who was always from his youth puritannically affected, (sufficiently evidenced in his satyrs) sided with the presb. in the beginning of the civil wars rais'd by them, an. 1642, became an enemy to the king and regality, sold the estate he had, and with the moneys received for it rais'd a troop of horse for the parliament, was made a captain and soon after a major, having this motto on his colours, *Pro Rege, Lege, Grege;* but being taken prisoner by the cavaliers, sir Jo. Denham the poet (some of whose land at Egham in Surrey Wither had got into his clutches) desired his majesty not to hang him, 'because that so long as Wither lived, Denham would not be accounted the worst poet in England.' About that time he was constituted by the said long parliament a justice of peace in quorum for Hampshire, Surrey, and Essex, (which office he kept 16 years) and afterwards was made by Oliver major gen. of all the horse and foot in the county of Surrey, in which employment he licked his fingers sufficiently, gaining thereby a great odium from the generous royalist. After the king's restoration in 1660,

he lost all the lands that had belonged to royalists and bishops, which he before had either bought, or had conferr'd upon him for the love and zeal he had to the blessed cause. And being then look'd upon as a dangerous person to the king and state, especially for a scandalous and seditious libel that he had then dispersed, was committed prisoner to Newgate; and afterwards, upon his own confession, and the oaths of two persons, that he was the author of it, he, by order of the house of commons, was sent in custody, and committed close prisoner to the Tower of London, to be debarr'd pen, ink, and paper, and about the same time (24 of March 1661/2) an impeachment was ordered to be drawn up against him. In both which prisons he continued three years and more, wrote several things by the connivance of the keeper, of which some were afterwards made public, yet could never refrain from shewing himself a presbyterian satyrist. He began very early, being precisely educated from his childhood, to express and publish those conceptions, which the affections and inclinations to youth had awakened in him, endeavouring to season them with morality and piety, as subjects of that nature are capable of; suiting them to the capacities of young men, who delight to see their own natural passions, represented as 'twere in a glass; wherein they not only meet with some better things than they looked for, but with such notions also therewith mixed, as insinuated into their hearts that seasoning which made them much delighted with his poems, and rendred him so generally known, that thousands, especially such youths that were puritannically educated, were desirous to peruse his future writings, and to take better heed of that, whereof else perhaps they had taken little or no notice, while others of generous education, and of more solid parts, looked upon them as the effects of a crazed brain, and esteemed Taylor the water-poet a fit match for him with his wild and rambling rhimes. The things that he hath written and published are very many, accounted by the generality of scholars mere scribbles, and the fancies of a conceited and confident, if not enthusiastical, mind.—ANTHONY À WOOD, *Athenae Oxonienses,* 1691–1721

George Wither was born June 11, 1588, and in his younger years distinguished himself by some pastoral pieces, that were not inelegant; but growing afterwards involved in the political and religious disputes in the times of James I. and Charles I. he employed his poetical vein in severe pasquils on the court and clergy, and was occasionally a sufferer for the freedom of his pen. In the civil war that ensued, he exerted himself in the service of the Parliament, and became a considerable sharer in the spoils. He was even one of those provincial tyrants, whom Oliver distributed over the kingdom, under the name of Major Generals; and had the fleecing of the county of Surrey: but surviving the Restoration, he outlived both his power and his affluence; and giving vent to his chagrin in libels on the court, was long a prisoner in Newgate and the Tower. He died at length on the 2d of May, 1667.—THOMAS PERCY, *Reliques of Early English Poetry,* 1765

General

George Withers; a most profuse pourer forth of English Rhime, not without great pretence to a poetical zeal against the vices of the Times, in his *Motto;* his *Remembrancer;* and other such like Satirical Works: besides which, he turned into English verse the *Songs of Moses*; and other *Hymns of the Old Testament*; in all which, and whatever else there is of his, dispersed up and down, (for his works, however voluminous, have been scarce thought worthy to be collected into a volume,) whoever shall go about to imitate his lofty style, may boldly venture to ride post and versify: yet, because vulgarly taken for a great poet, and by some for a prophet, in regard many things are fancied to have come to pass which he pretended to predict, he must not be omitted: but the most of poetical fancy which I remember to have found in any of his writings, is in a little piece of pastoral poetry, called *The Shepherd's Hunting*.—EDWARD PHILLIPS, *Theatrum Poetarum Anglicanorum*, 1675

Honest George Withers, though a rustic poet, hath been very acceptable; as to some for his prophecies, so to others, for his plain country honesty.—RICHARD BAXTER, *Poetical Fragments*, 1681

> Know, Eusden thirsts no more for sack or praise;
> He sleeps among the dull of ancient days;
> Safe, where no Critics damn, no duns molest,
> Where wretched Withers, Ward, and Gildon rest.
> —ALEXANDER POPE, *The Dunciad* (1728), 1742,
> Bk. 1, ll. 293–96

This beautiful old song 〈"The Shepherd's Resolution"〉 was written by a poet, whose name would have been utterly forgotten, if it had not been preserved by *Swift*, as a term of contempt. *Dryden* and *Wither* are coupled by him like the *Bavius* and *Mœvius* of Virgil. *Dryden*, however, has had justice done him by posterity: and as for *Wither*, though of subordinate merit, that he was not altogether devoid of genius, will be judged from the following stanzas. The truth is, *Wither*, was a very voluminous party-writer: and as his political and satyrical strokes rendered him extremely popular in his life-time; so afterwards, when these were no longer relished, they totally consigned his writings to oblivion.—THOMAS PERCY, *Reliques of Ancient English Poetry*, 1765

Amongst his numerous verses, which he seems to have scribbled with endless profusion, and with a total disregard to the art of blotting, there are entire compositions, which could not have proceeded, but from one, who was endowed with a strong poetical spirit. In those instances he is generally characterized by an easy elegance, and a copiousness of unaffected sentiment. A man of real taste, who has an opportunity of comparing all his publications, many of which can now seldom be met with, would do an acceptable service to the literary world, by giving a judicious selection from them.—SAMUEL EGERTON BRYDGES, "Preface" to *Censura Literaria*, 1806, Vol. 2, p. x

The poems of G. Wither are distinguished by a hearty homeliness of manner, and a plain moral speaking. He seems to have passed his life in one continued act of an innocent self-pleasing. That which he calls his *Motto* is a continued self-eulogy of two thousand lines, which we read it to the end without any feeling of distaste, almost without a consciousness that we have been listening all the while to a man praising himself. There are none of the cold particles in it, the hardness and self-ends which render vanity and egotism hateful. He seems to be praising another person, under the mask of self; or rather we feel that it was indifferent to him where he found the virtue which he celebrates; whether another's bosom, or his own, were its chosen receptacle. His poems are full, and this in particular is one downright confession, of a generous self-seeking. But by self he sometimes means a great deal,—his friends, his principles, his country, the human race.

Whoever expects to find in the satirical pieces of this writer any of those peculiarities which pleased him in the satires of Dryden or Pope, will be grievously disappointed. Here are no high-finished characters, no nice traits of individual nature, few or no personalities. The game run down is coarse general vice, or folly as it appears in classes. A liar, a drunkard, a coxcomb, is *stript and whipt*; no Shaftesbury, no Villiers, or Wharton, is curiously anatomized, and read upon. But to a well-natured mind there is a charm of moral sensiblity running through them which amply compensates the want of those luxuries. Wither seems every where bursting with a love of goodness and a hatred of all low and base actions.—At this day it is hard to discover what parts in the poem here particularly alluded to, *Abuses Stript and Whipt*, could have occasioned the imprisonment of the author. Was Vice in High Places more suspicious than now? had she more power; or more leisure to listen after ill reports? That a man should be convicted of a libel when he named no names but Hate, and Envy, and Lust, and Avarice, is like one of the indictments in the *Pilgrim's Progress*, where Faithful is arraigned for having "railed on our noble Prince Beelzebub, and spoken contemptibly of his honourable friends, the Lord Old Man, the Lord Carnal Delight, and the Lord Luxurious." What unlucky jealousy could have tempted the great men of those days to appropriate such innocent abstractions to themselves!

Wither seems to have contemplated to a degree of idolatry his own possible virtue. He is for ever anticipating persecution and martyrdom; fingering, as it were, the flames, to try how he can bear them. Perhaps his premature defiance sometimes made him obnoxious to censures, which he would otherwise have slipped by.

The homely versification of these Satires is not likely to attract in the present day. It is certainly not such as we should expect from a poet "soaring in the high region of his fancies with his garland and his singing robes about him;" nor is it such as he has shown in his *Philarete*, and in some parts in his *Shepherds Hunting*. He seems to have adopted this dress with voluntary humility, as fittest for a moral teacher, as our divines chuse sober grey or black; but in their humility consists their sweetness. The deepest tone of moral feeling in them, (though all throughout is weighty, earnest and passionate) is in those pathetic injunctions against shedding of blood in quarrels, in the chapter entitled "Revenge." The story of his own forbearance, which follows, is highly interesting. While the Christian sings his own victory over Anger, the Man of Courage cannot help peeping out to let you know, that it was some higher principle than *fear* which counselled his forbearance.

Whether encaged, or roaming at liberty, Wither never seems to have abated a jot of that free spirit, which sets its mark upon his writings, as much as a predominant feature of independence impresses every page of our late glorious Burns; but the elder poet wraps his proof-armour closer about him, the other wears his too much outwards; he is thinking too much of annoying the foe, to be quit easy within; the spiritual defences of Wither are a perpetual source of inward sunshine, the magnanimity of the modern is not without its alloy of soreness, and a sense of injustice, which seems perpetually to gall and irritate. Wither was better skilled in the "sweet uses of adversity," he knew how to extract the "precious jewel" from the head of the "toad," without drawing any of the "ugly venom" along with it.—The prison notes of Wither are finer than the wood notes of most of his poetical brethren. The description in the Fourth Eglogue of his *Shepherds Hunting*, (which was composed during his imprisonment in the Marshalsea) of the power of the Muse to extract pleasure from common objects, has been oftener quoted, and is more known, than any part of his writings. Indeed the whole Eglogue is in a strain so much above not only what himself, but almost what any other poet has written, that he himself could not help noticing it; he remarks, that his spirits had been raised higher than they were wont "through the love of poesy."—The praises of Poetry have been often sung in ancient and in modern times; strange powers have been ascribed to it of influence over animate and inanimate auditors; its force over fascinated crowds has been acknowledged; but, before Wither, no one ever celebrated its power *at home*, the wealth and the strength which this divine gift confers upon its possessor. Fame, and that too after death, was all which hitherto the poets had promised themselves from their art. It seems to have been left to Wither to discover, that poetry was a present possession, as well as a rich reversion; and that the Muse had promise of both lives, of this, and of that which was to come.—CHARLES LAMB, "On the Poetical Works of George Wither," c. 1815

From youth to age George continued to pour forth his lucubrations, in prophesy, remonstrance, complaint, and triumph, through good and evil report, through all vicissitudes of fortune: at one time in command among the saints, and at another scrawling his thoughts in jail, when pen and ink were denied him, with red ochre upon a trencher. It is generally allowed that his taste and genius for poetry did not improve in the political contest. Some of his earliest pieces display the native amenity of a poet's imagination but as he mixed with the turbulent times, his fancy grew muddy with the stream. While Milton in the same cause brought his learning and zeal as a partisan, he left the Muse behind him, as a mistress too sacred to be introduced into party brawlings; Wither, on the contrary, took his Muse along with him to the camp and the congregation, and it is little to be wondered at that her cap should have been torn and her voice made hoarse in the confusion. —THOMAS CAMPBELL, *Specimens of the British Poets*, 1819

It would have been very well to have republished the *Fair Virtue*, and *Shepherd's Hunting* of George Wither, which contain all the true poetry he ever wrote; but we can imagine nothing more dreary than the seven hundred pages of his *Hymns and Songs*, whose only use, that we can conceive of, would be as penal reading for incorrigible poetasters.—JAMES RUSSELL LOWELL, "Library of Old Authors," 1858–64

It is somewhat difficult to tell the student what may be considered the chief production of George Wither. His *Shepheards' Hunting* is generally associated with his name. But he was the author of more than a hundred works besides, the collection together of which no one has as yet been found sufficiently courageous to undertake. Very many of these productions are of a political nature. He was also the author of a number of religious pieces, of some very graceful songs and poems, and of some very biting satires under the title *Abuses Stript and Whipt*. *Britain's Remembrancer* is a long and able poem, written by him in London, during the plague of 1627, and is by some considered the most valuable of all his writings.—JAMES HAIN FRISWELL, *Essays on English Writers*, 1869, p. 76

Wither resembles Wordsworth in having written almost all his good work within a period of a few years. That period is from 1613 to 1623. The great exception is the *Hallelujah*—a collection of sacred poems, in which are some beautiful things written as late as 1641. On the whole, however, the collection of Wither's poems entitled *Juvenilia* contains nearly all his best writing. The enthusiasm with which he threw himself into politics damaged his genius. His nature was not large enough

to pour itself with equal power into the two channels of art and practical life. He became an eager partisan and sectary, retaining that moral elevation and dignity which ever honourably distinguishes him, but losing all sense of form and measure, perhaps indeed deliberately neglecting them as things indifferent. It is then to the early part of his life that we have to attend; and here we must remember his two years at Oxford, where he was a member of Magdalen College: two happy years, he himself has told us, which were unfortunately cut short by his sudden withdrawal from the University. In 1605, he went up to Lincoln's Inn, and there became acquainted with Browne, who was at that time a member of the Inner Temple. The friendship was a very important one for Wither. The two wrote in friendly rivalry, and often in intimate co-partnership, and we shall hardly err in laying great stress upon Browne's influence during the first period of Wither's poetry. Browne was a born artist, if ever there was one, and his example wooed the naturally ascetic and polemical genius of Wither into pleasanter paths for a while. Wither in later life expresses most unnecessary repentance for his early poems. He had no such reason for feelings of the kind as perhaps Chaucer had. Not a single line of his poetry is really corrupt or dishonourable to the writer. But he was young then, and could write of love and the beauty of nature and the beauty of woman, with a facile pen and an ardent delight in the fulness of his life and the power of his art, which seemed no doubt profane and dangerous trifling to the Puritan captain of the Civil War. But even in his youth life did not altogether smile upon him. His very harmless satires, published under the title *Abuses Stript and Whipt* in 1613, were rewarded by imprisonment in the Marshalsea. As Lamb says, it is wonderful that such perfectly general denunciations of the ordinary vices of Gluttony, Avarice, Vanity, and the rest of it in the abstract should have seemed offensive to any human being. But the cap fitted some one in high place, and Wither had to expiate his plain spokenness by a rigorous confinement. After his liberation he renewed more intimately than ever his friendship with Browne, and in 1615 wrote in conjunction with him the *Shepherd's Pipe*. His own *Shepherd's Hunting*, which he wrote in prison (see the extract here given) and which contains perhaps his very best work, appeared in the same year. To this date also must be assigned the first edition of his *Fidelia*, a poetical epistle from a forsaken fair one to her inconstant lover. At the end of this first edition of *Fidelia* is printed that famous song—'Shall I, wasting in despaire?'— which will always keep Wither's memory green, even if all else of his poetry is forgotten. The *Motto* followed in 1618, and met at once with great success. The poem is an amusingly egotistical performance, but the egotism is, as Charles Lamb said, of a sort which no one can resent. The motto is 'Nec habeo, nec careo, nec curo,' and the poem is divided into three parts, one treating of 'nec habeo,' another of 'nec careo,' and the third of 'nec curo.' In a preface addressed to 'Anybody,' he makes a statement which perhaps no one would wish to gainsay. 'The language is but indifferent, for I affected matter rather than words; the method is none at all: for I was loath to make a business of a recreation.' It is worth noticing that in the preface he alludes to the episode which, in spite of its uncouthness and exaggeration, is perhaps the most amusing part of his satires, in very uncomplimentary terms. 'The foolish Canterbury Tale in my Scourge of Vanity (which I am now almost ashamed to read over) even that hath been by some praised for a witty passage.' Whenever Wither gives himself liberty and has his fling, he is sure not long afterwards to repent. In 1623 appeared his first serious attempt at sacred poetry in the shape of his *Hymns and Songs of the Church*. Great part of this collection consists of metrical paraphrases of the Psalms and Song of Solomon, but there are also some hymns the inspiration of which is due to no one but Wither himself. Such are the 'Hymn for All Saints Day' and the 'Hymn for the Author,' which are not only interesting in themselves but because a close comparison with the form in which these same poems appeared in the collection entitled *Hallelujah* nearly twenty years afterwards reveals the notable fact that Wither was one of the very few poets who improved his work by retouching it, and that his second thoughts were always his best. I give nothing from his *Britain's Remembrancer* (1628) or from his *Emblems* (1634). The former seems to me a rather tedious political poem, and the latter is merely a collection written to order as text for a certain number of Dutch engravings. It is true that there are one or two of these latter poems which show qualities of thought and diction not to be disregarded, but on the whole I do not think he reaches his best anywhere in the collection. *Hallelujah* (1641) shows that great part of his old power still survives. The versification is flexible and musical in a very high degree, clothing the thought sometimes, as in the poem on 'All Saints' Day', in a form of subtle beauty and strangeness; in other poems, as in the verses 'For Those at Sea,' moving with a grand lilt and rapidity which fitly symbolize the theme. The verses on 'A Dear Friend Deceased' are of exquisite tenderness and beauty. They are written from the heart and to the heart, and affect us as they must have affected the writer himself. Wither has the same rare power of pathos that was possessed also by his friend Browne.

The limits of our space prevent us quoting even all of the few poems that we have specially named; but it is hoped that our selection will still be fairly representative of a poet who is certainly much less known than he deserves to be. Braithwaite wrote in 1615—

And long may England's Thespian springs be known
By lovely Wither and by bonny Browne

But the wish has hardly been fulfilled, and there are few readers who would not be a little surprised by the epithet here applied to the Puritan poet. No real lover of poetry will however grudge it him. He is one of the few masters of octosyllabic verse in our language. Lamb has dwelt lovingly on its curious felicities, and for compass and variety it would not be easy to name its superior. It is the one form of verse pre-eminently suited to Wither, who has achieved no such triumphs with the heroic couplet. But it is not only for beauty of poetic form that Wither deserved Braithwaite's enthusiastic epithet. Like the Charmides of Plato's dialogue, he has 'what is much more important, a beautiful soul.' Never was there a purer or more honourable spirit, or one which kept closer to the best it knew, and as Wither has revealed himself in his works in a way in which few poets have done, it is natural to read him not only with admiration but with sympathy.—W. T. ARNOLD, "George Wither," *The English Poets*, ed. Thomas Humphry Ward, 1880, Vol. 2, pp. 87–89

The comparative impotence of even the best criticism to force writers on public attention has never been better illustrated than in the case of George Wither himself. The greater part of a century has passed since Charles Lamb's glowing eulogy of him was written, and the terms of that eulogy have never been contested by competent authority. Yet there is no complete collection of his work in existence, and there is no complete collection even of the poems, saving a privately printed one which is inaccessible except in large libraries, and to a few subscribers. His sacred poems, which are not his best, were indeed reprinted in the Library of Old Authors; and one song of his, the famous "Shall I wasting in despair," is universally

known. But the long and exquisite poem of *Philarete* was not generally known (if it is generally known now, which may be doubted) till Mr. Arber reprinted it in the fourth volume of his *English Garner* three or four years ago. Nor can *Fidelia* and *The Shepherd's Hunting* be said to be familiar to the general reader. For this neglect there is but one excuse, and that an insufficient one, considering the immense quantity of very indifferent contemporary work which has had the honour of modern publication. What the excuse is we shall say presently. . . .

The defect in his work, . . . which is somewhat passed over in the criticisms of Lamb and others, is its amazing inequality. This is the more remarkable in that evidence exists of not infrequent retouching on his part with the rather unusual result of improvement—a fact which would seem to show that he possessed some critical faculty. Such possession, however, seems on the other hand to be quite incompatible with the production of the hopeless doggerel which he not infrequently signs. . . . Even in his earlier and purely secular work there is something, though less of this inequality, and its cause is not at all dubious. No poet, certainly no poet of merit, seems to have written with such absolute spontaneity and want of premeditation as Wither. The metre which was his favourite, and which he used with most success—the trochaic dimeter catalectic of seven syllables—lends itself almost as readily as the octosyllable to this frequently fatal fluency; but in Wither's hands, at least in his youth and early manhood, it is wonderfully successful. . . . Nor had he at times a less original and happy command of the rhymed decasyllabic couplet which he sometimes handles after a fashion which makes one almost think of Dryden, and sometimes after a fashion (as in the lovely description of Alresford Pool at the opening of *Philarete*) which makes one think of more modern poets still. Besides this metrical proficiency and gift, Wither at this time (he thought fit to apologise for it later) had a very happy knack of blending the warm amatory enthusiasm of his time with sentiments of virtue and decency. There is in him absolutely nothing loose or obscene, and yet he is entirely free from the milk-and-water propriety which sometimes irritates the reader in such books as Habington's *Castara*. Wither is never mawkish, though he is never loose, and the swing of his verse at its best is only equalled by the rush of thought and feeling which animates it. As it is perhaps necessary to justify this high opinion, we may as well give the "Alresford Pool" above noted. It is like Browne, but it is better than anything Browne ever did; being like Browne, it is not unlike Keats; it is also singularly like a poet of our own day, Mr. William Morris.

For pleasant was that Pool; and near it, then,
Was neither rotten marsh nor boggy fen.
It was not overgrown with boisterous sedge,
Nor grew there rudely, then, along the edge
A bending willow, nor a prickly bush,
Nor broad-leafed flag, nor reed, nor knotty rush:
But here, well ordered, was a grove with bowers;
There, grassy plots, set round about with flowers.
Here, you might, through the water, see the land
Appear, strewed o'er with white or yellow sand.
Yon, deeper was it; and the wind, by whiffs,
Would make it rise, and wash the little cliffs;
On which, oft pluming, safe, unfrighted then
The gagling wild goose, and the snow-white swan,
With all those flocks of fowl, which, to this day
Upon those quiet waters breed and play.

When to this gift of description is added a frequent inspiration of pure fancy, it is scarcely surprising that—

Such a strain as might befit
Some brave Tuscan poet's wit,

to borrow a couplet of his own, often adorns Wither's verse.
—GEORGE SAINTSBURY, *A History of Elizabethan Literature*,
1887, pp. 302–6

JOHN FYVIE
"George Wither"
Macmillan's Magazine, May 1890, pp. 39–46

John Bright is reported to have said to a friend, "If you come across a quotation in any speech of mine that you don't recognise, it is probably Wither." It is possible that to some of his friends the name might have been as unfamiliar as the quotations; they may even have taken it as a misprint for Whittier. Yet George Wither was a person of no inconsiderable note in his day, and among the voluminous writings which he has left behind him are several passages of rare grace and beauty. His career as an author commenced in 1613, the year which witnessed the production of the last of Shakespeare's dramatic creations, and it only terminated with his death in 1667, the year following the great fire of London. He may be said to have outlived his own fame. Pope refers to him in *The Dunciad* as "wretched Wither," sleeping "among the dull of ancient days, safe where no critics damn;" but he was in Pope's time only remembered as a renegade cavalier who, like all renegades, was extremely bitter against his old party. Ritson, the crusty collector of old ballads, called him the English Bavius, and the more genial Bishop Percy merely says that "he distinguished himself in youth by some pastoral pieces that were not inelegant." Subsequent critics, however, have adopted a much higher estimate of Wither's poetical work. Ellis, in his *Specimens of Early English Poets*, and Sir Egerton Brydges in his *Censura Literaria*, both quoted Wither extensively, and spoke enthusiastically of the sweetness and melody of his verse; while Charles Lamb, beyond question the most competent of all judges of our older literature, has devoted to his earlier poems an essay full of fine and felicitous praise.

George Wither was born in 1588, at Bentworth in Hampshire. His family was apparently of some position and wealth, for he records how in his youthful days hounds, hawks, and horses were at his command, and intimates that he might have required "without denial,"

The lute, the organ, or deep-sounding vial,

or indeed anything else he had a mind to, to cheer his spirits. In his sixteenth year he was sent up to Magdalen College, Oxford, where for some time he found more delight in "practice at the tennis-ball" than in practice at "old Scotus, Seton, and new Keckerman." Hardly, however, had he turned over a new leaf, and begun to love a learned college life, when he was removed from Oxford and taken home, much to his disgust, "to hold the plough." Though not altogether congenial to him, a farming life was far from unendurable, but a proposal to apprentice him to "some mechanick trade" was not to be thought of with equanimity, and the youth, then eighteen years of age, hurried off to London. Here he entered himself at Lincoln's Inn, and was fortunate enough to strike up a close friendship with William Browne, who was then meditating his *Britannia's Pastorals*, the influence of which powerfully affected all the earlier work of his friend. Wither's plans were not very definite, but he had a vague notion that he could push his fortune at court. Naturally therefore he dropped into the laureate vein, and we find him, in company with numerous other

bardlings, bewailing the untimely death of Prince Henry with a sheaf of elegies, and the next year composing *epithalamia* to celebrate the marriage of the Princess Elizabeth. There was apparently not enough of the sycophant in Wither's composition to ensure him a rapid rise in court favour, and failing to obtain any preferment, he turned satirical and in 1613 produced his *Abuses Stript and Whipt*, the dedication to which says that, having been provided with no work, he has employed his leisure in observing the vices of the times. Warton says the satires are severe but not witty. They certainly contain none of those pungent personalities such as Dryden and Pope loved to make their adversaries' ears tingle with. Hate, envy, revenge, covetousness, vanity and the rest of them, receive some hard knocks, but it is always abstract vice that he scourges, never particular men in whom such vices are presumed to be personified. Perhaps, however, it was more evident at the time than it is now what people in high places the cap fitted. At all events the satires sufficed to obtain for their author a lodging in the Marshalsea prison. Curiously enough, he appears to have thought that as satire got him in, satire might get him out. Accordingly in 1614 he composed another, written with much vigour, and addressed to the King, in which he shows himself altogether unrepentant for his former offence.

Perhaps it was thought wise to muzzle such an outspoken muse, or some other influence may have been at work; at any rate Wither was soon liberated, and moreover presented by the King with a patent for some *Hymns and Songs of the Church* which he proposed to write. But he had chosen the wrong road to fortune. The man who wrote the following lines had evidently mistaken his vocation when he proposed to rise in life by the arts of the courtier, though, as we have seen, he had at least tried his hand at the doleful elegies he now scorns, and apparently to no purpose.

I have no Muses that will serve the turn
At every triumph, and rejoice or mourn
Upon a minute's warning for their hire,
If with old sherry they themselves inspire.
I am not of a temper like to those
That can provide an hour's sad talk in prose
For any funeral, and then go dine,
And choke my grief with sugar-plums and wine.
I cannot at the claret sit and laugh,
And then, half tipsy, write an epitaph.

. . .

I cannot for reward adorn the hearse
Of some old rotten miser with my verse;
Nor, like the poetasters of the time,
Go howl a doleful elegy in rhyme
For every lord or ladyship that dies,
And then perplex their heirs to patronise
That muddy poesy.

So he will find out a more excellent way to success. During his imprisonment in the Marshalsea, he had composed *The Shepherd's Hunting*. This is a pastoral poem in five eclogues. In the first eclogue, Willie (William Browne) comes to lament his friend's imprisonment, and finds that he may save his labour, for Philarete (Wither) has discovered that "stone walls do not a prison make, nor iron bars a cage," and professes to have enjoyed more true bliss and content in the quiet prison than ever he knew in the contentious court. In the second and third eclogue Philarete relates, under the thin disguise of a shepherd's hunting, the whole story of his imprisonment and the cause of it. It is in the fourth eclogue that Wither first uses, and at once with consummate mastery, that seven-syllabled trochaic metre which so delighted Charles Lamb. Philarete advises his friend to produce more pastorals. Willy dejectedly replies that what he has done has not been very well received; that he has been told he is too young, and should "keep his skill in store till he has seen some winters more." Whereupon Philarete declares,

> That the sacred Muses can
> Make a child in years a man.

And then follows "that rapturous melody of praise and thanksgiving to poetry, which," says Mr. Swinburne, "has made the modest name and gentle genius of Wither immortal in the loving memory of all who know and cherish that 'best earthly bliss' which filled his prison-house with 'comfort and delight.'" This splendid panegyric, which extends to a hundred and twenty lines, has been more frequently quoted than anything else that Wither wrote, but it is not by any means so generally known that any apology need be offered for transcribing one of its finest passages again. She, he says of his Muse,

> She doth tell me where to borrow
> Comfort in the midst of sorrow;
> Makes the desolatest place
> To her presence be a grace;
> And the blackest discontents
> To be pleasing ornaments.
> In my former days of bliss
> Her divine skill taught me this,
> That from everything I saw
> I could some invention draw,
> And raise pleasure to her height
> Through the meanest object's sight.
> By the murmur of a spring
> Or the least bough's rusteling,
> By a daisy, whose leaves spread,
> Shut when Titan goes to bed,
> Or a shady bush or tree,
> She could more infuse in me
> Than all nature's beauties can
> In some other wiser man.

"The praises of poetry," says Charles Lamb, "have been often sung in ancient and in modern times; strange powers have been ascribed to it of influence over animate and inanimate auditors; its force over fascinated crowds has been acknowledged; but, before Wither, no one ever celebrated its power *at home*, the wealth and the strength which this divine gift confers upon its possessor. Fame, and that too after death, was all which hitherto the poets had promised themselves from their art. It seems to have been left to Wither to discover that poetry was a present possession, as well as a rich reversion; and that the Muse had promise of both lives, of this and of that which was to come."

Wither's "darling measure," in which the fourth eclogue of *The Shepherd's Hunting*, and the greater part of *The Mistress of Philarete* is written, has been sometimes spoken of by critics as octosyllabic verse, which plainly it is not. It is the seven-syllabled trochaic couplet, which Shakespeare lightly laughed at as the "butter-woman's rank to market," and which, as used at a later date by Ambrose Philips, roused Henry Carey (he "who lived a life free from reproach, and hanged himself October the 4th, 1743") to parody it and add a new adjective to our English vocabulary in calling it Namby-Pamby. Wither himself seems to anticipate some cavilling at it, for he says:

> If the verse here usèd be
> Their dislike; it liketh me.
> Pedants shall not tie my strains
> To our antique poets' vaines.

Doubtless it is a form of verse that readily runs into doggerel, and the fatal facility of its flow tends to the production of a

maximum of jingling sound with a minimum of sense. But in the hands of masters like Ben Jonson, Fletcher, Wither, and Milton it has proved itself an instrument of considerable compass, and they have drawn from it not only strains of "linked sweetness long drawn out," but notes of deeper harmony and power. In a note to the essay already quoted, Lamb cites the following lines from *The Shepherd's Hunting*:

> If thy birth doth bravely tower,
> *As she makes wing she gets power;*
> Yet the higher she doth soar,
> She's affronted still the more,
> Till she to the high'st hath past,
> Then she rests with fame at last,

and, remarking that "a long line is a line we are long repeating," he asks what Alexandrine could express "labour slowly but strongly surmounting difficulty" as it is done in the second of these lines? Again, he says, in more sweeping terms, "What metre could go beyond these, from *Philarete?*"

> Her true beauty leaves behind
> Apprehensions in my mind
> Of more sweetness than all art
> Or inventions can impart,
> *Thoughts too deep to be express'd*
> *And too strong to be suppress'd.*

In 1618 appeared *The Motto*, written, he says, by way of recreation after his liberation from the Marshalsea. It is a long poem (some two thousand lines) in the heroic couplet, and is divided into three sections corresponding to the three divisions of the motto, *Nec habeo, Nec curo, Nec careo*. It is in form a continuous self-eulogy, yet, as has been more than once remarked, it is singularly free from any offensive or distasteful egotism. The reason of this is supplied by Wither himself in his preface to *The Motto*. "My intent was," he says, "to draw the true picture of mine own heart; that my friends who knew me outwardly might have some representation of my inside also. And that, if they liked the form of it, they might (wherein they were defective) fashion their own minds thereunto. But my principal intention was, by recording those thoughts, to confirm mine own resolution; and to prevent such alterations as time and infirmities may work upon me." That is to say, he had no intention of holding up a likeness of himself for all men to admire and imitate, but of painting the picture of a man such as he fain would have himself to be. And, being endowed with a pure and healthy mind, his ideal is a high and noble one. Regarding *The Motto* as a work of art, we may, in spite of an occasional fine passage, adopt his own words. "The language," he says, "is but indifferent: for I affected matter more than words. The method is none at all: for I was loathe to make a business of a recreation."

In 1619 appeared *Fidelia*, and elegiac epistle of forty-four pages from a forsaken fair one to her inconstant lover. The lady, without any feigning, pours out her own love with all the ardour of an Eloisa and something of the plain-spokenness of a Juliet. There are some fine touches in the poem, but, though Wither seems to have been a master in the art of love, we have a shrewd suspicion that there is too strong a tincture of the masculine element in Fidelia's philtre.

Fair Virtue, though written some time before, did not see the light until 1622, and even then was published anonymously, because Wither had some, though perfectly groundless, fears that it would damage the credit of more serious work which he then had in hand. It was entitled *Fair Virtue: or, The Mistress of Philarete, written by Himself*; and in a preface the publisher says that he has entreated the author to explain his meaning in certain obscure passages, and to set down to what good purposes the poem would serve. All he could get from him was, however, that the first would take away the employment of his interpreters, and the second would be well enough found out by all such as had honest understandings. The reader is designedly left in doubt whether the poet is merely celebrating the charms of his own mistress, or laying his votive offering at the shrine of Virtue herself. The introductory epistle favours the latter view.

> On this glass of thy perfection,
>   If that any women pry,
> Let them thereby take direction
>   To adorn themselves thereby,
>   And if aught amiss they view,
>   Let them dress themselves anew.
>
>   . . .
>
> This thy picture therefore show I
>   Naked unto every eye.
> Yet no fear of rival know I,
>   Neither touch of jealousy.
>   For the more make love to thee
>   I the more shall pleasèd be.
> I am no Italian lover
>   That would mew thee in a jail;
> But thy beauty I discover
>   English-like, without a veil.
>   If thou mayst be won away,
>   Win and wear thee, he that may.

In another passage, however, he distinctly states that he is painting no imaginary portrait, but that a real love for a real lady is the font and inspiration of his song.

> For if I had never seen
> Such a beauty, I had been
> Piping in the country shades
> To the homely dairy maids,
> For a country fiddler's fees,
> Clouted cream and bread and cheese.

It is also probable that he would have remained in the embarrassing condition in which he found himself when, as he confesses, he simultaneously courted Amaryllis, Phyllis, Daphne, and Cloris,

> And in love with all together,
> Fearèd the enjoying either,
> 'Cause to be of one possest
> Bar'd the hope of all the rest.

But now the face of the whole round world is changed, and he is as constant as the needle to the pole. He proceeds to sing the praises of his mistress in his own rude way, as he modestly says, but really with many a delicate touch of dainty art, as in the following lines:

> When her ivory teeth she buries
> 'Twixt her two enticing cherries,
> There appear such pleasures hidden
> As might tempt what we're forbidden.
> If you look again, the whiles
> She doth part those lips in smiles,
> 'Tis as when a flash of light
> Breaks from heaven to glad the night.

Charles Lamb, with unerring taste, has pointed out two passages of *The Mistress of Philarete* as being of preeminent merit. They are indeed the fairest flowers in this lover's coronal. The first passage is that wherein he wonders that all men, even her servants, are not pleading love, and then explains, according to love's philosophy, why they are not. It is too long to be transcribed in this place, and the reader must be referred

to Lamb's essay, or to a copy of Wither's poems if haply he may find one.

The second passage is that in which he vindicates himself against the common charge of hyperbole by boldly denying the possibility of hyperbole, and justifying his "setting forth her glories by unheard-of allegories." The whole passage is fine, and the following six lines are among the loveliest of their kind in our literature.

> Stars indeed fair creatures be;
> Yet amongst us where is he
> Joys not more the whilst he lies
> Sunning in his mistress' eyes,
> Than in all the glimmering light
> Of a starry winter's night?

But he is not content only to celebrate his mistress's beauty of hand, and foot, of lip, and eye, and brow; he must also praise her spiritual perfections, for,

> This that I have here exprest
> Is but that which veils the rest.
> An incomparable shrine
> Of a beauty more divine.

And moreover,

> These are beauties that shall last
> When the crimson blood shall waste,
> And the shining hair turn grey,
> Or with age be worn away.

It is strange that any man capable of producing poetry of this high order should ever have felt called upon to apologize for it, as Wither did on more than one occasion. In his satire "Of the Passion of Love," after railing in good set terms at the absurdities commonly perpetrated by people in that undesirable condition, he bethinks himself of his own *Philarete*.

> How now; was't not you (says one) that late
> So humbly begg'd a boon at Beauty's gate?

Yes; he must admit it was; and all he can say for himself is that he has had his follies like other men, and doubtless cut quite as absurd a figure as any imaginary lover depicted in the present satire. And again, in a postscript to *The Shepherd's Hunting*, he anticipates a similar objection, though in this case he takes his stand boldly on the feelings natural to ardent youth; for he says, "Neither am I so cynical but that I think a modest expression of such amorous conceits as suit with reason will yet very well become my years; in which not to have feeling of the power of love were as great an argument of much stupidity, as an over sottish affection were of extreme folly." This is admirably put, and quite unimpeachable; but there was not the slightest necessity for him to apologize. Allowing for the change in manners since the seventeenth century, Wither's muse is as modest as Mr. Coventry Patmore's.

Nearly all Wither's best work was produced in the decade 1613 to 1623. Between these two dates were published his *Abuses Stript and Whipt, Fidelia, The Shepherd's Hunting, The Motto,* and *The Mistress of Philarete.* With these we take leave of Wither the poet, and in subsequent publications make acquaintance with Wither the preacher, the prophet, the puritan, and the politician. Wither was no exception to the general rule that those who abandon for public life the studies of poetry and philosophy suffer a steady degeneration, partaking like brooks and rivers, as Landor finely says, "the nature of that vast body whereunto they run, its dreariness, its bitterness, its foam, its storms, its everlasting noise and commotion." Not that Wither ever became quite the fanatic that he has been represented to have been. Up to the time of the outbreak of the civil war, he was an adherent of the established order both in church and state. His *Hymns and Songs of the Church* were approved by the Archbishop of Canterbury, and he says in his *Furor Poeticus*,

> The Royal Power I loyally obey'd
> And though it did oppress, was so afraid
> Of innovating, that a Reformation
> Thereof I wishèd, not an extirpation.

He never became a sectary, but described himself, like Milton, as a member of the Church Universal. One sentence from his *Answer to Some Objections* is worth quoting. "True faith," he says, "cannot be evidenced without good works, which being imperfect in the best of men, we have no such certain mark whereby unfeigned disciples may be known, as by their being loving to each other, and charitably affected towards all men; yea, although they are our personal enemies." His own charitableness was considerably tempered by an ineradicable contentiousness. He lived under eleven different forms of government, and he managed to be more or less at loggerheads with them all.

Wither was in London during the devastation caused by the plague of 1625. "When hundreds of thousands forsook their habitations" he remained, "to be a Remembrance both to this city and the whole nation." In his *Britain's Remembrancer* he describes his experience in walking the deserted streets. The Royal Change and St. Paul's Cathedral, usually crowded promenades, were avoided as places of certain danger; the Strand was as unfrequented as a country road; the Inns of Court were silent as the grave; smokeless chimneys betokened that numberless houses were uninhabited, and where pleasant women's faces were once to be seen, "the empty casements gapèd wide for air." Two poets, Thomas Lodge and John Fletcher, are said to have perished in this pestilence, but Wither had no belief in contagion, and notwithstanding that he awoke one morning with "round ruddy spots" (the fatal signs) on his breast and shoulders, he came through the danger unscathed.

In 1639 occurred his first experience of soldiering, when he was a captain of horse in the expedition against the Scots. On the outbreak of the war in England, Wither, according to Anthony Wood, sold his estate and raised a troop for the service of the Parliament. In 1643 he was appointed governor of Farnham Castle. He asserted that his superiors neglected to supply him with adequate means of defending the place; his enemies said that he deserted it. Anyhow, as Campbell remarks, the defence of his conduct which he afterwards published seems to have been far more resolute than his defence of the fortress. Wither's own house and farm were among the first to suffer during the war, for, as early as January 1642, we find the House of Commons making an order for the immediate payment to him of £328 6s., by way of compensation for the plunder by the King's cavaliers. But Wither claimed to have lost as much as £2,000, and he obtained an order empowering him to indemnify himself by seizing the goods of those who had plundered him. Among these was Sir John Denham, and Wither promptly seized upon his neighbour's property. Some time after this, as Aubrey tells the story, Wither was taken prisoner, and in great danger of his life; but Sir John Denham prayed the King not to hang him, for that while George Wither lived, he (Denham) could not be accounted the worst poet in England. Wither's life was accordingly spared. In 1643 we hear of him in poverty and distress, getting pecuniary aid from his generous friend Mr. Westron and from the Earl of Essex. He appears to have been perpetually petitioning Parliament for the redress of his grievances, and getting orders for his relief which were almost invariably of no benefit to him.

The energy which in happier circumstances might have given us permanent additions to our poetical literature, expended itself in cursory comments on current events, futile vaticinations, and profitless controversies. In 1653 his ever-restless mind produced a curious scheme for parliamentary reform. He declared the means of settlement to be an "Everlasting Parliament." Every city, shire, or borough, "on pain of being deeply fined," was to elect a representative annually, and this was to be done in such a manner that a twelfth part of the members retired, and new members took their places every month. The members were to be paid their wages regularly, and the House was to elect a fresh Speaker also every month. Undue influence in elections was to be punished by exile, and bribery in the public offices by death. There was to be a new Parliament House, "with towers adorned and strong walls fenced about," and having gardens and fair walks adjoining thereto. Members were to receive free lodging in twelve mansions to be erected close by the House, there was to be "a constant table of one meal a day" for all and sundry, and many other things arranged,

> So as they might,
> Pursue the public service with delight.

And "forasmuch as outward habits draw respect unto men's persons," the members were to be all alike attired in a peculiar robe or upper garment, and from each man's neck was to be suspended a golden tablet whereon was enamelled "the British Isles within the ocean placed." This poetico-political pamphlet may be commended to the attention of certain hon. members now at St. Stephen's.

Wither's own circumstances, however, were growing worse and worse. His enemies caused his name to be struck from the Commission of the Peace for Hampshire and from the militia, and he had become so poor that when it was proposed to rate him at two horses for the service of the militia, he pitifully protested that he was hardly able to find so much as the bridles. In August, 1661, his books and papers were seized by authority of a warrant from Secretary Nicholas; he was charged with publishing a seditious libel against members of the House of Commons, and in the course of a few days found himself a prisoner in Newgate. He was kept in confinement until July, 1663, when he was released, on giving to the Lieutenant of the Tower a bond to be of good behaviour. A second time he saw the plague ravage London, and although none of his household succumbed to it, the sickness and subsequent fire played such havoc among his friends that, some being dead, some impoverished, and the remainder scattered, neither he nor they knew where to find each other, and there were few or none to help him in the destitution of his latter days. He died on May 2nd, 1667.

Wither's poetry, at least all that was written between 1613 and 1623, before he sold his birthright for a mess of pottage, is characterized by fine feeling, delicate fancy, true pathos, and singularly sweet versification. He is at his best in the seven-syllabled trochaic measure of *Philarete* and *The Shepherd's Hunting*, but many of his lyrics are only below the best, and have that indescribable charm of the older Elizabethan manner, which he lived long enough to see evaporating into the courtly sprightliness of his later contemporaries. Only one of these keeps its place in the popular anthologies, the "Shall I wasting in despair," to which Mr. Palgrave in his *Golden Treasury* has prefixed the title of "The Manly Heart." But Wither has the true lyrical note, and the music of more than one song of his "beats time to nothing in the brain" of many a student who knows and loves the treasures that lie buried in worm-eaten volumes on the dustiest shelves of our great libraries.

Wither was not included in Chalmers' collection of the British Poets, neither has any complete edition of his works ever been published. In the early years of this century Sir Egerton Brydges edited a somewhat meagre selection from them, and in 1872 the Spencer Society published three handsome volumes entitled *Juvenilia*, containing nearly all his best work. But these are neither generally known nor easily accessible, and a popular reprint of some half-dozen of Wither's most notable performances would be a boon for which all true lovers of poetry would be deeply grateful.

EDMUND GOSSE
From *The Jacobean Poets*
1894, pp. 181–88

A very prominent figure among the Jacobean poets, yet one with which it is very difficult to deal, is that of George Wither. The time has passed when this voluminous writer can be treated by any competent critic with the contempt of the age of Anne. The scorn of Pope still clings, however, to the "wretched Withers," whose name he misspelt, and of whose works he had probably seen nothing but the satires. Nor would it be safe, on the score of exquisite beauties discoverable in the early lyrics of Wither, to overlook the radical faults of his style. One or two generous appreciators of Jacobean verse have done this, and have claimed for Wither a very high place in English poetry. But proportion, judgment, taste must count for something, and in these qualities this lyrist was deplorably deficient. The careful student, not of excerpts made by loving and partial hands, but of the bulk of his published writings, will be inclined to hesitate before he admits that Wither was a great poet. He will rather call him a very curious and perhaps unique instance of a tiresome and verbose scribbler, to whom in his youth there came unconsidered flashes of most genuine and exquisite poetry.

George Wither was born at Brantworth, in Hampshire, on the 11th of June, 1588. His parents were in independent and even affluent circumstances; his earliest education was found in the neighbouring village school of Colemore, and he was still but a boy when he was sent to Magdalen College, Oxford. His college career was abruptly terminated after two years, when he returned to "the beechy shadows of Brantworth," and, according to his own possibly hyperbolic statement, "to the plough." The general supposition has been, caused perhaps by some laxity in Anthony à Wood's information, that he went up to London of his own accord in 1605, to seek his fortune there, and entered himself of Lincoln's Inn. The date is probably much too early, for he was then only seventeen years of age, and we know that he spent a weary time in Hampshire. At all events, it is not until 1612 that we hear of him as a poet, and this was probably about the date of his appearance in London. In that year he published, on the theme which excited universal emotion at the moment, a little volume of *Prince Henry's Obsequies*, a series of nearly fifty sonnets, smoothly and volubly indited, and containing occasional phrases of some beauty.

It is understood that this little volume, and a still smaller quarto of *Epithalamia* which immediately followed it, introduced Wither to the company of young poets who at this time began to collect in the courts of law. In particular, it is certain that he gained the friendship of Browne and of Christopher Brooke. In 1613, however, Wither suddenly became prominent by the publication of a volume of satires entitled *Abuses Stript and Whipt*, of which four editions were rapidly exhausted. The scandal caused by this book was so great that the poet was thrown into the Marshalsea prison, where, as he tells us, he "was shut up from the society of mankind, and, as one unworthy the compassion vouchsafed to thieves and murderers, was neither permitted the use of my pen, the access or sight of acquaintance, the allowances usually afforded other close prisoners, nor means to send for necessaries. . . . I was for many days compelled to feed on nothing but the coarsest bread, and sometimes locked up four and twenty hours together without so much as a drop of water to cool my tongue." This severity must have been presently relaxed, for Wither wrote much in prison; but he was not suffered to leave the Marshalsea until many months had passed.

It is very difficult, with the text of *Abuses Stript and Whipt* before us, to understand why it should have caused such vehement official resentment. The book is really a collection of essays on ethical subjects, running to about ten thousand verses, all in the heroic couplet. The so-called "satires" deal with such themes as "Love," "Presumption," "Weakness," and "Vanity." There are more odd instances of suppression, of course, than this, that of Drayton's *Harmony of the Church*, being the most unaccountable of all. Wither's satire, however, is so anodyne and so impersonal, so devoid of anything which could, apparently, be taken as a home-thrust by any individual, that the scandal caused by *Abuses Stript and Whipt* is an enigma of literary history. Here are none of those direct portraits which passed almost unchallenged in the satires of Marston and Donne. There is, notwithstanding, a passage in the ninth satire of the first book which attacks the prelates of the English Church very sharply, and the imprudence of this outburst seems to have struck the poet himself, for he proceeds to a direct flattery of the Archbishop of Canterbury. In the absence of any other light, we may perhaps conjecture that the chapter on "Ambition" earned our young poet his cell in the Marshalsea.

These Satires are readable, and have none of the Persius-like obscurity and roughness of earlier English satire. The author, after some obliging traits of autobiography, essays to deal with the whole subject of the decay of Man's moral nature. We find lucid constructions and smooth verse throughout, and wherever a picture of manners is introduced, it is given with a Dutch precision and picturesqueness. Already, in this lively production of his twenty-fifth year, we are conscious of Wither's radical faults, his moral garrulity, his tedious length. It seems certain that the fine lyrical vein in his genius very soon dried up. In the opening of the *Abuses Stript and Whipt*, he speaks of having already indited "Aretophil's compliment, with many doleful sonnets." This collection, then, may be consigned to his very early youth, although, so far as we know, it did not make its public appearance until it was printed, as *Fair Virtue, The Mistress of Philarete*, in 1622. It may be safely dated ten years earlier.

Leaving this collection for awhile, we come to the books which Wither wrote in prison. It is not needful to dwell on his contributions, in 1614, to *The Shepherd's Pipe* of Browne, Christopher Brooke and Davies of Hereford; but in 1615 appeared two exquisite volumes, *Fidelia* and *The Shepherd's Hunting*. The former was privately printed, and of this edition but one copy is known to survive; the latter is not a common book. *Fidelia* is an "elegiacal epistle," in heroic couplet, addressed by a woman to her inconstant friend; it is a fragment of some huge poem probably carried no further. It possesses a great delicacy of passion, and a versification curiously and irresistibly suggestive of that of Dryden; *Fidelia* is by far the most attractive of the non-lyrical works of Wither.

In *The Shepherd's Hunting* all is lyrical in spirit, if not in form. It is divided into eclogues, in which the poet somewhat dimly recounts his woes and their alleviations, in exquisite verse of varied measures. He is not even gloomy long, and hastens to assure us that—

> though that all the world's delight forsake me,
> I have a Muse, and she shall music make me;
> Whose very notes, in spite of closest cages,
> Shall give content to me and after ages.

The fourth eclogue is the sweetest of all. Here, as has been said, "the caged bird begins to sing like a lark at Heaven's gate," and bids its free companions to be of good cheer.

> As the sun doth oft exhale
> Vapours from each rotten vale,
> Poesy so sometimes drains
> Gross conceits from muddy brains,—
> Mists of envy, fogs of spite,
> 'Twixt man's judgments and her light;
> But so much her power may do,
> That she can dissolve them too.
> If thy verse do bravely tower,
> As she makes wing, she gets power;
> Yet the higher she doth soar,
> She's affronted still the more;
> Till she to the highest hath past,
> Then she rests with Fame at last.
> Let nought therefore thee affright,
> But make forward in thy flight;
> For if I could match thy rhyme,
> To the very stars I'd climb,
> There begin anew, and fly
> Till I reached eternity.

In all the days of James I., no more unaffected melodies, no brighter or more aerial notes, were poured forth by any poet than are contained in this delicious little volume of *The Shepherd's Hunting*.

We may now come to the *Mistress of Philarete*. This as it was finally published, is a much more bulky affair. The form is decidedly unfortunate; the poem consists of lyrics, many of them of a somewhat miscellaneous character, set in a framework of recitative heroic couplets. The opening of *The Mistress of Philarete*, with its glowing description of the poet's Hampshire home, and in particular of Alresford Pool, has been greatly praised, but can scarcely be praised too highly. Where the contents of this volume are successful, it is in their use of the dancing measure, the true singing note. Nowhere is the octosyllabic used with more rapturous felicity than occasionally here. Often the poet rings out a pure sonorous cadence; still more often he is rapid, lucid, easy, and modern. If in

Fidelia we were reminded of Dryden, the double rhymes and reckless phrases in *Philarete* makes us think of Elizabeth Browning.

> Say, you purchase, with your pelf,
> Some respect, where you importune!
> Those may love me, for myself,
> That regard you for your fortune.
> Rich, or born of high degree,
> Fools, as well as you, may be!
> But that peace in which I live,
> No descent nor wealth can give.
>
> If you boast that you may gain
> The respect of high-born beauties,
> Know, I never wooed in vain,
> Nor preferrèd scornèd duties;
> She I love hath all delight,
> Rosy red with lily white;
> And, whoe'er your mistress be,
> Flesh and blood as good as she.

Wither's diction is curiously transitional here, and while with one hand he stretches up to Greene and Lodge, with the other he feels downwards towards the lyrists of the Restoration.

But it would be utterly uncritical to say this and this only. The purple passages are interwoven with the commonest sacking. Even in his own day, and thus early, it had been perceived that he possessed no powers of self-criticism. He is very indignant with those who censure the diffuseness, the length, the didactic dulness of his poems; he calls them "fools," and cries—

> Let them know . . .
> I make to please myself, and not for them!

It is a misfortune that he judged himself so ill, for the "fools" were perfectly right, and all these faults were patent in his poetry already. They were soon to become paramount, and the darnel was to kill the poetic wheat long before the harvest. The later career of Wither is deplorable. His political and religious tergiversations give the impression, not of hypocrisy in conscious error, but of hopeless blundering, of the wrong-headedness of a radically tactless man. He wrote hymns, which have been over-praised, and he published a multitude of pamphlets in prose and verse, which no one has dared to flatter, and few have tried to read. He outlived James I. by nearly forty years, reaped the reward of his malignant invectives by being lodged in Newgate and in the Tower, and died at last, dishonoured and obscure, on July 27, 1663, as melancholy an instance as we find in literary history of genius outlived, and a beautiful youth belied by a wretched and protracted old age.

JEREMY TAYLOR

1613–1667

Jeremy Taylor was baptized at Trinity Church, Cambridge, on August 15, 1613. His father, a barber, was evidently an educated man, for he taught his son grammar and mathematics before sending him to a grammar school. In 1626 Taylor entered Gonville and Caius college, Cambridge, becoming a fellow there in 1633. In the same year he took orders and became a lecturer at St. Paul's. When word of his eloquence reached Archbishop Laud, Taylor was invited to preach at Lambeth. Pleased with the young cleric's sermon, Laud nominated him to a fellowship at All Souls, Oxford, in 1635, but advised him to retain his Cambridge fellowship and make use of the opportunity for study afforded by it. Yet despite one fellowship in Oxford and another in Cambridge, Taylor evidently spent much of his time in London. He became chaplain to the archbishop and chaplain in ordinary to Charles I, and in 1638 was presented with the rectory of Uppingham, in Rutlandshire.

During the years preceding the Civil War Taylor gained a reputation for royalist sympathies and suspected leanings to Rome. Although he made efforts to allay such suspicions—his sermon on the Gunpowder Plot being a notable example—his friendships with Laud and Christopher Davenport, the Franciscan chaplain to Queen Henrietta Maria, and an inclination to asceticism, did little to reassure his opponents. When the Civil War broke out, Taylor's parish was sequestrated and Taylor went to fight with the Royalists; he was captured during the siege of Cardigan castle in 1645. After the Puritan victory, opposition to his alleged papist sympathies increased and led to his imprisonment on several occasions.

Between periods of imprisonment Taylor acted as chaplain to the Earl of Carbery, spending ten years at Golden Grove, the Earl's mansion in Carmarthenshire. The years in Wales were extremely productive; it was there that Taylor wrote most of his best-known works. A *Discourse of the Liberty of Prophesying* (1646) was the first of his theological works, followed by *Apology for Authorized and Set Forms of Liturgy* (1649), *The Real Presence* (1654), and *Unum Necessarium* (1655). He also wrote two cycles of sermons, published in 1651 and 1653, and several devotional and casuistical works, *Golden Grove* (1655), named for his benefactor's mansion, *The Rule and Exercise of Holy Living* (1651), *The Rule and Exercise of Holy Dying* (1651), and *Ductor Dubitantium* (1660).

Taylor left Golden Grove around 1655 and Wales altogether in 1657. With the assistance of his old friend, John Evelyn, he got an appointment as a lecturer in Lisburn, Ireland, in 1658. He spent the rest of his life in Ireland, first as lecturer and subsequently, after the Restoration, as a member of the Irish Privy Council, vice-chancellor of the University of Dublin, and as Bishop of Down, Connor, and Drumore. His final work, *Dissuasive from Popery*, published in two parts in 1664 and 1667, was written in response to the pastoral needs of the Irish dioceses. Taylor died at Lisburn on August 13, 1667, and was buried at Drumore cathedral.

Personal

But he had not only the accomplishments of a gentleman, but so universal were his parts, that they were proportion'd to every thing. And tho' his spirit and humour were made up of smoothness and gentleness, yet he could bear with the harshness and roughness of the schools, and was not unseen in their subtilties and spinosities. His skill was great both in the civil and canon law and casuistical divinity: And he was a rare conductor of souls, and knew how to counsel, and to advise; to solve difficulties, and determine cases, and quiet consciences. To these may be added his great acquaintance with the fathers and ecclesiastical writers, and the doctors of the first and purest ages both of the Greek and Lat. church; which he hath made use of against the Rom. catholics, to vindicate the church of England from the challenge of innovation, and to prove her ancient, catholic, and apostolical. Add to all these, he was a person of great humility, had nothing in him of pride and humour, but was courteous and affable and of easy access. He was withal a person of great charity and hospitality: and whosoever compares his plentiful incomes with the inconsiderable estate he left at his death, will be easily convinc'd that *Charity* was steward for a great proportion of his revenue. To sum up all in a few words of ⟨G. Rust⟩, 'This great prelate had the good humour of a gentleman, the eloquence of an orator, the fancy of a poet, the acuteness of a schoolman, the profoundness of a philosopher, the wisdom of a chancellour, the sagacity of a prophet, the reason of an angel, and the piety of a saint. He had devotion enough for a cloister, learning enough for an university, and wit enough for a coll. of virtuosi. And had his parts and endowments been parcel'd out among his poor clergy that he left behind him, it would perhaps have made one of the best dioceses in the world.'—ANTHONY À WOOD, *Athenae Oxonienses*, 1691–1721

In learning he was scarcely inferior to any theologian whatever; and in richness of imagination he is superior to all. On the subject of original sin, and of the justification of man before God, his sentiments differed from those of the established church of which he was a member; but on other points of Christian verity his views were generally correct. He is one of those few authors "the dust of whose works is gold;" and as long as the English language is understood, his volumes will constitute some of its choicest treasures. Through the whole of his numerous writings the flame of genius and of devotion burns with unabated and unexampled strength.—EDWARD WILLIAMS, *The Christian Preacher* (1800), 1843, p. 363

Those who have looked at Taylor's portraits will have been struck by the beauty and grace of his personal appearance. There is a ripe and somewhat soft freshness of health in his face, "with his hair long and gracefully curling on his cheeks, large dark eyes full of sweetness, an aquiline nose," and an open earnest expression. He is said not to have been without consciousness of his personal beauty, and to have frequently introduced his portraits in different attitudes in his various writings.—JOHN TULLOCH, "Jeremy Taylor," *Rational Theology and Christian Philosophy in England in the Seventeenth Century*, 1872, Vol. 1, p. 371

General

From this venerable and learned writer's Polemical Discourses, the Theological Student must derive the soundest instruction and most important advantages. It may not perhaps be generally known, but its nevertheless true, that partly from the 44th section or discourse of Dr. Taylor, and partly from Stillingfleet's *Irenicum*, Mr. Locke borrowed the plan of his *Letters on Toleration*.—WILLIAM BELOE, *Anecdotes of Literature and Scarce Books*, 1807–12, Vol. 1, p. 180

The writings of Bishop Jeremy Taylor are a perpetual feast to me. His hospitable board groans under the weight and multitude of viands. Yet I seldom rise from the perusal of his works without repeating or recollecting the excellent observation of Minucius Felix. *Fabulas et errores ab imperitis parentibus dis-*

cimus; et quod est gravius, ipsis studiis et disciplinis elab-oramus. —SAMUEL TAYLOR COLERIDGE, "Jeremy Taylor" (1812), *Literary Remains*, ed. Henry Nelson Coleridge, 1836, Vol. 1, p. 285

It would be worth your while to read Taylor's *Letter on Original Sin*, and what follows. I compare it to an old statue of Janus, with one of the faces, that which looks towards his opponents, the controversial phiz in highest preservation,—the force of a mighty one, all power, all life,—the face of a God rushing on to battle, and, in the same moment, enjoying at once both contest and triumph; the other, that which should have been the countenance that looks toward his followers, that with which he substitutes his own opinion, all weather eaten, dim, useless, a *Ghost in marble*, such as you may have seen represented in many of Piranesi's astounding engravings from Rome and the Campus Martius. Jer. Taylor's discursive intellect dazzle-darkened his intuition. The principle of becoming all things to all men, if *any* means he might save *any*, with him as with Burke, thickened the protecting epidermis of the tact-nerve of truth into something like a callus. But take him all in all, such a miraculous combination of erudition, broad, deep, and omnigenous; of logic subtle as well as acute, and as robust as agile; of psychological insight, so fine yet so secure! of public prudence and practical *sageness* that one ray of *creative Faith* would have lit up and transfigured into wisdom, and of genuine imagination, with its streaming face unifying all at one moment like that of the setting sun when, through an interspace of blue sky no larger than itself, it emerges from the cloud to sink behind the mountain, but a face seen only at *starts*, when some breeze from the higher air scatters, for a moment, the cloud of butterfly fancies, which flutter around him like a morning-garment of ten thousand colours—(now how shall I get out of this sentence? the tail is too big to be taken up into the coiler's mouth)—well, as I was saying, I believe such a complete man hardly shall we meet again.—SAMUEL TAYLOR COLERIDGE, Letter to John Kenyon (Nov. 3, 1814)

Jeremy Taylor was a writer as different from Sir Thomas Browne as it was possible for one writer to be from another. He was a dignitary of the church, and except in matters of casuistry and controverted points, could not be supposed to enter upon speculative doubts, or give a loose to a sort of dogmatical scepticism. He had less thought, less "stuff of the conscience," less "to give us pause," in his impetuous oratory, but he had equal fancy—not the same vastness and profundity, but more richness and beauty, more warmth and tenderness. He is as rapid, as flowing and endless, as the other is stately, abrupt, and concentrated. The eloquence of the one is like a river, that of the other is more like an aqueduct. The one is as sanguine as the other is saturnine in the temper of his mind. Jeremy Taylor took obvious and admitted truths for granted, and illustrated them with an inexhaustible display of new and enchanting imagery. Sir Thomas Browne talks in sum-totals: Jeremy Taylor enumerates all the particulars of a subject. He gives every aspect it will bear, and never "cloys with sameness." His characteristic is enthusiastic and delightful amplification. Sir Thomas Browne gives the beginning and end of things, that you may judge of their place and magnitude: Jeremy Taylor describes their qualities and texture, and enters into all the items of the debtor and creditor account between life and death, grace and nature, faith and good works. He puts his heart into his fancy. He does not pretend to annihilate the passions and pursuits of mankind in the pride of philosophic indifference, but treats them as serious and momentous things, warring with conscience and the soul's health, or furnishing

the means of grace and hopes of glory. In his writings, the frail stalk of human life reclines on the bosom of eternity. —WILLIAM HAZLITT, *Lectures on the Dramatic Literature of the Age of Elizabeth*, 1820

The heavenly-mindedness of Jeremy Taylor threw such a charm over his diction—exhibited such proofs of genius and of piety—that that great man may be considered as the founder of a school, (even of the opposite persuasion), in which enthusiasm was mistaken for inspiration, and where there was an equal glow of piety, but unsupported by such flights of genius and such demonstrations of learning.—THOMAS FROGNALL DIBDIN, *The Library Companion*, 1824, p. 49

Jeremy Taylor ⟨is⟩ restless, fervid, aspiring, scattering abroad a prodigality of life, not unfolding but creating, with the energy and the "myriad-mindedness" of Shakespere.

. . . ⟨O⟩ne remarkable characteristic of his style which we have already noticed ⟨is⟩ the everlasting strife and fluctuation between his rhetoric and his eloquence, which maintain their alternations with force and inevitable recurrence, like the systole and diastole, the contraction and expansion, of some living organ. For this characteristic he was indebted in mixed proportions to his own peculiar style of understanding and the nature of his subject. Where the understanding is not active and teeming, but possessed and filled by a few vast ideas (which was the case of Milton), there the funds of a varied rhetoric are wanting. On the other hand, where the understanding is all alive with the subtlety of distinctions, and nourished (as Jeremy Taylor's was) by casuistical divinity, the variety and opulence of the rhetoric is apt to be oppressive. But this tendency, in the case of Taylor, was happily checked and balanced by the commanding passion, intensity, and solemnity of his exalted theme, which gave a final unity to the tumultuous motions of his intellect. The only very obvious defects of Taylor were in the mechanical part of his art, in the mere *technique*. He writes like one who never revises, nor tries the effect upon his ear of his periods as musical wholes, and in the syntax and connexion of the parts seems to have been habitually careless of slight blemishes.

. . . The smooth monotony of the leading religious topics, as managed by the French orators, receives under the treatment of Jeremy Taylor at each turn of the sentence a new flexure, or what may be called a separate *articulation*; old thoughts are surveyed from novel stations and under various angles; and a field absolutely exhausted throws up eternally fresh verdure under the fructifying lava of burning imagery. *Human life*, for example, *is short; human happiness is frail*; how trite, how obvious a thesis! Yet, in the beginning of the *Holy Dying*, upon that simplest of themes how magnificent a descant! Variations the most original upon a ground the most universal, and a sense of novelty diffused over truths coeval with human life! Finally, it may be remarked of the imagery in the French rhetoric that it is thinly sown, commonplace, deficient in splendour, and above all merely ornamental; that is to say, it does no more than echo and repeat what is already said in the thought which it is brought to illustrate; whereas in Jeremy Taylor and in Burke it will be found usually to extend and amplify the thought, or to fortify it by some indirect argument of its truth. Thus, for instance, in the passage above quoted from Taylor upon the insensibility of man to the continual mercies of God, at first view the mind is staggered by the apparent impossibility that so infinite a reality, and of so continual a recurrence, should escape our notice; but the illustrative image, drawn from the case of a man standing at the bottom of the ocean, and yet insensible to that world of waters above him, from the uniformity and equality of its pressure, flashes upon us with a sense of something equally marvellous in a case which we know to be a physical fact. We are thus reconciled to the proposition by the same image which illustrates it.—THOMAS DE QUINCEY, "Rhetoric" (1828), *Collected Writings*, ed. David Masson, 1859, Vol. 10, pp. 105–8, 125–26

⟨January 31, 1830⟩ I have not got on with ⟨reading⟩ Jeremy Taylor, as I don't like it much. I do not like subdivisions of virtue, making a separate article of each particular virtue or crime: I much more like the general, and artless, commands of our Saviour. Who can say anything new after him? It seems to me absurd to attempt it, except as far as concerns stepping into a bishoprick.

⟨March 14, 1833⟩ After having read Herbert or Jeremy Taylor, and become suffused with their spirit, do you not wonder that you ever go back again to coldness and worldliness? Our good feelings are so entrancing while they last: but that is the reason they last so short a time: but our more paltry propensities are cold and rational, and so stay by us, and become part of our natures.

⟨May 23, 1835⟩ It seems to me that our old Divines will hereafter be considered our Classics—(in Prose, I mean)—I am not aware that any other nations have such books. A single selection from Jeremy Taylor is fine: but it requires a skilful hand to put many detached bits from him together: for a common editor only picks out the flowery, metaphorical, morsels: and so rather cloys: and gives quite a wrong estimate of the Author, to those who had no previous acquaintance with him: for, rich as Taylor's illustrations, and grotesque as his images, are, no one keeps a grander proportion: he never huddles illustration upon the matter so as to overlay it, nor crowds images too thick together: which these Selections (in Basil Montagu's *Thoughts of Divines and Philosophers*) might make one unacquainted with him to suppose. This is always the fault of Selections: but Taylor is particularly liable to injury on this score. What a man he is! He has such a knowledge of the nature of man, and such powers of expressing its properties, that I sometimes feel as if he had had some exact counterpart of my own individual character under his eye, when he lays open the depths of the heart, or traces some sin to its root. The eye of his portrait expresses this keen intuition: and I think that I should less like to have stood with a lie on my tongue before him, than before any other I know of.—EDWARD FITZ-GERALD, Letters to John Allen, 1830–35

Taylor's was a great and lovely mind; yet how much and injuriously was it perverted by his being a favorite and follower of Laud, and by his intensely Popish feelings of church authority. His Liberty of Prophesying is a work of wonderful eloquence and skill; but if we believe the argument, what do we come to? Why, to nothing more or less than this, that—so much can be said for every opinion and sect, so impossible is it to settle any thing by reasoning or authority of Scripture—we must appeal to some positive jurisdiction on earth, *ut sit finis controversarium*. In fact, the whole book is the precise argument used by the Papists to induce men to admit the necessity of a supreme and infallible head of the church on earth. It is one of the works which pre-eminently gives countenance to the saying of Charles or James II., I forget which:—"When you of the Church of England contend with the Catholics, you use the arguments of the Puritans; when you contend with the Puritans, you immediately adopt all the weapons of the Catholics." Taylor never speaks with the slightest symptom of affection or respect of Luther, Calvin, or any other of the great reformers—at least, not in any of his learned works; but he

saints every trumpery monk or friar, down to the very latest canonizations by the modern Popes. I fear you will think me harsh, when I say that I believe Taylor was, perhaps unconsciously, half a Socinian in heart. Such a strange inconsistency would not be impossible. The Romish church has produced many such devout Socinians. The cross of Christ is dimly seen in Taylor's works. Compare him in this particular with Donne, and you will feel the difference in a moment. Why is not Donne's volume of sermons reprinted at Oxford?

In the reign of Edward VI., the Reformers feared to admit almost any thing on human authority alone. They had seen and felt the abuses consequent on the Popish theory of Christianity; and I doubt not they wished and intended to reconstruct the religion and the church, as far as was possible, upon the plan of the primitive ages. But the Puritans pushed this bias to an absolute bibliolatry. They would not put on a corn-plaster without scraping a text over it. Men of learning, however, soon felt that this was wrong in the other extreme, and indeed united itself to the very abuse it seemed to shun. They saw that a knowledge of the Fathers, and of early tradition, was absolutely necessary; and unhappily, in many instances, the excess of the Puritans drove the men of learning into the old Popish extreme of denying the Scriptures to be capable of affording a rule of faith without the dogmas of the church. Taylor is a striking instance how far a Protestant might be driven in this direction.—SAMUEL TAYLOR COLERIDGE, *Table Talk*, June 4, 1830

With all his genius, learning, and industry, Jeremy Taylor never could be a poet, because he never went beyond himself—beside himself, it you will. He has put the question beyond doubt: he tried verse; but his lines are like petrifications, glittering, and hard, and cold; formed by a slow but certain process in the laboratory of abstract thought; not like flowers, springing spontaneously from a kindly soil, fresh, and fragrant, and blooming in open day. The erudite divine is always in his study.—JAMES MONTGOMERY, *Lectures on General Literature, Poetry, &c.*, 1833, p. 83

When Jeremy Taylor wishes to prove the insensible progress of "a man's life and reason," he does not set about it by a syllogism, but a picture. He is not contented with a simple illustration—he raises up an elaborate landscape.—EDWARD BULWER-LYTTON, "Sir Thomas Browne," *Edinburgh Review*, Oct. 1836, p. 11

> Old *Chrysostom*, best Augustine,
> And he who blent both in his line,
> The younger *Golden Lips* or mines,
> Taylor, the Shakspeare of divines.
> His words are music in my ear.
> —RALPH WALDO EMERSON, "The Problem," 1839

Jeremy Taylor stands altogether alone among churchmen. Who has ever manifested any portion of that exquisite intermixture of a yearning love with a heavenly fancy, which enabled him to embody and render palpable the holy charities of his religion in the loveliest and most delicate images? Who has ever so encrusted his subjects with candied words; or has seemed, like him, to take away the sting of death with "rich conceit;" or has, like him, half persuaded his hearers to believe that they heard the voice of pitying angels?—THOMAS NOON TALFOURD, "On Pulpit Oratory," *Critical and Miscellaneous Writings*, 1842, p. 226

Mr. Coleridge placed Jeremy Taylor among the four great geniuses of old English literature. I think he used to reckon Shakspeare and Bacon, Milton and Taylor, four-square, each against each. In mere eloquence, he thought the Bishop without any fellow. He called him Chrysostom. Further, he loved the man, and was anxious to find excuses for some weak parts in his character. But Mr. Coleridge's assent to Taylor's views of many of the fundamental positions of Christianity was very limited; and, indeed, he considered him as the least sound in point of doctrine of any of the old divines, comprehending within that designation the writers to the middle of Charles II.'s reign.—HENRY NELSON COLERIDGE, *Specimens of the Table Talk of the Late Samuel Taylor Coleridge*, 1853, pp. 328–29, Note

His very style—like the murmur of a deep sea, bathed in the sun—so richly coloured by an imagination that was never disunited from the affections, and at the same time so sweetly cadenced, so full of gentle and varied melodies, reflects his character; and not the less so because of a certain want of nervousness and consistency, a certain vagueness and almost feebleness which it occasionally displays.—W. E. H. LECKY, *History of the Rise and Influence of the Spirit of Rationalism in Europe*, 1865

At the head of our English divines stands Jeremy Taylor at least as regards eloquence and brilliancy of imagination. He has been by some called the Spenser, by others the Shakespeare, of our theological literature; and he deserves both titles. He is as learned, as sweet, and as alluring as Spenser, and he has sometimes the tragic force and power, now and then a glimpse of the humour, and in some degree the fertile imagery and copiousness of diction of Shakespeare.—JAMES HAIN FRISWELL, *Essays on English Writers*, 1869, p. 182

A kind of Spenser in a cassock.—JAMES RUSSELL LOWELL, "Spenser" (1875), *Works*, Riverside ed., Vol. 4, p. 325, Note

Taylor was the most eloquent of men, and the most facile of orators. Laden with thought, his books are read for their sweet and deep devotion (a quality which also belonged to his fellow-writer, Lancelot Andrewes), even more than for their impassioned and convoluted outbreaks of beautiful words.—STOPFORD A. BROOKE, *English Literature*, 1896, p. 153

But Taylor's theology, it must be admitted, is without symmetry; it is not a noble building; a very large portion of his writings reads like the essays and confession of Montaigne, expressed in most dazzling and ambitious language. His most religious writings are what we have called them, Divine contemplations; thought, in the more strict comprehension of the term, we have little or none; imagination and emotion we have in abundance. After a time we find the understanding is not firm beneath us, and we begin to perceive that if we demand from our author argumentative coherence, we shall deal unjustly with him, while we cut ourselves off from the possession of much pleasure. We learn that his gift is to teach us rather as a seer than as a philosopher; to lift us at once to the spiritual rather than debate with us the material reasons of things. When he attempts the latter we become angry with him; always, when he attempts the former, it is as if at his touch the tabernacle of the testimony is opened in heaven.—E. PAXTON HOOD, *The Throne of Eloquence*, 1885, p. 163

It is not true that, except by great complaisance of the reader, Jeremy Taylor's long sentences are at once understandable. They may, of course, and generally can be understood *kata to semainsmenon*, as a telegram with half the words left out may at the other end of the scale be understood. But they constantly withstand even a generous parser, even one who is to the fullest extent ready to allow for idiom and individuality. They abuse

in particular the conjunction to a most enormous extent—coupling by its means propositions which have no legal connection, which start entirely different trains of thought, and which are only united because carelessness and fashion combined made it unnecessary for the writer to take the little extra trouble necessary for their separation. Taylor will, in the very middle of his finest passages, and with hardly so much as a comma's break, change *oratio obliqua* to *oratio recta*, interrupt the sequence of tenses, make his verbs agree with the nearest noun, irrespective of the connection, and in short, though he was, while in Wales, a schoolmaster for some time, and author of a grammatical treatise, will break Priscian's head with the calmest unconcern.—GEORGE SAINTSBURY, *A History of Elizabethan Literature*, 1887, p. 332

He united learning and fervent eloquence perhaps more than any other English writer.—FRANCIS TURNER PALGRAVE, *The Treasury of Sacred Song*, 1889, p. 345, Note

He was saturated through and through with learning and with piety; and they gurgled from him together in a great tide of mellifluous language. The ardors and fervors of Elizabethan days seem to have lapped over upon him in that welter of the Commonwealth wars. He has been called the Shakespeare of the pulpit; I should rather say the Spenser—there is such unchecked, and uncheckable, affluence of language and illustration; thought and speech struggling together for precedence, and stretching on and on, in ever so sweet and harmonious jangle of silvery sounds.—DONALD G. MITCHELL, *English Lands, Letters, and Kings (From Elizabeth to Anne)*, 1890, p. 139

Those who claim for the Church of England one of the highest places amongst Christian bodies for literary eminence, would naturally put forward Jeremy Taylor as one of the leading witnesses in favour of their proposition; and certainly it may be doubted whether any English ecclesiastical writer would be entitled to take precedence of him in a literary point of view, though he has been surpassed again and again by writers on special subjects whose eloquence, versatility, learning, dexterity were greatly inferior to his.—SIR JAMES FITZJAMES STEPHEN, *Horae Sabbaticae*, 1892

English prose had perhaps lost its best chance of rising to the highest level when the Elizabethan age passed without leaving a standard warranted by its authority. The floods of controversy, of misdirected effort, of exaggerated individualism, passed over it. But in time it attained to a more serene atmosphere. In Jeremy Taylor, and we might add, in a lesser degree, in Leighton, we see the evolution of order from disorder. Taylor inherited something from the Euphuists: he caught his note of earnestness from such a man as Donne; but in his prose we have a sense of greater security and restfulness than in any that had gone before. The fretfulness of controversy, the restlessness of individualism, the perpetual pursuit of intricacy, and the ceaseless desire to startle the reader, all the seare calming down. The note of his books is earnestness; but it is earnestness which flows calmly. Contrast his prose with that of Milton, powerful as that is with the very heat of the fight, and sounding as it were with the echo of the war-trumpet. We cannot deny its power, we cannot resist its excitement. But yet we are compelled to hear in it rather the echoes of what had gone before than to recognise it as the harbinger of a new and more self-contained prose. . . .

On the whole the elements of greatest hopefulness for English prose—its earnestness, its dignity, its conscious grace—were perhaps best summed up, in that age, in Jeremy

Taylor: and to him more than to any other may be ascribed the handing on of the torch from the preceding to the next generation, and the preserving of its flame clear and undimmed amidst the heated struggles and cloudy controversies of the time.—HENRY CRAIK, "Introduction" to *English Prose*, 1893, Vol. 2, pp. 6–7

As a preacher and devotional writer, Bishop Jeremy Taylor stands in the very first rank among the great divines of the golden period of English theology. His sermons are, of their kind, unrivalled. They differ widely from those of his great contemporaries, Barrow, Sanderson, and South; but they are, in their way, quite equal to any of them. In wealth of illustration, exuberance of fancy grandeur of diction and style, it would be difficult to find their equals in the English language. When Taylor wrote, that language had outgrown the roughness—one might almost say, the grotesqueness—which sometimes marks the earlier prose, and had not degenerated into the commonplace tameness which marks the age of Tillotson. And besides having so noble a vehicle to convey his thoughts, Taylor had other elements of a great preacher. He had a very definite message to deliver, without which the most eloquent preacher will be futile; and there was a spirit of piety about him which gives his sermons an unction, a sweetness, and a tenderness which commend them to the heart as well as to the head. The unlearned reader may find a difficulty by being, as it were, pulled up constantly by some quotation from a Greek or Latin author; but Taylor almost always translates it at once, and when he does not, it may generally be ignored without losing the thread of the discourse. The burden of Taylor's teaching, both in his sermons and in his devotional works, is that, in his own words, "Theology is rather a Divine life than a Divine knowledge." He disliked controversy, and is not seen at his best in his controversial writings. He was not an accurate thinker, and it is sometimes hard to reconcile different passages in his writings. It was perhaps this looseness of thought rather than intentional heresy that led him in some of his works, notably the *Unum Necessarium*, to approach perilously near towards Pelagianism. Hence it is hazardous to appeal to his authority as a theologian, for he might frequently be contradicted by himself. His forte lay not so much in argument as in appeals to the moral and spiritual nature of his readers or hearers, expressed in pure and stately language, and illustrated by magnificent descriptions and apposite quotations from all kinds of authors, sacred and profane. He had a tendency to turn everything he touched to a practical and devotional purpose. Hence his *Life of Christ*, or, to give it its full title, *The History of our Blessed Redeemer, Jesus Christ, or the Great Exemplar*, is quite as much a devotional work as his *Holy Living* or *Holy Dying*. But he is more self-restrained and less ornamental in his devotional works than in his sermons, rarely diverging in them from his mother-tongue. One of his great merits as a devotional writer is the very rare faculty he possessed of composing prayers. His prayers are some of the very few which can bear a moment's comparison with those in the Book of Common Prayer. His light esteem of mere opinions when separated from practice led him to write one of the most remarkable of all his works, "A Discourse of the Liberty of Prophesying, with its just Limits and Temper: showing the unreasonableness of prescribing to other Men's Faith, and the iniquity of persecuting differing Opinions." The title tells its own tale. The theory which Taylor advances, and the arguments by which he supports it, are now so generally admitted that they sound like commonplaces; but at the time when Taylor wrote on the subject he was far in advance of his age.

We cannot complain that Bishop Taylor was sparing in the use of his powers in that direction in which he was most qualified to shine, for his printed sermons and devotional writings are very voluminous. But with that curious infelicity which great men sometimes show in estimating their own capacities, the work over which he took by far the greatest pains was one in which both his merits and his defects were alike hindrances to his success. In the seventeenth century the word "casuistry" had not yet acquired its evil meaning as almost equivalent to "sophistry." Some of our best casuists, such as Bishops Hall, Sanderson, and Barlow, belong to this period. Bishop Taylor was led, as usual, by purely practical motives to devote himself to this uncongenial work. He thought that "of books of casuistical theology we were almost wholly unprovided; and, like the children of Israel in the days of Saul and Jonathan, we were forced to go down to the forges of the Philistines, to sharpen every man his share and his coulter, his axe and his mattock. We had swords and spears of our own, enough for defence, and more than enough for disputation; but in this more necessary part of the conduct of consciences we did receive our answers from abroad, till we found that our old needs were very ill supplied, and new necessities did every day arise." To supply this want he took infinite trouble, devoting some of the best years of his life to elaborating his long work, entitled *Ductor Dubitantium, or Cases of Conscience*, which appeared in 1660. He was himself so far satisfied with the result that he prophesied that his reputation among posterity would rest upon this book—a prophesy which has been signally falsified by the event. For one person who is acquainted with the *Ductor Dubitantium*, there are probably a hundred who know something, at any rate, about the *Holy Living* and *Holy Dying*, the *Golden Grove*, the *Marriage Ring*, and the *Via Intelligentiæ*. One reason, no doubt, why Taylor's casuistical work had fallen into comparative oblivion is that the subject itself is an obsolete study—not, perhaps, to the advantage of morals. But apart from this, Bishop Taylor was out of his element. A casuist should be terse, logical, severely simple—in short, almost everything that Taylor was not. His illustrations and quotations from the learned languages are even more profuse in the *Ductor* than in the sermons. Bishop Taylor's habit of mind, no less than his style, was essentially of the florid order; one would have said also, the poetic, had it not been that he tried poetry, and was not very successful. But as a prose writer he was, in his proper department and in his own day, quite unrivalled; and there are few who have surpassed him since. —J. H. OVERTON, "Jeremy Taylor," *English Prose*, ed. Henry Craik, 1893, Vol. 2, pp. 525–28

Few theologians have left more mark on English religion than Jeremy Taylor. His sermons combine many of the merits of Andrewes and of William Law. They are extraordinarily fertile in conceit and in appropriate illustration, they are searching and intimate in their application, and removed from all possibility of dulness by their sparkling and abundant imagination. His controversial writings are less easy, but their style is vigorous. His *Ductor Dubitantium* is almost the only treatise on casuistry written by an English Churchman, and it has all the honesty, and more than the skill, that might be expected. Books such as these belong to the armoury of the theologians, but the prayers of the *Golden Grove* and the admonitions of *Holy Living* and *Holy Dying* belong by right to every man that can appreciate either literature or religion. Certainly no religious works in English possess the same rare combination of merits, and none have more powerfully affected English life. The acute insight and the intimate knowledge of human nature which they show on every page are only equalled by the marvellous imagination which illuminates the style as well as the matter. Of all English prose writers, Jeremy Taylor is the richest.—WILLIAM HOLDEN HUTTON, *Social England*, ed. H. D. Traill, 1895, Vol. 4, p. 292

Works

Taylor and Barrow are incomparably the greatest preachers and divines of their age. But my predilection is for Taylor. He has all the abundance and solidity of the other, with a ray of lightening of his own, which, if he did not derive it from Demosthenes and Tully, has, at least, as generous and noble an original. It is true they are both *incompti*, or rather exuberant. But it is for such little writers as the Preacher of Lincoln's Inn [himself] to hide their barrenness by the finicalness of culture.—WILLIAM WARBURTON, Letter 50, Note, *Letters from a Late Eminent Prelate*, ed. Richard Hurd, 1808

His *Holy Living and Dying* is a divine pastoral. He writes to the faithful followers of Christ, as the shepherd pipes to his flock. He introduces touching and heartfelt appeals to familiar life; condescends to men of low estate; and his pious page blushes with modesty and beauty. His style is prismatic. It unfolds the colours of the rainbow; it floats like the bubble through the air; it is like innumerable dew-drops that glitter on the face of morning, and tremble as they glitter. He does not dig his way underground, but slides upon ice, borne on the winged car of fancy. The dancing light he throws upon objects is like an Aurora Borealis, playing betwixt heaven and earth.—WILLIAM HAZLITT, *Lectures on the Dramatic Literature of the Age of Elizabeth*, 1820

On the whole, the *Ductor Dubitantium* is the work of a mind acute, vigorous, and imbued with an extent and variety of information which would have overburdened a meaner intellect, and by which Taylor himself is, perhaps, sometimes encumbered rather than adorned. A mind it is essentially poetical rather than critical, ardent in conceptions in themselves are almost always clear, though he overlays them not unfrequently with a profusion of words and metaphors, and though he is apt to derive his first principles from springs of action in themselves circumstantial and secondary. But though it offers in some respects, a less profound and original view of human motives than is to be met with in later writers; though its length renders it less readable, and the author's anxiety to say every thing on both sides of every question may lead a careless reader sometimes in suspense as to his final determination; it is still a work which few can read without profit, and none, I think, without entertainment. It resembles, in some degree, those ancient inlaid cabinets, (such as Evelyn, Boyle, or Wilkins might have bequeathed to their descendants,) whose multifarious contents perplex our choice, and offer to the admiration or curiosity of a more accurate age, a vast wilderness of trifles and varieties, with no arrangement at all, or an arrangement on obsolete principles; but whose ebony drawers and perfumed recesses contain specimens of every thing that is precious or uncommon, and many things for which a modern museum might be searched in vain.—REGINALD HEBER, *Life of Jeremy Taylor*, 1824, pp. 314–15

The most curious, and, perhaps, the ablest of all his compositions ⟨is⟩ his admirable *Liberty of Prophesying*; composed, as he tells his patron, Lord Hatton, . . . under a host of grievous disadvantages; in adversity and want; without books or leisure; and with no other resources than those which were supplied by a long familiarity with the sacred volume, and a powerful

mind, imbued with all the learning of past ages.—REGINALD HEBER, *The Life of Jeremy Taylor*, 1824, pp. 36–37

The most extensive and learned work on casuistry which has appeared in the English language is the *Ductor Dubitantium* of Jeremy Taylor, published in 1660. This, as its title shows, treats of subjective morality, or the guidance of the conscience. But this cannot be much discussed without establishing some principles of objective right and wrong, some standard by which the conscience is to be ruled. . . . The heterogeneous combination of things so different in nature and authority, as if they were all expressions of the law of God, does not augur well for the distinctness of Taylor's moral philosophy, and would be disadvantageously compared with the "Ecclesiastical Polity" of Hooker. Nor are we deceived in the anticipations we might draw. With many of Taylor's excellences, his vast fertility and his frequent acuteness, the *Ductor Dubitantium* exhibits his characteristic defects: the waste of quotations is even greater than in his other writings, and his own exuberance of mind degenerates into an intolerable prolixity. His solution of moral difficulties is often unsatisfactory: after an accumulation of arguments and authorities, we have the disappointment to perceive that the knot is neither untied nor cut; there seems a want of close investigation of principles, a frequent confusion and obscurity, which Taylor's two chief faults—excessive display of erudition, and redundancy of language—conspire to produce. Paley is no doubt often superficial, and sometimes mistaken; yet in clearness, in conciseness, in freedom from impertinent reference to authority, he is far superior to Taylor.—HENRY HALLAM, *Introduction to the Literature of Europe*, 1837–39, Pt. 4, Ch. 4, Pars. 3–4

It seems very certain that he was preeminently a poet amongst preachers. This apology and allowance must be made for him, that no other pulpit name is associated with so rich and rare a poetic exuberance. The epithet of the modern, or the English Chrysostom seems scarcely a fitting one; Chrysostom was essentially an orator. We do not think of Jeremy Taylor as an orator. We have already said, we cannot conceive those sermons preached to vast audiences; he who cannot preach to vast audiences is no orator; he may be a most delightful preacher with the audience fit and few, and the charm of cryptic thought and feeling; and this is the attraction and the pleasure of the devotions and contemplations of Jeremy Taylor.—E. PAXTON HOOD, *The Throne of Eloquence*, 1885, p. 154

In another, the *Unum Necessarium*, or Discourse on Repentance, his looseness of statement and want of care in driving several horses at once, involved him in a charge of Pelagianism, or something like it, which he wrote much to disprove, but which has so far lasted as to justify modern theologians in regarding his ideas on this and other theological points as, to say the least, confused.—GEORGE SAINTSBURY, *A History of Elizabethan Literature*, 1887, p. 331

⟨*Holy Living and Holy Dying* is⟩ his masterpiece. A series of sermons in simple paragraphs, eloquent and persuasive, exhorting to an upright and holy life. It has been a popular book even to the present time. All of Taylor's writings are marred by the style prevalent in his time, but accentuated and exaggerated by him; Latinized, but careless, florid, gorgeous, rapid, opulent of words.—FRED PARKER EMERY, *Notes on English Literature*, 1891, p. 42

⟨*Ductor Dubitantium* illustrates⟩ better almost than any other book in the language, a remarkable point in the history of speculation—the transition from moral theology to moral philosophy, from the textbooks of the confessional to the works of writers on morals, regarded as a matter of ordinary speculation.—Sir James Fitzjames Stephen, *Horae Sabbaticae*, 1892

Even Jeremy Taylor suffers from the imperfections of contemporary taste. His unction is too long-drawn, his graces too elaborate and gorgeous, and modern readers turn from the sermons which his own age thought so consummate in their beauty to those more colloquial treatises of Christian exposition and exhortation of which the *Holy Living* and the *Holy Dying* are the types.—Edmund Gosse, *A Short History of Modern English Literature*, 1897, p. 152

The style of ⟨*Ductor Dubitantium*⟩ is prolix and hazy, overloaded with quotations and references, and only rarely enriched by illustration or eloquence, for which, indeed, the subject gives little scope.—J. Howard B. Masterman, *The Age of Milton*, 1897, p. 183

It is generally admitted that the literary genius of Taylor is seen at its best in his sermons. A passage in a sermon by South (30 April 1668) is evidently aimed at the pulpit style of Taylor, whose "starched similitudes" he caricatures. But while Taylor's imagination travels far and wide, takes daring flights, and again treads homely ground, he employs his gift in real elucidation of his point; and by the vividness of his own conceptions redeems from commonplace the preacher's most obvious themes. Apart from the play of fancy, the singular neatness of his workmanship gives beauty to his writing. The appalling length of his periods is very much a matter of punctuation. His style is not involved; few writers have been better artists in clear and striking sentences. It is true that he is wanting in some of the higher qualities of eloquence. He arrests and delights rather than moves his reader, for he is not himself carried away. In the midst of splendours he never rises into passion, and bounds his meaning with even cautious care. In his piety there is little fervour, but all his writings give the deep impression of a chastened and consecrated spirit of devotion.—Alexander Gordon, *Dictionary of National Biography*, 1898, Vol. 55, p. 428

CHARLES LAMB
Letters to Robert Lloyd (1801)
Charles Lamb and the Lloyds, ed. E. V. Lucas
1898, pp. 148–55

April 6, 1801

I love the man ⟨Taylor⟩, and I love his paraphernalia, and I like to name him with all his attributions and additions. If you are yet but lightly acquainted with his real manner, take up and read the whole first chapter of the *Holy Dying*; in particular turn to the first paragraph of the 2 sect. of that chapter for a simile of a rose, or more truly many similes within simile; for such were the riches of his fancy, that when a beauteous image offered, before he could stay to expand it into all its capacities, throngs of new coming images came up, and justled out the first, or blended in disorder with it, which imitates the order of every rapid mind. But read all of the first chapter by my advice; and I know I need not advise you, when you have read it, to read the second.

Or for another specimen (where so many beauties crowd, the judgment has yet vanity enough to think it can discern the handsomest, till a second judgment and a third *ad infinitum* start up to disallow their elder brother's pretensions) turn to the Story of the Ephesian Matron in the second section of the 5th chapter of the same *Holy Dying* (I still refer to the *Dying* part,

because it contains better matter than the *Holy Living*, which deals more in rules than illustrations—I mean in comparison with the other only, else it has more and more beautiful illustrations—than any prose book besides)—read it yourself and show it to Plumstead (with my Love, and bid him write to me), and ask him if Willy ⟨Shakespeare⟩ himself has ever told a story with more circumstances of fancy and humour.

The paragraph begins, 'But that which is to be faulted,' and the story not long after follows. Make these references while P. is with you, that you may stir him up to the Love of Jeremy Taylor, and make a convertite of him. Coleridge was the man who first solemnly exhorted me to 'study' the works of Dr. Jeremy Taylor, and I have had reason to bless the hour in which he did it. Read as many of his works as you can get. I will assist you in getting them when we go a stall hunting together in London, and it's odds if we don't get a good Beaumt. and Fletcher cheap.

Bp. Taylor has more and more beautiful imagery, and (what is more to a Lover of Willy) more knowledge and description of human life and manners than any prose book in the language: he has more delicacy and sweetness than any mortal, the 'gentle' Shakespear hardly excepted,—his similies and allusions are taken, as the bees take honey, from all the youngest, greenest, exquisitest parts of nature, from plants, and flowers, and fruit, young boys and virgins, from little children perpetually, from sucking infants, babies' smiles, roses, gardens,—his imagination was a spacious Garden, where no vile insects could crawl in; his apprehension a 'Court' where no foul thoughts kept 'leets and holydays.'

> Snail and worm give no offence,
> Newt nor blind worm be not seen,
> Come not near our fairy queen.

You must read Bishop Taylor with allowances for the subjects on which he wrote, and the age *in* which. You may skip or patiently endure his tedious discourses on rites and ceremonies, Baptism, and the Eucharist, the Clerical function, and the antiquity of Episcopacy, a good deal of which are inserted in works not purely controversial; his polemical works you may skip altogether, unless you have a taste for the exertions of vigorous reason and subtle distinguishing on uninteresting topics. Such of his works as you should begin with, to get a taste for him (after which your Love will lead you to his Polemical and drier works, as Love led Leander 'over boots' knee-deep thro' the Hellespont), but read first the *Holy Living and Dying*, and his *Life of Christ* and *Sermons*, both in folio. And, above all, try to get a beautiful little tract on the *Measures and Offices of Friendship*, printed with his *opuscula* duodecimo, and also at the end of his Polemical Discourses in folio. Another thing you will observe in Bp. Taylor, without which consideration you will do him injustice. He wrote to different classes of people. His *Holy Living and Dying* and *Life of Christ* were designed and have been used as popular books of family Devotion, and have been thumbed by old women, and laid about in the window seats of old houses in great families, like the Bible, and the 'Queene-like-Closet or rare boke or Recipes in medicine and cookery, fitted to all capacities.'

Accordingly in these *the fancy* is perpetually applied to; any slight conceit, allusion, or analogy, any 'prettiness,' a story true or false, serves for an argument adapted to women and young persons, and 'incompetent judgments;' whereas the Liberty of Prophecy (a book in your father's bookcase) is a series of severe and masterly reasoning, fitted to great Clerks and learned Fathers, with no more of Fancy than is subordinate and ornamental.—Such various powers had the Bishop of Down and Connor, Administrator of the See of Dromore!

My theme and my story!

⟨Undated⟩

To your inquiry respecting a selection from Bp. Taylor I answer—it cannot be done, and if it could it would not *take* with John Bull. It cannot be done, for who can disentangle and unthread the rich texture of Nature and Poetry, sewn so thick into a stout coat of theology, without spoiling both *lace* and *coat*? How beggarly and how bald do even Shakespeare's Princely Pieces look when thus violently divorced from *connection* and *circumstance*! When we meet with To be or not to be, or Jacques' moralisings upon the Deer, or Brutus and Cassius' quarrel and reconciliation,—in an Enfield Speaker, or in Elegant Extracts,—how we stare, and will scarcely acknowledge to ourselves (what we are conscious we feel) that they are flat and have no power. Something exactly like this have I experienced when I have picked out similes and stars from *Holy Dying* and shown them *per se*, as you'd show specimens of minerals or pieces of rock. Compare the grand effect of the Star-paved firmament, and imagine a boy capable of picking out those pretty twinklers one by one and playing at chuck-farthing with them. Everything in heaven and earth, in man and in story, in books and in fancy, acts by Confederacy, by juxtaposition, by circumstance and place. Consider a fine family (if I were not writing to you I might instance your own) of sons and daughters, with a respectable father and a handsome mother at their heads, all met in one house, and happy round one table. Earth cannot show a more lovely and venerable sight, such as the Angels in heaven might lament that in their country there is no marrying or giving in marriage. Take and split this Body into individuals—show the separate caprices, vagaries, &c., of Charles, Rob, or Plum, one a Quaker, another a Churchman. The eldest daughter seeking a husband out of the pale of parental faith—another warping, perhaps—the father a prudent, circumspective, do-me-good sort of a man *blest* with children whom no ordinary rules can circumscribe. I have not room for all particulars—but just as this happy and venerable Body of a family loses by splitting and considering individuals too nicely, so it is when we pick out Best Bits out of a great writer. 'Tis the *sum* total of his mind which affects us.

REGINALD HEBER
From *The Life of Jeremy Taylor*
1824, pp. 189–92, 320–25

It may . . . excite our wonder that such sermons as ⟨those in Ἐνιαυτός⟩ should have been addressed to any but an audience exclusively academical. An university alone, and an university of no ordinary erudition, appears the fitting theatre for discourses crowded, as these are, with quotations from the classics and the fathers; with allusions to the most recondite topics of moral and natural philosophy; with illustrations drawn from all the arts and sciences, and from history ancient and modern, clothed in a language rich and harmonious, indeed, beyond all contemporary writers, but abounding in words of foreign extraction, and in unusual applications of those which are of native origin. Nor should I have hesitated to conclude, that most of Taylor's sermons had been really composed and intended only for an academical audience, had not the author himself informed us, in his title-page and his dedication to Lord Carbery, that they were preached at Golden Grove, to the family and domestics of his patron; or, at most, to a few gentlemen and ladies of that secluded neighbourhood, and to as

many of the peasantry on the estate as could understand English. It is true, perhaps, that in those days a learned style of preaching was not only more frequently affected by divines, but more generally popular with their auditories, than it has been during the last century; and that they who could least understand a sermon, were not, therefore, the least ready to applaud it. The popularity of some preachers has descended to our times, who seem to have had scarcely any other stock in trade than a quantity of good and sufficient Greek and Hebrew quotations; while, on the other hand, the simplicity and unaffected plainness of the admirably learned Pocock was regarded by the rustics of his parish, as a proof that, "though a kind and neighbourly man, he was no Latinist." Taylor, however, had no need of such arts, and was by far too conscientious to employ them. He was too good, as well as too wise; too earnestly intent on amending the hearts and saving the souls of his hearers, to have amused their ears with that which could not reach their understanding; and I am therefore much inclined to believe that in preparing his sermons for the press, he materially changed them from the compositions which he had delivered to his rustic auditory in South Wales: or, that they had really been, in the first instance, designed for the university pulpit; and that, when preaching them at Golden Grove, he had recourse to such extemporaneous omissions or alterations as suited the abilities and circumstances of his congregation.

Such omissions or alterations would, in fact leave the essential merits of the discourse in a great measure unimpaired. The tenour of its reasoning would remain unbroken, though the recondite illustrations were withdrawn. Those illustrations and images which, as is the case with no small number in Taylor's works, are borrowed from natural objects, would produce a yet more powerful effect in proportion as those objects were familiar to his hearers. The practical wisdom of his counsels; his awful denunciations of God's judgments against sin; his admirable topics of consolation to the penitent; his affectionate earnestness, and his yet more persuasive piety, would lose none of their power if delivered in more homely language; and those persons are mistaken, who apprehend that a congregation in the humble ranks of life are unequal to the task of following up the most accurate chain of reasoning, if conveyed in words of which they know the meaning. To lay down a general rule for the selection of such a popular language is not, indeed, very easy; but it will be found, for the most part, that words of Saxon or Teutonic derivation, as they are more forcible and expressive to all English ears, so to an uninstructed English ear they are usually far more intelligible than those terms, (however familiar to the educated part of the nation,) which, are of French or Latin origin.

But whatever the sermons of Taylor may have been as delivered from the pulpit and to a miscellaneous or vulgar auditory, it is certain that, as essays for the closet, and as intended for those into whose hands they usually fall, few compositions can be named so eminently distinguished by fancy, by judgment, by learning, and by powers of reasoning; few, where the mind is so irresistibly allured, if not to agree with the author, at least to think well of him; or where so much luxuriance of imagination, and so much mellowness of style, are made the vehicles of divinity so sound, and holiness so practical. Those persons will, in fact, be much deceived, (they may be, perhaps, deceived to their own infinite advantage,) who take up his sermons as a book of amusements only; in which little is to be found but quaint singularities of expression, and pedantic though brilliant and characteristic ornament. As little will those do justice to their merits, who draw back from their perusal in the expectation of finding precepts too rigid and ascetic for our nature, or the general frame of society; the dicta of one who had forgotten or never experienced the temptations of the world, or the inexpediency of laying down an impracticable measure of duty. No writer, with whose works I am acquainted, has spoken more wisely, or with a greater knowledge, of the human heart; none more moderately, or (except in those particulars where the souls of men are really endangered,) more indulgently, than Taylor in his Ἐνιαυτός ; and, while his sermons on "Godly Fear" lay bare with a needful and scrupulous austerity the ruinous self-deceptions of a pretended repentance, and of that transient sorrow for sin or its consequences, which too many mistake for amendment, no writer has given a more just and beautiful picture of the goodness and gentleness of our Almighty Parent, than may be found in his discourses on the Miracles of the Divine Mercy." Of the rest, the "House of Feasting," and the "Marriage Ring," are perhaps the most characteristic, and distinguished by the greatest liveliness of fancy; while a very curious and difficult question is acutely and profitably discussed in the sermon on "The Entail of Curses." And, (though some of his positions are here, as on former occasions, laid down with too great and unqualified severity,) many awful and alarming truths are powerfully expressed, where he is treating of what he considers "The Invalidity of a Death-bed Repentance." Of all, the most likely to be practically useful are, perhaps, the two on "The Flesh and the Spirit," and those on the "Growth of Sin, and the several Estates of Sinners." All, however, may be read with profit; and, by a man of genius, none can be read without delight and admirtion. . . .

Of the broader and more general lines of Taylor's literary character, a very few observations may be sufficient. The greatness of his attainments, and the powers of his mind, are evident in all his writings, and to the least attentive of his readers. It is hard to point out a branch of learning or of scientific pursuit to which he does not occasionally allude; or any other of eminence, either ancient or modern, with whom he does not evince himself acquainted. And it is certain, that as very few other writers have had equal riches to display, so he is apt to display his stores with a lavish exuberance, which the severer taste of Hooker or of Barrow would have condemned as ostentatious, or rejected as cumbersome. Yet he is far from a mere reporter of other men's arguments,—a textuary of fathers and schoolmen,—who resigns his reason into the hands of his predecessors, and who employs no other instrument for convincing his readers than a lengthened string of authorities. His familiarity with the stores of ancient and modern literature is employed to illustrate more frequently than to establish his positions; and may be traced, not so much in direct citation, (though of this, too, there is, perhaps, more than sufficient,) as in the abundance of his allusions, the character of his imagery, and the frequent occurrence of terms of foreign derivation, or employed in a foreign and unusual meaning.

It is thus that he more than once refers to obscure stories in ancient writers, as if they were, of necessity, as familiar to all his readers as himself; that he talks of "poor Attilius Aviola," or "the Lybian lion," that "brake loose into his wilderness, and killed two Roman boys;" as if the accidents of which he is speaking had occurred in London a few weeks before. It is thus that, in warning an English (or a Welsh) auditory, against the brief term of mortal luxury, he enumerates a long list of ancient dainties, and talks of "the condited bellies of the searus," and "drinking of healths by the numeral letters of Philenium's name." It is thus that one of his strangest and harshest similies, where he compares an ill-sorted marriage to "going to-bed with a dragon," is the suggestion of a mind familiar with those *Lamiæ* with female faces and extremities like a serpent, of whose enticements strange stories are told in the old dæmonologies. And thus that he speaks of the *"justice"* instead of the "juice" of fishes; of an "excellent" pain; of the gospel being preached, not to "the common people," but to "idiots;" and of "serpents" (meaning "creeping things,") devouring our bodies in the grave. It is this which gives to many of his most striking passages the air of translations, and which, in fact, may well lead us to believe that some of them are indeed the selected members of different and disjointed classics.

On the other hand, few circumstances can be named which so greatly contribute to the richness of his matter, the vivacity of his style, and the harmony of his language, than those copious drafts on all which is wise, or beautiful or extraordinary, in ancient writers or in foreign tongues; and the very singularity and hazard of his phrases have not unfrequently a peculiar charm, which the observers of a tamer and more ordinary diction can never hope to inspire.

One of these archaisms, and a very graceful one, is the introduction of the comparitive degree, simply and without its contrasted quantity, of which he has made a very frequent use, but which he has never employed without producing an effect of striking beauty.

Thus, he tells us of "a *more* healthy sorrow;" of "the air's *looser* garment, or the *wilder* fringes of the fire;" which, though in a style purely English, they would be probably replaced by positive or superlative epithets, could hardly suffer this change without a considerable detraction from the spirit and raciness of the sentence. The same observation may apply to the use of *"prevaricate,"* in an active sense; to "the *temeration* of ruder handlings;" and to many similar expressions, which, if unusual, are at least expressive and sonorous, and which could hardly be replaced by the corresponding vernacular phrases without a loss of brevity or beauty. Of such expressions as these, it is only necessary to observe, that their use, to be effectual or allowable, should be more discreet, perhaps, and infrequent, than is the case in the works of Taylor.

I have already noticed the familiarity which he himself displays, and which he apparently expected to find, in an almost equal degree, in his readers or hearers, with the facts of history, the opinions of philosophy, the productions of distant climates, and the customs of distant nations. Nor, in the allusions or examples which he extracts from such sources, is he always attentive to the weight of authority, or the probability of the fact alleged. The age, indeed, in which he lived, was, in many respects, a credulous one. The discoveries which had been made by the enterprise of travellers, and the unskillful, and as yet immature efforts of the new philosophy, had extended the knowledge of mankind just far enough to make them know that much yet remained uncertain, and that many things were true which their fathers had held for impossible. Such absence of scepticism is, of all states of the human mind, most favourable to the increase of knowledge; but for the preservation of truths already acquired, and the needful separation of truth from falsehood, it is necessary to receive the testimony of men, however positive, with more of doubt than Boyle, Wilkins, or even Bacon, appear to have been accustomed to exercise.

But Taylor was any thing rather than a critical inquirer into facts (however strange) of history or philosophy. If such alleged facts suited his purpose, he received them without examination, and retained them without scruple; and we therefore read in his works, of such doubtful or incredible examples as that of a single city containing fifteen millions of inhabitants;

of the Neapolitan manna, which failed as soon as it was subjected to a tax; and of the monument "nine furlongs high," which was erected by Ninus, the Assyrian.

Nor, in his illustrations, even where they refer to matters of daily observation, or of undoubted truth, is he always attentive to accuracy. "When men sell a mule," he tells us, "they speak of the horse that begat him, not of the ass that bore him." It is singular, that he should forget that, of mules, the ass is always the father. What follows is still more extraordinary, inasmuch as it shows a forgetfulness of the circumstances of two of the most illustrious events in the Old Testament. "We should fight," says he, "as Gideon did, with three hundred hardy brave fellows that would stand against all violence, rather than to make a noise with ram's horns and broken pitchers, like the men at the seige of Jericho." Had he thought twice, he must have recollected that "making a noise" was at least one principal part of the service required from Gideon's troops, and that the "broken pitchers" were their property alone, and a circumstance of which the narrative of the siege of Jericho affords not the least mention.

An occasional occurrence of such errors is indeed unavoidable; and, irrelevant as some of his illustrations are, and uncertain as may be the truth of others, there is none, perhaps, of his readers who would wish those illustrations fewer, to which his works owe so much of their force, their impressiveness, and their entertainment. As a reasoner, I do not think him matchless. He is, indeed, always acute, and, in practical questions, almost always sensible. His knowledge was so vast, that on every point of discussion he set out with great advantage, as being familiar with all the necessary preliminaries of the question, and with every ground or argument which had been elicited on either side by former controversies. But his own understanding was rather inventive than critical. He never failed to find a plausible argument for any opinion which he himself entertained; he was as ready with plausible objections to every argument which might be advanced by his adversaries; and he was completely master of the whole detail of controversial attack and defence, and of every weapon of eloquence, irony, or sarcasm, which was most proper to persuade or to silence. But his own views were sometimes indistinct, and often hasty. His opinions, therefore, though always honest and ardent, he had sometimes occasion, in the course of his life, to change; and instances have been already pointed out, not only where his reasoning is inconclusive, but where positions, ardently maintained in some of his writings, are doubted or denied in others. But, it should be remembered how much he wrote during a life in itself not long, and, in its circumstances, by no means favourable to accurate research or calm reasoning. Nor can it be a subject of surprise, that a poor and oppressed man should be sometimes hurried too far in opposition to his persecutors, or that one who had so little leisure for the correction of his works should occasionally be found to contradict and repeat himself.

I have already had occasion to point out the versatility of his talents, which, though uniformly exerted on subjects appropriate to his profession, are distinguished, where such weapons are needed, by irony and caustic humor, as well as by those milder and sublimer beauties of style and sentiment which are his more familiar and distinguishing characteristics. Yet to such weapons he has never recourse either wantonly or rashly. Nor do I recollect any instance in which he has employed them in the cause of private or personal, or even polemical hostility, or any occasion where their fullest severity was not justified and called for by crimes, by cruelty, by interested superstition, or base and sordid hypocrisy. His satire was always kept in check

by the depth and fervour of his religious feelings, his charity, and his humility.

It is on devotional and moral subjects, however, that the peculiar character of his mind is most, and most successfully, developed. To this service he devotes his most glowing language; to this his aptest illustrations: his thoughts, and his words, at once burst into a flame, when touched by the coals of this altar; and whether he describes the duties, or dangers, or hopes of man, or the mercy, power, and justice of the Most High; whether he exhorts or instructs his brethren, or offers up his supplications in their behalf to the common Father of all,—his conceptions and his expressions belong to the loftiest and most sacred description of poetry, of which they only want, what they cannot be said to need, the name and the metrical arrangement.

It is this distinctive excellence, still more than the other qualifications of learning and logical acuteness, which has placed him, even in that age of gigantic talent, on an eminence superior to any of his immediate contemporaries; which has exempted him from the comparative neglect into which the dry and repulsive learning of Andrews and Sanderson has fallen;—which has left behind the acuteness of Hales, and the imaginative and copious eloquence of Bishop Hall, at a distance hardly less than the cold elegance of Clark, and the dull good sense of Tillotson; and has seated him, by the almost unanimous estimate of posterity, on the same lofty elevation with Hooker and with Barrow.

Of such a triumvirate, who shall settle the precedence? Yet it may, perhaps, be not far from the truth to observe, that Hooker claims the foremost rank in sustained and classic dignity of style, in political and pragmatical wisdom; that to Barrow the praise must be assigned of the closest and clearest views, and of a taste the most controlled and chastened; but that in imagination, in interest, in that which more properly and exclusively deserves the name of genius, Taylor is to be placed before either. The first awes most, the second convinces most, the third persuades and delights most: and, (according to the decision of one whose own rank among the ornaments of English literature yet remains to be determined by posterity,) Hooker is the object of our reverence, Barrow of our admiration, and Jeremy Taylor of our love.

JOHN TULLOCH
From "Jeremy Taylor:
Liberty of Christian Teaching within the Church"
*Rational Theology and Christian Philosophy
in England in the Seventeenth Century*
1872, Volume 1, pp. 347–53, 406–10

Taylor is medieval, ascetic, casuistic in his mature type of thought. He is a scholastic in argument, a pietist in feeling, a poet in fancy and expression; he is not a thinker. He seldom moves in an atmosphere of purely rational light; and even when his instincts are liberal and his reasoning highly rational in its results, he brings but a slight force of thought, of luminous and direct comprehension, to bear upon his work. Stillingfleet, again, is antiquarian, formal, and controversial. His intellect is acute, hard, and ingenious, ready to cope with any subject and any opponent that may cross his path, or may seem to him inimical to the Church. He is alert alike against the Romanist, the Separatist, and the Rationalist—one of a common type of theologians bred by all Churches, who delight to go forth with weapons of war against all assailants of official orthodoxy and official privilege. They have their own merits, this class of writers; and Stillingfleet, as well as Jeremy Taylor, is a name of which the Church of England has reason to be proud. Her great roll of illustrious writers would be much poorer if they were gone. There are few names, upon the whole, which shine with a richer or grander lustre than that of Taylor.

. . . fertile and unrestrained as Taylor's mental activity was in many directions, there is no influence of which it bears more trace than that of the scholasticism still prevailing in his youth. He is one of several examples in his generation of a singular combination of poetic imaginativeness, exuberant in its wantonness, with an arid scholasticism tedious in its love of trifles and distinctions. A medieval culture overlaid his native richness of fancy and feeling, without moulding and educating it. The imaginative fruitfulness survives; but it is not well mixed—it is hardly mixed at all—with the harder intellectual grain developed by the scholastic discipline. And so, like some other writers of the seventeenth century,[1] he seems almost to have two minds: one tender, sweet, and luxuriant to excess; the other hard, subtle, formal, prone to definition and logomachy. He is, at the same time, poet and casuist, orator and ascetic. The poetic, rhetorical elements lie alongside the dialectic in his genius, without blending, or fusing and strengthening into a thorough rational faculty.

Taylor became Bachelor of Arts in 1631, and is stated by his panegyrist Rust to have been chosen Fellow of Caius immediately afterwards. There appear, however, to be some doubts of this circumstance, which is distrusted by Heber. It is not till 1633, when he became Master of Arts, that Taylor's name occurs in the list of Fellows. He had then been admitted into holy orders, and appears from the first to have attracted attention as a preacher. It was his powers in this respect that brought him under the knowledge of Laud, and opened up for him a new career. One of his fellow-students, of the name of Risden, had become lecturer in St Paul's Cathedral, and wished Taylor to supply his place for a short time. Here his eloquence and graceful person, aided, no doubt, by the interest attaching to his youth, made a lively impression, and speedily procured him friends and admirers. He appeared, in the language of Rust, as "some young angel newly descended from the visions of glory." The fame of the youthful preacher was carried to Laud, just then elevated to the see of Canterbury, and, with that remarkable appreciation of genius which we have already noticed both in the case of Hales and Chillingworth, he sent for Taylor to preach before him at Lambeth. He was highly satisfied with his sermon, and immediately interested himself in his advancement. The story is that he wished to rescue so promising a preacher from the snares of a premature popularity in London. He thought him too young for such a sphere as St Paul's, and that it was "for the advantage of the world that such mighty parts should be afforded better opportunities of study and improvement than a course of constant preaching would allow of."[2] Taylor, of course, begged his Grace's pardon for the fault of his youth, and promised, "if he lived, he would amend it." Such is the manner in which Bishop Rust represents this turning-point in Taylor's career; and there is no reason to doubt his substantial accuracy, however much his admiring fancy may have embellished the event. Laud was greatly attracted by Taylor, and used his influence in establishing him at Oxford. After some difficulty, he was able to secure him a Fellowship at All Souls'. Sheldon, who was warden of the college, interposed to prevent his immediate appointment, notwithstanding the choice of the Fellows at Laud's instance; but the nomination devolving in due course to the archbishop as visitor, he carried

out his intentions by his own authority: Taylor became a Fellow of All Souls' on the 14th of January 1636.

This is a curious and significant step in Taylor's career. It is singular, first of all, to find him, no less than Hales and Chillingworth, in immediate connection with Laud. At this early period, Taylor's mind had probably not opened to the deeper questions of his time. There was nothing about him, except his undoubted ability, to attract the archbishop. This credit must be given to Laud, whatever we may think of his ecclesiastical policy: he had an eye for theological genius. The active patron of Hales and Chillingworth and Taylor cannot be accused of intellectual meanness, or of entire misapprehension of the spiritual forces of his time. Probably, as is often found to be the case with extreme ecclesiastics, Laud had no objection to an active and even liberal spirit of theological inquiry, where there was no tendency to practical insubordination or political restlessness. He may have guessed instinctively that none of these men would be likely to prove keen opponents of his ritualistic policy. Their spirit of conciliatory doctrinism made them indifferent, if not in some degree disposed, to ceremonies which must have appeared to them mere matters of expediency, while to the Puritan they savoured of idolatry. Their broad sense acknowledged no reason for repudiating a certain richness and elaboration of worship. And in Taylor's case, while his speculative liberality can hardly have appeared as yet, there may have been already some trace of those casuistic tendencies which afterwards matured and gave complexion to his theological culture. There is no difficulty in understanding the sympathy between Laud and the author of the *Ductor Dubitantium*, and the *Holy Living* and *Holy Dying*, however imperceptible may seem the links of association between him and the author of the *Liberty of Prophesying*.

It will be seen, therefore, that the general position of Taylor in the 'Liberty of Prophesying' is identical with that of Chillingworth in the *Religion of Protestants*. The conclusions which the latter reaches in a special conflict with the resurgent spirit of Romanism in England in the time of Laud, the former maintains professedly in a treatise written with a view to still the strife of ecclesiastical bigotry and faction in the time of the civil war. Chillingworth shows a firmer mastery of principles, a more downright and vigorous thoughtfulness, in the midst of all the special details of his argument; but Taylor draws out his principles with a more comprehensive range and purpose, and sets the problem of his time—the reconstitution of the Church on an evangelical yet tolerant basis—in a more definite light. This problem appears in Chillingworth's pages only indirectly. But this is expressly the question which Taylor set himself to solve in the view of the jarring parties of his time. His solution is that the Church should rest on the Apostles' Creed—neither more nor less; and that there should be the widest toleration of opinions ranging from Anabaptism to Popery. He devotes a special section to the discussion of the case of the Anabaptists, and concludes that as "there is no direct impiety in their opinion," and so much which may be fairly urged in its defence, they are to be "redargued or instructed," but in no respect to be coerced. His liberality towards a sect so hateful to all classes of dogmatists in the seventeenth century, and the extremely impartial manner in which he had set forth what might tend in behalf of their opinions, involved him in special suspicion, and he felt himself under the necessity of answering, in an appendix, his own arguments on behalf of this sect. Nothing is more creditable to Taylor than his frank liberality in this case, as nothing can better illustrate the intolerant spirit of the seventeenth century dogmatism than the obligation under which he felt of showing that his "meaning" was "innocent;" and that while maintaining that an ample case could be made out for the toleration of the Anabaptists, he did not mean in any respect to weaken what he believed to be the truth, or "to discourage the right side." To Taylor there was no error intolerable which was not impious or licentious, opposed to the fundamental principles of the Christian religion or to good morals and government; and the Christian Church, instead of seeking to narrow its terms of communion, was bound by every consideration of Christian truth and policy to open its doors as widely as possible for all who would come in. The "faith of the apostles" entitles all who hold it to "the communion of saints." "To make the way to heaven straiter than God made it, or to deny to communicate with those whom God will vouchsafe to be invited, and to refuse our charity to those who have the same faith because they have not all our opinions, is impious and schismatical; it infers tyranny on one part, and persuades and tempts to uncharitableness and animosities on both."[3]

There is no reason why individual Christians should not communicate with Churches of "different persuasions." If they require no impiety or anything unlawful as the condition of their communion, communion with them merely implies that we acknowledge them "as servants of Christ, as disciples of His doctrine, and subjects to His laws," while their "particular distinguishing doctrine" has no effect with us.

Beyond the primitive *facts* of the Gospel, in short, Taylor does not recognise any valid basis for the Christian Church, or any valid terms of Christian communion. He was, no doubt, as we have seen, himself an earnest defender of Episcopacy. For the perfect order of the Church he would certainly have maintained the necessity of Episcopal government and of liturgical worship. His writings leave this beyond question. But that Episcopacy or a liturgy has anything to do essentially with a man being a Christian, or with the recognition of Christian brotherhood, is an opinion opposed to the whole spirit of his great treatise, and to many of its express statements. A Christian is one who accepts Christ as his Saviour and Lord, and orders his life under the inspiration of this simple but mighty faith; a Christian Church is a society of men who acknowledge the same faith and walk by the same rule. These are the essentials; all else is accidental. No error is damnable which may be held with an honest mind. "It concerns all persons to see that they do their best to find out truth; and if they do, it is certain that, let the error be never so damnable, they shall escape the error or the misery of being damned for it. And if God will not be angry with men for being invincibly deceived, why should men be angry one at another?"[4] "All opinions in which the public interests of the commonwealth, and the foundation of faith and a good life, are not concerned, are to be permitted freely. 'Let every one be persuaded in his mind,' was the doctrine of St Paul, and that is argument and conclusion too; and they were excellent words which St Ambrose said in attestation of this great truth,—'Imperial authority has no right to interdict the liberty of speaking, or sacerdotal authority to prevent the speaking of what you think.'"[5]

Nothing can be more beautiful than the close of Taylor's treatise. It condenses in a parable the whole pith of his argument; and the effect lingers in the memory as a lofty strain of music which has melted into pathos ere it dies. "I end with a story," he says, "which I find in the Jews' books." It was long doubtful whether Taylor did not mean under this indefinite nomenclature to hide an invention of his own rich and beautiful fancy; but, as Heber explains, the source of the story has at length been discovered, not in a Jewish work, but in a tale of the Persian poet Saadi. The story is as follows: "When Abraham sat at his tent-door, according to his custom, waiting to entertain strangers, he espied an old man stooping and leaning on his staff, weary with age and travail, coming towards him, who was an hundred years of age. He received him kindly, washed his feet, provided supper, caused him to sit down; but observing that the old man sat and prayed not, nor begged for a blessing on his meat, he asked him why he did not worship the God of heaven. The old man told him that he worshipped the fire only, and acknowledged no other God. At which answer Abraham grew so zealously angry that he thrust the old man out of his tent, and exposed him to all the evils of the night and an unguarded condition. When the old man was gone, God called to Abraham and asked him where the stranger was; he replied, 'I thrust him away because he did not worship Thee.' God answered him, 'I have suffered him these hundred years, although he dishonoured me; and couldst not thou endure him one night, when he gave thee no trouble?' Upon this, saith the story, Abraham fetched him back again, and gave him hospitable entertainment and wise instruction." "Go thou and do likewise," he adds, "and thy charity will be rewarded by the God of Abraham."

The lesson is one, unhappily, which requires constant repetition in the history of the Christian Church.

Notes

1. Samuel Rutherford, the well-known Scotch Puritan divine, who replied in an elaborate volume to Taylor and "other authors contending for lawless liberty or licentious toleration of sects and heresies," is an instance of the same poetic and scholastic qualities ill combined, or rather not combined at all. In Rutherford, indeed, both the poetry and the logic must be admitted to be of very inferior quality. Yet the same contrast of mental character is presented. He is scarcely the same writer in his 'Letters,' the only productions of his pen now known, and in his argumentative treatises. The 'Letters' are marked by the extravagances of a fancy lawless in its exuberance. The treatises are dull, barren, operose, and unillumined in argument to a frightful degree. Nobody without an effort can read them. And if it may seem too great a disparity to compare Rutherford in any respect with Taylor (although their controversial relation suggests the comparison), we may point to the greatest literary name of the age as illustrative of the same fact. Marvellous as are Milton's prose works, they are, especially the treatise on Divorce, lacking in lofty rationality and consistency of argument. The poet is revealed in the splendour of occasional thoughts and in passages of noble eloquence; but the imagination has not blended with the understanding so as to give insight, comprehension, and light to the general train of reasoning.
2. Rust.
3. Sect. xxi. I.
4. Sect. xxii. 3.
5. "Nec imperiale est, libertatem dicendi negare; nec sacerdotale quod sentias non dicere."—*Ibid.*

EDWARD DOWDEN
From "An Anglican and a Puritan Eirenicon: Jeremy Taylor: Baxter"
Puritan and Anglican
1901, pp. 197–213

A funeral panegyric is not and cannot be a complete criticism; but true sorrow may be keen-sighted for the characteristic virtue of a mind and life. No better word, when allowance has been made for the occasion, has been spoken of Jeremy Taylor than that found in the sermon preached a few days after his death by his friend and follower Dean Rust, himself a writer of some distinction, whose affinities were with the school of the Cambridge Platonists. Taylor was not a great or original thinker; he was not always as wise as he was learned; the spirit of authority sometimes overbore with him the spirit of conciliation. "He was not unseen," says Rust, "in the subtleties and spinosities of the schools, and upon occasion could make them serve his purpose." It was not always an advantage to Taylor that he delayed among these subtleties and spinosities, and the panegyrist adds with a half apologetic touch: "Yet, I believe, he thought many of them very near akin to the famous knight of La Mancha, and would make sport sometimes with the romantic sophistry, and fantastic adventures of school-errantry." We may remain unconvinced when Rust ascribes to his friend "the profoundness of a philosopher, the sagacity of a prophet, the reason of an angel." But when he speaks of the natural ardour of Taylor's temperament, the opulence of his endowment, the harmonious richness of his genius, and when he adds that this ardour and these great gifts were directed towards piety, we feel that he has found the centre, and said a final word: "Nature had befriended him much in his constitution; for he was a person of a most sweet and obliging humour, of great candour and ingenuousness; . . . his soul was made up of harmony; . . . all his words and his very tone and cadences were unusually musical. But that which most of all captivated and ravished his hearers was the gaiety and richness of his fancy; for he had much in him of that natural enthusiasm which inspires all great poets and orators; and there was a generous ferment in his blood and spirits, that forcibly excited his imagination, and raised it to such a degree of luxuriancy as nothing but the greatness of his wit and judgment could have kept within due bounds." The truth could hardly be better told. And Rust adds elsewhere in his *éloge*: "His humility was coupled with extraordinary piety; and, I believe, he spent the greatest part of his time in heaven; his solemn hours of prayer took up a considerable portion of his life; and we are not to doubt but he had learned of St Paul to pray continually; and that occasional ejaculations, and frequent aspirations, and emigrations of his soul after God, made up the best part of his devotions." There we have the whole man, his ardour, his rich endowments, his various learning, (of which Rust tells us also) and the zeal of his piety.

The restraint of Taylor's affluence, that which saved it from expanding into a luxuriant marsh, came less from his judgment than from his zeal. At his best he flows forward with a harmonious impetuosity, like a river that is wide, and is swifter than it seems, exultant, with many a refluent eddy which cannot check, but rather is part of, the sweep and progress of the stream. Nowhere perhaps does the natural ardour of Taylor's heart appear more attractively than in the discourse addressed to Mrs Katherine Philips—the matchless Orinda—on the nature, offices, and measures of Friendship. Orinda, whom Mr Gosse calls the first English sentimentalist, had erected friendship in her Arcady of the sweet shire of Cardigan into a kind of fine art. "The noble Palæmon," Jeremy Taylor, in his letter to her is passionate, with wise and sacred passion, but certainly is untouched by any effeminate sentimentality. He tells us how every common sorrow of the world, if brought home to the imagination, wounds the spirit of charity within him, yet he reserves his best affections for those whom kinship or circumstances have brought near: "I pray for all mankind; I am grieved at every sad story I hear; I am troubled when I hear of a pretty bride murdered in her bride-chamber by an ambitious and enraged rival; I shed a tear when I am told that a brave king was misunderstood, then slandered, then imprisoned, and then put to death by evil men;[1] and I can never read the story of the Parisian Massacre, or the Sicilian vespers, but my blood curdles, and I am disordered by two or three

affections. . . . But though we must pray for all men, yet we say special litanies for brave kings and holy prelates, and the wise guides of souls; for our brethren and relations, our wives and children."

Not even the poet of *Leaves of Grass* has sung more enthusiastically of comradeship than Taylor in this Discourse. Friendship is like the sun, the eye of the world; but men, according to their worth, differ in their capacity to receive its showers of warmth and light. The emanation of the beams of the sun is for all the world; for the scalded Indian and the poor boy that shakes at the foot of the Riphæean hills; but men receive of friendship only what they can; "and some have only a dark day and a long night, snows and white cattle, a miserable life, and a perpetual harvest of catarrhs and consumptions, apoplexies and dead palsies; but some have splendid fires and aromatic spices, rich wines and well-digested fruits, great wit and great courage; because they dwell in his eye, and look in his face, and are the courtiers of the sun, and wait upon him in his chambers of the East." Such splendid fires and aromatic spices were the gifts of the sun to Taylor in his best creations. Addressing in this Discourse a woman celebrated for her genius in friendship, he must needs touch upon the subject of friendships in which a woman bears a part, and he does so with a noble enthusiasm. Marriage in its ideal he conceives as friendship brought to perfection; and beyond this passage we have little to lead us to any inference as to the happiness which Taylor found in his first or his second wife:[2] "You may see how much I differ from the morosity of those Cynics who would not admit your sex into the communities of a noble friendship . . . I cannot say that women are capable of all those excellencies by which men can oblige the world; and therefore a female friend in some cases is not so good a counsellor as a wise man, and cannot so well defend my honour, nor dispose of reliefs and assistances, if she be under the power of another; but a woman can love as passionately, and converse as pleasantly, and retain a secret as faithfully, and be useful in her proper ministries; and she can die for her friend as well as the bravest Roman knight." Over which fine outbreak Orinda may well have given a sigh of satisfaction.

It is unfortunate for Taylor that he should be known chiefly by ornaments detached from his larger compositions. The lark rising from his bed of grass, and beaten back with the loud sighings of an eastern wind, the rose newly springing from the clefts of its hood, and dismantled of its too youthful and unripe retirements—these and the like are beautiful and memorable, but if read as elegant extracts they leave an impression that Taylor's excellence lay in filigree work, and that sweetness with him was not united with severity or strength. Nor, indeed, was it always. But Taylor's happiness of temper and his florid graces, growing freely like the little rings of the vine, were not inconsistent with habits of almost ascetic discipline and with an energy of imagination which shows itself in greatness of composition. The large ordonnance of some of his discourses will surely strike any reader of those which treat of Christ's advent to Judgment. There is in them a magnificence of terror, but of terror relieved by a solemn joy, which reminds one, if not of the splendid mastery of Tintoretto, yet, at least, of the constructive power of Poussin. The sweep and grandeur of the whole are the true evidence of the preacher's imaginative passion. He puts the trumpet to his lips, and it is a

> Tuba mirum spargens sonum
> Per sepulchra regionum,

such as might penetrate the ears, let us not say of the watchful dead, but rather of Hogarth's sleeping congregation.

Fervour in the pursuit of devout ends is what Taylor above all desires to breathe into his hearers. If we pray, let our prayers be as flames of fire ascending from the heart's altar. When you reckon up your prayers, "you must reckon, not by the number of the collects, but by your sighs and passions, by the vehemence of your desires, and the fervour of your spirit, the apprehension of your need, and the consequent prosecution of your supply." For cold prayers are not put into the account, but are laid aside "like the buds of roses, which a cold wind hath nipped into death, and the discoloured tawny face of an Indian slave." And again, without elaborated metaphor, yet in words no less characteristic of Taylor than the last: "He that is cold and tame in his prayers hath not tasted of the deliciousness of religion and the goodness of God; he is a stranger to the secrets of the Kingdom, and therefore he does not know what it is either to have hunger or satiety; and therefore neither are they hungry for God nor satisfied with the world; but remain stupid and inapprehensive, without resolution and determination, never choosing clearly, nor pursuing earnestly, and therefore never enter into possession, but always stand at the gates of weariness, unnecessary caution, and perpetual irresolution."

Three sermons are specially devoted to the subject of "Lukewarmness and Zeal; or Spiritual Fervour." Taylor's own fervour makes him courageous in his teaching. Contrasting the spirit of Christian worship with that of the Mosaic ritual, he utters words which we might rather have expected to hear from the lips of a Puritan divine. By the shadow of the ceremony, under the law of Moses, God did indeed require the substantial worship; "yet because they were to mind the outward action, it took much off from the intention and activity of the spirit; man could not do both busily." Milton has used the same argument against elaborate ceremony. The preacher again dares to declare boldly, though under the shadow of St Augustine's authority, that sin may be the cloudy porch which leads to sanctity; the loss of chastity by one—virgin or widow—who is chaste and proud, may be, in a true sense, a means to grace; to fall into offence is sometimes a remedy. He asserts that a lukewarm religion, if it be not in progress to a better state, is "much worse" than no religion at all. He does not scruple to say, that to give to the poor is better than to give to a church. And for one whose preaching, no doubt, was hung upon by many enraptured auditors of the sex that most looks up to a gracious pulpiteer, it needed, perhaps, yet higher courage to announce pretty plainly that certain of them had better be at home attending to their household duties. "Martha was troubled with much serving; that was 'more than needs,' and therefore she was to blame; and sometimes hearing in some circumstances may be 'more than needs'; and some women are 'troubled with over much hearing,' and then they had better have been serving the necessities of their house." It would be base to conjecture that a popular Puritan lecturer was holding forth in the neighbourhood of Golden Grove.

Easy ways to salvation were viewed by Taylor with distrust; strait is the gate; the Kingdom of Heaven suffereth violence, and the violent take it by force. In the second sermon on "Godly Fear" he had ventured to say that our sins are not pardoned easily and quickly; pardon fluctuates like the wave when the tide has turned, and only gradually invades the shore; we are to expect it upon such terms as are revealed, which include time, and labour, and uncertainty, and fear, and holy living. How shall we know that we have received the grace of forgiveness? Not by some sudden inward light, which may be a false phosphorescence sprung from our own heart. There is a surer way of knowledge: "If I have sinned against God in the shameful crime of lust, then God hath pardoned my sins, when, upon repentance and prayers, He hath given me the grace of chastity. My drunkenness is forgiven when I have acquired the grace of temperance and a sober spirit. My covetousness shall no more be a damning sin, when I have a loving and charitable spirit; loving to do good, and despising the world." In all things let us base our confidence on grounds that are solid and stable. "Let us proceed," says Taylor in one of his noblest words, "from causes to effects, . . . and believe felicity not to be a chance but a choice." And it is in such words as these rather than in the well-known decorative passages that we reach to the strength of the great preacher's spirit.

All the highest spiritual teachers have declared that a state of aridity is sometimes as profitable to the soul as a state of refreshment. Taylor exhorts his hearers to fill the dry places at least with duties well done: "This delight is not to be understood as if it were always required that we should always feel an actual cheerfulness and sensible joy; such as was that of Jonathan, when he had newly tasted honey, and the light came into his eyes, and he was refreshed and pleasant. This happens sometimes, when God pleases to entice, or reward a man's spirit, with little antepasts of heaven; but such a delight only is necessary, and a duty, that we always choose our duty regularly, and undervalue the pleasures of temptation, and proceed in the work of grace with a firm choice and unabated election." If we elect to go still forward under our load of difficulty and pain it is enough; what we choose, that we delight in.[3]

Out of the strong came forth sweetness; and here the strength is that of an eager, ardent nature. Let us see Taylor aright, and we shall perceive that his sweetness grows out of an inward severity, and that the blossoming passages of his writings mean often that the passion of his heart must break forth in beauty. The following, from the second sermon "Of Lukewarmness and Zeal," may serve as an example, which is highly characteristic of the writer; it is no ornament attached externally, but the flowering of sap ascending from roots that strike deep in earth: "You may observe it, that so long as the light shines bright, and the fires of devotion and desires flame out, so long the mind of a man stands close to the altar, and waits upon the sacrifice; but as the fires die, and desires decay, so the mind steals away, and walks abroad to see the little images of beauty and pleasure, which it beholds in the falling stars and little glow-worms of the world. The river that runs slow and creeps by the banks, and begs leave of every turf to let it pass, is drawn into little hollownesses, and spends itself in smaller portions, and dies with diversion; but when it runs with vigorousness and a full stream, and breaks down every obstacle, making it even as its own brow, it stays not to be tempted by little avocations, and to creep into holes, but runs into the sea through full and useful channels; so is a man's prayer, if it moves upon the feet of an abated appetite; it wanders into the society of every trifling accident, and stays at the corners of the fancy, and talks with every object it meets, and cannot arrive at heaven; but when it is carried upon the wings of passion and strong desires, a swift motion and a hungry appetite, it passes on through all the intermediate region of clouds, and stays not till it dwells at the foot of the throne where mercy sits, and thence sends holy showers of refreshment." The sermons on Lukewarmness and Zeal close with certain warnings, for Taylor's religious prudence was great and taught him that true zeal has its measures, and intemperate zeal its dangers. His age seemed to him an age of violent passions tending to strife, but of much lukewarmness towards what is sincerely good. He pleads therefore for a zeal according to knowledge, not for a *via media* of tameness, but for a pure ardour in the pursuit of what he terms a persevering, a great, a passionate religion.

In days of trouble and division Taylor put forth an Eirenicon in his *Liberty of Prophesying*. To reduce the essential articles of Christian belief to those of the Apostles' Creed, to maintain the prerogative of human reason, to exhibit the uncertainty of theological opinions, and to write in the temper of charity was certainly to serve the cause of toleration. But a man may widen the bounds of toleration, yet draw the line with a rigid pen. He may shrink from giving his fundamental principles their complete application. As an Irish bishop Taylor's action certainly did not result in peace; but it would be unjust not to bear in mind the difficulties of his position. He insisted on order and obedience within his own communion; and his opponents were not of a compliant temper. "We find," he writes in the dedication of his sermon preached at the opening of the Irish Parliament, "that all Christian churches kept this rule; they kept themselves and others close to the rule of faith, and peaceably suffered one another to differ in ceremonies, but suffered no difference amongst their own; they gave liberty to other churches, and gave laws, and no liberty, to their own subjects: and at this day the churches of Geneva, France, Switzerland, Germany, Low Countries, tie all their people to their own laws, but tie up no man's conscience; if he be not persuaded as they are, let him charitably dissent, and leave that government, and adhere to his own communion." Taylor's principles of conformity were rather defensive than designedly aggressive, yet in its result his action savours too much of Black Bartholomew day, and those who should celebrate his memory with most applause are the Presbyterians of the north of Ireland, who were gainers by his over-strained spirit of legality.

Yet to his Irish days belongs a second and a very admirable Eirenicon—the sermon which he named "Via Intelligentiæ," preached before "the little but excellent University of Dublin," and published in 1662. It is addressed to such earnest seekers for truth as a sanguine person might suppose would specially gather around a university, and the text is the conciliating one "If any man will do his will, he shall know of the doctrine." Such a text is indeed two-edged, and may lend itself to uncharitable handling. We, of this communion or of that, do God's will and know of the doctrine; those who maintain another doctrine have erred because of evil affections and unrighteous lives, and cannot be among the doers of God's will. There is something *naïve* in such sophistry as this; but Taylor in the sermon sophisticates his text with most sincere conviction. Kings and bishops are of divine ordinance; to submit to them is to be loyal to the will of God. What criminals therefore are they who oppose bishops and a king, men who "rise up against their fathers, and are cruel to their brethren, and stir up the people to sedition; and all this with a cold stomach and a hot liver, with a hard heart and a tender conscience, with humble carriage and a proud spirit." And in like manner consider, he cries, the "infinite unreasonableness" that is in the Popish religion, how against common sense their doctrine of transubstantiation is, how against the common experience of human nature is the doctrine of the Pope's infallibility, how against Scripture is the doctrine of indulgences and purgatory. How is belief in these absurdities possible? Simply enough; the devisers of the doctrines were not among those who did God's will; the doctrines were imposed upon the credulous for the sake of temporal ends. Every proposition of the Popish religion which differs from those held by us is meant "to serve the end of money or of power." Taylor does not raise the question whether a like argument could have been effectively used by a nonconformist against the Anglican establishment.

But putting aside matter of controversy, there is much that is of high excellence in the "Via Intelligentiæ." It admirably

describes the temper in which truth should be sought; it admirably distinguishes between a notional assent to propositions and the real and vital apprehension of truth; it justly rebukes some of the trifling or over-curious learning of the schools. The drift of the whole is that "theology is rather a divine life than a divine knowledge."

Men of his time, says Taylor, had been wrangling about peace, and seeking the ascertainment of some common body of truth as the ground of religious unity. Each rival communion was prepared to exhibit a system of belief, and tell you that is the true religion, and they are the Church, and the peculiar people of God. Of this, says Taylor, there will be no end—"for divide the Church into twenty parts, and, in whatsoever part your lot falls, you and your party are damned by the other nineteen." Another imagined way to reconcile the differences of Christendom is that of moderation, a way favoured by Erasmus, Grotius, and others. Let each sect abate its asperities, and pare away something of its distinctive doctrine, and let all join in common terms and phrases of accommodation. "From hence"—such is Taylor's remorseless statement of his conviction—"can succeed nothing but folly and a fantastic peace: this is but the skinning of an old sore; it will break out upon all occasions." Something, he thinks, may be gained by clearness of definition in questions of controversy; but, after all, this is nothing else but "a drawing up the armies in battalia with great skill and discipline"; it brings the combat to a precise issue, and the next thing the combatants do is to thrust their swords into one another's sides. What remedy, Taylor asks, after all this? Is it to be found in the complete toleration of all opinions? This is a way of peace rather than of truth. It is indeed a highly reasonable way; yet how can the intolerant, who seek not equality but absolute rule, be themselves tolerated? Complete toleration—Taylor spoke of his own time, and the words were spoken in Ireland—"is better in contemplation than in practice." Mere opinions certainly are not to be persecuted; but it is equally certain that opinions which lead to violence in states ought not to be made public and permitted.

The human ways towards truth and peace have failed and must fail. What is God's way? "If any man do His will he shall know of the doctrine. . . . The way to judge of religion is by doing of our duty: and theology is rather a divine life than a divine knowledge. In heaven, indeed, we shall first see, and then love; but here on earth, we must first love, and love will open our eyes as well as our hearts; and we shall then see, and perceive, and understand."

Taylor does not mean that one who does the duty that lies nearest to him will be enlightened by new revelations, and be conducted by ecstasy, and pray in a transfiguration, and live upon raptures. The spirit of God does not spend its holy influences "in disguises and convulsions of the understanding." It does not destroy but rather heightens reason. The process is simple; good men see what is good, and they lay hold of it; "half a word is enough to make them understand; a nod is a sufficient reproof; the crowing of a cock, the singing of a lark, the dawning of the day, and the washing their hands, are to them competent memorials of religion and warnings of their duty." Human learning, indeed, brings excellent aids to the true knowledge of religion; but by arguing and dispute we see no more than the shadow of God, in which are many dark appearances, little certainty, and much conjecture. If by human learning we have attained to the meaning of a divine word, there is still "a meaning of the meaning" (for the leaves of the book are written within and without), a living secret, which can only be made real for us through practice—"this is to be felt, and not to be talked of; and they that never touched it with their finger may secretly perhaps laugh at it in their heart, and be never the wiser." Taylor himself was a man of multifarious learning, a theologian and a casuist, but it seemed to him that scholars too often lived upon air and empty notions, troubling themselves, as he admirably puts it, with tying and untying knots, like hypochondriacs in a fit of melancholy, raising foolish questions, spending zeal in things unprofitable, making religion to consist of outsides. "No, no"; he cries, "the man that is wise, he that is conducted by the Spirit of God, knows better in what Christ's kingdom does consist than to throw away his time, and interest, and peace and safety—for what? for religion? no: for the body of religion? not so much: for the garment of the body of religion?" no, not for so much: but for the fringes of the garment of the body of religion. A word that has meanings for the nineteenth century as truly as for Taylor's own day.

Stated in a word, Taylor's teaching is that truth resides implicitly in goodness; it may never attain to an explicit statement in words or propositions, but it abides in the heart as a hidden wisdom, which regulates conduct and contains all that is needful for life and godliness. He does not shrink from illustrating his central thought by a striking example. Who is he that best knows, as far as it can be known to man, the unintelligible mystery of the Divine nature? Not he who can do no more than recite the "Quicunque vult," and brandish his sword in honour of the credenda. We may amuse ourselves,

says Taylor, with essences and hypostasies and personalities, distinctions without difference, priority in coequalities, and unity in pluralities, and may be none the wiser; we may build three tabernacles for the Trinity in our head, and may talk something, and know not what. But the good man, who feels "the power of the Father," he to whom "the Son" is become "wisdom, righteousness, sanctification and redemption," he in "whose heart the love of the Spirit of God is spread"; he— though he understands nothing of what is unintelligible— alone understands the mystery of the holy Trinity, for, vigorous in holy actions, he sees with his heart what his tongue can never express, and his metaphysics can never prove.

Such is Jeremy Taylor's "Eirenicon"; one which settled nothing, and could settle nothing immediately; one which could not on the instant avert grave errors of judgment or stay unhappy courses of action; but one which, if taken to heart, and made real to the conscience and to conduct, must in the end form a temper favourable both to truth and peace.

Notes

1. The reference seems to be to Charles I.; the discourse was published in 1657.
2. His second wife is believed to have been a natural daughter of Charles I.
3. "Of Lukewarmness and Zeal," Part II.

ABRAHAM COWLEY

1618–1667

Abraham Cowley was born on July 24, 1618, on Fleet Street, London. He attended Westminster School as a King's Scholar from 1628 to 1635, and entered Trinity College, Cambridge, in 1637, receiving a B.A. in 1639 and an M.A. in 1642.

Cowley had begun his literary activity at an early age, composing *Pyramus and Thisbe*, an epic romance, at age ten; the poem was included in a small volume entitled *Poeticall Blossomes* (1635), published when he was only fifteen. His collection of 1636, *Sylva*, shows the influence of Latin poets, especially Horace. During his college years he wrote several comedies, *Loves Riddle* (1636), *Naufragium Joculare* (1638), and *The Guardian* (1641; revised and republished in 1661 as *Cutter of Coleman-Street*).

He was forced to leave Cambridge in 1644 because of his Royalist sympathies. He fled first to Oxford and then to France with the exiled court. From 1646 to 1656 he was secretary to the Queen and served on several diplomatic missions. In 1647 he published a collection of love poetry, *The Mistress*, which was reprinted in 1656 in a complete volume of his mature poems, along with *Miscellanies*, *Pindarique Odes*, and *Davideis*, a sacred epic about King David.

In 1654 Cowley returned to England, and following a brief imprisonment studied medicine and botany at Oxford. After the Restoration he retired to Chertsey, Surrey, where he continued several poems in praise of Charles II's return to the throne. He also wrote scientific essays, including *The Advancement of Experimental Philosophy* (1661) and *A. Couleii Plantarum Libri Duo (A Book of Poems about Plants in Two Sections)* in 1662. In his later years he completed *Of My Life*, a vivid account of his early years. Cowley died on July 28, 1667, and was buried in Westminster Abbey.

Personal

We are therefore wonderful wise men, and have a fine business of it; we, who spend our time in poetry. I do sometimes laugh, and am often angry with myself, when I think on it; and if I had a son inclined by nature to the same folly, I believe I should bind him from it by the strictest conjurations of a paternal blessing. For what can be more ridiculous than to labour to

give men delight, whilst they labour, on their part, most earnestly to take offence?—ABRAHAM COWLEY, "Preface" to *Cutter of Coleman-Street*, 1663

Even when I was a very young Boy at School, instead of running about on Holy-days, and playing with my Fellows: I was wont to steal from them, and walk into the Fields, either alone with a Book, or with some one Companion, if I could find any of the same Temper. I was then too, so much an Enemy to all Constraint, that my Masters could never prevail on me, by any Persuasions or Encouragements, to learn without Book the common Rules of Grammar, in which they dispens'd with me alone, because they found I made a shift to do the usual Exercise out of my own Reading and Observation.

. . . I was even then acquainted with the Poets (for the Conclusion is taken out of *Horace*;) and perhaps it was the immature and immoderate Love of them which stamp'd first, or rather engrav'd these Characters in me: They were like Letters cut into the Bark of a young Tree, which with the Tree still grow proportionably. But, how this Love came to be produc'd in me so early, is a hard Question: I believe I can tell the particular little Chance that filled my Head first with such Chimes of Verse, as have never since left ringing there: For I remember when I began to read, and to take some Pleasure in it, there was wont to lye in my Mother's Parlour (I know not by what accident, for she her self never in her Life read any Book but of Devotion) but there was wont to lye *Spencer's* Works; this I happen'd to fall upon, and was infinitely delighted with the stories of the Knights, and Giants, and Monsters, and brave Houses, which I found every where there: (Tho my Understanding had little to do with all this) and by degrees with the Tinkling of the Rhyme and Dance of the Numbers, so that I think I had read him all over before I was twelve Years old, and was thus made a Poet as irremediably as a Child is made an Eunuch.—ABRAHAM COWLEY, "Of Myself," *Discourses by Way of Essays in Verse and Prose*, 1667

Went to Mr. Cowley's funerall, whose corps lay at Wallingford House, and was thence convey'd to Westminster Abbey, in a hearse with six horses, and all funeral decency; neeare an hundred coaches of noblemen and persons of qualitie following; among these all the witts of the towne, divers bishops and cleargymen.—JOHN EVELYN, *Diary*, Aug. 3, 1667

He was not so much respected by the cavaliers as he ought to have been, upon the restauration, which much troubled him, and made him fly off something, as appears partly from the preface to his poems. He was however a good natured man, of great candor and humanity, and no party ever spoke ill against him upon that score.—THOMAS HEARNE, *Reliquiae Hearnianae*, May 18, 1706

Cowley's allowance was, at last, not above three hundred a year. He died at Chertsey; and his death was occasioned by a mean accident, whilst his great friend, Dean Sprat, was with him on a visit there. They had been together to see a neighbour at Cowley's; who (according to the fashion of those times) made them too welcome. They did not set out for their walk home till it was too late; and had drank so deep, that they lay out in the fields all night. This gave Cowley the fever that carried him off. The parish still talk of the drunken Dean.—ALEXANDER POPE (1728–30), cited in Joseph Spence, *Anecdotes, Observations and Characters of Books and Men*, ed. S. W. Singer, 1820

When Cowley grew sick of the court, he took a house first at Battersea, then at Barnes; and then at Chertsey: always farther and farther from town. In the latter part of his life, he showed a sort of aversion for women; and would leave the room when they came in: 'twas probably from a disappointment in love. He was much in love with his Leonora; who is mentioned at the end of that good ballad of his, on his different mistresses. She was married to Dean Sprat's brother; and Cowley never was in love with anybody after.—ALEXANDER POPE (1742–43), cited in Joseph Spence, *Anecdotes, Observations and Characters of Books and Men*, ed. S. W. Singer, 1820

General

To him no author was unknown,
Yet what he wrote was all his own;
He melted not the ancient gold,
Nor with Ben Jonson, did make bold
To plunder all the Roman stores
Of poets and of orators.
Horace's wit and Virgil's state,
He did not steal, but emulate;
And when he would like them appear,
Their garb, but not their clothes, did wear.
He not from Rome alone, but Greece,
Like Jason, brought the golden fleece.
—SIR JOHN DENHAM, "On Mr. Abraham Cowley's Death, and Burial amongst the Ancient Poets," c. 1667

Cowley is an author extremely corrupted by the bad taste of his age; but had he lived even in the purest times of Greece or Rome, he must always have been a very indifferent poet. He had no ear for harmony; and his verses are only known to be such by the rhyme which terminates them. In his rugged untunable numbers are conveyed sentiments the most strained and distorted, long-spun allegories, distant allusions, and forced conceits. Great ingenuity, however, and vigour of thought, sometimes break out midst those unnatural conceptions; a few anacreontics surprise us by their ease and gaiety: his prose writings please, by the honesty and goodness which they express, and even by their spleen and melancholy. This author was much more praised and admired during his lifetime, and celebrated after his death, than the great Milton.—DAVID HUME, *History of England*, 1754–62

Ingenious Cowley! and though now, reclaim'd
By modern lights from an erroneous taste,
I cannot but lament thy splendid wit
Entangled in the cobwebs of the schools.
I still revere thee, courtly though retired;
Though stretch'd at ease in Chertsey's silent bowers
Not unemploy'd, and finding rich amends
For a lost world in solitude and verse.
—WILLIAM COWPER, "The Task," *The Winter Evening*, 1784

Abraham Cowley, a precocious child, a reader and a versifier like Pope, and who, like Pope, having known passions less than books, busied himself less about things than about words. Literary exhaustion has seldom been more manifest. He possesses all the capacity to say whatever pleases him, but he has precisely nothing to say. The substance has vanished, leaving in its place an empty form. In vain he tries the epic, the Pindaric strophe, all kinds of stanzas, odes, short lines, long lines; in vain he calls to his assistance botanical and philosophical similes, all the erudition of the university, all the recollections of antiquity, all the ideas of new science: we yawn as we read him. Except in a few descriptive verses, two or three graceful tendernesses, he feels nothing, he speaks only; he is a poet of the brain. His collection of amorous pieces is but a vehicle for a scientific test, and serves to show that he has read the authors, that he knows geography, that he is well versed in anatomy, that he has a smattering of medicine and astronomy, that he has at his service comparisons and allusions enough to rack the brains of his readers. He will speak in this wise:

Beauty, thou active—passive Ill!
Which dy'st thyself as fast as thou dost kill!

or will remark that his mistress is to blame for spending three hours every morning at her toilet, because

> They make that Beauty Tyranny,
> That's else a Civil-government.

After reading two hundred pages, you feel disposed to box his ears. You have to think, by way of consolation, that every grand age must draw to a close, that this one could not do so otherwise, that the old glow of enthusiasm, the sudden flood of rapture, images, whimsical and audacious fancies, which once rolled through the minds of men, arrested now and cooled down, could only exhibit dross, a curdling scum, a multitude of brilliant and offensive points. You say to yourself that, after all, Cowley had perhaps talent; you find that he had in fact one, a new talent, unknown to the old masters, the sign of a new culture, which needs other manners, and announces a new society. Cowley had these manners, and belongs to this society. He was a well-governed, reasonable, well-informed, polished, well-educated man, who after twelve years of service and writing in France, under Queen Henrietta, retires at last wisely into the country, where he studies natural history, and prepares a treatise on religion, philosophising on men and life, fertile in general reflections and ideas, a moralist, bidding his executor "to let nothing stand in his writings which might seem the least in the world to be an offence against religion or good manners." Such intentions and such a life produce and indicate less a poet, that is, a seer, a creator, than a literary man, I mean a man who can think and speak, and who therefore ought to have read much, learned much, written much, ought to possess a calm and clear mind, to be accustomed to polite society, sustained conversation, pleasantry. In fact, Cowley is an author by profession, the oldest of those, who in England deserve the name. His prose is as easy and sensible as his poetry is contorted and unreasonable. A polished man, writing for polished men, pretty much as he would speak to them in a drawing-room,—this I take to be the idea which they had of a good author in the seventeenth century. It is the idea which Cowley's Essays leave of his character; it is the kind of talent which the writers of the coming age take for their model; and he is the first of that grave and amiable group which, continued in Temple, reaches so far as to include Addison.—HIPPOLYTE TAINE, *History of English Literature*, tr. H. Van Laun, 1871, Vol. 1, pp. 328–30

Cowley was still mentioned with high respect during the eighteenth century, and was the first poet in the collection to which Johnson contributed prefaces. Johnson's life in that collection was famous for its criticism of the "metaphysical" poets, the hint of which is given in Dryden's *Essay on Satire*. It assigns the obvious cause for the decline of Cowley's fame. The "metaphysical poets" are courtier pedants. They represent the intrusion into poetry of the love of dialectical subtlety encouraged by the still prevalent system of scholastic disputation. In Cowley's poems, as in Donne's, there are many examples of the technical language of the schools, and the habit of thought is perceptible throughout. In the next generation the method became obsolete and then offensive. Cowley can only be said to survive in the few pieces where he condescends to be unaffected, and especially in the prose of his essays, which are among the earliest examples in the language of simple and graceful prose, with some charming poetry interspersed. —LESLIE STEPHEN, *Dictionary of National Biography*, 1887, Vol. 12, p. 382

Works

POETRY

These times have produced many excellent poets, among whom, for strength of wit, Dr. Abraham Cowley justly bears the bell.—RICHARD BAXTER, "Prefatory Address" to *Poetical Fragments*, 1681

One of our late great poets is sunk in his reputation, because he could never forgive any conceit which came in his way; but swept, like a drag-net, great and small. There was plenty enough—but the dishes were ill sorted; whole pyramids of sweetmeats for boys and women, but little of solid meat for men. All this proceeded not from any want of knowledge, but of judgment. Neither did he want that in discerning the beauties and faults of other poets, but only indulged himself in the luxury of writing; and perhaps knew it was a fault, and hoped to find it. For this reason, though he must always be thought a great poet, he is no longer esteemed a good writer; and for ten impressions which his works have had in so many successive years, yet at present a hundred books are scarcely purchased once a twelvemonth; for, as my last Lord Rochester said, though somewhat profanely, "Not being of God, he could not stand."—JOHN DRYDEN, "Preface" to *Fables*, 1700

> While *Celia's* tears make sorrow bright,
> Proud grief sits swelling in her eyes:
> The sun (next those the fairest light)
>   Thus from the ocean first did rise.
> And thus thro' mists we see the sun,
> Which else we durst not gaze upon.
> These silver drops, like morning dew,
>   Foretell the fervour of the day;
> So from one cloud soft show'rs we view,
>   And blasting lightnings burst away.
> The stars that fall from *Celia's* eye,
> Declare our doom in drawing nigh.
> The baby, in that sunny sphere
>   So like a *Phaëton* appears,
> That heav'n, the threaten'd world to spare,
>   Thought fit to drown him in her tears:
> Else might th' ambitious nymph aspire,
> To set, like him, heav'n too on fire.

> —ALEXANDER POPE, "Verses in Imitation of Cowley, I: Weeping," 1701

Cowley is a fine poet, in spite of all his faults.—He, as well as Davenant, borrowed his metaphysical style from Donne. —ALEXANDER POPE (1734–36), cited in Joseph Spence, *Anecdotes, Observations and Characters of Books and Men*, ed. S. W. Singer, 1820

> Who now reads Cowley? If he pleases yet,
> His moral pleases, not his pointed wit:
> Forgot his Epic, nay Pindaric art
> But still I love the language of his heart.

> —ALEXANDER POPE, *Imitations of Horace*, 1737, *Ep.* II. i. 75–78

We are even more pleased with some of the earliest of his juvenile poems, than with many of his later performances; as there is not every where in them that redundancy of wit; and where there is, we are more inclined to admire, than be offended at in the productions of a boy. His passion for studious retirement, which was still increasing with his years, discovered itself at thirteen, in an ode which a good judge thinks equal to that of Pope on a similar subject, and which was written about the same era of his life. The tenderness of some of his juvenile verses shews, that he was no stranger to another passion; and it is not improbable but Margarita, or one of her successors, might at fifteen, have had a full possession of his heart. —JAMES GRANGER, *Biographical History of England*, 1769–1824

To speak of this neglected writer, as a poet. He had a quick and ready conception; the true enthusiasm of genius, and vast materials, with which learning as well as fancy had supplied him for it to work upon. He had besides a prodigious command of expression, and a natural and copious flow of eloquence on every occasion, and understood our language in all its force and energy. Yet betwixt the native exuberance of his wit, which hurried him frequently on conceits, and the epidemical contagion of that time, which possessed all writers with the love of points, of affected turns, and hard unnatural allusion, there are few of his poems which a man of just taste will read with admiration, or even with pleasure. Some few there are and enough to save his name from oblivion, or rather to consecrate it, with those of the master spirits of our country, to immortality.—RICHARD HURD, *Commonplace Book*, c. 1808

He wrote verses while yet a child; and amidst his best poetry as well as his worst, in his touching and tender as well as extravagant passages, there is always something that reminds us of childhood in Cowley. . . . Misanthropy, as far as so gentle a nature could cherish it, naturally strengthened his love of retirement, and increased that passion for a country life which breathes in the fancy of his poetry, and in the eloquence of his prose.—THOMAS CAMPBELL, *Specimens of the British Poets*, 1819

In the next year, 1647, Cowley's *Mistress* appeared; the most celebrated performance of the miscalled metaphysical poets. It is a series of short amatory poems, in the Italian style of the age, full of analogies that have no semblance of truth, except from the double sense of words and thoughts that unite the coldness of subtility with the hyperbolical extravagance of counterfeited passion. . . .

The Pindaric odes of Cowley were not published within this period. But it is not worth while to defer mention of them. They contain, like all his poetry, from time to time, very beautiful lines; but the faults are still of the same kind: his sensibility and good sense, nor has any poet more, are choked by false taste; and it would be difficult to fix on any one poem in which the beauties are more frequent than the blemishes. Johnson has selected the elegy on Crashaw as the finest of Cowley's works. It begins with a very beautiful couplet, but I confess that little else seems, to my taste, of much value. "The Complaint," probably better known than any other poem, appears to me the best in itself. His disappointed hopes give a not unpleasing melancholy to several passages. But his Latin ode in a similar strain is much more perfect. Cowley, perhaps, upon the whole, has had a reputation more above his deserts than any English poet; yet it is very easy to perceive that some, who wrote better than he, did not possess so fine a genius.—HENRY HALLAM, *Introduction to the Literature of Europe*, 1837–39, Pt. 3, Ch. 5, Pars. 40–41

Cowley is one of the poets of remote and brilliant turns of thought, and elaborated literary distinction. One does not love his poetry; but one can admire it often—if only one would read it.—WILLIAM MICHAEL ROSSETTI, *Humorous Poems*, 1872, p. 132

Cowley's remarkable prose may be for the present put aside. In his verse he is not merely a most curious bridge of communication between the couplet poets, the "school of good-sense,"

and the metaphysicals, but almost more than Waller, and much more than Denham, the pair who usually go with him, a bridge between one whole period of poetry and another. He wrote in youth a play called *The Guardian*, which he did not then intend for the stage, but after the Restoration altered and had acted as *Cutter of Coleman Street*. But this requires no special notice. His purely poetical works, which are by no means so easily to be distinguished by mere chronological order as might be thought likely, fall pretty easily into three classes when judged from the point of view of form—namely, couplet verse, lyrics and stanza-poems of various kinds, and Pindarics.

Of the couplet verse the most important piece in size, as indeed it is of the whole, is the curious sacred epic of the *Davideis*, much of which was written at Cambridge, though it was continued (it never was completed) later. Four books exist; yet even this manageable length, assisted by Cowley's immense popularity, never made it generally read. There are unquestionably fine things in it—from the opening picture of Hell, earlier by much than that of Milton, through the sketch of the Priests' College, a favourite theme with the author, and worked out by him also in prose, to David's account of Saul and of Jonathan. And the passages of length are as a rule inferior to the single lines and couplets, which are sometimes wonderfully fine. But the miscarriage of the piece as a whole may be accounted for many times over. It is true, as Johnson urges, that the story, being merely begun, has no time to justify itself, that its amplification of familiar Scripture is felt as impertinent, and that the decorations exhibit the fatal fault of the "metaphysicals" almost in the worst degree. But there is more than this. The very accomplishment of the couplets now and then jars with the phraseology and imagery, as would not have been the case in stanza or blank verse; and, little story as the poet gives himself room to tell, he interferes with the interest even of what little there is by constant divagation. The book is a museum of poetic fragments tastelessly cemented together, not an organic whole.

In his other couplet pieces, from quite early things to the translations intercalated in the *Essays*, Cowley shows much better, or at any rate is much more accessible, as a pioneer in the path. The piece upon the "Happy Birth of the Duke of Gloucester" in 1640, though sometimes "enjambed," shows on the whole a great preference for, and a pretty complete command of, the authentic, balanced, self-contained couplet with the cracker of rhyme at the tail of it. We only want weight to give us Dryden, and polish to give us Pope: the form is there already.

In his stanza-poems and lyrics proper Cowley shows the retrospective side of his poetic Janus-head, though it is observable that even in *Constantia and Philetus*, one of the earliest of the *Juvenilia*, the concluding couplets of the sixain "snap" as they would not have done in Daniel or in Drayton. The lyrics are often quite Jonsonian, while sometimes they have a lightness which Ben rarely achieved, and which is chiefly proper to his "sons," of whom Cowley was born just too late to be one. The famous *Chronicle*, his best-known thing, is the very best of poetic froth; while the *Anacreontics* are often equal to Ben, and sometimes not very far below Milton. One is frequently inclined to give Cowley a really high place, when something—his shallowness or his frigid wit, or a certain "shadow before" of eighteenth-century prose—interferes, especially in his once-adored *Mistress*.

Undoubtedly, however, Cowley's *Pindarics* are the most peculiar efforts of his talent, and those which, upon his own time, produced most of the effect of genius. They are little read

now, and there can be no doubt that both their structure and the presumed necessity of imitating Pindar's style of obscure conceit encouraged the metaphysical manner very treacherously. But they would be interesting to us even were they far worse than they are intrinsically, because to the historian of literature nothing can ever be uninteresting which has, for a long time, supplied an obvious literary demand on the part of readers and provided employment for great writers. To Cowley we owe—in that sense of obligation which always presupposes remembrance, that the debt would have been due to another if this man had not been in case to lend—the really magnificent odes of Dryden, Gray, and Collins pretty directly; indirectly that still greater one of Wordsworth which is almost his solitary claim to have reached the highest summits of poetry; and many great things of Shelley and Tennyson, not to mention lesser men. And the eager adoption of the form, which for more than half a century produced libraries full of unreadable Pindarics (the most interesting and nearly the most hopeless examples being those of no less a man than Swift), shows us what the time wanted, how it was sick of the regular stanza, how blank verse was still a little too bold for it, while it had not yet settled down, or resigned itself to the regular tick of the couplet-clock. But as a matter of fact the things themselves are not contemptible. "Life and Fame," "Life," the "Ode to Mr. Hobbes," and others are, or at least contain, very fine things; and the chief drawback of the whole is that descent to colloquial abbreviations ("I'm," etc.) which was due partly to the slow vulgarising of popular taste on such points which we shall have to record, partly to the still-prevailing dread of slur and trisyllabic equivalence. On the whole, no doubt, Rochester was right when he said ("profanely," as Dryden very properly adds) that "Cowley was not of God, and so he could not stand." But the special reason of his fall was that he never could make up his mind whether to stand with the old age or with the new, with the couplet or with the wilder verse, with mystical fantasy or clear common sense, with lawless splendour or jejune decency.
—GEORGE SAINTSBURY, *A Short History of English Literature*, 1898, pp. 403–5

PROSE

In all our comparisons of taste, I do not know whether I have ever heard your opinion of a poet, very dear to me,—the now-out-of-fashion Cowley. Favour me with your judgment of him, and tell me if his prose essays, in particular, as well as no inconsiderable part of his verse, be not delicious. I prefer the graceful rambling of his essays, even to the courtly elegance and ease of Addison; abstracting from this the latter's exquisite humour.—CHARLES LAMB, Letter to Samuel Taylor Coleridge (Jan. 10, 1797)

Cowley's *Essays* are delightful reading. Nor shall I forgive his biographer for destroying the letters of a man of whom King Charles said at his interment in Westminster Abbey. "Mr. Cowley has not left a better in England." The friend and correspondent of the most distinguished poets, statesmen, and gentlemen of his day, his letters must have been most interesting and important, and but for the unsettled temper of affairs, would doubtless have been added to our polite literature.
—A. BRONSON ALCOTT, *Concord Days*, 1869, p. 62

Cowley's last request to his literary executor was to excise from his works any word or phrase that might give the least offence to religion or good manners. This sincere expression of the piety which was in him—for, notwithstanding the florid exuberance of his pen, Cowley was as a writer, whether of poetry or of prose, quite free from affectation—should be cited at the head

of any tribute, however slight, to his literary genius. Fortune plunged him in a long series of dubious activities from the day when he was driven from the gates of Trinity to that when he found refuge at last in his

  gentle, cool retreat
 From all th' immoderate heat,
 In which this frantic world doth burn and sweat

and he drank almost to the dregs the cup of tarnished gold, which is filled with the *miseriæ curialium*. Yet he thought nobly of life and its purposes, and, above all, of that pursuit of letters to which, as a boy, he had been attracted by the copy of Spenser that lay in his mother's parlour, and to which he remained true through all the vicissitudes of his career. Thus, while the decline of his poetic reputation is one which no revival awaits—for it is only out of the decay of another Elizabethan age that another fantastic epoch of literary taste could be generated,—the nearer we can come to him in his prose the more his individuality commends itself to our sympathies; and in this sense Pope's well-worn "Still I love the language of his heart," may fearlessly be cited once more.

Cowley's prose is but little in quantity, and some of it hardly comes into the category of pure literature. His *Proposition for the Advancement of Experimental Philosophy* is one of the London University—and more especially the London Professorial University—projects of his day, and a very ardent plea for the endowment of research, on conditions (including that of celibacy) which appeared to Cowley indispensable for its prosecution. He was, it should be remembered, not only a fellow, but, so to speak, the poet laureate of the Royal Society. In his discourse by way of *Vision concerning the Government of Oliver Cromwell* he held a brief of a different kind, and this time before a tribunal in little need of being convinced on his side of the question. This piece, though its opening possesses a certain charm, is so rhetorically commonplace in thought that its plan at once sinks from grandeur into grotesqueness, and the Tutelar Angel, to speak profanely, only appears at the wicket in order to be bowled over. Cowley's disposition, it is clear, was magnanimous; but the turbid political atmosphere of his times, of which not even a Milton could wholly escape the contagion, make it quite impossible for a henchman of the Stuarts to weigh the historic Cromwell. The attempt is a mere ambitious failure. Far happier, and deserving not to be altogether overlooked among its author's prose writings, is the preface to the comedy of *Cutter of Coleman Street* (the revised *Guardian* of Cowley's Cambridge days). He is here on firm ground, moving among the experiences and, it must be allowed, the convictions of his own career, with a temperate dignity commanding respect even for a comic dramatist of the Restoration.

There remain the *Discourses*—they are but eleven in number, and so far as the prose in them is concerned, not one of them is too long—*by way of Essays, in Verse and Prose.* They are rightly considered to form a sort of half-way house between Bacon and Addison, and are thus never likely to fall out of notice. But their chief attraction lies in the personal savour which pervades them all, and makes them, collectively and individually, their author's own. I cannot subscribe altogether to Johnson's *dictum*, that "no author ever kept his verse and prose at a greater distance from each other"; for though Cowley's prose is without the occasional turgidity of his verse, and without the occasional suggestion of a broken pinion in the midst of a Pindaric flight, it equally abounds in witty turns, while happily quotations, as a rule, do duty for mere conceits. Very manifestly (though I do not know that this has been pointed out) his immediate model as a prose essayist was

Montaigne, to whom he refers more than once in passing, and with whose ways of thinking and writing, inseparable as these necessarily are in essays of the personal type, he may be supposed to have familiarised himself in the long days of his French exile. Such pieces as those "Of Greatness" and "Of Myself" could hardly have been written except by a diligent student of this exemplar. For the rest, I hardly know why Cowley should be grudged full credit for "the vehement love of retirement," to use Johnson's phrase, announced by the very titles of these essays—"Of Liberty," "Of Solitude," "Of Obscurity," "The Garden," "The Dangers of an Honest Man in much Company." Professor Minto tells us that Cowley, in his constant enunciation of his philosophy of life, was "moved entirely by constitutional sentiment." To be sure there is a difference between weariness and moral indignation; but Cowley's desire for independence was not the less genuine because through most of his life he had been a bondsman, and he loved his fetters none the better because he had worn them till their rust had entered into his very soul.

Nothing further need, I think, be said by way of introduction to extracts which, in this instance, it is easy enough to make, but which can hardly do justice to the pleasant continuity which is one of the principal attractions of essays in Cowley's manner. He may himself have placed more value on the gems of wit glittering on the surface of everything he produced; did he not, forsooth, enter it as a count in his indictment against Oliver Cromwell that the Protector "left no wise or witty apophthegm behind him?" And he may have specially delighted in the echoes for which, in every one of these *Essays*, he found or made opportunity of those "chimes of verse" which "never left ringing in his head" since his boyhood; though, to our taste, this intermixture of prose and metre only serves to give to both something of the sprightly insincerity of the *vaudeville*. The familiar ease, never descending into what would misbecome either the man of breeding or the man of letters, is the true cause of the pleasure which cultivated readers have never ceased to derive from these *Essays*; and to enjoy this pleasure to the full, we should pace with their author the whole length of his modest garden walks; for his estate was not on the scale of his friend John Evelyn's.—A. W. WARD, "Abraham Cowley," *English Prose*, ed. Henry Craik, 1893, Vol. 2, pp. 573–76

THOMAS SPRAT
From "An Account of the Life of Mr. Abraham Cowley"
The Works of Abraham Cowley
1668, Volume 1, pp. xvi–xxiv

Of his Works that are Publish'd, it is hard to give one general Character, because of the Difference of their Subjects; and the various Forms and distant Times of their Writing. Yet this is true of them all, that in all the several Shapes of his Style, there is still very much of the Likeness and Impression of the same Mind; the same unaffected Modesty, and natural Freedom, and easie Vigour, and chearful Passions, and innocent Mirth, which appear'd in all his Manners. We have many things that he writ in two very unlike Conditions, in the University and the Court. But in his Poetry, as well as his Life, he mingled with excellent Skill what was good in both States. In his Life he join'd the Innocence and Sincerity of the Scholar, with the Humanity and good Behaviour of the Courtier. In his Poems he united the Solidity and Art of the one, with the Gentility and Gracefulness of the other.

If any shall think that he was not wonderfully curious, in the Choice and Elegance of all his Words: I will affirm with more Truth on the other side, that he had no manner of Affectation in them; he took them as he found them made to his Hands; he neither went before, nor came after the Use of the Age. He forsook the Conversation, but never the Language, of the City and Court. He understood exceeding well all the Variety and Power of Poetical Numbers; and practis'd all sorts with great Happiness. If his Verses in some Places seem not as soft and flowing as some would have them, it was his Choice, not his Fault. He knew that in diverting Mens Minds, there should be the same Variety observ'd as in the Prospects of their Eyes; where a Rock, a Precipice, or a rising Wave, is often more delightful than a smooth, even Ground, or a calm Sea. Where the Matter requir'd it, he was as gentle as any Man; but where higher Virtues were chiefly to be regarded, an exact Numerosity was not then his main Care. This may serve to answer those who upbraid some of his Pieces with Roughness, and with more Contractions than they are willing to allow. But those Admirers of Gentleness without Sinews, should know that different Arguments must have different Colours of Speech; that there is a kind of Variety of Sexes in Poetry, as well as in Mankind: That as the peculiar Excellence of the Feminine kind, is Smoothness and Beauty; so Strength is the chief Praise of the Masculine.

He had a perfect Mastery in both the Languages in which he writ: But each of them kept a just Distance from the other; neither did his *Latin* make his *English* too old, nor his *English* make his *Latin* too modern. He excell'd both in Prose and Verse; and both together have that Perfection, which is commended by some of the Ancients above all others, that they are very obvious to the Conception, but most difficult in the Imitation.

His Fancy flow'd with great Speed, and therefore it was very fortunate to him, that his Judgment was equal to manage it. He never runs his Reader nor his Argument out of Breath. He perfectly practises the hardest Secret of good Writing, to know when he has done enough. He always leaves off in such a manner, that it appears it was in his Power to have said much more. In the particular Expressions there is still much to be applauded, but more in the Disposition and Order of the whole. From thence there springs a new Comliness, besides the Feature of each Part. His Invention is powerful, and large as can be desir'd. But it seems all to arise out of the Nature of the Subject, and to be just fitted for the thing of which he speaks. If ever he goes far for it, he dissembles his Pains admirably well.

The Variety of Arguments that he has manag'd is so large, that there is scarce any Particular of all the Passions of Men, or Works of Nature, and Providence, which he has pass'd by undescrib'd. Yet he still observes the Rules of Decency with so much Care, that whether he inflames his Reader with the softer Affections, or delights him with inoffensive Raillery, or teaches the familiar Manners of Life, or adorns the Discoveries of Philosophy, or inspires him with the Heroick Characters of Charity and Religion: To all these Matters that are so wide asunder, he still proportions a due Figure of Speech, and a proper Measure of Wit. This indeed is most remarkable, that a Man who was so constant and fix'd in the Moral Ideas of his Mind, should yet be so changeable in his Intellectual, and in both to the highest Degree of Excellence.

If there needed any Excuse to be made, that his Love-Verses should take up so great a Share in his Works, it may be alledg'd that they were compos'd, when he was very young. But it is a vain thing to make any kind of Apology for that sort of

Writings. If Devout or Virtuous Men will superciliously forbid the Minds of the Young, to adorn those Subjects about which they are most Conversant; they would put them out of all Capacity of performing graver Matters, when they come to them. For the Exercises of all Mens Wits, must be always proper for their Age, and never too much above it: And by practice and use in lighter Arguments, they grow up at last to excel in the most weighty. I am not therefore asham'd to commend Mr. *Cowley's* Mistress. I only except one, or two Expressions, which I wish I could have prevail'd with those that had the Right of the other Edition, to have left out. But of all the rest I dare boldly pronounce, that never yet so much was written on a Subject so Delicate, that can less offend the severest Rules of Morality. The whole Passion of Love is inimitably describ'd, with all its mighty Train of Hopes, and Joys, and Disquiets. Besides this amorous Tenderness, I know not how in every Copy, there is something of more useful Knowledge very naturally and gracefully insinuated, and every where there may be something found, to inform the Minds of wise Men, as well as to move the Hearts of young Men, or Women.

The Occasion of his falling on the Pindaric way of Writing, was his accidental meeting with *Pindar's* Works, in a Place, where he had no other Books to direct him. Having then consider'd at leisure the Height of his Invention, and the Majesty of his Style, he try'd immediately to imitate it in *English*. And he perform'd it without the Danger that *Horace* presag'd to the Man who should dare to attempt it.

If any are displeas'd at the Boldness of his Metaphors, and Length of his Digressions, they contend not against Mr. *Cowley*, but *Pindar* himself; who was so much reverenc'd by all Antiquity, that the Place of his Birth was preserv'd as Sacred, when his Native City was twice destroy'd by the Fury of two Conquerors. If the Irregularity of the Number disgust them, they may observe that this very thing makes that kind of Poesie fit for all manner of Subjects: For the Pleasant, the Grave, the Amorous, the Heroic, the Philosophical, the Moral, the Divine. Besides this they will find, that the frequent Alteration of the Rhime and Feet, affects the Mind with a more various Delight, while it is soon apt to be tir'd by the settled Pace of any one constant Measure. But that for which I think this Inequality of Number is chiefly to be preferr'd, is its near Affinity with Prose: From which all other kinds of *English* Verse are so far distant, that it is very seldom found that the same Man excels in both ways. But now this loose, and unconfin'd Measure has all the Grace, and Harmony of the most confin'd. And withal, it is so large and free, that the Practice of it will only exalt, not corrupt our Prose; which is certainly the most useful kind of Writing of all others; for it is the Style of all Business and Conversation.

Besides this imitating of *Pindar*, which may perhaps be thought rather a new sort of Writing, than a restoring of an Ancient; he has also been wonderful happy, in Translating many difficult Parts of the Noblest Poets of Antiquity. To perform this according to the Dignity of the Attempt, he had, as it was necessary he should have, not only the Elegance of both the Languages; but the true Spirit of both the Poetries. This way of leaving Verbal Translations, and chiefly regarding the Sense and Genius of the Author, was scarce heard of in *England*, before this present Age. I will not presume to say, that Mr. *Cowley* was the absolute Inventor of it. Nay, I know that others had the good luck to recommend it first in Print. Yet I appeal to you, Sir, whether he did not conceive it, and discourse of it, and practise it as soon as any Man.

His *Davideis* was wholly written in so young an Age; that if we shall reflect on the vastness of the Argument, and his manner of handling it, he may seem like one of the Miracles, that he there adorns, like a Boy attempting *Goliah*. I have often heard you declare, that he had finish'd the greatest part of it, while he was yet a young Student at *Cambridge*. This perhaps may be the Reason, that in some few Places, there is more Youthfulness, and redundance of Fancy, than his riper Judgment would have allow'd. I know, Sir, you will give me leave to use this liberty of Censure; for I do not here pretend to a profess'd Panegyrick, but rather to give a just Opinion concerning him. But for the main of it, I will affirm, that it is a better Instance and Beginning of a Divine Poem, than I ever yet saw in any Language. The Contrivance is perfectly Ancient, which is certainly the true Form of Heroic Poetry, and such as was never yet outdone by any new Devices of Modern Wits. The Subject was truly Divine, even according to God's own Heart. The Matter of his Invention, all the Treasures of Knowledge and Histories in the Bible. The Model of it comprehended all the Learning of the East. The Characters lofty and various: The Numbers firm and powerful: The Digressions beautiful and proportionable: The Design to submit mortal Wit to heavenly Truths: In all there is an admirable mixture of Human Virtues and Passions, with religious Raptures.

The truth is, Sir, methinks in other Matters, his Wit excell'd most other Mens: But in his Moral and Divine Works it outdid itself. And no doubt it proceeded from this Cause, that in other lighter kinds of Poetry, he chiefly represented the Humours and Affections of others; but in these he sate to himself, and drew the Figure of his own Mind.

SAMUEL JOHNSON
From "Cowley"
Lives of the English Poets
1779–81

His Miscellanies contain a collection of short compositions, written some as they were dictated by a mind at leisure, and some as they were called forth by different occasions; with great variety of style and sentiment, from burlesque levity to awful grandeur. Such an assemblage of diversified excellence no other poet has hitherto afforded. To choose the best, among many good, is one of the most hazardous attempts of criticism. I know not whether Scaliger himself has persuaded many readers to join with him in his preference of the two favourite odes, which he estimates in his raptures at the value of a kingdom. I will, however, venture to recommend Cowley's first piece, which ought to be inscribed 'To my muse', for want of which the second couplet is without reference. When the title is added, there will still remain a defect; for every piece ought to contain in itself whatever is necessary to make it intelligible. Pope has some epitaphs without names; which are therefore epitaphs to be let, occupied indeed for the present, but hardly appropriated.

The ode on Wit is almost without a rival. It was about the time of Cowley that *Wit*, which had been till then used for *Intellection*, in contradistinction to *Will*, took the meaning, whatever it be, which it now bears.

Of all the passages in which poets have exemplified their own precepts, none will easily be found of greater excellence than that in which Cowley condemns exuberance of Wit:

> Yet 'tis not to adorn and gild each part,
> That shews more cost than art.
> Jewels at nose and lips but ill appear;
> Rather than all things wit, let none be there.
> Several lights will not be seen,

If there be nothing else between.
Men doubt, because they stand so thick i' th' sky,
If those be stars which paint the galaxy.

In his verses to lord Falkland, whom every man of his time was proud to praise, there are, as there must be in all Cowley's compositions, some striking thoughts; but they are not well wrought. His elegy on Sir Henry Wotton is vigorous and happy, the series of thoughts is easy and natural, and the conclusion, though a little weakened by the intrusion of Alexander, is elegant and forcible.

It may be remarked, that in this Elegy, and in most of his encomiastick poems, he has forgotten or neglected to name his heroes.

In his poem on the death of Hervey, there is much praise, but little passion, a very just and ample delineation of such virtues as a studious privacy admits, and such intellectual excellence as a mind not yet called forth to action can display. He knew how to distinguish, and how to commend the qualities of his companion; but when he wishes to make us weep, he forgets to weep himself, and diverts his sorrow by imagining how his crown of bays, if he had it, would *crackle* in the *fire*. It is the odd fate of this thought to be worse for being true. The bay-leaf crackles remarkably as it burns; as therefore this property was not assigned it by chance, the mind must be thought sufficiently at ease that could attend to such minuteness of physiology. But the power of Cowley is not so much to move the affections, as to exercise the understanding.

The *Chronicle* is a composition unrivalled and alone: such gaiety of fancy, such facility of expression, such varied similitude, such a succession of images, and such a dance of words, it is in vain to expect except from Cowley. His strength always appears in his agility; his volatility is not the flutter of a light, but the bound of an elastick mind. His levity never leaves his learning behind it; the moralist, the politician, and the critick, mingle their influence even in this airy frolick of genius. To such a performance Suckling could have brought the gaiety, but not the knowledge; Dryden could have supplied the knowledge, but not the gaiety.

The verses to Davenant, which are vigorously begun, and happily concluded, contain some hints of criticism very justly conceived and happily expressed. Cowley's critical abilities have not been sufficiently observed: the few decisions and remarks which his prefaces and his note on the *Davideis* supply, were at that time accessions to English literature, and shew such skills as raises our wish for more examples.

The lines from Jersey are a very curious and pleasing specimen of the familiar descending to the burlesque.

His two metrical disquisitions *for* and *against* Reason, are no mean specimens of metaphysical poetry. The stanzas against knowledge produce little conviction. In those which are intended to exalt the human faculties, Reason has its proper task assigned it; that of judging, not of things revealed, but of the reality of revelation. In the verses *for* Reason is a passage which Bentley, in the only English verses which he is known to have written, seems to have copied, though with the inferiority of an imitator.

The holy Book like the eighth sphere does shine
   With thousand lights of truth divine,
So numberless the stars that to our eye
   It makes all but one galaxy:
Yet Reason must assist too; for in seas
   So vast and dangerous as these,
Our course by stars above we cannot know
   Without the compass too below.

After this says Bentley:

Who travels in religious jars,
Truth mix'd with error, clouds with rays,
With Whiston wanting pyx and stars,
In the wide ocean sinks or strays.

Cowley seems to have had, what Milton is believed to have wanted, the skill to rate his own performances by their just value, and has therefore closed his Miscellanies with the verses upon Crashaw, which apparently excel all that have gone before them, and in which there are beauties which common authors may justly think not only above their attainment, but above their ambition.

To the Miscellanies succeed the *Anacreontiques*, or paraphrastical translations of some little poems, which pass, however justly, under the name of Anacreon. Of those songs dedicated to festivity and gaiety, in which even the morality is voluptuous, and which teach nothing but the enjoyment of the present day, he has given rather a pleasing than a faithful representation, having retained their spriteliness but lost their simplicity. The Anacreon of Cowley, like the Homer of Pope, has admitted the decoration of some modern graces, by which he is undoubtedly made more amiable to common readers, and perhaps, if they would honestly declare their own preceptions, to far the greater part of those whom courtesy and ignorance are content to style the Learned.

These little pieces will be found more finished in their kind than any other of Cowley's works. The diction shews nothing of the mould of time, and the sentiments are at no great distance from our present habitudes of thought. Real mirth must be always natural, and nature is uniform. Men have been wise in very different modes; but they have always laughed the same way.

Levity of thought naturally produced familiarity of language, and the familiar part of language continues long the same: the dialogue of comedy, when it is transcribed from popular manners and real life, is read from age to age with equal pleasure. The artifice of inversion, by which the established order of words is changed, or of innovation, by which new words or meanings of words are introduced, is practised, not by those who talk to be understood, but by those who write to be admired.

The Anacreontiques therefore of Cowley give now all the pleasure which they ever gave. If he was formed by nature for one kind of writing more than for another, his power seems to have been greatest in the familiar and the festive.

The next class of his poems is called *The Mistress*, of which it is not necessary to select any particular pieces for praise or censure. They have all the same beauties and faults, and nearly in the same proportion. They are written with exuberance of wit, and with copiousness of learning; and it is truly asserted by Sprat, that the plenitude of the writer's knowledge flows in upon his page, so that the reader is commonly surprised into some improvement. But, considered as the verses of a lover, no man that has ever loved will much commend them. They are neither courtly nor pathetick, have neither gallantry nor fondness. His praises are too far-sought, and too hyperbolical, either to express love, or to excite it: every stanza is crouded with darts and flames, with wounds and death, with mingled souls, and with broken hearts.

The principal artifice by which *The Mistress* is filled with conceits is very copiously displayed by Addison. Love is by Cowley, as by other poets, expressed metaphorically by flame and fire; and that which is true of real fire is said of love, or figurative fire, the same word in the same sentence retaining both significations. Thus, 'observing the cold regard of his mistress's eyes, and at the same time their power of producing love in him, he considers them as burning-glasses made of ice. Finding himself able to live in the greatest extremities of love, he concludes the torrid zone to be habitable. Upon the dying of a tree, on which he had cut his loves, he observes, that his flames had burnt up and withered the tree.'

These conceits Addison calls mixed wit; that is, wit which consists of thoughts true in one sense of the expression, and false in the other. Addison's representation is sufficiently indulgent. That confusion of images may entertain for a moment; but being unnatural, it soon grows wearisome. Cowley delighted in it, as much as if he had invented it; but, not to mention the ancients, he might have found it full-blown in modern Italy.

Aspice quam variis distringar Lesbia curis,
    Uror, & heu! nostro manat ab igne liquor;
Sum Nilus, sumque Aetna simul; restringite flammas
    O lacrimae, aut lacrimas ebibe flamma meas.

One of the severe theologians of that time censured him as having published a *book of profane and lascivious Verses.* From the charge of profaneness, the constant tenour of his life, which seems to have been eminently virtuous, and the general tendency of his opinions, which discover no irreverence of religion, must defend him; but that the accusation of lasciviousness is unjust, the perusal of his works will sufficiently evince.

Cowley's *Mistress* has no power of seduction; 'she plays round the head, but comes not at the heart.' Her beauty and absence, her kindness and cruelty, her disdain and inconstancy, produce no correspondence of emotion. His poetical account of the virtues of plants, and colours of flowers, is not perused with more sluggish frigidity. The compositions are such as might have been written for penance by a hermit, or for hire by a philosophical rhymer who had only heard of another sex; for they turn the mind only on the writer, whom, without thinking on a woman but as the subject for his task, we sometimes esteem as learned, and sometimes despise as trifling, always admire as ingenious, and always condemn as unnatural.

The Pindarique Odes are now to be considered; a species of composition, which Cowley thinks Pancirolus might have counted *in his list of the lost inventions of antiquity,* and which he has made a bold and vigorous attempt to recover.

The purpose with which he has paraphrased an Olympick and Nemeaean Ode is by himself sufficiently explained. His endeavour was, not to shew *precisely what Pindar spoke, but his manner of speaking.* He was therefore not at all restrained to his expressions, nor much to his sentiments; nothing was required of him, but not to write as Pindar would not have written.

Of the Olympick Ode the beginning is, I think, above the original in elegance, and the conclusion below it in strength. The connection is supplied with great perspicuity, and the thoughts, which to a reader of less skill seem thrown together by chance, are concatenated without any abruption. Though the English ode cannot be called a translation, it may be very properly consulted as a commentary.

The spirit of Pindar is indeed not everywhere equally preserved. The following pretty lines are not such as his *deep mouth* was used to pour:

Great Rhea's son,
If in Olympus' top where thou
Sitt'st to behold thy sacred show,
If in Alpheus' silver flight,
If in my verse thou take delight,

My verse, great Rhea's son, which is
Lofty as that, and smooth as this.

In the Nemeaean ode the reader must, in mere justice to Pindar, observe that whatever is said of *the original new moon, her tender forehead and her horns,* is superadded by his paraphrast, who has many other plays of words and fancy unsuitable to the original, as,

The table, free for every guest,
    No doubt will thee admit,
And feast more upon thee, than thou on it.

He sometimes extends his author's thoughts without improving them. In the Olympionick an oath is mentioned in a single word, and Cowley spends three lines in swearing by the *Castalian Stream.* We are told of Theron's bounty, with a hint that he had enemies, which Cowley thus enlarges in rhyming prose:

But in this thankless world the giver
Is envied even by the receiver;
'Tis now the cheap and frugal fashion
Rather to hide than own the obligation:
Nay, 'tis much worse than so;
It now an artifice does grow
Wrongs and injuries to do,
Lest men should think we owe.

It is hard to conceive that a man of the first rank in learning and wit, when he was dealing out such minute morality in such feeble diction, could imagine, either waking or dreaming, that he imitated Pindar.

In the following odes, where Cowley chooses his own subjects, he sometimes rises to dignity truly Pindarick, and, if some deficiencies of language be forgiven, his strains are such as those of the Theban bard were to his contemporaries:

Begin the song, and strike the living lyre:
Lo how the years to come, a numerous and well-
    fitted quire,
    All hand in hand do decently advance,
And to my song with smooth and equal measure
    dance;
    While the dance lasts, how long soe'er it be,
My musick's voice shall bear it company;
    Till all gentle notes be drown'd
    In the last trumpet's dreadful sound.

After such enthusiasm, who will not lament to find the poet conclude with lines like these!

But stop, my Muse—
Hold thy Pindarick Pegasus closely in.
    Which does to rage begin—
—'Tis an unruly and a hard-mouth'd horse—
'Twill no unskilful touch endure,
But flings writer and reader too that sits not sure.

The fault of Cowley, and perhaps of all the writers of the metaphysical race, is that of pursuing his thoughts to their last ramifications, by which he loses the grandeur of generality; for of the greatest things the parts are little; what is little can be but pretty, and by claiming dignity becomes ridiculous. Thus all the power of description is destroyed by a scrupulous enumeration; and the force of metaphors is lost, when the mind by the mention of particulars is turned more upon the original than the secondary sense, more upon that from which the illustration is drawn than that to which it is applied.

Of this we have a very eminent example in the ode intituled 'The Muse', who goes to *take the air* in an intellectual chariot, to which he harnesses Fancy and Judgement, Wit and Eloquence, Memory and Invention: how he distinguished Wit from Fancy, or how Memory could properly contribute to Motion, he has not explained; we are however content to suppose that he could have justified his own fiction, and wish to see the Muse begin her career; but there is yet more to be done.

> Let the *postilion* Nature mount, and let
> The *coachman* Art be set;
> And let the airy *footmen*, running all beside,
> Make a long row of goodly pride;
> Figures, conceits, raptures, and sentences,
> In a well-worded dress,
> And innocent loves, and pleasant truths, and useful lies,
> In all their gaudy *liveries*.

Every mind is now disgusted with this cumber of magnificence; yet I cannot refuse myself the four next lines:

> Mount, glorious queen, thy travelling throne,
> And bid it to put on;
> For long though cheerful is the way,
> And life, alas! allows but one ill winter's day.

In the same ode, celebrating the power of the Muse, he gives her prescience, or, in poetical language, the foresight of events hatching in futurity; but having once an egg in his mind, he cannot forbear to shew us that he knows what an egg contains:

> Thou into the close nests of Time dost peep,
> And there with piercing eye
> Through the firm shell and the thick white dost spy
> Years to come a-forming lie,
> Close in their sacred fecundine asleep.

The same thought is more generally, and therefore more poetically, expressed by Casimir, a writer who has many of the beauties and faults of Cowley:

> Omnibus mundi Dominator horis
> Aptat urgendas per inane pennas,
> Pars adhuc nico latet, & futuros
> Crescit in annos.

Cowley, whatever was his subject, seems to have been carried, by a kind of destiny, to the light and the familiar, or to conceits which require still more ignoble epithets. A slaughter in the Red Sea, *new dies the waters name*; and England, during the Civil War, was *Albion no more, nor to be named from white*. It is surely by some fascination not easily surmounted, that a writer professing to revive *the noblest and highest writing in verse*, makes this address to the new year:

> Nay, if thou lov'st me, gentle year,
> Let not so much as love be there,
> Vain fruitless love I mean; for, gentle year,
> Although I fear,
> There's of this caution little need,
> Yet, gentle year, take heed
> How thou dost make
> Such a mistake;
> Such love I mean alone
> As by thy cruel predecessors has been shewn;
> For, though I have too much cause to doubt it,
> I fain would try, for once, if life can live without it.

The reader of this will be inclined to cry out with Prior—

> —Ye Criticks, say,
> How poor to this was Pindar's style!

Even those who cannot perhaps find in the Isthmian or Nemeaean songs what Antiquity has disposed them to expect, will at least see that they are ill represented by such puny poetry; and all will determine that if this be the old Theban strain, it is not worthy of revival.

To the disproportion and incongruity of Cowley's sentiments must be added the uncertainty and looseness of his measures. He takes the liberty of using in any place a verse of any length, from two syllables to twelve. The verses of Pindar have, as he observes, very little harmony to a modern ear; yet by examining the syllables we perceive them to be regular, and have reason enough for supposing that the ancient audiences were delighted with the sound. The imitator ought therefore to have adopted what he found, and to have added what was wanting: to have preserved a constant return of the same numbers, and to have supplied smoothness of transition and continuity of thought.

It is urged by Dr. Sprat, that the *irregularity of numbers is the very thing* which makes *that kind of poesy fit for all manner of subjects*. But he should have remembered, that what is fit for every thing can fit nothing well. The great pleasure of verse arises from the known measure of the lines, and uniform structure of the stanzas, by which the voice is regulated, and the memory relieved.

If the Pindarick style be what Cowley thinks it, *the highest and noblest kind of writing in verse*, it can be adapted only to high and noble subjects; and it will not be easy to reconcile the poet with the critick, or to conceive how that can be the highest kind of writing in verse, which, according to Sprat, *is chiefly to be preferred for its near affinity to prose*.

This lax and lawless versification so much concealed the deficiencies of the barren, and flattered the laziness of the idle, that it immediately overspread our books of poetry; all the boys and girls caught the pleasing fashion, and they that could do nothing else could write like Pindar. The rights of antiquity were invaded, and disorder tried to break into the Latin: a poem on the Sheldonian Theatre, in which all kinds of verse are shaken together, is unhappily inserted in the *Musae Anglicanae*. Pindarism prevailed about half a century; but at last died gradually away, and other imitations supply its place.

The Pindarique Odes have so long enjoyed the highest degree of poetical reputation, that I am not willing to dismiss them with unabated censure; and surely though the mode of their composition be erroneous, yet many parts deserve at least that admiration which is due to great comprehension of knowledge, and great fertility of fancy. The thoughts are often new, and often striking; but the greatness of one part is disgraced by the littleness of another; and total negligence of language gives the noblest conceptions the appearance of a fabric august in the plan, but mean in the materials. Yet surely those verses are not without a just claim to praise; of which it may be said with truth, that no man but Cowley could have written them.

The *Davideis* now remains to be considered; a poem which the author designed to have extended to twelve books, merely, as he makes no scruple of declaring, because the Aeneid had that number; but he had leisure or perseverance only to write the third part. Epick poems have been left unfinished by Virgil, Statius, Spenser, and Cowley. That we have not the whole *Davideis* is, however, not much to be regretted; for in this undertaking Cowley is, tacitly at least, confessed to have miscarried. There are not many examples of so great a work, produced by an author generally read, and generally praised, that has crept through a century with so little regard. Whatever is said of Cowley, is meant of his other works. Of the *Davideis* no mention is made; it never appears in books, nor emerges in conversation. By the *Spectator* it has once been quoted, by *Rymer* it has once been praised, and by *Dryden*, in *Mac Flecknoe*, it has once been imitated; nor do I recollect much other notice from its publication till now, in the whole succession of English literature.

Of this silence and neglect, if the reason be inquired, it will be found partly in the choice of the subject, and partly in the performance of the work.

Sacred History has been always read with submissive reverence, and an imagination over-awed and controlled. We have been accustomed to acquiesce in the nakedness and simplicity of the authentick narrative, and to repose on its veracity with such humble confidence, as suppresses curiosity. We go with the historian as he goes, and stop with him when he stops. All amplification is frivolous and vain; all addition to that which is already sufficient for the purposes of religion, seems not only useless, but in some degree profane.

Such events as were produced by the visible interposition of Divine Power are above the power of human genius to dignify. The miracle of Creation, however it may teem with images, is best described with little diffusion of language: *He spake the word, and they were made.*

We are told that Saul *was troubled with an evil spirit*; from this Cowley takes an opportunity of describing hell, and telling the history of Lucifer, who was, he says,

Once general of a gilded host of sprites,
Like Hesper leading forth the spangled nights;
But down like lightning, which him struck, he came,
And roar'd at his first plunge into the flame.

Lucifer makes a speech to the inferior agents of mischief, in which there is something of heathenism, and therefore of impropriety; and, to give efficacy to his words, concludes by lashing *his breast with his long tail*. Envy, after a pause, steps out, and among other declarations of her zeal utters these lines:

Do thou but threat, loud storms shall make reply,
And thunder echo to the trembling sky.
Whilst raging seas swell to so bold an height,
As shall the fire's proud element affright.
Th' old drudging Sun, from his long-beaten way,
Shall at thy voice start, and misguide the day.
The jocund orbs shall break their measur'd pace,
And stubborn Poles change their allotted place.
Heaven's gilded troops shall flutter here and there,
Leaving their boasting songs tun'd to a sphere.

Every reader feels himself weary with this useless talk of an allegorical Being.

It is not only when the events are confessedly miraculous, that fancy and fiction lose their effect: the whole system of life, while the Theocracy was yet visible, has an appearance so different from all other scenes of human action, that the reader of the Sacred Volume habitually considers it as the peculiar mode of existence of a distinct species of mankind, that lived and acted with manners uncommunicable; so that it is difficult even for imagination to place us in the state of them whose story is related, and by consequence their joys and griefs are not easily adopted, nor can the attention be often interested in any thing that befalls them.

To the subject, thus originally indisposed to the reception of poetical embellishments, the writer brought little that could reconcile impatience, or attract curiosity. Nothing can be more disgusting than a narrative spangled with conceits, and conceits are all that the *Davideis* supplies.

One of the great sources of poetical delight is description, or the power of presenting pictures to the mind. Cowley gives inferences instead of images, and shews not what may be supposed to have been seen, but what thoughts the sight might have suggested. When Virgil describes the stone which Turnus lifted against Aeneas, he fixes the attention on its bulk and weight:

Saxum circumspicit ingens,

Saxum antiquum, ingens, campo quod forte jacebat
Limes agro positus, litem ut discerneret arvis.

Cowley says of the stone with which Cain slew his brother,

I saw him fling the stone, as if he meant
At once his murther and his monument.

Of the sword taken from Goliah, he says,

A sword so great, that it was only fit
To take off his great head who came with it.

Other poets describe death by some of its common appearances; Cowley says, with a learned allusion to sepulchral lamps, real or fabulous,

'Twixt his right ribs deep pierc'd the furious blade,
And open'd wide those secret vessels where
Life's light goes out, when first they let in air.

But he has allusions vulgar as well as learned. In a visionary succession of kings:

Joas at first does bright and glorious show,
In life's fresh morn his fame does early crow.

Describing an undisciplined army, after having said with elegance,

His forces seem'd no army, but a crowd
Heartless, unarm'd, disorderly, and loud;

he gives them a fit of the ague.

The allusions however are not always to vulgar things: he offends by exaggeration as much as by diminution:

The king was plac'd alone, and o'er his head
A well-wrought heaven of silk and gold was spread.

Whatever he writes is always polluted with some conceit:

Where the sun's fruitful beams give metals birth,
Where he the growth of fatal gold does see,
Gold, which alone more influence has than he.

In one passage he starts a sudden question, to the confusion of philosophy:

Ye learned heads, whom ivy garlands grace,
Why does that twining plant the oak embrace?
The oak, for courtship most of all unfit,
And rough as are the winds that fight with it.

His expressions have sometimes a degree of meanness that surpasses expectation:

Nay, gentle guests, he cries, since now you're in,
The story of your gallant friend begin.

In a simile descriptive of the Morning:

As glimmering stars just at th' approach of day,
Cashier'd by troops, at last drop all away.

The dress of Gabriel deserves attention:

He took for skin a cloud most soft and bright,
That e'er the midday sun pierc'd through with light;
Upon his cheeks a lively blush he spread,
Wash'd from the morning beauties' deepest red;
An harmless flattering meteor shone for hair,
And fell adown his shoulders with loose care;
He cuts out a silk mantle from the skies,
Where the most sprightly azure pleas'd the eyes;
This he with starry vapours sprinkles all,
Took in their prime ere they grow ripe and fall;
Of a new rainbow, ere it fret or fade,
The choicest piece cut out, a scarfe is made.

This is a just specimen of Cowley's imagery: what might in general expressions be great and forcible, he weakens and makes ridiculous by branching it into small parts. That Gabriel was invested with the softest or brightest colours of the sky, we might have been told, and been dismissed to improve the idea in our different proportions of conception; but Cowley could not let us go till he had related where Gabriel got first his skin, and then his mantle, then his lace, and then his scarfe, and related it in the terms of the mercer and taylor.

Sometimes he indulges himself in a digression, always conceived with his natural exuberance, and commonly, even where it is not long, continued till it is tedious:

> I' th' library a few choice authors stood,
> Yet 'twas well stor'd, for that small store was good;
> Writing, man's spiritual physic, was not then
> Itself, as now, grown a disease of men.
> Learning (young virgin) but few suitors knew;
> The common prostitute she lately grew,
> And with the spurious brood loads now the press;
> Laborious effects of idleness.

As the *Davideis* affords only four books, though intended to consist of twelve, there is no opportunity for such criticisms as Epick poems commonly supply. The plan of the whole work is very imperfectly shewn by the third part. The duration of an unfinished action cannot be known. Of characters either not yet introduced, or shewn but upon few occasions, the full extent and the nice discriminations cannot be ascertained. The fable is plainly implex, formed rather from the Odyssey than the Iliad; and many artifices of diversification are employed, with the skill of a man acquainted with the best models. The past is recalled by narration, and the future anticipated by vision: but he has been so lavish of his poetical art, that it is difficult to imagine how he could fill eight books more without practising again the same modes of disposing his matter; and perhaps the perception of this growing incumbrance inclined him to stop. By this abruption, posterity lost more instruction than delight. If the continuation of the *Davideis* can be missed, it is for the learning that has been diffused over it, and the notes in which it had been explained.

Had not his characters been depraved like every other part by improper decorations, they would have deserved uncommon praise. He gives Saul both the body and mind of a hero:

> His way once chose, he forward thrust outright,
> Nor turn'd aside for danger or delight.

And the different beauties of the lofty Merah and the gentle Michol are very justly conceived and strongly painted.

Rymer has declared the *Davideis* superior to the *Jerusalem* of Tasso, 'which,' says he, 'the poet with all his care, has not totally purged from pedantry.' If by pedantry is meant that minute knowledge which is derived from particular sciences and studies, in opposition to the general notions supplied by a wide survey of life and nature, Cowley certainly errs, by introducing pedantry far more frequently than Tasso. I know not, indeed, why they should be compared; for the resemblance of Cowley's work to Tasso's is only that they both exhibit the agency of celestial and infernal spirits, in which however they differ widely; for Cowley supposes them commonly to operate upon the mind by suggestion; Tasso represents them as promoting or obstructing events by external agency.

Of particular passages that can be properly compared, I remember only the description of Heaven, in which the different manner of the two writers is sufficiently discernible. Cowley's is scarcely description, unless it be possible to describe by negatives; for he tells us only what there is not in heaven. Tasso endeavours to represent the splendours and pleasures of the regions of happiness. Tasso affords images, and Cowley sentiments. It happens, however, that Tasso's description affords some reason for Rymer's censure. He says of the Supreme Being,

> Hà sotto i piedi e fato e la natura,
> Ministri humili, e 'l moto, e ch' il misura.

The second line has in it more of pedantry than perhaps can be found in any other stanza of the poem.

In the perusal of the *Davideis*, as of all Cowley's works, we find wit and learning unprofitably squandered. Attention has no relief; the affections are never moved; we are sometimes surprised, but never delighted, and find much to admire, but little to approve. Still, however, it is the work of Cowley, of a mind capacious by nature, and replenished by study.

In the general review of Cowley's poetry it will be found, that he wrote with abundant fertility, but negligent or unskilful selection; with much thought, but with little imagery; that he is never pathetick, and rarely sublime, but always either ingenious or learned, either acute or profound.

It is said by Denham in his elegy,

> To him no author was unknown;
> Yet what he writ was all his own.

This wide position requires less limitation, when it is affirmed of Cowley, than perhaps of any other poet—He read much, and yet borrowed little.

His character of writing was indeed not his own: he unhappily adopted that which was predominant. He saw a certain way to present praise, and not sufficiently enquiring by what means the ancients have continued to delight through all the changes of human manners, he contented himself with a deciduous laurel, of which the verdure in its spring was bright and gay, but which time has been continually stealing from his brows.

He was in his own time considered as of unrivalled excellence. Clarendon represents him as having taken a flight beyond all that went before him; and Milton is said to have declared, that the three greatest English poets were Spenser, Shakespeare, and Cowley.

His manner he had in common with others: but his sentiments were his own. Upon every subject he thought for himself; and such was his copiousness of knowledge, that something at once remote and applicable rushed into his mind; yet it is not likely that he always rejected a commodious idea merely because another had used it: his known wealth was so great, that he might have borrowed without loss of credit.

In his elegy on Sir Henry Wotton, the last lines have such resemblance to the noble epigram of Grotius upon the death of Scaliger, that I cannot but think them copied from it, though they are copied by no servile hand.

One passage in his *Mistress* is so apparently borrowed from Donne, that he probably would not have written it, had it not mingled with his own thoughts, so as that he did not perceive himself taking it from another.

> Although I think thou never found wilt be,
>   Yet I'm resolv'd to search for thee;
>   The search itself rewards the pains.
> So, though the chymic his great secret miss,
> (For neither it in Art nor Nature is)
>   Yet things well worth his toil he gains:
>   And does his charge and labour pay
> With good unsought experiments by the way.
>   (Cowley)

> Some that have deeper digg'd Love's mine than I,
> Say, where his centric happiness doth lie:
>   I have lov'd, and got, and told;
> But should I love, get, tell, till I were old,
> I should not find that hidden mystery;
>   Oh, 'tis imposture all:
> And as no chymic yet th' elixir got,

But glorifies his pregnant pot,
  If by the way to him befal
Some odoriferous thing, or medicinal,
  So lovers dream a rich and long delight,
But get a winter-seeming summer's night.

Jonson and Donne, as Dr. Hurd remarks, were then in the highest esteem.

It is related by Clarendon, that Cowley always acknowledged his obligation to the learning and industry of Jonson; but I have found no traces of Jonson in his works: to emulate Donne, appears to have been his purpose; and from Donne he may have learned that familiarity with religious images, and that light allusion to sacred things, by which readers far short of sanctity are frequently offended; and which would not be borne in the present age, when devotion, perhaps not more fervent, is more delicate.

Having produced one passage taken by Cowley from Donne, I will recompense him by another which Milton seems to have borrowed from him. He says of Goliah,

His spear, the trunk was of a lofty tree,
Which Nature meant some tall ship's mast should
  be.

Milton of Satan,

His spear, to equal which the tallest pine
Hewn on Norwegian hills, to be the mast
Of some great admiral, were but a wand,
He walk'd with.

His diction was in his own time censured as negligent. He seems not to have known, or not to have considered, that words being arbitrary must owe their power to association, and have the influence, and that only, which custom has given them. Language is the dress of thought; and as the noblest mien, or most graceful action, would be degraded and obscured by a garb appropriated to the gross employments of rusticks or mechanicks, so the most heroick sentiments will lose their efficacy, and the most splendid ideas drop their magnificence, if they are conveyed by words used commonly upon low and trivial occasions, debased by vulgar mouths, and contaminated by inelegant applications.

Truth indeed is always truth, and reason is always reason; they have an intrinsick and unalterable value, and constitute that intellectual gold which defies destruction: but gold may be so concealed in baser matter, that only a chymist can recover it; sense may be so hidden in unrefined and plebeian words, that none but philosophers can distinguish it; and both may be so buried in impurities, as not to pay the cost of their extraction.

The diction, being the vehicle of the thoughts, first presents itself to the intellectual eye: and if the first appearance offends, a further knowledge is not often sought. Whatever professes to benefit by pleasing, must please at once. The pleasures of the mind imply something sudden and unexpected; that which elevates must always surprise. What is perceived by slow degrees may gratify us with the consciousness of improvement, but will never strike with the sense of pleasure.

Of all this, Cowley appears to have been without knowledge, or without care. He makes no selection of words, nor seeks any neatness of phrase: he has no elegances either lucky or elaborate; as his endeavours were rather to impress sentences upon the understanding than images on the fancy, he has few epithets, and those scattered without peculiar propriety or nice adaptation. It seems to follow from the necessity of the subject, rather than the care of the writer, that the diction of his heroick poem is less familiar than that of his slightest writings. He has given not the same numbers, but the same diction, to the gentle Anacreon and the tempestuous Pindar.

His versification seems to have had very little of his care; and if what he thinks be true, that his numbers are unmusical only when they are ill read, the art of reading them is at present lost; for they are commonly harsh to modern ears. He has indeed many noble lines, such as the feeble care of Waller never could produce. The bulk of his thoughts sometimes swelled his verse to unexpected and inevitable grandeur; but his excellence of this kind is merely fortuitous: he sinks willingly down to his general carelessness, and avoids with very little care either meanness or asperity.

His contractions are often rugged and harsh:

One flings a mountain, and its rivers too
Torn up with 't.

His rhymes are very often made by pronouns or particles, or the like unimportant words, which disappoint the ear, and destroy the energy of the line.

His combination of different measures is sometimes dissonant and unpleasing; he joins verses together, of which the former does not slide easily into the latter.

The words *do* and *did*, which so much degrade in present estimation the line that admits them, were in the time of Cowley little censured or avoided; how often he used them, and with how bad an effect, at least to our ears, will appear by a passage, in which every reader will lament to see just and noble thoughts defrauded of their praise by inelegance of language:

Where honour or where conscience *does* not bind,
  No other law shall shackle me;
  Slave to myself I ne'er will be;
Nor shall my future actions be confin'd
  By my own present mind.
Who by resolves and vows engag'd *does* stand
  For days, that yet belong to fate,
Does like an unthrift mortgage his estate,
  Before it falls into his hand,
  The bondman of the cloister so,
And that he *does* receive *does* always owe.
And still as Time comes in, it goes away,
  Not to enjoy, but debts to pay!
Unhappy slave, and pupil to a bell!
Which his hours' work as well as hours *does* tell:
Unhappy till the last, the kind releasing knell.

His heroick lines are often formed of monosyllables; but yet they are sometimes sweet and sonorous.

He says of the Messiah,

Round the whole earth his dreaded name shall sound,
And reach to worlds that must not yet be found.

In another place, of David,

Yet bid him go securely, when he sends;
'Tis Saul that is his foe, and we his friends.
The man who has his God, no aid can lack;
And we who bid him go, will bring him back.

Yet amidst his negligence he sometimes attempted an improved and scientifick versification; of which it will be best to give his own account subjoined to this line,

Nor can the glory contain itself in th' endless space.

'I am sorry that it is necessary to admonish the most part of readers, that it is not by negligence that this verse is so loose, long, and, as it were, vast; it is to paint in the number the nature of the thing which it describes, which I would have observed in divers other places of this poem, that else will pass for very careless verses: as before,

And over-runs the neighb'ring fields with violent
course.

'In the second book,

> *Down a precipice deep, down he casts them all—*

'—And,

> *And fell a-down his shoulders with loose care.*

'In the third,

> *Brass was his helmet, his boots brass, and o'er*
> *His breast a thick plate of strong brass he wore.*

'In the fourth,

> *Like some fair pine o'er-looking all th' ignobler wood.*

'And,

> *Some from the rocks cast themselves down headlong.*

'And many more: but it is enough to instance in a few. The thing is, that the disposition of words and numbers should be such, as that, out of the order and sound of them, the things themselves may be represented. This the Greeks were not so accurate as to bind themselves to; neither have our English poets observed it, for aught I can find. The Latins (*qui musas colunt severiores*) sometimes did it, and their prince, Virgil, always: in whom the examples are innumerable, and taken notice of by all judicious men, so that it is superfluous to collect them.'

I know not whether he has, in many of these instances, attained the representation or resemblance that he purposes. Verse can imitate only sound and motion. A *boundless* verse, a *headlong* verse, and a verse of *brass* or of *strong brass*, seem to comprise very incongruous and unsociable ideas. What there is peculiar in the sound of the line expressing *loose care*, I cannot discover; nor why the *pine is taller* in an Alexandrine than in ten syllables.

But, not to defraud him of his due praise, he has given one example of representative versification, which perhaps no other English line can equal:

> Begin, be bold, and venture to be wise.
> He who defers this work from day to day,
> Does on a river's bank expecting stay
> Till the whole stream that stopp'd him shall be gone,
> Which runs, and as it runs, for ever shall run on.

Cowley was, I believe, the first poet that mingled Alexandrines at pleasure with the common heroick of ten syllables, and from him Dryden borrowed the practice, whether ornamental or licentious. He considered the verse of twelve syllables as elevated and majestick, and has therefore deviated into that measure when he supposes the voice heard of the Supreme Being.

The author of the *Davideis* is commended by Dryden for having written it in couplets, because he discovered that any staff was too lyrical for an heroick poem; but this seems to have been known before by May and Sandys, the translators of the *Pharsalia* and the *Metamorphoses*.

In the *Davideis* are some hemistichs, or verses left imperfect by the author, in imitation of Virgil, whom he supposes not to have intended to complete them: that this opinion is erroneous may be probably concluded, because this truncation is imitated by no subsequent Roman poet; because Virgil himself filled up one broken line in the heat of recitation; because in one the sense is now unfinished; and because all that can be done by a broken verse, a line intersected by a *caesura* and a full stop will equally effect.

Of triplets in his *Davideis* he makes no use, and perhaps did not at first think them allowable; but he appears afterwards to have changed his mind, for in the verses on the government of Cromwell he inserts them liberally with great happiness.

After so much criticism on his Poems, the Essays which accompany them must not be forgotten. What is said by Sprat of his conversation, that no man could draw from it any suspicion of his excellence in poetry, may be applied to these compositions. No author ever kept his verse and his prose at a greater distance from each other. His thoughts are natural, and his style has a smooth and placid equability, which has never yet obtained its due commendation. Nothing is far-sought, or hard-laboured; but all is easy without feebleness, and familiar without grossness.

It has been observed by Felton, in his *Essay on the Classicks*, that Cowley was beloved by every Muse that he courted; and that he has rivalled the Ancients in every kind of poetry but tragedy.

It may be affirmed, without any encomiastick fervour, that he brought to his poetick labours a mind replete with learning, and that his pages are embellished with all the ornaments which books could supply; that he was the first who imparted to English numbers the enthusiasm of the greater ode, and the gaiety of the less; that he was equally qualified for spritely sallies, and for lofty flights; that he was among those who freed translation from servility, and, instead of following his author at a distance, walked by his side; and that if he left versification yet improvable, he left likewise from time to time such specimens of excellence as enabled succeeding poets to improve it.

THOMAS HUMPHRY WARD
From "Abraham Cowley"
The English Poets, ed. Thomas Humphry Ward
1880, Volume 2, pp. 237–43

The Mistress (which had been printed in 1647) is a collection of about a hundred love-poems, explained by the author in the preface to the Folio as being mere feigned addresses to some fair creature of the fancy. 'So it is that Poets are scarce thought Freemen of the Company without paying some duties and obliging themselves to be true to Love.' The apology, even if true, was hardly required even by Puritan strictness; for with two or three exceptions the poems are as cold as icy conceits can make them. Johnson's characteristic judgment is hardly too severe: 'the compositions are such as might have been written for penance by a hermit, or for hire by a philosophical rhymer who had only heard of another sex.' It is as though in the course of a hundred years the worst fancies which Wyatt had borrowed from Petrarch had become fossilized, and were yet brought out by Cowley to do duty for living thoughts. What is love? he seems to ask: it is an interchange of hearts, a flame, a worship, a river to be frozen by disdain—he has a hundred such physical and psychological images of it; and the poetry consists in taking the images one by one and developing them in merciless disregard of taste and truth of feeling. Is love fire? (we may give two or three of his illustrations even after Addison's page-long summary):—

> Another from my mistress' door
>   Saw me with eyes all watery come;
> Nor could the hidden cause explore,
>   But thought some smoke was in the room:—
> Such ignorance from unwounded learning came;
> He knew tears made by smoke, but not by flame!

The lover writes his love-letters in lemon-juice, that the fire of his mistress' eyes may bring the letters to light. At another time he pictures his heart as not inflammable only, but explosive:—

> Woe to her stubborn heart if once mine come
>   Into the selfsame room!

> 'Twill tear and blow up all within,
>   Like a grenado shot into a magazine.

At another, the story of his love cut in the bark has burnt and withered up the tree. Again, if love is worship, his mistress, who has proved unfaithful, is like the idolators of old who sinned against light:—

> So the vain Gentiles, when they left t'adore
> One Deity, could not stop at thousands more . . .
> Ah, fair Apostate! could'st thou think to flee
> From Truth and Goodness, yet keep Unity?

Or again; is his mistress dressed out for conquest? Then her beauty, which had been a civil government before, becomes a tyranny. But we have said enough: *The Mistress,* Cowley's most elaborate and sustained effort, is clearly a failure. Nothing of what we require of love-poetry is there—neither grace nor glow nor tenderness nor truth. The passion is neither deeply felt nor lightly uttered.

We cannot judge so simply the *Pindarique Odes,* a form of composition of which Cowley was the inventor, and which found universal favour in England down to the time of Gray. He was well aware that in writing in this way, which he thought to be an imitation of Pindar, he was making a questionable innovation. 'I am in great doubt,' he says, 'whether they will be understood by most readers; nay even by very many who are well enough acquainted with the common roads and ordinary tracks of poesy. . . . The digressions are many and sudden, and sometimes long, according to the fashion of all lyrics, and of Pindar above all men living. The figures are unusual and bold, even to temerity, and such as I durst not have to do withal in any other kind of poetry; the numbers are various and irregular, and sometimes, especially some of the long ones, seem harsh and uncouth if the just measures and cadences be not observed in the pronunciation. So that almost all their sweetness and numerosity (which is to be found, if I mistake not, in the roughest, if rightly repeated) lies in a manner wholly at the mercy of the reader.' For himself, however, he had no doubts about the value of the new style of poetry; nay, he found a pleasure in comparing the 'liberty' of the ode with the moral liberty of which he was always a votary:—

> If Life should a well-ordered poem be
>   (In which he only hits the white
> Who joins true profit with the best delight)
> The more heroic way let others take,
>   Mine the Pindaric way I'll make.
> The matter shall be grave, the numbers loose and
>   free.

But the analogy was a very imperfect one with him; for while the moral liberty which he enjoyed led him to a life of great simplicity, unworldliness and charm, his liberty of verse led him too often into mere intellectual athleticism and display. 'That for which I think this inequality of number is chiefly to be preferred,' says Dr. Sprat with great artlessness, 'is its affinity with prose'; and that no doubt was the reason which induced the Flatmans and the Samuel Wesleys of the next generation to choose that mode of dress for their platitudes. But with Cowley the attractiveness of the Ode seems to have been the wealth of opportunity which it afforded for what he called 'bold figures,' that is, for imagery such as could and would have occurred to no one else than to himself. Only Cowley, and he only in an Ode, could have paused in the midst of a solemn address to the Muse and bidden her 'rein her Pindaric Pegasus closely in'—for

> *'Tis an unruly and a hard-mouthed horse.*

Only Cowley, and he only in an Ode, could have set the same

Muse in her chariot, with Eloquence and Wit and Memory and Invention in the traces and the 'airy footmen' of Conceits to run by her side, and then have suddenly turned to compare this Muse with the Creator:—

> Where never yet did pry
> The busy Morning's curious eye,
> The wheels of thy bold Coach pass quick and free,
>   And all's an open road to thee.
> Whatever God did say
> Is all thy plain and smooth uninterrupted way.
> Nay, even beyond his works thy voyages are known,
>   Thou'st thousand worlds too of thine own.
> Thou speak'st, Great Queen, in the same style as he,
> And a new world leaps forth when thou say'st, Let it
> be!

The very apparatus of notes with which it was permissible to issue the Odes enlarged the poet's opportunities. In the *Praise of Pindar,* for example, we have—

> So Pindar does new words and figures roll
> Down his impetuous dithyrambic tide.
>   Which in no channel deigns to abide,
>   Which neither banks nor dikes control;

on which the note is, '*Banks,* natural; *Dikes,* artificial. It will neither be bounded nor circumscribed by nature nor by art.' With such a means of interpretation at hand, what limit need the poet set on his invention?

And yet, when the subject is one that interests him, Cowley has something to say that we should not wish unsaid or said differently. Sonorousness counts for something, after all, in the treatment of such themes as the future of knowledge or the fate of a hero and a cause. The two odes which we have chosen for quotation—that 'To Mr. Hobbes' and that called 'Brutus'—are rightly grandiose, and are therefore successful. Like the other leading spirits of his age, Cowley looked across the passing troubles of the day to the new world to which Bacon had pointed, and which Bacon's followers were hastening to occupy; and of this feeling the 'Ode to Mr. Hobbes' is the best expression. Again, the dominant fact in contemporary history (the Odes were published in 1656) was the success of the new Cæsar, Cromwell. Conscientious royalists like Cowley, such at least as were men of contemplation not of action, threw themselves back on history and philosophy, and if they could not explain the evil they paralleled it with other evils from which good had seemed to flow. Brutus, the slayer of Cæsar, the avenger of his country's murder, is himself slain; but what then? Virtue is for all that not an idol or a name:—

> Hold, noble Brutus, and restrain
> The bold voice of thy generous disdain.
>   These mighty gulfs are yet
> Too deep for all thy judgment and thy wit.

The two odes are brilliant examples of what Cowley could do when he left what he was conventionally expected to feel for what he really felt.

About the *Davideis,* the epic of whose twelve books fortunately only four came to the birth, perhaps the less said the better. We do not altogether wish it away, on account of the vigorous pages which it inspired in the preface; the pages which contain Cowley's eloquent and almost Miltonic plea for sacred poetry:—

> It is not without grief and indignation that I behold
> that divine science employing all her inexhaustible
> riches of wit and eloquence, either in the wicked and
> beggarly flattery of great persons, or the unmanly
> idolizing of foolish women, or the wretched affecta-
> tion of scurril laughter, or at best on the confused

1608

antiquated dreams of senseless fables and meta-morphoses. Amongst all holy and consecrated things which the devil ever stole and alienated from the service of the deity; as altars, temples, sacrifices, prayers, and the like; there is none that he so universally, and so long usurped, as poetry. It is time to recover it out of the tyrant's hands, and to restore it to the kingdom of God who is the Father of it. It is time to baptize it in Jordan, for it will never become clean by bathing in the water of Damascus.

But if we ask how Cowley realised his aspirations, how he succeeded in 'elevating poesy' rather than 'abasing divinity,' the answer must be disappointing. The *Davideis* is a school exercise, no more. It is at least no injustice to take as a specimen the most famous of the descriptive passages, the picture of Hell:—

> Beneath the silent chambers of the earth,
> Where the sun's fruitful beams give metals birth,
> Where he the growth of fatal gold doth see,
> Gold which above more influence has than he;
> Beneath the dens where unfledged tempests lie,
> And infant winds their tender voices try;
> Beneath the mighty ocean's wealthy caves,
> Beneath th' eternal fountain of all waves,
> Where their vast court the mother-waters keep,
> And undisturb'd by moons in silence sleep;
> There is a place deep, wondrous deep below,
> Which genuine night and horror does o'erflow;
> No bound controls th' unwearied space, but hell
> Endless as those dire pains that in it dwell.
> Here no dear glimpse of the sun's lovely face
> Strikes through the solid darkness of the place!
> No dawning morn does her kind reds display;
> One slight weak beam would here be thought the day
> No gentle stars with their fair gems of light
> Offend the tyrannous and unquestion'd night.
> Here Lucifer the mighty captive reigns,
> Proud, 'midst his woes, and tyrant in his chains

We are driven in sheer despair to Milton:—

>   He views
> The dismal situation waste and wild;
> A dungeon horrible on all sides round
> As one great furnace flamed: yet from those flames
> No light, but rather darkness visible,
> Served only to discover sights of woe,
> Regions of sorrow, doleful shades

Here are two nearly contemporary pictures: the one full of gloom, profundity, terror, all coming directly from Milton's simple handling of simple elements. Fire and darkness—these are the physical materials of his hell, and they are left to produce their effect upon the reader by their own intensity and vastness, while the spiritual side of hell is presented in that ceaseless note of woe, 'Regions of sorrow, doleful shades.' In Milton, in effect, we have that 'union of simplicity with greatness' that marks the true epic. But Cowley's hell is shown to us as lying piled with imaginary cosmical lumber, under the caverns where metals are bred, under the nests of the callow crying

tempests, under the court of the waters. He cannot take us to it except through a labyrinth of details, on each of which he would dwell for a moment, losing sight of the end. 'Infant winds,' 'tender voices,' 'the vast court of the mother waters,' the influence of gold, the cause of tides and tidelessness—what have these to do with hell, that is, with the deepest conception of dread and darkness which the mind can form? But it is a consolation to be able to believe that Cowley was dissatisfied with the *Davideis*, and that in his maturity he regarded it as merely indicating to others the poetical capabilities of the Bible history. 'I shall be ambitious of no other fruit from this weak and imperfect attempt of mine,' he says at the end of the preface, 'but the opening of a way to the courage and industry of some other persons, who may be better able to perform it throughly and successfully.' Eleven years after these words were written appeared *Paradise Lost*.

The subsequent editions of the folio contain other writings, both verse and prose, that Cowley published in his later years, and some of the verse we give in our selections. There are no general features however by which we can distinguish these poems from the rest of his work: sometimes, as in the beautiful stanzas which we quote from the 'Hymn to Light,' or in the verses which close the 'Essay on Solitude,' or in the 'Ode on the Royal Society,' he rises to his highest point; sometimes, as in what he wrote on the death of 'the matchless Orinda,' and in the poem on 'The Garden,' he sinks to his lowest.

Addison's Essay[1] and Johnson's Life have said the last word on Cowley's 'mixed wit,' 'metaphysics,' or 'conceits'; and we need hardly dwell at any greater length on what is the first, most obvious, and most disastrous quality of his muse. He owes to it his poetical effacement with posterity, as he owed to it his first success with his contemporaries; and it would be ungracious as well as uncritical to fasten our attention solely upon that canker of his style. He lived at the end of one intellectual epoch and at the beginning of another; he held of both, and he was marred by the vices of the decadence as much as, but no more than, he was glorified by the dawning splendours of the new age. What had been the extravagance of a young and uncontrolled imagination in Lyly and Sidney became the pedantry of ingenuity in the sane and learned Cowley, the master of two or three positive sciences and of all the literatures of Europe. But this pedantry was not all. 'I cannot conclude this head of mixed wit,' says Addison, 'without owning that the admirable poet out of whom I have taken the examples of it had as much true wit as any author that ever writ, and indeed all other talents of an extraordinary genius.' Not, perhaps, all other talents of an extraordinary genius, but knowledge, reflection, calmness and clearness of judgment; in a word, the gifts of the age of science and of prose which set in with the Restoration; and with these a rhetorical and moral fervour that made him a power in our literature greater, for the moment, than any that had gone before.

Notes

1. *Spectator*, no. 62.

SIR WILLIAM DAVENANT

1606–1668

William Davenant was born in Oxford in February 1606. His father was an innkeeper there and legend has it that Shakespeare was his godfather. Davenant received his education at the Oxford grammar school. From 1622 to 1624 he served as a page to the Duchess of Richmond. Thereafter he worked in Fulke Greville's household until 1628. Around 1624 Davenant married his first of three wives. Several years after his first wife's death Davenant developed a severe case of syphilis. He was given mercury to cure the disease; however, the mercury badly disfigured his nose, leaving Davenant with a permanent reminder of his past lifestyle.

During the late 1620s Davenant began to write dramas. His earliest plays, both tragedies, were *The Cruell Brother* (1627) and *The Tragedy of Albovine* (1629). In 1634 Davenant's comic masterpiece, *The Witts*, was staged. Other notable plays include *Love and Honour* (1634), *The Platonick Lovers* (1635), *News from Plimouth* (1635), and *The Unfortunate Lovers* (1638). Davenant's 1635 court masque, *The Temple of Love*, and his volume of poetry, *Madagascar* (1638), attracted the favorable notice of Queen Henrietta Maria. In 1638 he succeeded Ben Jonson as Poet Laureate and in 1639 he became manager of the Cockpit Theatre. With the closing of the London theatres by Puritans, Davenant joined the Royalists at the siege of Gloucester. In 1643 he was knighted by the King for his efforts. Davenant lived in exile with the court until his appointment in 1650 as Lieutenant-Governor of Maryland. His ship to America was intercepted by the Puritans and he was jailed in the Tower for two years. While in prison he worked on his romantic epic, *Gondibert*, which was never completed.

He was eventually pardoned in 1654, and began to write so-called "operas," to avoid the Puritan restriction on theatrical productions. These "operas" include *The Siege of Rhodes* (1656), *The Cruelty of the Spaniards in Peru* (1658), and *The History of Sir Francis Drake* (1658). With the Restoration Davenant was granted one of two patents to produce theatre in London; the other patent went to Thomas Killigrew. Davenant revived English theatre which had been dormant for over fifteen years; he especially favored Shakespeare's plays. He died on April 7, 1668, and was buried in Westminster Abbey.

Personal

Will. *Davenant* asham'd of a foolish mischance
That he had got lately travelling in *France*,
Modestly hoped the handsomnesse of's Muse
Might any deformity about him excuse.
     And
Surely the Company would have been content,
If they could have found any President;
But in all their Records either in Verse or Prose,
There was not one Laureat without a nose.

—SIR JOHN SUCKLING, "The Wits," 1637

I up and down to the Duke of York's playhouse, there to see, which I did, Sir W Davenant's corps carried out toward Westminster, there to be buried. Here were many coaches, and six horses and many hackneys, that made it look, methought, as if it were the burial of a poor poett. He seemed to have many children by five or six in the first mourning-coach, all boys.
—SAMUEL PEPYS, *Diary*, April 9, 1668

Sir William Davenant, Knight, Poet Laureate, was borne in the City of Oxford, at the Crowne Taverne. He went to schoole at Oxon to Mr. Sylvester, but I feare he was drawne from schoole before he was ripe enough.

His father was John Davenant, a Vintner there, a very grave and discreet Citizen; his mother was a very beautifull woman and of a very good witt, and of conversation extremely agreable.

Mr. William Shakespeare was wont to goe into Warwickshire once a yeare, and did commonly in his journey lye at this house in Oxon, where he was exceedingly respected. (I have heard Parson Robert say that Mr. William Shakespeare

haz given him a hundred kisses.) Now Sir William would sometimes, when he was pleasant over a glasse of wine with his most intimate friends—e.g. Sam Butler, author of *Hudibras*, etc., say, that it seemed to him that he writt with the very spirit that did Shakespeare, and seemed contented enough to be thought his Son. He would tell them the story as above, in which way his mother had a very light report, whereby she was called a Whore.

He was preferred to the first Dutches of Richmond to wayte on Her as a Page. I remember he told me, she sent him to a famous Apothecary for some Unicornes-horne, which he resolved to try with a Spider which he incircled in it, but without the expected successe; the Spider would goe over, and thorough and thorough, unconcerned.

He was next a servant (as I remember, a Page also) to Sir Fulke Grevil, Lord Brookes, with whom he lived to his death, which was that a servant of his (that had long wayted on him, and his Lordship had often told him that he would doe something for him, but did not, but still putt him off with delayes) as he was trussing up his Lord's pointes comeing from Stoole (for then their breeches were fastned to the doubletts with points; then came in hookes and eies; which not to have fastened was in my boy-hood a great crime) stabbed him. This was at the same time that the Duke of Buckingham was stabbed by Felton, and the great noise and report of the Duke's, Sir William told me, quite drowned this of his Lord's, that 'twas scarce taken notice of. This Sir Fulke G. was a good witt, and had been a good Poet in his youth. He wrote a Poeme in folio which he printed not till he was old, and then (as Sir W. said) with too much judgement and refining, spoyled it, which was at first a delicate thing.

He writt a Play or Playes, and verses, which he did with so

much sweetnesse and grace, that by it he got the love and friendship of his two Mecaenasses, Mr. Endymion Porter and Mr. Henry Jermyn (since Earl of St. Albans) to whom he has dedicated his Poeme called *Madegascar*. Sir John Suckling was also his great and intimate friend.

After the death of Ben Johnson he was made in his place Poet Laureat.

He gott a terrible clap of a Black handsome wench that lay in Axe-yard, Westminster, whom he thought on when he speakes of Dalga in *Gondibert*, which cost him his Nose, with which unlucky mischance many witts were too cruelly bold: e.g. Sir John Menis, Sir John Denham, etc.

In the Civill Warres in England he was in the Army of William, Marquess of Newcastle (since Duke) where he was Generall of the Ordinance. I have heard his brother Robert say, for that service there was owing to him by King Charles the First 10,000 pounds. During that warre, 'twas his Hap to have two Alderman of Yorke his Prisoners, who were something stubborne, and would not give the Ransome ordered by the Councell of Warr. Sir William used them civilly and treated them in his Tent, and sate them at the upper end of his Table *à la mode de France*, and having donne so a good while to his chardge, told them (privately and friendly) that he was not able to keepe so chargeable Guests, and bad them take an opportunity to escape, which they did: but having been gon a little way they considered with themselves that in gratitude they ought to goe back and give Sir William their Thankes; which they did, but it was like to have been to their great danger of being taken by the Soldiers, but they happened to gett safe to Yorke.

After the King was beaten out of the field, Sir William Davenant (who received the honour of Knighthood from the Duke of Newcastle by Commission) went into France; resided chiefly in Paris, where the Prince of Wales then was. He then began to write his Romance in Verse called *Gondibert*, and had not writt above the first booke, but being very fond of it, prints it (before a quarter finished) with an Epistle of his to Mr. Thomas Hobbes, and Mr. Hobbes excellent Epistle to him printed before it. The Courtiers with the Prince of Wales could never be at quiet about this piece, which was the occasion of a very witty but satericall little booke of Verses writt by George Duke of Bucks, Sir John Denham, etc.:

> That thou forsak'st thy sleepe, thy Diet,
> And which is more then that, our quiet.

This last word Mr. Hobs told me was the occasion of their writing.

Here he layd an ingeniose Designe to carry a considerable number of Artificers (chiefly Weavers) from hence to Virginia; and by Mary the queen-mother's meanes, he got favour from the King of France to goe into the Prisons and pick and choose. So when the poor dammed wretches understood what the designe was, they cryed *uno ore* [with one voice] *Tout tisseran*, i.e. We are all weavers. Will picked 36, as I remember, if not more, shipped them, and as he was in his voyage towards Virginia, he and his Tisseran were all taken by the Shippes then belonging to the Parliament of England. The Slaves, I suppose, they sold, but Sir William was brought Prisoner to England. Whether he was first a Prisoner at Caresbroke Castle in the Isle of Wight or at the Tower of London, I have forgott; he was a Prisoner at Both. His *Gondibert* was finished at Caresbroke Castle. He expected no mercy from the Parliament, and had no hopes of escaping his life. It pleased God that the two Aldermen of Yorke aforesayd, hearing that he was taken and brought to

London to be tryed for his life, which they understood was in extreme danger, they were touched with so much Generosity and goodness, as, upon their owne accounts and meer motion, to try what they could to save Sir William's life, who had been so civill to them and a meanes to save theirs, to come to London: and acquainting the Parliament with it, upon their petition, etc., Sir William's life was saved.

'Twas Harry Martyn that saved Sir William Davenant's life in the Howse. When they were talking of sacrificing one, then said Henry that in Sacrifices they always offered pure and without blemish: now yee talke of making a Sacrifice of an old rotten rascall. *Vide* H. Martyn's life, where by this very jest, then forgott, the Lord Falkland saved H. Martyn's life.

Being freed from imprisonment, because Playes (*scil.* Tragedies and Comoedies) were in those Presbyterian times scandalous, he contrives to set up an Opera *stylo recitativo*, wherein Serjeant Maynard and severall Citizens were engagers. It began at Rutland howse in Charter-house-yard; next at the Cock-pitt in Drury-Lane, where were acted very well, *stylo recitativo, Sir Francis Drake,* and *the Siege of Rhodes*. It did affect the Eie and eare extremely. This first brought Scenes in fashion in England; before, at playes, was only a Hanging.

Anno Domini 1660 was the happy restauration of his Majestie Charles II. Then was Sir William made, and the Tennis-Court in Little Lincolnes-Inne-fielde was turn'd into a Play-house for the Duke of Yorke's Players, where Sir William had Lodgeings, and where he dyed.

I was at his funerall. He had a coffin of Walnutt-tree; Sir John Denham sayd 'twas the finest coffin that ever he sawe. His body was carried in a Herse from the Play-house to Westminster-abbey, where, at the great West dore, he was received by the Singingmen and Choristers, who sang the Service of the Church (I am the Resurrection, etc.) to his Grave, which is in the South crosse aisle, on which, on a paving stone of marble, is writt, in imitation of that on Ben Johnson: O *rare Sir Will. Davenant.*

But me thought it had been proper that a Laurell should have been sett on his Coffin—which was not donne.—JOHN AUBREY, "Sir William Davenant," *Brief Lives*, 1669–96

William D'Avenant made his first entry on the stage of this vain world in the parish of S. Martin within the city of Oxford, about the latter end of the month of Febr. and on the third of March following, an. 160%, he received baptism in the church of that parish. His father John Davenant was a sufficient vintner, kept the tavern now known by the name of the Crown, (wherein our poet was born) and was mayor of the said city in the year 1621. His mother was a very beautiful woman, of a good wit and conversation, in which she was imitated by none of her children but by this William. The father, who was a very grave and discreet citizen (yet an admirer and lover of plays and play-makers, especially Shakespeare, who frequented his house in his journies between Warwickshire and London) was of a melancholic disposition, and was seldom or never seen to laugh, in which he was imitated by none of his children but by Robert his eldest son, afterwards fellow of St. John's coll. and a venerable doct. of div. As for William, whom we are farther to mention, and may justly stile 'the sweet swan of Isis,' was educated in grammar learning under Edw. Sylvester, whom I shall elsewhere mention, and in academical in Linc. coll. under the care of Mr. Dan. Hough, in 1620, 21, or thereabouts, and obtained there some smattering in logic: but his geny, which was always opposite to it, lead him in the pleasant paths of poetry, so that tho' he wanted much of university learning, yet he made as high and noble flights in the poetical faculty, as fancy could advance, without it. After he had left the said coll. wherein, I presume, he made but a short stay, he became servant to (Frances) the first dutchess of Richmond, and afterwards to Foulk lord Brook, who being poetically given (especially in his younger days) was much delighted in him. After his death (an. 1628.) he being free from trouble and attendance, betook himself to writing of plays and poetry, which he did with so much sweetness and grace, that he got the absolute love and friendship of his two patrons Endimyon Porter and Hen. Jermyn afterwards earl of S. Alban's; to both which he dedicated his poem, which he afterwards published, called *Madagascar*. Sir John Suckling also was his great and intimate friend, who exercis'd his fancy on that book, and other of his poems, but could not let him pass without this censure in his *Session of Poets*.

> Will. Davenant, asham'd of a foolish mischance,
> That he had got lately travelling into France;
> Modestly hoped the handsomness of his muse
> Might any deformity about him excuse.

This sir John, son of Sir Joh. Suckling of Whitton in Middlesex knight, sometime one of the secretaries of state, afterwards controller of the houshold to king James and king Charles 1. to which last he was of the privy council: who dying 27 March 1627 (at which time sir John the poet was 19 years of age) was buried in the church of S. Andrew, in the city of Norwich. The said mischance which sir John mentions, hapned to D'avenant by lying with a handsome black girl in Axe-yard in Westminster, on whom he thought when he spoke of Dalga in his *Gondibert*, which cost him his nose; and thereupon some wits were too cruelly bold with him, and his accident, as sir Jo. Mennes, sir Jo. Denham, &c. After the death of Ben. Johnson he was created poet-laureat, an. 1637: At which time Tho. May the translator of Lucan, a candidate for that place, was put aside; which ever after, especially when the times were changed, caused him in his writings to be an enemy to the king and his cause. In the month of May, 1641, our author D'avenant being accused to be one of the conspirators to seduce the army against the parliament, he absconded, but upon the issuing out of a proclamation to have him and others taken, he was apprehended at Feversham in Kent, and committed to the custody of a serjeant at arms. Among the said conspirators Hen. Percy esq; brother to the earl of Northumberland was one, who "was originally of Ch. church, created lord Percy of Alnwick 19 Car. and" afterwards lived and died a perfect Hobbist at Paris. Hen. Jermyn esq. (afterwards earl of S. Alban's) sir John Suckling, Kt. &c. were two more, who all escaped: But D'avenant being bailed in July following, he fled towards France, and in his way thither was seized on by the mayor of Canterbury, and strictly examined; upon which sir John Mennes hath a pleasant poem. After he had spent some time there, he returned, was entertained by William marquess of Newcastle, and by him made pro-prefect or lieutenant-general of his ordnance. In Sept. 1643 he received the honour of knighthood from his majesty near to Glocester, that city being then besieged, at which time sir William was in great renown for his loyalty and poetry. But upon the declining of the king's cause, and all things thereupon, especially the church, being, visibly tending to ruine, he retir'd again into France, changed his religion for that of Rome, and setling for a time in Paris, where Charles prince of Wales then was, he began to write his romance in verse called *Gondibert*, and had not wrote scarce two books, but being very fond of them, did print them with a large epistle to Hobbes of Malmsbury, and Hobbes's excellent epistle to him, before them. The courtiers who were then with the said prince, could never be at quiet for the discourse had

about this piece, which was the reason why some there (George duke of Buckingham, sir John Denham, &c.) made satyrical verses on him and his poem. Afterwards having laid an ingenious design to carry a considerable number of artificers, chiefly weavers, from France to Virginia (being encouraged thereunto by Henr. Maria the queen mother of England, who got leave for him so to do from the king of France) he did effect it so far, that he and his company were ship'd in their way thither, and had got on the main ocean; but being soon after seized on by certain ships belonging to the parliament of England, he was carried prisoner, first to the isle of Wight an. 1650, and afterwards to the Tower of London, in order to be tried for his life in the high court of justice, an. 1651, but upon the mediation of Joh. Milton and others, especially two godly aldermen of York (to whom he had shewed great civility, when they had been taken prisoners in the north by some of the forces under William marquess of Newcastle) he was saved, and had liberty allow'd him as a prisoner at large. At that time tragedies and comedies being esteemed very scandalous by the presbyterians, and therefore by them silenced, he contriv'd a way to set up an Italian opera to be performed by declamations and music: And that they might be performed with all decency, seemliness and without rudeness and profaneness, John Maynard serjeant at law, and several sufficient citizens were engagers. This Italian opera began in Rutland-house in Charterhouse-yard, "May 23. 1656," and was afterwards translated to the Cock-pit in Drury-lane, and delighting the eye and ear extreamly well, was much frequented for several years. So that he having laid the foundation of the English stage by this his musical drama, when plays were, as damnable things, forbidden, did, after his majesty's restoration, revive and improve it by painted scenes, at which time he erected a new company of actors, under the patronage of James duke of York, who acted several years in a tennis-court in Little Lincoln's-inn Fields. . . . At length this noted and celebrated author having lived to about his grand climacterical year, made his last exit in his house in Little Lincoln's-Inn-Fields, in the parish of S. Clement's Danes near London, on the seventh day of April in sixteen hundred sixty and eight, and was two days after buried in the south cross isle, or south transcept of the abbey church of S. Peter within the city of Westminster, without any lawrel upon his coffin, which, I presume, was forgotten. His body was deposited in the very place, or near it, where his antagonist Tho. May the English Lucan had been buried.—ANTHONY À WOOD, *Athenae Oxonienses*, 1691–1721

That notion of Sir William Davenant being more than a poetical child only of Shakespeare, was common in town; and Sir William himself seemed fond of having it taken for truth. —ALEXANDER POPE (1728–30), cited in Joseph Spence, *Anecdotes, Observations and Characters of Books and Men*, ed. S. W. Singer, 1820

General

> Thou has redeem'd us, *Will*; and future Times
> Shall not account unto the Age's crimes
> Dearth of pure Wit; since the great Lord of it
> (*Donne*) parted hence, no Man has ever writ
> So neere him, in's owne way: I would commend
> Particulars, but then, how should I end
> Without a Volume? Ev'ry Line of thine
> Would aske (to praise it right) Twenty of mine.
> —SIR JOHN SUCKLING, "To my Friend Will. Davenant; on his other Poems," 1637

The writing of Prefaces to Plays was probably invented by some very ambitious Poet, who never thought he had done enough: Perhaps by some Ape of the *French* Eloquence, who uses to make a business of a Letter of gallantry, an examen of a Farce; and in short, a great pomp and ostentation of words on every trifle. This is certainly the talent of that Nation, and ought not to be invaded by any other. They do that out of gayety which would be an imposition upon us.

We may satisfie our selves with surmounting them in the Scene, and safely leave them those trappings of writing, and flourishes of the Pen, with which they adorn the borders of their Plays, and which are indeed no more than good Landskips to a very indifferent Picture. I must proceed no farther in this argument, lest I run my self beyond my excuse for writing this. Give me leave therefore to tell you, Reader, that I do it not to set a value on any thing I have written in this Play, but out of gratitude to the memory of *Sir William D'avenant*, who did me the honour to joyn me with him in the alteration of it.

It was originally *Shakespear's*: a Poet for whom he had particularly a high veneration, and whom he first taught me to admire. The Play it self had formerly been acted with success in the *Black-Fryers*: and our excellent *Fletcher* had so great a value for it, that he thought fit to make use of the same Design, not much varied, a second time. Those who have seen his *Sea-Voyage*, may easily discern that it was a Copy of *Shakespear's Tempest*: the Storm, the desart Island and the Woman who had never seen a Man, are all sufficient testimonies of it. But *Fletcher* was not the only Poet who made use of *Shakespear's* Plot: Sir *John Suckling*, a profess'd admirer of our Author, has follow'd his footsteps in his *Goblins*; his *Regmella* being an open imitation of *Shakespear's Miranda*; and his Spirits, though counterfeit, yet are copied from *Ariel*. But Sir *William D'avenant*, as he was a man of quick and piercing imagination, soon found that somewhat might be added to the Design of *Shakespear*, of which neither *Fletcher* nor *Suckling* had ever thought: and therefore to put the last hand to it, he design'd the Counterpart to *Shakespear's* Plot, namely that of a Man who had never seen a Woman; that by this means those two Characters of Innocence and Love might the more illustrate and commend each other. This excellent contrivance he was pleas'd to communicate to me, and to desire my assistance in it. I confess that from the very first moment it so pleas'd me, that I never writ any thing with more delight. I must likewise do him that justice to acknowledge, that my writing received daily his amendments, and that is the reason why it is not so faulty, as the rest which I have done without the help or correction of so judicious a friend. The Comical parts of the Saylors were also his invention, and for the most part his writing, as you will easily discover by the style. In the time I writ with him I had the opportunity to observe somewhat more neerly of him than I had formerly done, when I had only a bare acquaintance with him: I found him then of so quick a fancy, that nothing was propos'd to him, on which he could not suddenly produce a thought extreamly pleasant and surprizing: and those first thoughts of his, contrary to the old *Latine* Proverb, were not alwaies the least happy. And as his fancy was quick, so likewise were the products of it remote and new. He borrowed not of any other; and his imaginations were such as could not easily enter into any other man. His corrections were sober and judicious: and he corrected his own writings much more severely than those of another man, bestowing twice the time and labour in polishing which he us'd in invention. It had perhaps been easie enough for me to have arrogated more to my self than was my due in the writing of this Play, and to have pass'd by his name with silence in the publication of it, with the same ingratitude which others have us'd to him, whose Writings he

hath not only corrected, as he has done this, but has had a greater inspection over them, and sometimes added whole Scenes together, which may as easily be distinguish'd from the rest, as true Gold from counterfeit by the weight. But besides the unworthiness of the action which deterred me from it (there being nothing so base as to rob the dead of his reputation) I am satisfi'd I could never have receiv'd so much honour in being thought the Author of any Poem how excellent soever, as I shall from the joining my imperfections with the merit and name of *Shakespear* and Sir *William D'avenant*.—JOHN DRYDEN, "Preface" to *The Tempest, or the Enchanted Island,* 1670

To Sir William Davenant, the English theatre, on its revival after the interruption which we have so often mentioned, owes its new institution, if this term may be here used. He introduced the Italian system of decoration, the *costume,* as it was then well or ill understood, the opera music, and in general the use of the orchestra. For this undertaking Charles II. had furnished him with extensive privileges. Davenant was a sort of adventurer and wit; in every way worthy of the royal favour; to enjoy which, dignity of character was never a necessary requisite. He set himself to work in every way that a rich theatrical repertory may render necessary; he made alterations of old pieces, and also wrote himself plays, operas, prologues, &c. But of all his writings nothing has escaped a merited oblivion.—AUGUST WILHELM SCHLEGEL, *Lectures on Dramatic Art and Literature,* tr. John Black, 1809, Lecture 28

Devoid of all higher original genius, D'Avenant applied himself, in no vulgar spirit nor without taking full advantage of such lights as were vouchsafed to him, to the task of satisfying what to him was the supreme criterion of merit, viz. the most cultivated taste (or what appeared to him such) of his age. From this point of view the Preface to *Gondibert*—his most ambitious work, although it remained a fragment—well deserves study, more especially since it contains some interesting observations on the relations between dramatic and epic poetry. The epic itself proves its author to have been under the influence of one of the most finished of conceptions in the poetic drama, of which he was to survive to show his imperfect apprehension in a revision of notorious ineptitude.

In his pre-Revolution plays he succeeded in reproducing, more faithfully than a greater writer could have done, not only the tastes and sentiments, but as it were the very temper of mind and tone of morality of his age, so far as they were within his view. The enthusiasm which he dedicated to such a patron as Endymion Porter expressed his sympathy with a whole phase of social and artistic feeling of which 'his Endymion' was no unworthy representative. As a dramatist, D'Avenant may, in the earlier series of his plays, be described as a limb of Fletcher, whom he resembled in his audacious choice of subjects, in his roving rather than soaring flights of fancy, and in his love of warm descriptive colouring. On occasion, he reveals some traces of the tenderness and even of the poetic feeling of his predecessor; but of the humour in which Fletcher abounded D'Avenant seems to me to possess little or nothing. He is not incapable of passion; but he is in general so unmeasured in expression as to make it difficult to distinguish between his passion and his rant. Burying his characters beneath accumulations of incident, he seems to lose sight of them in the process; and although a certain advance is observable in the successive plays belonging to this earlier group, hardly one of them seems to possess an intrinsic title to special remembrance.—ADOLPHUS WILLIAM WARD, *A History of English Dramatic Literature* (1875), 1899, Vol. 3, pp. 167–69

There is not a more hopelessly faded laurel on the slopes of the

English Parnassus than that which once flourished so bravely around the grotesque head of Davenant. The enormous folio edition of his works, brought out in 1673 in direct emulation of Ben Jonson, is probably the most deplorable collection of verses anywhere to be found, dead and dusty beyond the wont of forgotten classics. The critic is inclined to say that everything is spurious about Davenant, from the legend that connects his blood with Shakespeare's to the dramatic genius that his latest contemporaries praised so highly. He is not merely a ponderous, he is a nonsensical writer, and having begun life by writing meaningless romantic plays in imitation of Massinger, and insipid masques in the school of Ben Jonson, he closed his long and busy career by parodying the style of Dryden. But he really deserves to be classed with none of these authors, but with Sir William Killigrew and Sir Robert Stapleton, the dullest crew of pedants and poetasters which our literature has seen. From this wide condemnation of the writings of Davenant, his romantic epic of *Gondibert* must be excepted. It is a poem of chivalry, the scene of which is laid in Lombardy, but which the author grew tired of before it had occurred to him to construct a plot. It is, accordingly, nothing but an incoherent, rambling fragment, through which the reader toils, as if through a quicksand, dragging his steps along, and rewarded every now and then by a firmer passage containing some propriety of thought or a beautiful single line. The form of *Gondibert* is borrowed from the *Nosce Teipsum* of Sir John Davies, and was soon afterwards employed again by Dryden for his *Annus Mirabilis*.
—EDMUND GOSSE, "Sir William Davenant," *The English Poets*, ed. Thomas Humphry Ward, 1880, Vol. 2, p. 289

Works

GONDIBERT

Methinks *Heroick Poesie* till now
Like some fantastick *Fairy Land* did show,
Gods, Devils, Nymphs, Witches and *Gyants race*,
And all but *Man* in *Mans chief work* had place.
Thou like some worthy *Knight* with sacred Arms
Dost drive the *Monsters* thence, and end the *Charms.*
Instead of those dost *Men* and *Manners* plant,
The things which that rich *Soil* did chiefly want.
Yet ev'en thy *Mortals* do their *Gods* excell,
Taught by thy *Muse* to *Fight* and *Love* so well.
   By fatal hands whilst *present Empires* fall,
Thine from the Grave *past Monarchies* recall.
So much more thanks from humane kind does merit
The *Poets Fury*, then the *Zelots Spirit.*
And from the *Grave* thou mak'est this *Empire* rise,
Not like some dreadful *Ghost* t'affright our Eyes,
But with more Luster and triumphant state,
Then when it *crown'd* at proud *Verona* sate.
So will our *God rebuild* mans perisht frame,
And raise him up much *Better*, yet the *same.*
So *God-like Poets* do past things reherse,
Not *change*, but *Heighten* Nature by their Verse.
   With shame, methinks, great *Italy* must see
Her *Conqu'erors* rais'ed to *Life* again by *Thee.*
Rais'd by such pow'erful *Verse*, that ancient *Rome*
May blush no less to see her *Wit o'recome.*
Some men their *Fancies* like their *Faith* derive,
And think all Ill but that which *Rome* does give.
The Marks of *Old* and *Catholick* would find,
To the same *Chair* would *Truth* and *Fiction* bind.
Thou in those beaten pathes disdain'st to tred,
And scorn'st to *Live* by robbing of the *Dead.*

Since Time does all things change, thou think'st not fit
This latter *Age* should see *all New but Wit.*
Thy *Fancy* like a *Flame* its way does make,
And leave bright *Tracks* for following Pens to take.
Sure 'twas this noble boldness of the *Muse*
Did thy desire to seek new *Worlds* infuse,
And ne're did Heav'n so much a *Voyage* bless,
If thou canst *Plant* but *there* with like success.
                —ABRAHAM COWLEY, "To Sir *William Dave-
                nant*, upon his two first Books of *Gondibert*,
                finished before his voyage to *America*," 1650

Thus the wise nightingale that leaves her home,
Her native wood, when storms and winter come,
Pursuing constantly the cheerful spring,
To foreign groves does her old music bring.
   The drooping Hebrews' banished harps, unstrung
At Babylon upon the willows hung;
Yours sounds aloud, and tells us you excel
No less in courage, than in singing well;
Whilst, unconcerned, you let your country know,
They have impoverished themselves, not you;
Who, with the Muses' help, can mock those fates
Which threaten kingdoms, and disorder states.
So Ovid, when from Cæsar's rage he fled,
The Roman Muse to Pontus with him led;
Where he so sung, that we, through pity's glass,
See Nero milder than Augustus was.
Hereafter such, in thy behalf, shall be
The indulgent censure of posterity.
To banish those who with such art can sing,
Is a rude crime, which its own curse does bring;
Ages to come shall ne'er know how they fought,
Nor how to love their present youth be taught.
This to thyself.—Now to thy matchless book,
Wherein those few that can with judgment look,
May find old love in pure fresh language told,
Like new-stamped coin made out of Angel gold;
Such truth in love as the antique world did know,
In such a style as courts may boast of now;
Which no bold tales of gods or monsters swell,
But human passions, such as with us dwell.
Man is thy theme; his virtue, or his rage,
Drawn to the life in each elaborate page.
Mars, nor Bellona, are not named here,
But such a Gondibert as both might fear;
Venus had here, and Hebe been outshined
By thy bright Birtha and thy Rodalind.
Such is thy happy skill, and such the odds
Betwixt thy worthies and the Grecian gods!
Whose deities in vain had here come down,
Where mortal beauty wears the sovereign crown;
Such as of flesh composed, by flesh and blood,
Though not resisted, may be understood.
                —EDMUND WALLER, "To Sir William Dave-
                nant, upon His Two First Books of *Gondibert*,"
                1650

Well, wee are rescued! and by thy rare Pen
Poets shall live, when *Princes* dye like men.
Th'hast cleer'd the prospect to our harmless *Hill*,
Of late years clouded with imputed Ill,
And the *Soft, youthfull Couples* there may move
As chast as *Stars* converse and smile above.
Th'hast taught their *Language*, and their *love* to flow
Calme as *Rose-leafes*, and coole as *Virgin-snow*,

Which doubly feasts us, being so refin'd
They both *delight*, and *dignifie* the mind,
Like to the watrie *Musick* of some Spring,
Whose pleasant flowings at once *wash* and *sing*.
    And where before *Heroick Poems* were
Made up of *Spirits*, *Prodigies*, and *fear*,
And shew'd (through all the *Melancholy flight*,)
Like some dark Region overcast with night,
As if the Poet had been quite dismay'd,
While only *Giants* and *Inchantments* sway'd,
Thou like the *Sun*, whose Eye brooks no disguise
Hast Chas'd them hence, and with *Discoveries*
So rare and learned fill'd the place, that wee
Those fam'd *Grandeza's* find out-done by thee,
And under-foot see all those *Vizards* hurl'd,
Which bred the wonder of the former world.
'Twas dull to sit, as our fore-fathers did,
At *Crums* and *Voyders*, and because unbid
Refrain wise appetite. This made thy *fire*
Break through the *ashes* of thy aged *Sire*
To lend the world such a Convincing light
As shewes his *fancy* darker than his sight.
Nor was't alone the *bars* and *length* of dayes
(Though those gave *strength* and *stature* to his *bayes*,)
Encounter'd thee, but what's an old Complaint
And kills the fancy, a *forlorn Restraint*;
How couldst thou mur'd in solitarie stones
Dresse BIRTHA'S smiles, though well thou might'st her
        grones?
And, strangely Eloquent, thy self divide
'Twixt *Sad misfortunes*, and a *Bloomie Bride*?
Through all the tenour of thy ample Song
Spun from thy own rich store, and shar'd among
Those fair *Adventurers*, we plainly see
Th' *Imputed* gifts, *Inherent* are in thee.
Then live for ever (and by high desert)
In thy own *mirrour*, matchless *Gondibert*,
And in *bright Birtha* leave thy *love* Inshrin'd
Fresh as her *Emrauld*, and *fair* as her *mind*,
While all Confesse thee (as they ought to doe)
The Prince of *Poets*, and of *Lovers* too.
        —HENRY VAUGHAN, "To Sir *William D'avenant*,
        upon his *Gondibert*," *Olor Iscanus*, 1651

The next for *Epick Poesie*, is Sir *William D'avenant*, his Wit is well known; and in the Preface to his *Gondibert*, appear some strokes of an extraordinary judgment. He is for *unbeaten tracks*, and *new wayes of thinking*; but certainly in his *untry'd Seas* he is no great discoverer.

    One design of the *Epick Poets* before him was to adorn their own Countrey, there finding their *Heroes*, and patterns of Virtue; whose example (as they thought) would have greatest influence and power over Posterity; but this Poet steers a different course, his *Heroes* are all Forreigners: He cultivates a Countrey that is nothing akin to him, 'tis *Lombardy* that reaps the honour of all.

    Other Poets chose some *Action* or *Heroe* so illustrious, that the name of the Poem prepared the Reader, and made way for its reception: but in this Poem none can divine, what *great action* he intended to celebrate; nor is the Reader obliged to know whether the *Heroe* be *Turk* or *Christian*. Nor do the first lines give any light or prospect into his *design*. Methinks, though his Religion could not dispense with an *Invocation*, he needed not have scrupled at the *Proposition*: yet he rather chooses to enter in at the top of an house, because the mortals of *mean* and *satisfied minds* go in at the door. And I believe the

Reader is not well pleas'd to find his Poem begin with the praises of *Aribert*, when the Title had promised a *Gondibert*. But before he falls on any other business, he presents the Reader with a description of each particular *Heroe*, not trusting their *actions* to speak for them; as former Poets had done. Their practice was fine and artificial, his (he tells us) is a *new way*. Many of his *Characters* have but little of the *Heroick* in them; *Dalga* is a Jilt, proper onely for *Comedy*; *Birtha* for a *Pastoral*; and *Astragon*, in the manner here described, yields no very great ornament to an *Heroick Poem*; nor are his *Battels* less liable to *Censure*, than those of *Homer*.

    He dares not, as other *Heroick Poets*, heighten the *action* by making Heaven and Hell interess'd, for fear of offending against *probability*; and yet he tells of

        Threads by patient *Parcæ* slowly spun.

And for being dead, his phrase is,

        Heaven call'd him, where peacefully he rules a Star.

And the *Emerald* he gives to *Birtha*, has a stronger *tang* of the Old Woman, and is a greater *improbability* than all the enchantments in *Tasso*. A just *medium* reconciles the farthest extremes, and due preparation may give credit to the most unlikely Fiction. In *Marino*, *Adonis* is presented with a *Diamond Ring*, where, indeed, the stone is much-what of the same nature; but this Present is made by *Venus*: and from a *Goddess* could not be expected a gift of ordinary virtue.

    Although a Poet is oblig'd to know all Arts and Sciences, yet he ought discreetly to manage this knowledge. He must have judgment to select what is noble or beautiful, and proper for his occasion. He must by a particular Chymistry extract the essence of things, without soiling his Wit with the gross and trumpery. But some Poets labour to appear skilful with that wretched affectation, they dote on the very terms and *jargon*: exposing themselves rather to be laught at by the Apprentices, than to be admir'd by Philosophers: But whether *D'Avenant* be one of those, I leave others to examine.

    The sort of Verse he makes choice of, might, I suppose, contribute much to the vitiating of his stile; for thereby he obliges himself to stretch every period to the end of four lines. Thus the sense is broken perpetually with *parentheses*, the words jumbl'd in confusion, and a darkness spread over all; that the sense is either not discern'd, or found not sufficient for one just Verse, which is sprinkl'd on the whole *tetrastick*.

    In the *Italian* and *Spanish*, where all the *Rimes* are dissyllable, and the percussion stronger, this kind of Verse may be necessary; and yet to temper that grave march, they repeat the same Rime over again, and then they close the *Stanza* with a *Couplet* further to sweeten the severity. But in *French* and *English*, where we rime generally with onely one syllable, the *Stanza* is not allow'd, much less the *alternate* Rime in long Verse; for the sound of the monosyllable Rime is either lost ere we come to its correspondent, or we are in pain by the so long expectation and suspense.

    This alternate *Rime*, and the downright *Morality* throughout the whole *Canto's* together, shew him better acquainted with the *quatrains* of *Pybrach*, which he speaks of, than with any true Models of *Epick Poesie*.

    After all, he is said to have a particular Talent for the *Manners*: his thoughts are great, and there appears something *roughly Noble* throughout this fragment; which, had he been pleased to finish it, would, doubtless, not have been left so open to the attack of Criticks.—THOMAS RYMER, *Preface to Rapin's Reflections on Aristotle's Treatise of Poesie*, 1694

Sir William Davenant's *Gondibert* is not a good poem, if you take it in the whole; but there are a great many good things in it.—He is a scholar of Donne's, and took his sententiousness and metaphysics from him.—ALEXANDER POPE (1734–36), cited in Joseph Spence, *Anecdotes, Observations and Characters of Books and Men*, ed. S. W. Singer, 1820

His heroic poem of *Gondibert* has, no doubt, great imperfections; but it intimates everywhere a mind above those laborious triflers, who called that poetry which was only verse; and very often exhibits a majestic, dignified, and manly simplicity, equally superior to the metaphysical school, by the doctrines of which Davenant was occasionally misled. Yet, if that author too frequently imitated their quaint affectations of uncommon sentiment and associations, he had at least the merit of couching them in stately and harmonious verse.—SIR WALTER SCOTT, *The Life of John Dryden*, 1808

One of the curiosities in the history of our poetry, is the *Gondibert* of D'Avenant; and the fortunes and the fate of this epic are as extraordinary as the poem itself. Never has an author deserved more copious memoirs than the fertility of this man's genius claims. His life would have exhibited a moving picture of genius in action and in contemplation. With all the infirmities of lively passions, he had all the redeeming virtues of magnanimity and generous affections; but with the dignity and the powers of a great genius, falling among an age of wits, he was covered by ridicule. D'Avenant was a man who had viewed human life in all its shapes, and had himself taken them. A poet and a wit, the creator of the English stage with the music of Italy and the scenery of France; a soldier, an emigrant, a courtier, and a politician:—he was, too, a state-prisoner, awaiting death with his immortal poem in his hand; and at all times a philosopher!

That hardiness of enterprise which had conducted him through life, brought the same novelty, and conferred on him the same vigour in literature.

D'Avenant attempted to open a new vein of invention in narrative poetry; which not to call *epic*, he termed *heroic*; and which we who have more completely emancipated ourselves from the arbitrary mandates of Aristotle and Bossu, have since styled romantic. Scott, Southey, and Byron have taught us this freer scope of invention, but characterised by a depth of passion which is not found in D'Avenant. In his age, the title which he selected to describe the class of his poetical narrative, was a miserable source of petty criticism. It was decreed that every poem should resemble another poem, on the plan of the ancient epic. This was the golden age of "the poet-apes," till they found that it was easier to produce epic writers than epic readers.

But our poet, whose manly genius had rejected one great absurdity, had the folly to adopt another. The first reformers are always more heated with zeal than enlightened by sagacity. The four-and-twenty chapters of an epic, he perceived, were but fantastical divisions, and probably, originally, but accidental; yet he proposed another form as chimerical; he imagined that by having only five he was constructing his poem on the dramatic plan of five acts. He might with equal propriety have copied the Spanish comedy which I once read, in twenty-five acts, and in no slender folio. "Sea-marks (says D'Avenant, alluding to the works of antiquity) are chiefly useful to *coasters*, and serve not those who have the ambition of *discoverers*, that love to sail in untried seas;" and yet he was attempting to turn an epic poem into a monstrous drama, from the servile habits he had contracted from his intercourse with the theatre! This error of the poet has, however, no material influence on the *Gondibert*, as it has come down to us; for, discouraged and ridiculed, our adventurer never finished his voyage of discov-

ery. He who had so nobly vindicated the freedom of the British Muse from the meanness of imitation, and clearly defined what such a narrative as he intended should be, "a perfect glass of nature, which gives us a familiar and easy view of ourselves," did not yet perceive that there is no reason why a poetical narrative should be cast into any particular form, or be longer or shorter than the interest it excites will allow. . . .

The *Gondibert* has poetical defects fatal for its popularity; the theme was not happily chosen; the quatrain has been discovered by capricious ears to be unpleasing, though its solemnity was felt by Dryden. The style is sometimes harsh and abrupt, though often exquisite; and the fable is deficient in that rapid interest which the story-loving readers of all times seem most to regard. All these are diseases which would have long since proved mortal in a poem less vital; but our poet was a commanding genius, who redeemed his bold errors by his energetic originality. The luxuriancy of his fancy, the novelty of his imagery, the grandeur of his views of human life; his delight in the new sciences of his age;—these are some of his poetical virtues. But, above all, we dwell on the impressive solemnity of his philosophical reflections, and his condensed epigrammatic thoughts. The work is often more ethical than poetical; yet, while we feel ourselves becoming wiser at every page, in the fulness of our minds we still perceive that our emotions have been seldom stirred by passion. The poem falls from our hands! yet is there none of which we wish to retain so many single verses. D'Avenant is a poetical Rochefoucault; the sententious force of his maxims on all human affairs could only have been composed by one who had lived in a constant intercourse with mankind.—ISAAC DISRAELI, "D'Avenant and a Club of Wits," *Quarrels of Authors*, 1812–13

Davenant's *Gondibert* is a tissue of stanzas, all aiming to be wise and witty, each containing something in itself, and the whole together amounting to nothing. The thoughts separately require so much attention to understand them, and arise so little out of the narrative, that they with difficulty sink into the mind, and have no common feeling of interest to recal or link them together afterwards. The general style may be judged of by these two memorable lines in the description of the skeleton-chamber.

> Yet on that wall hangs he too, who so thought,
> And she dried by him whom that he obeyed.

Mr. Hobbes, in a prefatory discourse, has thrown away a good deal of powerful logic and criticism in recommendation of the plan of his friend's poem. Davenant, who was poet-laureate to Charles II. wrote several masques and plays which were well received in his time, but have not come down with equal applause to us.—WILLIAM HAZLITT, *Lectures on the English Comic Writers*, 1818

As for *Gondibert*, those may criticise it who can read it. —THOMAS BABINGTON MACAULAY, "John Dryden" (1828), *Critical, Historical, and Miscellaneous Essays*, 1860, Vol. 1, p. 350

KARL ELZE
From "Sir William Davenant" (1869)
Essays on Shakespeare, tr. L. Dora Schmitz
1874, pp. 346–55

He differed from Shakespeare in the first place in his fundamental notion of the nature of dramatic poetry; he did not consider its object to lie in holding up a mirror to nature, but, as is evident from the various passages referred to, in promoting virtue and moral refinement by the representation of heroic examples. He repeatedly lays the greatest stress upon 'moral representations,' and his poetry in so far has a tendency. It may, perhaps, be imagined that he required a pretext like this to reconcile the Puritans to his attempts at reviving the theatre which they had suppressed, but the moralising tendency was in his blood, although it cannot be denied that these circumstances may have favoured it. One of his earliest plays, the tragi-comedy, *The Just Italian* (which appeared in 1630), is praised by William Hopkins as 'a legitimate poem,' in opposition to the pleasures of Paris Garden; and Thomas Carew contrasts it to the popular theatre, 'that adulterate stage,' and praises Beaumont and 'great Jonson,' without mentioning Shakespeare. Both of them evidently intend thus to console Davenant for the failure of his play. In Davenant's eyes the drama was only to represent the highest social life, and overstrained morals and court etiquette were to be introduced upon the stage. He found these things better ordered in France than at home. The French drama, however, was greatly influenced by the novels of Calprenède and Scudéri, both of them also widely read in England, which contain nothing but 'unnatural representations of the passions, false sentiments, false precepts, false wit, false honour, and false modesty, with a heap of improbable, unnatural incidents, mixed up with true history, and fastened upon some of the great names of antiquity.' 'Every king,' says Sir Walter Scott, 'was by prescriptive right a hero, every female a goddess, every tyrant a fire-breathing chimera, and every soldier an irresistible Amadis.'[1] This is the starting point of the erroneous way entered upon by the classic court drama, both in England and in France; from this all the defects of the characterisation, of the motives, and of the composition in general proceeded. In Shakespeare, action and conflict arise out of the inmost soul of the individual, out of the natural disposition of his mind, the peculiarities of his character and his passions, but in Davenant, individualisation gives place to typical characteristics which found their highest development in the French drama. In addition to this, the action is influenced and the conflict produced by circumstances which are beyond the control of the persons acting. Occurrence imperceptibly takes the place of action. The influence of such outward occurrences upon the composition is the characteristic sign of the decline of art; it is most closely connected with the development of the external theatrical resources, decoration and machinery.[2] This kind of composition and characterisation at the same time requires far less intuition on the part of the poet; it is the work of talent not of genius. Davenant, like all the rest of that school, was not concerned in representing men as they really are; he intends his characters to be above all things noble, great, and heroic, which to him was the *conditio sine qua non* of their admission to the stage. Their faults were only to serve as foils to their virtues, in the same way as shade is necessary to give light its full effect. This very naturally gave rise to high-flown and sententious declamations, to the pompousness of hollow feeling, to bombast instead of sublimity. Davenant, it is true, did not reach the height of this style; this was reserved for his younger friend, Dryden, for whose heroic plays he paved the way, as Dryden himself admits in his 'Essay on Heroic Plays.' His dramas, with the exception of the operas and some few pathetic scenes, are not yet written in rhymed couplets, but either in prose or in the blank verse imitated from Shakespeare. Like Shakespeare he has interspersed the latter not only with shorter or longer lines, but also with prose, and in his tragi-comedies has retained the mixture of the tragic and the comic. In several plays he more or less strictly observes the unities, as, for instance, in *The Man's the Master*, borrowed

from Scarron, where it is expressly stated that the scene is Madrid, and 'in one house.' Dryden, in *All for Love* (1678), has entirely submitted to the three unities. That the limitation of locality was rendered necessary by the introduction of moveable scenery has been said before; for although the latter did not necessitate the absolute unity of place, yet it was not capable of following the unlimited change of scene.

By way of example let us examine the tragi-comedy *Love and Honour* (the two pivots of the classic court-drama). The inhabitants of Savoy have routed the Milanese—why they have been at war with one another we are not told—and are preparing for a happy return home. Rich booty and numerous prisoners of war are carried to Turin; among the latter is a number of women, the most conspicuous of whom is Evandra, the daughter and heiress of the Duke of Milan, who has been captured by the young and valiant Count Prospero. Prospero, however, on account of this capture, incurs the severe reproaches of his friend Alvaro, son of the Duke of Savoy, who informs him that many years ago his father's brother has been taken prisoner and executed by the Duke of Milan, and that therefore his father will no doubt cruelly revenge himself upon Evandra. Prospero regrets his mistake, which threatens to deprive him of the prince's favour; but as it is too late to restore the fair princess to her family, he conceals her in a subterraneous vault in his house, which is unknown to everybody except himself. On the return of the army the Duke of Savoy issues an edict that, after the lapse of a year, all female prisoners shall be at liberty to return to Milan without ransom, if, up to that time, they have not consented to marry their conquerors, who are meanwhile to provide for them. Evandra alone, of whose arrival the Duke has heard in spite of every precaution, is not included in this number, but is to suffer immediate death as soon as found. When Prospero refuses to disclose her place of concealment he is sentenced to be executed on the following morning; Alvaro, however, who in the meantime has seen Evandra and become enamoured of her, intercedes for his friend, and is willing to take his father's anger to himself. Prospero, too, has fallen in love with Evandra, and so has Leonel, Prince of Parma, who like her has been brought to Turin as a prisoner of war. All these lovers visit Evandra in Prospero's house without showing a trace of jealousy. Prospero and Alvaro dispute with each other for the honour and happiness of dying for Evandra; one outbids the other in generosity and in the readiness to sacrifice himself, and such is their heroism that not even in a word they betray love of life or regret to leave the world. They are, however, surpassed by Evandra, who, with the assistance of her companion Melora (Leonel's sister, also a prisoner of war), locks them up in her grotto in order to save them. She then intends to deliver herself up to the Duke, but Melora is beforehand with her, and represents herself as Evandra. The contention of the lovers is now renewed between the girls, each one wishing to die for the other. They face death with greater equanimity than if they were going to a ball; they think of nothing but the heroic deed which they are about to accomplish, and of the renown which they will gain by it. This heroism on the part of the women, however, does not make the Duke swerve from his vow of revenge, any more than that of their lovers, or the ransom offered by Milan. Unable to find out the real Evandra, the Duke orders both girls to be put to death. At the last moment, Alvaro, Prospero, and their friends, propose to rescue the poor martyrs by force, but do nothing for the execution of such a plan. Leonel now discovers himself to be a son of that Duke of Parma who, while in the service of Milan, has taken the Duke of Savoy's brother prisoner; he thus attains his object of setting the girls free, and is now to die in their stead. How is all this to end? How can it end but by a *deus ex machina*? When the execution is just about to take place, two envoys appear from Milan, but even their entreaties and remonstrances make no impression upon the stubborn Duke; whereupon they suddenly take off their false beards, and behold, it is the Duke of Milan himself, with the Duke of Savoy's brother, who has not been executed, but has all this time been kept by the Duke of Milan rather as a friend than a prisoner. The revenge over which the Duke of Savoy has been brooding for ten long years is thus suddenly deprived of its object; why he has been allowed so long to believe in his brother's death remains unexplained. Universal rejoicing and the usual marriages form the conclusion.

As indicated by the title of tragi-comedy, the play is garnished with comic elements, but they are vulgar and rude. There is ribaldry, but no wit, and not a trace of Shakespeare's gracefulness. The fact is, that by the Puritanical persecution and sanctimoniousness, sensuality had been driven back into the minds of the people. It now broke out afresh, not however with the healthy and frank naïveté of the Shakespearean period, but as vicious wantonness. The comic personages of the play are Captain Vasco, and his retainers, Frivolo, Altosto, &c., as far as such fellows can be comic; they are evident copies of Falstaff and his crew. Vasco has captured a widow of eighty, who is said to be wealthy, and as he is penniless he resolves there and then to marry her in spite of her wrinkles, her cough, and her deafness, hoping that she will soon die. The old hag, inconceivable as it may be, gives her consent, and the marriage takes place. On the following morning the young couple are treated to a serenade which is unequalled in loathsomeness.

In spite of all these defects, *Love and Honour*, according to Cibber's statement, was the most successful of all Davenant's plays. As we learn from the title of the quarto edition, printed in 1649, it was acted at the Blackfriars, consequently before the closing of the theatres. After the Restoration it was revived with extraordinary splendour. Betterton played Prince Alvaro, and the King lent him his coronation robes for the occasion; the Duke of York and Lord Oxford lent theirs to Harris (Count Prospero) and to Price (Leonel). Mr. Halliwell's statement that in the folio edition of 1673 there are several omissions and alterations, justifies the supposition that the play itself was remodelled.

From the comic part of *Love and Honour* an inference may be drawn in regard to Davenant's comedies. After the Restoration comedy certainly occupied a different position from tragedy, which in a great measure was due to the personal bias of Charles II., who, according to the evidence given by Dryden, greatly influenced the reconstruction of the English drama. For although Charles II. from political motives was perfectly content that tragedy should be made harmless, yet it was by no means his wish that the Muse of Comedy should become a maid of honour. During his exile he had lived pretty much upon an equal footing with his companions in misfortune, and with them had tried to sweeten his hardships by taking part in popular, and too often licentious amusements. Even after he had ascended the throne he did not consider it a

degradation to seek pleasure in the low and dissolute pastimes of public exhibitions. It was the right food for his libertinism. Accordingly it was quite to his taste that comedy as far as possible should follow the beaten track of the Elizabethan era, and if it was to imitate any foreign model at all, he greatly preferred the Spanish comedy to the Parisian, as the intrigues, confusions, and disguises of the former were much more in accordance with his taste. He had evidently become acquainted with the Spanish comedy while abroad, and it was at his express recommendation that Sir Samuel Tuke's *Adventures of Five Hours* (1663) and Crowne's *Sir Courtly Nice* were translated from the Spanish. Dryden's *Wild Gallant*, and his *Maiden Queen*, with which the monarch was particularly pleased, resembled the Spanish comedy in character. Even where, exceptionally, the English comedy inclined to the French, this exception only served to confirm the rule, inasmuch as the respective French originals were themselves copies from the Spanish. This was, for example, the case with Davenant's *The Man's the Master* (published in 1669), the greater part of which is a literal translation of Scarron's *Jodelet, ou le maître valet*.[3] By depriving the play of its poetical dress (only in a few passages he rises to blank verse) Davenant has greatly lowered it, and the scenes between the servants, which he has added of his own invention, serve only to increase the coarseness, while in the French drama even the servants were obliged to study propriety of conduct and to keep in the background. Davenant has drawn out these very scenes with unmistakable partiality, because he knew that this would suit the taste of his public. The importance given to external occurrences in the composition is especially perceptible in this play, the levers of the action and of the conflict being the accidental confusion of two portraits, and the freak of the master—which arises out of it without an inner motive—to disguise himself as a servant and to let the servant play his part.

Notes

1. Scott, *Life of Dryden*, sect. 2. Compare Hallam, *Introd. Lit. Eur.*, iii. 518 seqq.
2. 'Sedulous study, deep reflection, and long and repeated correction and revision were not to be expected from a playwright by whom three dramas were to be produced in one season; and in their place were substituted adventures, surprises, rencontres, mistakes, disguises, and escapes, all readily accomplished by the intervention of sliding panels, closets, veils, masks, large cloaks, and dark lanterns.' Scott, *Life of Dryden*, sect. 2.
3. The introduction is borrowed from Scarron's *L'Héritier ridicule*. The dialogue has been considerably curtailed by Davenant, in accordance with a remark which he makes in his *Playhouse to be Let*, Act I.:

    > The French convey their arguments too much
    > In dialogue: their speeches are too long.

    Pepys saw the play on the 26th of March 1668, in the Duke's Theatre. 'The most of the mirth,' he says, 'was sorry poore stuffe, of eating of sack posset and slabbering themselves, and mirth fit for clownes; the prologue but poor, and the epilogue little in it but the extraordinariness of it, it being sung by Harris and another in the form of a ballet.'

SIR KENELM DIGBY

KATHERINE PHILIPS

JAMES SHIRLEY

GEORGE WITHER

THE
TENTH MUSE
Lately ſprung up in AMERICA.
OR
Severall Poems, compiled
with great variety of VVit
and Learning, full of delight.
Wherein eſpecially is contained a com-
pleat diſcourſe and deſcription of
The Four
Elements,
Conſtitutions,
Ages of Man,
Seaſons of the Year.
Together with an Exact Epitomie of
the Four Monarchies, viz.
The
Aſſyrian,
Perſian,
Grecian,
Roman.
Alſo a Dialogue between Old England and
New, concerning the late troubles.
With divers other pleaſant and ſerious Poems.
By a Gentlewoman in thoſe parts.
Printed at London for Stephen Bowtell at the ſigne of the
Bible in Popes Head-Alley. 1650.

Title page of Anne Bradstreet's *The Tenth Muse*

JEREMY TAYLOR

WILLIAM PRYNNE

1600–1669

William Prynne was born at Swainswick, Somerset, in 1600. He attended the Bath Grammar School before entering Oriel College, Oxford, in 1616. He received a B.A. in 1621, and subsequently read law at Lincoln's Inn, London. In 1628 he was called to the bar, but by this time Prynne already had embarked on his career as a Puritan pamphleteer. His first work, *The Perpetuity of a Regenerate Man's Estate* (1627), was a theological tract. It was his *Histriomastix: The Players Scourge or Actors Tragoedie* (1632) which made him notorious. In this 1100-page "pamphlet" Prynne attacks London theatres and their various productions. In it he also attacks women actors, referring to them as "notorious whores." Whether this reference was intentional or coincidental is unknown. However, at the time of the pamphlet's publication Queen Henrietta Maria was engaged in a dramatic production herself. Archbishop Laud decided that the reference to women actors was a direct offense against the Crown, and so in 1634 Prynne was sentenced by the Star Chamber to life imprisonment. In addition, he had to pay a huge fine, lost his law and university degrees, and lost his ears in the pillory. He continued to write while in the Tower, and his cheeks were later branded with the initials S.L., for seditious libeller. Prynne liked to refer to these initials as "Stigmata Laudis."

Pryne was released in 1640 by the Long Parliament. Immediately he began to gather evidence against Laud. Eventually Laud was convicted and beheaded in 1645, due largely to Prynne's efforts. In 1642 the theatres closed as Prynne had wished, and by 1648 he was serving as the Member of Parliament for Newport. In 1649 he again was imprisoned during Pride's Purge for his support of Charles I in Parliament. After spending several years in prison he regained his seat in the House of Commons and brought forward the bill dissolving Parliament and restoring the monarchy. He was rewarded by Charles II with the position of Keeper of the Tower Records. Prynne later dedicated his *Brevia Parliamentaria Rediviva* (1662) to Charles II.

Prynne was both a fanatical Puritan and an ardent Royalist. These conflicting political allegiances landed him frequently in jail, but did not inhibit his writing. He was the author of over 200 pamphlets and tracts. Never married, he died at his quarters at Lincoln's Inn on October 24, 1669. He was buried in the chapel there.

Personal

⟨Lord Treasurer Finch⟩ told me Mr. Prin's Character; that he is a man of mighty labour and reading and memory, but the worst judge of matters, or layer-together of what he hath read, in the world—(which I do not however believe him in); that he believes him very true to the King in his heart, but can never be reconciled to Episcopacy. That the House doth not lay much weight upon him or anything he says.—SAMUEL PEPYS, *Diary*, July 3, 1666

Anno 1637 he was stigmatized in the Pillorie, and then Banished to Cornet-castle in Guernsey, where he was very civilly treated by the Governour Carteret, a very ancient familie in that Island. His Eares were not quite cutt off, only the upper part, his tippes were visible. Bishop William Lawd, A. B. Cant., was much blamed for being a Spectator, when he was his Judge. Anno 1641 he was, with Burton and Bastwyck, called home by the Parliament, and hundreds mett him and them out of London some miles.

He was a learned man, of immense reading, but is much blamed for his unfaithfull quotations. He was of a strange Saturnine complexion. Sir C. W. sayd once, that he had the countenance of a Witch.

His manner of Studie was thus: he wore a long quilt cap, which came 2 or 3, at least, inches over his eies, which served him as an Umbrella to defend his Eies from the light. About every three houres his man was to bring him a roll and a pott of Ale to refocillate his wasted spirits: so he studied and dranke, and munched some bread; and this maintained him till night, and then, he made a good Supper: now he did well not to dine,

which breakes of one's fancy, which will not presently be regained: and 'tis with Invention as a flux, when once it is flowing, it runnes amaine: if it is checked, flowes but *guttim*: and the like for perspiration, check it, and 'tis spoyled.

He endured severall Imprisonments for the King's cause, and was (really) very instrumentall in his restauracion.

Upon the opening of the Parliament, viz. letting in the Secluded Members, he girt on his old long rustie Sword (longer then ordinary.) Sir William Waller marching behind him (as he went to the Howse) W. Prynne's long sword ranne between Sir William's short legges, and threw him downe, which caused laughter.—JOHN AUBREY, "William Prynne," *Brief Lives*, 1669–96

General

Mr. Prynne's books, having been made use of for wast paper, begin now to be scarce, and to be got into curious hands, purely for this reason, because he commonly cites his vouchers for what he delivers, and thereby gives his reader an opportunity of examining the truth of them. Mr. Baker, of Cambridge, believes his study hath more of Mr. Prynne's books than any one of that university, and he well remembers, that he sent up his "Anti-Arminianism" to Mr. Strype, which he could not meet with at London, when he was writing one of his books, and yet it has two editions.—THOMAS HEARNE, *Reliquiae Hearnianae*, Aug. 25, 1719

Vast erudition, without the tact of good sense, in a voluminous author, what a calamity! for to such a mind no subject can present itself on which he is unprepared to write, and none at the same time on which he can ever write reasonably. The name and the works of William Prynne have often come under the eye of the reader; but it is even now difficult to discover his real character; for Prynne stood so completely insulated amid all parties, that he was ridiculed by his friends, and execrated by his enemies. The exuberance of his fertile pen, the strangeness and the manner of his subjects, and his pertinacity in voluminous publication, are known, and are nearly unparalleled in literary history. . . .

The literary character of Prynne is described by the happy epithet which Anthony Wood applies to him, "Voluminous Prynne." His great characteristic is opposed to that axiom of Hesiod so often quoted, that "half is better than the whole;" a secret which the matter-of-fact men rarely discover. Wanting judgment, and the tact of good sense, these detailers have no power of selection from their stores, to make one prominent fact represent the hundred minuter ones that may follow it. Voluminously feeble, they imagine expansion is stronger than compression; and know not to generalise, while they only can deal in particulars. Prynne's speeches were just as voluminous as his writings; always deficient in judgment, and abounding in knowledge—he was always wearying others, but never could himself. He once made a speech to the House, to persuade them the king's concessions were sufficient ground for a treaty; it contains a complete narrative of all the transactions between the king, the Honses, and the army, from the beginning of the parliament; it takes up 140 octavo pages, and kept the house so long together, that the debates lasted from Monday morning till Tuesday morning! . . .

When we examine ⟨*Histriomastix*⟩, often alluded to, the birth of the monster seems prodigious and mysterious; it combines two opposite qualities; it is so elaborate in its researches among the thousand authors quoted, that these required years to accumulate, and yet the matter is often temporary, and levelled at fugitive events and particular persons; thus the very formation of this mighty volume seems paradoxical. The secret history of this book is as extraordinary as the book itself, and is a remarkable evidence how, in a work of immense erudition, the arts of a wily sage involved himself, and whoever was concerned in his book, in total ruin. The author was pilloried, fined, and imprisoned; his publisher condemned in the penalty of five hundred pounds, and barred for ever from printing and selling books, and the licenser removed and punished. Such was the fatality attending the book of a man whose literary voracity produced one of the most tremendous indigestions, in a malady of writing.—ISAAC DISRAELI, "A Voluminous Author without Judgment," *Calamities of Authors*, 1812–13

This *magnum opus* of Puritan enthusiasm and learning ⟨*Histriomastix*⟩—for it exhibits both qualities in a very extraordinary degree—appears to have been the fruit of seven years' labour. Its author, a young barrister of Lincoln's Inn, whose first published treatise is dated 1627, but who seems to have begun his book against stage-plays some three years earlier, may have been encouraged in his undertaking by the current of opinion in that Society. Unlike their brethren in the Temple and at Gray's Inn, the Benchers of Lincoln's Inn had prohibited the 'disorderly Bacchanalian Grand-Christmasses' which it was customary to celebrate by dramatic or quasi-dramatic entertainments. To them therefore in the first instance, to the students of the Inns of Court, too long known as the patrons of stage-plays, in the second, and finally to the Christian Reader in general, he dedicates his work. It is no light shaft which he directs against the object of his wrath; for the book consists of more than a thousand closely-printed small quarto pages—as why should it not, when the play-books which it denounces are

occasionally growing 'from Quarto into Folio,' and 'Shackspeers Plaies are printed in the best Crowne paper, far better than most Bibles.' Prynne's treatise is accordingly as solid as it is elaborate,—the work of an indefatigable reader who never fails to give chapter and verse for every one of the thousands of quotations constituting the bulk of his materials, who disposes his arguments in regularly arranged groups (grimly distributed into Parts, Acts, and Scenes), and who puts each argument forward in regular syllogistic form. Occasionally a 'Chorus' of reflexions is introduced, and a 'Catastrophe,' with a long quotation from the Jesuit Mariana and a short passage from St. Augustine, concludes the whole. The tone of the work is in general dry and calm; but the author is capable of rising to eloquence, as in the final exhortation in act v of the Second Part. In the choice of the arguments themselves, as will be seen from the brief sketch of the book appended below the text, there is nothing new; but they are nowhere else developed with anything like the same fulness; and for the historian of the drama Prynne's treatise furnishes an ample repository of much useful learning. It is to be observed that his acquaintance with the stage-plays of his own times was obviously of the most limited description. He states that on his first arrival in London he had 'heard and seene foure severall Playes, to which the importunity of some ill acquaintance drew me whiles I was yet a novice'; and in one passage he refers to a reflexion upon Puritan attacks against the stage made in a play produced at the opening of the new theatre (at Whitefriars). But he never quotes, or otherwise appeals to, illustrations from the English drama of his own or any other period. As to 'professed printed Play-Champions,' he observes that he only knows of two, both 'scribbling hackney Players'—*viz.* Lodge in his *Play of Playes* and (Thomas) Heywood in his *Apology for Actors*; and to the arguments of the latter he addresses himself at length. The treatise is intended to make good a conclusion—and nothing short of it—in favour of the total suppression of stage-plays; and from this point of view the whole of the argument is conducted.—ADOLPHUS WILLIAM WARD, A *History of English Dramatic Literature* (1875), 1899, Vol. 3, pp. 240–43

In 1627 Prynne's first book appeared: *The Perpetuity of a Regenerate Man's Estate.* Under the forms of theological argument, Prynne's contention is, in the main, a contention for the central idea of Calvinism, the immediate dependence of the individual soul upon God without the intervention of human or material agencies. But in Prynne's hands the theme was stripped of all the imaginative grandeur with which it has been so often clothed. His pages, with their margins crowded with references, afforded a palpable evidence how much he owed to his reading and his memory. He had no formative genius, no broad culture, no sense of humour. He had no perception of the relative importance of things distasteful to him. *Health's Sickness*, a violent diatribe on the supreme wickedness of drinking healths, was followed by *The Unloveliness of Lovelocks*, an equally violent diatribe on the supreme wickedness of the long lock of hair floating over the shoulder, which was the latest fashion amongst courtiers. The folly of the day was chastised with a torrent of learned objurgation which would not have been out of place in a harangue directed against the seven deadly sins. He had nothing worse to say when he sat down to prepare A *Brief Survey and Censure of Mr. Cosin's Cozening Devotions.*

It is easy to turn scornfully upon the aridity of Prynne's mind—far easier than it is to read his books. Yet hard and unintelligent as his assault upon Cosin was, he was but giving voice, in his own peculiar way, to the repugnance felt by strong men to the feminine neatness of Cosin's devotional exercises.

They threatened to 'take the imprisoned soul and lap it in Elysium,' to teach the ardent spirit to forego the stern wrestling for truth and to content itself with the passive acknowledgment of an order in the formation of which it was to take no part. Cosin would teach men to regard the State as dependent on the authority of the King, and the Church as dependent on the authority of the clergy.

The problem presented by these disputes was a hard one for a statesman to solve. To Prynne it presented no difficulty at all. No man was to be allowed to speak or write against the Calvinistic doctrines. The conclusions of the Synod of Dort were to be offered as a test to every clergyman in England. Those who refused to subscribe were to be at once excluded from holding any ecclesiastical office.—SAMUEL R. GARDINER, *History of England*, 1883, Vol. 7, pp. 13–14

ANTHONY À WOOD
From *Athenae Oxonienses*
1691–1721

William Prynne, a most noted and frequent writer of his time, was born at Swainswick near Bath in Somersetshire, an. 1600, at which time his father (as afterwards this his son whom we now mention) was a tenant to Oriel coll. educated in grammar learning (as I conceive) within the same city of Bath, became a commoner of the said coll. of Oriel under the tuition of Giles Widdowes, an. 1616, took one degree in arts in 1620, went afterwards to Linc. inn to obtain knowledge in the common law, where he was made successively barrester, utter barrester, bencher and reader. At his first coming to that inn he became a great follower and admirer of that noted puritan Dr. John Preston then lecturer there; who finding him to be of an enterprizing nature, hot-spirited, and eager in pursuit of any thing that was put into him, he was looked upon by Preston and his party as the fittest person to adventure upon such exploits, which a more sober and considerate man durst not have appeared in. Whereupon he was put into the road of writing, not without the helps and advice of Preston and the brethren, and having made or gotten a common-place-book, published several matters against the loosness and debauchery (so he took it) of the times, as against drinking of healths, long or womanish hair, stage-plays, wherein the queen (Henr. Maria) was in a gross manner reflected upon several times, and other matters relating to the church, discipline and members thereof; which were altogether looked upon as aliene from his profession, and pragmatical and impudent for him so to do. About the time of Christmas, an. 1632, he published a book entit. *Histriomastix*, &c. wherein breathing out nothing but disgrace to the nation, infamy to the church, reproaches to the court, dishonour to the queen, and some things which were thought to be tending to the destruction of his majesty's person, as Dr. Pet. Heylin an enemy to our author Prynne tells[1] us; great complaints therefore were made of that book, notwithstanding it had been licensed by Mr. Tho. Buckner chaplain to Dr. Abbot archb. of Canterbury. Before I go forward with this matter, you may be pleased to hear what a certain[2] author saith of it, thus—'About this time (meaning the latter end of 1632) Mr. Prynne published his book called *Histrio-mastix*, by license of archb. Abbot's chaplain, which being against plays, and a reference in the table of the book, to this effect,—women actors notorious whores, relating to some women actors mention'd in his book as he affirmeth.—It hapned, that about six weeks after this, the queen acted a part in a pastoral, at Somerset-house, and then the archbishop Laud, and other prelates, whom Prynne had angered, by some books of his against Arminianism, and against the jurisdiction of the bishops, and by some prohibitions which he had moved, and got to the high commission court.—These prelates and their instruments, the next day after the queen had acted her pastoral, shewed Prynne's book against plays, to the king, and that place of it, "Women actors notorious whores," and they informed the king and queen, that Prynne had purposely written this book against the queen and her pastoral, whereas it was published six weeks before that pastoral was acted. Yet the king and queen, though thus exasperated, did direct nothing against him, till Laud set Dr. Heylin (who bare a great malice to Prynne for confuting some of his doctrines) to peruse Prynne's books, and to collect the scandalous points out of them; which Heylin did, though (as Prynne affirms) not at all warranted by the text of his book; but these two gentlemen were well matched, and alike in other things, tho' so much different in divinity, or shew of it,' &c. Thus our author here quoted, of whom I shall hereafter make large mention. Upon the said complaints concerning that book, Heylin being appointed to collect such passages out of it that were esteemed scandalous to the king, queen, state, and government of the realm, did, after some time, deliver them in writing to sir John Coke or Cook secretary of state and to Dr. Laud bishop of London: the last of which did soon after, on a sabbath-day morning, go to Will. Noy attorney gen. and charged him to prosecute Prynne for the said book, which Noy did rigorously enough. Afterwards Prynne was sent for before the lords in the inner star chamber, where being examined about the said matters, was committed prisoner to the Tower of London, on the first day of Febr. 1632, where remaining without permission of bail till the month of Feb. 1633, was at last brought to a tryal in the court of star chamber, (having been first pre-condemned by the gentlemen of his own profession) and afterwards sentenced by that court on the 17th day of the said month, thro' the eager prosecution of the said Noy, to be fined 5000*l* to the king, expelled the university of Oxford and Lincolns-inn, degraded and disinabled from his profession in the laws, to stand in the pillory, first in the Palace-yard in Westminster, and three days after in Cheapside, in each place to lose an ear, (tho' this last part of his censure was much moderated in the execution) to have his book called *Histriomastix* publicly burnt before his face by the hand of the hangman, and remain prisoner during life. After this sentence was executed (which was in May an. 1634.) he was remitted to his prison: But all this was so far from working any remorse in him, that it rather hardned him in his ways, for on the 11th of June following, as soon as he could provide himself of pen, ink, and paper, he wrote[3] a most sharp and libellous letter to Dr. Laud then archb. of Cant. touching his censure in the said court, and that which the archb. in particular had declared against him. With this letter the archb. acquainted his majesty, who thereupon commanded him to refer it to attorney Noy. Noy sent for Prynne from his prison, and demanded of him, whether the letter was of his own handwriting or not: to which Prynne cunningly replied, that he could make no answer to that demand, unless he could see the letter, and might read the same. No sooner was the letter put into his hands, and Noy's back turn'd a little towards him, but presently he tore it to pieces, and flung the pieces out of the window, to the end that the said letter might not rise in judgment against him, if the attorney should proceed to an ore-tenus, as he meant to do. For this affront, and the principal passages of the letter, the attorney acquaints their lordships in open court, but there was no remedy: for being there was no proof of the misdemeanor but the letter it self, and that the letter could not be brought in evidence as it should have been, the archb. thought it a more noble act to remit the crime, than trouble the court, or any of his majesty's ministers in the prosecution of it. But herein Prynne sped better than some others, who had before been snarling at him, and laboured to expose him to scorn and danger. In Apr. the same year (which is a step back in this discourse) he was solemnly degraded in the univ. of Oxon, and his name dashed out of the *Matricular*. In 1636 he published two books at once, or immediately after each other. One of them was called *The Quench Coal*, in answer to that called A *Coal from the Altar; against placing the Communion-Table Altarwise*. The other named *The Unbishoping of Timothy and Titus, against the Apostolical Institution of Diocesan Bishops*. But that which was entit. to him by the name of a libel, was his pamphlet called *News from Ipswich*, intended chiefly against Dr. Wrenn then bishop of Norwich, who had taken up his dwelling in that town: and fell as scandalously foul on the archb. himself and some of the other bishops also, and such as acted under them in the present service. For therein he descants very trimly (as he conceived) on the archbishop himself with his arch-piety, arch-charity, arch-agent for the devil, &c. With like reproach he fell on the bishops generally, calling them Luciferian lord bishops, execrable traytors, devouring wolves, &c. with many other odious names not fit to be used by a Christian, and more particularly on Wrenn, &c. In midsummer term he was brought to his tryal in the star chamber, for what he had done; but his answer was so libellous and full of scandal, that no counsellor could be found to put his hand to it, according to the course of that court. So that instead thereof he exhibited a cross bill against the archbishop and his confederates, (as he called them) charging them with the greatest part of those reproaches which had been made the subject matter of his former libels: which being signed by no hands but by his own, and tendred so to the lord keeper, was by him rejected, and himself taken pro confesso, his obstinacy in not answering in due form of law, being generally looked upon by the court as a self conviction. On the 14th of June an. 1637, he received his sentence, which briefly was to this effect, that he be fined 5000*l* to the king, to lose the remainder of his ears in the pillory, to be branded on both cheeks with the letters S. L. for a schismatical libeller, and to be perpetually imprison'd in Caernarvan castle. At the pronouncing of which sentence the archb. made a long and elaborate speech in vindication of himself and the rest of the bishops from any design to bring in popery, or innovating in the government and forms of worship, here by law established. On the 30th of the said month the lord's censure was put in execution in the Palace-yard at Westminster; at which time suffer'd also by clipping of ears John Bastwick dr. of physic, not of this, but of another, university; and Hen. Burton, bac. of div. minister of S. Matthew's church in Friday-street in London. On the 27th of July following, our author Prynne was removed from the Tower to the Fleet, and the same day, being guarded, he began his journey towards Caernarvan castle in Wales: from which time till the 5th of Aug. when then he arrived at Caernarvan, he was met, saluted, bless'd and exhibited to, by the godly party in all chief towns that he passed thro'. But such a haunt there was to the said castle when he was there, that for the prevention of all intelligence and correspondence to be held between him and Burton in Lancaster castle, or with the said party, the state found it necessary to remove him to Mount Orgueil castle in the isle of Jersey. So that by virtue of a warrant dated the 27th of Aug. Prynne was conveyed thither, not without great danger, in January following: where being well used, tho' closely shut up, he exercised his pen in writing divine and profitable meditations. In 1640,

Nov. 7. an order issued out from the blessed house of commons (as by the said godly party it was called) for his releasement from his prison, as also for the releasement of Bastwick, who was then in S. Mary's castle in the isle of Scilly, and for Burton in Castle Cornet in the isle of Guernsey. So that our author Prynne and Burton, who were prisoners at no great distance, met together at Guernsey, and travelled in each others company to London: In whose passage thither, divers of the godly party met them at Dartmouth, Exeter, Lime, Dorchester, Salisbury, Andover, Basing, and elsewhere, visited them, blest them, and accompanied them on horse-back, some part of their way. On the 28th of the same month they triumphantly entred London, being then accompanied by thousands on foot, and horse-back, and in coaches, with rosemary and bays in their hats, crying 'Welcome home, welcome home, God bless you, God bethanked for your return,'&c. to the great defiance and contempt of authority and justice. On the 30th of the said month, they were both presented by their keepers, who came with them, to the commons house, where they had liberty granted to frame new petitions in their own names, according to their own liking, and to present them to the house as soon as they could prepare them. The 3d of Dec. following Prynne presented a large petition, fully shewing his sufferings, and the grand tyranny, as he call'd it, of the archbishop, &c. for which afterwards he had[4] a large requital. Not long after, upon the leaving of the house of commons by divers members, purposely to adhere to his majesty, he was elected a recruiter for Newport in Cornwall, to serve in that most unhappy parliament. So that being setled in the house, he became the most busy and pragmatical person of the herd, and so inveterate and implacable against the bishops, but more in an especial manner against Laud in private action and speech with him while he was prisoner in the Tower, in public speeches against him in the parliament-house, and in writing and publishing books and pamphlets of, and against, him, that he could scarce take quiet rest till he had fetch'd off his head, in requital of his ears, that he (as Prynne pretended) had taken off before. But of these matters when it was too late, and that he had fully seen to what great woe, misery and confusion the godly party had brought the king and the nation, he did heartily repent, and wished that when they had cut off his ears they had cut off his head. By order from a close committee he searched archbishop Laud's chamber in the Tower, took away many bundles of papers—— put his hand in the archbishop's pocket lying by his bed side, took away his *Diary* containing all the occurrences of his life; and his *Book of private Devotions*.[5] He was trusted with the providing of all the evidence against Laud at his tryal, and was relator and prompter and all. Never weary of any thing, so that he might do the archb. mischief, &c.[6] During the sitting of the long parliament he shew'd himself a zealous covenanteer in ordering and settling presbytery, but when the independents began to overtop the brethren, he shew'd himself a bitter enemy to them, and advanced much the king's cause, especially in his declension. In 1647 he was appointed one of the visitors for the univ. of Oxon by the said parliament, and how busily he behaved himself there, in Apr. 1648, I have told you elsewhere. See in *Hist. & Antiq. Univ. Oxon.* lib. 1. sub an. 1648. On the 6th of Dec. 1648, he, with other members of the H. of Com. were turn'd out from the house by the army, and imprison'd for that they were zealous for peace and in bringing the king to his parliament. Whereupon he became a bitter enemy to the said army, and Oliver their leader; doing them also much mischief by publishing divers pamphlets against them and their tyranny. Soon after he conveyed his estate away to one or more of his relations, and thereupon denied the paying of taxes, and stood in open defiance to Oliver; for which he was imprison'd in Dunster Castle in Somersetshire, and brought into trouble. He then stood much upon Magna Charta, the liberty of the subject (for which he was beloved by several cavaliers) and I know not what. But all that he did being to little purpose, he bent his mind and pen for some time against the papists, Jews, quakers, &c. and in writing books of divinity; which being not answer'd, or seem'd to be regarded, he grew, as 'twere, weary of himself, began to look up at last, and to settle on more moderate and quiet courses. Mr. Prynne's busy warm temper involved him in many difficulties, as will appear by this list of the places and times of his first imprisonments under his professed enemies the prelates. (1) Tower of London, to which he was committed for his *Histriomastix*, 1 Feb. 1632. (2) The Fleet, when his first sentence for his *Histriomastix* was exerted, 7 May 1634. (3) Tower of London, to which he was committed from the Fleet 1 June 1636. (4) Caernarvan castle in North-Wales, to which by his said sentence he was sent close prisoner to the tower, 5 August 1637. (5) Mount Orgueil castle in the isle of Jersey, where he was closely imprison'd, when remov'd from Caernarvan-Castle 17 Jan. 1637, whence he was sent for and enlarg'd by the parliament, 19 Nov. 1640.

Places and times of his second imprisonments under false brethren and pretended friends. (1) Hell in Westm. by the army officers, for speaking his conscience and discharging his duty in parliament, 6 December, 1648. (2) The Swan in the Strand by the Same officers, for the same cause, Dec. 7. an. 1648. (3) The King's-head in the Strand by the same power and for the same cause, 2 Jan. 1648. (4) Dunster-castle in Somersetshire, where he was close prisoner by a Whitehall warrant under Mr. Jo. Bradshaw's hand, expressing no particular cause, 1 Jul. 1650, which Whitehall warrant was dated 25 Jun. 1650. (5) Taunton castle and the Lamb tavern in Taunton, when remov'd from Taunton, by no particular warrant, 12 Jan. 1650. (6) Pendennis castle in Cornwall, where he remain'd close prisoner by a Whitehall warrant under Mr. Bradshaw's hand, mentioning no cause but Taunton's unfitness to restrain him in, 2 Jul. 1651. On the 21st of Feb. 1659, he, as a secluded member of the commons house, being restored to sit again, became instrumental for the king's restoration, and so forward and bold that he openly spoke in the house, when it was not then seasonable for such expressions, that if the king must come in, it was safest for them that he should come in by the votes, who had made the war against his father, &c. Which I say being then unseasonably spoken, he was sent for by general Monk and his privy counsellors, and admonished to be quiet; and then it was the business of Mr. Will. Morice to keep the then expiring parliament steddy and clear from intermeddling in the change of government; in which case he did excellent service, punctually observing the directions of the general, who passionately longed for their dissolution. In Apr. 1660 he the said Prynne was chose a burgess for the city of Bath to sit in the healing parliament that began at Westm. 25th of the said month; and after his majesty's restoration, he, instead of being made one of the barons of the exchequer, which, as 'tis said, he sought after, was made chief keeper of his maj. records in the Tower of London, with 500*l* per an. salary; (but afterwards much lessened) purposely to employ his head from scribling against the state and bishops. But so it was that he extracting thence several books, did in some of them, particularly in his two tomes of *An exact Chronological Vindication, &c.* endeavour to bring an odium upon the bishops and their function by giving an history in them of the pope's usurpations upon the king and subjects of England and Ireland. In Aug. the same year he was appointed one of the six commissioners for

appeals and regulating the excise; and in the month of Apr. 1661 he was again elected a burgess for Bath to sit in that parl. that began at West. the 8th of May the same year: But in July following being discontented at some proceedings in the house, he published a seditious paper against them entit. *Sundry Reasons tendred to the most honourable House of Peers, &c. against the new intended Bill for governing and reforming Corporations.* This pamphlet coming into the hands of several members of parliament who much complained against it, the house appointed a committee to examine and enquire after the author, the printer and publisher thereof. The committee met and soon found that Prynne was the author of it: And accordingly on the 15th of the said month of July the whole matter was reported to the house: who, thereupon, being highly provok'd, Prynne unable to conceal it any longer (for 'twas proved that he had sent that paper to the printing-house, and that he had corrected the proof sheet and revise with his own hand) he flew to the printing-house and commanded the compositors to distribute the form, for they would be searched. Which being done, Prynne desired to be heard, and (unable to evade the evidence) confessed himself to be the unhappy author. Then speaking largely, setting forth what service he had done for the king formerly, how kind and civil the king had been to him, &c. alledging that he had no mischievous intent, but was sorry for what he had done, and humbly craved their pardon; the house then unanimously called upon him to withdraw, and afterwards proceeded to debate it, and resolved upon the question, that the said printed paper entit. *Sundry Reasons, &c.* is an illegal, false, scandalous, and seditious pamphlet. Prynne afterwards was called in again to receive the sense of the house, which was as aforesaid. Then Mr. speaker (sir Edw. Turner) worthily told him, how sorry he was that a person of his years and experience should commit so foul an offence, and one that had formerly much, and yet now deserved to suffer all his punishments over again, as imprisonment, pillory, &c. But the house had considered his late services and hazards for his majesty, and in contemplation of them, and his expressions of his sorrow, (which truly seemed very great) the house shewed mercy unto him. Prynne then did thankfully acknowledge the justice of the house in their judgment of his great offence, that the said paper was an illegal, false, scandalous and seditious pamphlet, that he did humbly submit thereunto, and did render most humble thanks to the house and every member thereof for their mercy and favour to him: which words he spake with great sense of his own offence, and the house's goodness, not offering to justify the least line of his paper, which his conscience told him he could not. Whereupon the house being satisfied with his confession and recantation, they did remit his offence, and Prynne sat down in his place. From which time to the day of his death we heard of no more libels publish'd by him. The books and little pamphlets that he wrote, were theological, historical, political, controversial, &c. but very few of his own profession: all which are in number near 200, as the titles following shew, bound up in about 40 volumes in fol. and qu. in Linc. inn library: To which an eminent[7] sage of the law, who had little respect for those published in his time, promised to give the works of John Taylor the water-poet to accompany them. 'Twas not only he, but many others afterwards, especially royalists, that judged his books to be worth little or nothing, his proofs for no arguments, and affirmations for no testimonies, having several forgeries made in them for his and the ends of his brethren. They are all in the English tongue, and by the generality of scholars are looked upon to be rather rapsodical and confus'd, than any way polite or concise, yet for antiquaries, critics, and sometimes for divines, they are useful. In most of them he shews great industry, but little judgment, especially in his large folios against the pope's usurpations. He may be well intituled Voluminous Prynne, as Tostatus Albulensis was 200 years before his time called Voluminous Tostatus: for I verily believe, that if rightly computed, he wrote a sheet for every day of his life, reckoning from the time when he came to the use of reason and the state of man. His custom when he studied was to put on a long quilted cap which came an inch over his eyes, serving as an umbrella to defend them from too much light, and seldom eating a dinner, would every 3 hours or more be maunching a roll of bread, and now and then refresh his exhausted spirits with ale brought to him by his servant.

> Thou that with ale, or viler liquors,
> Did'st inspire Wythers, Prynne, and Vicars,
> And teach, though it were in despight
> Of nature and the stars, to write, &c.

Thus *Hudibras*, part 1.—He was a right sturdy and doughty champion for the cause, a puritan beautifew, an inveterate enemy against the hierarchy of bishops, especially upon his imprisonment and sufferings for his *Histrio-mastix*, a busy, pragmatical and meddling man without end, and one that had brought his body into an ill habit, and so consequently had shortned his days, by too much action and concernment day and night. M. Needham the weathercock tells[8] us, that he was one of the greatest paper worms that ever crept into a closet or library, &c. and others that he never intended an end in writing books, and that his study or reading was not only a wearisomness to the flesh, but to the ears: Nay a printed petition, whereby some wags, under the name of the peaceable and well-affected people of the three nations, did shew that whereas Will. Prynne bencher of Lincoln's-inn, had for many years last past (reckoning backward from 1659, in which year the said petition was published) been an indefatigable and impertinent scribler, and had almost nauseated the sober part of the said nations with the stench of his carion pasquils and pamphlets, for some whereof he had suffered under the hierarchy in the time of the late king, &c. that he might have an act of amnesty and pardon for all his treasons, seditions, Jesuitismes, contempts of government, misunderstanding of the scriptures, law and reason, misquotations and misapplications of authorities to his pasquils, &c. Which petition I say being published, and cried in Westm. hall and about London streets, did so extreamly perplex Prynne for a time, that he became in a manner craz'd. To conclude: I must now let the reader know, that there was no writer of his time, nor ever before, except Bale, that was given more to calumny and railing in his writings than he, especially against the bishops, true churchmen of England, episcoparians and papists, while in the mean time his brethren that deserved justly to be chastised by his pen, were omitted. As for his railing at the episcoparians, all readers of his books pen'd against Dr. Laud and the bishops may in a plentiful manner behold; and what he says against the papists, let it be truth or not truth, may also in them be easily discern'd. But for these last, the papists, let one of their[9] number, who is a grave writer, characterize our author Prynne for an egregious lye that he hath committed against a red-letter'd-man and against the English papists, when he would have them all massacred in 1666.—'Yet of late this poysonous humour of calumniating God's saints is become the principal character of the new reformed gospel. I will add one example more of a calumniator, at least parallel to these; viz. Mr. Will. Prynne a late stigmatized presbyterian, who in his not long since published censure of archb. Whitgift, charges S. Anselme[10] that he induced

sir Walt. Tyrrell to murder king Will. Rufus. Now by the consent of all historians, Tyrrell himself was no murderer, for it was by the unhappy casual glancing of an arrow that the king was slain. However it hapned, yet certain it is that at that time S. Anselme was an exil'd person in France: and whereas at the king's burial many noble-men met, but few mourn'd for his death, yet saith a late protestant[11] historian, of all mourners Anselme expressed most cordial sorrow at the news. That blasphemous tongue therefore must expect that such envenomed darts as these, shot against heaven it self, will, if he repent not, one day descend upon his own head, and the wounds made by them never be cured. But alas, what repentance can be expected in such a person who is inveteratus dierum malorum, when we see in his decrepit age his rancorous tongue against innocent catholics yet more violently set on fire of hell, so far as to solicite a general massacre of them by publishing himself, and tempting others to damn their souls also, by publishing through the whole kingdom that in the last fatal calamity by fire, hapning to London, (1666) they were the only incendiaries. This he did, tho' himself at the same time confessed that not the least proof could be produced against them: But, said he, it concerns us, that this report should be believed. Complaints of this most execrable attentate were made, and several oaths to confirm this were offer'd; but in vain. However surely there is a reward for the innocent oppressed. And whatsoever Mr. Prynne may think, doubtless there is a God who judges the world. Let him therefore remember what the spirit of God says, Quid detur, What must be given to thee, and what must be assigned to thee for thy portion, O deceitful tongue? Sharp darts cast by an almighty arm with devouring coals of juniper,' &c. . . . As for our voluminous author William Prynne, he died in his lodgings in Lincolns-Inn on the 24th of October in sixteen hundred sixty and nine, and was buried in the walk under the chappel there, which stands upon pillars. Over whose grave, tho' there is no epitaph, only his name and obit, which are now worn out, yet I shall venture to give you this epitaph that was then made upon him.

> Here lies the corps of William Prynne,
> A bencher late of Lincolns-Inn,
> Who restless ran through thick and thin.
> This grand scripturient paper-spiller,
> This endless, needless margin-filler,
> Was strangely tost from post to pillar.
> His brains career were never stopping,
> But pen with rheume of gall still dropping,
> Till hand o'er head brought ears to cropping.
> Nor would he yet surcease such theams,
> But prostitute new virgin-reams
> To types of his fanatic dreams.
> But whilst he this hot humour hugs,
> And for more length of tedder tugs,
> Death fang'd the remnant of his lugs.

Notes

1. In his *Life of William Archb. of Cant*. part 1. lib. 3. an. 1632.
2. Bulstr. Whitlock in his *Memorials of English Affairs*, under the year 1632.
3. In the *Life of William*, &c. as before part 1. lib. 4.
4. See Prynne's book entit. A *new Discovery of the Prelate's Tyranny*, p. 141. and elsewhere.
5. *Hist. of the Troubles and Tryal of Archb. Laud*, cap. 16. p. 205, 206.
6. Ibid. cap. 21. p. 216.
7. Will. Noy of Linc. inn attorn. gen.

8. In *Merc. Pol.* nu. 7.
9. Ser. Cressy in his *Church Hist. of Britanny*, book 14. chap. 4. p. 321.

10. See also in *Prynne's Antipathy of the English Lordly Prelacy*, &c. part 1. p. 10.
11. Thom. Fuller in his *Ch. Hist.* lib. 3. sect. 40.

SIR JOHN DENHAM

1615–1669

Of English parents, John Denham was born in Dublin in 1615. He attended Trinity College, Oxford, from 1631 to 1634. He read law at Lincoln's Inn, London, and was called to the bar in 1639. Denham succeeded to the family estate at Egham, Surrey, in 1638. A Royalist supporter, he aided in the unsuccessful defense of Farnham Castle in 1643. After a brief imprisonment Denham traveled to the Continent where he lived intermittently with the exiled court during most of the Commonwealth. In 1660 Denham returned to England permanently, and was appointed Surveyor-General of Works. He was criticized for his lack of architectural expertise, but he remained in office until his death. In 1661 Denham was knighted and he served until 1669 as the member of Parliament for Old Sarum.

Denham's best-known work, *Cooper's Hill* (1642), is a long topographical poem set near his Egham home. In 1641 his blank verse tragedy about the Turkish court, *The Sophy*, was staged. Denham is also responsible for a paraphrase translation of portions of the *Aeneid*. His other translations include *Of Prudence* and *Of Justice*, verse paraphrases of works by the Italian poet Mancini, and *Cato Major*, based on a work of Cicero. Towards the end of his life Denham completed Katherine Philips's unfinished play, *Horace* (1668), and wrote the poem "On Mr. Abraham Cowley's Death." Denham became ill in 1666, and briefly was confined to a mental asylum. Rumors that his young wife, his second spouse, was the mistress of the Duke of York, supposedly brought on Denham's fits of jealousy. He recovered after his wife's death in 1667, but he died shortly thereafter on March 10, 1669. He was buried in Westminster Abbey.

Personal

Sir John Denham was unpolished with the smallpox: otherwise a fine complexion. He was of the tallest, but a little incurvetting at his shoulders, not very robust. His haire was but thin and flaxen, with a moist curle. His gate was slow, and was rather a Stalking (he had long legges.) His Eie was a kind of light goose-gray, not big; but it had a strange Piercingness, not as to shining and glory, but (like a Momus) when he conversed with you he look't into your very thoughts.

He was admitted of Trinity Colledge in Oxford: I have heard Mr. Josias Howe say that he was the dreamingst young fellow; he never expected such things from him as he haz left the world. When he was there he would Game extremely; when he had played away all his money he would play away his Father's wrought rich gold Cappes. He was as good a Student as any in the House. Was not suspected to be a Witt.

He was much rooked by Gamesters, and fell acquainted with that unsanctified Crew, to his ruine. His father had some suspition of it, and chid him severely, wherupon his son John (only child) wrot a little Essay, *Against Gameing, and to shew the Vanities and Inconveniences of it*, which he presented to his father to let him know his detestation of it. But shortly after his Father's death (who left 2000 or 1500 pounds in ready money, 2 houses well furnished, and much plate) the money was played away first, and next the plate was sold. I remember about 1646 he lost 200 pound one night at New-cutt.

He was generally temperate as to drinking; but one time when he was a Student of Lincolne's-Inne, having been merry at the Taverne with his Camerades, late at night, a frolick came into his head, to gett a playsterer's brush and a pott of Inke, and blott out all the Signes between Temple-barre and Charing-crosse, which made a strange confusion the next day, and 'twas in Terme time. But it happened that they were discovered, and it cost him and them some moneys. This I had from R. Estcott, Esq., that carried the Inke-pott.

At last, viz. 1640, his Play of The Sophy came out, which did take extremely. Mr. Edmund Waller sayd then of him, that he *broke-out like the Irish Rebellion: three score thousand strong*, before any body was aware.

At the beginning of the Civill Warre he was made Governor of Farnham Castle for the King, but he was but a young Soldier, and did not keepe it. In 1643, after Edgehill fight, his Poeme called *Cowper's-hill* was printed at Oxford, in a sort of browne paper, for then they could gett no better.

1647 he conveyed, or stole away the two Dukes of Yorke and Glocester from St. James's (from the Tuition of the Earle of Northumberland) and conveyed them into France to the Prince of Wales and Queen-mother.

Anno 1652, he returned into England, and being in some straights was kindly entertayned by the Earle of Pembroke at Wilton, where I had the honour to contract an acquaintance with him. He was, as I remember, a yeare with my Lord of Pembroke at Wilton and London; he had then sold all the Lands his Father had left him.

The parsonage-house at Egham (vulgarly called The Place) was built by Baron Denham; a house very convenient, not great, but pretty, and pleasantly scituated, and in which his son, Sir John, (though he had better seates) did take most delight in. He sold it to John Thynne, Esq. In this parish is a place called Cammomill-hill, from the Cammomill that growes there naturally; as also west of it is Prune-well-hill (formerly part of Sir John's possessions) where was a fine Tuft of Trees, a clear Spring, and a pleasant prospect to the East, over the levell of Middlesex and Surrey. Sir John tooke great delight in this place, and was wont to say (before the troubles) that he would build there a Retiring-place to entertaine his muses; but the warres forced him to sell that as well as the rest. He sold it to Mr. Anstey. In this parish W. and by N. (above Runney-Meade) is Cowper's Hill, from whence is a noble prospect, which is incomparably well described by that Sweet Swan, Sir John Denham.

In the time of the Civill-warres, George Withers, the Poet, begged Sir John Denham's Estate at Egham of the Parliament, in whose cause he was a Captaine of Horse. It happened that G. W. was taken prisoner, and was in danger of his Life, having written severely against the King, &c. Sir John Denham went to the King, and desired his Majestie not to hang him, for that *whilest G. W. lived, he should not be the worst Poet in England.*

He was much beloved by King Charles the first, who much valued him for his ingenuity. He graunted him the reversion of the Surveyor of His Majestie's buildings, after the decease of Mr. Inigo Jones; which place, after the restauration of King Charles II he enjoyed to his death, and gott seaven thousand pounds, as Sir Christopher Wren told me of, to his owne knowledge. Sir Christopher Wren was his Deputie.

He burlesqued Virgil, and burnt it, sayeing that 'twas not fitt that the best Poet should be so abused. In the verses against *Gondibert*, most of them are Sir John's. He was satyricall when he had a mind to it.

His first wife was the daughter and heire of Mr. Cotton of Glocestershire, by whom he had 500 pounds per annum, one son, and two daughters.

He maried his 2nd wife, Margaret Brookes, a very beautifull young lady: Sir John was ancient and limping. The Duke of Yorke fell deeply in love with her (though I have been morally assured he never had any carnall knowledge of her). This occasioned Sir John's distemper of madness, which first appeared when he went from London to see the famous Free-stone quarries at Portland in Dorset, and when he came within a mile of it, turned back to London again, and did not see it. He went to Hounslowe, and demanded rents of Lands he had sold many yeares before; went to the King, and told him he was the Holy Ghost. But it pleased God that he was cured of this distemper, and writt excellent verses (particularly on the death of Mr. Abraham Cowley) afterwards. His 2nd lady had no child: was poysoned by the hands of the Countess of Rochester, with Chocolatte.—JOHN AUBREY, "Sir John Denham," *Brief Lives*, 1669–96

John Denham the only son of sir John Denham knight, sometime chief baron of the Exchequer in, and one of the lords justices or commissioners of, Ireland, by Eleanor his wife one of the daughters of sir Garret More knight, sometime baron of Mellifont in that kingdom, was born within the city of Dublin, but being brought thence very young, at what time his father was made one of the barons of the Exchequer in England, an. 1617, he was educated in grammar learning either in London or Westminster, and being made full ripe for the university, was sent to Trinity coll. where he became a gent. com. in Michaelm. term, an. 1631, aged 16 years. But being looked upon as a slow and dreaming young man by his seniors and contemporaries, and given more to cards and dice, than his study, they could never then in the least imagine, that he could ever inrich the world with his fancy, or issue of his brain, as he afterwards did. From Trin. coll. where he continued about three years, and had been examined in the public schools for the degree of bach. of arts, he went to Lincolns inn, where tho'

he followed his study very close to the appearance of all persons, yet he would game much, and frequent the company of the unsanctified crew of gamesters, who rook'd him sometimes of all he could wrap or get. But his father having received notice of these matters, took him severely to task, with many threatenings to cast him off, if he did not forbear from so doing. Whereupon he wrote a little *Essay against Gaming*, shewing the vanities and inconveniences, which he presented to his father to let him know his detestation, of it. After his father's death, (who died 6 Jan. 1638, and was buried in Egham church in Surrey) he fell to gaming again, and shortly after squandred away several thousands of pounds that were left him, &c. In the latter end of the year 1641 he published the tragedy called *The Sophy*, which took extremely much and was admired by all ingenious men, particularly by Edm. Waller of Beaconsfield, who then said of the author, that he broke out like the Irish rebellion, threescore thousand strong, when no body was aware, or in the least suspected it. Shortly after he was prick'd high sheriff for Surrey, and made governour of Farnham-castle for the king: But he being an inexpert soldier, soon after left that office, and retired to his maj. at Oxon, where he printed his poem called *Cooper's-Hill*: which hill is in the parish of Egham in Surrey above Runey Mead, hath a very noble prospect, and the author of it from thence doth admirably well describe several places in his view there, which he mentions in that most celebrated poem. In "April" 1648, he conveyed or stole away, James duke of York from S. James's in Westminster, then under the tuition of Algernon earl of Northumberland, and carried him into France to the prince of Wales and the qu. mother, and not long after was sent with William (afterwards lord) Crofts as envoies to the king of Poland by the said prince, then king Charles 2. In 1652 or thereabouts, he return'd into England, and being in some streights (for by gaming and the war he had squandred away much of his estate at Egham and elsewhere, and the rest ordered to be sold by the parliament 15 July 1651) he was kindly entertain'd by the earl of Pembroke at Wilton; where, and sometimes at London, he continued with that count more than a year: In which time he did translate one of *Virgil's Æneids* and burlesqu'd it, but whether he ever publish'd it, I know not. King Charles 1. did grant to him the reversion of the place of surveyor of his buildings after the decease of Inigo Jones: Which place he entring upon at the restoration of king Charles 2, an. 1660 (for the said Jones died 21 July 1651, aged 79 years or thereabouts, and was buried in the church of S. Bennet near to Pauls-wharf in London) he enjoyed it to the time of his death, and got by it 7000*l.* In the year following he was made knight of the Bath at the coronation of king Charles 2. and became much renown'd in the court of that king for his ingenuity; but upon some discontent arising from a second match, he became craz'd for a time, and so consequently contemptible among vain fops. Soon after being cured of his distemper, he wrote excellent verses on the death of Abr. Cowley the prince of poets, and some months after followed him.—ANTHONY À WOOD, *Athenae Oxonienses*, 1691–1721

General

Or lookt I back unto the Times hence flown,
To praise those Muses, and dislike our own?
Or did I walk those *Pean*-Gardens through,
To kick the Flow'rs, and scorn their odours too?
I might (and justly) be reputed (here)
One nicely mad, or peevishly severe.
But by *Apollo!* as I worship wit,

(Where I have cause to burn perfumes to it:)
So, I confesse, 'tis somwhat to do well
In our high art, although we can't excell,
Like thee; or dare the Buskins to unloose
Of thy brave, bold, and sweet *Maronian* Muse.
But since I'm cal'd (rare *Denham*) to be gone,
Take from thy *Herrick* this conclusion:
'Tis dignity in others, if they be
Crown'd Poets; yet live Princes under thee:
The while their wreaths and Purple Robes do shine,
Lesse by their own jemms, then those beams of thine.

> —ROBERT HERRICK, "To M. *Denham*, on His
> Prospective Poem" (c. 1642), *Hesperides*, 1648

A Poet of the first Form, whose Virtue and Memory will ever be as dear to all Lovers of Poetry, as his Person was to Majesty it self; I mean, King *Charles* the First, and Second.

. . . ⟨H⟩is Works . . . consist of Poems, part of which are Translations; as *The Destruction of Troy*, an *Essay on the Second Book of* Virgil's *Æneis*, *The Passion of* Dido *for Æneas*, being the later part of the Fourth Book; *Sarpedon's Speech to Glaucus*, being part of the Twelfth Book of *Homer*; Two Pieces from the Italian of *Mancini*, upon the two first Cardinal Virtues, *Prudence*, and *Justice*, &c. Others, are his own Productions, amongst which his *Coopers Hill* is most commended; *A Poem, which* (in the Opinion of Mr. *Dryden*, who is without contradiction a very able Judge in Poetry) *for the Majesty of the Stile, is, and ever will be, the exact Standard of good Writing*. His Verses on Sir *William Fanshaw's* Translation of *Il Pastor Fido*, and his Preface to the Destruction of Troy, shew sufficiently his Judgment, and his Translations themselves his Genius, for Performances of that nature: and admitting it true, that few Versions deserve praise; yet *His* are to be excepted from the general Rule. His Elegy on Mr. *Cowley*, (part of which we have transcribed already in the Account of that great Man), will make his Name famous to Posterity: and there wants nothing to eternise his Name, but a Pen equal to his, (if any such were to be found) to perform the like Friendly office to his *Manes*.

He has writ but one Play, but by that Specimen we may judge of his ability in Dramatick, as well as Epick Poesy; this Play being generally commended. 'Tis call'd *The Sophy*, a Tragedy, acted at the Private-house in *Black-friars* with good applause: 'Twas first printed in quarto *Lond.* 1642. but since publisht with his Poems and Translations; all which are dedicated to King *Charles* the Second. The last Edition being printed in octavo *Lond.* 1671. For the Plot of this Play, it is the same with that of *Baron's Mirza*, (which Story you may find in *Herberts Travels*) tho' differently handled by each Poet: and tho' it has been objected by Mr. *Baron*, that our Author kills *Abbas* in this Tragedy, who really surviv'd some years after the Murther of his Son; it may be answer'd, That he did only Poetical Justice, and took no other Liberty than what is allow'd by *Horace*: Pictoribus atque Poetis Quidlibet audendi semper suit æqua Potestas.—GERARD LANGBAINE, *An Account of the English Dramatick Poets*, 1691

Denham was the first writer to adopt the precise manner of versification introduced by Waller. His relation to that poet resembles that taken a century later by Mason with respect to Gray, but Denham is a more original writer than Mason. The names of Waller and Denham were first associated by Dryden, and the critics of the next sixty years were unanimous in eulogizing the sweetness of the one, and the strength of the other. It is quite true that the versification of Denham is vigorous; it proceeds with greater volume than that of Waller, and produces a stronger impression. But he is a very unequal and irregular writer, and not unfrequently descends to doggerel, and very dull doggerel too. His literary taste was superior to his genius; he knew what effect he desired to produce, and strove to conquer the difficulties of antithesis, but the result of his effort was rarely classic. He takes the same place in English poetry as is taken in French by Chapelain and other hard versifiers of the beginning of the seventeenth century, who had lost the romantic fervour and had not yet gained the classic grace. But, like those poets, he has his fine flashes of style.—EDMUND GOSSE, "Sir John Denham," *The English Poets*, ed. Thomas Humphry Ward, 1880, Vol. 2, p. 279

Works

THE SOPHY

The Sophy on its production met with extraordinary praise. Its celebrity is no doubt attributable in part to the impressive character of its versification. Denham's 'majesty' and 'strength' are acknowledged by Dryden and by Pope; and in these respects *The Sophy* is worthy of the poet of *Cooper's Hill*. But the more immediate success of this tragedy must have been chiefly due to the management of the action, which Denham had derived from the *Travels of Sir Thomas Herbert* (1634). The central situation of the plot is extremely pathetic in character. The machinations of Haly, the villainous favourite of Abbas, King of Persia, induce that monarch to imprison his noble son Merza, and to have his eyes put out. Half-maddened by his injuries, the Prince is about to revenge himself on his father by taking the life of his own little daughter, Fatyma, when he is recalled to his better self by the child's appeal to the love of her mother, his faithful wife, Erythaea. The Prince is poisoned by the intriguer, at the moment when deliverance is at hand, and the King dies haunted by the memory of his many crimes—while the task of wreaking vengeance upon the villainous Haly is left to the youthful Sophy, Prince Merza's son.

The style of this production is rhetorical, but sustained; its value was overrated by Denham's contemporaries, but it is certainly one of the best tragedies of its time, and had doubtless been produced under the inspiration of worthy models. In the political wisdom which it teaches in one of its most striking scenes, something nobler than party spirit reveals itself; and a lesson is enforced deserving the attention both of kings and of rebels who misuse religion as an instrument or as a pretext.—ADOLPHUS WILLIAM WARD, *A History of English Dramatic Literature* (1875), 1899, Vol. 3, pp. 148–49

COOPER'S HILL

Th⟨e⟩ sweetness of Mr. *Wallers* Lyrick Poesie was afterwards follow'd in the Epick by Sir *John Denham*, in his *Coopers-Hill*: a Poem which your Lordship knows for the Majesty of the Style, is, and ever will be the exact Standard of good Writing.—JOHN DRYDEN, Dedication to *The Rival Ladies*, 1664

> he whose Song rais'd *Cooper's Hill* so high,
>   As made its Glory with Parnassus vie.

> —SIR JOHN OLDHAM, "A Pastoral on the Death
> of the Earl of Rochester," c. 1684

Nor, Denham, must we e'er forget thy strains,
While *Cooper's Hill* commands the neighb'ring plains.

> —JOSEPH ADDISON, "An Account of the Greatest
> English Poets," 1694

Ye sacred Nine! that all my Soul possess,
Whose Raptures fire me, and whose Visions bless,

Bear me, oh bear me to sequester'd Scenes,
The Bow'ry Mazes and surrounding Greens;
To *Thames's* Banks which fragrant Breezes fill,
Or where ye Muses sport on *Cooper's* Hill.

(On *Cooper's* Hill eternal Wreaths shall grow,
While lasts the Mountain, or while *Thames* shall flow)
I seem thro' consecrated Walks to rove,
I hear soft Musick dye along the Grove;
Led by the Sound I roam from Shade to Shade,
By God-like Poets Venerable made:
Here his first Lays Majestick *Denham* sung;
There the last Numbers flow'd from *Cowley's* Tongue.
O early lost! what Tears the River shed
When the sad Pomp along his Banks was led?
His drooping Swans on ev'ry Note expire,
And on his Willows hung each Muse's Lyre.

—ALEXANDER POPE, *Windsor-Forest*, 1713

Sir John Denham, in his *Cooper's Hill*, (for none of his other poems merit attention), has a loftiness and vigour which had not before him been attained by any English poet who wrote in rhyme. The mechanical difficulties of that measure retarded its improvement. Shakspeare, whose tragic scenes are sometimes so wonderfully forcible and expressive, is a very indifferent poet when he attempts to rhyme. Precision and neatness are chiefly wanting in Denham.—DAVID HUME, *History of England*, 1754–62

This poem, by Denham, though it may have been exceeded by later attempts in description, yet deserves the highest applause, as it far surpasses all that went before it: the concluding part, though a little too much crowded is very masterly.—OLIVER GOLDSMITH, *The Beauties of English Poetry*, 1767

The plan is original, as far as our poetry is concerned: and I do not recollect any exception in other languages. Placing himself upon an eminence not distant from Windsor, he takes a survey of the scene; he finds the tower of St. Paul's on its farthest horizon, the Castle much nearer, and the Thames at his feet. These, with the ruins of an abbey, supply, in turn, materials for a reflecting rather than imaginative mind, and, with a stag-hunt, which he has very well described, fill up the canvas of a poem of no great length, but once of no trifling reputation. The epithet, *majestic* Denham, conferred by Pope, conveys rather too much; but *Cooper's Hill* is no ordinary poem. It is nearly the first instance of vigorous and rhythmical couplets; for Denham is incomparably less feeble than Browne, and less prosaic than Beaumont. Close in thought, and nervous in language like Davies, he is less hard and less monotonous; his cadences are animated and various, perhaps a little beyond the regularity that metre demands; they have been the guide to the finer ear of Dryden. Those who cannot endure the philosophic poetry must ever be dissatisfied with *Cooper's Hill*; no personification, no ardent words, few metaphors beyond the common use of speech, nothing that warms or melts or fascinates the heart. It is rare to find lines of eminent beauty in Denham; and equally so to be struck by any one as feeble or low. His language is always well chosen and perspicuous, free from those strange turns of expression, frequent in our older poets, where the reader is apt to suspect some error of the press, so irreconcilable do they seem with grammar or meaning.—HENRY HALLAM, *Introduction to the Literature of Europe*, 1837–39, Pt. 3, Ch. 5, Pars. 36–37

Cooper's Hill may be considered as belonging in point of composition to the same school with Sir John Davies's *Nosce Teipsum*; and, if it has not all the concentration of that poem, it is equally pointed, correct, and stately, with, partly owing to the subject, a warmer tone of imagination and feeling, and a fuller swell of verse. The spirit of the same classical style pervades both; and they are the two greatest poems in that style which had been produced down to the date at which we are now arrived.—GEORGE L. CRAIK, *A Compendious History of English Literature and of the English Language*, 1861, Vol. 2, p. 33

His best poem, *Cooper's Hill*, is the description of a hill and its surroundings, blended with the historical ideas which the sight recalls, and the moral reflections which its appearance naturally suggests. All these subjects are in accordance with the nobility and the limitation of the classical spirit, and display his vigor without betraying his weaknesses; the poet could show off his whole talent without forcing it. His fine language exhibits all its beauty, because it is sincere. We find pleasure in following the regular progress of those copious passages in which his ideas, opposed or combined, attain for the first time their definite place and full clearness, where symmetry only brings out the argument more clearly, expansion only completes thought, antithesis and repetition do not induce trifling and affectation, where the music of the verse, adding the breadth of sound to the fulness of sense, conducts the chain of ideas, without effort or disorder, by an appropriate measure to a becoming order and movement. Gratification is united with solidity; the author of *Cooper's Hill* knows how to please as well as to impress. His poem is like a king's park, dignified and level without doubt, but arranged for the pleasure of the sight, and full of choice prospects. It leads us by easy digressions across a multitude of varied thoughts. It shows us here a mountain, yonder a memorial of the nymphs, a classic memorial, like a portico filled with statues, further on a wide river-course, and by its side the ruins of an abbey; each page of the poem is like a distinct alley, with its distinct perspective. Further on, our thoughts are turned to the superstitions of the ignorant middle-ages, and to the excesses of the recent revolution; then comes the picture of a royal hunt; we see the trembling stag brought to a stand in the midst of the leaves:

He calls to mind his strength, and then his speed,
His winged heels, and then his armed head;
With these t' avoid, with that his fate to meet;
But fear prevails, and bids him trust his feet.
So fast he flies, that his reviewing eye
Has lost the chasers, and his ear the cry.

These are the worthy spectacles and the studied diversity of the grounds of a nobleman. Every object, moreover, receives here, as in a king's palace, all the adornment which can be given to it; elegant epithets are introduced to embellish a feeble substantive; the decorations of art transform the commonplace of nature: vessels are "floating towers;" the Thames is the most loved of all the Ocean's sons; the airy mountain hides its proud head among the clouds, whilst a shady mantle clothes its sides. Among different kinds of ideas, there is one kingly, full of stately and magnificent ceremonies, of self-contained and studied gestures, of correct yet commanding figures, uniform and imposing like the appointments of a palace; hence the classic writers, and Denham amongst them, draw all their poetic tints. From this every object and circumstance takes its coloring, because constrained to come into contact with it. Here the object and circumstances are compelled to traverse other things. Denham is not a mere courtier, he is an Englishman; that is, preoccupied by moral emotions. He often quits his landscape to enter into some grave reflection; politics, religion, come to disturb the enjoyment of his eyes; in reference to a hill or a forest, he meditates upon man; externals lead him inward; impressions of the senses to contemplations of the soul. The men of this race are by nature and custom esoteric. When he sees the Thames throw itself into the sea, he compares it with "mortal life hasting to meet eternity." The face of a mountain, beaten by storms, reminds him of "the common fate of all that's high or great." The course of the river suggests to him ideas of inner reformation:

> O could I flow like thee! and make thy stream
> My great example, as it is my theme!
> Though deep, yet clear, though gentle yet not dull;
> Strong without rage, without o'erflowing, full.

> But his proud head the airy mountain hides
> Among the clouds; his shoulders and his sides
> A shady mantle clothes; his curled brows
> Frown on the gentle stream, which calmly flows;
> While winds and storms his lofty forehead beat,
> The common fate of all that's high or great.

There is in the English mind an indestructible stock of moral instincts, and grand melancholy; and it is the greatest confirmation of this, that we can discover such a stock at the court of Charles II.—HIPPOLYTE TAINE, *History of English Literature*, tr. H. Van Laun, 1871, Vol. 1, Bk. 3, Ch. 1

THEOPHILUS CIBBER
From "Sir John Denham"
The Lives of the Poets
1753, Volume 3, pp. 1–6

An eminent poet of the 17th century, was the only son of Sir John Denham, knight, of Little Horsley in Essex, and some time baron of the Exchequer in Ireland, and one of the lords justices of that kingdom. He was born in Dublin, in the year 1615; but was brought over from thence very young, on his father's being made one of the barons of the Exchequer in England 1617.

He received his education, in grammar learning, in London; and in Michaelmas term 1631 he was entered a gentleman commoner in Trinity College, Oxford, being then 16 years of age; where, as Wood expresses it, 'being looked upon as a slow dreaming young man, and more addicted to gaming than study, they could never imagine he could ever enrich the world with the issue of his brain, as he afterwards did.'

He remained three years at the university, and having been examined at the public schools, for the degree of bachelor of arts, he entered himself in Lincoln's Inn, where he was generally thought to apply himself pretty closely to the study of the common law. But notwithstanding his application to study, and all the efforts he was capable of making, such was his propensity to gaming, that he was often stript of all his money; and his father severely chiding him, and threatning to abandon him if he did not reform, he wrote a little essay against that vice, and presented it to his father, to convince him of his resolution against it. But no sooner did his father die, than being unrestrained by paternal authority, he reassumed the practice, and soon squandered away several thousand pounds.

In the latter end of the year 1641 he published a tragedy called the *Sophy*, which was greatly admired, and gave Mr. Waller occasion to say of our author, 'That he broke out like the Irish rebellion, threescore thousand strong, when no body was aware, nor in the least expected it.' Soon after this he was pricked for high sheriff for the county of Surry, and made governor of Farnham-Castle for the King; but not being well skilled in military affairs, he soon quitted the post and retired to

his Majesty at Oxford, where he published an excellent poem called *Cooper's-hill*, often reprinted before and since the restoration, with considerable alterations; it has been universally admired by all good judges, and was translated into Latin verse, by Mr. Moses Pengry of Oxford. . . .

In the year 1647 he was entrusted by the Queen with a message to the King, then in the hands of the army, and employed in other affairs relating to his Majesty. In his dedication of his poems to Charles II. he observes, that after the delivery of the person of his royal father into the hands of the army, he undertook for the Queen-mother, to get access to his Majesty, which he did by means of Hugh Peters; and upon this occasion, the King discoursed with him without reserve upon the state of his affairs. At his departure from Hampton-court, says he, 'The King commanded me to stay privately in London, to send to him and receive from him all his letters, from and to all his correspondents, at home and abroad, and I was furnished with nine several cyphers in order to it. Which I trust I performed with great safety to the persons with whom we corresponded; but about nine months after being discovered by their knowledge of Mr. Cowley's hand, I happily escaped both for myself and those who held correspondence with me.

In April 1648 he conveyed away James duke of York, then under the tuition of Algernon earl of Northumberland, from St. James's, and carried him into France, to the prince of Wales and Queen-mother. This circumstance is related by Wood, but Clarendon, who is a higher authority, says, that the duke went off with colonel Bamfield only, who contrived the means of his escape. Not long after, he was sent embassador to the King of Poland, in conjunction with lord Crofts, to whom he addresses a poem written on their journey; from whence he brought ten thousand pounds for his Majesty, by the decimation of his Scottish subjects there.

About the year 1652, he returned into England, and was well received by the earl of Pembroke at Wilton, and continued with that nobleman about a year; for his own fortune by the expence he was at during the civil war, and his unconquerable itch of gaming was quite exhausted. From that year to the restoration, there are no accounts of our author; but as soon as his Majesty returned, he entered upon the office of surveyor of his Majesty's buildings, in the room of Inigo Jones, deceased; and at the coronation of King Charles II. was created a knight of the Bath. Upon some discontent arising from his second marriage he lost his senses, but soon recovering from that disorder, he continued in great esteem at court for his poetical writings. In the dedication of his poems to King Charles II. he tells us that he had been discouraged by King Charles I. from writing verses.

> One morning (says he) when I was waiting upon the King at Causham, smiling upon me, he said he could tell me some news of myself, which was that he had seen some verses of mine the evening before (being those to Sir Robert Fanshaw) and asking me when I made them, I told him two or three years since; he was pleased to say, that having never seen them before, he was afraid I had written them since my return into England; and though he liked them well he would advise me to write no more: alledging, that when men are young, and having little else to do, they might vent the over-flowings of their fancy that way, but when they were thought fit for more serious employments, if they still persisted in that course, it would look as if they minded not the way to any better; whereupon I stood corrected as long as I had the honour to wait upon him.

This is a strong instance of his duty to the King; but no great compliment to his Majesty's taste: nor was the public much obliged to the Monarch for this admonition to our author.

But King Charles II. being of an humour more sprightly than his father, was a professed encourager of poetry, and in his time a race of wits sprung up, unequalled by those of any other reign.

This monarch was particularly delighted with the poetry of our author, especially when he had the happiness to wait upon him, in Holland and Flanders; and he was pleased sometimes to give him arguments to write upon, and divert the evil hours of their banishment, which now and then, Sir John tells us, he acquitted himself not much short of his Majesty's expectation.

In the year 1688 Sir John Denham died, at his office in Whitehall, and was interred in Westminster-Abbey, near the tombs of Chaucer, Spenser, and Cowley.

SAMUEL JOHNSON
"Denham"
Lives of the English Poets
1779–81

Of Sir John Denham very little is known but what is related of him by Wood, or by himself.

He was born at Dublin in 1615; the only son of Sir John Denham, of Little Horsely in Essex, then chief baron of the Exchequer in Ireland, and of Eleanor, daughter of Sir Garret Moore, baron of Mellefont.

Two years afterwards, his father, being made one of the barons of the Exchequer in England, brought him away from his native country, and educated him in London.

In 1631 he was sent to Oxford, where he was considered 'as a dreaming young man, given more to dice and cards than study'; and therefore gave no prognosticks of his future eminence; nor was suspected to conceal, under sluggishness and laxity, a genius born to improve the literature of his country.

When he was, three years afterwards, removed to Lincoln's Inn, he prosecuted the common law with sufficient appearance of application; yet did not lose his propensity to cards and dice; but was very often plundered by gamesters.

Being severely reproved for this folly, he professed, and perhaps believed, himself reclaimed; and, to testify the sincerity of his repentance, wrote and published *An Essay upon Gaming*.

He seems to have divided his studies between law and poetry; for, in 1636, he translated the second book of the *Aeneid*.

Two years after, his father died; and then, notwithstanding his resolutions and professions, he returned again to the vice of gaming, and lost several thousand pounds that had been left him.

In 1631, he published *The Sophy*. This seems to have given him his first hold of the publick attention; for Waller remarked, 'that he broke out like the Irish rebellion three score thousand strong, when nobody was aware, or in the least suspected it': an observation which could have had no propriety, had his poetical abilities been known before.

He was after that pricked for sheriff of Surrey, and made governor of Farnham Castle for the king; but he soon resigned that charge, and retreated to Oxford, where, in 1643, he published *Cooper's Hill*.

This poem had such reputation as to excite the common

artifice by which envy degrades excellence. A report was spread, that the performance was not his own, but that he had bought it of a vicar for forty pounds. The same attempt was made to rob Addison of his *Cato*, and Pope of his *Essay on Criticism*.

In 1647, the distresses of the royal family required him to engage in more dangerous employments. He was entrusted by the queen with a message to the king; and, by whatever means, so far softened the ferocity of Hugh Peters, that, by his intercession, admission was procured. Of the king's condescension he has given an account in the dedication of his works.

He was afterwards employed in carrying on the king's correspondence; and, as he says, discharged this office with great safety to the royalists: and being accidentally discovered by the adverse party's knowledge of Mr. Cowley's hand, he escaped happily both for himself and his friends.

He was yet engaged in a greater undertaking. In April 1648, he conveyed James the duke of York from London into France, and delivered him there to the Queen and prince of Wales. This year he published his translation of *Cato Major*.

He now resided in France, as one of the followers of the exiled King; and, to divert the melancholy of their condition, was sometimes enjoined by his master to write occasional verses; one of which amusements was probably his ode or song upon the Embassy to Poland, by which he and lord Crofts procured a contribution of ten thousand pounds from the Scotch, that wandered over that kingdom. Poland was at that time very much frequented by itinerant traders, who, in a country of very little commerce and of great extent, where every man resided on his own estate, contributed very much to the accommodation of life, by bringing to every man's house those little necessaries which it was very inconvenient to want, and very troublesome to fetch. I have formerly read, without much reflection, of the multitude of Scotchmen that travelled with their wares in Poland; and that their numbers were not small, the success of this negotiation gives sufficient evidence.

About this time, what estate the war and the gamesters had left him was sold, by order of the parliament; and when, in 1652, he returned to England, he was entertained by the earl of Pembroke.

Of the next years of his life there is no account. At the Restoration he obtained, that which many missed, the reward of his loyalty; being made surveyor of the king's buildings, and dignified with the order of the Bath. He seems now to have learned some attention to money; for Wood says, that he got by this place seven thousand pounds.

After the Restoration he wrote the poem on Prudence and Justice, and perhaps some of his other pieces: and as he appears, whenever any serious question comes before him, to have been a man of piety, he consecrated his poetical powers to religion, and made a metrical version of the psalms of David. In this attempt he has failed; but, in sacred poetry who has succeeded?

It might be hoped that the favour of his master and esteem of the publick would now make him happy. But human felicity is short and uncertain; a second marriage brought upon him so much disquiet, as for a time disordered his understanding; and Butler lampooned him for his lunacy. I know not whether the malignant lines were then made publick, nor what provocation incited Butler to do that which no provocation can excuse.

His frenzy lasted not long; and he seems to have regained his full force of mind; for he wrote afterwards his excellent poem upon the death of Cowley, whom he was not long to survive; for on the 19th of March, 1668, he was buried by his side.

Denham is deservedly considered as one of the fathers of English poetry. 'Denham and Waller,' says Prior, 'improved our versification, and Dryden perfected it.' He has given specimens of various composition, descriptive, ludicrous, didactick, and sublime.

He appears to have had, in common with almost all mankind, the ambition of being upon proper occasions *a merry fellow*, and, in common with most of them, to have been by nature, or by early habits, debarred from it. Nothing is less exhilarating than the ludicrousness of Denham. He does not fail for want of efforts: he is familiar, he is gross; but he is never merry, unless the 'Speech against peace in the close Committee' be excepted. For grave burlesque, however, his imitation of Davenant shews him to have been well qualified.

Of his more elevated occasional poems there is perhaps none that does not deserve commendation. In the verses to Fletcher, we have an image that has since been often adopted:

But whither am I stray'd? I need not raise
Trophies to thee from other men's dispraise;
Nor is thy fame on lesser ruins built,
Nor need thy juster title the foul guilt
Of eastern kings, who, to secure their reign,
Must have their brothers, sons, and kindred slain.

After Denham, Orrery, in one of his prologues,

Poets are sultans, if they had their will;
For every author would his brother kill.

And Pope,

Should such a man, too fond to rule alone,
Bear like the Turk no brother near the throne.

But this is not the best of his little pieces: it is excelled by his poem to Fanshaw, and his elegy on Cowley.

His praise of Fanshaw's version of Guarini contains a very spritely and judicious character of a good translator:

That servile path thou nobly dost decline,
Of tracing word by word, and line by line.
Those are the labour'd births of slavish brains,
Not the effect of poetry, but pains;
Cheap vulgar arts, whose narrowness affords
No flight for thoughts, but poorly stick at words.
A new and nobler way thou dost pursue,
To make translations and translators too.
They but preserve the ashes, thou the flame,
True to his sense, but truer to his fame.

The excellence of these lines is greater, as the truth which they contain was not at that time generally known.

His poem on the death of Cowley was his last, and, among his shorter works, his best performance: the numbers are musical, and the thoughts are just.

Cooper's Hill is the work that confers upon him the rank and dignity of an original author. He seems to have been, at least among us, the author of a species of composition that may be denominated *local poetry*, of which the fundamental subject is some particular landscape, to be poetically described, with the addition of such embellishments as may be supplied by historical retrospection, or incidental meditation.

To trace a new scheme of poetry has in itself a very high claim to praise, and its praise is yet more when it is apparently copied by Garth and Pope; after whose names little will be gained by an enumeration of smaller poets, that have left scarce a corner of the island not dignified either by rhyme, or blank verse.

Cooper's Hill, if it be maliciously inspected, will not be found without its faults. The digressions are too long, the mo-

rality too frequent, and the sentiments sometimes such as will not bear a rigorous enquiry.

The four verses, which, since Dryden has commended them, almost every writer for a century past has imitated, are generally known:

O could I flow like thee, and make thy stream
My great example, as it is my theme!
Though deep, yet clear; though gentle, yet not dull;
Strong without rage, without o'erflowing full.

The lines are in themselves not perfect; for most of the words, thus artfully opposed, are to be understood simply on one side of the comparison, and metaphorically on the other; and if there be any language which does not express intellectual operations by material images, into that language they cannot be translated. But so much meaning is comprised in so few words; the particulars of resemblance are so perspicaciously collected, and every mode of excellence separated from its adjacent fault by so nice a line of limitation; the different parts of the sentence are so accurately adjusted; and the flow of the last couplet is so smooth and sweet; that the passage, however celebrated, has not been praised above its merit. It has beauty peculiar to itself, and must be numbered among those felicities which cannot be produced at will by wit and labour, but must arise unexpectedly in some hour propitious to poetry.

He appears to have been one of the first that understood the necessity of emancipating translation from the drudgery of counting lines and interpreting single words. How much this servile practice obscured the clearest and deformed the most beautiful parts of the ancient authors, may be discovered by a perusal of our earlier versions; some of them the works of men well qualified, not only by critical knowledge, but by poetical genius, who yet, by a mistaken ambition of exactness, degraded at once their originals and themselves.

Denham saw the better way, but has not pursued it with great success. His versions of Virgil are not pleasing; but they taught Dryden to please better. His poetical imitation of Tully on *Old Age* has neither the clearness of prose, nor the spriteliness of poetry.

The 'strength of Denham,' which Pope so emphatically mentions, is to be found in many lines and couplets, which convey much meaning in few words, and exhibit the sentiment with more weight than bulk.

On the Thames.

Though with those streams he no resemblance hold,
Whose foam is amber, and their gravel gold;
His genuine and less guilty wealth t' explore,
Search not his bottom, but survey his shore.

On Strafford.

His wisdom such, at once it did appear
Three kingdoms' wonder, and three kingdoms' fear;
While single he stood forth, and seem'd, although
Each had an army, as an equal foe.
Such was his force of eloquence, to make
The hearers more concern'd than he that spake;
Each seem'd to act that part he came to see,
And none was more a looker on than he;
So did he move our passions, some were known
To wish, for the defence, the crime their own,
Now private pity strove with publick hate.
Reason with rage, and eloquence with fate.

On Cowley.

To him no author was unknown,
Yet what he wrote was all his own;
Horace's wit, and Virgil's state,

He did not steal, but emulate!
And when he would like them appear,
Their garb, but not their cloaths, did wear.

As one of Denham's principal claims to the regard for posterity arises from his improvement of our numbers, his versification ought to be considered. It will afford that pleasure which arises from the observation of a man of judgement naturally right forsaking bad copies by degrees, and advancing towards a better practice, as he gains more confidence in himself.

In his translation of Virgil, written when he was about twenty-one years old, may be still found the old manner of continuing the sense ungracefully from verse to verse.

Then all those
Who in the dark our fury did escape,
Returning, know our borrow'd arms, and shape,
And differing dialect: then their numbers swell
And grow upon us: first Choroebeus fell
Before Minerva's altar; next did bleed
Just Ripheus, whom no Trojan did exceed
In virtue, yet the gods his fate decreed.
Then Hypanis and Dymas, wounded by
Their friends; nor thee, Pantheus, thy piety,
Nor consecrated mitre, from the same
Ill fate could save; my country's funeral flame
And Troy's cold ashes I attest, and call
To witness for myself, that in their fall
No foes, no death, nor danger I declin'd,
Did, and deserv'd no less, my fate to find.

From this kind of concatenated metre he afterwards refrained, and taught his followers the art of concluding their sense in couplets; which has perhaps been with rather too much constancy pursued.

This passage exhibits one of those triplets which are not infrequent in this first essay, but which it is to be supposed his maturer judgement disapproved, since in his latter works he has totally forborn them.

His rhymes are such as seem found without difficulty, by following the sense; and are for the most part as exact at least as those of other poets, though now and then the reader is shifted off with what he can get.

O how *transform'd!*
How much unlike that Hector, who *return'd*
Clad in Achilles' spoils!

And again,

From thence a thousand lesser poets *sprung,*
Like petty princes from the fall of *Rome.*

Sometimes the weight of rhyme is laid upon a word too feeble to sustain it:

Troy confounded falls
From all her glories: if it might have stood
By any power, by this right hand it *shou'd.*
—And though my outward state misfortune *hath*
Deprest thus low, it cannot reach my faith.
—Thus by his fraud and our own faith o'ercome,
A feigned tear destroys us, against *whom*
Tydides nor Achilles could prevail,
Nor ten years' conflict, nor a thousand sail.

He is not very careful to vary the ends of his verses: in one passage the word *die* rhymes three couplets in six.

Most of these petty faults are in his first productions, when he was less skilful, or at least less dexterous in the use of words; and though they had been more frequent, they could only have lessened the grace, not the strength of his composition. He is one of the writers that improved our taste, and advanced our language, and whom we ought therefore to read with gratitude, though, having done much, he left much to do.

ANNE BRADSTREET

1612–1672

Anne Dudley Bradstreet was born in Northampton, England, in 1612. During her childhood she lived in the house of the Earl of Lincoln, where her father, Thomas Dudley, was the Earl's steward. She read widely in the large library collected there, and in that same house also met her future husband, Simon Bradstreet, whom she married in 1628. In 1630 she, her husband, and her father embarked on the ship *Arbella,* bound for New England. Anne and Simon Bradstreet settled first at Ipswich and, in 1645, in North Andover, Massachusetts. The rest of Anne Bradstreet's life revolved around her combined duties as the daughter of one Deputy-Governor of the Massachusetts Bay Colony and wife of another (Thomas Dudley and Simon Bradstreet both held that office); as a housewife and mother of eight children in a frontier settlement; and as a conscientious Puritan religionist. In her copious spare time she wrote a substantial amount of poetry, and prose meditations as well.

Her early poetry was not intended for publication, but her admiring brother-in-law John Woodbridge took copies of her manuscripts with him to England in 1647, where they were published without her knowledge as *The Tenth Muse Lately Sprung Up in America* in 1650. In addition to "A Dialogue between Old England and New," an elegy for Sir Philip Sidney, and poems on other, mostly religious themes, the volume was largely made up of her "Quaternions." These lengthy poetic discourses on the four elements, four humours of man, four ages of man, four seasons, and four monarchies imitated the *Divine Weekes and Workes* and *Creation* of French poet Guillaume Du Bartas, and also show her familiarity with Ralegh's *History of the World* and the poetry of Sidney and Spenser. After the publication of *The Tenth Muse* Bradstreet wholly abandoned the encyclopedic style, thereafter writing either prose or lyric poetry. A second edition of *The Tenth*

Muse, with Bradstreet's numerous corrections and revisions inserted, was published posthumously in 1678. In it are a score of poems not present in the first edition, including "Contemplations," considered by many to be her best poem. The final addition to what we have of her work was a book of seventy-seven Meditations Divine and Morall bequeathed in manuscript to her son Simon along with copies of some unpublished poems.

Anne Bradstreet was one of the earliest women in English literature to have produced a substantial body of work, and also wrote the first poetry in the English-speaking New World that has proven to be of lasting interest. She died in North Andover, Massachusetts, in 1672.

General

Mercury shew'd Apollo, Bartas Book,
Minerva this, and wisht him well to look,
And tell uprightly, which, did which excell;
He view'd, and view'd, and vow'd he could not tell.
They bid him Hemisphear his mouldy nose,
With's crackt leering-glasses, for it would pose
The best brains he had in's old pudding-pan,
Sex weigh'd, which best, the Woman, or the Man?
He peer'd, and por'd, and glar'd, and said for wore,
I'me even as wise now, as I was before:
They both 'gan laugh, and said, it was no mar'l
The Auth'resse was a right Du Bartas Girle.
Good sooth quoth the old Don, tel ye me so,
I muse whither at length these Girls wil go;
It half revives my chil frost-bitten blood,
To see a woman, once, do ought that's good;
And chode buy Chaucers Boots, and Homers Furrs,
Let men look to't, least women weare the Spurs.

— NATHANIEL WARD, Untitled poem, *The Tenth Muse Lately Sprung Up in America*, 1650

There is one thing yet remaining, in which Women have excelled, that is, *Poetry*. Their excellency in this, tends as much to their vindication as any thing yet spoken to. To be a *Poetaster*, is no great matter; but to be a *Poet-Laureat*, requires great natural endowments, such as man cannot lend, if God doth not give; *Poeta nascitur, non fit.* If a man's natural parts be low, Industry, Education, Time, and Practice, may raise to some competent height in Oratory; therefore we say, *Orator fit:* But all the Instruction and Education in the World, all the pains, time, and patience imaginable, can never infuse that sublime Fancy, that strong Memory, and excellent Judgment required in one that shall wear the Bayes.

A good Poet, must know things Divine, things Natural, things Moral, things Historical, and things Artificial; together with the several terms belonging to all Faculties, to which they must allude. Good Poets must be universal Scholars, able to use a pleasing Phrase, and to express themselves with moving Eloquence. . . .

How excellent a Poet Mrs. *Broadstreet* is, (now in *America*) her Works do testifie. — BATHSUA MAKIN, "An Essay to Revive the Antient Education of Gentlewomen," 1673

Anne Broadstreet, a *New-England* poetess, no less in title; viz. before her *Poems, printed in Old-England anno* 1650; then *The tenth Muse sprung up in America*; the memory of which poems, consisting chiefly of Descriptions of the *Four Elements*, the *Four Humours*; the *Four Ages*, the *Four Seasons*, and the *Four Monarchies*, is not yet wholly extinct. — EDWARD PHILLIPS, "Women," *Theatrum Poetarum Anglicanorum*, 1675

Her virtues were so great, that they do raise
A work to trouble fame, astonish praise.
When as her Name doth but salute the ear,
Men think that they perfections abstract hear.

Her breast was a brave Pallace, a *Broad-street*,
Where all heroick ample thoughts did meet
Where nature such a Tenement had tane,
That others souls, to hers, dwelt in a lane.

— JOHN NORTON, "A Funeral Elogy, Upon That Pattern and Patron of Virtue, the Truely Pious, Peerless & Matchless Gentlewoman Mrs. Anne Bradstreet, Right Panaretes, Mirror of Her Age, Glory of Her Sex, Whose Heaven-Born-Soul Leaving Its Earthly Shrine, Chose Its Native Home, and Was Taken to Its Rest, Upon 16th Sept. 1672," *Several Poems Compiled with Great Variety of Wit and Learning*, 1678

If the rare learning of a *daughter*, was not the least of those bright things that adorned no less a Judge of *England* than Sir *Thomas More*; it must now be said, that a Judge of *New-England*, namely, *Thomas Dudley*, Esq. had a *daughter* (besides other children) to be a *crown* unto him. Reader, *America* justly admires the learned women of the other *hemisphere*. She has heard of those that were *tutoresses* to the old professors of all philosophy: she hath heard of *Hippatia*, who formerly taught the liberal arts; and of *Sarocchia*, who more lately was very often the moderatrix in the disputations of the learned men of *Rome*: she has been told of the three *Corinnæs*, which equalled, if not excelled, the most celebrated *poets* of their time: she has been told of the Empress *Endocia*, who composed poetical paraphrases on divers parts of the *Bible*: and of *Rosuida*, who wrote the *lives* of holy men; and of *Pamphilia*, who wrote other histories unto the life: the writings of the most renowned *Anna Maria Schurnian*, have come over unto her. But she now prays, that into such catalogues of *authoresses*, as *Beverovicius, Hottinger*, and *Voetius*, have given unto the world, there may be a room now given unto Madam Ann Bradstreet, the daughter of our governour *Dudley*, and the consort of our governour *Bradstreet*, whose *poems*, divers times printed, have afforded a grateful entertainment unto the ingenious, and a monument for her memory beyond the stateliest *marbles*. — COTTON MATHER, "Successors," *Magnalia Christi Americana*, 1702, Bk. 2

The first wife of Governor Bradstreet . . . was Anne, daughter of Governor Thomas Dudley, whom she married in England. She died 16th September, 1672, at the age of 60 years. "She is," says Savage, "the most distinguished of the early matrons of our land by her literary powers." A volume of her poems was published in 1678. It was dedicated to her father, in a copy of verses, dated 20 March, 1642, and is probably the earliest poetic volume written in America.

There is also in possession of one of her descendants, a manuscript volume, in the hand-writing of Mrs. Bradstreet, dedicated to her "Dear Son Simon Bradstreet," and containing seventy seven "Meditations, Divine and Moral," which she intended to continue through the volume, as we are told in a note written by her son, "but was prevented by death." Extracts from these Meditations are given in the History of the First

Church of Charlestown, Massachusetts.—JACOB BAILEY MOORE, "Simon Bradstreet," *Lives of the Governors of New Plymouth, and Massachusetts Bay*, 1851, p. 388

The first edition of Mrs. Bradstreet's poems was printed through the agency of her brother-in-law, Mr. John Woodbridge, and without her knowledge, in London, in 1650, under the title of *The Tenth Muse lately sprung up in America.* . . . *By a Gentlewoman in those Parts.* The second edition was printed in Boston in 1678, with the title *Several Poems compiled with great Variety of Wit and Learning, full of Delight.* . . . *By a Gentlewoman in New England.* A third edition was issued in Boston in 1758, with the same title, but without the name of the publisher or the printer.

From the fact that three editions of these poems were printed in those early days, we must infer that our ancestors read them with pleasure; but in our time the interest attached to them is other than literary. It is certainly a notable fact that such a volume was written and printed within the first twenty years after the settlement of the Massachusetts Colony, and under circumstances the most unfavorable for literary development. It is curious also to see what sort of poetic verdure could spring from such uncongenial soil.

The education and social position of Mrs. Bradstreet, the daughter of Thomas Dudley, and wife of Simon Bradstreet, both Governors of the Massachusetts Colony, and both eminent among its original founders, were excelled probably by those of no other lady in the Colony. That she was an affectionate wife, a devoted mother, and a pattern of piety after the best Puritan models, is evident from her writings. She was born at Northampton in England in 1612–13. Nothing is known of her early life, except what is gathered from a few allusions made to it by herself. "As I grew up," she says, "to be about 14 or 15, I found my heart more carnal, and sitting loose from God; vanity and the follies of youth took hold of me. About 16 the Lord laid his hand sore upon me and smote me with the small-pox. When I was in my affliction, I besought the Lord, and confessed my pride and vanity, and he again restored me. But I rendered not to him according to the benefit received. After a short time I changed my condition, and was married, and came into this country, where I found a new world and new manners, at which my heart rose. But after I was convinced it was the way of God, I submitted to it and joined to the church at Boston."

If her poems had been written before she renounced the pride and vanity of this world, and "joined to the church at Boston," they would doubtless have treated a class of topics of more interest to the modern antiquary than anything contained in the volume before us. Her carnal heart, it seems, rebelled at first against the early experiences and new manners of this Western world. What a contribution to our knowledge of those times would have been her description, in humorous or satirical verse, of the experiences and manners which ruffled the serenity of her worldly mind! Early piety is perhaps always to be commended; but in this instance it was not favorable for that kind of literary effort in which the present age is interested, as showing the manners and customs of our ancestors.

We are in the habit of extolling the wisdom and foresight of our progenitors; and yet they seem to have had little conception of the kind of information respecting themselves which would be sought for in subsequent ages. A third-rate antiquary of to-day, if, by some eddy in the stream of time, he could be set back two centuries, would give us a more satisfactory account of the "form and pressure" of the time in which they lived than the best of those early writers have recorded. The

incidents of every-day life they regarded as beneath the dignity of history and of poetry even.

Mistress Bradstreet's verses, not excepting the few on domestic themes, such as "the restoration of my dear husband from a burning ague," "upon my daughter Hannah Wiggin, her recovery from a dangerous fever," might as well have been written in England as in Boston, or Andover, so far as they shed light upon what was characteristic of New England. Even from her domestic verses she managed to exclude everything but her emotional piety and personal feelings. This excellent lady was doubtless one of the sixty or eighty principal women who, at first, attended the weekly preaching exercises of Mistress Anne Hutchinson, and she must have taken sides in the wordy and memorable Antinomian controversy of 1636. A woman's account of this woman's quarrel, in prose, rhyme, or blank verse, would have been precious; but, alas! there is no allusion to the subject in her writings. In the place of it we are treated with a rhythmical "Epitome of the three first Monarchies, viz. the Assyrian, Persian, Grecian, and the Roman Commonwealth." A hundred other topics founded on the events, the customs, the virtues, and the follies of that period might be suggested, of which her Muse, if it had anticipated the demands of this practical and degenerate age, would doubtless have sung. But hers was not the Muse of Colonial history, and we must be content with substitutes in the form of rhymes on "The Four Elements, the Four Constitutions, the Four Ages of Man, and the Four Seasons of the Year," which have as much relation to Massachusetts affairs of two centuries ago as they have with the Darwinian theory of to-day. . . .

It would, of course, be very unhandsome treatment to test the literary merits of Mistress Bradstreet's verses by the modern standard of criticism. The sole interest attached to them is that they were written and printed at that early period. With an antiquary the intrinsic merits of a book have nothing to do with its pecuniary value, which is the measure of a strange madness among collectors to possess it. The two early New England books which now command the highest price,—somewhere in the vicinity of a thousand dollars each,—the *Bay Psalm Book*, 1640, and *Eliot's Indian Bible*, 1663,—are intrinsically as worthless volumes as can be named. The latter no person living *can* read (unless we except one linguistic scholar), and the former no person would desire to read. Still, a few of Anne Bradstreet's poems can be read without doing penance, and in the elegant form in which they are here presented are positively attractive, especially when we compare them with the rhythmical jargon of their contemporary, the *Bay Psalm Book*. —UNSIGNED, *North American Review*, Jan. 1868, pp. 330–33

She was well read in the literature of the time, poetical, theological, and other, and without possessing genius, was a young woman of talents. It was the fashion to admire Sidney's "Arcadia," so she admired it, and wrote an elegy upon its chivalrous author, whom his contemporaries insisted on idolizing. She also admired Spenser's *Faerie Queene*, which was more read in the first half of the seventeenth century than it ever has been since; and she may be said to have doted upon Du Bartas, whom every body was reading then, through the lumbering version of Sylvester, though nobody can be persuaded to read him now. Her master was Du Bartas, whose "sugared lines" she read over and over, grudging that the Muses did not part their overflowing store betwixt him and her:

> A Bartas can do what a Bartas will,
> But simple I according to my skill.

—RICHARD HENRY STODDARD, "Richard Henry Dana," *Harper's New Monthly Magazine*, April 1879, p. 769

Mrs. Bradstreet's poems bear evidence of an intimate acquaintance with, and great admiration of, "Great Bartas' sugared lines." Sylvester's trans. of the *Divine Weeks* of Du Bartas had introduced this poet to a large circle of English Admirers.

Mrs. Bradstreet thus expresses her admiration of the Soldier-Poet:

But when my wandering eyes and envious heart
Great Bartas' sugared lines do but read o'er,
Fool! I do grudge the muses did not part
'Twixt him and me their over-fluent store
A Bartas can do what a Bartas will—
But simple I, according to my skill.

Nathaniel Ward, the author of *The Simple Cobbler of Agawam*, would have us to understand that, whatever might be Mrs. Bradstreet's opinion in the premises, yet Apollo was not by any means satisfied of the unquestionable precedence of Du Bartas:

Mercury showed Apollo Bartas' book,
Minerva this, and wished him well to look
And tell uprightly which did which excel,
He viewed and viewed and vowed he could not tell.
(see Griswold's *Female Poets of America*)

Dr. Cotton Mather considered her works to be

"A monument to her memory, beyond the stateliest marble."—*Magnalia Christi Americana*

Your only hand those poesies did compose;
Your head the source whence all those springs did flow.

(JOHN ROGERS: *President of Harvard College*)

Now I believe Tradition, which doth call
The Muses, Virtues, Graces, females all;
Only they are not nine, eleven, nor three:—
Our authoress proves them but one unity.

(BENJAMIN WOODBRIDGE, *first graduate of Harvard College*)

"*One* unity:" is it possible? How strange!

John Norton describes this "peerless gentlewoman, the mirror of her age and glory of her sex":

Praise her who list, yet he shall be a debtor,
For art ne'er feigned, nor nature formed, a better.

"These praises run into hyperbole, and prove, perhaps, that their authors were more gallant than critical: but we perceive from Mrs. Bradstreet's poems that they are not destitute of imagination, and that she was thoroughly instructed in the best learning of the age."—R. W. Griswold.

In the height of enthusiasm, good John Norton goes so far as to declare, that if Virgil could hear her works, he would condemn his own to the flames. As the Mantuan Bard is not likely to be gratified by hearing Mrs. Bradstreet's effusions, it is idle to discuss the position assumed by Norton, and argue whether Virgil would or would not be capable of such an act of philanthropic abnegation, or ebullition of disappointed rivalry, as the combustion of his verses would display to the eyes of an astonished and mourning world. Miserable as Virgil's effusions may be, when compared with the verses of Mrs. Bradstreet, yet somehow we have become accustomed to him, and could better spare a better poet,—even the famed "Tenth Muse" herself.—GEORGE W. CHILDS, *Critical Dictionary of English Literature and British and American Authors*, 1886, p. 236

No poet has enduring place whose work has not been the voice of the national thought and life in which he has had part. Theology, politics, great questions of right, all the problems of human life in any age may have, in turn, moulded the epic of the period; but, from Homer down, the poet has spoken the deepest thought of the time, and where he failed in this has failed to be heard beyond his time. With American poets, it has taken long for anything distinctively American to be born. With the early singers, there was simply a reproduction of the mannerisms and limitations of the school for which Pope had set all the copies. Why not, when it was simply a case of unchangeable identity, the Englishman being no less an Englishman because he had suddenly been put down on the American side of the Atlantic? Then, for a generation or so, he was too busy contending with natural forces, and asserting his claims to life and place on the new continent, to have much leisure for verse-making, though here and there, in the stress of grinding days, a weak and uncertain voice sounded at times. Anne Bradstreet's, as we know, was the first, and half assured, half dismayed at her own presumption, she waited long, till convinced as other authors have since been, by the "urgency of friends," that her words must have wider spread than manuscript could give them. Now and again it is asserted that the manuscript for the first edition was taken to London without her knowledge and printed in the same way, but there is hardly the slightest ground for such conclusion, while the elaborate dedication and the many friendly tributes included, indicate the fullest knowledge and preparation. All those whose opinion she most valued are represented in the opening pages of the volume.

Evidently they felt it necessary to justify this extraordinary departure from the proper sphere of woman, a sphere as sharply defined and limited by every father, husband and brother, as their own was left uncriticised and unrestrained. Nathaniel Ward forgot his philippics against the "squirrel's brains" of women, and hastened to speak his delight in the little book, and Woodbridge and John Rogers and sundry others whose initials alone are affixed to their prose or poetical tributes and endorsements, all banded together to sustain this first venture.—HELEN CAMPBELL, *Anne Bradstreet and Her Time*, 1891, pp. 224–25

Works

Kind Reader: Had I opportunity but to borrow some of the Authors wit, 'tis possible I might so trim this curious work with such quaint expressions, as that the Preface might bespeake thy further perusall; but I feare 'twil be a shame for a man that can speak so little, to be seene in the title page of this Womans Book, lest by comparing the one with the other, the Reader should passe his sentence, that it is the gift of women, not only to speak most, but to speake best; I shall leave therefore to commend that, which with any ingenious Reader will too much commend the Author, unless men turne more peevish then women, to envie the excellency of the inferiour Sex. I doubt not but the Reader will quickly finde more then I can say, and the worst effect of his reading will be unbeleif, which will make him question whether it be a womans Work, and aske, Is it possible? If any doe, take this as an answer from him that dares avow it; It is the Work of a Woman, honoured, and esteemed where she lives, for her gracious demeanour, her eminent parts, her pious conversation, her courteous disposition, her exact diligence in her place, and discreet mannaging of her family occasions; and more then so, these Poems are the fruit but of some few houres, curtailed from her sleep, and other refreshments. I dare adde little, lest I keepe thee too long, if thou wilt not beleeve the worth of these things (in their kind) when a man sayes it, yet beleeve it from a woman when thou seest it. This only I shall annex, I feare the displeasure of no person in the publishing of these Poems but the Authors, without whose knowledge, and contrary to her expectation, I have presumed to bring to publick view what she resolved should never in such a manner see the Sun; but I found that divers had gotten some scattered papers, affected them wel, were likely to have sent forth broken peices to the Authors prejudice, which I thought to prevent, as well as to pleasure those that earnestly desired the view of the whole.—JOHN WOODBRIDGE, "Introduction" to *The Tenth Muse Lately Sprung Up in America*, 1650

> Thou ill-form'd offspring of my feeble brain,
> Who after birth did'st by my side remain,
> Till snatcht from thence by friends, less wise then true
> Who thee abroad, expos'd to publick view,
> Made thee in raggs, halting to th' press to trudg,
> Where errors were not lessened (all may judg)
> At thy return my blushing was not small,
> My rambling brat (in print) should mother call,
> I cast thee by as one unfit for light,
> Thy Visage was so irksome in my signt;
> Yet being mine own, at length affection would
> Thy blemishes amend, if so I could:
> I wash'd thy face, but more defects I saw,
> And rubbing off a spot, still made a flaw.
> I stretcht thy joynts to make thee even feet,
> Yet still thou run'st more hobling then is meet;
> In better dress to trim thee was my mind,
> But nought save home-spun Cloth, i'th' house I find
> In this array, 'mongst Vulgars mayst thou roam
> In Criticks hands, beware thou dost not come;
> And take thy way where yet thou art not known,
> If for thy Father askt, say, thou hadst none:
> And for thy Mother, she alas is poor,
> Which caus'd her thus to send thee out of door.

> —ANNE BRADSTREET, "The Author to her Book," *Several Poems Compiled with Great Variety of Wit and Learning*, 1678

The volume of poems ⟨*The Tenth Muse*⟩, written by Mrs. Anne Bradstreet, was dedicated by her to her father, in a copy of verses, dated March 20, 1642. It is, therefore, undoubtedly, the first attempt made in the country to obtain the poetic laurel. . . .

From the topics treated of in this volume, the general character of it is apparent. By constitutions, the four temperaments are in fact intended, and they are described with tolerable accuracy. There is some good description in the several poems, especially in the account of the four seasons; and generally, the versification is not unharmonious. The historical poetry is little else than a chronological table turned into rhyme.

⟨John⟩ Norton, . . . declares her poetry so fine, that were Maro to hear it, he would again condemn his works to the fire; and the learned and accomplished editor of *Winthrop's Journal* praises the volume, and calls it a real curiosity.—UNSIGNED, "Early American Poetry," *American Quarterly Review*, Dec. 1827, pp. 494–95

Though it was only as a poet that Anne Bradstreet was known to her own time, her real strength was in prose, and the "Meditations, Divine and Morall," written at the request of her second son, the Rev. Simon Bradstreet, to whom she dedicated them, March 20, 1664, show that life had taught her much, and in the ripened thought and shrewd observation of men and manners are the best testimony to her real ability. For the

reader of to-day they are of incomparably more interest than anything to be found in the poems. There is often the most condensed and telling expression; a swift turn that shows what power of description lay under all the fantastic turns of the style Du Bartas had created for her.—HELEN CAMPBELL, *Anne Bradstreet and Her Time*, 1891, p. 288

EVART A. DUYCKINCK AND
GEORGE L. DUYCKINCK
From "Anne Bradstreet"
Cyclopaedia of American Literature
1855, Volume 1, pp. 48–49

The cares of married life would not appear to have interrupted Mistress Bradstreet's ⟨educational⟩ acquisitions, for she was married at the age of sixteen, and her poetry was written in the early part of her life. As she had eight children, and addressed herself particularly to their education, the cradle and the Muse must have been competitors for her attention. Her reading, well stuffed with the facts of ancient history, was no trifle for the memory; but we may suppose the mind to have been readily fixed on books, and even pedantic learning to have been a relief, where there were no diversions to distract when the household labors of the day were over. Then there is the native passion for books, which will find its own opportunities. The little volume of her poems, published in London, in 1650, is entitled *The Tenth Muse, lately sprung up in America; or, Several Poems, compiled with great variety of wit and learning, full of delight: wherein especially is contained a complete Discourse and Description of the Four Elements, Constitutions, Ages of Man, Seasons of the Year. Together with an Exact Epitome of the Four Monarchies, viz., the Assyrian, Persian, Grecian, Roman. Also a Dialogue between Old England and New concerning the late troubles, with divers other pleasant and serious Poems. By a Gentlewoman in those parts.* A more complete edition was published in Boston in 1678, which contains her *Contemplations*, a moral and descriptive poem, the best specimen of her pen; *The Flesh and the Spirit*, a dialogue, and several poems on family incidents, left among her private papers.

The formal natural history and historical topics, which compose the greater part of her writings, are treated with doughty resolution, but without much regard to poetical equality. The plan is simple. The elements of the world, fire, air, earth, and water; the humors of the constitution, the choleric, the sanguine, the melancholy, and phlegmatic; childhood, youth, manhood, and age; spring, summer, autumn, and winter, severally come up and say what they can of themselves, of their powers and opportunities, good and evil, with the utmost fairness. The four ancient monarchies are catalogued in a similar way. It is not to be denied, that, if there is not much poetry in these productions, there is considerable information. For the readers of those times they contained a very respectable digest of the old historians, and a fair proportion of medical and scientific knowledge. It is amusing to see this mother in Israel writing of the Spleen with the zest of an anatomist.

> If any doubt this truth, whence this should come,
> Show them the passage to the duodenum.

The good lady must have enjoyed the perusal of Phineas Fletcher's *Purple Island*, a dissecting theatre in a book, which appeared in 1633. Her descriptions are extremely literal. She writes as if under bonds to tell the whole truth, which she does without any regard to the niceties or scruples of the imagination. Thus her account of childhood begins at the beginning somewhat earlier than a modern poetess would tax the memory of the muse; and she thinks it necessary to tell us in her account of winter, how,

Beef, brawn and pork, are now in great'st request,
And solid'st meats our stomachs can digest.

When we come upon any level ground in these poems, and are looking round to enjoy the prospect, we may prepare ourselves for a neighboring pitfall. In "Summer" we set forth trippingly afield—

Now go those frolic swains, the shepherd lad,
To wash their thick-cloth'd flocks, with pipes full glad.
In the cool streams they labor with delight,
Rubbing their dirty coats, till they look white.

. . . In the historic poems, the dry list of dynasties is sometimes relieved by a homely unction and humor in the narrative, as in the picture of the progress of Alexander and the Persian host of Darius—though much of this stuff is sheer doggrel, as in the Life and Death of Semiramis:

She like a brave virago play'd the rex,
And was both shame and glory of her sex.

. . .

Forty-two years she reign'd, and then she dy'd,
But by what means, we are not certified.

If sighs for "imbecility" can get pardon for bad verses, we should think only of Mrs. Bradstreet's good ones—for her poems are full of these deprecatory acknowledgments.

The literary father of Mrs. Bradstreet was Silver-tongued Sylvester, whose translation of Du Bartas was a popular book among Puritan readers at the beginning of the seventeenth century. His quaint volumes, which will be remembered as favorites with Southey's simple-minded Dr. Daniel Dove, were both poetical and devout; and if they led our author's taste astray, they also strengthened her finest susceptibilities. She has left a warm poem "in his honor," in which there is an original and very pretty simile.

My Muse unto a child, I fitly may compare,
Who sees the riches of some famous fair;
He feeds his eyes, but understanding lacks,
To comprehend the worth of all those knacks;
The glittering plate, and jewels, he admires,
The hats and fans, and flowers, and ladies' tires;
And thousand times his 'mazed mind doth wish
Some part, at least, of that brave wealth was his;
But seeing empty wishes nought obtain,
At night turns to his mother's cot again,
And tells her tales (his full heart over glad)
Of all the glorious sights his eyes have had:
But finds too soon his want of eloquence,
The silly prattler speaks no word of sense;
And seeing utterance fail his great desires,
Sits down in silence.

Nathaniel Ward, the author of the Simple Cobbler of Agawam, in some comic fetches prefixed to the poems, says:—

The Authoresse was a right Du Bartas girle.

Mrs. Bradstreet was also a reader of Sir Philip Sidney's Arcadia, which she has characterized with more minuteness than others who have written upon it, in an Elegy which she penned forty-eight years after the fall of that mirror of knighthood at Zutphen.

Ann Bradstreet died 16th September, 1672, at the age of sixty. That she had not altogether survived her poetical reputation in England, is shown by an entry in Edward Phillips's (the nephew of Milton) *Theatrum Poetarum*, in 1674, where the

title of her Poems is given, and their memory pronounced "not yet wholly extinct."

JAMES ANDERSON
From "Anne Dudley, Wife of Simon Bradstreet"
Memorable Women of the Puritan Times
1862, pp. 256–84

Mrs. Bradstreet had been strictly indoctrinated in puritan principles; and, after the example of her father, she steadily professed and maintained them through the whole of her life. The Puritanism of her creed, both on religious and political questions, she fully brings out in her "Dialogue between Old England and New, concerning their present troubles, anno 1642," when the civil war between Charles I. and his parliament broke out.

In this poem she describes at length the *cause* of the troubled state of Old England, namely, England's sins. Sacred laws were broken. Idolatry, which has ever been the bane and the ruin of nations, was openly practised. The gospel was trodden down. Ecclesiastical offices were bought and sold. The tendency of Romanism to gain the ascendency was so great that the pope was exulting in the hope of soon seeing the old superstition restored in England. Scorn, injuries, calumnies, nicknames, were daily heaped on the saints of the Most High. How was the land profaned by blasphemies such as ear had never heard from Beelzebub himself! how was it desecrated by Sabbath-breaking, and debased by drunkenness, bribery, adultery, theft, falsehood, usury, extortion, and oppression! Nor was England yet cleansed from the blood of martyrs and of others who had been unjustly put to death. These were the hydras that were consuming her vitals, the bitter fountains whence flowed the bitter streams she was drinking, the root whence proceeded the deadly fruit she was eating. For all these enormities, and more than could be related, the ministers of the Word, in sermons which then stood upon record, had threatened a woful day of retribution—but she had mocked the preachers, and put the evil day far away. Yea, these prophets' mouths had been stopped. Some of them had been suspended; others deprived of their livings. Some had been heavily fined; others thrown into prisons. Some had been scourged; others driven into exile. Some had had their ears cropped; others their cheeks branded with a red-hot iron. Such were the sins which Mrs. Bradstreet represents as crying to Heaven for vengeance upon England.

In the same poem she next describes the *condition* of England in a strain of heartfelt sympathy with the parliament, and yet of fervent loyalty to the sovereign, opposed though she was to his arbitrary power. The ground of the dispute between the king and the parliament was simply whether the law or the king was supreme. The parliament stood up for law and right in opposition to royal prerogative, which the monarch, with a fatal infatuation, was determined to uphold. In the contest the Earl of Strafford had been beheaded, and Laud was now a prisoner in the Tower. The contention between the subjects and their master grew, till from words they fell to blows, and thousands lay wounded and dead on the field of battle. The bitterness of England's woes consisted in this, that now she was slaughtered by her own sons, and this might be only the beginning of her sorrows. Her towns were plundered; her houses were devastated; her virgins were ravished; her young men were slain; her flourishing trade was destroyed, and all the calamities of famine were impending. The poor were deprived of their wages; their children were in want of bread; and the tears of their unhappy mothers were unpitied. Yet all this, while calling forth commiseration, might issue in the regeneration of England—might issue in what had been so long hoped for and prayed for, "that right may have its right, though bought with blood."

On all who were engaged in that noble enterprise in support of the supremacy of law against prerogative, the blessing of Heaven is invoked—on the Nobles, who perilled their lives in defence of the truth; on the Commons, who boldly stood up for the common good, and for the infringed laws of their country; on the Counties, who assisted with hearts and estates; on the Preachers, who cheered on the patriotic bands; and should not Meroz' curse be imprecated on all who, in this great struggle for the right, helped not with prayers, arms, and purse? These, it is hoped, were the days when the church's foes would be crushed—when "prelates would be rooted out, head and tail, root and branch;" when "all their attire, Baal's vestments," "their mitres, surplices, copes, rochets, crossiers," would be brought out to make a bonfire, "the flash lighting Christendom," and letting "all the world see" that England "hated Rome's whore with all her trumpery." Brave Essex, the commander of the parliamentary army, is bidden go on and show whose son he was, not false in heart either to king or country, but expelling, and destroying, and treading down equally the enemies of the people and of the crown. The result, it is trusted, would be such glorious days that the sight would dazzle the eyes of the beholders, and excite their wonder at England's settled peace, at her wealth and splendour, at her church and commonwealth so established as to cause universal joy that she had displayed her banners, and set up a new order of things. Then impartial justice would be dispensed in her courts of law, high commissions would be abolished, the whole apparatus of persecution would be destroyed, and England, a happy nation, would flourish for ever, nourished in truth and righteousness.

These her puritanical sentiments, earnest and thorough, on the religious and political questions of her day, Mrs. Bradstreet introduces in the form of a dialogue between Old England and New. Old England is represented as the fairest of queens, now sitting in the dust in a mourning garb, with a drooping head and folded arms, wailing and heaving sighs, as if some mighty calamity had befallen her. New England, as the daughter of this queen, approaches her, and beholding her in this sorrowful plight, inquires what ailed her—what deluge of woes had overwhelmed her famous realm, what meant her wailing tone and mourning guise?

Ah! tell thy daughter, she may sympathize.

. . . The sequel of the civil convulsions in Old England we have already touched upon. Puritanism triumphed, though only for a time, and emigration to America ceased. The throne tottered and fell. The army gained the ascendency and brought Charles I. to the block. Though Mrs. Bradstreet's sympathies went along with the parliament in their struggles in the cause of liberty, yet her sentiments as to the civil constitution of England were too conservative, and her attachment to the sovereign was too sincere and ardent, to permit her to regard the tragedy of his execution with any other feelings than those of the strongest disapprobation, not unmingled with horror. In introducing in the "Four Ages of Man," "Old Age," recounting the history of the puritan period, after betokening her loyal attachment to the royal family in all their fortunes, and in all their branches, and expressing especially the sympathy excited in her breast by the calamities which had befallen Elizabeth, daughter of James I., and her worthy consort Frederick V., King of Bohemia, she indicates how deeply she deplored the fate of Charles I.; and it even seems, what in similar cases is not uncommon, as if her sympathy for his sufferings for a time made her forget, or weakened her sense of the wrongs he had done to his subjects, and the tyranny which had constrained her and her relatives and others to emigrate to the New World.

> I've seen from Rome an execrable thing,
> A plot to blow up nobles and their king;
> I've seen designs at Ru, and Cades crost,
> And poor Palatinate for ever lost;
> I've seen a prince to live on others' lands,
> A royal one, by alms from subjects' hands;
> I've seen base men advanc'd to great degree,
> And worthy ones put to extremity:
> But not their prince's love, nor state so high,
> Could once reverse their shameful destiny.
> I've seen one stabb'd, another lose his head,
> And others fly their country through their dread.
> I've seen, and so have ye, for 'tis but late,
> The desolation of a goodly state,
> Plotted and acted, so that none can tell
> Who gave the counsel, but the prince of hell.

Nothwithstanding Mrs. Bradstreet's decided Puritanism, she entertained the highest veneration for the memory of Queen Elizabeth and delighted to linger over her history, intolerant as was that queen to the Puritans. Elizabeth was the great protectress of Protestantism, both in England and throughout Europe during the whole of her reign. Had Mary Queen of Scots succeeded in obtaining the English throne she would at once have united with Spain and France in the conspiracy formed by these two great powers for the extirpation of the Protestant faith in every country of Europe. Elizabeth seemed to have been specially raised up by Providence to make England the bulwark of Protestantism, and, by thwarting the exterminating designs of Spain and France, to save Protestantism from extirpation in the whole of Europe. The Puritans understood this well, and this accounts for her popularity among them, notwithstanding her making them the victims of a persecuting policy. One of Mrs. Bradstreet's minor poetical compositions is, "in honour of that high and mighty princess, Queen Elizabeth, of most happy memory." In the poem she begins with thus addressing the queen:—

> Although, great queen, thou now in silence lie,
> Yet thy loud herald Fame doth to the sky
> Thy wondrous worth proclaim, in every clime,
> And so has vow'd, whilst there is world or time.

In the poem itself she thus eulogizes Elizabeth:—

> She hath wip'd off th' aspersion of her sex,
> That women wisdom lack to play the Rex,
> Spain's monarch says not so, nor yet his host—
> She taught them better manners to their cost.
> The Salic law had not in force now been,
> If France had ever hop'd for such a queen.

And contrasting the condition of England in her own days with its more enviable condition in the reign of that magnanimous queen, who by the masculine vigour of her government had raised it to a pitch of glory and prosperity which her feeble successors had failed to maintain, she breaks forth:—

> But happy England, which had such a queen,
> O happy, happy, had those days still been!

. . . Mrs. Bradstreet had a great liking for books, and many of her hours of relaxation from household duties and cares she devoted to reading, from which she derived much profit and enjoyment. Her father, in addition to his other qualities, was an epicure in books, as we learn from an epitaph to his memory, of which Cotton Mather gives a poetical translation:—

In books a prodigal, they say;
A living cyclopædia;
Of histories of church and priest,
A full compendium, at least;
A table-talker, rich in sense,
And witty, without wit's pretence.

The passion for book learning, which was so strong in Mrs. Bradstreet may thus have been acquired from the example and training of her father.

One of her favourite books was Sir Philip Sydney's *Arcadia*, "a continual grove of morality shadowing moral and political results under the plain and easy emblems of lovers." In early youth she had devoured this book, forming, like the author's countrymen and countrywomen, by whom it was greatly admired and extensively read, a very different opinion of the high place in literature to which it was entitled from that of the author himself, who is said some hours before his death to have enjoined some friend to consign it to the flames. To the celebration of Sidney and his work her muse has dedicated a lengthened poem in the form of an elegy, written in 1638, forty-eight years after this famed knight had died of his wounds at Zutphen. She thus eulogizes him as an honor to his country and age:—

When England did enjoy her halcyon days,
Her noble Sidney wore the crown of bays;
No less an honour to our British land
Than she that sway'd the sceptre with her hand:
Mars and Minerva did in one agree,
Of arms, and arts, thou should'st a pattern be.

And her epitaph upon him is:—

Here lies entomb'd in fame, under this stone,
Philip and Alexander, both in one;
Heir to the muses, the son of Mars in truth,
Learning, valour, beauty, all in virtuous youth.

History was to her a favourite study, and much of her leisure she dedicated to reading on this subject, particularly to the reading of the history of her own country, with which she was intimately acquainted, and the history of the great empires of antiquity—the Assyrian, the Persian, the Grecian, and the Roman, with the leading facts of which she was also familiar. Nor did she neglect works of science and medicine. Books in poetry were also the frequent companions of her vacant hours, as might have been anticipated from the imaginative and poetical elements which entered largely into her mental composition.

From her literary habits and tastes she sought expression, as we have seen, to the reflections and emotions which sprung up in her mind, in the language of poetry. Her father had made rhyme the vehicle or exponent of his feelings, and her poetical taste and talent, as well as her love of reading, she may have inherited from him. She indeed ranks as the earliest female poet which America produced.

Her great master and model in poetical composition was the French soldier poet, Du Bartas, who flourished in the reign of Henry IV. "The Divine Weeks" and other works of this poet, translated by the silver-tongued Sylvester from French into English, were so highly popular in the early days of New England that all who took up the pen to write poetry endeavoured to imitate them; and in the estimation of Mrs. Bradstreet they were a standard of taste so super-excellent that nothing could surpass or equal them. In her "Prologue" to her poem on the "Four Elements," she thus expresses her admiration of Du Bartas:—

But when my wond'ring eyes and envious heart

Great Bartas' sugar'd lines do but read o'er;
Fool, I do grudge the muses did not part
'Twixt him and me that over-fluent store;
A Bartas can do what a Bartas will,
But simple I, according to my skill.

And in a poem specially devoted to the celebration of his poetical genius she says:—

Amongst the happy wits this age hath shown,
Great, dear, sweet Bartas, thou art matchless known.

Her admiration and imitation of Du Bartas did not contribute to strengthen or to refine her poetical genius. Full of conceits, of forced unnatural comparisons, and far-fetched illustrations, his grotesque effusions vitiated her taste, which the study of better models would have raised to a high degree of perfection. . . .

If tried by an exact standard of æsthetics, her poetry in passing through the ordeal will reveal many blemishes. Its poetical merits are unequal. It is often prosaic, deficient in melody of versification, and betrays the common faults of the Du Bartas school. The historical portion is little more than a chronological table of facts, in which, if there is not much poetry, there is considerable historical information. It will not be difficult to find in her poems passages of bad taste and of sheer doggerel, should a reader examine them for such an ungallant purpose.

But notwithstanding such defects as these, there is traceable on every page of her poetry a warm heart, a cheerful, debonair disposition, genuine candour, and earnest piety; and some of her verses are very pleasing from their harmonious versification, their chaste and nervous diction, as well as their religious feeling and purity of sentiment. In her account of the seasons she shows good descriptive powers. . . .

Mrs. Bradstreet's "Contemplations" alone, which has been frequently reprinted in America, proves that she was a genuine poet, and affords perhaps the most favourable specimen of her poetical genius. From this poem it is evident that she had an eye to survey, and a heart to feel the beauties of nature. The rising and setting sun; the mighty forest of unknown antiquity, extending far beyond the eye's utmost reach; the trees clothed with foliage and laden with fruit; the blooming flowers, whether growing wild in the wilderness, or cultivated in the garden by the industry of man; the flowing river with its rocky banks; the fish frisking in the limpid stream; the mirthful melody and the mechanical instinct of birds—these had to her a magical power of attraction, and she describes them often in pleasing and beautiful strains. "The slow measure she adopts suits well the solemn majesty of her musing thoughts." . . .

This appreciation of the beauties of nature, and of the wonders of creation, raised her thoughts in solemn and admiring meditation to the great Creator. In her "Contemplations" she walks as it were through the august temple of creation, and everything which meets her eye carries her soul upward to the glorious Architect, to the realization of his presence and agency, of his power, wisdom, and goodness, and lays her prostrate before him in humble reverence and profound adoration.

Then higher on the glistening sun I gaz'd,
Whose beams were shaded by the leafy tree:
The more I look'd, the more I grew amaz'd,
And softly said, What glory's like to thee?
Soul of this world, this universe's eye,
No wonder some made thee a deity;
Had I not better known, alas! the same had I.

Art thou so full of glory that no eye
   Hath strength thy shining rays once to behold?
And is thy splendid throne erect so high,
   As to approach it can no earthly mould?
How full of glory then must thy Creator be,
Who gave this bright lustre unto thee!
Admir'd, ador'd for ever, be that majesty.

She then contrasts the frailty and evanescence of man as a terrestrial being with the greater durability of the other works of the material universe—a solemn and humbling thought. But taking a more comprehensive view of man—looking to the future restoration of his mortal body and to his high destiny as a rational and an immortal being, she contemplates him, notwithstanding the humiliating spectacle he presents with his sorrows and cares terminating in death, as rising immeasurably superior to all the other works of the material creation.

When I behold the heavens, as in their prime,
   And then the earth (though old) still clad in green,
The stones and trees, insensible of time,
   Nor age, nor wrinkle, on their front are seen;
If winter come, and greenness then do fade,
A spring returns, and they more youthful made;
But man grows old, lies down, remains where once
he's laid;
Nor youth, nor strength, nor wisdom, spring again
Nor habitations long their names retain,
But in oblivion to the final day remain.

Shall I then praise the heavens, the trees, the earth,
   Because their beauty and their strength last longer?
Shall I wish their, or never to had birth,
   Because they're bigger, and their bodies stronger?
Nay, they shall darken, perish, fade, and die,
And when unmade, so ever shall they lie,
But man was made for endless immortality.

Yet, while thus doing homage to the high destiny of man, she thinks mournfully over the tenaciousness with which he clings to the present state of existence, and the apathy or dread with which he turns away from the thought of that endless state, whither he is tending, notwithstanding all that he experiences of the emptiness, the insufficiency, the sinfulness, and the miseries of the present.

And yet this sinful creature, frail and vain,
   This lump of wretchedness, of sin and sorrow,
This weather-beaten vessel wreckt with pain,
   Joys not in hope of an eternal morrow:
Nor all his losses, crosses, and vexation,
In weight, in frequency, and long duration,
Can make him deeply groan for that divine
translation.

Her apostrophe to Time in the closing verse of her "Contemplations," is well conceived and expressed. It awakened in her sadness to think of the havoc committed by that sure though silent destroyer of all things earthly; but it mitigated, and even dispelled this sadness to think that the Christian shall survive all its ravages, and, emerging from the wreck of all things merely terrestrial, shall flourish vigorous and undecaying in the perpetual youth of immortality.

O Time! thou fatal wrack of mortal things,
That draws oblivion's curtains over kings,
Their sumptuous monuments, men know them not,
Their names without a record are forgot,
Their parts, their ports, their pomp's all laid in th'
dust,
Nor wit, nor gold, nor buildings 'scape time's rust;
But he whose name is graved in the white stone
Shall last and shine when all of these are gone.

JOHN HARVARD ELLIS
From "Introduction"
The Works of Anne Bradstreet in Prose and Verse
1867, pp. xi–lxxi

O f the merit of these ⟨poems⟩, I will say but little, leaving the reader to judge for himself on this point. I can hardly expect, however, that, after 'twice drinking the nectar of her lines,' he will "welter in delight," like the enthusiastic President Rogers.[1] Yet I am confident, that, if it is denied that they evince much poetic genius, it must, at least, be acknowledged that they are remarkable, when the time, place, and circumstances under which they were composed, are taken into consideration. They are quaint and curious; they contain many beautiful and original ideas, not badly expressed; and they constitute a singular and valuable relic of the earliest literature of the country. It is important that the reader should bear in mind the peculiarly unpropitious circumstances under which they were written. No genial coterie of gifted minds was near to cheer and inspire her, no circle of wits to sharpen and brighten her faculties; she had no elegant surroundings of rich works of art to encourage and direct her tastes: but the country was a wilderness, and the people among whom she dwelt were the last in the world to stimulate or appreciate a poet.

Notwithstanding her assurance to her father that

My goods are true (though poor) I love no stealth,[2]

Mrs. Bradstreet's longer poems appear to be, in many places, simply poetical versions of what she had read. Accordingly, her facts and theories are often discordant with what the more accurate and thorough investigation of recent years has made certain or probable. To point out these differences wherever they occur would be at once a difficult and a useless task. Her poems make it evident that she had been a faithful student of history, an assiduous reader, and a keen observer of nature and of what was transpiring both at home and abroad. She mentions many of the principal Greek and Latin authors, such as Hesiod, Homer, Thucydides, Xenophon, and Aristotle, Virgil, Ovid, Quintus Curtius, Pliny, and Seneca; but there is no reason to suppose that she had read their works, either in the originals or in translations. A few scraps of Latin are to be found scattered through her writings; but they are such as any one might have picked up without knowing the language. "The Exact Epitomie of the Four Monarchies," which takes up considerably more than half of the volume of *Poems*, was probably derived almost entirely from Sir Walter Raleigh's *History of the World*, Archbishop Usher's *Annals of the World*, the Hebrew writings, Pemble's *Period of the Persian Monarchie*,[3] and perhaps from other historical treatises. She frequently refers to Raleigh and Usher; but it was to Raleigh that she was chiefly indebted, and she follows him very closely. . . .

After the publication of the first edition of her *Poems*, Mrs. Bradstreet appears to have read Sir Thomas North's translation of Plutarch's *Lives*, and to have incorporated some of the facts which she thus obtained into the second edition. She does not mention Plutarch in the first edition; while, in the second, she refers to him twice by name. I will give a single instance of the way in which she made these additions. In place of the lines in the first edition, already quoted,—

   Alexander now no longer could containe,
     But instantly commands him to be slaine;—

are substituted in the second, the following:—

   Which *Alexanders* wrath incens'd so high,
     Nought but his life for this could satisfie;

From one stood by he snacht a partizan,
And in a rage him through the body ran.[4]

These last two lines must have come from Plutarch.

> Then *Alexander* taking a partisan from one of his
> guard, as *Clitus* was coming towards him, and had
> lift vp the hanging before the doore, he ranne him
> through the body, so that *Clitus* fell to the ground,
> and fetching one grone, died presently.[5]

So, notwithstanding her allusion to Galen and Hippocrates,[6] it is almost certain that she obtained her wonderfully exact
description of human anatomy from the "curious learned
Crooke,"[7] whose *Description of the Body of Man* had gone
through three editions in London in 1631.

Mrs. Bradstreet's familiarity with the Bible is apparent all
through her writings. There are traces of her having used the
Genevan Version, which, for many reasons, was more acceptable to the Puritans than the authorized one of King James.

Du Bartas, as translated by Joshua Sylvester, was her favorite author. However distasteful his writings may be to readers of
the present day, they were then exceedingly popular, and we
are told that Milton not only found pleasure in reading them,
but was to some extent indebted to them.[8] Mrs. Bradstreet,
besides her special tribute to his memory, constantly displays
her admiration for Du Bartas. This liking was known to her
friends; and in her dedication of her *Poems* to her father, she
felt it necessary expressly to disclaim having copied from him at
all. How much she really owed to him it is hard to tell. The
general idea of her longer poems may have been suggested by
reading his works, and her style and manner may have been
affected in the same way.[9]

Sir Philip Sidney was also a great favorite with Mrs.
Bradstreet, but she was not able to praise his works in such
unqualified terms as she does those of Du Bartas. Her criticisms are quite entertaining. She refers to the *Historie of Great
Britaine* by Speed, and to Camden's *Annales*,[10] as if she had
read them, and she probably derived some of the facts used in
the "Dialogue between Old-England and New" from the former. She was not ignorant of the works of Spenser,[11] but she
does not discuss their merits. . . .

Mrs. Bradstreet had eight children, four sons and four
daughters; a fact which she has recorded in some fanciful
verses, beginning,—

> I had eight birds hatcht in one nest,
> Four Cocks there were, and Hens the rest,
> I nurst them up with pain and care,
> Nor cost, nor labour did I spare,
> Till at the last they felt their wing.
> Mounted the Trees, and learn'd to sing;[12]

She goes on at some length, carrying out the simile, and describes their past life, their condition at that time, and her
solicitude for their future health and happiness. Prompted by
her love for her children, she wrote out her religious experiences, in a little book in which she also kept a record, partly in
prose and partly in verse, of her sicknesses, her religious feelings, and the most important incidents in her life.[13] The earliest date in it is July 8, 1656,[14] but it was undoubtedly begun
before that.

Having had from her birth a very delicate constitution,
prostrated when only sixteen years old by the small-pox, troubled at one time with lameness, subject to frequent attacks of
sickness, to fevers, and to fits of fainting, she bore these numerous inflictions with meekness and resignation. Recognizing the
inestimable blessing of health, she regarded it as the reward of
virtue, and looked upon her various maladies as tokens of the
divine displeasure at her thoughtlessness or wrong-doing. She

says that her religious belief was at times shaken; but her doubts
and fears were soon banished, if, indeed, they were not exaggerated in number and importance by her tender conscience. Her
children were constantly in her mind. It was for them that she
committed to writing her own religious experiences, her own
feelings of joy or sorrow at the various changes which brightened or darkened her life. Her most pointed similes are drawn
from the familiar incidents of domestic life, especially the
bringing-up of children. From some of these references it
would seem as if she had found among her own children the
most diverse traits of character; that some of them were obedient and easily governed, while others were unruly and headstrong; and that she derived an intense satisfaction from
contemplating the virtues of some, while she deplored the
failings of others. Notwithstanding the comfort she took in her
children, notwithstanding the happiness of her married life,
she continually dwells on the vanity of all worldly delights, the
shortness of life, and the great ills to which humanity is subject. She found, however, a never-failing solace for all her
troubles in prayer. "I have had," she writes, "great experience
of God's hearing my Prayers, and returning comfortable Answers to me, either in granting ye Thing I prayed for, or else,"
she adds, with a charming frankness, "in satissfying my mind
without it."[15]

In November, 1657, her son Samuel, her eldest child,
sailed for England.[16] He graduated at Harvard College in the
year 1653, but his age is not known, though at that time he
could not have been more than twenty. Mrs. Bradstreet says,
"It pleased God to keep me a long time without a child, which
was a great grief to me, and cost mee many prayers and tears
before I obtaind one."[17] Samuel was,—

> The Son of Prayers, of vowes, of teares,
> The child I stay'd for many yeares.[18]

and she was very loth to part with him, but she committed him
at last to the care of Providence, and was rewarded by welcom-
ing him home safe, in July, 1661.[19] . . .

Mrs. Bradstreet had from time to time been writing under
the name of "Meditations" some apothegms, suggested mainly
by the homely events of her own experience. This was done at
the request of her son Simon, to whom they were dedicated
March 20, 1664.[20] The "Meditations" display much more ability, much greater cultivation of mind, and a deeper
thoughtfulness than most of her other works. She shows in
them a more correct taste than in her *Poems*. We must take her
word for their originality. "I have avoyded," she says, "in-
croaching upon others conceptions because I would leave you
nothing but myne owne, though in value they fall short of all
in this kinde." And again she reminds him that "There is no
new thing vnder ye sun, there is nothing that can be sayd or
done, but either that or something like it hath been both done
and sayd before."

In July, 1666, by the burning of the house at Andover, her
papers, books, and many other things of great value to her,
were destroyed. She had intended to complete her poetical
account of "The Roman Monarchy," and had spent much time
in preparing a continuation of it, but the loss of what she had
already finished made her abandon the work altogether.[22] Her
son Simon thus notices this disaster in his diary, and represents
his father's loss as very great:—

> July. 12. 1666. Whilst I was at N. London my fathers
> house at Andover was burnt, where I lost my Books,
> and many of my clothes, to the valeiu of 50 or 60 lb
> at least; The Lord gaue, and the Lord hath taken,
> blessed bee the Name of the Lord. Tho: my own
> losse of books (and papers espec.) was great and my

fathers far more being about 800, yet ye Lord was pleased gratiously many wayes to make up ye fame to us. It is therefore good to trust in the Lord."

There could have been little of variety to call Mrs. Bradstreet aside from the daily routine of her quiet country life. Attendance on the frequent and long-protracted religious meetings, and the duties of her household, must have occupied her time when she was well. She had evidently exposed herself to the criticism of her neighbors by studying and writing so much. The fact of a woman's being able to compose any thing possessing any literary merit was regarded with the greatest surprise by her contemporaries, and was particularly dwelt upon by her admirers.[23] In the "Prologue" she says:—

> I am obnoxious to each carping tongue
> Who says my hand a needle better fits,
> A Poets pen all scorn I should thus wrong,
> For such despite they cast on Female wits:
> If what I do prove well, it won't advance,
> They'l say it's stoln, or else it was by chance.[24]

The forests were still stocked with wild beasts, and there was constant fear of assaults and depredations by the Indians. She wandered in the woods, however, and found great pleasure in meditating on their ever winning charms, their grand and quiet beauty. By far the best of all her *Poems* was the result of one of these rambles. It appeared for the first time in the second edition, under the name of "Contemplations."[25] She describes with great spirit the sights and sounds of the forest, the fields and the stream, and makes us wish that she had done more in this style, for which many of the poets of her time were distinguished. It was doubtless by the side of the untamed Merrimac, before its rushing waters were made to pour through the immense structures which now line its banks, that she sat and pondered. The great dam which now spans the river at Lawrence is only two miles from the spot where the first settlement of Andover was made, and where Mrs. Bradstreet lived when she wrote,—

> Under the cooling shadow of a stately Elm
>   Close fate I by a goodly Rivers side,
> Where gliding streams the Rocks did overwhelm;
>   A lonely place, with pleasures dignifi'd.[26]

This "Poem" proves that she had true poetic feeling, and shows to what she could rise when she was willing to throw aside her musty folios and read the fresh book of nature.

> And Wisdom's self
> Oft seeks to sweet retired solitude,
> Where, with her best nurse Contemplation,
> She plumes her feathers, and lets grow her wings,
> That in the various bustle of resort,
> Were all-to ruffled, and sometimes impair'd.[27]

The revision of her *Poems* must have been no small undertaking, and from some of the references in the many additions which she made, it is evident that she was engaged upon this work as late at least as 1666. Sympathizing, as she naturally did, with Parliament and the Puritans, she said much in the first edition, written at the outbreak of the Civil War, which she felt obliged to omit or modify to suit the state of things existing under the Restoration. Although she speaks of a *"Brittish bruitish Cavaleer,"* and dignifies him with the titles of "wretch" and "monster," yet she has to come down to calling Cromwell a "Usurper." Indeed, these alterations form one of the most diverting features of the book. It must be confessed, however, that she rather inclined from the first to be a Monarchist, and that her hatred of Papists admitted of not the slightest compromise.

She had never set a very great value on the pleasures of this world, and had always been ready to abandon them for the joys which she expected to find in another. In the last piece which we have in her writing, dated Aug. 31, 1669,[28] she represents herself as positively weary of life and longing to die. Three years after, her wish was granted, and she was released from suffering. Her son Simon's sad account of her sickness and death proves that it must have been in reality a blessing to her:—

September 16. 1672. My ever honoured & most dear Mother was translated to Heaven. Her death was occasioned by a consumption being wasted to skin & bone & She had an issue made in her arm bec: she was much troubled with rheum, & one of ye women y^t tended herr dressing her arm, s'd shee never saw such an arm in her Life, I, s'd my most dear Mother, but y^t arm shall bee a Glorious Arm.

I being absent fro her lost the opportunity of comitting to memory her pious & memorable xpressions vttered in her sicknesse. O y^t the good Lord would give vnto me and mine a heart to walk in her steps, considering what the end of her Conversation was, y^t so wee might one day haue a happy & glorious greeting.

Notes

1. *See The Works of Anne Bradstreet in Prose and Verse*, ed. John Harvard Ellis, 1867, pp. 93–96. All further citations of Bradstreet's works by page number will refer to this edition.
2. See page 98, last line.
3. See page 250, note. William Pemble, a learned divine, was born in Sussex, or at Egerton, in Kent, in 1591, and died April 14, 1623. One of his works was entitled, "THE PERIOD OF THE PERSIAN MONARCHIE, Wherein sundry places of *Ezra*, *Nehemiah*, and *Daniel* are cleered. Extracted, contracted, and englished (much of it out of Doctor *Raynolds*) by the late learned and godly Man Mr. WILLIAM PEMBLE, of *Magdalen Hall* in OXFORD." This is doubtless the book which Mrs. Bradstreet had seen. All of his works were separately printed after his death, and then collected in one volume, folio, in 1635, and reprinted four or five times.
4. See pages 283 and 284, note *i*, and page xlvii.
5. North's *Plutarch*. London: 1631, p. 700.
6. See page 143.
7. See page 144. Probably Helkiah Crooke, M.D., of whose works Watt has the following in his *Bibliotheca Britannica*, Vol. i., p. 272, w.:—"Μικροκοσμογραφία, or a Description of the Body of Man, collected and translated out of all the best Authors of Anatomy, especially out of Gaspar, Bauchinus, and A. Sourentius. Lond. 1615, 1618, 1631. fol. A large work, illustrated with the plates of Vesalius and others.—An Explanation of the fashion and use of three and fifty Instruments of Chirurgery. Lond. 1631, fol. The same Lond. 1634, 8vo. Taken chiefly from Parey." [Ambrose Paré, a French Surgeon.]
8. Craik's *English Literature*, Vol. i. p. 569, and note 2. Bohn's *Bibliographer's Manual, sub* Du Bartas.
9. Guillaume de Saluste du Bartas, born of noble parents near Auch about 1544, and brought up to the profession of war, distinguished himself as a soldier and negotiator. Holding the same religious views as Henry IV. before he became King of France, and attached to the person of that prince in the capacity of a gentleman in ordinary of his bed-chamber, he was successfully employed by him on missions to Denmark, Scotland, and England. He was at the battle of Ivry, and celebrated in song the victory which he had helped to gain. He died four months after, in July, 1590, at the age of forty-six, in consequence of some wounds which had been badly healed. He passed all the leisure which his duties left him at his château du Bartas. It was there that he composed his long and numerous poems: *La Première Semaine*, that is, the Creation in seven days, *L'Uranie*, *Judith*, *Le Triomphe de la Foi*, *Les Neuf Muses*, and *La Seconde Semaine*. The last work is very strangely

entitled, as it comprehends a great part of the Old Testament histories. His principal poem, *La Semaine*, went through more than thirty editions in less than six years, and was translated into Latin, Italian, Spanish, English, German, and Dutch. MICHAUD; BIOGRAPHIE UNIVERSELLE, *sub* Bartas.

Sylvester's translation of Du Bartas's works was first published in a quarto volume in London in 1605, the parts of which it was composed having previously appeared separately. The title of the edition of 1621 was "DU BARTAS. HIS DIUINE WEEKES AND WORKES, with a Complete Collection of all the other most delightfull Workes, Translated and Written by yᵉ famous Philomusus Josvah Sylvester, Gent." Others had also competed with Sylvester in this work.

10. See page 358.
11. See pages 348 and 358.
12. See page 400.
13. See pages 2–39.
14. See page 17.
15. See page 7.
16. See page 24.
17. See page 5
18. See page 24.
19. See page 28.
20. See page 47.
21. See page 53.
22. See pages 40 and 329.
23. See pages 83–92. There is a paragraph in Mr. and Mrs. S. C. Hall's sketch of Miss Hannah More (probably written by *Mrs.* Hall) which shows that public opinion changed quite slowly on this point.

"In this age, when female talent is so rife,—when, indeed, it is not too much to say women have fully sustained their right to equality with men in reference to all the productions of the mind,—it is difficult to comprehend the popularity, almost amounting to adoration, with which a woman writer was regarded little more than half a century ago. Mediocrity was magnified into genius, and to have printed a book, or to have written even a tolerable poem, was a passport into the very highest society."—*Art Journal*, London: 1866, p. 187.

24. See page 101.
25. See page 370.
26. See page 377.
27. Milton's *Comus*, 375–80.
28. See pages 42–44.

MOSES COIT TYLER
From "New England: The Verse-Writers"
A History of American Literature
1878, Volume 1, pp. 280–88

In the year 1650,—a full twelvemonth after the head of Charles the First had fallen upon the block in front of his palace at Whitehall, the very year in which Oliver Cromwell was giving to the Presbyterian Scots on the field of Dunbar a strong dose of English Congregationalism,—there was published, in London, a book of poems written by a gifted young woman of the New England wilderness, Anne Bradstreet by name. The book bore one of those fantastic and long-winded title-pages, at once a table of contents and a printer's puff, that the literary folk of the sixteenth and seventeenth centuries greatly delighted in. It reads thus: "The Tenth Muse lately sprung up in America; or, Several Poems, compiled with great variety of wit and learning, full of delight; wherein especially is contained a complete discourse and description of the four elements, constitutions, ages of man, seasons of the year; together with an exact epitome of the four monarchies, viz., the Assyrian, Persian, Grecian, Roman; also, a dialogue between Old England and New concerning the late troubles; with divers other pleasant and serious poems. By a gentlewoman in those parts. Printed at London, for Stephen Bowtell, at the sign of the Bible, in Pope's Head Alley, 1650."[1]

Perhaps that year, 1650, was not the friendliest year that could be imagined for any Tenth Muse to get the attention of the world, even though she had "lately sprung up in America," and even though the poems she sang were "compiled with great variety of wit and learning, full of delight." Not the Muses, one would say, but rather the Furies had the field just then; and the dulcet notes of any gentle word-music had little chance of being heard, amid the universal din of the crashing footsteps of Mars striding angrily up and down the island, while, in the pauses of his wrathful spasms, the politicians were bent on filling the air with their clamorous and sullen jargon. But whether the time were fortunate, or otherwise, for the publication of Anne Bradstreet's poems, not greatly did it concern Anne Bradstreet herself, far away from London in her rustic mansion, amid the picturesque hills and rough woods of Andover, and within sound of the murmurs of the Merrimac.

She was born in England, in 1612. Her father, Thomas Dudley, an austere Puritan, a man of much study and stern will, had settled down, after some military experience, as steward of the estates of the Puritan nobleman, the Earl of Lincoln. It was while he was in that responsible service, that his brilliant young daughter passed some of her girlhood in the earl's castle of Sempringham; and we may not doubt that a mind so eager for knowledge as was hers, made high festival over the various treasures of books that were gathered there. In the year 1628, when she had reached the age of sixteen, she married the man in whose loving and grave companionship she passed the remainder of her life, Simon Bradstreet, nine years older than herself, of a good family in Suffolk, a graduate of Emmanuel College, Cambridge, educated to business by her own father, and fearing no man. Two years later, the young people joined the great company of wealthy and cultivated Puritans who sailed away to New England, where, thenceforward, Simon Bradstreet steadily advanced in importance, and came to take a great part in matters of church and state, living out a long career there as colonial secretary, judge, legislator, governor, ambassador, and royal councillor, dying at last in great honor, at the great age of ninety-four, the white-haired and wise-tongued Nestor of the Puritan commonwealth.

This coming away from old England to New England was, for many of these wealthy emigrants, a sad sacrifice of taste and personal preference; and for none of them, probably, was it more so than for this girl-wife, Anne Bradstreet, who, with a scholar's thirst for knowledge, and a poet's sensitiveness to the elegant and the ugly, would have delighted in the antique richness and the mellow beauty of English life, as much as she recoiled from the savage surroundings, the scant privileges, the crude, realistic, and shaggy forms of society in America. "After a short time," she says in an autobiographic sketch, "I changed my condition and was married, and came into this country, where I found a new world and new manners, at which my heart rose. But after I was convinced it was the way of God, I submitted to it."[2] But though she thus submitted to her fate, the effort was one that had to be ever-renewed; and in her own writings, as in the writings of her contemporaries, one hears, between the lines, the plaintive cry of their consciousness of being, for a sacred duty and by God's unmistakable will, in a remote exile:

> Remember, Lord, thy folk, whom thou
> To wilderness hast brought.[3]

It took several years for her husband and herself to find

their way to their permanent home; but in 1644, after many settlements, they settled finally near Andover, where, upon a farm which is still pointed out as the Bradstreet farm, amid noble and inspiring natural scenery, and within the distance of only a mile and a quarter from the Merrimac, she passed the remainder of her life, dying in 1672, at the age of sixty.

So, whatever work this writer wrought, whether good or bad, she wrought in the midst of circumstances that did not altogether help her, but hindered her rather. She was the laborious wife of a New England farmer, the mother of eight children, and herself from childhood of a delicate constitution. The most of her poems were produced between 1630 and 1642, that is, before she was thirty years old; and during these years, she had neither leisure, nor elegant surroundings, nor freedom from anxious thoughts, nor even abounding health. Somehow, during her busy life-time, she contrived to put upon record compositions numerous enough to fill a royal octavo volume of four hundred pages,—compositions which entice and reward our reading of them, two hundred years after she lived.

Perhaps her prose writings, by no means many or long, are likely to be more attractive to the altered tastes of our time, than her poems can be. They consist of a brief sketch of her own life, called "Religious Experiences," and of a series of aphorisms bearing the title of "Meditations Divine and Moral." It is in the latter work that we find the best examples of her strength of thought, and of her felicity in condensed and pungent expression: "A ship that bears much sail, and little or no ballast, is easily overset; and that man whose head hath great abilities and his heart little or no grace, is in danger of foundering."[4] "Authority without wisdom, is like a heavy axe without an edge, fitter to bruise than polish."[5] "Iron, till it be throughly heat, is uncapable to be wrought; so God sees good to cast some men into the furnace of affliction, and then beats them on his anvil into what frame he pleases."[6] "We read in Scripture of three sorts of arrows,—the arrow of an enemy, the arrow of pestilence, and the arrow of a slanderous tongue. The two first kill the body, the last the good name; the two former leave a man when he is once dead, but the last mangles him in his grave."[7] "Sore laborers have hard hands, and old sinners have brawny consciences."[8] "We often see stones hang with drops, not from any innate moisture, but from a thick air about them. So may we sometimes see marble-hearted sinners seem full of contrition; but it is not from any dew of grace within, but from some black clouds that impends them, which produces these sweating effects."[9] "Dim eyes are the concomitants of old age; and short-sightedness in those that are eyes of a republic, foretells a declining state."[10] "Ambitious men are like hops, that never rest climbing so long as they have anything to stay upon; but take away their props, and they are of all, the most dejected."[11]

It was, however, as a poet only, that Anne Bradstreet was known in literature to her contemporaries. Our expectations of finding high poetic merit in her work, are not increased by ascertaining the lines of culture through which she trained herself for her calling as poet. Literature, for her, was not a republic of letters, hospitable to all forms of human thought, but a strict Puritan commonwealth, founded on a scheme of narrow ascetic intolerance, and excluding from its citizenship some of the sublimest, daintiest, and most tremendous types of literary expression. Evidently, in her mind, William Shakespeare, play-wright and actor, was an alien, and a godless person; and Ben Jonson, Massinger, Beaumont and Fletcher, Webster, Ford, Shirley, and all the rest of that superb group of masters, were sons of Belial. Furthermore, while her imagina-

tion thus lost the witchery and the stimulation of the great English dramatists, she was taught to seek for the very essence of poetry in the quirks, the puns, the contorted images, the painful ingenuities of George Wither and Francis Quarles, and especially of *The Divine Weeks and Works* of the French poet Du Bartas, done into English by Joshua Sylvester. In short, she was a pupil of the fantastic school of English poetry—the poetry of the later euphuists; the special note of which is the worship of the quaint, the strained, the disproportionate, the grotesque, and the total sacrifice of the beautiful on the altar of the ingenious. Harmony, taste, dignity, even decency, were by this school eagerly cast away, if only an additional twist could be given to the turn of a metaphor, or still another antithesis could be wrenched from the agonies of a weary epithet. It is easy enough to find in the writings of Anne Bradstreet grotesque passages, preposterous stuff, jingling abominations; but we shall only mislead ourselves, if we look upon these as traits peculiarly characteristic of this writer, or of American verse-writing in the seventeenth century. They were, rather, the symptoms of a wider and far deeper literary disease—a disease which, originating in Italy in the sixteenth century, swept westward and northward like the plague, desolating for a time the literatures of Spain, of France, and of England. The worst lines of Anne Bradstreet and of the other American verse-writers in the seventeenth century, can be readily matched for fantastic perversion, and for the total absence of beauty, by passages from the poems of John Donne, George Herbert, Crashaw, Cleveland, Wither, Quarles, Thomas Coryat, John Taylor, and even of Herrick, Cowley, and Dryden.[12] . . .

Of course, Anne Bradstreet had ample precedents in English literature for this form of poetry.[13] Of course, too, she was grossly misled; since poetry is nothing if it is nothing more than rhymed historical teaching. The fatal taint in all her poetical life was that, badly instructed by her literary guides, she too generally drew her materials from books rather than from nature. How much better, had she bravely looked within her own heart, and out upon the real world, and given voice to herself rather than to mere erudition! . . .

The traditional disparagement by men, of the intelligence of her sex, of course she felt,—the sting of it, the wrong of it; and she resented it, sometimes in the form of a sarcastic reference, sometimes in that ironical admission that hers was indeed "a less noble gender," and sometimes in that of a superb and defiant denial. For instance, as a woman, she seemed to take vast pleasure in the magnificent career of Queen Elizabeth:

> She hath wiped off the aspersion of her sex,
> That women wisdom lack to play the Rex.[14]

Appealing to the universal and enthusiastic pride of Englishmen in the imperial greatness of their recent woman-monarch, the poet, in a flash, retaliates upon masculine detraction, with this keen and glorious thrust:

> Now say, have women worth, or have they none?
> Or had they some, but with our Queen is't gone?
> Nay, masculines, you have thus taxed us long;
> But she, though dead, will vindicate our wrong.
> Let such as say our sex is void of reason,
> Know 'tis a slander now, but once was treason.[15]

Upon the whole, it is impossible to deny that Anne Bradstreet was sadly misguided by the poetic standards of her religious sect and of her literary period, and that the vast bulk of her writings consists not of poetry, but of metrical theology and chronology and politics and physics. Yet, amid all this lamentable rubbish, there is often to be found such an ingot of genuine poetry, as proves her to have had, indeed, the poetic endowment. Of her own claims as a writer of verse, she kept for herself a very modest estimate; and in the Prologue to her volume, she speaks of her writings in diffident lines, whose merit alone would prompt us to grant to her a higher poetic rank than she herself asks for:

> And oh, ye high flown quills that soar the skies,
> And ever with your prey still catch your praise;
> If e'er you deign these lowly lines your eyes,
> Give thyme and parsley wreaths: I ask no bays.
> This mean and unrefined ore of mine
> Will make your glistering gold but more to shine.[16]

Notes

1. The entire works of Anne Bradstreet, in prose and verse, edited by John Harvard Ellis, were published in sumptuous form at Charlestown, Mass., in 1867; to which volume I refer in the present chapter.
2. *The Works of Anne Bradstreet*, p. 5.
3. Ibid., p. 34.
4. Ibid., p. 48.
5. Ibid., p. 50.
6. Ibid., p. 54.
7. Ibid., p. 55.
8. Ibid., p. 56.
9. Ibid., pp. 58–9.
10. Ibid., p. 55.
11. Ibid., p. 55.
12. The later English euphuists were called by Dr. Johnson "the metaphysical poets," a description that does not describe them. Perhaps Milton's phrase is the best one—the "fantastics." What Donne and his poetic associates were to English literature, that were Marini to Italian literature, Gongora to Spanish, Du Bartas to French. For accounts of the "conceited" epoch in English Literature, see Henry Morley, *First Sketch of Eng. Lit.* 526–532; Thomas Arnold, *Manual of Eng. Lit.* 160–164; Hippolyte Taine, *Hist. Eng. Lit.* I. 201–206.
13. For example, *The Mirror for Magistrates*, Samuel Daniel's *History of the Civil Wars*, and Michael Drayton's *Barons' Wars*, to say nothing of the early chronicles, many of which were in verse.
14. *The Works of Anne Bradstreet*, pp. 340–341.
15. Ibid., p. 361.
16. Ibid., p. 102. In the last line but one I have substituted "ore" for "ure," which, in spite of the explanation of the latest editor of her works, I think to be a misprint in the first edition. This may be a suitable place in which to mention the interesting fact that among the lineal descendants of this noble personage—this "Gentlewoman of New England" as she was designated on the title-page of the first edition of her poems, this "peerless gentlewoman" as John Norton calls her—are included the Channings, the Buckminsters, Eliza B. Lee, Richard H. Dana the poet, Richard H. Dana the prose-writer, Wendell Phillips, and Oliver Wendell Holmes.